The Encyclopedia of Australian ROCK AND POP

The Encyclopedia of Australian
ROCK AND POP

Ian McFarlane

ALLEN & UNWIN

This book is dedicated to the memory of Lawrence Victor McFarlane 1929–1996
('Treasured memories and lessons for life')

First published in 1999 by
Allen & Unwin
9 Atchison Street,
St Leonards NSW 1590 Australia
Phone: (61 2) 8425 0100
Fax: (61 2) 9906 2218
E-mail: frontdesk@allen-unwin.com.au
Web: http://www.allen-unwin.com.au

National Library of Australia
Cataloguing-in-Publication entry:

McFarlane, Ian, 1959– .
The encyclopedia of Australian rock and pop.

ISBN 1 86508 072 1.
ISBN 1 86449 768 2 (pbk).

1. Rock music—Australia—History and criticism. 2. Popular music—Australia—History and criticism. 3. Rock groups—Australia. 4. Rock musicians—Australia. I. Title.

781.640994

Set in 9/10pt Caslon by DOCUPRO, Sydney
Printed by Brown Prior Anderson Pty Ltd, Burwood, Vic.

10 9 8 7 6 5 4 3 2 1

Foreword

From the wireless days of the 1950s, we now sit in front of a screen linked to the pulse and pace of the world via a thing called the Internet. From discs once played at variable speeds, we now let lasers guide us through the melodies of the day. Times they have been a-changin', and probably a mite too fast for everybody. And in amongst the push and rush of modern day living, we've left behind some damn fine things. Trodden right over some of the most talented people on earth in search of the next big thing. They've been buried and almost forgotten. So when an archaeologist comes along to shed some light where light has not shone for a long while, we should be thankful.

Recently we've marvelled at the music of the late twentieth century documented in the BBC's *Dancing in the Streets* series. We've also been able to flick through tomes like *The Wee Rock Discography* to remind us of the body of work from some of the all time greats. But the perspective has always come from an overseas angle. In this musical satellite known as Australia (where pop and rock music has always had a life of its own), it's time to stop, look and most importantly listen.

I'll always remember the time a friend passed on to me a cassette of The Loved Ones' *Magic Box*. He didn't say much, just that he thought I'd like it. As soon as I heard Gerry Humphreys' wail, with a force close to mach 10, I felt that tingle one gets when something new genuinely excites and thrills. This short-lived 1960s group from Melbourne was hardly new when its music crossed my path, but I wondered how such a treasure had remained so hidden from the public's view. To this day, radio gladly dishes out the hits and memories from overseas, and allows certifiable Australian gems like this to gather dust in vaults. That's cultural negligence.

In this encyclopedia (which shall never be more than a CD's reach away during my shifts), you can read what happened to The Loved Ones, but also find out where Spiderbait formed and how they've ridden the wave to platinum status. Do you know what Kids in the Kitchen (remember the annoyingly popular 'Change in Mood' from 1983?) has in common with the television series *Frontline*? And what was that Sydney band that sang about a cicada devouring a whole inner-west suburb? (It was Outline, by the way.)

What you're holding here is not endless lists of LP catalogue numbers and dates. What's before you is a sign of Australian times spread across four decades of musicians (over 800 bands and solo artists!). It's their history and it's your history as well. Rediscover how The Angels through to The Zoot got from A to Z, and how you travelled along with them. And if you've never travelled their route before, then buckle up and enjoy the ride because all the signposts you'll need are right before your eyes.

RICHARD KINGSMILL
TRIPLE J
18 DECEMBER 1997

Contents

Acknowledgements

There is an enormous number of people I need to thank for their help along the way. Firstly to my family for their continued support, and in particular to Mandy, James and Dylan for their love (and for putting up with my obsession). To my publisher at Allen & Unwin, Sophie Cunningham for believing in the project from the outset and for her continued support. To Colette Vella, my editor at Allen & Unwin, for her assistance throughout the production of the book. To Karen Stephens for taking the time and effort to read the first draft of the encyclopedia.

To the many musicians I have interviewed over the years or who provided me with information in other ways. They are (in alphabetical order): Russell Baresevic, Tony Biggs, Lindsay Bjerre, Kevin Borich, Philip Brophy (hey Phil, why didn't you get back to me? I gave up chasing you), Warwick Brown, Lindsay Brunsdon, Deborah Conway, Mick Conway, Bob Daisley (also his wife Vicki), Nic Dalton, Dannie Davidson, Leo De Castro, John Dowler, Andrew Duffield, Maurice Frawley, James Freud, Warwick Gilbert, Les Gock, Dave Graney, Roger Grierson, Kerrie Hickin, Ian Hill, Dave Hole, Mick Holmes, Simon Holmes, Rowland S. Howard, Shane Howard, Tony Joyce, Peter Jones, Spencer P. Jones, Jim Keays, Ron Keeley, Sean Kelly, Wally Kempton, Steve Kilbey, Maria Kozic, Ed Kuepper, Sleepy Greg Lawrie, Bill Leggett, Ian List, Mal Logan, Steve Lorkin, Lobby Loyde, Paul Lyneham, David McComb, Kerry McKenna, Nigel Macara, Rob MacKenzie, Phil Manning, Brenden Mason, Chris Masuak, Gil Matthews, Mario Millo, Clare Moore, Warren Morgan, Brett Myers, John Nolan, Paul O'Leary, Charlie Owen, Oxx (Simon Cooper), James Peirce, Ron Peno, Tex Perkins, Nick Philips, Bill Putt, Neil Rogers, Jo-Anne Roberts, Warren Rough, Mike Rudd, Ross Ryan, Kim Salmon, Harvey Saward, Chris Scheri, John 'Spider' Scholtens, Glen Sheldon, Brad Shepherd, Joel Silbersher, Scott Stephens, Iggy Stewart, Mia Stone, Dave Studdert, Mark Taylor, Matt Taylor, Deniz Tek, Dave Thomas, Doug Thomas, Billy Thorpe, Dave Tice, Andy Turner, Peter Tyrrell, Bill Walsh, Peter Wells, Davern 'Hoodoo' White, Dennis Wilson, Ross Wilson, Robyn Youlten, Gary Young and Rob Younger.

Thanks to the following for assistance in many ways (also in alphabetical order): J.J. Adams, Glenn A. Baker, Mark Burchett, Harry Butler (you are a legend Harry!), Dave Butterworth (Galactic Zoo, Triple R), Max Crawdaddy (Son Of Crawdaddy, Triple R), Tony Duke (Goldmine), Christie Eliezer, Steve Fraser (above and beyond the call of duty), Doug Garley, Stan Innes, Helen Jedwab, Richard Kingsmill (Triple J), Paul McHenry (keep up the good work Paul), Vicki Mau, the late Dean Mittelhauser and his wife Sue, Tony Mott for photos, Carmel Nunan (High Noon), Brian Priddy, Liz Reed, Bevan Roberts (Polyester), Neil Rogers (Australian Mood, Triple R), Peter Shillito, Gaynor Simpson and Leisel Woodward at *TV Week*, Chris Spencer, Glenn Terry, Dave Vodicka, Clinton Walker (thanks for all your encouragement and suggestions), Peter Wise and Terry Young.

Thanks to the following record company people: the Au-go-go crew (Bruce Milne, Greta Moon, Pat Monaghan, Dom Molomby, Scotti Henthorn, Richie Ramone and Shaun Bowman you guys have been great!), Alison Moore, Jenny Crowley, Sharon Ashworth, David Williams, Andrew McGee and Frank Falvo (Shock), Nic Dalton and Dave Chatfield (Half a Cow), Dave Laing (Dog Meat), Phil McDougall (Reactor), Jorge Munoz (Pink Flamingo), John Needham (Citadel/Kara Management), John Foy and Merran Morton (Red Eye), Libby Jones (ABC), David Peacock (Polydor), Marcus Seal (Mercury), Steve Cross (Infectious), Irene Saunders (BMG), Scott Murphy, Liza Birmingham and Jo Corbett (MDS), Shelley Thornley (TWA), Peter Billing (Universal), Michael Woods (Festival), Kathryn Taylor (Warner), Sarah Morgan (Mushroom), Trish Pavone (Sony/Epic), Katherine Markinson (Sony/Columbia).

IAN MCFARLANE
23 NOVEMBER 1997

Introduction

The Encyclopedia of Australian Rock and Pop is about the history of Australian rock'n'roll. It is not about the future. Like most people, I cannot predict the future, so what you have in front of you is 41 years of history. This book covers the period 1957 to 1997 in significant detail, with a Stop Press section to cover the major events of 1998. Of course, the Australian music industry is a living, breathing entity, and so it shall continue to unfold and evolve long after I have stopped writing and this book is on the shelf. If you approach *The Encyclopedia of Australian Rock and Pop* with that in mind, then you will be rewarded with a vibrant journey into our past.

As is the nature of any commercial enterprise, the Australian music industry is driven by new releases and the frantic search for the next chart-busting act. 'New product' is the great godhead of modern music. Scant regard is given to past events, as record companies and managers push successive generations of up-and-coming performers to the forefront at the expense of their predecessors. And, like most artists, rock musicians are driven by a desire to create, to produce new and more exciting music and to be accepted as successful in the eyes of fans and peers alike. Music keeps evolving at a rapid pace.

All of this is a way of asking you to delve now into our musical heritage and history. It is time to examine our musical roots in order to fully appreciate the present. Oddly enough, for the dedicated researcher like myself, the present informs the past in the future. My intention with this book was to take the historical perspective, and to do so I had to formulate the mind-set that the past was paramount. By and large, the British, Europeans and Americans love their music history; they positively bathe in its crystalline glow. Australians are a little less enthusiastic, more complacent about their past.

Aside from its entertainment value, music is an important social barometer. It informs our very existence. Local writers such as Glenn A. Baker, Clinton Walker, Stuart Coupe, Noel McGrath and a few others have always known the value of our musical heritage. Yet even the pioneering work of those writers has rarely benefited from a united front. This encyclopedia, then, is the most comprehensive and extensive examination of the history of Australian rock and pop published to date.

It took me a year to actually write *The Encyclopedia of Australian Rock and Pop*. Yet I have been a fan of Australian rock music for over 25 years, and have been writing about it since 1984. My basic premise was to include as many artists and bands who have issued records/CDs in the rock idiom (and its myriad forms) since 1957. It did not matter whether bands were perceived as mainstream or alternative, as long as they had made an impact either via chart success, on the live circuit or something less tangible like stirring an emotional response.

As to the time frame of 1957 to 1997, that was not simply an arbitrary decision. Popular music certainly existed in Australia pre-1957, but that year marked the dawning of the local rock'n'roll era. As a potent new musical force, rock'n'roll had been on the move in the USA since 'Rock Around the Clock' came out in 1954, but the devil's music took a while to filter down to Australia. 1957 was the year local heroes like Johnny O'Keefe entered the fray with debut records that defined an era. Likewise, 1997 was an appropriate year with which to draw this history to a close. One event that heralded the arrival of a new era in Australian rock'n'roll was the farewell Crowded House performance on the steps of the Sydney Opera House (24 November 1996) in front of an estimated crowd of 150 000 people.

I have excluded jazz artists (James Morrison, Vince Jones, John Sangster, Crossfire, Galapagos Duck, etc.) and country performers (Slim Dusty, Tex Morton, James Blundell, John Williamson, Reg Lindsay, etc.), not because their contribution to Australian music as a whole was unworthy of appraisal, but simply because they did not fall within the parameters set for the book. You will notice some country performers within these pages, but they were included by virtue of their grounding within the rock framework (e.g. Keith Glass, The Happening Thang).

I have refrained from covering New Zealand bands and performers, although there are exceptions (Dragon, Split Enz, La De Das, Max Merritt and Jenny Morris readily spring to mind). These acts are included because they worked and toured for significant periods of time within Australia, had their greatest successes in Australia and, to all intents and purposes, are accepted as an important part of the Australian rock industry. I would refer readers to John Dix's exhaustive and essential book, *Stranded in Paradise: New Zealand Rock'n'Roll 1956–1988*, for further examination on that subject (including the likes of Ray Columbus and the Invaders, Johnny Devlin, Dinah Lee, Mother Goose, Sharon O'Neill, etc.).

By virtue of its nature then, *The Encyclopedia of Australian Rock and Pop* is a reference work. While it does not function as a strict narrative history of Australian rock music, the encyclopedia's purpose is to create a detailed historical overview by way of individual entries. Likewise, the encyclopedia focuses on the musicians and bands that have made their mark on history, rather than the industry movers and shakers behind the scenes. There are also separate entries on the ABC-TV pop show *Countdown*, rock festivals, independent record labels and the Rock'n'Roll High School.

Noel McGrath issued his first *Australian Encyclopedia of Rock* in 1978. His rationale for inclusion was based on mainstream Top 40 chart success. A sound enough reason possibly, but many worthy bands were omitted as a consequence. The 1984 revised edition extended the basic premise, but even the inclusion of such 'independent' acts as The Moodists and Radio Birdman was not enough to provide a complete picture. This is not meant to denigrate McGrath's work; as a pioneering publication in the field, his 1984 edition still stands as a worthy reference guide.

Another important reference was *The Who's Who of Australian Rock* compiled by Chris Spencer, Zbig Nowra and Paul McHenry. The third edition of *The Who's Who of Australian Rock* featured a listing of almost every Australian rock music act (band, band member and solo performer) that ever existed. As such, the book simply listed band personnel and a range of record releases, with a brief description of the particular act. It is indeed a handy reference tool, yet it is a bit like reading the phone book (i.e. not much of a story, but a hell of a cast!). As a ready reckoner, it works well, although it is virtually impossible to fathom the history of a particular act by focusing on that entry per se. Certainly the book is compendious, but it does include many errors. As a starting point to glean surface information, *The Who's Who of Australian Rock* is fine, but any serious researcher into the history of Australian rock music must inevitably dig deeper. That called for an exhaustive process of cross-referring to establish the accuracy of facts and details.

As well as all the books listed in the References section, my research took me to the numerous local rock magazines that have been published over the years. I poured through the pages of every issue of *Go-Set*, *Juke*, *RAM (Rock Australia Magazine)*, *Rolling Stone*, *Roadrunner*, *Hot Metal*, *Vox* and *Juice* on which I could lay my hands. Fortunately, I have a significant collection of those magazines that I hoarded over the years. Then there were fanzines like *B-Side*, *DNA*, *Fast Forward*, *From the Vault*, *Lemon*, *Party Fears*, *Pulp*, *The Livin' End*, *Shakin' Street*, *Vicious Kitten*, *Australian Music Museum*, *It*, *Form Guide*, etc., all of which were an endless source of information. The street press, like Melbourne's *Beat Magazine* and *In-Press*, Sydney's *On the Street* and *Drum Media* also proved very handy. I consulted innumerable chart listings (the ARIA charts, the Kent charts, the *Juke* charts, the *RAM* 'Australia Now' alternative charts, various regional radio station charts, etc.) for chart placements. Until the early 1970s, there was no true national chart, so where possible I have indicated chart positions for the appropriate state/capital city.

I interviewed dozens of Australian musicians to pinpoint facts and detail (see full list in the Acknowledgements). I also visited many Internet Web sites. These sites were maintained variously by the bands themselves, record companies, fans or management. They were a good source of discographical detail. The sites I visited included The Angels, Christine Anu, The Badloves, The Birthday Party, Boxcar, The Cannanes, Nick Cave, Kate Ceberano, The Church, Clouds, Def FX, Hoodoo Gurus, Hunters & Collectors, Paul Kelly, Ed Kuepper, Mental as Anything, Midnight Oil, Kylie Minogue, Dannii Minogue, The Mark of Cain, Olivia Newton-John, The Plunderers, Pollyanna, Radio Birdman, Ratcat, Regurgitator, Archie Roach and Ruby Hunter, Severed Heads, silverchair, Spiderbait, Split Enz, Weddings, Parties, Anything and You Am I.

Also useful were all the record company biographies I've amassed that shed light on band histories. Record releases by local artists formed another important source of information. I trawled through my own extensive collection and that of my collector friends to confirm that elusive detail. I examined the credits, liner notes, fine print, song titles, track listings and catalogue numbers of an unbelievable number of records and CDs. I listened to Australian music day and night for months to gain deeper insight into the subject about which I was writing. In many cases, I re-acquainted myself with some fabulous material that I have always loved, as well as experiencing the rush of hearing new and exciting sounds.

Fortunately, having written about Australian music for so long, I was able to plunder my own thorough research and the articles that I have written for *Juke*, *Hot Metal*, *From the Vault*, *The Edge*, various album liner notes plus my own retro-zines *Prehistoric Sounds (Australian Independent Music, 1976–1990)*, *The Australian New Music Record Guide 1976–1980*, *Freedom Train (Australian Progressive Rock 1970–1976)* and *The Australian Progressive, Hard Rock and Blues Record Guide 1969–1977*. The search continues.

Australian Rock and Pop: A Brief History

The following section is not designed to be a detailed theoretical analysis of Australian rock and pop; rather it is a brief introduction brimming with all the signposts that mark 41 years of success and development.

Rock'n'roll was born in the mid-1950s, when American musicians combined Black rhythm and blues (R&B) with White country music to arrive at a new musical hybrid. While Elvis Presley, Bill Haley, Jerry Lee Lewis, Little Richard, Chuck Berry, Gene Vincent and Buddy Holly dominated the early days of American rock'n'roll, Australia boasted Johnny 'The Wild One' O'Keefe. J.O'K. is recognised as Australia's first genuine rock'n'roll star. Backed by The Dee Jays, and his own voracious will to succeed, J.O'K. made an enormous impact. He issued his debut single, '(You Hit the Wrong Note) Billygoat', in July 1957, to be followed by a run of 35 hits. In his wake came the likes of Alan Dale and the Houserockers, Col Joye and the Joy Boys, Warren Williams and the Squares, Dig Richards and the R'Jays, Johnny Rebb and the Rebels and Barry Stanton and the Belaires (all based in Sydney). Melbourne had Johnny Chester and the Chessmen, The Thunderbirds, Judy Cannon, The Planets, the Henri Bource All Stars, The Autocrats and Malcolm Arthur and the Knights.

As well as inspiring a generation of singers to believe in themselves, J.O'K. also helped pioneer rock music on national television when *Six O'Clock Rock* went to air in February 1959. *Bandstand* had actually premiered four months earlier, but initially was only broadcast in Sydney. *Bandstand* presented wholesome, family entertainment and pure pop confection. Its stable of regular stars included the likes of Bryan Davies, Noeleen Batley, Col Joye, Judy Stone, The Allen Brothers, The Delltones, The De Kroo Brothers, Patsy Ann Noble, Lucky Starr and Laurel Lea. The early 1960s were dominated by instrumental rock. Sydney bands like The Atlantics, The Denvermen and The Statesmen embraced the Californian surf music craze, while Melbourne's The Phantoms, The Strangers, The Breakaways and The Saxons took their cue from British and European instrumental combos like The Shadows, The Tornados and The Spotnicks.

Surf and instrumental music dominated local dances and charts from 1961 to 1963. After The Beatles burst dramatically on to the music scene in 1963, things were never quite the same. The Fab Four, and other British bands, helped usher in beat music which was essentially rock'n'roll played with renewed vigour and vocal harmonies. Australian bands learned fast, and by 1965 the country's foremost beat pop sensations included Billy Thorpe and the Aztecs, Ray Brown and the Whispers, The Easybeats, M.P.D. Limited and Bobby and Laurie. Solo stars like Ronnie Burns, Normie Rowe, Merv Benton and Lynne Randell also enjoyed chart success and its attendant fan hysteria. The Easybeats grabbed the international limelight when they took their classic working-class anthem 'Friday on My Mind' to #1 in Australia, #6 in the UK and #16 in the USA.

Just as The Beatles had inspired the beat music explosion, The Rolling Stones, The Pretty Things, The Animals and The Yardbirds sparked off the suburban R&B revival. Sydney boasted The Missing Links, The Creatures and The Throb, Brisbane had The Purple Hearts, Adelaide The Master's Apprentices and The Blues Syndicate, while Melbourne spawned The Loved Ones, The Rising Sons, The Spinning Wheels and schoolboy outfit The Pink Finks. While R&B's raucous energy generally remained the reserve of the dedicated aficionado (with a few exceptions), crisp, well-crafted pop music still dominated the charts. Bands of the calibre of The Twilights, Doug Parkinson In Focus, The Zoot, The Valentines, The Cherokees and The Flying Circus, plus solo performers like Johnny Farnham, Johnny Young and Russell Morris, all made their mark throughout the second half of the 1960s.

By 1969, the overseas advent of psychedelia, acid rock and progressive rock had heralded a new musical age. It was the age of Woodstock, Aquarius, and peace and love. While there were relatively few local bands playing in the psychedelic idiom (James Taylor Move, The Wild Cherries and The Haze spring to mind), Australia's burgeoning underground rock movement gave rise to the likes of Tully, Tamam Shud, Jeff St John's Copperwine and Levi Smith's Clefs in Sydney, and Spectrum, Chain and the newly reconstituted Billy Thorpe and the Aztecs in Melbourne. By the new decade, Company Caine, Sons of the Vegetal Mother, Fraternity, Healing Force, Blackfeather, Bakery, Pirana and Kahvas Jute had entered the fray. Local clubs and rock festival sites reverberated to the sound of heavy rock and unbounded guitar improvisations.

1971 was the year when Australia's heavies made the transition from underground demi-gods to chart-busters in their own right. Spectrum, Daddy Cool and Chain all enjoyed #1 hit singles, as well as producing adventurous and well-crafted albums. Daddy Cool's *Daddy Who? Daddy Cool!* sold 60 000 copies, which set a new yardstick by which Australian rock success could be measured. By 1972, Billy Thorpe was the unassailable monarch of Aussie rock, and his band The Aztecs the loudest and heaviest blues band of the day.

The Aztecs' legendary performance at the inaugural Sunbury festival spawned a best-selling album, while the autobiographical 'Most People I Know (Think that I'm Crazy)' became Thorpie's biggest hit since his mid-1960s heyday. The Aztecs, Chain, Carson, Coloured Balls and La De Das constituted a push towards the roots of rock, the blues, establishing a blueprint for the pub rock scene that was to follow. Furthermore, Sunbury 1972 was a defining moment in the history of Australian rock. It was the first time people realised it was not necessary to book overseas acts in order to pull 35 000 fans to a three-day outdoor event.

Thorpie's stranglehold on the local market was soon usurped by the brash and charismatic Skyhooks, whose groundbreaking debut album from 1974, *Living in the 70's*, sold in unprecedented quantities (saving the band's label Mushroom from financial collapse in the process). 1974 also saw the unveiling of the ABC-TV pop show *Countdown*. As well as Skyhooks, *Countdown* cultivated the growth and popularity of Sherbet, Hush, John Paul Young, Dragon, the Ted Mulry Gang, Ol'55, Supernaut, Marcia Hines, Jon English, Mark Holden and many other 1970s pop icons. By the late 1970s, AC/DC and the Little River Band had made their presence felt on the international market. AC/DC was the most significant and quintessentially Australian band to emerge during the *Countdown* era. Lead singer Bon Scott's death in February 1980 only spurred the band on to greater heights on the international stage.

Meanwhile, overseas bands like the Sex Pistols, The Damned, The Clash and The Ramones had created a musical revolution of a different kind: punk rock. While prototypal pioneers The Saints and Radio Birdman had been in operation since 1974, the 1977 punk explosion spawned The Thought Criminals, Rocks and X in Sydney, The Leftovers, The Fun Things and Razar in Brisbane, The Victims and The Scientists in Perth and The Boys Next Door, News, Negatives and Young Charlatans in Melbourne. While initially ignored at home, The Saints' howling, milestone debut single '(I'm) Stranded' (issued September 1976) was nominated Single of the Week by British rock paper *Sounds*. It has since been acknowledged as one of the greatest Australian songs of all-time.

While punk retained its grassroots following, the likes of Cold Chisel, Midnight Oil, The Angels, Rose Tattoo, Finch, The Hitmen, Kevin Borich Express and others were forging national identities on the thriving pub rock circuit. By the early 1980s, Split Enz, Jo Jo Zep and the Falcons, Mondo Rock, Australian Crawl, The Sports, Mental as Anything, Models and Moving Pictures came to the fore. Synth pop practitioners like Real Life and Pseudo Echo adapted the stylish precepts of UK bands Duran Duran and Human League and landed in the charts. Men at Work, Air Supply, INXS, Midnight Oil, Icehouse, The Angels and Divinyls turned their attentions overseas to varying degrees of success.

Men at Work and Air Supply each enjoyed #1 US hit singles. INXS became the biggest band to emerge from Australia, and lead singer Michael Hutchence our most adored rock star. Behind those international flagbearers, the likes of The Birthday Party, Hunters & Collectors, The Go-Betweens, The Triffids, Laughing Clowns, Scientists, The

Church, Hoodoo Gurus and Do Ré Mi created a sense of place and overseas identity on their own terms. At home, alternative bands as diverse as The Lime Spiders, Beasts of Bourbon, The Hard-Ons, Harem Scarem, The Screaming Tribesmen, Sacred Cowboys and Died Pretty worked the inner-city circuit for all its worth.

By 1986, Jimmy Barnes and John Farnham had become our most popular solo performers since J.O'K.'s reign in the late 1950s. Barnes scored six consecutive #1 albums. Farnham's *Whispering Jack* was the first Australian album to sell one million copies locally, while his #1 hit 'You're the Voice' reached #6 in the UK. Kylie Minogue and Crowded House likewise scored #1 hits at home and a string of record successes on the international market. Kate Ceberano and Paul Kelly kept the home fires burning with hit singles and critically acclaimed albums alike. Meanwhile, Nick Cave had become an icon and one of Australia's most respected musical ambassadors. Ed Kuepper and Dave Graney were not too far behind in the credibility stakes.

Daryl Braithwaite, James Reyne, Jenny Morris, Wendy Matthews, Craig McLachlan and Peter Andre emerged as our brightest pop stars during the late 1980s and early 1990s. Sydney bands Ratcat and The Hummingbirds became the first local outfits to bridge the gap between the alternative rock scene and the mainstream charts. With an entertaining blend of fuzz-pop and comic book aesthetics, Ratcat sent both the *Tingles* EP and single 'That Ain't Bad' to the national #1 spot. Very soon, one-time alternative heroes like The Cruel Sea, Clouds, Died Pretty, You Am I, Spiderbait, Tumbleweed and Regurgitator followed Ratcat into the national charts with a combination of incendiary guitar attack and nonchalant coolness.

In 1991, Yothu Yindi became the first Aboriginal band to taste mainstream success when the epochal 'Treaty' (Filthy Lucre mix) hit #11 nationally. The 1990s also saw the advent of the musical subculture known as grunge (as epitomised by Nirvana, Soundgarden, etc.) which found its most prominent local manifestation in silverchair. Following their Australian success, the three Newcastle lads that made up silverchair managed to achieve what many British bands first did in the 1960s: sell American music back to the Americans. In silverchair's wake, bands as diverse as Powderfinger, Grinspoon, Automatic, Ammonia and The Superjesus began to look overseas.

The most phenomenal success story of the 1990s, however, has been reserved for Brisbane duo Savage Garden, who won an unprecedented ten Australian Record Industry Association (ARIA) Awards, sold 600 000 copies of their debut album at home and scored a #1 US hit with 'Truly, Madly, Deeply'. On a sadder note, Michael Hutchence died on 22 November 1997, an apparent suicide.

How to Use this Book

The Encyclopedia of Australian Rock and Pop is presented in an A to Z format. You can either start reading at A and proceed through to Z, or simply thumb though each letter for your favourite groups and solo artists. Within the book, solo artists are listed under their surnames (e.g. John Farnham) and groups under group name (e.g. Radio Birdman). Each heading appears in bold type. The heading is followed by the year of formation (for groups), the general style to which they conform (pop, rock, punk, etc.) and then the original line-up for each group. The style designation in some cases may be contentious, and not everyone will agree with the description. In this case, the function of labelling is to establish a frame of reference within the wider system of which that artist is a part.

The biography beneath the heading outlines the career of the artist/group. Each entry is formulaic to some extent, giving a brief career overview, band personnel, line-up changes, records released, significant events and major achievements. Record release dates (as far as can be determined) and Top 40 chart placements (where applicable) are usually given in brackets following the title. At the end of each entry, there is an album discography, giving the album title and then, in brackets, the record label and year of release: e.g. *Whispering Jack* (Wheatley/BMG, 1986). For the purposes of this book, I refer to both vinyl LPs and CDs as albums. Albums listed in the discographies are not necessarily currently available.

Song titles appear within single inverted commas (e.g. 'Born Out of Time'), and album, book and film titles are in italics (e.g. *Diesel and Dust*; *For The Term of His Natural Life*; *Strictly Ballroom*). Where appropriate, 7-inch vinyl singles, Compact Disc singles (CD singles), 7-inch vinyl extended play (EP) records, 12-inch vinyl EP records and compact disc extended plays (CD EPs) are detailed separately. In most cases, both the A-sides and B-sides of 7-inch vinyl singles are given, with the two sides separated by a slash (e.g. 'Eagle Rock'/'Bom Bom'). For CD singles, only the main song title is usually given. Likewise for vinyl EPs and CD EPs, only the title appears, although other track details may be listed.

When another Australian artist is mentioned within the main text of a particular entry, and that artist also has a separate entry, the name appears in bold type for cross-referencing purposes. For example, under the entry for John Farnham the following sentence appears: In February 1982, Farnham replaced **Glenn Shorrock** in **Little River Band**. The reference may seem obscure in some instances, but by flicking to the appropriate entry you can make the connection.

It was not possible to include every Australian band and artist who has issued a record over the last 41 years (I will leave that to the compilers of the *Who's Who of Australian Rock*). Those unhappy with the exclusion of Johnny Dribble and the Wet Rocks will need to look elsewhere. Likewise, there have been numerous up and coming bands and artists that have emerged in the last year or so (e.g. The Onyas, Jebediah, Brown Hornet, Monique Brumby, Nikka Costa, Leonardo's Bride, etc.) that have yet to make a significant impact (either real or projected) and so therefore have not been included.

Bands, solo artists, managers, record companies and agents please note: if you believe there should be an entry in possible future editions of this book, please send all relevant band details to the author. I require the usual promotional folios—that is, a complete biography (formation, personnel, line-up changes, tour supports, achievements), discography, photos and all CD releases. I need to be kept informed!

Now it is time to start reading about your favourite bands. Enjoy! In the meantime, fact-checkers, well-wishers and others, you are invited to write to the author with praise, disagreements, additions, omissions and corrections (be polite about it please!).

Address all correspondence to:
Ian McFarlane
Stroll On Enterprises
PO Box 2250
Sunbury 3429
Victoria Australia

A

Chris Abrahams

Style: *Jazz, blues*

As one of the most respected musicians in Australia, Chris Abrahams regularly featured on 'Best Keyboard Player' listings in *Rolling Stone*. He was voted Best Keyboard Player for 1990. Abrahams spent time with The Benders, The Sparklers, **Peter Blakeley** and The Resurrection, The Necks, **Jackie Orszaczky** and The Godmothers and Mephisto Waltz (with **Ed Kuepper**).

The Benders were a popular Sydney jazz combo comprising Abrahams (keyboards), Dale Barlow (sax), Jason Morphett (sax), Lloyd Swanton (bass) and Louis Burdett (drums). They recorded three albums for the Hot label, *E* (1983), *False Laughter* (1984) and *Distance* (1985). Dance-pop band The Sparklers comprised Abrahams, Melanie Oxley (vocals; ex-Sweet Nothings), Peter Oxley (bass; ex-**Sunnyboys**), Bill Bilson (drums; ex-**Sunnyboys**), Gerard Corben (guitar; ex-**Lime Spiders**) and Ernie Finch (guitar).

The Sparklers issued one single on the Phantom label, 'Overworking'/'Baby Baby' (October 1986) and one on the Mighty Boy label, 'So Often Dreaming'/'Can't Take Anymore' (January 1987), before Abrahams left to be replaced by Phil Grove. The band continued on and issued the Leszek Karski-produced album *Persuasion* (1988) on Mighty Boy before breaking up in 1989. The Necks comprised Abrahams, Lloyd Swanton and Tony Buck (drums), and issued several albums of abstract, improvised, jazzy mood music, including *Sex* (1990) and *Next* (1991) on jazz label Spiral Scratch, and *Aquatic* (1994) and *Silent Night* (1997) on the Fish of Milk label.

Abrahams appeared as a session player on records by **Laughing Clowns**, **The Triffids**, **Ed Kuepper**, **The Lime Spiders** and **Stephen Cummings**, plus the soundtrack albums to television shows *Illusion* and *Dancing Daze* (both 1986). In 1989 he formed a partnership with ex-Sparklers singer Melanie Oxley which resulted in the 12-inch EP 'Resisting Calm' for Spiral Scratch. The duo issued two moody, emotive soul/pop albums, *Welcome To Violet* and *Coal*, on the Remote label. In 1993, Abrahams toured as keyboard player for **Midnight Oil** on the Earth and Sun and Moon world tour.

Solo albums: *Piano* (Hot, 1985), *Walk* (Hot, 1987); ***Chris Abrahams and Melanie Oxley albums:*** *Welcome To Violet* (Remote/MDS, 1992), *Coal* (Remote/MDS, 1994); ***Benders albums:*** *E* (Hot, 1983), *False Laughter* (Hot, 1984), *Distance* (Hot, 1985); ***Necks albums:*** *Sex* (Spiral Scratch, 1990), *Aquatic* (Fish of Milk, 1994), *Silent Night* (Fish of Milk, 1997).

Abramelin

Formed: *1993*
Style: *Death metal*
1991 line-up as Acheron: *Simon Dower (vocals), David Abbott (guitars), Tim Aldridge (guitars), Justin Wornes (bass), Jason Dutton (drums)*

Melbourne band Abramelin started life as Acheron in 1988. The band's dark, heavy sound owed much to European and American death metal groups such as Bathory, Entombed, Obituary, Therion, Immolation and General Surgery. Acheron was part of a small Melbourne death/grindcore/thrash metal scene that included Necrotomy, Damnatory, Sanctum, Toxaemia, Disembowelment, Hecatomb and Crepitus.

By 1991, only founder member David Abbott remained from the original line-up. Acheron issued a 7-inch single 'Deprived of Afterlife'/'Death of Millions' on French label Corpse Grinder Records. Mark Schilby replaced Abbott and Ewan Harriott replaced Jason Dutton in 1993, and Acheron became Abramelin to avoid confusion with an overseas band which had the same name. After that, Abramelin issued the CD EP *Transgression From Acheron* (1994) and the full-length album *Abramelin* (1995), as well as supporting overseas visitors Napalm Death (1995), Paradise Lost and Cathedral (March 1996) on their respective Australian tours. Abramelin's sound had taken on a sludge-like heaviness only matched by the likes of Brisbane band Misery.

Album: *Abramelin* (Thrust/Shock, 1995).

Absent Friends

Formed: *1989*
Style: *R&B, soul, funk*
Original line-up: *Sean Kelly (vocals, guitar; ex-***Models***),* **Wendy Matthews** *(vocals), Garry Gary Beers (bass; from* **INXS**), Nicole Ainslee (keyboards), Andrew Duffield (keyboards; ex-**Models***), James Valentine (sax; ex-***Models***), Michael King (guitar, ex-Danglin' Brothers,* **Jimmy Barnes** *Band), John MacKay (drums; ex-***Machinations***)*

Following the break-up of **Models** in 1988 and a short-lived solo career that resulted in the 'Thank You, Goodnight'/'Whatever You Say' single for the rooArt label (March 1989), Sean Kelly formed an ad-hoc band called Sean Kelly and His Absent Friends. Initially the floating line-up, as listed above, assembled for touring purposes in May 1989. An early showcase gig was as one of the supports to **Crowded House** at the Rock for Land Rights concert (July).

By the end of the year, Absent Friends had become a more permanent affair and issued the 'Hallelujah'/'Come Clean' single on rooArt. The players featured on that record were Kelly, Beers, Matthews, Duffield, MacKay, King, Ainslie and Valentine, plus guests Roger Mason (keyboards; ex-**Models**) and **INXS** drummer Jon Farriss. 1990 proved to be Absent Friends' most successful year with the release of the best-selling *Here's Looking Up Your Address* album (May) and three singles, 'Hullabaloo' (April), 'I Don't Wanna Be with Nobody But You' (June) and 'Harmony' (August). The soul-stirring cover of Eddie Floyd's 'I Don't Wanna Be With Nobody But You' featured **Wendy Matthews** on lead vocals and **Peter Blakeley** on background vocals. It reached #1 on the national singles chart (July 1990) and established the band as a headlining concert attraction across Australia.

When Absent Friends supported **INXS** on their 1990 European tour, bassist Ron Francois (ex-**Eurogliders**) replaced Garry Beers, and Geoff Stapleton (keyboards; ex-**Aliens**, **GANGgajang**) joined to fill in for the departing Duffield, Ainslie and Valentine. The band completed a successful 1990 by winning Best Single ('I Don't Wanna Be with Nobody But You') at the Australian Record Industry Association (ARIA) Awards. Absent Friends' last record was the live EP 'Networking' (1991), after which they broke up. Kelly and Stapleton formed **The Dukes** and **Wendy Matthews** pursued a highly successful solo career.

Album: *Here's Looking Up Your Address* (rooArt/PolyGram, 1990)

AC/DC

Formed: *1973*
Style: *Hard rock*
Original line-up: *Dave Evans (vocals), Malcolm Young (rhythm guitar, backing vocals; ex-Velvet Underground), Angus Young (lead guitar; ex-Tantrum), Larry Van Kriedt (bass), Colin Burgess (drums; ex-***Master's Apprentices***)*

As one of Australia's best known rock exports, AC/DC has quite a reputation to uphold. With worldwide album sales in the multi-millions and superstar status on the international hard music circuit, AC/DC's place in rock history is well assured. The band even overcame the potentially disastrous death of original lead singer Bon Scott in 1980 to surpass their previous achievements.

The guitar-packing Young siblings, Malcolm and Angus (both born in Glasgow, Scotland and younger brothers of ex-**Easybeats'** George Young), formed AC/DC in Sydney at the end of 1973. Older sister Margaret named the band after a warning sign she noticed on her sewing machine. She also suggested that Angus, who was 17 at the time, wear a school uniform on stage. Legend has it that AC/DC made its live debut on 31 December 1973 at Chequers discotheque in Sydney. The band's set comprised covers of Rolling Stones, Chuck Berry and Beatles songs, plus a smattering of old blues standards and tentative originals.

AC/DC

By April 1974, AC/DC comprised Malcolm, Angus, Evans, Rob Bailey (bass; ex-Natural Gas) and Peter Clack (who joined after Ron Carpenter had a short stint on drums). The new line-up issued 'Can I Sit Next to You Girl?'/'Rockin' in the Parlour' on Albert (July) and supported Lou Reed on his Rock'n'Roll Animal tour of Australia (August). AC/DC's original image was bisexual glam rock. With the departure of Dave Evans and the arrival of Ronald 'Bon' Scott (ex-Spektors, **Valentines**, **Fraternity**) in September 1974, AC/DC's working-class style, boogie-rock sound and earthy humour fell into place. Phil Rudd (drums; ex-**Buster Brown**) also joined in January 1975 (replacing Clack) and Malcolm switched to bass (replacing Bailey) until a suitable replacement could be found. Mark Evans (bass) completed the first classic AC/DC line-up when he joined in March 1975. During those formative stages, the redoubtable production team of Vanda and Young at Albert Productions guided the band and went on to oversee the first six albums.

AC/DC's initial achievement was to take the raw energy of Aussie pub rock, extend its basic guidelines, serve it up to a teenybop ***Countdown*** audience and still reap the benefits of the live circuit by packing out the pubs. The first evidence of the new AC/DC came with a thumping reworking of the Big Joe Williams blues standard 'Baby Please Don't Go'/'Love Song' (#10 in March 1975) and the Young–Scott–Young-penned 'High Voltage'/'Soul Stripper' (#6 in July). The albums *High Voltage* (March 1975) and *TNT* (December) also charted nationally (reaching #7 and #2 respectively).

When stacked up against the melodious pop of **Sherbet** and the glitter/glam of **Skyhooks** and **Hush**, AC/DC's brand of hard rock was rugged, outrageous and irrepressible. AC/DC were the bad boys, the brats who were not afraid to whoop it up a little on the ***Countdown*** stage. Bon Scott was the crude, lewd and tattooed larrikin who oozed a real macho sensuality. Angus was the manic guitarist in the schoolboy uniform who grabbed the girls' attention. AC/DC was not doing anything original at that stage (mostly recycling boogie-blues riffs and Chuck Berry licks at high volume) but it was the *way* they did it that got fans excited.

In 1976 AC/DC issued four classic hit singles 'It's a Long Way to the Top (If You Wanna Rock'n'Roll)'/'Can I Sit Next to You Girl?' (#5 in January), 'TNT'/'I'm a Rocker' (#11 in March), 'Jailbreak'/'Fling Thing' (#5 in June) and 'Dirty Deeds Done Dirt Cheap'/'R.I.P. (Rock In Peace)' (#21 in October). The band was huge in Australia, and Atlantic Records showed great foresight by signing AC/DC to an international deal. AC/DC left Australia in April 1976 bound for the UK, and Atlantic (UK) issued the *High Voltage* album (a combination of the first two Australian albums) in May. 'It's a Long Way to the Top (If You Wanna Rock'n'Roll)'/'Can I Sit Next to You Girl?' also appeared as the band's debut UK single in April.

The British rock press initially dubbed AC/DC street punks (and to a certain degree they were), but they earned a reputation as a hard-working rock band with a series of uncompromising, high-energy performances across the UK and Europe (including tour supports to Ritchie Blackmore's Rainbow and Black Sabbath). Rarely had audiences encountered the likes of leering, bare-chested madman Bon Scott and the hyperkinetic, blues guitar pyrotechnics of Angus Young.

The *Dirty Deeds Done Dirt Cheap* album (Australian #4 in October 1976) had been thrown together between heavy touring. Overall it lacked the bite and melodrama of *TNT*, although the manic 'Problem Child', the rough'n'raw 'Jailbreak' and the slow and insinuating 'Ride On' were the equal of any in the AC/DC canon. The second single from *Dirty Deeds*, 'Love At First Feel'/'Problem Child', reached #31 in February 1977.

Englishman Cliff Williams (ex-Home, Bandit) replaced Mark Evans in April 1977, and AC/DC set their sights on cracking the USA. Between 1977 and 1979 the band issued a series of phenomenal hard rock classics: *Let There Be Rock* (Australian #20 in May 1977; UK #17), *Powerage* (UK #26 in May 1978), the live *If You Want Blood, You've Got It* (UK #13 in October) and *Highway to Hell* (Australian #13 in October 1979; UK #8). Australian singles included 'Dog Eat Dog'/'Carry Me Home' (March 1977), 'Let There be Rock'/'Let There be Rock Part Two' (May), 'Rock'n'Roll Damnation'/'Cold Hearted Man' (UK #24 in June 1978), 'Whole Lotta Rosie'/'Dog Eat Dog' (live) (November) and 'Highway to Hell'/'If You Want Blood' (Australian #24 in October 1979).

Scott made 'Let There be Rock' his great personal statement; he appeared as a priest in the film clip, grinning lasciviously and preaching the rock'n'roll bible. In 1981, UK headbangers' bible *Kerrang!* voted 'Whole Lotta Rosie' the greatest heavy metal track of all time. In 1990, readers of UK magazine *Raw* voted 'Whole Lotta Rosie' as the greatest-ever rock riff.

Highway to Hell (produced by Robert 'Mutt' Lange) became AC/DC's breakthrough album in the USA (#17 in October 1979). Just as supergroup status loomed, tragedy struck on 19 February 1980 when Bon Scott died following a night of heavy drinking. He was found dead in a car with the official verdict being 'Acute alcoholic poisoning—Death by Misadventure'. The rest of the band decided to continue and recruited former Geordie lung-screamer Brian Johnson as Bon's replacement. AC/DC recorded a new album with Lange at Compass Point Studios, Nassau, Bahamas, and on release in July 1980 *Back in Black* became an immediate success. It reached #2 in Australia, #1 in the UK and #4 in the USA and remains one of the greatest rock albums ever issued.

It spawned three hit singles, 'You Shook Me All Night Long'/'What Do You Do For Money Honey' (Australian #8 in September 1980; UK #38; USA #35), 'Rock'n'Roll Ain't Noise Pollution'/'Hell's Bells' (Australian #7 in December 1980; UK #15) and 'Back in Black'/'What Do You Do for Money Honey' (USA only; #37 in March 1981). To date, *Back in Black* has sold over ten million copies, making it, alongside Def Leppard's *Hysteria* and Metallica's *Metallica*, one of the best-selling heavy metal albums of all time.

For Those About to Rock (We Salute You) (Australian #3 in December 1981; UK #3; USA #1) was another monster seller. It produced two singles, 'Let's Get It Up'/'Snowballed' (USA #44 in February 1982) and 'For Those About to Rock (We Salute You)'/'Let There Be Rock' (live) (UK #15 in June). *Flick of the Switch* (Australian #3 in September 1983, UK #4; USA #15) continued the formula with little variation. It yielded the singles 'Nervous Shakedown'/'Brain Shake' (September 1983), 'Flick Of The Switch'/'Badlands' (November) and 'Guns For Hire'/'Landslide' (March 1984).

Simon Wright (ex-Tytan) replaced Phil Rudd in 1984 and the new line-up issued *Fly on the Wall* (Australian #1; UK #7 in August 1985; USA #32), *Who Made Who* (*Maximum Overdrive* soundtrack; Australian #3, UK #11 in June 1986; USA #33) and *Blow Up Your Video* (Australian #1, UK #2 in March 1988; USA #12). 'Who Made Who'/'Guns For Hire' (live) (May 1986) and 'Heatseeker'/'Go Zone' (from *Blow Up Your Video*) (January 1988) were #16 and #12 UK hit singles respectively; otherwise this was a period of little advancement. *Fly on the Wall* included the singles 'Danger'/'Hell or High Water' (June 1985) and 'Shake Your Foundations'/'Stand Up' (January 1986). 'That's The Way I Wanna Rock'n'Roll'/'Kissin' Dynamite' (March 1988) was also lifted from *Blow Up Your Video*. 'Heatseeker' peaked at #5 in Australia.

During May 1988, cousin Steve Young (ex-Starfighters) deputised on tour for the briefly 'indisposed' Malcolm Young. In 1989, bald-headed drummer Chris Slade (ex-Gary Moore Band, Manfred Mann's Earth Band, The Firm) replaced Wright, who joined Dio. These changes ushered in a revival in the band's fortunes.

The albums *The Razor's Edge* (Australian #1, UK #4 in February 1991; USA #2), *Live* (Australian #1, UK #5 in November 1992; USA #15) and *Ballbreaker* (Australian #1, UK #6 in October 1995; USA #4) returned AC/DC to the charts in a big way. Likewise, the singles 'Thunderstruck'/'Fire Your Guns' (Australian #10; UK #13 in October 1990), 'Moneytalks'/'Mistress for Christmas' (UK #36; USA #23 in December), 'Are You Ready'/'Got You by the Balls' (UK #34 in April 1991), 'Highway to Hell' (live)/'Hell's Bells' (UK #14 in November 1992), 'Big Gun'/'Back in Black' (live) (from the Arnold Schwarzenegger film *The Last Action Hero*) (UK #23 in July 1993; USA #35) and 'Hard as a Rock'/'Caught with Your Pants Down' (UK #33 in November 1995) sold well. In 1996, Phil Rudd returned to the AC/DC drum stool after an absence of 12 years. The *1996 'Ballbreaker' Australian Tour* EP reached #49 on the national chart during September. EMI issued the five-CD box set *Bonfire* in October 1997. It contained *Back in Black*, *Live from the Atlantic Studios*, the two-album set *Let There Be Rock the Movie: Live in Paris* and the rarities set *Volts*.

To date, AC/DC's international standing has remained at a premium, with sell-out tours being the order of the day. AC/DC has toured Australia four times since Scott's death (1981, 1988, 1991, 1996), appearing with increasingly spectacular stage shows on each occasion. The sonic, frontal assault of an AC/DC concert was guaranteed to provide prime entertainment and value for money. On the international circuit, AC/DC had the distinction of headlining the UK's massive Donington Monsters of Rock Festival more times than any other band (three), as well as playing to 347 000 people at the 1985 Rock in Rio festival. Equally significant, but more tragic was the fact that, in January 1991, three youths were crushed to death at an AC/DC concert in Salt Lake City, USA.

Albums: *High Voltage* (Albert/CBS, 1975), *TNT* (Albert/CBS, 1975), *Dirty Deeds Done Dirt Cheap* (Albert/CBS, 1976), *Let There Be Rock* (Albert/CBS, 1977), *Powerage* (Albert/EMI 1978), *If You Want Blood, You've Got It* (Albert/EMI, 1978), *Highway to Hell* (Albert/EMI, 1979), *Back in Black* (Albert/EMI, 1980), *Box Set* (*High Voltage* to *Highway to Hell*, except *If You Want Blood*) (Albert/EMI, 1981), *For Those About to Rock (We Salute You)* (Albert/EMI, 1981), *Flick of the Switch* (Albert/EMI, 1983), *Fly on the Wall* (Albert/EMI, 1985), *Who Made Who* (*Maximum Overdrive* soundtrack, Albert/EMI, 1986), *Box Set II* (*Back in Black* to *Who Made Who*) (Albert/EMI, 1987), *Blow Up Your Video* (Albert/EMI, 1988), *The*

Razor's Edge (Albert/EMI, 1990), *Live* (Albert/EMI, 1992), *Ballbreaker* (Albert/EMI, 1995), *Bonfire* (box set, Albert/EMI, 1997).

Further reading: *Highway to Hell: The Life & Times of AC/DC Legend Bon Scott* by Clinton Walker (Sun/Pan Macmillan, 1994).

Geoff Achison

Style: *Blues*

Alongside **Phil Manning** and **Dave Hole**, guitarist Geoff Achison has been hailed as one of the finest blues players in Australia. He has been the recipient of several notable awards, including runner-up in the 1994 Australian Blues Performer of the Year contest and winner the following year, plus the Albert King Award for Most Promising Guitarist at the 1995 USA International Blues Competition.

Achison took his inspiration from Eric Clapton, Freddy King and Albert Collins. He played in Bob Sedergreen's Bluesbusters in the late 1980s, before forming his own band, Just Blues. He played with **Dutch Tilders** and The Blues Club for four years. He formed his own Geoff Achison Band with Keith Nolan (keyboards), John Arthur (bass) and Steve Nicel (drums) in 1993 in order to pursue a solo career. Achison issued several fine albums that combined elements of Joe Cocker and Little Feat with Achison's love for traditional blues. He also collaborated with Adrian Keating on the album *Classically Blue*. Mal Logan (keyboards; ex-**Healing Force**, **Renée Geyer** Band) joined the Geoff Achison Band in March 1996 and Bob Hornbuckle replaced Arthur on bass. Achison broke the band up in 1997 and travelled to the UK. Prior to leaving Australia, Achison issued a solo acoustic blues album, *Mystery Train*.

Albums: *Big Machine* (Jupiter II/Larrikin, 1994), *Genevieve* (Jupiter II/Larrikin, 1995), *Classically Blue* (with Adrian Keating, 1996), *Mystery Train* (Newmarket, 1997).

Acuff's Rose

Formed: *1991*
Style: *Country rock*
Original line-up: *Jeff Williams (vocals, guitar), Kay-Louise Patterson (keyboards, vocals), Martin Lewis (guitar), Jack Coleman (bass), James Hurst (drums)*

This Melbourne band's clean, laid-back country style was heard to good advantage on the EP *Long Past Dawn* (July 1992) and the album *Never Comin' Down* (June 1993). Ex-**Triffids** David McComb, Robert McComb and Graham Lee, plus Charlie Owen and **Chris Wilson**, augmented the band in the studio for *Never Comin' Down*. Acuff's Rose derived its name from legendary US country singer Roy Acuff ('Great Speckled Bird'). Although Acuff did not sing about a rose, he formed a music publishing partnership with songwriter Fred Rose. In 1995, Bruce Kane (ex-**Honeymoon in Green**, Dave Last's Boy Kings) joined on drums. The second Acuff's Rose album, *Son of the North Wind*, came out in November 1995. That time, Spencer P. Jones and Coral Snakes' Robin Casinader featured as guest players.

Albums: *Never Comin' Down* (Torn & Frayed/Shock, 1993), *Son of the North Wind* (Torn & Frayed/Shock, 1995).

Billy Adams

Style: *Pop*

Bouffant-haired singer Billy Adams (real name William Tregonning) first came to attention with Melbourne band The Checkmates whom he fronted between 1961 and 1963. At various times The Checkmates comprised Adams, Jeff Bedford (guitar), Tony Daly (guitar), Ian Allen (bass), Graham Bloomfield (sax), Roger Scott (sax), Ron Chapman (drums) and Eddie Chappell (drums). After Adams went solo, Ron Fletcher joined as lead singer. Adams went solo at the end of 1963, becoming a regular on the television pop show *The Go!! Show*. He recorded five pop singles for the Go!! label: 'Slow Down Sally'/'Alone' (1965), 'I Think I'm Gonna Kill Myself'/'Shirley Lee' (1965), 'Lookin' for Love'/'All Time Loser' (1966), 'Come Dance with Me'/'Dancing in Your Eyes' (1966) and 'Change Your Mind'/'I Fall to You' (1966), of which only 'Slow Down Sally' charted.

Adderley Smith Blues Band

Formed: *1964*
Style: *Blues*

Alongside Brisbane's **Bay City Union** and Sydney's **The Foreday Riders**, Melbourne's Adderley Smith Blues Band is recognised as one of the first authentic blues bands Australia ever produced. Blues enthusiasts Kerryn Tolhurst (guitar) and Mark Dindas (piano) formed the band, taking their inspiration from the Chicago blues masters like Muddy Waters, Jimmy Rogers, Junior Wells, Willie Dixon, Sonny Boy Williamson and Howlin' Wolf.

The line-up shifted constantly. **Broderick Smith**

(vocals, harp) joined in 1966, and over the years other members included Gary Collier (guitar), Fat Fred Bond (vocals), Joe Camilleri (vocals, sax), John O'Brien (vocals), Colin Graham (bass; future Australian Ballet lighting director), Ron Issac (drums), Paul Lever (vocals, harp) and Doug Stirling (bass). The band played regularly at dances and blues clubs around Melbourne. Smith and Tolhurst were called up for the army draft in 1968, but Tolhurst kept a line-up (with drummer Noel Herridge and bassist Mark Kozuch) going until 1970. Although the Adderley Smith Blues Band did not release any records, demo and live recordings are known to exist. Tolhurst and Smith teamed up again in 1973 with **The Dingoes**.

Addictive

Formed: *1988*
Style: *Thrash metal*
Original line-up: *Greg Smith (bass, vocals), Joe Buttigiey (guitar), Mick Sultana (guitar), Matt Coffey (drums)*

Addictive was part of the burgeoning Sydney thrash metal scene popularised by **Mortal Sin** and Slaughter Lord. The band's other Sydney contemporaries included **Massive Appendage**, **Massappeal**, **Ya Ya Choral**, Fester Fanatics, Enticer, Death Mission, Persecution and Precursor. In November 1989, Addictive issued the album *Pity of Man* on the Survival label. It revealed the band's heavily Metallica/Flotsam & Jetsam/Sacred Reich-influenced style. In 1990, Steve Moore (ex-Enticer) replaced Coffey and the band commenced work on its second album with producer Bob Daisley (ex-**Kahvas Jute**, Chicken Shack, Blackmore's Rainbow, Ozzy Osbourne Blizzard of Ozz). The album's release was held up for over a year when the master tapes mysteriously went missing. *Kick 'em Hard* eventually appeared in February 1993, by which time Addictive had run out of steam.

Albums: *Pity of Man* (Survival, 1989), *Kick 'em Hard* (Survival 1993).

Aesop's Fables

Formed: *1968*
Style: *Pop*
Original line-up: *Cheryl Blake (vocals), Jimmy Doyle (guitar; ex-Telstars), Gary Moberley (organ; ex-Ramrods), Michael Lawler (bass), Russell Dunlop (drums)*

Aesop's Fables was just one of a number of polished Sydney pop bands formed around 1968/1969 (**New Dream**, **The Affair**, The Clik, etc.). Initially the band played cover material (such as The 5th Dimension) before writing originals.

Gary Moberley's previous band, The Ramrods, is remembered for being managed by future Australian Prime Minister Paul Keating. Barry Connors (vocals), Barry Brady (guitar), Ken Kramer (bass) and Quentin Chadwick (drums) completed The Ramrods' line-up. The band issued two singles on EMI/Parlophone, 'Since I Don't Have You' (1966) and 'You Shoulda Held On'/'Get Back' (1966). In 1988, reissue specialists Raven combined the singles on the 12-inch EP *Enfield Energy*.

In 1969, Aesop's Fables were runners-up in the Hoadley's Battle of the Sounds competition, but split up without recording. In February 1970, Moberley and Russell Dunlop revived the band (initially as the New Aesop's Fables) with Brenda Glover (ex-Jet Set) replacing Cheryl Blake, Brian Holloway (guitar; ex-Dream, Image) replacing Jimmy Doyle and Owen Booth (bass) replacing Michael Lawler. Melbourne mainstay Les Stacpool (ex-**Chessmen**, **Merv Benton** and The Tamlas, **Levi Smith's Clefs**, **Rockwell T. James** and The Rhythm Aces, Browns, **Doug Parkinson** In Focus, Genesis) replaced Holloway after two months. Holloway joined **Ronnie Charles** (ex-**Groop**) in Captain Australia and the Honky Tonk, with whom he travelled overseas.

Glover was a blues belter in the vein of **Wendy Saddington**, **Bobbi Marchini** and **Alison McCallum**, and helped steer the band down a more rock-oriented path. Charlie Tumahai (bass; ex-Multiple Balloon) replaced Booth in mid-1970, but the band had broken up by October. Aesop's Fables' sole single, 'Little Yellow Pills'/'Sandman', came out on the Generation label in February 1971. 'Little Yellow Pills' was a Jackie Lomax cover; 'Sandman' was a Stacpool original. A month later, Brenda Glover issued a solo single on the Violet's Holiday label: The Rolling Stones' 'Jumpin' Jack Flash'/ 'Fanny Adams'.

With the break-up of Aesop's Fables, Stacpool and Tumahai made plans for a new band, but Tumahai joined Nova Express briefly before moving on to **Healing Force**. Stacpool issued a solo single on Generation in November 1971, Neil Young's 'Down by the River'/'Don't Go Away'. He went on to join Sasha, **Country Radio**, Gulliver's Travels, Living Legends and The Allstars (among many others). He also became an in-demand session player. Glover joined The John Rupert Group and Moberley joined Holloway in The Honky Tonk.

The Affair

Formed: *1967*
Style: *Pop*
Original line-up: *Gino Cunnico (vocals), Bruce Maddon (keyboards), James Kelly (guitar), Paul 'Sheepdog' Wheeler (bass), Tony Bolton (drums)*

Sydney band The Affair was originally known as The Gino Affair, led by 16-year-old singer/child actor Gino Cunnico. The late 1966 line-up of The Gino Affair comprised Cunnico, James Kelly, Tony Bolton, Tony Bowman (guitar, vocals; ex-Dennis Williams and the Delawares) and Bob Daisley (bass; ex-Dennis Williams and the Delawares). The Affair came into being at the start of 1967. Cunnico left mid-year to join **The Executives**, and his place was taken by Derek Fitton (ex-**Derek's Accent**) and then Kerrie Biddell.

With Mike Howlett replacing Wheeler on bass, a new line-up of The Affair formed in January 1968. The Affair was always a polished and professional pop band and won the Vocal Group final at the 1968 Hoadley's National Battle of the Sounds. Rory Thomas (ex-Questions, **Doug Parkinson** In Focus) replaced Maddon in August, adding his distinctive Hammond organ sound to the band's musical scope.

Festival issued two Affair singles, 'Shoeshine Boy'/'What Became of Mary' (July 1968) and 'Money Can't Buy Me Love'/'Sing a Simple Song' (October 1969). The band broke up at the end of 1969 after moving into a series of television Club Show and cabaret residencies. Biddell went on to a successful solo career in jazz; Wheeler joined **Billy Thorpe** and the Aztecs then **MacKenzie Theory**; Bolton played in Luke's Walnut, Traine, **Freshwater**, **Country Radio**, the **Stevie Wright** Band and Greg Quill's Southern Cross; Kelly was in **Levi Smith's Clefs**, Mother Earth and Crossfire; Howlett went to the UK where he joined Gong before becoming an in-demand producer.

The Affected

Formed: *1990*
Style: *Punk pop*
Original line-up: *Scott Crawford (guitar, vocals), Stui Thompson (guitar), Matt Landy (bass), Anthony Saunus (drums)*

The Affected's brand of melodic, guitar-driven pop-punk borrowed from the likes of Kiss, Hüsker Dü, Iggy and the Stooges, Redd Kross and Neil Young. Adam Adair replaced Matt Landy soon after formation. The band's label Rubber Records billed The Affected as 'Melbourne's uncrowned kings of wiener rock'. The Affected's contemporaries on the Melbourne independent scene included **Hoss**, **Powder Monkeys**, **The Meanies**, White Elephants and Rootbeer.

Rubber Records issued the four-track EP *The Affected* (March 1991), the CD EP *EP* ('Misjudge Me') (September 1992), and the album *Bleed* (May 1993). Janine Chung (bass) and Sean Snare (drums) joined Crawford in a new, three-piece Affected line-up at the end of 1993. The new line-up issued the CD EP 'A Fate Worse than a Fate Worse than Death' (February 1994), which had been produced by former Gun Club member Ward Dotson. The last Affected release was the CD single 'Dannii' (November 1994). The Affected became Acer in early 1995. Acer issued the album *Blonde* in October 1995.

Albums: *Bleed* (as The Affected, Rubber, 1993), *Blonde* (as Acer, Rubber, 1995).

The Aints

Formed: *1991*
Style: *Rock*
Original line-up: **Ed Kuepper** *(guitar, vocals; ex-*
Saints, Laughing Clowns*), Kent Steedman (bass; from* **Celibate Rifles***), Tim Reeves (drums)*

In between commitments to his solo career, former **Saints/Laughing Clowns** guitarist **Ed Kuepper** found time in April 1991 to play a series of gigs around Sydney with a band he dubbed The Aints. The name 'Aints' was derived from an old bass drum head that had belonged to former Saints drummer Ivor Hay. The 'S' in the lettering for **The Saints**' name had worn off, leaving 'aints'. The Aints was an opportunity for Kuepper to reclaim some of the electric intensity that had characterised his former bands.

The subsequent limited edition 'authorised bootleg' live album *S.L.S.Q.* (which stands for 'Strictly Low Sound Quality') featured manic renditions of Saints classics like 'Know Your Product', 'This Perfect Day' and 'Nights in Venice'. '(I'm) Stranded' was issued as a single. Within a year, The Aints (with Mark Dawson, drums, Artie Sledge, bass and Tim Hopkins, sax) had issued two fiery, distortion-drenched studio albums of original material, *Ascension* (November 1991) and *Autocannibalism* (June 1992). With blistering, guitar heavy tracks such as 'Like an Oil Spill', 'It's Still Nowhere', 'Ill Wind' and 'Linda and Abilene', these albums were the antithesis of Kuepper's solo work. *Ascension* paid dual homage to two of Kuepper's acknowledged influences: firstly, the record cover echoed that of

The Stooges' *Funhouse*; and secondly, the album title was borrowed from jazz pioneer John Coltrane.

A third Aints studio album, *Afterlife*, remains unissued, although Hot Records put out the five track CD EP sampler *Cheap Erotica* in November 1993 and the compilation *Shelflife Unlimited!!—Hotter Than Blazing Pistols!!!* in August 1995.

Albums: *S.L.S.Q.* (Hot, 1991), *Ascension* (Hot, 1991), *Autocannibalism* (Hot, 1992), *Shelflife Unlimited!!—Hotter Than Blazing Pistols!!!* (Hot/Shock 1995).

Air Supply

Formed: *1975*
Style: *Harmony rock*
Original line-up: *Graham Russell (guitar, vocals), Russell Hitchcock (vocals), Chrissie Hammond (vocals)*

With international acclaim and eight Top 10 hit singles (including a #1) in the USA to its credit, Air Supply was one of the most successful Australian bands of the 1980s. US *Billboard* magazine hailed Air Supply as the biggest selling chart act of the decade. To date, the group has sold over 15 million records worldwide. In Australia, the band's soft rock sound, tight harmonies and clean image have generally been ignored and derided, despite the success of many of the band's singles and albums on the local charts.

English-born singer/songwriter Graham Russell, Russell Hitchcock and Chrissie Hammond formed Air Supply when the three musicians were cast members of *Jesus Christ Superstar*. Jeremy Paul (bass, vocals; ex-Soffrock) replaced Chrissie in 1976. CBS issued Air Supply's successful debut single, 'Love And Other Bruises'/'If You Knew Me' (#6 in October 1976), and album, *Air Supply* (#17 in December). The second single, 'Empty Pages'/'Feel the Breeze' (February 1977), missed the national Top 40. The Air Supply line-up on the album comprised Hitchcock, Russell and Paul, plus Mark McEntee (lead guitar), Adrian Scott (keyboards) and Jeff Browne (drums). The band then set off on tour with a line-up of Hitchcock, Russell, Paul and Scott, plus newcomers Brenton White (guitar; ex-Skintight) and Nigel Macara (drums; ex-**Tamam Shud**, **Ariel**).

The line-up of Hitchcock, Russell, Paul, Scott, Macara and new lead guitarist Rex Goh recorded the album *The Whole Thing's Started* which came out in July 1977. The album produced the singles 'Do What You Do'/'It's Automatic' (June), 'That's How the Whole Thing Started'/'There's Nothing I Can Do' (October) and 'Do It Again'/'Who Will Love Me Now?' (February 1978). The band's concerts during the second half of 1977 took in supports for Rod Stewart's Australian, USA and Canadian tours and a performance at the annual CBS conference in London with Chicago and Boz Scaggs. Jeremy Paul left at the end of 1977; he later formed **Divinyls** with another ex-Air Supply alumnus Mark McEntee. The Air Supply touring line-up at that point comprised Hitchcock, Russell, Macara and Goh, plus Robin LeMesurier (lead guitar), Joey Carbone (keyboards) and Howard Sukimoto (bass).

The early 1978 touring line-up comprised Hitchcock, Russell, Macara, Ken Francis (guitar), Rick Mellick (keyboards) and Bill Putt (bass; ex-**Spectrum**, **Ariel**). Air Supply stabilised in late 1978 with the line-up of Hitchcock, Russell, David Moyse (guitar; ex-Sailor), Brian Hamilton (bass, vocals; ex-Sailor) and Ralph Cooper (drums; ex-Windchase). The new line-up issued the album *Life Support* (April 1979), which yielded the singles 'Bring Out the Magic'/'Just Another Woman' (November 1978), 'Lost in Love'/'Believer' (April 1979) and 'Just Another Woman'/'Bring Out the Magic' (October 1979). Helping out on the album sessions were Coz Russo and Frank Esler-Smith on keyboards, **Tommy Emmanuel** and Peter Walker (ex-**Bakery**) on guitars and Geoff Oakes and Mike Bukowsky on brass.

'Lost in Love' became the band's first Australian hit (#13 in June 1979) since 'Do What You Do' had reached #32 in August 1977. Air Supply's USA breakthrough came in 1980 when Arista issued the Robie Porter-produced album *Lost in Love* (June) and the single 'Lost in Love' (January). The line-up on the *Lost in Love* album featured Hitchcock, Russell, Moyse, Cooper and Criston Barker (bass, ex-Ash, **Freeway**, Hollywood), with guest players Esler-Smith and Sam McNally (ex-**Stylus**) on keyboards and Emmanuel on guitar.

With 'Lost in Love', Air Supply became the first Australian band to reach #3 in the USA. 'Lost in Love' also reached #4 in Japan. Air Supply followed up 'Lost in Love' with four more US Top 5 hits 'All Out of Love' (#2, June 1980), 'Every Woman to Me' (#5, November) and 'The One that You Love' (#1, July 1981) and 'Here I Am' (#5, September). 'All Out of Love' also reached #11 in the UK. Air Supply wrapped up its successful 1981 American tour with a concert at Los Angeles' renowned Greek Theatre. At the 1982 American Music Awards, Air Supply was voted Best Group for 1981.

The band's US chart run continued with the singles 'Sweet Dreams' (#5, January 1982), 'Even the Nights are Better' (#5, June), 'Young Love' (#38, October), 'Two Less Lonely People in the

World' (#38, November), 'Making Love out of Nothing at All' (#2, August 1983) and the albums *The One that You Love* (July 1981) and *Now and Forever* (June 1982). Both albums featured the line-up of Hitchcock, Russell, Moyse, Cooper, Rex Goh (guitar), Frank Esler-Smith (keyboards; ex-**Doug Parkinson** and The Southern Star Band) and David Green (bass).

Meanwhile, in Australia, 'All Out of Love'/'Old Habits Die Hard' reached #9 in August 1980, 'Every Woman To Me'/'My Best Friend' #8 in January 1981, 'The One that You Love'/'I Want to Give It All to You' #10 in July and 'Even the Nights Are Better'/'Taking the Chance' #35 in July 1982. The band's other Australian releases, 'Here I Am'/'I've Got Your Love' (September 1981), 'I'm Late Again'/'What Kind of Girl' (October 1982), 'Two Less Lonely People in the World'/'One Step Closer' (November), 'Now and Forever'/'Young Love' (May 1983) and 'Making Love Out of Nothing At All'/'What Kind of Girl' (August) did not reach the Top 40. *The One that You Love* peaked at #10 on the Australian album chart in September 1981, while *Now and Forever* went as high as #22 in August 1982. *Air Supply's Greatest Hits*, however, went on to become the band's biggest selling album in Australia, when it reached #1 during August 1983. The album also made the US Top 10, on its way to selling three million copies.

The line-up on the 1985 album *Air Supply* was Hitchcock, Russell, Esler-Smith, Cooper, Ken Rarick (keyboards), Wally Stocker (guitar; ex-Babys) and Don Cromwell (bass). The album produced one US hit, 'Just As I Am'/'Crazy Love' (#19, June 1985) and two flops, 'The Power of Love'/'Sunset' (1985) and 'Lonely is the Night'/'I'd Die For You' (1986) before the group disbanded. Hitchcock went solo for a time, issuing a cover of The Walker Brothers' 'The Sun Ain't Gonna Shine Anymore' backed by a cover of Jimmy Ruffin's 'What Becomes of the Broken Hearted' as a single, followed by the album *Russell Hitchcock* in 1988.

Little was heard from Air Supply until the early 1990s when the albums *The Earth Is . . .* and *The Vanishing Race* came out. Although they failed to chart in Australia, both sold well throughout Asia. Graham Russell and Russell Hitchcock continued to resurrect Air Supply periodically in order to play the American and (more lucrative) Asian concert circuit with great success. An example of the band's enduring appeal was the album *Now And Forever—Greatest Hits Live*, which had been recorded in Taipei, Taiwan on 15 and 16 June 1995. It sold 450 000 copies in the region, and in Hong Kong stayed at #1 for 15 weeks. Air Supply also played six sell-out concerts in mainland China, at 20 000 capacity auditoriums.

In July 1996, Russell and Hitchcock returned to Australia for Air Supply's first local tour in more than 15 years. The line-up included American musicians Guy Allison (keyboards), Cliff Rehrig (bass) and Mark Williams (drums). In June 1997, Russell Hitchcock joined **Yothu Yindi's** Mandawuy Yunupingu and **The Seekers'** Judith Durham for the joint single 'I Am Australian' (penned by Seeker Bruce Woodley and **The Bushwackers'** Dobe Newton) which made its debut at #17 on the national single chart.

Albums: *Air Supply* (CBS, 1976), *The Whole Thing's Started* (CBS, 1977), *Life Support* (Wizard, 1979), *Lost in Love* (Wizard/Big Time, 1980), *The One that You Love* (Big Time, 1981), *Love and Other Bruises* (reissue of first album, Harmony/CBS, 1981), *Now and Forever* (CBS, 1982), *Air Supply's Greatest Hits* (Big Time, 1983), *Air Supply* (Arista/BMG, 1985), *Hearts in Motion* (Arista/BMG, 1986), *The Earth is . . .* (Giant/BMG,1991), *Feel The Breeze* (CBS, 1992), *The Vanishing Race* (Giant/BMG, 1993), *News from Nowhere* (Giant/BMG, 1995), *Now and Forever—Greatest Hits Live* (Giant/BMG, 1995), *The Book of Love* (Giant/BMG, 1996).

Albatross (*see* Bjerre)

Alchemist

Formed: *1989*
Style: *Death metal*
1991 line-up: *Adam (vocals, guitar), Andrew (guitar), John (bass), Rodney (drums)*

In the pantheon of Australian death metal/grindcore that included the likes of **Armoured Angel**, **Abramalin**, Manticore, Misery and Persecution, Canberra techno-metal band Alchemist boasted the most diverse sound. In mixing elements of King Crimson and spacey Pink Floyd effects with the usual deathy vocal growls and intense riffs, Alchemist forged its own brand of 'progressive jazz thrash' or 'psychedelic death metal'.

By 1991, only founder-member Adam remained from the original line-up. Alchemist contributed the track 'Escapism' to Roadrunner Australia's *Redrum* compilation (June 1993), and European label Lethal issued the band's debut album *Jar of Kingdom* the same year. Roy replaced Andrew on guitar, and Melbourne label Thrust issued the band's second album, *Lunasphere*, in May 1995. The band's third album *Spiritech*, came out in August 1997. Over the years, Alchemist has played tour supports to international visitors Kreator, Bolt Thrower, Fear Factory, Pungent Stench, Cathedral, Paradise Lost and Napalm Death.

Albums: *Jar of Kingdom* (Lethal, 1993), *Lunasphere* (Thrust/Shock, 1995), *Spiritech* (Thrust/Shock, 1997).

Aleph

Formed: *1975*
Style: *Symphonic rock*
Original line-up: *Joe Walmsley (vocals), Dave Froggett (guitar), Mary Carpenter (keyboards), Mary Hansen (keyboards), David Highett (bass), Ron Carpenter (drums)*

Sydney-based symphonic rock band Aleph's one album, *Surface Tension,* featured full-blown, complex progressive rock in the Yes/Genesis/King Crimson vein. Joe Walmsley's high-pitched vocals recalled Yes singer Jon Anderson, while Dave Froggett's guitar style was in the manner of King Crimson's Robert Fripp. The only other local bands playing in a similar style at the time were **Sebastian Hardie** and Windchase. *Surface Tension* failed to chart. Prior to the album's release, Aleph issued a cover of The Yardbirds' 'Little Games'/'Of the Essence' as a single. Walmsley left before the album appeared at the end of 1977. Unable to find a suitable replacement, the band fell apart in early 1978. Later in the year, Ron Carpenter formed First Light, which issued a self-titled, self-financed album in 1979.

Album: *Surface Tension* (Atlantic, 1977).

The Aliens

Formed: *1978*
Style: *New wave*
Original line-up: *Danny Johnson (bass, vocals; ex-Riff Raff), Geoff Stapleton (guitar, vocals; ex-Riff Raff), Greg Webster (lead guitar, vocals; ex-Riff Raff), Graham Lewis (keyboards), Kevin Patricks (drums)*

The Aliens were one of the first 'uniformed' new wave bands of the late 1970s (black clothes and skinny, white ties). Originally from Adelaide and known as Riff Raff, The Aliens' sound embraced guitar-oriented pop rock with the emphasis on 1960s melodies. The band relocated to Melbourne in late 1978.

Graham Lewis and Kevin Patricks had left by the time Mushroom issued the singles 'Confrontation'/'Boys in Black' (#36 in December 1979), 'Follow That Girl'/'The Hiding of Dr Jekyll' (February 1980) and the album *Translator.* Rob Grosser played drums on the records. Webster left in June 1980, to be replaced by Randy Bulpin (ex-**Mondo Rock,** Hot Club) in September. A new line-up of Stapleton, Greg Trennery (bass), Malcolm Fogg (drums) and Pierre Baroni (guitar, synthesiser, ex-Power by Beat) issued the independent single 'I Don't Care'/'Over My Head' in February 1981, after which the band broke up. Stapleton went on to play with **GANGgajang, Absent Friends** and **The Dukes;** Baroni was in Field of Knives and **The Pony** before working in the art department at Mushroom Records for many years.

Album: *Translator* (Mushroom/Festival, 1980).

Allegiance

Formed: *1990*
Style: *Thrash metal*
Original line-up: *John Mihos (vocals), Jason Stone (guitar), Tony Campo (guitar), Dave Harrison (bass), Conrad Higson (drums)*

As Australia's foremost thrash metal band of the 1990s, Perth-based Allegiance has gained international acclaim and interest from several key figures in the heavy metal world. Allegiance's tight sound mixed the heavy riffs and complexities of San Francisco Bay Area thrash bands like Metallica, Testament, Slayer and Exodus with a touch of Sepultura, and has remained relatively unchanged since the band's formation in 1990.

When John Mihos left a couple of months after

Allegiance

formation, Conrad Higson took over lead vocals and Colin Butcher joined on drums. Over the next three years, Allegiance became the biggest drawcard on the West Australian rock scene. The band's three self-financed cassettes (*Make the Pledge*, *Torn Between Two Worlds* and *Studio Live*) sold over 3000 copies and garnered favourable reviews in the UK headbangers' bible *Kerrang!* and USA metal magazine *Metal Maniacs*. Allegiance won Most Popular Band at the 1992 West Australian (WA) Music Industry Awards, as well as taking out the WA finals of the 1992 Yamaha Rock Competition. In the national finals, Allegiance was awarded the *Juke* Encouragement Award. The band contributed 'Morally Justified' to Roadrunner Australia's compilation of local metal acts, *Redrum* (June 1993).

In early 1993, ex-Judas Priest frontman Rob Halford took an interest in Allegiance, with the view of setting up management and album distribution in the USA through his Los Angeles-based company Entertainment Management Advisory Services (EMAS). The arrangement eventually resulted in the release of the band's first album, *D.E.S.T.I.T.U.T.I.O.N.* in June 1994. Without mainstream radio support, the album topped the WA charts. Allegiance repeated that feat with its second album *Skinman* (November 1996). Allegiance's fierce live reputation resulted in several appearances on the Big Day Out festival bill, as well as supporting international visitors like Morbid Angel, Kreator, Faith No More, Fight and Fear Factory.

Albums: *D.E.S.T.I.T.U.T.I.O.N.* (Id/PolyGram 1994), *Skinman* (Id/PolyGram, 1996).

Christie Allen

Style: *Pop*

English-born singer Christie Allen (b. 1954) was voted Most Popular Female Performer at the 1979 and 1980 *TV Week*/***Countdown*** Awards. Her bright pop sound has always been appreciated by her fans. Her hit singles 'Falling in Love with Only You'/'Under Lock and Key' (#20, April 1979), 'Goosebumps'/'Ships that Pass Through the Night' (#3, October 1979) and 'He's My Number One'/ 'Count Me Out' (#4, February 1980) were among the most successful releases on the Mushroom label to that time. 'Goosebumps' alone sold 60 000 copies.

Allen had been singing in Perth band Pendulum when she came to the attention of ex-**Twilights** guitarist Terry Britten. Britten had co-written hit singles for Cliff Richard and Tina Turner ('What's Love Got to Do With It', 'We Don't Need Another Hero'). He returned to Australia to work with Allen. Her debut single was 'You Know that I Love You'/'Nashville Tennessee' (September 1978). When 'Goosebumps' took off, she toured with The Hot Band which comprised Greg Cook (guitar; ex-**Cam-Pact**, **Mondo Rock**), Max Chazan (guitar; ex-Rubes), Michael Hegerty (bass; **Richard Clapton** Band), Rick Puchala (drums; **Richard Clapton** Band) and Bruce Haymes (organ; ex-Rubes, **Richard Clapton** Band).

Christie's last four singles 'Magic Rhythm'/ 'Only Yes Will Do' (May 1980), 'Baby Get Away'/ 'Don't Stop' (August), 'Switchboard'/'Monday Through Friday' (November) and 'Don't Put Out the Flame'/'City Lights' (March 1981) were minor hits. Ill-health prevented her from touring and she retired from performing. By the 1990s she was back singing with country bands.

Albums: *Magic Rhythm* (Mushroom/Festival, 1979), *Detour* (Mushroom/Festival, 1980).

Daevid Allen

Style: *Avant-jazz, rock*

During the 1960s and 1970s, guitarist Daevid Allen was one of the most respected rock/avant-garde/jazz musicians working on the UK and European scene. His work with the original Soft Machine and Gong is still highly regarded by aficionados, but in Australia he remains relatively unknown.

Beatnik poet and musician Allen left Australia in 1960 to travel around Europe. He came into contact with the likes of poet Allen Ginsberg, novelist William S. Burroughs and poet Robert Graves. Daevid Allen provided the music for a dramatisation of Burroughs' *The Ticket that Exploded*. By 1966 Allen was living in the UK, and playing with a group of Canterbury musicians in Soft Machine. Being an experimentalist of some note already, Allen brought the influence of Terry Riley (free-form improvisation and tape-loops) into the band. Soft Machine was named after the Burroughs novel, and Allen is credited with contacting the author to obtain permission for its use. The band was at the forefront of the British psychedelic movement alongside Syd Barrett-era Pink Floyd, The Crazy World of Arthur Brown, Tomorrow and Dantalion's Chariot.

Allen recorded only one single with Soft Machine, 'Love Makes Sweet Music'/'Feelin' Reelin' Squeelin' (February 1967). Following the band's temporary move to France in late 1967, he was refused re-entry into England (due to an expired visa and appearance deficiencies apparently!) and Soft Machine continued as a three-piece. In Paris,

Allen set up a community of musicians that included his partner Gilli Smyth (space whisper) and recorded two solo albums, *Magick Brother Mystic Sister* and *Banana Moon*. By now referring to himself as Dingo Virgin or Bert Camembert, Allen formed Gong in 1970 and recorded *Camembert Electrique* and *Continental Circus* for the French label BYG.

Gong's music mixed space rock and psychedelia with avant-experimentation and hippy philosophy. In England, Gong became popular on the festival circuit (alongside Hawkwind, Pink Fairies, Skin Alley, etc.) and recorded the *Radio Gnome Invisible* album trilogy for Virgin Records (*The Flying Teapot, Angel's Egg* and *You*). The trilogy was full of eccentric detail and revolved around Allen's tale of Zero the Hero and The Pot Headed Pixies from the Planet Gong.

Allen left Gong in 1974 and recorded a series of well-received solo albums. Then, as Planet Gong, he recorded the single 'Opium for the People' and album *Live Floating Anarchy* 77 (1978); as New York Gong (Allen plus the band Material), he recorded the single 'Much Too Old' and *About Time* (1980). He returned to Australia in 1984 and teamed up with David Tolley (ex-Tolley and Dara) as The Ex. That collaboration resulted in the *Don't Stop* mini-album. Then, as The Invisible Opera Company Of Tibet, Allen issued the single 'Trial By Headline' and the albums *Oz Becoz* and *The Owl and the Tree*.

While in Australia, Allen also continued his pursuit of esoteric wisdom by working on Drones, training as a 'Conscious Connected Breath' therapist and organising Healing Festivals to put his various themes of self-advancement into communal practice. In January 1988, he returned to the UK, re-formed Gong as Gong Maison, toured and recorded a series of new albums: *Gong Maison* (1989), *Shapeshifter* (1992), *Live On TV 1990* (1993), *25th Birthday Party (Gong Live)* (1995) and *How to Nuke the Eiffel Tower (Gong Global Family)* (1995). Allen continued to record solo albums, most of which have only been issued in the UK or Europe.

Allen solo albums: *Magick Brother Mystic Sister* (BYG, 1970), *Banana Moon* (BYG, 1971), *Good Morning!* (Virgin, 1976; as Daevid Allen & Euterpe), *Now is the Happiest Time of Your Life* (Affinity, 1977), *N'Existe Pas!* (Charly, 1979), *Divided Alien Playbax '80* (Charly, 1981), *The Death of Rock'n'Roll and Other Entrances* (Shanghai, 1982), *Alien in New York* (Charly, 1983), *Don't Stop* (Shanghai, 1986; as The Ex), *Oz Becoz* (Invisible, 1988) and *The Owl and the Tree* (Demi Monde, 1989; both as The Invisible Opera Company of Tibet), *Australia Aquaria/She* (Demi Monde, 1990), *Stroking the Tail of the Bird* (Amp, 1990; with Gilli Smyth and Harry Williamson), *The Seven Drones* (Voiceprint, 1991), *Live at the Witchwood* (Voiceprint, 1992; as Daevid Allen & The Magick Brothers), *Invisible Opera Company of Tibet* (Voiceprint, 1992), *Twelve Selves* (Voiceprint, 1993), *Voiceprint Radio Session* (Voiceprint, 1994).

Peter Allen

Style: *Adult contemporary pop*

Peter Allen (b. 1944, d. 1992) was one of the most internationally acclaimed performers and songwriters of the Australian rock and pop era. Some of his most famous songs include 'I Go To Rio' (which topped the charts in Paris, Rio De Janeiro and Australia), 'I Honestly Love You' (recorded by **Olivia Newton-John**), 'Arthur's Theme (The Best That You Can Do)' (which won an Oscar as the title song for the film *Arthur*), 'Don't Cry Out Loud' (a hit for US singer Melissa Manchester) and 'I Still Call Australia Home'. Allen's glitzy, flamboyant stage show was a popular nightclub and concert attraction in the USA. His death at the age of 48 from AIDS-related throat cancer was a tragic loss.

Allen was born Peter Woolnough in the NSW country town of Tenterfield. The son of a violent, alcoholic father, Allen found solace in his music. From early on he was a gifted pianist, singer and dancer, and entertained the locals with his Fats Waller and Jerry Lee Lewis-styled performances. At 15 he moved to Sydney and joined Chris Bell as the folk-pop duo The Allen Brothers.

The Allen Brothers became regulars on television pop show *Bandstand*, and at 16 were signed by American impresario Lee Gordon to his Leedon label. The Allen Brothers issued two singles on Leedon, 'Bells Bells Bells'/'Summer Clouds' (April 1960) and 'There's No Need'/'Busy Lips' (June) before moving to EMI. EMI's Pye subsidiary label issued four Allen Brothers singles, 'First Kiss'/'My Secret' (July 1960), 'Pretty Keen Teen'/'There's No Need' (September), 'Too Much'/'Ever Since' (October) and 'No Hesitation'/'Knocking on the Right Front Door' (shared with The Barry Sisters) (December). On the Sydney charts, 'First Kiss' reached #11, 'Pretty Keen Teen' #14 and 'No Hesitation' #19. 'First Kiss' became the duo's only Melbourne Top 40 hit single when it reached #32 in August 1960.

From there, The Allen Brothers moved to EMI's HMV label for three singles, 'No Fooling'/'Be An Angel Darling' (December 1961), 'Baby Loves Me'/'Firefly' (February 1962) and 'There's

Never Been a Girl Like You'/'Ain't Misbehaving' (August). Allen had already set his sights overseas and the pair duly left Australia in April 1962 for a three-week booking in Tokyo. Two years later, the duo was still touring the Orient, having played in Japan, South Korea, Kowloon, the Philippines and Hong Kong. While performing their Las Vegas-styled nightclub act at the Hong Kong Hilton in May 1964, The Allen Brothers came to the attention of American actress/singer Judy Garland, who became their manager and took them to the USA. They toured America as Garland's opening act, and undertook their own tours of nightclubs around the country. On 3 March 1967, Allen married Garland's daughter Liza Minnelli. The Allen Brothers signed to Mercury and issued the album *Chris & Peter Allen's Album #1*.

By 1970, with encouragement from Liza, Allen had started writing songs. In March of that year, he dissolved his act with Chris Bell, as well as separating from Liza, whose star was on the rise. Allen moved to New York's Greenwich Village and mixed with the chic Andy Warhol/Manhattan art crowd (writing songs for Candy Darling to sing in Jackie Curtis's underground play *Vain Victory*). He began performing his solo act in the small clubs of the Village like The Bitter End and The Talkhouse. Allen also signed to Metromedia and issued his debut singer/songwriter album *Peter Allen* (August 1970).

In 1972, Allen made a brief return to Australia, the experience of which prompted him to write one of his best known songs, the autobiographical 'Tenterfield Saddler'. Allen issued his second American album, *Tenterfield Saddler*, in mid-1972. By the end of the year, he had moved to Los Angeles and was opening for Bette Midler at the Troubadour Club. In 1973 he collaborated with fellow Australian expatriate **Helen Reddy**, before returning to New York. Allen perfected his extravagant stage show with a year-long residency at the prestigious Reno Sweeney Club. He began collaborating with songwriters Carole Bayer Sager and Jeff Barry, as well as signing a new deal with A&M Records. In 1974, **Olivia Newton-John** took the Peter Allen/Jeff Barry composition 'I Honestly Love You' to #1 on the American singles chart. Allen also recorded a version of the song for his third American album, *Continental American*.

At the end of 1975, Allen supported **Helen Reddy** on her tour of Japan, Hong Kong and Australia. Although unknown in his homeland, Allen garnered consistently positive reviews at the expense of the better known headliner. Back in the USA, A&M sent Allen out on an ill-matched tour with flashy, theatrical rock band The Tubes. The tour was a disaster, but Allen was able to pick up the pieces when he linked up with powerful manager Dee Anthony (Peter Frampton, J. Geils Band, Gary Wright).

In 1976, Allen issued the *Taught by Experts* album which included his most famous song, the bright uptempo samba 'I Go to Rio'. The song was a minor hit in the USA. A year later, aided by regular airings of the video on the ABC's television pop show ***Countdown***, 'I Go To Rio'/'This Time Around' reached #1 on the Australian charts. 'I Go To Rio' became the highlight of his act, with Allen dancing in red sequined attire, shaking his maracas and creating a frenzied carnival atmosphere. Allen was now able to tour the world as a bona fide headlining superstar. He returned to Australia in September 1977 for a successful tour, which ended with a free concert in the Brisbane Botanical Gardens. His next single, 'The More I See You'/'I Honestly Love You' reached #11 in October, while the album *Taught by Experts* had also made the Australian Top 10.

Next Allen issued the in-concert double album *It is Time for Peter Allen* (October 1977) and the more reflective *I Could Have Been a Sailor* (February 1979). 'I Could Have Been a Sailor'/'Tenterfield Saddler' was issued as a single (January 1980). A&M also issued the *Tenterfield Saddler* album for the first time in Australia. In 1980 Allen opened on New York's Broadway with his most ambitious show *Up in One*. Allen toured Australia with *Up in One*, and his return provided the inspiration for another of his best known songs 'I Still Call Australia Home'. He performed the song in front of Queen Elizabeth for the Royal Command Variety Performance held at the Sydney Opera House. Australian airline QANTAS later adopted 'I Still Call Australia Home' as its signature song.

The *Bi-Coastal* album produced the singles 'Bi-Coastal'/'Simon' (September 1980), 'Fly Away'/'Planes' (January 1981) and 'One Step Over The Borderline'/'I Could Really Show You Around' (May 1981). The album title raised questions in the media about Allen's sexual preferences, but it was his way of describing to the press and public how and where he lived—in both Los Angeles *and* New York. Such was Allen's popularity by 1981 that he was able to perform to full houses at the Greek Theatre in Los Angeles, Manhattan's famed Copacabana Club and New York's prestigious Radio City Music Hall. His collaboration with composers Burt Bacharach, Carole Bayer Sager and Christopher Cross, 'Between The Moon And New York City:

Arthur's Theme' won the 1981 Oscar for Best Theme Song.

In August 1982, *The Very Best of Peter Allen* reached #9 on the Australian charts. He travelled to the UK to play the Pirate King in a British television production of Gilbert and Sullivan's *Pirates of Penzance*. Allen's ninth album, *Not the Boy Next Door*, came out in March 1983, which coincided with another Australian tour. *Not the Boy Next Door* reached #24 on the national chart and yielded the singles 'Not the Boy Next Door' and 'You Haven't Heard the Last of Me'. *Making Every Moment Count* (1984) and another in-concert album, *Captured Live at Carnegie Hall* (1985), followed.

Allen's second Broadway production, the ill-fated *Legs Diamond*, was lambasted by the critics. It closed after only two months. He returned to Australia for successful tours in August 1988, January 1990 and January 1992. Soon after that Allen was diagnosed with cancer; he died on 19 June 1992. He was inducted into the Australian Hall of Fame in 1993 at the sixth annual Australian Record Industry Association (ARIA) Awards ceremony.

Albums: *Peter Allen* (US only, Metromedia, 1970; reissued on Raven, 1994), *Tenterfield Saddler* (US only, Metromedia, 1972), *Continental American* (US only, A&M, 1974), *Taught By Experts* (A&M, 1977), *It is Time for Peter Allen* (A&M, 1977), *I Could Have Been a Sailor* (A&M, 1979), *Tenterfield Saddler* (A&M, 1980), *Bi-Coastal* (A&M, 1980), *The Very Best of Peter Allen* (A&M, 1982), *Not the Boy Next Door* (Arista, 1983), *Making Every Moment Count* (Arista, 1985), *Captured Live at Carnegie Hall* (Arista, 1985), *The Very Best of Peter Allen* (PolyGram, 1992), *The Boy from Oz* (Arista, 1995).

Allniters

Formed: *1980*
Style: *Ska pop*
Original line-up: *Peter Hill-Travis (vocals), Brett Pattinson (vocals), Martin Fabok (guitar), Stuart Crysell (guitar; ex-Bedhogs), Ted Ayers (sax), Mark Taylor (keyboards), Graham Hood (bass), Dave Betts (drums)*

During the late 1970s/early 1980s, the small Sussex Hotel in downtown Sydney was home to that city's mod scene. When the Bluebeat/2 Tone movement erupted in Britain (Madness, The Specials, Selector), it was only natural that ska too would end up there. One of Australia's first ska bands, Allniters got their start at the Sussex in 1980.

The band began as a loose-knit aggregation around guitarist Martin Fabok. The band's only ambition at that stage was to have fun, although early gigs were often marred by fights between skinheads, mods, rude boys and surfers. Allniters' first two independent singles, 'She Made a Monkey Out Of Me'/'Allniters Are Alrighters' (August 1981) and 'You Shouldn't Stay Out Late'/'What Gives You the Right?' (1982) for the GREEN label made only a marginal impression. At the same time, Fabok, Crysell, Taylor plus a host of other musicians formed an occasional studio band called The Igniters to play dub reggae. The band's only release was a 1982 four-track EP, *Igniters*.

By the time Allniters signed to Powderworks/RCA in 1983, the band's live reputation was formidable. The singles 'Hold On'/'Mr Unioshi-Yunioshi' (May 1983), Bobby Bloom's 'Montego Bay'/'Get It Together' (September) and 'Love and Affection'/'Juliette' (November), plus the album *D-D-D-Dance* (October) were national Top 40 hits ('Montego Bay' reached #16). On the Sydney chart, 'Hold On' peaked at #15, 'Montego Bay' at #10 and 'Love and Affection' at #21. The album's unique fusion of ska, dub and good-time pop garnered favourable reviews. By that time the line-up comprised Hill-Travis, Pattinson, Ayers, Fabok, Taylor, Crysell, plus Julie Conway (vocals), Stephen Luke (trombone), Perry Andronos (bass) and Dave Lennon (drums).

1983 to 1984 was to be the band's peak period. Following two more singles, 'Screaming Dreaming'/'Allniters Are Alrighters' (August 1984) and 'I Saw You First'/'Mexico' (December), the band split in January 1985. Crysell, Ayers and Taylor formed Castles in Spain with Nicholas Conroy (vocals), Cameron Giles (bass; ex-Mindsweepers) and John MacKay (drums; ex-Seamonsters, Vulgar Beatmen).

Then, in July 1985, Conway, Pattinson, Hill-Travis, Fabok and Luke revived Allniters with new members Mark Tanner (guitar), Peter Bolke (bass; ex-Honeydrippers), Dale Pandit (drums; ex-Leftovers), Mark Fuccilli (sax; ex-Chinless Elite) and Ralph Franke (sax; ex-**Strange Tenants**). By February 1986, the line-up comprised Conway, Pattinson, Hill-Travis and Franke, plus newcomers Michael Allen (keyboards), Mickey Marnie (guitar, ex-Treble Clefs), Troy Duncomb (bass) and Simon Knapman (drums, ex-Kam Sha). The new line-up recorded the Martin Plaza-produced 'All That Easy'/'The Party' single (July 1987) for Mushroom, but by that stage the band had run its course.

Album: *D-D-D-Dance* (Powderworks/RCA, 1983).

The Allusions

Formed: *1965*
Style: *Beat pop*
Original line-up: *Michael Morris (rhythm guitar, vocals; ex-Dennis Williams and the Delawares), Terry Hearne (lead guitar, vocals; ex-***Dave Bridge** *Trio), John Shaw (keyboards, vocals), Terry Chapman (bass), Kevin Hughes (drums)*

The Allusions were one of the most stylish and inventive of Sydney's 1960s beat pop bands. The band issued six singles 'Gypsy Woman'/'Fever (Burns in my Brain)' (March 1966), 'The Dancer'/'Roller Coaster Man' (July), 'Looks Like Trouble'/'97 Cigarettes' (October), 'Roundabout'/'I'll Be Home' (February 1967), 'Seven Days Of Rain'/'Two Of A Kind' (July) and 'Mr Love'/'And She's Mine' (January 1968), 'The Dancer' EP (April 1967), plus one rare and excellent self-titled album (January 1967) for EMI/Parlophone. Bruce Davis (ex-Dennis Williams and The Delawares) replaced Terry Chapman on bass in July 1966, in time to appear on the album. Chapman went on to join one of Australia's first psychedelic trios, The Knack, with drummer Craig Collinge (ex-Librettos and pre-**Procession**).

'Gypsy Woman' and the Michael Morris-penned 'The Dancer' were Top 10 hits in Sydney (#8 and #9 respectively), and are rightly regarded as Australian 1960s classics. 'The Dancer' owed a debt to The Beatles' arrangement of 'I'm Happy Just To Dance With You'. The Allusions also included a tough cover of The Kinks' R&B stomper 'I Gotta Move' on their album. **Chris Bailey** recorded a version of 'Gypsy Woman' with **The Saints** in 1981. Morris left in late 1967 to be replaced briefly by John Spence. The Allusions continued on as a four-piece until October 1968, when Terry Hearne joined Digger Revell's backing band. Morris returned but, having failed to adapt to the prevailing winds of psychedelia, the band finally split in 1969.

Album: *The Allusions* (EMI/Parlophone, 1967).

Ammonia

Formed: *1993*
Style: *Indie guitar rock*
Original line-up: *Dave Johnstone (guitar, vocals), Simon Hensworth (bass), Allan Balmont (drums)*

Perth-based band Ammonia started life as Fuzzswirl. With a name change, Ammonia supported **You Am I** and overseas visitors Redd Kross, and then signed to Sony's development label Murmur (home to **silverchair**). Ammonia issued the CD EP 'In a Box' (November 1994), which reached #15 on the West Australian mainstream charts and the national alternative Top 10. Like 'In a Box', the second CD EP, 'Sleepwalking' (March 1995), outlined the band's brand of guitar-driven power pop.

It was the success of the infectious CD singles 'Drugs' (September) and 'Suzi Q' (December), plus the Kevin 'Caveman' Shirley-produced album *Mint 400* (September) during 1995, however, that established the band at the forefront of national indie-pop. *Mint 400* showcased the band's uncanny pop sensibility. 'Drugs' reached #32 on the mainstream chart in November. 'Drugs' was later voted #27 on the 1995 Triple J Hottest 100 list. A spot on the 1996 Big Day Out national tour and the release of the third CD single from *Mint 400*, 'Ken Carter' (#50 in February 1996) followed.

Epic Records issued *Mint 400* and 'Drugs' in the USA, and the band toured the States to a positive response. 'Drugs' went on to sell over 50 000 copies in the USA. Ammonia issued a new CD single, 'Satin Only' (October 1996). In 1997 the band recorded a new album in New York with producer Dean Friedman (Flaming Lips), with the first CD single 'You're Not the Only One who Feels this Way' appearing in August. As with other contemporary three-piece bands like **silverchair**, **You Am I**, **Regurgitator**, **Spiderbait**, **Pollyanna** and **Even**, Ammonia combined pop economy, power, melody and rock intensity in equal measure.

Album: *Mint 400* (Murmur/Sony, 1995).

Angry Anderson

Style: *Hard rock*

Over the course of a lengthy career, gravel-throated vocalist Gary 'Angry' Anderson (b. 1949) has gone from attention-grabbing, rock'n'roll bad boy to all-round Australian media star. His position as youth affairs reporter on *The Midday Show* and *A Current Affair* was the perfect outlet for his hyperactive personality and gift of the gab.

Anderson earned the nickname 'Angry Ant' during his youth after his aggressive and volatile nature got the better of him. Anderson channelled his anger and energy into rock music as lead singer with Peace Power and Purity during 1971 and 1972. In 1973 he formed boogie band **Buster Brown** and in late 1976 joined **Rose Tattoo**. The Tatts forged an identity as one of Australia's peerless, street-level, hard rock bands. The band's hits like 'Bad Boy for Love' and 'We Can't be Beaten' became anthems for disaffected suburban youth, and

Anderson was seen as a spokesman for young outsiders. The band earned an international reputation on the heavy metal touring circuit.

In 1985 Anderson moved into feature film work. His first acting role was a bit part in *Bullamakanka.* He then took the part of Ironbar Bassey in the Kennedy–Miller film *Mad Max III: Beyond Thunderdome,* alongside Mel Gibson, Tina Turner and Frank Thring. The final Tatts album, *Beats from a Single Drum* (1986), had started out as an Anderson solo album when American producer Kevin Beamish (REO Speedwagon, Starship) was brought in to oversee recording. The album was a more polished affair than previous Tatts records.

It included the plaintive ballad 'Suddenly' which was used during the wedding of Charlene Mitchell (**Kylie Minogue**) and Scott Robinson (**Jason Donovan**) in the Ten Network's popular soapie *Neighbours.* 'Suddenly'/'Falling' became Anderson's first solo hit single when it reached #2 on the national charts the same week that Minogue's first single, 'Locomotion', sat at #1 (August 1987). The two singles swapped places a week later, with 'Suddenly' at the top and 'Locomotion' at #2.

Beats from a Single Drum was reissued in 1988 as an Anderson solo album. He took a three-year break from rock'n'roll before issuing his debut solo album proper, *Blood from Stone* (September 1990). Produced by American Beau Hill (ZZ Top), it yielded the singles 'Heaven'/'Motorbike Song' (August) and the anthemic 'Bound for Glory'/'Love Bites' (November). Anderson's backing band comprised Robin Riley (lead guitar; ex-**Redhouse**, **Rose Tattoo**, **Party Boys**), American Bobby Barth (guitar), Jim Hilbun (bass; ex-**Angels**) and Tim Powles (drums; ex-**Ward 13**, **Venetians**, **Divinyls**). Anderson performed 'Bound for Glory' at the opening ceremony of the 1990 AFL Grand Final in Melbourne, and the Angry Anderson Band supported US visitors Aerosmith on their October 1990 Australian tour.

During his break from rock music, Anderson appeared as Vladimir Lenin in the stage production of *Rasputin* (with **Jon English** and Terry Serio), and joined *The Midday Show.* In 1992, he took the role of King Herod in the revived Australian production of the Andrew Lloyd Webber/Tim Rice stage musical *Jesus Christ Superstar.* Alongside **John Farnham** (Jesus), **Kate Ceberano** (Mary Magdalene), Jon Stevens (Judas), John Waters (Pontius Pilate), **Russell Morris** (Simon Zealotes) and David Gould (Caiaphas), Anderson featured on the #1 charting *Jesus Christ Superstar: The Album* issued by Polydor in July.

Anderson also became involved with charities such as NAPCAN (National Association for the Prevention of Abuse and Neglect of Kids) and the Prince of Wales Hospital. As well as a stint with **The Party Boys** in 1987 and The Wild Colonial Boys (with co-vocalists **Dragon**'s **Marc Hunter** and Sharon O'Neill), Anderson has toured with his solo bands Angry and Double Trouble. Apart from touring with the reformed **Rose Tattoo** and a new line-up of the Angry Anderson Band in 1993, Anderson virtually gave up rock'n'roll to concentrate on his mainstream television career.

The 1993 version of Angry Anderson Band was essentially Anderson backed by **The Bombers**: John Brewster (lead guitar; ex-**Angels**, **Party Boys**), Steve Crofts (guitar; ex-Black Cat Moan), Alan Lancaster (bass; ex-Status Quo, **Party Boys**) and Peter Heckenberg (drums; ex-Black Cat Moan).

Albums: *Beats from a Single Drum* (Mushroom/Festival, 1988), *Blood from Stone* (Mushroom/Festival, 1990).

Further reading: *Angry: Scarred For Life* by Karen Dewey (Ironbark/Pan Macmillan), 1994.

Greg Anderson

Style: *Pop, country*

Singer/songwriter Greg Anderson began singing in the 1960s, doing country tours and making regular television appearances. He recorded two beat pop singles for the Kommotion label in 1966, 'I've Been Unfaithful'/'Mickey's Monkey' and 'I Feel Good'/'When It's Over'. In 1970 he represented Australia at Expo '70 in Osaka, Japan. His song 'No Roses For Michael' was the theme for a television drama about a drug addict. Festival issued the song as a single (with 'Ned Kelly' on the flip side) and it reached #21 in October 1970. Greg recorded four more singles for Festival: 'Just Come Running to Me'/'Live for Life' (1971), 'It's Over'/'Shame' (1971), 'Someone Somewhere'/'It's Over' (1972) and 'Thank Your Lucky Stars'/'It's Over' (1972), plus one album.

Albums: *Greg Anderson* (Festival, 1970), *Greg Anderson* (budget reissue, Festival/Harlequin, 1973).

Peter Andre

Style: *Dance funk*

British-born singer Peter Andre (b. 1973, real name Peter Andrea) first came to the nation's attention when his debut single, a cover of Brenton Wood's 1967 worldwide hit 'Gimme Little Sign', reached #3 on the national charts in March 1993. 'Gimme

Little Sign' went on to become the twelfth biggest selling single in Australia for the year. The follow-up, 'Funky Junky', reached #13 in July 1993, and Andre issued his debut, self-titled album in December. Andre scored well at the 1993 Australian Record Industry Association (ARIA) Awards by winning Best Pop Release for his *Peter Andre* album and Highest Selling Australian Single for 'Gimme Little Sign'.

His next single, 'Let's Get It On'/'Do You Wanna Dance', reached #17 in January 1994, by which time Andre was one of the hottest dance artists in the country. 'To The Top' only managed #46 (June 1994), but 'Mysterious Girl' restored him to the Top 10 (#8) in October 1995. Andre's collaboration with vocal harmony group Past to Present 'Get Down on it' resulted in another Top 10 placing (#5) during March 1996.

In 1993, Andre turned his attention to the UK market. Andre's family had emigrated to Australia from London in the early 1980s, and he returned to his homeland after a ten-year absence. In 1996, Andre broke into the UK dance/pop market in a big way. His debut UK single 'Turn it Up' managed the minor placing of #64 in June 1995, followed by 'Mysterious Girl' at #53 in September and 'Only One' at #16 in April 1996. Mushroom (UK) reissued 'Mysterious Girl' in June, whereupon it hit the #2 spot. Then the singles 'Flava' (September 1996) and 'I Feel You' (November), plus the album *Natural* (September), all made their debuts at the coveted #1 spot on the UK charts. 'I Feel You' had advance orders of 250 000 copies alone. In the era of boy band dance-pop (Take That, Boyzone), Andre became the ultimate pin-up idol. Andre's career also received a boost in the USA when the Hispanic community began playing and buying his records in large quantities.

Albums: *Peter Andre* (Melodian/Mushroom, 1993), *Natural* (Melodian/Mushroom, 1996).

The Angels

Formed: *1974*
Style: *Hard rock*
Original line-up: *Bernard 'Doc' Neeson (bass, vocals), John Brewster (rhythm guitar, vocals), Rick Brewster (lead guitar), Peter Christopoulos (aka Charlie King; drums)*

Alongside **Cold Chisel**, **Midnight Oil**, **The Hitmen** and **Rose Tattoo**, The Angels had a profound effect on the Australian live music scene of the late 1970s/early 1980s. The Angels helped redefine the Australian pub rock tradition, a tradition that had its kickstart at the hands of **Billy Thorpe** and The Aztecs, **Coloured Balls**, **AC/DC** and others earlier in the decade. The Angels' brand of no-frills, hard-driving boogie rock attracted pub goers in unprecendented numbers. In turn, The Angels' shows raised the standard expected of live music. After 20 years on the road, the band showed little sign of easing up on the hard rock fever.

Doc Neeson, The Angels

The Angels originally formed in 1970 as Moonshine Jug and String Band, playing coffee houses and university campuses around Adelaide, South Australia. The line-up included John Brewster (guitar, banjo, harp, washboard), Rick Brewster (violin, percussion), Craig Holden (guitar), Bernard 'Doc' Neeson (aka Doc Talbot; guitar, vocals), Bob Petchell (banjo, harp) and Pete Thorpe (tea chest bass). Moonshine Jug and String Band issued the independent single 'That's All Right with Me'/'She Belongs to Me' and the four-track EP 'Keep You on the Move' which was a Top 5 hit in Adelaide. Both records came out on manager John Woodruff's Sphere label. The band reformed in 1993 and recorded the album *Rent Party* (1994).

In 1974 the band turned electric and began playing 1950s rock'n'roll/R&B material on the pub circuit as The Keystone Angels. A national tour as backing band for Chuck Berry, a standing ovation at the 1975 Sunbury festival and a single, 'Keep on

Dancing'/'Good Day Rock'n'Roll' (also on Sphere, 1975), all followed. By 1976, the band had toughened its sound into a unique brand of beefy hard rock and, as The Angels, they were signed to the Albert label. Vanda and Young produced the band's first single, 'Am I Ever Gonna See Your Face Again?'/'Round We Go' (May 1976). Graham 'Buzz Throckman' Bidstrup replaced Charlie King on drums in August 1976, and Chris Bailey (ex-Red Angel Panic, **Headband**) joined on bass in January 1977. That allowed Neeson to concentrate on his duties as frontman. With renewed vigour, The Angels issued the single 'You're a Lady Now'/'Can't Get Lucky' (July 1977) and the album *The Angels* (September).

The Angels started 1978 with the release of the crunching single 'Comin' Down'/'Live it Up' (March), which was a sign of things to come. The band cracked the national charts for the first time with the buzzing 'Take a Long Line'/'Love Takes Care' (July 1978; #29 in November). Mark Opitz produced the band's watershed second album, *Face To Face* (August), which reached #16 in November. It stayed on the charts for 79 weeks to qualify for platinum status four times over (280 000 copies sold).

By that stage, The Angels were Australia's highest paid band, attracting record crowds wherever they played. As the consummate frontman, the charismatic Doc Neeson injected a strong theatrical edge into the band's on-stage antics. The Angels were often seen as a punk/new wave outfit, yet the high energy sound, powerful guitar riffing and muscular yet supple rhythm section took the band beyond such easy categorisations.

In November 1978, The Angels supported David Bowie on his first Australian tour, which coincided with the release of *The Tour* EP: 'After The Rain'/'Who Rings The Bell?' (live), 'Comin' Down' (live). On New Year's Eve 1979, The Angels played in front of close to 100 000 people on the steps of the Sydney Opera House. The night ended in a riot and rock music was banned from official Sydney New Year's Eve celebrations. Chris Bailey and Doc Neeson were both hit on the head with bottles and had to receive stitches to deep cuts.

The third album, *No Exit* (#8 in July 1979) produced one single 'Shadow Boxer'/'Planned Obsolescence' (#25 in June 1979). Alberts also issued the 12-inch EP 'Out of the Blue', 'Mr Damage' (live)/'Save Me' (live), 'Am I Ever Gonna See Your Face Again?' (1979 version)(#29 in November 1979) and the compilation album *The Angels' Greatest* (#5 in May 1980) before The Angels signed and American deal for five years with CBS/Epic. The first CBS/Epic album, *Dark Room* (#6 in June 1980), yielded three singles: 'No Secrets'/'Staring Voices' (#8 in May 1980), 'Poor Baby'/'I'm Scared' (live) (June) and 'Face the Day'/'Public Enemy' (September). Meanwhile, The Angels had toured the USA, billed as Angel City. The name change came about to avoid confusion with the US glam metal band Angel.

On their first US tour (supporting Cheap Trick), The Angels had all their equipment stolen in Chicago. Cheap Trick's Rick Neilson donated several guitars in order to help keep the band on the road. Angel City was kicked off a Kinks tour, so the story went, because the band was too good! US Epic issued the albums *Face to Face* (a compilation of the Australian albums *Face to Face* and *No Exit*), *Dark Room* and *Night Attack*. Although The Angels rarely charted in the USA, bands like Mötley Crüe (who covered 'Take a Long Line'), Guns N' Roses (who covered 'Marseilles') and Great White (who recorded 'Face The Day' and 'Can't Shake It') have cited them as a primary influence.

In March 1981, New Zealander Brent Eccles (ex-Space Waltz, Citizen Band) replaced Bidstrup who went on to **GANGgajang** and **The Party Boys**. That same month, the non-album single 'Into the Heat'/'Back on You' (later included on the compilation *Greatest Hits Vol. II*) reached #14 on the Australian chart. The new line-up issued the *Never So Live* 12-inch EP ('Fashion and Fame', 'Talk About You'/'Bad Dream', 'Angel') (#17 in October 1981) and the album *Night Attack* (November) which saw the songs moving into heavy metal territory. The album peaked at #11 on the national chart, and produced two further singles 'Night Attack'/'Devil's Gate' (February 1982) and 'Living on the Outside'/'Storm the Bastille' (May 1982). In April 1982, Los Angeles musician Jim Hilbun replaced Bailey, and the band toured the USA for the fourth time.

The albums *Watch the Red* (#6 in May 1983) and the American recorded *Two Minute Warning* (#2 in February 1985) were well received. *Watch The Red* produced the singles 'Stand Up'/'Chaplain's Drum' (#21 in November 1982), 'Eat City'/'Let Me In' (#22 in April 1983), 'Live Lady Live'/'Live Lady Live #2' (May) and 'Is That You?'/'Stay Away' (August). *Two Minute Warning* gave rise to 'Between the Eyes'/'Dead Man's Shoes' (October 1984), 'Look the Other Way'/'Run for Shelter' (February 1985), 'Sticky Little Bitch'/'Breakdown' (March) and the double single 'Underground'/'Underground' (live); 'Small Price' (live)/'Look The Other Way' (live) (June).

Despite the strong album sales, all was not well within The Angels' camp and long-serving member John Brewster left in February 1986. He was replaced by Bob Spencer (ex-**Finch**, **Skyhooks**,

Young Lions) in March. Brewster spent time with **The Party Boys** and then joined **The Bombers**.

The Angels came out of that difficult period of transition with the multifarious *Howling* album (October 1986) which reached #6 nationally in December. It produced four singles in 'Nature Of the Beast'/'All Night for You' (#22 in August 1986), 'Don't Waste My Time'/'Hide Your Face' (#25 in October), 'Can't Take Anymore'/'Stonewall' (April 1987) and a tenacious cover of the Mann/Weil song 'We Gotta Get Out Of This Place'/'Be With You' (January 1987) which reached #6 in March. The 12-inch version of 'Don't Waste My Time' added 'Don't Waste My Time' (extended mix), while the 12-inch of 'Can't Take Anymore' also contained the additional track 'Standing Over You'.

The double live album *Liveline* (February 1988) spanned ten years of Angels material. It peaked at #2 nationally, and yielded two singles, 'Am I Ever Gonna See Your Face Again'/'Marseilles' (#6 in March 1988; the 12-inch version added 'Shoot it Up') and 'Love Takes Care'/'Be with You' (May; the 12-inch added 'Eat City'). In May 1988 Spencer broke his wrist and 21-year-old **Jimi 'The Human' Hocking** deputised for him on the ambitious Liveline tour of Australia. The Angels also issued the non-album single 'Finger on the Trigger'/'Straight Aces' in November. Once again, the 12-inch version boasted an additional track, 'Living in the Bodyguard of Luxury'.

In 1989 The Angels signed with Chrysalis in the USA, and recorded *Beyond Salvation* in Memphis, Tennessee, with producer Terry Manning (ZZ Top, Led Zeppelin). During that time the band, with Manning on guitar, played fun gigs billed as Dancing Richard and the Dicks and The Cow Demons. The band members were also made honourary citizens of Memphis. Halfway through the sessions, Perth musician James Morley (ex-Strawberry Blonde) replaced Jim Hilbun. On its release in June 1990, *Beyond Salvation* went to #1 in Australia, remaining on the charts for 38 weeks and achieving platinum sales in the process. It was one of The Angels' best albums, Manning having stripped the band's sound back to basics and brought the guitars to the fore.

It spawned four popular singles: 'Let The Night Roll on'/'Junk City' (#17 in February 1990), 'Dogs are Talking' backed with demo tracks by **Baby Animals**, The Hurricanes and Desert Cats (#11 in May, and the band's first-ever gold single), 'Back Street Pick Up'/'Take It Easy' (#23 in October) and 'Rhythm Rude Girl'/'Beyond Salvation', 'Bitch' (live) (November). The US version of *Beyond Salvation* on Chrysalis featured a completely different track selection, including a number of alternative versions of songs on the Australian edition.

On 18 February 1990, The Angels, along with **Midnight Oil**, **Split Enz**, **Crowded House**, **Jimmy Barnes**, **Noiseworks** and **v Spy v Spy** played to over 40 000 people at the Earthquake Relief concert in Newcastle. In February 1991, The Angels issued the double single pack 'Bleeding with the Times'. It contained two previously unissued tracks from the Memphis *Beyond Salvation* sessions, 'Bleeding with the Times' and 'Blood on the Moon', plus two remixes from the *Howling* album 'Don't Waste My Time' and 'When the Time Comes'.

The band's thirteenth album, *Red Back Fever* (December 1991), produced the singles 'Some of that Love'/'Mercury Blues' (October 1991), 'Once Bitten Twice Shy'/'Don't Break Me Down' (January 1992) and 'Tear Me Apart'/'Tear Me Apart' (extended mix) (#33 in July). Mushroom reissued the album in July 1992 as a double CD pack with *Left Hand Drive* (an album of rare and previously unissued material) in time for another extensive national tour, the Alcohol and Violence Tears You Apart tour.

In 1993 John Brewster and Jim Hilbun returned to the fold, replacing Spencer and Morley. Spencer formed The Temple Gods with Liam Shields (vocals), John Conomos (guitar), Rick Grant (bass) and Peter Heckenberg (drums; ex-B.B. **Steal**, Black Cat Moan) with whom he issued the album *Tempted* (October 1995).

The Angels' sixteenth album, *Evidence* (December 1994), was a 'Best Of' collection with two new tracks, 'Turn It On' and 'Don't Need Mercy'. The tracks were issued as CD singles in November ('Don't Need Mercy'/'The Zoo-Name Dropping-Bow Wow', 'Stay Away') and March 1995 ('Turn It On'/'Man There') respectively. 'Turn It On' and 'Don't Need Mercy' also turned up on the *Hard Evidence Tour* CD EP (April) along with two other recent cuts, 'Spinning My Wheels' and 'Blue Light'.

At the end of 1995, The Angels announced their impending split. The Farewell Tour went so well that the band decided to stay together and continued touring throughout 1996. Finding themselves without a record deal, The Angels issued their next CD single, 'Call That Living' (July 1996) independently. In July 1997, The Angels set off on the Lounge Lizards tour (playing acoustic instruments) with guest singers **Angry Anderson** and **Ross Wilson**. By that stage the band had commenced work on a new album for release in 1998.

Albums: *The Angels* (Albert/EMI, 1977), *Face to Face* (Albert/EMI, 1978), *No Exit* (Albert/EMI, 1979), *The Angels' Greatest* (Albert/EMI, 1980), *Dark Room* (CBS/Epic, 1980), *Night Attack* (CBS/Epic,

1981), *Watch the Red* (CBS/Epic, 1983), *Two Minute Warning* (Mushroom/Festival, 1984), *Greatest Hits Vol. II* (CBS/Epic, 1984), *Howling* (Mushroom/Festival, 1986), *Their Finest Hour—and Then Some (Greatest Hits)* (Albert/EMI, 1986), *Liveline* (Mushroom/Festival, 1988), *The Angels' Box Set* (Albert/Epic, 1988), *Beyond Salvation* (Mushroom/Festival, 1990), *Red Back Fever* (Mushroom/Festival, 1991), *Red Back Fever/Left Hand Drive* (Mushroom/Festival, 1992), *Evidence* (Mushroom/Festival, 1994).

Christine Anu

Style: *Dance funk*

Singer/songwriter/dancer Christine Anu was born in 1970 in Cairns, Queensland to Torres Strait Islander parents. She first came to prominence as a graduate of the Aboriginal and Islander Dance Theatre. She also appeared as a guest of the Bangarra Dance Company in the ballet *Praying Mantis Dreaming*. Anu toured as backing vocalist with **Neil Murray** and The Rainmakers for a year, then issued her debut single, a dance-oriented remake of **Paul Kelly's** 'Last Train', in December 1993. Kelly sang backing vocals on the single. 1994 saw the release of her second single, 'Monkey and the Turtle' for the White label. An infectious mix of urban dance grooves, traditional Islander stories and funky riffs, it augured well for the future.

Not drowning, waving member David Bridie produced Anu's acclaimed debut album, *Stylin' Up* (May 1995), which spawned two hit singles in 'Party' and 'Come On'. With the album Anu won the Australian Record Industry Association (ARIA) award for the Best Aboriginal/Torres Strait Islander release of 1995. Her version of **Neil Murray's** 'My Island Home' won Song of the Year at the 1995 Australian Performing Rights Association (APRA) Awards ceremony. Anu saw out 1995 with successful tours of South East Asia and Australia. Her backing band comprised Bridie (keyboards), Leroy Cummings (guitar), Stephen Hadley (bass; ex-**Black Sorrows**), Peter Luscombe (drums; ex-**Black Sorrows**), Anita Spring (backing vocals) and Michelle Lee (backing vocals).

In May 1996, the ABC profiled the singer in a television special called *Saltwater Soul*, which also featured concert footage. At the tenth annual Australian Record Industry Association (ARIA) Awards (1996), Anu was named Best Female Artist, ahead of the likes of **Kylie Minogue**, **Tina Arena**, **Wendy Matthews** and **Kate Ceberano**. Anu also took out Best Indigenous Release for 'Come On'. Anu sang on 'Now Until the Break of Day' (September 1997), the first single lifted from the soundtrack to Baz Luhrmann's feature film, *A Midsummer Night's Dream*. She shared the vocals with Kiva's Royce Doherty and David Hobson.

Christine Anu

Album: *Stylin' Up* (White/Mushroom/Festival, 1995)

The Apartments

Formed: *1978*
Style: *Pop*
Original line-up: *Peter Milton Walsh (guitar, vocals), Michael O'Connor (guitar, vocals), Peter Whitby (bass, vocals), Peter Martin (drums)*

Like a number of Australian musicians who got their start during the late 1970s new wave movement—Simon Bonney (**Crime and the City Solution**), Rowland S. Howard (These Immortal Souls)—The Apartments' Peter Milton Walsh has received more acclaim in Europe than at home. Walsh's songs are full of bittersweet, lyrical imagery. His admirers include the likes of **Ed Kuepper**, **Dave Graney** (who covered Walsh's 'World Full of Liars') and UK band This Mortal Coil.

Walsh formed The Apartments in Brisbane. He was also briefly a member of the nascent **Go-Betweens** towards the end of 1978. The Apartments issued the pop-oriented *Return of the Hypnotist* EP on **The Go-Betweens'** Able Label (October 1979). By 1980 Walsh was playing with Out of Nowhere (one single: 'Remember, Remember'/'No Resistance' on the Prince Melon label) which included **Laughing Clowns** member Jeffrey Wegener on drums. Michael O'Connor joined Zero which included future **Go-Betweens** members Lindy Morrison and John Willsteed.

In 1982 Walsh moved to New York and joined power pop band The Colors (alongside another ex-Brisbane lad Robert Vickers, ex-Numbers and pre-**Go-Betweens**). Walsh then joined **Ed Kuepper**'s band **Laughing Clowns** in London, staying long enough to play bass on the acclaimed *Law of Nature* album. He reformed The Apartments in 1984 with Gary Warner (piano), Graeme Beavis (guitar, vocals; ex-**Fun Things**), Joe Borkowski (bass) and Bruce Carrick (drums), and issued the single 'All You Wanted'/'Fever Elsewhere' on Hot (November).

Walsh relocated to London and issued the 12-inch EP 'The Shyest Time' (June 1987), plus the cult classic album *The Evening Visits . . . And Stays For Years* on Rough Trade. Backing musicians on the album included Bruce Carrick and **The Triffids'** Graham Lee (lap steel), plus Clare Kenny (bass; ex-Orange Juice) and Ben Watt (guitar; from Everything But the Girl). 'The Shyest Time' was used on the soundtrack to the John Hughes teen film *Some Kind of Wonderful*. Just as interest in the band was beginning to escalate, Rough Trade went broke, which forced Walsh to return to Sydney.

The 1989 line-up of The Apartments included Michael Couvret (bass, ex-**Celibate Rifles**), Mark Dawson (drums), Astrid Munday (backing vocals) and guest **Ed Kuepper**. The 1993 line-up of Milton Walsh, Dawson, Greg Atkinson (guitar; ex-**Ups And Downs,** on loan from **Big Heavy Stuff**) and John Willsteed (bass; ex-Zero, **Go-Betweens**) recorded the album *Drift* and the CD EP 'Life'. Vocalists Carolyn Polley (from **Big Heavy Stuff**) and Clare Kenny (Shakespeare's Sister), plus violin player Kathryn Weimass, also contributed to the album.

Drift was issued in Europe on the New Rose label, and garnered generous reviews in France. It was so well received in France, in fact, that while *Drift* sold less than 200 copies in Australia, it reputedly sold 20 000 there. For the May 1995 album *A Life Full of Farewells*, The Apartments delivered all the right elements that make up a great pop record, but it still failed to sell in Australia. Nevertheless, Walsh flew to France to undertake a week's worth of television and press promotion, and to play three showcase gigs with The Apartments. In late 1996, Hot issued the mail-order only album *Fete Foraine* which consisted of acoustic reworkings of previously released Apartments material. Walsh recorded a new album, *Apart*, backed by Ken Gormly (bass; from **The Cruel Sea**) and Gene Maynard (drums) which came out in October 1997.

Albums: *The Evening Visits . . . And Stays For Years* (Rough Trade, 1985), *Drift* (Torn & Frayed/Shock, 1993), *A Life Full of Farewells* (Hot, 1995), *Fete Foraine* (Hot, mail-order only, 1996), *Apart* (Hot, 1997).

Aragon

Formed: *1987*
Style: *Symphonic rock*
Original line-up: *Les Dougan (vocals), Tom Behrsing (keyboards), John Poloyannis (guitar), Tony Italia (drums)*

Symphonic rock, by and large, has not been a popular genre in Australia. During the 1970s, Sydney bands **Sebastian Hardie**, Windchase and **Aleph** found some success. Melbourne bands Product, Mandrake Garden and Aragon continued the tradition during the 1980s.

Scottish-born Les Dougan, Italian-born Tony Italia, German-born Tom Behrsing and Greek-born John Poloyannis joined forces as Aragon in 1987. The band obviously had a very European sound that also drew on the complexities and sense of theatre displayed by British bands like Genesis and Marillion. The band's May 1988 independent mini-album *Don't Bring The Rain* (with session bassist Rob Bacon) was hailed as a progressive rock masterpiece by British and European underground music magazines. It was virtually ignored in Australia except by a hardcore following. Californian label Progressive Records issued the album in the USA with additional material the band recorded in 1990. Dutch label Si Music Records put out Aragon's next album, *The Meeting,* in 1992. *The Meeting* comprised Act V of the band's ambitious concept piece *Mouse.* The band's European popularity resulted in French fans setting up the Aragon fan club The Cradle (named after a track on *Don't Bring The Rain*).

Albums: *Don't Bring The Rain* (Aragon Music, 1988), *Don't Bring The Rain* (Progressive, 1990; USA only), *The Meeting* (Si Music, 1992; Europe only).

The Arctic Circles

Formed: *1983*
Style: *Garage-punk, R&B*
Original line-up: *Leo Kelly (vocals), Alex Plegt (guitar), Greg Baxter (bass), Steven Danko (drums)*

1960s-influenced band The Arctic Circles played the Melbourne independent scene circa mid-1980s, alongside the likes of Inner Sleeves, **The Gas Babies**, **The Bo-Weevils**, **Shindiggers**, etc. The band's sound mixed garage-punk, psychedelia and tough R&B riffs. The Arctic Circles issued the single 'Angel'/'My Baby Said That' (October 1985) and the mini-album *Time* (March 1987) on Mr Spaceman Records. The band also contributed three tracks, 'Walk Away', 'You Satisfy Me' and 'Why?', to 2JJJ's 1985 Various Artists compilation *Cooking With George Mark Too*. Plegt later played with beat pop band Forbidden Planet.

Mini-album: *Time* (Mr Spaceman, 1986).

Tina Arena

Style: *Adult contemporary pop*

Tina Arena

Singer Tina (Filippina) Arena (b. 1969) got her start in show business as a team member of Melbourne television variety show *Young Talent Time* during the late 1970s. Often referred to by compere **Johnny Young** as 'Tiny' Tina Arena, it took her many years to shake off the stigma attached. Undaunted she has gone on to become one of Australia's most popular performers of the 1990s.

Arena issued her first dance-pop single, 'Turn Up The Beat', in 1987, and appeared as support for Lionel Ritchie on his Australian tour. She began playing the Melbourne pub and club circuit with a nine-piece group called Network, and co-starred with David Atkins in his stage show *Dynamite*, which ran for ten months. Arena scored her first hit single with the uptempo 'I Need Your Body'/'Stage Fright' (#3 in June 1990). At that stage Arena was projecting a raunchy disco-diva persona, with the video clip to 'I Need Your Body' flaunting a pouting rock starlet with bouncing cleavage and attitude to burn. She followed up with 'The Machine's Breaking Down' (#23 in September 1990) and 'Strong as Steel' (#30 in November 1990), plus the Ross Inglas-produced album *Strong as Steel*. Arena's fifth single, 'Woman's Work', appeared in March 1991.

In 1991, dissatisfied with the way her career was progressing, Arena moved to Los Angeles to take singing lessons and commence songwriting. She returned to Australia and toured with the 1993 local production of Andrew Lloyd Webber and Tim Rice's musical *Joseph and the Amazing Technicolor Dreamcoat* in the role of The Narrator. Arena adopted a more mature, sophisticated, soul-tinged style and approach for her second album, the David Tyson-produced *Don't Ask*. Arena co-wrote ten of the album's 11 tracks, and her powerful, crystal clear voice more than adequately matched the material on offer. The album was a huge success, and spawned five hit singles: 'Chains' (#4 in November 1994), 'Sorrento Moon (I Remember)' (#7 in April 1995), 'Heaven Help My Heart' (#22 in August 1995), 'Wasn't It Good?' (#11 in November 1995) and 'That's the Way a Woman Feels' (#31 in March 1996). Surprisingly, the album only reached #1 on the national charts in November 1995—a year after its release.

Not only was *Don't Ask* the best selling Australian album for 1995, but also the best selling album for the year, ahead of Celine Dion, The Cranberries, Michael Jackson, Mariah Carey and **silverchair**. It stayed in the Top 50 for 84 weeks and went on to sell over 600 000 copies (eight times platinum) in Australia alone, the most ever by an Australian female recording artist. Arena also took out the 1995 Australian Record Industry Association (ARIA) Awards for Best Australian Album, Best Female

Artist, Best Pop Release (for 'Chains') and Song of the Year (for 'Chains'). When issued in Europe, *Don't Ask* sold 70 000 copies in its first week of release, and the soulful 'Chains' reached the Top 10 in Britain (#6), Ireland (#9), Holland (#7) and Israel (#8).

'Heaven Help My Heart' followed 'Chains' into the UK Top 20, and Arena earned a nomination for Best International Newcomer at the BRIT Awards, the UK equivalent of the Grammys. In December 1995, Arena married her long-time manager Ralph Carr. March 1996 saw the release of 'Chains' in the USA, with *Don't Ask* following a month later. The album also came out in Japan. Arena based herself in Los Angeles, poised to make her presence felt on the vast American market. By 1997, *Don't Ask* had sold two million copies around the world. Arena re-emerged in August 1997 when her third album, *In Deep*, made its debut at #1 on the Australian chart. The album's first single, 'Burn', had reached #2 a month earlier. 'If I Didn't Love You' followed in November. By that stage *In Deep* was on its way to selling triple platinum (210 000 copies).

Albums: *Strong As Steel* (Sony/Columbia, 1990), *Don't Ask* (Sony/Columbia, 1994), *In Deep* (Sony/Columbia, 1997.)

Ariel

Formed: *1973*
Style: *Rock*
Original line-up: *Mike Rudd (guitar, vocals; ex-Chants R&B,* **Party Machine**, **Sons of the Vegetal Mother**, **Spectrum***), John Mills (keyboards; ex-***Spectrum***),* **Tim Gaze** *(guitar, vocals; ex-***Tamam Shud**, **Kahvas Jute**, *Miss Universe), Bill Putt (bass; ex-Lost Souls,* **Spectrum***), Nigel Macara (drums; ex-***Tamam Shud**, *Miss Universe)*

Ariel was the brainchild of Mike Rudd and Bill Putt following on from the break-up of their previous band, **Spectrum**, in April 1973. Ariel's more direct approach encompassed progressive rock, blues, hard rock and pub-rock with country overtones. The band derived its name from the fairy messenger Ariel in Shakespeare's *The Tempest.*

The joyous reggae-rock single 'Jamaican Farewell'/'Red Hot Momma' (September 1973; #34 in October) and the accomplished *A Strange Fantastic Dream* album (December 1973) set the tone for the band's work. The original line-up broke up in April 1974, leaving only Rudd and Putt. John Lee (drums; ex-Sayla, **Blackfeather**, **Dingoes**) joined in May, followed by Harvey James (guitar; ex-Sayla, **Mississippi**) who joined in July. The sturdy 'Yeah Tonight'/'(I am the) Laughing Man (for Leo)' single came out in August, and two months later Ariel left for the UK. EMI (England) issued *A Strange Fantastic Dream* on the Harvest offshoot label, and then booked the band into London's Abbey Road Studios (December 1974). Because EMI (Australia) had rejected Rudd's projected science-fiction concept album *The Jellabad Mutant*, Ariel came up with the *Rock & Roll Scars* set. Rudd viewed the album as retrogressive because it mixed re-recorded versions of old **Spectrum** and Ariel material with only three all-new songs. Nevertheless, the album stood up remarkably well with the band boosting the old songs with a hard rock edge, and delivering the new tunes in the same robust vein. 'Keep on Dancing (with Me)'/'I'll Be Gone' came out as a single (March 1975).

Glyn Mason (guitar, vocals; ex-Rebels, **Chain**, Copperwine, **Home**) joined in January 1975. Following a UK tour, Nigel Macara returned to replace Lee (who joined UK band Dirty Tricks) in June 1975. The three guitar line-up of Ariel recorded the single 'I'll Take You High'/'I Can't Say what I Mean' (December 1975), and appeared on the live, Various Artists album *A-Reefer-Derci* on the Mushroom label (1976). In March 1976 Ariel brought in Tony Slavich (keyboards; ex-**Richard Clapton** Band) to replace Harvey James, who left to join **Sherbet**. The new line-up recorded 'I Can Do Anything'/'Cypherland Blues' and *Goodnight Fiona.* The album was a fine showcase for Ariel's pub-rock, blues and country sound, but it found the band treading water rather than progressing. Nevertheless, it peaked at #19 in Melbourne during October 1976. That same month, Iain McLennan (ex-**Richard Clapton** Band) replaced Macara on drums.

The band's popularity on the pub circuit did little to bolster record sales. 'Disco Dilemma'/'How Do You Do It?' (April 1977) and 'It's Only Love'/'It's Time We Said Our Goodbyes' (August 1977) were minor hits. Ariel called it a day with a lavish concert (called Island Fantasia) held at Melbourne's Dallas Brooks Hall on 21 August 1977. The concert resulted in the live albums *Aloha Ariel* and *Ariel Alive!!—More From Before.* Rudd produced Melbourne band Daniel's debut album *Last Night in the City* (August 1978), before teaming up again with Bill Putt in Mike Rudd's Instant Replay, **Mike Rudd and The Heaters**, W.H.Y., Number 9 and The Burwood Blues Band. Rudd and Putt issued the album *Living on a Volcano* in 1995. Putt was also part of the 1978 **Air Supply** touring band. In August 1997, Rudd and Putt reformed the *Rock & Roll Scars*

Ariel line-up (with John Lee and Harvey James) for a series of gigs.

Mason toured briefly with **Richard Clapton**, and played with the short-lived Loose String Band. He formed The Stockley See Mason Band in late 1978 with fellow veterans Chris Stockley (guitar, vocals; ex-**Axiom**, **Dingoes**, Greg Quill's Southern Cross) and Sam See (guitar, vocals; ex-**Sherbet**, **Flying Circus**, **Fraternity**, Greg Quill's Southern Cross). Mason left in May 1980, and went on to play with Tour De Force, **The Fabulous Zarsoff Brothers** and the Doc Span Blues Band.

Albums: *A Strange Fantastic Dream* (EMI, 1973), *Rock & Roll Scars (Before The Mutant)* (EMI/Harvest, 1975), *Goodnight Fiona* (CBS, 1976), *Aloha Ariel* (Image, 1977), *Ariel Alive!!—More from Before* (Image, 1978), *Live in Concert* (double repackage of *Aloha Ariel* and *Ariel Alive!!—More from Before*, Avenue, 1980).

The Armchairs (*see* North 2 Alaskans)

Armoured Angel

Formed: *1987*
Style: *Death metal*
Original line-up: *Glen 'Lucy' Luck (bass), Matt Green (guitar), Joel Green (drums, vocals)*

That Australia's conservative national capital, Canberra, should give rise to one of the country's first death metal bands in Armoured Angel has long been cause for amazement. The band's earliest influences included UK bands such as Motorhead and Venom. Armoured Angel's cassette demos, *Wings of Death* and *Communion*, reached metal fans across the world and garnered favourable reviews in UK metal magazines like *Kerrang!* and *Metal Hammer*. *Wings of Death* was later issued in the UK as a 12-inch EP by CCG Records.

At the start of 1993, the band played on the Sydney bill of the inaugural national Big Day Out tour. PolyGram's development label Id issued the CD EPs *Stigmatyr* (December 1992) and *Mysterium* (April 1994), which further displayed the band's brutally heavy sound. The band supported international death metal visitors Morbid Angel, Bolt Thrower and Carcass. In 1995, Armoured Angel toured the UK, Europe and America. For many years, Armoured Angel was one of the driving forces behind Canberra's annual *Metal for the Brain* benefit concert.

Ray Arnott

Style: *Hard rock*

Veteran drummer Ray Arnott's professional career extends back to The Chelsea Set, **Cam-Pact** and The Browns during the 1960s. Throughout the 1970s he played in **Company Caine**, Genesis, **Spectrum**, **Mighty Kong**, **The Dingoes**, One Nite Stand and the Ray Arnott Band. His 1980s work has encompassed time with **Cheetah**, **John Paul Young** and The All Stars, **Cold Chisel**, the **Jimmy Barnes** Band and the Ray Arnott Group (R.A.G.).

Arnott started out in 1964 as lead singer with the South Town Moods. He played drums until 1977 when he formed R&B band One Nite Stand in which he was frontman. The original One Nite Stand line-up comprised Nick Head (guitar), Dennis Millar (guitar), Peter Howell (bass; ex-**Margret Roadknight**) and Trevor Young (drums; ex-**Coloured Balls**). By August 1977, the line-up comprised Arnott, Peter Laffy (guitar; ex-Fox, **Freeway**, **Mondo Rock**), Randy Bulpin (guitar; ex-Toads, Ready Rubbed), Bruno De Stanislo (bass; ex-**Bandicoot**) and Peter Reed (drums; ex-**New Dream**, Hot Dog, **Bandicoot**).

Renowned producers Vanda and Young then signed Arnott to a solo deal with the Albert label. The Leszek Karski-produced hard rock album *Rude Dudes* (October 1979) included the singles 'Need Your Love'/'Boogie on' (August) and 'On the Run'/'Boogie on' (November). The Ray Arnott Band included Warren Morgan (piano, ex-**Chain**, **Billy Thorpe** and The Aztecs, **John Paul Young** and the All Stars), Ronnie Peel (bass, ex-**La De Das**, **Rockwell T. James** and The Rhythm Aces, J.P.Y. and the All Stars), Les Karski (guitar, ex-Supercharge), Ace Follington (drums, ex-**Chain**, the **Richard Clapton** Band, Australia) and back-up singers Harry Tate and Joey Diamond.

Arnott continued his solo career with R.A.G. in 1984 for the singles 'Flaming Heart'/'Girls' (November) and 'Slow Dance'/'Christine' (June 1985) and album *Rock'n'Roll* (all Albert).

Albums: *Rude Dudes* (Albert/EMI, 1979), *Rock'n'Roll* (Albert/EMI, 1985)

Doug Ashdown

Style: *Folk*

Adelaide-born singer/songwriter Doug Ashdown first came to public attention during the 1960s with a series of folk/country albums for CBS, and the singles 'Something Strange' (1968) and 'Whole Lotta Shakin' Going On'/'Marcie' (1969) for Philips.

In 1970 he signed to the newly founded independent label Sweet Peach and issued the singles 'The Day They Freed the Noise'/'I've Come to Save the World' and 'Saddest Day of All'/'Georgetown', plus one of Australia's first double albums, *The Age of Mouse*. Backing musicians for the album included members of the nascent **Fraternity**.

Ashdown issued the album *Live* during 1972. MCA issued *The Age of Mouse* in the USA which prompted Ashdown and his producer Jimmy Stewart's move to Nashville, Tennessee. Ashdown concentrated on songwriting, and after some success (including a #1 country hit, 'Just Thank Me', for American David Rogers) the pair returned to Australia. They set up the Billingsgate label, and in 1974 issued Ashdown's sixth album, *Leave Love Enough Alone*, which yielded the singles 'They Always Seem to Look Like Marianne'/'Tomorrow is the Last Time' (February) and 'Leave Love Enough Alone'/'Skid Row' (September). The evocative 'Leave Love Enough Alone' was not successful until reissued as 'Winter in America (Leave Love Enough Alone)', when it reached #14 in Melbourne during October 1976, and #30 in Sydney during February 1977.

Ashdown released a batch of strong singles (including 'You're the Song'/'You Are All I Need to Know', 'The Band Played Waltzing Matilda'/'Tell Me Honey', 'Fraser for a Day'/'Promised Land' and 'World for the Right Kind of Man'/'Like a Highway') and albums throughout the late 1970s and early 1980s, with minor chart success. His most recent album, *No Cheap Grace* came out in March 1996.

Albums: *This is Doug Ashdown* (CBS, 1965), *The Real Thing* (CBS, 1966), *Source* (CBS, 1968), *The Age of Mouse* (Sweet Peach, 1970), *Doug Ashdown Live* (Sweet Peach, 1972), *Leave Love Enough Alone* (Billingsgate, 1974), *Winter in America* (reissue of *Leave Love Enough Alone*, Festival/Infinity, 1976), *Trees* (Ash, 1977), *Empty Without You* (Festival, 1977), *The World for the Right Kind of Man* (CBS, 1983), *Love Lives Love Grows* (Larrikin, 1987), *No Cheap Grace* (NashWest/Roadshow, 1996).

Asteroid B-612

Formed: *1992*
Style: *Hard rock*
1993 line-up: *Grant McIver (vocals), John Spittles (guitar), Michael Gibbons (guitar), Scott Nash (bass), Darren Pierce (drums)*

Asteroid B-612 began playing its brand of hard-edged Detroit-inspired 'sonic rock action' around Sydney during 1992. Without falling prey to the pitfalls of such an established form, the band overlayed its bedrock of raunchy 12 bar blues with textbook riffs and searing, dual lead guitar work-outs. Asteroid B-612 played it lean and mean without sounding tired or regressive in the process. Reference points included MC5, **Radio Birdman** and Sonic's Rendezvous Band.

The above line-up recorded the band's 1993 self-titled debut album. Asteroid B-612 shared a single, 'I've Had You', with fellow Sydney outfit Brother Brick. In late 1994, Stewart 'Leadfinger' Cunningham replaced Gibbons and Ben Fox replaced Pierce. Canadian label Lance Rock issued the single 'I've Had You'/'Gimme Some Truth' in 1995. Asteroid issued the album *Forced into a Corner* before signing to Melbourne label Au-go-go for the CD EP *Teen Sublimation Riffs* (1995). Cunningham left Asteroid B-612 while the band was on tour across the USA with Gashuffer in late 1996. He nevertheless appeared on the band's third and best album, *Not Meant for This World*, which came out during October. Ken 'Killer' Watts (ex-Valvolux) replaced Cunningham and the band recommenced touring in early 1997. A new single, 'September Crush', appeared in November.

Albums: *Asteroid B-612* (Destroyer, 1993), *Forced into a Corner* (Destroyer, 1994), *Not Meant for This World* (Au-go-go, 1996).

Asylum

Formed: *1985*
Style: *Hard rock*
Original line-up: *Marc 'Catweazle' Welsh (guitar, vocals), Jason Breitfuss (bass), Brad Foster (drums)*

Gold Coast band Asylum played a tough but melodic mix of hard rock, punk and power pop that drew on Kiss, Cheap Trick, The Ramones and The Stooges for inspiration. Asylum formed in March 1985, quickly outgrowing its local following before relocating to Sydney in 1986. Asylum shared inner-city Sydney gigs with the likes of **Happy Hate Me Nots, The Hard-Ons, Massappeal, Ratcat, The Psychotic Turnbuckles**, etc. Asylum swiftly assumed headlining status by earning a reputation as the band few others wanted to follow on stage. Marc Welsh also began moonlighting with Jed Starr's glam rock band Kings Cross.

Asylum recorded the single 'Leopards'/'Ode to Belial' (November 1987) and mini-album *Home Sweet Home* (January 1989) for the Waterfront label. Au-go-go Records included Asylum's fierce rendition of The Stooges' 'TV Eye' on the Stooges' tribute album *Hard To Beat* (1988). Asylum moved to Melbourne in 1989 and subsequently split up. Welsh joined **Have a Nice Day (HAND)** in 1990. Welsh left **HAND** in 1994 to join Jed Starr's Starworld. By 1996 he was playing bass with hard-rock band Floor Thirteen which comprised Winston Giles (guitar, vocals) and Venom Brown (drums; ex-**Massive Appendage,** Starworld). Floor Thirteen issued the CD EP *The World* on the Pink Tone-Ales label in February 1997. The band's sound mixed Beatles and Cheap Trick-styled melodicism with Jane's Addiction and Stone Temple Pilots-inspired grunge riffs. In May the band headed off to the US for a tour, but Welsh left soon after.

Mini-album: *Home Sweet Home* (Waterfront, 1989).

The Atlantics

Formed: *1961*
Style: *Surf to garage punk*
Original line-up: *Theo Penglis (guitar), Eddy Matzenik (guitar), Bosco Bosonac (bass), Peter Hood (drums)*

Glenn A. Baker has referred to The Atlantics as 'one of the most extraordinarily talented rock groups Australia has ever produced'. The band's sound encompassed surf instrumentals and sneering garage-punk and, as well as issuing 18 singles under its own name, the band also backed **Johnny Rebb** and **Russ Kruger** for a series of fine singles between 1964 and 1969.

The Atlantics formed in Sydney during 1961. Jim Skaithitis replaced Matzenik a year later. The band's first single for CBS 'Moon Man'/'Dark Eyes' (February 1963) echoed The Shadows' twanging guitar sound. 'Bombora'/'Greensleeves' (#1 in Sydney, #5 in Melbourne, July 1963) and 'The Crusher'/'Hootenanny Stomp' (#4 in Sydney, #21 in Melbourne, November 1963) established the band as bona fide leaders of the burgeoning surf instrumental craze. CBS issued 'Bombora' (an Aboriginal word for large waves breaking over rock shelves) in the USA, UK, Europe, Japan and New Zealand. Alongside the likes of The Ventures' 'Walk—Don't Run', The Surfaris' 'Wipe Out', The Chantays' 'Pipeline', The Pyramids' 'Penetration' and Dick Dale's 'Misirlou', 'Bombora' is considered a classic of the surf genre.

The Atlantics cut seven more singles for CBS (including the vocal single 'Surfin' Queen'/'Count Down Stomp', billed as Kenny Shane and The Atlantics) before moving to the Sunshine label in 1966. Over the next year, The Atlantics cut three remarkably tough rock singles, 'It's a Hard Life'/'Why Do You Treat Me Like You Do?' (July 1966), 'I Put a Spell on You'/'By the Glow of a Candle' (January 1967) and 'Come on'/'You Tell Me Why' (March 1967), all of which are highly regarded by aficionados of 1960s garage-punk. Reissue specialists Raven Records included 'Come on' on *Ugly Things* (1980), the seminal collection of Australian 1960s punk artefacts. Sydney band Wet Taxis issued an authentic rendition of 'Come on' as a single on Hot in 1984.

The Atlantics recorded five singles for the Ramrod label, 'Waiting Here for Someone'/'That Lovin' Feeling' (September 1967), 'Sunshine and Roses'/'When I Look Into My Life' (December), 'A Girl Like You'/'Baby Blue' (April 1968), 'What is Love'/'I'll Never Let You Go' (September) and 'Light Shades of Dark Part 1'/'Light Shades of Dark Part 2' (September 1969). The band's last recording was the **Johnny Rebb** single 'Ding Dong'/'Summertime Blues', before they called it quits at the end of the decade.

Albums: *Bombora* (CBS, 1963), *Now It's Stomping Time* (CBS, 1963), *The Explosive Sounds of the Atlantics* (CBS, 1964), *Greatest Hits* (CBS, 1965), *The CBS Singles Collection 1963–65* (Canetoad, 1988), *The Complete CBS Recordings* (Canetoad, 1989), *The Legendary JRA/Ramrod Sessions* (Canetoad 1989).

Atlas Strings

Formed: *1992*
Style: *Pop, folk*
Original line-up: *Ben Mullins (guitar, lead vocals; ex-Benedicts, Roadhead), Michael Armiger (bass; ex-10,000 Guitars,* **Paul Kelly** *Band,* **John Kennedy's Love Gone Wrong, Johnnys, Go-Betweens, Cleopatra Wong,** *Roadhead), Andrew Axton (drums)*

Ben Mullins and Michael Armiger first came together in Sydney band Roadhead, before linking up with Andrew Axton as Atlas Strings. The band's sound mixed melodic pop with a contemporary folk outlook. Reference points for the band's songs included Van Morrison, Bob Dylan and Tim Buckley. Atlas Strings signed to Polydor's Eternity label, alongside **Rebecca's Empire, Blue Million Miles** and Charlotte Grace.

Mullins' first band, The Benedicts, formed in Brisbane during 1988 before moving to Sydney. Tim Hagen (bass) and Leo Mullins (drums) completed the line-up. The band issued two singles on the Waterfront label, 'On the Air'/'Cold Comfort' (1989), and 'Shout Me Down'/'Praying For You' (1990), plus the album *Hoon* (1991). Leo Mullins joined **The Welcome Mat** in May 1991, and Ben Mullins formed Roadhead with Armiger.

Atlas Strings issued the CD EPs *Atlas Strings* (1994) and 'Carelessly' (1994) before Greg Throsby joined on guitar. Two further CD EPs, 'Miss Judas' and 'Needs', followed in July and November 1995 respectively. The band made a greater impact with the release of its debut, full-length album *Dagger Stare* and the CD single 'Blackwater' (May 1997), which were full of richly woven ballads and pop songs. Just prior to the album's release, Throsby and founder member Armiger left the band, and Atlas Strings supported Scottish visitors Texas on their May Australian tour as a three-piece.

Album: *Dagger Stare* (Eternity/Polydor, 1997).

Australian Crawl

Australian Crawl

Formed: *1978*
Style: *Pop rock*
Original line-up: **James Reyne** *(vocals), Simon Binks (lead guitar), Brad Robinson (rhythm guitar), Paul Williams (bass), David Reyne (drums)*

The image of Australian Crawl as fun-loving, sun-worshipping, playboy musicians radiating a healthy aura and rebellious charm did much to instil a deep attraction and sense of loyalty into the band's many fans. That, and a series of finely crafted, accessible albums and singles, ensured that Australian Crawl became one of the most successful bands of the 1980s.

The members of Australian Crawl all hailed from the Mount Eliza area on the Mornington Peninsula, Victoria. Australian Crawl came together in late 1978 after **James Reyne** and Simon Binks' first band Spliff Rouch broke up. Cheerful, gangling guitarist Brad Robinson was the son of Justice James Robinson. Bill McDonough (ex-Loose Trousers) replaced David Reyne. The band's accessible sound bore a particular Melbourne resonance, with its fresh and appealing combination of wry social observation, bright guitar licks and vital energy welded to a sweaty backbeat. EMI Records put the Crawl in the studio with producer David Briggs from the **Little River Band**. The sessions yielded the debut single 'Beautiful People'/'Man Crazy' (#22 in November 1979) and the album *The Boys Light Up* (April 1980).

The Crawl made one of the most memorable debuts on the ABC-TV pop show ***Countdown*** (performing 'Beautiful People') when **James Reyne** appeared with both his arms encased in plaster. He had been hit by a car, an episode chronicled in the track 'Indisposed' on the debut album. Reyne also became noted for his idiosyncratic, clipped vocal style which the lyrics to 'Beautiful People' tended to accentuate. *The Boys Light Up* reached #4 on the national album charts and went on to become one of the most successful Australian debut albums of the 1980s. It remained on the charts for an unbroken 104 weeks, eventually selling over 280 000 copies (four times platinum). Two further singles were hits: the raunchy 'The Boys Light Up'/'Boot Hill' (#22 in May 1980) and the reflective 'Downhearted'/'Why I've Been' (#12 in July 1980).

Singer/guitarist Guy McDonough (Bill's younger brother) joined in October 1980, adding his songwriting and vocal flair to the band's established sound. The Peter Dawkins-produced *Sirocco* (named after Errol Flynn's yacht) reached #1 in July 1981 (also achieving four times platinum sales). 'Things Don't Seem'/'Big Fish' (#11 in June 1981), 'Errol'/'Easy On Your Own' (#18 in October) and 'Oh No, Not You Again'/'Lakeside' (November) kept the band on the national chart.

Sons of Beaches (recorded in Hawaii with expatriate Australian producer Mike Chapman) boasted a rougher, rock'n'roll edge than its glossy pop rock predecessors. It reached #1, but of its three singles, 'Shut Down'/'Creating Monsters' (June 1982), 'Daughters of the Northern Coast'/'King Sap (and Princess Sag)' (August) and 'Runaway Girls'/'Santa Claus is Back in Town' (November), only 'Shut Down' reached the Top 40 (#17 in July). EMI issued the album in the USA.

Around 1982–83, **James Reyne** undertook extra-curricular activities. First he sang with **The Party Boys**, then starred with Rebecca Gilling and Wendy Hughes in the television miniseries *Return to Eden*, which was screened in September 1983. Reyne appeared in the role of playboy tennis professional

Greg Marsden, and later declared he was not very good in the part, declining many acting offers since. His only other acting role to date was playing the part of Australian manager Roger Davies in the US telemovie *Tina*, based on the life of singer Tina Turner.

Bill McDonough left the Crawl in 1983. Ex-**Angels** drummer Buzz Bidstrup played on the *Semantics* EP which contained the sparse and chilling 'Reckless (Don't Be So . . .)'. *Semantics* reached #1 on the national singles chart during October. John Watson (ex-**Kevin Borich Express**) came in as a permanent replacement for McDonough. The live mini-album *Phalanx* was something of a stop-gap measure between studio albums, but it reached #4 during December nevertheless. The Crawl's biggest overseas break came when English new romantics Duran Duran took the band as support on a UK tour.

In early 1984, prestigious US label Geffen signed the Crawl and issued *Semantics* (a compilation of tracks from past records) for the American market. The band was forced off the road when Guy McDonough was admitted to hospital. He died in June 1984 of viral pneumonia. Prior to his death, he had recorded demos with his brother Bill, Sean Higgins (synthesisers), Nigel Spencer (bass, synth), Mick Hauser (sax) and Michael Bright (lead guitar). Bill assembled the tapes and Wheatley Records issued Guy's album, *My Place* (April 1985), and singles 'My Place'/'Things Don't Seem' and 'What's in It for Me'/'Hook, Line and Sinker' in honour of his memory.

Australian Crawl re-grouped, adding Mark Greig (guitar; ex-**Runners**) for live dates in late 1984. The band recorded *Between a Rock and a Hard Place* with English producer Adam Kidron. As well as costing a staggering $400 000 to produce, the album was a mishmash of styles *and* a commercial disaster (it peaked at #12 in August but slipped out of the Top 40 two weeks later). The band had to tour for the next year to pay off the debt. The album produced the flop singles 'Two Can Play'/'Two Can Play' (June 1985), 'If This Is Love'/'You Told Me' (September), 'Trouble Spot Rock'/'Newly Weds in the Morning' (November) and 'Two Hearts'/'Across the Way' (January 1986). Harry Brus (ex-**Kevin Borich Express**) replaced long-standing bass player Paul Williams in May 1985. Nevertheless, the band had run its course and Australian Crawl broke up at the beginning of 1986. The band's final concert on 27 January 1986 produced the album *The Final Wave* which came out in October.

In seven years, Australian Crawl sold over a million records in Australia. **James Reyne** went on to pursue a successful solo career. Brad Robinson moved into television, first as a presenter with the *Page One* current affairs show, then as a presenter and co-producer of documentaries. In the 1990s he managed James and David Reyne, and worked as an agent for the Advantage Sports Management Group. He died on 13 October 1996 following a three-year battle with lymphoma, only weeks after Australian Crawl had been inducted into the Australian Record Industry Association (ARIA) Hall of Fame.

Australian Crawl albums: *The Boys Light Up* (EMI, 1980), *Sirocco* (EMI, 1981), *Sons of Beaches* (EMI, 1982), *Phalanx* (EMI, 1983), *Crawl File: Their Greatest Hits* (EMI, 1984), *Between a Rock and a Hard Place* (Freestyle/RCA, 1985), *The Final Wave* (Freestyle/RCA, 1986); ***Guy McDonough album:*** *My Place* (Wheatley/RCA, 1985).

Autohaze

Formed: *1990*
Style: *Indie guitar pop*
Original line-up: *Tim Jackson (vocals, guitar), Chris Chapple (guitar), Kerrie Hickin (bass; ex-Lynching Party,* **Ku Klux Frankenstein**, *Fire,* **Sunset Strip***), David Ledere (drums)*

Melbourne band Autohaze played a brand of pop that featured languid melodies and ragged vocals, overlaid with bursts of squalling guitar. Reference points abounded, from UK art pop (Ride) and noisy USA guitar pop (Sugar, Dinosaur Jr) to Neil Young.

Autohaze built up a cult following on the Melbourne inner-city pub circuit. The band issued a trio of rough-hewn singles, 'Undecided'/'Guess It's More' (1991), 'Hanging Around'/'Coode Island Baby' (demo) (March 1992) and the gig giveaway, 'Dive into the Sun'/'Put it Together' (May), plus the mini-album *Mild Steel Flat* (April 1992) on the Summershine label. Later in the year, Adam Fennessy replaced Kerrie Hickin who went on to form **Holocene**. The '27 Air' EP appeared in September 1992, followed by the 'Spanish' CD EP in April 1993. *Mild Steel Flat* had garnered glowing reviews in UK music papers like *New Musical Express*, which resulted in Autohaze becoming the first Australian band to sign a deal with the much vaunted Creation label (home to Ride, My Bloody Valentine, Primal Scream, Sugar and others). The band's first overseas album *Stumblebum* (October 1993) combined *Mild Steel Flat*, the two EPs and the early singles.

In Australia, Autohaze signed a deal with Mercury's development label Id and issued the single

'Way Out There' (August 1994). The band spent the early part of 1994 touring overseas and recording a second album with American producer Tim O'Heir (Belly, Dinosaur Jr). *Magneto* was a flawed offering, but it more than fulfilled the band's early promise with a range of moods and styles. The album yielded the singles 'Light of Day' (April 1995) and 'White Bird' (September). Prestigious US label SubPop also issued 'White Bird' as a 7-inch single for the American market. Autohaze issued a third single from *Magneto*, 'Satellite City', in 1996.

Albums: *Mild Steel Flat* (mini-album, Summershine/Shock, 1992), *Stumblebum* (Creation/Shock, 1993), *Magneto* (Id/Mercury, 1995).

Automatic

Formed: *1993*
Style: *Indie guitar rock*
Original line-up: *Matt Fenton (guitar, vocals; ex-Spinouts), Alex Jarvis (guitar; ex-Spinouts), Richard Taylor (bass), Leigh Marlow (drums)*

The Victorian harbourside city of Geelong gave rise to a number of aggressive independent guitar bands during the 1980s, such as **Bored!**, **The Sunset Strip**, **Magic Dirt**, Poppin' Mommas and Seaweed Goorillas. Automatic has continued that tradition into the 1990s with a combination of commercial hooks and guitar-heavy pop songs.

Matt Fenton and Alex Jarvis started out in high school band The Spinouts, playing a range of covers by the likes of **The Lime Spiders**, The Exploited, the Dead Kennedys and Joy Division. Fenton and Jarvis then formed Automatic with Richard Taylor and Leigh Marlow. Automatic issued its debut, independent CD EP *Automatic* in early 1995, and then contributed a version of 'You Shook Me All Night Long' to BMG's **AC/DC** tribute album *Fuse Box: The Alternative Tribute* (May 1995). By August of that year, Automatic had signed to Sony's Murmur label (home to **silverchair** and **Ammonia**). Murmur issued the CD EP 'Sister K' (October 1995), plus the CD singles 'What If . . . ' (April 1996) and 'It's Like Sound' (August) to a positive response. While the material on the singles veered between fuzz-pop and full-tilt hard rock, Automatic nevertheless revealed itself to be a band with the strengths of its convictions.

Nick Launay (**Models**, **Midnight Oil**, **silverchair**) produced Automatic's debut album *Transmitter* which came out in May 1997. The songs mixed American progressive rock noise (à la Soundgarden and Smashing Pumpkins) with British guitar pop in the vein of Teenage Fanclub or Elastica. *Transmitter* included the band's previous singles 'What If . . . ' and 'It's Like Sound', with 'Another Up' being issued as the album's third CD single in March 1997. By that stage, Danny Plant (ex-**Custard**) had replaced Marlow on drums. Sony/Columbia also issued *Transmitter* in the USA, plus the CD singles 'What If' and 'It's Like Sound'. Automatic then toured from New York to Los Angeles as support to **silverchair**. The fourth CD single from *Transmitter*, 'Five', came out in August 1997.

Album: *Transmitter* (Murmur/Sony, 1997).

Autumn

Formed: *1969*
Style: *Pop*
August 1970 line-up: *Tony Romeril (vocals), Steve McMurray (guitar), Greg Jacques (organ), Rick Graham (bass), Glen Beatson (drums)*

Following a tradition set by the likes of **The Executives**, **The Affair**, **New Dream** and **The Zoot**, Sydney-based Autumn was unashamedly a pop band. The band's debut single 'Mr Henry's Lollipop Shoppe'/'Today' for EMI/Columbia at the start of 1970 set the tone for subsequent releases. The band's second single, 'Yellow River' (on Chart), was a cover of English band Christie's hit. The song was also covered by Melbourne band **Jigsaw** and the two shared a joint national #1 hit in August 1970.

Three more pop singles on Chart, 'Looking Through the Eyes of a Beautiful Girl'/'Song to Raymondo' (#3 in Sydney, November 1970), 'She Works in a Woman's Way'/'Midnight Special' (a collaboration with cabaret singer Dave Allenby; February 1971) and 'Miracles'/'Lady Jane' (March), and the album *Song to Raymondo* saved the band from becoming a one-hit wonder. Autumn also shared an EP with Barrie McAskill and **Levi Smith's Clefs** called *The Best of Whisky A-Go-Go* on the Chart label. The Autumn tracks were The Beatles' 'Day Tripper' and Jimmy Webb's 'By the Time I Get to Phoenix'.

In April 1971, Allan Marshall (guitar; ex-**Hot Cottage**) replaced Jacques. The new line-up issued the singles 'Falling'/'Miracles' (#10 in Sydney, May 1971), 'Goblin's Gamble'/'Lady Anne' (July) and 'Just Couldn't Believe It'/'Bye Bye to You' (September), the EP *A Patch Of Autumn* and the album *Comes Autumn* (all on Warner). Charlie Wright (piano, organ; ex-Harry Young and Sabbath) joined at the end of 1971. Autumn travelled to the UK in 1972, but split up six weeks after arriving in the Old Dart. McMurray, Beatson and Marshall formed Mecca, moved to Canada and went on to join

Canadian band Wireless. That band issued three albums of bluesy hard rock, *Wireless* (1976), *Positively Human, Relatively Sane* (1979) and *No Static* (1980), on the Anthem label. Romeril ended up in Italy for a time, recording under the pseudonym of Andy Foxx. Romeril and Graham re-formed Autumn briefly in Sydney during 1976 to minimal response. The new line-up comprised Dave Hallard (guitar), James Caulfield (keyboards) and Con Westaberg (drums).

Albums: *Song to Raymondo* (Chart, 1971; reissued on Summit, 1973), *Comes Autumn* (Warner, 1971).

Avalanche

Formed: *1975*
Style: *Hard rock*
Original line-up: *Adrian Campbell (vocals; ex-Raw Glory), Tony Naylor (guitar; ex-Ida May Mack,* **Band of Talabene, Bootleg Family Band***), Clive Harrison (bass; ex-***Kush**, **Bootleg Family Band***), Geoff Cox (drums; ex-***Bootleg Family Band***)*

With the break-up of **The Bootleg Family Band** in November 1975, Tony Naylor, Geoff Cox and Clive Harrison recruited Adrian Campbell and began gigging as Avalanche in early 1976. The band's catchy pop rock sound was displayed on the singles 'Wizard Of Love'/'The Climb' (February 1976; #23 in Melbourne during May), 'Sweet Baby Brown Eyes'/'Bermuda Triangle' (July 1976), 'Landslide'/'Overnight Sensation' (October 1976) and 'Good for Me Good for You'/'Mr Jones' (March 1977) and the album *Avalanche* (September 1976).

Cox and Harrison left in early 1977, to be replaced by John Barnes (who was in turn replaced quickly by Barry Cram, ex-Michael Turner In Session, **Pantha**) and Graham Thompson (ex-**Stars**) respectively. Gerard McCabe (keyboards) also joined and that line-up issued a cover of The Beatles' 'Got To Get You into My Life' as a single (November 1977). Clive Harrison went on to issue a solo album, *Once Bitten*, on RCA in 1982. By 1978, Naylor and Campbell had revamped the band as Front Page with a line-up of Phil Wood (bass), Tony Thornton (drums; ex-Clean Cut) and Bruce Haymes (keyboards). James Black (keyboards, guitar, vocals; ex-Rum Jungle) then replaced Haymes. Front Page issued the single 'I Thought I'd Never Fall in Love Again'/'Rockin' Hollywood' in August 1978, but by 1979 it was over. Naylor joined **Jon English**'s band Baxter Funt in 1980.

In 1981 Campbell formed Ada's Persuaders who issued one single, 'Let the Girl Dance'/'Break the Ice' on the Full Moon label. In 1985 Campbell then joined forces with Larry Groves (keyboards; ex-Jefferson Blues, Ticket, **Cheetah**, Echoes, **Broderick Smith** Band) and Michael Den Elzen (guitar; ex-**Broderick Smith** Band) in modern funk outfit Adrian's Wall. That band issued four singles, 'Reach Out'/'Run into the Night' (October 1986), 'Night People'/'Better Late than Never' (March 1987), 'Afraid to be Afraid'/'I'm what You're Looking for' (July) and 'Time Standing Still'/'Dancer' (October), plus the album *Caught in the Web* (April) for the Zoom label. None of the records was successful.

Album: *Avalanche* (Bootleg, 1976).

The Avengers

Formed: *1967*
Style: *Pop*
Original Line-up: *Ross Bentley (vocals), Roger Gellicoe (guitar), Graeme Rabnott (guitar), Garth Austin (bass), Mick Monaghan (drums)*

Not to be confused with New Zealand band The Avengers, the Brisbane-based Avengers initially plied their wares on the club and discotheque circuit, doing mainly Top 40 pop covers. The band's swinging 1960s pop sound was heard on the singles recorded for EMI/Columbia: 'What Price Love?'/'Only Once in My Lifetime' (June 1968) and 'Listen Listen'/'Just One More Chance' (January 1969). Ex-**Twilights** singer **Glenn Shorrock** managed the band at the start of 1969. Ex-**Twilights** guitarist Terry Britten wrote the band's third single, 'Tweedelee Dee'/'Caroline Court' (May 1969), which was a minor hit in Brisbane.

The line-up by that stage comprised Julian Jones (vocals; ex-Breed), Roger Hicks (guitar; ex-**Zoot**), Keith Kerwin (guitar), Andy Tait (bass) and Don Lebler (drums). The band broke up in September 1969. Lebler joined **Axiom**. By the end of 1969, Tait had The (New) Avengers in operation which also included Jeff Black, Bobby Jacobson, Rick Matson and David Briggs. John Bush replaced Briggs on guitar in May 1970, but the new line-up was short lived. Briggs joined the **Little River Band** as lead guitarist in 1976.

Avion

Formed: *1981*
Style: *Rock*
Original line-up: *Randall Waller (vocals, guitar), Martin Toole (guitar), Evan Murray (keyboards), Kendall Waller (bass), John Waller (drums)*

Outside a strong cult following, Sydney band Avion's brand of melodic, American-influenced

Adult Oriented Rock (AOR) met with virtual indifference at home. RCA issued the band's eponymous, debut album in the USA and Canada before it came out in Australia (September 1983). Randall Waller had issued two solo albums *Oasis* (1978) and *Midnight Fire* (1980) before forming Lionheart, which became Avion in 1981.

The three singles lifted from *Avion*, 'I Need You'/'Once Bitten Twice Shy' (March 1983), 'Diamond Eyes'/'Warrior' (September) and 'Never Let Me Go'/'Where Do We Go From Here?' (October) were not successful. 'Still The Night'/'Southern Cross' came out as a single in August 1984.

For the 1987 album, *White Noise*, Paul Gannell replaced Toole on guitar. *White Noise* spawned three singles, 'We've Got Secrets'/'Bigger They Are' (September 1985), 'Celebration'/'Ransom' (September 1986) and 'Berlin Wall'/'On and On' (April 1987). In late 1987, Evan Murray died in a car accident while the band was on tour. His death, and a lack of airplay for the band's singles, precipitated Avion's break-up at the end of the year. Following the break-up, Randall Waller was a member of the Sharon O'Neill Band for a year. He worked as a producer and engineer in the UK between 1988 and 1993. He was a member of the Bonnie Tyler Band in 1989.

Back in Australia, Randall joined **Billy Thorpe**'s new band in 1996. Randall then wrote and recorded 'Side by Side' which was a dedication to the victims of the 1996 Port Arthur massacre. 'Side by Side' was issued as a single in February 1997 with all proceeds going to the Port Arthur Appeal Fund.

Albums: *Avion* (RCA, 1983), *White Noise* (EMI, 1987).

Axiom

Formed: *1969*
Style: *Country, rock*
Original line-up: **Glenn Shorrock** *(vocals; ex-***Twilights***)*, **Brian Cadd** *(vocals, piano; ex-***Groop***)*, *Chris Stockley (guitar, vocals; ex-***Cam-Pact***)*, *Don Mudie (bass; ex-***Groop***)*, *Doug Lavery (drums; ex-***Doug Parkinson** *In Focus*, **Valentines***)*

Axiom was deservedly touted as Australia's first 'supergroup'. The band's formation in May 1969 brought together five experienced and talented musicians. One of the main inspirations behind Axiom's blend of rock and country was The Band's landmark *Music from Big Pink* album. Axiom achieved three Top 10 hit singles, and issued arguably the first local rock album that embraced Australian lyric themes (*Fool's Gold*).

The band's chart success was instant when the Cadd/Mudie-penned singles 'Arkansas Grass'/'Samantha' (December 1969) and 'A Little Ray of Sunshine'/'Ford's Bridge' (April 1970) reached #7 and #5 respectively. Don Lebler (ex-**Avengers**) replaced Lavery and the band left for the UK in April 1970. Axiom's third single 'Father Confessor'/'Time and Time Again' (July) and debut album *Fool's Gold* both failed to chart, perhaps due to the band's absence from the local scene.

In London, Axiom signed a three-year deal with Warner Reprise who flew the band to Los Angeles in September 1970 to record the album *If Only . . .* Upon returning to Australia in October, Axiom toured and issued a fourth single, the exceptional 'My Baby's Gone'/'Hold the Phone' (#8 in February 1971). *If Only . . .* was a more polished album than *Fool's Gold* but it received little attention when issued later in the year. *If Only . . .* and 'My Baby's Gone' were both issued in the USA.

Axiom returned to England during February 1971, but broke up a month later. Before the final split, Axiom recorded one of the first colour film clips by an Australian band (for 'My Baby's Gone'). In Australia, Parlophone issued the year-old 'Ford's Bridge'/'Yesterday, Today and Tomorrow' as a final single. Lebler joined **The Mixtures**. Cadd and Mudie wrote and recorded as a duo before **Brian Cadd** embarked on a successful solo career. Shorrock joined international-flavoured band Esperanto before returning to Australia and joining **Little River Band**. Stockley went on to work with a succession of bands like Sunshine, Wizard, Winchester and Ceduna (which included Don Mudie and ex-**Mixtures** drummer Mick Holden) before joining **The Dingoes** in 1973 and The Stockley See Mason Band in 1978.

Albums: *Fool's Gold* (EMI/Parlophone, 1970), *If Only . . .* (Warner Reprise, 1971).

Ayers Rock

Formed: *1973*
Style: *Rock, jazz*
Original line-up: **Ray Burton** *(guitar, vocals; ex-***Dave Bridge Quartet**, *Executives*, **Friends***)*, *Jimmy Doyle (lead guitar; ex-Silhouettes,* **Aesop's Fables**, *Moonstone,* **King Harvest***)*, *Duncan McGuire (bass; ex-Phantoms, Epics, Questions,* **Doug Parkinson** *In Focus*, **King Harvest**, **Friends***)*, *Mark Kennedy (drums; ex-***Spectrum**, **King Harvest**, **Doug Parkinson** *In Focus*, **Friends***)*

For a period during the 1970s, the members of Ayers Rock were seen as 'musician's musicians'. The band issued a series of technically proficient

Ayers Rock

recordings, but in the long run any quest for commercial acceptance was marred by the seriousness of the music.

Ayers Rock evolved out of the trio Burton McGuire and Kennedy. The three musicians had all been members of the final version of **Friends**. They left singer **Leo De Castro** high and dry when they formed the eponymous trio in June 1973. With the arrival of Jimmy Doyle in August, Ayers Rock was born. Col Loughnan (sax, flute, clarinet, piano; ex-**Crescents**, **Delltones**, Kala) had been living in London for a few years, and he accepted the band's offer to join in October 1973. The band members had a wealth of experience in the industry. **Ray Burton** co-wrote **Helen Reddy's** international hit 'I am Woman' while working in the USA. He returned to Australia in early 1973 and joined **Friends**. McGuire started out with The Phantoms in 1959.

Ayers Rock's first single, 'Rock'n'Roll Fight (Going On)'/'Sorrowful Eyes', was one of the first releases on the Mushroom label (December 1973). Burton returned to the USA in March 1974 and Chris Brown (ex-**Python Lee Jackson**, Kala) joined. The band's sound took on a more jazz-rock edge as displayed on the live-in-the-studio album *Big Red Rock* and 'Lady Montego'/'Going Home' single (November 1974). One of the band's showcase live songs included on the album was a cover of Weather Report's 'Boogie Woogie Waltz'.

American label A&M Records signed the band and issued the album in the USA. During September 1975, the label booked Ayers Rock into the Record Plant in Los Angeles to record its second album, *Beyond*. Kennedy left in February 1976 to join **Marcia Hines'** band. He was replaced initially by session drummer Doug Gallacher and then Russell Dunlop (ex-**Aesop's Fables, Levi Smith's Clefs**, SCRA, Mother Earth, **Johnny Rocco Band**) in May. *Beyond* (April 1976) gave rise to two unsuccessful singles, 'Little Kings'/'Get Out to the Country' (October 1975) and 'Song for Darwin'/'Place to Go' (May 1976).

That same month, Ayers Rock returned to the USA to promote *Beyond*. Ayers Rock was the first Australian band to play to massive crowds on the USA touring circuit (predating **Little River Band, AC/DC, Air Supply, Men At Work** and **INXS**). In the long run, however, the band only achieved limited success overseas.

Back in Australia during August 1976, McGuire, Loughnan and Dunlop all left. McGuire initially joined Windchase and then concentrated on production. He died in July 1989 after a long battle with cancer. Doyle and Brown put Ayers Rock on hold for a year until they recruited new players John Young (bass; ex-De Castro), Bermudian Keith Casey (percussion) and Joe Tattersall (drums; ex-**Healing Force**, Barry Leef Band). By 1978 the line-up had changed again to be Doyle, Brown, Casey, Andy Cowan (keyboards, vocals; ex-**Madder Lake**), Steve Hogg (bass; ex-**Bakery**) and Hamish Stewart (drums). The band toured constantly but did not appear on record again until 'On the Avenue'/'Sister Feels' came out in March 1980. The final Ayers Rock album was *Hot Spell* (May 1980), followed by the single 'Lies'/'Feel the Heat' (July 1981).

Albums: *Big Red Rock* (Mushroom/Festival, 1974), *Beyond* (Mushroom/Festival, 1976), *Hot Spell* (Red Rock/RCA, 1980).

The Aztecs (*see* Billy Thorpe)

B

Baby Animals

Formed: *1989*
Style: *Hard rock*
Original line-up: *Suze DeMarchi (vocals, guitar; ex-Photoplay, Kind, DD and the Rockmen), Dave Leslie (guitar; ex-Swingshift), Eddie Parise (bass; ex-***Boys***, Bel Aires, Bamboo Curtain), Frank Celenza (drums; ex-***Boys***, Bamboo Curtain)*

Husky-voiced singer Suze DeMarchi recorded three soft-metal singles in the UK for EMI during the late 1980s, including 'Dry Your Eyes'/'Big Wednesday', 'Me and You'. DeMarchi co-wrote 'Big Wednesday' with Simon Climie of pop duo Climie Fisher. The deal with EMI came about through demos DeMarchi had recorded with guitarist Kevin Peek (ex-**James Taylor Move**, Quartet, Sky) and drummer Trevor Spencer (ex-**James Taylor Move**, Quartet, Tarney Spencer Band). Prior to that, DeMarchi had sung in Perth bands Photoplay (circa 1982), The Kind (which also featured her sister Denise and guitarist Mark Lizotte aka **Johnny Diesel**) and DD and the Rockmen.

Photoplay comprised DeMarchi, Cath Fletcher (keyboards, vocals), Mark Fletcher (guitar), Pat Quinn (bass) and Bryce Buckley (drums). The band's influences included U2, The Cure, Simple Minds and Martha and the Muffins. Two Photoplay tracks, 'Hit Me' and 'No Escape', appeared on the Various Artists album *Demowest* on the Tempo label. DD and the Rockmen also contained ex-**Boys** drummer Celenza.

Upon returning to Australia in July 1989, DeMarchi linked up with Celenza to form a new band. The pair relocated to Sydney, recruited Parise and Leslie and in October 1989 Baby Animals were born. The unsigned Baby Animals came to widespread attention when **The Angels** picked them up for support on the Dogs are Talking national tour. **The Angels** included Baby Animals' demo 'Break My Heart' (plus demos by The Hurricanes and The Desert Cats) as the B-side to the 'Dogs are Talking' single (April 1990). **The Angels'** long-serving manager John Woodruff eventually left that band to concentrate on managing Baby Animals. He was

Baby Animals

also instrumental in getting the band signed to former Chrysalis boss Terry Ellis's international label Imago.

Woodruff's faith in Baby Animals paid off with the release of the band's eponymous debut album in September 1991. Recorded at Bearsville Studios, Woodstock, USA with expatriate Australian producer Mike Chapman (Sweet, Suzi Quatro, Blondie, **Divinyls**), the album reached #1 in Australia, sold 300 000 copies and spawned four hit singles, 'Early Warning'/'Baby Animals' (#21, June 1991), 'Rush You'/'Big Time Friends' (#30, September), 'Painless' (#49, November) and 'One Word' (#10, February 1992). The songs showcased the band's confident and melodic brand of hard rock and, in particular, highlighted DeMarchi's provocative vocal growl. 'Ain't Gonna Get' appeared as the fifth single lifted from the album (April 1992).

Baby Animals became the second biggest selling album for 1992 (behind **Jimmy Barnes'** *Soul Deep*).

The band won three Australian Record Industry Association (ARIA) Awards in 1991 (Best Debut Single for 'Early Warning', Best Debut Album and Best Album). 'One Word' was later nominated for 1992 Australian Song of the Year at the Australian Performing Right Association (APRA) Awards. Baby Animals then turned their attention overseas. With the release of the album in the USA, it charted well in places like New York and Boston. The band toured the USA and Europe, taking in support slots to Bryan Adams (on his successful 1991 UK tour) and Van Halen. To coincide with the band's return to Australia, Imago reissued *Baby Animals* as a Limited Tour Souvenir Edition (July 1992) with four previously unreleased live tracks added.

Shaved and Dangerous (August 1993) produced by American Ed Stasium (Ramones, Living Colour, **Hoodoo Gurus**), was a more adventurous progressive rock album. It had less of a commercial feel, and Leslie layered the songs with snaking guitar solos. Nevertheless, it made its debut at #2 on the national chart. Guitarist Nuno Bettencourt (from US band Extreme) co-wrote and played guitar on one song 'Because I Can' and produced 'Life From a Distance'. The CD singles 'Don't Tell Me What to Do' (#24, July), the double A-sided 'At the End of the Day'/'Backbone' (#60, November) and 'Lights Out at Eleven' (#54, February 1994) were minor hits.

Baby Animals spent the second half of 1993 on the road across the USA, including a lengthy support slot to Robert Plant and two months headlining a club tour of their own. The band returned to Australia in early 1994 for the God Shave the Queen tour, but since that time there has been very little activity. In August 1994 DeMarchi married Nuno Bettencourt and moved to Boston, Massachusetts.

Albums: *Baby Animals* (Imago/BMG, 1991), *Shaved and Dangerous* (Imago/BMG, 1993).

Bachelors from Prague

Formed: *1985*
Style: *R&B, jazz, funk*
Original line-up: *Henry Maas (vocals; ex-Buddy Lowenstein Big Band), Bruce Haymes (keyboards; ex-* **Russell Morris** *and The Rubes,* **Richard Clapton** *Band), Chris Minko (trumpet), Andrew Philipp (sax), Jeff Raglus (trumpet; ex-Escalators), Tom Roberts (guitar), Justin Stanford (percussion), George Frimil (bass), Russell Cook (drums)*

Melbourne-based Bachelors from Prague came to the public's attention in the mid-1980s playing a stylish and infectious blend of 1940s jazz, 1950s R&B, 1970s funk and salsa. Lead singer Maas had been a member of 1970s cabaret duo The Busby Berkeleys (which originated out of the Pram Factory in Carlton) and The Buddy Lowenstein Big Band. His love of jazz and musical theatre formed the basis for the Bachelors' entertaining style and energetic approach.

Bachelors From Prague established themselves as *the* band to see while cruising the cafes and clubs of Brunswick Street, Fitzroy, inner-city Melbourne. Setting sights further afield, the band issued its debut album, *The Energetic Cool* (August 1988), on its own 3333 label. The album produced two excellent singles, 'Go'/'Even Dishwashers Get the Blues' (July) and 'Tightrope'/'The Outsider' (February 1989). *Birth of the Fool* (March 1990) was preceded by the single 'Get Smart'/'Theme for Two Beds' (October 1989). The next album, *The Essentials,* yielded the double A-sided single 'Trouble'/'The Irvin Rockman Affair'. Thiery Fossemalle replaced Frimil on bass in 1991. At the end of the year, the band issued the 12-inch single/CD single 'Great!'. The band never achieved widespread commercial success, but always lived up to its audience's high expectations.

Albums: *The Energetic Cool* (3333/Musicland, 1988), *Birth of the Fool* (3333/PolyGram, 1990), *Live at the Sing Sing* (Larrikin, 1989), *The Essentials* (Mercury, 1990).

Lisa Bade

Style: *Pop rock*

Melbourne singer Lisa Bade got her start singing back-up vocals on **Mark Gillespie's** 1980 album *Only Human*. Bade's debut single, a cover of Gillespie's 'Traveller in the Night'/ 'Stormy Red', came out on the Wheatley Brothers' label later in the year. Bade recorded her debut album *Suspicion* in Los Angeles with American producer David Kershenbaum during 1982. *Suspicion* highlighted Bade's husky vocal delivery, and included two singles, '(That Ain't) No Way to Treat a Lady'/'Losin' Feelin' (July 1982) and 'Willow'/'Pile Up on the Highway' (November 1992). The Lisa Bade Band toured with the **Little River Band** at the end of 1982. Since then, Bade has issued one single, 'Walk Away'/'Never Looked So Good', on Freestyle (1985) and has sung with Wilbur Wilde's Blowout, the **Mark Gillespie** Band and Pink Cadillac. She also formed popular covers trio The Love Stars with Nikki Nicholls (vocals) and Harry Mulaney (guitar).

Album: *Suspicion* (Wheatley, 1982).

The Badloves

Formed: *1990*
Style: *R&B, soul*
Original line-up: *Michael Spiby (guitar, vocals; ex-Screen Idols,* **Daryl Braithwaite** *Band), John Spiby (keyboards, sax), John Housden (lead guitar; ex-***Daryl Braithwaite** *Band), Stephen 'Irish' O'Prey (bass; ex-***Daryl Braithwaite** *Band), Chris Tabone (drums)*

Michael Spiby formed The Badloves in Melbourne during January 1990. Spiby, John Housden and Stephen O'Prey had all been part of **Daryl Braithwaite's** 1989 touring band. A year later, Michael's brother John left The Badloves to be eventually replaced by Tony Featherstone on Hammond organ and guitar. The band became a popular live attraction courtesy of regular gigs and a fine set of laid-back, 1970s-styled blues, Memphis soul and New Orleans R&B material. The band's sound was simple, soulful and very funky. The Badloves were immediately labelled as 'organic', 'neo-hippies' and 'retro', which may have been the case, but at least it showed a band working within a rich musical tradition.

The Badloves signed a deal with Mushroom Records at the end of 1992 after label head Michael Gudinski saw them supporting Hall and Oates at the Melbourne Concert Hall. Initially the band's debut album *Get on Board* (June 1993) sold moderately, and the first two CD singles, 'Lost'/'Green Limousine', 'Stop' (March) and 'I Remember' (July), were only minor hits. Months of touring and opening for bands like **The Sharp, Weddings, Parties, Anything** and **Baby Animals** did not help sales. The band's fortunes began to change at the end of 1993 when they collaborated with **Jimmy Barnes** on his *Flesh and Wood* album.

In partnership, they recorded a cover version of The Band's classic 'The Weight', which reached #6 in December 1993. Following the success of 'The Weight' and the release of 'Green Limousine' as a single, *Get on Board* eventually made the Australian Top 5 (selling in excess of 140 000 copies), and the band won three 1993 Australian Record Industry Association (ARIA) Awards (Best Debut Album for *Get on Board*, Best Debut Single for 'Lost' and Best New Talent).

In early 1994, The Badloves toured Europe with **Jimmy Barnes**, after which bassist O'Prey left the band to be replaced by John 'Bullfrog' Favarro. The CD single 'Memphis' appeared in March. The band then undertook the successful Travelling Salvation tour which saw The Badloves playing to packed houses across Australia. The beginning of 1995 was taken up with recording a new album with producer Doug Roberts, and the whole project was documented by filmmaker Clayton Jacobsen. Black Crowes producer Jack Joseph Puig mixed the album *Holy Roadside* in Los Angeles.

Holy Roadside came out in September 1995, preceded by the CD single 'Caroline' in August. A limited edition collectors' album, *Live In Amsterdam* (recorded at 'The Paradiso' while the band was touring Europe with **Jimmy Barnes**), was also available for a short time with the purchase of *Holy Roadside*. The soulful 'Slave' appeared as the album's second CD single in November. The 'Barefoot Bride' CD single (May 1996) featured a live rendition of Paul Simon's 'Love Me Like a Rock'. The Badloves issued the live album *Everybody Everywhere* in April 1997.

Albums: *Get on Board* (Mushroom/Festival 1993), *Holy Roadside* (Mushroom/Festival 1995), *Everybody Everywhere* (Mushroom/Sony, 1997).

Chris Bailey

Style: *R&B, soul*

Since the mid-1970s, Chris Bailey (b. 1956) has shaped a persona as the world-weary, insouciant, wine-sipping, bohemian troubadour. Born of Irish Catholic parents in Kenya and raised in Belfast, Bailey immigrated to Australia with his family in 1967. He got his start with **The Saints** in Brisbane during the early 1970s. During the mid-1990s, he moved to Sweden, and continued to spend most of his time touring Europe, where he is held in high esteem.

When the original version of **The Saints** imploded in England at the end of 1978, **Ed Kuepper** returned to Australia and eventually put together **Laughing Clowns**. Bailey stayed in England, retained the Saints name and formed a new line-up with Barrington Francis (guitar), Bruce 'Cub' Callaway (guitar, ex-X-Men), Janine Hall (bass, ex-Young Charlatans) and Ivor Hay (drums). The four-track EP *Paralytic Tonight Dublin Tomorrow* came out on Lost Records in Australia (March 1980) and New Rose in France. It contained one of Bailey's early classics in 'Simple Love'.

Hay and Callaway left straight after the recording session and returned to Australia. Bailey's Saints toured Australia for the first time in March 1980. The line-up featured Bailey, Barrington, Callaway, Hall and Hay. Mark Birmingham took over on drums, Callaway left again and The Saints recorded the single 'In The Mirror'/'Always' (issued November 1980) in London and *The Monkey Puzzle* album

Chris Bailey

(issued February 1981) in Sydney. The single 'Let's Pretend'/'Gypsy Woman' followed in April 1981.

Bailey returned to England and The Saints issued *Casablanca* (July 1982) on New Rose in Europe and Lost in Australia. The Saints' line-up on the album was a basic three-piece of Bailey (vocals and guitars), Hall and Iain Shedden (drums). The band was augmented by a horn section of Paul Neiman (trombone), Steve Sidwell (trumpet) and Roger Crankwell (sax, clarinet), plus Jess Sutcliffe (piano), Denis Haines (piano) and The Damned's Brian James (lead guitar) guesting on two tracks. The Saints toured Australia in November and December 1982 with a line-up of Bailey, Hall, Shedden, Laurie Cuffe (guitar) and Chris Burnham (guitar; ex-**Supernaut**). Bailey's transitional solo album *What We Did on Our Holidays* (1984) included covers of old soul, folk and blues material (including songs from Jimmy Reed and Jacques Brel), plus an early rendition of 'Ghost Ships'.

By 1984, Bailey was living and recording in Sydney, as well as touring as a solo acoustic act. In July RCA issued a new Saints album, *A Little Madness to be Free*, preceded by the classic single 'Ghost Ships'/'Wrapped Up and Blue' (May). The album was more rock-oriented, with extensive use of acoustic guitar, brass and strings set among tightly focused arrangements. With Bailey's booming, bluesy voice in fine form, it may well constitute his most fully realised project. Bailey put together another touring line-up of The Saints that included Burnham, Shedden and Tracy Pew (bass, ex-**Birthday Party**). Original Saints guitarist **Ed Kuepper** also toured with the band (replacing Pew on bass) for a couple of weeks during July, but old conflicts arose and he left. Two further singles were lifted off the album, 'Imagination'/'Heavy Metal' (August 1984) and 'Angels'/'(Don't Send Me) Roses' (March 1985). In March 1985, ex-**Laughing Clowns** members Louise Elliot (sax) and Jeffrey Wegener (drums) joined The Saints for a national tour. Bailey, Richard Burgmann (guitar, ex-**Sunnyboys**) and Arturo 'Archie' Larizza (bass, ex-Innocents) completed the line-up.

Bailey formed a more permanent Saints line-up with Burgmann, Larizza and Ivor Hay. Larizza's previous band, Adelaide post-punk pop outfit The Innocents, issued four singles 'Identikit Girl'/'Let's Get Pissed' (1980), 'Think About Tomorrow, Tomorrow'/'Cold Hard Cash', 'Rat Race' (as The Noise, 1981), '(I Am Not) a Magic Man'/'Staying at Home' (December 1983) and 'After a Fashion'/'Strange Cults and Customs' (1985).

The Saints signed with Mushroom in Australia and Polydor in the UK, and issued the acclaimed *All Fools' Day* album (April 1986). Recorded at Rockfield Studios in Wales, the album became the band's most successful to that time. It produced the singles 'Just Like Fire Would'/'Storm' (February 1986), the gospel tinged 'Temple of the Lord'/'East is East' (May) and 'See You in Paradise'/'Casablanca' (September). Such was The Saints' standing that the band was included on the bill of the massive Australian Made tour in early 1987. The April 1988 album *Prodigal Son* (recorded in London and New York) and singles 'Grain of Sand'/'Mad Race' (February) and 'Stay'/'Idiot Blues' (May) featured the line-up of Bailey, Larizza, Iain Shedden, Barrington Francis and Joe Chiofalo (organ). TVT Records issued *Prodigal Son* in the USA and The Saints toured there for the first time.

The Saints' cover of **The Easybeats**' 'The Music Goes Round My Head'/'Tomorrow' was issued as a single in December 1988. The A-side was included on the soundtrack to the Yahoo Serious film *Young Einstein*. *Permanent Revolution* (March 1992) was the last Saints album for four years. Bailey issued *Demons* (May 1991) and the singles 'Bridges'/'Midnight Run' (April) and 'Marie Antoinette'/'Marie Antoinette' (dub version) (August) under his own name. He recorded *Demons* in Memphis, Tennessee, with the results ranging from boisterous rock to blues. Despite its title, *Savage Entertainment* (October 1992) offered up simpler material with less cluttered production values than heard on *Demons*. It yielded the CD EP 'Do They Come from You?'. At the end of 1993, Bailey wrote and recorded several songs (including a reworking of 'All Fools' Day') with Concrete Blonde's Johnette Napolitano.

Bailey recorded his fourth solo album *54 Days . . . at Sea* in his adopted hometown of Malmö, Sweden. It was one of his most interesting albums, as it featured contributions from Bolivian folk musicians Victor Salazar (on charango) and Oscar Salazar (on traditional flute) in a breezy rock setting. Swedish musicians Eddie Nystrom (guitar), Magnus Borjeson (bass) and Stellan Colt (drums) provided the rock base for the album. Bailey also contributed a cover of **Tim Finn's** 'Not Even Close' to the Various Artists compilation *Earth Music* issued on Mushroom (June 1994).

Bailey revived The Saints' name at the end of 1996 for the tough rock album *Howling*, and toured Australia for the first time in eight years (February 1997) with a line-up comprising English and Danish musicians. Bailey's mocking Oscar Wilde tone of voice and sly lines of patter have often gone over the collective heads of audiences. He has been involved in the release of several brilliantly conceived albums, and he remains one of Australia's most intriguing performers.

Saints albums: *The Monkey Puzzle* (Lost/EMI, 1981), *Casablanca* (Lost/EMI, 1982), *A Little Madness to be Free* (RCA, 1984), *Live in a Mud Hut* (New Rose, import only, 1985), *Out in the Jungle* (New Rose, import only, 1985), *All Fools' Day* (Mushroom/Festival, 1986), *Prodigal Son* (Mushroom/Festival, 1988), *The New Rose Years (Greatest Hits)* (Fan Club/New Rose, import only, 1990), *Songs of Salvation 1976–1988* (Raven, 1991), *Permanent Revolution* (Mushroom/Festival, 1992), *Howling* (Roadshow/Warner, 1996); ***Chris Bailey solo albums:*** *What We Did on Our Holidays* (New Rose, import only, 1984), *Demons* (Mushroom/Festival, 1991), *Savage Entertainment* (Aurora/Mushroom/Festival, 1992), *54 Days . . . at Sea* (Aurora/Mushroom/Festival, 1994).

Merril Bainbridge

Style: *Folk, pop*

Melbourne singer/songwriter Merril Bainbridge (b. 1968) was the first Australian female artist to attain a national #1 chart position with a self-penned debut single. 'Mouth' reached the top of the charts in May 1995 and stayed there for six weeks. When originally issued in October 1994 (backed with an acoustic version of the Pet Shop Boys' 'Being Boring'), the single was rejected by radio programmers.

The directors of Bainbridge's label Gotham, Ross Fraser and **John Farnham**, were aware of the song's potential and re-released 'Mouth' as a four-track CD EP in March 1995 to an overwhelming response. 'Mouth' also made the Top 15 when issued in Japan in early 1996. 'Under the Water' was a second Australian hit (#4 in August 1995) and Bainbridge issued her debut album, *The Garden*, in September. 'Under the Water' became the most played Australian song on local radio during 1996. Bainbridge formed the Merril Bainbridge Band with Andrew Bryant (guitar), Rejin Field (violin), Peter Whitehead (bass), Atlanta Cougan (keyboards, backing vocals) and Angus Burchill (drums) and hit the road. 'Power of One' reached #21 in December 1995 and 'Sleeping Dogs' came out in February 1996.

Album: *The Garden* (Gotham/BMG, 1995).

Dorothy Baker

Style: *Pop*

Dorothy Baker was a successful cabaret and television singer during the late 1950s and early 1960s. Her biggest pop success was a cover of Jo Ann Campbell's 'Girl from Wolverton Mountain' on W&G Records. According to Noel McGrath, the release of 'Girl from Wolverton Mountain' must be one of the country's fastest single releases. He wrote: 'Dorothy was contacted on a Tuesday, the song was recorded on the Wednesday, at the radio stations by Friday, and in the shops the following Monday.' Baker had two other hit singles 'Darling' (#27 in January 1963) and 'A Little Like Lovin'' (#26 in August 1963). She recorded two other singles for W&G, 'There's No One in the Whole World'/'If You Were Losing Him to Me' and 'Just Like Taking Candy from a Baby'/'The Fir'.

Album: *Dorothy Baker* (W&G, 1962).

Bakery

Formed: *1970*
Style: *Progressive rock*
Original line-up: *John Worrall (vocals, flute), Peter Walker (guitar; ex-Jelly Roll Bakers), Mal Logan (keyboards; ex-Rebels), Eddie McDonald (bass; ex-[NZ] Avengers), Hank Davis (drums; ex-[NZ] Avengers)*

Perth band Bakery is best known for its *Rock Mass for Love* album which was *not* indicative of the band's style of progressive hard rock. When Bakery recorded the album live at a mass held at St George's Cathedral on 21 March 1971, it was the era of 'Jesus Rock' (*Jesus Christ Superstar* and *Godspell*).

Bakery's two thunderous singles, 'Bloodsucker'/'Leave Scruffy Alone' (February 1971; on RCA) and 'No Dying in the Dark'/'Trust in the Lord' (July 1971; on Astor) actually revealed the band's true influences (Deep Purple, Black Sabbath and Led Zeppelin). 'No Dying in the Dark' peaked at #9 on the Perth singles chart.

New Zealanders Hank Davis and Eddie McDonald formed Bakery at the start of 1970. By mid-year, the line-up comprised Davis, McDonald, wild-haired guitarist Peter Walker, Tom Davidson (vocals) and Rex Bullen (keyboards; ex-**Bitter Lemons**). Mal Logan only played with Bakery for four months. He joined **Healing Force** in October 1970, and original lead singer John Worrall joined Ssarb before forming Fatty Lumpkin in 1972.

Fatty Lumpkin became another Perth institution. The name Fatty Lumpkin was derived from J.R.R. Tolkien's fantasy novel *The Hobbit* (Fatty was the dwarf Tom Bombadil's pony). The first line-up of Fatty Lumpkin included Worrall, Roy Daniels (bass; ex-Ssarb), Lindsay Wells (guitar; ex-**Healing Force**) and Tom Watts (drums). Latter-day members included Rex Bullen (keyboards; by then ex-Bakery, Natural Gas), Phil Pruiti (guitar), John Meyer (guitar), Bob Fortescue (bass; ex-**Blackfeather**, Ssarb), Warren Ward (bass), Jon Rider (bass, vocals), David Little (drums) and Al Kash (drums; ex-**Blackfeather**).

Fatty Lumpkin issued the singles 'Don't Knock My Boogie'/'Got to Get Back T' Nellie' (October 1973), 'Millionaire'/'Man Who Owns the Sea' (July 1974). 'Movin''/'One Way Road' (June 1976) and 'Lemme Rock'/'Freedom' (December 1976) before breaking up. The singles balanced jazzy hard rock with lofty, flute-led progressive ballads (somewhere between Jethro Tull and Focus) replete with quasi-Santanaesque lead guitar from Meyer. Meyer went on to Everest, Saracen (who issued one independent, self-titled album in 1986), **Rose Tattoo** and a latter-day line-up of **Chain**.

In the meantime, the 1971 line-up of Bakery recorded the *Rock Mass for Love* album (issued during August) and the two singles, before Mark Verschuer (ex-Barrelhouse) replaced Davidson on vocals. Verschuer sang lead vocals on the album *Momento* (August 1972), which was a fine example of European-influenced, heavy progressive rock. More line-up changes occurred in 1972 when Steve Hogg (bass, vocals; ex-Juke, King Biscuit Company, Nostra Damus) and Peter Ewing (organ, vocals) replaced McDonald and Bullen respectively; Verschuer also left. Davis, Walker, Hogg and Ewing shared vocal duties. Eddie McDonald initially joined ex-**Levi Smith's Clefs** singer Barry McAskill's new band McAskill and then the **Phil Manning** Band in May 1975. Bullen went on to work with **Jim Keays'** Southern Cross and the **Marc Hunter** Band. He died in March 1983.

As a four-piece, Bakery earned acclaim on the eastern states festival/concert circuit playing alongside **Billy Thorpe** and the Aztecs, **MacKenzie Theory**, **Chain**, **Carson**, **Madder Lake**, **Sid Rumpo** and the like. The live version of the jazz-infused 'Living with a Memory' (the studio version appeared on *Momento*) appeared on Mushroom's triple album set *The Great Australian Rock Festival Sunbury 1973* (April 1973). Phil Lawson (bass) replaced Hogg in February 1973 and New Zealand-born Barry Leef (ex-Simple Image, Hunger) joined as lead singer. In August, **Jackie Orszaczky** (ex-Syrius) replaced Lawson on bass.

Barry Leef came to the attention of Frank Zappa when The Mothers of Invention toured Australia during June 1973 (Bakery covered Zappa's 'Road Ladies' on stage). Zappa was impressed with Leef's vocal abilities, and invited the singer to join The Mothers of Invention. Visa and work permit problems arose when it came time for Leef to join The Mothers in the USA, and he reluctantly had to decline the offer. Bakery continued playing live until February 1975, but did not record again. Reissue specialists Raven included Bakery's 'No Dying in the Dark' on the definitive collection of Australian progressive rock, *Golden Miles: Australian Progressive Rock 1969–1974* (1994).

Walker became in-house studio engineer at Trafalgar Studios, and later produced albums for **Cold Chisel**, **Catfish** and **Ian Moss**. Leef formed the Barry Leef Band (with Walker) and recorded a couple of singles for Festival/Infinity, 'Last Song'/'Three Minute Hero' (May 1975) and 'To Be Back Home'/'What Do You Want?' (February 1976). Orszaczky joined the **Marcia Hines** Band as musical director.

Steve Hogg went on to play with Baiyana, the Chuck McKinney Band, the **Ray Burton** Band, **Ayers Rock** and others. In the late 1980s, he formed The Rhythm Snakes which comprised Bob Thorne (guitar), Clayton Black (drums) and Howie Smallman (harp). In 1989, Hogg assembled a studio band to record an album of his own material. The band comprised Thorne, Bob Patient (piano), Ian Ironside (drums), Mark Alderman (harp) and Bernie Payne (sax). Hogg died on 20 July 1990, before the album was completed. His mother and the musicians involved arranged for the tapes to be issued as the Steve Hogg album *Various Fools & Vices*, which appeared in 1992.

Albums: *Rock Mass For Love* (Astor, 1971), *Momento* (Astor, 1972).

The Bam Balams

Formed: *1984*
Style: *Rock'n'roll*
Original line-up: *Brendan Kibble (vocals, guitar), Brad Fitzpatrick (guitar, vocals), Steve Cole (bass, vocals), Matt Manchester (drums, vocals)*

While many of their Sydney-based contemporaries exploited Detroit-inspired hard rock (**Trilobites**), 1960s acid-punk (**Lime Spiders**) or 1960s psychedelia (**Moffs**), The Bam Balams were practitioners of a lively brand of rock'n'roll that mixed R&B, blues, rockabilly, country and pop.

The band's name was derived from a track on The Flamin' Groovies' album *Supersnazz*, and other influences ranged from Chuck Berry, Gene Vincent, Jerry Lee Lewis, The Rolling Stones and The Byrds to Creedence Clearwater Revival and Gram Parsons. Singer/songwriter Brendan Kibble formed The Bam Balams during April 1984. The line-up of Kibble, Brad Fitzpatrick, Steve Cole and Matt Manchester recorded the singles 'Deliver My Love'/'Mean Thang' (November 1985) and 'No-One Else'/'Gettin' Over You' (June 1986) for the Citadel label. Ex-**Radio Birdman** singer Rob Younger produced the records and Citadel in-house engineer Alan Thorne (**Died Pretty**, **Lime Spiders** and **Screaming Tribesmen**) worked the desk.

Kibble broke up the band at the end of 1986 and formed a new line-up with Steve Carlin (guitar), Amr Z. Abdallah (bass) and Warren Elford (drums). Citadel's sister label Green Fez issued the band's next single 'Surfin' in the Swamp'/'Fire in My Soul' in March 1988. The band broke up again, and Kibble received an invitation from ex-Long Ryders singer/guitarist Syd Griffin to join his new band in Los Angeles. Kibble declined the offer and decided to reform The Bam Balams with Ian Little (ex-**Grooveyard**) replacing Carlin and Joe Breen (ex-Coupe DeVille) replacing Elford. Abdallah remained from the previous line-up. The lavishly packaged album *The Genuine Rock & Roll Medicine Show* (December 1988) and its single 'Wheel of Fortune'/'Rock it to the Moon' (November) were strong records. Abdallah left in 1989 and Greg Marchant came in as replacement. The band's next single, 'Hellfire'/'Hold on Me' (November 1989), was written about one of the band's heroes, 'The Killer' (Jerry Lee Lewis).

Dave Castellari replaced Marchant in 1990, and The Bam Balams put out their final record that year on the Pink Flamingo label, the 12-inch EP *Extended Play* ('10 000 Miles'). The Bam Balams never gained commercial success, but the independent charts indicated that all their records sold well.

Album: *Genuine Rock & Roll Medicine Show* (Green Fez, 1988).

The Bamboos

Formed: *1984*
Style: *Swamp rock*
Original line-up: *Craig Hallsworth (guitar, vocals), Roger Russell (guitar), Mark Gelmi (bass), Tony Chiallella (drums)*

Craig Hallsworth formed The Bamboos in the West Australian township of Collie. The Bamboos issued the cassette album *Rarer than Rocking Horse Shit* in 1986 and toured the eastern states. The Cleopatra label reissued *Rarer than Rocking Horse Shit* on vinyl. The band's brand of raw guitar trash and country/swamp rock caught the attention of Citadel Records boss John Needham.

In 1986, Shakir Pichler replaced Tony Chiallella on drums and Greg Hitchcock (ex-Go Starts, Grave Robbers) replaced Roger Russell on guitar. Citadel issued the single 'Virginia'/'Snuff' (September 1986) and the mini-album *Born Killer* (May 1987). By the time the mini-album came out, Russell Hopkinson (ex-**Vicious Circle**) had replaced Pichler on drums. The Bamboos' final single, 'With Which to Love Her'/'Winded', came out in October 1987, after which the band split.

Hopkinson played with **The Kryptonics** in Perth and **Nursery Crimes** in Melbourne before joining Sydney band **You Am I** in 1992. Hitchcock was in a variety of bands, including The Stonefish, The Neptunes, **The Kryptonics**, **The New Christs** and **The Verys** before joining **You Am I** in 1995 as a hired gun. The Neptunes comprised Hitchcock, Jamie Parry (vocals), Rocky Mason (guitar), Rob Findlay (bass) and Ian Chater (drums). They described their music as 'psychedelic amphetamine surf groove'. The band issued the mini-album *Hydrophobia* (1988) and the album *Godfish* (1991) on the Citadel label.

Hallsworth went on to form The Healers with Tony Vespoli (lead guitar), Jim Butterworth (bass, vocals) and Miles Hitchcock (drums). The Healers played driving rock'n'roll with Johnny

Thunders-inspired lead guitar laid over the top. The band issued two 12-inch EPs, 'Wildfire' and 'Dark Country' (both 1990), plus the album *Secret Show* on the Rattlesnake label.

Bamboos albums: *Rarer than Rocking Horse Shit* (Cleopatra, 1986), *Born Killer* (mini-album, Citadel, 1987); ***Healers album:*** *Secret Show* (Rattlesnake, 1991).

Band of Light

Formed: *1972*
Style: *Blues rock*
Original line-up: *Phil Key (vocals, guitar; ex-***La De Das***), Norm Roue (slide guitar; ex-Gutbucket,* **Lotus,** *Wolfe), Peter Roberts (bass; ex-***Freshwater, La De Das***), Tony Buettel (ex-***Bay City Union, Levi Smith's Clefs, Fraternity, Band of Talabene***)*

Phil Key had spent eight years with **La De Das** before forming Band of Light in October 1972 as a more introspective, personal venture. Ian Rilen replaced original bass player Peter Roberts after only three gigs. Master slide guitarist Norm Roue and drummer Tony Buettel completed the line-up.

Band of Light immediately established a slow, heavy blues style dominated by Roue's stinging slide work. Key also introduced a quasi-religious philosophy into the band's lyrics that espoused racial equality, social justice and spiritual harmony. Band of Light was one of the first local bands to use a symbol (a yin-and-yang-like circle set within two contrasting yet harmonious triangles) to represent the bands philosophy and approach. The band worked the Sydney and Melbourne pub/festival circuit alongside **Billy Thorpe** and the Aztecs, **Carson, Coloured Balls, Chain, Madder Lake, Buffalo,** etc.

Band of Light scored a national #18 hit single in July 1973 with the infectious boogie rocker 'Destiny Song'/'Over 'B'' which was taken from the album *Total Union* (August). Mostly the album was standard hard rock, slow 12-bar blues and boogie, but the best tracks revealed Band of Light to be an energetic and funky rock band. The second single 'Free Them From Hunger'/'The Cat' (August) and the non-album 'Moonstruck'/'If' (November) failed to chart. 'Destiny Song', 'Moonstruck', 'Free Them From Hunger' and 'If' were later combined on the rare *Band of Light* EP. Roue, Rilen and Buettel all left Band of Light in mid-1974. Roue went on to join **Buffalo,** Rilen helped form **Rose Tattoo** in 1976 and Buettel went into production work. Key was ready to record the band's second album and called in Bill Williams (bass) and Dannie Davidson (drums; ex-**Tamam Shud, Kahvas Jute**) to complete *The Archer.*

That album had a much drier sound than the debut and failed to chart. The single, 'The Archer, A Sagittarian Rhapsody'/'Silus The Sun', was not successful. Ray Vanderby (keyboards) and Eddie Hansen (lead guitar; ex-Ticket) filled out the basic three-piece line-up for live dates, but by the end of 1974 the band had broken up. Key ended up driving taxis in Sydney for many years. He died in May 1984 as a result of a congenital heart condition.

Albums: *Total Union* (WEA/Warners, 1973), *The Archer* (WEA/Warners, 1974).

Band of Talabene

Formed: *1972*
Style: *Blues rock*
Original line-up: **Phil Manning** *(guitar, vocals; ex-***Bay City Union, Chain,** *Pilgrimage,* **Friends***), Tony Naylor (guitar, vocals; ex-Ida May Mack), Phil Gaunt (bass; ex-Ida May Mack), Tony Buettel (drums: ex-***Bay City Union, Levi Smith's Clefs, Fraternity***)*

In April 1972, ex-**Chain** guitarist **Phil Manning** launched his new rock-blues band Willy and the Philtones. The name was in homage to bands like Derek and the Dominoes (i.e. no-one called Willy in the band) and because it comprised two Phils (Manning and Phil Gaunt) and two Tonys (Tony Naylor and Tony Buettel).

By July, the band had evolved into Band of Talabene with Gus Fenwick (ex-**Pleazers**) replacing Gaunt. The band's new name derived from a dream Manning's daughter Kim had one night in which she saw a band called 'Talabene' that featured pumpkins playing guitars! That version of Band of Talabene lasted until December 1972 and issued one single, 'Herbert's Boogie'/'Tell It Like It Is' (November), on the Bootleg label. Manning left to join Mighty Mouse, which evolved into a new version of **Chain** at the start of 1973.

Naylor kept the Band of Talabene name alive with a new line-up comprising ex-**La De Das/Band of Light** bassist Peter Roberts on guitar, Fran Kelly (bass) and Peter Curtain (drums, ex-**Party Machine**). The new line-up issued the single 'Oh, Darling'/'Blind Man' (April 1973) on Bootleg. The June 1973 line-up featured Naylor, Roberts, Paul 'Sheepdog' Wheeler (bass; ex-**Billy Thorpe** and the Aztecs) and Dallas Royal (drums). Steve Webb (ex-**Blackfeather,** Wolfe, **Duck,** Tramp) then replaced Royal on drums. By the end of the year, Band of Talabene had been incorporated into **The Bootleg Family Band,** which provided back-up for singers like **Brian Cadd.**

The Band Who Shot Liberty Valance

Formed: 1987
Style: Rock
Original line-up: *Fred Negro (vocals; ex-Editions,* **I Spit on Your Gravy**, *Gravybillies), Phil 'Grizzly' Miles (guitar; ex-***I Spit on Your Gravy**, *Gravybillies), Trevor Pennington (bass; ex-***Corpse Grinders***), Terry Fosters (harmonica), Phil 'Good-One' Bryant (drums; ex-***Corpse Grinders***)*

Melbourne-based lager louts The Band Who Shot Liberty Valance were the ultimate charmless, inner-city party band. The band grew out of three of Melbourne's most notorious groups of the 1980s, **I Spit on Your Gravy**, The Gravybillies and **Corpse Grinders**.

Cartoonist/St Kilda identity Fred Negro's previous band, **I Spit on Your Gravy**, had managed to score a deal with Virgin Records, as did The Band Who Shot Liberty Valance. Virgin issued the album *Outlaw Death Lager Drinkers from Hell* in October 1988. A couple of song titles gave an indication of the band's nefarious intentions: 'Gravybillies in the Sky' (a reworking of 'Ghost Riders in the Sky') and 'I Fought the Slab' (formerly 'I Fought the Law'). The Band Who Shot Liberty Valance courted controversy rather than record sales and broke up in 1989. Trevor Pennington and Phil Bryant joined **Intoxica**, while Negro and Fosters continued the drunken hillbilly theme with The Brady Bunch Lawnmower Massacre. That band comprised Negro, Fosters, Garry Mansfield (guitar), Paul Barnett (bass) and Scotti 'Stix' Simpson (drums; ex-**I Spit on Your Gravy**).

The band's crude, artless cacophony was once described as a cross between The Butthole Surfers and the Beverly Hillbillies. Certainly the band never let any notions of taste get in the way of a rollicking, drunken good time. Shock Records issued the mini-album *Contact Pool* and single 'Bourbon Bound' in 1991. The last Brady Bunch Lawnmower Massacre records were the album *Desperate Football* (August 1992) and single 'Drink Myself to Life'/'Inca Cave' (July).

The Brady Bunch Lawnmower Massacre broke up in 1993 and Negro formed The Fuck Fucks. That subversive lot comprised Negro, Tristan Miller (guitar), Dave Moll (guitar; ex-**Harem Scarem**, Relics, Teddy Turner and the Bunsen Burners), Paddy Chong (bass; ex-**Nursery Crimes**) and Tony Biggs (drums; ex-Black Assassins, **Hell to Pay**). The band became legendary around the Melbourne inner-city circuit due to Negro's penchant for dropping his pants on stage and carrying out unspeakable acts on pieces of fruit and cans of baked beans!

The Fuck Fucks had three tracks included on the independent compilation *Here Come Eleven Nuns* (on the Buggertoe label) alongside The Shonky Tonks, Fatty Cramps and Teddy Turner and the Bunsen Burners. There was also the track 'Burgershop Slaughter' included on the *Vulgar Tongue* double compilation (1996). *The Who's Who of Australian Rock* (4th edition) listed The Fuck Fucks as having issued the album *Bring Out the Gimp* in December 1994, but that is not the case. (Negro was, however, involved in the revue-styled *Dog Fiction* around that time which was based on Quentin Tarantino's film, *Pulp Fiction*, in which the 'Gimp' character appeared.) The band issued its debut album *Here* in August 1997.

Band Who Shot Liberty Vallance album: *Outlaw Death Lager Drinkers from Hell* (Virgin, 1988); ***Brady Bunch Lawnmower Massacre albums:*** *Contact Pool* (mini-album; Shagpile/Shock 1991), *Desperate Football* (Shagpile/Shock, 1992); ***The Fuck Fucks album***: *Here* (Shock, 1997).

Bandicoot

Formed: 1976
Style: Pop, rock
Original line-up: *Mick Fettes (vocals; ex-***Madder Lake***), Shane Bourne (vocals)*

In 1976, tall, gangly stand-up comedian Shane Bourne formed a songwriting partnership with pudgy, moon-faced singer Mick Fettes (the Laurel and Hardy of Australian rock). They decided to get together with a bunch of musicians, record an album, have a few drinks and laughs and then break-up. The sessions proved so enjoyable that a full-time band was born.

Helping out in the studio were **Gary Young** (drums, ex-**Daddy Cool**, Hot Dog), Danny Bourne (keyboards; ex-Hot Dog, on loan from **Pantha**), Kerry McKenna (on guitar; from **Madder Lake**) and Ross Davis (guitar). The band's self-titled album mixed good-time rock'n'roll, blues, country and pop but failed to chart. The radio-friendly Beatlesque single 'Living Off the Radio'/'Who Am I to Say?' (March 1976) was not successful.

Bandicoot toured for a year with a line-up that comprised Fettes, Bourne, Mick Elliot (guitar; ex-**Sid Rumpo**, Wild Beaver Band, **Jim Keays'** Southern Cross), Tony Vikaris (guitar; ex-Left of Centre), Bruno De Stanislo (bass; ex-North Wind) and Peter Reed (drums; ex-**New Dream**, Hot Dog). Bandicoot broke up in May 1977, and Bourne and

Elliot continued on for a while with a new band called Hound Dogs. Bourne was resident funny man on Channel Nine's *Hey Hey It's Saturday* television variety show during the 1980s. In 1996 he compered a revival of Graham Kennedy's 1970s television quiz show *Blankety Blanks*.

Album: *Bandicoot* (Rainbird, 1976).

Bang the Drum

Formed: *1989*
Style: *Pop, rock*
Original line-up: *Steve Driver (vocals), Jim Reece (guitar, vocals), Jeremy Cole (keyboards), Geoff Robson (bass, vocals), J.J. Harris (drums; ex-*Divinyls*)*

This Sydney-based band evolved out of Tasmanian outfit Bigger than Texas. The band signed to WEA and issued the single 'Only You'/'Back Tomorrow' at the end of 1989. 'Only You' cracked the national Top 30. Charles Fisher produced the band's self-titled debut album (June 1990) which yielded the singles 'Passion' (May) and 'Stay Forever' (August). The album showed the band to be working in the same idiom as the likes of **Icehouse** and **Noiseworks**, but this did not translate into record sales. With the album's release, Bang the Drum supported overseas visitors Fleetwood Mac on an Australian tour.

Album: *Bang The Drum* (WEA, 1990).

The Barbarellas

Formed: *1990*
Style: *Pop*
1991 line-up: *Eleanor Rodgers (vocals), Matt Galvin (guitar), Jon Robertson (guitar), Dave Keys (bass), Mike Vlack (drums)*

Eleanor Rodgers and Matt Galvin formed The Barbarellas in Sydney. The band's name was derived from the 1968 science-fiction feature film *Barbarella* starring Jane Fonda. The above line-up recorded the band's first single for Citadel, 'Dying Inside'/'Forget About You'. Chris Hampston replaced Vlack in 1992. The band's brand of jangly, melodic (yet tough) guitar pop was at odds with most of the material issued by Citadel (Detroit-flavoured hard rock). Nevertheless, Citadel issued The Barbarellas' 12-inch EP, 'Fringe', and mini-album, *Quit Skylarking*, in 1991. The band's debut album, *Slumber* (June 1992), was a compilation of the single, the EP and the mini-album. It made for a strong release as a whole. The Barbarellas broke up in 1993.

Albums: *Quit Skylarking* (mini-album; Citadel, 1991), *Slumber* (Citadel, 1992).

Tony Barber

Style: *Beat pop*

1960s aficionado (the late) Dean Mittelhauser described guitarist/singer/songwriter Tony Barber in the fanzine *The Livin' End* as 'definitely one of our most underrated performers from the sixties . . . He played a bigger part in the success of Billy Thorpe & The Aztecs than is generally credited.'

English-born Barber (not to be confused with one-time *Sale of the Century* presenter Tony Barber) was born in 1940 and immigrated to Australia in 1964. He had played with a small-time band in England called The Electrons. Within a month of arriving in Australia, he had joined **Billy Thorpe** and the Aztecs. He wrote the songs that made up The Aztecs' first single, 'Blue Day'/'You Don't Love Me' (April 1964). Two days before The Aztecs were to record two more of his songs for the next single, Barber received The Rolling Stones' first British EP, *Rolling Stones*, sent over by his brother from England.

The Aztecs heard The Stones' version of Leiber and Stoller's 'Poison Ivy' and decided to record it themselves. It became The Aztecs' first #1 hit single in June 1964. Barber stayed with The Aztecs long enough to appear on three further singles, 'Mashed Potato', 'Sick and Tired' and 'Over the Rainbow'. When the original Aztecs broke up, Barber joined forces with the band's other guitarist, Vince Maloney, in the short-lived Vince and Tony's Two (with John Shields on bass and Jimmy Thompson on drums).

Barber split from Maloney, and made an immediate impression with his debut solo single 'Someday'/'Is It Raining?' (February 1966) on the Spin label. 'Someday' was a direct copy of The Aztecs' sound which no doubt helped propel it to #7 on the Melbourne chart and #11 in Sydney. Barber had four more minor hit singles, 'Wait By The Water'/'What Now?' (April 1966), 'Wondrous Place'/'No, No, No' (July), 'Lookin' for a Better Day'/'I Don't Want You Like That' (January 1967) and 'Bird's Eye View'/'Women of Stone' (April). Barber used **Steve & the Board** and **The Bee Gees** as backing musicians for his solo album (all were signed to Nat Kipner's Spin label). Barber then slipped from view. During the early 1980s, Barber formed a partnership with **Billy Thorpe** in the *Sunshine Friends* soft toy project.

Album: *Someday . . . Now!* (Spin, 1966).

Nick Barker and the Reptiles

Formed: *1988*
Style: *Rock, blues*
Original line-up: *Nick Barker (vocals, guitar; ex-Curse, Reptile Smile, Freak Power,* **Wreckery***), Adrian Chynoweth (guitar; ex-Curse, Reptile Smile, Freak Power), Drew Basford (bass), David Pinder (drums)*

Nick Barker served a long apprenticeship on the Melbourne independent scene of the 1980s before embarking on a successful mainstream career with Nick Barker and the Reptiles. Barker played bass in The Curse, Reptile Smile, Freak Power and inner-city angst kings **The Wreckery** before forming The Reptiles in March 1988. A series of acoustic shows Barker undertook with **Hunters & Collectors'** Mark Seymour during 1987 gave him the confidence to form his own band.

The Reptiles' sassy brand of commercial rock'n'blues found immediate acceptance on the pub rock circuit. By the end of 1988, White/Mushroom had issued the band's **Chris Bailey**-produced debut single, 'Another Me'/'Spirit Level' (December). The singles '(Sure Beats) Goin' to Pieces'/ 'Hell to Pay' (July 1989) and a cover of Steve Harley and Cockney Rebel's 1975 classic 'Make Me Smile (Come Up and See Me)'/'Resurrection Time' (October) were hits in Melbourne. 'Make Me Smile (Come Up and See Me)' also reached #25 nationally in November 1989. American producer Jim Farrachi flew out to Australia to work on the band's debut album, *Goin' to Pieces*, which came out in August 1989. By that stage, Chris 'Houn'dog' Harris had joined on harmonica.

The Reptiles embarked on a rigorous touring schedule around the country (200 gigs a year), becoming one of the archetypal Oz Rock pub bands of the era. Matthew Heydon (keyboards) joined the band in 1990. Marc Scully (ex-Love Rodeo, **Deadly Hume**) also replaced original bass player Drew Basford. It was not until March 1991, however, that the band issued a second album, *After the Show*. Produced by Los Angeles native Joe Hardy (best known for his work with Steve Earle), it was a diverse collection of songs, ranging from tough rock'n'roll and bar-room boogies to ballads. The album spawned three singles, 'Won't Get You Loved' (February, 1991), 'Can't Hold on' (May) and 'Miles to Go'/'Before I Go' (live) (September).

The Reptiles broke up in 1993, following the release of a final single 'Out in the Open' (February 1992) and the CD EP 'Loose' (April). Following a year spent travelling overseas, Barker formed a new band called Barker. Barker comprised Nick Barker, ex-Reptile Matt Heydon, Anthony Ragg (bass, ex-**Kings of the Sun**), Tim Henwood (guitar; on loan from Supermann) and Venom Brown (drums; ex-**Massive Appendage**). The band issued the singles 'Heard So Much About You' (March 1994), 'World's a Peach' (July) and 'Time Bomb' (September), plus the album *Happy Man* (August). 'Time Bomb' logged an impressive #20 placing on the 1994 Triple J Hottest 100 list.

Nick Barker

The CD EP *Son of Happy Man* followed in April 1995. The *Happy Man* album was not commercially successful and Barker went solo. His debut solo album, *Damn Mermaids* (August 1996), produced the CD singles 'Imogen' (June) and 'Someone Like You' (October). Barker's backing band at that stage (dubbed The Damn Mermaids) comprised Lincoln Jones (bass) and Craig Whitelock (drums).

Nick Barker and the Reptiles albums: *Goin' To Pieces* (White/Mushroom/Festival, 1989), *After The Show* (White/Mushroom/Festival, 1991); ***Barker album:*** *Happy Man* (White/Mushroom/Festival, 1994); ***Nick Barker solo album:*** *Damn Mermaids* (White/Mushroom/Festival, 1996).

Jimmy Barnes

Style: Rock

As the elder statesman of Oz Rock, Jimmy Barnes has carved out the most successful solo career of any performer in Australian rock history (with the possible exceptions of **Johnny O'Keefe** and **John Farnham**). Popularly known as 'Barnsey', the gravel-voiced blues belter has been feted by prominent Australians of all persuasions and was the first local musician to be interviewed on *60 Minutes* (March 1988). He retained his popularity due to a down-to-earth, 'just one of the boys' charm.

Barnes was born James Swan in Glasgow, Scotland during 1956. His family emigrated to Australia when he was four years old. The Swan family (including his brother John, aka **Swanee**) settled in the tough migrant working-class suburb of Elizabeth in Adelaide, South Australia. His mother remarried and Jim Swan adopted his stepfather's surname of Barnes. Barnes's first band was called Tarkus, but he rose to national prominence as frontman for **Cold Chisel**, one of Australia's best loved bands. Driven by a voracious will to succeed, he launched his solo career immediately after **Cold Chisel** broke up in late 1983.

His #1 album *Bodyswerve* (September 1984) was basically a reworking of the **Cold Chisel** 'barnstorming' pub-rock approach. Barnes wrote all the tracks on the album's three singles 'No Second Prize'/'I've Got News for You' (#11 in August), 'Promise Me You'll Call'/'Boys Cry Out for War' (November) and 'Daylight'/'Paradise' (#14 in February 1985). His backing band on the album comprised Malcolm Eastick (guitar; ex-**Stars, Broderick Smith**'s Big Combo), Chris Stockley (guitar, mandolin; ex-**Cam-Pact, Axiom, Dingoes**, Stockley See Mason Band), Bruce Howe (bass, ex-**Fraternity**) and **Ray Arnott** (drums, ex-**Spectrum, Dingoes**). With the addition of backing vocalists Maggie McKinney and Shauna Jenson, the Jimmy Barnes Band took to the road. Robin Riley (ex-**Redhouse**, **Rose Tattoo**, **Party Boys**, Beast) later replaced Stockley, and keyboard player Peter Kekel (ex-Gillian Eastoe and King Dog, **Swanee**, Beast) joined at the end of 1985.

The December 1985 album *For the Working Class Man* was a double 12-inch EP set featuring five new songs recorded in New York and Los Angeles, plus a bonus disc containing seven remixes from *Bodyswerve*. The new songs utilised the services of many top American session players (Waddy Wachtel, Billy Burnette, Charlie Sexton, Mick Fleetwood, Randy Jackson, Jonathan Caine and members of Little Feat). Although aimed at the vast American market, the album was a huge success locally. It reached #1 on the national chart in February, and went on to sell over 350 000 copies. The album's string of anthemic singles, 'I'd Die to Be with You Tonight'/'Vision' (#4 in October 1985), 'Working Class Man'/'No Second Prize' (#7 in February 1986) and 'Ride the Night Away'/'Paradise' (Top 40 in April 1986), were chart successes. The Jonathan Caine-penned 'Working Class Man' was used as the theme song to Ron Howard's feature film of the same name (called *Gung-Ho* in the USA).

By that stage, Barnes was dividing his time equally between Australia and America (where he had signed to Geffen Records). He formed a songwriting partnership with Jim Vallance (also Bryan Adam's songwriting partner) and was using Jonathan Caine as his producer. On the jingoistic Australian Made tour of January/February 1987, Barnes's backing band comprised Canadian musicians (with the sole exception of Australian Peter Kekel). The Barnes/**INXS** joint recording of **The Easybeats'** rocker 'Good Times' was adopted as the unofficial anthem of the tour. The single crashed in at #1 first week on the national chart during January 1987. It also appeared on the soundtrack to the movie *The Lost Boys*.

The *Freight Train Heart* album (December 1987) and the double live LP *Barnestorming* (November 1988) continued the US-styled stadium rock tradition. *Freight Train Heart* made its debut at #1 on the national chart, and went on to sell 200 000 copies in Australia. It yielded five singles, 'Too Much Ain't Enough'/'Do or Die' (#1 in November 1987), 'Driving Wheels'/'Different Lives' (#4 in February 1988), 'I'm Still on Your Side'/'Going to Mexico' (March), 'Waiting for the Heartache'/'Seven Days' (July) and 'When a Man Loves a Woman'/'I'd Die to be With You Tonight' (#2 in December 1988). Likewise, *Barnestorming* made its debut at #1 on the Australian chart, while the single 'Last Frontier'(live)/'Many Rivers To Cross' peaked at #31 in February 1989.

The Don Gehman-produced *Two Fires* (July 1990) was another #1 album which contained five hit singles: 'Lay Down Your Guns'/'Broken Hearts' (#4 in August 1990), 'Let's Make it Last All Night'/'Bad News' (#12 in November 1990), 'Little Darling' (#39 in February 1991), 'When Your Love is Gone' (#11 in May) and 'Love is Enough' (#48 in August). *Two Fires* became the fourth biggest selling album in Australia for 1990 *and* the fifth biggest selling for 1991 (over 400 000 copies sold all up). It came out on Atlantic in the USA.

Barnes's sixth #1 album *Soul Deep* (October 1991), was the singer's tribute to his favourite soul/R&B performers of the 1960s. It produced the singles Joe Tex's 'I Gotcha' (#6 in October 1991) and Marvin Gaye/Ashford/Simpson's 'Ain't No Mountain High Enough' (#28, February 1992). The Barnsey and Farnsey (**John Farnham**) duet on the Hayes/Porter song 'When Something is Wrong with My Baby' was also a #3 hit (November 1991), despite being considered an overwrought example of two grown men screaming their lungs out at each other! Nevertheless, *Soul Deep* went on to become the biggest selling Australian album issued on Mushroom (more than 600 000 copies sold). Barnes won Best Male Artist and Highest Selling Album at the 1991 Australian Record Industry Association (ARIA) Awards.

Members of Barnes's recording and touring bands circa 1989–92 included Australian guitarists **Kevin Borich**, **Johnny Diesel** and Mick King; American guitarists Charlie Sexton, Todd Sharp and Jeff Neill; American keyboard players Jonathan Caine (ex-Babys, Journey), Tom Lang and Michael Mani; English keyboard player Allan Mansfield (from **Dragon**); Australian keyboard players Peter Kekel and Mal Logan (ex-**Renée Geyer** Band); Australian bass players Chris Bailey (ex-**Angels**) and Michael Hegerty (ex-**Richard Clapton** Band); American drummers Tony Brock (ex-Babys) and Walfredo Reyes; Australian drummers Buzz Bidstrup (ex-**Angels**, **GANGgajang**) and Angus Burchill (from **John Farnham** Band); and backing vocalists **Deni Hines**, Debbie Harwood, Marcie Levy and Sharon O'Neill.

Heat (#2 in April 1993) produced the hits 'Sweat it Out' (#11 in January), 'Stand Up' (#41 in March) and 'Stone Cold' (#4 in June). Once again produced by Gehman (best known for his work with R.E.M. and John Cougar Mellencamp), *Heat* featured writing contributions from **Ross Wilson** and Saint **Chris Bailey**. Barnsey's 1993 touring band comprised Jeff Neill (guitar), Matt Heydon (keyboards; ex-**Nick Barker and the Reptiles**), Michael Hegerty (bass), Angus Burchill (drums) and Lisa Hunt (backing vocals).

Barnes worked with a number of artists such as **The Badloves**, **Deborah Conway**, **Archie Roach**, **Diesel** and Joe Cocker on his album of acoustic duets *Flesh and Wood* (December 1993). The album produced the Top 10 hit cover of The Band's 'The Weight' shared with **The Badloves**. The next two singles lifted from the album, 'You Can't Make Love Without a Soul' (February 1994) and 'Still Got a Long Way to Go' (with **Diesel**) were not chart hits. Barnes contributed a version of **Chain's** 'Black and Blue' to the Various Artists compilation *Earth Music* (June 1994).

Jimmy Barnes

In 1994 Barnes found himself in financial difficulties. Success was a double-edged sword. He certainly made a lot of money from touring and record sales, but essentially the more he worked to pay off debts, the more he had to pay out to cover the costs of touring and recording, let alone paying his taxes. Leaving his Bowral NSW country estate, Barnes took his family to live in Europe. Barnes returned to Australia in mid-1995 to promote his ninth album *Psyclone*. It produced the hit single 'Change of Heart' (#17 in May 1995). His next single, the ballad 'Come Undone' (July), was not a chart success. At the end of 1995, Barnes supported overseas visitors Bon Jovi on that band's Australian tour. Barnes's hit for 1996 was 'Lover Lover' (#6 in October), followed by 'Never Give You Up' (#33 in March 1997). His biggest latterday album was the 1996 triple platinum, #1 collection *Hits*. In October 1997, Barnes teamed up with his erstwhile **Cold Chisel** companions in the recording studio with the view to reforming the band.

As well as collaborations with **INXS**, **John Farnham** and **The Badloves**, Barnes has recorded successful duets with Tina Turner '(Simply) the Best'/'River Deep Mountain High' (which reached

#14 in June 1992) and **Nathan Cavaleri** ('Gonna See My Baby Tonight', September 1993). Jimmy Barnes is an Australian phenomenon. He has sold over six million records in a country of 17 million people. To date, major overseas success has eluded him. Nevertheless, Barnes looms large as the admirable journeyman musician who has consistently revitalised his career with quality input and earnest execution.

Albums: *Bodyswerve* (Mushroom/Festival, 1984), *For the Working Class Man* (Mushroom/Festival, 1985), *Freight Train Heart* (Mushroom/Festival, 1987), *Barnestorming* (Mushroom/Festival, 1988), *Two Fires* (Mushroom/Festival, 1990), *Soul Deep* (Mushroom/Festival, 1991), *Heat* (Mushroom/Festival, 1993), *Flesh and Wood* (Mushroom/Festival, 1993), *Psyclone* (Mushroom/Festival, 1995), *Hits* (Mushroom/Festival, 1996).

Further reading: *Too Much Ain't Enough* by Toby Creswell (Random House, 1993).

Yvonne Barrett

Style: *Pop*

Pop singer Yvonne Barrett appeared on *The Go!! Show* television series in 1965, and then recorded three singles for the Go!! label. 'Little People'/'You're the One', 'Send Her Away'/'Won't Someone Say' and 'Don't Bother Callin''/'I'm Takin' Him Back' were minor hits in Melbourne. She recorded a single for Columbia in 1970, 'Lu'/'Picture Me Gone', and then moved into club and television work. She was tragically murdered in 1985.

Noeleen Batley

Style: *Pop*

During the early 1960s, pop singer Noeleen Batley (born in 1944 and dubbed 'Australia's Little Miss Sweetheart') was a regular on television pop shows like *Six O'Clock Rock* and *Bandstand*. She scored a hit single for Festival's Rex label with 'Barefoot Boy'/'When My Blue Moon Turns to Gold Again', which reached the Top 5 in most states during November 1960. Her debut single was actually 'Starry Eyes'/'Soldier Soldier Won't You Marry Me' in February 1960.

She recorded two more moderately successful singles for the Rex label, 'Rendezvous'/'Fickle Fingers' (February 1961) and 'Tammy'/'Little Sir Echo' (August 1961), and then signed direct to Festival for 'Ice Cream Man'/'Over in that Happy Land' (September 1961). Throughout that time, Batley toured with artists like **Johnny O'Keefe**, **Col Joye** and the Joy Boys, **Johnny Chester**, **Lucky Starr** and The Allen Brothers. She was named Australia's Top Female Vocalist of 1961.

Following four more singles, 'Steady Johnny'/'Letter Full of Tears' (March 1962), 'Don't Play No. 9'/'Crying Fool' (June), 'Ten Lonely Weekends'/'My Boy' (March 1963) and 'Surfer Boy'/'Forgive Me' (February 1964), Batley scored her second biggest hit with 'My Little Treasure from Japan' (#24 in October 1964). The original Japanese version of the song, 'Kon Nichi Wa Akachan', had already sold over a million copies in Japan. Batley's version was issued in Japan and sold over 60 000 copies. When Batley toured there during 1965, she was well received. 'Tears Of Farewell' also sold 60 000 copies in Japan.

Batley began to move into cabaret, and recorded seven more singles for Festival in Australia before travelling to the UK in 1969. She recorded one single in England ('Seabird'/'Let It Stay this Way'), toured throughout Europe and represented Australia at the Brazil Popular Song Festival held in Rio de Janeiro. Batley later settled in the USA and retired from regular performing.

Albums: *Rendezvous* (Festival/Rex, 1961), *You Made Me Love You* (Festival, 1964), *Christmas Album* (Festival, 1965), *Little Treasure from Japan: The Festival File Volume One* (Festival, 1988).

Billy Baxter (*see* The Hollowmen)

Bay City Union

Formed: *1966*
Style: *Blues*
Original line-up: *Paul 'A.P.' Johnson (vocals),* **Matt Taylor** *(rhythm guitar, vocals, harmonica), Jimmy Brelsford (lead guitar), Trevor Bagnall (bass), Peter Miles (drums; ex-***Purple Hearts***)*

Alongside Melbourne's **Adderley Smith Blues Band** and Sydney's **The Foreday Riders**, Brisbane-based Bay City Union is generally acknowledged as one of the earliest traditional Chicago blues bands formed in Australia. The band grew out of the same scene that also gave rise to Black Cat Circle, The Chelsea Set, Thursday's Children and Mick Hadley's Coloured Balls.

Led by master bluesman **Matt Taylor**, Bay City Union existed between March 1966 and July 1968. There were a number of line-up changes throughout the band's history. Original lead singer Paul Johnson left in mid-1966. Taylor abandoned rhythm guitar to concentrate on lead vocals and harmonica, while Glenn Wheatley was installed as rhythm guitarist. At the end of 1966, Peter Miles left to join Mick Hadley's Coloured Balls (and later **Bulldog**), and Tony Buettel (ex-South Town Moods) took his place. With the departure of original guitarist Jimmy Brelsford at the beginning of 1967, the band relocated to Melbourne. There **Phil Manning** (lead guitar; ex-**Tony Worsley and the Fabulous Blue Jays**) joined the band, giving a line-up of Taylor, Manning, Wheatley, Bagnall and Buettel. Bagnall left the band in December 1967. Wheatley switched to bass, and the four-piece line-up stayed together long enough to record the single 'Mo'reen'/'Mary Mary' for Festival (April 1968).

Joey Maiorano (ex-Gas Company) joined on keyboards around the time of the single's release, but Bay City Union disbanded in June 1968 due to a general lack of interest in blues bands. Manning joined The Laurie Allen Revue and Wheatley joined **The Master's Apprentices**. Taylor and Buettel attempted to keep Bay City Union alive with the addition of two ex-members of New Zealand band Chants R&B, Matt Croke (aka Max Kelly, lead guitar) and Neil Young (bass), but the line-up was short-lived. **Matt Taylor** went on to blues bands like Genesis and Meating before teaming up again with Manning in **Chain**. Wheatley later headed the Wheatley Organisation and found success as manager for **Little River Band** and **John Farnham**.

B.B. Steal

Formed: *1987*
Style: *Hard rock*
Original line-up: *Craig Csongrady (vocals; ex-Boss), Kevin Pratt (guitar; ex-Boss), Warren Mason (guitar), Peter Waterank (bass), Peter Heckenberg (drums; ex-Boss,* **Swanee***)*

Commercial hard rock band B.B. Steal emerged from the ashes of Sydney heavy metal band Boss. Singer Craig Csongrady fronted that band for four years (1983 to 1986). Boss recorded four singles, 'Strange Games'/'The Woman is Hot' (May 1984), 'Dancin' Queen'/'Kick Ass (Rock'n'Roll)' (December 1984), 'Shake It'/'Free Wheelin'' (March 1985) and 'Cry Cry'/'Take It or Leave It' (July) and the album *Step on It* (October 1984) for RCA.

The line-up on the album was Csongrady, Kevin Pratt (guitar), Peter Sutcliffe (guitar), Scott Ginn (bass) and Joe Tatts (drums). The band built a solid live reputation in Sydney but could not sell records in Australia. *Step on It*, however, managed to sell 20 000 copies in Germany and Japan. Scott Ginn issued a solo album, *One Man Army*, on the independent Montreaux imprint in 1986. In early 1987, Csongrady was asked to audition as frontman for US heavy metal band Quiet Riot. Nothing came of the offer, so retaining guitarist Pratt and drummer Peter Heckenberg from the final version of Boss (which also included ex-**Heaven** bass player Laurie Marlowe), Csongrady formed B.B. Steal. Peter Waterank and Warren Mason completed the line-up.

B.B. Steal recorded three singles for PolyGram over the next three years: 'I Believe'/'Love's on the Rocks' (November 1988), 'Heartbeat Away'/'Hold on' (March 1989) and 'Don't You Love Me and Leave Me'/'Heartbeat Away' (1990). None was successful. The band's biggest break came when Def Leppard's guitarist Phil Collen produced the album *On the Edge*. The line-up featured on the album was Csongrady, Pratt, Mason and James Young (drums) with Andy Cichon (ex-**Rose Tattoo**) filling in on bass. *On The Edge* (June 1992) was a polished AOR album but neither it nor the singles 'Big Love' (May) and 'Live it Up' (August) proved successful. By the time the album came out, the line-up comprised Csongrady, Pratt, Mason, Richard Grant (bass) and Craig Rosevear (drums). Cichon had formed **Judge Mercy** and Young had joined **The Poor Boys**. Rosevear went on to replace Brad Heaney in **The Screaming Jets**. B.B. Steal toured with different line-ups until 1995.

B.B. Steal album: *On the Edge* (Phonogram, 1992); ***Boss album:*** *Step on It* (RCA, 1984).

Beargarden

Formed: *1981*
Style: *Glam pop*
Original line-up: *Sam Sejavka (vocals; ex-***Ears***), Gus Till (keyboards; ex-***Ears***), Ross Farnell (bass; ex-Daily Planet), Carl Manuel (drums; ex-***Ears***)*

Beargarden grew out of the ashes of inner-city Melbourne, post-punk band **The Ears**. Beargarden adopted a sophisticated, quasi-decadent look and style that drew from English antecedents like Roxy Music, Japan and Psychedelic Furs. The original version of Beargarden made little headway and broke up in mid-1982. By December, Sejavka, Till, Farnell and Manuel had reformed the band with Shane Andalou on guitar. The band wrote commercial songs and signed to Virgin, but could not attract the record-buying public.

Beargarden's debut single, 'The Finer Things'/'West', came out in September 1984. It was followed by 'I Write the News'/'Go Perfect Windows' (June 1985) and 'Drink Drink Drink'/'Lounge' (October). The 12-inch version of 'I Write the

News' also featured the instrumental 'A Dog Barks in a Blizzard of Tickertape'. For its debut album, the band replaced Farnell with Simon Polinski and added Shaun Anderson (guitar).

All that Fall (November 1986) and the single 'A Seaside Song'/'A Year in the Shade' (March 1987) made little impression. The band broke up not long after without making any commercial impact. Anderson, Andalou, Polinski and Larry Thang (keyboards, trumpet) formed the short-lived Singing Bone. Sejavka, Till and Polinski also worked together as The Index, exploring African rhythms and other world music styles. Sejavka has written, directed and performed for local theatre productions (including the plays *Quintessence*, *In the Service of Beauty* and *Angel Gear*) since Beargarden's split.

Album: *All that Fall* (Chase, 1986).

Beasts of Bourbon

Formed: *1983*
Style: *Blues rock*
Original line-up: Tex Perkins *(vocals; ex-Dum Dums), Spencer P. Jones (guitar;* **Johnnys***),* **Kim Salmon** *(guitar;* **Scientists***), Boris Sujdovic (bass;* **Scientists***), James Baker (drums;* **Hoodoo Gurus***)*

Over the course of 13 years, numerous permutations and six albums, Beasts of Bourbon have proven themselves to be masters of uncompromising gut-bucket blues and hard-edged rock'n'roll. Red Eye label manager John Foy has been quoted as describing Beasts of Bourbon as 'the closest thing this country has ever come to a band like The Rolling Stones, at their peak, with genuine roots and an incredible range'.

Gregory 'Tex' Perkins formed his first band, psychobilly/cow-punks The Dum Dums, in Brisbane during 1982 when he was 16 years old. The band's influences included The Cramps, The Meteors, **The Birthday Party**, Johnny Cash and Merle Haggard. As Tex Deadly and the Dum Dums, the band moved to Sydney before breaking up in July 1983. When Perkins had to fulfil a couple of Dum Dum gig commitments, he called on Spencer Jones and Boris Sujdovic to help out, and Beasts of Bourbon were born.

The band was named Beasts of Bourbon in honour of the drunken party atmosphere generated. By September 1983, **Kim Salmon** and James Baker had expanded the line-up. The Beasts cut their debut album, *The Axeman's Jazz*, in one drunken, eight-hour session with engineer Tony Cohen during October 1983. Legend has it that the session was fuelled by 72 cans of beer and one bottle of

Beasts of Bourbon

Scotch, and that it only ended when the band members began passing out! In January 1984, a Beasts line-up of Perkins, Salmon (replaced by Jones), Sujdovic, Tony Thewlis (guitar; **Scientists**) and Brett Rixon (drums; **Scientists**) played a round of gigs in Perth. A month later, Perkins and Salmon, plus **The Church** drummer Richard Ploog, found time to play gigs in Sydney as Salamander Jim before Salmon left for the UK with **Scientists** in March. Perkins formed a permanent line-up of Salamander Jim that same month.

The Axeman's Jazz came out in July 1984 on the GREEN label. With tracks like 'Evil Ruby', 'Lonesome Bones', 'Drop Out' and a cover of Creedence Clearwater Revival's 'Graveyard Train', it remains a classic of Australian garage/swamp rock. It was the best-selling Australian alternative album for 1984. It also went on to sell over 30 000 copies in Europe. The single, Leon Payne's 'Psycho'/'Good Times', 'Sometimes Goodguys' (also issued in July), was the best-selling Australian alternative single for 1984. The Beasts' line-up of Perkins, Baker, Jones, Stu Spasm (bass; ex-Zulu Rattle, Salamander Jim) and Brad Shepherd (guitar; **Hoodoo Gurus**) came together for the Sultans of Swig tour in order to promote the release of *The Axeman's Jazz*. The good-time nature of the event was disturbed when Baker was unceremoniously sacked from **Hoodoo Gurus**; in response, the Beasts sacked Shepherd. Spasm moved to rhythm guitar and Graham Hood (from **The Johnnys**) joined on bass for the remainder of the tour.

For the next four years, the individual members pursued their own projects. Perkins worked with Salamander Jim, the abortive Fur Bible in the UK (with ex-Gun Club guitarist Kid Congo Powers), The Bush Oysters, Thug, Hot Property and The Butcher Shop. Spencer had **The Johnnys**, Salmon and Sujdovic **Scientists**. Baker recorded a one-off single for Red Eye, 'I Can't Control Myself'/'Born to be Punched' (June 1985), as The James Baker Experience (with Perkins, Stu Spasm and **Roddy 'Ray'da' Radalj**).

With the return in April 1987, and subsequent break-up of **Scientists**, Baker, Sujdovic and Ray'da formed **The Dubrovniks**. Salmon formed **Kim Salmon and The Surrealists**. In March 1988, the Beasts (Perkins, Salmon, Jones, Baker and Sujdovic) decided to reconvene and cut *Sour Mash* with engineer/producer Phil Punch. *Sour Mash* (December 1988) virtually redefined the parameters of guitar-based rock'n'roll. The Cramps-influenced swamp-rock of old had been discarded for a more adventurous slab of gutbucket blues and avant-garde weirdness. Perkins' voice had matured into an authentic blues growl that showed the influence of Howlin' Wolf, Captain Beefheart and Tom Waits. The thundering cover of the Jack Nitzsche/Ry Cooder song 'Hard Work Drivin' Man' backed with 'Elvis Impersonator Blues' and 'I Love You Because' (November 1988) became a #1 independent hit single, as did the double single 'The Hate Inside' (August 1989).

The Beasts toured Europe and then recorded a third album, *Black Milk*. Issued in July 1990, the album yielded two singles, the double 7-inch set Hound Dog Taylor's 'Let's Get Funky' (June) and 'Words from a Woman to Her Man'/'I Hope You Find Your Way Home' (November). For the band's Kick Arse Australian tour of February/March 1991, The Surrealists' rhythm section of Brian Henry Hooper and Tony Pola had replaced Sujdovic and Baker. The Tony Cohen-produced *The Low Road* (December 1991) consolidated the Beasts' position as one of the country's pre-eminent rock bands. It was an album brimming with urgency, surrealism, atmosphere, myth, illusion and honesty, but above all, hard-nosed rock riffs. Among the album's nefarious delights were the blistering 'Chase the Dragon' (about heroin smuggling), a cover of **AC/DC**'s slow and insinuating 'Ride on' and the Hendrix-flavoured CD EP 'Just Right' (January 1992).

The Beasts took part in the inaugural Big Day Out (BDO) on 25 January 1992 and then toured Europe for the third time. The double live album/video *From the Belly of the Beasts* came out in January 1993 to coincide with the band's appearance on the first national bill of BDO. Two months later, the music/lyric book *10 Years Behind Bars* appeared, complete with a bonus CD EP which contained two cuts from the *Belly* album and two previously unissued live tracks. The Beasts went their separate ways during 1993, and did not work together again until September 1996. In the interim, Perkins fell in with **The Cruel Sea**, recorded and toured with Don Walker and Charlie Owen as Tex Don and Charlie and issued a solo album, *Far be It from Me* (August 1996).

Salmon remained with The Surrealists when the Beasts reconvened in September 1996. His place was taken by journeyman guitarist Charlie Owen (ex-**Louis Tillett** and The Aspersion Caste, **New Christs**, **Divinyls**, Tex Don and Charlie). Spencer Jones produced Owen's 1994 solo album on Red Eye, *Vertigo and Other Phobias*. The Beasts' sixth album, *Gone*, came out in January 1997, in time for the band's third appearance on the Big Day Out national bill. The band had broken up again by the end of the year.

Albums: *The Axeman's Jazz* (GREEN, 1984; reissued on Red Eye, 1988), *Sour Mash* (Red Eye, 1988), *Black Milk* (Red Eye/Polydor, 1990), *The Low Road* (Red Eye/Polydor, 1991), *From the Belly of the Beasts* (Red Eye/Polydor, 1993), *Gone* (Polydor, 1997).

Beatfish

Formed: *1990*
Style: *Dance pop*
Original line-up: **James Freud** *(keyboards, vocals, bass; ex-***Models***), Martin Plaza (guitar, vocals;* **Mental as Anything***)*

James Freud and **Mental as Anything**'s Martin Plaza were the driving forces behind Beatfish. The Beatfish concept mixed traditional styles of songwriting with dance music and techno grooves. The duo's debut CD single, 'All Around the World'/'Out of Control' was a minor hit single.

'Wheels of Love'/'I Want to be Bad Part II' cracked the Top 30 in September 1991. Renowned DJ/mixer/producer Robert Racic (**Boxcar**, **Severed Heads**, **Rockmelons**) worked with the duo on their debut album *Beatfish*, which came out in November. Beatfish's next two singles, 'Out Of Control'/'Whatchoolookinat' (April 1992) and 'Get Together'/'Son', 'Wheels of Love' (July) were not successful. The Beatfish touring line-up comprised Freud, Plaza, Scott Saunders (keyboards; from **Bellydance**), Natalie Gabatski (backing vocals) and John MacKay (drums; ex-**Machinations**, **Absent Friends**).

At the start of 1992, Beatfish was invited to play on the Wizards of Oz showcase series of gigs in Los Angeles, alongside **The Angels**, **Kate Ceberano**, **Deborah Conway**, **The Black Sorrows** and **The Poor**. The idea was to attract the attention of interested record companies in the USA, but no offers were forthcoming. Beatfish broke up at the end of 1992 when **Mental as Anything** resumed activities. **James Freud** re-emerged in 1996 with Moondog and the single 'Postcard to Hawaii'.

Album: *Beatfish* (BMG, 1991).

Beathoven

Formed: *1975*
Style: *Power pop*
Line-up: *David Minchin (guitar, vocals), Charles Touber (guitar, vocals), Greg Cracknell (bass, vocals), Brent Jeffrey (drums)*

During the late 1970s, when power pop was being vilified overseas as a vibrant and relevant music form, Tasmanian power poppers Beathoven went by largely unnoticed. The band's crisp, urgent sound encompassed Beatles melodies, Raspberries harmonies and the Searchers' jangly guitar lines. While the likes of **Hush**, **Sherbet** and **Skyhooks** held sway on the mainland, Beathoven attained a similar level of teen adulation in Hobart by playing the suburban and high school dance circuit. Beathoven issued one single, 'Do You Remember the Time?', and then moved to Melbourne in 1977.

EMI issued the band's second single, 'Shy Girl'/'Does it Matter?' in 1978. Visiting American rock svengali-figure Kim Fowley produced demos for the band but failed to secure label interest. By 1980, Beathoven had become The Innocents. **Ol'55** pop purist Jim Manzie produced the singles 'Sooner or Later'/'The "B" Side' (June 1980) and 'Come Tonight'/'Absence' (March 1981) for the Trafalgar label. The singles were then leased and issued through RCA. Jarryl Wirth (ex-**News**, Lonely Boys) played guitar on the sessions, and he began to work closely with the band. David Minchin and Greg Cracknell left The Innocents when the singles failed to take off. Touber and Wirth continued on with new bass player Bob Smith (ex-Affections). The Innocents broke up in late 1981. Raven issued a posthumous album that drew together various Beathoven/Innocents singles, unissued tracks and demos.

Innocents (aka Beathoven) album: *Here We Come!* (Raven, 1984).

The Bee Gees

Style: *Pop, R&B, disco*
Line-up: *Barry Gibb (vocals, guitar), Maurice Gibb (vocals, bass, keyboards), Robin Gibb (vocals)*

The Bee Gees' place in the history of Australian pop is well assured. The Gibb brothers recorded in Australia between 1963 and 1966, during which time they struggled for recognition. Thereafter they became an international phenomenon.

The Gibb brothers were born on the Isle of Man in the Irish Sea (Barry in 1946 and twins Robin and Maurice in 1949) and grew up in Manchester. The Gibb family migrated to Australia in 1958. After settling in Brisbane, The Bee Gees began appearing on local television shows like *Anything Goes*, *Brisbane Tonight* and *Cottee's Happy Hour* and radio. Even at an early age, the brothers were accomplished singers and songwriters, with their forte being impeccable three-part harmonies. The brothers signed to Festival and issued 11 singles, two EPs and one album on the Leedon label, plus three singles, one EP and two albums on the Spin label. Producer Ozzie Byrne was an important catalyst in The Bee Gees' early career, letting the Gibbs have free time in his small Hurstville studio.

The Leedon singles were: 'The Battle of the Blue and Grey'/'The Three Kisses of Love' (March 1963), 'Timber!'/'Take Hold of that Star' (June), 'Don't Say Goodbye'/'Peace of Mind' (February 1964), 'Claustrophobia'/'Could It Be?' (August), 'Turn Around Look at Me'/'Theme from the Travels of Jamie McPheeters' (October), 'House Without Windows' (with Trevor Gordon)/'I'll Be Happy' (December), 'Every Day I Have to Cry'/'You Wouldn't Know It' (April 1965), 'Little Miss Rhythm and Blues' (with Trevor Gordon)/'Here I Am' (May 1965), 'Wine and Women'/'Follow the Wind' (August), 'I Was a Lover and a Leader of Men'/'And the Children Laughing' (November 1965) and 'Cherry Red'/'I Want Home' (March 1966). The EPs were *The Bee Gees* (1964) and 'Wine and Women' (1966).

The Spin singles were: 'Monday's Rain'/'All My Life' (June 1966), 'Spicks and Specks'/'I am the World' (September 1966) and 'Born a Man'/'Big Chance' (January 1967). The EP was 'Spicks and Specks' (1967). The Bee Gees also backed other local artists such as Johnny Devlin and **Tony Barber**. Many of the singles were local hits in Brisbane or Sydney, but the only one to crack the national Top 40 was 'Spicks and Specks' (#4 in October 1966). By that time, however, The Bee Gees had become frustrated with the lack of recognition in Australia. The family returned to the UK in January 1967.

In the UK, The Bee Gees recruited Aussie expatriates Vince Melouney (aka Maloney; guitar, ex-**Billy Thorpe** and the Aztecs, Vince Melouney Sect) and Colin Petersen (drums; ex-**Steve & the Board**). Petersen had been a child actor in films such as *Smiley* and *The Scamp*. The two musicians remained with The Bee Gees until early 1970.

Geoff Bridgeford (ex-**Steve & the Board**, **Groove**) replaced Petersen, although Melouney was not replaced. He formed **Fanny Adams**.

Upon arrival in the UK in early 1967, The Bee Gees immediately fell on their feet when Australian expatriate businessman Robert Stigwood (of NEMS Enterprises) offered them a management deal. NEMS was headed by The Beatles' manager Brian Epstein. Stigwood got The Bee Gees signed to Polydor in the UK and ATCO in the USA. Initially, The Bee Gees were compared with The Beatles, but undaunted, the brothers went on to score an extraordinary run of best-selling singles and albums across the world.

The Bee Gees' work during the late 1960s and early 1970s is still highly regarded. Evocative songs like 'New York Mining Disaster 1941' (Australian #3, UK #12, US #14, 1967), 'To Love Somebody' (Australian #6, UK #41, US #17, 1967), 'Massachusetts' (Australian #1, UK #1, US #11, 1967), 'Words' (Australian #11, UK #8, US #15, 1968), 'I've Got to Get a Message to You' (Australian #4, UK #1, US #8, 1968), 'First of May' (Australian #13, UK #6, 1969), 'I Started a Joke' (Australian #3, US #6, 1969), 'Lonely Days' (Australian #8, UK #33, US #3, 1970), 'How Can You Mend a Broken Heart?' (Australian #2, US #1, 1971), 'My World' (Australian #4, UK #16, 1972) and 'Run to Me' (Australian #3, UK #9, 1972) featured striking harmonies and quality arrangements.

'Massachusetts', 'I've Got to Get a Message to You' and 'How Can You Mend a Broken Heart?' all sold a million copies each. The ballad 'To Love Somebody' is one of the trio's most enduring songs, as evidenced by the vast number of cover versions, most notably Nina Simone, Eric Burdon and the Animals, Janis Joplin and Rod Stewart. The Bee Gees' UK debut album, *Bee Gees' 1st* is a classic of the period, on a par with the best that The Beatles, The Rolling Stones, The Kinks, The Who and The Small Faces produced at the time.

Three hitless years in the UK (July 1972 to May 1975) saw The Bee Gees' popularity at an all-time low. They were reduced to playing the English cabaret circuit. Australian fans remained faithful to the band by sending 'Saw a New Morning' to #26 in June 1973 and 'Mr Natural' to #7 in October 1974. Eventually the brothers travelled to the USA where they recorded in Miami, Florida. The R&B/soul-flavoured albums *Main Course* and *Children of the World* brought about a change in their fortunes. *Main Course* and *Children of the World* produced the US #1 hit singles 'Jive Talkin'' and 'You Should Be Dancing' respectively (also Australian #16 and #14). That inevitably led to the trio's move into straight disco for the 50 million-selling *Saturday Night Fever* soundtrack album.

Between October 1977 and April 1979, The Bee Gees scored an unbroken run of six consecutive US #1 hit singles: 'How Deep is Your Love?', 'Stayin' Alive', 'Night Fever', 'Too Much Heaven', 'Tragedy' and 'Love You Inside Out'. That made them the only artists during the 1970s to have nine #1 hits in the USA. 'Night Fever' and 'Tragedy' also made #1 in the UK, while 'Stayin' Alive' and 'Too Much Heaven' also peaked there at #4 and #3 respectively. Here in Australia, 'How Deep is Your Love?' reached #4, 'Stayin' Alive' #1, 'Night Fever' #5, 'Too Much Heaven' #5 and 'Tragedy' #2. The band's reputation, however, was damaged somewhat by the ill-advised film venture *Sgt Pepper's Lonely Hearts Club Band*.

The Bee Gees have been resurrected over and over again. During the late 1980s and early 1990s, they were back in the Top 10 with hits like 'You Win Again' (UK #1, 1987), 'One' (US #7, 1989), 'Secret Love' (UK #5, 1991) and 'For Whom the Bell Tolls' (UK #4, 1993). The Bee Gees issued a new album in April 1997, *Still Waters*, after which they were inducted into the American Rock'n'Roll Hall of Fame. *Still Waters* reached #6 in Australia during June, while its single 'Alone' peaked at #9 a month later. 'Still Waters Run Deep' appeared as the second single in September. The Bee Gees were inducted into the Australian Record Industry Association (ARIA) Hall of Fame at the 1997 awards ceremony.

As well as writing all The Bee Gees' songs, Barry Gibb has provided hits for many artists, including the Kenny Rogers/Dolly Parton duet 'Islands in the Stream' (the most successful country song of all time) and Diana Ross's 'Chain Reaction'. Throughout their career, The Bee Gees have shown a remarkable diversification of their talents and an uncanny ability to continually reinvent themselves. Their strengths remain their vocal dexterity, a consummate grasp of pop melodies and an innate ability to render seamless arrangements. The Bee Gees have produced one of the richest legacies of songwriting, performance and production in the history of popular music.

Albums: *The Bee Gees Sing and Play 14 Barry Gibb Songs* (Leedon, 1965), *Monday's Rain* (Spin, 1966), *Turn Around, Look at Us* (Spin, 1967), *Bee Gees' 1st* (Polydor, 1967), *Horizontal* (Polydor, 1968), *Idea* (Polydor, 1968), *Odessa* (Polydor, 1969), *Cucumber Castle* (television film soundtrack including other artists, Polydor, 1970), *Marley Purt Drive* (Polydor, 1970), *Two Years on* (Polydor, 1970), *Melody* (film soundtrack, Polydor, 1971), *Trafalgar* (Polydor, 1971), *To Whom it May Concern* (Polydor, 1972), *Life* *in a Tin Can* (RSO, 1973), *Mr Natural* (RSO, 1974), *Main Course* (RSO, 1975), *Children of the World* (RSO, 1976), *Here at Last . . . Bee Gees . . . Live* (RSO, 1977), *Saturday Night Fever* (film soundtrack including other artists, RSO, 1978), *Sgt Pepper's Lonely Hearts Club Band* (film soundtrack including other artists, Polydor, 1978), *Spirits Having Flown* (RSO, 1979), *Living Eyes* (RSO, 1981), *Staying Alive* (film soundtrack, RSO, 1983), *E.S.P.* (RSO, 1987), *One* (RSO, 1989), *High Civilisation* (RSO, 1991), *Size Isn't Everything* (RSO, 1994), *Still Waters* (Polydor, 1997); ***Barry Gibb solo albums:*** *Now Voyager* (Polydor, 1984), *Hawks* (film soundtrack, Polydor, 1988); ***Robin Gibb solo albums:*** *Robin's Reign* (Polydor, 1970), *How Old Are You?* (Polydor, 1983), *Secret Agent* (Polydor, 1984), *Walls Have Eyes* (Polydor, 1985); ***Bee Gees' compilations:*** *Rare, Precious and Beautiful* (Polydor, 1968), *Rare, Precious and Beautiful Vol. 2* (Polydor, 1968), *Rare, Precious and Beautiful Vol. 3* (Polydor, 1969), *The Best of the Bee Gees* (Polydor, 1969), *The Best of the Bee Gees Vol. 2* (RSO, 1973), *Bee Gees Gold, Volume One* (RSO, 1976), *Birth of Brilliance (1963–1966)* (Festival, 1978), *Bee Gees Greatest* (RSO, 1979), *Bee Gees Collection* (14-album box set, RSO, 1979), *Bee Gees Bonanza—The Early Days* (Pickwick, 1979), *The Early Days Vol.1, Vol. 2 and Vol. 3* (Hallmark, 1979), *The Very Best of the Bee Gees* (Polydor, 1990), *Tales from the Brothers Gibb: A History in Song 1967–1990* (Box set, Polydor, 1990), *The Very Best of the Bee Gees* (reissue, Polydor, 1997).

Bell Jar

Formed: *1985*
Style: *Rock, folk*
1986 line-up: *Raoul Graf (vocals, acoustic guitar), David Price (keyboards), Ben Whatmore (guitar), Simon Roy (bass), Steve Munro (drums)*

Sydney band Bell Jar's brand of melodramatic, earthy, folk-influenced rock was at odds with prevailing trends on the Sydney scene. Bell Jar issued two singles on the Chase label, 'Run and Run'/'Laughing Holiday' (1986) and 'In Sanctuary'/'Blood Red Roses' (1987), before signing to Hot Records. Hot issued two 12-inch EPs in 1988, 'Beauty Was the Beast' and 'Cut'. The band's album *Glass* (August 1990) and its singles, 'Love Like Rain' (November 1989), 'Burn' (March 1990) and 'Bitter Taste'/'This Country' (June), came out on Festival. When Bell Jar broke up, Graf formed country/folk band The Infidels, which issued an album, *3 In The Morning* (1994), and a CD EP, 'Precious Stuff' (1995).

Album: *Glass* (Festival, 1990).

Bellydance (*see* d.i.g.)

The Benders (*see* Chris Abrahams)

Bengal Tigers

Formed: *1980*
Style: *Heavy metal*
Original line-up: *Gordon Heald (vocals), Barnie Fakhouri (guitar), Steve Tyler (bass), Mick Egan (drums)*

Melbourne band Bengal Tigers took their inspiration from European heavy metal bands like Judas Priest, Accept and The Scorpions. Bengal Tigers were one of the few traditional heavy metal bands working the Melbourne scene of the early to mid-1980s, alongside Axatak, Blackjack, Ion Drive, Stingray, Crossmember and Taipan. The band issued the independent mini-album *Metal Fetish* in 1983. Mushroom reissued *Metal Fetish* in 1984.

Mushroom also issued the singles 'Break and Bend'/'Fallen Idol' (October, 1983) and 'Cheat on'/'Burn it Up' (September 1984). Fakhouri left in 1984 to be replaced by Yuri Linzew (ex-Axatak). The band broke up a year later, but reformed in 1993. Along with Heald and Fakhouri, the new line-up included Keith Peter-Budge (guitar), James R. Powers (bass) and Noel Tenny (drums). Bengal Tigers issued a five-track CD EP, *Painclinic* (1995), the CD single 'In One Ear' (August 1997), and a full-length album, *In the Blood* (September), on their own SM label.

Albums: *Metal Fetish* (mini-album, SM, 1982; reissued Mushroom, 1984), *In the Blood* (SM, 1997).

Merv Benton

Style: *Pop*

During the 1960s, Merv Benton (born in 1945 as Mervyn Bonson) was the epitome of the good-looking, clean-cut pop idol. At the height of his popularity, only **Billy Thorpe, Ray Brown, Normie Rowe, Bobby and Laurie** and **Ronnie Burns** rivalled Benton for sheer audience attention.

Benton got his start on the early 1960s Melbourne dance circuit with The Ramrods. He signed to W&G Records in 1964 and for the next two years enjoyed an amazing run of 12 Top 40 hit singles in Melbourne. His biggest hits were 'Baby Let's Play House'/'Endless Sleep' (#17 in April 1964), 'I Got Burned'/'Cincinatti Fireball' (#13 in May 1965), 'Yield Not to Temptation'/'Twenty Flight Rock' (#11 in August 1965), 'Don't Destroy Me'/'Can I Believe It's True?' (#19 in October 1965) and

'You've Got What it Takes'/'Shake Rattle and Roll' (#20 in February 1966).

Benton's backing band, The Tamlas, originally comprised Charlie Gauld (guitar; ex-**Thunderbirds**), Noel Watson (guitar; ex-Tridents), Ian Allen (bass; ex-**Planets**) and Eddie Chappell (drums; ex-Checkmates). For most of Benton's hit-making period, The Tamlas featured Chappell, Les Stacpool (guitar; ex-**Chessmen**), Ron Gilbey (guitar) and Dennis Tucker (bass; ex-Rondells). In August 1966, the singer was literally struck dumb with a disabled larynx. The tragedy befell the singer just as he was voted Australia's third top male vocalist (behind **Normie Rowe** and **Ronnie Burns**) in *Go-Set*'s inaugural Pop Poll. The problem hampered Benton for 18 months, and he eventually returned to his pre-showbiz job in a bank. He did record a country album in 1969 but never returned to full-time singing.

Albums: *Come on and Get Me* (W&G, 1964), *Sounds Great* (W&G, 1965), *The Best of Merv Benton* (W&G, 1966), *Great Country Songs (Movin' on)* (W&G, 1969), *Fabulous* (compilation, Raven, 1985).

The Bhagavad Guitars

Formed: *1987*
Style: *Pop*
Original line-up: *Jeremy Butterworth (guitar, vocals), John Underwood (guitar, vocals), Kynan Hughes (bass), Matt Kerr (drums)*

This Sydney-based band originally formed in Canberra as Inner Circle during 1985, springing from the same setting that spawned **Falling Joys** and **The Plunderers**. The name The Bhagavad Guitars was derived from a pun on the title of the Hindu book *The Bhagavad-Gita*. The band's brand of spacious, chiming guitar-based pop called to mind the likes of **The Crystal Set**, **The Church** and UK band Simple Minds. The Red Eye label issued two mini-albums in 1988, *Foreverglades* (July) and *Headland* (November).

The Church's **Steve Kilbey** produced *Foreverglades*, and its featured track, 'Just to be Sure' became a radio hit in Sydney. New Zealander Adrian Workman had replaced original bass player Kynan Hughes by the time the band recorded *Headland* in October 1988. In July 1990, Red Eye combined the two mini-albums on the one compilation, also called *Foreverglades*. The band also issued the CD EP/double 7-inch single 'Party' during October. The Bhagavad Guitars recorded a new album *Introversion* in 1991, but it remained unissued until March 1997 when Kilbey put it out on his Karmic Hit label as a double set with a bonus 14-minute CD EP *Extraversion*. In the meantime, the band had issued the album *Hypnotised* (July 1993) and the CD EP 'Hypnotise Me' (March).

Albums: *Foreverglades* (mini-album, Red Eye, 1988), *Headland* (mini-album, Red Eye, 1988), *Foreverglades* (CD compilation of first two mini-albums, Red Eye, 1990), *Hypnotised* (Karmic Hit/Shock, 1993), *Introversion* (Karmic Hit/MDS, 1997).

Big Heavy Stuff

Formed: *1990*
Style: *Indie guitar rock*
Original line-up: *Greg Atkinson (guitar, vocals; ex-***Ups and Downs***), Carolyn Polley (guitar, vocals; ex-Toys Went Beserk), Darren Jones (bass), Darren Atkinson (drums; ex-***Ups and Downs***)*

In the late 1980s, the Atkinson brothers, Greg and Darren, were members of neo-psychedelic outfit **Ups and Downs**. In 1990, the two musicians formed a decidedly more noisy outfit called Big Heavy Stuff, taking their cue from the likes of Slint, Nirvana, Teenage Fanclub and My Bloody Valentine. Atkinson and Carolyn Polley's combination of blistering guitar noise was tempered by classic pop melodies.

Big Heavy Stuff signed to the Volition label and issued the CD EP 'Pops Like Crazy' (December 1991) and the CD singles 'Chaos' (November 1992) and 'North by Night'/'Skin a Cat' (October 1993). Following the release of the band's debut album *Truck* in November 1993, Nick Kennedy replaced Darren Atkinson on drums, and Eliot Fish (ex-Templebears) replaced Darren Jones on bass.

Big Heavy Stuff issued four more noisy, upfront CD EPs, 'Trouble and Desire' (November 1994), 'Covered in Bruises' (August 1995), 'Big Mouth' (October 1996) and 'May' (March 1997). 'Big Mouth' and 'May' were lifted from the band's first album for the Hypnotised label, *Maximum Sincere* (May 1997). By the time the album appeared, Polley had left to be replaced by Adam Young, (ex-**Daisygrinders**). Big Heavy Stuff issued two more CD singles from the album, 'Maximum Sincere' and 'Cheating on a Dead Wife', during November 1997. Meanwhile, in 1994 Darren Atkinson had formed Atticus with Paul Martin (guitar, vocals), Josh Morris (guitar, vocals) and Alex Ronayne (bass). The band played well-crafted pop rock, and issued a trio of CD EPs, 'Super',

'Same Shovel Different Spade' and 'Smart Casual' in 1995.

Albums: *Truck* (Volition/Sony, 1993), *Maximum Sincere* (Hypnotized/Shock, 1997).

Big Pig

Formed: *1986*
Style: *Funk, rock*
Original line-up: *Oleh Witer (vocals, percussion; ex-Bang), Sherine (vocals, percussion; ex-Editions, Bang), Nick Disbray (vocals, percussion), Tony Antonaides (vocals, harmonica), Tim Rosewarne (vocals, keyboards; ex-Bang), Neil Baker (drums), Adrian Scaglione (drums)*

Melbourne band Big Pig burst on to the scene with a unique style and image. The band's percussion-driven funk sound was almost entirely rhythmic based, with harmonica, a smattering of keyboards and Sherine's smouldering gospel-infused vocals providing the melody. The band wore distinctive leather aprons which enhanced the austere/semi-industrial nature of the music.

Big Pig was the brainchild of percussionist/singer Oleh Witer. Dispensing with the Grace Jones-styled funk of his previous band, Bang, Witer took Big Pig down a more avant-funk-meets-disco route while still retaining a feel for pop economy. The band issued an independent, self-titled, 12-inch EP containing the thumping, wailing 'Hungry Town'. Mushroom reissued the record in October 1986 as a double 12-inch EP which included extended dance mixes of 'Hungry Town' and 'Money God'. Coupled with a striking film clip directed by Richard Lowenstein, 'Hungry Town' scored the band immediate attention. It reached #14 on the national chart in December. Yahoo Serious included 'Hungry Town' on the soundtrack to his feature film *Young Einstein*.

Englishman Nick Launay (Public Image Ltd, **Midnight Oil**, **Models**) produced and engineered the band's second single, 'Boy Wonder'/'Hellbent Heaven' (April 1987) and the debut album, *Bonk*. The album yielded the singles 'Breakaway'/'Hellbent Heaven' (February 1988), 'Big Hotel'/'Fine Thing' (June) and 'Iron Lung'/'Iron Lung' (December). Launay was renowned for pioneering the huge drum sound that was prevalent in mid-1980s rock productions. It tends to make the records sound dated, but *Bonk* was successful at the time and reached #4 on the national chart in July. Big Pig's cover of Chuck Jackson's 'Breakaway' also became the band's biggest hit single when it peaked at #4 in April. Later it was used on the soundtrack to the American feature film *Bill and Ted's Excellent Adventure*.

Big Pig toured constantly, at home and overseas, but things were quiet on the recording front until 1990. Over the next year, the band put out three 12-inch singles 'Justifier'/'Taste' (August 1990), 'Hanging Tree' (January 1991) and 'King of Nothing' (April) and a new album *You Lucky People*. Big Pig enlisted the services of Daddy O (Stetasonics) and Femi Jaya (Prince) on the album in its quest for the ultimate in dance grooves.

Albums: *Big Pig* (mini-album, Mushroom/Festival, 1986), *Bonk* (Mushroom/Festival, 1988), *You Lucky People* (Mushroom/Festival, 1990).

Big Storm

Formed: *1985*
Style: *Rock*
Original line-up: *Stewart D'Arrietta (keyboards, vocals; ex-Lifesavers), Don Miller-Robinson (guitar; ex-Gunther's G-Force, Lifesavers,* **Dragon***), Jeremy Cole (keyboards), Bjarn Ohlin (guitar, keyboards; ex-***Divinyls***), Dario Bertoli (bass), Hughie Benjamin (drums; ex-Lifesavers)*

Sydney-based Big Storm was a stadium-rock styled band formed by a bunch of experienced musicians. Stewart D'Arrietta had already issued a solo album on PolyGram, *Side Effects*, and three singles, 'Man in Love' (September 1985), 'After the Storm' (April 1986) and 'Wouldn't Be Dead for Quids' (July). Don Miller-Robinson had also pursued a solo career, issuing three singles 'There Was a Girl'/'Ghosts of Love' (WEA, October 1982), 'Who Kissed the Usherette'/'Just Can't Stop' (Mushroom, January 1984) and 'Which Way Is Up?'/'Rebels in the Mountains' (Mushroom, September 1984). Hughie Benjamin (ex-Lifesavers) had recorded with both D'Arrietta and Miller-Robinson.

Despite such an array of talent and the push from WEA, Big Storm's records were not successful. The band's singles were 'Rubber Love'/'Not Guilty' (October 1988), 'Happy New Year'/'Rubber Love' (January 1989), 'Not Guilty'/'Rubber Love' (February 1989) and 'Once in Bed'/'Not Waiting' (August 1989). In 1992, D'Arrietta worked with John Waters on the stage show *Glass Onion*, which featured the songs of John Lennon.

Album: *Living in Exile* (WEA, 1988).

Bigger than Jesus (*see* X)

Billy T

Formed: *1976*
Style: *Soul, funk, reggae*
Original line-up: **Ross Hannaford** *(guitar, vocals; ex-***Pink Finks, Party Machine,** *Quinn,* **Sons of the Vegetal Mother, Daddy Cool, Mighty Kong***), Russell Kinross-Smith (guitar, vocals; ex-***Cam-Pact, Company Caine, Duck, Mighty Kong***), Joe Creighton (bass, vocals; ex-***Melissa,** *Band of Angels), Mick Holden (drums; ex-***Mixtures, Hot City Bump Band***)*

Melbourne band Billy T was never commercially successful, despite the presence of so many acclaimed musicians within its ranks. The band came together in April 1976. **Ross Hannaford** and Irishman Joe Creighton were devotees of Satguru Maharaj Ji and the Divine Light Mission, and much of their religious philosophy came through in the band's lyrics. The band also played some of the most vibrant dance music of the day.

Billy T signed to CBS and issued two singles, 'Gotta Keep on Dancing'/'I'm In a Dancing Mood' (August 1977) and the Four Tops' 'Baby I Need Your Lovin''/'Live Together' (November 1977). Hannaford and Creighton left Billy T at the end of the year in order to travel to the USA to attend various religious festivals. While in the US, they formed One Foundation with Geoff Bridgeford (drums; ex-**Steve & the Board, Groove, Bee Gees**) to play at Mission conventions. Upon his return to Australia in 1978, Hannaford worked with Bambu, Lucky Dog, the **Mark Gillespie** Band, The Rocking Emus, **Goanna, The Black Sorrows,** Dianna Kiss and a host of others. Creighton has since become one of the most in-demand journeyman session players in the country.

The new Billy T line-up of Kinross-Smith, Holden, Geoff Maling (percussion), Neal MacPherson (keyboards), Gene Cendrillon (bass) and Shirley Reid (vocals; ex-**Company Caine**) was on the road by the time a third Billy T single, 'I Am What You Are' (radio edit)/'I Am What You Are' (album version) came out in February 1978. CBS finally issued the Billy T debut album *No Definitions* in March 1978 (recorded by the Hannaford/Creighton/Kinross-Smith/Holden line-up), but the band broke up a month later. The final Billy T line-up had been Kinross-Smith, Holden, Cendrillon and Greg Cook (guitar, keyboards; ex-**Cam-Pact**, Skylight, **Phil Manning** Band, **Mondo Rock**). Kinross-Smith joined **Leo De Castro's** Heavy Division, before travelling to Perth in 1979 where he and Shirley Reid joined a band called Zeroes. He teamed up again with Hannaford in a version of **Goanna** around 1983.

Album: *No Definitions* (CBS, 1978).

The Birthday Party

Formed as The Boys Next Door: *1975*
Style: *Post-punk rock*
Original line-up: *Nick Cave (vocals), Mick Harvey (guitar), Tracy Pew (bass), Phill Calvert (drums)*

The Birthday Party is recognised as one of the most influential, creative and inspirational rock bands Australia has ever produced. Perhaps the band's most enduring legacy was the way in which it re-acquainted British post-punk audiences with noise, anger, intensity and sheer passion. The Birthday Party folded at a time when, having exhausted its distinctive sound, the band was beginning to widen its musical horizons.

The Birthday Party had its roots in new wave band The Boys Next Door. Nick Cave, Mick Harvey, Tracey Pew and Phill Calvert were attending Caulfield Grammar School in Melbourne's eastern suburbs when they formed the band in 1975. Initial inspiration came from British 1960s R&B/pop (Them, The Who) and 1970s glam rock (David Bowie, Roxy Music), plus a few American icons (Alice Cooper, Lou Reed, The Ramones). By 1978, The Boys Next Door were part of a thriving alternative new music scene centred on the Crystal Ballroom in the inner-city Melbourne suburb of St Kilda.

The Boys Next Door issued a single 'These Boots Were Made for Walking'/'Boy Hero' (April 1978) and appeared on Suicide Records' *Lethal Weapons* compilation (with **Teenage Radio Stars**, Negatives, **JAB**, Wasted Daze, Survivors and **X-Ray-Z**). Rowland S. Howard (ex-Young Charlatans) joined

The Boys Next Door, later known as The Birthday Party

in December 1978, bringing his distinctive guitar sound and songwriting abilities. *Door Door* (April 1979) on Mushroom Records was a transitional album and contained Howard's 'Shivers', now recognised as an Australian classic. 'Shivers' came out as a single backed with 'Dive Position' (May 1979).

Later in the year, The Boys Next Door signed to manager **Keith Glass**'s Missing Link label and put out the 12-inch EP *Hee Haw* (December). It was a sign of things to come. The band had moved into more abstract pastures, with the simple, shifting song arrangements offset by lots of jagged edges and Howard's patented, abrasive guitar noise. The influence of overseas bands like The Pop Group, Pere Ubu, The Fall and Gang of Four had also started to take hold. In February 1980 The Boys Next Door transformed into the more artfully malevolent The Birthday Party and left for the UK.

In London, the band found little affinity with the likes of The Human League, Joy Division or Echo and the Bunnymen, but soon made its presence felt on the English scene. Influential BBC DJ John Peel became an early and long-serving convert. 4AD issued 'The Friend Catcher' EP in the UK, and Missing Link issued the bold and audacious, yet nimble and funky single 'Mr Clarinet'/'Happy Birthday' (July 1980). Missing Link also put out an album *The Boys Next Door/The Birthday Party* (November 1980) which was a mix of previously issued EP and singles tracks with a couple of unissued cuts. It marked the band's move into more experimental, hitherto uncharted territory.

The Birthday Party returned to Australia in November 1980 to tour and record. It was during this time that the band cemented its reputation as a peerless live act, with its omnipresent influence settling over the Melbourne scene. The Tony Cohen-produced *Prayers on Fire* album (May 1981) and the slow, lurching single 'Nick the Stripper'/'Blundertown' (June) were issued to universal acclaim. The records were a sign of the band irrevocably and unashamedly changing for the better, being more aggressive than anything they had ever recorded. The band's steady diet of Stooges, Pere Ubu, Captain Beefheart, Suicide and The Fall was reflected in the twisted sounds heard on tracks like 'Zoo-Music Girl', 'Nick the Stripper', 'King Ink', 'Dull Day' and 'Figure of Fun'.

Back in London, the band issued the groundbreaking 'Release the Bats'/'Blast Off' single (August 1981) which spent three weeks at the top of the British independent charts. Its brooding juxtaposition of sex/vampire/horror unwittingly tied the band in with the emergent Goth sub-culture. One of the band's legendary UK shows at London's The Venue in November 1981 produced the *Drunk on the Pope's Blood* live EP (issued February 1982). Subtitled '*16 Minutes of Sheer Hell!*', it formed one half of the shared album with New York siren Lydia Lunch's *The Agony is the Ecstasy*. Howard and Harvey went on to record the 12-inch EP 'Some Velvet Morning'/'I Fell in Love with a Ghost' with Lunch. It came out credited to Rowland S. Howard and Lydia Lunch. Howard has featured on much of Lunch's subsequent recorded output, including the excellent 1991 album *Shotgun Wedding*.

Back in Australia in December 1981 to tour and record, Pew was imprisoned following his third drink driving charge. Barry Adamson (ex-Magazine), Harry Howard and Chris Walsh (from **The Moodists**) helped out on the new record and the ensuing UK tour. With bleak tracks like '6" Gold Blade', 'She's Hit' and 'Kiss Me Black', the pivotal *Junkyard* album (July 1982) surpassed the extreme sound of *Prayers of Fire*. It also sported a cover by American cartoonist Ed 'Big Daddy' Roth (creator of Rat Fink). The recording session also produced the one-off single with members of **The Go-Betweens** 'After the Fireworks'/'After, After the Fireworks' (credited to the Tuff Monks).

In August 1982, The Birthday Party shifted base to Berlin in order to escape the constant exposure and expectations of them in the UK. Calvert was dropped (moving on to Psychedelic Furs) and Harvey took over on drums. As an intense and tightly focused four-piece, the band recorded two extraordinary EPs, *The Bad Seed* and the posthumously released *Mutiny!* With tracks like 'Sonny's Burning' and 'Deep in the Woods', *The Bad Seed* (March 1983) remains the band's most fully realised and enduring recording.

The seeds for the band's break-up had been sown by early 1983. Rivalries within the group had intensified, and the prodigious consumption of drugs and alcohol by various members began to undermine any sense of unity. Matters came to a head when Harvey refused to undertake a tour of Australia at the end of May 1983. Des Hefner deputised, but the band played its final gig in Melbourne on 9 June 1983. Cave and Harvey went on to form **Nick Cave and the Bad Seeds**. Pew returned to Australia and enrolled in university. Harvey and Howard collaborated on **Crime and the City Solution** with singer Simon Bonney. Howard split from that band in 1986 and formed his much-heralded 'supergroup', These Immortal Souls, with whom he recorded two albums of dark, ominous, challenging rock music *Get Lost (Don't Lie!)* (1987)

and *I'm Never Gonna Die Again* (1992). He returned to live in Australia in 1994.

There has been enough continued interest in The Birthday Party in the intervening years for Shock Records to reissue the band's material on CD. *The Birthday Party* box set from late 1994 contained *Hee Haw*, *Prayers on Fire*, *Junkyard*, *Drunk on the Pope's Blood* and *It's Still Living*, plus a 24-page booklet. In October 1996, Shock reissued *Hee Haw*, *Prayers on Fire*, *Junkyard*, *The Bad Seed/Mutiny!* and *Hits* as individual releases.

Albums: *Door Door* (Mushroom/Festival, 1979), *Hee Haw* (Missing Link, 1979), *The Boys Next Door/The Birthday Party* (Missing Link, 1980), *Prayers on Fire* (Missing Link, 1981), *Drunk on the Pope's Blood* (Missing Link, 1982), *Junkyard* (Missing Link, 1982), *The Bad Seed* (4AD, 1983; import only), *Mutiny!* (Mute, 1983; import only), *It's Still Living* (Missing Link, 1985), *A Collection—Best and Rarest* (Missing Link, 1986), *Hits* (Missing Link/Shock, 1993), *The Birthday Party* (box set) (Missing Link/Shock, 1994).

Further reading: *Nick Cave—The Birthday Party and Other Epic Adventures* by Robert Brokenmouth (Omnibus Press, 1996).

The Bitter Lemons

Formed: *1965*
Style: *R&B*
Original line-up: *Paul Lyneham (vocals), Dave Kain (guitar; ex-Phantoms), Nicky Arndt (guitar), Rex Bullen (guitar, keyboards), Graeme Harding (bass), Steve Senz (drums)*

Canberra's mid-1960s beat/R&B scene comprised the likes of The Bitter Lemons, The Casuals, The Roadrunners, The Second Movement, The Brothers Grimm, The Action, Bobby Knight and the Nightbeats, The Chosen Few and The Five Just Men, among others. The Bitter Lemons' influences included The Rolling Stones, Them and The Pretty Things, and they were seen as the bad boys on the scene.

The Bitter Lemons ran their own dances at the Lemon Tree discotheque. It was closed down by the police after one too many fights between the local rockers and the band's fans. In 1965 The Bitter Lemons issued a slice of primitive garage R&B on the EMI Custom label 'Canberra Blues'/'One More Chance'. Dennis Flynn (rhythm guitar) replaced Bullen, who joined The Five Just Men with Ian Winter (ex-Brothers Grimm). Winter's band The Brothers Grimm had issued two singles on EMI/HMV, Chuck Berry's 'Beautiful Delilah'/'Happiness Street' (February 1966) and 'All My Dreams Come True'/'You Were the One' (April 1966). Winter went on to **Carson** and **Daddy Cool**, while Rex Bullen later played in **Bakery**, Natural Gas, **Jim Keays'** Southern Cross and **Ray Burton** and the Nightflyers. He died in March 1983.

The Bitter Lemons toured interstate, and broke up around 1967. Kain went on to The Five Just Men, The Untamed, The Square Circle, Dr Kandy's Third Eye and **Company Caine**. Singer Paul Lyneham moved into journalism, and then television current affairs reporting with the ABC's *Four Corners* and *The 7.30 Report*. He later moved to the Nine Network. In recent years, Graeme Harding drowned in a boating accident, and Dennis Flynn was shot dead in Los Angeles.

Bjerre

Style: *Pop, rock*

Singer/songwriter Lindsay Bjerre had fronted acclaimed bands The Sunsets, **Tamam Shud** and Albatross before he launched his solo career in 1977. Albatross formed in September 1972 and comprised Bjerre, Peter Barron (bass; ex-**Tamam Shud**), Kim Bryant (drums; ex-**Country Radio**) and Simone Bjerre (vocals). Richard Lockwood (sax, flute, clarinet; ex-**Tully**, **Tamam Shud**) joined in April 1973.

Albatross's brand of gentle, tasteful country-flavoured rock was at odds with the then-prevailing trends in Australian music such as boogie, blues, pub rock or pop. Accordingly, Albatross shared an affinity with only a handful of like-minded bands such as **Country Radio** and **Home**. Bjerre eschewed **Tamam Shud's** progressive rock approach to sing acoustic-based songs about the ecology, outdoor life and the sea. By the time *A Breath of Fresh Air* came out in November 1973, Bjerre had split the band. He had developed an interest in eastern religions and lived with the Hare Krishnas for six months. He wrote a rock opera which never saw the light of day, and then spent most of 1975 travelling throughout Europe and the USA.

He decided to become a 'performer' and under the influence of Lindsay Kemp studied mime in the UK. Out of that experience, the singer developed his bizarre and romantic Bjerre character, which was a cross between a French Charlie Chaplin and a cabaret-styled David Bowie. Bjerre signed with Phonogram and issued the theatrical *Stealing the Hours* album (May 1977) which combined sophisticated pop funk with melodramatic touches and a whimsical feel. Following exposure on the ABC-TV's pop show ***Countdown***, the airy, seductive

'She Taught Me How to Love Again'/'Youthful Charlie' became a Top 20 hit in October 1977. The album's second single, 'I'll Take You Higher'/'Old Soul', failed to chart.

Bjerre formed a touring band which comprised Paul Radcliffe (guitar), Steve Isoardi (keyboards), Wayne Roundtree (bass; replaced by Phil Hitchcock), Ace Follington (drums; ex-**Chain**, Australia), Jason Morphett (sax) and Greg Taylor (sax). Australian pub rock audiences of the day found Bjerre's theatrical approach difficult to appreciate. By 1978, Bjerre had formed a more rock-oriented band which comprised Follington, Paul 'Sheepdog' Wheeler (bass, ex-**Billy Thorpe** and the Aztecs, **MacKenzie Theory**), Greg Hooke (keyboards; ex-Odyssey), while he handled guitar duties. The new line-up recorded the punchy rock album *Hard Times* (issued July 1978). The singles 'Not So Easy'/'Wasting the Magic' (June 1978) and 'You Won't Dance With Me'/'Down the Ghetto' (July 1979) were not successful. Bjerre dropped from view until **Tamam Shud** re-formed in 1993.

Bjerre solo albums: *Stealing the Hours* (Philips/Phonogram, 1977), *Hard Times* (Philips/Phonogram, 1978); ***Albatross album:*** *A Breath of Fresh Air* (WEA/Reprise, 1973).

Black Alice

Formed: *1982*
Style: *Heavy metal*
Original line-up: *Rob Hartley (vocals), Jamie Page (guitar), Vince Linardi (bass), Joe Demasi (drums)*

Black Alice was a little-known Perth heavy metal band that recorded its debut album in Singapore, and had it issued in the UK and reviewed in British HM bible *Kerrang!* before anyone was the wiser in Australia. The band's brand of UK-influenced heavy metal was well suited to an overseas market. The *Endangered Species* album (October 1984) saw the band indulge in the world of sword and sorcery with tracks like 'Blade of Slaughter', 'In the Hall of the Ancient Kings' and 'Man of Metal' (an ode to bushranger Ned Kelly).

In late 1984, Jamie Page joined forces with fellow Perth musicians Jon Ryder (vocals, bass, keyboards; ex-Saracen) and Pete Thompson (drums, vocals; ex-Saracen) in power trio Trilogy. The band issued an album, *Life on Earth,* on the Bonsai label (1985) which drew comparisons with Canadian outfit Rush. Page then left to be replaced by Peter Jenkins. Trilogy issued its second album, *Next in Line* (which only appeared on French label Axe Killer, 1986), before reverting to the Saracen moniker for a third album *Saracen* (1987). For that album Saracen's original guitar player John Meyer (also ex-**Rose Tattoo**) had returned to the fold to replace Jenkins.

In 1988, singer Rob Hartley appeared in a post-apocalyptic, science fantasy feature film called *Sons of Steel,* written and directed by Gary Keady who had co-produced the *Endangered Species* album with Englishman Steve James. Naturally enough, Hartley appeared in the role of Black Alice and also sang on the soundtrack which was written by Gary and Rod Keady. *Sons of Steel* grew out of a 1984 short film called *Knightmare* co-directed by Keady and Yahoo Serious. The rooArt label issued two tracks from the *Sons of Steel* soundtrack as a single in 1989: 'Fighting for You!'/'Hard Lover'. Musicians on the album included Hartley (vocals), Jamie Page (guitars), Andy Cichon (bass; ex-**Rose Tattoo**), Scott Johnson (drums; ex-**Jimmy and the Boys, Rose Tattoo**) and Paul Radcliffe (keyboards, guitar; ex-**Bjerre** Band).

Black Alice albums: *Endangered Species* (Street Tunes/Big Island, 1983; reissued on RCA, 1984), *Sons of Steel* (original soundtrack album, Big Island/rooArt, 1989); ***Trilogy albums:*** *Life on Earth* (Bonsai, 1985), *Next in Line* (Axe Killer, France only, 1986).

The Black Diamonds

Formed: *1965*
Style: *Garage punk*
Original line-up: *Glenn Bland (vocals, harmonica), Alan 'Olly' Oloman (guitar, vocals), Brian 'Felix' Wilkinson (organ, piano), Alan Keogh (bass), Colin McAuley (drums)*

The Black Diamonds will be remembered as one of the most ferocious garage/punk outfits Australia ever produced in the 1960s. The band's snarling 'I Want, Need, Love You' takes pride of place as one of the best cuts on Raven's seminal Aussie 1960s punk collection *Ugly Things*.

The Black Diamonds formed in the Blue Mountains area around Lithgow (NSW). Lithgow is a coal town, and 'black diamond' is a term for coal. Alan Oloman and Alan Keogh first worked together in Lithgow rockabilly band Johnny Kett's Black Diamonds. As The Black Diamonds, the band issued two singles, 'See The Way'/'I Want, Need, Love You' and 'Outside Lookin' in'/'Not this Time' on Festival during 1967. Like The D-Coys, The Black Diamonds were equally adept at producing both jubilant pop and tough garage-punk on either side of the one single. In 1968 Darcy Rosser replaced

Alan Keogh on bass, the band changed its name to Tymepiece and made the permanent move to Sydney. At that point, producer Pat Aulton approached the band to record as **Love Machine**.

Love Machine's version of The Tokens' 'The Lion Sleeps Tonight' was a hit, but the band members soon tired of the **Love Machine** pop trappings and moved on. Tymepiece issued three singles, 'Bird in the Tree'/'I Gotta Know What You're Like' (August 1968), 'Become Like You'/'Give a Little More' (November 1969) and 'Won't You Try?'/'Down and Out' (October 1970) on Festival before moving to the progressive subsidiary label Infinity. The band's rare debut album, *Sweet Release* (February 1971), offered a diverse range of moods and styles, from psychedelic pop ('Why?'), folk ('Reflections') and country ('Sweet Release') to R&B ('I Love, You Love') and heavy progressive blues ('Shake Off'). Tymepiece broke up soon after the album's release. Oloman appeared in the 1974 line-up of **The Executives**. Reissue specialists Raven later included the pulsating, eight-minute 'Shake Off' on the essential collection *Golden Miles: Australian Progressive Rock 1969–1974* (1994).

Tymepiece album: *Sweet Release* (Festival/Infinity, 1971).

The Black Sorrows

Formed: *1984*
Style: *R&B, soul, zydeco*
Original line-up: *Joe Camilleri (aka Joey Vincent, vocals, sax; ex-***Pelaco Brothers**, **Jo Jo Zep and the Falcons***), Paul Williamson (clarinet, sax), George Butrumlis (piano accordion), Wayne Burt (guitar, vocals; ex-***Jo Jo Zep and the Falcons***), Jeff Burstin (guitar; ex-***Company Caine**, **Jo Jo Zep and the Falcons***), Steve McTaggart (violin), Wayne Duncan (bass; ex-***Daddy Cool**, *Living Legends),* **Gary Young** *(drums; ex-***Daddy Cool**, **Jo Jo Zep and the Falcons***)*

Any examination of The Black Sorrows inevitably comes down to one person. Joe Camilleri (singer, songwriter, saxophonist, producer and the brains behind The Black Sorrows) is one of the most genuinely talented figures in Australian music. Maltese-born (in 1948), Camilleri got his start on the Melbourne soul and R&B circuit during the 1960s with bands like The King Bees and **Adderley Smith Blues Band**.

His appearances with Lipp and the Double Dekker Brothers, Sharks and **The Pelaco Brothers** in the early 1970s may have been legendary, but it was not until the formation of **Jo Jo Zep and the Falcons** in 1975 that Camilleri achieved national

Joe Camilleri, The Black Sorrows

prominence. The Falcons earned a reputation as a red-hot live band and recorded a series of highly acclaimed albums and singles. Jo Jo Zep broke up in 1983 and Camilleri launched The Black Sorrows a year later. From humble beginnings playing zydeco, R&B and soul-inspired semi-acoustic music around Melbourne's inner-city cafes, Camilleri transformed the band into one of the most sophisticated ensembles in the country.

For the first couple of years, Camilleri steered a shifting line-up of musicians (which included three ex-Falcons) through several relaxed and pleasant albums like *Sonola*, *Rockin' Zydeco* and *A Place in the World*. These early records concentrated on material such as Van Morrison's 'Brown Eyed Girl', John Lee Hooker's 'Don't Look Back' and Ray Peterson's 'Corrina, Corrina', plus an increasing number of Sorrows' originals. The band's early singles included: 'What a Difference a Day Makes'/'Brown Eyed Girl' (June 1984, from *Sonola*), 'Shape I'm in'/'My Negress in Black' (March 1985, from *Rockin' Zydeco*), 'Sons of the Sea'/'Gypsy Heart' (November 1985) and 'Country Girls'/'A Place in the World' (March 1986, both from *A Place in the World*), 'Daughters of Glory'/'Foolish Girl' (April 1987), 'Maybe Tomorrow'/'Dear Children' (June) and 'The Last Frontier'/'Wild Street Girls' (November, all from *Dear Children*).

Nick Smith (vocal harmonies, lyrics; ex-**Millionaires**, **Kevins**) and Peter Luscombe (drums) joined The Black Sorrows prior to recording *A Place in the World*, although the band still essentially featured a floating line-up. Guest musicians on that album included Joe Creighton (bass; ex-**Billy T**), **Ross Hannaford** (guitar; ex-**Daddy Cool**, **Billy T**), **Andrew Pendlebury** (guitar; ex-**Sports**), Ed Bates (guitar; ex-**Sports**) and The Blackberries (vocal harmonies). Johnny Charles (bass) and Mick 'The Reverend' O'Connor (Hammond organ) joined for *Dear Children*. Mick Girasole then replaced Charles on bass.

Dear Children represented a turning point in the band's career. Originally issued independently and sold only at the band's gigs, it reached the national Top 20 (#18 in June 1987) once CBS stepped in with a distribution deal. With the arrival of backing vocalists **Vika and Linda Bull**, and the establishment of a permanent line-up, The Black Sorrows issued the finely crafted albums *Hold on to Me*, *Harley and Rose* and *Better Times*. As well as Camilleri and the Bull sisters, the line-up around *Hold on to Me* (September 1988) featured Jeff Burstin, Wayne Burt, Mick Girasole and Peter Luscombe (Smith had left the touring band, but still contributed lyrics).

Hold on to Me peaked at #6 on the national chart in May 1989. It stayed on the chart for a year and sold 250 000 copies, as well as a respectable 150000 units when issued in Europe and the USA. It produced five singles: 'Hold on to Me'/'Safe in the Arms of Love' (August 1988), 'The Chosen Ones'/'Mercenary Heart' (October), 'Chained to the Wheel'/'Waiting for the Rain' (February 1989), 'The Crack Up'/'The Story Never Changes' (April) and 'Fire Down Below', 'Daughters of Glory' ('89 remix)/'Come on in My Kitchen' (August). 'Hold on to Me' reached #24 on the national chart in October 1988, 'Chained to the Wheel' reached #9 in May 1989 and 'The Crack Up' reached #40 in June. The Black Sorrows also won Best Group at the 1989 Australian Record Industry Association (ARIA) Awards.

Richard Sega replaced Girasole on bass, and Jen Anderson (violin; ex-Kings of the World) joined for the classic *Harley and Rose* (November 1990). The album yielded the excellent singles 'Harley and Rose'/'The Calling' (#24 in September 1990), 'Never Let Me Go'/'Never Let Me Go' (Swamp Mix) (#30 in April 1991) and 'Hold It Up to the Mirror' (June). Later on, Jen Anderson issued a solo CD EP, 'Seek', on the Chapel of Change label (1992). Anderson toured with the Jen Anderson Band, which comprised Tony Faehse (guitar, vocals; ex-**Jo Jo Zep and the Falcons**), Tim Henwood, (guitar, vocals), Pat Quinn (bass, vocals) and Terry Bartholemew (drums). In 1993 she wrote, recorded and then performed the soundtrack to the classic German silent film *Pandora's Box* during its Australian art-house run. In 1994, Anderson produced **Ruby Hunter's** debut album *Thoughts Within*, as well as contributing tasteful violin and viola fills to a couple of the tracks.

With heavy overseas touring (seven tours in 18 months) taking its toll on the band's resolve and stability, Burt and Girasole left The Black Sorrows in late 1991. Michael Barker (percussion) and Stephen Hadley (bass; ex-**Kate Ceberano** and The Ministry of Fun) came in as replacements. During May 1992 The Black Sorrows joined **Beatfish**, **Deborah Conway**, **The Poor Boys**, **Kate Ceberano**, **Club Hoy** and **The Angels** for the Wizards of Oz series of showcase gigs in Los Angeles. The band's next album, *Better Times* (October 1992), produced the singles 'Better Times' (May), 'Ain't Love the Strangest Thing?' (#46 in September) and 'Come on, Come on' (February 1993). Lyricist Laurie Polec had taken over from Nick Smith for *Better Times*. Like *Hold on to Me* before them, *Harley and Rose* and *Better Times* (Top 10 in April 1993) both sold over 200000 copies.

In between his commitments to The Black Sorrows, Camilleri found time to issue the album *Amazing Stories* (December 1991) with his occasional country/R&B outfit The Revelators. The Revelators comprised Camilleri, Burstin, Luscombe, Joe Creighton (bass, vocals; ex-**Billy** T) and James Black (keyboards, guitar; ex-**Mondo Rock**), with help from the Bull sisters, Anderson, Barker, Garrett Costigan (pedal steel) and Venetta Fields (vocals). *Amazing Stories* produced two singles, 'What Does It Take (to Win Your Love)?' (November 1991) and Bob Dylan's 'Caribbean Wind' (April 1992). Also included on the album was an elegant reworking of the Gram Parsons/Chris Etheridge tender-sad love song 'Hot Burrito #1'. For a short time, *Amazing Stories* and The Black Sorrows' *Better Times* were available as a Limited Edition two-for-one CD collector's pack.

In 1993, The Black Sorrows issued the CD EPs 'Sweet Inspiration' (July) and 'Stir It Up' (#58 in November). At the end of 1993, Camilleri dismantled the Bull sisters/Burstin/Luscombe/Anderson/Barker/Hadley version of The Black Sorrows, and reconstituted the band as a solo act with supporting musicians. After a chance meeting with Kerryn Tolhurst (ex-**Country Radio**, **Dingoes**), Camilleri travelled to New York to record the *Lucky Charm* album, with Tolhurst co-producing.

Lucky Charm was a more reflective, rootsier collection than previous band efforts. It produced the CD EP 'Snakeskin Shoes' (#16 in August 1994) and the singles 'Last One Standing for Ya' and 'Lucky Charm'. Ex-**Noiseworks'** frontman Jon Stevens sang a duet with Camilleri on 'Last One Standing for Ya', which reached #46 nationally in December. Camilleri also contributed a cover of **Country Radio's** 'Gypsy Queen' to the Various Artists compilation *Earth Music* issued on the Mushroom label (June 1994). 'Gypsy Queen' was issued as a CD single, backed with the non-album track **The Church** doing **The Radiators'** 'Room Full Of Diamonds'.

In December 1995, Camilleri issued a solo CD EP, 'All Saints Hotel'. It was the only release since the 1986 cover of Kool and the Gang's 'Celebration'/'Wha'cha Gonna Do About It?' and 1989's 'Angel Dove' single to come out under his own name rather than The Black Sorrows' moniker. The CD EP contained a zydeco reworking of Chuck Berry's 'Run Rudolph Run', a song which Camilleri had previously recorded for release as the first **Jo Jo Zep** single in late 1975.

In 1996, The Black Sorrows released the triple live album *Radio Waves* which presented the ultimate Black Sorrows gig (36 tracks!). Also available was *The Black Sorrows* box set, containing the albums *Sonola*, *Rockin' Zydeco*, *Dear Children* and *A Place in the World*, plus *Not for Production* an exclusive 11-track compilation of rarities and never-before-released tracks. The box set brought The Black Sorrows story full circle. In early 1997, Camilleri established a new, eight-piece line-up of The Black Sorrows that was inspired by a late 1960s New York-style of jazz/funk/blues as pioneered by Ramsey Lewis and Les McCann. The first release from the new Black Sorrows was the CD EP 'New Craze' (August 1997).

Black Sorrows albums: *Sonola* (Spirit, 1984; reissued by White/Mushroom/Festival, 1984), *Rockin' Zydeco* (White/Mushroom/Festival, 1985), *A Place in the World* (Virgin, 1986), *Dear Children* (Spirit, 1987; reissued by CBS, 1987), *Hold on to Me* (CBS, 1988), *Harley and Rose* (CBS, 1990), *Better Times* (Sony/Columbia, 1993), *The Chosen Ones Greatest Hits* (Sony/Columbia, 1993), *Lucky Charm* (Sony/Columbia, 1994), *Radio Waves* (three CD live album) (Head/Mushroom/Festival, 1996), *The Black Sorrows* (box set; Head/Mushroom/Festival, 1996), *The Very Best of The Black Sorrows (Johnny Gumbo's Nude Lounge)* (Mushroom/Sony, 1997); ***Revelators album:*** *Amazing Stories* (Sony/Columbia, 1991).

The Blackeyed Susans

Formed: *1989*
Style: *Country, folk*
Original line-up: *David McComb (guitar, vocals; from* **Triffids***), Robert Snarski (guitar, vocals; ex-***Chad's Tree***), Ross Bolleter (keyboards), Phillip Kakulas (bass, guitar, vocals; ex-***Triffids, Martha's Vineyard***), Alsy MacDonald (drums; from* **Triffids***)*

The Blackeyed Susans came about as a sideline venture for members of the so-called 'Perth-expat Mafia' (David McComb, Phil Kakulas, Rob Snarski and Alsy MacDonald) when they decided to put together a loose outfit to play covers. As befits the talents of the collaborators, the band's sound was a rich musical blend of country, folk and soulful ballads.

The aggregation played a few shows in Perth during late 1988 as The Bottomless Schooners of Old before becoming The Blackeyed Susans in the new year. McComb and McDonald were on sabbatical from **The Triffids** at the time. At the end of 1989, Sydney-based independent label Waterfront issued The Blackeyed Susans' four-track, 12-inch vinyl EP *Some Births are Worse than Murders*. It included rearrangements of Pomus/Shuman's 'Viva Las Vegas' and the traditional 'Cripple Creek'. McComb and McDonald had returned to the UK with **The Triffids**, and principal songwriters Snarski and Kakulas employed a floating line-up of musicians (including members of **The Jackson Code**) for the next year. It was only after **The Triffids** broke up, and McComb returned from London in 1991, that the band became an ongoing concern.

At the start of 1992, Waterfront issued two more four-track, 12-inch vinyl-only EPs 'Anchor Me' (January) and 'Depends What You Mean by Love' (February). Waterfront combined the 12 tracks from the EPs, plus four additional cuts, to make up the band's 16-track debut album *Welcome Stranger* (August 1992). After settling on a line-up of Snarski, Kakulas, McComb, Graham Lee (guitar, pedal steel; ex-**Triffids**, **Dave Graney** and the White Buffaloes), Warren Ellis (violin, piano accordion) and Jim White (drums; ex-**Venom P. Stinger**), The Blackeyed Susans set off on a national tour. Ellis and White had just formulated **Dirty Three**, and Ellis was also moonlighting in Kim Salmon's STM and Charles Marshall and the Body Electric at that stage.

At the end of 1993, The Blackeyed Susans issued their debut album proper, *All Souls Alive*, which contained 'A Curse on You', a piece of gothic high-drama-set-in-song that recalled a William Faulkner novel. The album also produced two CD

EPs, 'This One Eats Souls' and 'Dirty Water'. After that, McComb concentrated on his band The Red Ponies while Ellis and White did the same with **Dirty Three**. Snarski, Kakulas and Lee toured as The Blackeyed Susans Trio in order to promote the album's release.

The Blackeyed Susans' third album, *Mouth to Mouth* (July 1995), produced two CD EPs, 'Let's Live' (June) and 'Mary Mac' (September). Alongside the core of Kakulas, Snarski and Lee, the album featured contributions from new keyboard player Kieran Box, Kathy Wemyss (vocals; from **Jackson Code**), Jen Anderson (violin; ex-**Black Sorrows**), Helen Mountford (cello), Dan Luscombe (guitar) and Ashley Davies (drums; ex-**White Cross**, **Wild Pumpkins at Midnight**). The Blackeyed Susans then consolidated with the line-up of Kakulas, Snarski, Box, Luscombe and new drummer Mark Dawson (ex-**John Kennedy's Love Gone Wrong**, **Ed Kuepper** Band). The Blackeyed Susans' fourth album, *Spin the Bottle* (August 1997), included the CD singles 'Smokin' Johnny Cash' (May) and 'Spin the Wheel' (September).

Albums: *Welcome Stranger* (Waterfront, 1992; reissued by Torn & Frayed in 1993), *All Souls Alive* (Torn & Frayed/Shock, 1993), *Mouth to Mouth* (Hi-Gloss/MDS, 1995), *Spin the Bottle* (Hi-Gloss/MDS, 1997).

Blackfeather

Formed: *1970*
Style: *Progressive rock*
Original line-up: *Neale Johns (vocals), John Robinson (guitar; ex-Lonely Ones, Monday's Children,* **Dave Miller Set***), Leith Corbett (bass; ex-***Heart 'n' Soul**, **Dave Miller Set***), Mike McCormack (drums; ex-***Dave Miller Set***)*

The story of Blackfeather is one of the most convoluted in the entire history of Australian rock. Something in the vicinity of 50 musicians passed through the Blackfeather ranks down the years. The band left behind two genuine classic singles in 'Seasons of Change' and 'Boppin' the Blues'.

The original line-up of Blackfeather emerged out of the ashes of the **Dave Miller Set** in April 1970. Even at that stage, 18-year-old Neale Johns was a singer of great power and conviction, and John Robinson was a nascent guitar hero on par with **Lobby Loyde** and **Kevin Borich**. Leith Corbett and Mike McCormack moved on quickly to be replaced by Bob Fortesque and Al Kash respectively. The band built up a following on the Sydney and Melbourne hard rock circuit and cut *At the Mountains of Madness*. It remains a highly regarded progressive rock album, highlighted by Robinson's fluid, inventive guitar technique and a swag of adventurous songs. *At the Mountains of Madness* came out in April 1971 and reached #7 on the national chart a month later. Reissue specialists Raven later included the epic 'Long Legged Lovely' on the essential Various Artists compilation *Golden Miles: Australian Progressive Rock 1969–1974* (1994).

The soaring, seductive 'Seasons of Change'/'On this Day that I Die' (May 1971) was a national #15 hit (#9 in Sydney) during June. Johns and Robinson had originally written 'Seasons of Change' for **Fraternity**, but the Blackfeather version was strong enough to be issued in its own right. Meanwhile, Terry Gascoigne had replaced Al Kash on drums in March 1971. By the time the single came out, Harry Brus (bass; ex-Amazons, **Dave Miller Set**, **Jeff St John's** Copperwine) and Steve Webb (drums) had replaced Fortesque and Gascoigne respectively. A further split occurred in August 1971 when Robinson, Brus and Webb carried on without Johns under the name of Blackfeather.

The singer formed his own version of Blackfeather with Zac Zytnik (guitar; ex-**Tamam Shud**, Bootleg), Paul Wylde (piano; ex-Starving Wild Dogs, **Hannagan**), Warren Ward (bass; ex-**Flying Circus**, **Maple Lace**) and Jim Penson (drums; ex-Plastic Tears, **Maple Lace**). Paul Conyngham from the Nova Agency held legal rights to the Blackfeather name and Robinson's Blackfeather soon broke up. Robinson joined Sydney club band Hunger with singer **Bobbi Marchini**. He then became a part of studio band **Duck** in 1972, reunited briefly with **Dave Miller Set**, formed Tramp in 1973 and then issued a solo album, *Pity for the Victim*, on Festival/Infinity in 1974.

Zytnik left Blackfeather in December 1971, as did Penson at the start of 1972. Billy Taylor (ex-**Flake**) joined on guitar and the band recorded a new single, 'Boppin' the Blues'/'Find Somebody to Love' with The Aztecs' Gil Matthews filling in on drums. By the time the single became a national #1 hit in August, Trevor Young had joined as temporary drummer. He was replaced by Greg Sheehan, and guitarist Taylor also left to return to **Flake**. The new four-piece line-up relied on dominant boogie-woogie piano as a substitute for guitar, and issued the live album *Boppin' the Blues* (December 1972) and new single 'Slippin' and Slidin''/'Fly on My Nose' (February 1973).

By January 1973, Wylde had left, and guitarists Lindsay Wells (ex-**Healing Force**, One Ton Gypsy) and Tim Piper (ex-**Chain**, One Ton Gypsy) joined. Once again, Blackfeather was playing hard rock and the band's set at Sunbury 1973 was issued as the live album *Blackfeather Live! (Sunbury)* in 1974. The Blackfeather track, 'I'm Gonna Love You', also appeared on Mushroom's triple live set *The Great Australian Rock Festival Sunbury 1973* (April 1973). John Lee (ex-Sayla) then replaced Sheehan on drums after Sunbury, but by April Blackfeather had split. Johns initially went solo before joining **Flake** in July. **Flake** at that stage comprised guitarists John Russell and Billy Taylor, plus two other ex-Blackfeather alumni, Warren Ward and Jim Penson. **Flake** lasted until the end of 1974.

A short-lived Blackfeather line-up in 1975 comprised Johns, Billy Taylor (guitar), Ray Vanderby (keyboards; ex-**Band of Light**), Billy Rylands (bass) and Doug McDonald (drums). Johns re-emerged in early 1976 with a new Blackfeather featuring Vanderby, Lee Brossman (bass), Warwick Fraser (drums) and 14-year-old Stewart Fraser (guitar). That was a more pop-oriented line up, but only lasted until November when Johns left to travel to the UK. The rest of the band recruited singer John Swan and guitarist Wayne Smith to became **Feather**.

In the UK, Johns teamed up with guitarist Con Gallin and recorded an album with session players. Johns and Gallin returned to Australia in 1977 and put together a band called Fingerprint (with drummer Trevor Young and bassist Mark Smith) to promote the upcoming album. In the end, only the single 'Play Roulette'/'When I Get Out of Here' (August 1977) came out and Fingerprint broke-up. Johns and Young re-formed Blackfeather in June 1978 with Paul Wylde (piano) and Warren Ward (bass). By October, the line-up had changed to Johns, Ray Oliver (guitar; ex-**Friends**), Rick Rankin (guitar), Jeff Rosenberg (bass; ex-Hot Air Band) and Huk Treloar (drums, ex-**Pantha**, **Bleeding Hearts**, Living Legends). John Strangio (ex-**Dingoes**, **Chariot**) came in for a while to replace Rosenberg, but the band was defunct by the end of the year.

By 1980, Johns and Young were playing around the Melbourne pub circuit with Brenden Mason (guitar, ex-**Madder Lake**) and Kerrie McKenna (bass, ex-**Madder Lake**) as Claude Rains. Ever the opportunist, Johns revived the Blackfeather name one more time in 1983 with Russell Hinton (guitar; ex-**Country Radio**), Andy Cowan (keyboards, ex-**Madder Lake**, **Ayers Rock**), Cleve Judge (bass) and Joe Vizzone (drums). By then, the band had well and truly run its course and that line-up was short-lived.

Albums: *At the Mountains of Madness* (Festival/Infinity, 1971), *Boppin' the Blues* (Festival/Infinity, 1972), *Blackfeather Live! (Sunbury)* (Festival/Calendar, 1974).

Peter Blakeley

Style: *Soul*

Peter Blakeley (b. 1960) is recognised as one of the most unique Australian singers ever. His sweet, versatile vibrato is equally at home around soul standards, country ballads, upbeat dance tunes and even rock and blues songs. The founder of Atlantic Records, Ahmet Ertegun, called him 'the best white soul singer I've ever heard'. Writer Clinton Walker wrote that Blakeley was 'simply the most beautiful singer I'd ever heard up so close, and I wasn't alone in my opinion'. For someone with such high accolades, Blakeley is vastly underrated in Australia, with only two hit singles to his credit.

Blakeley's first band was Peter Black and the Reds, but he came to wider prominence while singing with Sydney bands Rat Tat Tat, Paris Green and **Rockmelons**. Blakeley sang on **Rockmelons'** second single 'Sweat it Out'/'If Tomorrow Ever Comes' in 1986. He formed his own band, The Resurrection, in 1986 and signed to True Tone Records. True Tone issued the singles 'Must be Chemical'/'When I was a Little Boy' (March 1986), Marvin Gaye's 'Ain't That Peculiar'/'Ain't Nothing Like the Real Thing' (May), 'Caterina'/'Cattle Train' (March 1987) and 'Bye Bye Baby'/'One of the Family' (August), plus the mini-album *Vicious* (April 1987). The Resurrection comprised **Chris Abrahams** (bass, piano), Jim Benjamin (drums), Mark Punch (guitar; ex-**Renée Geyer** Band) and **Wendy Matthews** (backing vocals).

The Resurrection recorded an album for True Tone which was never issued, and Blakeley was without a record deal. By 1988, Blakeley had signed an American deal with Capitol Records and was living and recording in Los Angeles. That resulted in the acclaimed *Harry's Cafe de Wheels* album which was issued in March 1990. With production duties shared by one-time 1960s British pop singer Peter Asher (10,000 Maniacs, Linda Ronstadt) and Stewart Levine (Simply Red), and featuring the cream of Los Angeles session players, the album was a confident and contemporary release.

The jubilant 'Crying in the Chapel'/'Caterina' reached #3 in February 1990, and *Harry's Cafe de Wheels* made its debut in the national Top 5. Blakeley's gorgeous reading of Ewan MacColl's 'First Time Ever I Saw Your Face'/'Bye Bye Baby' was issued as a second single and made #17 in April. Two other singles, 'Quicksand' (May) and the upbeat 'You Never Heard It from Me' were minor hits. 'Crying in the Chapel' attained platinum status (over 70 000 copies sold) and was the 18th biggest selling single in Australia during 1990; *Harry's Cafe de Wheels* eventually attained triple platinum status (over 210 000 copies sold) and was the 21st biggest selling album for 1990. Blakeley also won Best Australian Single for 'Crying in the Chapel' at the 1989 Australian Record Industry Association (ARIA) Awards.

Blakeley toured Australia with a band comprising Junior Baillie (drums), Hopeton Hibbert (bass), Mabon Hodges (guitar), Roger Mason (keyboards, ex-**Models**) and **Deni Hines** (backing vocals). 'Crying in the Chapel' was to be Blakeley's commercial peak in Australia. He spent the next couple of years fighting Capitol in order to get out of his contract.

Blakeley recorded his next album, *The Pale Horse*, at Prince's Paisley Park Studios with producer David Z. *The Pale Horse* was a more sophisticated and polished release but it failed to match the success of its predecessor. Likewise, the album's two singles, 'God's Little Elvis' and 'I've Been Lonely', failed to reach the national Top 40. Nevertheless, Blakeley's own psychedelic-soul gem 'Through the Looking Glass', his beautiful interpretation of Curtis Mayfield's 'Ain't No Love Lost' and the punchy, rhythmic funk of Johnny 'Guitar' Watson's 'A Real Mother for Ya' demonstrated the maturity evident in the singer's voice.

Albums: *Vicious* (mini-album, True Tone/PolyGram, 1987), *Harry's Cafe de Wheels* (Capitol/EMI, 1990), *The Pale Horse* (Giant/BMG, 1994).

Jon Blanchfield

Style: *Pop*

Singer Jon Blanchfield recorded nine pop singles and an album for RCA during the 1960s. The singles were: 'Upstairs Downstairs'/'Town of Tuxley Toymaker' (1965), 'You've Got a Lot of Living'/'Time' (1967), 'Lavender Girl'/'Look What I've Got' (1968), 'Somebody to Love'/'Pray for Love' (1968), 'Baby, Get in the Groove'/'Reach for The Sun' (1969), 'She's a Baby'/'I Get so Excited' (1969), 'Son of a Simple Man'/'Waltzing Matilda' (1969), 'Lucy's Place'/'Is it True?' (1971) and 'Let the Good Times Roll'/'Shenandoah' (1972). None was successful at a national level. Blanchfield compered the television pop show *Up Tight* and then moved on to the club and cabaret circuit. In 1976, he launched the short-lived Rainbird label which issued albums by **Bandicoot**, **Coloured Balls** and **Lobby Loyde**.

Album: *Jon Blanchfield* (RCA, 1969).

The Bleeding Hearts

Formed: *1976*
Style: *Pub rock*
Original line-up: *Martin Armiger (guitar, vocals; ex-Toads), Eric Gradman (violin, vocals; ex-Sharks, Toads), Chris Worral (guitar; ex-***Pelaco Brothers**, **Captain Matchbox Whoopee Band***), Laurie Tunnecliffe (bass), Huk Treloar (drums; ex-***Pantha***)*

Between 1976 and 1977, The Bleeding Hearts were at the forefront of a thriving Melbourne pub rock scene that included the early **Sports**, **Jo Jo Zep and the Falcons**, Gulliver's Travels, **Mondo Rock**, **Stiletto**, **Redhouse** and **Millionaires**.

In early 1977, Rick Grossman replaced Tunnecliffe on bass and Keith Shadwick (ex-**Sun**, Uncle Bob's Band) joined on sax and backing vocals. Following a national tour support to American singer Country Joe McDonald during April 1977, Chris Worral left the band. He went on to join **Stiletto** and **Paul Kelly** and the Dots. The Bleeding Hearts attracted a good deal of attention, but were unable to fulfil their early promise before breaking up in August 1977. The limited edition album *What Happened!* and single 'Hit Single'/'Boys' came out a year later. The album featured one side of rough studio demos and one side of live material. (The EMI Custom single 'Can't Let You Go'/'Out on the Streets Again' that came out in 1981 was by an unrelated Bleeding Hearts.)

Armiger joined Flying Tackle and High Rose Bombers, before replacing Ed Bates in **The Sports** during 1978. Treloar joined **The Little Heroes** and The Hot Club, and Grossman joined **Parachute**. Gradman produced recordings for a couple of Melbourne punk/new wave bands, including The Negatives, Two Way Garden and Kikx. In November 1978, he and Grossman formed Eric Gradman: Man & Machine with Mick Holmes (guitar; ex-Negatives), Robert Kretschmer (guitar; ex-Spare Change, **Parachute**) and Graeme Perry (drums; ex-Spare Change, **Parachute**).

Eric Gradman: Man & Machine became one of the leading lights on the late 1970s Melbourne independent scene, although the band collapsed as quickly as it rose to prominence. The band's only recordings were the 'Crime of Passion' 12-inch EP and one side of a gig giveaway single 'The Bath' shared with Tch Tch Tch. The band broke up at the start of 1980. Gradman went on to form Eric Gradman's Enjoy, Sound of Music, Funkanation and The Ugly Sisters. Journeyman bassist Grossman went to **Matt Finish**, **Divinyls**, **Hoodoo Gurus** and **Ghostwriters**. Holmes joined **The Zimmermen** and

Dirt. Kretschmer became an integral part of the 1980s line-up of **Icehouse**.

Album: *What Happened!* (Missing Link, 1978).

Blekbala Mujik

Formed: *1988*
Style: *Rock, reggae*

Arnhem Land-based Koori band Blekbala Mujik formed in 1988. Bandleader Peter Miller (vocals, guitar) was the youngest member of the Northern Land Council. The Central Australian Aboriginal Media Association (CAAMA) recorded the band, and Blekbala Mujik issued the seven-track cassette sampler *Come-N-Dance* in 1993 followed by its eponymous debut album in May 1996.

Blekbala Mujik was a mix of catchy Aboriginal pop, reggae, techno-tribal dance material and bright funky rock. American Allen Murphy (ex-**Warumpi Band**, Village People, **Yothu Yindi**) pushed the band along with his solid drumming. The four traditional pieces included on the record featured yidaki (didjeridoo) player Lazarus Murray. Other members of Blekbala Mujik have included Thomas Valandhu (drums), Lachlan Gela Lawrence (bass, vocals), Wayne Kala Kala (drums), Jason Fuller (percussion), Johnny Blanasi (guitar) and Dwayne Billy (percussion). The CD EP 'Walking Together' came out in June 1997. Blekbala Mujik has followed in the footsteps of **Warumpi Band**, **No Fixed Address**, **Coloured Stone**, **Yothu Yindi** and others in establishing a place for Koori and Murri music on the local scene.

Album: *Blekbala Mujik* (CAAMA/Shock, 1996).

Blitz Babies

Formed: *1993*
Style: *Punk pop*
Original line-up: *Joanne Lanzon (vocals), Ziad (guitar), Jamie (guitar), Errol (bass), Grant (drums)*

Sydney band Blitz Babies played a blend of punkish noise and melodic pop somewhere between **The Meanies** and X-Ray-Spex. Ian replaced Errol in 1994. Blitz Babies built up a strong live following on the Sydney scene and the band's 7-inch self-titled EP on the No Deal label sold out in a matter of weeks. The album *On the Line* came out in November 1994, after which the band toured Europe at the invitation of its European record distributor. The band issued the CD EP 'Feel This' in December 1995. By that stage, the band was down to a four-piece of Joanne, Ziad, Grant and Ian, issuing a second album, *Thought Spawn*, a year later. *Thought Spawn* produced the CD EP 'Worlds Apart' (August 1996).

Albums: *On the Line* (Spent Music, 1994), *Thought Spawn* (Onefoot, 1997).

Bloodloss

Formed: *1982*
Style: *Post-punk grunge*
Original line-up: *Sharron Weatherill (vocals, guitar), Jim Selene (bass; ex-Spell), Renestair E.J. (guitar, sax; ex-Head On), Martin Bland (drums; ex-Chaos, Head On, Crawling Eye, Acid Drops)*

Adelaide band Bloodloss has existed in three separate incarnations. Renestair E.J. and Martin Bland formed the basis of the band when they worked together in Head On, a loud, Detroit-fuelled punk band in the vein of The Stooges and MC5. Renestair E.J. moved to Sydney in late 1982 where he formed Bloodloss with Sharron Weatherill and another ex-Adelaidian, Jim Selene. In the meantime Bland stayed in Adelaide where he joined Crawling Eye and then The Acid Drops.

Bloodloss went through a number of fill-in drummers until Bland joined in 1983. With the addition of Stuart Grey (aka Stu Spasm, guitar, vocals) later in the year, Bloodloss became Zulu Rattle. Zulu Rattle's only release was 'Terror Train' on the Various Artists *Strawberry Hills* compilation on GREEN Records. Zulu Rattle lasted until March 1984 when Spasm and Bland joined **Tex Perkins'** new band, Salamander Jim. Salamander Jim broke up a year later and Spasm and Bland formed **Lubricated Goat**. Selene returned to Adelaide and joined The Spikes. Bland returned to Adelaide in 1985 and joined Primevils with Dave Mason (guitar, vocals; ex-Head On, Acid Drops), Su Severin (guitar; ex-Crawling Eye) and Selene. Primevils issued the single, 'I Saw My Name (Written on a Tombstone)'/'Hammer Yourself Senseless' (November 1986) and the album *Chicken Factory* (May 1987) on the Greasy Pop label. Renestair E.J. joined Primevils in time to appear on the album.

Meanwhile, the reconstituted Bloodloss with Weatherill, Renestair E.J., Chris Wiley (bass; from **Fear and Loathing**), Charlie Tolnay (guitar; ex-**Grong Grong**, concurrently in **King Snake Roost**) and Andrew Stosch (aka Andrew Foley, drums) had issued the *Bloodloss* cassette on Greasy Pop during 1986. Tolnay was only briefly a member of Bloodloss. With the breakup of Primevils in 1987, Bland rejoined Bloodloss as dual drummer alongside Stosch. As displayed on the album *Human Skin Suit* (June 1988), that version of Bloodloss played a jazzy brand of pre-grunge noise. By that stage, Tolnay was concentrating on **King Snake Roost** and only contributed guitar as a guest player to one track on the album. Weatherill left in 1988 and Bland moved up front on guitar and vocals. The new line-up issued the single 'Smell Machine'/'Shake Your Leaves' (March 1989). Wiley left and Selene rejoined on bass. Bloodloss broke up in 1990 after issuing a second album, *The Truth is Marching in*, on the Aberrant label.

Bland and Renestair E.J. joined Stu Spasm's **Lubricated Goat**. Bland also played as a guest on Tolnay and Peter Hill's proto-grunge studio project Bushpig before moving to the home of grunge (Seattle, USA) in 1992. Steve Turner (guitar) and Mark Arm (vocals, guitar) from Seattle grunge band Mudhoney had also been involved in the Bushpig line-up during Mudhoney's Australian tours. Bland joined Turner and Arm in their studio band The Monkey Wrench. In 1992, SubPop issued the Monkey Wrench single 'Bottle Up and Go' and album *Clean as a Broke Dick Dog*.

In 1993, Bland and Renestair E.J. reactivated Bloodloss with Mark Arm and another Aussie expatriate, Guy Maddison (bass; ex-**Lubricated Goat**, Monroe's Fur, Greenhouse Effect). As displayed on the album *Live My Way* (March 1996), that version of Bloodloss played delta blues by way of Captain Beefheart and Jon Spencer Blues Explosion. *Misty* on the Au-go-go label contained material from 1993–1994 which displayed echoes of Pere Ubu, Thug and all manner of jazz and blues. By 1994, Bland and Renestair E.J. were members of Maddison's band Monroe's Fur.

In the meantime (1992), Jim Selene had switched to guitar and formed a new band called FreeMovingCurtis (FMC) which comprised Steve Collinson (vocals; ex-Shanks), Stuart Silcox (guitar; ex-Filthy Scumbags, **Hot Tomatoes**), Dave Christopher (bass; ex-Plague, **Meanies**) and Warwick Savvas (drums; ex-Shanks). FMC practised a rough-hewn blend of punk-rock attitude and heavy guitar riffs. The band issued two CD EPs, 'Blind' (October 1993) and 'Persuader' (1994) on the Hippy Knight label before the original line-up called it quits in June 1995. Collinson, Selene and Silcox relocated to Sydney, recruited a new rhythm section and issued a full-length, self-titled album (which had been recorded by the original line-up).

Bloodloss albums: *Human Skin Suit* (Greasy Pop, 1988), *The Truth is Marching in* (Aberrant, 1990), *In-a-Gadda-Da-Light* (US import, Sympathy For The Record Industry, 1993), *Live My Way* (Warner/Reprise, US import, 1996), *Misty* (Au-go-go, 1996); ***Primevils album:*** *Chicken Factory* (Greasy Pop, 1987); ***FreeMovingCurtis album:*** *FreeMovingCurtis* (Hippy Knight, 1995).

Blue Million Miles

Formed: *1990*
Style: *Pop*
Original line-up: *Mark Foster (guitar, vocals; ex-Samurai Trash), Mark Bradridge (guitar, vocals, keyboards; ex-Jump Vision, Watusi Now)*

Sydney musicians Mark Foster and Mark Bradridge formed Blue Million Miles in 1990, primarily as a recording venture. Since Foster's first band Samurai Trash broke up in 1986, he had concentrated on songwriting and video production, winning two Australian Film Institute (AFI) awards for short films.

Samurai Trash comprised Foster, Jerome McClintock (bass) and Philip Beckett (drums). The band signed to Virgin Australia and issued three singles, 'Come and Play'/'Seaside', 'Tell Me'/'Green' and 'Samurai Stomp'/'That Old Country Rock', before breaking up. Bradridge formed Jump Vision in Wollongong (NSW) during 1980. The line-up was completed by Richard Knott (bass, vocals) and Dave Rowley (drums). The band's brand of 1960s-influenced soul and ska was readily accepted on the Sydney mod circuit, where the band played alongside the likes of **Allniters**, The Introverts and **Fast Cars**. The band issued one single 'Can't Get Used to You'/'The Jump' on the Basilisk label (March 1981) before breaking up. Rowley joined **The End** and Bradridge formed Watusi Now.

Watusi Now comprised Knott, Rebecca Hancock (vocals) and Peter Megende (guitar, percussion). Watusi Now issued one single on Hot 'Sound of God'/'Letter to God' in 1983 which reflected the band's strong dance music leanings. The band broke up a year later. Megende later travelled to the USA, where he joined highly rated New York hardcore band Helmet and played on the 1992 album *Meantime*. Bradridge went on to work as editor for *Countdown* magazine. In 1994, Blue Million Miles signed to PolyGram's Eternity label alongside **Rebecca's Empire**, **Atlas Strings** and Charlotte Grace. Eternity issued two Blue Million Mile CD EPs, *Blue Million Miles* (1994) and 'Big Big Place' (June 1995).

Blue Ruin

Formed: *1985*
Style: *Blues rock*
Original line-up: *Ian 'Quincy' McLean (vocals; ex-Scrap Museum), Mulaim Vela (guitar; ex-Scrap Museum), Adam Learner (bass, ex-***International Exiles**, **Little Murders**, *Scrap Museum), Phill Calvert (drums; ex-***Birthday Party**, *Psychedelic Furs)*

Centred around the imposing presence and vocal growl of frontman Ian 'Quincy' McLean, Blue Ruin formed out of the ashes of Melbourne band Scrap Museum. Scrap Museum issued the single 'Say Die'/'That Dirty, Stink'n', Unclean, Love Affair' (1984) on the Rampant label. Ex-**Birthday Party** member Phill Calvert returned to Australia in 1985, fresh from his stint with UK band Psychedelic Furs, and replaced drummer Frank Borg. Scrap Museum became Blue Ruin.

The albums *Such Sweet Thunder* (January 1986) and *Flame* (May 1987), and the singles 'Venus'/'Hey Bo' (November 1986), 'Bad Gin'/'Two Sleepy People' (March 1987) and 'What A Hell'uva Woman'/'I Hit the Big Time in a Bottle' (December) established the band's hard-edged blues-based style. The band contributed the Jimi Hendrix-infused 'Bad Gin' to the Rampant label's Various Artists album *Running Rampant Volume 1* (1987). Simon Capp replaced Learner on bass, and Blue Ruin moved to the UK in an attempt to gain wider acceptance. For 12 months the band did the rounds of the London pub and club circuit, issuing an EP 'Lighthouse Girl' on the Imaginary label.

With the band overseas, the rooArt label issued the live album *Strange Things in the Corner* (February 1989), which showcased McLean's raw, bluesy vocals and Mulaim Vela's astonishing guitar technique. Back in Australia, Blue Ruin issued its third album *I'm Gonna Smile* (December 1990), which produced the singles 'Don't Go No More' (September) and 'Shotgun Hips' (February 1991). Following the release of *I'm Gonna Smile*, Calvert left to be replaced by John Hall, who in turn was replaced by Greg Heynes. Adam Learner also returned to the fold in place of Capp, and that line-up issued a final album, *Tattoo Tears*, in late 1993. By the end of 1995, Blue Ruin had broken up.

Albums: *Such Sweet Thunder* (Major, 1986), *Flame* (Rampant, 1987), *Strange Things in the Corner* (rooArt, 1989), *I'm Gonna Smile* (Foghorn/MDS, 1990), *Tattoo Tears* (Foghorn/MDS, 1993).

The Blue Echoes

Formed: *Late 1960s*
Style: *Pop*

During the late 1960s and early 1970s, The Blue Echoes were one of the most popular bands playing the Melbourne cabaret and club circuit. By 1973, the band's line-up was Phil Golotta (vocals), Ray Eames (guitar, vocals), Ray Quon (keyboards, vocals), Chris Studdard (bass, vocals) and Ron Chapman (drums, vocals).

The band issued five singles, the most successful being 'Going to a Party'/'Don't You Want Me?' (October 1973). In May 1977, The Blue Echoes briefly became The Echoes when Golotta and Studdard were replaced by solo singers Robin Jolley and Rod Kirkham. Jolley had scored a #4 hit single in 1972 with the **Brian Cadd**/Don Mudie song 'Marshall's Portable Music Machine' on the Fable label. Jolley continued to issue singles like 'Where the Music's Playing', 'Do You Wanna Boogie', 'Baby What's Getting to You' and 'Midnight Woman', but failed to reach the charts again. Likewise, Rod Kirkham had issued a hit single in 1973, 'I Can't Get Sunday Out of My Mind', but had been unable to sustain a solo career. Original members Golotta and Studdard returned in late 1977 and The Blue Echoes continued until November 1983.

Albums: *High Heeled Rock & Roll* (Image 1975), *Dancing in the Streets* (Hammard 1976), *Clap Your Hands and Stamp Your Feet* (Hammard 1980), *At the Hop* (Hammard, 1981).

The Blues Syndicate

Formed: *1965*
Style: *R&B*

Adelaide band The Blues Syndicate grew out of the same mid-1960s R&B scene that gave rise to **The Master's Apprentices**, The Others, Blues Rags'n'Hollers, Dust'n'Ashes and The Harts. Like Blues Rags'n'Hollers, who issued a gutsy version of Willie Dixon's 'I Just Want to Make Love to You'/'Got Love If You Want It' as a single for the Leedon label (July 1966), The Blues Syndicate cut one single for Leedon 'Tired Of Trying'/'Baby Please Don't Go' (October 1966), before breaking up.

Around 1966–67, The Blues Syndicate made regular appearances at the popular Big Daddy's discotheque, alongside many other bands on the scene. In late 1966, the independent Gamba Records imprint recorded eight bands (including The Blues Syndicate) live at the disco, for a proposed album, *Live at Big Daddy's Discotheque*, which never saw the light of day at the time. All that survived of the idea was a sole acetate disc which changed hands many times over the years, eventually ending up in the possession of Adelaide DJ David Day. In 1986, reissue specialists Raven issued this fascinating, long-lost artefact. The bands featured on the album were Little Sammy & The In People, The Bentbeaks, The Blues Syndicate, The Others, The Y?4, The Harts, The Third Party and **The Chosen Few**.

The Blues Syndicate covered Robert Johnson's 'Crossroads' and Wilson Pickett/Steve Cropper's 'In the Midnight Hour'. Some of the tracks covered by the other bands included: Bonnie Rice's 'Mustang Sally' (The Bentbeaks), Walter Jacobs' 'Blues With a Feeling' (The Others), Marvin Gaye/et al.'s 'Dancing In The Streets' (The Y?4), Bobby Troup's 'The Girl Can't Help It' (The Harts), Chip Taylor's 'Wild Thing' (The Third Party) and James Brown's 'I'll Go Crazy' (**The Chosen Few**).

Bluebottle Kiss

Formed: *1993*
Style: *Grunge*
Original line-up: *Jamie Hutching (guitar, vocals), Ben Fletcher (bass, vocals), Peter Noble (drums)*

This young Sydney three-piece played a melancholy brand of guitar grunge that was heavy on atmosphere and lengthy feedback solos. Dinosaur Jr, Palace and Neil Young were reference points, as opposed to the fuzz pop of (then) in vogue US bands like Sebadoh, Buffalo Tom and Pavement. The band's contemporaries on the Sydney scene included **Crow**, **Pollyanna**, **Big Heavy Stuff**, **Drop City** and **Daisygrinders**.

One of the band's early demos, *Sonic Elevator Music for the Masses*, attracted some interest. Eighteen months after formation, Bluebottle Kiss signed a deal with Sony's Murmur label (home to **silverchair**) and issued the album *Higher Up the Firetrails* (April 1995). In recording the album, the band eschewed the relatively sterile confines of the studio, and set up in Sydney's Bondi Pavilion Theatre with producer Wayne Connolly (**Welcome Mat**) in order to capture a certain ambience. The album ran the gamut of sounds from quiet dirge to chaotic noise. The band saw out 1995 with the release of the seven-track, 46-minute CD EP *Double Yellow Tarred*.

For the band's second full-length album, *Fear of Girls* (August 1996), Bluebottle Kiss utilised the services of famed American producer Jack Endino (Nirvana, Mudhoney, Afghan Whigs). Once again the 14-track, 65-minute album covered a lot of ground, from tough, noisy art-rock to bleak ballads. 'Autumn Comes Too Soon' (June) and 'Helping You Hate Me' (November) came out as CD singles. Bluebottle Kiss issued a new CD EP, 'Somnambulist Homesick Blues', in June 1997.

Albums: *Higher Up The Firetrails* (Murmur/Sony, 1995), *Fear of Girls* (Murmur/Sony, 1996).

Bluestone

Formed: *1972*
Style: *Country rock*
Original line-up: *Terry Dean (vocals, guitar), Mike Burke (guitar, banjo), Edward Fry (bass), John Creech (drums; ex-***Mixtures***)*

Melbourne singer Terry Dean formed country rock band Bluestone. He had enjoyed a semi-successful solo career during the 1960s, having recorded two singles for the Go!! label, 'It's You'/'Stagger Lee' (June 1965) and 'The Answer to Everything'/'Git It!' (April 1966). Dean's backing band around that time was the original **Mixtures** line-up.

Brian Cadd signed Bluestone to Bootleg Records, which issued eight singles and a self-titled album. 'Wind and Rain'/'Road to Nowhere' (May 1973), 'The Singer Sang the Song'/'Sing Me a Rainbow' (October 1973), 'Ride on'/'The Only Girl' (August 1975) and 'Rock and Roll Crazy'/'Say That You Need Me' (April 1977) were minor hits in Melbourne. Laurie Arthur and Nigel Thompson replaced Mick Burke and Edward Fry respectively in 1975. By the early 1980s, the band had made the move into straight country. The band's last three singles were 'Single Again'/'Keep on Dancing' (July 1981), 'Remember'/'Oh, How She Loves Me' (April 1982) and 'Same Party'/'Time Won't Change' (1984).

Albums: *Bluestone* (Bootleg, 1974), *The Closer You Get* (Avenue, 1982).

Bluetile Lounge

Formed: *1991*
Style: *Rock, country*
Original line-up: *Dan Erickson (guitar, vocals), Gabrielle Cotton (slide guitar), Howard Healy (bass, vocals), Alex Stevens (drums)*

This young Perth, Western Australia band perfected a brand of countryish rock that relied on meandering atmospherics, lengthy build-ups and gentle climaxes. 'Slow and quiet' was an apt description for the band's music, which drew inspiration from such disparate overseas sources as Cowboy Junkies,

Sonic Youth (more specifically the extended coda sections to that band's songs), Galaxie 500 and Codeine.

Bluetile Lounge played its first gig in May 1993. By the time it played at the Perth leg of the 1996 Summersault festival tour, the band had received praise from US visitors like Sonic Youth, Pavement and Foo Fighters. The band's debut, five-song, 46-minute album *lowercase* was issued locally on the Summershine label and then issued in the USA by Seattle's SubPop label. US critics came up with descriptions like 'Sonic Youth on valium' and 'Neil Young on disprin' to describe the band's sound.

Album: lowercase (Summershine/Shock, 1996).

Bobby and Laurie

Formed: *1964*
Style: *Beat pop*
Original line-up: *Bobby Bright (vocals), Laurie Allen (vocals)*

If anyone captured the spirit of the Australian pop scene of the 1960s in all its foot-stomping, hand-clapping, mane-shaking, fun-loving glory then it was the duo of Bobby and Laurie. Supported by their crack backing band The Rondells, Bobby and Laurie cut a series of vibrant hit singles that helped usher in the Australian beat movement (alongside **Billy Thorpe** and the Aztecs, **M.P.D. Limited** and **The Easybeats**).

Laurie Allen started out in 1959 as lead guitarist with Malcolm Arthur and the Knights, which also included Malcolm Arthur (guitar, vocals), Phil Blackmore (piano), Gordon Onley (bass) and Graeme Trottman (drums). Malcolm Arthur had worked with the Henri Bource All Stars and The Autocrats before forming The Knights. The band was one of the first rock'n'roll outfits on the Melbourne scene. Arthur released one solo single on the W&G label, 'Why', before The Knights issued the single 'Cross My Heart' on Crest. Trottman and Blackmore later backed **Normie Rowe** as members of The Playboys. After leaving The Knights, Allen joined The Blue Jays as organist/vocalist (one single for Crest in 1962, 'Wolfman'). Bobby Bright recorded two solo singles for W&G in 1963, 'Girls Never Notice Me' and 'Defeated by His Heart'. Bobby and Laurie first teamed up as members of revue act The Roulettes, before striking out on their own at the end of 1964.

Bobby and Laurie became regulars on the teen-formatted *Go!! Show* in Melbourne, which resulted in the Go!! label signing the duo. The duo's pop star status was established when they had four hit singles in Melbourne during 1965: 'I Belong with You', with its foot-stomping middle-eight ('Trouble In Mind' appeared on the flip) was #2 in March, 'Someone'/'You Are Gone' (#4 in June), 'Judy Green'/'Mojo Queen' (#8 in September) and 'Crazy Country Hop'/'It Ain't Fair' (#25 in December).

The original Rondells line-up that backed Bobby and Laurie on 'I Belong with You' comprised Bernie O'Brien (lead guitar), John Sullivan (rhythm guitar), Dennis Tucker (bass) and Dennis Collins (drums). Once 'I Belong with You' became a hit, Bobby and Laurie formed a touring line-up of The Rondells which comprised John Sullivan, Roger Treble (lead guitar; ex-Silhouettes, Lincolns), Wayne Duncan (bass; ex-Lincolns) and **Gary Young** (drums; ex-Silhouettes, Lincolns). Barry Rodgers later replaced Sullivan on rhythm guitar. In June 1965, The Rondells enjoyed their own, minor hit single on the Go!! label when a cover of Chuck Berry's 'Talkin' 'Bout You'/'Baby Don't Hide' reached #31 in Melbourne.

Bobby and Laurie signed to Albert Productions (home of **The Easybeats** and **Billy Thorpe** and the Aztecs) in 1966. Albert/Parlophone issued the singles 'Sweet and Tender Romance'/'Down in the Valley' (February 1966), a plaintive version of Roger Miller's 'Hitchhiker'/'You'll Come Round' (March), 'High Noon'/'Tonight when I Come Home' (June) and 'Every Second Day'/'First Street Blues' (October). In the wake of the #1 chart success of 'Hitchhiker', Bobby and Laurie were given their own ABC-TV show *It's a Gas*, a more sedate, sophisticated version of the *Go!! Show*. *It's a Gas* soon became *Dig We Must* and the show's 'young adult' trappings turned the fans off the show and away from Bobby and Laurie. Frustrations came to a head, and Bobby and Laurie split in February 1967. The duo's final album, *Exposaic*, featured almost entirely country music, except for an inventive piece of swirling psychedelia in 'Every Second Day'.

Bobby started acting (*Start Living*, *Homicide*), did adult cabaret, formed Penny Arcade, recorded a solo single for CBS ('Would You Believe'/'Love') and became a DJ on 3XY in Melbourne. Laurie formed the ambitious soul revue (based on his Stax/Volt idols) The Dice. Later renamed the Laurie Allen Revue, that band included ex-Rondells Barry Rodgers (bass, soon replaced by Wayne Duncan) and **Gary Young**, guitarist Harry Henri (replaced by **Phil Manning**) and backing vocalists Glenys and **Colleen Hewett** (The Creations). The Laurie Allen Revue recorded three singles for Festival: 'Beautiful Brown Eyes'/'Saved' (August 1967), 'Any Little Bit'/'Cool Jerk' (April

1968) and 'As Long as I Got You'/'Born to Follow' (June 1968).

In 1969, Bobby and Laurie teamed up again for the singles 'The Carroll County Accident'/'A Hole in the Ground' (December 1969), 'Through The Eyes Of Love'/'Trouble on the Turnpike' (December 1970) and 'I'm Gonna be a Wheel Someday'/ 'The Train of Love' (October 1971). By late 1971, the reunion had run its course. Bright continued acting (including an appearance in the local stage production of The Who's *Tommy*), wrote and recorded commercials and recorded *Bobby Bright* for RCA (1975).

Laurie Allen immersed himself totally in straight country music, which resulted in two solo albums on ATA, *Once Upon a Song* (1972) and *Any Other Man* (1976). Allen also issued a weeping, country treatment of 'I Belong with You' as a single in 1972. Allen collaborated with ex-boxer turned country singer Lionel Rose on his 1972 album for Festival, *Jackson's Track*. Bobby and Laurie appeared periodically on the nostalgia circuit and even popped up on Melbourne television in an advert for Guests Furniture during December 1996. Bright also took a film role in Ana Kokkinos's gritty urban drama *Only The Brave* (1994). The duo's mercurial relationship may have overshadowed the music to a certain extent. Yet there is no denying that Bobby and Laurie songs like 'I Belong with You', 'You'll Come 'Round', 'Jump Back' and 'Every Second Day' are the equal of anything recorded during the 1960s.

Albums: *Bobby and Laurie* (Go!!, 1965), *Hitchhiker (Cum Sunt Ambulant)* (EMI/Parlophone, 1966), *Exposaic* (EMI/Parlophone, 1966), *The Very Best of Bobby and Laurie* (Astor, 1980), *Jump Back!* (Raven, 1985), *I Belong with You* (Canetoad, 1990).

Bodyjar

Formed: *1994*
Style: *Punk rock*
Original line-up: *Cameron Baines (vocals, guitar), Ben Peterson (vocals, guitar), Grant Relf (vocals, bass), Ross Hetherington (drums; ex-Bastard Squad)*

During 1995–96, Melbourne punk outfit Bodyjar emerged as one of the most popular bands within Australia's all-ages touring circuit. As with like-minded bands such as One Inch Punch, Bodyjar drew inspiration from Californian skate-punk bands on the Epitaph label (Offspring, Bad Religion, Pennywise, NOFX), as well as their mid-1980s forebears Descendants and All (plus local bands like **The Hard-Ons**), for their brand of forceful yet melodic punk rock.

Bodyjar formed as Helium in 1992. Helium issued one album, *You Can't Hold Me Down* (October 1993), before changing names. Bodyjar's two albums, *Take a Look Inside* and *Rimshot* (on the Shagpile label through Shock), sold well on an independent level in Australia. *Take a Look Inside* yielded the CD EPs 'Time to Grow Up' and 'Gee and Al', while *Rimshot* spawned the CD EPs 'Glossy Books' and 'Don't Tell Me'. Both albums have also been issued worldwide on Real Cool Records (Japan), Burning Heart (Europe) and Revelation (America). The band issued a new CD EP 'Strange Harvest' in August 1997. Bodyjar has toured Japan (October 1995), Europe (March 1996) and the USA (April 1997).

Albums: *Take a Look Inside* (Shagpile/Shock, 1995), *Rimshot* (Shagpile/Shock, 1996).

The Bombers

Formed: *1988*
Style: *Hard rock*
Original line-up: *Tyrone Coates (vocals, sax), John Brewster (guitar, ex-***Angels***,* **Party Boys***), Angelo Salter (guitar), Alan Lancaster (bass; ex-Status Quo,* **Party Boys***), John Coughlan (drums; ex-Status Quo)*

This much-vaunted hard rock 'supergroup' came together in 1988. In October 1989, Peter Heckenberg (ex-Boss, **B.B. Steal**) replaced John Coughlan, and a few months later Steve Crofts replaced Angelo Salter. Heckenberg and Crofts were also members of the side project Black Cat Moan with **Angels** guitarist Bob Spencer. In 1990, Black Cat Moan issued the album *Black Cat Moan*, which was full of blues and bar-room boogie, on the Arika label (through Larrikin).

The Bombers toured solidly for a year (close to 300 gigs) and signed a worldwide deal with A&M Records along the way. The band's debut album, *Aim High* (April 1990), and three singles, 'Running into the Shadows' (October 1989), 'World's on Fire'/'Get Up and Get It On' (June 1990) and 'Flash in Japan'/'Don't Come Easy' (September 1990), were not successful. The band set off on tour with the likes of **The Radiators** and **De Mont**, as well as landing a couple of choice support slots to international visitors like Alice Cooper (April 1990) and Skid Row (May). Despite being an Oz Rock pub band in the classic **Cold Chisel/Angels** mould, The Bombers could not entice the record-buying public. In 1993, The Bombers (sans Tyrone Coates) backed

Angry Anderson on tour, before John Brewster rejoined **The Angels**.

Album: *Aim High* (A&M, 1990).

Grahame Bond (aka Aunty Jack) and Rory O'Donoghue (aka Thin Arthur)

Style: *Parody*

Grahame Bond and Rory O'Donoghue were the principal stars and the force behind the successful ABC-TV comedy *The Aunty Jack Show*. Aunty Jack was the 300-pound, Harley Davidson-riding protagonist with one golden boxing glove and the 'I'll rip yer bloody arms off!' catchcry. Thin Arthur was the laconic, philosophising straightman in black and white striped tights, complete with braces, dicky, walking cane and straw boater.

Together with other characters like Kid Eager (played by Garry McDonald, who also developed his **Norman Gunston** character while appearing on the show) and Flange Desire, the duo forged a genuinely funny, original and memorable Australian comedy show. *The Aunty Jack Show* only ran for two series (1972–73), but it is fondly remembered by those who were seduced by its enduring charms. After the show was axed, the Aunty Jack team recorded an album, *Aunty Jack Sings Wollongong*, and single, 'Farewell Aunty Jack'/'Doin' the Aunty Jack', for Polydor. The single was credited to Cool Bananas and had originally been issued by Picture Records. It was the first Australian picture disc. The single was a #1 hit in January 1974 and eventually sold over 100 000 copies.

Bond and O'Donoghue were both accomplished musicians. O'Donoghue got his start as guitarist in The Pogs during the mid-1960s when he was still at school. In 1972 he took the part of Peter in the Sydney production of Andrew Lloyd-Webber and Tim Rice's *Jesus Christ Superstar*. For most of 1973, O'Donoghue worked with his band Cool Bananas, issuing the single 'Been and Gone' on the Albert label (October 1973). Cool Bananas comprised O'Donoghue, Don Reid (flute, sax), Wayne Findlay (keyboards), Stein Bottington (bass) and Rob Dearlove (drums), who was replaced by Russell Dunlop (ex-**Levi Smith's Clefs**, SCRA, Mother Earth) in time for the single.

Bond and O'Donoghue wrote all the music and lyrics on the *Aunty Jack Sings Wollongong* album and, together with Garry McDonald (harmonica), Jamie McKinley (piano), Jeff Oakes (sax), Bruce Worrall (bass) and Greg Henson (drums), played on the records. Bond, O'Donoghue, McDonald and Maurice Murphy wrote the comedy material. Another of Bond's characters on the album was Kev Kavanagh the heavy metal butcher! In May 1974, Bond and O'Donoghue formed Aunty Jack and the Gong for a successful national tour. The Gong comprised four members of Sydney funk outfit **Johnny Rocco Band** (Tony Buchanan, sax; Mark Punch, guitar; Tim Partridge, bass; and Russell Dunlop, drums), plus Ian Clyne (keyboards; ex-**Loved Ones, Levi Smith's Clefs, Chain**) and Denni Gordon (backing vocals).

The pair continued writing and performing shows, including the short-lived *The Off Show* (the one pilot episode was immediately erased when an ABC executive took offence to the 'Leave it to Jesus' theme song!), *Wollongong The Brave*, *Flash Nick From Jindavick* and the *Grahame Bond Show*. In 1980, Bond and O'Donoghue composed the music for the feature film *Fatty Finn*. That year, Bond also presented his popular stage production *Boys Own McBeth* with help from musical director Red Symons (ex-**Skyhooks**). In May 1984, Bond staged the rock'n'roll comedy show *Captain Bloody*. Shock Records reissued *Aunty Jack Sings Wollongong* on CD in May 1996 with a bonus disc containing previously unissued material.

Album: *Aunty Jack Sings Wollongong* (Polydor, 1974; reissued on Shock in 1996), *Boys Own McBeth* (Dunsinan, 1980).

The Bondi Cigars

Formed: *1989*
Style: *R&B*
Original line-up: *Shane Pacey (vocals, guitar; ex-U-Turn,* **Foreday Riders***), Leszek Karski (guitar, vocals; ex-Supercharge,* **Hippos***), Alan Britton (bass; ex-***Dynamic Hepnotics, Foreday Riders***), Ace Follington (drums; ex-***Chain***, Australia,* **Hippos***)*

The term 'Bondi Cigar' is a colloquialism for those brown nasties that are flushed into the sea, to float around the surf off Sydney's famous Bondi Beach. Rather than aspiring to such pong-inducing depths, Sydney band The Bondi Cigars is actually one of the great blues/R&B outfits of the 1990s.

The band's energetic, no-frills, bar-room blues (in the Buddy Guy/B.B. King/Albert Collins vein) have found many devotees. The Bondi Cigars started out in late 1989 as a temporary diversion for the musicians from their own bands. The combination worked so well that The Bondi Cigars began touring and recording on a regualar basis. Declan Kelly (ex-Beefs) replaced Follington in 1991 in time for the band's second album, *Bad Weather Blues* (June 1992). The band issued a third album, *After Closing Time*, in late 1995. Les Karski left in 1996.

Pacey also issued an album *Got the News* (1993) under the moniker Shane Pacey and the Cigars. The line-up comprised Pacey, Britton, Clayton Doley (organ; ex-Double Whammy) and Matthew Morrison (drums; ex-Double Whammy). Pacey actually got his start with Sydney pop band U-Turn which also comprised Chris Fitzgibbon (vocals), George Steffe (guitar), Shane Rogers (bass) and Rob Grant (drums). U-Turn issued two singles, 'Traffic Lights'/'Long Lost Years' (June 1977) and 'One Day Love Affair' (September) plus one album, *Living in the City*, before disappearing in a cloud of indifference.

Albums: *Bondi Cigars* (ABC, 1990), *Bad Weather Blues* (Larrikin/Festival, 1992), *After Closing Time* (Larrikin/Festival, 1995).

Simon Bonney (*see* Crime and the City Solution)

Boom Crash Opera

Formed: *1985*
Style: *Rock*
Original line-up: *Dale Ryder (vocals), Peter Farnan (guitar; ex-Serious Young Insects), Greg 'Spock' O'Connor (keyboards), Richard Pleasance (bass; ex-Government Drums, Bang), Peter Maslen (drums; ex-One Hand Clapping)*

Almost from its inception in 1985, Boom Crash Opera was the subject of competition between major record companies in a bid to snare the band. Boom Crash Opera eventually signed to WEA with immediate results.

Peter Farnan had been a member of quirky, three-piece Melbourne new wave band Serious Young Insects. Michael Vallance (bass, vocals) and Mark White (drums, vocals) completed the line-up. That band issued one album, *Housebreaking*, and three singles, 'Trouble Understanding Words'/'On Time' (June 1981), 'Be Patient'/'Nerve' (May 1982) and 'Faraway Places'/'Music to Watch Girls By' (September) on the Native Tongue label (through Epic) before breaking up.

Farnan and Richard Pleasance then formed Boom Crash Opera in Melbourne with Peter Maslen, Greg O'Connor and newcomer Dale Ryder. Ryder became a pin-up idol, and it seemed Boom Crash Opera would become a case of contrived form over substance. The band's first two exuberant singles, 'Great Wall'/'Caught Between Two Towns' (#7 in May 1986) and 'Hands Up in the Air'/'Leave' (#11 in August) put paid to that when each hit the national Top 20. The singles established the hallmarks of the Boom Crash Opera sound: the tight, funky rock of the music, the boom-like crack of the drums and the work song chant of the vocals.

American Alex Sadkin (Grace Jones, James Brown, Simply Red, Talking Heads) produced the band's eponymous debut album, which came out in September 1987. Sadkin was killed in a motor accident in Nassau immediately following the completion of *Boom Crash Opera*. 'City Flat'/'Spirit of Progress' (July 1987), 'Her Charity'/'Face that I'm Living in' (September) and 'Love Me to Death'/'Bombshell' (February 1988) were minor hits, while the album peaked at #17 in November.

These Here are Crazy Times (October 1989) reached #7 on the national chart in November, and yielded the hits 'Onion Skin'/'Rocks in My Head' (#11 in August), 'Get Out of the House'/'Thinking in Slow Motion' (#24 in October) and 'The Best Thing'/'Flying a Kite in the Rain' (December). *Look! Listen!* featured the jubilant 'Dancing in the Storm' (#21 in May 1990) and 'Talk About It' (#35 in July). At the end of 1990, Pleasance had to step out of the group due to health problems (tinnitus). He produced six tracks on **Deborah Conway**'s successful debut solo album, *String of Pearls*, and issued his acclaimed solo album, *Galleon*, on East West in 1991. It contained the singles 'Sarah (I Miss You)' (May) and 'Don't Cry' (August). Pleasance issued a new CD single, 'Love is All', in August 1994, followed by his second solo album, *Colour Blind*, in 1995

Various bass players stepped in to replace Pleasance: Mick Vallance, Dorian West (ex-Wildland) and finally Ian Tilley. Boom Crash Opera's only release for 1991, the *Dreams on Fire* EP ('Holy Water'), only managed #44 in December. The band started 1992 with an Australian tour support slot to Canadian singer/songwriter Bryan Adams. Keith Forsey (Simple Minds, Billy Idol) produced the next album, *Fabulous Beast* (March 1993), which could not halt the band's further chart slide. Of its three CD singles, only 'Bettadaze' (#43 in November 1992) and 'In the Morning' (#36 in April 1993) made the charts. The third single was 'This Isn't Love' (June).

'Gimme' (#14 in October 1994) and 'Tongue Tied' (#25 in February 1995), both from the fifth album *Born* (March 1995), were the band's biggest latter-day hits. *Born* was a tougher affair which found the band embracing hi-tech pop, techno-metal and all manner of sound effects and cyberpunk studio trickery. Not only did the *Born* CD feature the band's album, it also provided computer interactivity (via any CD-ROM-equipped PC or Mac) with video clips and a Boom Crash Opera discography. Two more singles came from *Born*, 'Dissemble' (April) and 'Soundtrack (So Lonely)' (June). Over the years, Boom Crash Opera's strong visual image and the uncanny ability of its principal songwriters to pen catchy, commercial songs ensured a string of successful releases.

In 1997 Farnan toured with a reformed version of **The Master's Apprentices**. Ryder also took time out to play Frank N. Furter in the Australian and Hong Kong stage productions of *The Rocky Horror Show*. As a four-piece (Farnan, Ryder, Maslen and Tilley), Boom Crash Opera issued a new single 'Dreaming Up a Fire' in September 1997. The single saw a return to the rock-solid rhythms that had driven the band's early hits. It was lifted from the album *Gizmo Mantra* (November).

Albums: *Boom Crash Opera* (WEA, 1987), *These Here are Crazy Times* (WEA, 1989), *Look! Listen!* (WEA, 1990), *Fabulous Beast* (East West/Warners, 1993), *Born* (BMG, 1995). *Gizmo Mantra* (BMG, 1997).

The Bootleg Family Band

Formed: *1973*
Style: *Pop rock*
Original line-up: *Tony Naylor (guitar; ex-Ida May Mack,* **Band of Talabene***), Brian Fitzgerald (keyboards), Russell Smith (trumpet; ex-***Ram Jam Big Band, Levi Smith's Clefs***), Gus Fenwick (bass; ex-***Healing Force***), Geoff Cox (drums), Angela Jones (vocals), Penny Dyer (vocals), Louise Lincoln (vocals)*

Singer/songwriter **Brian Cadd** formed The Bootleg Family Band with the express purpose of having them back himself and other artists on his Bootleg label. The enterprise was drawn along similar lines to that employed by American singer/producer Leon Russell when he gathered together all-star ensembles for such tours and albums as Joe Cocker's *Mad Dogs and Englishmen* and *Leon Russell and the Shelter People* (on his own Shelter label). If not quite so grandiose and overblown in its execution, the Bootleg Family venture was successful.

The band had its own Top 5 hit singles with covers of Loggins and Messina's 'Your Mama Don't Dance'/'Honky Tonk Woman' (February 1973) and Betty Everett's 'Shoop Shoop Song'/'Walking Home in the Morning' (July 1974). The singles were combined for the four-track *Bootleg Family Band* EP (February 1975). There were two more Bootleg Family Band singles: 'Wake Up Australia'/'Ballad of Billy Clover' (June 1973) and 'Green Door'/'Kenny' (February 1975).

The band toured the USA with **Brian Cadd** in 1974. Cadd and The Bootleg Family Band were the first Australian artists to perform on the American television shows *Midnight Special* and Don Kirshner's *Rock Concert*. In May 1975, however, the extended Bootleg Family Band line-up was trimmed back to a four-piece known as The Bootleg Band which was used for touring purposes only: Naylor, Cox, Ian Mason (keyboards, ex-Mason's Cure) and Clive Harrison (bass; ex-**Kush**). The Bootleg Band issued a single, 'How Do I Try?'/'Rockin' Hollywood' (October 1975). When Cadd moved to the States at the end of 1975, Mason left and the others reconvened as **Avalanche**.

Bored!

Formed: *1987*
Style: *Punk rock*
Original line-up: *Dave Thomas (guitar, vocals; ex-Bodies, Slaughter House), John Nolan (guitar; ex-Behind The Magnolia Curtain), Adrian Hann (keyboards), Grant Gardner (bass), Justin 'Buzz' Munday (drums)*

Seminal Geelong guitar band Bored! was at the forefront of that Victoria harbourside city's push to make a mark on the Australian independent scene. In the wake of Bored!'s gut-level and explosive approach to music making, the Geelong floodgates opened to spawn the likes of **The Sunset Strip**, **The Dirty Lovers**, Seaweed Goorillas, Amba Fear, Poppin' Mommas, Warped, She Freak, **Magic Dirt**, **Automatic** and Food, all garage rock exponents of considerable power and conviction.

Dave Thomas had been a member of Geelong punk band Bodies (circa 1983), and in 1985 played with Melbourne band Slaughter House which comprised Mike Chrystal (guitar; ex-**Gas Babies**, White Elephants), Mark Ivey (vocals; ex-White Elephants), Geoff Martyr (bass; ex-Sick Things) and Jim Smith (drums; ex-White Elephants). Thomas put the first version of what became Bored! together in late 1986. For the first year, the band was variously known as International Rescue, Sister Anne or White Noise. When the line-up stabilised with Thomas, Nolan, Munday, Gardner and Hann, the band settled on Bored!. Thomas dispensed with the keyboards to concentrate on a finely honed, guitar-heavy, punk/metal hybrid. The band's influences ranged from **The Saints**, **Radio Birdman**, **Coloured Balls**, **AC/DC** and **Rose Tattoo** to The Stooges, MC5, the Sex Pistols, Black Sabbath, Mudhoney, Motorhead and Blue Cheer. The band's name was derived from a song by US band Destroy All Monsters.

The band's self-titled mini-album (on Grown

Up Wrong, October 1988) included a cover of **Coloured Balls'** 'Human Being'. *Bored!* was issued in Germany on the Glitterhouse label. The single 'Little Suzie'/'Heartbreaker' came out in the USA on the Sympathy for the Record Industry label. Dog Meat Records issued *Negative Waves* and the single 'Satisfaction'/'Round and Round', 'You Make Me Sick' in October 1989. The album included a hot wired cover of **AC/DC**'s 'Whole Lotta Rosie', which was also included on the Various Artists tribute album *Used and Recovered By . . .* (1990). The title *Negative Waves* was taken from a line in Gary Young's (not the **Daddy Cool** drummer) cult biker/road movie *Cosy Cool*. Around that time, Bored! also appeared on a single by studio band Sabotage (brainchild of ex-**God** guitarist Joel Silbersher): 'Take Some Drugs Tonight'/'Search and Destroy'. By late 1989, Tim Hemensley (ex-Royal Flush, **God**) had taken over from Gardner. Hemensley added much to the band's charisma and sense of arrogance. The new line-up recorded *Take It Out on You* (issued on Glitterhouse in Germany) and toured Europe in 1990.

As soon as Bored! returned to Australia, Nolan and Hemensley split to form **Powder Monkeys**. Thomas recruited bassist Russell Baricevic (ex-**Gas Babies**, Macho Clowns) and concentrated on a more stripped-down punk rock attack. During 1991, Tas Blizzard, from fellow Geelong band Seaweed Goorillas, filled in for Thomas when he was unable to play guitar due to a broken arm. Survival Records issued the albums *Feed the Dog* (1991), *Junk* (1992) and *Scuzz* (March 1993), plus the single 'People Say' (November 1991). **The Celibate Rifles'** guitarist, Kent Steedman, produced eight of the tracks on *Junk* and **Peter Wells** produced four. *Scuzz* mopped up nine live tracks and 13 studio outtakes.

Bored! contributed the tracks 'There's a Lot of It Going Around' (by Melbourne punk band **The Chosen Few**) and 'Descender' to Thomas' 1992 Geelong compilation *Check this Action . . . Let the Fun Begin* on his own Destroyer label. By that stage, Bored! was on its last legs, and eventually broke up in 1993. Thomas has always been an enormous influence on, and source of encouragement for, young bands on the Geelong independent scene. Through his tireless efforts over the years he did much to foster the growth of that scene. He lived in Europe for a year, and on his return in 1995 joined fellow Geelong band **Magic Dirt**. Following his 18-month tenure with that band, Thomas re-formed Bored! during November 1997. Baricevic, Munday and new member Matt Randall (rhythm guitar; ex-Trigger) completed the line-up.

Albums: *Bored!* (mini-album; Grown Up Wrong, 1988), *Negative Waves* (Dogmeat, 1989), *Take It Out on You* (mini-album; Dogmeat, 1990), *Feed the Dog* (Survival, 1991), *Junk* (Survival, 1992), *Scuzz* (Survival, 1993).

Kevin Borich Express

Formed: *1976*
Style: *Hard rock, blues*
Original line-up: *Kevin Borich (guitar, vocals; ex-***La De Das, John Paul Young** *and the All Stars), Harry Brus (bass; ex-Amazons,* **Jeff St John's** *Copperwine,* **Blackfeather***), Barry Harvey (drums; ex-Thursday's Children,* **Wild Cherries, Chain***)*

New Zealand-born Kevin Borich is one of the most celebrated guitar players in the history of Australian rock. He also remains an underrated songwriter, and his live reputation has rarely been reflected in record sales despite producing strong releases down the years. He spent 11 years with **La De Das,** and a short spell with **John Paul Young** and the All Stars during 1975 before forming the first version of his Kevin Borich Express in early 1976. The original line-up listed above was short-lived. The only recording that line-up put down, 'The End of Me', later turned up on the Various Artists compilation *Australian Guitar Album* (Razzle/Festival, 1979), which also featured **Lobby Loyde, Mario Millo, Ian Moss, Phil Manning, Rockwell T. James,** Chris Turner, Mick Elliott, Russell Smith, Ian Miller and Harvey James.

Reuben San Fiansco (bass) and Gil Matthews (drums; ex-**Billy Thorpe** and the Aztecs) then replaced Harry Brus and Barry Harvey. Matthews stayed for only a handful of gigs before returning to The Aztecs, so in July 1976 John Annas (drums; ex-Atlas, **Wendy Saddington** Band) joined. The Express issued its scorching debut single, 'Goin' Somewhere'/'Scene from Starcrossed Lovers', on Image in October 1976. Tim Partridge (ex-Clockwork Oringe, Island, **Mighty Kong, Johnny Rocco Band**) took over from San Fiansco and the new line-up completed the debut album, *Celebration!* Issued in March 1977, the album produced a second single, 'Goin' Down Town' (single edit)/'Going Down Town' (May).

Celebration! peaked at #28 on the national chart, and was the perfect showcase for Borich's exceptional blues-based heavy rock technique. It contained the seven-minute, guitar tour-de-force 'Celebration' which boasted some of the most dazzling fretwork Borich has ever committed to vinyl. Borich earned further accolades when he jammed with international visitors like Carlos Santana and

Ritchie Blackmore. Kevin Borich Express also supported UK guitar legend Jeff Beck in early 1977, and took part in the ambitious Rockarena tour (October 1977) supporting Fleetwood Mac, Santana and the Little River Band.

Lonely One (November 1977) and the singles 'Tango Queen'/'I Just Wanna Love You' (also November) and 'Tell Me Why'/'White Ship' (February 1978) were less supercharged affairs. By that stage, Borich had set his sights on the USA and the album featured a very polished production sound which tended to gloss over his guitar playing. By the time the album came out, Partridge had been replaced by American Tim Ayers and then Bob Jackson. Before Kevin Borich Express left for the USA in May 1978, Paul Christie (ex-Loose Booty) had replaced Jackson.

In the USA, the band toured (including an opening spot for AC/DC), added American keyboard player Tim Schafer (ex-Gary Wright Band) to the line-up and recorded a new album, *No Turning Back*, at Cherokee Studios, Los Angeles. *No Turning Back* (March 1979) included the singles 'No Turning Back'/'I Can't Wait' (November 1978), 'Mama is a Jazza'/'Social Disease' (March 1979) and 'Silver Dime'/'Caught in the Middle' (June 1979). In April 1979, Schafer and Christie left. Lindsay Osbourne came in temporarily until Tim Partridge rejoined on bass. The Borich/Partridge/Annas line-up recorded *Live!*, appeared on Renée Geyer's album *Blues License* (July 1979) and toured Europe. A compilation album of tracks from *Lonely One* and *No Turning Back* came out in Germany, and the Express appeared on Munich television. Following the overseas tour, Annas left to be replaced by John Watson. The Express line-up of Borich, Partridge and Watson recorded a new album, *Angel's Hand*, in London with English producer Chris Tsangarides during November 1979. Partridge left in April 1980 and Michael Deep joined.

Angel's Hand (November 1980) and the single 'One More Dream'/'Angel's Hand' (also November) featured a tough rock sound, and were the first Express records for the Mushroom label. The Express line-up of Borich, Watson and Deep collaborated with bluesman Dutch Tilders on the album *The Blues Had a Baby* (issued November 1980) and single 'Bad Books'/'The Blues Had a Baby' (April 1981). For the 10-inch mini-album *Shy Boys/Shy Girls* (November 1981) and the singles 'Shy Boys, Shy Girls'/'Going Fishing' (also November) and 'Getting So Excited'/'Theme X' (February 1982), ex-Dragon drummer Kerry Jacobson had replaced Watson.

John Annas returned to the fold in mid-1982. Steve Balbi (ex-Rupert B.) replaced Deep on bass, and Andy Cowan (keyboards; ex-Madder Lake, Ayers Rock) also joined. By mid-1984, the line-up was back to a trio of Borich, Balbi and Adrian Cannon (drums; ex-Full Circle). That line-up recorded three songs, 'Fever', 'World's on Fire' and 'Slinky'. Borich issued 'World's on Fire/'Slinky' as a solo single in October 1986. 'Fever' remained unissued until it and 'World's on Fire' were included on the 1993 compilation album *Kevin Borich Collection*. Borich put the Express on hold in 1985. He did not stop touring, however, and spent most of the 1980s in Paul Christie's band The Party Boys. He joined the Jimmy Barnes Band for the 1990 Two Fires tour of Australia and New Zealand.

Borich has reactivated the Express on several occasions throughout the 1990s. John Annas and Ian Lees (bass; ex-Moving Pictures) have been members, but the strongest line-up featured John Watson and Harry Brus. Although Borich has not had a solo record deal since his days with Mushroom, he remains one of the most accomplished guitar players in the country. He issued the independent, mail-order album *Live at the Big Kahuna* in 1995.

Albums: *Celebration!* (Image, 1977), *Lonely One* (Image, 1977), *No Turning Back* (Mercury, 1979), *Live!* (Avenue/Festival, 1979), *Best of Kevin Borich Express* (Avenue/Festival, 1980), *Angel's Hand* (Mushroom/Festival, 1980), *Rock Legends* (reissue of *No Turning Back*, Mercury, 1980), *Shy Boys/Shy Girls* (10-inch mini-album, Mushroom/Festival, 1981), *Kevin Borich Collection* (Mushroom/Festival, 1993), *Live at the Big Kahuna* (KB, 1995), *Going Down Town* (reissue of *Celebration* and *Lonely One*, Avenue/EMI, 1996); ***With Renée Geyer:*** *Blues License* (RCA, 1979); ***Borich'n'Tilders album:*** *The Blues Had a Baby* (Eureka, 1980).

Boss (*see* B.B. Steal)

Lindsay Bourke

Style: *Classical, ambient*

Lindsay Bourke (b. 1945) was a German-descended, classically trained musician, painter and poet. His earliest musical influences ranged from Beethoven, Chopin and Mahler to Bob Dylan. In 1966, he held his first solo painting exhibition in a small North Sydney gallery, and gave the first mixed media (sight and sound) show in Sydney at the Cell Block Theatre. As a solo organist (backed by his own quadraphonic sound system and light show), Bourke played concerts during 1969 alongside celebrated underground band **Tully** and jazz pianist John Sangster. In 1970, noted German experimentalist Karl-Heinz Stockhausen invited Bourke to stay with him in Germany.

Following his well-publicised concert at the Sydney Town Hall, 'Homage to Beethoven', Bourke issued his own custom-pressed album *Wilderness Awakening* in 1971.The entire album had been composed and played by Bourke. It was basically a piano improvisation in five movements: 'Discovery', 'Contemplation', 'Joy', 'Absorption' and 'Being'. In September of that year, Bourke toured Australia as support to international visitors Pink Floyd.

During that period, Bourke also composed and recorded the soundtrack to an obscure, 11-minute silent feature made by film-maker Chris Löfven. Called *The Beginning* (and loosely influenced by the book *Chariots of the Gods*), the film depicted a peaceful, New Age hippie society set in an indeterminate time and space being visited by extraterrestrial life. Bourke's heavy organ score gave the film a chilling ambience, which only enhanced the more bizarre aspects of this fascinating underground film venture. In 1975, an artist called Lindsay Blue issued an independently pressed album *Love All Life*. Although the true identity of Blue has always been shrouded in mystery, it is likely that it was Bourke under a pseudonym. By today's parlance, *Love All Life* would be classified as ambient or New Age relaxation music, with its emphasis on electronic instrumentation and natural sounds. There was also a distinct religious leaning in tracks like 'Rejoice in the Kingdoms', 'Praise the Creator' and 'Love All Life'.

Albums: *Wilderness Awakening* (Spore/AAVR Custom, 1971); ***As Lindsay Blue:*** *Love All Life* (Custom pressing, 1975).

The Bo-Weevils

Formed: *1985*
Style: *Garage rock*
Original line-up: *Ian Hill (vocals, keyboards, guitar; ex-Fizzpops,* **Crackajacks**, **Olympic Sideburns**, *Big Fans of Jesus), Steve Anderson (guitar), Neil Rogers (bass), Mark Jenkinson (drums)*

This Melbourne combo was one of the first Australian bands of the 1980s to play wild, 1960s-inspired garage-punk (alongside the likes of **Wet Taxis** and **The Lime Spiders**). During their formative years (in true garage band fashion), the band members were barely able to play their instruments, but that did not put a dampener on their enthusiasm. Over the course of 12 years, the band embraced a more varied approach by incorporating psychedelic and hard rock elements.

Ian Hill and Neil Rogers formed the band in early 1985. The Bo-Weevils shared stages around inner-city Melbourne pubs with other 1960s-influenced bands like **Shindiggers**, plus harder-edged outfits like **Cosmic Psychos**, **Ku Klux Frankenstein**, **Exploding White Mice** and Pizza Sluts. The Bo-Weevils' early singles on Kavern 7, 'Lies', 'Come on Back'/'You Drive Me Wild', 'All I Want' (August 1986) and 'That Girl'/'I Want You' (November), showed their garage-punk roots. Hill and Anderson left to be replaced by Davern White (keyboards, guitar, vocals; ex-Undecided) and Nino Spadaro (guitar, vocals) in April 1987. The mini-album *The Vortex Took Them* (March 1988) continued in the same garage vein.

Where Particular People Congregate (March 1989), *Destroyer of Worlds* (May 1990), the live *If God was an Astronaut* (August 1992) and the singles 'Middle of Nowhere'/'Cheap Wine' (March 1991) and 'Jay's Song'/'I was Young', 'Grandmaster of Disaster' (September 1991) saw the band stretching out under the influence of Green on Red, the Rain Parade and other roots-rock influenced contemporary American outfits. *Reap* (October 1992), *Burn* (November 1995) and the 'Into Sunshine' CD EP were straight-ahead, guitar rock releases. The compilation *Trapped in the Garage* (December 1996) drew together the band's early garage-band material. Ian Hill rejoined for a tour in early 1997 to promote the compilation.

White has moonlighted with **The Breadmakers**, The Way Gone Frantics and A.1 Mining Company (with Rogers). Likewise, Hill, Jenkinson and Spadaro (plus bassist Theresa Hambrook) formed The Fizzleheads, and have issued two albums, *The Fizzleheads* (1993) and *Shoot the Stars* (1994).

Albums: *The Vortex Took Them* (mini-album; Kavern 7, 1987), *Where Particular People Congregate* (Mr Spaceman, 1989), *Destroyer of Worlds* (Mr Spaceman, 1990), *If God was an Astronaut* (Rubber, 1992), *Reap* (Rubber, 1992), *Burn* (Rubber, 1995), *Trapped in the Garage* (Corduroy, 1996).

Box of Fish

Formed: *1982*
Style: *Gothic punk*
Original line-up: *Andrew Johnson (vocals), Carol Anderson (guitar; ex-Girlfriends), Bill Quarry (bass), Craig Rossi (drums)*

Box of Fish grew out of the Sydney, inner-city punk scene of the early 1980s alongside **The Kelpies**,

World War XXIV, Vigil-Anti, What?!!, Vellocette, Queen Anne's Revenge, Wrong Kind of Stoneage and Positive Hatred. All of those bands were documented on Aberrant Records, essential 1983 punk compilation *Flowers from the Dustbin*. The Box of Fish tracks on that album were 'The Good, the Bad, the Ugly' and 'Our Father'.

The band's original name was A Box of Fish with Tartare Sauce with a drum machine providing the beat. Box of Fish came into being with the arrival of Craig Rossi in June 1982. Rossi also moonlighted with Ian Rilen's band Sardine v between July 1982 and June 1983. Box of Fish's debut single 'Sex Cat Killer'/'Erosion' on the Method label (November 1983) bears the influence of early Bauhaus, especially in Anderson's brooding vocals. Chris Royal (guitar) joined in July 1984, and the new line-up issued the mini-album *Slap 'em Around The Gills* (July 1985) which mixed grinding punk guitarwork with gothic overtones.

Box of Fish broke up in September 1985. Ross went on to join **King Snake Roost**, while Johnson and Quarry formed The Fester Brothers with Stephen 'Bones' Martin (guitar). By December, Quarry had formed Toys Went Beserk with Leslie 'Coo' Bennett (vocals, piano; ex-Lavender Disaster), Andy Jarvis (guitar; ex-Dusk Furrow), Steve (guitar) and Mark Nicholson (drums; ex-**Happy Hate Me Nots**). Toys Went Beserk derived its moniker from a lyric line in the Siouxsie and The Banshees song 'Spellbound'. The band was adept at playing powerful, noisy guitar pop.

The band contributed its first recording, 'One Day (My Head is Gonna Explode)', to the Various Artists *Trousers In Action No. 2* EP. Toys Went Beserk signed to the Aberrant label, issuing the single 'Don't Run Away'/'Guns at My Head' (October 1986) and the double 12-inch EP *Pieces* (June 1987), after which Carolyn Polley replaced Steve on guitar. Aberrant later issued *Pieces* as an album.

Toys Went Beserk issued two singles in 1988, 'No Warning'/'Inseparable' (June) and 'Forever and a Day'/'Something Better' (October). In 1989, the band issued the 12-inch single 'Have No More'/'Salvation', 'See the Man' and the album *Smiler with a Knife* (December). 'Brand New Life' was issued as a single in April 1990. Polley left to join **Big Heavy Stuff**. In August 1990, Toys Went Beserk travelled to Boston in order to record a new album with American producer Gary Smith (Throwing Muses, Pixies, The Chills) at his Fort Apache studios. The resultant album, *Sensory* (February 1991), included the powerful single 'Wheels in Motion'.

Box of Fish mini-album: *Slap 'em Around the Gills* (Method, 1985); ***Toys Went Beserk albums:*** *Smiler with a Knife* (Aberrant, 1989), *Pieces* (Aberrant, 1989), *Sensory* (Aberrant, 1991).

Box the Jesuit

Formed: *1986*
Style: *Rock*
Original line-up: *Goose (born Stephen Gray, vocals; ex-Madroom), Susie Beauchamp (violin, percussion; ex-Madroom), Patrick Kavanagh (guitar, sax, organ; ex-Smack of Jellyfish), Phillip Clifford (bass), Chris Baker (drums)*

The main protagonists in Sydney band Box the Jesuit, rambunctious frontman Goose and violinist Susie Beauchamp, had previously worked with Madroom. Madroom formed in 1981 under the influence of English bands like Joy Division, Bauhaus and the whole emergent Goth sub-culture. Braying sax and Beauchamp's discordant desecrations on the violin (sort of like The Velvet Underground on Prozac) only added to the general melee.

Madroom issued a 12-inch EP in August 1982, *Cruelty of Beauty*, and an album in 1984. The album bears one of the longest titles ever bestowed upon a record (courtesy of writer Claes Oldenburg, 1961): *I am for an art that takes its form from the lines of life itself, that twists and extends and accumulates and spits and drips and is heavy and coarse and blunt and sweet and stupid as life itself.* The album featured the line-up of Goose, Beauchamp, David Belial (bass), Kevin Lewis-Black (drums) and Kym Tonkes (guitar). The track 'The Lever' appeared on the UK compilation of Australian bands, *Beneath the Southern Cross* which also featured **Sunday Painters**,

Box the Jesuit

Whirlywirld, **Tactics**, **The Triffids** and **Severed Heads**. By October 1986, Madroom had evolved into Box the Jesuit.

Goose derived the band's name from an eighteenth century English seafaring euphemism for masturbation (the full expression was 'To box the Jesuit and get cockroaches'). As rock writer Mark Demetrius put it, Box the Jesuit was one of Australia's 'most genuinely exotic and original bands'. The band's early records, such as the mini-album *Bloody Mary* (August 1987), the 12-inch EP *Cut* (1988) and the album *Punch Out that Looney Sappy Tune* (April 1989), reflected the influence of US bands like Swans, Big Black and The Butthole Surfers.

Box the Jesuit contributed a twisted cover of **Freshwater's** 'Satan' to the Black Eye Various Artists album *Waste Sausage*, alongside the likes of **Lubricated Goat**, **Grong Grong**, The Bush Oysters, Real Fucking Idiots, Purple Vulture Shit and Smack of Jellyfish. As well as recording a live performance for the Japanese television rock show *Rock Around The World*, Box the Jesuit supported the likes of **Nick Cave and the Bad Seeds** and Chicago band Big Black.

Box the Jesuit contributed 'The Buckle and the Beard' to the Timberyard Various Artists yuletide album *Rockin' Bethlehem* (December 1989). The line-up on the October 1990 album *Murdercycle* and its single 'Angel Flame'/'Whore Me' was Goose, Beauchamp, Kavanagh, Clifford, Stuart Olsen (drums, guitar) and new member John Murphy (drums; ex-Whirlywirld, Slub, No, **Max Q**). With the release of the album, Paul Stothard (ex-Bird Dissolves) replaced Kavanagh on guitar.

In 1991, Goose and Beauchamp collaborated with singer Victoria as Ripe for You; they issued one 12-inch EP which included a cover of Noosha Fox's 1970s hit 'S-S-S-Single Bed' backed with 'Cocksure' and 'Topless Mother of Eight'. The results mixed electronic effects with glam sleaze. By 1993, Box the Jesuit had evolved into a flat-out hard rock band, with rootsy Chicago blues clashing headlong with the obligatory avant-garde noise. The band's fourth and last album, *Guide Dogs for the Spiritually Impaired* (July 1993), even included a cover of Mott the Hoople's 'Roll Away the Stone', plus Goose's swansong 'You've Got to Know Your Limitations'. The line-up included Goose, Beauchamp, Clifford, Nathan Keating (drums) and Paul Wonderlick (aka Stothard; guitar).

The flamboyant Goose always entertained audiences with his melodramatic, theatrical performances. For the band's Stark Raving Elvis extravaganzas, Goose would don full Elvis Presley garb, replete with spangled jumpsuits and capes. He died on 1 August 1993 following a long battle with lymphoma. Ben Brown from fellow Sydney outfit **Hellmenn** filled in as frontman for Box the Jesuit initially, until Goose's brother Martin took over permanently. The band continued as Guide Dogs for the Spiritually Impaired. By 1995, the band had run its course.

Albums: *Bloody Mary* (Snoyd, 1987), *Punch Out that Looney Sappy Tune* (Timberyard, 1989), *Murdercycle* (Timberyard, 1990), *Guide Dogs for the Spiritually Impaired* (Kosmic Ganda/Siren, 1993).

Boxcar

Formed: *1986*
Style: *Electronic dance pop*
Original line-up: *David Smith (vocals, guitar, keyboards), Carole Rohde (vocals, keyboards; ex-Ironing Music)*

When musicians David Smith and Carole Rohde formed dance band Boxcar, the intention was to combine noise with a beat, technology with a decent song, along the lines of UK experimentalists Cabaret Voltaire and local electronic heroes **Severed Heads**. The fact that the band hailed from Brisbane, Queensland (a city not known for its electronic heritage) did not deter them in their quest.

Smith and Rohde recruited Brett Mitchell (keyboards) and Crispin Trist (percussion) and began playing live on a regular basis. The band made little headway, mostly due to a general lack of interest in electronic dance-pop within the rock milieu, rather than any lack of talent on the musicians' part. Boxcar came to the attention of Sydney-based independent label Volition, who issued the band's debut, 12-inch single 'Freemason'/'Comet' in November 1988. The single was unfairly dismissed by critics as too derivative of New Order, but it took off in the dance clubs. When issued in the USA on Arista, 'Freemason' had been remixed by New York dance maestro Arthur Baker. It reached #8 on the American *Billboard* dance chart, a first for an Australian band, let alone one virtually unknown in its homeland. The band's US follow-up, 'Insect', fared almost as well when issued at the start of 1990.

For its debut album on Volition, *Vertigo*, the band utilised the services of redoubtable DJ/mixmaster/producer (the late) Robert Racic. *Vertigo* (November 1990) was a very accessible collision of sound, song and dance beats. Reference points were many, ranging from New Order (without being a rip-off), Yello, Future Sound of London and **Severed**

Heads. 'Gas Stop (Who Do You Think You Are?)' (October 1990) and 'Lelore' (March 1991) were all issued as singles: 'Gas Stop (Who Do You Think You Are?) made the Top 20 (#13) on the American *Billboard* dance chart. The band's second album, *Revision* (December 1992), featured one new track 'Ultrasonic' plus nine remixes from the debut. 'Hit & Run' appeared as a single in October.

In 1992, founder member Rohde and percussionist Trist left the band to be replaced by Stewart Lawler (keyboards). Boxcar was in heavy demand as remixers for bands as diverse as **Single Gun Theory** ('I Am What I Am', 1992), **Severed Heads** ('Tingler', 1992; 'Heart of the Party', 1994), **Models** ('I Hear Motion', 1993) and **Falling Joys** ('Amen', 1994). In 1994 the band played the Boiler Room on the national Big Day Out tour, and signed a new international deal with Dave Stewart's Anxious label.

Boxcar issued the CD EPs 'Universal Hymn' and 'What Are You So Happy About?' in 1994. At the end of the year, the band recorded a version of **AC/DC**'s 'Highway to Hell' for inclusion on Polydor's tribute album *For Those About to Rock: We Salute AC/DC*. Boxcar's second album proper, *Algorhythm*, came out in late 1994. It was another modern-sounding album without being too clean or sterile. Lisa Maxwell and Amanda Brown (ex-**Go-Betweens**) contributed lead vocals alongside Smith. Boxcar supported UK visitors The Grid and M People on Australian tours. At the start of 1996, Boxcar signed a new deal in the UK with Pulse8 Records for the release of an overseas version of *Algorhythm* plus the single 'People Get High'.

Albums: *Vertigo* (Volition/Sony, 1990), *Revision* (Volition/Sony, 1992), *Algorhythm* (Volition/Sony, 1994).

The Boys

Formed: *1978*
Style: *Hard rock*
Original line-up: *Brent Lucanus (vocals), Lino del Roio (guitar) Camillo del Roio (guitar), Robbie Salpietro (bass), Tony Cimino (drums)*

Guitar-playing siblings Lino and Camillo del Roio formed The Boys in Perth while still at high school. Originally known as Rockhouse Corporation, the band's punchy and appealing brand of hard rock (somewhere between early **AC/DC** and **The Angels**) attracted a fanatical following in Perth. The Boys were often able to pull 1000 fans to their pub gigs.

Carmelo Sallazzo replaced original drummer Tony Cimino in 1979. Festival signed the band and issued the singles 'You Better Move on'/'Schoolgirls' (June, 1980) and 'When You're Lonely'/'It Doesn't Matter' (August 1980) on the Parole label. 'When You're Lonely' reached #1 on the Perth charts and attracted interest in the eastern states. The band toured Melbourne and Sydney in 1981. Meanwhile, Frank Celenza replaced Sallazzo on drums. In November 1981, Festival issued the album *The Boys* which yielded two further singles, 'Hurt Me Babe'/'Coming Home' (March) and 'Weoh Weoh Weoh'/'One Way' (September).

At the end of 1981, The Boys supported **AC/DC** at Perth's Entertainment Centre. Paul McCarthy replaced Brent Lucanus as frontman, only to be replaced by Wayne Green in early 1982. *Inside the Cage* (November 1982) and the singles 'Don't Say No'/'Why'd Ya Do That?' (September) and 'Lonely Dreamers'/'Cold Mind' (March 1983) failed to match the success of the band's earlier releases. Nevertheless, with the release of the album, The Boys supported UK heavy metal visitors Iron Maiden on that band's November 1982 Australian tour. The Boys broke up in 1983. Lino and Camillo, with Celenza, resurrected The Boys in 1987 with a new line-up of Tony Celiberti (keyboards), Eddie Parise (bass) and Tony Newman (vocals). The Boys became Boyschool in 1988, but a year later had broken up. Celenza and Parise moved on to **Baby Animals**.

Albums: *The Boys* (Festival/Parole, 1981), *Inside the Cage* (Festival/Parole, 1982).

The Boys Next Door (*see* The Birthday Party)

Mike Brady

Style: *Pop*

Mike Brady (b. 1948) is one of the most successful songwriters in the history of Australian pop, although his biggest hit appealed to football fans rather than strictly music fans. During the 1960s, English-born singer/guitarist Mike Brady carved out a career as a member of **The Phantoms**, **M.P.D. Limited**, **Johnny Young's** Kompany and The Mike Brady Group. In 1970 he signed to Fable Records as a soloist and issued the singles Rare Bird's 'Sympathy'/'Look at Me' (November 1970) and 'Oh Lord, Why Lord'/'I Have Changed' (August 1971).

Throughout the 1970s, Brady concentrated on writing and recording commercials. In 1979 Brady wrote a commercial for the Seven Network in Melbourne. The one-minute commercial was to help promote Seven's television coverage of the Victoria Football League (VFL) season. Brady recorded the rousing 'Up There Cazaly' (centred around 1930s footballer Roy Cazaly) with his partner Peter Sullivan. Brady and Sullivan reworked the song and issued it as a single on Fable (June 1979) under the name of The Two Man Band. It hit #1 and eventually sold over 280 000 copies.

Brady returned to his recording career and issued the album *Invisible Man* and singles 'Dreamer'/'How Does It Feel?' (February 1980), 'The Cube'/'The Headless Horsemen' (September 1981; credited to Mike Brady and the Cubettes) and 'You're Here to Win'/'Advance Australia Fair' (July 1982). Subsequent Two Man Band singles have included 'One Day in September'/'Look up in the Sky' (September 1980), 'There's a Little Bit Of Cazaly in Us All'/'Twenty Five Years in the Outer' (June 1981) and 'We're Gonna Grab that Cup'/'Hobart' (August 1983). Brady moved into writing soundtrack music for the feature films *Blue Fire Lady* (1977) and *The Club* (1980). In 1980, Brady also produced, published and released (on his Full Moon label) the **Joe Dolce** Music Theatre's single 'Shaddap You Face'. The single reached #1 in Australia during November, #1 in the UK during February 1981 and went on to sell over three million copies worldwide.

In 1994, Brady collaborated with **Greg Champion** to write sports-related songs. The collaboration resulted in three CD singles on the Massive label (credited to **Greg Champion** and the Music Men) 'Shane Warne'/'Our Don Bradman', 'We Want a Wicket!' and 'That's the Thing About Football' (co-written with **Paul Kelly**). 'That's the Thing About Football' was heard regularly as part of the Seven Network's coverage of games during the Australian Football League (AFL) season.

Albums: *Invisible Man* (Full Moon, 1980), *The Songs of Football's Greatest Sons* (Full Moon, 1981), *Up There* (Full Moon, 1982), *Winners and Sinners* (Full Moon, 1994).

The Brady Bunch Lawnmower Massacre (*see* The Band Who Shot Liberty Valance)

Daryl Braithwaite

Style: *Pop, rock*

Singer Daryl Braithwaite (b. 1949) has proven his resilience by overcoming several major setbacks during his career. Such extraordinary lows, among the highs, would have finished a lesser performer. Born in Melbourne, Braithwaite moved to Sydney in the mid-1960s where he fronted a succession of pop bands: Bright Lights, House of Bricks and Samael Lilith.

He got his first big break when he joined **Sherbet** in early 1970. **Sherbet** went on to become one of the country's biggest bands over the next ten years. In March 1973, Braithwaite took the lead role in the local stage production of The Who's rock opera *Tommy*. Other cast members included **Billy Thorpe, Linda George, Colleen Hewett, Broderick Smith, Doug Parkinson, Jim Keays** and Keith Moon. Although the show was only staged twice, it helped facilitate Braithwaite's subsequent solo career.

Over the next six years, Braithwaite enjoyed seven solo hit singles: 'You're My World'/'Princess' (#1 in November 1974), 'Cavalry'/'Simple Song' (#10 in September 1975), 'Old Sid'/'Time' (#5 in May 1976), 'Love Has No Pride'/'Fly Away' (#4 in April 1977), The Small Faces's 'Afterglow (Of Your Love)'/'Let's Go Dancing' (#29 in October 1977), 'If You Walked Away'/'I'm Feeling Lonely' (#14 in June 1978) and 'Why Do I Break It Up?'/'See' (#35 in January 1979). During that time, Braithwaite won the *TV Week* King of Pop Award twice (1975 and 1976) but did not leave **Sherbet** as had been rumoured. His last two solo singles to that time 'Love Like a Child'/'Slowed Down' (September 1979) and 'Prove Your Love'/'Lips That Taste Like Wine' (January 1980) were minor hits.

Following the break-up of **Sherbet** in 1984, Braithwaite spent several years reassessing his position. He hit an all-time low when he was forced to go on to the dole, and then had to work as a labourer on a road gang for Bulla Shire Council. With the help of managers Nathan Brenner and Simon Fenner, plus producer Simon Hussey, Braithwaite found his feet, signed to CBS/Sony and issued the album *Edge* in November 1988.

Braithwaite had already made a strong comeback with his national #1 hit single 'As the Days Go By'/'In My Life' (September 1988). *Edge*, however, straggled around the lower reaches of the national Top 20 for several months before finally attaining the #1 spot in June. It went on to become CBS/Sony's biggest selling Australian album to that time, and produced three more hit singles in the process: 'All I Do'/'Promised Land' (#12 in December 1988), 'One Summer'/'Pretending to Care' (#8 in April 1989) and 'Let Me Be'/'It's All in the

Music' (#26 in June). The album and its singles certainly captured a wonderful summer-filled mood, and a sense of freedom and happiness. Braithwaite's 1989 touring band comprised John Housden (lead guitar), Michael Spiby (rhythm guitar, vocals), Laurence Maddick (keyboards; ex-**Strange Tenants**), Stephen O'Prey (bass) and John Corniola (drums).

Braithwaite formed a new touring line-up that included guitarist Chuck Hargreaves. His second #1 album, *Rise* (July 1991), produced two further hit singles, 'Rise' (#23 in December 1990) and a cover of Rickie Lee Jones' 'The Horses' (#1 in May 1991). The next three singles, 'Don't Hold Back Your Love', 'Scarred' and 'Nothing to Lose', were not chart successes. 'The Horses' was the fourth biggest selling single in Australia for 1991, and was named Song of the Year at the 1991 Australian Music Awards. *Rise* attained triple platinum status (over 210 000 copies sold) and became the biggest selling album in Australia for 1991.

That was to be Braithwaite's commercial peak, because of the singles lifted from *Taste the Salt* (December 1993), only 'The World as It Is' managed to reach the national Top 50 (#35 in November 1993). *Taste the Salt* was Braithwaite's least successful album, having sold less than 30 000 copies. Its three other singles were 'Barren Ground' (January 1994), 'Breaking the Rules' (March) and 'Higher than Hope' (with **Tommy Emmanuel**). *Six Moons: The Best of Daryl Braithwaite 1988–1994* (November 1994) produced one new song, 'How Can I Be Sure?' which was issued as a single (October).

The glow was further taken off his achievements by legal action that culminated in a Supreme Court judge ruling in favour of his two former business associates, Nathan Brenner and Simon Fenner, who had claimed they were owed $600 000. Mr Justice Byrne ruled that they were entitled to $57 446 and Braithwaite had to pay court costs estimated at $500 000. Undaunted, Braithwaite hosted a television special called *Dreams Can Come True* for the Ten Network in 1995. Then, in 1996, at the age of 48, Braithwaite scored a role in the Australian production of the Tim Rice/Björn Ulvaeus and Benny Andersson collaboration *Chess.*

Albums: *Daryl Braithwaite . . . Best of* (Razzle/Festival, 1978), *Out on the Fringe* (Razzle/Festival, 1979), *Edge* (CBS/Sony, 1988), *Rise* (CBS/Sony, 1990), *Taste the Salt* (Sony, 1993), *Six Moons: The Best of Daryl Braithwaite 1988–1994* (Sony, 1994).

The Breadmakers

Formed: *1989*
Style: *R&B*
Original line-up: *Richard 'Lazy Dik' Whelan (vocals, harmonica; Cracked Jaffers), Clive 'Smokey' Shephard (keyboards), 'Homesick' Gordon Johns (guitar; ex-Cracked Jaffers, Unheard), Davern 'Hoodoo' White (guitar, vocals; also in* **Bo-Weevils***), Nick 'Cadillac Slim' Phillips (bass; ex-Puritans), Scott 'Bootpolish' Lacey (drums; ex-Puritans)*

The Breadmakers were one of the rockin'est combos ever to grace a Melbourne stage. The band comprised a bunch of 1950s R&B/blues enthusiasts who derived their collective name from the Slim Harpo song '(I'm Your) Breadmaker'.

Scott Lacey and Nick Phillips' previous band The Puritans comprised Julios Doyle (lead vocals), Cameron Peter (organ, piano, rhythm guitar) and Michael Poynter (lead guitar, backing vocals). The Puritans played tough R&B in the Pretty Things/Rolling Stones vein. The band issued the single 'Grace Hotel' and the 10-inch mini-album *The Puritans* on the Mr Spaceman label before issuing the album *(My Baby's Mind is Like a) Beach House* (December 1991) through Shock and *Have an R&B Party with the Puritans* (1992) on the Corduroy label. *Beach House* yielded the single 'Hey Frank!'/'Blues for J.T.'.

Richard Whelan and Gordon Johns' other band, The Cracked Jaffers, also played R&B. The band issued the 7-inch EP 'Drop In' on the Kavern 7 label before Johns left. The line-up of Whelan, David Grabau (guitar), Joe McGrath (bass) and Justin Ward (drums) issued the single 'Soft Rain' (March 1991) and the mini-album *Hip Pocket Nerve* on the Honk label before calling it quits in 1992. Johns was also a member of The Unheard, who issued the 'Don't Stand in My Sunshine' EP on Kavern 7 in 1988.

In 1994, Michael 'Mick Tall' Brierley (guitar; ex-Mathmos) replaced Johns in The Breadmakers. Whelan left in 1995 and 'Hoodoo' White became lead vocalist. White and Shepherd left in the middle of a European tour during 1996 and Whelan briefly came back into the fold. Between 1990 and 1996, The Breadmakers recorded four entertaining albums of authentic, Louisiana swamp R&B (all in glorious mono!).

The Breadmakers albums: *Hoodoo Nightspot* (Corduroy, 1990), *Twelve More Miles to Midnight* (Corduroy, 1991), *The Night the Moon Forgot to Rise (Corduroy, 1994), Cool!* (Corduroy, 1996); ***Puritans***

albums: *The Puritans* (10-inch mini-album, Mr Spaceman, 1988), *(My Baby's Mind is Like a) Beach House* (Shock, 1991), *Have an R&B Party with the Puritans* (Corduroy, 1992).

Dave Bridge Quartet

Formed: *1961*
Style: *Instrumental*
Original line-up: *Dave Bridge (lead guitar; ex-Joy Boys),* **Ray Burton** *(rhythm guitar), Ken White (bass), Warren Foley (drums)*

Dave Bridge was the original lead guitarist with **Col Joye's** backing band, The Joy Boys. Bridge joined The Joy Boys in 1957, and stayed with the band until he formed the Dave Bridge Quartet in 1961. By that stage he had earned a reputation as Australia's most accomplished guitarist.

The Dave Bridge Quartet became regulars on *Bandstand* and *The Johnny O'Keefe Show*, and recorded two successful singles for HMV: 'Skip to My Lou'/'Sunday Morning' (1961) and 'San Fernando Valley'/'Town Hall Shuffle' (1962). Bridge had two solo hit singles, 'Tornado'/'The Tide' and 'The Swan'/'Preacher' in 1963. 'The Swan' was his rearrangement of Tchaikovsky's *Swan Lake*. He formed The Dave Bridge Trio in 1963 with Terry Hearne (bass) and Bruce Jackson (drums). The Trio had hits with 'Trail Blazer'/'On the Town' (June 1963), 'Bondi Stomp'/'Riding the Bower' (October 1963) and 'Surfie Guitar'/'Fly Over' (January 1964). Bridge had one more solo single on CBS, 'High Noon'/'I Who Have Nothing', in 1966 before he concentrated on session, production and arrangement work.

Solo albums: *Surfin' Down Under* (HMV, 1964), *The Dave Bridge Album* (CBS, 1972), *Guitar Sounds of the Seventies* (CBS, 1980).

David Bridie and John Phillips (*see* not drowning, waving)

Philip Brophy

Style: *Somewhere between art and pop*

Melbourne musician/writer/artist/film-maker/conceptualist Philip Brophy (b. 1957) is one of the true unheralded geniuses of Australia's post-punk underground. Between 1977 and 1983, he was leader of an esoteric experimental outfit →↑→ (pronounced by three clicks of the tongue as Tch Tch Tch), and a core member of the group of musicians centred on the Clifton Hill Community Music Centre in inner-city Melbourne. He was involved in Innocent Records which issued records by →↑→, **David Chesworth**, Essendon Airport and others.

At the same time, he moonlighted with Chesworth as the Dave and Phil Duo, playing light jazz and 'dinner muzak'. He was drummer of acclaimed big band the **Hot Half Hour** in 1982, and joined rock band **Olympic Sideburns** briefly in 1985. He was credited with playing drums on that band's self-titled 1985 album, but it had been recorded before he actually joined. He was also heard on the airwaves of Melbourne community radio station 3RRR-FM, co-presenting the 'popular culture' show EEEK! with Au-go-go Records head Bruce Milne.

→↑→ was one of the most original and adventurous groups to emerge from the late 1970s Melbourne new wave scene. The group was a collection of musicians and artists coordinated by Brophy who, at various times and in various guises, performed music, staged plays, produced literature, screened films and exhibited artwork. Often referred to as an electronic band, →↑→ was never bound by genre restrictions. The group functioned as a way of taking an art form or concept of music, re-stating it, questioning it and exposing the way it worked. Indeed, the group's name challenged conventional approaches: →↑→ can be written in only one way and said only one way and those two ways are totally unrelated, although they advertise the same thing. The name of one of the group's tours, Fuck Dance, Let's Art, said a lot about the approach on offer.

The group began performing in late 1977. An early gig was as part of the Melbourne Punk Gunk concert on New Years Eve 1977 (also organised by →↑→), which took place on a footpath in the inner-Melbourne suburb of Carlton. Also on the bill that night were The Boys Next Door, Babeez and Spred. The group also played at pubs, art galleries and the Clifton Hill Community Music Centre. While the music was based around the synthesiser, the group readily embraced rock structures. The original line-up of Philip Brophy (drums, synthesiser, piano), Alan Gaunt (synthesiser), Ralph Traviato (sax, vocals) and Leigh (guitar, synthesiser) was known to perform a whole set of punk covers by the likes of Sex Pistols and The Clash (as they did at Punk Gunk).

The group also tackled material like 'Rock'n'Roll' by Led Zeppelin and 'God' by Yoko Ono. On record, the group's music consisted of immediately appealing, well-arranged and snappily played instrumentals with primitive use of keyboards in the tradition of UK groups like XTC. The first three EPs formed a trio of concept records that contained seven minutes of music a side. *Venetian Rendezvous* (May 1979) was muzak-based, *Nice Noise* (October 1979) was rock, while →↑→ (February 1980) was 'minimal' music. One piece, 'One Note Song', was re-created on each of the EPs in the appropriate style. A fourth EP, *Caprice,* (November 1980) explored a swing-like mode. The line-up on the EPs comprised Brophy, Leigh, Traviato and Anthe (synth).

The track 'Pop Art' appeared on a gig giveaway split single shared with Eric Gradman: Man & Machine (December 1979). The album *Spaces* (1981) comprised soundtrack music for original videos (by Robert Randall and Frank Bendinelli). The promotional only 12-inch EP 'L'Acrostique D'Amour'/'The Crush' on Missing Link (February 1981) was credited to Asphixiation. The project was part of the →↑→ show/tour/album *Asphixiation: What is This Thing Called Disco?* which brought the group to a wider audience. The 1982 line-up comprised Brophy (drums, electronics), Traviato (sax, synthesiser), Maria Kozic (synthesiser, vocals) and Jane Stevenson (synthesiser, vocals). →↑→ contributed the tracks 'Oomgawa Wana Tuba Bibi' and 'Various Levels' to the Innocent compilation albums *New Music 1978/79* and *New Music 1980* respectively.

Throughout 1982 and 1983, the group produced *Stuff* magazine, a forum for anyone with something to say. The film *No Dance* concerned itself 'directly with the ever-growing phenomenon of cross-over audiences, in this case, rock and film', and the group screened it at rock venues. At the end of 1983, Brophy, Maria Kozic and Philip Moreland, representing the group, set off on a world tour, initiated by an invitation to present work at the Museum of Modern Art in Paris. After that, Brophy folded the group concept to concentrate of other areas.

Since the mid-1980s, Brophy has lectured in Visual Communications and written key theoretical articles in the areas of horror cinema and popular culture. In 1987 he directed the independent 16-millimetre film *Salt Saliva Sperm and Sweat*, a highly visceral depiction of the human condition. The film was screened at the 1988 Edinburgh Film Festival, and won the Erwin Rado/Film Victoria Award for Best Australian Short at the 1988 Melbourne Film Festival. Brophy also wrote and recorded the film soundtrack. He also presented an exhibition, *Trash and Junk Culture an All-Consuming Consumption*, in 1988. In 1990, Brophy's Present Records issued a series of albums, including his soundtrack to *Salt Saliva Sperm and Sweat*, and *The Abdominal Wall of Noise* which was Brophy working under the guise of Instrumentless. His other music project around that time was the duo Colossus with Bill McDonald on bass. In 1992 he produced the album *Viral Pulse* for Maria Kozic and The MK Sound.

In 1993 Brophy co-wrote (with Rod Bishop) and directed the squirm-inducing but hysterically funny cult horror/exploitation film *Body Melt.* The film was acclaimed in Europe, but its release (June 1994) was marred by limited distribution in Australia (i.e. mainstream distributors would not touch it). It remains highly underrated, one of the purest pieces of cinema ever produced in Australia.

→↑→ ***albums:*** *Spaces* (Innocent, 1981), *Asphixiation: What is This Thing Called Disco?* (Innocent 1981), *Muzak, Rock and Minimalism* (compilation of early EPs, Present, 1985), *Soundtracks* (Present, 1985), *No Dance* (mini-album Present, 1988), *Club Video* (soundtrack mini-album, Present, 1988); ***Philip Brophy album:*** *Salt Saliva Sperm and Sweat* (Present, 1990).

Ray Brown and the Whispers

Formed: *1964*
Style: *Beat pop*
Original line-up: *Ray Brown (vocals), Al Jackson (lead guitar), Lawrie Barclay (rhythm guitar), John Manners (bass), Pat Jeffrey (drums)*

With the arrival of The Beatles on the worldwide pop scene in 1963, Shadows-styled instrumental bands the world over went looking for lead singers. In Australia, The Mustangs became **The Master's Apprentices** (with **Jim Keays**), The Vibratones became **Billy Thorpe** and the Aztecs and The Nocturnes became Ray Brown and the Whispers.

By late 1964, Ray Brown and the Whispers had become the resident band at the premier discotheque of the day, Surf City (in Sydney's Kings Cross), having replaced **Billy Thorpe** and the Aztecs who were enjoying national hits and touring interstate. Ray Brown and the Whispers signed to the Leedon label, and scored four Top 5 hits in a row in hometown Sydney during 1965: '20 Miles'/'Devoted To You' (#1 in January), 'Pride'/'Say It Again' (#1 in April), 'Fool Fool Fool'/'Go to Him' (#1 in July) and 'In the Midnight Hour'/'Now is the Time' (#2 in October). The singles also charted well in Melbourne: '20 Miles' (#26), 'Pride' (#7), 'Fool Fool Fool' (#7) and 'In the Midnight Hour' (#4).

All the A-sides were cover versions (Chubby Checker's '20 Miles', Billy J. Kramer's 'Pride', Roosevelt Greer's 'Fool, Fool, Fool' and Wilson Pickett/Steve Cropper's 'In the Midnight Hour'). Ray's boyish appeal made him, alongside **Normie**

Rowe, **Stevie Wright** and **Billy Thorpe**, one of the most popular singers of the day. The album *Hits & Brass* pulled together the band's hits on one side, with the second side featuring five new, brass-laden songs. Four more singles followed in 1966: 'Tennessee Waltz'/'I Am What I Am' (#6 in Sydney, February), 'I Can't Get Enough'/'A.B.C. Song' (May), 'Ain't It Strange?'/'I Can't Get Enough' (September) and 'Respect'/'Too Late to Come Home' (October) before Ray Brown and the Whispers parted company.

Brown formed a 'New Whispers' with Dave Russell (guitar; ex-Ray Columbus and the Invaders), Ronnie Peel (bass; ex-**Missing Links**, **Pleazers**) and Steve Hardy (drums), but this was short-lived. Brown's 1967 album *Same Old Song . . . Brand New Beat* featured **Max Merritt and The Meteors** on four tracks. It yielded his final Sydney hit, 'Same Old Song'/'New Kind of Love' (#6 in March). Brown then spent two years in the USA where he cut a solo album *Just Ray Brown* and single 'Don't Fall in Love'/'I'm Gonna be a Country Boy' (July 1969) with producer David Axelrod for Capitol Records. The album was a flop and, as Brown explained in a *Go-Set* article at the time, 'Capitol spent $30 000 on it, put in a 30-piece orchestra and then wouldn't let me pick my own material'.

Having absorbed all the prevailing musical trends of the day in the States, Brown returned home in late 1969 and formed country rock band Moonstone with Mal Clarke (guitar; ex-**Tony Worsley and the Fabulous Blue Jays**) and Jimmy Doyle (guitar; ex-**Aesop's Fables**). The single 'Oh, Sarah'/'King Velvet' (April 1970) and album *Mad House* (October) featured an esoteric blending of country, folk, psychedelia and Eastern influences. Aside from Brown, Clarke and Doyle, other musicians on the album included Russell Hinton (guitar), John Carr (guitar, bass), Ed Gaston (bass), Eligio Sincic (sitar, tablas), Jimmy Thompson (drums; ex-**Billy Thorpe** and the Aztecs), Pee Wee Clark (pedal steel guitar) and various musicians on wind and string instruments.

Brown spent another year in the USA and, on his return in November 1971, formed the adventurous, 'Mad Dogs and Englishmen'-styled, eight-piece jazz-rock band One Ton Gypsy. The original line-up included three vocalists: Ray, **Alison McCallum** (ex-**Freshwater**) and **Graham Lowndes** (ex-Bootleg). One Ton Gypsy suffered many line-up changes. Some of the more prominent musicians within the band's ranks included: Dave Fookes (keyboards), Peter Martin (guitar; ex-SCRA), Ray Oliver (guitar, ex-**Friends**), Ronnie Peel (bass; ex-**Missing Links**, Whispers, **Rockwell T. James** and The Rhythm Aces, Browns), Tim Piper (guitar; ex-**Chain**, Savage Rose Blues Band), Margaret Piper (backing vocals), Laurie Pryor (drums, ex-**Twilights**, **Healing Force**), Ray Rivamonte (percussion, vocals), Lindsay Wells (guitar, ex-**Healing Force**) and Paul Wylde (piano; ex-**Blackfeather**). Rivamonte later recorded an interesting concept album in the USA called *Birth of the Sun* which came out on the Image label in November 1976. It produced the single 'Only a Crazy Man Knows'/'Birth of the Sun' (June 1977).

Brown eventually had a solo single issued on Mushroom, 'Steel Guitar'/'Covered Wagon' (November 1973), but by that stage the potentially brilliant One Ton Gypsy had run its course. Brown continued to perform solo, and travelled throughout outback Australia absorbing Aboriginal culture. Throughout the 1980s, Brown reformed The Whispers (with various new line-ups) for several rock'n'roll revival concerts. He died in August 1996 as a result of a heart attack.

Ray Brown and the Whispers albums: *Ray Brown and the Whispers* (Leedon, 1965), *Hits & Brass* (Leedon, 1965), *Heading for the Top* (Leedon, 1966), *Dance Dance Dance* (Leedon, 1966), *Same Old Song . . . Brand New Beat* (Festival, 1967), *Miles of Hits—The Festival File Volume Seven* (Festival, 1988). ***Ray Brown solo album:*** *Just Ray Brown* (Festival, 1969); ***Ray Brown and Moonstone album:*** *Mad House* (Festival, 1970).

Buffalo

Formed: *1971*
Style: *Heavy rock*
Original line-up: *Dave Tice (vocals; ex-Head), Alan Milano (vocals; ex-Mandala), John Baxter (guitar; ex-Head),* **Peter Wells** *(bass; ex-Head), Paul Balbi (drums; ex-Bootleg, Head)*

Sydney band Buffalo was one of Australia's pioneering heavy rock outfits. There was nothing subtle about Buffalo's primal, heavyweight sound, but it was delivered with a great deal of conviction. And by virtue of the band's appearance on Phonogram's prestigious and collectable Vertigo label, Buffalo's sound became familiar to record collectors around the world. Indeed, by the late 1980s (long after the band's break up), Buffalo's popularity in territories such as France and Germany far exceeded that experienced by the band in Australia during the 1970s.

Buffalo was the first Australian band signed to Vertigo. In combining the dense, occult riffing of Black Sabbath with the progressive blues chops of other British groups like Free and May Blitz, the band certainly captured the arrogant disposition of the times in a bold and thunderous fashion. The beginnings of Buffalo can be traced back to blues band Head which formed in Brisbane during 1968. The line-up comprised expatriate Englishman Dave Tice, **Peter Wells**, Neil Jensen (guitar) and Steve Jones (drums). Head moved to Sydney during mid-1970, and by 1971 had issued one single on Phonogram/Philips 'Hobo'/'Sad Song', 'Then'. Jones and Jensen were edged out to make way for Paul Balbi and John Baxter. With the arrival of co-vocalist Alan Milano in August 1971, Buffalo was born.

Alongside **Billy Thorpe** and the Aztecs and **Blackfeather**, Buffalo was one of the loudest and heaviest bands of the day. *Dead Forever . . .* (June 1972) and the single 'Suzie Sunshine'/'No Particular Place' (May) sold well, with the album eventually selling 25 000 copies. The credits on the cover advised: 'Play this album LOUD'. Milano left and Jimmy Economou replaced Balbi on drums. *Volcanic Rock* (July 1973) and *Only Want You for Your Body* (June 1974) kept up the scorching, heavy metal mayhem, with Baxter's savage guitar work and Tice's demented vocals well to the fore.

Aside from absurdly macho song titles like 'I'm a Skirtlifter, Not a Shirt Raiser', the band's controversial album cover designs raised more than a few eyebrows. *Dead Forever . . .* featured a mournful, blood-soaked face peering through the eyesocket of a skull (classic heavy metal imagery). *Volcanic Rock* boasted a graphic yet hilarious depiction of the female form as a menstruating volcano. *Only Want You for Your Body* depicted an obese, screaming woman shackled to a torture rack while the back cover showed the band as leering, lascivious Aussie yob rockers! The last two cover credits advised 'Play *this* album even louder!' and 'Now blow your speakers out!'

Buffalo's singles on Phonogram's Philips label during 1973 and 1974 were: 'Just a Little Rock'n'Roll'/'Barber Shop Rock' (July 1973), 'Sunrise (Come My Way)'/'Pound of Flesh' (September 1973, from *Volcanic Rock*) and 'What's Going On'/'I'm Coming On' (May 1974, from *Only Want You for Your Body*), plus the rare *Buffalo* EP ('Suzie Sunshine', 'Dead Forever'/'Barbershop Rock', 'Sunrise Come My Way') on Vertigo. In mid-1974, Buffalo recruited Norm Roue (slide guitar; ex-**Band of Light**), but a few months later Baxter was sacked from the band. Although Buffalo recorded two more albums, the band had lost one of its most valuable and distinctive assets and its spirit simply dwindled. Baxter joined Boy Racer and then formed **Southern Cross** with ex-Buffalo vocalist Alan Milano.

Karl Taylor joined and the band issued *Mother's Choice* (March 1976), plus the singles 'Little Queenie'/'Girl Can't Help It' (August 1975), 'Lucky'/'On My Way' (November) and 'Sweet Little Sixteen'/'Essukay' (April 1976). The band originally wanted to call the album either *Songs for the Frustrated Housewife* or *Thieves, Punks, Rip-offs and Liars* but cautious executives at Phonogram rejected the titles as being too sexual and too controversial respectively.

By the time the album appeared, both Roue and Taylor had left to be replaced by Chris Turner (ex-Drain). Taylor issued a solo album on Polydor, *Taylor Maid*, later in the year, and went on to form blues-rock outfit Huntress. For a while, Colin Stead (ex-Lloyd's World, Sweet Wine) joined Buffalo as second guitarist, but the line-up proved incompatible. The Tice/Wells/Economou/Turner line-up issued a new single, 'Rollin''/'Hotel Ladies' (August), but by the end of 1976 Wells had quit to form **Rose Tattoo**. Ross Simms came in as the band's new bass player. The Tice/Economou/Turner/Simms line-up supported UK visitors Ritchie Blackmore's Rainbow on tour during November 1976, and then recorded a new album, *Average Rock'n'Roller.*

The album and second single, 'Sailor'/'Average Rock'n'Roller' (May 1977), were Buffalo's attempt at a more commercial sound, but lacked the coherent direction of their predecessors. By the time the album came out in July 1977, Buffalo had broken up. Tice had received an invitation to join English pub rockers The (Count) Bishops. Former Buffalo drummer Paul Balbi had joined that band in London during 1975. Tice left for the UK in March 1977 and Buffalo dissolved. Tice returned to Australia in the early 1980s and formed **The Headhunters** with Mick Cocks (ex-**Rose Tattoo, Heaven**) and Mark Evans (ex-**AC/DC, Finch, Heaven**).

In late 1977, Turner played with **Rose Tattoo** as guest guitarist. He went on to rejoin **Pete Wells** during 1983 in Scattered Aces. Turner also issued a solo album, *My Guitar and Me,* and single, 'I'm Crazy'/'Motel Gypsy' in 1981 on the Big Rock label (through RCA). He issued a second album on Big Rock, *Exile* (1990).

Albums: *Dead Forever . . . (Vertigo, 1972), Volcanic Rock* (Vertigo, 1973), *Only Want You for Your Body* (Vertigo, 1974), *Mother's Choice* (Vertigo, 1976), *Average Rock'n'Roller* (Vertigo, 1977), *Rock Legends* (Phonogram, 1980), *Skirtlifters: Highlights and Oversights 1972–1977* (Raven, 1991; reissued on Phonogram in 1992).

Bughouse

Formed: *1988*
Style: *Rock*
Original line-up: *Lea Cameron (vocals), Steve Campbell (guitar), Genevieve Maynard (bass), Peter Brookes (drums)*

Sydney band Bughouse was a difficult band to pigeonhole. Even the band members themselves admitted to not knowing how to describe their sound, which incorporated wiry funk rhythms, punk tempos, folksy touches and big rock guitar riffs. Bughouse built up a following on the Sydney scene and issued its debut single, 'V For Vendetta'/'Burn It Back', on its own Ursula label in November 1989.

The band followed up its debut with a single that combined an idiosyncratic cover of Jefferson Airplane's 'Somebody to Love' on the A-side with a funky rendition of **Radio Birdman's** 'New Race' on the flip. The *Bughouse* EP from 1990 highlighted singer Lea Cameron's commanding voice and the band's assured backing. The band issued two more independent singles, 'Hell for Leather' and 'Rare Occasion', before signing to Mushroom's subsidiary label White. The band's debut album *Every Fool in Town* was uncharacteristically restrained and, following its release, the band left White.

The sessions for the proposed second album were truncated, which resulted in a CD EP, 'Bardo', issued through Mushroom Distribution Services (MDS). The term 'Bardo' was taken from the *Tibetan Book of the Dead*, describing a state of nothingness, being trapped in limbo. The band almost broke up at that stage, but persevered. Nick Fisher (ex-Wet Taxis, **New Christs**, **Louis Tillett**) replaced Brookes. After a difficult phase in Bughouse's career, the second album, *Fink Tank* (June 1994), gave full vent to the band's fiery passion.

Albums: *Every Fool in Town* (Ursula/White/Mushroom/Festival, 1991), *Fink Tank* (Ursula/MDS, 1994).

Vika and Linda Bull

Style: *Jazz, R&B*

Born of a Tongan mother and an Australian father, singing siblings Vika and Linda Bull are considered, along with Rugby great Jonah Lomu, to be the most famous Tongans in the world. The sisters also happen to be two of Australia's most popular performers, by virtue of their productive solo careers and as featured vocalists in **The Black Sorrows**.

Before coming to prominence with **The Black Sorrows**, Vika and Linda sang with Sophisticated Boom Boom and The Sacred Hearts of Sweet Temptation. Vika also issued two solo singles in 1988 'Living Hell' and 'My House'. The sisters' debut album, *Vika and Linda*, featured songwriting contributions from **Paul Kelly**, **Stephen Cummings**, Joe Camilleri and Nick Smith, Mark Seymour, **Nick Barker** and Wayne Burt. It contained the singles 'Hard Love' and 'When Will You Fall for Me?'.

In 1996, Vika and Linda made a return visit to Tonga where they paid their respects to the nation's monarch King Taufa'ahu Tupou. While in Tonga, Vika and Linda managed to get some of that country's finest musicians, including the Mosi Mosi Kava Club (whose sweet harmonies were a delight), to contribute to their second album. Whereas *Vika and Linda* was based on a proven hit formula, *Princess Tabu* (September 1996) was a purer reflection of the cultural strains and rich diversity of their heritage. The album produced the single 'Love Comes Easy' (July). Helping out were friends **Paul Kelly**, **Tim Finn**, Barry Palmer, Michael Barker and **Diesel**. The album was recorded in England with producer Jeremy Allom (Massive Attack) and engineer Marc Ramaer (kd lang).

For their solo live appearances, Vika and Linda were joined, at various times, by Jeff Burstin (guitar; from **The Black Sorrows**), Bruce Haymes (keyboards), Peter Luscombe (drums; from **The Black Sorrows**), Stuart Speed (bass) and Jex Saarelaht (keyboards). Vika and Linda Bull's first release for 1997 was the CD single 'The Parting Song' (February), lifted from *Princess Tabu*.

Albums: *Vika and Linda* (Mushroom/Festival, 1995), *Princess Tabu* (Mushroom/Festival, 1996).

Bulldog

Formed: *1970*
Style: *Progressive blues*
Original line-up: *Mick Rogers (guitar, vocals; ex-***Procession**, **Doug Parkinson** *In Focus), Bob Dames (bass; ex-***Purple Hearts**, *Black Cat Circle, Coloured Balls), Peter Miles (drums; ex-***Bay City Union**, *Coloured Balls)*

Led by English-born Mick Rogers, Bulldog was an adventurous, but short-lived, blues power trio. With Bob Dames and Peter Miles on board, Rogers was able to steer the band through an accomplished mix of hard rock, blues and avant-jazz material. Rogers had spent time with respected outfit **Procession** and a short two months (December 1969 to January 1970) with **Doug Parkinson** In Focus. He formed Bulldog in February.

Just as Bulldog's only single, 'Man of Constant

Sorrow'/'Inner Spring', came out on the Fable label at the end of 1970, Rogers responded to Manfred Mann's beckoning call to join his Chapter III (with ex-**Procession** member Craig Collinge on drums) in the UK, effectively ending Bulldog's career. Chapter III became Manfred Mann's Earth Band and Rogers stayed on board until the 1975 album *Nightingales and Bombers*. While Rogers was working with the Earth Band, Manfred Mann was instrumental in his band cutting versions of **Chain's** 'Black and Blue' (included on the 1973 album *Messin'*) and **Spectrum's** 'I'll Be Gone' and 'Launching Place' (on the 1974 album *The Good Earth*). Manfred Mann's Earth Band toured Australia at the end of 1971 on a package tour that also included Free and Deep Purple.

On his return to Australia in 1976, Rogers put in a short stint with the **Renée Geyer** Band before forming Mick Rogers and Eclipse. Peter Jones (electric piano), Mike Clarke (bass; ex-Skylight, **Mándu**, Silver Sun) and Graham Morgan (drums) completed the line-up. Jones and Morgan had played on **Jackie Orszaczky's** progressive-jazz album *Beramiada*. Eclipse's only single, a cover of Bob Dylan's 'Get Your Rocks Off'/'T.C.S.' (September 1976), featured a mix of John McLaughlin, Manfred Mann's Earth Band and Weather Report elements; in short, hard rock with jazz-rock leanings. Once again, Eclipse was short-lived. Rogers returned to the UK, where he joined Greenslade and Aviator.

Ray Burgess

Born: *1952*
Style: *Pop rock*

Melbourne-born singer Ray Burgess (b. 1952) was a member of Redtime between 1970 and 1973. The band was a popular club attraction in Melbourne and Perth. Burgess launched his solo career in late 1974 with the punchy hit singles 'Touch Me'/'Keep on Rocking' (#3 in January 1975) and 'Love Fever'/'You Really Got Me' (#11 in July 1975).

He was a regular on ***Countdown*** around that time, and then became compere of the Melbourne television series *Rock'n'Roll Circus* in late 1975. In July 1976, he moved to Sydney to host the ABC-TV national weekday afternoon pop show *Flashez*. **Ross Wilson** produced Burgess's debut album, *Not So Pretty*, which contained the Greg Macainsh-penned 'Sad Rock'n'Roll'. *Flashez* was wrapped up in November 1977 and Burgess formed the Ray Burgess Band to play the pub circuit. After his band broke up, Burgess concentrated on club, cabaret and television appearances. Aside from 'Touch Me' and 'Love Fever', Burgess's only other charting single was 'Gloria'/'Dancing Shoes' (#23 in July 1977).

His other singles were: 'Rock'n'Roll Lightning'/'Give Me What You've Got' (July 1975), 'Little Boy Sad'/'Business of Nothing' (May 1976), 'Sad Rock'n'Roll'/'Hot Cookie' (September 1976), 'Midnight Cowboy'/'Lightning's Child' (September 1977), 'Black is Black'/'Drift Away' (January 1978), 'Love Stealer'/'When You Lose Somebody You Love' (July 1978), 'Lover Boy'/'When You Lose Somebody You Love' (April 1979) and 'Eve of Destruction'/'When You Lose' (September 1989).

Albums: *Not So Pretty* (Festival/Infinity, 1976), *Final Mix* (Festival/Infinity, 1978), *Gloria—Best Of Ray Burgess* (Festival/Infinity, 1992).

Ronnie Burns

Style: *Pop*

During the mid-1960s, Ronnie Burns (b. 1946) vied with **Normie Rowe** and **Merv Benton** as the most popular solo singer on the pop scene. In 1967 he was voted Most Popular Australian Male Vocalist in the *Go-Set* Pop Poll, and the ABC filmed a documentary called *The Life of Ronnie Burns*.

Burns' first group, The Flies, was the first Australian band to consciously ape The Beatles. The band comprised Burns (vocals, rhythm guitar), John Thomas (lead guitar), Themi Adams (bass) and Hank Wallis (drums). The Flies supported The Rolling Stones' first Australian tour. The Flies' singles were 'Tell Her That'/'I'll be in Love with You' (July 1964), 'Doin' the Mod'/'Ain't that Just Like Me' (July 1965) and 'Can't You Feel?'/'I'll Pass on by' (September 1965). Burns left The Flies in August 1965 to go solo, and was replaced by Peter Nicol (ex-Wild Colonials).

Over the next five years, Burns had nine hit singles in Melbourne: 'The Very Last Day'/'Let It Be Me' (#19 in June 1966), 'True True Lovin''/'Too Many People' (#17 in September), 'Coalman'/'All the King's Horses' (#7 in January 1967), 'Exit Stage Right'/'In the Morning' (#19 in June), 'We Had a Good Thing Going'/'Can't You Feel' (#36 in October), 'When I Was Six Years Old'/'So Good' (#28 in March 1968), 'Age of Consent'/'Piccadilly Pages' (#16 in December), 'Smiley'/'Jodie' (#2 in December 1969) and 'The Prophet'/'Maggie Mine' (#25 in March 1971). 'Coalman' and 'Smiley' also charted well in Sydney at #7 and #3 respectively. 'Coalman' and 'Exit Stage Right' were written by **The Bee**

Gees; 'Age of Consent' was written by **The Twilights'** Terry Britten.

By the early 1970s, Burns had ditched the pop trappings for a more middle-of-the-road sound and a new nightclub image. He became a regular on the club and cabaret circuit, and on television variety shows such as *Young Talent Time*. His last single was 'Brand New Number One'/'I Want You' (December 1980), written by **Johnny Young**. During 1996, Burns joined up with fellow 1960s veterans **Russell Morris** and Darryl Cotton to play the revival circuit. The three singers issued a self-titled album during the year which comprised nine original solo recordings, plus three new recordings by the trio.

Albums: *Smiley* (Festival/Spin, 1969), *Ronnie* (Festival/Spin, 1970), *Best of Ronnie Burns* (Festival/Spin, 1971), *Virgo* (Festival/Spin, 1971), *We've Only Just Begun* (Festival, 1972), *For You* (Summit, 1974), *Enter Stage Left: The Festival File Volume 23* (Festival, 1994).

Ray Burton

Style: *Rock*

Singer/songwriter/guitarist Ray Burton (b. 1945) was not well known in Australia, but he has been a professional musician for over 30 years. He got his start at 17 as guitarist with the **Dave Bridge Quartet**. He then joined **The Delltones** and, briefly, The Questions before joining **The Executives** in early 1968. He remained with **The Executives** for three years, during which time the band relocated to the USA where they became known as Inner Sense. In 1971, Burton co-wrote the song 'I Am Woman' with expatriate **Helen Reddy**.

'I Am Woman' was used as the theme song to the 1972 feature film *Stand Up and Be Counted*, and went on to become a US #1 hit single for Reddy. Burton returned to Australia in March 1973 and joined **Leo De Castro's Friends**. He then formed an eponymous trio with ex-**Friends** members Duncan McGuire (bass) and Mark Kennedy (drums) which had evolved into **Ayers Rock** by the end of 1973. Burton left **Ayers Rock** at the start of 1974 and returned to the USA. His return was in order to push his claim for unpaid royalties due from the sales of 'I Am Woman'. While in the States, Burton worked as a session player for the likes of Billy Joel, Dave Mason and Jimmy Webb. He also wrote the theme song 'Best Friend' for the feature film *Airport '75*. Burton returned to Australia in late 1977 and formed The Nightflyers.

The line-up comprised John Pugh (guitar; ex-**Eighteenth Century Quartet**, **Cam-Pact**, **James Taylor Move**, **Healing Force**, Baiyana, Silver Sun), Rex Bullen (keyboards; ex-**Bakery**, Natural Gas, **Jim Keays'** Southern Cross), Ian Davidson (guitar, synthesiser), Gus Fenwick (bass; ex-**Pleazers**, **Band of Talabene**, **Healing Force**) and Steve Hopes (drums). Burton issued his album *Dreamers and Nightflyers*, plus two singles 'Too Hard to Handle'/'Lady of the Morning' and 'Paddington Green'/'Ain't It Funny' in 1978. In 1979 he worked with Crossfire, toured Australia as support to Joan Armatrading and then returned to the USA to concentrate on songwriting.

Album: *Dreamers and Nightflyers* (Warner, 1978).

The Bushwackers

Formed as The Original Bushwackers and Bullockies Bush Band: *1970*
Style: *Bush, folk*
Original line-up: *Jan Wositzky (vocals, harmonica, banjo, percussion), Dave Isom (guitar, vocals, mandolin), Bert Kahanoff (lagerphone)*

As Australia's foremost interpreters of traditional Australian bush and folk music, The Bushwackers have existed for over 25 years. Other bands to have played in the bush/dance idiom include Uncle Bob's Band, early **Redgum** and The Cobbers, but none has been able to capture the vitality of the form in the same way. The band's albums from the late 1970s and early 1980s remain classics of the genre.

Jan Wositzky, Dave Isom and Bert Kahanoff formed The Original Bushwackers and Bullockies Bush Band in 1970. Mick Slocum (piano accordion, vocals) and Dave Kidd (fiddle) joined in 1971. Dobe Newton (lagerphone, vocals), Tony Hunt (fiddle) and Peter Howell (bass) all joined around 1973. By then the band was known as The Bushwackers Band. Newton has since assumed leadership of the band, mainly because he is the longest-standing member. The Bushwackers augmented their traditional instrumentation with electric guitars and drums, which helped to define the band's varied and enthusiastic style. The 1976 line-up comprised Wositzky, Slocum, Kidd, Newton, Louis McManus (fiddle, guitar, mandolin) and Englishman (the late) Pete Farndon (bass), who went on to become a member of UK new wave band The Pretenders in 1978. Other late 1970s members included Chris Duffy (guitar), Steve Groves (guitar, vocals; ex-**Kinetics**, Tin Tin), Fred

Kuhnl (bass), Greg Martin (drums) and Michael Harris (fiddle).

The 1982 line-up was Newton, McManus, Danny Bourke (fiddle, vocals), Roger Corbett (bass, vocals), **Tommy Emmanuel** (guitar, vocals; ex-Southern Star Band, Goldrush) and Freddie Strauks (drums, ex-**Skyhooks**, **Sports**). Tony O'Neill (mandolin, guitar, vocals) then replaced McManus, Michael Harris rejoined in 1983 and Robbie Ross (ex-**Goanna**) replaced Strauks on drums. The band's singles during the early 1980's included: 'The Flying Pieman'/'The Kangaroo Hop' (June 1980), 'Les Darcy'/'Weevils in the Flour' (March 1981), 'Marijuana Australiana'/'Ned Kelly's Tunes' (September 1981), 'When Britannia Ruled the Waves'/'Hanging Rock' (June 1983, 'Warrigul Morning'/'Goanna Stew' (December 1983) and Lime Juice Tub'/'Marijuana Australiana' (May 1984). Amoung the band's other classic tunes are 'Lachlan Tigers', 'Flash Jack from Gundagai' and a version of Eric Bogle's 'And the Band Played Waltzing Matilda'.

Newton disbanded The Bushwackers in 1984, but continued to bring various line-ups together for annual reunion tours. In late 1993, Newton and Corbett revived the band on a permanent basis as The Bushwackers Band (after a few gigs as The Range Rovers), with a new line-up of Melanie Williamson (piano accordion, guitar, vocals), Michael Fix (guitar, ex-Hat Trick), Mark Oats (fiddle) and Pete Drummond (drums). Peter Malone replaced Fix on guitar later in the year, and the band issued the EP 'Billy of Tea' and the new album *Jubilee*. Brad Johns then took over from Malone, Johns in turn was replaced by journeyman guitarist **Tim Gaze** (ex-**Tamam Shud**, **Ariel**, **Rose Tattoo**) for the band's 1997 line-up.

The Bushwackers recorded a live album, *Oz Rock Salute*, in January 1997, covering classic Oz Rock from **Cold Chisel** ('Choir girl') to **Goanna** ('Solid Rock') and **Daddy Cool** ('Eagle Rock'). The album featured guest players like **Tommy Emmanuel** and **Greg Champion**.

Albums: *A Shearer's Dream* (Larrikin, 1974), *And The Band Played Waltzing Matilda* (Image, 1976), *Murrumbidgee* (Image, 1977), *Bushfire* (Image, 1979), *The Bushwackers Band Dance Album* (Image, 1980), *Faces in the Street* (Avenue, 1981), *Beneath the Southern Cross* (CBS, 1981), *The Bushwackers Collection* (Avenue, 1981), *Down There for Dancing* (CBS, 1982), *Warrigul Morning* (CBS, 1983), *Lively* (CBS, 1984), *Celebration* (CBS, 1988), *Shoalhaven Man* (1989), *So Far . . . 1974–1994* (ABC/EMI, 1995), *Jubilee* (ABC/EMI, 1996), *Oz Rock Salute* (ABC, 1997).

Buster Brown

Formed: *1973*
Style: *Rock, boogie*
Original line-up: **Gary 'Angry' Anderson** *(vocals; ex-Peace Power and Purity), John Moon (guitar), Paul Grant (guitar), Chris Wilson (keyboards), Ian Ryan (bass; ex-Ash, Chook), Phil Rudd (drums)*

Alongside **Coloured Balls**, Melbourne band Buster Brown was one of the most notorious streetlevel/boogie outfits of its day. Led by the tiny but terrifying **Angry Anderson**, Buster Brown built up a solid following around the pubs, and among the skinheads on the suburban dance circuit.

Buster Brown played at the 1974 Sunbury Festival and live recordings of 'Roll Over Beethoven' and 'Buster Brown' appeared on the Various Artists budget album *Highlights of Sunbury '74 Part 1* issued on the Mushroom anti-Ripoff label. Geordie Leach replaced orginal bass player Ian Ryan in early 1974. The album *Something to Say* (January 1975) and the singles 'Buster Brown'/'Rock'n'Roll Lady' (July 1974) and 'Something to Say'/'Let Me In' (January 1975) did not reflect the band's live strengths. At the end of 1974, the original Buster Brown line-up split, and for the next year line-up changes prevented the band from achieving greater progress. Phil Rudd left to join **AC/DC**. The next line-up (April to June 1975) comprised Anderson, Wilson, Leach, Dennis Miller (guitar) and Trevor Young (drums; ex-**Coloured Balls**).

Anderson formed Buster Brown Mark III in July 1975, when he was joined by Billy Miller (guitar, vocals), Dave Springfield (guitar) and Ken Firth (bass; ex-**Tully**) all from **The Ferrets**, plus drummer Dallas 'Digger' Royal (ex-**Band of Talabene**). The band finally dissolved in November 1975. Miller, Springfield and Firth reconvened **The Ferrets**. Anderson attempted to get a band off the ground with guitar legend **Lobby Loyde** who had produced *Something to Say*. He then went on to join **Rose Tattoo** in late 1976.

Album: *Something to Say* (Mushroom/Festival, 1974).

The Butcher Shop (*see* Tex Perkins)

Debra Byrne

Style: *Pop*

Singer/actor Debra Byrne (b. 1957) first came to prominence as one of the original team members of television variety show *Young Talent Time* on the Ten

Network in Melbourne. The show first went to air in 1971, and Byrne remained until 1974. At 16 she issued her debut solo single, 'He's a Rebel'/'I Am Woman' (March 1974), which became Australia's biggest hit for the year after it shot to #1 on the Melbourne charts and #35 in Sydney.

Another Crystals oldie, 'Da Doo Ron Ron'/'The Boogie Man' followed (#7 in Melbourne during January 1975) and Byrne was voted *TV Week* Queen of Pop for 1974 and 1975. In September 1975, she travelled to London and appeared on *The Cliff Richard Show*. 'You Promised Me the Love'/'There'll Never Be a Way' returned her to the Melbourne charts in February 1977 (#31), and she continued her regular television appearances. Her last single for the 1970s was 'Dirty Ol' Man'/'Ain't No Sunshine' (June 1977).

During 1980 and 1981, Byrne worked with **John Farnham** on the ABC-TV variety show *Farnham and Byrne*. She issued one single in 1981, a cover of The Crocodiles' 'Tears'/'Something to Remember' (May). During the early 1980s, Byrne battled heroin addiction, spending time in Melbourne drug rehabilitation centre Odyssey House. She recovered to make her film debut in *Rebel* (1985), playing the part of Kathy McLeod opposite American actor Matt Dillon. That same year she took the part of Grizabella in the Australian stage production of the Andrew Lloyd-Webber musical *Cats*. She appeared on the Australian Cast recording album of *Cats* (on EMI) alongside Marina Prior, **Jeff Philips**, David Atkins and John Wood. In 1988, Byrne was in *Les Miserables*.

Byrne's only album for the 1980s, *Persuader* (1985) produced the singles 'The Persuader'/'So Sad the Song' (June) and 'Heroes'/'Memory' (December). In the early 1990s Byrne issued two mature, adult contemporary pop albums, *Caught in the Act* (April 1991) and *Sleeping Child* (1994), the CD singles 'Diamond in the Rough' and 'So Soon' plus the CD EP 'Heaven Down Here'. In 1996 she took the part of aging film star Norma Desmond in the Australian production of the Andrew Lloyd-Webber musical *Sunset Boulevard*. The show was struck by a number of setbacks even before opening night. Firstly, Byrne suffered back problems and it seemed the show would be cancelled. Then, on the eve of the show's premiere (25 October 1996), musical director and arranger Brian Stacey was killed in a hit-and-run accident. The show did go on, its run finishing in June 1997. Byrne recorded her fifth album, *New Ways to Dream* in February 1997.

Albums: *She's A Rebel* (as Debbie Byrne, Festival, 1974), *Persuader* (EMI, 1985), *Caught in the Act* (Mushroom/Festival, 1991), *Sleeping Child* (Mushroom/Festival, 1994), *New Ways to Dream* (Polydor, 1997).

C

CACTUS CHiLD

Formed: *1994*
Style: *Folk, pop*
Original line-up: *Gemma Deacon (vocals), Ian Shadwell (guitar), Chris Miller (bass), Angus Diggs (drums)*

Sydney band CACTUS CHiLD issued its first CD EP, 'On', in 1994. In 1996, CACTUS CHiLD supported international visitors Lisa Loeb, Ronnie Jordan, Jeff Buckley and Luka Bloom, and issued the Craig Porteils-produced album *diaphon*es which sold 2000 copies. In late 1996, Universal Music Australia's subsidiary label Grudge signed the band and reissued *diaphones*, which came repackaged with 'On' as a bonus disc. The band also re-recorded the track 'Fall' as 'Fall '97', which came out as a CD single in March 1997. Carolyn Shine (keyboards, vocals) joined to fill out the band's sound.

Album: *diaphon*es (Independent, 1996), *diaphones* (reissue; Grudge/Universal/BMG, 1997).

Brian Cadd

Style: *Pop rock*

Throughout the early to mid-1970s, Brian Cadd (b. 1946) was one of Australia's foremost singer /songwriter/impresarios. With the help of Fable Records' manager Ron Tudor, he set up the Bootleg label in 1972. Much in the fashion of American musician/producer Leon Russell, Cadd gathered around him a 'family' of musicians, dubbed **The Bootleg Family Band**, to back him and other artists on the label. Cadd enjoyed a successful solo career, and achieved some attention in the USA.

Cadd's early forays into music included stints with the Beale Street Jazz Band and The Castaways. In 1965, The Castaways became R&B band The Jackson Kings with a line-up of Brian Caine (aka Cadd), Carl Bennett (vocals), Chas Brown (guitar), Ray Neville (bass) and Bill Turgeon (drums). **Ronnie Charles** (vocals) was also a member at the end of the band's life. The Jackson Kings recorded two singles for CBS, 'Watch Your Step'/ 'Come On Now' (February 1966) and 'Watermelon Man'/'Lawdy Miss Clawdy' (April 1966).

In October 1966, Cadd and Charles joined **The Groop**. The band split up in May 1969. During that time, Cadd developed his songwriting, and as well as penning many of **The Groop's** songs, **The Master's Apprentices** covered his 'Silver People', which they rearranged and issued as 'Elevator Driver'. Cadd's next band was **Axiom**. In partnership with ex-**Groop** bass player Don Mudie (who also joined **Axiom**), and under the influence of The Band's landmark *Music from Big Pink* album, Cadd co-wrote virtually everything **Axiom** recorded, including the hits 'Arkansas Grass', 'A Little Ray of Sunshine' and 'My Baby's Gone'.

With the break-up of **Axiom** in 1971, Cadd and Mudie issued the single 'Show Me the Way'/'Rolling and Tumbling Down' on Fable (December; #15 in February 1972). Having set up Bootleg, Cadd was able to launch his solo career. In the meantime, three of Cadd's earliest solo recordings, 'Sure Feels Good', 'Making It on Your Own' and 'Come With Me', appeared on the Various Artists soundtrack album *Morning of the Earth* (May 1972). Cadd's debut solo single, 'Ginger Man'/'Fairweather Friend', was an immediate national success (#16 in October 1972). His eponymous debut album reached #2, and spent 20 weeks on the album charts.

Cadd won the composer's section of the 1972 Hoadley's National Battle of the Sounds with 'Don't You Know It's Magic'. Cadd also performed the song at the Tokyo World Popular Song Festival and took out the Most Outstanding Composition Award. **Johnny Farnham** later released the song as a single. In 1973, Cadd's second album, *Parabrahm*, reached #5, and he issued the singles 'Every Mother's Son'/'Pappy's Got the Blues' (March), 'Silver City Birthday Celebration Day' (July), 'Keep on Rockin''/'Handy Man' (October) and 'Alvin Purple'/ 'Sometime Man' (November). 'Alvin Purple' was the theme song to Tim Burstall's feature film of the same name starring Graeme Blundell. As well as the theme song, Cadd wrote the entire musical scores for *Alvin Purple*, and its sequel *Alvin Rides Again*.

Bootleg issued the *Brian Cadd* EP which

featured 'Ginger Man', 'Show Me the Way', 'Every Mother's Son' and 'Silver City Birthday Celebration Day'. Cadd was also heard singing lead vocals on **The Bootleg Family Band's** hit 'Your Mama Don't Dance'. Cadd's solo career continued apace during 1974 with *Moonshine* (#16 in September), and the singles 'Class Of '74'/'School Days' (April), 'Let Go'/'Think It Over' (#14 in September) and 'Boogie Queen'/'All in the Way' (December). Cadd signed an American deal and the albums *Parabrahm* and *Moonshine* came out on Chelsea Records.

He toured the USA with **The Bootleg Family Band**, and became the first Australian artist to perform on the American television shows *Midnight Special* and *Don Kirshner's Rock Concert*. 1975 saw the Australian release of the single 'Gimme Good Lovin''/'Fire At Shepherd's Flat' (recorded in the USA) and the compilation *The Magic of Brian Cadd*. Having signed a new deal with Interfusion in the USA, Cadd spent the next six years working in the States. Interfusion issued the albums *White on White* and *Yesterday Dreams*, plus the singles 'White On White'/'El Dorado', 'Longest Night' (1976), 'Yesterday Dreams'/'1,000 Different Ways' (October 1978), 'Skating on Thin Ice'/'Ol'55' (April 1979) and 'Very Very Long Time'/'Move Me' (May 1980). While in the USA, Cadd had his songs covered by Gene Pitney ('Let Go'), the Pointer Sisters ('Love is Like a Rolling Stone', which was the flip to their hit 'Fire'), Glen Campbell, Dobie Gray, Cilla Black, Wayne Newton, Yvonne Elliman, Bonnie Tyler and Paul Jones.

Cadd returned to Australia in late 1981. Mushroom issued a one-off single, 'My Baby (Loves To Hurt Me)'/'For the Love of a Woman' (September 1982). Cadd set up his production company Shameless Productions, then issued an album and two singles, 'Land of the Video'/'Real to Me' (March 1985) and 'Still Hurting Me'/'Writing's on the Wall' (June 1985) for the Graffiti label. In 1993, Cadd formed a partnership with **Glenn Shorrock** as The Blazing Salads. The duo worked the cabaret and club circuit, and issued an album and three singles, 'When It All Comes Down', 'De-Emphasize' and 'Little Ray of Sunshine'. The duo's backing band included Rex Goh (guitar; ex-**Air Supply**), Kirk Lorange (guitar; ex-**Richard Clapton** Band) and Mark Kennedy (drums; ex-**Spectrum**, **Ayers Rock**, **Marcia Hines** Band).

As well as pursuing his solo career, Cadd produced albums for **Hans Poulsen**, Frieze (aka Darryl Cotton and Beeb Birtles from **The Zoot**), **New Dream**, **Dutch Tilders**, **Bluestone**, Kerrie Biddell and Daryl Somers. He also branched into film soundtracks, contributing to the likes of *Fatal Vision*, *Vampires at Death Beach* and *Return of the Living Dead*.

Albums: *Brian Cadd* (Bootleg, 1972), *Parabrahm* (Bootleg, 1973), *Moonshine* (Bootleg, 1974), *The Magic of Brian Cadd* (Bootleg, 1975), *White on White* (Festival/Interfusion, 1976), *Yesterday Dreams* (Festival/Interfusion, 1978), *The Best of Brian Cadd* (Summit, 1979), *Keep on Rockin'* (J&B, 1980), *No Stone Unturned* (Graffiti, 1985), *Sweet Rock & Roll* (compilation, Fable/EMI, 1996); ***With Glenn Shorrock:*** *The Blazing Salads* (EMI, 1993).

Caligula

Formed: *1990*
Style: *Techno grunge*
Original line-up: *Ashley Rothschild (vocals), Mitchell Foley (vocals, synth), James Fonti (vocals, synth; ex-My Heart Bleeds for You), James MacKinnon (guitar), Sean Fonti (bass; ex-My Heart Bleeds for You,* **Massappeal***), David Ross (drums; ex-***Massappeal***)*

Sydney band Caligula juxtaposed funk bass lines, heavy metal guitar riffs, hip-hop beats, techno keyboards and acid-house grooves to come up with a unique musical stew. Caligula's approach was similar in some ways to that of **Def FX**. Other reference points were UK bands KLF and Pop Will Eat Itself, or early (pre-'Epic') Faith No More. Certainly, from early on, the band's eccentric sound was the focus of a great deal of attention. Caligula even cracked the mainstream charts with a series of challenging releases.

Having taken its blend of electronic noise, samples and pop smarts as far as it could on the Sydney scene, Caligula made regular tours around Australia, including a support slot to UK visitors Pop Will Eat Itself (1992) and Depeche Mode (1994). In quick succession, Caligula issued the mini-album *Caligula*, and the CD EPs 'Got One' (December 1991), 'Bluff' (August 1992), *I.C.U.* ('Before') (April 1993) and 'Tears of a Clown' (a 1990s updating of the old Smokey Robinson hit). As well as scoring well on the independent charts, the last two reached #55 (June 1993) and #25 (February 1994) respectively on the mainstream national charts. The album *Rubenesque* (March 1994) was a reaffirmation of the band's techno experimentation and more earthy pop roots.

Albums: *Caligula* (mini-album, Timberyard, 1991), *Rubenesque* (Id/Mercury, 1994).

Mark 'Cal' Callaghan (*see* GANGgajang; The Riptides)

Joe Camilleri (*see* The Black Sorrows; Jo Jo Zep and the Falcons)

Cam-Pact

Formed: *1967*
Style: *Soul, psychedelic pop*
Original line-up: **Keith Glass** *(vocals, guitar; ex-Rising Sons,* **Eighteenth Century Quartet***), Chris Stockley (guitar; ex-Roadrunners, Delta Set), John Pugh (guitar, vocals, autoharp; ex-Roadrunners, Delta Set,* **Eighteenth Century Quartet***), Mark Barnes (bass; ex-Moppa Blues, Roadrunners, Delta Set), Bob Lloyd (drums)*

Cam-Pact was one of the most important breeding grounds for rock musicians of note on the Melbourne scene of the late 1960s/early 1970s. Cam-Pact became a cornerstone band with a genuine cult following. The band's name was originally the tongue-in-cheek The Camp Act, but that was considered too outrageous for the time.

Cam-Pact started as a Stax/Tamla Motown soul group in April 1967, before progressing through teenybopper and psychedelic stages and on to heavy blues. The band suffered many line-up changes, with the final version (circa early 1970) eventually evolving into **Company Caine** with the addition of **Gulliver Smith** (ex-Dr Kandy's Third Eye). The second line-up comprised Glass, Stockley and Barnes, with Trevor Courtney (drums; ex-Chants R&B) and Greg Cook (guitar; ex-Silk'n'Dreams) replacing Lloyd and Pugh respectively. Lloyd went on to Carnival, **Extradition** and Forest. Pugh spent the next few years jumping from one band to the next in quick succession: **James Taylor Move**, The News, The Avengers, **Healing Force**, Baiyana, Silversun, **Ray Burton** Nightflyers and the **Renée Geyer** Band.

The second line-up of Cam-Pact was the most consistent and popular combination. The band's four singles for Festival were all fine examples of late 1960s psychedelic pop: 'Something Easy'/'Michael' (March 1968), 'Drawing Room'/'I'm Your Puppet' (May 1968), 'Good Good Feelin''/'And It Won't Be Long' (September 1968) and 'Potion of Love'/'Cry My Heart Out' (June 1969). By late 1968, Barnes had left and Glass was playing bass. Glass and Stockley had also left Cam-Pact by the middle of 1969. Stockley joined **Axiom** and then **The Dingoes**. Initially **Keith Glass** appeared in the Australian production of *Hair*, after which he went on to become something of a legendary figure in his own right. Cam-Pact's last single was 'Zoom Zoom Zoom'/'Getting Myself Together' (September 1969).

Latterday members included Bill Blisset (organ, vocals), Russell Smith (guitar; ex-Nineteen87), Chris Löfven (bass; ex-19th Generation, Carnival) who was replaced by Cliff Edwards (bass) and **Ray Arnott** (drums; ex-Chelsea Set, Browns). Bluesman **Matt Taylor** also filled in as lead singer for a two-week tour of Sydney during early 1970. By March 1970, the final, three-piece Cam-Pact line-up of Smith, Arnott and Edwards had formed the backbone of **Company Caine**. Löfven went on to become a leading underground film-maker. He directed groundbreaking filmclips for **Daddy Cool's** 'Eagle Rock' and **Spectrum's** 'I'll Be Gone'. In 1972 he filmed an intriguing 11-minute silent short called *The Beginning* which featured a heavy organ score by musician **Lindsay Bourke**. In 1976, Löfven wrote, produced and directed the feature film *Oz*, an Australian adaption of the *Wizard of Oz* storyline.

In 1977, Glass issued the four-track Cam-Pact EP *Living in the '60s* on his Missing Link label. The EP included 'Drawing Room', 'I'm Your Puppet' and two previously unissued tracks from 1968 'Wasted (on a Fantasy)' and '(You Don't Have to) Break it to Me Gently'.

Candy Harlots

Formed: *1987*
Style: *Hard rock*
Original line-up: *Mark Easton (vocals; ex-Suicide Squad,* **Kelpies**, *Soggy Porridge, Glam Savages), Ron Barrett (aka Ron B. Gypsy, guitar; ex-Glam Savages), Marc Lee De Huger (guitar), Leeno Dee (bass), Tony Cardinal (drums; ex-What??!!, Soggy Porridge)*

Sydney band Candy Harlots were an unashamedly macho, decadent lot. With a black leathers'n'chains and gutter-rock image played out over an entertaining brand of hard-edged rock'n'roll, the Harlots drew inspiration from US outfits like New York Dolls and Mötley Crüe.

Independent label Au-go-go issued the band's debut single 'Red Hot Rocket'/'When Will I Know?' in April 1989. The first pressing of 500 copies came on red vinyl with a pair of lace panties wrapped around each single. The band issued its second single, 'Danger'/'Wrap to Arms', on the Timberyard label (May 1990). The band suffered several blows that year, when first Marc Lee De Huger left and then Ron Barrett died from an asthma attack (allegedly precipitated by drug/alcohol abuse) in October. Mark Easton also left at the end of the year. Leeno Dee and Tony Cardinal decided to continue and recruited new members Phil Bowley (guitar), Peter Masi (guitar) and Aiz Lynch (vocals; ex-Backstreet Shuffle).

The band signed to Virgin Records and then supported **AC/DC** on several dates of its October 1991 Razor's Edge Australian tour. Flamboyant frontman Lynch stayed long enough to sing on the singles 'Danger' (re-recorded version)/'Hot Love Child' (October 1991), 'Sister's Crazy' (April 1992) and 'What are We Fighting for?' (August), the EP *Foreplay* (which reached the national Top 30 and #6 in Sydney during March 1992) and the sleaze-rock album *Five Wicked Ways* (national #31 in May 1992).

In June 1992, Candy Harlots dispensed with Lynch's services (he formed Angry Snuff Puppet) and replaced him with 18-year-old Hayden Watt (ex-Triple X). In mid-1993, Masi and Cardinal left (leaving Dee as the sole original member). Tubby Wadsworth (drums, ex-Fester Fanatics, Killing Time) joined Dee, Bowley and Watt, and the band became known as Helter Skelter. Helter Skelter issued a new single, Iggy Pop's 'Cry for Love', but by April 1994 had become The Harlots with the addition of a new singer Jordan Howe. The band issued the CD EP *The Harlots* (October 1994), which contained a cover of Kiss's 'Detroit Rock City'. By the end of 1995, the band had broken up. Leeno Dee and Phil Bowley formed a new band called Dearly Beloved with drummer Steve Aubey. The band issued a self-financed CD EP, *Pushover*, in late 1996.

Album: *Five Wicked Ways* (Virgin, 1992).

The Cannanes

Formed: *1984*
Style: *Pop, folk*
Original line-up: *Annabel Bleach (vocals), Michelle Cannane (recorder, percussion), Stephen O'Neill (guitar, trumpet; ex-Guthugga Pipeline, Particles,* **Lighthouse Keepers***), Frances Gibson (bass), David Nichols (drums; ex-BFMF, Pious Eggs)*

The Cannanes' brand of wide-eyed, bittersweet, simple folksy pop bore the influence of **The Go-Betweens** and the softer side of The Velvet Underground. The band has actually received more interest from the USA and Europe than here in Australia. The band's recording output has been erratic but prolific. The Cannanes' first release was the self-produced cassette *The Cannanes Come Across with the Goods* in 1985.

David Nicholls issued the band's wilfully amateurish four-track EP, *Bored Angry and Jealous* (January 1987), on his independent label Distant Violins (which was also the name of his self-published fanzine). English music paper *New Musical Express* gave the EP a glowing review, in which the reviewer (under the moniker of 'The Legend') declared it to be 'Single of the Year!' The band took such hyperbole in its stride and continued to work. Randall Lee (guitar, vocals) and Susan Grigg (violin; ex-**Chad's Tree**) joined in early 1987, after which time Annabel left. The Cannanes issued their debut album, *African Man's Tomato*, in November 1987. Michelle and Susan left before the album was issued. As a four-piece (Lee, Nichols, Gibson and O'Neill), the band issued two singles in 1988, 'I Think The Weather's Affected Your Brain'/'Stories' (April) and 'Cardboard'/'Woe' (May).

The Cannanes completed the album *A Love Affair with Nature* with assistance from Susan Grigg. In 1990, with Nick Kidd (bass, French horn) on board, The Cannanes recorded *Caveat Emptor*, which did not come out until 1993. In May 1991, The Cannanes undertook a low-key tour of the USA. In August 1992, the Bi Joopiter label in the UK issued the *Broken Bottles* EP and Ajax in the USA issued the *Stumpvision* EP. The US album *Witchetty Pole* was a compilation of *African Man's Tomato* and the *Bored Angry and Jealous* EP. In late 1992, Gavin Butler (bass, vocals, guitar; ex-Guthugga Pipeline, Teapot) joined. In 1994, Francesca Bussey replaced Butler on bass, giving a line-up of O'Neill, Gibson, Nichols and Bussey. *Short Poppy Syndrome* came out in 1994. The band's US release, *A Love Affair with Nature* (May 1995), was a compilation of the album of the same name and the 'Cardboard' and 'Weather' singles. The Cannanes issued a new album, *The Cannanes* (August 1996), which added a discernible sense of professionalism to the band's usually whimsical and shambolic charm. The Cannanes toured Australia for the first time in a number of years.

After leaving The Cannanes in 1991, Randall Lee formed Nice with Susannah Stuart-Lindsay (bass) and Jo Packer (drums). Stuart-Lindsay later moved to rhythm guitar to make way for new bass player Mark King. Like The Cannanes, Nice played baroque, romantic pop that also recalled **The Go-Betweens** and The Velvet Underground's third album. US label Feel Good All Over issued two Nice albums, *Nice* (1992) and *Apple Pie* (1993). Lee then formed Ashtray Boy with Thomas Tallis (bass) and Neil Johnson (drums). To confuse matters, Lee moved to Chicago, where he formed a separate-but-equal incarnation of Ashtray Boy. The album *The Honeymoon Suite* (on Feel Good All Over, 1993) featured the American line-up, while *Macho Champions* (on Ajax, 1994) was split between the two combos. *Candypants Beach* (on Ajax, 1995) and *The Everyman's Fourth Dimension* (on Ajax, 1996) were mostly recorded in Australia. The band's diverse musical palate incorporated jangly folk pop and more surreal moments.

Albums: *African Man's Tomato* (no label, 1987), *A Love Affair with Nature* (no label, 1989), *Caveat Emptor* (Feel Good All Over, US import only, 1993), *Witchetty Pole* (Feel Good All Over, US import only, 1993), *Short Poppy Syndrome* (Ajax, US import only, 1994), *A Love Affair with Nature* (Ajax/MDS, 1995), *The Cannanes* (Ajax/MDS, 1996).

Judy Cannon

Style: *R&B, pop*

Melbourne singer Judy Cannon (b. 1939) is recognised as one of Australia's first and best female rock'n'rollers. Unlike other female performers from the early 1960s, like **Noeleen Batley** (dubbed 'Australia's Little Miss Sweetheart'), **Judy Stone** and **Patsy Ann Noble**, who presented wholesome, soft images, Cannon was an out-and-out blues belter. Her earliest influences included Johnny 'Mr Cry' Ray, Elvis Presley, Jerry Lee Lewis and LaVern Baker. Perhaps only **Betty McQuade** and Laurel Lea approached Cannon in style. Cannon's career in Australia was relatively short, as she went to the UK in 1963 and began performing in musicals.

Cannon's career got under way in 1957 when she sang at 50:50 dances at Coburg Town Hall. She appeared on television shows like *Stairway to the Stars* and *Teenage Mailbag*, and in late 1958 joined crack Melbourne instrumental outfit **The Thunderbirds** as one of its featured vocalists (alongside Billy Owens and Billy O'Rourke). **The Thunderbirds** became resident group at Earl's Court in St Kilda. In late 1959, **The Thunderbirds** signed to Festival's Rex label, which resulted in the release of two EPs and two singles. Owens, O'Rourke and Cannon sang a song each on the band's debut EP *Rex 4 Star* (completed by a rendition of Duane Eddy's instrumental 'Peter Gunn'). Cannon sang 'Laughing on the Outside'. Owens and O'Rourke sang two songs each on the second EP, *The Thunderbirds*, and the debut single 'Running Bear'/'Blue Woman' (1959). Cannon took vocal honours on the second single 'Ma, He's Making Eyes at Me'/'Laughing on the Outside' (April 1960).

Cannon made regular appearances on Brian Henderson's *Bandstand*, after which **Johnny O'Keefe** invited her to sing on *Six O'Clock Rock*. Having made the move to Sydney, Cannon's debut performance on *Six O'Clock Rock* (23 April 1960) became the first of many until the show's demise in mid-1962. In early 1961, Cannon issued her second single for Rex, 'If She Should Come to You', which featured backing provided by **Dig Richards** and The R'Jays. The single was issued backed by a track from Perth singer Les Meade. 'If She Should Come to You' later appeared on the Rex album *All Australian Hit Parade*. By that stage, Cannon was touring Australia with the likes of **Johnny O'Keefe** and the Dee Jays, **Col Joye** and the Joy Boys and **Dig Richards** and the R'Jays. She supported Cliff Richard and the Shadows on their October 1961 Australian tour. A month later, Cannon issued her third single 'That Funny Feeling'/'Shanghai'. With the demise of *Six O'Clock Rock* in mid-1962, Cannon moved on to regular appearances on the Seven Network's *Sing Sing Sing* (again with O'Keefe) and *Star Time*, then on to the ABC for *The Bryan Davies Show*.

In July 1963, Cannon left Australia bound for the UK. She had intended to stay in London for six months, but that extended into 13 years. Soon after her arrival in the UK, Cannon landed a television role on Terry O'Neill's *One O'Clock Show*. One of her greatest successes was stepping into the lead role of Mama Rose in the hit musical *Gypsy*. With her return to Australia in 1976, Cannon joined children's television show *Play School* as a presenter. That was short-lived, however, because a few months later Cannon returned to the UK.

Cannon came back to Australia in the early 1980s and moved into selling real estate. In 1983, she performed at a 1960s revival concert which also featured **The Thunderbirds, Betty McQuade**, Malcolm Arthur and Billy Owens. In late 1996, the Canetoad label issued a compilation *Girls! Girls! Girls! (Australian Female Performers of the Sixties: Volume 1)* which included Cannon's 'Hello Heartache'. Other singers featured were **Betty McQuade, Noeleen Batley, Yvonne Barrett**, Carolyn Young, The Taylor Sisters, Vicki Forrest, Lee Sellers, Pam Oakley, Del Juliana, The Field Twins and Joy Lemmon.

Captain Cocoa

Formed: *1984*
Style: *Pop*
Original line-up: *Glen O'Neil (vocals), Evan Ong (percussion, vocals), Mark Murphy (guitar), Andre Elhay (sax, flute, vocals), Leon Le Bruin (trumpet), David O'Neil (bass, vocals), David Wookey (drums)*

On a mid-1980s Melbourne scene besotted by post-**Birthday Party** angst or heavy gothic grunge, the clean-cut lads who made up Captain Cocoa came on like Haircut 100. In other words, Captain Cocoa played pure, unadulterated pop music. Other influences included Orange Juice, The Housemartins, Madness and a touch of 'Oliver's Army'-era Elvis Costello.

Captain Cocoa formed in the Melbourne suburb of Mitcham. The band members displayed their sense of humour by riding their bikes to a gig at ID's in Prahran to launch their debut single 'Bicycle Thieves'/'Sympathy Vote', 'Kite' as a part of Bike Week (August 1988). Adam Dennis replaced Le Bruin in 1988. The band celebrated its suburban roots on *Kite* (January 1989), an album full of pure pop confection like 'To My Dancing Queen', 'Butterflies', 'Young Conservative' and 'Now She Works in a Bank'. The band broke up in 1990 after issuing a final single, 'Paul Weller (Was Formerly Yours)' (May). David O'Neil went on to a successful career in stand-up comedy, and as a member of the *Osso Buco* comedy team and the *Breakfasters* on Melbourne public radio 3RRR-FM and as a writer for television comedy shows *Full Frontal* and *Eric* (with Eric Bana).

Album: *Kite* (Cleopatra, 1989).

Captain Matchbox Whoopee Band

Formed: *1969*
Style: *Jug-band pop, jazz*
Original line-up: *Mick Conway (vocals, washboard, ukelele), Jim Conway (harmonica, kazoo, vocals), Dave Hubbard (guitar), Peter Inglis (guitar, vocals), Peter Scott (tea chest bass), Mick Fleming (banjo, mandolin, guitar, vocals), Jim Niven (piano, pedal organ)*

As one of the most unusual aggregations ever assembled in Australia, Captain Matchbox Whoopee Band played jug-band blues enlivened with sideshow entertainment and vaudeville lunacy. An overseas equivalent would perhaps be Bonzo Dog Doo Dah Band.

Captain Matchbox was centred around the Conway brothers, Mick and Jim, who formed the band in 1969. The Conways' early inspiration came from the likes of Fats Waller, Jelly Roll Morton and other 1930s jazz exponents. Captain Matchbox's theatrical style found much favour with Melbourne's underground scene, and the band became a regular at the Much More Ballroom, supporting **Spectrum**, **Daddy Cool**, etc.

Captain Matchbox's first mainstream exposure came with an appearance in Tim Burstall's 1971 film *Stork* starring Bruce Spence and Jackie Weaver. Image Records issued the singles 'My Canary Has Circles Under His Eyes'/'Nagasaki' (a Top 40 hit in November 1972) and 'I Can't Dance (Got Ants in My Pants)'/'Jungle Dance' (April 1973) and the album *Smoke Dreams* (June). The album was comprised entirely of 1930s and 1940s jazz, blues and jug-band standards. Image licensed the album to the ESP-Disk label (home to Tom Rapp's Pearls Before Swine) for release in the USA.

In November 1973, the line-up had changed to the Conway brothers, Niven and Fleming with new members Geoff Hales (drums, washboard), Fred Olbrei (violin, vocals) and Dave Flett (electric bass, slide dobro, backing vocals, ukelele; ex-Lipp and The Double Dekker Brothers). Jon Snyder (guitar) joined at the beginning of 1974, and the band issued 'Your Feets Too Big'/'Wait for Me Juanita' (February 1974) and 'Hernando's Hideaway'/'Down Undergroundsville' (July 1974). 'Wait For Me Juanita' was one of the band's first original compositions (written by Mick Conway and Dave Flett) to see release on record.

Another Conway–Flett song 'Wangaratta Wahine' became the title track to the band's breakthrough album which came out at the end of 1974. The band appeared on the ABC-TV's pop show ***Countdown*** playing 'Wangaratta Wahine', and by August 1975 the album had reached #4 on the national charts. Another of the album's distinguishing features was the Michael Leunig cartoon on the cover. In 1975, Fleming and Hales left to be replaced by Chris Worral (ex-**Pelaco Brothers**) and Manny Paterakis. Mushroom signed the band and issued 'Australia'/'Christopher Columbus' (October 1975) and the album *Australia*. Once again, it was an entertaining mix of originals and covers like 'Cocaine Habit', 'Sweeny Todd the Barber' and Noel Coward's '20th Century Blues'. In keeping with the band's sense of humour, in the album credits Mick was listed as Microphone Conway while Chris Worral was Christmas Worral.

There were more line-up changes in 1976 with Jack Saram replacing Olbrei, Graeme Isaacs replacing Paterakis and Gordon McLean replacing Worral. Niven also left to join **The Sports**. The band's old label, Image, issued the compilation album *Making Whoopee* (October 1976). By November 1976, Captain Matchbox had evolved into The Soapbox Circus when it was incorporated in the Australian Performing Group. Flett had left and two new members, Peter Mulheissen (bass) and Rick Ludbrook (guitar, sax), joined. The new line-up recorded the live album *The Great Stumble Forward*, the single 'If I Can't Hav-Anna in Cuba'/'Chiropodist Shop', and appeared in the play *Smackin' the Dacks*.

By 1978 the band was known as Matchbox with a line-up of Mick, Jim, Ludbrook, Mulheissen, McLean, Tony Burkys (guitar; ex-Original Battersea Heroes) and Stephen Cooney (guitar), who was replaced by Louis McManus (ex-**Bushwackers**). Matchbox released *Slightly Troppo*, which produced the singles 'Sleep'/'Victims of Circumstance' (June 1978) and 'Love is Like a Rainbow' (January 1979). Matchbox also appeared in Tim Burstall's 1979 feature film *Dimboola*.

By mid-1979, the line-up of Mick, Jim, McManus and Mulheissen had been augmented by Robert Ross (drums; ex-Manning), Eric McCusker (guitar) and Chris Coyne (sax, flute). That version of the band introduced a more rock-oriented sound, but by September 1980 Matchbox had broken up. McCusker joined **Mondo Rock** and the Conway brothers embarked on a series of new ventures. The first was The Hotsie Totsie Band in 1981, then Carnival in 1983 and The Conway Brothers Hiccups Orchestra in 1984. Carnival comprised Mick, Jim, Palz (lead vocals), Jim Niven (ex-**Sports**), Kim Cook (guitar), Kim Constable (bass; ex-Ratbags of Rhythm) and Warwick Kent (drums; ex-Ratbags of Rhythm). The Hiccups Orchestra issued a self-titled album on Larrikin in 1987 which mixed old (1930s and 1940s) favourites with contemporary satire. 'Cho Cho Ch' Boogie' was the single. Mick worked with Mick Conway's Whoopee Band in 1989. When Avenue/CBS reissued *Wangaratta Wahine* in 1983, Captain Matchbox Whoopee Band re-formed for a one-off national tour. The line-up featured Mick, Jim, Flett, McManus, Hales, Niven and Jim Pennell (drums).

In the late 1980s, Jim Conway was diagnosed with Multiple Sclerosis (MS). Despite being wheelchair-bound he has continued to play, most notably in The Backsliders. The Backsliders comprised Conway (harmonica), Peter Burgess (drums; ex-Stumblers) and Dominic Turner (guitar, vocals; ex-Stumblers). The band's brand of purist acoustic blues and R&B appealed to a hardcore following that has been rewarded with the release of five albums, *Preachin' Blues* (MBS, 1988), *Sittin' on a Million* (Sandstock, 1989), *Hellhounds* (Sandstock, 1991), *Live at the Royal* (Blues Club, 1992) and *Wide Open* (Blues Club, 1995).

Captain Matchbox Whoopee Band albums: *Smoke Dreams* (Image, 1973), *Wangaratta Wahine* (Image, 1974; reissued 1983), *Australia* (Mushroom/Festival, 1975), *Making Whoopee* (compilation, Image, 1976; reissued on CD, Avenue/EMI, 1996). ***As Soapbox Circus:*** *The Great Stumble Forward* (Mushroom/Festival, 1976); ***Matchbox album:*** *Slightly Troppo* (Mushroom/Festival, 1979); ***Conway Brothers Hiccups Orchestra album:*** *The Conway Brothers Hiccups Orchestra* (Larrikin, 1987).

Captain Rock

Style: *Musical comedy*

Comedian Bob Brown took the stage name Captain Rock. He was one of the first Australian performers to combine comedy with rock music, much in the fashion of US satirists Cheech and Chong. Captain Rock signed to Mushroom and issued the singles 'Give Me a Home Among the Gum Trees'/'Can't Stop Rock'n'Rollin'' (November 1975) and 'Steamed Vegetables'/'Shape I'm in' (March 1976) and the album *Buried Treasure*. He next surfaced in 1981 on Fable with 'I Do Love Saturday Arvo'/'Can We Do It Again?'. He issued a new album in 1990. In the early 1980s, bush band Bullamakanka recorded a version of Captain Rock's 'Home Among the Gum Trees'. Bullamakanka's rendition of the song was later adopted as the theme song to popular television gardening show *Burke's Backyard*.

Albums: *Buried Treasure* (Mushroom/Festival, 1975), *Living in Australia* (Independent, 1990).

Glenn Cardier

Style: *Folk, soft rock*

Sydney singer/songwriter Glenn Cardier was a popular solo performer on the early 1970s scene. In much the same vein as James Taylor, **Doug Ashdown** and **Ross Ryan**, Cardier played a brand of gentle and reflective acoustic folk and soft rock that gained him a strong cult following. Cardier actually started out playing lead guitar in Brisbane acid-rock band The Revolution before taking to the road as a folkie.

He signed to Festival's progressive Infinity label, with which he issued two albums and five singles: 'See My Way'/'Teach Me How to Fly' (March 1972), 'Every Wounded Bird'/'The Juggler' (July 1972), 'Ulysses'/'Minstrel' (February 1973), 'Oh Dear Saint Peter'/'I Am the Day' (July 1973) and 'I See a Comedy'/'Lovers Alias Fools' (June 1974). Never content to be seen as just a sensitive folkie, Cardier toured with rock bands like **La De Das**, **Country Radio**, **Sherbet** and **Daddy Cool**. He also made an appearance at the 1972 Sunbury Festival, and supported overseas visitors Frank Zappa and Manfred Mann's Earth Band.

In 1974, Cardier became one of the first musicians in Australia (along with Rob MacKenzie from **MacKenzie Theory** and Greg Quill from **Country Radio**) to receive a travel grant from the Australia

Council for the Arts (under the auspices of Gough Whitlam's Labor government). He travelled to England where he toured for several years, recording the *Glenn Cardier* album and a single 'Till the Fire Dies'/'Christopher Columbus' (June 1976) for Interfusion along the way.

On his return to Australia in late 1978, Cardier recorded 'Establishment Blues' under the psuedonym of Sydney Hill. The song appeared as the B-side to the Mojo Singers' #1 hit 'C'mon Aussie C'mon'. Cardier's 1979 band, the Bel-Aires, comprised Brad Alick (lead guitar), Eddie Parise (bass, who later joined **Baby Animals**) and Vince Crae (drums). Cardier issued the single 'Expectations'/'I Saved Annette from Drowning' in February 1980. He has also recorded the Christmas track 'Reindeers on the Rooftops' under the alias Riff Raff.

Albums: *Days Of Wilderness* (Festival/Infinity, 1972), *Only When I Laugh* (Festival/Infinity, 1974), *Glenn Cardier* (Interfusion, 1976), *Everyday Maniac: The Festival Files Volume 20* (Festival, 1991).

Kev Carmody

Style: *Folk, country, blues*

Koori singer/songwriter Kev Carmody (b. 1946) grew up in a droving family in the Toowoomba region of southern Queensland. He was forcibly separated from his family at nine years of age and sent to school in Toowoomba. He never completed his senior school years, but at the age of 33 he enrolled at Darling Downs Institute of Advanced Education to study colonial history. He then completed a PhD in History at The University of Queensland.

In December 1988, Carmody issued his acclaimed debut album, *Pillars of Society*, on the Rutabagas label (distributed by Larrikin). Songs like 'Black Deaths in Custody' and 'Thou Shalt Not Steal' highlighted the oppression and ignorance facing Australia's Aboriginal people. Carmody's music was influenced by his own Murri culture, as well as the protest songs of Woody Guthrie, Bob Dylan and Leadbelly (Huddie Ledbetter). Steve Connolly (from **Paul Kelly** and the Messengers) produced Carmody's second album, *Eulogy (for a black person)* (December 1991). The album's songs like 'Cannot Buy My Soul', 'River of Tears' and 'Droving Women' were fleshed out by guest appearances from **Paul Kelly** and members of Mixed Relations. Carmody issued the CD EP 'Street Beat' in December 1992.

Kelly again appeared on Carmody's 1993 album *Bloodlines*, which included the CD single 'Freedom' (August) and a version of 'From Little Things Big Things Grow'. Co-written with Kelly, and originally included on The Messengers' album *Comedy*, 'From Little Things Big Things Grow' told the story of the Gurindji drovers' walk-out at Windy Hill, Northern Territory during the 1960s—which sparked off the land rights movement in Australia. In 1993, Carmody was also featured as one of four black profiles in the SBS-TV documentary series called *Bloodlines*.

The Church's Steve Kilbey produced Carmody's fourth album, *Images & Illusions*, which featured guest appearances from Linda Neal (violin), Greg Sheehan (percussion) and **Tiddas** and Arramaieda (backing vocals). The album came out in September 1995, and yielded the single 'The Young Dancer is Dead'. Carmody has performed at prisons around the country, and supported international visitors Bob Dylan, Bonnie Raitt and Billy Bragg on their respective Australian tours.

Albums: *Pillars of Society* (Rutabagas/Larrikin, 1989), *Eulogy (for a black person)* (Festival, 1991), *Bloodlines* (Festival, 1993), *Images & Illusions* (Festival, 1995).

Pat Carroll

Style: *Pop*

Melbourne-born pop singer Pat Carroll was a regular on *Bandstand* and *The Go!! Show* during the mid-1960s. She issued seven singles on W&G between 1964 and 1966: 'He's My Guy'/'He Loves Me Too', 'Where Have You Been?'/'That's All', 'Why Do Fools Fall in Love?'/'End of the World', 'I Know'/'Chained to a Melody', 'Did He Call Today Mama?'/'Here I Am', 'You're No Good'/'Don't Come Running Back' and 'He's a Rebel'/'Talk About Love'.

In 1967 she won an award and travelled to England. She teamed up with **Olivia Newton-John** (at the suggestion of **The Seekers'** Athol Guy) as Pat and Olivia. The duo became successful on television and in clubs. In 1969, after she was unable to renew her working visa, Carroll returned to Australia. She recorded 'All Kinds of Everything'/'In Your World' for Fable and it became her only national hit (#19 in June 1970). That year she married ex-**Strangers** guitarist John Farrar (then part of Marvin, Welch and Farrar). Carroll recorded three singles for the Interfusion label, 'To the Sun'/'Out of my Mind' (September 1972), 'Live Love'/'To the Sun' (October 1972) and 'Now I'm Stuck on You'/'I'm Not Ready' (October 1973). Throughout most of the 1970s, Carroll was based in the UK and the USA, where Farrar was a top composer and producer. Farrar composed 'Hopelessly Devoted to You', which **Olivia Newton-John** sang on the *Grease* soundtrack.

Carson

Formed: *1970*
Style: *Blues, boogie*
Original line-up: *Sleepy Greg Lawrie (slide guitar, dobro; ex-***Creatures***, Chocolate), John Capek (piano, vocals; ex-Leo and Friends), Ian Ferguson (bass, vocals), Tony Lunt (drums)*

Along with **Billy Thorpe** and the Aztecs and **Chain**, **Carson** was one of the leading blues bands on the early 1970s Melbourne scene. Other blues bands on the Melbourne scene at the time included Genesis, **Bulldog** and **Adderley Smith Blues Band**. The original version of Carson formed as Carson County Band in January 1970.

By late 1970, Carson had dropped the County Band part of the name to avoid the country image with which the band was being tagged. Prior to that, Carson County Band issued a single on the Rebel label, 'On the Highway'/'Resting Place' which was a good example of the band's clattering Chicago blues/Canned Heat-influenced sound. Even at that early stage, Greg Lawrie was one of the foremost slide guitar players in the country. Around the same time (May 1970), Lawrie and Capek collaborated with Genesis members **Matt Taylor**, Tim Piper and Yuk Harrison, plus Trevor Courtney, on a one-off recording session as The Meating. The resultant single, 'Bad Luck Feeling'/'Back Home' on Rebel (August 1970), was another fine example of Australian hard blues.

Capek left Carson at the end of 1970; he went on to join **King Harvest**, Flite and **Hannagan**. He issued a single on Philips in 1972, 'Blue Jean Baby'/'Annabelle', after which he left to work overseas. According to the *Who's Who of Australian Rock*, Capek has had his songs recorded by Rod Stewart, Chicago, Toto, Manhattan Transfer, Don Johnson, **Olivia Newton-John**, Dan Hill, Marc Jordan, the **Little River Band**, **John Farnham**, Patty Austin and Diana Ross. His songs have also appeared on the soundtracks to the overseas feature films *Cocktail* and *Youngblood*, plus a trio of Pino Amenta's Australian films, *Boulevard of Broken Dreams* (1988), *Heaven Tonight* (1990) and *What the Moon Saw* (1990). In 1991, Capek issued a solo album, *Indaba*.

In the meantime, **Broderick Smith** (vocals, harp, ex-**Adderley Smith Blues Band**, Sundown) and Ian 'Willy' Winter (guitar; ex-Brothers Grimm, Five Just Men, Pigface) joined Carson in time to record a single for the Havoc label, 'Travelling South'/'Moonshine', which came out in August 1971. Havoc reissued the single in November 1972, by which time Carson had signed to EMI/Harvest. Reissue specialists Raven included 'Travelling South' on the *Golden Miles: Australian Progressive Rock 1969–1974* compilation (1994).

In July 1971, Ferguson left to join Island, and his place was taken by Barry Sullivan (ex-**Chain**) for three months. When Sullivan left to join Capek and ex-**King Harvest** singer **Leo De Castro** in Flite, Gary Clarke (ex-**King Harvest**) became Carson's new bass player. In November, Mal Logan (keyboards; ex-**Healing Force**) also joined. By that stage Carson was celebrated as one of the great jamming bands of the day. Occasionally the band was augmented by a three-piece brass section.

In March 1972, Ian Winter left Carson to join **Daddy Cool** as second guitarist. With the break-up of **Daddy Cool** in August, Winter returned to the Carson fold. During early 1972, the band's manager, Rhett Walker, decided to promote **Broderick Smith** as a solo artist. Smith recorded two singles for Image, 'Goin' on Down to the End of the World'/'She's Gone' (May 1972) and 'Yesterday It Rained'/'About Life' (March 1973). All four tracks had been written and produced by **Brian Cadd** (Smith did co-write 'About Life').

Carson's first commercial success came with the single 'Boogie Part One'/'Boogie Part Two', which reached #30 in September 1972. It was followed in November by the powerful *Blown* album, which was full of free-flowing, bluesy hard rock. By that stage sax player Mal Capewell (ex-Dr Kandy's Third Eye, **Company Caine**) had joined the touring line-up. Capewell had made a name for himself in the UK as a member of such bands as Dada and Graham Bond's Holy Magick. Carson appeared at Sunbury 1973, over the January Australia Day weekend, and then promptly broke up. The Carson track 'Friday Night Groove' appeared on Mushroom's triple live album of the event, *The Great Australian Rock Festival Sunbury 1973* (April 1973). EMI/Harvest issued the band's Sunbury set later in the year as the live album *On the Air*.

Broderick Smith formed **The Dingoes** with Kerryn Tolhurst and Chris Stockley. Sleepy Greg Lawrie appeared on the **Chain** album *Two of a Kind*, as well as playing on **Matt Taylor's** albums *Straight as a Die* and *Music*, plus his hit single 'I Remember When I Was Young'. Lawrie then turned up in Gulliver's Travels, **Broderick Smith's** Hired Hands, The Whittle Family and Last Chance Band. Mal

Logan formed Alta Mira, then joined **The Dingoes** and the **Renée Geyer** Band.

Albums: *Blown* (EMI/Harvest, 1972), *On the Air* (EMI/Harvest, 1973).

Catchcry (*see* The Riptides)

Catfish (Don Walker)

Style: *Blues, rock*

Between early 1984 and 1987, former **Cold Chisel** pianist/songwriter Don Walker stepped away from the Australian music industry. After ten years on the road with **Cold Chisel**, he deserved a break. He travelled extensively across Australia and overseas, and prepared the songs that would make up his next project.

Under the guise of Catfish, Walker signed to WEA and issued an album and three singles, 'The Early Hours'/'Electric Man' (October 1988), 'When You Dance'/'See You Again' (December) and 'Hiwire Girl'/'My Backyard' (February 1989). In keeping with his preference, Catfish was a low-key affair. Even when **Cold Chisel** was at the height of its popularity, Walker was always content to stand in the shadows, half-obscured. Yet it was Walker's vibrant songs like 'Khe Sanh', 'Star Hotel', 'Choir Girl' and 'Cheap Wine' that helped make **Cold Chisel** so successful. Catfish was a more personal project for Walker, but a lot of the material on *Unlimited Address* (October 1988) had a similar late-night, smoky blues feel to **Cold Chisel**. Helping out on the record were Dave Blight (harmonica), **Cold Chisel's Ian Moss** (guitar), co-producer Peter Walker (guitar; ex-**Bakery**) and South African producer Ricky Fataar (drums; ex-Beach Boys, Rutles).

In 1989 Walker took Catfish on tour with a line-up that included Blight, Charlie Owen (guitar; ex-**New Christs**), Andrew Reid (guitar), Paul Burton (bass) and Buzz Bidstrup (drums; ex-**Angels**). That same year, Walker worked with **Ian Moss** on his solo debut album, *Matchbook*. Walker contributed keyboards and bass, and wrote or co-wrote with Moss nine of the album's ten tracks including the hit singles 'Tucker's Daughter' and 'Telephone Booth'.

In 1991, Walker issued a second Catfish album, *Ruby* (October), and the singles 'Johnny's Gone' and 'Crooked Smile'. The touring Catfish line-up at that stage comprised Blight, Owen, Burton and new member Paul DeMarco (drums; ex-Scattered Aces, Heart Attack). In 1993, Walker formed a partnership with Charlie Owen and **Beasts of Bourbon/Cruel Sea** frontman **Tex Perkins** as Tex Don and Charlie. The union produced the album *Sad but True* (November 1993), a rootsy collection of acoustic country-blues tunes full of steel guitar and sparse piano.

Catfish (Don Walker)

The standout tracks included Don's 'Sitting in a Bar', Charlie's 'Dead Dog Boogie' and Tex's 'I Must be Getting Soft'. Produced by Tony Cohen, the album featured guest players like **Kim Salmon** (guitar; Surrealists, **Beasts of Bourbon**), steel guitar player Garrett Costigan, and Warren Ellis (violin) and Jim White (drums), both from **Dirty Three**. Tex Don and Charlie undertook an Australian tour which resulted in the *Monday Morning Coming Down (Live)* album, plus the CD single 'What I Done to Her' (September 1994). Walker was on the promotional trail again with the release of the **Cold Chisel** rarities collection *Teenage Love* in November.

Walker issued his second solo album *We're All Gunna Die* in September 1995. In 1996, WEA reissued on CD the Don Walker-penned soundtrack for the 1982 film *Freedom* (which had produced the single 'Speed Kills'/'Fascist Sounds' featuring Michael Hutchence from **INXS**). The album had originally come out in March 1982.

Catfish albums: *Unlimited Address* (WEA, 1988), *Ruby* (EastWest/WEA, 1991); ***Don Walker solo albums:*** *Freedom* (film soundtrack; WEA, 1982; reissued 1996), *We're All Gunna Die* (Salt/Shock, 1995); ***Tex Don and Charlie albums:*** *Sad But True* (Red Eye/Polydor, 1993), *Monday Morning Coming Down (Live)* (Red Eye/Polydor, 1994).

Cattletruck

Formed: *1984*
Style: *R&B, country*
Original line-up: *Paul Janovskis (vocals, guitar), Charles Todd (sax), Tony Dennis (bass), James Martin (drums)*

Melbourne outfit Cattletruck started life as Caught in a Cattletruck, a small-time St Kilda bar band playing in an acoustic country-blues idiom. Paul Janovskis and Tony Dennis formed the band out of a mutual love of the roots music of Johnny Cash, Screamin' Jay Hawkins and early Elvis Presley.

Paul Janovskis and Tony Dennis decided to take on a more electric sound. Phil Viggiano (keyboards) and Peter Knight (trumpet) joined in early 1985. With the departure of Todd, who joined **The Wreckery**, the band recruited Nick Cross on sax. Cattletruck issued the independent single 'Never Is'/'Crawfish' which was given away at a headlining gig at the Prince of Wales Hotel in December 1985. Following support slots to **Hoodoo Gurus**, **The Saints**, **Australian Crawl**, **Models** and international visitors Los Lobos, The Violent Femmes and Lloyd Cole and The Commotions, Cattletruck signed to the Regular label.

By that stage, the line-up had consolidated with Janovskis, Dennis, Viggiano, Knight, Cross and Bruce Coombs (drums). The band's first singles for Regular were 'Change'/'Roadhouse Girl' (October 1986) and 'Leave Me'/'Head' (March 1987). Englishman Dave Courtnay (Eric Clapton, Three Dog Night, Paul McCartney) produced the band's debut album, *Ready to Believe*, (December 1987), which yielded the singles 'Rain'/'Riding Out Tonight' (August 1987), Ashton, Gardner & Dyke's 'Resurrection Shuffle'/'Concrete And Diesoline' (November) and 'Reason to Believe'/'Personal Battle' (March, 1988). The album mixed rock, pop, country, R&B and blues, but was perhaps too diverse to appeal to the record-buying public. Cattletruck's last single was '(It's Not Such a) Bad Life'/'She Is' (June 1988).

At the end of 1988, Janovskis left Cattletruck. He became Paul Dean and formed Gas with Brett Kingman (guitar; ex-**Uncanny X-Men**, **James Reyne** Band), Greg Tailby (drums) and Rick Tailby (bass). Kingman had played in pop bands but was an accomplished rock guitarist. The jazz-trained Tailby brothers added a swing-like rhythm to the band's hard rock sound. Gas signed to Mushroom and issued the album *Burn So Bright* (June 1990) and the singles 'Burn So Bright' and 'Empty Dreams'. The records were not successful. Kingman and the Tailby brothers left in 1991 to be replaced by Brett Goldsmith (guitar; ex-**Chantoozies**), Brett Luton (drums; ex-**Geisha**) and Peter Dickson (bass). The band broke up soon after. Kingman went on to join Bigger than Jesus.

In the meantime, Cattletruck toured throughout 1989 with a new line-up which comprised Tony Dennis, Peter Knight and Bruce Coombs, plus newcomers Gary Young (vocals), Scott Kingman (guitar, brother of Brett) and Steve Colebrook (sax). The new line-up made little headway and broke up at the end of the year.

Cattletruck album: *Ready to Believe* (Regular/Festival, 1987); ***Gas album:*** *Burn So Bright* (Mushroom/Festival, 1990).

Nathan Cavaleri

Style: *Rock, blues*

Guitar prodigy and blues aficionado Nathan Cavaleri (b. 1982) had achieved an enormous amount by the time he was 14. At the age of nine he jammed with Dire Straits' lead guitarist Mark Knopfler, who called him 'unbelievable'. Then he played with guitar legend B.B. King, who called him 'the future of the blues'.

Following an appearance at the 25th Anniversary Concert for US magazine *Guitar Player* in San Francisco, Cavaleri acted in the Disney film *Camp Nowhere* and recorded two albums, *Jammin' with the Cats* and *Nathan*. Buzz Bidstrup (ex-**Angels**) produced Cavaleri's debut album. Cavaleri's debut single was a cover of Elvis Presley's 'Little Egypt' (May 1992). *Jammin' with the Cats* produced the single 'Sleepwalk' (July 1993), while *Nathan* yielded two singles, 'Workin' on It' (September 1994) and 'If Loving You is Wrong' (March 1995). Cavaleri also collaborated with **Jimmy Barnes** on the CD single **La De Das'** 'Gonna See My Baby Tonight' (September 1993). A total of 50 000 copies of the single were packaged inside Uncle Toby's cereal boxes.

Backing the guitarist on *Nathan* were the likes of Andrew Strong (vocals; of *The Commitments* fame), Sweet Pea Atkinson (vocals), Randy Jacobs (guitar), Teddy Andreadis (keyboards), Jeff Berlin (bass) and Curt Bisquera (drums). At 14, Cavaleri travelled to the White House and met US president Bill Clinton. The youngster introduced himself: 'G'day, I'm Nathan Cavaleri' to which Clinton replied: 'Yeah, I recognise you'. In early 1997, Cavaleri won the Medibank Private Arts Award at the Young Australian of the Year Ceremony. He also completed his first role in an Australian movie, *Paws*, to which he contributed two songs on the soundtrack.

Cavaleri has also had to battle ill-health. At the age of six he was diagnosed with leukaemia. It was The Starlight Foundation that made his wish to jam with Mark Knopfler come true. Remarkably, Cavaleri overcame the life-threatening illness and at 13 was declared free of the disease.

Nathan Cavaleri album: *Jammin' with the Cats* (Mushroom/Festival, 1993), ***Nathan Cavaleri Band album:*** *Nathan* (Mushroom/Festival, 1994).

Nick Cave and the Bad Seeds

Formed: *1983*
Style: *Rock, blues*
Original line-up: *Nick Cave (vocals; ex-***Birthday Party***), Mick Harvey (guitar, drums; ex-***Birthday Party***), Barry Adamson (bass, keyboards; ex-Magazine), Blixa Bargeld (guitar, on loan from Einsturzende Neubauten), Hugo Race (guitar; ex-Plays with Marionettes), Anita Lane (synthesiser)*

Nick Cave is one of the most celebrated and enigmatic performers of the post-punk rock era. He boasts an unrivalled international reputation in his field. His avant-garde take on rock is rooted in the blues, yet he has bypassed expectations constantly by transcending stylistic constraints. Although in recent years Cave has explored a more traditional ballad form, he has lost none of the passion and tension that earmarked his early work. With his long-time musical director Mick Harvey, Cave has fashioned a superb body of work.

Melbourne-born Cave and Harvey first came to prominence with post-punk legends **The Birthday Party**. After that band imploded in 1983, Cave assembled his first solo band. Cave recorded one side of his debut solo album in the UK (September 1983) with Harvey, Barry Adamson and Blixa Bargeld. Early solo shows around that time were billed as Nick Cave and the Cavemen. Cave joined other underground luminaries Marc Almond, Lydia Lunch and Clint Ruin (collectively known as The Immaculate Consumptive) for a short tour of the US east coast at the end of 1983. He assembled Nick Cave: Man or Myth with Harvey, Adamson, Hugo Race and Tracy Pew (bass; ex-**Birthday Party**) for a brief Australian tour at the start of 1984.

Kylie Minogue and Nick Cave

With Harvey, Adamson, Bargeld and Race (now dubbed The Bad Seeds), plus Anita Lane, Cave completed his debut solo album *From Her to Eternity* (issued in June 1984). The Bad Seeds' sparse, twisted blues setting provided much scope for Cave's passionate bellowing. Cave also recorded a startling interpretation of the Elvis Presley classic 'In the Ghetto', which was issued as a non-album single (June) backed with 'The Moon is in the Gutter'. As well as being a #1 hit on the independent charts, *From Her to Eternity* reached #40 on the mainstream British charts. Although Anita Lane did not stay with The Bad Seeds, Cave and Harvey contributed to her 1995 CD single, 'The World's a Girl', and album, *Dirty Pearl*. Harvey also sang a duet with Lane on the CD single 'Harley Davidson'. The single was lifted from Harvey's album of Serge Gainsbourg covers *Intoxicated Man* (November 1995). Harvey issued a second collection of Gainsbourg interpretations, *Pink Elephants*, in November 1997.

The First Born is Dead (July 1985) took Cave's fixations with the blues and Elvis Presley one step further, this time with mixed results. While Cave's emotional range was intact, he left himself open to accusations of romanticising a culture he's never known. Fortunately tracks like 'Tupelo', 'Train Long-Suffering', 'Black Crow King' and a cover of Bob Dylan's 'Wanted Man' did not sound like a man singing out of ignorance. 'Tupelo' was issued as a single (June) with a radically different version of the old **The Birthday Party** live staple 'The Six Strings that Drew Blood' on the flip.

Race had left prior to recording *The First Born is Dead* to form his own band **The Wreckery**. Cave added Thomas Wydler (drums; ex-Die Haut) so that Harvey could concentrate on guitar. *Kicking Against the Pricks* (September 1986) featured all cover versions, from The Velvet Underground's 'All Tomorrow's Parties' to **The Seekers**' 'The Carnival is Over'. The album and its single, 'The Singer'/ 'Running Scared' (August 1986), displayed Cave's ability as a gifted interpreter of other artists' material. The album's title, *Kicking Against the Pricks*, was derived from a chapter in the book *For the Term of His Natural Life*.

Your Funeral . . . My Trial contained all original

material. The album title took on a sense of irony when, on the eve of its release in November 1986, Cave faced a somewhat tenuous vagrancy charge in New York and his former **The Birthday Party** compadre Tracy Pew died as a result of a brain haemorrhage. Over the next year, Cave wrote *And the Ass Saw the Angel*, a southern gothic novel full of brooding imagery, which was eventually published by Black Spring Press in 1989. Black Spring also issued *King Ink*, a well-received collection of poems, prose and song lyrics. Cave and The Bad Seeds made a cameo appearance playing 'From Her to Eternity' in Wim Wenders' 1987 feature film *The Wings of Desire*.

In late 1987, Cave took his first acting role in director John Hillcoat and producer Evan English's feature film *Ghosts . . . of the Civil Dead*. The film was set in the fictional Central Industrial Prison. Cave played the part of psychotic inmate Maynard, with co-star Dave Mason (from **The Reels**) playing the prison queen Lilly. Cave received a script co-credit (along with Hillcoat, English and Hugo Race). Cave, Harvey and Bargeld composed the film soundtrack which was issued by Mute in June 1989. *Ghosts . . . of the Civil Dead* also made its debut in early 1989.

In early 1988, Cave recalled Harvey, Bargeld and Wydler for The Bad Seeds' Your Funeral My Trial Australian tour (February/March). The Bad Seeds included new members Roland Wolf (bass) and Kid Congo Powers (guitar; ex-Cramps, Gun Club). For some time, Harvey had moonlighted with **Crime and the City Solution**, which was fronted by singer Simon Bonney and also included ex-**The Birthday Party** guitarist Rowland S. Howard. *Tender Prey* (September 1988) was a powerful return to form. It yielded the taut, violent single 'The Mercy Seat'/'New Day' (June), and the milder 'Deanna'/'The Girl at the Bottom of the Glass' (September). The UK edition of *Tender Prey* included a limited edition 12-inch EP which featured Cave narrating excerpts from *And the Ass Saw the Angel*. By that stage, Cave had been in the depths of heroin addiction for some years. He eventually recovered, to take on his career with renewed vigour. By 1989, Cave had left London and Berlin to live in Brazil. The Bad Seeds recorded a new album in São Paulo, Brazil during October 1989.

The Good Son (April 1990) featured less forceful material, but did display a quiet, mournful intensity. It spawned two classic singles, 'The Ship Song'/'The Train Song' (March) and 'The Weeping Song'/'Cocks'n'Asses' (October). 'The Ship Song' continued Cave's exploration of the more traditional ballad form. In Australia, middle-of-the-road ballad singer Denis Walter issued his version of the song as a single to a positive response. *The Good Son* was the best-selling Australian alternative album for 1990. By that stage, Martyn Casey (bass; ex-**Triffids**) and Conway Savage (keyboards; ex-Boy Kings, White Buffaloes) had joined The Bad Seeds. 'Straight to You'/'Jack the Ripper' (April 1992) and 'I Had a Dream, Joe'/'The Good Son' (October) from *Henry's Dream* (May) followed in the same vein, but with more spectacular results. *Henry's Dream* became Cave's most successful album to date when it reached #25 on the Australian mainstream chart and #29 in the UK national listing during June.

'Straight to You' was the best-selling Australian alternative single for 1992 (and overall second behind Nirvana's 'Smells Like Teen Spirit'). Likewise, *Henry's Dream* was the best-selling Australian alternative album for the year (and third overall behind Nirvana's *Nevermind* and the Red Hot Chili Peppers' *Blood Sugar Sex Magic*). In November 1992, Cave and ex-Pogues frontman Shane McGowan issued a joint single 'What a Wonderful World'/'A Rainy Night in Soho', 'Lucy 2'.

Nick Cave and the Bad Seeds toured Australia in January 1993 as part of the Big Day Out national bill. Other international acts on the bill included Sonic Youth and Iggy Pop. Cave also made an appearance as pop star Freak Storm in Tom DiCillo's feature film *Johnny Suede* (with Brad Pitt). The full impact of The Bad Seeds' performance craft to that point was captured on the gritty *Live Seeds* album (September 1993), which included a photo-diary by Peter Milne. The next CD single, 'Do You Love Me?'/'Cassiel's Song', 'Sail Away' followed in March 1994, while the album *Let Love in* (April) continued Cave's drive into the mainstream consciousness. Full of dramatic, richly woven compositions, *Let Love in* reached #12 in Britain. The album produced two further singles, 'Loverman'/'(I'll Love You) Till the End of the World' (July 1994) and 'Red Right Hand'/'That's What Jazz is to Me' (October 1994). 'Red Right Hand' was included on the soundtrack of popular American television show *The X-Files*, as well as appearing on the soundtrack to the 1994 Jim Carrey comedy *Dumb and Dumber*.

Cave and The Bad Seeds were back in Australia during December 1994 for the Let Love in tour. Cave stayed around long enough into 1995 to play a few gigs with **Dirty Three**. His next single was as unexpected as it was inspired. His duet with **Kylie Minogue**, 'Where the Wild Roses Grow', reached #2 on the Australian national mainstream chart during October 1995. It also peaked at #11 in the UK that same month. 'Where the Wild Roses

Grow' was awarded Song of the Year and Best Pop Release at the tenth annual Australian Record Industry Association (ARIA) Awards. Minogue's guest spot with Nick Cave and the Bad Seeds singing 'Where the Wild Roses Grow' was a highlight of the 1996 Big Day Out tour.

The song was lifted from the concept album *Murder Ballads* (January 1996), which focused on death and the blues inspired by it. Minogue also sang on the Bob Dylan cover, 'Death is Not the End'. *Murder Ballads* included Cave's version of the traditional 'Stagger Lee', which has been praised as the definitive interpretation of the song. The second single from the album was Cave's duet with P.J. Harvey on the traditional 'Henry Lee'/'King Kong Kitchee Kitchee Ki-Mi-O'. Cave was named Songwriter of the Year by the Australian Performing Right Association (APRA).

Cave's next CD single, 'Into My Arms', came out in February 1997, followed by *The Boatman's Call* a month later. The gospel-tinged 'Into My Arms' peaked at #26 on the Australian national chart in its first week of release. *The Boatman's Call* made its debut at #5, and stayed in the national Top 40 for eight weeks. The CD single '(Are You) The One that I've Been Waiting for?' followed in June. Bargeld, Cave and Harvey wrote the original score for the feature film *To Have and to Hold* which came out in mid-1997. Cave and the Bad Seeds returned to Australia during November for the Boatman's Call national tour.

Nick Cave and the Bad Seeds albums: *From Her to Eternity* (Mute/EMI, 1984), *The Firstborn is Dead* (Mute 1985), *Kicking Against the Pricks* (Mute, 1986), *Your Funeral . . . My Trial* (Mute, 1986), *Tender Prey* (Mute, 1988), *The Good Son* (Mute/Liberation, 1990), *Henry's Dream* (Mute/Liberation, 1992), *Let Love in* (Mute/Liberation, 1994), *Murder Ballads* (Mute/Liberation, 1996), *The Boatman's Call* (Mute/Liberation, 1997); ***Blixa Bargeld, Nick Cave, Mick Harvey albums:*** *Ghosts . . . of the Civil Dead* (soundtrack, Mute/BMG, 1989), *To Have and to Hold* (soundtrack, Icon Soundtracks/PolyGram, 1997). ***Mick Harvey solo albums:*** *Intoxicated Man* (Mute/Liberation, 1995), *Pink Elephants* (Mute/Liberation, 1997).

CDB

Formed: *1991*
Style: *Vocal harmony*
Original line-up: *Andrew De Silva (vocals), Gary Pinto (vocals), Brad Pinto (vocals), Danny Williams (vocals)*

In an era when boy-band dance-pop (Take That, Boyzone, Boyz II Men, Past to Present) was popular on the charts around the world, CDB became the first local harmony quartet to make an impact. The members of CDB drew inspiration from vocal stylists like Stevie Wonder, The Commodores, Sam Cooke and Teddy Riley. The group's sound combined elements of R&B, soul and New Jack Swing tied to dexterous vocal harmonies and arrangements.

CDB

After three years of live work in clubs around Melbourne, CDB signed to Sony. The group's debut album, *Glide with Me* (October 1995), produced four national hit singles, 'Hook Me Up' (#11 in December 1994), 'Hey Girl (This is Our Time)' (#14 in July 1995), a cover of Earth Wind and Fire's 'Let's Groove' (#2 in November 1995) and 'Don't Stop' (#28 in April 1996). *Glide with Me* went on to attain platinum status in Australia (over 70 000 copies sold). 'Let's Groove' won Highest Selling Single at the 1996 Australian Record Industry Association (ARIA) Awards. CDB toured Korea, Thailand, Malaysia, Singapore, Taiwan, Hong Kong, the Philippines and Fiji, where the album also sold well. The group's fifth CD single, 'Good Times', came out in July 1997 (#24 in August), to be followed by the album *Lifted* in October, and a new single, 'Back Then', in November.

Albums: *Glide With Me* (Sony, 1995), *Lifted* (Sony, 1997).

Kate Ceberano

Style: *Pop, blues, jazz*

Renowned for her soulful and powerful vocal style, Kate Ceberano (b. 1966) first came to prominence as singer for popular mid-1980s dance/funk outfit **I'm Talking**. Following the break-up of that band in 1987, Ceberano has gone on to become Australia's most popular jazz, blues and contemporary pop singer.

Ceberano's first solo album was the live set *Kate Ceberano and Her Septet* (March 1987), which featured the singles 'I'm Beginning to See the Light' (March) and 'The Masquerade is Over'/'Memory Serves' (May). Ceberano's Septet comprised her brother Phil Ceberano (guitar), Jex Saarelaht (piano), Robert Burke (sax), Stuart Speed (bass), Russell Smith (trumpet), Peter Jones (drums) and Alex Pertout (percussion). In 1987 she collaborated with **Wendy Matthews** on the soundtrack to the ABC-TV drama series *Stringer*. The album *You've Always Got the Blues* (April 1988) was a mix of torch song standards and new songs contributed by a variety of writers like Don Walker and Steve Prestwich ('The Girl in the Picture') and the album's producer Martin Armiger ('Stringer'). It reached #4 on the national chart, and produced the singles 'You've Always Got the Blues'/'3=2+1 (Shame)' (March) and 'Guilty (Through Neglect)'/'Danger Zone' (May). Ceberano's work on *You've Always Got the Blues* earned her the 1988 Australian Record Industry Association (ARIA) Award for Best Female Artist.

Ceberano's celebrated debut solo album, *Brave* (September 1989), gave rise to four exuberant and soulful dance-pop singles, 'Bedroom Eyes'/'Kate's Blues' (#2 in June 1989), 'Love Dimension'/'Like Now' (#14 in September), 'Brave'/'Young Boys are My Weakness' (#17 in November) and 'That's What I Call Love'/'Catalonia Knights' (#30 in April 1990). Produced by Nick Launay (**Midnight Oil, Models**), the album made its debut at #8 on the national charts before hitting the top spot in November. The album also featured an atmospheric rendering of **The Reels** classic 'Quasimodo's Dream'. For her live shows, Ceberano assembled The Ministry of Fun which included Jex Saarelaht, Phil Ceberano, Stephen Hadley (bass), Bruce Pawsey (drums) and Lisa Maxwell (backing vocals). Prior to the release of *Brave*, Kate appeared in an off-beat short film, *Arguing the Toss of a Cat*, as a jazz singer struggling with her career, her boyfriend, her neighbours and their cat.

Ceberano won the 1989 ARIA Awards for Best Female Artist and Highest Selling Single ('Bedroom Eyes'). At the end of 1990, she received three prestigious MO Awards for Rock Performer, Female Rock Performer and Contemporary Concert Performer of the Year. The release of *Brave* overseas also led to successful concerts in the UK, the USA and at the Midem Festival in France. In 1990, Kate issued a new album with her Sextet (the Septet minus Pertout), *Like Now* (August) and new single 'Dindi'/'Samba Minha' (also August). In early 1991 she moved to New York to record with hip-hop mixmaster Arthur Baker, which resulted in her fourth album, *Think About it!* (October, 1991). The album peaked at a relatively disappointing #24 on the charts and its three singles, 'Every Little Thing'/'Losing You' (#34 in August), 'Satisfied' (October) and 'See Right Through'/'Everything Will Be Alright' (#33 in December 1991), were minor hits.

Kate Ceberano

In early 1992, Ceberano appeared on the bill of the Wizards of Oz showcase tour of Los Angeles alongside the likes of **The Angels**, **Beatfish**, **The Black Sorrows** and **Club Hoy**. Next Ceberano joined the Australian cast of the revived stage musical *Jesus Christ Superstar*, in the role of Mary Magdalene. Alongside **John Farnham** (Jesus), Jon Stevens (Judas), **Angry Anderson** (Herod), John Waters (Pontius Pilate), **Russell Morris** (Simon Zealotes) and David Gould (Caiaphas), Ceberano featured on the #1 charting *Jesus Christ Superstar the Album* issued by Polydor in July. She sang on the hit singles 'I Don't Know How to Love Him' (#38 in

February 1992) and 'Everything's Alright' (a #6 duet with **John Farnham** during September).

Such was Ceberano's popularity by 1993 that she was afforded her own television series on the ABC, *Kate Ceberano & Friends*. It was a relaxed mix of songs and interviews, and her guests included Angie Hart from **Frente!**, Vince Jones, Margaret Urlich, **Debra Byrne, Paul Kelly, Deborah Conway** and Jon Stevens. Performances from the series were featured on the album *Kate Ceberano & Friends* (1994). Ceberano contributed a cover of **Hunters & Collectors'** 'Throw Your Arms Around Me' to the Various Artists compilation CD *Earth Music* issued on the Mushroom label (June 1994).

At the end of 1993, Ceberano recorded a new album, *Globe*, in New York with producer Fred Maher (best known for his work with Lloyd Cole, Matthew Sweet and Lou Reed), but only the CD single 'All That I Want is You' (June 1994) appeared at that time. A week before the album's scheduled release, Ceberano's US label Elektra dropped her from its roster. *Globe* was refined, remixed, partially rerecorded, retitled (to *Blue Box*) and eventually issued in July 1996 (national #18 in August). It was preceded by the CD singles 'Change' (March) and a cover of Joan Armatrading's 'Love And Affection' (June). On 5 February 1996 Ceberano married Australian producer/director Lee Rogers. She worked on *Dust Off the Wings*, her husband's latest film project, at the end of 1996. In 1997, Ceberano recorded a new album, *Pash*, for release in 1998. The title track, 'Pash', appeared as the album's first CD single in November 1997.

Albums: *Kate Ceberano and Her Septet* (Regular/Festival, 1987), *Brave* (Regular/Festival, 1989), *Like Now* (Regular/Festival, 1990), *Think About It!* (Regular/Festival, 1991), *Kate Ceberano & Friends* (ABC/Regular/Mushroom/Festival, 1994), *Blue Box* (Regular/Mushroom/Festival, 1996); ***With Wendy Matthews:*** *You've Always Got the Blues* (ABC, 1988); ***Australian cast recording album:*** *Jesus Christ Superstar the Album* (soundtrack, Emerald City/Polydor, 1992).

The Celibate Rifles

Formed: *1979*
Style: *Punk rock*
Original line-up: *Kent Steedman (guitar), Dave Morris (guitar), Michael Couvret (bass), Phillip Jacquet (drums)*

When The Celibate Rifles burst forth from Sydney's northern beach suburbs in 1980, the members described themselves as 'the best high school band ever in the history of the world'. The band's garage rock sound was directly descended from the first generation of Australian punk, **The Saints** and **Radio Birdman**. Since expanding on their proto-punk roots, the Rifles have forged an incisive rock'n'roll identity.

Kent Steedman, Dave Morris, Michael Couvret and Phillip Jacquet conceived the band in 1979 when they were still at high school. Singer Damien Lovelock joined in 1980. He was almost ten years their senior, but he gave the Rifles a much needed lyrical focus for the band's unremitting energy. Celibate Rifles issued the four-track EP *But Jacques the Fish* independently in March 1982. Hot signed the band and reissued the EP in March 1983. James Darrock (bass; ex-Trans Love Energy, Fifth Estate, Slaughterhouse 5) replaced Couvret (who joined Mushroom Planet) and the band issued its debut album, *Sideroxylon* (May 1983).

The early records were raw and undisciplined, but they did display the band's flair, humour and commitment. As the album came out, Steedman joined **The New Christs** when that band supported Iggy Pop on his June 1983 Australian tour. Steedman stayed with **The New Christs** until October, when his commitment to the Rifles beckoned. He appeared on **The New Christs'** 'Born Out of Time' single. With the Rifles on hold, Lovelock formed an acoustic studio band with **Louis Tillett** (Wet Taxis) and Brett Myers (**Died Pretty**). No Dance issued the *Carnival of Souls* EP on Hot in March 1984.

The Rifles' singles 'Pretty Pictures'/'Out in the West Again' (October 1983) and 'Merry Xmas Blues'/'Summer Holiday Blues' (December) were departures for the band as they featured acoustic guitars instead of the all-out electric attack. Darrock left in January 1984 to form **The Eastern Dark**. He died in a car accident in March 1986. Couvret returned for the album *The Celibate Rifles* (May 1984) and the singles 'Wild Desire'/'I'm Waiting for the Man' (April) and 'Sometimes'/'$E=MC^2$' (November). The album was still rough-hewn but with more variation, style and power than the debut. Around that time, visiting American critic David Fricke from *Rolling Stone* was prompted to describe the Rifles as 'urban teen frenzy with lyricist Lovelock's adult fears erupting in a glowing atomic fireball of bazooka guitars and terminal volume'.

The band's only release for 1985 was 'Six Days on the Road'/'Groupie Girl' (July). *The Turgid Miasma of Existence* came out in June 1986. A limited edition EP featuring 'Eddie', 'Ice Blue' and 'Thank

You America' was given away with the first 500 copies of the album. The Rifles undertook an extensive tour of the USA, where their records had garnered much praise from the underground press. The band arranged and financed the tour independently. Issued in November 1986, *Kiss Kiss Bang Bang* (recorded live at New York's legendary CBGB's bar, July 1986) captured the band's sound in all its blistering glory.

Couvret and Jacquet left the band in September 1986 to be replaced by Rudy Morabito (bass; ex-Amused) and Paul Larsen (drums; ex-Funhouse, Gun Control). The band toured Europe and recorded *Roman Beach Party* in Holland during June 1987. The album appeared in November. Morabito left in 1988 to be replaced by Jim Leone (ex-**No Man's Land**). By that stage, Couvret was playing with **The Lime Spiders**, and Jacquet had joined Voodoo Lust. The Rifles' last release on Hot to that time was a 12-inch EP featuring a cover of Patti Smith's 'Dancing Barefoot' (May 1988). The Rifles signed to True Tone and issued *Blind Ear* (April 1989), which contained several of the band's best singles, the riff-happy 'Johnny'/'El Salvador' (February 1989), the rollicking 'O Salvation!'/'Fish and Trees' (June) and the double 7-inch 'Wonderful Life'/'5 Lamps'; 'Where the Action Is', 'She's So Fine'/'Hot Stuff' (March 1990).

The band also contributed a cover of **John Paul Young's** 'Where the Action Is' to the Various Artists album *Used and Recovered By* (1990). Hot closed its Rifles account with the double retrospective set *Platters du Jour* (October 1990), a selection of rare early singles and EP sides with a limited edition 7-inch EP containing three unreleased tracks included. The band members undertook various extra-curricular activities between 1988 and 1990. Lovelock had already written and produced a one-off single in 1984, 'Summertime (All Round the World)'/'Sunnyboyfriend', for Australian world female surfing champion Pam Burridge (issued under the name of Pam and the Pashions during October). In June 1988 he issued his debut solo album *It's a Wig Wig Wig Wig World* followed by the single 'Disco Inferno'/'Sisters' (April 1990).

Lovelock's studio band included Peter Koppes (guitar; from **The Church**), Rick Grossman (bass; from **Hoodoo Gurus**), Joe Latty (guitar; ex-Itchy Rat) and Richard Ploog (drums; from **The Church**). Guitarist Reeves Gabrels, from David Bowie's band Tin Machine, also appeared on 'Disco Inferno'. Lovelock formed a touring line-up of Damien Lovelock's Wigworld which comprised Joe Latty, Clyde Bramley (bass; ex-**Hoodoo Gurus**), Patrick Polnov (guitar) and Hamish Stuart (drums). During 1991, Lovelock issued the single 'The Dalai Lama' (October) and album *Fishgrass* (December) on Festival. Away from the torrid overdrive of the Rifles, the album found Lovelock in a more reflective and melodic mood.

Steedman formed Crent with Chris Townsend (from **Kiss My Poodles Donkey**). Crent issued the singles 'A.I.D.S.' and '9K.?' plus the mini-album *Crent* on Waterfront. Crent's music was more in the bayou/boogie tradition of John Lee Hooker fleshed out by Steedman's bursts of Frank Zappaesque wah wah guitar. Crent issued a second album, *Pink Album*, on the Shagpile label (through Shock) at the end of 1993. Steedman also guested on bass with **Ed Kuepper's** band **The Aints**, playing on the live album *S.L.S.Q.* Jim Leone and Paul Larsen joined Roddy Rayda and The Surfin' Caesars for the album *Orgazmatazz*.

In October 1990, Larsen left The Rifles to join **The Screaming Tribesmen**. Nik Rieth took Larsen's place. At the end of 1991, the Rifles signed to Festival. They issued the double album *Heaven on a Stick* (March 1992), the single 'Groovin' in the Land of Love' (December 1991) plus the double 7-inch single *Where the Wild Things Are . . .* (March 1992). The Rifles shared *Where the Wild Things Are . . .* with **The Hard-Ons** to coincide with a joint Australian tour the two bands undertook mid-year. The Rifles' tracks were '5 Lamps' and 'Electric Flowers'. Straight after that, The Rifles embarked on the Live Stick '92 world tour which took in dates across the UK, Europe and the USA. Festival issued a second, double 7-inch single from *Heaven on a Stick*, 'Cold Wind', in May 1992.

1992 ended for the Rifles with Hot issuing re-mastered CD versions of the band's first five albums. The Rifles returned to Hot for *Yizgarnnoff* (a second live album) and *Sofa* (a 20-track 'Best of' compilation) which came out in May and December 1993 respectively. In late 1993, Steedman and Rieth joined **Deniz Tek** to record his *Outside* album. Steedman and Rieth toured extensively with The **Deniz Tek** Group over the next few years and recorded a new album in 1996, *Le Bonne Route*. *Spaceman in a Satin Suit* (May 1994) was The Celibate Rifles' best studio album since *Blind Ear*. The band also contributed a cover of **The Sports'** 'Boys! (What Did the Detective Say?)' to the Various Artists project *Earth Music*. 'Boys! (What Did the Detective Say?)' appeared on the *Earth Music* CD EP (August 1994) along with **Died Pretty** covering

The Celibate Rifles

Laughing Clowns' 'Eternally Yours' and **Painters and Dockers** doing **Mental as Anything's** 'The Nips Are Getting Bigger'.

In late 1996, Hot issued the mail-order only *On the Quiet*, a selection of acoustic reworkings of previously released material. *On the Quiet* came with a limited edition bonus all-electric CD EP of Australian covers (including **The Sports'** 'Boys!, What Did the Detective Say?' and **Rose Tattoo's** 'Astra Wally') that showed The Celibate Rifles still to be a peerless hard rock band.

Celibate Rifles albums: *Sideroxylon* (Hot, 1984), *The Celibate Rifles* (Hot 1984), *The Turgid Miasma of Existence* (Hot, 1986), *Kiss Kiss Bang Bang* (Hot, 1986), *Roman Beach Party* (Hot, 1987), *Blind Ear* (True Tone/EMI, 1989), *Platters du Jour* (Hot, 1990), *Heaven on a Stick* (Festival, 1992), *Yizgarnnoff* (Hot, 1993), *Sofa* (Hot, 1993), *Spaceman in a Satin Suit* (Hot, 1994), *On the Quiet* (Hot mail-order only, 1996); ***Damien Lovelock albums:*** *It's a Wig Wig Wig Wig World* (Hot, 1988), *Fishgrass* (Festival, 1991).

Chad's Tree

Formed: *1983*
Style: *Country, folk*
Original line-up: *Mark Snarski (vocals), Robert Snarski (guitar, vocals), Kim Bettenay (bass), James Hurst (drums)*

This Perth, Western Australia band was the direct ancestor of both **The Blackeyed Susans** and **The Jackson Code**. The Snarski brothers were the driving forces behind Chad's Tree. The band's brittle, off-kilter sound evoked the sense of distance, desolation, harshness and loneliness of the Nullarbor Plain (but also its fragile nature), much in the same fashion as fellow Perth outfit **The Triffids**.

Chad's Tree relocated to Sydney and issued its debut 7-inch single 'Crush the Lily'/'Toll for Josephine' (November 1985) on the Hot label. Subsequent singles, 'Sweet Jesus Blue Eyes'/'To the Highest Bidder' (February 1987) and 'Stroller in the Rain'/'The Orchard' (March 1988), plus the album *Buckle in the Rail* (January 1987) came out on the Nude label. The 'Crush the Lily' and 'Sweet Jesus Blue Eyes' singles were also combined on the four-track, 12-inch EP *Chad's Tree* for release in the UK through Rough Trade.

There were a number of different line-ups over the course of six years. As well as Kim Bettenay, the band's bass players included Mark Hemery, Peter Michael, Barry Turnbull and Simon Kain. Susan Grigg (ex-**Cannanes**) joined on piano and violin in 1987, and was replaced by Kathy Wemyss in 1989. Jason Kain (lead guitar, ex-Wet Taxis) also replaced Robert Snarski, who went off to form **The Blackeyed Susans**. The band issued a second album, *Kerosene*, in March 1989. With the break-up of Chad's Tree a month later, Mark Snarski and Wemyss formed **The Jackson Code**.

Albums: *Buckle in the Rail* (Nude, 1987), *Kerosene* (Waterfront, 1989).

Chain

Formed: *1968*
Style: *Blues*
Original line-up: **Wendy Saddington** *(vocals, ex-Revolution,* **James Taylor Move***), Warren Morgan (keyboards, vocals; ex-Beaten Tracks),* **Phil Manning** *(guitar, vocals; ex-***Tony Worsley and the Fabulous Blue Jays, Bay City Union***, Laurie Allen Revue, Beaten Tracks), Murray Wilkins (bass; ex-Beaten Tracks), Ace Follington (drums; ex-Beaten Tracks)*

Since the late 1960s, the name Chain has been synonymous with Australian blues of the highest quality and integrity. The band's history spans a quarter of a century and at least 40 musicians can lay claim to having been a member of Chain over the years.

In the beginning (1967), there was The Beaten Tracks out of Perth, comprising Warren Morgan, Ace Follington, Murray Wilkins, **Dave Hole** (guitar) and Ross Partington (vocals). The Beaten Tracks played a mix of Vanilla Fudge, The Beatles, Paul Butterfield and Motown material. At the start of 1968, Hole (now recognised as one of Australia's blues guitarists *par excellence*) left the band. Partington also left at the end of the year.

With new guitarist **Phil Manning** on board, The Beaten Tracks moved to Melbourne in December 1968. There singer **Wendy Saddington** joined and The Chain was born. Saddington named the band after the soul classic 'Chain of Fools'. By May 1969, Saddington had moved on to work for *Go-Set* magazine and then to sing with **Jeff St John's** Copperwine. Wilkins left The Chain in August to be replaced by New Zealander Tim Piper (bass; ex-Chants R&B, Electric Heap). Fellow New Zealander, blind organist Claude Papesch (ex-Electric Heap), also joined, and the new five-piece line-up recorded the single 'Show Me Home'/'Mr Time' (October 1969) for Festival Records. It was one of the first progressive blues records ever issued in Australia.

Follington, Piper and Papesch all left The Chain in October 1969 to be replaced by Barry 'Big Goose' Sullivan (bass; ex-Thursday's Children, **Wild Cherries**) and Barry 'Little Goose' Harvey (drums; ex-Thursday's Children, **Wild Cherries**). Soon after, the band's name was shortened from The Chain to Chain. New Zealander Glyn Mason (guitar, vocals; ex-Rebels) joined Chain in January 1970. In June, Chain travelled to Sydney to record the seminal *Live Chain* album at Caesar's Palace discotheque. By that time, the Melbourne blues scene was beginning to burgeon and Chain joined the likes of **Billy Thorpe** and the Aztecs, **Carson** and **Adderley Smith Blues Band** as the leaders of the movement. In July (three months before *Live Chain* came out in October 1970), Morgan left Chain to join **Billy Thorpe** and the Aztecs and Mason left to travel overseas.

Following a month working as a three-piece (Manning, Big Goose, Little Goose), the most famous line-up of Chain came into being during September 1970, when **Matt Taylor** (vocals, harp; ex-**Bay City Union**, Genesis, Meating) joined. The new line-up signed to Festival's new progressive subsidiary label Infinity and issued the classic single 'Black and Blue'/'Lightning Ground' (March 1971) and the ground-breaking album *Toward the Blues* (September). 'Black and Blue' (with its famous 'we're groaning' vocal refrain) was a #1 hit in Melbourne and enjoyed a five-month stay in the Top 40. Although oddly ignored by Sydney radio, the single managed to reach the national #10 position in May 1971.

Toward the Blues reached #6 on the national album chart, and remains one of the greatest blues albums ever issued in Australia. As a follow-up, Chain issued the complex, imaginative blues single 'Judgement'/'Blow in 'D'' (July 1971) which went to #6 in Melbourne and #13 in Sydney (#31 nationally). These records established Chain as the nation's leading progressive blues outfit, but this period of success came to an end when Manning, Little Goose and Big Goose all left the band around July 1971. Manning joined Morgan in the short-lived duo Pilgrimage, Big Goose joined **Carson** temporarily and Little Goose joined **King Harvest**.

Meanwhile, Taylor kept the Chain name alive with a new line-up comprising Kevin Murphy (drums; ex-**Wild Cherries**, Rush, **Billy Thorpe** and the Aztecs, **King Harvest**) and two ex-members of **Healing Force** (Charlie Tumahai, bass and Lindsay Wells, lead guitar). Murphy left in September, and another ex-**Healing Force** alumnus Laurie Pryor (drums) joined for a month until Taylor split the band at the end of October. **Matt Taylor** later enjoyed a successful solo career with hit singles like 'I Remember when I was Young'/'Krishna Loves You, Too' and 'Fair Dinkum Aussie Blues'/'Alone' and albums *Straight as a Die* and *Music*.

In November 1971, the *Live Chain* version of Chain (Manning, Morgan, Mason, Little Goose and Big Goose) re-formed. Once again, this was a short-lived venture (three months), but the band did manage to record the *Chain Live Again* album which was not issued until October 1972. In the meantime, Warren Morgan had formed a three-piece line-up of Chain with Big Goose and Laurie Pryor (quickly replaced by Little Goose), which relied on dominant piano as a substitute for guitar. The Morgan/Big Goose/Pryor line-up appeared on the bill of the inaugural Sunbury Festival (January 1972). The Morgan/Big Goose/Little Goose line-up existed for six months (February to July), and recorded one single, 'Sunny Day'/'I Was Born' (issued in October 1972), for Festival/Infinity.

For most of 1972, **Phil Manning** had been working with his new outfit the **Band of Talabene**, but by the end of the year he had reunited with the two Gooses in Mighty Mouse. The Mighty Mouse line-up comprised Manning, Ian Clyne (organ; ex-**Loved Ones**, **Ram Jam Big Band**, **Levi Smith's Clefs**), Mal Capewell (sax, flute;

ex-Dr Kandy's Third Eye, Dada, **Company Caine, Levi Smith's Clefs**), Big Goose (bass), Little Goose (drums) and Kevin Murphy (drums; by then ex-**Levi Smith's Clefs**). In February 1973, Mighty Mouse (sans Murphy) simply changed its name and Chain line-up #15 came into being. The line-up of Manning, Big Goose, Little Goose, Clyne and Capewell remained stable for a year.

The band's manager, Michael Gudinski, immediately signed Chain to a deal with his fledgling Mushroom label. Mushroom issued two Chain singles, 'I Thought You Weren't My Friend'/'Elephant' (May 1973) and 'I'm Gonna Miss You Babe'/'Hey, Baby' (November) and one album, *Two of a Kind* (December). The first side of the album featured contributions from members of the Muddy Waters Band (with whom Chain toured during May 1973), while the other contained the side-long, live track 'How to Set Fire to an Elephant'.

The last line-up of Chain to that time, Manning, Big Goose, Mal Logan (keyboards; ex-**Healing Force, Carson**) and Tony Lunt (drums; ex-**Carson**), formed in February 1974 and broke up in July. In October, Mushroom issued the essential double retrospective set *History of Chain*, which contained previously unissued material including a crunching live version of 'Black and Blue' recorded at the Odyssey Pop Festival, Wallacia in January 1971.

For the next six years, **Phil Manning** pursued a solo career, forming various bands along the way (including Manning and the Phil Manning Band). He also spent six months during 1977 as a member of **John Paul Young** and the All Stars, alongside Warren Morgan. Likewise, **Matt Taylor** had been touring the country with various line-ups of his Matt Taylor Band, as well as spending two years as a member of **Western Flyer** with ex-**Procession** member Brian Peacock. At the beginning of 1981, Manning and Taylor joined forces again, this time as the Matt Taylor Phil Manning Band. That band recorded the excellent *Oz Blues* album (June 1981) and a single, 'Spring Hill'/'The Line'. At that time, interest in Chain was still strong. Over the Australia Day weekend in January 1982, the re-formed 'Black and Blue' version of Chain (Manning, Taylor, Big Goose and Little Goose) performed at the Mushroom Evolution Concert to celebrate the Tenth Anniversary of Mushroom Records. A couple of songs from the band's performance appeared on the triple album set *The Mushroom Evolution Concert.*

Chain re-formed on a permanent basis in December 1983 with Manning, Taylor, Big Goose and Little Goose. The line-up existed for nearly three years and recorded the album *Child of the Street* (October 1985) and singles 'I Don't Wanna Be Like Anyone Else'/'Messages' (October) and '(Doin') The Highway 31 Shuffle'/'Missile' (June 1986).

After Manning and Big Goose left Chain towards the end of 1986, Taylor and Little Goose kept the band going with new members. These included brilliant guitarist John Meyer (ex-Fatty Lumpkin, Everest, Saracen, **Rose Tattoo**) who contributed significantly to the band's sound and development over the next four years. Meyer had appeared on the Tatts' 1984 album *Southern Stars*, and recorded one accomplished hard rock set with Saracen, *Saracen* (1986), which sold well in Europe via a release on the French label Axe Killer. Jon Ryder (vocals, bass, keyboards; ex-Everest, Trilogy) and Pete Thompson (drums, vocals; ex-Trilogy) completed the Saracen line-up. With Roy Daniel (bass; ex-Fatty Lumpkin) on board, Chain issued the album *Australian Rhythm and Blues* and single 'Harmonica'/'Spring Hill' (both April 1988). The next line-up of Taylor, Meyer, Bob Fortesque (bass; ex-**Blackfeather**, Fatty Lumpkin, True Colours) and Michael Burn (drums) issued the album *Blue Metal* (May 1990). Following Meyer's departure, **Phil Manning** rejoined Chain for a short time at the beginning of 1991.

In April 1991, Taylor and Manning joined **Broderick Smith** (vocals, harp; ex-**Carson**, **Dingoes**, Big Combo), Mick 'The Reverend' O'Connor (organ; ex-Big Combo), Peter 'Brolga' Coughlan (bass; ex-**Goanna**) and Robbie Dillon (drums; ex-**Mike Rudd and the Heaters**) and undertook an Australian tour as Blues Power. By the end of 1991, **Matt Taylor** had formed a new version of Chain, this time billed as Matt Taylor's Chain. The line-up of Taylor, Jeff Lang (guitar), Dirk Du Bois (bass), Bob Patient (piano) and Gus Warberton (drums) recorded a new album *Walls 2 McGoo (Trouble in the Wind),* which came out in 1992. Lang went on to work as a solo blues guitarist in his own right, issuing several albums along the way: *Ravenswood* (1994), *Native Dog Creek* (on the Black Market label, 1996) and *Live at the Vineyard* (with **Chris Finnen**, 1996).

After 1992, Taylor employed a floating line-up of musicians whenever he toured the country as Matt Taylor's Chain (including ex-**Stars** guitarist Malcolm Eastick, and members of **The Giants** in Melbourne). Taylor, Manning and Little Goose (plus Dirk Du Bois on bass) reactivated the Chain name in June 1995 for a national tour. Big Goose rejoined Taylor, Manning and Little Goose when Chain played the annual East Coast Blues Festival at Byron Bay in April 1996 (25 years after the release of 'Black and Blue'). The Taylor/Manning/Little Goose/Du Bois Chain line-up was working again at the start of 1997. By the end of the year, the band had laid plans for the release of a new live album in early 1998.

Albums: *Live Chain* (Festival, 1970), *Toward the Blues* (Festival/Infinity, 1971), *Chain Live Again* (Festival/Infinity, 1972), *Two of a Kind* (Festival/Mushroom), *History of Chain* (Festival/Mushroom, 1974), *Best of Chain* (Festival/Infinity, 1980), *Child of the Street* (EMI/Team, 1985), *Australian Rhythm and Blues* (BMG/Ariola/RCA, 1988), *Blue Metal* (Forever/BMG/Arista, 1990), *Trouble in the Wind (aka Walls 2 McGoo)* (as Matt Taylor's Chain; Forever/Aim, 1992).

Greg Champion

Style: *Country, folk*

Singer/songwriter/commentator/sports fan Greg Champion has had a long, but relatively low-key career. Aside from his forays into the world of country and rock, he was heard on the airwaves as a member of the sharp-witted and popular sports/satire radio team *The Coodabeen Champions*. The irreverent sports show started in 1981 on Melbourne community radio station 3RRR-FM before moving to the ABC for a three-hour Sunday night national timeslot in 1989. The show featured Champion's lighthearted and always entertaining songs. The Coodabeen line-up comprised Champion, journalist Ian Cover, barrister Simon Whelan, tertiary lecturer Jeff Richardson and public servant Tony Leonard. The show remained on air until late 1996.

Champion's early bands included country-rock outfits Tidewater and Bank of France. Tidewater formed as a three-piece acoustic group in 1973, comprising Champion, Brooke Mostyn-Smith (guitar, vocals) and Paul Ziesing (bass). Dean Nielsen (drums) and Graham Davidge (lead guitar, vocals, flute; ex-Superlemon, **Little River Band**) joined in 1975 and Tidewater issued an album, *Wild Horse Plains*, in 1976. James Black (keyboards, guitar) joined after the album came out. Tidewater broke up a year later.

By 1979, Champion was a member of **The Fabulaires**, before joining The Young Homebuyers. His solo band, Greg Champion's Eternal Struggle Between Good and Evil, included Wayne Burt (guitar; ex-**Daddy Cool, Jo Jo Zep and the Falcons**), John James (J.J.) Hackett (drums; ex-**Fabulaires, Mondo Rock**) and Ian McDonald (bass). His other bands were Manic Rockers from Hell, The Possum Hunters and The Important Brothers. Champion supported Scottish comedian Billy Connelly in 1986.

In 1985, Champion issued his debut single 'I Made a Hundred in the Backyard at Mum's'/'Somebody's Going to Get Hurt' on the small Team label. ABC radio host Ian 'Macca' McNamara adopted 'I Made a Hundred . . . ' as the theme for his popular show *Australia All Over*. This eventually led to Champion recording his debut, self-titled album in 1990. It produced the single 'Now She's Living in Innisfail' which appeared in June. Songs like 'I Made a Hundred . . . ', 'Now She's Living in Innisfail', 'Old Station Wagon with the Lights on Out the Front' and his third single '88ks From Alice' (1992), from the album *Champs*, reflected the distinctly Australian flavour of Champion's songwriting style.

In 1994 Champion collaborated with **Mike Brady** to write sports-related songs. The collaboration resulted in three CD singles on the Massive label (credited to Greg Champion and the Music Men) 'Shane Warne'/'Our Don Bradman', 'We Want a Wicket!' and 'That's the Thing about Football' (co-written with **Paul Kelly**). 'That's the Thing About Football' was heard regularly as part of the Seven Network's television coverage of games during the Australian Football League (AFL) season.

In early 1997, Champion released his third album of country-style Australiana, *Australian Music*.

Albums: *Greg Champion* (ABC, 1990), *Champs* (ABC, 1992), *That's What I Like About Football* (Massive/Warner, 1995), *Football Is A Funny Game* (Massive/Warner, 1996), *Australian Music* (Massive/Warner, 1997).

The Champions (*see* The Elks)

The Chantoozies

Formed: *1986*
Style: *Pop*
Original line-up: *Ally Fowler (vocals), Tottie Goldsmith (vocals), Angie LaBozzetta (vocals), Eve Von Bibra (vocals), Scott Griffiths (keyboards), Frank McCoy (guitar, vocals), Brett Goldsmith (bass, guitar), David Reyne (drums; ex-***Australian Crawl***, Cats Under Pressure)*

Melbourne pop sensations The Chantoozies formed as a good-time covers band to play at Tottie Goldsmith's 25th birthday party. The band's debut club gig attracted 600 people, which was encouragement enough for the musicians to continue. The band's exuberant and clean-cut style was ultra-commercial and resulted in a great deal of success.

Vocalists Ally Fowler and Goldsmith were best known as television actresses with credits in *Prisoner*, *Sons and Daughters* and *Neighbours*, and *The Henderson Kids* respectively. Eve Von Bibra and Angie LaBozzetta were from the theatre and modelling respectively. Brett Goldsmith had worked as a club DJ and Reyne was an original member of **Australian Crawl** alongside his brother James. In 1983, David acted in the popular ABC-TV series *Sweet and Sour* and the 1986 film *Frenchmen's Farm*, after which he formed studio outfit Cats Under Pressure. Simon Hussey (guitar, keyboards) and Mark Greig (guitar; ex-**Runners, Australian Crawl**) completed the line-up. The band issued the 7-inch single 'Let Me Be'/'Polar Notch' and the 12-inch 'On Again Off Again'/'Ping Pong'. When Reyne joined The Chantoozies in 1986, Hussey joined the **James Reyne** Band. Later he became part of another studio project **Company of Strangers**, with Reyne and **Daryl Braithwaite**.

Four months after formation, The Chantoozies signed a deal with Mushroom Records which resulted in a disco version of Redbone's 1970s hit 'Witch Queen'/'The Chantoozie Shuffle' as the band's debut single. 'Witch Queen' reached #3 in March 1987 and suddenly the band was in big demand. The follow-up single, John Kongos' 'He's Gonna Step on You Again'/'26 Oz' (June 1987), vied with **The Party Boys'** hard rock version for a place on the charts simultaneously, although The Chantoozies' rendition was the least successful. Brett Goldsmith and Von Bibra co-penned the band's third single, 'Wanna be Up'/'Little Women' (May 1988) and Goldsmith also took over the reins as the band's musical director. 'Wanna be Up' reached #8 on the national chart in August. The band's debut album, *Chantoozies* (produced by American Mark Berry), featured predominantly self-penned cuts with the two previously released covers thrown in.

Another Goldsmith/Von Bibra co-write, 'Kiss'n' Tell'/'Want to Go' (August 1988) came out as the band's fourth single. The album reached #13, while 'Kiss'n'Tell' peaked at #24 in October. By that stage, Greg Millikan had replaced Griffiths on keyboards. The Chantoozies toured with **James Reyne** and **Daryl Braithwaite**, and just as their live profile was at a premium they decided to take a break. The Chantoozies returned to the charts in late 1989 with their fifth single, the pop ballad 'Come Back to Me'. Griffiths and Tottie Goldsmith left the band in mid-1990. Goldsmith later presented the television series *Sex/Life* in 1996. Meanwhile, with just the three vocalists Fowler, Von Bibra and LaBozzetta, the band issued the single 'Walk on' (October 1990) and the album *Gild the Lily* (April 1991). The band's final singles were a cover of Stephen Stills' 'Love the One You're With' (March) and 'I'll be There' (September). Fowler returned to acting, appearing in the Ten Network's television drama series *Big Sky* (1996). Reyne also returned to television as a presenter on lifestyle/travel show *Getaway*.

Albums: *The Chantoozies* (Mushroom/Festival, 1988), *Gild the Lily* (Mushroom/Festival, 1991).

Chariot

Formed: *1974*
Style: *Hard rock*
Original line-up: *Dennis Wilson (guitar, vocals; ex-Mecca,* **Kahvas Jute***), Peter Roberts (guitar; ex-***La De Das**, **Band of Light**, **Kahvas Jute***), John Strangio (bass; ex-St James Infirmary, Middle Earth,* **Dingoes***), Steve Webb (drums; ex-***Blackfeather**, **King Harvest**, *Tramp)*

Dennis Wilson was one of Australia's pre-eminent guitar heroes. He formed Chariot with ex-bass player Peter Roberts, who switched to guitar. Chariot earned a reputation as one of the country's hardest working bands (upwards of 300 gigs per year for three years). Unfortunately there was very little recorded evidence to attest to the band's fierce live reputation. Chariot formed in May 1974 with the demise of Wilson's previous band **Kahvas Jute**. Persistent line-up changes thwarted the band's chances at the big time. In late 1974, Nevin 'Loppy' Morris (ex-**Home**) replaced Steve Webb. In early 1975, Rick Sutton replaced Roberts. In mid-1975, Jim Penson (ex-Plastic Tears, **Maple Lace, Blackfeather, Flake**) replaced Morris, and in late 1975, Jim Hilson joined as lead singer.

The Wilson/Strangio/Sutton/Penson/Hilson line-up was the most consistent, and was basically the recording group. The band issued the singles 'I'll Keep on Loving You'/'On the Line' (January 1976) and 'Set Me Free'/'Take Me Home' (December 1976) on the Wizard label. Both singles featured commercial hard rock tunes, but they failed to chart. Chariot actually recorded an album's worth of material (at Trafalgar Studios with producer Charles Fisher) which has never seen the light of day. In 1977, Rick Sutton left to join **Jimmy and the Boys** and Hilson left to join country band Stockade. Mal Clarke (guitar, vocals; ex-**Tony Worsley and the Fabulous Blue Jays**) and Glenn Ford (keyboards) joined to fill out the sound. Wilson eventually disbanded Chariot in December 1977. Jim Penson joined Hilson in Stockade, but he died in a car accident in 1979.

Wilson formed the Dennis Wilson Band, but split that aggregation in 1980. He received an offer to do a commercial to promote the Space Invaders video game. The offer fell through, but he recorded the gimmicky 'Johnny and the Space Invaders' anyway with Fisher. Regular Records issued it as a single (February 1980). The B-side 'Runaway' was more in keeping with Wilson's hard rock style. Wilson's next venture was the commercially minded *Walking on Thin Ice* album on RCA (December 1980). Wilson had recorded six tracks at Trafalgar Studios with Fisher, then recorded four more songs with American session players at the House of Music Studios in New Jersey. The album was very Americanised, with less emphasis placed on Wilson's guitar playing. Influences ranged from Bruce Springsteen to John Mellencamp.

The single 'Walking on Thin Ice'/'Let it Slip' (December 1980) initially received radio airplay. Then Yoko Ono released her 'Walking on Thin Ice' single (March 1981) and album (in the wake of John Lennon's murder) and media attention immediately shifted to the most newsworthy personality. Wilson's last single was 'Heartbeat'/'Paradise' (March 1981). Wilson toured in support of the album with The Deltoids, which comprised two ex-Chariot members John Strangio and Loppy Morris. Since that time Wilson has toured with **Swanee** and the Doc Span Blues Band, appeared on **Jackie Orszaczky's** *Jump Back Jack* album, formed a part-time band called Thin Ice and recorded demos for a proposed new solo album. Wilson worked with a temporarily re-formed **Kahvas Jute** in 1993, but since then has gigged as a solo acoustic act around northern New South Wales.

Dennis D. Wilson solo album: *Walking on Thin Ice* (RCA, 1980).

Ronnie Charles

Style: *Pop*

Singer Ronnie Charles Boromeo had been in The Jackson Kings and **The Groop** with **Brian Cadd**. With the break-up of **The Groop** in May 1969, Charles went solo. Prior to his solo career getting off the ground, Charles sang backing vocals on 'Love Machine' by **Pastoral Symphony**, a studio group which also comprised **The Twilights**, **The Strangers'** Terry Walker and the Johnny Hawker Singers. Charles' two solo singles for Festival echoed the big, booming pop sound of 'Love Machine'. They were 'Katy Jane'/'No Face, No Name, No Number' (December 1969) and 'It's Been So Long'/'Natural Man' (March 1970).

Charles then formed Captain Australia and the Honky Tonk with Brian Holloway (guitar; ex-Dream, Image, **Aesop's Fables**), Graham Jones (bass; ex-**Iguana**), Richard Wright (drums; ex-**Groop**) and Steve Yates (keyboards; ex-Rush, **Expression**). In August 1970, Eric Cairns (ex-Somebody's Image, Image, **Heart'n'Soul**, **Company Caine**) replaced Wright and Les Gough (bass; ex-Somebody's Image, Image, **Heart'n'Soul**) replaced Jones. Gary Moberley (ex-**Aesop's Fables**) also replaced Yates who joined **King Harvest**. Captain Australia issued the single 'Excerpts from Muses'/'Everybody I Love You' on Havoc in early 1971.

Just as the single came out, Charles, Cairns, Holloway, Gough and Moberley travelled to the UK. By 1972, Charles had formed a new band called Atlas which comprised Gough and two English musicians, Terry Slade (drums; ex-Sunshine) and Glen Turner (guitar), who had been an early (pre-recording) member of Wishbone Ash. Holloway joined Esperanto with **Glenn Shorrock** (ex-**Twilights**). Moberley went on to work with English singer/songwriter John Miles, who had a UK hit single in 1976 with 'Music'. Atlas was a hard rock/boogie outfit, fitting in with contemporary English bands like Wishbone Ash, Free, Status Quo, etc. Warner/Reprise issued the band's eponymous debut album and two fine hard rock singles 'Rock 'n'Roll Wizards'/'Military Rag' and 'They Don't Know'/'The Knowing' before Atlas broke up in 1974.

Charles recorded two solo singles, 'Yesterday's Witness'/'Can You See?' and 'Layla Part 1'/'Layla Part 2' and an album for the 20th Century label in 1976. The ambitious *Prestidigitation* album featured contributions from the London Symphony Orchestra and the English Chamber Choir. Charles returned to Australia in the late 1970s. In 1980 he recorded a single backed by Melbourne band **The Runners**, 'Rock and Roll Hoodlum'/'Aim for the Stars', which came out on the Full Moon label. As well as issuing a second solo album, *Hands Off*, in 1983, Charles sang with White Light Orchestra, Turbo Luv Nuns, Running Scared and Post Mortem throughout the 1980s.

Albums: *Prestidigitation* (20th Century, 1976), *Hands Off* (Arctic, 1983).

Cheek

Formed: *1976*
Style: *Pop*
Original line-up: *Lee Emmett (vocals; ex-Jasper), Robin Jackson (guitar; ex-***Hush***, Ricochet), Randy Hall (lead guitar), Felix Maslin (bass, vocals; ex-Jasper), Bud Mangion (drums; ex-Jasper)*

Although based on a seemingly foolproof formula, it was probably the ultra-commercial pop image that contributed to Cheek's eventual break-up. The mainstays of Cheek (Lee Emmett, Felix Maslin and Bud Mangion) first joined forces in 1974 as Jasper. The other members of Jasper were Peter Emmett (vocals, guitar) and Steve Hall (guitar). Jasper issued one single, 'Lola', in early 1976 before calling it a day.

Emmett, Maslin and Mangion formed Punkz with the addition of Robin Jackson (original lead guitarist with **Hush**) and Randy Hall, who was quickly replaced by Ray Goodwin (ex-**Dragon, John Paul Young** and the All Stars). The band came to the attention of **Ol'55** manager Glenn A. Baker, who helped mould Punkz's 1960s pop image. Mushroom issued the singles 'Anyway You Want It'/'I Can't Control Myself' (December 1976) and 'Take Me for What I'm Worth'/'Good Times' (June 1977), neither of which was successful. Goodwin left soon after and the band changed its name to Cheek to avoid any punk rock connotations.

A cover of the Mighty Avengers' 'So Much in Love' backed with **The Easybeats'** 'Do You Have a Soul?' was Cheek's debut single for Mushroom (January 1978). It reached #23 in Melbourne during April. Troy Richards (keyboards, guitar, sax; ex-Raw Glory, Rainbow) joined and Cheek commenced recording an album (which never eventuated). 'Leave My Heart Alone'/'Still in Love' came out in June. It was not successful and the band broke up in August 1978. The four single tracks later appeared as an EP on Greg Shaw's Bomp label in Los Angeles. Jackson and Mangion joined the Chris Turner Band and Maslin joined Adelaide's Fat Lip. Maslin died as a result of an asthma attack in 1988.

Cheetah

Formed: *1977*
Style: *Pop rock*
Original line-up: *Chrissie Hammond (vocals), Lyndsay Hammond (vocals)*

The English-born, Melbourne-bred Hammond sisters Chrissie and Lyndsay were the archetypal 1970s sex bombs with big hair. They had tremendous, booming rock voices and were in constant demand as session vocalists. Between the two, they appeared on albums by **Jo Jo Zep and the Falcons, Stars, Jon English, Daryl Braithwaite, Marc Hunter,** the **Ted Mulry Gang, Graham Lowndes, Flash and the Pan** and Anne Kirkpatrick. As a vocal duo, they toured behind the **Ted Mulry Gang, Mark Holden, Stevie Wright, Norman Gunston, Daryl Braithwaite** and Shirley Strachan.

Chrissie first came to prominence in the role of Mary Magdalene in the second Australian stage production of *Jesus Christ Superstar*. In 1975 she worked with the original version of **Air Supply** before embarking on a career with her sister. Lyndsay fronted Skintight for three years before forming Cheetah with Chrissie. Philips issued a single, 'Love Ain't Easy to Come by'/'Shake it to the Right', in 1977 without the duo's consent or that of their manager Brian de Courcy. Ian 'Molly' Meldrum produced the duo's official debut single, a cover of The Ronettes' 'Walking in the Rain'/'Desperado', which reached #12 in October 1978. 'Deeper than Love'/'I Believe in You' (February 1979) was the duo's first single for the Albert label. The record featured a lavish and dramatic production sheen which was perfect for radio, but it failed to chart. It did, however, take off in Germany and went on to sell 100 000 copies across Europe.

Under the production guidance of Albert's resident gurus Vanda and Young, the Hammond sisters turned their attentions to **AC/DC**-styled hard rock with some success. Cheetah's debut album *Rock'n'Roll Women* (April 1982) yielded a string of anthemic rock singles: 'Spend the Night'/'I'm Yours' (September 1980; #31 in December), 'Love You to the Limit'/'Let the Love Begin' (February 1981), 'Bang Bang'/'Suffering Love' (August 1981) and 'My Man'/'Come and Get It' (April 1982). The musicians on the album were Ian Miller (lead guitar; ex-**Chetarca, John Paul Young** and the All Stars), Ronnie Peel (rhythm guitar; ex-**Missing Links, Rockwell T. James** and the Rhythm Aces, **La De Das**, J.P.Y. and the All Stars), Leszek Karski (bass; ex-Supercharge), Mike Peters (keyboards) and **Ray Arnott** (drums; ex-**Cam-Pact, Spectrum, Dingoes**). Cheetah toured across Australia and the UK (including a slot on the 1982 Reading festival bill) but disappeared from the recording scene. Lyndsay re-emerged in 1997 with the CD single 'Shattered' and the album *The Raven* on Warner's East West label.

Cheetah album: *Rock'n'Roll Women* (Albert/EMI, 1981); ***Lyndsay Hammond album:*** *The Raven* (East West/Warner, 1997).

The Cherokees

Formed: *1961*
Style: *Beat pop*
Original line-up: *Billy Dale (lead guitar; ex-***Chessmen***), Barry King (rhythm guitar), Paul (surname unknown; bass), Barry Windley (drums; ex-***Chessmen***)*

Melbourne-based The Cherokees emerged from singer **Johnny Chester's** regular backing band **The Chessmen**. When Billy Dale and Barry Windley left **The Chessmen**, Chester suggested they name their new band The Cherokees after a popular ice-cream of the period. The Cherokees' Shadows-styled instrumental sound found much favour on the Melbourne dance circuit. In 1962, Doug Trevor (ex-Marksmen) replaced the mysterious Paul, and Lindsay Morrison replaced Barry King. The Marksmen were another Melbourne-based instrumental group; they had hit singles with 'Lost Guitar'/'Beachcomber' (July 1961), 'Pinocchio'/'Rock Lomond' (March 1962) and 'Triangle'/'Gunshot' (February 1963).

W&G Records signed The Cherokees and issued the singles 'Moon in the Afternoon'/'Running Wild' (1964) and 'I've Got Something to Tell You'/'It's Gonna Work Out Fine' (May 1965) and the ultra-rare *Here Come the Cherokees* album. By 1965, the band had made the successful transformation from Shadows instrumentals to Beatles-styled beat pop. By that stage, Billy Dale had left, so Trevor switched to lead guitar and Peter Tindal (ex-Dymonds) joined on bass. Tindal and Windley shared lead vocals. The band found a manager in Carol West (**Lynne Randell** and The Spinning Wheels) and signed to the Go!! label, now one of the most collectable of all Australian 1960s record labels.

Covers of The Impressions' 'I've Been Trying'/'Only if I Care' (#36 in August 1965), The Beau Brummels' 'That's if You Want Me to'/'Stop this Misery' (#39 in December 1965), The Crests' 'The Angels Listened in'/'Shame on You Baby' (#22 in March 1966) and 'A Woman with Soul'/'I'll Give You Love' (#24 in July 1966) were all hits in Melbourne. 'A Woman with Soul' was a reworking of The Impressions' song 'Woman's Got Soul' which was written by Curtis Mayfield. The Cherokees' fifth Go!! single, 'Little Lover'/'The Thought of You' (September 1966), was their best release of all. Both tracks were out-and-out beat stompers. Line-up problems around the time of the single's release prevented the band from playing live, and the record sank without a trace. First Windley left to be replaced by Peter 'Max' Bilney (ex-Secrets), while Kevin Smith (ex-Viscounts, D-Coys) joined on lead vocals. Then, when Morrison left, Trevor moved to rhythm guitar and Marty Van Wynk (ex-**Throb**) took over on lead guitar.

Smith had been co-lead singer with Adelaide R&B band The D-Coys. Led by singer/songwriter Alistair Innes, The D-Coys issued three singles on EMI/Columbia in 1966: 'Come Running to Me'/'I Don't Want' (January), 'Leaving Here'/'Now Comes a Day' (July) and 'Bad Time'/'You're Against' (October). Like **The Black Diamonds**, The D-Coys were equally adept at producing both jubilant pop and tough garage-punk on either side of the one single. The band's singles are highly prized by collectors of 1960s Australian pop. 'Bad Time' was one of the many standout tracks on Raven's Australian 1960s garage-punk collection *Ugly Things*. 'You're Against' appeared on Raven's collection of 1960s pop gems, *Kicks (The Great Lost Australian 60s Pop Album)*.

1967 saw The Cherokees become virtually a pop jug-band with swing era overtones. Memorable covers of Ted Weems' 'Oh Monah!'/'Ain't Gonna Cry No More' (Melbourne #18, Sydney #12 in January 1967) and Cab Calloway's 'Minnie the Moocher'/'I've Gone Wild' (Melbourne #17 in May 1967) became the band's biggest hits. Like 'The Thought of You', the generally neglected B-side 'I've Gone Wild' was one of the band's toughest beat tracks. The success justified an album *Oh Monah!*, but soon after that the Go!! label collapsed and the band was without a deal. Van Wynk left to be replaced by Mike McGuire. The band issued a one-off single on Festival 'Sally'/'Grey Sunday Morning' (August 1968). It was not successful, but then the band scored the coveted support spot on The Monkees' Australian tour of October 1968. Unfortunately, the band was on its last legs and by the end of the year had broken up. Although The Cherokees did not achieve major status, the band remains one of the finest, yet most underrated, exponents of beat music that Australia produced during the 1960s.

In 1977 Doug Trevor and Paul O'Gorman co-wrote 'Ride, Ride America' which won the Australian Popular Song Contest that year. O'Gorman also performed the song at the World Contest in Tokyo, winning the Outstanding Song Award and Outstanding Song Performance Award. O'Gorman issued 'Ride, Ride America' as a single and it made the Australian charts in December 1977. Trevor produced O'Gorman's debut album, *The Poet and the Painter*, which came out on Festival in May 1978. Trevor now manages country superstars Gina Jeffreys and Troy Cassar-Daley.

Albums: *Here Come the Cherokees* (W&G, 1964), *Oh*

Monah! (Go!!, 1967), *The Legendary Go!! Sessions* (Canetoad, 1990).

The Chessmen

Formed: *1960*
Style: *Rock'n'roll*
Original line-up: **Johnny Chester** *(vocals), Bert Stacpool (piano), Les Stacpool (sax), Huey Fryer (guitar), Jeff Cason (upright slap bass), Len Woodhouse (drums)*

The Chessmen were one of the most proficient rock'n'roll bands on the early 1960s Melbourne scene. The band originally formed as The Jaywoods. With **Johnny Chester** the obvious star, the band became known as Johnny Chester and his Chessmen. There were regular line-up changes throughout 1960–61. Barry Windley replaced Woodhouse on drums; Ken Branchflower (electric bass) replaced Cason; Frank McMahon replaced Branchflower. Billy Dale (lead guitar), George Dale (rhythm guitar) and Laurie Arthur (lead guitar) were members for a while. When Huey Fryer left Les Stacpool took over lead guitar. Billy Dale and Barry Windley formed **The Cherokees** in 1961.

Johnny Chester formed a more permanent Chessmen line-up in 1961 with Les Stacpool (guitar), Albert Stacpool (piano), Frank McMahon (bass) and Graeme Trottman (drums). Mike Lynch replaced Trottman in 1962. The band backed Chester on most of his single sides, but Chester was generally backed by other bands while on tour (such as **The Thunderbirds**). The Chessmen maintained their own career, recording four instrumental singles and an album for W&G between 1963 and 1966. The singles were 'The Rebel'/'Outer Sanctum' (1963), 'Rock and Roll Music'/'Like, Long Hair' (1964), 'Wild Little Willie'/'Twistified' (1965) and 'Bop-a-Lena'/'Hound Dog' (1966). 'The Rebel' and 'Like, Long Hair' were later included on the collection *The W&G Instrumental Story*, put out by the Canetoad label in 1989.

The Chessmen were the resident group on Chester's ABC-TV national show *Teen Scene*, which first went to air in October 1964. For the show, the band was augmented by Henri Bource (sax; ex-Allstars, **Thunderbirds**) and Don Wright (sax). After the band split in 1965, Les Stacpool went on to join **Merv Benton** and the Tamlas, **Levi Smith's Clefs**, **Doug Parkinson** In Focus, **Aesop's Fables, Country Radio,** The Living Legends and Blacksmith Hopkins, among many others.

Album: *The Chessmen Play and Sing Dance Favourites* (W&G, 1964).

Johnny Chester

Style: *Rock'n'roll, country*

Johnny 'Ches' Chester (b. 1941) is remembered as one of Melbourne's first and best rock'n'roll singers of the early 1960s. While Sydney already had the likes of **Johnny O'Keefe**, **Alan Dale** and **Col Joye**, Chester was able to grab the monopoly down south. During the 1960s, Chester enjoyed a successful run of hit singles in Melbourne. He moved into straight country in the 1970s, but his earliest heroes included Buddy Holly, Elvis Presley, Eddie Cochran, Gene Vincent and **Johnny O'Keefe**.

Johnny Chester and his **Chessmen** began promoting their own dances at Preston Town Hall in 1960. Chester came to the attention of popular DJ Stan Rofe, who introduced him to W&G Records' A&R manager, Ron Tudor. With backing provided by **The Thunderbirds**, Chester issued his first two Melbourne hit singles, 'That's How it's Gonna Be'/'The Hokey-Pokey'(#8 in May 1961) and the *4 on 1 Super Disc* single, 'Can Can Ladies'; 'What a Night'/'The Hokey-Pokey'; 'That's How it's Gonna Be' (#5 in July). Around that time, Chester appeared as one of the supports (backed by The Joy Boys) on the Connie Francis Big Show, The Hi-Fi Club Presents Johnny O'Keefe: The Wild One tour (backed by the Hi-Marks), and the All Star Rock Show (backed by **The Thunderbirds**).

Chester's third single with backing by **The Thunderbirds** was 'Shakin' All Over'/'California Sun' (#4 in January 1962). Rock'n'roll aficionados consider this version of 'Shakin' All Over' to be the definitive Australian rendition. Chester recorded with his **Chessmen** for the next eight singles on W&G: 'Shy Away'/'A Funny Little Feeling' (#35 in August 1962), Chris Montez's 'Let's Dance'/'Forty Days' (#18 in October), Eddie Cochran's 'Summertime Blues'/'I Love Mary' (#6 in December), 'Nick Nack Paddy Wack'/'Butterflies' (#27 in May 1963), Cochran's 'C'Mon Everybody'/'The Old Copper Kettle' (#12 in August), 'Teeny'/'Do the Stomp' (#11 in January 1964), Chuck Berry's 'Bye Bye Johnny'/'Miss Anne' (May 1964) and 'Unless You Care'/'(You're So Square) Baby I Don't Care' (#25 in November 1964). His last single on W&G was 'Your Cheating Heart'/'Adios My Darling'. Chester also issued an album, *Wild and Warm*, and two EPs, *Johnny Chester's Hit Parade* and the rare *My Blues and I* on W&G.

Chester's biggest break came when he supported The Beatles on the band's July 1964 Australian tour. Once again, he was not able to use his **Chessmen** and backing was provided by **The Phantoms.** In October, Chester became compere of his own national television show, *Teen Scene*, which lasted for two seasons. Chester recorded three singles for W&G's In label: 'When Will I be Loved?'/'Shop Around' (July 1965), 'Something's Got a Hold on Me'/'It's Too Late' (October) and 'Steppin' Out'/'I Feel Good All Over' (February 1966), plus the rare EP 'Goodnight Irene', none of which charted. He parted company with his **Chessmen** and formed The Johnny Chester Trio with Bert Stacpool (piano), Johnny Marco (guitar) and Tom Vigushin (bass). In 1966, Chester became a DJ on Melbourne's 3UZ, where he stayed for eight years. His last pop single was 'Heaven Help the Man'/'I'm Gonna have a Real Good Time' on Astor (1968).

In 1969 Chester issued two singles on Philips, 'Green Green'/'It Works Out Easier that Way' and 'Highway 31'/'I Just Don't Know How to Say Goodbye'. By that stage Chester had moved into the country music field. Next he signed to Fable and formed **Jigsaw**. Johnny Chester and Jigsaw had hits with 'Gwen (Congratulations)'/'A Lonely Man Like Me' (national #26 in October 1971), 'Shame and Scandal'/'Billy's Coming Home for Christmas' (#12 in February 1972), 'Midnight Bus'/'Highway 31' (#25 in December 1972), 'World's Greatest Mum'/'Three Jobs Down' (#9 in August 1973) and 'She's My Kind of Woman'/'Won't You Send Your Sweet Lovin' to Me' (#17 in June 1974). By 1977 he was touring with The Blue Denim Country Band and back on television with the ABC-TV's national show *Country Road*.

In 1979, Chester signed to WEA and formed a new band, Hotspur. Chester continued to issue counry albums and singles, and made his mark on the Tamworth Country Music Festival by winning the Male Vocalist of the Year for three years in a row, 1981–83.

Albums: *Wild and Warm* (W&G, 1963), *Best of Ches* (W&G, 1964), *Johnny Chester Sings His Greatest Hits* (W&G, 1965), *Johnny Chester and Jigsaw* (Fable 1971), *Going Places (Just For Fun)* (Fable, 1972), *The Best of Johnny Chester* (Fable, 1974), *For the World's Greatest Mum* (Fable, 1974), *Greensborough Music* (Fable, 1975), *Into Country* (Bullet, 1976), *Country Salute* (RCA, 1978), *Johnny Chester* (Image, 1978), *Johnny Chester and Hotspur* (WEA, 1980), *My Kinda Country* (Velvet, 1980), *Love in the Meantime* (WEA, 1981), *From Under the Influence* (WEA, 1983), *The Hits of Johnny Chester* (J&B, 1984), *Songmaker* (1995).

David Chesworth

Style: *Electronic*

Synthesiser player David Chesworth was active on the Melbourne experimental/electronic music scene of the late 1970s/early 1980s. He was involved in coordinating the Clifton Hill Community Music Centre, a collective of artists and musicians (including **Philip Brophy's** band →↑→), who at various times and in various guises performed music, staged plays, screened films and exhibited artwork.

Chesworth co-edited (with Brophy) *New Music* magazine which documented Melbourne's electronic and experimental music scene. Chesworth worked with his own band, Essendon Airport, as well as collaborating with Brophy under the guise of the Dave and Phil Duo. Chesworth's self-produced debut album, *50 Synthesiser Greats*, actually contained 39 instrumentals of mildly diverting synth noodlings. Three tracks were later re-released on the *Signal-to-Noise Set, Volume 1* on Cleopatra in 1981. The Dave and Phil Duo performed light, electric piano music which might be termed 'dinner muzak'. The duo issued one EP, *Present Themselves*, on the Innocent label in 1980.

Essendon Airport (with guitarist Robert Goodge) was another vehicle for 'new music' of the electronic and experimental kind. The band issued an EP, *Sonic Investigations (of the Trivial)*, in 1979, as well as teaming up with singer Anne Cessna for the 'Talking to Cleopatra'/'Lost in Madagascar' single (both on Innocent). The 1982 line-up of Chesworth, Goodge, Ian Cox (sax; ex-**Hot Half Hour**), Barbara Hogarth (bass; ex-Government Drums) and Paul Fletcher (drums) played a hybrid of modern jazz, rock and funk. Essendon Airport issued a mini-album, *Palimpsest*, in late 1982, and disbanded in mid-1983. Goodge, Cox and Hogarth formed popular funksters **I'm Talking**. Essendon Airport, →↑→, the Dave and Phil Duo, Laughing Hands and others appeared on Innocent Records' two 1981 compilations *New Music 1978/79* and *New Music 1980*.

Chesworth's second album, *Layer on Layer*, was later repackaged with his debut as *Spiral Rebound*. In 1985 Chesworth formed Whaddya Want? with Phillip Jackson (synthesiser), Warwick Bone (synthesiser), Bill McDonald (bass) and Michael Tinney (guitar). The band issued the single 'Life on TV'/'Involved with You' and the mini-album *Skippy Knows* (1986) on the Correct label. In 1987, Chesworth recorded the soundtrack album to the independent film *No Particular Place*. In 1993, he formed the experimental David Chesworth Ensemble with Hope Csutorus (violin), John McCall (keyboards), Bill McDonald (bass), Helen Mountford (cello), Simon Myers (trombone), Xenia Hanusiak (percussion) and Peter Neville (percussion). The album *Exotica Suite* worked as incidental or theme-based music for a 'soundtrack without visuals'. Much of the album also recalled the wry, gently rhythmic fun of the UK band Penguin Cafe Orchestra.

Albums: *50 Synthesiser Greats* (Musicland, 1979), *Layer on Layer* (Innocent, 1981), *Spiral Rebound* (Innocent, 1982), *No Particular Place* (Correct, 1987), *Tantrum* (Correct, 1988), *Risky Business* (Correct, 1990); ***With David Chesworth Ensemble:*** *Exotica Suite* (Warner Classics, 1995).

Chetarca

Formed: *1974*
Style: *Progressive blues*
Original line-up: *Paul Lever (vocals, harp; ex-Langford Lever), Andrew Vance (piano, Hammond organ; ex-Langford Lever), Bruce Bryan (synthesiser; ex-Langford Lever), John Rees (bass; ex-Langford Lever), Geoff Gallent (drums; ex-Langford Lever)*

Chetarca had previously worked for three years as Langford Lever, playing blues rock on the Melbourne pub circuit. When guitarist Ian Miller left in 1974, Chetarca was born. Chetarca issued one refined and very underrated progressive album in 1975. The album boasted an accomplished dual keyboard attack (no guitars), and Lever's bluesy vocals and wailing harp. Its centrepiece was the side-long, 24-minute 'Oceanic Suite'. Emerson Lake and Palmer was an obvious reference point for the band's music, although more obscure UK progressive bands like Spring and Nektar came to mind. The frantic 'Another Day'/'Fisherman's Nightmare' was issued as a single but, like the album, it sank without a trace. Ian Miller (who also produced the album) re-joined the band, but Chetarca had broken up by early 1976. While the other members disappeared from view, Miller joined **John Paul Young** and the All Stars and John Rees later turned up in **Men at Work**.

Album: *Chetarca* (Atlantic, 1975).

The Chevelles

Formed: *1989*
Style: *Power pop*
Original line-up: *Richard Lane (guitar, keyboards, vocals; ex-***Stems***), Duane Smith (guitar; ex-Freuds), Jeff Halley (bass; ex-***Kryptonics***), Guy Douglas (drums)*

The Chevelles hailed from Perth, Western Australia, and followed in the tradition of **The Stems** and Someloves (i.e. classic garage power pop but with added atmosphere). Two important overseas reference points would be The Smithereens and The Replacements. Richard Lane had been a member of **The Stems** for five years. The Chevelles issued the single 'Be My Friend'/'She Don't Come Around' (August 1990) and the EP 'The Kids Ain't Hip' (November) on Sydney independent label Zero Hour before Adrian Allen replaced Lane.

By that stage, The Chevelles were one of the premier independent bands on the Perth scene, scoring regular gigs and high-profile support slots to the likes of **The Church**, **Hunters & Collectors** and **Baby Animals**, plus overseas visitors Billy Bragg and The Smithereens. The band issued *The Kids Ain't Hip* throughout Europe as a full-length compilation album. That sparked off a great deal of European interest in the band. The Chevelles signed to Survival in 1992 and issued the CD EP 'Girl for Me' during October. The single 'Murder on her Mind' (January 1993) and the CD EP *Memories* (April 1993) were tasters for the band's debut album, *Gigantic*, which came out in June. Rather than concentrating on traditional 1960s jangly guitar pop, *Gigantic* showcased the band's heavier and more textured, but still tuneful, approach.

Just as The Chevelles were gearing up for their first national tour, they replaced original drummer Guy Douglas with Mario Frisino (on loan from fellow Perth power poppers The Calhoons). Eventually Martin Moon came in as a permanent replacement. At the end of 1993, The Chevelles undertook a joint, six-week, 27-date European tour with **The Screaming Tribesmen** and **Screamfeeder**.

Album: *Gigantic* (Survival, 1993).

Jimmy Chi

Style: *Reggae*

Koori singer/songwriter Jimmy Chi (b. 1948) was born in Broome, Western Australia. In 1981 he enrolled at the Centre For Aboriginal Studies in Music (CASM) in Adelaide, where he formed calypso reggae band The Kuckles. The band released an independent cassette album *Milluja Rumurra* (or *Brand New Day*), the songs of which formed the basis of Chi's musical play *Bran Nue Dae*.

Bran Nue Dae premiered at the Octagon Theatre on 22 February 1990 for the Festival of Perth. Andrew Ross directed the play, and Bran Nue Dae Productions in association with the West Australian Theatre Company produced it. The company took the play around Australia during the year. Based on Chi's own experiences, *Bran Nue Dae* centred around the travels of Aboriginal boy Willy as he went on a search for his identity. Although focusing on tragic events, it was nevertheless funny and entertaining. The play featured 22 original Kuckles songs which were performed by members of that band and fellow Broome outfit **Scrap Metal**. Chi collaborated with Michael Manolis and the play's musical director Steven Pigram (from **Scrap Metal**) on the music.

Chicks Inc

Formed: *1976*
Style: *Disco funk*
Line-up: *Safanya (vocals), Wendy Knudson (keyboards, vocals), Pam Withnell (sax, flute, clarinet), Chris Mitchell (guitar), Sue Nielson (bass, vocals), Miriam Curtis (drums), Jenny Bowman (dancer), Wendy Dowsett (dancer)*

Brisbane band Chicks Inc drew its American-styled disco-funk sound from the likes of The Commodores, Rufus, Kool and the Gang and Wild Cherry. Reputedly, Chicks Inc also presented a wild and sexy stage act. Chris Mitchell was the band's token male musician. Other predominantly female bands during the late 1970s included Garbo, **Sweet Jayne** and then, later on, The Party Girls.

The 1978 line-up included Curtis, Robyn Krupski (keyboards), Robyn McKie (guitar), Jack Wilson (bass), Mardi (vocals) and Tina Rae (dancer). The last line-up included Curtis, Finn Christian (vocals), Paula Williams (vocals), Jennifer Kelly (guitar), Danny Patchin (bass), Kim Wheeler (keyboards) and Peter Wragg (synthesiser). Chicks Inc issued an album and four singles on RCA, 'Jive to Stay Alive' (1977), 'Inside Information'/'Let Me Take You There' (1978), 'I'm on Fire'/'Bside the Cside' (1978) and 'Movie Star'/'Can't Take it with Me' (1978; as Chicks).

Album: *Security* (RCA, 1980).

Chocolate Starfish

Formed: *1992*
Style: *Rock*
Original line-up: *Adam Thompson (vocals; ex-Show of Hands, Gravity), Zoran Romich (guitar, vocals; ex-Gravity), Norman Flavo (keyboards, vocals), Craig Harnath (bass; ex-***Kids in the Kitchen***, Gravity), Bruce Pawsey (drums; ex-Battle Happy, Ministry of Fun)*

Melbourne band Chocolate Starfish came to the nation's attention in 1993 with a booming cover of Carly Simon's 1973 hit 'You're so Vain'. As a single, 'You're so Vain' reached #11 on the national charts during September and established the band's mainstream credentials.

Chocolate Starfish had been playing the Melbourne club and pub scene for 18 months prior to signing to EMI. It was deemed necessary to choose a cover song with which to launch the band on to the national market. Inevitably, that stamped the Starfish as simply a covers band in the eyes of critics and the public alike. Nevertheless, the members of Chocolate Starfish had enough belief in their own songwriting skills and natural abilities to transcend such easy categorisations. And in singer Adam Thompson, the band possessed an entertaining frontman who lent the music an air of much-needed theatricality and melodrama.

The band's debut release was the CD EP *Seafood* in March 1993, by which time John Stone (aka John Nixon, bass; ex-**Roxus**) had replaced Harnath and Darren Danielson (drums; ex-**Roxus**) replaced Pawsey. As a follow-up to the 'You're so Vain' hit, the band issued the self-penned 'All Over Me' which reached #33 in December 1993. By that stage, Chocolate Starfish had supported the likes of **INXS** and **Baby Animals**, and toured as headliners in their own right. Chocolate Starfish scored a third hit (and second gold single after 'You're so Vain') with the power ballad 'Mountain' (#12 in April 1994). The band's self-titled album (produced by former **Pseudo Echo** frontman Brian Canham) made its debut at #2 on the national album chart. It showcased the band's confident and punchy, if overwrought, delivery. *Chocolate Starfish* surpassed platinum status (100 000 copies sold), making it the most successful debut album for 1994. 'Four Letter Word' (#41 in July) was the band's fourth single.

Chocolate Starfish issued three CD singles during 1995, 'Accidently Cool' (#39 in August), 'April the Fool' (#45 in October) and 'Motherless' (December), plus a second full-length album *Box*. Mixed by American Thom Panunzio (U2, Soundgarden), *Box* followed the commercial formula set by the band's debut. Like *Chocolate Starfish*, it mixed strong vocals with grungy riffs, anthemic choruses with moody ballads, and accessible 1970s-influenced rock with tight 1990s production values. In early 1996, 'Holy Water' was lifted as the fourth CD single from *Box*. By 1997, Danielson was working in Brill with Brian Canham.

Album: *Chocolate Starfish* (EMI, 1994), *Box* (Virgin, 1995).

Choirboys

Formed: *1979*
Style: *Hard rock*
Original line-up: *Mark Gable (vocals, guitar), Brad Carr (lead guitar), Ian Hulme (bass), Lindsay Tebutt (drums)*

Sydney band Choirboys was the archetypal hard-rocking pub outfit of the early 1980s. No doubt due to the band's close affinity with the **AC/DC** and **Rose Tattoo** style of guitar noise, the Albert label signed the band in 1983.

Choirboys issued the album *Choirboys* (July 1983; #19 in October) and three singles on Albert: 'Never Gonna Die'/'Bullshit' (#30 in August), 'Talk Big' (September) and 'Boys in the Band'/'Bought and Paid for' (November). With the release of the album, the band toured as support to **The Angels** and **Rose Tattoo**. Choirboys had also been picked to support **Cold Chisel** on its historic Last Stand tour at the end of 1983, but because Gable had ruptured his vocal chords, which rendered him speechless, the band had to bow out. Gable's affliction prevented the band from touring and recording for most of 1984 and 1985.

The band bounced back in 1986 with a new record deal on Mushroom. 'Fireworks'/'We Can Dance' (May 1986) was the band's Mushroom debut. Brett Williams (ex-Brakes) replaced Brad Carr and Choirboys supported Bon Jovi on the American band's 1987 Australian tour. The Peter Blyton/Brian McGee (Rolling Stones, Cyndi Lauper) produced *Big Bad Noise* album peaked at #2 in April 1988 and went on to sell over 100 000 copies. It yielded the hit singles 'Run to Paradise'/'Struck by Lightning' (#3 in January 1988), 'Boys will Be Boys'/'Last Night of My Life' (#12 in March 1988) and 'Struggle Town'/'Let's Prey' (May 1988).

By that stage, however, a number of other bands had come through playing in a similar style, such as **Noiseworks**, **Kings of the Sun** and **Johnny Diesel** and the Injectors. Choirboys were eventually lost in the rush. *Midnight Sun* and the singles 'Place with No Love', 'Rendezvous'/'Sweet Seduction' and 'All Night' followed. Brad Heaney (drums; ex-**Screaming Jets**) and Steve Williams (guitar; ex-**Wa Wa Nee**) joined in 1993. Barton Price (ex-**Models**, Lost Angels) replaced Heaney in 1994 and Choirboys issued the album *Dancing on the Grave of Rock'n'Roll* and single 'Drops Like a Stone' (May 1995).

By 1996 the line-up was Gable, Hulme, Price and Richard Lara (guitar; ex-**Screaming Jets**). That line-up recorded *Yo-Yo* in Cologne, Germany with producer Peter Blyton, after which Price left the band. *Yo Yo* produced the CD single 'Solo' (December 1996). Choirboys ended the year as support act to US hard rock legends Cheap Trick on that band's Australian tour.

Albums: *Choirboys* (Albert/EMI, 1983), *Big Bad Noise* (Mushroom/Festival, 1988), *Midnight Sun* (Mushroom/Festival, 1991), *Decade 1983-1993* (Mushroom/Festival, 1993), *Dancing on the Grave of Rock'n'Roll* (Camouflage, 1994), *Yo-Yo* (Camouflage/TWA, 1996).

The Chosen Few

Formed: *1965*
Style: *R&B*
Original line-up: *Mike Siegele (keyboards, vocals), Dean Schubert (rhythm guitar), Bob van Amstel (lead guitar), Rod Schubert (bass), Brian Fechner (drums)*

There was a Canberra band also called The Chosen Few around the same time, but this Chosen Few began as The Outcasts in the small South Australian grape growing/winemaking township of Nuriootpa (just north of Adelaide). The members were all of German and Dutch descent. Being the only rock band in town, The Outcasts began running their own dances at Bentley Court discotheque. The band's influences included The Zombies, The Animals, the Spencer Davis Group, James Brown and Wilson Pickett.

In 1966, The Outcasts became The Chosen Few and began playing Adelaide. The Chosen Few won the South Australian heat of the Hoadley's Battle of the Sounds in June 1966. At the national final held in Melbourne, they were beaten by another Adelaide band, **The Twilights**, who had entered as a Melbourne band. As a result of winning the state final, The Chosen Few recorded a single for the Go!! label The Zombies' 'Is this a Dream?'/'Let Me Down Easy' (December 1966). In 1967, The Chosen Few broke up, so Mike and Bob teamed up with Martin McAvenna and John Hudson (both ex-Bentbeaks) as the short-lived The Force.

The Chosen Few

Formed: *1977*
Style: *Punk*
Original line-up: *Ian Weaver (vocals), Bruce Friday (guitar), Ian Cunningham (bass), Cal MacAlpine (drums)*

The Australian late 1970s punk movement spread its tentacles far and wide. The Chosen Few hailed from Hastings, on the Mornington Peninsula, south of Melbourne. The band's Stooges/MC5/**Radio Birdman**-influenced sound was heard on the ultra-rare six-track 7-inch EP *The Joke's On Us* (September 1978). 'Disco Tek Wrek' was dedicated to **Radio Birdman**'s **Deniz Tek**. **Bored!** later covered the track 'There's a Lot of It Going Around'. Alongside **News**'s 'Dirty Lies' single, *The Joke's on Us* was the only genuine Melbourne punk record issued in 1978. The band later became Bohdan and the Instigators when ex-**JAB** frontman Bohdan X joined. A couple of the members continued as Rah Rah the Flag in the early 1980s. MacAlpine later turned up as a member of **Olympic Sideburns** and Dirt.

Chosen Few

Formed: *1986*
Style: *Pop*
Original line-up: *Abe Elshaikh (guitar, vocals), Danny McCarthy (guitar, vocals), Paul Reed (bass), Rex Mansfield (drums, vocals)*

Sydney band Chosen Few won the 1987 Sydney Battle of the Bands. Mushroom signed the band and issued the singles 'Get it Right'/'With Barely a Whisper' (November 1988) and 'Rise'/'One Mistake' (May 1989). Chosen Few's debut album, *Friends, Foes and Firewood,* yielded the singles 'Days Like These'/'Bleed Me' and 'When the Boat Comes in'/'Unofficial'. None of the band's records was a chart success, although **Daryl Braithwaite** later covered 'Rise' as the title track for his #1 album.

Album: *Friends, Foes and Firewood* (Mushroom/Festival, 1990).

Christbait

Formed: *1990*
Style: *Industrial metal*
Original line-up: *Jason Vasallo (vocals), Craig (guitar), Jason (guitar), Nadia (bass), Lenny (drums)*

This aggressive Melbourne band started out as a generic death metal outfit before opting for a slower, down-tuned, more industrial-strength grunge noise. Early reference points included UK bands like Napalm Death, Fudge Tunnel and Carcass. As the band's sound evolved, other influences (Godflesh, Black Sabbath, Cathedral) made an impact. The band earned a cult following on the small Melbourne death/grindcore scene alongside the likes of **Abramelin** and Blood Duster, issuing the CD EP *Yeast* on the Dr Jim's label in late 1992. Christbait supported overseas visitors like Fear Factory, Bad Brains, Helmet and Morbid Angel before slipping from view. Christbait returned in late 1996 with the album *dirtypunkmutha.*

Album: *dirtypunkmutha* (Shock, 1996).

Ana Christensen

Style: *Folk pop*

Singer/songwriter Ana Christensen (b. 1960) was born in California and raised in Papua New Guinea before relocating to Townsville, north Queensland in the late 1970s. She issued her debut album *Deep in the Night* on the independent Nicholls 'n' Dimes label in 1988. It was not until Christensen signed to CBS in early 1990 that her career proper was under way.

Produced by former **Sherbet** keyboard player Garth Porter, the *Brave New World* album yielded the singles 'Isolate Your Heart' (August 1990) and 'Brave New World' (November). Leading session players like South African producer Ricky Fataar (drums; ex-Beach Boys) and Rex Goh (guitar; ex-**Air Supply**) contributed to the album. The sweet, sensitive and soulful sounds with which Christensen embued her album drew comparisons with the likes of Melanie, Tracey Chapman and Joni Mitchell. The songs ranged from Celtic ballads and country-tinged pop to laid-back rock.

In 1991, Christensen formed the all-electric Ana Christensen Band with Mike Caen (guitar; ex-Street Talk, Pink Slips, Scribble), Mike Woodcock (guitar), Lee Borkman (keyboards; ex-Pink Slips, Scribble), Steve Bull (bass, keyboards) and Tim Powles (drums; ex-**Venetians**). At the end of 1991 Christensen issued a version of Bob Dylan's classic 'Like a Rolling Stone' as a prelude single to the recording of her third album. The song reflected her move into more of a rock'n'roll style. Christensen did not issue her third album until 1994. *Not All Monkeys are Right Handed* produced the singles 'Cultivate the Wild' (July) and 'I Will Hold You Up' (November).

Albums: *Deep in the Night* (Nicholls 'n' Dimes, 1988), *Brave New World* (CBS, 1990), *Not All Monkeys are Right Handed* (CBS, 1994).

The Church

Formed: *1980*
Style: *Rock*
Original line-up: **Steve Kilbey** *(bass, vocals), Peter Koppes (guitar), Nick Ward (drums)*

From its beginnings as a 1960s-inspired neo-psychedelic pop band (all jangly, Byrds-like guitar riffs and mystical imagery) to an international standing based

Steve Kilbey, The Church

on a series of exceptional album releases, The Church created a unique and distinctive style. With enthusiastic press and respectable sales around the world, the band spent a considerable amount of the 1980s touring the UK, Europe and the USA.

English-born singer/songwriter **Steve Kilbey** formed The Church in Sydney during April 1980. Liverpool, UK-born Marty Willson-Piper (guitar) joined one month later. That line-up recorded a four-song demo which they sent to Chris Gilbey at ATV/Northern. A publishing deal and a recording contract with EMI/Parlophone quickly followed. The band's first release was the low-key 'She Never Said'/'In a Heart Beat' single (November, 1980). The band's debut album *Of Skins and Heart* (May 1981; #30 in June) and second single 'The Unguarded Moment'/'Busdriver' were more indicative of an emerging style. 'The Unguarded Moment' reached #22 and, despite Kilbey's dislike of the song, it remains the band's signature tune in Australia.

Eighteen-year-old Richard Ploog replaced Ward at the start of 1981, and the delightful five-track double single 'Too Fast for You' followed in July. The double single initially came in a pressing of 5000 copies, after which the tracks were also issued as separate singles: 'Tear it All Away'/'You've Got to Go', 'Fraulein' and 'Too Fast for You'/'Sisters'. The band's international debut album *The Church* (on Carrere in the UK and Capitol in the USA) omitted various tracks from the local release and added several from 'Too Fast for You'. *The Blurred Crusade* (February 1982; #10 in March) was a smoother, fuller release than the debut and spawned two singles, 'Almost with You'/'Life Speeds Up' (#21 in March) and 'When You Were Mine'/'The Golden Dawn' (May). Around that time, Kilbey declared to *RAM (Rock Australia Magazine)* that he was the 'best songwriter in the world'. Whether he meant it seriously or otherwise, this resulted in a local backlash that persisted for some years.

Meanwhile, *The Blurred Crusade* was issued in the UK and Europe, and in October 1982 the band commenced an extended tour of those territories. In November, Carrere issued the collectable 10-inch, four-track EP *Temperature Drop in Down Town Winterland* ('The Unguarded Moment', 'Sisters'/'An Interlude', 'Golden Dawn') for the UK market. The five-track *Sing-Songs* EP, which included a cover of Paul Simon's 'I Am a Rock', followed in December. The EP featured a sparser sound and pointed towards the next album, *Seance*, which reached # 18 in June 1983. That stark release explored the band's darker side, and tracks like the singles 'It's No Reason'/'Someone Special' (May 1983) and 'Electric Lash'/'Autumn Soon' (September) were awash with strings and other effects. In 1984, The Church added ex-**Reels** keyboard player Craig Hooper as an auxiliary member. Hooper contributed to the band's excellent 1984 EP *Persia* (August), which yielded such radiant Church moments as 'Constant in Opal' and 'Shadow Cabinet'. *Persia* had been preceded by the equally impressive *Remote Luxury* EP (March). The two EPs made up the international album version of *Remote Luxury* (issued in August) and, following strong reviews in the USA, the band undertook its first American tour (October/November 1984).

1985 was a quiet year for The Church, and Kilbey took the opportunity to issue his first solo single ('This Asphalt Eden'/'Never Come Back', 'Shell'). The first Church single in two years, 'Already Yesterday'/'As You Will', came out in October 1985. It was a taster for the acclaimed *Heyday* album (produced by Englishman Peter Walsh), which reached #14 on the national chart in March 1986. Songs such as 'Myrrh', 'Night of Light' and the singles 'Tantalized'/'The View' (January) and 'Columbus'/'Trance Ending' (May) were among the richest moments in the Church canon. With the album selling well overseas, the band left for its third international tour in April 1986.

While the band was on the European leg of the tour, Willson-Piper quit. Tensions had arisen over Kilbey's authority within the band (he wrote nearly all the band's material), and Willson-Piper only came back into the fold under the agreement that future Church compositions would be collaborative efforts. This new-found unity immediately revealed itself on *Starfish* (March 1988), which yielded the sumptuous ballad 'Under the Milky Way' and the taut rocker 'Reptile'. Both were issued as singles ('Under the Milky Way' backed with 'Warm Spell' and 'Musk' in February 1988; 'Reptile' backed with the non-album 'Texas Moon' in July). These were the band's first local hit singles since 'Almost with You' in 1982. In fact, 'Under the Milky Way' became the band's biggest hit ever when it peaked at #5 on the national chart in April. It also won Best Single at the 1988 Australian Record Industry Association (ARIA) Awards. 'Destination'/'We Both Know You're Here' (November) was the third single lifted from *Starfish*.

'Under the Milky Way' also reached #24 in the USA, which led to more international touring. *Starfish* was the band's first release for Mushroom (and Arista worldwide), and EMI brought its Church era to a close with the double retrospective album *Hindsight* (July 1988). *Starfish* was the band's most successful album ever, peaking at #7 in Australia, while in the USA it sold 600 000 copies. The *Gold Afternoon Fix* album (April 1990) was a disappointment, despite heady moments with the singles 'Metropolis'/'Much Too Much' (March), 'You're Still Beautiful'/'Hunter' (June) and 'Terra Nova Cain'/'Desert' (September). In Australia, 'Metropolis' and *Gold Afternoon Fix* both peaked at #10 on their respective national chart the same week. The album also sold 250 000 copies in the USA on pre-sale orders alone.

Long-serving member Ploog left at that point to be replaced by ex-Patti Smith Band drummer Jay Dee Daugherty. The new line-up issued the 65 minute *Priest=Aura* album (April 1992), which concentrated on long, atmospheric pieces like 'Aura', 'Mistress' and the CD singles 'Ripple' (March) and 'Feel' (July). It sold over 200 000 copies in the USA. Koppes and Daugherty left prior to further touring and The Church emerged as a duo (Kilbey and Willson-Piper) with the 75-minute *Sometime Anywhere* album (June 1994). That rich, dark, epic release picked up where *Priest* left off with lush, lengthy tracks like 'Day of the Dead', 'Fly Home' and the CD single 'Two Places at Once' (June). Early copies of the album came with a bonus, seven-track collection, *Somewhere Else*. The Church also contributed a cover of **The Radiators**' 'Room Full of Diamonds' to the Various Artists *Earth Music* project (June). 'Room Full of Diamonds' did not appear on the album, but emerged as a bonus cut on the CD single of Joe Camilleri's 'Gypsy Queen' (originally recorded by **Country Radio**).

After the patchy *Magician Among the Spirits* album and its CD single 'Comedown' (May 1996), Kilbey put The Church on hold to concentrate on production work and his solo career. The September 1996 touring line-up featured Kilbey, Willson-Piper, Peter Koppes and Tim Powles (drums; ex-**Venetians**). A year later, The Church signed a new deal with UK label Demon Records (home to Elvis Costello), and recommenced recording and touring. The last two albums in the Church *oeuvre* were the collection of B-sides and oddities *A Quick Smoke at Spot's (Archives 1986–1990)* and the superb *Almost Yesterday 1981–1990* compilation on Raven.

Since the mid-1980s, the individual members of The Church have issued many solo outings. The most prolific was **Steve Kilbey** with four albums, a mini-album, several singles and a CD EP, *Narcosis*; he has also collaborated with former **Go-Betweens** member **Grant McLennan** as **Jack Frost** which resulted in two albums (*Jack Frost* in 1990 and *Snow Job* in 1996). Kilbey's solo work tended to be more adventurous, with a definite avant-garde feel. Willson-Piper has released four albums of stirring, atmospheric pop which yielded four singles 'She's King'/'Frightened Because of You' (August 1988), 'Questions Without Answers' (June 1990), 'Melancholy Girl'/'On the Tip of My Tongue' (October 1990) and 'Luscious Ghost' (October 1992). He also toured as a part-time member of UK band All About Eve in 1991–92. Koppes has released two albums and two mini-albums, and has also toured with his band The Well, which comprised Anthony Smith (keyboards; ex-Flowers/**Icehouse**), Jim Leone (bass; from **Celibate Rifles**) and Richard Ploog (drums; ex-Church).

The Church albums: *Of Skins and Heart* (EMI/Parlophone, 1981), *The Blurred Crusade* (EMI/Parlophone, 1982), *Seance* (EMI/Parlophone, 1983), *Heyday* (EMI/Parlophone, 1986), *Hindsight* (EMI/Parlophone, 1988), *Starfish* (Mushroom/Festival, 1988), *Gold Afternoon Fix* (Mushroom/Festival, 1990), *A Quick Smoke at Spot's (Archives 1986–1990)* (Mushroom/Festival, 1991), *Priest=Aura* (Mushroom/Festival, 1992), *Sometime Anywhere* (Mushroom/Festival, 1994), *Almost Yesterday 1981–1990* (Raven, 1995), *Magician Among the Spirits* (Deep Karma/Mushroom/Festival, 1996); ***Marty Willson-Piper solo albums:*** *In Reflection* (Chase, 1987), *Art Attack* (Survival/CBS, 1988), *Rhyme* (Rykodisc/ Festival, 1990), *Spirit Level* (Rykodisc/Festival, 1992); ***Peter Koppes solo albums:*** *When Reason Forbids* (mini-album, Session, 1987), *Manchild and Myth* (Session, 1988), *From the Well* (TVT/Mushroom/Festival, 1990), *Iridescence* (mini-album, Session, 1991).

Richard Clapton

Style: Rock

Singer/songwriter Richard Clapton (b. 1949) spent his formative years as a travelling troubadour, working in the UK and Germany during the late 1960s/early 1970s. He played with a few rock bands, as well as working solo in folk clubs. He returned to Australia in 1972 with a batch of songs based on his experiences overseas.

Clapton signed a record deal with Festival/Infinity and a publishing deal with Essex Music. He issued his debut single, 'Last Train to Marseilles'/'High Train Girl' (October 1972). Backing musicians were Red McKelvie (lead guitar; ex-**Flying Circus**, Powderhorn, Third Union Band), Kenny Kitching (pedal steel) and John Capek (piano; ex-**Carson**), plus the **Country Radio** rhythm section John Du Bois (bass) and Tony Bolton (drums). The single was not successful, and Clapton joined Sydney jazz-rock band Sun for six weeks (he left in January 1973). He eventually completed his debut album, *Prussian Blue*, which came out in November 1973. The album produced two more singles, 'All the Prodigal Children'/'Hardly Know Myself' (October) and 'I Wanna Be a Survivor'/'Prussian Blue' (July 1974). Clapton utilised the services of **La De Das** on two tracks 'Hardly Know Myself' and 'I Wanna Be a Survivor', plus a number of other session players like McKelvie, **Glenn Cardier** (guitar), Russell Dunlop (drums; ex-**Levi Smith's Clefs**, SCRA), Mike Perjanik (organ), Trevor Wilson (bass; from **Home**), Mike Lawler (bass; ex-Rajahs) and Ian Bloxham (percussion) on the rest of the album.

Clapton's first chart success came with the single 'Girls on the Avenue'/'Travelling Down the Castlereagh' (January 1975). 'Girls on the Avenue' came adorned with a gorgeous guitar refrain provided by McKelvie which no doubt added to its success. Interestingly, Festival had shown little faith in 'Girls on the Avenue' initially by issuing it as the B-side. Strong radio support resulted in the song becoming a national #2 hit during March. The *Girls on the Avenue* album produced a second single, 'Down the Road'/'Rose Wine Cafe' (June) which was not successful. The non-album single 'Please Come Home'/Burn Your Bridges' came out in October. Clapton's third album, *Main Street Jive* (July 1976), gave rise to one single, 'Suit Yourself'/'Kicking the Moon Around' (June 1976). At the end of the year, Clapton undertook a European tour.

The Richard Clapton Band at that stage comprised Canadian Kirk Lorange (lead guitar), Tony Slavich (keyboards), Michael Hegerty (bass) and Jim Penson (drums; ex-**Blackfeather**). Clapton's next big hit, 'Capricorn Dancer'/'Babe Rainbow' (February 1977), was lifted from the *Highway One* soundtrack album, which also featured tracks by **Ol'55, Skyhooks, The Dingoes** and The Bilgola Bop Band. The enchanting 'Capricorn Dancer' reached #20 in May. Clapton's third album, *Goodbye Tiger* (August 1977), remains his most celebrated work, an album full of rich, melodic and accessible rock with a distinctly Australian flavour. It established Clapton's reputation as one of the most important Australian songwriters of the 1970s.

Goodbye Tiger reached #5 during November, and produced the singles 'Deep Water'/'Factory Life' (September) and 'Down in the Lucky Country'/'Wintertime in Amsterdam' (January 1978). 'Deep Water' reached #28 in November. Clapton's backing band on the album comprised Lorange, Hegerty, Gunther Gorman (guitar; ex-**Home**), Cleis Pearce (viola; ex-**MacKenzie Theory**), Diane McLennan (backing vocals) and Greg Sheehan (drums; ex-**Blackfeather, MacKenzie Theory**), with assistance from Tony Buchanan (sax; ex-**Thunderbirds, Johnny Rocco Band**), Tony Ansell (keyboards) and Jim Penson on a number of tracks. For a brief period at the end of 1977, Clapton's touring band comprised Lorange, McLennan, plus three ex-members of **Ariel**, Tony Slavich, Glyn Mason (guitar, vocals) and Iain McLennan (drums, vocals). In early 1978, he was back to the line-up of Lorange, Diane McLennan, Ansell, Hegerty and Sheehan. Lorange issued a solo album in October 1983, *No Apostrophe*, on WEA.

Clapton spent most of 1978 touring and recording overseas. He recorded a new album in Los Angeles at the end of the year with help from a host of L.A. session players including Ritchie Zito (guitar), Reggie McBride (bass), Rita Jean Bodine (backing vocals) and Aussie expatriate Doug Lavery (drums; ex-**Valentines, Axiom**). Two tracks from the American sessions, 'Steppin' Across the Line' and 'When the Heat's Off', appeared on the compilation album *Past Hits and Previews* (November). 'Steppin' Across the Line'/'Suit Yourself' also appeared as a single.

Clapton's American-recorded album, *Hearts on the Nightline* yielded two singles, 'Hearts on the Nightline'/'When the Heat's Off' (April 1979) and 'Ace of Hearts'/'Down the Tracks' (June). The album coincided with a 75-date national tour which began in April. While the album peaked at #17 on the chart, neither single was successful. Clapton's seventh album, *Dark Spaces* (July 1980; #23 in September), featured the line-up of Tony Ansell, Mark Moffatt (lead guitar; ex-Carol Lloyd Band), **Stars'**

Andrew Durant (rhythm guitar), Clive Harrison (bass; ex-**Kush**, **Avalanche**) and **Dragon's** Kerry Jacobsen (drums), plus contributions from Cleis Pearce (viola), Tony Buchanan (sax), Sam McNally (synthesiser; ex-**Stylus**) and Mark Meyer (drums). The album's singles were 'Get Back to the Shelter'/'Metropolis' (June) and 'High Society'/'Le Club Des Fools' (September). Clapton dedicated *Dark Spaces* to Durant, who had died in June. Clapton sang three songs, 'Look After Yourself', 'Innocent Bystander' and 'Ocean Deep', on the *Andrew Durant Memorial Concert* album (1981).

In 1982, Clapton signed a new record deal with WEA which resulted in one of his strongest albums, *The Great Escape* (February). Produced by Mark Opitz, the album gave rise to the singles 'I Am an Island'/'Walk on Water' (February), 'Spellbound'/'Syncopation Train (April) and 'The Best Years of Our Lives'/'Flow in Motion' (September). The hard rocking 'I Am an Island' became Clapton's first national hit since 'Deep Water', when it reached #20 during March. *The Great Escape* went as high as #7 the same month. Clapton set off on another extensive national tour in support of the album's release.

His backing band included Harvey James (lead guitar; ex-**Ariel**, **Sherbet**), Coz Russo (piano), Graham Thompson (bass; ex-**Stars**, **Avalanche**, **Russell Morris** Band, **Broderick Smith** Big Combo), Mark Meyer (drums; ex-**Stylus**, **Mark Gillespie** Band) and Mary Bradfield (backing vocals). All the players had contributed to the album, alongside Lorange, Clive Harrison, Tony Slavich and Mick 'The Reverend' O'Connor (organ; ex-**Broderick Smith** Band), plus Garry Gary Beers (bass) and Jon Farriss (drums) from **INXS**. The **INXS** connection came about when Clapton produced the band's 1981 album, *Underneath the Colours*. With *The Great Escape* still in the national Top 20 during May, the compilation *The Very Best of Richard Clapton* managed to peak at #15.

In 1983, Clapton joined **The Party Boys** for a tour, taking over from **James Reyne**. Clapton appeared on the album *Greatest Hits (of Other People)* and single Bobby Fuller Four's 'I Fought the Law'/'The Stealer' (November 1983). In 1984, Clapton signed a new deal with Mushroom Records for the album *Solidarity*. Once again, Clapton utilised the services of a stellar array of session players, including Graham Thompson, South African Ricky Fataar (drums), Allan Mansfield (keyboards; from **Dragon**), **Kevin Borich** (guitar; ex-**La De Das**), Buzz Bidstrup (drums; ex-**Angels**), James Black (keyboards; ex-**Mondo Rock**) and backing vocalists Venetta Fields, Mark Williams and Mary Bradfield.

Solidarity (September 1984) included the singles 'The Heart of It'/'Atom Bomb' (August), 'Solidarity'/'New World' (October) and 'Feelin' Alright Tonight'/'Goodbye Barbara Anne' (February 1985). Clapton's music had always displayed a very soulful edge, and that was particularly evident on tracks like 'The Heart of It', 'Feelin' Alright Tonight' and 'Cry Mercy Sister'. His touring band in support of the album featured Thompson, Slavich, Venetta Fields, Trevor Reading (guitar; ex-**Runners**) and Gil Matthews (drums; ex-**Billy Thorpe** and the Aztecs, **Mondo Rock**). Clapton was back with WEA for the 1987 album *Glory Road* (October) and its singles 'Glory Road'/'Love is Strong' (September), 'Trust Somebody'/'Homeland' (December) and 'Angelou'/'The Underground' (January 1988). Jon Farriss produced *Glory Road* as a return favour for Clapton's production work on *Underneath the Colours*.

In September 1989, Clapton issued the live album *The Best Years of Our Lives*, which featured many of his best songs. 'Deep Water'/'Blue Bay Blues' (July) and 'Ace of Hearts'/'Solidarity' (September) were issued as singles. Recorded in concert on 16 April 1989, Clapton's backing band for the night comprised Lorange (guitar), Moffatt (guitar), Hegerty (bass), Ben Butler (guitar), Jeff Bartolomei (keyboards) and Steve Sowerby (drums), with Fields and Bradfield on backing vocals. Beers (bass), Farriss (drums) and **Jimmy Barnes** (backing vocals) also appeared as guest players.

Clapton spent the next four years in contractual limbo. A new record deal with East West fell through, and he went through four changes in management. Finally he signed a five-album contract with Sony, with the first release being *Distant Thunder* (May 1993). Infused with genuine passion, the album recalled Clapton's finest works such as *Goodbye Tiger*, *Dark Spaces* and *The Great Escape*. The album produced four CD singles, 'Happy Valley' (December 1992), 'Distant Thunder' (April 1993), 'All Fall Down' (October) and 'Oceans of the Heart' (January 1994). Backing musicians on the album included **Ian Moss** (guitar; ex-**Cold Chisel**), Roger Mason (keyboards; ex-**Models**), Kirk Pengilly (sax; from **INXS**), Graham Thompson (bass) and Mark Meyer (drums). Although Clapton had been without a record deal between 1990 and 1993, he continued to draw huge crowds on the touring circuit. He set off on tour again with the release of *Distant Thunder*. Clapton's second album for Sony, *Angeltown* (May 1996), included the single 'Dixieland' (March).

Albums: *Prussian Blue* (Festival/Infinity, 1973), *Girls on the Avenue* (Festival/Infinity, 1974), *Main Street Jive* (Festival/Infinity, 1976), *Goodbye Tiger* (Festival/Infinity, 1977), *Past Hits and Previews*

(Festival/Infinity, 1978), *Hearts on the Nightline* (Festival/Infinity, 1979), *Dark Spaces* (Festival/Infinity, 1980), *The Very Best of Richard Clapton* (Festival/Infinity, 1982), *Great Escape* (WEA, 1982), *Solidarity* (Mushroom/Festival, 1984), *Glory Road (WEA, 1987), Best Years of Our Lives* (WEA, 1989), *Distant Thunder* (Sony, 1993), *Angeltown* (Sony, 1996).

Cleopatra Wong

Formed: *1990*
Style: *Pop*
Original line-up: *Amanda Brown (vocals, violin, oboe, guitar; ex-***Go-Betweens***), Lindy Morrison (vocals, drums; ex-***Go-Betweens***)*

With the break-up of the critically acclaimed, but commercially unsuccessful **Go-Betweens**, the female portion of that band formed Cleopatra Wong. The duo's hesitant, if heartfelt, early live performances bore testimony to the fact that Amanda Brown had stepped out as lead vocalist and frontperson for the first time in her life. Likewise, Brown and Morrison's first attempts at songwriting were tentative.

Cleopatra Wong signed to the rooArt label, and issued the debut CD EP *Egg* in February 1992. With assistance from Mark Moffatt (guitar), Michael Armiger (bass; ex-**Johnnys, Go-Betweens**), David Lane (keyboards) and Colin Bloxsom (percussion), Cleopatra Wong began to play on a regular basis. The band's second CD EP, *Cleopatra's Lament* (March 1993), maintained the lush, melodic pop of the debut, but with greater development in the songwriting department. The CD single 'Baby for You' featured **Wendy Matthews** on backing vocals and former **Laughing Clowns'** member Louise Elliot on sax. Warner Music Asia invited Cleopatra Wong to represent Australia in the Golden Kite Song Awards in Kuala Lumpur. Entrants from different countries were expected to write a song specifically for the occasion. Cleopatra Wong co-wrote the song 'Family Tree' with English songwriter Jonathan Male, who was also responsible for **Wendy Matthews'** 'The Day You Went Away'.

The Cleves

Formed: *1968*
Style: *Pop, rock*
Original line-up: *Gaye Brown (vocals, organ), Ron Brown (guitar), Milton Lane (bass), Graham Brown (drums)*

The Brown siblings Gaye, Ron and Graham had formed The Clevedonaires in New Zealand during the mid-1960s. They relocated to Sydney, where they formed The Cleves. The Cleves were just one of a number of 'quality' Sydney pop bands formed around 1968/9 (**The Executives, The Affair, Aesop's Fables**, The Clik, etc.).

The Cleves issued two pop singles on Festival, 'Sticks and Stones'/'Don't Turn Your Back' (September 1969) and 'You and Me'/'Cassie' (May 1970), plus the EP *Music from Michael* on Festival's Infinity label (1971). The EP featured songs recorded for the soundtrack to the 'Michael' episode (directed by Peter Weir) from the short film anthology *Three to Go*. By late 1970, the band was pursuing a more diverse musical path. The band's rare and collectable album *Cleves* (January 1971) was a prime example of where psychedelic pop gave way to a more progressive aesthetic.

The album was dominated by lengthy tracks, atmospheric organ/fuzzed guitar interplay and tight vocal harmonies (similar to UK bands on the Vertigo label like Cressida and Affinity). The highlights included an impressive rendering of the George Gershwin chestnut 'Summertime'. Before the album appeared, The Cleves backed Sydney DJ Donnie Sutherland on the sugary pop single 'Bonnie Bonnie Bonnie';'Na Na, Kiss Him Goodbye'/'I Don't Mind', which came out on the Violet's Holiday label. The Cleves were subsequently joined by Vince Melouney (guitar; ex-**Billy Thorpe** and the Aztecs, **Bee Gees, Fanny Adams),** and Rob Aitkin who replaced Lane on bass. Ace Follington (ex-**Chain, Country Radio**) then replaced Graham Brown on drums. In October 1971, The Cleves moved to the USA (sans Melouney who had formed Flite with **Leo De Castro**), where they became known as Bitch. The band issued three singles in the US, 'Laughing', 'Good Time Coming' and 'Wildcat' on Warner Brothers, before slipping from view.

Album: *Cleves* (Festival/Infinity, 1971).

Cloud Nine (*see* Taste)

Clouds

Formed: *1989*
Style: *Indie guitar pop*
Original line-up: *Jodi Phillis (vocals, guitar; ex-Nu-Genes), Robert Phelan (guitar), Tricia Young (vocals, bass), Stuart Eadie (drums; ex-Humdingers)*

Sydney band Clouds attracted a great deal of attention courtesy of their brand of raucous, yet tuneful, guitar pop. Reference points ranged from influential US outfit The Pixies to UK bands like The Cocteau

Twins, Lush and My Bloody Valentine. Alongside **The Cruel Sea, Ratcat, The Hummingbirds, The Underground Lovers** and **Falling Joys**, Clouds helped refresh the local commercial scene of the early 1990s.

Phillis' first band, The Nu-Genes, issued one single, 'Level with Me'/'Straight from the Heart', on the Giant label in 1988. Stuart Eadie's previous band, The Humdingers, played a hard-edged brand of rock. The original line-up comprised Eadie, Tim Oxley (vocals, guitar), John Mitting (guitar, vocals) and Karl Bergensen (bass). Jeff Ryan replaced Bergensen in 1987. The band issued the single 'A Little Love on the Side'/'We Have Got It All' (October 1987), the mini-album *Sign in the City* (1988) and the 12-inch EP *Big Brutha* (1988) on the Waterfront label.

Clouds formed in December 1989, and less than a year later had secured a contract with Red Eye Records. There have been several line-up changes over the years: David Easton replaced Robert Phelan in late 1990; Andrew Byrne replaced Eadie in early 1992 and Raphael Whittingham (ex-Daisychains) replaced Byrne in late 1992; and in November 1996 Ben Nightingale (ex-Vincent Stone, Psyclone Smyle) replaced Easton on guitar. Eadie went on to play with **Died Pretty** for a time and then joined The Olive Branch. That band also comprised Tim Freedman (keyboards), Nick Freedman (guitar; ex-**Sunnyboys**), Andy Lewis (bass; ex-**Gadflys**), Paul Jensen (trumpet) and Andy Kell (sax). The band's one CD EP, 'Time Flies Over Central' (March 1993), mixed indie guitar pop and jazz with pleasant results. Tim Freedman went on to form **The Whitlams**.

Meanwhile, Clouds issued its debut release on Red Eye, the four-track, double 7-inch single/CD EP *Clouds* (lead track 'Cloud Factory') during October 1990. The 12-inch EP/CD EP *Loot* (April 1991), the #1 alternative hit single 'Hieronymus'/'Lucy's Eyes' (August) and the band's acclaimed debut album, *Penny Century* (October), followed. *Penny Century* took the band into the mainstream Top 20 for the first time when it peaked at #14 on the national chart during November. 'Anthem' was lifted from the album as a 7-inch vinyl EP and a CD EP in March 1992, by which time Clouds had appeared on the bill of the inaugural Big Day Out festival held in Sydney. Consolidating the success of *Loot*, which had skirted the lower reaches of the national mainstream charts, 'Anthem' reached a respectable #47 in March (#24 in Sydney). 'Anthem' had the curious distinction of simultaneously sounding like The Pixies' 'Wave of Mutilation' and The Trogg's 'Wild Thing'.

Clouds

The band's eight track mini-album *Octopus* (October 1992) produced the CD single 'Say It' (September). *Octopus* returned the band to the mainstream chart when it reached #25 during November. In early 1993, the band undertook a successful British tour in support of the release of *Penny Century* there. The CD EP 'Bower of Bliss' (August 1993) was a prelude to the excellent *Thunderhead* album (October), which also produced the CD single 'Alchemy's Dead' (November). While *Thunderhead* boasted a harsher guitar sound courtesy of Easton, the songs still featured the band's trademark melodic flair, rich harmonies and off-kilter lyrical twists. The last song on the album was the 11-minute epic 'The Rocket'.

Clouds spent most of 1994 touring the USA and Europe. It was a quiet year on the recording front with only the CD EP *Beetroot* (October) seeing the light of day. Clouds had recorded *Beetroot* with producer Harvey Swift at Fortress Studio, London, during August. During March 1995, Elektra issued an expanded version of *Thunderhead* plus the CD single *3 Songs* ('Bower of Bliss', 'Blade', 'Universal') in the USA. The band's American deal looked promising, but three months later Elektra shed its entire overseas roster and A&R department, leaving Clouds without record company push in the USA. Meanwhile, Red Eye issued the CD EPs 'Aquamarine' (August 1995) and 'Panel Van' (November 1995) in Australia. In May 1996, Red Eye issued a remastered version of the *Penny Century* album, which also came with a limited edition compilation *Pre-Raphaelite* that drew together 14 tracks culled from the band's early EPs. The album attained gold status (35 000 copies sold) soon after.

Jodi Phillis was the first Clouds member to record

a solo album. Under the moniker Lounge-O-Sound, she issued her solo debut *Lounge-O-Sound* in September 1996. Clouds' 'Down from the Sky'/'Here Now' CD single/7-inch vinyl single (September 1996) was a taster for the band's fourth album, *Futura* (November). The album produced a second CD single, 'Never Say Forever' (January 1997). In May 1997, Clouds announced their imminent break-up and undertook a final national tour during June.

Albums: *Penny Century* (Red Eye/PolyGram, 1991), *Octopus* (mini-album, Red Eye/PolyGram, 1992), *Thunderhead* (Red Eye/PolyGram, 1993), *Futura* (Red Eye/PolyGram, 1996).

Club Hoy

Formed: *1985*
Style: *Folk pop*
Original line-up: *Penny Flanagan (acoustic guitar, vocals), Julia Richardson (acoustic guitar, vocals)*

Sydney folk pop duo Club Hoy were never 'hip' in terms of musical credibility on the local scene, but they did achieve a sustained level of success with the release of several interesting records. The pair joined up while still at high school when they attempted to form a rebel church choir. They played at various folk clubs, supporting Flanagan's father's folk group.

By the time the duo started playing the Sydney pub circuit in 1989, they had perfected their playing and winsome two-part harmonies. Former **Go-Betweens** member **Grant McLennan** produced the duo's debut single, 'On and On'/'Lucy, with Me' (March 1990), on the Waterfront label. Tim Hagen (bass) and Leo Mullins (drums) from The Benedicts provided backing on the recording session. From there, Club Hoy established its own label, Hoyden, under the banner of Regular Records. Former **Radio Birdman** member Rob Younger produced the duo's second single, 'Da Da Da Da' (1991). Former **Sports** member Martin Armiger produced the duo's October 1991 debut album, *Thursday's Fortune*, which produced the singles 'House on Fire' (September) and 'Not Like That' (February 1992). The album presented the duo's ethereal, folksy pop backed by strong melodies, subtle playing and full arrangements. Backing for the album was provided by Armiger and other session musicians like Kirk Lorange.

The girls recruited an electric rhythm section comprising Bernie Hayes (bass) and Vince Sheehan (drums) in order to present the album in the live forum. Club Hoy made an appearance at the inaugural Big Day Out festival held in Sydney during January 1992. The duo also travelled to Los Angeles to take part in the Wizards of Oz showcase tour alongside **Beatfish, The Angels, The Poor, The Black Sorrows** and **Kate Ceberano.**

Club Hoy issued two CD EPs in 1992, 'Walk Away' (August) and 'Trumpet' (October). The duo then unwittingly became the centre of controversy when *Lemon* fanzine editor (the late) Louise Dickinson printed certain disparaging remarks of a sexual nature directed at the girls when she reviewed 'Trumpet'. There was a great deal of discussion on radio and in the music press (Stuart Coupe called the offending lines 'a true low point in music journalism'), and there was the possible threat of legal action. Television current affairs programs like *A Current Affair* and *The Today Show* even got in on the act. *A Current Affair* host Mike Munro called the report 'a truly disturbing story' (shades of *Frontline* no less). When the fuss had died down, Club Hoy quietly slipped from view.

Flanagan emerged as a solo artist in 1994 with the release of her debut album *Bravado* and single 'Lap It Up'. She also published a novel *Changing the Sky*. In 1995 Flanagan formed a touring line-up of her band The New Moon which comprised David Barrowclough (guitar, vocals), Andrew Bett (keyboards), Steve Bull (bass) and Mark Dawson (drums). She issued two CD EPs during 1995, 'Piece of You' and 'The Sky' (remixed by techno-dance outfit **Boxcar**).

Club Hoy album: *Thursday's Fortune* (Hoyden/Regular/Festival, 1991); ***Penny Flanagan and the New Moon album:*** *Bravado* (Regular/Festival, 1994).

The Cockroaches

Formed: *1979*
Style: *R&B, pop*
Original line-up: *Paul Field (vocals), John Field (vocals, guitar), Tony Field (vocals, guitar), Jeff Fatt (keyboards), Phil Robinson (bass), Tony Henry (drums)*

The Cockroaches took their name from an obscure *nom de plume* favoured by The Rolling Stones during the 1960s. It was a fitting choice, due mostly to the good-time R&B material that The Cockroaches played during their formative years.

The Field brothers formed the nucleus of the band while still at boarding school, St Joseph's College at Hunter's Hill (NSW). The brothers were also noted for their cricketing skills. John Field was selected as Under 19 NSW Cricketer of the Year. From very early on, The Cockroaches were an in-demand pub band, building a sweaty, frenzied atmosphere with good old-fashioned showmanship and unpretentious, energetic rock'n'pop. As original material began to replace covers in the band's set, The Cockroaches issued a string of singles on a variety of independent labels. In 1986 the band signed a deal with Regular Records (home to **Icehouse** and **Mental as Anything**).

The band's first seven singles were 'I Want a Leather Jacket'/'Blue Moon of Kentucky' (June 1980), 'Through with Her'/'Bingo Bango' (June 1981), 'Used to Be'/'She Goes on and on' (August), 'Empty Heart'/'Apartment #9' (October), 'Shake Jump and Shout'/'Last Night', 'Empty Heart' (November 1982), 'See You in Spain'/'I've Been Thinking About You' (June 1984), 'My Whole World's Falling Down'/'Groovin' in the Graveyard' (June 1985) and 'Another Night Alone'/'My Type of Girl' (December).

By that stage, Phil Carson had replaced Phil Robinson on bass. The band's first single on Regular, 'Wait Up'/'Henry's Lizard' (September 1986), became a national Top 40 hit and #13 in Sydney. Produced by Charles Fisher and mixed by Jim Bonneford (Kool and the Gang, Jimmy Cliff), the band's debut album *The Cockroaches* (March 1987) produced three further singles, 'She's the One'/'Can in the Hand' (January), 'Some Kind of Girl'/'Dr Richmond' (May) and 'Double Shot (of My Baby's Love)'/'Something Good' (August). *The Cockroaches* reached #9 on the national chart, on its way to selling over 100 000 copies and 'She's the One' became the band's biggest hit when it peaked at #7 during April 1987. 'Some Kind of Girl' and 'Double Shot (of My Baby's Love)' also made the Top 30.

Peter Mackie replaced Carson before the band recorded its second album, *Fingertips*. The album produced the band's next four singles, 'Hey What Now!'/'Marie' (#30 in June), 'You and Me', 'So Wild'/'Some Kind of Girl', 'Can't Sit Down' (#35 in October), 'Permanently Single'/'Rudolph Had a Baby' (January 1989) and 'Another Saturday Night'/'I've Got to Hang on' (August). In early 1989, The Cockroaches undertook a national tour with their Regular label mates **Mental as Anything**. The band's third album on Regular, *Positive* (June 1991), produced three singles, the gospel-flavoured 'Hope'/'Soul to Soul' (August 1990), 'I Must Have Been Blind' (May 1991) and a cover of Brenda Lee's 'Here Comes the Feeling' (August), which also appeared on the soundtrack to the feature film *The Crossing*. By the end of the year, however, The Cockroaches as a band concept had run its course.

Tony Field and Jeff Fatt then embarked on a project called The Wiggles with Murray Cook (bass) and Greg Page (vocals), which turned out to be one of the most successful ventures of the 1990s. The initial idea behind The Wiggles was to produce fun and creative musical projects for Early Childhood Education at Sydney's Macquarie University (the four musicians were qualified pre-school teachers). By combining music, song and dance with characters like Dorothy the Dinosaur, Henry the Octopus, Captain Feathersword and Wags the Dog, The Wiggles came up with a winning formula that was a hit with the kids. The band's debut album, *The Wiggles*, and its CD single, 'Here Comes a Song', immediately attained Gold Record status (35 000 copies sold). *The Wiggles* eventually attained platinum status (70 000 copies), as did the follow-ups *Here Comes a Song* (1992), *Yummy Yummy* (1993), *Big Red Car* (1995) and *Wiggly Wiggly Christmas* (1996).

The Wiggles toured to an enormous response. The Wiggles also had the honour of creating some of the biggest selling children's videos when *Wiggle Time*, *Yummy Yummy* and *Big Red Car* all achieved double platinum status. The band's fourth video, *Wake Up Jeff!*, sold over 200 000 copies between August and December 1996. The band's fifth video, *The Wiggledance*, came out in early 1997. By mid-1997, The Wiggles had sold over 965 000 videos. The two Wiggles books, *Let's Wiggle* and *Dorothy the Dinosaur's Picture Book*, were in their sixth editions at the time of writing.

The Wiggles have also won a number of awards, including two Australian Performing Right Association (APRA) songwriting awards for Best Children's Song of 1994 and 1995. *Big Red Car* won the 1995 Australian Record Industry Association (ARIA) Award for Best Children's Release. The Wiggles also released a feature film based on their adventures with Dorothy the Dinosaur. In 1997, The Wiggles were estimated to be a $40 million retail business in Australia, which placed them second only to Bananas in Pyjamas in the children's market. Unlike their counterparts, however, whose popularity rose out of a successful television show, The Wiggles' success grew from their creative songwriting skills.

Cockroaches albums: *The Cockroaches* (Regular/Festival, 1987), *Fingertips* (Regular/Festival, 1988), *Positive* (Regular/Festival, 1991); ***Wiggles albums:*** *The Wiggles* (ABC, 1991), *Here Comes a Song* (ABC, 1992), *Yummy Yummy* (ABC, 1993), *Big Red Car* (ABC, 1995), *Wiggly Wiggly Christmas* (ABC, 1996).

Cold Chisel

Formed: *1973*
Style: *R&B, hard rock*
Original line-up: **Jimmy Barnes** *(vocals), Don Walker (piano),* **Ian Moss** *(guitar, vocal), Les Kaczmarek (bass), Steve Prestwich (drums)*

In late 1983, after ten years on the road, Cold Chisel called it a day. Not that the band split up for want of success; by that stage Cold Chisel had built up a reputation previously uncharted in Australian rock history. By virtue of the profound effect the band's music had on the many thousands of fans who witnessed its awesome power, Cold Chisel remains one of Australia's best-loved groups. As one of the best live bands of its day, Cold Chisel fused a combination of rockabilly, hard rock and rough-house soul'n'blues that was defiantly Australian in outlook.

Songwriter Don Walker, **Ian Moss** and Les Kaczmarek formed Cold Chisel in Adelaide during September 1973. The line-up was completed by volatile, Glasgow-born singer **Jim Barnes** (as he was known throughout his tenure with the band) and Liverpool-born drummer Steve Prestwich. Cold Chisel's early repertoire was peppered with Free and Deep Purple covers which earned the band a cult following around the local pubs. When Walker went to The University of New England in Armidale, NSW to complete an honours degree in quantum mechanics, such was the close-knit nature of the band that the other members went with him. The band returned to Adelaide, but in mid-1975 Barnes left for several months to join his brother John Swan (**Swanee**) in **Fraternity**. **Fraternity** was already an established institution on the scene, but well and truly on its last legs by that stage.

Frontman Bon Scott had left **Fraternity** to join **AC/DC**, and **Swanee** came in as his replacement. **Swanee** moved to drums and invited Barnes to be lead singer. With **Fraternity** falling apart, Barnes took his leave and was accepted back into the Cold Chisel fold. Phil Small replaced Kaczmarek on bass, and the band moved to Melbourne for three months before finally settling in Sydney at the start of 1977.

The band signed to Warner/Atlantic and issued the single 'Khe Sanh'/'Just How Many Times?' (April 1978). *Cold Chisel* failed to capture the band's renowned live firepower, despite the presence of such crowd favourites as 'Khe Sanh', 'Home and Broken Hearted' and 'One Long Day'. It achieved gold status, however, and launched the band on to the major league. The single 'Goodbye (Astrid Goodbye)'/'Georgia on My Mind' (September 1978) failed to chart, but the live EP *You're Thirteen, You're Beautiful and You're Mine* reached #35 on the singles chart in December. It captured the band in its favoured element, fired by raucous versions of Walker's 'Merry-Go-Round' and Chip Taylor's 'Wild Thing'. *Breakfast at Sweethearts* reached #4 in March 1979, achieved platinum status (over 70 000 copies sold) and was the top-selling Australian album for the year. It went on to sell over 140 000 copies. Its two singles both missed the Top 40 charts: 'Breakfast at Sweethearts'/'Plaza' (February 1979) and 'Shipping Steel'/'Showtime' (May 1979).

The Mark Opitz-produced *East* (June 1980) was a confident, fully realised work of tremendous scope. Among its delights were the singles 'Choir Girl'/'Conversations' (#14 in December 1979), 'Cheap Wine'/'Rising Sun' (#8 in May 1980) and 'My Baby'/'Misfits' (August 1980). (There was also the highly collectable 12-inch release of 'Choir Girl'/'Khe Sanh' (live).) *East* went as high as #2 on the national chart, and by May 1981 had sold over 200 000 copies (on its way to the 350 000 mark). *East* also marked a first for the band, with all members contributing songs (instead of Walker taking the lion's share). In particular, **Ian Moss** shone with his contribution 'Never Before'. He also sang on two other tracks, Phil Small's 'My Baby' and Steve Prestwich's 'Best Kept Lies'. The first pressing of 10 000 copies of *East* contained a bonus single of Bob Dylan's 'Knockin' on Heaven's Door' (live)/ 'Party's Over'.

The double live set *Swingshift* (March 1981) had been recorded during the Youth in Asia tour the previous May. The album made its debut at #2 on the national chart (on its way to #1 and 210 000 sales) and yielded the 12-inch single 'Don't Let Go'/'Four Walls'. In April 1981, Cold Chisel caused havoc at the 1980 ***Countdown*** Awards ceremony by smashing up the stage set in protest. In July 1981, Cold Chisel toured the USA where *East* (with a different track selection) and the single 'My Baby' had already been issued. *East* peaked at #173 on the US Billboard chart, and the band supported the likes of Cheap Trick, Joe Walsh, Ted Nugent, Heart and the Marshall Tucker Band across the States.

The Barnes-penned 'You Got Nothing I Want'/ 'Numbers Fall' (#12 in December 1981) was the first single from the band's second classic album *Circus Animals* (March 1982). The album also made #1 nationally (with over 210 000 copies sold), and produced two more singles: Steve Prestwich's 'Forever Now'/'Bow River' (#4 in April 1982) and 'When the War Is Over'/'Wild Colonial Boy' (#25 in August). During May 1982, Cold Chisel returned to the States and then toured Europe and the UK for the first time. Ultimately, Cold Chisel achieved little impact outside of Australia. The band's failed attempts to break into the American market represented a major blow. At that time, America was besotted by vacuous stadium rock bands like Styx, Journey and REO Speedwagon, and Cold Chisel's earthy, high-energy rock was overlooked. Ironically, Cold Chisel's musical roots were almost entirely based in American blues, soul and rock'n'roll of the 1950s and 1960s, which only contributed to the overall disillusionment.

In early 1983, Prestwich was forced to leave the band due to back injuries sustained in a car accident. His place was taken by journeyman drummer **Gary Young** (ex-**Daddy Cool**, **Jo Jo Zep and the Falcons**) who filled in for a six-week tour. By June Prestwich had announced his departure from the band and **Ray Arnott** (ex-**Spectrum**, **Dingoes**) took over. Then in August, Cold Chisel announced its break-up. Prestwich re-joined for The Last Stand tour of October, which marked the band's tenth anniversary. On 12 December 1983, at the Sydney Entertainment Centre, Cold Chisel played its last show together.

The band's monumental series of farewell shows yielded *The Barking Spiders Live* album (1985), *The Last Stand* video and *The Last Stand* soundtrack which came out in October 1992. *The Last Stand* reached #7 on the national album chart during November. Cold Chisel had occasionally played gigs under the delightfully monikered pseudonym of The Barking Spiders, and *The Barking Spiders Live* album was packaged in the style of a bootleg.

The newly recorded double A-sided single 'Hold Me Tight'/'No Sense' came out in October 1983 and reached the national Top 10 (#8). With touring commitments out of the way, the band settled in to complete the lacklustre *Twentieth Century* album. Nevertheless, the album was strong enough to make its debut at #1 on the national chart during April 1984 (eventually selling over 140 000 copies, as well as producing three further singles: 'Saturday Night'/'Painted Doll' (March; #5 in April), 'Only One'/'Twentieth Century' (May) and 'Flame Trees'/'River Deep Mountain High' (August; #21 in September).

Before the dust had even settled, **Jimmy Barnes** launched his solo career with the release of his debut solo album *Bodyswerve*. The other members took a little longer to get going. Don Walker (with **Catfish**) and **Ian Moss** had solo success during the late 1980s/early 1990s. Steve Prestwich joined **Little River Band** for two years (during which time the band covered his 'When the War is Over'), and later turned up in **Ian Moss**'s solo band. Phil Small played in a couple of small-time pub bands, Pound, The Earls of Duke and The Outsiders.

The Cold Chisel story, however, did not end there. In 1985 WEA issued *Radio Songs (Best of)* which was a collection of the band's more frantic moments such as 'Conversations', 'My Turn to Cry', 'Hound Dog', 'Painted Doll', 'Rising Sun' and three tracks from *You're Thirteen . . .* It reached #1 during December. The Cold Chisel compilation *Chisel* came out in October 1991 with the previously B-side only 'Misfits' released as a CD single (with live versions of 'Mona and the Preacher' and 'Four Walls'). *Chisel* peaked at #3 on the national chart (selling over 210 000 copies), while 'Misfits' managed #25. With the release of *Chisel*, the members of Cold Chisel reconvened briefly in order to receive awards for sales of two million records. There was something of a Cold Chisel revival with the November 1994 release of the archival collection *Teenage Love*. Chisel manager Rod Willis and the band members had dusted off 33 unissued tracks for possible inclusion. They selected 24 for release on the 16-track *Teenage Love* and the three collector-orientated singles that accompanied it.

Teenage Love proved to be a remarkable collection of songs that were brimming with loose ends and vibrant spontaneity. Outstanding tracks like 'Metho Blues', 'Nothing but You', 'Teenage Love Affair' and the boogie 'Drinkin' in Port Lincoln' (recorded in 1976 at Pepper Studios in Adelaide) possessed more grit and fire than most of the debut album or *Twentieth Century*. The three singles, 'Hands out of My Pocket' (#9 in September 1994), 'Nothing but You' (#16 in November) and 'Yesterdays' (#23 in March 1995), made the band chart darlings all over again. The band regrouped in the recording studio during October 1997.

Cold Chisel's achievements can never be underestimated. For starters, the band has sold over three million records, two-thirds after disbanding in 1983. It was not just the high-intensity, yet melodic and intelligent nature of the band's songs, which rock writer Murray Engelheart praised for their 'desperation and savage grace'. It was not just **Jimmy Barnes'** menacing, self-destructive performance skills, or **Ian Moss'** hard-edged blues guitar work. Nor was it just Don Walker's deft, intuitive and gut-wrenching songwriting skills. For Cold Chisel, the whole was always greater than the sum of its parts, and the band's aura continues to expand.

Albums: *Cold Chisel* (Atlantic, 1978), *Breakfast at Sweethearts* (Elektra, 1979), *East* (WEA, 1980), *Swingshift* (WEA, 1981), *Circus Animals* (WEA, 1982), *Twentieth Century* (WEA, 1984), *Radio Songs*

(Best of) (WEA, 1985), *Razor Songs* (WEA, 1988), *Chisel* (East West/Warner, 1991), *The Last Stand* (East West/Warner, 1992), *Teenage Love* (East West/Warner, 1994).

Collette

Style: *Disco, pop*

Sydney-based singer Collette Roberts first came to the nation's attention when she signed to CBS and issued a cover of Anita Ward's 1979 disco hit 'Ring My Bell'/'Save Yourself' as her debut single. 'Ring My Bell' reached #3 on the national charts in May 1989. Collette followed this up with two further hits, 'All I Wanna Do Is Dance'/'Push' (#12 in August) and 'That's what I Like About You'/'Hot-house' (#35 in December).

DJ Stephen 'Pee Wee' Ferris (ex-Flotsam Jetsam) produced Collette's debut album *Raze the Roof*. In 1990, Collette returned to the studio with producer Mark S. Berry for her second album, *Attitude*, which produced the singles 'Who do You Think You Are?' (#71 in October), 'Upside Down' and a cover of Natalie Cole's 'This Will Be' (1991). 'Who do You Think You Are?' featured New Jack Swing beat stylings (a mix of funk, soul and hip hop) and its lyrics were aimed at Collette's critics.

Albums: *Raze the Roof* (CBS, 1989), *Attitude* (CBS, 1991).

Coloured Balls

Formed: *1972*
Style: *Progressive rock*
Original line-up: **Lobby Loyde** *(guitar, vocals; ex-***Purple Hearts, Wild Cherries, Billy Thorpe** *and the Aztecs), Andrew Fordham (guitar, vocals), Janis Miglans (bass), Trevor Young (drums)*

With an aesthetic push that fused hippie philosophy to explosive rock'n'roll, Coloured Balls were one of the most misunderstood bands of the early 1970s. The mainstream media branded Coloured Balls as anti-social misfits, due in no small degree to their single-minded performances, the adoption of the (then prevalent) sharpie haircut and the aggressive nature of their skinhead following. Coloured Balls tapped into the same kind of vital and direct energy that fired the punk onslaught four years later. Less a case of being ahead of their time, Coloured Balls were merely a symptom of it. Like **Radio Birdman** soon after, Coloured Balls were never part of the musical establishment. In a perfect world, Coloured Balls would be recognised as Australia's version of legendary Detroit outfit MC5 (minus the rabble-rousing politics).

The redoubtable **Lobby Loyde** was already a veteran of the Australian music scene by the time he formed Coloured Balls in March 1972. As well as his tenures with **The Purple Hearts**, **The Wild Cherries** and **Billy Thorpe** and the Aztecs, Loyde cut a remarkable solo album, *Plays with George Guitar*, in 1971 which remains a hard rock milestone. Coloured Balls' first single 'Liberate Rock'/'Slowest Guitar on Earth' (August 1972) had actually been recorded before Loyde formed the band. Several Aztecs (Warren Morgan, Gil Matthews and Paul 'Sheepdog' Wheeler) lent a hand in the studio and the single hit the Top 20 in both Melbourne and Sydney. In late 1972, the original line-up recorded an album called *Rock Your Arse Off*. The album was deemed unsuitable for release by cautious record companies and the tapes remained on the shelf until the independent Rainbird label released them as *The First Supper Last (Or Scenes We Didn't Get to See)* in May 1976.

With Ian 'Bobsie' Millar having replaced Andrew Fordham in early 1973, the band issued three hard rock singles and two albums during the year. 'Mr Mean Mouth'/'Love Me Girl' (March), the Pomus/Schuman tune 'Mess of the Blues'/'Devil's Disciple' (September) and 'Flash'/'Dave the Rave' (November) were all minor hits in hometown Melbourne. 'Mess of the Blues' also reached #39 nationally. Coloured Balls supported UK visitors Marc Bolan and T-Rex on an Australian tour (November 1973), and issued their debut album, *Ball Power*, a month later. It reached #13 on the national album chart at the beginning of 1974.

Ball Power remains one of the classic Oz Rock guitar albums of the early 1970s. Ranging in style from simple, raw rock'n'roll ('Flash', 'Won't You Make Up Your Mind') and sleazy blues ('Something New') to hard driving progressive rock ('Human Being', 'That's What Mama Said'), the album boasted considerable depth and a singularity of direction. The expansive, riff-heavy 'Human Being' was one of the album's highlights. It was later covered by bands like the White Elephants and **Bored!**. Reissue specialists Raven included the track on the essential compilation *Golden Miles: Australian Progressive Rock 1969–1974* (1994).

The Balls were also heard on the live, budget-priced album *Summer Jam* (recorded at the 1973 Sunbury Festival; issued in November), which featured the 16-minute, cosmic heavy metal epic 'GOD' (which stands for 'guitar overdose'). Grunge heroes **Cosmic Psychos** later covered 'GOD' on their CD EP *Palomino Pizza*. Coloured Balls issued a second album, *Heavy Metal Kid*, and two more singles, 'Love You Babe'/'Shake Me Babe' (Melbourne #16 in June 1974; national #38) and 'Bama Lama Baby'/'By Your Lover' (October), before calling it a day. With the escalation of violence between various sharpie and non-sharpie factions at the band's concerts, the media accused the Balls of inciting riots, which did little for their resolve and strength of purpose. Loyde simply walked away from the violence and media barrage and quietly dissolved the band.

Following Coloured Balls' premature split at the end of 1974, Loyde initially went solo, issuing the single 'Do You Believe in Magic'/'Love Lost on Dream Tides' (December 1975) on the Bootleg label and the *Obsecration* album (May 1976) on Rainbow. In May 1976, Loyde left Australia bound for the UK. On his return to Australia in 1979, he joined **Rose Tattoo** as bass player. That line-up of the Tatts recorded an album in Los Angeles which remains unissued. Loyde went on to work with a revived version of Southern Electric before devoting his time to production duties and live sound mixing for the likes of **Sunnyboys**, **Machinations**, **X** and **Painters and Dockers**.

Albums: *Ball Power* (EMI, 1973), *Heavy Metal Kid* (EMI, 1974), *First Supper Last (or Scenes We Didn't Get to See)* (Rainbird, 1976), *Liberate Rock!* (compilation; Raven, 1989), *The Best of Ball Power and More* (compilation, Siren, 1996), *Lobby Loyde and the Coloured Balls* (CD reissue of *First Supper Last* and *Obsecration*, Fable/EMI, 1997).

Coloured Stone

Formed: *1978*
Style: *Rock, country*
Original line-up: *Bruce Lawrie (lead guitar), Neil Coaby (rhythm guitar), Mackie Coaby (bass, vocals), Buna Lawrie (drums, vocals)*

Alongside **Yothu Yindi**, Coloured Stone was one of the most prolific of Australia's Aboriginal bands. Originally from the Koonibba Aboriginal community near Ceduna on the Great Australian Bight, South Australia, Coloured Stone moved to Adelaide where its mix of reggae, rock and country won a strong following. The band came into contact with **No Fixed Address** at the Centre for Aboriginal Studies in Music (CASM), and was inspired to replace the covers in its set with the original material Buna Lawrie had been writing.

The band's debut single, 'Black Boy'/'Kapi Pulka' (May 1984), on the Imparja label (through Hot Records) was an independent hit. It also sold well in a number of African and Asian-Pacific countries (#1 in Fiji), eventually selling 120 000 copies with minimal support from commercial radio networks. Coloured Stone recorded two rough-hewn albums for the Hot label *Koonibba Rock* (cut in just five hours; issued April 1985) and *Island of Greed* (October) before signing to Powderworks. In 1986, Coloured Stone toured Germany, France, the UK and the US east coast to a positive response. The album *Island of Greed* won the 1986 Australian Record Industry Association (ARIA) award for Best Indigenous Album. The band issued two albums on Powderworks, the compilation *Black Rock from the Red Centre* and *Human Love* (April 1987) plus two singles, the hard-rocking 'Dancing in the Moonlight'/'When You Gonna Learn?' (March 1987) and 'Human Love'/'Waiting for the Tide' (July). The band later contributed 'Dancing in the Moonlight' to the Various Artists album *Building Bridges* on CBS (1989).

For the *Human Love* album, Bart Willoughby (drums, vocals; ex-**No Fixed Address**) had replaced Buna on drums (allowing Buna to concentrate on lead vocals and rhythm guitar), and Selwyn Burns had replaced Bruce Lawrie on lead guitar. Robbie Fletcher replaced Willoughby in 1987. The band's first album for BMG/RCA, *Wild Desert Rose* (January 1989), yielded the singles 'Stay Young'/'Love is for Life' (December 1988), 'Kiss the Days Goodbye'/'Dreamtime Stories' (March 1989) and the wistful 'Wild Desert Rose' (October 1989). *Wild Desert Rose* was named Record of the Week in New York's *Village Voice*, and the album went on to reach #10 on the New York charts. Despite pockets of success like that overseas, the band continued to spend up to ten months a year on the road in the bush playing to local Aboriginal communities. For the sixth album, *Crazy Mind* (April 1990), Buna continued to draw on his experiences of Australia's heartland as displayed on songs like 'Nullarbor' and 'It Never Rains'.

In 1991, **Yothu Yindi** scored a hit single with the epochal 'Treaty'. Although **Yothu Yindi** itself might not have been possible without Coloured Stone's pioneering efforts, the dance-oriented sound of 'Treaty' influenced Buna's writing. Coloured Stone's seventh album, *Inma Juju*, (simply translated as 'dance music') and the single 'Love is the Medicine' (July 1992) were fine pieces of dance-rock. Russell Guy had also joined on keyboards, giving the music a fuller sound. By 1993, Selwyn Burns was playing with Blackfire.

Albums: *Koonibba Rock* (Imparja/Hot, 1985), *Island of Greed* (Imparja/Hot, 1985), *Black Rock from the Red Centre* (Powderworks, 1987), *Human Love*

(Powderworks, 1987), *Wild Desert Rose* (BMG/RCA, 1989), *Crazy Mind* (BMG/RCA, 1990), *Inma Juju (Dance Music)* (BMG/RCA, 1992).

Company Caine

Formed: *1970*
Style: *Progressive psychedelic blues*
Original line-up: **Gulliver Smith** *(vocals, ex-Little Gulliver and the Children, Dr Kandy's Third Eye), Russell Smith (guitar, vocals; ex-***Cam-Pact***), Jeremy Noone (aka Jeremy Kellock, sax, keyboards; ex-Leo and Friends), Cliff Edwards (bass; ex-***Cam-Pact***),* **Ray Arnott** *(drums; ex-Chelsea Set, Browns,* **Cam-Pact***)*

Legendary Melbourne progressive band Company Caine emerged from the ashes of psychedelic pop bands **Cam-Pact** and Dr Kandy's Third Eye. The final version of **Cam-Pact** circa early 1970 included Cliff Edwards, **Ray Arnott** and Russell Smith. Delightfully eccentric singer/songwriter **Gulliver Smith** joined the three musicians in March and, with Jeremy Noone on board, the first line-up of Company Caine was complete.

Before joining Company Caine, Gulliver had already been a cult performer on the Melbourne dance circuit with his band Little Gulliver and the Children, and the Sydney psychedelic underground with Dr Kandy's Third Eye. In July 1970, Arnott left Company Caine to join **Matt Taylor's** new blues band, Genesis. Two months later, Arnott replaced Mark Kennedy in **Spectrum**. Meanwhile, Eric Cairns (ex-Somebody's Image, Image, **Heart'n'Soul**) joined Company Caine as Arnott's replacement. Cairns left two months later to join **Ronnie Charles'** band Captain Australia and the Honky Tonk. Tim Partridge (ex-Clockwork Oringe) also replaced Edwards around that time. By then the band had built a reputation as one of the most adventurous avant-garde outfits of the day. The band's contemporaries on the Melbourne 'head' circuit included **Spectrum**, **Chain**, **Sons of the Vegetal Mother**, **Healing Force** and **Billy Thorpe** and the Aztecs.

The 1971 line-up of Company Caine comprised the two Smiths, Noone, Ian Mawson (keyboards), Arthur Eizenberg (bass; ex-Square Circle, Dr Kandy's Third Eye, **Heart'n'Soul**) and John 'Ernie' McInerny (drums). In June, that line-up recorded the single 'Trixie Stonewall's Wayward Home for Young Women'/'It's Up to You' (issued in September 1971) and the groundbreaking album *A Product of a Broken Reality* (issued in November). By that stage, the band's music was more expansive, more 'out there' than just about every band of the day. *A Product of a Broken Reality* remains a milestone of

Gulliver Smith and Russell Smith, Company Caine

the early 1970s progressive rock era. Reissue specialists Raven included 'The Day Superman Got Busted' on the collection *Golden Miles: Australian Progressive Rock 1969–1974* (1994). **The Church**'s **Steve Kilbey** later covered the album track 'Woman with Reason' on his 1987 solo album, *The Slow Crack*.

In August 1971, Noone left Company Caine to join **King Harvest** before moving on to **Daddy Cool** a month later. At the end of 1971, Mal Capewell (sax, flute) joined. As well as having played with Australian 1960s bands **Phil Jones and the Unknown Blues** and Dr Kandy's Third Eye, Capewell travelled to the UK where he cut a dashing figure as a member of Dada (behind vocalists Robert Palmer and Elkie Brooks) and Graham Bond's Holy Magick. Following Capewell's arrival, Company Caine relocated to Sydney where they began billing themselves as Co. Caine. Another ex-Dr Kandy's Third Eye alumnus, Dave Kain (also ex-Space), joined as rhythm guitarist in early 1972. The only other Company Caine record to that time was the single 'Dear Caroline'/'Now I'm Together'. **The Sports** later covered 'Now I'm Together', as well as another Gulliver Smith/Russell Smith song, 'Don't Hold Back that Feeling', with considerable aplomb.

Co. Caine split up in October 1972. Russell Smith joined the touring line-up of studio band **Duck**. Capewell joined Mighty Mouse and began guesting with **Carson**. After a short time spent trying to get a new band together with ex-**Daddy Cool** members **Ross Wilson** and **Ross Hannaford**, **Gulliver Smith** launched his solo career with the album *The Band's Alright but the Singer Is . . .* Not long after, Russell Smith joined Wilson and Hannaford in their new band, **Mighty Kong**.

In 1975, the Real label reissued *A Product of a Broken Reality*, which prompted Gulliver and Russell to regroup. Initially the pair performed as Metropolis, until they re-formed Company Caine with help from rock writer David 'Dr Pepper' Pepperell. The new line-up comprised John Power (bass; ex-**Foreday Riders**), Jeff Burstin (guitar; ex-Gutbucket, Rock Granite and the Profiles) and co-lead singer Shirley Smith (ex-**Lizard**). The new line-up was superior in some respects to the original, and played the Melbourne and Sydney concert/dance circuit for a year before calling it quits again. The band recorded enough material (half studio, half live) to fill the excellent and ultra-rare *Doctor Chop* album (1976). Dr Pepper contributed liner notes to the album, and **Ross Wilson** produced three tracks ('Doctor Chop', 'Buzzin' with My Cousin' and 'The Golden Boogie') on the studio side. The two other cuts on that side, 'Now I'm Together' and 'Dear Caroline', were previously unreleased, long versions of the band's 1972 single.

In mid-1976, **Gulliver Smith** formed Gulliver's Travels. A year later, Smith travelled to the UK where he worked for many years with the Gulliver Smith Band. He returned to Australia in the late 1980s, and in 1996 issued the album *Deux Poètes* as Gullifer Smith. Russell Smith joined **Ross Hannaford** in **Billy T**, then went on to Heavy Division (with singer **Leo De Castro**), The Zeroes and **Goanna**. He also composed the soundtrack to the film *Rainbow Farm*. Geoff Burstin and John Power joined **Jo Jo Zep and the Falcons**.

Albums: *A Product of a Broken Reality* (Generation, 1971), *A Product of a Broken Reality* (Rock Masterworks Volume One) (Real/Electric, 1975; reissue), *Doctor Chop* (Lamington/Electric, 1976).

Company of Strangers

Formed: *1991*
Style: *Rock, pop*
Original line-up: **James Reyne** *(vocals, guitar; ex-***Australian Crawl***),* **Daryl Braithwaite** *(vocals, guitar; ex-***Sherbet***), Simon Hussey (keyboards, drums; ex-Cats Under Pressure, James Reyne Band), Jef Scott (guitar, vocals; ex-James Reyne Band, Daryl Braithwaite Band)*

Company of Strangers commenced as a songwriting venture for producer Simon Hussey and American-born guitarist Jef Scott. The pair recorded an album in December 1991 with assistance from **James Reyne** and **Daryl Braithwaite** in between commitments to their own successful solo careers. Scott had worked with Reyne and Braithwaite since 1987. Likewise Hussey was instrumental (in his role as producer) in the success of Braithwaite's 1989 comeback album *Edge*. Company of Strangers signed to Sony and issued *Company of Strangers* in November 1992. The album contained commercial rock pop and produced the singles 'Sweet Love' (June 1992), 'Motor City (I Get Lost)' (September), 'Daddy's Gonna Make You a Star' (January 1993) and The Beatles' 'Baby You're a Rich Man' (June 1993). 'Sweet Love' peaked at #24.

Album: *Company of Strangers* (Sony, 1992).

Conway Brothers Hiccups Orchestra (*see* Captain Matchbox Whoopee Band)

Deborah Conway

Style: *Pop*

Charismatic and outspoken singer/songwriter Deborah Conway (b. 1959) first came to prominence during the mid-1980s as frontperson for agit-funk band **Do Ré Mi**. Conway had previously sung in Melbourne punk band The Benders and taken the part of Julie in John Clark's 1982 feature film *Running on Empty* with Terry Serio. **Do Ré Mi** scored a hit with the provocative 'Man Overboard' single before splitting up at the end of 1988. Conway was also named Best Australian Female Singer by *Rolling Stone* magazine that year.

After **Do Ré Mi** split, Conway initially spent time in the UK and sang on Peter Townsend's *Iron Man* album. In 1990 she took a small role (as a goddess) in the Peter Greenaway film *Prospero's Books*, which opened in December 1991. She also sang on Michael Nyman's soundtrack to the film. In the meantime, Conway had returned to Australia and worked with pub band Rose Amongst Thorns and semi-acoustic performance collective The Drawcards. Her solo career took a long time to get off the ground. Her acclaimed 1991 album *String of Pearls* finally came together after two years, six producers, four false starts, three continents and two record companies.

Producer Richard Pleasance (ex-**Boom Crash Opera**) was the catalyst in completing the album. He produced six of the album's 12 tracks in Melbourne, including the singles 'It's Only the

Beginning' (#19 in August 1991) and 'Release Me' (#58 in February 1992). Michael Den Elzen (from Schnell Fenster) contributed guitar to the Melbourne-recorded tracks. Another single 'Under My Skin' (#34 in December 1991) had been produced by Joe Hardy at Ardent Studios in Memphis, Tennessee. *String of Pearls* peaked at #15 on the national album chart in November 1991, and went on to attain platinum status (70 000 copies sold). The fourth single from the album 'White Roses' (July 1992) was not successful. Nevertheless, Conway won Best Female Artist at the 1991 Australian Record Industry Association (ARIA) Awards.

During May 1992 Conway joined **The Black Sorrows**, **Beatfish**, **The Angels**, **The Poor**, **Club Hoy** and **Kate Ceberano** in the Wizards of Oz showcase gigs in Los Angeles. *Bitch Epic* (with its eye-catching cover featuring a naked Conway covered in chocolate Nutella and cream) and the single 'Alive and Brilliant' came out in November 1993. The CD EP 'Today I am a Daisy' (April 1994) and the live album *Epic Theatre* followed. The Deborah Conway Band at that stage comprised Willy Zygier (guitar; ex-Tootiville), Al Harding (keyboards), Bill McDonald (bass; ex-**Hot Half Hour**) and Hughie Benjamin (drums; ex-Lifesavers, **Big Storm**, **Yothu Yindi**).

Conway then formed studio outfit Ultrasound with ex-**Crowded House** drummer Paul Hester, Bill McDonald and Willy Zygier, which resulted in the self-titled *Ultrasound* album. Conway and Zygier relocated to London at the end of 1995 in order to establish the singer's solo career in the UK. She returned to Australia in mid-1997 after completing her fourth solo album, *My Third Husband* (issued in October). The album yielded the singles 'Only the Bones (Will Show)' (September) and 'Ultrasound 2001' (November).

Deborah Conway albums: *String of Pearls* (Mushroom/Festival, 1991), *Bitch Epic* (Mushroom/Festival, 1993), *Epic Theatre* (Mushroom/Festival, 1994); *My Third Husband* (Mushroom/Sony, 1997); ***Ultrasound album:*** *Ultrasound* (Mushroom/Festival, 1995).

Colin Cook

Style: *Pop*

Sax player/singer Colin Cook was born in Dacca, Bangladesh and moved to Australia with his parents in 1952. In 1957 he joined his first band, The Sapphires, but by 1958 was playing with Melbourne's most respected rock'n'roll combo, **The Thunderbirds**. Cook stayed with **The Thunderbirds** for two years, and played on the band's early EPs for the Rex label, *Rex 4 Star* and *The Thunderbirds*.

Upon leaving **The Thunderbirds**, Cook established himself as a singer on the Melbourne dance circuit, appeared on *Bandstand* and supported US teen idol Fabian on his Australian tour. In late 1962, Cook signed to Ron Tudor's W&G label, and issued 13 singles with that label over the next four years. The singles were Ricky Nelson's 'It's Up to You'/'Just Another Rumour' (December 1962), 'Crying Over You'/'C'mon Pretty Baby' (June 1963), 'Come on Back Baby'/'Blues Baby' (November), Kenny Chandler's 'Heart'/'Surfin' Holiday' (January 1964), Phil Philips' 'Sea of Love'/'High School Romance' (June), 'A Teenager Feels it Too'/'Put Me Down' (August), 'My Gal'/'Handsome Guy' (November), Tommy Sands' 'Blue Ribbon Baby'/'Heebie Jeebies' (February 1965), 'Funny'/'Stop Sneakin' Around' (July), Crash Craddock's 'Well, Don't You Know?'/'Trying to Get to You' (September), Carl Perkins' 'Boppin' the Blues'/'Hey Pretty Baby' (1966), 'Ain't Got You'/'Foolish Little Boy' (1966) and 'Wanted'/'I'll Always Be in Love with You' (1966).

'It's Up to You', 'Blue Ribbon Baby' and 'Well, Don't You Know?' were all Top 30 hits in Melbourne. 'Heart' was Cook's biggest hit when it peaked at #8 in January 1964. In early 1967, Cook moved to the Clarion label for three singles 'Pocket Full of Rainbows'/'Everybody's Talking 'Bout a Thing Called Love' (February 1967), 'You Baby'/'Cry I Do' (August) and 'Riot in Cell Block #9'/'I Have My Friends' (March 1968). In the late 1960s, Cook moved to the UK where he worked in the London stage productions of *Hair* and Andrew Lloyd Webber and Tim Rice's *Jesus Christ Superstar*. He issued a single on the Philips label in 1972, 'Take Your Time Little Girl'/'Love for Living'. In 1979, he formed vocal group The Rainer Brothers, followed by rock'n'roll combo The Jealous Guys.

The Jealous Guys comprised Englishmen Robin McPherson (guitar) and Jim Twomey (drums; ex-Tourists), plus Aussie expatriates Mick Flynn (bass; ex-**Mixtures**), Fred Wieland (guitar; ex-**Strangers**, **Mixtures**) and Billy Kristian (guitar; ex-**Max Merritt and the Meteors**, **Billy Thorpe** and the Aztecs). Cook moved back to Australia in 1982. He issued one single on the Southern Cross label in 1984 'Brylcream and Blue Suede Shoes'/'Be Bop and Blue Suede Shoes'.

Albums: *Here's Colin Cook* (W&G, 1964); ***Album shared with The Strangers:*** *Colin Cook and the Strangers* (W&G, 1965).

Bobby Cookson

***Style:** Rock'n'roll, pop*

Melbourne singer Bobby Cookson started out singing and playing guitar with local rock'n'roll combo The Premiers. Stan Azzopardi (piano accordion, guitar), Tony Buchanan (sax), Colin James (sax) and Ken Merandis (tea-chest bass) completed the line-up. Cookson decided to go solo, performing at suburban dances around Malvern, Springvale and Mordialloc. Cookson possessed a powerful, Roy Orbison-style voice which made him a popular attraction.

In 1961 Cookson signed to Astor Records, for whom he issued six singles. The singles were 'Flutter Flutter'/'That's Alright' (#20 in Melbourne, November 1961), 'True and Faithful'/'Slow Motion' (June 1962), 'Timber'/'Ding Dong' (#29 in October), Ray Peterson's 'I Could Have Loved You So Well'/'Fourteen Carat Gold' (#14 in November), 'One Last Kiss'/'She's My Southern Belle' (January 1963) and 'Rona'/'Gone for the Summer' (#31 in March). By that stage The Premiers had also made a name for themselves as a popular group around Melbourne. The line-up comprised Stan Azzopardi (lead guitar), Colin James (sax), Noel Tresider (piano), Lee Conway (bass) and Joe Gatt (drums). As well as backing Cookson, The Premiers backed other Astor artists like **Betty McQuade**. The Premiers issued one single on Astor, 'Mary Had a Little Lamb'/'Song of India', which graced the lower reaches of the Melbourne Top 40 chart for one week.

Bobby Cookson and the Premiers also issued the single 'I'm from New Orleans'/'I've Had My Moments' in 1963. The Premiers continued on into the late 1960s, after which Conway became a successful country singer, and Azzopardi, Tresider and latter-day sax player Ken Semple joined the Paul McKay Sound. In June 1964 Cookson issued one single on Leedon (through Festival) 'Money Honey'/'Freedom to Love'. He also issued one single on the Go!! label, 'Funny Man'/'That Lucky Old Sun' (August 1965), before disappearing from view.

Corpse Grinders

***Formed:** 1982*
***Style:** Psychobilly*
***Original line-up:** Tony 'Bonehead' Shaw (vocals), Arthur Matsakos (guitar), Pete Andrews (guitar; ex-Twangin' Heartthrobs), Trevor Pennington (bass), Phil 'Good One' Bryant (drums; ex-Zorros)*

Rough-house Melbourne combo Corpse Grinders had a fondness for old EK Holden station wagons and bad horror movies. They showed impeccable 'bad taste' by deriving their band name from Ted V. Mikels' 1971 horror exploitation flick *The Corpse Grinders*. Corpse Grinders were the city's premier exponents of psychobilly, a mutant strain of rock'n'roll that mixed rehashed rockabilly riffs and swampy blues licks with punk attitude and voodoo imagery. Influences ranged from Link Wray, Carl Perkins, Screamin' Jay Hawkins and Gene Vincent to Sex Pistols, The Gun Club and The Cramps. And, like The Cramps, Corpse Grinders' gloriously sloppy gigs provided prime entertainment.

In early 1983, Warren Rough (ex-Autodrifters, **Crackajacks**) replaced Andrews who formed **Shindiggers**. During August, the Grinders supported visiting Los Angeles hardcore outfit the Dead Kennedys on one of their Melbourne concerts. Lead singer Jello Biafra described Corpse Grinders as the most entertaining band in Australia. In 1984, the band issued two gig-giveaway singles, 'I Eat Babies'/'I Go Crazy' and (with **Olympic Sideburns**) 'I Eat Babies'/'7 & 7 Is', plus the mini-album *Corpse Grinders* (September). The band also contributed 'I Go Crazy' to Au-go-go Records' 1984 Various Artists compilation *Asleep at the Wheel.*

Corpse Grinders broke up in 1985. Tony Shaw, Phil Bryant and Trevor Pennington later reunited in **Intoxica**. Rough joined **The Paramount Trio** in 1987. Corpse Grinders reunited in late 1991 for a riotous round of Melbourne gigs (including a support to international visitors Dread Zeppelin), which resulted in the live album *Corpse Grinders.*

Albums: *Corpse Grinders* (mini-album, Man Made, 1984); *Corpse Grinders* (Shock, 1992).

Cosmic Psychos

***Formed:** 1985*
***Style:** Punk rock*
***Original line-up:** Peter Jones (guitar, vocals; ex-Spring Plains), Ross Knight (bass, vocals), Bill Walsh (drums, vocals; ex-Spring Plains)*

Melbourne band Cosmic Psychos were the self-styled 'blokes you can trust'. They looked like the average Joe Blow you would have a beer with at a backyard barbecue, or the motor mechanic down the road. Yet, after 13 years, the Psychos have travelled the world several times over, shared festival stages with Mudhoney, Nirvana, L7, Helmet and Motorhead, released seven albums and garnered international acclaim as grunge pioneers. In 1995, Pearl Jam's Eddie Vedder joined them on stage for a jam. Rock royalty or what?!

On the post-**Birthday Party** pre-grunge world of

inner-city Melbourne circa 1985, Cosmic Psychos combined equal parts Stooges riffs, Ramones tempos, lashings of wah wah guitar, American 1980s hardcore attitude and a healthy dose of yobbo humour. Cosmic Psychos played no-frills, stripped-down punk rock. Between 1982 and 1984, Cosmic Psychos were known as Spring Plains with Steve Morrow (vocals) and Neal Turton-Lane (bass). Spring Plains played an arty kind of punk noise, somewhere between **The Birthday Party** and a more narcotic sounding Ramones. The band's only recorded legacy was 'American Hymn' (included on Au-go-go's 1984 Various Artists compilation *Asleep at the Wheel*) and a self-financed cassette release.

With the departures of Morrow and Turton-Lane, and the arrival of Ross Knight at the end of 1984, Spring Plains evolved into Cosmic Psychos. The band issued its debut, mini-album *Down on the Farm* in December 1985. The band's #1 independent single 'Lead Me Astray'/'No Money' appeared in October 1987, followed by the full-length, self-titled album in December. The band signed to Survival and issued *Go the Hack* (December 1989) and the single 'Lost Cause'/'Rambo'. The album was also issued in Europe on Normal Records. Al Secher-Jensen (ex-**Venom P. Stinger**) deputised for the unavailable Ross Knight on a European tour during 1989. Peter Jones left in 1990 and his place was taken by Robbie Watts (ex-**I Spit on Your Gravy**, Quivering Quims). Jones went on to join Sydney band Enter the Vortex. Cosmic Psychos' sound altered very little with the new addition, as the albums *Slave to the Crave* (November 1990) and *Blokes You Can Trust* (produced by American Butch Vig, 1991) and the singles 'Dead Roo'/'You Can't Come in' (October 1991) and 'Back at School'/(L7's) 'Shove' (May 1992) showed.

On the May 1993 CD EP *Palomino Pizza*, Cosmic Psychos paid homage to their Oz Rock forebears by covering **Coloured Balls'** 'G.O.D.', **Billy Thorpe** and the Aztecs' 'Most People I Know (Think that I'm Crazy)' and **Buffalo's** 'Sunrise'. Cosmic Psychos appeared on the national bill of the 1995 Big Day Out tour. The band continued its unique style with the 1995 album *Self-Totalled* and the CD singles 'Neighbours' (August 1994) and 'Whip Me' (Unplugged) (June 1996). Following another appearance on the 1997 Big Day Out tour, the band completed a new album, *Oh What A Lovely Pie*, which came out in August. UK techno band The Prodigy included a cover version of the L7/Cosmic Psychos song 'Fuel My Fire' (which LZ adapted from the Psychos' 'Lost Cause', and hence the co-writing credit) on its 1997 album *The Fat of the Land*.

Albums: *Down on the Farm* (Mr Spaceman, 1985), *Cosmic Psychos* (Mr Spaceman, 1987), *Go the Hack* (Survival, 1989), *Slave to the Crave* (Survival, 1990), *Blokes You Can Trust* (Survival, 1991), *Down on the Farm/Cosmic Psychos* (reissue, Shagpile/Shock, 1994), *Self-Totalled* (Shagpile/Shock, 1995), *Oh What a Lovely Pie* (Shagpile/Shock, 1997).

Darryl Cotton (*see* The Zoot)

Countdown

With the advent of television pop show *Countdown* in 1974, Australian music entered a new era. There had been pop shows before on Australian television but, like *Ready Steady Go!* and *Top of the Pops* in Britain, *Countdown* became the yardstick by which everything was measured. *Countdown* was the cultural backdrop for the generation of Australian music fans that grew up in the 1970s. If you were a music fan, you never missed an episode.

Johnny O'Keefe pioneered rock music on Australian television with *Six O'Clock Rock*, *Sing Sing Sing* and *The Johnny O'Keefe Show*. Then there was the bespectacled, respectable Brian Henderson fronting the wholesome, family entertainment styled *Bandstand* which lasted from November 1958 until August 1972. Based on the American show *Bandstand* (hosted by fresh-faced Dick Clark), Australia's *Bandstand* built up a stable of regular stars that included the likes of **Bryan Davies, Noeleen Batley, Col Joye, Judy Stone, The Allen Brothers, The Delltones, The De Kroo Brothers, Patsy Ann Noble, Lucky Starr**, Laurel Lea and Sandy Scott.

Throughout the 1960s and early 1970s, television shows like *The Go!! Show*, *Teen Scene*, *Uptight*, *Kommotion*, *It's All Happening*, *Happening '70* and *Happening '71* provided a modicum of interest. There was even a show called *Countdown* during the 1960s on regional Queensland television. In August 1969, ABC-TV launched its ten-minute, non-hits format show *GTK* ('Get To Know'), which introduced Australia to an emerging rock counterculture. *GTK* ran until 1974. The ABC was also behind *Countdown*, but this was to be a pure pop, hits-all-the-way show. Executive producers Ted Emery and Michael Shrimpton chose former *Go-Set* writer Ian 'Molly' Meldrum as the show's talent coordinator, an inspired choice given Molly's propensity for strangling the English language.

Molly's *Humdrum* segment became a riot of non sequiturs and unjustified hyperbole. In between all the 'ums' and 'ahs', occasionally Molly managed to tell the viewers about a good album he had just heard. 'Mollyisms' like 'So watch out for that one', 'So there you go!' and 'Do yourself a favour' became part of the venacular. Comedian **Norman Gunston** celebrated Molly's quirks in the gloriously funny 'Normdrum'. As writer Peter Wilmoth pointed out in his book *Glad All Over*, in many ways Molly *was* a bumbler, and people liked him for that. If he ever got through an interview with Rod Stewart, Elton John or Billy Joel without making a complete fool of himself, it was a miracle. Yet, underneath it all, Molly was a music fanatic, totally committed to, and passionate about, his work. Ultimately it was his drive that helped make *Countdown* so popular.

Countdown started life as six half-hour black-and-white episodes which went to air in late 1974. Its first hour-long colour edition, hosted by **Johnny Farnham**, aired in early 1975. Farnham announced the first band, **Skyhooks**, and it was straight into 'Horror Movie'. **Skyhooks** led Australia's glam-rock explosion, and the band looked outrageous on camera. Lead singer Shirley Strachan appeared in a blue-and-yellow satin jumpsuit with a hand painted on the crotch. Guitarist Red Symons was wrapped in a red cape, his tongue poking out for all to see. Meanwhile, drummer Freddie Strauks wore a Roman centurion's helmet and tunic straight out of *Epic Theatre*.

Countdown was the perfect forum not only for **Skyhooks**, but also **Sherbet**, **AC/DC**, **Hush**, the **Ted Mulry Gang**, **Supernaut**, **Dragon**, **Ol'55**, **The Ferrets**, **Little River Band**, **John Paul Young**, **William Shakespeare**, **Ray Burgess**, **Mark Holden**, **Marcia Hines**, **Jon English**, **Christie Allen** and countless others to strut their stuff. Throughout the 1980s, bands as diverse as **INXS**, **Real Life**, **Pseudo Echo**, **Moving Pictures**, **Do Ré Mi**, **The Uncanny X-Men**, **The Church**, **Split Enz**, **Men at Work**, **Eurogliders**, **Models** and **Australian Crawl** benefitted from *Countdown's* patronage.

Not all bands were welcome. **Rose Tattoo** was banned after singer **Angry Anderson** kissed guitarist Mick Cocks smack on the lips during 'Bad Boy for Love'. Perhaps Angry was just passing on his chewing gum! Likewise, **The Saints** were banned when the English rock papers printed certain disparaging remarks made by singer **Chris Bailey** and guitarist **Ed Kuepper**. Then there was the time **Cold Chisel** smashed up the set of the 1980 *Countdown* Awards ceremony (April 1981) in protest against the show's vacuous nature. **Midnight Oil** steadfastly refused to ever grace a *Countdown* stage, much to Molly's chagrin. In the end, none of these bands' careers suffered as a consequence.

Countdown came to an end in 1987. Molly tried to keep the flame alive when ABC-TV launched its new youth program, *Countdown Revolution*, on 3 July 1989. Molly was the new show's producer. Despite promises from executive producer Richard Reisz that *Countdown Revolution* would be a 'trendsetter and a fully fledged entertainment program', the show was a disaster and short-lived. Presenters Tania Lacey and Mark Little attempted an on-air coup as some kind of protest, and the show was axed.

There were many memorable occasions on the original *Countdown* series. Here are just a few:

- Bon Scott leaping around in pigtails and schoolgirl's uniform as **AC/DC** powered through 'Baby Please Don't Go';
- **William Shakespeare** squeezed into a sequined, extravagantly flared jumpsuit with puffed sleeves, tottering on platform shoes singing 'My Little Angel' in a quaint, high-pitched voice, surely one of the most gruesome sights of the era;
- Iggy Pop spitting at Molly and calling him 'Dogface' after which Iggy terrorised the young audience with the microphone stand during 'I'm Bored', finally shoving the mic down the front of his pants;
- English singer Billy Idol announcing 'I've had some really hot sex since arriving in Australia' at one of the awards ceremonies;
- **Hush** performing the #1 hit single 'Bony Moronie' as singer Keith Lamb thrust out his crotch and leered at the camera and guitarist Les Gock leaped around in glam threads and peroxided streaks in his flowing, jet-black hair;
- one of the first punk bands of the day, The Boys Next Door, performing 'These Boots were Made for Walking' in 1978;
- Perth band **Scientists** doing 'Last Night' in 1981 on a set replete with 44 gallon drums and cyclone fencing;
- the aforementioned stage trashing at the hands of **Cold Chisel**;
- Molly Meldrum disappearing under the table after too much champagne while celebrating the show's 100th episode;
- **John Paul Young** punching Molly on the nose during the same show;
- Molly's famous non-interview with Prince Charles (after messing up the introduction, an extremely nervous Molly says; 'I saw your mum in an open carriage in London the other day', to which Prince Charles replied: 'You mean Her Majesty the Queen);
- Molly pawing all over **Olivia Newton-John** much to her disbelief ('Oh, I can't stop kissing her, smooch!'); and

- Molly removing his cowboy hat to reveal a shaved cranium at the close of the last episode of *Countdown* at Sydney's Entertainment Centre on 19 July 1987.

Molly went on to present *Molly's Melodrama* on the popular Melbourne television variety show *Hey Hey It's Saturday*, but his name will forever be linked with *Countdown*. He took out the Lifetime Achievement Award in 1993 at the sixth annual Australian Record Industry Association (ARIA) Awards ceremony.

Countdown's mark on Australian popular culture can best be summed up in a scene from Richard Lowenstein's 1987 film *Dogs in Space* which was set in grimy inner-city Richmond circa 1978–79. **INXS**'s singer Michael Hutchence, playing monosyllabic, wanna-be punk musician Sam, breaks off a conversation, stumbles into the living room muttering: 'I've got to watch *Countdown*.'

Albums: Various Artists—*Countdown Silver Jubilee LP* (Countdown, 1977); Various Artists—*10 Years of Countdown* (ABC, 1984); Various Artists—*Do Y'self a Favour!* (Raven, 1993).

Further reading: *Glad All Over—The Countdown Years 1974–1987* by Peter Wilmoth (McPhee-Gribble, 1993).

Country Radio

Formed: *1970*
Style: *Country rock*
Original line-up: *Greg Quill (vocals, guitar), Chris Anderson (harmonica), Orlando Agostino (guitar), John Walsh (bass), Dave Hannagan (percussion, vocals)*

During the early 1970s, Country Radio was one of the most accomplished Australian bands playing in an electric country-rock vein. Other bands of a similar ilk included the (post-bubblegum) **Flying Circus**, **Axiom**, **Albatross**, **Home**, Quinn, Sundown, Powderhorn and Third Union Band.

Singer/songwriter (and *Go-Set* journalist) Greg Quill had run the folk hangout The Shack in the Sydney beachside suburb of Narrabeen during the late 1960s. In 1970 he recorded a solo album *Fleetwood Plain* and single 'Fleetwood Plain'/'Song to David' with help from John Walsh (bass), Chris Anderson (harmonica) and rock band **Pirana**. Out of that grew the first version of Country Radio when Orlando Agostino and Dave Hannagan joined in June 1970. By May 1971, the line-up comprised Quill, Chris Blanchflower (harmonica), John A. Bird (piano), Mal Algar (bass, ex-Chorus) and Ace Follington (drums; ex-**Chain**, Savage Rose Blues Band, Powderhorn). That line-up recorded 'Listen to the Children'/'Last Time Around' for Festival/Infinity. A month before the single appeared in November 1971, Kim Bryant replaced Follington (who joined **The Cleves**). Tony Bolton (ex-**Affair**, Luke's Walnut, **Freshwater**) then replaced Bryant. In January 1972, John Du Bois (bass; ex-**New Dream**) replaced Algar and Kerryn Tolhurst (guitar, mandolin; ex-**Adderley Smith Blues Band**) joined.

The new line-up issued the delightful singles 'Gypsy Queen'/'Radio Rag' (#12 in August 1972) and 'Wintersong'/'Observations from a Second Storey Window' (#37 in December), plus the album *Country Radio Live* (December), which had been recorded before an invited audience at TCS Studios in Melbourne on 4 October 1972. The band undertook a short tour of Canada at the end of the year, and then appeared at the second annual Sunbury Festival over the Australia Day weekend in January 1973. The live track 'Silver Spurs' was included on the Various Artists triple album on Mushroom *The Great Australian Rock Festival Sunbury 1973* (April 1973).

Tolhurst left soon after the band played Sunbury, and set about forming **The Dingoes** with **Broderick Smith** (ex-**Carson**). Quill formed a new Country Radio line-up with Bolton, Du Bois and Russ Johnson (guitar; ex-**Mississippi**). Les Stacpool and Russell Hinton (ex-Moonstone) took turns playing guitar with the band throughout the year. Du Bois left the band in August to join **The Dingoes**. After Country Radio's fourth single, 'Bound for South Australia'/'I Need Women' (August 1973), failed to chart, Quill abandoned the band concept in December. The 1974 compilation album *Gypsy Queen* drew together several non-album singles and previously unissued tracks.

In 1974 Quill recorded the accomplished John Sayers-produced album *The Outlaw's Reply*. Helping out in the studio were Kerryn Tolhurst (electric guitar, steel guitar, mandolin), Peter Walker (lead guitar; ex-**Bakery**), Peter Jones (electric piano), Russ Hinton (guitar, vocals), John Du Bois (bass), Tony Bolton (drums), Barry Leef (background vocals), Chris Neal (synthesiser) and Chris Blanchflower (harmonica). By the time the album and its singles, 'She Do It to Me'/'Terry's Tune' (April 1975) and 'Blackmail'/'The Outlaw's Reply' (September), came out, Quill was working in Canada. He had received a travel grant from the Australian Arts Council. In 1977 Quill formed Southern Cross with Chris Stockley (guitar; ex-**Axiom**, **Dingoes**), Sam See (guitar; ex-**Flying Circus**, **Fraternity**), Bruce Worrall (bass, ex-**Sherbet**) and Tony Bolton. Southern Cross toured Australia in August 1978 and issued one single, 'Been So Long'/'I Wonder Why' (October 1978).

Following that, Quill returned to Toronto, Canada to work as a solo artist while Stockley and See formed The Stockley See Mason Band with Glyn Mason (guitar, vocals; ex-**Ariel**). In 1982, Quill quit performing and by the 1990s was one of Toronto's leading rock music and television journalists. He has also written books on Michael Jackson (1988) and The Rolling Stones (*The Rolling Stones 25th Anniversary Tour*, 1989).

Country Radio albums: *Country Radio Live* (Festival/Infinity, 1972), *Gypsy Queen* (Festival/Calendar, 1974), *Wintersongs—The Festival File Volume 22* (Festival, 1992); ***Greg Quill solo albums:*** *Fleetwood Plain* (EMI/Harvest, 1970), *The Outlaw's Reply* (Festival/Infinity, 1975).

The Crackajacks

Formed: *1979*
Style: *Rockabilly*
Original line-up: *Rick Newton (vocals, rhythm guitar; ex-Offbeats), Warren Rough (lead guitar, ex-Autodrifters), Charlie Paine (slap bass), Mick Lyons (drums)*

Taking inspiration from the original 1950s Sun rockabilly cats like Carl Perkins, early Elvis Presley and early Roy Orbison, plus Gene Vincent, Dale Hawkins, Link Wray and lesser lights such as Charlie Feathers, the Burnette Brothers and Sleepy La Beef, The Crackajacks were the first Australian band to play in that genre.

Warren Rough formed The Crackajacks following the break-up of The Autodrifters. Au-go-go Records issued The Crackajacks' debut single, 'Long Blonde Hair'/'Stranger than Fiction' (March 1980), which sold out its pressing of 1000 copies. Astor reissued the single in September 1980 and Missing Link did so a third time in September 1981 with a new B-side, 'Wash Machine Boogie'. Missing Link also issued 'Can't Do Without You'/'Go Cat Go' (June 1981).

'Long Blonde Hair' was then issued a fourth time as part of the band's debut album, *Little Heart Attacks* (January 1982). Charlie Paine played bass on eight of the album's 12 tracks, with Peter Patter appearing on the other four. Jack Cracka joined on bass after the album sessions. At the start of 1982, Ian Hill joined on rhythm guitar. Peter Jones then replaced Hill mid-year, and Troy Fenton replaced Jack Cracka. After The Crackajacks broke up in late 1982, Rough joined **Corpse Grinders** and then **The Paramount Trio.** Newton formed El Prezzos and Crummy Cowboys. By 1988 he was billing himself as Rick O'Shea, fronting The Everlovin' O'Sheas and then Rick O'Shea's Flaming Stars. In 1989, Rough and O'Shea reformed The Crackajacks for a tour. Graham Thomas (bass) and **Gary Young** (drums) completed the line-up.

Album: *Little Heart Attacks* (Missing Link, 1982).

Cranky

Formed: *1994*
Style: *Funk, jazz*
Original line-up: *Bruce Clark (vocals, flute), Dave Power (guitar, vocals), Dr Pain (synthesiser, samples), Satch (sax), Dave Morris (bass), Ivan (drums)*

The members of Melbourne-based six-piece funk outfit Cranky were all former students of the Victorian College of the Arts jazz improvisation course. The band's frantic fusion of funk, jazz and rap immediately drew a following on the inner-city Melbourne pub circuit. The band was traversing similar territory to the likes of **Skunkhour**, Brown Hornet and Capital F. The band signed to Polydor and issued the CD EP *Two Bugs* (June 1995) which featured the shanking funk-rap 'Australia Don't Become America'. A second CD EP, *Cranky*, ('Redheads'), and the band's debut full-length album, *Cranky*, followed at the end of 1995.

Album: *Cranky* (Polydor, 1995).

Crash Politics

Formed: *1983*
Style: *Rock*
Original line-up: *Stuart Paton (guitar, vocals), Michael Wood (guitar, keyboards), James Riff (bass), Andrew Reefman (drums)*

Sydney band Crash Politics played a strident, rhythmic brand of rock that drew inspiration from the likes of U2 and Simple Minds. The band signed to Chase Records and issued the mini-album *A Taste of Things to Come* (October 1986), which produced the singles 'The Same'/'Silence in the Air' (October) and 'Stronger than My Will'/'Sheep' (March 1987).

Ross Farnell (ex-**Beargarden**, Gangland) replaced Riff in 1987. A year later the band signed to the rooArt label, alongside **The Hummingbirds, Tall Tales & True, The Trilobites, Hipslingers** and **Martha's Vineyard.** Initially, Crash Politics contributed the track 'Bitter Rain' to rooArt's Various Artists compilation *Youngblood* (September 1988), before issuing its debut album, *Mother's Intention*, in 1989. The album yielded the singles 'Stop'/'Metal Face' (September 1988) and 'Great Smell of Freedom'/'Yidypb' (November). **INXS** guitarist Tim

Farriss produced Crash Politics' next single, 'Never Too Popular', which ended up on the band's second album, *Tales of the Freshmen*. After the release of a fourth album, *Kiss My Mind* (December 1991), Crash Politics slipped from view.

Albums: *A Taste of Things to Come* (mini-album, Chase, 1986), *Mother's Intention* (rooArt/PolyGram, 1989), *Tales of the Freshmen* (rooArt/PolyGram, 1990), *Kiss My Mind* (rooArt/PolyGram, 1991).

Crashland

Formed: *1988*
Style: *Rock*
Original line-up: *Lyn Gordon (vocals, guitar; ex-Modern Jazz), Ash Wednesday (synthesiser, bass; ex-***JAB**, **Models**, *Metronomes, Modern Jazz), Phil Sutherland (bass), Ray Moore (drums)*

This Melbourne band started out as a wild and trashy covers outfit having fun on the inner-city circuit. The songs the band covered ranged from the Jerry Lee Lewis chestnut 'Whole Lotta Shakin' Goin' on' to The Runaways' teen anthem 'Cherry Bomb'. Gradually the band began to introduce self-penned songs into the set.

Ash Wednesday had a good deal of experience on the pub circuit under his belt with **JAB**, **Models**, The Metronomes and Modern Jazz. The Metronomes were a studio electronic outfit that comprised Wednesday, rock journalist Al Webb (guitar, synthesiser; ex-Streetlife) and Andrew Picouleau (bass, synthesiser). The band issued two singles, 'Saturday Night'/'Sunday Morning' (May 1980) and 'A Circuit Like Me'/'A Closed Circuit' (November 1980), plus two interesting albums, *Multiple Choice* (1981) and *Regular Guys* (1985), on the Cleopatra label.

Wednesday produced Melbourne singer Karen Marks' single 'Cold Cafe'/'Won't Wear It for Long' (January 1981). Modern Jazz featured a fluid line-up that included Lyn Gordon (vocoda), Andrew Phillpott (synthesiser) and Ted Thornbury (vocals). The band played 1980s techno music and issued one album, *The Nude*, on the Cleopatra label in 1986. A year after formation, Crashland signed a deal with Regular Records which resulted in the 'Cherry Bomb'/'Elvis Working' single (October 1989). Crashland's self-titled debut album comprised half original material and half covers, performed in the band's inimitable fashion. The band's second single featured a demented electro remodelling of John Lee Hooker's 'Boom Boom'/'On T.V.' (April 1990).

Album: *Crashland* (Regular/Festival, 1990).

Craven Fops

Formed: *1985*
Style: *Rock*
Original line-up: *Daniel Morphett (vocals, harmonica), James A. Scanlon (lead guitar), Penny Quarry (rhythm guitar), Bryan King (bass), Kit Quarry (drums)*

Sydney band Craven Fops was at turns eclectic, anarchic and imaginative. The band's music ran on manic, nervous energy that recalled a cross between The Velvet Underground, Television and Gram Parsons over an abrasive yet always hummable garage-R&B backing.

The band issued its debut four-track 12-inch EP, *When a Whiskey* on the obscure Bulb label, followed by the 'Epic Merriment'/'Chemical Blues' single on its own Craven imprint (July 1987). In 1987, Scanlon moonlighted with country band **The Killer Sheep**. That band also comprised Astrid Munday (vocals), Michael O'Connell (guitar; ex-**Apartments**), Clinton Walker (bass) and James McKay (drums). Munday had worked as backing vocalist for a number of years, and she contributed her pure tones to records by **Paul Kelly** and the Coloured Girls, **Died Pretty** and **Nick Cave and the Bad Seeds**. Walker was a well-known rock music journalist who had contributed to the likes of *RAM (Rock Australia Magazine)* and *Rolling Stone*, among others.

The Killer Sheep adopted a grunge-country sound that mixed Jesus and Mary Chain with bluegrass elements. The band made a disastrous appearance at the 1987 Tamworth Country Music Festival where its style was met with bemused indifference. The band managed one single on Au-go-go, 'Wild Down Home'/'Don't Turn Your Back' (1988), before disintegrating. Since then, Walker has written several books, including *Highway to Hell: The Life and Times of AC/DC Legend Bon Scott* and *Stranded: The Secret History of Australian Independent Music 1977–1991*.

By the time The Craven Fops issued the four-track, 10-inch EP *Pleasure* in early 1990 on the Half a Cow label, Belinda Cape had replaced Kit Quarry on drums and Matthew Crosby had joined on sax. Neil Johnson replaced Cape in 1990, and Crista Hughes joined as backing vocalist for the recording of the band's debut album, *Spin the Bottle* (January 1992). Singer Daniel Morphett also moonlighted with part-time outfit The Godbotherers. The rest of the band, Greg Hassell (guitar), Tony Locke (bass) and Rob Shannon (drums), were all members of Living with Robert. The Godbotherers issued one four-track EP in 1990 called *Jesus Christ—It's . . . The Godbotherers* (on the Phantom label), which featured simple, trashy guitar pop tunes.

Album: *Spin the Bottle* (Half a Cow, 1992).

The Creatures

Formed: *1965*
Style: *Garage punk*
Original line-up: *Eric Marcic (guitar), Keith Matcham (vocals), Michael Parnis (rhythm guitar), Herman Marcic (bass), Rudolph Marcic (drums)*

Like **The Missing Links, The Pink Finks, The Elois, The Throb, The Black Diamonds**, The Running Jumping Standing Still and many others, The Creatures were a product of the mid-1960s suburban R&B boom. Armed with cheap guitars, Vox amps, the latest Pretty Things and Yardbirds singles, a six-pack and a mess of attitude to spare, these bands got their start in garages across the nation.

When they hit dance stages, they were as tough and uncompromising as The Stones and The Pretty Things, or any of their American contemporaries like The Standells, The Seeds, Count Five, The Sonics and The Shadows of Knight. The wild, uninhibited Creatures can lay claim to one of the most sublime pieces of garage-punk mania ever in 'Ugly Thing'. Reissue specialists Raven included the song on the first *Ugly Things* compilation of Australian 1960s garage-punk bands. As co-compiler, Glenn A. Baker wrote in his liner notes: 'At a time when moderate long hair was becoming acceptable, (The Creatures) dyed their tatty locks to bilious pastel shades and invited the media to react with appropriate horror.'

The Creatures formed in Mildura (Victoria) as The Beagle Boys during 1965. In February 1966, The Beagle Boys became The Creatures and relocated to Sydney where they regularly supported **The Easybeats** at Beatle Village. Richard White replaced Michael Parnis and The Creatures issued their impossibly scarce debut single 'Mona'/'All I Do is Cry' on the obscure Sound-66 imprint. At the end of 1966, Eric left to be replaced by Greg Lawrie. RCA stepped in and issued 'Ugly Thing'/'Your One and Only Man' in December 1967. By that stage, The Creatures had moved to Melbourne, and having tired of the dyed hair became The Chocolate. The Chocolate recorded one single for Festival, 'I'm an Animal'/'It's Been a Long Time Coming' (September 1969), by which time the band had broken up. Lawrie formed **Carson** County Band and Herman joined Toby Jugg. Keith Matcham was shot to death on the premises of his panel-beating business in the late 1970s.

The Crescents

Formed: *1958*
Style: *Vocal trio*
Original line-up: *Colin Loughnan (vocals), Mike Downes (vocals), Kel Palace (vocals)*

Colin Loughnan, Mike Downes and Kel Palace were all 17 years old when they came together in Sydney during 1958. The trio took its inspiration from American harmony groups like The Diamonds, The Jordanaires, Danny and the Juniors, The Fleetwoods and The Four Aces. Singer **Johnny O'Keefe** took the young singers under his wing.

As well as backing O'Keefe and his band at local dances, the trio made its television debut on his show *Six O'Clock Rock* in March 1959. The trio became regulars on *Six O'Clock Rock*, *Teen Time* and *Bandstand*. The Crescents began to rival **The Delltones** as the most popular vocal group in Sydney. They were selected as one of the many supports to Johnny Ray's August 1959 and Fabian's October 1959 Australian tours. Promoter Lee Gordon was impressed enough to sign the trio to his Leedon label. The Crescents recorded seven singles and two EPs for Leedon.

The singles were (the O'Keefe/Loughnan-penned) 'Everlovin''/'You Broke My Heart' (December 1959), 'Mr Blue'/'How Important Can It Be?' (Top 10 in Sydney during February 1960), 'When You Wish upon a Star'/'Hand of God' (April 1960), 'One More Kiss'/'Picture of Love' (November 1960), 'Stars will Remember'/'Love Love Love' (January 1961), 'Way of the Cross'/'Story of the Cross' (June 1961) and 'Get a Job'/'Silhouettes' (August 1961). The EPs were *Rock Time* (1960) and *Hit It for Six* (1961).

In October 1961, The Crescents appeared on the bill for the third Lee Gordon Big Show, as one of the support acts for Ricky Nelson. By that time, Alan Roberts had replaced Downes. The demise of The Crescents ironically came when the lead singer of **The Delltones**, Noel Widerberg, died in July 1962. Colin Loughnan was offered the job of replacing Widerberg as **The Delltones'** lead singer, which he accepted. He remained with **The Delltones** for five years. In the late 1960s, he travelled to England where he joined Kala. On his return, he played sax in the Daly-Wilson Big Band and **Ayers Rock**.

Crime and the City Solution

Formed: *1977*
Style: *Rock*
Original line-up: *Simon Bonney (vocals), Harry Zanteni (guitar), Dave MacKinnon (sax), Phil Kitchener (bass), Don McLennan (drums; ex-Particles)*

Simon Bonney is highly regarded in Europe, where his band Crime and the City Solution built up a strong cult following during the 1980s. In Australia, Bonney and his crew have attracted minimal interest which actually says nothing about the quality of the music on offer.

Bonney formed the original version of Crime and the City Solution in Sydney at the height of late 1977's punk explosion. He had sung occasionally with Don McLennan's band The Particles. Peter Nelson described Crime in *Pulp* fanzine (#5) as: 'An exciting blend of fuzzed monotone guitar runs and squawking saxophone riffs . . . [like] the drone songs on Wire's 'Pink Flag'.' Although Crime and the City Solution attracted some interest in Sydney, Bonney moved to Melbourne in late 1978, where his more arty pretentions were better accepted. Retaining McLennan, he assembled a new version of Crime and the City Solution with Chris Astley (keyboards), Kim Beissel (sax), Lindsay O'Meara (bass; ex-Voigt/465) and Dan Wallace-Crabbe (guitar).

Bonney was befriended by members of The Boys Next Door, an association that served him well later on. By all accounts, Bonney had a strong influence on **Nick Cave's** stage craft. Crime and the City Solution broke up in 1979 without having recorded anything for posterity. Wallace-Crabbe later joined **Laughing Clowns**, and Beissel later appeared in **Hot Half Hour** and formed a series of his own bands such as The Whites, The Fallen Angels and Mouse.

Following a period in a psychiatric hospital, Bonney travelled to London in late 1983. When **The Birthday Party** broke up at the same time, Mick Harvey encouraged Bonney to revive Crime and the City Solution. The pair brought in another ex-**Birthday Party** alumnus, Rowland S. Howard, on guitar and keyboards, and his brother Harry on bass; Harvey played drums and keyboards. The band's debut, 12-inch four-track EP *The Dangling Man* (June 1985) picked up where **The Birthday Party** had left off with a gloomy, stripped-down, blues-flavoured sound. The mini-album *Just South of Heaven* (October 1985) featured a cleaner, more powerful set of songs dominated by Bonney's dramatic vocals and chilling instrumentation. Epic Soundtracks (ex-Swell Maps) then took over on drums, allowing Harvey to concentrate on guitar and keyboards. Bronwyn Adams also joined on violin. The new line-up recorded *Room of Lights* and the 12-inch single 'Adventure', 'It Takes Two to Burn'/'The Kentucky Click' (both 1986).

While all this activity was going on, Harvey was dividing his time between **Nick Cave and the Bad Seeds** and Crime and the City Solution. As a consequence, Crime only functioned around Harvey's commitments. Rowland and Harry Howard left in late 1986 to put together their long-heralded 'supergroup' These Immortal Souls with which they recorded two albums of dark, ominous, challenging rock music, *Get Lost (Don't Lie!)* (1987) and *I'm Never Gonna Die Again* (1992). They also issued two 12-inch singles, 'Marry Me (Lie! Lie!)' and 'King of Kalifornia'.The original line-up comprised Rowland, Harry, Epic Soundtracks and Genevieve McGuckin (keyboards). Rowland Howard returned to live in Melbourne during 1994. He joined Spencer P. Jones' band The Holy Spirits before reviving These Immortal Souls to play the Melbourne pub circuit. The line-up comprised Howard, Jones, McGuckin, Chris Walsh (bass; ex-**Moodists**) and Peter Jones (drums; ex-**Harem Scarem**).

In the meantime, Thomas Stern (bass), Alexander Hacke (guitar) and Chrislo Haas (synthesiser) joined Crime and the City Solution, giving a line-up of Bonney, Harvey, Adams, Stern, Hacke and Haas. The promise of *Just South of Heaven* and *Room of Lights* was realised on *Shine* (August 1988) and *The Bride Ship* (June 1989). In Australia, the Rampant label put together a compilation of *Just South of Heaven* and *Room of Lights* (under the title *Room of Lights*) for local release (March 1988). In the UK, *The Bride Ship* yielded the 12-inch EP 'The Shadow of No Man' (1989). The last Crime and the City Solution records were the album *Paradise Discotheque* (October 1990) and the 10-inch EP 'The Dolphins and the Sharks' (1991). By the time the EP came out, Crime and the City Solution had fallen apart. The band's legacy includes several haunting and art-infused releases.

Having left Europe, Bonney moved to Los Angeles in 1991, where he developed an interest in American country music (in the vein of Gram Parsons). His solo albums, the introspective *Forever* and the observational *Everyman*, were greeted with much critical acclaim. *Forever* produced the single 'There can Only be One', while *Everyman* included the single 'Don't Walk Away from Love' and a cover of Willie Nelson's 'Blue Eyes Cryin' in the Rain'. Bonney spent most of 1995 and 1996 touring throughout the USA to an ever-increasing cult following.

Albums: *Just South of Heaven* (mini-album, UK only, Mute, 1985), *Room of Lights* (UK only, Mute, 1987), *Room of Lights* (Australian only compilation, Rampant, 1988), *Shine* (UK Mute; Rampant in Australia, 1988), *The Bride Ship* (UK Restless/Mute; BMG/Arista/Mute in Australia, 1989), *Paradise Discotheque* (UK only Mute, 1990), *The Adversary—Live* (UK Mute, 1994); ***Simon Bonney solo albums:*** *Forever* (Mute/MDS, 1992), *Everyman* (Mute/Liberation/Festival, 1994); ***These Immortal Souls albums:*** *Get Lost (Don't Lie!)* (Mute, 1987), *I'm Never Gonna Die Again* (Mute, 1992).

Crow

Formed: *1988*
Style: *Rock*
Original line-up: *Peter Fenton (guitar, vocals), Peter Archer (guitar, vocals), Paul Gormack (bass), John Fenton (drums), Christopher Baz (percussion)*

Peter and John Fenton grew up in Canberra (ACT) before relocating to Sydney in 1988. Crow picked up a strong following on the inner-city circuit where its dark, gothic imagery and reckless, unsettling music was well appreciated. Writing in *Rolling Stone*, reviewer John Encarnacao described the band's early sound as 'akin to a beast that hasn't washed itself for a week and wears its odour like a badge of individuality'. Reference points ranged from local heroes like **Tactics** and **The Birthday Party** to New York band Sonic Youth.

Crow signed to the Phantom label for the release of the mini-album *Sunburnt Throats and Happy Thunderclouds* (May 1990) and the single 'Confection'/'Ravine' (August 1991). By that stage, Jim Woff had replaced Paul Gormack on bass, and percussionist Baz was appearing less frequently with the band. In October 1992, Crow linked up with the Half a Cow label for the release of the five-track CD EP *Crow* (which also included 'Confection' and 'Ravine'), followed by the CD single 'Railhead'/'How and Why Wonder' (May 1993) and album *My Kind of Pain* (July).

Crow recorded *My Kind of Pain* with American producer Steve Albini, best known for his work with Nirvana, The Pixies, Helmet and P.J. Harvey, plus his own bands Big Black, Rapeman and Shellac. Sydney engineer Tim Whitten remixed the album in Australia because the band was unhappy with Albini's final mix. As was to be expected, however, the album was full of potent songs backed by a muscular wall of guitar noise. Once the band had completed work on the album in Chicago in late 1992, drummer John Fenton left to be replaced by Tina Stevens (ex-Plug Uglies). Crow supported US visitors Pavement on their May 1993 Australian tour, during which Andy Marks (ex-Lunarcide) replaced Stevens on drums. The band commenced 1994 with a spot on the Sydney bill of the Big Day Out. Half a Cow issued one more Crow CD EP, *The Helicon Days* (April 1994), before the band moved to rooArt's Ra label for the CD single 'Privilege' (August 1995) and second full-length album *Li-Lo-ing* (September).

Produced by Tim Whitten, *Li-Lo-ing* took the best elements of *My Kind of Pain*, while adding layers of burning intensity to create a deeper and darker mood. Guest musicians on the album included **Chris Abrahams** (keyboards) and Warren Ellis (violin; from **Dirty Three**). *Li-Lo-ing* produced a second CD single, 'Paper Eyes' (January 1996). Shortly after the band had completed the album at the end of 1994, Richard Andrew (ex-**Underground Lovers**) replaced Marks on drums. Crow contributed a cover of **Tactics'** 'Second Language' to the soundtrack of David Caesar's feature film *Idiot Box* (February 1997).

Albums: *Sunburnt Throats and Happy Thunderclouds* (mini-album, Phantom, 1990), *My Kind of Pain* (Half a Cow, 1993), *Li-Lo-ing* (Ra/rooArt/Sony, 1995).

Crowded House

Formed: *1985*
Style: *Pop*
Original line-up: *Neil Finn (vocals, guitar; ex-***Split Enz***), Nicholas Seymour (bass; ex-Plays with Marionettes, Bang, Horla), Paul Hester (drums, ex-Cheks,* **Deckchairs Overboard, Split Enz***)*

On 24 November 1996, Crowded House, one of Australia's most successful and best-loved groups ever, was laid to rest. In front of an estimated crowd of 150 000 people, Crowded House played a farewell concert on the steps of the Sydney Opera House. The demise of Crowded House effectively heralded the arrival of a new era in Australian rock'n'roll.

When **Split Enz** broke up in December 1984, Neil Finn and Paul Hester decided to form a new band. With Nick Seymour and auxiliary member Craig Hooper (guitar, keyboards; ex-**Reels**) on board, the band took the moniker The Mullanes (after Neil's middle name). In late 1985, the band bypassed Australian record companies and signed directly to Capitol in the USA. The band relocated to Los Angeles (minus Hooper) and commenced work on its debut album with producer Mitchell Froom. The band was rechristened Crowded House in homage to the cramped conditions the members (and friends) endured while living in a rented Hollywood bungalow.

With the help of a host of session players (including Froom on keyboards), *Crowded House* (August 1986) proved to be a very polished affair. It also revealed the extraordinary breadth of Neil Finn's songwriting talents. It included at least five certified classics in 'Mean to Me', 'World Where You Live', 'Don't Dream It's Over', 'Love You 'Til the Day I Die' and 'Something so Strong'. *Crowded House* produced five singles in Australia: 'Mean to Me'/'Hole in the River' (July 1986), 'Now We're Getting Somewhere'/'Recurring Dream' (September), 'Don't Dream It's Over'/'That's What I Call Love' (November), 'World Where You Live'/'Hole in the River' (March 1987) and 'Something so Strong'/'I Walk Away' (June).

Although the first UK single, 'World Where You Live'/'That's What I Call Love' (August 1986), failed to chart, American success followed soon after. On release the same month, the album rose to #12 in the US. The singles 'Don't Dream It's Over' and 'Something so Strong' peaked there at #2 (January 1987) and #7 (April) respectively. The next US single, 'World Where You Live'/'Hole in the River', however, only managed a relatively poor placing of #65 during August. Nevertheless, American critics hailed Neil Finn as the successor to the songwriting crown of Lennon/McCartney. Certainly, the band's romantic guitar pop had a similar effect on listeners to that created by The Beatles.

In Australia it was a different story. 'Mean to Me' peaked at a modest #18 during August 1986. *Crowded House* lingered around the lower reaches of the Australian album charts for almost a year before it reached #1 (June 1987). The catalyst was Australian radio finally getting behind 'Don't Dream It's Over' and 'Something so Strong'. 'Don't Dream It's Over' went to #7 in March 1987 and 'Something so Strong' peaked at #12 during July. *Crowded House* remains one of the most impeccably crafted, timeless Australian albums of the 1980s.

With the success of the album in the USA, Crowded House launched into a punishing schedule of American concert tours. Inevitably the band played to packed auditoriums. Not only were American audiences seduced by the band's consummate musical skills, but they were also won over by the affable sense of humour on offer. In particular, Paul Hester's on-stage court jester antics were the focus of much attention. It was not unusual, for example, for Hester to stop the show, order takeaway and happily chomp on hamburgers while all around waited!

In the UK, success also took a little longer in coming, but 'Don't Dream It's Over' reached #27 there during April 1987. 'Better be Home Soon'/'When You Come' (July 1988) was a strong follow-up single with its simple acoustic arrangement and three-part 'round-the-campfire' harmonies. Both the single and the band's second album, *Temple of Low Men*, went to #1 in Australia during the same week in August 1988. The album won Best Album and Best Cover Artwork at the 1988 Australian Record Industry Association (ARIA) Awards. 'Better Be Home Soon' was named Song of the Year. Overseas audiences, however, were unprepared for *Temple of Low Men*.

The album's lush sound was deceptive because tracks like 'When You Come', 'I Feel Possessed', 'Into Temptation' and 'Never Be the Same' uncovered the band's darker side. *Temple of Low Men* only managed #40 in the USA, despite bearing the hallmarks of another classic album. Likewise, 'Better be Home Soon'/'Kill Eye' peaked at #42 in the US during August, but failed to reach the UK chart. 'Into Temptation'/'Mansion in the Slums' (live), 'This Is Massive' (live) (December 1988) and 'Sister Madly'/'Love this Life' (April 1989) came out as singles in Australia. The band also contributed 'Mansion in the Slums' to the Various Artists album *Building Bridges* on CBS (1989).

Neil's older brother, and another ex-**Split Enz** alumnus, **Tim Finn**, joined Crowded House in 1990. *Woodface* (July 1991) and the sardonic single 'Chocolate Cake'/'As Sure as I am' fared poorly in the USA (*Woodface* only reached #83). In Australia, the band was as popular as ever ('Chocolate Cake' reached #20 upon release in June and *Woodface* peaked at #2), and in the UK its star was on the rise. *Woodface* made #34 there at the end of 1991. Likewise, the band enjoyed four more hits from *Woodface*, 'Fall at Your Feet' (Australian #31 in October 1991; UK #17), 'It's Only Natural' (Australian #15 in March 1992; UK #24 in September), 'Weather with You' (UK #7 in February 1992; Australian #27 in June) and 'Four Seasons in One Day' (UK #26 in June 1992; Australian #47 in August). All these CD singles featured alternative, usually live, bonus tracks in the different territories. 'Fall at Your Feet'/'Whispers and Moans' was the last Crowded House single issued on vinyl in Australia.

At the end of 1992, Crowded House took out Best International Group at the prestigious UK Music Awards, the BRITS, beating Pearl Jam, Nirvana, R.E.M. and U2 in the process. The group also won Best Band at the 1992 ARIA Awards. **Tim Finn** had left in late 1991, and American Mark Hart (keyboards, guitar; ex-Supertramp) joined as a hired hand in order for the band to continue touring. In early 1993, Crowded House began recording a new album in the isolated environment of Kare Kare beach on the North Island of New Zealand with UK producer Youth.

Together Alone (October 1993) was another classic album, reaching #1 in Australia and #4 in the UK. Its CD singles 'Distant Sun' (UK #19 in October 1993; Australian #23 in November), 'Nails in My Feet' (UK #22 in November 1993; Australian #34 in February 1994) and 'Locked Out' (UK #12 in February 1994) sold well. All was not well, however, within the band. Following the Together Alone Australian tour of February 1994, Hester announced his departure in May. He returned to Melbourne to be with his family and to tend his garden. He played drums with studio outfit Ultrasound fronted by **Deborah Conway**. Melbourne drummer Peter Jones (ex-**Harem Scarem,** Vince Jones, **Kate Ceberano's** Septet) came in as replacement and Crowded House continued to tour.

Finn and Seymour recorded demos with Hart and Jones in Auckland at the end of 1994 for the proposed fifth Crowded House album. The project was shelved when Neil joined Tim for the *Finn* album (UK #15 in October 1995). *Finn* produced two singles, 'Suffer Never'/'Weather with You' (demo) (UK #29 in October 1995) and 'Angels Heap'/'It's Only Natural' (demo), 'Chocolate Cake' (demo) (UK #41 in November 1995).

The Crowded House singles 'Fingers of Love' and 'Private Universe' came out in May 1994 and May 1995 respectively. By the beginning of 1996, Crowded House was on its last legs. Hester rejoined briefly to record three new songs with Mitchell Froom: 'Not the Girl You Think You Are', 'Instinct' and 'Everything is Good for You'. 'Everything is Good for You' appeared as a CD single and peaked at #9 in Australia during June 1996. 'Not the Girl You Think You Are' came out in September, and reflected its more melancholy demeanour by only reaching #37. All three songs were included on *Recurring Dream—The Very Best of Crowded House,* which came out in July 1996. *Recurring Dream* was the band's most successful album to date. It made its debut at #1 on the Australian *and* the UK album charts. By the beginning of 1997, it had sold over 400 000 copies in Australia (six times platinum) and 600 000 in the UK. By the end of June 1997, it had spent 50 weeks in the Australian Top 40 album listing and sold a staggering 500 000 copies. It went on to take the Best-Selling Australian Album award at the 1997 ARIA ceremony.

With *Recurring Dream* in the shops, Neil Finn announced the break-up of Crowded House. Hester rejoined the band for the farewell show in November 1996, and **Tim Finn** made a guest appearance. With the demise of the band, Neil considered his options, Seymour joined **deadstar**, Hester worked with a band called The Fez (with Mike Rudd and Bill Putt) and Mark Hart rejoined Supertramp.

Crowded House contributed a number of songs to film soundtracks, including 'Recurring Dream' in the Australian feature film *Rikki and Pete*, and 'Locked Out' and 'Something so Strong' in *Reality Bites* (1994). The band also rerecorded 'Recurring Dream' for the *Tequila Sunrise* (1989) soundtrack. 'Don't Dream It's Over' appeared during pivotal scenes in the US television miniseries *The Stand* (1994), which was based on the book by Stephen King.

Albums: *Crowded House* (EMI/Capitol, 1986), *Temple of Low Men* (EMI/Capitol, 1988), *Woodface* (EMI/Capitol, 1991), *Together Alone* (EMI/Capitol, 1994), *Recurring Dream—The Very Best of Crowded House* (EMI/Capitol, 1996).

Further reading: *Private Universe* by Kerry Doole and Chris Twomey (Omnibus Press, 1996).

Crown of Thorns (*see* Chris Wilson)

Jeffrey Crozier

Style: *Magician*

Magician/illusionist/actor/musician Jeffrey Crozier (b. 1948, d. 1981) was one of the most enigmatic, yet bewildering and totally underrated performers this country has ever produced. Crozier's influence and reputation were felt more overseas than in Australia. After more than a decade of perfecting his stage craft, he died in May 1981 in his hometown of Seymour, Victoria. He reputedly died while rehearsing the illusion of self-hanging.

Crozier got his start as a magician on Melbourne television during the late 1960s. In 1969 he formed The Magik Word, and then The Indian Medicine Magik Show, a radical and visual combination of magic, pyrotechnics, lighting effects, on-stage menagerie and loud rock music. He was accompanied by his assistant Lady Air (Andrea Ewing) and musicians Jan Sardi (guitar), Phil Stone (bass) and Tom Riley (drums). The Indian Medicine Magik Show was popular at 'head' venues like the T.F. Much Ballroom in Fitzroy, where the troupe shared stages with **Spectrum** and performance artists The Tribe.

Crozier became frustrated with his lack of success and acceptance in Australia, and in July 1971 travelled to the USA. In 1974 he toured the US with The Moon Rock Circus, an extension of what he was doing in Australia. Instead of being branded a freak, Crozier was hailed as a genius. A review in the *New York Times* declared 'Crozier's demented Merlin is a triumphant creation'. The Moon Rock Circus comprised musicians Danny Chambers, Steve Germinder and Peter Giordano. In 1977, Crozier's new troupe The Kongress was closer to Alice Cooper-styled shock rock, replete with electric chairs, smoke bombs and anarchic rock music.

Crozier returned to Australia in 1978, where he continued to be ignored by all but a dedicated few. He was even voted Australia's top magician at the twelfth Annual Wizards Convention. In 1979 he teamed up with The Generator, which comprised David Mow (guitars), Robert Greaves (synthesiser) and Keith Casey (percussion). The Generator had already issued an independent album, *Dance of the Spheres* on the private Fission Chips label.

With Crozier on board, the group's shows became almost entirely improvisational, although Crozier remained totally exacting in his stage craft. Crozier was often billed as the 'voodoo psychedelic magician'. In January 1981, Crozier and the Generator recorded enough material to fill a double album, which Mow assembled and issued following the magician's death. The haunting *Tranceformer* featured Crozier's monologues and incantations set to a heady tapestry of synthesisers, guitars, rhythm machines and treated percussion. The sound was somewhere between Brian Eno circa *Another Green World* (1975), the Gothic overtones of Tangerine Dream's synthesiser explorations and the space rock of Arthur Brown's Kingdom Come.

Crozier and the Generator album: *Tranceformer* (Fission Chips, 1983).

The Cruel Sea

Formed: *1988*
Style: *Surf, blues, funk*
Original line-up: *Danny Rumour (aka Danny Aitkins, guitar; ex-Blackrunner, Ugly Mirrors,* **SPK**, *Urban Guerillas, Sekret Sekret), Ged Gorben (guitar), Dee Gorben (bass), Jim Elliot (drums; ex-Sekret Sekret; Spectre's Revenge)*

For a band that started out as a purely instrumental outfit in 1988, it is of some note that The Cruel Sea went on to become one of Australia's most popular outfits. The catalyst was singer **Tex Perkins,** who initially joined on a part-time basis in 1989, to add his broad brushstroke lyrics to the band's swelling melodies. Later on, with Perkins on board as a full-time member, the band gained widespread acclaim.

The Cruel Sea

The original Cruel Sea line-up grew out of Sydney independent band Sekret Sekret. Fronted by singer David Virgin (ex-Broken Toys, Ugly Mirrors), Sekret Sekret itself grew out of the late 1970s Sydney punk scene centred around the Grand Hotel. The band played a sprightly brand of punky power pop with psychedelic overtones. Sekret Sekret issued four independent singles, 'Charity'/'Hope You Can' (June 1980), 'New King Jack'/'Moose Beach' (December 1980), 'Girl with a White Stick'/'Chimes' (June 1984) and 'Just to Love You'/'Waterbirds' (October 1984), before breaking up in 1987. Under the name of David Verjin, frontman Virgin later issued an interesting folk/country album, *Landlord Green* (1991), which included guitar contributions from Danny Rumour.

The Cruel Sea took its name from a song by 1960s US surf instrumental band The Ventures (it was also the title of the novel by Nicholas Monsarrat). The original line-up was short-lived and Rumour and Elliot recruited Ken Gormly (bass; ex-Sekret Sekret) and James Cruickshank (keyboards, guitar; ex-Widdershins, **Neil Murray** and the Rainmakers). For a time, Rumour and his compatriots were content to explore their own instrumental surf sound (epic rather than twangy), but at the start of 1989, Perkins began joining the band on stage. It was not without irony that the band's atmospheric music evoked the feel of wide open spaces, yet they commanded a fanatical following on the Sydney inner-city pub circuit. The band signed to the Red Eye label and Perkins sang on the 12-inch EP 'Down Below' (September 1989) and the band's debut album, *Down Below* (December). Due to his commitments to **Beasts of Bourbon** at that stage, however, he was precluded from becoming fully involved.

The singles 'I Feel'/'Help Me' (September 1991), the CD EPs *4 x 4* (March 1992) and 'This is Not the Way Home' (August 1992) plus the album *This is Not the Way Home* (December 1991) followed. *This is Not the Way Home* garnered critical acclaim and was an indication of things to come. The music ranged from funky Louisiana swamp blues to sweet soul, with Perkins' laconic vocals recalling the spirit of Captain Beefheart, Tony Joe White and John Lee Hooker in the process. With the release of *This is Not the Way Home*, The Cruel Sea embarked on a European tour supporting **Nick Cave and the Bad Seeds**. With the suspension of **Beasts of Bourbon** activities in early 1993, Perkins was able to join The Cruel Sea as a full-time member. This new-found unity resulted in the classic album *The Honeymoon is Over* (May 1993), which yielded the singles 'Black Stick' (December 1992), 'The Honeymoon is Over' (July 1993), a cover of Tony Joe White's 'Woman with Soul' (October) and 'Seems Twice' (February 1994). 'Black Stick' reached #25 on the national charts during May, and 'The Honeymoon is Over' peaked at #41 in August.

The Honeymoon is Over made its debut at #4 on the mainstream charts, eventually reaching the coveted #1 spot (and selling over 140 000 copies in the process). On the album, Perkins dubbed himself the 'Delivery Man'. The super funky 'The Honeymoon is Over' went on to log a #9 placing on Triple J's 1993 Hottest 100 list (the highest placing for an Australian band that year). At the 1993 Australian Record Industry Association (ARIA) Awards ceremony, The Cruel Sea took out the honours for the Best Group, Best Album (*The Honeymoon is Over*), Best Single and Song of the Year ('The Honeymoon is Over'). The shine was taken off the evening somewhat when, at one of the post-awards parties, Perkins was involved in a fracas with a drunken guest who had attacked his girlfriend, photographer Krystina Higgins. To top the night off, two of the band's ARIA trophies were stolen.

The Cruel Sea ended 1994 with another tour throughout Europe supporting **Nick Cave and the Bad Seeds**, followed by their own headlining jaunt across Europe and Canada. Four singles were lifted from the band's second #1 album, *Three Legged Dog* (November 1994), 'Better Get a Lawyer' (#29 in January 1995), 'Just a Man' (#39 in April), 'Anybody but You' (#49 in July) and 'Too Fast for You' (August). The band commenced 1995 by supporting The Rolling Stones on their massive Voodoo Lounge tour of Australia. Following the release of *The Honeymoon is Over* in Europe (on Polydor) and the USA (on A&M), the band then undertook its third overseas tour. The Cruel Sea completed another successful year with its second award for Best Group at the 1995 ARIA ceremony.

Rock'n'Roll Duds (November 1995) mopped up a batch of B-sides, demos and studio out-takes. The band toured constantly until early 1996, after which Perkins completed his solo album, *Far be It from Me* and reactivated **Beasts of Bourbon**. At the start of 1997, The Cruel Sea returned to its instrumental roots (sans Perkins) for a series of gigs, including an appearance at the Sydney leg of the Big Day Out tour. With the break-up of the Beasts later in the year, Perkins rejoined The Cruel Sea.

Albums: *Down Below* (Red Eye, 1989), *This is Not the Way Home* (Red Eye/Polydor, 1991), *The Honeymoon is Over* (Red Eye/Polydor, 1993), *Three Legged Dog* (Red Eye/Polydor, 1994), *Rock'n'Roll Duds* (Red Eye/Polydor, 1995).

The Cruisers

Formed: *1979*
Style: *Pub rock*
Original line-up: *Andrew Denholm (guitar, vocals), Tony Persic (guitar, vocals), Allan Webster (bass, vocals; ex-Streetlife), Johnny Walker (drums)*

Carlton pub band The Cruisers formed out of Streetlife. Streetlife existed between 1977 and 1978, and comprised Allan Webster, Al Webb (guitar), John Hunter (guitar) and Frank Borg (drums). Streetlife had one track, 'Streetlife', included on the Missing Link Various Artists album *The Melbourne Club* in 1979. Webster was editor of *Juke* magazine between 1976 and 1980. Al Webb was a *Juke* staff writer. Webster formed The Cruisers in 1979. The Cruisers issued one single in 1980, 'You Don't Know Me'/'Motorway', on Slipt Discs Records. This Cruisers is different from another Melbourne band called The Cruisers which existed between 1977 and 1978, comprising Shane Day (vocals), Chris Dyson (guitar), Roger Hart (guitar, vocals), John Lloyd (drums), Derek McCathie (bass) and Frank Savage (guitar).

The Crusaders

Formed: *1994*
Style: *Garage punk*
Original line-up: *James McDonald (guitar, vocals, harmonica), Chris Malters (guitar, vocals, harmonica), James Kendall (bass), Mick Baty (drums)*

Sydney band The Crusaders served up a brand of twanging, fuzzed-out, rabble-rousing music that was firmly rooted in the American 1960s garage/R&B tradition. During the 1980s, bands such as Wet Taxis, **The Lime Spiders**, **The Stems** and **The Bo-Weevils** pioneered a similar brand of garage/punk.

The band's CD EP, *Wylde Times at the Castle*, and full-length albums *Keep it Up* and *Fat, Drunk and Stupid* featured a sound comparable to contemporary US 1960s-inspired combos like The Mummies, The Gories and Jack O' Fire and Japanese band Teengenerate. Naturally enough, The Crusaders decked themselves out in chain mail and medieval smocks sporting the Maltese Cross. As well as playing gigs around Australia with other garage rock exponents like **Asteroid B-612**, The Raouls, Planet of the Apes and **The Hekawis**, in early 1997 The Crusaders undertook a tour of Spain, where loud 1960s garage/surf is well appreciated. Dionysus Records in Europe issued the band's single 'Yeah Yeah' and the 10-inch EP *Addicted to Fuzz*.

Albums: *Keep it Up* (Larsen, French import only, 1995), *Fat, Drunk and Stupid* (Swivel Disc, 1996).

The Crystal Set

Formed: *1984*
Style: *Rock*
Original line-up: *Russell Kilbey (bass, vocals), Phil Maher (guitar, vocals), Davey Ray Moor (keyboards, vocals), Charles Ratcliffe (drums)*

The Crystal Set emerged with a refined, atmospheric brand of psychedelia and rock that drew influences from UK artists as diverse as The Cure and Brian Eno. Crystal Set also suffered comparisons with local favourites **The Church**. The connection was that The Crystal Set's Russell Kilbey was the younger brother of **The Church**'s **Steve Kilbey**. The comparisons ended there because The Crystal Set's music had an identity of its own.

The Crystal Set issued its debut single, 'A Drop in the Ocean'/'She Counts Up the Days', on the Set label in December 1984. Red Eye reissued the single in November 1985, by which time The Crystal Set had built up a strong cult following around Sydney. For the finely crafted single 'Benefit of the Doubt'/'Don't be Surprised' (May 1985), Kilbey, Davey Moor and Phil Maher were augmented in the studio by drummers Mark Evans (on 'Don't be Surprised') and John Lloyd (on 'Benefit of the Doubt'). The line-up consolidated with the arrival of Tim Seckold (drums; ex-Catchcry) in time for the singles 'Wholly Holy'/'Hubble Bubble' (April 1987) and 'Who Needs Who Now?'/'From Now on' (December 1987), the confident debut album *From Now on* (May 1987) and the 12-inch EP *Cluster* (July 1988). Moor left the band in April 1988. The band broke up at the end of the year. Maher worked with Melbourne big band Mouse, while Kilbey played gigs with Floyd Vincent and the Child Brides.

In May 1989, Maher, Kilbey and Seckold reformed The Crystal Set with Luke Blackburn on bass, which allowed Kilbey to concentrate on vocals and acoustic guitar. The band issued the singles 'A Furious Mess'/'Some Attention' (June 1990), 'She Spits Out Stars'/'Gargoyle' (December 1990) and 'Thrive' (July 1991), the CD EP *Mixed Bag* ('Like a Treasure') (December), plus the album *Almost Pure* (April 1991). The *Umbrella* album (June 1990) was a 'Best of' collection. Following the Crystal Set's final break-up in 1991, Russell Kilbey worked with the short-lived Sex Industrie, then Warp Factor 9 with another brother John Kilbey. Warp Factor 9 issued the album *Five Days in a Photon Belt* in 1994. Russell then formed Turkeyneck Lasso and issued a self-titled album in 1996 on Id/PolyGram. In 1997, he collaborated with brother Steve on the ambient album *Gilt Trip* (Vicious Sloth Collectables). Russell remains active recording film soundtracks.

Albums: *From Now on* (Red Eye, 1987), *Cluster* (mini-album, Red Eye, 1988), *Umbrella* (Red Eye/Polydor, 1990), *Almost Pure* (Red Eye/Polydor, 1991).

The Cuckoos

Formed: *1982*
Style: *Pop rock*
Original line-up: *Graeme Forsythe (guitar, vocals), Alastair Wallace (guitar), Simon Kafas (bass, vocals), Stephen Kane (drums)*

The Cuckoos began life in Adelaide during 1979 as the Beat Detectives. The band specialised in a sunny brand of pop rock. Following a move to Melbourne, the Beat Detectives became The Cuckoos, and in 1983 The Cuckoos moved base once again to Sydney. The Hot label distributed the band's debut, four-track EP, 'On the Ghost Train', which appeared in August 1984. Barry Carter joined on bass to allow Simon Kafas freedom to concentrate on his frontman duties. The Cuckoos signed to Survival and issued the singles 'Wax Works'/'You Were a Devil' (1985) and 'Wheels of Your Heart' (1986) plus the *Sticks and Stones* album. The records were not successful and the band broke up in the late 1980s.

Album: *Sticks and Stones* (Survival, 1986).

Stephen Cummings

Style: *R&B, soul, funk*

Respected Melbourne singer Stephen Cummings (b. 1954) has enjoyed a long and successful career. His first band in the mid-1970s was Carlton cult outfit **The Pelaco Brothers** (with Joe Camilleri, Ed Bates and Johnny Topper). He fronted **The Sports** for six years before launching his solo career in 1982. Cummings reached a peak in the late 1980s with acclaimed albums like *Lovetown* and *A New Kind of Blue*, although his latter-day albums reflected a more adventurous spirit.

The Sports broke up at the end of 1981. Cummings issued his debut single 'We All Make Mistakes'/'Accordion to Mao' in January 1983. 'Stuck on Love'/'I Won't Give Up' (September 1983) and a cover of The O'Jays' 'Backstabbers'/'Hardly Working' (November) followed. The Martin Armiger-produced *Senso* album (August 1984) featured an all-star cast of studio musicians, including Peter Luscombe (drums), South African Ricky Fataar (percussion), Joe Creighton and Mark Ferrie (bass), Robert Goodge, Martin Armiger and **Andrew Pendlebury** (guitars), Vince Jones (cornet), Joe Camilleri and Wilbur Wilde (saxes), Jantra DeVilda, Duncan Veall and Stephen Bigger (keyboards) and backing vocalists Venetta Fields, Nick Smith, Stephanie Sproul and Linda Nutter.

Senso was aimed at the dance floor and yielded the soul/funk singles 'Gymnasium'/'Much Too Much' (July 1984) and 'Another Kick in the Head'/'Look Again Lovers' (October). Cummings issued one more dance pop single in 1985, 'What am I Going to Do?'/'Not Afraid' (August 1985). *This Wonderful Life* (September 1986) was a less boisterous, more intimate offering that included the singles 'Speak with Frankness'/'Ten Very Sad Songs' (July) and 'Love is Crucial'/'Things that I Have Done Wrong' (October). In 1987, Cummings collaborated with ex-**Sports'** guitarist **Andrew Pendlebury** on the single 'She Set Fire to the House'/'Country Joy' (September).

To promote his third album, *Lovetown* (January 1988), Cummings formed Stephen Cummings' Lovetown with Rebecca Barnard (backing vocals), Shane O'Mara (guitar), **Andrew Pendlebury** (guitar), Mick Girasole (bass; from **Black Sorrows**) and Peter Luscombe (drums; also **Black Sorrows**). Like *This Wonderful Life*, *Lovetown* was a very subtle, alluring, personal and mostly acoustic album. It was full of conversational, narrative vignettes from a world where the ironic title *Lovetown* certainly referred to Melbourne. Two singles were lifted from the set, 'Some Prayers be Answered'/'Last Round Up' (February 1988) and 'My Willingness'/'Time to Kill' (May).

Cummings then signed to True Tone and issued *A New Kind of Blue* (March 1989), the final instalment in a trilogy of albums that seduced the senses, rather than bludgeoned the eardrums. It contained three singles, 'Love is a Life'/'Here is Where the Sky is Blue' (October 1988), 'Your House is Falling'/'Question' (February 1989) and 'When the Day is Done'/'Who Listens to the Radio' (July). *A New Kind of Blue* won the 1989 Australian Record Industry Association (ARIA) Award for Best Adult Contemporary Album.

Cummings' fifth solo album, *Good Humour* (1990), and its three singles, 'Hell (You Put Me Through)', Sly Stone's 'Family Affair' and 'Stand Up (Love is the Greatest)', harked back to his funky dance-oriented *Senso* period. His backing band on *Good Humour* comprised O'Mara, Barnard and Nick Smith (ex-**Kevins**), with contributions from members of Sydney jazz outfit The Necks and Robert Goodge (guitar; ex-**I'm Talking**). For the 1992 album *Unguided Tour*, Cummings went for a more traditional rock approach. *Unguided Tour* yielded the singles 'Keep the Ball Rolling' (August) and 'Didn't Anybody Ever Say No to You' (October). Cummings' band on that album included regular collaborators O'Mara, Barnard and Luscombe, plus Bill McDonald (bass) and **Chris Abrahams** (keyboards). Cummings also issued his version of Elton John's 'Teacher I Need You' as a single in May 1993.

The Church's **Steve Kilbey** produced Cummings' seventh solo album, *Falling Swinger* (August 1994). Kilbey's input was heard to good effect on the adventurous CD singles 'September 13' (July) and 'The Big Room' (October). In 1994, Cummings dueted with Toni Childs on the single 'Fell from a Great Height'. Cummings enlisted Kilbey again for his eighth solo album, *Escapist* (September 1996), which continued the experimentation of *Falling Swinger*. Fellow Church members Marty Willson-Piper and Peter Koppes appeared as guests. The songs ranged from the countrified ballad 'Everything Breaks Your Heart' to the psychedelic-tinged mantra 'Sometimes'. In 1996, Minerva/Reed published Cummings' first novel, *Wonder Boy*. In October 1997, Cummings issued the compilation album *Puppet Pauper Pirate Poet Pawn & King*, which featured three new songs, including a cover of **Flash and the Pan**'s 'Waiting for a Train'.

Cummings remains a critically acclaimed artist whose records, despite being modest hits, have never reached a mass audience in the way that

James Reyne, **Daryl Braithwaite** and **John Farnham**'s have done. Interestingly, this perceptive and passionate songwriter is best known as the voice behind the television jingle 'I Feel Better Now' (which he co-wrote with Robert Goodge) for the Medibank Private health fund.

Albums: *Senso* (Regular, 1984), *This Wonderful Life* (Centre, 1986), *Lovetown* (Rampant, 1988), *A New Kind of Blue* (True Tone/EMI, 1989), *Good Humour* (True Tone/Polydor, 1990), *Unguided Tour* (Polydor, 1992), *Rollercoaster* (compilation, Polydor, 1993), *Falling Swinger* (Polydor, 1994), *Escapist* (Polydor, 1996) *Puppet Pauper Pirate Poet Pawn & King* (compilation, Polydor, 1997).

Peter Cupples (*see* Stylus)

CURIOUS (yellow)

Formed: *1987*
Style: *Pop*
Original line-up: *Karin Jansson (vocals, guitar), Phil 'Filthy' Hall (guitar; ex-Dropbears, Sardine v), Les White (bass; ex-Subterraneans), Michael 'Snapper' Knapp (drums; ex-Dropbears)*

Swedish-born Karin Jansson formed CURIOUS (yellow) as a vehicle for her singing and songwriting. Jansson took her band's name from the Swedish 1960s art-house soft-porn film *I Am Curious (yellow)*. She had previously been a key member of all-girl Swedish pop sensations Pink Champagne, and came to Australia in 1986 with **The Church**'s **Steve Kilbey**. Jansson co-wrote The Church's biggest hit 'Under the Milky Way' with Kilbey.

Kilbey also produced CURIOUS (yellow)'s debut 12-inch EP, *i am curious*, which came out in March 1988. Phil Maher from **The Crystal Set** contributed guitar to one track. With the release of the EP, CURIOUS (yellow) undertook an east coast tour with fellow Red Eye bands **The Crystal Set**, **The Bhagavad Guitars** and The Mexican Spitfires. Jansson issued two singles, 'Taken By Surprise' (August) and 'Love Itself' (November), and the album *Charms & Blues* (September) under the CURIOUS (yellow) moniker during 1990. Kilbey produced the album and co-wrote much of the material, which combined airy ambience with melancholy pop. Joining Jansson around that time were Les White, Mike Caen (guitar), Jim Bowman (guitar) and Mark Dawson (drums).

Album: *Charms & Blues* (Red Eye, 1990).

Custard

Formed: *1990*
Style: *Power pop*
Original line-up: *David McCormack (guitar, vocals; ex-Who's Gerald), Paul Medew (bass; ex-Who's Gerald), Shane Braun (drums)*

Brisbane band Custard combined fresh and energetic power pop with a quirky sense of humour and just a hint of kitsch. Frontman David McCormack displayed a ready grasp of the pop form, with a fine ear for catchy melodies and neat arrangements. Reference points ranged from US bands like Talking Heads, Devo, The Pixies and Pavement to UK popsters XTC.

Custard actually formed in 1989 under the name of Custard Gun. The line-up comprised David McCormack, Paul Medew, Shane Braun and James Straker (guitar). When Straker left at the start of 1990, Custard came into being, although the band did not get off the ground until Mat Strong (guitar) joined at the end of the year. With Custard in its formative stages, McCormack moonlighted with Brisbane artists Robert Moore (bass) and Glenn Thompson (drums) in the improvisational country band Cow. McCormack, Moore and Thompson backed ex-**Go-Between Robert Forster** on his second solo album, *Calling from a Country Phone* (June 1993), as well as backing him on tour (when they were known as Robert Forster's Silver Backwash). Cow issued the wildly eclectic album *Beard* in May 1996.

Meanwhile, Danny Herrenberg had replaced original Custard drummer Braun in December 1991. Danny Plant then replaced Herrenberg during April 1993. Custard issued its debut EP, 'Rockfish Anna', in late 1991. The band also contributed a re-recorded version of 'Rockfish Anna' to rooArt's *Youngblood 3* compilation. The EP *Bedford* ('Buttercup') and the band's first release on the Ra label, the CD EP *Gastanked*, came out in May and October 1992 respectively. The CD EP *Brisbane* (May 1993) and two more CD singles followed, 'Casanova' (November) and 'Singlette' (March 1994). 'Singlette' was the first single lifted from the band's debut, full-length album *Wahooti Fandango* (July 1994). The album yielded three more CD singles, 'Aloha Trombonist', 'Pack Yr Suitcases' and 'Alone'.

In 1995, Custard travelled to the USA to record its second album, *Wisenheimer*, at San Francisco's Hyde Street Studio with US producer Eric Drew Feldman (Captain Beefheart, Pere Ubu, P.J. Harvey, Frank Black). The first CD single lifted from the album, 'Apartment' (October 1995), was one of the

Custard

most popular independent hits of the year. It logged a #7 placing on the 1995 Triple J Hottest 100 list (the highest placing for an Australian band that year). *Wisenheimer* yielded three further CD singles, 'Lucky Star' (February 1996), 'Sunset Strip' (June) and 'Leisuremaster' (September). At the end of 1996, Cow's drummer, Glenn Thompson, replaced Plant. Custard then travelled to the USA again to record its third album (second with producer Feldman). Recorded at Easley Studios in Memphis, Tennessee (birthplace of quality albums from the likes of Sonic Youth, Jon Spencer Blues Explosion, Jeff Buckley and Pavement), the album *We Have the Technology* appeared in August 1997. The first CD single, 'Nice Bird', preceded it in June. The second, 'Anatomically Correct', followed in September.

Albums: Wahooti Fandango (Ra/rooArt/BMG, 1994), *Wisenheimer* (Ra/rooArt/BMG, 1995), *We Have the Technology* (Ra/rooArt/BMG, 1997).

Cybotron

Formed: *1976*
Style: *Electronic*
Original line-up: *Steve Maxwell Von Braund (synthesiser, sax), Geoff Green (synthesiser, organ, piano, mellotron)*

Steve Maxwell Von Braund was one of the first musicians in Australia to be influenced by the singular sounds emanating from Germany during the early 1970s. (Labelled 'krautrock', the German 'kosmische musik' movement encompassed Tangerine Dream, Ash Ra Tempel [sic], the Cosmic Jokers, Can, Neu!, Amon Düül II, etc.) The German-descended Von Braund was reputedly an associate of the likes of Hawkwind and Tangerine Dream.

In 1975, Von Braund recorded possibly Australia's first wholly 'electronic' album, *Monster Planet.* Von Braund played an array of synthesisers, electronic percussion and treated saxophones. Ex-**Master's Apprentices** frontman **Jim Keays** sang on the title track and ex-Aztecs member Gil Matthews engineered the album as well as playing drums and bass. Henry Vynhal played violin. In 1976, Von Braund unveiled the krautrock-inspired Cybotron with fellow electronic musician Geoff Green. Cybotron was a bona fide experimental outfit, and the band's eponymous debut album featured a mix of heavy synthesiser kinetics, organ drones and pulsating electronic beats ('mind-expanding brain food', to use the vernacular of the day).

Colossus (also engineered by Gil Matthews) featured a more progressive edge backed by a massive symphonic sound. Colin Butcher (drums, percussion, synthesiser) augmented the line-up for *Colossus. Implosion* followed the symphonic route, but with a pop tinge to a couple of tracks like the single 'Encounter'/'We'll be Around' (December 1980). Mark Jones (bass, guitar, keyboards) joined for *Implosion*, and engineer Matthews was back playing drums and keyboards. Other Cybotron singles were 'Colossus'/'Ride to Infinity' (May 1978) and 'Ride to Infinity'/'Xmas Hills' (May 1980). Green also contributed keyboards to the track 'Earthrise' on the cosmic concept album *Back from Beyond* by electronic musician Ian MacFarlane (no relation to the author). The album appeared on the Neutron Star label in 1980. MacFarlane issued one more album, *Void Spirit*, in the same ambient/progressive fusion vein.

Steve Maxwell Von Braund solo album: *Monster Planet* (Clear Light of Jupiter, 1975); ***Cybotron albums:*** *Cybotron* (Clear Light of Jupiter, 1976), *Saturday Night Live* (No label, 1976), *Colossus* (Champagne, 1978), *Implosion* (Cleopatra, 1980).

D

Daddy Cool

Formed: 1970
Style: Rock'n'roll
Original line-up: **Ross Wilson** *(vocals, guitar; ex-***Pink Finks, Party Machine, Procession, Sons of the Vegetal Mother***)*, **Ross Hannaford** *(lead guitar; ex-***Pink Finks, Party Machine,** *Quinn,* **Sons of the Vegetal Mother***), Wayne Duncan (bass; ex-Rondells,* **Sons of the Vegetal Mother***)*, **Gary Young** *(drums; ex-Silhouettes, Rondells,* **Ram Jam Big Band, Sons of the Vegetal Mother***)*

Daddy Cool

Up until 1971 in Australia, if a local album sold anywhere near the 10 000 mark there was almost cause for national celebration. That mark was shattered in fine style when Daddy Cool issued its bold, exuberant debut album *Daddy Who? Daddy Cool!* The album set a new yardstick by which Australian rock success could be measured by selling an unprecedented 60 000 copies.

Ross Wilson launched Daddy Cool as a bit of a joke. Daddy Cool was basically a rock'n'roll revival outfit, a humorous and entertaining diversion from the serious business of advancing the horizons of rock music. Wilson took the band's name from The Rays' 1957 hit, and it was a chance for him to indulge his passion for vintage Los Angeles rock'n'roll. The public caught on quickly and Daddy Cool soon became Australia's top group. Wilson and his partner **Ross Hannaford** first worked together in teenage R&B outfit **The Pink Finks**, before moving on to **The Party Machine**. Wilson was a member of **Procession** in England between March 1969 and early 1970. In the interim, Hannaford formed country-rock band Quinn.

It was while they were attempting to get their esoteric, special occasion progressive band **Sons of the Vegetal Mother** off the ground during 1970, that Wilson and Hannaford decided to play around with the rollicking, good-time Daddy Cool concept. **Gary Young** and Wayne Duncan completed the line-up. Daddy Cool's first gigs were in November 1970, at such notorious 'head' venues of the day as Melbourne's T.F. Much Ballroom. The Vegetal Mother concept was abandoned when Daddy Cool became a hit at the Odyssey Pop Festival, Wallacia in January 1971. By June Daddy Cool was #1 on the singles chart with the Australian dance classic 'Eagle Rock'/'Bom Bom'. Two months later, the band topped the album charts with *Daddy Who? Daddy Cool!*

The Wilson-penned 'Eagle Rock' was promoted by one of the first Australian rock film clips (made by Chris Löfven). It became the best-selling Australian single for 1971. 'Eagle Rock' has been reissued several times since, reaching the national Top 20 (#19) again in 1982 as a 12-inch EP (with 'Daddy Rocks Off' and 'Bom Bom' on the flip). 'Eagle Rock' reputedly inspired Elton John to write 'Crocodile Rock'. *Daddy Who? Daddy Cool!* has likewise been repackaged innumerable times, most recently on CD as part of the 1992 Daddy Cool box set *Totally Cool.* The box set was issued to commemorate the 21st anniversary of the release of *Daddy Who? Daddy Cool!* 'Eagle Rock' (1992 Dance Mix) came out as a CD single (July 1992).

In August 1971, Wilson took Daddy Cool to the US West Coast to tour, which included a week of dates at Los Angeles' famed Whisky A-go-go club. The band undertook two further USA tours

(October 1971 and March to May 1972), playing with the likes of Linda Ronstadt, Captain Beefheart, Flash Cadillac and the Continental Kids, Little Feat and Fleetwood Mac. While well received in certain regional pockets, the band did not make a national breakthrough. The American versions of *Daddy Who? Daddy Cool!* and *Teenage Heaven* on Warner/Reprise, plus a handful of singles, sold to a cult following.

In September 1971, 'Come Back Again'/'Just as Long as We're Together' reached #2 in Australia. That same month, Jeremy Noone (ex-**Company Caine**) joined. With Noone on board, Wilson was able to steer the band down a more progressive rock path. Noone contributed to the delightful five-track *D.C.E.P.* (#11 in December) and the single 'Hi Honey Ho'/'Don't Ever Leave Me' (#13 in December). The heavier sounding 'Hi Honey Ho' was a taster for the band's more adventurous second album.

By 1972, only **Billy Thorpe** and the Aztecs rivalled Daddy Cool in overall popularity. Daddy Cool's controversial *Sex, Dope, Rock'n'Roll: Teenage Heaven* album made the Top 10 in January 1972. Church and government leaders took offence at the album's title, plus the tracks 'Baby Let Me Bang Your Box' and 'Sixty Minute Man'. Interestingly, both songs had been hits in the USA during the 1950s for The Penguins and Billy Ward and the Dominoes respectively. *Sex, Dope, Rock'n'Roll: Teenage Heaven* possessed a more progressive rock edge, as displayed on material like the *Teen Love* extravaganza ('Teen Love', 'Drive in Movie' and 'Love in an F.J.') and 'Make Your Stash'. Reissue specialists Raven included 'Make Your Stash' on the essential Various Artists compilation *Golden Miles: Australian Progressive Rock 1969–1974* (1994).

Noone left in March 1972, and Ian Winter (guitar; ex-Pig Face, **Carson**) joined just in time for the third American tour. Winter gave the band a heavier, more blues-based sound which was heard on 'Teenage Blues'/'At the Rockhouse' (September 1972). The single had been recorded at Warner Studios in Los Angeles. Meanwhile, 'I'll Never Smile Again'/'Daddy Rocks Off' reached #27 in July. Then, in August, Wilson announced the band's break-up. Daddy Cool played its final concert at the Much More Ballroom on 13 August 1972. The band's final single for 1972 was 'Rock'n'Roll Lady'/'Cadillacin"(October 1972). The songs had been written by **Gary Young** and he also sang lead vocals. The single was credited to **Gary Young** with Daddy Cool. **Gary Young** and Wayne Duncan formed rockabilly/country outfit Hot Dog and issued two singles, 'Rock-A-Billy Beating Boogie Band'/'You Can't Shake the Boogie in Worn Down Rockin' Shoes' (April 1973) and 'The Saga of the Three Pigs'/'With You Tonight' (October 1973).

Rosses Wilson and Hannaford formed **Mighty Kong**, which lasted until December 1973. In September 1973, Wizard issued the double live album *Daddy Cool Live! The Last Drive-in Movie Show*, which had been recorded at the farewell concert a year before. It reached #20 on the national charts. Wizard also issued three singles from the album, 'One Night'/'Cadillacin" (February 1973), 'Flash in My Head'/'Little Darlin", 'Boy You're Paranoid' (June) and 'Duke of Earl'/'Jambalaya' (September). The heavier tracks like 'Flash in My Head' and 'Boy You're Paranoid' were an indication of where Wilson and Hannaford would head with **Mighty Kong**.

Following a 'one-off' re-formation for Sunbury 1974, Wilson decided to re-form Daddy Cool permanently. The band issued two singles on Wizard, 'All I Wanna Do is Rock Part I'/'All I Wanna Do is Rock Part II' (March 1974) and 'The Boogie Man'/'I Was a Teenage Creature' (July). Wizard also issued the *D.C. Hits EP*. By early 1975, new bands like **Skyhooks** and **AC/DC** were stealing Daddy Cool's thunder. Wilson had already produced **Skyhooks'** debut album, *Living in the 70's*. Daddy Cool's days were numbered. In April 1975, Wilson added Ian 'Gunther' Gorman (guitar; ex-**Home**) in an attempt to revitalise the band's sound. In June 1975, a car accident put Wayne Duncan out of action, so Hannaford switched to bass while Wayne Burt (ex-Rock Granite and the Profiles) joined on guitar. The band made its final Melbourne appearance at Reefer Cabaret on 13 September 1975 and, following two weeks of gigs in Sydney, called it quits.

The Daddy Cool legend has lived on with the release of several 'Best of' collections over the years, including the popular *Daddy's Coolest* (#10 in October 1982) and the *Totally Cool* box set (September 1992). One of the most interesting posthumous albums was the *The Missing Masters* compilation (March 1981), which drew together one side of rare studio selections with a side of previously unissued live recordings.

With the break-up of Daddy Cool, Wilson set up the Oz Records label with Glenn Wheatley. Wilson launched his solo career with the single 'Living in the Land of Oz'/'Who's Gonna Love You Tonight?' (from the soundtrack to the Chris Löfven film *Oz*). He formed **Mondo Rock** in 1976 and has continued to record as a solo artist since. **Ross Hannaford** attempted to form a new band with Joe Camilleri (ex-**Pelaco Brothers**) before the singer went off to join **Jo Jo Zep and the Falcons**. Hannaford went on to work with **Billy T**, One Foundation, Bambu, Lucky Dog, The Rocking Emus, **Goanna**, Dianna Kiss and many others. **Gary Young** became a long-term member of **Jo Jo Zep and the Falcons** before fronting The Rocking Emus. Since then he has played with Rock Doctors, the **Phil Manning** Trio, **Dancehall Racketeers**, **The Black Sorrows**, Andy Baylor's Cajun Combo, etc. Wayne Duncan went to Gulliver's Travels, The Living Legends, Bambu, The Rocking Emus, The Gentlemen, Wilbur Wilde's Blowout etc.

In 1994 Daddy Cool re-formed in order to record two new songs for the 'Ballad of Oz' CD single. When combined with **Skyhooks'** 'Happy Hippy Hut', it reached #35 nationally (August 1994). In 1996, Hannaford and Duncan joined forces with Frankie J. Holden and Wilbur Wilde (both ex-**Ol'55**), Bongo Starkie and Freddy Strauks (both ex-**Skyhooks**) as Ol' Skydaddys to play the cabaret circuit.

Albums: *Daddy Who? Daddy Cool!* (Sparmac, 1971), *Sex, Dope, Rock'n'Roll: Teenage Heaven* (Sparmac, 1972), *Daddy Cool's Golden Hits* (Sparmac, 1972), *Daddy Cool Live! The Last Drive-in Movie Show* (Wizard, 1973), *The Daddy Cool Story* (Music For Pleasure, 1973), *The Best of Daddy Cool* (Summit, 1974), *The Greatest Hits* (Wizard, 1976), *Daddy Who? Daddy Gold* (reissue of first album; Wizard, 1977), *The Missing Masters* (Wizard, 1981), *The Daddy Cool Collection* (Axis, 1982), *Daddy's Coolest* (Wizard, 1982), *Daddy's Coolest Volume II* (Wizard, 1986), *Totally Cool* (21st anniversary box set; Mega/Sony, 1992), *Daddy's Greatest and Coolest Hits* (Mega/Sony, 1994).

The Dagoes

Formed: *1978*
Style: *Rock*
Original line-up: *Ron Dago (real name Ron Putens, vocals), Tony Rome (real name Neil Perryman, guitar), Frankie Thomas (real name Doug Thomas, guitar), Rickie Gee (real name Rick Gac, bass), Johnny Tomato (real name Beau Kostyszyn, drums)*

The South Australian capital of Adelaide (the City of Churches) is well known for its rock'n'roll tradition. After all, **The Master's Apprentices**, **The Twilights**, **The Angels** and **Cold Chisel** all got their start there, and the city helped foster the growth and success of Bon Scott's pre-**AC/DC** band **Fraternity**. Less well known is the history of the city's independent scene of the late 1970s/early 1980s.

The first generation of Adelaide punk/new wave bands included **Young Modern**, **JAB**, **X-Ray-Z**, Black Chrome, Warm Jets, The Accountants and The Dagoes. The nucleus of The Dagoes came together in early 1978 as Daryl Breakaway and the Niggers. The band became The Dagoes in May 1978 with the arrival of Doug Thomas. Dick Dago (real name Richard Cant, vocals) replaced Ron Putens in October 1978 and Otis (real name Quentin Lynne, bass) replaced Rick Gee in March 1979. The Dagoes became The Tony Rome Band in May 1979 after Lilly Pointless (real name Lucy Potter, backing vocals) and Gina Maria Dago (real name Cathy Fargher, backing vocals) joined. They reverted to The Dagoes moniker when Spiro Aggro (real name Ian Reedy, guitar) joined in September. Aggro left in October and Turk Nancarrow (real name Geoff Short, drums) replaced Johnny Tomato who switched to keyboards. The Dagoes broke up in December 1979.

The Dagoes appeared on two of the first independent cassette releases in 1978, *Live At the Marryatville* (with The Accountants and The U-Bombs) and *An Evening with the Dagoes*. Both had been recorded live. Having dubbed themselves The 'Legendary' Dagoes, the band became a veritable institution in Adelaide. The December 1979 line-up reconvened in February 1980 and recorded the three-track EP *The Dagoes Sell Soul* which showed the band's US-influenced garage roots (the EP included a cover version of Roky Erickson's pre-13th Floor Elevators band The Spades' 'We Sell Soul').

Doug Thomas financed the EP's release for his newly formed Greasy Pop label. At that stage, Greasy Pop existed solely for The Dagoes and was the perfect outlet for the band's American-oriented rock'n'roll. For most of 1980, The Dagoes comprised Cant, Rome, Thomas, Tomato, Nancarrow, Pointless, Lou Ouji (real name Ian List, bass) and Arna Terrazzo (real name Arna Eyers-White, backing vocals). Gino Earthquake (real name Nigel Sweeting, bass) replaced List and that line-up recorded the double single 'It's You'/Kid's Got Style' (live), 'This Perfect Band' (live); 'Rollin' on'/'Somehow', 'Ten Years on' (July 1981). Sydney-based independent label Phantom reissued two tracks ('Ten Years on' and 'Somehow') from the double set as a single in August 1981. Cant and Sweeting left in late 1981, and the line-up of Rome, Thomas, Tomato, Nancarrow, Dean Martin (real name James Tizard, bass) and Di Palma (vocals) recorded the single 'Daunting'/'Blood on My Face' (August 1982). Geoff Pin (real name Geoff Simpson, bass) replaced Martin but the band broke up at the end of 1982.

Thomas, Nancarrow and Ian List recorded the

single 'Assassination'/'Suicide' as The Assassins which came out in February 1983. At the same time, Thomas, List, Tizard and Greg Swanborough (drums) were in the process of forming The Spikes. Taking their name from one of Lou Reed's pre-Velvet Underground bands The (Falling) Spikes, List's Spikes played hard-edged, swampy acid-pop. Other members who passed through the band's ranks included Mick Brown (vocals), Jim Selene (bass), Chris Willard (bass), Sheree Goldsworthy (bass) and Paul Sharman (drums). The Spikes issued three singles, 'She's Melting'/'Theme from Acid Beach' (December 1983), 'A Bloody Mess'/'The Meaning of Life', 'Bang Shang A Lang' (June 1985) and 'River of Love'/'Pass Myself' (June 1986), the mini-album *6 Sharp Cuts* (July 1985) and the album *Colour in a Black Forest* (September 1986) on Thomas' Greasy Pop label. Vic Conrad from **The Garden Path** contributed keyboards to *Colour in a Black Forest.*

Meanwhile, back in 1984, Tony Rome, Richard Cant and Johnny Tomato re-formed The Dagoes with Peter Roth (lead guitar), Phil Hannaford (bass) and Andrew Griffiths (drums). That line-up was short-lived but did record the single 'Heartbeat'/'Hey Man' for Greasy Pop (August 1984). Ian List went on to form The UVs with such Adelaide luminaries as Doug Thomas, Jeff Stephens (guitar; on loan from **Exploding White Mice**), Chris Willard (bass; from **Lizard Train**) and David Bunney (drums; from **Exploding White Mice**). Ian List and The UVs issued one self-titled 12-inch EP on Greasy Pop (shared with The Assassins' 'Kill the Prime Minister'; 1990). US label Sympathy For The Record Industry issued the UVs single 'Dropping Bombs' (1989), while UK label Zinger issued the album *Crayon Jungle* (1989).

In 1988, The Dagoes with Doug Thomas re-formed for a run of tenth anniversary shows. In 1990, Greasy Pop issued the *Ten Years on 1980–1990* single ('Vatican Stomp'/'I Can Do What I Want'). In September 1994, Ian List and Neil Perryman compiled all The Dagoes' material on the CD collection *Hot & Tasty Supreme.* In 1995, Doug Thomas formed power pop band Satellite 5 with John Rushin (vocals), Phil Bradley (guitar; ex-Jackals), Howard Shawcross (bass; ex-**Elks**, Howard I Know, Jackals) and James Baker (drums; ex-**Victims**, **Scientists**, **Hoodoo Gurus**, **Beasts of Bourbon**, **Dubrovniks**).

Dagoes album: *Hot & Tasty Supreme* (Greasy Pop, 1994); ***Spikes albums:*** *6 Sharp Cuts* (mini-album, Big Time/EMI, 1985), *Colour in a Black Forest* (Greasy Pop, 1986; reissued on CD in 1994 with the mini-album and early single cuts added).

The Daisygrinders

Formed: *1991*
Style: *Indie guitar rock*
Original line-up: *Andrew Hunter (bass, vocals), Rosie (guitar, vocals), Adrian (guitar, vocals), Drew Beaman (drums, vocals)*

The Daisygrinders formed in the New South Wales country town of Bathurst, relocating to Sydney a year later. The band's debut CD EP/10-inch vinyl EP, 'Throwlilly' (December 1992), displayed a ready grasp of heavy riffs but suffered from poor sound quality. The second CD EP, 'Roamin' Bruce' (June 1993), featured stronger production. Rohan Bridge and Adam Young replaced Rosie and Adrian in time for the limited edition CD EP 'Previval' (which included a mellifluous cover of Neil Young's 'Down By the River') and the CD single 'Cardriver'. The band's sonic blast full-length, debut album *Joe Velocity* and its CD single 'Yo Yo' came out in early 1995.

Album: *Joe Velocity* (Half a Cow, 1995).

Erl Dalby and Pyramid

Formed: *1969*
Style: *Pop*
Original line-up: *Erl Dalby (vocals), George Kent (vocals), Jim Squadrito (vocals), Russell Bayne (guitar), Roy Giles (bass), Bob Jourdan (drums)*

Singer Erl Dalby fronted Wollongong band Erl's Court between 1967 and 1969. Erl's Court recorded the Vanda and Young song 'Can't Wait for September' but broke up following the session. Dalby joined Sydney band Pyramid and, having taken the tapes of 'Can't Wait for September' with him, Pyramid then recorded over the original backing tracks.

The DuMonde label issued the track as a single with 'Let Me Be Yours Till Tomorrow' on the flip, and it became a minor hit in Sydney during November 1970. Dalby issued a solo single 'Send Suzanna Home'/'Teach Me How to Fly' on the Banner label (August 1971), followed by another Pyramid single, 'Fisherman'/'Celebrate'. Dalby left Pyramid at the end of 1971 and recorded a second solo single with producer Rory Thomas (ex-**Questions**, **Affair**) 'Candy'/'Pasadena' (April 1972). The B-side was another Vanda and Young composition also covered by **John Paul Young**. Dalby travelled to the UK where he studied at the Royal Academy of Dramatic Arts (RADA). He returned to Australia in 1977, did some acting in soapies and then became fully involved in martial arts.

Alan Dale and the Houserockers

Formed: *1956*
Style: *Rock'n'roll*
Original line-up: *Alan Dale (vocals), Bobby Broome (guitar), John Bolton (sax), John Carter (piano), Keith Sharrat (bass), Don Prouse (drums)*

Alongside **Johnny O'Keefe** and **Col Joye**, Alan Dale was one of Sydney's original rock'n'rollers. Inspired by the film *Blackboard Jungle* and its opening song, Bill Haley and the Comets' 'Rock Around the Clock', Dale formed his first band, The Houserockers, in late 1956. Soon The Houserockers were competing with the only other rock'n'roll bands around, **Johnny O'Keefe** and the Dee Jays and **Col Joye** and the Joy Boys.

The Houserockers promoted their own dances and appeared on television shows *Accent on Youth* and *Tonight*. They belted out all Haley's hits of the day like 'Razzle Dazzle', 'Shake, Rattle and Roll' and 'Rock Around the Clock'. By the end of 1957, the Houserockers line-up comprised Sharrat, Prouse, Sonny Neville (guitar), Bob Bertles (sax) and Brian Turvey (piano). Johnny Burns replaced Prouse soon after. In 1958, Dale dispensed with The Houserockers to form The Casuals with Brian Turvey, Gordon Holmes (sax), John Dodds (drums), Ken Anderson (bass, sax) and John Cameron (guitar). That line-up remained stable for five years.

Alan Dale and the Casuals made regular appearances on **Johnny O'Keefe's** *Six O'Clock Rock* television show, and then signed to EMI/Columbia. The Casuals' debut single was a cover of Bo Diddley's 'Crackin' Up' backed by Chuck Berry's 'Back in the USA' (August 1959). The Casuals recorded four more singles: 'Love Me All the Time'/'Dance the Kangaroo Hop', 'Torment'/'You Threw a Dart', 'Very Young'/'Chewing Gum' and 'Two Innocent Lovers'/'Tiara'. The Casuals broke up in 1962. In 1983, Raven Records compiled the 15-track Alan Dale and the Houserockers album *Crackin' Up*, which also contained two previously unissued songs and five live tracks.

Album: *Crackin' Up* (Raven, 1983).

Dancehall Racketeers

Formed: *1981*
Style: *Rockabilly, western swing*
Original line-up: *Andy Baylor (fiddle, guitars, mandolin, vocals), Donal Baylor (fiddle, mandolin), Peter Baylor (fiddle, guitar, vocals)*

The Baylor brothers Andrew, Donal and Peter formed the nucleus of Melbourne band Dancehall Racketeers. The band mixed rockabilly with western swing to produce a unique combination. The band issued two EPs, 'Bottle Baby Boogie' and 'Rocket 88', and two singles, 'I've Got a Hole in My Pocket'/'Zydeco Cha Cha' and 'Alons a Layfayette'/'Deep Elm', on the local Preston label.

The 1984 line-up of the three Baylor brothers joined by Rick Dempster (steel guitar, harmonica, vocals; ex-Autodrifters) and Eddie Colbourne (drums) contributed the tracks 'We're Gonna Teach You to Rock' and 'In the Mood' to the Various Artists album *Regular Rockabilly* on the Regular label (1984). The 1986 line-up of Dancehall Racketeers included Andy, Donal, Dempster, Ian Hayes (double bass, vocals) and **Gary Young** (drums; ex-**Daddy Cool, Jo Jo Zep and the Falcons**). The band's self-titled debut album (October 1986) featured a mix of swing and rockabilly covers, with three Andy Baylor originals in the same style.

Since 1990, Andy Baylor has worked with his Cajun Combo, drawing on a more varied New Orleans-styled sound. The line-up has included Young, Wayne Duncan (another old **Daddy Cool** alumnus on bass), Peter Linden (steel guitar), George Butrumlis (piano accordian; ex-**Black Sorrows**) and Lisa Miller (vocals) among others. Cajun Combo issued one self-titled album in 1991.

Albums: *Dancehall Racketeers* (Nicholls'n'Dimes/RCA, 1986), *Andy Baylor's Cajun Combo* (1991).

Bryan Davies

Style: *Pop*

As Noel McGrath has pointed out, British-born, Sydney-based singer Bryan Davies (b. 1944) was Australia's answer to the American teen-idol trend of the early 1960s. The US teen-idols included the likes of Bobby Rydell, Fabian, Frankie Avalon, Paul Anka, Bobby Vee and Brian Hyland. Inevitably, these charming, wholesome, well-mannered (with just a teasing hint of wildness) teenage dreamboats offered the kind of safe, bland image that wild rockers like Jerry Lee Lewis, Gene Vincent, Chuck Berry and Eddie Cochran had revolted against in the first place.

Davies appealed to teenagers and mums alike, and for that reason became popular on *Bandstand* and scored a couple of teendream pop hit singles, including 'Dream Girl'/'Then I'll Know' (#1 in Sydney, July 1961) and 'Five Foot Two'/'Ladder of Love' (#4 in October 1961). All up, he recorded ten singles for HMV and Columbia between 1961 and 1964; 'Sad Sixteen'/'Don't Love' (March 1961), 'Slicin' Sand Twist'/'Twist'n'Twirlin'' (February

1962), 'Ten Pin Bowling'/'You're Gonna Fall' (Sydney #18, July), 'Without a Shoulder to Cry on'/'Don't Ever, No Never' (August), 'My Dream of You'/'Tell the Other Guy' (January 1963), 'Biggity Big'/'Rich Boy' (May), 'Raincoat in the River'/'In Your Shoes' (May 1964) and 'I Don't Like to Be Alone'/'Love and Money' (November).

Also, at the age of 17, Davies became the youngest compere of a national television show when the *Bryan Davies Show* went to air on the ABC during March 1962. Davies appeared in the Christmas 1963 'surfing musical' *Once Upon a Surfie*. Also in the cast were **Dig Richards**, Jackie Weaver, **Lucky Starr**, Jay Justin, **Rob E.G.**, Jan Green and **The Delltones**. In 1964, Davies travelled to London and recorded with British composer and producer Norrie Paramour.

On his return to Australia, Davies had adopted a more Beatles-influenced style and appearance. Between 1965 and 1968, he recorded a further eight singles for HMV, 'I'm Gonna Make You Cry'/'Watch What You Say' (February 1965), 'Skinny Minnie'/'Should Have Stayed in Bed' (April 1965), 'I Need You'/'The Girl I Love' (November 1965), 'Do You Mind?'/'Ginny Come Lately' (1966), 'My Name is Mud'/'Why?' (1966), 'Alberta'/'I Only Dream of You' (Sydney #18, February 1967), 'Night and Day'/'Together By Myself' (August) and 'You Won't Be the Last'/'End of Another Day' (February 1968). By the late 1960s, Davies had moved into cabaret and television work.

Albums: *On My Way* (EMI/HMV, 1965), *Together by Myself* (EMI/Columbia, 1968).

Leo De Castro

Style: *Funk, soul, country*

For most of the 1970s and 1980s, New Zealand-born Leo De Castro was one of the best soul singers working in Australia. During the 1970s in particular, Leo was a permanent fixture of the pub/concert/festival circuit and was praised for his vocal abilities. De Castro was always able to gather quality musicians around him, but unfortunately he was under-recorded. He returned to New Zealand in 1995.

De Castro's first band was The Dallas Four in New Zealand. He came to Australia in 1969 and joined The Browns, which comprised Les Stacpool (guitar; ex-**Chessmen**, **Merv Benton** and the Tamlas), Ronnie Peel (bass; ex-**Missing Links**, **Pleazers**, **Rockwell T. James** and the Rhythm Aces) and **Ray Arnott** (drums; ex-Chelsea Set). The Browns also worked with singer Bernadette O'Neill, and were variously referred to as Leo and the Browns or Bernadette and the Browns.

Leo and Friends comprised De Castro, John Capek (piano, vocals), Rob MacKenzie (guitar), Jeremy Noone (sax) and Kevin Murphy (drums; ex-**Wild Cherries**). In September 1970, De Castro formed **King Harvest**. When that band broke up in September 1971, he formed the short-lived Flite with Barry Sullivan (bass; ex-Thursday's Children, **Wild Cherries**, **Chain**, **Carson**), Barry Harvey (drums; ex-Thursday's Children, **Wild Cherries**, **Chain**, **King Harvest**), Vince Melouney (guitar; ex-**Billy Thorpe** and the Aztecs, **Bee Gees**, **Fanny Adams**, **Cleves**) and John Capek (piano; ex-**Carson**, Meating, **King Harvest**).

In December 1971, De Castro formed **Friends** with Charlie Tumahai (vocals, percussion; ex-**Healing Force**, **Chain**). **Friends** broke up two years later and, after a brief period with New King Harvest, Leo formed De Castro in early 1974. Moving away from the progressive rock of **Friends**, the band played a mix of funk, soul, rock and blues. It was a style De Castro would pursue for the rest of his career. The line-up was completed by Rob Grey (keyboards), Ian 'Willy' Winter (guitar; ex-**Carson**, **Daddy Cool**), John Young (bass) and Steve Webb (drums; ex-**Blackfeather**, **Duck**, Tramp). Later in the year, De Castro joined Sydney funk outfit **Johnny Rocco Band**. The band recorded the first version of 'Heading in the Right Direction', co-written by Rocco guitarist Mark Punch and Garry Paige. Singer **Renée Geyer** later made the song famous via her definitive reading.

In 1976, De Castro formed Cahoots with Tui Richards (guitar; ex-New King Harvest, **Johnny Rocco Band**, Powerhouse), Billy Rylands (guitar; ex-**Freshwater**, **Stevie Wright** Band), Phil Pritchard (guitar; ex-Highway, Miss Universe), George Limbidis (bass; ex-**Freshwater**, Highway, Miss Universe) and Doug McDonald (drums; ex-Powerhouse). In May 1977, the band was billed as Leo De Castro and Rocco with Mark Punch back in the line-up. By the end of the year, it was the Leo De Castro Band. Then came Heavy Division in 1978 with Tui Richards, Russell Smith (guitar; ex-**Cam-Pact**, **Company Caine**, **Mighty Kong**, **Billy T**), Tim Partridge (bass; ex-Clockwork Oringe, **Mighty Kong**, **Kevin Borich Express**) and John Watson (drums).

By December 1978, it was Leo De Castro and Babylon with Tui Richards, Billy Rylands, Thomas Reid (bass) and John McInerney (drums; ex-**Company Caine**, **Foreday Riders**). Babylon recorded one single for Warner in 1979, a cover of Elvis Presley's 'Suspicious Minds'/'Hindley Street'. In the early 1980s, De Castro moved to Tasmania and formed Toots and the Legmen with Tim Partridge, Peter Hutchinson (guitar), David McLeod (keyboards) and Conrad Parkes (drums). By 1985, it was Leo and Friends with Leigh Taafe (guitar), Damien Bernard (bass) and Frank Bernard (drums).

Next came The Early Kookas with Tim Partridge, Ross Kerr (guitar) and Roger Pickering (drums), followed by The Kingpins with Partridge, Dave Berry (guitar), Derek Trehair (sax) and Steve Marskell (drums). De Castro continued to perform solo around Tasmania. In October 1987, De Castro assembled a group of musicians under the Friends banner for a series of shows at The Basement in Sydney. The line-up comprised Jimmy Doyle (guitar), Mark Punch (guitar), Dave McRae (piano), Dave Green (bass), Mark Kennedy (drums), Andy Thompson (sax), Jason Brewer (sax), Jason McDermid (trumpet) and Sally King (guest vocals). The shows produced the cassette album *Live at the Basement*.

In 1995, De Castro returned to New Zealand with the purpose of reuniting with his former **Friends** comrade Charlie Tumahai. Charlie had been playing bass with The Herbs for the previous ten years. Sadly, Tumahai died in December 1995 from a heart attack. Leo De Castro remains but a footnote in the history of Australian rock. Over the course of 25 years, Leo recorded just seven singles (two with **King Harvest**, two with **Friends**, two with **Johnny Rocco Band** and one with Babylon) plus one album (with **Johnny Rocco Band**). The records reveal De Castro to be the owner of a passionate, soulful voice.

The De Kroo Brothers

Formed: *1959*
Style: *Harmony pop*
Original line-up: *Leo De Kroo (vocals, guitar), Doug De Kroo (vocals, guitar)*

Dutch-descended, Perth-raised siblings Leo and Doug De Kroo joined rock'n'roll band The Roulettes in 1958. Stepping out as a singer/songwriter/guitar playing duo, Leo and Doug became The De Kroo Brothers (in the manner of The Everly Brothers). The duo moved to Sydney in 1960 and signed to EMI/Columbia.

Columbia issued the duo's debut single, 'On the Job Too Long'/'Head Over Heels', in February 1960, and then six days later released a second single, 'Loveland'/'Cause I Like It'. The De Kroo Brothers were singing a mix of rockabilly, country and pop harmonies, but on the sessions for the singles they were backed by jazz band the Billy Antman Quintet and female back-up singers The Rock-a-Belles. Oddly, the self-penned B-side 'Head Over Heels' was simply credited to Leo De Kroo. The duo began appearing on television shows *Six O'Clock Rock*, *Bandstand* and *Teen Time*. It was another year before Columbia issued the third De Kroo single 'Cave in'/'Love's a Funny Little Game' (March 1961). Backing for this session was provided by The Dee Jays with Warren Carr on piano and George Golla on lead guitar.

The De Kroo Brothers signed to Festival and issued 'Don't Let the Stars Get in Your Eyes'/'All for the Love of You' (September 1961). After two further singles, 'Road to Gundagai'/'Peggy Sue' (March 1962) and 'Tears of Pity'/'It Never Came True' (February 1963), the duo finally had a Top 40 hit with '(And Her Name is) Scarlet'/'All Right, Be That Way' (#4 in Sydney, September 1963). Festival issued three more singles, 'Foggy Mountain Top'/'Movin' Out' (February 1964), 'Buena Suerte'/'Love is a Meaningless Word' (May 1964) and 'Oh Suzie Darling'/'I Run in Circles' (January 1965), plus a self-titled album. By 1965, The De Kroo Brothers had retired and set up a guitar school in Sydney.

Albums: *The De Kroo Brothers* (Festival, 1964), *Scarlet: The Festival File* (Festival, 1988), *Collector's Album* (Canetoad, 1988).

De Mont

Formed: *1987*
Style: *Hard rock*
Original line-up: *Craig Morrison (vocals), Terry Mandryk (guitar), Peter James (keyboards), Grant Byrne (bass), Rod Willner (drums)*

Craig Morrison was the son of 1960s Australian rock'n'roll/country music stalwart **Lucky Starr**. At a young age he began working with his father's travelling shows, before turning his hand to acting in television soapies like *Sons and Daughters*. In 1987, he moved to the New South Wales Central Coast, two hours north of Sydney, where he formed De Mont as a covers band to play the local pub circuit.

De Mont began to attract a following on the Sydney suburban pub scene. The band's first big break came when offered a support slot with **John Farnham**, playing in front of 27 000 people. The band came to the attention of producer Peter Dawkins (via **Lucky Starr**), who drew up a deal with his Giant label. The band's debut single, 'I Want Your Body'/'Strange World', came out in April 1989, followed by the *Body Language* album and a second single, 'Close to the Edge'/'Too Late', in September.

The album highlighted the band's anthemic, melodic Adult Oriented Rock (AOR) style, but it lacked the outstanding songs required to attract attention further afield. De Mont toured as support act to ex-**Cold Chisel** guitarist **Ian Moss**, plus visiting US glam rockers Mötley Crüe (April 1990). The band issued a third single, 'So Easy', later in the year. De Mont broke up a year later without having made a lasting impact. The posthumous album *R.I.P. PED* combined a selection of unissued studio tracks and live cuts.

Albums: *Body Language* (Giant, 1989), *R.I.P. PED* (M Records, 1993).

Lucy De Soto Band (*see* Peter Wells)

Dead Can Dance (DCD)

Formed: *1981*
Style: *Ambient*
Original line-up: *Lisa Gerrard (vocals; ex-Microfilm), Brendan Perry (vocals), Paul Erikson (bass), Simon Monroe (aka Des Hefner, drums; ex-Marching Girls)*

In the tradition of UK bands like The Cocteau Twins and This Mortal Coil, Dead Can Dance (DCD) constructed soundscapes of mesmerising grandeur and solemn beauty. The DCD sound is often referred to as 'world music', with its embracement of African polyrhythms, Gaelic folk, Gregorian chants, Middle Eastern mantras and art-rock. DCD boasts a strong following in Europe and America, but in Australia the duo remains something of a mystery.

The original DCD came together in Melbourne during August 1981 when Lisa Gerrard and UK-born Brendan Perry joined forces. The original line-up listed above only lasted a short time. Gerrard had previously sung with new wave band Microfilm. The line-up of Microfilm was Gerrard, Marshall Butters (guitar), Gordon Pitt (guitar), Nique Delaney (bass) and Shane Brown (drums). Microfilm issued one independent single, 'Centrefold'/'Window' (July 1980), and had the track 'Summer House' included on the Various Artists album *From Belgrave with Love* (Cleopatra, 1981). Gerrard's solo track 'Mossaic' also appeared on that compilation. Even at that stage, Gerrard's voice sounded eccentric. With the break-up of Microfilm, Gerrard joined DCD and she and Perry moved to the UK in May 1982. Gordon Pitt went on to **Dorian Gray** and **John Justin and the Thunderwings**. Nique Delaney became actor Nique Needles who had parts in Richard Lowenstein's feature film *Dogs in Space* (1987) plus the ABC-TV drama series *The Four Minute Mile* (as athlete John Landy) and *Janus*.

Once settled in the UK, DCD signed to 4AD (home to **The Birthday Party**, The Cocteau Twins and This Mortal Coil) and issued the four-track EP *Garden of the Arcane Delights* plus the albums *Dead Can Dance* and *Spleen and Ideal*. The first album featured drum-driven, ambient guitar music with chanting, singing and howling from Gerrard and Perry. The original UK DCD line-up also included Peter Ulrich, Scott Rogers and James Pinker. For the second album, DCD was down to the singing duo, with ethereal keyboards replacing guitars, and with cello, tympani and trombones blended. The duo's sixth album, *Into the Labyrinth*, sold 500 000 copies worldwide. (Indeed, DCD is the biggest selling act on the 4AD label.) DCD songs have featured in the US art-house film *Baraka* ('The Host of the Seraphim'), the Spanish film *El Nino de la Luna* (in which Gerrard also took a role), and the French film *Sahara Blue*, as well as a chase sequence in US cop show *Miami Vice*.

In 1994, during a world tour, DCD recorded the double live album *Toward the Within* in California before an invited audience. The concert was also released on video. DCD toured Australia briefly in 1995 and issued the compilation *A Passage of Time*. DCD issued its ninth album, *Spiritchaser*, in 1996. Gerrard issued a solo album, *The Mirror Pool*, in 1995.

Albums: *Dead Can Dance* (4AD, 1984), *Spleen and Ideal* (4AD, 1985), *Within the Realms of A Dying Sun* (4AD, 1986), *The Serpent's Egg* (4AD, 1988), *Aion* (4AD, 1990), *Into the Labyrinth* (4AD, 1993), *Toward the Within* (4AD, 1994), *A Passage of Time* (4AD, 1995), *Spiritchaser* (4AD, 1996); ***Lisa Gerrard solo album:*** *The Mirror Pool* (4AD, 1995).

The Deadly Hume

Formed: *1985*
Style: *Rock, blues*
Original line-up: *Greg Perano (vocals, guitar; ex-*__Hunters & Collectors,__ *Love Rodeo), Stephen 'Bones' Martin (guitar; ex-Playful Kittens, Fester Brothers), Marc Scully (bass; ex-Love Rodeo), Stuart Brown (drums)*

Greg Perano was one of the founder-movers of the original version of Melbourne institution **Hunters & Collectors**. When he left that band at the end of 1983, he relocated to Sydney. Initially he joined short-lived country trio Love Rodeo with **Roddy Radalj** (guitar, vocals; ex-**Scientists**, Rockets, Le Hoodoo Gurus, **Johnnys**) and Marc Scully (bass).

A year later, Love Rodeo had run its course and Radalj moved on to his next project which eventually became **The Dubrovniks**. Love Rodeo did reconvene briefly at the start of 1989 to record the 'Love Yodel No. 9'/'Would You Believe?' single (July 1989) for the Timberyard label. Meanwhile, at the end of 1985, Perano and Scully formed The

Deadly Hume with Bones Martin from The Fester Brothers. The Deadly Hume played a ragged brand of angst-ridden blues driven by a manic, rhythmic sense of urgency. The band's music had something in common with Melbourne counterparts like **The Wreckery**, **Blue Ruin** and even **Hunters & Collectors**. The first Deadly Hume record was an unofficial 12-inch EP on the Bulb label called *Starving Whipped*.

The band signed to the Phantom label and issued its debut single, 'Passenger Blues'/'Bed as Big as a Boat', in December 1986. Next came the band's debut album, *Me, Grandma, Iliko and Hilarian* (September 1987), plus the promotional single 'Fine Line' (250 copies only). Having been recorded live on to a two-track machine, the album featured a raw, brutal sound that tended to bludgeon rather than entice. Perano's monotone vocals, Martin's spiky guitar and the rumbling rhythm section certainly contributed to the uneasy listening. In October 1988, The Deadly Hume appeared on a rare gig giveaway album *Assorted Desecrations and Magnificent Mutations*, as part of Phantom's tenth anniversary celebrations. The band covered a song by former Phantom group Sardine v ('I Hate You').

The band's mini-album *Lonely Mr Happy* (August 1988) continued in the same low-fi, angst-ridden, post-punk mould. Ron Hadley replaced Martin that same year, but the band then slipped from view. Martin formed Las Empaladoras. In February 1990, Perano toured Australia as percussionist in the backing band for pop sensation **Kylie Minogue**. Perano resurrected The Deadly Hume and issued the single 'The Hokey Pokey'/'Afterhours'. 'The Hokey Pokey' was the children's song given a sinister edge. The band resumed live work but broke up soon after.

Albums: *Me, Grandma, Iliko and Hilarian* (Phantom, 1987), *Lonely Mr Happy* (mini-album; Phantom, 1988).

deadstar

Formed: *1995*
Style: *Pop*
Original line-up: *Caroline Kennedy (vocals, guitar; ex-***Plums***), Barry Palmer (guitar, bass; ex-Soul Twisters,* **Harem Scarem**, *Crown of Thorns,* **Hunters & Collectors***), Peter Jones (drums; ex-***Harem Scarem**, *Crown of Thorns,* **Kate Ceberano's** *Septet,* **Crowded House***)*

Towards the middle of 1996, deadstar emerged as one of the most highly feted and individual bands of the decade. The band came about soon after Barry Palmer and Peter Jones (who had played together in the blueswailing **Harem Scarem**) were asked to write the score for a projected film called *The Baby Bath Massacre*. The pair recruited Caroline Kennedy in August 1995 and recorded an album.

The film never eventuated, but deadstar was born. Quickly signing to White Records, deadstar issued the CD singles 'Going Down', 'She Loves She' and 'Sister', plus an eponymous debut album (April 1996). The album's mix of trashy pop and indie guitar rock found a ready-made market. There were plenty of loose arrangements in the songs, with Palmer's guitar and Kennedy's quavering, imperfect vocals laid down rough and raw.

In November 1996, ex-**Crowded House** bassist Nick Seymour joined deadstar, and the band began playing live. deadstar appeared as part of the Big Day Out tour in January 1997, and issued *Milk* (another album of garagey pop gems) in August. *Milk* produced the CD singles 'Don't It Get You Down?' (September 1996) and 'I've Got Something to Tell You' (June 1997). In between her deadstar commitments, Kennedy performed with her other band, Salon Baby. At the end of 1996, Palmer produced the **Hunters & Collectors'** Mark Seymour's debut solo album, *King Without a Clue*.

Albums: *deadstar* (White/Mushroom/Festival, 1996), *Milk* (White/Mushroom/ Festival, 1997).

Liz Dealey and the Twenty Second Sect

Formed: *1986*
Style: *Garage rock*
Original line-up: *Liz Dealey (vocals, guitar; ex-Sputniks, Acid Drops), Chris Willard (guitar; from* **Lizard Train***), Shane Bloffwitch (bass; from* **Lizard Train***), David Creese (drums; from* **Lizard Train***)*

Liz Dealey is one of the most underrated, yet challenging female singers Australia has ever produced. She would give Fiona Horne (**Def FX**) and Christina Amphlett (**Divinyls**) a run for their money, but she remains unknown outside a strong cult following.

Adelaide-based Dealey got her start in music as bassist for Sputniks. Sputniks' quorum comprised Dave Graney, Steve Miller and Clare Moore, who went on to form **The Moodists**. Dealey joined Captain Scarlett and then The Acid Drops, an archetypal 1960s-inspired garage trash outfit that also comprised David Mason (guitar; ex-Head On), Chris Willard (bass, vocals; ex-Head On) and Martin Bland (drums; ex-Chaos, Head On, Crawling Eye). Bland left soon after The Acid Drops' formation to join **Bloodloss** in Sydney. Phil Rady (drums; ex-Head On) came in as his replacement. The Acid Drops' 7-inch EP 'Surfin' Prostitute Beat'/'Rattle

My Zulu', 'Outta Sight Outta Mind' (October 1984) on the Greasy Pop label was a blast of frantic noise and garage-punk energy.

The band broke up in 1985. Dealey joined Revenge of the Gila Monsters briefly, before forming The Twenty Second Sect in 1986. Willard joined **The Lizard Train** and Mason went on to Primevils and **Exploding White Mice**. Martin Bland continued his notorious career with Salamander Jim and **Lubricated Goat**. He moved to the USA in 1992 and worked with The Monkey Wrench and a revived **Bloodloss** with Mark Arm from Mudhoney.

The original line-up of The Twenty Second Sect comprised members of **The Lizard Train** (as listed above). They backed Dealey on The Twenty Second Sect single 'The Wailing House'/'Tell Me Go', '(Don't) Give Me That' on Greasy Pop (December 1986). By 1987, Dealey had formed a more permanent line-up of The Twenty Second Sect with Orietta (guitar), Michael Tohl (bass), Andrew Foley (guitar) and David Creese. The new line-up issued the mini-album *Get that Charge* (November 1988) which was full of revved-up, proto-grunge rock'n'roll. The Megadisc label issued *Get that Charge* in Europe with the three tracks from the first single plus the band's previously unissued cover of the Union Carbide Production song 'Ring My Bell' added.

By 1989, Scott had replaced Creese due to his commitments to **The Lizard Train**. The Twenty Second Sect's second album, *Unexploded*, lacked the drive of *Get that Charge*. By 1990, The Twenty Second Sect had gone as far as it could, and Dealey played in the short-lived Motherfuckers. Tohl later joined up with David Mason to form Easy Action. By 1994 Dealey had linked up with **The Lizard Train** again, this time as the Liz Dealey Band. The band recorded 'The Witching Hour' which was issued on a compilation. By 1996 Dealey was based in Melbourne and fronting a band called Peppershield.

Albums: *Get that Charge* (mini-album; Greasy Pop, 1988), *Get that Charge* (import only Megadisk, 1989), *Unexploded* (Greasy Pop, 1989).

Dear Enemy

Formed: *1982*
Style: *Pop*
Original line-up: *Ron Martini (vocals), Chris Langford (guitar), Les Barker (guitar; ex-Benders), Martin Fisher (keyboards; ex-Innocents,* **Little Heroes**, **Swanee***), Peter Leslie (bass; ex-***Little Heroes***), Ian Morrison (drums)*

Melbourne band Dear Enemy suffered the fate of having one successful single, 'Computer One', and being unable to capitalise on that success, despite significant media attention. The band derived its name from popular Australian comic strip 'Ginger Meggs'. Whenever Ginger received letters from his rival Eddie Coogan, they were always addressed to 'Dear Enemy'.

The band signed to EMI/Capitol and recorded *Ransom Note* in the USA with producer Peter McIan (best known for his work with **Men at Work** and **Mondo Rock**). *Ransom Note* spawned three singles, 'Computer One'/'Day to Day' (#16 in December 1983), 'Good Life'/'On the Line' (February 1984) and 'Kids on the Street'/'Talking to You' (May). Two more singles followed, 'New Hero'/'Billy's Theme' (1984) and 'Stay'/'Looking for Love' (1986), before Joey Amenta (ex-**Taste**, **Redhouse**, **Russell Morris** Band) replaced Barker. 'New Hero' was the theme song to the 1984 film *Street Hero* starring Vince Colisimo. Jerry Leigh then replaced Amenta and Dear Enemy issued a final, independent single, 'You're Right You're Right'/'Love Flows' in December 1988 before calling it quits.

Album: *Ransom Note* (EMI, 1983).

Deckchairs Overboard

Formed: *1982*
Style: *Funk, pop*
Original line up: *Ken Campbell (guitar, vocals; ex Cheks), John Clifforth (keyboards, guitar, vocals; ex-True Wheels, Cheks), Cathy McQuade (bass; ex-***Ears***), Paul Hester (drums; ex-Cheks)*

Sydney funk band Deckchairs Overboard emerged out of the ashes of Melbourne-based power pop band The Cheks. The Cheks formed in 1980 with Ken Campbell, John Clifforth, Paul Hester and Steve Carter (bass). The band did not release a record, but recorded a promotional theme song for community radio station 3RRR-FM.

In August 1981, Cheks signed to Regular Records. In January 1982, Cathy McQuade (ex-**Ears**) replaced Carter and the band became Deckchairs Overboard. The band's crisp, minimalist pop-funk sound began to gel. With the move to Sydney in May 1982, the band built up a strong following around the inner city. The four-track, 12-inch EP *Deckchairs Overboard* (produced by Cameron Allen who had worked with **Icehouse** and **Mental as Anything**) came out in November 1982.

Deckchairs Overboard issued the singles 'That's the Way'/'Carried Away' and 'Shout'/'Shout' in 1983. Hester left towards the end of the year to join **Split Enz** and later **Crowded House**. His place was taken by Dennis Flannery (ex-Agents), who was swiftly replaced by Matthew Wenban. Michael Hoste (keyboards; ex-**Icehouse**) also joined. By the time 'Walking in the Dark'/'Over and Over' (June 1984) and 'Fight for Love'/'Can't Stop the Motor' (August 1985) came out, Deckchairs Overboard comprised the duo of Clifforth and McQuade plus new members.

Helping Clifforth and McQuade out on their debut album *Deckchairs Overboard* (October 1985) were Wenban, Gordon Sullivan (guitar), Scott Saunders (keyboards), Jimmy Doherty (drums) and Tim Brosnan (guitar; ex-**Paul Kelly** and the Dots, **Runners**). The touring line-up comprised Clifforth, McQuade, Sullivan, Saunders and Peter Ciobo (drums). Sullivan dropped out soon after. Regular reissued the 'Walking in the Dark' single in November 1985. The band broke up soon after. Saunders went on to form **d.i.g. (directions in groove)**.

Album: *Deckchairs Overboard* (Regular/Festival, 1985).

Decline of the Reptiles

Formed: *1983*
Style: *Garage rock*
Original line-up: *Mark Roxburgh (vocals; ex-Trans 262), Dean Coulter (guitar, vocals; ex-Trans Love Energy), Bruce Tatham (keyboards), Bruce Tindale (guitar; ex-Professors, Room 101, Coupe de Ville), Stephen Mather (bass; ex-Playboy Lords,* **Lipstick Killers***), Michael Charles (drums; ex-Shy Impostors,* **Lipstick Killers,** *Angie Pepper Band)*

On the post-punk Sydney scene of the early 1980s, there were a number of bands playing **Radio Birdman**/MC5/Stooges/Ramones-inspired garage rock'n'roll. Included in that coterie were the likes of ME 262 (aka The Ruse and Trans 262) and Trans Love Energy (aka Fifth Estate and Slaughterhouse 5).

Trans Love Energy was a three-piece comprising Dean Coulter (guitar, vocals), James Darrock (bass, vocals) and Murray Engleheart (drums). That band did not release any records. Darrock joined **The Celibate Rifles** at the start of 1982, and later formed **The Eastern Dark**. Engleheart became a long-time rock journalist with *Juke*, *Drum*, *Hot Metal*, *Metal Hammer* and countless other publications.

ME 262 comprised Mark Roxburgh (vocals), Tony Gibson (guitar), Andy Newman (bass) and Alan Marr (drums). As Trans 262, the band issued a four-track independent EP, 'Don't Hold Me Down', in early 1982 and then broke up. In late 1983, Roxburgh and Coulter teamed up with ex-**Lipstick Killers** rhythm section Michael Charles and Stephen Mather, plus Bruce Tatham and Bruce Tindale to form Decline of the Reptiles.

Gibson joined garage-rock band The Howling Commandos with John Dennison (vocals; ex-Guests), Andrew Dennison (bass; ex-Guests) and Michael McCallum (drums). The Commandos failed to build up the same fanatical following as Decline of the Reptiles or **The Eastern Dark**, but they did issue the 12-inch EP *90 Days* on the Waterfront label (1984) and the single 'Walk on By'/'Pick Me Up' on the ViNil label (1985). Andy Newman (another ex-Trans 262 alumnus) joined on keyboards for the single, but the band broke up a year later.

In the meantime, Decline of the Reptiles continued in the same Detroit/garage vein with large doses of tough, melodic pop and 1960s psychedelia added. The band built up a strong following around the Darlinghurst/inner-city scene alongside like-minded Sydney outfits such as **The Trilobites**, **Hoi Polloi**, Melting Skyscrapers, The Spectre's Revenge, Mushroom Planet, The Conspirators and later **The Psychotic Turnbuckles** and **The Eastern Dark**. By the time Decline of the Reptiles recorded 'What I Feel'/'Flesh' in May 1984, the line-up comprised Roxburgh, Coulter, Tatham, Tindale, Phil Kerney (bass) and Garry Munro (drums). When Waterfront issued the single during August, the picture sleeve came embossed with a reptile skin texture. The single reached #1 on the alternative chart.

Tindale left in October 1984 and Decline of the Reptiles recorded the mini-album *The Hammer Speaks* a month later. Munro left in April 1985, and he was eventually replaced by Mark Welch (ex-**No Man's Land**). *The Hammer Speaks* came out in September 1985. The title of the band's second mini-album, *Too Much Armour (Not Enough Brains)* (January 1987), proved to be a prophetic one. It was the band's last record, as Decline of the Reptiles broke up in 1986.

In mid-1987, the original line-up of ME 262 (Roxburgh, Gibson, Newman and Marr) regrouped for a weekend to record the latter-day Iggy and the Stooges' song 'I Got Nothin'' for inclusion on Au-go-go's Stooges tribute album *Hard to Beat* (1988). Mark Roxburgh co-produced (with Phil Kerney, Steve Clark and the band) **Ratcat's** eponymous debut mini-album of 1987.

In 1986, Gibson formed Rattlesnake Shake with

Peter Patterson (vocals; ex-Melting Skyscrapers, Naked Lunch), Anthony Kolinac (guitar), Ed Johnson (bass) and Jason Boylan (drums). That line-up issued one single, 'Beyond Belief'/'Some Kinda Love', on Waterfront during 1987. By 1990 the line-up had altered to include Gibson, Patterson, Andy Newman (bass; ex-Trans 262, Howling Commandos), Steve Beves (guitar; ex-Melting Skyscrapers, Naked Lunch) and Brett Ford (drums; ex-**Kryptonics**, **Lubricated Goat**, Punjabbers).

The new Rattlesnake Shake line-up issued a self-titled, 12-inch EP in August 1990 (on the Rattlesnake label through Survival). In March 1991, the band changed names to Dark Carnival and a month later to Thrill Killers. By the end of the year, only Gibson and Patterson remained from the previous line-up. Thrill Killers issued the album *Thrill Killers* in 1992 through Mushroom Distribution Services (MDS).

Mini-albums: *The Hammer Speaks* (Waterfront, 1985), *Too Much Armour (Not Enough Brains)* (Waterfront, 1986).

Grantley Dee

Style: *Pop*

In 1963, at the age of 16, blind singer Grantley Dee (b. 1947) became the youngest disc jockey on Australian radio at that time when he joined Melbourne's 3AK. Dee later signed with HMV and had hit singles with 'Let the Little Girl Dance'/'Answer Me' (#2 in Melbourne during May 1966) and 'Wild One'/'You Thrill Me' (#17 in September 1966). Dee recorded an album and four more singles, 'You're Sixteen'/'Every Breath I Take' (November 1966), 'Lonely One'/'We Must be Doing Something Right' (April 1967), 'Stop Where You Are'/'It Hurts Me' (August 1967) and (with **Little Pattie**) 'We Must be Doing Something Right' 'Lonely One' (1966).

Albums: *Grantley Dee* (HMV, 1966), *Let the Little Girl Dance* (EMI, 1982).

Def FX

Formed: *1990*
Style: *Techno*
Original line-up: *Fiona Horne (vocals, ex-Mothers), Blake Gardner (guitar; ex-Bezerk), Sean Lowry (synthesisers, sequencers, samples; ex-King Prawn), Martyn Basha (bass; ex-Bezerk)*

Def FX grew out of the late 1980s Sydney punk/techno scene. The band's intention from the outset

Def FX

was to mix energetic dance beats with hardcore grungy rock. Add to the equation lead singer Fiona Horne's captivating, feline stage presence, and it equalled a spiralling, trance-inducing blast of electronic dance music.

Various descriptions like 'techno-metal-hiphop-pop' and 'sonic fusionists' only told part of the story. Unbeknown to the band at the time of formation, the term Def FX was a mathematical formula: 'Definition of function X is the fusion of two qualities at point X'. Aside from the four main musicians, Def FX boasted a hidden fifth member, Larry Van Kriedt (sax, sequencers; ex-**AC/DC**, **Non Stop Dancers**) who also co-wrote much of the band's early material.

The Mothers line-up of Fiona Horne (vocals, guitar), Nat (guitar), Jo Collings (bass) and Rick (drums) issued the single 'Drives Me Wild'/'Get Outta My Life' (October 1987). The 1988 line-up of Horne, Rick, Luke (guitar) and Cristina Calero (bass) issued the mini-album *12 Incher* before breaking up in 1989. Both releases were on the independent Waterfront label.

Soon after formation, Def FX set about touring extensively around Australia. The band issued three CD EPs, *Water* (featured tracks 'Surfers of the Mind' and a cover of **Daddy Cool's** 'Make Your Stash') (June 1991), *Surge* (featured track 'Under the Blue') (November) and *Blink* (featured track 'Sex/Game/Sucker') (June 1992) on the Phantom label before signing to EMI. Dave Stein replaced Blake Gardner, and EMI issued the album *Light Speed Collision* (December 1992) and three CD EPs 'No Time for Nowhere' (March 1993), 'Space Time Disco' (June) and 'Post Moronic' (September 1994). 'Post Moronic' was the band's first mainstream Australian chart entry, reaching #43 in October 1994. By that stage, Def FX had toured the USA three times and signed an American deal with RCA/BMG. The US version of *Light Speed Collision* (July 1993) included a remix of 'Surfers of the Mind'.

Phantom issued the compilation album *Baptism* (November 1993), which included the early EPs, plus the remixes of 'Surfers of the Mind' and 'Walk on Water'. The band appeared on the national bill of the 1994 Big Day Out tour. Def FX left EMI in 1995 and issued the over-ambitious *Ritual Eternal* on the independent Cicada label (May). In late 1995, Sean Fonti (bass; ex-**Caligula**) joined, and Def FX signed to Universal Music Australia's subsidiary label Grudge. 'Psychoactive Summer' (#42 in March 1996) was another minor hit. Def FX's third album, *Majick*, made its debut at #21 on the national chart in July 1996. The album's second CD single, 'I'll be Your Majick', reached #47 in August, and the third CD single 'Spell on You' was a radio hit. The fourth CD single lifted from the album, 'Deja Vu', appeared in October.

With the release of *Majick*, Def FX supported US band Smashing Pumpkins' Australian tour, and then toured South-East Asia and Japan to positive reviews. MCA issued *Majick* in New Zealand, Japan, the UK and Germany. Charlie McMahon (didjeridoo; ex-**Gondwanaland Project**) joined the band as an auxiliary player, adding a new slant to the Def FX sound. Def FX broke up in 1997. Fiona Horne has been the subject of much attention from the tabloid press and television current affairs shows due to her interest in witchcraft. She practised Wicca, a form of earth magic described as a 'feminine-based religion'. In 1997, she wrote a book on the subject.

Albums: *Light Speed Collision* (EMI, 1992), *Baptism* (Phantom, 1993), *Ritual Eternal* (Cicada/MDS, 1995), *Majick* (Grudge/Universal/BMG, 1996).

Defryme

Formed: *1990*
Style: *Hard rock*
Original line-up: *Quinn Gardener-Kane (vocals), Rob Dexter (guitar), Mike Richardson (bass), John Hall (drums), Jade Burton (backing vocals)*

When the highly touted Defryme formed in Frankston, Victoria during February 1990, the intention was to sound like American heavyweights Living Colour. The members of Defryme had been inspired by the funk/metal hybrid of such Living Colour tracks as 'Cult of Personality'. Ultimately, the band's sound settled into a full-frontal hard rock attack, with one reference point perhaps being Rage Against the Machine (sans the rap-styled vocals).

Within a year of formation Jade Burton had left, Grant Millen (keyboards) had joined and Glenn Millen had replaced John Hall on drums. Frankie Bazar also joined on sax, and Defryme issued its debut CD EP, *Stylo Curiae* (August 1992), on the R Dog label (through MDS). The brutal singles 'God Inside a Man' (June) and 'Purekiller' (September) followed during 1993. 'God Inside a Man' reached #51 on the national chart in July. 'Purekiller' had been inspired by a serial killer operating in the Frankston area, its lyric thrust arguing for the reintroduction of capital punishment. The *Purekiller* album came out in May 1994. It was an ambitious debut, and the single, LL Cool J's 'Mama Said Knock You Out', reached #38 in April. There was an expectation that the album would be a big seller, but in the end it sold only moderately. The last Defryme single was 'Sanity' (July 1994), after which the band broke up.

Album: *Purekiller* (BMG, 1994).

The Degenerates

Formed: *1987*
Style: *Hard rock*
Original line-up: *Jamie Durrant (guitar, vocals), Robert MacKay (bass), David Klenjans (drums)*

Benalla (Victoria) hard rock band The Degenerates originally formed as The Degens. The Degens issued the single 'Out of My Head'/'Get It on' on the Amputated Hand label in 1989. By the time the band issued its second single, 'Play Dinosaur' (May 1992), and debut album, *Play Dinosaur* (June), the name had been expanded. The Degenerates recorded a second album, then a single in 1995, 'Life Expectancy'. By late 1995, The Degenerates had evolved into Box of Anger with Jamie Durrant,

David Klenjans and Julian Chick (bass). The band issued the CD EP 'Clean' (November 1995) and the album *Box of Anger* (June 1996). Durrant also ran the Bent Records label. He issued a solo CD single on Bent, 'Goodbye' (November 1994).

Albums: *Play Dinosaur* (Bent/Shock, 1992), *Outspoken* (Bent/Shock, 1993), *Box of Anger* (Bent, 1996).

Delaney Venn

Formed: *1980*
Style: *Pop*
Original line-up: *Michael Delaney (vocals, guitar; ex-Syliva and the Synthetics), Chris Venn (vocals, guitar; ex-Simon and the Diamonds)*

Sydney-based actors/musicians Michael Delaney and Chris Venn first joined forces in the band Neon Hearts which also comprised Chris Raggett (lead guitar; ex-**Matt Finish**), Paul Wheeler (bass; ex-**Billy Thorpe** and the Aztecs, **MacKenzie Theory**, **Bjerre**) and Tony Doyle (drums). Delaney and Venn added a very theatrical touch to their style of pop rock. As Delaney Venn, the band signed to Mercury and issued the singles 'Prisoner'/'Fix It Up' (February 1979) and 'No Expectations'/'Dub Dub' (June 1979), plus the album *Neon Hearts*. At the end of 1980, Delaney Venn issued its third single, 'White Reggae'/'Lucky Number', and by 1981 the pair had gone their separate ways. Michael Delaney died in a car accident on 7 September 1982.

Album: *Neon Hearts* (Mercury/PolyGram, 1980).

The Delltones

Formed: *1959*
Style: *Vocal harmony*
Original line-up: *Noel Widerberg, Warren Lucas, Ian 'Pee Wee' Wilson, Brian Perkins*

In the pantheon of Australian rock'n'roll, The Delltones remain unrivalled in the vocal group genre. Taking their cue from American vocal groups such as The Diamonds and Elvis Presley's The Jordanaires, The Delltones formed in January 1959.

Rock'n'roll impresario Lee Gordon signed the group to his Leedon Records and issued the singles The Crows' 'Gee'/'Why' (June 1959), 'Tonight'/'Everything I Do' (October), 'Yes Indeed'/'Tell Me that You Care' (February 1960) and 'White Cliffs of Dover'/'Land of Beauty' (May), plus the EP *Digging with the Delltones* (June). The singles were minor hits in Sydney. The Delltones backed local rock'n'rollers like **Johnny O'Keefe**, **Johnny Rebb** and Johnny Devlin, and began appearing on Six O'Clock *Rock* and *Bandstand*. Lee Gordon also booked The Delltones for his Big Show tours.

In June 1960, The Delltones signed to Coronet/CBS for the singles 'Little Miss Heartbreak'/'Take My Heart' (November 1960) and 'You're the Limit'/'Girls Were Made for Boys' (January 1961). 'You're the Limit' was the group's first Sydney Top 10 hit (#4). HMV/EMI issued 'Wonder'/'A Teenager in Love' (April 1961) and 'String Along'/'Even Tho'' (July). The Delltones then re-signed to Leedon, by that stage owned by Festival, and issued 'Get a Little Dirt on Your Hands'/'A Happy Pair' (January 1962). Just as the single entered the charts, Noel Widerberg died in a car accident. The single eventually peaked at #3 in Sydney and Top 20 in most states. Following two months of inactivity, The Delltones invited Colin Loughnan from **The Crescents** to replace Noel. The Delltones then scored their biggest hit with 'Come a Little Bit Closer'/'Joanie' (#3 in Sydney, January 1963). 'Sitting by the Moonlight'/'Mary Ann' (June 1963) was the group's eighth chart entry in Sydney.

Next The Delltones jumped on the surf music bandwagon with the tongue-in-cheek 'Hangin' Five'/'Surf City' (#2 in Sydney, #14 in Melbourne, November 1963) and 'Out the Back'/'That's How Many Tears' (February 1964). Covers of The Diamonds' 'Walkin' Along'/'Paper Doll' (July 1964) and The Tams' 'Hey Girl, Don't Bother Me'/'The Wonder of You' (October 1964) were uptempo beat-styled singles. The Delltones issued two more singles, 'Lonely Boy'/'The Walk' (March 1965) and 'Tonight We Love'/'Don't You Care?' (September), plus their sixth album, *The Dellies Burst Out*, before being dropped by Leedon.

Following the novelty single 'I'm a Boomerang Bender'/'Is it Any Wonder?' on CBS (March 1967), The Delltones travelled to East Asia and Europe. Col Loughnan stayed in the UK and joined Kala. He returned to Australia in 1973 and joined **Ayers Rock** as sax player. Back in Australia during 1970, The Delltones issued 'Give Me Some Loving'/'Have a Little Talk' on Fable (October), 'Billy's Rock'n'Roll will Stand'/'Rock'n'Roll will Stand' on Festival (November 1971) and 'Birmingham'/'Tears Begin to Fall' on HMV (1973). The Delltones' albums *London Sessions*, *Rock'n'Roll will Stand* and *Rock'n'Rollin' with The Delltones* coincided with the rock'n'roll revival. By 1973, The Delltones had retired from the scene.

Pee Wee Wilson revived The Delltones in 1981 (with all new members) and toured the Sydney club circuit. The Delltones issued 'Mr Bassman'/'Leaving on a Jet Plane' on Seven (1981) and 'The Hucklebuck'/'Get a Job' on RCA (1982). The television-promoted K-Tel album *Bop Til Ya Drop!* sold 65 000 copies and precipitated a revival in the group's fortunes. The Delltones issued a string of albums and eight singles on the Chase label. The singles included 'Papa-Oom-Mow-Mow' (1984), 'I Wonder Why'/'Hit and Run Love' (1985), The Drifters' 'Saturday Night at the Movies'/'Blue Moon' (1985), 'Love will Find a Way'/'So in Love' (1986) and 'Forever Now'/'Touch and Go' (1988). While The Delltones' heyday had well and truly passed, the group was still issuing singles as late as 1993 ('Stole My Heart Away' and 'Burn Like a Rocket').

Albums: *The Delltones* (Leedon, 1962), *Come a Little Bit Closer* (Leedon, 1963), *Surf 'n' Stomp* (Leedon, 1964), *Best of* (Leedon, 1964), *Golden Hits of the Golden Groups* (Leedon, 1964), *The Dellies Burst Out* (Leedon, 1965), *London Sessions* (Parlophone, 1971), *Rock'n'Roll will Stand* (Summit, 1972), *Rock'n'Rollin' with the Delltones* (Summit, 1973), *20 Golden Greats* (Festival, 1978), *Over the Years* (Seven, 1979), *Bop Til Ya Drop!* (K-Tel, 1983), *Tickled Pink* (Chase, 1984), *Out in the Open* (Chase, 1986), *All These Things and More* (Chase, 1987), *Oasis* (Chase, 1988), *The Delltones Live* (1993), *The Sunshine Club* (1995).

The Denvermen (with Digger Revell)

Formed: *1961*
Style: *Instrumental*
Original line-up: *Digger Revell (born Gary Hildred, vocals), Les Green (lead guitar), Tex Ihasz (rhythm guitar), Peter Burbidge (sax), Allan Crowe (bass), Phil Bower (drums)*

The Denvermen were the first Australian group to achieve chart success in the instrumental craze of the early 1960s. The band grew out of the ashes of two Sydney rock'n'roll bands, Paul Dever and the Denvermen and Digger Revell and the Lonely Ones. Guitarist Les Green was a member of The Denvermen and, when that band broke up in 1961, he retained the name and joined singer Revell as Digger Revell and the Denvermen.

Although credited to Digger Revell's Denver Men, the band's first single, 'Outback'/'The Mexican', for HMV (September 1962) was an instrumental in the Shadows mode. Green was one of the first guitarists in Australia to use effects boxes like an echolette, which was the same type as that used by Hank Marvin of The Shadows. Another influence on Green at that stage was American Duane Eddy. New Zealand rock'n'roller Johnny Devlin wrote and produced the band's first hit single, 'Surfside'/'Lisa Maree' which reached #1 in Sydney and #6 in Melbourne during April 1963. 'Surfside' was issued in the USA (on Capitol) and in the UK. Devlin became the band's manager. He wrote and produced two further hit singles for the band: the vocal cuts 'Building Castles in the Air'/'The Habit of Loving You' (as Digger Revell with the Denver Men; May 1963) and the instrumentals 'Blue Mountains'/'Night Rider' (as The Denvermen).

Peter Burbidge left in early 1963. Green wrote the band's next hit, 'Avalon Stomp'/'Harbour Cruise' (#5 in Sydney, August 1963). The Denvermen signed to RCA and issued their fourth Devlin-penned single 'Stomp Fever'/'The Sun Seeker' (#31 in Sydney, #32 in Melbourne, October 1963). In September 1963, Digger Revell and the Denvermen issued their second vocal single, a version of Judy Garland's 'Over the Rainbow' backed with Devlin's 'I'm Gonna Make You'. It was not a hit, but a year later **Billy Thorpe** and the Aztecs issued a similar version of 'Over the Rainbow' and reached #1 in the process. The Denvermen showed their versatility by backing Johnny Devlin on his hit 'Stomp the Tumbarumba'/'I Beg of You' (#30 in Melbourne, November 1963).

'Spanish Sands'/'Mystery Wave' (#37 in December) was taken from The Denvermen's debut album, *Let's Go Surfside with the Denvermen.* The Denvermen backed singer Tony Weston for the innane single 'The Hootenanny Stomp'/'Forever Mine', then issued another Digger Revell and the Denvermen single, 'My Little Rocker's Turned Surfie'/'Tip of My Tongue' (January 1964). The single reached the Sydney Top 10 (#9), and was the last surf music hit by an Australian band in the face of The Beatles' onslaught. By that stage, Revell was being pushed more and more as a solo singer, so he left to work the nightclub circuit. There was one more Digger Revell and the Denvermen vocal single, 'Just Call on Me'/'Mr Moon, Mr Cupid and Me' (May 1964). While they had started singing on stage, The Denvermen persisted with their instrumental sound on record for the singles 'The Rebel'/'Varquero', 'The Proud Ones'/'Surfer's Blues' and 'She's Gone'/'Route No. 1'.

Revell and the Denvermen joined up again for covers of Ritchie Valens' 'Come on, Let's Go'/'Don't You Know?' (July 1964) and Little Richard's 'Jenny Jenny'/'I Love the Way You Love Me'

(September 1964). By that stage, Revell and the Denvermen had turned 'mod' and were playing mostly Merseybeat-related material. The Digger Revell and the Denvermen single 'A Shot of Rhythm and Blues'/'Take Your Time' (November 1964) was followed by the first vocal effort by The Denvermen (sans Revell) on The Everly Brothers' 'Bird Dog'/'Without You' in early 1965. The final Digger Revell and the Denvermen single was The Platters' 'My Prayer'/'High School Confidential' (the Jerry Lee Lewis rocker), which reached #4 in Sydney and #12 in Melbourne during May 1965.

That same month Crowe departed to be replaced by Kenny Kramer (ex Bluedogs). Revell went solo again with the singles 'Twilight Time'/'I'm Gonna Send You Back to Georgia' (March 1965) and 'You'd Better Move on'/'As Long as She Needs Me' (June). Les Green then left to join The Sundowners. He was replaced by Mick Liber, and The Denvermen issued a final single, 'I Can Tell'/'Time will Bring Everything' (November 1965).

Digger Revell continued to pursue a solo career, issuing increasingly middle-of-the-road singles for RCA such as 'You've Got What It Takes'/'Worried Man' (1966), 'You Won't Find that Kind in Me'/'My Mammy' (1966), 'All Our Love is Slipping Away'/'It's So Easy' (December 1966), 'All for the Love of a Girl'/'Sunshine on My Shoulder' (1967) and 'Funny How Time Slips Away'/'Who Cares?' (1967). His last chart entry was 'You Won't Find that Kind in Me', which reached #38 in October 1966. In the early 1980s, Revell re-emerged with an outlaw country image. He issued the album *Alive and Kicking* and the single 'The World's Gone Crazy'/'Let's Hear It for the Working Man' (September 1982) on RCA.

The Denvermen albums: *Let's Go Surfside with the Denvermen* (RCA, 1963), *'Surfside' and Other Great Instrumentals* (Canetoad, 1989). ***Digger Revell albums:*** *My Prayer* (RCA, 1965), *Alive and Kicking* (RCA, 1982), *You Just Get Better All the Time* (RCA, 1985), *Reachin' for the Stars* (compilation, Canetoad, 1989).

Depression

Formed: *1982*
Style: *Hardcore punk*
1983 line-up: *Spike (vocals), Smeer (real name Stephen Lazaros, guitar; ex-Lois Lane,* **Desert Rat***), Liddy (bass), Danny (drums)*

Once the original punk movement of the late 1970s (Sex Pistols, Clash, Ramones, etc.) had dissipated, a whole new genre grew out of its ashes in the early 1980s. Hardcore was based around distorted, metallic guitar riffs, frantic tempos and rasping, rapid-fire vocals barking out politically motivated lyrics that focused on government corruption, police brutality and social inequality. The UK had Discharge, Charged GBH, The Exploited, Vice Squad, Crass and Abrasive Wheels; California had the Dead Kennedys, Black Flag, Circle Jerks, Subhumans, Bad Brains and Angry Samoans; Canada had D.O.A.

The first two Melbourne bands to embrace the hardcore approach were Sick Things and Depression. Others followed, including **Vicious Circle**, Murder Murder Suicide, Civil Dissidents, Permanent Damage, End Result, Arm the Insane, Children of Sorrow, Death Sentence, etc. The attendant hardcore sub-culture was populated by disaffected youth who were fanatical about the music on offer.

Depression's original guitarist John Feedback left at the end of 1982 to form End Result. That band contributed two tracks to the rare Melbourne punk compilation *Eat Your Head* (1984), alongside **Vicious Circle**, **I Spit on Your Gravy**, Civil Dissident, Murder Murder Suicide, Scum, Royal Flush, Charred Remains, Bodies, Permanent Damage and Madflowers. Four years after End Result broke up, the track 'National Service' appeared on the Reactor label's 35-track Various Artists hardcore compilation *The Not So Lucky Country* (1988). John Feedback joined thrash metal band Renegade which issued the *Total Armageddon* album on the Cleopatra label in March 1988.

Feedback's replacement in Depression, Smeer, had already gigged around the late 1970s Melbourne pub scene with Lois Lane and **Desert Rat**. Depression was an entirely different proposition. The band became the centre of a socially and politically aware sub-culture based around Smeer's abode, 'Hardcore House'. Depression came to the attention of the Dead Kennedys' leader, Jello Biafra, when it supported that American band on its 1983 Australian tour. Jello included Depression's first recording, 'What a Strange World', on the hardcore compilation album *Welcome to 1984* issued in the US on the Alternative Tentacles label.

The newly formed Reactor label issued Depression's three-track, debut EP, 'Money Chain' (January 1984), followed by the 26-track *Depression* album (May 1985) and the **Lobby Loyde**-produced, nine-track *Australia Australia* mini-album (November 1985). Californian label Flipside issued *Australia Australia* in the USA during 1987. It was released under the title *Australia and More* and was a split album with fellow Melbourne hardcore band GASH.

In 1986, Spike left the band and Smeer took over lead vocals. Sham also replaced Danny on drums; 17-year-old Dakka replaced Sham in 1987. Depression made its boldest statement with the aptly titled *Ultra Hardcore Mega Heavy Punk Metal Thrash* album (recorded live at the Seaview Ballroom in January 1987; issued in July) and the 'Big Brother' 7-inch EP on the Cleopatra label. Cleopatra issued Depression's fourth album, *Thrash Till Death—Studio Tapes,* in April 1988 before the band called it a day. Smeer assembled the double, 42-track *Hardcore History 1982–1986* album for release on the Funnel Web label (March 1989).

Smeer also moonlighted on drums with femme hardcore band GASH (Girls Against Sexist Hype). Anna (lead vocals), Liz (guitar, vocals) and Vera (bass) comprised GASH. Anna left in 1985 and Liz took over lead vocals. The band's simplistic punk thrash was heard on the single 'God is Dead'/'Aquarious' (sic) and the *GASH* album in 1986 (both issued on Reactor). The Cleopatra label issued the GASH EP 'Lesson' in 1987 and the album *Positive Change* in 1988.

Albums: *Depression* (Reactor, 1985), *Australia Australia* (Reactor, 1985), *Ultra Hardcore Mega Heavy Punk Metal Thrash* (Cleopatra/Musicland, 1987), *Thrash Till Death—Studio Tapes* (Cleopatra/Musicland, 1988), *Hardcore History 1982–1986* (Funnel Web/Dreamtime, 1989).

Derek's Accent

Formed: *1966*
Style: *Beat pop*
Line-up: *Derek Fitton (vocals), Tony Wilkinson (lead guitar), John Wilkinson (rhythm guitar), Ron Morgan (bass), David Miles (drums)*

Derek's Accent was a short-lived Sydney beat band comprising five teenage British migrants. In late 1965, **The Bee Gees'** producer Nap Kipner was promoting singer Derek Fitton as a solo artist. Fitton teamed up with the above line-up at the start of 1966. Derek's Accent played the local scene and appeared on a few television shows (*Be My Guest, Saturday Date*) before breaking up in July 1966. Fitton joined **The Affair** briefly in 1967.

The band left behind one great single, 'Ain't Got No Feeling'/'That is Life Today' on the Downunder label. Other bands on the Downunder stable included **Marty Rhone** and the Soul Agents, The Mystics, Rick and the Bad Boys, The Second Thoughts, Kevin Bible and the Book and Barrington Davis. The tough 'Ain't Got No Feeling' was comparable to other beat/garage singles from bands such as **The In-Sect** and **The Atlantics**. Reissue specialists Raven included 'Ain't Got No Feeling' on *Ugly Things #2.*

Desert Rat

Formed: *1978*
Style: *Hard rock*
Original line-up: *Jerome Speldwinde (vocals), Denny Stibbard (guitar, vocals), John Moon (guitar, vocals; ex-***Buster Brown***), Ian Ryan (bass, vocals; ex-Chook,* **Buster Brown***), John Dee (drums)*

Melbourne pub-rock band Desert Rat started life as Da Boys in 1976 with the above line-up. Da Boys issued one single in 1977 before changing its name to Desert Rat in January 1978. Desert Rat issued the album *Home from the Front* and the single 'Need Your Love'/'Reaching for the Sky' (March 1978) on the Champagne label. By the time the album came out in May 1978, John Moon, Denny Stibbard and Ian Ryan had all left. They were replaced by Stephen Lazaros (guitar; ex-Lois Lane), Skeeta Pereira (guitar; ex-**Finch**) and Tom 'Two Bob' Johnson (bass). Desert Rat continued to play the hard rock pub circuit until 1979, but broke up without having progressed much further. In the early 1980s, Lazaros re-emerged as Smeer, the driving force behind hardcore punk outfit **Depression**.

Album: *Home from the Front* (Champagne, 1978).

Died Pretty

Formed: *1983*
Style: *Rock*
Original line-up: *Ron Peno (vocals; ex-Hellcats, 31st), Brett Myers (guitar, vocals; ex-***End***, No Dance), Frank Brunetti (keyboards; ex-Super K)*

Sydney band Died Pretty has produced some of the most inspirational rock music heard in Australia. By drawing on an eclectic and diverse range of influences (The Velvet Underground, Television, vintage Bob Dylan and Neil Young, 1960s psychedelia and 1970s progressive rock), Died Pretty unashamedly plundered rock's past to arrive at an original sound that was always passionate, atmospheric and uplifting.

Velvet Underground devotee Brett Myers and rock journalist Frank Brunetti formed an experimental Suicide-styled duo during April 1983. With Ron Peno added, the aggregation took the name Died Pretty. When Jonathan Lickliter (bass; ex-**End**) and Colin Barwick (drums; ex-**End**) joined a month later, the band began playing the inner-city circuit. Ron Peno already had a considerable underground reputation via his stints with The Hellcats (a tough New York Dolls-inspired covers band) and Brisbane hard rock outfit The 31st (with future **Screaming Tribesmen** leader Mick Medew, and future **Hitmen** and **Hoodoo Guru's** guitarist Brad Shepherd). Died Pretty's early contemporaries included **The Screaming Tribesmen, The Flaming Hands, Hoodoo Gurus, The Celibate Rifles, The New Christs, Sunnyboys, The Lime Spiders, Beasts of Bourbon,** Wet Taxis and many other celebrated independent bands.

Having signed to the Citadel label, Died Pretty issued three classic singles: 'Out of the Unknown'/ 'World Without' (April 1984), 'Mirror Blues' Part I/ 'Mirror Blues' Part II (October, 1984) and 'Stoneage Cinderella'/'Yesterday's Letters' (June 1986), plus the compelling *Next to Nothing* 12-inch EP (August 1985). 'Out of the Unknown' and 'Stoneage Cinderella' combined sombre, evocative backing with intense guitar scree, while the 10-minute 'Mirror Blues' was a driving psychedelic epic that packed an incredible punch. All reached #1 on the alternative charts. 'Out of the Unknown', 'Stoneage Cinderella' and 'Final Twist' (from *Next to Nothing*) later appeared on Citadel's essential double album compilation *Take Everything Leave Nothing* (March 1988). By the time Died Pretty came to record the Rob Younger-produced *Free Dirt*, Mark Lock (ex-Phantom Agents) had replaced Lickliter and Chris Welsh (ex-31st) had replaced Barwick. *Free Dirt* came out in August 1986.

What Goes On issued the singles and album in the UK while Closer issued *Free Dirt* in Europe. While the band's records sold well on an alternative level in Australia, interest in the band was at a premium overseas by that stage. Died Pretty left for its first tour of Europe and the USA in October 1986. In France and Italy, in particular, Died Pretty was treated as rock'n'roll royalty, which was a far cry from the complacency the band often experienced with homegrown audiences.

Lost (June 1988) was a more expansive and versatile album than *Free Dirt. Lost* became the second biggest-selling alternative album for 1988 (between **Ed Kuepper's** *Everybody's Got to* and **The Church's** *Starfish*). It yielded the singles 'Winterland'/'Wig-out' (Acoustic) (October 1987), 'Towers of Strength'/ 'From a Buick 6' (June 1988) and 'Out of My Hands'/ 'When You Dance' (November 1988). 'Winterland' was the best-selling alternative single for 1987. In between the year it took for the album to be released, Steve Clark (ex-Glass) had replaced Lock. Long-serving member Frank Brunetti left in April 1988. Before he left, Died Pretty undertook its second tour of the USA and Europe. The last record to feature Brunetti was the #1 alternative hit 'Everybody

Died Pretty

Moves'/'In Love Prison' (March 1989). John Hoey (ex-X-Men, **Thought Criminals, New Christs**) came in as his replacement. Hoey's first major assignment with the band was a third tour of Europe and the USA. Once the tour was over, the band recorded *Every Brilliant Eye* in Los Angeles with producer Jeff Eyrich (The Gun Club, The Plimsouls).

Every Brilliant Eye (April 1990) was one of the finest Australian releases of 1990. It included the single 'Whitlam Square'/'Sink or Swim' (February) and the double single set 'True Fools Fall'/'A Ballad'; 'Is There Anyone?'/'Kingpin' (May). Died Pretty's fourth album, *Doughboy Hollow* (August 1991), followed the formula set by *Lost* and *Every Brilliant Eye*, but with more spectacular results. Brimming with passionate, dramatic and alluring musical vistas, the album took the band into the national mainstream Top 20 for the first time when it peaked at #19 during September. It produced three, near-perfect pop singles 'Stop Myself'/'Godbless' (July 1991), 'D.C.'/ 'Wonder' (September) and 'Sweetheart'/'Time' (February 1992). One of the band's showcase gigs around that time was as part of the inaugural Big Day Out held in Sydney on 25 January 1992.

It was to be another two years before the next Died Pretty album, *Trace*, appeared (September 1993). In the interim, both Clark and Welsh had left the band. Robbie Warren replaced Clark. Murray Shepherd, Warwick Fraser (both ex-**Screaming Tribesmen**) and Stuart Eadie (ex-**Clouds**) filled in for Welsh until he returned to the fold in late 1992. While all that activity was going on, Died Pretty's manager John Needham had sorted out a new, worldwide deal with Sony/Columbia. *Trace* made its debut at #11 on the national mainstream chart (although it slipped out of the Top 40 three weeks later). It yielded four strong singles, the four-track

7-inch EP/CD EP 'Caressing Swine', 'This Reason'/'A Song for Me', 'The Cross' (June 1993), and three CD singles, 'Harness Up' (August), 'Headaround' (November) and 'A State of Graceful Mourning' (December). While the singles scored well on the alternative chart, 'Harness Up' was the band's only national mainstream Top 40 hit single (#35 during September). Died Pretty contributed a cover of **Laughing Clowns'** 'Eternally Yours' to the Various Artists compilation *Earth Music* (June 1994). 'Eternally Yours' also appeared on the *Earth Music* CD EP along with **The Celibate Rifles** covering **The Sports'** 'Boys! (What Did the Detective Say?)' and **Painters and Dockers** doing **Mental as Anything's** 'The Nips Are Getting Bigger'.

Died Pretty's last release for 1994 was the *Days* CD EP which came out in December. *Days* featured new drummer Nick Kennedy. By the time the *Sold* album came out in February 1996, Kennedy had been replaced by Shane Melder (on loan from **Sidewinder**). The Rob Younger-produced *Sold* album and its CD singles 'Cuttin' Up Her Legs' (September 1995) and 'Good at Love' (November) failed to chart, and Sony dropped the band from its roster in April 1996. Simon Cox (ex-**Juice**) replaced Melder in May 1996, and Died Pretty returned to the Citadel label for the CD EP *Deeper* (November 1996). Died Pretty recorded a new album, *Using My Gills as a Roadmap* (slated for release in early 1998), which produced another classic slice of pop in the new CD single 'Radio' (November 1997). Lack of widespread commercial success has not blunted the acclaim that Died Pretty has always garnered from the music press and dedicated fans. Likewise, the band's remarkable recorded legacy has stood the test of time.

Albums: *Free Dirt* (Citadel, 1986), *Pre-Deity* (compilation, Citadel, 1988; reissued on CD in 1992), *Lost* (Blue Mosque/Festival, 1988), *Every Brilliant Eye* (Blue Mosque/Festival, 1990), *Doughboy Hollow* (Blue Mosque/Festival, 1991), *Trace* (Sony/Columbia, 1993), *Sold* (Sony/Columbia, 1996).

Diesel (aka Johnny Diesel, Mark Lizotte)

Style: *R&B, soul*

American-born, Australian-raised singer/guitarist Mark Lizotte (b. 1967) paid his dues on the Perth pub circuit playing with the likes of The Kind, Innocent Bystanders and Close Action. Lizotte appeared on two singles by Innocent Bystanders, 'Lebanon'/'Young Hearts' (A.I.R., 1984) and 'Dangerous'/'I Don't Care' (Chase, July 1986). The line-up on the first single was Lizotte, Brett Keyser (vocals), John 'Yak' Sherritt (drums), John 'Tatt' Dalzell (bass) and Cliff Kinneen (keyboards). After Lizotte's departure, Keyser recruited new players John Heussanstamm (guitar) and Al Kash (drums; ex-**Blackfeather**) and issued the album *Don't Go Looking Back* on the Chase label.

Lizotte assumed the identity of Johnny Diesel, and formed R&B outfit Johnny Diesel and the Injectors in June 1986. The original line-up comprised Diesel, Dalzell, Sherritt, George Dalstrom (guitar) and Bernie Bremond (sax, vocals). Dalstrom left at the end of the year. The Injectors' vibrant blend of Southern rock, soul and R&B (not to mention Diesel's sharp guitar playing and pin-up idol looks) earned them a reputation as the hottest live band on the Perth scene. In September 1987, the Injectors relocated to Sydney, and under the guidance of **The Angels'** drummer Brent Eccles began touring the Eastern states. **Jimmy Barnes** offered The Injectors the opening slot on his Freight Train Heart tour, with Diesel doubling up to play with both bands each night.

Johnny Diesel and the Injectors signed a worldwide deal with Chrysalis Records, and in August 1988 travelled to Memphis, Tennessee to record with famed American producer Terry Manning (Joe Cocker, Fabulous Thunderbirds, ZZ Top). The band's eponymous debut album (March 1989) was bursting with raw and exciting material. It produced the national hit singles 'Don't Need Love'/'Never Last' (#8 in January 1989), 'Soul Revival'/'Thang One', 'Who's for Better?' (#9 in March), 'Cry in Shame'/'Dry Tears' (#10 in May) and 'Looking for Love'/'Get Back' (#28 to August). The band won Best New Talent at the 1989 Australian Record Industry Association (ARIA) Awards. *Johnny Diesel and the Injectors* made its debut at #2 on the national chart in April 1989, and won the ARIA Award for the best-selling album of the year (over 280 000 copies). The Injectors also toured the UK, where they cut the mini-album *Live in London*.

After four years' solid work on the road with The Injectors, Diesel tired of the band format. In early 1991 he broke up The Injectors, split from his long-serving management team of Brent Eccles and John Woodruff and dropped 'Johnny', to re-launch himself as solo artist Diesel with a new deal through EMI. Diesel's debut solo single, 'Love Junk', was a #19 hit in July 1991. Diesel appeared on **Jimmy Barnes**'s 1991 album *Soul Deep* and spent most of the second half of the year touring with Barnes. For his own Rock'n'Soul tour in early 1992, Diesel's backing band comprised Jim Hilbun (bass; ex-**Angels**), Leslie Barlow (backing vocals), Matthew

Branton (guitar) and Roger Mason (keyboards; ex-**Models**).

Diesel's debut solo album, *Hep Fidelity* (March 1992), was full of sassy rock-funk and soul. It yielded the hit singles 'Come to Me' (#8 in January), 'Tip of my Tongue' (#4 in March), 'Man Alive' (#20 in July) and 'One More Time' (#59 in October). The album reached #1 on the national chart and went on to sell over 200 000 copies in Australia. Diesel won Best Male Artist and Best Album (*Hep Fidelity*) at the 1992 ARIA Awards ceremony.

The Lobbyist (August 1993) featured a mix of new songs (recorded at George Martin's AIR Studios in London) and live acoustic and electric reworkings of material from *Hep Fidelity* along with a couple of covers. As well as reaching #1 on the national chart, the album produced three singles William Bell's 'Never Miss Your Water' (#12 in August), 'Masterplan' (#42 in October) and Otis Redding's 'I've Been Loving You Too Long' (#41 in January 1994). Diesel won Best Male Artist for the second year in a row at the 1993 ARIA Awards ceremony.

Diesel contributed a cover of **Richard Clapton's** 'Underground' to the Various Artists compilation *Earth Music* issued on the Mushroom label (June 1994). Diesel's hit-making run continued with his third album *Solid State Rhyme* (November 1994), which spawned the singles 'All Come Together' (#17 in November), 'Fifteen Feet of Snow' (#29 in April 1995) and 'Get It on' (June). At the end of 1995, Diesel and renowned blues singer **Chris Wilson** entered the studio to record an album of blues standards, obscure covers and one Diesel original. *Short Cool Ones* (April 1996) contained the CD singles Ann Peebles' 'I Can't Stand the Rain' (March) and 'Strangelove' (June).

Johnny Diesel and the Injectors albums: *Johnny Diesel and the Injectors* (Chrysalis/Festival, 1989), *Live in London* (Chrysalis/Festival, 1990); ***Diesel albums:*** *Hep Fidelity* (EMI, 1992), *The Lobbyist* (EMI, 1993), *Solid State Rhyme* (EMI, 1994), *Rewind—The Best of Diesel* (EMI, 1996); ***Diesel and Chris Wilson album:*** *Short Cool Ones* (Aurora/White/Mushroom, 1996).

d.i.g. (directions in groove)

Formed: *1991*
Style: *Jazz, funk*
Original line-up: *Scott Saunders (keyboards; ex-***Deckchairs Overboard**, **Beatfish***), Tim Rollinson (guitar), Rick Robertson (sax), Alexander Hewetson (bass), Terepai Richmond (drums)*

Sydney band d.i.g. (directions in groove) was one of Australia's finest exponents of acid jazz. Acid jazz was pioneered in the UK by bands like Brand New Heavies, Young Disciples, Galliano, Mother Earth, Corduroy, James Taylor Quartet and Jamiroquai. Essentially acid jazz fused the traditional structures and sense of melody of jazz with an infectious and hypnotic blend of 1970s black funk'n'soul (James Brown, Curtis Mayfield, Herbie Hancock, Funkadelic, etc.), 1980s hip hop and even Latin rhythms. Although acid jazz was a fashionable catch-all phrase used to introduce listeners to a new musical fusion, d.i.g. eventually transcended such easy categorisations.

d.i.g.

d.i.g. was amongst a clutch of new bands at that time exploring diverse musical avenues on the traditional Australian pub-rock scene: **Juice's** hard funk, **Swoop's** soulful funk grooves, **Def FX's** techno-metal, **Skunkhour's** funk'n'rap and **Caligula's** techno-pop. d.i.g. gigged regularly on the Sydney pub circuit (including appearances at that bastion of Sydney jazz traditionalism The Basement) before signing to PolyGram's Id label. d.i.g. issued its debut CD EP *Directions in Groove* (featured track 'Re-Invent Yourself') in April 1993.

The band's accomplished full-length debut album *Deeper* reached #7 on the national album chart during March 1994. It produced the imminently danceable CD single 'The Favourite'. Sydney diva Toni Mott sang lead vocals on that inspired slice of jazz-funk. The band's second CD single, 'Dreamtime', was a musical and lyrical nod to Koori culture. *Deeper* went on to sell over 50 000 copies in Australia (something of a record for jazz-based music locally) and 80 000 copies overseas. Sam Dixon replaced Alexander Hewetson in 1994, and the band signed an international deal with prestigious jazz label Verve (on the off-shoot Forecast imprint) and toured Europe. While in Europe, d.i.g. performed at the prestigious Montreaux Jazz Festival.

Co-produced with Jeremy Allom (Incognito, Bjork, East 17, Massive Attack), the band's second album, *Speakeasy* (August 1995), was a more mature, confident and ultimately more durable album than its debut. It was a fine collection of sweet, funky jazz-grooves backed up by impeccable musicianship. 'Futures' was issued as a CD single in July. A limited edition version of *Speakeasy* came with a bonus six-track live CD which documented a gig at The Basement, when the band was joined on stage by Gerard Presencer, sax player with the Brand New Heavies. Guitarist Tim Rollinson issued his debut solo album, *Cause + Effect*, on Mercury in June 1997.

Scott Saunders also worked in Sydney-based dance-funk outfit Bellydance. At its biggest, that ensemble numbered 12 members. The band originally formed as Bellydance Disco, issuing its debut single 'Spittin' Bullets' in July 1987. Bellydance built up a strong following on the Sydney dance/pub circuit, and first came to national prominence with the release of the topical single 'Green Revolution' in mid-1992. Bellydance recorded its 16-track debut album, *One Blood*, with DJ/producer Stephen 'Pee Wee' Ferris in 1992, but the album did not see the light of day until October 1993. The album contained a mix of hard funk, smooth soul-pop, dub reggae and jazz-funk. The 'Fun Dopin'' CD EP preceded the album in May 1993. That same month, the band supported overseas visitor Maxi Priest on his Australian tour.

Bellydance issued one CD EP during 1994, 'The Joker'. The band issued its second album, *Babylon Mixed Business*, in late 1995, once again preceded by a CD single, 'Bubbles' (May), and a CD EP, 'Ain't No Use' (November). There have been numerous line-up changes within Bellydance's ranks. The band's other mainstays since inception were Tony Hughes (vocals) and Ted Cavanagh (guitar).

d.i.g. albums: *Deeper* (Id/Mercury, 1994), *Speakeasy* (Id/Mercury, 1995); ***Bellydance albums:*** *One Blood* (Regular/Festival, 1993), *Babylon Mixed Business* (Regular/Festival, 1995).

The Dingoes

Formed: *1973*
Style: *R&B, country*
Original line-up: **Broderick Smith** *(vocals, ex-***Adderley Smith Blues Band**, *Sundown*, **Carson***), Kerryn Tolhurst (guitar, mandolin; ex-***Adderley Smith Blues Band, Country Radio***), Chris Stockley (guitar; ex-***Cam-Pact, Axiom***), John Strangio (bass; ex-St James Infirmary, Middle Earth), John Lee (drums; ex-Sayla,* **Blackfeather***)*

Virtually from the moment The Dingoes formed in April 1973, the band was hailed as one of the most important new bands in the country. The Dingoes certainly had an impressive pedigree, yet in retrospect the band remains one of the most underrated outfits this country has ever produced. Right from the outset the band's spirited combination of R&B, country and red-hot rock'n'roll was imbued with a delightful sense of time and place. Kerryn Tolhurst and **Broderick Smith** were not afraid to infuse their songs with uniquely Australian themes and imagery. The band's debut album *The Dingoes* remains a genuine Australian rock classic.

The first change in The Dingoes' line-up occurred when John Du Bois (ex-**New Dream, Country Radio**) replaced John Strangio on bass during August 1973. The first example of the band's craft was 'Way Out West'/'Shine a Light' (November 1973). The single reached #26 in Melbourne. As a reflection of life in the Australian outback, 'Way Out West' has rarely been bettered. **James Reyne** and country singer James Blundell scored a hit in 1992 with their revival of the song.

One week before the single came out, Chris Stockley was admitted to hospital as a result of being shot in the stomach at a party. The episode was a mystery at the time, but many years later it transpired that notorious criminal Dennis Allen (son of Kath Pettingill) had shot Stockley while attempting to gatecrash the party. While Stockley was recuperating, Mal Logan (keyboards; ex-**Healing Force, Carson**) joined. Logan stayed with the band until the end of 1974. The Dingoes' debut album and second single, 'Boy on the Run'/'The Last Place I Wanna Be', came out in June 1974. 'Boy on the Run' went as high as #30 in Melbourne while *The Dingoes* reached #18. The Federation of Australian Broadcasters awarded *The Dingoes* Album of the Year.

John Lee left The Dingoes in May 1974 (he joined **Ariel**), to be replaced by **Ray Arnott** (ex-Browns, **Cam-Pact**, **Company Caine**, Genesis, **Spectrum, Mighty Kong**). The non-album song

'Smooth Sailing' backed with the album track 'Dingoes' Lament' came out as the band's third single (October 1974). 'Smooth Sailing' did not chart until the band re-recorded it for single release in 1977. Over the next year, with help from Rod Stewart's road manager, Australian Billy McCartney, the band negotiated with Peter Rudge (tour manager with The Rolling Stones and Lynyrd Skynyrd) to take over management in the USA. It was to be another year before The Dingoes travelled to Canada. In the meantime, The Dingoes contributed two tracks, 'Marijuana Hell' and Percy Sledge's 'When a Man Loves a Woman' to the Various Artists live album *Live at the Station* (Lamington, 1976).

Just prior to leaving Australia, former drummer John Lee (by then ex-**Ariel**, Dirty Tricks) replaced Arnott, who pursued a solo career. In 1977, The Dingoes settled in Mill Valley near San Francisco and recorded the album *Five Times the Sun* with producer Elliot F. Mazer. It was a strong rock album with a prominent American production sound, although the band retained its earthy Australian roots. The Rolling Stones' session pianist Nicky Hopkins and The Band's Garth Hudson contributed to the album. The re-recorded single 'Smooth Sailing'/'Way Out West' (September 1977) made its way to #35 on the national chart during October, while *Five Times the Sun* peaked at #19 the same month.

Chris Stockley left in early 1978 to join Greg Quill's Southern Cross. He later returned to Australia and joined The Stockley See Mason Band (with Glyn Mason, ex-**Home** and **Ariel** and Sam See, ex-**Fraternity**), Rock Doctors, the **Jimmy Barnes** Band, The Blue Heelers and country ensemble The Vic State Opry. Los Angeles session players Andrew Jeffers Hardin (guitar, vocals) and Smiggy (keyboards, guitar, vocals) joined The Dingoes. The band recorded *Orphans of the Storm* and the single 'Into the Night'/'Since You've Been Gone' at the Hit Factory in New York City. *Orphans of the Storm* (February 1979) went as high as #36 on the national chart; however, by the time it appeared, The Dingoes had broken up. After six years of hard slog with little commercial success to show for it, the *Five Times the Sun* track 'Waiting for the Tide to Turn' seemed all the more prophetic.

Broderick Smith returned to Australia and formed The Hired Hands, Big Combo and various line-ups of his **Broderick Smith** Band. Tolhurst initially stayed in the USA and carved out a career as a songwriter. With his return to Australia in 1986, he formed The Tremors and then Rattling Sabres with Robert Price (vocals), Lindsay Hodgson (bass) and ex-Dingoes drummer John Lee, who replaced Leyton Greening. Rattling Sabres issued one of the songs Tolhurst had written in the USA as a single, 'All Fired Up'/'Nothing Sacred', on the Mighty Boy label (August 1987). It was a minor hit in Australia for the band. A year later, American singer Pat Benatar issued a version of the song as a single. It was a major hit in Australia (#3 in October 1988), as well as reaching #19 in the USA. Benatar included the song on her album *Wide Awake in Dreamland.*

Albums: *The Dingoes* (Mushroom/Festival, 1974), *Five Times the Sun* (A&M, 1977), *Orphans of the Storm* (A&M, 1979), *Way Out West: The Best of The Dingoes* (compilation, Mushroom/Festival, 1992).

Thc Dirty Lovers

Formed: *1988*
Style: *Garage punk*
Original line-up: *Shane 'Buddy Love' Anderson (singer), Nozza (slop guitar), Arch (rockin' rhythm guitar), Rudi (bass), Sash 'Cha-Cha' Illevski (skins)*

Geelong's favourite sons The Dirty Lovers took their inspiration from 1950s rockabilly, Nuggets-styled 1960s garage punk, 1960s sexploitation film soundtracks and trashy pulp paperbacks (much in the manner of The Cramps). The band built up a solid following around Melbourne, and the Dog Meat label issued the band's debut, four-track 7-inch EP *Shanty Tramp* in August 1990.

Tragedy struck on 10 January 1991, when Shane Anderson and Sash Illevski died in a car accident en route to a gig in Melbourne. The accident also claimed the life of ex-Hangmen singer Dean Smith. (The Hangmen had issued a four-track, 7-inch EP 'Only Get What You Give' in September 1986 on the independent Trapdoor imprint.) Californian label In the Red Records issued The Dirty Lovers' single 'Teenage Love Bomb'/'All I Want' posthumously. **Bored!** frontman Dave Thomas also included The Dirty Lovers tracks 'Check This Action' and 'Straight to Hell' on his compilation of Geelong bands *Check this Action . . . Let the Fun Begin* (Destroyer, 1992).

Dirty Three

Formed: *1992*
Style: *Instrumental rock*
Original line-up: *Mick Turner (guitar; ex-Sick Things,* **Moodists, Venom P. Stinger, Fungus Brains***), Jim White (drums; ex-People with Chairs Up Their Noses,* **Feral Dinosaurs, Venom P. Stinger***), Warren Ellis (violin; ex-These Future Kings)*

Around 1995–1996, mercurial, mesmeric Melbourne three-piece Dirty Three emerged as the band 'most

Dirty Three

likely to'. For an instrumental three-piece band led by an electric violin-wielding maniac, Dirty Three has since garnered an extraordinary amount of international praise and attention. Among all the easily digestible **You Am I**'s, **silverchairs**, **Spiderbaits** and **Regurgitators**, Dirty Three came up with a sound that was almost unclassifiable.

Essentially, Dirty Three's rumbling, dynamic sound incorporated open-ended, improvisational, electric rock reminiscent of 1970s band **MacKenzie Theory** minus the jazz-rock histrionics. By the same token, as writer Clinton Walker has pointed out, the band had as much in common with traditional folk forms, 1960s free jazz and contemporary techno trance. The members of Dirty Three had honed their skills playing the thriving Melbourne independent scene of the 1980s. Ellis played briefly with These Future Kings around 1986. That band comprised Charles Caldas (guitar, vocals), Perry White (guitar), Steven Johansen (sax, keyboards), Claudia White (bass) and Mark Freeman (drums). When Ellis left, Jennifer McCutchen joined on viola. These Future Kings issued the mini-album *These Future Kings* (1987) and the album *Carnival* (March 1989) on the Rampant label.

While Dirty Three was getting off the ground, White and Ellis were moonlighting with three bands: **The Blackeyed Susans**, Kim Salmon's STM and Charles Marshall and the Body Electric. Ellis also joined ex-**Triffids** member David McComb in his band The Red Ponies, which undertook a European tour in late 1993. Throughout 1994, Dirty Three toured constantly, playing supports to international visitors like Pavement, The Beastie Boys and Jon Spencer Blues Explosion. White and Ellis also toured with Tex Don and Charlie. The Torn & Frayed label issued Dirty Three's eponymous debut album in July 1994. Brimming with Ellis's alternately subtle and dramatic violin flourishes, Turner's tensile guitar lines and White's sympathetic drumming, the album was a strong introduction to the band's atmospheric musical palate. Dirty Three's reputation continued to build. At the 1995 Melbourne Big Day Out, **Nick Cave** joined the trio on stage. Recorded as a demo, the *Sad and Dangerous* album was initially only issued in the USA through Boston-based label Poon Village (just 1000 copies on vinyl in hand-screened covers).

Then in true do-it-yourself fashion, with only a handful of gigs lined up and very little money, Dirty Three flew to San Francisco in March 1995. By the end of the year, the band had played over 200 shows on four continents, including the prestigious alternative Lollapalooza festival and a tour of Israel with **Nick Cave and the Bad Seeds**. The band also collaborated with Cave on the live music for the classic silent film *The Passion of Joan of Arc* (as part of the London Film Festival). *Dirty Three* was subsequently released in the USA on Touch & Go, and in the UK on Big Cat. *Sad and Dangerous* came out locally during July 1995.

Dirty Three consolidated its local standing with another spot on the 1996 Big Day Out tour, then headed overseas again for tours across Europe (with **Nick Cave**) and the USA. Ellis collaborated with Cave on the music for the stage play *Billy the Kid* in Vienna, Austria. The band's third album, *Horse Stories*, came out during September 1996. In January 1997, the American edition of *Rolling Stone* voted *Horse Stories* among the top three albums of 1996 (ahead of discs by R.E.M. and Nirvana). Dirty Three recorded a new album (slated for release in 1998), while Mick Turner also found time to issue his debut solo album, *Tren Phantasma* (September 1997), on the US label Drag City. Dirty Three's record sales have not necessarily reflected the critical acclaim afforded the band. Yet, as Clinton Walker has observed, Dirty Three's phenomenal success is testament not only to the power of the band's music, but also to the members' sheer force of will.

Albums: *Dirty Three* (Torn & Frayed/Shock,

1994), *Sad and Dangerous* (Torn & Frayed/Shock, 1995), *Horse Stories* (Hope & Anchor/Shock, 1996).

Divinyls

Formed: *1980*
Style: *Rock, pop*
Original line-up: *Christina Amphlett (vocals), Mark McEntee (guitar; ex-*Air Supply*), Bjarn Ohlin (keyboards, guitar, vocals), Jeremy Paul (bass; ex-*Air Supply*), Richard Harvey (drums; ex-Farmer John)*

Led by provocative singer Christina Amphlett, whose songwriting with guitarist Mark McEntee is the basis of the band, Divinyls have recorded a wealth of excellent material. The band's sound has ranged from commercial hard-pop and driving arena rock to alluring ballads. As the band's focal point, Amphlett has strutted her stuff across stages the world over, astounding or bewildering audiences with her displays of school uniform-clad bump'n'grind burlesque, unrestrained sexuality and animal grace.

By the time Divinyls formed in 1980, Amphlett had been singing in bands since the early 1970s. Her early bands included Daisy Clover (which she joined at age 14), One Ton Gypsy and Steamhammer. She had also spent three years travelling throughout Europe, during which time she spent a period in a Spanish gaol. Her travels no doubt gave her a wealth of experience from which to draw her lyrics.

Divinyls emerged out of inner-city Sydney and quickly built up a national following. In September 1981 WEA issued the band's debut single, 'Boys in Town'/'Only One' which reached #8 during October. It was lifted from the mini-album *Music from Monkey Grip* (#27 in June 1982), the soundtrack to the film of the same name directed by Ken Cameron. Amphlett took the small speaking part of Angela in the film. The band supported UK band Simple Minds and **Icehouse** on an Australian tour. In March 1982, Rick Grossman (bass; ex-**Bleeding Hearts**, **Parachute**, **Matt Finish**) replaced Jeremy Paul. With the help of astute manager Vince Lovegrove (ex-**Valentines**) Divinyls signed to Chrysalis and recorded the punchy *Desperate* album in New York with producers Mark Opitz and Bob Clearmountain. *Desperate* (January 1983) peaked at #3 on the national chart, and produced the singles 'Science Fiction'/'I'll Make You Happy' (November 1982), 'Siren (Never Let You Go)'/'Elsie' (April 1983) and 'Casual Encounter'/'Gonna Get You', 'Only Lonely' (live) (August). Only 'Science Fiction' charted (#13 in January 1983).

Christina Amphlett, Divinyls

Divinyls continued to tour extensively, both locally and overseas. 'Good Die Young'/'9.50' (August 1984) and 'In My Life'/'Don't You Go Walking' (November) followed. In 1985, J.J. Harris replaced Richard Harvey on drums. Producers Mike Chapman (Suzi Quatro, Sweet, Blondie), Mark Opitz (**Cold Chisel**, **Midnight Oil**) and Art of Noise's Gary Langan guided the band through the confident *What a Life!* album (November 1985). *What a Life!* made its debut on the national chart at #5, and reached #2 a week later. The Chapman/Holly Knight-penned single 'Pleasure and Pain'/'What a Life' peaked at #5 in Australia during November, and also cracked the American Top 40. Two further singles were lifted off *What a Life!*, 'Sleeping Beauty'/'Motion' (December 1985) and 'Heart Telegraph'/'Guillotine Day' (May 1986).

Following months of extensive touring across the USA, Divinyls were invited to participate in the enormous Australian Made tour in early 1987. By that stage, the line-up featured Amphlett, McEntee, Grossman and three Americans, Frank Infante (guitar, ex-Blondie, Iggy Pop Band), Tom Caine (drums) and Kenny Lyon (keyboards). Such was the band's arena rock experience that it consistently lived up to audience expectations on the tour.

By the time Divinyls recorded the second Mike

Chapman-produced album, *Temperamental*, the band was basically the duo of Amphlett and McEntee. Helping out were Lyon, Warren McLean (drums; ex-**Machinations**) and Tim Millikan (bass; ex-Tootieville). *Temperamental* peaked at #9 on the national chart during May 1988. Its three singles, 'Back to the Wall'/'Fighting' (#20 in March), Syndicate of Sound's 'Hey Little Boy'/'Para Dice' (#24 in July) and 'Punxsie'/'Victoria' (October) were minor hits. In late 1990, Divinyls signed to Virgin and issued the biggest album of their career. Produced by Englishman David Tickle (**Split Enz**), and aided by American session players like Benmont Tench (Hammond organ), Randy Jackson (bass) and Charlie Drayton (drums), *diVINYLS* (February 1991) ushered in a revival of the band's fortunes. It spawned the #1 Australian hit single 'I Touch Myself'/'Follow Through' (January).

The second single, 'Love School'/'Love School' (instrumental), was not quite so successful, having stalled at #43 during April. Likewise the third and fourth singles, 'Make Out Alright' (May) and 'I'm on Your Side'/'I Touch Myself' (live) (September), were not chart hits. Nevertheless, the provocative 'I Touch Myself' (a blatant paean to masturbation) took Divinyls into the US Top 10 (#4) and UK Top 10 (#10). Likewise, *diVINYLS* went Top 5 in Australia and #15 in the US. 'Ain't Gonna Eat Out My Heart' (Australian #19 in January 1993), Chip Taylor's 'Wild Thing' (#39 in May) and Roxy Music's 'Love is the Drug' (November) continued the hit run. Director Yahoo Serious used 'Wild Thing' on the soundtrack to his feature film *Reckless Kelly*. 'Ain't Gonna Eat Out My Heart' appeared on the *Buffy the Vampire Slayer* soundtrack, while 'Love is the Drug' was heard on the *Super Mario Bros* soundtrack.

For the *Divinyls Live* album (recorded in 1991), the line-up featured the omnipresent Amphlett and McEntee, plus Charlie Owen (rhythm guitar; ex-**New Christs**), Jerome Smith (bass), Lee Borkman (keyboards) and Charlie Drayton (drums, by then also playing bass with Keith Richards' X-Pensive Winos). Divinyls' first album for BMG/RCA, *Underworld* (#47 in August 1996), yielded the singles 'I'm Jealous' (#14 in April 1995), 'Hard on Me' (March 1996), 'Human on the Inside' (June) and 'Heart of Steel' (October). Drayton played on the album and also produced nine tracks. Divinyls' first release for 1997, 'For a Good Time', was the fifth CD single lifted from *Underworld*.

Albums: *Music from Monkey Grip* (mini-album soundtrack; WEA, 1982), *Desperate* (Chrysalis/Festival, 1983), *What a Life!* (Chrysalis/Festival, 1985), *Temperamental* (Chrysalis/Festival, 1988), *diVINYLS* (Virgin, 1991), *The Essential Divinyls* (compilation, Chrysalis/EMI, 1991), *The Collection* (compilation, Virgin, 1993), *Divinyls Live* (Massive, 1994), *Underworld* (BMG/RCA, 1996), *Make You Happy 1981–1993* (Raven, 1997).

DM Three (*see* The Stems)

Do Ré Mi

Formed: *1981*
Style: *Rock, funk*
Original line-up: **Deborah Conway** *(vocals; ex-Benders), Helen Carter (bass; ex-Friction), Stephen Philip (guitar; ex-***Thought Criminals***), Dorland Bray (drums; ex-***News***, Benders)*

Throughout the mid- to late-1980s, Sydney band Do Ré Mi was one of Australia's most successful and respected post-punk outfits. Initially adhering to its punk roots, the band recorded two 12-inch EPs on the independent GREEN label, *Standing on Wires* and *The Waiting Room* (issued through EMI). *The Waiting Room* (January 1983) contained an early version of what became the band's most distinctive song, 'Man Overboard'.

The band earned a strong live following courtesy of what writer Clinton Walker once described as 'stringent, slicing, funky, politically-motivated rock'. Do Ré Mi signed with Virgin Records and the band's chart run commenced in July 1985 when 'Man Overboard'/'Fish Tank', 'Black Crocodiles' reached #4 on the national chart. The brutally honest anti-love song 'Man Overboard' featured **Deborah Conway** at her compelling best. It was also the first chart hit to mention the words 'penis envy' and 'pubic hair' in its lyrics. The band's debut album *Domestic Harmony* (recorded at Townhouse III Studios in London with producer Gavin McKillop) also reached the national Top 10 (#6 in September 1985).

It was to be a peak that the band could not duplicate. Six further singles made the Top 100 by 1988, but none did better than Top 30: 'Idiot Grin'/'No Fury' (September 1985, #43), 'Warnings Moving Clockwise'/'Disneyland', 'Standing on Wires' (May 1986, #72), 'Guns and Butter'/'Bill the Cat' (October 1986, #48), 'King of Moomba'/'Tearing Up the Carpet' (May 1987, #52), 'Adultery'/'Deep Blue Sea' (October 1987, #22) and 'Haunt You'/'Sweet Nothing' (June 1988, #91).

Another English producer Martin Rushent (Buzzcocks, Human League) produced the band's next album, *The Happiest Place in Town* (February 1988). It was a strong second album with an accessible pop sound, but following bouts of international touring the band broke up at the end of 1988. Conway was named Best Australian Female Singer by *Rolling Stone* magazine that year. **Deborah Conway** went solo while Stephen Philip and Helen Carter formed Lupi. Dorland Bray could be found in **Ghostwriters** with Rick Grossman (**Hoodoo Gurus**) and Rob Hirst (**Midnight Oil**).

Albums: *Domestic Harmony* (Virgin, 1985), *Happiest Place in Town* (Virgin, 1988).

Dog Trumpet

Formed: *1991*
Style: *Pop*
Original line-up: *Reg Mombassa (born Chris O'Doherty, guitar, keyboards, harmonica, vocals), Peter O'Doherty (guitar, vocals)*

What began as a sideline project for **Mental as Anything** siblings Reg Mombassa and Peter O'Doherty at the start of 1991 eventually took on a life of its own. With **Mental as Anything** in recess, it was a good opportunity for the pair to record a collection of songs they had been stockpiling over the years. The Dog Trumpet sound reflected a sincere affection for classic 1960s pop and whimsical psychedelia.

Under the name of Peter & Reg, Reg & Peter, the duo issued the single 'Jean'/'Nobody Home' (March 1991), before assuming the name Reg & Peter's Dog Trumpet for the album *Two Heads One Brain*. Two singles were lifted from the album, 'Made of Wood'/'Red Brick Home' (June 1991) and 'I'm So Handsome'/'Dream' (October). Helping out in the studio were Mike Gubb (keyboards; ex-**Dynamic Hepnotics**, **Mental as Anything**), John Bliss (drums; ex-**Reels**) and Mark Honeybrook (bass). The next two years saw the release of the CD EPs *Kiss a Gun Down* (October 1992) and 'Strange Brew' (October 1993). 'Strange Brew' was an inspired reworking of the old Cream song. Tony Martin had replaced Honeybrook on bass.

After that, **Mental as Anything** re-emerged to tour and record, with Dog Trumpet put on the back-burner. In 1996, Reg and Pete revived Dog Trumpet and issued the album *Suitcase*. Backing the duo in the studio were Tony Martin, Andy Travers (drums; ex-**Happening Thang**) and Amanda Brown (violin, backing vocals; ex-**Go-Betweens**). Reg and Peter are also known for their paintings, and for their poster, T-shirt and record cover designs.

Albums: *Two Heads One Brain* (Regular/Festival, 1991), *Suitcase* (TWA, 1996).

Dog Trumpet

Joe Dolce

Style: *Folk, pop*

American-born Joe Dolce is one of the great one-hit-wonders of Australian pop. Produced by **Mike Brady**, Dolce's single 'Shaddap You Face'/'Ain't in No Hurry' (as Joe Dolce Music Theatre) was one of the biggest selling Australian singles of all time. In Australia, the single sold 300 000 copies, and worldwide sales are estimated to be over three million copies. There have been 25 cover versions of the song. 'Shaddap You Face' was an Australian #1 in November 1980, and a UK #1 in February 1981. The single also charted well throughout Europe, Canada, New Zealand and the USA, and Joe Dolce Music Theatre toured overseas to some success.

Dolce had started his musical career in the USA with a band called Headstone Circus. He moved to Australia during the 1970s. Following the success of 'Shaddap You Face' Dolce continued to issue singles, including 'If You Want to be Happy (For the Rest of Your Life)'/'Ain't Been Missing You' (April 1981), 'Christmas in Australia'/'The Twelve Days of Christmas' (November 1981) and 'You

Toucha My Car I Breaka You Face'/'Dolciato' (June 1982).

He signed to PolyGram, but never graced the charts again. He formed Skin the Wig with singer/performance artist Lynn Van Hecke, who had been part of Joe Dolce Music Theatre. In fact, Van Hecke's debut single 'Ain't Been Missin' You'/'Walking the Dog' (September 1981) had been lifted from Dolce's *Shaddap You Face* album. By the mid-1980s, Dolce was working on the folk circuit. In 1988, Dolce turned his talents to acting, taking the role of travelling salesman Nino Patrovita in Marc Gracie's feature film *Blowing Hot and Cold*. Dolce issued a new single, 'Vaffanculo Polka', in February 1989. During 1993, Dolce appeared in Van Hecke's performance piece *Difficult Women*. In 1997 he completed a new album, *Memoirs of a Mouth Organ*.

Albums: *Shaddap You Face* (Full Moon/Astor, 1981), *Christmas in Australia* (PolyGram, mini-album, 1981), *Pizza Pizza* (PolyGram, 1984), *Memoirs of a Mouth Organ* (JD, 1997).

Jason Donovan

Style: *Pop*

Internationally renowned singer/actor Jason Donovan (b. 1968) is the son of actor Terence Donovan and television presenter Sue MacIntosh. Donovan first came to prominence playing Scott Robinson in the Ten Network's television soapie *Neighbours* during the mid-1980s. *Neighbours* became one of the most popular television shows in the UK and, like his co-star **Kylie Minogue**, Donovan came to the attention of British hit-making producers Stock Aitken Waterman (SAW).

The producers promoted him as a teen idol. Donovan enjoyed the Australian hit singles 'Nothing Can Divide Us'/'Nothing Can Divide Us' (Instrumental) (#4 in November 1988), 'Too Many Broken Hearts'/'Wrap Your Arms Around Me' (#7 in March 1989), Brian Hyland's 'Sealed with A Kiss' (#8 in July), 'Every Day (I Love You More)' (#43 in October), 'When You Come Back to Me' (#40 in March 1990) and The Cascades' 'Rhythm of the Rain'/'Story of My Life' (#44 in November 1990). His duet with **Minogue** 'Especially for You'/'All I Wanna Do is Make You Mine' was also a #1 hit in January 1989. His next single, 'I'm Doing Fine' (February 1991), was not successful. Donovan's debut album, *Ten Good Reasons*, also peaked at #5 on the national chart in July 1989.

Donovan's greatest successes, however, were to be in the UK (including three #1 hits in a row), where he now enjoys megastar status. He has been based there since the early 1990s. Donovan's chart hits in the UK were: 'Nothing Can Divide Us' (#5, September 1988), 'Especially for You' (#1, December), 'Too Many Broken Hearts' (#1, March 1989), 'Sealed with A Kiss' (#1 in June), 'Every Day (I Love You More)' (#2, September), 'When You Come Back to Me' (#2, December), 'Hang on to Your Love' (#8, April 1990), 'Another Night' (#18, June), 'Rhythm of the Rain' (#9, September), 'I'm Doing Fine' (#22, October), 'RSVP' (#17, May 1991), 'Any Dream will Do' (#1, June), 'Happy Together' (#10, August), 'Joseph Mega Mix' (#13, December), 'Mission of Love' (#26, July 1992), 'As Time Goes By' (#26, November) and 'All Around the World' (#41, August 1993).

In 1990, before he left Australia, Donovan took the small role of Private Talbot in film director Stephen Wallace's war-time courtroom drama *Blood Oath* which starred Bryan Brown. Donovan was also seen in the Australian television miniseries *The Heroes* (1989) and the film *Shadows of the Heart* (1990). While pursuing his solo singing career in the UK, Donovan appeared in the successful revivals of the stage musicals *Joseph and the Amazing Technicolor Dreamcoat* and *The Rocky Horror Show* (as Frank N. Furter). Donovan has suffered at the hands of the British music press, and successfully sued *The Face* for libel. He continues to pursue a highly lucrative career in show business.

Albums: *Ten Good Reasons* (Mushroom/Festival, 1989), *Between the Lines* (Mushroom/Festival, 1990), *Greatest Hits* (Mushroom/Festival, 1991).

Dorian Gray

Formed: *1981*
Style: *Goth rock*
Original line-up: *Gordon Pitt (bass, vocals; ex-Microfilm, Bleú Scooters), David Mast (guitar; ex-Bleú Scooters), Chuck Meo (drums; ex-***Ears***, Dresden War Crimes)*

The three musicians that made up Melbourne based Dorian Gray had been around in small-time new wave bands for a couple of years. **The Ears** and Microfilm had issued singles. The Bleú Scooters were one of the first mod bands on the Melbourne scene, but did not issue any records. The post-**Birthday Party**/Joy Division-influenced Dresden War Crimes had issued a self-financed cassette, *Solution*. They had also been one-time roadies for The Boys Next Door. Dorian Gray supported UK visitors Echo and the Bunnymen in 1981. The band's debut single, 'Emperor's New

Clothes'/'Bloodlust', came out on Au-go-go in June 1982. Its moody sound was somewhere between Joy Division and Bauhaus with dark lyrical themes.

By the time the single appeared, Marshall Butters (ex-Mircofilm) had joined on rhythm guitar. The band broke up in 1983 and Pitt went on to join **John Justin and the Thunderwings**. Chuck Meo joined **Olympic Sideburns** and later appeared in Richard Lowenstein's feature film *Dogs in Space*. He played in Melbourne band Taking the Veil, which comprised Glenys Osbourne (vocals; she also appeared in *Dogs in Space*), Randall Thain (guitar), Rusty Teluk (guitar) and Vincent Kramer (bass). The band issued one mini-album, *Brick by Brick*, in 1987.

Dove

Formed: *1973*
Style: *Soft rock*
Original line-up: *Sharyn Cambridge (vocals), Jim Sifonios (guitar, keyboards, vocals), Warwick Thomas (bass, vocals), Steve Gill (drums, vocals)*

Melbourne band Dove signed to the Sunrise label (distributed by WEA) in mid-1973, and issued the singles, 'It Might as Well Rain Until September'/'I Can't Get to You' (August 1973) and 'Little Honda'/'Twenty Years' (November 1973). The singles were minor hits in hometown Melbourne.

Dove's debut album *Magic to Do* included two more singles, 'Magic to Do'/'Ready for the Truth' (May 1974) and 'Amazing Grace'/'Country Girl' (#8 in November 1974). Two further singles came out through WEA, 'Play Something Sweet'/'Night Time Lover' (December 1974) and 'Just One Look'/'Long Live Love' (July 1975), before the band signed to the Image label. Image issued 'Let's Hang on'/'River of Flames' (December 1975) and 'The Lion Sleeps Tonight'/'Paper Face' (April 1976), plus the band's second album.

Another label change to Crystal Clear resulted in the *Dove* album and single 'Gotta Get Away'/'Since You've Been Gone' (July 1976). One of Dove's showcase gigs was at the Melbourne Moomba Festival in March 1976 when the band appeared before 65 000 people backed by a 60-piece orchestra. Dove broke up in 1978, after which Sharyn formed the Sharyn Cambridge Band, then the Sharyn Cambridge–Colin Who Band.

Albums: *Magic to Do* (Sunrise, 1974), *Love Harmony and Understanding* (Image, 1975), *Dove* (Crystal Clear, 1976).

John Dowler (*see* Young Modern; The Zimmermen)

Peter Doyle

Style: *Pop*

Pop singer Peter Doyle (b. 1949) has enjoyed a remarkably varied and successful career that has taken him from Australia to the UK, the USA and back again. He started singing aged nine on the television talent show *Swallow's Juniors*. By 14 he was appearing on Sunday afternoon pop shows at Melbourne's Festival Hall. At 16 he scored a record deal with Ivan Dayman's Sunshine label and began appearing on television pop show *The Go!! Show*.

Matched with dependable backing group The Phantoms, Doyle recorded six singles for Sunshine: Conway Twitty's 'Speechless (The Pick Up)'/'Like I Love You' (#14 in May 1965), Solomon Burke's 'Stupidity'/'Heigh Ho!' (#11 in July), Small Faces' 'What'cha Gonna Do About It?'/'Do It "Zulu Style"' (#35 in November), The Platters' 'Great Pretender'/'Everybody Loves a Lover' (#22 in January 1966), 'Something You Got Baby'/'Go Away' (May) and 'Mr Good Time'/'Tweedle Dee' (November 1966). In 1967, Doyle moved to the Astor label and issued two further singles 'You Can't Put That in a Bottle'/'I'm Not the Boy You're After' (April) and Neil Sedaka's 'Plastic Dreams and Toy Balloons'/'You're My Reason' (June). He also utilised the services of Grandma's Tonic as his backing band (which included ex-members of **Tony Worsley's** backing band The Fabulous Blue Jays).

In May 1968, with his solo career at a low ebb, Doyle joined Rob Lovett (ex-**Wild Cherries, Loved Ones**) and Malcolm McGee (ex-**Wild Cherries, Python Lee Jackson**) in the heavily hyped would-be Walker Brothers, The Virgil Brothers. The vocal trio issued three singles, a cover of The Knight Brothers' 'Temptation's 'Bout to Get Me'/'I See Her Face' (June 1968), 'Here I Am'/'Shake Me Wake Me' (September) and 'When You Walk Away'/'Good Love' (September 1969). Danny Robinson (ex-**Wild Cherries**) replaced McGee for the last single, which had been recorded in the UK with producer David MacKay. In 1970, with the vocal trio format virtually stagnant, Doyle accepted entrepreneur David Joseph's offer to join The New Seekers. The ultra-commercial New Seekers found the chart success for which Doyle had been searching so long.

The band enjoyed hit singles in the UK with the likes of 'What Have They Done to My Song Ma?', 'Never Ending Song of Love', 'I'd Like to Teach the World to Sing (in Perfect Harmony)' (a #1), 'Beg Steal Or Borrow', 'Circles', 'Come Softly to Me' and 'You Won't Find Another Fool Like Me' (their second UK #1). Doyle left The New Seekers in June 1973, and continued to work in the UK until 1981. In 1977, he issued his first solo album in more than ten years, *Skin Deep*. On his return to Australia, Doyle worked with a band called Standing Room Only. By 1982, Doyle was working in the USA with a band called Regis at the invitation of former Wings drummer Steve Holly. Doyle eventually returned to Australia, and has continued to perform on the club and nostalgia circuit.

Albums: *Peter's First Album* (Sunshine, 1966), *Skin Deep* (RCA, 1977).

Dr Fruitworld

Formed: *1991*
Style: *Punk rock*
Original line-up: *Alan 'Big Al' Creed (vocals, guitar; ex-Government Downfall, Aberration, Heresy), Phil Van Rooyen (guitar, vocals), Ken Archbold (bass; ex-Climate of Fear, Itchy Rat), Andrew Warren (drums)*

Sydney band Dr Fruitworld drew its influences from mid-1980s US melodic hardcore (Descendants, Bad Religion, Hüsker Dü) and late 1970s British punk (Stiff Little Fingers, Clash). The band worked the Sydney inner-city circuit for two years before issuing the CD EP *Noise Fix* (May 1993) on the Tunnel label. Charlie O'Neill replaced Archbold and Simon Lazarus (real name Simon Cooper, aka Oxx; ex-**Massive Appendage**, Slampacker, Lazarus) replaced Warren. The band shortened its name to Fruitworld, and issued the Damien Lovelock-produced CD EP 'Pain' (January 1994). After touring with the likes of **Powder Monkeys** and **Front End Loader**, the band called it a day later in the year. Creed, Archbold and Van Rooyen formed The Panadolls with Matt Banneman (bass) and Ashley Thomson (drums). The band issued one CD EP *Beyond the Valley of the Panadolls* in October 1995. In early 1997, Creed was a member of **The New Christs**.

Dragon

Formed: *1972*
Style: *Rock, pop*
Original line-up: *Graeme Collins (piano, vocals), Ray Goodwin (guitar, vocals; ex-Jacob Manning, OK Dinghy, Staff), Todd Hunter (bass; ex-OK Dinghy, Staff), Neil Reynolds (drums)*

During the late 1970s, New Zealand band Dragon was one of the most popular and notorious acts on the Australian scene. Led by the charismatic Hunter brothers (Marc and Todd), the band earned a reputation for fierce live shows, arrogant behaviour and a decadent lifestyle which resulted in unprecedented media attention. The rock'n'roll lifestyle, however, also eventually contributed to the deaths of two members, Neil Storey and Paul Hewson. Among the tragedies, Dragon created a legacy of perfectly constructed rock and pop songs, a number of which had sprung from the pen of the erudite Hewson.

Todd Hunter and Ray Goodwin formed Dragon in Auckland during January 1972. By the beginning of 1973, Neil Storey (ex-Mandrake, Billy TK's Powerhouse) had replaced Neil Reynolds, and Ivan Thompson (ex-Mandrake) had replaced Graeme Collins. Todd's brother Marc also joined around that time as lead singer. By the end of 1974, Dragon was New Zealand's top live attraction. Dragon recorded two progressive art-rock albums for Phonogram's Vertigo label, *Universal Radio* (June 1974) and *Scented Gardens for the Blind* (March 1975). 'Vermillion Cellars'/'Rock'n'Roll Ponsonby' was Dragon's first single. The records sold steadily without charting.

With Robert Macklin Taylor (guitar; ex-Mammal) having replaced Thompson in December 1974, Dragon eschewed the art-rock trappings for raunchier dance music. Vertigo issued a second Dragon single, 'Education'/'Swell Foot Sue' in early 1975, but once again it failed to chart. Setting its sights overseas, Dragon relocated to Sydney in May 1975. The move, however, was fraught with mishaps. Within weeks of arriving, most of the band's equipment had either been stolen or damaged in a road accident. Vertigo issued Dragon's third single, 'Star Kissed'/'Crystal Dove' (both tracks written by Goodwin) in September, and a month later the band supported UK visitors Status Quo on an Australian tour. Another New Zealander, Paul Hewson (ex-Freedom Express, Cruise Lane), joined on keyboards to fill out the sound, but in January 1976 Goodwin departed.

Throughout 1976, Dragon staked out Sydney's famed Bondi Lifesaver club as its own territory. CBS signed the band and issued the singles 'Wait Until Tomorrow'/'Show Danny Across the Water' (July 1976) and 'This Time'/'The Dreaded Moroczy Bind' (October 1976). Just as 'This Time' began to chart (it eventually reached #26 nationally), Neil Storey died from a drug overdose. Wellington-born Kerry Jacobson (ex-Mammal, Quincey Conserve) came in as Storey's replacement. With renewed vigour, Dragon spent the next two years touring and eventually achieved the status of Australia's most popular band.

The new line-up recorded 'Get that Jive'/'On the Beachhead' (#16 in April 1977) and *Sunshine* (#18 in June). *Sunshine* confirmed the band's uncanny ability to craft both anthemic pop songs and tight, funky rock'n'roll. Combined with an arrogant attitude that they were already stars, this showed Dragon to be a band of almost limitless possibilities. Like **AC/DC** before them, the members of Dragon were the bad boys on the block, able to outclass the likes of **Sherbet** and **Skyhooks** at their own game.

As the single 'Sunshine'/'New Machine' reached #33 in September 1977, Dragon signed with CBS's US West Coast subsidiary label Portrait. *Sunshine* came out in the USA as the retitled *Same Old Blues*. The Australian Top 10 (#6) album *Running Free* yielded the Paul Hewson-penned classic single 'April Sun in Cuba'/'Telephone' (#2 in November 1977), which remains Dragon's most identifiable song. It was only kept from the top spot by Paul McCartney and Wings' huge hit 'Mull of Kintyre'. In New Zealand, it also provided Dragon with its first-ever chart hit when it peaked at #9 during March 1978. Both follow-up singles, 'Shooting Star'/'Some Strange Dream' (December 1977) and 'Konkaroo'/'Mr Thunder' (April 1978), missed the national Top 40. Dragon supported US singer Boz Scaggs on his February 1978 Australian tour.

Dragon's second Australian Top 10 (#4) album, *O Zambezi*, included the #1 hit 'Are You Old Enough?'/'Company' (August 1978) and another archetypal Dragon song in the funky title track 'O Zambezi'. The album's second single, 'Still in Love with You'/'Politics', reached the Top 30. By the end of 1978, both *Running Free* and *O Zambezi* had achieved double platinum status (in excess of 140 000 copies of each album sold). In November 1978, Portrait issued Dragon's second US album, *Dragon*, and the band toured America with the mismatched Johnny Winter Band. The US sojourn culminated in an infamous episode during a gig in Dallas, Texas during which Marc incited the audience to wreck tables and chairs and smash glasses.

In February 1979, **Marc Hunter** was sacked due to his unreliable behaviour and escalating drug addiction. Richard Lee (violin, guitar, vocals) took Hunter's place in Dragon. Lee had been a member of Melbourne pub bands Issac Aaron and Sidewinder. The second-named band issued one independent EP, *Sidewinder*. Perth musician Billy Rogers (sax, piano, harmonica; ex-Last Chance Café) also joined in March. The new line-up released the singles 'Love's Not Enough'/'Four Short Solos' (April 1979), 'Counting Sheep'/'Now that Daddy's Home' (August) and 'Motor City Connection'/'Same Old Lies' (October), plus the album *Power Play* (September). Although the new album failed to reached the national Top 40, *Dragon's Greatest Hits Volume 1* had peaked at #8 during July. The new Dragon aimed for a more sophisticated audience, but by that stage the magic had faded. Dragon broke up in December 1979.

Dragon

Meanwhile, **Marc Hunter** had launched a successful solo career. Todd moved into production before joining **XL-Capris** as guitarist. Hewson enjoyed success back in New Zealand with The Pink Flamingos. Taylor joined pub band The Magnetics. Jacobson joined the Willy Winter Band and then **Kevin Borich Express**.

In August 1982, the classic Dragon line-up of Marc and Todd Hunter, Robert Taylor, Paul Hewson and Kerry Jacobson reconvened for the national Class Reunion tour. Ostensibly run to pay off outstanding debts, the tour proved so successful that the band re-formed on a permanent basis. Dragon issued the tentative one-off single 'Ramona'/'Blacktown Boogie' (October 1982) on EMI, but it failed to chart. The band hit its stride with the follow-up singles on the Mercury label 'Rain'/'It's Too Late' (national #2 in August 1983) and 'Magic'/'April Sun in Cuba' (#24 in December).

Around that time, Jacobson had fallen ill and Englishman Terry Chambers (ex-XTC) took his place. English keyboards player Alan Mansfield (ex-Robert Palmer Band), who had produced 'Rain' and 'Magic', also joined the band. This resulted in a much fuller, more rock-oriented sound. The Carey Taylor-produced album *Body and the Beat* (June 1984) was a polished, contemporary sounding Adult Oriented Rock rock album. It reached #5 in July and produced three more strong singles,

'Cry'/'What Am I Gonna Do?' (#12 in June), 'Body and the Beat'/'Are You Old Enough?,' (July) and 'Wilderworld'/'Easy Street' (August). 'Wilderworld' also appeared on the *Street Hero* film soundtrack. At the end of 1984, Dragon travelled to the USA to tour and record. That resulted in the 'Speak No Evil'/'Witnessing' single (#16 in March 1985). The band was forced to change its name to Hunter for the US market, in order to avoid any heavy metal connotations the name Dragon implied.

Tragedy struck the band again on 10 January 1985 when Paul Hewson died in New Zealand. The live album *Live One* (June 1985) was a stop-gap measure until Dragon could sort out a number of pressing problems. Coupled with Hewson's death, both Robert Taylor and Terry Chambers left the band. Eventually Don Miller-Robinson (ex-Lifesavers) replaced Taylor and English drummer Doane Perry (from Jethro Tull) replaced Chambers. Respected guitarist **Tommy Emmanuel** replaced Miller-Robinson in 1986.

Dragon bounced back with the Todd Rundgren-produced, pure pop album *Dreams of Ordinary Men* (August 1986), which reached #15 on the chart in October. The album sold close to 100 000 copies and produced the singles 'Dreams of Ordinary Men'/'Start It Up' (#12 in September), 'Western Girls'/'When I'm Gone' (November) and 'Nothing to Lose'/'Intensive Care' (March 1987). Dragon undertook an extensive European tour (as Hunter), which took in festival dates and supports to Tina Turner across Germany and Austria. The album sold 40 000 copies in those territories. The joyous cover of Kool and the Gang's 'Celebration'/'Blue Blue is the Radio' (November 1987) returned the band to the Australian charts (#12 in January 1988).

In early 1988, guitarists Peter Grimwood and Randall Waller (ex-**Avion**), plus drummer Barton Price (ex-**Models**) complemented the basic Dragon line-up of Marc, Todd and Mansfield temporarily. Dragon's only release for 1988 was the non-album single 'River'/'Bottom to the Top' (May). *Bondi Road* (April 1989) yielded the singles 'Young Years'/'Runaway' (#18 in May), 'Here Am I'/'Good Time Girl' (July), 'Summer'/'Heart of Fire' (October) and 'Book of Love' (February 1990). Emmanuel appeared as a session player on some tracks, while New Zealander Mike Caen (ex-Pink Slips, Scribble) had joined as the band's new guitar player. Mitch Farmer and John Watson (ex-**Australian Crawl**) played drums on the album. *Bondi Road* peaked at #14 on the album chart in May. By early 1990, Dragon had effectively disbanded, but not for long.

The 1995 album *Incarnations* featured the single 'Chains of Love'/'Still in Love' (September), plus re-recorded versions of some of Dragon's most memorable songs including 'Are You Old Enough?', 'April Sun in Cuba' and 'Rain'. As well as Marc, Todd, Mansfield, Caen and Peter Northcote (guitar), the album featured an array of guest musicians (including **Kevin Borich**, **Renée Geyer**, **Tommy Emmanuel** and Kirk Lorange). Dragon was still creating radio-friendly, corporate pop, but with Australian radio more interested in **silverchair**, Oasis or Green Day, there was little chance of airplay.

The 1996 touring line-up featured Marc, Mansfield, Caen, Ange Tsoitoudis (guitar), Dario Bortolin (bass; ex-**Scary Mother**) in place of Todd and Mick O'Brien (drums). In October 1996, Sony issued the 'best of' CD EP *Dragon* which featured the tracks 'Get that Jive', 'This Time', 'April Sun in Cuba' and 'Are You Old Enough?'. In 1997 Marc Hunter was diagnosed as suffering throat cancer. He died in July 1998.

Albums: *Universal Radio* (Vertigo, 1974), *Scented Gardens for the Blind* (Vertigo, 1975), *Sunshine* (CBS, 1977), *Running Free* (CBS/Portrait, 1977), *O Zambezi* (CBS/Portrait, 1978), *Power Play* (CBS, 1979), *Dragon's Greatest Hits Volume 1* (CBS, 1979), *Body and the Beat* (Polydor, 1984), *Live One* (PolyGram, 1985), *Are You Old Enough* (compilation, K-Tel/CBS, 1985), *Dreams of Ordinary Men* (PolyGram, 1986), *Bondi Road* (Wheatley/BMG, 1989), *So Far: Their Classic Collection* (compilation, J&B, 1990), *Cuts from the Tough Times* (compilation, PolyGram, 1990), *Incarnations* (Roadshow/Warner, 1995).

Dreamkillers

Formed: *1991*
Style: *Hardcore*
Original line-up: *Les Jobson (vocals; ex-Mystery of Sixes), Phil 'Sid' Roberts (guitar; ex-Reality Damage, Disorderly Public Outbreak, Insane Hombres), Shaun Witcher (guitar), Terry McDougall (bass; ex-Pictish Blood, Psycho Circus, Insane Hombres), Paul McCallum (drums)*

Brisbane-based, tattooed heavyweights Dreamkillers grew out of the ashes of a number of infamous underground punk/thrash bands of the 1980s. Hardcore/skate-thrash outfit Insane Hombres occupied Terry McDougall and Sid Roberts between 1988 and 1990. As well as McDougall and Roberts, Insane Hombres included John Bryant (vocals) and Ian Cranfield (drums; ex-Reality Damage, Psycho Circus) and the band issued one mini-album, *To the Core* (June 1989), on its own Non-Regulation imprint.

Jobson's band Mystery of Sixes issued two rare

punk EPs 'Mystery of Sixes'/'Totally Me', 'Black Magic' (1982) and *Mystery of Sixes* (1983). Mystery of Sixes came to the attention of the Dead Kennedys' Jello Biafra when that American hardcore band toured Australia. Biafra reportedly re-engineered and reissued the *Mystery of Sixes* EP on the Alternative Tentacles label.

The name Dreamkillers was taken from an old Insane Hombres song. Dreamkillers' sound mixed heavy metal riffs and hardcore punk attitude in equal measure (akin to US bands like Black Flag and Suicidal Tendancies). In 1993, Dreamkillers issued the CD EPs *Poison in the Soup* and *Carnival of Skin* on the Velvet Urge label (through Siren). Roberts and McCallum left the band mid-1993. Roberts was not replaced, but Lindsay Tsdmanin came in as McCallum's replacement. The new line-up issued the CD EP *Fairgrounds for Insanity* (August 1994), which included live favourites 'Homophobia' and 'Latent Karma'.

It was not until March 1995, however, that the band followed those releases with the single 'Sarah'/'Unbearable Light' and the full-length album *Scorched Earth Policy*. By the time the album came out, stalwart member McDougall had moved on to be replaced by Dave Smith (ex-A.I.M.). Dreamkillers supported US visitors L7 on an Australian tour, but slipped from view until mid-1997 when they signed to Roadrunner Australia. Roadrunner issued the CD single 'Dry Reach' in August, followed by the album *Character Building Hell-Trip* in October.

Albums: *Scorched Earth Policy* (Velvet Urge/Siren, 1995), *Character Building Hell-Trip* (Roadrunner/Sony, 1997).

Drop City

Formed: *1993*
Style: *Indie guitar pop*
Original line-up: *Matt Tow (guitar, vocals), Conner Grennan (bass), Chris Cobb (drums)*

Sydney band Drop City played melodic indie-guitar pop that fitted somewhere between UK bands like Ride, Spaceman 3 and early Primal Scream. The band's contemporaries on the Sydney scene included **Pollyanna, Big Heavy Stuff, Bluebottle Kiss** and **The Verys**. Lucas Steurewald replaced Chris Cobb in 1995. Drop City signed to the Red Eye label and issued the full-length album *A Revolution of Purely Private Expectations* (June 1994) and the CD EP *Chiaroscuro* (November).

Drop City appeared on the Sydney leg of the 1995 Big Day Out tour. The CD single 'Setting Sun' (August 1995) and the band's second album, *Magic Transistor Radio* (September), combined mood and melody with an epic sense of purpose. Drop City recorded the album in the UK with producer Andy Wilkinson (Stereolab, Boo Radleys). Red Eye lifted two further CD singles from the album, 'Apple Tree' (February 1996) and a remixed version of 'Cool Times' (May). Drop City supported the **Hoodoo Gurus** and American band The Posies on an Australian tour throughout July 1996. Drop City issued two new CD singles, 'Fools Rush in' (October 1996) and 'Living in the Machine' (March 1997), which were lifted from the album *This Heavenly Machine* (March).

Albums: *A Revolution of Purely Private Expectations* (Red Eye/Polydor, 1994), *Magic Transistor Radio* (Red Eye/Polydor, 1995), *This Heavenly Machine* (Polydor, 1997).

The Dubrovniks

Formed: *1987*
Style: *Rock*
Original line-up: **Roddy Radalj** *(guitar, vocals; ex-Exterminators,* **Scientists**, *Rockets, Le Hoodoo Gurus,* **Johnnys**, *Love Rodeo, James Baker Experience), Peter Simpson (guitar, vocals; ex-Teeny Weenies, Super K, Spectre's Revenge,* **Hoi Polloi**), *Boris Sujdovic (bass; ex-Exterminators,* **Scientists**, **Rockets**, **Beasts of Bourbon**), *James Baker (drums; ex-***Victims**, **Scientists**, **Hoodoo Gurus**, **Beasts of Bourbon**, *James Baker Experience)*

When Sydney band The Dubrovniks emerged in 1987, the individual members had personal histories in Australian music stretching back a decade. James Baker, Roddy 'The Raj' Radalj, Peter Simpson and Boris Sujdovic comprised an inner-city 'supergroup' of sorts right from the outset.

Originally known as The Adorable Ones (formed August 1986), the band had to change names due to a Brisbane outfit already operating under that moniker. The name Dubrovniks was derived from the fact that both Radalj and Sujdovic were born in the (former) Yugoslavian village of Dubrovnik. The band's clattering, yet accessible rock'n'roll was drawn along the lines of The Troggs meets T-Rex by way of New York Dolls. Radalj was also known for his stylish attire and his guitar made from a pine cheeseboard!

Citadel issued the singles 'Fireball of Love'/'If I Had a Gun' (April 1988) and a cover of Alvin Stardust's 'My Coo Ca Choo'/'Girls Go Manic' (November 1988). By the time the band recorded and issued the single 'Speedway Girls'/'Freezin' Rain' (June 1989) and the album *Dubrovnik Blues*

(August), the ever-restless Radalj had left. In late 1988, Radalj formed the sideline band The Punjabbers with Brett Ford (drums; ex-**Kryptonics**, **Lubricated Goat**), Tony Robertson (bass; ex-**Hitmen**, **New Christs**, Naked Lunch) and Tony Thewlis (guitar; ex-**Scientists**) and issued the single 'Rock'n'Roll Loveletter' on Timberyard (December 1988). Radalj then formed The Surfin' Caesars and recorded several albums.

Chris Flynn (guitar, vocals; ex-**Headstones**) eventually replaced Radalj, and the band signed to Mushroom. The band's releases on Mushroom maintained the revved-up, trashy rock'n'roll tradition. *Audio Sonic Love Affair* (September 1990) included the singles 'She Got No Love'/'Got this Far' (June) and 'Love is on the Loose'/'Something's not Right in the World' (October). Glen Armstrong (guitar; ex-**Girlies**) replaced Simpson in 1991, and the new line-up issued *Chrome* in June 1992. It produced two cracking singles in 'Saigon Rose' (February) and 'French Revolution' (June). In between albums, Baker and Sujdovic toured and recorded with **Beasts of Bourbon**. In early 1991, the two severed their commitments to the Beasts in order to concentrate on The Dubrovniks. Mushroom dropped the band in 1993. German label Normal issued *Medicine Wheel* in Europe, and Mushroom Distribution Services (MDS) distributed it in Australia.

The Dubrovniks broke up in 1995 and Baker returned to Perth. He joined power pop band Satellite 5 with John Rushin (vocals), Phil Bradley (guitar; ex-Jackals), Doug Thomas (guitar; ex-**Dagoes**, Spikes) and Howard Shawcross (bass; ex-**Elks**, Howard I Know, Jackals).

Albums: *Dubrovnik Blues* (Timberyard, 1989), *Audio Sonic Love Affair* (Mushroom/Festival, 1990), *Chrome* (Mushroom/Festival, 1992), *Medicine Wheel* (Normal/MDS, 1994).

Duck

Formed: *1972*
Style: *Rock*
Original line-up: **Jon English** *(vocals; ex-***Sebastian Hardie***)*, **Bobbi Marchini** *(vocals; ex-Hunger), John Robinson (guitar; ex-***Dave Miller Set**, **Blackfeather**, *Hunger), Bobby Gebert (keyboards; well-known jazz session player), Larry Duryea (percussion; ex-***Tamam Shud***), Teddy Toi (bass; ex-***Billy Thorpe** *and the Aztecs,* **Fanny Adams**, **Wild Cherries***), Steve Webb (drums; ex-***Blackfeather**, *Wolfe)*

Sydney-based band Duck was an all-star 'supergroup' assembled by producer G. **Wayne Thomas** in order to record a studio-only album of cover versions. The nucleus of Duck grew out of Sydney club band Hunger which John Robinson formed following his departure from **Blackfeather**. The Duck venture proved so enjoyable for all concerned that the band also toured briefly once the album came out.

Danny Robinson (vocals; ex-**Wild Cherries**, Virgil Brothers) joined Duck for the live shows, because **Jon English** was already playing Judas Iscariot in the stage production of *Jesus Christ Superstar* and was unavailable to tour. Russell Smith (guitar; ex-**Company Caine**) also joined for tours. The collectable *Laid* album (July 1972) was padded out with some ordinary songs, but was buoyed by strong renditions of Neil Young's 'Southern Man', Bill Withers' 'Ain't No Sunshine', Frank Zappa's 'Dog Breath' and Nick Gravenites' (as covered by Janis Joplin) 'Burned Alive in the Blues'. Two singles were lifted from the set 'Sweet Inspiration'/'Southern Man' (May 1972) and Paul McCartney's 'Maybe I'm Amazed'/'The Man in Me' (September).

On the evidence of tracks like the blueswailin' 'Burned Alive in the Blues' and 'Southern Man', **Bobbi Marchini** was a flat-out, blues-belter in the Janis Joplin/Maggie Bell mould. She later recorded several delicate soul-pop singles for the Albert label, which did little to reflect her tougher blues style. She also sang on Robinson's 1974 solo album, *Pity for the Victim*. Once Duck's touring commitments were out of the way, Robinson reunited with singer Dave Miller in a revived version of **Dave Miller Set**, which also comprised Steve Hogg (bass; ex-**Bakery**) and Steve Webb (drums). The reunion was short-lived and Robinson formed Tramp with Webb, Len Pitt (vocals) and Benny Kaika (bass; ex-**McPhee**). Webb and Kaika contributed to Robinson's 1974 solo album, *Pity for the Victim*, alongside Marchini.

Duck album: *Laid* (Warner, 1972); ***John Robinson solo album:*** *Pity for the Victim* (Festival/Infinity, 1974).

Jeff Duff

Style: *Pop*

Eccentric singer Jeff (aka Geoff) Duff (b. 1950) first came to prominence with the jazz-rock styled **Kush**, best known for the album *Snow White . . . and the Eight Straights*, which contained a brilliant version of Jimmy Webb's 'McArthur Park'. With the break-up of **Kush** in 1975, Duff went solo and issued a cover of The Knight Brothers' 'Temptation's 'Bout to Get Me' (also issued by The Virgil Brothers in the 1960s) as a single in April 1977 (backed with 'Where will I be Tomorrow?'). Duff showed his theatrical bent by donning Rudolph Valentino garb (à la *The Sheik*) in order to promote the single.

Duff travelled to the UK, where he signed up with the Beggar's Banquet label. The British readily accepted his eccentricities, although he did cause a stir with the mainstream media. As the waif-like androgynous oddball Duffo, he fitted in with the weirder end of the new wave scale. His eponymous debut album bore the legend 'Maybe god's a genius too!' Musically *Duffo* had hints of Bonzo Dog Doo Dah Band, The Tubes, The Kinks and Monty Python. Duffo sang the witty lyrics with a pronounced strine inflection. The single 'Give Me Back Me Brain' managed to reach #60 on the UK mainstream charts in May 1979. His band on the album included expatriates Mike Howlett (bass; ex-Gong) and David Herzog (guitar; ex-**Kush**).

The PVK label issued Duffo's next two albums and four singles, 'After the Subsequent Inquiry'/ 'Mumbo Jumbo', 'John and Betty Go to LA'/'Lost in My Room', Lou Reed's 'Walk on the Wild Side' and 'I Want to be the Pilot'. His last UK release was the 12-inch EP 'Gonna Send the Boys Round' on Cherry Red. Duff also recorded as Ivor Biggin before returning to Australia in 1986, and issuing the single 'Walk on the Wild Side'/'Killing this Affair' on the Powderworks label (May 1987). Powderworks had also issued Duff's third album, *Bob the Birdman*, in Australia.

In 1988 Duff took the part of Secta in the post-apocalyptic science fantasy feature film *Sons of Steel*, written and directed by Gary Keady. The soundtrack album featured the Duff song 'Here Come the Freaks'. Later in the year Duff formed The Jeff Duff Orchestra (an all-girl group of classically trained musicians). Duff's Orchestra combined violins, cellos and Sergeant Pepper uniforms with a rock backing. Duff must have held his arrangement of 'Walk on the Wild Side' in high regard, as he recorded it a second time, this time with The Jeff Duff Orchestra on the Captain Vimto label (May 1989). Promoted by an innovative film clip, the single gained attention and became a turntable hit. The Jeff Duff Orchestra issued a self-titled, live album, *Jeff Duff Orchestra* (July 1989), and a second single, 'Venice'/'New Boy', on Captain Vimto.

Duff's next band was jazz-funk outfit Duffhead with Peter Head (piano; ex-**Headband**), Harry Brus (bass; ex-**Kevin Borich Express**) and Greg Henson (drums). By 1990, the line-up was Duff, Head, Chris Bailey (bass; ex-**Angels**), Peter Figures (drums; ex-**Jeff St John** and Copperwine), **Jackie Orszaczky** (bass; ex-Syrius, Jump Back Jack) and Andy Thompson (sax). Soon after, Duff was working with Duff and Rhodes which comprised Glenn Rhodes (vocals), Rex Goh (guitar; ex-**Air Supply**), Greg Henson (drums), Col Loughnan (sax, flute; ex-**Ayers Rock**) and Helen Lutz (violin). Duff continued to issue records into the 1990s, including the singles 'Never Too Late' (1990) and 'Don't You Feel Sexual?' (August 1992), plus the album *Angels and Rascals* in 1994. In 1995 he unveiled his new band, Prophets of Groove, playing jazz, soul and funk. Although generally perceived in Australia as being too left-field, the ever-optimistic Duff liked to see himself as 'more like Julio Inglesias or Barry Manilow'.

Albums: *Duffo* (Beggar's Banquet in the UK, WEA in the USA, import only, 1979), *The Disappearing Boy* (PVK import only, 1980), *Bob the Birdman* (PVK, import only, 1981), *Bob the Birdman* (Powderworks, 1983), *Jeff Duff Orchestra* (Captain Vimto/BMG, 1989), *Angels and Rascals* (MDS, 1994).

The Dugites

Formed: *1978*
Style: *Pop rock*
Original line-up: *Lynda Nutter (vocals), Peter Crosbie (keyboards), Gunther Berghoffer (guitar), Phillip Bailey (bass), Clarence Bailey (drums)*

The Dugites emerged from Perth, Western Australia, playing a vibrant blend of 1960s-influenced pop, funk and soul. The band issued the self-financed single 'Hit Single'/'Bruce' in 1979, toured as backing band for **Dave Warner** in mid-1979 and then signed to the Sydney-based Deluxe label. In 1980 Paul Noonan (bass; ex-**Dave Warner's from the Suburbs**) replaced Phillip Bailey.

British keyboardist Bob Andrews (from Graham Parker and the Rumor) produced the band's eponymous debut album which mixed catchy pop tunes ('In Your Car', 'Mama Didn't Warn Me') with darker moments ('No God No Master', 'Gay Guys'). The single 'In Your Car'/'13 Again' combined a pinch of Sandie Shaw, The Shangri-Las and Blondie. It reached #34 in July 1980. *The Dugites* (August) reached Top 10 in Perth, and peaked at #22 nationally. It went on to attain gold status (35 000 copies sold).

Deluxe lifted two further singles from the album, 'Goodbye'/'No God No Master' (July 1980) and 'South Pacific'/'Gay Guys' (October). The Dugites next charted with the plaintive 'Waiting'/'Who Loves You More?' (#40 in August 1981), which was taken from the album *West of the World* (July; #33 in August). 'Part of Me'/'Never Touch' came out in

September. Rough Diamond issued the single 'No Money'/'Decide' (July 1982) and the mini-album *No Money* (August). By that stage, **Andrew Pendlebury** (guitar; ex-**Sports**) had replaced Berghoffer. Pendlebury was then replaced by Bob Fallovic (aka Boris Garter; ex-Stockings). Paul Williamson also joined on sax. By mid-1983, the line-up was down to Nutter, Crosbie, Bailey and Noonan.

The Dugites signed to Mercury/PolyGram, but their brief chart run had ended. *Cut the Talking* (April 1984) was a polished album that mixed bright synth-pop and funk, but it failed to chart. Likewise, the singles 'Cut the Talking'/'Michael and Rodney' (November 1983), 'Juno and Me'/'Everything Must Change' (April 1984) and 'It Ain't Like That'/'All that I Want' (August) were not successful. With the release of the album, The Dugites added Peter Kaldor (sax) and John Crosbie (trombone, trumpet) for touring purposes, but by the end of 1984 the members had gone their separate ways.

Albums: *The Dugites* (Deluxe, 1980), *West of the World* (Deluxe, 1981), *Cut the Talking* (Mercury, 1984).

The Dukes

Formed: *1990*
Style: *R&B, soul, funk*
Original line-up: *Sean Kelly (guitar,vocals; ex-***Teenage Radio Stars**, **Models**, **Absent Friends***), Geoff Stapleton (keyboards, guitar; ex-***Aliens**, **GANGgajang***), Peter Willersdorf (bass; ex-***Tim Gaze** *Band,* **Gyan***), Tony Georgeson (drums), Kevin Dubber (trumpet), Mark Dennison (sax) (aka The Brasstards)*

Prior to forming The Dukes in late 1990, Sean Kelly had enjoyed chart success with **Models** and **Absent Friends**. When The Dukes started gigging in March 1991, their sassy mix of R&B, soul and funk earned them a strong following on the Australian pub/club circuit. Sony signed The Dukes and issued the CD singles 'Gonna Get High' (#60 in August, 1992) and 'Faith' (#28 in December), plus the album *Harbour City* (December). 'Gonna Get High' reached the Top 10 in Perth. The album highlighted some fine ensemble playing and Kelly's wry lyrical sense of humour.

The band's third single from the album, 'Nothing Can Bring Me Down' (February 1993), was not successful. Yahoo Serious commissioned The Dukes to record versions of the Bobby Fuller Four's 'I Fought the Law' and The Beatles' 'Happiness is a Warm Gun' for his film *Reckless Kelly*. Serious also included 'Faith' on the *Reckless Kelly* soundtrack. The Dukes subsequently issued those three tracks (plus a live version of 'Gun in My Hand') on the CD EP 'I Fought the Law' which came out in August 1993. The Dukes broke up just as the CD EP hit the shops.

Album: *Harbour City* (Sony, 1992).

Robyne Dunn

Style: *Pop*

Sydney-based singer/songwriter/pianist Robyne Dunn (b. 1963) began her professional career with a role in the stage musical *Pearls Before Swine*. Her formative influences included singer/songwriters like Kate Bush, Joni Mitchell, Carole King and Burt Bacharach. With the aid of her brother Michael, she recorded a series of demos at Trackdown Studios.

Studio manager Jeff Watson was so impressed with her songs that he immediately took over her management. Watson and Dunn sent the demos to various record companies. Mushroom offered Dunn a deal on the strength of the demos, making her the first act on that label signed on the basis of an unsolicited tape. Mushroom issued Dunn's debut self-titled mini-album in October 1987, and she scored the support slot to overseas visitor Billy Joel on his 1988 Australian tour. English producer Gil Norton (**Triffids**, Echo and the Bunnymen, Pixies) worked with Dunn on her full-length debut album, *Labour of Liberty* (September 1989) which produced two singles, 'My Spark and Me' (April) and 'History' (September). The album showcased Dunn's soaring vocals and finely crafted, keyboard-laden songs.

Despite its strengths, the album was not successful and Dunn slipped from view. She re-emerged in late 1994 with the low-key, self-produced album *Stowaway*. Eschewing the sumptuous production values of *Labour of Liberty*, the album mostly featured just Dunn's voice and keyboards, giving full vent to the warmth and beauty of her stylish brand of pop.

Albums: *Robyne Dunn* (mini-album, Mushroom/Festival, 1987), *Labour of Liberty* (Mushroom/Festival, 1989), *Stowaway* (MDS, 1994).

Judith Durham (*see* The Seekers)

The Dynamic Hepnotics

Formed: *1979*
Style: *Soul, R&B*
Original line-up: *Continental Robert Susz (vocals, harmonic; ex-Rugcutters, Humdinger Dogs), Andrew Silver (guitar; ex-Big Town Playboys), Tim Martin (sax; ex-***Friends***), Manuel Patti (bass), Richard Ruhle (drums)*

Throughout the early 1980s, Sydney-based The Dynamic Hepnotics was the premier soul/R&B

outfit in the land. Fronted by the stylish Continental Robert Susz, the band boasted an authentic repertoire of 1950s and 1960s roots-based favourites, and a swag of quality originals in the same vein.

The original line-up recorded the four-track EP 'Shakin' All Over' for the fabulous Mambo label which came out in May 1980. By that stage, Bruce Allen (sax; ex-**Jeff St John** Band, **Ol'55**), Allen Britton (bass; ex-Mangrove Boogie Kings) and Robert Souter (drums; ex-**Lizard**, Gulliver's Travels, Living Legends) had joined Susz and Andrew Silver. The new line-up recorded the Susz-penned 'Hepnobeat'/'Funky Turban' single (September 1981). It initially came out on Mambo, then was reissued by Missing Link. Jim Niven (organ; ex-**Sports**) also played on the record. 'Hepnobeat'/ 'Funky Turban' was issued a third time in August 1982, this time as a 12-inch on Stateside (through CBS). The single was also issued in Europe (on the Statik label), the USA and Japan. Having established the connection with Missing Link, The Dynamic Hepnotics issued the *Strange Land* mini-album (August 1982). 'Hepnobeat' and 'Funky Turban' were again included on that excellent six-track release.

The Dynamic Hepnotics looked further afield, and in 1984 signed to Mushroom's White label. The first release on White was 'I'll Make You'/'The Meaning of Life' (May 1984), followed by 'Soul Kind of Feeling'/'Last to Know' (September) and 'Gotta be Wrong'/'Motley Crusaders' (March 1985). The singles launched the band into the premier league when 'Soul Kind of Feeling' peaked at #4 on the national chart in December 1984 and 'Gotta be Wrong' reached #7 in May 1985. In between came the album *Live*, which was a mix of originals and cover versions such as Scott/Malone's 'Turn on Your Lovelight' and Holland/Dozier/Holland's '(I'm a) Roadrunner' recorded live in the studio at A.A.V. Melbourne. By that stage, New Zealander Mike Gubb (keyboards; ex-Rough Justice) had joined the band.

The Dynamic Hepnotics recorded *Take You Higher* in early 1985. 'Whenever You're Ready'/ 'Blue Kind of Feeling' was lifted from the album as a single in July 1985. *Take You Higher* peaked at #19 on the national chart in June. At the end of 1985, Mark Simmonds replaced Bruce Allen on sax and Dave Brewer (ex-**Elks**) replaced Andrew Silver. Peter Bishop (trumpet) also joined the band, and the new line-up recorded 'On Our Way Now'/'The Work It Out' (March 1986).

It was to be the band's final release. Following further line-up changes with Duncan Archibald replacing Souter, Chris Pascoe replacing Gubb and Lloyd Swanton (ex-Benders) replacing Britton, the band broke up at the end of 1986. Continental Robert Susz concentrated full-time on his sideline band The Mighty Reapers (of Vengeance), which also included Dave Brewer, Richard Ruhle, Vito Portolesi (bass), Duncan Archibald (drums) and Sammila Sitole (percussion). As The Mighty Reapers, the band issued three albums of stylish soul/ R&B material, *The Mighty Reapers* (1993) *Trouble People* (1994) and *The Hurt is On* (1997), plus the cassette *You Gotta Reap* (1990).

Britton joined **The Foreday Riders** and then **The Bondi Cigars**. Gubb joined **Mental as Anything**, The Layabouts, **Dog Trumpet** then **The Headhunters**. Silver joined Wild Blue Yonder. Bruce Allen toured with **Ross Wilson's** Rockhouse, the **Fabulous Zarzoff Brothers** and The Eddys.

Dynamic Hepnotics albums: *Strange Land* (mini-album, Missing Link, 1982), *Live* (Mushroom/ Festival, 1984), *Take You Higher* (Mushroom/Festival, 1985); ***Mighty Reapers albums:*** *The Mighty Reapers* (Rufus/Polydor, 1993), *Trouble People* (Rufus/Polydor, 1994), *The Hurt is On* (Rufus/Polydor, 1997).

E

The Ears

Formed: *1979*
Style: *Art-punk*
Original line-up: *Sam Sejavka (vocals), Mick Lewis (guitar), Cathy McQuade (bass), Charles 'Chuck' Meo (drums)*

Alongside The Boys Next Door, **Models**, Whirlywirld, The Fabulous Marquises, etc., art-punk outfit The Ears became one of the most popular bands on the Melbourne inner-city/Crystal Ballroom scene. The Ears issued the independent single 'Leap for Lunch'/'The Crater' in early 1980.

Soon after, Carl Manuel replaced Charles Meo (who joined **Dorian Gray**) and Gus Till joined on keyboards. Missing Link issued The Ears' second single, 'Scarecrow'/'The Lollyhater' in early 1981. The songs echoed the sounds of David Bowie and Brian Ferry crossed with Magazine and The Boys Next Door. The band broke up at the end of 1981. Sejavka, Till and Manuel formed **Beargarden**, and Cathy McQuade joined **Deckchairs Overboard.** The Ears also had the tracks 'Perennial Boogie' and 'One Light' included on the Various Artists album *From Belgrave with Love* (Cleopatra, 1981).

The Ears had so influenced film-maker Richard Lowenstein (he shared a house with them) that he based his 1987 feature film *Dogs in Space* around their story. A couple of old Ears songs ('Dogs in Space' and 'Golf Course') were re-recorded for the film soundtrack. **INXS**' frontman, the late Michael Hutchence, appeared in the part of Dogs in Space singer 'Sam', and Charles Meo played the part of Dogs in Space drummer Chuck.

The Earthmen

Formed: *1991*
Style: *Pop*
Original line-up: *Scott Stevens (vocals), Aaron Goldberry (guitar), Stephen Nash (guitar), Eric Prentice (bass), Glen Peters (drums)*

Melbourne-based, 1960s-influenced pop band The Earthmen initially formed as a loose jamming outfit. By the time they recorded the single 'Stacey's Cupboard'/'Roll' towards the end of 1991, The Earthmen had yet to play live. The above line-up appeared on the single which came out on the Summershine label in April 1992.

Nick Betterham (also a member of Blindside) replaced Nash in December 1991, which coincided with The Earthmen's earliest gigs. Two more singles, 'Flyby'/'Too Far Down' (August 1992) and 'Cool Chick #59'/'Elephant' (demo) (October), plus the mini-album *Teen Sensations* (April 1993) came out on Summershine. The band's final release on Summershine was the EP 'The Fall and Rise of My Favourite Sixties Girl' (May 1994), featuring songs that were full-bodied and tuneful. By that stage, Ben Bleechmore had replaced Glen Peters and Robert Cooper had replaced Eric Prentice.

The Earthmen began to attract interest from overseas. The US label Slumberland had already issued 'Cool Chick #59'/'Momentum' as a single, after which The Earthmen signed to Atlantic's subsidiary Seed label. Seed issued *Teen Sensations* as a full-length album (with early singles added) in the USA and Europe, plus the EP 'The Fall and Rise of My Favourite Sixties Girl' (July 1994). That same month The Earthmen embarked on a US and UK tour. With the band's return, Aaron Goldberry left to be temporarily replaced by Stephen Moffatt (on loan from **The Plums**). The band contributed 'Kinder' to rooArt's Various Artists album *Youngblood 4* (September 1994).

In early 1996, The Earthmen signed to Warner Australia's East West label. The band's local releases for the year were the CD singles 'Scene Stealer' (April) and 'Hug Me Tighter' (August). By the time the band came to record its debut album, the line-up was down to Stevens, Betterham and Matt Sigley (bass, keyboards). **Underground Lovers**' drummer Derek Jon Yuen filled in for the album sessions. The release of the CD single 'Whoever's Been Using This Bed' (January 1997) and the album *Love Walked in* (April 1997) confirmed The Earthmen's ability to craft articulate, melodic pop music. 'Coloured in' came out as the album's second

CD single in June, followed by 'Love Walked in' during November,

The line-up stabilised once more at the end of 1996 with Stevens, Betterham, Sigley, Nick Murray (guitar, organ) and Craig Mitchell (drums; ex-Push of Love). Mitchell's previous band, Push of Love comprised Tony Tomorrow (guitar, vocals), Jock McCoy (guitar, vocals), Robert Murraylee (keyboards) and Mik Findlay (bass). Push of Love issued the single 'Strange Big City'/'Every Day' (September 1986) and the mini-album *Shake the Tree* (October) on the Chase label. Greg Hynes and Russell Bradley played drums on the album before Mitchell joined.

The Earthmen also contributed 'The House that Jack Kerouac Built' to the **Go-Betweens** tribute album *Right Here* on Hippy Knight Records (1996). The band has supported international visitors like Alanis Morrisette, Buffalo Tom and Lemonheads.

Albums: *Teen Sensations* (mini-album, Summershine, 1993), *Love Walked in* (Warner/East West, 1997).

The Eastern Dark

Formed: *1984*
Style: *Punk rock, pop*
Original line-up: *James Darrock (guitar, vocals; ex-***Celibate Rifles***), Bill Gibson (bass, piano, guitar, vocals), Geoff Milne (drums; ex-Sigh of Relief)*

Of all the legendary Sydney-based independent guitar bands of the 1980s (**The New Christs**, **The Screaming Tribesmen**, **Beasts of Bourbon**, **The Hard-Ons**, etc.), The Eastern Dark will be remembered as the most talented, all-encompassing and passionate bunch of the lot. The band was one of the pioneering power trios on the Australian alternative scene. Unfortunately, the band never got the chance to fulfil its early promise because guiding light James Darrock died in a car accident on 4 March 1986. It was a tragic end to a classic band.

Darrock formed The Eastern Dark in January 1984, after two years as **The Celibate Rifles'** bass player. One of the band's earliest ambitions was to play every Ramones song ever recorded. Accordingly, over the next two years, the band opened each gig with a Ramones song (in chronological order) until the catalogue had been exhausted! The Waterfront label issued the band's classic debut single, 'Julie is a Junkie'/'Johnny and Dee' (August 1985), which became a #1 alternative hit. Although it reflected Darrock's Ramones/**Radio Birdman** fixation, it also revealed his ability to craft perfectly structured, neo-guitar pop. At the time, rock writer J.J. Adams described The Eastern Dark as the epitome of inner-city cool.

The Eastern Dark completed its debut, Rob Younger-produced mini-album, *Long Live the New Flesh*, in February 1986, just days before setting off for its third tour of Melbourne. Tragedy struck on the Hume Highway when the band's van (driven by Darrock) left the road near Wagga Wagga, NSW. As well as killing Darrock, the accident put Billy Gibson, Geoff Milne and the band's sound engineer, Tim Pittman, in hospital. Darrock was 26 years old. Waterfront issued the mini-album in July, complete with a dedication to James Darrock. In June 1990, Waterfront issued the double retrospective album *Girls on the Beach (with Cars)*, which compiled live material (including one of Darrock's best songs, 'Whore') and unissued studio cuts. Steven Danno included The Eastern Dark's 'Stay Alone' on the Sydney compilation *Swingin' from the Trees*, which came out on Au-go-go Records (1988).

Once fully recovered from the accident, Gibson went on to join The Smelly Tongues, The Surfin' Caesars, **The Hellmenn**, **The New Christs** and, in 1996, Evan Dando's band Lemonheads. At the end of 1996, Gibson returned to Australia and joined Hey! Charger. Milne played with **The Plunderers** and The Red Planet Rocketts.

Albums: *Long Live the New Flesh* (mini-album, Waterfront, 1986), *Girls on the Beach (with Cars)* (Waterfront, 1990).

The Easybeats

Formed: *1964*
Style: *Beat pop*
Original line-up: **Stevie Wright** *(vocals; ex-Chris Langdon and the Langdells), George Young (guitar), Harry Vanda (born Johannes Vandenberg, guitar, ex-Starfighters, Starlighters), Dick Diamonde (born Dingernam Vandersluys, bass), Gordon 'Snowy' Fleet (drums; ex-Mojos)*

The history of The Easybeats spans more than two decades, with the band becoming one of Australia's most successful music exports. During the mid-1960s, amid scenes of screaming teenage girls and mass hysteria ('Easyfever'), The Easybeats managed to issue a legacy of fine beat pop. The band's classic working-class anthem, 'Friday on My Mind', remains one of the most exciting singles issued during that, or any other, era.

The Easybeats formed in 1964 around five European migrants. Dutch-born Harry Vanda and Dick Diamonde were living at the Villawood Migrant Hostel when they met 15-year-old English-

The Easybeats

born **Stevie Wright** and Scottish-born George Young. Young was the younger brother of Alex (aka George Alexander) who found success in the UK with The Big Six and Grapefruit. The last member to join was English-born Snowy Fleet. Unlike most other local bands of the day, The Easybeats donned neat matching suits and quickly made an impact at Sydney's most popular discos like Beatle Village, Surf City and Havana Village. Music publisher Ted Albert signed the band to Albert Productions and EMI/Parlophone. Over the next two years, The Easybeats became Australia's top band, notching up a string of exceptional hit singles and undertaking hugely successful tours. The wild hysteria experienced at Easybeats concerts shocked and outraged civic officials.

Initially, the songwriting chores were taken on by Wright and Young. They wrote the early hits 'For My Woman'/'Say that You're Mine' (Melbourne #5 in July 1965), 'She's So Fine'/'The Old Oak Tree' (Sydney and Melbourne #1 in June), 'Women (Make You Feel Alright)'/'In My Book' (Sydney #1, Melbourne #7 in January 1966), 'Come and See Her'/'I Can See' (Sydney #1, Melbourne #10 in May 1966) and 'Sorry'/'Funny Feelin'' (Sydney and Melbourne #4 in November 1966). Gradually Vanda and Young came to prominence as the band's hit-making, songwriting team. Their hits were 'Wedding Ring'/'Me or You' (Sydney #6, Melbourne #13 in September 1965), 'Sad Lonely and Blue'/'Easy as Can be' (Sydney #4, Melbourne #24 in November 1965), 'I'll Make You Happy' (*Easyfever* EP) (Sydney #1, Melbourne #7 in August 1966) and 'Friday on My Mind'/'Made My Bed, Gonna Lie in It' (Sydney and Melbourne #1 in December 1966).

By 1966, The Easybeats had also issued three strong albums. Having achieved as much as they could, The Easybeats left Australia bound for the UK on 14 July 1966. United Artists had already issued 'Come and See Her'/'Make You Feel Alright (Women)' as a single in the UK. The band recorded 'Friday on My Mind' with producer Shel Talmy who had already moulded hits for The Who and The Kinks. Talmy also produced the band's first UK album, *Good Friday* (retitled *Friday on My Mind* for the US market). 'Friday on My Mind' immediately reached #1 across Australia, but it took a little longer for the British to catch on. It finally achieved a #6 placing. As the single reached the Top 10 in Germany, Holland, France and Italy during March 1967, The Easybeats undertook a European tour supporting The Rolling Stones. 'Friday on My Mind' also made #16 in the USA. The single went on to sell over a million copies worldwide.

The Easybeats returned to Australia in May 1967 for a successful homecoming tour. The hits continued with 'Who'll be the One?'/'Do You Have a Soul?' (Sydney #19, Melbourne #12 in April 1967) and 'Heaven and Hell'/'Pretty Girl' (Sydney #11, Melbourne #14 in July 1967). As with The Who's 'Waltz for a Pig', 'Do You Have a Soul?' was reputedly directed at Shel Talmy. Snowy Fleet left the band once the tour was completed. Back in the UK, The Easybeats took on English-born Australian Tony Cahill (ex-**Purple Hearts**) as his replacement. In August 1967, the band commenced a two-month American tour supporting Gene Pitney and The Buckinghams.

During early 1968, Vanda and Young began to craft a series of epic pop productions for The Easybeats that ranged from classic psychedelia and screaming rockers to Tom Jonesian ballads. 'The Music Goes Round My Head'/'Come in You'll Get Pneumonia' (Sydney #34, Melbourne #25 in January 1968), 'Hello, How Are You?'/'Falling Off the Edge of the World' (Sydney #23, Melbourne #26 in March 1968) and 'Land of Make Believe'/'Good Times' (Sydney #22 in August 1968) were all Australian hits. 'Hello, How Are You?' returned The Easybeats to the UK charts for the first time in nearly 18 months when it reached #20. The glorious rocker 'Good Times' was later covered with much success by **INXS** and **Jimmy Barnes**.

After initial recording sessions had been aborted, a second overseas album on United Artists finally came out in June 1968. In the UK it was titled *Vigil* (as it was also called in Australia on

Parlophone); in the USA it was *Falling Off the Edge of the World*. From that stage onwards, The Easybeats were effectively Vanda and Young's backing band. The group spirit had deteriorated by late 1968. The last group singles were 'Lay Me Down and Die'/'See Line Woman' (November 1968) and 'St Louis'/'Can't Find Love' (national #21 in August 1969). 'St Louis' was another fine rocker in the 'Good Times' mould, and was the band's first release on the Polydor label.

The *Friends* album was actually a batch of Vanda and Young demos (with 'St Louis' added) that Polydor issued in November 1969. The last Australian single to that time was 'I Love Marie'/'Gonna Make It' (November 1969), while the UK also got 'Friends'/'Rock & Roll Boogie' (May 1970). Meanwhile, as 'St Louis' was making its minor chart rise, The Easybeats reluctantly undertook a five-week Australian tour. Parlophone/Albert also issued the year-old, psychedelic-tinged 'Peculiar Hole in the Sky'/'HP Man' as a (failed) single (September 1969). As the lacklustre tour ground onwards, it was obvious the band was on its last legs. Once the tour was completed, The Easybeats went their separate ways. Ironically, as Vanda and Young were left with debts amounting to $85 000, 'St Louis' made an appearance in the lower reaches of the USA charts.

Stevie Wright stayed in Australia, formed a band called Rachette and joined the cast of *Jesus Christ Superstar*. Cahill returned to the UK and joined **Python Lee Jackson**. Likewise, Vanda and Young returned to the UK to work for three years as freelance songwriters/producers/musicians. They returned to Sydney in 1973 and set up home in the Albert studio complex. Throughout the mid-1970s, as Australia's top producers, Vanda and Young proceeded to swamp the local charts with a seemingly endless string of hits for **John Paul Young**, **AC/DC**, **Ray Burgess**, **William Shakespeare**, **The Angels**, **Cheetah** and **Rose Tattoo**. Their finest effort was reserved for **Stevie Wright**, for whom they crafted the epic #1 hit 'Evie' in 1974. Vanda and Young also enjoyed chart success here and overseas with their own alter-ego project **Flash and the Pan**.

Interest in The Easybeats continued into the 1970s and 1980s. In 1977 EMI issued the Glenn A. Baker-compiled *The Shame Just Drained*, which comprised most of the tracks from the band's aborted, and previously unissued, second British album. Baker also compiled the essential *Absolute Anthology* in 1980, which was strong enough to reach #35 on the national chart. The Raven label (also co-run by Baker) issued the EPs *Mean Ol' Loving* (1979), *Son of Easyfever* (1980) and *Son of Son of Easyfever* (1981), plus the album *EP LP Volume 2* (which compiled all the EP cuts). The television-advertised compilation *The Easybeats* put the band back on the charts briefly in 1981. The Albert label issued the singles 'Friday on My Mind'/'She's So Fine', 'Wedding Ring' (October 1980) and 'Good Times'/'Land of Make Believe' (1981).

In October 1986, the Vanda/Young/Wright/Diamonde/Fleet line-up of The Easybeats reunited for a successful Australian tour. Albert issued the *Histor-Easy* EP in November as a souvenir of the tour. One side featured a clumsily edited medley of the band's biggest hits, backed by a live version of 'She's So Fine' from 1966 and the 1968 track 'Hello, How Are You?'. Raven later included five tracks from the band's 7 November 1986 concert at the Sydney Entertainment Centre on the album *Live—Studio and Stage*.

Albums: *Easy* (EMI/Parlophone, 1965), *It's 2 Easy* (EMI/Parlophone, 1966), *Easybeats Volume 3* (EMI/Parlophone, 1966), *Best of + 'Pretty Girl'* (EMI/Parlophone, 1967), *Friends* (EMI/Parlophone, 1968), *Vigil* (EMI/Parlophone, 1968), *The Shame Just Drained* (EMI, 1977), *Absolute Anthology* (EMI, 1980), *EPLP Volume 2* (Raven, 1981), *The Easybeats* (Hammard, 1981), *The Definitive Series* (Albert/EMI, 1992), *Live—Studio and Stage* (Raven, 1995).

Rob E.G.

Style: *Pop*

As Glenn A. Baker has noted, Rob E.G. (real name Robert George Porter) was, by any criterion, a curious sensation. Amidst Australia's frantic rock'n'roll boom of the early 1960s, clean-cut Rob E.G. appeared on stage with a lap steel guitar, playing novelty instrumentals with titles like 'Whiplash' and 'Railroadin''. As such, he was a permissible teen idol for the young girls of the community.

Rob E.G. learnt the lap steel while still at school. He first came to record company attention in 1959 when he played a version of the Santo and Johnny hit 'Sleepwalk' on Sydney television. He signed to the Rex label and issued the minor hit singles Hank Williams' 'Your Cheatin' Heart'/'Seven Foot Two' (February 1960), 'Whiplash'/'Do You Love Me?' (Sydney #12 in August 1960), 'Railroadin''/'My First Love' (Sydney #31 in October 1960) and 'Comanche Sunset'/'China Doll' (March 1961).

His career almost came to an end when he suffered spinal injuries in a car accident. He returned to active work in 1962, compered *Opportunity*

Knocks for Channel Nine and signed to Festival. Over the next three years, he scored major hits with 'Si Senor (I Theenk)'/'Swan River (Twist)' (Sydney #1, Melbourne #2 in May 1962), '5-4-3-2-1 Zero'/'Jamaican Farewell' (Melbourne #3 in October), 'Jezabel'/'Stage to Cimmaron' (Sydney #2, Melbourne #8 in May 1963), '55 Days at Peking'/'Greenhorn' (Sydney and Melbourne #1 in July), 'Soul'/'Cottin' Pickin" (Sydney #27, Melbourne #25 in November) and the vocal single 'When You're Not Near'/'Aloha Oe' (Sydney #7, Melbourne #12 in August 1964).

Some of his singles that missed the Top 40 included 'Carmen'/'Senorita' (March 1964), 'Tim-Buc-Too'/'Adventures in Paradise' (May 1964) and 'Hawaii Tattoo'/'Peter Gunn' (December 1964). By 1964, Porter was a *Bandstand* regular and also hosting *Surf Sound*. With the arrival of Beatlemania, the first phase of his career ended. Beatles manager Brian Epstein encouraged Porter to travel to England, which he did with little success. As Robie Porter, he continued recording singles for Festival: 'Either Way I Lose'/'Born' (July 1966), 'I Haven't Got Anything Better to Do'/'No One Lives in My World' (March 1967), 'You Could End the World'/'Sure Has Been Good Lovin' You Baby' (January 1968), and 'Writing's on the Wall'/'If You'd Let Me' (April 1968).

Porter then travelled to the USA to write and record. He returned to Australia in 1970 and issued three singles on his independent Sparmac label, 'Gemini'/'He is Not Me' (August 1970), 'Santa Claus'/'Funky Version' (December) and a cover of the Joe Cocker/Chris Stainton song 'Try to Find More Love (There Must be a Reason)'/'Empty' (March 1971). He turned his attention to production, management and promotion. Over the 1971–72 period, he produced hits for **Daddy Cool**, **Rick Springfield** and **Healing Force**. In 1973, he set up the Wizard label with Stephen Binder and began producing hit singles and albums for **Hush** and **Marcia Hines**. A number of Hines' most memorable tracks, including 'Shining' and 'A Love Story', were written by Porter. Although remembered as a novelty act from the 1960s, Porter was a successful music businessman throughout the 1970s and 1980s.

Rob E.G. albums: *Jezabel* (Festival, 1963), *Best of Rob E.G.* (Festival, 1964), *Rob E.G. Plays Hawaiian* (Festival, 1964), *Guitar Sounds of Rob E.G.* (Summit, 1965), *5-4-3-2-1 The Festival File Volume Three* (Festival, 1988); ***Robie Porter albums:*** *Songs* (Festival, 1968), *Heart of the Matter* (MGM, 1969).

Lisa Edwards

Style: *Pop*

Vocalist Lisa Edwards was primarily known as a regular back-up singer with **John Farnham**, alongside the likes of Venetta Fields and Lindsay Field. Edwards has sung on most of Farnham's solo albums, as well as numerous other sessions. She has also pursued a sporadic solo career which has resulted in at least one massive hit, a sensual cover of Godley and Creme's 'Cry'.

Lisa's debut solo single was 'Centre Spread'/'Power' on Mushroom (September 1981). In 1985 she issued a duet with Adrian Campbell, 'You Are My Melbourne'/'Melbourne the Beginning', on Powderworks. Throughout the mid-1980s, Edwards sang with White Light Orchestra, the Turbo Luv Nuns and dance/disco outfit Short Circuit before joining the **John Farnham** Band in 1987.

Edwards sang on the Short Circuit album *Waiting for the Big One* (1988) and the singles 'He's Got It' (May 1987), 'Waiting for the Big One' (May 1988) and 'Burning for You' (December 1988). In 1992, Edwards scored her biggest hit with 'Cry' (#5 in July). Her second single was 'So Dangerous' (1992). In August 1993, Edwards issued her debut album *Thru the Hoop*, which featured 'Cry', as well as yielding two further singles, 'Until the Day' (June) and 'Lose Myself in You' (September). Neither was a chart success, and Edwards concentrated on her work with **John Farnham**.

Album: *Thru the Hoop* (Emerald City/Polydor, 1993).

Mark Edwards (*see* The Runners)

Effigy

Formed: *1993*
Style: *Gothic pop*
Original line-up: *Peter Hardman (guitar, vocals), Annie Beckerling (bass), Jason Stacy (drums)*

Highly touted Perth band Effigy's influences ranged from The Cure and The Stone Roses to Smashing Pumpkins and Garbage. Effigy signed to Roadrunner Australasia in 1995, becoming the first local act on the roster of that international record company. Effigy relocated to Melbourne. The CD singles 'Lovers' (October 1996) and 'Small' (February 1997) attracted attention, which was consolidated with the release of the album *Effigy* (April 1997). The third CD single, 'I Give in', followed in May.

Album: *Effigy* (Roadrunner/Sony, 1997).

Eighteenth Century Quartet

Formed: *1966*
Style: *Folk, 'baroque' rock*
Original line-up: **Hans Poulsen** *(guitar, vocals, bouzouki, mandolin),* **Keith Glass** *(guitar, vocals; ex-Rising Suns), John Pugh (guitar, violin, autoharp, harmonica, vocals; ex-Roadrunners), Frank Lyons (bass), Dennis Forster (drums, ex-Rising Suns)*

Melbourne band Eighteenth Century Quartet was essentially a manufactured group, put together by promoter Ian Oshlack to capitalise on the American trend towards folk and baroque pop as practised by The Lovin' Spoonful ('Do You Believe in Magic?') and The Left Banke ('Walk Away Renee').

Before the other members joined, **Hans Poulsen** had already issued his own custom-pressed single 'The World Goes on'/'I'm Gonna Treat You Good' (on the East label) under the name of 18CQ. That line-up also comprised Steve Dunstan and the wonderfully named Baarda. Poulsen was a prolific songwriter, and Eighteenth Century Quartet played an almost totally original set which was virtually unheard of at that stage. The band signed to the Go!! label and issued two singles, 'Rachel'/'Distant Relative' (October 1966) and 'Am I a Lover?'/ 'Drawing Room' (December 1966). The first two songs were Poulsen compositions, the second two were written by **Keith Glass**. By the end of 1966, Poulsen had left to concentrate on his songwriting. He enjoyed a string of solo hits in the early 1970s.

By the time the second single came out, the band's live repertoire bore no relationship to the earlier folk-rock trappings. Glass and John Pugh had come from an R&B background, so the band began playing more uptempo soul/R&B/rock material. In March 1967, Glass and Pugh abandoned the Eighteenth Century Quartet concept to form **Cam-Pact**. Glass later re-recorded 'Drawing Room' with **Cam-Pact**.

The Eighty Eights

Formed: *1979*
Style: *Pop, rock*
Original line-up: *Maurice D'Abruzzio (vocals, guitar), Larry Van Kriedt (guitar; ex-***AC/DC***), Kent Jackson (bass), John Bartram (drums)*

The Eighty Eights (formerly known as The Motels) were an energetic pop/rock band hailing from Newcastle, NSW. Larry Van Kriedt had a background of some note; born in San Francisco, his father was a renowned jazz sax player; he was also the original bass player for the nascent **AC/DC**. Likewise, American-born John Bartram was a jazz drummer of solid reputation. Kent Jackson was from New Zealand.

The band's debut single was a snappy little pop/reggae song by the title of 'She Fell in Love with James Bond'/'What's Coming to You' (October 1980). Initially released on the small Result label, it was reissued in January 1981 when the band signed to PolyGram Records. In 1981, Result/PolyGram issued two singles, 'Don't Call Us'/'Chinese Opera' (July), 'Time Machine'/'Light Year' (September), the EP *Live Pop* (May) and the album *Top of the World*. The records were not successful nationally, and the band broke up in early 1982. D'Abruzzio formed Getaway Plane and Van Kriedt formed **Non Stop Dancers**. Getaway Plane comprised D'Abruzzio (guitar, vocals), Malcolm Toft (guitar, sax, keyboards), Bruce Feltham (bass) and Tony Ball (drums). The original line-up issued one single on the Powderworks label in 1987, 'Love Without Danger'/'Wasted'.

By 1989, the line-up had changed completely, with only D'Abruzzio remaining from the original. The new players were Wayne Miller (keyboards), Jeff Gordon (bass) and John Prior (drums). The new line-up issued 'Premonition'/'Rising Voices' on the Vision label in September 1989. By that stage, Getaway Plane had run its course and the band broke up soon after.

Album: *Top of the World* (Result/PolyGram, 1981).

Electric Hippies

Formed: *1993*
Style: *Psychedelic pop*
Original line-up: *Justin Stanley (guitar, keyboards, vocals; ex-***Noiseworks***), Steve Balbi (bass, guitar, vocals; ex-***Noiseworks***)*

With the break-up of **Noiseworks**, ex-members Justin Stanley and Steve Balbi formed the production and recording venture known as Electric Hippies. The duo's first release was the CD EP *It's Cool* (featuring the track 'Jonny Courageous' which was reputedly a swipe at former **Noiseworks** frontman Jon Stevens) (October 1993). The CD singles 'Greedy People' (#29 in June 1994) and 'I Believe in You' (September) preceded the album *Electric Hippies* in October.

The album mixed *Revolver*-era Beatles melodies with a *Ziggy Stardust*-period David Bowie glam rock aesthetic. There was also a limited edition version of the album which featured three-dimensional artwork à la The Rolling Stones' 1967 psychedelic album *Their Satanic Majesties Request*. 'Jonny Courageous'

Electric Hippies

was then reissued as a CD single in December 1994. Electric Hippies issued a fifth CD single, 'Didn't Mean to Make You Cry', in early 1995. Electric Hippies have produced records for Pearls & Swine, Vincent Stone (the 'Sunshine' and 'Best of My Love' CD singles and the *Vincent Stone* album, all 1993), **Juice**, **Jenny Morris** and Nikka Costa (the excellent 1996 album *Butterfly Rocket* and its single 'Master Blaster').

In early 1997, Balbi unveiled his new band, Universe which comprised former **X** drummer Cathy Green on bass, Big Bird (real name Matt McCormack, guitar; ex-Starworld), Jim Denley (flute) and Cath Synnerdahl (drums; ex-Wrecking Crew, Mother Hubbard). Synnerdahl's previous band, Mother Hubbard, played a powerful blend of rootsy blues, Southern soul and hard rock. In 1996, the band issued the CD EP 'Pain', the full-length album *You Me Him She* and the CD singles 'River', 'Two Weeks' and 'Running Away' on Festival's Outlaw label. Universe issued its debut CD EP, *Above Water*, on the Phantom label during September.

Album: *Electric Hippies* (rooArt/Warner, 1994).

Electric Pandas

Formed: *1983*
Style: *Pop, rock*
Original line-up: *Lin Buckfield (vocals, guitar), Tim 'Pretty Boy' Walter (guitar), Warren Slater (bass), Mark 'Hips' Stinson (drums)*

For a while around 1984/1985, Electric Pandas were genuine pop stars. Led by the energetic Lin Buckfield, the band played a punchy, melodic and commercial brand of pop rock. Many predicted a rosy future for the band, but things fell apart in late 1986.

Electric Pandas signed to Regular and issued the hit single 'Big Girls'/'TV Dogs' (#8 in Sydney during May 1984). It launched the band on to the Australian touring circuit in a big way. The 12-inch EP 'Let's Gamble' followed at the end of the year, after which the band went into the studio to record an album. By that stage, Buckfield had replaced the rest of the band en masse: Craig Karl Wacholz (ex-Dee Minor and The Dischords) replaced Tim Walter on lead guitar, Marcel Chaloupka (ex-Smith, Moving Parts) replaced Warren Slater on bass and Phillip Campbell replaced Mark Stinson on drums.

Point Blank (September 1985) and its singles 'Missing Me'/'Twenty Revolutionaries' (July) and 'Italian Boys'/'Johnny' (October) were not as successful as the debut single. *Point Blank* peaked at #22 on the national chart during November. It was enough, however, to keep the band in the public eye. There were other line-up changes (Brad Holmes replacing Campbell, Neil McDonald replacing Chaloupka and Charlie Chan joining on keyboards) before the band broke up in April 1987.

Lin Buckfield also issued a duet single with **James Reyne** for the Freestyle label in April 1985 'R.O.C.K.'/'Under My Thumb'. After the Pandas broke up, Buckfield formed F.O.O.D. with Craig Wacholz, Ray Spole (bass) and Glen Patterson (drums). F.O.O.D. issued the 12-inch single 'Happy House' in 1990. With new members added, including two sax players, Neil McKenzie and Dieter Pruggo, Buckfield then transformed F.O.O.D. into Happy House. The band's dance-funk was heard on the 12-inch single 'What U Wanna Do That For?', the CD EP 'Shelter Down' and the album *Happy House* in 1993. Happy House issued a final CD EP, 'Passion', in June 1995.

Electric Pandas album: *Point Blank* (Regular/Festival, 1985); ***Happy House album:*** *Happy House* (Shock, 1993).

Maureen Elkner

Style: *Pop*

As Noel McGrath has noted, Maureen Elkner's one big hit single, 'Rak Off Normie'/'Norman', had the effect of categorising her as a comedy/novelty artist. The song was a sequel to **Bob Hudson's** #1 hit 'The Newcastle Song', and in that regard it was successful. It did, however, mean that Elkner's other pop-oriented records were neglected.

Elkner started out in the late 1960s with the female vocal trio The Chiffons, which also contained Sue Brady and Judy Condon. The trio sang back-up vocals for **Johnny Farnham**, and toured Vietnam around 1969 with The Gallery, entertaining Australian troops stationed there. The Chiffons recorded one single for Astor, 'Secret Love'/'It Hurts Like 16' (April 1970), before Elkner left to be replaced by Pauline Brady. In 1974, Elkner issued two Suzi Quatro-styled pop rock singles on Festival/Infinity 'Dynamite'/'Barley Rye' (January) and a cover of The Troggs' 'Wild Thing'/'Sweet Morning' (May). She signed to M7 Records (which also issued Hudson's records) and issued five singles and two albums, *Maureen Elkner* and *Love Tracks* (1977).

The **Bob Hudson**/Chris Neal-penned 'Rak Off Normie' reached #6 in June 1975. Her other singles were 'Leo from Cleo'/'Some Girls Do Some Girls Don't' (February 1976), 'Hello in There'/'What are We Fighting For?' (May), 'Love Suite' (September), and 'The Loving Song'/'You Don't Love Me' (December 1977).

Albums: *Maureen Elkner* (M7, 1976), *Love Tracks* (M7, 1977).

The Elks

Formed: *1976*
Style: *R&B*
Original line-up: *Ivan Zar (harmonica), Terry Serio (vocals), John Hood (guitar; ex-***Sid Rumpo***), Dave Brewer (guitar), Keith Jacobs (bass), Reg Zar (drums)*

Perth-based R&B band The Elks formed in 1976 around the Zar brothers Ivan and Reg. The pioneering Zar brothers had been playing R&B around Perth since the late 1960s. Some of their early bands included King Biscuit Company, Uncle Meat, Tampa Red, Mr Pig, Lucy Crown, Bitch and Last Chance Café. Very much in the style of bands such as Sydney's **Foreday Riders** and Adelaide's Smokestack Lightnin', The Elks initially drew on Chicago electric blues for inspiration. Gradually, the band adopted a more commercial R&B sound. In December 1977, American-born Howard Shawcross (ex-Last Chance Café) replaced Keith Jacobs on bass. The band toured the Eastern States four times between 1977 and 1979.

In July 1979, Missing Link issued the band's debut **Matt Taylor**-produced album, *Refer to Drawer*. Prior to that, the band issued the independent cassette album *FM Live*, which was taken from a radio broadcast by Melbourne community radio station 3RRR-FM in April 1978. The Zar brothers left in mid-1978. Tim Coyle (keyboards), Michael Fagan (harmonica) and Gary Masel (drums; all ex-Zephyrs) joined. Masel fell ill in August. Howie Johnson and Gil Matthews (ex-**Billy Thorpe** and the Aztecs) filled in until Masel recovered in November. Coyle left in December and Serio took up rhythm guitar. The band continued to tour throughout 1980 and 1981. Vinnie Crea replaced Masel in 1980. The Perth-based Parole label issued 'Party Girl'/'Fast Buck' in July 1981, but by the end of the year The Elks had broken up.

Brewer went on to work with **The Dynamic Hepnotics** and popular Sydney R&B bands The Champions and The Mighty Reapers (of Vengeance), while Shawcross joined **The Riptides** and then The Champions. In 1984, Shawcross formed pub-rock band Howard I Know, with which he issued two singles, 'Orwell Street'/'Days of Our Lives' (August 1985) and 'Standby Flight'/'Failure' (June 1986), on the Red Eye label. In the early 1990s, he joined Perth hard rock band The Jackals. The Jackals line-up comprised Shawcross, Paul McCarthy (vocals), Phil Bradley (guitar) and Howie Johnson (drums). The band had already issued the single 'Faint Aroma of Performing Seals'/'Power' (1987) and the 12-inch EP 'Lucy's Falling Backwards' (1988) on the Modern label by the time Shawcross joined. The Jackals issued the album *Pheal* in 1992

Serio turned to acting, taking the part of Mike in John Clark's 1982 feature film *Running on Empty* with **Deborah Conway**. He also issued a solo single in August 1982, 'It All Comes Running Back'/'Sitting in the Dark', which was lifted from the film soundtrack. His biggest break came in 1986 when he portrayed **Johnny O'Keefe** in the Seven Network's miniseries *Shout! The Story of Johnny O'Keefe*. He has since appeared in the miniseries *Fields of Fire* (1987), plus the drama series *Rafferty's Rules* (1987) and *GP* (1995). Serio kept his vocal chords active with The Champions, which also featured Brewer and Shawcross. Other members of The Champions over the years included Robert Brooks (guitar, keyboards), Vicki Kennedy (vocals), Sally King (vocals, guitar), Graeme Gibb (bass), Tim Martin (sax), Richard Ruhle (drums) and Daryl Jacobs (drums). The Champions issued an album, *Dancing is Crazy*, and single, 'Eye to Eye'/'Get Away' (August 1984) on the Arika label. Brewer later joined jazz band The Catholics.

Elks album: *Refer to Drawer* (Missing Link, 1979); ***Champions album:*** *Dancing is Crazy* (Arika, 1984).

The Elois

Formed: *1964*
Style: *Garage punk*
Original line-up: *Doug Blair (vocals, rhythm guitar), Dennis Fiorini (lead guitar, vocals), Michael Dzuirek (bass), Bill Van Berkel (drums)*

As with **The Creatures, The Throb, The Missing Links, The Black Diamonds, The In-Sect, The Atlantics,** The D-Coys, The Morlocks and The Running Jumping Standing Still, The Elois can lay claim to one of the most extraordinary Australian garage-punk singles of the 1960s. The Elois' 'I'm a Man'/'By My Side' came out on W&G's In label in April 1967. The single actually reached #38 on the Melbourne charts, but as soon as the Spencer Davis Group's version of 'I'm a Man' became a hit, The Elois' version sank without a trace. The manic 'By My Side' later appeared on Raven's seminal *Ugly Things* compilation (1980).

The Elois formed in the Victorian township of Maryborough in 1964. Inspired by The Rolling Stones, The Who, The Pretty Things and The Yardbirds, the band played revved-up R&B. The band's name was taken from H.G. Wells' sci-fi novel *The Time Machine*, in which the peace-loving race of future humans, The Elois (pronounced E-loys) were often attacked by the brutal Morlocks. Alan Rowe (vocals) replaced Blair in 1965. Fiorini began to adopt a tougher guitar sound, introducing the 'all-new' Echolet fuzzbox as his stock-in-trade. The Elois competed in the Melbourne heats of the 1966 Hoadley's National Battle of the Sounds. Greg Heenan then replaced Dzuirek, and the band moved to Melbourne. The In label issued the 'I'm a Man' single, after which The Elois recorded four tracks for a prospective EP. Before In could issue the EP, however, The Elois broke up.

Tommy Emmanuel

Style: *Country, rock, blues*

Guitarist Tommy Emmanuel (b. 1955) is one of Australia's most respected musicians. For many years Emmanuel was a session player and sideman known for his versatility and easy-going personality. He has played on dozens of albums, from the likes of **Air Supply, Swanee** and **Dragon** to **John Farnham, Doug Parkinson** and **Daryl Braithwaite**.

As a songwriter (co-writing with 1960s star Steve Kipner), his compositions have been recorded by **Olivia Newton-John**, Al Jarreau and Sheena Easton. With his brother Phil in Goldrush and The Emmanuel Brothers Band, he established a reputation as a guitar virtuoso. It is for his successful solo career, however, that he is best known. As well as having produced a series of exceptional albums, Emmanuel is the only instrumentalist in the country consistently drawing capacity audiences in the live forum. Over the years, Emmanuel has toured as support to overseas visitors like Bob Marley and the Wailers, Eric Clapton, Stevie Wonder, Albert Lee and Chet Atkins.

As a child prodigy during the 1960s, Tommy and his brother Phil formed their own bands like The Emmanuel Quartet, The Midget Safaries and The Trailblazers (completed by siblings Chris on drums and Virginia on slide guitar). Tommy commenced his session career during the 1970s; some of his most notable appearances were on the **Air Supply** hit singles 'Lost in Love', 'All Out of Love', 'Every Woman in the World' and 'Now and Forever'.

In 1978 Emmanuel joined **Doug Parkinson** and the Southern Star Band, playing on the album *I'll be Around*. With the break-up of The Southern Star Band in late 1980, Emmanuel joined **John Farnham's** backing band, which also comprised Sam McNally (keyboards; ex-**Stylus**), Barry Sullivan (bass; ex-**Chain**) and David Jones (drums). That line-up appeared on Farnham's 1981 solo album *Uncovered*. In 1982, Emmanuel joined his brother Phil's band Goldrush as drummer; the rest of the line-up included Mark Collins (banjo, mandolin, guitar, vocals), Dave Mare (vocals, guitars) and Chris Haigh (bass, vocals; ex-Gillian Eastoe and King Dog). Goldrush issued one album, *Live at Last* (Oz/EMI, June 1983). Tommy and Phil also toured throughout 1982 as The Emmanuel Brothers Wiz Band, which comprised Chris Haigh, Shauna Jensen (vocals), Graham Nevnepia (percussion) and Steve Hopes (drums).

During 1983 and 1984 Tommy toured with **The Bushwackers**. In 1985, he played drums in the Sharon O'Neill Band, and in 1986 replaced Robert Taylor in **Dragon**. He played guitar on **Dragon's** platinum selling *Dreams of Ordinary Men* album and toured the world with the band. He also played sessions on **Dragon's** 1989 *Bondi Road* album. Emmanuel finally got his solo instrumental career off the ground with the release of the gentle and textural *Up from Down Under* album and single 'Up from Down Under' in June 1988.

In order to promote the album, he formed the first version of the Tommy Emmanuel Band, which comprised Jim Kelly (guitar; ex-**Levi Smith's Clefs**, Crossfire), Sam McNally (keyboards; ex-**Stylus**), Victor Rounds (bass) and Mitch Farmer (drums). In 1989, Emmanuel toured with Malcolm Eastick (guitar; ex-**Stars**, **Broderick Smith's** Big Combo, **Jimmy Barnes** Band) under the Joint Forces banner. The rest of the band line-up comprised Adrian Campbell (vocals; ex-**Avalanche**, Adrian's Wall), Mal Logan (keyboards; ex-**Healing Force**, **Renée Geyer** Band), Victor Rounds (bass) and Mitch Farmer (drums).

Prior to recording *Up from Down Under* (which eventually sold 70 000 copies) Emmanuel had actually issued *From Out of Nowhere*, an album of country swing and bluegrass tunes recorded with American pedal steel guitar player Pee Wee Clark. It was reissued in 1989 following Emmanuel's solo success. Emmanuel's second solo album, *Dare to be Different* (July 1990), produced the singles Rodrigo's 'Guitar Concierto de Aranjuez' and 'Country Wide'. The album reached the national Top 5 and attained platinum status (70 000 copies sold). Emmanuel's third platinum-selling album, *Determination* (November 1991), reached #14 on the national chart, and yielded the singles 'Stevie's Blues' and 'Determination'. 'Stevie's Blues' also won Emmanuel the 1991 Australian Performing Right Association (APRA) Songwriting Award.

His September 1993 album, *The Journey*, included four singles, 'The Journey' (August), 'Villa Anita' (November), 'Big Brother' (February 1994) and 'Since We Met' (May). *The Journey* made its debut at #5 on the national chart, and Emmanuel won Best Adult Contemporary Record at the 1993 Australian Record Industry Association (ARIA) Awards. In 1993 Emmanuel also issued a guitar tuition video, *Guitar Talk*, through Sony. Emmanuel appeared on the **Daryl Braithwaite** single 'Higher than Hope' (1994), which had been lifted from the singer's *Taste the Salt* album.

In 1995, Emmanuel recorded the album *Terra Firma* with his brother Phil. 'Love Gone West' was issued as the single (June 1995). The pair toured with The Phil and Tommy Emmanuel Band, which comprised Rex Goh (guitar; ex-**Air Supply**), James Roche (keyboards), Rob Little (bass) and Kevin Murphy (drums). As well as working with Goldrush and Gillian Eastoe and King Dog, Phil Emmanuel issued a solo album in 1992, *Kakadu Sunrise*.

In November 1995, Tommy Emmanuel issued his sixth solo album, *Classical Gas*, which included his reworking of Mason Williams' 1968 international hit single 'Classical Gas'. Emmanuel recorded the album in collaboration with the Australian Philharmonic Orchestra. For his seventh solo album, *Can't Get Enough* (#26 in March 1997), Emmanuel travelled to the USA, where he utilised the services of famed guitarists Larry Carlton, Chet Atkins and Robben Ford. His eighth album was a collection of duets with US guitar legend Atkins, *The Day Fingerpickers Took Over the World* (1997).

Albums: *From Out of Nowhere* (with Pee Wee Clark and Friends, Trafalgar 1980; reissued by WEA, 1989), *Up from Down Under* (Artful Balance, 1988), *Dare to be Different* (Mega/EMI, 1990), *Determination* (Mega/EMI, 1991), *The Journey* (Sony/Columbia, 1993), *The Journey Continues The Platinum Edition* (reissue, Sony/Columbia, 1994), *Terra Firma* (with Phil Emmanuel, Sony/Columbia, 1995), *Classical Gas* (Sony/Columbia, 1995), *Can't Get Enough* (Sony/Columbia, 1996), *The Day Fingerpickers Took Over the World* (with Chet Atkins, Sony/Columbia, 1997).

The End

Formed: *1979*
Style: *Rock*
Original line-up: *Brett Myers (guitar, vocals), Murray Davis (keyboards), Andrew Massey (bass), Colin Barwick (drums)*

Brisbane-born Brett Myers was a Velvet Underground devotee who formed The End during February 1979, in order to fulfil his desire to play a heavily Velvet Underground-influenced brand of rock. Jonathan Lickliter replaced Massey soon after formation.

The band's early repertoire consisted largely of covers of material by The Velvet Underground, Nico, The Stooges, New York Dolls, The Modern Lovers, Wire, Eno, Pere Ubu and even The Ronettes. The End played gigs around Brisbane with **The Go-Betweens**, **The Riptides**, **The Apartments**, **The Fun Things** and The 31st. The End issued the independent single 'My Confession'/'White World' (September 1981) in a pressing of just 300 copies. Myers decided to relocate the band to Sydney following a tour there in October. Within months Barwick, Davis and Lickliter had left to be replaced by Jonathan Purcell (guitar; ex-Moving Parts), Cameron Hulme (bass; ex-Hope is a New Coat) and David Rowley (drums; ex-Jump Vision). That version of The End was less unique in a way, but the band continued to tour until May 1983. In early 1984, the Hot label prepared a self-titled cassette of End material for release, but despite a handful of pre-release copies being sent out for promotion the cassette mysteriously never eventuated.

By that stage, Myers had collaborated with **The Celibate Rifles'** Damien Lovelock and Wet Taxis' **Louis Tillett** on the No Dance acoustic EP

'Carnival of Souls'. He was also in the process of forming **Died Pretty** with Frank Brunetti and Ron Peno. The original **Died Pretty** line-up was completed by Myers' old End compadres Colin Barwick and Jonathan Lickliter.

Buddy England

***Style:** Pop*

British-born 1960s pop singer Buddy England (real name Ian Kilgower) was one of the first artists to appear on television's *The Go!! Show*. He did not sign to the Go!! label, however, instead going straight to Festival before signing with EMI.

Festival issued his debut single, 'I've Come of Age'/'I'm Gonna Find Myself a Girl' in June 1965. EMI/HMV issued seven singles: 'If I Never Get to Love You'/'Matter of Moments' (April 1966), 'If You'll Stay'/'Question' (June), 'Doll House'/'Looking for Me' (August), 'There Goes My Baby'/'Your Eyes Tell on You' (November), 'Movin' Man'/'Get Away' (March 1967), 'Sunny'/'Lonely Avenue' (July) and 'I'm Going for You'/'Never Do Tomorrow' (November).

'Sunny' coincided with England's departure for the UK. He worked and recorded in England and Europe before returning to Australia. EMI/Columbia issued the singles 'Name of My Sorrow'/'Coralanne' (September 1968) and 'What a Wonderful World'/'In Need of a Friend' (May 1969). England recorded one more single, this time on the Air label, 'Josephine'/'Sunday Child' (1970). He then joined **The Mixtures** briefly, before joining the Astor label as A&R manager. In June 1977, England replaced Bruce Woodley in **The Seekers**. In 1993, England issued an album, *Fate's a Fiddler, Life's a Dancer*.

***Album:** Fate's a Fiddler, Life's a Dancer* (Astor, 1993).

Jon English

***Style:** Pop, rock*

Singer Jon English (b. 1949) was one of Australia's most successful solo performers. Like **John Farnham**, English has enjoyed an across-the-board appeal. He has been able to divide his time between rock music, stage musicals, television and cabaret without fear of over-exposure. His biggest chart successes came during the 1970s, but his talents continue to be highly regarded and sought after into the 1990s.

The English-born singer fronted the original **Sebastian Hardie** (when it was an in-demand suburban dance band) until January 1972. English then joined the Australian stage production of Andrew Lloyd Webber and Tim Rice's *Jesus Christ Superstar* (directed by Jim Sharman) in the role of Judas Iscariot. He remained with the musical for a lengthy and successful run (705 performances between May 1972 and February 1974), appearing on the Original Cast album issued on MCA during 1972. During that time he had also sung with studio band **Duck**, appeared on the soundtrack to the rock opera *Ned Kelly* and recorded his first solo album.

English's debut album, *Wine Dark Sea*, contained the singles Mike D'Abo's 'Handbags and Gladrags'/'Horsehair and Plastic' (March 1973) and 'Close Every Door'/'Summer Song' (July 1973). Backing musicians on the album included Mike Wade (guitars), Michael Carlos (keyboards; ex-**Tully**), Ken Firth (bass; ex-**Tully**), Jamie McKinley (piano), Bobby Gebert (piano), Teddy Toi (bass; ex-**Fanny Adams**, **Wild Cherries**, **Duck**), Steve Webb (drums; ex-**Blackfeather**, **Duck**) and Greg Henson (drums). *It's All a Game* yielded English's first hit, 'Turn the Page'/'Just the Way I Am' (#7 in February 1975). English then joined a new production of *Jesus Christ Superstar*, after which he recorded his third album, *Hollywood Seven*.

Following on from 'Turn the Page', the next single, 'Hollywood Seven'/'Sandcastles' (a #17 hit in May 1976), established English's penchant for dramatic rock ballads. The album's other two singles were 'Lovin'Arms' (July 1975) and 'I'm A Survivor'/'Walk Across the World' (August 1976). **Sebastian Hardie** (at that time enjoying success with the album *Four Moments*) backed English on the album's title track. *Minutes to Midnight* yielded three singles in 'Lay It All Down'/'Whole Lot More' (December 1976), 'Behind Blue Eyes'/'Hey Moonshine' (May 1977) and 'Everytime I Sing a Love Song'/'Don't Let Me be Misunderstood' (August). English formed the Jon English Band for touring purposes. The line-up comprised Mike Wade (guitar), Eric Macitchka (guitar), Steve Doran (keyboards), Rick Mellick (keyboards), James Rattray (bass) and Danny Grose (drums). *Words are Not Enough* produced the hits 'Words Are Not Enough'/'Up to No Good' (#5 in July 1978) and 'Nights in Paradise'/'Fantastic' (#21 in October).

1978 and 1979 were to be English's most successful years. With *Words are Not Enough* selling well, English starred in the television miniseries *Against the Wind* in the role of convict Jonathan Garrett. English and **Sebastian Hardie** guitarist **Mario Millo** composed, recorded and produced the *Against the Wind* soundtrack album, which went on to become the best-selling middle-of-the-road album for 1979. The single 'Six Ribbons'/'Mary's Theme' (#5 in January 1979) was the best-selling male pop single for the year. English was voted Best New Television Talent at the 1979 Logie Awards. *Against the Wind* later became a hit series when screened on UK and Scandinavian television.

The 'Best of' album *English History* reached #4 on the charts in August 1979. 'Get Your Love Right'/'He Could Have Been a Dancer' (#27 in May 1979) and 'Hot Town'/'Show No Weakness' (#11 in December 1979) were hits. English toured nationally and overseas with his new band, Baxter Funt. At that stage, the band comprised Mike Wade, Tony Naylor (guitar; ex-**Band of Talabene**, **Bootleg Family Band, Avalanche**), Peter White (keyboards), John Coker (bass) and Greg Henson (drums). English's association with Wade and Henson extended back to 1972 when the musicians were part of the *Jesus Christ Superstar* backing band.

Following up such a flurry of successes must have been a daunting prospect. English kept up the pace with *Calm Before the Storm* (#17 in April 1980) and its singles 'Carmilla'/'Survivor' (#27 in April) and 'Little by Little'/'I Hope It Turns Out Right' (June 1980). *Inroads* contained the singles 'Hold Back the Night'/'King of the Blind' (January 1981), 'Ask No Questions'/'Straight from the Heart' (June) and 'The Shining'/'Josephine (Too Many Secrets)' (September 1981).

In early 1981, English undertook a sold-out Scandinavian tour. English's backing band comprised **Mario Millo** (guitar), **Jackie Orszaczky** (bass; ex-Syrius, **Bakery**, **Marcia Hines** Band), Coz Russo (keyboards), Richard Gawned (tenor sax, flute; ex-**Marcia Hines** Band) and Nick Lister (drums; ex-**Kush**). As well as *Against the Wind* being popular on television, the single 'Against the Wind' reached #1 in Sweden, while the follow-up, 'Hollywood Seven', roared into the Top 5. The *Against the Wind* soundtrack album peaked at #2 and sold over 100 000 copies.

English's next album, the live double set *Beating the Boards* (May 1982; #22 in June), yielded the single 'Beating the Boards'/'Turn the Page' (April). English's backing band, The Foster Brothers, at that stage contained Keith Kerwin (guitar, vocals; ex-Southern Star Band), John Dallimore (guitar, flute, vocals; ex-**Redhouse**), Peter Deacon (keyboards, vocals), John Coker (bass) and Greg Henson (drums). *Some People* included 'Some People (Have All the Fun)'/'Beating the Boards' (July 1983) and 'Waterloo'/'Oh Paris' (November). English's duet with **Renée Geyer**, 'Every Beat of My Heart', came out in 1984. Previously he had recorded 'Jokers and Queens'/'Best of Me' and the *Jokers and Queens* mini-album with **Marcia Hines** (1982).

In 1984 English joined the stage production *The Pirates of Penzance* in the role of the Pirate King. Over the next decade he appeared in a number of successful stage musicals, including *Rasputin* (with Terry Serio and **Angry Anderson**), *The Mikado* and *H.M.S. Pinafore*. English also collaborated with producer David MacKay on an elaborate adaptation of Homer's *Illiad* under the title of *Paris*. WEA issued the double album of the *Paris* opera in late 1990, which featured contributions from such musical luminaries as John Parr, Demis Roussos and Doc Neeson, plus Barry Humphries. Despite lacklustre reviews, *Paris* won English and MacKay the Best Original Soundtrack or Cast Recording at the 1990 Australian Record Industry Association (ARIA) Awards.

English kept up his solo recording schedule with the singles 'Emotion'/'Best in Me' (September 1985), 'Dark Horses'/'I Can Do Better than That' (May 1986), 'Another Brand New Day'/'Best in Me' (August 1987), 'Younger Days'/'Carmilla' (April 1988) and 'We'll be There'/'Glass Houses' (October 1988), plus the album *Dark Horses* (May 1987). The Foster Brothers circa 1985 comprised Kerwin, Deacon and Henson plus newcomers Peter Greenwood (guitar; ex-**Marc Hunter** Band) and Tony Mitchell (bass; ex-**Sherbet**).

The 1990 album *Always the Busker* contained the singles 'Always the Busker', 'High Windows' and 'Love Has Power'. In 1993, English starred in the television comedy series *All Together Now*. Playing the part of absent-minded, washed-up rock star Bobby Rivers was a good example of English's talents and the self-deprecating sense of humour that has made him a popular figure for so long. English issued 'All Together Now' as a single. A new 'Best of' album came out in July 1993, and English issued a single in September 1994, 'Stand by Me'.

Albums: *Jesus Christ Superstar* (Original Cast recording shared with other artists, MCA, 1972), *Wine Dark Sea* (Warm & Genuine/Phonogram, 1973), *It's All a Game* (Warm & Genuine/Phonogram, 1975), *Hollywood Seven* (Polydor, 1976), *Minutes to Midnight* (Polydor, 1977), *Words are Not Enough* (Polydor, 1978), *Against the Wind* (television miniseries soundtrack with **Mario Millo**, Polydor, 1978), *English History* (compilation, Polydor, 1979), *Calm Before the Storm* (Mercury, 1980), *Inroads* (Mercury, 1981), *Jokers and Queens* (mini-album with **Marcia Hines**, Midnight, 1982), *Some People Can Do What They Like* (Mercury, 1983), *Beating the Boards* (Mercury, 1983), *Modern English* (J&B, 1983), *Dark*

Horses (Midnight/Chase, 1987), *Always the Busker* (BMG/RCA, 1990), *Paris* (Original Cast recording, WEA, 1990), *Best of Jon English 20th Anniversary Album* (BMG/RCA, 1993).

Equal Local

Formed: *1980*
Style: *Jazz-rock*
Original line-up: *Dean Richards (guitar; ex-Whirlywirld), Philip Jackson (synthesisers, trumpet, rhythm generator; ex-Whirlywirld), Melissa Webb (synthesiser, piano), Bryce Perrin (acoustic bass), Mick Hauser (sax)*

For a brief period circa 1980 to 1981, instrumental outfit Equal Local was the 'Next Big Thing' on the Melbourne inner-city/Crystal Ballroom circuit. Clinton Walker referred to Equal Local as the most important band to emerge from Melbourne in the wake of **The Birthday Party's** relocation to London. Dean Richards and Philip Jackson had worked with **Ian 'Ollie' Olsen** in pioneering electronic outfit Whirlywirld.

Richards formed Equal Local in early 1980. The band's pioneering brand of post-punk jazz-rock was bright, inventive, intricate and irresistible. Utilising a funky, pulse-like beat as a base, the band was free to lay hypnotic textures and a rich tapestry of styles over the top. Missing Link issued the 12-inch EP *Madagascar* and the 12-inch single 'Yank'/'12 Ways' in 1981. The band toured interstate and began picking up interest further afield. Having decided that the concept had run its course, however, Richards disbanded Equal Local in early 1982 to form neo-big band **Hot Half Hour**. He later formed 100 Flowers in Bloom with Mick Hauser. Hauser died in 1985 from a brain tumour.

Euphoria

Formed: *1992*
Style: *Dance pop*
Original line-up: *Andrew Klippel (keyboards), Keren Minshull (vocals, dancer), Holly Garnett (vocals, dancer)*

Euphoria was one of the first local outfits of the 1990s to embrace a lightweight, techno dance-pop ethic as espoused in the USA by the likes of C + C Music Factory, Black Box and 2 Unlimited. American-born Andrew Klippel was the son of famous Australian sculptor Robert Klippel.

He spent his formative years in the UK where he became a jazz purist. He began playing live with his own small bands around Sydney, including Andrew Klippel and Electric Soul. British-born Keren Minshull had sung backing vocals on album sessions for **Swanee**, Noni Hazelhurst and Jade Hurley, before joining Klippel in Electric Soul. She also came to the nation's attention in 1988 as co-lead singer of the Bicentennial anthem 'Celebration of a Nation' (the other singer being **Rick Price**).

In the early 1990s, Klippel formed a songwriting/production company called ESP with Melbourne DJ Ean Sugarman. Klippel and Sugarman co-wrote Euphoria's debut single, 'Love You Right', which became a national #1 hit when issued by EMI in December 1991. Follow-up single 'One in a Million' (May) also reached #1, while 'Do for You' (August) peaked at #5. Euphoria was in big demand. The *Total Euphoria* album made its debut on the national chart at #14 in November and the group's future seemed bright. 'Love You Right' ended up as one of the most played singles on Australian radio for 1992, as well as the 24th biggest selling single for the year.

All was not harmonious within the group, however, and Holly Garnett left under a cloud citing 'musical differences' as the cause. As it transpired, part of the problem was that, although Garnett appeared in the film clip to 'Love You Right', she was only miming to Minshull's vocals. It had been decided that the blonde Garnett was a more appropriate face with which to launch and market Euphoria than the dark-haired Minshull. The whole thing backfired, various tensions and bitterness arose within the group, the next singles 'I will Never Leave You' (February 1993) and 'Elated' (July) barely scraped into the Top 40, and Euphoria subsequently disappeared from view. Klippel went on to work as a writer and producer in the USA. He worked with vocal harmony group **Human Nature** on the triple platinum selling album *Telling Everybody* (1996).

Album: *Total Euphoria* (ARE/EMI, 1992).

Eurogliders

Formed: *1980*
Style: *Pop, soul*
Original line-up: *Bernie Lynch (guitar, vocals; aka Rip Torn, ex-Stockings),* **Grace Knight** *(vocals), Amanda Vincent (keyboards), Crispin Ackerman (guitar), Jeff Rosenberg (bass; ex-Hot Air Band, Stockley See Mason Band), John Bennetts (drums; ex-Stockings)*

Perth band Eurogliders represented the accessible face of post-punk new wave music. The band's sophisticated brand of pop was traditional in its structure, but displayed the decidedly 'modern veneer' (hip clothes, heavy use of synthesiser) of the day. This resulted in a good deal of success and chart action for the band.

Bernie Lynch formed the original version of Eurogliders (then known as Living Single) during 1980 with his partner, UK-born vocalist **Grace Knight**. Prior to that he had fronted new wave band The Stockings as Rip Torn. The Stockings comprised Frank Lee (guitar), Lon Gerae (bass) and Fred A'Snare (real name John Johnson, drums). Lynch left in 1980 to be replaced by Boris Garter (real name Bob Fallovic, guitar, vocals). The Stockings issued the 12-inch EP 'Street Talking' (April 1980), the singles '(She's a) Devil'/'Tiny Voices' (May 1981), 'Good Luck'/'Make You Cry' (August) and 'Limbo'/'Boy Girls' (January 1982), plus the albums *Red Tango* (September 1981) and *Limbo* (April 1982) on the Rough Diamond label.

In late 1981, Eurogliders travelled to the Philippines to record their debut album for PolyGram. Even though the airfares and recording costs were cheaper, the experiment proved costly in the long run. Unhappy with the results, the band eventually re-recorded several songs and remixed the whole album. Despite such misgivings, *Pink Suit New Day* and the singles 'Without You'/'No Goodbyes' (#32 in August 1982) and 'Laughing Matter'/'Sharpening Knives' (September) provided Eurogliders with a strong foothold in the Australian market.

In 1983, Eurogliders signed an international deal with CBS. The first single on CBS was 'No Action'/'All this Rain' (March). Jeff Rosenberg left at that stage, and the band travelled to the UK in July 1983 to record the all-important second album. Ron Francois (ex-Teardrop Explodes, Lene Lovich Band) joined as the band's new bass player. Eurogliders' return in December coincided with the release of their fourth single, 'Another Day in the Big World'/'Simon'.

The band found success with the UK-recorded, Nigel Gray-produced album *This Island* which concentrated on a funky, dance-oriented sound. The album reached #5 in July 1984 and produced two of the band's most memorable singles, the national #1 hit 'Heaven (Must be There)'/'Heliograph' (April 1984) and 'Maybe Only I Dream' (August). 'Heaven (Must be There)' also charted in the US Top 50, and the band was invited to play at the MTV Awards in New York.

Absolutely (October 1985) featured a smoother soul-influenced sound. It made the national Top 5, sold over 130 000 copies and yielded four singles, 'We Will Together'/'Wildlife' (#8 in May 1985), 'City of Soul'/'When the Stars Come Out' (#16 in September), 'Can't Wait to See You'/'I Like to Hear It' (#11 in January 1986) and 'Absolutely'/'Learning How to Swim' (#19 in April 1986). In early 1987, Amanda Vincent, John Bennetts and Ron Francois all left the band. Lynch, Knight and Ackerman continued on with new players Guy Le Claire (guitar), Rex Goh (guitar; ex-**Air Supply**), Lindsay Jehan (bass) and Steve Sowerby (drums).

1988's *Groove* was the band's most overtly soul/R&B/funk influenced album to date, and it peaked at #18 on the national chart. It contained the singles 'Groove'/'Groovethang' (#9 in April), 'It Must be Love'/'Ain't Nothing' (June), 'Listen'/'Christmas in Kings Cross' (September) and 'Precious' (March 1989). The band called it a day in 1989. **Grace Knight** pursued a successful career as a jazz singer.

Albums: *Pink Suit Blue Day* (PolyGram, 1982), *This Island* (CBS, 1984), *Absolutely* (CBS, 1985), *Groove* (CBS, 1988).

Dave Evans and Thunder Down Under (*see* Rabbit)

Even

Formed: *1994*
Style: *Indie guitar pop*
Original line-up: *Ashley Naylor (vocals, guitar; ex-Swarm), Wally Kempton (bass, vocals;* **The Meanies***), Matthew Cotter (drums; ex-Swarm)*

Ashley Naylor was the closest thing the Melbourne independent scene of the mid-1990s had to a song craftsman in the classic mould. His ready grasp of melody and harmony, plus an ability to craft catchy guitar riffs, resulted in his band Even producing one of the best Australian debut albums of 1996.

Naylor and Matthew Cotter had previously played with The Swarm, which also included Francis Leach (vocals) and David Rowland (bass). The band issued three independent singles, 'Fifteen Minutes'/'Gutter Glory' (November 1988), 'Do You Believe Me' (April 1990) and 'Gutless Wonder'/'Jesus Freak' (April 1991), before calling it quits. The Swarm also contributed 'Charlotte' to rooArt's Various Artists compilation *Youngblood II* (1990). Latter-day members of The Swarm included Tim Aylward (bass) Damian Percy (bass) and Andrew Harrison (keyboards). Percy also played with **Pray TV** and Naylor appeared as a guest player on that band's *Paydirt* album.

Within a year of its formation in March 1994, Even boasted support slots with local bands like **You Am I** and **Kim Salmon and the Surrealists**, plus overseas visitors Beck, Urge Overkill, Superchunk, NOFX, Sebadoh and Pavement. The band's

Even

Melbourne contemporaries included **Autohaze**, **Holocene**, **The Earthmen**, **The Fauves**, **Snout** and **Dirty Three**. Naylor also played guitar with Danny Vertessy's band Fragment (later called **Rail**), while Kempton was a member of punky power poppers **The Meanies**. Even signed to independent label Rubber and issued the CD EPs *In Stereo* (May 1995) and *Ten to Forty-Six* ('Stupid Dream') (November). National youth radio station Triple J added the track '24 Hour Cynic' (from *In Stereo*) to high rotation, and the EP went on to sell out five pressings. The band's shining debut album, *Less is More*, came out in July 1996. It was brimming with exceptional tunes ('Karmic Flop', 'Stop and Go Man', 'Dear Morris', 'She Told Me So' and 'Eternal Teen' to name but a handful), a timeless feel and pop hooks by the truckload.

Even's brash, honest and exhilarating guitar-driven power pop may have drawn inspiration from The Who, The Beatles, Badfinger, Big Star, etc., but it also managed to give contemporary international names like The Presidents of the United States, The Posies, Ash and Everclear a run for their money. *Less is More* produced two CD singles during 1996, 'Don't Wait' (June) and 'Stop and Go Man' (September), which included a cover of The Beatles' 'And Your Bird Can Sing'. Even appeared on the bill of the 1997 Big Day Out in January, and then issued a third CD single from *Less is More*, 'Peaches and Cream' (February). A month later, Even left Australia for US and European tours. The new CD EP, *One Side Not*, appeared in November.

Album: *Less is More* (Rubber/Shock, 1996).

The Every Brothers

Formed: *1986*
Style: *Pop, folk*
Original line-up: *Terry Every (real name Terry Bradford; guitar; vocals; ex-Instamatix), Greg Every (real name Greg Williams; guitar, vocals; ex-Young Homebuyers)*

Adelaide band The Every Brothers began as an acoustic duo comprising Terry Bradford and Greg Williams. Bradford was an ex-folkie, then currently playing in **July 14th**. Williams was a member of Play Loud. Bradford had also written songs with **Little River Band's Glenn Shorrock** during the late 1970s.

The Every Brothers' debut mini-album *Picks and Pens* came out on Greasy Pop in August 1986. It featured the duo's tongue-in-cheek (yet consummately played) take on the Simon and Garfunkel/ Everly Brothers' pop-folkie muse, plus a cover of Bob Dylan's 'Absolutely Sweet Marie'. With the break-up of **July 14th** in 1987, The Every Brothers became a full-time band. Robyn Habel (bass; ex-**July 14th**) and Andy Mills (drums; another ex-**July 14th** alumnus) joined the band. Setting their sights higher, The Every Brothers signed to Polydor and issued the singles 'This Town'/'Swim' (January 1988), 'Paved with Gold'/'Don't Blame the Weather' (July) and 'Eyes for the Blind'/'Don't Blame the Weather' (December). Changing the name to just The Everys, the band issued the album *Everyone* and a final single, 'Stranger than You Are'/'I Can't Breathe' (February 1989).

Albums: *Picks and Pens* (mini-album, Greasy Pop, 1986), *Everyone* (Polydor, 1989).

The Executives

Formed: *1966*
Style: *Pop*
Original line-up: *Carole King (vocals), Brian King (keyboards), Keith Leslie (vocals, sax), Garry King (sax, vocals), Dudley Hood (guitar), Rhys Clark (drums)*

Of all Australia's popular bands during the 1960s, The Executives earned the honour of being the country's top sophisticated pop group. Producing crisp, harmony-drenched sounds not unlike The Mamas and the Papas and dressed in smart suits, The Executives looked more at home on the cabaret circuit than playing the discotheques of the day. As Noel McGrath has noted, the band's musical expertise was unequalled, and between them the members could play a total of 31 instruments.

Festival signed the band and issued its debut single, 'Wander Boy'/'You're Bad' (January 1967), after which **Ray Burton** (ex-**Dave Bridge Quartet**) replaced Hood and Gino Cunnico (ex-Gino Affair) replaced Leslie. Brian Patterson (guitar; ex-**Tony Worsley and the Fabulous Blue Jays**) also came on board once the band had established itself. By the time The Executives left for the USA in 1968, they had scored a run of hit singles: Kenny Young's 'My Aim is to Please You'/'Bad Reputation' (June 1967), Stephen Stills' 'Sit Down I Think I Love You' /'Don't You Sometimes, Baby, Find That I'm on Your Mind?' (August), Mann/Weil's 'It's a Happening World'/'Moving in a Circle' (March 1968), 'Windy Day'/'This Town Isn't the Same Anymore' (June) and 'Summerhill Road'/'Christopher Robin' (December). 'My Aim is to Please You' and 'Sit Down I Think I Love You' were both #4 hits in Sydney, while 'Windy Day' went Top 10 (#7) there as well.

In the USA, the band signed to the Buddah label. Success was not forthcoming, so the band returned to Australia. The Executives' last two singles on Festival were 'Parenthesis'/'Got My Woman' (August 1969) and 'Hey Man'/'You're Gonna Love Me' (November 1969). The Executives returned to the USA at the end of 1969, whereupon they changed their name to Inner Sense. By that stage, however, Inner Sense's breezy pop had become outmoded in the face of rock's new progressive phase and the band quietly folded. Burton co-wrote 'I am Woman' with **Helen Reddy** before returning to Australia in 1973. Cunnico later issued an eponymous solo album on Buddah.

Carole and Brian formed a new band called Transition, which they renamed The Executives in June 1974. Jonne Sands (vocals), Ron Smith (guitar; ex-Chapter Three), Alan Oloman (bass, vocals; ex-**Black Diamonds**, Tymepiece) and Brian Kirby (drums; ex-Clik) completed the line-up. The Executives played the cabaret circuit and issued three singles on Polydor, 'On the Road Back'/ 'Uptown 'n'Down' (July 1974), 'Let the World Go Round'/ 'Country Lady' (April 1976) and 'Tinker Tailor'/ 'Songs of Love' (October). The band also recorded the theme song to the Nine Network's soapie *Young Doctors*.

Albums: *The Executives* (Festival, 1968), *On Bandstand* (Festival, 1968), *Executives . . . Now!* (Summit, 1969), *The Happening World of the Executives: The Festival File Volume Twelve* (compilation, Festival, 1988).

Exploding White Mice

Formed: *1984*
Style: *Punk rock*
Original line-up: *Paul Gilchrist (vocals), Gerry Barrett (guitar), Andy McQueen (bass), Craig Rodda (drums; on loan from* **Screaming Believers***)*

On the post-**Radio Birdman** independent scene of the mid-1980s, Adelaide band Exploding White Mice was the right band, at the right time, playing the right kind of music. Taking inspiration from The Ramones, **Radio Birdman**, MC5, The Stooges, Johnny Thunders and American 1960s garage punk, the Mice played high energy, melodic, hard-edged rock'n'roll.

Inevitably that led to accusations of unoriginality and, worse still, pure retrogression. Yet that hardly mattered to fans of that style of music. Exploding White Mice became one of the most popular bands on the Australian independent scene of the day. The original line-up of Exploding White Mice came together in mid-1984 to play a one-off gig at a party. In the spirit of the event, the band took its name from the cult film *Rock'n'Roll High School*. The initial live repertoire was all cover versions. Two weeks later, the band began playing pub gigs and decided to keep going.

Soon after, Giles Barrow (rhythm guitar) joined and Jeff Stephens (lead guitar; ex-Firm Grip, Spitfires, Tombstone Shadows) replaced Gerry Barrett. At the end of 1984, the band recorded enough songs to fill a mini-album which came out as *A Nest of Vipers* on Greasy Pop (October 1985). By that stage, David Bunney (ex-Zippy and the Coneheads) had replaced Rodda, who had returned to his commitments with **Screaming Believers**.

A Nest of Vipers featured a mix of originals and covers of The Chantays' 'Pipeline', The Wheels' 'Bad Little Woman' and Bo Diddley's 'Let the Kids Dance' (as covered by **Radio Birdman**). The record spent eight months on the Australian independent charts after having reached #2. The track 'Dangerous' appeared on the soundtrack to the US feature film *The Allnighter*. The band's version of The Stooges' 'Down on the Street' also appeared on Greasy Pop's Various Artists' album *An Oasis in A Desert of Noise*, plus Au-go-go's 1988 Stooges tribute album *Hard to Beat*.

The band became regulars on the interstate touring circuit. 'Blaze of Glory'/'He's Gonna Step on You Again' came out in March 1987. *Brute Force and Ignorance* (August 1988) continued The Ramones/Birdman fixation with its buzz-saw riffs and breakneck tempos. It contained the singles 'Fear (Late at Night)'/'Without Warning' (May 1988) and 'Breakdown #2'/'Bury Me' (November). David Mason (ex-Acid Drops, Primevils) replaced Barrow at the end of 1988.

The new line-up recorded the single 'Make It Right'/'Ain't It Sad?' (July 1989) before Mason left to be replaced by Jack Jacomas. One of Jacomas's earliest gigs with the band was supporting the Mice's New York heroes The Ramones in Adelaide. The band spent the early months of 1990 touring Europe, returning to Australia in May for live dates to support the release of the album *Exploding White Mice* and single 'I Just Want My Fun'/'First Time is the Best Time', 'Do the Crunch'. The album included one side of fresh studio recordings and one side of live cuts, including covers of **The Saints'** 'Misunderstood' and Alex Chilton's 'Bangkok'.

Long-serving frontman Paul Gilchrist called it a day in 1991, and the band was down to a four-piece. Stephens took over vocal duties in addition to lead guitar. Andrew Bunney (ex-Coneheads) replaced Jacomas in 1991. Fellow Adelaide band The Coneheads had recorded a couple of tough guitar pop singles, 'Barn Burnin''/'Action', 'Evil Little Elmer' (October 1986), 'Chewy Chewy'/'Skippin', Skippin', Skippin'' (January 1988), the EP *Burned Again* (1987) and the album *Bum* (1990) on Greasy Pop.

By 1991, Exploding White Mice's standing in Australia had subsided. Interest in Europe, however, was still at a premium. The band's next album, *Collateral Damage* (August 1992), came out on German label Normal, and was imported into Australia via Shock Records. In 1994, Au-go-go issued the band's fifth album, *We Walk Alone.* Among the album's tempered guitar riffs and rough-hewn harmonies, reference points still abounded, and included The Ramones, The Stooges, The Beach Boys, The Beatles, DMZ, Bad Religion and New York Dolls. The band made an appearance in Bill Young's 1994 black comedy *The Roly Poly Man*, playing—what else but—a 'punk-rock bar-band from Hell'.

Albums: *A Nest of Vipers* (mini-album, Greasy Pop, 1985), *Brute Force and Ignorance* (The Greasy Record Company/Festival, 1988), *Exploding White Mice* (The Greasy Record Company/Festival, 1990), *Collateral Damage* (Normal/Shock, 1992), *We Walk Alone* (Au-go-go/Shock, 1994), *A Nest of Vipers* (CD reissue with extra tracks, Bastard, 1995).

The Expression

Formed: *1968*
Style: *Blues, pop*
1969 line-up: *Don Sellers (vocals), Mick Bohl (bass, guitar), Peter Gregory (guitar, bass), Ron Sellers (drums)*

The Expression formed in Adelaide during 1968 as a blues band. With a move to Melbourne a year later, the band began playing a more pop-influenced bubblegum style of music on the local discotheque/club circuit. In early 1970, the band changed direction again, adding a tougher hard rock edge to proceedings.

The band's one and only single, 'Quicksand'/'Remember the Times', came out on the Rebel label in June 1970. The A-side was written by **The Master's Apprentices'** Doug Ford and **Jim Keays.** Alongside **The Wild Cherries'** 'Krome Plated Yabby' and 'That's Life', this record ranks as one of the most astonishing hard guitar/psychedelic singles of the period. The band added Steve Yates (keyboards) and began playing Led Zeppelin, Guess Who and Mountain covers on stage. The Expression broke up in late 1970. Gregory joined The Ash, and Yates joined Rush and Captain Australia and the Honky Tonk before moving on to **King Harvest**.

The Expression

Formed: *1981*
Style: *New wave pop*
Original line-up: *Tom Haran (vocals; ex-Visitor), Neville Dowling (keyboards; ex-Visitor,* **Dave Warner Band***), Andrew Wong-Yen (guitar; ex-Visitor), Stephen Manassah (bass), Steve Hopes (drums; ex-Nightflyers)*

Like **Eurogliders, Kids in the Kitchen** and **Real Life**, Sydney band The Expression proffered a smooth, commercial brand of chart-oriented pop rock. Despite a big push from the band's record company, The Expression failed to make a lasting impact.

Tom Haran, Neville Dowling and Andrew Wong-Yen had all played in Perth band Visitor during the late 1970s. They met up again in Sydney and formed The Expression in late 1981. Mushroom Records signed the band and issued the singles 'With Closed Eyes'/'Nothing Changes' (February 1983), 'Decisions'/'More Like a Feeling Than a Taste' (August) and 'Total Eclipse'/'Round and Round' (October), plus the album *The Expression.*

The singles were minor hits in Melbourne ('With Closed Eyes' peaked at #18 and 'Total

Eclipse' at #26). 'With Closed Eyes' also went as high as # 22 nationally. By the time the album came out, Guy Slingerland (ex-**Renée Geyer** Band) had replaced Steve Hopes on drums. The working line-up of The Expression broke up in late 1983. Haran and Dowling then recorded a second album with English session players. The singles 'Present Communication'/'Three Folk Day' (March 1984) and 'Small Brave Land'/'Old Mankind' (July 1985), from *Conscience* (August 1985), were not successful. Haran and Dowling continued on briefly with a new line-up, but by that stage interest in the band's style of music had completely dried up.

Albums: *The Expression* (Mushroom/Festival, 1983), *Conscience* (Mushroom/Festival, 1985).

The Exserts

Formed: *1980*
Style: *Punk*
Original line-up: *Steven Demsey (bass), Charlie Sammut (drums), Greg Suptut (guitar, vocals)*

The Exserts emerged from Sydney's early 1980s punk scene. Two years after formation, Simon Holmes replaced Greg Suptut. In May 1983, Holmes was replaced by Andrew Thomas. Holmes later joined **The Hummingbirds**. The new line-up contributed three tracks ('Business Man', 'Countdown' and 'Stranglehold') to Bruce Griffith's second Aberrant Sydney punk compilation *Not So Humdrum* (1984). Other bands featured on that collection were **Rocks, Happy Hate Me Nots**, Suicide Squad, Vigil-Anti, Wrong Kind of Stoneage and Itchy Rat. The Exserts continued playing the local pub network without scoring interest further afield. Aberrant finally issued the band's self-titled debut album in 1987, after which The Exserts broke up.

Album: *The Exserts* (Aberrant, 1987).

Extradition

Formed: *1969*
Style: *Folk*
Original line-up: *Shayna Karlin (vocals), Colin Dryden (vocals, guitar), Colin Campbell (vocals, guitar), Jim Stanley (bass), Bob Lloyd (drums; ex-***Cam-Pact***)*

The basis of Extradition dated back to the mid-1960s, when long-time folkies Colin Dryden and Colin Campbell teamed up to play the folk hang-outs around Sydney. In 1969, the duo recruited Shayna Karlin, Bob Lloyd and Jim Stanley in order to form Extradition.

That line-up received a standing ovation at the Fourth National Folk Festival in March 1970. The band came to the attention of **Tully** (at that time one of Australia's top concert attractions), with which they toured. Soon after, Dryden left the band and Campbell and Karlin were absorbed into the ranks of **Tully**. The Extradition line-up of Campbell, Lloyd and Karlin, plus Richard Lockwood (flute, woodwind) and Ken Firth (bass) from **Tully**, recorded the debut Extradition album at the end of 1970 with producer Gus McNeil.

The ultra-rare *Hush* album (June 1971) remains one of the most elegant and beautiful folk albums ever recorded in Australia. It mixed the delicate, acoustic textures of English folk music (Bert Jansch, Mellow Candle, Pentangle) with jazz and Eastern elements. Karlin's nightingale vocals were a stand-out feature. The single 'A Love Song'/'Minuet' (March 1971) was lifted from the album. *Hush* remains a true folk artefact of great interest to collectors. By the time the album came out, Extradition had ceased to exist, with the members concentrating on **Tully**.

Album: *Hush* (Sweet Peach, 1971).

F

The Fabulaires

Formed: *1979*
Style: *R&B*
Original line-up: Greg Champion *(guitar, vocals; ex-Tidewater, Bank of France), Mick Teakle (guitar; ex-Clean Cut), Jo Moore (vocals; ex-Bank of France), Jane Lewis (vocals), Ian McDonald (bass; ex-***Stars***), John James (J.J.) Hackett (drums; ex-Rum Jungle,* **Stars***)*

The Fabulaires formed in Adelaide with the above line-up. The band started out doing covers of soul, reggae, country and 1960s pop songs before relocating to Melbourne in 1980. It was there that Wayne Burt (guitar, vocals; ex-**Jo Jo Zep and the Falcons**, Living Legends, Sneakers) joined, and he steered the band into a more R&B/rockabilly-oriented direction.

By that stage, the band's repertoire included a number of Burt and Champion's originals. In early 1981, Geoff Hassell (ex-Lucky Dog) replaced Hackett who joined **Mondo Rock**. Just as the band's live following was picking up, tragedy struck in April when Jo Moore died in a car accident while the band was on tour. The Fabulaires broke up, with the posthumous mini-album *Apocalypso* coming out later in the year.

The mini-album mixed three studio tracks and three live cuts from a 3CR-FM Live-to-Air broadcast. **Greg Champion** and Mick Teakle joined ex-Adelaide pop band The Young Homebuyers. The line-up comprised Champion, Teakle, Nigel Lawrence (lead vocals; ex-Nasty Nigel and the Teenage Hellcats), Greg Williams (guitar), Paul Zeising (bass; ex-Tidewater, Bank of France, Redeye) and Tony Thornton (drums; ex-Front Page, **Paul Kelly** and the Dots). Nasty Nigel and the Teenage Hellcats had issued an independent single, 'Jonestown Suicide'/'A.K.A.', on the Criminal label in 1979.

The Young Homebuyers signed to the Rough Diamond label and issued two singles, 'Take One Step'/'Work Hard (Polish Reggae)', 'Laughing Clown' (May 1982) and 'She's a Girl'/'Showbiz Revolution' (September), plus the mini-album *Young Homebuyers* (October 1982). Later on, **Greg Champion** became a member of 3AW/3LO's radio team the *Coodabeen Champions*, and pursued a successful solo career. Burt went on to the Rock Doctors and **The Giants,** among others.

Fabulaires mini-album: *Apocalypso* (Rough Diamond, 1981); ***Young Homebuyers mini-album:*** *Young Homebuyers* (Rough Diamond, 1982).

The Fabulous Zarsoff Brothers

Formed: *1979*
Style: *R&B*
Original line-up: *Peter Knox (aka Izzy Foreal, bass, vocals, kazoo; ex-***69ers***), Greg Deane (aka Bernie Zarsoff, piano, vocals, kazoo), Tony Grose (aka Bluey Zarsoff, guitar, sax, vocals), Tony Verhoeven (aka Terry Zarsoff, drums)*

The Fabulous Zarzoff Brothers played R&B, blues and rock mixed with lowbrow, cabaret-styled, schoolboy humour. Dubbing themselves 'The Marx Brothers of rock'n'roll' the band became a popular Sydney attraction before breaking up in late 1988. *The Who's Who of Australian Rock* (3rd edn) lists at least 13 different line-ups. The original line-up lasted from October 1979 until May 1981. Deane and Grose later formed The Eddys.

Some of the other, numerous members included Garry Dale (aka Smoky Zarsoff, lead guitar), Warwick Kennington (aka Rocky Zarsoff, drums; ex-Fabulous Nudes), Danny Haynes (aka Rory Zarsoff, guitar, vocals), Daryl McKenzie (aka Lefty Zarsoff, drums; ex-Nutwood Rug), Dave Wray (aka Rudi Zarsoff, sax), Peter Kekel (aka Cranky Zarsoff, keyboards), Peter Northcott (aka Arfur Zarsoff, guitar), Sam See (aka Smoky Zarsoff II, guitar; ex-**Fraternity**, Stockley See Mason Band) and Bruce Allen (aka Zippy Zarsoff, sax; ex-**Ol'55**, **Dynamic Hepnotics**). The Fabulous Zarsoff Brothers recorded two EPs, *Bumsweat and Other Popular Filth* (Pirana Bros. label, 1981) and 'Nose Picking Boogie' (Pirana Bros, 1981), one single, 'Handy Man'/'Workin' It Out' (Pirana Bros, 1983), plus two albums.

Albums: Rude Awakening (Browneye Gramophonics, 1984), *Chockablock Full of Live Zarsoffs* (Browneye Gramophonics, 1985).

Fair Warning (*see* S.A.S.)

Falling Joys

Formed: 1985
Style: Indie guitar pop
1986 line-up: Suzie Higgie (guitar, vocals), Stuart G. Robertson (bass, vocals), Ken Doll (drums)

During Falling Joys' formative years, various descriptions, such as 'pop with muscle' and 'maximum pop', were bandied around in an attempt to get to grips with the band's muse. Neither term necessarily captured the band's wide-eyed, melodic appeal. Formed as a three-piece outfit in Canberra during late 1985, Falling Joys did not sign a recording deal until 1988. The band preferred a slow evolution and control over its own destiny.

Various Falling Joys line-ups came and went in the early days. Some of the early players included Anthony Merriless (drums), Robin Miles (keyboards, vocals) and Andrew McFarlane (sax). The line-up of Higgie, Robertson and Doll (plus Craig Adam guesting on keyboards) recorded the independent single 'Burnt So Low'/'Kiss the World Goodbye' in August 1986, not long after relocating to Sydney. The single came out in January 1987. After that the band signed to Volition Records. By the end of 1988, the line-up had stabilised with Higgie, Robertson (who switched to guitar), Pat Hayes (bass) and Pete Velzen (aka Pete Plunder, drums; ex-**Plunderers**).

Falling Joys' next singles, 'Nearly a Sin'/'In Time' (June 1988), the much revered 'You're in a Mess'/'Oyster Hill' (December 1988) and 'Tunnel Vision' (July 1989), plus the 12-inch EP *Omega* (1989), gained the band many new fans. Higgie's breathy vocals on these records were just one of the band's trademark sounds. The lush debut album *Wish List* was the breakthrough release for which the band had been waiting. It featured the summery hit single 'Lock It', which not only topped the alternative charts, but also made the lower reaches of the mainstream listing (#55 in February 1991). The live CD EP 'Jennifer' followed in September 1991 (#60). The Nettwerk label issued the album in the USA.

Following a European tour during 1991, the band recorded a second album with the Wonderstuff production team of Pat Collier and Jessica Corcoran (Ned's Atomic Dustbin) in the UK. The harder edged *Psychohum* (June 1992) yielded three singles: the noisy, guitar-driven pop of 'Black Bandages' (May) and 'Incinerator' (September), plus the ballad 'A Winter's Tale' (March 1993). Alongside **Clouds**, **Ratcat** and **The Cruel Sea**, Falling Joys were helping to refresh the local commercial scene.

It was to be another two years before the band's third album, *Aerial,* came out (September 1993). The Paul McKercher-produced album was the band's most accomplished, varied and cohesive release to date. It took the band into the lower reaches of the mainstream Top 40 album chart for the first time. Like its predecessor, *Aerial* yielded three singles, 'Fiesta!' (August), 'Breakaway' (November) and 'Make It Soon' (May 1994). At the end of 1993, the band undertook the Aerial national tour in order to promote the album. Falling Joys contributed a cover of **The Eastern Dark's** 'Over Now' to the Various Artists compilation *Earth Music* issued on the Mushroom label (June 1994).

Volition labelmates **Boxcar** produced Falling Joys' 'Amen (Remix)' (1994) single, which attracted a new audience. The band was quiet again until the CD EP 'Universal Mind' came out in August 1995. By that stage, Jason Morrisby had replaced Pat Hayes on bass. In 1996, Higgie recorded a low-key and low-fi album of soft-hued country'n'blues tunes with Bad Seed pianist Conway Savage which had yet to see the light of day at the time of writing.

Albums: Wish List (Volition, 1990), *Psychohum* (Volition, 1992), *Aerial* (Volition/Sony, 1993).

Fanny Adams

Formed: 1970
Style: Progressive rock
Original line-up: **Doug Parkinson** *(vocals, rhythm guitar; ex-Questions, In Focus), Vince Melouney (aka Maloney, guitar; ex-***Billy Thorpe** *and the Aztecs, Vince Maloney Sect,* **Bee Gees***), Teddy Toi (bass; ex-***Max Merritt and the Meteors**, **Billy Thorpe** *and the Aztecs, Little Sammy and the In People), Johnny Dick (drums; ex-***Max Merritt and the Meteors**, **Billy Thorpe** *and the Aztecs,* **Doug Parkinson** *In Focus)*

The story of Fanny Adams encapsulates one of the great disasters of Australian rock music. What sounded like a brilliant idea in theory turned out to be an ill-fated and short-lived affair for all concerned.

Guitarist Vince Melouney had spent three and a half years with **The Bee Gees** in the UK. Having tired of **The Bee Gees'** commercial pop sound, he put in a short stint with Ashton Garner and Dyke (of 'Resurrection Shuffle' fame) before landing a solo record deal with MCA in mid-1970. Before he left Australia, Melouney had been a member of **Billy Thorpe** and the Aztecs. When he split from that band in 1965, he formed Vince and Tony's Two with another ex-Aztecs alumnus **Tony Barber** (with John Shields on bass and Jimmy Thompson on drums); Barber soon left. Retaining Shields and Thompson, Melouney recruited Billy Taylor (guitar) and formed The Vince Maloney Sect. The Sect became resident house band on the Melbourne television pop show *Kommotion* and issued one single on the Kommotion label, 'She's a Yum Yum'/'No Good Without You' (March, 1966). The second single, 'I Need Your Lovin' Tonight'/'Mystery Train' (October), appeared as a Vince Maloney solo release, as did the EP *This is the EP*. Both releases were on Kommotion.

Melouney travelled to London, where he joined **The Bee Gees** during early 1967. In 1970 Melouney decided to form a hard rock band with which to record his album for MCA. His first recruit was New Zealander Teddy Toi, who was doing session work in London. 1970 was the heyday of progressive rock with Led Zeppelin, Deep Purple and Black Sabbath starting to dominate the UK charts, and Fanny Adams was an attempt at creating an antipodean hard rock supergroup. In June 1970, Melouney invited Johnny Dick and **Doug Parkinson** to join him in the UK. Toi and Dick had played together in the second version of The Aztecs during the mid-1960s. Parkinson, who conveyed considerable charisma with his imposing presence and gruff, raspy voice, had spent several years fronting respected psychedelic pop outfit In Focus. Dick was also a member of In Focus at that time.

Fanny Adams cut an album of adventurous, heavy, progressive blues-rock. There were a couple of ponderous, over-long tracks (like the 10-minute 'In A Room'), but Melouney's crunching, multi-layered Jimmy Page-styled guitar riffs kept the whole thing together. The album appeared posthumously in June 1971, and MCA lifted 'Got to Get a Message to You'/'They're All Losers Honey' as the single. Reissue specialists Raven later included the album track 'Ain't No Loving Left' on the 1994 compilation *Golden Miles: Australian Progressive Rock 1969–1974*.

Fanny Adams returned to Australia in December 1970, but simply fell apart within a month of arriving. The catalyst for the band's demise was a combination of ill-advised boasts of their imminent success ('In three weeks Fanny Adams will be the best band that ever trod this earth' Parkinson declared to *Go-Set* magazine), internal dissent and high audience expectations. The straw that broke the camel's back, however, occurred when a fire at Sydney's Caesar's Palace discotheque destroyed all the band's equipment. Parkinson left the band amidst much acrimony. Such was MCA's dissatisfaction with the split that the label effectively prevented Parkinson from recording for two years.

In the meantime, Parkinson assembled a new version of In Focus, and later pursued a successful solo career. Throughout the 1970s, Melouney worked with a succession of bands, including **The Cleves**, Flite, **Levi Smith's Clefs**, the **Jeff St John** Band, **John Paul Young** and the All Stars and **Rockwell T. James** and the Rhythm Aces. Toi and Dick played on **Lobby Loyde's** classic hard rock album *Plays with George Guitar*, and then joined Loyde in a new version of **The Wild Cherries**. The pair later re-joined **Billy Thorpe** and the Aztecs, before Dick moved on to J.P.Y. and the All Stars.

Album: *Fanny Adams* (MCA, 1971).

Fantasy

Formed: *1967*
Style: *Pop*
Original line-up: *Dave Studdard (guitar, vocals), Jeff Buzaglo (keyboards, vocals), Chris Studdard (bass, vocals), Colin Ross (drums, vocals)*

Melbourne band Fantasy is primarily remembered for the novelty hit 'The Marrow Song', which reached #29 in May 1973. 'The Marrow Song' was the band's rearrangement of Billy Cotton's 1930 hit 'Oh! What a Beauty'. The band's history actually stretched over 12 years. Fantasy formed in 1967 and quickly found an audience as **Johnny Farnham's** touring band. Mal Nichols (guitar, vocals) replaced Dave Studdard in 1972. Fantasy played the cabaret and club circuit, and recorded three singles for EMI: 'Universal Sun'/'Suzie' (May 1971); 'The Marrow Song'/'Forty Days of Rain' (April 1973) and 'Just Another Pretty Face'/'Look Around' (August 1973). The band enjoyed some success with the television-promoted album *A Tribute to Australian Rock'n'Roll* in 1977. By that stage, David Sholson had replaced Chris Studdard and Lloyd Poole had replaced Buzaglo.

Album: *A Tribute to Australian Rock'n'Roll* (Hammard, 1977).

John Farnham

Style: *Adult contemporary pop*

Without doubt, John Farnham (b. 1949) is *the* most successful solo artist in the history of Australian rock and pop. He is a true pop phenomenon. The singer's first flush of success (when he was known as Johnny Farnham) came during the 1960s in the wake of his #1 hit, the innocuous novelty song 'Sadie, the Cleaning Lady'. He was crowned King of Pop for five years in a row from 1969 to 1973. His subsequent stature as Australia's pre-eminent, adult contemporary performer of the 1990s outweighs his squeaky-clean pop idol image in terms of credibility.

Farnham's across-the-board appeal ensured sell-out concerts whenever he toured. Likewise, his albums invariably headed the best-seller lists. Yet, underneath all the trappings of success, Farnham has retained an affable sense of humour and a simple, unpretentious 'everyman' charm which also makes him one of the most respected celebrities in Australian entertainment history.

The English-born singer's first job was as a plumber's apprentice. He began his musical career in the mid-1960s fronting Melbourne bands The Mavericks and Strings Unlimited. Farnham came to the attention of manager Darryl Sambell, who scored him a solo deal with EMI Records in September 1967. Over the next ten years, Johnny Farnham issued a string of enormous hit singles. He also tried his hand at musical theatre (*Dick Whittington and His Cat*, *Charlie Girl* and *Pippin*) and television (*Opportunity Knocks*, *Bobby Dazzler* and *Survival with Johnny Farnham*).

Farnham's singles discography to 1977 incorporates 'Sadie, the Cleaning Lady'/'In My Room' (#1 in December 1967), 'Underneath the Arches'/'Friday Kind of Monday' (#6 in March 1968), 'Jamie'/'I Don't Want To Love You' (#8 in July), 'Rose Coloured Glasses'/'Scratchin' My Head' (#19 in October), 'I Saw Mommy Kissing Santa Claus'/'The Little Boy that Santa Forgot' (November), 'One'/'Mr Whippy' (#4 in August 1969), 'Raindrops Keep Falling on My Head'/'Two' (#1 in December), 'Comic Conversation'/'Pretty Things' (#10 in November 1970), 'Happy Christmas'/'Ringing Reindeer' (December 1970), 'Acapulco Sun'/'As Long as Life Goes On' (#21 in July 1971), 'Walking the Floor on My Hands'/'My Favourite Occupation' (#25 in December), 'Baby Without You'/'That's Old Fashioned' (duet with Allison Durbin; #16 in December), 'Rock Me Baby'/'Nobody's Fool' (#4 in October 1972), 'Don't You Know It's Magic'/'Sweet Cherry Wine' (#12 in January 1973), 'Everything is Out of Season'/'It's Up to You' (#8 in April), 'I Can't Dance to Your Music'/'Beautiful City' (#12 in September), 'Shake a Hand'/'If You Would Stay' (#24 in January 1974), 'Corner of the Sky'/'Morning Glow' (May), 'One Minute Every Hour'/'Baby Don't Get Hooked on Me' (August), 'Things to Do'/'To Be or Not to Be' (November), 'Don't Rock the Boat'/'Running to the Sea' (October 1975), 'You Love Me Back to Life Again'/'Call Me Back' (January 1977) and 'Rock & Roll Hall of Fame'/'Monkey See Monkey Do' (July 1977).

John Farnham

By the late 1970s, Farnham had moved into the cabaret/nightclub field, having lost his pop star footing. He had also become known as John Farnham. In 1980 he signed to the Wheatley Brothers organisation, a move which brought a reversal of his fortunes. The Graham Goble-produced *Uncovered* album included a dramatic rearrangement of The Beatles' 'Help' which was issued as a single with 'Back to the Back Wood' on the flip side. The single reached #8 in August 1980, while the album peaked at #20 in October. 'She's Everywhere'/'On My Own' (September) and 'Please Don't Ask Me'/'I Never Did Get Through' (December) followed, but neither made the Top 40.

Farnham's touring band at that stage comprised **Tommy Emmanuel** (guitar; ex-Southern Star Band), Mal Logan (keyboards; ex-**Renée Geyer** Band), Barry Sullivan (bass; ex-**Chain**) and Derek Pellici (drums; on loan from **Little River Band**), all of whom had played on the album. When Pellici and Logan had to return to their commitments with **LRB**, Sam McNally (keyboards; ex-**Stylus**) and David Jones (drums) joined the John Farnham Band. During 1980, Farnham also appeared in the ABC-TV series *Farnham and Byrne* with **Debra Byrne**. His two singles for 1981 were 'Too Much Too Soon'/'Jillie's Song' (March) and 'That's No Way to Love Someone'/'Blame It on the Weather' (September).

In February 1982, Farnham replaced **Glenn Shorrock** in **Little River Band**. Coincidentally, Farnham's manager Glenn Wheatley also managed **LRB**. Farnham stayed with that band for four years. While a member of **LRB**, Farnham issued one solo single through RCA, 'Justice for One'/'The Quiet Ones' (September 1984). At the end of 1985, **LRB** collapsed in disarray and Farnham was without a record deal. With his fortunes at something of a low ebb, Farnham embarked on a new solo career that would take him to the top in his field.

First up was the enormously successful *Whispering Jack* album (October 1986), which went on to become the first local album to sell over one million copies in Australia alone. *Whispering Jack* and its first single, 'You're the Voice'/'Going Going Gone' (September), topped their respective charts simultaneously during November 1986. The album produced three more singles, 'Pressure Down'/'Let Me Out' (#4 in February 1987), **Gulliver Smith** and **Ross Wilson's** 'Touch of Paradise'/'Help' (#18 in March 1987) and 'Reasons'/'One Step Away' (May 1987). The anthemic 'You're the Voice' had been written by Chris Thompson (Manfred Mann's Earth Band), Andy Qunta (**Icehouse**), Keith Reid (Procol Harum; he wrote the lyrics to 'A Whiter Shade of Pale') and New York session singer Maggie Ryder. When issued in Europe, 'You're the Voice' sold over a million copies. It reached #6 in the UK during April 1987.

At the end of 1986, Farnham hit the road with the John Farnham Band which comprised **David Hirschfelder** (keyboards; ex-**Little River Band**), Brett 'Rambo' Garsted (lead guitar), Greg Macainsh (bass; ex-**Skyhooks**) and Angus Burchill (drums). Farnham won the 1987 Australian Record Industry Association (ARIA) Award for Best Male Artist. In Australia's Bicentennial year, 1988, Farnham was nominated Australian of the Year. It was the first time a pop artist had ever been elevated into the national consciousness in such a way.

Farnham followed up *Whispering Jack* with *Age of Reason* (August 1988), another #1 album of polished, high-tech synth pop with little in the way of lyrical depth. It went on to become the best-selling Australian album for 1988. It also yielded the singles 'Age of Reason'/'When the War is Over' (#1 in July 1988), 'Two Strong Hearts'/'It's a Long Way to the Top (If You Wanna Rock'n'Roll)' (#5 in October), 'Beyond the Call'/'Blow by Blow' (November) and 'We're No Angels'/'Listen to the Wind' (April 1989). Farnham's next hit was the duet 'Communication'/'Attitude' with **Danni'elle Gaha** (#13 in September 1989). In March 1989, Farnham travelled to Moscow in order to join Peter Gabriel, The Pretenders' Chrissie Hynde, U2's The Edge, Eurythmics' Annie Lennox, Talking Heads' David Byrne and other top musicians for the launching of Greenpeace's album *Rainbow Warriors* in the USSR.

Farnham's fifteenth album, *Chain Reaction*, marked a departure for the singer. Gone were the slick, electronic sounds and occasionally overwrought arrangements which characterised its two predecessors. There was an emphasis placed on acoustic instrumentation and ensemble vocals. The title track was an almost threadbare rockabilly shuffle. Material for *Whispering Jack* and *Age of Reason* had also been commissioned from outside writers. Nine of the 12 tracks on *Chain Reaction* were co-written by Farnham in conjunction with long-time producer Ross Fraser and musical director **David Hirschfelder**. Guitarists Brett Garsted and Phil Buckle (from **Southern Sons**) also contributed strong rootsy rock backing.

Like *Age of Reason* before it, *Chain Reaction* made its debut at #1 on the national charts in October 1990, and was the biggest selling album in Australia for the year. It featured the hit singles 'Chain Reaction' (#6 in September), 'That's Freedom' (#6 in November), 'Burn for You' (#5 in December) and 'In Days to Come' (#49 in April 1991). Farnham completed 1990 by taking out his second Best Male Artist trophy at the ARIA Awards. 'Burn for You' also won ARIA Song of the Year. Next up was the live album *Full House* from which came the single 'Please Don't Ask' (#21 in December). *Full House* managed a relatively disappointing chart position of #2 in November 1991 (kept off the top spot by **Jimmy Barnes**'s *Soul Deep* album). As it was, Farnham sang a duet with Barnes on *Soul Deep*, 'When Something is Wrong with My Baby', which reached #3 when issued as a single (November).

In 1992, Farnham joined the Australian cast of the revived stage musical of Andrew Lloyd Webber and Tim Rice's *Jesus Christ Superstar*, in the role of Jesus. Alongside **Kate Ceberano** (Mary Magdalene), Jon Stevens (Judas), **Angry Anderson** (Herod), John Waters (Pontius Pilate), **Russell Morris** (Simon Zealotes) and David Gould (Caiaphas), Farnham featured on the #1 charting *Jesus Christ Superstar The*

Album issued by Polydor in July. He also sang on the hit single 'Everything's Alright' (a national #6 duet with Ceberano during September).

Then Again . . . included the hits 'Seemed Like a Good Idea' (#16 in September 1993), 'Angels' (#36 in December), 'Talk of the Town' (February 1994) and 'The Reason Why' (May). Farnham won the Highest Selling Australian album (for the fourth time) at the 1993 ARIA Awards. *Romeo's Heart* (#2 in July 1996) produced the hits 'Have a Little Faith (in Us)' (#3 in March) and 'A Simple Life' (#29 in June). The album's third single, 'Romeo's Heart' (August) was not successful. The album won Best Adult Contemporary release at the 1996 ARIA Awards. Farnham's first CD single for 1997 was 'All Kinds of People' (June). His duet with vocal harmony group **Human Nature**, 'Every Time You Cry', reached #3 in October. That same month the compilation *Anthology 1 (Greatest Hits 1986–1997)* hit #1 on the national chart.

John Farnham has always been able to surround himself with mature, seasoned musicians who added to his appeal. Throughout the late 1980s, as well as the members already listed, his backing band included the likes of John Clarke (percussion), Joe Creighton (bass; ex-**Billy T**), **Lisa Edwards** (backing vocals), Venetta Fields (backing vocals), Lindsay Field (backing vocals, guitar), Nikki Nicholls (backing vocals), Wayne Nelson (bass; ex-**Little River Band**), Bruno De Stanislo (bass), Derek Pellici (drums) and Sam See (guitar; ex-**Flying Circus**, **Fraternity**, Stockley See Mason Band). Since 1990, Jack Jones (guitar, backing vocals; **Southern Sons**), Phil Buckle (guitar; **Southern Sons**), Steve Housden (guitar; ex-**Little River Band**), Chuck McKinney (backing vocals; ex-**Hot City Bump Band**), Jamie Paddle (keyboards), Lisa Maxwell (backing vocals), Stuart Fraser (guitar; ex-**Feather**, **Noiseworks**) and Chong Lim (keyboards) have toured and recorded with Farnham.

Johnny Farnham albums: *Sadie* (EMI/Columbia, 1968), *Looking Through a Tear* (EMI/Columbia, 1970), *Christmas is Johnny Farnham* (EMI/Columbia, 1970), *Everybody Ought to Sing a Song* (EMI/Columbia, 1971), *Together* (with Allison Durbin, EMI/HMV, 1971), *Johnny Farnham Sings Hits from the Movies* (EMI/Columbia, 1972), *Johnny* (EMI/Columbia, 1972), *Hits Magic & Rock 'N Roll* (EMI, 1973), *Johnny Farnham Sings the Big Hits of '73* (EMI, 1973), *J.P. Farnham Sings* (EMI, 1975), *Best of Johnny Farnham* (EMI/Axis, 1981), *Another Side of John Farnham* (compilation of early material, EMI, 1987), *Where Do I Begin?* (compilation, EMI, 1996). ***John Farnham albums:*** *Uncovered* (W.B.E./EMI, 1980), *Whispering Jack* (Wheatley/ BMG, 1986), *Age of Reason* (Wheatley/BMG, 1988), *Chain Reaction* (Wheatley/BMG/RCA, 1990), *Full House* (Wheatley/BMG/RCA, 1991), *Then Again . . .* (Wheatley/BMG/RCA, 1993), *The Classic Gold Collection—Through the Years (1967–1985)* (EMI, 1995), *Romeo's Heart* (Wheatley/BMG/RCA, 1996), *Anthology 1 (Greatest Hits 1986–1997)* (Gotham/BMG/RCA, 1997, *Anthology 2 (Classic Hits 1967–1985 Recorded Live)* (Gotham/BMG/RCA, 1997), *Anthology 3 (Rarities)* (Gotham/BMG/RCA, 1997).

Further reading: *Whispering Jack: The John Farnham Story* by Clark Forbes (Hutchinson Australia, 1989).

Fast Cars

Formed: *1980*
Style: *Pop*
Original line-up: *Fabian Byrne (guitar, organ), Dianah Levy (guitar, vocals), Dave Pye (bass, trumpet), Andy Southam (drums)*

Although not strictly a mod band, Fast Cars' earliest gigs were at the mod hangout the Sussex Hotel in inner-city Sydney. The mods accepted the band because it played a reckless brand of dance pop in the Blondie/Penetration mould.

In 1981, **Mental as Anything's** Martin Plaza produced the band's debut 12-inch EP, *Annual*, and single, 'Saturday's Girl'/'No Love Today'. Both records came out on the Method label. Fast Cars broke up soon after, but reconvened a year later. The band issued the cassette *Fast Cars* and a second single on Method, 'Love Child'/'Dave's Song', 'Now or Never' (June 1984), before splitting for good. Method also included 'Love Child' on the Various Artists album *Sound of Sydney Volume 3*.

In late 1983, Di Levy formed Helter Skelter. The band issued one single, 'Make Believe'/'The Party' (March 1984) on the Hot label. It was produced by ex-**Laughing Clown** Peter Doyle. Byrne formed Fiction Romance with the remnants of fellow Sydney band Warm Jets. The line-up was completed by Prue Rheuben (vocals), Tracey Allen (keyboards), Anthony Perrott (guitar), Peter Bennett (bass) and Doug Lees (drums). Fiction Romance issued the single 'All of This is New'/'So Close to You' on the Method label (September 1984). The band played infrequently, and it was not until 1988 that the album *Marching Orders* and its single, 'Troubled World'/'Disarm the Cowboys', came out. The band broke up a year later.

Fiction Romance album: *Marching Orders* (Method, 1988).

The Fauves

Formed: 1989
Style: Rock
Original line-up: *Andrew Cox (guitar, vocals), Philip Leonard (guitar, vocals, brass), Andrew 'Jack' Dyer (bass), Adam Newey (drums)*

Four school friends from the Mornington Peninsula (Victoria) formed The Fauves. The band took its name from the art movement Fauvism, which was characterised by both its intensity and infatuation with colour. Andrew Cox and Philip Leonard were entirely self-taught, managing to eschew standard musical formats and conventional guitar tunings in the process. The band's early sound was an energetic distillation of garage-punk rock riffs and surreal lyrics.

The band's first release was the independent single 'Fireman 451'. The five-track EP 'This Mood has Passed' (June 1990) reflected the frantic, primal elements of early **Hunters & Collectors** or **Moodists**. The band issued two singles during 1991, 'When Luck Ran Out' and 'Daughter Aboard'. The band kept up the experimental energy and humour with the 1992 CD single 'Misguided Modelling Career' plus the CD EPs 'The Scissors Within' (April) and 'Tight White Ballhugger' (September) on Shock Records.

The Fauves came to wider attention when they appeared on the bill of the first Big Day Out national tour in early 1993. By October, The Fauves had signed to Polydor and issued their debut album *Drive Through Charisma*. Recorded in a mud-brick house in Daylesford with producer Robbie Rowlands, the album featured such memorable titles as 'Let Me Be Your Toilet', 'Hitler Youth' and 'Orgamasarion'. The album's single was 'Thin Body Thin Body' (September 1993). Simon Holmes (**Hummingbirds**) and Wayne Connolly (**Welcome Mat**) co-produced The Fauves' second album *The Young Need Discipline* and its three CD singles 'The Driver is You' (November 1994), 'Caesar's Surrender' (April 1995) and 'Dwarf on Dwarf' (June). Without diluting the band's strengths, the album featured a more streamlined rock'n'roll approach (something akin to Pavement or latter-day R.E.M.). The band's third CD single for 1995 was the knowing 'Everybody's Getting a 3 Piece Together' (November).

The confident *Future Spa* album (October 1996) yielded the popular CD singles 'Dogs Are the Best People' (June) and 'Self Abuser' (October). The singles logged #20 and #30 respectively on the 1996 Triple J Hottest 100 list. The Fauves commenced

The Fauves

1997 with a slot on the bill of the Big Day Out tour. The band followed that up with the third CD single lifted from *Future Spa*, 'Don't Get Death Threats Anymore' (April 1997). The Fauves recorded a new album (slated for release in 1998), and the first CD single, 'Sunbury '97', appeared in November 1997.

Albums: *Drive Through Charisma* (Polydor, 1993), *The Young Need Discipline* (Polydor, 1994), *Future Spa* (Polydor, 1996).

Fear and Loathing

Formed: 1981
Style: Punk, grunge
Original line-up: *Agravaine McLachlan (vocals), Chris Wiley (guitar, bass), Harry Butler (guitar, bass, vocals)*

Taking inspiration from Hunter S. Thompson's seminal 'gonzo journalism' tome *Fear and Loathing in Las Vegas*, Adelaide band Fear and Loathing played a frantic clash of punk and gothic proto-grunge. Of the original members, Harry Butler is the editor of long-running Adelaide punk fanzine *D.N.A.*

There have been at least 20 other musicians who have passed through the band over the years. Some of the early members included Andrew Cappo (vocals; ex-Human Crash); Marek Urbanski (vocals; ex-Ribcage Wrestlers), who replaced Agravaine McLachlan in 1984; Dave Williams (drums; ex-Human Crash); Mark Ferguson (drums; ex-Ribcage Wrestlers); Paul Smith (drums); Steve Amos (drums); and Chris Haynes (drums; ex-Skunks). The core of the band between 1986 and

1989 was Chris Wiley, Harry Butler, David Ormsby (guitar), Hermann Lauss (bass, who joined in 1984) and John Scott (drums; from **Mark of Cain**). That line-up issued the album *Wait 'Til the Cat Licks It Up* (1989), and contributed 'Fur Burger' and 'B.F.A.' to the UK-released, *Raw Cuts Volume 4: Australian Nitro* (1987), '44VD' to the Reactor label's compilation, *The Not So Lucky Country* (1988), and 'Steam Shit' to the Dominator collection, *Are We Still Here?*.

Terry Rowe replaced Scott on drums in 1989, and the band recorded a second album *The Odyssey of the Trojan Meatball* after which Butler left. Jonas Dawson (vocals) joined in 1993. The band continued in to 1997. Wiley found time to play with a number of different bands including Screaming Wombats from Hell, Sleaze Patrol, Love Fever, **Bloodloss**, Megalon's Eggs and Hack, while Butler has also been a member of Human Crash, Raw Power, Void, Hack and Grog. Between 1986 and 1989, Fear and Loathing issued four self-financed cassettes of demo material on Butler's El Crappo label *A Box Full of Fluffy Ducks* (1986), *Seven Slugs on a Dinner Plate* (1987), *Beer Fat is Good Fat, But Cider Fat is Better, But Who Cares We All Drink Flagons Anyway* (*Beer Fat* for short; 1988) and *An Army of Thalidomides Armed with Axes and Aardvarks* (1989).

Albums: *Wait 'Til the Cat Licks It Up* (Waterfront, 1989), *The Odyssey of the Trojan Meatball* (Thalidomide Octopus/Waterfront, 1990).

Fear of Falling

Formed: *1989*
Style: *Pop*
Original line-up: *Kerry Lee (vocals), Neil Coombe (guitar, vocals), Caroline Grubb (bass), Mark McElligott (drums)*

Brisbane band Fear of Falling formed in 1989. Cas Simpson replaced Grubb and Adam Cole replaced McElligott during 1991. Fear of Falling signed to the Phantom label and issued the single 'Your Place'/'Slave', 'Fear . . . ', which showcased the band's ethereal brand of layered pop. The band relocated to Sydney and issued two further singles in 1991 'Butler to Your Masquerade' and 'For the Tourist'/'South of Nowhere', as well as contributing 'Your Place' to rooArt's Various Artists set, *Youngblood II* (1990). The debut album came out a year later, plus a final single 'Crossroads of Reality'/'Acid Rain'.

Album: *Welcome to Wonderland* (Phantom, 1992).

Feather

Formed: *1976*
Style: *Hard rock*
Original line-up: *John Swan (vocals; ex-***Fraternity**, **Jim Keays'** *Southern Cross), Stuart Fraser (guitar; ex-Streetlife,* **Blackfeather***), Wayne Smith (guitar; ex-Bullett), Lee Brossman (bass; ex-Highway,* **Blackfeather***), Warwick Fraser (drums; ex-Streetlife,* **Blackfeather***)*

The nucleus of Sydney band Feather came together in early 1976 under the name **Blackfeather**. Lead singer Neale Johns had fronted various incarnations of **Blackfeather** since 1970. The 1976 **Blackfeather** line-up was more pop-oriented and featured Johns, Ray Vanderby (keyboards), Lee Brossman, Warwick Fraser plus Warwick's 14-year-old brother Stuart.

That line-up only lasted until November 1976 when Johns left to travel to the UK. Vanderby also left, and the rest of the band recruited singer John Swan and Wayne Smith to became Feather. The band's first break came that same month when it supported UK visitors Ritchie Blackmore's Rainbow on an Australian tour. Feather settled into the local pub rock circuit and issued the pop rock single 'Girl Trouble'/'Sweet Melinda' (May 1977) on CBS. Feather reputedly recorded an album, *Going Through Changes*, around that time, but the LP has never surfaced.

Jimmy Barnes (ex-**Cold Chisel**) joined as co-lead singer in July 1977, but a few weeks later returned to his old band. In November 1977, Brossman and Smith left to be replaced by Mark Mitchell (bass) and Chris Jones (guitar; ex-**Finch**). In April 1978, on the eve of Feather's support slot to **Ted Mulry Gang's** three-month Disturbing the Peace national tour, Swan left. Nineteen-year-old Gary Conlan (ex-Class) stepped in as Swan's replacement. Feather contributed two tracks, 'Here with Me' and 'Bad Blood', to the live, Various Artists album *Canned Rock* (on Albert) which had been recorded at Parramatta Gaol. By 1980, Feather was working under the name of Kid Colt. By the end of the year, Warwick and Stuart Fraser, plus Mark Mitchell, had joined singer Karen Smith as Smith.

Marcel Chaloupka replaced Mitchell on bass, and Smith issued two hard rock singles on the WBE label, 'Nightlights'/'Life in the Fast Lane' (April 1981) and 'Lonely Man'/'Stepping Time', 'Intensive Care' (June). The band broke up in 1982. Warwick Fraser later played with The Change, **The Screaming Tribesmen**, Flying Tigers, the **Peter Wells** Band and **Died Pretty**, among others. Likewise, Stuart Fraser has enjoyed regular employment within the ranks of The Change, **Swanee**, **Noiseworks**, the **Renée Geyer** Band and the **John Farnham** Band. John Swan was the most successful ex-member of Feather under the guise of **Swanee**.

feedtime

Formed: *1979*
Style: *Punk rock*
Original line-up: *Rick Johnson (guitar, vocals), Alan Larkin (bass)*

Sydney band feedtime was one of the most uncompromising and influential groups to emerge from that city's early 1980s inner-city scene. The band started out as a duo in December 1979, soon adding drummer Dave Carter, who was then replaced by Nella Mobbs. Tom Sturm joined as drummer in 1982, and that line-up remained stable until 1989. By the time feedtime established an identity on the Sydney scene, there was only one other band that could match them for sheer sonic force and rhythmic density: the notorious **X**.

Feedtime issued its debut 14-track album *feedtime* at the end of 1985. The band's music mixed grinding guitars and driving beats with an unsettling ambience. Two non-album tracks from the same recording session, 'Don't Tell Me' and 'Small Talk', appeared on the Aberrant label's third compilation of Sydney punk bands, *Why March When You Can Riot?* (1985). Aberrant later issued 'Don't Tell Me' and 'Small Talk' as a single (September 1987). In the meantime, Aberrant issued feedtime's debut single 'Fractured'/'Safari', 'Rumble' (September 1986), followed by the album *Shovel* in February 1987. The band's second album, *Cooper S* (May 1988), featured all cover versions done in the inimitable feedtime style of raw and heavy thrash. Highlights included The Beach Boys' 'Fun Fun Fun', The Rolling Stones' 'Play with Fire' and Slade's 'Hear Me Calling'. The band also shared a split single ('Buffalo Bob') with Adelaide band **King Snake Roost** ('More than Love') (March 1988).

The band called it a day in February 1989, following the release of the album *Suction*. In 1995, Rick Johnson and Alan Larkin revived feedtime with Larkin's younger brother Paul on drums. In the intervening years, feedtime had come to be seen as pioneers of grunge, with American bands as diverse as Sonic Youth, Nirvana and White Zombie citing the Sydney trio as a key influence. In April 1996, feedtime issued a new album, *Billy*, on Sydney independent label Black Hole. The album also saw release in the USA on the Amphetamine Reptile label. Feedtime supported New York hardcore trio Unsane on an East Coast Australian tour, after which the band toured North America. Feedtime then supported UK group The Damned and local heroes **X** on a national tour in April 1997.

Albums: *feedtime* (feedtime, 1985), *Shovel* (Aberrant, 1987), *Cooper S* (Aberrant, 1988), *Suction* (Aberrant, 1989), *Billy* (Black Hole, 1996).

Feral Dinosaurs

Formed: *1982*
Style: *Country*
Original line-up: *Nick Danyi (sax, vocals), Jim Shugg (guitar; ex-People with Chairs Up Their Noses), Conway Savage (piano), Dave Last (double bass, vocals), Jim White (drums; ex-People with Chairs Up Their Noses)*

Country music has never been big on the inner-city Melbourne pub circuit. Possibly the only two Melbourne bands of the early 1980s with a passing interest in Hank Williams Jr, Don Gibson or Merle Haggard were Feral Dinosaurs and The King Jerklews.

Au-go-go Records included Feral Dinosaurs' version of Don Gibson's 'Blue Day' on the Various Artists album *Asleep at the Wheel* (1984). Feral Dinosaurs then issued two independent singles, 'Ramblin' Man' and '50 Miles from Home', plus the mini-album *You've All Got a Home to Go to* (December 1985). Andrew Crowder also joined in 1985 on bass. When the band broke up, Crowder joined **Honeymoon in Green.** Last formed rockabilly band Dave Last's Boy Kings with Conway Savage, Manny Markogiannakos (guitar), Shane Walsh (bass) and Bruce Kane (drums). White joined **Venom P. Stinger** and later **Dirty Three.**

Savage was also heard in **Dave Graney and the White Buffaloes** and **Nick Cave and the Bad Seeds.** He issued a self-titled CD EP in late 1992. In 1996, Savage recorded a low-key and low-fi album of soft-hued country'n'blues tunes with **Falling Joys'** Suzie Higgie which has yet to see release.

Mini-album: *You've All Got a Home to Go to* (Major, 1985).

The Ferrets

Formed: *1975*
Style: *Pop*
Original line-up: *Billy Miller (guitar, vocals), Dave Springfield (guitar), Ken Firth (bass; ex-***Tully***)*

As Noel McGrath put it, The Ferrets came to the nation's attention in a blaze of publicity for the 1977 single 'Don't Fall in Love' and album *Dreams of a Love*. Under the patronage of ***Countdown*** compere and talent coordinator Ian 'Molly' Meldrum (who produced the album), it seemed inevitable The Ferrets would find long-term success, but due to line-up changes and a general lack of acceptance the band split in 1979.

The Ferrets came together in Sydney during early 1975. Billy Miller, Ken Firth and Dave Springfield then put the band on hold while they joined the final version of **Buster Brown** (July to November 1975). When **Buster Brown** dissolved, Philip Eisenberg (guitar) joined Miller, Firth and Springfield and The Ferrets relocated to Melbourne. Miller, Firth and Eisenberg had previously worked together in the *Jesus Christ Superstar* stage production. The band came to the attention of Meldrum and he introduced them to Rick Brewer (drums; ex-**Zoot**, I'Tambu, **Jim Keays'** Southern Cross) who joined in April 1976. Meldrum was also instrumental in getting the band signed to Mushroom Records. He took the band into the studio in July 1976 to start work on an album. (When the album finally appeared, Meldrum's credit read 'Producer: Willie Everfinish'.) Meanwhile, Miller's sisters Pam and Jane had joined as back-up singers.

The Ferrets' first single, 'Robin Hood'/'The Lemming Song' (April 1977) was not successful, but 'Don't Fall in Love'/'Lies' (June 1977) made #1 in Melbourne and #3 nationally. The band's long-awaited debut album was eventually 'rush-released' in October. Initial copies of the album were issued in a plain white cardboard sleeve only bearing The Ferrets' name, because the artwork had not been finalised. The release was deemed necessary in order to satisfy buyer demand. When the proper sleeves were made available, the purchaser could make the swap. As it transpired, *Dreams of a Love* climbed no higher than #20 on the album charts. The band's third single, 'Janie May'/'Just Like the Stars', reached # 25 in November.

In December, Pam and Eisenberg left and Jane switched to keyboards. Following the release of the unsuccessful 'Are You Looking at Me?'/'Holloway' single (April 1978), Jane and Firth both left. George Cross (bass; ex-**Jim Keays'** Band) replaced Firth, giving a line-up of Miller, Springfield, Brewer and Cross. That line-up recorded 'This Night'/'Tait's Run' (September 1978) and *Fame at Any Price* (October 1978). Neither record was successful. Cross was replaced by Ric Petropolis (ex-Last Chance Café) in September. In late 1978, Charisma Records issued *Dreams of a Love* and 'Don't Fall in Love' in the UK and Europe.

The Ferrets' last single, 'Tripsville'/'It's Not Over', came out in January 1979 and two months later the band broke up. Miller and Firth formed The Great Blokes; Springfield, Petropolis and Brewer joined Miller's younger brother Kenny in The Motivators. That band issued the album *The Motivators* and the singles 'So Scared', 'Kicks' (shared with the Jukes' 'Let You Know' and 'We All Know By Now') (July 1980), 'After the Fall'/'Slipping', 'Coming Up' (October 1980), 'Summer'/'Just Don't Care' (January 1981) and 'New Blood'/'At This Point in Time' (May 1981) on the Result label.

Eisenberg formed **Mighty Guys**. In 1983, Billy Miller formed The Spaniards with Mick Pealing (vocals; ex-**Stars**, Ideals) and Mark Mannock (keyboards; ex-Ideals). The Spaniards utilised other players as required, including Dave Springfield (guitar), Kevin Purcell (keyboards), Russell Brown (bass) and John Annas (drums; ex-**Kevin Borich Express**). The Spaniards issued three singles, 'God is a Shield' (1984), 'Angel' (1985) and 'What Can I Do?' (1985), plus the mini-album *Locked in a Dance* (EMI, 1986). Miller has continued to work with various bands ever since.

Albums: *Dreams of a Love* (Mushroom/Festival, 1977), *Fame at Any Price* (Mushroom/Festival, 1978).

Fester Fanatics (*see* Massive Appendage)

Festivals

The history of rock festivals in Australia echoes much of what went on overseas. The most famous American rock festivals of the 1960s, the Monterey International Pop Festival (June 1967) and Woodstock (August 1969), were the main inspirations for Australia's first rock festivals held during the early 1970s. Woodstock, in particular, was an important manifestation of the hippy philosophy of peace, love and harmony through rock music.

In Australia, the effect of Woodstock was twofold. Firstly the naivety of the 1960s was cast aside. As Clinton Walker put it, Australia's new progressive bands were engendered with a sense of where they could take their music, of stripping away old inhibitions, of exploring their roots in order to expand their horizons. Secondly, it allowed young and enterprising, if inexperienced, promoters the opportunity to make their mark on the industry.

Australia's first rock festival, *Pilgrimage for Pop*, was held at a farm near Ourimbah, NSW over the Australia Day weekend, January 1970. The organisers were a group of expatriate Americans called Nutwood Rug Band. That acid-rock band had emigrated from Los Angeles in 1967 so that the members could escape the Vietnam War draft (or so the story goes). Dennis Wilson from **Kahvas Jute** recalled that the band was originally known as Captain Reefer and the Desert Siren. **Billy Thorpe** also called the band the 'stonedest bunch of guys I'd ever met'. Ourimbah drew 6333 paying customers and featured the likes of **Billy Thorpe** and the Aztecs, **Jeff St John's** Copperwine, **Tully**, **Wendy Saddington**, **Doug Parkinson** In Focus, **Leo De Castro** and Friends, **Max Merritt and the Meteors**, **Levi Smith's Clefs** and Nutwood Rug Band.

Victoria's first festival at Launching Place was held New Year's Eve 1970. Only 3000 people turned up at Launching Place, and it rained most of the time. Nevertheless, **Billy Thorpe**, **Healing Force**, **Wendy Saddington**, **Spectrum**, **King Harvest** and **Jeffrey Crozier** entertained the crowd in fine style. Neither of the festivals made any money, but as Adrian Rawlings (who compered Ourimbah) wrote, they did provide a sense of real adventure, a sense of fulfilment, and 'despite their many ragged edges, they were transcendentalist's paradise'.

January 1971 saw the advent of the 'The Odyssey' Festival, Wallacia (NSW) and Myponga Festival in South Australia. Rawlings was the compere again. Wallacia drew 14 000 people and Myponga 15 000. The stars of the day were **Daddy Cool**, **Spectrum**, **Chain**, Thorpie and the Aztecs, **King Harvest**, **Fanny Adams**, **Healing Force**, **Fraternity** and **Wendy Saddington** and Copperwine. Black Sabbath and Cat Stevens were flown in to boost Myponga's bill, but the promoters still did not make any money. Another festival held in January 1971 was Fairlight (NSW) which featured bands like **The Cleves**, **La De Das**, **Blackfeather**, **Pirana**, **Tully** and **Kahvas Jute**.

In late 1971, Odessa Promotions organised (with decent publicity) what was to be the first profitable Australian rock festival at Sunbury, Victoria. Held over the Australia Day Weekend, January 1972, the inaugural Sunbury Festival was a defining moment in the history of Australian rock. It was the first time people realised it was not necessary to book overseas acts in order to pull 35 000 fans to a three-day outdoor event. **Billy Thorpe** was the unassailable monarch of Sunbury 1972. The Aztecs' legendary performance spawned a Top 5 album, *Aztecs Live! at Sunbury*. 'Whoooaa-yeeaah!' and 'Suck more piss!' resounded around the hills of Sunbury like a call to arms. Ex-**Loved One** Gerry Humphreys compered the event. Other stars on the Sunbury bill included **Max Merritt and the Meteors**, **Spectrum**, **Chain**, **The Wild Cherries**, **SCRA**, **Pirana**, **Tamam Shud**, **Company Caine**, **Friends**, **Carson** and **La De Das**. Film-maker John Dixon produced a documentary of the event *Sunbury* which is of great historical significance. Buoyed by the success of Sunbury 1972, the promoters repeated Sunbury in 1973, 1974 and 1975.

1973 and 1974 were good years. At Sunbury 1973, rock'n'roll legend **Johnny O'Keefe** appeared and, after the initial boos and heckles had died away, had the audience of hippies eating out of the palm of his hand. **Billy Thorpe** and the Aztecs headlined again each year. Comedian Paul Hogan compered Sunbury 1973, while **Jim Keays** took the honours in 1974. Other bands making their mark included **Coloured Balls**, **Madder Lake**, **Carson**, **Matt Taylor**, **Healing Force**, **Country Radio**, **Band of Light**, **Bakery**, **MacKenzie Theory**, **Friends**, **Flying Circus** and **Sid Rumpo** in 1973, while **Skyhooks**, **The Dingoes**, **Kush**, **Buster Brown**, **Chain**, **Madder Lake**, **MacKenzie Theory**, **Ayers Rock**, **Ross Ryan** and the re-formed **Daddy Cool** went down well at 1974.

Mushroom Records launched itself with the first triple-album set of Australian rock when it released *The Great Australian Rock Festival Sunbury 1973* in April 1973. Queen was the only overseas band booked for Sunbury 1974. The band was booed off the stage with calls of 'go back to Pommyland, ya pooftahs!' Freddie Mercury responded with 'when we come back to Australia, Queen will be the biggest band in the world', and they were. Sunbury 1975 was a disaster. It rained constantly, only 16 000 paying customers turned up and Deep Purple walked away with an enormous purse for its exclusive performance. None of the local bands were paid, the members of **AC/DC** got into a punch-up with Deep Purple's roadies, Odessa Promotions went into liquidation and that was the end of Sunbury. On a brighter note, The Keystone Angels were the only act to receive a standing ovation. Other acts that played Sunbury 1975 included **Sherbet**, **Skyhooks**, **Daddy Cool**, **Ariel**, **Ayers Rock**, **The Dingoes**, **Madder Lake**, **Renée Geyer** and Sanctuary, **La De Das**, **Captain Matchbox Whoopee Band**, **Kush** and **Ross Ryan**.

Meanwhile, other regional festivals came and went. In April 1972, Mulwala, held on the banks of the Murray River inland from Albury, was a disaster. Canned Heat and Stephen Stills' Manassas took the money and ran. The local bands hardly got a look in. Hillcrest Festival held in South Australia in October 1974 no doubt helped boost The Keystone Angels' confidence for their slot at Sunbury 1975. With the demise of Sunbury, the Australian Rock Festival almost became extinct. In 1977, biker gang the Hell's Angels organised the first of many festivals held at Broadford, Victoria. Broadford's scope ran the gamut of hard rock and boogie bands, to the virtual exclusion of everything else. Needless to say, **The Angels**, **Chain**, **The Giants**, Canned Heat and even Uriah Heep reigned supreme. In 1996, Broadford celebrated its twentieth year in operation, the longest-running rock festival event in the world.

The only mainstream festival until 1981 was the national Rockarena tour in October 1977, which featured Fleetwood Mac, Santana, **Little River Band**, **Kevin Borich Express** and Japanese band Creation. In October 1981, the three-day Tanelorn Festival of Transition (held near Stroud, NSW) drew 28 000 fans but still lost money. As well as featuring **Redgum**, **The Church**, **Moving Pictures**, **Kevin Borich Express**, **Men at Work**, **Sunnyboys**, **Broderick Smith's** Big Combo, **Midnight Oil** and **Split Enz**, the festival saw the return of **Billy Thorpe**, then based in the USA. Narara (Somersby, NSW) was another step ahead, with 25 000 people in attendance over the three-day Australia Day weekend, January 1983.

Narara '83 featured **Cold Chisel**, **Australian Crawl**, **The Angels**, **Men at Work**, **Moving Pictures**, **The Church**, **Richard Clapton**, **Jo Jo Zep**, **Rose Tattoo**, **Dragon**, **Goanna** and **The Hitmen**, among others. Some 33 000 fans attended Narara '84 to see local bands such as **Hoodoo Gurus**, **The Dynamic Hepnotics**, **Mondo Rock**, **Mental as Anything**, **Eurogliders**, **Models**, **INXS**, **The Radiators**, **Sunnyboys**, **Real Life** and compere Austen Tayshus. The organisers upped the ante with international visitors The Pretenders, Simple Minds, Talking Heads, Def Leppard, Eurythmics and Sandii and the Sunsetz. Despite persistent rain over the three days, it was a success. The smaller-scaled Werrikimbe Festival (Forbes River, NSW) during September drew 10 000 people to see **Dragon**, **The Angels**, **Jimmy Barnes**, **Rose Tattoo**, **Eurogliders**, **Allniters**, **Swanee** and **Redgum**.

In January 1987, four promoters (Mark Pope, Richard MacDonald, Gary Grant and Chris Murphy) ran the massive Australian Made event. Boasting a solid bill of **Mental as Anything**, **The Triffids**, **The Saints**, **I'm Talking**, **Divinyls**, **Models**, **Jimmy Barnes** and **INXS**, the tour drew record crowds across the country. It was the first travelling festival tour to feature exclusively Australian bands. Likewise, in 1987, the inaugural Livid Festival was held in Brisbane. It was the first event to lock into the alternative scene, a vast, previously untapped audience making its own identity and waiting for an event to call its own. In 1996, Livid celebrated its tenth anniversary. In 1990, a group of enterprising promoters also instigated the annual East Coast Blues and Roots Festival (held in Byron Bay), which played host to local blues artists like **Chain** and The Backsliders, as well as many international acts.

During the early 1990s, events in Australia again began to run in parallel with those in America. Jane's Addiction/Porno for Pyros' lead singer Perry Farrell, manager Ted Gardner (Porno for Pyros, Tool) and others organised the enormous travelling festival known as Lollapalooza, an alternative venture that became an almost exclusive domain for the likes of Nirvana, Soundgarden, Jane's Addiction, etc. In Australia, promoters Ken West and Vivian Lees had similar, lofty ideals. Together they launched the Big Day Out (BDO). The inaugural (one-day) event was held at the Sydney Showground (Hordern Pavilion) in January 1992 and drew a respectable crowd of 9000 fans. The bill included overseas visitors Nirvana (right on the cusp of an international breakthrough), Violent Femmes and Henry Rollins, plus local acts like **The Celibate Rifles**, **Died Pretty**, **Cosmic Psychos**, **The Hellmenn**, **Massappeal**, **You Am I**, **Beasts of Bourbon**, **The Meanies**, **Clouds**, **Club Hoy**, **Ratcat**, **The Hard-Ons** and **Yothu Yindi**.

Despite being a logistical nightmare, BDO became a national event with concerts in Sydney, Melbourne, the Gold Coast, Adelaide, Perth and Auckland (New Zealand) each year. BDO 1993 featured Iggy Pop, Sonic Youth, Mudhoney, the Disposable Heroes of Hiphoprisy and **Nick Cave and the Bad Seeds**, as well as the cream of upcoming local acts. Over the next four years, BDO played host to international acts like The Ramones, Urge Overkill, Soundgarden, Smashing Pumpkins, Ministry, The Cult, Screaming Trees, Hole, Primal Scream, The Offspring, Elastica, Rage Against the Machine, Jesus Lizard, Porno for Pyros, Patti Smith, The Prodigy, Shonen Knife, Fear Factory and the Jon Spencer Blues Explosion.

Likewise, BDO provided the perfect launching pad for homegrown talent like **Spiderbait**, **Def FX**, **silverchair**, **Magic Dirt**, **Tumbleweed**, **TISM**, a reformed **Radio Birdman**, **You Am I**, **Regurgitator**, **Powderfinger**, **Dirty Three**, **Dave Graney 'n' the Coral Snakes**, **Even**, **Powder Monkeys** and a host of others. Of the many highlights over the years, the time **Kylie Minogue** sang a duet with **Nick Cave** on 'Where the Wild Roses Grow' to the delight of the crowd at BDO 1996 must be a sentimental favourite. Then, after finally being taken seriously by the big wigs, promoters Lees and West announced that BDO 1997 would be the last. Naturally, BDO 1997 drew the biggest crowds (37 000 people in Melbourne, for example). It was the end of an era.

Another popular festival (albeit on a smaller scale) that coincided with BDO was the Meredith Music Festival, held in rural Victoria. The festival came about when local farmer Jack Nolan discovered a natural amphitheatre on his property. The first Meredith Music Festival was held in December 1991, and in 1997 it turned seven. Meredith mostly featured Australian bands. Meanwhile, in the wake of BDO's runaway national success, other promoters took the plunge. So far there has been Alternative Nation, Steve Pav's Summersault, Homebake at Byron Bay (which drew 13 000 fans in 1996), Rock Above the Falls, Peaches'n'Cream, Offshore, Mudslinger and others.

Once seen as an anachronism and/or a forum for ageing hippies to indulge in misty-eyed nostalgia, the rock festival has become an essential part of the Australian music scene. The Australian summer festival season became a viable and creative alternative to the pub circuit. The summer would not have been the same without at least half-a-dozen festivals competing for ever-escalating attendance figures.

Sunbury albums: *Sunbury* (EMI/HMV, 1972), *Aztecs Live! At Sunbury* (Havoc, 1972), *The Great Australian Rock Festival Sunbury 1973* (Mushroom/Festival, 1973), *Summer Jam* (Mushroom anti-Rip Off/Festival, 1973), *Carson on the Air* (EMI/Harvest, 1973), *Blackfeather Live! (Sunbury)* (Festival/Infinity, 1974), *Francis Butler's 69ers Live* (Festival/Infinity, 1974), *Highlights of Sunbury '74 Part 1* (Mushroom anti-Rip Off/Festival, 1974), *Highlights of Sunbury '74 Part 2* (Mushroom anti-Rip Off/Festival, 1974).

Videos: *Sunbury* (Directed by John Dixon; Siren Entertainment, 1994), *Australian Made* (Directed by Richard Lowenstein, Hoyts PolyGram, 1988), *Ritual Habitual Big Day Out 1996 A Documentary* (PolyGram Video, 1996).

Further reading: *Festivals in Australia, An Intimate History* by Adrian Rawlings (D.T.E. Publications, 1983); *Australian Made* by Glenn A. Baker (Fontana/Collins, 1987).

Fiction Romance (*see* Fast Cars)

Billy Field

Style: *Jazz pop*

In 1981, husky voiced singer/piano player Billy Field (b. 1953) was one of the most popular acts on the Australian scene. His two jazz-pop singles, 'Bad Habits' and 'You Weren't in Love with Me', were big hits, registering #4 and #1 respectively on the national chart. His debut album, *Bad Habits*, also made #1 and became one of the year's Top 5 selling albums.

Field got his start with Sydney schoolboy band King Fox. The line-up comprised Field, Paul Radcliffe (guitar, flute), Peter Muller (organ), David King (bass) and Andrew Evans (drums). The band members came from the affluent suburb of Vaucluse and, as Glenn A. Baker has noted, got their career underway when various parental patrons supplied them with the very best musical instruments and equipment. The band's debut single on the Du Monde label, 'Unforgotten Dreams'/'Alone, So Alone' (April 1970), became a Top 10 hit in Sydney (#7), staying on the charts for 17 weeks.

The follow-up, 'Tymepiece'/'Will You Love Me Tomorrow?' (August), was a minor hit. Both singles were fine pieces of inventive psychedelic pop bordering on progressive rock. King Fox commenced recording an album, but when all five members failed their end-of-year exams as a result of their extra-curricular activities, the parents who had helped start their career neatly terminated it. The album never saw the light of day. Radcliffe, Muller, King and Evans revived King Fox in 1972 and issued one final single on Festival, 'I Think You're Fine'/'We're Gonna Think of a Name' (June).

Field spent five years working in the country before establishing Paradise Studios in Sydney during 1979. Following the success of *Bad Habits*, he recorded a follow-up, *Try Biology*. Neither it, nor the singles 'True Love' (October 1982; #16 in December) and 'Try Biology' (February 1983) were quite so successful. As well as continuing to manage Paradise Studios and maintaining an interest in R&B, Field has recorded three jazz albums.

Albums: *Bad Habits* (WEA, 1981), *Try Biology* (WEA, 1982), *Say Yes* (Agape, 1989), *Rock & Roll Memories* (J&B, 1989), *Western Light* (J&B, 1993).

Finch

Formed: *1973*
Style: *Hard rock*
Original line-up: *Owen Orford (vocals), Bob Spencer (guitar), Tony Strain (bass), Peter McFarlane (drums)*

By the time Sydney band Finch (previously known as Stillwater) issued its debut single in 1974, it was already one of the best hard rock outfits on the local scene. Lead guitarist Bob Spencer was still in high school at that stage.

Owen Orford was a flashy frontman with a confident rock voice and a neat line in microphone-stand acrobatics. Bob Spencer's guitar heroes were Jimmy Page and Paul Kossoff, and the band was renowned for slipping Led Zeppelin, Free and Bad Company covers into its set. Finch won the 1973

2SM/Pepsi Pop Poll for which the prize was a contract with Picture Records. This resulted in the picture disc single 'And She Sings'/'Out of Control' (January 1974). Finch also appeared on the soundtrack album to the surfing film *Drouyn*. Finch's three rock tracks, 'Sail Away', 'Lady of Truth' and 'Roses', appeared alongside jazzy incidental material written by Peter Martin (ex-SCRA).

The band settled into the pub rock circuit and issued the underrated, self-financed *Thunderbird* album in May 1976. The band members still had a good deal of English-flavoured blues and hard rock buzzing around in their systems when they recorded the album. The band's confident sound was also heard to good advantage on the singles 'Stay'/'Roses' (April 1976) and 'Short Changed Again'/'One Nighter' (December). 'Short Changed Again' peaked at #29 on the Sydney chart. Finch moved to Melbourne at the end of 1976, and embarked on a successful tour with **Supernaut**. In March 1977, just as Finch was making commercial headway, 19-year-old Spencer left to replace Red Symons in **Skyhooks**. Tony Strain also left the band.

Finch went through a rash of new players (guitarists Gary Quince, ex-**Redhouse**, Skeeta Pereira and Sam Mallett, plus bass player Graham Thompson, ex-**Stars**), before the line-up stabilised with the arrival of Mark Evans (bass; ex-**AC/DC**) in June 1977 and Graham Kennedy (guitar, vocals) and Chris Jones (guitar; ex-White Heat) a month later. Finch signed to CBS/Epic and issued the single 'One More Time'/'Mean Machine' (October 1977). Dave Hinds (ex-**Rabbit**) replaced Jones (who joined **Feather**) in December 1977.

The band was moving in a more commercial hard rock direction, and its next single, 'Where Were You?'/'Leave the Killing to You' (February 1978), reached #14 in Melbourne and #33 in Sydney. The album *Nothing to Hide* (March) produced a second single, 'Nothing to Hide'/'Foolin'' (May). Finch then signed with CBS's US West Coast subsidiary label Portrait. Due to the presence of a Dutch band also called Finch, the band became Contraband. Portrait issued Contraband's debut single, 'That's Your Way'/'Dreamer', in October 1978. That same month, Barry Cram (ex-**Pantha**, **Avalanche**, **Russell Morris** Band) replaced McFarlane, who joined **Swanee**. The *Contraband* album came out in May 1979, accompanied by the singles 'Rainin' Again'/'Too Drunk to Know' (March 1979) and a cover of the Spencer Davis Group's 'Gimme Some Lovin''/'C 61' (July 1979). The album created some interest in the USA, but was not successful in Australia.

Portrait dropped Contraband later in the year, and the band broke up. Orford joined Toys and later moved into band management and promotion. Cram and Hinds joined Mick Pealing and the Ideals. Evans went on to the likes of Beast, **Swanee**, **Heaven** and **The Headhunters**, among others.

Finch albums: *Thunderbird* (Eagle, 1976), *Nothing to Hide* (CBS/Epic, 1978); ***Contraband album:*** *Contraband* (CBS/Portrait, 1979).

Fini Scad

Formed: *1995*
Style: *Indie guitar pop*
Original line-up: *Dave Thomas (guitar, vocals), Billy Coupland (guitar), Lincoln Beecroft (bass), Jonathan McPhee (drums)*

As with bands like **Automatic**, **Gaslight Radio** and **Paradise Motel**, Sydney-based Fini Scad emerged in 1996 in the wake of the breakthrough commercial success of **silverchair**, **You Am I**, **Regurgitator**, **Spiderbait** and **Powderfinger**. Fini Scad signed to Mushroom's development label, Bark, and issued its debut CD EP 'Testrider' (October 1996). With its lead track, the stirring 'Coppertone', Fini Scad made an immediate impact (supported by airplay from Triple J). The song's melodic rock edge echoed US bands such as The Posies, Everclear, Pavement and Sebadoh. 'Coppertone' registered #42 on the 1996 Triple J Hottest 100 list. In early 1997, Fini Scad toured as support to **The Fauves**, **deadstar** and **The Saints**, and set about recording its debut album with producer Paul McKercher (**You Am I**, **Tumbleweed**). The CD single 'Furious' came out in June 1997.

Neil Finn (*see* Crowded House; Split Enz)

Tim Finn

Style: *Pop, rock*

New Zealand-born singer/songwriter Brian Timothy Finn (b. 1952) spent over 12 years as the driving force behind **Split Enz**, one of the most successful bands on the Australian scene of the early 1980s. He launched his solo career in June 1983 with the release of the acclaimed *Escapade* album, and has pursued an erratic path since.

Finn issued *Escapade* on Mushroom while still a member of **Split Enz**. Produced by Mark Moffatt and Ricky Fataar, *Escapade* reached #7 in August 1983. It was still in the national Top 20 in January 1984, the same week Split Enz's *Conflicting Emotions* peaked at #13. *Escapade* yielded three hit singles,

Neil and Tim Finn

'Fraction Too Much Friction'/'Below the Belt' (#8 in June 1983), 'Made My Day'/'Another Chance' (#22 in September) and 'Staring at the Embers'/ 'Through the Years' (#35 in December), plus the unsuccessful 'In a Minor Key' (February 1984).

Flushed with the success of his debut album, Finn left **Split Enz** in June 1984. His departure certainly contributed to the band's demise at the end of the year. Finn issued one last single for Mushroom in August 1985, 'Home for My Heart'/ 'Strange Night' (included on *The Coca-Cola Kid* film soundtrack and produced by Phil Manzanera) before signing to Virgin. Finn's first international album, *Big Canoe* (April 1986), and its two singles, 'No Thunder No Fire No Rain'/'Searching the Street' (March) and 'Spiritual Hunger'/'So Deep' (July), were not successful.

In 1987 Finn moved to WEA for the *Les Patterson Saves the World* soundtrack and the singles 'You Saved the World'/'Les Fanfare' (April 1987) and 'With You I'm Alive'/'Hacia El Sol' (September). Finn continued his flirtation with film when he made a fleeting appearance as a singer in his (then) partner Greta Scacchi's film *White Mischief*. Finn spent two years of songwriting and collaboration with producer Mitchell Froom (**Crowded House**) in preparation for his fourth solo album, *Tim Finn* (May 1989). It was a very deep and highly personal album. 'How'm I Gonna Sleep?'/'Cruel Black Crow' (March) and 'Crescendo'/'Six Months in a Leaky Boat', 'Show a Little Emotion' (July) were lifted as singles. One track, 'Parihaka', was about racial harmony, and addressed the subject of the rise of Maori nationalism in New Zealand. He cut the track with Maori group The Herbs.

Just as he was bringing his solo career back on track, Finn joined his brother Neil in **Crowded House**. Finn contributed to the album *Woodface* and the sardonic single 'Chocolate Cake' before leaving the band at the end of 1991. After travelling around the world for most of his career, Finn settled in Melbourne and built his own studio, Periscope. Nevertheless, the peripatetic Finn could not stand still for long. He recorded his fifth solo album, *Before & After*, in four different locations (Dublin, London, Los Angeles and Melbourne) with seven different producers. Despite the piecemeal nature of its genesis, *Before & After* proved to be Finn's strongest, most cohesive and most positive statement to date.

Released in July 1993, the album included the singles 'Persuasion' (June), 'Hit the Ground Running' (October) and 'Many's the Time' (recorded with Hothouse Flowers) (April 1994). The album's songs traversed an eclectic array of styles and feels, from country-flavoured ballads to reggae-tinged and soul-inflected pop. *Before & After* went on to reach #29 on the UK charts, a first for Finn. At the end of 1994, Finn teamed up with British solo singer Andy White and former Hothouse Flowers singer/guitarist Liam O'Maonlai in the studio project ALT (Andy, Liam and Tim). The collaboration resulted in the *Altitude* album, which managed to reach #67 in the UK at the end of 1995.

Finn kept busy throughout 1995 by teaming up again with his brother Neil to record an album. No doubt buoyed by his recent success in the UK, the *Finn* album reached #15 on the British charts in October 1995. *Finn* also produced two UK hit singles, 'Suffer Never'/'Weather with You' (demo) (#29 in October) and 'Angels Heap'/'It's Only Natural' (demo), 'Chocolate Cake' (demo) (#41 in November). In between commitments to his solo career, Finn also toured with the re-formed **Split Enz** (1989 and 1993) and appeared on the *Enzso* album (1996) of orchestrated **Split Enz** material.

Tim Finn solo albums: *Escapade* (Mushroom/Festival, 1983), *Big Canoe* (Virgin, 1986), *Les Patterson Saves the World* (film soundtrack; WEA, 1987), *Tim Finn* (EMI/Capitol, 1989), *Before & After* (EMI/Capitol, 1993); ***With ALT:*** *Altitude* (EMI/Parlophone, 1995); ***With Neil Finn:*** *Finn* (EMI/Capitol, 1995).

Chris Finnen

Style: Blues

Alongside **Dave Hole**, **Phil Manning**, **Kevin Borich** and **Geoff Achison**, Adelaide-based Chris Finnen is considered to be one of the best electric blues guitarists in Australia. Finnen's career stretches back to the likes of St James Infirmary in 1970, through Concrete Wellington in 1972, Offering and Redeye during the mid-1970s, the **Matt Taylor** Band circa 1982 and many others. In 1979, Finnen issued a self-financed cassette entitled *Journey and Dream Suite*.

Finnen contributed to the **Matt Taylor** Band's 1983 album *Always Land on Your Feet*. Finnen left the **Matt Taylor** Band at the end of 1983, due to the clash of a heavy touring schedule and his own commitments. The near-blind Finnen had been offered a job as Counsellor and PR person for the Blind Institute in Melbourne. He formed his own three-piece Chris Finnen Band in 1985 which comprised Peter Howell (bass) and Mick Patterson (drums), who was replaced by Robin Andrews. The 1994 line-up of The Chris Finnen Blues Band included Michael Winter (bass), who was replaced by Dirk Du Bois (ex-**Chain**), and John Freeman (drums; ex-**Fraternity**). The Chris Finnen Blues Band issued the album *Live* in June 1995. In 1996, Finnen collaborated with another fine blues guitarist, Jeff Lang (ex-**Matt Taylor's Chain**) for the limited edition album *Live at the Vineyard*. Backing the two guitarists were Dirk Du Bois (bass) and Steve Peterka (drums) with guest player Kerryn Tolhurst (ex-**Dingoes**) on lap steel guitar.

Albums: *Live* (Festival/Exile, 1995), *Live at the Vineyard* (Crossing Records, 1996).

The Fireballs

Fire (*see* Ku Klux Frankenstein)

The Fireballs

Formed: *1990*
Style: *Rockabilly/heavy metal fusion*
Original line-up: *Matt Healey (guitar), Joe Phantom (bass, vocals), Eddie Fury (drums, vocals)*

With a style based around slaphappy rockabilly roots welded to hyperactive speed metal guitar riffs and gravity-defying mohawk haircuts, Melbourne band The Fireballs appealed to metal, punk and Cramps fans alike. The Fireballs had the distinction of breaking house attendance records at a number of inner-city Melbourne pubs.

The band's debut release was the 'Terminal Haircut Blistered' CD EP in 1992. The 'Fall of the Damned' CD EP (September 1993), two singles 'Go Go Go' (June 1994) and 'Don't Bother Me' (October), and the album *Life Takes Too Long* (June 1994) came out over the next year. The Fireballs also shared a single with **Front End Loader**, 'Big Black Hearse'. The subject matter of the band's songs ran the gamut of fast cars ('Go Go Go'), aliens and horror films ('Spaceman Rock'n'Roll'), sex ('Bondage'), drugs ('Something to Think About') and not much else. In 1994, The Fireballs recorded a version of **AC/DC**'s 'Rocker' for inclusion on Polydor's tribute album *For Those About to Rock: We Salute AC/DC* (1995). In 1995, cartoonist Dillon Naylor (who had drawn graphics for the band since its inception) issued the first of his *Fireballs Comic Book*. In the tradition of Kiss, the comic focused on the band's ridiculously hectic lifestyle with plenty of guaranteed laughs.

The Fireballs' second album, *So Bad It's Good* (July 1996), contained a feast of distorted guitars, bone-rattling percussion and sprinting bass lines. With titles like 'The Killer Within', 'Vampire Envy', 'I Got No Brain' and the single 'Voodoo', it gave The Cramps a run for their psychobilly money. In 1996, The Fireballs supported overseas visitors Supersuckers and Dick Dale.

Albums: *Life Takes Too Long* (MDS, 1994), *So Bad It's Good* (MDS, 1996).

The Fish John West Reject

Formed: *1985*
Style: *Country, rockabilly*
Original line-up: *Mark Narkowicz (guitar, vocals), Mark Adams (guitar, vocals)*

Tasmanian band The Fish John West Reject played an energetic blend of music that incorporated country, folk, acoustic R&B and rockabilly (not unlike the Violent Femmes). The band started out as an acoustic duo before adding the rhythm section of Andrew Viney (bass) and Graham Rankin (drums) in 1986. Rankin also played in **The Odolites**. The band issued the independent cassette album *Canned* (1986) before breaking up in 1987. Rankin relocated to Melbourne with **The Odolites**. The Fish John West Reject reconvened in early 1988, moved to Melbourne and issued the cassette album *Shy but Wild* (1988), plus the single 'Left'/'Childless Mother' (April 1989). Other players joined, including Martin Witheford (guitar, vocals), Michael Witheford (bass, vocals) and Stanley Paulzen who replaced Rankin on drums in 1991.

The band's debut vinyl album *Swim* yielded the EP 'The Orchard'/'Minute', 'Ezekiel Saw that Wheel' (April 1990). The boisterous cover of Woody Guthrie's 'Ezekiel' was one example of the band's eclectic tastes. The Fish contributed a cover of fellow Tasmanian band The Innocents' 'Sooner or Later' to the Various Artists tribute album, *Used and Recovered by . . .* (1990) They issued a second album, *Fin* (July 1991), another single, 'Exile', and a 12-inch EP, 'Sick Inside', on the Shock label before calling it a day in 1992. In 1993 Michael Witheford formed power pop outfit Lust in Space with Alex Lynch (guitar) and Rod Fulton (drums). Phil Lally replaced Fulton on drums. Lynch and Lally also played with fellow Tasmanian outfit Fridge. Lust in Space issued two CD EPs, 'Glamnesia' (1994) and 'Speed Queen' (1995).

Albums: *Swim* (River Filf, 1989), *Fin* (Shock, 1991).

Flake

Formed: *1968*
Style: *Pop, rock*
Original line-up: *Sharon Sims (vocals), Denise Gaines (vocals), Geoff Gray (vocals; ex-Eli), Lindsay Askew (guitar), Rob Toth (keyboards), Mick Gaul (bass), Wayne Thomas (drums; ex-Plastic Tears)*

From swinging 1960s pop'n'soul to early 1970s progressive rock, Sydney band Flake tried its hand at just about every musical genre of the day. Flake was one of the first Sydney club bands to play note-for-note renditions of early Traffic, Spooky Tooth, Deep Purple and Vanilla Fudge material. Certainly possessed of a wealth of talent, the band mostly found success with a string of glossy pop singles.

From 1969 onwards, there were regular line-up changes within the band's ranks: Ross Jeffries replaced original guitarist Lindsay Askew; John Russell (ex-Amber, Plastic Tears) replaced Jeffries; and Denis Moore (ex-Him and the Others) replaced Gaul on bass. Dave Allen (sax, flute) also joined, and Shauna Jensen (vocals) was a member briefly at the end of 1970. That year, Flake signed to Martin Erdman's independent Du Monde label (home to King Fox, **Erl Dalby and Pyramid**, Samael Lilith, Elm Tree, Clapham Junction, **The 69ers**, Toby Jugg, Wheelbarrow and Ben Turpin). Flake's rise on the pop charts coincided with the 1970 radio ban on British and major-label Australian records which lasted for six months.

As a consequence, Flake enjoyed a run of memorable hit singles: a cover of Bob Dylan's (by way of Julie Driscoll) 'This Wheel's on Fire'/'You've Got Me Thinking' (Sydney #4, #20 nationally; July 1970), Marmalade's 'Reflections of My Life'/'Teach Me How to Fly' (Sydney #11, Top 30 nationally; January 1971), Vanda and Young's 'Life is Getting Better'/'Down in Rio' (Sydney #15; June 1971) and 'Under the Silent Tree'/'Say Goodbye' (Sydney #35; November 1971).

By early 1971 the line-up had stabilised with Sims, Gray, Russell and Thomas plus newcomers Billy Taylor (guitar; ex-Purple Vision) and Greg Higgs (bass, vocals). Taylor was an accomplished slide guitarist, and he added considerable weight to the band's sound. Flake's schizophrenic debut album, *How's Your Mother!* (December 1971), on Du Monde's sister label Violet's Holiday, featured one side of the band's lightweight pop hits and one side of hard rock tracks spiced with touches of fuzz-drenched psychedelia (including Vanda and Young's solid 'Quick Reaction'). The album sank without a trace and is very scarce these days. Just prior to the album's release, Mick Meehan (ex-Cinnamon) replaced Taylor on lead guitar.

Flake's live popularity continued into 1972, but the band only issued one single that year, 'See the Light'/'Where are You?' (December). Sharon Sims also issued a solo single on Violet's Holiday, 'To Be the One You Love'/'Where are You?' (February 1972). By the end of 1972, Flake had fallen apart with Wayne Thomas leaving to form a new band called Mr Madness featuring three ex-Flake alumni, Lindsay Askew (guitar), Mick Gaul (bass) and Rob

Toth (keyboards). Roy Richie joined on guitar and vocals.

Flake re-emerged in early 1973 with a new line-up of Billy Taylor, John Russell, Ted Atkinson (bass) and Jim Penson (drums; ex-**Blackfeather**). By July 1973, the line-up had become Taylor, Russell and Penson plus newcomers Neale Johns (vocals; ex-**Blackfeather**) and Warren Ward (bass; ex-**Flying Circus**, **Blackfeather**). As a consequence Flake was more **Blackfeather** than Flake at that stage. The band's one single, 'Scotch on the Rocks'/'Breadalbane' on Festival's Infinity label (February 1974) boasted out-and-out hard rock riffs. Flake finally came to an end later in the year. Taylor joined Johns in a new **Blackfeather** line-up at the start of 1975.

In 1989, Festival issued the Glenn A. Baker-compiled *Reflections* retrospective set, which prompted a Flake re-formation. The line-up of Lindsay Askew (guitar), Rob Askew (bass), Anna Medley (vocals), Gordon Sheard (guitar) and Wayne Thomas (drums) played the Sydney pubs until 1991.

Albums: *How's Your Mother!* (Violet's Holiday/Festival, 1971), *Reflections: The Festival File Volume Thirteen* (Festival, 1989).

The Flaming Hands

Formed: *1980*
Style: *Soul, pop*
Original line-up: *Julie Mostyn (vocals; ex-Kamikaze Kids), Jeff Sullivan (guitar; ex-*Passengers*), Steve Harris (keyboards; ex-*Passengers*, Visitors), Richard Allen (bass), Michael Hiron (drums; ex-*Leftovers*)*

Led by charismatic singer Julie Mostyn and astute songwriter/guitarist Jeff Sullivan, The Flaming Hands were one of the great inner-city Sydney bands of the early 1980s. The band's intense yet tuneful blend of 1960s soul, R&B and psychedelic pop attracted a loyal following.

The band signed to the Phantom label and issued the delightful 'I Belong to Nobody'/'The Stranger' single in September 1980. The single featured soul covers originally recorded by Soul Incorporated and The Marvelettes respectively. By the time the first single came out, Paul 'Sluggo' Maheno had joined (sax, vocals). The new line-up issued the **Lobby Loyde**-produced 'Wake Up Screaming'/'Sweet Revenge' single in March 1981. That coincided with another line-up change, with Sullivan, Mostyn and Sluggo being joined by newcomers Grant Conner (bass; ex-Idiot Savant), Peter Bull (keyboards) and Alan Brown (drums; ex-**Passengers**, Proteens).

The new line-up supported UK band The Clash at its epic seven-night stand at Sydney's Capitol Theatre during February 1982. The Clash's manager, Bernie Rhodes, became something of a Flaming Hands fan. The Flaming Hands issued a new single, 'It's Just that I Miss You'/'Go or Stay', a month later. By the end of the year, however, Sullivan and Mostyn had grown dissatisfied with their lack of progress and inability to gain a major record deal and broke up the band. Bull later joined **Paul Kelly** and the Coloured Girls. Sullivan and Mostyn started to put together a new band called Tunnels and Trains, but a year later had reverted to the name The Flaming Hands. The band signed to Big Time (through EMI) and prepared to record an album. With the help of **INXS** members Andrew Farriss and Garry Beers, Sullivan and Mostyn recorded the 12-inch single 'Cast My Love'/'Kismet' (October 1983) and the 7-inch single 'The Edge'/'Sacrifice' (March 1984).

By early 1984, Flaming Hands consisted of Sullivan, Mostyn and Sluggo. With assistance from session players like Sam McNally (keyboards; ex-**Stylus**) and Rex Goh (guitar; ex-**Air Supply**), The Flaming Hands completed their debut, self-titled album. Issued during October 1984, it contained 'Cast My Love' and 'The Edge', as well as two more singles, 'Break Down and Cry'/'Open Windows' (July) and 'Out of Our Hands'/'Wild Boy' (March 1985). By mid-1984, The Flaming Hands had returned to the live arena with a line-up of Sullivan, Mostyn, Sluggo, Tim Leitch (keyboards), D.C. Robertson (bass; also in **Scattered Order**) and Michael Prowse (drums; also in **Scattered Order**). At the end of 1985, after five and a half years of perseverance, with little chart success and only a cult following to show for it, Sullivan and Mostyn finally laid The Flaming Hands to rest.

Album: *The Flaming Hands* (Big Time/EMI, 1984).

Penny Flanagan and the New Moon (*see* Club Hoy)

Flash and the Pan

Formed: *1976*
Style: *Pop rock*
Original line-up: *Harry Vanda (guitar, keyboards), George Young (guitar, keyboards, vocals)*

The venerable production/songwriting team of Harry Vanda and George Young enjoyed considerable success during the 1960s as members of **The Easybeats**. While working in the UK as freelance producers/songwriters/musicians, Vanda and Young issued the single 'Lazy River'/'Free and Easy' on the Albert label (October 1971).

They also issued a series of obscure singles in the UK under various pseudonyms, including Paintbox ('Get Ready for Love'/'Can I Get to Know You?', October 1971), Haffy's Whisky Sour ('Shot in the Head'/'Bye Bye Bluebird' in November 1971) and Marcus Hook Roll Band ('Natural Man'/ 'Boogalooing is for Wrong' in August 1972 and 'Louisiana Lady'/'Hoochie Coochie Har Kau' in March 1973). Vanda and Young had their songs covered in the UK by David Bowie ('Friday on My Mind' on *Pin-Ups*), Rod Stewart ('Hard Road' on *Smiler*), Savoy Brown ('I'll Make You Happy' on *Hellbound Train*) and Warhorse ('St Louis' on *Warhorse*).

The duo returned to Sydney in late 1973 and set up home in the Albert studio complex. They recorded a raucous, booze-soaked rock album for EMI as Marcus Hook Roll Band. The *Tales of Old Grand-Daddy* album reputedly featured the first studio venture for George's younger brothers Malcolm and Angus, who had just formed **AC/DC**. 'Can't Stand the Heat'/'Moonshine Blues' was issued as a single. EMI re-issued the album as *Full File* in 1981 with the first two, previously non-album, singles added. Throughout the mid-1970s, as Australia's top producers, Vanda and Young proceeded to swamp the local charts with a seemingly endless string of hits for **John Paul Young**, **AC/DC**, **Ray Burgess**, **William Shakespeare**, **The Angels**, **Cheetah** and **Rose Tattoo**. Their finest effort was reserved for **Stevie Wright**, for whom they crafted the epic #1 hit 'Evie' in 1974.

In January 1977, Vanda and Young issued the single 'Hey! St Peter'/'Walking in the Rain' under the alter-ego concept name of Flash and the Pan. Originally intended as an engaging diversion from the real job of record production for other artists, Vanda and Young found themselves with a hit on their hands when 'Hey! St Peter' reached #3 on the Australian charts. The music was based around an accessible, yet inventive synthesiser-based pop rock sound with an emphasis on George's spoken-word vocals and shouted chorus. Grace Jones later issued a version of 'Walking in the Rain' as a single.

Flash and the Pan re-entered the Australian Top 5 in August 1978 with 'Down Among the Dead Men'/'Man Who Knew the Answer'. When issued in the UK as 'And the Band Played on (Down Among the Dead Men)', it peaked at a respectable #54. The album *Flash and the Pan* and a third single, 'American Shuffle'/'Hole in the Middle', followed in December. *Flash and the Pan* reached #80 on the US charts in July 1979, as well as reaching #1 in Scandinavia. Vanda and Young received numerous offers to tour, but preferred the sanctity of their 24-track Albert Studio enclave.

Vanda and Young added studio cohorts Leszek Karski (bass), **Ray Arnott** (drums) and Warren Morgan (piano) to flesh out the second Flash and the Pan album. *Lights in the Night* yielded the singles 'Welcome to the Universe'/'Lights in the Night' (July 1980) and 'Media Man'/'Captains Beware' (December 1980). For their third Flash and the Pan album, Vanda and Young brought in ex-**Easybeats** frontman **Stevie Wright** and Lyndsay Hammond from **Cheetah** to carry the vocal chores.

Headlines and its singles, 'Where Were You?'/ 'Hey Jimmy' (July 1982) and 'Waiting for a Train'/ 'Don't Vote' (December 1982), featured a more basic rock approach, but with no loss of power or originality. When issued overseas during April 1983, 'Waiting for a Train'/'"A"' became a smash hit, reaching #7 in the UK. *Headlines* was Flash and the Pan's third #1 album in Scandinavia. The UK-only album *Panorama* reached #69 there in July 1983. For *Early Morning Wake Up Call* and its singles 'Midnight Man'/'Fat Night' (November 1984) and 'Early Morning Wake Up Call'/'Look at that Woman Go' (February 1985), Flash and the Pan was back to the duo of Vanda and Young. *Nights in France* (October 1987) included the singles 'Ayla'/'Your Love is Strange' (September) and 'Money Don't Lie'/ 'Bones' (April 1988).

Just when it seemed that Vanda and Young had dispensed with the Flash and the Pan concept, they re-emerged in 1992 with *Burning Up the Night* and the CD singles 'Burning Up the Night' (October) and 'Living on Dreams' (March 1993).

Flash and the Pan albums: *Flash and the Pan* (Albert, 1978), *Lights in the Night* (Albert, 1980), *Headlines* (Albert, 1982), *Early Morning Wake Up Call* (Albert, 1984), *Nights in France* (Albert, 1987), *Burning Up the Night* (Albert, 1992), *Flash and the Pan Hits Collection* (Castle/Albert, 1993); ***Marcus Hook Roll Band albums:*** *Tales of Old Grand-Daddy* (EMI, 1974), *Full File* (reissue, EMI, 1981); ***Vanda and Young albums:*** *The Vanda and Young Story* (featuring Various Artists, Albert/Drum, 1976), *Their Music Goes Round* (featuring Various Artists, Albert, 1992).

The Flies

Formed: *1984*
Style: *Pop*
Original line-up: *Michael De La Motte (guitar, vocals), John Encarnacao (guitar, piano, vocals), Peter Marley (bass, vocals), Peter Kelly (drums, trumpet)*

There was a Melbourne band from the 1960s fronted by **Ronnie Burns** called The Flies, but these Flies hailed from Sydney and formed in 1984. The band toured for three years and issued the four-track EP 'Turtle Monster' (October 1985) and the single 'Lunch'/'I Can Feel Me' (September 1986) on the Pagan label.

The Flies' bright, quirky pop style was at odds with most other bands on the Sydney scene, but they did command a cult following. After the band broke up in 1987, Encarnacao joined Smelly Tongues, which comprised Bill Gibson (bass, vocals; ex-**Eastern Dark**) and Jess Ciampa (drums). Smelly Tongues played a raw mix of rock, jazz and hardcore, and issued a single 'Just Look Like They Feel'/'Why on Earth' (December 1989), and two mini-albums, *The Sound of Slapping Skin* (1988) and *Pickle* (1989), on the Waterfront label. Encarnacao also turned up in the first version of Nic Dalton's band **Godstar** and was a long-time rock journalist for *RAM* and *Rolling Stone* magazines. Kelly joined **Vanilla Chainsaws, No Man's Land** and **The New Christs**. Gibson went on to **The New Christs** and Lemonheads.

Flowers (*see* Icehouse)

The Flying Circus

Formed: *1968*
Style: *Pop, country*
Original line-up: *Doug Rowe (guitar, vocals; ex-NZ Castaways), Jim Wynne (vocals, guitar), Bob Hughes (bass, vocals), Colin Walker (drums)*

It is possible that The Flying Circus was one of the most misunderstood bands that Australia has ever produced. No doubt the fact that the band's biggest hit singles were pure bubblegum pop, when underneath it all dwelt an exceptional country-rock band, added to the confusion. Likewise, the band tried its hand at so many divergent music styles that an identity crisis was the only possible result.

Entirely unrelated to the Monty Python comedy crew, Australia's Flying Circus came together in August 1968 when four country and folk-rock devotees joined forces. The band originally played harmony-rich covers of Byrds, Bob Dylan and Dillards country songs. Hughes departed in early 1969 to become a DJ and actor, and The Flying Circus recruited Greg Grace (vocals, harmonica) and Warren Ward (bass). Having signed to EMI, the band issued the singles 'Hayride'/'Early Morning' (February 1969) and 'La La'/'Last Train' (May 1969). Both A-sides were formula pop hits written by the American team of Buzz Cason and Mac Gayden, and naturally they made The Flying Circus into pop stars.

'Hayride' peaked at #24 nationally (#5 in Sydney) and 'La La' hit the national Top 10 (#8 in Sydney). The band's debut album was an odd collection of the pop hits, Byrds' covers, an ill-conceived medley of songs from the rock musical *Hair* and a couple of Rowe's country-rock tunes. The Rowe-penned 'Run Run Run'/'All Fall Down' (December 1969) echoed the 'Hayride'/'La La' formula to achieve another Top 20 placing on the Australian charts and #7 in Sydney. The hit singles essentially sealed the band's fate. As Glenn A. Baker has noted, teenybopper dance audiences roared at the familiar hits, but were bemused by the delicate country-rock songs. Likewise, country-rock fans only saw a bubblegum pop band and dismissed The Flying Circus out of hand.

Grace left in June to form **Hot Cottage**. Ward fell ill in September and was replaced by Terry Wilkins (ex-Quill). Ward later joined **Blackfeather**. Both Wynne and Rowe also suffered bouts of ill-health at the end of the year, which hampered touring commitments. The *Frontier* EP (April 1970) featured all country songs, including covers of Dylan's 'I'll Be Your Baby Tonight' and Merle Haggard's 'The Day the Rains Came'. Noted country picker Red McKelvie (ex-Dark Ages, Starving Wild Dogs, Quill, Savage Rose Blues Band) joined in April, which facilitated the band's move in a pure country direction.

The excellent *Prepared in Peace* album was well received, and McKelvie's The Band-influenced 'Israel'/'Giselle' (October 1970) made for a fine single. The Flying Circus's controversial win at the 1970 Hoadley's National Battle of the Sounds (favourites **The Zoot** were placed second) only succeeded in ending the band's chances for wider mainstream acceptance. The Flying Circus ditched the country sound (and McKelvie in the process) for a more rock-oriented direction (akin to Crosby Stills Nash and Young). McKelvie formed a series of fine country-rock bands including Chant, Powderhorn and Third Union Band. He issued two solo singles, 'She's So Fine'/'Papa Joe' (October 1971) and 'Another Country Town'/'Surry Hills Sunshine' (May 1972), on Festival's Infinity label, and two singles with Third Union Band on the ATA label, 'Johnny Don't Sing in a Rock'n'Roll Band No More'/'Movin' On' (May 1972) and 'Hyway Ryder'/'Movin' On' (August 1972).

Meanwhile, Sam See (guitar, keyboards; ex-**Sherbet**) joined Flying Circus in time to record the rock album *Bonza Beaut & Boom Boom Boom*. The singles 'Turn Away'/'The Longest Day' (February 1971) and 'It Couldn't Happen Here'/'Somerville' (April 1971) were two of the band's best, but neither charted. By that time, disillusioned with the lack of acceptance on home turf, The Flying Circus had relocated to Toronto, Canada. The band's last single for 1971 was 'The Ballad of Sacred Falls'/'Finding My Way' (September).

Towards the end of 1971, Wynne and See both left the band. See joined **Fraternity**. Greg Grace returned to the fold, and the band spent most of 1972 touring Canada where audiences were more receptive. The superb *Gypsy Road* album (issued in America as *Flying Circus* on Capitol) delivered everything the past years had promised. 'Old Enough (to Break My Heart)' reached #8 on the Canadian charts and 'Maple Lady' graced the lower reaches of the US Top 100. 'Train Ride'/'Old Enough (to Break My Heart)' (May 1973) came out as a single in Australia, but sank without a trace.

The Flying Circus returned to Australia to play the 1973 Sunbury Festival, but the lukewarm reception did little to bolster the band's regard for local audiences. Back in Canada, Sam See rejoined (having quit **Fraternity** in the UK) and Grace left for the second time. *Last Laugh* was another strong rock album which produced one US-only single, 'Jabber Jabber'/'Gypsy Road', on Capitol. By the end of 1974, the band had split for good. Wilkins and See toured and recorded with Canadian band Lighthouse (*Good Day* on Polydor, 1974), Rowe concentrated on songwriting and setting up a recording studio in Toronto, and Grace became a roadie for Canadian band Wireless (which included three ex-**Autumn** members).

Sam See later returned to Australia as a member of Greg Quill's Southern Cross, before joining The Stockley See Mason Band in 1978. The Flying Circus's original bass player Bob Hughes appeared in the 1976 Australian-made film *ABBA The Movie* and later played Martin Kelly in popular television sit-com *Hey Dad!*. The Glenn A. Baker-compiled *Steam Trains & Country Days* was a lovingly assembled anthology of the band's EMI material.

Albums: *The Flying Circus* (EMI/Columbia, 1969), *Prepared in Peace* (EMI/Columbia, 1970), *Bonza, Beaut & Boom Boom Boom* (EMI/Harvest, 1971), *Gypsy Road* (Warner, 1973), *Last Laugh* (Warner, 1974), *Steam Trains & Country Days* (EMI, 1977), *Best of The Flying Circus 1969–1971* (compilation, EMI, 1995).

The Foreday Riders

Formed: *1966*
Style: *Blues*
Original line-up: *Ron King (vocals, harmonica), Jeff King (guitar, dobro)*

In the pantheon of Australian blues, names like **Chain**, **Matt Taylor** and **Dave Hole** are well known. Not so well known, but of equal relevance, is Sydney band The Foreday Riders. As well as being one of the first traditional blues bands in the country (alongside **Adderley Smith Blues Band** and **Bay City Union**), The Foreday Riders had the distinction of being one of the longest running blues bands in the country. As with **Chain**, there have been constant line-up changes over the years.

Brothers Ron and Jeff King have steered the band since putting the first line-up together in 1966. As blues enthusiasts of impeccable taste, the brothers drew inspiration from Chicago electric blues masters like Muddy Waters, Little Walter Jacobs, Jimmy Rogers and Howlin' Wolf. It is difficult to pin-point the original line-up, but members during the late 1960s included Rick Lock (drums), Peter Anson (guitar; ex-**Missing Links**, **Jeff St John** and the Id), Rolli Utzinger (piano), John Murphy (bass), Mark Punch (guitar), Jill Drury (vocals) and Dave Drury (bass).

Since the early 1970s, other members have included Phil Colson (guitar), Tony Pedroza (guitar), Andrew Reid (guitar), Harvey Fisk (guitar), Leszek Karski (guitar), Ian Winter (guitar), Shane Pacey (guitar), Billy Rylands (guitar), Ron Tabuteau (guitar), Graeme Gibbs (bass), John Power (bass), Harry Brus (bass), Alan Britton (bass), Andrew Ross (sax), Ernie McInerney (drums) and John Simone (drums).

Recording-wise, The Foreday Riders issued one of the first independent limited edition albums, *Foreday Riders Blues Band*, in 1969 (on the Muff label). The Riders' first official album, the live set *Blues Live at "French's"* appeared in 1974. The line-up on that album comprised the King brothers, Harvey Fiske, Rick Lock and John Murphy (bass). The Riders also backed **Jeannie Lewis** on a version of 'Cocaine Blues' on her 1974 live album *Looking Backwards to Tomorrow (In and Out of Concert)*.

The band signed to blues label Eureka and issued *Once a Week* and *Playin' Up*. The albums showcased the band's gritty, authentic approach to roadhouse blues. As well as recording a swag of original tunes, the band covered T-Bone Walker's 'Stormy Monday' and 'T-Bone Shuffle', Willie Dixon's 'I'm Ready' and Taj Mahal's 'Good Morning Miss Brown' among others. The line-up on *Once a Week* was Ron and Jeff, Lock, Phil Colson and Graeme Gibbs. *Playin' Up* featured Ron and Jeff, Gibbs, Andrew Ross, Ernie McInerney and Adelaide guitarist Ron Tabuteau (ex-Smokestack Lightning).

Smokestack Lightning issued an independent album in 1976, *Don't Nobody Know* (on the EMS label), that mined a similar vein of authentic

Chicago blues. Tabuteau's slow-rollin' blues 'Cold Cold Feeling' appeared on both Smokestack Lightning's album and The Riders' *Playin' Up*. He went on to head a number of blues bands in Melbourne, including Chickenhead. That band issued a self-titled album on the Blue Tongue label in 1997. The Riders continued to tour, but it was to be another ten years before the band issued a fifth album, *Riders' Digest*, on the Avan Guard label. *Riders' Groove* came out in 1993. Never driven by commercial gains, The Foreday Riders have remained true to their urban electric blues roots.

Albums: *Foreday Riders Blues Band* (Muff, 1969), *Blues Live at "French's"* (EMI, 1974), *Once a Week* (Eureka, 1976), *Playin' Up* (Eureka, 1977), *Riders' Digest* (Avan Guard/Larrikin, 1987), *Riders' Groove* (Avan Guard/Larrikin, 1993).

Robert Forster

Style: *Pop, country*

Following the demise of the highly acclaimed **Go-Betweens** in 1989, singer/songwriter/guitarist Robert Forster (b. 1957) settled into a low-key solo career. His debut solo album, *Danger in the Past* (1990), and single, 'Baby Stones' (November 1990), were recorded in Germany with substantial assistance from The Bad Seeds' Mick Harvey.

There were rumours of a **Go-Betweens** reunion when Forster teamed up with his erstwhile partner **Grant McLennan** for a support slot to UK outfit Lloyd Cole and the Commotions during 1991, but nothing eventuated. Forster returned to his hometown of Brisbane and recorded the bustling country-pop album *Calling from a Country Phone* (June 1993). The album produced the CD single 'Drop' (May). His touring band (known as Robert Forster's Silver Backwash) comprised David McCormack (guitar; on loan from **Custard**), Robert Moore (bass) and Glenn Thompson (drums). McCormack, Moore and Thompson also worked together as improvisational country band Cow.

For his third album, *I Had a New York Girlfriend* (1994), Forster utilised the services of Conway Savage (piano; from **Nick Cave and the Bad Seeds**), Charlie Owen (guitar; ex-**New Christs**), Graham Lee (pedal steel; ex-**Triffids**) and various members of **Dave Graney's** Coral Snakes. The album consisted of all covers, with the standouts including Guy Clark's 'Broken Hearted People', Bill Anderson's '3am' and Keith Richards' 'Locked Away'. Forster returned to the UK but was quiet on the recording front until the *Warm Nights* album came out in September 1996. Produced by ex-Orange

Robert Forster

Juice singer Edwyn Collins, the album was a laid-back collection of summery pop. The single 'Cryin' Love' featured one of the most entertaining film clips for the year. In mid-1997, Forster reunited with **Grant McLennan** for a series of showcase gigs across the UK as **The Go-Betweens**.

Albums: *Danger in the Past* (Beggars Banquet, 1990), *Calling from a Country Phone* (Shock, 1993), *I Had a New York Girlfriend* (Concubine/Shock, 1994), *Warm Nights* (Concubine/Shock, 1996).

Fragile (*see* The Hummingbirds)

John J. Francis

Style: *Folk, country*

During the early 1970s, John J. Francis joined the likes of **Ross Ryan** and **Glenn Cardier** as one of the country's foremost singer/songwriters. Although not as successful as Ryan or Cardier, Francis boasted a unique, husky voice and a pleasant country-blues style.

Francis was born in 1945 and started out in the early 1960s with Newcastle pop outfit The Sorrows, who issued the single 'Someday'/'I'm Lonely' (1964) on the Big Sound label. The John Francis Collexion issued one single on RCA in 1967, 'I Talk to the Trees'/'You Tell Me'. His next band, Magic, issued two singles, 'I Want to Fly' (1969) and 'The Carpenter's Song'/'Vintage Wine' (1970), on Philips.

During the early 1970s, he went solo and issued four albums, four singles, 'Play Mumma, Sing Me a Song'/'What to Do' (#22 in Sydney, July 1973), 'Simple Ben'/'Embarrassing Situation' (1973), 'City Lights, Saturday Night 1959'/'Liberated Roadside Lady' (1974) and 'Lucky Star'/'Money Honey' (1974), plus the EP 'Play Mumma' for Warner. Francis also contributed The Band-inspired 'Simple Ben' to the Various Artists soundtrack album *Morning of the Earth.*

Albums: *Rock'n'Roll Refugee* (Warner, 1972), *Breaks Words Thoughts* (Warner, 1973), *Open Fist* (Warner, 1974), *Wassa Matta* (Warner, 1974).

Fraternity

Formed: *1970*
Style: *Rock, blues*
Original line-up: *Mick Jurd (guitar; ex-***Levi Smith's Clefs***), John Bisset (keyboards, vocals; ex-***Levi Smith's Clefs***), Bruce Howe (bass, vocals; ex-***Levi Smith's Clefs***), Tony Buettel (drums; ex-***Levi Smith's Clefs***)*

The name Fraternity is well known to many Australian rock fans, but very few people are familiar with the band's music (aside from the hardened collector). Of course, the band is famous for the fact it featured the pre-**AC/DC** Bon Scott as its frontman. The band was a popular live attraction but made little impact on the local charts.

The four members of the original Fraternity were all part of Sydney R&B band **Levi Smith's Clefs** circa 1969. Led by Adelaide legend Barrie McAskill, **Levi Smith's Clefs** issued one of the first Australian progressive rock albums in *Empty Monkey* (March 1970). **Levi Smith's Clefs** (sans McAskill) also backed singer/songwriter **Doug Ashdown** on his double album *Age of Mouse*. At the beginning of 1970, buoyed by their recording ventures, the four musicians decided to form their own band. Left high and dry by the split, McAskill relocated to Melbourne and assembled a new version of **Levi Smith's Clefs**.

Fraternity issued the single 'Why Did It Have to Be Me?'/'Question' on the Sweet Peach label (October 1970). By the time the single came out, Bon Scott (vocals; ex-Spektors, **Valentines**) had joined, while John Freeman (another ex-**Levi Smith's Clefs** alumnus) had replaced Tony Buettel on drums. **The Valentines** had been a straight teenypop band, and Fraternity was a chance for Scott to indulge in his passion for tougher rock'n'roll. The new line-up recorded its debut album, *Livestock*, at Sydney's United Sound Studios with producers **Doug Ashdown** and Jimmy Stewart. Although the album featured a patchy mix of rock/pop tunes and metaphysical, art-rock ramblings, it revealed a band attempting to approach a uniquely Australian sound.

With financial support from businessman/manager Hamish Henry, Fraternity moved to Hemming's Farm on the outskirts of Adelaide in order to 'get it together in the country' in the time-honoured communal fashion of The Band and Traffic. Fraternity issued four collectable singles during 1971, 'Livestock', 'Why Did It Have to Be Me?'/'Cool Spot' (January), 'Seasons of Change'/'Sommerville' (March) and 'The Race Part I'/'The Race Part II' (October) on Sweet Peach, plus 'If You Got It'/'Raglan's Folly', 'You Have a God' (October) on the Raven label. The band's version of the John Robinson/Neale Johns-penned 'Seasons of Change' reached #1 in Adelaide, but was overshadowed on the national charts by **Blackfeather's** more powerful rendition.

In May 1971 'Uncle' John Ayers (harmonica) joined Fraternity. The band won the 1971 Hoadley's National Battle of the Sounds, beating out all comers with its thumping rock'n'roll. Sam See (piano, slide guitar; ex-**Sherbet, Flying Circus**) joined in September, and the band recorded its second album, the collectable *Flaming Galah*. With See on board, Fraternity achieved a sound similar to The Band's celebrated dual keyboard approach. Despite serving up a bevy of bluesy hard rock, *Flaming Galah* only featured three all-new songs, next to re-recorded (albeit stronger) versions of old material. 'Welfare Boogie' (one of the new songs) was issued as a single, backed with 'Annabelle' (March 1972).

By the time the album came out in April 1972, Fraternity had taken advantage of its Battle of the Sounds prize and relocated to London. The UK scene circa 1972 was besotted by glam rock, and Fraternity's brand of blues/country rock hardly set the place alight. Fraternity became known as Fang and undertook the odd tour, but any confidence and arrogance the band had amassed in Australia soon dissipated. The first to leave was Sam See, who rejoined **Flying Circus** in Canada. Fraternity limped back to Adelaide in disarray at the end of 1973.

Soon after returning home, Scott was involved in a motorbike accident which nearly claimed his life. Howe, Ayers and Freeman formed a new line-up of Fraternity in late 1974 with Mauri Berg (guitar; ex-**Headband**), John Swan (lead vocals; ex-Hard Time Killing Floor) and Peter Bersee (violin). In mid-1975, Freeman left, and Swan took over the drums with his younger brother **Jimmy Barnes** (ex-**Cold Chisel**) joining as lead singer. Barnes' stay was brief and he returned to **Cold Chisel**. Swan also left to join **Jim Keays'** Southern Cross and the rest of the band struggled on. Swan later fronted **Feather** and his own band **Swanee**.

By the end of 1975, Fraternity had changed names to Some Dream before evolving into Mickey Finn by 1978. Mickey Finn comprised Howe, Ayers, Berg and Joff Bateman (drums; ex-**Headband**). The 1980 line-up of Howe, Ayers, Berg, John Freeman (drums) and Stan Koritni (guitar) issued the album *Mickey Finn* on the Eureka label (October 1980). It produced the singles 'I'm a Man'/'Quick Release' (November) and 'So Many Lies'/'Baby Please Don't Go' (May 1981). Howe later turned up in the ranks of the **Jimmy Barnes** Band (1984) and The Mega Boys (1985).

Meanwhile, Bon Scott had recovered from his injuries and found fame with **AC/DC**. Before he joined **AC/DC** in late 1974, however, Scott sang with an ad hoc collection of Adelaide musicians dubbed The Mount Lofty Rangers, led by ex-**Headband** member Peter Head (aka Peter Beagley). Scott also cut a demo of a song called 'Round and Round' written and produced by Peter Head. The song remained unreleased until December 1996, when Head Office Records (through EMI) issued it on CD EP.

The CD EP also included a ghastly 1990s remake of the song called 'Round and Round and Round' that combined Scott's original vocal tracks with slick, new studio backing (à la The Beatles' reworking of John Lennon's demos for 'Free as a Bird' and 'Real Love'). As it transpired, the original recording possessed a rough-hewn charm that should have been left well alone.

Fraternity albums: *Livestock* (Sweet Peach, 1971), *Flaming Galah* (RCA, 1972), *Bon Scott Seasons of Change 1968–72* (included **Valentines** material; Raven, 1987), *Bon Scott & Fraternity Complete Sessions 1971–72* (double compilation; Raven, 1997); ***Mickey Finn album:*** *Mickey Finn* (Eureka, 1980).

Maurice Frawley and the Working Class Ringos

Formed: *1993*
Style: *Country, blues*
Original line-up: *Maurice Frawley (guitar, vocals; ex-Japanese Comix,* **Paul Kelly** *and the Dots,* **Olympic Sideburns***), David Sanford (sax, piano, vocals), Charlie Owen (guitar; ex-***New Christs***), Spencer P. Jones (guitar; ex-***Johnnys, Beasts of Bourbon***), Shane Walsh (double bass; ex-***Honeymoon in Green***), Des Hefner (drums; ex-Marching Girls,* **Slaughtermen***)*

Singer/guitarist Frawley was involved in the Melbourne pub circuit for many years as a member of Japanese Comix (1979–80), **Paul Kelly** and the Dots (1980–82), **Olympic Sideburns** (1983–86) and The Working Class Ringos.

Japanese Comix comprised Frawley, Shane Day (vocals; ex-Cruisers, High Rise Bombers), James Williams (guitar; ex-High Rise Bombers), Chris Jobson (bass) and Greg Simpkins (drums). The band played the late-1970s Carlton pub scene alongside the likes of **Paul Kelly** and the Dots, Wrecked Jets and Cuban Heels. The band's brand of power pop was heard on the four-track, 7-inch EP *Japanese Comix* which came out on the Mambo label in 1980. Michael Barclay replaced Simpkins that same year, but the band broke up not long after. Barclay later played with **The Runners** and **Paul Kelly** and the Coloured Girls.

In 1990 Frawley formed Maurice Frawley's Big City Burnout with Jack Abeyratne (guitar), Nigel Hartford (bass; ex-**White Cross**), David Sanford (sax, piano, vocals) and Paul Wall (drums). Frawley's next venture was country-blues band Maurice Frawley and the Working Class Ringos. As well as the above line-up, guest players included Rosie Westbrooke (double bass) and Sean Kelly (bass). The Ringos issued the CD EP *Woop Woop* in 1994. Tony Cohen produced the band's debut full-length album *Livin' Lazy* (May 1995). Among a host of strong original tunes, it featured a cover of The Rolling Stones' 'Sweet Black Angel'.

Album: *Livin' Lazy* (Id/Mercury, 1995).

Freaked Out Flower Children

Formed: *1991*
Style: *Flower pop*
Original line-up: *Gumpy Phillips (vocals, guitar; ex-Battle Happy), Tricky J (synth programmer), Sophie Lee (sax, vocals), Nicole Love (backing vocals), Fiona Ruttelle (backing vocals)*

This enterprising bunch of musicians/scene stealers appeared in 1991 playing dance music versions of 1960s flower power hits. Gumpy Phillips had previously been a member of mid-1980s Melbourne band Battle Happy along with Phil Ceberano (guitar). The band issued one independent single 'Evil Donald'/'Decline and Fall' on the Rampant label in 1985 before disappearing. Phillips and Tricky J had also worked as a rap act and issued one single. Sophie Lee was a television presenter (*Bugs Bunny, Sex*) and actor (*Flying Doctors*).

The Freaked Out Flower Children's first and only hit was a reworking of Eric Burdon and War's 'Spill the Wine' (#31 in February 1992). The band's debut album, *Love In* (December 1991), was full of syncopated beats and breezy melodies wrapped around tunes like Barry McGuire's 'Eve of Destruction', Five Man Electric Band's 'Signs' and Jimi Hendrix's 'Purple Haze'. 'Beautiful People' was issued as the second single. The retro-cabaret and day-glo focus of the ensemble, however, did little to foster a sense of longevity and the concept had run its course by 1993. Sophie Lee later appeared in the 1996 Australian feature film *The Castle*.

Album: *Love In* (Virgin, 1992).

The Freeloaders (*see* The Philisteins)

Chris Freeman

Style: *Classical, flamenco, folk*

Gifted multi-instrumentalist Chris Freeman was noted for his exacting six- and 12-string guitar technique, although he was also adept at playing bass, organ, piano and synthesiser. His main influences included guitar virtuosos like Manitas de Plata and Paco Pena. Freeman garnered considerable praise for his work, but he never embraced the notion of mainstream acceptance. He recorded a series of independent albums that earned him a cult following.

Freeman commenced guitar lessons at the age of eight, and by 16 had begun to experiment with multi-track recording and electronic sound effects combined with guitar. He lost the top of his left middle finger when it was severed in a car accident at 17. To compensate, he had a sterling silver cap fitted, hence the title of his 1976 album *Thesilger* (i.e. silver finger). He often performed with orchestral backing tapes (created using a Fairlight CMI), or with contributions from noted orchestral arranger and synthesiser player John Shaw. As well as issuing several independent albums, Freeman put out the 7-inch EP *Chris Freeman* ('Autumn', 'Song for a Lost Friend'/'Disco Flamenco', 'Astrida'). Freeman died in 1992 as a result of an asthma attack.

Albums: *Thesilger* (T.S.F., 1976), *Shifting Sands... Night & Day* (T.S.F., 1978), *Best of Chris Freeman* (compilation, T.S.F., 1991); ***With John Shaw:*** *Chris Freeman and John Shaw* (Chris Freeman Records/EMI, 1981), *Synthesized Orchestration* (Chris Freeman Records, 1983), *Synthesized Orchestration Vol. 2* (Chris Freeman Records, 1984).

FreeMovingCurtis (*see* Bloodloss)

Freeway

Formed: *1974*
Style: *Hard rock*
Original line-up: *Frank Chic (vocals), Steve Welch (guitar), John Grant (keyboards), Criston Barker (bass, vocals; ex-Ash, Island), Bill Lincoln (drums)*

Commercial hard rock band Freeway formed in Melbourne. The band took its main inspiration from bands such as Free, while frontman Frank Chic possessed a voice that resembled Paul Rodgers mixed with Bobby 'Blue' Bland. The band built up a following on the Melbourne pub circuit alongside the likes of the **Little River Band**, **Madder Lake**, **Buster Brown**, **AC/DC**, **The Dingoes**, **Ariel** and **Company Caine**.

Criston Barker had previously fronted hard rock band The Ash under the name of Criston Somerset. The rest of the band comprised George Edwards (guitar), Ian Ryan (bass) and Dennis Johns (drums). The Ash was one of the first local bands to embrace an English-flavoured hard rock sound. The band's two singles for the Havoc label, 'Avignon'/'Sable' (1970) and 'Midnight Witch'/'Warrant' (1971), combined Led Zeppelin and Jethro Tull elements (except for 'Avignon', which was closer to **The Bee Gees**).

Early in its career, The Ash signed to **The Master's Apprentices'** booking agency Drum. Masters guitarist Doug Ford wrote 'Midnight Witch' for The Ash. It is possible he also played on the record, as his guitar style was stamped all over the songs. The original Ash line-up came together in January 1970. By 1971, guitarists Peter Gregory (ex-**Expression**) and Ron Hood had replaced Edwards. Various line-ups came and went; by 1972, Ash included Somerset, Kim Dawson (guitar; ex-**Lotus**), Warwick Wilkes (keyboards; ex-**Lotus**), Gary Porterhouse (bass) and Derek Pellici (drums). With the break up of The Ash in 1972, Barker joined Island with Leith Corbett (bass; ex-**Heart 'n' Soul**) before moving on to Freeway in 1974.

Freeway came to the attention of **Skyhooks'** Greg Macainsh (then the most respected songwriter in Australia), who offered the band a couple of his songs to record. The band included a cover of Macainsh's 'Sad Rock'n'Roll' on its debut album, the **Jim Keays**-produced *Ridin' High*. The album yielded two singles, 'Same Old Story'/'Down that Freeway' and 'Ridin' High'/'Lot of Lovin' to Do', neither of which was successful on the charts.

Welch and Chic left after the album came out; Peter Laffy (ex-Fox) and Greg Cook (guitar, vocals; ex-**Cam-Pact**, Skylight, **Mándu**, the **Phil Manning**

Band) came in as replacements. As well as Laffy, Fox had comprised Michael Upton (vocals), Neil Hodgson (bass, vocals) and Les Oldman (drums). Fox formed a songwriting partnership with John Brownrigg (ex-**Sect**, Star Spangled Banger) who wrote or co-wrote five songs on the band's debut album *What the Hell is Going On?* (EMI, 1974). The album included the singles 'Who Do'/'Jean Sea' and 'I Said'/'Ziggy Stardust'. On the album, Fox sounded like a lighter version of Free or **AC/DC**.

Freeway planned its next album but broke up in late 1976. Chic formed Hollywood and Laffy joined **Jim Keays'** Southern Cross, **Mondo Rock** and The Hot Club. Barker joined The New Hush and **Air Supply**, with which he toured for two years. Barker issued a solo album, *Side by Side*, and single, 'Prisoner (Without a Name)'/'Thrill of It All', on the Rumur label during 1984.

Album: Ridin' High (Philips/Phonogram, 1975).

Frente!

Formed: *1989*
Style: *Folky pop*
Original line-up: *Angie Hart (vocals), Simon Austin (guitar, vocals), Tim O'Connor (bass), Mark Picton (drums, recorder)*

When Melbourne quartet Frente! rose to national prominence via the release of a series of whimsical, off-kilter pop gems like 'Ordinary Angels' and 'Accidentally Kelly Street', few people could have foreseen the level of success the band would go on to attain. Frente!'s quirky, irreverent, acoustic-based sound was at odds with the usual guitar-heavy, grunge trends of the day. The band's presentation had a tweeness about it that could have been off-putting if not for its genuine freshness and honesty.

Simon Austin, Tim O'Connor and Mark Picton formed the basis of the band, but the Frente! line-up was not complete until the arrival of 17-year-old high school student and aspiring actor Angie Hart. Quite aside from Austin's ready grasp of pop melodies and the band's gentle rhythms, the key to the Frente! sound lay in Hart's breathy ingenue vocals. The band took its name from the Spanish word for 'forehead'. With two years of constant gigging on the Melbourne inner-city scene under its collective belt, Frente! issued the self-financed CD EP *Whirled* (on the Thumb Print label) in August 1991. The EP track 'Labour of Love' logged a #69 placing on Triple J's inaugural Hot 100 (Songs of All Time) list.

The band signed to Mushroom's White label and issued the CD EP *Clunk* (April 1992). With the

Frente!

melancholy 'Ordinary Angels' as its featured track, the CD EP reached #3 on the national singles chart in June. *Clunk* went on to sell 65 000 copies. Aided by a breezy, slightly kooky video clip, the summery sugar-pop single 'Accidentally Kelly Street' (October) reached #3 on the national charts during December. The band was so popular that television comedy troupe the D-Generation was compelled to produce a spot-on send-up of the video.

US producer/engineer Michael Koppelman (Prince) worked the mixing desk on the band's debut full-length album, *Marvin the Album*, which came out in December 1992. It reached #1 on the independent chart and #4 on the national mainstream chart, eventually achieving platinum status (over 70 000 units sold) in the process. The group capped off a successful 1992 by winning Best Debut Single ('Ordinary Angels') and Best Debut Album (*Marvin the Album*) at the Australian Record Industry Association (ARIA) Awards. The single 'No Time' reached a relatively disappointing #50 during March 1993.

The usually shy Hart caused a near-sensation when she stripped for a cover story in Sydney-based magazine *Juice* (issue #5, July 1993). The cover shot featured a naked Hart tastefully covered by a plethora of beads and a strategically placed hand in the manner of Bob Seidemann's famous photo of Janis Joplin.

Alistair Barden (ex-Maelstrom) replaced Picton mid-year, after which Frente! left for Europe and America in order to promote the international version of *Marvin* which featured two new tracks. While overseas, Frente! opened a couple of dates on **Crowded House's** sellout European tour, recorded a BBC Radio One live session in Manchester, and supported Counting Crows in the USA.

Marvin the Album eventually went on to sell over 750 000 copies worldwide. 'Ordinary Angels' appeared on the soundtrack album to popular US soapie *Melrose Place*. Frente!'s soft version of New Order's 'Bizarre Love Triangle' also created a lot of interest. 'Lonely'/'Bizarre Love Triangle' had reached #7 in Australia during July 1994.

Frente! eventually spent over a year skipping back and forth across the Atlantic on tour, the strain of which almost split the band at the end of 1994. O'Connor did leave, to be replaced by Bill McDonald (ex-**Hot Half Hour**, **Deborah Conway** Band, **Rebecca's Empire**). During the early months of 1995, Austin and Hart started writing together again for the first time in two years. Frente! spent two months recording (in Spain) and mixing (in London) a new album, *Shape*, with producers Dave Allen (The Cure, Sisters of Mercy) and Cameron McVey (Neneh Cherry).

Shape (July 1996) was more sophisticated and textured than its naive (yet still classy) predecessor. The album produced two CD singles, 'Sit on My Hands' (June) and 'What's Come Over Me?' (October). Upon the album's release in August 1996, Frente! toured Europe, Asia and the USA. Instead of repeating the 1994 marathon effort, the jaunt was restricted to a more manageable three months. Back in Australia, the band supported overseas visitor Alanis Morrisette on her December 1996 tour. Frente! performed on the Melbourne leg of the Big Day Out (January 1997), and issued a new CD single 'Goodbye Goodguy', in July.

Albums: *Marvin the Album* (White/Mushroom/Festival, 1992), *Shape* (White/Mushroom/Festival, 1996).

Frenzal Rhomb

Formed: *1992*
Style: *Punk*
1993 line-up: *Jason Whalley (vocals), Ben Whalley (guitar), Alexis Feltham (bass), Nat Nykyruj (drums)*

Power-punk outfit Frenzal Rhomb formed in Sydney. Taking inspiration from Californian melodic hardcore bands like Bad Religion, The Descendants, All, Fugazi, etc., the Rhomb built a huge all-ages following around the country. There were various line-ups until the band stablised as above. Lindsay McDougall replaced Ben Whalley in late 1996.

Frenzal Rhomb appeared on the Sydney bill of the 1994 Big Day Out. The band's debut CD EP *Dick Sandwich* (March 1995) sold 2000 copies, a more than respectable number for an independent release. Frenzal Rhomb supported Californian tourists NOFX on that band's national tour in the middle of 1995. NOFX's Fat Mike was so impressed with the band's rugged punk style that he issued the CD EP on his own Fat Wreck Chords label in the USA. Shock Records' Shagpile label issued Frenzal Rhomb's single 'Genius' (1995), plus the CD EP *Coughing Up a Storm* (1995) and the album *Not So Tough Now* (July 1996). The CD EP 'Punch in the Face' came out in November 1996, and the band commenced 1997 with an appearance on the national bill of the Big Day Out. Toward the end of the year, the band undertook a US tour (supporting Blink 182) and issued its second album, *Meet the Family* (October) and CD single, 'There's Your Dad' (September).

Albums: *Not So Tough Now* (Shagpile/Shock, 1996), *Meet the Family* (Shagpile/Shock, 1997).

Freshwater

Formed: *1968*
Style: *Blues, pop*
1970 line-up: *Ian Johnson (vocals), Murray Partridge (guitar, vocals), Peter Sheehan (organ, vocals; ex-***Heart 'n' Soul***), Dallas McDermott (bass), Joe Vella (drums)*

In May 1969, unknown New Zealand blues band Freshwater arrived in Australia. Murray Partridge originally formed the band. A number of New Zealand musicians passed through Freshwater's ranks, including Billy Rylands (guitar), Milton Parker (guitar, vocals), Phil Jacobs (vocals, flute), George Limbidis (bass), Paul Reid (bass), Peter Roberts (bass) and Daryl Jacobs (drums). Peter Sheehan joined at the end of 1969.

In Australia, Freshwater issued the pop singles 'Together, Till the End of Time'/'It's in Your Power' (August 1969) and 'Son of a Loving Man'/'People Gotta Live Together' (October) on the W&G label. Taking a cue from the likes of Cream, Traffic and Blood Sweat and Tears, Freshwater then started to play a more progressive style of music. The Caesar's International label issued the single 'Satan'/'Satan's Woman' in May 1970. Caesar's was a popular Sydney discotheque of the day, as well as being a management company and independent record label.

'Satan' (written by Sheehan) and 'Satan's Woman' (written by Partridge) formed a quasi-concept suite based around the Manson Family murder of actress Sharon Tate. The staid local radio networks of the day promptly called for the single to be banned. It managed to register #28 on the Sydney charts nevertheless. The record's brooding, organ-based sound did make for a somewhat subversive offering. In 1990, Sydney band **Box the Jesuit** covered 'Satan' for inclusion on the Various Artists album *Waste Sausage* on the Black Eye label.

At the start of 1971, **Alison McCallum** (ex-Dr Kandy's Third Eye) joined as lead vocalist. By September, the line-up had changed again to feature Partridge, McCallum, David Fookes (keyboards), Rod Coe (bass) and Tony Bolton (drums). The band's last single, 'I Ain't Got the Time'/'Hello Sunshine' (November 1971), featured commercial soul/pop with McCallum's sweet vocals up front. The single peaked at #19 in Sydney, but Freshwater had broken up by the end of 1971. McCallum went solo and scored a big hit with a cover of Vanda and Young's 'Superman'.

Partridge formed Wolfe with Andrew Parata (lead vocals, guitar; ex-Hunger), Norm Roue (slide guitar; ex-Gutbucket, **Lotus**), Billy Rylands (bass; ex-Freshwater, **Lotus**) and Steve Webb (drums; ex-**Blackfeather**). The band was short-lived; by the end of 1972, Webb had joined **Duck** and Roue was touring with **Band of Light**. Partridge returned to New Zealand where he joined Living Force.

James Freud

Style: Pop

It has been a long, diverse career for singer James Freud (born in 1959 as Colin McGlinchy). Although rarely accepted in supposedly 'hip' circles, Freud has enjoyed chart and live success in four different guises: as a solo artist, as a member of **Models**, with dance-pop act **Beatfish** and most recently with surf-pop outfit Moondog.

James Freud (lead vocals, guitar) got his start with glam-punk band **Teenage Radio Stars**, which he formed at the end of 1977 with school friend Sean Kelly (guitar, vocals). The band lasted until the end of 1978. At the start of 1979, Freud took a young band called Colt and formed James Freud and the Radio Stars. The line-up was Bryan Thomas (guitar), Roger Mason (keyboards), Murray Doherty (bass) and Glen McGrath (drums). Tony Lugdon (guitar, keyboards; ex-Steeler) replaced Thomas mid-year. Freud signed to Mushroom and began recording an album. By the time the album was completed at the end of 1979, James Freud and the Radio Stars comprised Freud, Mason, Peter Cook (guitar, vocals), Mick Prague (bass) and Tommy Hosie (drums).

In May 1980, Mushroom issued James Freud and the Radio Stars' debut single, 'Modern Girl'/ 'Tragic Tales', which reached #12 nationally and Top 5 in Melbourne. That same month, the band supported UK synth wunderkid Gary Numan on his Australian national tour. The album *Breaking Silence* (credited to James Freud on the cover, but to James Freud and the Radio Stars on the record label) followed in June. It reflected Freud's carefully cultivated, new wave, glam-pop image and his ready grasp of the three-minute pop framework. Numan had been so impressed that he invited Freud to record an album in the UK under his aegis. Neither party was happy with the result, and the album has never seen the light of day. While in London, the band became known as James Freud and Berlin due to the fact there was already an English band called The Radio Stars. When Freud and Berlin returned to Australia at the end of 1980, Randy Bulpin (ex-**Mondo Rock, Aliens**) replaced Cook. The next single taken from *Breaking Silence* 'Enemy Lines'/'Only the Young' (October 1980) was credited to James Freud's Berlin.

The Gary Numan-produced 'Automatic Crazy'/ 'While We Worship Oxygen' came out in March 1981 credited to James Freud and Berlin. (The band had recorded the single in Sydney with Numan prior to the English trip.) One month later, Freud broke up Berlin. He and Mason returned to England and formed a band called Orient-R. The band played one London gig before Mason joined Gary Numan's touring band. At the beginning of 1982, Freud returned to Australia with the express purpose of rejoining his old partner Sean Kelly in his band **Models**. After much success, **Models** broke up in June 1988, and Freud relaunched his solo career. He travelled to New York and recorded *Step into the Heat* with Chic/Powerstation mastermind (the late) Bernard Edwards at Powerstation Studios. *Step into the Heat* yielded three singles, 'Hurricane'/'Everything's Alright' (March 1989), 'One Fine Day'/'Holy War' (July) and 'Let's Get It On'/'The Long Good Friday' (November). Of the three singles, only 'Hurricane' reached the national Top 20 when it peaked at #15 in June.

Freud formed a touring band which comprised Steve Williams (guitar; ex-**Wa Wa Nee**), Paul Williamson (sax), Lee Borkman (keyboards; ex-Pink Slips, Scribble), Nero Swan (bass; ex-**Machinations**), Warren McLean (drums; ex-**Machinations, I'm Talking, Divinyls**) and Sandi Chick (backing vocals), who was replaced by Toni Mott. *Step into the Heat* was reputedly the most expensive album Mushroom Records ever issued. It managed to peak at #16 on the national chart in June, but swiftly dropped out of the Top 40 a few weeks later. With his solo career at a low ebb, Freud played bass in **Kylie Minogue's** backing band during 1990. At the end of 1990, he formed a partnership with **Mental as Anything's** Martin Plaza as dance-pop duo **Beatfish.** The duo scored a couple of minor hits, after which Freud began writing and producing music for television commercials.

In January 1996, Freud started recording a new solo album, *Big Mouth,* which he eventually scrapped. Only one track, the summery surf-pop 'Postcard to Hawaii' met his expectations. With the aid of collaborator Phil Ceberano (guitar), Freud formed Moondog and completed a whole album in the 'Postcard to Hawaii' vein. 'Postcard to Hawaii' was issued as a single and became one of the most played tracks on the Australian regional commercial radio network over the 1996 Christmas period. The *Postcard to Hawaii* album came out in January 1997, and Moondog played a month of shows around Sydney. The Moondog line-up was Freud, Ceberano, Colin Bloxsom (lap steel guitar), Tony Hunt (acoustic guitar), Greg Royal (bass) and Warren Trout (drums).

James Freud solo albums: *Breaking Silence* (Mushroom/Festival, 1980), *Step into the Heat* (Mushroom/Festival, 1989); ***Moondog album:*** *Postcard to Hawaii* (TWA, 1997).

Friends

Formed: *1971*
Style: *Progressive rock*
Original line-up: **Leo De Castro** *(vocals, guitar; ex-Browns,* **King Harvest**, *Flite), Charlie Tumahai (vocals, percussion; ex-***Aesop's Fables, Healing Force, Chain***), Tim Martin (sax, flute), Duncan McGuire (bass; ex-Epics, Questions,* **Doug Parkinson** *In Focus,* **King Harvest***), Mark Kennedy (drums; ex-***Spectrum, King Harvest, Doug Parkinson** *In Focus)*

New Zealand-born musicians Leo De Castro and Charlie Tumahai were the driving forces behind Friends. The duo joined forces in December 1971. Guitarists Rob MacKenzie (on loan from **MacKenzie Theory**) and then **Phil Manning** (in between versions of **Chain**) filled in until Billy Green (ex-**Doug Parkinson** In Focus, **King Harvest, Gerry and the Joy Band**) and Ray Oliver (ex-Light, **King Harvest**) joined in April 1972 to provide an accomplished, dual-guitar attack.

The new line-up recorded the exceptional hard rock single 'B-B-Boogie'/'Freedom Train' (August 1972) for the ATA label. Reissue specialists Raven included the jubilant jazz-tinged 'Freedom Train' on the essential compilation *Golden Miles: Australian Progressive Rock 1969–1974* (1994). Friends built up a strong following on the Melbourne pub/club circuit alongside the likes of **Chain, Billy Thorpe** and the Aztecs, **Carson, Company Caine, Spectrum,** etc. Tumahai left at the start of 1973 to return to the re-formed **Healing Force.** Friends appeared at Sunbury 1973 as a six-piece comprising De Castro, McGuire, Kennedy, Green, Oliver and Martin.

The live cuts 'Bird on the Wire' and 'La La Song' appeared on Mushroom's triple album set *The Great Australian Rock Festival Sunbury 1973* (April 1973). Mushroom also issued the band's raucous bar-band renditions of Little Richard's 'Lucille' and Willie McTell's 'Statesboro Blues' (as made famous by The Allman Brothers) as a single in February 1973. Soon after that, Green, Oliver and Martin left the band. **Ray Burton** (guitar; ex-**Delltones, Executives**) had recently returned from the USA and he joined Friends in April making it a four-piece line-up. The De Castro/McGuire/Kennedy/Burton line-up of Friends appeared on the Various Artists live album on Mushroom, *Garrison the Final Blow Unit I,* with impressive versions of 'Lady Montego' and 'Freedom Train'.

Not long after those songs had been recorded (June 1973), Burton, Kennedy and McGuire left **Leo De Castro** to form an eponymous trio which had evolved into **Ayers Rock** by the end of the year. De Castro formed a new, short-lived, version of **King Harvest** before joining **Johnny Rocco Band.**

Frieze (*see* The Zoot)

Front End Loader

Formed: *1991*
Style: *Hard rock*
Original line-up: *Davis Claymore (vocals, guitar; ex-Edelweiss), Bowden Campbell (guitar, vocals; ex-Edelweiss), Richard Corey (bass; ex-***Kryptonics***), Peter Kostic (drums; ex-***Kryptonics***)*

Heavy duty Sydney four-piece Front End Loader (formed December 1991) could never be considered subtle. Its debut single was called 'Weak as Piss', backed with 'All-Star Jam' and 'Strange Tools' (February 1993). Front End Loader signed to the Survival label and issued the EP *'Fraid Knot* (May 1993) and its debut self-titled album (June). The album highlighted the band's sense of humour and gritty, unrestrained brand of thrash rock. The CD EP *Adolescent Fantasy World* (June 1994) kept up the momentum, while the split single ('Heightened State of Awareness') shared with **The Fireballs** was a ragged free-for-all. In late 1993, Front End Loader toured nationally with American visitors No Means No, a favour that was reciprocated when the

Sydneysiders were invited on a European tour in October 1994.

Let's Ride! and its single 'Be-Jesus' (March 1995) mixed brawn with irony, complex riffs with eccentric humour. Front End Loader contributed a track to the **AC/DC** tribute album on BMG *Fuse Box: The Alternative Tribute* (July 1995). As well as undertaking the Heavy Weight Kings of Rock national tour with **The Superjesus** and awesome New Zealand band Shihad (August 1996), Front End Loader appeared on the bill of the Big Day Out for three years in a row (1993–95). The band's third album, *Last of the V8 Interceptors*, and its CD EP, 'Pulse', appeared in August 1997.

Albums: *Front End Loader* (Survival, 1993), *Let's Ride!* (Shagpile/Shock, 1995), *Last of the V8 Interceptors* (Shagpile/Shock, 1997).

Frozen Doberman

Formed: *1989*
Style: *Thrash metal*
Original line-up: *Adam Marsh (vocals), Peter 'Red' Fortune (guitar), Tim West (bass), Shaun Barry (drums)*

As one of the Sydney heavy metal scene's most consistent thrash bands, Frozen Doberman was revered by a fanatical few and overlooked in general. Frozen Doberman issued a self-financed 12-inch EP, 'Dying Phase', in 1991. The band supported international visitors Sepultura and Metallica at a concert each in Sydney. Warhead Records issued the band's debut album, *Bonsai*, in September 1994. Jason Garito replaced Shaun Barry in August 1995. Frozen Doberman tracks appeared on the metal compilations *Redrum* ('Dying Phase') and *While My Guitar Gently Kills Your Mother* ('Apparition').

Album: *Bonsai* (Warhead, 1994).

The Fuck Fucks (*see* The Band Who Shot Liberty Valance)

The Fun Things

Formed: *1978*
Style: *Punk*
Original line-up: *Brad Shepherd (guitar, vocals), John Hartley (bass), Murray Shepherd (drums)*

That arguably the most conservative city in Australia gave rise to some of the most anarchistic bands of the Australian punk rock era has long been cause for amazement. Brisbane's **The Saints**, **The Leftovers**, Razar and The Fun Things were an obvious backlash to an oppressed society in the mid- to late 1970s.

The Fun Things formed as The Aliens in 1978 with the above line-up. When Graeme Beavis (guitar) joined the three-piece Aliens in 1979, the band became The Fun Things. The band's sound and style were modelled almost exclusively on the **Radio Birdman**/Stooges/Sex Pistols mould of punk rock. The band's contemporaries included **The Go-Betweens**, **The Riptides**, **The Apartments** and **Young Identities**. The Fun Things issued what has emerged as one of the most collectable artefacts of the Australian punk rock era, the *Fun Things* EP which came in a pressing of only 500 copies. The four killer tracks, 'Lipstick', 'Savage', 'When the Birdmen Fly' and '(I Ain't Got) Time Enough for Love', mixed gutsy guitar riffs, breakneck tempos, punk attitude and youthful exuberance in equal measure, even if at times the lyrics wallowed in a mire of purile teen angst cliches.

During 1986, when interest in Australian independent music was at a premium throughout Europe, French label Sonic Records issued an illegitimate 7-inch single that combined two tracks from the EP 'Lipstick' and 'Savage'. The Fun Things broke up just as the EP came out in May 1980. Brad Shepherd went on to The 31st, Super K, **The Hitmen** and **Hoodoo Gurus**. Murray Shepherd and John Hartley joined **The Screaming Tribesmen**, before Shepherd went on to Four Horsemen. Beavis was a member of **The Apartments** circa 1984.

Fungus Brains

Formed: *1982*
Style: *Proto-grunge/punk*
Original line-up: *Geoff Marks (vocals, sax), Mick Turner (guitar; ex-Sick Things), Peter Maddick (trumpet), Simon Adams (bass), Simon Sleigh (guitar, drums), Andrew Walpole (drums, guitar)*

Fungus Brains was one of the most original bands playing the early 1980s Melbourne inner-city scene. The band grew out of the ashes of pioneering hardcore outfit Sick Things which, alongside Mick Turner, comprised Dugald McKenzie (vocals), Geoff Martyr (bass) and Gary Hirst (drums).

Sick Things broke up in 1981 before issuing any records. The single 'Committed to Suicide'/'Police' appeared in 1986 on the Max Music label, while the Shock label issued the album *The Sounds of Silence* in March 1990. Consisting of material recorded between 1980 and 1981, the records featured ferocious guitar riffs and distorted vocals, displaying the band's penchant for flat-out, Black Flag-style hardcore punk. McKenzie later sang with Ollie Olsen's Orchestra of Skin and Bone before rejoining Turner in **Venom P. Stinger**. Geoff Martyr played with Slaughter House and The White Elephants, and later formed Legend Killers with Mick Francis (vocals), Paul Waste (guitar; ex-Extremes) and Geoff Simmons (drums; ex-Extremes).

In the meantime, Fungus Brains issued the independent album *Ron Pistos Real World* in 1983. It was a stylistic collision of punk, **Birthday Party** trappings, avant no-wave jazzy noise and a dozen other reference points. Fungus Brains broke up in April 1983 when Turner joined **The Moodists.** Over the next 18 months, various members played in bands like Brainshack. When Turner left **The Moodists** in January 1985, Fungus Brains lumbered back to life.

The reconstituted Fungus Brains issued a self-titled album on the Crash label in 1986. Jeff Lea replaced Marks as lead singer soon after. Fungus Brains came to an end for the second time when Turner left to concentrate on his new band, **Venom P. Stinger**. When that band wound down in about 1990, Turner revived Fungus Brains yet again. The line-up at that stage was Turner, Walpole, Peter Villiger (bass), Ricky Howell (vocals) and Paula Henderson (sax; ex-**White Cross**). That line-up issued another independent album, *I'm So Glad,* before breaking up. Turner has since found worldwide acclaim as a member of **Dirty Three**.

Fungus Brains albums: *Ron Pistos Real World* (Max Music, 1983), *Fungus Brains* (Crash, 1986), *I'm So Glad* (Frock, 1990); ***Sick Things album:*** *The Sounds of Silence* (Shock, 1989).

Fur

Formed: *1993*
Style: *Grunge*
Original line-up: *Kim Myer (guitar, vocals), Mindy Mapp (bass), Michelle (drums)*

Abrasive three-piece, guitar-fuzz/grunge band Fur hailed from Tugan on Queensland's Gold Coast. Fur issued the self-financed single 'Fix It' at the end of 1993 and then signed to the Fellaheen label for the EP *Find What You Like and Let It Kill You* (September 1994). Michelle left the band to be replaced by Simon and then Peter Werth; Michelle returned to the fold in 1996.

Meanwhile Fur had relocated to Sydney, where the band got lumped in with the network of local 'femrock' or 'grot grrrl' bands (with some justification) that included **Nitocris**, Mace, Gravelrash, SPDFGH, Sulk, Bittersweet and others. Fur contributed a version of **AC/DC**'s 'Ride On' to BMG's **AC/DC** tribute album *Fusebox: The Alternative Tribute* (May 1995). Fellaheen issued the band's CD EP *Losin' Your Marbles* in August 1995, followed by the Rob Younger-produced *Neon Pressure* CD EP in August 1996. *Neon Pressure* included a raw cover of Janis Joplin's 'Move Over'. Fur played shows with overseas visitors Fugazi, Bikini Kill, Luscious Jackson and The Offspring.

Fur issued its debut, full-length album *The Betty Shakes* in May 1997. It highlighted the band's continuing quest for a raw and abrasive sound, backed by better songs and tighter playing. *The Betty Shakes* produced the excellent CD single 'Blondi' which was a driven slice of grunge pop.

Album: *The Betty Shakes* (Fellaheen/Shock, 1997).

Mike Furber

Style: *Beat pop*

Mike Furber (b. 1948) is one of the tragic figures of the Australian pop world. As a member of The Bowery Boys, he sang on three of the most collectable Australian singles of the 1960s. As a solo artist during the late 1960s, he was constantly compared with **Normie Rowe** (unfavourably), which did little to boost his confidence. During the early 1970s, with his solo career in tatters, the sensitive Furber fell into depression and committed suicide.

In late 1965, at the age of 17, the English-born Furber joined Brisbane band The Bowery Boys. The Bowery Boys were an accomplished beat group, comprising Robbie Van Delft (lead guitar), Greg Walker (rhythm guitar), Paul Wade (bass) and Neville Peard (drums). When The Bowery Boys came to the attention of promoter Ivan Dayman (manager of **Normie Rowe** and owner of Sunshine Records), he launched the band as Mike Furber and the Bowery Boys. This gave the impression that Furber was the solo star and that The Bowery Boys were merely his backing band, which was not the case.

Indeed, Mike Furber did possess dashing good looks, and the 'little boy lost' image he adopted for his early promotional photos certainly endeared him to masses of female fans. Nevertheless, Mike Furber and the Bowery Boys issued three remarkable singles in 1966, which 1960s aficionado (the late) Dean Mittelhauser regarded as among the very best to come out of Australia during that period. 'Just a Poor Boy'/'Mailman Bring Me No More Blues' (January), a cover of The Mockingbirds' 'You Stole My Love'/'It's Gonna Work Out Fine'

(February) and 'That's When Happiness Began'/ 'You' (July) made the lower reaches of various regional charts. Mike Furber promoted the singles on *The Go!! Show* and *Kommotion* (usually without The Bowery Boys).

The band also issued two EPs, 'Just a Poor Boy' and 'You Stole My Love', plus the album *Just a Poor Boy*. In the collectors' magazine *From the Vault*, Mittelhauser rated this as one of the rarest and very best Australian albums of the 1960s. Furber left The Bowery Boys at the end of 1966 to further his solo career. By 1968 his popularity had slipped, despite three strong solo singles, 'Where Were You?'/ 'Second Hand People' (January 1967), 'I'm So Glad'/'It's Too Late' (August 1967) and 'Bring Your Love Back Home'/'If You Need Me' (October 1967). In 1969, Furber resurfaced with 'There's No Love Left'/'Keep a Little Love' (September) and the custom-penned Vanda and Young song suite 'I'm on Fire'/'Watch Me Burn' (November).

In the early 1970s, Furber did a stint of National Service and appeared in the stage musicals *Godspell* and *Nuclear*. Never a strong-willed person to begin with, Furber continued to suffer bouts of depression. Apparently the straw that broke the camel's back occurred when Furber was sacked from *Nuclear*. Reputedly in the depths of depression, he hanged himself on 10 May 1973. It has been suggested, however, that Furber was actually murdered because he had befriended a King's Cross prostitute. The truth may never be known.

Album: *Just a Poor Boy* (Kommotion, 1966).

G

Gina G

Style: *Dance pop*

In 1995 Australian singer Gina Gardener was working in the UK, where as a hopeful young starlet she scored a minor hit with Bass Culture's 'Love the Life'. During 1996, the re-styled Gina G put the 'glamour' back into Australian pop music. Gina G entered the Eurovision Song Contest as the UK entrant with the dance-floor friendly 'Ooh . . . Ahh, Just a Little Bit'. Issued as a single, it became a UK #1 hit in April 1996, thereby placing Gina G alongside Sandie Shaw ('Puppet on a String'), Cliff Richard ('Congratulations'), Brotherhood of Man ('Save all Your Kisses for Me') and Bucks Fizz ('Making Your Mind Up') as the only UK Eurovision entries to have topped the UK charts.

'Ooh . . . Ahh, Just a Little Bit' peaked at #5 in Australia during July, as well as reaching #12 in the USA. The follow up, 'I Belong to You', made the UK Top 10 (#6) in November and the Australian Top 30 in December. Gina G's third single 'Fresh!' was #1 in the UK at the start of 1997. It began its Australian chart run during April and reached a peak of #23 in May. 'Fresh!' sold over one million copies worldwide. Gina G issued her debut album *Fresh!* in May 1997.

Album: *Fresh!* (Eternal/Warner, 1997).

The Gadflys

Formed: *1984*
Style: *Roots-rock*
Original line-up: *Mick Moriarty (guitar, vocals), Phil Moriarty (clarinet)*

Canberra-based band The Gadflys mixed the busking flavour of the Violent Femmes with all manner of American roots music (rockabilly, country, R&B, jazz). The late 1984 line-up comprised Mick and Phil Moriarty, Anthony Hayes (guitar), Nic Dalton (bass) and Pete Velzen (drums). Hayes, Dalton and Velzen all left in 1985 to form **The Plunderers**. The Gadflys broke up for a time, but the Moriarty brothers revived the name a few years later.

The Gadflys have utilised the services of a number of bass players since that time, including Andy Lewis, Nathan Nancarrow and Jonathan Nix. The band issued its rough-hewn debut EP *The Gadflys* in October 1991 on the Phantom label. It was followed by the full-length album *Take Your Medicine* (December 1992), and the CD EPs 'Don't Get Me Wrong' (November 1993) and 'Guru' (November 1994). The band travelled overseas in 1994, 1995 and 1996 for appearances at the prestigious Edinburgh Festival, and tours throughout Holland and Germany. Other than that, The Gadflys were quiet on the recording front, finally issuing a new album, *Dimitri's Bungalow*, and CD single, 'Don't Leave Me a Fool', on the Larrikin label in April 1997. The Gadflys also appeared as house band for the 1997 Melbourne Comedy Festival.

Albums: *Take Your Medicine* (Phantom, 1993), *Dimitri's Bungalow* (Larrikin/Festival, 1997).

Kiley Gaffney

Style: *Rock*

Brisbane performance artist/singer Kiley Gaffney (b. 1970) emerged out of the loose Brisbane collective that spawned bands such as **Regurgitator** and Pangaea. It was Gaffney, in fact, who told Quan Yeomans the Eskimo fairytale that became **Regurgitator's** 'Blubber Boy'. Gaffney's style was in the vein of overseas artists like Diamanda Galas. In 1996, Gaffney signed to Warner and issued her debut CD EP 'Punk Rok Chik'.

Subtitled *Beauty, Glamour and Personality with Kiley Gaffney*, the CD EP took in the mocking, X-Ray-Specs-inspired title track and a cover of The Buzzcocks' teen-sex anthem 'Orgasm Addict'. The EP also posed as the soundtrack to a non-existent film, *Bitter Fluff*. Gaffney ended 1996 with the CD single 'Postman'. In 1997, she recorded her debut album, *Bitter Fluff (The Theme from the Movie)* for release in August. Gaffney has toured with local bands like **TISM**, **Regurgitator**, **Dirty Three**, **Powderfinger** and **Dave Graney**, plus overseas acts like Bikini Kill, Shonen Knife and Skunk Anansie.

Album: *Bitter Fluff (The Theme from the Movie)* (Warner, 1997).

Danni'elle Gaha

Style: *Soul, pop*

Singer Danni'elle Gaha (b. 1967) has a number of claims to fame: she scored a hit single with a duet shared with **John Farnham** ('Communication'); she was the first Australian to make the soul charts in London; and she made regular appearances on the ABC-TV's Saturday night variety show *Club Buggery* (presented by hosts 'Rampaging' Roy Slaven and H.G. Nelson) as part of the singing duo The Nissan Cedrics.

Gaha's duet with Farnham, 'Communication', reached #13 on the national chart during September 1989. It spent ten weeks in the Top 40. All profits ($80 000) from the sales were donated by BMG Records and the song's publisher (Peer International Music) to the Get Real Project. In 1990, Gaha toured with the **Jason Donovan** Band as a back-up vocalist, singing the **Kylie Minogue** duet 'Especially for You' with Donovan each night. In 1991, Gaha signed a deal with Epic/Sony. Ex-**Wa Wa Nee** frontman Paul Gray produced her debut solo single, 'I Like It'. Gaha then scored three minor UK hit singles with 'Stuck in the Middle' (#68 in August 1992), 'Do It for Love' (#52 in February 1993) and 'Secret Love' (#41 in June).

In 1994, Gaha joined the team of the ABC's Saturday night television variety show *Club Buggery*. Along with Louise Anton as vocal duo The Nissan Cedrics, Gaha provided the glamour-girl vocals which welcomed each guest. Gaha and Anton also acted in the comedy segment *Star Search* in which they played the parts of Sheets Afyre and Muff Merkin respectively. In early 1997, The Nissan Cedrics recorded an album of cover versions *Going for a Song*, with producer Paul Gray, which appeared in September.

Nissan Cedrics album: *Going for a Song* (East West/Warner, 1997).

Galadriel

Formed: *1969*
Style: *Progressive rock*
Original line-up: *John 'Spider' Scholtens (vocals), Garry Adams (guitar, vocals; ex-House of Bricks), Gary Lothian (lead guitar; ex-Elliot Gordon Union), Mick Parker (bass, flute; ex-Samael Lilith), Doug Bligh (drums; ex-House of Bricks)*

This Sydney band issued one of the rarest major label progressive rock albums of the early 1970s. Twenty years after its initial release, *Galadriel* became a highly sought-after collectors' item among European progressive rock circles.

Galadriel grew out of the ashes of two Sydney suburban dance bands. House of Bricks comprised Garry Adams, Doug Bligh, **Daryl Braithwaite** (vocals) and Bruce Worrall (bass). That band's only claim to fame was being pipped at the winners' post in the 1969 2SM/Pepsi Pop Poll contest by schoolboy outfit The Menu (led by 14-year-old guitarist **Mario Millo**). As a member of Samael Lilith, Mick Parker played bass and flute on the band's one and only single on the independent Du Monde label, The Moody Blues' 'Nights in White Satin'/'Sitting in the Park' (February 1970). 'Nights in White Satin' reached #14 on the Sydney chart. The band took its name from the mythical Hebrew demon Samael and his principal female cohort Lilith. The line-up on the single comprised Parker, Ray Ferguson (vocals, guitar), Brent Thurlow (organ) and Greg Wilder (drums). With the break-up of House of Bricks and the departure of Parker to join Galadriel, Braithwaite and Worrall joined Samael Lilith and from there went on to great success with **Sherbet**.

Galadriel took its name from the golden-haired Lady Galadriel (the powerful guardian of the elves of Lorien) in J.R.R. Tolkien's fantasy masterpiece *The Lord of the Rings*. The band's contemporaries included **Tamam Shud**, **Kahvas Jute**, **Blackfeather** and **Spectrum**. Du Monde issued Galadriel's country-tinged debut single 'Lady was a Thief'/'Girl of Seventeen' (February 1971). The band signed to Polydor and issued *Galadriel* (produced by American Tom Lubin) and the single 'Standing in the Rain'/'Working' (May 1971). The songs ranged in style from bluesy hard rock ('Amble On', 'Girl of Seventeen') to jazzy ballads ('Standing in the Rain'). The records sank without a trace. Bruce Belbin (ex-Gutbucket) replaced Parker and the band commenced work on a second album. Due to complications beyond the band's control, the master tapes for the work-in-progress were erased. The band broke up in early 1972.

Garry Adams and Doug Bligh joined **Mario Millo's** (pre-**Sebastian Hardie**) band The Clik. Bligh later played with Stuart and McKay, Goldrush, the **Richard Clapton** Band, the **Ross Ryan** Band and Windchase. Lothian went on to the Cyril B. Bunter Band and the Chris Turner Band. Reissue specialists Raven included 'Girl of Seventeen' on the *Golden Miles: Australian Progressive Rock 1969–1974* compilation (1994) while Vicious Sloth Collectables reissued *Galadriel* on CD during 1995.

Album: *Galadriel* (Polydor, 1971; reissued Vicious Sloth, 1995).

GANGgajang

Formed: *1983*
Style: *Pop rock*
Original line-up: *Mark 'Cal' Callaghan (guitar, vocals; ex-***Riptides***), Geoffrey Stapleton (guitar, keyboards; ex-***Aliens***), Chris Bailey (bass; ex-Red Angel Panic,* **Headband**, **Angels***), Buzz Bidstrup (drums, ex-***Angels***)*

This popular Sydney outfit originally came together as a loose collection of seasoned musicians out for a bit of fun. The band's name was derived from the onomatopoeic word for a loud, open chord struck on a guitar. Mark Callaghan and Buzz Bidstrup recorded 'Gimme Some Loving' initially as a demo. Chris Bailey and Geoffrey Stapleton joined the pair. By that stage, Callaghan, Bidstrup and Chris Bailey had also worked on the music for the ABC-TV series *Sweet and Sour*. When Mercury issued 'Gimme Some Loving'/'Noisy Talking' as a single (November 1984) it became a minor hit (#33).

Suddenly in demand, GANGgajang went back into the studios with American producer Joe Wissert (Lovin' Spoonful, The Turtles, Boz Scaggs) in order to complete its debut album. Augmented by Gordon Sullivan (lead guitar; on loan from **Deckchairs Overboard**), Kayellen Bee (vocals, percussion) and Marilyn Delaney (vocals, keyboards), the band went on tour. Robert James then replaced Sullivan on lead guitar.

The album (issued November 1985) yielded the singles 'House of Cards'/'From the Top to the Bottom' (March), 'Giver of Life'/'Mysterious' (August), 'Sounds of Then'/'House of Cards' (live) (December) and 'The Bigger They Are'/'Giver of Life' (live) (April 1986). 'Giver of Life'/'Mysterious' also appeared as a six-track double single pack, with four bonus live tracks on the additional single. GANGgajang also contributed a track, 'Dream at Night', to the soundtrack of the Australian feature film *Emoh Ruo*; 'Dream of Night' appeared as a single in October 1985.

Although not a big hit at the time (#21 in Sydney), the wonderfully evocative 'Sounds of Then' became well known ten years later when it was used to advertise Coca-Cola and then picked up by the Nine Network as its promotional signature tune. *GANGgajang* achieved gold status (35 000 copies sold), and the band toured for two years. *GangAGAIN* (October) and its singles 'Initiation'/'Sounds of Then' (January), 'American Money'/'Roof Only Leaks When It's Raining' (August) and 'Tree of Love'/'Luck of the Irish' (December) followed in 1987.

Callaghan put GANGgajang on hold while all the members worked on other projects. Callaghan revived **The Riptides**, as well as producing a solo album, *Sailors and Mermaids*, and three singles, 'I Will Be with You'/'Changing Times' (July 1988), 'Do It Rite'/'Golden Years' (September) and 'Golden Years'/'Spooky' (July 1989). Bidstrup, Stapleton, James, Bailey, Bee and Delaney were all involved in C&W combo The Stetsons. Stapleton joined **The Dukes** in 1990.

Bidstrup, Callaghan, Bailey and James (with new keyboard player Mark O'Connor) revived GANGgajang in 1993 to record *Lingo* for the rooArt label. The album (issued in May 1994) included the CD singles 'Hundreds of Languages' (December 1993) and 'Talk to Me' (April 1994). The reunion was short-lived. PolyGram issued the compilation *The Essential GANGgajang* in 1996. Over the course of ten years and three albums, GANGgajang produced a healthy legacy of joyous pop music.

Albums: *GANGgajang* (True Tone/PolyGram, 1985); *GangAGAIN* (Mercury/PolyGram, 1987); *Lingo* (rooArt, 1993), *The Essential GANGgajang* (PolyGram, 1996).

The Garden Path

Formed: *1985*
Style: *Psychedelic pop*
Original line-up: *Victor Conrad (vocals, guitar, keyboards; ex-Fools Apart), Rohan Belton (organ, vocals; ex-Verge), Graeme Burdett (guitar; ex-Shreds,* **Screaming Believers***), Colin Gellard (bass; ex-Fools Apart), Terry Aldridge (drums)*

Before forming The Garden Path, Victor Conrad had been a member of Adelaide power pop band Fools Apart. The band comprised Conrad, Jeremy Bruer (guitar, vocals), Rees Hughes (bass) and Craig Rodda (drums). Hughes and Rodda left in 1981 to join **Screaming Believers**. David Quinn and George Satanovic took their places. Dave Andrews replaced Quinn in 1983.

In early 1984, Colin Gellard replaced Andrews, and John Gazzola became the band's latest drummer. The single 'On the Beach'/'Ruins' on Greasy Pop displayed the band's powerful yet melodic style. Fools Apart also shared a split single with **Screaming Believers**, 'Within An Inch'. Fools Apart broke up in late 1984. Conrad, Gellard and Aldridge formulated plans for a new band, and with the arrival of Graeme Burdett and Rohan Belton in March 1985, The Garden Path line-up was complete. The Garden Path sound and style was almost entirely based on 1960s neo-psychedelic pop, with influences drawn from *Revolver*-period Beatles and 'See Emily Play'-era Pink Floyd to more contemporary bands such as The Soft Boys and Green On Red.

The band's earliest recordings appeared on various compilations: 'Night and Day' on SA-FM's *Brewing* album, 'This Place' on Greasy Pop's *An Oasis in a Desert of Noise*, and 'What Do You Want to Hear?' and 'Times (Out of Mind)' to Double J's *Cooking with George, Mark Too*. The Garden Path issued one of the classic independent albums of the 1980s in *5 Reasons* (June 1986). The album was brimming with finely crafted, ethereal psychedelia, as displayed on tracks like 'This Place', 'Into the Clouds', 'Little Pieces' and 'Times (Out of Mind)'. The band maintained the quality with second album *Blue* (August 1987), although tracks like 'In the Dark' and 'Statues of a Man' boasted a harder edge.

Conrad and Belton also moonlighted with occasional band The Dust Collection covering obscure 1960s psychedelic and garage-punk songs. The line-up comprised Conrad (keyboards), Belton (bass), Travis Underdog (vocals), Scott Allen (guitar, vocals), Gerry Barrett (guitar) and Andrew Geue (drums). The line-up of Belton, Underdog, Allen, Geue and Barrett recorded the single '10 Til 13 O'clock'/'Green (When She Says)', 'The Light' for the Greasy Pop label (December 1986).

Belton and Burdett left The Garden Path in 1987 to join The Psycho Daisies, so the band was down to a four-piece of Conrad, Gellard, Aldridge and newcomer Dave Lokan (guitar) for the 1989 album *All the Things*. By that stage, The Garden Path had dispensed with the psychedelic pop flavour for a tougher guitar sound, although the album sounded more like a second-rate Church record. The album yielded the single 'Just Like You'/'Take It All Back'. Aldridge left in 1990 to be replaced by Craig Rodda (ex-**Screaming Believers**), but the band broke up soon after.

Meanwhile, Belton had joined The Handmedowns as bass player. Prior to that, the line-up comprised Trevor Comley (guitar, vocals), Tony Dyer (guitar, vocals), Dave Gray (bass) and Jason Kilic (drums). The Handmedowns played a vibrant brand of 1960s-inspired power pop. For the mini-album *Back to Yourself* on Greasy Pop, the band was down to a three-piece comprising Comley, Kilic and Belton. It was to be the band's only record. Conrad was an auxiliary member of The Spikes (appearing on the band's 1986 album *Colour in a Black Forest*) and The Acid Birds (1987). Likewise, Gellard and Aldridge were involved in The Acid Birds.

Garden Path albums: *5 Reasons* (Greasy Pop, 1986), *Blue* (Greasy Pop, 1987), *All the Things* (CC Music, 1989); ***Handmedowns mini-album:*** *Back to Yourself* (Greasy Pop, 1988).

Gas (*see* Cattletruck)

The Gas Babies

Formed: *1983*
Style: *Garage punk*
Original line-up: *Steve Fusezi (guitar, vocals; ex-Young Savages, Virgins,* **Little Murders**, *White Elephants), Mike Chrystal (lead guitar; ex-Young Savages, Virgins, White Elephants), Russell Baricevic (bass, vocals; ex-Jets), Rod McMurrich (aka Rodney Modney, drums; ex-Jets)*

During the early 1980s, The Gas Babies were one of the first Melbourne inner-city bands to play a predominantly 1960s-influenced brand of music. The band's set was peppered with obscure Yardbirds, MC5 and *Nuggets*-styled American garage-punk tunes (The Seeds, Mouse and the Traps, Count Five, 13th Floor Elevators, etc.). The Gas Babies were also big fans of The Flamin' Groovies.

Fusezi and Chrystal had been in three legendary (i.e. obscure) Melbourne punk bands, Young Savages, The Virgins and The White Elephants. Another ex-Virgins alumnus, Simon Smith (also ex-Z-Cars), replaced McMurrich in The Gas Babies during late 1984, after which the band broke up. The Gas Babies played the inner-city circuit for only ten months (December 1983 to September 1984) and failed to record anything comprehensive before breaking up. The original line-up re-formed in 1986 to record a cover of The Flamin' Groovies' 'Headin' for the Texas Border' for release as a single, backed with 'DmF (Ready to Go)', on the Grown Up Wrong! label (December 1986). The band also contributed 'Slow Death' (also by The Groovies) to Au-go-go Records' second Melbourne compilation, *A Slab of Vic* (1986). McMurrich later played with LSD and **Sunset Strip**.

At the end of 1985, Baricevic joined Ramones tribute band The Marones which comprised Russie Marone, Tony 'Bonehead' Shaw (aka Boney Marone, vocals, **Corpse Grinders**), Arch Law (aka Archie Marone, drums, **Huxton Creepers**) and Paul Thomas (aka Paulie Marone, guitar, **Huxton Creepers**). The band played a couple of fun-packed, showcase gigs around the Melbourne inner-city pub circuit before calling it quits. Baricevic, Chrystal and Smith formed Macho Clowns in 1986, and issued the 12-inch EP *Humbuck* on Au-go-go during

1988. Dean Muller (ex-Voodoo Lust) replaced Smith on drums. Baricevic later played with **Bored!** and **Pray TV**. In 1990, Chrystal revived The White Elephants with Mark Ivey (vocals; ex-Virgins), Geoff Martyn (guitar; ex-Sick Things) and Rick Ferrara (drums; ex-Beach Nuts, Stone Circus), and issued the single 'Vic Morrow's Head'/'You Endanger Us' on the Dog Meat label.

Gaslight Radio

Formed: *1995*
Style: *Indie guitar pop*
Line-up: *Rory Cooke (vocals, guitar), Martin Cooke (guitar), Phil Rouben (bass), Simon Piper (drums)*

Gaslight Radio hailed from Burleigh Heads on Queensland's Gold Coast. With influences drawn from US bands like The Pixies, Pavement and The Breeders, the band fashioned a compelling brand of low-fi indie guitar pop. The band recorded its debut CD EP, *Torchin' Towns, Hankerin' Homes*, four months after formation. The CD EP came out on the independent Lonely Guy label in August 1996, earning the band across-the-board praise. Gaslight Radio spent a year touring Australia with other like-minded bands such as **Autohaze, Drop City** and Pollen. The band signed to Mushroom Distribution Services (MDS) and issued a second CD EP, *. . . our dolelove* (June 1997). The featured track 'The Singer's a Liar' highlighted the band's off-kilter inventiveness. A new CD single, 'Is by Bus', appeared in November 1997.

Tim Gaze

Style: *Blues, hard rock*

Tim Gaze (b. 1954) has enjoyed a long career as one of Australia's pre-eminent guitar players. Although never held in the esteem bestowed on **Kevin Borich** or **Ian Moss**, for example, Gaze's exacting technique and songwriting skills have kept him in demand for many years. Gaze's early influences ranged from Eric Clapton, Peter Green and Jimi Hendrix to many jazz players. He formed Stonehenge in 1968 when he was 14 years old. By the time he was 16, he was playing in one of Australia's first progressive rock bands, **Tamam Shud**. He appeared on the band's classic album, *Goolutionites and the Real People*. By the time the album came out at the end of 1970, Tim had recorded an album with **Kahvas Jute** *Wide Open* which came out in January 1971.

Gaze spent several months with **Kahvas Jute** (mid-1970) before returning to **Tamam Shud** just as *Goolutionites* came out. **Tamam Shud** broke up in August 1972, after which Gaze and Shud's drummer Nigel Macara formed Miss Universe. New Zealanders Phil Pritchard (guitar; ex-Highway) and George Limbidis (bass; ex-Highway) completed the line-up. In early 1973, Gaze and Macara joined Rosses Wilson and Hannaford (then fresh from the break-up of **Daddy Cool**) in their new band. The band never got off the ground. (Wilson and Hannaford's band soon evolved into **Mighty Kong**.) In April, Gaze and Macara joined Mike Rudd and Bill Putt (then fresh from the break-up of **Spectrum**) in their new venture, **Ariel**.

Gaze and Macara played on **Ariel's** debut album, *A Strange Fantastic Dream*. Gaze co-wrote (with Rudd) **Ariel's** first single 'Jamaican Farewell', as well as writing other outstanding album tracks like 'Miracle Man'. Gaze and Macara stayed with **Ariel** until April 1974. Gaze toured with **Stevie Wright** and the All Stars until the end of the year. He formed a band called Dayride in 1976 which evolved into, firstly, the Tim Gaze Rock Ensemble and then the Tim Gaze Band by 1977. Members of the band around that time included Peter Bolton (keyboards), Peter Blyton (bass) and Robbie France-Shaw (drums). Harry Curtis (bass) and Andy Cowan (keyboards; ex-**Madder Lake**) were also members at one stage. In 1982, the Tim Gaze Band appeared on the soundtrack of the surfing film *Band on the Run*.

Festival/Infinity prepared an album for *Band on the Run* (featuring a mix of tracks by Tim Gaze Band and J.J. Cale) for release. Due to copyright restrictions, however, the album never officially came out, although a number of copies did escape on to the market. Gaze kept a version of the Tim Gaze Band (with John Barnes on drums and Peter Willersdorf on bass) going until the end of 1984, after which he joined seminal pub rockers **Rose Tattoo** as slide guitarist. Gaze appeared on the singles 'Born to Be Wild', 'Calling' and 'Suddenly', plus the album *Beats from a Single Drum*. **Rose Tattoo** split in 1987.

Gaze set up his own studio, and played with a number of bands (including Skin Game, Brothers of the Bell and Big Secret) over the next three years. He also backed solo singer **Gyan** on a regular basis. In 1990 Gaze and Phil Graham (guitar, vocals) co-wrote, recorded and produced the soundtrack to the surfing film *Sultans 2—The Power Strikes Back*. The soundtrack was only ever issued on cassette on the Upuze label. In 1991 Gaze toured with the **Peter Wells** Band. In March 1993, **Tamam Shud** re-formed, recorded the album *Permanent Culture* and scored a hit with 'Stay'. The band broke up two years later and Gaze returned to his studio and session work. In late 1996 he joined **The Bushwackers**.

Geeza

Formed: *1974*
Style: *Hard rock*
1975 line-up: *Alan Watt (vocals), Gaby Marshall (guitar), Lee Martin (bass), Ian Webb (drums), Alan Fraiel (drums)*

Sydney band Geeza started life as The Geeza Rock'n'Roll Show, presenting a cabaret-style act replete with all manner of stage props, theatrics (including exploding telephone boxes) and uptempo rock'n'roll. By 1976, Martin and Fraiel had dispensed with the theatrics, shortened the name to Geeza, and formed a new line-up with Terry Halliday (vocals) and Gabriel Vendetti (guitar). Steve Gronow replaced Martin in 1977. The band signed to the Living Sound label and issued a single, Sensational Alex Harvey Band's 'Vambo'/ 'Get It On' (April 1976). In 1977, Geeza issued the **Mario Millo**-produced album *Streetlife* and the singles 'Run'n'Hide'/'Sydney City Ladies' and 'Song to Warilla'/'Dragon Queen'. None of the records was successful and the band broke up a year later.

Album: *Streetlife* (Laser/RCA, 1977).

Joe Geia

Style: *Reggae*

Koori musician Joe Geia (b. 1960) began his full-time performance career when he joined the Kuku-Yalanji Dance team during the late 1970s. He recorded *Rebel Voices* in 1979 with assistance from the Central Australian Aboriginal Media Association (CAAMA). Originally from Palm Island in northern Queensland, Geia moved to Adelaide, South Australia to attend the Centre for Aboriginal Studies in Music (CASM).

There he joined reggae band **No Fixed Address** as singer, percussionist and didgeridoo player. He toured locally and overseas with the band, and appeared on the acclaimed *From My Eyes* mini-album. Geia left **No Fixed Address** in 1983 to form reggae band Nya Nunga in Sydney. In 1985 he moved to Melbourne, where he joined Prince Nyah and the Slaves of Sin. The band comprised Koori Brother William (vocals), John Petros (guitar), Peter Camm (guitar), Rob Dixon (keyboards), Chris Coyne (sax), Steve Hewitt (trumpet), Barry Denik (bass) and Des McKenna (drums; ex-Lavidia Sage). McKenna was better known as 'Animal' from the studio band of television variety show *Hey Hey It's Saturday*.

In 1986, Prince Nyah and the Slaves of Sin toured South Australia and the Northern Territory to coincide with the symbolic handover of Uluru (Ayers Rock). Geia also toured briefly with **Shane Howard** as a guest member of his band, **Shane Howard** and Friends. In 1987, Geia took a position as Cultural Officer with the Aboriginal Advancement League of Victoria. One of his roles was to visit local schools to play didgeridoo, teach dance and demonstrate traditional cooking. In 1988, the Australia Council granted Geia $90 000 to record his own songs which resulted in the *Yil Lull* album on the Aboriginal artists label Only Gammin'. The Council also sent Geia on a six-month tour around Australia with a six-piece band.

In 1989, Geia contributed 'Yil Lull' to the Various Artists album *Burning Bridges* on CBS. Since that time, Geia has continued to work through Only Gammin', and has gigged with a number of different bands, including Gospel Choir, Art Attack and Joe Geia and the Heads. **Paul Kelly** included his cover of 'Yil Lull' on The Messengers' 1992 rarities collection, *Hidden Things*. Geia continued to tour, and issued a new album in 1996 *Tribal Journey*. He toured Germany to some acclaim. Back in Australia, he teamed up with Simon Hewitt (guitar) for gigs.

Albums: *Yil Lull* (Only Gammin', 1988), *Tribal Journey* (Larrikin/Festival, 1996).

Geisha

Formed: *1983*
Style: *Pop, rock*
Original line-up: *Chris Doheny (guitar, vocals), Ken Sheppard (guitar), John Nyman (keyboards), Donoghue Doheny (bass, vocals), Peter Robertson (drums)*

This Melbourne band formed as Geisha Detail. The band drew its inspiration from 1970s glam rock and early 1980s English New Romantic bands such as Duran Duran and Spandau Ballet.

As Geisha, the band signed to EMI and issued the singles 'Fool's Way'/'Heartfall' (April 1985), 'Rainy Day'/'Not the Same' (July) and 'Kabuki'/ 'Moving to the Rhythm' (September), plus the album *Geisha* (October). The singles were hits in Melbourne ('Kabuki' peaked at #20 in December) and the band became popular around the suburban pub circuit. EMI reissued 'Rainy Day' in March 1986 (as a 7-inch single with a new B-side, 'Night Games'), plus as a 12-inch 'Rainy Day'/'Kabuki'. Geisha scored its biggest hit single when 'Part Time Love Affair'/'Girl Like You' (August 1986) peaked at #3 on the Melbourne chart during September.

By late 1986, Geisha was working as a three-piece of Chris Doheny, Ken Sheppard (bass) and Brett Luton (drums). In the new year, Doheny completely revamped the line-up with new members Steve Carter (bass), Laurence Maddick (keyboards; ex-**Strange Tenants**), Tommy Hosie (drums; ex-**James Freud's** Berlin) and Englishman Rob Dean (guitar; ex-Japan). *Midnight to Dawn* (October 1987) yielded the singles 'Calling Your Name'/'Don't Come Knocking' (August), 'Normal People'/'Paranoid Street' (October) and 'Never Tell You Why'/'Shining Star' (December). Geisha broke up in April 1988. Chris Doheny went on to covers bands Diamond Dogs, All the Young Dudes and Dragonfly. He continued to record, singing lead vocals on 'It's More Than a Game' which was the theme song to the Nine Network's *The Footy Show*. In September 1997, Doheny issued his debut solo single, The Beatlesque 'Can You Hear the Rain?'.

Albums: *Geisha* (EMI, 1985); *Midnight to Dawn* (EMI, 1987).

Linda George

Style: *Soul, pop*

Alongside **Colleen Hewett** and **Renée Geyer**, singer Linda George (b. 1951) was one of the most popular solo performers on the early 1970s pop scene. The English-born singer migrated to Australia with her family in 1964. She joined her first band, The Nova Express, in 1969. The Nova Express was a jazz-rock styled big band (similar to **Heart 'n' Soul** and **Kush**). During the period George was with the band, The Nova Express comprised Ken White (guitar), Peter Walsh (organ), Wayne Lanham (bass), Craig Forbes (drums), Dave Clark (sax), Ken Schroder (sax) and Ian Hellings (trumpet). The band won the Victorian final of the Hoadley's National Battle of the Sounds and issued one single on EMI/Columbia, a cover of 'Take Another Little Piece of My Heart'/'Around the Block' in 1970 before George left to go solo.

George toured with The Marlboro Big Band, The Barry Veith Big Band, The ABC Showband and Opus Big Band before turning to session work. She signed a solo deal with the Image label in 1972 and developed a soul-pop style. Image issued her debut single, 'Let's Fly Away'/'Song to Save the World', in May. Her first chart hits were covers of Gladys Knight and The Pips' 'Neither One of Us'/'If It's Alright with You' (national #16, July 1973) and Ruby and the Romantics' 'Our Day will Come'/'Yesterday and You' (#36, January 1974). During March 1973, George also appeared as the Gypsy Queen in the local stage production of The Who's rock opera *Tommy*. Other cast members included **Billy Thorpe**, **Daryl Braithwaite**, **Colleen Hewett**, **Broderick Smith**, **Doug Parkinson**, **Jim Keays** and Keith Moon.

In 1974, Image issued the album *Miss Linda George*, plus the singles 'Mama's Little Girl'/'Between Her Goodbye and My Hello' (#9 in August) and 'Give It Love'/'Yesterday and You' (December). *Step by Step* produced the singles 'Shoo Be Doo Be Doo Dah Day'/'I Wanna Hear Music' (September 1975) and 'Step by Step'/'Wake Up' (May 1976). George's last single for Image was 'Sitting in Limbo'/'Hard to Be Friends' (November 1976). From the late 1970s onwards, she concentrated on session work. She recorded three singles during the early 1980s for **Mike Brady's** Full Moon label, 'Love is Enough'/'You are Mine Tonight' (with Paul McKay, April 1980), 'Telephone Lines'/'Physical Things' (June 1981) and 'Face to Face'/'Up Until Now' (August 1982).

Albums: *Miss Linda George* (Image, 1974), *Step by Step* (Image, 1975).

Lisa Gerrard (*see* Dead Can Dance)

Gerry and the Joy Band

Formed: *1971*
Style: *Rock'n'roll*
Original line-up: *Gerry Humphreys (vocals, ex-***Loved Ones***), ***Billy Green*** (guitar; ex-***Doug Parkinson*** In Focus, ***King Harvest***), Brian Peacock (bass; ex-Playboys, Librettos, ***Procession***)*

Respected singer Gerry Humphreys formed Gerry and the Joy Band in late 1971. **Daddy Cool** members **Ross Wilson** (guitar, vocals), **Ross Hannaford** (guitar), **Gary Young** (drums) and Jerry Noone (sax, keyboards) augmented the basic line-up of Humphreys, Green and Peacock in the studio. Humphreys compered the inaugural Sunbury Pop Festival in January 1972.

Gerry and the Joy Band recorded a cover of Buddy Holly's 'Rave On' for its debut single, backed with 'Oh Lonesome Me' (March 1972). The single made the lower reaches of the Top 40 chart in April, encouragement enough for the band to record a follow-up, 'Ongo Bongo'/'My Name is Earl (I Need a Girl)' (September 1972). The entertaining 'Ongo Bongo' featured a novelty 'jungle' flavour. Green had already recorded 'My Name is Earl' as the B-side to his 1970 solo single 'This Must Be the End'. Although only a part-time venture for all concerned, the band made live appearances throughout 1972 with various line-ups. By mid-1972, Green was playing with **Friends**. At the end of the year, Humphreys travelled to Brazil, the UK and the USA where MGM issued 'Ongo Bongo' as a single.

Renée Geyer

Style: Jazz, blues, soul

Long recognised as Australia's foremost jazz, blues and soul singer, Renée Geyer (b. 1952) has issued 14 albums over the course of a 25-year career. Best known for her rich, soulful, passionate and husky vocal delivery, Geyer has also been in demand as a session singer. She has sung back-up vocals on numerous album sessions, ranging from **La De Das, Dragon** and **Men at Work** to **Richard Clapton** and **Jimmy Barnes**. Geyer has worked and recorded in the USA, as well as singing back-up vocals for international artists such as Sting, Joe Cocker and Chaka Khan.

Geyer's earliest bands included Sydney-based jazz-blues outfits Dry Red and Sun. Sun comprised Geyer, Keith Shadwick (sax, flute, clarinet, vocals), Chris Sonnenberg (guitar, who replaced original guitarist Steve Phillipson), George Almanza (piano), Henry Correy (bass) and Garry Nowell (drums). The band issued one collectable, progressive jazz-rock album, *Sun 1972*, on RCA (August 1972) before Geyer moved on. Starlee Ford took her place and the band continued on until late 1974.

In mid-1972, Geyer sang with two short-lived bands, Free Spirit and Nine Stage Horizon, before joining another jazz-blues band, Mother Earth. Mark Punch (guitar, vocals; ex-Nine Stage Horizon), Jim Kelly (guitar; ex-**Affair**, **Levi Smith's Clefs, SCRA**), David Lindsay (bass) and John Proud (drums; ex-Nine Stage Horizon) completed the original Mother Earth line-up. By the beginning of 1973, Harry Brus (bass; ex-Amazons, **Jeff St John's** Copperwine, Third Union Band, **Blackfeather**, Hunger) and Russell Dunlop (drums; ex-**Aesop's Fables, Levi Smith's Clefs, SCRA**) had taken over from Lindsay and Proud. As the co-writer of 'Heading in the Right Direction' (with Garry Paige), Punch featured prominently in Geyer's subsequent career. Mother Earth backed Geyer on her self-titled debut album (produced by Gus McNeil) and the singles 'Space Captain'/'If Only You Believe' (June 1973) and 'Oh! Boy'/'No Such Thing as Love' (September). Geyer split from Mother Earth at the end of the year.

Tweed Harris (ex-**Groove**) produced Geyer's second album, *It's a Man's Man's World* (#16 in October 1974), which yielded the singles 'What Do I Do on Sunday Morning?'/'Scarlet Ribbons' (June), 'It's Been a Long Time'/'Take Me Where You Took Me Last Night' (August) and a cover of James Brown's 'It's a Man's Man's World'/'Once in a Lifetime Thing' (November). Backing musicians on the album included Tweed Harris (keyboards), **Phil Manning**, Steve Murphy, **Tim Gaze** and Tony Naylor (guitars), Barry 'Big Goose' Sullivan (bass; **Chain**) and Geoff Cox (drums; **Bootleg Family Band**).

Renée Geyer

Geyer's gorgeous rendering of Brown's 'It's a Man's Man's World' became her first charting single when it reached #29 in Melbourne during December 1974. By that time, she had teamed up with jazz-funk band Sanctuary. The original Sanctuary line-up (August 1974) comprised Mal Logan (keyboards; ex-**Healing Force**, **Chain**, **Dingoes**, Silver Sun), Barry Sullivan (bass; ex-**Chain**, Silver Sun), Barry Harvey (drums; ex-**Chain**) and **Billy Green** (guitar; ex-**Doug Parkinson** In Focus, **King Harvest**, **Friends**). As well as Logan and Sullivan, the short-lived Silver Sun (July to August 1974) comprised John Pugh (guitar; ex-**Cam-Pact**, **Healing Force**), Sam McNally (keyboards) and Sunil De Silva (drums; ex-Skylight).

There were a number of line-up changes (guitarists Green, John Pugh, Lindsay Wells and Tim Piper came and went) before Sanctuary stabilised with Logan, Sullivan, Mark Punch (guitar; ex-Mother Earth, **Johnny Rocco Band**) and Greg Tell (bass) in June 1975. When they came to record the *Ready to Deal* album, Sanctuary became known as the Renée Geyer Band. *Ready to Deal* (November 1975) was a success, reaching #12 on the Melbourne album chart and #21 nationally in December. It spawned three singles, '(I Give You) Sweet Love'/ 'Love's Got a Hold' (issued in October, but then swiftly withdrawn), 'Heading in the Right Direction'/'Love's Got a Hold' (#15 in Melbourne during December) and 'If Loving You is Wrong' (March 1976). During that period, the Renée Geyer Band supported overseas visitors like Eric Clapton, Freddy King, Sonny Terry and Brownie McGee and Houndog Taylor.

Mick Rogers (ex-**Procession**, **Bulldog**, Manfred Mann's Earth Band) replaced Punch in the early months of 1976. The Renée Geyer Band recorded the live album *Really . . . Really Love You* (issued August 1976) and single 'Shaky Ground'/'It Only Happens' (September 1976) before Geyer travelled to the USA to record *Moving Along* in Los Angeles with Motown producer Frank Wilson and a host of American session players, including members of Stevie Wonder's band. 'Stares and Whispers'/'Be There in the Morning' (national #12 in May 1977) and 'Tender Hooks'/'We Had It All' (July) were issued as singles. *Moving Along* peaked at #10 in Melbourne during June 1977, and #11 nationally a month later. Geyer's final single for 1977 was the theme song to the television soapie *Restless Years*, backed with 'Theme from *Restless Years*' which was by The Mike Perjanik Orchestra. In the meantime, Logan and Sullivan had re-formed Sanctuary to work the Melbourne pub circuit. In late 1977, the band backed **Doug Parkinson**.

Geyer spent the next decade or so dividing her time between Australia and the USA. She recorded *Winner* in Los Angeles (again produced by Wilson) with the Renée Geyer Band line-up of Mark Punch, Greg Tell and Tim Partridge (bass), plus session players. 'Money (That's What I Want)'/'Moving Along' (April 1978) and 'Baby Be Mine'/'Baby I'm the One' (October 1978) were issued as singles. The excellent *Blues License* album (July 1979) and the single B.B. King's 'The Thrill is Gone'/'Bellhop Blues' (June) featured the **Kevin Borich Express**, augmented by Mal Logan, Tim Piper (ex-Chants R&B, **Chain**, **Blackfeather**, Alta Mira, the **Ray Burton** Band), Mark Punch, Kerrie Biddell and others. In 1980, Geyer signed to Mushroom Records. She recorded with rock band The Ideals, which resulted in the hard-edged 'Hot Minutes'/'Tangled Up in Trechery' single (July 1980). Her biggest hits came with the salsa/reggae-styled 'Say I Love You'/'Bad Side of the Blues' single (national #5 in July 1981) and the Rob Fraboni/Ricky Fataar-produced *So Lucky* album (November).

The album produced two further singles, 'Do You Know What I Mean?'/'Good Lovin'' (December 1981; #29 in February 1982) and 'I Can Feel the Fire'/'Come On' (February 1982). Geyer issued three more singles on Mushroom: the non-album 'Love So Sweet'/'I've Got News for You' (July 1982), a cover of Goffin/King's 'Goin' Back'/'(We Got the Makings of a) Fever' (shared with **Glenn Shorrock**; February 1983) and 'Trouble in Paradise'/'Life Begins at Thirty' (October). Geyer's last albums on Mushroom were *Renée Live* (April 1983) and the 'Best of' set *Faves* (December).

In 1984 Geyer recorded a duet with **Jon English**, 'Every Beat of My Heart'. Her first album for WEA, *Sing to Me* (June 1985), included the singles 'Faithful Love'/'Memory' (February), 'Every Day of the Week'/'Without Love' (April) and 'All My Love'/'Guess Who I Saw Today' (June). Her 1985 touring band comprised Jim Gannon (guitar), Tony Backhouse (guitar), Jamie McKinley (keyboards), Geoff Oakes (sax), Ian Belton (bass; ex-QED) and Mark Kennedy (drums; ex-**Spectrum**, **Ayers Rock**, **Marcia Hines** Band). *Live at the Basement* (1986) was Geyer's last solo album for the next eight years, during which time she lived in Los Angeles. While in the USA, Geyer joined Californian band Easy Pieces, appearing on the album *Easy Pieces* (A&M, 1988). Easy Pieces also featured Hamish Stuart (guitar, vocals), Anthony Jackson (bass) and Steve Ferrone (drums).

In 1993, Geyer contributed 'Crazy' and 'Foggy Highway' to the Martin Armiger-produced soundtrack of the ABC-TV drama series *Seven Deadly Sins*. The **Paul Kelly**-produced *Difficult Woman* album came out in late 1994. It featured a strong set of R&B, jazz and soul tunes, including the Kelly-penned 'Difficult Woman', 'Foggy Highway' and 'Sweet Guy'. By that stage, Geyer had resumed touring, and she worked with **Paul Kelly** throughout 1995 and 1996. Her 1995 solo backing band comprised Paul Berton (guitar), George Powers (keyboards), Hal Tupaea (bass) and Mark Kennedy (drums). Geyer has contributed a great deal to Australian music over the years, and her voice and stage presence remain vibrant and powerful.

Albums: *Renee Geyer* (RCA, 1973), *It's a Man's Man's World* (RCA, 1974), *Ready to Deal* (RCA, 1975), *Really, Really Love You* (RCA, 1976), *At Her Very Best* (RCA, 1977), *Moving Along* (RCA, 1977), *Winner* (RCA, 1978), *Blues License* (with the **Kevin Borich Express**, RCA, 1979), *So Lucky* (Mushroom/Festival, 1981), *Renée Live* (Mushroom/Festival, 1983), *Faves* (Mushroom/Festival, 1983), *Sing to Me* (WEA, 1985), *Live at the Basement* (ABC, 1986), *Difficult Woman* (Larrikin/Festival, 1994).

Ghostwriters

Formed: *1991*
Style: *Pop, rock*
Original line-up: *Rob Hirst (drums, vocals, guitar; from* **Midnight Oil***), Rick Grossman (bass; from* **Hoodoo Gurus***), Dorland Bray (drums, guitar; from Popstuds, ex-***Do Ré Mi***)*

Ghostwriters was essentially a studio band put together by Rob Hirst, Rick Grossman and Dorland Bray. The three friends met in 1979, and had planned to record together for a number of years. Such were the demanding schedules of their respective bands that the opportunity did not arise until early 1991. By that stage, Bray had switched from drums to guitar and was playing bluegrass with his band The Popstuds. Rob Hirst financed the recording sessions. He also invited New Zealander Andy Dickson (guitar, vocals; ex-Narcs) to flesh out the sound.

The Leszek Karski/Rob Hirst-produced *Ghostwriters* came out in December 1991, and included the single 'Someone's Singing "New York New York"'. Initially there had been some resistance from the **Midnight Oil** camp to Hirst recording away from the band. Accordingly, in order for the album to come out, Hirst agreed that neither his name nor his likeness appear on the record, the video or any of the promotional material. Likewise, he agreed that Ghostwriters not perform live.

Two further singles were lifted from the album during 1992, 'Runaway Bay' (February) and 'World is Almost at Peace' (May). It was to be another three years until Hirst and Grossman worked together again as Ghostwriters. Bray was not involved that time. The album *Second Skin* and single 'International Rules of Love'/'Tears of St Lawrence' came out in August 1996. For the album, Ghostwriters was augmented by session players like Mark Moffatt (guitar), **Chris Abrahams** (Hammond organ, mellotron), Jan Preston (piano) and the **Hunters & Collectors'** horn section.

Albums: *Ghostwriters* (Virgin, 1991), *Second Skin* (Mercury/PolyGram, 1996).

The Giants

Formed: *1983*
Style: *Blues, boogie*
1990 line-up: *Stuart Wood (guitar, vocals, harp), Mick Riley (lead guitar, backing vocals), Iain Hergstrom (sax, harmonica), Chris Van Bakel (bass, backing vocals), James Kearns (drums, backing vocals)*

Melbourne band The Giants played a timeless brand of hard rocking blues. The band was held in high esteem among the local biker community. The Giants had the distinction of playing at the annual biker rock festival Broadford 14 times. The band issued two independent cassette albums, *Gigantic* (1990) and *Boots'n'All* (1991), before its debut album *Live at Broadford* (March 1993).

The driving force behind the band was Stuart Wood. There have been many line-up changes over the years. The one listed above recorded the 1990 cassette *Gigantic*. The 1991 line-up comprised Wood, Riley, Keanes, Chris Wilson (keyboards; ex-**Buster Brown**) and Martin Coogan (keyboards). By 1992 the line-up was Wood, Wilson, Kearns, Wayne Burt (guitar; ex-**Jo Jo Zep and the Falcons**, **Black Sorrows**) and Glen Suckling (bass). The line-up of Wood, Wilson, Burt, Suckling and new drummer Paul Keane recorded the album *Live at Broadford*.

In 1993, Robert Tronca (ex-Taipan) replaced Wilson on keyboards, Michael Strangel replaced Keane and Paul Williams (ex-**Australian Crawl**) replaced Suckling. Wilson and Keane returned to the band in 1994. Geordie Leach (bass; ex-**Rose Tattoo**, **Peter Wells** Band) replaced Williams in August 1995. By 1997, the line-up was Wood, Burt, Wilson, Leach and Rick Puchala (drums; ex-**Russell Morris** and the Rubes). Whenever bluesman **Matt Taylor** toured Melbourne during the early 1990s, he utilised The Giants as his backing band. Usually billed as Matt Taylor and The Giants Chain Show, the nights encompassed a solo set by Taylor, a set by The Giants, then the musicians would combine for a set as **Matt Taylor's Chain**. The Giants have issued four albums of immaculately played rock 'n' boogie and gritty roadhouse blues.

Albums: *Live at Broadford* (Independent, 1993), *Freedom Road* (New Market, 1994), *The Nature of the Beast* (Black Market, 1996), *Working Underground* (Black Market, 1997).

Barry Gibb (*see* The Bee Gees)

Andy Gibb

Style: *Pop*

Following the international success of his three older brothers in **The Bee Gees**, Andy Gibb (b. 1958, d. 1988) appeared as a star in his own right during 1977. He died in 1988 of myocarditis, a rare inflammatory virus of the heart muscle. Gibbs' drug addiction and financial bankruptcy during the 1980s were widely reported. He had not recorded since 1981, but at the time of his death was reputedly about to sign a new contract with Island Records.

Gibb was born in Manchester, England. His family emigrated to Australia in 1958 when he was only months old. Then in 1967, when Andy was nine, the Gibb family returned to the UK so **The Bee Gees** could further their careers. Gibb returned to Australia in late 1974, on the advice of his brother Barry, to make a start on his solo career. He formed a band called Andy Gibb and Zenta, and signed a publishing deal with **Col Joye's** publishing company Joye Music. Gibb scored support slots to overseas visitors The Sweet and The Bay City Rollers in 1975. In 1976, Gibb travelled to Florida to record his debut album, *Flowing Rivers*, under the direction of Barry Gibb and producer Albhy Galuten.

He toured America as support to **The Bee Gees**, and scored three consecutive #1 US hits with 'I Just Want to Be Your Everything'/'In the End' (August 1977), '(Love is) Thicker than Water'/'Words and Music' (1978) and 'Shadow Dancing' (1978). 'I Just Want to Be Your Everything' was also #1 in Australia. Gibb scored his two biggest UK hits in 1978 with 'An Everlasting Love' (#10 in August) and '(Our Love) Don't Throw It All Away' (#32 in December). By that stage, Gibb had almost eclipsed his illustrious brothers in popularity.

Further minor hits followed, including 'Desire'/'Waiting for You' (February 1980), 'Time is Time'/'I Go for You' (January 1981), 'Me (Without You)'/'Melody' (June 1981) and a duet with **Olivia Newton-John**, 'I Can't Help It'/'Someone I Ain't' before Gibb moved into television work and musical theatre. He co-hosted the US pop show *Solid Gold*, but was fired at the end of the second season for missing too many tapings. He landed the lead role in the Broadway production of *Joseph and the Amazing Technicolor Dreamcoat*, but lost that after skipping a dozen performances in a month.

With his drug and financial problems resolved, Gibb began working on a return to the music scene. Tragedy struck on 10 March 1988 when Gibb died in Oxford, England. He was 30 years old.

Albums: *Flowing Rivers* (Interfusion/Festival, 1977), *Shadow Dancing* (RSO, 1978), *After Dark* (RSO, 1980), *Andy Gibb's Greatest Hits* (RSO, 1980).

Robin Gibb (*see* The Bee Gees)

Mark Gillespie

Style: Roots rock

Singer/songwriter/guitarist Mark Gillespie commanded a strong cult following on the Melbourne scene. His heartfelt roots-rock style mixed R&B, soul, funk and a touch of reggae. His tracks 'I'm a Kite (Won't You Be My Hurricane?)' and 'The Joke's on You' appeared on the Oz label's Various Artists album *The Debutantes* (1977). Gillespie also issued *Make Up*, a collection of prose and poetry published by Outback Press.

Gillespie's debut single 'Savanarola'/'Just Wanna Ball' came out credited to Mark Gillespie and the Victims in 1978. His band at that point comprised Mick 'The Reverend' O'Connor (keyboards), Bruno De Stanislo (bass; ex-One Nite Stand) and Peter Reed (drums; ex-Hot Dog, One Nite Stand). Gillespie issued a single on Festival/Infinity, 'Coming Back for More'/'Alligator Music' (April 1979), before coming to wider attention when he supported Maria Muldaur, Tom Waits and Rodriguez on their respective Australian tours. Gillespie's touring band comprised O'Connor, **Broderick Smith** (vocals, harmonica, guitar; ex-**Dingoes**), Stephen Cooney (guitar), Clive Harrison (bass, backing vocals; ex-**Kush, Avalanche**), Trevor Courtney (drums; ex-Chants R&B, **Vibrants**, Skylight), Stewart Watson (fiddle, mandolin, guitar) and Pat and Gay L'Nane (backing vocals).

Gillespie recorded his brilliant debut album, *Only Human*, with assistance from Joe Creighton (bass; ex-**Billy** T), **Ross Hannaford** (guitar, backing vocals; ex-**Daddy Cool**), Rex Bullen (keyboards; ex-**Bakery**), Mark Meyer (drums) and **Lisa Bade** (backing vocals). Gillespie sang as well as playing guitar, keyboards and mandolin. The album produced the singles 'Only Human'/'Long & Strong' (June 1980) and 'Small Mercies'/'Black Angels' (September). 'Deep as You'/'Stronger Together', 'Together' followed in April 1981. Gillespie travelled throughout Asia before recording his second album, *Sweet Nothing*. His backing band again included Hannaford, Meyer and Bade, plus Tim Partridge (bass), Andrew Thompson (sax), Gary Lyon (backing vocals) and Nikki Nicholls (backing vocals). *Sweet Nothing* (March 1982) took Gillespie into the national Top 40 for the first time when it peaked at #32. The album also reached #9 in Melbourne. *Sweet Nothing* yielded three singles, 'Nothing Special'/'Passing' (February), 'Traveller in the Night'/'Swing Tonight' (June) and 'Night & Day'/'Looking for You' (October).

Gillespie's third album, *Mark Gillespie* (aka *Ring of Truth*) (January 1984) produced the singles 'Ring of Truth'/'All for Your Love' (November 1983), 'You'/'Thanks' (also November 1983) and 'Letting Go'/'Animal' (May 1984). Backing Gillespie on the album was drummer Geoff Bridgeford (ex-**Groove**, **Bee Gees**). Little was heard from Gillespie on the music scene for some time. He returned to Asia and founded an orphanage in Bangladesh. He re emerged in Australia during 1992 and issued the album *Flame*, the CD single 'Long Time' and the CD EP 'Don't Wait' on the Aurora label.

Members of his backing band around that time included old mates Joe Creighton and **Ross Hannaford**, plus James Black (keyboards; ex-**Russell Morris** Band, **Mondo Rock**, Revelators), Angus Burchill (drums; **John Farnham** Band), Alex Pertout (percussion), John Watson (drums; ex-**Australian Crawl**, **Kevin Borich Express**), Shane O'Mara (guitar; ex-**Stephen Cummings** Band) and Bill McDonald (bass; ex-**Hot Half Hour**, **Deborah Conway** Band).

Albums: *Only Human* (W.B.E./EMI, 1980), *Sweet Nothing* (Wheatley/EMI, 1981), *Mark Gillespie* (Wheatley/EMI, 1983), *Best of Mark Gillespie (Small Mercies)* (Wheatley/EMI, 1985), *Flame* (Aurora/Mushroom/Festival, 1992).

Girl Monstar

Formed: *1988*
Style: *Trash pop*
Original line-up: *Sherry Valier (real name Sherry Rich, vocals, rhythm guitar; ex-Cactus Fever), Anne McCue (lead guitar, vocals), Damian Child (bass), Sue World (drums, vocals; ex-Wet Ones)*

Melbourne all-girl band Girl Monstar took its inspiration from bands like The Runaways, Girlschool, The Bangles and The Pandoras. The band's trash pop style mixed tough guitar riffs with strong harmonies.

Sue World had previously played with The Wet Ones, a delightful Melbourne all-girl combo that played tongue-in-cheek, 1960s-inspired guitar pop (sort of like The Shangri-Las by way of The Buzzcocks and The Pandoras). The Wet Ones formed in 1984 and comprised Sue World, Kelly Brimacombe (guitar, vocals), Rosi Joy (guitar, vocals) and Genevieve Hassall (bass). The band issued the gig giveaway single 'Next Summer'/'Alligator' (December 1986), the 12-inch EP *It's a Premoistened World* (October 1986) and the mini-album *Crack Up* (October 1988) on the Polyester label before calling it quits. The Wet Ones also contributed a cover of **The Loved Ones'** 'Everlovin' Man' to Au-go-go's Various Artists compilation *A Slab of Vic* (1986).

Girl Monstar signed to the Timberyard label and issued the single 'Surfing on a Wave of Love'/'He's Hell' (October 1989). The band came to wider attention at the start of 1990 after scoring support slots to Danish hard rockers D.A.D. and American heavy metal bad boys Skid Row on their respective Australian tours. Later tour supports included shows with The Buzzcocks and The Ramones. The single 'Joe Cool'/'Egomaniac' followed later in the year. Girl Monstar contributed a cover of the Hanoi Rocks song 'Dead by Christmas' to Timberyard's yuletide Various Artists compilation *Rockin' Bethlehem* (1990), plus a cover of 'Is that You?' to the Kiss tribute album *Hard to Believe* on the Waterfront label (1990).

The band issued the album *Monstereo Delicio* in July 1992 by which time Janene Abbott had replaced Damian Child, who joined Velocity. Girl Monstar broke up a year later. Sue World joined The Exotics. Sherry Valier reverted to her real name and formed feisty country-rock band Sherry Rich and the Grievous Angels in early 1994. The Grievous Angels comprised Steve Connolly (lead guitar; ex-**Paul Kelly** and the Coloured Girls/Messengers), Matt Heydon (keyboards; ex-**Nick Barker and the Reptiles**), Doug Lee Robertson (bass; ex-Ice Cream Hands) and Steve Morrison (drums).

Rich issued the CD EPs *Sherry Rich and the Grievous Angels* (January 1995) and 'Trying to Write a Love Song' (January 1996) on the Rubber label. Also helping out on *Sherry Rich and the Grievous Angels* were Charlie Owen (guitar; ex-**New Christs**, Tex Don and Charlie) and Jen Anderson (violin; ex-**Black Sorrows**). In early 1997, Rich recorded her debut album in Nashville, Tennessee, *Sherry Rich and Courtesy Move*, for release in October. The first CD single 'Polite Kisses', came out in August.

Girl Monstar album: *Monstereo Delicio* (Timberyard, 1992); ***Sherry Rich album:*** *Sherry Rich and Courtesy Move* (Rubber/BMG, 1997).

Girl Overboard

Formed: *1988*
Style: *Pop, rock*
Original line-up: *Lisa Schouw (vocals), Robin Gist (guitar), Brett McNaughton (keyboards), Dean Hilson (sax), Jenny Milroy (percussion and backing vocals), Lee Davidson (drums)*

This Melbourne pop band started life in 1985 as Separate Tables. Initially formed as a trio of Lisa Schouw, Robin Gist and Brett McNaughton, the band played the pub circuit accompanied by a drum machine before adding the other members as above. John Favaro joined on bass in 1988. Separate Tables scored the support slot to **John Farnham's** Jack's Back tour of 1987, and signed a deal with BMG. The band issued three singles, 'When the Word Came Down'/'Mist' (December 1987), 'Change My Sex'/'Blue Hat', 'Unanswerable' (May 1988) and

'Wrap Your Arms Around Me'/'Wrap Your Arms Around Me' (March 1989), before changing its moniker to Girl Overboard.

Girl Overboard's debut album, *Paint a Picture* (March 1990), yielded the minor hits 'I Can't Believe'/'Blue Falls the Rain' (#43 in December 1989) and 'The Love We Make'/'When the Word Came Down' (#23 in March 1990). *Paint a Picture* reached #16 on the national chart in April. As displayed on the album, the band's sound was a safe mix of dance pop, light jazz and American-styled hard rock. Two further singles were lifted from the set, 'Some Things Never Change' and 'In the Evening', but neither charted. 'I Can't Believe' was issued in the USA, but was not successful.

Tony Day replaced Lee Davidson in 1991, and a cover of Creedence Clearwater Revival's 'Who'll Stop the Rain?' returned the band to the lower reaches of the charts (#59) in September. *Go* and its singles 'Chain of Fools', 'Your Love' and 'Jackie' offered lushly textured rock and pop with Schouw's rich contralto well to the fore.

Albums: *Paint a Picture* (BMG, 1989), *Go* (BMG, 1993).

Girlfriend

Formed: *1991*
Style: *Pop*
1992 line-up: *Melanie Alexander (vocals), Jackie Cowell (vocals), Siobhan Heidenreich (vocals), Robyn Loau (vocals), Lorinda Noble (vocals)*

The idea behind teeny-pop sensations Girlfriend came from five Sydney schoolfriends attending singing and dance classes. There have been many all-girl groups in pop (think The Crystals, The Shangri-Las, Bananarama and more recently The Spice Girls, plus in Australia The Chiffons and The Cookies), but Girlfriend filled a gap in the early 1990s teen market.

Girlfriend made a demo of the song 'Take It from Me' and signed a management deal and record contract in double-quick time. Of the five founding members, only Melanie Alexander, Jackie Cowell and Siobhan Heidenreich remained. They were joined by Samoan-descended, New Zealand-born Robyn Loau and Lorinda Noble who appeared on the debut album *Make It Come True* (December 1992). The album peaked at #4 during January 1993, and yielded three national Top 20 hit singles during 1992, 'Take It from Me' (a #1 in June), 'Girl's Life' (#12 in August) and 'Without You' (#19 in October). A fourth single, 'Bad Attitude', made it as high as #22 in January 1993.

Girlfriend took to the road with a backing band, playing sell-out concerts around Australia. The girls released and promoted a range of Girlfriend clothing, of which department stores could not get enough. The first release of clothing sold out within four weeks. The group's second album, *It's Up to You* (December 1993), featured the singles 'Not a Day Goes By', 'Wishing on the Same Star' and 'Heartbeat' (#37 in October 1993). Loau left Girlfriend in mid-1994 and the others continued as GF4. Two further singles came out, 'Sooner or Later' (#10 in October 1994) and 'Need Love to Make the Sex Right' (September 1995), but GF4 slipped from view. Loau played the part of Lani in the 1997 David Caesar feature film *Idiot Box*. She issued her debut solo album, *Malaria*, in October 1997. The first CD single, 'Sick with Love', reached #23 during September. Loau also sang on the first single, 'Mana (Part II)', from producer Anthony Copping's Siva Pacifica (Spirit of the Pacific) project.

Albums: *Make It Come True* (BMG, 1992), *It's Up to You* (BMG, 1993).

The Girlies

Formed: *1986*
Style: *Punk rock*
Original line-up: *Tony Brassington (vocals; ex-Prince of Weasels), Mark Wilkinson (guitar; ex-Strange Glory), Glen Armstrong (guitar), Shane Cooke (bass; ex-*Vampire Lovers*, Four Horsemen), Heyden Wilson (drums; ex-Hellfire Club)*

This Brisbane guitar band formed in June 1986, originally playing all Stooges and Ramones-styled covers. Mark Hayman (ex-Butler Groove) replaced Glen Armstrong after three months. The new line-up issued the single 'Pussycat'/'The Feeling's Gone' on the Petite label (September 1987).

Au-go-go Records also included The Girlies' version of 'Tight Pants' on The Stooges' tribute album *Hard to Beat* (1988). After that, the band's line-up changed regularly, with Brian Mann (guitar; ex-Headstones) and Glenn James (lead guitar; ex-Horny Toads) replacing Mark Wilkinson and Hayman, and singer Darren Russell replacing Tony Brassington. Wilkinson went on to The Lime Spiders and The New Christs. Other guitar players within the band's ranks included Dazy Robinson and Murray Belcher. The Girlies' long-awaited mini-album, *Common Thing*, finally came out in 1990, by which time the band was on its last legs.

Glenn James' previous band, The Horny Toads, comprised Marky Toad (vocals), Joel James (rhythm guitar), Dennis Anderson (bass) and Mikey J. Horny Toad (drums). With a sound that mixed *Raw Power*-era Iggy and the Stooges with The Dictators, The Horny Toads played it hard and fast with tongues firmly planted in cheeks. Sydney label Green Fez (a Citadel offshoot) issued the band's debut mini-album, *Con Anima Con Forza*, in 1988. The band's second mini-album, *Wired* (on the Amplexus label), featured manic guitar freakouts on songs like 'Switch Bitch'.

Mini-album: *Common Thing* (Timberyard, 1990).

Keith Glass

Style: *Country, R&B*

Singer/guitarist/songwriter Keith Glass is one of the unsung legends of Australian rock music. He was prominent in several bands during the 1960s: The Rising Sons, **Eighteenth Century Quartet** and **Cam-Pact**. Glass has also made his mark on the Australian country music scene. Some of his songs, like 'This Country of Mine', 'When Stan was the Man', 'Outback (in Our Backyard)' and the satirical 'Victoria Bitter (She Made Me that Way)' have attracted considerable interest.

When Glass left **Cam-Pact** in 1969, after three years and four singles, he took the role of Berger in the original Australian stage production of the American 'tribal love-rock musical' *Hair* directed by Jim Sharman (later acclaimed as the director of the feature film version of *The Rocky Horror Show*). *Hair* had its Australian premier on 5 June 1969. Glass was heard on the *Hair* Australian Cast album issued by Spin at the end of 1969. His version of 'Donna' from the musical was the flipside to Sharon Redd's rendition of 'Easy to be Hard'. The single came out in October 1969.

Under the influence of Merle Haggard, Hank Williams and Gram Parsons, Glass formed pioneering country-rock band Sundown in 1970. The original Sundown line-up was Glass, Mark Barnes (bass; ex-Moppa Blues, Delta Set, Roadrunners, **Cam-Pact**), **Broderick Smith** (vocals, harmonica; ex-**Adderley Smith Blues Band**), Kerryn Tolhurst (guitar; ex-**Adderley Smith Blues Band**) and Barry Windley (drums; ex-**Chessmen**, **Cherokees**, Quinn). Later members included Mike Edwards (pedal steel), Steve Edwards (bass), David Green (guitar), Dave Redapple (guitar) and Richard Wright (drums; ex-**Groop**). Sundown issued one single on Image, 'This Country of Mine'/'Outback Dan' (June 1972), before breaking up. Country legend Slim Dusty later recorded 'This Country of Mine'.

Glass then went into record retail and pioneered the import record boom in the early 1970s with his shop Archie & Jughead's. By the late 1970s, as well as playing in the Keith Glass Band (KGB) and The Living Legends, Glass was running the Missing Link retail outlet and independent record label. As with **Cam-Pact** during the 1960s, Missing Link was a cornerstone organisation on Melbourne's independent scene of the late 1970s.

As a record shop, Missing Link was one of the first in Australia to stock independent punk and new wave records. As a record label, it provided an important outlet for the recordings of The Boys Next Door/**The Birthday Party**, Whirlywirld, **Laughing Clowns**, **La Femme**, **The Go-Betweens** and others. The first two releases on Missing Link were actually 1960s R&B band The Union's *Ultimate Garage Band* EP (The Union had been fronted by respected 1970s rock journalist David 'Dr Pepper' Pepperell) and **Cam-Pact's** *Living in the '60s* EP.

As manager of **The Birthday Party**, Glass did much to foster the band's growth and independence. It was with his assistance (financial and morale-wise) that the band got to England in the first place. Glass should be recognised as one of the grand patrons of the Australian new wave movement.

In 1977, the Keith Glass Band (KGB) comprised Glass, Wayne Duncan (bass; ex-**Daddy Cool**), Robert Souter (drums; ex-**Lizard**) and Les Stacpool (guitar; ex-**Chessmen**, **Merv Benton** and the Tamlas, **Doug Parkinson** In Focus, **Aesop's Fables**). The band played R&B and country-tinged rock. With the arrival of Wayne Burt (guitar; ex-**Jo Jo Zep and the Falcons**) during October 1977, KGB became The Living Legends. Huk Treloar (drums; ex-**Pantha**, **Bleeding Hearts**) replaced Souter, who went to **The Dynamic Hepnotics**. The Living Legends had two tracks, 'Hopeless Case' and 'Baby Doll', included on the Various Artists album *The Melbourne Club* on Missing Link.

After a stint songwriting in Nashville, Tennessee, Glass returned to Melbourne and opened the country record store Deep South. In 1986 he issued a mini-album, *God, Guns and Guts*, on Au-go-go under the pseudonym Onie J. Holy. By the late 1980s, Glass was again exploring urban Australian themes over country/blues rhythms with the Keith Glass Honky Tonk Band and Keith Glass and the Tumblers. In 1988, Glass signed a solo deal with Virgin Records and issued two well-received country albums, *Going Over Old Ground* and *Living Down My Past*, plus a series of singles, 'When Stan Was the Man', 'Home and Away Game', 'Victoria Bitter (She Made Me that Way)', 'Going Over Old Ground' and 'Walking Off the Land'.

Backing on the albums was by The Tumblers: Mark Mealin (guitar), Peter Scholz (pedal steel), Nick Pitman (bass) and Noel Herridge (drums; ex-**Sid Rumpo**), plus guests like Glass's songwriting collaborator Mick Hamilton (guitar), **Broderick Smith** (vocals, harp) and former Asleep at the Wheel steel-player Lucky Oceans. Keith Glass and the Tumblers made several appearances at the Tamworth Country Music Festival during the early 1990s. Glass also co-hosted the country music show *High in the Saddle* with Dave Dawson on Melbourne community radio station 3RRR-FM. In 1988 he contributed songs to the soundtrack for the film *Rikky & Pete*.

Glass recorded three albums with the Hamilton Glass and Young trio (comprising Glass, Mick Hamilton and Gary Young) in the mid-1990s. He released a new solo album, *Smoke and Mirrors*, in 1997.

Keith Glass albums: *Going Over Old Ground* (Virgin, 1989), *Living Down My Past* (Virgin, 1991), *Smoke and Mirrors* (Straight Up/Shock, 1997); ***Hamilton Glass and Young albums:*** *Rocking Cowboy* (Larrikin, 1993), *Songs the Radio Taught Us* (Larrikin, 1995), *Unidentified Playing Objects* (Larrikin, 1996).

Glide

Formed: *1990*
Style: *Indie guitar pop*
Original line-up: *William Arthur (guitar, vocals), Tim Scott (guitar), Marc Lynch (bass), Jason Kingshott (drums)*

This Sydney-based band first came to prominence after winning a Triple J-FM demo competition. Taking inspiration from UK bands such as Swervedriver, Ride and Teenage Fanclub, Glide served up an eclectic mix of melodic guitar noise, fuzzed-out pop and deep emotion. The band was hailed as a leading light on the 1990s independent music scene.

Glide debuted with the 1992 CD EPs 'Pretty Mouth' (May) and 'Shuffle Off to Buffalo' (December) on the Medical label, followed by the 1993 CD EPs 'Wake' (July) and 'Why You Asking?' (October) on MDS. Paul McDonald replaced Tim Scott for those releases. The band signed to the Hypnotized label (through Shock) and issued the full-length album *Open Up and Croon* and the CD EP 'Something' in 1995. By 1996 Glide was down to a three-piece line-up of William Arthur, Jason Kingshott and Andy Kelly (bass, vocals). That line-up issued the album *Disappear Here* (June 1996), which yielded the CD EPs 'What Do I Know?' (May) and 'Here She Comes' (November). Glide appeared on the Sydney bill of the Big Day Out in 1997. In November, the band issued *Shrink Wrapped Real Thing* which compiled the first three CD EPs with four new tracks, including the CD single, 'Something of Me Inside'.

Albums: *Open Up and Croon* (Hypnotized/Shock, 1995), *Disappear Here* (Hypnotized/Shock, 1996), *Shrink Wrapped Real Thing* (Hypnotized/Shock, 1997).

The Globos

Formed: *1981*
Style: *Cabaret pop*
Line-up: *Wendy de Waal (vocals), Mark Trevorrow (vocals)*

Wendy De Waal and Mark Trevorrow were the driving forces behind this good-time cabaret act. Initially the duo (plus extras) mimed and danced to backing tapes of pop hits from the late 1950s and early 1960s. Complete with kitsch 1960s gear, The Globos based their act on Australian pop shows such as *Bandstand*, *Kommotion* and *Shindig*. After they came to the attention of ex-**Skyhook** Red Symons, The Globos signed to the White label and issued two singles. Symons produced and played on 'Tintarella Di Luna'/'Twisto Globo' (#30 in September 1982) and a cover of Sonny and Cher's 'The Beat Goes on'/'Kiss and Tell' (#28 in April 1983). After The Globos' concept had run its course, Trevorrow launched himself as the ultimate plastic cabaret star and television host Bob Downe.

Go 101

Formed: *1987*
Style: *Funk, pop*
Original line-up: *David Wilson (vocals; keyboards; ex-Hue & Cry), Daniel Alan (drums; ex-Hue & Cry), Steven Brooks (guitar), Simon Kershaw (keyboards), Peter Badenoch (bass; ex-Software Seduction)*

This Melbourne band came together around Singapore-born singer David Wilson and Daniel Alan, after they broke up their old band Hue & Cry. The pair formed a songwriting partnership, and later brought in Steven Brooks, Simon Kershaw and Peter Badenoch. Ruthven Martinus also contributed on synthesiser. James Almond replaced Kershaw on keyboards in 1987.

Go 101 signed to PolyGram's Mercury label and issued the singles 'Build It Up'/'Walls' (December 1988), 'Room for Love'/'Falling (Down a River)' (March 1989) and 'Jealous Heart'/'Jealous Heart' (November), plus the album *Tempting Fate* (produced by American John Potoker). The records were full of smooth, sophisticated funk'n'soul with the emphasis on dance beats. Go 101 supported international visitors George Michael and Whitney Houston, and issued only one more single, 'Message to a Broken Heart', before slipping from public view.

Album: Tempting Fate (Polydor, 1989).

The Go-Betweens

Formed: *1977*
Style: *Pop, folk*
Original line-up: **Grant McLennan** *(guitar, bass, vocals),* **Robert Forster** *(guitar, vocals)*

In 1996, French magazine *Les Inrockuptibles* voted The Go-Betweens' 1988 album *16 Lovers Lane* the third best album of the 1980s (behind The Smiths' *The Queen is Dead* and The Pixies' *Doolittle*). Such is the band's standing in European music circles that its memory remains cherished nearly ten years after splitting. Here in Australia, the band's passing was mourned by only a dedicated few.

The one thing that eluded The Go-Betweens during their 12 years together was commercial success. As with a number of Australian independent bands over the last 20 years (**The Saints**, **The Birthday Party**, **Laughing Clowns** and **Scientists** to name but a few), The Go-Betweens' record sales never equated to their position in the first division of credibility.

When two would-be singer/songwriters (Forster and McLennan) formed The Go-Betweens in Brisbane during December 1977, their only concern was to amuse themselves. Yet, within two years, The Go-Betweens were living and recording in England. Although inspired by the British punk explosion, Forster and McLennan took more from such disparate sources as Bob Dylan, The Velvet Underground, Patti Smith, Talking Heads, Jonathan Richman and The Monkees than the Sex Pistols. With Forster on guitar and McLennan on bass, the band's first, temporary drummer was Bruce Anthon from fellow Brisbane band The Survivors. With help from guest drummer Dennis Cantwell (on loan from **The Riptides**), The Go-Betweens recorded 'Lee Remick'/'Karen'. (**The Apartments'** leader Peter Milton Walsh was a member of The Go-Betweens briefly over the 1978/1979 summer.)

A year later, with help from the band's first permanent drummer, Tim Mustafa (drums), Malcolm Kelly (organ, piano) and Candice and Jacqueline on tambourine and go-go dancing, The Go-Betweens recorded 'People Say'/'Don't Let Him Come Back'. Both singles were issued on the Able label (in September 1978 and September 1979 respectively). Incidentally, Candice and Jacqueline were Forster and McLennan's little in-joke; they were the pair's imaginary girlfriends, or more likely their alter-egos.

Both singles were sparsely produced, poorly played yet passionately performed folksy, post-punk pop songs. They were sunny, catchy and hopelessly romantic, earning the band immediate local and international acclaim. The UK office of US independent label Beserkley offered the band a deal on the strength of 'Lee Remick'. True Tone/PolyGram repackaged the singles as the 12-inch EP *The Able Label Singles* in 1986.

Encouraged by the UK response, Forster and McLennan left Australia in November 1979. They eventually signed a deal with Scottish neo-pop independent label Postcard (run by Alan Horne and home to Josef K, Aztec Camera and Orange Juice). Postcard reissued 'People Say' in the UK, followed by 'I Need Two Heads'/'Stop Before You Say It' (November 1980), which was recorded with Orange Juice drummer Steven Daly. 'I Need Two Heads' reached #6 on the UK independent charts. Missing Link issued 'I Need Two Heads' in Australia upon the band's return (February 1981).

With a permanent drummer, Lindy Morrison (ex-Zero), on board, The Go-Betweens cut 'Your Turn My Turn'/'World Weary' (September 1981), 'Hammer the Hammer'/'By Chance' (March 1982) and *Send Me a Lullaby* (February). The album was tentative and clumsy, its brittle, rough-hewn sound hardly setting the charts alight. Morrison also played drums on fellow Brisbane band Four Gods' single 'Enchanted House'/'Restless' (September 1981), which appeared on the Able label. Two years on, and after returning to the UK, *Before Hollywood* (May 1983) was a lot more world-weary. It was full of deceptively simple yet accomplished songs like 'A Bad Debt Follows You', 'Dusty in Here', 'On My Block', 'That Way' and the title cut. The album's centrepiece was 'Cattle and Cane', a brilliant evocation of McLennan's youth over subtle yet powerful backing. It was issued as a single backed with 'Heaven Says' (also May 1983).

Spring Hill Fair (September 1984), for the Sire label, was another quantum leap, boasting such exemplary Go-Betweens moments as 'Bachelor Kisses', 'Part Company' and 'Man O' Sand to Girl O' Sea'. With the addition of Robert Vickers (bass; ex-Numbers, Colors), McLennan had moved to guitar so the sound was bolder and more confident. 'Man O' Sand to Girl O' Sea'/'This Girl, Black Girl' (November 1983), 'Part Company'/'Just a King in a

Mirror' (August 1984) and 'Bachelor Kisses'/'Rare Breed' (November 1984) were lifted as singles.

After being on six different record labels over the previous eight years, The Go-Betweens signed a substantial deal with True Tone (through PolyGram) in 1985. *Liberty Belle and the Black Diamond Express* (March 1986) remains the band's most cohesive and finely crafted statement. Tracks like 'Spring Rain', 'Head Full of Steam', 'Twin Layers of Lightning' and 'The Wrong Road' positively glowed with beauty and atmosphere. *Liberty Belle* spawned the singles 'Spring Rain'/'Life at Hand' (February 1986) and 'Head Full of Steam'/'Little Joe' (June 1986).

Tallulah (June 1987), while not quite so cohesive, contained two of the band's most winsome and hummable songs, 'Right Here' and 'Bye Bye Pride'. New member Amanda Brown's violin, oboe, guitar and keyboards added extra lustre. The album yielded three singles, 'Right Here'/'When People are Dead' (March 1987), 'I Just Get Caught Out'/'Don't Let Him Come Back' (May) and 'Bye Bye Pride'/'Time in the Desert' (August). In November 1987, The Go-Betweens relocated to Sydney after spending six years in London.

Vickers left at that time to be replaced by John Willsteed (bass, guitar, organ; ex-Zip, Zero, **Catchcry**). *16 Lovers Lane* (September 1988) was the band's most polished and accessible release. 'Love Goes On!' was lush and transcendent pop, the breezy sound of 'Streets of Your Town' belied its subject matter (domestic violence) and Forster's pastoral 'Love is a Sign' was as eloquent as he ever got. The album actually registered #81 on the UK mainstream charts in September. The album's two singles were 'Streets of Your Town'/'Wait Until June' (August 1988) and 'Was There Anything I Could Do?'/'Rock and Roll Friend' (October). To coincide with the album's release in Australia, the band undertook The Birds and the Bees national tour.

Throughout 1989, The Go-Betweens played headlining shows in the UK and USA, and toured the world as support to R.E.M.. In October 1989, Michael Armiger (ex-10,000 Guitars, **Paul Kelly** Band, **John Kennedy's Love Gone Wrong, Johnnys**) replaced Willsteed. Then, in December 1989, Forster and McLennan decided to split the band. There was no warning, no acrimonious bouts of feuding, just a decision to stop the band. Forster and McLennan went solo, while Morrison and Brown formed **Cleopatra Wong**.

Interest in The Go-Betweens has increased over the years. The album *The Go-Betweens: 1978–1990* (December 1990) was a double compilation put together by the band's main protagonists, Forster and McLennan. In March 1996, the Hippy Knight label issued The Go-Betweens' tribute album *Right Here*, which featured contributions from bands as diverse as **Frente!**, **Snout**, **Pray TV**, **The Earthmen** and **The Meanies**. In June 1996, the Silk Screen label (through MDS) issued remastered CD versions of the band's six albums. The sound was immaculate, and each CD featured a detailed booklet plus a separate insert with the original artwork. In April 1997, Allen & Unwin published David Nichols' book *The Go-Betweens*. Forster and McLennan reunited The Go-Betweens for a series of showcase gigs in the UK during mid-1997.

Albums: *Send Me a Lullaby* (Australia: Missing Link; UK: Rough Trade, 1981), *Before Hollywood* (Stunn/Rough Trade, 1983), *Spring Hill Fair* (Sire, 1984), *Very Quick on the Eye Brisbane 1981* (early demo material, Man Made, 1985), *Metal and Shells* (compilation, PVC UK import only, 1985), *Liberty Belle and the Black Diamond Express* (True Tone/PolyGram, 1986), *Tallulah* (True Tone/PolyGram, 1987), *16 Lovers Lane* (Mushroom/Festival, 1988), *The Go-Betweens: 1978–1990* (Beggars Banquet, 1990).

Further reading: *The Go-Betweens* by David Nichols (Allen & Unwin, 1997).

Goanna

Formed: *1977*
Style: *Rock, folk*
Original line-up: **Shane Howard** *(vocals, guitar), Mike Biscan (guitar), Richard Griffiths (bass), Rod Hoe (drums)*

Goanna first rose to national prominence in 1982 with the release of the hit single 'Solid Rock' and the confident album *Spirit of Place*. The band toured constantly and issued a second album in 1985, *Oceania*. The group had actually come together in Geelong, Victoria, six years prior to the release of 'Solid Rock'. Although the line-up was constantly shifting, the group essentially evolved around ex-folkie **Shane Howard**.

Singer/songwriter/guitarist Howard formed The Goanna Band in late 1977. An important member, Rose Bygrave (keyboards, vocals), joined in 1979, after which the line-up became Howard, Bygrave, Warwick Harwood (lead guitar, vocals), Ian Morrison (vocals, harmonica), Carl Smith (bass) and Gary Crothall (drums, ex-**Redhouse Roll Band**). That line-up of The Goanna Band recorded the independent **Broderick Smith**-produced four-track

12-inch EP 'Livin' on the Razor's Edge' (issued on the EMI Custom Press label).

In 1981, Goanna signed to WEA and scored the support slot to James Taylor's Australian tour. Goanna issued the anthemic 'Solid Rock'/'Four Weeks Gone' in October 1982. 'Solid Rock' was a damning indictment of the European invasion of Australia. WEA was reluctant to issue it as the first single, and indeed the band felt it had little commercial appeal. Howard insisted on its release to make a statement, the public caught on and it reached #3 on the national charts. Much later Goanna contributed 'Solid Rock' to the Various Artists album *Building Bridges* on CBS (1989).

In December, the album *Spirit of Place* (produced by **Trevor Lucas**) entered the Melbourne charts at #1 first week in, as well as reaching #3 on the national charts. The second single, 'Razor's Edge'/'On the Platform', reached #30 in April 1983. The Goanna line-up on *Spirit of Place* was Howard, Bygrave, Harwood, Marcia Howard (backing vocals), Graham Davidge (lead guitar; ex-**Little River Band**, Stephen Foster Band), Mick 'The Reverend' O'Connor (Hammond organ; ex-**Broderick Smith's** Big Combo), Peter 'Brolga' Coughlan (bass) and Robert Ross (drums), with Billy Inda contributing on didgeridoo. In the meantime, Harwood had left the band, and Suzie Dickinson joined as backing vocalist. In May 1983, Goanna issued the single 'Let the Franklin Flow' under the pseudonym of Gordon Franklin and the Wilderness Ensemble. The single was in support of the Tasmanian Wilderness Society's campaign against the proposed damming of Tasmania's Franklin River. The single reached #12 on the national charts. By late 1983, journeyman guitarists **Ross Hannaford** and Russell Smith (ex-**Billy** T) had replaced Davidge and O'Connor, while Geoff Bridgeford (ex-**Groove**, **Bee Gees**) took over from Robert Ross. Bart Willoughby (ex-**No Fixed Address**) also joined on percussion and didgeridoo.

Goanna's third single was 'That Day (is Coming Sooner)'/'Comes the Rain' (October 1983). The album *Oceania* (April 1985) produced the singles 'Common Ground'/'Oceania' (December 1984), 'Dangerous Dancing'/'Shadow of Your Love' (May 1985) and 'Song for Africa'/'Zanzibar' (September). The line-up for that album was Shane Howard, Marcia Howard, Bygrave, Brolga, Hannaford, Bridgeford, Brian Holloway (guitar; ex-Somebody's Image, Esperanto) and ex-Little Feat member Billy Payne (who also produced the album) on keyboards. Mal Logan (keyboards; ex-**Healing Force**, **Renée Geyer** Band) appeared on one track and toured with the band upon the album's release.

Oceania managed a relatively disappointing #20 on the national chart during May. The final two Goanna touring line-ups were a): Shane, Marcia, Bygrave, Simon Curphy (lead guitar), Spiro Phillipas (bass) and Derek Pellici (drums; ex-**Little River Band**); and b): Shane, Marcia, Bygrave, Curphy, Joe Imbrol (bass), Dave Stewart (drums; ex-**Daniel**) and **Coloured Stone** member Bart Willoughby who was a guest on didgeridoo and percussion.

In September 1985, while Goanna was still on tour promoting *Oceania*, Shane Howard was reported missing. The band had to cancel $20 000 worth of bookings. It was believed that Howard became disillusioned with the marathon touring schedules the band undertook in order to pay off debts caused by high overheads, to say nothing of the band's unstable line-up. It transpired that Howard had travelled to South Australia with Willoughby. His departure naturally signalled the end of Goanna. He went on to pursue a solo career. Rose Bygrave issued a solo single, 'Maybe Midnight'/'Protection' (June 1989). She commenced work on a solo album but nothing eventuated.

Albums: *Spirit of Place* (WEA, 1982), *Oceania* (WEA, 1985).

God

Formed: *1986*
Style: *Punk rock*
Original line-up: *Tim Hemensley (bass, drums, vocals), Joel Silbersher (guitar, vocals), Sean Greenway (guitar, vocals), Matthew Whittle (bass, drums, vocals)*

The members of God were all still in their mid-teens when they got together in 1986. Tim Hemensley (aka Meatcleaver Boy) had played in various Melbourne punk bands since the age of ten. One band, Royal Flush, had two tracks ('Christian Bullshit' and 'Coppers Around the Corner') included on the Melbourne punk compilation *Eat Your Head* (1984). In the 1990s, Royal Flush guitarist Roman Tucker formed punk rock pranksters The Martians with David Archdall (bass) and Daniel Dempster (drums).

Matthew Whittle (aka Matty Mustang) and Sean Greenway (aka Sean Scorpion) formed their first band, Foot and Mouth, in 1984. The band issued a mini-album, *The Prophecy of Fossos*, on the No Penis No God label (1986). Joel Silbersher (aka Joel Rock'n'Roll) had been a DJ on community radio station Triple RRR-FM. God's influences ranged from Kiss, Motorhead, Black Sabbath and The Rolling Stones to The Stooges, The Ramones and The

Dictators. These guys were in love with the whole notion of youth as counter-cultural revolutionary, of rock'n'roll as pure trash. They even called their fan club the 'God Army' in emulation of Kiss.

God came to the attention of Bruce Milne at Au-go-go Records who issued the band's astonishing Hüsker Dü-styled debut single 'My Pal'/'A Man Without a Woman is Like a Nun Without a Jackhammer' in January 1988. Suddenly the members of God had an alternative #1 hit on their hands before they were even old enough to get beer riders at their gigs! 'My Pal' was the third biggest selling alternative single for 1988. **Magic Dirt** later covered 'My Pal' on the *Idiot Box* soundtrack (1997). God issued the mini-album *Rock is Hell* (December 1988) in four different covers, one each designed by the individual band members. The record itself suffered from slop-bucket production values, but was another statement in God's quest for the ultimate 'so bad it's good' trash aesthetic. The album *For Lovers Only* boasted stronger production and songs, but just before it came out in December 1989, God decided to break-up. Hemensley joined **Bored!** before forming **Powder Monkeys**. Whittle formed Patterson's Curse. Greenway played with Butt Ugly and **The Freeloaders**. Silbersher formed **Hoss**.

Albums: *Rock is Hell* (mini-album, Au-go-go, 1988), *For Lovers Only* (Au-go-go, 1989).

Godstar

Formed: *1991*
Style: *Psychedelic pop*
Original line-up: *Nic Dalton (guitar, vocals; ex-***Plunderers***), John Encarnacao (lead guitar; ex-***Flies***), Tom Morgan (bass, vocals), Alison Galloway (drums; ex-Jupiter)*

For Sydney-based musician Nic Dalton, the prospect of working on one project at any given time was unthinkable. He started out with mid-1980s thrash pop three-piece **The Plunderers**, and since that time he has recorded with 23 bands. In 1990, he set up his Half a Cow record label and bookshop in the Sydney inner-city suburb of Glebe. The label became an outlet for the likes of Sneeze, Hippy Dribble, **Sidewinder**, **The Daisygrinders**, **Crow**, **Smudge**, **Swirl** and many others.

In January 1991 he formed the first version of Godstar with Tom Morgan, Alison Galloway and rock writer John Encarnacao. Morgan and Galloway worked so well together that Dalton suggested they form their own band which became **Smudge**. Dalton derived the Godstar name from Psychic TV's 1986 single 'Godstar', which was about Brian Jones of The Rolling Stones. Dalton's intention for Godstar was to mix uplifting Todd Rundgren/Nazz-styled psychedelic pop with a sombre Velvet Underground flavour. Despite the ever-evolving nature of Godstar's muse, and the diverse range of musicians on hand, Dalton has managed to retain a sense of stylistic continuity over several releases. Dalton included the Godstar track 'It's My Turn' on the Half a Cow 7-inch giveaway compilation single alongside **Smudge** and **Swirl**. Dalton put Godstar on hold when he joined **The Hummingbirds** in 1991 as temporary replacement for Robyn St Clare. In 1992 Dalton reactivated Godstar. The core line-up of the second version of Godstar was Dalton (guitar, vocals), Robyn St Clare (bass, vocals), Tom Morgan (guitar, vocals) and Alison Galloway (drums).

Godstar

At the same time, Dalton received an offer to join Evan Dando's band Lemonheads. Before Dalton jetted off with Lemonheads to tour internationally and record the album *Come on Feel the Lemonheads*, Godstar recorded two CD EPs, 'The Brightest Star' and *Chemcraze* (featuring 'Bad Bad Implications'). The CD EPs were issued in November 1992 and May 1993 respectively. Godstar recorded its debut album, *Sleeper*, in Boston, Massachusetts during two one-week breaks in Lemonheads' hectic schedule (August 1992).

Alongside Morgan and Galloway, helping out on the sessions were Juliana Hatfield Band bass player Bob Weston (deputising for St Clair) and Evan Dando, who played drums on three tracks. Issued in August 1993, *Sleeper* was full of rough-hewn and basic, yet boisterous, psychedelic pop. It gave rise to the CD EP 'Lie Down Forever' (July), which also included previously unreleased material. Godstar toured the Australian east coast during September 1993 with Dando in tow.

Two years later, Dalton issued the second Godstar album, *Coastal* (July 1995), which featured the usual backing musicians and Boston band Fuzzy on several tracks. *Coastal* mixed fiesty pop and psychedelic sound collages with dancefloor grooves. It yielded the CD single 'Pushpin'/'Seeing Stars' (June 1995) and the CD EP 'Table for One' (October). The CD EP 'Love and Death' was a limited edition bonus disc included with early copies of *Coastal*. As well as appearing on CD format, *Coastal* came out as a double vinyl album. The Godstar track 'Ambient Groupie' also appeared on the compilation *Rock'n'Roll is Here to Pay* on the P-76 label through Shock (1995).

Godstar undertook its second Australian tour to promote the release of *Coastal*, but by the end of 1995 Dalton had split the band. He formed a new band called The Kombi Nation (TKN). He also worked with Tom Morgan in Sneeze and, in early 1997, a pseudo-soul band called The Ultimate Vanilla. In October 1996 Dalton issued the final Godstar recordings as *The Godstar Reminder* EP on the Blind label. The last Godstar-related release was the *September* album (April 1997), credited to The Godstar Reminder which featured unreleased Godstar material recorded in September 1993. Godstar also had records issued overseas on several labels, including Taang! (*Sleeper* and the EPs 'Lie Down Forever' and 'Single'), Bus Stop (the 'Four Seventy' EP), Rugger Bugger (the 'Glasgow' EP) and 100 Guitar Mania (the 'Way Out Jim' single).

Albums: *Sleeper* (Half a Cow, 1993), *Coastal* (Half a Cow/Mercury, 1995), *September* (as The Godstar Reminder; Half a Cow, 1997).

Gondwanaland Project

Formed: *1982*
Style: *Ambient*
Original line-up: *Charlie McMahon (didgeridoo, vocals), Peter Carolan (synthesiser)*

Gondwanaland was the hypothetical continental landmass of the prehistoric Mesozoic era that included Antartica, South America, Africa, India and Australia. Sydney musician Charlie McMahon formed the band Gondwanaland Project in order to combine his love for the Australian outback and his didgeridoo playing.

McMahon took up the didgeridoo as a teenager and perfected his technique over the years he spent working in Central Australia. Much of McMahon's music was inspired by landscapes, in particular the endless horizons of the desert. To achieve the unique sound McMahon required for his desert tunes, he joined up with synthesiser player Peter Carolan in 1982. Eddie Duquemin (percussion) joined the duo in 1986. Gondwanaland issued a self-financed cassette in 1983 *Didgeridu-Synth*. The Hot label issued Gondwanaland's debut album, *Terra Incognita*, and single, 'Danger'/'Drought', in May 1984. The Powderworks label issued *Let the Dog Out* in 1986, before Gondwanaland signed to WEA for the *Gondwanaland* album. McMahon introduced his vocals to the overall sound on that album.

Gondwanaland achieved its strongest combination of ambient and avant-garde experimentation on the album *Wildlife*. Tracks like 'Highway' and 'Deja Vu' evoked the vastness and loneliness of Central Australia. The band contributed 'Bullant' to the Various Artists album *Building Bridges* on CBS (1989). Gondwanaland played intermittently, but continued to record appealing music.

Albums: *Terra Incognita* (Hot, 1984), *Let the Dog Out* (Powderworks, 1986), *Gondwanaland* (WEA, 1987), *Wildlife* (WEA, 1989), *Wide Skies* (WEA, 1992), *Big Land* (WEA, 1994).

Trevor Gordon

Style: *Pop*

Television host/singer Trevor Gordon signed to the Leedon label in 1964 and issued the single 'Like the Big Guys Do'/'Going to the Church on Sunday' (May 1964). In late 1964, Gordon teamed up with **The Bee Gees**, who lent their names, voices and songs to his next two singles 'House Without Windows'/'And I'll Be Happy' (January 1965) and 'Little Miss Rhythm'n'Blues'/'Here I Am' (March 1965). Reissue specialists Raven included the tough sounding 'Little Miss Rhythm'n'Blues' on the inaugural *Ugly Things* compilation (1980).

In 1967, Gordon joined The Gathering. The band issued a couple of singles, 'Portobello Road' (1968) and 'Lovely Loretta' (1969), by which stage Gordon had left the country to live in England. There he renewed his friendship with **The Bee Gees**. He formed a vocal duo with Graham Bonnet. As The Marbles, the duo made an immediate impression on the UK charts with **The Bee Gees**-penned singles 'Only One Woman'/'By the Light of a Burning Candle' (#5) and 'The Walls Fell Down' (#28).

The Marbles issued a third single, 'Breaking Up is Hard to Do'/'I Can't See Nobody' and a self-titled album (only issued in Germany and the USA) before breaking up in early 1970. *The Marbles* album was issued in Australia during 1981 as part of PolyGram's budget *Rock Legends* series. Following the break-up, Bonnet went solo ('Warm Ride', Dylan's 'It's All Over Now, Baby Blue') and later joined heavy metal bands Ritchie Blackmore's Rainbow and the Michael Schenker Group as lead vocalist. Gordon issued a solo album, *Alphabet*, in the UK on Polydor circa 1972.

Album: *Alphabet* (Polydor, 1972).

Gotham City

Formed: *1982*
Style: *Rock*
Original line-up: *Rob Tillett (guitar, synthesiser, vocals)*

Although Gotham City did exist as a band for a short time at the end of 1982, the project was essentially a solo effort by Rob Tillett. Tillett had been active on the Adelaide rock scene since the mid-1960s. His first band was Tattered Sole, followed by Brunswick Blues Vision.

Tillett formed psychedelic/cosmic blues rock band Red Angel Panic (RAP) in 1968 when director Doug Anders recruited Tillett to provide the musical backing for his stage play *Rites Underground*. RAP provided the musical backing for Anders' second stage play, *Viet Rock*, in late 1969. The association resulted in RAP's debut single, 'Viet Rock'/'Private Investigator', for the Nationwide label in late 1970. The A-side was a scathing attack on the futility of the Vietnam War, while the flip side was a ballad with a sprawling organ arrangement.

By that stage, the band's line-up comprised Tillett (guitar, vocals), Ron Anderson (vocals), Ken Skinner (organ), Chris Bailey (bass; ex-Tattered Sole), Chris Timms (violin) and Peter McCormack (drums). The band's contemporaries on the early 1970s Adelaide scene included **Fraternity**, Rashamra, Musik Express, Moonshine Jug and String Band, Buffalo Drive and Glassweb. RAP was one of the first outfits of the day to espouse a social and political agenda. The band played the college circuit, as well as the usual round of moratoriums and protest marches.

RAP issued a second single on the Nationwide label, 'Good Old Rock'n'Roll'/'I'm Swinging', in 1971 before calling it quits. Chris Bailey joined **Headband** and later turned up in Oz rock favourites **The Angels** and **GANGgajang**. Meanwhile, Tillett ploughed on with a variety of bands including Sheep in Fog, Johnny Ego and the Allstars, Rock'n'Roll Express and The Gods. Tillett very briefly joined **The Angels** as bass player in 1976 before the band relocated to Sydney. By 1980, Tillett had written enough of his own material to record an entire album. Tillett issued his solo album, *Radioactive*, and its single, 'Don't Call Me'/'Give Me the Part' (October 1982), under the Gotham City banner on his own Boulevard label. Helping out in the studio were Chris Bailey and fellow Angel Buzz Bidstrup (drums), plus English session players Simon Eyre (guitar) and Carlos Morales (guitar).

Radioactive featured mainstream rock and pop, ranging in sound from the Alan Parsons Project to REO Speedwagon, **Icehouse** to **Mondo Rock**. The touring version of Gotham City comprised Tillett, Steve Reinthal (guitar), Matthew Hughes (synthesiser), Trevor McSweeney (bass), Ralph Hooper (sax) and Anthony Smythe (drums). The album was not successful and the band was short-lived. Tillett continued to work with a variety of bands and in 1993 he formed acoustic folk outfit The Meercats with Mick Bradley (vocals, flute), Tony Becze (guitar), Moses Carmen (keyboards) and Taliska Hollow (bass). The Meercats issued a cassette album, *Urban Swamp*, in 1994.

Album: *Radioactive* (Boulevard/EMI, 1982).

Dave Graney 'n' the Coral Snakes

Formed: *1988*
Style: *Country-flavoured R&B*
Original line-up: *Dave Graney (aka The Australian Stallion, The Golden Wolverine, The Housewife's Choice, Son of the Morning Star, The Savage Sportsman, Lord David, The King of Pop; vocals, guitar; ex-*__Moodists__*), Clare Moore (drums; ex-*__Moodists__*), Malcolm Ross (guitar; ex-Orange Juice), Gordy Blair (bass), Louis Vause (keyboards).*

At the 1996 Australian Record Industry Association (ARIA) Awards ceremony, Dave Graney was named Best Australian Male Artist. With characteristic style, Dave's wardrobe for the occasion consisted of a hot pink, crushed velvet suit and a wig that would have made any self-respecting 1970s porno star jealous. By announcing tongue-in-cheek 'the King is dead, long live the King', Graney accepted his rightful place alongside **John Paul Young**, **John Farnham** and **Daryl Braithwaite** in the King of Pop pantheon.

Of course, it had only taken the local music industry 16 years to acknowledge one of the most enigmatic and genuinely talented rock showmen this country has ever known. If paying one's dues is the way to stardom, then Graney's time was well overdue.

Graney started out in The Slunks, a punk band he put together in 1978 with a few friends in his hometown of Mount Gambier, South Australia. He moved to Adelaide and formed Sputniks with Clare Moore (drums), Steve Miller (guitar), Phillip Marks (guitar) and **Liz Dealey** (bass). Graney, Moore and Miller moved to Melbourne as **The Moodists** in 1980. **The Moodists** relocated to London in October 1983, and broke up in 1986. At the end of 1987, Graney and Moore unveiled their new band, Dave Graney with the Coral Snakes. The rest of the band comprised British musicians Louis Vause, Gordy Blair and Malcolm Ross. The Coral Snakes replaced the unsettling thump'n'grind of **The Moodists** with a more refined, lyrical style of rock with a noticeable Gram Parsons flavour.

Graney and his band recorded their debut 12-inch EP, *Dave Graney with the Coral Snakes at His Stone Beach*, with producer Barry Adamson in August 1988. Just as the EP came out in the UK on the Fire label, Graney and Moore had to leave the country at the behest of the Immigration Department. Once settled back in Australia, Graney and Moore formed The White Buffaloes with Rod Hayward (guitar; ex-**Little Murders**), Chris Walsh (bass; ex-**Moodists**) and Conway Savage (from Boy Kings) on keyboards. Martin Lubran (ex-**Hunters & Collectors**) augmented the line-up on pedal steel guitar.

My Life on the Plains (March 1990) revealed Graney's love of romantic, country-flavoured R&B, and included covers of Gram Parson's 'Brass Buttons' and Fred Neil's 'Dolphins' (as covered by Tim Buckley). The album title was derived from the autobiography of Lt. Col. George Custer. Graney also developed his Buffalo Bill Cody persona around that time, replete with waxed goatee and ostrich-skin jacket. By the time the album appeared, Graham Lee (ex-**Triffids**) had replaced Lubran on pedal steel, and Savage had departed to tour with **Nick Cave and the Bad Seeds**. The new line-up recorded the live in the studio mini-album *Codine*, which came out in late 1990.

Graney and Moore returned to the UK in June 1990 with The White Buffaloes to record a second album *I Was the Hunter . . . And I Was the Prey*. The album was held up for over a year due to business problems with the band's English label, Fire. By the time it came out in May 1992, the band had transformed into Dave Graney with the Coral Snakes and had returned to Australia. The new line-up of Graney, Moore, Hayward, Gordy Blair and Robin Casinader (keyboards; ex-**Wreckery**) came together in mid-1991. That line-up recorded the live album *Lure of the Tropics*, issued by the Torn & Frayed label (July 1992). Casinader also issued a solo album in August 1991, *All This will Be Yours*.

Dave Graney

At the end of 1992, Graney scored a publishing deal with PolyGram Publishing, and the Coral Snakes entered the studio with engineer/producer Tony Cohen to record their breakthrough album *Night of the Wolverine*. Helping out were Andrew Picouleau (bass; ex-**Sacred Cowboys**), Amanda Mitchell (backing vocals) and **Tex Perkins** who guested on one track. *Night of the Wolverine* (April 1993) was a certified Australian rock classic. It captured Graney at the peak of his songwriting powers. Tracks like 'You're Just Too Hip Baby', 'Night of the Wolverine', 'I'm Just Havin' One O' Those Lives' and 'Three Dead Passengers' were full of elegant and eccentric detail. The album was issued in the UK during July 1996.

With Gordy Blair back in the bass seat, Dave Graney with the Coral Snakes consolidated their new-found success with the album *You Wanna Be*

There But You Don't Wanna Travel (June 1994) which made its debut at #10 on the national mainstream chart. It included the CD singles 'I'm Gonna Release Your Soul' (April) and 'You Wanna Be Loved' (August). Initial copies of the album came packaged with a limited edition bonus disc, *Unbuttoned*, which featured seven previously unissued tracks.

The Dave Graney 'n' the Coral Snakes' album *The Soft 'n' Sexy Sound* (#15 in July 1995) included the singles 'I'm Not Afraid to Be Heavy' (June), 'Rock'n'Roll is Where I Hide' (August) and 'I'm Gonna Live in My Own Big World' (February 1996). The album also contained one of the sharpest observations on the machinations of rock music in 'Morrison Floor Show'. The limited edition bonus disc that time was titled *Music for Colourful Racing Identities*. 'Rock'n'Roll is Where I Hide' registered #16 on the 1995 Triple J Hottest 100 list. The White Buffaloes/Coral Snakes' albums were remastered and repackaged for CD release in November 1996. The reissued *Soft 'n' Sexy Sound* included a different bonus disc, *Simply the Best 'El Supremo'*. The Coral Snakes first single for 1997 was 'Feelin' Kinda Sporty' (April) from the album *The Devil Drives* (May). The album reached #18 in June, and produced a second CD single, 'A Man on the Make', in September.

Albums: *My Life on the Plains* (with The White Buffaloes; Fire/MDS, 1990), *Codine* (mini-album with The White Buffaloes, Fire/MDS, 1990), *I Was the Hunter . . . And I Was the Prey* (with The White Buffaloes; Fire/MDS, 1992), *Lure of the Tropics* (as Dave Graney with the Coral Snakes, Torn & Frayed/Shock, 1992), *Night of the Wolverine* (as Dave Graney with the Coral Snakes, Id/Mercury, 1993), *You Wanna Be There But You Don't Wanna Travel* (as Dave Graney with the Coral Snakes, Id/Mercury, 1994), *The Soft 'n' Sexy Sound* (as Dave Graney 'n' the Coral Snakes, Id/Mercury, 1995; repackaged in 1996 with bonus disc *Simply the Best 'El Supremo'*), *The Devil Drives* (as Dave Graney 'n' the Coral Snakes, Id/Mercury, 1997).

Gravity Pirates

Formed: *1983*
Style: *Gothic rock*
Original line-up: *Steven Hinds (guitar, vocals), Paul Hindes (keyboards), Mark Sillis (bass), Keith Boots (drums)*

This Sydney band had much in common with other outfits of the day such as Madroom and **Box of Fish**. **Lobby Loyde** produced the band's debut 12-inch EP, *This Way to the Cargo Cult* (1983), which boasted Killing Joke/Joy Division-styled Gothic rock. Sharon Von Tromp (vocals) joined in 1986. Pierre Della-Putta replaced Boots and Alistair Stevenson replaced Sillis. *New Age Dreams* featured a less cluttered, more textured and melodic approach (somewhere between Japan and This Mortal Coil). It included a cover of The Velvet Underground's 'Femme Fatale'.

Album: *New Age Dreams* (Survival, 1987).

Billy Green

Style: *Rock, jazz*

Journeyman guitarist Billy Green was one of the most inventive and distinctive players on the local scene during the 1960s and early 1970s. Dutch-born Green (born Wilhelmus Groenwagon) played a key role in bands like The Epics, The Questions, **Doug Parkinson** In Focus, Rush, **King Harvest**, **Gerry and the Joy Band** and **Friends**.

He was noted for writing, and providing the dazzling acid guitar fireworks on outstanding In Focus tracks like 'Then I Run', 'Without You', 'Pour Out All You've Got' and the experimental 'Today (I Feel No Pain)'. Green also played the gorgeous, haunting wah wah guitar lines that graced **King Harvest's** version of Jim Webb's 'Wichita Lineman' (1971). Rush was a would-be blues 'supergroup', and one of the shortest lived 'supergroups' in Australian rock history at that (December 1969 to January 1970). The band comprised Green, Malcolm McGee (vocals; ex-**Wild Cherries**, **Python Lee Jackson**, Virgil Brothers), Steve Yates (keyboards), Duncan McGuire (bass; ex-Questions, **Doug Parkinson** In Focus) and Kevin Murphy (drums; ex-**Wild Cherries**).

Green also played on numerous sessions during the early 1970s. He issued a solo single in 1970 on EMI/Columbia, 'This Must Be the End'/'My Name is Earl'. Alongside tracks from **Hans Poulsen** and **The Seekers'** Bruce Woodley, Green contributed 'Double Stroke', 'Bell's Beach Stomp', 'The Crowd at Bell's', 'Soul Surfing' and 'Speed' to the soundtrack of Tim Burstall's 1970 surfing film *Getting Back to Nothing*. The Fable label issued the *Getting Back to Nothing* soundtrack album in 1971.

In 1974, Green composed and produced the soundtrack to Sandy Harbutt's cult Australian biker film *Stone*. The material ranged from incidental background music and hard rock, to aggressive jazz-fusion (in the vein of Al Di Meola) and beyond. Helping out in the studio were Peter Jones (piano), Barry Sullivan (bass), Graham Morgan (drums) and

Andy Cowan (keyboards). Green's former partner **Doug Parkinson** also sang on two tracks, 'Cosmic Flash' and 'Do Not Go Gentle' (with lyrics derived from the Dylan Thomas poem *Do Not Go Gentle in that Good Night*), a song which In Focus also performed. In 1976, Green travelled to Los Angeles, where he worked as a session player. He later moved to Texas, where he formed a blues power trio, Greenstreet, and a free-form jazz outfit, Aquaviva.

Album: *Stone* (soundtrack, WEA, 1974).

James Griffin and the Subterraneans

Formed: *1984*
Style: *Rock, country*

Singer/songwriter James Griffin has expressed himself as a musician, playwright, poet and painter. In 1979, he issued the self-financed four-track *James Griffin* EP which combined uptempo satirical numbers with wistful country ballads. A year later, Griffin formed The Agents with Lindy Allen (bass), James McIntyre (keyboards) and Robin Walsh (drums).

The original Agents line-up recorded the independent single 'Suburbs of the Heart'/'Night People', 'Behind the Noise'. A second line-up of Griffin, Kydric Shaw (guitar, keyboards), Karl May (bass) and Gye Bennets (drums) issued 'Merciless Cinema'/'Manhattan Project' in 1981. Further line-up shuffles ensued, with James McIntyre returning, Kim Knight replacing May on bass and Dennis Flannery replacing Bennets on drums. The Agents issued the mini-album *No Adjustments to the Face* and a third single, 'Seven Samurai'/'Pictures of You and Me', in 1983 before Griffin took the band off the road in order to form James Griffin and the Subterraneans. Griffin issued his second solo EP, *Panic*, in December 1984.

The idea behind The Subterraneans was to have a floating line-up, with Griffin inviting musicians who had no touring or recording commitments with their own bands to join at any given time. Musicians who passed through the band's ranks during the first year included Rick Grossman (bass; **Divinyls**), Tim Brosnan (guitar; **Paul Kelly** and the Dots, **Runners**), Louise Elliot (sax; **Laughing Clowns**), Andrew Thompson (sax), Dorland Bray (drums; **Do Ré Mi**), Michael Barclay (drums; **Zimmermen**), Jeremy Cook (drums), Eddy Duquemin (drums) and Neville Dowling (keyboards; **Expression**).

The line-up for the mini-album *The Immigrant Tango* and singles 'Angel Run'/'My Heart for You' (November 1985) and 'Surf City'/'Blood of the Poet' (July 1986) included Griffin (vocals, guitar), Peter Crosbie (keyboards; ex-**Dugites**), Peter Coutanche (guitar; ex-Kamikaze Kids, **X**), Peter Kaldor (bass, sax), **Steve Kilbey** (bass on three tracks), Marty Willson-Piper (guitar on one track; from **The Church**) and John Lloyd (drums; from **Icehouse**).

The basic line-up for *A Cure for Snakebite* (October 1986) was Griffin, Coutanche, Kaldor, Lloyd and Crosbie, plus contributions from Chris 'Klondike' Masuak (guitar; from **The Screaming Tribesmen**), Paul Noonan (bass; ex-**Dugites**), Richard Burgman (guitar; from **The Saints**), Michel Rose (pedal steel), Alistair Jones (piano accordion) and backing vocalists Tracey Callander, Toni Allaylis, **Peter Blakeley** and **Deborah Conway**. The album yielded the singles 'No Surrender'/'Bridge Like the Wind' (October 1986) and 'The Road to the Rodeo'/'Bridge Like the Wind' (March 1987). Griffin issued the solo single 'Suburb of the Heart'/'Posterity' in October 1987.

For the album *True Love and the Many Meanings of Invisibility* (December 1987), Griffin used the truncated line-up of Coutanche (guitar, bass) and Ian Nelson (drums). The album encompassed folk, pop and country elements. *Land of a Thousand Dances* (subtitled *A Rock'n'Roll Novel*) was a double, spoken-word album based on a novel Griffin wrote. The album also featured four songs from Griffin's previous records 'The Wild Years', 'The Blood of the Poet', 'The Land of a Thousand Dances' and 'Mary and the Kid Leave Home'. In 1991, Griffin was working with a band called The Shadow Gang, which comprised Roger Hart (guitar, vocals), Rowan McKinnon (bass) and Peter Harrison (drums).

At the end of 1992, Griffin produced and assembled the Various Artists album *Moon Over Melbourne* as part of ABC Melbourne Radio's celebration of that city's diverse folk, rock and jazz heritage. Featured singers included **Vika and Linda Bull** (**Paul Kelly's** 'Melbourne Girls'), **Stephen Cummings** (Kelly's 'From St Kilda to King's Cross'), **Paul Kelly** (**Archie Roach's** 'Charcoal Lane'), Jane Clifton (**Skyhooks'** 'Carlton'), Bernadette Robinson (Griffin's 'Moon Over Melbourne'), **James Reyne** ('My Day at the Beach') and **Greg Champion** ('Never Turn Right at Burke Road, Malvern').

Albums: *The Immigrant Tango* (mini-album, Chase, 1985), *A Cure for Snakebite* (Chase, 1986), *True Love and the Many Meanings of Invisibility* (Chase, 1987), *Land of a Thousand Dances (A Rock'n'Roll Novel)* (Chase, 1987).

Grinspoon

Formed: *1995*
Style: *Grunge*
Original line-up: *Phil Jamieson (vocals), Pat Davern (guitar), Joe Hansen (bass), Kris Hopes (drums)*

Lismore (NSW) band Grinspoon shot to national attention (and airplay) in 1995 as the winners of Triple J's inaugural *Unearthed* competition. Not bad for a band that recorded its two-song demo three weeks after formation, and in only three hours! The song that won the competition for the band, 'Sickfest', was the first the members had ever written together. 'Sickfest' logged the #74 placing on the 1995 Triple J Hottest 100 list.

In the wake of that success, Grinspoon toured with **Frenzal Rhomb**, **Def** FX and **The Screaming Jets** and opened the inaugural Homebake Festival at Byron Bay in January 1996. Grinspoon recorded the self-financed five-track CD EP *Licker Bottle Cozy* in July 1996. The band then signed to MCA's Australian subsidiary label Grudge (the second signing after **Def** FX), which issued the CD EP in December 1996. The lead track, 'Post Enebriated Anxiety' was a good example of the band's grinding, de-tuned yet polished sound (imagine Helmet crossed with Bush). Grinspoon's debut album, *Guide to Better Living*, appeared in September 1997, preceded by the CD singles 'Pedestrian' (July) and 'DC x 3 (Dead Cat 3 Times)' (August). The album made #12 nationally in October, and produced a third CD single, 'Repeat', in October.

Album: *Guide to Better Living* (Grudge/Universal/MCA, 1997).

Grinspoon

Grong Grong

Formed: *1982*
Style: *Swamp rock*
Original line-up: *Michael Farkas (vocals, sax, synth), Charlie Tolnay (guitar), Dave Taskas (bass; ex-Blood Sport), George Klestinis (drums; ex-Perdition)*

This Adelaide-based crew were the original post-punk, grunge noise terrorists. Grong Grong's brand of psychotic, swamp rock was akin to a Mac truck driving slowly through a china shop while The Cramps' 'I Ain't Nothing But a Gorehound' blasted out over a nearby PA system! Grong Grong operated in much the same fashion as like-minded Adelaide bands such as **Bloodloss**, **Fear and Loathing** and Primevils. The band took its name from the New South Wales township of Grong Grong, which provided little clue as to the *modus operandi* at work. Grong Grong supported Californian hardcore band the Dead Kennedys when they toured Australia in 1983.

Grong Grong fell apart at the end of 1984 when Farkas was hospitalised following a drug overdose that led to him enduring a six-month coma. Tolnay and Klestinis joined **King Snake Roost**. Tolnay was later a member of **Lubricated Goat** and American band Tumor Circus. Sydney-based independent label Aberrant issued a posthumous Grong Grong album (June 1986), which featured one side of studio demos and one side of live cuts (including a cover of The Meteors' 'Hills Have Eyes'). Dead Kennedys' lead singer Jello Biafra also issued the *Grong Grong* album on his Alternative Tentacles label in the USA.

Farkas eventually recovered and went on to join Hack, which comprised Harry Butler (guitar, vocals, bass; ex-**Fear and Loathing**), Nathan Dale (guitar, vocals, bass), Lynda Staunton (bass, viola, clarinet) and Peter Birkill (drums). The band formed with the express purpose of playing original, intense, slow grunge music in the vein of John Murphy's Slub and New York noise makers The Swans.

By the time Hack issued its debut album, *The Rotten World Around Us*, in 1991, Dave Williams (ex-Perdition, **Fear and Loathing**) had replaced Birkill (who died in 1995), Staunton had left and Chris Wiley (guitar, keyboards; ex-**Fear and Loathing**, **Bloodloss**) had joined. Williams had previously replaced Klestinis in hardcore outfit Perdition. With Williams as drummer, that band issued the 7-inch EP *Intoxicated* (1984) and the album *How to Teach Your Budgie to Talk* (1985) on Melbourne-based hardcore label Reactor. Hack broke up in 1993 after recording a second album which remains unreleased. Butler is editor of long-running Adelaide fanzine *D.N.A.*, and has also played in Void, Human Crash, Raw Power and Grog.

Grong Grong album: *Grong Grong* (Aberrant, 1986); ***Hack album:*** *The Rotten World Around Us* (Seaside/Waterfront, 1991).

The Groop

Formed: *1964*
Style: *Pop to R&B*
Original line-up: *Peter McKeddie (vocals), Peter Bruce (guitar), Max Ross (bass), Richard Wright (drums)*

The history of Melbourne band The Groop is divided into two distinct periods. The original line-up issued several novelty-type singles, while the second, more successful line-up boasted a stronger R&B style. The original version of The Groop, however, was also an accomplished live band. McKeddie, Ross and Wright had worked together in the short-lived folk group The Wesley Trio, before forming The Groop in 1964. They recruited English-born Peter Bruce (guitar). The band's early publicity boasted that Bruce had been a member of the (then popular) Dave Clark Five in the UK. Bruce had indeed played with Dave Clark, but it was with one of his pre-Dave Clark Five skiffle groups.

The Groop became popular at debutante balls and society functions. CBS signed the band and issued the novelty singles 'Ol' Hound Dog'/'Cry Cry Baby' (September 1965), 'Best in Africa'/'Gloria' (January 1966) and 'I'm Satisfied'/'Bad Times' (May 1966), all of which made the Melbourne Top 20. The Groop also recorded two albums before McKeddie and Bruce left in August 1966. The last single from the original line-up was 'Empty Words'/'The Gun and Flowerpot Trick' (October 1966).

By that time the revised Groop line-up was in operation. Ross and Wright had recruited **Ronnie Charles** (vocals; ex-Jackson Kings), Brian Caine (aka **Brian Cadd**, keyboards; ex-Jackson Kings) and Don Mudie (guitar), and the band moved in a more adventurous R&B direction. The new line-up's first single included covers of Solomon Burke's 'Sorry' and Bo Diddley's 'Who Do You Love?', but it was to be the band's next single, 'Woman You're Breaking Me'/'Mad Over You', which became an Australian 1960s classic.

'Woman You're Breaking Me' reached #6 in Melbourne and #12 in Sydney during July 1967. At the same time, The Groop took out first prize in the 1967 Hoadley's National Battle of the Sounds. The prize was return tickets to the UK on a Sitmar cruise. Before the Groop left for the UK in January 1968, CBS issued the singles 'Seems More Important'/'Annabelle Lee' (November 1967) and 'Lovin' Tree'/'Night Life' (January 1968), plus the album *Woman You're Breaking Me.*

In the UK, The Groop gigged regularly, but made little headway. Paul Jones (from Manfred Mann) did issue the Caine/Ross-penned 'When I was Six Years Old' (also covered in Australia by **Ronnie Burns**) as a single, although it failed to chart. CBS UK issued two Groop singles during 1968, 'Woman You're Breaking Me'/'Mad Over You' and 'Lovin' Tree'/'Night Life'. While in the UK, The Groop recorded two tracks, supposedly for release in Germany only, but which were never issued: 'Mandrake Wine' and 'Maid of Iron'. CBS did issue 'Lovin' Tree'/'Night Life' in Germany, where it became a minor hit. The Groop toured there in July to some acclaim.

Meanwhile, Max Ross had fallen ill and left the band. Mudie moved to bass, and the band returned to Australia in October 1968 as a four-piece. The new line-up issued the singles 'Such a Lovely Way'/'We Can Talk' (Melbourne #13 in February 1969) and 'You Gotta Live Love'/'Sally's Mine' (June 1969), both of which bore the influence of English bands like Traffic and The Beatles. The Groop had actually broken up in May 1969, and 'You Gotta Live Love' was not a hit. The actual last track The Groop ever recorded was not even credited to the band. It was The Groop that provided the instrumental backing to **Russell Morris**'s psychedelic pop classic 'The Real Thing'.

With the break-up of The Groop, Cadd and Mudie formed a songwriting partnership. Under the influence of The Band's landmark *Music from Big Pink* album, the pair set about forming **Axiom. Brian Cadd** later pursued a successful solo career. Charles and Wright formed Captain Australia and the Honky Tonk, after which Charles returned to the UK and formed hard rock band Atlas. In early 1989, The Groop re-formed for a tour. The line-up comprised Peter McKeddie, Peter Bruce and Richard Wright from the original line-up, Ronnie Charles and Don Mudie from the second version, plus ring-ins Rob Glover (bass; ex-**Sports**) and Tweed Harris (keyboards; ex-**Groove**).

Albums: *The Groop* (CBS, 1965), *I'm Satisfied*

(CBS, 1966), *Woman You're Breaking Me* (CBS, 1967), *Great Hits from the Groop* (Music for Pleasure, 1968).

The Groove

Formed: *1967*
Style: *Pop, soul*
Original line-up: *Peter Williams (vocals, guitar; ex-*Max Merritt and the Meteors*), Rod Stone (guitar; ex-Librettos,* Normie Rowe *and the Playboys), Tweed Harris (keyboards; ex-Clefs), Jamie Byrne (bass; ex-Running Jumping Standing Still, Black Pearls), Geoff Bridgeford (drums; ex-*Steve & the Board*)*

Like The Groop, The Groove was one of the most respected local bands of the late 1960s. The Twilights' manager, Garry Spry, formed the band in May 1967 with the intention of creating the most accomplished group of its day. As well as having led Adelaide 1960s institution The Clefs, Tweed Harris was an assistant musical director at Channel Seven and one of EMI's house producers.

EMI/Columbia signed The Groove, and the band had immediate success with covers of The Isley Brothers' 'Simon Says'/'With This Ring' (Sydney #6, Melbourne #17 in October 1967) and Sam Cooke's 'Soothe Me'/'I See a New Day' (Sydney #8, Melbourne #14 in March 1968). The band's third single, 'What is Soul?'/'Goin' Back', reached #36 in August 1968. One month previously, The Groove won first prize in that year's Hoadley's National Battle of the Sounds. The band's last single for 1968 was 'You are the One I Love'/'Merry Go Round' (October).

The band made use of its Battle of the Sounds prize of boat tickets to the UK in March 1969, just as 'Relax Me'/'Dance to the Music' reached the national Top 40. While in the UK, the band recorded its sixth single, 'The Wind'/'Play the Song', which came out on Columbia in Australia (June) and Parlophone in the UK. It was not successful in either territory. The Groove made little headway in the UK and broke up. The band re-formed as Eureka Stockade and issued the single 'Sing No Love Songs'/'Jump Down and Turn Around' on Decca in 1970. Following that, Harris returned to Australia to resume his production work. Bridgeford replaced Colin Petersen in The Bee Gees, and played on the albums *Trafalgar* (1971) and *To Whom It May Concern* (1972). He returned to Australia in the late 1970s and went on to play with Goanna and the Mark Gillespie Band.

Album: *The Groove* (EMI/Columbia, 1968).

Grooveyard

Formed: *1982*
Style: *Pop*
Original line-up: *John Schofield (guitar, vocals), Geoff Rhoe (vocals, guitar; ex-Minuteman), Ian Little (aka 'Rev' Ian Paisley; guitar, vocals), Robert Hood (aka Bob Wackley, bass; ex-Razar, Buddies), Sean Maguire (drums; ex-Coupe De Ville, Minuteman)*

Sydney band Grooveyard was one of that city's early exponents of jangly, 1960s-inspired paisley pop. The members had come from a variety of different backgrounds. Bob Wackley had been a member of notorious Brisbane punk band Razar, which also comprised Marty Burke (vocals), Steve Mee (guitar) and Greg Wackley (drums). Razar issued two collectable punk artefacts, the 'Task Force (Undercover Cops)'/'Stamp Out Disco' single and the *Razar* EP before imploding in 1980.

Sean Maguire and Geoff Rhoe had been members of Detroit-inspired group Minuteman, which also comprised Doug Lonsdale (vocals), John Needham (guitar) and Clyde Bramley (bass; ex-Hitmen, Other Side, New Christs, Super K). Minuteman issued one single on Needham's Citadel label, 'Voodoo Slaves'/'I Wanna Be Your Minuteman' (September 1982). Steve Lorkin replaced Bramley for gigs. Maguire's previous band, Coupe De Ville, also put out the *Live at the Leichhardt* EP on the Lost label during 1981.

Not long after Grooveyard formed, Rhoe left to pursue an acting career (he had already appeared in the role of Garry in Bruce Beresford's 1981 feature film, *Puberty Blues*). The Hitmen's Chris Masuak produced the band's debut single, 'Avalanche of Love'/'I Told You So', which appeared on the GREEN label in May 1984. By that stage, Richard Lawson (concurrently in The Lime Spiders) had replaced Maguire on drums. The band toured until splitting up in September 1984. Lawson returned to his duties with the Spiders. Hood joined The Screaming Tribesmen and Schofield joined Chinless Elite.

Toward the end of 1985, the Schofield/Little/Hood/Lawson line-up reconvened briefly for a run of gigs around Sydney. They also took the opportunity to record a mini-album, which did not see the light of day until issued on the Waterfront label in 1989. By that stage Schofield was working with Paul Kelly and the Coloured Girls, Little had joined The Bam Balams and Lawson had toured the world with The Lime Spiders. In 1994, Schofield, Little and Maguire, plus Tom Czarnota (bass), Katrina Sandberg (keyboards) and Jacqui Bliss (percussion) formed studio band Deep End and recorded the album, *Hysteria Hits the Ham Wheel.*

Mini-album: *Grooveyard* (Waterfront, 1989).

Norman Gunston

Style: *Satire*

The 'Little Aussie Bleeder' Norman Gunston (played by actor Garry McDonald) was one of the most famous Australian media personalities of the 1970s. The original *Norman Gunston Show* (circa 1975 and 1976) remains a genuinely funny and innovative television variety show. Gunston's hysterical interviews with the likes of Frank Zappa, Paul and Linda McCartney, Sally Struthers (from US sitcom *All in the Family*), Keith Moon (where Moon's response was to pour champagne over Norman's head) and later on Kiss are the stuff of legend.

McDonald was an accomplished character actor; he played Dave Rudd in the ABC-TV comedy series *Snake Gully with Dad and Dave* during 1972. He first developed the Norman Gunston character while a member of the cast of ABC-TV's *The Aunty Jack Show*. Norman's *What's on in Wollongong* segment became a popular part of the show. Norman appeared on the *Aunty Jack Sings Wollongong* album, along with McDonald's other character Kid Eager. In 1975, McDonald starred in his own television variety series *The Norman Gunston Show*.

McDonald was never afraid to make Norman the fall guy, the sap who always managed to send himself up, as well as all those around him. Norman's real talent was in being able to bamboozle and confound his interview subjects. His interviewees were either completely dumbstruck, or caught on and joined in all the fun. Another of Norman's specialities was musical satire. Norman's debut single, 'Salute to ABBA'/'Hors D'Oeuvre', reached #12 on the national charts in December 1976. Norman's debut album, *The Popular Ballad Animal*, also included his reworkings of Tom Jones' 'Delilah', Shirley Bassey's 'I (Who Have Nothing)', Elvis Presley's 'Jailhouse Rock', Billy Joel's 'Piano Man' among others.

Mushroom Records issued Norman's topical 'I Might Be a Punk (But I Love You Baby!)'/'Love Me Tender' in May 1977. The A-side was co-written by **Ross Wilson** and David 'Dr Pepper' Pepperell. *Nylon Degrees* featured live performances from Norman's tours over the previous year when he was backed by The Gunstonettes and The Norman Tabernacle Choir (i.e. **Cheetah**). A cover of **Sherbet's** 'Howzat' was issued as a single (June 1978). 'Kiss Army'/'Normdrum' was a national #13 hit single during November 1980. Comedy writer Trevor Farrant wrote much of Gunston's material (such as 'Normdrum'), which McDonald delivered with impeccable timing and madcap style.

McDonald then 'retired' the Norman Gunston character to concentrate on his acting career (two of his best roles were in the movie *Ginger Meggs* and as the hapless Arthur in the ABC-TV show *Mother and Son*). Norman re-emerged in 1990. His first triumph was performing a version of **INXS**'s 'Suicide Blonde' with the Salvation Army Band at a variety extravaganza. Next Norman recorded a send-up of 'Amigos Para Siempre' (the theme song to the 1992 Barcelona Olympic Games) as a duet with Effie (Mary Coustas) from television sitcom *Acropolis Now*. McDonald commenced a new series of *The Norman Gunston Show*, but after only a few episodes he suffered a much publicised nervous breakdown. McDonald finally laid the Norman Gunston character to rest.

Albums: *The Popular Ballad Animal* (Lamington/Electric, 1976), *Nylon Degrees* (Mushroom/Festival, 1978), *Join the Dots* (EMI, 1984).

Guttersnipes

Formed: *1990*
Style: *Punk, pop*
Original line-up: *Andrew Rice (aka Ricey, guitar, vocals), Paul Brockhoff (aka, Brocky, guitar, vocals), Michael McManus (aka Macca, bass), Ian MacKaye (drums)*

Taking their cue from the likes of Hüsker Dü, Lemonheads, Fugazi and other 1980s US guitar bands, Melbourne's Guttersnipes traded in guitar-heavy pop. 'Melodic grunge' was a term often used to describe the band's loud, distorted yet tuneful approach. Mark Hurst (aka Hursty) replaced Ian MacKaye very early on.

Guttersnipes issued their debut single, 'It's Over'/'Tide', 'How Can I?' on the Au-go-go label in 1991. Au-go-go issued the band's debut album, *Blurred*, on 10-inch vinyl as well as CD in July 1992. The CD version included the three tracks from the single as bonus cuts. The band supported international visitors Lemonheads, Fugazi and Nirvana during 1992, as well as sharing stages with fellow Melbourne bands **Spiderbait**, **The Meanies** and The Throwaways. Guttersnipes contributed a track to rooArt's heavy grunge compilation *Crack in the Sun or Fade in the Shade* (November 1992) alongside the likes of **You Am I**, **Nursery Crimes**, **Screamfeeder**, **Massappeal**, **The Meanies**, **Tumbleweed** and

Headache. Guttersnipes were quiet for several years until they issued a self-titled CD EP in April 1996.

Album: Blurred (Au-go-go, 1992).

Gyan

Style: Pop

Sydney-based singer/songwriter Gyan first came to prominence with the release of her self-titled debut album which yielded the hit singles 'Wait'/ 'Love in Question' (#19 in September 1989) and 'It's Alright'/'Don't Touch' (November 1989). Gyan co-wrote 'Wait' with **GANGgajang's** Geoffrey Stapleton and **1927** guitarist Garry Frost. Producer Charles Fisher had signed her to Trafalgar Productions (home to **Radio Birdman** and **1927**), which resulted in a record deal through WEA. *Gyan* peaked at #21 on the national chart in November.

Gyan put together her first touring band which featured some of the musicians who contributed to her album, including Hanuman Das (drums), Mark O'Connor (keyboards), **Jackie Orszaczky** (bass), David Sparks (guitar) and Geoffrey Stapleton (guitar, keyboards). **Tim Gaze** (guitar) also backed Gyan for her solo shows. She was voted Best New Talent at the 1989 Australian Record Industry Association (ARIA) Awards. For her second album, Gyan spent three years writing the material. Again produced by Fisher, *Reddest Red* made less use of the synthesised textures of Gyan's debut. It included the CD singles 'Something's Gotta Give' (August 1992) and 'Visualise' (December). Her touring band in 1992 included Ian Belton (bass; ex-QED), Tony Deveaux (guitar) and Chris Sweeney (drums). In 1995, Gyan travelled to Europe to work and record.

Albums: Gyan (Trafalgar/WEA, 1989), *Reddest Red* (Trafalgar/WEA, 1992).

H

Hack (*see* Grong Grong)

Chris Hall and the Torquays

Formed: *1965*
Style: *R&B, pop*
Line-up: *Chris Hall (real name Chris Higgs, vocals), Bob Jones (rhythm guitar), Billy Taylor (lead guitar), Warren Jaeger (bass), Peter Sutherland (drums)*

Siblings Chris, Ken and Greg Higgs worked as The Hall Brothers before Chris teamed up with crack instrumental outfit The Torquays. Not long after Chris joined the band, his brother Greg replaced Warren Jaeger and Dave Longmore replaced Billy Taylor, who left to join The Vince Maloney Sect. Chris Hall and the Torquays held down a residency at Sydney's famed Star Club, and shared in all the mass hysteria of the day alongside **Billy Thorpe** and the Aztecs, **Ray Brown and the Whispers** and **The Easybeats**. All that eluded Chris Hall and the Torquays was an all-important hit single.

The band only recorded one single for the Spin label, 'Don't Ask Me Why'/'A Little Lovin'' (May 1966). By the end of the year, the band comprised Chris, Greg, Jones, Ray White (organ) and Peter 'Peewee' Sutherland (drums). There were a number of other line-up changes over the years. Chris Hall and the Torquays stayed intact until 1970 by promoting their own dances.

The Handmedowns (*see* The Garden Path)

The Hangovers

Formed: *1987*
Style: *Rock*
Original line-up: *Clifford Palmer (vocals), Russ Johnson (guitar, vocals; ex-***Mississippi**, **Country Radio**, *Sultan Brothers), Ian Nancarrow (bass, harmonica; ex-Others, Bucket), Piet Collins (drums; ex-Blooze Muthas, Others)*

Originally known as Cliff and the Hangovers, this Adelaide band comprised a bunch of seasoned musicians. Ian Nancarrow had led Adelaide R&B legends The Others since the mid-1960s. Over 30 musicians have passed through The Others' ranks. The 1987 line-up comprised Nancarrow, Piet Collins and **Chris Finnen** (guitar). The Others line up of Nancarrow (harmonica, slide guitar, vocals), Brian Cain (lead vocals), Terry Osmond (lead guitar, vocals) and Pete Smith (drums), with guest player Ken Skinner (keyboards), recorded the album *Collector's Item*, which came out on the EMI Custom label in early 1982. Another of Nancarrow's late 1960s bands was the psychedelic outfit The Bucket, which issued the Mick Bower-penned 'I Can't Help Thinking of You' as a single on Festival (March 1969).

Nancarrow and Collins joined forces with Palmer and Johnson in late 1987 as Cliff and the Hangovers. In 1989 Joff Bateman (ex-**Headband**) replaced Collins, who later went on to work with **The Sharp**. The band added Shaun Nancarrow (guitar) and became The Hangovers. The Hangovers issued the single 'I Hate Summer' and the album *You're Not So Bad Yourself* (August 1990). With the demise of The Hangovers in 1991, Nancarrow revived The Others with Palmer, Pete Smith, Shaun Nancarrow and Jeff Gurr (guitar).

Album: *You're Not So Bad Yourself* (The Greasy Record Company/Festival, 1990).

Ross Hannaford

Style: *R&B, reggae, funk*

Journeyman guitarist Ross Hannaford (b. 1950) is one of the unsung giants of the Australian music industry. The genuinely media shy Hannaford has rarely been in the spotlight, but he has made an indelible mark on the music scene. As well as being a member of many well-known bands, Hannaford has played on countless sessions for artists as diverse as **Mark Gillespie**, **Steve Hoy**, **Joe Geia**, **Shane Howard**, **John Farnham** and **Tina Arena**. Hannaford is a natural musician with the ability to combine R&B, soul, funk, reggae and rock into an homogeneous whole. His guitar style is both versatile and unique.

Hannaford got his start in the 1960s with schoolboy R&B band **The Pink Finks**. From there he progressed through **The Party Machine**, Quinn, **Sons of the Vegetal Mother**, **Daddy Cool**, **Mighty Kong** and **Billy T**. Quinn issued one single in January 1970, which featured covers of Bob Dylan's 'Mighty Quinn'/'I'll Be Your Baby Tonight'. During the mid-1970s, Hannaford became a devotee of Satguru Maharaj Ji and the Divine Light Mission. In 1977, he travelled to the USA to attend various religious festivals. While in the US, he formed One Foundation with Joe Creighton (bass; ex-**Melissa**, **Billy T**) and Geoff Bridgeford (drums; ex-**Steve & the Board**, **Groove**, **Bee Gees**) to play at Mission conventions. On his return to Australia in 1978, Hannaford formed reggae bands Bambu and Lucky Dog. The original Lucky Dog line-up comprised Margot Barrett (vocals; ex-Small Axe), Martin Kellock (rhythm guitar, vocals), Mike Krelle (keyboards), Wayne Duncan (bass; ex-**Daddy Cool**) and Geoff Hassall (drums; ex-Paul Madigan and the Humans). The band issued one independent single, 'Why Do Fools Fall in Love?'/'Mr Bones', 'Wake Up', in December 1980.

As the perennial 'gun-for-hire' throughout the 1980s, Hannaford played with everyone from the **Mark Gillespie** Band, **Gary Young** and the Rocking Emus, **Ross Wilson's** Rockhouse, the **Ian Moss** Band and the **Steve Hoy** Band to **Goanna**, **The Black Sorrows** and Yu-En. His Ross Hannaford Trio circa 1988 comprised Wayne Duncan and John James (J.J.) Hackett (drums; ex-**Mondo Rock**). In 1989, Hannaford assembled roots rockers Dianna Kiss, which has included the likes of Paul Gadsby (bass), Stuart Speed (bass), Peter Jones (drums), Ray Pereria (percussion), Neon Leon (guitar), Jex Saarelaht (piano) and Russell Smith (trombone; ex-**Ram Jam Big Band**) over the years. The band built up a grassroots following on the inner-city Melbourne scene, and issued an independent, self-titled album in October 1994. The band's music ranged from rock and soul to New Orleans funk and reggae.

In 1996, Hannaford was part of revival band Ol' Skydaddys which also comprised Wayne Duncan, Frankie J. Holden (**Ol'55**), Wilbur Wilde (**Ol'55**), Bongo Starkie (**Skyhooks**) and Freddie Strauks (**Skyhooks**). He also issued the *Ross Hannaford Trio* album (September 1996) which featured backing from Howard Cairns (bass) and Nicky Bomba (drums).

Albums: *Dianna Kiss* (Espy Recorders, 1994), *Ross Hannford Trio* (Noah's Ark, 1996).

Hannagan

Formed: *1971*
Style: *Country, folk*
Line-up: *Terry Hannagan (guitar, vocals; ex-Turnstile), Bobbie Turnbull (vocals), Tim Piper (guitar; ex-Chants R&B,* **Chain***), John Capek (piano; ex-***Carson***), Tim Partridge (bass; ex-Clockwork Oringe), Laurie Pryor (drums; ex-***Twilights***, Genesis)*

Hannagan evolved around singer/songwriter Terry Hannagan, who issued his debut single, a cover of Bob Dylan's 'It's All Over Now, Baby Blue'/'Song for Allan', in February 1971. Hannagan's debut album, *Tired from the Trip*, came out on EMI's Harvest label later in the year. The personnel on the album comprised Red McKelvie (guitar; ex-**Flying Circus**, Powderhorn), Paul Wylde (piano), Chris Duffy (fiddle, mandolin), Robbie Bryce (flute), Ian Young (harp), Tim Partridge (bass) and John McInerny (drums).

The album featured a delightful mix of singer/songwriter folk and country rock material, highlighted by McKelvie's nimble-fingered guitar picking. It comprised eight Terry Hannagan original compositions, plus covers of Leonard Cohen's 'Suzanne' and Don Henderson's 'Albion St'. The title track, 'Tired from the Trip', appeared as a single (backed with 'You Took the Best') in August 1971. Prior to recording his solo album, Hannagan had fronted a band called Turnstile that comprised Ian Clyne (keyboards; ex-**Loved Ones**, **Ram Jam Big Band**), Wayne Duncan (bass; ex-Rondells), **Gary Young** (drums; ex-Rondells, **Ram Jam Big Band**) and Terry Villis (guitar; ex-**Ram Jam Big Band**). Hannagan contributed the track 'It'll Be Alright' to the Various Artists *Morning of the Earth* soundtrack album in 1972. He sang backing vocals on **Doug Parkinson's** 1973 album *No Regrets*, but after that he disappeared from view.

Album: *Tired from the Trip* (EMI/Harvest, 1971).

The Happening Thang

Formed: *1988*
Style: *Country pop*
Original line-up: *Andy Travers (guitar, vocals, harmonica; ex-Spitfires, Milky Bar Kids), Rose Pearse (vocals), Cathy Wearne (fiddle, vocals), Jeff Mercer (guitar, mandolin, dobro), David Patterson (bass, vocals), Ricky Cole (drums)*

The Happening Thang combined Hank Williams-style country roots with pop melodies to produce an uplifting, Australian urban and western sound.

Other influences included Gram Parsons, Jimmy Rodgers and early Elvis Presley.

Travers had originally been a drummer in Adelaide roots rockers The Spitfires before switching to guitar with Sydney rockabilly band The Milky Bar Kids. The Spitfires comprised Travers, Ted 'Stickman' Keeley (vocals), Jeff Stephens (guitar, vocals), Greg Ryan (guitar), Rick Gac (bass; ex-**Dagoes**) and Jeff Karutz (sax, harmonica). The band issued one mini-album, *I Was a Teenage Teenager*, and one single, 'Rumble in the Jungle'/'Why Do I Feel I'm Gonna Cry?' (April 1983) on the Rivet label before breaking up. The Milky Bar Kids comprised Travers, John Hilliard (guitar, vocals), Paul Burton (bass) and Patrick Loughney (drums, vocals). The band contributed the tracks Elvis Presley's 'Flaming Star' and 'If You Remember Me' to the compilation album *Regular Rockabilly* (Regular, 1984). Regular also issued the two tracks as a single. Murray Lock replaced Burton, but The Milky Bar Kids broke up in 1986.

Travers formed The Happening Thang with the above line-up. In 1989, the band signed to the Trafalgar label and issued the singles 'I Don't Wanna Go to Work'/'Let's Pretend' (February) and 'Drive Away'/'Saddle Up and Say Goodbye' (July), plus a self-titled album (June). A year later the band issued the 'Losing End' single and *Saddlepop* album (produced by **Hoodoo Gurus'** Dave Faulkner). Also in 1990, the band won New Talent of the Year at the Australasian Country Music Awards.

Albums: *The Happening Thang* (Trafalgar/WEA, 1989), *Saddlepop* (Trafalgar/WEA, 1990).

Happy Hate Me Nots

Formed: *1983*
Style: *Power pop*
Original line-up: *Paul Berwick (guitar, vocals; ex-Cambridge Rapists, Positive Hatred), Tim McKay (guitar), Peter Lennon (bass, vocals; ex-Lepers), Neil Toddie (drums; ex-London Noise, Hilton Bombers, Cambridge Rapists, Positive Hatred)*

Sydney band Happy Hate Me Nots emerged out of the early 1980s Sydney punk scene which also fostered the growth of bands like **The Kelpies**, **Box of Fish**, Suicide Squad, Wrong Kind of Stoneage, World War XXIV and others. Being more attuned to less anarchistic, more melodic musical pursuits, the band quickly moved beyond such confining parameters. Nevertheless, Happy Hate Me Nots contributed two of their earliest recordings, 'The Build Up' and 'When the Chips are Down', to the second Aberrant Records Sydney punk compilation *Not So Humdrum*.

In May 1984, Mark Nicholson replaced Neil Toddie, who joined Itchy Rat. The original Itchy Rat incarnation of Toddie, Dean Driscoll (vocals; ex-What?!!, Anti-Hierarchy), Owie (guitar; ex-What?!!, Anti-Hierarchy) and Ken Archbold (bass; ex-No God No Dog, Climate of Fear) only lasted six months. The band contributed three tracks, 'Jack Junk', 'A Homely Situation' and 'The Sky is Falling', to *Not So Humdrum* (1984). Driscoll and Owie revived Itchy Rat in early 1985 with new guitarist Joe Latty. The new line-up issued the single 'Save the Labels for Tins of Peas'/'One Man's Brains' on the Waterfront label. Itchy Rat issued a second single, 'Train of Death'/'Silent Footsteps', on the Exposure label (November 1986) before splitting for good.

In the meantime, the Waterfront label issued Happy Hate Me Nots' self-titled EP ('Won't Do Any Good') and the single 'You're an Angel'/'What Did They Say?' in 1985. The ringing 'You're an Angel', with its energetic blast of Jam-styled power pop, was one of the year's best independent singles. It was to be almost two years before the band's next records appeared. By that stage, Mick Searson had replaced Nicholson and French-born Christian Houllemare replaced Peter Lennon. The mini-album *Scrap* (May 1987) and single 'Salt, Sour and Brighton'/'Inside' (October) maintained the frantic pace and boundless energy of the band's earliest singles. One of the mini-album's highlights, 'Blue Afternoon', was more inventive and revealed a band capable of moving beyond the garage thrash aesthetic.

Rob Younger produced Happy Hate Me Nots' debut, full-length album *Out* (August 1988). It was a varied and well-rounded set of songs, including the singles 'Don't Move Too Far'/'Livey Up Yourself' (June) and 'Soul Rejection'/'Resistance' (December). A couple of the album's songs featured horn sections that called to mind **The Saints** circa *Eternally Yours*. By that stage, the band had played with just about every other band on the Sydney scene, including **The Eastern Dark**, **The Headstones**, **Asylum**, **The Hummingbirds**, **The Hard-Ons**, etc.

The band was quiet again on the recording front for another two years. The singles 'Something' and 'I Could See It Coming', plus the mini-album *A Place to Live* came out in 1991. The album retained the rough-hewn quality and edginess of previous efforts, but with more control and space evident in the sound. By the end of 1991, however, the band had run its course. Houllemare joined **The New Christs** in January 1992.

Albums: *Scrap* (mini-album, Waterfront, 1987), *Out* (Waterfront, 1988), *A Place to Live* (Waterfront/Festival, 1991).

Hard Candy

Formed: *1991*
Style: *Rock*
Original line-up: *Erika Bach (vocals, guitar), Demetri Vlass (bass)*

Originally known as Ape the Cry, this Melbourne band has issued four albums of hard-edged, challenging rock music. Ape the Cry also issued a self-titled mini-album (1988), an album, *And The* (1989), and a single, 'Push' (1990), on its own Ape label. Other members of Ape the Cry between 1987 and 1991 included Melinda Davies (vocals, who has also sung with Hard Candy), Kevin Aberg (drums), Bryce Buckley (drums) and Terry Bartholomew (drums).

Erika Bach and Demetri Vlass became Hard Candy in November 1991. They derived their new name from a short story by US writer Tennessee Williams. Hard Candy's albums have been issued in European territories such as Germany, France and Greece where the band enjoys a strong cult following. Hard Candy issued three albums in quick succession, *Tattoo* (June 1992), *Amplifier* (May 1993) and *Lick* (July 1994), but then took three years to put out a new album, *Speed Crash Burn* (April 1997). In between, the band issued just one CD single, 'Junior' (March 1996).

Hard Candy has mostly played as a three-piece with drummer Garry Bainbridge, although Reno Lalli (bass) and Melinda Davies (backing vocals) joined for a European tour in 1992. Jodge Wheelahan (guitar) joined in early 1997 to help lift the pressure off Bach. Hard Candy's sound has often been compared with US band Concrete Blonde and English singer P.J. Harvey.

Albums: *Tattoo* (Loud/MDS, 1992), *Amplifier* (Loud/MDS, 1993), *Lick* (Loud/MDS, 1994), *Speed Crash Burn* (MDS, 1997).

The Hard-Ons

Formed: *1982*
Style: *Punk rock, pop*
Line-up: *Peter Black (guitar, vocals), Ray Ahn (bass), Keish De Silva (drums, vocals)*

The Hard-Ons put the noise back into the beat. Call them heavy metal if you want; they have been called worse: smutty schoolboys, racists, gypsies, tramps and thieves. It is possible that The Hard-Ons were the only band to realise rock'n'roll was about having fun, meeting girls and getting beaten up (in that order). Their music was cheap and potent, their appeal selective. Yet never has so much been owed by so many to so few chords.

The Hard-Ons

The Hard-Ons certainly packed a lot into their 12-year existence. The trio met at Punchbowl High School, in Sydney's vast Western suburbs. Peter Black was of Yugoslavian extraction, Ray 'What's Goin" Ahn was from Korea and Keish De Silva was Sri Lankan. As far as they were concerned, being young, from multicultural backgrounds and in love with rock'n'roll were all assets. The band's sound and approach fused punk tempos, hardcore attitude, heavy metal riffs and surf-pop melodies into a seamless ball of energy.

They began playing as The Plebs before settling on the name The Hard-Ons at the end of 1982. That immediately set the tone for their future. Audiences either reacted to their shows with wild enthusiasm, or shocked outrage and sheer anger. Likewise, the band's song lyrics, plus their poster and record cover artwork (mostly drawn by

Ahn), polarised opinions. Were they puerile, racist, sexist, misogynist and every other 'ist' in the English language, or the work of irreverent geniuses? Swimming against the tide was a way of life for The Hard-Ons. Never critics' darlings, The Hard-Ons built up a strong local and international following. The band's records on the Waterfront label sold in unprecedented numbers for an independent act. The Hard-Ons played in every conceivable venue throughout Australia, toured Europe, Japan and America (several times), recorded with American hardcore godfather Henry Rollins, shared stages with The Ramones, Iggy Pop, Faith No More, Nirvana (the list is endless).

The Hard-Ons' recorded output was prodigious. Their earliest records were the 'Surfin' on My Face' EP (ViNil Records, August 1985) and the flexi-disc featuring covers of **The Elois'** 'By My Side' and The Legends' 'I'll Come Again' which was included with Issue #6 of *The Livin' End* fanzine (July 1986). The band contributed three tracks, 'School Days', 'Squat House' and 'Coffs Harbour Blues', to the third Aberrant Sydney punk compilation *Why March When You Can Riot?!* (1985). The singles 'The Girl in the Sweater'/'I Heard Her Call My Name' (July 1986) and 'All Set to Go'/'Ferdi's Song' (April 1987), plus the mini-album *Smell My Finger* (November 1986) on the Waterfront label were full of manic energy, distorted guitar riffs, low-brow humour and melodic power. 'All Set to Go' was the best-selling alternative single for 1987. The compilation album *Hot for Your Love, Baby* (December 1987) had been assembled for overseas release, but there was sufficient demand for Waterfront to issue it locally.

The band kept up the mayhem with the singles 'Suck'n'Swallow'/'Busted' (January 1988) and 'Just Being with You'/'Growing Old' (March 1989), the 12-inch single 'Don't Wanna See You Cry' (June 1989), the gig giveaway EP 'Sick of Being Sick' (July 1989), the 10-inch mini-album *No Cheese* (shared with UK band The Stupids; March 1989), plus the albums *Dickcheese* (April 1988) and *Love is a Battlefield of Wounded Hearts* (June 1989). The Hard-Ons also contributed a cover of '1970' to Au-go-go's Stooges tribute album *Hard to Beat* (1988), and 'Lick It Up' to Waterfront's Kiss tribute album *Hard to Believe* (1990).

In 1990, Waterfront signed a distribution deal with Festival Records which resulted in the album *Yummy!* (December 1990) and the singles 'Where Did She Come from?'/'Get Out of My House' (November) and 'Dull'/'Sri Lanka' (February 1991). During May 1990, The Hard-Ons recorded a collaboration with Henry Rollins, which resulted in the 10-inch single featuring a cover of **AC/DC's** 'Let There Be Rock', backed with The Hard-Ons/Rollins-penned 'Carry Me Down' (July 1991). The first pressing of 2000 copies included a bonus 10-inch record with the Rollins spoken-word track 'I Know You' backed by a cover of Cheech and Chong's 'Earache My Eye'. At the inaugural Big Day Out, held in Sydney in January 1992, Rollins joined the band on stage for four songs.

The Hard-Ons shared the split, double single *Where the Wild Things Are . . .* (March 1992) with **The Celibate Rifles** to commemorate their joint national tour. The Hard-Ons contributed the tracks 'Sorry' and 'Lose It' which had been produced by The Damned's Captain Sensible in London during June 1991. Thee Slayer Hippy (from heavyweight US punk band Poison Idea) mixed the CD single 'She's a Dish' (August 1992) and mini-album *Dateless Dudes' Club* (August), then produced the band's final album, *Too Far Gone* (July 1993). That album contained the CD single 'Crazy Crazy Eyes' (June 1993) and the CD EP 'Test' (January 1994), plus a contribution from Poison Idea's Jerry A on the track 'The Blade'.

In October 1994, The Hard-Ons announced their break-up. The band members explained that, after more than ten years of playing the same songs, they were just not interested in doing so any more. *A Decade of Rock*, a 48-track, double-CD package complete with extensive biography and photobook, chronicled the band's evolution in detail. One disc contained all the singles, the other featured live cuts and rarities. Following the band's final national tour, Peter Black and Ray Ahn formed Nunchuka Superfly while Keish De Silva launched Malibu Stacey. The Hard-Ons re-formed for a round of gigs in late 1997.

To appreciate The Hard-Ons' impact, just consider the following facts: they had 17 consecutive #1 placings on the Australian alternative charts, they sold twice as many records in Australia as **Beasts of Bourbon,** they were mobbed while touring in Japan and they spawned a London tribute band called Suck'n'Swallow!

Albums: *Smell My Finger* (mini-album, Waterfront, 1986), *Hot for Your Love, Baby* (compilation, Waterfront, 1987), *Dickcheese* (Waterfront, 1988), *No Cheese* (mini-album shared with The Stupids; Waterfront, 1988), *Love is a Battlefield of Wounded Hearts* (Waterfront, 1989), *Yummy!* (Waterfront/Festival, 1990), *Dateless Dudes' Club* (mini-album, Waterfront/Festival, 1992), *Too Far Gone* (Waterfront/Festival, 1993), *A Decade of Rock* (includes *Singles* and *Rarities*, Waterfront/Festival, 1994).

Harem Scarem

Formed: *1982*
Style: *Blues rock*
Original line-up: *Christopher Marshall (vocals), Charles Marshall (bass), Philip Wales (guitar)*

Over the course of six years and three albums, Harem Scarem became a veritable institution on the Melbourne inner-city scene. In the early days, Harem Scarem played raucous, swampy blues rock fleshed out by wild Stooges guitar riffs. Frontman Christopher Marshall was capable of taking his dynamic voice from a guttural roar to a breathy whisper, and back to an anguished howl in the space of one phrase. Later on, the band tempered the manic riffs somewhat to arrive at an innovative brand of rock.

By the time Harem Scarem played its first gig in February 1983, Glen Sheldon (guitar) and Clifford Booth (drums) had joined the line-up. The band contributed 'Love Attraction' to Au-go-go Record's Melbourne compilation *Asleep at the Wheel.* 'Dirty' Kurt Lindtner (harmonica) and David Moll (who replaced Phil Wales on guitar) then expanded the line-up, and the band issued the mini-album *Dogman* (March 1985). It contained one of the band's stage favourites, the epic 'Fever Rock', which was also issued as a gig giveaway single, spread over two sides of a 7-inch record.

In February 1985, Peter Jones replaced Booth on drums. In September 1985, the band underwent a complete overhaul: Barry Palmer (lead guitar; ex-Soul Twisters) replaced Moll, **Chris Wilson** (harmonica, sax; ex-Soul Twisters) replaced Lindtner and Charles Marshall and Glen Sheldon swapped instruments. Few alternative bands of the day could ever hope to match that line-up for muscular bravado and sheer instrumental firepower. Harem Scarem issued the classic *Pilgrim's Progress* album (December 1986) and the single 'Hard Rain'/'Sweet Thing' (September) to great critical acclaim. 'Miracle Mile'/'Dead of the Night' from the album followed as a single in June 1987. The band's version of Iggy and the Stooges' 'Open Up and Bleed' from *Pilgrim's Progress* also appeared on Au-go-go's Stooges' tribute album *Hard to Beat* (1988).

By 1988, the band's line-up had changed considerably. **Chris Wilson** left in May 1987 to pursue a solo career. The band began to concentrate on a tough, lean rock'n'roll sound. With the departure of frontman Christopher Marshall in December (to undertake a Masters Degree in Art History), the band's future looked in doubt. Charles Marshall took over lead vocals and assumed leadership of Harem Scarem. Peter Hall (ex-Head Undone) replaced Sheldon on bass in May 1988. By that stage, Barry Palmer was also working concurrently with **Hunters & Collectors**.

Harem Scarem

The stripped-down four-piece line-up issued the album *Lo & Behold* on Citadel Records (December 1988; only the third Melbourne band ever signed to that Sydney-based label). It was another strong release with a more varied approach (rock, blues and soul influences mixed with The Band-like country elements). The album yielded the singles 'Long Time Between Drinks'/'Honeyman' (December 1988) and 'Rub Me the Right Way'/'Peace of Mind' (April 1989).

With the album's release Jex Saarelaht (ex-**Kate Ceberano** Septet) joined Harem Scarem on piano. The band broke up a year later. Charles Marshall formed The Body Electric which comprised Lindsay Brunsdon (guitar; ex-**Ku Klux Frankenstein**, Fire), Matt Heydon (keyboards), Stuart Speed (bass) and Terry Bartholomew (drums). The line-up of Marshall, Warren Ellis (violin), Jim White (drums; both from **Dirty Three**) and Brian Henry Hooper (bass; from **Kim Salmon and the Surrealists** and **Beasts of Bourbon**) issued the debut CD EP *Charles Marshall and the Body Electric* (November 1994) plus the album *I Don't Want It* (1995).

Palmer concentrated on **Hunters & Collectors**, and later formed **deadstar**. Jones became an in-demand gun-for-hire, appearing in **deadstar,** with his most notable assignment being Paul Hester's replacement in **Crowded House**. Christopher Marshall re-emerged in 1997 with the Christopher Marshall Band, which featured **Stephen Cummings** (rhythm guitar, vocals; ex-Sports), Barry Palmer (lead guitar; on loan from **deadstar**), Mark Ferrie (bass; ex-**Models**, **Sacred Cowboys**) and John Watson (drums; ex-**Australian Crawl**). Marshall issued the CD EP 'Kiss Me Ether' in September.

Albums: *Dogman* (mini-album, Au-go-go, 1984), *Pilgrim's Progress* (Au-go-go, 1986), *Lo & Behold* (Citadel, 1988).

Harpoon (*see* The Kryptonics)

Bev Harrell

Style: *Pop*

Alongside **Lynne Randell**, Bev Harrell was one of the most popular female solo singers on the mid-1960s pop scene. She was a regular on television shows like *Bandstand* and *Kommotion*, and issued eight singles on EMI (three for the HMV label and five for the Columbia label).

The singles were: 'What Am I Doing Here with You?'/'You Really Didn't Mean It' (#6 in Sydney, January 1967), 'Come on Over to My Place' (Sydney #31, March), 'You Baby'/'You are the Love of My Life' (June), 'One in a Million'/'Give Me Time' (Sydney #28, February 1968), 'Mon Pere'/'At Times Like These' (July), 'One Way Ticket'/'I am the World' (October), 'Everybody Needs Love'/'My Little One' (April 1969) and 'The Looking Glass'/'Yes I'm Ready' (February 1970). In 1970, she travelled to the UK, where she recorded for the Bell label. Arriving back in Australia during 1972, she signed to RCA and issued three singles, 'It Was Easy'/'The Right Thing to Do' (June 1973), 'Carols by Candlelight'/'You've Got to Save Me' (October) and 'Mon Pere'/'I Believe in Music' (March 1974). Her last single, 'Bring Back Those Memories'/'Sing', was on Polydor. Harrell continued to work on the club circuit.

Albums: *This is Bev* (EMI/HMV, 1967), *I Believe in Music* (RCA, 1974).

Rolf Harris

Style: *All-round entertainment*

All-round entertainer and multi-instrumentalist Rolf Harris (b. 1930) has been charming people around the world for more than 35 years. He is recognised for his natural abilities as a television presenter, folk singer, painter and wobble-board player!

Over a period of ten years, Harris scored six Australian hit singles: 'Tie Me Kangaroo Down, Sport' (Sydney #1, Melbourne #2 in May 1960), 'Six White Boomers' (Sydney #2, Melbourne #29 in December 1960), 'Sun Arise' (Melbourne #30 in April 1961), 'Court of King Caractacus' (Melbourne #13 in June 1964), 'Jake the Peg' (Sydney #5, Melbourne #8 in March 1966) and 'Two Little Boys' (Sydney #1, Melbourne #8 in January 1970). Such was the all-pervasive nature of these songs during the 1960s and early 1970s that baby Australians across the land took them in with their mother's milk. The British appreciated Harris as well, and he enjoyed hit success with 'Tie Me Kangaroo Down, Sport' (#9 in July 1960), 'Sun Arise' (#3 in October 1962), 'Johnny Day' (#44 in February 1963), 'Bluer than Blue' (#30 in April 1969) and 'Two Little Boys' (#1 in November 1969). He even enjoyed a cult following in the USA, as exemplified by Alice Cooper recording a version of 'Sun Arise' for the album *Love It to Death* (1970).

Harris spent many years working in the UK as a performer and television presenter, to the extent that he was not above being satirised on British comedy shows such as *The Goodies*. Harris's greatest success, however, occurred in 1993 when his unlikely cover of Led Zeppelin's 'Stairway to Heaven' became a chart hit in the UK. The single came about after Harris had been approached to sing his arrangement of the song on the ABC-TV show *The Money or the Gun* (1989). Each week, presenter Andrew Denton introduced an artist doing a version of 'Stairway to Heaven' in their own style. Thus **The Whipper Snappers** played it as a harmony drenched power pop song, the Australian Doors Show as a brooding, druggie epic and **Robyne Dunn** as a dramatic torch song. Harris gave the song a semi reggae beat and featured the wobble board prominently. Above all, it was his off-the cuff ad-libs and throwaway sense of fun that made Harris's version interesting.

Vertigo issued the single and it reached #7 on the UK charts (February 1993). Harris became something of a cult figure on the heavy metal scene, appearing at the big rock festivals of the day such as Reading. He issued a new album, *Rolf Rules OK!*, which, as well as 'Stairway to Heaven', also featured his interpretations of the likes of The Rolling Stones' '(I Can't Get No) Satisfaction', Lou Reed's 'Walk on the Wildside', Deep Purple's 'Smoke on the Water', The Troggs' 'Wild Thing' and Jerry Lee Lewis's 'Great Balls of Fire'.

Selected album discography: *All Together Now!* (EMI), *There's a Party on with Rolf Harris* (EMI), *The Party's on Again with Rolf Harris* (EMI), *This is Rolf Harris* (EMI), *The Australian Album* (Festival), *Two Little Boys* (Festival), *Instant Music* (Festival), *Rolf Harris* (Festival), *Rolf Harris Live at the Sydney Opera House* (Festival), *The Boy from Bassendean* (Festival),

Rolf Rules OK! (Phonogram/Mercury, 1993), *The Definitive Rolf Harris* (compilation, EMI, 1994).

Mick Harvey (*see* The Birthday Party, Nick Cave and the Bad Seeds)

Have a Nice Day (HAND)

Formed: *1989*
Style: *Power pop*
Original line-up: *Fiona Lee Maynard (bass, vocals), Glenn Lewis (guitar), Glenn Maynard (drums)*

Fronted by the confident and talented Fiona Lee Maynard, this Melbourne band was essentially a power pop outfit with a metallic edge. The band's influences ranged from Cheap Trick, Kiss and The Ramones to Suzi Quatro and The Buzzcocks. The original line-up lasted about a year before Marc 'Catweazle' Welsh (ex-**Asylum**, Kings Cross) replaced Glenn Lewis on guitar. Within the space of a year, HAND supported overseas visitors like Mudhoney, Concrete Blonde, Faith No More and Suzi Quatro. The band scored an avid fan in Concrete Blonde's Johnette Napolitano, and also signed a record deal with White/Mushroom.

Meanwhile, the band's debut single 'Fill Me Up'/'Jannifer' (August 1990) and self-titled mini-album for the Shock label were full of energetic and passionate pop. Kevin 'Caveman' Shirley (later known for his work with **silverchair** and **Tumbleweed**) produced the band's debut full-length album *Explore* (September 1991). The album mixed melodic power pop ('Comfort and Solitude', 'These are Memories', the single 'Get to Know You') with crunching heavy rock ('Lady of the Lake'). The band toured constantly for most of 1992, as well as issuing the CD EP 'Slipped Away' (March). Fiona travelled to the USA, where she wrote songs with Napolitano.

HAND supported US band Extreme on its Australia tour during April 1993, then issued a new single, 'All of Me', in May. The band's second album, *Handlelight* finally came out in October 1993, preceded by the CD single 'You Understand' (September). Produced by American Mark Dearnley (**Kings of the Sun**, Mother Love Bone, Motorhead, XTC), *Handlelight* featured a mellower sound overall, with ballads like 'Not Crying Anymore' being the most effective tracks. Two months after the album's release, Welsh left HAND to join Jed Starr's Starworld. James Lomas replaced Welsh and the band also added Monique Boggia on keyboards. HAND played its final gigs during March 1994. That effectively paved the way for Fiona to launch her solo career, which commenced with the release of her debut single 'Not Crying Anymore' (August 1994) and album *My Time* (essentially a reworking of *Handlelight*; November).

In late 1994, Welsh was in F.R.O.G.; in 1996 he joined Floor Thirteen as bass player. In 1995, Fiona Lee Maynard formed a new band, In Vivo, with members of Concrete Blonde. In Vivo issued a self-titled album in January 1996 which had been produced by Johnette Napolitano. In Vivo toured Australia in early 1997.

Albums: *Have a Nice Day* (mini-album, Shock, 1990), *Explore* (White/Mushroom/Festival, 1991), *Handlelight* (Mushroom/Festival, 1993). ***Fiona Lee Maynard solo album:*** *My Time* (Mushroom/Festival, 1994); ***In Vivo album:*** *In Vivo* (TWA, 1996).

Colin Hay

Style: *Rock, folk*

Scottish-born singer/songwriter Colin Hay (b. 1953) came to the world's attention as frontman for mega-successful band **Men at Work**. From humble beginnings at the tiny Cricketer's Arms pub in the working-class, inner-city Melbourne suburb of Richmond, to filling stadiums across the USA, **Men at Work** attained a level of success previously uncharted by an Australian band. **Men at Work** scored two international #1 singles with 'Who Can It Be Now?' and 'Down Under', while the band's debut album, *Business as Usual*, sold a staggering ten million copies worldwide.

Following the break-up of **Men at Work** in December 1985, and time spent recording in London, Hay launched his solo career with the rootsy album *Looking for Jack* (March 1987). Hay took an acoustic quartet (including latter-day **Men at Work** bass player Jeremy Alsop) on the road around Australia, but neither the album nor its singles, 'Hold Me'/'Home Sweet Home' (January 1987) and 'Can I Hold You?'/'Nature of the Beast' (May), were chart successes. Once where people had been clamouring to see **Men at Work**, Colin Hay could barely fill a country pub. From international multi-platinum success to solo ignominy was a bitter pill to swallow, but Hay persevered.

In March 1988, he formed the Colin Hay Band with Bryce Philby (guitar), Paul Gadsby (bass; ex-**Paul Kelly** and the Dots, **Broderick Smith** Band), Robert Dillon (drums; ex-**Mike Rudd and the Heaters, Broderick Smith** Band) and Gerry Hale (mandolin, fiddle). The *Wayfaring Sons* album (April 1990) featured a mix of acoustic Celtic folk and rock music, with Hay rediscovering his Scottish roots. It yielded the singles 'Into My Life' (March), 'Wayfaring Sons' (May) and 'Storm in My Heart' (August). Hay spent most of 1991 in Los Angeles, before returning to Melbourne to record his third solo album.

The title *Peaks and Valleys* was not without irony. That time around it was just Hay, his voice, his sister Carol Hay and two acoustic guitars. *Peaks and Valleys* (March 1992) was an evocative collection of earthy folk and pop songs. In September 1993, Hay appeared for a solo stint at the Edinburgh Festival in Scotland. He issued his fourth solo album, *Topanga*, in March 1994. It sold well in Canada, Germany and Brazil. In July, Hay set off on his solo Man at Work Australian tour. Hay spent the next couple of years working in the USA. He turned his talents to acting and scored roles in the Australian films *Cosi* and *Heaven's Burning*. In mid-1996, Hay and his old comrade in **Men at Work**, Greg Ham, took a re-formed version of the band on a sell-out tour of Brazil. Hay returned to Australia in late 1996 to tour.

Albums: *Looking for Jack* (CBS, 1987), *Wayfaring Sons* (as Colin Hay Band; MCA, 1990), *Peaks and Valleys* (East West/Warner, 1992), *Topanga* (East West/Warner, 1994).

Headband

Formed: *1971*
Style: *Progressive rock*
Original line-up: *Mauri Berg (guitar, harmonica, vocals; ex-Silhouettes, Ides of March, Resurrection, W.G. Berg, War Machine), Peter Beagley (keyboards; ex-Johnny Mac and the Macmen, Peter Beagley Trio, Boz), Chris Bailey (bass, vocals; ex-Red Angel Panic), Joff Bateman (drums, vocals; ex-Resurrection, W.G. Berg, War Machine)*

Adelaide progressive/blues rock group Headband comprised a bunch of experienced musicians. Finnish-born Mauri Berg had started out playing Shadows material in The Silhouettes. Peter Beagley was a member of Adelaide's first rock'n'roll band Johnny Mac and the Macmen. During the 1960s, he played jazz and travelled to the UK where he toured with Boz Burrell (later a member of Bad Company). Beagley returned to Australia and played avant-garde jazz before joining Headband.

Headband played everything from blues and jazz to folk and country. The band's debut single for RCA, 'Scratch My Back'/'Musical Man' (1972) featured straight pop, but by the time the band came to record the album *A Song for Tooley*, the sound was more adventurous. Nevertheless the album (issued September 1973) was erratic, with the material ranging from Uriah Heep-styled heavy rock to psychedelic pop and progressive jazz. It yielded three singles, 'Land of Supercars'/'How Much I Miss the Country' (1972), 'Country Lady'/'Stay with Me' (1973) and 'A Song for Tooley'/'Brand New Morning' (1973). In the early 1990s, *A Song for Tooley* became something of a collectable progressive rock artefact.

Headband supported The Rolling Stones in Adelaide during the band's February 1973 Australian tour. Headband broke up in 1974. Berg and Bateman later joined a couple of ex-**Fraternity** members in Mickey Finn. Chris Bailey issued a solo single on RCA, 'Sunday Too Far Away'/'Bushranger Song' (March 1975) before joining pub rockers **The Angels** in January 1977. He later played with the likes of **GANGgajang**, The Stetsons and the **Jimmy Barnes** Band. Peter Beagley began to work under the name of Peter Head. He formed ad hoc country rock outfit The Mount Lofty Rangers, which featured many Adelaide rock luminaries such as Bon Scott.

Head produced the rock musical *Lofty*, and wrote soundtrack music for films like *The Nostradamus Kid* and *Les Patterson Saves the World*. He moved to Sydney and issued a series of cassette albums under his own name and ran his own Head Office Records. Head issued a mini-album in 1997, *King of the Cross*. (Note: this Headband is not to be confused with a New Zealand band from the same period with the same name.)

Album: *A Song for Tooley* (Polydor, 1973)

Header

Formed: *1994*
Style: *Power pop*
Original line-up: *Ian Freeman (vocals; ex-Fallen Angels, Palisades, Mars Bastards), Dave Chadwick (guitar; ex-Rainyard), Brad Bolton (guitar; ex-Rainyard), Liam Coffey (bass, vocals; ex-Rainyard), Dean Willoughby (drums)*

Perth-based band Header was a guitar pop outfit in the enduring British tradition (from The Beatles, The Kinks and The Who to The Faces, The Buzzcocks and The Smiths). English-born singer Ian Freeman had also been influenced by T-Rex and Slade before discovering The Smiths in the early 1980s.

The genesis of the Header sound can actually be found in earlier Perth bands The Palisades and The Rainyard. The Palisades formed in 1985 and comprised Freeman (vocals), Jeff Baker (guitar, vocals; ex-Fallen Angels), Guido Berini (guitar, vocals; ex-Fallen Angels), Velo Zupanovich (bass; ex-Gostarts, Grave Robbers, Fallen Angels) and Richard Nash (drums; ex-Fallen Angels). The band issued the single 'A Month Too Soon'/'Today of All Days' (June 1987) and the mini-album *A Month Too Soon* on the Easter label.

By the end of 1987, the line-up comprised Freeman, Baker and Zupanovich plus new drummer Dave Hale. The 1988 line-up had shifted to include Freeman and Zupanovich, plus newcomers Gil Bradley (guitar) and Duncan McMillan (drums). Mandy Haines replaced Zupanovich (who joined Someloves) in 1989, after which the band broke up. Freeman and Baker then formed studio outfit The Mars Bastards, and began recording with help from the likes of Bradley, Liam Coffey, Cliff Kent (bass), Mark Scarparolo (bass) and Shaun Lohoar (drums; ex-Beekeepers). The Mars Bastards issued the singles 'Ricky Dixon' (1989) and 'This Windy City' (1990) plus the mini-albums *Six* (1990), *Crazy* (1990) and *Roller Coaster* (1990).

The original Rainyard line-up (circa 1989) comprised Coffey (vocals), Brad Bolton (guitar), Jeff Baker (guitar; ex-Palisades), Martin Gamble (guitar), Michael Zampogna (bass) and Adrian McMillan (drums). David Chadwick replaced Baker on guitar in 1990. Rainyard issued two independent singles, 'So Happy Now' (1989) and 'Hellbent Suicidal Over You', plus three mini-albums, *Icecream Overdrive* (1989), *Worth Hating for* (1990) and *Let It Speed* (1993), before calling it a day.

Freeman, Coffey, Chadwick, Bolton and Willoughby formed Header in 1994. The band issued two independent singles, 'Not Proud' and 'Rat', plus the CD EP *Header* (on the Fish Bowl label through MDS) before signing to Mushroom's development label Bark. Bark issued the band's second CD EP, 'Sugafix' (July 1995), which was produced by UK expatriate Chris Dickie (Morrissey, Pogues, Kirsty MacColl). The band's ringing guitar work and well-crafted pop melodies provided a sweet alternative to the prevailing, heavy sound of grunge.

Header relocated to Melbourne and recorded its debut album, *On High St* (again with Dickie). 'Restoration' was lifted as the CD single (April 1996). The album also yielded two CD EPs, 'Crazy Head' (June) and 'Brazen Head' (October). *On High St* (July) was full of tough guitar hooks and bright harmonies in the Britpop tradition. Yet, before the Oasis/Teenage Fanclub rip-off accusations take hold, consider that the Header sound harks back to the kind of music The Palisades and The Rainyard were playing throughout the late 1980s.

Album: *On High St* (Bark/MDS, 1996).

The Headhunters

Formed: *1980*
Style: *R&B*
Original line-up: **Marc Hunter** *(vocals; from* **Dragon***), Mick Cocks (guitar; ex-***Rose Tattoo***),* **Kevin Borich** *(guitar; from* **Kevin Borich Express***), Todd Hunter (bass; from* **Dragon***), John Watson (drums; from* **Kevin Borich Express***)*

Sydney band The Headhunters was essentially an ad hoc aggregation of musicians who were drawn together by a love of playing raucous R&B. The band has not toured constantly, only assembling as the need arose. There have been many different line-ups over the years, with the likes of Mark Evans (guitar, ex-**AC/DC, Heaven**), Dave Tice (vocals; ex-**Buffalo**, Count Bishops), Greg Skehill (drums; ex-Sardine v), Ian Lees (bass; ex-**Moving Pictures**) and Paul DeMarco (drums; ex-Illustrated Men) passing through the band's ranks. Dave Tice sang on the band's 1986 single, 'I Believe in Love'/ 'Buy Me a Ticket'. The 1992 line-up of Tice, DeMarco, Lees, Steve Edmonds (guitar) and Mike Gubb (keyboards) recorded the album *Outlaw Boogie Vol. 1.*

Album: *Outlaw Boogie Vol. 1* (Oz Bike, 1993).

The Headstones

Formed: *1985*
Style: *Hard rock*
Original line-up: *Chris Flynn (guitar, vocals), Anthony Schoenwald (guitar, vocals), Brendan Flynn (bass, vocals), Neil McCarthy (drums)*

The Headstones formed in Brisbane before relocating to Sydney during 1986 where their brand of 1960s inspired, hard-edged guitar pop found much favour on the inner-city circuit. The band signed to the Waterfront label and issued the singles 'When You're Down'/'All the Things You Do' (December 1986) and *Love Songs* ('You Got Love'/'Gimme Love') (August 1987). Following a tour support to UK hard rockers The Cult, Anthony Schoenwald left to be replaced by Brian Mann (ex-**Girlies**).

The 12-inch EP *Lovers' Web* (January 1989) featured a rawer R&B sound (à la The Pretty Things), with guest player Steve Flynn blowing harmonica on two tracks, 'Maharaji Baby' and 'Low Down Dirty Man'. It was The Headstones' final record. The band fell apart at the end of 1988 and Chris Flynn joined **The Dubrovniks**. Mann went on to **The Screaming Tribesmen** and **The Lime Spiders**. Brendan Flynn joined Lovecraft. Lovecraft comprised Flynn, Rusty James (guitar), Tim Dalton (keyboards), Russell Jones (bass) and Ben Doolan (drums). The band issued three CD EPs, 'Love' (1992), 'Live Forever' (1993) and 'Busker Blues' (1995).

The Healers (*see* The Bamboos)

Healing Force

Formed: *1970*
Style: *Progressive rock*
Original line-up: *Lindsay Wells (guitar), Mal Logan (keyboards; ex-Rebels,* **Bakery***), John Pugh (bass, vocals; ex-Roadrunners,* **Eighteenth Century Quartet, Cam-Pact,** *News,* **James Taylor Move** *guitarist), Laurie Pryor (drums; ex-Johnny Broome and the Handels,* **Twilights,** *Genesis)*

In a career spanning a mere 12 months, Healing Force cut just one extraordinary single. Written by Lindsay Wells, the rhapsodic 'Golden Miles' captured the sense of loneliness and sadness of a life spent on the road. Its crisp, rhythmic organ-based sound enveloped a flowing melody line and dramatic chorus. To top it off, Charlie Tumahai's majestic vocal delivery packed an incredible punch. 'Golden Miles' remains one of the best Australian singles of the 1970s.

Healing Force formed in October 1970 with a line-up of Wells, New Zealander Mal Logan, Laurie Pryor and John Pugh. Pugh quit before the band played live. New Zealander Charlie Tumahai (bass, vocals; ex-Multiple Balloon, **Aesop's Fables,** Nova Express) took his place. Alongside the likes of **Billy Thorpe** and the Aztecs, **Chain, King Harvest** and **Spectrum**, the band became a major force on the Melbourne 'head' scene. Following the release of 'Golden Miles'/'The Gully' on the Sparmac label (June 1971), Tumahai, Wells and Pryor all quit one by one to join **Chain.** Tumahai left in July, Wells in August and Pryor in September. Logan re-recruited John Pugh to play guitar, Ray Findlay (bass; ex-**Lost Souls,** Nineteen87) and a young drummer called Joey Tattersalls (who was swiftly replaced by the more experienced Eric Cairns, ex-Somebody's Image, **Heart 'n' Soul, Company Caine**, Captain Australia and the Honky Tonk).

While all these changes were going on, 'Golden Miles' reached #8 in Melbourne and Top 30 nationally (#22). By the end of November 1971, the band had collapsed and Logan joined **Carson**. Meanwhile, Wells and Pryor were playing in **Ray Brown's** One Ton Gypsy and Tumahai had joined fellow New Zealander **Leo De Castro** in Friends. In November 1972, Logan, Pugh and Pryor re-formed Healing Force, with Gus Fenwick (ex-**Pleazers, Band of Talabene**) on bass.

By the beginning of 1973, Tumahai had rejoined on vocals and percussion and the band quickly regained its old following. Healing Force appeared at Sunbury 1973 but by the end of April that year, the band had split for good. The live track 'Erection' appeared on Mushroom Record's triple album set *The Great Australian Rock Festival Sunbury 1973* (April 1973). Logan and Tumahai next teamed up with Tim Piper (guitar; ex-Chants R&B, **Chain,** Genesis, Savage Rose Blues Band, **Blackfeather**) and Tony Lunt (drums; ex-**Carson**) in the short-lived Alta Mira. The band played tight, funky hard rock and blues (in the vein of Harvey Mandel and Johnny Winter), and only existed for six months (May to October 1973).

A punchy live rendition of the Sugarcane Harris/Harvey Mandel song 'My Soul's on Fire' from the Mushroom album *Garrison the Final Blow Unit 1* (1973) was the only recorded document of Alta Mira's existence. When the band broke up, Logan joined **The Dingoes** as a part-time member. He later played with **Chain**, Silver Sun, Sanctuary and the **Renée Geyer** Band, and continues to work as an in-demand session player to this day. Tumahai joined **Mississippi** as bass player in December 1973. That band went to London in 1974 and Tumahai decided to stay.

In the UK he joined famed art-rock outfit Be Bop Deluxe (led by Bill Nelson), with which he remained for several years, playing on the albums *Futurama, Sunburst Finish, Modern Music* and *Live in the Air Age.* During the late 1970s, he formed The Dukes with Jimmy McCulloch (guitar; ex-Thunderclap Newman, Stone the Crows, Wings) and Miller Anderson (vocals, guitar). On his return to New Zealand in the mid-1980s, Tumahai joined his cousin Dilworth Karaka in popular reggae-rock band The Herbs. He remained with The Herbs until his death (from a heart attack) in December 1995.

Heart 'n' Soul

Formed: *1967*
Style: *Pop, jazz-rock*
Original line-up: *Graeme Willington (vocals, percussion), Ian Willington (guitar), Philip Prideaux (trumpet, French horn), Percy Ohrling (sax), Rory Thomas (organ; ex-***Questions***), Leith Corbett (bass), Graham Lewis (drums)*

As Glenn A. Baker wrote, Heart 'n' Soul, like **The Ram Jam Big Band**, began as a white-suited club band, but swiftly gained acceptance in the rock world via superb, innovative musicianship and a genuinely exciting sound. As Australia's first jazz-rock 'big band', Heart 'n' Soul enthralled festival audiences with rock versions of 'The 1812

Overture', 'Brandenburg Concerto', 'Also Sprach Zarathrustra' and 'MacArthur Park'.

Other contemporary Australian bands that mined a similar jazz-rock vein included Nova Express, **Southern Contemporary Rock Assembly (SCRA)** and **Kush**. Heart 'n' Soul issued three jazz-pop singles on Festival: 'Who Could Be Loving You?'/'She's Got the Time' (1968), 'Lazy Life'/ 'Good Things Come to Those Who Wait' (Sydney #17 in May 1969), which were combined on the rare 'Lazy Life' EP, and 'Let Me Sing in Your Band'/ 'Lights of Cincinatti' (1970).

Many noted musicians (over 25 members all up) passed through the band's ranks over the years, including Keith Barr (tenor sax, oboe, piano; ex-Nutwood Rug, Quill), Bobby Gebert (piano), Peter Sheehan (piano, organ), Eric Cairns (drums; ex-Somebody's Image), John Pouche (drums), Lindsay Farr (baritone sax, flute; ex-Carnival), Bernie McCann (alto sax), Allan Blakers (alto sax), Greg Foster (trombone, harmonica), Richard Price (violin, recorder), Larry Taylor (aka Larry Duryea, percussion), Geoff Oakes (sax), Les Gough (bass) and Arthur Eisenberg (bass; ex-Dr Kandy's Third Eye) among others.

Of the original members, Leith Corbett joined the **Dave Miller Set** in 1969. He later collaborated with Dave Miller on the interesting *Reflections of a Pioneer* album and its single, 'Reflections of a Pioneer'/'353527 Charles' (November 1970), which were issued on the Spin label. By the time Heart 'n' Soul came to record the ambitious *Hot Boogie Band* album in late 1970, the band numbered 12 musicians. The strain of supporting such an unwieldy ensemble took its toll, and the album and its single 'Hot Boogie Band'/'Earthrise' (January 1971) were issued posthumously. The album combined uptempo R&B ('Hot Boogie Band'), classical elements ('Earthrise'), percussion-driven rock ('Yeah Go-1-2 Are You Ready?') and pure jazz-rock fusion ('Dance of the Pigs').

***Album:** Hot Boogie Band* (Festival/Infinity, 1971).

Heaven

***Formed:** 1980*
***Style:** Heavy rock*
Original line-up:** Allen Fryer (vocals; ex-Heroes, Fat Lip), Kelly Haese (lead guitar; ex-Swanee***), John Haese (rhythm guitar, ex-Fat Lip), Laurie Marlow (bass; ex-Heroes, Almost Human, Fat Lip), Joe Turtur (drums, ex-Fat Lip)*

At a time when heavy metal/heavy rock was considered passé (the early 1980s), this Sydney (by way of Adelaide) band embraced the genre with a passion and sense of purpose. Managed by former **AC/DC** right-hand man Michael Browning for many years, the ambitious Heaven set its sights on the American rock market almost from the outset. Bands like **AC/DC** and **Rose Tattoo** had already made significant inroads into the international heavy rock touring circuit, and Heaven simply followed suit.

Heaven grew out of Adelaide band Fat Lip. The original Fat Lip line-up comprised Allen Fryer, Felix Maslin (bass; ex-**Cheek**), Steve Francis (guitar) and Aldo Civitcio (drums; ex-**Scandal**). Maslin and Francis left to join Fast Foods, so Fryer and Civitico formed a new line-up with John Haese and Laurie Marlow. Joe Turtur then took over from Civitico on drums. Marlow had previously played in heavy metal band Almost Human, led by singer Damien Kelly. In 1986 Kelly formed a new Almost Human line-up with David Kennedy (guitar), Michael Dryden (guitar), Louis Saez-Sanches (bass) and Howard Kehl (drums). That line-up developed a more textured AOR style. Almost Human issued a single, 'Hold On', which reached #35 in Adelaide and #82 nationally in October 1987. Chris Tucker returned to the band in early 1988 to replace Kehl.

Before Heaven formed, Scottish-born Fryer had been under consideration as a possible replacement for the recently deceased Bon Scott in **AC/DC**. He left Fat Lip and moved to Sydney in early 1980 in order to follow up the interest. By the time he arrived in Sydney, **AC/DC** had offered the job to Englishman Brian Johnson. With the arrival of Haese, Marlow and Turtur in Sydney, and the recruitment of Kelly Haese, Fat Lip became known as Heaven. Heaven issued two singles 'Fantasy'/ 'One Nighter' (December 1981) and 'In the Beginning'/'Storm' (June 1982), plus the album *Twilight of Mischief* on the Deluxe label. Mick Cocks (ex-**Rose Tattoo**) replaced John Haese in May 1982, and Heaven relocated to Los Angeles. In L.A., the band adopted a studded leather'n'chains look straight out of a *Mad Max* movie. Heaven supported Judas Priest, Kiss and Black Sabbath on American tours, and issued the album *Where Angels Fear to Tread* (March 1984) and single 'Rock School'/'Sleeping Dogs' (February). A number of well known heavy metal luminaries such as Glenn Hughes (Deep Purple), Lita Ford and Ronnie James Dio (billed as 'Evil Eyes') contributed backing vocals to the album. *Where Angels Fear to Tread* garnered positive reviews in UK heavy metal magazines such as *Kerrang!*

In the meantime, Cocks and Turtur had been ousted from Heaven in September 1983 to be replaced by former **AC/DC** bass player Mark Evans (guitar; also ex-**Finch**, Beast) and John Lalor (drums; ex-Dallimore, **Swanee**, Beast) respectively. A year later, Scottish-born Fryer was the only remaining original member. In July 1984, he had formed a new Heaven line-up that comprised American Mitch Perry (guitar; ex-Steeler), plus Australians Bruno Renzella (bass; ex-Dukes) and Tommy Dimitroff (drums; ex-Dukes). By the end of the year the band comprised Fryer, Perry and Dimitroff, plus Americans Mark Cunningham (guitar; ex-Rick Derringer Band) and Dennis Feldman (bass; ex-Michael Schenker Group). Heaven continued to tour across the States, issuing a final album, *Knockin' on Heaven's Door*, and single, Bob Dylan's 'Knockin' on Heaven's Door'/'Burn', on RCA before fading from view.

In the end, Heaven could only go so far, its brand of mainstream heavy rock usurped eventually by the more decadent glam-sleaze approach of other Los Angeles bands like Guns N' Roses, Mötley Crüe, Ratt and L.A. Guns. Nevertheless, Heaven should be remembered for its obstinate determination to succeed in a field where very few dared to tread. As a postscript to the Heaven story, during 1986, four ex-members, Mark Evans, Kelly Haese, Laurie Marlow and Joe Turtur, plus singer Rob Hartley (aka **Black Alice**), toured briefly as The Hellcats, playing exclusively Heaven songs! In 1989, Evans, John Haese, Robin Riley (guitar; ex-**Redhouse, Rose Tattoo, Party Boys, Jimmy Barnes** Band), Stuart Cave (vocals; ex-Tough Luxury) and Scott Johnson (drums; ex-**Jimmy and the Boys**, **Rose Tattoo**) teamed up as Mama's Darlings. In 1991, Kelly formed Freight Train with Steve Williamson (vocals; ex-Virgin Soldiers).

Albums: *Twilight of Mischief* (Deluxe/RCA, 1982), *Where Angels Fear to Tread* (Deluxe/RCA, 1984), *Knockin' on Heaven's Door* (RCA, 1985).

The Hekawis

Formed: *1993*
Style: *Garage-surf*
Original line-up: *'Screamin'' Steve Zillman (lead vocals, organ; ex-Bluebirds of Happiness, Steve and the Disciples), Rob 'Kid Regal' Zillman (sax), Brett 'Rotten Eagle' Barton (guitar, vocals; ex-Bluebirds of Happiness, Earwigs), James 'Scarlet Eagle' Peirce (bass, vocals; ex-Bluebirds of Happiness, Apaches), Dave 'The Spook' Hogan (drums; ex-Bluebirds of Happiness, Steve and the Disciples)*

Brisbane band The Hekawis played twangin', American-inspired, garage-tinged 'frat-rock' and surf instrumentals with a sense of fun and showmanship not seen since Sam the Sham and the Pharaohs sang about the 'Woolly Bully'. The band embraced everything American 1960s culture had to offer, from surf music, Farfisa organs and 'Louie Louie' to hotrods, B-grade movies and television sitcoms (after all, the band derived its name from the wayward Indian tribe in *F-Troop*; choice quote: 'Where the heck are we?').

The pre-Hekawis bands The Bluebirds of Happiness, The Disciples and The Apaches all played 1960s-inspired garage-punk. The Apaches issued one single, 'I'm Leaving Town', on the Sundown label in 1992. There have been a number of different Hekawi line-ups: Dave Hogan and Mick 'Thunderbolt' McIntyre (ex-Earwigs) have swapped the drum stool several times; Rob Zillman and Brett Barton left in 1994; Gavin 'Sheik' Ross (guitar; ex-Steve and the Disciples) replaced Barton; Adriano P. Regano (guitar; ex-Apaches) replaced Ross in 1995; Ross replaced Regano in 1997. The Steve Zillman/Peirce/McIntyre/Regano line-up recorded enough material to fill two albums (due for release in 1997).

The Hekawis issued the 'Indian Giver' EP on the Giant Claw label (1994), 'The Spook' EP on the Corduroy label (1995), the 'Scalp Surfin'' EP on American label Telstar (1995) and the 'Flowers in the Night'/'On this Day' single on the Wild Eagle label (1996). Perhaps the quote that appears on the sleeve of 'The Spook' EP best sums up The Hekawis' appeal: 'Four twangin' tropical tunes for your next Frat Party or Surfin Safari'.

The Helicopters

Formed: *1980*
Style: *New wave pop*
Line-up: *Deidre Baude (aka Deidre Baude De Bunnetatte; bass, vocals), Peter Stafford (guitar), Kevin Rooney (aka Kevin Kavanah; drums)*

Perth band The Helicopters formed in August 1980, existed for four years and issued a self-titled mini-album and a cassette, *Great Moments in Aviation*. Tony Thewlis (guitar) and Phil Bennett (keyboards, vocals) replaced original guitarist Peter Stafford in April 1981. Stafford went on to Vicious Yo-Yos and Big Red Tractor.

George B. Rushmore (aka George O'Brien) replaced Thewlis, who left at the end of 1981 to join **Scientists**. The Helicopters' English-influenced new wave sound was revealed in the cover versions they played live (i.e. U2, Altered Images, Siouxsie and the Banshees). The line-up of Baude, Rushmore,

Bennett and Kavanah recorded *The Helicopters* and then broke up in August 1982. Rushmore joined Perfect Strangers, a popular Perth outfit fronted by Andy Clayton-Smith. Baude, Bennett and Rooney played in glam-rock covers band Lazerblades for six months. In early 1983, the three musicians plus Vic Reynolds (guitar; ex-Change Alley) revived The Helicopters, which lasted for another year. As well as Perfect Strangers and Big Red Tractor, The Helicopters' Perth contemporaries included Photoplay, Scant Regard, Silent Type, The Frames and Go-Starts.

With the band's break-up, Baude and Kavanah travelled to the UK, while Bennett joined Lick the Lizard. The Helicopters also contributed the track 'Tag Along' to the Various Artists album *West* (1981), which also included **Eurogliders**, **Manikins**, The Essentials, The Invaders, The Rockets and Barrelhouse.

Album: *The Helicopters* (Warped/Tempo, 1982).

Hell to Pay

Formed: *1990*
Style: *Rock*
Original line-up: *Ian Rilen (guitar, vocals; ex-***Band of Light**, **Rose Tattoo**, **X**, *Sardine v), Spencer P. Jones (guitar, vocals; ex-Cuban Heels,* **Johnnys**, **Beasts of Bourbon***), Cathy Green (bass; ex-Cough Cough,* **X***), Tony Biggs (drums; ex-Black Assassins)*

In between their commitments to the peripatetic X, Ian Rilen and Cathy Green formed Hell to Pay as a more melodic (yet still tough) rock outfit. Spencer Jones fleshed out the guitar department with characteristic bluesy flair, while ex-Double J presenter Tony Biggs kept the beat tight and simple. Hell to Pay issued the single 'Saints and Kings'/'Would You Believe It?', 'Starting All Over' (May 1991), the album *Steal It* (August 1992) and the CD EP 'Two Days Off (Five Days On)' (November 1992) on the Red Eye label.

By the time the album came out, Jon Schofield (bass, ex-**Grooveyard**, **Paul Kelly** and the Messengers) had replaced Green. The album revealed the band's preoccupation with a Stones/Faces neo-boogie and 1980s swamp-rock amalgam, while tracks like 'Two Days Off (Five Days On)' and 'Booze to Blame' were paeans to hard drinking and hard living. Hell to Pay broke up not long after the album came out. Rilen revived X, while Biggs joined Melbourne's own booze hounds The Fuck Fucks.

Album: *Steal It* (Red Eye, 1992).

The Hellmenn

Formed: *1986*
Style: *Punk rock*
Original line-up: *Ben Brown (vocals), David 'Spiff' Hopkins (lead guitar), Tony (rhythm guitar), Anthony Bross (bass), Steve Heald (drums)*

The Hellmenn came blasting out of Sydney's northern beaches' skate-punk scene like a rocket from the tombs of hell. The band's fierce sound mixed Black Flag with Black Sabbath by way of an environmental manifesto. The band's original image was of drug-crazed surf-punks looking for good times and loud rock'n'roll, which said more about a desire to create mayhem as opposed to creating great art. On the other hand, singer Ben Brown was also well known for his grotesque, demented artwork which was an extension of the band's frantic approach to music making. The Hellmenn's contemporaries included the likes of **Asylum**, **The Hard-Ons**, **Massappeal** and **Ratcat**.

The Hellmenn signed to the Waterfront label and issued the hardcore mini-albums *Herbal Lunacy* (December 1987) and *Bastard Sons of 10 000 000 Maniacs* (November 1988). The second record was populated by such unhinged characters as the 'Tripping Priest' and 'Sluggo'. Yet, among the chaos,

The Hellmenn

there was some semblance of order. The title *Herbal Lunacy*, for example, reflected the band's interest in herbal medicine (Hopkins is a qualified naturopath). The band contributed a cover of 'Search and Destroy' to Au-go-go's Stooges tribute album *Hard to Beat* (1988).

In 1989, Victor Levi (ex-**Ratcat**) replaced Tony, and the band supported American hardcore godfather Henry Rollins on his Australian tour. The Hellmenn issued one single during 1989, *Blubber Soul* ('Daydreaming'/'The Trip'), after which Levi left the band. A year later, The Hellmenn issued the album *Mourning of the Earth* and the single 'Anyone'/'Possums' (May 1990). The album featured a mellower set of songs, and the title was a pun highlighting the seriousness of the worldwide environmental issue. The Hellmenn contributed a cover of 'The Deuce' to the Kiss tribute album *Hard to Believe* on the Waterfront label (1990). The band's last release for the year was the single 'Homegrown' (December), which had been lifted from *Mourning of the Earth*. Around the same time, Bill Gibson (ex-**Eastern Dark**) joined on guitar.

The EP 'Electric Crazy Land' (October 1991) boasted a broad range of sounds, from Hendrix-like psychedelia to Sonic Youth-styled noise. The description 'sonic surf sounds' was an appropriate one. The band, however, had fallen into a rut and broke up at the end of the year. A few weeks later, Brown, Hopkins and Heald revived The Hellmenn with new member Ken Archbold (bass; ex-Climate of Fear, Itchy Rat, **Dr Fruitworld**). That line-up appeared on the bill of the inaugural Big Day Out (January 1992). In March 1992, Waterfront combined the 'Electric Crazy Land' EP with the band's first two mini-albums plus the previously B-side only 'Possums', and issued the compilation on CD under the title *Electric Crazy Land*.

The band then signed to Phonogram's development label Id, which issued the CD EP 'Meltdown' (September 1992). The EP mixed three studio tracks with three bonus live cuts. The CD EP 'Absolute Filth' (June 1993) was another strong studio release (described by the band as 'thermonuclear-sonic-burn-out'). Although The Hellmenn had progressed over the years, they continued to be dogged by references to their skate/surf/thrash beginnings. After eight years of noise making, The Hellmenn called it a day in April 1994.

Albums: *Herbal Lunacy* (mini-album, Waterfront, 1987), *Bastard Sons of 10 000 000 Maniacs* (mini-album, Waterfront, 1988), *Mourning of the Earth* (Waterfront, 1990), *Electric Crazy Land* (Waterfront, 1992).

The Henchmen

Formed: *1964*
Style: *Pop*
Original line-up: *Doug Osbourne (guitar), Duncan MacKellar (guitar), David Mann (keyboards), Del Smeeton (bass), Malcolm Payne (drums)*

The Henchmen hailed from the Melbourne bayside suburb of Altona, and were originally known as Kevin Thompson and the Pacifics. The band played at local surf dances. When Thompson left in mid-1964, the band became The Henchmen (or The Stenchmen as they referred to themselves!). A couple of months later, the band recruited Rick Diamond (aka Rick McDiarmid) as lead vocalist.

The Henchmen won the 1964 3UZ Battle of the Sounds, with the prize being a contract with the Go!! label. Go!! issued the singles 'Rockin' Robin'/'Baby What's Wrong?' (#5 in April 1965) and 'Can't You Hear Me Callin?'/'Easy Money' (#36 in July 1965). The Henchmen became regulars on television shows like *Bandstand*, *Saturday Date*, *The Go!! Show* and *Kommotion*. At the end of 1965, Osbourne and Diamond left the band.

In 1966, The Henchmen came second to **The Twilights** in the Melbourne finals of the Hoadley's National Battle of the Sounds, and issued a new single on EMI/HMV, The Rolling Stones' 'Stupid Girl'/'Keep on Going Back' (September). By that stage, only Mann remained from the original line-up. The new members were Barry Roy (lead guitar, vocals), Roger Forward (rhythm guitar, vocals), Sperri Goupetta (bass) and Chris Riddell (drums). The Henchmen issued a final single on EMI/Columbia in December 1968, a cover of Joe Tex's 'Baby I Need You'/'Come on Down to My Boat', before calling it a day.

Tony Henry

Style: *Pop*

Tony Henry was a popular Melbourne solo singer during the mid-1960s. Backed by The Breakaways, Henry built up a following on the local dance and discotheque circuit, as well as appearing on the *Go!! Show*. Between 1963 and 1965, The Breakaways recorded an album, *Meet the Breakaways* (1963), and six singles for W&G: 'Rockin' Frog'/'Blowing in the Wind', 'You're Just in Love'/'Bonaparte's Retreat', 'World is Waiting for Sunrise'/'Granada', 'The Flipper'/'The Wheel', 'I Walk the Line'/'Dominique' and 'Johnny B. Goode'/'It's a Lie'.

The Breakaways also backed Henry on his first three singles for the W&G label: 'Every Way

Out'/'Baby Blue' (1965), Buddy Holly's 'Heartbeat'/'One Sided Love Affair' (1966) and 'What to Do'/'You Can Have Her' (1966). Henry recorded three more singles, 'Searchin''/'This Time' (August 1966), 'Wild One'/'Honey Love' (October 1966) and 'She Cried'/'Standing Watch' (February 1967), before fading from view.

Heroes (*see* Rabbit)

Colleen Hewett

Style: Pop

During the 1970s, Colleen Hewett (b. 1950) was one of Australia's most popular female singers. She was born in Bendigo, Victoria and began singing at 12 years of age. In 1967 she joined vocal trio The Creations, backing solo singers like **Billy Adams** and **Buddy England**. From there, Hewett worked with The Laurie Allen Review (joined by her sister Glenys) and The Ian Saxon Sound.

In 1970, she stepped out as a solo singer, winning that year's *Bandstand* Best Female Newcomer of the Year award. She signed to Festival Records and issued her debut single, a cover of the Leon Russell/Bonnie Bramlett song 'Superstar'/'More Today than Yesterday' (June 1971). The single peaked at #30 on the national chart, and soon after Hewett joined the cast of the Melbourne production of the musical *Godspell*. She took her next single from the show, 'Day by Day'/'By My Side' (November 1971).

The single became a national #1 hit, sold over 50 000 copies and established Hewett as the country's leading female performer. She completed a successful 1971 by winning the *Bandstand* Best Female Singer award. Her next single, a cover of The Beatles' 'Carry that Weight'/'Danny Boy' (#29 in November 1972), was lifted from her debut album, *Colleen Hewett*. She travelled to the USA and the UK at the end of 1972, and completed the year by being crowned *TV Week* Queen of Pop and winning the *Go-Set* national Pop Poll as Best Female Singer.

In March 1973, Hewett appeared in the role of the Mother in the local stage production of The Who's rock opera *Tommy*. Also in the cast were **Billy Thorpe**, **Daryl Braithwaite**, **Broderick Smith**, **Doug Parkinson** and Keith Moon. Hewett issued three singles during 1973, 'Waltzing Matilda'/'Mother' (June), 'A Wish a Wish'/'It's Gonna Be a Long Time' (September) and the lavish 'Sit Yourself Down'/'Can't Sit Down' (November). Despite her high profile, none of the singles was a national success. At the end of the year, Hewett won the *TV Week* Queen of Pop award for the second year in a row.

Hewett joined **John Farnham** as co-star in the stage show *Pippin*, which opened in Melbourne during February 1974. 'Pippin (Finale)'/'I Can't Fly' appeared as her seventh single in March. Hewett remained with the show for a year, after which she headed to the USA. She had signed a deal with Atlantic Records which resulted in one fine album, *M'Lady* (June 1974). The album produced the single 'I Believe When I Fall in Love' (July). *M'Lady* was moderately successful, and Hewett returned to Australia in May 1977. In September, she took a role in the ABC-TV series *The Truckies* which ran for two seasons.

During the early 1980s, Hewett returned to the limelight with a hit single on the Wizard label, 'Dreaming My Dreams with You'/'One Eyed Man'. It became the second biggest hit single of her career when it reached #2 in March 1980. She followed that up with the single 'Gigolo'/'You Keep Walking Back' (October 1981) on Festival. The single reached #25 in January 1982. After that, Hewett signed to the Avenue label, for which she issued four singles: 'Hearts'/'Take Me in Your Arms' (September 1982), 'Wind Beneath My Wings'/'Constantly' (February 1983), Tim Finn's 'I Hope I Never'/'Sleepless Nights' (July 1983) and 'If You Ever Feel the Need'/'Love is Not Easy' (1984), plus the album *Colleen*. 'Wind Beneath My Wings' reached #21 in Melbourne during April. It later became a huge hit for Bette Midler from the *Beaches* soundtrack. Hewett continued performing, and in the 1990s she worked in radio broadcasting with Melbourne station Gold-FM.

Albums: *Colleen Hewett* (Festival, 1972), *M'Lady* (Atlantic, 1974), *Hits* (Summit, 1974), *Colleen* (Avenue/CBS, 1983), *Power of Love* (J&B, 1988).

Deni Hines

Style: Soul, pop

Deni Hines (b. 1971) is the daughter of **Marcia Hines**, one of the most popular singers in Australia during the 1970s. Coming from a showbusiness family, it was inevitable that Hines would follow the path set by her mother. Hines gained valuable experience during the early 1990s by touring as a backing vocalist for **Wa Wa Nee**, **Peter Blakeley**, **Jimmy Barnes** and **Kylie Minogue**. She followed that with a part in the stage musical *Big River*.

From there, Hines joined Sydney dance-funk outfit **Rockmelons**, singing lead vocals on three of their biggest hits: Bill Withers' 'Ain't No Sunshine' (#5 in January 1992), 'That Word (L.O.V.E.)' (#4 in June 1992) and 'It's Not Over' (#15 in September 1992). Hines embarked on a solo career, but it took four years, three continents and two record companies before her debut album reached the record shops. In 1993, she signed to American label Interscope (home to Helmet, Nine Inch Nails, Snoop Doggy Dogg and Tupac Shakur) and commenced recording in New York and Los Angeles. The sessions were not fruitful. Hines left Interscope and returned to Australia to sign with Mushroom Records.

While waiting for studio time, Hines played the part of Mary Magdalene in the revived stage musical *Jesus Christ Superstar* (the same theatre role her mother had made famous during the early 1970s). Hines and producer Ian Green eventually spent seven months in London recording her debut album. At the end of 1995, Hines issued her debut single, 'It's Alright', which reached #4 nationally. It was followed by her second single, the silky-smooth 'Imagination' (#37 in March 1996), and the *Imagination* album in August. The third single lifted from the album, 'I Like the Way', came out in May, followed by a slow groove rendition of 10CC's 'I'm Not in Love' (September), on which Hines overdubbed 340 takes of backing vocals (the same number as on the 10CC original). 'It's Alright' won Best Debut Single at the 1996 Australian Record Industry Association (ARIA) Awards.

Albums: *Imagination* (Mushroom/Festival, 1996).

Marcia Hines

Style: *Pop, soul*

Boston-born Marcia Hines (b. 1953) arrived in Australia in April 1970 at the age of 16 to appear in promoter Harry M. Miller's local production of the American 'tribal love-rock musical' *Hair* (directed by Jim Sharman). That in turn led to her taking the role of Mary Magdalene in Miller and Sharman's next production, Andrew Lloyd Webber and Tim Rice's *Jesus Christ Superstar* (taking over from Michelle Fawdon). When that show ended in February 1974, Hines joined the Daly-Wilson Big Band, with which she toured Australia, the USA and Soviet Russia.

Hines signed a solo deal with Robie Porter's Wizard label in July 1974. Porter produced a string of hit albums and singles for Hines that saw her elevated to the position of Australia's top female performer during the late 1970s. Hines was crowned Australia's Queen of Pop for three consecutive years (1976–78), and her albums sold in excess of 500 000 copies all up. Hines' 1977 touring band included Stephen Housden (guitar), Frank Esler-Smith (keyboards), Tony Hedges (keyboards), Warren Ford (keyboards), Mike Cleary (trumpet), Mike Bukovsky (trumpet), Richard Gawned (tenor sax, flute), Steve Parkinson (baritone sax, flute), Monalisa and Terry Young (backing vocals), **Jackie Orszaczky** (musical director, bass; ex-Syrius), Sunil De Silva (percussion) and Mark Kennedy (drums; ex-**Spectrum**, **King Harvest**, **Doug Parkinson** In Focus, **Friends**, **Ayers Rock**). Hines and Kennedy were engaged for a number of years before the relationship fell apart.

Hines' singles on Wizard were: James Taylor's 'Fire and Rain'/'You' (#9 in May 1975), 'From the Inside'/'Jumping Jack Flash' (#8 in November 1975), 'Don't Let the Grass Grow'/'You Gotta Let Go' (May 1976), Burt Bacharach/Hal David's 'I Just Don't Know What to Do with Myself'/'Trilogy' (#3 in September 1976), 'Until Your Love Broke Through'/'Whatever Goes Round' (December), 'What I Did for Love'/'A Love Story' (#7 in June 1977), 'You'/'In a Mellow Mood' (#1 in November), 'Music is My Life'/'Empty' (#19 in April 1978), 'Imagination'/'Shining' (June), 'Let the Music Play'/'Empty' (October), 'Something's Missing in My Life'/'Moments' (#10 in April 1979), 'Dance You Fool, Dance'/'Trilogy' (live) (August) and 'Where Did We Go Wrong?'/'Dance You Fool, Dance' (November).

She enjoyed hit albums with *Marcia Shines* (#10 in November 1975), *Shining* (#4 in December 1976), *Ladies and Gentlemen . . . Marcia Hines* (#5 in September 1977), the double album *Live Across Australia* (#6 in March 1978) and *Ooh Child* (#15 in June 1979). *Shining* and *Live Across Australia* were the most successful, selling in excess of 150 000 and 100 000 copies respectively. In 1978, Hines appeared in her own ABC-TV series *Marcia Hines Music*, which was so successful that she returned for a second season in 1979. She also reprised her role of Mary Magdalene in the Sydney club circuit revival of *Jesus Christ Superstar*, but her return was brief. She was forced to miss several performances due to throat and respiratory problems.

In 1980, Marcia left Wizard and signed a new deal with the Midnight label (through WEA). Her singles on Midnight were: 'Your Love Still Brings Me to My Knees'/'Till It's Too Late' (#10 in August 1981), 'What a Bitch is Love'/'It Don't Take Much' (September), 'Take It from the Boys'/'Taking It All In' (February 1982), 'Jokers and Queens'/'The Best of Me' (shared with **Jon English**) (June 1982), 'Love Side'/'The Best of Me' (September), 'Heart Like a Radio'/'She Got You' (March 1983) and 'Shadow in the Night'/'You Never Told Me Love Hurts' (November). Her fifth studio album, *Take It from the Boys*, reached #16 nationally in October 1981, while the compilation album *Greatest Hits Volume 1* reached #2 in February 1982. *Love Sides* (May 1983) and its singles 'Love Side', 'Heart Like a Radio' and 'Shadow in the Night' were not so successful. Hines revived her Mary Magdalene role for the second time in the late 1983 Melbourne season of *Jesus Christ Superstar*.

Hines remained quiet on the recording front for more than a decade while she concentrated on being with her daughter, **Deni Hines**. During 1993, she returned to the stage with The Masters of Rhythm and Taste. In 1994 she issued her first album in 12 years, *Right Here and Now*. It featured a mix of gospel and soul tunes such as 'Common Mind' and big production ballads like 'Point of No Return', plus the singles 'Rain (Let the Children Play)' (August 1994) and 'Give It All You've Got' (October). In March 1994, Hines toured nationally for the first time in seven years.

Albums: *Marcia Shines* (Wizard, 1975), *Shining* (Wizard, 1976), *Ladies and Gentlemen . . . Marcia Hines* (Wizard, 1977), *Live Across Australia* (Wizard, 1978), *Ooh Child* (Wizard, 1979), *Take It from the Boys* (Midnight, 1981), *Greatest Hits Volume 1* (compilation, Wizard, 1981), *Love Sides* (Midnight, 1982), *Jokers and Queens* (mini-album shared with **Jon English**, Midnight, 1982), *Greatest Hits Volume 2* (compilation, Wizard, 1982), *With All My Love* (compilation, Wizard, 1983), *The Marcia Hines Collection* (compilation, Axis, 1984), *The Complete Marcia Hines* (compilation, Hammard, 1984), *Greatest Hits* (Mega, 1992), *Right Here and Now* (Warner, 1994).

The Hippos

Formed: *1985*
Style: *R&B*
Original line-up: *Leszek Karski (guitar, vocals; ex-Supercharge,* **Ray Arnott** *Band), Bridie King (keyboards; ex-Ratbags of Rhythm), Ian Jones (sax, percussion), John Power (bass, vocals; ex-***Company Caine**, **Foreday Riders**, **Jo Jo Zep and the Falcons**, *Rock Doctors), Ace Follington (drums; ex-***Chain**, **Richard Clapton** *Band, Australia)*

The Hippos started out as an ad hoc, good-time bar band playing a loose, timeless and entertaining brand of Memphis soul and New Orleans R&B. The members boasted an impressive pedigree that stretched back to the early 1970s.

Leszek Karski first came to Australia in 1977 as a member of UK band Supercharge. He decided to stay, and worked as an engineer/producer/musician for Albert Productions. He also played in **Ray Arnott** Band, **Cheetah**, **Flash and the Pan** and **The Foreday Riders**, as well as producing **Midnight Oil** and **v Spy v Spy**. Bass player John Power had been plucking the blues for more than a decade, and he possessed an extravagant vocal growl unmatched in these parts. The Hippos signed to WEA and issued the singles 'Dark Age'/'Rodent Operative' (June 1988) and 'Breaking Up Somebody Else's Home'/'The Tiny Blues' (October), plus the album *Hippocracy* (July). The Hippos issued a second album *Hippocalypse* (with the second bad pun in an album title) at the end of 1989. The album yielded the singles 'Time and Motion'/'Ded Fred' (October 1989) and 'Eat at Home' (March 1990).

Karski and Ace Follington left The Hippos during 1990 in order to join **The Bondi Cigars**, while Bridie King also made her exit. They were replaced by Rory McKibbon, Richard Harvey (ex-**Divinyls**, **Party Boys**) and Phil Grove respectively. The Hippos were quiet on the recording front for another two years, until they re-emerged in September 1993 with *Creatures from the Back Saloon* (yep, third corny pun, but at least it raised a chuckle). The album featured contributions from bluesman Earl King.

Albums: *Hippocracy* (WEA, 1988), *Hippocalypse* (WEA, 1989), *Creatures from the Back Saloon* (Exile/Festival, 1993).

Hipslingers

Formed: *1983*
Style: *Psychedelic pop*
Original line-up: *Stuart St Hill (trumpet, cornet, vocals), John Di Gravio (vocals, guitar, keyboards; ex-Mansons), David Brett (bass, vocals; ex-Mansons)*

This Hunter Valley (NSW) band formed in April 1983. Hipslingers mixed tough, Church-like psychedelic pop with an oblique jazzy touch (not that far removed from **Laughing Clowns**) courtesy of St Hill's trumpet/cornet flourishes. By the time the band came to record its debut single, 'Just My State of Mind'/'I Want a School Girl' (1984), Nick Cecire had replaced Tom Masi and Frank Rosetti on the drum stool.

'Heavenly Blue'/'Wilderness' came out in September 1985. The uptempo 'Heavenly Blue' was reminiscent of The Byrds' 'Artificial Energy' (from *The Notorious Byrd Brothers* album), which was a good indication of the band's intent. Darren Rowe replaced David Brett on bass in late 1986. The new line-up recorded a third single, 'Pilgrim'/'Chimes'

(February 1987) and the debut album *Panoramic* (December 1987). 'What's the Matter?'/'Never the Twain' also came out in 1988. Hipslingers contributed the track 'Psycho' to rooArt's inaugural *Youngblood* compilation (September 1988), alongside material from **The Trilobites**, **Martha's Vineyard**, **Crash Politics**, **Tall Tales & True**, **The Hummingbirds**, Violet Town and others.

There were more line-up changes: Michael Thompson replaced Rowe on bass; Kyri Frame replaced Thompson; and Garry Koski (trombone) joined. The curiously titled single 'Life Was Meant to Enjoy' (life was meant to enjoy what?) came out in late 1991, followed by the CD EP *Somnium* in January 1992.

Album: *Panoramic* (Shoot the Sax Player, 1988).

David Hirschfelder

Style: *Rock, pop*

Well-known session keyboard player David Hirschfelder has provided backing for the likes of **John Farnham**, **Peter Cupples**, the **Little River Band**, Wilbur Wilde's Blowout and Yu-En. He has appeared on recording sessions for Cupples, Farnham, LRB, **Girl Overboard**, **Southern Sons**, plus the *Jesus Christ Superstar* stage show during 1992.

Hirschfelder grew up in the Victorian regional city of Ballarat. He completed a Bachelor of Music degree at Melbourne University. In 1980 he worked with acclaimed jazz-rock outfit Pyramid and joined the **Peter Cupples** Band, playing funky US West Coast rock. In 1983, Hirschfelder toured with the **Little River Band** as an auxiliary player, eventually joining during October as replacement for Beeb Birtles. Hirschfelder appeared on the LRB albums *Playing to Win* and *No Reins*.

When lead singer **John Farnham** left LRB at the end of 1985 to reactivate his solo career, he invited Hirschfelder to record and tour with him. Hirschfelder remained Farnham's musical director for many years, appearing on the #1 albums *Whispering Jack*, *Age of Reason* and *Chain Reaction*. In between the Farnham recording/touring schedule, Hirschfelder worked with **Dragon** on the album *Bondi Road*, composed the theme to the *Page One* television current affairs program, scored the soundtracks to the television documentaries *Suzi's Story*, *Never My Child* and *Macrene's Theme* and issued the solo album *Welcome to the Nightclub of My Mind* (March 1990).

In 1992, Hirschfelder worked as composer/arranger on the soundtrack to director Baz Luhrmann's internationally acclaimed feature film *Strictly Ballroom*. More recently, Hirschfelder composed, arranged and produced the soundtrack to the multi-award winning Australian film *Shine*, for which he earned an Oscar nomination at the 1997 Academy Awards ceremony. Following the film's international success, Hirschfelder sued the film company, Momentum Films, for royalties owing from sales of the soundtrack album.

Album: *Welcome to the Nightclub of My Mind* (Wheatley Bros, 1990)

Carol Hitchcock

Style: *Disco funk*

In 1987, it seemed possible that bald-headed disco diva Carol Hitchcock would become Australia's own version of Grace Jones. After establishing an identity on the Melbourne inner-city dance club scene with funk bands Bang and Cat People, Hitchcock signed to Mushroom Records. The label flew her to London to record her debut single with the UK hit-making team of Stock Aitken Waterman (SAW) (famous for their work with Mel and Kim, Bananarama, Dead or Alive, Rick Astley and later The Spice Girls and **Kylie Minogue**). Hitchcock's single, a disco-funk reworking of The Temptations' 1969 dance hit 'Get Ready'/'More than Words Can Say' (June 1987), reached #12 on the national chart in August. A&M issued the single in the UK, where it reached #56. The gutsy singer had made her mark but, unfortunately, there was no follow-up and Hitchcock slipped from view.

The Hitmen

Formed: *1977*
Style: *Hard rock*
Original line-up: *Johnny Kannis (vocals), Charlie Georgees (guitar; ex-Hellcats), Chris Masuak (guitar; on loan from* **Radio Birdman***), Warwick Gilbert (bass; on loan from* **Radio Birdman***), Ron Keeley (drums; on loan from* **Radio Birdman***)*

Sydney band The Hitmen never achieved the commercial success for which they so obviously strived. The band's records were tough, melodic and catchy, and the live shows were consistently impressive displays of high energy rock'n'roll. Lack of record company push, and a constant shifting of membership, made it difficult for the band to sustain a concerted attack, despite a relentless touring schedule right across Australia. The Hitmen's greatest hindrance, however, seems to have been the fact that they were the first band from the punk/new

The Hitmen

wave era that aimed to break out of the inner-city circuit by taking its music to the general Australian public. With blind faith in their own abilities, the band members set a tough agenda and inevitably they were forced to pay the price.

The first incarnation of The Hitmen, then known as Johnny and the Hitmen, came together in November 1977 for a series of fun gigs. The Hitmen reflected Johnny Kannis's taste in music by covering Elvis Presley, Rolling Stones and Ramones songs, plus various surf and punk tunes. The band played shows between Masuak, Gilbert and Keeley's commitment to **Radio Birdman**. Kannis was also Birdman's 'Master of Ceremonies'. **Radio Birdman** guitarist Deniz Tek produced Kannis's debut solo single, a cover of The Drifters' 'Under the Boardwalk'/'King of the Surf', which came out on WEA in November 1978.

When **Radio Birdman** travelled overseas in early 1978, Kannis assembled a new, short-lived line-up as Johnny Kannis and the Hitmen, which was a seven-piece Las Vegas-styled revue. The line-up was Kannis, Georgees, Steve Harris (keyboards), Angie Pepper (vocals), Lynne Phillips (vocals), Clyde Bramley (bass) and Alan Brown (drums). Harris, Pepper and Brown went on to form **The Passengers**, while Bramley and Georgees joined Rob Younger and Mark Kingsmill in The Other Side. In July 1978, following **Radio Birdman's** disbandment, Masuak revived The Hitmen with Kannis, Ivor Hay (drums; ex-**Saints**) and Phil Sommerville (bass). In September, Warwick Gilbert joined on rhythm guitar, fuelling rumours that The Hitmen were attempting to become **Radio Birdman** Mark II.

This was far from the case, because while Birdman had operated outside the mainstream music industry, The Hitmen insisted on becoming a commercial proposition. The band toured constantly and signed to WEA in March 1979. WEA issued the singles 'Didn't Tell the Man'/'I Am the Man' (July 1979) and 'I Want You'/'Tell Tale Heart' (March 1980). The galvanising Kiss-like rocker 'I Want You' was a good indication of the band's intent.

Mark Kingsmill (ex-Hellcats, Other Side) replaced Hay in August 1979 (after Geoff Peterkin from **Ol'55** had filled in for a month). Sommerville then left, Gilbert moved back to bass and Tony Vidale joined on guitar. In December 1980, The Hitmen recorded their debut album with producer Mark Opitz (**The Angels**, **Cold Chisel**). The 'I Don't Mind'/'Rock'n'Roll Soldiers' single (June 1981) and *Hitmen* album (July) were excellent slices of melodic hard rock. Opitz had achieved a full-throated production sound in the studio that did justice to the band's fierce live reputation. Vidale had left before the album sessions were completed. Brad Shepherd (ex-**Fun Things**, 31st) joined the band, re-recorded all Vidale's guitar parts in a day and then made his live debut a couple of weeks later. Throughout November 1981, The Hitmen supported US visitors Steppenwolf on tour. Gilbert left during the tour to be replaced by Tony Robertson (ex-Credits, 31st).

Robertson's first band The Credits had comprised Greg Williamson (guitar; ex-Survivors) and Bruce Anthon (drums; ex-Survivors). The Credits issued one tough power pop single, 'It's You'/'Fazed Dazed' (on Thunder Productions, 1979), before splitting up. Anthon went on to The Shakers and Les Bon Bons. After that, Robertson was a member of the 31st alongside Shepherd. In early 1982, The Hitmen signed a new deal with RCA and issued the singles 'Everybody Knows (I Don't Like Love)'/'Dancin' Time' (April 1982) and 'Bwana Devil'/'I Didn't Want to Love You' (November), plus the album *It is What It is* (November).

One month before the album came out, Shepherd jumped ship (in order to join **Hoodoo Gurus**), and The Hitmen continued as a four-piece. The band continued to draw big crowds on tour, but could not sell records. Consequently, RCA dropped The Hitmen and the band went into hibernation. In June 1983, Rob Younger used Masuak, Robertson and Kingsmill as the basis for his band **The New Christs** (along with Kent Steedman from **The Celibate Rifles**) in order to support Iggy Pop on his Australian tour.

In the meantime, Kannis formed a soul revue called Johnny Kannis and Night Train with Steve Harris (keyboards; ex-**Passengers**, Visitors) and Lynne Phillips (backing vocals), plus Rohan Cannon (guitar), Paul Reed (bass), Mick Thornton (trumpet), Don Raffaele (sax, percussion) and Michael Buckley (drums) who were all on loan from Rupert B. On the way to a Night Train gig during July, Kannis, Harris and Phillips were severely injured in a car accident. Kannis spent months in hospital recuperating, and such were his injuries that it put an end to The Hitmen's future plans. Masuak, Robertson and Kingsmill continued with **The New Christs**.

By June 1984, Kannis had recovered sufficiently to re-form The Hitmen for a farewell tour. Masuak, Robertson and Kingsmill brought in new member Richard Jakimyszyn (guitar; ex-**Lime Spiders**, **New Christs**), and the tour yielded the live album *Tora Tora DTK* (November 1984). Following the June tour dates, Masuak, Robertson and Kingsmill all joined **The Screaming Tribesmen**. Kingsmill left a month later in order to join **Hoodoo Gurus**, while Robertson had rejoined Kannis by the end of the year in the short-lived Johnny Kannis Band. Jakimyszyn, Raffaele, Tony Jukic (guitar), Melanie Oxley (backing vocals) and Brett 'The Destroyer' Luton (drums) completed the line-up. The band played predominantly Hitmen material, plus covers from The Doors, The Dictators, The Flamin' Groovies and Elvis Presley. After that, Jakimyszyn returned to **The Lime Spiders** and Robertson formed Naked Lunch.

Naked Lunch comprised Robertson, Steve Beves (vocals, guitar; ex-Melting Skyscrapers), Peter Patterson (vocals; ex-Melting Skyscrapers) and Gary Cross (drums), with guitarists like Tony Gibson, Mick Medew, Richard Burgmann and Roger Gold helping out. The band issued the single 'Little Too Late'/'Teenage Blues' (Waterfront, November 1986) and the mini-album *Things Grow* (Green Fez, 1988). Beves and Patterson's previous band, Melting Skyscrapers, issued one single on Waterfront, 'Strange Device'/'Beyond the Grave' (May 1985). Kannis turned to managing **The Screaming Tribesmen**, **The Psychotic Turnbuckles** and Voodoo Lust, as well as forming The Johnny Kannis Explosion. Kannis formed a new Hitmen line-up (Ivor Hay, Tony Robertson, plus guitarists Peter Banesevic and Tony Jukic) for a brief tour during January and February 1988.

With the break-up of **The Screaming Tribesmen** in April 1989, Masuak and Kannis re-formed The Hitmen as Hitmen DTK with Matt Le Noury (aka Matt Nasty, guitar; ex-**Vampire Lovers**, Flying Tigers), Brad Ferguson (bass; ex-Voodoo Lust) and Gye Bennetts (drums; ex-Terminal Twist, Johnny Kannis Explosion). The new line-up issued the 12 inch EP *U.E.L.A.* (which stands for 'Utopian Emotional Love Aura') on Survival (November 1989). Survival also reissued the *Tora Tora DTK* live album in December. Hitmen DTK toured throughout 1990, including the joint Buncha Brats tour with Voodoo Lust and **Peter Wells'** Heart Attack. The next line-up of Masuak, Kannis, Bob Sattler (guitar; ex-Johnny Kannis Explosion, Roddy Ray'da and The Surfin' Caesars), Shane Cooke (bass; ex-**Vampire Lovers**, Four Horsemen) and Gerald Presland (drums) issued the album *Moronic Inferno* (November 1991) and CD single 'Surfing in Another Direction'.

Hitmen DTK supported ex-Stooges' guitarist Ron Asheton's band Dark Carnival on its Australian tour of December 1991, after which Masuak and Kannis broke up the band. The Dogmeat label reissued 'King of the Surf' as a single (backed with the previously unissued cover of The Seeds' 'Pushin' Too Hard') in May 1992, and Kannis used **The Trilobites** to back him on a number of promotional gigs. Masuak formed **Juke Savages**, and then was involved in the **Radio Birdman** reunions of 1996.

Albums: *Hitmen* (WEA, 1981), *It is What It is* (RCA, 1982), *Tora Tora DTK* (ABC, 1984; reissued on Survival, 1989), *Hitmen 78–82* (compilation of the first album and early singles; Survival, 1988), *Moronic Inferno* (Zeus/Shock, 1991).

Hobbs' Angel of Death

Formed: *1987*
Style: *Thrash metal*
Original line-up: *Peter Hobbs (guitar, vocals; ex-Tyrus); Mark Woolley (lead guitar; from Nothing Sacred), Karl Lean (bass; from Nothing Sacred), Sham (drums; from Nothing Sacred)*

Hobbs' Angel of Death was one of the first Australian bands to play a distinctly European form of thrash metal (in the manner of bands like Kreator, Destruction and Celtic Frost). Peter Hobbs conceived the band in January 1987, recording two demo tapes, *Angel of Death* and *Virgin Metal Invasion from Down Under*, with help from three members of fellow Melbourne band Nothing Sacred. The demos attracted the interest of German label Steamhammer.

Steamhammer signed Hobbs' Angel of Death, and flew the band over to West Berlin to record its debut album at Musiclab Studios with producer Harris Johns. Hobbs and Woolley recruited fellow Melbourne musicians Phil Gresik (bass; from Mass Confusion) and Darren McMaster-Smith (drums; ex-New Religion) for the album sessions. The resultant self-titled album (issued July 1988) became a best-seller in Europe, but was only available locally on import. With the release of the album, Hobbs' Angel of Death made its live debut in Melbourne (supporting Sydney thrashers **Mortal Sin**). In 1989, Hobbs and Woolley recruited a new rhythm section comprising Dave Frew (bass) and Bruno Canziani (drums) and began touring. It was to be another six years before Hobbs' Angel of Death delivered a follow-up album, *Inheritance*. In the meantime, Woolley and Frew had formed their own band, Hatred.

Of the original band members, Woolley (ex-Heresy), Karl Lean (ex-Vengeance, Heresy) and Sham (ex-Vengeance, Heresy) had played with one of Melbourne's most popular heavy metal bands, Nothing Sacred. Mick Burnham (vocals; ex-Vengeance, Heresy) and Richard 'Buddy' Snape (lead guitar; ex-Heresy) completed the line-up. The band's influences included Motorhead, Judas Priest, Ted Nugent, Hawkwind, Venom, Van Halen and Metallica. Nothing Sacred recorded an excellent 12-inch EP, *Death Wish* (1986), and the album *Let Us Pray* before Woolley left to join Angel of Death. Snape also left and Nothing Sacred recruited guitarists George Larin (ex-New Religion) and Terry Cameron (ex-Nemesis). *Let Us Pray* came out in May 1988 on the Cleopatra label. Larin later joined **Taramis**. Buddy Snape went on to join progressive metal band Mandrake Garden, which issued one impressive mini-album, *Picturesque*, in early 1990.

Phil Gresik also played with Melbourne thrash/hardcore band Mass Confusion which comprised Darren 'Dog' Walsh (vocals), Steve 'Slob' Maidment (lead guitar) and Chris Phillips (drums; ex-Tyrus). Mass Confusion issued a self-financed album, *Confusion Intrusion*, in 1991, supported overseas visitors like Motorhead and Sepultura, added James Morse on bass (Gresik switched to rhythm guitar), but broke up in 1993 without making significant headway.

Albums: *Hobbs' Angel of Death* (Steamhammer, import only, 1988), *Inheritance* (Def/Shock, 1995).

Jimi 'The Human' Hocking

Style: *Hard rock*

Guitarist Jimi 'The Human' Hocking first came to prominence in Melbourne band The Aströs, who issued a self-titled mini-album on the Robot label in 1986. The Aströs comprised Hocking, Peter German (bass; ex-Phantom Band) and Greg Pedley (drums; ex-Phantom Band). Hocking was an exceptional guitar player, and in May 1988 he established his ability to play with the big guns when he deputised on tour for **The Angels'** ailing guitarist Bob Spencer.

Hocking went on to become a permanent fixture on the Melbourne pub circuit with his band Jimi 'The Human' and Spectre 7 and as a solo acoustic performer. Spectre 7 comprised Hocking, Josie Jason (guitar, vocals; ex-Butterfly, Final Outcome, Dirty Rats, Mars Needs Women), Didi Kies (bass; ex-Adventure, Honeythieves) and Christian Muehike (drums; ex-Honeythieves). The band issued the singles 'Quicksand' and 'Edge of Insanity'/'Robot Man', plus the album *No Turning Back* (March 1990) on the Avenue label. *No Turning Back* reached the Melbourne Top 30. Josie Jason went on to lead her own band, Josie Jason and the Argonauts, for many years. That band comprised Peter Wanliss (guitar), Kevin Hunt (bass) and Greg Aldridge (drums). Graham Maddicks replaced Aldridge on drums and the band issued the CD EP *Medusa Goes to Market* (May 1992) and the album *Big Green Water* (1995).

Jimi 'The Human' and Spectre 7 issued a second album in 1993, before Hocking replaced Richard Lara in **The Screaming Jets** in early 1994. He toured internationally with the band and played on the albums *The Screaming Jets* (1995) and *World Gone Crazy* (1997). During his tenure with The Jets, Hocking also found time to issue the mail order acoustic album *The Ultimate Bootleg* (August 1996). When he left the Jets in May 1997, Hocking returned to playing the Melbourne pub scene. He formed a new band, The Human Condition, and issued the album *The Great B-Grade Remake*.

Albums: *No Turning Back* (Avenue/EMI, 1990), *Living in Luxury* (Primitive, 1993), *The Ultimate Bootleg* (Feral, 1996), *The Great B-Grade Remake* (Blah Blah Blah, 1997).

Ray Hoff and the Off Beats

Formed: *1959*
Style: *R&B*
Original line-up: *Ray Hoff (born Ray Hough, vocals), Jimmy Taylor (piano; ex-Warren William and the Squares), Darby Wilson (guitar), John Ryan (bass), Leon Isackson (drums)*

Singer Ray Hoff formed the first version of Ray Hoff and the Off Beats in Sydney during the late 1950s. The band's style of rock'n'roll was raw with a strong R&B base. The band made little headway, despite several years of slogging around the Sydney dance/discotheque circuit. There were a number of different line-ups during the band's early days. John Ryan and his brother Vince (sax) were temporary members. In 1960, Jimmy Taylor left to join Johnny Devlin and the Devils, and Leon Isackson joined **Dig Richards** and the R'Jays.

RCA issued one single in 1964, a cover of Chuck Berry's 'Little Queenie'/'Baby What Do You Want Me to Do?', before Hoff dissolved The Off Beats and headed over to Perth in Western Australia. The final version of The Off Beats contained Jimmy Taylor, Col Risby (lead guitar) and Mike Downes (rhythm guitar), all of whom joined **Billy Thorpe** and the Aztecs. In Perth, Hoff formed a new Off Beats line-up, a seven-piece band comprising Graham Bartlett (guitar), John Gray (bass), Basil V'Delli (keyboards), Warwick Findlay (drums), Robert Baxter (sax), Roger Bloom (sax) and David Birkbeck (trumpet). As Perth's premier R&B outfit, Ray Hoff and the Off Beats signed to the Clarion label and issued the singles 'Let's Go, Let's Go, Let's Go'/'Bama Lama Bama Loo' (May 1966) and 'Tossin' and Turnin''/'Looking for My Pigs' (October 1966).

Ray Hoff and the Off Beats' rare, self-titled debut album featured one side of live cuts and one side of studio material. Among obligatory covers of 'Got My Mojo Working', 'In the Midnight Hour' and 'Mercy Mercy' was the wild instrumental 'My Good Friend Mary Jane'. Ray Hoff and the Off Beats issued one more single, 'Love Love Love'/'I've Got to Get to You', this time on the Action label (August 1967). With the final break-up of The Off Beats, Hoff formed a duo with Andre De Moller (ex-Blue Dogs) before travelling to the UK. In late 1971, Hoff joined an ambitious rock'n'roll revue band in Perth called Likefun. The line-up also included **Stevie Wright** (vocals; ex-**Easybeats**), Shirley Reid (vocals), Morri Pierson (vocals), John Tucak (bass) and Alan Wilkes (organ).

Albums: *Ray Hoff and the Off Beats* (Clarion, 1966), *Let's Go: The Festival File* (Festival, 1988).

Hoi Polloi

Formed: *1982*
Style: *Rock*
Original line-up: *Darcy Condon (vocals; ex-Playboy Lords, Hey Pineapple), Paul Thirkell (guitar, vocals; ex-Playboy Lords, Super K), Len Samperi (bass), Tony Samperi (drums)*

Darcy Condon and Paul Thirkell led The Playboy Lords to minor acclaim on the Sydney independent scene (circa 1979–80). As well as Condon and Thirkell, who formed Hoi Polloi, The Lords comprised Bill Bilson (drums), who went on to **Sunnyboys**, and Stephen Mather (bass), who joined **The Lipstick Killers**. Bilson and Mather teamed up again in the 1990s as members of Doctor Stone.

The Hoi Polloi line-up as above issued two singles in 1984: the gig giveaway 'Zig Zag Wanderer'/'Club Terranean' and 'Kid Octane'/'Shake Loose' (October). The next line-up was Condon, Thirkell, Arthur 'Tuck' Hatzakos (bass, vocals), Marcus Phelan (guitar) and Julian Clarke (drums). The Hoi Polloi line-up of Condon, Thirkell, Hatzakos, Mark Stinson (drums) and Peter Simpson (keyboards; ex-Spectre's Revenge) recorded the mini-album *Soul of Discretion.* Warwick Fraser replaced Stinson in 1985, but the band broke up in 1986. Condon went on to form The Vindaloonies with Ron Blake (piano accordian), Rob Luckey (guitar), Gerry Kortegast (bass) and Anthony Parrot (drums). The band played an eclectic blend of country rock, gypsy folk and rock'n'roll. The Citadel label issued two Vindaloonies singles 'Shine on'/'Red Light Go Green' (March 1987) and 'Live Another Day'/'Like a Child' (September) before the band called it a day.

Mini-album: *Soul of Discretion* (Correct/Hot, 1985).

Mark Holden

Style: *Pop*

Adelaide-born singer Mark Holden (b. 1954) will always be remembered for his clean-cut image, his white dinner suit and his penchant for handing out carnations to girls on the set of the popular television show ***Countdown***. Holden's successful solo career encompassed four hit singles between 1976 and 1977, two double-gold status albums (50 000 copies sold of both *Let Me Love You* and *Encounter*), a *TV Week* King of Pop award for Best Newcomer

(1976), plus a number of television and film acting roles.

Holden's singles have included 'Never Gonna Fall in Love Again'/'There'll Come a Day' (#12 in June 1976), 'I Wanna Make You My Lady'/'Never Ever Monday' (#9 in September 1976), 'Last Romance'/'Hurricane Rider' (#14 in November 1976), 'Hey My Love'/'We Have Love' (February 1977), 'Reach Out for the One Who Loves You'/'Stay with Me' (#23 in October 1977), 'Let's Go Dancing'/'Easy Street' (January 1978), 'First Thing in the Morning'/'Where are You Girl?' (March 1978), 'Stay'/'Another Night' (1979), 'For You'/'I'll Rock You to Sleep Tonight' (March 1983) and 'Who Do You Love?' (August 1983).

His acting roles have included parts in television soapie *Young Doctors* and the feature films *Blue Fire Lady* (1977) and *Newsfront* (1977). He also compered the television shows *Target* (1975) and *Reach for the Stars* (1978). Since the 1980s, Holden has been based in Los Angeles, where he established himself as a songwriter. He has had his material covered by Meatloaf, Joe Cocker, Gladys Knight, Bob Welch and ex-Sex Pistol Steve Jones. Holden recorded his fourth solo album in Los Angeles utilising session musicians.

Albums: *Dawn in Darkness* (EMI, 1975), *Let Me Love You* (EMI, 1976), *Encounter* (EMI, 1977), *Moments (Best of)* (EMI, 1979), *Mark Holden* (Mercury, 1983).

Dave Hole

Style: *Blues, R&B*

English-born Dave Hole (b. 1948) is the most acclaimed blues guitarist Australia has ever produced. Hole has built up an international reputation courtesy of his unorthodox slide guitar style, his rousing live shows and a series of hard-rocking, roadhouse blues albums. Hole has earned the respect of musicians such as Gary Moore, yet it took two decades of slogging around the Australian touring circuit before the local industry sat up and took notice.

Hole's family immigrated to Australia, settling in the Western Australian capital of Perth when he was four years old. He formed his first band, Broken Habits, in 1965. A year later, he formed the first version of the Dave Hole Band with Denis Crake (vocals), Daryl Upson (bass; ex-Broken Habits) and Jim Morris (drums). In 1968, he joined local heroes The Beaten Tracks, comprising Warren Morgan (piano, organ), Ross Partington (vocals), Murray Wilkins (bass) and Ace Follington (drums). The Beaten Tracks won the Perth heat of the 1968 Hoadley's National Battle of the Sounds, and toured the Eastern states. While in Melbourne, Hole left the band to return to university in Perth. With new guitarist **Phil Manning** on board, The Beaten Tracks relocated to Melbourne, linked up with new singer **Wendy Saddington** and made the transition into the first line-up of legendary blues band **Chain**.

Hole formed the Dave Hole Blues Band before travelling to London in 1972 with Upson and Al Kash (drums; ex-**Blackfeather**). The three-piece band played local pubs for a year. Hole returned to Australia and, over the next decade, honed his masterful slide technique and established himself on the Perth pub circuit with various line-ups of the Dave Hole Band.

Hole's unconventional method of playing over the top of his guitar's fretboard, with the slide on his index finger, came about because he broke his little finger. He was unable to fit a slide comfortably on the little finger. The 1977 Dave Hole Band line-up of Phil Bailey (bass) and Ian Ironside (drums) contributed two tracks, 'Country Town' and 'Still in Love with You', to a Perth compilation album *The 6WF Rock Group Album* (1979). In 1979, Hole teamed up with noted bluesman **Matt Taylor** (ex-**Bay City Union, Chain, Western Flyer**) as the **Matt Taylor** Band Featuring Dave Hole. Paul Poole (bass; ex-Manteca) and Ric Whittle (drums; ex-Fatty Lumpkin, Manteca) completed the line-up. For the next year, the band toured the country to packed houses. At the height of the new wave movement (when anything pre-1976 was considered passé), Hole and Taylor were playing some of the most electrifying blues rock ever heard in this country. The band had the potential to be as famous as **Chain** itself, but unfortunately never got the chance to record. By late 1980, the **Matt Taylor** Band Featuring Dave Hole had come to a natural end.

Hole resumed his slow conquest of the local blues scene. In 1988, he formed blues power trio Short Fuse with John 'Hambone' Wilson (bass) and Ronnie 'Greystroke' Parker (drums). The band recorded the album *Short Fuse Blues* with Bob Patient (ex-**Matt Taylor's Chain**) contributing keyboards to the album sessions. Patient later toured with the band. *Short Fuse Blues* (August 1992) was full of Hole's sinuous, hot-wired guitar work, which evoked the spirit of Elmore James and Blind Willie Johnson. On the strength of that album, Hole landed a contract with America's largest blues label, Chicago-based Alligator Records (home to Albert Collins, Katie Webster, Koko Taylor, Lonnie Mack and Johnny Winter among others). *Short Fuse Blues* also caught the attention of Gary Moore, who invited Hole to tour as his support throughout Europe. Further accolades came with a feature in the slide guitar issue of *Guitar Player* magazine (November 1992).

Since then, Hole has toured overseas constantly and issued one great blues album after another. The autobiographical 'You Don't Have to Be Pretty to Sing the Blues' (from the 1993 album *The Plumber*) came out as a single. His 1993 touring band comprised Wilson, Patient and Rudi Miranda (drums). In 1996, Hole travelled to Chicago to record with several of that city's most experienced blues players. They included Ray 'Killer' Allison (drums; James Cotton, Muddy Waters, Buddy Guy), Johnny B. Gayden (bass; Koko Taylor, Son Seals, Albert Collins' Icebreakers), Tony Z (keyboards; Ronnie Earl, Larry McCray, Buddy Guy), Billy Branch (harmonica; Willie Dixon, Sons of Blues) and Gene Barge (sax; Gary U.S. Bonds, Little Milton). The sessions resulted in the album *Ticket to Chicago*.

Hole's touring band circa 1996 and 1997 comprised Patient, Ric Whittle (drums; ex-**Matt Taylor** Band, Manning–Taylor Band) and Roy Daniel (bass; ex-Fatty Lumpkin, Manning–Taylor Band, **Chain**)

Albums: *Short Fuse Blues* (Festival, 1991), *The Plumber* (Festival, 1993), *Working Overtime* (Festival, 1994), *Steel on Steel* (Festival, 1995), *Whole Lotta Blues* (compilation of first four albums, Festival, 1996), *Ticket to Chicago* (Festival, 1997).

The Hollow Men

Formed: *1985*
Style: *Folk, pop*
Original line-up: *Billy Baxter (vocals; ex-Ghetto Blasters, Big Fans of Jesus), Mal Stanley (vocals, guitar, organ; ex-Burning Souls), Jon Von Goes (guitar), Danny Butler (bass), Paul Johnstone (drums)*

Led by Melbourne cult identity Billy Baxter, The Hollow Men emerged during the mid-1980s playing a tuneful, chiming amalgam of folk, pop and rock. Baxter was probably best known as the person **Paul Kelly** immortalised in his 1980 single '(I Wanna Be Like) Billy Baxter'.

The Hollow Men issued the 12-inch EP *Blue Trains and Gravel Lanes* on the Rampant label (October 1986), after which the original line-up split. The Hollow Men track 'Nights Like These' appeared on Rampant's Various Artists album *Running Rampant Volume 1* (1987). In between auditioning new members, Baxter and Stanley began work on the mini-album *This is Cactus Land* at Joe Camilleri's home studio. In 1988, The Hollow Men moved to the Au-go-go label for their debut, full-length album *Broken Stuff* (March) and the 12-inch EP *Live and Otherwise* (October).

The line-up on the album was Baxter, Stanley, Barbara Waters (guitar, vocals; ex-Broken Hearts), John Drayton (bass) and Archie Cuthbertson (drums; ex-Never Never Band, Ghetto Blasters), with embellishment from guest players James Singleton (cello) and Peter Scholtz (pedal steel). In early 1989, Gina Hearnden (vocals, guitar) replaced Waters, who formed Barb Waters and the Rough Diamonds. The *So Long* album (credited to The Hollowmen) yielded the single 'Human Wreck'/'(You're the Only One) Can Make Me Cry' (February 1990). *So Long* contained a diverse range of appealing tunes, including a gentle treatment of Hüsker Dü's 'Don't Want to Know if You are Lonely'. At the end of 1990, Baxter put The Hollowmen on hold and issued his debut solo album *Holler* a year later.

The last Hollowmen release was the band's version of **God's** 'My Pal' which was issued as a split single with **The Whipper Snappers**. 'My Pal' also appeared on the Various Artists tribute album *Used and Recovered by* on the White label (1990), in which various bands covered classic Australian songs by other artists. By that stage, The Hollowmen had gone their separate ways. Baxter pursued his solo career while Stanley, Drayton and Cuthbertson formed pop rock band Pale Blue Eyes. The other members of Pale Blue Eyes included Liz Aldridge (vocals, guitar), Dave Vandenberg (guitar, vocals) and Sarah Wells (violin). Pale Blue Eyes issued the CD EP 'Rainy Day' in 1992. Hearnden went on to work with The Snow Leopards and The Catalinas.

Prior to dissolving The Hollowmen, Baxter had issued the singles 'It's Too Late to Turn Back Now'/'Bernadette' (on Joe Camilleri's Spirit label, April 1987) and a cover of **The Bee Gees'** 'To Love Somebody'/'Tourists in Heaven' (a duet with **John Kennedy** on the Mighty Boy label, September 1988). Baxter recorded half of his second album, *Speedhump/Thump*, in Melbourne with members of **Autohaze**, **Ripe**, **The Killjoys** and The Somerfields, and the other half in Sydney with members of **The Hummingbirds**, **Smudge** and **The Welcome Mat**. Baxter was also heard as a DJ on Melbourne community radio station 3RRR and the ABC's 3LO on the *Sunday Night Live* show.

Hollowmen albums: *Broken Stuff* (Au-go-go, 1988), *So Long* (Au-go-go, 1990); ***Billy Baxter albums:*** *Holler* (Au-go-go, 1991), *Speedhump/Thump* (Chip Chop/MDS, 1994).

Holocene

Formed: *1993*
Style: *Celestial pop*
Original line-up: *Kerrie Hickin (bass, vocals; ex-***Ku Klux Frankenstein**, **Sunset Strip**, **Autohaze***), Jo-Anne Roberts (guitar, vocals; ex-***Ripe***), Mick Sim (guitar, vocals; ex-Beekeepers), Duncan Hamilton (drums; ex-Squad)*

Holocene was a brief Melbourne delight that flew in the face of that city's penchant for heavy/grunge bands of all descriptions. Holocene's blend of boisterous, harmony-driven guitar pop and intergalactic imagery was punchier, brighter and more fun than any one had a right to expect. Reference points abounded, from The Go-Gos and Badfinger to Redd Kross and The Breeders.

Perth musician Mick Sim's previous band, The Beekeepers, broke up in 1991. The Beekeepers formed out of the ashes of The Fate which comprised Sim, Alan McNeill (vocals, guitar), Mal Secourable (bass, vocals) and Guy Brewster (drums). The Fate had formed in 1986 as De Verks. The Fate issued one self-titled mini-album for the Modern label in 1987. That year, Shaun Lohoar replaced Brewster on drums. The Fate broke up in 1988. Sim and Lohoar formed The Beekeepers with Nick Tweedie (acoustic guitar) and Darren Leitch (bass). Alana Hunt joined on vocals and violin in 1989, and former Fate bass player Mal Secourable replaced Tweedie on acoustic guitar in 1990. Later in the year, Bernice Smith replaced Hunt on violin and vocals. The Beekeepers' independent releases included two EPs, *The First Session* (1989) and *Beefarm Road* (Zero Hour Records, 1991), and a single, 'Take Me Back' (1990). The band's spirited, winsome folk-pop sound called to mind early **Go-Betweens**, **Triffids** and **Hollow Men**.

Holocene

Holocene spent a year building up a cult following on the Melbourne inner-city pub circuit before issuing a trio of fine CD EPs, 'Pop Astronauts' (March 1994), 'Flying' (May) and 'Guitarbarella' (October), in quick succession. Each was brimming with melodic pop hooks, exquisite guitar work and just a hint of kitsch. Alongside self-penned gems like 'Pop Astronauts', 'Antimatter Eon' and 'Guitarbarella', Holocene showed impeccable taste by covering such obscure songs as Badfinger's 'Flying', Opal's 'Supernova' and The 5th Dimension's 'Who Do You Think of?' (to say nothing of the band's dynamic live rendition of The Move/E.L.O. chestnut 'Do Ya'). The band supported overseas visitors Superchunk and Buffalo Tom on their Australian tours.

American Robert Weston produced Holocene's debut album, *Spurr* (March 1995). Despite its joyous immediacy, it was not the commercial breakthrough release for which the band had been hoping. Sim and Hamilton left towards the end of 1995 to be replaced by John Freeman-Baxter and Adam Newey (on loan from **The Fauves**) respectively. The band found a permanent drummer in Geoff Pennington, who joined during December. Holocene's days were numbered, however, and in May 1996 the band called it quits.

Album: *Spurr* (Concubine/Shock, 1995).

Home

Formed: *1972*
Style: *Country rock*
Original line-up: *Glyn Mason (guitar, vocals; ex-Rebels,* **Chain**, *Copperwine), Ian 'Gunther' Gorman (guitar, vocals; ex-Salty Dog), Trevor Wilson (bass, vocals; ex-***La De Das***), Nevin 'Loppy' Morris (drums; ex-***Hot Cottage***)*

Like **Axiom**, **Country Radio**, Powderhorn and a few others, Home was one of the first local bands to embrace an American West Coast-influenced brand of country rock and infuse it with uniquely Australian imagery. Glyn Mason, Trevor Wilson and Gunther Gorman were also devotees of Satguru Maharaj Ji and the Divine Light Mission. Mason formed Home in late August 1972, following the break up of Copperwine. Home signed to Atlantic and issued the album *Home—At Last!* and the single 'Maureen'/'Forget Me Not' (October 1973). The album was full of light and nimble country rock with a clean blues edge.

Phil Lawson (ex-**Bakery**) replaced Wilson on bass during September, and the band continued in the same country-blues rock vein for its second album *Long, Long Way to Nowhere* (1974). It was a pleasant sound, but not slick in an Eagles/Poco kind of way. The single 'Bang Bang Bang' (backed with the title track) was actually reminiscent of The Byrds circa 1971 ('Gunga Din' and 'Chestnut Mare'). Not long after the album came out, Mason accepted an offer to join **Ariel**, which precipitated Home's break-up in January 1975. Gorman did short-term stints with **Daddy Cool** (April to September 1975), **Sherbet** (January to March 1976) and the **Richard Clapton** Band before forming his own band, Gunther's G-Force, in 1978 with guitarist Don Miller-Robinson. In 1980, Gorman issued a solo album on WEA, *Infectious Rhythm*, and the single 'I Was Seduced'/'Oh J.B.' (December 1980). In 1982, he worked with ex-members of **Ol'55** as The Fives.

With the break-up of **Ariel** in August 1977, Mason toured briefly with the **Richard Clapton** Band and played with the short-lived Loose String Band. He formed The Stockley See Mason Band in late 1978 with fellow veterans Chris Stockley (guitar, vocals; ex-**Axiom**, **Dingoes**, Greg Quill's Southern Cross) and Sam See (guitar, vocals; ex-**Sherbet**, **Flying Circus**, **Fraternity**, Greg Quill's Southern Cross). Jeff Rosenberg (bass; ex-Hot Air Band) and Dave Stewart (drums; ex-Daniel) completed the line-up. The Stockley See Mason Band signed to Mushroom and issued the maxi-single 'Endless Love'/'Blue Horizons', 'The Last One to Know' (September 1979), the single Lonnie Mack's 'Lucy'/'Paradise for Fools' (January 1980) and the album *Beg Steal or Borrow* (November 1979). Mason left in May 1980, to be replaced by Englishman Chris Copping (keyboards; ex-Procol Harum) and Brian Cappuno (vocals; ex-Hotspur, Ace Novelty Company). Three months later, Copping and Cappuno both left. The Stockley See Band broke up in March 1981.

Stewart joined Mason's new band, Tour De Force, which broke up in 1983. Mason went on to **The Fabulous Zarsoff Brothers** and the Doc Span Blues Band. Stockley went on to Rock Doctors, **The Tinsley Waterhouse Band**, the **Jimmy Barnes** Band, The Blue Heelers and country ensemble The Vic State Opry. Rosenberg joined **Eurogliders**. See played with the **John Farnham** Band and the **Broderick Smith** Band among others.

Home albums: *Home—At Last!* (Atlantic, 1973), *Long, Long Way to Nowhere* (Atlantic, 1974); ***Stockley See Mason Band album:*** *Beg Borrow or Steal* (Mushroom/Festival, 1979).

Honeymoon in Green

Formed: *1982*
Style: *Pop*
Original line-up: *John Danyi (vocals, guitar), Amanda Fox (keyboards), David Elliot (bass), Rick Ferrara (drums)*

This Melbourne inner-city band mixed moody pop, Dylanesque lyrics and a Joy Division-like ambience. By eschewing a 'rock' approach early on, the band preferred to create a mood with its subtle use of haunting atmospherics and a chiming guitar/keyboard interplay. Honeymoon in Green issued a self-financed single, 'Acrobat in Love'/'Good Mood', in June 1983, and then was quiet for a year or so.

In 1985 the band issued the four-track 12-inch EP *Temperature Here* on the Rampant label, followed by the single 'Eve'/'Wheel Girl' (December 1986), which was produced by Whirlywirld founder **Ollie Olsen**. By that stage, Shane Walsh (ex-Dave Last's Boy Kings) had replaced David Elliot, Bruce Kane (ex-Dave Last's Boy Kings) had joined on drums and Andrew Crowder (keyboards, guitar; ex-**Feral Dinosaurs**) had replaced Amanda Fox. A year later, the band issued its debut album, *Angels Bringing* (September 1987). *Angels Bringing* was a punchy rock album, far removed from the band's esoteric early sound. Honeymoon in Green broke up in 1989. Walsh later worked with **Maurice Frawley and the Working Class Ringos**, and Kane joined country rock band **Acuff's Rose**.

Album: *Angels Bringing* (Rampant, 1987).

The Honeys

Formed: *1987*
Style: *Country, folk*
Original line-up: *Andrea Croft (vocals), Michael 'Blue' Dalton (slide guitar, harmonica; ex-***Lighthouse Keepers***), Bruce Begley (guitar, vocals; ex-Slaybells), Grant Shanahan (bass, vocals; ex-Slaybells), Philip Rawlinson (drums; ex-Rabbit's Wedding)*

The Honeys formed in Sydney, New South Wales during September 1987. The band had its roots in Perth, Western Australia from where Andrea Croft, Bruce Begley, Grant Shanahan and Philip Rawlinson all originally hailed. The band's fresh blend of country and folk rock elements was fleshed out by silky smooth harmonies, bluesy harp, a subtle rhythm, delicate washes of slide guitar and Croft's warm and soulful voice. It was a very pleasant sound, and surprisingly the band found favour with Sydney-based independent label Waterfront (home to **The Hard-Ons**, **Massappeal**, **The Eastern Dark** and **Hellmenn**, but also **The Lighthouse Keepers** and The Widdershins).

Rawlinson's previous band, Rabbit's Wedding, issued the singles 'Rideout'/'Someone as' (April 1986) and 'Coming Like Summer'/'Mandarins' (November 1987), plus the mini-album *In Truth About Road* (August 1987). With the aid of a Western Australian Arts Council Grant, The Honeys recorded their debut album, *Goddess*, at Poons Head Studio, East Fremantle only three months after formation.

The Honeys returned to Sydney where Waterfront issued the album in May 1988. Begley wrote all the tracks bar one, 'Bells of Spring', penned by Shanahan. By the time the album came out, Brett Thomson had replaced Rawlinson. The Honeys issued two more singles 'The Man Who was Through with the World'/'Sick' (December 1988) and 'Gone Away'/'Monster' (July 1989) before breaking up at the end of 1989. Croft, Shanahan and Thomson formed Catherine Wheel with Stephen 'Biff' Smith (guitar), while Dalton joined The Bluemeninthals. Catherine Wheel issued two pure pop singles, 'Blue Avenue'/'Lost Explanation' (1990) and 'Almost Blind' (1991), plus the CD EP *Self Portraits* (1992). With the break-up of Catherine Wheel, Croft and Begley were reunited in The Snow Leopards.

With backing provided by a number of musicians, including Kylie Adams (vocals), Lisa Partington (vocals), Magdelaine Chase (vocals), Peter Nagle (guitar), James Lockett (keyboards), Andrew Ingram (bass) and Peter Kelly (drums; ex-**Flies**, **Vanilla Chainsaws**, **No Man's Land**), The Snow Leopards recorded the mini-album *Snow Leopards* (May 1991) and the CD EP 'Sweet Sweet Dreams' (February 1992) for the Waterfront label. The 1992 Snow Leopards line-up comprised Begley, Adams, Partington, Kelly, Peter 'D.J.' Kelly (bass; ex-**Vanilla Chainsaws**) and Gina Hearnden (vocals; ex-**Hollow Men**).

Albums: *Goddess* (Waterfront, 1988), *Ultimo* (compilation, Waterfront, 1995).

Hoodoo Gurus

Formed: *1981*
Style: *Pop, rock*
Original line-up: *Dave Faulkner (guitar, vocals; ex-***Victims**, **Manikins***), Kimble Rendall (guitar, vocals; ex-***XL-Capris***),* **Roddy Radalj** *(guitar, vocals; ex-Invaders,* **Scientists**, *Rockets), James Baker (drums; ex-***Victims**, **Scientists***)*

Hoodoo Gurus were one of the great singles bands of the Australian rock and pop era (right up there with **The Easybeats** and **Mental as Anything**). Yet, over the course of 15 years and 28 singles, only four of those reached the national Top 30. Of those four, only one, 'What's My Scene?', went Top 5.

Statistics like that actually say very little about the band's music. From perfect 1960s power pop ('I Want You Back', 'What's My Scene?') and wild garage punk ('Leilani', 'Like Wow-Wipeout'), to driving hard rock ('Axegrinder', 'The Right Time') and funky psychedelic kitsch ('Miss Freelove '69'), the Gurus' music knew no bounds. And as main songwriter Dave Faulkner has noted, many of the Gurus' most popular songs live were often their least successful singles.

The genesis of the Hoodoo Gurus' sound lies in Perth punk bands **The Victims** and **Scientists**. After a stint with fellow Perth punk-popsters **Manikins**, Faulkner travelled to the USA. Upon his return Faulkner, Baker and Radalj relocated to Sydney where the three musicians formed Le Hoodoo Gurus on 1 January 1981. The band's heroes, as quoted in one of the band's early classics '(Let's All) Turn on' were The Cramps, The Fleshtones, New York Dolls, The Ramones, The Flamin' Groovies, Sky Saxon, Gene Vincent, The Rolling Stones, T. Rex and The Troggs—all garage rock'n' roll exponents.

With the unorthodox line-up of three guitars and drums (no bass), Le Hoodoo Gurus immediately stood out from Sydney's Detroit-inspired fraternity. By fusing classic pop melodies, punkish guitars and an American junk culture aesthetic with an absurd sense of humour, the Gurus built up a fanatical following. The band's debut single, 'Leilani'/'Leilani Part II' (October 1982), was an instant classic. Powered by a whomping, Gary Glitteresque back-beat provided by Baker, and lots of 'umgawas' in the vocal department, 'Leilani' was inspired by those Hollywood south seas melodramas like *Bird of Paradise* (1951) in which the maiden was sacrificed to the erupting volcano in order to appease the gods, leaving her hapless lover bereft on the sand. It was pure pulp, but glorious fun all the same.

Just before the single came out, Rendall left the band to concentrate on his film-making career. Dropping the 'Le' part of the name, Faulkner drafted in Clyde Bramley (ex-**Hitmen**, Other Side, **New Christs**, Minuteman, Super K) to play bass. The change in format was too much for Radalj, who left to form **The Johnnys**. His place was taken in October 1982 by Brad Shepherd (ex-**Fun Things**, 31st, **Hitmen**, Super K) who added his considerable guitar prowess to the overall sound. Bramley had formed Super K as a 1960s bubblegum tribute band, covering material by such eminent creations as The 1910 Fruitgum Co., The Lemon Pipers, The Ohio Express, The Archies and The American Breed. Super K was the production banner under which bubblegum whiz kids Jerry Kasenetz and Jeff Katz worked. Super K (the band) played a few shows around Sydney in 1982 and issued the single 'Recurring Nightmare'/'Go-Go' on the GREEN label. Citadel reissued the single in 1986. Super K on the single comprised Bramley, Shepherd, Tracey Landing (vocals), Catherine Wade (vocals), Paul Thirkell (guitar), Frank Brunetti (organ) and Ken Doyle (drums).

Having established themselves as one of the country's finest live bands, Hoodoo Gurus issued the essential *Stoneage Romeos* album in March 1984. *Stoneage Romeos* remains one of the finest debut albums issued by an Australian band. The Gurus dedicated the album to such 1960s television sitcom icons as Larabee (*Get Smart*), Larry Storch (*F-Troop*) and Arnold (the pig) Ziffel (*Petticoat Junction*). They even tipped their hat to Larry, Curly and Moe by deriving the album title from a Three Stooges short!

The album yielded the singles 'Tojo'/'(Let's All) Turn on' (June 1983), 'My Girl'/'Be My Guru' (#35 in October 1983) and 'I Want You Back'/'Who Do You Love?' (March 1984). As the band was riding its first wave of success, Baker was sacked amid a blaze of ill-feeling during August 1984. He went on to concentrate on **Beasts of Bourbon** and **The Dubrovniks**. Mark Kingsmill (ex-Hellcats, Other Side, **Hitmen, New Christs**) came in as replacement. *Mars Needs Guitars!* (#3 in September 1985) spawned two of the band's best singles in 'Bittersweet'/'Mars Needs Guitars!' (#16 in June) and 'Like Wow-Wipeout'/'Bring the Hoodoo Down' (#15 in October), as well as 'Death Defying'/'Turkey Dinner' (February 1986) and 'Poison Pen'/'In the Wild', 'Teenage Head' (September 1986). This time the album was dedicated to Jonathan Harris (who played *Lost in Space* villain Dr Zachary Smith).

The band toured the USA (where *Stoneage Romeos* and *Mars Needs Guitars!* had topped the Alternative/College charts) and Europe. The band's third album, *Blow Your Cool!*, was full of energetic pop songs like the singles 'What's My Scene?'/'Heart of Darkness' (#3 in May 1987), 'Good Times'/'Hell for Leather' (#36 in August) and 'In the Middle of the Land'/'Hayride to Hell II', 'The Showdown' (December). Members of The Bangles and The Dream Syndicate contributed backing vocals to several songs on the album. *Blow Your Cool!* made its debut on the national charts at #2 in May, and went on to sell over 70 000 copies.

Dave Faulkner, Hoodoo Gurus

At that point, the band opted out of its record contract with Big Time, amid protracted legal wranglings. Then, in March 1988, long-serving member Bramley left the band. The Gurus' future looked bleak, but Rick Grossman (ex-**Bleeding Hearts, Matt Finish, Divinyls**) eventually replaced Bramley. Later in the year, the Gurus signed a new deal with RCA, with the first fruits of the liaison being the single 'The Generation Gap'/'Jungle Bells' (December 1988). RCA lifted three singles off *Magnum Cum Louder* (June 1989): 'Come Anytime'/'Cajun Country' (#26 in June), 'Axe Grinder'/'Spaghetti Western' (August) and 'Another World'/'Cover for a Friend' (October). *Magnum Cum Louder* reached a peak of #4 on the national chart in July. It was not a big seller in the long run, despite another clutch of outstanding tunes and extensive local and international touring in support of its release.

The Gurus bounced back two years later with one of their best albums, *Kinky* (May 1991). Mixed by American Ed Stasium (Ramones, Living Colour, **Baby Animals**) *Kinky* peaked at #10 on the national chart in June. It produced four singles, 'Miss

Freelove '69'/'Stomp the Tumbarumba' (#17 in April 1991), '1000 Miles Away'/'I Think You Know' (#33 in July), 'A Place in the Sun'/'The Doctor is in' (August) and 'Castles in the Air'/'Little Drummer Boy' (December). Another gruelling world tour followed the album's release. In August 1992, the Gurus issued the compilations *Electric Soup* (single A-sides) and *Gorilla Biscuits* (single B-sides and rarities). *Electric Soup*, in particular, confirmed the band's consistent ability to craft timeless, diamond-hard pop gems. It reached #6 on the national album listing, and went on to sell over 140 000 copies. The band recorded its sixth studio album in Los Angeles with Stasium.

Crank (March 1994) was a much rawer rock album, and the first CD single, 'The Right Time' (November 1993), was one of the band's hardest rocking songs *ever*. The album made its debut at #2 on the national album charts. Three more CD singles followed, 'You Open My Eyes' (January 1994), 'Less than a Feeling' (April) and 'Nobody' (June). The Crank world tour took the Gurus through the USA, Canada, Europe and Brazil, where they commanded a fanatical following. Faulkner also composed the soundtrack to Laurie McInnes' 1994 feature film *Broken Highway*.

In 1995, the Gurus collaborated with **The Master's Apprentices** frontman **Jim Keays** on an updated rendition of 'Turn Up Your Radio'. The song was included on a new Masters' Best of album, as well as being issued as a single. In 1996 the Gurus signed a new deal with Mushroom Records and issued *Blue Cave* (June). The album made the national Top 20, and spawned three CD singles, 'Waking Up Tired'/'Quicksand' (April), 'If Only' (August), 'Down on Me'/'Big Deal' (December) plus the *Hoodoo Voodoo* CD EP (February 1997), which featured dance remixes of tracks like 'Down on Me' and 'Son of a Gun'.

The band set off on an Australian tour with US outfit The Posies and local band **Drop City**. Touring commitments were curtailed when Kingsmill severed tendons and nerves in his arm as a result of an onstage accident. Once Kingsmill recovered, the Gurus completed their Circus Maximus Australian tour at the end of 1996. In January 1997, Dave Faulkner announced that the band would be breaking up at the end of the year. Two months later, the Gurus undertook another tour of Brazil, where they played a concert in front of 40 000 people. The Gurus commenced their final Australian tour, the three-month Spit the Dummy jaunt, in October 1997. The tour coincided with the release of the double compilation album *Armchair Gurus/Electric Gurus*, which made #29 on the national chart. The 34-track collection contained two previously unissued tracks, plus five new songs, including the band's final CD single 'The Real Deal'. After 16 years on the road, and one and a quarter million album sales worldwide, it was all over for Hoodoo Gurus.

Albums: *Stoneage Romeos* (Big Time/EMI, 1984), *Mars Needs Guitars!* (Big Time/EMI, 1985), *Blow Your Cool!* (Big Time/EMI, 1987), *Magnum Cum Louder* (Big Time/EMI, 1988), *Kinky* (BMG/RCA, 1991), *Electric Soup* (BMG/RCA, 1992), *Gorilla Biscuits* (BMG/RCA, 1992), *Crank* (BMG/RCA, 1994), *Blue Cave* (Mushroom/Festival, 1996), *Armchair Gurus/Electric Chair* (Mushroom/Sony, 1997).

Horsehead

Formed: *1992*
Style: *Hard rock*
Original line-up: *Andy McLean (vocals; ex-21 Guns), Cameron McKenzie (guitar; ex-21 Guns), Scott Kingman (guitar; ex-***Chantoozies***), Mick Vallance (bass; ex-***Boom Crash Opera***), Craig Waugh (drums; ex-***Uncanny X-Men**, *RAW)*

The members of Melbourne-based band Horsehead had all played in a variety of pop rock outfits before joining forces in a harder edged venture. Andy McLean and Cameron McKenzie's previous band 21 Guns issued one self-titled album and three singles, 'I Believe', 'Save Me' and 'Hard Luck Story', on WEA during 1990. McLean had also appeared as a compere on the ABC-TV's ill-fated pop show *Countdown Revolution* in 1989.

Horsehead's take on stadium rock mixed a Led Zeppelinesque bottom-end kick with gut-thumping Faith No More-styled riffs. Nothing subtle or innovative, but everything delivered with great force and conviction. The band played its debut gig in March 1992, and within months had built up a strong following on the Melbourne pub and club scene. US label Maverick (home to Madonna) took an interest in Horsehead, but the band signed to Mushroom instead. Mushroom issued the single 'Oil and Water' and the band's acclaimed, self-titled debut album (November 1993), after which Horsehead set out on an Australian tour as support to **Hoodoo Gurus**. The band's touring commitments were put on hold at the end of 1994 when McLean wound up in hospital as a result of his over-enthusiastic stage activities. The band laid low for most of 1995 before bouncing back with a new album a year later.

Onism (May 1996) and the CD singles 'Strange' (April), 'Ever' (June) and 'Shine' (October) reflected the band's move into territory already mapped out by US heavyweights like Tool, Stone Temple Pilots and Alice in Chains. This was partially facilitated by the album's producer Sylvia Massey, who had also worked with Tool and Skunk Anansie. The band slipped from view for a year before re-emerging in mid-1997 with a tour support to US visitors Live and a new CD EP, *The Golden Cow Collection*, on the independent Stubble label (through Shock). Horsehead supported US visitor Alice Cooper on his Australian tour during September.

Albums: *Horsehead* (ATI/Mushroom/Festival, 1993), *Onism* (Mushroom/Festival, 1996).

Hoss

Formed: *1990*
Style: *Hard rock*
Original line-up: *Joel Silbersher (guitar, vocals; ex-***God***), Mick Weber (guitar; ex-Seminal Rats, Slush Puppies), Scott Bailey (bass), Todd McNeair (drums; ex-Seminal Rats)*

Former **God** member Joel Silbersher was the driving force and main songwriter behind hard-rocking Melbourne quartet Hoss. The band earned a solid reputation by consistently living up to audience expectations with well-honed songs and uncompromising gigs. By taking inspiration from the likes of The Rolling Stones, Kiss, The Stooges, **AC/DC** and Black Sabbath, Hoss came up with a near-perfect blend of melodic power chords, hyper-kinetic guitar riffs and hard driving rock beats.

Hoss' debut album *Guzzle* was a rushed affair (recorded in one session, the day before the band played its debut gig), and consequently lacked appealing ideas. 'Green' was lifted as the single. It was backed by two, non-album cover songs, Aerosmith's 'Bright Light Fright' and Bob Dylan's 'It's All Over Now, Baby Blue', which were proof of the band's eclectic approach. The band was at its best on the album *You Get Nothing* (April 1992), which mixed Detroit rock action with *Exile on Main Street*-era Rolling Stones raunch. The single 'It's Everywhere'/'Ark' (February) showed a poppier side to the band without sacrificing an ounce of distortion or power in the process. Occasional sax and piano fleshed out the arrangements. Silbersher also brought in extra guitarists Paul Ryan (ex-**Sunset Strip**) and John Nolan (from **Powder Monkeys**) to boost the overall sound.

Before the album came out, Jimmy Sfetsos (guitar; ex-Nice Girls from Cincinnati) and Michael 'Captain Kaos' Glenn (drums; ex-Joysticks, Forbidden Planet) had replaced Weber and McNeair respectively. Weber and McNeair returned to Seminal Rats, which also comprised Michael Harley (vocals), Reuben Pinkster (guitar) and David Balsamo (bass). The Rats played a solid brand of punk rock, and all up issued the mini-albums *Seminal Rats* (1987) and *Omnipotent* (1988), the album *Life in the Necropolis* (1990) and the single 'La Grande Bouffe'/'Head Rush' (November 1991).

In 1993 Hoss issued the CD EP 'Cave Me in' (June), the album *Bring on the Juice* (August) and the single 'The Tiredest Man Awake'/'Token Kiss' (on the Death Valley label). The album title was derived from the James Brown song 'Funky Drummer' in which Brown shouts out the instruction to his band to 'pump it up'. Journeyman guitarist Charlie Owen contributed lap slide and dobro to the meandering blues 'Lip from Lip' on the album. Silbersher and Owen later collaborated on the *Tendrils* album (June 1995), which featured 'last-record-of-the-night-kind-of-music' as epitomised by a sombre cover of Richard Thompson's 'Night Comes in'.

Hoss issued the CD EP 'Gentle Claws' in March 1994, but it was to be another 18 months before a new album, *Everyday Lies*, arrived (November 1995). Silbersher kept busy in the meantime by issuing his debut solo album under the moniker of Melonman. The album was a ramshackle collection of country-tinged tunes and garage trash-pop. Dean Muller (ex-Voodoo Lust, Macho Clowns) replaced Glenn in Hoss during 1995. Hoss contributed 'The Bullshit Never Ends', 'Winter Salsa' and a cover of **The Saints'** 'Simple Love' to the *Idiot Box* soundtrack which was issued on rooArt/BMG in February 1997.

Hoss albums: *Guzzle* (Au-go-go, 1990), *You Get Nothing* (Dog Meat, 1992), *Bring on the Juice* (Dog Meat, 1993), *Everyday Lies* (Dog Meat, 1995); ***Joel Silbersher solo album as Melonman:*** *Melonman* (Rubber, 1994); ***Joel Silbersher and Charlie Owen as Tendrils:*** *Tendrils* (Dog Meat, 1995).

Hot City Bump Band

Formed: *1973*
Style: *Soul, funk*
Original line-up: *Chuck McKinney (vocals), Margaret McKinney (vocals), John Adolphus (guitar), David McMaster (organ), Robert Ellis (congas), David Green (bass), Mick Holden (drums; ex-***Mixtures***)*

Chicago-born Chuck McKinney and his wife Margaret worked in the Melbourne season of the stage musical *Hair*. At the end of 1973, they formed Hot

City Bump Band with four local musicians and West Indian percussionist Robert Ellis. Hot City Bump Band was one of the first soul/funk bands ever assembled in Australia, and local audiences (having been brought up on a steady diet of rock, boogie and pop) took a while to warm to the band's dance-oriented sound.

The band signed to the Wizard label, and issued the singles The Beatles' 'Come Together'/'Ain't Nobody' and 'Time is on Your Side'/'Trying Times' in 1974. A year later the band issued its debut album, *Come Together*, and third single, 'Do What You Wanna Do'/'Let's Fly', which peaked at #13 in Melbourne during August 1975. By that stage, Noel Davies had replaced original guitarist John Adolphus. The band supported international visitors Osibisa, Gladys Knight and the Pips and The Temptations during the year. Then, in January 1976, Hot City Bump Band announced its break-up, issuing a final single, 'Ain't No Use'/'I Really Love You', the same month.

Chuck, Margaret and David Green initially formed City Strut before Chuck issued a solo single, 'If You Don't Know Me by Now'/'Mighty Mighty', on the Miracle label (December 1976). Chuck formed the Chuck McKinney Band with Frank Esler-Smith (keyboards), David McMaster (keyboards), Phil Leisenberg (guitar), Steve Hogg (bass; ex-**Bakery**) and Sunil de Silva (drums; ex-Skylight). Margaret issued a duet single with Danny McMaster in 1981, 'Back to Where We Started'/'True Kind of Loving'. Chuck and Margaret both went on to become in-demand session singers. Chuck appeared on **John Farnham's** 1990 album *Chain Reaction* and also toured as back-up singer in the **John Farnham** Band. In 1993, Margaret worked as tour manager for pop sensations **Girlfriend**.

Album: *Come Together* (Wizard, 1975).

Hot Cottage

Formed: *1969*
Style: *Country rock*
Original line-up: *Greg Grace (vocals; ex-***Flying Circus***), Kim Humphreys (guitar; ex-Paper Grape), Dick Huxley (keyboards), Steve Hart (bass; ex-Paper Grape), Nevin 'Loppy' Morris (drums; ex-Paper Grape)*

Singer Greg Grace left **Flying Circus** in June 1969 to form Hot Cottage with ex-members of Paper Grape. The early **Flying Circus** had played country rock prior to recording a series of ultra-commercial, bubblegum pop singles. Hot Cottage allowed Grace to return to the harmony-laden, American West Coast-influenced country rock sound of The Byrds, Buffalo Springfield and the newly formed 'supergroup' Crosby Stills and Nash. Hot Cottage's debut single for EMI/Columbia featured two Buffalo Springfield covers, 'Mister Soul'/'Bluebird' (January 1970).

In mid-1971, Grace rejoined **Flying Circus**, by then based in Canada and immersing themselves fully in the country rock genre. Hot Cottage recruited new singer Barry Dominey, who had previously played drums in psychedelic band The Wright of Waye. The Wright of Waye issued two ultra-rare singles, 'Penelope Play'/'You Can't do it Alone' (on Natec, 1968) and 'Sun God'/'Dollar Song' (on Philips, 1969). Reissue specialists Raven later included 'Sun God' on the various artists compilation *Ugly Things 4 Down Under Dreamtime (Australasian Sixties Psychedelia)* (1989). In the meantime, the new Hot Cottage moved in a heavier blues rock direction, issuing a second single 'Made to Love You'/'Sour Lovin'' on EMI/HMV (October 1971).

Latter-day Hot Cottage singer Jim Willebrandt had previously sung with Clapham Junction (one single for the Du Monde label, 'Emily on Sunday'/'Good Time Music' in November 1970) and Stafford Bridge (two singles for Festival/Infinity 'Song for a Blind Man'/'Passing Lines', February 1972 and 'Poor Soul'/'Welcome to the Court', October 1972). With the break-up of Hot Cottage in 1973, Kim Humphreys formed Stumble and Loppy Morris joined country rock outfit **Home**, before turning up in hard rock band **Chariot** at the end of 1974.

Hot Half Hour

Formed: *1982*
Style: *Swing jazz*
Original line-up: *Dean Richards (guitar; ex-Whirlywirld,* **Equal Local***), Trish Viggiano (piano), Stephen Lys (trumpet), Geoff Campbell (trumpet), John Crosbie (trombone), Kim Beissel (baritone sax), Mick Hauser (tenor sax), Ralph Traviato (tenor sax), Paul Holleman (alto sax), Ian Cox (alto sax, soprano sax), Chris Parslow (alto sax, clarinet), Andrea Jones (vocals), Bryce Perrin (double bass; ex-***Equal Local***),* **Philip Brophy** *(drums; ex-→↑→)*

Dean Richards was something of a pioneer on the Melbourne new wave scene during the late-1970s, having been a member of seminal electronic outfit Whirlywirld and leader of post-punk jazz-rock band **Equal Local.** Bryce Perrin and Mick Hauser had also been members of **Equal Local. Philip Brophy** was another pioneer, with his esoteric experimental band →↑→. With the neo-big band Hot Half Hour, the musicians played swing-jazz in the tradition of The Glenn Miller Orchestra, Tommy Dorsey and the Count Basie Big Band.

The 14-member big band appeared on stage wearing dinner suits, seated behind podiums with Richards acting as conductor, arranger and guitar player. Hot Half Hour impressed audiences willing to seek a live experience beyond pub rock. The band's only recording, a self-titled 12-inch EP on the Man Made label, suffered from a harsh production sound, although it conveyed enough of the band's uptempo live feel to be a successful statement. Andrea Jones also appeared at live gigs as the band's chanteuse, but she was absent from the recording. Brophy and Perrin left at the end of 1982 to be replaced by Graeme Perry (ex-**Parachute,** Eric Gradman: Man & Machine) and Bill McDonald respectively. Hot Half Hour continued for another year before Richards and Hauser moved on to 100 Flowers in Bloom. Mick Hauser died from brain cancer in February 1985.

Hot Tomatoes

Formed: *1988*
Style: *Punk*
Original line-up: *Mark Bell (vocals), Scott Burnett (guitar), Stu (guitar), Giles Bettison (bass), Michael Pittman (drums)*

This Adelaide band played flat-out, distorted punk-thrash in the manner of US skate-punks Suicidal Tendencies. The band issued an album, *With a Pinch of Salt,* on the Dominator label. In 1990, Kelly Hewson (guitar; ex-Funhouse, Order of Decay) and Neil Cook replaced Scott Burnett and Mark Bell respectively. Hewson remained with Hot Tomatoes for three years. Hot Tomatoes issued the four-track 7-inch EP 'Stalwart Carousel' before breaking up in 1992.

Hewson's previous band, Funhouse, was based in Sydney, but grew out of Adelaide band Gun Control. Funhouse comprised Phil McTaggert (bass), Rip Savage (vocals) and Paul Larsen (drums). Funhouse issued one single, 'Conspicuous Consumption'/'Retaliation', in 1984 before splitting up. At the same time he joined Hot Tomatoes, Hewson was also a member of hardcore band Grunter which comprised Aaron Hewson (drums; ex-Order of Decay), Michael Feeney (bass; ex-Order of Decay) and Dave Scunge (vocals). Grunter grew out of the ashes of hardcore band Order of Decay, which had occupied Kelly, Aaron and Michael at the end of the 1980s.

'Filthy' Phil Partridge was Order of Decay's lead singer. Order of Decay issued a 7-inch EP and a self-titled album on the Dominator label before transforming into Grunter at the end of 1990. Grunter shared the *Do It* album (on Dominator) with Melbourne band Arm the Insane. By 1995, Grunter's line-up included Kelly Hewson, Scunge, Rob Bryant (bass) and Adam Messenger (drums), who was then replaced by Damien Shepherd. Aaron Hewson had joined **The Mark of Cain.** Grunter issued a new album, *Long Gone Wastage*, on Dominator in December 1996.

Album: *With a Pinch of Salt* (Dominator, 1989).

Shane Howard

Style: *Folk, country*

Singer/songwriter Shane Howard (b. 1955) is best known for his work with **Goanna,** whose 1982 hit single 'Solid Rock' remains a staple of the 'classic hits' radio format. Following the break-up of **Goanna** at the end of 1985, Howard has pursued a successful solo career, mainly on the folk circuit. He has toured overseas and issued five albums.

Howard's first touring band, Shane Howard and Friends, comprised members of the last **Goanna** line-up: Simon Curphy (guitar), Joe Imbrol (bass), Dave Stewart (drums) and his sister Marcie (backing vocals), plus guest player **Joe Geia** (guitar, vocals). Since then he has formed numerous line-ups of the Shane Howard Band. In 1987, Howard relocated to the Gulf of Carpentaria (Northern Territory) where he spent time playing with Aboriginal musicians such as members of **Coloured Stone.** In May 1989, he issued his debut album, *Back to the Track*, which yielded the singles 'Back to the Track'/'Mother Earth' (March) and 'Just a Feeling'/ 'Big City Blues' (June). Howard issued the album initially on his own Uluru label before RCA stepped in with a distribution deal.

Howard signed a new deal with BMG and issued the album *River,* which included three singles, 'Walk on Fire', 'If the Well Runs Dry' and 'Escape from Reality'. Mark Moffatt produced the album, and Howard employed the services of guest musicians like Ricky Fataar (drums), Mark Punch (guitar) and **Ross Hannaford** (guitar). Tracks like 'Heart of the Country' and 'If the Well Runs Dry' reflected Howard's environmental concerns. Howard supported overseas visitors Clannad and Hothouse Flowers on their respective Australian tours. Howard's third album, *Time will Tell* (August 1993), included the singles Bob Dylan's 'I Shall Be Released' and 'Flesh and Blood'. In 1993, Howard

Shane Howard

toured Ireland, as a guest of Irish folk singer Mary Black. Black recorded a cover of Howard's 'Flesh and Blood', which became a major hit for her. A second tour of Ireland for Howard resulted in the 1995 album *Live in Ireland.* Howard issued the album on his own label Big Heart.

John Farnham issued the Shane Howard-penned 'Talk of the Town' as a single in 1994. Howard collaborated with **Archie Roach** on a cover of **Scrap Metal's** 'Nhyul Nhyul Girl' which they contributed to the Various Artists compilation *Earth Music* issued on the Mushroom label (June 1994). In 1996, Howard worked with Koori artists such as **Archie Roach**, Bart Willoughby, **Kev Carmody** and **Tiddas**. In early 1997, Howard was working in Broome, Western Australia where he produced an album *Saltwater Country* for The Pigram Brothers (previously known as **Scrap Metal**). Howard's fifth solo album, *Clan*, came out through the ABC. Many of the songs on the album explored Howard's Irish heritage, paying homage to the culture of his ancestors. Juxtaposed against that were songs focusing on the plight of Australia's Aboriginal people.

Albums: *Back to the Track* (Uluru Music/RCA, 1989), *River* (BMG, 1990), *Time will Tell* (BMG, 1993), *Live in Ireland* (Big Heart, 1995), *Clan* (Big Heart/ABC, 1997).

Steve Hoy

Style: *Roots rock*

Newcastle-born singer/songwriter Steve Hoy started his career singing acoustic folk and blues in pubs and wine bars around Sydney. He moved to Canberra in 1983, where he formed rockabilly outfit The Hoy Boys. Hoy first came to widespread attention when Joe Camilleri's Spirit label issued his debut album, *Anticipation*, and single 'Your Heart on My Sleeve'/'Blowing 'Round Here' in 1985. Camilleri also produced the album, and was instrumental in assembling a crack backing band for the session featuring himself, **Ross Hannaford**, Wayne Duncan and **Gary Young**. Hoy's music embraced elements of country, R&B and rock'n'roll, with the singer citing such influences as Robert Johnson, Muddy Waters, Hank Williams, Chuck Berry and Bob Dylan.

Hoy relocated to Melbourne and toured with a new version of The Hoy Boys which comprised Mark Greig (guitar; ex-**Runners**), Paul McNaughton (bass; ex-**Runners**) who later emerged as a solo performer in his own right under the name **Paul Norton**, and Grant Hamston (drums; ex-**Runners**). Hoy joined Chris Stockley's country ensemble, The Vic State Opry, which also included noted pedal steel player Garrett Costigan. Hoy continued his solo career with the mini-album *Possession* (October 1987) and single 'Where I Come from'/'Good for a Laugh' (August 1988) on the Mighty Boy label. In 1989 Hoy signed a deal with A&M/Polydor.

His first two singles for A&M were 'Raindance'/'Blowin' Round Here' (June 1989) and 'Break Up Fall Out'/'I'll Be with You', followed by the Mark Moffatt-produced album *Life Next Door* in August 1990. Helping out on the album sessions were the likes of Stockley (guitar, mandolin, dobro), Costigan (pedal steel), Chong Lim (keyboards), Graham Thompson (bass; ex-**Stars**) and Peter Luscombe (drums; **Black Sorrows**). The Steve Hoy Band supported US visitor Melissa Etheridge on her first Australian tour. Hoy issued his fourth album in October 1994 and continued to tour.

Albums: *Anticipation* (Spirit/Virgin, 1984), *Possession* (mini-album, Mighty Boy, 1987), *Life Next Door* (A&M/Polydor, 1990), *Self Defence* (Siren, 1994).

Bob Hudson

Style: *Folk, comedy*

Bob Hudson was essentially a folk singer, although the comedy monologues he incorporated into his act proved too much for the purists. Hudson came to the attention of ABC musical director Chris Neal who arranged for him to record the in-concert album *The Newcastle Song.* Chris Neal produced and played on the album. The album spawned the national #1 hit single 'The Newcastle Song'/'Ventriloquist Love' (March 1975), which had been edited down from the ten-minute album version.

Aside from its topical humour and catchy chorus, the song was an incisive piece of social commentary. Hudson had been performing the song for several years before recording it. Hudson wrote a straight novelty sequel to 'The Newcastle Song' called 'Rak Off Normie', which **Maureen Elkner** recorded. The single reached #6 in June. Folk/blues singer **Margret Roadknight** covered another of Hudson's social-observations-set-in-song, 'Girls in our Town' (from *The Newcastle Song*) and scored a minor hit in the process. Hudson and Roadknight later toured together.

Hudson was reluctant to become a full-time performer, however, opting instead to concentrate on his job as producer/announcer for Sydney community radio station Double J (the precursor to the national youth radio network Triple J). Meanwhile, as a follow-up to 'The Newcastle Song', Hudson issued the album *After Me Cat Left Home* and the single 'Waltzing Matilda Rock'/'Heartsmasher'. Hudson issued his third album, *Party Pieces*, in 1980. Since then, he has concentrated on writing and DJ work.

Albums: *The Newcastle Song* (M7, 1975), *After Me Cat Left Home* (M7, 1975), *Party Pieces* (Larrikin, 1980).

Benjamin Hugg

Style: *Folk*

Melbourne-based folk singer Benjamin Hugg had a brief brush with pop fame in 1974 when his single 'Thank God You're Here with Me'/'Silly Minded People' reached #35 on the national charts during August. Hugg's second single, 'Minchinberry Walk'/'My Jenny', came out in January 1975. His album *Early One Morning* was a pleasant collection of folk and pop tunes. Session musicians like Peter Robinson (guitar, bass), Bill Pyman (guitar), Barry Sullivan (bass; ex-**Chain**), Joe McLaughlin (piano) and Kerryn Tolhurst (steel guitar; **Dingoes**) contributed to the album.

Hugg's second album, *What's Been Happening?*, featured a rockier sound as displayed on the single 'What's Been Happening?'/'Needle of Misfortune'. Backing musicians that time included Peter Walker (guitar; ex-**Bakery**), Peter Roberts (bass; ex-**La De Das**), Tim Partridge (bass; ex-**Mighty Kong**), Michael Bart (keyboards), Russell Dunlop (drums; ex-**Levi Smith's Clefs**, SCRA, Mother Earth, Cool Bananas), Joe Tattersalls (drums), Geoff Oakes (sax; ex-**Heart 'n' Soul**), John Sayers (piano) and Barry Leef (backing vocals; ex-**Bakery**). Hugg formed the Benjamin Hugg Band which comprised Greg Johnson (guitar), Keith Miller (bass) and David Pitt (drums) in order to tour, after which he slipped from public view.

Albums: *Early One Morning* (Astor, 1974), *What's Been Happening?* (Wizard, 1975).

Human Nature

Formed as the 4Trax: *1991*
Style: *Harmony pop*
Original line-up: *Phil Burton (vocals), Andrew Tierney (vocals), Mike Tierney (vocals), Toby Allen (vocals)*

Like Melbourne-based vocal quartet **CDB**, Human Nature's pin-up idol looks and harmony-drenched sound created a great deal of interest. In an era when boy band dance-pop (Take That, Boyzone, Boyz II Men, Past to Present) was popular on the charts around the world, Human Nature made an impact on the local charts. Human Nature started out in 1991 as The 4Trax. With a name change, the quartet signed to Sony for its debut album *Telling Everybody*. The album brimmed with silky smooth dance-pop and blue-eyed soul, and duly reached the national Top 10 in January 1997. It went on to sell over 210 000 copies, and produced four hit singles: 'Got It Goin' On' (Top 40 in May 1996), 'Tellin' Everybody' (#30 in August), 'Wishes' (#8 in December) and 'Don't Say Goodbye' (#8 in April 1997).

In mid-1997, Human Nature toured internationally as support to Michael Jackson and Celine Dion. The quartet's fifth single, 'Whisper Your Name', peaked at #34 in August, while their duet with **John Farnham**, 'Every Time You Cry', hit #3 in October 1997. Human Nature ended the year with the release of a cover of Curtis Mayfield's 'People Get Ready' as a single (November).

Album: *Telling Everybody* (Sony, 1996).

The Hummingbirds

Formed: *1986*
Style: *Pop*
Original line-up: *Simon Holmes (guitar, vocals; ex-Bug Eyed Monsters,* **Exserts***), John Boyce (bass; ex-Bug Eyed Monsters), Mark Temple (drums; ex-Bug Eyed Monsters)*

The Hummingbirds were one of the most highly touted outfits to emerge from Sydney's inner-city scene during the late 1980s. Yet, unlike **The Lime Spiders** and **The Celibate Rifles** for example, the band steered clear of Detroit-inspired garage rock, opting instead for vocal harmonies and classic guitar-pop melodies. The band's stated aim was to be the 'ultimate pop band'. In their quest for the perfect pop song, however, the musicians were not afraid to make their sound a little rough around the

The Hummingbirds

edges (somewhere between The Velvet Underground, R.E.M., The Buzzcocks and Big Star).

After a few months of initial rehearsal as a three-piece, Alannah Russack (guitar, vocals) joined. In early 1987, John Boyce left to be replaced by Robyn St Clair. The band signed to independent label Phantom and issued four impressive singles, 'Alimony'/'Three in the Morning' (July 1987), 'Everything You Said'/'Get on Down' (January 1988), 'Swim to Shore'/'Be Careful' (July) and 'Hindsight'/'Dragged Over the Coals' (November). In October, the band appeared on a rare gig giveaway album *Assorted Desecrations and Magnificent Mutations*, as part of Phantom's tenth anniversary celebrations. The Hummingbirds covered songs by former Phantom bands Le Hoodoo Gurus ('Leilani') and **The Flaming Hands** ('It's Just that I Miss You').

The Hummingbirds contributed 'Hindsight' to the fledgling rooArt label's inaugural *Youngblood* compilation (September 1988), alongside material from **The Trilobites**, **Martha's Vineyard**, **Crash Politics**, **Hipslingers**, **Tall Tales & True**, Violet Town and others. That led to a full recording contract with rooArt, which the band signed in a blaze of publicity at the start of 1989. The Hummingbirds recorded their debut album with American producer Mitch Easter (noted for his work with bands like R.E.M. and Game Theory, plus his own outfit Let's Active).

The 14-track *loveBUZZ* album (March 1990) yielded the singles 'Blush'/'Let Her Down Gently' (August 1989) and 'Word Gets Around'/'Today of All Days' (November). All the media attention afforded the band was vindicated when 'Blush' not only reached #1 on the alternative chart, but also peaked at #25 on the national mainstream list. The band's first single for 1990 was a new version of 'Alimony' (March).

In early 1990, St Clair collaborated with **The Plunderers'** Nic Dalton on the studio project Love Positions, which yielded the album *Billiebeebup* (on Dalton's Half a Cow label). Dalton also deputised on tour for St Clair, who was taken ill and admitted to hospital in May. Meanwhile, 'Blush' had come out as a single in the UK where *Melody Maker* listed it as Single of the Week. A year later, The Hummingbirds issued a second album, *va va voom* (April 1991). If *loveBUZZ* revelled in its naive enthusiasm, *va va voom* was a more mature, complex work. The punchy, keyboard-driven 'If a Vow' (March) and '2 Weeks with a Good Man in Niagara Falls'/'Don't Fall Down' (July) appeared as singles. Both showed the band's growth and willingness to move onwards. The Hummingbirds spent most of the early months of 1991 on tour across Australia, Europe and North America.

In early 1992, Dalton once again deputised for St Clair. The Holmes/Russack/Temple/Dalton line-up recorded the CD EP *You Just Gotta Know My Mind*, which appeared in May. The EP featured a remodelling of Donovan's 'Know My Mind'. Later in the year, Shane Melder replaced the long-serving Temple on drums. The band also split from rooArt, issuing two final CD EPs, *Gone* (February 1993) and *Tail* (July 1993), independently before calling it a day.

Holmes moved into production work (**The Fauves**) and formed ambient outfit Coloursound with **Drop City's** Matt Tow. In 1995 he joined forces with Wayne Connolly (guitar, vocals, ex-**Welcome Mat**, Knievel), Shane Melder (then in **Sidewinder**) and Martin Craft (bass; also from **Sidewinder**) as studio band Fragile. The Half a Cow label issued Fragile's album *Airbrushed Perfection* (March 1996), which ran the gamut of sounds from jangly pop ('Dream Come True') to noisy Hüsker Dü-inspired rockers ('She Really Means that Much to Me', 'Resolving Conflict Situations').

In 1994, Temple switched to guitar and vocals, and formed Growl with Paula Bray (bass, vocals) and Pete Bennett (drums; ex-**Welcome Mat**). Growl played noisy, low-fi guitar pop, as displayed on the band's debut 7-inch vinyl single 'Seems'/'Deserve' (May 1995). The band's next release, the five-track CD EP *Feel This Way* (March 1996), was more of the same.

Hummingbirds albums: *loveBUZZ* (rooArt/PolyGram, 1989), *va va voom* (rooArt/Warner, 1991); ***Fragile album:*** *Airbrushed Perfection* (Half a Cow/Mercury, 1996).

Marc Hunter

Style: *Rock, pop*

New Zealand-born Marc Hunter (b. 1953) launched his solo career after being sacked from his frontman duties with **Dragon** in February 1979. He initially travelled to Morocco and London on holiday before signing a deal with CBS. Hunter's debut album, *Fiji Bitter* (November 1979), yielded the breezy hit single 'Island Nights'/'East to the Winter' (#20 in July), plus two non-hits, 'Don't Take Me'/'My Mystery' (November) and 'When You Walk in the Room'/'Thrill Has Gone' (January 1980). Backing musicians on the album included Marc's brother Todd Hunter (bass), Harvey James (guitar; from **Sherbet**), Terry Wilson (guitar; ex-Original Battersea Heroes, Wasted Daze) and John Annas (drums; ex-**Kevin Borich Express**).

Hunter moved to PolyGram/Mercury for his second album, *Big City Talk* (August 1981), and the singles 'Big City Talk'/'Old Fashioned Love Affair' (July; #25 in August), '(Rock'n'Roll is) a Loser's Game'/'Midnight Knocks' (September), 'Side Show'/'Slow Down Baby' (November) and 'Nothing but a Lie'/'Echoes' (May 1982). By that stage, Marc and his brother Todd were in the process of reactivating **Dragon**, and as a consequence Hunter put his solo career on hold. Following three years of recording and touring with Dragon, Hunter issued his third solo album, *Communication* (September 1985), a polished set of Adult Oriented Rock (AOR) songs. As with his previous solo ventures, Hunter employed the cream of session musicians for the album, including Mark Punch, Peter Walker, Kirk Lorange and Jeff 'Skunk' Baxter on guitars, Todd Hunter and Phil Scorgie on bass, Allan Mansfield and Don Walker on keyboards and Mark Kennedy and South African producer Ricky Fataar on drums.

The album included the singles 'Communication'/'Hollywood' (1984) and 'The Empty Beach'/'Simple Words' (August 1985). The Don Walker-penned 'The Empty Beach' was the theme song to the Bryan Brown film of the same name. In May 1992, Hunter issued his fourth solo album, *Night & Day*, which featured a collection of jazz and pop standards. His fifth solo album, *Talk to Strangers*, included the singles 'Get So Rough' and 'One of the Good Guys'. In 1997 Marc Hunter was diagnosed as suffering throat cancer. He died in July 1998.

Albums: *Fiji Bitter* (CBS, 1979), *Big City Talk* (PolyGram, 1981), *Communication* (PolyGram, 1986), *Night & Day* (PolyGram, 1992), *Talk to Strangers* (PolyGram, 1994).

Ruby Hunter

Style: *Folk*

Koori singer/songwriter Ruby Hunter released her debut album, *Thoughts Within*, in May 1994. Produced by Jen Anderson (ex-**Black Sorrows**), the album contained songs written and developed over a period of 15 years. Tracks like the single 'Let My Children Be', 'A Change Gonna Come' and 'Kurongk Boy, Kurongk Girl' told of the survival of her people, as well as focusing on her own tragic past of forced separation. With roots in gospel, country, R&B and folk, the individual songs on *Thoughts Within* made for a satisfying whole.

With the album's release, Ruby and her band embarked on the successful Modern Day Girls tour across Australia. Ruby has also toured locally and internationally with her spouse **Archie Roach**, and has contributed several songs (such as 'Down City Streets' and 'From Paradise') to his solo albums. At the end of 1995, Ruby made her television debut with a speaking part and concert performance on the ABC-TV miniseries *Corelli*.

Album: *Thoughts Within* (Aurora/Mushroom/Festival, 1994).

Hunters & Collectors

Formed: *1981*
Style: *Art-funk to pub rock*
Original line-up: *Mark Seymour (guitar, vocals; ex-Jetsonnes), Ray Tosti-Gueira (guitar, vocals; ex-Jetsonnes), Geoff Crosby (keyboards), Greg Perano (percussion; ex-True Wheels), John Archer (bass; ex-Jetsonnes), Doug Falconer (drums; ex-Jetsonnes), Robert Miles (live sound, art director)*

The journey that has taken Hunters & Collectors from esoteric art-funk innovators to Australia's greatest pub-rock exponents has been a fascinating one to say the least. The band's early records were full of challenging, noisy rock, bleak imagery, gripping drama and slithery funk. By the 1986 album

Human Frailty and single 'Say Goodbye', the band had stripped away unnecessary excess to arrive at a sound that combined equal parts refried boogie-rock and lyric paradoxes.

Frontman Mark Seymour became the 'thinking woman's sex symbol' with his blue labourer's singlet, bulging biceps, introspective angst and impassioned vocals. There was a double irony in the sight of beer-soaked boys in suburban pubs across the land bellowing about not feeling like a woman any more, while the girls danced relentlessly up the back. Hunters & Collectors' great achievement was to lay bare human emotions in the intensely ritualistic milieu of the pub-rock gig.

The foundation stone of the Hunters & Collectors' sound can be found in Melbourne band The Jetsonnes which comprised Seymour, John Archer, Doug Falconer, Ray Totsi-Gueira and Margot O'Neill (vocals). The Jetsonnes played the inner-city scene circa 1980. As Clinton Walker put it, the band's clever post-punk pop sound was lighter, bouncier (rather than funkier) and more infectious than other like-minded bands such as **Models** and **International Exiles**. The only recorded evidence of the band's brief existence was the track 'Newspaper' which was combined with **International Exiles'** 'Miniskirts In Moscow' as one side of a gig giveaway 7-inch single. Not long after that, Seymour and the others abandoned The Jetsonnes for a far more radical and unremitting concept.

Seymour introduced new members Geoff Crosby and Greg Perano, whose inspired contribution was to utilise an empty gas tank as percussion, which gave the sound its clattering, metallic edge. Perano also derived the band's name from the track 'Hunters and Collectors', on the German band Can's 1975 album *Landed*, which was a good indication of the influences and intentions at work. The extended line-up also included a massed horn section (eventually known as The Horns of Contempt) that comprised John Howard (trumpet), Andy Lynn (trumpet), Chris Malherbe (trumpet), Nigel Crocker (trombone), Michael Waters (trombone) and Jeremy Smith (French horn). Also integral to the band's approach was live sound mixer Robert Miles, hence the credit as a band member.

Right from the outset, Hunters & Collectors were hailed as the hip 'Next Big Thing' and *the* band to experience live. Mushroom Record's subsidiary label White signed the band and issued the 12-inch EP 'World of Stone'/'Watcher', 'Loinclothing' (January 1982) and the combined mini-album/12-inch EP *Hunters & Collectors* (July 1982). *Hunters & Collectors* took the band into the national Top 20 for the first time when it peaked at #14 during September. The mini-album contained one of the band's early classics in the seven-minute 'Talking to a Stranger'. Combined with Richard Lowenstein's radical film clip, 'Talking to a Stranger' was an expression of alienation and sheer anguish. It was also issued on 7-inch as an edited single version backed with the full-length rendition (July 1982).

By that stage, Martin Lubran had replaced Tosti-Gueira on guitar, and The Horns of Contempt was down to a trio of Howard, Waters and Smith. The band saw out 1982 with the release of the Mike Howlett-produced *Payload* 12-inch EP (December). Hunters & Collectors spent six futile months in the UK during 1983, then travelled to West Germany to record *The Fireman's Curse* with renowned producer Conny Plank (Can, Cluster, Kraftwerk). *The Fireman's Curse* (September 1983) was overly ambitious and cluttered, and generally suffered from a lack of fresh ideas. 'Judas Sheep'/'Eggheart' (on 12-inch only, August) and 'Sway'/'Mr Right' (November) were issued as singles. At that point, the band nearly broke up, although only Perano and Lubran left.

Following a period of re-evaluation, the brilliant *The Jaws of Life* album (also recorded with Plank; issued July 1984) featured a stripped-down rock sound, a driving rhythm, more concise arrangements and stronger songs. 'Betty's Worry or the Slab'/'Carry Me' was an inspired choice as a single (August 1984). As Toby Creswell wrote in *Rolling Stone*, the album's aesthetic push ranged from the barrenness and isolation of outback Australia to the beer-swilling machismo of the suburbs. The poignant (non-album) 'Throw Your Arms Around Me'/'Unbeliever' was another classic single (November 1984). The live album *The Way to Go Out . . .* (May 1985) captured all the ferocious power and muscular energy that characterised the band's pub gigs. Crosby left after that, and Waters took over keyboards.

The Gavin McKillop-produced album *Human Frailty* (May 1986) was a further refinement of the sinewy and dynamic approach established on *The Jaws of Life*. The album saw the band become what Ed St John in *Rolling Stone* called 'a truly accessible, street-credible rock & roll band'. *Human Frailty* reached #10 on the national chart in June. It yielded the singles 'Say Goodbye'/'Follow Me' (#20 in April 1986), 'Throw Your Arms Around Me' (new version)/'When the Truth Comes Out', 'Who's on Left' (#32 in June), 'Everything's on Fire'/'This Morning' (August) and 'Is There Anybody in There?'/'Dog' (October).

Following the release of *Human Frailty*, the

band toured the USA twice and issued the three-track, 12-inch EP 'The Living Daylights' (April 1987). This was something of a stop-gap measure before the band returned with the Greg Edward-produced *What's a Few Men?* album in November. Seymour derived the album's title from Albert Facey's memoir, *An Unfortunate Life*. 'Do You See What I See?'/'Give Me a Reason' (#25 in November 1987), 'Still Hanging Around'/'John Riley' (February 1988) and 'Back on the Breadline'/'Real World' (June) were issued as singles.

The newly recorded 'Back on the Breadline' actually came from the US release (on IRS) of the *What's a Few Men?* album which had been renamed *Fate*. As well as 'Back on the Breadline', *Fate* featured several other new tunes in place of tracks from the Australian release. The White label did not issue *Fate* locally until April 1991. Accomplished blues guitarist Barry Palmer (concurrently in **Harem Scarem**) joined in early 1988, allowing Seymour greater freedom as frontman. *Ghost Nation* (March 1990) was perhaps the band's finest album to date. It produced the singles 'When the River Runs Dry'/'Price of Freedom' (#23 in December), 'Turn a Blind Eye'/'Two Roads' (#42 in March 1990), 'The Way You Live'/'Do You See What I See?' (acoustic) (May) and 'Love All Over Again' (August). The band also contributed the track 'Breakneck Road' to the Various Artists album *Building Bridges* on CBS (1989).

Ghost Nation peaked at #5 on the national chart, and broke the 70 000 unit platinum award threshold (eventually selling 130 000 copies) for the first time in the band's career. To coincide with this new-found success, the band signed a new worldwide deal with Atlantic Records, scored the coveted support slot on **Midnight Oil's** 1990 international tour and was named Australian Band of the Year in *Rolling Stone*. 1990 ended with the release of 'Throw Your Arms Around Me' (another new version) for a third time as a single (#34 in February 1991) and the compilation album/video *Collected Works 1982–1990*.

American producer Don Gehman (R.E.M., John Mellencamp) incorporated electronic percussion and drum loops into the sound on the band's seventh studio album *Cut* (#6 on the national album charts in August). It featured the singles 'Where Do You Go?' (#33 in October 1991), 'Head Above Water' (July 1992), 'We the People' (September) and 'True Tears of Joy' (#14 in February 1993). The CD EP 'Holy Grail' became another hit for the band (#20 in July 1993). The Nick Mainsbridge-produced album *Demon Flower* featured a stronger emphasis on guitars. It reached #2 nationally and spawned the singles 'Easy'/'Panic in the Shade' (March 1994), 'Back in the Hole' (August) and 'Drop in the Ocean' (November). Hunters & Collectors also contributed a cover of **The Saints'** 'Know Your Product' to the Various Artists compilation *Earth Music* issued on Mushroom during June 1994.

The band toured Europe, after which Palmer formed **deadstar**. He did, however, remain a member of Hunters & Collectors. The band continued its release schedule with the CD EP *Live Demons* (March 1995) and its second live epic, the 25-track double album *Living in Large Rooms and Lounges* (December 1995). At the end of 1996, Seymour undertook a solo tour and recorded the Barry Palmer-produced debut solo album *King Without a Clue*. Seymour's debut CD single, 'Last Ditch Cabaret', appeared in April 1997, to be followed by the album and second single, 'The Ghost of Vainglory', in October. By that time Hunters & Collectors had recorded a final studio album, *Juggernaut* (slated for release in early 1998), and announced their imminent split.

Hunters & Collectors albums: *Hunters & Collectors* (White/Mushroom/Festival, 1982), *The Fireman's Curse* (White/Mushroom/Festival, 1983), *The Jaws of Life* (White/Mushroom/Festival, 1984), *The Way to Go Out . . .* (White/Mushroom/Festival, 1985), *Human Frailty* (White/Mushroom/Festival, 1986), *What's a Few Men?* (White/Mushroom/Festival, 1987; reissued as *Fate* in 1991), *Ghost Nation* (White/Mushroom/Festival, 1990), *Collected Works 1982–1990* (White/Mushroom/Festival, 1990), *Skin, Bones & Bolts* (box set, White/Mushroom/Festival, 1991), *Cut* (White/Mushroom/Festival, 1992), *Demon Flower* (White/Mushroom/Festival, 1994), *Living in Large Rooms and Lounges* (White/Mushroom/Festival, 1995); ***Mark Seymour album:*** *King Without a Clue* (Mushroom/Sony, 1997).

Hush

Formed: *1971*
Style: *Glam pop*
Original line-up: *Keith Lamb (vocals), Robin Jackson (guitar), Chris Nolan (keyboards), Rick Lum (bass), John Koutts (drums)*

One of the defining moments of Australia's 1970s pop legacy was undoubtably Hush performing 'Boney Moroney' on the ABC-TV pop show ***Countdown***. The updated version of the old Larry Williams' rocker was a #1 hit for Hush in September 1975, and was the perfect vehicle for the band's flashy hi-jinks.

Hush

Lead singer Keith Lamb wiggled his satin flares-encased bum, thrust out his crotch and leered at the camera with a mischievous look in his eyes (and all the little girls understood). Guitarist Les Gock dashed around the set in stack-heeled boots and glam threads, with peroxided streaks in his flowing, jet-black hair. Bassist Rick Lum hammed it up in a serious kind of way. Drummer Chris 'Smiley' Pailthorpe cheerfully revealed his goofy, gap-toothed grin whenever the camera panned across his face.

These guys loved to put on a show. It was all a little contrived, but glorious entertainment just the same. Hush was Australia's answer to Slade, T-Rex or The Sweet. They had the sound (basic, sassy glam-pop and refurbished 12-bar boogie), the looks *and* the songs to make a grab for stardom. For three years (1974–76) Hush were genuine scream-dream pop sensations. In the pantheon of 1970s pop, only **Skyhooks**, **Sherbet**, **Supernaut** and **John Paul Young** rivalled Hush for the attention of hordes of howling, weeping teenyboppers.

English-born Lamb formed the first version of Hush in 1971 as a light pop band. The band issued one unsuccessful single on Phonogram's Philips label, 'Over You'/'Rainy Day Bells'. In April 1972, Gock (ex-Chariot) and Pailthorpe joined Lamb and Lum for the classic Hush line-up. Gock gave the band a tougher sound in the guitar department. His influences included the likes of Rory Gallagher, John Mayall and The Rolling Stones. Hush made the finals in the New South Wales heats of the 1972 Hoadley's National Battle of the Sounds, and then issued a reggae version of 'White Christmas' as a single (December 1972).

The first evidence of the hard-rocking Hush style came with the singles 'Get the Feeling'/'Take Us Home' (#11 in Sydney, October 1973) and 'Man Eater'/'Black Skinned, Blue-Eyed Boys' (February 1974) and the live-in-the-studio album *Aloud'n' Live!*. The album reached #20 on the national chart, attained gold status and from that point on, the Hush machine just exploded. Concert supports to overseas visitors like The Jackson Five and Status Quo during 1973 brought the band to larger audiences.

'Get Rocked'/'Linda Lee' (May 1974), 'Walking'/'Exit' (#10 in August), 'C'Mon We're Taking Over'/'Paradise' (September), 'Boney Moroney'/'Rocking Gypsy King' (#1 in September 1975), the Dave Clark Five's 'Glad All Over'/'Get What?' (#9 in October), 'You Really Gotta Hold on Me'/'Rough, Tough'n'Ready' (February 1976), 'Too Young to Know'/'Lies' (#21 in October 1976) and 'Sunday'/'How Do You Feel? Alright!' (December 1976) were classic pop singles. Likewise, album titles like *Get Rocked*, *C'mon We're Taking Over*, *Rough Tough'n'Ready* and *Nothing Stays the Same Forever* were statements of intent. In August 1976, Jacques De Jongh (ex-**Redhouse**) joined on rhythm guitar. Three months later Lum left so De Jongh moved to bass. The band's next break came with the support slot to Alice Cooper on his March 1977 Australian tour. By that stage, however, Hush's popularity had begun to slide.

When the band tried to make a serious affirmation of its abilities (the July 1977 album *Touché* featured a rock side, *A Touch of Decadence*, and a slow side, *A Touch of Class*) prospects were grim. The singles 'Nothing Stays the Same Forever'/'Sunday' (June 1977) and 'Messin' Around'/'Only Love' (August) were not successful. Around that time, Gock issued a solo single on Wizard, 'Everywhere I Go'/'(I Think I'm) Falling in Love' (August), as did Lamb with Cole Porter's 'Who Wants to Be a Millionaire?'/'9 to 5er' (September). 'Everywhere I Go' was actually a track from *Touché*.

Pailthorpe left Hush at the end of 1977, followed by Gock a few months later. Lamb and De Jongh attempted to keep the flame alight with The New Hush, but by then the screaming had faded. In April 1978, De Jongh left to join **John Paul Young** and the All Stars. The New Hush line-up became Lamb, Con Gallin (guitar; ex-Fingerprint), Paul Grant (guitar; ex-**Buster Brown**, Hollywood), Criston Barker (bass; ex-Ash, **Freeway,** Hollywood) and Nat De Palma (drums; ex-20th Century). That line-up only lasted two months, and Lamb continued with the Keith Lamb Band which comprised Alex O'Hara (lead guitar; ex-Chook), John Kaling (rhythm guitar, keyboards), Graeme Sayers (bass) and Shane Dorrington (drums). Keith Lamb Band issued the single 'In the City'/'Didyava Goodweekend' (July 1978), after which the band became known as Larry. The Larry line-up of Lamb, Kaling, Tony Harvey (lead guitar; ex-**James Freud's** Radio Stars), Kerry Bennett (bass) and Canadian Brian Pitcher (drums; ex-**Jim Keays** Band) issued one single, a cover of The Rolling Stones/ Chris Farlowe hit 'Out of Time'/'Lay Down'(June 1979).

By the end of 1979, the band was known as Airport, with a line-up of Lamb, Harvey, Pitcher and Robin Jackson (bass, vocals, ex-Hush, Punkz). Airport issued three singles, 'Short Skirts'/'Parlez Vous' (1981), 'Sure Means Something'/'People's Rock'n'Roll' (1981) and 'Gimme Rock'n'Roll'/'In Love' (1982) on Festival/Infinity, but none was successful. Airport broke up in 1982, and Lamb disappeared from view. In 1987 he was admitted to a psychiatric hospital after being found unfit to face a $4 million fraud charge (he had written out a cheque for $4 million when he only had $200 in his bank account). He was later diagnosed as suffering from schizophrenia.

It would be too easy to heap derision on to the memory of Hush. They were simply the right band in the right place at the right time. After all, it was all pop music (as in popular) and Keith, Les and the boys probably had the ride of their lives. Underneath it all, Les Gock really did know how to handle his white Stratocaster and, besides, his business acumen has come to the fore. In the lucrative world of advertising, Les has established himself as one of the country's foremost music and sound designers. He has also produced the soundtracks for the film *Puberty Blues* and the television drama *Water Rats*.

Albums: *Aloud'n'Live!* (WEA, 1973), *Get Rocked* (Wizard, 1974), *C'mon We're Taking Over* (Wizard, 1974), *Rough, Tough'n'Ready* (Wizard, 1975), *Nothing Stays the Same Forever—Best of* (Wizard, 1976), *Touché* (Wizard, 1977), *The Best of Hush* (Castle/BMG, 1995).

Huxton Creepers

Formed: *1983*
Style: *Garage pop*
Original line-up: *Rob Craw (guitar, vocals), Paul Thomas (guitar, vocals), Matthew Eddy (bass, vocals), Archie Law (drums)*

Huxton Creepers was one of the first Melbourne bands to play a brand of melodic, 1960s-influenced garage-pop. The band spent three years touring the national pub/club circuit before issuing its debut album. The Creepers' records boasted tuneful songs and bright instrumentation, but somehow never captured the sweaty atmosphere and exuberant sense of fun they generated on stage.

The members of Huxton Creepers formed the band while still at high school. The band's name was derived from a character in the Basil Rathbone/Nigel Bruce Sherlock Holmes film *Pearl of Death* (1944); however, the band got it wrong as the character was actually called the Hoxton Creeper (as played by actor Rondo Hatton). The Creepers attracted attention almost from the outset with their energetic, guitar-based rock'n'roll. The band contributed the track 'King of the Road' to Au-go-go's Various Artists album *Asleep at the Wheel* (1984). In early 1985, the band issued its debut, limited edition single 'Wishing Well'/'Iceman', which was only given away at a gig.

Not long after, the band signed a deal with the Big Time label. The band's first official single was the Rob Younger-produced 'The Murderess'/ 'Happy Days' (April 1985). At the end of the year, the band entered the studios with producers/engineers Ian 'Mack' McKenzie and Steve Berlin (from US band Los Lobos) to record *12 Days to Paris*. The album yielded the singles 'My Cherie Amour'/'True Love Baby' (April 1986), 'I will Pursuade You'/'I've Been Around' (July) and 'Autumn Leaves'/'Don't Even Think About It' (March 1987). Despite garnering positive reviews and selling well on an independent level, the album failed to make a dint on the mainstream charts.

The Creepers' next single, a cover of Manfred Mann's 'Pretty Flamingo'/'25 Words or Less' (August 1987), was the band's best shot at commercial acceptance. One-time member of UK hit-makers Procol Harum, Chris Copping (then residing in Australia), contributed organ to the single. The band recorded its second album with producer Alan Thorne at Trafalgar Studios. *So This is Paris* (March 1988) was a stronger effort than the debut, with the songs fleshed out by ringing guitar work. It spawned two of the band's best singles, 'Skin of My Teeth'/'Come Another Day' (November 1987) and 'Rack My Brains'/'When You Leave' (March 1988).

While the Creepers went into hibernation for a time, Craw and Thomas worked as the acoustic duo Rob Knows Paul, issuing a self-titled mini-album in early 1990 (on the Beealzebob label). The Creepers then called it a day with the release of the mini-album *Small Mercies* (April 1990). The title track saw the band moving away from its power pop roots to incorporate a more country/R&B flavour.

Craw formed an acoustic trio called The Disciples of Hanuman, and contributed a solo track, 'When It's Christmas Time' to the Timberyard label's second yuletide Various Artists compilation album *Rockin' Bethlehem: The Second Coming* (1990). Craw also contributed a version of **The Angels'** 'Am I Ever Gonna See Your Face Again?' to 3RRR-FM's Various Artists tribute album *Used and Recovered by* (1990). In the early 1990s, Craw formed a number of bands, including The Harlequins and The Victory Girls. The Harlequins comprised Adam Duncan (violin, mandolin, keyboards, vocals), Phil Wales (guitar; ex-**Harem Scarem**), Pat Quinn (bass) and Terry Bartholomew (drums). Paul Thomas joined **Weddings, Parties, Anything**. The 1996 'Best of' compilation, *Afterlife*, included unreleased material and a live track. It generated enough interest for the band to undertake a one-off reunion tour.

Albums: *12 Days to Paris* (Big Time, 1986), *So This is Paris* (Big Time, 1988), *Small Mercies* (mini-album, Musicland, 1990), *Afterlife—Best of* (Shock, 1996).

Hyperion

Formed: *1990*
Style: *Progressive metal*
Original line-up: *Jim Georgopoulos (vocals), Corey Romeo (guitar), Anthony Brereton (guitar), Steve Cole (bass), Mark Wylie (drums)*

In Greek mythology, Hyperion was one of the Titans (the offspring of Uranus and Gaia, the Earth Mother), the race of gods who held sway before Zeus and the Olympians emerged. Melbourne band Hyperion played a suitably majestic brand of progressive metal in the vein of Canadian outfit Rush. Hyperion built up a cult following on the local heavy metal circuit, and issued two well-received demos. In 1993, the band added Lara Jorgacevic (keyboards). In November 1994, the Def label issued the band's well-honed, melodic debut album *Inundation*, which reached the top of the Melbourne heavy metal charts. Cruze (ex-Despised) replaced Steve Cole in 1995 and Hyperion issued the CD EP *Primal Storm* in June 1996.

Album: *Inundation* (Def/Shock, 1994).

I

I Spit on Your Gravy

Formed: *1983*
Style: *Punk*
Original line-up: *Fred Negro (vocals, drums; ex-Editions), Jason 'The Big J' Banner (guitar), Mark 'Sausage Fingers' Carson (bass), Scotti 'Stix' Simpson (vocals, drums)*

By deriving their name from the 1979 revenge/exploitation film *I Spit on Your Grave*, the members of this notorious Melbourne band made their intentions clear from the outset. They were in it to cause mayhem, ruffle a few feathers and have fun in the process.

Fred Negro had already played the inner-city new wave scene as a member of post-punk band The Editions. The original Editions line-up (1979) comprised Negro (drums), Roz Dear (vocals), John Durr (guitar) and Urban Skyline (real name Bryce Collie; bass). The Editions recorded two tracks, 'You're Nice' and 'Cheapness', for a prospective single which never saw the light of day. They did, however, put out three cassette albums, *Aggression*, *Recession* and *Obsession* (on their own Orgasm imprint) between 1981 and 1982. Sherine replaced Dear in 1980. Other line-up changes included Ben Harmsen replacing Skyline and Wayne Tait replacing Negro in 1983, plus Elly Mantzaris (keyboards) joining in 1983. The band broke up in 1984. Sherine went on to **Big Pig** and Negro formed I Spit on Your Gravy. Durr set up blues label Black Market in the 1990s.

In the true spirit of punk, I Spit on Your Gravy's early live shows were shambolic, drunken affairs, replete with on-stage brawls and members barely able to stand upright, let alone play their instruments! Negro also had a penchant for dropping his pants in public (still does!), to say nothing of other on-stage obscenities, which naturally drew the wrath of the local police. Within their inner-city Melbourne enclave of St Kilda, however, The Gravies commanded a loyal following.

The Gravies paid homage to their roots with the title of the mini-album *St Kilda's Alright* (February 1985). Once again, the record drew controversy when the police deemed the booklet that came with it to be obscene and confiscated all copies. Basically, the booklet was a few sheets of paper stapled together featuring Negro's debauched cartoons and photocopied images from various pornographic magazines. All that tended to detract from the actual music, which was desperately inept and sounded like it had been recorded at the bottom of a dam. Prior to that, The Gravies contributed two tracks, 'Violent Fluff' and 'Done to Death', to the 1984 Melbourne punk compilation *Eat Your Head* (No Master's Voice) alongside tracks by **Vicious Circle**, Civil Dissident, Charred Remains, End Result, Royal Flush, Bodies, Permanent Damage, Murder Murder Suicide and others.

In 1985, Phil 'Grizzly' Miles (rhythm guitar, vocals) joined and, later in the year, Robbie 'The Love Pig' Watts (ex-Quivering Quims) replaced Carson on bass. The band also added a duo of back-up singers, Sindy Virtue and Di Jones. The Gravies persisted in their quest for the ultimate in bad taste, eventually signing a deal with Virgin Records. Virgin issued the 'double B-sided' single 'Pirahna'/'Man's Not a Camel' (May 1987) and the album *Fruit Loop City* (June). 'Pirahna' was an unsubtle rewrite of the Monkees' '(I'm Not Your) Stepping Stone'.

Eventually, The Gravies tired of the constant harassment from the constabulary and called it a day in 1988. Negro and Miles worked as the country-spoof outfit the Gravybillies, and later had the last laugh when they resurrected I Spit on Your Gravy for the odd 'farewell gig' or two. Negro went on to **The Band Who Shot Liberty Vallance**, The Brady Bunch Lawnmower Massacre and The Fuck Fucks. Watts joined **Cosmic Psychos** as guitarist in 1990.

Albums: *St Kilda's Alright* (mini-album, Man Made, 1985; reissued on Polyester, 1989), *Fruit Loop City* (Virgin, 1987).

The Icecream Hands (*see* The Mad Turks from Istanbul)

Icehouse

Formed as Flowers: *1978*
Style: *Pop, rock*
Original line-up as Flowers: *Iva Davies (guitar, vocals), Adam Hall (keyboards), Keith Welsh (bass), Don Brown (drums)*

The name Icehouse is ostensibly a front for classically trained musician Iva Davies. He has been responsible for directing the band's career, and has assembled musicians under the Icehouse banner as required. During the band's formative years, Davies' brand of modernist pop rock was compared unfavourably with that of UK artists like David Bowie, Roxy Music and Ultravox. Nevertheless, Davies is a natural pop craftsman who helped pioneer the use of The Fairlight CMI (Computer Musical Instrument) in this country, scoring intermittent international success along the way.

Iva Davies was actually born *Ivor* Davies (in 1955). He began his musical career as a teenager studying oboe at the New South Wales Conservatorium of Music and playing in The ABC National Training Orchestra. He signed to RCA in 1975 as a solo artist and issued two glam-pop singles, 'Leading Lady'/'Gonna Give You All My Love' (credited incorrectly to *Iva* Davies, July 1975) and 'Back to California'/'I Can't Reach You' (as Iva Davies and Afghan; October 1975). At the time, Davies cited his influences as mainly from 'classical structures', but admitted that Led Zeppelin, Marc Bolan, George Harrison and Elton John had also had their effect on his music. The singles were not successful and Davies made a living writing transcripts for music publishing companies.

With the advent of punk/new wave circa 1977, Davies acquired an electric guitar, and reinvented himself as the black leather-clad, black Les Paul-slinging frontman of Sydney pub dance band Flowers. The lightweight band name was deliberately misleading because Flowers was a heavy glitter-punk band that established a reputation by playing note-for-note covers of classic rock songs by T-Rex, Lou Reed, David Bowie, The Kinks, Sex Pistols and the like. Someone coined the phrase 'punk jukebox' to describe Flowers.

In mid-1979, John Lloyd (ex-High Rise Bombers, **Paul Kelly** and the Dots) and Michael Hoste replaced Don Brown and Adam Hall respectively. The band supported UK visitors XTC and Magazine, and toured nationally with **The Angels** and **Cold Chisel**. By that stage, Flowers had begun playing original material, mostly written by Davies, but some co-written with Hoste. Flowers signed to the Regular label and began recording an album. Anthony Smith replaced Hoste halfway through the sessions.

Iva Davies, Icehouse

Flowers' first two 7-inch singles, 'Can't Help Myself'/'Send Somebody' (also issued on 10-inch format; May 1980) and 'We Can Get Together'/'Paradise Lost' (July), were national hits, peaking at #10 and #16 respectively. The Cameron Allen/Iva Davies-produced *Icehouse* album (October) was full of dramatic and brooding, yet accessible rock. The album hit the national Top 5 (#4) and by the end of 1981 had sold over 100 000 copies, establishing Flowers as a major new band. A third single, 'Walls'/'All the Way' came out in January 1981 (#20 in March).

New-found success began to take its toll on the band's solidarity. Following tours of Europe and Canada, and not long after the commencement of recording for a follow-up album to *Icehouse*, the band broke up. Only the 'Love in Motion'/'Goodnight Mr Matthews' single (#10 in November 1981) featuring the old line-up emerged. By that stage, the band had become known as Icehouse because of a legal restriction outside Australia. The business-minded Keith Welsh went on to become part of the Dirty Pool management team, and managed **Do Ré Mi** and **Boom Crash Opera**.

Davies recorded the *Primitive Man* album virtually as a solo release. Its three singles, 'Great

Southern Land'/'Uniform' (August 1982), 'Hey Little Girl'/'Glam (October) and 'Street Cafe'/'Over the Line' (February 1983), were major national hits (peaking at #5, #6 and #18 respectively). *Primitive Man* reached #1 in October 1982, and went on to sell over 100 000 copies. Icehouse later contributed 'Great Southern Land' to the soundtrack of Yahoo Serious's 1988 film *Young Einstein*.

Meanwhile, in early 1983, Davies assembled a new Icehouse line-up comprising Hoste, Lloyd, Robert Kretschmer (guitar; ex-**Parachute**, Eric Gradman: Man & Machine), plus Englishmen Guy Pratt (bass; ex-Killing Joke) and Andy Qunta (keyboards). In May, 'Hey Little Girl' reached #17 in the UK, #14 in Sweden, #13 in Holland, #5 in Germany and #1 in Switzerland. *Primitive Man* also hit the Top 10 in Germany, Sweden and Switzerland. Icehouse toured as support to David Bowie on the European leg of his Serious Moonlight tour.

The *Sidewalk* album reached #4 in Australia during July 1984. It yielded the singles 'Taking the Town'/'Dance on' (#22 in May), 'Don't Believe Anymore'/'Java' (#22 in August) and 'Dusty Pages'/'Stay Close Tonight' (November). At that point, Davies wrote (entirely on the Fairlight Music Computer) and recorded the soundtrack to video-clip director Russell Mulchay's debut feature film *Razorback*. In 1985, the Sydney Dance Company approached Davies to write the soundtrack to the ballet *Boxes*. Davies collaborated with Icehouse guitarist Robert Kretschmer on the project. The ballet premiered on 7 November 1985 at the Sydney Opera House. Davies, Kretschmer and a guest percussionist from Japan, Masaki Tanazawa, performed the music. *Boxes* was issued as a rare soundtrack album.

For the Rheet Davies/David Lord-Alge produced *Measure for Measure* album, the Icehouse line-up was Davies (vocals, guitar, keyboards, Fairlight), Kretschmer (guitar), Pratt (bass), Qunta (keyboards), Simon Lloyd (sax, trumpet, keyboards), Steve Jensen (drums; ex-Japan) and Tanazawa (drums), with Brian Eno (ex-Roxy Music and later known for his work with U2) treating the keyboard parts and singing backing vocals. *Measure for Measure* reached #8 in May 1986, and featured the singles 'No Promises'/'Perfect Crime' (#19 in January), 'Baby You're So Strange'/'Too Late Now' (#12 in May), 'Mr Big'/'Sister' (#14 in August) and 'Cross the Border'/'The Flame' (October). The *Measure for Measure* touring band comprised Davies, Kretschmer, Qunta, Lloyd, Vito Portolesi (bass) and Paul Wheeler (drums). Icehouse toured the USA, where *Measure for Measure* had reached #55 on the Billboard chart. Glenn Krawezyk then replaced Portolesi on bass in late 1986.

Stephen Morgan replaced Krawezyk, and the band entered its most successful phase with the release of the #1 album *Man of Colours* (September 1987). The album went on to sell 540 000 copies in Australia alone, making Icehouse second only to **John Farnham** in the popularity stakes at that time. It yielded three Top 5 hit singles, 'Crazy'/'Completely Gone' (#3 in July), 'Electric Blue'/'Over My Head' (#1 in October) and 'My Obsession'/'Your Confession' (#5 in December), plus two Top 40 hits, 'Man of Colours'/'Komsaka B' (February 1988) and 'Nothing Too Serious'/'No' (June).

Man of Colours won the 1987 Australian Record Industry Association (ARIA) Awards for the Best Album and Highest Selling Album. It also made #43 in the USA, while 'Crazy' (which Davies co-wrote with John Oates from Hall and Oates) became a massive US hit when it reached #7 during April 1988. 'Electric Blue' followed 'Crazy' into the US Top 10 when it peaked at #10 during June. The only Icehouse records for 1989 were the single 'Touch the Fire'/'The Last Out' (#13 in Australia during November) and the double compilation album and video collection *Great Southern Land*. The album peaked at #12 on the national chart in January 1990. The other new track included with the compilation, 'Jimmy Dean', reached #47 when issued as a single in February 1990.

Qunta left at that stage. Icehouse's seventh album, *Code Blue* (October 1990), was Davies' most ambitious (but flawed) work to date. The album yielded the singles 'Big Fun' (#47 in August 1990), 'Miss Divine' (#16 in October), 'Anything is Possible' (#49 in January 1991) and 'River Meets the Sea' (March 1991). The album featured the basic Icehouse line-up of Davies, Lloyd, Wheeler and Morgan, while Paul Gildea (guitar) and Roger Mason (keyboards; ex-**Models**) were added for touring purposes. *Code Blue*, however, barely sold platinum (70 000 copies) and Davies slipped from view. In 1992, EMI issued a new Icehouse compilation, *Masterfile,* which also contained a new version of 'Love in Motion' (a duet between Davies and Christina Amphlett), which was issued as a single.

After two years of recording inactivity, Davies re-emerged with a new Icehouse album, *Big Wheel* (November 1993), and the CD singles 'Spin One' (July), 'Satellite' (October) and 'Big Wheel' (March 1994). With the basic line-up of himself, Lloyd, Wheeler and David Chapman (guitar), Davies came up with one of the strongest Icehouse albums of all. Nevertheless, it failed to reach the national

Top 40. *Big Wheel* also furthered Davies' interest in computer technology. A limited edition run of the album came with one of the first dual interactive computer disk/CD packages available in Australia. The Apple-compatible disk contained lyrics, album credits, animated graphics, artwork, an Icehouse history and discography and storyboard for the 'Satellite' video clip. There was talk of a double album of Icehouse remixes at that stage called *Full Circle*, but its release was shelved until 1997.

In 1995, Davies recorded an album of cover songs as the score for the Sydney Dance Company's ballet production of *Berlin*. *The Berlin Tapes* (November 1995) included songs by a number of Davies' acknowledged influences such as David Bowie, Lou Reed and Roxy Music, plus seminal new wave outfits Psychedelic Furs, The Cure, Talking Heads, Public Image Ltd, Killing Joke, XTC and Simple Minds.

Albums: *Icehouse* (as Flowers; Regular/Festival, 1980), *Primitive Man* (Regular/WEA, 1982), *Sidewalk* (Regular/WEA, 1984), *Measure for Measure* (Regular/Festival, 1986), *Man of Colours* (Regular/Festival, 1987), *Great Southern Land* (Regular/Festival, 1989), *Code Blue* (Regular/Festival, 1990), *Masterfile* (EMI, 1992), *Big Wheel* (Diva/Massive/EMI, 1993), *The Berlin Tapes* (Diva/Roadshow, 1995), *Full Circle* (Diva/EMI, 1997); ***Iva Davies solo albums:*** *Razorback* (soundtrack; 1984); *Boxes* (soundtrack, 1985).

The Iguana

Formed: *1967*
Style: *Harmony pop*
Original line-up: *Gary Sweetman (vocals), Clive Littlewood (guitar), Gary Littlewood (guitar), Graham Jones (bass), Peter Saunders (drums)*

This Melbourne suburban band displayed a tight vocal harmony sound. The Iguana issued its debut single on the W&G label (through Festival) 'Imagine This'/'Dreaming Away to Myself' (October 1967). Festival issued the band's second single, a cover of The 5th Dimension's 'California, My Way'/'Mary Go Round' (February 1968), which made the Top 10 in Melbourne. Festival issued two more singles, The Beatles' 'Ticket to Ride'/'Sunshine People' (August) and 'Good News'/'Requiem: 820 Latham' (March 1969) and the EP 'California, My Way' (1968). Neither record charted. Russell McGregor replaced Saunders in 1968. The band broke up at the end of 1969 and McGregor was later awarded an Opera scholarship.

I'm Talking

Formed: *1983*
Style: *Funk, soul*
Original line-up: **Kate Ceberano** *(vocals; ex-Expozay, Hoagy Cats), Robert Goodge (guitar; ex-Essendon Airport), Ian Cox (sax; ex-Essendon Airport,* **Hot Half Hour***), Stephen Charlesworth (keyboards), Barbara Hogarth (bass; ex-Essendon Airport), Cameron Newman (drums)*

In some ways, Melbourne band I'm Talking was an odd phenomenon. Firstly, with a couple of members drawn from an experimental background (Robert Goodge and Ian Cox) it was unusual for the band to play silky-smooth disco, funk and soul. Goodge and Cox's previous band, Essendon Airport, played a hybrid of modern jazz and funk with art-rock leanings, but the musicians eschewed the experimental approach in favour of a more commercial route. Indeed, I'm Talking was one of the first bands to introduce sophisticated dance beats to a pub-rock audience *and* to win them over. Secondly, with two vivacious singers out front, the band's appeal extended beyond the standard constraints of the pub-rock milieu.

I'm Talking played the Melbourne pub/club circuit for a year, and had already issued a self-financed 12-inch EP, 'Someday' (May 1984), before coming to the attention of Regular Records. The band added Zan (ex-Grand Wazoo, Bang) as co-lead singer, and found national chart success with the singles 'Trust Me'/'Take It to the Bridge' (#6 in February 1985), 'Lead the Way'/'Disko', 'Love Don't Live Here Anymore' (#20 in August 1985) and Rose Royce's 'Love Don't Live Here Anymore'/'Cry Me a River' (#17 in September). 'Lead the Way' impressed drummer Fred Maher from UK band Scritti Politti so much that he offered to produce the band's debut album *Bear Witness*. Issued in August 1986, the accomplished album reached #5 on the national chart, and yielded three hits, 'Do You Wanna Be?' (#9 in May 1986), 'Holy Word' (sung by Zan, #8 in August) and 'How Can It Be?' (October). International interest followed, and I'm Talking undertook a 36-date UK tour supporting Five Star. Warren McLean (ex-**Machinations**) replaced Cameron Newman and Kevin Wiltshire joined as second keyboardist. That line-up appeared on the national Australian Made tour of January 1987.

It was to be I'm Talking's last major engagement. Zan, Charlesworth, McLean and Wiltshire had all left by March. Finding the new four-piece format unworkable, I'm Talking announced its

I'm Talking

break-up in July. **Kate Ceberano** and Zan both launched solo careers. Zan issued two solo dance/pop singles in 1989, 'It's Your Move' and 'Good Love' (produced by Todd Hunter), plus the 12-inch single 'Nobody Else' in March 1991. Zan also worked with a number of bands, including Mercy Mercy (with her sister Sherine from **Big Pig**). Goodge went on to work as part of the Filthy Lucre production team which was responsible for the remix on **Yothu Yindi's** epochal chart hit 'Treaty'.

Albums: *Bear Witness* (Regular/Festival, 1986), *Dancing* (compilation, Regular/Festival, 1988).

Indecent Obsession

Formed: *1987*
Style: *Pop rock*
Original line-up: *David Dixon (vocals), Andrew Coyne (guitar), Mick Szumowski (keyboards), Daryl Sims (drums)*

Teen pop sensations Indecent Obsession came together in Brisbane when main songwriters David Dixon and Mick Szumowski were 16 and 17 years old respectively. Andrew Coyne and Daryl Sims joined, after which the band spent 18 months touring the Queensland club/pub circuit and recording demos. Indecent Obsession came to the attention of Ian 'Molly' Meldrum, who signed the band to his Melodian label (through Mushroom).

Indecent Obsession relocated to Melbourne, where its mix of pop rock and dance-pop songs gained more attention. The band's debut single, 'Say Goodbye'/'Take Me Higher' (July 1989) reached #6 on the national singles chart, without the support of the commercial radio networks. The second single, 'Tell Me Something'/'Why Do People Fall in Love?' (October), also went Top 20 (#12). Indecent Obsession ended 1989 as tour support to popular American singer Debbie Gibson. Just as the band hit the crest of a wave of popularity among teenagers, Melodian issued the *Spoken Words* album (November 1989). The songs on the album were patchy, ranging from the polished synth-pop of 'Tell Me Something' to the contrived, melodramatic ballad 'Come Back to Me', which was issued as the third single in December. 'Never Gonna Stop'/'Say Goodbye' (live) was the album's fourth single.

Spoken Words eventually attained platinum status in Australia (over 75 000 copies sold), but when issued overseas that figure rose to over 250 000 copies worldwide. 'Tell Me Something' reached #1 in Indonesia, #1 in Hong Kong, #31 in the USA, Top 10 in Japan and Top 10 in South Africa. 'Come Back to Me' also went to #1 in Hong Kong. In Europe, the band was compared favourably to **INXS** and Duran Duran. Indecent Obsession spent most of 1991 writing and recording its second album, *Indio*, in Los Angeles with producer Peter Wolf (Escape Club, Go West, Wang Chung). With *Indio* (August 1992), the band made the transition from naive pop to mature, radio-friendly dance music. The album yielded the singles 'Rebel with a Cause', 'Kiss Me', 'Indio' and 'Gentleman Style'. For most of 1992, Indecent Obsession toured Latin America, Europe and the Asia-Pacific region, with the result that *Indio* sold over 200 000 copies. 'Kiss Me' and 'Gentleman Style' both went to #1 in Indonesia and Malaysia, with 'Kiss Me' also a Top 5 hit in Japan.

The band's biggest success, however, was reserved for South Africa, where 'Kiss Me' topped the charts for five weeks in early 1992. As the bonds of apartheid were slowly being broken, Indecent Obsession made history by becoming the first Western act to tour South Africa since the lifting of the cultural boycott. The band was greeted by screaming fans and scenes of mass hysteria the likes of which South Africa had rarely experienced before (**John Paul Young** was the only other Australian act to achieve chart success there). While in South Africa, the band was given the blessing of James Mange, one-time African National Congress (ANC) military leader, who had spent many years in gaol alongside future South African Prime Minister Nelson Mandela.

With the American release of *Indio*, and subsequent US tour, Indecent Obsession added Mark Gray (bass; ex-**Wa Wa Nee**) to the touring line-up. In April 1993, Dixon took the lead role in the local production of Andrew Lloyd Webber and Tim Rice's stage musical *Joseph and the Amazing Technicolor Dreamcoat.* In 1994 he and Coyne left the band to be replaced by Richard Hennassey (vocals) and Graham Kearns (guitar). That same year, Indecent Obsession issued its third album, *Relativity*, which spawned the singles 'Fixing a Broken Heart' and 'Fall from Grace'.

Albums: *Spoken Words* (Melodian/Mushroom/Festival, 1990), *Indio* (Melodian/Mushroom/Festival, 1992), *Relativity* (Melodian/Mushroom/Festival, 1994).

Independent record labels

There is a long-held assumption that independent record labels only emerged in the wake of the late 1970s punk movement. While that is a noble concept ('independent' certainly went hand-in-hand with punk's Do-It-Yourself ethos), the reality is somewhat more widespread. In the USA, for example, all manner of self-financed independent labels had been issuing blues, R&B and country records since the 1920s.

Likewise in Australia, country artists have been issuing and distributing their own records for decades. With the dawning of the rock'n'roll era in the late 1950s, the major record companies lacked an understanding of the emergent form, and were ill-equipped initially to deal with the youth culture phenomenon. Since that time, independent labels have continued to spring up as a viable alternative to the major record companies. These days, the majors comprise EMI, BMG (formerly RCA), PolyGram, Sony Music (CBS, Epic) and Warner Music (formerly WEA). Australia's own label Festival was formed in 1952 and became a major player as manufacturer and distributor for many important labels right up to the early 1990s.

As the term implies, independent labels existed outside the mainstream music industry, thereby creating an outlet for the bands and artists that the majors considered inappropriate to their focus, commercially unviable or that they simply had no knowledge of how to market and promote. Locally, some of the first independent rock'n'roll labels included Prestophone, Leedon, Crest, Planet (run by Bob King Crawford) and Rex. Leedon and Rex were distributed by Festival, and were later absorbed whole into that company's business affairs. American Lee Gordon set up Leedon in order to issue overseas records, and to facilitate local releases by artists like **Johnny O'Keefe**, **The Crescents**, **Lonnie Lee**, **Warren Williams** and **The Delltones**. Often considered to be the 'midwife' of Australian rock'n'roll, Leedon cut an imposing figure in his role as label manager, tour promoter and all-round music entrepreneur.

During the early 1960s, Melbourne label W&G began issuing records by instrumental groups such as **The Thunderbirds**, **The Phantoms**, The Saxons and The Breakaways, plus rock'n'roller **Johnny Chester** and folkies **The Seekers**. With the advent of Beatlemania and the explosion of the beat boom, independent labels like Sunshine, Kommotion, Go!!, In, Spin, Orbit, Scope, Clarion, Astor, Ramrod, Mojo and Linda Lee satisfied the demand for local product by the likes of **Billy Thorpe** and the Aztecs, **Bobby and Laurie**, **M.P.D. Limited**, **The Loved Ones**, **Normie Rowe**, **Ronnie Burns**, **Johnny Young** and countless others.

With the arrival of the progressive rock era circa 1969–70, new independent labels came to the fore. The 1970 'radio ban', in which major label records by local and overseas artists were denied airplay, left a gap for small, enterprising local labels to act quickly and get their records played. Labels like Havoc, Rebel, Fable, Du Monde, Caesar's International, Violet's Holiday, Air, Generation, Sparmac, Raven, Nationwide, Edition One, M7, Banner and Chart sprang up to fill the vacuum. Havoc went on to have great success with **Billy Thorpe** and the Aztecs and **Coloured Balls**. Other labels like Sweet Peach, Bootleg, Image, Wizard and Warm & Genuine also grabbed a corner of the market.

Two of the most successful independent labels throughout the 1970s were Mushroom and Albert. Set up in 1972 by impresario Michael Gudinski, Mushroom caught the mood of the times by issuing records by **Chain**, **The Dingoes**, **Madder Lake** and **Skyhooks**. **Skyhooks** were the most successful band of the 1970s. The band's debut album, *Living in the 70s*, sold an unprecedented 226 000 copies (it eventually reached the 375 000 mark), thereby launching Mushroom as a premier league player in the record company game. Mushroom dominated the Australian industry right into the 1990s, having nurtured the careers of bands such as **Split Enz** and **Models**, and solo artists like **Jason Donovan** and **Kylie Minogue**.

One of Mushroom's earliest coups was to ensure major distribution through Festival, and many would argue that the label quickly outgrew its independent status. All the same, the Mushroom subsidiary label White (set up in 1981) was one of the first of its kind to focus on (then) 'alternative' bands such as **Hunters & Collectors**, **Machinations** and **Sacred Cowboys**. Likewise, Albert had distribution through EMI. Albert Productions had been in operation since the 1960s, churning out hits for **Billy Thorpe** and the Aztecs, **The Easybeats**, **John Paul Young**, **Stevie Wright** and **William Shakespeare**. Albert's greatest contribution was to immortalise Aussie pub rock via the streetwise swagger of **AC/DC** and **Rose Tattoo**

Just prior to the advent of punk, independent labels like Clear Light of Jupiter, Real/Electric, Champagne, Rainbird, Oz, Eagle, Living Sound, Laser and Eureka were catering to eclectic tastes. The punk/new wave explosion of 1976–77 has been described as the 'big bang' of the independent universe. Almost overnight, bands began issuing and distributing their own limited edition singles, sometimes with homemade production values and picture sleeves to match. **The Saints** and **Radio Birdman** kicked the Australian new wave movement off with a shower of teenage sweat and pure adrenalin. **The Saints** issued their howling, milestone debut single '(I'm) Stranded' on their own Fatal Records imprint (October 1976). The record scored a glowing review in UK music paper *Sounds*, which led to EMI signing the band.

Likewise, **Radio Birdman** set up the Trafalgar label to issue its mail order 7-inch EP *Burn My Eye* and debut album *Radios Appear*. Later on, WEA stepped in with a distribution deal for the album, but Birdman remained fiercely independent and openly cautious of major label concerns. Like many pioneers, **The Saints** and **Radio Birdman** set up their own labels simply because the major labels were just not interested in the kind of music those bands created. As the late 1970s rolled on, independent labels proliferated. Often set up and driven by enthusiasts who knew the value of the music that the major labels rejected outright, these labels operated out of small backrooms, working within shoestring budgets, with low margins but boundless enthusiasm all the same. Quite often the people who ran the labels, and the bands involved, also packaged and distributed the records themselves (i.e. took them around to the record shops that stocked independent releases).

Melbourne had **Keith Glass**'s Missing Link (also a record shop), Bruce Milne's Au-go-go, Zak, Reverse, Innocent, Mambo, Unforgettable and Cleopatra; Sydney had Remand, Powderworks, Wallaby Beat, Point Blank, Doublethink, Lost, Regular, Deluxe, Larrikin, Lost in Space, Prince Melon, Local, M-Squared, Axle, Terse and Result; Brisbane had **The Go-Betweens'** Able label (with its cute motto 'If it's Ready, it's Able') and Savage/Shake; Perth had Bicton, D.N.A. and White Rider; Adelaide had Tomorrow.

The 1980s saw the fullest flowering of the Australian independent movement. Often records on these independent labels sold more than major label releases, but still the mainstream industry refused to take any notice. As well as Missing Link and Au-go-go in particular, some of the independent labels taking Australian music to the world included Phantom, GREEN, Waterfront, Citadel, Greasy Pop, Survival, Red Eye, Method, Sundown, Hot, True Tone, Aberrant, Grown Up Wrong/Dog Meat, Doc, Rampant, Reactor, Mr Spaceman, Polyester, Chase, Timberyard, Volition, Summershine and sundry others. Many of these labels operated right throughout the 1980s and into the 1990s. In some cases (Citadel, Greasy Pop, Red Eye, True Tone and Waterfront), the only way for them to survive was to establish distribution through a major label.

Several events occurred during the late 1980s/early 1990s which facilitated the further growth of the independent ethos. The rooArt label (with distribution through PolyGram initially) made an assault on the mainstream charts with bands like **Ratcat** and **The Hummingbirds**. In Melbourne, three shrewd entrepreneurs (David Williams, Andrew McGee and Frank Falvo, all of whom had a grounding in independent music retailing) set up the Shock Records label, distribution service and export arm. Shock provided a viable and lucrative alternative to major label distribution and, by focusing on local and overseas independent labels, began to show the majors how it should be done. Shock's market share eventually outstripped that of a number of the major labels. The majors had to sit up and take notice.

In the USA, labels such as SubPop, SST and Slash had already openly challenged the majors. Then staunchly independent bands such as Nirvana, Hüsker Dü, Soundgarden, Sonic Youth and Soul Asylum began to sign deals with major labels. In Australia, the likes of Sony, PolyGram and Mushroom set up their own development labels such as Murmur, Id and Bark. These sub-labels were run on an independent basis while having the obvious benefits of major label infrastructure. Almost overnight, the music culture changed, and suddenly the likes of **The Cruel Sea**, **silverchair**, **You Am I**, **Regurgitator** and **Spiderbait** were dominating the Australian Record Industry Association (ARIA) Awards *and* the charts. Indeed, Murmur's first release was **silverchair's** 'Tomorrow', which became a Top 10 mainstream hit.

The distinction between what constitutes an independent or 'alternative' band and a mainstream band has now become blurred. Such labelling and categorisation have become redundant. Nevertheless, the independent ethos remains relevant as a means to an end, with names such as Aim, Bent, Corduroy, TWA, Dominator, Dr Jims, Fellaheen, Half a Cow, Newmarket, Rubber, Siren and Shock's inhouse labels like Shagpile, Concubine, Hypnotized and Thrust continuing to emerge. Sadly, as alternative became mainstream, one-time leaders in the field like Red Eye, Volition and Dogmeat shut down operations in 1996.

iNFeCTeD

Formed: *1992*
Style: *Industrial/death metal*
Original line-up: *Joe Kapiteyn (vocals), Matthew Jefferson (guitar), James Campbell (bass), Gareth Morris (drums)*

This highly rated Perth death metal band attracted a loyal following in its hometown, supported overseas visitors Morbid Angel, Fear Factory, Pungent Stench and Carcass and issued two self-financed cassettes *Infected* and *Prick* before coming to the attention of audiences in the eastern states during late 1993. iNFeCTeD signed a deal with Shock Records' heavy metal label Thrust, which issued the band's debut album, *Crawlspace* (December 1993).

iNFeCTeD toured the eastern states in 1994. In early 1995, the band added Bjorg Saetre (keyboards) to its line-up and issued a second album, *Control* (April). The band undertook a second national tour during May. With its commitments to Thrust completed, iNFeCTeD issued a three-track demo cassette, *TRiAl* (March 1996), but broke up at the end of the year. Kapiteyn and Morris formed a new experimental band called iMAJ (pronounced Image).

Albums: *Crawlspace* (Thrust/Shock, 1993), *Control* (Thrust/Shock, 1995).

Glen Ingram and the Hi-Five

Formed: *1965*
Style: *Pop*
Original line-up: *Glen Ingram (vocals), Terry Walker (vocals), Kevin Reddington (guitar), Alan Ingram (bass, vocals), Jim McRobertson (drums)*

By sheer tyranny of distance, the Perth pop scene of the mid-1960s was a far cry from the frantic environment of the eastern states where pop hysteria was the order of the day. The Perth scene was dominated by a handful of bands like **Ray Hoff and the Off Beats**, The Times and Glen Ingram and the Hi-Five. Ingram and the Hi-Five issued one single on the local Clarion label (through Festival) which was a beat rendition of the traditional 'Skye Boat Song'. Glen Ingram sang lead vocals on the A-side while co-lead vocalist Terry Walker sang the flip 'Long Time Gone'.

The single became a national Top 10 hit, but The Hi-Five never toured the eastern states. By 1967, Ingram was fronting a new band called The Clan which issued the single 'That It's Me'/'Take this Hammer' (again on Clarion). Ingram issued a couple of solo singles, 'I'll Be Doggone'/'You Don't Know' (1967) and 'Let Me Be Free'/'I Want You Again' (1971), before working as a club performer. Alan Ingram joined **Jeff St John's** Copperwine in 1968.

Walker joined The Times, and then sang lead vocals on the psychedelic exploitation single 'Hypnotic Suggestion'/'Even Stevens' by Perth studio outfit The Vegetable Garden. The single came out on the Clarion label (September 1969) but sank without a trace. Reissue label Raven included 'Hypnotic Suggestion' on its 1989 Various Artists album *Ugly Things 4 Down Under Dreamtime (Australasian Sixties Psychedelia)*. Walker subsequently travelled to Melbourne, where he joined **The Strangers** and sang on the **Pastoral Symphony** hit, 'Love Machine'.

The Innocents (*see* Beathoven)

The In-Sect

Formed: *1965*
Style: *R&B*
Original line-up: *Frank Sebastyan (vocals), Phil Wooding (guitar), Peter Manuel (organ), Allan Sands (bass), Geoff Pretty (drums)*

Adelaide band The In-Sect began life as Dave Thunder and the Macmen around 1961. The In-Sect played the local dance scene for a number of years, and were a musically substantial bunch indeed. On any given night, the band could be heard playing Top 40 covers or middle of the road muzak on the showband/cabaret circuit (where the good money was to be earned), or wild R&B and garage-punk on the discotheque/dance circuit.

As Dave Thunder and the Macmen, the band issued its dire debut single, 'Clap Your Hands'/'Forgive Me Darlin', on the W&G label (February 1966). Not long after the single's release, the band became The In-Sect in homage to The Beatles. The band's first classic single, 'Let This Be a Lesson'/'Take It Easy' (June), was a tough R&B raver in The Yardbirds vein. The even wilder 'I Can See My Love'/'More than I Can Say' (August) and 'I am Waiting'/'Down and Out' (December) followed. Each single featured Wooding's trademark 'buzzing' guitar solos, and all made the Top 10 in Adelaide.

Still unknown in the other states, the band issued the ultra-rare album *In-Sect A-Sides*. The band hedged its bets either way by including the singles tracks, a cover of the Yardbirds' 'Over Under Sideways Down' and five tacky pop/cabaret songs. Nevertheless, the album was of sufficient quality for 1960s aficionado (the late) Dean Mittelhauser to rate it as one of the best and rarest albums of the 1960s. Raven reissued the album in 1985, ditching two of the weaker tracks for a later single.

The band then issued two novelty singles with local DJ John Vincent on vocals "Ow Yer Goin"/'Over Under Sideways Down' (August 1967) and 'Madge's Charity Badges'/'Choko Brandy' (December 1968). Both these singles also reached the Top 10 in Adelaide. In 1967, Steve Lada (ex-**Ram Jam Big Band**) replaced Sands, and in late 1968 Wooding left to join **Jeff St John's** Copperwine in Sydney. The In-Sect issued one final novelty single, 'The Ballad of Andy Capp'/'Window', in 1969 before Pretty left to join The Going Thing. John Bywaters (ex-**Twilights**) then replaced Lada, and the band mutated into The Frank Sebastyan Entertainment Revue, which played the cabaret circuit right through the 1970s.

Albums: *In-Sect A-Sides* (W&G, 1967), *In-Sect A-Sides* (reissue; Raven, 1986).

iNsuRge

Formed: *1994*
Style: *Techno-metal*
Original line-up: *Chris Dubrow (guitar, vocals; ex-Soulscraper), Monique Wakelin (keyboards), Jan Sebastian (percussion), Mattieu MacRoth (bass), Matt Richmond (drums)*

Melbourne band iNsuRge mixed Chris Dubrow's vitriolic, politically motivated lyrical tirades with hardcore guitar riffs, heavy-duty percussion and thudding samples (a la Front 242 or Ministry). Writing in *Rolling Stone*, reviewer Mark Demitrius called the band's sound 'St Vitus dance-music'. The outspoken Dubrow had already explored similar territory with his previous band Soulscraper.

As well as Dubrow, Soulscraper comprised Sarah Lord (bass), James Lynch (drums), Eleanor Rayner ('rhythm' samples) and Jim Shnookal ('lead' samples). Soulscraper was alternatively considered to be a techno outfit or a grunge band. With the release of its debut EP, 'Heard It All Before', in early 1993, Soulscraper was unfairly written off as a Nine Inch Nails clone. Dubrow broke up Soulscraper and launched his new outfit, iNsuRge, in early 1994. iNsuRge issued a trio of CD EPs, 'I.M.F.' (1994), 'Political Prisoners' (1995) and 'Speculator' (February 1996), before debuting with its full-length album, *Power to the Poison People*, in August 1996 (national #16 in September). 'Time Bomb' (September) was also lifted as a CD single.

Album: *Power to the Poison People* (East West/Warner, 1996).

International Exiles

Formed: *1978*
Style: *Pop*
1979 line-up: *Laine McCready (vocals), Andy Calender (keyboards, vocals), Rob Wellington (guitar; ex-Fiction), Adam Learner (bass), David Adams (drums)*

Alongside **Models**, **Little Murders** and The Jetsonnes, International Exiles were one of the first bands to rise out of Melbourne's hothouse punk, new wave explosion playing an exuberant brand of neo-pop. Wellington had been a member of the first line-up of **Little Murders** when they were still known as Fiction. Fiction recorded the songs 'Things will Be Different' and 'Take Me I'm Yours' which comprised **Little Murders'** debut 1979 single on the Au-go-go label. International Exiles issued two singles in 1980.

The first, 'Miniskirts in Moscow', was shared as one side of a gig giveaway 7-inch with The Jetsonnes. The second, 'Let's Be Sophisticated'/'Note to Roger', came out on the Missing Link label. Shane Middleton replaced Adams in 1981, but the band broke up a year later. Wellington formed Wild Dog Rodeo before pursuing a career in rock video production (he directed **John Farnham's** 'You're the Voice' and **Models'** 'Big on Love') and later in multimedia production.

The Interstellar Villains

Formed: *1988*
Style: *Grunge pop*
Original line-up: *Tony Thewlis (guitar, vocals; ex-***Helicopters**, **Scientists***), Richard Walsh (guitar), Alan Hislop (drums; ex-***Moffs***)*

Following the proto-grunge/noise he explored with **Scientists**, Tony Thewlis formed The Interstellar Villains as a more 1960s-influenced garage-pop band. The band signed to the Timberyard label and issued the mini-album *Right Out in the Lobster Quadrille* (January 1989), plus the singles 'Sex Kittens'/'I Wanna Gun', 'Lost Cause' (June) and Jackie De Shannon's 'Baby That's Me'/'(Sometimes Think I am Just Another One of) Dylan's Dreams' (November). The album mixed Troggs humour, Big Star pop-raunch and Syd Barrett-era Pink Floyd experimentation. Alison Handley (vocals) joined for the singles.

The album *Revolver* and singles 'Caught My Death' (1990) and 'Big Head'/'Like Flies on Sherbet' (September 1991) were more of the same. 'Like Flies on Sherbet' was a deranged Alex Chilton cover from a Chilton tribute album. The Villains reputedly took up exile in Spain (due to local apathy), where they had the single 'My Boyfriend is an Outlaw' issued on Madrid-based label Munster. The band also contributed the track 'Christmas Chimes (are Here Already)' to the Timberyard Various Artists album *Rockin' Bethlehem* (1989).

Albums: *Right Out in the Lobster Quadrille* (mini-album, Timberyard, 1989), *Revolver* (Timberyard, 1990).

Intoxica

Formed: *1989*
Style: *Garage rock, psychobilly*
Original line-up: *Tony Shaw (vocals; ex-***Corpse Grinders***), George Spencer (guitar; ex-***Olympic Sideburns***), Nick DelRey (guitar; ex-King Jerklews), Trevor Pennington (bass; ex-***Corpse Grinders, Band Who Shot Liberty Valance***), Phil 'Good One' Bryant (drums; ex-Zorros,* **Corpse Grinders, Band Who Shot Liberty Valance***)*

With a pedigree drawn from such infamous Melbourne inner-city legends as **Corpse Grinders**, **Olympic Sideburns** and The King Jerklews, there was only one style of music Intoxica could have ever played: Cramps-styled psychobilly mixed with garage-swamp rock. Hardly original, but full of beer-swilling humour, urban sleaze, re-fried boogie riffs, distorted bass lines and Screamin' Jay Hawkins-like vocal yelps and growls nonetheless. Intoxica issued the album *Intoxica* and single 'Brandivino Party'/'Raging Sea' in 1990. The band gigged sporadically and issued a second single, 'I Wanna Wear Your Skin'/'Mad Man', 'Squad Car' on the Giant Claw label (March 1993), before signing off with a second album in 1994. Tony Shaw went on to front The Exotics, who issued a single in August 1997, 'You Drive Me Coo Coo Baby!'. Intoxica re-emerged in November 1997 with the album, *Dragstripper*.

Albums: *Intoxica* (Shock, 1990), *Suburban Roulette* (Shock, 1994), *Dragstripper* (Shock, 1997).

INXS

Formed: *1977*
Style: *Rock, funk*
Original line-up: *Michael Hutchence (vocals), Tim Farriss (guitar), Andrew Farriss (keyboards), Kirk Pengilly (guitar, sax), Garry Gary Beers (bass), Jon Farriss (drums)*

Before the tragic death of lead singer Michael Hutchence on 22 November 1997 at the age of 37, INXS had not suffered one line-up change in 20 years of operation! INXS can lay claim to being the most internationally successful Australian rock band of all time. The band's success can be attributed to many factors, including the unchanging line-up, an inordinate amount of self-belief, unstinting touring schedules, consistently strong and fresh production for each album, a distinctive hard rock sound that incorporated funk and dance influences and frontman Hutchence's sultry good looks.

Indeed, Hutchence was the archetypal rock showman. He exuded an overtly sexual, macho cool with his flowing locks, and lithe and exuberant stage movements. Having grown up in Hong Kong, California and Sydney, Hutchence came to epitomise the globe-trotting, superstar rock singer, with all the attendant trappings of international fame. Hutchence also had to deal with his fair share of tabloid scandals, such as when he and Paula Yates (proud parents of Heavenly Hiraani Tiger Lily) were at the centre of drug and pornography accusations, plus custody battles with Yates' former husband Sir Bob Geldof.

INXS formed in Sydney during 1977 as The Farriss Brothers. The band relocated to Perth, Western Australia in 1978 when the Farriss family moved there taking the underage Jon with them. A year later the band was back in Sydney with a new name: INXS. In 1980, the band linked up with manager Chris Murphy (soon to head the powerful MMA organisation). The independent Deluxe label issued the band's debut single, 'Simple Simon'/'We are the Vegetables' (May 1980), followed by the album *INXS* (October 1980) and its single, 'Just Keep Walking'/'Scratch' (September).

Those early records displayed a jaunty, new wave/ska-pop sound and were not indicative of the band's future directions. The records sold poorly ('Just Keep Walking' managed to reached #38 on the national charts), but the band quickly gained a reputation as one of the country's best live acts. Constant touring across the country during 1981 (almost 300 shows) kept INXS in the public eye, and subsequent records began to sell. The band's third single, a revival of **The Loved Ones'** 'The Loved One'/'The Unloved One' reached #18 in April 1981. The **Richard Clapton**-produced *Underneath the Colours* album (October 1981; #15 in November) yielded the singles 'Stay Young'/ 'Lacavocal' (September; #21 in November) and 'Night of Rebellion'/'Prehistoria' (January 1982). INXS then signed a new deal with WEA. The budget-priced collection INXS*ive* on Deluxe mopped up various album tracks and early singles sides.

Shabooh Shoobah (October 1982) was the band's first album to reach the Top 10 nationally (#5 in

November). Backed by booming production values courtesy of Mark Opitz and a selection of confident, well-crafted rock songs, it was the band's strongest to date. The album spawned four singles, 'The One Thing'/'Space Shuttle' (#14 in August 1982), 'Don't Change'/'Go West' (#15 in November), 'To Look at You' (double single pack, #36 in March 1983) and the 12-inch EP *Dance:* 'Black and White' (#24 in July). *Shabooh Shoobah* was the band's first international release (on Atlantic/ATCO in the USA and Mercury in the UK). Both the album and single 'The One Thing' charted in the Top 30 in the USA, and the band spent much of 1983 touring the country (including support slots to The Kinks and Adam Ant). Things were a little slower to take off in the UK, where the 'hip' music press dismissed the band's music as unimaginative MTV rock.

While in New York, the band entered Power Station studios with Chic leader Nile Rogers to record 'The Original Sin'. The track showcased the band's new fascination for melding rock, funk and modern dance rhythms. It became the band's first Australian #1 single in January 1984. INXS later contributed 'The Original Sin' to the Various Artists album *Building Bridges* on CBS (1989). The Nick Launay-produced album The Swing made its debut at #1 on the Australian album chart (April 1984), and remained on the chart for over a year. The album boasted all the confident swagger and accomplished rock hooks of a band on the cusp of international acceptance; it reached #52 in the USA during mid-1984. Three further singles were lifted from the set for release in Australia: 'I Send a Message'/'Mechanical' (#2 in March 1984), 'Burn for You'/'Johnson's Aeroplane' (#3 in July) and 'Dancing on the Jetty'/'The Harbour' (#39 in October). The *Dekadance* cassette compilation (March 1985) featured six extended and/or remixed versions of songs from *The Swing* plus the previously unavailable cover of 'Jackson' (featuring a duet between Hutchence and **Jenny Morris**). The compilation reached #3 on the national chart in May. The promotional, 12-inch vinyl edition of *Dekadance* is one of the band's rarest releases.

In 1985, INXS took out seven awards at the ***Countdown*** Awards ceremony. *Listen Like Thieves* came out in August and made its debut at #1 on the national chart, having attained platinum status on advance orders alone (unprecedented in Australia). The album yielded four singles in Australia: 'What You Need'/'I'm Over You' (#1 in August 1985), 'This Time'/'Sweet as Sin' (#19 in December), 'Kiss the Dirt (Falling Down the Mountain)'/'Six Knots', 'The One Thing' (live) (#15 in March 1986) and 'Listen Like Thieves'/'Different World' (#28 in June). Producer Chris Thomas (Sex Pistols, Pretenders, Roxy Music) gave the album a much harder sound than heard on previous INXS records, but somehow it lacked the pop smarts that had made *The Swing* so appealing. Nevertheless, *Listen Like Thieves* went on to sell over a million copies worldwide (US #11; UK #48). 'What You Need' became the band's first Top 5 (#5) hit in the USA, but when issued in the UK it only managed #51.

Michael Hutchence, INXS

Such was INXS's live standing in the UK, however, that the band was able to sell out London's prestigious Albert Hall, which led to two appearances supporting Queen at Wembley Stadium. Worldwide success continued to grow after the band's performance at the Australian Live Aid concert was beamed across the globe in July 1986. At the end of 1986, INXS recorded a rousing rendition of the old **Easybeats'** rocker 'Good Times'/'Laying Down the Law' with **Jimmy Barnes**. To coincide with the massive Australian Made tour of early 1987 (which **Jimmy Barnes** and INXS headlined), the single reached #1 nationally. 'Good Times' also reached #47 in the USA and was later included on the soundtrack to the film *The Lost Boys*.

Hutchence was the first member of INXS to release any records under his own name when he issued a solo single, a cover of Whirlywirld's 'Rooms for the Memory'/'Golfcourse' (#11 in February 1987). Both songs were taken from the soundtrack to Richard Lowenstein's feature film *Dogs in Space*. Set in the post-punk wasteland of inner-city Melbourne, the film featured Hutchence in the part of Sam, lead singer with the band Dogs in Space.

The next album, *Kick* (November 1987; again with Thomas as producer), became the band's most enduring release by mixing the hard rock sound of *Thieves* with a looser approach to dance grooves. It made its debut at #2 in Australia and went on to hit the top spot. It was the second biggest selling album on the Australian charts for 1988. INXS won Best Group at the 1988 Australian Record Industry Association (ARIA) Awards. *Kick* also reached #9 in the UK and #3 in the USA and went on to sell nine million copies worldwide. The first single from the album 'Need You Tonight'/'I'm Coming (Home)' (October 1987) reached #3 in Australia, and by January 1988 it was #1 in the USA. When issued in the UK, however, 'Need You Tonight' only reached #58. After two sold-out UK tours, however, Mercury reissued 'Need You Tonight' a year later, which resulted in a #2 placing. 'Mystify'/'Devil Inside' followed suit, reaching #14 in the UK during March 1989. The next brace of singles lifted from *Kick* were big hits in Australia, but did even better Stateside: 'Devil Inside'/'On the Rocks' was #2 in March 1988 (Australian #5), 'New Sensation'/'Do Wot You Do' reached #3 in May (Australian #8) and 'Never Tear Us Apart'/'Guns in the Sky' ('Move on' was the B-side in Australia) hit #7 in September (Australian #8). 'Do Wot You Do' also appeared on the soundtrack to the popular teen feature film *Pretty in Pink*.

During October/November 1988, INXS undertook the massive Calling All Nations tour of Australia, after which the band members scattered across the globe to pursue individual projects for a year. Hutchence collaborated with **Ian 'Ollie' Olsen** on the **Max Q** album and appeared in cult film director Roger Corman's *Frankenstein Unbound*, in which he played the part of Percy Bysshe Shelley. His co-stars were Raoul Julia, John Hurt and Bridget Fonda. Andrew Farriss produced **Jenny Morris'** *Shiver* album and Beers toured with **Richard Clapton** and **Absent Friends**.

The band's eighth album, *X*, returned INXS to the charts in October 1990 (Australian #4; UK #2; US #5). It yielded the hit singles 'Suicide Blonde'/'Everybody Wants U Tonight' (Australian #2 in October; UK #11; US #9), 'Disappear'/'Middle Beast' (Australian #23 in January 1991; UK #21; US #8), 'Bitter Tears'/'The Other Side' (Australian #36 in March; UK #30; US #46) and 'By My Side'/'Soothe Me' (Australian #23 in June; UK #42).

Hutchence's much publicised romance with **Kylie Minogue** around that time also brought the group to the attention of a whole new generation of potential fans. Hutchence was later quoted as saying that his favourite pastime was 'corrupting Kylie'. *Live Baby Live* (Australian #3; UK #8; US #72) was a document of the band's triumphant concert at Wembley Stadium in front of 74 000 fans during July 1991. It also contained one previously unreleased studio track, 'Shining Star', which was issued as a single backed with three live cuts, 'I Send a Message', 'Faith in Each Other' and 'Bitter Tears' (Australian #21 in November 1991; UK #27). *Live Baby Live* was the band's least successful album in eight years. 'Shining Star' spent only one week in *Billboard*'s Hot 100, breaking the band's run of US hits.

Nevertheless, the band's perseverance in the face of initial UK apathy was vindicated when INXS walked away with Best International Group award and Best International Artist honour for Hutchence at the 1991 BRIT presentations. The band also helped organise (with co-manager Gary Grant and Mark Pope) the ambitious Concert for Life, which was held in Sydney's Centennial Park on 28 March 1992. The concert drew approximately 65 000 fans and raised $600 000 for St Vincent's Hospital.

The Mark Opitz-produced *Welcome to Whatever You Are* (August 1992) saw the band experimenting in the studio. In Australia it peaked at #2 during September, but went one better in the UK, where it hit the top spot. It went on to sell two and a half million copies worldwide. It yielded five singles: 'Heaven Sent'/'It Ain't Easy' (Australian #13 in July 1992; UK #31), 'Not Enough Time'/'Deepest Red' (US #28 in August), 'Baby Don't Cry'/'Baby Don't Cry Part 2'(Australian #30 in September; UK #20), 'Taste It'/'Light the Planet' (Australian #36 in December; UK #21) and 'Beautiful Girl'/'In My Livingroom' (Australian #34 in May 1993; UK #23; US #46).

INXS followed up a year later with *Full Moon, Dirty Hearts* (Australian #18; UK #3; US #53), in which the band members re-acquainted themselves with their pub-rock roots. The first single was the hard rocking 'The Gift'/'Need You Tonight' (Australian #16 in October 1993; UK #11), followed by 'Please (You Got that)' (with Ray Charles)/'Born to Be Wild' (Australian #37 in December; UK #50) and 'Time'/'Communication' (Live) (Australian #36 in February 1994). The band's version of Steppenwolf's 'Born to Be Wild' also appeared on the soundtrack to the Yahoo Serious film *Reckless Kelly*.

INXS—The Greatest Hits peaked at #3 in the UK and the Australian Top 10 during December 1994. It included one new song, 'The Strangest Party (These are the Times)' which was issued as a single backed with 'Wishing Well' (Australian #34 in October; UK #15). Ironically, *INXS—The Greatest Hits* did not chart well in the USA, where previously the band had been treated as conquering heroes. No doubt the arrival of grunge in general, and the emergence of bands like Nirvana, Soundgarden and Smashing Pumpkins in particular, contributed to INXS' lower profile in the US. Nevertheless, Hutchence kept busy by contributing to a number of feature film soundtrack and tribute album projects. These included singing 'Under My Thumb' on the *Symphonic Music of the Rolling Stones* album, 'Baby Let's Play House' on the Elvis Presley tribute album *It's Now or Never*, a cover of Iggy Pop's 'The Passenger' on the *Batman Forever* soundtrack and a version of Eric Burdon and War's 'Spill the Wine' on the *Barb Wire* soundtrack.

In 1996, INXS split from long-time manager Chris Murphy, and left Atlantic/ATCO for a lucrative new deal with Mercury in the USA. March 1997 saw the release of the first new INXS album in three years, *Elegantly Wasted*. With the likes of **Savage Garden**, **silverchair** and **Human Nature** dominating the charts, the album could only manage an Australian Top 40 stay of four weeks after peaking at #14. Likewise the first CD single, 'Elegantly Wasted' charted at #48 for only one week during April and then disappeared. Nevertheless, *Elegantly Wasted* sold almost a million copies worldwide. The second single 'Don't Lose Your Head' (as featured in the film *Face/Off*) came out in June. The members of INXS had returned to Australia during November, for their 20th anniversary national tour when Hutchence died by hanging himself at the Ritz-Carlton Hotel in the Sydney suburb of Double Bay. An inquest into his death found it was suicide, although some believe it was an accident.

Albums: INXS (Deluxe/RCA, 1980), *Underneath the Colours* (Deluxe/RCA, 1981), *Shabooh Shoobah* (WEA, 1982), INXS*ive* (Deluxe/RCA, 1982), *The Swing* (WEA, 1984), *Listen Like Thieves* (WEA, 1985), *Kick* (WEA, 1987), *X* (WEA, 1990), *Live Baby Live* (East West/Warner, 1991), *Welcome to Whatever You Are* (East West/Warner, 1992), *Full Moon, Dirty Hearts* (East West/Warner, 1993), INXS—*The Greatest Hits* (East West/Warner, 1994), *Elegantly Wasted* (Mercury/Polydor, 1997).

Itch-E & Scratch-E

Formed: *1992*
Style: *Techno dance*
Original line-up: *Andy Rantzen (Itch-E; keyboards, samples), Paul McDermott (Scratch-E; keyboards, samples)*

The Australian techno-rave/electronic-dance scene of the early 1990s was small in comparison to its overseas role model. Electronic wizz kids Itch-E & Scratch-E virtually had a stranglehold on the scene from the outset. Paul McDermott had been working with ambient outfit **The Lab** and Andy Rantzen with Pelican Daughters when they decided to start Itch-E & Scratch-E as a joke. They were joined by Sheriff 'Dub Man' Lindo for live shows.

The duo recorded a demo which came to the attention of the Volition label. Volition's offshoot label, Second Nature, issued the CD EP 'Irritable' (August 1992) and the album *Itch-E Kitch-E Koo* (October 1993). The CD single 'Sweetness and Light' won the 1995 Australian Record Industry Association (ARIA) Award for best dance release. Itch-E & Scratch-E followed this up with the sprawling double album *Itch-E & Scratch-E . . . and Friends* (1996) which covered the gamut of electronic dance. The *and Friends* part comprised the high-energy house of CrackerJack, the funky bleeps of Event Horizon, the electronic jazz of Alien Headspace and the hypnotic dub of Sheriff Lindo. Itch-E and Lindo were also involved in Event Horizon and Scratch-E was one half of CrackerJack. Itch-E & Scratch-E's 'Bouncing Chamber' and 'Howling Dog' were issued as CD EPs.

At the end of 1996, Itch-E & Scratch-E were forced to take a new name, due to two acts overseas going by the same name, to say nothing of the cat and mouse team of Itchy and Scratchy that appeared in popular television cartoon show *The Simpsons*. The duo came up with Boo Boo and Mace (or Boo Boo, Mace 'n' Nutcase when joined onstage by Lindo). Boo Boo, Mace 'n' Nutcase appeared on the national bill of the Big Day Out (1997) as headlining act in the techno-based Boiler Room. Boo Boo and Mace issued the CD EP 'Flowers in the Sky' in February 1997, to be followed by the Boo Boo, Mace 'n' Nutcase CD single, 'Gotta Move On', in November.

Albums: *Itch-E Kitch-E Koo* (Second Nature/Volition, 1993), *Itch-E & Scratch-E . . . and Friends* (Second Nature/Volition, 1996).

J

JAB

Formed: *1976*
Style: *Experimental, punk*
Original line-up: *Bohdan X (guitar, vocals), Ash Wednesday (synthesiser, bass), Boris (guitar), Janis Freidenfelds (aka Johnny Crash, drums)*

Adelaide band JAB started out as an experimental outfit, taking inspiration from the likes of Eno, David Bowie and certain German electronic artists such as Kraftwerk, Neu!, Faust and Can. With the advent of punk/new wave circa 1977, the band took on a brasher punk stance. Alongside the likes of **The Dagoes**, **Young Modern**, **X-Ray-Z**, Black Chrome, Nasty Nigel and the Teenage Hellcats, Sputniks, The U-Bombs, The Warm Jets and The Accountants, JAB was part of the first wave of new bands on the Adelaide scene.

JAB backed frontman Bohdan X on his solo single 'Time to Age'/'You Got Soul' which came out on the Tomorrow label in late 1977. The single was not punk, however, being almost acoustic in a Roy Harper vein. By the time the single came out, JAB had relocated to Melbourne. Bobby Stopa replaced Boris on guitar. JAB became part of the Melbourne new wave scene, and got swept up, along with The Boys Next Door, **Teenage Radio Stars**, **X-Ray-Z**, The Negatives and others, as part of the Suicide Records package. JAB contributed two tracks, 'Blonde and Bombed' and 'Let's Go', to the label's 1978 Various Artists compilation *Lethal Weapons*.

Pierre Voltaire (bass; ex-**Teenage Radio Stars**) joined JAB in May 1978, but three months later the band broke up. Bohdan X joined members of **The Chosen Few** to form Bohdan and the Instigators. He later issued several solo records, including the four-track, 12-inch EP *Bohdan* ('Fear of Flying') (Rumour, December 1983) and the mini-album *Kingsnake* (Rampant, 1988). He became a DJ on community radio station 3RRR-FM. Wednesday, Crash and Voltaire linked up with Sean Kelly (guitar, vocals; ex-**Teenage Radio Stars**) to form **Models**. Wednesday stayed with **Models** for a year, after which he played with The Metronomes, Modern Jazz and **Crashland**. He also issued a solo single in 1980, 'Love by Numbers'/'Boring Instrumental'.

Jack Frost

Formed: *1990*
Style: *Rock*
Original line-up: Grant McLennan *(vocals, guitar, bass; ex-***Go-Betweens***)*, **Steve Kilbey** *(vocals, guitar, bass, keyboards, drums; from* **The Church***)*

Jack Frost was a collaboration between **Grant McLennan** and **Steve Kilbey** that began on 'a rainy Friday afternoon' when Kilbey suggested the two musicians write a song. The duo cut a complete album in two weeks. The songs on *Jack Frost* ranged from romantic ballads to tough rock, with the two singers' voices fitting together well. Bryce Surplice helped out on drums and synth. 'Every Hour God Sends' (November 1990) and 'Thought That I was Over You' (April 1991) were issued as singles. Due to commitments to their own bands and solo projects, it took until late 1995 for the pair to work together again. The resultant album, *Snow Job*, came out to little fanfare and duly sank without a trace.

Albums: *Jack Frost* (Red Eye, 1990), *Snow Job* (Karmic Hit, 1996).

The Jackson Code

Formed: *1988*
Style: *Country, folk*
Original line-up: *Mark Snarski (guitar, vocals; ex-***Chad's Tree***), Jason Kain (guitar; ex-Wet Taxis), Kathy Wemyss (vocals, trumpet; ex-Wet Taxis), Kenny Davis Jr (accordion, keyboards)*

Perth musician Mark Snarski spent several years with **Chad's Tree**, a band that also included his brother Robert. Robert formed **The Blackeyed Susans**, and Mark began to develop his songwriting with The Jackson Code. The band featured a nucleus of Snarski, Kain, Wemyss and Davis. For the band's debut album, Snarski utilised the services of Amanda Pearson (vocals, percussion), Barry Turnbull (bass) and Mark Dawson (drums). The band's critically acclaimed debut album, *del musical del mismo nombre*, came out in August 1989.

The band recorded the album in four days on a budget of $1000. The lush romanticism of the songs had critics searching for superlatives. Writing in *Rolling Stone*, reviewer Jon Casimir called the album one of the minor masterpieces of 1989. As Casimir put it, the band took inspiration for its 'self-styled urban Romantic Cabaret' from German writers such as Brecht and Weill, as well as Tom Waits. Rather than capitalise on such acclaim, Snarski chose to take a break, spending two years travelling in Spain and the USA. He revived The Jackson Code in 1992 and recorded a new album. Helping out in the studio again were Pearson, Turnbull and Dawson, plus string, brass and 'hand-clap' sections. The band issued *Strange Cargo* (August 1992) on the Citadel label. Once again, Snarski's songs were melodramatic vignettes, detailing a range of emotions and shady characters. The music ranged from rock to pop to country to jazz to European folk.

The band's third and fourth albums, *Draggin' the River* (December 1993) and *The Things You Need* (September 1995), offered further vivid splashes of literary colour amid a world of grunge and techno. These albums spawned the CD EPs 'Who's Watching Who?' (September 1993), 'Poison Berries' (January 1994) and 'Bring Yourself Home to Me' (July 1995). In the early days, Snarski kept The Jackson Code's live appearances to a minimum, but as the band's profile rose via a deal with Ra/rooArt, he was prepared to tour more often.

Albums: *del musical del mismo nombre* (Waterfront, 1989), *Strange Cargo* (Citadel, 1992), *Draggin' the River* (Ra/rooArt, 1993), *The Things You Need* (Ra/rooArt, 1995).

Rockwell T. James

Style: *Pop, R&B*

Rockwell T. James was the alter ego of journeyman bass player Ronnie Peel. Peel got his start in the 1960s with the original line-ups of **The Missing Links** and **The Pleazers**, plus the second version of **Ray Brown and the Whispers**. In 1967, he formed the first incarnation of Rockwell T. James and the Rhythm Aces, which became the house band at Sydney's famed Whisky A-Go-Go discotheque. The line-up comprised Peel, Lance Dixon (organ), Les Stacpool (guitar; ex-**Chessmen**, **Merv Benton** and the Tamlas), Mike Freeman (trumpet), Ron Freeman (sax) and Roger Felice-Andrews (drums; ex-**Marty Rhone** and the Soul Agents).

The Rhythm Aces issued the single 'Love Power'/'New Orleans Funk' on the Festival label (February 1968). When the band folded mid-year, Peel and Stacpool formed The Browns with **Ray Arnott** (drums; ex-Chelsea Set) and New Zealand vocalist **Leo De Castro**. In 1970, Peel and Felice-Andrews travelled to the UK where they landed a job as rhythm section for hit-makers Thunderclap Newman (of 'Something in the Air' fame). Peel returned to Australia in late 1971 and joined **Ray Brown's** new band, One Ton Gypsy. From there he joined **La De Das**, then on the rise to becoming one of the country's finest boogie-rock outfits. **La De Das** folded in late 1975 and Peel joined **John Paul Young** and the All Stars as rhythm guitarist.

In 1976, with the help of **Sherbet's** Garth Porter, Peel revived his Rockwell T. James persona for two singles on Festival/Infinity: 'Come on Home (a Song for Anna)'/'Belinda' (May 1976; #22 in Melbourne during August) and 'Roxanne'/'Hey Mama' (October; #26 in Melbourne during December). In October 1977, Peel issued a Rockwell T. James album, *Shot of Rhythm & Blues*, on Sherbet's Razzle label. 'Lady Blue' (August 1977) was issued as the single. In July 1978, Peel issued a fifth Rockwell T. James single, 'Rollin' on'/'On My Mind'. The studio band comprised Peel, **Sherbet's** Garth Porter (keyboards) and Tony Mitchell (bass), Mark Kennedy (drums) and Tony Buchanan (sax), plus **Cold Chisel's Ian Moss** (lead guitar).

Peel then formed a touring line-up of Rockwell T. James and the Rhythm Aces which comprised himself (vocals, rhythm guitar), Vince Melouney (slide guitar; ex-**Billy Thorpe** and the Aztecs, **Bee Gees**, **Fanny Adams**), Chris Turner (lead guitar; ex-Drain, **Buffalo**), John Strangio (bass; ex-**Dingoes**, **Chariot**) and Jim Penson (drums; ex-Plastic Tears, **Blackfeather**, **Chariot**). Peter Roberts (bass; ex-**La De Das**, **Chariot**) and Ace Follington (drums; ex-**Chain**, Australia) then replaced Strangio and Penson respectively. Razzle reissued the *Shot of Rhythm & Blues* album as *Rollin' on* with both sides of the last single added.

The last Rockwell T. James record was the single 'Let It Go' (November 1979) which Peel shared with **Mario Millo's** 'Rebecca' on the flip side. Both tracks had been lifted off the Various Artists *Australian Guitar Album*. Peel then laid the Rockwell T. James concept to rest. He has since worked with **Ray Arnott** Band, **Cheetah** and Scattered Aces. Scattered Aces comprised Peel (bass, vocals), Chris Turner, **Peter Wells** (slide guitar; ex-**Buffalo**, **Rose Tattoo**) and Fred Zeppelin (real name Paul DeMarco, drums). The band toured throughout 1984 and issued the mini-album *Six Pack* and the single Eddie Cochran's 'C'mon Everybody'/'Waltzing Matilda' on the Big Rock label.

Albums: *Shot of Rhythm & Blues* (Razzle/Festival, 1977), *Rollin' on* (Razzle/Festival, 1978).

James Taylor Move

Formed: *1967*
Style: *Psychedelic pop*
Original line-up: *Robert (R.J.) Taylor (vocals, bass), Kevin Peek (guitar; ex-Hurricanes,* **Twilights**, *Johnny Broome and the Handels), Allan Tarney (organ; Johnny Broome and the Handels), Trevor Spencer (drums)*

The year 1967 will forever be remembered as the 'Summer of Love', the year psychedelia rose to prominence around the world. In the UK, Cream, The Jimi Hendrix Experience and Pink Floyd were setting trends in the world of acid-rock. Australia followed suit a little while later with a number of Hendrix-influenced bands such as The Haze, The Trip, The Knack, The Revolution, and the most memorable of the lot, James Taylor Move. The band came together in Adelaide when a sharp discotheque owner decided to assemble a band to capitalise on the new sound of psychedelia.

Two local 'name' musicians, Robert Taylor and Trevor Spencer, teamed with Kevin Peek and Allan Tarney who had just returned from trying their luck in the UK with R&B outfit Johnny Broome and the Handels. The Handels had issued one single on the W&G label, 'Dos and Don'ts'/'Don't Know Her Name', in 1965 before travelling to the UK. Before that, Peek had been a member of The Hurricanes with John Perry (vocals), Peter Brideoake (rhythm guitar), John Bywaters (bass) and Frank Barnard (drums), plus the nascent **Twilights**. James Taylor Move supported **The Twilights**, moved to Melbourne and issued two fascinating psychedelic singles, 'And I Heard the Fire Sing'/'Magic Eyes' (August 1967), and 'Baby Jane'/'Still I Can Go On' (October) on Festival. The Hendrix-derived 'And I Heard the Fire Sing' was too much for local radio of the day, but programmers flipped the single over to reveal the more radio-friendly psychedelic pop of 'Magic Eyes', which eventually gave James Taylor Move a southern states hit (#33 in Melbourne).

In May 1968, Kevin Peek left to be replaced by John Pugh (guitar, ex-Roadrunners, Delta Set, **Eighteenth Century Quartet**, **Cam-Pact**) and Lance Dixon (organ, sax; ex-**Rockwell T. James** and the Rhythm Aces). A month later, Taylor also left the band to be replaced by 18-year-old blues belter **Wendy Saddington** (ex-Revolution). Taylor fronted a series of bands under the names of R.J. Taylor, as well as one called Traine. R.J. Taylor issued a single, 'Can't Shoot Your Brother Down'/'Ups and Downs' on the Caesar's International label (June 1970). By the end of 1968 James Taylor Move had dissolved completely. Saddington joined **The Chain** and Copperwine, Pugh went on to The Avengers, **Healing Force**, Baiyana, Silversun, **Ray Burton** and the Nightflyers and the **Renée Geyer** Band. Lance Dixon joined **The Ram Jam Big Band**.

Peek, Spencer and Tarney formed The Kevin Peek Trio. The band travelled to the UK and, with the arrival of Terry Britten (guitar; ex-**Twilights**), became known as Quartet. Quartet recorded two singles for Decca, 'Now'/'Will My Lady Come?' (December 1969) and 'Joseph'/'Mama Where Did You Fall?' (May 1970). The band also recorded an album which has never seen the light of day. With the break-up of Quartet, Peek became an in-demand session player for the likes of Cliff Richard, Shirley Bassey, Mary Hopkin and Hank Marvin before joining John Williams' enormously successful classical rock band Sky in 1978. Peek issued three solo albums, *Guitar Junction* (1980), *Awakening* (1982) and *Life and Other Games* (1982).

Britten also worked as a session player for the likes of Cliff Richard (for whom he co-wrote 'Devil Woman'), Tina Turner and Mike Hugg. In 1977, Britten returned to Australia to write and produce songs for **Christie Allen**. He later co-wrote two of Tina Turner's biggest hits 'What's Love Got to Do with It?' and 'We Don't Need Another Hero'. Tarney and Spencer became session players for **Olivia Newton-John** and The New Seekers. In 1976 they formed The Tarney Spencer Band and issued three albums *Tarney Spencer* (1976), *Three's a Crowd* (1978) and *Run for Your Life* (1979). Tarney wrote several of Cliff Richard's biggest latter-day hits, including 'We Don't Talk Anymore' (1977), 'Dreamin'' (1980) and 'Wired for Sound' (1981), as well as producing his *Wired for Sound* album and others. In the early 1980s, Tarney formed a songwriting partnership with UK singer Leo Sayer.

Janz

Formed: *1988*
Style: *Funk, pop*
Original line-up: *David Janz (vocals), David Carr (guitar), Robert Parde (keyboards), Debbie Lavell (backing vocals), Phil Martin (bass), Miles Stewart-Howie (drums)*

Melbourne band Janz shot to international attention in 1988 when it won the Yamaha International Song

Contest (after winning the Australian *Juke*/Yamaha Rock 1988 final). The band's funk-oriented dance music was uptempo and very infectious. Janz issued two singles on CBS in 1989, 'Crime'/'Hold on' (June) and 'Picture'/'Twelve Years' (October). By that stage, lead singer David Janz had assembled a new line-up comprising Miles Stewart-Howie, Phil Martin and Vinnie Demore (guitar), which concentrated on a tougher pop sound.

J.F.K. and the Cuban Crisis (*see* John Kennedy's Love Gone Wrong)

Jigsaw

Formed: *1968*
Style: *Country pop*
Original line-up: *Ray Eames (lead guitar; ex-*Tony Worsley and the Fabulous Blue Jays*), Ron Gilby (rhythm guitar; ex-*Merv Benton *and the Tamlas), Dennis Tucker (bass; ex-*Merv Benton *and the Tamlas), Alan 'Ollie' Fenton (drums; ex-*Phantoms, *Rockhouse)*

Melbourne singer **Johnny Chester** formed Jigsaw in May 1968 to be his new backing band. Chester was one of Melbourne's first rock'n'roll singers, and he had previously used **The Chessmen** as his backing band. By 1968, Chester was moving in a country-pop direction. Jigsaw backed Chester on his early 1970s hits like 'Gwen (Congratulations)' (1971), 'Shame and Scandal' (1972), 'Midnight Bus' (1972), 'World's Greatest Mum' (1973) and 'She's My Kind of Woman' (1974), plus the album *Going Places*.

Jigsaw also worked the Melbourne pub circuit in its own right, and signed a deal with Ron Tudor's Fable Records. Before the band made the charts, however, Ollie Fenton was killed in a car accident. Eddie Chappel (ex-All Stars, Tamlas) came in as his replacement. Jon Calderwood also replaced Ray Eames around the same time. Jigsaw's biggest hit was a cover of UK band Christie's 'Yellow River'/'Baby Give Me a Smile'. Sydney group **Autumn** also issued 'Yellow River' at the same time; consequently, the two groups were credited with a joint national #1 hit in August 1970. 'Yellow River' stayed on the charts for 24 weeks.

Jigsaw's other singles were 'To Love Means to be Free'/'Marilyn Jones' (May 1970), 'Albert the Albatross'/'There's a Sign Girl' (March 1971), 'So I Tell You'/'Sweet Little Rock'n'Roller' (September), 'How Do You Do?'/'Like Ya Brother' (#11 in April 1972), 'Mademoiselle Ninette'/'Mystery Man' (#20 in November), 'Singalong'/'Sylvania' (April 1973), 'Clap Your Hands'/'Marilyn Jones' (August), 'Sunday Girl and You'/'You' (January 1974), 'A Rose Has to Die'/'Music Man' (#9 in August), 'Light Up the World'/'Take Me Daddy' (December), 'Teach Me How to Rock and Roll'/'You' (November 1975) and 'Every Day, Every Night'/'Music Man' (January 1977).

Album: *Best of Jigsaw* (Fable, 1975).

Jimmy and the Boys

Formed: *1976*
Style: *Shock rock*
1977 line-up: *Ignatius Jones (vocals), Joylene Thornbird Hairmouth (born William O'Riordan, keyboards, vocals), Andrew de Teliga (guitar), Jason Morphett (sax), Tom Falkinham (bass), Scott Johnson (drums)*

Led by vocalist/contortionist Ignatius Jones and Joylene Hairmouth (the kitchiest of transvestites), Jimmy and the Boys were one of the most popular live acts on the Australian scene at the end of the 1970s. Much in the vein of US theatrical rock act The Tubes, Jimmy and the Boys pioneered the use of shock theatrics in Australia. Rock writer Jenny Hunter-Brown described the band as a 'high voltage package of filth, glorious filth'. The band's gigs mixed S&M trappings, sex shop props, mock rape and other depravities with sub-Zappaesque humour, hard rock, jazz, reggae and disco.

Jones and Hairmouth regularly changed membership as the need arose. By late 1978, the line-up comprised Steven Hall (guitar, vocals; ex-Jasper), Danny Damjanovic (sax, flute), Michael Parks (bass, vocals) and Barry Lytten (drums; ex-**Rabbit**). The release of the band's debut album *Not Like Everybody Else* was held up because Astor Records (the band's distributor) deemed the material to be 'too obscene'. The album eventually came out on Festival's new label Avenue during November 1979, replete with such choice songs as 'Dr Cairo', 'Butchy Boys' and 'Cops are Coming'. One month previously, the band's debut single The Kinks' 'I'm Not Like Everybody Else'/'Wild Boys' came out.

In April 1980, Jones and Hairmouth unveiled a new Jimmy and the Boys line-up which comprised Joe P. Rick (real name Rick Sutton, guitar, vocals; ex-**Chariot**), Michael Vidale (bass, vocals) and Scott Johnson (drums). The new line-up undertook the I Just Wanna be Rude to You national tour, and issued two singles, 'Products of Your Mind'/'Komputer Song' (May 1980) and the **Tim Finn**-penned 'They Won't Let My Girlfriend Talk to Me'/'Brave New World' (#8 in May 1981). The band's second album, *The Teddy Boys' Picnic*, spawned two further singles, 'Mirror Mirror'/'Love is Cheap' (July 1981) and a cover of The Rolling Stones' 'Get Off My Cloud'/

'Dr Cairo' (November). In January 1982, Jimmy and the Boys broke up, and Jones joined the stage production of the *Rocky Horror Show* in the dual roles of Eddy and Dr Scott.

Jones also issued two solo singles, 'Like a Ghost'/'Seductive Ways' (April 1982) and 'Whispering Your Name'/'It's No Reason' (March 1983). 'Like a Ghost' and 'It's No Reason' were written by **The Church**'s **Steve Kilbey**. The singles became hot dance club favourites among the gay community on the American west coast. In mid-1982, Jones and Hairmouth temporarily re-formed Jimmy and the Boys for a national tour. This resulted in the live album *In Hell with Your Mother*, after which Jimmy and the Boys ceased to exist. Jones was reported to have signed a six-album American deal with Warner Brothers, but nothing eventuated. In 1984, Jones formed Arms & Legs with Andrew Ross (keyboards; ex-**Ward 13**), Kirk Godfrey (guitar; ex-Big Red Tractor), Steve Harris (bass; ex-**Passengers**, Visitors) and Jeremy Cook (drums), which lasted a year. Jones and O'Riordan then formed sophisticated swing jazz/cabaret band Pardon Me Boys with Jones' sister Monica Trapaga on lead vocals.

Jones contributed regularly to rock papers such as *RAM (Rock Australia Magazine)* and *The Edge*, and he went on to be editor of *Stiletto* magazine. In 1991, he published a book called *The 1992 True Hip Manual*. He contributed a re-working of **John Paul Young's** 'Yesterday's Hero' to the soundtrack of director Baz Luhrmann's internationally acclaimed feature film *Strictly Ballroom*.

Albums: *Not Like Everybody Else* (Avenue/Festival, 1979), *Teddy Boys' Picnic* (Avenue/Festival, 1981), *In Hell with Your Mother* (Avenue/Festival, 1982), *Out of Phaze* (compilation, Avenue/EMI, 1988).

Jo Jo Zep and the Falcons

Formed: *1975*
Style: *R&B, soul, reggae*
Original line-up: *Wayne Burt (guitar, lead vocals; ex-Rock Granite and the Profiles), Joe Camilleri (vocals, sax; ex-King Bees, Lipp and the Double Dekker Brothers, Sharks,* **Pelaco Brothers***), Jeff Burstin (guitar, vocals; ex-Gutbucket, Rock Granite and the Profiles,* **Company Caine***), John Power (bass, vocals: ex-***Foreday Riders**, **Company Caine***),* **Gary Young** *(drums, vocals; ex-Rondells,* **Daddy Cool**, *Hot Dog)*

Any examination of Jo Jo Zep and the Falcons inevitably comes down to one person, Joe Camilleri, one of the most genuinely talented figures in Australian rock music. Although he was not the instigator of The Falcons, he named the band and became its leader and focal point. Camilleri was born in Malta (1948) and got his start on the Melbourne 1960s soul and R&B circuit in bands like The King Bees.

His appearances with Lipp and the Double Dekker Brothers, Sharks and **The Pelaco Brothers** in the early 1970s may have been legendary, but it was not until the formation of The Falcons in 1975 that Joe achieved national prominence. The original Jo Jo Zep and the Falcons was a funky, energetic R&B band based around guitarist/singer/songwriter Wayne Burt, with Joe lending his distinctive vocals and sax work to the band's sound.

The Falcons came together in late 1975 with the break-ups of **Daddy Cool**, **The Pelaco Brothers** and **Company Caine**. **Gary Young** and John Powers immediately became the tightest rhythm section in the land. All members shared backing vocals, while Power possessed an extravagant vocal growl virtually unmatched in the southern hemisphere (his singing on Young's 'I'm a Madman' was astonishing). The first Jo Jo Zep single (virtually a Joe Camilleri solo release produced by **Ross Wilson** and credited to Jo Jo Zep and His Little Helpers) was a cover of Chuck Berry's 'Run Rudolph Run'/'Guess Who' on Mushroom (November 1975). The band signed to Wilson's Oz label (through EMI) and issued the singles 'Beatin' Around the Bush'/'Glad I'm Living Here' (July 1976), Otis Redding's 'Security'/'Run, Run, Rudolph' (November) and 'If It's Love that You Want Darling'/ 'Dancing Shoes' (April 1977), plus the album *Don't Waste It* (February 1977). 'Beatin' Around the Bush' and 'Glad I'm Living Here' also appeared on the soundtrack to Chris Löfven's debut feature film *Oz*.

In early 1977, Burt left to be replaced by Tony Faehse (guitar, vocals; ex-Musik Express, Alvin Stardust Band). In June 1977 Wilbur Wilde (sax, vocals; ex-**Ol'55**) also joined, bringing the band's number to six. The Wilson-produced album *Whip It Out* yielded the single '(I'm in a) Dancing Mood'/'I Remember' (October 1977). None of The Falcons' records had charted nationally, but by that stage the band was one of the most acclaimed live attractions in Australia. The live, 12-inch EP *Loud and Clear* reached #28 in August 1978. The EP also spawned the single 'Honey Dripper'/'Girl Across the Street', which managed to capture some of the band's live fervour. One of the band's most memorable singles, 'So Young'/'Long Distance Call', also charted, reaching #29 in November 1978. The single had been lifted from the mini-album *So Young*, which also included a wonderful rendition of Ray Charles' 'I Believe to My Soul'. Elvis Costello later covered 'So Young'.

The band left Oz/EMI and signed with Mushroom. EMI issued the album *Let's Drip Awhile*, which was the *Loud and Clear* EP plus seven other live tracks recorded in 1977. For the band's most accomplished and successful album *Screaming Targets* (#13 in August 1979), Camilleri infused the music with a large dose of reggae rhythms which resulted in two hit singles 'Hit and Run'/'Not a Woman Not a Child' (#12 in August 1979) and 'Shape I'm in'/'So Young' (New Version), 'Shape I'm in' (Dub Version) (#22 in November). The album also caught the mood of the times with outstanding tracks like 'Don't Wanna Come Down', 'You Made a Fool Out of Me', 'Close to the Bone' and 'Thin Line'. Initial copies of *Screaming Targets* included a bonus, limited edition live album of material recorded in Melbourne during April 1979.

Hats Off Step Lively (July 1980; #17 in August) and the singles 'All I Wanna Do'/'Too Hot to Touch' (#34 in June) and 'Puppet On a String (Let Her Go)'/'Ain't Going to Spend Another Night Without You' (July) were more pop oriented. The Falcons still tore it up on stage, and while touring overseas in mid-1980 were invited to play at the prestigious Montreaux Jazz and Blues Festival. The band's next single included two versions of 'I will Return' (from *Hats Off Step Lively*), one being a live rendition recorded at New York's Bottom Line. The limited edition, double single version of that release also included two tracks recorded at the Montreaux Festival, 'Don't Wanna Come Down' and 'I Need Your Loving'.

The Falcons' most unusual releases were the single 'Sweet'/'Rub Up Push Up' (February 1981), which mixed heavy metal guitars with falsetto vocals, and the 10-inch mini-album *Dexterity* (July). In June, Camilleri took The Falcons off the road. In August, he launched a new line-up of Burstin and Faehse plus newcomers Simon Gyllies (bass; ex-**Mondo Rock**, Imports) and Freddy Strauks (ex-**Skyhooks, Sports**). Young and Power joined Rock Doctors and Wilde formed his Big Kombi.

In 1982, Camilleri instigated more changes, re-emerging with a brass-driven, latin-styled big band simply called Jo Jo Zep. The album *Cha* (October 1982) was a bold move. It ran the gamut of sounds from the tongue-in-cheek, Kid Creole and the Coconuts-styled salsa melodrama of 'Taxi Mary' to a gorgeous rendition of the Burt Bacharach/Hal David song 'Walk on by'. Those two songs were issued as singles, backed by 'This is Our Time' (September) and 'Lonely Man' (December) respectively. 'Taxi Mary' reached #11 on the national chart and #6 in Melbourne. The last Jo Jo Zep single was 'Losing Game'/'Slave for Love' (July 1983).

At its peak, the Jo Jo Zep big band numbered 11 members: Camilleri, Burstin, Gyllies, Jane Clifton (vocals), Bill Canty (keyboards), Ray Pereira (percussion), Keith Pereira (percussion), James Valentine (sax), Paul Williamson (brass), Stephen Ewart (brass) and Des McKenna (drums). Such an unwieldy ensemble proved impossible to keep on the road and, by 1983, Jo Jo Zep was laid to rest. In December, Mushroom issued the excellent anthology album *The Sound of Jo Jo Zep*. Although not a big seller, it was inspiration enough for Camilleri to take The Falcons line-up of Burstin/Faehse/Wilde/Power/Young out on the road for a national tour in March 1984. With that out of the way, Camilleri threw his lot in with his new band, the R&B/soul/zydeco-influenced **Black Sorrows**.

Albums: *Don't Waste It* (Oz/EMI, 1977), *Whip It Out* (Oz/EMI, 1977), *So Young* (mini-album, Oz/EMI, 1978), *Let's Drip Awhile* (EMI, 1979), *Screaming Targets* (Mushroom/Festival, 1979), *Hats Off Step Lively* (Mushroom/Festival, 1980), *Dexterity* (10-inch mini-album, Mushroom/Festival, 1981), *Cha* (Mushroom/Festival, 1982), *The Sound of Jo Jo Zep* (Mushroom/Festival, 1983), *Shape I'm In* (compilation, Mushroom/Sony, 1997).

Johnny Rocco Band

Formed: *1974*
Style: *Funk, soul*
Original line-up: *Mark Punch (guitar, vocals; ex-Mother Earth), Tony Buchanan (sax; ex-***Thunderbirds***, Daly-Wilson Big Band), Tim Partridge (bass; ex Clockwork Oringe,* **King Harvest**, *Island,* **Mighty Kong***), Russell Dunlop (drums; ex-***Aesop's Fables**, **Levi Smith's Clefs**, *Mother Earth)*

Sydney-based group Johnny Rocco Band formed in February 1974, and was one of the first Australian bands to incorporate funk and soul into the pub-rock forum. Three months after formation, a nightclub fire destroyed the band's PA, amps, microphones and drums. Nevertheless, the members regrouped to back **Grahame Bond and Rory O'Donoghue** (aka Aunty Jack and the Gong) for a successful national tour.

Toward the end of 1974, **Leo De Castro** (vocals; ex-**King Harvest**, Flite, **Friends**, De Castro) and Mick Kenny (keyboards; ex-**Levi Smith's Clefs**) expanded the band's line-up. The band signed to the Ritz Gramophone label, and recorded the single 'Heading in the Right Direction'/'Funky Max'. Before the single appeared in August 1975, Harris Campbell had replaced Mark Punch, who went on to join the **Renée Geyer** Band. Geyer later recorded the definitive version of the Mark Punch/Garry Paige composition 'Heading in the Right Direction'. Johnny Rocco Band issued the album *Rocco* (May 1976), which yielded the singles 'We're Gonna Have a Good Time'/'Who's this Guy?' (April). The album was not successful, and the band broke up. **Leo De Castro** formed Cahoots. In May 1977, the band was billed as Leo De Castro and Rocco with Mark Punch and Tony Buchanan back briefly in the line-up. Partridge joined the **Kevin Borich Express** and Dunlop joined **Ayers Rock**.

Album: *Rocco* (Ritz Gramophone/Festival, 1976).

Johnny Teen and the Broken Hearts

Formed: *1987*
Style: *Rock*
Original line-up: *Johnny Teen (real name Robert Gale, vocals), Garth Lucas (real name Garth Freudenstein, guitar), Steve Watson (guitar, synthesiser), Tony Wiltshire (bass), James Sullivan (drums)*

Much like contemporary Sydney band **Candy Harlots**, Johnny Teen and the Broken Hearts took the whole decadent, sleaze-rock ethic to its logical limits. The band's music was a primitive amalgam of re-fried Eddie Cochran riffs (via New York Dolls), sassy glam-rock moves and punk snarl, all topped off by Teen's tuneless croak.

Citadel's offshoot label Green Fez issued the band's debut, live single which featured a cover of **Supernaut's** 'I Like It Both Ways'/'She Stinks of Sex' (April 1988). From there the band moved to the Timberyard label for the four-track *Extremely Mini* EP (which featured the songs 'Bubblegum Witch' and 'McDonald's Girl') (December 1988), plus the singles 'Dig It'/'Stardom Ain't Easy' and Wanda Jackson's 'Funnel of Love'/'Dear Santa'. 'Dear Santa' also appeared on Timberyard's yuletide Various Artists album *Rockin' Bethlehem* (1990). By that stage, the band was without a rhythm section. The last Johnny Teen and the Broken Hearts record was the compilation *Greatest Picks*.

By the start of 1991, Johnny Teen had reverted to his real name of Robert Gale and formed Pearls and Swine with Mark Ward (guitar), Ronnie Neal (bass) and Ken Wheeler (drums). The band played a funk/metal hybrid as displayed on the CD EP *Eat This* (November 1991), the single 'No More Room in Heaven' (April 1992) and debut album *Far King Great* (August). In May 1992, Pearls and Swine took part in the Wizards of Oz series of Los Angeles showcase gigs alongside **The Poor Boys**, **The Angels**, **Kate Ceberano**, **Beatfish** and **The Black Sorrows**. Mick Vawdon then replaced Neal on bass, and the band supported US visitors Ugly Kid Joe in early December 1992. Pearls and Swine broke up soon after.

Meanwhile, Freudenstein had formed hard rock band Alien Grey with Ronnie Neal (bass; ex-Pearls and Swine), Mark Budd (vocals, guitar; ex-Junkmale) and Ben Paul (drums; ex-Wendells). At the first gig Alien Grey played, **Electric Hippies** (Justin Stanley and Steve Balbi) offered to produce the band's debut recording, which resulted in the CD EP 'Number Five 5' in late 1993. Alien Grey came to the attention of American manager Ted Gardner (Porno for Pyros, Tool and major organiser of the Lollapalooza festival) who offered to manage the band in the USA. Alien Grey recorded enough material for a second EP (including a proposed single, 'Devolution') with producer Jed Starr. Nothing came of all the interest shown in Alien Grey because by the end of 1994 the band had broken up.

Johnny Teen album: *Greatest Picks* (Timberyard, 1990); ***Pearls and Swine album:*** *Far King Great* (Big Stars/Mushroom/Festival, 1992).

The Johnnys

Formed: *1982*
Style: *Rock*
Original line-up: *Roddy Ray'da (real name* **Roddy Radalj**, *guitar, vocals; ex-Exterminators, Invaders,* **Scientists**, *Rockets, Le* **Hoodoo Gurus**), *Graham 'Hoody' Hood (bass, vocals; ex-***Allniters***), Billy Pommer Jr (drums; ex-Cry)*

Sydney band The Johnnys came together more as a good-time, fun band than anything else. The joke was good enough for the band to stretch it out for seven years, fuelled by endless touring and countless gallons of beer along the pub-rock road to hell. Early on, the press dubbed The Johnnys' style as 'cow-punk', which was a convenient handle to describe the band's blend of punk attitude, rock'n'roll riffs, country-honk beats, leather chaps and stetson hats.

Formed by **Roddy Radalj**, one of the true originals of Australia's punk rock heritage, the band started out as a three-piece. In early 1983, New Zealand born Spencer P. Jones (guitar, vocals; ex-Cuban Heels, Beats Working, **North 2 Alaskans**, **Olympic Sideburns**) joined. Cuban Heels had comprised Jones, Steve Connolly (guitar, vocals), Brian Allamby (drums), Chris Hunter (bass) and Graham Lewis (keyboards). The band played the Melbourne pub-rock scene circa 1979–81, and issued one single, 'Little Girl'/'Fast Living Friend'

(August 1980). Connolly later joined **Paul Kelly** and the Coloured Girls.

The new, four-piece Johnnys line-up issued a one-off single on the Regular label, 'I Think You're Cute'/'Mountain Man' (October 1983). The single's picture cover bore the legend 'The Johnnys are Regular Little Monsters', which summed the band up perfectly. Radalj wandered off in early 1984 to form Love Rodeo (from whence he joined The James Baker Experience before instigating **The Dubrovniks**, The Punjabbers and The Surfin' Caesars). Paul 'Slim' Doherty replaced Radalj, and Jones assumed lead vocals. The band signed to manager Roger 'Pa' Grierson and Stuart Coupe's GREEN label for the 7-inch single 'My Buzzsaw Baby (Really Cut Me Up)'/'Slip Slap Fishin" (produced by Steve Nieve of UK band The Attractions), and the 12-inch EP *The Johnnys* (both November 1984), which also contained 'My Buzzsaw Baby (Really Cut Me Up)'.

From there The Johnnys signed to Mushroom Records for their first hit singles, 'Injun Joe'/'Cannonball' (November 1985), Gamble and Huff's '(There's Gonna Be a) Showdown'/'Rebel Yell' (March 1986) and 'Bleeding Heart'/'My Buzzsaw Baby (Really Cut Me Up)' (June). All three single A-sides were lifted from the band's debut, **Ross Wilson**-produced album *Highlights of a Dangerous Life* (August 1986), which concentrated on a straighter rock'n'roll approach. Two non-album singles followed: 'Elvisly Yours'/'Black Bart' (March 1987) and 'Don't Put the Blame on Me'/'Logan Girls' (February 1988).

Wilson also produced the band's second album, *Grown Up Wrong* (August 1988) which yielded the band's last two singles, a cover of Chris Spedding's bubblegum punk classic 'Motorbikin"/'Shameless Girl' (July) and 'Anything Could Happen'/'Bounty Hunter' (November). *Grown Up Wrong* was a rollicking (if flawed), good-time, country-flavoured rock'n'roll record, but it failed to chart. Michael Armiger (ex-10,000 Guitars, **Paul Kelly** Band, **John Kennedy's Love Gone Wrong**) replaced Hood on bass at that point. Despite being one of the most popular bands on the pub-rock circuit, The Johnnys never crossed over into the premier league. The band broke up in 1989. Jones had already expended a great deal of effort as a member of the (until then) part-time **Beasts of Bourbon**. When that band lumbered into life as a full-time proposition in 1989, Spencer threw in his lot with the Beasts.

Since then, Spencer has worked with fellow **Beasts of Bourbon** member **Tex Perkins** in The Butcher Shop and Minced Meat, with Ian Rilen in **X** and **Hell to Pay**, with **Maurice Frawley** in The Working Class Ringos, with Rowland S. Howard in These Immortal Souls and with **Paul Kelly**. He produced Mick McGinley and the Sinners' 1993 album *Lapsed* and Charlie Owen's 1994 solo album *Vertigo and Other Phobias*. He also assembled his own band, The Holy Spirits, utilising the services of Rowland S. Howard and others.

After ten albums to his credit with various bands, perennial gun-for-hire Jones finally issued his debut solo album, *Rumour of Death*, on Red Eye/PolyGram in November 1994. The album mixed a timeless rock'n'roll feel with country elements, and yielded the single 'The World's Got Everything in It' (March 1995). Guests on the album included Warren Ellis (violin; **Dirty Three**), Graham Lee (pedal steel; ex-**Triffids**), Nick Rischbieth (guitar; **Sacred Cowboys**), Conway Savage (piano; **Nick Cave and the Bad Seeds**), Bryan Henry Hooper (bass; **Beasts of Bourbon**, **Surrealists**) and Peter Jones (drums; ex-**Harem Scarem**). In late 1996, Spencer Jones linked up again with the reunited **Beasts of Bourbon**.

Johnnys albums: *Highlights of a Dangerous Life* (Mushroom/Festival, 1986), *Grown Up Wrong* (Mushroom/Festival, 1988); ***Spencer P. Jones album:*** *Rumour of Death* (Red Eye/PolyGram, 1994).

Kevin Johnson

Style: *Folk, country*

Singer/songwriter Kevin Johnson will always be remembered for his two biggest hit singles 'Bonnie, Please Don't Go' and 'Rock and Roll (I Gave You the Best Years of My Life)'. 'Rock and Roll' reached #4 in Australia (October 1973) and #23 in the UK (January 1975), as well as charting in many parts of Europe. Johnson consolidated his international reputation through extensive touring, as well as issuing a series of well-crafted albums.

'Rock and Roll' went on to become one of the most covered songs written by an Australian artist. 27 different artists covered the song during 1975. Mac Davis, who changed the end verses slightly to give the song a 'happy ending', made it a hit in the USA (#15), as did Terry Jacks in Canada. In late 1976, Johnson received a Citation of Achievement for Outstanding Airplay across the USA from the American song publishing organisation Broadcast Music Inc. (BMI). Johnson also received an Australian Performing Right Association (APRA) award for Outstanding Services to Australian Music.

Johnson got his start as a songwriter for **Col Joye** and others during the mid-1960s. He issued two singles on Joye's ATA label, 'Hayman Island'/

'Heartache Man' (February 1967) and 'Woman You Took My Life'/'You've Lost the Power' (March 1968). In 1969 he signed with the independent Sweet Peach label and issued his debut album *In the Quiet Corners of My Mind* a year later. 'It Was Good While It Lasted'/'Sometimes' was lifted as a single.

'Bonnie, Please Don't Go'/'I Came to Somerset' reached #15 nationally (#2 in Sydney) in March 1971, but his fifth single, 'All Our Favourite Songs'/'Younger Days', failed to make the national Top 40. Johnson spent the next two years writing songs for the American publishing company Tree International. He re-emerged in February 1974 with the album *Rock and Roll I Gave You the Best Years of My Life* on the Good Thyme label. 'Rock and Roll (I Gave You the Best Years of My Life)'/'There's Nothing I Would Rather Do' (September 1973) and 'Kedron Brook'/'Life is What You Make It' (March 1974) were issued as singles.

Johnson supported overseas visitor Roberta Flack in 1975. He issued two singles in 1975, 'Man of the 20th Century'/'Sunday Morning Roses' (February 1975) and 'Someday Sam'/'I Knew You Sunset' (November 1975). His last records for the Good Thyme label were the single 'Over the Hills and Far Away'/'Taking the Long Way Home' (August 1976) and album *Man of the 20th Century*. Helping out on the album were well-known session players such as Mark Punch, Jim Kelly and Rory O'Donoghue on guitars, Wayne Findlay (keyboards), Tim Partridge (bass) and Russell Dunlop (drums).

When Johnson toured Europe in late 1976, he was the subject of a television special that was broadcast in Switzerland, France, Italy and Germany. In Ireland, he did five concerts in the biggest venues available (2000 seaters), drawing more people than the Bay City Rollers in the process! His single 'Grab the Money and Run'/'Over the Hills and Far Away' made the Irish charts. He returned to Europe in 1977. Meanwhile, Johnson signed a new deal in Australia with Festival's Infinity label, issuing his first single with that company 'All I Ever Needed'/'State of Mind' in December 1977. The album *Journeys* included the singles 'Next Plane to New Mexico'/'The Comeback Trail' (January 1979) and 'Paraguyan Sunset'/'Love Knows Where to Find You' (August 1979). 'He Was Just a Boy'/'I Knew You Sunset' followed in March 1980. During the early 1980s, Johnson continued to undertake European tours where his records received positive reviews and encouraging sales.

The *Night Rider* album plus the singles 'Night Rider'/'Tonight I'll Be Part of the Crowd' (February 1981) and 'Reasons'/'For the Good of the Nation' (1982) kept Johnson in the public eye. The album *Spirit of the Times* (August 1985) gave rise to the singles 'Hard Act to Follow'/'The Fires Within' (December 1984) and 'Night Comes'/'Further Down the Line' (October 1985). The J&B label issued a 'Best of' album in 1992, *Now and Then*, which included four new tracks. In September 1996, Johnson issued his first studio album in over ten years, *The Sun will Shine Again*. The album contained a reworking of 'Rock'n'Roll' called 'Aussie Rules (I Thank You for the Best Years of Our Lives)', which came about at the request of the Australian Football League (AFL). It became the official AFL Centenary song.

Albums: *In the Quiet Corners of My Mind* (Sweet Peach, 1970), *Rock and Roll I Gave You the Best Years of My Life* (Good Thyme, 1974), *Man of the 20th Century* (Good Thyme, 1976), *Journeys* (Festival/Infinity, 1978), *Best of Kevin Johnson* (Festival/Infinity, 1979), *Night Rider* (Festival/Infinity, 1981), *Spirit of the Times* (Festival/Infinity, 1985), *Now and Then* (J&B, 1992) *The Sun will Shine Again* (Festival, 1996).

Phil Jones and the Unknown Blues

Formed: *1965*
Style: *Blues, pop*
Original line-up: *Phil Jones (vocals), Chris Brown (guitar), Andrew Blundell (keyboards), Bill Hodgkisson (bass), Dave Rowland (drums)*

Singer Phil Jones formed The Unknown Blues as a schoolboy band. In early 1967, the band signed to Festival Records and issued 'If I Had a Ticket'/'300 Pounds of Joy' (March) which became a Top 20 hit in Sydney. 'If I Had a Ticket' was a traditional song which the band rearranged and wrote new lyrics. **Ed Kuepper** revived the song in 1994 when he issued it as a CD single.

The Unknown Blues earned a reputation as a fine blues band. They followed up 'If I Had a Ticket' with another traditional song, 'Pick a Bale of Cotton'/'Sylvie' (August) and 'Lovin' You, is Better, Baby'/'Brave New World (of Fairy Tales)' (November). By that stage, new members had arrived, including Mal Capewell (sax), King Fisher (trumpet; ex-Id), Vaughan Brus (keyboards) and Ian Sullivan. The band broke up and Jones issued two solo singles on Festival, 'I Really Love You'/'This Time' (September 1968) and 'I Feel Like a King'/'Blue Laroo' (December 1968).

In 1969, Phil Jones, Chris Brown and Mal Capewell headed to the UK, where they became involved in the burgeoning underground/progressive rock community based around London's Ladbroke Grove/Notting Hill Gate area. Jones joined the Eastern tinged jazz-rock band Quintessence, alongside another Australian, Ron Rothfield, who had assumed the name Raja Ram (flute, violin, percussion). Jones took the name Shiva Shankar Jones. Shiva appeared on four Quintessence albums for the Island label, *In Blissful Company*, *Quintessence*, *Dive Deep* and *Self*.

Shiva left the band in late 1971 to form the like-minded Kala with Quintessence guitarist Maha Dev (Dave Coding). Kala issued one self-titled album on the Bradleys label (1972). Expatriates Dave Bentley (ex-**Python Lee Jackson**), Chris Brown and Col Loughnan joined Kala following the album's release, but soon after Brown and Loughnan returned to Australia to join **Ayers Rock**. Shiva travelled to the USA before returning to Australia in 1975. He formed a succession of bands, including Phil Jones Band and Cisco Kids. He effectively retired from performing. In the early 1990s, his sons Amarnath and Krishna formed rock-funk band **Juice**.

Meanwhile, Mal Capewell worked in the UK where he cut a dashing figure as a member of Manfred Mann's Chapter III, Dada (which included singers Robert Palmer and Elkie Brooks; one album *Dada* on Atlantic, 1970) and Graham Bond's Holy Magick. He returned to Australia in 1972 and worked with the likes of **Company Caine**, **Levi Smith's Clefs**, Mighty Mouse, **Chain**, **Carson** and **Healing Force**.

Spencer P. Jones (*see* Beasts of Bourbon; The Johnnys)

Col Joye

Style: Rock'n'roll, pop

Col Joye has enjoyed one of the longest careers of any artist in Australian rock'n'roll. In 1997, he celebrated 40 years in the business. Alongside the likes of **Johnny O'Keefe**, **Lonnie Lee**, **Alan Dale**, **Johnny Chester** and **Digby Richards**, Joye was one of the stars of the country's early rock'n'roll days.

Yet, unlike O'Keefe, who was referred to as the 'Wild One', Joye presented a carefully cultivated and wholesome 'teen idol' image. Like Pat Boone in the USA, Joye has enjoyed a steady career path, and consequently his popularity remained strong. This was shown in 1989 when he shared major concert stages with the likes of Chuck Berry, Jerry Lee Lewis, The Everly Brothers and Bo Diddley as part of the Legends of Rock tour. Since 1959, when he became the first Australian pop performer to reach the #1 position on the local charts, Joye has issued a steady stream of records. His tally of over 50 singles, 30 EPs and 30 albums is impressive by any standards.

Joye was born Colin Frederick Jacobsen. In 1957 he joined The K.J. Quintet as rhythm guitarist and singer alongside his brother Kevin (piano), plus **Dave Bridge** (lead guitar), Laurie 'Zeke' Erwin (sax) and Johnny Bogie (drums). With their first major engagement at promoter Bill McColl's *Jazzorama* concert in October, the band became known as Col Joye and the Joy Boys. The band began running its own dances at the Bankstown Capitol, and Joye's younger brother Keith completed The Joy Boys line-up on bass.

A&R manager Ken Taylor signed the band to Festival Records, and Col Joye and the Joy Boys made their record debut with the EP *Joyride* (April 1958). The band's second EP, *Sweet Beat* (October 1958) included an early Col Joye/Kevin Jacobsen composition 'Goin' Down Town (to See Miss Brown)'. These records were fairly primitive outings and failed to make the charts. Likewise, the band's debut single, a cover of Loyde Price's 'Stagger Lee' backed with The Crests' 'Sixteen Candles' (February 1959), failed to chart. It was single number two that set the ball rolling. 'Bye Bye Baby'/'I Miss You So' reached #3 in Melbourne and #1 in Sydney during June 1959, and was Festival's first national hit with a local artist.

The band then scored three further Top 10 hits in a row: 'Rockin' Rollin' Clementine'/'Fools Like Me' (Sydney #1, Melbourne #2 in September 1959), 'Oh Yeah Uh Huh'/'Living Doll' (Sydney and Melbourne #1 in October 1959) and 'Teenage Baby'/'Half as Much' (Sydney #4, Melbourne #10 in January 1960). Joye and the Joy Boys were in hot demand for shows at the Sydney Stadium, where they shared the billing with the likes of Little Richard, Gene Vincent, The Everly Brothers, Ricky Nelson, Conway Twitty, Fabian and **Johnny O'Keefe**. The band became regulars on television shows like *Bandstand* and O'Keefe's *Six O'Clock Rock*. They also began touring overseas.

In the studio, Joye and the Joy Boys were recording anything that took their fancy, from Cliff Richard to Chuck Berry. Later in his career, Joye moved towards a country-tinged, light pop sound which suited his 'gentle' image. The Jacobsens also developed their business interests by setting up Joye Enterprises and their own publishing company, Joye Music. During the mid-1960s, the brothers established the ATA label and talent agency. Over the years, this grew to include Kevin Jacobsen Productions (which has toured artists as diverse as John Denver, **The Bee Gees** and Placido Domingo) and Kevin Jacobsen Rock Management.

Meanwhile, back in 1959, Festival issued Joye's first album, the 10-inch *Jump with Joye. Col Joye Sings Songs that Rocked the Stadium* and *The Golden Boy* followed in 1960. Over the years 1960–62, Joye continued his run of hit singles with 'Bad Man'/'Dreamy Eyes' (Sydney #7, Melbourne #16 in April 1960), 'Yes Sir, That's My Baby'/'Just Give Me Love' (Sydney #1, Melbourne #13 in September), Faron Young's 'Goin' Steady'/'Naughty Girls' (Sydney #8, Melbourne #15 in May 1961), '(The Bells are Ringing) for Me and My Gal'/'Honky Tonk Girl' (Sydney and Melbourne #24 in August), 'Sweet Little Sixteen Twist'/'What About Me' (Sydney and Melbourne #21 in January 1962), Gene Pitney's 'Today's Teardrops'/'If You Love Her' (Sydney #7 in May; shared with Ricky Nelson) and 'Sweet Dreams of You'/'Please Give It a Chance' (Sydney #29, Melbourne #23 in August). Festival also issued ten Col Joye EPs during that period.

On the other hand, Festival was more moderate with Joye's album releases, content to issue collections like *Col Joye Sings His Solid Gold Hits* and *Col Joye and the Ballad*, which found him in a decidedly mellow mood. Joye also teamed up with singer **Judy Stone** for the EPs 'The I's Have It' and 'Clap Your Hands', and albums *Col and Judy* and *The Best of Col and Judy*, which contained cutesy material like 'Young and Healthy', 'Angry' and 'Side by Side'.

It was also around that time that The Joy Boys began to assert themselves as a successful chart outfit in their own right. Concentrating on a light, chirpy instrumental sound, the band enjoyed a run of hit singles with 'Istanbul'/'Hen-pecked' (credited to Col Joye's Joy Boys) (Sydney #6, Melbourne #31 in February 1961), 'Hindustan'/'Feelin' Blue' (March), 'Smokey Mokes'/'Kurrawatha' (Sydney #1, Melbourne #19 in August), 'Whistlin' Rufus'/'Joye Guitar Boogie' (Melbourne #30 in January 1962), 'Southern 'Rora'/'Night Coach to Cairo' (Sydney and Melbourne #5 in June), 'Waltz of the Flowers'/'Gavotte Espresso' (Sydney #11 in September), 'Xmas Guitar'/'Wild Love' (Sydney #19 in December) and 'Murphie the Surfie'/'Zambesi Stomp' (Sydney #6, Melbourne #30 in November 1963). Meanwhile **Dave Bridge** had left in 1961, to be replaced by Norm Day. The Joy Boys issued 11 EPs and five albums from 1961 to 1963.

Joye's only hit singles for 1963 were '(Underneath the) Starlight of Love'/'Put 'Em Down' (Melbourne #31 in May) and a cover of Gene Vincent's 'Be Bop A-Lula'/'I Need Your Love Tonight' (Sydney #21 in September). 'Starlight of Love' had been written by the young Barry Gibb of **The Bee Gees**, and it featured the three Gibb brothers on backing vocals. Joye had 'discovered' **The Bee Gees** in a Surfer's Paradise church hall during 1961, brought them to Sydney to be managed by his brother Kevin and signed them to Joye Music.

During the years 1963 and 1964, Joye made less impact on the charts, but remained as popular as ever on television and the stage. Then, as if to remind his fans of his roots, Joye released a run of singles, EPs and albums that predominantly featured rock'n'roll revivals. The singles included covers of 'Be Bop A-Lula' (August 1963) and Johnny Burnette's 'Just a Little Too Much'/'She's Got It' (July 1964). The EPs carried titles like 'Be Bop A-Lula', 'Shake, Rattle and Roll', 'All Shook Up' and 'Rock Around the Clock', while the albums included *Classics of Rock*, *Stomp Around the Clock*, *Rock Classics No. 2* and *Rhythm'n'Blues Session*. Early in 1965 Joye spent two months touring Japan. Joye and the Joy Boys enjoyed considerable Japanese popularity, even though Joye's voice was never heard on the three all-instrumental albums recorded by King Records for the Japanese market.

During 1965, the Jacobsens set up the ATA label and recording studio, and Joye's subsequent releases were on that label. Joye's last three Festival singles contained some of his most interesting cover versions: Burt Bacharach/Hal David's 'From Rocking Horse to Rocking Chair'/'Moonlight will Come' (February 1965), Steve Cropper/Rufus Thomas' 'Can Your Monkey Do the Dog?'/'Down the Line' (June) and Petula Clark/Tony Hatch's 'You're the One'/'You're Never Off My Mind' (October).

Joye's first ATA single was 'I Don't Care If the Sun Don't Shine'/'They Fell In Love' (May 1965), followed by 'Long Long Time'/'Mary Anne' (September). The B-side of the latter single had been written by singer/songwriter **Kevin Johnson** who went on to enjoy great success with his hits 'Bonnie Please Don't Go' and 'Rock and Roll (I Gave You the Best Years of My Life)'. Joye recorded several more of Johnson's songs over the years, including 'You Know How I Feel' (B-side to 'There Goes My Everything', February 1967), 'You Brought Out the Best In Me' (B-side to a cover of Jimmy Cliff's 'Come Into My Life', March 1970) and 'Woman You Took My Life' which was a single A-side (backed with 'Simple Words and Music', October 1975).

Joye scored the biggest hit of his career in July 1973 when 'Heaven is My Woman's Love'/'Happy Days' reached #1 on the national chart. He followed that up with the Laurie Allen (of **Bobby and Laurie** fame) song 'Sunshine in My Face', backed with 'If

It Feels Good Do It' (June 1974), but it failed to chart. Nevertheless, as with Johnson, Joye continued to record more of Allen's songs, including 'Swaggering' (B-side to 'My Wife's House', August 1974), 'Through Children's Eyes' (B-side to 'A Mother as Lonely as You', May 1977) and 'Concert in the Sky' (B-side to 'Catch a Little Love Light', January 1980).

Throughout the 1970s and into the 1980s, many of Joye's albums were compilations, issued on budget labels such as Summit, Horizon, Rainbow, J&B and Universal. Joye continued to record and perform, although his records rarely appeared on the charts. Some of his more prominent latter-day singles were 'She's a Gypsy'/'Be Bop A-Lula' (25th Anniversary issue; March 1983), 'Take Me Back to Rock'n'Roll'/'Teddy Bear' (June 1989) and 'Ain't that Too Much'/'Nothin' to Lose' (September 1989). He included a cover of the **Russell Morris** song 'Beautiful You' on his 1995 album *Oh Yeah.*

Also of interest was the Glenn A. Baker compiled 30th Anniversary box set, *Thirty Years of Rock'n'Roll.* It contained a selection of 104 Joye songs spread over five albums. There was also a bonus 12-inch, 45 RPM, Col Joye interview disc included.

Col Joye albums: *Jump with Joye* (10-inch album, Festival, 1959), *Col Joye Sings Songs that Rocked the Stadium* (Festival, 1960), *The Golden Boy* (Festival, 1960), *Col Joye Sings His Solid Gold Hits* (Festival, 1961), *Joy to the World* (Festival, 1961), *Joyride* (Festival, 1961), *Col Joye and the Ballad* (Festival, 1962), *Col and Judy* (with **Judy Stone**, Festival, 1962), *The Best of Col and Judy* (with **Judy Stone**, Festival, 1963), *Classics of Rock* (Festival, 1963), *Stomp Around the Clock* (Festival, 1963), *Rock Classics No. 2* (Festival, 1964), *Rhythm'n'Blues Session* (Festival, 1965), *The Col Joye Show (Songs for Swingin' Mums and Dads)* (Festival, 1966), *Let's Rock with Col Joye* (Summit, 1970), *The Best of Col Joye* (Horizon, 1971), *For the Good Times* (ATA/Festival, 1972), *Rockin' and Stompin' with Col Joye* (Summit, 1973), *Heaven is My Woman's Love* (ATA/Festival, 1974), *The Col Joye Story* (Festival, 1974), *The Rock Goes On with Col Joye* (Summit, 1974), *For You* (ATA/Festival, 1975), *Col Joye Rocks and Stomps* (Summit, 1975), *A Little Bit Country* (with **Little Pattie**, Pisces, 1977), *21 Years of Rock'n'Roll* (ATA/Festival, 1978), *Col Joye Rocks and Stomps* (Rainbow, 1979), *The Very Best 22 Golden Hits* (J&B, 1984), *20 Most Requested* (J&B, 1984), *Rockin' On* (J&B, 1986), *Rockin' and Stompin'* (Universal, 1987), *Greatest Hits* (J&B, 1988), *Rocky Road Blues* (Festival, 1989), *Thirty Years of Rock'n'Roll* (30th Anniversary Box Set) (ATA/Festival, 1989), *Truckstop* (ATA/Festival, 1990), *Oh Yeah* (ATA/Festival, 1995). ***Joy Boys albums:*** *Col Joye's Joy Boys* (Festival, 1961), *New Old Time* (Festival, 1962), *Joy Boys' Fabulous Hits* (Festival, 1962), *Cooking Up a Party* (Festival, 1963), *Surfin' Stompin' Joys* (Festival, 1964), *On Top of the World* (ATA/Festival, 1974), *Instrumentally Yours—20 Fabulous Hits* (ATA/Festival, 1977).

Judge Mercy

Formed: *1990*
Style: *Hard rock*
Original line-up: *Andy Cichon (rhythm guitar, vocals; ex-***Rose Tattoo, Swanee, James Reyne** *Band), Ismet 'Izzy' Osmanovich (lead guitar), Craig Foster (bass), Mick O'Shea (drums; ex-***Swanee***)*

Andy Cichon had cut his teeth playing bass with **Rose Tattoo**, **Swanee** and **James Reyne**. In August 1990, he drew together three young musicians in order to form hard rock band Judge Mercy. The band got its first big break opening for **AC/DC** on two dates (Brisbane and Sydney) of that band's October 1991 Razor's Edge Australian tour.

Judge Mercy earned a reputation as one of the hardest working Oz rock bands around, touring the pub rock circuit with everyone from **The Angels** and **The Screaming Jets** to **The Poor Boys**. The band issued the live, five-track EP *Live with It!* on the Massive label (headed by Laurie Dunn) in August 1992. The EP's featured track 'Mr Attitude' summed up the band's brand of hard-driving blues rock. The band utilised the services of American producer John Jansen (TSOL, Faster Pussycat, Love/Hate) for its debut album *Protocol So Holy,* which was issued in June 1993. In March 1994, Judge Mercy issued a CD single 'Open It Up', which also included three bonus live tracks. After Judge Mercy broke up in 1995, Cichon went on to work with the **Peter Wells** Band and Romeo Dog. In mid-1997, Osmanovich replaced Jimi Hocking in **The Screaming Jets**.

Album: *Protocol So Holy* (Massive, 1993).

Juice

Formed: *1991*
Style: *Hard funk*
Original line-up: *Amarnath Jones (guitar, vocals), Krishna Jones (guitar, vocals), David Kyle (bass), Lucius Borich (drums)*

This Sydney band played a fiery fusion of hard funk, aggressive rock, psychedelia and soul (somewhere between Funkadelic, Led Zeppelin, Jimi Hendrix and the 'stoned soul picnic' stylings of Sly and the Family Stone). Juice was one of a number of young bands at that time exploring diverse musical avenues on the traditional Australian pub-rock scene: **d.i.g.**'s acid jazz, **Swoop**'s soulful funk grooves, **Def FX**'s techno-metal, **Skunkhour**'s funk'n'rap and **Caligula**'s techno-pop. Amarnath and Krishna are the sons of **Phil Jones** who worked with The Unknown Blues in the 1960s, before travelling to the UK where he joined progressive band Quintessence. Lucius Borich is the son of guitar legend **Kevin Borich**.

Juice supported the likes of **Hoodoo Gurus** and **INXS** and issued its debut, self-titled CD EP 'Movin' on' (April 1993), which stayed on the alternative chart for 15 weeks. The band issued its full-length album *Wine of Life* in May 1994. *Wine of Life* yielded the CD singles 'Skyhigh'/'One Thing' (April 1994) and 'Paper World' (November). David Kyle left before the album's release, to be replaced by Ben Rosen. Likewise, Borich left in early 1995 to form heavy progressive blues band The Hanging Tree. The line-up comprised Borich, Emmy Walters (vocals), Flynn Gower (guitar), Rohan Mellick (guitar) and Daniel Parkinson (bass). The band fused crunching, down-tuned, blues-derived guitar riffs with a rhythmic swing to arrive at a sound reminiscent of retro-metal masters Monster Magnet and Kyuss.

The Hanging Tree issued a self-financed, self-titled album on the Scratch 'M label (August 1996) and toured with **The Screaming Jets**. Paul Ermer replaced Mellick at the end of 1996; Dave Romeo then replaced Ermer. Meanwhile, Chris Simms had replaced Borich in Juice, and the band supported overseas visitors Radiohead and The Tea Party on their Australian tours. Juice issued the CD single 'Never Enough' in June 1995, followed by the CD EP 'Fractured' in September. Simon Cox replaced Simms on drums, but by early 1996 Juice had split.

Album: *Wine of Life* (Dr J/Polydor, 1994).

Juke Savages

Formed: *1992*
Style: *R&B, country*
Original line-up: *Chris 'Klondike' Masuak (guitar, vocals; ex-Jackals,* **Radio Birdman**, **Hitmen**, **New Christs**, **Screaming Tribesmen**, *Roddy Ray'da and the Surfin' Caesars), Brad Ferguson (bass; ex-Voodoo Lust,* **Hitmen***), Paul Larsen (drums; ex-***Celibate Rifles**, *Roddy Ray'da and the Surfin' Caesars)*

Chris Masuak spent many years with four of the classic Australian high-energy, guitar rock bands **Radio Birdman**, **The Hitmen**, **The New Christs** and **The Screaming Tribesmen**. The Canadian-born guitarist grew up in the far-flung township of Kamloops, and his roots actually lay in country music and R&B. Masuak's first forays into country-rock (under the moniker of Klondike) were the 12-inch EP *Chris Boy King and the Kamloops Swing* (September 1987), the single '(Take Me) Back to Country' (October) and the mini-album *Cowboy Angel* (May 1989) on the Rattlesnake label. Helping out were fellow **Screaming Tribesmen** Bob Wackley (bass) and Warwick Fraser (drums). Masuak put his solo projects on hold while he toured with **Hitmen DTK** and Roddy Ray'da and the Surfin' Caesars between 1989 and 1991. At the start of 1992, Masuak joined **Deniz Tek**'s studio backing band (dubbed The World Shakers), which Tek had assembled in order to record his debut album *Take It to the Vertical*.

In April 1992 Masuak, with the above line-up, formed the country/R&B-flavoured Juke Savages, issuing a self-titled CD EP on the Phantom label during December. In late 1993, Red Porter (bass) and Gerard Presland (drums; ex-**Hitmen** DTK) replaced Ferguson and Larsen respectively. The Juke Savages issued the full-length album *Pagan Rites and Big Juju On the Road to Ascension* in 1994. In early 1996, Masuak joined the re-formed **Radio Birdman** for the national Radios On! tour. The 1996 Juke Savages line-up included Tubby Wadsworth (drums; ex-Fester Fanatics, Killing Time, Harlots). Masuak also played drums in surf outfit The Raouls, which featured another ex-Birdman alumnus, Warwick Gilbert, on guitar.

Album: *Pagan Rites and Big Juju On the Road to Ascension* (Phantom, 1994)

July 14th

Formed: *1984*
Style: *Rock, folk*
Original line-up: *Terry Bradford (guitar, vocals; ex-Instamatix), Rod Ling (guitar, vocals; ex-Empty Vessels), Robyn Habel (bass, vocals; ex-False Alarm, Empty Vessels), Roy Ezinger (drums; ex-U-Bombs, Mutes)*

Ex-folkie Terry Bradford formed July 14th in Adelaide during April 1984. The band came about when Bradford scored the support slot to US visitors the Violent Femmes. The band became July 14th due to the fact that Bradford, Rod Ling and Robyn Habel all shared the same birth date. July 14th is also Bastille Day, the anniversary of the storming of the Bastille which launched the French Revolution. July 14th mixed rock, folk and politics in equal measure. The band was often joined on stage by the Holy Wind Brass section.

July 14th issued the classic independent single 'Me and My Gun'/'We Kiss' on the Greasy Pop label in September 1984. Ezinger left soon after to be replaced by Tom Cowsill (ex-Odyssey, Montage). The album *Australian Bite* followed in July 1985. The band also recorded the soundtrack to the ABC-TV documentary *Searching for Women In History*. In early 1986, Cowsill left to be replaced by Andrew Mills (ex-Desperate Measures, Speedboat). July 14th issued the cassette album *Cut It Live* in late 1986. At the same time, Bradford began working with guitarist Greg Williams (ex-Young Homebuyers, Play Loud) as acoustic duo **The Every Brothers**. July 14th recorded a second album in 1987, after which the band broke up. *Till We Meet Again* came out posthumously. Habel and Mills joined Bradford in **The Every Brothers**.

In 1993, Robyn Habel issued her debut, self-titled album on the Rounder label. In August 1995, she issued her second album, *Red*, and the single 'Turn Me On'. The music encompassed folk, blues and funk, all of which provided a good showcase for Habel's clear vocal style. Habel formed backing band The Rain in order to tour. The line-up comprised James Aujard (guitar), Tim O'Donnell (keyboards), Trent Edwards (bass) and Nick Southgate (drums).

Albums: *Australian Bite* (Greasy Pop, 1985), *Till We Meet Again* (Greasy Pop, 1988).

Jump Incorporated

Formed: *1985*
Style: *Rock*
Original line-up: *Mark Woods (guitar, vocals; ex-Moving Parts, Sirens), Nada Sinkovic (keyboards, vocals; ex-Moving Parts, Sirens), Geoff Gray (bass, vocals, ex-Moving Parts, Sirens), Martin Sinkovic (drums, vocals; ex-Moving Parts, Sirens)*

Jump Incorporated grew out of the ashes of Sydney dance-flavoured pop band Moving Parts. Jonathan Purcell also played guitar in that band. Moving Parts issued two 7-inch EPs in 1980, *Moving Parts* and 'Living China Doll'/'Heart of Darkness', 'Tell Me Why'. Moving Parts broke up in 1981, but reconvened a year later. In 1984 the band became known as The Sirens, and then Jump Incorporated in 1985.

Jump Incorporated signed to Mushroom Records, and Mark Opitz (**Cold Chisel**, **Hitmen**) produced the debut single 'Sex and Fame'/'Baby Switchblade' (January 1986). 'Sex and Fame' mixed heavy guitars, anthemic choruses and glam-rock sleaze over a throbbing disco beat. Opitz also produced the band's debut album, *Push Push One Day Too Far*, which produced the singles 'Never Needed You More'/'Gun for Love' (September 1986), 'Turn It On'/'Make Me Scream' (April 1987) and 'Jagged'/'Midnight Action' (June 1987). At the end of 1986, the band expanded with the additions of Lee Borkman (keyboards; ex-Pink Slips, Johanna Pigott's Scribble) and Finbar O'Hanlen (lead guitar). The band played for another year or so before breaking up. In 1992, O'Hanlen was in a band called Lost Angels with ex-**Models** drummer Barton Price.

Album: *Push Push One Day Too Far* (Mushroom/Festival, 1987).

John Justin and the Thunderwings

Formed: *1985*
Style: *Glam pop*
Original line-up: *John Justin (guitar, vocals; ex-Modesty, An Affair), Paul Hines (keyboards; ex-Adventure), Gordon Pitt (bass, vocals; ex-Microfilm, Bleú Scooters,* **Dorian Gray***), Carl Manuel (drums; ex-***Ears**, **Beargarden***)*

Frontman John Justin was well known on the early 1980s Melbourne scene via his New Romantic glam rock bands Modesty and An Affair. Modesty comprised Justin, Shane Hayton (keyboards), Anthony Tavasz (bass) and Peter Black (drums). By August 1982, Modesty had evolved into An Affair when Stu Storm (keyboards) took over from Hayton, guitarist Peter Cook (ex-**James Freud** and the Radio Stars) took over from Black on drums and Anthony Moore (bass, synthesiser) replaced Tavasz. Early influences included Ultravox, Japan, Spandau Ballet and Duran Duran. An Affair broke up in 1983.

Justin signed to Wheatley Records and issued his debut, solo single 'It's Magic'/'Only with You' in October 1984. For his next step towards commercial acceptance, Justin drew heavily on Marc Bolan and T. Rex for inspiration. Indeed, the name of his new band, The Thunderwings, was derived from a 1972 T. Rex B-side (to 'Metal Guru'). John Justin and the Thunderwings' debut album, *Justice* (September 1986), was brimming with swaggering glam-pop material like the singles 'Flash King Cadillac'/'So Far So Good' (August 1986), 'Justice'/'Only with You' (November) and 'Little Miss Love'/'Outback' (February 1987). 'Flash King Cadillac' peaked at #20 on the Melbourne chart.

In 1987, Tony Featherstone (bass) and Robert Woodrow (drums) replaced Pitt and Manuel respectively. Justin issued one more single, a cover of David Essex's 'Rock on'/'Ride to Live' (August 1987), on BMG before The Thunderwings broke up. Justin went on to play with Melbourne covers bands The Party Animals and The Rock Dogs.

Album: *Justice* (Wheatley/RCA, 1986).

K

Kahvas Jute

Formed: 1970
Style: Progressive rock
Original line-up: *Dennis Wilson (lead guitar, vocals; ex-Riddles, Kevin Bible and the Book, Barrington Davis and the Power Pact, Mecca),* **Tim Gaze** *(lead guitar, vocals; ex-Stonehenge,* **Tamam Shud***), Bob Daisley (bass; ex-Dennis Williams and the Delawares, Gino Affair,* **Throb***, Barrington Davis and the Power Pact, Mecca), Dannie Davidson (drums; ex-Strangers, Sunsets,* **Tamam Shud***)*

Sydney band Kahvas Jute was an archetypal progressive hard rock band. The band's music was expansive and free flowing, strong on rhythm and melody and bristling with exceptional guitar work. Kahvas Jute's album *Wide Open* is an Australian progressive rock milestone. During the 1980s and early 1990s, it was a highly sought after artefact in European progressive rock circles.

Dennis Wilson appeared on one single with Kevin Bible and the Book, 'Rockin' Pneumonia'/'I Found a New Love' (August 1966), on the Down Under label. He and Bob Daisley first worked together in beat-pop band Barrington Davis and the Powerpact. Sydney-based singer Barrington Davis had already recorded one solo single, 'Dear Lady'/'Complicated Riddle' (October 1966) for Down Under and one for the Spin label, 'Raining Teardrops'/'As Fast as I Can' (May 1967) *before* forming The Powerpact with Wilson, Daisley and Brian Boness (drums). 'Raining Teardrops' featured a kinetic, punkish edge which precipitated its inclusion on Raven's second *Ugly Things* compilation (1982).

By the end of 1968, The Powerpact had transformed into hard rock outfit Mecca. Davis, being a cabaret singer at heart, had opted out of the new venture and travelled to England. The original three-piece Mecca line-up of Wilson, Daisley and Robin Lewis (drums) was joined by Clive Coulson (vocals; ex-Dark Ages) in early 1970. New Zealander Coulson had already travelled the world as road manager for The Pretty Things, The Yardbirds and Led Zeppelin.

Mecca earned a reputation as proficient practitioners of the Cream/Jeff Beck Group-styled school of hard blues-rock, and issued one excellent single on the Festival label, 'Black Sally'/'Side Street Man' (March 1970). By that stage, Wilson had emerged as one of the country's foremost guitar players extant. New Zealand progressive band Human Instinct later covered 'Black Sally' on its *Stoned Guitar* album. Not long after the single's release, Coulson responded to the beckoning call from Peter Grant and Jimmy Page to rejoin the Led Zeppelin entourage for a European tour. Mecca broke up at the end of June 1970, and Wilson and Daisley formed Kahvas Jute with Dannie Davidson and Tim Gaze. Davidson had spent most of the 1960s working with **Lindsay Bjerre** in The Strangers, The Sunsets and **Tamam Shud**. Sixteen-year-old guitar prodigy Gaze had been playing with **Tamam Shud** for six months when he followed Davidson into the new band. Kahvas Jute immediately earned a reputation as an exceptional live band.

Kahvas Jute signed to Festival's new progressive subsidiary label Infinity (alongside **Billy Thorpe** and the Aztecs, **The Cleves**, **Tymepiece**, **Heart 'n' Soul** and **Blackfeather**) and issued *Wide Open* in January 1971. The album was redolent of UK blues rock bands such as Cream, Blodwyn Pig and The Jeff Beck Group (with a touch of US West Coast rock added). Yet, rather than being a slavish copy of the overseas role model, the album bore a uniquely Australian flavour. Tracks like 'Free', 'She's So Hard to Shake' and the blazing nine-minute epic 'Parade of Fools' benefitted from Wilson and Gaze's dual lead guitar attack. Furthermore, Daisley's restlessly exploratory bass playing (in the manner of Jack Bruce) and Davidson's steady, hard beat formed a solid bedrock for all the guitar fireworks. 'Free'/'Ascend' was issued as a single (July 1971).

Gaze had returned to **Tamam Shud** by the time the album came out, and Kahvas Jute continued as a three-piece. In June 1971, Wilson and Davidson travelled to the UK. Daisley did not make the trip at that stage. His place had been filled by Scott Maxey (ex-Nutwood Rug Band). Daisley joined his fellow musicians in the UK during July 1971. Kahvas Jute played a number of club dates in London but made little headway and broke up.

Daisley joined Stan Webb's Chicken Shack in February 1972, and Wilson also signed on as the band's roadie and front-of-house mixer. Daisley appeared on the Chicken Shack album *Unlucky Boy* (1973) before leaving to join Mungo Jerry in June 1973. He played on such Mungo Jerry hits as 'Alright Alright Alright', 'Long Legged Woman in a Black Dress' and 'Wild Love'. Daisley rejoined Stan Webb in Broken Glass, which also comprised Robbie Blunt (guitar) and Bob Clouter (drums).

From there, Daisley won international acclaim as a journeyman bass player with heavy metal acts Widowmaker (playing on *Widowmaker*, 1976; *Too Late to Cry*, 1977), Ritchie Blackmore's Rainbow (*Long Live Rock'n'Roll*, 1978), Ozzy Osbourne (*Ozzy Osbourne's Blizzard of Ozz*, 1980; *Diary of a Madman*, 1981; *Bark at the Moon*, 1983; *No Rest for the Wicked*, 1988), Uriah Heep (*Abominog*, 1982; *Head First*, 1983), Gary Moore Band (*Victims of the Future*, 1984; *Run for Cover*, 1985; *Wild Frontier*, 1987; *After the War*, 1989, *Still Got the Blues*, 1990), Black Sabbath (as a session player on *The Eternal Idol*, 1987) and Mother's Army (*Mother's Army*, 1993; *Planet Earth*, 1997). He has also appeared as a session player for noted guitarists like Yngwie Malmsteen and Stevie Vai.

Meanwhile, Wilson had been invited to replace Jeff Beck in the remnants of The Jeff Beck Group (comprising Max Middleton, Bobby Tench and Clive Charman). The project fell through, but that band eventually went on to work as Hummingbird with guitarist Bernie Holland. Wilson returned to Australia in May 1973 and revived Kahvas Jute with Davidson and Maxey. Kahvas Jute supported US visitor Bo Diddley on his second Australian tour (October 1973). In March 1974 Maxey left to be replaced by Peter Roberts (ex-**La De Das**, **Band of Light**, **Band of Talabene**). By May 1974, Kahvas Jute had evolved into **Chariot**.

Album: *Wide Open* (Festival/Infinity, 1971; re-issued on CD, 1994).

Tom Kazas (*see* The Moffs)

Jim Keays

Style: *Rock*

Scottish-born singer Jim Keays (b. 1946) fronted the acclaimed **Master's Apprentices** for seven years. When The Masters broke up in the UK at the end of 1971, Keays returned to Australia. He became *Go-Set* magazine's Adelaide correspondent, formed the Rock On Agency and compered the Mulwala Rock Festival in April 1972. In March 1973, Keays appeared as The Lover, alongside **Billy Thorpe**, **Daryl Braithwaite**, **Colleen Hewett**, **Broderick Smith**, **Doug Parkinson** and Keith Moon, in the Australian stage production of The Who's *Tommy*. In January 1974, he compered the third annual Sunbury Festival.

After that, Keays recorded his debut solo album *The Boy from the Stars*. It was an ambitious science fiction concept album based around the story of an extraterrestrial visitor who attempts to warn the earth of its impending doom through the misuse of various sources of power. It was an oft-trodden science fiction story-line (shades of *The Day the Earth Stood Still* and *This Island Earth*), but the album was put together with a great deal of skill and attention to detail.

The album featured an all-star cast of musicians, including members of **Ayers Rock**, **Chain** and **Sid Rumpo**, plus **Billy Green** (guitar), **Marcia Hines** (backing vocals) and **Lobby Loyde** (guitar) among others. Keays wrote most of the music, and all of the lyrics, assuming the role of the boy from the stars. 'Kid's Blues'/'Inter-Planetary Boogie' (December 1974) and 'The Boy from the Stars'/ 'Take it on Easy' (#35 in Melbourne during February 1975) were issued as singles. *The Boy from the Stars* also peaked at #13 on the Melbourne album chart during February. Keays mounted an elaborate stage production for *The Boy from the Stars*, but due to the enormity of the show he only performed three concerts (including Sunbury 1975).

For his next single, the reggae-tinged, anti-drug song 'Give it Up'/'Love is' (June 1975), Keays utilised the services of **Ross Hannaford** and Joe Creighton (ex-**Melissa**). Keays' touring band at that time comprised Creighton, Mick Elliot (guitar; ex-**Sid Rumpo**), Dennis Garcia (keyboards), David Allardis (piano) and Geoff Bridgeford (drums; ex-**Bee Gees**). He then formed Jim Keays' Southern Cross with Mick Elliot, Rex Bullen (keyboards; ex-**Bakery**, Natural Gas), George Cross (bass; ex-Clydehouse) and Rick Brewer (drums; ex-**Zoot**). Jim Keays' Southern Cross issued a re-working of The Masters' 'Undecided'/'For Someone' as a single on CBS (December 1975), which peaked at #36 in Melbourne during January 1976. By the end of 1975, the Southern Cross line-up featured Peter Laffy (guitar; ex-Fox), Ron Robinson (bass) and John Swan (drums; ex-**Fraternity**).

In 1977 Keays linked up with **Phil Manning** (ex-**Chain**) for the short-lived Manning/Keays Band. In 1978, Keays formed the Jim Keays Band with

Ron Robinson, James Black (guitar; ex-Rum Jungle) and David Rowe (drums). Soon after, John Moon (guitar; ex-**Buster Brown**) and Geoff Spooner (guitar; ex-Barrelhouse, **Levi Smith's Clefs**) replaced Black. By early 1979, the band had evolved into The Keays with a revamped line-up of Moon, Bruce Stewart (guitar; ex-Loose Trousers), Peter Marshall (bass) and Nigel Rough (drums; ex-Loose Trousers).

In early 1980, the band commenced recording an album with producer John Sayers at Music Farm Studios. The album sessions were never completed due to Stewart's ill-health. The band broke up and only the 'Lucifer Street'/'The Living Dead' single saw release at that stage. The album *Red on the Meter* eventually came out in 1983 as a Jim Keays solo release, along with a reissue of 'Lucifer Street' backed with 'Australian Blues' on the Rumur label (October). Dissatisfied with the turn of events, Keays began work as a club DJ. In 1987, Keays signed to Virgin Records and flew to the UK to record with producer Craig Leon (The Ramones, The Bangles) and ex-Sweet guitarist Andy Scott. The sessions resulted in two singles featuring radical reworkings of **The Master's Apprentices'** 'Undecided'/'Dubcided' (July 1987) and The Count Five's 'Psychotic Reaction'/'Bates Motel' (October).

From that point, Keays was involved in various **Master's Apprentices** reunions. In 1993, Keays issued his second solo album, *Pressure Makes Diamonds*, on the Gemstone label. BMG reissued the album in mid-1994, after which Keays revived **The Master's Apprentices** again.

Albums: The Boy from the Stars (EMI, 1974), *Red on the Meter* (Rumur/CBS, 1983), *Pressure Makes Diamonds* (Gemstone, 1993; reissued Possum/BMG, 1994).

Paul Kelly

Style: Rock, folk

From very early on in his career, Paul Kelly (b. 1955) was recognised as one of the most significant singer/songwriters in the country. Inspired initially by the likes of Bob Dylan, Hank Williams, Lou Reed and Robert Johnson, Kelly's narrative songwriting style was infused with wry observations, bittersweet emotions and enormous appeal. As well as issuing an enduring body of work with his own bands, Kelly has co-produced **Archie Roach's** acclaimed *Charcoal Lane* album, and had his songs covered by many artists including, among others, **Jenny Morris** ('Beggar on the Street of Love'), **Jo Jo Zep and the Falcons** ('Only the Lonely Hearted'), **Renée Geyer** ('Difficult Woman', 'Foggy Highway'), **Christine Anu** ('Last Train') and **Wendy Matthews** ('Take Your Time') .

Kelly began his career writing poetry and learning guitar. He travelled around the country before settling in Melbourne in late 1976. In 1977 he joined R&B pub band the High Rise Bombers, which comprised Kelly (guitar, vocals), Martin Armiger (guitar, vocals; ex-Toads, **Bleeding Hearts**), Chris Dyson (guitar; ex-Cruisers), Keith Shadwick (sax; ex-**Sun**), Sally Ford (sax; ex-Flying Tackle), Lee 'Fred' Cass (bass; ex-Lip Arthur, Superlemon) and John Lloyd (drums, ex-Relaxed Mechanics, Cruisers). Chris Langman (guitar, vocals; ex-Spare Change, **Parachute**) replaced Dyson in early 1978.

The band built up a cult following on the Carlton pub circuit, but the strain of maintaining such a large ensemble (which included three songwriters) proved too much. In August 1978, Armiger left to join **The Sports** and Ford joined **The Kevins**. The only recorded evidence of the band's existence were the tracks 'She's Got It' and 'Domestic Criminal', which appeared on Missing Links' Various Artists album *The Melbourne Club* in 1981.

Meanwhile, Kelly, Langman and Lloyd formed the first line-up of Paul Kelly and the Dots with Paul Gadsby (bass) and Chris Malhebe (guitar). Chris Worral (guitar; ex-**Captain Matchbox**, **Pelaco Brothers**, **Bleeding Hearts**, **Stiletto**) replaced Malhebe in February 1979. The Dots quickly became one of the most popular bands on the Melbourne scene. Lloyd left in June to join Flowers in Sydney, and Tony Thornton (drums; ex-Sidewinder, Front Page) took his place. Chris Dyson (guitar; ex-Cruisers, High Rise Bombers, **Stiletto,** Romantics) also took over from Langman.

Paul Kelly and the Dots' independent debut 7-inch EP (late 1979) combined one studio track, 'Recognition', with three live cuts, 'Lowdown', 'Faster than Light (Our Love)' and 'I See Red'. It was a good display of Kelly's earthy pop rock roots. In early 1980, the band signed to Mushroom Records and issued 'Seeing is Believing'/'Angel in Me' (May). By that stage, the line-up comprised Kelly, Worral, Dyson, Thornton and newcomer Alan Brooker (bass; ex-Clean Cut). The delightful, ska-tinged 'Billy Baxter'/'Hard Knocks' (November 1980) became the band's only national Top 40 charting single in March 1981. Further line-up changes had occurred in late 1980 when Tim Brosnan (guitar; ex-**Millionaires**, True Wheels, Romantics) and Mick Holmes (guitar; ex-Negatives, Eric Gradman: Man & Machine, Romantics) replaced Dyson and Worral. Dyson joined Beats Working. Meanwhile, it had taken three producers (Martin

Armiger, Joe Camilleri and **Trevor Lucas**) and several months to complete The Dots' debut album *Talk*. The album appeared in March 1981 and yielded the single 'Lowdown'/'Want You Back' (April).

In late 1981, Kelly and the Dots travelled to the Philippines to record their second album, *Manilla*. The album's release was delayed until August 1982 due to further line-up changes. **Maurice Frawley** (ex-Japanese Comix) replaced Holmes on guitar, and Huk Treloar (ex-**Bleeding Hearts**, Sneakers, **Little Heroes**) replaced Thornton on drums. Kelly also spent a period recovering from a broken jaw, which was the result of being mugged in Melbourne. *Manilla* included the singles 'Clean this House'/'Touchy Babe' (April 1982) and 'Alive and Well'/'Some Guys' (July 1982). In early 1982, Kelly also issued a joint single with Jo Kennedy, 'Rocking Institution'/'Body and Soul' (both songs from the *Starstruck* soundtrack).

Alex Formosa replaced Treloar in mid-1982. By August 1983, Kelly had broken up The Dots to form the Paul Kelly Band with Frawley, Michael Armiger (bass; ex-10,000 Guitars) and Greg Martin (drums). By late 1984, the line-up included Armiger, Steve Connolly (guitar; ex-Cuban Heels, Rare Things, **Zimmermen**) and Michael Barclay (drums; ex-Japanese Comix, **Little Murders, Runners, Zimmermen**).

Following a period of re-evaluation, Kelly moved to Sydney, played solo dates and teamed up with Connolly and Barclay to record his debut solo album. *Post* (May 1985) was a stark, highly personalised collection of acoustic songs that showcased the extraordinary breadth of Kelly's songwriting skills. 'From St Kilda to King's Cross'/ 'Blues for Skip' was issued as a single (May). By that stage, Kelly had assembled The Coloured Girls with Connolly, Barclay and Armiger.

Initially the band was a loose aggregation, incorporating the likes of Rick Grossman (bass; from **Divinyls**), Spencer P. Jones (from **The Johnnys**), Chris Coyne (sax) and others. By the end of 1985, the line-up had consolidated with Connolly, Barclay, Peter 'Pedro' Bull (keyboards; ex-**Flaming Hands, Grooveyard**) and Jon Schofield (bass; ex-**Grooveyard**). The Coloured Girls were an essential part of Kelly's musical development, a band capable of great empathy, adaptability and above all adept at producing energetic, intelligent rock'n'roll. Connolly in particular contributed a great deal to Kelly's sound and style.

In September 1986, Paul Kelly and the Coloured Girls issued the sprawling, 24-track double set *Gossip*, one of the genuine classics of Australian

Paul Kelly

rock. The album produced the singles 'Before too Long'/'White Train' (#15 in July 1986), 'Darling It Hurts'/'Preaching to the Converted' (#16 in October), 'Leaps and Bounds'/'Bradman' (January 1987) and 'Look So Fine, Feel So Low'/'Somebody's Forgetting Somebody (Somebody's Letting Somebody Down)', 'Pastures of Plenty' (April 1987). *Gossip* reached #7 on the national chart and attained gold status in Australia (over 35 000 copies sold). It was issued in the USA on A&M as a single album. In the USA, The Coloured Girls became known as The Messengers (in deference to racial sensitivities). The band toured the USA, initially as the support to **Crowded House** then as a headlining act.

The band's second album, *Under the Sun*, reached #17 on the Australian chart in December 1987, eventually attaining platinum status (70 000 copies sold). It was one of the best Australian albums for the year. *Under the Sun* yielded four singles, 'To Her Door'/'Bicentennial' (#6 in December 1987), 'Forty Miles to Saturday Night'/'Little Decisions' (February 1988), 'Don't Stand So Close'/'Hard Times' (May 1988) and the double 7-inch set 'Dumb Things'/'Deportees'; 'Rock'n' Soul'/'Reckless' (#36 in February 1989). 'Dumb Things' was included on the soundtrack to the Yahoo Serious feature film *Young Einstein*. Kelly also contributed a cover of **Australian Crawl**'s 'Reckless' to the Various Artists tribute album, *Used and Recovered by* (1990).

With the release of *So Much Water So Close to Home* (July 1989), the band also became known as Paul Kelly and the Messengers in Australia. *So Much Water . . .* featured some of Kelly's most passionate and world-weary songs. The album title appeared in the song 'Everything's Turning to White', which was inspired by the Raymond Carver short story 'So Much Water So Close to Home'. The album spawned the singles 'Sweet Guy'/'Ghost Town' (June 1989) and 'Careless'/'Special Treatment' (November), plus the four-track EP 'Most Wanted Man in the World', 'I Had Forgotten You'/'Beggar on the Street of Love' (live), 'I Won't Be Your Dog Anymore' (live) (March 1990). Kelly also contributed 'Special Treatment' to the Various Artists album *Building Bridges* on CBS (1989).

Kelly and the Messengers undertook another US tour where A&M had continued to issue the band's albums. The next Messengers album was the 18-track *Comedy* (November 1990). It featured the singles 'Pouring Petrol on a Burning Man'/'Other People's Houses' (October), 'Don't Start Me Talking'/'From St Kilda to King's Cross' (January 1991), 'Keep It to Yourself'/'Brand New Ways' (May) and 'Wintercoat'/'Special Treatment' (September). One of the album's highlights was the seven-minute epic 'From Little Things Big Things Grow' (co-written with **Kev Carmody**), a documentary narrative of one of the first Aboriginal land rights claims. Kelly had tackled similar topics before on tracks like 'Maralinga (Rainy Land)' from *Gossip* and 'Bicentennial' from *Under the Sun*.

Paul Kelly and the Messengers played their final gigs together during August 1991. The fifth and final Messengers album was *Hidden Things* (May 1992), a collection of rare recordings and B-sides made between 1986 and 1991. The album gave rise to the single 'When I First Met Your Ma'/'Rally Round the Drum' (April). Also included were covers of 'Reckless', Woody Guthrie's 'Pastures of Plenty' and **Joe Geia's** 'Yil Lull'. With the break-up of The Messengers, Kelly travelled to the USA in order to establish a base in Los Angeles. Guitarist Steve Connolly produced **Kev Carmody's** *Eulogy (for a black person)* as a follow-up to his co-credit with Kelly on **Archie Roach's** *Charcoal Lane*. Connolly later worked with Sherry Rich and the Grievous Angels before forming his own band. He died in 1995 from heart problems following surgery.

Before Kelly left for the USA, he took his first acting role in the stage play *Funerals and Circuses* for the Adelaide Fringe Festival, and recorded the solo, double live album *Live, May 1992* (October 1992). He also contributed several songs to the soundtrack of the 1993 ABC-TV drama series *Seven Deadly Sins*. In the USA, Kelly toured as a solo artist, signed to the Vanguard label and worked on **Renée Geyer's** album *Difficult Woman* in Los Angeles. Back in Australia in late 1993, he produced **Vika and Linda Bull's** debut album *Vika and Linda*, recorded a new album, *Wanted Man*, and issued his book *Paul Kelly Lyrics* (Angus & Robertson). He also recorded the soundtrack to Alkinos Tsilimidos' feature film *Everynight . . . Everynight* (1994).

Kelly's third solo album, *Wanted Man* (July 1994), mixed a wide range of styles, from country and reggae to R&B and pop. It included the CD singles 'Song from the Sixteenth Floor' (January 1994), 'Love Never Runs on Time' (May) and 'God's Hotel' (September). His 1995 album, *Deeper Water* (August), yielded the singles 'Summer Rain' (February), 'Give in to My Love' (August) and 'Deeper Water' (November). Kelly also issued a second live album in October 1995, *Live at the Continental and the Esplanade*.

Kelly's 1996 band included Shane O'Mara (guitar; from **Rebecca's Empire**), Bruce Haymes (keyboards; ex-**Bachelors from Prague**), Stephen Hadley (bass; ex-**Black Sorrows**) and Peter Luscombe (drums; ex-**Black Sorrows**), with Spencer P. Jones (**Beasts of Bourbon**) joining as an auxiliary member. That line-up issued the CD EP 'How to Make Gravy' at the end of the year. In May 1997, Kelly issued a new CD single, 'Tease Me'/'It Started with a Kiss', followed by the 20 track 'Best of' album *Songs from the South: Paul Kelly's Greatest Hits* which was the perfect anthology of his work. The album made its debut at #2 on the national chart in June, and went on to sell double platinum (over 140 000 copies). Kelly was named Best Male Artist at the 1997 Australian Record Industry Association (ARIA) awards ceremony, as well as being inducted into the ARIA Hall of Fame.

Paul Kelly and the Dots albums: *Talk* (Mushroom/Festival, 1981), *Manilla* (Mushroom/Festival, 1982); ***Paul Kelly solo albums:*** *Post* (Mushroom/Festival, 1985), *Live, May 1992* (Mushroom/Festival, 1992), *Wanted Man* (White/Mushroom/Festival, 1994), *Deeper Water* (White/Mushroom/Festival, 1995), *Live at the Continental and the Esplanade* (White/Mushroom/Festival, 1996), *Songs from the South: Paul Kelly's Greatest Hits* (White/Mushroom/Sony, 1997); ***Paul Kelly and the Coloured Girls albums:*** *Gossip* (Mushroom/Festival, 1986), *Under the Sun* (Mushroom/Festival, 1987); ***Paul Kelly and the Messengers albums:*** *So Much Water So Close to Home*

(Mushroom/Festival, 1989), *Comedy* (Mushroom/Festival, 1991), *Hidden Things* (Mushroom/Festival, 1992).

The Kelpies

Formed: *1981*
Style: *Punk*
Original line-up: *James Gelding (vocals; ex-Blackrunner, Bedhogs), Mark Easton (lead guitar; ex-Suicide Squad, Bedhogs), Brian Connolly (rhythm guitar; ex-Swankers, Aftermath), Con Murphy (bass; ex-Suicide Squad), Ashley Thompson (drums; ex-Mayhem)*

The Kelpies grew out of Sydney's early 1980s punk scene. In their brief existence (March 1981 to September 1981, and then March 1982 to August 1982), The Kelpies went from being one of the most popular bands on the inner-city scene to being locked out of virtually every gig in town due to the amount of violence at their shows.

Mark Easton and Con Murphy formed Suicide Squad in April 1978. Mick Adams (vocals) and Steve Cord (drums) completed the line-up. Annie Barrett replaced Adams and Suicide Squad issued one single on the Doublethink label, 'I Hate School'/'New Kids' Army' (January 1980). The single was reminiscent of UK punk outfits like X-Ray Spex. Barrett left to join Miss Australia. Suicide Squad continued on for another year with different line-ups. Throughout 1980, Easton also played with James Aitkins' (aka James Gelding) band The Bedhogs.

Suicide Squad broke up in early 1981, and Easton, Gelding and Murphy formed The Kelpies. The Phantom label issued The Kelpies' single 'Take Me Away'/'Second by Second' posthumously in November 1982. 'Take Me Away' also appeared on Phantom's 1983 Various Artists album *Paths of Pain to Jewels of Glory*. Three tracks from the band's first demo recordings ('My Wall', 'Truro Murders' and 'Television') also appeared on the Aberrant label's seminal collection of Sydney punk bands, *Flowers from the Dustbin* (1983). Aberrant also included three Suicide Squad tracks, 'Unwanted', 'Gossip Column' and a cover of Roger Whittaker's 'New World in the Morning', on its second punk compilation, *Not So Humdrum* (1984). Aberrant later issued The Kelpies album *Official Bootleg* (October 1986).

With the break-up of The Kelpies, Gelding and Connolly joined The Undertakers. Easton, Murphy and Thomson formed Soggy Porridge with Daniel Coumbe (guitar). Soggy Porridge issued a mini-album, *Slurp Tracks* (August 1983) on the New Zealand label Jayrem, plus two singles, 'How Can I Tell You?'/'Theme from Soggy Porridge' (1984) and 'Call My Name'/'Rip this Soul Apart' (1986), on the Method label. For the second single, Easton and Murphy were joined by Jonathan Purcell (guitar; ex-Moving Parts, **End**) and Tony Cardinal (drums). Easton and Cardinal formed The Glam Savages and then **Candy Harlots** in 1987.

Album: *Official Bootleg* (Aberrant, 1986).

John Kennedy's Love Gone Wrong

Formed: *1984*
Style: *Country, R&B*
Original line-up: *John Kennedy (vocals, guitar; ex-J.F.K. and the Cuban Crisis), Graham Lee (pedal steel, acoustic guitar, backing vocals; ex-Lawson Square Infirmary), Peter Kennard (bass, keyboards; ex-***Rockmelons***), Peter Timmerman (drums; ex-Cheatin' Hearts)*

Liverpool-born, Brisbane-raised singer/songwriter John Kennedy was Australia's foremost performer of 'Urban and Western' roots music. Kennedy coined the phrase 'Urban and Western' to describe his music, which combined contemporary production values and lyrics relevant to living in urban Australia over a traditional country music backing. Overseas equivalents would be *My Aim is True* period Elvis Costello and American bands like The Blasters and Rank and File. Kennedy's earliest influences ranged from 1960s pop to the country music of Johnny Cash, Patsy Cline, Bob Dylan, Gram Parson and Merle Haggard.

Kennedy formed his first band, J.F.K. and the Cuban Crisis, in Brisbane, Queensland during October 1980. Following on from other Brisbane bands like **The Go-Betweens** and **The Apartments** (i.e. the 'Brisbane sound'), J.F.K. and the Cuban Crisis played a brand of jangly guitar pop with country overtones. The original line-up comprised Kennedy, James Pattinson (vocals, mandolin), Holger Maschke (slide guitar), Paul Hardman (keyboards), John Downie (bass) and Stephen Pritchard (drums).

J.F.K. and the Cuban Crisis issued one independent single, 'Am I a Pagan?'/'That Alarming Sound' (March 1982), on the Two Possibilities label before moving to Sydney in May. One of the band's early fans, Steve Stavrakis, set up the Waterfront label specifically to issue the four-track EP *Careless Talk Costs Lives* (December 1982). One track from the EP, 'The Texan Thing', attracted a good deal of attention and alternative radio airplay. In 1983, the line-up comprised Kennedy, Pattinson, Greg Hall (bass) and Paul Rochelli (drums). By 1984, J.F.K. and the Cuban Crisis had moved away from its pop roots, allowing the country elements to dominate proceedings.

Waterfront issued the band's second EP, 'The Ballad of Jackie O'/'The Texan Thing' (live), 'Jackson' (April 1984) and the album *The End of the Affair* (May). The album title proved prophetic, as a month later Kennedy disbanded J.F.K. and the Cuban Crisis due to the age-old 'musical differences'. Kennedy entered the studio to record his debut solo single with Graham Lee (acoustic guitar, pedal steel, vocals), Peter Kennard (percussion), Martin Tucker (piano), Ike (double bass), Adrian Bingham (sax) and Peter Timmerman (drums).

'Forget'/'The End of the Affair' came out on Waterfront in September 1984, by which time Kennedy had formed his new band, John Kennedy's Love Gone Wrong, with the line-up listed above. The original line-up was conceived as a casual group assembled to promote Kennedy's solo releases. Kennedy took the band back into the studio to record his second single, 'Miracle (in Marrickville')/'Two People'. By the time the single came out in March 1985, Kennedy had added Colin Bloxsom (lead guitar; ex-Pop Rivets) to the Love Gone Wrong line-up.

In April, John Kennedy's Love Gone Wrong entered the Ten Network's television talent show *Starsearch*, and surprised themselves (and their audience) by winning four heats and progressing all the way to the series final. Although beaten in the final, the experience gained the band a great deal of exposure. Retaining Bloxsom, Kennedy formed a permanent Love Gone Wrong line-up with Barry Turnbull (bass; ex-**Chad's Tree**), Mark Dawson (drums) and Margaret Labi (harmony vocals). Kennedy took the band on the road across the eastern states, and recorded a new single in September.

'King Street'/'To Forget' (November 1985) was Kennedy's first single for the Red Eye label, and the first to bear the John Kennedy's Love Gone Wrong credit. The band's next release was the Christmas gig giveaway 7-inch single 'A Time for Giving' (December). In early 1986, Kennedy spent two months travelling across the USA and Mexico, and upon his return found that Dawson had joined **Ed Kuepper's** band The Yard Goes on Forever and Bloxsom was no longer interested in playing with Love Gone Wrong.

While auditioning for new players, Kennedy, Turnbull and Cory Messenger (acoustic guitar) formed the casual band John Kennedy's Sweet Dreams to play a small number of shows around Sydney. Sweet Dreams played the country-inspired originals from the Love Gone Wrong repertoire and country favourites from people like Patsy Cline, Willie Nelson, Johnny Cash, Bob Dylan and The Byrds. With assistance from Turnbull, Messenger, Mark Dawson, Ian Simpson (banjo, pedal steel), Sandy Chick (harmony vocals) and **The Go-Betweens'** Amanda Brown (violin), Kennedy recorded a new single.

By the time 'Big Country'/'You Brought It All Back to Me' came out in July 1986, Kennedy had formed a new Love Gone Wrong with Turnbull, Messenger, Wayne Connolly (lead guitar, vocals) and Vincent Sheehan (drums). Kennedy had written 'Big Country' with Slim Dusty in mind, and indeed the song captured an authentic country truckin' feel. The band embarked on its Big Country tour, taking in shows with the likes of **Weddings, Parties, Anything** and **The Hollowmen**. In October, Red Eye issued the eight-track mini-album compilation *From Woe to Go*, which charted Kennedy's progress since 1984. It included the American version of 'Big Country' with alternative lyrics in which Tully and the Alice became Tulsa and Dallas.

Love Gone Wrong ended the year with another Christmas gig giveaway single, Chuck Berry's 'Run Rudolph Run'/'Rudolph's Talking Christmas Blues'. In early 1987, Michael Armiger (ex-10,000 Guitars, **Paul Kelly** Band) replaced Turnbull on bass. Love Gone Wrong signed a deal with the Mighty Boy label, issuing a new single 'The Singing City'/'Love Gone Wrong', 'Theme from Love Gone Wrong' (instrumental) in September 1987. The album *Always the Bridegroom* (December) and its second single, 'World Upside Down'/'Better Days' (May 1988), followed.

In August 1988, Kennedy decided to break up Love Gone Wrong after Armiger accepted an offer to join **The Johnnys**. Kennedy undertook a solo acoustic tour, and issued a duet with **The Hollowmen's** Billy Baxter as his next single, **The Bee Gees'** 'To Love Somebody'/'Tourists in Heaven' (October). That same month, Kennedy flew to Berlin, where he had been invited to perform at the Berlin Independence Day (BID) Music Festival.

Back in Australia, Kennedy issued his debut solo album *One Day* (February 1989), which yielded the single 'Out of Town'/'Miracle', 'You Brought It All Back to Me' (January 1989). Following his Out of Town Farewell Tour during February, Kennedy left Australia bound for the USA and the UK before finally settling in Berlin. In 1990, Kennedy recorded an acoustic retrospective of some of his finest songs, dating back to J.F.K. and the Cuban Crisis, for the US-based Furnace label. Sydney-based Red Eye issued the retrospective *Have Songs will Travel* set on CD in Australia, and Kennedy returned for an

Australian tour during November. Back in Berlin, Kennedy formed a new band called The Honeymooners. With The Honeymooners, Kennedy issued the CD single 'By the Light of the Day' (February 1994), the CD EP *The Honeymooners* and the album *Fiction Facing Facts* (May 1993). Highlights on the album included 'Johnny Does Jazz' and the simple elegy 'The Rain that Breaks the Drought'.

J.F.K. and the Cuban Crisis album: *The End of the Affair* (Waterfront, 1984); ***John Kennedy's Love Gone Wrong album:*** *From Woe to Go* (Red Eye, 1986); ***Love Gone Wrong album:*** *Always the Bridegroom* (Mighty Boy, 1987); ***John Kennedy solo albums:*** *One Day* (Mighty Boy, 1989), *Have Songs will Travel* (compilation, Red Eye, 1990); ***John Kennedy and the Honeymooners album:*** *Fiction Facing Facts* (PolyGram, 1993).

The Kevins

Formed: *1978*
Style: *Pop*
Original line-up: *Anne Harkin (guitar, vocals; ex-Flying Tackle), Sally Ford (sax; ex-Flying Tackle, High Rise Bombers), Nick Smith (aka Nick Lafayette, vocals, guitar; ex-***Millionaires***), Steve 'Buzz' Leeson (bass, vocals; ex-***Millionaires***), Michael Davis (drums)*

Melbourne band The Kevins grew out of the ashes of 'sophisticated rock' outfit **Millionaires** and all-girl band Flying Tackle. The band played the late 1970s Carlton scene alongside **Models**, **Paul Kelly** and the Dots, The Armchairs and the like. The band's debut single, 'And So We Meet'/'Out at Night', on the Missing Link label (September 1979) combined pop, soul and funk with a large dose of good humour.

The Kevins continued to gig, but it was almost two years before the band appeared on record again. The appealing 'Romeo Romeo'/'Fool's Paradise' single (August 1982) on the White label was the band's best shot at the commercial charts, and it managed to peak at #22 in Melbourne. The single was lifted from the band's debut mini-album, *Club of Rome* (produced by **The Sports'** Martin Armiger). David Hicks (ex-**Millionaires**) had replaced Davis on drums by that stage. The Kevins issued a final single with Armiger producing 'Ululation (Here It Comes Again)'/'Little Sister' (September 1983) before splitting up.

Smith issued a solo single, The Young Rascals' 'Groovin''/'Shake It', on Joe Camilleri's Spirit label (1984), and later collaborated with Camilleri as lyricist on **The Black Sorrows** albums *A Place in the World*, *Hold on to Me* and *Harley and Rose*. Ford worked with The Escalators and **The Black Sorrows** among others.

Mini-album: *Club of Rome* (White/Mushroom/Festival, 1982).

Kids in the Kitchen

Formed: *1983*
Style: *Pop, funk*
Original line-up: *Scott Carne (vocals), Greg Woodhead (keyboards), Greg Dorman (guitar), Craig Harnath (bass), Bruce Curnow (drums)*

From very early on, Melbourne band Kids in the Kitchen attracted a great deal of attention. Kids in the Kitchen had the right sound (contemporary synth pop with a dash of funk inspired by the likes of Duran Duran, Spandau Ballet and Chic), the right looks and plenty of youthful appeal to make a grab for the charts. The Kids had only been playing live for eight months when Mushroom's White label snapped them up.

Indeed, the interest was vindicated when the band's first two singles, 'Change in Mood'/'Far from Where' (produced by Ricky Fataar and Tim Kramer, October 1983) and 'Bitter Desire'/'Hunting and Haunting' (April 1984), charted in the national Top 10. 'Change in Mood' and 'Bitter Desire' also peaked at #2 and #9 respectively in Melbourne. The band toured constantly, initially as support to the likes of **Models**, and then as headliners. In 1984 the band was dogged by a number of line-up changes. Eventually Alistair Coia (keyboards) replaced Woodhead and Claude Carranza (guitar) replaced Dorman.

The band completed its debut album, *Shine* (June 1985), which yielded three further singles, 'Something that You Said'/'Cruel Time' (#16 in May), 'Shine'/'Hard' (June) and 'Current Stand'/'Current Stand' (Instrumental) (#14 in August). *Shine* peaked at #6, attained platinum status (70 000 copies sold) and the band undertook several national tours. The band's next two singles were non-album 'My Life'/'Fun', 'Frog' (November 1985) and 'Out of Control'/'Stop' (June 1986).

In late 1986, drummer Bruce Curnow was ousted from the band. Renowned New York session drummer 'Sterling' Silver came in as Curnow's replacement, but left after just one showcase gig to join the Cyndi Lauper Band. Jason Stonehouse eventually joined as the band's new drummer. The Kids completed a second album *Terrain*. With tracks produced by four different producers (David Kershenbaum, Richard Gottehrer, Andy Wallace and the band's own Craig Harnath), *Terrain* was patchy, but it displayed a more mature dance approach. It produced the singles 'Say It'/'White Love' (August 1987) and 'Revolution Love'/'Cry' (November). At the end of 1987, newcomer Simon Kershaw (ex-**Go 101**) joined on keyboards. 'Say It' became the band's last national hit when it peaked at #20 in October.

With the break-up of Kids in the Kitchen in 1988, Carne joined rockabilly band Priscilla's Nightmare, which comprised Matt Sanford (guitar; ex-Bwana), Chris Wilson (keyboards), Graeme Thomas (bass) and David Hicks (drums; ex-**Millionaires, Kevins**). Priscilla's Nightmare issued the single 'She Ain't No Woman'/'Wearing that Loved on Look' and a self-titled mini-album in 1989 on White. In 1990, Carne issued two solo dance-pop singles on Mushroom, 'All I Wanna Do' and 'Freedom'. He supported overseas visitors Soul II Soul on an Australian tour.

Harnath moved into production work for the likes of **Chocolate Starfish**. He had previously co-produced (with Mike Duffy) **Kylie Minogue's** 'Glad to Be Alive', which was the B-side to her debut single, 'Locomotion'. In fact, Harnath and Carranza co-wrote 'Glad to Be Alive'. Harnath later worked on the soundtracks to ABC-TV shows like *Frontline* and *Funky Squad*.

Kids in the Kitchen albums: *Shine* (White/Mushroom/Festival, 1985), *Terrain* (White/Mushroom/Festival, 1987); ***Priscilla's Nightmare mini-album:*** *Priscilla's Nightmare* (White/Mushroom/Festival, 1989).

Steve Kilbey

Style: *Rock*

Singer/songwriter/bassist Steve Kilbey was the driving force behind internationally acclaimed band **The Church**. Aside from issuing 11 albums with **The Church**, the prolific Kilbey has pursued his own esoteric solo career. Inevitably played, engineered and produced by himself (with numerous guest musicians helping out), Kilbey's solo recordings were challenging and evocative. They ran the gamut of sounds and emotions from electronic and avant-garde to acoustic and symphonic, joyous and dreamy to saturnine and sardonic.

Kilbey issued his debut solo single, 'This Asphalt Eden'/'Never Come Back', 'Shell', in July 1985. Originally issued by EMI/Parlophone, the Red Eye label reissued the single in November 1987. That same year Red Eye issued Kilbey's first two solo albums, *Unearthed* (January) and *Earthed* (June), the mini-album *The Slow Crack* (December) and his second single, 'Fireman'/'Forgetfulness', 'Nonapology' (November). Issued simultaneously with *Earthed* was a book of Kilbey's prose and poetry under the same title. The *Earthed* album was conceived as a possible soundtrack to the reading of the book, which had come first in terms of conception.

Following the worldwide success of **The Church's** *Starfish* album and 'Under the Milky Way' single, Kilbey returned to his solo career with the single 'Transaction'/'No Such Thing' (June 1989) and the 12-inch version of 'Transaction' with two extra tracks (July 1989). 'Transaction' was from *The Slow Crack* and 'No Such Thing' was lifted from Kilbey's third album, the CD/double album *Remindlessness* (December 1989). The double album version contained two tracks ('Random Pan' and 'Pain in My Temples') not included on the later CD version. Also in 1989, Kilbey collaborated with singer Donette Thayer on the album *Hex*.

In 1990, Kilbey collaborated with one-time **Go-Between Grant McLennan** as the duo **Jack Frost,** which resulted in the album *Jack Frost* (December) and the single 'Every Hour God Sends' (November) on Red Eye. **Jack Frost** issued a second album, *Snow Job,* in 1996. In December 1991, Kilbey issued the scarce CD EP *Narcosis*, his last solo release for the Red Eye label.

Kilbey set up his Karmic Hit studio and label and continued to be involved in a wide range of projects. These included Margot Smith's *Sleeping with the Lion* album (as player and producer), Fake's self-titled album (as producer), **CURIOUS (yellow)** (as writer and producer), the Brett Whiteley tribute album *Strange Brew* (as contributor of the poem 'Season in Hell'), **Stephen Cummings'** *Falling Swinger* and *Escapist* albums (as producer, co-writer and player), **Kev Carmody's** *Images and Illusions* album (as producer and player) and as writer and producer of the soundtrack for the 1997 feature film *Black Rock*. In May 1997, the Vicious Sloth label issued the Kilbey CD *Narcosis Plus* (a reissue of the *Narcosis* CD EP plus three unissued tracks from the same sessions). Kilbey also collaborated with his brother Russell on the ambient instrumental/electronic album *Gilt Trip*.

Albums: *Unearthed* (Red Eye, 1987), *Earthed* (Red Eye, 1987), *The Slow Crack* (mini-album, Red Eye, 1987), *Remindlessness* (Red Eye, 1989), *Narcosis Plus* (Vicious Sloth, 1997), *Gilt Trip* (in collaboration with Russell Kilbey, Vicious Sloth, 1997).

Killing Time (*see* Mantissa)

The Killjoys

Formed: *1987*
Style: *Pop, folk*
Original line-up: *Anna Burley (vocals, guitar; ex-Wild Science), Craig Pilkington (guitar, vocals; ex-Wild Science), Carolyn Schwerkolt (vibraphone, keyboards), Jeremy Craigie-Smith (bass), Will Larsen (drums)*

Classically trained guitarist Craig Pilkington and singer Anna Burley first worked together in Melbourne band Wild Science. The pair decided to form their own band when the other members of Wild Science wanted to go in a hard rock direction. The Killjoys sound mixed appealing pop melodies and bittersweet folk harmonies with a jazzy edge.

In 1989, the band issued the EP 'Audrey' (March) and single 'Fall Around Me' (November) on the independent Audrey label. 'Audrey' was named after the Melbourne landmark the 'Skipping Girl' neon sign in inner-city Richmond. The Killjoys contributed a cover of **The Seekers**' 'Another You' to the Various Artists tribute album, *Used and Recovered by* (1990). Their debut album *Ruby* (October 1990) won the 1990 Australian Record Industry Association (ARIA) Award for Best Independent Release. At one of the parties after the official ceremony, Carolyn Schwerkolt accidently dropped the award into Sydney Harbour! That incident created interest further afield, and the band signed to the Mushroom off-shoot label MXL (presumably on the strength of the music).

Ruby produced the single 'Michael Told Me'. Michael Hohnen replaced Daniel Palamara who had replaced Craigie-Smith, and The Killjoys issued a new EP, *Spin* (featured track 'Calling Me On'), in November 1991. At the end of 1992, The Killjoys travelled to the UK and recorded their second album, *A Million Suns*, with producer Craig Leon (Ramones, Pogues, Bangles). The album came out in March 1993. It was a collection of breezy, uplifting folksy pop songs including the singles 'Beauty + Danger' (February 1993) and 'I Lied' (June).

The Killjoys

The band suffered several line-up changes, including Dave Foley replacing Larsen on drums during 1993, Dave Nelson replacing Hohnen in 1995 and the departure of Schwerkolt. Gary Aspinall (guitar, vocals; ex-**Odolites**, Somerfields) joined in early 1995. The band issued the CD EP 'Love and Uncertainty' in May 1994 and the CD single 'Come Around' in October 1995. The Killjoys also contributed a cover of **Cold Chisel's** 'Flame Trees' to the Various Artists compilation *Earth Music* issued on the Mushroom label (June 1994). A new CD single, 'Stupid Waste', appeared in March 1996. They were quiet for another 18 months until the release of the CD single 'Save Me' in November 1997.

Albums: *Ruby* (Audrey, 1990), *A Million Suns* (MXL/Mushroom/Festival, 1993).

The Kinetics

Formed: *1965*
Style: *Beat pop*
Original line-up: *Steve Groves (vocals, guitar, harmonica), John Vallins (guitar, drums, clarinet), Ken Leroy (bass), Ian Manzie (drums, piano, banjo)*

The members of Melbourne beat pop band The Kinetics were all of about 16 years old when they issued the single 'Excuses'/'I Know Where You're Hiding' (September 1966) on CBS. 'Excuses' reached #19 on the Melbourne chart, but the follow-ups 'Gone to Work It Out'/'Feduping Day' (December) and 'Tomorrow Today'/'You're So Good to Me' (March 1967) were not successful.

The Kinetics had broken up by the end of 1967, and Steve Groves joined up with erstwhile **Steve & the Board** frontman Steve Kipner as vocal harmony act the Steve and Stevie Duo. Steve and Stevie issued one single on Festival, 'Remains to Be Seen'/'Merry Go Round' (1968). With the arrival of former Kinetic John Vallins, the act became known as Rombo's World. From there, Groves and Kipner travelled to the UK and became known as Tin Tin.

Tin Tin adopted a very British-influenced pop sound and signed to Polydor. Tin Tin issued nine singles on Polydor: 'Only Ladies Play Croquet'/'He Wants to Be a Star' (1969), 'Toast and Marmalade for Tea'/'Manhattan Woman' (1970), 'Come on Over Again'/'Back to Winona' (1970), 'Is That the Way?'/

'Swans on the Canal' (1971), 'Talking Turkey'/'The Cavalry are Coming' (1972) and 'I'm Afraid'/'Handle Me Easy' (1973), plus two albums, *Tin Tin* and *Astral Taxi*. Decca issued a final Tin Tin single in 1973, 'It's a Long Way to Georgia'/'Can't Get Over You'. The Steve Groves-penned, Maurice Gibb-produced 'Toast and Marmalade for Tea' reached #10 in Australia (June 1971) and #20 in the USA. Ex-Kinetic Vallins joined Tin Tin in May 1971.

Groves returned to Australia in 1975. He co-wrote 'On the Loose Again' which, when performed by **Marty Rhone**, won the 1976 Popular Song Festival in Tokyo. Groves later also recorded the song with the Steve Groves Band. The Bootleg label issued two Steve Groves Band singles, 'On the Loose Again'/'Star Maker' (November 1976) and 'Here I am'/'Slippery Shoes' (April 1977).

In the meantime, Vallins had formed a songwriting partnership with Steve Kipner's father Nat (who ran the Spin label in the 1960s, which was responsible for many of the early **Bee Gees** records, plus those by his son's band **Steve & the Board**). Johnny Mathis and Deniece Williams enjoyed a worldwide hit in March 1978 with the Kipner/Vallins composition 'Too Much Too Little Too Late'.

King Harvest

Formed: *1970*
Style: *Progressive rock*
Original line-up: **Leo De Castro** *(vocals, guitar; ex-Leo and the Browns, Leo and Friends), Jimmy Doyle (guitar; ex-Silhouettes,* **Aesop's Fables**, *Moonstone), Steve Yates (keyboards; ex-Rush,* **Expression***), Duncan McGuire (bass; ex-Phantoms, Epics, Questions,* **Doug Parkinson** *In Focus, Rush), Mark Kennedy (drums; ex-***Spectrum***)*

New Zealand-born singer **Leo De Castro** possessed one of the most soulful blues voices to be heard on the Australian scene during the early 1970s. Although he never achieved widespread success, the redoubtable De Castro surrounded himself with musicians of quality and distinction, as the above line-up of King Harvest attests.

In 1969 De Castro worked with Leo and Friends which comprised Rob MacKenzie (guitar), Jeremy Noone (sax), John Capek (piano) and Kevin Murphy (drums; ex-**Wild Cherries**). That band broke up at the start of 1970. King Harvest came together in September 1970, and immediately earned acclaim as one of the leading 'heavy' bands on the burgeoning Melbourne progressive rock circuit. The band shared stages with the likes of **Billy Thorpe** and the Aztecs, **Chain**, **Carson**, **Company Caine**, **Bulldog** and **Spectrum**. The band suffered a number of line-up changes in its brief 12-month existence.

Only a matter of weeks after formation, **Billy Green** (ex-**Doug Parkinson** In Focus) replaced Jimmy Doyle. Green had also left by the beginning of 1971, and Rob MacKenzie filled in until Ray Oliver (ex-The Light) joined permanently. In March 1971, Mark Kennedy and Duncan McGuire left to rejoin with Parkinson and Green in **Doug Parkinson** In Focus. Kennedy and McGuire teamed up again with De Castro in **Friends** before forming **Ayers Rock**. Gary Clarke (bass) and Kevin Murphy (ex-Rush, **Billy Thorpe** and the Aztecs) became the new King Harvest rhythm section. Ray Oliver also left in March to be replaced by New Zealander John Williams (ex-Rebels).

By August 1971, the King Harvest line-up comprised De Castro, Rob MacKenzie, John Capek (piano; ex-**Carson**), Jeremy Noone (piano, sax; ex-**Company Caine**), Tim Partridge (bass; Clockwork Oringe) and Barry Harvey (drums; ex-Thursday's Children, **Wild Cherries, Chain**). Clarke had joined **Carson** and Murphy joined **Chain**. The new line-up lasted until September, when De Castro, Capek and Harvey formed the short-lived Flite with Vince Melouney (guitar; ex-**Billy Thorpe** and the Aztecs, **Bee Gees, Fanny Adams, Cleves**) and Barry Sullivan (bass; ex-Thursday's Children, **Wild Cherries, Chain**). By early December 1971, De Castro had formed **Friends** with Charlie Tumahai.

King Harvest concentrated on rearranging well-known songs of the day, at the expense of writing original material. The band excelled in the live situation, but its two singles on RCA were safe, if passionately performed, cover versions. 'Wichita Lineman'/'Summer in the City' (January 1971) is the band's crowning achievement. 'Wichita Lineman' is one of the most beautifully elegiac and timeless ballads ever written. King Harvest's enthralling arrangement of this oft-covered Jimmy Webb classic was highlighted by De Castro's soulful vocals and Green's haunting wah wah guitar lines. The single reached #35 in March 1971.

In total contrast to the delicate 'Wichita Lineman', King Harvest's version of The Rolling Stones' 'Jumping Jack Flash (Part 1)'/'Jumping Jack Flash (Part 2)' (April 1971) was a potent, six-minute rave-up fired by blazing guitars and crashing drums. That single failed to chart. Ian 'Molly' Meldrum produced both records. Reissue specialists Raven included 'Wichita Lineman' on the essential collection *Golden Miles: Australian Progressive Rock 1969–1974* (1994).

In mid-1973, with the break-up of **Friends**, De Castro formed the short-lived New King Harvest with Tui Richards (guitar), Lindsay Wells (guitar; ex-**Healing Force**, One Ton Gypsy, **Blackfeather**), Ben Kaika (bass; ex-**McPhee**, Tramp) and Steve Webb (drums; ex-**Blackfeather**, **Duck**, Tramp). By the end of the year De Castro had formed a new band called De Castro.

King Snake Roost

Formed: *1985*
Style: *Grunge*
Original line-up: *Alan O'Neill (vocals), Charles Tolnay (guitar; ex-***Grong Grong**, **Bloodloss***), Michael Raymond (bass), George Klestinis (drums; ex-***Grong Grong***)*

Adelaide band King Snake Roost (KSR) was the obvious inheritor of the **Grong Grong** mantle of the ultimate 'garage-noise' outfit. The band's sound was based around abrasive, feedback-heavy guitar riffs, a relentless rhythm section and manic, tuneless vocals and harp playing (not that far removed from a band such as **Lubricated Goat**). The band members cited an eclectic range of influences, from jazz (Miles Davis) and blues (Sonny Terry and Brownie McGee, Screamin' Jay Hawkins) to **The Birthday Party** and The Pop Group.

The original KSR line-up was short-lived. By the time KSR recorded its debut mini-album for the Aberrant label, *From Barbarism to Christian Manhood*, in 1987 the line-up was Tolnay, Raymond, Peter Hill (vocals, harp) and Bill Bostle (drums). David Quinn replaced Raymond on bass, and the new line-up relocated to Sydney. There KSR recorded three singles, 'Top End Killer'/'A Storm Brewin'' (May 1988), Alice Cooper's 'School's Out' (shared with **Bloodloss**'s cover of Ike and Tina Turner's 'Nutbush City Limits') and 'More than Love' (shared with **feedtime's** 'Buffalo Bob'), plus the full-length album *Things that Play Themselves* (March 1989).

In late 1989, KSR undertook a two-month tour of the USA, playing with the likes of Babes in Toyland, Helmet and fellow Sydneysiders **The Hard-Ons**. While in the USA, the band recorded a new album with famed producer Butch Vig, who went on to worldwide acclaim for his work with Nirvana, Smashing Pumpkins and Sonic Youth, plus his own band Garbage. At the end of KSR's American tour, Tolnay worked with the Dead Kennedys' lead singer Jello Biafra and members of US band Steel Pole Bathtub as studio outfit Tumor Circus. The KSR album *Ground into the Dirt* (1990) was issued on the Amphetamine Reptile label in the USA and Megadisc in Europe. The Aberrant label imported copies into Australia. Following the album's release, Quinn and Bostle left KSR to be replaced by Paul Kitten (ex-Space Juniors) and Craig Rossi (ex-**Box of Fish**) respectively. KSR broke up at the end of 1990. KSR re-formed in 1993 to record but nothing eventuated.

Tolnay and Hill formed studio band Bushpig and issued the album *Bushpig* (June 1992). Also included in the Bushpig line-up at various stages were Paul Kitten (guitar), Guy Maddison (bass, keyboards; ex-**Lubricated Goat**), Stephen 'Bones' Martin (guitar; ex-Fester Brothers, **Deadly Hume**) and John Murphy (drums; ex-Whirlywirld, Slub, **Box the Jesuit**). Steve Turner (guitar) and Mark Arm (vocals, guitar) from Seattle grunge band Mudhoney also augmented the Bushpig line-up when they toured Australia.

In the meantime, Quinn formed industrial duo Deathless with Damian Bennett (bass, synthesiser, vocals). The duo's radically detuned soundscapes were pushed along by two basses, abrasive synthesiser noises and a melange of pounding drum machines. Deathless took its influences from the likes of UK industrial metallers Godflesh and Swiss techno-death band Celtic Frost. With little interest in Deathless's chosen genre locally, the duo relocated to London in 1992. The duo recorded the album *Anhedonia* with assistance from Godflesh's Justin Broadrick. It came out in February 1993 on the UK label Electrip. The duo's second album *Antilectual-Non Deathless*, came out on Electrip in 1995.

King Snake Roost albums: *From Barbarism to Christian Manhood* (Aberrant, 1987), *Things that Play Themselves* (Aberrant, 1989), *Ground into the Dirt* (Amphetamine Reptile, US import only, 1990); ***Bushpig album:*** *Bushpig* (PGK/Waterfront, 1992).

Kings Cross (*see* Massive Appendage)

Kings of the Sun

Formed: *1986*
Style: *Hard rock*
Original line-up: *Jeffrey Hoad (vocals, guitar; ex-Young Lions), Ron Thiessen (guitar; ex-***Uncanny X-Men***), Anthony Ragg (bass; ex-Ballistics), Clifford Hoad (drums; ex-Young Lions)*

Sydney band Kings of the Sun started life as a pop rock outfit, but made a name for themselves on the international touring circuit as an out-and-out hard rock band. The band's brand of southern-fried boogie rock combined the raunchiness of Aerosmith, the earthiness of **Rose Tattoo** and the gritty swagger of The Rolling Stones in one powerhouse unit. Lead singer Jeffrey Hoad was the archetypal flamboyant rock showman with his cascading blond locks, sassy stage moves and macho cool. Clifford Hoad was a flashy drummer whose ability to drive the music ever onwards was never in doubt.

The Hoad brothers got their start with ex-**Skyhooks'** guitarist Bob Spencer's band The Young Lions. When Spencer was offered the gig as replacement for John Brewster in **The Angels** at the start of 1986, he jumped at the opportunity. The Hoads formed their own band, Kings of the Sun, and signed to Mushroom Records. The band's debut single, 'Bottom of My Heart'/'Bad Love' (October 1986), created some interest, eventually reaching the national Top 20.

By the end of 1986, Kings of the Sun were on the verge of breaking up, but as luck would have it, RCA (America) executive Simon Lowe saw the band in Sydney and made them an offer on the spot. The band spent most of 1987 touring the US hard rock circuit before booking into the studio with famed producer/engineer Eddie Kramer (Jimi Hendrix, Led Zeppelin, Rolling Stones). Ron Thiessen had left the band by that stage and Jeffrey Hoad handled all of the guitar parts on the album, until Glen Morris arrived to add his touch in the live situation. *Kings of the Sun* (October 1988) was a no-frills, hard rock album with a raw feel for pop economy. It produced two singles, the tongue-in-cheek swamp-stomp 'Serpentine'/'Wild Cat' (July) and the playful 'Black Leather'/'Bad Love' (October). The music was hardly innovative, but it did provide the jagged link between the fullsome heavy metal racket of Guns N' Roses and the brazen retro feel of The Georgia Satellites, while also avoiding the pitfalls of the glam-metal fraternity (Poison, etc.) in the process. Kings of the Sun toured the USA (supporting Joe Satriani) and Europe (supporting Kiss), only returning to Australia at the end of 1988.

The band ran foul of the corporate rock machine when it supported American visitors Guns N' Roses at the Sydney Entertainment Centre. Jeffrey Hoad took to the stage with a leather whip and dropped his pants in front of the audience. He also let his opinions on Guns N' Roses be known. Guns N' Roses frontman Axl Rose wasted no time in denigrating Kings of the Sun, apologising for allowing them to open the show. This sealed the band's fate in the eyes of local audiences, despite the fact that Kings of the Sun were one of *the* classic Australian hard rock bands in the tradition of **AC/DC**, **Rose Tattoo** and **The Angels**.

Nevertheless, Kings of the Sun continued to tour overseas. Morris left in mid-1989, only to return eight months later after having played with **The Screaming Tribesmen**. Kings of the Sun issued their second album, *Full Frontal Attack*, in August 1990. It produced the singles 'Drop the Gun'/'Haunt You Baby' (July) and the ballad 'I Get Lonely' (October). The band returned to the USA for the opening slot on guitarist Lita Ford's American tour, before embarking on an Australian jaunt with **The Screaming Jets** in early 1991.

Morris and Ragg left Kings of the Sun in 1992 (Morris formed Bloodshot and Ragg went on to form disco/funk covers band Stone Cold Boners). The Hoads recruited American Brad Spurr (bass) and continued as a three-piece. The band's third album, *Resurrection* (May 1993), and the singles 'Trapped Inside Your Heart' (April) and 'Road to Nowhere' (July) offered further doses of raunchy rock'n'roll. Kings of the Sun supported **Jimmy Barnes** on his 1993 Australian tour. American Phil Soussan replaced Spurr and Kings of the Sun issued the single 'Bombs Away' in September 1995.

Albums: *Kings of the Sun* (Mushroom/Festival, 1988), *Full Frontal Attack* (Mushroom/Festival, 1990), *Resurrection* (Mushroom/Festival, 1993).

Kiss My Poodles Donkey

Formed: *1991*
Style: *Rock*
Original line-up: *Paul Kidney (vocals), Chris Townsend (guitar, vocals), Doug Ironside (guitar), Dave Bullock (percussion, samples), Glenda (bass), Richard Berckelman (drums)*

This Sydney band produced a curious blend of hard rock, mutant funk, swamp-blues and free-form jazz. The combination did not always work in the live situation, being too monochromatic to carry the weight. On the other hand, the band developed an adventurousness in the studio that overcame such restrictions. Very much in the vein of that other unclassifiable Sydney band, **Box the Jesuit**, Kiss My Poodles Donkey appealed to eclectic tastes.

Hot issued the band's eponymous mini-album in late 1991. Angela Chenowyth (bass; ex-Stone Circus) replaced Glenda in 1992. The band's full-length debut album *New Hope for the Dead* (October 1993) was patchy, ranging from noisy hard rock ('The Lizard', 'Psychoman') to dreary funk (a cover of Prince's 'Gett Off'). Townsend also worked with **The Celibate Rifles'** guitarist Kent Steedman under the moniker Crent. With the break-up of Kiss My Poodles Donkey in 1994 Townsend (bass, clarinet, percussion, vocals) formed improvised noise/free-form jazz/ambient band Whore with Peter Jones (guitar, vocals) and Paul Larson (drums). The band issued one self-titled album on the Black Hole label in April 1996.

Albums: *Kiss My Poodles Donkey* (Hot, 1991), *New Hope for the Dead* (Hot, 1993).

Knievel (*see* the Welcome Mat)

Grace Knight

Style: *Pop, jazz*

UK-born singer Grace Knight first came to national prominence with **Eurogliders**. That band's smooth blend of synth pop, dance-funk and soul garnered positive reviews, hit singles and a strong following. With the band's demise in 1989, Knight initially sang back-up vocals in the Tania Bowra Band, before launching a solo career in the jazz-pop field.

With little experience in singing jazz, Knight recorded the soundtrack to the ABC-TV miniseries *Come in Spinner* with acclaimed jazz musician Vince Jones. The soundtrack album featured 1940s jazz standards and produced three singles, 'I've Got You Under My Skin' (sung by Jones), 'The Man I Love' and 'Sophisticated Lady'. The album reached #5 on the national chart in May 1990. Knight also took a small acting role in the series. Knight's debut solo single was another standard, 'Fever', which was lifted from her debut album, *Stormy Weather* in September 1991. *Stormy Weather* peaked at #14 on the national chart in October.

In contrast to the low-key *Stormy Weather*, Knight's second solo album, *Gracious*, featured a total of 43 session musicians. It contained big, brassy and busy arrangements of standards like 'On a Clear Day', 'Moondance', 'Cry Me a River' and 'Papa Was a Rolling Stone'. Knight returned in February 1996 with the album *Live*.

Albums: *Come in Spinner* (soundtrack shared with Vince Jones, ABC, 1990), *Stormy Weather* (Sony/Columbia, 1991), *Gracious* (Dino, 1993), *Live* (1996).

Peter Koppes (*see* The Church)

The Kravats

Formed: *1958*
Style: *Beat pop*
Original line-up: *Norm Walker (vocals), Noel Best (lead guitar), Ray Woodruff (rhythm guitar, vocals), Richard Millhouse (bass), Max Johns (drums)*

Alongside The Planets and Chaos & Co., The Kravats were Tasmania's premier rock'n'roll combo of the early 1960s. The Kravats held the residency at Hobart's first teen dance, The Spook Club, for many years. Although the band made frequent trips to the mainland, sustained success elsewhere was limited. Then again, having been dubbed 'Tasmania's answer to The Beatles' and The 'Mighty' Kravats in their home state, there seemed little need to venture further afield.

The Kravats' original lead singer, Norm Walker, left before the band became famous in Hobart. Ray Woodruff took over the vocal chores. By 1963, The Kravats were perfecting their own 'Shadows sound' and signed to the W&G label. The band's debut instrumental single, 'Puppet Strings'/'Bei Mir Bist Duschoen' (August 1964) reached #2 on the Tasmanian charts and #5 on the Perth charts. The Perth success was down to the fact that one-time Tasmanian DJ Keith McGowan had moved to the Western Australian capital and plugged The Kravats' single regularly on the local 6PR radio station. The band made a successful tour of Perth in 1965, scoring a few appearances on **Johnny Young's** *Club 17* television pop show.

Meanwhile, the band's second instrumental single, 'Fred'/'Jindivick', reached the Tasmania Top 5 in early 1965. At that stage, the band added Barry Woodruff as lead vocalist and developed a more contemporary beat-pop sound. The band's cover of The Animals' 'Baby Let Me Take You Home'/'Balai Hai' reached #1 in Tasmania, holding out The Beatles' 'Help' from the top spot for three weeks. The Kravats were regulars on local television shows like *Saturday Stomp* and *Saturday Party*. The band recorded four more singles, 'It Must Be Jelly'/'Stavark' (September 1965), 'Come on Back'/'Well All Right' (May 1966), 'We're Gonna Howl Tonight'/'The Pain is Here' (October 1966) and 'That's What I Want'/'It's Unlikely' (March 1967), plus the EP *We the Kravats* (1965) before parting company with W&G.

According to Dean Mittelhauser's article on The Kravats in his *Livin' End* fanzine (Issue #7), the band continued to gig right up until the late 1980s, although no further records were forthcoming.

Russ Kruger

Style: *Beat pop*

Singer Russ Kruger was the younger brother of famed rock'n'roller **Johnny Rebb**. With his blond hair and clean-cut good looks, Kruger was often dismissed as a lightweight teen idol pop star. Nevertheless, he boasted heavyweight backing for his eight solo singles from redoubtable hit-makers **The Atlantics**. **The Atlantics** had made a name for themselves as the country's foremost surf instrumental band, scoring hits with the likes of 'Bombora' and 'The Crusher'. By 1966, **The Atlantics'** chart run had come to an end. Although the band continued to produce quality singles under its own name, it became better known for providing studio backing for the abovementioned singers.

According to the discography in Dean Mittelhauser's *The Livin' End* fanzine, Kruger's singles backed by **The Atlantics** were: 'Well, That Ain't Nice'/'Tallahassie Lassie' (January 1966, Leedon), 'Baby, Baby Don't Go'/'Little Bit O' Soul' (March 1966, Leedon), 'Splish Splash'/'Separate the Men from the Boys' (May 1966, Leedon), 'Keep Me Satisfied'/'Tell the Truth' (October 1966, Sunshine), 'Look at My Baby'/'Little Girl' (February 1967, Sunshine), 'I'm a Little Boy'/'My Way of Thinking' (October 1967, Ramrod), 'I Don't Love You No More'/'Move It Baby' (February 1968, Ramrod) and 'Rainbow Ride'/'Money to Burn' (July, 1969, Ramrod). Raven included the Kruger track 'Keep Me Satisfied' on the Various Artists compilation *Ugly Things #3* (1987).

The Kryptonics

Formed: *1985*
Style: *Garage rock*
Original line-up: *Michael Reynolds (vocals), Ian Underwood (guitar, vocals), Cathy Webb (bass), Shakir Pichler (drums)*

The Kryptonics formed in Perth, Western Australia, during August 1985. Early on The Kryptonics boasted a primitive Cramps-inspired edge to their garage-punk sound. The band adopted the black leather/guitar-grunge look of their Sydney forebears like **The Lime Spiders** and **The Trilobites**. By 1988, the band had evolved into a tough yet melodic power pop outfit. Over the course of seven years, Ian Underwood was the only constant member.

The Kryptonics issued the single 'Baby'/'Plastic Imitation' on the local Cherry Top label (January 1986). By mid-1986, the band's line-up was Underwood, Cathy Webb, Peter Hartley (guitar; ex-Rockafellas, X-Offenders, Lavender Disaster) and Brett Ford (drums; ex-Exhibit A, Rockafellas, Kansas City Killers). The new line-up recorded the second single, 'Land That Time Forgot'/'She's Got Germs' (on the Easter label, January 1987), and the flexi-single 'Cyclops'/'Rock Me to Sleep' which came with issue #6 of *Vortex* fanzine

The Kryptonics fell apart in mid-1987, and Underwood assembled a new line-up comprising Greg Hitchcock (guitar; ex-**Bamboos**, Neptunes), Jeff Halley (bass; ex-Sunstones) and Russell Hopkinson (drums; ex-**Vicious Circle**, Cremator, **Bamboos**). That line-up recorded the mini-album *69*, issued by Sydney-based label Waterfront in May 1989. Meanwhile, ex-members Hartley and Ford had joined Stuart Gray (aka Stu Spasm) in the first line-up of noise terrorists **Lubricated Goat**. Hopkinson and Hitchcock later joined forces again in **You Am I**.

By 1989, The Kryptonics line-up was Underwood, Halley, Tony Rushan (guitar, vocals; ex-Ritual) and Andrew Robinson (drums; ex-Ritual) who was soon replaced by Peter Kostic. The Underwood/Halley/Rushan/Kostic line-up toured and issued the single 'When It's Over'/'Oedipus Complex' on Waterfront (September 1989). The next line-up of Underwood, Rushan, Kostic and Greg Brennan (bass) recorded a new single for the Seaside label, 'Bad September'/'Another Girl Another Planet' (live), 'Telephone Line' (live) which appeared in November 1990. Richard Corey replaced Brennan in July 1990, and the band relocated to Sydney in August. The Kryptonics issued a 12-inch EP, 'Tonka Tuff', on the Zero Hour label in 1991 before parting company.

Rushan went on to form Sydney sludge rock band Harpoon. James McCann (vocals), Sabrina Collins (bass), Gavin Lewis (bass), Allan Miller (drums) and Tim Fagen (sax) completed the line-up. Harpoon created brooding, experimental soundscapes, with an ambient, industrial-strength edge pushed along by two bass players. The original line-up lasted about a year. Rushan left but was not replaced. Murray Shepherd (drums; ex-**Fun Things**, **Screaming Tribesmen**) and Dave Bullock (percussion) replaced Miller. That line-up of Harpoon issued the seven-track album *Fork Tongued Pressed and Greasy* in March 1996.

Meanwhile, Ian Underwood formed a new band Challenger 7 in 1994 with help from two other ex-Kryptonics, Peter Kostic and Richard Corey, who by then were also members of **Front End Loader**. Greg Hitchcock (by then in **The Verys**) completed the Challenger 7 line-up. The band recorded one CD EP, 'Morris', before breaking up; the CD EP appeared in August 1995.

Kryptonics mini-album: *69* (Waterfront, 1989); ***Harpoon album:*** *Fork Tongued Pressed and Greasy* (Black Hole, 1996).

Ku Klux Frankenstein

Formed: *1983*
Style: *Gothic acid-rock*
Original line-up: *Neild Schneider (aka Neild Stein, vocals, sax), Lindsay Brunsdon (aka Lindsay Storm, guitar, vocals; ex-Hear Hear), Kerrie Hickin (aka Kerrie Van Lewin, bass; ex-Lynching Party), Andrew Flossos (aka Andrew Frank, drums)*

Melbourne inner-city band Ku Klux Frankenstein had a propensity to be inspirational and wildly erratic in the space of one performance. The band's sound was built around a rumbling rhythm section, Lindsay Brunsdon's abrasive acid-rock guitar fireworks and Neild Schneider's gravel-pit vocals overlaid with a sinister Gothic atmosphere. The band played the inner-city circuit alongside other like-minded outfits such as **Cosmic Psychos, Venom P. Stinger**, Tombstone Hands, Gothic Farmyard and Pizza Sluts.

Ku Klux Frankenstein recorded a demo, 'Baby You Light Up My Cigarette', which became a favourite on public radio station 3PBS-FM. The band's self-titled 12-inch EP on the Crash label (1985) featured slop-bucket production values and a murky sound that did little to entice the unsuspecting listener. In 1986, Ku Klux Frankenstein became known as Fire, perhaps as a result of having burnt its bridges in terms of acceptance beyond its inner-city enclave. In early 1987, Fire issued the album . . . *A Frame of Purple Roses* and single 'Rosemary Rosary'/'Savage Summer', 'Baby You Light Up My Cigarette' on the Cleopatra label. Album cuts like 'Lion of Love' and 'Make It Through the Night' revealed a band with the strength of its convictions. Rodney Kuna replaced Hickin on bass, but by the end of 1987 Fire had broken up.

Following Fire's break-up, Brunsdon played with The Wet Ones, Dirty Strangers and Charles Marshall and the Body Electric. Hickin went on to **The Sunset Strip, Autohaze** and **Holocene**. Schneider turned his hand to acting and took bit parts in television shows like *Blue Heelers*. Flossos went on to complete his medical studies.

Fire album: . . . *A Frame of Purple Roses* (Cleopatra, 1987).

Ed Kuepper

Style: Rock

With 18 solo albums to his credit (not to mention 15 as a member of **The Saints, Laughing Clowns** and **The Aints**), Ed Kuepper (b. 1955) is one of Australia's most prolific and respected recording artists. He is also one of the most adventurous and distinctive Australian songwriters of recent decades.

German-born Kuepper's career commenced in Brisbane during 1973 with **The Saints**. He formed **Laughing Clowns** following the split of the original Saints in 1978. The Clowns lasted until December 1984, after which Kuepper recorded his first solo album, the stark and angular *Electrical Storm* (October 1985), on which he played most of the instruments. In 1986 he formed The Yard Goes on Forever, which comprised Louis Burdett (drums; ex-Powerhouse), who was replaced a month later by Mark Dawson (ex-**John Kennedy's Love Gone Wrong**), Michael Arthur (guitar) and Paul Smith (bass; ex-**Laughing Clowns**). Kuepper derived the band's name from the title of the Richard Harris album *The Yard Went on Forever*. Stalwart drummer Dawson remained Kuepper's musical sidekick for many years.

The 1987 line-up of The Yard Goes on Forever featured Smith, Dawson, Jim Bowman (keyboards) and Rebecca Hancock (backing vocals). The albums *Rooms of the Magnificent* (January 1987) and *Everybody's Got to* (June 1988) consolidated the band's impressive live standing and contained many fine examples of guitar/horn-driven rock. *Rooms* produced the singles 'Also Sprach the King of Euro-Disco'/'Without Your Mirror' (December 1986) and 'Sea-Air'/'I'm Your Prince' (May 1987). *Everybody's Got to* cracked the mainstream Top 40. It gave rise to five singles: 'Not a Soul Around'/ 'Rooms of the Magnificent' (June 1987), 'Nothing Changes in My House'/'At Times So Emotional' (November 1987), '(When There's) This Party'/ 'One Good Reason' (April 1988), 'Too Many Clues'/ 'Spartan Spirituals' (July) and 'Burned My Fingers'/ 'Sixteen Days', 'Sentimental Jokes' (September), all of which performed well on the independent charts.

Michael Couvret (ex-**Celibate Rifles, Lime Spiders**) replaced Smith on bass at the end of 1988. The Yard Goes on Forever's final release was the limited edition *Happy as Hell* EP in 1989. The EP contained the band's versions of one **Saints** ('Everything's Fine') and three **Laughing Clowns** tracks ('Sometimes', 'Ghost of an Ideal Wife' and 'New Bully in Town'). It was only ever available for one month. Following 11 rock albums, Kuepper returned to basics with his acoustic album *Today Wonder* (October 1990). Recorded on a shoestring budget, using unconventional guitar effects and an unusual drumkit, Kuepper and Mark Dawson proved that less is more with a mix of new tunes and covers (including a re-working of **Laughing Clowns'** 'Eternally Yours').

From there, Kuepper's work rate increased threefold. He formed **The Aints**, with whom he issued three fiery, distortion-drenched albums *S.L.S.Q.* (May 1991), *Ascension* (December 1991) and *Autocannibalism* (June 1992). With blistering, guitar-heavy tracks like 'Like an Oil Spill', 'It's Still Nowhere', 'Ill Wind' and 'Linda and Abilene', these albums were the antithesis of Ed's solo work. In early 1991, Kuepper also formed the ambient instrumental band Mephisto Waltz with Mark Dawson and jazz pianist **Chris Abrahams**. The band toured but did not issue any records. In between, Kuepper

Ed Kuepper

found time to release a direct follow up to *Today Wonder*. Featuring the hook-laden single 'The Way I Made You Feel' (April 1992), *Honey Steel's Gold* (November 1991) was Ed's most successful album to date. It reached #28 on the national album chart at the start of 1992, the highest mainstream placement for an independent album to that time.

In August, 1992, two months after **The Aints'** *Autocannibalism* appeared, Kuepper issued *Black Ticket Day*. Radio-friendly songs like the hypnotic 'Real Wild Life' and 'Black Ticket Day' (both issued as singles in June and December 1992 respectively) sat alongside fully orchestrated, lengthy pieces like 'Blind Girl Stripper' and 'Walked Thin Wires'. The album received the 1992 Australian Record Industry Association (ARIA) Award for Best Independent Album.

By April 1993, Kuepper was back at the top of the alternative chart with *Serene Machine*, an album of 12 sparse, pop-oriented songs including the single 'Sleepy Head (Serene Machine)' (May) that emphasised his melodic guitar playing and songwriting skills. Kuepper set off on tour again with his new band The Serene Machine. *Serene Machine* earned Kuepper his second ARIA Award in a row for Best Independent Album. 1993 drew to a close for Kuepper with the release of *The Butterfly Net* compilation (November). That hand-picked retrospective set drew together 14 tracks from *Electrical Storm* to *Black Ticket Day*, plus the four cuts from the rare *Happy as Hell* EP.

After more than a year away from the studio, Kuepper returned with *Character Assassination* (July 1994). Once again the album highlighted his ability to work with different arrangements. It contained a re-working of **The Aints'** 'Ill Wind', and a cover of the **Phil Jones and the Unknown Blues'** late 1960s hit 'If I Had A Ticket' which was issued as a CD single (March 1994). Early copies of *Character Assassination* contained a bonus disc called *Death to the Howdy-doody Brigade* which featured the original undubbed masters of the album. Kuepper contributed a cover of **The Loved Ones'** 'Sad Dark Eyes' to the Various Artists *Earth Music* album issued on the Mushroom label (June 1994). Kuepper dubbed his 1994 band The Institute of Nude Wrestling after a sign on the cover of Alice Cooper's 1974 album *Muscle of Love*. The line-up comprised Kuepper, Dawson, Brian Mann (guitar; ex-**Girlies, Headstones, Screaming Tribesmen, Lime Spiders**), Barry Turnbull (bass; ex-**John Kennedy's Love Gone Wrong**, Widdershins) and Linda Neil (violin).

In early 1995, Kuepper embarked on his first solo, overseas tour which took in dates across the USA, Canada and Europe. His tenth solo album, *A King in the Kindness Room* (October 1995), included the wry CD single 'Wasn't I Pissed Off Today?' (August), the orchestrated epic 'Messin' Part II' and Kuepper's tortured rendition of **AC/DC's** 'Highway to Hell', which also appeared on the **AC/DC** tribute album *Fuse Box: The Alternative Tribute* (on BMG, May 1995). 'Highway to Hell' appeared as a CD single in October. Kuepper also issued two limited edition mail order only albums in 1995, and ended the year with another compilation, *Sings His Greatest Hit for You*.

With its tongue-in-cheek title and a cover with which Kuepper paid tribute to the likes of Richard Harris, this was another worthy release featuring tracks drawn from *Serene Machine*, *Character Assassination* and *A King in the Kindness Room*. Kuepper issued a new CD single, 'Fireman Joe', in July 1996, followed by 'All of These Things' and the ambitious *Frontierland* album (one of Kuepper's very best records) during October. Initial copies came with an extra disc, the 13-track compilation *Samplerland*. In March 1997, Kuepper issued a third mail order album *Starstruck . . . Music for Films & Adverts*, which featured 28 diverse instrumentals. The album appeared commercially under the truncated title of *Starstruck*, and with two tracks deleted.

Kuepper followed this up with the third CD single lifted from the *Frontierland* album, 'Weepin' Willow' (May). That same month he left Australia for a solo tour of Europe. The tour resulted in the live album *With a Knapsack on My Back* (October 1997), which had been recorded in Germany. Kuepper's fourth compilation album, *The Wheelie Bin Affair* (an odds-and-sods collection culled from recent singles), came out in September. By that stage Kuepper had his new band on the road, The Oxley Creek Playboys (Alex Compton, bass; Simon Cox, drums; ex-**Juice**, **Died Pretty**). They recorded a new album, *Cloudland*, which was due for release in early 1998.

Albums: *Electrical Storm* (Hot, 1985), *Rooms of the Magnificent* (True Tone/Hot, 1987), *Everybody's Got to* (True Tone/Hot, 1988), *Today Wonder* (Hot, 1990), *Honey Steel's Gold* (Hot/Shock, 1991), *Black Ticket Day* (Hot/Shock, 1992), *Serene Machine* (Hot/Shock, 1993), *The Butterfly Net* (Hot/Shock, 1993), *Character Assassination* (Hot/Shock, 1994), *A King in the Kindness Room* (Hot/Shock, 1995), *I Was a Mail Order Bridegroom* (limited edition mail order, Hot, 1995), *Exotic Mail Order Moods* (limited edition mail order, Hot, 1995), *Sings His Greatest Hit for You* (Hot/Shock, 1995), *Frontierland* (Hot/TWA, 1996), *Samplerland* (Hot/TWA, 1996), *Starstruck . . . Music for Films & Adverts* (limited edition mail order, Hot, 1997), *Starstruck* (Hot, 1997), *The Wheelie Bin Affair* (Hot, 1997), *With a Knapsack on My Back* (Hot, 1997).

Kush

Formed: *1971*
Style: *Jazz rock*
Original line-up: *Geoff Duff (aka* **Jeff Duff**, *vocals), Roger Pell (guitar), John Ellis (sax, clarinet, flute), Ron Anderson (piano, sax, flute), Colin Chapman (trumpet, flugel horn), John Hughes (trumpet, trombone), Rob Mathews (bass), Graham McDonald (drums)*

Melbourne band Kush established a reputation as one of the most entertaining outfits on the Australian early 1970s pub rock scene. Fronted by the androgynous Geoff Duff, the band mixed appealing Blood Sweat and Tears/Chicago-styled jazz-rock with outrageous and bizarre stage antics. One of the band's more notable on-stage escapades managed to incur the wrath of various religious and societal groups of the day. During the band's deliberately blasphemous (but tongue-in-cheek) 'Satanic Deity', the waif-like, fish-net-stocking-clad Duff would assume the role of Beelzebub himself while ripping up the Bible! It was all in the name of good fun, but not everyone took it that way. Nevertheless, Kush produced a number of interesting records including the album *Snow White . . . and the Eight Straights.*

Kush evolved out of club band Clickety Clack. Duff was the last to join. Other bands like Nova Express, SCRA and **Heart 'n' Soul** had already mined a similar vein of brass-laden big band rock. Dave Herzog and Ian Mason replaced Roger Pell and Ron Anderson respectively not long after formation. Pell went on to form **Pantha**. Kush signed to Warner Brothers in 1973. The loud and brassy cover of Henry Mancini's 'Peter Gunn'/'Sky is Falling' (July) was an obvious choice for a debut single, but it was not really indicative of the band's overall style.

The second single, 'Wait'/'Can't You Hear Me Calling?' (November 1973), worked better as a re-recorded album track on the band's debut LP *Snow White . . . and the Eight Straights*. By the time the band came to record the album in early 1974, Steve Ball had replaced Mason, Nick Lister had replaced McDonald, John Santos had replaced Chapman, Ian Hellings (ex-Nova Express) had replaced Hughes and Bill Harrower (ex-**Levi Smith's Clefs**) had replaced Anderson. *Snow White . . . and the Eight Straights* (September 1974) mixed campy jazz-pop ('Easy Street') and hard jazz-rock ('All Right in the City', 'Satanic Deity', 'Klue') with dramatic, orchestrated epics ('Christopher John' and Jim Webb's 'McArthur Park'). 'Easy Street'/'All Right in the City' (#17 in Melbourne during October 1974) and 'McArthur Park'/'Klue' (April 1975) were issued as singles. The album also peaked at #5 on the Melbourne chart.

At the end of 1974, Ellis left and Clive Harrison replaced Mathews on bass. By early 1975, the line-up comprised Duff, Herzog, Ball, Harrison, Lister and Arthur Robinson (sax, flute, clarinet, violin). That line-up recorded the desultory *Nah, Tellus Wh't Kush Means Yer Great Sausage* album and single 'I'm Your Football'/'Out of My Tree' (February 1975), both of which sank without a trace. The band's final single, 'Banana Song'/'Whatever Happened to the Good Ol' Days' (June 1975), was credited to Geoff Duff and Kush. One month later, Kush broke up, and Duff formed the Geoff Duff Survival Band. Duff re-formed Kush in March 1977, ostensibly to help promote his debut solo single, a cover of The Knight Brothers' 'Temptation's 'Bout to Get Me'/'Where Will I Be Tomorrow?'.

The line-up was Duff, Ellis, Anderson, Santos, Ted Joiner (trumpet), Dave Sterry (guitar), Peter Sullivan (keyboards), Gary Costello (bass) and Bob Bickerton (drums; ex-Rock Granite and the Profiles,

Mondo Rock). Other players came and went, including Richard Zartorski (keyboards); Zartorski and Sterry later went on to **Real Life**. The re-formed Kush only performed for a matter of months before breaking up permanently. **Jeff Duff** concentrated on his solo career, eventually travelling to the UK and assuming the eccentric Duffo persona.

Albums: *Snow White . . . and the Eight Straights* (Warner Bros, 1974), *Nah, Tellus Wh't Kush Means Yer Great Sausage* (RCA, 1975).

L

La De Das

Formed: *1964*
Style: *R&B, boogie*
Original line-up: *Phil Key (lead vocals, guitar), Trevor Wilson (bass, vocals), Kevin Borich (lead guitar, vocals), Brett Neilson (drums)*

From their beginnings as a tough garage/R&B band to their final years as an exciting hard rock/boogie outfit, New Zealand's La De Das did it all. Over the course of ten years together, La De Das recorded five albums, toured Britain and Europe, scored hit singles and established themselves as one of the most innovative bands in Australia.

When a bunch of idealistic 16-year-old musicians formed La De Das (originally called The Mergers) in Auckland during 1964, they had immediate designs on following in the footsteps of national heroes like Ray Columbus and the Invaders and **Max Merritt and the Meteors**. Alongside the likes of **The Pleazers**, Chants R&B, The Avengers, The Gremlins, The Underdogs, Larry's Rebels and Human Instinct, La De Das were at the forefront of a vibrant New Zealand pop scene. La De Das' debut single, 'Little Girl'/'Ever Since that Night' (June 1965), was a low-key slice of Rolling Stones-derived R&B issued on the local Talent City label. Bruce Howard (organ, vocals) joined La De Das in 1965 and the band turned professional. La De Das signed to Philips and issued the classic single, The Blues Magoos' 'How is the Air Up There?'/'The Pied Piper', which reached #4 on the New Zealand charts in May 1966. The single also topped the Sydney charts.

From there the band issued one tough garage-punk single after another: 'Don't You Stand in My Way'/'I Take What I Want' (June 1966), Chester Burnett's 'On Top of the World'/'Hey Girl' (November), Bruce Channel's 'Hey Baby'/'Other Love' (a New Zealand #1 in March 1967), 'All Purpose Low'/'My Girl' (June) and 'Rosalie'/'Find Us a Way' (September). The band's first two albums, *La De Das* and *Find Us a Way*, plus the EP 'Stupidity', are also highly regarded by 1960s aficionados. Having conquered New Zealand, La De Das set their sights on Australia. La De Das made one tentative foray on to the Australian scene in mid-1967, but their brand of R&B made little impact. By the time La De Das arrived back in Australia at the start of 1968 (with new drummer Bryan Harris, ex-Action), they had changed direction. La De Das were one of the first local bands to include covers of Vanilla Fudge, Doors and Traffic (and later The Band) material in its repertoire. Billed as 'The Beautiful La De Das', the band was at the forefront of the Australian flower power movement.

With new drummer Keith Barber (ex-**Wild Cherries**) on board, the band set about recording its ambitious concept album *The Happy Prince* (based on the Oscar Wilde fairytale). 1969 was the year of the rock opera (The Pretty Things' *S.F. Sorrow*, The Who's *Tommy*, The Kinks' *Arthur*) and, upon its release in April, *The Happy Prince* was praised for its quality musicianship and production values. Despite the fine playing, it was an overly serious and flawed album, and duly sank without a trace. 'Come and Fly with Me'/'Swallow Little Swallow' was lifted as a single in May.

La De Das flew to the UK in April 1969. By that stage, psychedelia had been replaced by Led Zeppelin-style heavy blues, and La De Das' brand of soft psychedelic pop was outdated. La De Das did record a version of The Beatles' 'Come Together'/'Here is Love' as a single (September 1969), but the disastrous nine-month UK sojourn did little for the band's confidence. Back in Australia, La De Das changed direction again, and were eventually hailed as one of the funkiest, hard-driving rock outfits in Australia. It was this concept of straightforward, gutsy rock'n'roll which resulted in La De Das, **Billy Thorpe** and the Aztecs and **Daddy Cool** becoming the country's three top groups by 1972.

Meanwhile, Wilson had not returned from the UK. In disarray, the band recruited fellow New Zealander Reno Tehei (bass; ex-Compulsion, Luke's Walnut, Genesis). Wilson eventually returned to the fold as guitarist, but the three-guitar line-up just did not work. The band's tenth single, the delicate, flute-led ballad 'Sweet Girl'/'I Can't

Find a Reason' (January 1971) bombed. 1970 had been a transitional year for the band, and by the end of it Howard had left to join **Levi Smith's Clefs** (and later **Billy Thorpe** and the Aztecs), Wilson had also departed (later to join **Home**) and Tehei had been deported back to New Zealand. With the addition of Peter Roberts on bass (ex-**Freshwater**), La De Das spent 1971 consolidating their position as one of the hardest working bands on the scene.

The funky, infectious singles 'Gonna See My Baby Tonight'/'Fare Thee Well' (September 1971) and 'Morning Good Morning'/'You and Me' (March 1972) were national hits, reaching #12 and #24 respectively. Key and Roberts left in October 1972 to form **Band of Light**, and as a three-piece (with new bass player Ronnie Peel; ex-**Missing Links**, **Pleazers**, **Rockwell T. James** and the Rhythm Aces, Browns, One Ton Gypsy), La De Das pulled out all stops. The band featured prominently at the inaugural Sunbury Pop Festival, January 1972, and alongside The Aztecs and **Friends** managed to attract one of the largest crowds ever assembled in Australia at a concert at Melbourne's Myer Music Bowl (estimated at over 200 000 people).

Borich was now firmly entrenched as Australia's guitar hero supremo; his superb rendition of Jimi Hendrix's workout on Dylan's 'All Along the Watchtower' became a signature, and the band was never allowed to finish a gig until delivering it. The fiery *Rock and Roll Sandwich* (the band's first album in five years, issued November 1973) remains a classic boogie rock album. The singles 'I'll Never Stop Loving You'/'It's the Beginning' (December 1972) and 'The Place'/'No Law Against Having Fun' (March 1974) maintained the pace but were not chart hits. The band's final singles, punchy, commercial covers of Chuck Berry's 'Too Pooped to Pop'/'She Tell Me What to Do' (#26 in July 1974) and Hank Williams' 'Honky Tonkin''/'Temple Shuffle' (August 1974), were minor national hits. 'Too Pooped to Pop' also peaked at #13 in Melbourne. La De Das supported UK glam-rocker Gary Glitter on his July 1974 Australian tour.

In March 1975, EMI gathered up the band's recent singles and four unissued tracks for the compilation album *Legend* as something of a contractual obligation. By May 1975, the band had run its course. After playing with **John Paul Young** and the All Stars for several months, Borich re-formed La De Das briefly with a line-up comprising Peel, Warren Morgan (piano; ex-**Billy Thorpe** and the Aztecs) and Johnny Dick (drums; ex-**Billy Thorpe** and the Aztecs), all of whom were also concurrently in The All Stars. By early 1976, Borich had formed the **Kevin Borich Express**, an outfit that he fronted well into the 1990s.

Albums: *La De Das* (Philips, 1966), *Find Us a Way* (Philips, 1967), *The Happy Prince* (EMI, 1969), *Rock and Roll Sandwich* (EMI, 1973), *Legend* (EMI, 1975), *La De Das Anthology—Rock'n'Roll Decade 1964–74* (EMI, 1981).

La Femme

Formed: *1978*
Style: *Punk, rock*
Original line-up: *Chane Chane (vocals), Brett Walker (guitar), Graham Schiavello (bass; ex-***Teenage Radio Stars***), Peter Kidd (drums; ex-***Teenage Radio Stars***)*

Led by a confident frontman in Chane Chane and a flashy guitarist in Brett Walker, Melbourne band La Femme was essentially a heavy metal band in glitter/punk trappings. The band played the inner-city scene alongside all the other new bands of the day like **Models**, The Boys Next Door, **The Ears**, **Little Murders** and **News**.

As Bruce Milne has pointed out, La Femme had a strong rapport with audiences, and for that reason was readily accepted on the suburban pub circuit where many other punk bands of the day would have been despised. La Femme signed to **Keith Glass**'s Missing Link label and issued the single 'Chelsea Kids'/'I Wanna Be Your Man' (June 1979). La Femme scored an appearance on ***Countdown***, but because the show's producers took exception to the lyrical content of 'Chelsea Kids', the band went to air miming to the inferior cover of Lennon/McCartney's 'I Wanna Be Your Man'.

Bob Furst (keyboards; ex-Liners) joined La Femme in January 1980, appearing on the band's second single, 'I Don't Want to Go Home'/'All Day and All of the Night' (May 1980). Missing Link issued the band's debut album, *La Femme*, in June. The album contained a number of fine examples of the band's confident, swaggering punk-metal sound ('Chelsea Kids', 'Doe See Doe', 'Boys Next Door').

In early 1981, Walker and Furst left the band to form Shy Boys; Schiavello also departed. The remaining two members recruited brothers Shaun (guitar) and Mark Gardener (bass) plus Gary McFarlane (keyboards). The new line-up recorded a final single, 'Looking for a Laugh'/'No-one Talks' (November 1981) before breaking up at the end of 1982. In 1983, Chane and Kidd recruited Colin Trott (guitar), Grant McDonough (guitar) and Andrew McDonough (bass), but that line-up was short-lived. Since that time, the Chane/Walker/

Kidd/Schiavello line-up has re-formed on at least two occasions (1988 and 1992) for tours. Bob Furst later became publisher of Melbourne street music paper *Beat*.

Album: *La Femme* (Missing Link/7 Records, 1980).

The Lab

Formed: *1991*
Style: *Electronic dance*
Original line-up: *Yolanda Podolski (vocals), Paul McDermott (keyboards, samples), Warwick Factor (bass, vocals)*

Sydney-based trio The Lab played a catchy brand of electronic pop that mixed bold, mesmerising beats with layered dance-pop, all wrapped up in rhythmic washes of textured keyboard sounds and Podolski's operatic vocals (not that far removed from UK bands like Portishead). McDermott also moonlighted with his other band, techno-dance outfit **Itch-E & Scratch-E**, but unlike them The Lab concentrated on a more emotional and accessible sound.

The Lab signed to the Ra label and issued the CD EP *Ultra* in November 1992. With **Itch-E & Scratch-E** taking up much of McDermott's time, The Lab did not follow up until the *Terminal* CD EP came out in March 1994. *Terminal* contained 'Lifetime', an infectious slice of dance-pop. The band's debut album, *Labyrinth* (September 1997), was a diverse release that yielded the lush and uplifting CD singles 'Beautiful Sadness' (1996) and 'I Will Find You' (August 1997).

Album: *Labyrinth* (Ra/BMG, 1997).

The Last Words

Formed: *1977*
Style: *Punk*
Original line-up: *Malcolm Baxter (vocals), Andy Groome (guitar), Mick Smith (bass), Jeffrey Wegener (drums; ex-***Saints***)*

Alongside **X**, **The Thought Criminals**, **Rocks**, Psycho-Surgeons, Johnny Dole and the Scabs, Filth, Blackrunner and The Hellcats, The Last Words were one of the first punk bands on the late 1970s Sydney scene. As such, the band's level of musical proficiency was somewhat crude and raw, but they persisted and eventually issued several singles and an album.

The original line-up only lasted a few months. Jeffrey Wegener went on to join Young Charlatans in Melbourne and then **Laughing Clowns** in Sydney. The Last Words recorded their debut single, 'Animal World'/'Wondering Why', which appeared on the independent Remand label (March 1978). 'Animal World' was a poorly recorded, self-produced effort (with Baxter playing drums and singing, and Groome on guitar and bass). With a new rhythm section of Leigh Kendall (bass) and Ken Doyle (drums), The Last Words re-recorded 'Animal World' and reissued it on the Wizard label in early 1979, with a new B-side, 'Every Schoolboy's Dream' (pressed on blue vinyl). That version appeared later in the year as a UK-only single on Rough Trade, again with a new B-side ('No Music in the World Today').

With a new drummer, John Gunn, The Last Words travelled to the UK where they issued two more UK-only singles 'Today's Kidz'/'There's Something Wrong' (January 1980) and 'Top Secret'/'Walk Away' (August 1980) and an album, *The Last Words*, before breaking up. Malcolm Baxter returned to Australia in 1981 and, after much effort and the aid of a Commonwealth government grant, set up the Liverpool Music Resource Centre in June 1984. The Centre and its record label Tribal were created to help aspiring musicians in Sydney's vast western suburbs to organise gigs, make industry contacts and to record and release material.

Album: *The Last Words* (UK only; Armageddon, 1980).

Laughing Clowns

Formed: *1979*
Style: *Rock, soul, avant-jazz*
Original line-up: **Ed Kuepper** *(guitar, vocals; ex-Kid Galahad and the Eternals,* **Saints***), Bob Farrell (sax), Ben Wallace-Crabbe (bass), Jeffrey Wegener (drums; ex-***Saints**, **Last Words**, *Young Charlatans)*

With the collapse of **The Saints** in the UK at the end of 1978, **Ed Kuepper** was ready to retire from music. Following three classic albums with **The Saints** *(I'm) Stranded*, *Eternally Yours* and *Prehistoric Sounds*, Kuepper was faced with the problem of where to head next. He was writing less commercial, more cerebral material; *Prehistoric Sounds* certainly paved the way for what lay ahead for Kuepper.

Following his return to Australia in late 1978, Kuepper formed Laughing Clowns with the above line-up in April 1979. From the outset, the band's music was diverse yet moody, at turns melodic or dissonant. It ranged from rock and soul to avant-jazz (inspired by Archie Shepp and Pharoah Sanders) and because no one instrument dominated proceedings, the sound was very rhythmic and percussive. The band made its live debut in Sydney during August 1979 and was met with almost total bemusement. Part of the problem was that the band's sound defied categorisation. Having to overcome such ludicrous labels as 'jazz-punk', Laughing Clowns went on to be one of the most innovative independent bands of the early 1980s.

The band recruited Dan Wallace-Crabbe (piano; ex-**Crime and the City Solution**), signed to Melbourne label Missing Link and issued the mini-album *The Laughing Clowns* (May 1980). The result was a record unlike any other made in Australia to that point. The music's only parallel lay in latter-day Saints as a logical progression from *Prehistoric Sounds*, but at the same time it was a departure, a foray into new territory. The open-ended song arrangements were stirring and provocative, but also disconcerting. The production values were cavernous and echoey; a fascinating sound, but very cold and detached.

The *Sometimes the Fire Dance* 7-inch EP appeared on the band's own Prince Melon label (October 1980). 'Holy Joe' from the mini-album and the powerhouse 'Sometimes (I Couldn't Live with Anyone)' from the EP were later coupled as a 7-inch single on Hot Records (1984). Hot also put out a 12-inch version which added the epic jazz-infused 'I Don't Know What I Want'. Peter Doyle joined on trumpet, which heralded the Clowns' more expansive big-band phase. In November 1980, Laughing Clowns joined **The Birthday Party** and **The Go-Betweens** for two landmark gigs at Sydney's Paris Theatre. At the end of the year, both Ben Wallace-Crabbe and Bob Farrell left the band; Dan Wallace-Crabbe followed a few months later.

The band's second mini-album, *Laughing Clowns 3*, appeared in March 1981. The three tracks from *Sometimes the Fire Dance* plus all of *Laughing Clowns 3* then made up the *Reign of Terror/Throne of Blood* compilation album (July 1981). The album effectively marked the end of the first phase in the band's career. The depleted line-up of Kuepper, Wegener and Doyle played a few gigs until Louise Elliot (sax, flute) and Leslie 'Biff' Millar (fretless bass; upright bass) joined in the middle of 1981. The new line-up issued the ambitious album *Mr Uddich-Schmuddich Goes to Town* (March 1982). 'Theme from "Mad Flies Mad Flies"'/'Mr Uddich-Schmuddich Goes to Town' was lifted as a single.

Following a national tour to promote the album, Laughing Clowns flew to the UK where the Red Flame label had already issued a compilation album, *The Laughing Clowns*. That album sold well enough for Red Flame to issue a second compilation in July 1983 called *Laughter Around the Table*, which contained new material the band had recorded in London. Laughing Clowns toured with **The Birthday Party** and The Fall, and were starting to make some headway in the UK when the band broke up at the end of 1982.

The new line-up of Kuepper, Wegener, Elliot and Peter Milton Walsh (bass; ex-**Apartments**, **Go-Betweens**, Out of Nowhere, Colors) returned to Australia in May 1983. The London-recorded EP *Everything that Flies . . .* came out in Australia during July 1983, and the band toured to a positive response. In October 1983, Laughing Clowns returned to the UK to tour for several months. Laughing Clowns signed a new deal with Hot Records and issued the 12-inch EP 'Eternally Yours' (March 1984) and the *Law of Nature* album (April). Both records immediately went to the top of the independent charts and they remain amongst the band's very finest works. There were moments of great beauty on *Law of Nature* such as 'Law of Nature', 'Written in Exile' and 'Eternally Yours', where Elliot's soulful and epic sax riff danced majestically in the air.

At the end of 1984, Hot Records put together a compilation album of old Clowns material, bearing the audaciously tongue-in-cheek title of *History of Rock'n'Roll Volume One*. By the time the album came out in December, Laughing Clowns had broken up. The band fell apart in the studio amid much acrimony while recording their new album, *Ghosts of An Ideal Wife*. For the album sessions, the basic core of Kuepper, Elliot, Wegener and bassist Paul Smith (who had replaced Milton Walsh) was joined by **Louis Tillett** (piano), Glad Reed (trombone) and Dianne Spence (sax), the last two also joining the band for the final live shows.

The band's final single was 'Just Because I Like'/'Crystal Clear' (February 1985). By the time *Ghosts of an Ideal Wife* came out in June 1985, Kuepper was already in the process of recording his debut solo album, *Electrical Storm*. Elliot and Wegener joined **Chris Bailey's** Saints for a tour; Elliot moved on to **James Griffin** and the Subterraneans and Kings of the World, and much later joined Dave Studdert's Mumbo Jumbo in the UK.

Albums: *The Laughing Clowns* (mini-album, Missing Link, 1980), *Laughing Clowns 3* (mini-album, Prince Melon, 1981), *Reign of Terror/Throne of Blood* (compilation, Prince Melon, 1981), *Mr Uddich-Schmuddich Goes to Town* (Prince Melon, 1982), *Law of Nature* (Hot, 1984), *History of Rock'n'Roll Volume One* (compilation, Hot, 1984), *Ghosts of an Ideal Wife* (Hot, 1985), *Golden Days—When Giants Walked the Earth* (compilation, Hot, 1995).

Lawson Square Infirmary (*see* The Triffids)

Le Club Foote

Formed: *1980*
Style: *Pop, rock*
Original line-up: *Rodney Freeman-Smith (vocals), Kim Gyngell (keyboards), Phillip Hyde (guitar), Neil Kelly (bass), Shane Sampson (drums)*

This satirical Melbourne pop band played the local pub circuit for several years before signing a deal with EMI. In 1984, **Men At Work's Colin Hay** produced the band's debut album, *Cinema Qua*. It produced two singles, 'Party'/'Happy' and 'Warning'/'Life in Ice'. The album sold only moderately and a year later Le Club Foote broke up.

Gyngell turned his talents to acting and comedy. During the late 1980s, he was a member of the popular television show *The Comedy Company*. Gyngell's absent-minded simpleton Col'n Carpenter proved such a popular character that he was afforded his own television series in 1990, *Col'n Carpenter*. Gyngell originally developed the character when he was writing for Sydney's Double J (the precursor to the ABC national youth radio network Triple J).

Since then, Gyngell has appeared in feature films like *Wills and Burke* (1985), *With Love to the Person Next to Me* (1986), *Bushfire Moon* (1987), *What the Moon Saw* (1990), *Heaven Tonight* (1992) and *Love and Other Catastrophes*. He won the 1988 Australian Film Institute (AFI) award as Best Supporting Actor for his role as Ian McKenzie in Pino Amenta's *Boulevard of Broken Dreams*. His other television appearances have included *Fast Forward* and the ABC miniseries *Seven Deadly Sins* (1993) and *Kangaroo Palace* (1997).

Album: *Cinema Qua* (EMI, 1984).

Ben Lee

Style: *Indie pop*

Teenage cult performer Ben Lee (b. 1978) first came to public attention in 1993 as a member of Sydney band Noise Addict. With an average age of 14, Noise Addict impressed rock promoter Steve Pavlovic, who signed the band to his Fellaheen label on the strength of a self-recorded and distributed demo. Noise Addict's line-up included Lee, Doran Kalinko (bass) and Josh Zoldan (drums). Later members included Saul Smith (drums) and Daniel Kohn (guitar).

Noise Addict's second-ever gig was supporting overseas visitors Sonic Youth which immediately established the band's credentials amongst the indie cognoscenti. There were some parallels to be drawn with another teenage band, **silverchair**, which was just about to hit with the best-selling 'Tomorrow' single, although Lee preferred to see Noise Addict as infinitely more 'punk rock'. Fellaheen issued Noise Addict's debut single, 'I Wish I was Him' (a wry semi-acoustic ode to Lemonheads' Evan Dando), in October 1993. The band supported US bands like Pavement and Fugazi, and played a string of all-ages shows. Noise Addict's April 1994 CD EP *The Taste in My Eyes* displayed plenty of low-fi charm and youthful exuberance among the stylised Jonathan Richmanesque songs. Other early Noise Addict recordings appeared in the US on two 10-inch mini albums, *Young & Jaded* (on Grand Royal) and *DEF* (on Estatic Peace!), plus the 7-inch single 'The Frail Girl'/'Poison 1080', 'Spritz' (on Grand Royal, 1995).

Lee recorded his debut solo album *Grandpaw Would* (April 1995) with US producer Brad Wood (Sebadoh, Liz Phair) in Chicago and Sydney. The album showcased Lee's nascent songwriting talents and his ability to craft simple, snappy, sparse tunes like 'Pop Queen' and 'I Wrote a Song for You'. The album produced the CD EP 'Away with the Pixies'. Lee saw out 1995 by touring the USA with an American backing band, hanging out with the Beastie Boys (after having signed to their label Grand Royal), supporting cult favourite Alex Chilton on his Australian tour and issuing the debut Noise Addict album *Meet the Real You* (also produced by Brad Wood). In true punk rock style, as soon as the album came out, Lee broke up the band.

Having turned 18, Lee issued his second solo album *Something to Remember Me By* (recorded with Wood in Los Angeles) in May 1997. The album's best songs like 'New Song' and 'Career Choice', were rough diamonds in the ever evolving career of this indie prodigy.

Lee solo albums: *Grandpaw Would* (Fellaheen/Shock, 1995), *Something to Remember Me By* (Fellaheen/Shock, 1997); ***Noise Addict album:*** *Meet the Real You* (Fellaheen/Shock, 1995).

Lonnie Lee

Style: *Rock'n'roll*

Rock'n'roll singer Lonnie Lee (b. 1940) was born David Laurence Rix in Rowena (NSW) on his parents' sheep farm. With aspirations from an early age to be a performer, Lee's earliest idols included Johnny Ray and Elvis Presley. In 1958, Lee came to the attention of Australia's first rock'n'roll hero,

Johnny O'Keefe, when the young singer won an Elvis Presley competition at Sydney's Trocadero Ballroom.

O'Keefe became Lee's manager and entrepreneur Lee Gordon signed him to a five-year deal with Leedon Records on J.O.K.'s recommendation. Lonnie Lee's debut single, O'Keefe's 'Ain't It So'/'Shame on You Miss Johnson', reached #9 on the Sydney charts during November 1959. Following performances on television shows like *Bandstand* and J.O.K.'s *Six O'Clock Rock*, the single reached #4 nationally. Lee formed a backing band, The Leemen, comprising Derby Wilson (lead guitar), Peter Bazley (rhythm guitar), Dave Scott (sax), Johnny Ryan (bass) and Tony Gaha (drums) and toured the country. His second single, 'Starlight Starbright'/'She's Doin' Me Wrong' (February 1960), reached #3 in Sydney and Top 5 in Melbourne. 'Yes Indeed I Do'/'Lover Doll' (May 1960) was Lee's third Sydney Top 10 hit.

The double A-sided hit 'Defenceless'/'I Found a New Love' was Lee's most successful single to date as both sides made the Sydney Top 40 in September 1960. Firstly Otis Blackwell's 'Defenceless' peaked at #17, then Nat Kipner's 'I Found a New Love' rose to #2. By that stage, Lee had been voted Australia's #1 performer by the viewers of *Six O'Clock Rock*, just ahead of his mentor **Johnny O'Keefe**. Lee's debut album, *A Night Out with Lonnie Lee*, and subsequent singles, 'Sit Around and Talk to Me'/'Baby Baby Bye Bye' (another double-sided hit in March 1961) and 'You're Gonna Miss Me'/'Sitting by the River' (June) kept him in the charts. Lee's second album, *Starring Lonnie Lee*, compiled his first six singles, and was reissued under the title of *Lonnie Lee's Greatest Hits* in 1972.

Lee's first single for 1962, 'When the Bells Stop Ringing'/'Sunday', was to be his last chart hit when it reached #15 in January. He issued four more singles on Leedon 'Don't You Know (Pretty Baby)'/'Sure Fire Bet' (March), 'Marilyn'/'Too Soon to Know' (September), 'She is the One Girl for Me'/'Fun in the Summer Sun' (February 1963) and 'Acres of Everything but Love'/'I'd Like to Leave If I May' (August) before signing to EMI. Lee's EP releases on Leedon were *This is Lonnie Lee*, *Lonnie's Golden Record*, *Frankfurt Special*, *Walkin' with Lonnie Lee*, *Sitting by the River*, *I Found a New Love* and *In the Middle of an Island*.

EMI's HMV label issued four Lee singles over the next 18 months, but none charted: 'Free Free Man'/'I Need You Now' (April 1964), 'My Baby Don't "Low"'/'On the Run' (January 1965), 'Love's Gonna Live Here'/'More than Yesterday' (February) and 'Little White House'/'Waltz You Saved for Me' (September). For most of that period The Leeman comprised Jeff Denton (bass, piano), Lance Ransome (lead guitar), Graham Dunn (rhythm guitar) and Frank Griffith (drums).

At the age of 26, Lee was considered too old for new television pop shows like *Saturday Date* and *The Go!! Show*, so he moved into the country field. His country album *A Country Boy at Heart* was not successful. In 1967 he headed overseas to earn a living on the club circuit in England, Europe and South East Asia. Returning to Australia in 1969, Lee signed a new deal with the Sunshine label. His two Sunshine singles, 'Hello Love'/'Sad Over Someone (SOS)' (1970), and (the re-recorded) 'Starlight Starbright'/'The Traveller' (1971) were flops and he slipped back into his club career.

In 1974, Lee joined **Johnny O'Keefe's** successful package show The Good Old Days of Rock'n'Roll (alongside **Barry Stanton**, Tony Brady, Jade Hurley, Johnny Devlin and Laurel Lea), which toured Australia throughout 1974 and 1975. Lee relocated to Hendersonville, Tennessee where he set up a promotional firm, Lee Pro. He recorded a couple of albums of country songs in Nashville, which only ever appeared on cassette, *Holding on* and *Elvis—A Tribute*. Lee returned to Australia in 1983 and issued one single on the small Starlite label 'Johnny Rock'n'Roll'/'I'm Holding on' (1986). Throughout the 1980s, Lee toured with his own package show which included the likes of **Barry Stanton** and Johnny Devlin.

Albums: *A Night Out with Lonnie Lee* (Leedon/Festival, 1960), *Starring Lonnie Lee* (Leedon/Festival, 1961), *A Country Boy at Heart* (EMI/HMV, 1965), *Lonnie Lee's Greatest Hits* (Calendar/Festival, 1972).

The Leftovers

Formed: *1976*
Style: *Punk*
Original line-up: *Warren Lamond (vocals), Jim Shoebridge (guitar), Glenn Smith (bass), Ed Wreckage (real name Ed Dzidrch, drums). Other members: Johnny Burnaway (real name Johnny Gorman, guitar), Michael Hiron (drums)*

That what was arguably the most conservative city in Australia gave rise to some of the most anarchistic bands of the Australian punk rock era has long been cause for amazement. Brisbane's **The Saints**, **The Fun Things**, Razar and The Leftovers were an obvious backlash to an oppressed society in the mid-to-late 1970s. Writer Clinton Walker described The Leftovers as Australia's first true punks in the Sex Pistols mould: obnoxious, anarchic, anti-social, powerful, violent and with a strong self-destructive bent. The Leftovers suffered all the setbacks befitting a band of their nature (including continuous harassment from the local constabulary), but were persistent enough to plough on and finally release a single in June 1979.

'Cigarettes and Alcohol'/'No Complaints', 'I Only Panic when There's Nothing to Do' (500 copies) rates along with the first records from **The Victims**, **The Saints**, **Radio Birdman**, **News**, **Scientists** and **The Fun Things** as one of the classics of the late 1970s Australian punk rock era. In keeping with the spirit of the band's muse, some of the singles had 'The Fucken Leftovers Hate You' rubber-stamped on the plain white sleeve. Not long after the single came out, The Leftovers fell apart. 'No Complaints' later appeared on the 1989 compilation of Brisbane punk bands *At The Solicitor's Request.*

Michael Hiron went on to **The Riptides**, **The Flaming Hands**, Catchcry and Pineapples from the Dawn of Time. Johnny Gorman formed The Plug Uglies in 1986, but died in 1988. Hiron replaced Gorman (who was his brother) in Plug Uglies. Hiron produced the band's debut mini-album *Knock Me Your Lobes* (1989). The album line-up comprised Gorman, Roger Norris (vocals; ex-Other Voices), Mark Lock (bass) and Tina Stevens (drums). After that the line-up became Norris, Stevens, Hiron (guitar, bass), Clem Lukey (guitar; ex-Dum Dums, Pineapples from the Dawn of Time) and John Willsteed (bass, guitar; ex-Zero, **Go-Betweens**). That line-up contributed 'All Done In' to rooArt's Various Artists album *Youngblood II* (1990).

Following The Leftovers' disintegration, Ed Wreckage spent time in gaol. Warren Lamond almost lived up to his death wish when he attempted suicide in the early 1990s. Glenn Smith died in 1995.

Levi Smith's Clefs

Formed: *1967*
Style: *R&B*
Original line-up: *Barrie McAskill (vocals), Les Tanner (guitar), Bob Jeffrey (sax), Bruce Howe (bass), Vince Jones (drums)*

During the 1960s, Scottish-born Barrie McAskill earned a reputation as one of the country's pioneering soul/R&B singers. A great bear of a man with a commanding presence and gravelly voice to match, McAskill led numerous line-ups of his band Levi Smith's Clefs between 1967 and 1975.

Levi Smith's Clefs initially earned a reputation on the disco/club circuit as a gutsy R&B band in the vein of **Max Merritt and the Meteors**, eventually proving to be a breeding ground for the swelling ranks of Australia's progressive scene. **Tully**, **Fraternity** and **Southern Contemporary Rock Assembly** (SCRA), for example, all sprang almost intact from the bosom of the Clefs. Smith's philosophy was to encourage his band members to improve as musicians, and for them to move on as the urge arose. Accordingly, more than 60 musicians passed through the band's ranks over the years.

The Levi Smith's Clefs story actually began in Adelaide, South Australia during 1963 when Tweed Harris (organ) formed The Clefs. The early line-up included Trevor Pridham (vocals), Les Tanner (guitar), Michael Atkins (drums), Dennis Marshall (sax) and Bruce Howe (bass). The Clefs became an in-demand dance band on the city's thriving club circuit. McAskill (ex-Fabulous Drifters) joined in 1965 and the line-up became Harris, Howe, Tanner, McAskill, Bob Jeffrey (sax) and Vince Jones (drums; ex-Fabulous Drifters).

The Clefs issued three singles in 1966, 'I Can Only Give You Everything'/'Roberta' (on EMI/Columbia), 'A Boy Like Me'/'Bring It to Jerome' (on the Phono Vox label) and 'House of the Rising Sun'/'We'll Meet Again' (on the Peace label). When Harris accepted an invitation to join supergroup-in-the-making **The Groove** in early 1967, McAskill assumed leadership of the band. The Clefs' manager Peter Raphael suggested the band be renamed Levi Smith's Clefs (which in a roundabout way had been inspired by the name of the Four Tops' lead singer Levi Stubbs).

As a five-piece, Levi Smith's Clefs moved to Melbourne and then to Sydney where they took up an 18-month residency at the Whisky A Go Go club. The line-up shifted constantly along the way, with Inez Amaya (vocals), Les Stacpool (guitar; ex-**Chessmen**, **Merv Benton** and the Tamlas), Ian Walsh (organ), Michael Carlos (organ), Doug Stirling (bass), John Blake (bass), John 'Yuk' Harrison (bass), John Helman (bass), Gil Matthews (drums; ex-Max Hamilton and the Impacts) and Jimmy Thompson (drums) passing through the ranks, some for the second time.

By 1968, the line-up had stabilised with McAskill, Amaya, Carlos, Blake, Mick Jurd (guitar), Richard Lockwood (flute, sax) and Robert Taylor (drums). At the end of the year, Carlos, Lockwood, Blake and Taylor all left to form **Tully**, before joining the Australian stage production of the American 'tribal love-rock musical' *Hair* in June 1969 as resident backing band. Amaya also joined the cast of *Hair*. McAskill and Jurd assembled a new Levi Smith's Clefs with John Bissett (organ), Bruce Howe (bass) and Tony Buettel (drums; ex-**Bay City Union**).

That line-up recorded the adventurous *Empty Monkey* album for the Sweet Peach label. It was one of the first local albums to combine soul/R&B/pop with a more progressive rock outlook.

Despite being a groundbreaking release in many ways, the music was somewhat ponderous and the album failed to take off. The standout cut was an 11-and-a-half minute arrangement of The Beatles' 'We Can Work it Out'. Sweet Peach also lifted two singles from the album, 'Lisa'/'Roadrunner' (January 1970) and a cover of Junior Walker's 'Shotgun'/'Who is it that Shall Come?' (April 1970). By the time the album came out in March 1970, Jurd, Bissett, Howe and Buettel had all left to form **Fraternity**.

Having been left high and dry by the departures, McAskill had no recourse but to assemble a new Levi Smith's Clefs line-up that comprised Linda Cable (vocals), Ken Deacon (vocals), Steve Doran (keyboards), Peter Karlenick (guitar), Doug Stirling (bass), John Freeman (drums; soon to be lured away to join **Fraternity** when Buettel quit, and to be replaced by Michael Darby), Mike Cousins (trombone), Steve Bowden (trombone), Bill Harrower (sax) and Mike Kenny (trumpet). As Barrie McAskill's Levi Smith's Clefs, the band issued two brassy R&B singles, 'Live Like a Man'/'Piece of My Heart' (September 1970), and 'Gonna Get a Seizure'/'Dancing and Drinking' (April 1971), plus an EP, *Best of Whisky A Go Go* (shared with **Autumn**), on the Chart label. The Barrie McAskill and Levi Smith's Clefs tracks were 'Down in the Valley' and 'Lawdy Miss Clawdy'.

Throughout 1971, the band held down the residency at the famed Chequers club in Sydney. Line-up changes continued apace with Julie Robinson (vocals), Bruce Howard (organ; ex-**La De Das**), Michael Carlos (organ; ex-**Tully**), Jim Kelly (guitar; ex-**Affair**), Billy TK (guitar; ex-Human Instinct), Ted 'The Head' Yanni (guitar), Yuk Harrison (bass; by then ex-Genesis), Doug Stirling (bass), Russell Dunlop (drums; ex-**Aesop's Fables**), Allan Turnbull (drums), Greg Henson (drums) and Bob Jeffrey (sax) passing through. Kelly, Dunlop and Kenny formed the basis of **Southern Contemporary Rock Assembly** (SCRA) when they left McAskill's band.

The late 1971 line-up of McAskill, Carlos, Stirling, Henson and Jeffrey became known variously as Barrie McAskill's Bear Brigade or McAskill's Marauders. Carlos and Henson then joined the backing band for the local production of the Andrew Lloyd Webber and Tim Rice rock musical *Jesus Christ Superstar*. Barrie McAskill's People comprised Vince Melouney (guitar; ex-**Billy Thorpe** and the Aztecs, **Bee Gees**, **Fanny Adams**, **Cleves**, Flite), Michael Barnes (guitar; ex-Nutwood Rug), Ken Firth (bass; ex-**Tully**) and Kevin Murphy (drums; ex-**Wild Cherries**, The Aztecs, **King Harvest**, **Chain**).

In mid-1972, McAskill reverted to the Levi Smith's Clefs name for the line-up of Doug Stirling, Kevin Murphy, Les Stacpool and Ian Clyne (keyboards; ex-**Loved Ones**, **Ram Jam Big Band**). By October 1972, McAskill was working with a line-up which comprised Murphy, Clyne, Mal Capewell (sax, flute; ex-Dr Kandy's Third Eye, Dada, **Company Caine**), Russell Smith (trumpet, vocals; ex-**Ram Jam Big Band**), Barry Sullivan (bass; ex-**Chain**) and Barry Harvey (drums; ex-**Chain**). A month later, Murphy, Clyne, Capewell, Sullivan and Harvey broke away from McAskill and Smith, recruited **Phil Manning** (guitar, vocals; ex-**Chain**, **Band of Talabene**), and became Mighty Mouse.

Having been left high and dry once again, McAskill formed a new band called McAskill which occupied him until 1976. The members of that band at various times included Alvin Tutin (guitar), Lindsay Wells (guitar; ex-**Healing Force**, **Chain**, **Blackfeather**), Jeff Spooner (guitar), Ian Mawson (keyboards; ex-**Company Caine**), Howie Morgan (keyboards), Eddie McDonald (bass; ex-**Bakery**), Doug Stirling (bass; ex-Levi Smith's Clefs), Warren Ward (bass; ex-**Flying Circus**, **Blackfeather**), Bob Fortesque (bass; ex-**Blackfeather**), Roger McLachlan (bass), Dallas 'Digger' Royal (drums) and Paul Johnson (drums). McAskill returned to Adelaide in 1977 and formed an ever-evolving series of bands including East End Street Band, Barrie McAskill's on Fire, Barrie McAskill and Friends, Barrie McAskill's Levi Smith's Clefs, Barrie McAskill's Soul Survivors, Who Dat Dere and Topsy and the Bear.

Album: *Empty Monkey* (Sweet Peach, 1970).

Jeannie Lewis

Style: *Rock to jazz*

Jeannie Lewis (b. 1945) is one of the most enigmatic and expressive, yet underrated singers Australia has ever produced. At the expense of detracting from Lewis's redoubtable talents, try to imagine a cross between UK vocalists Sandy Denny and Kate Bush for at least one reference point. Always able to adapt her emotional and dramatic voice to suit a range of moods and styles, whether it be folk, rock, blues, opera or avant-jazz, Lewis was a fine interpreter of other people's material.

During the 1960s, Lewis sang in folk clubs and with the Ray Price Jazz Quintet and the Alan Lee Jazz Quintet. She appeared on the Ray Price Jazz Quintet album *Spectrum* (1971). One of Lewis's early bands was the 1970 Sydney-based outfit

Gypsy Train which comprised Bobby Gebert (piano), Kydric Shaw (guitar), Terry Wilson (vocals), John Helman (bass; ex-**Levi Smith's Clefs**) and Daryl McKenzie (drums). In 1972, Lewis sang the title song to Jim Sharman's debut feature film *Shirley Thompson Versus the Aliens*. A year later, Lewis issued her debut album, *Free Fall Through Featherless Flight*. With music arranged and directed by Michael Carlos (ex-**Tully**, **Levi Smith's Clefs**), the album included a breathtaking array of material like **Graham Lowndes'** 'Till Time Brings Change', **Gulliver Smith** and Jeremy Noone's 'It's Up to You' and **Billy Green's** adaptation of the Dylan Thomas poem 'Do Not Go Gentle'.

Backing musicians included Carlos (moog, organ, harpsichord), Mike Wade (guitar), Mike Reid (guitar), Ken Firth (bass; ex-**Tully**), Jamie McKinley (piano), Greg Henson (drums), Alan Lee (percussion), **Marcia Hines** (backing vocals), Shayna Stewart (backing vocals; ex-**Tully**), The Fidelio String Quartet and a wind section. The album won the Australian Radio Record Award for the Best Australian LP of 1974, despite receiving no radio support whatsoever. Lewis's second album, the in-concert set *Looking Backwards to Tomorrow (in and out of concert)*, featured the singer's renditions of songs by Ray Davies ('Celluloid Heroes'), Dory Previn ('Scared to Be Alone'), Stephen Sondheim ('Ladies Who Lunch'), **Graham Lowndes** ('The House is Burning') and the Rev. Gary Davies ('Cocaine Blues' with backing provided by **The Foreday Riders**). 'Celluloid Heroes'/'Rocelli Kabarunta' was issued as a single. American label Mainstream issued the album in the USA.

Lewis's most adventurous album, the double set *Tears of Steel & the Clowning Calaveras* recreated her series of concerts held in November 1975. The initial inspiration for the project was the poem *Tears of Steel* by Chilean writer Pablo Nerunda, and the Mexican Day of the Dead (All Soul's Day) festivities in which people paraded 'Calaveras' (mock skeletons) in a burlesque parody of life and death. Once again, Lewis and musical director Carlos drew on an eclectic and sometimes astonishing range of songs encompassing Phil Ochs' 'The Crucifixion', **Graham Lowndes'** 'Rising of the Tide', Jimmy Webb's 'The Moon's a Harsh Mistress', The Fugs' 'When the Mode of the Music Changes', David Bowie's 'All the Madmen' and Dory Previn's 'The Game'.

In late 1975, Lewis won a study grant from the Australia Arts Council (under the auspices of Gough Whitlam's Labor government) and headed overseas. She spent three years in South America, where she studied the politics and music of the continent. She returned in late 1978, and supported John McLaughlin on his Australian tour (July 1979). Next, Lewis presented a show called *Krazy for You* which featured material from Nick Lowe, Noel Coward and Bruce Springsteen. In 1981, Lewis took the lead role in the stage production *Piaf*, which resulted in the album *Piaf, the Songs and the Story* (January 1982). She continued in musical theatre with roles in *Three Penny Opera* and her own show, *For A Dancer*. In 1983, Lewis appeared in the show *So U Want Blood*; backing for the show was provided by the All Singing All Dancing Orchestra which comprised Red Symons (guitar, musical director; ex-**Skyhooks**), Paul Grabowsky (piano), George Worontshak (keyboards), Ian McDonald (bass) and Eddie Van Roosendael (drums; ex-**Stiletto**). EMI issued the *So U Want Blood* album and the single 'Big Cliches (are the Best)'/'Just One Spark' (September 1983).

Since that time, Lewis has appeared in a theatre production of Bizet's *Carmen* (1984), represented Australia at the Festival International Cervantino in Mexico (1987), presented her own shows, *For a Dancer* (1985), *Voxy Lady* (1990) and *Dangerous Lovers* (1992), joined the cast of the Paul Robeson stage show *Deep Bells Ring* (1987), appeared on the album *Cinderella a Cappella* alongside **Margret Roadknight**, Moya Simpson and Blaire Greenberg (1994), and toured with a revival of *Piaf* (1996). EMI issued a compilation in April 1995 called *Classic Tracks 1973–76*.

Albums: *Free Fall Through Featherless Flight* (EMI, 1973), *Looking Backwards to Tomorrow (in and out of concert)* (EMI, 1974), *Tears of Steel & the Clowning Cavaleras* (EMI, 1976), *Till Time Brings Change* (compilation, EMI, 1980), *Piaf, the Songs and the Story* (WEA, 1982), *So U Want Blood* (Larrikin/EMI, 1983), *Classic Tracks 1973–76* (compilation, EMI, 1995).

The Lighthouse Keepers

Formed: *1982*
Style: *Country, folk*
Original line-up: *Greg Appel (acoustic guitar, bass, keyboards, vocals), Juliet Ward (vocals, bass, keyboards), Mike 'Blue' Dalton (slide guitar, dobro, bass, harmonica), Stephen O'Neil (drums, bass, guitar, sax)*

The Lighthouse Keepers' tasteful, jangly brand of country-tinged folk rock was at odds with prevailing trends on Sydney's early 1980s, Detroit-besotted independent scene. The band nevertheless issued a number of albums and singles, and always lived up to audience expectations.

In 1983, The Lighthouse Keepers issued their debut single, 'Gargoyle'/'Demolition Man', 'Quick Sticks', and the low-fi mini-album *The Exploding*

Lighthouse Keepers on their own independent Guthugga Pipeline label. For the mini-album, the band added drummer Steven Williams (ex-Particles), allowing Stephen O'Neil to concentrate on bass, guitar and sax. O'Neil also moonlighted with his other band, The Particles. The Particles had been around in various incarnations since 1977, fronted at various times by singers Simon Bonney (pre-**Crime and the City Solution**), Astrid Spielman and Michael Wood. The band managed to sustain a cult following around the inner-city Sydney scene courtesy of its delightful, melodious pop sound. The Particles issued three independent EPs, *Advanced Colouring* (1979), *Colour in* (1980) and *I Love Trumpet* (1983).

Sydney independent label Hot reissued The Lighthouse Keepers' 'Gargoyle' single (August 1984), as well as putting out the band's full-length debut album *Tales of the Unexpected* (November). 'Ocean Liner'/'Sad Tale' was lifted as a single (November). Hot issued a third single, 'Ode to Nothing'/'Seven Years', in August 1985, and the band flew to the UK for a series of shows (including supporting fellow Australians **The Triffids** in London). The Lighthouse Keepers broke up in early 1986. As a farewell gesture, the band compiled the 'Gargoyle' and 'Ode to Nothing' singles, the *Exploding* mini-album and two previously unissued tracks, 'Mr Wicked' and 'Lair', on the album *Imploding* (November 1986). Greg Appel and Juliet Ward went on to The Rainlovers, which became The Widdershins; Dalton joined **The Honeys**; O'Neil joined **The Cannanes**.

The Widdershins comprised Appel, Ward, James Cruickshank (guitar, keyboards, vocals), Barry Turnbull (bass; ex-**John Kennedy's Love Gone Wrong**) and Peter Timmerman (drums). The band issued the singles 'Now You Know'/'Dishwashing Liquid' (September 1987) and 'Return of the King' (March 1989), the mini-album *Bottleman's Wife* (June 1988) and the album *Ascension* (May 1989) on the Waterfront label. With the break-up of The Widdershins in 1989, Ward and Cruickshank formed Juliet Hammerhead and Friends. Cruickshank went on to work with **Neil Murray** and the Rainmakers and **The Cruel Sea**. The 35-track Lighthouse Keepers retrospective album *Lipsnipegroin* (1993) combined all the band's material plus three previously unissued tracks. At the same time, Appel's new band, One Head Jet, issued its debut CD EP, *Snickedy Palace*.

Lighthouse Keepers albums: *The Exploding Lighthouse Keepers* (mini-album, Guthugga Pipeline, 1983), *Tales of the Unexpected* (Hot, 1984), *Imploding* (Waterfront, 1986), *Lipsnipegroin* (Phantom, 1993); ***Widdershins albums:*** *Bottleman's Wife* (mini-album, Waterfront, 1988), *Ascension* (Waterfront, 1989).

Peter Lillie (*see* The Pelaco Brothers).

The Lime Spiders

Formed: *1981*
Style: *Acid punk, hard rock*
Original line-up: *Mick Blood (vocals), Daryl Mather (guitar), Dave Guest (bass), Geoff Cleary (drums)*

When Jello Biafra, lead singer with Californian band the Dead Kennedys, was quoted as saying 'I never thought I'd hear a psychedelic slime band more hardcore than the Green Fuzz, but here they are', he was referring to The Lime Spiders' fanatical embracement of 1960s American garagemania. As Australia's premier exponents of 1960s neo-psychedelia, The Lime Spiders took their cue from The 13th Floor Elevators, The Moving Sidewalks, The Standells, The Haunted, The Sonics, The Litter, The Count Five, The State of Mind, The Seeds and numerous other bands gathered on US compilations like *Nuggets*, *Pebbles*, *Boulders* and *Psychedelic Unknowns*. The band's raucous sound mixed screaming vocals and wild, fuzz-tone guitar riffs to arrive at a mutant strain of acid punk that bordered on heavy metal.

Mick Blood and Daryl Mather formed The Lime Spiders in Sydney's vast western suburbs during February 1981. After an initial period of development the band added 17-year-old, hot-shot guitarist Richard Jakimyszyn during August. The new line-up played its debut gig at the Southern Cross Hotel, inner-city Sydney (September 1981). The Spiders broke up in February 1982, but reconvened during September with a new drummer, Stephen Rawles. The main inspiration for the reformation was the massive, 64-band Battle of the Bands competition held at the Southern Cross Hotel (later to be renamed the Strawberry Hills). The Spiders went on to take out first place, with the prize being a recording deal with the independent GREEN label which resulted in the '25th Hour' double single set (June 1983).

Produced by ex-**Radio Birdman** frontman Rob Younger, the double single boasted over-the-top covers of The Haunted's '1-2-5' and Liberty Bell's 'That's How It will Be' plus two killer originals in the same vein, '25th Hour' and 'Can't Wait Long'. Warwick Gilbert (bass; ex-**Radio Birdman, Hitmen**) played on the singles in place of the departed Dave Guest. Bruce Tatham and Bill Gibson contributed keyboards and backing vocals respectively.

The Lime Spiders broke up again before '25th Hour' came out, but by August 1983 Blood and Jakimyszyn were fronting a new rhythm section of

Tony Bambach (bass, vocals; ex-Most) and Richard Lawson (drums, vocals; ex-Most). The Most had been the Spiders' main rival in the 1982 Battle of the Bands Grand Final. In March 1984, the new line-up recorded the classic single 'Slave Girl'/ 'Beyond the Fringe', which came out on the Citadel label in October. It went on to become one of the biggest selling independent singles of the 1980s, and even scaled the lower reaches of the national mainstream charts. The single also established the band's reputation in European countries like France, Germany, Spain and Sweden, where fans in those territories became hooked on its wild acid-punk sound.

By September 1984, Gerard Corben (another ex-Most alumnus) had boosted the sound as rhythm guitarist, and the band began to tour consistently. The five-piece line-up, however, was short-lived. Jakimyszyn had already moonlighted with **The New Christs** and **The Hitmen**, but decided to leave The Spiders at the end of 1984. He later formed The Warm Jets and briefly rejoined The Lime Spiders in May 1987 (in time for the release of the band's debut album). Back to a four-piece, The Lime Spiders issued another best-selling independent single, 'Out of Control'/'Save My Soul' (December 1985), on Citadel before Blood left the band to travel overseas for a year. The rest of The Spiders continued on with singer Mark Green under the name Adolphus; Corben also worked with The Sparklers. With Blood's return in September 1986, The Lime Spiders reconvened and signed to Virgin Records.

The band's debut release on Virgin was the 'Weirdo Libido'/'Here with My Love' single (January 1987), which also appeared on the soundtrack to the Yahoo Serious feature film *Young Einstein*. The 12-inch version of 'Weirdo Libido' added a side of four live cuts that included versions of The Remains' 'Time of Day' and Love's 'My Flash on You'. 'Weirdo Libido' peaked at #25 on the Sydney mainstream chart. The band's debut album, *The Cave Comes Alive* (June 1987), produced the singles 'My Favourite Room'/'Blood from a Stone' (7-inch; May), 'My Favourite Room'/'Blood from a Stone', 'I Heard Her Call My Name' (12-inch; June), 'Just One Solution'/'Drip Out' (August) and 'Jessica'/'Sparks' (October). With the album out, the band supported UK hard rockers The Cult on an Australian tour. At the end of 1987, the Lime Spiders embarked on a tour of the US, where 'Slave Girl' had been a #1 hit on the College/Alternative chart. The tour took in support slots to Public Image Ltd and Faith No More. Jakimyszyn left after the US jaunt. Virgin reissued *The Cave Comes Alive* in 1988 with a bonus, four-track, live USA tour EP (on green vinyl).

The *Volatile* album (May 1988) contained a decent array of riff-heavy, hard rock tracks, but lacked the raw spark that had characterised the band's earlier output. *Volatile* yielded the singles 'Volatile'/'Working for a Living' (May 1988) and 'The Other Side of You'/'Can't You Read My Mind?' (August). The same sessions produced the four-track 12-inch EP imaginatively titled *EP* (March 1989). By the time *Volatile* appeared, the line-up featured Blood, Lawson, Corben, Bambach and ex-**Celibate Rifles** bass player Michael Couvret on rhythm guitar. In December 1988, Phil Hall (ex-Sardine v, Dropbears, Joeys) replaced Bambach on bass, with Mark Wilkinson (concurrently in Brisbane outfit **The Girlies**) replacing Couvret on guitar. That line-up supported US visitor Iggy Pop on his January 1989 Australian tour. Wilkinson contributed guitar to a couple of tracks on the band's underrated hard rock album *Beethoven's Fist*, but had left before the album appeared in 1990. The album produced the single 'Cherry Red'/'Mr Big Mouth' (October 1990), as well as containing at least one bona fide Lime Spiders classic in the breakneck '9 Miles High'.

Not long after that, The Lime Spiders fell apart, but Blood revived the band in 1992 with the line-up of Lawson, Hall, Brian Mann (guitar; ex-**Girlies, Headstones, Screaming Tribesmen**), Peter Murphy (guitar) and Luke Mason (drums). The new line-up supported US visitors The Black Crowes on their Australian tour during June 1992. A month later, The Lime Spiders issued the CD single 'Blood Sugar Sex Lawson'. By 1993, Blood had folded the band. Yet, as they say, you can't keep a good band down: Blood and Hall were back at the start of 1997 with a new Lime Spiders line-up featuring David Sparks (guitar), Stephen Waters (guitar) and Stuart Wilson (drums).

Albums: *Slave Girl* (UK-only mini-album of early singles; Hybrid/Big Time, 1985), *The Cave Comes Alive* (Virgin, 1987), *Headcleaner* (compilation; Virgin, 1988), *Volatile* (Virgin, 1988), *Beethoven's Fist* (Virgin, 1990).

The Lipstick Killers

Formed: *1978*
Style: *Punk rock*
Original line-up: *Peter Tillman (vocals; ex-Filth), Mark Taylor (guitar; ex-Psycho-Surgeons), Kim Giddy (bass; ex-Precious Little), David Taylor (drums; ex-Psycho-Surgeons)*

The Lipstick Killers grew out of the ashes of two of Sydney's most notorious late 1970s punk bands, Psycho-Surgeons and Filth. Inspired by The Ramones' first album (issued July 1976), import record shop owner Mark Taylor formed a band called the Frozen Stiffs with Ronnie Pop (vocals), Charlie Georgees (guitar), Craig Amiet (bass) and David Taylor (drums).

After a few months of rehearsals, Pop and Georgees wandered off to form The Hellcats. Pop later re-emerged as Ron Peno in **Died Pretty**. At the start of 1977, Taylor, Amiet and Taylor recruited singer Paul Gearside and began to play gigs. Rechristened Psycho-Surgeons after a newspaper headline, the band's street-level punk credentials were based around a crude measure of musical proficiency and a full quota of Stooges-derived material in the live set. Until Filth came along a year later, Psycho-Surgeons earned a reputation as the most despised band in Sydney. Alongside The Hellcats and Johnny Dole and the Scabs, Psycho-Surgeons were one of the first bands to become associated with the scene that grew up around the Oxford Funhouse, the legendary venue in inner-city Sydney run by **Radio Birdman**.

Gearside left the band in late 1977 after being severely beaten up by three Hell's Angels during a gig at the Oxford Funhouse. As a result of the violence, which was not symptomatic of the Funhouse itself, the owners closed the venue's doors to rock gigs. Psycho-Surgeons issued their debut single in September 1978. 'Horizontal Action'/'Wild Weekend' was a crudely recorded but intriguing release pushed along by Taylor's thumping hard beat. Its collectability as a punk artefact was assured from the outset due to its limited edition of 500 copies, and because the band members splattered real cow's blood over all the sleeves!

Not long after the single's release, Psycho-Surgeons mutated into The Lipstick Killers with the arrival of Peter Tillman and Kim Giddy. Tillman had sung with Filth alongside teenage guitarist Bob Short for a year. To many observers, Filth was the most nihilistic band on the scene, and Short was known to take his Iggy Pop obsession to unhealthy extremes. The Lipstick Killers' Americanised brand of glitter/hard rock drew as much on late 1960s acid-punk as The Stooges and New York Dolls circa 1973 for inspiration. Another of the band's stated musical influences was UK glam star Gary Glitter. The Lipstick Killers played the Sydney scene alongside **The Passengers**, **The Flaming Hands**, **The Hitmen**, **Sunnyboys** and The Visitors. In November 1979, the band issued the classic **Deniz Tek**-produced independent single 'Hindu Gods (of Love)'/'Shakedown USA', which was atmospheric, hard'n'fast rock at its best.

In late 1980, Michael Charles (ex-Shy Impostors) replaced David Taylor on drums. The Lipstick Killers then spent a year living in Los Angeles, and became involved in the burgeoning Californian hardcore scene that had already thrown up the likes of Black Flag, Circle Jerks and Flesh Eaters. During that time, Stephen Mather (ex-Playboy Lords) replaced Giddy on bass. The band, however, made little headway and was living in poverty. Following a Christmas dinner that consisted of boiled onions and refried beans, the band broke up and the members limped home to Australia at the start of 1982. Mark Taylor moved into computer graphics, Mather joined **Decline of the Reptiles** and Charles joined the Angie Pepper Band and later on **The Screaming Tribesmen**.

Citadel Records issued the live album *Mesmerizer* in December 1984. It had been taken from a cassette recording of one of the band's infrequent Los Angeles gigs (in the manner of The Velvet Underground's *Live at Max's Kansas City*). As such, the sound quality was rough'n'ready but the energy and atmosphere were enough to gain an insight into the band's true spirit. The independent Vi-Nil label also issued the 'Sockman'/'Pensioner Pie' single in January 1985 from demos the band had recorded at the end of 1978.

The Lipstick Killers re-formed for a brief Sydney tour in January 1989. In April 1995, Mark Taylor, Tillman and Mather formed 1960s acid-punk revivalists Doctor Stone. Bil Bilson (drums; ex-**Sunnyboys**) and Chris Willing (Farfisa organ) completed the line-up. The band played a few gigs around Sydney during 1995. Doctor Stone issued the CD EP *Purple Slice* in December 1996 on the Appointment label. It contained three new songs and a re-recording of The Lipstick Killers' 'Hindu Gods (of Love)'.

Album: *Mesmerizer* (Citadel, 1984).

The Little Heroes

Formed: *1980*
Style: *Pop*
Original line-up: *Roger Hart (aka Roger Wells, vocals, guitar; ex-Cruisers, Secret Police), David Crosbie (keyboards), John Taylor (bass, vocals; ex-Secret Police), Bruce Pumpa (drums; ex-Secret Police)*

Melbourne band The Little Heroes evolved out of Carlton pub-rock band Secret Police which occupied Roger Hart, John Taylor and Bruce Pumpa during 1978 and 1979. The line-up was completed by Andrew Callender (guitar, vocals), Peter Linley (sax) and original bass player Neil Walker. Prior to Secret Police, Hart played in The Cruisers which comprised Shane Day (vocals), Chris Dyson (guitar), Frank Savage (guitar), Derek McCathie (bass) and John Lloyd (drums). Secret Police did not issue any records, although posthumously the band contributed the tracks 'Emotion' and 'Everybody Looks Lonely at Night' to Missing Links' 1981 Various Artists album *The Melbourne Club*. The Little Heroes came second in the Victorian heat of the 1980 Battle of the Sounds, and then took out first place in the national final with prize money of $5000. The band issued its debut independent single 'She Says'/'Coming Home' in November 1980.

Huk Treloar (ex-**Bleeding Hearts**, High Rise Bombers, Living Legends, Sneakers) replaced Bruce Pumpa and the band issued the album *The Little Heroes* (August 1981). The album produced three singles, 'For a Bleeding Heart'/'She Says' (March 1981), 'Last Number One'/'Catch Me' (June) and 'India was Calling Me'/'Pretty Shadow' (September). At the end of 1981, Alan 'Clutch' Robertson replaced Treloar on drums. The new line-up issued the *Play by Numbers* album (August 1982) which peaked at #25 on the national chart during September. The album yielded the band's only national Top 20 hit single, 'One Perfect Day'/'Just Can't Wait' (#12 nationally and #6 in Melbourne during May 1982). Two further singles were lifted from the album, 'Young Hearts'/'Please Don't Wear that Hat' (#35 in September) and 'Saturday (Afternoon) Inside'/'To Be Her Cat' (October).

By that stage, Martin Fisher (ex-Breakers) had replaced Crosbie on keyboards, and Peter Leslie had replaced Taylor on bass. At the end of 1982, Fisher and Leslie both left to join **Dear Enemy**, and Paul Brickhill (keyboards; ex-MEO-245) and Rick Loroit (bass; ex-Inserts) came in as replacements. Anthony Tavasz (ex-Modesty) replaced Loroit after four weeks. Paul Bell also joined on guitar to allow Hart more freedom as lead vocalist. Through all the changes, the band travelled to the UK to record its third album with producer Rupert Hine. The polished *Watch the World* album (September 1983) included three singles, 'Watch the World'/'Whose Turn to Cry?' (August), 'Bon Voyage'/'Let It Go' (November) and 'Modern Times'/'Painting Pictures' (March 1984). *Watch the World* reached #24 on the national chart in October, but by June 1984 The Little Heroes had called it a day. In 1997, Roger Hart wrote a book on meditation

Albums: *The Little Heroes* (Giant/CBS, 1981), *Play by Numbers* (EMI, 1982), *Watch the World* (EMI, 1983), *Play by Numbers/Watch the World* (double CD reissue, EMI, 1993).

Little Murders

Formed: *1979*
Style: *Power pop*
Original line-up: *Rob Griffiths (guitar, vocals; ex-Subway, Fiction), Clint Small (guitar, vocals), Ken Hamilton (bass; ex-Subway, Fiction), Rod Flegg (drums)*

Rob Griffiths named his band Little Murders after a 1971 film directed by Alan Arkin and starring Elliot Gould. As an English expatriate, Griffiths embraced 1960s English pop culture (The Who, The Troggs, The Kinks, Union Jacks draped over amplifiers) and accordingly Little Murders became the premier mod band on the late 1970s/early 1980s Melbourne independent scene.

The band's debut single, 'Things will Be Different'/'Take Me I'm Yours', on Au-go-go Records (December 1979) was actually recorded by Rob's old band Fiction, prior to the formation of the first Little Murders line-up listed above. Fiction comprised Griffiths, Hamilton, Rob Wellington (guitar; ex-Obsessions) and Vic Bolgarow (drums). Wellington moved on to **International Exiles** and Wild Dog Rodeo. 'Things will Be Different' was an excellent debut single, a blast of punchy, danceable pop, and it rapidly sold out its pressing of 1000 copies. 'Things will Be Different' ranks alongside **The Riptides**' 'Sunset Strip' and **Young Modern**'s 'She's Got the Money' as one of the classics of Australian new wave power pop.

By May 1980, the band's line-up comprised Griffiths, Flegg, Stuart Beatty (guitar) and Steve Fusezi (bass). Two further singles for Au-go-go followed: 'High School'/'Trouble with Love' (which featured Clint Small) and 'She Lets Me Know'/'It's Over'. During the sessions that produced 'She Lets Me Know', Griffiths took time off to record a single with other musicians. 'Melody'/'Waiting' came out under the name Dance Set in 1981. Clint Small went on to record solo and issued two EPs on Au-go-go, 'Crack in the Wall', 'Have You Got the Feeling?'/'Wyvern Parsons Where are You?' (1979) and 'On the Fourth Floor'/'Daeng', '(I'm) Hep Up to Here' (1980), plus two mini-albums *Steel* (1986) and *Loners* (1987), and a single, 'Love Has Taken Me'/'While You Sleep' (1988), on the Fourth Floor label.

Line-up changes plagued Little Murders for the next couple of years. The mid-1981 line-up featured Griffiths, Beatty, Kim Holmberg (guitar, vocals; ex-Leftovers), Paul Holmberg (drums, vocals; ex-Leftovers) and Alan Brooker (bass; ex-**Paul Kelly** and the Dots). The Holmbergs' previous band, The Leftovers, were popular in the Victorian rural township of Bendigo, and had issued one independent single, 'Killing Time'/'Trudy Vasiline', in 1980. The 1982 line-up of Little Murders, which comprised Griffiths, Rod Hayward (guitar; ex-Frank Savage and the Citizens), Chris Hunter (bass; ex-Cuban Heels) and Michael Barclay (drums; ex-Japanese Comix), was the most accomplished and consistent to date. Unable to secure a major record deal for his efforts, however, Griffiths eventually broke up Little Murders in December 1983. Barclay went on to join **The Runners**, **The Zimmermen**, **Paul Kelly** and the Coloured Girls and **Weddings, Parties, Anything**; Haywood joined cabaret kings Pete Best Beatles and much later turned up in **Dave Graney 'n' the Coral Snakes**.

Griffiths made an unsuccessful attempt to revive the Little Murders name in 1985, and independent label Polyester Records issued the '100 Drugs'/'The Beat Goes On' single (the tracks had been recorded in 1983 and 1979 respectively). Au-go-go issued the retrospective set *Stop!* in 1986, which drew together various singles tracks and unissued studio cuts. In late 1995, Rob Griffiths revived the Little Murders name, and over the next 18 months recorded a new album. Backing musicians included Rod Hayward, Phil Wales (guitar; ex-**Harem Scarem**), Craig Pilkington (guitar; from **The Killjoys**), Tony Ennis (bass) and Dave Foley (drums; also from **The Killjoys**). The album *. . . and stuff like that* (June 1997) comprised the new material (including the single 'Love and Stuff Like That'/'100 Drugs') plus six previously released cuts. By that stage, Griffiths had a new Little Murders line-up on the road with Ennis, plus Paul Thomas (guitar) and Michael Barclay (drums) on loan from **Weddings, Parties, Anything**.

Albums: *Stop!* (Au-go-go, 1986), *. . . and stuff like that* (Swerve, 1997).

Little Pattie

Style: *Surf pop*

During the early years of Australian rock'n'roll, the scene was almost entirely male dominated. As the beat softened and the frantic momentum diminished during the early 1960s, the first female solo singers began to emerge. These included **Noeleen Batley** (dubbed 'Australia's Little Miss Sweetheart'), **Judy Stone**, **Patsy Ann Noble**, **Betty McQuade**, Patti Markham, Lana Cantrell, Lee Grant, Candy and Mandy, Laurel Lea and Patricia 'Little Pattie' Amphlett (b. 1949).

By the age of 13, Amphlett had already appeared on the television show *Opportunity Knocks*. She then became a regular at Sydney's southern beaches surf club dances, singing with The Statesmen. Singer Jay Justin is credited with having discovered Amphlett. He recommended her to EMI after seeing her perform at Bronte Surf Club, and co-wrote (with Joe Halford) her debut single. As Little Pattie, Amphlett issued 'He's My Blonde Headed Stompie Wompie Real Gone Surfer Boy'/'Stompin' at Maroubra' and it became a hit (Sydney #2, Melbourne #25 in December 1963). As Bob Rogers wrote in *Rock'n'Roll Australia*, the Australian summers of 1961, 1962 and 1963 were dominated by the surfing craze both musically and physically. Little Pattie's sweet personality and chirpy surf-pop caught the tempo of the times, and she instantly became the heroine of Australian surf music.

At 15, Little Pattie left Sydney Girls High School to concentrate on her singing career. She scored three more hit singles during 1964 and made regular appearances on television pop shows like *Bandstand*, *Saturday Date* and *Sing, Sing, Sing*. She followed up 'We're Gonna Have a Party Tonight'/'Dear Judy' (Sydney #18 in March 1964), 'Drag Race Johnny'/'He's My Boy' (July) and 'Surfin' Time Again'/'Everybody Keeps Telling Me' (December) with more Sydney hits: 'Pushin' a Good Thing Too Far'/'Ladies Man' (#28 in March 1965) and 'Dance Puppet Dance'/'I Just Need Your Love' (#9 in October). She rounded out 1965 with 'My Love'/'It's You Babe' (November).

By 1966, Little Pattie had moved upmarket. She left the dances behind to make club and cabaret appearances. She continued to issue singles for EMI up until 1970: 'Game of Love'/'Raindrops Fall Like Teardrops' (1966), 'Will Ya or Won't Ya?'/'Never Gonna Love Again' (1966), 'Don't Walk Away'/'Your Kind of Lovin'' (1966), 'Let Me Dream'/'Love will Come Back' (1966), 'With Love from Jenny'/'It's All Over Now' (1967), 'I'll Eat My Hat'/'Nothin'' (1967), 'If He Would Care'/'Thrill is Gone' (1967), 'I Knew Right Away'/'In Time' (1967), 'Sunshine Boy'/'24th Day of July' (1968), 'Love is a Happy Thing'/'Nothing You Can Do' (1968), 'Someone Out There' (1969), 'Gravitation'/'Let the Music Start' (as Pattie, 1969) and 'The Penthouse'/'We're Not Gonna Take It' (1970).

In the meantime, Little Pattie had married **Col Joye's** brother Keith and signed to the Joye Organisation's ATA label. She issued seven singles on ATA: 'April Fool'/'Seen It All Before' (April, 1971), 'Save Me'/'So Softly' (as Pattie, 1972), 'Carolina'/'Two Different Things' (1972), 'What's Your Mama's Name?'/'Since You're Not Around' (as Pattie, 1973), 'Kentucky Blues'/'Without You' (1974), 'Only If You Want to'/'It's All for You' (September, 1976) and 'What Am I Gonna Do?'/'Blue

Jean Baby' (December 1977). By 1977, Little Pattie had moved into a country direction as displayed on her seventh album, *Only If You Want To*. In 1980 she issued 'Ain't Nothing Gonna Keep Me from You'/'Love is' on Polydor.

Albums: *Little Things Like This* (EMI/HMV, 1964), *Pattie* (EMI/HMV, 1965), *The Many Moods of Pattie* (EMI/HMV, 1965), *The Best of Little Pattie* (EMI/Columbia, 1968), *Beautiful in the Rain* (EMI/Columbia, 1969), *I will Bring You Flowers* (ATA/Festival, 1972), *Only If You Want To* (ATA/Festival, 1977), *20 Wompy Stompy Hits!* (EMI, 1981), *Moments Like These* (Labrava, 1995).

Little River Band

Little River Band

Formed: *1975*
Style: *Harmony rock*
Original line-up: **Glenn Shorrock** *(lead vocals; ex-***Twilights**, **Axiom**, *Esperanto), Graham Goble (guitar, vocals; ex-Alison Gros,* **Mississippi***), Beeb Birtles (guitar, vocals; ex-***Zoot***, Frieze,* **Mississippi***), Graham Davidge (lead guitar; ex-Superlemon), Dave Orrams (bass), Derek Pellici (drums; ex-***Mississippi***)*

As a group of highly competent rock musicians, Little River Band's aim was to create a textured, harmony-dominant, mass-appeal sound and style. Indeed, the band's sophisticated brand of West Coast-influenced harmony rock was ideally suited to the vast American market. Little River Band (LRB) was the first Australian band of the 1970s to gain significant international success, paving the way for **AC/DC**, **Air Supply**, **Men at Work** and **INXS** across the USA in the process. Under the careful guidance of manager (and ex-**Master's Apprentices** bass player) Glenn Wheatley, the band undertook a punishing schedule of American tours which helped push albums like *Sleeper Catcher* and *First Under the Wire* over the million sales mark.

LRB evolved out of the ashes of **Mississippi** which broke up in the UK at the end of 1974. Graham Goble and Beeb Birtles had already laid the foundation for the LRB sound with the tight, intricate harmonies they developed in **Mississippi**. Right from the outset, LRB was Goble and Birtles' band, the product of a shared and ambitious vision given a tangible focus by Wheatley's managerial skills. Goble and Birtles brought in the experienced **Glenn Shorrock** to front the band. As lead singer, Shorrock provided the perfect counterpoint to Goble and Birtles' backing harmonies. Since the demise of **Axiom** in the UK during March 1971, Shorrock had spent the previous four years working overseas. As a songwriter, Shorrock also contributed the likes of 'Emma', 'Statue of Liberty', 'Seine City', 'Help is on Its Way', 'Cool Change', 'Shut Down, Turn Off' and 'Long Jumping Jeweller' to the band's repertoire.

Original lead guitarist Graham Davidge left early in the piece (he played on the band's very first, unreleased recording, a cover of the Everly Brothers' 'When Will I Be Loved?'). LRB then snared classically trained guitarist/arranger Rick Formosa to complete the line-up. Roger McLachlan also replaced original bass player Dave Orrams. LRB took its name from a signpost on the road from Melbourne to Geelong where the band played its first engagement. By the end of 1975, the band had made the national charts with 'Curiosity (Killed the Cat)'/'I Just Don't Get the Feeling Anymore' (#8 in October) and *Little River Band* (#12 in November). 'Emma'/'Love is a Feeling' (#20 in January 1976) and 'Everyday of My Life'/'Days on the Road' (#24 in May), plus *After Hours* (#4 in May) followed. In August 1976, both Formosa and McLachlan left the band to be replaced by David Briggs (ex-**Avengers**) and George McArdle respectively.

In September, the band left for its first international tour, taking in the UK (including a support slot to Queen in London), Europe and the USA (as support to the Average White Band). In November, an edited version of the eight and a half minute 'It's a Long Way There' (from the debut album, backed with 'Time to Fly') reached the American Top 30 (#28) and the Dutch Top 10. The band's self-titled US debut album (a compilation of the first two Australian LPs) sold a healthy 200 000 copies. The band's third album, *Diamantina Cocktail* (April 1977), sold over 100 000 copies in Australia; by the end of the year, it had achieved gold status in the USA (500 000 copies sold), the first time that an Australian band had managed such a feat.

Diamantina Cocktail produced the hit singles 'Help is on Its Way'/'Inner Light' (Australian #1 in April; US #14 in May), 'Witchery'/'L.A. in the Sunshine' (Australian #26 in August), 'Happy Anniversary'/'Lady' (US #16 in October) and 'Home on Monday'/'Raelene' (November 1977). The album reached #2 in Australia and #49 in the USA.

The band's second US tour took in support slots to the Doobie Brothers, America and Supertramp, plus a series of headlining dates. *Sleeper Catcher* reached #17 in the USA, and LRB became the first band to locally record an album which sold one million copies (platinum) in the USA. It also sold 100 000 copies in both Australia (#3 in May 1978) and Canada. Three singles were lifted from the album: 'Shut Down, Turn Off'/'Days on the Road' (Australian #11 in April 1978), 'Reminiscing'/'Take Me Home' (Australian #31 in July; US #3 in May) and 'Lady' (US #10 in January 1979).

LRB's first 'Best of' compilation, *It's a Long Way There—Greatest Hits* reached #2 in Australia during November 1978, and sold over 200 000 copies. For the band's next American tour, session drummer Geoff Cox (ex-**Bootleg Family Band**, **Avalanche**) deputised for the unavailable Pellici, who was recovering in hospital after an exploding gas cylinder caused burns to his hands and chest. During the tour, LRB supported Boz Scaggs, Jimmy Buffett and The Eagles. The band's sixth album (and second US million seller), *First Under the Wire*, reached #2 in Australia (August 1979) and Top 10 in the US. 'Lonesome Loser'/'Another Runaway' became the band's eighth Australian hit single (#19 in July 1979). 'It's Not a Wonder'/'The Rumour' (September 1979) and 'Red Shoes'/'Let's Dance' (May 1980) failed to reach the Top 40. *First Under the Wire* also gave LRB two more US Top 10 hits with 'Lonesome Loser' (#6) and 'Cool Change' (#10).

For LRB's fifth US tour in August 1979, Barry Sullivan (bass; ex-**Chain**, **Renée Geyer** Band) and Mal Logan (keyboards; ex-**Healing Force**, **Renée Geyer** Band) joined the band. American Wayne Nelson joined LRB as permanent bass player in early 1980. In between their commitments to LRB, Birtles, Goble and Shorrock found time to issue solo records. Birtles and Goble collaborated on the singles 'Lonely Lives'/'Megan' (February 1978), 'I'm Coming Home'/'You'll Never Change Your Mind' (#8 in April 1979) and 'How I Feel Tonight'/'Netherlands' (June 1980), plus the album *Last Romance*. Shorrock scored a Top 10 hit in April 1979 with a cover of Bobby Darin's 'Dream Lover'/'Spin Me Round'.

The live albums *Backstage Pass* (recorded with the Adelaide Symphony Orchestra; #18 in January 1980) and *Live in America* (April 1980) kept LRB on the local charts until the band could undertake its first Australian tour in three years (summer 1980/81). 'Long Jumping Jeweller'/'Don't Worry No More' reached #32 in March 1981. In July 1981, Briggs left the band to be replaced by English-born Steve Housden (ex-Imports). Briggs' last album with LRB was *Time Exposure* (September 1981; Australian #9 in October) which produced the hits 'Night Owls'/'Suicide' (Australian #18, US #6, October), 'Man on Your Mind'/'Love will Survive' (US #14, December) and 'Take It Easy on Me'/'Orbit Zero' (US #10, February 1982).

In February 1982, Shorrock left LRB to pursue a solo career. His place was taken by one of Australia's most popular singers, **John Farnham**. The new line-up of LRB scored hit singles with 'Down on the Border'/'No More Tears' (Australian #7 in August 1982), **The Easybeats'** 'St Louis'/'Easy Money' (October 1982) and 'The Other Guy'/'Take It Easy on Me' (Australian #18, February 1983; US #11), plus the best-selling album *The Net* (Australian #10 in June 1983). 'We Two'/'Falling' (May 1983) and 'You're Driving Me Out of My Mind'/'Mr Socialite' (August 1983) were not successful.

In October 1983, founder member Birtles left LRB to be replaced by **David Hirschfelder** (keyboards). Birtles turned his hand to writing theme songs for feature films like *Something Great* and *Rio*. Pellici also left the band; his replacement was Steve Prestwich (ex-**Cold Chisel**). *Playing to Win* (February 1985) was a strong album but it failed to halt the band's slide in popularity. 'Playing to Win'/'Through Her Eyes' (December 1984), 'Blind Eyes'/'The Butterfly' (May 1985) and 'Time for Us' (April 1986) were issued as singles. **John Farnham** left LRB at the end of 1985 to reactivate his solo career. The last LRB album that Farnham sang on was *No Reins*, which yielded three singles in 'No Reins on Me'/'Paper Paradise' (June 1986), 'Face in the Crowd'/'Thin Ice' (September) and Prestwich's 'When the War is Over'/'How Many Nights?' (February 1987).

In 1988, with the band's fortunes at a low ebb, former members Shorrock and Pellici rejoined LRB. The new line-up of Goble, Shorrock, Pellici, Nelson and Housden recorded the album *Monsoon* (June 1988). *Monsoon* peaked at #7 on the Australian chart, and gave rise to the singles 'Love is a Bridge'/'Inside Story' (May 1988), 'Son of a Famous Man'/'Lyin' Eyes' (August), 'Soul Searching'/'The Great Unknown' (October) and 'When will I Be Loved?'/'D' (1989). 'Love is a Bridge' became the band's second biggest Australian hit single when it peaked at #7 in June. The 1989 album *Too Late to Load* featured early demos and studio out-takes.

The *Get Lucky* album (April 1990) featured the line-up of Goble, Shorrock, Pellici, Nelson, Housden and Tony Scuito (keyboards). 'If I Get Lucky'/'Piece of My Heart' (1990) and 'Every Time I Look Around' (1990) were issued as singles. Founder member Goble left the touring line-up in order to concentrate on his splinter project Broken Voices. American Peter Beckett (vocals, guitar; ex-Player) took Goble's place on the band's 1990 American tour. Goble later issued a European-only album, *Nautilus*, under the guise of the Graham Goble Experience. Goble remains one of the most lauded Australian songwriters of the rock era, clearly demonstrated by his commendation for Three Million US Airplay for 'Reminiscing'.

LRB called it a day in 1991. Over the course of 16 years, the band achieved a level of international success that was only surpassed by **AC/DC**, **Men at Work** and **INXS**. LRB's latter years were particularly lean, but the band's willingness during the early days to tour the USA constantly (13 tours between 1976 and 1983) ensured a string of best-selling records.

Albums: *Little River Band* (EMI, 1975), *After Hours* (EMI, 1976), *Diamantina Cocktail* (EMI, 1977), *Sleeper Catcher* (EMI, 1978), *It's a Long Way There—Greatest Hits* (EMI, 1978), *First Under the Wire* (EMI, 1979), *Backstage Pass* (EMI, 1980), *Live in America* (EMI/Capitol, 1980), *Time Exposure* (EMI/Capitol, 1981), *Greatest Hits Volume 2* (EMI/Capitol, 1983), *The Net* (EMI/Capitol, 1983), *Playing to Win* (EMI/Capitol, 1985), *No Reins* (EMI/Capitol, 1986), *Monsoon* (WEA, 1988), *Too Late to Load* (EMI, 1989), *The Farnham Years* (compilation, EMI, 1989), *Get Lucky* (MCA, 1990), *The Classic Collection* (EMI, 1992), *The Classics Live* (EMI, 1993), *Reminiscing* (compilation, EMI, 1995).

Lizard

Formed: *1972*
Style: *Progressive rock*
Original line-up: *Dave Conners (sax; ex-Jamieson Battery, White Wine), Mick Tulk (lead guitar), Greg Hill (bass; ex-White Wine), Robert Souter (drums; ex-Jamieson Battery, White Wine)*

The original line-up of Sydney progressive rock band Lizard grew out of a project called White Wine which had been instigated by Gus McNeil (ex-**Nomads**). Dave Conners, Greg Hill and Robert Souter were part of White Wine when the band travelled to the UK in 1970. Once White Wine had run its course, Conners, Hill and Souter recruited English-born guitarist Mick Tulk in a fledgling group that also included another Australian expatriate, Mitch Byrnes (sax; ex-Gus and the House).

Conners, Hill, Souter and Tulk returned to Australia at the start of 1972, which coincided with John Wheeler (keyboards) and Shirley Reid (vocals; ex-Nine Stage Horizon) joining Lizard. Reid left at the end of 1972 and Lizard signed to EMI's progressive Harvest label. The band issued the ultra-rare *Bad Companions* album and the single 'Rosalyn'/'Cecil' in 1973. The album highlighted a confident brand of progressive jazz-blues that drew comparisons with **Company Caine**, with which Lizard shared a level of cosmic affinity. Lizard broke up at the end of 1973, and Tulk and Conners appeared on erstwhile **Company Caine** frontman **Gulliver Smith's** solo album *The Band's Alright but the Singer is . . .* Tulk, Conners and Hill then joined Smith's solo band, The Dead End Kids. Shirley Reid joined the re-formed **Company Caine** as co-lead vocalist with Smith in 1975. Souter joined **Keith Glass**'s Living Legends and **The Dynamic Hepnotics**.

Album: *Bad Companions* (EMI/Harvest, 1973).

The Lizard Train

Formed: *1985*
Style: *Rock*
Original line-up: *Chris Willard (guitar, vocals; ex-Head On, Crawling Eye, Acid Drops, Revenge of the Gila Monsters), Phil Drew (guitar, vocals), Shane Bloffwitch (bass, vocals; ex-Risque Humour), David Creese (drums, vocals; ex-Risque Humour)*

The Lizard Train was part of the thriving, late 1980s Adelaide independent scene that also gave rise to **Exploding White Mice**, **Screaming Believers**, **The Garden Path**, **Liz Dealey** and the Twenty Second Sect, The Spikes and **July 14th**. The Lizard Train played an adventurous brand of hard-edged rock that drew on US 1960s acid-punk and early 1980s Gun Club swamp-blues for inspiration.

The band's first recording venture involved backing **Liz Dealey** (ex-Acid Drops) on the debut single by Liz Dealey and the Twenty Second Sect, 'The Wailing House'/'Tell Me No', '(Don't) Give Me That' (1986). That set the tone for The Lizard Train's debut release, the four-track, 12-inch EP *Thirteen Hour Daydream* (August 1986), on which a melange of screaming guitars did battle over a rumbling rhythm section. Yet, beneath the distorted riffs and lyrical angst, the band boasted a melodic and harmonic sensibility usually disregarded in such aggressive music.

The record immediately drew interest in European territories like France and Germany. In

1987, The Lizard Train undertook its first overseas tour. The band's debut full-length album, *Slippery* (September 1987), featured a slightly less supercharged (though still effective) approach overall as epitomised by the single 'Beauty Underground'/'The Day the Sky Went Black' (June) and the chiming Neil Young-like 'Ever Been There?' Drew left in December 1987 and the band continued as a three-piece. The Lizard Train toured Europe again before issuing a second album, *The Ride*, and the 12-inch single 'She Gets Me' in 1990. *The Ride* stands as the high point in the band's career, a work brimming with powerful, dark songs and inspired musicianship.

In 1992, The Lizard Train signed to Shock Records' Shagpile subsidiary label for the aptly named *Get Yer Wah Wahs Out* album. True to the album's title, songs like 'Such a Nice Girl' and 'Harry the Dirty Dog' featured an unsettling sonic assault of wah wah and fuzzed guitar effects that was remarkably intriguing by the same token. The albums *Couch* (October 1993) and *Everything Moves* (March 1995), plus the CD single 'It All Came from Nothing' (February 1995) maintained the noise factor as well as the song quality. US producer Steve Albini (Nirvana, Breeders, Jesus Lizard) worked with the band on *Everything Moves*. By the time the band's last release, the CD EP *Inertia* (May 1995), came out, The Lizard Train had relocated to Melbourne and evolved into The Dumb Earth.

The Dumb Earth comprised Willard (who switched to bass), Creese, Mark Ford (sax) and Adam Kyle (guitar). Writer Andy Turner described the band's sound as a 'brain-melting amalgamation of avant-garde jazz and slide guitar'. The Dumb Earth issued one single in 1996, 'Taxi Me Through', and the album *Walk the Earth* in June 1997.

Albums: *Slippery* (Greasy Pop, 1987), *The Ride* (Greasy Pop, 1990), *Get Yer Wah Wahs Out* (Shagpile/Shock, 1992), *Couch* (Shagpile/Shock, 1993), *Everything Moves* (Shagpile/Shock, 1995), *Walk the Earth* (as The Dumb Earth, Rubber, 1997).

Carol Lloyd Band (*see* Railroad Gin)

Lotus

Formed: *1970*
Style: *Rock, pop*
Original line-up: *Shane Hewitt (vocals), Kim Dawson (lead guitar, vocals), Warwick Wilkes (organ, vocals), Ian Every (bass, vocals), Ray Smedley (drums)*

Like a number of Sydney bands that earned a living on the suburban dance/discotheque circuit of the early 1970s, Lotus was always destined to be trapped somewhere between minor pop star status and the dedicated progressive rock devotee. When the members of Lotus first came together at the start of 1970, they lived on a farm on the outskirts of Sydney where they grew their own food.

Lotus moved to Melbourne later in the year, and established a reputation for energetic live shows. In December 1970, the band issued its one and only single, 'Lotus 1 (I'll Be Gone)'/'Epoch' on EMI/Parlophone. This impressive hard rock single graced the lower reaches of the national top 40 (peaking at #33) in May, but a month later Lotus broke up. Dawson and Wilkes played in Melbourne band The Ash for a time. By the end of 1971, Dawson, Wilkes and Smedley had returned to Sydney and re-formed Lotus with newcomers Norm Roue (slide guitar; ex-Gutbucket) and Billy Rylands (bass; ex-**Freshwater**). That line-up was short-lived. By early 1972, Roue and Rylands had joined Wolfe; from there Roue joined **Band of Light** and **Buffalo**. Ian Every returned to the fold, and the Dawson/Wilkes/Smedley/Every line-up kept active until August 1973. Reissue specialists Raven included 'Lotus 1' on the 1994 compilation *Golden Miles: Australian Progressive Rock 1969–1974* (1994).

Love Gone Wrong (*see* John Kennedy's Love Gone Wrong)

Love Machine

Formed: *1968*
Style: *Pop*
Original line-up: *Glenn Bland (vocals, harmonica), Alan 'Olly' Oloman (vocals, guitar), Brian 'Felix' Wilkinson (keyboards), Darcy Rosser (bass), Colin McAuley (drums)*

Love Machine was a studio creation working under an assumed name for producer Pat Aulton. The musicians Aulton used actually comprised Sydney band Tymepiece, who had formed as **The Black Diamonds** in 1965. Love Machine came about when Aulton revived The Tokens' 1962 hit 'The Lion Sleeps Tonight' to coincide with the opening of the Warragamba Lion Park near Sydney.

'The Lion Sleeps Tonight'/'The Lonely Hearts Club Christmas Party' reached #11 on the Sydney chart and #26 in Melbourne during October 1968. Love Machine issued a follow-up single, 'Keep Searchin'/'May My Heart Cast into Stone (January 1969), and an album, *The Lion Sleeps Tonight* (1969). The strain of making appearances as both Love Machine and Tymepiece proved too much for the musicians involved, and they moved on. Aulton kept the Love Machine name alive with a new batch of studio musicians. A revival of **The Delltones'** 'Get a Little Dirt on Your Hands'/'Just Like Romeo and Juliet' reached #38 on the chart in June 1969. Two further singles followed, 'My Little Chickadee'/'The Devil Came from Kansas' and 'Mr DJ Play Me a Song'/'Love at First Sight', before Aulton laid the concept to rest.

Album: *The Lion Sleeps Tonight* (Calendar/Festival, 1969).

Love Positions (*see* The Plunderers)

The Loved Ones

The Loved Ones

Formed: *1965*
Style: *R&B, pop*
Original line-up: *Gerry Humphreys (vocals; ex-Red Onions Jazz Band), Rob Lovett (guitar; ex-***Wild Cherries***), Ian Clyne (organ, piano; ex-Red Onions Jazz Band), Kim Lynch (bass; ex-Red Onions Jazz Band), Gavin Anderson (drums; ex-***Wild Cherries***)*

The Loved Ones remain one of the most revered of all Australia's 1960s groups. In Gerry Humphreys, the band possessed a singer of remarkable flair and vitality whose dexterous, blueswailin' voice set standards other vocalists of the day could only ever hope to match. The band was equally adept at playing tough R&B or reflective pop. The Loved Ones issued at least three bona fide Australian rock classics in 'The Loved One', 'Everlovin' Man' and 'Sad Dark Eyes'.

Until R&B filtered down to Australia in 1964, Humphreys, Ian Clyne and Kim Lynch made a living playing jazz in The Red Onions Jazz Band. The band issued one rare album on W&G's Blue Label, *The Red Onions Jazz Band* (1964), before breaking up in early 1965. Likewise, Rob Lovett and Gavin Anderson were playing jazz with **The Wild Cherries** before that band also turned to R&B. The Loved Ones formed in October 1965 and by early 1966 had signed to W&G's pop subsidiary label In. The band's debut single, 'The Loved One'/'This is Love' (May 1966), immediately hit #15 in Melbourne and #2 in Sydney. 'Everlovin' Man/'More than Love' (July 1966) fared even better in Melbourne, reaching #2 in August and staying on the charts for 19 weeks. In Sydney it peaked at #9. The 'Blueberry Hill' EP reached #11 in Melbourne and #16 in Sydney during December. Meanwhile, Clyne had left the band to be replaced by Reg 'Treva' Richardson. Clyne worked with The Black Pearls, **The Ram Jam Big Band**, Excalibur, **Levi Smith's Clefs** and **Chain**. He also spent most of 1970 and 1971 overseas.

The hits continued with 'Sad Dark Eyes'/'The Woman I Love' (Melbourne #20, Sydney #33 in January 1967) and 'A Love Like Ours'/'Lovely Car' (Melbourne #21 in April). In May 1967, Lynch left the band; Lovett moved over to bass and American-born Danny De Lacy came in on lead guitar. The Loved Ones' fifth single, 'Love Song'/'Magic Box' (August 1967), failed to chart and the band broke up in October. Humphreys went into management and then formed **Gerry and the Joy Band** at the end of 1971. He also compered the inaugural Sunbury Pop Festival in January 1972. In 1977, he settled in London where he reputedly worked as a hospital orderly.

In May 1968, Lovett joined **Peter Doyle** and Mal McGee (ex-**Python Lee Jackson**) in the heavily hyped, would-be Walker Brothers, The Virgil Brothers. The vocal trio issued three singles: a cover of The Knight Brothers' 'Temptation's 'Bout to Get Me'/'I See Her Face' (June 1968), 'Here I Am'/ 'Shake Me Wake Me' (September) and 'When You Walk Away'/'Good Love' (September 1969), and travelled to the UK. The Virgil Brothers failed to make an impact, and Doyle joined The New Seekers. Lovett stayed in the UK where The New Seekers covered one of his songs, 'When There's No Love Left' (co-written with Brian Peacock).

In 1981, **INXS** revived The Loved Ones' 'The Loved One' for its second hit single. **INXS** later re-recorded the song for inclusion on its multi-platinum selling album *Kick* (1988). By that stage, continuing interest in The Loved Ones had prompted the group to re-form for a national tour in September 1987. Drummer Peter Luscombe deputised for the unavailable Anderson. The tour resulted in the live album *Live on Blueberry Hill* (April 1988). Lovett went on to work with R&B outfit The Fudds, issuing an album in June 1994, *Meet the Fudds*, on the Lavish label. The Loved Ones' *Magic Box* album has been reissued on several occasions; Raven's 1985 reissue added three live cuts from 1967 and the previously non-album track 'This is Love' (from the 'Blueberry Hill' EP).

Albums: *Magic Box* (W&G, 1967; reissued on Astor in 1975 and on Raven in 1985), *Live on Blueberry Hill* (Mushroom/Festival, 1988).

Damien Lovelock (*see* The Celibate Rifles)

Graham Lowndes

Style: *Folk, rock*

Singer/songwriter Graham Lowndes was a veteran of the late 1960s folkie scene, having played in the Currency Blues Band with **Mike McClellan**. During the early to mid-1970s, Lowndes sang in a number of rock bands including R.J. Taylor, Bootleg, Powderhorn and One Ton Gypsy. Lowndes contributed vocals to **Lobby Loyde's** classic 1971 hard rock album *Plays with George Guitar*.

Bootleg comprised Lowndes (vocals, guitar), Zac Zytnik (lead guitar; ex-**Tamam Shud**), John Jackson (bass) and Nigel Macara (drums; ex-Stonehenge). The band issued one obscure single, 'Whole World Should Slow Down'/'Lost Love', in the second half of 1970, after which Macara left to join **Tamam Shud**. Paul Balbi replaced Macara, and Phil Hitchcock also replaced Jackson on bass. In November 1970, Lowndes left to join Red McKelvie's country-rock outfit Powderhorn and Zytnik joined **Blackfeather**. Powderhorn comprised Lowndes, McKelvie (guitar; ex-**Flying Circus**), Bill Twyman (bass; ex-R.J. Taylor) and Ace Follington (drums; ex-**Chain**, R.J. Taylor). The band had broken up by the end of 1971 and Lowndes joined **Ray Brown's** new band One Ton Gypsy. He left in 1972 to pursue a solo career which eventually resulted in the 1973 album *Survival's a Song* and single 'Survival's a Song'/'Town of Fear' on the Albert label.

His 1975 album, *Mouth Music* (on the independent Jambone imprint), was a more rock-oriented effort and featured contributions from musicians like **Ray Arnott** (drums; ex-Chelsea Set, **Company Caine**, **Spectrum**, **Mighty Kong**), Sam McNally (keyboards), Mike Burke (pedal steel guitar), Steve Murphy (lead guitar) and Russell Smith (brass; ex-**Ram Jam Big Band**). Singer **Jeannie Lewis** recorded a number of Lowndes' songs, including 'Till Time Brings Change', 'The House is Burning', 'The Rising of the Tide' and 'Loser'.

Albums: *Survival's a Song* (Albert/EMI, 1973), *Mouth Music* (Jambone, 1975).

Lobby Loyde

Style: *R&B, rock*

The redoubtable Lobby Loyde (b. 1946) is one of the true legends of Australian rock'n'roll. During the 1960s, when the guitar became the dominant symbol in rock, Loyde emerged as Australia's first true guitar hero. As Glenn A. Baker put it, Loyde was busy blowing up speaker boxes years before high volume and feedback became a rock staple.

Lobby Loyde was born John Baslington Lyde in the central Queensland town of Longreach. He studied classical music as a child, before taking up electric guitar in his teens. In 1963, as Barry Lyde, he joined Brisbane band The Stilettos, playing Shadows-styled instrumentals. In 1964, he joined a young R&B band called The Impacts fronted by expatriate Englishman Mick Hadley. Along with fellow Englishman Bob Dames (drums), Hadley had experienced the burgeoning London R&B club scene first hand. With a name change to **The Purple Hearts**, the band became one of the hottest R&B outfits in Australia. In early 1967, Barry Lyde became Lobby Loyde and began transforming a one-time jazz/R&B band called **The Wild Cherries** into one of the most relentlessly experimental psychedelic groups Australia ever witnessed. He remained with **The Wild Cherries** until the end of 1968, when he accepted an offer to join emergent blues hero **Billy Thorpe** in his band The Aztecs.

Under Loyde's influence, The Aztecs spearheaded the burgeoning blues, boogie and heavy rock movement of the day. It was on that foundation that **Billy Thorpe** earned his position as the unassailable king of Australia's early 1970s rock scene. Loyde stayed with The Aztecs until October 1970. At the start of 1971, he recruited the former **Fanny Adams** rhythm section of Teddy Toi (bass) and Johnny Dick (drums) in order to record his outstanding solo album, *Plays with George Guitar* (issued in September). That album remains a progressive rock milestone, one of the most remarkable heavy guitar records of the period. Out of that association, Loyde, Toi and Dick formed a new, three-piece line-up of **The Wild Cherries**. Loyde kept the band going until February 1972, after which he formed a new band called **Coloured Balls**.

That band lasted for three years. Following the band's premature split at the end of 1974, Lobby initially went solo, issuing the single 'Do You Believe in Magic?'/'Love Lost on Dream Tides' (December 1975) on the Bootleg label.

Loyde issued his second solo album, *Obsecration* (May 1976), which was an impressive work of guitar explorations and thematic textures. Backing Loyde on the album was a loose aggregation of musicians which he dubbed Southern Electric. The line-up comprised two ex-**Coloured Balls** members, Andy Fordham (rhythm guitar) and Janis Miglans (bass), plus **Mándu** (vocals), John Dey (keyboards) and James Thompson (drums; ex-**Billy Thorpe** and the Aztecs). With the release of *Obsecration*, Loyde moved to the UK with a couple of Southern Electric members (Fordham, Dey, Thompson). The Virgin label had shown interest in issuing *Obsecration* in the UK, although a deal never eventuated. The UK was then in the thick of the punk movement, and Loyde was not able to get Southern Electric off the ground. Loyde ran the front-of-house sound for a few new wave bands and worked in a studio learning production skills. On his return to Australia in 1979, Loyde formed a new band with Gil Matthews (drums; ex-**Billy Thorpe** and the Aztecs), Gavin Carroll (bass) and **Mándu**, initially dubbed The Empty Halls Band but later renamed Southern Electric. That potentially brilliant line-up recorded the masterful hard rock album, *Live with Dubs*, which eventually saw release in October 1980.

In 1979, Loyde also contributed the track 'John's Song' to the Various Artists *Australian Guitar Album* (Festival/Razzle), which also featured **Kevin Borich, Mario Millo, Ian Moss, Phil Manning, Rockwell T. James,** Chris Turner, Mick Elliott, Russell Smith, Ian Miller and Harvey James. In the meantime, Loyde had joined **Rose Tattoo** as bass player. That line-up of the Tatts recorded an album in Los Angeles which remains unissued. Loyde toured with the Tatts for a year (October 1979 to September 1980).

He then devoted his time to production duties and live sound mixing for the likes of **Sunnyboys, Machinations, X** and **Painters and Dockers**. In 1990, he played bass in a short-lived band called Dirt alongside Jex Byron (vocals, ex-**Olympic Sideburns**), Mick Holmes (guitar, ex-**Zimmermen**), Geordie Leach (bass, ex-**Rose Tattoo**) and Cal MacAlpine (drums; ex-**Chosen Few**). In 1997, Loyde formed a new band called Fish Tree Mother.

Lobby Loyde solo albums: *Plays with George Guitar* (Festival/Infinity, 1971), *Lobby Loyde* (reissue of debut album, Festival/Calendar, 1974), *Obsecration* (Rainbird, 1976); ***Southern Electric album:*** *Live with Dubs* (Mushroom/Festival, 1980).

Lubricated Goat

Formed: *1986*
Style: *Rock*
Original line-up: *Stu Spasm (real name Stuart Gray, vocals, guitar, synthesiser, bass; ex-Exhibit A, Zulu Rattle, Salamander Jim,* **Beasts of Bourbon**, *James Baker Experience, Death in Vegas, Hot Property), Martin Bland (drums, vocals; ex-Head On, Crawling Eye, Acid Drops,* **Bloodloss**, *Zulu Rattle, Salamander Jim, Primevils), Pete Hartley (bass, guitar; ex-***Kryptonics***), Brett Ford (drums; ex-***Kryptonics***)*

The driving force behind the anarchistic Lubricated Goat was one Stu Spasm, a musician not known for subtlety and restraint. As a member of a group of like-minded musicians (**Tex Perkins**, Lachlan McLeod, Martin Bland and Peter Read), Stu Spasm conceived Lubricated Goat as a subversive take on all things complacent and facile in rock music circa 1986.

For the musicians involved, it was simply a chance to exist on the very edges of the Sydney rock scene, and to play out a sick joke for their own entertainment. John Foy at Red Eye Records liked the joke and formed the Black Eye label specifically as an outlet for the recorded works of this bunch of noise terrorists. The first batch of Black Eye records issued in July 1987 included Lubricated Goat's *Plays the Devil's Music* album, Thug's *Mechanical Ape/Proud Idiots Parade* album and the notorious 'Dad' single, plus the Various Artists album *Waste Sausage* which had been compiled by McLeod. *Plays the Devil's Music* comprised recordings Spasm had made with Bland in Adelaide and with Pete Hartley and Brett Ford in Perth during September 1986. As such, the original Lubricated Goat line-up was a transient one at best. The consolidated line-up of Spasm, Hartley, Ford and Guy Maddison (bass) issued the album *Paddock of Love* (July 1988).

Lubricated Goat will forever be remembered for its infamous appearance on the ABC-TV's late-night variety show *Blah Blah Blah* in late 1988. That particular episode dealt with the issue of censorship, and the band members performed the cacophonous 'In the Raw' completely naked. The sight of the Goats' real (and imagined) body parts was enough to prompt scores of irate callers to jam the ABC's switchboard for 30 minutes, for the *Daily Mirror* to run a front-page exposé and for current affairs shows like the *Midday Show*, *Hinch* and *Newsworld*, plus radio commentators like Ron Casey, to call for an end to such moral depravity.

The line-up of Spasm, Maddison, Charlie Tolnay (guitar; ex-**Grong Grong**, **King Snake Roost**) and Gene Ravet (drums; ex-Ragadoll, concurrently in Space Juniors) produced the 12-inch EP *Schadenfreude* (May 1989). That year, Lubricated Goat undertook a low-budget, two-month tour of the USA which saw the band supporting the likes of The Butthole Surfers and Killdozer. While in Seattle, Washington, Lubricated Goat issued a limited edition single for the SubPop label 'Meeting My Head'/'20th Century Rake'. The next line-up of Spasm, Renestair E.J. (guitar, sax; ex-**Bloodloss**, Primevils), Lachlan McLeod (bass, sampling; ex-Salamander Jim) and Martin Bland (drums, synthesiser) issued the album *Psychedelicatessen* (August 1990). *Psychedelicatessen* featured a variety of styles (from noisy free-form jazz to noisier hard rock), with tortured guitars and raw vocals being the band's characteristic mode of operation.

Lubricated Goat undertook a European tour in 1990 that came to an abrupt halt when Spasm was stabbed in a drug deal gone wrong in Berlin. Spasm relocated to New York where he married Babes in Toyland bassist Kat Bjelland. The pair formed Crunt with Jon Spencer Blues Explosion drummer Russell Simms. Crunt played grungy roots-rock fleshed out by violent, sex-obsessed lyrics. The band issued a self-titled album in 1994. That same year Spasm reactivated Lubricated Goat and recorded *Forces You Don't Understand* in New York with guest players from US bands like The Swans and Cop Shoot Cop. After that the band fell apart, as did Spasm's marriage. He fell deeper into the depths of heroin addiction, but by 1996 had again reactivated Lubricated Goat with new players.

Lubricated Goat albums: *Plays the Devil's Music* (Black Eye, 1987), *Paddock of Love* (Black Eye, 1988), *Psychedelicatessen* (Black Eye, 1990), *Forces You Don't Understand* (Independent, 1994); ***Crunt album:*** *Crunt* (Shagpile/Shock, 1994).

Steve Lucas (*see* X)

Trevor Lucas

Style: *Folk*

Trevor Lucas (b. 1943) was one of the most acclaimed singer/songwriters Australia ever produced and although he was held in high regard in UK folk-rock circles, he remained virtually unknown in his homeland. The deep-voiced singer issued his ultra-rare, debut folk album *See that My Grave is Kept Clean* on the East label in 1964. He also contributed a studio version of Gary Shearston's 'Voyager' to the otherwise live Various Artists album *Australian Folk Festival* on the obscure Score label. Also on the album, recorded in August 1964, were other folkies like Tina Lawton, Martin Wyndham-Read, Brian Mooney, Paul Marks and Lenore Somerset. A single 'Folk Attic'/'Presents' also appeared that year.

Even before Lucas had made a name for himself in Australia, he travelled to the UK in late 1964 and settled in London. He established himself on the folk circuit, performed at the International Folk Fest at the Royal Albert Hall and recorded another rare and highly sought after solo album, *Overlander* (1966). The album included the single 'Waltzing Matilda'/'It's On'. In August 1967, he formed cosmopolitan folk-rock group Eclection; the band's contemporaries on the burgeoning UK electric folk scene included Fairport Convention and The Pentangle. Eclection recorded one self-titled album for Elektra in 1968 but, despite an excellent reputation, the band failed to break through. Lucas dissolved the group at the end of 1969 to form Fotheringay with his lady Sandy Denny. Denny had just left Fairport Convention following the recording of the seminal British electric folk album *Liege and Lief*. In 1970, Denny was voted Britain's number one female singer. She was most widely known, in rock music circles, for her duet with Robert Plant on Led Zeppelin's 'Battle of Evermore'.

Fotheringay lasted until January 1971 and issued one self-titled, UK Top 20 album on the Island label. Denny launched her solo career, and Lucas worked with her on the albums *The North Sea Grassman and the Ravens* (1971), *Sandy* (1972) and *Like An Old Fashioned Waltz* (1973) for Island. Lucas established himself as an in-demand session player and producer, appearing on albums by Bronco, Julie Covington, Al Stewart, The Strawbs and Richard and Linda Thompson. At the start of 1972, he assembled a bunch of English folk musicians (including Sandy Denny, Richard Thompson and other members of Fairport Convention) under the collective title of The Bunch, in order to record a studio album for Island. *Rock On* featured vintage rock'n'roll covers performed with a folk-rock slant. The album was received so well that, in August 1972, Lucas was invited to join Fairport Convention as producer, singer and guitarist.

The Fairport line-up of Lucas, Jerry Donahue (guitar), Dave Pegg (bass, vocals), Dave Swarbrick (fiddle, vocals) and Dave Mattacks (drums) issued the albums *Rosie* (1973) and *Nine* (1973) on Island. Lucas and Denny were married on 20 September

1973. In March 1974, Denny rejoined Fairport Convention, and she and Lucas remained with the band until January 1976. During that time, the Fairports recorded the albums *Live Convention (a Moveable Feast)* (1974) and *Rising for the Moon* (1975). Denny resumed her solo career with the *Rendezvous* album (May 1977), but she died from a brain haemorrhage in April 1978 after falling down a staircase at a friend's house.

Lucas returned to Australia and, following a period of re-evaluation, formed the film company Andromeda Productions to produce documentaries and children's dramas. He returned to music production at Music Farm Studios in northern NSW. He produced albums for **Paul Kelly** and the Dots (*Talk*), **The Bushwackers** (*Faces in the Street*), **Goanna** (*Spirit of Place*), **Redgum** (*Frontline*) and **Strange Tenants** (*Movin' In*). Lucas also began to make sporadic live appearances at venues like Melbourne's Troubadour Cafe. He co-composed, with Ian Mason, the soundtracks to the feature films *Jenny Kissed Me* (1986) and *Slate Wyn and Me* (1987). In 1987, Lucas and his family moved to Epping, NSW and he came into contact with one of Fairport Convention's early managers, John Penhallow, who had also relocated to Australia. Lucas and Penhallow began to issue a series of limited edition, private-sale cassette releases, *Attic Tracks Volumes I to IV*.

The tapes contained previously unissued, or rare, alternate takes of material that Lucas and/or Denny had recorded between 1972 and 1984. Lucas died on 4 February 1989 and Penhallow assumed custodianship of his and Denny's musical legacy. In 1995, reissue specialists Raven compiled 18 of the best tracks for release on the essential collection *The Attic Tracks 1972–1984*. Among the tracks Lucas performed were a gently soulful version of **Richard Clapton's** 'Girls on the Avenue' (from 1977) and the original rendition of the self-penned 'The Ballad of Ned Kelly' (from 1974), which **Redgum** later recorded under the title 'Poor Ned'.

Albums: *See that My Grave is Kept Clean* (East, 1964), *Overlander* (Reality, 1966), *The Attic Tracks 1972–1984* (compilation credited to Sandy Denny, Trevor Lucas and Friends, Raven, 1995).

M

Machinations

Formed: *1980*
Style: *Dance pop*
Original line-up: *Fred Loneragan (vocals), Tim Doyle (guitar), Tony Starr (keyboards, vocals, drum machine)*

Sydney band Machinations was one of the most popular outfits working the mid-1980s independent scene. The band's music successfully melded pop smarts and rock cool to a dance-funk backing. Starting out as a three-piece electro-pop outfit on the Sydney inner-city circuit, Machinations soon added Nick 'Nero' Swan on bass. In late 1980, the band entered the studio with producer **Lobby Loyde**, which resulted in the single 'Average Inadequacy'/'Arabia' (September 1981) and the four-track, 12-inch EP *Machinations* ('Jets', 'Arabia', 'John Wane', 'Edge') on the Phantom label (December).

'Average Inadequacy' created enough interest for Mushroom's White label to sign the band and reissue the single with a new B-side, 'Machinations of Dance' (March 1982). A year later, Machinations issued a new single, 'Jack'/'Be Double' (February 1983), followed by 'Pressure Sway'/'Pushbike' (June). 'Pressure Sway' became the band's first national mainstream charting single when it peaked at #21 during July. Both singles had been lifted from the album *Esteem* (April 1983), as was the next one, 'Jumping the Gap'/'Terminal Wharf' (October). With the album's release, and an Australian tour support slot to English visitor Joe Jackson, Machinations added Warren McLean on drums. The band entered Rhinoceros Studios with English producer Julian Mendelshon, emerging with the smoothest and most fully realised album of its career, *Big Music* (July 1985).

The album produced four hit singles, 'No Say in It'/'Man Overboard' (September 1984; #11 in October), 'My Heart's on Fire'/'Spark' (May 1985; #18 in June), 'You Got Me Going Again'/'I Ain't Waiting for No Train' (August) and 'Execution of Love'/'Dusted Down' (December). Naomi Star sang backing vocals on most of the album, although Inez Anthony was featured on 'No Say in It'. In 1986, White issued the mini-album *The Big Beat*, a collection of dance remixes of singles like 'No Say in It', 'Execution of Love', 'Pressure Sway' and 'You Got Me Going Again'. That year, Warren McLean left Machinations to join Melbourne funk-pop outfit **I'm Talking**. Henry Downes took his place on drums. Downes was then replaced by John MacKay (ex-Sea Monsters) in early 1987. The band was back in the studios soon after with American producer Andy Wallace (Prince, Run DMC), recording a new album.

Uptown (October 1988) produced four singles spread out over 18 months: 'Do to You'/'Looking Out for You' (August 1987, #18 in October), 'Intimacy'/'Hit by a Missile' (May 1988) 'Do It to Me'/'Normal' (October) and 'Cars & Planes'/'Cars & Planes' (February 1989). By that stage, Machinations had established themselves as a popular band on the Australian touring circuit. Unfortunately, the band's activities were curtailed in early 1989 when a hit-and-run accident left frontman Loneragan unconscious and with a broken back. He spent several months recuperating in hospital. The band intended writing while Loneragan recovered from his injuries, but eventually the other members decided to go their separate ways. Swan toured with the **James Freud** Band. In early 1997, Machinations with Loneragan reconvened for a tour which they hoped would lead to new recordings.

Albums: *Esteem* (White/Mushroom/Festival, 1983), *Big Music* (White/Mushroom/Festival, 1985), *The Big Beat* (mini-album, White/Mushroom/Festival, 1986), *Uptown* (White/Mushroom/Festival, 1988).

MacKenzie Theory

Formed: *1971*
Style: *Jazz rock*
Original line-up: *Rob MacKenzie (lead guitar; ex-Leo and Friends,* **King Harvest**, *Great Men), Cleis Pearce (electric viola), Mike Leadabrand (bass), Andy Majewski (drums)*

Formed in September 1971 by multi-talented guitarist Rob MacKenzie, and featuring the flying elbows of electric viola player Cleis Pearce, MacKenzie Theory forged an identity as one of

Australia's truly mind-blowing progressive rock bands. The band consistently enthralled festival and concert audiences with a dynamic instrumental sound that embraced elements of Santana (circa *Caravanserai*), King Crimson, John Coltrane and Mahavishnu Orchestra.

While Rob MacKenzie was getting MacKenzie Theory off the ground, he played as a guest guitarist with a number of bands, including **Friends** and **Billy Thorpe** and the Aztecs. As the band's popularity grew, MacKenzie Theory made regular appearances alongside the likes of **Spectrum**, **Madder Lake**, **Chain**, The Aztecs and **Band of Light**. The first MacKenzie Theory recording, the eight-minute 'New Song and', appeared on the live Various Artists triple album *The Great Australian Rock Festival Sunbury 1973*, issued on Mushroom (April 1973). Although the live-in-the-studio album *Out of the Blue* (July 1973) did not do justice to the band's powerful stage presence, it did combine classical elements, majestic jazz-fusion and hard rock in a suitably cosmic fashion. In September 1973, both Leadabrand and Majewski left the band to be replaced by Paul 'Sheepdog' Wheeler (bass; ex-**Billy Thorpe** and the Aztecs, **Band of Talabene**) and Greg Sheehan (drums; ex-**Blackfeather**). Peter Jones also joined on electric piano.

In 1974, MacKenzie became one of the first musicians in Australia (along with folkie **Glenn Cardier** and Greg Quill from **Country Radio**) to receive a travel grant from the Australia Council for the Arts (under the auspices of Gough Whitlam's Labor government). MacKenzie and Pearce travelled to the UK, which effectively ended MacKenzie Theory's career. To mark the band's demise, Mushroom Records recorded the farewell concert (Melbourne's Dallas Brooks Hall, 15 May 1974) and issued the results as *Bon Voyage*. Once again, the album only offered a superficial glimpse into the band's live power. Nevertheless, epic tracks like 'Clouds' and 'Supreme Love' were at times sweet and dreamy, at others frantic and chaotic.

Mushroom included a different version of 'Supreme Love' on the budget album *Highlights of Sunbury '74 Part 2*. In 1994, reissue specialists Raven included 'Extraterrestrial Boogie' (from *Out of the Blue*) on the Various Artists collection *Golden Miles: Australian Progressive Rock, 1969–1974*. In the 1980s, MacKenzie moved to the USA, where he has since earned a respectable living as guitarist with rock'n'roll revival act Sha Na Na.

Albums: *Out of the Blue* (Mushroom/Festival, 1973), *Bon Voyage* (Mushroom/Festival, 1974).

Alison McCallum

Style: *Pop*

During the early 1970s, Alison McCallum (b. 1951) was one of the most popular female singers on the Sydney scene. Like **Wendy Saddington**, **Renée Geyer**, **Bobbi Marchini**, Sheryl Black (from SCRA) and Janice Slater, McCallum was a soul/blues stylist of considerable flair and passion. She listed blues singers Bessie Smith and Ma Rainey, and gospellers Clara Ward and Marianne Williams, among her strongest influences.

McCallum began her career in the late 1960s with Sydney-based bands like Big Apple Union, Dr Kandy's Third Eye and Chorus, before joining **Freshwater** at the end of 1970. McCallum recorded one soul-pop single with **Freshwater** 'I Ain't Got the Time'/'Hello Sunshine' (November 1971), which featured her sweet vocals up front. McCallum left **Freshwater** at the end of the year to sing with **Ray Brown's** One Ton Gypsy for one month before going solo. Her debut single, a stirring version of Vanda and Young's 'Superman'/'Take Me Back', reached #12 on the national charts in April 1972. Visiting English producer Simon Napier-Bell (Yardbirds, Move, T-Rex) worked on McCallum's debut album, *Fresh Water*. The album's mix of rock, jazz and blues material proved to be a fine showcase for her expressive voice.

At the end of 1972, McCallum sang lead vocals on the Gough Whitlam-led Labor Party's election campaign theme song, 'It's Time'. She also appeared in the television advertisements that went to air at that time, and 'It's Time' came out as a single (backed with 'Hippy Gumbo'). McCallum recorded three more singles for RCA, 'Ol' Rock'n' Roll Boogie Woogie Blues'/'Have You Seen Your Mother, Baby?', 'Would You Believe?'/'Lonely' and 'Teach Me How to Fly'/'Fire' before travelling to Europe to work. She performed 'Superman' at the 1973 Midem Conference in Cannes, France. On her return to Australia in 1974, McCallum signed to Albert Productions. At the start of 1975, she scored her second hit single, 'Excuse Me'/'Honk Honk' (#15 in January).

She recorded two more singles with Albert, 'Her Kind of Guy'/'If Your Eyes Could Smile' (September 1975) and 'Love Grows Cold'/'Lunatic Love' (February 1976), plus the album *Excuse Me*. The album included two Vanda and Young songs, 'Cry for Me' and 'Things to Do' plus an elegant reworking of the Flying Burrito Brothers' tender-sad love song 'Hot Burrito'. While signed to Albert, McCallum recorded a single, 'So Tough'/'To Know

Him is to Love Him' (October 1974), as one-third of the vocal group The Hooter Sisters (alongside Janice Slater and **Bobbi Marchini**). McCallum then concentrated on session work, appearing on albums by **Billy Thorpe**, **Ross Ryan**, **Jeff St John** and Anne Kirkpatrick among others.

In an opportunistic piece of record company marketing, RCA reissued 'Superman'/'Take Me Back' during 1979 in order to capitalise on the release of *Superman: The Movie* starring Christopher Reeves. RCA also issued a Best of collection called *Superman*. Since that time, McCallum has disappeared from public view. An Alison McCallum rarity appeared on the 1979 Glenn A. Baker-assembled collection *Albert Archives*. In 1969, McCallum had recorded a version of **The Bee Gees'** oft-covered 'To Love Somebody' with backing provided by **Tully**. The song had been aired as part of the ABC-TV series devoted to **Tully** called *Fusions*.

Albums: *Fresh Water* (RCA, 1972), *Any Way You Want Me* (reissue of debut LP, RCA, 1973), *Excuse Me* (Albert/EMI, 1975), *Superman—Best of* (RCA, 1979).

Mike McClellan

Style: *Folk, country*

Singer/songwriter Mike McClellan became interested in folk music during the mid-1960s after Bob Dylan and Joan Baez came to the attention of a wide audience. McClellan formed the Currency Blues Band with **Graham Lowndes** and Derek Robinson. With the break-up of the band in 1969, McClellan won a series final of television talent show *New Faces*.

He made regular appearances on the television series *Sound of Music*, played the folkie circuit alongside the likes of **Graham Lowndes**, **Doug Ashdown**, **Glenn Cardier**, **Jeannie Lewis** and **Margret Roadknight** and in 1972 signed to Col Joye's ATA label. McClellan's debut album *Mike McClellan* produced two singles, 'Some Other Sunrise'/'Nursery Rhyme' (August 1972) and 'Susie Get Me Off this Train'/'Fiddler' (1973). McClellan issued one more single on ATA, 'Country Morning'/'Playing It by Ear' before signing to EMI. McClellan's debut album for EMI, *Ask Any Dancer*, yielded his only hit single, 'Song and Dance Man'/'Another Grey Day', which reached #33 on the national chart in November 1974. 'Rock'n'Roll Lady'/'Catfish Rag' came out as a second single in March 1975. American country singer Rick Nelson issued a cover version of 'Rock'n'Roll Lady' as a single in October 1975.

In 1975, McClellan worked on an album written, conceived and produced by Peter Dawkins. *The Star Suite* was an interpretation of the four elements of the Zodiac. The studio band Patch assembled by Dawkins comprised McClellan (acoustic guitar), **Mike Rudd** (electric guitar; **Ariel**), Rod Coe (bass), Tony Esterman (keyboards) and Doug Gallacher (drums). Support players included Bill Putt (bass; **Ariel**), **Tim Gaze** (lead guitar), Tony Ansell (organ) and Mike Perjanik (ARP synthesiser). McClellan co-wrote the tracks 'Air' and 'Earth'. The release of McClellan's third album *Until the Song is Done* during March 1976 coincided with his support to American singer Melanie on her Australian tour. The album featured a more varied sound, from country-pop ('The Gamble') and jazz-tinged pop ballads ('Takin' the Tide') to dramatic, orchestrated epics ('Sail Tonight'). Melanie later recorded 'Carry Me (Until the Song is Done)' and invited McClellan to support her on a US tour. As it turned out, the Melanie tour support fell through and McClellan focused his attention back on the local scene.

An Evening with Mike McClellan: Live (recorded at EMI's Studio A) came out in November 1977. In 1979, McClellan recorded an album under the aegis of executive producers Vanda and Young. The *Laughing in the Dark* album included the singles 'Good Companions'/'Sad Songs' (April 1980) and 'Rock'n'Roll Man'/'Hold Tight' (November). The *Repeat Prescription* album on RCA produced the single 'Face to Face'/'Fallen Again' (1986). McClellan's most recent album, *Heartland*, included the singles 'Heartland' and 'Murmur of the Heart' (1988). McClellan has always been a relatively low-key performer, but very little has been heard from him since that time.

Albums: *Mike McClellan* (ATA/Festival, 1972), *Ask Any Dancer* (EMI, 1974), *Until the Song is Done* (EMI, 1976), *An Evening with Mike McClellan: Live* (EMI, 1977), *Laughing in the Dark* (Albert/EMI, 1980), *Repeat Prescription* (RCA, 1986), *Heartland* (RCA, 1989).

David McComb (*see* The Triffids)

Guy McDonough (*see* Australian Crawl)

Craig McLachlan

Style: *Rock, pop*

Craig McLachlan (b. 1965) first came to public attention during 1986 with the long-running role of the likeable larrikin Henry Ramsay in the popular television soapie *Neighbours*. In 1989, McLachlan won the coveted Gold Logie for his performance in *Neighbours*. McLachlan was also an accomplished singer/guitarist and in 1988 he formed a band to play the Melbourne pub circuit. Craig McLachlan and the Y-Fronts comprised McLachlan, his high school mate Mark Bain (bass) and Dave Williams (drums). In 1989, McLachlan quit *Neighbours* to appear in another popular soapie, *Home and Away*. He relocated to Sydney where he formed Craig McLachlan and Check 1-2 with Bain and John Clarke (drums; ex-**John Farnham** Band).

Check 1-2 signed to CBS and issued its debut single, 'Rock the Rock' (November 1989), which peaked at #23 on the national chart during January 1990. The Garth Porter-produced album *Craig McLachlan and Check 1-2* (May 1990) yielded the hit singles Bo Diddley's 'Mona'/'I Don't Mind' (#4 in June), 'Amanda'/'Baby Loves Funky' (#29 in August) and 'I Almost Felt Like Crying' (October). *Craig McLachlan and Check 1-2* reached #4 on the national chart during July. 'Mona' took out the 1990 Australian Record Industry Association (ARIA) Award for the Highest Selling Single of the Year. 'Mona', 'Amanda' and 'I Almost Felt Like Crying' also performed well in the UK, where they reached #2 (June 1990), #19 (August) and #50 (November) respectively. His popularity had no doubt been given a boost by the runaway success of *Neighbours* over there.

In 1991 McLachlan appeared in the television miniseries *Heroes II: The Return*, and the New Zealand feature film *Absent Without Leave*. He enjoyed a minor solo hit single in Australia when 'On My Own' peaked at #25 during September 1991. His second solo album, *Hands Free* (March 1992), produced two minor UK hit singles in 'One Reason Why' (#29 in April) and 'On My Own' (#59 in November). Another single lifted from *Hands Free*, a cover of Dave Edmunds' 'I Hear You Knocking' (July), was not successful.

In June 1992, he showed his versatility by playing the role of Frank N. Furter in the Australian revival of Richard O'Brien's stage musical *The Rocky Horror Show*. At the end of the year he took the role of Danny Zuko in the UK production of the stage musical *Grease*. McLachlan's duet with Debbie Gibson (as Sandy) on the perennial favourite, 'You're the One that I Want', reached #13 on the UK charts in July 1993. His single of the *Grease* theme song also reached #44 in December. McLachlan then concentrated on his acting career, with roles in the British drama series *Bugs* and the British/German feature film *Catherine the Great*. His most recent UK hit single, 'Every Day' (#65 in July 1995), came out under the moniker of Craig McLachlan and the Culprits.

Albums: *Craig McLachlan and Check 1-2* (CBS, 1990), *Hands Free* (Sony, 1992).

G.W. McLennan

Style: *Folk, rock*

G.W. (aka Grant) McLennan (b. 1958) spent 12 years as a member of the highly regarded **Go-Betweens**. His first post-**Go-Betweens** recording venture was the self-titled **Jack Frost** album (1990) in collaboration with **The Church**'s **Steve Kilbey**. He also produced the debut single by Sydney folk-pop duo **Club Hoy** 'On and on'/'Lucy, with Me' (1990).

McLennan launched his solo career with a series of tentative live shows around Sydney, with backing provided by Phil Kakulas (from **The Blackeyed Susans**) on double bass. In 1991, McLennan issued the critically lauded *Watershed* album which was produced by New Zealander Dave Dobbyn. That ambitious and highly personalised collection of songs charted McLennan's emotions in the wake of **The Go-Betweens'** break-up. It yielded the CD singles 'Easy Come, Easy Go' and 'Word Gets Around'. The album revealed McLennan to be, in turns, the introspective singer/songwriter or the carefree and gregarious performer.

McLennan's second solo album, *Fireboy* (November 1992) was an even more melancholy set of songs that boasted fuller (though never obtrusive) arrangements. 'Surround Me' was issued as a CD EP (October) which also included McLennan's renditions of 'Moon River', The Monkees' 'Listen to the Band' and Bruce Springsteen's 'If I Should Fall Behind'. In 1993, McLennan toured with a band that comprised **Maurice Frawley** (guitar; ex-**Paul Kelly** and the Dots), Phil Kakulas (bass), Pedro Bull (keyboards; ex-**Paul Kelly** and the Messengers) and Michael Barclay (drums; ex-Messengers). McLennan issued a new CD single, 'Lighting Fires', in October 1993. Grant (no longer G.W.) McLennan issued his third solo album, *Horsebreaker Star* in December 1994.

That sprawling 24-track double album consisted of songs recorded with producer John Keane in Athens, Georgia. With its wide-screen outlook, the album shifted from country rock to bright acoustic pop with a great deal of optimism and passion. 'Simone and Perry' and 'Don't You Cry' were lifted as CD singles. In mid-1997, McLennan reunited with **Robert Forster** in **The Go-Betweens** for a series of showcase gigs in the UK. Following that, he issued his fourth solo album, *In Your Bright Ray*, and its CD single 'Comet Scar' (July).

Albums: *Watershed* (White/Mushroom/Festival, 1991), *Fireboy* (White/Mushroom/Festival, 1992), *Horsebreaker Star* (Concubine/Shock, 1994), *In Your Bright Ray*, (Concubine/Shock, 1997).

McPhee

Formed: *1970*
Style: *Progressive rock*
Original line-up: *Faye Lewis (vocals; ex-Luke's Walnut), Tony Joyce (lead guitar), Jim Deverell (Hammond organ), Benny Kaika (bass; ex-Bitter End, Compulsion, Multiple Balloon), Terry Popple (drums; ex-Tramline)*

Obscure Sydney-based group McPhee issued one ultra-rare but magnificent progressive rock album. During the late 1960s, Tony Joyce and New Zealand-born Jim Deverell had worked as session players backing artists like **Digby Richards**, **The Delltones** and Little Sammy and the In People. Benny Kaika was also from New Zealand. Singer Faye Lewis had done session work (she was a member of Luke's Walnut, the second Sydney *Hair* stage group after **Tully**). English-born Terry Popple had been a member of late 1960s UK blues-boom band Tramline, which issued a couple of albums on the Island label.

Popple linked up with McPhee when he travelled to Australia in early 1970. The band played the local club and wine bar circuit around Sydney, and in 1971 recorded an album for the independent Violet's Holiday label. The seven-track album contained heavy renditions of Spooky Tooth's 'The Wrong Time', Neil Young's 'Southern Man', Ritchie Haven's 'Indian Rope Man' and The Beatles' 'I am The Walrus', plus a couple of original tunes including the lengthy jazz-rock instrumental 'Out to Lunch'.

The album's *piece de resistance* was the surging rendition of 'Indian Rope Man' (as recorded by British soul/R&B act Julie Driscoll and Brian Auger's Trinity) in which Deverell delivered one of the most driven, transcendent Hammond organ solos ever committed to vinyl! That frantic rollercoaster ride of a song stands as one of the defining moments in the history of early 1970s Australian progressive rock.

Not long after the album came out, McPhee broke up. Popple returned to the UK where he joined SNAFU. Lewis returned to session work and sang in an outfit called the Bondi Bitch Band. Kaika played with **Jeff St John**, John Robinson's band Tramp and **Leo De Castro's** New King Harvest. Deverell travelled to the USA. Joyce relocated to Darwin, where he joined a number of Aboriginal bands like Under the Spell of Trees, Life on Mars and Dogboy. Dogboy featured American-born drummer Allen Murphy, who had worked with **Warumpi Band** and **Yothu Yindi**. For a number of years during the early 1990s, Joyce ran the Northern Territory office of the AusMusic organisation.

Album: *McPhee* (Violet's Holiday/Festival, 1971).

Betty McQuade

Style: *R&B, pop*

Scottish-born Betty McQuade migrated to Australia with her family at the age of eight. The family settled in Brisbane, and in 1960 McQuade relocated to Melbourne where she joined **The Thunderbirds** as replacement for **Judy Cannon**. Unlike other female singers of the day, such as **Noeleen Batley** (dubbed 'Australia's Little Miss Sweetheart'), **Judy Stone** and **Patsy Ann Noble**, who were distinctly middle-of-the-road pop, McQuade developed a tough R&B style in the manner of Wanda Jackson. She went on to cover a couple of Jackson's songs, notably 'Tongue Tied' and 'You Make Me Mad'.

After working with **The Thunderbirds** for a year, McQuade signed to the Astor label and issued her debut single, a cover of John D. Loudermilk's 'Midnight Bus'/'Tongue Tied', which reached #6 in Melbourne during December 1961. McQuade cut two more singles, Loudermilk's 'Blue Train'/'Summer Love' (January 1962) and 'Doggie in the Window'/'Have You Ever Been Lonely?', before she joined another popular Melbourne group, The Premiers. With backing provided by The Premiers, McQuade recorded her fourth single, Jo Ann Campbell's 'Bobby, Bobby, Bobby'/'You Make Me Mad'. It was her final single for Astor, and after making regular appearances on television pop show *The Go!! Show*, McQuade signed to the Go!! label.

Her two singles for Go!! were reissues of 'Midnight Bus'/'Tongue Tied' (September 1965) and 'Blue Train'/'Summer Love' (March 1966), plus the EP *Betty McQuade Sings*. McQuade issued one final single 'Dum Dum'/'Beauty is Just Skin Deep', for the W&G label (1967) before slipping from view. In 1981 the Raven label issued the six-track McQuade EP *Midnight Bus*. During the mid-1980s she began appearing in a series of rock'n'roll revival concerts such as The Happy Days of Rock'n'Roll in Melbourne. In late 1996, the Canetoad label issued a compilation *Girls! Girls! Girls! (Australian Female Performers of the Sixties: Volume 1)*, which included McQuade's 'Midnight Bus', 'Tongue Tied', 'Blue

Train' and 'Bobby Bobby Bobby'. Other singers featured were **Judy Cannon, Noeleen Batley, Yvonne Barrett**, Carolyn Young, The Taylor Sisters, Vicki Forrest, Lee Sellers, Pam Oakley, Del Juliana, The Field Twins and Joy Lemmon.

The Mad Turks from Istanbul

Formed: *1984*
Style: *Power pop*
Original line-up: *Chuck Skatt (real name Charles Jenkins, vocals), Hank M. Turk (real name Matthias Eckhardt, guitar), Martyn La Merde (real name Martyn Christopher, bass), Dom Benedictine III (real name Dominic Larizza, drums, guitar, vocals)*

Adelaide band The Mad Turks from Istanbul played a tough brand of 1960s-infused power pop that called to mind the likes of The Flamin' Groovies, The Kinks, Elvis Costello and The Ramones. The band's melodic disposition was at odds with other Adelaide bands of the era such as **Exploding White Mice**, The Spikes and **The Lizard Train**; nevertheless, The Mad Turks from Istanbul signed to the Greasy Pop label, which was also home to the aforementioned groups.

The band contributed the song 'Yet You Wonder Why' to Greasy Pop's 1985 Various Artists compilation *An Oasis in a Desert of Noise*. With the arrival of Steve Caon on drums in early 1986, Dom Benedictine moved over to guitar. The Mad Turks' debut single, the charming 'Lolene'/'Seeing was Believing', came out in October 1986, followed by 'Holding My Breath'/'All Those Words', 'Prostitute My Brain' (November 1987). The second single coincided with the release of the band's debut album, *Cafe Istanbul*. 'Looking Forward to Destroy'/ 'Given My Number' was lifted as the third single from the album (May 1988). In 1989, Hank Turk left the band, and with a move to Melbourne the band shortened its name to The Mad Turks. The band's second album, *Toast*, included three singles, 'Tempers Flare'/'American Hearthrob' (May 1989), 'The Last Time'/'Elusive Dream' (November) and 'Walking Disaster'/'Holding My Breath (Again)' (March 1990).

By 1992, the band had evolved into The Icecream Hands with a line-up of Skatt, Benedictine, Arch Larizza (bass; ex-Innocents, **Saints**), Derek Smiley (drums) and David Milne (keyboards). The Icecream Hands continued to play classic pop melodies in the tradition of The Beatles, The Kinks, Big Star, The Replacements and The Only Ones. The Rubber label issued the band's CD EPs *The Icecream Hands* (1992), 'Supermarket Scene' (1994), 'Olive' (November 1995) and 'Here We Go 'Round Now' (July 1997), plus the full-length albums, *Travelling Made Easy* (1993) and *Memory Lane Traffic Jam* (August 1997).

Mad Turks albums: *Cafe Istanbul* (The Greasy Record Company/Festival, 1987), *Toast* (The Greasy Record Company/Festival, 1990); ***Icecream Hands albums:*** *Travelling Made Easy* (Rubber, 1993), *Memory Lane Traffic Jam* (Rubber, 1997).

Madden and Harris

Formed: *1972*
Style: *Folk*
Original line-up: *David Madden (vocals, guitars, bass), Peter Harris (vocals, guitars, bass, mandolin, piano, organ, mellotron, harpsichord, bassoon, sax, zither, cello)*

Multi-instrumentalist Peter Harris was working as a guitar teacher when he joined forces with his pupil David Madden as folk duo Madden and Harris. The duo drew inspiration from such disparate sources as sixteenth-century chamber music, English folk and light jazz. The duo's progressive-folk sound was at odds with prevailing trends (pop, blues'n'boogie) on the local scene; the only other Australian band at the time playing in a similar style was **Extradition**.

Madden and Harris issued their delicate debut single, 'A Simple Song'/'Remember Me', on the Albert label in 1974. In 1975 Madden and Harris issued the ultra-rare *Fools Paradise* album on their own private Jasmine Records imprint. This carefully crafted songcycle was full of fragile, refined songs in the vein of UK folk acts like Nick Drake and Mellow Candle, the softer side of The Moody Blues and the quieter, pastoral moments to be found on the early albums by King Crimson.

For the album sessions, the duo was backed by Paul Baker (bass) and a trio of drummers including Doug Gallacher. Tracks like 'Wishes', 'The Wind at Eve', 'Margaret O'Grady' and the four-suite, side-long title cut 'Fools Paradise' combined gently swelling melodies, strummed guitars, ethereal mellotron backing, rippling pianos and soft shimmering harmonies. Harris also issued an interesting solo album, *Ruby*, around that time on the Ritz Gramophone label, but the duo was never heard from again. Vicious Sloth Collectables reissued the *Fools Paradise* album on CD in 1994 due to overseas collector demand for that folk artefact.

Madden and Harris album: *Fools Paradise* (Jasmine Records, 1975; Vicious Sloth Collectables CD reissue, 1994); ***Peter Harris solo album:*** *Ruby* (Ritz Gramophone/Festival, 1975).

Madder Lake

Formed: *1971*
Style: *Progressive rock*
Original line-up: *Mick Fettes (vocals), Brenden Mason (guitar), John McKinnon (keyboards), Kerry McKenna (bass), Jack Kreemers (drums)*

As one of the first bands signed to Michael Gudinski's fledgling Mushroom label, alongside **Chain**, **Matt Taylor**, **MacKenzie Theory**, **Ayers Rock** and **The Dingoes**, Melbourne group Madder Lake was best remembered for its infectious hit single '12lb Toothbrush'. Yet there was much more to Madder Lake than that song hinted; it eventually became something of a millstone around the band's collective neck.

Madder Lake originally worked under the name San Sebastian, but took a new moniker to reflect the band members' art school/graphic design backgrounds (madder lake is the colour obtained by mixing madder dye with oils or water). The band's brand of progressive psychedelic blues found much favour on the Melbourne pub and club circuit. One of Madder Lake's first major engagements was as opening act at the inaugural Sunbury Pop Festival in January 1972. A year later, the band was one of the headlining acts at Sunbury 1973. The live track 'Down the River'/'12lb Toothbrush' appeared on Mushroom's triple album of the event, *The Great Australian Rock Festival Sunbury 1973* (April 1973).

Meanwhile, the band issued its debut single (also the very first single on Mushroom), 'Goodbye Lollipop'/'Bumper Bar Song' (February 1973), and supported overseas visitors The Rolling Stones at their Melbourne concert held at the Kooyong Tennis Centre. 'Goodbye Lollipop' reached #13 in Melbourne and #35 nationally. The band was vying with **Chain**, **Billy Thorpe** and the Aztecs and **Coloured Balls** as one of the top live drawcards on the Melbourne scene by that stage. The band's best-selling debut album *Stillpoint* (August 1973) was an adventurous work brimming with superbly arranged material, appealing sounds and imaginative lyric themes. It reached #2 in Melbourne and #11 nationally, achieved gold status (35 000 copies sold) and established the band's standing as one of the most innovative outfits of the day.

By the time the band had issued its next single, the funky '12lb Toothbrush'/'Country Blues' (August 1973), Andy Cowan had replaced John McKinnon on keyboards. No doubt helped by its nagging vocal hook, the single reached the Top 10 in Melbourne and #35 nationally. The band's second album, *Butterfly Farm* (#18 in April 1974), was a worthy effort but it lacked the focus of the debut. The album sold well, but its two singles, 'Butterfly Farm'/'Back Seat Song' (April) and 'Booze Blues'/'One Star and the Moon' (May), were not successful. Even the band's next single, 'It's All in Your Head'/'Slack Alice' (November), which had been written and recorded specifically with radio airplay in mind, was a flop.

Madder Lake

At the end of 1974, Madder Lake left the Mushroom label and the band's fortunes were at a low ebb. Things picked up again when Madder Lake met visiting conductor David Meecham, who commissioned the band to write, record and perform a concept piece based around Aldous Huxley's *Brave New World*. The project was to be funded by the Australian Broadcasting Corporation (ABC) with Meecham providing the orchestrations. The band recorded demos but, due to financial cutbacks at the ABC and Meecham's other commitments across the world, the project was eventually shelved two years after commencement. In the meantime, Fettes and Cowan had left the band in late 1975. Fettes had contributed much to the band's sound and style with his gruff vocals, manic moonface persona and demented Joe Cockeresque stage movements.

The band continued on as a three-piece until McKinnon rejoined in early 1976. Fettes formed **Bandicoot** while Madder Lake went through three further line-up changes over the next year. Kerry McKenna left for three months to be replaced by Ian Holding (bass; ex-Sunshine, Sayla); on his return, McKenna rejoined on second guitar and Tony Lake also joined as lead singer. The band's sixth single, 'I Get High'/'Rodney's Birthday' (sung by McKinnon, July 1976), was not successful and Lake left in May 1977. By that stage the band existed in name only and rarely performed. In April 1978, Fettes rejoined and the band undertook a successful tour. Mushroom issued *The Best of Madder Lake* album in May; it sold well enough for the label to consider re-signing the band. The reunion looked permanent and the band laid plans for a new album, but Fettes left again in January 1979.

Madder Lake never officially split, just stopped playing gigs. Mason and McKenna formed Claude Rains with Neale Johns (vocals; ex-**Blackfeather**) and Trevor Young (drums; ex-**Coloured Balls**) and gigged sporadically into the late 1980s. Madder Lake re-formed for the Mushroom Evolution Concert over the Australia Day weekend in January 1982, which was held to celebrate Mushroom's tenth anniversary. Three Madder Lake tracks, 'Goodbye Lollipop', 'Song for Little Ernest' and '12lb Toothbrush', appeared on the triple live album of the event, *The Mushroom Evolution Concert* (1982). Since then, Madder Lake has re-formed for the odd gig or two (with new drummer Luke McKinnon), and in late 1996 began to record a new album.

Albums: *Stillpoint* (Mushroom/Festival, 1973), *Butterfly Farm* (Mushroom/Festival, 1974), *Best of Madder Lake* (Mushroom/Festival, 1978).

Liv Maessen

Style: *Pop*

Liv Maessen's brief, but highly successful solo career began in 1969 when she gained second place in the final of Channel Nine's popular talent show *New Faces*. Her prize was a contract with Ron Tudor's Fable Records. Within a year, the Danish-descended singer had scored three national hit singles: 'The Love Moth'/'Don't Forget About Me' (#39 in April 1970), a cover of the Mary Hopkin hit 'Knock Knock Who's There?'/'Just a Little Lovin'' (#2 in June) and Anne Murray's 'Snowbird'/'Are You Going My Way?' (#16 in October). Fable also combined the 'Knock Knock Who's There?' and 'The Love Moth' singles for the 'Knock Knock Who's There?' EP. Maessen's fourth single, 'Hurry on Down'/'Suddenly It's Sunny', came out in March 1971. In 1972 she issued two more Fable singles, 'New Love Day'/'Part of What You Hear' (July) and 'Taste of Honey'/'Amber Light' (October) before turning her attention to club and cabaret work.

Albums: *Liv for Life* (Fable, 1971), *Best of Liv Maessen* (Fable, 1973).

Magic Dirt

Formed: *1992*
Style: *Indie guitar rock*
Original line-up: *Adalita Srsen (vocals, guitar), Daniel Herring (guitar), Dean Turner (bass), Adam Robertson (drums)*

Highly touted Geelong (Victoria) band Magic Dirt started life in 1991 as Dear Bubbles. The band's contemporaries on the Geelong scene included **Bored!**, Amba Fear, She Freak, Seaweed Goorillas, Warped, Supergrass and Poppin' Mommas. As The Jim Jims, the band contributed a version of The Velvet Underground's 'Heroin' to Dave Thomas's 1992 Geelong compilation *Check this Action . . . Let the Fun Begin* (which also featured the abovenamed bands, plus others like **The Dirty Lovers**).

With another name change to Magic Dirt, the band issued a one-off single, 'Super Tear'/'Sea', on the independent Fellaheen label (July 1993) before signing to Melbourne label Au-Go-Go. The band's penchant for feedback improvisation, distorted guitar riffs and unusual tunings drew comparisons with The Stooges, Dinosaur Jr and New York indie veterans Sonic Youth. Magic Dirt scored support slots to US bands Sonic Youth and Pavement when they toured Australia. The CD EPs *Signs of Satanic Youth* (March 1994) and *Life was Better* (November 1994) established the band's reputation as bona fide alternative rock heroes. The band appeared on the

Magic Dirt

1995 Big Day Out tour and supported US visitors Hole around the country. Ex-**Bored!** frontman Dave Thomas (who had previously been Magic Dirt's manager) replaced Daniel Herring on lead guitar, and the band issued the 10-inch EP 'I was Cruel' (February 1996).

1996 was a busy year for Magic Dirt: the band signed a major deal with Warner Brothers in the USA, toured North America with the Archers of Loaf and issued the full-length album *Friends in Danger* (September). Produced by Paul McKercher (**You Am I**, **Tumbleweed**), the album matched the band's fearless experimentation with a dark, unhinged sound that went from moments of eerie near-silence to full-tilt guitar noise. 'Sparrow' was lifted as a CD single/double 7-inch vinyl single set in March 1997. Magic Dirt contributed a version of **God's** 'My Pal' to the *Idiot Box* soundtrack issued on rooArt/BMG in February 1997. Following that, Thomas left to be replaced by Spanish-born Raoul Sanchez (guitar; ex-Muffcake). Magic Dirt recorded a new album, *Young and Full of the Devil* (slated for release in early 1998), which yielded the CD EP 'Rabbit with Fangs' (November 1997).

Album: *Friends in Danger* (Au-go-go, 1996).

Makers of the Dead Travel Fast

Formed: *1980*
Style: *Experimental*
Original line-up: *Shane Fahey (synthesiser, vocals), Tim Schultz (sax, vocals, percussion), Greg Addison (guitar, vocals), Peter Richardson (piano, percussion, vocals), Steve Couri (bass), David Bullock (percussion)*

Sydney experimentalists Makers of the Dead Travel Fast derived their name from a quote in Bram Stoker's *Dracula*. The band created evocative washes of electronic soundscapes punctuated by all manner of percussion, eerie vocals, fluttering guitar and delicate sax. The band's contemporaries in the experimental stakes included Sydneysiders The Systematics, **Scattered Order** and **Severed Heads**, plus Melbourne's →↑→, Laughing Hands and **Equal Local**.

Makers of the Dead Travel Fast issued their debut single on **Scattered Order's** M-Squared label in 1981. The resonant 'Tael of a Saeghors'/'The Dumb Waiter' became something of a cult hit, and the band made its first live appearances. The band's debut album *The Vessels* mixed atmospheric, uncluttered sound textures with understated dynamics. The music drew certain parallels with the work of Brian Eno and the second side of David Bowie's *Low* album. The band issued the *Why Won't We Wake?* EP at the end of 1981 and promptly retired from live performances. The band only re-emerged for one more album, *Zoom is Less than Man*, in 1983 before breaking up. Shane Fahey went on to join **Scattered Order**. The Dead Travel Fast compilation *G'arage D'Or* came out in 1991. The title said a lot about the band's esoteric yet reverential approach to music making, having been derived from Luis Buñuel's classic surrealistic film *L'Age D'Or* (1930, *The Golden Age*).

Albums: *The Vessels* (M-Squared, 1981), *Zoom is Less than Man* (M-Squared, 1983), *G'arage D'Or* (Extreme, 1991).

Mándu

Style: *Rock*

Eccentric singer Mándu was something of an enigma and a sadly overlooked talent. He had a distinctive and emotional voice, but only issued one album that was received with bemused indifference. Nevertheless, the cosmic concept album *To the Shores of His Heaven* stands as a worthwhile period piece, a work graced with elegant songs, soaring arrangements and fine musicianship.

Some of the best musicians of the day played on the album (**Phil Manning**, Barry Sullivan, Steve Cooney, **Gary Young**, Peter Sullivan). The story-line told of an extraterrestrial visitor who, saddened by the state of the earth, opened his heart to the benign indifference of the universe. The fatalistic sense of despair in the lyrics was offset by just a glimmer of hope for a better future. It was a similar theme to that used by **Jim Keays** for his album *The Boy from the Stars* which came out at the same time, although Mándu infused his album with a more understated, intuitive sense of purpose. Mándu toured with The Mándu Band, which comprised Steve Cooney (guitar), Greg Cook (guitar; ex-**Cam-Pact**, **Mixtures**, Skylight), Peter Sullivan (keyboards), Mike Clarke (bass; ex-Skylight) and Bob Bickerton (drums; ex-Rock Granite and the Profiles).

Mándu issued two singles, 'We Ran Across the Sky'/'Traveller' (September 1974), and The Rolling Stones' 'Gimme Shelter'/'To the Shores of His Heaven' (September 1975), before joining **Lobby Loyde's** band Southern Electric. Mándu sang on the *Obsecration* album, and in 1976 travelled to the UK. He returned to Australia at the end of the decade and was on hand again when Loyde reactivated Southern Electric for the *Live with Dubs* album (1980). Mándu disappeared from view, re-emerging briefly during the mid-1980s with a band called Mándu Bándu.

Albums: To the Shores of His Heaven (Image/Astor, 1974), *We Ran Across the Sky* (reissue, Image/Astor, 1980).

Manikins

Formed: *1977*
Style: *Punk pop*
Original line-up: *Robert Porritt (vocals), Neil Fernandez (guitar), Ken Seymour (bass), Mark Betts (drums)*

One of the very first punk bands formed in Australia was Perth-based outfit The Cheap Nasties. Formed in August 1976 (one month after the first Ramones album came out), The Cheap Nasties comprised **Kim Salmon** (guitar, vocals), Robert Porritt, Neil Fernandez, Mark Betts and Dan Dare (bass). By 1977, the band had been joined by like-minded outfits Beheaded, **The Victims** and The Exterminators.

Formed in total isolation (like so many other primeval punk bands of the era), The Cheap Nasties made little headway. Salmon left in December 1977 to join The Invaders and then to form **Scientists**. The other members, with Ken Seymour replacing Dare, continued on as Manikins. Manikins leaned towards a cleaner, yet still tough, post-punk power pop sound. The band issued two independent singles, 'I Never Thought I'd Find Someone Who Could Be So Kind'/'Radio World' (November 1978) and 'Premonition'/'Laugh Too Loud' (August 1979). The band undertook a tour of the eastern states, but was met with virtual indifference. Dave Flick (real name Dave Faulkner, guitar, vocals; ex-**Victims**) joined in late 1979 and Manikins issued a third punky power pop single 'Love at Second Sight'/'Nuisance', 'All I Care About' (October 1980). Faulkner then left the band and travelled to Sydney, where he formed Le **Hoodoo Gurus**. At the end of 1981, having missed the opportunity to snare wider acclaim, Manikins called it quits.

Betts and Porritt re-formed Manikins in 1982 with Paul Blackbee (guitar, keyboards; ex-Screaming Fits) and Bradley Clark (guitar, bass; ex-Billy Orphan's Tears). The new line-up relocated to Melbourne and issued the cassette-only album *Live Locally*. By 1985, the vivacious Christine Bodey had replaced Porritt. Alexander Nettelbeck (keyboards) replaced Blackbee, and the band headed in a more commercial direction. Manikins signed to CBS and issued the single 'What are You on?'/'Dictator's Dream' (July 1986). The album *Manikins* came out in February 1988, with the singles 'Cruel World'/'Dracula's Slut' (November 1987) and 'Scent'/'Life Underground' (May 1988). 'Scent' had the distinction of being the very first CD single issued in Australia. In early 1988, Mick Prague (ex-**Teenage Radio Stars**, **James Freud's** Radio Stars) joined on bass. Manikins toured regularly, replaced Bodey with Christine Anne Trent but did not progress beyond their second-division status before breaking up in the early 1990s.

Album: Manikins (CBS, 1988).

Phil Manning

Style: *Blues*

Alongside **Dave Hole** and **Geoff Achison**, Phil Manning (b. 1948) is recognised as one of the best blues guitarists Australia has ever produced. Tasmanian-born Manning's earliest influences included The Beatles, The Rolling Stones, The Yardbirds, The Pretty Things and John Mayall's Bluesbreakers. From there he exploded Chicago electric blues (Muddy Waters, Howlin' Wolf, Elmore James, Jimmy Rogers, etc.) and Mississippi Delta acoustic blues (Son House, Robert Johnson, Tommy Johnson, Sonny Boy Williamson, etc.).

Manning had spells in Anonymous Incorporated, Cocaine Spell, **Tony Worsley and the Fabulous Blue Jays**, **Bay City Union** and the Laurie Allen Revue before joining Perth band The Beaten Tracks as replacement for the departing **Dave Hole**. In December 1968, The Beaten Tracks relocated to Melbourne where the band evolved into the first line-up of the legendary **Chain**. Manning left **Chain** for the first time in July 1971. He formed a duo with Warren Morgan (keyboards; ex-**Chain**, **Billy Thorpe** and the Aztecs) called Pilgrimage (named after the first track on the *Live Chain* album). The duo only worked together for four months and issued one single on Festival/Infinity, 'Walk in the Light'/'Just for You' (November 1971). Pilgrimage supported UK visitors Pink Floyd (September) and Elton John (October).

In November, Manning rejoined **Chain** for three months, after which he joined **Leo De Castro's Friends** on a freelance basis. In April 1972, he formed Willy and the Philtones which had evolved into **Band of Talabene** by July. By December 1972, Manning was playing with Mighty Mouse; in February 1973, with a simple name change, that band became **Chain** line-up #15. **Chain** stayed together until July 1974, and with the band's break-up Manning commenced his solo career. Throughout that period, Manning also worked as an in-demand session player, appearing on albums by the likes of **Russell Morris**, Frieze, **Ted Mulry**, **Brian Cadd**,

Dutch Tilders, **Matt Taylor**, **Jim Keays**, **Renée Geyer** and **Mándu**.

Manning issued his debut solo album, *I Wish there was a Way*, in December 1974. The album featured Manning in mellow, reflective singer/songwriter mode and it produced two singles, 'Love is the Mender'/'Take Your Chances' (December) and 'I Wish there was a Way'/'Aborigine Song' (March 1975). In May 1975, Manning launched the first Phil Manning Band which comprised Greg Cook (guitar, synthesiser; ex-**Cam-Pact**, **Mándu** Band), Eddie McDonald (bass; ex-**Bakery**) and Bruce Devenish (drums). The band recorded the commercial pop rock single 'Train to Ride'/'Tend to My Friend' which came out in October 1975. By September 1975, The Phil Manning Band line-up comprised Steve Cooney (guitar), Paul 'Sheepdog' Wheeler (bass; ex-**Billy Thorpe** and the Aztecs, **MacKenzie Theory**) and Tony Doyle (drums). Trevor Courtney (drums; ex-Chants R&B, **Cam-Pact**, **Vibrants**, Skylight) replaced Doyle in November 1975 but the band folded in March 1977.

Between April and June 1977, Manning was a member of **John Paul Young** and the All Stars alongside his old sparring partner in **Chain**, Warren Morgan. In July, Manning and **Jim Keays** (ex-Master's Apprentices) formed The Manning Keays Band with John Grant (keyboards; ex-**Freeway**), Andrew Kay (violin, keyboards), New Zealander Peter Cuddily (bass; ex-Space Waltz) and Robert Ross (drums). The band commenced recording an album, but Keays left early in the sessions. Rather than shelve the project, the guitarist renamed the band Manning and issued the undistinguished soul-pop album *Manning* in May 1978. The album yielded the singles Percy Sledge's 'When a Man Loves a Woman'/'Loudspeaker' (December 1977) and 'Call Me'/'Loudspeaker' (April 1978).

By July 1978, The Phil Manning Band comprised Grant, Cuddily, Midge Marsden (lead guitar) and John James (J.J.) Hackett (drums; ex-Rum Jungle). This was a more roots'n'blues-oriented outfit capable of playing blistering blues-rock. Manning's brother Dennis joined on keyboards to fill out the sound. In May 1979, PolyGram issued the single 'Just the Way It Goes'/'I Believe It's Over'. Marsden was something of a guitar hero in his native New Zealand, and the line-up of Manning, Marsden, Grant, Robbie Geappon (bass) and Bob Bickerton (drums; ex-Rock Granite and The Profiles, **Mándu** Band) issued the New Zealand-only album *Live* on Polydor (1979). By early 1980, the band had broken up and Manning returned to Tasmania for a brief holiday. That extended into a nine-month hiatus during which time he played a few solo club dates. At the end of the year, **Matt Taylor** invited Manning to join him in a blues band he was forming in Perth.

The Matt Taylor Phil Manning Band (with Roy Daniel, bass and Ric Whittle, drums) issued the exceptional *Oz Blues* album and the rare 'Spring Hill'/'The Line' single (both June 1981). The album featured a strong blend of R&B material, raunchy boogies and purist blues tracks. The band toured across the country but dissolved in December 1981. Manning formed a new Phil Manning Band with Englishman Chris Copping (keyboards; ex-Procol Harum), who was replaced by Mick 'The Reverend' O'Connor, Kerryn Tolhurst (guitar; ex-**Dingoes**), Wayne Duncan (bass; ex-**Daddy Cool**) and **Gary Young** (drums; ex-**Daddy Cool**). By 1983, The Phil Manning Band had been trimmed to The Phil Manning Rock'n'Roll Trio with just Duncan and Young remaining. The Trio broke up at the end of the year after touring constantly but getting nowhere. They had also spent time backing soul/jazz/blues singer **Renée Geyer**.

Manning and Taylor re-formed **Chain** in December 1983; Manning stayed with the band until the end of 1986. Manning settled into country Queensland with his family, and issued a solo acoustic album, *It's Blues*, at the start of 1988 on his own Tamborine Music imprint. In 1990, Manning issued the cassette-only release *Live at the Storey Bridge*. Both albums were enjoyable romps through a selection of Manning originals and covers of material by Robert Johnson, Muddy Waters, Blind Blake, Big Bill Broonzy and Paul Simon. In 1991, Manning formed a new band with Paul Cheeseman (bass) and Don Lebler (drums; ex-**Axiom**), and issued his fourth solo album, *Can't Stop* (November 1992). His fifth solo album, *The Back Shed* (March 1995) featured all instrumental, acoustic country blues material. By that stage Manning was a regular performer at the annual East Coast Blues Festival, either with his own band or backing the likes of ex-Rolling Stones guitarist Mick Taylor and **Renée Geyer**. In May 1995, Manning and Taylor re-formed **Chain** once again; since then, Manning has divided his time between touring commitments with **Chain** and performing solo shows. Manning issued a new album, *Two Roads*, in August 1997.

Phil Manning solo albums: *I Wish There was a Way* (Mushroom/Festival, 1974), *It's Blues* (Tamborine, 1988), *Live at the Storey Bridge* (Tamborine, 1990), *Can't Stop* (Tamborine, 1992), *The Back Shed* (Tamborine, 1995), *Two Roads* (Tamborine/Blackmarket, 1997); ***Manning album:*** *Manning* (Indigo, 1978); ***Phil Manning Band album:*** *Live* (as Phil Manning Band Featuring Midge Marsden, NZ only,

Polydor, 1979); ***Matt Taylor Phil Manning Band album:*** *Oz Blues* (Full Moon/Astor, 1981).

Brian Mannix (*see* Uncanny X-Men)

Mantissa

Formed: *1992*
Style: *Hard rock*
Original line-up: *Adam Pringle (vocals; ex-Compressed Heads), Nina Grant (bass, vocals; ex-Good and Evil), Chris Paine (guitar; ex-Utter Stench), Chris Collins (guitar; ex-Greg Brady Overdrive), Sid Green (drums; ex-Scoundrel)*

The highly touted Mantissa originally formed in 1989 under the name of Killing Time. That band comprised Adam Pringle, Nina Grant, Chris Paine, and a number of drummers (Arnie Prazz, Russell Hopkinson) until Tubby Wadsworth (real name Alex Nikolzew; ex-**Massappeal**, Fester Fanatics) joined as a permanent member at the end of the year.

Killing Time played the Melbourne inner-city circuit for a year. With the arrival of ace guitarist Jed Starr (real name Darren McCormack, ex-**Massive Appendage**, Fester Fanatics) in June 1990, the band's sound shifted from Stooges-style grunge to a more adventurous contemporary hard rock stance. Reference points extended from Led Zeppelin to Red Hot Chili Peppers and Living Colour. Killing Time swiftly outgrew its fanatical live following around Melbourne with the release of the independent 'Ruby's Mind' 12-inch EP in February 1991. With its crunching guitar riffs and funkified bass lines, the anthemic 'Ruby's Mind' launched Killing Time as a band with enormous potential and crossover appeal. After a modest initial pressing of just 800 copies sold out, the EP went on to sell an impressive 10 000 units and reached the national Top 20 in August.

The band supported overseas visitors like Faith No More, Mudhoney, Scatterbrain and Jane's Addiction, and became the subject of a furious bidding war between every major record company in Australia. Killing Time eventually signed a deal with Sydney-based independent label Red Eye. Red Eye reissued 'Ruby's Mind' (July), followed by the CD EP *The Mandlebroth Set* in October 1991. Wadsworth left the band at the end of 1991 to be replaced by Sid Green. The band issued the CD single 'Dream Alone'/'Mystery Line' (February 1992), after which Starr left to re-form Fester Fanatics. His place was taken by Chris Collins. Killing Time then signed an international deal with Polydor

Nina Grant, Mantissa

Records, and entered the studio with American producer Terry Date (Soundgarden, Pantera) in May to commence work on a debut album.

Due to a band also called Killing Time in the USA and another in Japan, the local Killing Time became Mantissa in August 1992. The name was inspired by John Fowles' novel *Mantissa* in which Mantissa was deemed the goddess of creativity. Mantissa's debut album *Mossy God* came out in October, which coincided with the band's national tour support to US visitors the Red Hot Chili Peppers. Two CD singles were lifted from the album, 'Mary Mary' (#55 in November) and 'Land of the Living' (#60 in March 1993). The album mixed grinding, heavy riffs, Grant's rumbling bass lines and Pringle's dramatic vocals with a mystical feel and all manner of psychedelic touches. Following the release of *Mossy God* and the single 'Land of the Living' in the USA mid-1993, Mantissa spent nine months touring across America. The band returned to Australia and issued a new CD single 'Sanctify' (June 1994), then supported visiting US heavyweights Pantera on an Australian tour (November).

In January 1995, Mantissa took part in the Big Day Out national tour, and issued a new CD EP

Interalia. August 1995 saw the release of the band's second album, *Thirst.* The album was not successful, despite the many years of groundwork the band had put in prior to its release. Having been tagged 'The Next Big Thing' and 'The Band Most Likely To' very early in its career, Mantissa was unable to sustain a high profile and slipped from view.

Albums: *Mossy God* (Red Eye/Polydor, 1992), *Thirst* (Polydor, 1995).

Maple Lace

Formed: *1969*
Style: *Pop*
Original line-up: *Ken Teasdale (vocals), Geoff Kanter (guitar), Ross Lalor (guitar), Paul Mumford (bass), John Newirth (drums)*

This Sydney pop band was the resident outfit at popular discotheque Caesar's Palace. In order to promote the disco, and to capitalise on the 1970 radio ban of overseas records, the management suggested the band record a version of the novelty song 'Gimme Dat Ding' for release as a single. 'Gimme Dat Ding' had been a Top 10 hit in the USA for Pipkins. Maple Lace's version of 'Gimme Dat Ding' came out on the Caesar's label backed with 'Comes a Time'. Singers on the single were Jerry Anderson and George Blanche, and the band shared a #7 chart placing in August 1970 along with another version by comedian Frankie Davidson.

By that stage, the band's line-up was Anderson, Blanche, Lindsay Askew (guitar; ex-**Flake**), Rob Toth (organ; ex-**Flake**), Doug Rae (bass; ex-**Sherbet**) and Mike Derey (drums). Maple Lace issued a second single, this time on the Chart label, 'Can't Stay Away from You'/'It's a Beautiful Day' (April 1971). Anderson and Toth revamped the band's line-up to include Ted 'The Head' Yanni (guitar), Warren Ward (bass; ex-**Flying Circus**) and Jim Penson (drums; ex-Plastic Tears). That was a strong line-up, but before the year was out Ward and Penson had left to join **Blackfeather** and Maple Lace folded.

Bobbi Marchini

Style: *Soul, pop*

Bobbi Marchini (nee Roberta Turnbull) was a versatile singer from the early 1970s who was adept with both soul pop material and flat-out blues rock. She sang with Sydney club band Hunger and appeared on the *Laid* album by studio outfit **Duck**. Her gutsy vocal contribution to tracks like Nick Gravenites' 'Burned Alive in the Blues' (in the manner of Janis Joplin) and Neil Young's 'Southern Man' added considerably to the record's appeal.

In 1973 English producer Simon Napier-Bell (Yardbirds, Move, T-Rex, **Alison McCallum**) took an interest in Marchini. She signed to Albert Productions with whom she issued several soul pop singles: 'Working My Way Back to You'/'I've Found My Way' (March 1973), 'Show and Tell'/'Voodoo Woman' (November), 'You're the Hand that Feeds My Love'/ 'London Town' (March 1974) and 'Home'/'I Love You Lord' (August). While signed to Albert, Marchini also appeared on the single 'So Tough'/'To Know Him is to Love Him' (October 1974) as one-third of the vocal group The Hooter Sisters (alongside Janice Slater and **Alison McCallum**). Marchini contributed vocals to a number of albums, including **Graham Lowndes'** *Survival's a Song* (1973), **La De Das'** *Rock and Roll Sandwich* (1973) and ex-**Blackfeather** guitarist John Robinson's solo album *Pity for the Victim* (1974), but since that time she has disappeared from public view.

Marcus Hook Roll Band (*see* The Easybeats; Flash and the Pan)

The Mark of Cain

Formed: *1984*
Style: *Punk rock*
Original line-up: *Rod Archer (vocals), John Scott (guitar, vocals; ex-Spiral Collapse), Kim Scott (bass), Gavin Atchison (drums; ex-Spiral Collapse)*

The long saga of Adelaide band The Mark of Cain revolves around the Scott brothers, John and Kim, whose shared vision encompassed the sum of the band's parts. Gloomy, monotonous vocals and bleak slabs of metallic guitar did battle over a lurching rhythm section to arrive at a harsh sound that drew on The Stooges, Joy Division, Big Black and Henry Rollins for inspiration.

Although referring to the Biblical story of Cain and Able (the first murder), the band's name The Mark of Cain was actually inspired by the Hermann Hesse novel *Demian.* The band's penchant for militaristic imagery and lyric themes (to say nothing of the members' close-cropped, marine-styled looks) only added to the sense of desperation and solitude displayed in the band's music. In The Mark of Cain's case, such overworked descriptions as 'intense', 'brutal', 'belligerent' and 'heavy-going' were entirely appropriate. After formation, the band went through a string of drummers (Gavin Atchison, Roger Crisp, John Rickett, Neil Guiver) before settling on Campbell Robinson at the end of 1988.

The Mark of Cain

John Scott had also taken over lead vocals from the departing Rod Archer.

Sydney-based independent label Phantom issued the band's debut single, 'The Lords of Summer'/'Can You See Now?', in September 1988. In October, The Mark of Cain appeared on a rare gig giveaway album, *Assorted Desecrations and Magnificent Mutations*, as part of Phantom's tenth anniversary celebrations. The Mark of Cain covered songs by former Phantom bands The Visitors ('Journey by Sledge') and Shy Impostors ('Seein' Double'). The band then signed to Adelaide independent label Dominator for the *Battlesick* album in August 1989. The title track 'Battlesick', also appeared on rooArt's Various Artists compilation *Youngblood II* (1990). The album *The Unclaimed Prize* (March 1991) offered up more sonic blasts of rough-hewn guitar riffs and booming drums. By the time the album appeared, John Scott had travelled overseas for the start of 18 months on a work-related project. Kim followed suit in 1991. Both brothers have Bachelor degrees in Engineering, John in Electronic and Kim in Mechanical. In the meantime, German label Normal had issued both *Battlesick* and *The Unclaimed Prize* in Europe.

While in Chicago, the brothers reunited in order to record with famed US producer Steve Albini (later to work with Nirvana and Jesus Lizard). The Mark of Cain's relationship with Albini went back to 1987 when the band supported his outfit Big Black on its tour of Australia. The sessions appeared in June 1993 as the CD EP *Incoming*. With Aaron Hewson (ex-Order of Decay, Grunter) on drums, The Mark of Cain re-formed in mid-1992 when John and Kim returned from their overseas sojourn. In early 1994, The Mark of Cain appeared on the bill of the Big Day Out tour, and issued the limited edition single 'Tell Me'/'Viet Vet' (February) on the Insipid Vinyl label.

By that stage, the band's influences had broadened to include Sonic Youth, Godflesh and Helmet. During that period, the band supported overseas visitors like Rollins Band, Fugazi, Helmet, Steve Albini's Shellac, The Butthole Surfers, Killdozer, All, Pavement and Primus. In early 1995, US hardcore godfather Henry Rollins helped finance and produce the band's third album, *Ill at Ease*. Rollins had long been an admirer of the band's work, and has gone on record as saying that he 'should have written "Battlesick"'. Rollins also made arrangements to issue the band's back catalogue worldwide on his 2.13.61 label. The *Ill at Ease* album (on the Ra label) reached #1 on the independent charts (December 1995) and produced the CD single 'First Time' (September). The band's final release on Dominator had been the CD EP *The Killer is Within* ('Hindsight'), which came out in July 1995.

In December 1996, The Mark of Cain issued the album *Rock and Roll*. It featured off-kilter remixes (from producers like **Itch-E and Scratch-E's** Paul Mac and the Young Gods' Franz Treichler) of such band favourites as 'Pointman', 'Hindsight' and 'The Hammer'. The 'Interloper' CD EP (May 1997) featured remixes of 'Interloper', 'The Contender' and 'You Let Me Down'. The Mark of Cain also contributed 'Hindsight' and a rampaging cover of **X**'s 'Degenerate Boy' to the soundtrack of David Caesar's feature film *Idiot Box* (February 1997). 'Degenerate Boy' also came out as a CD single.

Albums: *Battlesick* (Dominator, 1989), *The Unclaimed Prize* (Dominator, 1991), *Ill at Ease* (Ra/Warner, 1995), *Rock and Roll* (Ra/BMG, 1997).

Martha's Vineyard

Formed: *1986*
Style: *Folk rock*
Original line-up: *Peggy Van Zalm (vocals), Anthony Best (guitar, vocals), Norman Parkhill (guitar), Lisa Jooste (violin), Catherine McAuliffe (bass), Aidan D'Adhemar (drums)*

Martha's Vineyard shared a similar sound and outlook to that of fellow Perth, Western Australia, bands like **The Triffids**, **The Honeys** and **Chad's**

Tree. The band's brand of reflective folk rock mixed melancholy vocals, acoustic and electric guitars, gentle percussion and spacious arrangements to arrive at a harmonious and intriguing whole. Peggy Van Zalm's strong vocals drew comparison with the likes of Patti Smith, Chrissie Hynde and Joni Mitchell.

The band took its name from the famous holiday resort off the coast of Massachusetts, in the New England area of the USA. Not long after forming in May 1986, the band issued a self-titled cassette and shared a single 'Our Day' with Errol H. Tout's 'Sounds of Swimming'. The mini-album *For a Small World* followed in October 1987. Stuart Fenner replaced Lisa Jooste on violin, and Phil Kakulas (ex-**Triffids**) took over on bass. The line-up of Best, Van Zalm, Kakulas and D'Adhemar relocated to Sydney in 1988. In 1989, the fledgling rooArt label signed up Martha's Vineyard alongside **The Trilobites, Crash Politics, Tall Tales & True, Hipslingers** and **The Hummingbirds**. Martha's Vineyard contributed the track 'Unravelling' to the first of rooArt's *Youngblood* compilations (September 1988).

RooArt issued the debut Martha's Vineyard album *Old Beach Road* and single 'Old Beach Road'/'Trying Too Hard' in June 1989. There was a second single on rooArt, 'More of the Same', before the band disappeared from view in 1990. Kakulas joined **The Blackeyed Susans**. At the end of 1994, Van Zalm launched her solo career with the release of the album, *Shine*.

Martha's Vineyard albums: *For A Small World* (mini-album, Monkey, 1987), *Old Beach Road* (rooArt/PolyGram, 1989); ***Peggy Van Zalm solo album:*** *Shine* (Creative Arts, 1994).

Massappeal

Formed: *1985*
Style: *Hardcore punk*
Original line-up: *Randy Reimann (vocals), Brett Curotta (guitar, ex-Bedspreads), Kevin McCrear (bass), Darren Gilmour (drums; ex-***Rocks***, Climate of Fear)*

Alongside the likes of **The Hard-Ons** and **The Hellmenn**, Massappeal was at the forefront of the late 1980s Sydney hardcore scene. The band mixed breakneck punk tempos with unrelenting heavy metal guitar riffs to arrive at a potent and rough-hewn sound. As rock writer J.J. Adams pointed out, the band's early influences were American hardcore heroes like Black Flag, Suicidal Tendencies and Gangrene, as opposed to the English flavour (Charged GBH, Discharge, Exploited, Crass) of most early 1980s Sydney punk bands. Massappeal infused its incendiary live shows with a positive attitude that espoused a think-for-yourself ethos. Inevitably the sheer intensity and volume within which the band worked often masked such a thought-provoking and personal frame of reference.

In October 1986, the independent Waterfront label issued the band's debut release, the mini-album *Nobody Likes a Thinker* followed by the single *The Bar of Life* ('Fun Again'/'Are You Alright?') (August 1987). Alex Nikolzew (aka Tubby Wadsworth) played drums on the single. In 1988, Sean Fonti (ex-My Heart Bleeds for You) replaced McCrear on bass and David Ross (ex-**Vicious Circle**) replaced Wadsworth on drums. The band issued the excellent full-length album *Jazz* in November 1989. The initial pressing included a bonus four-track 12-inch EP, *Extra Jazz*. In April 1990 Ross left to be replaced by Peter Allen (drums), and the band supported US thrash outfit Anthrax at its Sydney concert. In October Fonti left to concentrate full-time on his other band, **Caligula** (which also included David Ross on drums). Adrielle came in as replacement bass player, and the band added second guitarist Ashley Chatto at the start of 1991. Massappeal supported US bands Scatterbrain and Fugazi, and then issued the CD single 'Chrysalidz' and second album *The Mechanic* (March 1992).

By that stage, the band had incorporated such diverse elements as Ministry, Treponem Pal, Revolting Cocks and Monster Magnet into its sound. A support slot to Brazilian thrash/hardcore heroes Sepultura during July 1992 highlighted a curious dilemma for the band: in spite of delivering a blistering set, Massappeal was not considered 'heavy metal' enough by the partisan Sydney crowd. Massappeal contributed a track to rooArt's Australian heavy grunge-pop compilation, *Crack in the Sun or Fade in the Shade* (November 1992), alongside the likes of **You Am I, Guttersnipes, Screamfeeder, Nursery Crimes, The Meanies, Tumbleweed** and Headache. Massappeal disappeared from view for a time, only re-emerging in early 1994 with a new line-up (Reimann, Curotta, Allen and bass player James), a new CD EP, *The Zesty Charismatic Personality Chamber* (January 1994), and new album, *Nommo Anagonno* (August). It was a strong album full of unsettling riffs and flat-out power grooves, but again the band slipped from view.

Albums: *Nobody Likes a Thinker* (mini-album, Waterfront, 1986), *Jazz* (Waterfront, 1989), *The Mechanic* (Survival/Sony, 1992), *Nobody Likes a Thinker* (CD reissue, Survival, 1993), *Jazz* (CD reissue, Survival, 1993), *Nommo Anagonno* (Shagpile/Shock, 1994).

Massive Appendage

Formed: *1986*
Style: *Heavy metal*
Original line-up: *Jed Starr (real name Darren McCormack, guitar, vocals), Big Bird (real name Matt McCormack, guitar, vocals), Snuff Beastley (real name Shawn McCormack, bass), Venom Brown (drums)*

Massive Appendage was just one of a number of different bands that Jed Starr has steered across a rocky road over the years. In the early 1980s, the McCormack family relocated to Los Angeles for a time; it was there that the McCormack siblings formed a band under the name of Kings Cross and recorded a self-titled, three-track 12-inch EP ('Gimme', 'Back Street Theatre'/'Love Machine'). Kings Cross became involved in the burgeoning Los Angeles glam-metal scene and came into contact with the likes of the nascent Guns N' Roses, Mötley Crüe, Ratt, etc.

The McCormack family returned to Sydney and the brothers formed the first version of Massive Appendage in 1986. The band's flashy sound was characterised by heavy riffs set in counterpoint to vocal harmonies and melodic guitar lines. The band's influences ranged from Black Sabbath and **AC/DC** to Kiss and the Sweet. In 1989, Oxx (real name Simon Cooper) replaced Brown on drums, and Massive Appendage issued its debut, self-financed album, *The Severed Erection*. The album cover artwork by Criss Hades caused a wave of controversy due to its vivid depiction of sexual ecstasy and drug paraphernalia. The band claimed the artwork to be 'pro-feminist and a statement against drug abuse, alcoholism, homosexuality, evangelism, child molestation, communism and the threat of nuclear war' but somehow its lurid contextualisation only served to dilute the message.

While working with Massive Appendage, Starr and Snuff moonlighted with their other bands, Kings Cross and Fester Fanatics. The revived Kings Cross also included Tubby Wadsworth (real name Alex Nikolzew, drums, vocals; ex-**Massappeal**) and Marc 'Cat Weazle' Welsh (on loan from **Asylum**) on guitar. Kings Cross issued its self-financed debut album *Psychedelic World* in 1989. Starr, Snuff and Wadsworth formed Fester Fanatics in September 1987 with Aldo Rubernik (aka Fester, vocals). With an 18-stone, bald-headed shouter by the name of Fester as its frontman, the band could never be accused of taking itself too seriously.

Fester Fanatics toured interstate on a regular basis and issued two self-financed albums, *What Choice Do We Have?* and *Fester Fanatics' Greatest Cocktail Party Hits*. The second album featured all 1970s covers, ranging from Black Sabbath's 'Hole in the Sky' to **Ted Mulry Gang's** 'Jump in My Car'. Both albums were indicative of the band's rough-hewn but heavy approach. By 1989, the line-up was Fester, Starr and Oxx (also in Massive Appendage) plus newcomer Squire Anderson (bass). The band broke up in March 1990. Starr and Oxx continued with Massive Appendage, while Fester and Squire formed Moron Appeal. In June 1990, Starr moved to Melbourne and joined Killing Time which already included Tubby Wadsworth as its drummer.

Starr contributed significantly to Killing Time's sound; he also wrote the songs 'Ruby's Mind' and 'Dream Alone' that helped establish the band's reputation. Starr left Killing Time in March 1992 to revive Fester Fanatics; Killing Time later evolved into **Mantissa**. At the end of 1992, Starr formed Starworld with Big Bird, Venom Brown and Anthony Ragg (bass; ex-**Kings of the Sun**). Marc Welsh replaced Ragg in 1993. The band's sound mixed such disparate influences as Cream, Funkadelic, MC5, Thin Lizzy and the Raspberries. Starworld issued the CD EP *Starworld '93* in November 1993. By that stage, Starr was also working in ex-**Noiseworks** frontman Jon Stevens' new band.

Massive Appendage album: *The Severed Erection* (Original, 1989); ***Fester Fanatics albums:*** *What Choice Do We Have?* (Original, 1988), *Fester Fanatics' Greatest Cocktail Party Hits* (Original, 1989); ***Kings Cross album:*** *Psychedelic World* (Original, 1989).

The Master's Apprentices

Formed: *1965*
Style: *R&B, progressive rock*
Original line-up: **Jim Keays** *(vocals, harmonica), Mick Bower (rhythm guitar), Rick Morrison (lead guitar), Gavin Webb (bass), Brian Vaughton (drums)*

The Master's Apprentices are remembered as one of Australia's best-loved bands of the 1960s. Between 1965 and 1972, the band embraced almost every trend in pop music, from raw R&B and psychedelic pop to full-blown progressive rock.

The Master's Apprentices began life in Adelaide as The Mustangs, playing Shadows-styled instrumentals. The line-up consisted of Mick Bower, Gavin Webb, Rick Morrison and Brian Vaughton. At the start of 1965, the band recruited **Jim Keays** as singer, adopted a rawer R&B-derived sound and became The Master's Apprentices. The band members chose the name because they were

The Master's Apprentices

as much influenced by the blues masters such as John Lee Hooker, Muddy Waters, Elmore James and Jimmy Reed as they were by the current crop of British R&B bands like The Rolling Stones, The Animals, The Pretty Things and The Yardbirds.

In 1966, The Masters were placed third in the Adelaide heat of the Hoadley's National Battle of the Sounds. A year later, Astor issued the band's debut single, the compelling 'Undecided', which had been written by Bower and Morrison. The flip featured Bower's extraordinary anti-war song, 'Wars or Hands of Time'. That classic single hit the Top 10 in Adelaide, Melbourne and Sydney during April, and the band commenced a hectic schedule of touring. The sudden success was too much for Vaughton and Morrison, who were replaced by Steve Hopgood and Tony Sommers (ex-**Johnny Young's** Kompany) respectively. The band's second raucous R&B single, 'Buried and Dead'/'She's My Girl', was a Top 20 hit in Sydney during June 1967, and coincided with the release of the debut album *The Master's Apprentices*. The band's next single was the blissful psychedelic pop of 'Living in a Child's Dream' (another Bower original)/'Tired of Just Wandering' which peaked at #4 in Sydney and #9 in Melbourne during September. The song scored *Go-Set*'s Song of the Year Award and Most Successful Australian Group of 1967 Award for the Masters.

The pressures of major success began to take its toll and Mick Bower left the band after suffering a nervous breakdown. He was replaced briefly by Rick Harrison before Peter Tilbrook (ex-Bentbeaks) came in as a permanent member. Without Bower's songwriting skills on which to call, the band had to search for suitable songs from outside sources. For their next single, The Masters chose a Brian Caine (later Cadd) song called 'Silver People'. The band rearranged the song and released it as 'Elevator Driver'/'Theme for a Social Climber'. Before the single's release in February 1968, Sommers and Hopgood were replaced by Doug Ford (hot-shot guitarist from **The Missing Links** and The Running Jumping Standing Still) and Colin Burgess (ex-Untamed and Haze).

In May 1968, Webb left to be replaced by Glenn Wheatley (bass; ex-**Bay City Union**). In June, the band issued the single 'Brigette'/'Four Years of Five', which was the first Ford/Keays collaboration. This was another pleasant dose of flower power pop and became The Masters' fifth hit in a row. The new line-up contested the 1968 Hoadley's National Battle of The Sounds final in July. The band came such a close second to **The Groove** that they were awarded a complimentary prize of boat tickets to England. 1968 ended with Tilbrook leaving, Astor releasing the two-year-old 'But One Day'/'My Girl' as a farewell single, the band signing on with influential manager Daryl Sambell and being voted Most Original Group and Second Most Popular Group (behind **The Twilights**) in the *Go-Set* Pop Polls. The Masters' first single for 1969 (on EMI/Columbia) was the vapid bubblegum song 'Linda Linda' (the B-side 'Merry-Go-Round' was tougher).

By the end of the year, the band had scored two Top 20 hits with the hard rock singles '5-10 Man'/'How I Love You' (July) and 'Think About Tomorrow Today'/'A Dog, a Siren and Memories' (December). The Masters also issued their second album, *Masterpiece*, in 1969 and set up the Drum Agency (motivated by the business-minded Glenn Wheatley) to manage acts like **Sect** and **The Expression** and promote concerts. 'Turn Up Your Radio'/'Jam It Up' became the band's biggest hit to date (peaking at #7 nationally in May 1970). 'Turn Up Your Radio' has since become an Australian rock classic. Just as the single peaked, the band left for England. Once in London, The Masters began to absorb all the heavy trends of the English scene and the results were heard on the evocative 'Because I Love You'/'I'm Your Satisfier' single (December 1970) and *Choice Cuts* album (May 1971).

Recorded at Abbey Road Studios with producer Jeff Jarrett, the masterful *Choice Cuts* was brimming with complex, shifting arrangements. Powerful material like 'Because I Love You', 'Death of a King', 'Rio De Camero', 'Song for a Lost Gypsy' and 'Michael' highlighted Doug Ford's exemplary guitar technique. *Choice Cuts* stood out like a diamond in the rough at the time, and it remains one of the finest Australian progressive hard rock albums ever issued. With the band's return to Australia in December, 'Because I Love You' reached #12 and *Choice Cuts* #11 in July 1971. The album was issued in England (renamed *The Master's Apprentices*) and when news arrived that it had garnered positive reviews in *NME* and *Melody Maker*, The Masters set off again for the UK in May.

One month later, the live *Nickelodeon* album and single 'Future of Our Nation'/'New Day' came out in Australia. The album had been recorded at Perth's Nickelodeon Theatre in December 1970, on the first date of the band's national tour, and was one of the first live albums ever issued in Australia. In England, the band recorded a final album, *A Toast to Panama Red*, and single, 'Love is'/'Southern Cross'. Like *Choice Cuts* before it, *A Toast to Panama Red* was a groundbreaking album of rarefied skill and tremendous scope yet, upon release in January 1972, it sank without trace. It was simply too musically advanced for the local industry of the day to comprehend. *A Toast to Panama Red* is one of the great lost treasures of the Australian progressive rock era. Reissue specialists Raven included the transcendent 'Melodies of St Kilda'/'Southern Cross' on the essential Various Artists compilation *Golden Miles: Australian Progressive Rock 1969–1974* (1994).

Even before the album came out, The Masters had broken up. Keays and Wheatley returned to Australia but Ford and Burgess kept The Masters' name alive for another year as a three-piece (with Denny Burgess, ex-**Throb** on bass). The three-piece line-up's only studio recording, 'Freedom Seekers', later appeared on the rarities compilation *Jam It Up!* (April 1987). Colin and Denny Burgess returned to Adelaide at the start of 1973. They attempted to form a new band, Hard Rock Theatre, with Keays (vocals), Peter Jesser (guitar) and Peter Staben (keyboards), but the venture never got off the ground. Colin moved to Sydney, where he joined the nascent **AC/DC** as its original drummer.

Jim Keays worked as a staff writer for *Go-Set* magazine before launching a successful solo career. Wheatley went into band management and proved his business acumen by becoming one of the most successful rock entrepreneurs in Australia during the 1980s. He formed the Wheatley Brothers Organisation and was instrumental in the local and international success of **Little River Band** and **John Farnham.** In 1974, EMI issued the *Now that It's Over (Best of)* compilation and a farewell single, 'Rio De Camero'/'Thyme to Rhyme' (August). Raven Records kept interest in the band alive during the 1980s with the release of the essential *Hands of Time (1966–72)* compilation and the *Jam It Up!* rarities collection. Raven reissued *Choice Cuts* in 1988 with the previously B-side only track 'New Day' added.

In 1983, Colin and Denny Burgess formed hard rock band His Majesty with Japanese singer Yukiko Davis and Spike Williams (guitar). His Majesty launched itself in a blaze of publicity, but neither the singles 'Glory Boys'/'Champagne Cocaine' (November 1983) and 'C Me Comin''/'Randy' (February 1985) on the Regal label nor the band's live shows attracted sufficient interest from the public. The band broke up in 1987.

In March 1988, Keays, Ford, Webb and Colin Burgess re-formed The Master's Apprentices and set off on the successful Birth of the Beat national tour. Roger Faynes (guitar, keyboards; ex-Koo De Tah) joined in order to fill out the live sound. The band signed a new deal with Virgin Records and, to promote the tour, the label issued *The Very Best of the Master's Apprentices*. In November 1988, The Masters released their first new album in 17 years, *Do What You Wanna Do,* which featured one side of live cuts and another of studio tracks. A re-recorded and rearranged version of 'Because I Love You'/'I'm Your Satisfier' (live) was issued as a single (October) and became a hit all over again to a whole new generation of fans. The Masters' last single was 'The Birth of the Beat'/'Birth of the Beat' (November).

Although Keays and Ford recorded demos in 1990, no new records were forthcoming. The two songwriting partners collaborated on Keays' third solo album, *Pressure Makes Diamonds,* which came out in 1993. In April 1995, Keays re-recorded a version of 'Turn Up Your Radio' with the aid of Australia's finest trash-pop exponents, **Hoodoo Gurus**. EMI issued the *Greatest Hits* compilation on CD with the new track added. Keays and Ford re-formed The Masters again in 1997 for several tours. The line-up also featured Peter Farnan (guitar, keyboards; on loan from **Boom Crash Opera**, John Favarro (bass; from **The Badloves**) and Tony Day (drums; ex-**Girl Overboard**).

Albums: *The Master's Apprentices* (Astor, 1967), *Masterpiece* (EMI/Columbia, 1969), *Choice Cuts* (EMI/Columbia, 1971), *Nickelodeon* (EMI/Columbia, 1971), *A Toast to Panama Red* (EMI/Columbia, 1972), *Now that It's Over (Best of)* (EMI, 1974), *Hands of Time 1966–72* (Raven, 1981), *Jam It Up! (A Collection of Rarities 1965–1973)* (Raven, 1987), *Very Best of the Master's Apprentices* (Virgin, 1988), *Do What You Wanna Do* (Virgin, 1988), *Greatest Hits (30th Anniversary)* (EMI, 1995).

Matchbox (*see* Captain Matchbox Whoopee Band)

Matt Finish

Formed: *1979*
Style: *Rock*
Original line-up: *Matt Moffitt (vocals, guitar), Glen White (bass), John Prior (drums)*

Sydney band Matt Finish played a melodic brand of guitar-based pub-rock that garnered critical acclaim and a wide fan base. Frontman Mark Moffitt was hailed as a fine songwriter of considerable insight and potential. Initially Matt Finish spent a year on the Australian pub circuit, establishing a solid reputation as a band to watch, before signing with producer Peter Dawkins' Giant label.

Jeff Clayton replaced original bass player Glen White, but then had to leave the band due to illness. In early 1980, Rick Grossman (bass; ex-**Bleeding Hearts**, **Parachute**, Eric Gradman: Man & Machine) came in as Clayton's replacement. Once Clayton had recovered his health, he rejoined on rhythm guitar during May and the band began touring to a positive response. Giant issued the band's debut single, *Matt Finish Play Africa* ('Mancini Shuffle'/'CIA') in November 1980. The band's excellent debut album, *Short Note* (March 1981), and second single, 'Short Note'/'Layman's Day' (February), reached #33 and #18 respectively on the national charts. Matt Finish toured constantly throughout 1981 and issued the five-track EP *Fade Away* in October 1981. Unfortunately, Moffitt succumbed to ill-health and the band split up at the end of the year. Grossman joined **Divinyls** while Moffitt spent a year recuperating and writing new material. Moffitt relaunched Matt Finish in May 1983 with the three-piece line-up of himself, Prior and Clayton (back on bass), before adding newcomer Bert Dorset on rhythm guitar at the end of the year.

The band immediately resumed touring and issued two 12-inch EPs, 'Out of These Moments'/'High Times for the Poor', 'Blind and Running' (October 1983) and *Matt Finish* (November). The album *Word of Mouth* (May 1984) confirmed that Matt Finish had lost none of its original spark. It produced three impressive singles, 'Always Another'/'Forecast' (March), 'Words and Wars'/'Still Roads' (June) and 'Come on Over'/'Light Up My Days' (September). Dorset left the band in late July while on tour. Matt Finish continued touring as a three-piece until 1985, after which Moffitt split the band to launch his solo career. Moffitt recorded his debut solo album, *As Little as a Look*, in Brussels, Belgium during March 1985. It produced the singles 'Miss This Tonight'/'Save Your Worry' (#17 in June 1986) and 'All that Stuff'/'Fever Pitch' (August). Moffitt's backing band for the sessions included Englishman Pete Glenister (guitar), Nicky Graham (bass, keyboards) and John Prior (drums).

Moffitt's touring band in support of the album's release was Glenister, Graham, Prior and Rob Fisher (keyboards). By the end of the 1980s, Moffitt was touring overseas with a band called The Blue Max and began writing songs with members of Keith Richards' X-Pensive Winos. In April 1992, Moffitt issued the limited edition acoustic CD EP *Euroka*. He then re-formed Matt Finish with stalwart member Prior plus Jennifer Barrett (guitar, vocals; ex-Blue Max), Guy Le Claire (guitar; ex-**Eurogliders**, **Ian Moss** Band, Guy Le Claire Band) and Lindsay Jehan (bass; ex-**Eurogliders**) and recommenced touring. 'One Day at a Time' (June 1992) was the first Matt Finish single for eight years. By 1993 the line-up comprised Moffitt, Paul Dawkins (keyboards), Rohan Cannon (guitar), Bobby Christian (bass) and Adrian Cannon (drums). *By Heart* (September 1993) was only the band's third album in a career that spanned 15 years. It yielded the CD EP 'Earthbound' (July) plus the CD singles 'Blue' (September) and 'Will I Ever Know?' (May 1994).

Matt Finish albums: *Short Note* (Giant/CBS, 1981), *Word of Mouth* (CBS, 1984), *By Heart* (BMG, 1993); ***Matt Moffitt solo album:*** *As Little as a Look* (CBS, 1985).

Wendy Matthews

Style: *Soul, pop*

During the 1990s, Canadian-born Wendy Matthews (b. 1961) was hailed as one of the finest singers in Australia. Matthews has cited her influences as the likes of Peter Gabriel, Daniel Lanois, Bobby Womack and Robbie Robertson. Her extraordinary, crystal-clear vocals also displayed a soulfulness that was the mark of a truly gifted singer.

Matthews left her hometown of Montreal, Quebec at 17 and spent the next two years busking across Canada, the USA and Mexico before landing in Los Angeles. There she sang with a number of local bands and scored work on the session circuit. In 1983, **Glenn Shorrock** invited Matthews to sing back-up vocals on his Australian solo tour. Smitten with Australia, she decided to stay. Initially Matthews became one of the most in-demand session singers in Sydney, appearing on dozens of commercials (L.J. Hooker, Coca-Cola, CCs, David Jones, Aus-

Wendy Matthews

tralian sugar, Qantas, etc.). In 1985, she contributed backing vocals to **Models'** breakthrough album *Out of Mind Out of Sight* and became a semi-permanent member of the band. She also sang on albums by **Jimmy Barnes**, **Tim Finn**, **Richard Clapton** and **Icehouse**.

In 1987, Matthews collaborated with **Kate Ceberano** on the soundtrack to the ABC-TV drama series *Stringer*. The album *You've Always Got the Blues* (April 1988) was a mix of torch song standards and new songs contributed by a variety of writers like Don Walker and Steve Prestwich ('The Girl in the Picture') and the album's producer, Martin Armiger ('Stringer'). It reached #4 on the national chart, and produced the singles 'You've Always Got the Blues'/'3=2+1 (Shame)' (March) and 'Guilty (Through Neglect)'/'Danger Zone' (May). She then assisted **Rockmelons** and **Peter Blakeley** on their respective debut albums, and helped form and define the sound of **Absent Friends**. Matthews sang on **Absent Friends'** soul-stirring #1 hit single, Eddie Floyd's 'I Don't Wanna Be with Nobody But You' and the best-selling *Here's Looking Up Your Address* album.

With the completion of **Absent Friends'** touring commitments in mid-1990, Matthews went into the studio with long-time friend and producer Ricky Fataar (ex-Beach Boys, Rutles) to record her debut solo album. Helping out in the studio were the likes of **Absent Friends** members Sean Kelly, Roger Mason, Garry Gary Beers, James Valentine, Mick King and Andrew Duffield, plus **Tim Finn** and **Peter Blakeley**. The resultant album, *Emigré*, defined the journey the singer had taken since leaving Canada 13 years previously. Highlights included the traditional ballad 'Goin' Back to My Roots' and 'Long Way from Home', plus the hit singles 'Token Angels' (#18 in November 1990), Bobby Womack's 'Woman's Gotta Have It' (#34 in February 1991) and 'Let's Kiss (Like Angels Do)' (#14 in June). As well as winning Best Female Artist and Best Debut Single ('Token Angels') at the 1990 Australian Record Industry Association (ARIA) Awards, Matthews was voted Best Female Singer in the 1990 *Rolling Stone* Readers' Poll.

Matthews assembled a touring band that included Paul Abrahams (bass), Robbie James (guitar; ex-**GANGgajang**), Michael King (guitar; ex-Danglin' Brothers, **Absent Friends**), Amanda Brown (oboe, violin; ex-**Go-Betweens**), James Valentine (sax; ex-**Models**), Mark O'Connor (keyboards), Lisa Maxwell (backing vocals) and Mark Meyer (drums; ex-**Mark Gillespie** Band, **Moving Pictures**). In October 1991, she issued the live mini-album *The Way It Has to Be* and toured as support to overseas visitors The Neville Brothers. Matthews ended a busy 1991 by recording her second full-length album *Lily* with American producer T-Bone Burnett. The album appeared in October 1992 which coincided with her support slot to UK visitors Simply Red. *Lily* initially reached #6 on the national album listing, but eventually went as high as #2 in May 1993. By that stage it had sold double platinum (140 000 copies).

It produced the hit singles 'The Day You Went Away' (#2 in November 1992), 'Friday's Child' (#15 in February 1993) and 'If Only I Could' (#41 in May). Matthews scored well in the 1992 ARIA Awards by taking out Best Female Artist and Best Single ('The Day You Went Away'). She won Best Female Artist for the third time at the 1993 Awards ceremony. *The Witness Tree* appeared at the end of 1994 and included the minor hit single 'Standing Strong' (#37 in December). Two further singles were lifted from the set, 'Love will Keep Me Alive' (March 1995) and 'Say a Prayer' (August), but neither reached the national Top 40. Since that time Matthews has continued to tour both locally and internationally. She issued a new CD single, 'Then I Walked Away', in June 1997, followed by her fifth album, *Ghost* (September). The second CD single, 'Big', came out in August.

Solo albums: *Emigré* (rooArt/Phonogram, 1990), *The Way It Has to Be* (rooArt/Phonogram, 1991), *Lily* (rooArt/Warner, 1992), *The Witness Tree* (rooArt/Warner, 1994), Ghost (BMG/RCA, 1997); ***With*** **Kate Ceberano**: *You've Always Got the Blues* (ABC/Festival, 1988).

The Mavis's

Formed: *1987*
Style: *Rock*
Original line-up: *Matt Thomas (vocals, guitar), Becky Thomas (vocals, keyboards), Katherine McNulty (bass), Andrea Vendy (drums)*

Fronted by the wide-eyed brother and sister team of Matt and Becky Thomas, The Mavis's hail from the Victorian regional township of Ballarat. Initially formed as a four-piece, the band added friend Andrew Craw as a floating member who would contribute his guitar playing in the live forum. In 1990, The Mavis's relocated to Melbourne, and gradually built up a cult following on the inner-city circuit. Nick Gill joined on guitar, and the Giggle label issued the band's debut, 7-inch vinyl single, 'Rollercoaster'/'Witch Hunt' in 1991.

The Mavis's issued two CD EPs, *Spindrift* (1993) and *Poseidon* (May 1994), through Mushroom Distribution Services (MDS). By that stage Josh Alexander had joined as replacement on bass for Katherine McNulty. In 1995, The Mavis's signed a deal with Mushroom's White label, which resulted in the CD single 'Moon Drone Gold' (December). The band's debut album, *Venus Returning* (July 1996), reached #33 on the national mainstream chart, and spawned three CD singles in the process: 'Box', 'Thunder' and 'Lost'. 'Thunder' scored enough airplay on national youth radio network Triple J to log the #92 position on the 1996 Hottest 100 list.

The album highlighted the band's brash sound, which mixed the Thomas siblings' idiosyncratic, imperfect vocal blend, crashing guitars, sugar-frosted melodies, goofy keyboard embellishments and odd instrumentation (sitar, Tibetan bells and Indian banjo). Writing in *Rolling Stone* magazine, reviewer Brett Woodward suggested the band resembled early 1980s acts like The Vaselines and The Raincoats. In 1997, the band commenced work on its second album, *Pink Pills*, which was scheduled for release in early 1998. The first single lifted from the album, the raunchy 'Naughty Boy', appeared in November 1997.

Album: *Venus Returning* (White/Mushroom/Festival, 1996).

Max Q

Formed: *1989*
Style: *Acid-house, pop*
Original line-up: *Michael Hutchence (vocals;* **INXS**), **Ian 'Ollie' Olsen** *(keyboards, programming; ex-Reals, Young Charlatans, Whirlywirld, Hugo Klang, Orchestra of Skin and Bone, No), Arnie Hanna (guitar; ex-Whirlywirld), Michael Sheridan (guitar; from No), Bill McDonald (bass; ex-***Hot Half Hour***), Gus Till (piano, programming; ex-***Beargarden***), John Murphy (drums, percussion; ex-***News***, Whirlywirld, Slub), Marie Hoy (backing vocals), Peggy Marley (backing vocals), Pat Powell (backing vocals)*

In 1989, **INXS** frontman Michael Hutchence collaborated with one of Australia's foremost avant-garde musicians, **Ian 'Ollie' Olsen**, in a studio project called Max Q. The pairing of Hutchence the pop idol and international superstar with Olsen the struggling underground cult personality was one of the most controversial in Australian rock history. Yet the combination of Hutchence's commercial nous and Olsen's eclectic approach resulted in a very interesting and adventurous album.

Hutchence and Olsen first met in 1986 on the set of the Richard Lowenstein film *Dogs in Space*, for which Olsen was musical director and Hutchence the star. Hutchence took the main song, 'Rooms for the Memory', into the national Top 20; Olsen wrote and originally played the song with his band Whirlywirld. With the completion of **INXS**'s 15-month Kick world tour at the end of 1988, Hutchence flew Olsen to Los Angeles to record a couple of his songs. The collaboration took off from there. Hutchence and Olsen named the project Max Q after Olsen's dog, a deaf, psychotic Queensland Blue Heeler. Olsen gathered together musicians from his regular circle in Melbourne and the band completed the album at Sydney's Rhinoceros Studios. American mix-master Todd Terry completed the final mixes on the album in New York.

Max Q the album (issued October 1989) featured a unique hybrid of tough acid-house grooves, pop melodies, funk guitar, electronic fills and soaring strings. Olsen wrote five of the songs; the other six were Hutchence/Olsen co-credits. The album produced the hit singles 'Way of the World'/'Zero-2-0' (#8 in October 1989) and 'Sometimes'/'Loveman' (#31 in December). A third single, 'Monday Night by Satellite'/'Ot-Ven-Rot', failed to reach the national Top 40. The album peaked at #20 in November. With the project completed, Hutchence appeared in cult director Roger Corman's film *Frankenstein Unbound* and then returned to his duties with **INXS**. Olsen continued to work on his Psy-Harmonics label and his techno band Third Eye with Gus Till.

Album: *Max Q* (CBS, 1989).

Maybe Dolls (*see* The Numbers)

Fiona Lee Maynard (*see* Have a Nice Day)

Sister Janet Mead

Style: *Religious pop*

Sister Janet Mead (of The Sisters of Mercy) has the distinction of being the first Australian recording artist to sell over one million copies of a locally produced record in the USA. Sister Janet's toe-tapping rendition of 'The Lord's Prayer' (with music arranged by Arnold Strauls) reached #4 in the USA, after having peaked at #3 in Australia during January 1974. The single (backed with 'Brother Sun and Sister Moon') was issued in 31 countries and went on to sell almost two million copies.

Sister Janet's debut album for Festival, *With You I Am* (which contained the single), also sold well, reaching #19 on the national chart in July 1974. Sister Janet had studied piano at the Adelaide Conservatorium, and her pop career grew out of the successful series of Rock Masses she conducted at Adelaide Cathedral. In fact, her second album, *Rock Mass*, featured a Mass recorded in its entirety. The genuinely media shy (with good cause) Sister Janet resisted the call to further her pop career, despite the barrage of requests for press, radio and television interviews that came her way. 'The Lord's Prayer' has been reissued on a number of occasions.

Albums: *With You I Am* (Festival, 1974), *Rock Mass* (Festival, 1975).

The Meanies

Formed: *1988*
Style: *Punky power pop*
Original line-up: *Link Meanie (real name Lincoln McLennan, vocals, guitar), D.D. Meanie (lead guitar), VB Meanie (bass, vocals), Ringo Meanie (drums)*

During the early 1990s, Melbourne four-piece The Meanies were the undisputed kings of the inner-city/all-ages circuit. The band's frantic, Ramones-inspired power pop and hyperactive live shows drew capacity audiences of alacritous fans. The Meanies were also one of the most productive independent recording bands of the day.

In 1989, Kinky Meanie (real name Wally Kempton) replaced original bass player VB Meanie.

The Meanies

VB (real name Dave Christopher) went on to play with Adelaide outfit FreeMovingCurtis. After establishing a solid live reputation, The Meanies made their record debut with three tracks on Au-go-go Records' 1990 Various Artists album *Boogie Wonderland* (shared with The Throwaways and Nice Girls from Cincinnati). The Meanies weighed in with the best track, the short, sharp and very catchy 'Our New Planet'. Between November 1990 and March 1991, the band issued (and sold out) a series of limited edition 7-inch vinyl EPs on Au-go-go: 'Darkside of My Mind'/'The Meanie Way', 'You're Pathetic' (500 copies), 'Lyin'/'The Meanie Twist', 'I'm Amazed' (750 copies), 'The Reason Why'/'Groove Meanies', 'Don't Smile (You Might Crack Your Face)' (750 copies) and 'Paranoid'/'What am I to Do?', 'Welcome Back to Me', 'Meanie Surprise' (1000 copies).

A fifth EP, 'Never'/'Steve Sex God', 'Sorry About the Violence', appeared in June 1991, followed by the gig giveaway EP 'Probe TV'/'Record Sale', 'Macho Wankers' at the end of the year. Most of these tracks were written by the prolific Link Meanie. Another vinyl EP, 'Scum'/'The Meanie Way', 'You're Pathetic' was issued in the USA on the Sympathy for the Record Industry label. The band also contributed a live track to the 10-inch, four-track gig giveaway EP *Teeth* (December 1991) shared with Au-go-go labelmates **Spiderbait**, **The Guttersnipes** and The Throwaways. The Meanies continued their releases in quick succession with the six-track mini-album/CD EP *Gangrenous* (September 1991), the full-length album *Come'n'See* (April 1992) and the CD EP *In Search of . . .* (October 1992).

Writing in *Hot Metal* magazine, Jeremy Sheaffe described The Meanies' music as 'a sort of four chord overdrive on a fully-throttled amphetamined fuzz'. There was little in the way of variation in the band's music (bubblegum harmonies over fast, simple and melodic guitars and a relentless back-beat), but that never stopped the band members from having fun. As well as playing their own shows and appearing on the bill of the inaugural Big Day Out festival in Sydney (January 1992), The Meanies scored tour supports to overseas visitors like Nirvana, Lemonheads, Pop will Eat Itself, Redd Kross and The Beastie Boys. The Meanies contributed 'Rubber Man' to rooArt's Australian heavy grunge-pop compilation *Crack in the Sun or Fade in the Shade* (November 1992), alongside the likes of **You Am I**, **Guttersnipes**, **Screamfeeder**, **Nursery Crimes**, **Mass-appeal**, **Tumbleweed** and Seaweed Goorillas.

At the end of 1992, Link Meanie issued an EP, *Ramonic Verses,* under the name of The Cranium Croutons. It featured Link playing all instruments, performing grindcore versions of Ramones songs. During January 1993, The Meanies added Tas Blizzard (from Geelong band Seaweed Goorillas) as second guitarist in time for their spot on the Melbourne leg of the inaugural national Big Day Out tour. Later in the year, The Meanies toured Japan, the USA and Europe. While in the USA, the band spent a week recording a new album with producer Conrad Uno in the home of grunge: Seattle, Washington. As well as the aforementioned 'Scum' single, the band also had records issued in the USA on the EmpTY, Merge and Get Hip labels, as well as the Time Bomb label in Japan, Vince Lombardi and Subway in Germany and Munster Records in Spain.

In September 1993, The Meanies issued a new CD single, 'Cruelty's Fun', followed closely by the 25-track anthology *The Meanie of Life* (November), which compiled all the band's early singles and rare cuts. The Meanies appeared on the national bill of the 1994 Big Day Out tour, after which Blizzard left the band. He returned to the Seaweed Goorillas in order to issue the CD EP 'Ode to Pain' and the album *Seaweed Goorillas* on the Destroyer label. 1994 also saw the release of The Meanies' Seattle-recorded album *10% Weird* (August) which produced the CD EPs 'Conan' (June) and '10% Weird' (October). The band toured as support to US rasta-hardcore veterans The Bad Brains throughout August 1994.

After five years of continuous touring and recording, the various band members became involved in side projects. Link played guitar with his brother Ross McClennan's band **Snout**; the pair later issued a self-titled album under the name of Meuscram (Au-go-go, October 1995). Wally moonlighted with Ashley Naylor's band **Even** and DD played with Crack, which featured members from Fridge and **The Affected**. In 1995, The Meanies contributed their glorious romp through 'It's a Long Way to the Top (If You Wanna Rock'n'Roll)' to BMG's **AC/DC** tribute album *Fuze Box: The Alternative Tribute* (May). 'It's a Long Way to the Top' also appeared as a CD single. The Meanies undertook a second tour of Europe in June/July 1995 after which Tas Blizzard rejoined. The Meanies' next CD single, 'Ton of Bricks' (also from *10% Weird*), came out in October 1995. The band followed that by contributing a version of 'Lee Remick' to the **Go-Betweens** tribute album *Right Here* on the Hippy Knight label (1996). The Meanies played their final shows in January 1996. Link Meanie formed The Tomorrow People (issuing the album *Shining* in June 1997) while Wally Kempton concentrated on **Even**, and his regular day job as a booking agent.

Albums: *Come'n'See* (Au-go-go, 1992), *The Meanie of Life* (compilation of early singles, Au-go-go, 1993), *Televolution* (US-only compilation, EmpTY, 1994), *10% Weird* (Au-go-go, 1994).

Medicine Show (*see* No Man's Land)

Melissa

Formed: *1969*
Style: *Rock*
Original line-up: *Robert Gunn (flute, vocals), Rick Barrett (guitars), Ken Frazier (bass, vocals), Warren 'Wal' Sparke (drums)*

Originally known as Molten Hue, Melissa was one of the first bands on the Sydney 'head' scene of the early 1970s to include obscure West Coast material in its live set. As Glenn A. Baker wrote, the band was caught between the totally dedicated flower children and the simple popsters. At its peak, the band was able to play concerts at Paddington Town Hall and Sydney's famed Arts Factory alongside **Tully**, as well as command a large following on the suburban dance circuit. Not long after the band's formation, Irishman Joe Creighton replaced original bass player Ken Frazier. From early beginnings playing acid-rock, Melissa developed into an innovative rock band with subtle country and jazz-blues overtones. The band's debut single, 'Mississippi Mamma'/'Too Much for Nothing' (March 1970), was a raucous slice of blues-rock with little concession to commercial gains.

In 1971, Melissa signed a management and recording deal with local entrepreneur Dal Myles. The band's debut album appeared to little response at the end of the year. The underrated *Midnight Trampoline* album serves as a worthwhile period piece, combining esoteric, folksy rock redolent of Jethro Tull ('Matalla', 'Getting Through'), Moody Blues-styled pastoral pop ('Out in the Country', 'Jennifer in New York'), progressive blues-rock ('Cuckoo') and two Van Morrison covers ('Young Lovers Do', 'Madame George'). The band was obviously much taken with Morrison's *Astral Weeks* album, and indeed Creighton bore a remarkable vocal resemblance to Van the Man. One of Melissa's highest-profile gigs at the time was as one of the Sydney supports to UK visitor Elton John (October 1971).

Prospects looked promising, but various pressures and frustrations brought to bear over the album severely undermined any sense of unity. By the time the album appeared, Rick Barrett and Wal Sparke had a new Melissa line-up on the road with Chris Keystone having replaced Robert Gunn on vocals, Ken Hanley taking over from Creighton on bass, and Glen Farley joining on keyboards. Melissa continued to tour but broke up at the end of 1972. Creighton returned to Ireland for a time before forming **Billy T** in Melbourne with **Ross Hannaford.** Creighton has since toured with Venetta Fields and **John Farnham,** and remains one of the most in-demand session players in the country. He also issued a solo album, *Holywell* (August 1992), on the Innisfree label which reflected his Celtic folk roots mixed with gospel and New Orleans R&B influences.

Album: *Midnight Trampoline* (Banner/Festival, 1971).

Melissa ('Tkautz)

Style: *Dance pop*

In July 1991, teenage soap-star turned chanteuse Melissa (b. 1974) was thrown into the deep end of pop stardom when her debut single 'Read My Lips' reached #1 on the national charts. The chart success was no doubt helped by the popularity of television soapie *E Street* in which Melissa played the part of Nikki Spencer.

With the soap opera/pop chart route already opened up by the likes of **Kylie Minogue**, **Jason Donovan** and Toni Pearen ('In Your Room'), Melissa was a natural to step into the fray. Her second single, 'Sexy (is the Word)', went to #2 in October. She took honours for Highest Selling Single ('Read My Lips') at the 1991 Australian Record Industry Association (ARIA) Awards. In 1992, Melissa scored with the album *Fresh* (#10 in July), and the singles 'Skin to Skin' (#19 in May) and 'My House' (November). She issued her fifth single in July 1993, 'Is It', and starred in a new television soapie, *Paradise Beach*. She later joined the cast of *Pacific Drive*.

Album: *Fresh* (Mercury/Phonogram, 1992).

Men at Work

Formed: *1979*
Style: *Rock, reggae, pop*
Original line-up: **Colin Hay** *(vocals, guitar), Greg Ham (flute, sax, keyboards, vocals; ex-Sneak Attack), Ron Strykert (lead guitar, vocals), John Rees (bass; ex-***Chetarca***), Jerry Speiser (drums)*

Glenn A. Baker called it a success saga even Hollywood could not have invented. Five scruffy pub musicians become international household names with a flippant, irresistible style of 1980s pop. The debut album sells ten million copies around the world and the band tours to great acclaim. The pressures of mega-stardom mercilessly break the unit's resolve. A third album sells less than one-tenth as many copies as the first and an infatuated world looks elsewhere for amusement.

Irrespective of the band's fairytale rise to prominence, Men at Work's phenomenal success inextricably created worldwide interest in Australia and Australian music. **Little River Band, Air Supply** and **AC/DC** paved the way in the USA; Men at Work simply opened the floodgates with little more than a clutch of great songs. Until **INXS** claimed the mantle of international superstars in the late 1980s, Men at Work was Australia's most famous group. The band's achievements during 1982 have ensured a place in the record books.

Scottish-born singer-songwriter **Colin Hay** met guitarist Ron Strykert when they worked on the stage musical *Heroes* in Sydney during 1978. The pair formed the nucleus of Men at Work when they began working around Melbourne as an acoustic duo. In mid-1979, Hay and Strykert (then on bass) recruited drummer Jerry Speiser. With Greg Sneddon (ex-Alroy Band) on keyboards, one of the band's earliest gigs was providing the backing for the West Community Theatre's amateur rock musical *Riff Raff*. An album of the songs and dialogue from *Riff Raff* (on the W.E.S.T. imprint) comprised the band's first recording venture. Sneddon had issued an impressive symphonic rock album on Mushroom Records in 1974 called *Mindstroll* which featured Speiser on drums. Sneddon did not remain with Men at Work, but by the end of 1979 Greg Ham and John Rees had joined. With Rees on bass, Strykert switched to lead guitar. Over the next 12 months, Men at Work built up a grassroots following, initially playing to modest crowds in small, dank Melbourne pubs like the Grace Darling and Richmond's Cricketer's Arms.

In 1980, Men at Work issued a self-financed, independent single, 'Keypunch Operator'/ 'Downunder' on their own M.A.W. imprint. The record sold in limited quantities and became a highly collectable item once the Men became famous. 'Keypunch Operator' was a fast-paced country-styled rocker with a clean sound and quirky rhythm. The flip was an acoustic prototype version of the later hugely successful international hit single. By the end of 1980, Men at Work had grown in stature to become the most in-demand and highly paid, unsigned band of the year. In early 1981, CBS signed Men at Work on the recommendation of A&R man Peter Karpin. American producer Peter McIan worked on the band's debut single, 'Who Can It Be Now?'/'Anyone for Tennis?' which reached #2 on the national charts in June. It stayed on the charts for 16 weeks. The band's second single, 'Down Under'/'Crazy', did even better by reaching #1 in November and staying on the charts for 18 weeks. The band's third single, 'Be Good Johnny'/'F 19', reached #8 in April 1982.

The debut, the Peter McIan-produced album *Business as Usual* (October 1981), immediately hit #1 on the national chart. At the end of its six-month Top 40 run, the album had sold over 300 000 copies. It eventually went on to sell over 400 000 copies in Australia. The album also made its debut at #1 on the New Zealand charts, becoming the first Australian album to achieve that honour. Aside from the strength of the music, part of the album's appeal was its economy. The production sound was low-key, but clean and uncluttered. Indeed, the songs stood by themselves with little embellishment save for a bright, melodic, singalong quality. By the end of 1981, Men at Work had also notched up #1 singles in Holland and Germany, a #2 in France and had scored a platinum album in Canada. The Americans and British took a little longer to catch on. In fact, CBS America had turned the album down twice before capitulating and issuing it in June 1982 (on Columbia). CBS/Epic also issued the album in the UK that same month. 'Who Can It Be Now?' came out in May and in August the band toured across the USA as support to Fleetwood Mac.

By October, 'Who Can It Be Now?' was #1 in the USA and #45 in the UK. In February 1983, Men at Work achieved a grand slam when both 'Down Under' and *Business as Usual* held down the #1 spots in the USA and UK. Only the mega-star likes of The Beatles, Rod Stewart and Simon and Garfunkel had done so in the past. *Business as Usual* became the longest running #1 debut album in American chart history (15 weeks), shattering The Monkees' 16-year-old record in the process. Men at Work's American success coincided with the introduction of the revolutionary 24-hour-a-day television rock service called *MTV* (Music Television). The video image of five irreverent, self-effacing young musicians who sang about Vegemite sandwiches and fried-out Kombis struck a responsive chord with viewers. Men at Work were named Best New Artist of the Year at the 1982 Grammy Awards, and Best New Artist in the *Rolling Stone* (US) Readers' Poll. The band spent most of 1983 touring the USA and Europe.

Meanwhile, back in Australia, Men at Work picked up Most Outstanding Achievement at the 1982 ***Countdown*** Awards. The first single, 'Dr Heckyll & Mr Jive'/'Shintaro', from the band's second album, *Cargo*, had already reached #6 in October 1982. 'Overkill'/'Til the Money Runs Out' reached #5 in April 1983; *Cargo* went straight to #1 upon release that same month. 'It's a Mistake'/'No Restrictions' was relatively unsuccessful having stalled at #34 in August. Likewise, the 12-inch 'Highwire'/'Fallin' Down', 'I Like to' single was only a minor hit. 'Down Under' made a return to the Australian Top 40 in October 1983, and again in January 1987, when it was used as the theme song for the Alan Bond/Ben Lexcen/Australia II syndicate's successful America's Cup challenge.

The band's international success continued. *Cargo* reached #8 in the UK and #3 in the USA (selling one million copies on advance orders alone and four million all up). 'Overkill' (US #3, UK #21), 'It's a Mistake' (US #6, UK #33) and 'Dr Heckyll & Mr. Jive' (US #28, UK #31) were all hits. On 4 August 1983, CBS awarded Men at Work the Crystal Globe Award in honour of generating $100 million worth of record business (five million albums sold) outside of their home country. The award put Men at Work in the same category at that time as other CBS artists like Santana, Simon and Garfunkel, Earth, Wind and Fire and Bob Dylan. From there, the band's downhill slide was slow but inevitable.

Once the 1983 world tour was over, the band returned to Australia for a year's break. Hay got married, went to France on his honeymoon and then produced Melbourne band **Le Club Foote**'s debut album. Strykert travelled to Europe and Ham moonlighted with Melbourne pub band Relax with Max. Internal pressures within the band came to a head and Rees and Speiser received their marching orders. At the start of 1985, Hay, Ham and Strykert were joined in the studio by session players Jeremy Alsop (bass) and Mark Kennedy (drums; ex-**Spectrum**, **Ayers Rock**, **Marcia Hines** Band) for the band's self-produced third album, *Two Hearts* (June 1985). Upon release in the USA, the album stalled at #50, barely selling 750 000 copies. In Australia, it peaked at #16 during June before dropping from sight.

Of its four singles, 'Everything I Need'/'Sail to You' (May 1985), 'Maria'/'Snakes and Ladders' (August), 'Hard Luck Story'/'Snakes and Ladders' (October 1985) and 'Sail to You'/'Children on Parade' (November), only 'Everything I Need' cracked the US Top 50 (at #47). It also reached #20 in Australia. The band's first American tour in 18 months was cancelled due to poor ticket sales. Strykert resigned from the band even before 'Everything I Need' came out. Hay and Ham recruited a new line-up comprising Alsop, James Black (keyboards, guitar; ex-**Mondo Rock**), Colin Bayley (guitar, ex-**Mi-Sex**) and Chad Wackerman (drums; ex-Frank Zappa) and prepared to tour. Eventually Ham also left and Hay brought in Paul Williamson (ex-**Black Sorrows**) on sax.

With Hay determined to keep the band alive, Men at Work undertook the Back To Business tour of the Australian pub circuit to a positive response. The tour extended briefly to South East Asia, but it was all over for Men at Work by the end of 1985. **Colin Hay** made no secret of wanting to return to his Gaelic soul roots and set off on an often interesting, but relatively low-key, solo career. Men at Work were inducted into the Hall of Fame at the 1993 Australian Record Industry Association (ARIA) Awards. In various parts of the world, interest in Men at Work has grown, and in mid-1996 Hay and his old comrade Greg Ham took a re-formed version of the band on a sell-out tour of Brazil.

Albums: *Business as Usual* (CBS, 1981), *Cargo* (CBS, 1983), *Two Hearts* (CBS, 1985), *Men at Work '81–'85* (compilation, CBS, 1986), *The Works* (CBS, 1992), *Contraband: The Best of Men at Work* (compilation, Columbia/Legacy, 1996).

Mental as Anything

Formed: *1976*
Style: *Pop, R&B*
Original line-up: *Martin Plaza (real name Martin Murphy, vocals, guitar), Reg Mombassa (real name Chris O'Doherty, guitar, vocals), Peter 'Yoga Dog' O'Doherty (bass, vocals), Andrew 'Greedy' Smith (keyboards, harmonica, vocals), Wayne 'Bird' Delisle (real name David Twohill, drums)*

For many years, Mental as Anything was the ultimate party band. The multifarious Mentals played a brand of rock'n'roll that mixed summery pop, gritty R&B and psychedelic ballads with an irrepressible sense of humour and bright instrumentation. It made for perfect entertainment in sweaty pubs across the land. The Mentals were also one of the most consistent and prolific hit singles bands Australia has ever produced. By the end of 1996, Mental as Anything had scored 22 national Top 40 hit singles.

Martin Murphy, Andrew Smith, David Twohill and New Zealand-born Chris O'Doherty met at art college where they formed the band during 1976. For its first gig, the band was without a name and the promoter suggested Mental as Anything. In August 1977, O'Doherty's brother Peter took over on bass and the line-up was finalised. The new line-up made its debut on 17 August 1977 (the day after Elvis Presley died) with a gig at the Cell Block Theatre. The Mentals' residency at the tiny inner-Sydney pub the Unicorn Hotel (where they played on a stage perched on top of a pool table) became so popular they had to look farther afield. Next stop was an 18-month residency at the Civic Hotel, during which time the Mentals drew consistent crowds. In September 1978, two Mentals fans, Martin Fabinyi and Cameron Allen, formed Regular Records in order to issue the band's records.

Regular issued the Mentals debut EP *Mental as Anything Plays at Your Party* which became an instant cult classic. The band managed to sell 1100 copies at gigs and from the boot of their car. In January 1979, Festival Records took over distribution of Regular. The band remixed a track from the EP, 'The Nips are Getting Bigger' (a sly, skiffle-like ode to drinking), for release as a single backed with 'Instrumental as Anything' (July 1979). It became the band's first national hit when it reached #16 in August. The Mentals were aiming for a national market with the release of their Cameron Allan-produced debut album *Get Wet* (September 1979). It was brim-full of simple, bouncy, melodic and well-crafted tunes which accurately summarised the band's good-natured wit and pop rock earthiness. With the aid of a support slot to UK visitors Dave Edmunds and Rockpile, the album reached the national Top 20 (#19 in November 1979). Virgin issued the album in the UK where 'The Nips are Getting Bigger' reached #1 on the alternative charts.

For their second Australian single, the Mentals pitched a cheesy instrumental bit with twangin' guitar and Sam the Sham organ as a 'Possible Theme for a Future TV Drama Series'/'Typical Romance' (#57 in November 1979). The band's third single was a love song to a foreign country based on travel brochures 'Egypt'/'Pork is Not a Gift' (January 1980). The singles were not hits, but with four songwriters in the band (Plaza, Smith, Mombassa, O'Doherty), the Mentals were never short of good material. The band's second album *Espresso Bongo* (#37 in July 1980) was not as instantly appealing as the debut, but it was still full of quality, entertaining tunes. Standouts included 'Harmonic Visions', 'Missing Plane', 'Troop Movements in the Ukraine', 'Insect Liberation' and the fourth single, 'Come Around'/'DC 10' (#18 in September 1980).

The album's title was taken from a 1960 Cliff Richard movie, and the band's photo on the front cover was pure kitsch. The album failed to chart in the Top 40, but the Mentals maintained a strong rapport with audiences and their standing as the #1 good-time outfit was confirmed with sell-out pub tours. The band's fifth (non-album) single, a cover of Michael and the Messengers' '(Just Like) Romeo and Juliet'/'Go Down', was a minor hit (#36 in January 1981).

The band's biggest success to that time came with the *Cats and Dogs* album which reached #3 in October 1981. The album's three singles, 'If You Leave Me, Can I Come Too?'/'Assault and Flattery' (#4 in June), 'Too Many Times'/'Holiday in Auckland' (#6 in October) and 'Berserk Warriors'/'L'Amore No More' (#30 in January 1982) were hits. In June 1982, the Mentals persuaded Elvis Costello (who was on tour) to produce their next single, 'I Didn't Mean to Be Mean'/'Yoga Dog Sunset', which reached #25 in September. That same month, A&M issued a compilation album, *If You Leave Me*, in the USA and Canada. The band toured the USA as support to **Men at Work**, as well as playing headlining gigs in Canada where 'Too Many Times' had made the Top 20.

The band's fourth album, *Creatures of Leisure* (#8 in April 1983) produced the hit single 'Spirit Got Lost'/'Not Enough' (#20 the same month). The album also yielded the minor hit singles 'Close Again'/'Homing Pigeon' (#55 in November 1982) and 'Brain Brain'/'Drinking of Her Lips' (#82 in June 1983). The Mentals returned to the USA and Canada for a second, gruelling tour during which they made an appearance on popular television pop show *Solid Gold* performing 'Brain Brain'. The band rounded out a busy 1983 with a new single Roy Orbison's 'Workin' for the Man'/'Seems Alright to Me' (#20 in November). 1984 was a quiet year, with the release of only one single 'Apocalypso (Wiping the Smile off Santa's Face)'/'Wouldn't Try to Explain' (#37 in December).

The Mentals leapt back into action in April 1985 with the release of the best-selling *Fundamental as Anything* album (#3 in July). Produced by American Richard Gottehrer (Blondie), the album featured a slicker, more high-tech sound than previous albums. It yielded the hit singles 'You're So Strong'/'Three Steps to Your Place' (#10 in March), 'Live It Up'/'Good Friday' (#1 in June) and 'Date with Destiny'/'Surf & Mull & Sex & Fun' (#13 in September). *Fundamental as Anything* attained double platinum status and was the highest selling Australian album for the year. The album saw the emergence of Greedy Smith as the band's most prominent hit songwriter; all three single A-sides were his compositions. Paul Hogan and John Cornell included the imminently hummable 'Live It Up' on the soundtrack to their enormously successful film *Crocodile Dundee*. Sony/Epic issued 'Live It Up' in Europe, where it reached #3 in the UK and #1 in Scandinavia during February 1987. It eventually sold 500 000 copies worldwide. 'You're So Strong' also reached #10 in the USA.

Meanwhile, back in November 1985, Regular/WEA, issued *Greatest Hits* which reached #2 in April 1986. The initial pressing came with a bonus, limited edition single, 'Big Wheel'/'Apocalypso', tucked inside the sleeve. 'Big Wheel' was issued as a single in its own right and reached #75 in December. The band issued a one-off single in June 1986, 'Sloppy Croc'/'Sloppier Croc', which was also taken from the *Crocodile Dundee* soundtrack. At the start of 1987, the Mentals took part in the ambitious Australian Made national tour. Billed as 'Special Guest Stars', the Mentals played the opening slot and paved the way for **The Triffids**, **I'm Talking**, **The Saints**, **Divinyls**, **Models**, **Jimmy Barnes** and **INXS**. The band hit the stage each show wearing a dazzling array of customised suits designed by the Mambo clothing company.

Mike Gubb (ex-**Dynamic Hepnotics**) had joined the band on keyboards to allow Greedy Smith freedom of movement across the stage. The shine was taken off the festivities somewhat when trombonist Peter Trotter, a member of the Mentals' brass section The Semi-Erect Horns, suffered a heart attack on stage during the Sydney concert. He died a few days later in Sutherland Hospital. The band's seventh album (and first for CBS), *Mouth to Mouth* (August 1987), produced the singles 'Let's Go to Paradise'/'My Hands are Tied' (#15 in December 1986), 'He's Just No Good for You'/'Ruby Baby' (#15 in June 1987), 'Don't Tell Me Now'/'I'm Glad' (#36 in September) and Elvis Presley's 'Love Me Tender'/'Wandering Through Heaven' (#34 in November).

Yahoo Serious included the Mentals' next single, a cover of Chuck Berry's 'Rock and Roll Music'/'Apocalypso' (live), on the soundtrack to his film *Young Einstein*. The single became a #6 national hit in February 1989. Serious later included the Mentals' track 'Ride' on the soundtrack to his 1993 film *Reckless Kelly*. 'Rock and Roll Music' also appeared on the Mentals' next album, *Cyclone Raymond*. It was a fine album of accessible, well-crafted pop songs including the singles 'The World Seems Difficult'/'Get You Back' (#19 in September 1989), 'Baby You're Wild'/'Wish I Could Believe' (#75 in November) and 'Overwhelmed'/'Walls of the World' (April 1990). Other highlights included Mombassa's 'Big Things in Life' and one of Plaza's best-ever songs, 'Some Feelings'.

In spite of its collection of strong tunes, the album failed to impress the record-buying public and only managed #38 on the charts. The Mentals themselves had become jaded with the whole band concept, and it came as no surprise when the band decided to come off the road. The individual members pursued their own careers: Reg and Peter O'Doherty launched their band **Dog Trumpet**; Smith played with his sideline project Greedy's on the Loose; Delisle returned to art college to finish his degree; and Plaza linked up with **James Freud** as one-half of dance-pop outfit, **Beatfish**.

Plaza also issued a solo single 'Labour of Love' (August 1990), which in fact was his fourth solo single. His March 1986 album on CBS, *Plaza Suite*, had produced three singles: a cover of Unit 4 + 2's 'Concrete and Clay'/'New Suit' (#2 in March), 'Best Foot Forward'/'Rollerina' (April) and 'Use Me All Over'/'Ruby Baby' (July). In May 1994, Plaza issued his acclaimed second solo album, *Andy's Chest*, a collection of Lou Reed covers (mostly from his *Transformer*/*Berlin* period, plus The Velvet Underground's 'I'm Waiting for the Man'). The album contained a sole Plaza original, 'My Salvation'. 'Satellite of Love'/'My Salvation' was issued as a CD single (also in May). Plaza's next CD single, 'Women', came out in August 1994.

The only Mental as Anything album to appear during the early 1990s was the odds'n'sods collection *Chemical Travel* (November 1993), which drew together overlooked B-sides and album tracks. The collection was heavily slated towards the band's early career, with only three of the album's 23 tracks coming from *Fundamental as Anything*, *Mouth to Mouth* or *Cyclone Raymond*.

Mental as Anything as a whole re-emerged at the end of 1994 with the CD EP *Bicycle* which the band members financed themselves and gave away to punters on their summer tour. The band signed a new deal with BMG and issued the glorious T. Rex pastiche 'Mr Natural' (originally on *Bicycle*) as a CD single. It restored the band to the national Top 30 (#27 in April). The CD singles 'Nigel' (June) and Wreckless Eric's 'Whole Wide World' (October), plus the album *Liar, Liar, Pants on Fire* (August) followed. The album was classic Mentals, full of wry, catchy and razor-sharp pop songs. 'Marianne' came out as a CD single in March 1996. Later in the year, Greedy Smith issued his debut solo album, *Love Harmonica*, a collection of his own easy-listening love songs that featured latin, pop and jazz rhythms with lush harmonica as the lead instrument.

As well as their music, the members of Mental as Anything were renowned for their artwork. The Mentals held the first painting and art exhibition of their own work in May 1982. It attracted a lot of interest, with buyers including Elton John, Mary Travers and Australian novelist Patrick White. In 1990, the Mentals staged the Mental as Anything Touring Art Exhibition with works by all five members. Reg Mombassa in particular has risen to fame as a painter of great distinction. His colourful, idiosyncratic designs have graced clothing (for the Mambo agency), calendars, posters and record covers (for the likes of the Mentals themselves, **Dog Trumpet**, **Crowded House**, **Mondo Rock** and PiL).

Over the course of 20 years, Mental as Anything has crafted a rollcall of deceptively simple yet classic pop songs. The band's characteristic approach to music-making appealed to an astonishingly broad cross-section of music lovers. Yet the band made its greatest mark by elevating the ordinary in life to the extraordinary in art. As writer Clinton Walker put it, any band that deified such everyday phenomena as dogs and Valiant Hemi Pacers must have something going for it!

Mental as Anything albums: *Get Wet* (Regular/Festival, 1979), *Espresso Bongo* (Regular/Festival, 1980), *Cats and Dogs* (Regular/Festival, 1981), *Creatures of Leisure* (Regular/WEA, 1983), *Fundamental as Anything* (Regular/WEA, 1985), *Greatest Hits* (Regular/WEA, 1985), *Mouth to Mouth* (CBS, 1987), *Cyclone Raymond* (CBS, 1989), *Chemical Travel* (Regular/Festival, 1993), *Liar, Liar, Pants on Fire* (BMG, 1995); ***Martin Plaza solo albums:*** *Plaza Suite* (CBS, 1986), *Andy's Chest* (BMG, 1994); ***Greedy Smith solo album:*** *Love Harmonica* (TWA, 1996).

MEO 245

Formed: *1978*
Style: *Pop rock*
Original line-up: *Paul Northam (guitar, vocals), Paul Brickhill (keyboards, guitar, vocals), Mick Wilson (bass), Campbell Laird (drums)*

MEO 245 evolved out of Tasmanian new wave band Guided Tour. The band relocated to Melbourne in

February 1979, where Mark Kellett replaced original bass player Mick Wilson. The band signed to Mushroom Records and issued the single 'Lady Love'/'Letters and Numbers' in October 1980. The singles 'Marching Feet'/'Somebody's Time' (March), 'Other Places'/'So Far Away' (July) and 'Jewels (for Your Love)'/'Closing in' (October), plus the Peter Dawkins-produced album *Screen Memory* followed in 1981. The album title was taken from *A Critical Dictionary of Psychoanalysis* and the record itself was full of English-influenced pop rock (not that dissimilar to Flowers/**Icehouse**).

During April and May 1982, the band recorded the powerful mini-album *Rites of Passage* which produced the singles 'Sin City'/'Dance' (September 1982) and 'Summer Girl'/'Other Places' (live) (November). Not long after recording *Rites of Passage* Kellett left the band to be replaced by Anthony Moore. In January 1983, Paul Brickhill departed to join **The Little Heroes**. That signalled the end of MEO 245 and a few months later the band broke up. Campbell Laird joined Soldiers of Fortune and later on Paul Northam turned up in a band called Luxury Device.

Albums: *Screen Memory* (Mushroom/Festival, 1980), *Rites of Passage* (mini-album, Mushroom/Festival, 1982).

Max Merritt and the Meteors

Formed: *1956*
Style: *R&B, soul*
Original line-up: *Max Merritt (vocals, guitar), Clancy Ross (sax), Peter Patene (piano), Ian Glass (bass), Pete Sowden (drums)*

New Zealand-born Max Merritt was one of rock'n'roll's great pioneers. He was already well established on the New Zealand scene long before he travelled across the Tasman Sea to take Australia by storm. At the age of 15, Merritt formed his first band to play the youth clubs around Christchurch. In 1958 he had a local hit single with the amusing 'Get a Haircut'.

With a move to Auckland, Max Merritt and the Meteors became the second most popular band in New Zealand (behind Ray Columbus and the Invaders). While The Invaders were masters of pure beat pop, The Meteors were more diverse, being able to tackle rock'n'roll, soul and R&B at will. Max also possessed a fine, gravelly voice which lent credibility to his own compositions in that vein. Between 1958 and 1964, The Meteors issued ten singles, two EPs and two albums. The band also backed Dinah Lee on her string of ska-bluebeat

Max Merritt and the Meteors

hits. The Meteors' line-up of Merritt, Peter Williams (guitar), Teddy Toi (bass) and Johnny Dick (drums) recorded the second album, *Max Merritt's Meteors*, and then relocated to Sydney at the end of 1964. The Meteors swiftly became *the* band to experience live on the eastern states discotheque and club circuit. Few Australian bands could match The Meteors' peerless mix of rock, soul and R&B.

Throughout 1965, The Meteors issued three singles, 'So Long Baby'/'You're Treating Me Bad' (April), 'Zip-A-Dee-Doo-Dah'/'I've Been Trying' (July) and 'You Deserve What You Got'/'I Want So Much to Know You' (December). In September 1965, Toi and Dick left to join **Billy Thorpe's** new Aztecs. Initially Merritt recruited Sydneysiders Bill Flemming (drums; ex-Midnighters, Chessman, Roland Storm and the Statesmen) and John Blake (bass), before settling on Kiwis Billy Kristian (who had been in an earlier Meteors line-up on bass) and Jimmy Hill (drums, ex-Invaders), who was soon replaced by the notorious Bruno Lawrence.

The band toured with UK visitors The Rolling Stones and The Searchers at the start of 1966. The Meteors issued two great singles on EMI/Parlophone during 1966: covers of Sam Cooke's 'Shake'/'I Can't Help Myself' (June) and Buster Brown's 'Fannie Mae'/'Baby Come Home' (October). In early 1967, stalwart members Williams (who left to join **The Groove**), Kristian and Lawrence all departed. Merritt assembled a new line-up with which he intended to tackle the UK market. The band comprised Bob Bertles (sax; ex-**Alan Dale and**

The Houserockers, R'Jays, **Jeff St John** and the Id), John 'Yuk' Harrison (bass; ex-**Levi Smith's Clefs**) and veteran jazz drummer Stewart Speer.

The new-look Meteors made their debut in May 1967, but the band's plans for the overseas jaunt were dashed on 24 June by a car accident in which Merritt lost an eye and Speer ended up in hospital for four months. The Meteors reassembled with strong support from their many fans and all sections of the music industry. By 1968, Merritt had established himself as the finest soul singer in Australia, outclassing such heavyweights as **Jeff St John**, Barrie McAskill and **Doug Parkinson** in the process. In June 1968, Max Merritt and the Meteors came in third to **The Groove** and **The Master's Apprentices** in the Hoadley's National Battle of the Sounds final.

In 1969 the ABC featured the band in a four-part 'in-concert' television series, *Max Merritt and the Meteors in Concert.* That same year the band signed a new deal with RCA Records and recorded a long overdue album. *Max Merritt & the Meteors* was an impressive collection of brassy, bluesy soul, including the Philly-soul cover 'Hey, Western Union Man' which was issued as a single backed with 'Home is Where the Heart is'. The single reached #13 on the national chart in December 1969, while the album performed even better by reaching #8 in June 1970. By that stage, Dave Ross (ex-Ray Columbus and the Invaders) had replaced Yuk Harrison on bass.

The Meteors recorded a new album, and then in October 1970 set off for an extended stay in the UK. The *Stray Cats* album produced the singles 'Good Feelin''/'I Can't Wait' (February 1971) and 'Hello L.A. Bye Bye Birmingham'/'Live Levis' (May 1971), none of which charted due to the band's absence from the local scene. The Meteors made little headway in the UK, and returned to Australia for a triumphant appearance at the inaugural Sunbury Festival, January 1972. Back in the UK, The Meteors went from strength to strength as their confidence built up with regular live work on the London pub circuit. They eventually scored national support slots on tours by the likes of Slade and The Moody Blues. In 1974, The Meteors fell on hard times when manager Peter Raphael left the band with no money and mounting debts. Bertles joined UK jazz-rock band Nucleus, Speer toured Europe with Alexis Korner and Merritt was forced to work as a bricklayer.

By 1975, Merritt and Speer had assembled a new, more professional-sounding Meteors which comprised British musicians John Gourd (guitar, slide guitar, piano), Howard Martin Deniz (bass) and Barry Duggan (sax, flute). The band became the first signing to the UK arm of Arista Records. The long-awaited new album, *A Little Easier,* became a best-seller, reaching #4 on the Australian charts in November 1975. It yielded the singles 'A Little Easier'/ 'Long Time Gone' (August) and the classic ballad 'Slipping Away'/'I Keep Forgetting' (Australian #2 and New Zealand #5 in November). The band's next album, *Out of the Blue* (#13 in August 1976) included the singles 'Let It Slide'/ 'Coming Back', 'Whisper in My Ear' (#29 in May) and 'Take Part of Me'/ 'Blame It on the Reggae' (August). The Meteors returned to Australia for a tour during May and June 1976. Lance Dixon (ex-**Rockwell T. James** and the Rhythm Aces, **Ram Jam Big Band**) had replaced Duggan on sax and keyboards by that stage. The band returned for another tour in February 1977 which yielded the in-concert album *Back Home Live* (recorded at Melbourne's Dallas Brooks Hall).

In 1978 Merritt dispensed with The Meteors (save for Stewie Speer) and signed a new deal with Polydor. He recorded the album *Keeping in Touch* in Nashville, Tennessee with producer Don Shroeder. Merritt then based himself in Los Angeles. Merritt's first single for Polydor was 'Wish You'd Never Come Into My Life'/'Draggin Chains' (July 1978). On release in February 1979, *Keeping in Touch* produced the singles Steely Dan's 'Dirty Work'/'Fat Man' (February), 'It's Over'/'Keeping in Touch' (May) and a gutsy reworking of 'Slipping Away'/ 'Rock'n'Roll Hobo' (July).

In May 1979, Merritt was back in Australia for a tour with a 12 piece band. His second American-recorded album, *Black Plastic Max,* boasted a soulful reworking of Clyde McPhatter's 'A Lover's Question' plus the single 'Tryin' Too Hard'/'Rock'n'Roll Mole' (February 1980). Merritt's touring band for his late 1980 Australian visit comprised Speer, Paul Grant (guitar), John Williams (keyboards) and Phil Lawson (bass). Merritt continued to work in Los Angeles and had sporadic releases over the next few years, including the singles 'Prove It'/'Growing Pains' (November 1982) and 'Mean Green Fighting Machine'/'My Best Friend' (November 1986). The last named was a sports-related promotion recorded for the Mojo advertising agency. Speer died of a heart attack in September 1986.

In 1991, Merritt returned to Australia to tour with The Brian Cadd and Max Merritt Band. The line-up comprised Merritt, **Brian Cadd** (vocals, piano), John Dallimore (guitar; ex-**Redhouse**, Dallimore, **Jon English** Band), Craig Reeves (keyboards), Des Scott (bass) and Dave Stewart (drums; ex-Daniel). In late 1996, Merritt returned to Australia for a number of tours around the club and pub circuit.

Albums: *C'Mon Let's Go* (Viking, 1960), *Max Merritt's Meteors* (RCA, 1965), *Max Merritt & the Meteors* (RCA, 1970), *Stray Cats* (RCA, 1971), *A Little Easier*

(Arista, 1975), *Out of the Blue* (Arista, 1976), *Back Home Live* (Arista, 1977), *Keeping in Touch* (Polydor, 1979), *Black Plastic Max* (Polydor, 1980), *17 Trax of Max!* (Raven, 1986), *23 Trax of Max!* (CD reissue, Raven, 1991).

Mickey Finn (*see* Fraternity)

Midnight Oil

Formed: *1976*
Style: *Rock*
Original line-up: *Peter Garrett (vocals), James Moginie (guitar, keyboards), Andrew 'Bear' James (bass), Robert Hirst (drums)*

Midnight Oil has long been regarded as Australia's most politicised rock'n'roll band. In voicing socio-political and environmental concerns with great effect through their music, the Oils turned the entertainment they provided into the message. Backed by penetrating and resolute manager Gary Morris, the band also changed the rules by which the music industry operated. Much to the frustration of record companies and promoters alike, The Oils wrote their own contracts which allowed them a maximum of creative control. Yet, underneath the radical politics and lean, driving guitar rock, Midnight Oil remained an honest and compassionate group of optimists with a strong pride in their own country.

The nucleus of Midnight Oil (James Moginie, Andrew James and Rob Hirst) came together in 1972 under the name of Farm. The band played around Sydney's northern beaches, building up a modest following among the surfing fraternity. By 1975, with a line-up of Peter Garrett, Moginie, James and Hirst, Farm had already undertaken a number of east coast tours. Farm's music combined elements of Focus, Yes, Jo Jo Gunne, Gun and Jethro Tull with their own material. Although the band members admitted to a heavy influence from Focus and Yes, they said at the time that 'the influence is used only as an extension of their individual style'. That style encompassed an energetic hard rock sound underscored by a uniquely Australian outlook and fiercely independent spirit.

Until Garrett completed his law degree at Canberra University and moved to Sydney permanently at the end of 1976, Farm/Midnight Oil was a part-time concern. Martin Rotsey (guitar) completed the Midnight Oil line-up when he joined in early 1977, and the band stepped up its live work. Midnight Oil swiftly earned a fierce reputation on the suburban pub circuit for its tenacious live shows. The gigantic, bald-headed, rampaging Garrett also began to emerge as one of the most compelling and outspoken frontmen of the era.

In 1978, Midnight Oil formed the Powderworks label in order to issue its eponymous debut album. Unlike the power of the band's live shows, the album lacked a decent punch. The production sound was shallow, at times the playing was self-effacing and undemanding and Garrett's vocals sounded stilted and merely adequate. Only a handful of tracks like 'Powderworks', 'Used and Abused' and the single 'Run by Night'/'Dust' (December 1978) revealed any promise. And the band was yet to present any firm political notions. By 1979 the Oils were one of the top live draws in the land.

The second album, *Head Injuries* (October 1979), highlighted the band's growth and strength of purpose. The dynamic singles 'Cold Cold Change'/'Used and Abused' (October) and 'Back on the Borderline'/'Section 5 (Bus to Bondi)' (February 1980) made a strong impact. The album managed to reach #36 on the national chart, and by mid-1980 had attained gold status (35 000 copies sold). In April, bass player Peter Gifford (ex-Huntress, **Ross Ryan** Brothers) replaced Andrew James who had to leave due to ill-health. The band issued the 12-inch EP *Bird Noises* in October 1980; it reached #28 on the national singles chart in December, and was Top 20 in Sydney and Melbourne. The EP continued the development heard on *Head Injuries*, with 'No Time for Games' and 'I'm the Cure' being particularly impressive. *Bird Noises* also boasted the anomalous, but delightful Shadows-like instrumental 'Weddingcake Island'.

With the release of the UK-recorded, Glyn Johns-produced *Place Without a Postcard* album (November 1981), the Oils began to reach a wider audience. The album made #12 on the national charts and produced the singles 'Don't Wanna Be the One'/'Written in the Heart' (#40 in November 1981) and the 12-inch 'Armistice Day'/'Stand in Line' (#31 in May 1982). In mid-1982, the Oils returned to the UK to record a new album with young, hot-shot producer Nick Launay (Public Image Ltd, Gang of Four, **Birthday Party**). The union resulted in the uncompromising and state-of-the-art *10,9,8,7,6,5,4,3,2,1* album which marked a significant departure for the band. While retaining the Oils' live energy, it bore no relation to anything they had previously performed or recorded. That the Oils' most adventurous and radical album to that time should also become their most popular was testament to their emerging status as Australian cultural icons.

The album reached #3 on the national chart in December 1982. It stayed in the Top 20 for ten months and by the end of 1983 had sold close to

250 000 copies. (The album eventually stayed on the chart for 186 weeks.) The album produced the hit singles 'US Forces'/'Outside World' (Instrumental) (#20 in December 1982) and 'Power and the Passion'/'Power and the Passion' (Dub Version) (#8 in April 1983). The Oils celebrated their first overseas album release (for *10 . . . 1*) when they signed to CBS in the UK and Columbia in the USA. 'Power and the Passion'/'Glitch Baby' came out as a single in both territories. The UK also got 'US Forces'/'Outside World', while the USA instead got 'Tin Legs and Tin Mines'/'Power and the Passion' and 'Outside World'/'Read About It'.

With the success of *10 . . . 1* Midnight Oil began to exert a great deal of political clout and pressure. In February 1983, the Oils helped organise the Stop the Drop Nuclear Disarmament concert (which they also headlined) at Melbourne's Myer Music Bowl. In October, the organisers of the concert and the producers of the subsequent television simulcast received a United Nations Media Peace Prize Award for their work. In 1984, the band travelled to Tokyo, Japan to record its next album with producer Nick Launay. *Red Sails in the Sunset* (October) perhaps overstepped the mark with its reliance on high-tech studio wizardry, but the band's optimistic lyric stance shone through. 'Best of Both Worlds'/'Kosciusko' and 'When the Generals Talk'/'Who Can Stand in the Way' were only issued as singles in the UK and USA.

Garrett confirmed his commitment to political and social change by running for the NSW Senate as the candidate for the Nuclear Disarmament Party at the 1984 federal elections. He was unsuccessful in his bid for a political career, but it signified to all and sundry that he was now a nationally recognised public figure. In August 1987, Garrett again turned his attention to public affairs when he joined the likes of Senator Janine Haines and Australia II designer Ben Lexcen in a forum against the introduction of the Australia Card. During January 1985, Midnight Oil played a one-off showcase gig on tiny Goat Island (in the middle of Sydney Harbour) to help celebrate the tenth anniversary of radio station 2JJJ (precursor to the national Triple J network). Billed as *Oils on the Water*, the concert was later issued on video.

In December 1985, the four-track 12-inch EP *Species Deceases* crashed into the singles chart at #1 on its first week of release. Ostensibly as a reaction against the studio sheen of *Red Sails in the Sunset*, the EP featured a stripped-back pub-rock sound. In terms of sheer sonic firepower, it was one of the band's hardest hitting works. In the winter of 1986, Midnight Oil embarked on the unprecedented

Peter Garrett, Midnight Oil

Blackfella/Whitefella tour playing to remote Aboriginal communities in the Northern Territory accompanied by Koori outfit **Warumpi Band**. Writer Andrew McMillan documented the tour in his book *Strict Rules*, an insightful look at Australian music and how it interacts with, reflects and changes our culture.

While the band was on the tour, the 12-inch EP 'The Dead Heart' (which had been written for the film *Uluru: An Anangu Story*) reached #1 on the national chart. The flip side featured **Warumpi Band's** 'Blackfella/Whitefella' and **Coloured Stone's** 'This Land'. In August 1987, Midnight Oil reached the peak of its powers with the release of the groundbreaking *Diesel and Dust* album. Inspired by the Blackfella/Whitefella tour, *Diesel and Dust* is arguably one of the greatest Australian albums of all time. Powerful, dynamic and passionate songs like 'Beds are Burning', 'Put Down that Weapon', 'Dreamworld', 'The Dead Heart' and 'Sell My Soul' were statements of intent and a call to action backed by the strength of their convictions.

Before the album's release, New Zealand-born Dwayne 'Bones' Hillman (ex-**Swingers**) had replaced Gifford on bass. 'Beds are Burning'/'Gunbarrel Highway' (#5 in September 1987), 'Put Down that

Weapon'/'Peace, Love and Understanding' (November) and 'Dreamworld'/'Arctic World' (August 1988) were issued as singles. After reaching #1 in Australia, *Diesel and Dust* heralded the Oils' international breakthrough by peaking at #19 in the UK, #1 in France and #21 in the USA. It went on to sell close to three million copies worldwide. 'Beds are Burning' also reached #6 in the UK (after being reissued in March 1989) and #17 in the USA.

Following the 1988 American tour to promote *Diesel and Dust* (with **Yothu Yindi** and American Indian activist/poet John Trudell aka Graffiti Man as supports), the Oils helped launch the Various Artists album *Burning Bridges*. The double album featured tracks by Midnight Oil ('Warakurna'), **Paul Kelly**, **Scrap Metal**, **Coloured Stone**, **Hunters & Collectors**, Areyonga Desert Tigers, **James Reyne**, **The Saints**, **Crowded House**, **INXS** and **Yothu Yindi**. All proceeds from sales went to the National Coalition of Aboriginal Organisations (NCAO). In 1989, Garrett was appointed President of the Australian Conservation Foundation (ACF).

The Oils' March 1990 album, *Blue Sky Mining* (produced by Warne Livesey), was their most defiant and outspoken work to date. The first single, 'Blue Sky Mine' (backed by 'You May Not Be Released'), was inspired by Ben Hills' book *Blue Murder* which detailed the history of the blue asbestos mine in Wittenoom, Western Australia. 'Blue Sky Mine' reached #8 on the national chart in March 1990. *Blue Sky Mining* made its debut at #1 on the national chart the same month. It yielded a further four minor hit singles, 'Forgotten Years'/'Shakers and Movers' (#26 in June), 'King of the Mountain' (#25 in October), 'Bedlam Bridge' (#46 in November) and 'One Country' (#51 in April 1991). As well as reaching #1 in Australia, the album peaked at #28 in the UK and #20 in the USA. Although it went on to sell over two million copies worldwide, it was not the massive chart smash the band had expected. The Oils spent most of 1990 touring across Europe and the USA in support of *Blue Sky Mining*.

While in the USA, the Oils staged one of their most infamous protest gigs on a Manhattan street. The unannounced lunchtime gig was to express their disgust over the Exxon Valdez oil spill in Alaska, and the band made its views felt by playing outside the company's headquarters. The protest attracted international attention to the cause, and the subsequent documentary of the concert *Black Rain Falls* raised funds for Greenpeace.

The Oils returned to Australia in November for their first full concert tour in three years. Columbia awarded the band the Crystal Globe Award in recognition of sales of five million albums outside Australia. The Oils also took out Best Group and Best Album (*Blue Sky Mining*) at the 1990 Australian Record Industry Association (ARIA) Awards. In 1991, the band took a year-long sabbatical, during which Rob Hirst recorded an album, *Ghostwriters*, with Dorland Bray and Rick Grossman, Moginie played on the new **Neil Murray** record and Garrett tended to his duties with the ACF. In 1993, Garrett resigned from the ACF and took up a position with the International Board of Greenpeace.

The Oils' in-concert album *Scream in Blue Live* (June 1992) featured the band in all its rough-edged, on-stage fury. The album's tracks were culled from concerts over an eight-year period (1982–90), plus 'Progress' which was taken from the band's lunchtime protest gig outside Exxon Valdez. 'Sometimes' (live)/'Beds are Burning' (live) was issued as a single and reached #33 in May 1992. A month earlier, Midnight Oil headlined the prestigious, annual Earth Day concert in Boston, Massachusetts. Then, under the guidance of Nick Launay (for the first time in eight years), the band recorded its ninth album, *Earth and Sun and Moon*. The album produced the singles 'Truganini' (Australian #10 in March 1993; UK #29 in April), 'My Country' (#52 in July), 'Outbreak of Love' (#57 in September) and 'In the Valley' (November). For their global tour in support of the album, the Oils added acclaimed keyboards player **Chris Abrahams**.

The Oils undertook the Breaking the Dry tour of Australia at the start of 1995, but it was to be another year and a half before they issued a new album, *Breathe* (October 1996), and single, 'Underwater' (#22 in September). The songs on *Breathe* featured a loose, raw feel but were mostly gentle and low-key. The album reached #3 on the national chart, but was the band's least successful album to date. It sold 50 000 copies before slipping out of the national Top 50. 'Surf's Up Tonight' was issued as a second single in November 1996. The Oils returned to the national album chart in November 1997, when the compilation *20,000 Watt R.S.L.* reached #4.

Albums: *Midnight Oil* (Powderworks, 1978), *Head Injuries* (Powderworks/7 Records/RCA, 1979), *Place Without A Postcard* (CBS, 1981), *10,9,8,7,6,5,4,3,2,1* (CBS, 1982), *Red Sails in the Sunset* (CBS, 1985), *Diesel and Dust* (CBS, 1987), *Blue Sky Mining* (CBS, 1990), *Scream in Blue Live* (Sony/Columbia, 1992), *Earth and Sun and Moon* (Sony/Columbia, 1993), *Breathe* (Sony/Columbia, 1996), *20,000 Watt R.S.L.* (Sony/Columbia, 1997).

Further reading: *Strict Rules* by Andrew McMillan (Hodder and Stoughton, 1988).

The Mighty Guys

Formed: 1980
Style: Rockabilly, R&B
Original line-up: *Mick Hamilton (guitar, vocals; ex-Moods,* **Vibrants***), Phil Eisenberg (bass, vocals; ex-***Ferrets***), Leon Isackson (drums; ex-***Digby Richards** *and the R'Jays, Stoneagers, Rajahs)*

The Mighty Guys were often lumped into The Stray Cats-styled rockabilly category for convenience sake. Yet the band's sound encompassed not only rockabilly but also R&B, pop, rootsy rock'n'roll and beatnik rhythms into a lean, mean and loose-limbed whole. The description 'Maynard G. Krebbs Beatabilly' seemed an appropriate one.

The three members of The Mighty Guys had a wealth of experience under their collective belts when they joined forces in mid-1980. Mick Hamilton got his start with 1960s Melbourne garage-beat band The Moods. The band comprised Hamilton (rhythm guitar, vocals), 14-year-old John Livi (lead guitar), Kevin Fraser (vocals), Peter Noss (bass) and Carl Savona (drums). Noss was later replaced by Ian Ferguson. The Moods supported The Rolling Stones on the Melbourne date of their 1966 Australian tour. The band had signed to EMI/HMV and issued two singles in 1966, 'Cos' of You'/'Say Hello to Me' (March) and 'Rum Drunk'/'I Love You So' (June). The band had broken up by the time 'Rum Drunk' appeared. Hamilton joined Adelaide band **The Vibrants** when they relocated to Melbourne. Raven Records included The Moods' gritty R&B stomper 'Rum Drunk' on the seminal collection of Australian 1960s garage-punk tracks *Ugly Things* (1980). During the 1970s, Hamilton worked in the British-based Springfield Revival.

Phil Eisenberg had stints in the backing bands for stage productions of *The Rocky Horror Show* and *Jesus Christ Superstar*, and played on **The Ferrets'** 1977 hit single 'Don't Fall in Love' and the album *Dreams of a Love*. He also toured South-East Asia for two years with Sorcery. Leon Isackson's career began way back in the late 1950s. He got his start in Sydney R&B combo **Ray Hoff and the Off Beats**. Next he joined The Stoneagers, who are credited with issuing one of the very first rock'n'roll EPs in Australia. Elvis Presley's 'Jailhouse Rock', 'Rock It Up'/'Too Much', 'Jenny Jenny' appeared on the Prestophone Olympic label in 1958. (It is claimed by some collectors that the record was recorded in 1956, but Presley did not release 'Jailhouse Rock' until the end of 1957.)

Isackson joined The Stoneagers in 1959, after the EP came out, and took the place of original drummer Devy Grace. The other members of The Stoneagers were Teddy Lees (guitar) and Roger Keys (piano). From there, Isackson joined **Digby Richards** and the R' Jays. In 1964 The R' Jays became The Rajahs with a line-up of Isackson, Jon Heyton (lead guitar, vocals), Lindsay 'Nosmo' King (rhythm guitar, vocals) and Michael Lawler (bass). The Rajahs were billed as 'Australia's Beatles', and just to perpetuate the correlation the band issued a rare EP, *Beatlemania* (March 1964), which contained renditions of six Beatles hits. In the meantime, The Rajahs had signed to the Leedon label and issued the singles 'Kiss Me Now'/'You'll Get Over It' (March 1964), 'Cathy's Clown'/'I Like the Look of You' (September) and 'Let Me Tell You About a Guy'/'Oh' (June 1965), plus the EP 'Kiss Me Now'. The band also backed **Johnny O'Keefe** and **Noeleen Batley** on some of their recordings.

In 1981, The Mighty Guys signed to Glenn A. Baker's Rivet label and issued the 10-inch mini-album *Rockin' All Through the Night*. They followed that up with the singles Red Foley's 'Old Shep'/'Something Else', 'One Night' (December 1981), 'Be Cool, Be Smart'/'Crying Lonely Sad and Blue' (August 1982), 'When I Walk You Home'/'Nervous Breakdown' (1983) and The McCoys' 'Hang on Sloopy'/'Landslide (1983), plus the album *Be Cool, Be Smart* (October 1982). Brian Dean replaced Eisenberg on bass in 1985. Bob Howe also joined on guitar, but The Mighty Guys broke up soon after. In 1986, Rivet issued the compilation album *The Rest of the Mighty Guys*, which pulled together non-album singles tracks, a few choice album cuts and two tracks recorded as Patti and the Mighty Guys, 'It's Love Baby' and 'Keep Your Hands Off Me'.

Albums: *Be Cool, Be Smart* (Rivet/Festival, 1982), *The Rest of the Mighty Guys* (Rivet/Festival, 1986).

Mighty Kong

Formed: 1973
Style: Rock
Original line-up: Ross Wilson *(vocals, guitar; ex-***Pink Finks, Party Machine, Procession, Sons of the Vegetal Mother, Daddy Cool***)*, **Ross Hannaford** *(guitar, vocals; ex-***Pink Finks, Party Machine,** *Quinn,* **Sons of the Vegetal Mother, Daddy Cool***), Russell Smith (guitar, vocals; ex-***Cam-Pact, Company Caine, Duck***), Tim Partridge (bass; ex-Clockwork Oringe,* **Company Caine***), Ray Arnott (drums; ex-Chelsea Set, Browns,* **Company Caine**, *Genesis,* **Spectrum***)*

With the break-up of **Daddy Cool** in August 1972, Rosses Wilson and Hannaford set about forming a new band. The pair decided to move away from the stylistic constraints that had bound **Daddy Cool** and to concentrate on a heavier style of rock. Latter-day **Daddy Cool** songs like 'Make Your Stash', 'Love in an FJ', 'Boy, You're Paranoid' and 'Flash in My Head' had been indicative of that emergent style. Initially ex-**Company Caine** singer **Gulliver Smith** was involved in the project, but by the end of 1972 he had wandered off to pursue a solo career.

Next Wilson and Hannaford recruited **Tim Gaze** (lead guitar; ex-Stonehenge, **Tamam Shud**, **Kahvas Jute**, Miss Universe) and Nigel Macara (drums; ex-Stonehenge, Bootleg, **Tamam Shud**, Miss Universe). After a month or two spent rehearsing and trying to get the band off the ground, Gaze and Macara left to join Mike Rudd's new band, **Ariel**. Wilson and Hannaford finally unveiled their new band, Mighty Kong, in April 1973. It comprised Russell Smith, Tim Partridge and **Ray Arnott**. Wilson had a lot of faith in his new venture, but he never got the chance to capitalise on the band's formidable potential. By the time the band's debut album, *All I Wanna Do is Rock*, and single, 'Callin' All Cats'/'Hard Drugs (are Bad for You)', came out in December 1973, Mighty Kong had folded.

Nevertheless, the album was a worthwhile release, with funky hard rockers like 'Jungle in My Blood', 'Homesick and Horny', 'Hard Drugs (are Bad for You)' and 'Got My Beliefs' standing out. Elsewhere the gorgeous Russell Smith/**Gulliver Smith**-penned ballad 'With a Smile Like That (How Could We Refuse?)' found Wilson in fine voice. Wilson and Hannaford went on to re-form **Daddy Cool** among many other bands. Arnott joined **The Dingoes**.

Album: *All I Wanna Do is Rock* (Wizard, 1973).

The Mighty Reapers (of Vengeance) (*see* The Dynamic Hepnotics)

Dave Miller Set

Formed: *1967*
Style: *Pop, rock*
Original line-up: *Dave Miller (vocals; ex-Byrds), John Robinson (lead guitar; ex-Lonely Ones, Monday's Children), Harry Brus (bass; ex-Amazons), Ray Mulholland (drums)*

New Zealand-born singer Dave Miller arrived in Sydney during 1966 with his band The Byrds. (Not to be confused with the McGuinn/Clarke/Crosby/Hillman Byrds.) That band soon fell apart and Miller formed the Dave Miller Set. The Spin label signed up the Dave Miller Set and issued three pop singles, 'Why? Why? Why?'/'Hard, Hard Year' (November 1967), 'Hope'/'Having a Party' (May 1968) and 'Let's Get Together'/'A Bread and Butter Day' (September 1968).

Bob Thompson (bass) replaced Harry Brus in 1968; Leith Corbett (bass; ex-**Heart 'n' Soul**) replaced Thompson; and Mike McCormac (ex-**Sect**) replaced Ray Mulholland in 1969. By 1969, John Robinson had emerged as a fluid and inventive guitarist, and the Dave Miller Set attained prominence as one of the first heavy rock bands on the local scene in the Led Zeppelin mould. Under the direction of Festival's in-house producer Pat Aulton, the band cut its fourth single, 'Mr Guy Fawkes'/ 'Someone is Sure to' (July 1969). The cover of English band Eire Apparent's 'Mr Guy Fawkes' ranks alongside the **Russell Morris** psychedelic classic 'The Real Thing' as the high-water mark of Australian pop production in the late 1960s. It reached #6 on the Sydney charts during November, by which time the Dave Miller Set was on its last legs. Miller issued a cover of Chicago's 'Does Anyone Really Know What Time It Is?'/'No Need to Cry' (March 1970) as a solo single. Robinson, Corbett and McCormac then formed **Blackfeather** with 18-year-old singer Neale Johns.

Corbett and McCormac soon abandoned **Blackfeather** to work with Miller on an album. Issued at the end of 1970, the *Reflections of a Pioneer* album was credited to Dave Miller/Leith Corbett and Friends. The album's diverse sound was exemplified by the single 'Reflections of a Pioneer'/'353527 Charles' (November 1970), which mixed country-tinged psychedelic pop (A-side) with heavy rock (B-side). In 1971, Miller formed a band called 2000. In February 1973 he reunited briefly with John Robinson (by then ex-**Blackfeather**, Hunger, **Duck**) in a revived version of the Dave Miller Set which also comprised Steve Hogg (bass; ex-**Bakery**) and Steve Webb (drums; ex-**Blackfeather, Duck**). Corbett travelled to the UK for a time and then, on his return in 1972, joined Island as lead guitarist.

Dave Miller/Leith Corbett and Friends album: *Reflections of a Pioneer* (Spin/Festival, 1970).

Millionaires

Formed: *1975*
Style: *Rock, pop*
Original line-up: *Nick Lafayette (real name Nick Smith, guitar, vocals), Jimmy Tomorrow (real name Henry Vynhal, violin), Boyd Compact (real name Tim Brosnan, lead guitar), Buzz Deluxe (real name Steve Leeson, bass, vocals), Karl Wolfe (real name Karl Segnit, drums; ex-Sharks)*

Melbourne band Millionaires billed itself as a 'sophisticated' rock outfit, which basically meant that they dressed in stylish attire and played snappy, accessible pop rock. The band played alongside the likes of **The Sports**, **Jo Jo Zep and the Falcons**, Gulliver's Travels, **Mondo Rock**, **Stiletto**, **Redhouse**, and **The Bleeding Hearts** on the thriving mid-1970s Melbourne pub scene. Henry Vynhal had played violin on Steve Maxwell von Braund's 1975 album *Monster Planet*.

Millionaires signed to Mushroom Records and issued the appealing single 'It's a Deal'/'Gossip' in September 1976. In early 1977, David Hicks replaced Karl Wolfe, who joined The Autodrifters, and Reynold Barton Walters (aka Rex Wailer) replaced Tim Brosnan who joined True Wheels. Jimmy Tomorrow also left and was not replaced. Millionaires called it a day in July. As a final gesture, the band issued the one-sided single, 'Please Don't Mention the Junta' on its own Soviet label in November 1977. By 1978, Nick Smith and Buzz Leeson had formed **The Kevins**. By 1980, Brosnan was a member of **Paul Kelly** and the Dots. Vynhal issued a solo single in 1979 on the Cleopatra label, 'Wake Up Tania'/'Punk Power'. In 1984, Smith issued a solo single, featuring a cover of The Young Rascals' 'Groovin''/'Shake It', on Joe Camilleri's Spirit label. Smith then formed a songwriting partnership with Camilleri, contributing lyrics to **Black Sorrows'** albums like *Hold on to Me* and *Harley and Rose*.

Mario Millo

Style: *Symphonic/classical rock*

Acclaimed guitarist/songwriter/composer Mario Millo (b. 1955) was something of a child prodigy. He learned to play the mandolin at age five, the guitar at eight and by 12 was fronting his first band, The Menu, formed with friends from Mitchell High School in Sydney's Western suburbs. By the time he was 14, Millo's band, then renamed The Clik, had issued its first, bubblegum single 'La De Da'/'Yes Sir' (November 1969) on Festival Records.

The contract with Festival was part of the prize awarded to the band for taking out first place in the 1969 2SM Pepsi Battle of the Bands held at the Sydney Stadium. The Menu's line-up was Millo (vocals, guitar), Brian Nicholls (organ), Vince Moult (bass) and Mark Friedland (drums). The Menu also scored a $5000 contract with the Cordon Bleu booking agency. The agency renamed the band The Clik, decked them out in cute, matching uniforms, and lined up work on the lucrative suburban dance circuit. Festival issued the band's second single, 'Mary Mary'/'Uptight Basil', in March 1970. Coca-Cola/McCann-Ericksons then chose the band to promote Fanta soft drink. As part of the advertising campaign, the band became The Fantasy, recorded a series of television commercials ('Fancy Nancy') and toured Australia and New Zealand.

Millo soon tired of the exploitation, and broke up The Fantasy in 1971. He travelled to Europe for six months, and then on his return in early 1972 re-formed The Clik as a more serious, rock-oriented venture. The line-up comprised Millo, Garry Adams (lead guitar; ex-**Galadriel**), Phil Cogan (bass) and Doug Bligh (drums; ex-**Galadriel**). By 1973, Justin McCoy had replaced Adams, but Millo broke up the band in October 1973 when he received an offer to join up-and-coming dance band **Sebastian Hardie**.

Sebastian Hardie eventually established a reputation as Australia's first symphonic rock band. Millo stayed with the band until the end of 1976. He then formed Windchase with **Sebastian Hardie** keyboards player Toivo Pilt, but that band only lasted for a year. Millo then joined **Jon English**'s backing band, Baxter Funt. At that stage, English was one of Australia's most popular solo singers. In 1978 English starred in the television miniseries *Against the Wind*. He and Millo composed, recorded and produced the *Against the Wind* soundtrack album, which went on to become the best-selling MOR album for 1979. The single 'Six Ribbons'/'Mary's Theme' (#5 in January 1979) was the best-selling male pop single for the year. *Against the Wind* later became a hit series when screened on UK and Scandinavian television.

Millo and English toured Scandinavia to great acclaim; *Against the Wind* went on to sell over 500 000 copies worldwide. In 1979, Millo contributed the track 'Rebecca' to the Various Artists *Australian Guitar Album* (Razzle/Festival) which also featured **Kevin Borich**, **Ian Moss**, **Lobby Loyde**, **Phil Manning**, **Rockwell T. James**, Russell Smith, Mick Elliott, Ian Miller, Chris Turner and Harvey James. 'Rebecca' was issued as a single backed with Harvey James' 'Let It Go'.

Flushed with the success of his venture with **Jon English**, Millo produced, composed, engineered and arranged his own album, *Epic III*, which came out in September 1979. It was a highly orchestrated work, brimming with classical themes and overtones that showcased Millo's characteristic soaring guitar technique. Master bass player **Jackie Orszaczky** and drummer Mark Kennedy helped out on the sessions. Neither the album nor its single, 'Life in Our Hands'/'Sogno D'Amore' (August 1979), reached the charts. It was a fate that befell Millo's next two singles, 'You'/'People Like Us' (October 1982) and

'Breaking Away'/'People Like Us' (February 1983), plus his second album, *Human Games* (May 1983).

By 1984, Millo had embarked on a successful career in soundtrack composition and production. Millo has scored the soundtracks to film and television productions like *World Safari II*, *Joh's Jury*, *Brides of Christ*, *The Lighthorsemen*, *Shame*, *Tanamera: The Lion of Singapore*, *A Fortunate Life*, *Bullwinkle*, *Lola Montes*, *The High Country*, *People Like Us*, *The Body Business*, *Shame* and *G.P.* Millo won the 1991 Australian Record Industry Association (ARIA) Award for Best Australian Soundtrack and APRA Awards for Best Television Theme and Best Television Score for *Brides of Christ*. *The Lighthorsemen* won an AFI Award for Best Original Music Score.

Albums: *Against the Wind* (television miniseries soundtrack with **Jon English**, Polydor, 1978), *Epic III* (Polydor, 1979), *Human Games* (EMI/Wheatley, 1983), *World Safari II* (film soundtrack, Powderworks/BMG, 1984), *A Fortunate Life* (television soundtrack, Polydor, 1986), *The Lighthorsemen* (film soundtrack, Festival, 1989), *Brides of Christ* (television soundtrack, ABC, 1991).

Dannii Minogue

Style: *Dance pop*

Dannii Minogue

Internationally famous singer Dannii Minogue (b. 1971) started acting at the age of seven in the national television drama series *Skyways*. She also had a small role in the popular Australian war-time soapie *The Sullivans*. In 1982, the then Dannielle joined the Ten Network's prime-time variety show *Young Talent Time* as a regular team member alongside **Tina Arena**. She remained with the show for six years. In 1988, she joined the Crawford Productions television drama series *All the Way*, followed by a long-running role as the character Emma in popular soapie *Home and Away*. Following the international success of *Neighbours* (which starred Dannii's sister **Kylie Minogue**), *Home and Away* brought Dannii to the attention of British and European audiences.

In 1990, Dannii returned to music and signed to the Mushroom label. Her debut single, 'Love and Kisses', became an instant hit, peaking at #4 on the national chart during April. Dannii's debut album, *Success* (November 1990), spawned three further hit singles: 'Success' (#28 in October), Stacey Latislaw's 'Jump to the Beat' (#48 in October 1991) and 'Baby Love' (#26 in April 1992). Under the supervision of hip New York producers Alvin Moody and Vinnie Bell (Neneh Cherry), the album displayed Dannii's bubbly combination of dance pop, rap and bubblegum funk.

Dannii began concentrating her efforts on the UK market where she scored five hit singles during 1991: 'Love and Kisses' (#8 in March 1991), 'Success' (#11 in May), 'Jump to the Beat' (#8 in July), 'Baby Love' (#14 in October) and 'I Don't Wanna Take this Pain' (#40 in December). She made numerous appearances on British television, including *Top of the Pops* and the *Royal Variety Performance*. Dannii's debut album was retitled *Love and Kisses* in the UK; it made its debut at #8 on the charts and remained in the Top 40 for three months. In 1991, UK's *TV Hits* magazine readers voted Dannii Best Female TV Star and London's Radio One and *Fast Forward* magazine awarded her #1 Woman of the Year. *Smash Hits* magazine voted her Best New Artist and runner-up in the Most Fanciable Singer and Best Female Singer sections.

In 1992, Dannii starred in her first feature film, an Australian/New Zealand co-production *Secrets* (in the role of Didi) which was set against the backdrop of The Beatles' 1964 Australian tour. Dannii contributed a version of The Jacksons' 'Show You the Way to Go' to the *New Musical Express* charity album *Ruby Trax* (1992). The royalties from the album's sales were donated to the British Spastics Society. 'Show You the Way to Go' became Dannii's sixth UK hit single when it reached #30 in August 1992. She ended the year with a minor hit in 'Love's on Every Corner' (#44 in December).

Dannii's 1993 album *Get Into You* yielded the hit singles 'This is It' (Australian #13 in September; UK #10 in July), 'This is the Way' (Australian #45 in November; UK #27 in October) and 'Get into You' (UK #36 in June 1994). In 1994, Dannii toured Japan as lead singer of dance pop group Euro-Groove. The group had Japanese hit singles with 'Rescue Me' and 'Boogie Woogie'. In 1995, Dannii added a *Playboy* pictorial to her list of credits. In 1996, she returned to television work when she co-hosted the popular British music/entertainment show *It's Not Just Saturday*.

Dannii had already hosted a number of national television programs, including the annual pop quiz series *Fan TC* on the BBC. She also made appearances on *The Big Breakfast*, which was co-hosted by another expatriate Australian, Mark Little. In 1997 Dannii signed a new record deal with Warner Music and issued her first solo single 'All I Wanna Do' (September), and album, *Girl* (October), in nearly four years. The album peaked at #36 on the national chart, while 'All I Wanna Do' went as high as #12 in October. The second single, 'Everything I Wanted' appeared in November.

Albums: *Success* (Mushroom/Festival, 1990), *Love and Kisses and . . .* (dance remixes of debut album, Mushroom/Festival, 1992), *Get into You* (Mushroom/Festival, 1993), *Girl* (Warner, 1997).

Kylie Minogue

Style: *Dance pop*

As one of Australia's most successful pop exports ever, singer/actor Kylie Minogue (b. 1968) was the subject of much derision throughout her early career. 'The Singing Budgie' was one of the lesser put-downs. While she remained the epitome of non-cool for many years, Kylie's fans bought her records by the truckload and lapped up any press or television coverage. Nevertheless, Kylie has remained steadfast in her career and successfully transcended the critical backlash. Along the way, she developed a new sound and new attitude to match, and more importantly gained a new audience in the process.

Kylie began her career with roles in television shows *The Sullivans*, *Skyways*, *The Henderson Kids* and *Fame and Misfortune* during the early to mid-1980s. With a new role as tomboy mechanic Charlene Mitchell in popular television soapie *Neighbours* during 1986, she came to the attention of a much wider audience. In 1987, Mushroom issued Kylie's first single, a cover of the Little Eva 1960s hit 'Locomotion'/'Glad to Be Alive', which became a #1 Australian hit (and the best-selling single for the year). In the process, Kylie opened up the soap opera/pop chart route, with everyone from **Melissa (Tkautz)** to Bruce Samazan, Toni Pearen to Noelene Donaher following suit.

In 1988, Kylie signed a deal with the British hit-making team of Stock Aitken Waterman (SAW). Her international success was immediate with the release of the single 'I Should Be So Lucky'/'I Should Be So Lucky' (instrumental) which simultaneously went to #1 in Australia, the UK and Japan during January 1988. Kylie followed that with the hits 'Got to Be Certain'/'Got to Be Certain' (instrumental) (which made history by making its debut at #1 on the Australian charts in July; also UK #2 in May), a re-recorded version of 'Locomotion' (UK #2, US #3 in August), 'Je Ne Sais Pas Pourquoi'/'Made in Heaven' (Australian #12, UK #2 in October) and her duet with **Jason Donovan,** 'Especially for You'/'All I Wanna Do is Make You Mine' (Australian #1, UK #1 in December). She also issued the best-selling *Kylie* album in July 1988 (Australian #2, UK #1).

Kylie quickly outsold all other SAW acts (like Bananarama, Mel & Kim and Rick Astley) put together. 'Especially for You' sold 750 000 copies alone, making it one of the biggest selling UK singles of the 1980s. With continuing worldwide success beckoning, Kylie left *Neighbours* after winning a Gold Logie. *Business Review Weekly* ran a story on Kylie Minogue Pty Ltd in which it forecast a possible 1988/89 income of $100 million, 98 per cent of it generated from outside of Australia. During 1989, the SAW hit-making machine continued with the singles 'Hand on Your Heart'/'Just Wanna Love You' (Australian #4, UK #1 in May), 'Wouldn't Change a Thing'/'It's No Secret' (Australian #6, UK #2 in August), 'Turn it Into Love/'Made in Heaven' (Japanese only release, #1) and 'Never Too Late'/'Made in Heaven' (Australian #14, UK #4 in November) plus the *Enjoy Yourself* album (Australian #7 in November).

Kylie capped off a successful 1989 by winning the Outstanding Achievement Award at the Australian Record Industry Association (ARIA) Awards. She starred as Lola Lovell in the $10 million movie *The Delinquents* (shot in Brisbane) with US actor Charlie Schlatter as co-star. After touring the UK, she started dating **INXS** frontman Michael Hutchence. Hutchence would later state that his favourite pastime was 'corrupting Kylie'. Kylie enjoyed hit singles throughout 1990 with 'Tears on My Pillow'/ 'We Know the Meaning of Love' (from *The Delinquents*; Australian #20, UK #1 in January), 'Better the Devil You Know'/'I'm Over Dreaming (Over You)' (Australian #4, UK #2 in May) and 'Step Back in Time'/'Step Back in Time' (instrumental) (Australian #5, UK #4 in November).

Following the success of the third SAW album, *Rhythm of Love*, which reached #10 in Australia during December, 1990 culminated in the sold-out Rhythm of Love Australian tour. Kylie had already toured Australia earlier in the year (February) with a backing band which included **James Freud** (bass; ex-**Models**), Greg Perano (percussion; ex-**Hunters & Collectors**, **Deadly Hume**) and **Deni Hines** (backing vocals).

Kylie responded to her critics in 1991 with the more mature-sounding album *Let's Get to It* (Australian #13 in December) and singles 'What Do I Have to Do?'/'What Do I Have to Do? (instrumental) (Australian #11, UK #6 in February), 'Shocked' (DNA Mix)/'Shocked' (Harding/Curnow Mix) (Australian #7, UK #6 in June) and 'Word is Out'/'Say the Word, I'll Be There' (Australian #10, UK #16 in September). In October she undertook a UK/European tour with a risqué show that featured revealing costumes (designed by John Galliano) and seductive moves. The media viewed this as a blatant Madonna rip-off. Kylie said of her new raunchy image, 'I'm not trying to do Madonna. No-one can do Madonna except Madonna. I'm just being me.'

By 1992 media acceptance had fallen into place. *Who* magazine placed her on the front cover, UK dance music bible *Mixmag* voted her 'Sexiest Person on the Planet' and *The Face* called her 'the new cultural icon'. Bobby Gillespie of UK band Primal Scream and James Dean Bradfield from the Manic Street Preachers both professed their adoration for the singer, while Teenage Fanclub recorded a song called 'Kylie's Got a Crush on Us'. Meanwhile, she continued to build-up a strong gay following across the world.

The hits continued into 1992–93 with 'If You Were with Me Now' (a duet with Keith Washington)/'I Guess I Like what I Like' (Australian #23, UK #4 in December 1991), 'Give Me Just a Little More Time'/'Do You Dare?' (Australian #24, UK #2 in January), 'Finer Feelings'/'Closer' (Australian #60, UK #11 in April), 'What Kind of Fool (Heard It All Before)'/'Things Can Only Get Better' (Australian #17, UK #14 in August) and Kool and the Gang's 'Celebration'/'Too Much of a Good Thing' (Australian #12, UK #20 in November). Kylie's 1993 *Greatest Hits* album (Australian #3, UK #1) was her final set for the SAW team and the PWL label.

Kylie's 1994 hits 'Confide in Me'/'Where Has the Love Gone?' (her first Australian #1 since 'Got to Be Certain' in 1988; also UK #2 in September) and 'Put Yourself in My Place' (UK #11 in November), plus the album *Kylie Minogue* (November) were the singer's first releases for the hip UK dance label deConstruction (outside Australia). Her third deConstruction single was 'Where is the Feeling?' (UK #16 in July 1996). Her limited edition (600 copies) book which featured exotic photographs and semi-nudity was instantly compared with Madonna's *Sex* book. In her next film, Steven de Souza's $38 million action film *Street Fighter*, Kylie starred in the role of Cammy (a kickboxing army Lieutenant) opposite Jean-Claude Van Damme. Kylie's third movie, the flop Hollywood comedy *Bio Dome* with American comedian Pauly Shore, was released direct to video in Australia during 1995.

In 1995, **Nick Cave** invited Kylie to record two duets, 'Where the Wild Roses Grow' and 'Death is Not the End', for his album *The Murder Ballads*. 'Where the Wild Roses Grow' was issued as a single, reaching #2 on the Australian charts in October 1995. It also peaked at #11 in the UK the same month. Kylie's performance of 'Where the Wild Roses Grow' with **Nick Cave and the Bad Seeds** was a highlight of the 1996 Big Day Out tour. 'Where the Wild Roses Grow' was awarded Song of the Year and Best Pop Release at the tenth annual Australian Record Industry Association (ARIA) Awards. Kylie recorded her second deConstruction album with producers Brothers In Rhythm, which was due for release in early 1998 as *Impossible Princess*. The album's first CD single, 'Some Kind of Bliss', peaked at #25 in October 1997, while the playful follow-up 'Did it Again' made #21 in December.

Kylie's achievements on the UK charts speak for themselves. She scored 13 Top 10 hit singles in a row (including four #1s). She stands as one of the most popular female chart performers in British pop history alongside the likes of Madonna, Dusty Springfield, Petula Clark, Kate Bush, **Olivia Newton-John**, Shirley Bassey, Tina Turner, Diana Ross, Aretha Franklin and Whitney Houston.

Albums: *Kylie* (Mushroom/Festival, 1988), *Enjoy Yourself* (Mushroom/Festival, 1989), *The Kylie Collection* (double reissue of first two albums, Mushroom/ Festival, 1989), *Rhythm of Love* (Mushroom/Festival, 1990), *Let's Get to It* (Mushroom/Festival, 1991), *Greatest Hits* (Mushroom/Festival, 1992), *Kylie's Remixes* (Mushroom/Festival, 1993), *Kylie's Remixes Volume 2* (Mushroom/Festival, 1993), *Greatest Remix Hits Volume 1* (Mushroom/Festival, 1993), *Greatest Remix Hits*

Volume 2 (Mushroom/Festival, 1993), *Kylie Non-Stop History 50+1* (Mushroom/Festival, 1993), *Kylie Minogue* (Mushroom/Festival, 1994).

Further reading: *Kylie* by Dino Scatena (Penguin Books, 1997).

Mi-Sex

Formed: *1978*
Style: *New wave rock*
Original line-up: *Steve Gilpin (vocals; ex-Fragments of Time), Kevin Stanton (guitar; ex-Think, Brigade, Fragments of Time), Murray Burns (keyboards; ex-Red Rose, Fragments of Time), Don Martin (bass; ex-Freeway, Father Thyme; Fragments of Time), Richard Hodgkinson (drums)*

During the early 1980s, New Zealand band Mi-Sex was one of the most popular groups on the Australian scene. The band mixed competently played, but derivative, new wave rock (somewhere between Ultravox and **The Angels**) and futuristic imagery with a carefully choreographed stage act and laser light show. Mi-Sex found a ready-made audience via appearances on ***Countdown***, but was also able to draw capacity crowds on the pub-rock circuit.

The members of Mi-Sex all had a solid grounding on the New Zealand scene. In 1972, 22-year-old Steve Gilpin came to prominence as a *New Faces* winner. Over the next five years, he became a regular on the hotel and cabaret circuit. In 1977, he decided to ditch the cabaret for rock'n'roll and linked up with Kevin Stanton, Don Martin, Murray Burns and Phil Smart (drums) in Fragments of Time. With the arrival of Richard Hodgkinson, a name change to Mi-Sex (from an Ultravox song) and the adoption of a leather pants/tough guy, new wave look and sound, the band set its sights on Australia. EMI New Zealand issued the band's debut single 'Straight Laddie'/'High Class Dame', but it sank without a trace. Mi-Sex arrived in Australia during August 1978. Within six months, the band was the fourth biggest drawcard on the Sydney scene (behind **Cold Chisel**, **The Angels** and **Midnight Oil**) and had signed to CBS.

CBS issued 'But You Don't Care'/'Burning Up' (#25 in June 1979), followed by the Peter Dawkins-produced *Graffiti Crimes* album in July. Backed by the band's national support slot to Talking Heads and a tour as headliners, *Graffiti Crimes* reached the Top 20 in September. Then came the band's biggest hit, the electro-pop anthem 'Computer Games'/'Wot Do You Want?' which hit #1 in October. With its simplistic, brain-teasing riff and Gilpin's mannered vocal yelps, 'Computer Games' boasted little substance but was constructed for maximum effect. It came to epitomise the one word which has plagued the memory of Mi-Sex: 'contrived'. That hardly mattered because, by April 1980, the single had charted Top 10 in Canada, France, Austria, Italy, West Germany and South Africa. *Graffiti Crimes* was also issued internationally during September 1979 on Columbia (except for Epic in the USA). The album eventually sold over 500 000 copies worldwide.

In November 1979, Mi-Sex performed at the Concert of the Decade on the steps of the Sydney Opera House in front of 160 000 people. The band played alongside **The Angels**, **Cold Chisel**, **Dragon**, **Renée Geyer**, **Skyhooks** and **Split Enz**. In April 1980, Mi-Sex commenced a month-long American tour that took the band from Los Angeles to Canada to New York. The band supported Iggy Pop, The Ramones and 999 along the way, as well as headlining a number of club dates. In the band's absence, Mi-Sex was honoured with three awards at the 1979 *TV Week*/***Countdown*** Awards ceremony: Most Popular Record ('Computer Games'), Best Australian Single ('Computer Games') and the Johnny O'Keefe Memorial Award for Most Promising New Talent.

The band's second album, *Space Race*, reached #6 on the national chart in June 1980. It produced two hit singles, 'People'/'Pages and Matches' (#6 in April 1980) and 'Space Race'/'Living in September' (#28 in June). A third single from the album, 'It Only Hurts When I'm Laughing'/'I Don't Know', failed to chart in the Top 40. The album's success was no doubt helped by CBS's massive promotional campaign for which 'Are you a clone? . . . No, I'm in the Space Race' was the slogan, and little rubber mannequins of the alien featured on the front cover popped up all over the place. *Space Race* also attained the #1 spot in New Zealand, just as the band undertook a triumphant homecoming tour.

Mi-Sex toured Australia and New Zealand for the next year but found its popularity in slow decline. *Shanghaied* (arguably the band's best album) and its singles, 'Falling In and Out'/'Round and Round' (April 1981), 'Missing Person'/'Water' (August) and 'Shanghaied'/'The Bend' (November) failed to impress the record-buying public. Only 'Falling In and Out' charted in the Top 20 (#20 in June). By that stage, the likes of **Split Enz**, **The Angels**, **Cold Chisel**, **INXS** and **Men at Work** had grabbed the public attention, and Mi-Sex barely got a look in.

During November 1981, fellow New Zealander Paul Dunning-Ham (ex-Coup D'Etat) replaced Hodgkinson on drums. 'Castaway'/'Young Maniacs'

(#23 in July 1982) and 'Down the Line (Making Love on the Telephone)'/'Calling' (#37 in December) kept the band members' heads above water. At the end of 1982, Stanton was forced to leave the band due to ill-health. His place was taken by Ted 'The Head' Yanni on lead guitar. When Stanton returned four months later, Yanni remained until Colin Bayley (guitar; ex-Silent Movies) replaced him in July 1983. Mi-Sex continued to issue singles like 'Lost Time'/'Antipodes Army' (May 1983) and 'Only Thinking'/'The Name Game' (October) to little effect. American producer Bob Clearmountain worked with the band on its fourth album, *Where Do They Go?* which produced two more (flop) singles, 'Blue Day'/'Lady Janice' (March 1984) and 'Five O'Clock in the Morning'/'Why Did You Leave?' (June).

The album had a definite American slant, and indeed 'Blue Day' tickled the lower reaches of the Billboard Top 100 for a week or two. In the end, 'Blue Day' and *Where Do They Go?* sank without a trace and Mi-Sex disbanded at the end of 1984. For a few years, Mi-Sex were bona fide pop stars, having hit on a winning formula that attracted a wide fanbase. Gilpin remained in Australia and worked with a number of bands including Under Rapz. In November 1991, Gilpin was involved in a car accident as he was returning home from an Under Rapz gig in northern NSW. He lapsed into a coma from which he never recovered. He died in Southport Hospital on 6 January 1992.

Albums: *Graffiti Crimes* (CBS, 1979), *Space Race* (CBS, 1980), *Shanghaied* (CBS, 1981), *Where Do They Go?* (CBS, 1983), *Greatest Hits* (CBS, 1984).

The Missing Links

Formed: *1964*
Style: *R&B*
Original line-up: *Bob Brady (vocals), Peter Anson (guitar), Dave Boyne (guitar), Ronnie Peel (bass; ex-Mystics), Danny Cox (drums)*

If the myths and legends are to be believed, The Missing Links were the wildest Australian R&B band of the entire 1960s. Just one listen to the band's recorded legacy is confirmation enough of the band's pioneering status. Certainly The Links were the first band here to play guitars 'like The Rolling Stones used', the first to grow long unruly hair, the first to destroy their instruments on stage and the first to utilise feedback. The Links also issued one of the rarest Australian albums of all-time.

The band came into being at the start of 1964 when Danny Cox and Peter Anson decided to form an R&B outfit with Ronnie Peel, Dave Boyne and Bob Brady. When one Sydney venue owner said the new band looked like a cross between man and ape, The Missing Links were named. The original line-up recorded the 'We 2 Should Live'/'Untrue' single (March 1965) for EMI/Parlophone but broke up in July 1965. New Zealand-born Andy James (real name Neville Anderson, vocals) and John Jones (guitar, who had been in The Missing Links right at the end) decided to re-form the band. They recruited Doug Ford (guitar), Baden Hutchens (bass; ex-Showmen), Ian Thomas (drums; ex-Showmen) and Chris Gray (keyboards) for an even more fierce version than the first.

The band immediately signed a deal with Philips and cut two epochal slices of R&B/garage-mania 'You're Drivin' Me Insane'/'Something Else' (January 1966) and 'Wild About You'/'Nervous Breakdown' (February 1966). Neither single charted but such is their reputation that reissue specialists Raven Records included 'You're Drivin' Me Insane' on the essential Australian 1960s punk compilation *Ugly Things* (1980) while **The Saints** covered 'Wild About You' on their seminal *(I'm) Stranded* album. **Ross Wilson** later included a re-working of 'You're Drivin' Me Insane' on the soundtrack to Chris Löfven's 1976 feature film *Oz*.

Philips issued the legendary *The Missing Links* album, and an impossibly rare single 'H'tuom Tuhs (Pt.1)'/'H'tuom Tuhs (Pt.2)' (March 1966). 'H'tuom Tuhs' was the final track on the album, and was actually the five and a half minute 'Mama Keep Your Big Mouth Shut' (also on the album) played backwards! Thomas and Baden quit to rejoin The Showmen midway through 1966 and the four-piece Links cut the rare EP *The Links Unchained*. By August 1966, the band had split for good with Ford and James moving to Melbourne to form The Running Jumping Standing Still (The RJSS). The original RJSS line-up comprised Ford, James, Rick Dalton (bass; ex-**Pink Finks**) and Ian Robinson (drums). The band members made a name for themselves as the feedback kings of the Melbourne scene, and alongside **The Purple Hearts**, the RJSS was one of the most exciting live acts of the day.

James quit in January 1967 in order to form the short-lived Andy James Asylum with Stewie Brian (guitar), Michael Durin (organ), Allan Jones (bass) and Doug Lavery (drums). Dennis Garcia (ex-**Mixtures**) replaced Durin in late 1967. A brain haemorrhage in 1968 slowed Anderson down somewhat, but he returned to performing when he took a part in the 1969 Sydney production of the American 'tribal-love rock musical' *Hair*. Anderson returned to New Zealand in late 1971 where he joined legendary, though unrecorded, Wellington group Arkastra. Wellington at that point was the centre of a thriving underground movement which also gave rise to Highway, Gutbucket, Mammal and the Bruno Lawrence Electric Revelation and Travelling Apparition (BLERTA).

In the meantime, Peter Newing (ex-**Pleazers**) came in as The RJSS's new lead singer and the band issued two gritty R&B singles on the Sunshine label, covers of 'Diddy Wah Diddy'/'My Girl' (March 1967) and 'She's So Good to Me'/'Little Girl' (August). By the time the second single appeared, Lavery (ex-Andy James Asylum) had replaced Robinson on drums and Jamie Byrne (ex-Black Pearls) had replaced Dalton on bass. John Phillips then replaced Byrne, but by the end of 1967 The RJSS had called it a day.

Ford joined **The Master's Apprentices** and Lavery went on to **Doug Parkinson** In Focus, **The Valentines** and **Axiom**. In the 1970s, Andy James became television actor Andy Anderson with a long-running part in *The Sullivans*; recently he has been seen in *The Great Bookie Robbery* (1986), *Phoenix* (1991) and *Fire* (1995). Of the original Links, Anson joined The Id, Peel ended up in **The Pleazers**, **Rockwell T. James** and the Rhythm Aces, **La De Das** and **John Paul Young** and the All Stars, Brady played in **Python Lee Jackson** and Cox joined The Lost Souls. Raven Records put out the *The Missing Links (Australian Rock Archives)* EP in 1980 and reissued *The Missing Links* album and *The Links Unchained* EP in 1986.

Albums: *The Missing Links* (Philips, 1966; reissued on Raven, 1986), *The Raven EP LP Vol. 1* (compilation shared with **The Purple Hearts**, **The Throb** and **The Wild Cherries**; Raven, 1982).

Mississippi

Formed: *1971*
Style: *Harmony rock*
Original line-up: *John Mower (lead vocals; ex-Alison Gros), Graham Goble (vocals, guitar; ex-Alison Gros), Russ Johnson (vocals, guitar; ex-Alison Gros)*

The precursor to Mississippi was Adelaide soft-rock band Alison Gros which included Graham Goble, Englishman Russ Johnson and John Mower. Alison Gros issued its debut single, 'Naturally'/'Would You Really Have to Go?' on the independent Gamba label in 1970. The band then signed to Fable and issued two more singles, 'If I Ask You?'/'So Good' (May 1971) and 'All the Days'/'Weaver of Life' (December 1971).

None of these singles was successful; however, Alison Gros made the charts with a novelty song under the guise of Drummond. The group's gimmicky trademark was to utilise chipmunk voices mixed in with normal vocal sounds. Drummond issued four singles for the Fable label: The Beatles' 'For You Blue'/'The Grasshopper' (June 1970), 'Daddy Cool'/'Hot Mumma' (June 1971), 'You Talk Too Much'/'Scotty' (January 1972) and 'Singin' the Blues'/'I Have Changed' (November 1972). 'Daddy Cool' was a massive hit for Drummond when it hit the national #1 spot in August 1971, and stayed on the charts for 22 weeks. Once Goble, Johnson and Mower had moved on, Fable employed studio musicians for two more singles, 'The Bump'/'Listen to the Song' (March 1975) and 'Who Wants to Be a Millionaire?'/'Shall We Dance?' (September 1977).

In 1972, Mississippi relocated to Melbourne and recorded a self-titled album for the Bootleg label. Helping out in the studio were the likes of Peter Jones (piano), Geoff Cox (drums), Barry Sullivan (bass) and Graeme Lyall (flute). The album featured a harmony-rich rock sound heavily influenced by Crosby Stills Nash and Young and The Band. One of the highlights was the lush, orchestrated epic 'Save the Land'. Another of the album's standouts, 'Kings of the World', was issued as a single backed with 'City Sunday'. With 'Kings of the World' sitting at #10 on the national charts during October 1972, Goble, Johnson and Mower recruited Beeb Birtles (vocals, guitar; ex-**Zoot**, Freize), Colin DeLuca (bass; ex-Fugitives) and Derek Pellici (drums; ex-Ash) in order to tour. 'Mr Moondog'/'All Through the Day' was issued as a single in December. One of the band's early showcase gigs was at the 1973 Sunbury rock festival backed by a full orchestra.

In February 1973, Johnson left to join **Country Radio**. Kerryn Tolhurst (guitar, mandolin; ex-**Adderley Smith Blues Band**, **Country Radio**) stepped in until March when he left to form **The Dingoes**. Harvey James (lead guitar; ex-Clydehouse, Sayla) joined as a permanent member and the band supported US visitors The Jackson Five on a national tour. The band issued 'Early Morning'/'Sweet World' as a single during July. In October, DeLuca and Mower both left to be replaced by Andre Santos (bass, vocals). Two months later, Charlie Tumahai (bass, vocals; ex-**Healing Force**, **Chain**, **Friends**, Alta Mira) replaced Santos and the line-up remained stable for six months. It was during that time that Goble and Birtles developed the tight harmony sound that was to characterise their later work with **Little River Band**.

'Will I?'/'Where in the World?' took the band back into the national Top 40 during May 1974 (#31). By that stage, the band had travelled to the UK where the *Mississippi* album had been issued to some interest. The band made little headway, however, and by mid-year had begun to stagnate. James was the first to leave when he returned to Australia during June in order to join **Ariel**. That same month, 'When You're Old'/'Do I?' came out as a single in Australia. Fable also combined the singles cuts 'Will I?', 'Mr Moondog', 'Kings of the World' and 'Early Morning' for the *Mississippi* EP (August 1974). Tumahai left at the end of 1974 to join British art-rock outfit Be Bop Deluxe. In early 1975, Goble, Birtles and Pellici returned to Australia, having formulated plans for a new band. The aim was to create a textured, harmony-dominant, mass-appeal sound and style. Having recruited frontman **Glenn Shorrock** (ex-**Twilights, Axiom**), **Little River Band** was underway.

Album: *Mississippi* (Bootleg, 1972).

Mixed Relations (*see* No Fixed Address)

The Mixtures

Formed: *1965*
Style: *Pop*
Original line-up: *Rod DeClerck (vocals, bass), Laurie Arthur (vocals, guitar; ex-***Strangers***), John Creech (drums, vocals)*

The Mixtures were a curious phenomenon in some ways. After forming during the mid-1960s as a beat-pop band, they scored Top 5 hits with three ultra-commercial, novelty pop songs, made headway in the UK with a #2 hit and by 1971 comprised a group of musicians that bore no relationship to the original line-up.

The line-up of Rod DeClerck, Laurie Arthur and John Creech issued three singles on EMI/HMV: 'Koko Joe'/'I've Been Wrong' (September 1965), 'Come on Out'/'Lose Your Money' (December 1966) and 'Music Music Music'/'Maria' (March 1967). At the start of 1967, The Mixtures supported The Walker Brothers on their Australian tour. That year, Dennis Garcia (organ) and Fred Weiland (lead guitar; ex-**Strangers**) joined to fill out the band's sound. Then Laurie Arthur took over the band's management and Mick Flynn (ex-Wild Colonials) replaced DeClerck on bass. Flynn's previous band, The Wild Colonials, comprised Lindsay Shah (guitar, vocals), Frank Main (guitar), Peter Nicol (guitar) and Dave Panther (drums). The band issued three beat-pop singles on EMI/HMV: 'I Only Have Eyes for You'/'Downtown Blues' (September 1965), 'Roses are Red'/'Ain't that Loving You Baby?' (October) and 'You are My Destiny'/'Get the Picture?' (December).

At the end of 1967, Garcia left The Mixtures and Idris Jones joined as lead singer. Garcia joined Andy James Asylum. As an accomplished keyboards player, Garcia later explored the field of bio-feedback by combining synthesisers, drum machines and computers to create what he termed 'bio-electronic music'. That resulted in the (proto-new wave) synthesiser album *Jive to Stay Alive* (Seabird/Indigo, 1977) and the single 'You Can Be Anything'/'IBM Boogie'. In mid-1969, former solo pop star **Buddy England** replaced Jones in The Mixtures and the band signed to CBS. The Mixtures issued two singles on CBS, 'Here Comes Love Again'/'Fancy Meeting You Here' (October 1969) and 'Ten Thousand Children'/'Call Me Do' (March 1970). By that stage, Jones had returned as lead singer and Gary Howard replaced Creech, thereby leaving not one original member in the line-up.

In mid-1970, The Mixtures signed to the Fable label and issued a cover of Mungo Jerry's 'In the Summertime'/'Where You Are' as a single. Coinciding as it did with the 1970 radio ban on certain major labels and overseas records, The Mixtures' version of the song hit the #1 spot during August unchallenged by the original. The band followed up with an original composition in the same jaunty vein, 'The Pushbike Song'/'Who Loves You'. 'The Pushbike Song' was a prime summer ditty and caught the tempo of the time by also leaping to the coveted #1 spot. As the single peaked in Australia, Polydor issued it in the UK and Sire in the USA. The British showed their appreciation by sending the single to #2 at the start of 1971, while the Americans placed it at #44 on the *Billboard* chart.

The Mixtures took that opportunity to travel to the UK with two new members in tow: Greg Cook (vocals, guitar; ex-**Cam-Pact**) replacing Jones and Mick Holden (drums) replacing Howard. For a short time, the band was feted by UK press, radio and television, and the future looked rosy. In April, Don Lebler (drums; ex-**Axiom**) replaced Holden and former Mixtures singer Idris Jones returned to the fold by replacing Cook. Meanwhile, 'Henry Ford'/'Home Away from Home' became a modest hit, reaching #29 on the Australian chart in July 1971. Further changes occurred in The Mixtures' ranks when Peter Williams (vocals, guitar; ex-**Max Merritt and the Meteors, Groove**) replaced Idris Jones. The Mixtures returned to Australia at the end of the year, issuing two singles in quick succession, 'Never Be Untrue'/'She's Gone Away'

(October) and 'Captain Zero'/'I Wanna Go Home' (November).

The airy, giddy 'Captain Zero' reclaimed The Mixtures' magic and reached #5 in December. At the start of 1972, The Mixtures were back in the UK where, although no further hit singles were forthcoming, they made a respectable living on the club circuit. During 1972, Fable issued the EP *The Mixtures* and the album *The Best of the Mixtures*. In May 1972, Chris Spooner replaced Flynn on bass and the band issued two singles on the UA label, 'Dazzle Easy, Diane'/'Found Out Where It's at' (November 1973) and 'Slow Train'/'My Home on the Murrumbidgee' (May 1974). By that stage the band had returned to Australia and the Weiland/Lebler/Williams/Spooner line-up signed a new deal with Festival Records. The Mixtures issued a self-titled album and a new single, 'Down Under Girls'/'My Neck of the Woods' (October 1974). One more single appeared in April 1975, 'Skateboard Jive'/'Come Together for the Games', before the band called it quits in 1976.

Albums: *In the Summertime* (Fable, 1970), *The Pushbike Song* (Summit, 1971), *Best of the Mixtures* (Fable, 1972), *The Mixtures* (Festival, 1974).

Models

Formed: *1978*
Style: *Pop*
Original line-up: *Sean Kelly (guitar, vocals; ex-***Teenage Radio Stars***), Ash Wednesday (synthesiser; ex-***JAB***), Pierre Voltaire (real name Peter Sutcliffe, aka Mr Pierre, bass; ex-***Teenage Radio Stars, JAB***), Janis Friedenfelds (aka Johnny Crash, drums; ex-***JAB***)*

Alongside The Boys Next Door/**The Birthday Party**, Models were one of the first Melbourne bands to rise out of the ashes of that city's hothouse punk/new wave explosion of the late 1970s with a clear vision and wider appeal. While **The Birthday Party** was hell-bent on kicking down the established parameters of rock music, Models were more clearly pop-oriented, and eventually reaped the benefits of their vision.

The band came together in August 1978 when Sean Kelly joined up with the remnants of **JAB**: Ash Wednesday, Pierre Voltaire and Janis Friedenfelds. Voltaire was quickly replaced by Mark Ferrie (ex-Carrl Myriad Band, Leisuremasters). Wednesday left the band in August 1979 to be replaced by Andrew Duffield (ex-Whirlywirld). Many of the band's early live classics like 'Body Shop', 'Whisper Through the Wall', 'Years Ago', 'The Other People Incident' and 'Brave New World' did not see release on record. The new line-up issued two independent, gig giveaway singles, 'Early Morning Brain (It's Not Quite the Same as Sobriety)' (shared with The Boys Next Door's 'Scatterbrain' on the flip side, October 1979) and 'Owe You Nothing'/'Progressive Office Pools' (August 1980). The band actually broke up in November 1979, but resumed touring after a successful reunion gig on New Year's Eve 1979. Models undertook an exhaustive schedule of local gigs and interstate tours, with support slots to international visitors like The B52s, The Vapours, The Ramones, XTC and Magazine.

Models

By mid-1980, the band's off-beat pop sound and live popularity had attracted the attention of several major record companies. Mushroom Records eventually signed Models and issued the band's independently recorded debut album *Alphabravocharliedeltaechofoxtrotgolf* in November 1980. The band refused to issue a single from the album, but Mushroom put out 'Two People Per Sq Km'/'Uncontrollable Boy (I'm Just an)', 'Young Rodents' as a promotional only 12-inch EP which was sent to radio stations. 1981 commenced with the departure of drummer Friedenfelds, who joined **Sacred Cowboys**. Ex-Swingers member Buster Stiggs joined in time for a national tour support slot to The Police. Derek Green, vice-president of A&M Records (home to The Police) was so impressed with Models that he offered the band an international deal.

Models flew to the UK and recorded the album *Local &/or General* at Farmyard Studios with producer Steve Tayler. *Local &/or General* (October 1981) reached #32 on the national chart, and produced the single 'Local &/or General'/'Telstar' (November). Prior to leaving for the UK, the band recorded demos at Richmond Records with producer Tony Cohen. The tracks combined spontaneous experimentation with economic arrangements and turned out so well that Mushroom issued them as the 10-inch mini-album *Cut Lunch* in July. Buoyed by the whimsical pop tune 'Two Cabs to the Toucan', *Cut Lunch* sold well enough to register #32 on the national chart.

A series of line-up changes plagued the band throughout 1982. First Stiggs and Ferrie quit to be replaced by Graham Scott (drums), John Rowell (guitar, both ex-Curse) and **James Freud** (bass). Freud had already enjoyed a relatively successful solo career as leader of **James Freud** and the Radio Stars and **James Freud** and Berlin. 'Modern Girl' had been a #12 national hit for Freud in August 1980, and the album *Breaking Silence* had sold well. Freud brought a great deal of commercial pop savvy and confidence into the band. Scott and Rowell both left in May, closely followed by long-term member Duffield. Kelly and Freud then recruited New Zealand-born Barton Price (ex-Crocodiles, Sardine v) to fill the drum spot. In the meantime, Mark Ferrie had issued a remixed version of 'Unhappy' (from the *Local &/or General* album) as a solo single backed with 'The Ton' (May 1982).

The band's next single, 'On'/'The Whole Story' (August 1982) was produced by **Lobby Loyde**. It reached #1 on the independent charts and was accompanied by a bizarre video produced by the Rich Kids. Gus Till (keyboards; ex-**Ears**, **Beargarden**) joined Models briefly toward the end of 1982, but by December a revitalised Duffield had rejoined. Models then hit their commercial stride with the release of the album *The Pleasure of Your Company . . .* (October 1983) which rose to #12 on the national chart (#6 in Melbourne). Producer Nick Launay (Public Image Ltd, **Birthday Party**, **Midnight Oil**) placed a greater emphasis on the rhythm section to provide a more flexible, dance-oriented sound.

The band was being referred to as a 'crossover' act and certainly sold more records than the other two best-known unconventional Melbourne bands of the day, **The Birthday Party** and **Hunters & Collectors**. The ebullient 'I Hear Motion'/'No Talking' (September 1983) single reached #16 nationally (#10 in Melbourne) during October. Hot on the heels of the album's success, Models scored the prestigious support slot to David Bowie's Serious Moonlight tour of Australia. Oddly enough, the band's next three singles, 'No Shoulders No Head'/'A Rainy Day' (December 1983), 'God Bless America'/'Watch Your Mouth' (April 1984) and 'Big on Love'/'Preacher from the Black Lagoon' (produced by American Reggie Lucas; October 1984), failed to chart convincingly. 'Big on Love' was the most successful when it peaked at #21 in December. 1984 ended with the recruitment of sax player James Valentine and the departure of Duffield in controversial circumstances. His place was taken by ex-Berlin member Roger Mason. Duffield issued a solo album, *Ten Happy Fingers*, on his own Retrograde label in 1988. **Wendy Matthews** joined Models as back-up vocalist and her input added significantly to the band's sound.

1985 saw the band attain its commercial zenith with the release of the *Out of Mind Out of Sight* album (#2 on the national chart in September). The single 'Barbados'/'Tropic of Cancer' also made #2 nationally (March 1985). 'Barbados' was a reggae-tinged pop ballad written by Duffield and sung by Freud, and despite its sunny title was a morbid tale of alcoholism and impending suicide. The video, directed by Richard Lowenstein, was influenced by *The Deer Hunter* and several scenes had to be edited out in order for it to be aired on prime-time television.

The band's next single, 'Out of Mind Out of Sight'/'Seeing is Believing' (July 1985) shot to #1 on the national chart during August, establishing Models as certified pop stars. The song was written and sung by Freud, and was an energetic distillation of his glam-pop roots and the band's brassy R&B predilections. It was the only Australian-recorded single to attain #1 status during 1985. The band's next two singles, 'Cold Fever'/'Another Rainy Day' (October) and Kelly's reflective 'King of Kings'/ 'Down in the Garden', 'Out of Mind' (live) (December), were minor hits. In 1986 Models flew to the UK to record *Models' Media* with producers Julian Mendelsohn and Mark Opitz, at Trevor Horn's state-of-the-art Sarm West Studios in London. Meanwhile, the Geffen label had released the 'Out of Mind Out of Sight' single in the USA (where it peaked at a respectable #36 in June), and the band toured there during November as special guests of English synth-pop band Orchestral Manoeuvres in the Dark (OMD).

Models' Media came out in December 1986 and reached #12 at the start of 1987. Its three singles, the R&B flavoured 'Evolution'/'Hell to Breakfast' (August 1986), 'Let's Kiss'/'A Man in a Boat' (November) and 'Hold on'/'Some Kind of Anger' (March 1987) reached #21, #27 and #21 respectively. 'Evolution' was included on the soundtrack to the American film *Soul Man*. Its inclusion was quite an honour for a white, Australian rock band because the rest of the soundtrack comprised black, American soul artists. In January, Models took part in the monumental Australian Made tour across the country. Also on the bill were **Mental as Anything**, **The**

Triffids, **I'm Talking**, **The Saints**, **Divinyls**, **Jimmy Barnes** and **INXS**. Models issued a version of The Beatles' 'Oh! Darling'/'Echoes in a Town Called Yamaha' as a single in September 1987. It was not successful and proved to be the band's final single. The Thank You Goodnight tour at the start of 1988 was ostensibly run to cover debts and it was obvious Models were on their last legs. The band's break-up was not made official until June 1988.

Kelly initially went solo before forming the popular **Absent Friends** with Duffield, Valentine, singer **Wendy Matthews** and **INXS** bassist Garry Gary Beers. After **Absent Friends** split in 1990 (the band was never designed to be a long-term venture), Kelly formed the critically acclaimed R&B/soul/funk outfit **The Dukes** which lasted until 1994. **Wendy Matthews** has enjoyed a successful career as a vocalist in her own right. James Valentine moved into television work (as presenter of the ABC-TV's *Afternoon Show* and *Racket*) and later radio broadcasting with the ABC's Radio National.

James Freud relaunched his solo career in 1989 with the Bernard Edwards' produced *Step Into the Heat* album. It was Mushroom's most expensive album ever, but it was not successful. Freud then teamed up for two years with **Mental as Anything's** Martin Plaza as dance pop duo **Beatfish**. Mushroom issued the retrospective *Models' Collection* in November 1993. That same month, Mushroom also reissued 'I Hear Motion' as a CD single which featured four remixes of the song courtesy of techno-dance outfit **Boxcar**.

Albums: *Alphabravocharliedeltaechofoxtrotgolf* (Mushroom/Festival, 1980), *Cut Lunch* (10-inch mini-album, Mushroom/Festival, 1981), *Local &/or General* (Mushroom/Festival, 1981), *The Pleasure of Your Company . . .* (Mushroom/Festival, 1983), *Out of Mind Out of Sight* (Mushroom/Festival, 1985), *Models' Media* (Mushroom/Festival, 1986), *Models' Collection* (compilation, Mushroom/Festival, 1993).

Matt Moffitt (*see* Matt Finish)

The Moffs

Formed: *1984*
Style: *Psychedelia*
Original line-up: *Tom Kazas (guitar, vocals), Nick Potts (organ), David Byrnes (bass), Alan Hislop (drums)*

Sydney band The Moffs was one of the first local groups of the 1980s to play a very English-derived, 1960s-influenced brand of psychedelia. The band's ethereal soundscapes placed them somewhere between (Syd Barrett-era) Pink Floyd and more obscure outfits like Kaleidoscope. The Moffs also incorporated esoteric, Middle Eastern elements into their songs.

Singer/guitarist Tom Kazas was the band's leading light. He wrote the bulk of the band's material and it was his melancholy vocals, flighty guitar riffs and dreamy mellotron washes that defined the sound. John Needham issued the debut Moffs' single 'Another Day in the Sun'/'Clarodomineaux' on his Citadel label during May 1985. By the time The Moffs recorded their debut album at the end of the year Mick Duncan had replaced Nick Potts on organ. *The Moffs* (June 1986) was dominated by lengthy mood pieces like 'I Once Knew' and the sumptuous, 12-minute instrumental 'The Meadowsong'. The line-up had changed again for the band's second single, 'Flowers'/'By the Breeze' (December 1986); Damon Giles had replaced Duncan on organ and Andrew Byrnes had replaced Alan Hislop on drums. In mid-1987, Scott Barnes replaced Giles and the band issued a third single, 'The Traveller'/'Quaker's Drum' (October).

The Kazas/Byrnes/Byrnes/Barnes line-up recorded the excellent *Labyrinth* album (July 1988), which furthered the band's atmospheric flights of fancy with tracks like 'Desert Sun' and 'Stealing Cake (to Eat the Moon)'. It was to be the band's last recording, although Citadel did compile the early singles and some choice album cuts on the 'Best of' set *Entomology* (December 1988). With the break-up of the band in 1989, Kazas launched his solo career and David Byrnes joined hard rock band Lazarus. Steve Casey (vocals; ex-Blood Guts'n'Beer), Drazan Peko (guitar, ex-Government Downfall, Aberration, Blood Guts'n'Beer) and Paul Mueller (drums) completed the Lazarus line-up. This heavyweight (in more ways than one) outfit drew inspiration from a variety of sources, ranging from British heavy metal (Motorhead, Tank) to Jimi Hendrix.

The band's adventurous brand of riff-rock was heard to good advantage on the CD EP *Cherokee* which came out on the Shagpile label at the end of 1991. Around that time, Oxx (real name Simon Cooper; ex-**Massive Appendage**) replaced Mueller on drums. The band's debut album, *Loud and Hairy*, came out posthumously in September 1993 (on the Shagpile label through Shock). It featured the band's cover of the Tank song 'Filth Hounds of Hades', plus other live favourites like the original tunes 'Piledriver' and 'Burn in Hell'.

In the meantime, Red Eye's off-shoot label Third Eye issued Kazas's debut solo album *Delinquenescence*. In 1991, Kazas formed Taj Orange which comprised Jim Hatzis (bass) and ex-Moffs member Andrew Byrnes (drums). The band issued a mini-album, *In a Sea with Taj Orange.* In 1992, Kazas produced **You Am I's** 'Can't Get Started' CD EP. In March 1993, he issued the album *Book of Saturdays* and assembled the ambitious Saturday Septet in order to tour. The band comprised Kazas on vocals, guitar and synthesiser, Tatjana Grujic (vocals), John Hollowell (keyboards), Lenid Marks (guitar), Vangelis Papageorgiou (flute, sax), Stella Bakopoulos (violin), Jim Hatzis (bass) and Andrew Byrnes (drums). In 1994, Citadel issued The Moffs' compilation *Psychedelicatessen*, and Kazas revived the band for a one-off national tour. In 1995, Kazas issued the album *Tom Kazas.*

Moffs albums: *The Moffs* (Citadel, 1986), *Labyrinth* (Citadel, 1988), *Entomology* (compilation, Citadel, 1988), *Psychedelicatessen* (compilation, Citadel, 1994); ***Tom Kazas solo albums:*** *Delinquenescence* (Third Eye, 1989), *Book of Saturdays* (Shock, 1993), *Tom Kazas* (Ravenswood/MDS, 1995).

Moir Sisters

Formed: *1970*
Style: *Pop, folk*

The Scottish-born Moir sisters (Jean, Margo and Lesley) migrated to Australia with their parents during the early 1960s. The girls developed the tight, three-part harmony style for which they became known. EMI signed the Moir Sisters following their successes on television talent shows like *New Faces* and *Showcase.*

Moir Sisters' debut single 'Good Morning How are You?'/'We will Never Change' reached #6 on the national charts during August 1974. It was to be the girls' only national hit single. The album *Lost: Somewhere Beyond Harmony* displayed the girls' confident style and strong original material. 'Harmony Blues'/'Stop the Music' (January 1975) was issued as a second single, followed by 'Don't Tell Mama'/'Wandering Hope' (April). In 1978, the Moir Sisters travelled to Los Angeles and then to the UK to record. The album *State of Shock* appeared later in the year under the name The Moirs. In the early 1980s, The Moirs signed to WEA and issued two singles , 'So Excited'/'You Won't Get Me' (September 1982) and 'Running Scared'/'See You Coming' (October 1983). The sisters continued to perform, and Margot Moir issued a solo single, 'Scarlet Skies'/'Tightrope' (1989), and album, *Loving You* (1996).

Albums: *Lost: Somewhere Beyond Harmony* (EMI, 1974), *State of Shock* (as The Moirs, Rocket, 1978), *Loving You* (Margot Moir solo, Newmarket, 1996).

Moler

Formed: *1994*
Style: *Indie guitar pop*
Original line-up: *Helen Cattanach (bass, vocals; ex-T-Bones, Kick House, The Stiff Kittens), Julien Poulson (guitar; ex-Snappers, Kick House, The Stiff Kittens), David Peacock (drums)*

Melbourne trio Moler originally came together under the name of Snuff in 1993. Prior to that, Helen Cattanach and Julien Poulson had worked together in The Stiff Kittens with Rob Lastdrager (drums, vocals; ex-Snappers, T-Bones). After playing gigs around Melbourne, the members travelled overseas. Cattanach and Poulson formed Kick House in Hong Kong, and Lastdrager played in a blues combo in Amsterdam. The three reunited in London during 1992 with Richard Webb (vocals, guitar; ex-Strange Fruit, T-Bones). As The Stiff Kittens, the band issued the CD EP 'As You Walk' on the UK independent label Psychic Records before returning to Australia.

As Snuff (Cattanach, Poulson and David Peacock), the band issued the CD EP *Driven* in 1995. Following that, Snuff became Moler and signed to Mushroom Records' subsidiary label Infectious in early 1996. Moler swiftly built-up a buzz around the Melbourne independent scene with its mix of noisy

Moler

guitar fuzz, hard-driving beats, strident pop melodies and Cattanach's alternately sweet'n'purring and aggressive vocals. There were a number of parallels to be drawn between other contemporary three-pieces like **Spiderbait**, **silverchair**, **Pollyanna** and **Regurgitator**, although Moler never strayed too far from its pop base. The band's influences included seminal American bands of the calibre of The Ramones, Hüsker Dü, Blondie and Sonic Youth.

Moler's debut CD EP for Infectious, *On Special*, appeared in June 1996. The lead-off track, 'Shopping Trolley', displayed plenty of appeal. Moler followed that up with the CD EP *Coaster* (September) which included the fiesty 'Parallel Lines'. The band toured with local bands like **Snout** and **Magic Dirt**, as well as supporting overseas visitors Ash, Garageland and Weezer.

Steve Boyle replaced Peacock on drums in early 1997. Moler continued with the release of its third CD EP *Infatuation* (May 1997). The lead track, 'Infatuation', became an alternative favourite courtesy of regular airplay on Triple J. The CD EP included three bonus cuts, the screaming 'In the Sun', a supercharged cover of The Buzzcocks' 'Ever Fallen in Love?' and the sugar-coated but assertive 'Perfect World'. The band completed work on its debut album, *Golden Duck*, with producer Lindsay Gravina. It came out in October 1997, preceded by the CD single 'Invite Me to Your Party'.

Album: *Golden Duck* (Infectious/Mushroom/Sony, 1997).

The Moles

Formed: *1989*
Style: *Pop*
Original line-up: *Richard Davies (vocals, guitar), Glen Fredericks (bass, keyboards), Carl Zadro (drums)*

Enigmatic Sydney band The Moles emerged in 1989 playing a sparse, divergent and restless brand of folk pop and vintage psychedelia set to a quirky backing. Reference points included New Zealand bands on the Flying Nun label like The Clean, The Bats and Tall Dwarfs, very early Pixies, the softer side of The Velvet Underground and even The Beach Boys. The original three-piece line-up had formed in 1988 as Warm Guns, before changing names to Five Acre Virgin and then finally the Moles in 1989.

The band's debut single, 'Propellor'/'With Body Wife Seven Days' (February 1990), and two releases on the Seaside label (via Waterfront), the album *Untune the Sky* (February 1991) and the four-track, 12-inch EP *Tendrills and Paracetamol* (September 1991), sounded fresh and playful enough to garner considerable cult praise. That extended to the UK when the Fire label issued *Untune the Sky* in 1992. Just prior to the local release of *Untune the Sky*, Warren Armstrong took over on bass and Shasha Kwa joined on keyboard and vocals, while Glenn Fredericks travelled to the UK for six months. The Davies/Fredericks/Zadro/Armstrong line-up recorded *Tendrills and Paracetamol* in mid-1991, with assistance from Kwa, Ben Ker (guitar) and Jillian Cordeiro (keyboards, vocals).

Richard Davies travelled to New York where he recorded four songs for release as the double 7-inch set, *The Moles: Double Single*, on the Ringers Lactate label in the US and Seaside locally. Having developed his interest in Americana, Davies teamed up with classically trained arranger Eric Matthews to record under the name of Cardinal. The Flydaddy label issued the Cardinal EP *Toy Bell* in late 1993, to be followed a year later by the full-length album *Cardinal* (November 1994). With Davies writing and singing most of the material, and Matthews concentrating on the meticulous arrangements, the pair produced layered, orchestral pop that recalled Love, The Beach Boys, The Left Banke and latter-day Zombies.

The Moles' second album, *Instinct* (issued as a companion piece to *Cardinal*), featured Davies backed by various guest musicians. Davies recorded his debut solo album, *There's Never Been a Crowd Like This*, with Ronald Jones from US avant-pop outfit The Flaming Lips. Avoiding the baroque constructs of *Cardinal*, Davies created an engaging album that mixed English-influenced, rustic folk pop with US country leanings.

Albums: *Untune the Sky* (Seaside/Waterfront, 1991), *Cardinal* (with Eric Matthews, Hypnotized/Shock, 1994), *Instinct* (Hypnotized/Shock, 1994), *There's Never Been A Crowd Like This* (Richard Davies solo, Flydaddy, 1996).

Mondo Rock

Formed: *1976*
Style: *Rock*
Original line-up: **Ross Wilson** *(vocals, guitar; ex-***Pink Finks, Party Machine, Procession, Sons of the Vegetal Mother, Daddy Cool, Mighty Kong***), Peter Laffy (guitar; ex-Fox,* **Freeway***), Greg Cook (keyboards, guitar; ex-***Cam-Pact***, Skylight,* **Phil Manning** *Band), Mike Clarke (bass; ex-Mick Rogers and Eclipse), Bob Bickerton (drums; ex-Rock Granite and the Profiles)*

The venerable **Ross Wilson** can take pride of place as one of the most important musicians Australia has ever produced. He commenced his career during the mid-1960s with teenage R&B band **The Pink Finks**, and was still active into the 1990s. By way of ceaseless touring and the release of a series of sophisticated pop rock albums, Wilson was able to establish Mondo Rock as one of the most popular acts in Australia during the early 1980s.

With the final break-up of **Daddy Cool** in September 1975, Wilson took time off to sort out legal wranglings with his former record company Wizard, and to get his own label Oz (formed with Glenn Wheatley) off the ground. Wilson also issued his debut solo single, 'Living in the Land of Oz'/'Who's Gonna Love You?' in August 1976. In November, he unveiled his new band, Ross Wilson's Mondo Rock, with the above line-up. By February 1977, the Mondo Rock line-up featured Wilson, Peter Laffy, Ian 'Willie' Winter (guitar; ex-**Carson**, **Daddy Cool**, **John Paul Young** and the All Stars), Barry Sullivan (bass; ex-**Chain**, **Renée Geyer** Band, Silver Sun) and Trevor Courtney (drums; ex-Chants R&B, **Cam-Pact**, **Vibrants**, Skylight, **Stylus**). The band attracted a strong following on the Melbourne pub circuit, but broke up mid-year.

In November 1977, Wilson formed a new line-up of Gunther Gorman (guitar, vocals; ex-**Home**, **Daddy Cool**, **Richard Clapton** Band), Tony Slavich (keyboards; ex-**Richard Clapton** Band, **Ariel**), Simon Gyllies (bass) and Iain McClennan (drums; ex-**Richard Clapton** Band, **Ariel**). Gorman left before the band played live and his place was taken by jazz guitarist Chris Jones (ex-Zoo). By mid-1978, the line-up comprised Wilson, Slavich, Gyllies and McClennan, plus the returning Peter Laffy (by then ex-One Nite Stand) and newcomer Randy Bulpin (guitar; ex-Toads, Ready Rubbed, One Nite Stand). In August 1978, Mondo Rock issued its excellent debut single, 'The Fugitive Kind'/'The Breaking Point' (on the Oz label), which reached #26 on the national chart during October 1978. 'The Fugitive Kind' appeared on the Oz label's Various Artists album *Living in the Land of Oz* (as did Wilson's 'Living in the Land of Oz').

Slavich left in November to join **Mike Rudd's** Instant Replay and Mondo Rock continued as a five-piece. That line-up issued the singles 'Love Shock'/'The Mood' (May 1979), 'Searching for My Baby'/'Send Me Someone' (September) and 'Primal Park'/'Live Wire' (November) plus the album *Primal Park* (October). Just as the band was stepping up its gig schedule to promote the release of *Primal Park*, McLennan contracted hepatitis and was forced to leave. Eddie Van Roosendael (ex-**Stiletto**) took his place initially, followed by Gil Matthews (ex-**Billy Thorpe** and the Aztecs). McLennan recovered and joined **The Sports**. He went on to issue a couple of solo records, including the albums *Through the Roof* (1989) and *Mauve* (1991).

Wilson split Mondo Rock in February 1980, but had launched a revised line-up by April. Initially retaining Matthews, the band also comprised Eric McCusker (guitar; ex-**Matchbox**), James Black (guitar, keyboards; ex-Rum Jungle, **Russell Morris** Band) and Paul Christie (bass; ex-**Kevin Borich Express**). McCusker was a songwriter of considerable skill and attention to detail, and he proved to be a valuable addition to Mondo Rock. Indeed, he wrote many of the band's biggest hit singles. Mondo Rock issued a new single, 'State of the Heart'/'Mona Lisa (She Smiles)' in October 1980, after which Andy Buchanan (ex-Darryl Cotton Band) replaced Matthews on drums. The gorgeous ballad 'State of the Heart' reached #6 on the national chart during November. John James (J.J.) Hackett (ex-**Stars**, **Fabulaires**) then replaced Buchanan on drums during March 1981. The next month, the single 'Cool World'/'Back on the Outside' reached #8 nationally.

Mondo Rock was now one of the biggest bands on the national touring circuit. The band consolidated its premier status with the release of the best-selling *Chemistry* album (#2 in August 1981) and two further hit singles, 'Chemistry'/'Searching for My Baby' (#20 in August) and 'Summer of '81'/'Mona Lisa (She Smiles)', 'The Fugitive Kind' (#31 in December). Atlantic Records issued the *Chemistry* album worldwide during February 1982. Atlantic also issued an edited version of 'State of the Heart' as the band's debut single in the USA, which caused a great deal of anguish on the part of Wilson and the song's writer, McCusker. The pair had faith in the song as a whole, but Atlantic executives felt that four minutes 20 seconds was too long for a radio-friendly single. 'State of the Heart' failed to chart, but expatriate **Rick Springfield** later enjoyed a considerable US hit with a rendition of the song that was almost identical to Mondo Rock's original, full-length version.

Meanwhile, the band continued its hit run at home with the *Nuovo Mondo* album (July 1982; #7 in August) and its three singles, 'No Time'/'Il Mondo Cafe' (#11 in July), 'The Queen and Me'/'Domination' (#40 in November) and 'In Another Love'/'Is It Any Wonder?' (February 1983). Christie left the band in September 1982 to form **The Party Boys**. His place was taken by James Gillard (ex-**Western Flyer**, **Russell Morris** and the Rubes, **Broderick Smith's** Big Combo). Mondo Rock started work on a new album in August 1983. The band scored its biggest hit when the single 'Come Said the Boy'/'Gotta Get Out' reached #2 on the national chart in March 1984. The *Modern Bop* album made its debut on the chart at #5 during April, attaining the #2 spot a week later. The second single lifted off the album, 'Baby Wants to Rock'/ 'Winds Light to Variable' made #18 during May, but the next single, 'Modern Bop'/'Cost of Living', just missed the Top 40.

In 1985, Mondo Rock signed to Polydor for the compilation album *Up to the Moment* (June) which also featured the new singles 'Good Advice'/'Dark Secrets' (December 1984) and 'The Moment'/'Take Me Away' (May 1985). *Up to the Moment* reached #5 in July. The band's sixth album, *Boom Baby Boom* (September 1986), featured the line-up of Wilson, McCusker, Hackett, Gillard, Andrew Ross (sax; ex-Arms & Legs) and Duncan Veall (keyboards). The album produced three singles, 'Rule of Threes'/ 'Roman Holiday' (August 1986), 'Primitive Love Rites'/'Under Lights' (November) and 'Boom Baby Boom'/'Do It Yourself' (June 1987). None of the singles was a big chart hit locally, but 'Primitive Love Rites' managed to reach the Top 10 in certain regional pockets in the USA. It peaked there nationally at #73. Mondo Rock issued the hard-edged *Aliens* 12-inch EP in November 1987, but by 1988 the band had run its course. Wilson took a break from Mondo Rock, and issued his debut solo album, *Dark Side of the Man* in 1989. A year later he revived Mondo Rock for a new album, *Why Fight It?*

The studio band that appeared on the album comprised Wilson, McCusker, New Zealander Ian Belton (bass; ex-QED, **Ian Moss** Band) and South African producer Ricky Fataar (drums; ex-Beach Boys, Blondie Chaplin, Rutles), plus American session players Bernie Worrell (keyboards; ex-James Brown, Funkadelic) and Waddy Wachtel (guitar; ex-Linda Ronstadt). Wachtel also produced the album. *Why Fight It?* (May 1991) yielded three CD singles, 'Why Fight It?' (November 1990), 'I Had You in Mind' (February 1991) and 'Soul Reason' (May). The album was not successful and Wilson was unable to re-establish his band at the forefront of Australian music. He dissolved Mondo Rock in order to work the local pub circuit with his new venture RAW.

Albums: *Primal Park* (Oz/EMI, 1979), *Chemistry* (Avenue/Festival, 1981), *Nuovo Mondo* (WEA, 1982), *Modern Bop* (WEA, 1984), *Up to the Moment* (Polydor, 1985), *Boom Baby Boom* (Polydor, 1986), *Aliens* (mini-album, Polydor, 1987), *Why Fight It?* (BMG, 1991).

The Monitors

Formed: *1980*
Style: *Pop*
Original line-up: *Mark Moffatt, Terry McCarthy*

The Monitors were a studio outfit put together by producer Mark Moffatt and advertising creative director Terry McCarthy. The Monitors' simplistic, synthesised pop drew parallels with UK outfit The Buggles, who had a hit around the same period, 'Video Killed the Radio Star'. Moffatt had played bass during the mid-1970s with The Carol Lloyd Band. He moved into engineering and production work, and one of his first efforts was working with **The Saints** on their milestone debut independent single, '(I'm) Stranded'. Since then he has produced albums for **Swanee**, **Mondo Rock**, **Jimmy and the Boys**, **Jenny Morris**, **Mental as Anything**, **Shane Howard**, **The Cockroaches** and **Yothu Yindi**, plus the soundtrack to the feature film *Starstruck*.

The Monitors' debut single, 'Singing in the '80s'/'Nautilus', reached the national Top 20 (#16) in September 1980. They followed that up with 'Nobody Told Me'/'Wishful Thinking' (#32 in June 1981), 'Who Do You Think It Was?'/'Midnight Club' (August 1982) and 'Having You Around'/'Last One to Know' (December 1982). The Monitors also issued the album *Back from Their Recent Illness* in October 1982. For the album, Moffatt and McCarthy were joined by Ricky Fataar. South African-born drummer/producer Fataar had worked internationally with the likes of The Beach Boys, Blondie Chaplin, Eric Idle's Beatles pastiche band The Rutles, Joe Walsh and Jennifer Warnes. He settled in Australia during the early 1980s and swiftly became a popular figure on the session/production circuit.

Moffatt and Fataar played on, and produced, **Tim Finn's** debut solo album *Escapade*. Since then, Fataar's credits have included work with **Renée Geyer**, **Marc Hunter**, **Jenny Morris**, **Ross Wilson**, **Mondo Rock** and **Crowded House** to name a few. Incidentally, the video for 'Singing in the '80s' featured the 11-year-old Blakeney twins Gillian and Gayle, who later went on to play sisters Caroline and Christina Alessi in popular television soapie *Neighbours*. The sisters followed the lead of **Kylie Minogue** and **Jason Donovan** and recorded a single, 'All Mixed Up' (1991), as The Twins with the British hit-making team Stock Aitken Waterman (SAW).

Album: *Back from Their Recent Illness* (Festival, 1982).

The Moodists

Formed: 1980
Style: Rock
Original line-up: **Dave Graney** *(vocals; ex-Sputniks), Steve Miller (guitar; ex-Sputniks), Steve Carmen (bass), Clare Moore (drums; ex-Sputniks)*

During the 1980s, The Moodists were something of a well-kept secret. In fact, over six years of existence the band spent only half that time in Australia. In the UK, where the band based itself for three years, it was a different matter. There The Moodists were acknowledged as proto-grunge noisemakers. The band's name is often mentioned in the same breath as **The Birthday Party**, **Laughing Clowns**, **The Go-Betweens**, **The Triffids** and **Scientists** when assessing Australia's contribution to 1980s British music. Nevertheless, The Moodists were an important band in the history of Australian rock, not least of all for giving us the wonderful **Dave Graney**.

The nucleus of The Moodists grew out of Adelaide band Sputniks, which comprised Graney, Clare Moore, Steve Miller, Phillip Marks (guitar) and **Liz Dealey** (bass). Sputniks' contemporaries on the Adelaide independent scene included **The Dagoes**, **Young Modern**, The Accountants and Bad Poets. Sputniks issued one independent single, 'Second Glance'/'Our Boys', in 1979 before relocating to Melbourne at the end of 1980. Only Graney, Moore and Miller made the move to Melbourne, where they were joined by Chris Walsh (ex-Negatives, Fabulous Marquises) who replaced original bass player Steve Carmen.

Walsh's previous band, The Fabulous Marquises, virtually had 'inner-city supergroup' status from the outset. As well as Walsh, the band comprised Mr Pierre (real name Peter Sutcliffe; vocals, guitar; ex-**Teenage Radio Stars**, **JAB**, **Models**), Edward Clayton-Jones (guitar, synth) and Katherine Denney (piano, organ). The band formed after Mr Pierre had been ousted from the nascent **Models** in late 1978. The Marquises' sound was sparse and electronic. The band's solitary single, 'Honeymoon'/'1,2,3, Factory' (September 1980), was initially included as part of the Unforgettable Music Box Set of three singles, alongside Ron Rude's Piano Piano and Microfilm. Ron Rude (head of the Unforgettable Music label) produced The Marquises' single. Rude also included the Marquises' track 'From My Heart to My Hands' on the Various Artists album *From Belgrave with Love* (1981). Clayton-Jones was later in **The Wreckery**.

The Moodists played gigs on the St Kilda/Carlton inner-city circuit alongside the likes of **Models**, Whirlywirld, **International Exiles**, **Little Murders** and the nascent **Hunters & Collectors**. Au-go-go Records boss Bruce Milne recognised the band's potential and issued the singles 'Where the Trees Walk Downhill'/'I Should have Been There' (October 1981) and 'Gone Dead'/'Chad's Car' (June 1982), plus the mini-album *Engine Shudder* (January 1983). In April 1983, Mick Turner (guitar; ex-Sick Things, **Fungus Brains**) joined, adding his squalling guitar work to the band's unnerving, avant-garage rock noise. *Engine Shudder* garnered positive reviews in the UK music press, and the Red Flame label issued it at the end of 1983. Even before The Moodists had established a reputation beyond the independent scene in Australia, they had decided to relocate to the UK. The band left for London in October 1983, where they played gigs with fellow expatriates **The Go-Betweens** and **Nick Cave**.

In 1984, Red Flame issued the band's full-length debut album *Thirsty's Calling* (April), plus the singles 'Runaway'/'Chevrolet Rise' (April) and 'Enough Legs to Live on'/'Can't Lose Her' (October). The album again drew favourable reviews, although the fickle UK music press tended to harp on about **The Birthday Party** comparisons. Even such ludicrous descriptions as 'garage jazz-punk' only hinted at the band's powerful sound. The Moodists toured Europe and the USA before returning to Australia in November 1984. In the meantime, Red Flame issued the band's second mini-album, *Double Life*, which contained tracks like the rumbling 'Six Dead Birds'. Following a support slot to UK visitors Public Image Ltd in January 1985, Mick Turner left the band. By May, The Moodists had returned to the UK and recruited new guitarist Malcolm Ross (ex-Orange Juice).

With the change of personnel, The Moodists underwent a musical transformation as well. The 12-inch EP *Justice and Money Too* (on the Creation label; August 1985) featured light, bluesy pop augmented with strings and piano. The band issued two more 12-inch EPs (on the Time/Abstract label), *Take the Red Carpet Out of Town* (October 1985) and *The Moodists* (February 1986). They revealed that, while The Moodists had toned down somewhat, the band had lost none of its ability to craft unique and compelling songs. By that stage, Walsh had left the band to return to Australia, and The Moodists recruited another ex-Orange Juice alumnus, Dave McClymont, as replacement. By the middle of 1986, The Moodists had split up. Miller became tour manager for **The Triffids** and Graney abandoned the band concept for a year. In 1987, he launched his new band, **Dave Graney** with the Coral Snakes.

Walsh later rejoined Graney in The White Buffaloes; by 1996, Walsh was playing in a band called Love Moods with Bruce Milne.

Albums: *Engine Shudder* (mini-album, Au-go-go, 1983), *Thirsty's Calling* (UK only, Red Flame/Virgin, 1984), *Double Life* (UK only, Red Flame/Virgin, 1985).

Moondog (*see* James Freud)

Jenny Morris

Style: *Pop, soul*

New Zealand-born singer Jenny Morris (b. 1956) started out with Wellington neo-feminist girl group Wide Mouthed Frogs. In 1980 she joined new wave pop outfit The Crocodiles, who had a Top 20 hit in their homeland with 'Tears'. The Crocodiles flew to Sydney in February 1981 but by July, with the band in tatters, Morris had launched her solo career. One of the other Crocodiles members who made the fateful move to Sydney was drummer Barton Price who went on to join Sardine v and **Models**. **Debra Byrne** later issued a cover version of 'Tears' as a single.

Morris sang the theme song to the feature film *Puberty Blues*. 'Puberty Blues' was issued as her debut solo single backed with 'Adolescent Angst' (December 1981). She then formed QED with Rex Goh (guitar; ex-**Air Supply**) and Ian Belton (bass). With the help of session players like Amanda Vincent, Sam McNally and Glen Muirhead (keyboards), Tony Buchanan (sax) and South African Ricky Fataar (drums, who also co-produced with Mark Moffatt), QED recorded a quite respectable pop album, *Animal Magic* (EMI; November 1984). The album contained a couple of old Crocodiles songs, including 'Animal Magic', 'Everywhere I Go' and 'You're So Hip'. The album produced three singles, 'Everywhere I Go'/'Checkmate' (national #21 in December 1983), 'Solo and More'/'I'll Get It Right' (March 1984) and 'This One'/'Hush Sweet Charlotte' (August). Although 'Everywhere I Go' peaked at #6 in Sydney, QED never really took off.

Morris issued a tentative solo single, 'Get Some Humour'/'Get Some Humour' in November 1985. In the meantime, Morris had sung backing vocals on **INXS**'s 1984 breakthrough album *The Swing*. At the end of 1985 she accepted an offer to sing backing vocals on **INXS**'s massive Listen Like Thieves world tour. **INXS**'s Andrew Farriss wrote and produced Morris's next single, 'You're Gonna Get Hurt'/'Cool' (September 1986), before he returned to his commitments on the international touring circuit. Producers Ricky Fataar and Mark Moffatt completed Morris's debut solo album, *Body and Soul*. Issued in July 1987, it was a promising release and yielded three singles, 'Body and Soul'/'Animal Magnetism' (April), 'You I Know'/'Broke the Leather' (August) and 'Lighthearted'/'Are You Ready?' (November).

Body and Soul reached #12 on the national chart, sold platinum (over 70 000 copies) and established Morris as one of the best singer/songwriters in the country. The Neil Finn-composed torch-ballad 'You I Know' became her biggest hit (#13 in September) and Morris won the 1987 Australian Record Industry Association (ARIA) Award for Most Popular Female Performer. In 1988 Morris married photographer Paul Clarke and took a break to start a family. Two years later she was back with the accomplished Andrew Farriss-produced album *Shiver* (August 1989). Morris co-wrote ten of the album's 11 tracks; the 11th track was a cover of **Paul Kelly**'s '(Beggar on the) Street of Love'. Four singles were lifted from the album: 'Saved Me'/'Drown' (#27 in August 1989), 'She Has to Be Loved'/'Conscience' (#5 in November), '(Beggar on the) Street of Love'/'Conscience' (February 1990) and 'Self Deceiver'/'Pass It Over' (Live) (April). 'Saved Me' and 'She Has to Be Loved' highlighted Morris's growing confidence by fusing funk rhythms with pop hooks.

Shiver reached #2 on the national chart in October, and went on to sell over 250 000 copies in Australia. Morris embarked on an international tour that took in US dates supporting Prince. Morris's 1990 touring band included Dweezil Zappa (son of Frank) on lead guitar. At the start of 1991, Morris issued a version of 'Piece of My Heart' (made famous by Janis Joplin) as a single (backed with a live version of 'She Has to Be Loved') and it reached #24 on the chart during February. With the help of co-producer Nick Launay and the master rhythm section of Jamaicans Sly Dunbar and Robbie Shakespeare, Morris crafted a cohesive, dynamic and emotion-charged third solo album, *Honeychild* (October 1991). The album reached #4 on the national chart and included her biggest hit single to date, the funky 'Break in the Weather' (#2 in October).

The album's second single, the haunting 'I've Had You' (co-written with **Paul Kelly**) was not quite so successful and peaked at #39 in January 1992. A third single, 'Crackerjack Man' (May 1992), missed the national Top 40. The 16-track compilation album *The Best of Jenny Morris: The Story So Far* (November 1992) drew together all Morris's hit singles, plus her rare duet with **INXS**'s Michael

Hutchence on 'Jackson' and a re-recorded version of 'Tears' which also came out as a CD single (October). *The Story So Far* peaked at #12 in April 1993, one month after Morris supported ex-Beatle Paul McCartney on an Australian tour.

Morris's next run of singles was spread over a period of almost two years: 'Only We Can Hear' (May 1994), 'Rhythm and Flow' (June 1995), 'In Too Deep' (October 1995) and 'What I Do Now' (February 1996). The album from which these singles were culled, *Salvation Jane*, appeared in August 1995 on the rooArt label. Among the production credits for the album were long-time collaborator Andrew Farriss, **Electric Hippies** and hot-shot engineer Jeremy Allom (Massive Attack).

Albums: *Body and Soul* (WEA, 1987), *Shiver* (WEA, 1989), *Honeychild* (East West/Warner, 1991), *The Best of Jenny Morris: The Story So Far* (compilation, Warner, 1992), *Salvation Jane* (rooArt/Warner, 1995).

The Russell Morris Band

Russell Morris

Style: *Pop, rock*

Melbourne-born singer/songwriter Russell Morris (b. 1948) remains one of the best performers to emerge from the Australian 1960s scene. Morris's distinctive voice graced a string of exceptional, fondly remembered hit singles, but in a career spanning over 30 years he has been sadly under-recorded, with only eight albums to his credit.

Morris got his start in 1966 when he sang lead vocals for pop/R&B band Somebody's Image. The rest of the band comprised Phillip Raphael (lead guitar), Kevin Thomas (rhythm guitar), Les Allen (aka Les Gough, bass) and Eric Cairns (drums). The band came to the attention of *Go-Set* writer and budding pop guru Ian 'Molly' Meldrum, who produced the first two singles for W&G's subsidiary label In Records. A cover of the Holland/Dozier/Holland soul hit 'Heat Wave'/'When I Come Home' (September 1967) failed to chart, but Joe South's 'Hush'/It's All Over Now, Baby Blue' reached #14 in Melbourne and #15 in Sydney during December 1967. The band's third single, 'Hide and Seek'/'Livin' in Style', reached #32 in Melbourne during May 1968; despite its moderate chart placing, it was the band's best release.

In September 1968, Morris left Somebody's Image to pursue a solo career. Thomas, Allen and Cairns continued as The Image with new singer/guitarist Brian Holloway (ex-Dream). Meldrum became Morris's manager, and together they transformed a modest **Johnny Young** composition into one of the most astonishing pop productions of the entire 1960s. The seven-minute, psychedelic epic 'The Real Thing' matched Meldrum's audacious wizard's brew of swirling studio embellishment with driving backing from **The Groop.** With the gentle 'It's Only a Matter of Time' on the B-side, 'The Real Thing' became a national #1 hit single in May 1969. 'The Real Thing' stayed on the chart for 23 weeks and is recognised as a bona fide Australian rock classic. The small Diamond label issued 'The Real Thing' in the USA and, despite only reaching #98 on the Billboard charts, it made #1 in Chicago, Houston and New York.

Morris's second solo single, 'The Girl that I Love'/'Part Three into Paper Walls', also reached #1 in Australia during August 1969. In September, Morris joined the cream of Aussie pop of the day, **Ronnie Burns, Johnny Farnham, The Zoot, Johnny Young, The Valentines, Doug Parkinson** In Focus and **The Master's Apprentices** in the national Operation Starlift tour. A month later, Morris left for the UK where Decca had issued 'The Real Thing' to virtual indifference. Morris returned to Australia in December 1969 and entered the studio with producer Howard Gable for his next single, 'Rachel'/'Slow Joey' (#23 in May 1970). The hard-rocking 'Mr America'/'Stand Together' (#9 in January 1971) was Morris's first songwriting venture. It won him Composer of the Year in the *TV Week* Music Awards.

With the assistance of **Brian Cadd, Billy Green, Rick Springfield**, members of **Chain** and producer Gable, Morris recorded his debut solo album, *Bloodstone.* It was one of the best pop albums of 1971, and displayed Morris's growing confidence as a songwriter and singer. It produced the hit single

'Sweet Sweet Love'/'Jail Jonah's Daughter' (#7 in July 1971). The album also reached #12 during September. In 1971, Morris formed a touring band, Cycle, and supported **The Bee Gees** on their Australian and New Zealand tour. During Easter 1972, Morris and Cycle appeared at the Mulwala Rock Festival, playing alongside local heavyweights like **Billy Thorpe** and the Aztecs, **La De Das**, **Chain**, **Carson** and **Coloured Balls**, plus international visitors Stephen Stills and Manassas and Canned Heat.

Morris issued two singles during 1972, 'Live with Friends'/'Alcohol Farm' (#13 in April) and the elegant 'Wings of an Eagle'/'Satisfy You' (#13 in December). He then turned his attention overseas, first travelling to London before settling in New York. In 1975, Morris issued his second solo album, *Russell Morris*, which came out on Wizard in Australia and RCA in the USA. The album featured top American session players like Hugh McCracken (guitar), David Spinozza (drums), Ken Archer (keyboards), Will Lee (bass), Rick Marotta (drums) and Michael and Randy Becker (horns). Among the ten Morris-penned compositions were rerecordings of 'Wings of an Eagle' and 'Sweet Sweet Love', and the single 'Let's Do It'/'Don't Rock the Boat' (#14 in November 1975). 'Sail with Me'/'Hard Road' was issued as a second single in May 1976. Morris's second American-recorded album, *Turn It On* (*Russell Morris 2* in the USA) was another strong release, but the singles 'R.J.S.S. (Running Jumping Standing Still)'/'Cloudy Day' (August 1976) and 'Wolves in White'/'Two Wheeled Flyer' (November) were not successful.

By the time Morris's Green Card (which allowed him to tour in the USA) came through in 1978, he was servicing fire extinguishers for a living and selling subscriptions to the Los Angeles *Examiner* door-to-door. He decided to return home in early 1978. He formed The Russell Morris Band and hit the Melbourne pub rock circuit. The band, which comprised Joey Amenta (lead guitar; ex-**Taste**, **Redhouse**), Ralph White (keyboards, sax; ex-**Renée Geyer** Band), Graham Thompson (bass; ex-**Stars**, **Avalanche**) and Barry Cram (drums; ex-Michael Turner in Session, **Pantha**, **Avalanche**), added a raunchier, hard rock edge to the likes of 'Sweet Sweet Love', 'Let's Do It' and 'The Real Thing'.

Morris signed to Mushroom Records and issued the singles 'Thunder Ground'/'Two Minute Warning' (March 1979), 'Hot Love'/'I'm Just a Writer' (June) and 'Surprise Surprise'/'Love Stealer' (September), followed by the album *Foot in The Door* (October). Prior to the album sessions, James Black (keyboards; ex-Rum Jungle) and Bruce Sandell (sax; ex-Rum Jungle) had replaced Ralph White. Following the album sessions, Barry Cram left to join Contraband. Keith Elliot (ex-Instant Replay) took his place, only to be replaced himself by Rick Puchala in late 1979.

1979 was a busy year for The Russell Morris Band. As well as touring in support of the release of *Foot in the Door*, the band supported overseas visitors Santana, Eddie Money, Hall and Oates, Dr Hook and Bob Marley on their respective Australian tours. In April 1980, Amenta left to join The Darryl Cotton Band, and Black left to join **Mondo Rock**. Max Chazan (guitar; ex-Hot Band) and Bruce Haymes (keyboards; ex-Front Page, **Richard Clapton** Band, Hot Band) came in as replacements. Chazan, Haymes and Puchala had also previously played in a band called The Rubes, so with the line-up change The Russell Morris Band became known as Russell Morris and the Rubes. The Rubes' February 1981 album *Almost Frantic* (produced by **Little River Band's** David Briggs) yielded the singles 'Hush'/'In the Heat of the Night' (September), 'The Roar of the Wild Torpedoes'/'Just Another Night' (February 1981) and 'So Tough'/'4 RPM' (April 1981). Only the reworking of 'Hush' made the national chart when it reached #35 in December 1980. The album peaked at #28 on the national chart.

In March 1981, James Gillard (ex-**Western Flyer**, Tremors) replaced Thompson, who joined **Broderick Smith's** Big Combo. In January 1982, Robbie Geappon (ex-**Phil Manning** Band, Ideals) replaced Gillard, who also joined **Broderick Smith's** Big Combo (replacing Thompson). That same month, Russell Morris and the Rubes appeared at the ambitious Mushroom Evolution concert which was held over the Australia Day weekend. The subsequent triple album live set, *The Mushroom Evolution Concert*, included The Rubes performing 'In the Heat of the Night' and 'Roar of the Wild Torpedoes'. Russell Morris and the Rubes issued only one single during 1982, 'Get It Right'/'You Wanted Fame' (July). Spiro Philipas replaced Geappon on bass. In May 1983, Morris and the Rubes parted company, and the singer went solo again. His next single was 'I'll Stay with You'/'Turn to Stone' (June 1983), which featured the singer doing a fine Tom Waits impersonation.

Morris returned to the Melbourne pub circuit with a new Russell Morris Band line-up of Vinnie Monea (lead guitar), Spiro Philipas (bass), Duncan Veall (keyboards) and Keith Elliot (drums). Alex Formosa replaced Elliot on drums. Morris then took the part of Riff Raff in the Melbourne stage production of *The Rocky Horror Show*. He played with 1960s covers band The Lonely Boys (Col Tipping, guitar; Dave Russell, bass; and Ron Mahony, drums) for three years, followed by Russell Morris and the Word (Steve Joyce, guitar; Chris Wilson, keyboards; Rob Gray, bass; and Ron Mahony, drums). During the early 1990s, there was something of a Russell Morris revival. In 1990, EMI issued a remixed version of 'The Real Thing' as a 12-inch single backed with 'Rachel'. That same year, Sydney-based pop outfit, **The Whipper Snappers**, contributed a version of 'Sweet Sweet Love' to the Various Artists album *Used and Recovered by* on Mushroom's White label. White also issued 'Sweet Sweet Love' as a **Whipper Snappers** single. **Ollie Olsen's** Third Eye reworked 'The Real Thing' into an epic techno/trance rave up.

In November 1991, Morris issued a new album, *A Thousand Suns* (produced by Mark Moffatt). The album included three singles, 'Tartan Lines'/'Over Excited' (February 1991), 'A Thousand Suns'/'This Bird has Flown' (May), and 'Stay with You'/'She's Leaving' (August). The album boasted a contemporary studio sheen, and featured guest musicians like Mark Punch, Ricky Fataar, Chong Lim and Venetta Fields. In 1992 Morris took on one of the highest profile roles of his career when he played Simon Zealotes in the Australian stage revival of *Jesus Christ Superstar*. He appeared alongside **John Farnham**, **Kate Ceberano**, **Angry Anderson**, John Waters and Jon Stevens on the #1 charting *Jesus Christ Superstar the Album* issued on Polydor in July. Farnham later covered the Russell Morris composition 'Diamonds' on his 1993 album *Then Again . . .*

Morris returned to the Australian touring circuit in 1994 with a new Russell Morris Band that comprised Trevor Reading (guitar; ex-**Runners**), Chong Lim (keyboards), Tim Milikan (bass) and Iain McLennan (drums; ex-**Ariel**, **Mondo Rock**, **Sports**). One of the band's showcase gigs was supporting the revived **Billy Thorpe** and the Aztecs at the Melbourne Myer Music Bowl in November 1994. During 1996, Morris joined up with fellow 1960s veterans Darryl Cotton and **Ronnie Burns** to play the revival circuit. The three singers issued a self-titled album during the year which comprised nine original solo recordings, plus three new recordings by the trio.

Albums: *Bloodstone* (EMI/Columbia, 1971), *Wings of an Eagle and Other Great Hits* (EMI/Columbia, 1973), *Russell Morris* (Wizard, 1975), *Turn It On* (Wizard, 1976), *Retrospective* (EMI, 1978), *Foot in the Door* (Mushroom/Festival, 1979), *Almost Frantic* (Mushroom/Festival, 1980), *A Thousand Suns* (Festival, 1991).

Mortal Sin

Formed: *1985*
Style: *Thrash metal*
Original line-up: *Mat Maurer (vocals), Keith Krstin (guitar), Paul Carwana (guitar), Andy Eftichiou (bass), Wayne Campbell (drums)*

During the mid-1980s, Sydney's vast western suburbs gave rise to a small, but fervent underground thrash/speed metal scene. The two leading lights on that scene were Mortal Sin and Slaughter Lord. Inspired by San Franciscan Bay Area bands such as Metallica, Exodus, Death Angel and Slayer, plus European groups like Kreator, Destruction, King Diamond and Celtic Frost, the two local bands developed in complete isolation outside the Australian mainstream. Slaughter Lord broke up without issuing any records.

In July/August 1986, Mortal Sin recorded its self-financed, self-produced debut album, *Mayhemic Destruction*. When issued on the band's own Mega Metal Productions label in May 1987, the album attracted a great deal of interest from overseas thrash metal fans. UK rock magazine *Metal Forces* rated the album as one of the best of its genre ever issued. The magazine's rating of 99 out of 100 (previously only awarded to Metallica's landmark *Master of Puppets* album) attracted a flurry of record company interest. Mortal Sin eventually signed to Phonogram's Vertigo label (home to heavyweights like Metallica, Kiss and Def Leppard in Europe). Vertigo repackaged the band's debut album, which subsequently became a best-seller throughout Europe. And all that before most Australians even knew Mortal Sin existed!

Meanwhile, Mortal Sin had started touring along the eastern states. Founding member Keith Krstin left the band at the end of 1987 to be replaced by Mick Burke (ex-Slaughter Lord). The band recorded a new album with famed American producer Randy Burns (Dark Angel, Megadeth), but its release was held up for over a year. *Face of Despair* finally appeared in May 1989 to coincide with the band's support slot to Metallica's Australian tour. With its greater attention to song arrangements and quality production, the album vindicated the overseas interest shown in the band. In July 1989, the band replaced Wayne Campbell with another ex-Slaughter Lord alumnus Steve Hughes and prepared to undertake an overseas tour. Mortal Sin supported the likes of Testament and Faith No More across Europe at the end of 1989.

In early 1990, lead singer Mat Maurer left Mortal Sin to form his own band, Omega. Steve Sly came in as Maurer's replacement. By September, Paul Carwana, Burke and Hughes had all left the band. Burke and Hughes formed Presto with Aaron Hodge (bass) and Luke Pittman (vocals). Sly and Eftichiou kept Mortal Sin alive by recruiting Dave DeFrancesco (guitar; ex-Enticer), Alex Hardy (guitar; ex-Rags'n'Riches) and Nash Hall (drums; ex-White Widow). That line-up supported US visitors Megadeth on its Australian tour during February 1991. Hardy left soon after, to be replaced by Tom Doustopil.

The band recorded a new album, *Rebellious Youth*, with producer Kevin 'Caveman' Shirley that saw release during November 1991. 'Every Dog Has Its Day' was issued as a single in October. The album was retitled *Every Dog Has Its Day* for release in Europe on Music for Nations. The band's sound had moved away from its thrash origins to embrace a more traditional power metal style akin to Iron Maiden or Armoured Saint. By that stage, however, Mortal Sin had lost its fanbase and the band broke up in 1992. Andy Eftichiou formed hard rock band Who's Guilty with Sean Bosco (vocals), Bruno Gerace (guitar), Bob Wheatley (keyboards) and Nick Pansini (drums). The band issued one CD EP in 1994, *Revenge*, before breaking up a year later.

In the meantime, original drummer Wayne Campbell had formed White Trash with Brendan Grimes (vocals), Troy Scerri (guitar), Anthony Roach (guitar) and Paul Miller (bass). By 1992, Campbell had moved on to Grungeon which comprised Doug Dalton (guitar, vocals; ex-**Suiciety**), Greg Morley (guitar) and Glen Sullivan (bass). The band's main inspirations were Sepultura and Slayer. Grungeon shared the Sydney metal scene with the likes of Manticore and Persecution, and had the tracks 'Rise Above' and 'Infernal Shelter' included on the compilations *Redrum* (on Roadrunner Australia) and *While My Guitar Gently Kills You Mother* (on Studio 52) respectively. Dalton and Sullivan left Grungeon in early 1994 and the band was quiet for some time. Dave Collis (bass) and Anthony Hoffman (guitar) joined and Grungeon re-emerged. In January 1996, Grungeon supported visiting New York metal band Brutal Truth, after which the band broke up. By the end of 1996, Mortal Sin had re-formed with a line-up of Mat Maurer, Andy Eftichiou, Paul Carwana, Wayne Campbell and Anthony Hoffman.

Albums: *Mayhemic Destruction* (Mega Metal, 1987; reissued by Vertigo/Phonogram, 1988), *Face of Despair* (Vertigo/Phonogram, 1989), *Rebellious Youth* (Virgin, 1991).

Mortification

Formed: *1990*
Style: *Death metal*
Original line-up: *Steve Rowe (vocals, bass), Michael Carlisle (guitar), Jayson Sherlock (drums)*

During the early 1990s, Mortification became internationally known as Australia's foremost Christian-inspired death metal band. Christian death metal: surely a contradiction in terms; but only for the uninitiated. Mortification successfully infused the down-tuned, sledgehammer riffs and gruff vocal style usually associated with the death/thrash metal genre with positive and spiritually uplifting lyric themes.

The forerunner to Mortification was a traditional heavy metal band known as Lightforce which Steve Rowe formed in Melbourne during 1987. The line-up comprised Rowe (bass, vocals), Steve Johnson (vocals), Murray Adams (guitar) and Errol Willenberg (drums). The band played the small local metal scene alongside the likes of **Taramis** and Mass Confusion. American label Pure Metal Records issued the band's debut album, *Mystical Thieves* (May 1989), which provided Lightforce with an effective stepping stone on to the international market. Lightforce supported visiting American Christian metal band Stryper on its 1989 Australian tour. By 1990, Rowe had decided to move in a heavier direction (influenced by Morbid Angel and Napalm Death) and formed Mortification. The band's local contemporaries in that field included **Acheron**, **Sadistik Execution**, **Armoured Angel**, Necrotomy and Sanctum. Mortification signed an international deal with American label Intense and issued its debut, self-titled album in 1991.

Over the next year, Intense issued the band's second and third albums, *Break the Curse* and *Scrolls of Megilloth*, plus the tour video *Grind Planets*. The band also signed a deal with the German-based Nuclear Blast label for the release of its albums across Europe. In 1992, Mortification undertook a successful North American tour with new drummer Johnny Vasquez (ex-Vengeance Rising). Nuclear Blast issued the band's fourth album, *Post Momentary Affliction*, in late 1993, swiftly followed by the live album and video *Live Planetarium* a few months later. With these releases, Mortification became one of the biggest selling Australian heavy metal bands ever (*Post Momentary Affliction* sold a respectable 30 000 copies in Europe alone). By 1994, Mortification comprised Rowe, Carlisle and newcomer Phil Gibson (drums). The band issued its sixth album, *Bloodworld*, in October 1994; Rose also published his first novel, *Minstrel*, which was described as a medieval music adventure.

By that stage, Mortification had toured the USA three times and Europe three times. In early 1995, Rowe flew to North America without Carlisle and Gibson. He recruited two stand-in members from Canada, Jason Campbell (guitar) and Bill Price (drums), in order to fulfil the band's touring commitments. With the aid of ex-Deliverance guitarist George Ochoa, Mortification recorded a new album, *EnVision EvAngelene*, for release in April 1996. In late 1996, Rowe was diagnosed with a form of blood cancer known as 'acute lymphatic leukemia'. Since that time, Mortification has slipped from public view.

Albums: *Mystical Thieves* (as Lightforce; Pure Metal, US only, 1989), *Mortification* (Intense, 1991), *Break the Curse* (Intense, 1991), *Scrolls of Megilloth* (Intense, 1992), *Post Momentary Affliction* (Nuclear Blast, 1993). *Live Planetarium* (Nuclear Blast, 1994), *Bloodworld* (Nuclear Blast, 1994), *Best of Lightforce* (Rowe Productions/ Nuclear Blast, 1994), *EnVision EvAngelene* (Rowe Productions/Nuclear Blast, 1996).

Moscos and Stone (*see* Railroad Gin)

Ian Moss

Style: *R&B, soul*

Ian Moss (b. 1954) came to prominence as guitarist with the highly revered **Cold Chisel**. When that band split at the end of 1983, singer **Jimmy Barnes** immediately leapt into a successful solo career. The media-shy Moss preferred to take his time in relaunching himself in solo mode. Moss formed the first version of The Ian Moss Band in October 1986. It comprised Andy Cowan (keyboards; ex-**Madder Lake**, **Ayers Rock**, **Kevin Borich Express**), Joe Imbroll (bass; ex-**Goanna**) and John Watson (drums; ex-**Kevin Borich Express**, **Australian Crawl**). By April 1987, the line-up comprised Watson, Peter Walker (guitar, synthesiser; ex-**Bakery**) and Joe Creighton (bass; ex-**Melissa**, **Billy T**).

It then took Moss until 1989 before he was ready to record his debut solo album. He spent nine months during 1988 in Los Angeles picking his way through hundreds of song demos from which to select a debut single. Eventually Moss called on his old **Cold Chisel** compadre Don Walker, with whom he co-wrote 'Tucker's Daughter' for release as a single. 'Tucker's Daughter'/'Islands' became an immediate smash hit when it reached #1 on the national chart during March 1989. With further writing help from Walker, plus production guidance from New Yorker Chris Lord-Alge (James Brown), Moss completed a polished album of sophisticated soul and radio-friendly R&B. *Matchbook* (September 1989) reached #1, sold over 210000 copies and produced two further national hit singles, 'Telephone Booth'/'Answer Machine Blues' (#7 in August) and 'Out of the Fire'/'Angel Eyes' (#29 in October). The album's fourth single, 'Mr Rain', failed to reach the Top 40.

Ian Moss

The album demonstrated Moss's exemplary, controlled guitar technique, but also highlighted his soulful voice. As **Cold Chisel's** foremost instrumental soloist, Moss had rarely taken the vocal spotlight. His superb voice was heard on a handful of **Cold Chisel** cuts like 'Bow River', 'My Baby' and 'One Long Day', plus the live showcase 'Georgia'. On *Matchbook*, Moss handled all lead vocals with considerable style and authority. Moss scored well in the 1989 Australian Record Industry Association (ARIA) Awards by taking out Male Artist of the Year, Best Debut Album, Best Album, Best Debut Single and Song of the Year ('Tucker's Daughter').

With the album's release, Moss hit the road with a touring band that included Ian Belton (bass; ex-QED), Randy Bulpin (rhythm guitar; ex-**Mondo**

Rock), Steve Fearnley (drums), Danny D'Costa (keyboards) and Mark Williams (backing vocals). He returned to the studio in 1991 for his second album. Produced by Peter Walker, *Worlds Away* (October 1991) again featured songs largely co-written with Don Walker in the soul/R&B vein, plus a re-working of Moss's classic **Cold Chisel** song 'Bow River'. The album featured the then current Ian Moss Band line-up of Claude Caranza (rhythm guitar; ex-**Kids in the Kitchen**), Chris Bekker (bass), Ricky Edwards (keyboards) and Davey Porter (drums). *Worlds Away* was not as successful as *Matchbook*. of its three singles 'Slip Away' (May), 'She's a Star' (September) and 'Never Give Up' (November), only 'Slip Away' made the national charts, and then only peaking at #59 during July 1991.

Moss effectively disappeared from public view for another five years. He reappeared in 1996 with a new record deal (with TWA) and his best-ever album, *Petrolhead* (August). That time the studio band, which featured Don Walker (keyboards), the venerable Ian Rilen (bass; from **X**), Paul DeMarco (drums; ex-**Rose Tattoo**) and Trent Williamson (harmonica), was a down'n'dirty blues-rock outfit. By replacing the studio gloss of previous albums with gritty, hard-edged tracks like 'Petrol Head', 'Two Seconds Two Long', 'It Ain't Easy', 'Poor Boy' and '80 MPH Blues', Moss was able to concentrate on his finely honed guitar work. The most commercial tracks, Walker's 'All Alone on a Rock' and 'Poor Boy', were issued as singles but neither made the charts. In 1997, TWA reissued *Petrolhead* with a bonus album, *Ian Moss Live*. Featured players on the live album were Moss, Walker, DeMarco, Rilen and Paul Wheeler, who replaced Rilen on bass halfway through the Petrolhead tour. By the end of the year, Moss had rejoined his fellow **Cold Chisel** members in the recording studio.

Albums: *Matchbook* (Mushroom/Festival, 1989), *Worlds Away* (Mushroom/Festival, 1991), *Petrolhead* (TWA, 1996), *Petrolhead/Ian Moss Live* (reissue, TWA, 1997).

Moving Pictures

Formed: *1978*
Style: *Rock*
Original line-up: *Alex Smith (vocals, guitar; ex-Bilgola Bop Band, This Side Up), Garry Frost (guitar, keyboards, vocals), Charlie Cole (keyboards), Andrew Thompson (sax; ex-Bilgola Bop Band), Ian Lees (bass; ex-This Side Up), Paul Freeland (drums)*

Sydney band Moving Pictures came to prominence in 1982 with the melodramatic power ballad 'What About Me?' written by Garry Frost. The single shot to #1 and established the band as one of the most popular acts on the Australian music scene. Despite a couple of further minor hit singles and years of solid touring, Moving Pictures was never able to replicate the runaway success of 'What About Me?'

Hyperactive lead singer Alex Smith and Frost formed Moving Pictures, and immediately set about establishing the band's reputation as a hard working, R&B-inspired pub-rock outfit. The main inspirations for the band's sound and style were Bruce Springsteen, Graham Parker and Van Morrison. The band signed to the Wheatley management organisation and issued two singles during 1981, 'Walls'/'All the Way' (July) and 'Bustin' Loose'/'Saturday Love' (October). Initially the band's debut album, *Days of Innocence* (October 1981), failed to reach the national Top 40, but it was a steady seller over the 1981/82 summer. With the release of 'What About Me?'/'Round Again' in January 1982, interest in the album picked up and both records hit the #1 spot simultaneously on their respective charts during February.

'What About Me?' became one of the biggest hits of the year, and it won Best Single Award at the 1982 ***Countdown*** Awards. The band's next single, 'Sweet Cherie'/'Nothing to Do', was not successful, although the follow-up 'Winners'/'Pay the Piper' reached #12 during November. In the meantime Mark Meyer (ex-**Stylus**, **Richard Clapton** Band, **Mark Gillespie** Band) had replaced original drummer Paul Freeland. US label Elektra signed Moving Pictures and issued 'What About Me?', which reached the American Top 20 (#19). Meanwhile, the album sold well enough to register in the US Top 60. Unfortunately, on the eve of a US tour that would have taken in support dates with Tom Petty, Hall and Oates and REO Speedwagon, Elektra collapsed and the band was unable to follow up on the interest generated.

Moving Pictures issued its second album, *Matinee*, in October 1983. It reached #16 on the national chart and produced the minor hit single 'Back to the Streets'/'Spies' (#37 in September). The album yielded three more singles, 'Where They Belong'/'Pleasure and Pain' (November), 'Back to Booze and Blues'/'Sisters of Mercy' (December) and 'Never'/'We Share Our Love' (March 1984), but none charted in the national Top 40. The band maintained a strong live following, and at the end of 1983 undertook a successful tour of Japan. By 1984, problems within the band had come to a head and founding member Frost left. He went on to form **1927**. Initially Joey Amenta (ex-**Taste**, **Redhouse**, **Russell Morris** Band, **Wendy and the**

Rocketts) took Frost's place, until Kevin Bennett came in as a permanent replacement.

Moving Pictures continued touring for another three years. Following the Last Picture Show tour in May 1987, the band members went their separate ways. The tour resulted in the live album *Last Picture Show* (December 1987). With Moving Pictures' break-up, Smith formed Alex Smith and the Volunteers, which had transformed into Alex Smith and DBM by 1989. DBM comprised Ben Little (guitar), Lee Borkman (keyboards; ex-Pink Slips, Scribble), Dave Carter (bass) and Mark O'Shea (drums). In 1991 he fronted The Blues Liners, and by 1992 was working in the UK where he recorded a single, 'This Time Tomorrow', under the aegis of Asia's bass player John Wetton. The single came out on the Emerald City label in July 1992. Meanwhile, Ian Lees, Kevin Bennett and Mark Meyer formed blues band Chasin' the Train with Canadian guitar ace Kirk Lorange (ex-**Richard Clapton** Band).

Albums: *Days of Innocence* (Wheatley, 1981), *Matinee* (Wheatley, 1983), *Last Picture Show* (Wheatley, 1987).

M.P.D. Limited

Formed: *1965*
Style: *Beat pop*
Original line-up: **Mike Brady** *(vocals, guitar; ex-***Phantoms***), Pete Watson (bass; ex-***Phantoms***), Danny Finley (drums; ex-Saxons,* **Sonics***)*

M.P.D. Limited had one of the most meteoric rises in the history of Australian rock and pop. As Glenn A. Baker put it, the band appeared out of the sky like Haley's Comet, flared brightly and then disintegrated, but within 18 months had helped alter the face of rock'n'roll in Australia. The genesis of M.P.D. Limited came about when 17-year-old, UK-born **Mike Brady** replaced the temporarily indisposed Dave Lincoln in successful Melbourne, Shadows-styled instrumental band **The Phantoms**. Brady was only with **The Phantoms** for two months, but in that time he and bass player Pete Watson had decided to form their own beat pop band.

Brady and Watson recruited Danny Finley in May 1965, and within three weeks M.P.D. (Mike, Pete and Danny) Limited was supporting UK visitors the Dave Clark Five on their Australian tour. In July 1965, M.P.D. Limited signed to the Go!! label and the band's debut single, Johnny Burnette's 'Little Boy Sad'/'Wendy Don't Go', immediately hit the #1 spot in Melbourne upon release during August. It also peaked at #5 in Sydney during October. The single's success thrust M.P.D. Limited into the limelight alongside the biggest acts of the day like **The Easybeats**, **Normie Rowe**, **Bobby and Laurie** and **Billy Thorpe** and the Aztecs. The band appeared on television shows like *The Go!! Show* and *Saturday Date* and toured the country. In November, M.P.D. Limited generated, with **The Easybeats** and **Tony Worsley** and **The Fabulous Blue Jays**, a wild riot at Brisbane Festival Hall.

M.P.D. Limited's dynamic stage act left their fans screaming for more. It revolved around a frantic, non-stop, 20-minute barrage of songs, Brady and Watson's carefully choreographed gymnastics and Finley's flamboyant drumming antics. The band's second single, Paul Anka's 'Lonely Boy'/'Wild Side of Life', was another hit, reaching #7 in Melbourne during November. A cover of The Shangri-Las' 'Remember (Walkin' in the Sand)'/'If You Were Mine' reached #19 in February 1966. 'Remember (Walkin' in the Sand)' was the band's final chart hit. 'No Regrets'/'I Won't Be Back' (June 1966) and 'Absence Makes the Heart Grow Fonder'/'I Am What I Am' (August) featured quality, self-penned compositions, but they were not successful. The Go!! label also issued two M.P.D. Limited EPs, 'Little Boy Sad' and *M.P.D. Limited*. 'Absence Makes the Heart Grow Fonder', which featured **The Bee Gees** on backing vocals, was issued as a single in Germany on the Ariola label.

In August 1966, M.P.D. Limited travelled to the UK, but after four months had made little headway and decided to return home. During January 1967, M.P.D. Limited undertook a successful homecoming tour, but rivalries within the band were such that the end was in sight. There was one more single on Go!!, 'Paper Doll'/'You Might as Well Forget Him' (March 1967), by which stage the band had broken up. After the split, both Brady and Finley formed short-lived bands called M.P.D., while Watson assembled the highly regarded Pete Watson's Rockhouse. In August 1967, he formed the original Wickedy Wak which comprised **Rick Springfield** (guitar), Phil Blackmore (organ; ex-**Normie Rowe** and the Playboys) and Dick Howard (drums). Wickedy Wak issued one single, **Johnny Young's** 'Billie's Bikie Boys'/'Chitty Chitty Bang Bang' on the Sunshine label (August 1969), by which time Springfield had joined **The Zoot**. Watson died in 1972 following a long illness.

In the meantime, Brady and Finley had toured with **Johnny Young's** Kompany. Brady then formed the Down Under Trio with Wayne Duncan (bass; ex-Rondells) and Gary Howard (drums; ex-**Mixtures**). Next he formed The Mike Brady Band, and issued a couple of solo singles on the Fable label. During the 1970s, he pursued a very successful career in songwriting/production/jingle writing. In 1979, **Mike Brady** wrote and recorded the enormously successful 'Up There Cazaly' under the name of The Two Man Band (with Peter Sullivan).

Albums: *Best of M.P.D. Limited* (Go!!, 1967), *The Wild Side of Life* (Raven, 1983).

Ted Mulry

Style: *Pop rock*

English-born pop balladeer Ted Mulry (b. 1949) first made an impression when his debut single 'Julia'/'So Much in Love' made the lower reaches of the national Top 40 chart in May 1970. The single was a Top 10 hit in his adopted hometown of Sydney. The shy, amateur songwriter had been driving a bulldozer for the Main Roads Department when he decided to submit demos of his songs to J. Albert and Son Publishers.

Tony Geary at EMI Records was impressed enough to issue 'Julia' as a single. Mulry then moved to the Albert label for his biggest hit single, 'Falling in Love Again'/'Louisa' (#11 in March 1971) and the album *Falling in Love Again*. His third single, 'Marsha'/'I Love You', was a regional hit in October 1971. That month Mulry returned to the UK as a result of obtaining a contract with Island Records' subsidiary label Blue Mountain. Blue Mountain issued Mulry's single, 'Ain't It Nice?'/'If You Should Ever Change Your Mind', under the pseudonym of Steve Ryder! It was not a hit and Mulry returned to Australia to pick up his career in Sydney. 'Memories'/'Remember Me' became Mulry's third hit single when it reached #30 in February 1972. Albert issued the UK single 'Ain't It Nice'/'If You Should Ever Change Your Mind' during May (as Ted Mulry of course), but it was not successful.

In October 1972, Mulry issued his last solo single, 'I Won't Look Back'/'Just Another Day', followed by the album *I Won't Look Back* (November). The album featured a rockier sound than heard on Mulry's early singles, and augured well for the future. **Sherbet** had also taken a cover version of one of the tracks, 'You're All Woman', into the National Top 20. Mulry formed a backing band from the remnants of popular suburban dance band The Velvet Underground. The band became known as the Ted Mulry Gang and set off on the tour-record-tour-record treadmill that saw them elevated to a position as one of the top pop outfits in the country.

Albums: *Falling in Love Again* (Albert/EMI, 1970), *I Won't Look Back* (Albert/EMI, 1971).

Ted Mulry Gang

Formed: *1972*
Style: *Pop boogie*
Original line-up: *Ted Mulry (vocals, bass), Les Hall (guitar; ex-Velvet Underground), Herman Kovacs (drums; ex-Velvet Underground)*

Within the confines of the Ted Mulry Gang (TMG), frontman Ted Mulry was able to make the transition from pop balladeer to certified rock'n'roller. Between 1974 and 1980, TMG racked up seven best-selling albums of good-time boogie'n'pop. During that time, TMG also undertook some of the most extensive national tours ever by an Australian band. Even when the band's hits dried up during the 1980s, the TMG machine rolled on with regular tours on the pub circuit.

When Mulry formed the Ted Mulry Gang, he was already a well-known pop star. His backing band was drawn from the remnants of suburban dance band The Velvet Underground. The original Velvet Underground formed in Newcastle (NSW) during 1967. The band claimed complete ignorance of any American usage of their moniker, having lifted it (like Lou Reed, John Cale and company) from the book of the same name which was essential 'head' reading in 1967. The original line-up comprised Steve Phillipson (vocals), Russell Bayne (guitar), David Schofield (organ), Mark Priest (bass) and Herman Kovacs (drums). Bayne, Priest and Schofield all left in 1969 to be replaced by Les Hall (guitar), Steve Crothers (bass) and Tony Heads (Hammond organ). As Newcastle's premier rock act of the day, The Velvet Underground offered quality versions of material by Love, Jefferson Airplane and The Doors. Phillipson was also a pioneer in the use of 'lighter fluid theatrics' (combustible fluid applied to the sleeves of his leather jacket and set alight).

The band issued one single on Festival, a cover of Jefferson Airplane's 'Somebody to Love'/'She Comes in Colours' (January 1970). By 1971, the band had relocated to Sydney. Heads and Crothers left, later forming Hiawatha, which was one of the first organ-driven rock bands in Australia (à la The Nice and Emerson Lake and Palmer) with Peter Shean (drums). The final Velvet Underground line-up of Kovacs, Hall, Andy Imla (vocals; ex-Elmtree), Malcolm Young (rhythm guitar) and Michael Szchefswick (bass) earned a moderate living as an in-demand suburban dance band. It was during the latter half of 1972 that Ted Mulry began to use The Velvet Underground as his regular backing outfit. By that stage, Young had left to lay plans for his next band, **AC/DC**. In September 1972, Hall and Kovacs joined Mulry for a performance at Newcastle's Waitara Festival and the Ted Mulry Gang was born.

Following up on Mulry's previous connection with Albert Productions, the Ted Mulry Gang signed to the label and issued its debut album, *Here We Are* (November 1974). Just prior to its release, Mulry added Gary Dixon (rhythm guitar; ex-Fat Harry) to fill out the band's sound. The album only sold moderately at first, and its first single, 'Sunday Evenings'/'Here We are' (March 1975), was not successful. In September 1975, Alberts issued 'Jump in My Car'/'I'm on Fire' as a single and a month later it had shot to #1 on the national chart. The single set the tone for subsequent releases with its simplistic, 12-bar boogie guitar riffs, thumping beat, Mulry's gravelly, gregarious vocals and tongue-in-cheek lyrics. The single sold 80 000 copies, and by 1976 the band was rubbing shoulders with the likes of **Sherbet**, **Skyhooks**, **Hush**, **Ol'55** and **John Paul Young** as one of the darlings of the Aussie pop scene.

In 1976 TMG issued two best-selling albums *Struttin'* (#9 in June) and *Steppin' Out* (#24 in November), plus three hit singles, 'The Darktown Strutter's Ball'/'She's for Me' (#3 in February 1976), 'Crazy'/'Help Me Out' (#13 in June) and 'Steppin' Out'/'It's All Over Now' (#25 in November). The band's rollicking remake of the 60-year-old 'The Darktown Strutter's Ball' had originally been a hit for the Original Dixieland Jazz Band in 1917. 'Jamaican Rum'/'Wanted Man' was the band's fifth hit single (#22 in March 1977) and last release for Albert Productions. In April 1977, TMG signed to the Mushroom label and issued a new album in June, *The TMG Album* (#24 in August). It produced two hit singles, 'My Little Girl'/'You've Got It' (#10 in June) and 'Naturally'/'Sha La La Lee' (#25 in September).

Disturbing the Peace included the singles 'Lazy Eyes'/'Set Me Free' (#21 in May 1978), 'Heart of Stone'/'I Miss You' (#20 in August) and '(You've Got the) Devil in You'/'Disturbing the Peace' (November). In April, the band set off on its three-month Disturbing the Peace tour across Australia (supported by **Feather**). At the end of 1978, TMG signed an American deal with Atlantic Records, and the band's records were also issued in New Zealand, South Africa, Canada, New Guinea and South-East Asia.

The *TMG Live* album featured one of the band's stage favourites in the bawdy 'Dyna', which had already established the band's reputation as lovable rogues. The Eddie Leonetti-produced *Locked In* album included three singles 'Save Me'/'How Long?' (February 1980), 'Can't Take It All'/'Home to You' (May) and 'Captured'/'I'm Down' (September), but none was successful. Thus ended TMG's love affair with the pop charts, but the band's place in Australian music history is well assured. The 1989 *Re-Union* album produced the single 'Old Habits'. Herman Kovacs went on to set up his own recording studio. He produced his brother Hank Kovacs' band Tall Stories' 1992 debut album *Different Worlds*.

Ted Mulry Gang albums: *Here We are* (Albert/EMI, 1974), *Struttin'* (Albert/EMI, 1976); ***TMG albums:*** *Steppin' Out* (Albert/EMI, 1976), *Greatest Hits* (Albert/EMI, 1977), *The TMG Album* (Mushroom/Festival, 1977), *Disturbing the Peace* (Mushroom/Festival, 1978), *TMG Live* (Mushroom/Festival, 1979), *Locked In* (Mushroom/Festival, 1980), *Re-Union* (CBS, 1989).

Neil Murray

Style: *Rock, country*

Singer/songwriter Neil Murray was raised on a farm at Lake Bolac, near Ararat in western Victoria. Murray's upbringing no doubt shaped his fascination for wide open spaces and a closeness to the Australian bush. In 1980, Murray travelled to the Northern Territory on a quest to discover the real Australia. He worked as a teacher, supply truck driver and outstation worker in the remote Western Desert Aboriginal communities of Papunya and Kintore. With George Rurrambu and Sammy and Gordon Butcher, Murray formed **Warumpi Band**. The band achieved significant success around Australia, touring with **Midnight Oil** on the 1986 Blackfella/Whitefella outback tour and issuing the acclaimed albums *Big Name, No Blankets* (1985) and *Go Bush!* (1987).

In 1988, Murray relocated to Sydney to record his debut solo album, *Calm and Crystal Clear*, with producer Mark Moffatt. With help from the likes of **Midnight Oil's** Peter Gifford and Andy Travers from **The Happening Thang**, Murray constructed an impressive debut. The music mixed rock and country in equal measure, which Murray described as 'outback rock with a slab of transcontinental drivin' thrown in'. *Calm and Crystal Clear* (April 1989) produced three singles, 'Calm and Crystal Clear'/'Too Many Love Songs' (March), 'Let's Fall in Love Again'/'Wild Country' (August) and 'Ocean of Regret', 'Clever Man'/'Silver City', 'Seven Days of Rain' (March 1990). Murray's songs were based around his outback experiences, and addressed the importance of Aboriginal people to Australia.

In order to tour, Murray formed The Rainmakers, which comprised James Cruikshank (keyboards, guitar; ex-Widdershins), Alex Hodgson (bass) and Bill Heckenberg (drums). The band completed 160 gigs around the country before Murray took a four-month break in the desert to take stock. Cruikshank went on to join **The Cruel Sea**. Neil Murray and the Rainmakers were back in action in mid-1990 as support for **Midnight Oil** on a national tour. Murray's second solo album, *These Hands*, included the singles 'Far Away' (February 1993), 'Holy Road' (May) and 'Sing Your Destiny' (October). In 1993 Murray issued a novel, *Sing for Me, Countryman*, which became something of a cult classic. Former Rainmakers backing vocalist **Christine Anu** featured three Neil Murray songs on her debut album, *Stylin' Up*, including 'My Island Home', which won Song of the Year at the 1995 Australian Performing Right Association (APRA) Awards ceremony.

In 1995, Murray toured Europe with the reconstituted **Warumpi Band**, and the band issued a new album, *No More Humbug* (June 1996). In May 1996, Murray issued his third solo album, *Dust*, as part of the ABC Music Songwriter Series. 'This Bliss' was issued as a single. The album featured contributions from musicians like David Bridie (**not drowning, waving**), **Chris Abrahams** and Jim Moginie (**Midnight Oil**), plus backing vocalists **Archie Roach**, **Christine Anu** and Sally Dastey and Amy Saunders from **Tiddas**.

Albums: *Calm and Crystal Clear* (Festival/Infinity, 1989), *These Hands* (Aurora/Mushroom/Festival, 1993), *Dust* (ABC Music/EMI, 1996).

My Friend the Chocolate Cake

Formed: *1991*
Style: *Chamber pop*
Original line-up: *David Bridie (vocals, keyboards), Andrew Caswell (mandolin), Hope Csutoros (violin), Helen Mountfort (cello), Andrew Richardson (guitar), Russell Bradley (percussion)*

David Bridie, Russell Bradley and Helen Mountfort formed My Friend the Chocolate Cake as a sideline project away from their main band **not drowning, waving**. The band's gentle, whimsical and mostly acoustic sound bore the influence of Simon Jeffes' Penguin Cafe Orchestra, John Cale and nineteenth-century classical music (Mountford has a degree in classical composition).

My Friend the Chocolate Cake was designed to be a fun venture for a bunch of friends, to sidestep **not drowning, waving's** deep, layered work for a more relaxed approach. All the same, in *Rolling Stone*, Bruce Elder described the band's debut, self-titled album as one of the best albums of high-art pop ever recorded in Australia. 'A Midwife's Tale' was issued as a CD single (February 1992). By the time the band issued its second album, *Brood*, two years later, there was a more serious aesthetic at work. *Brood* had been recorded with a generous budget and mixed in New York.

The album featured an intimate, accessible sound that ranged from the uptempo pop of the single 'Throwing It Away' to the gentle ballad 'The Old Years'. Michael Barker had replaced Bradley on percussion. 'I've Got a Plan' (November 1994) and 'Songs from Under the Floorboards' (March 1995) were issued as CD EPs. My Friend the Chocolate Cake's third album, *Good Luck*, and its CD singles, 'Lighthouse Keeper' (August 1996) and 'Your Ship has Gone' (May 1997), were among the band's most accomplished and direct statements to date. The group ended the year by winning Best Adult Contemporary release at the 1997 Australian Record Industry Association (ARIA) awards ceremony.

Albums: *My Friend the Chocolate Cake* (East West/Warner, 1991), *Brood* (White/Mushroom/Festival, 1994), *Good Luck* (White/Mushroom/Festival, 1996).

N

The Nauts (*see* Supernaut)

The Necks (*see* Chris Abrahams)

The New Christs

Formed: *1980*
Style: *Hard rock*
Original line-up: *Rob Younger (vocals; ex-***Radio Birdman***, Other Side), Clyde Bramley (bass; ex-***Hitmen***, Other Side), Bruce 'Cub' Callaway (guitar; ex-X-Men,* **Saints***), John Hoey (keyboards; ex-X-Men), Don McGlone (drums; ex-Bedhogs)*

Sydney band The New Christs has existed in several different incarnations, with the only constant factor being redoubtable frontman Rob Younger. Although the **Radio Birdman** legacy has continued to overshadow Younger's subsequent work, The New Christs remain one of the most important independent bands that emerged during the 1980s.

With the break-up of **Radio Birdman** in 1978, Younger initially formed the short-lived The Other Side with Clyde Bramley, Charlie Georgees (guitar; ex-Hellcats, **Hitmen**) and Mark Kingsmill (drums; ex-Hellcats). The Other Side played predominantly covers of 1960s garage-punk and R&B material, with a smattering of Younger originals in the same vein. Georgees was a rock-solid guitar player of tremendous skill, and Kingsmill was, even then, one of the best drummers in Australia. The Other Side earned a reputation as the archetypal, hard-driving, inner-city rock band, but the odds always seemed to be stacked up against any notions of sustained success. Just as the band was hitting its stride, Kingsmill left to join **The Hitmen**. Ron Keeley (ex-**Radio Birdman**, Visitors) took his place, but by the end of 1979 the band had fallen apart.

In early 1980, Younger and Bramley formed the first version of The New Christs with the above line-up. The original line-up was short-lived and never performed live, but did record the searing acid-punk single 'Face a New God'/'Waiting World' for the GREEN label. **The Thought Criminals**' Ken Doyle played drums on the recording session. Issued in August 1981, the single has since emerged as one of the most collectable artefacts of the Australian punk/new wave era. The New Christs' name did not appear again until June 1983 when Younger pulled together three members of **The Hitmen** (Chris Masuak, guitar, Mark Kingsmill, drums and Tony Robertson, bass), plus **The Celibate Rifles'** guitarist Kent Steedman, in order to support Iggy Pop on his Australian tour.

Initially, it was intended that The New Christs would only exist for the duration of the tour, but the aggregation proved so potent that they decided to work as a full-time band. Richard Jakimyszyn (guitar, ex-**Lime Spiders**) replaced Steedman, whose commitments to The Rifles precluded any lengthy stay. The new line-up recorded two consummate, guitar-driven, hard rock singles for the Citadel label, 'Like a Curse'/'Sun God' (April 1984) and 'Born Out of Time'/'No Next Time' (April 1986). 'Like a Curse' and 'Born Out of Time' later appeared on Citadel's essential double album compilation *Take Everything Leave Nothing* (March 1988).

Following the band's break-up in May 1984, Younger spent the next two and a half years producing a number of Sydney independent bands (including **Lime Spiders**, **Died Pretty**, **Eastern Dark**, **Psychotic Turnbuckles** and **Hard-Ons**, plus **Stems** from Perth). Of the other members, Masuak joined **The Screaming Tribesmen**, Kingsmill joined **Hoodoo Gurus** and Jakimyszyn re-joined **The Lime Spiders**. Younger revived the New Christs' name in February 1987, for the third time, with a line-up comprising Charlie Owen (guitar; ex-Tango Bravo), string-bean bass player Jim Dickson (ex-**Railroad Gin**, Survivors, **Passengers**, Barracudas) and Louis Burdett (drums; ex-Powerhouse, **Ed Kuepper** Band). Nick Fisher (ex-Wet Taxis, Paris Green) replaced Burdett and that line-up recorded four singles for Citadel: 'The Black Hole'/'Addiction' (July 1987), the double 7-inch 'Dropping Like Flies'/'Dead Girl'; 'I Swear'/'You'll Never Catch My Wave' (December), 'Headin' South'/'I Saw God' (November 1988) and 'Another Sin'/'The Burning of Rome' (June 1989).

The New Christs' explosive debut album *Distemper* (August 1989) remains the definitive

The New Christs

statement on the band's sound and style. It contained a wealth of powerful tracks like 'No Way on Earth', 'Afterburn', 'Circus of Sour' and 'The Burning of Rome'. The album attained the #1 spot on the alternative chart. As well as touring constantly across Australia, The New Christs also undertook two successful tours of Europe, where the band's records sold exceedingly well. The band broke up in late 1989, but there was a short-lived reunion at the start of 1991 when The New Christs were booked as support for The Ramones at that band's Sydney concert. Dickson went on to work closely with ex-**Radio Birdman** guitarist **Deniz Tek**, while Owen has worked with everyone from Don Walker and **Tex Perkins** (as Tex Don and Charlie) to **Beasts of Bourbon**. Owen also issued a solo album in 1994, *Vertigo and Other Phobias* (Red Eye/Polydor), which featured the old New Christs rhythm section of Jim Dickson (bass) and Nick Fisher (drums).

The next New Christs line-up appeared in January 1992 when Younger recruited Billy Gibson (guitar, organ; ex-**Eastern Dark**), Christian Houllemare (bass; ex-**Happy Hate Me Nots**), Stevie Plunder (guitar; ex-**Plunderers**) and Peter Kelly (drums; ex-**Flies, No Man's Land, Vanilla Chainsaws**). Plunder left at the end of the year to join **The Whitlams**; he died in 1996. Tony Harper (ex-Viscounts, Voodoo Lust) joined on guitar. Harper's previous band, Voodoo Lust, also comprised Gary Slater (vocals), Brad Ferguson (bass) and Dean Muller (drums). Voodoo Lust issued the singles 'Shake Shake, Hey Yey'/'No No No No' (August 1986), 'Stop Breakin' My Heart'/'Gossip' (July 1987) and 'Cathy's on Heat'/'How Do You Sleep?' (May 1988), plus the mini-albums *Voodoo Lust* (August 1987) and *Life, Love, Booze and Bitterness* (June 1988; both on Rattlesnake). The line-up on the latter comprised Slater, Harper, Steve King (bass) and Phil Jacquet (drums; ex-**Celibate Rifles**). Originally from Brisbane, the band broke up in Sydney in late 1989. Ferguson joined **The Hitmen**; Muller later turned up in Melbourne band **Hoss**.

The New Christs issued the *Pedestal* CD EP in October 1994. A month later, Gibson left (he later joined Lemonheads) to be replaced by Mark Wilkinson (guitar; ex-**Girlies, Lime Spiders**). That gave a tenacious line-up of Younger, Houllemare, Kelly, Harper and Wilkinson. The New Christs issued a new CD EP, *Woe Betide*, in November 1995. At the same time, Lance Rock Records in Canada put out the retrospective album *Born Out of Time* that drew together 13 tracks of prime New Christs aural mayhem. Younger also produced **Died Pretty's** *Sold* album in 1995. He toured with the re-formed **Radio Birdman** in early 1996 and then reactivated The New Christs again for the powerful *Lower Yourself* album at the start of 1997. The line-up on the album comprised Younger, Wilkinson, Houllemare and Kelly with assistance from John Hoey (keyboards; from **Died Pretty**). In April 1997, The New Christs toured Europe with newcomer Al Creed (ex-**Fruitworld**, Hey Charger!) on guitar and vocals.

Albums: *Distemper* (Blue Mosque/Festival, 1989), *Divine Rites* (mini-album compilation of early singles, Citadel, 1988), *Born Out of Time* (Canadian compilation, Lance Rock Records, 1995), *Lower Yourself* (Citadel, 1997).

New Dream

Formed: *1967*
Style: *Pop*
Original line-up: *Alex Kadell (aka Alex Opitz, vocals; ex-Changing Times), Jenny Johnson (keyboards; ex-Changing Times), Jack McGrath (guitar; ex-Final Four), Peter Nicoll (guitar; ex-Final Four), Terry Stirzker (bass; ex-Final Four), Mark Archer (drums; ex-Final Four)*

Following in the overseas tradition as forged by the likes of The Archies, The Lemon Pipers, The Ohio Express and The 1910 Fruitgum Co, New Dream was one of Australia's foremost bubblegum pop bands of the early 1970s. The band formed as The Dream in late 1967 when singer Alex Kadell and Jenny Johnson from The Changing Times joined forces with The Final Four. The Changing Times had been a popular Melbourne discotheque band of the mid-1960s that comprised Alan 'Edgell' Walker (bass), Allan Elliot (drums), Willy Ferris (lead guitar) and Barry Gallagher (rhythm guitar). To attract attention, the guys dressed up in black capes and dyed their hair blond.

The band recorded two singles for RCA, 'Mary Lou'/'I'm Going Away' (May 1965) and 'It Ain't So'/'Wonderful Wonderful' (August 1965). The sturdy cover of Ronnie Hawkins' 'Mary Lou' reached #12 on the Sydney chart. By early 1966, only Allan Elliot remained. He was joined by Alex Opitz (bass, vocals), Lyn Thomas (lead guitar) and Jenny Johnson (keyboards). That version of The Changing Times was more pop oriented. In early 1967, Roger Treble (guitar; ex-Silhouettes, Rondells), Wayne Duncan (bass; ex-Rondells) and **Gary Young** (drums; ex-Silhouettes, Rondells) joined Opitz and Johnson in the final version of The Changing Times. Opitz/Kadell and Johnson broke up the band when they formed The Dream.

In early 1968, Brian Holloway replaced Peter Nicoll on guitar. Holloway left later in the year to join the remnants of Somebody's Image (with the departure of **Russell Morris**) as The Image. The Dream became New Dream in March 1969 when the band's booking agency decided to pit them against two other emergent bubblegum bands, **The Flying Circus** and **The Zoot**. New Dream signed with Festival and issued the singles 'Yours Until Tomorrow'/'Turn Around' (April 1969) and 'Catching Up on Fun'/'You've Got that Certain Style' (July). The band's first national hit was 'Groupie'/'It's So Good to Be with You' (#28 in March 1970), written by Buzz Cason who had also penned hits for **The Flying Circus**. By that stage, the band consisted of Kadell, Johnson, Jack McGrath, John Du Bois (bass) and Peter Reed (drums).

The band's next three singles, 'Soft Delights'/'You Got Me Singing' (May 1971), 'Candy Love'/'Do You Think You Can Make Me Happy?' (September 1971) and 'Turned 21'/'Someone Like You' (March 1972) all made the charts, with 'Soft Delights' being the biggest hit (#21). In January 1972, Du Bois left to join **Country Radio** and he was replaced by Graham Jones (ex-**Iguana**, Captain Australia and the Honky Tonk). The new line-up completed the band's eponymous debut album (produced by **Brian Cadd**) and issued the singles T-Rex's 'Ride a White Swan'/'The Weak End' (December 1972) and 'Girl I'm Gonna Get You'/'Gene's Song' (February 1973). The album was a gloriously camp mix of the band's bubblegum hits, easy listening pop fluff replete with sweet harmonies and schmaltz strings, plus a cover of Joni Mitchell's 'Chelsea Morning'. New Dream broke up at the end of 1972; Peter Reed joined **Gary Young**'s Hot Dog and Kadell went solo.

Kadell and Johnson revived the New Dream name in 1974 for two singles, the Steve Groves-produced, Andy Fairweather Low-penned 'I Can't Stop Dancing (Dancing in the Dark)'/'Musical Lovin' Man' (July) and the **Buddy England**-produced 'Schlick Schlack Boom Boom'/'Country Life' (November). By that stage, the band's bubblegum pop sound had become outmoded.

Album: *New Dream* (Festival, 1973).

New Race

Formed: *1981*
Style: *Hard rock*
Original line-up: *Rob Younger (vocals; ex-***Radio Birdman***, Other Side,* **New Christs***),* **Deniz Tek** *(guitar, vocals; ex-***Radio Birdman***, Visitors), Warwick Gilbert (bass; ex-***Radio Birdman, Hitmen***), Ron Asheton (guitar; ex-Stooges, New Order, Destroy All Monsters), Dennis Thompson (drums; ex-MC5, New Order)*

New Race existed for six weeks and in that time played a total of 16 gigs. The New Race tour of April–May 1981 was designed to be a special event, a one-off opportunity for the band to assemble, burn brightly and then disintegrate like a falling star. The band left behind one of the greatest live albums in the history of Australian rock'n'roll.

The idea for the brief supergroup came about when Rob Younger and **Deniz Tek** were preparing the posthumous **Radio Birdman** album *Living Eyes* for release at the start of 1981. Having roped in another ex-Birdman alumnus, Warwick Gilbert, Tek invited Americans Ron Asheton and Dennis Thompson to join. Asheton and Thompson were part of the legendary Detroit rock scene that had spawned The Stooges, MC5, New Order, Sonic's Rendezvous Band and Destroy All Monsters, and which had so influenced the Sydney inner-city rock fraternity in particular.

American-born Tek had come into contact with Asheton and Thompson while he was completing his internship at a Detroit hospital, and the Americans were willing to help out on the tour. Over the course of the 16-date Australian east coast tour, New Race played to approximately 12 000 fans. The band played a mix of **Radio Birdman**, Visitors, Stooges, MC5 and Destroy All Monsters' classics, plus one original song, 'Columbia', which had been written during rehearsals especially for the tour. Once the tour was over, the members dispersed: Asheton and Thompson returned to the USA; Tek played with the Angie Pepper Band before returning to the USA to commence a career as a jet pilot and squadron doctor with the US navy; Younger re-formed **New Christs**; and Gilbert rejoined

Hitmen before moving into a career in graphic design/computer animation.

WEA issued the blistering live album *The First and Last* in September 1982. It was hard'n'fast Detroit rock'n'roll at its very best, with Tek and Asheton's incendiary guitar interplay well to the fore. In April 1983, the Citadel label (run by one-time Birdman cohort John Needham) issued The New Race single 'Crying Sun'/'Gotta Keep Movin''. The album has been reissued on at least four occasions. In the late 1980s, the French-based Revenge label issued two unauthorised, sub-standard albums (*The First to Pay* and *The Second Wave*) of live New Race material dubbed from cassette tapes owned by Asheton.

Album: *The First and the Last* (WEA/Trafalgar, 1982; reissued Big Time/EMI, 1984).

New World

Formed: *1967*
Style: *Vocal pop*
Original line-up: *John Kane (vocals), John Lee (vocals), Mel Noonan (vocals)*

New World was a middle-of-the-road vocal trio in the manner of Irish 1960s hit-makers The Bachelors. The group scored a hit with the release of its debut single, 'Try to Remember'/'The World I Used to Know' (#12 in January 1969). The group issued one more single, 'Feed the Birds'/'The Water is Wide' (December 1969) before travelling to the UK.

Initially New World's pleasant, innocuous and out-dated sound found little favour on a UK music scene otherwise preoccupied with heavy rock and the burgeoning glam-rock movement. New World then appeared on the prestigious British television talent show *Opportunity Knocks* and became an instant success. The trio signed to the fledgling RAK label and scored a run of British hit singles, including Joe South's 'Rose Garden'/'Ain't Nobody Ever Gonna Wonder?' (#15 in February 1971), 'Tom Tom Turnaround'/'Lay Me Down' (#6 in July), 'Kara Kara'/'Lord of the Dance' (#17 in December 1971), 'Sister Jane'/'First Steps' (#9 in May 1972) and 'Roof Top Singing'/'Lady Sunshine' (#50 in May 1973).

Oddly enough, the band's version of the expatriate Chinn-Chapman writing team's 'Living Next Door to Alice'/'Something to Say' failed to chart in the UK. Another RAK band, Smokie, later reached the UK Top 5 with its rendition of the song. New World issued one more single on RAK, 'Old Shep'/'Sally's a Lady', before signing to EMI for two final singles in 1974, 'Do It Again'/'Guitar Happy' (May) and 'Sweet Dreams'/'Happiness is You' (August). Meanwhile, New World also scored three hit singles in Australia with 'Tom Tom Turnaround' (#24 in September 1971), 'Sister Jane' (#16 in August 1972) and 'Living Next Door to Alice' (#35 in March 1973).

Albums: *New World* (EMI/Parlophone, 1969), *New World* (reissue of debut, EMI/Columbia, 1971), *I Believe in Music* (UK only, RAK, 1973), *Welcome to My World* (budget reissue of *New World*, EMI/Axis, 1975), *Yesterday's Gone* (EMI, 1975).

News

Formed: *1977*
Style: *Punk*
Original line-up: *Adam Punk (real name Gavin Quinn, vocals), Jarryl Circus (real name Jarryl Wirth, guitar), Joy Relentless (real name Julie Jordan, bass), John Smith-from-the-Suburbs (real name John Murphy, drums)*

The late 1970s punk movement manifested itself in the inner-city enclaves of the nation's capital cities around 1976. One of the original Melbourne punk bands (alongside The Boys Next Door and The Reals) was Babeez, which Gavin Quinn and Jarryl Wirth formed at the end of 1976. The original incarnation of Babeez was actually called Antennae and the TV Kids and also included Bruce Milne on bass and Graeme Pitt on guitar.

Babeez's line-up was Quinn, Wirth, Julie Jordan and a number of drummers including Paul Makeshift, Greg Perano and Alan (someone). There was also a number of additional guitarists like Ian Forrest and Lenny (someone) who played occasionally. Babeez issued the first Melbourne punk single 'Nobody Wants Me'/'Hate', 'Dowanna Love' in November 1977. The band recorded the single in a lounge room on cheap equipment so the sound was rough'n'ready to say the least. The single came in a pressing of 500 copies, packaged in a brown paper bag with lyrics crudely mistyped on the back and a picture of an aborted foetus printed on the front. Like a number of other primordial punk bands of the era, Babeez found little acceptance beyond a faithful few, and by the end of 1977 had evolved into News. The Babeez track 'Nobody Wants Me' later appeared on Missing Link's *Inner Sanctum* compilation credited to News.

News was at the centre of a spray-painting campaign at the time which saw the band's moniker adhered to just about every flat surface around inner-city Melbourne. News issued the single 'Dirty

Lies'/'Chop Chop Chop' in May 1978. The single ranks with the first recordings of **The Saints**, **Radio Birdman**, **The Victims**, **Scientists**, **The Leftovers** and **The Fun Things** as one of the classics of the late-1970s Australian punk movement. 'Chop Chop Chop' was actually announced as 'Fuck Fuck Fuck' on some copies of the screen-printed labels. By that stage, News was Melbourne's answer to The Ramones with a political conscience. The band was one of the few Melbourne punk bands of the day (alongside Young Charlatans, **The Chosen Few** and →↑→) to resist the lure of Suicide Records.

In 1979, News issued the *Dirty Secrets* double single which contained the one-sided 'Dowanna Love', 'Hate' (reissued from Babeez's single), plus the flexi-disc of 'Sweet Dancer'/'Tell Me Why'. In early 1979, two ex-members of **Stiletto**, Chris Dyson (guitar) and Eddie Van Roosendael (drums), played with News briefly, before they joined The Romantics. By May 1979, only singer Quinn remained from the original News line-up. Russell Urban (real name Russell Irvine, guitar), Kim Morton (bass) and Dorland Bray (drums) completed the new line-up. The band's sound was more power pop-based by that stage. Graham Lewis (keyboards; ex-**Aliens**) joined later in the year.

News bowed out with a final single in 1980 on the Missing Link label, 'That Girl'/'I'm So Confused'. Quinn teamed up with Dave Forward (synthesiser) as (Adam Five and) the Spies. Of the other News members, Dorland Bray joined The Benders and then **Do Ré Mi**; John Murphy joined Whirlywirld; and Jarryl Wirth joined **The Innocents** and The Breakers, and had tracks released internationally on the Kim Fowley-compiled *Vampires from Outer Space* sampler (1979) disguised as The Lonely Boys. The Spies issued a five-track, self-titled EP in 1980 which featured a poorly recorded electro-pop sound as displayed on the brattish 'The Rat Spat Back'. Quinn and Forward also recorded under the name of The Microtechs (the track 'Chant of the Pigdon Tribe' appeared on the Various Artists album *From Belgrave with Love*).

By 1982, Quinn and Forward had formed New Five with Dave Jacobs (guitar), Bob Reinking (bass) and Billy King (drums). New Five issued its self-financed debut single, 'Life without Lulu'/'Latin America', on the Au Fait label in June 1983. Mushroom's White label reissued the whimsical 'Life without Lulu' (an ode to a dead dog) a month later, and then again in 1984 with a new B-side, 'No Time'. New Five issued one more single, 'Every Minute'/'Philosophy of Hate', on White (September 1984) before calling it a day.

Olivia Newton-John

Style: *Pop, country*

During the 1970s and 1980s, Olivia Newton-John (b. 1947) was one of the most successful female singers in the world. Although Newton-John only spent the very earliest years of her career in Australia, she is considered to be an important member of the local entertainment community. Originally known for her breathy and delicate interpretations of ballads and country songs, Newton-John moved into a more upfront Adult Oriented Rock (AOR) style during the early 1980s.

Newton-John was born into an academic family in Cambridge, England; her grandfather on her mother's side was Nobel Prize-winning physicist Max Born. At the age of four, she immigrated with her family to Australia and settled in Melbourne. During her early teens, she formed The Sol Four with three school friends in order to work at local functions and jazz clubs. She began singing folk songs as a soloist in clubs and coffee lounges. In 1964, Newton-John appeared in a talent quest on **Johnny O'Keefe's** television show *Sing, Sing, Sing* and took out first prize. The prize was a trip to the UK, and she left Australia in 1965. Before she left, Newton-John sang the title song to the film *A Funny Thing Happened Down Under*. Not long after arriving in the UK, Newton-John teamed up with fellow Australian Pat Carroll as Pat and Olivia.

The duo appeared on BBC television and on the cabaret circuit. After Carroll was unable to renew her work permit, Newton-John took the plunge as a solo artist. (Carroll later married Newton-John's record producer John Farrar.) She issued her debut solo record, a cover of Jackie De Shannon's 'Til You Say You'll Be Mine'/'For Ever Before', as part of a one-single deal with Decca Records. The single was not successful, and before she could get her solo career off the ground, Newton-John became part of an abortive manufactured group called Toomorrow. The group was the brainchild of American Don Kirshner who was seeking a replacement for The Monkees. Toomorrow appeared in an innocuous, musical-comedy feature film of the same name (directed by Val Guest, 1970) in which the group was kidnapped by aliens who needed music for their home planet. Newton-John sang the track 'Goin' Back' on the soundtrack.

In 1971, Newton-John became engaged to The Shadows' Bruce Welch, who produced her debut solo album *Olivia Newton-John* (retitled *If Not for You* in Australia). The album produced the singles Bob Dylan's 'If Not for You'/'The Biggest Clown' (Australian #14, UK #7, US #25 in May) and 'Banks of the Ohio'/'Love Song' (Australian #1, UK #6 in October). Newton-John made frequent appearances on Cliff Richard's BBC television variety show around that time, and toured throughout Europe as his support act.

In 1972, Newton-John issued her second album, *Olivia*, which featured her version of George Harrison's 'What is Life?'. When issued as a single backed with 'I'm a Small and Lonely Light', 'What is Life' reached #16 in the UK during March 1972. The second single lifted from the album, 'Just a Little Too Much'/'My Old Man's Got a Gun' (August, 1972) was not successful. The album *Let Me Be There* (issued as *Music Makes My Day* in the UK) was her first to attain gold status in the USA (500 000 copies sold). It produced the singles John Denver's 'Take Me Home, Country Roads'/'Sail into Tomorrow' (UK #15 in January 1973), 'Let Me Be There'/'Maybe Then I'll Think of You' (Australian #16, US #6 in December 1973) and 'Music Makes My Day'/'Rosewater' (February 1974). 'Let Me Be There' won her a US Grammy Award for Best Country Female Vocal.

By 1974, Newton-John had relocated to the USA and rapidly established herself as one of the top-selling country artists of the day. Newton-John's fourth album, *Long Live Love*, included the hit singles 'Long Live Love'/'Angel Eyes' (Australian #15, UK #11 in July 1974) and 'I Honestly Love You' /'Home Ain't Home Anymore' (Australian #2, UK #22 and US #1 in October 1974). The **Peter Allen**/Jeff Barry composition 'I Honestly Love You' won Newton-John two Grammy awards: Record of the Year and Best Pop Vocal Performance. She also took out the Female Vocalist of the Year as voted by both the American and British Country Music Associations.

In March 1975, Newton-John's first 'Best of' collection, *Great Hits First Impressions*, reached #1 on the Australian charts. 'If You Love Me (Let Me Know)'/'Brotherly Love' was lifted as a single and it reached #2 in Australia during February and #5 in the US during June. 'If You Love Me (Let Me Know)' was also included on her next album, *Have You Never Been Mellow?*, which gave rise to her second US #1 single (also Australian #12 in April 1975), 'Have You Never Been Mellow?'/'Water Under the Bridge'. The album's third single was 'Please Mr Please'/'And in the Morning' (US #3, August).

Have You Never Been Mellow? made #1 in the USA, #17 in Australia and #37 in the UK. Her fourth single for 1975 was 'Richard's Window'/'Richard's Window—Piano Solo' taken from the movie soundtrack *The Other Side of the Mountain*. *Clearly Love* and its singles, 'Something Better to Do'/'He's My Rock' (September 1975) and 'Let It Shine'/'He Ain't Heavy . . . He's My Brother' (December) were not big successes, but Newton-John finished the year by winning the four major female pop and country awards in *Billboard* magazine. *Come on Over* (June 1976) included the Barry and Robin Gibb composition 'Come on Over' which was issued as a single backed with 'Small Talk and Pride' (February 1976). With the release of the album, Newton-John returned to Australia to star in a locally made television special for the Nine Network along with **Sherbet** and Glenn Campbell. Another track from the *Come on Over* album, a cover of Dolly Parton's 'Jolene', came out as a single much later (backed with 'Changes', March 1978) and it reached #10 in Australia during July that year.

Newton-John maintained her hectic recording schedule with the album *Don't Stop Believin'*, which yielded the singles 'Don't Stop Believin''/'Greensleeves' (July 1976) and 'Sam'/'I'll Bet Your a Kangaroo' (UK #6 in June 1977). Her tenth album, *Making a Good Thing Better*, included the single 'Making a Good Thing Better'/'I Think I'll Say Goodbye' (May 1977). By that stage, Newton-John had been chosen to co-star (in the role of Sandy) with John Travolta in the Robert Stigwood-produced film of the Broadway play *Grease*. It was the most important step in the singer's career. *Grease* was one of the most popular films of 1978, and the soundtrack album reached #1 worldwide (selling 520 000 copies within six months in Australia, and 25 million worldwide all up).

It provided Newton-John with the three biggest hit singles of her career to that time: 'You're the One that I Want' (a duet with Travolta) (Australian #1, UK #1, US #1 in May 1978), 'Hopelessly Devoted to You' (Australian #4, UK #1, US #3 in September) and 'Summer Nights' (with Travolta) (Australian #8, UK #2, US #5 in October). Newton-John returned to Australia for the local debut of *Grease* in August, which she followed up with a national tour. By the end of 1978, her next solo album *Totally Hot* had reached #7 in Australia and #30 in the UK. It produced three singles, 'A Little More Love'/'Borrowed Time' (Australian #9, UK #4 in December 1978), 'Deeper than the Night'/'Please Don't Keep Me Waiting' (May 1979) and 'Totally Hot'/'Dancin' Round and Round' (September). In the Queen's New Year Awards 1979, Newton-John was awarded an Order of the British Empire (OBE) for her contribution to entertainment.

Newton-John's next film (in the role of Kira) was the musical-fantasy *Xanadu* with the Electric Light Orchestra and Gene Kelly. The *Xanadu* soundtrack gave rise to two massive hit singles, 'Magic'/'Fool Country' (Australian #4, UK #32 and US #1 in July) and 'Xanadu' (with ELO)/'Whenever You're Away from Me' (Australian #2, UK #1, US #1 in August), plus the UK hit 'Suddenly' (with Cliff Richard)/'You Made Me Love You' (UK #15, US #20 in October). Her other single for 1980 was 'Don't Cry for Me Argentina'/'Gimme Some Lovin'' (Australian #34 in July).

1981 was another big year for the singer: the *Physical* album became the biggest of her career when it reached #3 in Australia, #11 in the UK and #1 in the USA during October. The album presented a raunchier image than Newton-John's fans had come to expect. The singles lifted from the album were Steve Kipner's 'Physical'/'The Promise (the Dolphin's Song)' (Australian #1, UK #7, US #1 in October), 'Make a Move on Me'/'Falling' (Australian #8, UK #43 in April 1982) and 'Landslide'/'Recovery' (UK #18 in June). The song 'Physical' was later used in the television commercial for PhysiCAL milk.

Newton-John's last two singles for 1982 were 'Heart Attack'/'Stranger's Touch' (Australian #22, UK #46 in October) and 'Tied Up (in Promises)'/'Silvery Rain' (December). She enjoyed her fourth Australian #1 album when *Greatest Hits Volume 3* went to the top in November 1982. The soundtrack to Newton-John's next movie, *Two of a Kind* (with John Travolta), spun off two charting singles, 'Twist of Fate'/'Coolin' Down' (Australian #2, UK #57, US #5 in December 1983) and 'Livin' in Desperate Times' (US #31, 1984). The 1985 *Soul Kiss* album produced the single 'Soul Kiss'/'Electric'. Newton-John was quiet on the recording scene for the next three years.

During that time, she concentrated on her career as co-proprietor of the Californian-based store Koala Blue, as well as bringing up daughter Chloe. She co-wrote a children's book called *A Pig Tale* which featured an environmental theme. She returned in September 1988 with the album *The Rumour* which featured the singles 'The Rumour', 'Can't We Talk It Over in Bed' and 'It's Always Australia for Me', plus a heartfelt interpretation of the David and David hit 'Walk Through Fire'. The December 1989 collection of children's songs, *Warm and Tender*, included the single 'Reach Out for Me'/'The Flower that Shattered the Stone'. She also revived her film career with roles in the American telemovies *A Mom for Christmas* (1990) and *A Christmas Romance* (1992).

In late 1991, Polygram reissued the *Grease* soundtrack on CD and it immediately leapt to #1 on the Australian and UK charts. The *Grease Mega-Mix* also registered #1 on the local singles chart and #3 in the UK. Newton-John's 1992 best of collection *Back to Basics* included the new single 'I Need Love' which became a minor hit in the UK (#75 in July). *Back to Basics* peaked at #10 on the Australian chart during September. The singer returned to Australia in the early 1990s, and in 1992 came the announcement that she had breast cancer.

She underwent successful treatment for the disease, and recorded a highly personalised album, *Gaia*, on which she wrote or co-wrote all the tracks. (In Greek mythology, Gaia is the nearest equivalent to Mother Earth.) *Gaia* charted in the Australian Top 10 album listing (#9) and the single 'No Matter What You Do' in the Top 40 (#35) during October 1994. Newton-John's most recent film appearance was in *It's My Party* (1995). She returned to Australian television as the presenter of *Wild Life with Olivia Newton-John* and in a series of advertisements for Panasonic.

Albums: *If Not for You* (Interfusion/Festival, 1971), *Olivia* (Interfusion/Festival, 1972), *Olivia Newton-John* (double reissue of first two albums, Interfusion/Festival, 1973), *Let Me Be There* (Interfusion/Festival, 1973), *Long Live Love* (Interfusion/Festival, 1974), *Great Hits First Impressions* (Interfusion/Festival, 1975), *Have You Never Been Mellow?* (Interfusion/Festival, 1975), *Clearly Love* (Interfusion/Festival, 1975), *Come on Over* (Interfusion/Festival, 1976), *Don't Stop Believin'* (Interfusion/Festival, 1976), *Making a Good Thing Better* (Interfusion/Festival, 1977), *Grease* (film soundtrack shared with Various Artists, RSO/PolyGram, 1978), *Greatest Hits Volume 2* (Interfusion/Festival, 1978), *Totally Hot* (Interfusion/Festival, 1978), *Xanadu* (film soundtrack shared with ELO, Jet/CBS, 1980), *Physical* (Interfusion/Festival, 1981), *Love Performance (Live In Japan)* (Interfusion/Festival, 1981), *Greatest Hits Volume 3* (Interfusion/Festival, 1982), *Two of a Kind* (film soundtrack, Festival, 1983), *Soul Kiss* (Festival, 1985), *The Rumour* (Festival, 1988), *Warm and Tender*

(Festival, 1989), *Back to Basics: The Essential Collection 1971–1992* (Festival, 1992), *Gaia* (Festival, 1994).

1927

Formed: *1987*
Style: *Pop rock*
Original line-up: *Eric Weideman (vocals, guitar), Garry Frost (guitar, keyboards, vocals; ex-***Moving Pictures***), Bill Frost (bass, vocals), James Barton (drums, vocals)*

Alongside **Men at Work's** *Business as Usual*, Sydney band 1927's album . . . *Ish* was one of the most successful Australian debut albums of the 1980s. The album . . . *Ish* attained five times platinum status by racking up sales of more than 400 000 copies. From there, it was a slow downhill run for the band, and a protracted end that saw its final album disappear without a trace.

Garry Frost was best known for his role as guitar player/songwriter with **Moving Pictures**. He penned the band's massive hit single 'What About Me?' before leaving the band after its second album. He formed a short-lived duo, Roberts Frost, with singer Brenton Roberts, but when that project failed to warm any hearts he retired to his home studio in Sydney to write. In late 1986, he saw vocalist Eric Weideman performing The Police's 'Roxanne' on the *Red Faces* segment of popular Melbourne television variety show *Hey Hey It's Saturday*. Frost knew that Weideman was the perfect singer for his unrecorded songs, and the ideal frontman for his new band. Frost drove all the way to Melbourne in order to snare the singer. With Frost's youngest brother Bill on bass and drummer James Barton, the line-up of 1927 was complete.

Frost spent a year attempting to get a deal for the band and every record company in the country knocked him back. Eventually producer Charles Fisher (who had worked on **Moving Pictures'** *Days of Innocence* album) signed 1927 to Trafalgar Productions which he ran in conjunction with **Hoodoo Gurus'** Dave Faulkner and the Gurus' manager Michael McMartin. Fisher produced 1927's debut album, . . . *Ish* (December 1988) which was brimful of stirring, stately pop rock anthems. The album reached #1 on the national chart during April 1989. In the interim, it had produced two Top 5 hit singles 'That's when I Think of You'/'Alright' (July 1988; #4 in September) and 'If I Could'/'No Talking' (October; #3 in December). Two further hit singles, 'You'll Never Know'/'Willing and Able' (#17 in February 1989) and 'Compulsory Hero'/'Propaganda Machine' (#8 in April) followed. The fifth single, 'To Love Me'/'All the People' (June), was not a chart success. . . . *Ish* stayed on the chart for a year. 'That's when I Think of You' also made the UK charts when it peaked at #46 in April 1989.

Eric Weideman, 1927

The band won the 1988 Australian Record Industry Association (ARIA) Awards for Best Debut Single ('That's When I Think of You') and Best Debut Album (shared with **Rockmelons'** *Tales of the City*). By that stage, Weideman had become something of a pin-up idol courtesy of his photogenic appearance and boyish good looks. Frost added Charlie Cole (keyboards; ex-**Moving Pictures**) to the line-up, and the band toured for a year in support of . . . *Ish*. In late 1989, as 1927 was in the process of commencing work on its new album, founder member and principal songwriter Garry Frost left the band. The parting was an amicable one, and the songwriting emphasis shifted to Weideman.

The Other Side (co-produced by Fisher and Frost) was full of lush, ambitious arrangements and well-crafted pop, but it lacked the charm and rousing choruses that had made its predecessor so accessible. The album made its debut at #3 but swiftly plummeted out of the chart. Its three singles, 'Tell Me a Story'/'Call on Me', 'Don't Forget Me'/'Seventeen' and 'The Other Side'/'Final Split', all made the lower reaches of the national Top 40. Two years later, 1927 was back with its third album, *1927* (November 1992). In the meantime, Barton and

Cole had left the band to be replaced by Phil Campbell (drums) and Dave Dwyer (guitar) respectively. The *1927* album revealed the band to be a competent, if mediocre, rock outfit trotting out blustery, by-rote hard rock numbers like the singles 'Scars' (October 1992) and 'It Ain't Love' (February 1993). By 1993, the band was in serious financial and artistic difficulties, and broke up with little fanfare.

Weideman slipped from public view, but re-emerged in September 1996 with his debut solo single 'Nothing I Can Do' (produced by Fisher). 'Nothing I Can Do' appeared as the last track on the 1927 'Best of' album *The Very Best of . . . 1927* which was a way of announcing his impending rise as a solo artist.

Albums: *. . . Ish* (Trafalgar/WEA, 1988), *The Other Side* (Trafalgar/WEA, 1990), *1927* (Trafalgar/Warner, 1992), *The Very Best of . . . 1927* (East West/Warner, 1996).

The Nissan Cedrics (*see* Danni'elle Gaha)

Nitocris

Formed: *1992*
Style: *Punk rock*
Original line-up: *Morgana Ancone (vocals), Kira Taylor (guitar), Jessie Finlayson (guitar), Sara Anderson (bass), Andrea Stanway (drums)*

The mid-1990s saw the rise of a number of all-girl, agit-rock bands like **Fur**, Mace, Bittersweet, Sulk, Dolljuice, Gravelrash, SPDFGH and Nitocris. Loosely combined under the collective banner of 'grot grrrls' (similar to the American 'riot grrrl' movement that encompassed Hole, Bikini Kill, Babes in Toyland, L7, etc.), it gave a focus for the musicians to address topics that affected them deeply.

In true punk-rock style, the members of Sydney-based Nitocris were unable to play their instruments when they formed the band in 1992. Eventually the band forged an energetic punk rock/heavy metal hybrid that drew on the likes of Slayer, Black Sabbath, The Clash, Patti Smith, L7, Joan Jett and The Blackhearts and Guns N' Roses for inspiration. (Nitocris, the goddess, was queen of the underworld in Egyptian mythology.) The girls' style was effective and anarchic enough for them to share stages with bands as diverse as **Armoured Angel**, **Frenzal Rhomb** and **Blitz Babies**. After appearing on the Sydney bill of the 1994 Big Day Out, Nitocris issued its debut, four-track CD EP 'Ten Stories Down' on the Phantom label (June).

'Ten Stories Down' also appeared on the band's debut album *Screaming Dolorous* (November 1994), as did a cover of Black Sabbath's 'N.I.B' which had become a live favourite. The band also shared a 7-inch single with fellow Sydney all-girl band Purr (the Nitocris track was 'Suxciety'), and contributed a track to rooArt's compilation *Youngblood 4* (September 1994). Nitocris spent most of 1995 touring constantly, and issued the CD EPs 'Epic Voyage' (lifted from *Screaming Dolorous*, October 1995) and 'Hyperland' (April 1996). 'Epic Voyage' included a live rendition of **AC/DC**'s 'Dirty Deeds Done Dirt Cheap', a version of which Nitocris also contributed to the **AC/DC** tribute album *Fuse Box: The Alternative Tribute* (BMG, June 1995). Nitocris returned in March 1997 with a new CD EP, *Butter*, and a national tour support to US punk band Sprung Monkey.

Album: *Screaming Dolorous* (Phantom, 1994).

No (*see* Ian 'Ollie' Olsen)

No Fixed Address

Formed: *1979*
Style: *Reggae, rock*
Original line-up: *Veronica Rankine (vocals, sax, flute), Les Graham (lead guitar), Ricky Harrison (rhythm guitar), John John Miller (bass), Bart Willoughby (drums, vocals, didgeridoo)*

Bart Willoughby was a member of the Pitjantjatjara tribe from Ceduna, on the Great Australian Bight, South Australia. He formed Koori band No Fixed Address while attending the Centre for Aboriginal Studies in Music (CASM) in Adelaide, South Australia. The band played local gigs, and then appeared in Ned Landers' groundbreaking, quasi-documentary film *Wrong Side of the Road* (1981), which dramatised the gritty experiences of two Aboriginal bands on tour.

The other band was fellow CASM outfit Us Mob which comprised Peter Butler (guitar, vocals), Carol Karpanny (guitar, vocals), Ronnie Ansell (bass) and Wally McArthur (drums). No Fixed Address and heavy rockers Us Mob appeared on one side each of the soundtrack album to *Wrong Side of the Road* (November 1981), becoming the first contemporary Aboriginal bands to be recorded in the process. By 1982, No Fixed Address and Us Mob had both relocated to Sydney. Us Mob found the going tough, and disbanded when a fire destroyed all their equipment. No Fixed Address managed to avoid any such setbacks, and toured constantly (including support slots to **Cold Chisel**, The Clash and US bluesman Taj Mahal).

The line-up that appeared on the band's David Briggs-produced mini-album *From My Eyes* (August 1982) and single 'From My Eyes'/'We Have Survived' was Willoughby, Graham, Chris Jones (rhythm guitar), Joe Hayes (bass), **Joe Geia** (vocals, percussion, didgeridoo) and Billy Inda (percussion, didgeridoo). The album featured strident, heartfelt songs like 'We Have Survived', 'Pigs' and 'Stupid System', which pulled no punches on the issue of racism. On the other hand, 'Sunrise' was a tale of lost love set to a gorgeous reggae-pop backing. The band later contributed 'We Have Survived' to the Various Artists album *Building Bridges* on CBS (1989). By September 1983, the line-up was down to a three-piece of Willoughby, Jones and Nicky Moffott (bass). Geia had left to form reggae band Nya Nunga in Sydney. Les Graham later joined Aroona. In July 1984, No Fixed Address left for the UK where the band appeared at the annual Notting Hill reggae festival, and undertook low-key tours. Upon returning to Australia at the end of the year, Louis McManus (ex-**Captain Matchbox**, **Bushwackers**) joined No Fixed Address as guest guitarist, but the band broke up a year later.

Towards the end of 1985, Willoughby toured with **Goanna** as a guest player on didgeridoo and percussion. Billy Inda had also played didgeridoo on **Goanna's** 1982 hit single 'Solid Rock'. In 1986, Willoughby joined fellow Koori band **Coloured Stone** as drummer. He appeared on the album *Human Love*, plus two singles: the hard rocking 'Dancing in the Moonlight'/'Kapi Pulka' (April 1987) and 'Human Love'/'Waiting for the Tide' (August 1987). By then, Willoughby had re-formed No Fixed Address with John John Miller (bass), Les Lovegrove (guitar) and Rick Lovegrove (guitar). The band made plans to return to Europe for another tour. There was also talk of a retrospective album called *Rough Cuts*, but nothing eventuated. In 1988, Willoughby toured with **Yothu Yindi** and by 1989 had formed Mixed Relations.

Mixed Relations played an infectious and funky hybrid of reggae, pop, rock and jazz. The band established a solid live reputation, but it took until October 1992 before the CD EP 'Take It or Leave It' appeared on the Red Eye label. The CD single 'Aboriginal Woman' and the album *Love* followed in February 1993 and April 1993 respectively. The line-up on *Love* comprised Willoughby (vocals, guitar, percussion, didgeridoo), Murray Cook (keyboards, bass; ex-**Warumpi Band**, **Happening Thang**), Leroy Cummings (guitar), Alvin Duffin (drums, percussion; ex-Mantaka), Alice Haines (vocals, percussion), Vanessa Lucas (bass, violin, backing vocals; ex-**Tall Tales & True**) and Brenda Gifford (sax, backing vocals), plus guest player Cliff Grigg (congas; ex-**v Spy v Spy**). A number of other musicians have passed through the band's ranks, including Sharon Carpenter (percussion, vocals), Suzanne Irvin (keyboards) and Megan Briansky (keyboards, vocals).

No Fixed Address albums: *Wrong Side of the Road* (film soundtrack shared with Us Mob; Black Australia/EMI Custom, 1981), *From My Eyes* (mini-album, Rough Diamond/Astor/PolyGram, 1982); ***Mixed Relations album:*** *Love* (Red Eye/Polydor, 1993).

No Man's Land

Formed: *1984*
Style: *Heavy rock*
Original line-up: *David Slade (vocals; ex-Mercy Killers), Mark Rostron (guitar), Peter Bennett (keyboards), Jim Leone (bass; ex-Mercy Killers), Mark Welsh (drums)*

Sydney heavy rock band No Man's Land drew inspiration from such disparate sources as heavy metal, glitter rock, psychedelia and blues. The band's contemporaries on the mid-1980s Sydney inner-city scene included The Naked Lunch, Mushroom Planet, The Sweet Ride, The Spectre's Revenge, **The Psychotic Turnbuckles**, **The Eastern Dark**, **The Hard-Ons** and **Hoi Polloi**. No Man's Land issued two singles, 'I Need More'/'Inside Your Heart' (August 1986) and 'Anything at All'/'Heartbreak Hotel' (December 1988), plus the mini-album *Savage Brides* (November 1987) on the Au-go-go label. The line-up on the album was Slade, Leone, Nick Potts (keyboards, harmonica; ex-**Moffs**), Dario Bicego (guitar, vocals) and Rod Bain (drums). Leone left in 1988 to join **The Celibate Rifles**.

No Man's Land contributed the track 'Into the Now' (which dated from the band's first recording session with the original line-up) to the Steven Danno-compiled Various Artists album *Swingin' from the Trees* (Au-go-go, 1988). The band suffered a number of line-up changes, and latter-day members included Michael Cullen (guitar), Peter Heywood (guitar), Mick Duncan (keyboards), Duilio Hernandez (drums), Peter Kelly (drums; ex-**Flies**, **Vanilla Chainsaws**) and Phil Kerney (bass). The band broke up in 1989. Hernandez joined **Vanilla Chainsaws** (taking Kelly's place) and later played in Wolfgang. Kelly returned to **Vanilla Chainsaws** (taking Hernandez's place) for a year before joining **The New Christs**.

Dave Slade went on to form heavy metal outfit Medicine Show which comprised Ross McDonald (rhythm guitar), Beggsy (slide guitar), Andrew McRoberts (bass) and Adam Gathercole (drums). The band issued one self-titled album on the Timberyard label (1993). Medicine Show came to the attention of visiting US heavyweights Slash and Gilbey Clark (from Guns N' Roses) and Sebastian Bach (from Skid Row), who joined the band for an on-stage jam while they toured Australia in 1993.

No Man's Land mini-album: *Savage Brides* (Au-go-go, 1987); ***Medicine Show album:*** *Medicine Show* (Timberyard, 1993).

No Nonsense

Formed: *1981*
Style: *Ska pop*
Original line-up: *Dicky Diver (real name Richard Bruce, vocals), Peter Bonett (organ, vocals), Rockin' Eugene (real name Eugene McQueen, guitar, vocals), Tony Tenor (real name Tony Walton, sax, percussion), Maurice Aggro (real name Maurice Argiro, bass), Drinker the Thinker (real name Rob Drinkwater, drums)*

Alongside the likes of Sydney's **Allniters**, Canberra's Naughty Rhythms and fellow Melbourne band **Strange Tenants**, No Nonsense was one of the first Australian bands to bring the sunny delights of ska-pop to local pub audiences. The burgeoning ska movement of the early 1980s was inspired by the UK Bluebeat/2-Tone phenomenon (Madness, The Specials, The Selector), which in turn had drawn on the original Jamaican ska pioneers like Prince Buster, Desmond Dekker and The Skatalites.

On any given night, in tiny, dank Melbourne pubs around Richmond, Collingwood or St Kilda, ska exponents like No Nonsense, Looney Tunes and **Strange Tenants** would play to their rowdy rude boy following. The scene was small, but the audiences were dedicated and passionate about their music. No Nonsense issued the four-track, 12-inch EP *Utter Nonsense* on the Man Made label during 1982. The band formed its own label, No Nonsense, and had its subsequent releases issued through EMI on a lease deal. These included the mini-album *Around Tuit* (September 1984) and the singles 'Changes Must Be Made'/'Hawaii Five-O' (1984) and 'Simple Needs'/'March in Time' (1985).

The line-up on *Around Tuit* was Bruce, McQueen, Argiro, Bonett, Walton, Graham Sullivan (sax, vocals) and Tommy McEwan (drums), plus guest players Jeff Raglus (trumpet, flugel horn) and Laurence Maddick (trombone; ex-**Strange Tenants**). By the time the mini-album appeared, Maddick had joined as a full-time member, replacing Bonett on keyboards. No Nonsense broke up in 1986. Argiro went on to join acclaimed outfit **The Underground Lovers**.

Mini-album: *Around Tuit* (No Nonsense/EMI, 1984).

Patsy Ann Noble

Style: *Pop*

Alongside the likes of **Bryan Davies**, **Lucky Starr**, **Noeleen Batley**, **Col Joye**, **Judy Stone**, **The Allen Brothers**, **The Delltones**, **The De Kroo Brothers**, Laurel Lea and Sandy Scott, Sydney-born pop singer Patsy Ann Noble (b. 1944) was one of the regular stars of popular television show *Bandstand* during the early 1960s. Noble's wholesome image was in keeping with the family entertainment values proffered by *Bandstand.*

Noble signed a deal with the HMV label and issued her debut single, 'I Love You So Much It Hurts'/'Like I'm in Love', in November 1960. She issued three more singles on HMV: 'Busy Lips'/'It's Always the Way' (January 1961), 'Good Looking Boy'/'The Guy Who Can Mend a Broken Heart' (November) and 'Once in a Lifetime'/'Don't Love and Run' (March 1962). 'A Good Looking Boy' became Noble's biggest hit when it reached #6 in Melbourne and #16 in Sydney. She rounded out 1961 by winning a Logie Award as Australia's best female singer.

In 1962 Noble travelled to the UK where she eventually signed to EMI/Columbia. Under the direction of producers like Norrie Paramour, Noble cut several singles, including 'Don't You Ever Change Your Mind'/'Sour Grapes' (February 1963), 'Heartbreak Avenue' (April), 'I was Only Fooling Myself'/'Ordinary Love' (July), 'Oh My Little Baby Darling'/'I'm Not Supposed to Know' (December), 'I Did Nothing Wrong'/'Better Late than Never' (May 1964) and 'Tied Up with Mary' (November). HMV also issued the single 'When You Find Your True Love'/'I'll be Thinking of You' in December 1963. By 1965, Noble had turned to acting, taking the role of Francesca in the low-budget, British thriller *Death is a Woman.*

Following a one-off single on Polydor, 'He Who Rides a Tiger' (1966), Noble relocated to the USA where she became known as Trisha Noble. She issued one more single, 'Live for Life' (1967), before concentrating on her acting career. With guest parts in *Columbo*, *Baretta* and *Buck Rogers* under her belt, Noble then appeared as Yvonne Holland in the long-running soapie *Executive Suite* during the late 1970s. She followed that with the role of Rosie in the crime series *Strike Force* (1982) alongside Robert Stack. Noble later returned to Australia and took a small role in the television miniseries *Body Business* (1986).

Album: *Just for You* (HMV, 1961)

Noise Addict (*see* Ben Lee)

Noiseworks

Formed: 1986
Style: Rock
*Original line-up: Jon Stevens (vocals; ex-Change), Stuart Fraser (guitar; ex-***Feather***, Smith, Change), Justin Stanley (keyboards), Steve Balbi (bass; ex-Rupert B.,* **Kevin Borich Express***), Kevin Nicol (drums; ex-Dial X, Change)*

During the late 1980s, Sydney band Noiseworks made an impact with a tightly focused sound that was tailor-made for commercial radio. By presenting just the right balance of tough pub-rock, anthemic choruses and lush production, the band produced three multi-platinum selling albums. Towards the end of its career, the band added supercharged funk and soul to the brazen white rock mix, but it was not enough to prevent the inevitable split.

Frontman Jon Stevens had been a successful solo pop star in his native New Zealand during the late 1970s/early 1980s. His older brother Frankie Stevens was a popular cabaret performer. Jon Stevens cut an album for CBS (NZ), *Jezabel*, which produced three hit singles 'Jezabel' (a New Zealand #1 in December 1979), Bobby Bloom's 'Montego Bay' (a second NZ #1 in January 1980) and 'Loving You' (Top 40). Stevens enjoyed another hit single, 'Don't Let Love Go', a duet with fellow CBS (NZ) artist Sharon O'Neill, that reached #5 in mid-1980. In 1981, Stevens relocated to Sydney where he signed a deal with the Big Time label. He cut his second, self-titled solo album in Los Angeles with American session players. It yielded two singles in 1982, a re-working of 'Jezabel' and 'Lover My Love', but neither was successful.

Stevens then formed The Change with Stuart Fraser who had been playing in bands since he was 14, when he and his older brother Warwick joined **Blackfeather** during 1976. **Blackfeather** was well past its prime by that stage, and when lead singer Neale Johns left, the rest of the players recruited singer John Swan (**Swanee**) and reconvened as **Feather.** When **Feather** broke up, Stuart and Warwick joined Smith which also comprised Karen Smith (vocals) and latter-day **Feather** bass player

Jon Stevens, Noiseworks

Mark Mitchell who was replaced by Marcel Chaloupka. Smith issued two independent singles, 'Nightlights'/'Life on the Line' (April 1981) and 'Lonely Man'/'Steppin' Time', 'Intensive Care' (June), before breaking up.

The Change played the occasional Sydney pub gig, and with the help of bass player Steve Balbi (on loan from **Kevin Borich Express**) recorded an independent single 'Forever Young'/'Out There' in 1984. By 1985, drummer Kevin Nicol had joined Stevens and Fraser, who began to lay plans for their new band which would combine Stevens' early love for Motown, Tom Jones and David Bowie material with Fraser's penchant for heavy rock riffs. They recruited Balbi as a permanent member. Balbi had played with funk band Rupert B. (or Rupert B. Funkified Filth Band as it was originally known) before joining the **Kevin Borich Express** in 1982. Balbi spent three years with the Express during a time when Borich was without a record deal.

Newcomer Justin Stanley completed the Noiseworks line-up in early 1986. He had been writing songs with Balbi. Noiseworks built up a grassroots following on the Australian pub-rock circuit and then, with the help of former **AC/DC** manager Michael Browning, signed to CBS. The band's debut, self-titled album peaked at #2 on the national chart in July 1987, sold over 210 000 copies (triple platinum) and produced five hit singles: 'No

Lies'/'Learning to Swim' (#19 in December 1986), 'Take Me Back'/'Don't Wait' (#6 in May 1987), 'Love Somebody'/'Love Somebody' (September), 'Welcome to the World'/'No Lies' (live) (November) and 'Burning Feelings'/'River of Tears' (1988).

The band enlisted the services of English producer Chris Kimsey (Rolling Stones) for the second album, *Touch* (November 1988). The album reached #4 on the national chart, sold 150 000 copies and yielded four hit singles: 'Touch'/'5 More Days' (#11 in December 1988), 'Voice of Reason'/'Walk with Me' (#43 in March), 'Simple Man'/'Letter' (#47 in May) and 'In My Youth'/'I Can't Win' (#44 in September). While Noiseworks barely made a dint in the Top 40 for the whole year, the band's position as one of the most popular live acts in Australia remained unchallenged.

By the end of 1989, the band had commenced work on its third album. This time the members handled production duties, which allowed them to stretch out in the studio. When the band's new label, Sony, rejected the completed album, American session ace Randy Jackson was brought in to work with the group in the studio. Only the singles 'Freedom'/'Believer' (#30 in June 1990) and 'Miles and Miles'/'Be Someone' (#26 in December) from the original sessions came out at that time. Neither was a big hit, but they did add a more innovative, almost hypnotic dance-groove to the band's standard FM rock formulae. The completed album, *Love Versus Money*, finally appeared in July 1991. It mixed tracks from the original sessions with straight-ahead, mainstream rock songs like 'Hot Chilli Woman', 'R.I.P. (Millie)' and 'Liberty Bell', which had been recorded with Jackson.

Love Versus Money made its debut at #1 on the national chart and 'Hot Chilli Woman' became the band's biggest hit when it reached #7 during July 1991. The emotion-charged power ballad 'R.I.P. (Millie)' peaked at #26 in October. A fifth single from the album, a cover of Sly and the Family Stone's 'Take You Higher' (also from the original sessions), failed to chart. At the start of 1992, Stevens joined the Australian cast of the revived stage musical *Jesus Christ Superstar*, in the role of Judas. Alongside **John Farnham** (Jesus), **Kate Ceberano** (Mary Magdalene), **Angry Anderson** (Herod), **Russell Morris** (Simon Zealotes), John Waters (Pontius Pilate) and David Gould (Caiaphas), Stevens featured on the #1 charting *Jesus Christ Superstar the Album* issued by Polydor in July, as well as the CD single 'Superstar' (October).

Stevens' spell with *Superstar* also heralded the end of Noiseworks. The band played its last gig at Selinas in Sydney during March 1992. The show produced the band's final single, a cover of The Beatles' 'Let It Be' (live), which came out in October, along with the *Greatest Hits* package (#6 in November). Stanley and Balbi formed production/recording duo **Electric Hippies** and Stevens relaunched his solo career. With the help of Stuart Fraser, Jed Starr (guitar; ex-**Massive Appendage**, Killing Time), **Nick Barker** (guitar, vocals; ex-**Nick Barker and the Reptiles**), Paul Gray (keyboards; ex-**Wa Wa Nee**), Roger McLaughlin (bass; ex-**Little River Band, Stars**) and Virgil Donati (drums; ex-**Taste, Southern Sons**), Stevens recorded his third solo album.

Issued in October 1993, *Are U Satisfied?* produced three singles, 'Going Down', 'Reflections' and 'I Wish It Would Rain'. In 1994, Stevens sang on **The Black Sorrows'** single 'The Last One Standing for You', which reached #46 on the national chart during December. In 1996, Stevens travelled to Los Angeles to record his next solo album under the direction of producer Randy Jackson. The R&B/MOR (Middle of the Road) styled *Circle* appeared in January 1997, preceded by the CD single 'When?' in September 1996. Stevens' next CD single, a cover of Frankie Goes to Hollywood's 'Two Tribes' (March 1997), was used as the theme song to Foxtel's Rugby Super League contest. By 1995, Stuart Fraser was a member of the **John Farnham** Band; he appeared on the album *Romeo's Heart* and the hit single 'Have a Little Faith (in Us)' (#3 in March 1996).

Noiseworks albums: *Noiseworks* (CBS, 1987), *Touch* (CBS, 1988), *Love Versus Money* (Sony, 1991), *Greatest Hits* (Sony, 1992); ***Jon Stevens solo albums:*** *Jezabel* (CBS, NZ only, 1980), *Jon Stevens* (Big Time, 1982), *Are U Satisfied?* (Sony/Columbia, 1993), *Circle* (Sony/Columbia, 1997).

The Nomads

Formed: *1962*
Style: *R&B*
1964 line-up: *Gus McNeil (vocals, sax), John Millyard (guitar), Tony Edye (guitar), Graeme Thompson (bass), Jim Yonge (drums)*

Originally known as The Casuals, then variously as The Nomads or Gus and the Nomads, this band was a popular attraction on Sydney's mid-1960s discotheque circuit. Frontman Gus McNeil was known for his energetic performances, and was regarded as one of the 'wild men of rock' at the time. The Nomads issued two R&B singles on EMI/Parlophone, 'If You Let Me'/'It's Alright' (November 1966) and 'Good Times'/'Don't You

Fret' (March 1967). As Gus and the Nomads, the band issued a self-titled EP at the end of 1967.

A year later, McNeil formed The Music Machine with Howard Page and travelled to the UK. The others continued on as The Nomads. On his return, McNeil formed Gus and the House with Barry Farrell (bass), Tony Hamilton (guitar), Mitch Byrne (sax; ex-Jamieson Battery) and Laurie Kemp (drums). Gus and the House issued the single 'The Bed'/'I Wish I Knew How It Would Feel to be Free' on Festival (June 1969). The Nomads' final single was 'Time to Get It Together'/'Don't Come Knockin'' (April 1970). By mid-1970, The Nomads had transformed into **Pirana**.

Meanwhile, McNeil had secured a recording deal and assembled a studio band called White Wine. The band comprised McNeil, Laurie Kemp, Bill Twyman (bass), Graham Conlan (guitar, vocals), Angela Jones (backing vocals) and Leonie Goodwin (backing vocals). The album *Overflow* (on Festival) and its single, The Flying Burrito Brothers' 'The Train Song'/'Look Around' (November 1969), achieved some success, which prompted McNeil to take the band on tour. Tony Hamilton and Al Jackson (guitar; ex-**Ray Brown and the Whispers**) joined the studio line-up on stage.

McNeil then took a new line-up of White Wine to the UK. That line-up included Frank Lewis (vocals, guitar), Greg Hill (bass), Dave Conners (sax; ex-Jamieson Battery), Robert Souter (drums; ex-Jamieson Battery) and Sandra Heinman (vocals). Once that project had run its course, Conners, Hill and Souter returned to Sydney and formed **Lizard**, while McNeil concentrated on production work and music publishing. During the 1970s, he produced albums for **Company Caine**, **Extradition**, **Pirana**, **Renée Geyer**, **Gulliver Smith**, **Home**, **Redhouse**, Syrius and Albatross.

Non Stop Dancers

Formed: *1983*
Style: *Pop, funk*
Original line-up: *Larry Van Kriedt (sax, guitar, vocals; ex-***AC/DC**, **Eighty Eights***), Kevin Jones (guitar, vocals), Jane Stewart (keyboards), Karen Steains (bass), Brett Van Kriedt (drums)*

Sydney dance outfit Non Stop Dancers played an energetic blend of pop, funk and soul. Larry Van Kriedt had a background of some note: born in San Francisco, his father was a renowned jazz sax player; he was also the original bass player for the nascent **AC/DC**. He formed Non Stop Dancers with his brother Brett following the break-up of his previous band, **The Eighty Eights**.

Non Stop Dancers issued *The Independent Single* ('Only One'/'Blow by Blow') in May 1984 before signing to EMI. The album *Surprise Surprise* (December 1984) produced three energetic singles, 'Shake this City'/'Spellbound' (October), 'Mobbing Me'/'Too Young to Die' (March 1985) and 'Dancing'/'Armadillo Rumba' (June). 'Shake this City' peaked at #22 in hometown Sydney during November. The band issued one more single, 'Lost and Found'/'Strive' (August 1986), before breaking up. Larry Van Kriedt concentrated on session work, and then in the early 1990s teamed up with **Def FX** as a hidden fifth member. He co-wrote much of the band's early material.

Album: *Surprise Surprise* (EMI, 1984).

North 2 Alaskans

Formed: *1981*
Style: *Psychedelic cabaret*
Original line-up: *Frank Savage (guitar, vocals; ex-Cruisers, Frank Savage and the Citizens), Johnny Topper (bass, vocals; ex-***Pelaco Brothers***, Autodrifters, Armchairs), Spencer Jones (guitar, vocals; ex-Cuban Heels, Beats Working), Jimi Williams (organ), Steve Watson (drums; ex-Frank Savage and the Citizens)*

For the final word in 1960s revivalism, look no further than Melbourne's self-styled kings of psychedelic cabaret, North 2 Alaskans. By taking musical satire to its logical limits, the band came up with a clever and always entertaining stage show. The band derived its name from the 1960 John Wayne adventure film *North to Alaska,* which said a lot about the irreverent aesthetic at work.

North 2 Alaskans played the early 1980s Melbourne pub circuit with a set comprised almost entirely of 1960s pop songs. As co-conspirators in this charade of outrageous proportions, Johnny Topper and Frank Savage could never be accused of taking themselves too seriously. Topper was already a Melbourne cult identity of some renown when he teamed up with Savage. As well as having played the inner-city circuit (Carlton, Fitzroy, Richmond, Prahran) with **The Pelaco Brothers**, The Fabulous Nudes, The Autodrifters and The Armchairs, Topper had issued his own single on the Big Girls label, 'Beatnik Twist'/'Frankie's Goat', under the guise of Johnny Topper and his Beatnik Buddies. The Armchairs comprised Topper (bass), Ian Stephen (piano, vocals), Gerry Joyce (guitar; ex-Gulliver's Travels) and Andrew Snow (drums, electronics).

That nifty little combo issued the EP 'Ski-Lo-Lo' and the satirical album *Party Time*, which drew on popular Australian culture and good old-fashioned rock'n'roll for inspiration. Stephen had already issued his own EP, *I'm Still in Two Minds About the Title*, as Ian Stephen's Schizophrenia during 1978. Topper went on to become an on-air identity with Melbourne community radio station 3RRR-FM, and Stephen fronted country-gospel band **The Slaughtermen** in 1985. Likewise, Savage had his own band, Frank Savage and the Citizens, which comprised Rod Hayward (guitar), Kim Blay (bass) and Steve Watson (drums). The Citizens issued one single on the Mambo label, 'Little Boy Lost'/'Helicopter', in 1980. Hayward later played in **Little Murders** and **Dave Graney 'n' the Coral Snakes**.

North 2 Alaskans issued two singles in 1982, a cover of **Pastoral Symphony's** 'Love Machine'/'Take a Letter Maria' (on Missing Link) and 'Gonks Go Beat' (Tommy James and the Shondells' 'Crimson and Clover', 'Incense'/'That Freaky Gonk Thang'). By the end of the year, the band had run its course. Spencer went on to join **Olympic Sideburns, The Johnnys** and **Beasts of Bourbon**. Almost immediately, Savage and Topper re-emerged with a new cabaret outfit, Pete Best Beatles, which also comprised Williams, Hayward and Gary Adams (drums). Warren Rough (guitar; concurrently in **Corpse Grinders**) replaced Hayward briefly for one season of gigs during early 1983. Pete Best Beatles issued the EP *Sounds for the Sophisticated Cabaret Music Lover* ('Alamein Train') (November 1984) and the mini-album *Stench of Wealth* (1985), by which time Andrew Picoleau (ex-X-Ray-Z, Metronomes, **Sacred Cowboys**) had replaced Topper on bass.

Armchairs album: *Party Time* (Reverse, 1980); ***Pete Best Beatles mini-album:*** *Stench of Wealth* (Major, 1985).

Paul Norton

Style: *Rock, country*

Melbourne singer/songwriter Paul Norton (real name Paul McNaughton) played bass with early 1980s band **The Runners**. That band issued a couple of near-hit singles and always seemed to be on the verge of breaking through but never did. For most of the mid-1980s, Norton concentrated on songwriting and playing the odd gig around Melbourne. Norton's influences ranged from David Bowie and Elvis Costello to Bruce Springsteen and **Paul Kelly**. In 1987, he issued an independent single, 'Larapinta'/'State She's In' before signing a solo deal with Mushroom Records. Norton's solo career got off to a flying start when his first single for Mushroom, 'Stuck on You'/'Don't Say a Word', raced up to #3 on the national chart during May 1989. Norton completed an album in the UK with the help of English producer Paul Muggleton and seasoned musicians like Elton John's drummer Charlie Morgan.

The album *Under a Southern Sky* (October 1990) showed promise and a down-home earthiness in the songwriting, but suffered from a certain blandness overall. It yielded four more singles, 'I Got You'/'Handshakin' Boy' (#31 in November 1989), 'Southern Sky'/'Southern Sky' (acoustic version) (#37 in August 1990), 'Billy Billy' (September) and 'Shake that Devil'/'Southern Sky (live) (February 1991). Norton formed a band in order to tour; the line-up comprised Mark Greig (guitar; ex-**Runners**), Tim Millikan (bass; ex-**Chantoozies**), Derek Pellici (drums; ex-**Little River Band**) and Norton's spouse Wendy Stapleton (backing vocals; ex-**Wendy and the Rocketts**). While Norton garnered positive reviews for his live shows, his hit single run was already over. His second Mushroom album, *Let It Fly* (October 1992), produced two singles, 'When We Were Young' (August) and 'Lil' Red Riding Hood' (October), but neither was successful.

Albums: *Under a Southern Sky* (Mushroom/Festival, 1990), *Let It Fly* (Mushroom/Festival, 1992).

not drowning, waving

Formed: *1983*
Style: *World music*
Original line-up: *David Bridie (vocals, piano, synthesiser, percussion), John Phillips (guitar)*

Acclaimed Melbourne group not drowning, waving presented a sweeping, multifaceted sound that was a cross pollination of everything from Brian Eno's *Another Green World* (1975) and the Eno/David Byrne collaboration *My Life in the Bush of Ghosts* (1983) to a variety of world musics. Classically trained David Bridie and John Phillips were not averse to incorporating African and other Third World rhythms into their muse. Likewise, they placed an emphasis on natural acoustic and atmospheric dynamics rather than an electronic approach.

Bridie and Phillips began working together as not drowing, waving in 1983. The duo issued its debut single on the Rampant label, 'Moving Around', 'Untouched'/'Unhappy as Can Be' (April 1984). The duo's debut album, *Another Pond* (January 1985), presented unique aural soundscapes full of weaving vocal melodies, mellifluous piano figures, gentle percussion and delicate guitar effects. The album showed the duo's early debt to UK 'group' Durutti Column (guitarist Vini Reilly). 'Hunting for Nuggets'/'Perfect Design', 'Away' was lifted as a single. In early 1985, Bridie teamed up with Rowan McKinnon (bass), Russell Bradley (drums), Tim Cole (vocals), James Southall (congas) and Greg Simmons (guitar) to form ambient-pop outfit Easter. The band played gigs around Melbourne and issued the single 'Cheesecloth'/'Pilon and the Tum Tum Tree' (August 1985) on Rampant. After that, Bridie concentrated on not drowning, waving. Bradley also issued a mini-album, *No Hands for the Preacher* (1987), with his own ambient band, An Ordinary Field (which included Chris Burns and Warren Siebert).

For not drowning, waving's second album, *The Little Desert* (January 1986), the basic line-up was augmented by Russell Bradley, Tim Cole, James Southall, Amanda Brotchie (vocals), Tanya Plack (flute) and Phillip Wale (cello). *The Little Desert* was a landmark release that expanded on the promise shown with the debut album. The expanded band line-up of Bridie, Phillips, Bradley, Cole, McKinnon and Southall also issued a dance single in September 1985, 'Mr Pooh, (Do Be a Don't Be)'/'Wooden Box', 'Prison'. Cole became the band's live sound engineer and record producer, as well as singer. At the end of 1985, Bridie and Phillips recorded the soundtrack for Melbourne filmmaker Mark Worth's documentary *Canoe Man*, which was about tribal canoe makers from Manus Island off the Papua New Guinea coast. That resulted in the six-track mini-album *The Sing Sing* which inspired Bridie's abiding passion for the music of Papua New Guinea.

Cold and the Crackle (June 1987) picked up where *The Sing Sing* had left off with the likes of the billowing 'Yes Sir, I Can Boogie' and the Afro-meets-techno-beats of 'Little Kings'. In December 1987, not drowning, waving also issued a four-track, 12-inch EP with Robby Douglas Turner, 'I Did', which included 'Little Kings' and a rearrangement of Canned Heat's 'Goin' Up the Country'. Not drowning, waving moved to the Mighty Boy label for the breakthrough album *Claim* (May 1989), which placed greater emphasis on more orthodox song structures at the expense of the usual experimental mood pieces. The album produced the singles 'Willow Tree'/'Claim' (March) and 'Fishing Trawler'/'Overlay' (August). Although not a big hit, 'Willow Tree' received commercial airplay, and the band began playing to sell-out concert audiences. *Claim* was also voted Best Australian Album in the 1989 *Rolling Stone* Critics Poll.

In late 1989, not drowning, waving made a trip to Rabaul, Papua New Guinea where the band recorded with local musicians and began to absorb new influences into their own material. This resulted in the band's fifth full-length album (and its first international release on Warner's Reprise label), *Tabaran*, which came out in March 1991. PNG superstar George Telek (from the Moab Stringband and rock band Painim Wok) co-wrote and sang a couple of songs on *Tabaran*. The album was credited to not drowing, waving and the musicians of Rabaul, Papua New Guinea featuring Telek. Two CD singles were lifted from the album, 'Pila Pila' and 'The Kiap Song'.

In 1990, classically trained cellist Helen Mountfort joined Bridie, Phillips, Bradley, Cole, McKinnon and Southall, helping to expand the band's scope in the process. The new line-up contributed a cover of The Reels' 'Kitchen Man' to the Various Artists tribute album *Used and Recovered by* (1990). With the release of *Tabaran* in 1991, not drowning, waving undertook a successful tour of Papua New Guinea which culminated in a Port Moresby concert in front of 25 000 people. Following the PNG tour, Bridie, Bradley and Mountfort formed off-shoot band **My Friend the Chocolate Cake**. Not drowning, waving completed a busy 1991 by recording the soundtracks to the feature films Jocelyn Moorhouse's *Proof* (issued April 1992) and Richard Lowenstein's *Say a Little Prayer. Tabaran* won the group Best Independent Release at the 1991 Australian Record Industry Association (ARIA) Awards.

In 1992, the band played an arts festival in Japan, and then travelled to the UK in order to record its sixth album, *Circus*, at Rockfield Studios, Wales. By that stage, Tim Cole had left the band and they used an outside producer for the first time, in this case Englishman Hugh Jones (Simple Minds, Echo and the Bunnymen). *Circus* (October 1993) produced the CD singles 'Crazy Birds' (July) 'Spark' (September) and 'Penmon' (December). In early 1994, David Bridie and John Phillips compiled a selection of their film, television and theatre soundtracks on the album *Projects 1983–1993* (April). Tracks were drawn from such works as the television series *Labor in Power*, the short films *Body Work*, *Greenkeeping* (both by David Caesar) and *Hungry Heart* (Luigi Acuisto) and the music and dance festival *South East*.

At the end of 1994, Bridie and Mountford collaborated on the soundtrack to Ann Turner's low-key feature film *Hammers Over the Anvil*. The project featured a number of guests like Jen Anderson (violin; ex-**Black Sorrows**) and **Hunters & Collectors'** horn section. The soundtrack appeared as the *Hammers* album credited to not drowning, waving. Following on from the release of *Circus*, Bridie had scaled down not drowning, waving's workload to concentrate on other projects. He moved into production work for **Archie Roach** (*Jamu Dreaming*) and **Christine Anu** (*Stylin' Up*), and toured in Anu's backing band throughout 1995. In May and June 1996, Bridie coordinated the trans-Pacific cultural event *Sing Sing*. With concerts in Melbourne, Sydney, Brisbane and Port Moresby, the collaborative event pulled together 30 musicians, including the Torres Strait Buia dancers, the re-formed not drowning, waving, **Archie Roach**, **Ruby Hunter**, **Kev Carmody**, George Telek, Pius Wasi's Kaiwosi group, Frances Williams, **Dave Steel** and the former members of PNG's Sanguma Ben Hakilits and Buruka Tau who had since joined **Yothu Yindi**.

Albums: *Another Pond* (Rampant, 1985), *The Little Desert* (Rampant, 1985), *The Sing Sing* (mini-album, Rampant, 1986), *Cold and the Crackle* (Rampant, 1987), *Claim* (Mighty Boy, 1989), *Tabaran* (Warner/Reprise, 1991), *Proof* (film soundtrack, Rougues Gallery/MDS, 1992), *Circus* (White/Mushroom/Festival, 1993), *Hammers* (film soundtrack, Rougues Gallery/MDS, 1994). ***David Bridie and John Phillips album:*** *Projects 1983–1993* (White/Mushroom/Festival, 1994).

The Numbers

Formed: *1978*
Style: *Power pop*
Original line-up: *Annalise Morrow (bass, vocals), Chris Morrow (guitar, vocals), Marty Newcombe (drums)*

The sister/brother team of Annalise and Chris Morrow was the driving force behind power pop outfit The Numbers. The band emerged from the post-punk Sydney scene with a clean sound and a strong sense of direction. In spite of a regular touring schedule and a brace of accessible pop releases, the band never made the commercial breakthrough for which they so vigorously strived.

The Morrows formed The Numbers in early 1978. Simon Vidale replaced Marty Newcombe in January 1979, and the band supported UK visitors XTC on that band's Australian tour. In September, The Numbers issued the EP, 'Govt Boy'/'Private Eyes', 'Guerilla' on the Local label. The EP featured three dazzling blasts of tough guitar pop reminiscent of The Jam or The Buzzcocks. Somehow the band never sounded quite so energetic on record again. At the end of 1979, the band signed to the Deluxe label (home to **INXS** and **The Dugites**) and issued the single 'The Modern Song'/'Take Me Away' in March 1980. It sold well in Sydney (#30) and just missed making the national Top 40. The band's next single, 'Five Letter Word'/'Alone', graced the lower reaches of the national Top 40 for two weeks. The band's third single, 'Mr President', backed with the previously released 'Private Eye' and 'Guerilla' (February 1981), failed to chart.

The band's Cameron Allen-produced debut album *The Numbers* came out in October 1980 (#29 in November), and in January 1981 Russell Handley (ex-Popular Mechanics) joined on keyboards. The arrangement lasted just one month before Handley made his exit. Soon after, Vidale departed and the Morrows added Gary Roberts (bass; ex-Moving Parts) and original drummer Marty Newcombe. With Roberts on bass, Annalise was free to concentrate on singing and playing rhythm guitar. That line-up issued the single 'Jericho'/'Turn Back' (August 1982). The band returned to the studio at the end of 1981 to record a new album with producer Graham 'Buzz' Bidstrup (ex-**Angels**). Newcombe and Roberts soon departed, and with Annalise back on bass and Bidstrup behind the drums, the band completed the album *39.51*. The album and single 'Big Beat'/'Telephone' both appeared in April 1982. The album's title was a veiled reference to criticisms the band endured over the brevity (28 minutes) of its debut album.

The Numbers returned to the road with a new line-up of Annalise, Chris, Colin Newham (keyboards; ex-**Reels**) and John Bliss (drums; ex-**Reels**). Newham and Bliss left the band in September 1982, just as a new single, 'Dreams from Yesterday'/'Again', emerged. The band went into hibernation until March 1983 when Craig Bloxom (bass; ex-**v Spy v Spy**), Marcus Phelan (guitar) and old drummer Simon Vidale all joined. By August 1983, The Numbers were back to a three-piece of Annalise, Chris and Vidale. With few prospects of making an indelible mark on the Australian scene, Annalise and Chris decided to dissolve the band. Annalise sang in jazz and blues clubs, and Chris issued a solo single on WEA, 'Just What I Needed'/'Big Money' (March 1987). Apart from that very little was heard from the Morrows until 1990.

That year Annalise and Chris re-emerged as MPM with Barton Price (ex-**Models**) on drums. MPM toured for three weeks before Price left. A year later, Annalise and Chris formed Maybe Dolls with Paul Wheeler (drums; ex-**Icehouse**). The band made an impact with the infectious single 'Nervous Kid' which reached #23 on the national chart in September 1991. The *Propaganda* album (October

1991) and three more singles, 'Cool Jesus' (March), 'Never Look Back' (May) and 'Only Love' (October), followed. The band toured to a positive response (including a support slot to UK visitors Big Audio Dynamite in March 1992) but it was all over again for the Morrows by 1993.

Numbers albums: *The Numbers* (Deluxe, 1980), *39.51* (Deluxe, 1982); ***Maybe Dolls album:*** *Propaganda* (BMG, 1991).

Nursery Crimes

Formed: *1989*
Style: *Punky power pop*
Original line-up: *Phil Rose (vocals; ex-Slush Puppies), David Dixon (guitar, backing vocals), Caine Knight (lead guitar), Paddy Chong (bass), Russell Hopkinson (drums; ex-***Vicious Circle, Bamboos, Kryptonics,** *Cremator)*

Melbourne band Nursery Crimes grew out of the same inner-city scene that spawned the likes of **Hoss, The Meanies, The Guttersnipes,** The Seminal Rats and The Slush Puppies. The Nursery Crimes' sound was built around melodic yet crunching guitar riffs, frenetic arrangements, rapid fire lead vocals and sweet harmonies. The band's antecedents in the melodic hardcore power pop stakes included The Ramones, The Buzzcocks, Bad Religion and Sydney's own funaddicts, **The Hard-Ons**.

Phil Rose fronted The Slush Puppies, which comprised Mick Weber (guitar) and Todd McNeair (drums; both from The Seminal Rats) and Shane Grubb (bass). Melbourne independent label Au-go-go issued The Slush Puppies' debut single, 'You're So Perfect'/'I Don't Like Anybody', in December 1988. Not long after the single's release, Rose broke up The Slush Puppies and formed Nursery Crimes. Au-go-go also issued Nursery Crimes' debut single, 'All Torn Up Inside'/'What Do You Know (Anyway)?' and mini-album *No Time for that Crime* in late 1990. By the time the mini-album came out Davage Thomas had replaced Paddy Chong on bass. Chong later joined The Fuck Fucks.

Nursery Crimes signed to the Survival label and issued a new single, a cover of The Beatles' 'Eleanor Rigby'/'Eleven Hours a Day' (April 1991). By the time that came out, James Mason had replaced Caine Knight on lead guitar. Later in the year, Survival reissued the 'Eleanor Rigby' single on CD and added one extra studio cut and two live songs. Nursery Crimes rounded out 1991 with the release of the four-track CD EP 'Marked by Time' which was taken from the band's amphetamine-charged, full-length debut album *Fun Hurts* (May 1992). Nursery Crimes contributed a track to rooArt's Australian grunge-pop compilation *Crack in the Sun or Fade in the Shade* (November 1992) alongside the likes of **You Am I, Guttersnipes, Screamfeeder, Massappeal, The Meanies, Tumbleweed** and Headache. At the end of 1992, James McInnes replaced Mason on lead guitar and Chris Latham replaced Russell Hopkinson, who went on to join **You Am I**. Nursery Crimes 1993 release was the CD EP *Something's Wrong with Our Heroes* (August). With its release, the band undertook the Ticket to Riot national tour with fellow Melbourne act **The Fireballs**.

Nursery Crimes broke up in early 1994, but Rose and McInnes swiftly re-surfaced in Shreen. Scott MacArthur (bass) and James Lynch (drums; ex-Soulscraper) completed the Shreen line-up. Like Nursery Crimes, Shreen's sound combined melodic pop hooks, incisive guitar riffs, tight harmonies and rapid tempos. David Dixon joined Shreen at the end of 1995. The band issued one album, *Accelerate*, in November 1995 (recorded before Dixon joined), and one CD single, 'Jesus Machine' (July 1996), on the Hypnotized label before falling apart.

Nursery Crimes albums: *No Time for that Crime* (mini-album, Au-go-go, 1990), *What Do You Know (Anyway)?* (European compilation, Normal, 1991), *Fun Hurts* (Survival, 1992); ***Shreen album:*** *Accelerate* (Hypnotized/Shock, 1995).

O

The Odolites

Formed: *1984*
Style: *Pop*
Original line-up: *Harvey Saward (guitar, vocals), Andrew Lethborg (guitar), Gary Aspinal (bass, vocals), Graham Rankin (drums)*

Tasmanian band The Odolites relocated to Melbourne in 1985. Often compared with **The Go-Betweens** and **The Triffids**, plus New Zealand acts on the Flying Nun label like The Chills, The Bats and The Clean, The Odolites played reflective, accessible guitar pop. The band's contemporaries on the Melbourne mid-1980s scene included **Sea Stories, not drowning, waving, Captain Cocoa, Blue Ruin** and **The Hollowmen.**

In 1986, The Odolites signed to the independent Rampant label and issued the five-track mini-album *Persistence of Memory* (August) plus the single 'Chimes'/'As Fresh as Monday', 'Room with No View' (January 1987). The band contributed 'Chimes' to Rampant's Various Artists album *Running Rampant Volume 1* (1987). The album *Face Down in the Violets* (August 1988) was a more diverse release; the single 'Kathleen's Tantrum'/'Call It What You May' (January 1988) featured members of **Sea Stories** and **not drowning, waving** guesting on viola and piano.

The Odolites split up in December 1988. Harvey Saward formed a partnership with Andrew Viney (bass; ex-**Fish John West Reject**) as The Tender Engines. That outfit issued the singles 'Clinging to the Wreckage'/'A Legend Never Fails' and 'With Regret'/'Under the Same Roof', plus the CD EP *With Regret* on the Summershine label in 1992. Two years later The Tender Engines issued two more singles, 'Something Wicked'/'The Final Kiss', 'Leaving Town' and 'Ex-Pop Song'/'A Night at the Fair', on Summershine. In the meantime, Gary Aspinal switched to guitar and formed The Somerfields with Dennis McGrath (guitar, vocals), Rupert Beaumont (bass) and Adrian Swallow (drums). The Somerfields issued the 12-inch EP *Somerfields* and the album *Medicine Ride* before breaking up in 1993. Aspinal joined **The Killjoys** in 1995. Rankin went to **The Fish John West Reject** and **Dave Steel.**

Albums: *Persistence of Memory* (mini-album, Rampant, 1986), *Face Down in the Violets* (Rampant, 1988).

Johnny O'Keefe

Style: *Rock'n'roll*

'The Wild One', The King of Australian Rock'n' Roll: Johnny O'Keefe (J.O'K.) (b. 1935) was all that and more. He was Australia's first rock'n'roll star, an inspiration to many other local singers and a national icon. J.O'K. was the first to admit he was a limited singer, but he possessed an incredible drive, a fierce ambition to succeed, a tireless facility for self-promotion, a tremendous flair for showmanship and a larrikin spirit that was irrepressible. He was also a person beset by inner demons; a near-fatal car crash, a much-publicised series of nervous breakdowns and bouts of alcoholism and drug addiction contributed to his slow decline. J.O'K. died from a heart attack on 6 October 1978 at the age of 43.

In June 1955, Australia discovered rock'n'roll. Like thousands of other young Australians, J.O'K. went to see Richard Brooks' juvenile delinquent film *The Blackboard Jungle.* With Bill Haley and His Comets' 'Rock Around the Clock' as its theme song, the American film had a profound effect on popular culture. For a start, it ensured that rock'n' roll would be forever associated with teenage drop-outs and hoodlums, which did wonders for its lexicon. 'Rock Around the Clock' certainly turned J.O'K.'s head. By day he worked at his father's furniture store in Pitt Street, Sydney; at night he made the occasional appearance as a Johnny Ray impersonator. By the end of 1956, having absorbed Haley's influence and that of other emergent rock'n'rollers like Little Richard and Jerry Lee Lewis, J.O'K. was recognised as Australia's first genuine rock'n'roll singer. J.O'K. equipped himself with a flamboyant wardrobe and a fine backing band: The Dee Jays.

The original line-up, formed in January 1957, consisted of American-born Dave Owens (tenor sax), John Balkins (baritone sax), Kevin Norton (guitar), Keith Williams (bass) and Johnny 'Catfish' Purser (drums). Not long after, Johnny Greenan and Lou Casch replaced Balkins and Norton respectively. Mike Tseng also joined on piano. There was no precendent for rock'n'roll in Australia, and the band had to make up the rules as they went along. Johnny O'Keefe and the Dee Jays began promoting their own dances in suburban halls and Police Boys Club rooms. J.O'K. made an enormous impact with his brash, uninhibited, spectacular and totally convincing performances. The other main attractions on the burgeoning Sydney rock'n'roll scene were **Alan Dale and the Houserockers** and **Col Joye** and the Joy Boys.

Expatriate American entrepreneur Lee Gordon booked The Dee Jays as support to Bill Haley and his Comets on their Australian tour in the middle of 1957. Gordon is regarded as being the midwife of Australian rock'n'roll, and he became one of J.O'K.'s closest allies. The Haley support was J.O'K's big break. He spent many hours talking to Haley, who gave the Australian singer a song to record '(You Hit the Wrong Note) Billygoat'. Haley also recommended Johnny O'Keefe and the Dee Jays to Festival's Artist and Repertoire manager Ken Taylor, who was slow on the uptake. J.O'K. simply took matters into his own hands. In what became a legendary episode characteristic of J.O'K.'s cocky persona, he announced to the local press that he had signed a deal with Festival Records. Taylor was forced into action, quickly set up an audition and only then did he sign J.O'K. Festival issued J.O'K.'s debut single, '(You Hit the Wrong Note) Billygoat'/'The Chicken Song', as a 78 RPM record (July 1957). It sold poorly, as did the follow-up 'Love Letters in the Sand'/'Am I Blue?' (which J.O'K. described as the worst recording of his life).

In the meantime, J.O'K. and the Dee Jays virtually became the resident Australian act on Lee Gordon's legendary Big Shows at Sydney Stadium. The first featured Little Richard, Gene Vincent and Eddie Cochran, followed by Buddy Holly, Jerry Lee Lewis and Paul Anka. J.O'K.'s first EP, the live *Shakin' at the Stadium*, produced 'Wild One' (co-written by The Dee Jays' Dave Owens and Johnny Greenan, with J.O'K. and Sydney DJ Tony Withers), which became J.O'K.'s first hit when it peaked at #20 on the Sydney charts during March 1958. The media dubbed him 'The Wild One', a designation the singer carried with him like a royal title for the rest of his career. J.O'K. issued three more Sydney Top 40 hits during 1958: Johnny and Joe's 'Over the Mountain'/'Lawdy Miss Clawdy', The Cuff Links' 'So Tough'/'That'll Be Alright' (#12) and 'I Ain't a Gonna Do It'/'Could this Be Magic?'.

Johnny O'Keefe

In February 1959, J.O'K. and the Dee Jays became the resident act on Australia's first national television rock program, the ABC's *Six O'Clock Rock*. After the first six episodes, J.O'K. took over as compere from Ricki Merriman. Alongside Brian Henderson's *Bandstand*, which had been broadcasting in Sydney only since November 1958, *Six O'Clock Rock* finally gave the local rock and pop industry a definite focus. Both shows created a virtual court of artists who began to dominate the Australian charts. J.O'K. issued two more Top 40 hit singles on Festival, 'What Do Ya Know?'/'Peek-a-Boo' (#12 in March 1959) and 'Why Do They Doubt Our Love?'/'You Excite Me' (#9 in May), before switching to Lee Gordon's Leedon label. On Leedon, the hits continued with 'Swanee River'/'The Steady Game' (#12 in October), The Isley Brothers' 'Shout'/'What I'd Say' (#3 in November) and J.O'K.'s first national #1, 'She's My Baby'/'Own True Self', in January 1960.

J.O'K. had recorded 'She's My Baby' under the direction of producer Ernie Freeman in Los

Angeles during his first trip to the USA (October 1959). Convinced he had achieved all he could in Australia, J.O'K. had set his sights on cracking the vast American market. In Los Angeles, J.O'K. met record executive Mickey Shaw, who signed the Australian to a deal with Liberty Records. J.O'K. returned to the USA in February 1960 for a promotional tour. Liberty had concocted a campaign based around J.O'K. being billed as 'The Boomerang Kid'. He was also required to give boomerang throwing exhibitions, at which Liberty offered five dollars to anyone who could throw further than the singer. At one particular exhibition, J.O'K. turned up drunk, for which Liberty had to pay out handsomely!

J.O'K. undertook a 35-state American tour but unfortunately made little impact. Although 'She's My Baby' reputedly sold over 100 000 copies in the USA, and 'It's Too Late' hit #1 in New Orleans for a week, J.O'K.'s American campaign eventually fell apart. On his return to Australia, 'It's Too Late'/'Jubilee' became J.O'K.'s eleventh Australian hit single. Following his American tour, however, J.O'K. was flat broke and suffering from depression. So that no one suspected he was broke, he bought a big Plymouth Belvedere on hire purchase, and in order to pay for the car he had to go on tour. He drove everywhere, and returned to Sydney every Saturday for *Six O'Clock Rock*. His June tour featured **Lonnie Lee**, **Barry Stanton**, Laurel Lea, Booka Hyland and **Ray Hoff**.

In the early morning hours of 27 June 1960, 20 kilometres north of Kempsey (NSW), J.O'K. fell asleep at the wheel of his Belvedere and collided with a gravel truck. J.O'K. sustained serious injuries, as did his passengers Johnny Greenan and his pregnant wife Jan, who suffered a miscarriage as a result (she died from cancer a few months later). J.O'K. received 64 stitches in his head, 26 in his hands and lost four teeth. In August, only six weeks after the wreck J.O'K. was back on *Six O'Clock Rock*. The fans tuned in each week to witness the changes to J.O'K.'s face as he underwent a series of facial reconstructions with plastic surgery. Although he was never the same person again (some believe J.O'K never really recovered from the accident), J.O'K. continued to score hits like 'Don't You Know'/'Come on and Take My Hand' (#1 in August 1960) and 'Ready for You'/'Save the Last Dance for Me' (#4 in November).

In January 1961, J.O'K. tried his luck again in the USA with even less success than before. On an impulse he flew to London, where he collapsed in the Park Lane Hotel. He woke up three days later in St George's Hospital suffering from nervous exhaustion. With Lee Gordon's help, he returned to Australia, but his tenure with *Six O'Clock Rock* had come to an end. By October he was hosting his own show, *The Johnny O'Keefe Show*, on the Seven Network in Sydney. With the show's success came more pressure for an overworked J.O'K. He suffered another breakdown in August 1962 and spent a month in the psychiatric ward of the Royal Prince Alfred Hospital. His show continued in his absence, and on his return it had been renamed *Sing, Sing, Sing*. J.O'K.'s popularity remained strong well into 1964.

His hit singles run continued with 'Swing Low Sweet Chariot'/'I Believe' (June 1961), 'I'm Counting on You'/'Right Now' (#1 in August 1961), 'Sing (and Tell the Blues So Long)'/'To Love' (#1 in March 1962), 'Yes Indeed I Do'/'Keep a Walkin'' (#30 in October), 'I Thank You'/'Heaven Sent' (#22 in December), 'Move Baby Move'/'You'll Never Cherish a Love So True' (#1 in June 1963), 'Shake Baby Shake'/'Good Luck Charm' (#8 in October), 'Twist It Up'/'Twist and Shout' (#32 in December), 'She Wears My Ring'/'Let's Love Tonight' (#2 in April 1964) and 'Rock'n'Roll will Stand'/'Will You Still Love Me Tomorrow?' (#30 in November).

With the arrival of Beatlemania in Australia during 1964, J.O'K.'s star began to dim. Beatlemania ushered in the end of an era for J.O'K. and his many contemporaries. It also heralded the dawning of an exciting new movement (beat music) with the likes of **The Easybeats**, **Billy Thorpe** and the Aztecs, **Ray Brown and the Whispers**, **Bobby and Laurie** and **Normie Rowe**, etc. stealing J.O'K.'s crown. J.O'K. banned 'long-hairs' from appearing on the family-styled *Sing, Sing, Sing*, but by the end of 1964 the show had ceased production. J.O'K. scored only three minor hits over the next five years, 'Sun's Gonna Shine Tomorrow'/'Mansion Over the Hilltop' (#38 in May 1966), 'Be Careful of Stones that You Throw'/'My Heart Belongs to Only You' (#28 in August 1966) and a re-release of 'She's My Baby'/'She Wears My Ring' (#22 in September 1969).

Aside from the short-lived television show, album and single *Where the Action Is* in 1967, J.O'K. spent most of 1965 through 1969 concentrating on the club and cabaret circuit. He also performed in a show tent on Sideshow Alley around Australia for a time. His only album releases were compilations and one live set, *Johnny O'Keefe Live on the Gold Coast*. He continued to battle depression, drug and alcohol dependency, more car accidents and divorce from his long-suffering wife Marianne. His non-charting singles throughout that time included 'Shout (Parts One and Two)'/'Come on and Take My Hand' (June 1964), 'Cry Cry Baby'/'Nobody

Loves Me (Everybody Hates Me)' (February 1965), 'Don't Be Cruel'/'Hey Girl' (November 1966), 'Ooh Poo Pah Doo'/'Ecstasy' (March 1967), 'Buzz Buzz Buzz'/'Where the Action is' (March 1967) and 'Just a Closer Walk with Thee'/'Why Do They Doubt Our Love?' (October 1967).

At the end of 1969, J.O'K. re-signed with Festival Records and began issuing new singles: 'Come on and Take My Hand'/'Right Now' (September 1969), 'Confessions of a Lonely Man'/'To Love Somebody' (February 1970), 'I am Blessed'/'I'm Counting on You' (February 1971), 'You've Got Me Dangling on a String'/'Keep on Smiling' (December 1971) and a re recorded version of 'So Tough'/ 'Holly Holy' (July 1972). Festival stepped up its promotional campaign and 'So Tough' returned J.O'K. to the national charts (#7 in September 1972) for the first time in three years. The follow-up single, a cover of Neil Diamond's 'High Rollin' Man'/'My Lady by the River' (December 1972), failed to reach the national Top 40 despite capturing the tempo of the times with a great deal of panache. (After all, **Blackfeather** had just made #1 with a similarly styled barrelhouse piano-led rocker 'Boppin' the Blues'.)

Still, J.O'K.'s time had come again. He appeared at the 1973 Sunbury rock festival and went down a storm. Compere Paul Hogan introduced him to the assembled crowd as a 'newcomer, so give him a go', J.O'K. walked on stage in a white suit and, ignoring the inevitable boos and jeers from the partisan audience, began to perform with all his heart. By the end of his set, J.O'K. had 35 000 hippies eating out of the palm of his hand. In early 1974, J.O'K. scored another Top 10 hit with his duet with Margaret McLaren on Inez and Charlie Foxx's 'Mockingbird'/'Soulshake' (#8 in April). It was his 29th hit. In August 1974, J.O'K. assembled a package tour called The Good Old Days of Rock'n'Roll with his old friends Johnny Devlin, **Barry Stanton**, Jade Hurley, Tony Brady, **Lonnie Lee** and Laurel Lea. From its opening at the St George's Leagues Club in Sydney, the tour was a success, and J.O'K. was still presenting it four years later.

He also continued to issue singles periodically, including 'Rock'n'Roll Music'/'Mary Lee' (April 1974), Vanda and Young's 'Saturday Night'/'Over and Over' (August 1974), 'On the Road'/'Rock'n' Roll Boogie' (February 1975), 'Full Blooded Natural Man'/'Taste the Wine' (October 1975), 'One of These Nights'/'Rock'n'Roll will Stand (It will Stand)' (December 1977) and a reissue of 'Move Baby Move'/'I Thank You' (May 1976). In the wake of J.O'K.'s death in October 1978, there was a revival of interest in his records. Festival reissued 'High Rollin' Man'/'I'm Counting on You' (November) and the album *22 Golden Greats*, followed by 'Ready for You'/'(You Hit the Wrong Note) Billygoat' (December 1981). In 1982, John Bryden-Brown's book *J.O'K. The Official Johnny O'Keefe Story* came out. The interest in J.O'K. didn't stop there.

In 1986, the Seven Network screened the mini-series *Shout! The Story of Johnny O'Keefe* with Terry Serio in the role of J.O'K. In 1987, American singer Iggy Pop issued a version of 'Wild One' under the title of 'Real Wild Child' as a single lifted from his album *Blah Blah Blah*. In 1994, the Powerhouse Museum opened its exhibition of Australian rock'n'roll under the title of *Real Wild Child* in celebration of J.O'K's contribution to popular culture. Festival has done much to keep the music of J.O'K. alive over the years. In October 1992 the label issued two 7-inch singles 'I'm Counting on You' and 'Sing (and Tell the Blues So Long)'. In 1996, the label issued the digitally remastered, three-CD (75 track) box set, *The Birth of Australian Rock'n'Roll*, which saw his music re-presented with a great deal of care and attention to detail. The box set was divided into *The Hits*, *The Ballads* and *The Rarities*.

Albums: *Johnny's Golden Album* (10-inch only, Festival, 1959), *Shout!* (Leedon/Festival, 1959), *The Big Show (Lee Gordon Presents the Big Show Starring Johnny O'Keefe)* (Leedon/Festival, 1960), *Shout! Shout! Shout!* (reissue of *Shout!*, Leedon/Festival, 1960), *I'm Still Alive* (Leedon/Festival, 1961), *The Wild One's Kingsize Hits* (Leedon/Festival, 1962), *Twist* (Leedon/Festival, 1963), *Come on* (Leedon/ Festival, 1963), *About Love* (Leedon/Festival, 1963), *The Best of Johnny O'Keefe* (Leedon/Festival, 1964), *Shake Baby Shake* (Leedon/Festival, 1964), *The J.O'K. Sound* (Leedon/Festival, 1964), *Ooh Poo Pah Doo* (Leedon/Festival, 1964), *The J.O'K. Story* (Leedon/Festival, 1964), *The Sun's Gonna Shine Tomorrow and Other J.O'K. Hits* (Leedon/Festival, 1965), *J.O'K. Ballads* (Leedon/Festival, 1966), *Where the Action is* (Leedon/Festival, 1966), *She's My Baby* (reissue of *The Sun's Gonna Shine Tomorrow*, Leedon/Festival, 1969), *Collectors' Items from the Rockin' '50s* (Festival, 1969), *Johnny O'Keefe Live on the Gold Coast* (Calendar/Festival, 1969), *Be Careful of Stones that You Throw* (reissue of *J.O'K. Ballads*, Calendar/Festival, 1970), *The Great J.O'K.* (Universal, 1970), *The Good Old Days of Rock and Roll* (Calendar/Festival, 1972), *Johnny O'Keefe at the Waltzing Matilda* (Calendar/Festival, 1973), *Johnny B. Goode Featuring Mockingbird* (Festival, 1973), *The Wild One Rocks Again* (Summit, 1973), *Peppermint Twist* (reissue of *Twist*, Festival, 1974), *King of Rock* (Calendar/Festival, 1975), *The Living Legend of J.O'K.*

(K-Tel, 1976), *20th Anniversary Album* (Festival, 1979), *A Tribute to Johnny O'Keefe: 22 Golden Greats* (Festival, 1978), *Real Wild Child* (10-inch double album, Festival, 1981), *Sing (and Tell the Blues So Long)* (10-inch album, Festival, 1986), *Shout! The Story of Johnny O'Keefe* (television miniseries soundtrack shared with Various Artists; Festival, 1986), *The Last Concert* (Canetoad, 1988), *So Tough* (eight album box set, Festival, 1989), *Real Wild Child* (CD reissue of 10-inch double album, Festival, 1990), *The Very Best of J.O'K.* (Rainbow, 1992), *The Birth of Australian Rock'n'Roll* (box set, Festival, 1996).

Further reading: *J.O'K. The Official Johnny O'Keefe Story* by John Bryden-Brown (Doubleday, 1982); *Shout! The Story of Johnny O'Keefe* by Robert Caswell (Currency Press, 1986).

Ol'55

Formed: *1975*
Style: *Rock'n'roll revival*
Original line-up: *Frankie J. Holden (real name Peter Bryan, vocals), Rockpile Jones (rhythm guitar, vocals), Patrick Drummond (lead guitar, vocals), Jimmy Manzie (bass, vocals), Geoff 'Stovepipe' Plummer (drums, vocals)*

Like Sha Na Na and Flash Cadillac and the Continental Kids in the USA, Australia's own rock'n'roll revival act, Ol'55, enjoyed enormous popularity with a style that bordered on parody. Under the direction of astute manager Glenn A. Baker, however, the band managed to combine novelty kitsch with clever theatrics, a keen sense of pop dynamics and an acute understanding of the rock'n'roll form.

Ol'55 emerged out of Sydney band Fanis which had formed in 1972. Former chartered accountant Peter Bryan joined Fanis at the start of 1975, and rock writer Baker created a whole new image for the band based around good-time American rock'n'roll. The band took its new name from the Tom Waits song (as covered by The Eagles), dressed in authentic rocker gear, and played vintage 1950s material and appealing originals in the same style (mostly written by Manzie). Having created the flamboyant Frankie J. Holden persona (FJ Holden, geddit?), Bryan proved to be a hyperactive, motormouthed frontman with a natural flair for outrageous showmanship. Ol'55 made its live debut in July 1975 and by September had issued its first single on the Mushroom label, Paul Anka's 'Diana' backed with The Spaniels' 'Goodnight Sweetheart'. Wilbur Wilde (sax) completed the classic Ol'55 line-up when he joined in October 1975.

Ol'55

'Diana' had been a minor hit in Sydney, but the follow-up, 'On the Prowl'/'This Little Girl', took the band into the national Top 20 (#18) during June 1976. At the same time, the band's debut album *Take It Greasy* peaked at #2 on the national album chart, eventually attaining double platinum status (over 140 000 copies sold). With two more hit singles, 'Looking for an Echo'/'Doin' Fine' (#14 in August) and '(I Want a) Rockin' Christmas'/'Little Saint Nick' (#8 in November), Ol'55 took its place alongside **Skyhooks**, **Sherbet**, **Hush**, the **Ted Mulry Gang**, **John Paul Young** and **Supernaut** in the vanguard of Australian mid-1970s pop. Plummer left Ol'55 in January 1977 to be replaced by Geoff 'Spud' Peterkin (ex-Springwater). One month later, the band's fifth single, 'C'Mon Let's Do It'/'Teenager in Love', reached #18 on the national chart. Frankie J. Holden also issued his debut solo single, 'My Right of Way'/'Chartered Accountant Blues', in April. Written by Jimmy Manzie, it was the theme song to the Australian feature film *The FJ Holden*.

Frankie J. Holden left the band in May 1977, followed one month later by Wilbur Wilde who joined **Jo Jo Zep and the Falcons**. Ol'55 unveiled its revamped line-up in August with new singer Mikey Raffone (microphone, geddit?; real name Paul Stevens, ex-**Silver Studs**). The band's second album *Fiveslivejive* (featuring the original line-up) failed to chart. In the meantime, the new line-up's debut single, 'Stay (While the Night is Young)'/'Caught in the Curl', reached #11 in November 1977. Bruce 'Tangles' Allen (sax) expanded the line-up at the end of 1977, but by February 1978 Mikey Raffone had left. The band continued as a five-piece with Jones, Drummond and Manzie sharing lead vocals. '(Feels Like a) Summer Night'/'He's Gotta Go' reached #23 in May 1978, but the band's next single, 'Time to Rock'n'Roll'/'Homework's Done', on the Junction label (October 1978) failed to chart. Likewise, the band's third album, *Cruisin' for a Bruisin'*, was not successful.

'Ruby'/'Nobody Should be Kissing My Baby' returned Ol'55 to the national Top 40 (#36) in February 1979, followed by the unsuccessful 'Living for Your Smile'/'Shaggy English Sheepdog' (April 1979). In March Ol'55 signed overseas deals with PolyGram for the release of *Cruisin' for a Bruisin'* in Europe and with CBS for release in Canada. Unfortunately, a split in the band's ranks prevented any follow-up on the deal. For some time, Manzie had been steering the band in a more pop-oriented direction, and this caused friction with Rockpile Jones and Patrick Drummond, who wanted to continue in the rock'n'roll vein. The two guitarists left the band in June 1979 amid much acrimony, taking with them the rights to the name of Ol'55.

Jones and Drummond recruited original Ol'55 drummer Geoff Plummer, Rob Drummond (bass) and Bob Tawney (guitar) in a new line-up and started from scratch. By the end of the year, Ol'55 had signed a new deal with RCA. Terry Bellew replaced Rob Drummond on bass. Ol'55 issued the unsuccessful single 'Comic Book World'/'Peek-a-Boo' (February 1980), followed by its eighth hit, Lou Christie's 'Two Faces Have I'/'The Fool' (issued on the Leo label through PolyGram), which reached #15 on the national chart during September (Top 10 in Melbourne and Sydney). *The Vault* album produced one more single, 'Anywhere the Girls are'/'You've Got What It Takes' (December), but Ol'55 split up soon after.

Meanwhile, Manzie and Peterkin had formed a more contemporary-sounding rock band by the name of The Breakers. Jarryl Wirth (guitar; ex-**News**, The Lonely Boys), Scott Douglas (rhythm guitar, vocals; ex-Class) and Martin Fisher (keyboards) completed the line-up. The Breakers were described as 'heavy metal pop that combined Beach Boys vocals, Ramones guitar riffs and Buggles synthesisers'. From early on, the band was highly touted; indeed, the single 'When I'm on TV'/'Lipstick and Leather' (August 1980) was tough guitar pop in the style of UK outfit The Motors. Nevertheless, The Breakers did not get the chance to fulfil any early promise because the band broke up a year later. Manzie concentrated on his production duties (**Innocents**, Loaded Dice, **Choirboys**).

Of the other members, Frankie J. Holden issued a second solo single in October 1980, 'Boomerang'/'Dinkie Di (Bob's Your Uncle)', and was the narrator for the stage musical *Best Little Whore House in Texas*. Bruce Allen joined Sydney R&B band **The Dynamic Hepnotics** in 1980. In April 1981, Patrick Drummond issued a solo single, 'The Chippendale Song'/'The Lucky Country', and in 1982 joined Skool Daze. In December 1981, RCA issued an Ol'55 12-inch single containing three medleys, 'Ol'55 on 45', 'Four Seasons Medley' and 'Summer of Ol'55'. In January 1982, Holden, Manzie, Wilde, Jones, Plummer and newcomer Gunther Gorman (guitar; ex-**Home**, **Daddy Cool**, **Sherbet**) reconvened as The Fives to appear at the Mushroom Evolution Concert to celebrate the tenth anniversary of the label. Three tracks, 'C'mon Let's Do It', 'On the Prowl' and 'Goodnight Sweetheart', appeared on the live, triple album of the event, *The Mushroom Evolution Concert*.

Since then, there have been various re-formations under the monikers of Ol'55, Frankie J. Holden and the Fives, and in the mid-1990s Ol' Skydaddys. The last named comprised Holden and Wilde from Ol'55 plus Bongo Starkie and Freddy Strauks from **Skyhooks** plus Wayne Duncan and Ross Hannaford from **Daddy Cool**. Holden has also pursued an acting career which has taken in television roles in *C/o the Bartons* (1988), *Embassy* (1990), *Late for School* (1992) and *Police Resuce* (1995), plus roles in the feature films Gillian Armstrong's *Hightide* (1987) and Ray Argall's *Return Home* (1990). He showed his cabaret/television variety skills when he took on the compere role for the Nine Network's *In Melbourne Tonight* (IMT) in 1995. As well as working with his own jazz band, Wilbur Wilde's Blow-Out, Wilde appeared in Brian Trenchard's low-budget feature film *Dead End Drive-In* (1986). He has also been a member of the studio band for popular television variety show *Hey Hey It's Saturday* since the mid-1980s.

Albums: *Take It Greasy* (Mushroom/Festival, 1976), *Fiveslivejive* (Musrhoom/Festival, 1977), *Cruisin' for a Bruisin'* (Junction/Powderworks, 1978; reissued 1983 on RCA), *The Vault* (Leo/7 Records, 1980), *Open Top Cars and Girls in Tight T-Shirts* (J&B, 1986), *Grease Works* (K-Tel compilation, 1987).

Ian 'Ollie' Olsen

Style: *Electronic, techno-dance*

Norwegian-born, Melbourne-bred musician Ian 'Ollie' Olsen is recognised as one of the key figures in the Australian post-punk electronic movement of the late 1970s. Ever the experimentalist, Olsen's eclectic career in avant rock has taken him from The Reals, one of the original Melbourne punk combos of the late 1970s, through to the acid-house/techno/trance outfit Third Eye. He was also the driving force behind the innovative Psy-Harmonics label.

The Reals comprised Olsen (guitar), Gary Gray (vocals), Chris Walsh (bass) and Peter Cave (drums). The band played the odd gig around Melbourne, and alongside The Boys Next Door, Babeez/**News**, →↑→ and The Obsessions were the only punk bands in town. At the end of 1977, Olsen left The Reals, and Gray, Walsh and Cave recruited Mick Holmes (guitar) to form The Negatives. Meanwhile, Olsen assembled the now legendary Young Charlatans which comprised Rowland S. Howard (guitar; ex-Obsessions), Jeffrey Wegener (drums; ex-**Saints**) and Janine Hall (bass). As Clinton Walker pointed out, Young Charlatans had inner-city 'supergroup' status from the outset and helped pioneer post-punk rock in Australia.

Young Charlatans' existence was brief but intense. They played a total of 13 gigs and earned a considerable reputation on the inner-city scene in the process. Olsen left and rejoined a number of times and by May 1978 the band had fallen apart. Young Charlatans did not record anything comprehensive, although a version of the Rowland S. Howard song 'Shivers' (later made famous by The Boys Next Door) appeared on the cassette-zine *Fast Foward* (#4). Howard went on to join The Boys Next Door/**Birthday Party**, Wegener played with **The Last Words** before joining **Ed Kuepper**'s new band **Laughing Clowns** in April 1979, and Hall later turned up in **The Saints** and **Weddings, Parties, Anything**. Olsen had moved on again, forming the equally legendary Whirlywirld.

Whirlywirld grew out of Olsen's dissatisfaction with conventional guitar-based rock, and his desire to transcend its limitations. Like Suicide in New York and Throbbing Gristle and Cabaret Voltaire in the UK, Whirlywirld was a pioneer in the field of post-punk synthesiser electronics. Whirlywirld was not the first electronic band in Australia (**Cybotron** has that distinction), but it was the first to apply the form to the punk ethos. The original Whirlywirld line-up (August 1978) comprised Olsen (vocals, electronics, sax), John Murphy (drums, electronics; ex-**News**), Dean Richards (guitar), Andrew Duffield (electronics) and Simon Smith (electronics). Olsen refused to play live, but Whirlywirld did issue the three-track maxi-single *Whirlywirld* ('Window to the World', 'Moto'/'Signals') on the Missing Link label in April 1979.

The record's startling, hard-edged electronic sound was embellished by Richard's 'electrical' guitar work and with Murphy bashing away on a variety of percussive devices, electronic and otherwise. By January 1979 Philip Jackson had replaced Duffield (who later joined **Models**) and the band commenced playing gigs. By mid-1979, Richards, Smith and Jackson had left (Richards went on to front cult combos **Equal Local** and **Hot Half Hour**). Greg Sun (bass) and Arnie Hanna (guitar) joined and the band issued the four-track 12-inch EP *Whirlywirld* (the first 500 copies of which contained a bonus 7-inch single 'Sextronics'/'Eyebrows Still Shaved'). By the end of 1979, after having played only 14 gigs, Whirlywirld had run its course. Olsen and Murphy left Australia in early 1980 bound for the UK.

In London, Olsen and Murphy formed The Beast Apparel, played a few gigs and eventually issued a single, 'Grand Life for Fools and Idiots'/'Beat Up the Old Shack' (on the Prince Melon label, 1982), which came out under the name Hugo Klang. The band recorded a second single, 'The Wheel of Fat'/'Mouse Runner' in Berlin. The Au-go-go label issued the single in Australia, by which time Olsen had split Hugo Klang. Olsen and Murphy returned to Australia in 1984 (after Murphy had played with a number of UK outfits like The Associates and Shriekback).

They formed avant-garde outfit Orchestra of Skin and Bone and issued a self-titled album on the Major label in 1985. The line-up on the album included Olsen (vocals, guitar), Murphy (drums), Arnie Hanna (guitar), Marie Hoy (keyboards; ex-Thrust and the Cunts), David Hoy (cello), Tom Hoy (sax), Lochie Kirkwood (vocals, sax), James Rogers (trumpet), Peter Scully (guitar) and Dugald McKenzie (vocals, harmonica). Orchestra of Skin and Bone proved incomprehensible to local audiences and rarely played live. By 1986, Olsen was working as musical director on Richard Lowenstein's feature film *Dogs in Space*, which was set in the Melbourne post-punk wasteland of the late 1970s. Murphy went on to form The Slub and Stress of Terror, and to play in bands as disparate as **The Wreckery**, **Box the Jesuit** and Dumb and the Ugly.

Olsen included two Whirlywirld songs on the

Dogs in Space soundtrack (January 1987): a re-recorded version of 'Win/Lose' and the previously unrecorded 'Rooms for the Memory'. 'Win/Lose'/'Win/Lose' (re-mix) was issued as an Olsen solo single (April), and 'Rooms for the Memory'/'Golfcourse' came out as a Michael Hutchence (star of the film) solo single. When Hutchence took 'Rooms for the Memory' to #11 on the national mainstream chart in February 1987, it only confirmed the commercial potential of Olsen's Whirlywirld material.

Next up, Olsen rejected virtually all musical precepts to form No, a band described as the ultimate crossover act due to its confrontational fusion of hardcore energy, abrasive heavy metal guitar riffs, electro-funk beats and acid-house grooves. The band comprised Olsen (vocals, keyboards, samples), Marie Hoy (keyboards, samples), Michael Sheridan (guitar) and Kevin McMahon (bass). No issued the mini-album *Glory to the Shit-for-Brains* (November 1987), a self-titled 12-inch EP (which included an incendiary reworking of Jimi Hendrix's 'Are You Experienced?') and the album *Once We were Scum Now We are God* (April 1989) on the Au-go-go label. Sheridan later joined Melbourne singer Kerri Simpson's band Vévé, which also comprised Bill McDonald (bass; ex-**Hot Half Hour**) and Justin Stanford (drums; ex-**Bachelors from Prague**). That line-up of Kerri Simpson and Vévé issued the CD EP *Vévé* (May 1993) and album *The Arousing* (June 1995). Simpson issued a second album, *Speak*, in September 1996. Sheridan was also a member of noise terrorists Peril.

At the end of 1989, Olsen collaborated on the **Max Q** project with **INXS**'s Michael Hutchence, which resulted in the best-selling *Max Q* album. Olsen also had studio outfit EXP with Kerri Simpson on the go at one stage, but by late 1990 he had launched his most radical project yet, Third Eye. In collaboration with Gus Till (keyboards; ex-**Beargarden**, **Max Q**), Olsen issued a techno-house dance version of the **Russell Morris** psychedelic classic 'The Real Thing' (backed with 'Behold the Angel of Frequency') as a single on the Regular label (September 1990). Olsen described Third Eye's rendition of 'The Real Thing' as 'a cyberdelic version featuring much sampling of Timothy Leary' and as 'an absolute acid nightmare'. With film- and video-maker Jeff Jaffers on percussion and visual environment creator DVO on hand, Third Eye undertook a series of shows in early 1992. Jaffers' video clip to 'The Real Thing' was nominated for an MTV Award in the USA.

The collective's second single, 'Pray' (June 1991), and the *Third Eye* album (January 1992) showed even more diversity. Bluesman **Chris Wilson** contributed harmonica to one track, 'Confusion'. As well as issuing the *Third Eye* album on CD, Olsen and Till also came up with the novel marketing idea of packaging it as five separate 12-inch singles in a black plastic canister with a booklet. The *Ancient Future* album followed in July 1993, then *Dance of Creation* in June 1994. In 1993, Olsen formed acid-house label Psy-Harmonics and techno-trance label Psychic Harmonies. Many of the acts on the labels (Third Eye, LumuKanda, Mystic Force and Zen Paradox) scored international distribution deals through some of Europe's leading dance labels. Third Eye contributed 'Dying (Hard)' and a remix of Kerri Simpson's 'Vévé' to the Various Artists album *Psy-Harmonics Volume One* (1994). In 1997, Olsen wrote the theme music for the ABC-TV's youth-oriented television drama series *RAW-FM*. Third Eye issued a new CD single, 'New Life', in October 1997.

Whirlywirld album: *Complete Studio Works* (Missing Link, 1986); ***Orchestra of Skin and Bone album:*** *Orchestra of Skin and Bone* (Major, 1985); ***No albums:*** *Glory to the Shit-for-Brains* (mini-album, Ultimate, 1987), *Once We were Scum Now We are God* (Au-go-go, 1989); ***Max Q album:*** *Max Q* (CBS, 1989); ***Third Eye albums:*** *Third Eye* (Regular/Festival, 1992), *Ancient Future* (Psy-Harmonics/MDS, 1993), *Dance of Creation* (Psy-Harmonics/MDS, 1994).

Olympic Sideburns

Formed: *1982*
Style: *Shockabilly*
Original line-up: *Peter 'Jex' Byron (vocals; ex-Glamstars), David 'George' Spencer (lead guitar; ex-Glamstars), Spencer P. Jones (guitar, vocals; ex-Cuban Heels, Beats Working,* **North 2 Alaskans***), Ian Hill (keyboards; ex-***Crackajacks***), Lindy Allen (bass), Tom McEwan (drums)*

The Melbourne, inner-city independent scene of the early 1980s was besotted by the earthy sounds of the seminal **Birthday Party**, The Cramps, The Stooges, Captain Beefheart and the solo Alex Chilton. The combination of Americanised garage-punk, swamp blues, 1950s rockabilly, 1960s psychedelia and voodoo imagery produced a mutant strain of music that came to be known as shockabilly or psychobilly.

Melbourne's foremost exponents in the shockabilly stakes included the likes of Olympic Sideburns, **Corpse Grinders**, Tombstone Hands and **Sacred Cowboys**. Olympic Sideburns, who came together in late 1982, added a rock'n'roll edge to proceedings. The original line-up did not last long: by the start of 1983 Jones had relocated to Sydney with **The Johnnys**; he was replaced initially by Jimmy Williams and later in the year by Maurice Frawley (ex-**Paul Kelly** and the Dots). Likewise, Allen and McEwan were replaced by Paul Bryant (ex-Corporate Body) and Chuck Meo (ex-**Dorian Gray**) respectively. The new line-up recorded the *Drunkyard* mini-album at the end of 1983 (issued May 1984), after which Meo was replaced by Maurice Molletta. The new line-up recorded the single '13th Floor'/'Fire It Up', 'She's Comin' Home' and (after Hill left) the debut, full-length album *Olympic Sideburns*. Olympic Sideburns also shared a gig giveaway single with **Corpse Grinders** '7 and 7 is'/ 'I Eat Babies'

By the time the album came out in May 1985, **Philip Brophy** (ex-→↑→) had replaced Molletta on drums (Brophy was given drumming credit on the album instead of Molletta). According to the band, *Olympic Sideburns* went on to sell 25 000 copies worldwide. Towards the end of 1985, Calum McAlpine (ex-**Chosen Few**, Rah Rah the Flag) replaced Brophy, which resulted in the most stable line-up of the band's history. In August 1987, Olympic Sideburns signed to Mushroom's Doc/White subsidiary label. The band issued a new album *Dixie Truck Stop!* (September), and single, 'Here Comes the Rain'/'Sorrento', 'Underworld' (February 1988). The album boasted a more authentic Rolling Stones/Creedence Clearwater Revival sound as opposed to the previous punk/psychedelic/ shockabilly hybrid. Alan Brooker (ex-**Paul Kelly** and the Dots, **Little Murders, Zimmermen**) replaced long-standing bass player Bryant. Olympic Sideburns continued to play to a cult following on the Melbourne scene, but split up at the end of 1988. Frawley later formed **Maurice Frawley and the Working Class Ringos**.

Albums: *Drunkyard* (mini-album, Strine, 1984), *Olympic Sideburns* (Major, 1985), *Dixie Truck Stop!* (Doc/White/Mushroom/Festival, 1987).

Orchestra of Skin and Bone (*see* Ian 'Ollie' Olsen)

Jackie Orszaczky

Style: *Jazz-rock, funk*

Hungarian-born master bass player Miklos 'Jackie' Orszaczky (b. 1948) arrived in Australia during 1970 with jazz-rock band Syrius. The highly regarded Syrius was Hungary's top rock attraction, and had already issued several albums of jazz fusion before relocating to Australia. The band's line-up comprised Orszaczky (bass, guitar, vocals), Zoltan 'Joel' Baronits (piano, oboe, sax), Latsi 'Les' Pataki (organ, piano, drums), Mihalt 'Michie' Radulty (sax, flute, violin) and Andras 'Andrew' Veszelinov (drums, guitar, trombone).

Syrius lived in Australia for a year and issued one ambitious, multi-layered album, *Syrius*, and single, 'I've Been this Down Before'/'Concerto Part II', on the Spin label in 1971. The band's influences ranged from John Coltrane, Chicago and Colosseum to Jimi Hendrix and Blood Sweat and Tears. The album mixed free-form jazz, progressive rock and epic jazz-fusion with interesting results. The band played all the 'head' venues of the day and backed a number of Australian musicians, including **Phil Manning** and Warren Morgan (Pilgrimage) and **Wendy Saddington**. Syrius returned to Hungary in October 1971, but Orszaczky came back to live in Australia during August 1973. He joined **Bakery**, with which he stayed until the band broke up in February 1975. Orszaczky formed a studio band comprising John Robinson (guitar; ex-**Blackfeather**), Peter Jones (electric piano) and Graham Morgan (drums) in order to record his debut solo album, *Beramiada*. The album came out in December 1975 on the Real label. It featured accomplished progressive jazz-fusion in the vein of Weather Report, George Duke and *Caravanserai*-era Santana.

By the time the album appeared, Orszaczky had joined the **Marcia Hines** Band (May 1975) as bass player and musical director. Orszaczky issued a solo single, 'Let's Go and Make It'/'Friend of Mrs S', on the Wizard label (December 1976). He remained with Hines for two years, after which he went on to become an in-demand session player. In 1987, Orszaczky formed Jump Back Jack with Phil Colson (guitar, vocals), Linda Bacon (trumpet, vocals), Mike Bukowsky (trumpet), Brad Child (sax), James Greening (trombone), Phillip Campbell (drums; ex-**Electric Pandas**) and Hamish Stewart (drums; ex-**Ayers Rock**). Later members included Rick Morrison (guitar), Mark Simmonds (sax) and Jason Morphett (sax). The band played West Coast rock and funk in the vein of Cold Blood, Tower of Power and Blood Sweat and Tears. Jump Back Jack issued two albums, *Jump Back Jack* (1987) and *Double Take* (1988).

In 1990, Orszaczky formed The Godmothers with **Chris Abrahams** (keyboards) and Greg Sheehan (drums; ex-**Blackfeather**, **MacKenzie Theory**, **Richard Clapton** Band) in order to play Ray Charles, R&B and funk covers. In 1992 he formed bass trio The Bass with Steve Hunter and Lloyd

Swanton (ex-Benders, Necks, Catholics). Orszaczky issued his next album, *Family Lore*, in August 1994 with backing provided by The Grandmasters, who included long-time collaborators Abrahams and Arnie Hanna (guitar; ex-Whirlywirld, **Max Q**), plus Tina Harrod (vocals), Cathy Harley (piano) and Geoff Lundgren (synthesiser). Orszaczky's supple bass playing provided a rock-solid foundation for the album's blend of soul, funk and jazz.

Albums: *Syrius* (with Syrius, Spin/Festival, 1971), *Beramiada* (Real/Electric, 1975), *Jump Back Jack* (mini-album with Jump Back Jack, ABC, 1987), *Double Take* (with Jump Back Jack, ABC, 1988), *Family Lore* (with The Grandmasters, Wright/Shock, 1994).

Outline

Formed: *1979*
Style: *Rock, jazz*
Original line-up: *Phil Rigger (lead vocals, trumpet; ex-Skintight), John Sammers (guitar, vocals), Alex Lakajev (keyboards), Mike Mead (trombone, vocals), Harry Ladamatos (bass), Mark Azzopardi (drums)*

Within six months of formation, Sydney band Outline was attracting a great deal of media interest and had signed to CBS. Co-founded by Phil Rigger and John Sammers, the band started out playing jazz-rock covers and Frank Zappa-styled material before injecting more contemporary new wave, synth-rock influences into the music.

In early 1980, Jeff Barrett replaced Harry Ladamatos on bass and Paul Ryan replaced Mark Azzopardi on drums. Outline issued its debut single, 'Cities'/'Look Inside Yourself' (July 1980), and set off on a national tour. In August the band entered the studio with producer Peter Dawkins to record its debut album. Outline issued three singles during 1981: the quirky, B-grade science fiction movie-inspired 'The Cicada (that Ate Five Dock)'/ 'Power and Control' (April), 'How Can I Get Out of Here?'/'Sleep' (August) and 'Maybe It's a Game'/ 'Body Race' (October).

Danny Damjanovic (ex-**Jimmy and the Boys**) replaced Mike Mead on sax in early 1982. By mid-year the line-up comprised mainstays Rigger, Sammers and Ryan, plus newcomers Michael Gray (keyboards; ex-**Jeff St John's** Asylum) and Chris Ford (bass; ex-Flex). The band's debut album, *Maybe It's a Game*, finally came out in August 1982. The album was not the commercial breakthrough expected, and interest in the band began to fall away. Outline issued only one more single, 'Stay with Me'/'She's Welcome' (October 1982), before splitting at the end of the year.

Album: *Maybe It's a Game* (Powderworks, 1982).

P–Q

Painters and Dockers

Formed: *1982*
Style: *Rock*
Original line-up: *Chris O'Connor (vocals, guitar), Paul Stewart (vocals, trumpet), Vladimir 'Steig' Juric (lead guitar), Phil Nelson (bass), Andy Marron (drums)*

For most of the 1980s, the irreverent Painters and Dockers were something of a Melbourne institution. The band was renowned for its forthright opinions, and hell-for-leather, uninhibited live shows that drew capacity audiences of slam-dancing fans. The band also pledged its support to, and helped organise, benefit gigs for such worthwhile causes as the Salvation Army, East Timorese refugees and the South West African Peoples Organisation (SWAPO).

The band originally formed for a one-off benefit gig (to help cover a friend's parking fines!), held in a Port Melbourne pub usually attended by members of the militant waterside Painters and Dockers Union. The gig was a sign of things to come: a drunken, machete-wielding maniac attacked the band's mixing desk, after which the police arrived, much to the annoyance of the real painters and dockers who started a riot! The band's next five gigs were banned and the sixth gig was a sell-out. Painters and Dockers never looked back. The band's first recording, 'Mohawk Baby', appeared on Au-go-go's *Asleep at the Wheel* Melbourne independent band compilation (1984). Colin Buckler replaced original drummer Andy Marron soon after. The band issued its debut album, *Love Planet*, on the Big Time label. It revealed the Dockers' fondness for local popular culture with such songs as 'Basia' (an ode to television presenter Basia Bonkowski) and 'The Boy Who Lost His Jocks on Flinders Street Station'. 'Basia'/'Virgin Child' came out as a single (March 1985).

The band used a brass section (dubbed the Brassholes) on the album; soon after, Dave Pace (trumpet) and Mick Morris (tenor sax) joined the line-up, adding an earthy R&B edge to the band's raucous, punk-infused power pop. The four-track, 12-inch EP 'Kill Kill Kill' (1985) featured cover versions originally done by some of the band's formative influences: the Sacred Cows' 'Kill, Kill, Kill' (from the Groovy Guru episode of American sitcom *Get Smart*), **Supernaut's** 'I Like It Both Ways', The Ramones' 'Do You Remember Rock'n'Roll Radio?' and **The Saints'** 'Know Your Product'. The live album *Bucket* (October 1986) featured in-concert favourites like 'Kill, Kill, Kill', 'Pull Me Off (My Silly Pedestal)', 'In My Mind' and 'Love on Your Breath' and just about approximated one of the band's sweaty gigs. The band's first two minor hit singles were 'Nude School'/'Dung Di (Don't Go)' (#21 in June 1987) and 'Die Yuppie Die'/'That's It' (September). Vietnamese vocalists Duc-Dzung, Dinh-Hy and Phyong-Trinh contributed to 'Dung Di (Don't Go)'

'Nude School' and 'Die Yuppie Die' appeared on the band's third album, *Kiss My Art* (August 1988), as did the next two singles, 'Love on Your Breath'/'Love Factory' (April 1988) and 'Safe Sex'/'Soul Child' (October). *Touch One, Touch All* (December 1989) and its singles 'Dirty Filthy Rock'n'Roll'/'Willoughby' (November) and 'Eat Shit Die' (May 1990) lacked the barbed humour so prevalent on previous albums. With the release of the album in Canada, Painters and Dockers undertook a Canadian tour which was sponsored by the King Kong Condom company! Darren Garth replaced original lead guitarist Steig at the start of 1990. The December 1991 mini-album *Hickory Dickory Dock* contained the yuletide-infused 'Merry Christmas, Carol' and the single 'New World Order'. *Nervous '90s* (August 1992) featured six studio tracks and three live cuts (including 'Jack's Car' and 'Die Yuppie Die') recorded with the Salvation Army Brass Band.

In 1992, Painters and Dockers were involved with PRICS (Performers Releasing Information about Clean Syringes). PRICS was a Melbourne-based collective intent on spreading safe sex and drug use messages through a series of gigs and workshops. After 1992, Painters and Dockers continued to tour (including the 16-date, three-week, 6500 kilometre Return to the Love Planet tour across Western Australia and the Northern Territory), but record releases became scarce. The band issued the pro-gay 'I Know Better Queens than That' CD EP in December 1993, and contributed a rendition of the **Mental as Anything** song 'The Nips are Getting Bigger' to the Various Artists *Earth Music* album. The band's final album, *The Things that Matter* contained the acerbic and topical 'Rape Judge'.

Albums: *Love Planet* (Big Time, 1984), *Bucket* (Doc/Big Time, 1986), *Kiss My Art* (Doc/White/Mushroom/Festival, 1988), *Touch One, Touch All* (Musicland, 1989), *Hickory Dickory Dock* (mini-album, MDS, 1991), *Nervous '90s* (MDS, 1992), *The Things that Matter* (MDS, 1994), *Bucket/Kill Kill Kill* (CD reissue, Shock, 1996).

Pantha

Formed: *1973*
Style: *Rock, jazz*
Original line-up: *Paul Curtis (lead vocals, percussion), Roger Pell (lead guitar, percussion, backing vocals; ex-***Kush***), Dannie Bourne (electric piano, percussion, backing vocals; ex-Hot Dog), Peter Lee (congas, percussion), Jack Wilson (bass, percussion), Adrian Payne (drums, percussion)*

Melbourne band Pantha was one of the most unusual aggregations on the Australian mid-1970s recording scene. The band played a unique hybrid of rock, jazz, Latin-American and West African music which called to mind Santana or Osibisa (by way of The Crusaders). The joyous, heavily percussive nature of the band's music actually belied a remarkable depth of musicianship and sense of character and place. Pantha commanded a loyal following on the Melbourne pub circuit. When it came to selling records, however, Pantha was not successful.

The *Doway Do Doway Do* album included the single 'I am Not Afraid'/'All Things Below' (November 1975) and the sweeping, Weather Report-styled 'Blue House'. By the time the album came out, Barry Cram (ex-Michael Turner in Session) had replaced Adrian Payne on drums and Jose McLaughlin had replaced Dannie Bourne on keyboards. Pantha issued two more singles in 1976, 'Happiness'/'Life Dreams' (February) and 'Melinda'/'Doway Do Doway Do' (December), but neither charted. Pantha supported US visitors The Doobie Brothers in early 1976, and made regular appearances on the ABC-TV's rock show *Radio with Pictures*. By early 1977, Peter Lee had moved to drums, and Merry Took had come in on percussion. Robert Ellis had also taken over from Jack Wilson on bass. The band continued to play the Melbourne pub circuit before breaking up in late 1977.

Album: *Doway Do Doway Do* (Wizard, 1975).

Parachute

Formed: *1977*
Style: *Rock*
Original line-up: *Chris Langman (guitar, vocals; ex-Spare Change), Robert Kretschmer (lead guitar; ex-Spare Change), Tony Murray (piano, vocals; ex-Spare Change), Rick Grossman (bass; ex-***Bleeding Hearts***), Graeme Perry (drums; ex-Spare Change)*

The origins of Melbourne pub band Parachute can be found in Adelaide outfit Spare Change, which comprised Chris Langman, Robert Kretschmer, Tony Murray, Graeme Perry and frontman John Dowler. Perry had replaced original Spare Change drummer Jon Wilkinson, who went on to join Rufus Red which later evolved into X-**Ray-Z**.

Spare Change moved to Melbourne in 1976 and recorded an album, *Lonely Suits*, which was not issued until December 1979 on the Cleopatra label. The single 'The Big Beat'/'Classified Ad' had come out in November 1976 on the Champagne label, but it created very little interest. Spare Change broke up in mid-1977. Dowler returned to Adelaide and formed **Young Modern**. Langman, Kretschmer, Murray and Perry recruited Rick Grossman to form Parachute, and threw themselves in amongst the Melbourne pub scene alongside the likes of **The Sports**, **Jo Jo Zep and the Falcons**, **Mondo Rock**, **Stiletto**, Gulliver's Travels and Living Legends.

Langman left at the end of 1977 to join High Rise Bombers. He later teamed up with another ex-High Rise Bombers alumnus, **Paul Kelly**, to form the first version of **Paul Kelly** and the Dots. By the end of 1978, Kretschmer, Grossman and Perry had joined Eric Gradman: Man & Machine. Two Parachute tracks, 'The Big Beat' and 'Falling', appeared on Missing Links' Various Artists album *The Melbourne Club* (1981). Kretschmer later became an integral member of **Icehouse** and journeyman bass player Grossman went on to play with **Matt Finish**, **Divinyls** and **Hoodoo Gurus**.

The Paradise Motel

Formed: *1995*
Style: *Rock*
Original line-up: *Merida Sussex (vocals), Charles Bickford (acoustic guitar), Mark BJ Austin (Hammond organ), Matthew Aulich (electric guitar), Matthew Bailey (bass), Tim O'Shannassy (drums)*

Melbourne band The Paradise Motel has been described as a cross between UK acts like Portishead and The Cocteau Twins, and the soundtrack to

The Paradise Motel

American television miniseries *Twin Peaks*. Other comparisons thrown the band's way included Nico, Mazzy Star and The Cowboy Junkies. Add to that the band's existentialist lyrical angst and the members' penchant for wearing neat suits and ties, and it all added up to an arty, shimmering tableau.

Whatever the case, The Paradise Motel managed to polarise critical opinions as to the worth of its dramatic, haunting, minor key soundscapes. Some declared Paradise Motel to be the most interesting new band of 1996, others found them insufferably pretentious and solemn. The CD EP/10-inch vinyl EP *Left Over Life to Kill* on the Infectious label contained a number of melancholy pieces like 'German Girl', 'Ashes' and 'North of God'. *Left Over Life to Kill* spent over 20 weeks on the local alternative chart after peaking at #2. Bickford reworked (looped, scratched, respliced, reconfigured) and remixed two tracks ('German Girl' and 'Jack Star') from *Left Over Life to Kill* for release as the band's second CD EP, *Some Deaths Take Forever*, with four new tracks added. *Some Deaths Take Forever* came in a pressing of 2000 copies.

The Paradise Motel supported **Tex Perkins** on a national tour throughout September. The band's debut, full-length album *Still Life* produced the CD single 'Bad Light' (October 1996) and the CD EP *(Please Keep Me Safe)* (March 1997). *(Please Keep Me Safe)* included the album track 'Calling You', plus five new songs recorded in February. *Still Life* initially came packaged with a limited edition CD EP, *Junk Mail*, comprising 32 minutes of album outtakes.

Album: *Still Life* (Infectious/Mushroom/Festival, 1996).

The Paramount Trio

Formed: *1987*
Style: *Electric country blues*
Original line-up: *Dave Hogan (vocals, harmonica; ex-Unknown Blues Band, Southern Lightning), Warren Rough (guitar; ex-Autodrifters,* **Crackajacks**, **Corpse Grinders***), Ken Farmer (drums; ex-Percolators, Echo Vampers,* **Dancehall Racketeers***)*

The three members who comprised Melbourne blues band The Paramount Trio possessed a pedigree that stretched back to the 1960s. New Zealand-born Dave Hogan fronted The Unknown Blues Band in his home country for five years before relocating to Australia in the early 1970s. He joined boogie/blues outfit Southern Lightning in 1977, with which he recorded two abums, *Down the Road* (1986) and *Southern Lightning* (1987), and two singles, 'Down the Road'/'Stones in My Passway' (October 1986) and 'Moonlight Street'/'Don't Call Me Mister' (October 1987), for the Cleopatra label. Alongside Hogan, Southern Lightning comprised Manny Seddon (guitar), Nik Guselev (bass) and Louie Black (drums).

Warren Rough's background was more diverse, taking in stints playing R&B, rockabilly and country with The Autodrifters, rockabilly with **The Crackajacks** and a mutant strain of rockabilly (psychobilly) with **Corpse Grinders**. The Paramount Trio's sound mixed authentic Chicago electric blues with Mississippi delta country blues. Like a number of other Melbourne roots-rock bands (**The Breadmakers**, Crown of Thorns), The Paramount Trio recorded in glorious mono. The band issued its debut single 'Tuff'/'Rollin' and Tumblin'' on the independent Preston label, followed by *The Paramount Trio* album on the Loser label in 1992. Since then, the band has issued the albums *Step It Up and Go* (1994), *The Paramount Trio Live* (1996) and *Electric Country Blues* (1997).

Farmer, Rough and Hogan also comprised one half of part-time R&B 'supergroup' Blues Hangover which featured master slide guitarist **Peter Wells** (ex-**Buffalo**, **Rose Tattoo**), Lucy De Soto (keyboards) and John Stax (original bass player with 1960s UK R&B kings The Pretty Things). The band's passionate, gritty brand of R&B was heard to good effect on two albums issued on the Dog Meat label, *Blues Hangover* (1995) and *Roadrunner* (1996). Hogan has also continued to moonlight on a part-time basis with Southern Lightning after the band re-formed in 1991. The line-up comprised Hogan, Manny Seddon (guitar), Geordie Leach (bass; ex-**Buster Brown**, **Rose Tattoo**) and **Gary**

Young (drums; ex-**Daddy Cool**, **Jo Jo Zep and the Falcons**).

Albums: *The Paramount Trio* (Loser, 1992), *Step It Up and Go* (Loser, 1994), *The Paramount Trio Live* (Loser, 1996), *Electric Country Blues* (Loser, 1997).

Doug Parkinson

Style: *Pop, rock*

As Glenn A. Baker put it, Doug Parkinson (b. 1949) is recognised as one of the great, distinctive Australian voices and one of the country's most respected musical mainstays. Indeed, Parkinson conveyed considerable charisma with his imposing presence, 'Lucifer' beard and gruff, raspy voice. He also surrounded himself with mature, seasoned musicians who added to his appeal. Yet between 1966 and 1997, Parkinson only scored six hit singles.

Parkinson's first amateur band was Strings and Things, which he formed in 1965 while still at high school. By the end of the year, the band had evolved into amateur folk group The 'A' Sound. The line-up comprised Parkinson, David Lee (guitar), Helen Barnes (bass) and Syd Barnes (drums). Syd (junior) and Helen were the son and daughter of cricketer Syd Barnes. In 1966, The 'A' Sound issued one pleasant folk single (in **The Seekers** vein) for Festival 'Talk About That'/ 'Tomorrow I Meet You' before breaking up at the end of that year. Parkinson went on to join The Questions which comprised Duncan McGuire (bass), **Billy Green** (guitar), Rory Thomas (Hammond organ) and Bill Flemming (drums; ex-Midnighters, Roland Storm and the Statesmen, **Max Merritt and the Meteors**). McGuire had started out in the late 1950s in The Phantoms before joining Roland Storm and the Statesmen in 1963.

McGuire first teamed up with Green in instrumental band The Epics during 1964. Peter Maxworthy (drums) completed the line-up. As well as backing singer Roland Storm on the single 'Zip a Dee Doo Dah'/'Shakin' All Over' and Peter Wright on 'I Couldn't Keep Your Heart'/'Once I had Your Love', The Epics recorded two singles for HMV 'Caravan'/'Around and About' (September 1964) and 'Too Late'/'Please Tell' (June 1965). By the end of 1965, McGuire and Green had moved on to The Questions. The Questions were a musically substantial bunch, but their one album, *What is a Question?*, and single, 'Karelia'/'Wheels' (October 1966), were sub-Herb Alpert pastiches and failed to chart. Parkinson joined in early 1967. With his facility for soul and blues, he immediately lifted The Questions into the premier league of Australian mid-1960s pop alongside the likes of **Max Merritt and the Meteors** and **The Groop**. In July 1967 The Questions were placed second to **The Groop** in the Hoadley's National Battle of the Sounds final.

The Questions with Parkinson issued three singles that remain minor psychedelic pop classics, 'Sally Go Round the Roses'/'Hey Gyp (Dig the Slowness)' (#14 in Sydney, July 1967), 'And Things Unsaid'/'I Can't Hear You' (October) and 'Something Wonderful'/'We Got Love' (February 1968), plus the EP 'Sally Go Round the Roses' ('Sally Go Round the Roses', 'Hey Gyp (Dig the Slowness)'/'Deep Purple', 'How High the Moon') (all on Festival). In January 1968, **Ray Burton** (guitar; ex **Delltones**) and Les Young (bass; ex-Chessmen) replaced Green and McGuire respectively. The new, short-lived Questions line-up toured as support band to the 'Big Show' tour of UK visitors The Who, The Small Faces and Paul Jones. By February 1968, The Questions had disbanded; a month later, Parkinson, Green, McGuire, Thomas and newcomer Doug Lavery (drums; ex-Andy James Asylum, Running Jumping Standing Still) relaunched themselves as Doug Parkinson In Focus.

The band swiftly issued the psychedelic-tinged 'I Had a Dream'/'Advice' single (May 1968), and then came in third at the 1968 Hoadley's National Battle of the Sounds final (behind **The Groove** and **The Master's Apprentices**). Doug Parkinson In Focus Mark I fell apart in August 1968; Thomas joined **The Affair** and Lavery joined **The Valentines**. By September 1968, Parkinson had In Focus Mark II on the road with Green, McGuire and Johnny Dick (drums; ex-**Max Merritt and the Meteors**, **Billy Thorpe** and the Aztecs). Fired by Green, McGuire and Dick's superb musicianship, the new In Focus was perfectly in sync with the tempo of the times. The band became one of the most popular outfits on the Melbourne suburban dance/ inner-city discotheque circuit.

Doug Parkinson In Focus signed a new deal with EMI/Columbia, and the band's version of The Beatles' 'Dear Prudence'/'This Must Be the End' (May 1969) shot to #5 on the national chart in June. A month later, the band took out Australia's premier pop prize as first placegetters in the Hoadley's National Battle of the Sounds final. EMI deemed the band's proposed new single, 'Today (I Feel No Pain)'/'Theme from Twelfth House', to be non-commercial and withdrew it from release. 'Today (I Feel No Pain)' was an inventive slice of psychedelia replete with Green's backwards guitar, and it duly appeared on the rare *Doug Parkinson In Focus* EP alongside 'Dear Prudence' and the band's next single, 'Without You'/'Hair'. 'Without You' returned the band to #5 on the chart in October. A month later, just as the band was riding the crest of a wave of popularity, Green and McGuire left to form short-lived 'supergroup' Rush with Malcolm McGee (vocals; ex-**Wild Cherries**, **Python Lee Jackson**, Virgil Brothers), Steve Yates (keyboards) and Kevin Murphy (drums; ex-**Wild Cherries**).

In December 1969, Parkinson and Dick recruited two guitarists, Englishman Mick Rogers (ex-**Procession**) and Melbourne legend Les Stacpool (ex-**Chessmen**, **Merv Benton** and the Tamlas, **Levi Smith's Clefs**, **Rockwell T. James** and the Rhythm Aces, Browns), for a new line-up. With Rush having unceremoniously folded, Green returned to the fold in January 1970 and the reconstituted In Focus line-up appeared at Australia's first rock festival, Pilgrimage for Pop at Ourimbah (NSW). In February, McGuire also returned, and Rogers and Stacpool duly departed. The band issued another excellent slice of psychedelic pop as its next single, 'Baby Blue Eyes'/'Then I Run', but it only reached #36 on the national chart during May 1970. In June, guitarist Vince Melouney (ex-Aztecs, **Bee Gees**) invited Dick and Parkinson to join his new band, **Fanny Adams**, in the UK. Green and McQuire joined **Leo De Castro** in **King Harvest**.

When the ill-fated **Fanny Adams** fell apart in February 1971, Parkinson recalled Green and McGuire for a new In Focus line-up. McGuire brought in drummer Mark Kennedy (ex-**Spectrum**, **King Harvest**), and the band picked up where it had left off the previous August. Fable Records issued a new In Focus single, the adventurous hard rock outing 'Purple Curtains'/'Pour Out All You've Got', which had already been in the can for a year and featured the previous line-up. The Fanny Adams break-up meant that Parkinson was unable to record for two years. This effectively hampered In Focus's progress, and in December 1971 McGuire and Kennedy left to join **Friends** and Green joined **Gerry and the Joy Band**. Parkinson spent the next two years attempting to get his solo career off the ground. He issued one single in August 1972, 'Lonely'/'Taking It Easy'. In March 1973, he appeared in the Australian stage production of The Who's rock opera *Tommy* alongside **Billy Thorpe**, **Daryl Braithwaite**, **Colleen Hewett**, **Broderick Smith**, **Jim Keays** and Keith Moon.

With the help of John Capek (piano; ex-**Carson**), drummers Graham Morgan, Peter Figures and Russell Dunlop, Tim Partridge (bass), guitarists **Kevin Borich**, **Billy Green**, Ross East and Jimmy Doyle, Roger Sellers (percussion), Don Reid (flute, sax) and Terry Hannagan (vocals), Parkinson completed his debut solo album, *No Regrets* (May 1973). Parkinson also formed Life Organisation to play 1940s-styled big band jazz. The line-up included the likes of Teddy Toi, Graham Morgan, Peter Martin (guitar; ex-SCRA), Warren Ford (guitar, piano), Bill Motzing (trombone, keyboards) and briefly **Wendy Saddington** (vocals). The Life Organisation single 'In the Mood (Forties Style)'/'Beyond the Blue Horizon' (June 1973) reached #36 in Sydney. The second single, 'Boogie Woogie'/'Little Brown Jug' (November), was not successful. Life Organisation also backed Parkinson on his second solo single (lifted from *No Regrets*), 'Love Gun'/'Dear Prudence' (April 1973). Parkinson also worked as A&R manager for WEA during this period.

In 1974, Parkinson contributed vocals to two songs, 'Cosmic Flash' and 'Do Not Go Gentle' (based on a Dylan Thomas poem, and a song In Focus had also played), on **Billy Green's** film soundtrack to Sandy Harbutt's cult Oz biker film *Stone*. Parkinson's 1974 touring band comprised Mick Liber (guitar; ex-**Python Lee Jackson**), Ray Vanderby (keyboards), Rod Coe (bass) and New Zealander Bruno Lawrence (drums, ex-**Max Merritt and the Meteors**, BLERTA). Lawrence later earned acclaim as an actor in such films as *The Quiet Earth* and *The Delinquents*, plus television series *Frontline*. Parkinson enjoyed his first solo hit single with a cover of Love Affair's 'Everlasting Love'/'All I Need is a Song' (November 1974). The single peaked at #22 in Sydney and #14 in Melbourne during March 1975. He issued two singles in 1975, a cover of Vanda and Young's 'Love is Like a Cloudy Day'/'One Track Mind' (May) and 'Raised on Rock'/'I'm Gonna Get You' (September), but neither charted.

In 1977, Parkinson appeared in the stage production of *Ned Kelly*. He also toured with backing provided by a re-formed version of Sanctuary which comprised ex-**Renée Geyer** Band members Mal Logan and Barry Sullivan. In early 1978, he formed The Southern Star Band which comprised Duncan McGuire (by then ex-**Friends**, **Ayers Rock**, Windchase), Mark Kennedy (by then ex-**Friends**, **Ayers Rock**, **Marcia Hines** Band), Frank Esler-Smith (keyboards; ex-**Marcia Hines** Band) and Englishman Jim Gannon (guitar; ex-Black Widow, Yellow Dog). **Tommy Emmanuel** soon replaced Gannon. Keith Kirwin (guitar, bass, vocals; ex-**Avengers**) joined in September 1979. The band played slick, funky jazz over an R&B foundation. Of the band's four singles 'Hungry Years'/'Soon as Your Thing is Done' (July 1978), 'I'll Be Around'/'Riff Raff' (January 1979), 'In My Life'/'Shuffle Up' (April) and 'You Ain't Going Nowhere Without Me'/'Now You're on Your Own' (September), only 'I'll Be Around' charted nationally (#22 in March). The album *I'll Be Around* was a steady seller but failed to reach the Top 40.

In 1980, Parkinson issued two solo singles, 'Arcade'/'Theme from Arcade' (instrumental by the Mike Perjanik Orchestra; theme song to the short-lived television soapie *Arcade*) and 'Under the Influence of Love'/'Flying South', on Festival before signing to CBS. By early 1981, The Southern Star Band had broken up and Parkinson formed a new Doug Parkinson Band in March. It comprised Dave Richard (guitar), Tim Piper (guitar; ex-**Chain**, **Blackfeather**), George Limbidis (bass; ex-Highway) and Adrian Payne (drums; ex-**Pantha**, **Broderick Smith's** Hired Hands).

Over the next three years, Parkinson issued one album, *Heartbeat to Heartbeat* (March 1983), and seven singles: 'Small Talk'/'Lady Luck' (March 1981), The Walker Brothers' 'The Sun Ain't Gonna Shine Anymore'/'Gonna Shake It' (July), 'Solitaire'/'Go While the Going's Good' (November), 'Better Keep Your Hands Off (My Potential New Girlfriend)'/'Lady Luck' (July 1982), 'Don't Let Love Go'/'Can't Live Without You' (January 1983), 'It's Your Move'/'I Don't Unlove You' (May) and 'Let Sleeping Dogs Lie'/'Thanks to You' (September). 'The Sun Ain't Gonna Shine Anymore' reached #18 in September 1981. In late 1983, Parkinson took a role in the revived stage production of *Jesus Christ Superstar*. He issued two more solo singles, 'Sailing'/'The Kites' (December 1984) and 'Willing and Abel'/'Endlessly' (May 1987), but since that time he has concentrated on musical theatre. His work has taken in roles with the stage productions *Big River*, *The Hunting of the Snark* and as the Big Bopper in the very successful *Buddy*. Parkinson issued the CD single 'Where Would We Be Without A.B.?' (Allan Border) in March 1994.

Doug Parkinson solo albums: *No Regrets* (Polydor, 1973), *Rock Legends* (reissue of *No Regrets*, Polydor, 1980), *Heartbeat to Heartbeat* (CBS, 1983), *Reflections* (Hammard, 1986), *In and Out of Focus 1966–75* (compilation, Raven, 1996); ***Southern Star Band album:*** *I'll Be Around* (Southern Star/Festival, 1979).

The Party Boys

Formed: *1982*
Style: *Rock*
Original line-up: **James Reyne** *(vocals; from* **Australian Crawl***), Kevin Borich (guitar, vocals; from* **Kevin Borich Express***), Harvey James (guitar; ex-***Mississippi, Ariel, Sherbet, Swanee***), Paul Christie (bass; ex-***Kevin Borich Express, Mondo Rock***), Buzz Bidstrup (drums; ex-***Angels***)*

Paul Christie formed good-time rock'n'roll band The Party Boys initially for a one-off, two-week tour. The tour was so successful that two weeks extended into ten years, with major hit singles, best-selling albums and sell-out tours along the way. When Christie left **Mondo Rock** in late 1982, he called up a few old mates with the idea of putting together a covers band for a fun tour. The Party Boys played all cover versions in order to maximise their impact on the pub circuit. The band received enormous media coverage, and recorded a live album on the fourth gig. *Live at Several 21st's* reached #9 on the national chart in March 1983 and produced the single The Rolling Stones' 'Bitch'/'Brand New Cadillac'.

Reyne went back to his commitments with **Australian Crawl** and **Richard Clapton** took his place. The new line-up issued a second live album, *Greatest Hits (of Other People)*, and single, Bobby Fuller Four's 'I Fought the Law'/'The Stealer' (November 1983). The album reached #25 on the charts. Robin 'The Beast' Riley (ex-**Rose Tattoo**) replaced Harvey James on guitar, and Shirley Strachan (ex-**Skyhooks**) replaced Clapton as lead singer. The new line-up issued another live album, *No Song Too Sacred*, and the single, Led Zeppelin's 'Kashmir'/'The Sea and I' (1984). The Paul Christie-penned B-side, 'The Sea and I' was a sea shanty he recorded with Borich, Steve Balbi (bass) and Andy Cowan (keyboards; both from **Kevin Borich Express**).

In 1985, Christie contacted American guitar legend Joe Walsh (ex-James Gang, Eagles) and invited him to tour with The Party Boys. The new line up of Christie, Borich, Walsh, **Marc Hunter** (vocals; **Dragon**) and Richard Harvey (drums; ex-**Divinyls**) undertook the sold-out The Great Bars of Australia tour and recorded a fourth live album, *You Need Professional Help*. In 1986, **Angry Anderson** (from **Rose Tattoo**) became the band's fifth lead singer. He fronted a reconstituted line-up that comprised Christie (who had moved from bass to second drums), Borich, Harvey, John Brewster (guitar; ex-**Angels**) and Alan Lancaster (bass; ex-Status Quo). Oddly enough, that line-up did not issue a live album.

John Swan (from **Swanee**) took over lead vocals, and his arrival ushered in the band's most popular phase. The line-up of Swan, Christie, Borich, Harvey, Lancaster and Brewster went into the studio to cut an album. *The Party Boys* (December 1987) marked a departure for the band, as it included six original songs among the covers. It became a best-seller and produced four hit singles: John Kongas' 'He's Gonna Step on You Again'/'Small Talk' (#1 in June 1987), Argent's 'Hold Your Head Up'/'She's a Mystery' (#19 in November), 'Is This the Way to Say Goodbye?'/'B-Side Shuffle' (December) and Them's 'Gloria'/'Rising Sun' (March 1988).

Just as the band's success was peaking, Swan

left to work on a feature film called *Chase the Moon* (which did not eventuate). At the end of 1987, Christie invited UK singer Graham Bonnett (ex-Marbles, Blackmore's Rainbow, Michael Schenker Group) to join The Party Boys, but after only five gigs Bonnett proved incompatible and he left. Swan returned for The Party Boys' support to **AC/DC**'s February 1988 Australian tour. In late 1988, Joe Walsh came back for another tour with The Party Boys. The new line-up comprised Christie, Borich, Walsh, American Calvin Welch (bass) and Hamish, Fergus and Angus Richardson (backing vocals). Walsh also appeared on the band's next studio single, 'Follow Your Heart' (March 1989), which had been written and sung by Borich. Later in the year, respected UK bluesman Eric Burdon became the band's seventh lead singer.

The new line-up comprised Christie, Burdon, Malcolm Eastick (guitar; ex-**Stars**, **Jimmy Barnes** Band), Mal Logan (keyboards; ex-**Healing Force**, **Renée Geyer** Band) and Warren McLean (drums; ex-**Machinations**, **I'm Talking**). Once again, that line-up did not record. At the end of 1989, Christie assembled a new, studio-only line-up of The Party Boys in order to record a single. The line-up comprised **Ross Wilson** (vocals), Stuart Fraser (guitar; from **Noiseworks**), Rick Mellick (keyboards), Dorian West (bass), Adrian Cannon (drums), Kevin Bennett (backing vocals) and Alex Smith (backing vocals; ex-**Moving Pictures**). Due to contractual reasons, the band was unable to use Wilson's original lead vocal on the cover of the Manfred Mann hit 'Doo Wah Diddy Diddy' and unknown singer Vince Contarino (from Adelaide covers band The Zep Boys) redid the vocal.

When issued as a single in early 1990, 'Doo Wah Diddy Diddy' (backed with 'Where's the Party? . . . Boys!' which was sung by Swan) reached #24 on the national chart. With the help of Swan, American producer and bass player Leon Gaer and a host of session players, Christie recorded a final Party Boys single, Billy Preston's 'That's the Way God Planned It'/'Just Like We Should'. It came out in September 1992. After ten years, Christie finally laid The Party Boys to rest. He wrote a book based on his experiences in the rock business, *The Rock Music Self Management Manual*, and moved into band management (The Breed, Julieanne Henry, **Tamam Shud**).

Albums: *Live at Several 21st's* (Oz/EMI, 1983), *Greatest Hits (of Other People)* (Oz/EMI, 1983), *No Song Too Sacred* (Oz/EMI, 1984), *You Need Professional Help* (CBS, 1985), *Rage (Best of the Party Boys)* (J&B, 1986), *The Party Boys* (CBS, 1987), *Greatest Hits, Misses, Rarities and 'B' Sides* (Sony/Columbia, 1992).

The Party Machine

Formed: *1967*
Style: *Rock*
Original line-up: **Ross Wilson** *(vocals; ex-***Pink Finks***)*, **Ross Hannaford** *(lead guitar; ex-***Pink Finks***), Mike Edwards (sax, flute), Joe Gorski (bass; ex-***Ram Jam Big Band***), Peter Curtain (drums)*

The enterprising **Ross Wilson** was the driving force behind the innovative Party Machine. Wilson and **Ross Hannaford** first worked together in Melbourne teenage R&B outfit **The Pink Finks**. At the beginning of 1967, the two Rosses formed the altogether more radical The Party Machine. Chris Kinman replaced original bass player Joe Gorski not long after formation.

In June, Mike Edwards left to join **The Ram Jam Big Band** and Kinman also left. His place was taken by ex-Chants R&B guitarist Mike Rudd, who switched to bass. For the material he was writing with The Party Machine, Wilson drew on Frank Zappa and Howlin' Wolf for inspiration. The band issued the now impossibly rare single 'You've All Gotta Go'/'Gentle Art' on EMI/Columbia in early 1969. The Party Machine found notoriety rather than success, in particular when the Victorian Vice Squad deemed the band's printed songbook (which contained such choice Wilson-penned songs as 'I Don't Believe All Your Kids Should Be Virgins') to be obscene and seditious.

The Party Machine ended in March 1969 when Wilson received an S.O.S. call from **Procession**, then based in England. Wilson joined **Procession** in an effort to salvage the band from imminent stagnation. The scheme did not work and Wilson returned to Australia in early 1970. In the interim, Hannaford and Edwards had formed the country-influenced Quinn and Rudd had formed **Spectrum**. Back in Australia at the start of 1970, Wilson formed esoteric, special-occasion, progressive band **Sons of the Vegetal Mother** with Hannaford and Rudd. The Sons had evolved into **Daddy Cool** by the end of 1970.

The Passengers

Formed: *1978*
Style: *Rock*
Original line-up: *Angie Pepper (vocals; ex-Johnny and* **The Hitmen***), Jeff Sullivan (guitar), Steve Harris (keyboards), Jim Dickson (bass; ex-***Railroad Gin***, Survivors), Alan Brown (drums)*

The Passengers were just one of a number of bands fronted by female singers that made their presence felt on the late 1970s Sydney, inner-city scene. Like **The Flaming Hands'** Julie Mostyn, Shy Impostors' Penny Ward and **The Numbers'** Annalise Morrow, The Passengers' Angie Pepper was a singer of considerable power and conviction.

Jim Dickson had started out in Brisbane-based, commercial rock band **Railroad Gin** before forming R&B outfit The Survivors. Greg Williamson (guitar, vocals) and Bruce Anthon (drums) completed the line-up and the band issued one power pop single, 'Baby Come Back'/'Mr Record Man', on the Real label (December 1977). Melbourne label Suicide reissued the single in June 1978, and included 'Baby Come Back' on the Various Artists punk compilation *Lethal Weapons* (April 1978). Williamson and Anthon formed The Credits when Dickson moved to Sydney.

The Passengers derived their name from the Iggy Pop song 'The Passenger', and played a balance of melodic 1960s pop and tough rock. Jerry Jones (ex-TV Jones) replaced Brown on drums in mid-1979. The band existed for just over a year, and only issued one single, 'Face with No Name'/'Girlfriend's Boyfriend', on the Phantom label (April 1980). The band had already broken up by the time the single appeared. 'Face with No Name' and the previously unissued 'Sad Day' appeared on the Phantom Records compilation *Paths of Pain to Jewels of Glory* (1983). During The Passengers' lifetime, Harris also moonlighted in **Deniz Tek's** band The Visitors. Sullivan and Harris went on to form **The Flaming Hands**. Dickson travelled to the UK where he joined neo-pop band The Barracudas. He returned to Australia in the mid-1980s and joined **The New Christs** and later the **Deniz Tek** Group.

Pepper travelled to the USA with Tek (also ex-**Radio Birdman**); she returned a year later and formed the Angie Pepper Band. Although The Passengers never issued an album, French label Revenge put out an unauthorised LP, *The Passengers with Angie Pepper* (1990), which consisted of various demos and live cuts. The Angie Pepper Band comprised Tek, Harris, Clyde Bramley (bass; ex-**Hitmen**, Other Side, **New Christs**) and Ivor Hay (drums; ex-**Saints**) who was later replaced by Michael Charles (ex-Shy Impostors, **Lipstick Killers**). In early 1982, the band started to record an album, but the sessions were never completed. Only two songs from the sessions ever saw the light of day when the Citadel label issued the evocative 'Frozen World'/'Why Tell Me?' as an Angie Pepper solo single (February 1984). 'Frozen World' reached #1 on the alternative charts, and was one of the best independent singles of 1984.

'Frozen World' appeared on the Hot Records compilation *No Worries* (1985) and the essential Citadel compilation *Take Everything Leave Nothing* (March 1988). Pepper sang on a re-recorded version of The Visitors' 'Miss You Too Much' which turned up on an album of Deniz Tek solo out-takes, *Orphan Tracks*, put out by Revenge (1990). 'Miss You Too Much' also appeared on an obscure American compilation called *Third Coast Underground* on the Challenge label. Following the Citadel release of 'Frozen World', Pepper returned to the USA with Tek and has remained away from the limelight ever since.

Pastoral Symphony

Formed: 1968
Style: Pop

Pastoral Symphony was never a group as such, merely a bunch of musicians assembled under a collective name. The Pastoral Symphony name did, however, register one hit single with the ultra-commercial pop ditty 'Love Machine'.

The story began with the arrival of English producer Jimmy Stewart in Australia during early 1968. Together with local producer Geoffrey Edelsten, Stewart set up a studio session to record a single under an assumed name. It was a common practice at the time in the UK (for example The New Vaudeville Band, The Flowerpot Men), but unheard of in Australia. The studio band comprised Terry Walker (lead vocals; from **The Strangers**), all of **The Twilights**, **Ronnie Charles** (harmonies; from **The Groop**), Johnny Hawker (harmonies) and the Johnny Hawker Orchestra's string and brass sections. Buoyed by Stewart's superb production techniques (for the time), the resultant single, 'Love Machine'/'Spread a Little Love Around', was strong enough to reach #10 in Melbourne and #16 in Sydney during June 1968. Stewart and Edelsten set about putting together a 'proper' Pastoral Symphony, but in the meantime a young Melbourne band had registered the name. The ensuing legal battle did little to further Stewart's cause, and Pastoral Symphony was never heard from again.

Stewart became involved in Adelaide independent label Sweet Peach as house producer. He formed a partnership with folkie **Doug Ashdown** as co-writer, co-producer and co-performer. In the early 1970s, Stewart set up the Billingsgate label. Meanwhile, Edelsten travelled to the USA where he made his fortune. He later earned a great deal of attention as the first (ill-fated) private owner of an Australian Rules Football team when he helped set up the Sydney Swans Football Club during the early 1980s.

Pearls and Swine (*see* Johnny Teen and the Broken Hearts)

Pel Mel

Formed: *1979*
Style: *Post-punk pop*
Original line-up: *Judy McGee (vocals, synthesiser, sax, clarinet), Jane McGee (guitar), Graeme Dunne (guitar, vocals), Glen Hill (bass), Dave Weston (drums)*

Newcastle band Pel Mel grew out of Australia's late 1970s post-punk movement. Early influences included UK bands like The Cure, Wire, Joy Division, The Fall and Gang of Four, although Pel Mel always mixed the avant-garde with a deceptively simple blend of bright dance beats and catchy new wave pop. With its idiosyncratic sound and style, Pel Mel made little headway on the hard rock-besotted Newcastle pub circuit. As a consequence, the band moved to Sydney in 1980.

Having established a reputation as one of the most progressive new music bands on the Sydney inner-city scene (alongside **Laughing Clowns**, Voigt/465 and **Machinations**), Pel Mel set about issuing a single. Sydney FM station Double J recorded the band for a new music special, and the tracks 'No Word from China'/'Ipaneema Mon Amour' comprised the band's debut single on their own independent Primate label (January 1981). New bass player Lindsay O'Meara (ex-Voigt/465, **Crime and the City Solution**) had taken over from Hill by the time the single came out. Voigt/465 had comprised O'Meara, Rae Macron Cru (vocals, keyboards), Rob Pobestek (guitar), Phillip Turnbull (keyboards, vocals) and Mark Boswell (drums). The band recorded one self-financed single, 'Secret West'/'State' (November 1978), and an album, *Slights Unbroken* (issued posthumously), before splitting.

Pel Mel's 'No Word from China' won instant favour among discerning critics and new wave fans. Gap Records issued a remastered version of the single (through EMI) in June, followed by 'Head Above Water'/'Heartbeat' in December. By that stage, Jane McGee and O'Meara had left the band. Craig Robertson (bass) completed the new, four-piece line-up. Pel Mel's debut album *Out of Reason* (produced by Tony Cohen, December 1982) boasted an appealing sound as displayed on the singles 'Blind Lead the Blind'/'Water' (November) and 'Shoes Should Fit'/'Lost My Appetite' (June 1983). The band toured to increasingly positive responses (including supports to UK visitors Elvis Costello and The Fall), but Robertson left in early 1983. Dunne moved to bass and newcomer Paul Davies came in on guitar.

Pel Mel's second album, *Persuasion* (October 1983), highlighted the band's increasing confidence and maturing songwriting skills. It featured a couple of the band's most captivating songs, the title track 'Persuasion', 'Footloose', 'That Girl Had a Gun' and the classic dance-pop single 'Pandemonium'/'Theme from *Splash*' (September 1983). The band toured until the end of 1984, but ran out of steam without breaking into the mainstream consciousness. The Pel Mel quorum of Judy and Jane McGee, Dunne and Weston had also comprised part of off-shoot band The Limp. There were a number of other players involved, including Tim McGee (synth). The band existed only briefly, but did issue one single, 'Marked Man'/'Ghost Train', 'Humans Beware', on the Primate label (1981), as well as having recorded 'Lost My Appetite', which was the B-side to Pel Mel's 'Shoes Should Fit'.

Albums: *Out of Reason* (Gap/EMI, 1982; reissued Gap/CBS, 1983), *Persuasion* (Gap/CBS, 1983).

The Pelaco Brothers

Formed: *1974*
Style: *Rockabilly*
Original line-up: **Stephen Cummings** *(vocals; ex-Ewe and the Merinos), Peter Lillie (guitar, vocals), Chris Worral (guitar), Joe Camilleri (sax, vocals; ex-King Bees, Lipp and the Double Dekker Brothers, Sharks), Johnny Topper (bass), Karl Wolfe (drums; ex-Sharks)*

The Pelaco Brothers were one of those seminal, inner-city Melbourne bands that never achieved commercial success, but were assigned legendary status by virtue of the personnel who passed through their ranks. In a career lasting less than 18 months, The Pelaco Brothers virtually defined a scene that encompassed a new musical aesthetic.

The band sang about truck drivers, roadhouses and endless highways, and played a brand of rockabilly, country swing and R&B that recalled American outfits like Commander Cody and his Lost Planet Airmen and Dan Hicks and his Hot Licks. Yet, the band's delivery presented a fiercely Australian outlook. The Pelaco Brothers played small, dank pubs like the Station Hotel (Prahran), the Tiger Room (Richmond), Martinis (Carlton) and the Champion Hotel (Collingwood) to a modest yet fanatical following. Chris Worral left early in the piece to be replaced by Ed Bates. Peter Martin also contributed slide guitar. Although the band never issued any records during its lifetime, the Ralph label put out the three-track, live EP *The Notorious Pelaco Brothers Show* ('Truckdrivin' Queen', 'Conga Line' and 'Cat Clothes') in June 1977. A year later, Missing Link included the band's only studio recordings, a cover of **Gary Young's** 'Rockabilly Heaven', 'Truckdrivin' Queen' and Truckdrivin' Guru' on the Various Artists album *The Autodrifters and The Relaxed Mechanics Meet The Fabulous Nudes and The Pelaco Bros* (June 1978).

The band broke up in late 1975. **Stephen Cummings** and Ed Bates formed **The Sports** and Joe Camilleri formed **Jo Jo Zep and the Falcons.** Of the other members, Peter Lillie formed Relaxed Mechanics with **Dave Steel** (vocals), Nick Rischbieth (guitar; ex-Sharks), Ian Coloquon (bass) and John Lloyd (drums). Relaxed Mechanics contributed two tracks, 'Shakin' the Blues' and 'Gooseball Brown', to Missing Links' Autodrifters/Relaxed Mechanics/Fabulous Nudes/Pelaco Brothers album. Steel later joined **Weddings, Parties, Anything**; Rischbieth was in **Sacred Cowboys**; and Lloyd joined High Rise Bombers followed by Flowers/**Icehouse.** Johnny Topper formed redneck C&W/rockabilly band The Fabulous Nudes with Pierre Jaquinot (guitar, vocals; ex-Spo-Dee-O-Dee), Jimmy Jessop (vocals, harmonica; ex-Spo-Dee-O-Dee), Peter Morrison (guitar, harmonica) and Warwick Kennington (drums; ex-Uncle Bob's Band). Fabulous Nudes contributed 'Come Back Baby', 'I'll Be a Dag for You Baby' and 'Harry's Cafe "de" Wheels' to the Missing Link album.

When The Relaxed Mechanics and The Fabulous Nudes both broke up, Lillie and Topper joined forces in The Autodrifters. Warren Rough (guitar) and Karl Wolfe (drums; by then ex-**Millionaires**) completed the line-up. Rick Dempster (vocals, harmonica) also joined. The band spiced its brand of rockabilly and R&B with touches of blues, bossanova and country elements. The Autodrifters issued the *Best Bets* EP (on the independent Zak label, May 1978) which was one of the first 12-inch EPs ever issued in Australia (alongside **Skyhooks'** 'Women in Uniform' and **Jo Jo Zep and the Falcons'** *Loud & Clear*). Lillie left The Autodrifters in mid-1978, and the band expanded its base with the arrival of Pierre Jaquinot (guitar; ex-Fabulous Nudes) and Andy Baylor (lap steel, fiddle, mandolin). Des Hewitt replaced Wolfe, and Mick Bowden also added sax for the occasional gig.

Missing Link included four Autodrifters' tracks 'Locked Out of Love', 'Santa's Joined a Disco', 'Big Jim' and 'Mr Whizz', on the 1978 album. The Autodrifters broke up in 1979. Topper joined The Armchairs and **North 2 Alaskans.** Rough went on to **The Crackajacks, Corpse Grinders** and **The Paramount Trio.** Baylor formed **Dancehall Racketeers** and Cajun Combo. Lillie formed The Leisuremasters and issued three solo singles, 'Hangin' Around the House'/'Holiday House' (1979), 'Samurai Star'/'Dangerman Theme' (1980) and 'Homicide'/'Division 4', 'Pain in Paradise' (1981) plus an album, *Guitar Method* (1981) for Missing Link. The Pelaco Brothers, Relaxed Mechanics, Autodrifters, Fabulous Nudes and Leisuremasters material was later combined on the 1993 compilation *Rough & Ready Rockabilly.* Lillie remained a cult figure on the Melbourne music scene for many years, re-emerging in early 1997 with the country album *Poetry & Western* on the Rhythms/Greasy Pole label (through Shock).

Various Artists album: *The Autodrifters and The Relaxed Mechanics Meet The Fabulous Nudes and The Pelaco Brothers* (Missing Link, 1978); ***Peter Lillie albums:*** *Guitar Method* (Missing Link, 1981), *Poetry & Western* (Rhythms/Greasy Pole/Shock, 1997).

Andrew Pendlebury

Style: Rock, R&B

Journeyman guitarist Andrew Pendlebury (b. 1952) was the son of artist L. Scott Pendlebury who won both the Archibald and Wynn art prizes. Pendlebury has pursued a career that garnered him much critical acclaim, but little in the way of mainstream success. Although occasionally compared with **Tommy Emmanuel**, Pendlebury has preferred to follow a more low-key, highly specialised path away from the limelight.

After leaving school, Pendlebury concentrated on his art career; he even held a number of successful exhibitions of his mainly impressionistic-style landscapes. Pendlebury's musical career got underway during the mid-1970s when he joined Melbourne R&B/country combo the Carrl Myriad Band which comprised Carrl Myriad (vocals, guitar), Chris Wilson (organ), Mark Ferrie (bass) and Phil Smith (drums). There were a number of different Myriad line-ups, but the above contributed three tracks, 'Ballad of The Station Hotel', 'Rock'n'Roll Highway' and 'Glenrowan', to the Various Artists album *Live at the Station* (Lamington, 1976). Previously Carrl and Janie Myriad had issued the folk album *Of All the Wounded People* in 1972. Pendlebury left the band in August 1977 to join R&B/rockabilly outfit **The Sports.** During his tenure with that band, Pendlebury moonlighted with good-time band The Gentlemen, which comprised Ed Bates (guitar; ex-

Sports), Wayne Duncan (bass; ex-**Daddy Cool**) and Freddy Strauks (drums; ex-**Skyhooks**).

Pendlebury remained with **The Sports** until 1981, after which he spent a year with **The Dugites**. In 1983, Pendlebury was part of the **Stephen Cummings** Band alongside Martin Armiger (guitar; ex-**Sports**), Nick Smith (guitar, vocals; ex-**Millionaires**, **Kevins**), Mark Ferrie (bass; ex-Myriad, **Models**), Peter Luscombe (drums) and Lynda Nutter (backing vocals; from **The Dugites**). Pendlebury appeared on Cummings' debut solo album *Senso*; he maintained his association with Cummings by playing on subsequent albums like *This Wonderful Life*, *Lovetown* and *A New Kind of Blue*, as well as touring with Stephen Cummings' Lovetown. Cummings returned the favour by collaborating with Pendlebury on the guitarist's debut single 'She Set Fire to the House'/'Country Joy' (September 1987).

The single came from Pendlebury's debut solo album *Between the Horizon and the Dockyard* (July 1987) for the Cleopatra label. With backing provided by Mark Ferrie (bass) and Peter Jones (drums), the album featured an eclectic mix of styles that encompassed country swing, Spanish, bluegrass, jazz and rock. Pendlebury mostly played acoustic guitar, with a smattering of restrained electric guitar filling out the sound. Pendlebury had also put in time with Ian Stephen's gospel/rockabilly outfit **The Slaughtermen** by that stage. The band issued the albums *Still Loving You* (1986) and *Melbourne, Memphis and a Mansion in the Sky* (1988).

Pendlebury returned to his solo career with the albums *Tigerland* (1988) and *Zing Went the Strings* (June 1990). For *Zing Went the Strings*, Paul Grabowsky (piano), Pete Linden (pedal steel), Doug de Vries (guitar), Stephen Hadley (bass) and John James (J.J.) Hackett (drums; ex-**Mondo Rock**) provided understated backing to Pendlebury's contemplative, instrumental guitar sounds. For his fourth solo album, *Don't Hold Back that Feeling* (May 1992), Pendlebury enlisted the services of an all-star cast of singers including **Deborah Conway**, **Chris Wilson**, **Dave Steel** and **Kate Ceberano**. Also helping out were the core of Ceberano's Ministry of Fun, Stephen Hadley (bass), Peter Jones (drums) and Jex Saarelaht (keyboards). Ceberano sang on 'Calling You', a cover of the theme song to the feature film *Bagdad Cafe*, which was issued as a CD single (April). The album's title track, a cover of **Company Caine's** smouldering R&B-infused 'Don't Hold Back that Feeling' (written by **Gulliver Smith** and sung by Wilson), had been a staple of **The Sports'** early live shows.

In 1993, Pendlebury collaborated with master jazz guitarist Doug de Vries (ex-Vince Jones Band, *Tonight Live with Steve Vizard* studio band) on the album *Karaté*. Once again, the album encompassed blues, jazz, gypsy, folk and boogie stylings played exclusively on acoustic guitars. Pendlebury continued to work as a backing musician for Tess McKenna and **Dave Steel**. He and de Vries issued a second collaborative album, *Trouble and Desire*, in September 1995.

Albums: *Between the Horizon and the Dockyard* (Cleopatra, 1987), *Tigerland* (Cleopatra, 1988), *Zing Went the Strings* (WEA, 1990), *Don't Hold Back that Feeling* (Gallery/East West/Warner, 1992), *Karaté* (with Doug De Vries, ABC/PolyGram, 1993), *Trouble and Desire* (with Doug De Vries, ABC/EMI, 1995).

Tex Perkins

Style: *Blues, country*

There is little doubt that Gregory 'Tex' Perkins (b. 1966) stands as one of the most lauded frontmen in the history of Australian rock'n'roll. The singer has risen from the depths of the early 1980s country-swamp underground to become a mainstream rock icon. He fronted two of the most popular bands of the late 1980s/early 1990s, **Beasts of Bourbon** and **The Cruel Sea.**

Perkins got his start in Brisbane psychobilly/cow-punk band The Dum Dums, which he formed in 1982 when he was 16 years old. The original Dum Dums line-up comprised Perkins, Ian Wadley (guitar), Greg Wadley (bass) and Greg Gilbert (drums). The band took its cue from the likes of **The Birthday Party**, The Cramps, Merle Haggard and Johnny Cash. Due to his interest in country music, Greg Perkins was given the nickname Tex and the band became known as Tex Deadly and the Dum Dums. The band did not issue any records, although the track 'This Here Country' appeared on the *Castrak #3* cassette (given away with *Ratsack* fanzine #3, 1983), while 'Crazy' and 'Cheap Funerals' appeared on the *Leaving Home for the Party on the Roof* cassette (1983). There were a number of line-up changes (Peter Jetnikov replaced Ian Wadley on guitar; Marco Halstead (ex-Disposable Fits) replaced Jetnikov; Steve Timms replaced Greg Gilbert on drums; Clem Lukey replaced Timms; and Cyril replaced Greg Wadley on bass) before The Dum Dums fell apart in Sydney during July 1983.

Halstead returned to Brisbane to form tongue-in-cheek country/bluegrass/punk band The Kingswood Trio with Peter Krool (bass) and John Downie (drums). The Kingswoods issued a C&W version of

Sex Pistols' 'Pretty Vacant' as the single 'Purty Vacant'/'Commissar's Song' on the GREEN label (1984). The band also issued the single 'Think of Me'/'Rock Billy Boogie' on the Sundown label (1985) before Halstead joined The Pineapples from the Dawn of Time. Under the name Mark C. Halstead, he later issued the acclaimed country album *Before and After Love* (produced by ex-Triffid Graham Lee) on the W. Minc label (through Shock, 1994).

In the meantime, when Perkins had to fulfil a couple of gig commitments after The Dum Dums split, he called upon Spencer P. Jones from **The Johnnys** and Boris Sudjovic from **Scientists** to help out. The band was named **Beasts of Bourbon** in honour of the drunken party atmosphere generated. By September 1983, **Kim Salmon** from **Scientists** and James Baker from **Hoodoo Gurus** had expanded the line-up and the band toured and recorded the album *The Axeman's Jazz* which came out in July 1984. In February 1984, Perkins and Salmon, plus drummer Richard 'Stix' Ploog (on loan from **The Church**), found time to play gigs around Sydney as Salamander Jim. The band played a stripped-down, mutant swamp-blues which suited Perkins' braying vocals. When Salmon left Australia in March 1984, to join **Scientists** in the UK, Perkins formed a more permanent Salamander Jim line-up with Lachlan McLeod (guitar), Stu Spasm (guitar, bass; ex-Exhibit A, Zulu Rattle) and Martin Bland (drums; ex-Chaos, Head On, Crawling Eye, Acid Drops, Zulu Rattle).

Salamander Jim built up a cult following, but had broken up by the time the mini-album *Lorne Green Shares His Precious Fluids* appeared on the Red Eye label in August 1985. Before leaving Salamander Jim, Perkins (on bass) and Spasm (guitar) joined ex-**Hoodoo Gurus** drummer James Baker and **Roddy Radalj** (ex-**Scientists**, Le **Hoodoo Gurus**, **Johnnys**) for a one-off studio recording as The James Baker Experience. That resulted in the single The Troggs' 'I Can't Control Myself'/'Born to Be Punched' (June 1985) on the Red Eye label. Spasm and Bland went on to form **Lubricated Goat** among other bands. In May 1985, Perkins left Australia for the UK in order to join ex-Cramps/Gun Club guitarist Kid Congo Powers in his new band the Fur Bible. Instead of the outrageous disco-funk outfit Perkins had in mind, the Fur Bible was an out-and-out Goth rock band. Somewhat disillusioned and completely broke, Perkins returned to Australia. For the next year, he played in a variety of ad hoc bands like The Bush Oysters, Vertigo, Toilet Duck and Hot Property (with Spasm), before forming Thug with McLeod and Peter Read.

Thug was a purely experimental noise outfit.

Don Walker, Charlie Owen and Tex Perkins

The word thug derived from Thuggee, which was the methods and practices of a violent organisation of robbers and assassins in colonial India of the late nineteenth century. The Thuggees worshipped the goddess Kali and performed ritual killings in her honour. Thug's incendiary frame of reference suited Perkin's purposes at that time. Alongside Spasm and Bland's band, **Lubricated Goat**, Thug presented a subversive take on all things complacent and facile. It was a chance for the musicians involved to exist on the very fringes of the Sydney rock scene, and to play out a sick joke for their own entertainment. John Foy at Red Eye liked the joke and formed the Black Eye label specifically as an outlet for this bunch of noise terrorists.

In July 1987, Black Eye issued the Thug album *Mechanical Ape/Proud Idiots Parade* and the #1 alternative hit single 'Dad'/'Thug', **Lubricated Goat's** *Plays the Devil's Music* album and the Various Artists album *Waste Sausage* (compiled by McLeod). *Waste Sausage* included contributions from Thug, The Bush Oysters, **Lubricated Goat**, **Box the Jesuit**, **Grong Grong** and others. In *Rolling Stone*, Clinton Walker described Thug's single 'Dad' as 'like a grinding stone turning in time to an Oedipal howl' (it was a compliment!). The second Thug album, *Electric Woolly Mammoth* (October 1988), was another set of strange electronic noises, nightmarish sound effects and toilet-bowl humour. McLeod issued another collection of low-fi tracks as *Leather Donut* (July 1988), which contained contributions from Salamander Jim, Thug, Read, Spasm, Bland and others.

Perkins next venture, The Butcher Shop, was a noisy, hard rock collaboration between Perkins, Spencer P. Jones, Kid Congo Powers (ex-Fur Bible), Billy Pommer (from **The Johnnys**) and Phillip Clifford (ex-Madroom, **Box the Jesuit**). The Butcher Shop issued the 'Hard for You' 12-inch EP on Black Eye (July 1988). For the *Pump Action* album, Lachlan McLeod (ex-Salamander Jim, Thug) replaced Powers on guitar and Pete Hartley (ex-**King Snake Roost**, **Lubricated Goat**) replaced Pommer on bass. The band never really took off as a live or studio venture because Perkins and Spencer each had full-time bands with which to contend: **Beasts of Bourbon** and **The Johnnys**.

Beasts of Bourbon reconvened in 1988, and toured and recorded until 1993. In the interim, Perkins also found time to tour and record two albums, *Down Below* and *The Honeymoon is Over*, with **The Cruel Sea**. In 1993, Perkins also formed a partnership with Don Walker (ex-**Cold Chisel**) and Charlie Owen (ex-**New Christs**, **Louis Tillett**'s Aspersion Caste) as Tex Don and Charlie. That union produced the album *Sad but True* (November 1993), a rootsy collection of acoustic, country-blues songs full of steel guitar and sparse piano. The standout tracks included Walker's 'Sitting in a Bar', Owen's 'Dead Dog Boogie' and Perkins' 'I Must Be Getting Soft'. Produced by Tony Cohen, the album featured guest players like **Kim Salmon** (guitar; Surrealists, **Beasts of Bourbon**), Garrett Costigan (steel guitar), plus Warren Ellis (violin) and Jim White (drums), both from **Dirty Three**.

Tex Don and Charlie undertook an Australian tour which resulted in the *Monday Morning Coming Down (Live)* album, plus the single 'What I Done to Her' (September 1994). Perkins returned to his post with **The Cruel Sea**, with which he toured until the beginning of 1996. With his commitments to **The Cruel Sea** completed, Perkins recorded his debut solo album, *Far Be It from Me*, which appeared in August. The album produced two CD singles, 'You're Too Beautiful' (July 1996) and 'Splendid Lie' (November), plus the radio hit 'Real Love'. The album radiated a mellow ambience with bittersweet, off-kilter melodies coming to the fore. It featured musical contributions from Owen and Ellis. Perkins undertook a solo tour to promote the album, and his band included Jim Elliot (drums) and Ken Gormly (bass) from **The Cruel Sea**, Charlie Owen (guitar) and **Louis Tillett** (keyboards, vocals). In September 1996, **Beasts of Bourbon** reconvened again, and recorded a new album *Gone* (January 1997). Perkins was back working with **The Cruel Sea** by the end of the year.

Tex Perkins solo album: *Far Be It from Me* (Polydor, 1996); ***Thug albums:*** *Mechanical Ape/Proud Idiots Parade* (Black Eye, 1987), *Electric Woolly Mammoth* (Black Eye, 1988); ***Butcher Shop album:*** *Pump Action* (Black Eye, 1990); ***Tex Don and Charlie albums:*** *Sad but True* (Red Eye/Polydor, 1993), *Monday Morning Coming Down (Live)* (Red Eye/Polydor, 1994).

Pete Best Beatles (*see* North 2 Alaskans)

The Phantoms

Formed: *1960*
Style: *Instrumental*
Original line-up: *Dave Lincoln (lead guitar), Gene Taylor (rhythm guitar), Pete Watson (bass), Alan 'Ollie' Fenton (drums)*

Alongside **The Thunderbirds**, **The Strangers**, **The Chessmen**, The Breakaways, The Saxons, The Fabulous Blue Jays, The Marksmen and The Playboys, instrumental combo The Phantoms were one of the bastions of Melbourne's early 1960s rock scene. Rather than embrace the surf craze that had enthralled their Sydney counterparts like **The Atlantics**, **The Denvermen** and The Statesmen, The Phantoms took their cue from British and European instrumental masters like The Shadows, The Tornados and The Spotnicks.

The European leaning was due to the fact that all four original members were expatriate Englishmen who had arrived in Australia during 1960. Gene Taylor returned to the UK in 1961. He was replaced by Bob Garde, and at the end of 1962 the band signed to the W&G label. The band issued a series of instrumental singles, 'Stampede'/'Midnight' (#27 in October 1962), 'The Rumble'/'The Two Forty Two' (#29 in March 1963) and 'Havanagila'/'Round and Round' (1963), plus the EP *Instrumental Hits*, before Beatlemania hit Australia and relegated instrumental groups to the scrapheap. The Phantoms were adaptable enough to embrace vocal and beat pop, and indeed were selected as one of the support bands for The Beatles' July 1964 Australian tour. The Phantoms' debut album, *Two Sides of the Phantoms*, and next two singles, 'I Want You'/'Move It' (1964) and 'The Cruel Sea'/'My Babe' (1965), showcased both their vocal and instrumental abilities.

In March 1965, 17-year-old, UK-born Mike Brady replaced the temporarily indisposed Dave Lincoln on lead guitar. Brady was only with The Phantoms for two months, but in that time he and bass player Pete

Watson had decided to form their own beat pop band which became M.P.D. **Limited.** Watson's departure in May 1965 effectively ended The Phantoms' career. Watson and Lincoln were later reunited in Pete Watson's Rockhouse. Ollie Fenton became **Jigsaw's** original drummer, but died in a car accident in 1969. Watson died in 1972 following a long illness, and Lincoln died in an industrial accident.

Albums: *The Two Sides of the Phantoms* (W&G, 1964), *The Legendary W&G Sessions* (Canetoad, 1990).

Jeff Phillips

Style: *Pop*

Western Australian-born pop singer Jeff Phillips first came to public attention in 1966 when he compered Perth television show *Club 17* (following original compere **Johnny Young's** departure). In 1968, he relocated to Melbourne and signed to Festival Records. His debut single, a cover of The Shirelles' 'Baby It's You'/'I Want to Meet Her', reached #21 in Melbourne and #34 nationally during December 1968.

Phillips was unable to sustain his chart career, but remained in the public eye as compere of his own television series, *Sounds Like Us*, for the ABC. The series lasted until the end of 1970. Then, in April 1971, Phillips took over from **Ross D. Wyllie** as compere of the O-Ten Network's *Happening '71*. In the meantime, Phillips had issued two more singles on Festival, 'Everything I Touch'/'I'm Coming Home Cindy' (March 1969) and 'I'm in Love with You'/'Wrong or Right' (April 1970), and one for the Generation label, 'I Want to Be Famous Like My Dad'/'A Love of Your Kind' (September 1970).

Phillips continued as host of *Happening '72*, but then in 1973 travelled to the UK where he concentrated on club work. He issued a version of the **John Paul Young** hit single 'Yesterday's Hero' for the UK market. In all, he issued three singles on the Philips label, 'Yesterday's Hero', 'Crying in the Middle of the Night'/'Saturday' (1976) and 'Here You Come Again' (1977), plus two on United Artists, Vanda and Young's 'Superman'/'The Other Side' and 'Shake a Hand'/'Watch My Baby Rock'n'Roll'. He achieved a modicum of success with appearances on television variety shows like the *Rolf Harris Show* and *Seaside Special*. During the late 1970s, Phillips spent time in Los Angeles before returning to Australia. He issued two more singles, 'L.A. Reggae'/'Just Another Pretty Face' (May 1980) and 'Desire'/'Sleep with the Angels' (November 1981). Since that time, Phillips has appeared in television and radio commercials.

In 1985, he scored a role in the Australian stage production of the Andrew Lloyd-Webber musical *Cats*. He appeared on the Australian Cast recording album of *Cats* (on EMI) alongside Marina Prior, **Debra Byrne**, David Atkins and John Wood.

The Philisteins

Formed: *1985*
Style: *Garage-punk*
Original line-up: *Aydn Hibberd (guitar, vocals, harmonica), Guy Lucas (guitar, vocals, organ), Scott Harrison (bass), Charlie Shackloth (drums)*

The members of the peripatetic Philisteins came together in Hobart, Tasmania for a one-off party gig under the name of The Cheesemongers. Legend has it that they were disliked by all and sundry, which set the tone for much of the band's subsequent career. By early 1986, the band members had become more serious, acquired a new name, The Philisteins (courtesy of band friend Stewart Tabert), and a more committed drummer in Konrad Park.

The band's influences ranged from 1960s UK R&B bands like The Pretty Things, The Yardbirds and The Rolling Stones to American garage-punk bands like Love, Music Machine, The 13th Floor Elevators, The Flamin' Groovies, The Stooges and MC5. The Philisteins issued a limited edition cassette (200 copies) called *Reverberations*, but by all accounts the band's raucous blend of punk/R&B/psychedelia was soundly despised outside a small cult following around Hobart. During June 1987, inspired by the bands they heard on Adelaide label Greasy Pop, The Philisteins relocated to the South Australian capital where their sound met with a more positive response. The line-up of Hibberd, Lucas, Harrison and Mark Coombes (drums) immediately fell in with the likes of **Exploding White Mice, Lizard Train**, The Spikes and Primevils. Harrison and Coombes soon left to be replaced by Ian Wettenhall and Nick Bruer respectively.

Bruer stayed long enough to appear on the band's debut, eight-track mini-album, *Bloody Convicts*, which Greasy Pop issued at the end of 1988. The material fell neatly between 1970s punk and 1960s psychedelia, with plenty of guitar riffs to the fore. The Philisteins also contributed one track, 'Early Morning Memory', from the mini-album to Greasy Pop's Various Artists compilation *Oasis 2* (1989). By that stage, the band's old Hobart compadre Stewart Tabert had replaced Bruer on drums. In May 1989, The Philisteins recorded their second mini-album, *Some Kind of Philisteins*, but a month later decided to move on again. They returned to

Hobart until November 1989, after which they relocated to Sydney.

By that stage, Greasy Pop had issued *Some Kind of Philisteins*, which boasted a more punkish edge compared with the band's first release. It featured two covers, The Downliner Sect's 'Outside' and The Nomads' 'Thoughts of a Madman'. In Sydney, the band made little headway, and by the end of 1990 had relocated once again, this time to Melbourne. On the thriving Melbourne inner-city scene, the band found kindred spirits among the likes of **Hoss**, **The Dirty Lovers**, The Puritans, The Cracked Jaffas, Seminal Rats and The Surfin' Poobahs. The Dog Meat label issued the band's debut, full-length album, *Lifestyles of the Wretched and Forgettable*, in 1991. One of the standout tracks was a cover of The Pretty Things' 'Can't Stand the Pain'.

By 1992, Lucas, Wettenhall and Tabert had dispensed with The Philisteins name and format in order to form The Freeloaders with Sean Greenway (guitar, vocals; ex-**God**). The Freeloaders' mix of heavy, Detroit-inspired garage rock and melodic rock'n'roll (in The Flamin' Groovies vein) met with some success on the Melbourne inner-city circuit. The Freeloaders contributed a cover of 'I Want You' to the Dog Meat label's Troggs tribute album *Groin Thunder* (1992). That compilation also contained The Philisteins' rendition of 'From Home', which had been recorded in 1990. Dog Meat issued The Freeloaders' 'Something for Nothing' CD EP (1993) and the full-length album *Squalifications* (1994) before Greenway and Wettenhall left. Damien Smith (guitar, vocals) and Dave Gray (bass) joined, and the band issued the raucous *Dead Before My Time* album. The Freeloaders operated in the same sphere as the likes of **Powder Monkeys**, **Hoss**, **The Sunset Strip**, etc., all of whom also happened to record for Dog Meat.

Philisteins albums: *Bloody Convicts* (mini-album, Greasy Pop, 1988), *Some Kind of Philisteins* (mini-album, Greasy Pop, 1989), *Lifestyles of the Wretched and Foregettable* (Dog Meat, 1991). ***Freeloaders albums:*** *Squalifications* (Dog Meat, 1994), *Dead Before My Time* (Dog Meat, 1996).

The Pink Finks

Formed: *1965*
Style: *R&B*
Original line-up: Ross Wilson *(vocals, harmonica), Rick Dalton (rhythm guitar),* **Ross Hannaford** *(lead guitar), Geoff Ratz (bass), Richard Franklin (drums)*

During the summer of 1964–65, the first rumblings of R&B began emanating from suburban garages and dank, dark clubs around Australia. The Pretty Things, The Rolling Stones, The Kinks and The Yardbirds had made their mark, and young local musicians became enamoured with the raucous sounds coming across from the UK.

Like **The Purple Hearts** in Brisbane, **The Missing Links** in Sydney, **The Master's Apprentices** in Adelaide plus fellow Melbourne bands (**Keith Glass**'s) The Rising Sons, The Union and The Spinning Wheels, schoolboy outfit The Pink Finks were a product of that suburban R&B boom. At 16 years of age, singer **Ross Wilson** was already an R&B devotee. He joined an instrumental band called The Fauves and they soon renamed themselves The Pink Finks. Once the band started to play local dances and clubs at weekends, Wilson began to dig deeper into the blues for songs by masters like Howlin' Wolf and Muddy Waters. David Cameron replaced original rhythm guitarist Rick Dalton in early 1965. Dalton went on to play with **The Missing Links** and The Running Jumping Standing Still.

During June 1965, The Pink Finks issued their debut single, a cover of Richard Berry's (via The Kingsmen) 'Louie Louie'/'Got Love If You Want It', on their own Mojo imprint. That raunchy, primitive slice of R&B-mania peaked at #16 on the 3DB charts in Melbourne, making the band members instant celebrities at school. The band had less success with its three subsequent singles for W&G's In subsidiary label: Joe South's 'Untie Me'/'Nowhere to Run', Willie Dixon's 'Backdoor Man'/'Something Else' and **Johnny Chester's** 'You're Good for Me'/'Comin' Home Baby'. Was it any wonder the records failed to chart? On the sinister 'Backdoor Man', Wilson sounded like a slimy, depraved 60-year-old guy with nefarious intentions. Not bad for a 17-year-old kid! The song also featured snappy guitar licks from the 14-year-old Hannaford. On the other hand, 'You're Good for Me' was a great little Rolling Stones rip somewhere between 'Oh, Carol' and '19th Nervous Breakdown'.

Mike Edwards (trumpet, sax) joined in August 1966, but the band folded at the end of the year when Franklin, Cameron and Ratz left to attend university. By early 1967, Wilson, Hannaford and Edwards had unveiled their new band, **The Party Machine**. In 1979, reissue specialists Raven put out the seven-track *Let's Meet the Pink Finks* EP, which contained the previously unissued 'Rub My Root'. In 1987 record collector's magazine *From the Vault* issued a flexi disc which contained the unissued tracks 'Drop Down Mama' and 'It Hurts Me So'. **Ross Wilson** went on to work with **Procession**, **Sons** of the Vegetal Mother, Daddy Cool, Mighty Kong, Mondo Rock, as well as pursuing a successful solo career. Ross Hannaford was in Quinn, Sons of the Vegetal Mother, Daddy Cool, Mighty Kong, Billy T, Bambu, Lucky Dog, Goanna, Dianna Kiss and Ol' Skydaddys among many others.

Richard Franklin later became a film director. His Australian feature credits included the sexual fantasy *The True Story of Eskimo Nell* (1975), the soft-porn film *Fantasm* (under the alias of Richard Bruce, 1976) and two under-rated gothic thrillers, *Patrick* (1978) and *Roadgames* (1981). He made the move to Hollywood in 1982 and went on to direct the American films *Psycho II* (1983), *Cloak and Dagger* (1984), *Link* (1986), and *FX2: The Deadly Art of Illusion* (with Australian actor Bryan Brown, 1991).

David Cameron graduated from the National Institute of Dramatic Arts (NIDA) in 1968 and pursued an acting career. His television credits have included stints in the ABC-TV series *Bellbird* (1969), the miniseries *Against the Wind* (1978), *Golden Soak* (1979), *Water Under the Bridge* (1980) and *Grim Pickings* (1989), plus the adventure series *The Keepers* (with Bill Hunter, 1984). His feature film roles have included *Raw Deal* (1977), James Ricketson's *Third Person Plural* (1978) and *Dawn!* (1979).

Pirana

Formed: *1970*
Style: *Rock*
Original line-up: *Tony Hamilton (lead guitar; ex-Gus and the House,* Nomads*), Stan White (Hammond organ, vocals), Graeme Thompson (bass; ex-*Nomads*), Jim Duke-Yonge (drums; ex-*Nomads*)*

Sydney band Pirana grew out of the ashes of 1960s band The Nomads. Leaving behind the obvious R&B/pop stylings of the earlier band, Pirana embraced a more progressive aesthetic. One of the band's biggest influences was Santana. Pirana employed the same mix of jazz and blues, soaring guitar lines, driving guitar/organ interplay, exotic percussion and a strong Latin flavour. Indeed, the band's workout on Santana's 'Soul Sacrifice' was an in-concert favourite.

Pirana was a concert/festival mainstay of the early 1970s, and always impressed with its lengthy free-form jams (or, to use the vernacular of the day, 'man, they could really blow!'). The band's albums and singles were also worthwhile progressive gems that possessed a lively outdoors feel. The band's first recording venture, however, soon after formation was backing folkie Greg Quill on his debut solo album *Fleetwood Plain* and single 'Fleetwood Plain'. In 1971, Pirana signed to EMI's new, progressive subsidiary label Harvest alongside Spectrum and Tully.

During 1971, Pirana issued two singles 'Here It Comes Again'/'Find Yourself a New Girl' (May) and 'I Hope You Don't Mind'/'Funny Games' (November), plus the album *Pirana* (April). 'Here It Comes Again' was the first local single processed in stereo. Reissue specialists Raven included 'Here It Comes Again' on the Various Artists compilation *Golden Miles: Australian Progressive Rock 1969–1974* (1994). At the end of the year, Pirana supported UK visitors Manfred Mann's Earth Band, Free and Deep Purple. In January 1972, Pirana was a hit at the inaugural Sunbury Pop Festival. By that stage, Keith Greig had replaced Stan White on organ. The band's rendition of 'Soul Sacrifice' appeared on the Various Artists album *Sunbury* (EMI, 1972). In November, the band issued its second album, *Pirana II*, which featured a classic slice of Australian progressive rock in the atmospheric, nine-minute 'Thinking of You'.

The band saw out its days to 1974 on the suburban dance and inner-city pub circuit, but did not record again. There were a number of line-up changes: in late 1972, Richard McEwan replaced Hamilton on guitar; Andy James (organ, flute) replaced Greig in 1973; and Phil Hitchcock replaced Thompson on bass in 1974. Hitchcock had previously played in Sydney band Eight Day Clock which played a brand of brassy jazz-pop in the vein of Blood Sweat and Tears or Chicago. Duke-Yonge went on to work with a number of bands, including Corroborree, the Anne Kirkpatrick Band and Bullamakanka

Albums: *Pirana* (EMI/Harvest, 1971), *Pirana II* (EMI/Harvest, 1972).

The Planets

Formed: *1958*
Style: *Rock'n'roll*
Original line-up: *Johnny Edwards (vocals), Graeme Howie (piano, sax, vocals; ex-House Rockers), Ben E. Joyner (guitar), Ron Fewster (guitar), Brian James (tenor sax, clarinet), Leon Basil (double bass), Brian Anderson (drums)*

The Planets were one of the very first rock'n'roll bands formed in Melbourne. The band played local dances in various town halls and RSL Clubs alongside the likes of Mickey Borg and the Tempests, Billy Owens and The Thunderbirds, Judy Cannon, The Moontones, the Henri Bource All Stars, The Autocrats and Malcolm Arthur and the Knights.

As well as Edwards, the band employed a number of featured vocalists including Barry Greenwood, Beverley Dick, Ron Patrick and Billy Dodds. Edwards, Dick, Patrick and Dodds formed vocal group The Planetones (in the manner of The Diamonds, Elvis Presley's The Jordanaires and Sydney group **The Delltones**) to accompany The Planets. In 1959, Graeme Howie, Brian Anderson and Beverley Dick split from The Planets to form The Big Beat Band. Greenwood and Joyner continued on as Barry and the Planets with newcomers Tony Lee (guitar, vocals), Johnny Fink (sax), Graham Lyall (sax), Laurie Arthur (bass) and John Rochee (drums).

In 1960, Barry and the Planets issued a single 'Remember Your Kissin''/'Sitting on Top of the World' on the Astor label. The B-side was a cover of the old Chester Burnett country-blues song. The two groups continued to play local rock'n'roll dances, but by the end of 1960 they had reunited under The Planets' banner. Alongside Dick and Edwards, Neil Andrews joined as featured vocalist. In 1961 The Planets became the resident band at the popular Hi-Way Klub which operated out of the Moorabbin Youth Club. The Planets appeared on the Seven Network's rock'n'roll show *Teenage Mailbag*, and recorded an EP, 'Express Eleven', for the AWA label. Beverley Dick sang on the rendition of Connie Francis's 'Lipstick on Your Collar'. By that stage, Allan Pope had joined The Planets on electric bass. In August 1961, Brian Lyons replaced James on sax.

By 1961, other Melbourne rock'n'roll and instrumental bands such as **Johnny Chester** and **the Chessmen**, **The Cherokees**, **The Strangers**, **The Phantoms** and The Premiers had come to the fore, but the rock'n'roll dance scene was undergoing a change. Outside forces (including the police, local councils and 'concerned' members of the public) forced many of the local promoters to present 60/40 dances which mixed rock'n'roll with ballroom dancing. The Planets fell in with the ballroom 60/40 circuit and began to tone down their sound and style. In late 1961, Malcolm Hope replaced Allan Pope on bass; Geoff Wightman soon replaced Malcolm Hope. In April 1962 The Planets recorded the backing to vocal group The Thin Men's debut single 'Can't Get You Out of My Mind'/'Learning the Twist' on the W&G label. The Thin Men had evolved from The Planetones and The Moontones and comprised Johnny Edwards, Ron Partick, Adrian Usher and Tony Lee.

At the end of 1962, Henri Bource (ex-Henri Bource All Stars, **Thunderbirds**) replaced Lyons on sax. Henri Bource had recorded an early rock'n'roll single with his All Stars, 'Reet Petite'/'Your Book of Life', in 1958 on the Planet label. The Henri Bource All Stars are also credited with having issued possibly the very first Australian rock'n'roll album, *Rock'n'Roll Party*, on the Planet label (1958). As well as Bource, Tony Buchanan and Graham Bloomfield played tenor sax for the The Planets until Lyons returned in August 1963. Other vocalists who worked with The Planets around that time included **Peter Doyle**, Max Jolly, Frankie Davidson, Peter McLean and Judy Kerzay.

Ian B. Allen (bass, vocals; ex-Ramrods, Checkmates) replaced Wightman in 1963. The new line-up of Howie, Joyner, Lyons, Anderson and Allen remained stable for eight years. The Planets continued on the 60/40 dance circuit, but with the emergence of Beatlemania during 1964 the band's sound became outdated. By 1967, Dick, Andrews and Lyons had all left the band. By the late 1960s, The Planets had moved into the suburban pub circuit. Once again, by 1970, with groups like **Billy Thorpe** and the Aztecs and **Chain** moving into the pubs, The Planets' rock'n'roll sound met with little favour. The Planets then moved on to the more upmarket cabaret and club circuit, and began to incorporate a more country-oriented sound into their shows. Ian Allen left The Planets in April 1972 to be replaced by Allan Pope. In March 1973, The Planets finally disbanded, and Joyner, Anderson and Pope moved into straight country music.

By 1983, the rock'n'roll nostalgia circuit was beginning to burgeon, and The Planets re-formed to take advantage of this. Promoter Greg Lynch presented a show called *The Happy Days of Rock'n' Roll* which featured Beverley Dick, The Planets, Malcolm Arthur, Colin Cook, Billy Owens and The Henri Bource All Stars. The re-formed Planets comprised Howie, Joyner, Allen, Lyons and Anderson. Later in the year, **Betty McQuade** deputised for Dick, who was recuperating from surgery. Allen continued with the rock'n'roll revival concept when he formed The Allstars which comprised himself, Henri Bource (sax), Murray Robertson (keyboards), Les Stacpool (guitar) and Mike Lynch (drums). Not to be confused with **John Paul Young** and the All Stars, The Allstars described themselves as 'Australia's most authentic '50s group'. With members hailing from The Planets, **The Thunderbirds**, **The Blue Echoes**, **The Chessmen** and Henri Bource All Stars, the band had some right to such a claim.

Latter-day Allstars members have included Graham Bloomfield (sax), Jon Calderwood (guitar), Ron Chapman (drums) and Stan Azzopardi (guitar; ex-Premiers). The band recorded five albums of rock'n'roll material, *The Allstars Featuring Grantley Dee* (1987), *Rock, Rock, Rock!* (1989), *Good Rockin'*

Tonight! (1991), *Still Rockin' On* (1992) and *Let the Little Girl Dance* (1994). The Allstars mostly toured the cabaret, rock'n'roll dance and nostalgia circuit, backing singers like **Merv Benton, Lonnie Lee, Barry Stanton, Betty McQuade, Grantley Dee, Peter Doyle, Colin Cook**, Dinah Lee, Bobby Bright and Johnny Devlin. The band has also toured with international performers like Rick Nelson, Del Shannon, Buddy Holly's Crickets, Gene Pitney, The Shadows, Chubby Checker, The Coasters and Freddy and the Dreamers.

Martin Plaza (*see* Mental as Anything)

The Pleazers

Formed: *1965*
Style: *R&B*
Original line-up: *Bobby Bacon (vocals), Billy London (vocals), Bruce 'Phantom' Robinson (lead guitar; ex-G-Men), Peter 'Bunt' Newing (rhythm guitar; ex-G-Men), Ronnie Peel (bass; ex-Mystics,* **Missing Links***), Dennis 'Speedy' Gilmour (drums; ex-G-Men)*

The Pleazers were an odd phenomenon in some ways. Although formed in Australia, they were almost completely ignored on home turf, but by circumstance came to be highly revered in New Zealand. Like a number of other bands around at the time (Larry's Rebels, **The In-Sect**), The Pleazers played a combination of commercial, novelty pop and wild R&B. It was for the latter style that The Pleazers earned their reputation.

In early 1965, Canadian-born Bobby Bacon and New Zealander Billy London were working around Auckland, NZ as The London Brothers. They won first prize in a talent quest which enabled them to work on promoter Ivan Dayman's Queensland band circuit. In Brisbane, the duo teamed up with the remnants of The G-Men and, with the addition of Ronnie Peel in mid-1965, The Pleazers came into being. At the end of the year The Pleazers travelled to New Zealand for a three-month stint at Auckland's Galaxie Club. Three months turned into 13 months and five New Zealand hit singles. Alongside Ray Columbus and the Invaders, Larry's Rebels and **La De Das**, The Pleazers were a favourite band in the land of the Long White Cloud. In early 1966, Bacon left to be replaced by English expatriate Shane Hale (aka Trevor Hales). Having signed to the Zodiac label, The Pleazers issued a string of singles, 'Last Night'/'In the Pines (Poor Girl)', Them's 'Gloria', 'Like Columbus Did', 'Hurtin' All Over' and 'Guilty'/'Can't Pretend'. The Pleazers also cut an album, *Definitely Pleazers*, and an EP, *A Midnight Rave with the Pleazers*.

In late 1966, The Pleazers returned to Australia with new bass player, Gus Fenwick (ex-Layabouts). Peel went on to join a revived version of **Ray Brown** and the Whispers in Sydney before forming **Rockwell T. James** and the Rhythm Aces and The Browns (with **Ray Arnott** and Les Stacpool). In 1972, he joined **La De Das** and by 1975 was a member of **John Paul Young** and the All Stars. In the mid-1980s, he was a member of The Scattered Aces with **Peter Wells**. In the meantime, The Pleazers picked up a small following on the Melbourne suburban dance and discotheque circuit and even cut two more singles, The Beach Boys' 'Here Today' and Leiber and Stoller's 'Three Cool Cats'. The band made little headway, however, and in 1967 London and Hale took a new line-up back to New Zealand. By the end of the year, it was all over. Robinson went on to The Troubled Minds, Newing joined Andy James and Doug Ford in the famed Running Jumping Standing Still and Fenwick turned up in **Band of Talabene, Healing Force, Bootleg Family Band, Ray Burton's** Nightflyers and **Swanee**.

Albums: *Definitely Pleazers* (Zodiac, NZ only, 1966), *A Midnight Rave with the Pleazers* (Raven, 1987).

The Plums

Formed: *1992*
Style: *Indie guitar pop*
Original line-up: *Caroline Kennedy (vocals, guitar; ex-Jack and the Beanstalk), Stephen Moffatt (guitar; ex-Jack and the Beanstalk), Peter McCracken (bass), Shamus Goble (drums; ex-Jack and the Beanstalk)*

Melbourne band The Plums had its basis in the quaintly named Jack and the Beanstalk. That band issued one independent single, 'Evolution', on its own Beanstalk imprint (1991) before evolving into The Plums. Taking a cue from US bands like The Pixies, The Plums mixed strident guitar riffs with melodic pop roots. Kennedy was the band's focal point with her tough-but-graceful presence, opinionated views and emotion-charged, if imperfect, vocals.

The band issued two CD EPs on the Temptation label (through Mushroom Distribution Services), *Au Revoir Sex Kitten* (November 1992) and *Read All Over* (May 1993), before signing to Mushroom's White subsidiary. The Plums supported US visitors Throwing Muses, Belly and Juliana Hatfield, then issued their acclaimed debut, full-length album *Gun* (April 1994). It produced the CD single

'Find this Anywhere' (May). The Plums issued a new CD EP, 'Heavenly', in June 1995, but two months later Kennedy had linked up with Barry Palmer in **deadstar**.

Album: Gun (White/Mushroom/Festival, 1994).

The Plunderers

Formed: *1984*
Style: *Power pop*
Original line-up: *Nic Dalton (bass, vocals), Stevie Plunder (real name Anthony Hayes, guitar, vocals), Lyndsey Dunbar (drums)*

The enterprising Nic Dalton has pursued an eclectic and generally low-key career that has, nevertheless, seen him play in 23 bands and issue an impressive number of releases under his own terms. After moving to Sydney in the late 1980s with The Plunderers, he set up his Half a Cow record label and bookshop in the Sydney inner-city suburb of Glebe. The label became an outlet for the likes of **Godstar**, **Sidewinder**, **The Daisygrinders**, **Smudge**, **Swirl**, Sneeze, Hippy Dribble and many others.

The Plunderers came together in Canberra (ACT) during 1984, playing a punky brand of power pop that mixed frantic guitar riffs, sharp harmonies and diamond-hard pop melodies. Reference points included The Buzzcocks, The Mekons, Big Star, The Stooges, The Strangeloves and The Banana Splits! After only a handful of gigs Lyndsey Dunbar left to study art overseas. Dalton and Stevie Plunder put The Plunderers on hold while they toured with fellow Canberra outfit **The Gadflys** for six months. Taking **The Gadflys**' drummer Pete Pillage (real name Pete Velzen, drums, lead vocals) with them, Dalton and Plunder revived The Plunderers in June 1985. In October 1985, the band issued the independent single 'Strange Affection'/'Into the Ice' on its own Rattlesnake label before making the move to Melbourne. By that stage, the band had added Andy Waterhole (real name Andy Lewis) on keyboards, guitar and harmonies. In July 1986, The Plunderers moved on again, this time to Sydney. As a three-piece (sans Waterhole), the band found instant favour on the inner-city circuit, playing alongside the likes of **The New Christs**, **The Hard-Ons** and **Died Pretty**.

In 1988, Citadel's offshoot label Green Fez issued the Charlie Owen-produced mini-album *Trust Us* (June) and the Rob Younger-produced second single 'I Don't Mind'/'Dying' (November). The band contributed a hard-hitting cover of The Stooges' 'No Fun' to Au-go-go Records, Stooges tribute album *Hard to Beat* (1988), plus a cover of

The Plunderers

'Charisma' to Waterfront's Kiss tribute album *Hard to Believe* (1990). In December 1988, original drummer Pillage/Velzen left to be replaced by Geoff Milne (ex-**Eastern Dark**). Velzen joined fellow Sydneysiders **Falling Joys**. The Plunderers issued the singles 'I Didn't Even See Them at All'/'Clean Hands', 'Trouble Struck' (June 1989) and 'Christo'/'Peggy' (November 1990) plus two 10-inch mini-albums, *Sarah's Not Falling in Love* (April 1990), and *Home Movies* (July 1991), on Citadel. The mini-albums saw The Plunderers moving beyond their three-minute, power pop roots to explore a more tripped-out kind of psychedelic revivalism on the eight-and-a-half minute 'The Shining' (from *Sarah's Not Falling in Love*) and the 12-minute 'Slide Show' (from *Home Movies*).

Dalton and his Plunderers compadres also conceived Hippy Dribble in 1989 as a one-off live event for the twentieth anniversary of Woodstock. Using the pseudonyms Nic Dribble, Stevie Dribble and Geoff Dribble, Hippy Dribble then issued a tongue-in-cheek, thrashy neo-psychedelic pop 12-inch EP, *Wild Strawberri*, on the Trip label (November 1990). They revived the joke in 1993 for the 7-inch vinyl single 'Cheerleader' (September) and the split album *Silver Apples* which they shared with another of Dalton and Plunder's bands Captain Denim: *Fade* (April 1995).

In January 1991, Dalton formed the first version

of **Godstar** with Tom Morgan, Alison Galloway and rock writer John Encarnacao. **Godstar** went on to issue a number of psychedelic pop releases, but Dalton put the band on hold later in the year when he joined **The Hummingbirds** as temporary replacement for Robyn St Clair. In 1992, Dalton revived The Plunderers for the full-length album *Banana Smoothie Honey* on Citadel. That effectively brought The Plunderers' era to a close. By the end of 1992, Dalton had joined Evan Dando's band Lemonheads, with which he toured internationally and appeared on the album *Come on Feel the Lemonheads*. He stayed with the band until August 1994. In 1993, Dalton reactivated **Godstar**. At the end of 1995, Dalton broke up **Godstar** and formed a new band called The Kombi Nation (TKN). He also worked with Sneeze and, in early 1997, a pseudo-soul band called The Ultimate Vanilla.

Another of Dalton's side projects was the delightfully eccentric Love Positions, which was a studio outfit he formed with **The Hummingbirds'** Robyn St Clair. Love Positions issued the single 'Light of Day'/'Kiss', 'Underworn' and the album *Billiepeebup* (both 1990) on the Half a Cow label. With the break-up of The Plunderers, Stevie Plunder joined **The New Christs**. He left a year later to form **The Whitlams** with Tim Freedman (keyboards, vocals; ex-Olive Branch) and Andy Lewis (double bass; ex-**Gadflys,** Plunderers). Plunder died on 24 January 1996 at the age of 32. Freedman kept **The Whitlams** going with new members and issued a new CD single, 'You Sound Like Louis Burdett', in May 1997.

Plunderers albums: *Trust Us* (mini-album, Green Fez, 1988), *Sarah's Not Falling in Love* (10-inch mini-album, Citadel, 1990), *Home Movie* (10-inch mini-album, Citadel, 1992), *Banana Smoothie Honey* (Citadel, 1992) *13.7.91 Live! Live! Live!* (10-inch mini-album, Club/Shock, 1991); ***Love Positions album:*** *Billiepeebup* (Half A Cow, 1990).

Pollyanna

Formed: *1993*
Style: *Pop*
Original line-up: *Matt Handley (guitar, vocals; ex-Catherine Wheel), Maryke Stapleton (bass, vocals), Serge Luca (drums, vocals)*

Sydney band Pollyanna played a brand of punky power pop which garnered a good deal of attention on the alternative scene. In 1994, Pollyanna signed with Mushroom subsidiary label Bark (home to **Header** and Manic Suede) and issued the CD EPs *Fordgreensilverocket* (October 1994), *Junior* (May 1995) and *Lemonsuck* (September 1995). *Junior* and *Lemonsuck* reached #1 on the national alternative charts, with tracks like 'Pale Grey Eyes' and 'Lemonsuck' becoming live favourites.

Pollyanna supported international visitors like the Jesus and Mary Chain, Teenage Fanclub, Sebadoh and Paw during 1995, and appeared on the bill of the 1996 Big Day Out tour. The 7-inch single 'Piston' (February 1996), the CD singles 'Keep Me Guessing' (April) and 'Potomac' (July), plus the band's debut, full-length album *Long Player* (March) maintained the quality of earlier releases. *Long Player* was an appropriate title as it featured an hour's worth of music over 14 songs. It reached #31 on the national mainstream chart. Just prior to the album's release Pollyanna toured as support to **Hoodoo Gurus**, and then in May supported Irish band The Cranberries on their Australian tour. Bark combined the CD EPs *Fordgreensilverocket* and *Junior* for release as the ten-track album *Junior Rock* (February 1997). By that stage, Glenn Maynard (ex-**Have a Nice Day**) had replaced Serge Luca on drums. Pollyanna's third album, *Hello Halo* (produced by Paul McKercher), came out in September

Pollyanna

1997. Two CD singles, 'Effervesence' and 'Peachy Keen', preceded the albums release in April and August respectively.

Album: *Long Player* (Bark/Mushroom/Festival, 1996), *Junior Rock* (Bark/Mushroom/Festival, 1996), *Hello Halo* (Bark/Mushroom/Sony, 1997).

The Pony

Formed: *1986*
Style: *Pop*
Original line-up: *Pierre Baroni (vocals, guitar), John O'Beirne (guitar), Dean Baroni (bass), Dale Hamilton (drums)*

Singer/guitarist/songwriter Pierre Baroni started out in the mid-1970s with young Melbourne pub band Carmine. Gee Deluca (lead guitar), Gino Deluca (bass, vocals) and Mario Baroni (drums) completed the Carmine line-up. Ian 'Molly' Meldrum was quoted as describing Carmine on the ABC-TV's pop show ***Countdown*** as 'one of the future top bands in Australia'.

Needless to say, Carmine did not become a top band and soon broke up. By late 1977, Baroni had formed new band P.X.B. (Power by Beat!!) which comprised Sam Mallet (guitar, vocals; ex-**Finch**), Graeme Elkins (bass, vocals) and Kevin Fitzpatrick (drums, vocals). In 1978, the band issued an independent record, *The P.X.B. EP,* which mixed good ol' pub-rock with polite power pop (reminiscent of UK outfit Eddie and the Hotrods). In late 1980, Baroni joined new wave band **The Aliens**, appearing on their final single, 'I Don't Care'/'Over My Head' (February 1981). With the break-up of **The Aliens** later in the year, Baroni formed Field of Knives. The band made little headway on the Melbourne pub scene, and by 1986 had evolved into The Pony.

The Pony proffered a jangly, 1960s-inspired guitar-pop sound and style with a dark, petulant edge as displayed on the single 'I Lied'/'Minutes in My Head', 'Fortunate Life' (April 1987). The band shared a gig giveaway single, 'In the Background', with fellow Melbourne band **Shindiggers** ('Good Golly Miss Molly'). The Pony's debut album, *Thorns and Cutlery* (May 1987), featured tunes mostly in The Beatles/Byrds idiom with the odd dash of Stonesy raunch. At the end of 1987, The Pony signed to Mushroom's subsidiary White label.

White issued a series of Pony singles that sold well on an independent level but failed to crack the mainstream charts. The singles were 'Alienation'/'My Window', 'Afterwords' (November 1987), 'The Heart is a Lonely Hunter'/'Empty Suits', 'Unanswerable' (April 1988), 'The Big Picture'/'Hope', 'Rules of the Game' (February 1989), 'Heaven'/'The Sounds of Silence' (July 1989) and 'Flatter'/'Yes', 'It Couldn't Happen Again' (November). The band issued a second album, *Memoirs of Daydreams* (July 1989), that fared little better. By 1990, The Pony had called it a day. Baroni went on to work as art director for Mushroom Records.

Albums: *Thorns and Cutlery* (Cleopatra, 1987), *Memoirs of Daydreams* (White/Mushroom/Festival, 1989).

The Poor

Formed: *1994*
Style: *Hard rock*
Original line-up: *Anthony 'Skenie' Skene (vocals, rhythm guitar), Julian Grynglas (guitar), Matt Whitby (bass), James Young (drums; ex-***B.B. Steal***)*

The Poor played raw, driving rock'n'roll in the tradition of Oz pub-rock forebears **AC/DC**, **Rose Tattoo** and **The Angels**. The band started life as The Poor Boys in the Northern Territory capital of Darwin during 1988. The Poor Boys originally comprised Anthony Skene, Julian Grynglas, Matt Whitby and drummer Chris Risdale. The band picked up a loyal following in the watering holes around its home state, before coming to the attention of Oz rock veterans **The Angels**.

The Poor Boys impressed **The Angels'** drummer Brent Eccles so much that he became their manager. The band relocated to Sydney in 1991, toured the west coast of the USA with **The Angels** as part of the Wizards of Oz showcase, and signed an American deal with Epic Records. **The Angels'** Rick Brewster and Bob Spencer produced The Poor Boys' Australian debut CD EP for Sony/Columbia, the dirty, grungy *Rude, Crude & Tattooed* (June 1992). By that stage, James Young had taken over the drum position. The Poor Boys supported **The Angels** on their massive Tears You Apart national tour (July–August 1992), and a year later issued a second CD EP, *Underfed.* Under the direction of English producer Paul Northfield (Suicidal Tendencies), the band recorded its debut, full-length album, *Who Cares?* The Poor Boys supported American visitors Alice in Chains and Suicidal Tendencies on their joint Australian tour (October 1993).

In March 1994, The Poor Boys officially became The Poor due to an American outfit also called The Poor Boys. Three months later, The Poor crashed into the national Top 10 with the frantic CD single 'More Wine Waiter Please'. *Who Cares?* made its debut at #4 on the national chart, the same week that one-time touring partners **The Screaming Jets** held down the #3 spot with their album *Tear of Thought*. The American release of *Who Cares* and 'More Wine Waiter Please' (March 1994) was greeted with much fuss. 'More Wine Waiter Please' was one of the most added tracks to US radio that month, and the rock press responded with raves like 'a romping, stomping, foot-thumping, sweat soakin' good time', 'ass-kicking rock and roll that breaks all barriers' and 'the best hard rock song to come out in a long time'. The album made its debut on the *Billboard* rock chart at #38.

The Poor toured Australia, the USA, Europe and Japan, but the band was unable to maintain the chart success rate at home when the next CD single, 'Poison', only managed a desultory #48 during September 1994. In early 1996, The Poor embarked on an international tour with **AC/DC**, which involved playing to over 750 000 people across America. The band returned to Australia at the end of 1996 and laid plans to record a second, long-overdue album.

Album: *Who Cares?* (Sony/Columbia, 1994).

Porcelain Bus

Formed: *1985*
Style: *Rock, R&B*
Original line-up: *Ian James (vocals), Robert McKiernan (guitar, vocals), Paul Patrick (bass), John Nolan (drums)*

Sydney band Porcelain Bus grew out of the same scene that spawned **Died Pretty**, **The Moffs**, **The Trilobites** and **The Bam Balams**, all of whom also recorded for the Citadel label. Schoolfriends Ian James, Robert McKiernan and Paul Patrick formed Mr Pharmacist in early 1985. The name was in homage to the band's 1960s acid-punk/R&B roots, being the title of a song written by Texan band The Other Half.

With the arrival of John Nolan at the end of the year, the band became known as Porcelain Bus, which was a tongue-in-cheek euphemism for throwing up in the toilet (i.e. 'driving the porcelain bus'). Rob Younger (ex-**Radio Birdman**) produced Porcelain Bus's debut single 'Indignation'/'My Family' (August 1986), which defined the band's sound (sparse, melodic guitar and husky vocals laid over a dark, rumbling rhythm section). A year later, Citadel issued the band's second single, 'The Well is Dry'/'The Hands Have Control' (July 1987) and the mini-album *Steel Bros*, both of which had been produced by **Died Pretty's** Brett Myers.

Myers also produced the band's full-length, debut album, *Talking to God* (October 1988), and the third single, 'Own Little World'/'Clockwork'. Citadel lifted a second single from the album, 'Rats'/'Hanging Back', 'Old Soldiers' (June 1989), and the album came out in Europe to positive reviews. Nolan left the band in November 1989 to be replaced by Adam Toole for the recording of the band's second, Myers-produced album, *Fragile*, in February 1990. The band's next single, 'Blue on Blue'/'Vertigo Man', appeared in June 1990, followed by *Fragile* a month later. Citadel licensed a compilation of the band's early material entitled *Sacred Relics* for release in Europe, which paved the way for a tour there in late 1990. The band continued to tour the east coast of Australia but broke up in 1991.

Albums: *Steel Bros* (Citadel, 1987), *Talking to God* (Citadel, 1988), *Fragile* (Blue Mosque/Festival, 1990), *Sacred Relics* (Blue Mosque/Festival, 1990).

Robie Porter (*see* Rob E.G.)

Hans Poulsen

Style: *Folk, pop*

During the late 1960s and early 1970s, Danish-descendant, singer/songwriter Hans Sven (born Brian Gordon) Poulsen (b. 1945) was Australia's resident hippie eccentric. His music was a pleasant and idealistic blend of soft-rock, pop, country, folk and even bluegrass elements. His melodies were always enchanting and his lyrics delved into social and environmental issues, alternative lifestyles, the meaning of life and good old-fashioned love. Throughout his lengthy career, Poulsen has maintained a positive and optimistic outlook on life.

Poulsen was a prolific songwriter, and reputedly wrote more than 300 songs while still in his teens. He was also a multi-instrumentalist, with the ability to play more than ten different instruments including the mandolin, recorder, balalaika, bouzouki, harpsichord, guitar and piano. In 1965, Poulsen formed 18CQ which evolved into **Eighteenth Century Quartet** with the addition of **Keith Glass** (guitar, vocals; ex-Rising Suns), John Pugh (guitar, violin, autoharp, harmonica, vocals), Frank Lyons (bass) and Dennis Forster (drums, ex-Rising Suns).

Poulsen left the band at the end of 1966 to concentrate on his songwriting and to get his solo career off the ground. He signed to EMI/Parlophone and issued two unsuccessful singles, 'Rocking Chair'/'After Dinner Evening Stroll' (January 1968) and 'Coming Home Late Again'/'Run

Away Children' (December). By 1969, Poulsen had written hit songs for **Johnny Farnham** ('Jamie', 'Rose Coloured Glasses'), **The Strangers** ('Lady Scorpio'), **The Zoot** ('Monty and Me'), **Russell Morris** ('It's Only a Matter of Time', B-side of the #1 single 'The Real Thing') and New Zealand band Larry's Rebels ('Everybody's Girl').

In 1970, Poulsen signed a new deal with Ron Tudor's Fable label. His debut album, *Natural High,* yielded the hit singles 'Boom Sha La'/'Mister Curiosity' (#6 in May) and 'There's a Light Across the Valley'/'Jenny Come Out of Hiding' (#30 in December). The title track, 'Natural High', is an underrated psychedelic pop gem. During 1971, two further singles were lifted from the set, but failed to chart: 'Stick of Incense'/'Getting Back to Nothing' (April) and 'Sweetest Girl I've Ever Seen (is Always Crying)'/'Seagull' (October). It was a measure of Poulsen's standing that a number of well-known rock musicians contributed to the album, including **Billy Green** (guitar; **Doug Parkinson** In Focus), Mick Rogers (guitar; **Procession, Bulldog**), Duncan McGuire (bass; **Doug Parkinson** In Focus), Mick Flynn (bass; **Mixtures**), Graham Morgan (drums), Peter Jones (keyboards) and Geoff Hales (sax).

The 'Stick of Incense' B-side, 'Getting Back to Nothing' was the theme song to Tim Burstall's 1970 surfing film of the same name. As well as 'Getting Back to Nothing', Poulsen also contributed 'Surf's Up' and 'Bomb Out Baby' to the *Getting Back to Nothing* soundtrack album (Fable, 1971) which also included contributions from **Billy Green** and ex-**Seeker** Bruce Woodley. Poulsen's third single for 1971, 'Stork's Song'/'Bikie Theme' (December), was the theme song to Tim Burstall's feature film *Stork*, starring Bruce Spence in the titular role. By that stage, Poulsen had made appearances at a number of pop festivals, including Ourimbah (January 1970), Wallacia (January 1971) and Launching Place (March 1971). Poulsen also appeared as support act, alongside **Billy Thorpe** and the Aztecs and Pilgrimage, for Elton John's outdoor, rain-soaked Melbourne concert (October 1971).

Poulsen's 1972 album *Lost and Found, Coming Home the Wrong Way Round* produced two singles, 'Meet Me in the Valley'/'Lost and Found' (June) and 'Sleepy Town Girl'/'Wanderer's Song' (November). Helping out on the album were members of **Captain Matchbox Whoopee Band** and the Hamilton County Bluegrass Band, plus **Brian Cadd** and Duncan McGuire. In early 1972, Poulsen travelled to Europe and the UK where he eventually settled at the Findhorn Foundation, a self-contained community in Scotland. He stayed with the Findhorn Foundation for three years, and contributed material to their albums *Can't Be Described in Words* and *What A Way to Look at Life.*

In London, Poulsen recorded an album, *Peace and Plenty*, under the aegis of expatriate Australian producer David Mackay. Mackay was also producer for UK pop act The New Seekers, and the connection led to the band recording a number of Poulsen's songs, 'The Wanderer's Song', 'There's a Light Across the Valley' and 'Don't Want to Lose You'. In 1975 Poulsen travelled to the USA where he remained until 1982. While living stateside, Poulsen performed solo dates and issued two cassette albums, *Dancing Shoes* (1975) and *The Wonderchild Family Singalong Songbook* (1977). A third album, *Bitter Beauty*, was not released. In the early 1980s, Poulsen contracted cancer, which precipitated his return to Australia. In 1983, Poulsen toured and recorded with Brendan Hanley's group Bahloo.

During the mid-1980s, Poulsen returned to the UK, where he contributed eight songs to the West End stage musical *Time.* The songs appeared on the soundtrack album *Dave Clark's Time the Album* (EMI/Capitol, 1986). Poulsen's songs were sung by the likes of Leo Sayer ('I Know I Know'), Ashford and Simpson ('Starmaker'), Julian Lennon and Stevie Wonder ('Time will Teach Us All') and Cliff Richard ('She's So Beautiful'). Back in Australia, Poulsen issued the cassette album *Sacred Games (A Prelude)* (Wonderchild, 1989). He suffered a stroke in 1992 but recovered sufficiently to record and issue an album, *Carry You in My Heart*, during 1993. The album featured contributions from seasoned session players like Mark Punch (guitar), Sunil De Silva (percussion), Mark Kennedy (drums) and Tony Buchanan (sax).

Albums: *Natural High* (Fable, 1971), *Lost and Found, Coming Home the Wrong Way Round* (Fable, 1972), *Carry You in My Heart,* (Independent, 1993).

Powder Monkeys

Formed: *1991*
Style: *Punk rock*
Original line-up: *Tim Hemensley (bass, vocals; ex-Royal Flush,* **God**, **Bored!**), *John Nolan (lead guitar; ex-Behind the Magnolia Curtain,* **Bored!**), *Adyn Hibberd (rhythm guitar, vocals; ex-***Philisteins***), Jed Sayers (harmonica), Timmy Jack Ray (drums)*

On the thriving Melbourne inner-city scene of the mid-1990s, Powder Monkeys were *the* band to experience in the live arena. The band's hard-driving, seething, strung-out, incendiary blend of punk, high energy rock'n'roll and heavy metal came on like a cross between The Stooges (circa 1973), Motorhead (circa 1976), **Rose Tattoo** (circa 1978) and US hardcore heroes Black Flag (circa 1980).

Volatile singer/songwriter/bass player Tim Hemensley wrote primal, street-level songs like 'Another Nite in Hell', 'I Stand Bare', 'Straight Until Morning' and 'In the Doldrums' that were reflections of his life. Very few independent outfits of the day could hope to match Powder Monkeys' live firepower, but inevitably the band's records failed to capture the essence of that live experience. Nevertheless, the band's handful of worthwhile recordings were backed by the brazen blare of guitars, gruff vocals, a taut and blunt rhythm section and barely contained rock energy.

Hemensley and John Nolan laid plans for the formation of Powder Monkeys when they were members of **Bored!** Following **Bored!**'s 1990 European tour, both Hemensley and Nolan left the band. It took a few months for them to get Powder Monkeys off the ground. In the interim, Nolan played with **Hoss**, appearing on that band's 1992 album *You Get Nothing*. The original, five-piece Powder Monkeys line-up proved incompatible and Adyn Hibberd left at the start of 1992. Hibberd did play on the title track to Powder Monkeys' debut CD single 'Yin Yang' (with 'Another Nite in Hell' and 'Atomic Resolution') which finally came out in February 1993 on the Dog Meat label.

Dog Meat also issued the band's debut album, *Smashed on a Knee*, in March 1994, almost two years after it had been recorded. Despite its uneven, rough-hewn quality, *Smashed on a Knee* possessed enough moments of sheer excitement and blazing energy to catapult the band to the forefront of the independent scene. Powder Monkeys consolidated their position with constant touring and support slots to the likes of the **Deniz Tek** Group and **Billy Thorpe** and the Aztecs. The band appeared on the bill of the 1995 Melbourne Big Day Out, then issued the CD EP 'Straight Until Morning' (February 1995) which featured material recorded for a Triple J live broadcast. By that stage, the band was down to a streamlined three-piece of Hemensley, Nolan and Ray. Later in the year, the band headed back into the studio to record a new album with producer Chris Thompson.

As well as supporting American hardcore hero Henry Rollins in November 1995, Powder Monkeys supported the re-formed **Radio Birdman** in January 1996. The band then issued its powerful second album, *Time Wounds All Heels* (February), which produced the three-track CD single 'The Supernova that Never Quits' (December 1995). The album was almost the definitive example of the band's

Powder Monkeys

skilful, diamond-hard blues thrash. The CD single also contained a studio rendition of Motorhead's 'Built for Speed' which had long been a staple of the band's live set. During 1996, Hemensley and Ray found time to play gigs with **Pete Wells** Band, as well as to play on that band's 1996 album *Go Ahead, Call the Cops*. With the release of *Time Wounds All Heels*, there was talk of a US tour and a lucrative recording deal for Powder Monkeys with the influential American label (formerly Def American run by Rick Rubin, and home to the likes of Slayer, Black Crowes and the Jayhawks). Nothing eventuated, and Powder Monkeys spent the first six months of 1997 in hibernation. They re-emerged in August with the limited edition (400 copies), red vinyl 7-inch single 'Get the Girl Straight'/'Wasn't Born Yesterday' on the Death Valley label.

Albums: *Smashed on a Knee* (Dog Meat, 1994), *Time Wounds All Heels* (Dog Meat, 1996).

Powderfinger

Formed: *1990*
Style: *Hard rock*
Original line-up: *Bernard Fanning (vocals, guitar, harmonica), Darren Middleton (guitar, vocals), Ian Haug (guitar, vocals), John Collins (bass), Jonathan Coghill (drums)*

Brisbane-based, hard rock band Powderfinger first came to the nation's attention in late 1993 when its CD EP *Transfusion* went straight to #1 on the Australian Record Industry Association (ARIA) alternative music chart, dislodging Nirvana's 'Heart-shaped Box' from the top spot in the process. The band went on to register a number of mainstream chart hits.

Deriving its name from the Neil Young song 'Powderfinger', the band made its mark with an earthy, blues-based sound that combined soaring, 1970s-influenced riff-rock with 1990s studio technology. With the added textures of folk, country and a soulful groove, the band was able to head in any direction. And in Bernard Fanning, Powderfinger possessed a rock vocalist of considerable power and conviction. Powderfinger grew out of a fledgling three-piece comprising Ian Haug, John Collins and Steven Bishop (drums). Fanning, Darren Middleton and Jonathan Coghill joined in 1990 (replacing Bishop) to form Powderfinger. The band started off covering pub-rock classics by The Rolling Stones, The Doors, Led Zeppelin, Steppenwolf, Rodriguez and Neil Young. Powderfinger emerged out of the same scene that gave rise to the likes of **Regurgitator**, **Custard**, **Screamfeeder**, Pangaea, Emporium and Brasilia.

Powderfinger issued its debut, independent CD EP *Powderfinger* in early 1993 before signing a major deal with Polydor. *Transfusion* (September 1993) vindicated Polydor's interest in the band when it registered high on the independent chart. The band appeared on the national bill of the 1994 Big Day Out tour. Powderfinger's full-length debut album, *Parables for Wooden Ears* (August 1994), produced the CD singles 'Tail' (June) and 'Grave Concern' (September). The Tony Cohen-produced *Parables for Wooden Ears* featured complex, meticulously crafted rock but was somewhat ponderous and sombre, which did little to fulfil the promise displayed on *Transfusion*. It did, however, place the band in the same territory as American groups like Living Colour and Soundgarden. Powderfinger supported US visitors Pantera on their 1994 Australian tour.

The band issued two CD EPs during 1995, 'Save Your Skin' (March) and 'Mr Kneebone' (August), before recording a new album at the end of 1995. The more self-assured and textured *Double Allergic* consolidated the band's position at the forefront of the alternative rock scene, alongside the likes of **You Am I**, **Spiderbait**, **silverchair**, **Regurgitator** and **Tumbleweed**. *Double Allergic* (September 1996) was full of accessible, spirited rock like the dynamic CD singles 'Pick You Up' (#22 in June) and 'D.A.F. (Cascading Down)' (#39 in September). 'Living Type' (November) was the third CD single lifted from *Double Allergic*. The album lept straight into the national Top 10, eventually peaking at #4 during February 1997.

Powderfinger

The album stayed in the Top 40 for 34 weeks and sold over 150000 copies (double platinum; a figure almost twice that of contemporaries like **You Am I** and **Spiderbait**). 'Pick You Up' was nominated as Song of the Year at the 1996 Australian Record Industry Association (ARIA) Awards. 'Pick You Up', 'D.A.F. (Cascading Down)' and 'Living Type' also registered #6, #18 and #32 respectively on the 1996 Triple J Hottest 100 list. Powderfinger appeared on the national bill of the Big Day Out tour (January 1997). In April, 'Take Me In' appeared as the fourth CD single lifted from *Double Allergic*. The album also came out in Canada, and Powderfinger undertook a North American tour.

Albums: *Parables for Wooden Ears* (Polydor, 1994), *Double Allergic* (Polydor, 1996).

Pray TV

Formed: *1988*
Style: *Pop*
Original line-up: *Aidan Halloran (vocals), Matt Scully (guitar, bass), Martin Kennedy (guitar, bass), Pat Burke (drums)*

Melbourne independent band Pray TV played a low-fi brand of melodic, sombre, fuzzy guitar power pop that called to mind overseas bands as disparate as The Buzzcocks, Hüsker Dü, Swervedriver, The Replacements and Ride. Joseph Kennedy replaced original drummer Pat Burke in 1989. The band issued its debut single, 'In My Street'/'A Foreign Land', 'Surf Nazi', on the Mr Spaceman label, followed by the *Pray TV* mini-album (both 1989).

Pray TV recorded one single for Au-go-go Records, 'Spent'/'She Fell' (May 1990), before signing to the Shock label. Shock issued the band's debut album, *Flux*, and the single 'Cold Dog Stew' in 1991, after which Scully left the band and Damian Percy joined on bass. The *Paydirt* album (August 1992) and the CD EP 'Aftermath' confirmed the band's ability to utilise distorted, whirring guitars and languid vocals within a solid, refreshing pop framework. Percy had left Pray TV by the time *Paydirt* came out; Russell Baricevic (ex-**Gas Babies**, **Bored!**) joined on bass at the end of 1992. In 1994, **Ed Kuepper** produced the band's third album, *Swinger's Paradise*, which came out in November. It was the first time that Kuepper had produced an album for another band, and the first time Pray TV had used an outside producer. The experiment was a success on both counts.

The album produced the CD single 'Sucker Punch'. At the end of 1994, Vicky Guglielmo replaced Joseph Kennedy on drums. The band issued one more CD EP, 'All the Way' (May 1995), and a final album, *Westona*, before splitting up at the end of 1996. Two of the band's latter-day recordings came out in 1997 as the surf instrumental single 'The Lost Wave'/'The Dreamer' under the moniker of Tsunami. The line-up comprised Martin Kennedy, Halloran (credited with encouragement), Baricevic, Guglielmo and Colin Rivenell (lead guitar).

Albums: *Pray TV* (mini-album, Mr Spaceman, 1989), *Flux* (Shock, 1991), *Paydirt* (Shock, 1992), *Swinger's Paradise* (Shock, 1994), *Westona* (Hypnotized/Shock, 1996).

The Press (*see* Southern Cross)

Rick Price

Style: *Pop*

Singer/songwriter Rick Price started performing at the age of nine, appearing with his family at country dances and local clubs around southern Queensland and northern New South Wales. Price then cut his professional teeth during the late 1980s as a backing vocalist for the likes of **Marica Hines**, **Jon English**, **Dragon**, Kerrie Biddell and Jade Hurley, as well as putting in a stint with the **Tommy Emmanuel** Band circa 1988. Price cited his main influences as Stevie Wonder and James Taylor.

Price first came to the nation's attention in 1988 as co-singer of the Bicentennial anthem 'Celebration of a Nation'. (Keren Minshull, the other singer later joined **Euphoria**.) In 1991, he launched his solo career by signing a deal with Sony Records. Price travelled to Los Angeles where he entered the studio with producer Chris Lord-Alge (best-known for his work with Bruce Springsteen, Roxette and Elton John). Helping out on Price's debut album, *Heaven Knows*, was a group of hot US session players who had collectively worked with everyone from Michael Jackson and Madonna to Steve Winwood and Barbra Streisand.

Price immediately found Australian chart success with his first three singles, 'Not a Day Goes By' (#5 in April 1992), 'Heaven Knows' (#6 in August) and 'What's Wrong with that Girl?' (#45 in December). *Heaven Knows* featured a well-crafted blend of radio-friendly Adult Oriented Rock (AOR), pop and soul material. It made its debut on the national album listing at #2 during July. Price formed a touring band which comprised Mike Caen (guitar), Peter Northcote (guitar), Shauna Jensen (backing vocals), P.J. Becker (backing vocals), Victor Rounds (bass) and Mitch Farmer (drums) in order to tour. By the end of the year, the line-up comprised P.J. Becker, Robert Parde (keyboards), Phil Gildea (guitar), Chris Becker (bass) and David Porter (drums).

The fourth single lifted from *Heaven Knows*, 'House Divided', failed to chart. Price returned to the Top 40 with a cover of the Left Banke/Four Tops chestnut 'Walk Away Renee' (also from the album, #16 in June 1993) and his duet with New Zealand vocalist Margaret Urlich, 'Where is the Love?' (#31 in December). Price's records began to sell throughout Asia and Europe where he was compared with American singer/songwriters like Bryan Adams and Richard Marx. At the end of 1993, Sony/Epic issued *Heaven Knows* in Japan. In November, he appeared as part of the highly successful Wizards of Oz series of showcase gigs in Japan (Tokyo, Osaka, Nagoya and Fukuoka) with Margaret Urlich and **Yothu Yindi**.

A month later, Price topped the Malaysian and Philippines single charts with 'Heaven Knows'. It was voted Song of the Year at the Singapore Music Awards, and went on to sell over 250 000 copies in South-East Asia alone. Price consolidated his chart success with sell-out tours in that territory. For his second album, *Tamborine Mountain*, Price eschewed the studio slickness of his debut. The album contained a more personalised and reflective collection of songs that encompassed a wider range of musical tastes. The album's first single, 'River of Love', reached #18 on the national chart during June 1995, although the two follow-ups, 'Bridge Building Man' (August) and 'To Be with You' (October), were not successful.

Albums: *Heaven Knows* (Sony, 1992), *Tamborine Mountain* (Sony, 1995).

Primevils (*see* Bloodloss)

Primitive Calculators

Formed: *1978*
Style: *Electronic*
Original line-up: *Stuart Grant (guitar, vocals), Denise Rosenberg (keyboards), David Light (bass, keyboards), Frank Lovece (drum machine, vocals)*

Alongside **Ollie Olsen's** band Whirlywirld, Primitive Calculators were leading lights of the so-called Melbourne 'Little Bands' movement of the late 1970s. The 'Little Bands' concept was based around the premise that anyone could get up on stage and perform for 15 minutes. As a consequence, many small-time bands like Morpions, Too Fat to Fit Through the Door, Thrush and the Cunts, Use No Hooks, The Alan Bamford Musical Experience and The J.P. Satre Band played a handful of shows to a small but enthusiastic following.

Primitive Calculators were the most musically forthright of the bunch. As writer Clinton Walker put it, Primitive Calculators delivered a raw, savage, kinetic sound that could only be compared with the New York No Wave (which encompassed the likes of Teenage Jesus and the Jerks and James Chance and the Contortions). The band built up a strong inner-city following and issued one independent single in 1979, 'Do that Dance'/'I Can't Stop It'. At the end of 1980, Primitive Calculators left for the UK and broke up soon after.

By 1983, Grant and Light had teamed up with Arnie Hanna (guitar, drums; ex-Whirlywirld who was later replaced by Phil Nicholls) and Terry Dooley (vocals; ex-Teenbeat) as The Bum Steers. That band was known for its radical, improvised, distortion-heavy reworkings of such Australian rock classics as **Russell Morris**'s 'The Real Thing' and **Coloured Balls'** 'GOD'. The band played regular gigs on the Melbourne inner-city circuit, and then contributed a version of 'Ol' Man River' to Au-go-go's Various Artists compilation album *Asleep at the Wheel* (1984). Stuart and Denise Grant also worked as cocktail jazz duo Mr Bum and Miss Ruby.

In early 1986, Primitive Calculators reassembled to record two tracks with producer/musical director **Ollie Olsen**, for the soundtrack to Richard Lowenstein's feature film *Dogs in Space*. Set in the post-punk wasteland of inner-city Melbourne, the film centred around the exploits of fictitious band Dogs in Space on the 'Little Bands' scene. Stuart Grant (vocals, guitar, drum machine), Denise Grant (keyboards), David Light (bass), Terry Dooley (backing vocals) and Marie Hoy (backing vocals) recorded the tracks 'Pumping Ugly Muscle' and 'Do the Icepick'. The band appeared in the film performing 'Pumping Ugly Muscle'; that track was also issued on the *Dogs in Space* soundtrack album (on Chase) and the single 'Pumping Ugly Muscle'/'Do the Icepick' (August 1987). As a result of their involvement in the film, the band members issued the album *Primitive Calculators*, which had been culled from a live performance recorded in 1979. The album came with a bonus, 7-inch re-pressing of the single 'Do that Dance'/'I Can't Stop It'.

Album: *Primitive Calculators* (No label, 1987).

Priscilla's Nightmare (*see* Kids in the Kitchen)

Procession

Formed: *1967*
Style: *Psychedelic pop, jazz*
Original line-up: *Mick Rogers (lead guitar, vocals; ex-Playboys), Trevor Griffin (organ; ex-Playboys), Brian Peacock (bass, vocals; ex-Librettos, Playboys), Craig Collinge (drums; ex-Librettos, Knack)*

Glenn A. Baker described Procession as the most publicity ambitious (some may say pompous) of all Australian late 1960s rock ensembles. Music writers like Ian Meldrum and Lily Brett at *Go-Set* magazine treated Procession's every action with gushing reverence, and national television rock show *Uptight* (coincidentally produced by Procession's manager David Joseph) featured the band in a special segment each week.

The band's game plan was to make everything it did an Australian 'first'. The band recorded its debut single, 'Anthem', a cappella; *Procession 'Live' at Sebastians* was the first live debut album in the country; a 40-piece choir backed the band for its debut television appearance; the second single, 'Listen', was the first to be recorded on freshly installed eight-track equipment at Armstrong Studios. Yet, for all its innovations and the attention afforded Procession, none of the band's records found chart success.

The Procession story began with two early 1960s bands, The Playboys and New Zealand's The Librettos. Melbourne instrumental combo The Playboys formed in 1963 with members drawn from **The Chessmen** and The Roulettes (Graeme Trottman, drums; Phil Blackmore, organ, piano, guitar; both also ex-Malcolm Arthur and the Knights) and The Impostors (John Cartwright, rhythm guitar; Bill Billings, lead guitar; and Ron Blaine, bass). Neil McArthur soon replaced Blaine on bass. The Playboys supported UK visitors Gerry and the Pacemakers and The Tremeloes during 1964; the exposure landed the band a contract with the Sunshine label. The band issued one album, *The 'Sound Award' Album* (1965), and five singles: 'Exodus'/'Sabre Dance' (January 1965), 'Swan Lake'/'Campdown Races' (February), 'Desperado'/'The Mean One' (June), 'He's Awright'/'Torture' (August) and 'Happy Organ'/'The High and the Mighty' (February 1966). Cartwright left in June 1965 and The Playboys became Sunshine's resident backing band for artists like Marcia Jones, **Billy Adams** and **Normie Rowe**.

In June 1966, Rod Stone (lead guitar) and Brian Peacock (bass, vocals; both ex-Librettos) replaced Cartwright, Billings and McArthur. New Zealand beat-pop outfit The Librettos had comprised Stone, Peacock, Craig Collinge (drums) and Lou Parun (guitar). The band recorded two singles for HMV (NZ), 'Great Balls of Fire'/'Twilight Time' (April 1965) and 'Ella Speed'/'I Want Your Love' (August), before arriving in Australia as a three-piece around Stone, Peacock and Collinge. The Librettos established themselves on the Melbourne discotheque circuit, and issued three fine pop singles on the Sunshine label: 'I Cried'/'She's a Go Go' (October), 'Rescue Me'/'What Do You Want to Make Those Eyes at Me?' (February 1966) and Paul Revere and the Raiders' 'Kicks'/'Wha'cha Gonna Do About It?' (May). None of the singles charted, and the band split. With Stone and Peacock ensconced in The Playboys, Collinge formed one of Australia's first psychedelic trios (à la Cream, Jimi Hendrix Experience), The Knack, with Wayne Roundtree (guitar) and Terry Chapman (bass; ex-**Allusions**).

The Playboys (Trottman, Blackmore, Stone, Peacock) travelled to the UK in November 1966 to meet up with **Normie Rowe**. In March 1967, Blackmore returned to Australia and Englishman Trevor Griffin (organ; ex-Question) took his place. Former Adam Faith sideman Mick Rogers also replaced Stone on guitar in the middle of the year. **Normie Rowe** failed to make a major impression in the UK charts, but The Playboys (sans Rowe) signed a deal with Andrew Loog Oldham's Immediate label for a one-off single. The Playboys' Immediate single (issued on Sunshine in Australia), 'Black Sheep R.I.P.'/'Sad', came out in August 1967. The Brian Peacock-penned 'Sad' is now justly celebrated as a minor classic of UK freakbeat (where beat-pop cross-pollinated with psychedelia), featuring great harmonies and Rogers' dazzling pysch-inflected guitar fireworks. It later appeared on the UK compilation of 1960s freakbeat rarities *Chocolate Soup for Diabetics Volume 3*, and Raven's pop collection *Kicks* (alongside The Librettos' 'Kicks' and Procession's 'One Day in Every Week').

Buoyed by a desire to create an original and progressive band, Peacock, Griffin and Rogers left **Normie Rowe** in October to form Procession. Peacock recalled Collinge, and Procession made its live debut on 17 December 1967 at Sebastians disco in Melbourne. Despite the media attention afforded the band, the singles 'Anthem'/'Take Time' (January 1968) and 'Listen'/'Minuet for Moderns' (April) failed to chart. Likewise, *Procession 'Live' at Sebastians*, which revealed the band's predilection for modern jazz, was not successful. Procession abandoned Australia, and returned to the UK to sign a deal with Philips/Mercury. Manfred Mann's Mike Hugg produced the band's self-titled second album, a sophisticated collection of jazz-tinged psychedelic pop material. In a repeat of the Australian experience, both the album and its two singles, 'Every American Citizen'/'Essentially Susan' (October 1968) and 'One Day in Every Week'/'Wigwam City' (February 1969), sank without a trace. 'One Day in Every Week' was a fully backed, re-recorded version of 'Anthem'.

By 1969, Procession's initial creative surge had been dampened somewhat and, in an attempt to revive the band's flagging fortunes, Peacock invited singer **Ross Wilson** (ex-**Pink Finks**, **Party Machine**) to join. Wilson flew to the UK, but by the end of the year Procession fell apart. Peacock returned to Australia and joined **Gerry and the Joy Band** in late 1971. Collinge remained in the UK where he worked with Manfred Mann Chapter III (playing on the 1970 Vertigo label album *Manfred Mann Chapter III*), Third World War (appearing on the highly rated 1971 album *Third World War*) and Shoot (one album for EMI, *On the Frontier*, 1973). Back in Australia, Rogers formed short-lived power-trio **Bulldog**, before responding to Mann's beckoning call to join Chapter III in the UK at the end of 1970. Griffin joined Wilson's new, special occasion progressive band **Sons of the Vegetal Mother**, but dropped out of the scene when Wilson formed **Daddy Cool**.

At the start of 1971, Chapter III became Manfred Mann's Earth Band and Rogers stayed on board until 1975 and the *Nightingales and Bombers* album. On his return to Australia in 1976, Rogers formed Mick Rogers and Eclipse with Mike Clarke (bass), Graham Morgan (drums) and Peter Jones (electric piano). Once again, Eclipse was short-lived and, after a stint with the **Renée Geyer** Band, Rogers returned to the UK. He joined the final, touring-only version (circa 1977) of UK art-rock band Greenslade with Dave Greenslade (keyboards), Tony Reeves (bass) and Jon Hiseman (drums; ex-

Colosseum). In 1978, Rogers formed Aviator with John Perry (bass, vocals), Jack Lancaster (woodwinds; ex-Blodwyn Pig) and Clive Bunker (drums; ex-Jethro Tull). Aviator issued two albums for EMI/Harvest, *Aviator* (1979) and *Turbulence* (1980).

In the meantime, Collinge had achieved rock infamy for his part in the bogus Fleetwood Mac put on the road by manager Clive Davies when the real Fleetwood Mac had to cancel its autumn 1973 American tour. The phony Fleetwood Mac tour was curtailed when Messers Fleetwood and McVie intervened with legal action. The band utilised by Davies later evolved into Stretch. Collinge returned to Australia in 1975 and played on **Marcia Hines'** debut album *Marcia Shines*.

Peacock dropped out of sight during the mid-1970s, only to emerge in 1977 as a member of country rock band **Western Flyer** with **Matt Taylor** (ex-**Chain**). He then moved into band management via **The Dugites, Eurogliders, Redgum** and **Wa Wa Nee**. In the early 1990s, Peacock became managing director of Export Music Australia (EMA), which launched the Wizards of Oz showcase in 1993. The final irony in the Procession story is that the David Joseph-managed New Seekers made the UK Top 20 during July 1978 with their version of Peacock's 'Anthem (One Day in Every Week)'.

Albums: *Procession 'Live' at Sebastians* (Festival, 1968), *Procession* (Festival, 1969), *Minuets for Moderns* (Raven, 1988).

Pip Proud

Style: *Pop*

Only a period as musically fertile, socially heady and culturally diverse as the late 1960s could have fostered the growth of a performer as unique as Phillip 'Pip' Proud (b. 1947). This shy singer/songwriter/poet was a true anomaly on the Australian 1960s pop scene. Proud sang his gentle pop songs in a quaint, quavering voice while strumming or tapping the strings of his (unamplified) electric guitar. Writer David Nichols later called Proud 'Australia's first pop primitive'. Overseas equivalents of the day would be the solo Syd Barrett and Pearls Before Swine's Tom Rapp. Proud was also compared with Bob Dylan, Donovan and Tiny Tim, comparisons which were spurious at best.

With help from financier Michael Hobbs, Proud recorded his limited edition, debut album *De Da De Dum* in 1967. One of the 50 or so copies pressed up came to the attention of Bob Cooley at Phonogram Records, who signed Proud to a deal with the Philips label. Proud re-recorded *De Da De Dum* which Philips issued as *Adreneline and Richard* in 1968. The album garnered positive reviews in *Go-Set*, and Proud made a few television appearances as well as doing a handful of live gigs. The album contained such sparse, idiosyncratic and evocative songs as 'De Da De Dum', 'Purple Boy Gang', 'Into Elizabeth's Eyes', 'An Old Servant' and 'Adreneline and Richard'.

Proud issued one more album on Philips, *A Bird in the Engine*, before travelling to the UK. Although the album contained several more captivating songs like 'Eagle-Wise', 'Hey Sue', 'Vida', 'A Bird in the Engine' and 'She Dwindles Her Fingers', Philips dropped Proud upon his return from the UK in 1970. Proud spent most of the 1970s writing poems, novels and plays. None of his novels was ever published, although Sydney radio station Double J aired two adaptations of his plays *Vlort Phlitson, Intergalactic Trouble Shooter* and *Don Coyote*. In 1995, David Nichols (from Sydney band **The Cannanes**) tracked down Proud and, with support from Nic Dalton at the independent Half a Cow label re-issued *Adreneline and Richard* and *A Bird in the Engine* on the *Eagle-Wise* CD (July 1996). Nichols and Dalton also took Proud into the studio for the first time in over 25 years to record a batch of new songs that may see the light of day in the near future on Half a Cow.

Albums: *De Da De Dum* (Grendel, 1967), *Adreneline and Richard* (Philips/Phonogram, 1968), *A Bird in the Engine* (Philips/Phonogram, 1969), *Eagle-Wise* (compilation, Half a Cow, 1996).

Pseudo Echo

Formed: *1982*
Style: *Synth pop*
Original line-up: *Brian Canham (vocals, guitar), Tony Lugton (synthesiser, vocals; ex-Steeler,* **James Freud** *and the Radio Stars), Pierre Pierre (real name Pierre Gigliotti, synthesiser, bass, vocals)*

Melbourne band Pseudo Echo was one of the first local pop bands of the early 1980s to take inspiration from the then fashionable UK New Romantic movement (Duran Duran, Spandau Ballet, Ultravox). Pseudo Echo combined flash clothes, blow-wave hairstyles, youthful exuberance and accessible synth-pop to arrive at a winning combination. Very nearly a case of form and style over content, Pseudo Echo nevertheless made an impact on the charts, and found a ready-made audience among teenagers who fawned on the band's every move.

Before Pseudo Echo formed, Tony Lugton had some experience under his belt playing on the late-1970s Melbourne pub circuit. He was lead guitarist with hard rock band Steeler, after which he joined **James Freud** and the Radio Stars. His stay was brief, but he remained long enough to play guitar on Freud's hit single, 'Modern Girl'. Brian Canham and Pierre Pierre had played in small-time bands together. The original three-piece Pseudo Echo line-up used a drum machine. Drummer Anthony Argiro joined in July 1983. Pseudo Echo came to the attention of Ian 'Molly' Meldrum, and the band became the first unsigned group to appear on the ABC-TV pop show ***Countdown***. As a result of the band's performance of the song 'Listening', EMI snapped them up. Pseudo Echo entered the studio with UK producer John Punter (Roxy Music, Japan) to record its debut album, *Autumnal Park*. The album reached the Top 10 in June 1984 and produced the Top 20 hit singles 'Listening'/'In Their Time' (#2 in January) and 'A Beat for You'/'Autumnal Park' (#11 in June), plus 'Stranger in Me'/'Turning the Page' (November) and 'Dancing Until Midnight'/'Scripts' (February 1985).

Meanwhile, Lugton left in October 1984 to be replaced by James Leigh (keyboards). The band's second album, *Love an Adventure* (November 1985), produced three hit singles, 'Don't Go'/'Living in a Dream' (#4 in November), 'Love an Adventure'/'All Tied Up' (#5 in February 1986) and 'Living in a Dream'/'Loose Ends' (#15 in May), plus the non-hit 'Try'/'Lonely Without You' (August). *Love an Adventure* peaked at #8 in December 1985 and went on to attain platinum status (70 000 copies sold). By the time the album appeared, Leigh's brother Vince Leigh (ex-Marginal Era) had replaced Argiro on drums and the band was a major live attraction.

In 1986, Pseudo Echo issued a rocked-up cover of Lipps Inc.'s disco hit 'Funky Town'/'Lies are Nothing' (October), which became one of the most successful Australian singles on an international level during 1987. As well as reaching #1 in Australia, it peaked at #6 in the USA, #8 in the UK, #2 in Canada and was Top 20 in Germany. In October 1987, Pseudo Echo won the Yamaha World Popular Song Contest (held in Japan) with the song 'Take on the World'. The prize money was US$10 000. While the band attended to its overseas touring commitments, EMI issued the compilation album *Long Plays 1983–1987*.

Pseudo Echo returned to the studio in 1988 with English producer Julian Mendelshon (Frankie Goes to Hollywood, **Models**) and American audio engineer Bob Clearmountain for the album *Race*. Issued in March 1989, the album featured a more mature rock sound (with Bon Jovi being one reference point), although it fared poorly with both the record-buying public and music critics. The album produced three singles, 'Fooled Again'/'Take on the World' (October 1988), 'Over Tomorrow'/'Wings' (February 1989) and 'Eye of the Storm'/'Don't You Forget' (July). Complete with the new arena rock sound came a new look: long, flowing hair, torn jeans and leather jackets.

By 1990, the Pseudo Echo sound had fallen from favour and the band called it a day. Canham moved into production work; his credits included **Chocolate Starfish's** self-titled debut album. Gigliotti played with covers band All the Young Dudes. In 1996, the Leigh brothers formed Vertigo with another brother, Gerry (guitar), and Hugh Wilson (vocals). Gotham/BMG issued the band's debut CD single, 'Forever Lately' (#46 in July 1997), and it was 1983 all over again. Canham also re-emerged in 1997 with his new band, Brill, (a collaboration with **Chocolate Starfish** drummer Darren Danielson) and album *Brill* (August).

Albums: *Autumnal Park* (EMI, 1984), *Love an Adventure* (EMI, 1985), *Long Plays 1983–1987* (EMI, 1987), *Race* (EMI, 1989), *Best Adventures* (compilation, EMI, 1995).

The Psychotic Turnbuckles

Formed: *1984*
Style: *Garage-punk, R&B*
Original line-up: *Jesse 'The Intruder' (real name Colin Caldwell, vocals), The Grand Wizard (real name Vince Cuscuna, guitar), El Sicodelico (real name Jay Younie, guitar), The Creep (bass, vocals), The Spoiler (drums)*

Sydney band The Psychotic Turnbuckles were only in it for the good times. After all, The Turnbuckles wore puke-green fright wigs and declared themselves to be the 'Inter-Continental Rock'n'Roll Tag Team Champions'. Their three main inspirations were *Wrestlemania*, *Bugs Bunny* and Handsome Dick Manitoba, frontman with 1970s New York heavyweights The Dictators. The Turnbuckles were the ultimate party band, a pure cartoon rock'n'roll creation, The Banana Splits of Australian rock'n'roll. By the same token, The Turnbuckles were deadly serious about their music, a melange of prototypal acid-punk/R&B guitar riffs and gruff vocals welded to a rumbling rhythm section. Not exactly pretty, not exactly subtle but a true celebration of the trash aesthetic. After six or seven singles and four albums, however, the joke wore thin. Like their wigs, The Turnbuckles were consigned to the back of the cupboard, to crawl out only for the occasional re-formation gig.

The genesis of The Psychotic Turnbuckles sound can be found in Conspirators, a tough 1960s garage-punk inspired band that played around Sydney during 1982–84. Conspirators comprised Colin Caldwell and Vince Cuscuna, plus Angelo Antidormi (guitar, vocals), Phil Tuchscherer (bass, vocals) and Phil 'The Bat' England (drums). The band issued one single, 'Twilight Zone'/'She's Gone', on the Suspect label during 1984 before Caldwell and Cuscuna left at the end of the year to form The Turnbuckles. The Vi-nil label issued Conspirators' four-track EP, *Expressway to Your Brain*, in April 1985, almost a year after it had been recorded. By that stage, The Turnbuckles had been in operation for six months, and Antidormi, Tuchscherer and England had recruited Tim Younie (lead vocals) to form The Sweet Ride. Taking their name from the title of the 1969 American film, The Sweet Ride continued in the Conspirators' garage vein.

The Dog Meat label issued The Sweet Ride's debut single, 'On the Line'/'Nothing to Lose' (1988), and the band contributed the track 'Room Full of Fools' to the Various Artists compilation *Swingin' from the Trees* (1988). Conspirators also appeared on the same album with the track 'Don't Leave Me', as did The Turnbuckles with 'Mr Zepplin Man'. The Turnbuckles' first two singles, 'The Creeps'/'Energy' (May 1985) and 'Psychotic Situation'/'The Crusher' (November), on the Vi-nil label were primitive slices of buzzing R&B/garagemania. Only **The Lime Spiders** and Wet Taxis rivalled The Turnbuckles for that authentic 1960s sound and sheer acid-guitar firepower. The cover of The Novas' desperately inept 'The Crusher' was proof of the band's cartoon approach to rock 'n 'roll. The Rattlesnake label later reissued the singles as a 12-inch EP, *The Psychotic Turnbuckles* (1987), with a bonus cut, the previously unissued 'Hey Eric'.

The band kept up the mayhem with the August 1986 mini-album *Destroy Dull City* (produced by Rob Younger), the 'Go Go Gorilla'/'Escape My Mind', 'Ode to Eclipso' 12-inch EP and the album *Beyond the Flipout* (both 1987). With song titles like 'Albuquerque (Wild Scenes)', 'Groove to the Eye', 'Wanna Ride the Wild Seas', 'Pismo Beach' and 'Rock'n'Roll Wrestling', the band members could never be accused of taking themselves too seriously. In 1987, The Unknown replaced The Creep on bass and the band contributed the track 'Mr Zepplin Man' to the *Swingin' from the Trees* compilation. Bud 'The Sledgehammer' Slater replaced El Sicodelico on guitar and the new line-up contributed '1969' to Au-go-go's Stooges tribute album, *Hard to Beat* (1988). Kid Sunshine replaced Slater and the new line-up recorded the single 'The Goodtimes (Outweigh the Bad Times)'/'The Sudan Butcher' (November 1988).

A new four-piece line-up of Jesse the Intruder, The Grand Wizard, The Unknown and Mr Ultimate (drums) recorded the album *Pharoahs of the Far Out* and the 12-inch EP 'Lunar Chik', 'Strychnine'/ 'Wiseguy', 'Hot Generation' (1989) for the Survival label. Gorgeous Karl Domah replaced Mr Ultimate before the album came out (November 1989), and the line-up remained stable for the next five years. The Turnbuckles signed to the Shock label and issued a run of records that included the singles 'Rock'n'Roll Terrorist'/'Hero Mountain' (April 1991), MC5's 'American Ruse'/'I Want Love' (live), 'You Really Got Me' (live) (limited edition 250 copies white label pressing, October 1991) and 'She's Afraid to Love Me'/'Slow Death', 'High Energy' (December 1992) and the album *Figure Four Brain Trance* (October 1993). The last two records were issued on Shock's hard rock subsidiary label Shagpile. 'She's Afraid to Love Me' also came out as a seven-track CD EP with different songs.

In August 1993, American label Sympathy for the Record Industry issued the single 'Crazy Times Ahead'/'Eye Surf Alone' (demo), 'She Put a Spell on Me' (demo) for the US market. At the end of 1994, Chuck the Rock (bass) replaced The Unknown for a final national tour. The original Turnbuckles line-up also re-formed for that tour, after which the band called it a day. On 14 June 1997, the line-up of Jesse the Intruder, The Grand Wizard, The Unknown (guitar), Chuck the Rock (bass) and Domah appeared for a one-off re-formation gig. The band pressed up a limited edition (350 copies) gig giveaway vinyl EP for the occasion, *Louder than Distortion*, which featured 'Teenage Crush Affair' (demo), 'Groove to the Eye' (live)/ 'Slow Death' (four-track version), 'Hero Mountain' (four-track version).

Albums: *Destroy Dull City* (mini-album, Rattlesnake, 1986), *Beyond the Flipout* (Rattlesnake/ Survival, 1987), *Pharaohs of the Far Out* (Survival, 1989), *Figure Four Brain Trance* (Shagpile/Shock, 1993), *Ride the Wild Sounds* (compilation of early material, Shagpile/Shock, 1994).

The Puritans (*see* The Breadmakers)

The Purple Hearts

Formed: *1964*
Style: *R&B*
Original line-up: *Mick Hadley (lead vocals; ex-Impacts), Barry Lyde (lead guitar; ex-Stilettos), Fred Pickard (rhythm guitar), Bob Dames (bass; ex-Impacts), Adrian 'Red' Redmond (drums)*

Pioneering Brisbane band The Purple Hearts issued a series of tough, incomparable R&B singles that remain classics of their type. The band's uncompromising approach to music-making was unrivalled in its day. Even the band's name (derived from the pep-pills favoured by the English mods of the mid-1960s, not the medal of valour) was a brash and outrageous statement.

Expatriate Englishmen Mick Hadley and Bob Dames had experienced the burgeoning London R&B club scene (Cyril Davies Allstars, Graham Bond, John Mayall, the nascent Rolling Stones) first hand before emigrating to Australia in 1963. Hadley and Dames formed The Impacts, but with the addition of Scottish-born Fred Pickard plus local musicians Barry Lyde and Adrian Redmond in 1964 the band became known as The Purple Hearts. The Hearts swiftly made an impact on the staid Brisbane scene with their uncompromising, gritty R&B. They issued a single, Graham Bond's 'Long Legged Baby'/'Gloria', on the obscure, independent label Soundtrack before signing to the Sunshine label (home to **Normie Rowe**, **Peter Doyle** and other pop stars of the day). Sunshine reissued 'Long Legged Baby' in October 1965 with a new B-side, 'Here 'Tis'. 'Long Legged Baby' reached the Top 10 in Brisbane, but by that stage the band had relocated to Sydney where Tony Cahill replaced Redmond.

The band's stay in Sydney was short; by the beginning of 1966, The Hearts had moved on to Melbourne. For the next year, The Hearts ruled over the city's discotheque circuit. They enjoyed two hit singles with 'Of Hopes and Dreams and Tombstones'/'I'm Gonna Try' (February 1966) and the memorable 'Early in the Morning'/'Just a Little Bit' (August 1966). Sunshine also issued the EP *The Sounds of the Purple Hearts*, which combined the 'Long Legged Baby' and 'Of Hopes and Dreams and Tombstones' singles. Then, on 23 January 1967, The Hearts issued a press release stating that they had ceased to progress musically, were becoming stagnant and, therefore, had decided to split. Lyde became **Lobby Loyde** and joined **The Wild Cherries**. The rest of the band continued on as a four-piece for a month, in order to honour outstanding touring commitments. The band's last two singles were the frantic 'You Can't Sit Down'/'Tiger in Your Tank' (January 1967) and 'Chicago'/'Bring It on Home' (April).

In 1979, reissue specialists Raven issued the six-track EP *Let's Meet the Purple Hearts* ('Of Hopes and Dreams and Tombstones', 'You Can't Sit Down', Chicago'/'Tiger in Your Tank', 'I'm Gonna Try', 'Early in the Morning'). Raven also included 'Just a Little Bit' on *Ugly Things Volume 2* (1982).

With the break-up of The Purple Hearts, Cahill travelled to the UK were he replaced Snowy Fleet in **The Easybeats**. In early 1968, Hadley joined Rob Lovett (ex-**Wild Cherries, Loved Ones**) and Malcolm McGee (ex-**Wild Cherries**, **Python Lee Jackson**) in the heavily hyped would-be Walker Brothers, The Virgil Brothers. After only a couple of weeks' rehearsal, Hadley left to be replaced by **Peter Doyle**. Hadley reunited with Bob Dames in Brisbane to form a new R&B band called Coloured Balls. Sam Shannon (vocals), Robbie Van Delft (guitar; ex-**Mike Furber** and the Bowery Boys) and Peter Miles (drums; ex-**Bay City Union**) completed the line-up. Coloured Balls emerged from the same blues scene that had also given rise to **Bay City Union**, Black Cat Circle, The Chelsea Set and Thursday's Children.

Coloured Balls played gigs around Brisbane until the end of 1969, but did not record anything for posterity. In 1970, Dames and Miles moved to Melbourne where they joined Mick Rogers (ex-**Procession**) in the short-lived power trio **Bulldog**. In an odd postscript to the Coloured Balls story, **Lobby Loyde** adopted the name for the band he formed in Melbourne during March 1972 that was totally unrelated to Mick Hadley's version. Throughout the 1970s and 1980s, Mick Hadley formed a succession of R&B bands. He recorded the album *Let's Dance* (comprising all R&B covers) with Mick Hadley's Last Shout in 1988, and *Butt Out* in 1995 with Mick Hadley and the Shakers.

Album: *The Raven EP LP Vol. 1* (compilation shared with **The Wild Cherries**, **The Throb** and **The Missing Links**; Raven, 1982).

Python Lee Jackson

Formed: *1966*
Style: *Soul, R&B*
Original line-up: *Malcolm McGee (vocals; ex-***Wild Cherries***), David Bentley (organ, vocals; ex-***Jeff St John** *and the Id), Mick Liber (guitar; ex-***Denvermen***), Lloyd Hudson (bass), David Montgomery (drums,* **Jeff St John** *and the Id)*

Alongside **Jeff St John** and the Id, **Max Merritt and the Meteors** and **Levi Smith's Clefs**, Python Lee Jackson was one of the first local bands to play soul and R&B. David Bentley and David Montgomery formed the band in Sydney after splitting from The Id. Malcolm McGee completed the line-up after he joined in Melbourne during June 1966.

The band issued two singles, 'Emergency Ward'/'Who Do You Love?' (November 1966), and Major Lance's 'Um-Um — Um-Um-Um-Um'/'Big City Lights' (December) before Bentley left to be replaced by Bob Welsh (piano). Virgil East replaced Lloyd Hudson in early 1967. The band issued two more singles, Sam and Dave's 'Hold on, I'm

Coming'/'Your Mother Should Have Warned You' and 'It's a Wonder'/'I Keep Forgetting', before splitting in mid-1967. Liber played with a short-lived re-formation of **Jeff St John's** old band the Id before backing **Billy Thorpe,** and then joining **Gulliver Smith** in The Noyes. East joined **Jeff St John's** Yama while McGee joined would-be Walker Brothers trio The Virgil Brothers with Rob Lovett (ex-**Loved Ones**) and **Peter Doyle**. In the meantime, Bentley had formed The David Bentley Trio with Montgomery and Hamish Hughes (bass) to play jazz and soul on the Melbourne discotheque circuit. Sometime during 1969, Bentley, Montgomery and Liber travelled to the UK where they revived the Python Lee Jackson name.

Tony Cahill (bass; ex-**Purple Hearts, Easybeats**) completed the line-up while UK jazz guitar player Gary Boyle (ex-Brian Auger Trinity) became a regular guest. In 1970, the band recorded an album, *In a Broken Dream,* for the Young Blood International label. The album remained unissued until 1972 when the brooding 'In a Broken Dream'/'Doing Fine' became a surprise #3 UK hit during September. Featured singer on 'In A Broken Dream' was Rod Stewart, who by 1972 was one of the UK's most famous rock'n'roll stars. Yet, in 1970 when he sang on the Python Lee Jackson album as an uncredited session singer, he was not so famous. Stewart had already sung with Shotgun Express, The Jeff Beck Group and the nascent Faces, but had yet to establish his solo career. Stewart's vocals were the perfect complement to the song's smouldering soul/blues base. He also appeared on two other tracks on the album, 'Blues' and a cover of the Whitfield/Strong song 'Cloud Nine'. 'In a Broken Dream'/'Blues' later appeared as a single on the Bellaphon label in Germany (1974).

By 1972, however, Python Lee Jackson had broken up and was unable to capitalise on the single's success. Liber had worked with UK bands Ashton Garner and Dyke (of 'Resurrection Shuffle' fame, although he joined after it was a hit) and Third World War (appearing on the band's highly rated *Third World War* album in 1971). He returned to Australia in 1973 and joined **G. Wayne Thomas**'s Crystal Voyager Band (1973) and the **Doug Parkinson** Band (1974). Liber went on to work as a highly sought-after country guitarist. Bentley worked for a time with Kala before also returning to Australia in 1974. Since that time, he has formed a succession of bands including Bentley's Boogie Band, Jazz and Blues Collection and The Hot City Band. He issued two solo albums, *Hot City Songs* (1980) and *Cap Sizes and Waiting* (1990), on his own Hot City label.

Album: *In a Broken Dream* (Young Blood International, UK only, 1972).

Q.E.D. (*see* Jenny Morris)

Greg Quill (*see* Country Radio)

R

Rabbit

Formed: *1973*
Style: *Glam rock*
Original line-up: *Mark Tinson (guitar, vocals), Jim Porteus (bass, vocals), Phil Screen (drums)*

Newcastle (NSW) band Rabbit originally formed as a three-piece performing material by the likes of Alice Cooper, The Who and The Move, plus tentative originals in the same vein. In 1974, Greg Douglas joined as lead singer. The more outrageous Dave Evans, who had just been ousted from **AC/DC**, replaced Douglas as lead singer in October 1974. Evans was known for his self-proclaimed 'rampant heterosexuality' and over-the-top theatrical performances. Rabbit adopted a thumping brand of commercial glam-boogie (somewhere between US groups like Kiss and Brownsville Station) and the members decked themselves out in bare-chested silk blouses, spandex leggings and stack-heeled boots.

Rabbit swiftly became Newcastle's foremost rock attraction. The climax of the band's shows came with Phil Screen's spectacular fire-breathing displays (à la Gene Simmons from Kiss). The band moved to Sydney and soon rivalled **Hush** in the glam stakes. Rabbit signed to CBS and issued the album *Rabbit*, which produced two singles, 'Lady La Di Da'/'Marvel Man' (October 1975) and 'Running Bear'/'Let's Go Rock'n'Rollin' Tonight' (December). With the release of the album, Dave Hinds (ex-Marshall Brothers) expanded the band's line-up by joining as lead guitarist. Rabbit followed up its tentative debut with the Australian glam-rock apotheosis (or nadir, depending on your viewpoint), *Too Much Rock'n'Roll*. The album produced two hard-rockin' singles, 'Too Much Rock'n'Roll'/ 'Shake that Thing' (February 1976) and 'Wildfire'/'Bad Girls' (July). Rabbit appeared on the ABC-TV's pop show ***Countdown***, and set off on a national tour with the **Ted Mulry Gang**.

In early 1977, founder members Mark Tinson and Phil Screen left the band. Only Screen was replaced (by Barry Lytten) and the band continued as a four-piece. Rabbit issued one more single, a cover of Paul Revere and the Raiders' 'Let Me'/'Kiss Me Goodnight' (July 1977), but by the end of the year was on shaky ground. With the departure of Evans in October 1977, Jim Porteus rejoined Tinson and Screen. They dispensed with the tacky glam-rock gear, recruited Peter De Jong (guitar, vocals) and renamed themselves Heroes. The band placed greater emphasis on the music, which was melodic hard rock.

Heroes based themselves in Newcastle, but signed to the Sydney-based Albert Productions. The band's debut album, *Heroes* (October 1980), yielded the singles 'Baby's Had a Taste'/'Waiting for You' (August) and 'The Star and the Slaughter'/'End of the Road' (January 1981). Heroes were Newcastle's top rock attraction, with both 'Baby's Had a Taste' and 'The Star and the Slaughter' making the Top 10 there. The album did even better by reaching #1. Heroes' other claim to fame is that they were the last band to play at Newcastle's Star Hotel, the controversial closure of which sparked off street violence and rioting that night. Heroes broke up in 1982. In 1983, Tinson and Screen joined **Swanee**, appearing on the album *Ready for Action! Live in the Snow*. They formed a band called the Tex Pistols in the early 1990s. In the meantime, Dave Hinds had joined popular Sydney hard rock outfit **Finch**. He remained with that band until the end of 1979, appearing on the albums *Nothing to Hide* (1978) and *Contraband* (1979). Hinds went on to join Mick Pealing and the Ideals.

During the early 1980s, frontman Dave Evans re-emerged in Melbourne with his new band, Hot Cockerel. The line-up included Simon Crofts (lead guitar), Nello Franceschini (rhythm guitar), Paul Walsh (bass) and John Mele (drums). The band never got the chance to record anything comprehensive before breaking up in 1984. Crofts was an exceptional heavy rock guitarist, and he went on to Melbourne bands like Fair Warning, **S.A.S.** and Back in Black. Meanwhile, at the end of 1985, Evans formulated the basis for his new band, Dave Evans and Thunder Down Under. The early line-up included Franceschini, Kevin Green (lead guitar), Steve Craven (bass) and Graham Owen (drums). By the time Evans came to record an album in April 1986 with English producer/engineer Mark Dearnley (**AC/DC**, Joan Armatrading, Def Leppard), he decided to use well-known session musicians.

These included John Dallimore (guitar), Sam See (guitar, keyboards), Joe Creighton (bass), Joe Camilleri (sax), Danny Simcic (drums), Robyn Payne (keyboards) and Alex Pertout (percussion) with Penny Dyer, Wendy Stapleton and Lindsay Field on backing vocals. *Dave Evans and Thunder Down Under* mixed hard rock with big production ballads. The album produced three singles, 'Hot Nights'/'It's Alright' (October 1986), 'Waltzing Matilda'/'Nice Guys' (November) and 'Another Day'/'It's Alright' (March 1987). Evans formed a touring version of Thunder Down Under with Dallimore, Payne, Geoff Warner (guitar), Rob Calvert (sax, keyboards; ex-**Strange Tenants**), Bones Hillman (bass; ex-**Swingers**) and Graham Owen (drums). Evans toured with the band until late 1988. Hillman went on to join **Midnight Oil**. Evans also had an acting role in the film *Coming of Age* and wrote or co-wrote four songs on the soundtrack.

Rabbit albums: *Rabbit* (CBS, 1975), *Too Much Rock'n'Roll* (CBS, 1976); ***Heroes album:*** *Heroes* (Albert/EMI, 1980); ***Dave Evans and Thunder Down Under album:*** *Dave Evans and Thunder Down Under* (Reaction/RCA, 1986).

Hugo Race The True Spirit (*see* The Wreckery)

Roddy Radalj (aka Roddy Ray'da, The Raj)

Style: *Punk rock*

Yugoslavian-born, Perth-raised musician Roddy Radalj (b. 1960) was one of the true originals of the Australian punk and post-punk scene. As a member of such popular bands as **Scientists**, Le **Hoodoo Gurus**, **The Johnnys** and **The Dubrovniks**, Radalj left his mark on the development of Australian music. By courtesy of his heritage, Radalj's formative influence was Eastern European gypsy music. As a consequence, Radalj became Australia's own rock'n'roll gypsy, wandering from one project to the next with little direction in his never-ending search for passion, spontaneity, fire and intensity.

Radalj joined his first band, The Exterminators, in mid-1977. The line-up comprised Radalj (guitar, vocals), Mark Demetrius (vocals), Boris Sujdovic (bass) and John Dowlings (drums). In true punk fashion, The Exterminators could barely play their instruments. Legend has it that the band's one and only gig consisted of six drunken attempts at playing Jonathan Richman and the Modern Lovers' 'Pablo Picasso' before they got bored and gave up! The Exterminators became The Invaders with the arrival of **Kim Salmon** (guitar, vocals; ex-Cheap Nasties), who replaced Demetrius in December 1977. The Invaders became **Scientists** in May 1978 when James Baker (ex-**Victims**) joined on drums. Radalj remained with **Scientists** until April 1979. He played on the band's debut, independent single 'Frantic Romantic'/'Shake (Together Tonight)' (June 1979), which became one of the most collectable artefacts of the Australian punk rock era.

Radalj and Sujdovic formed The Rockets with Allan Stewart (vocals), Peter Johnson (guitar) and John Cole (drums). The Rockets played a fast, edgy, tough form of rock'n'roll in the Ramones/Iggy Pop/New York Dolls vein. The band issued one independent single, 'Mean Mistress'/'Little Donna' (February 1980), on the White Rider label before Radalj and Sujdovic left. Stewart and Johnson recruited new players and continued on until 1985. In late 1980, Radalj relocated to Sydney where he formed Le **Hoodoo Gurus** with Dave Faulkner (ex-**Victims**), James Baker and Kimble Rendall (ex-**XL-Capris**). Radalj remained with the Gurus long enough to appear on the band's classic debut single, 'Leilani'/'Leilani Part II' (October 1982), for the Phantom label. Radalj co-wrote several of the songs with Faulkner, including 'Leilani', '(Let's All) Turn on', 'Arthur' and 'Death Ship', which appeared on the Gurus' debut album *Stoneage Romeos*. Just as the single appeared Radalj left the band to form **The Johnnys**. Once again, Radalj only remained long enough to appear on one Johnnys single, 'I Think You're Cute'/'Mountain Man' (October 1983) on the Regular label.

Radalj was ousted from **The Johnnys** in early 1984. He formed irreverent country trio Love Rodeo with Greg Perano (drums; ex-**Hunters & Collectors**) and Marc Scully (bass). A year later, Love Rodeo had run its course and Radalj moved on to his next project which eventually became **The Dubrovniks**. Love Rodeo did reconvene briefly at the start of 1989 to record the single 'Love Yodel No. 9'/'Would You Believe?' (June 1989) for the Timberyard label. Meanwhile, at the end of 1985, Perano and Scully had formed **The Deadly Hume** with Bones Martin from The Fester Brothers. In early 1985, James Baker (ex-**Hoodoo Gurus**) invited Radalj, **Tex Perkins** (**Beasts of Bourbon**, Salamander Jim) and Stu Spasm (Salamander Jim) to join him in the studio to record a one-off single, 'I Can't

Roddy Radalj

Control Myself'/'Born to Be Punched' as The James Baker Experience. The single appeared in June 1985 on the Red Eye label and reached #1 on the independent chart.

In August 1986, Radalj, Baker and Sujdovic (ex-**Scientists**, **Beasts of Bourbon**) formed The Adorable Ones with Peter Simpson (ex-Spectre's Revenge). Spectre's Revenge had been a popular band on the Sydney inner-city guitar scene, and alongside Simpson had comprised Lyn Lee (guitar, vocals), Steve Lorkin (bass; ex-Minuteman) and Andy McPherson (drums). The band had issued one single, 'No Moon at Midnight'/'I Wanna Be Like Maynard G. Krebbs', on the Au-go-go label (February 1985). In 1987, The Adorable Ones renamed themselves **The Dubrovniks** in honour of the fact that both Radalj and Sujdovic were born in the Yugoslavian village of Dubrovnik. The band's clattering, yet accessible rock'n'roll was drawn along the lines of The Troggs meets T-Rex by way of New York Dolls. Radalj also became known for his stylish attire and his guitar made from a wooden cheeseboard!

Citadel issued the singles 'Fireball of Love'/'If I Had a Gun' (April 1988) and a cover of Alvin Stardust's 'My Coo Ca Choo'/'Girls Go Manic' (December 1988). By the time the band recorded and issued the single 'Speedway Girls'/'Freezin' Rain' (July 1989) and the album *Dubrovnik Blues*, the ever-restless Radalj had been ousted yet again. Radalj's eviction from the band came as a consequence of an on-stage punch-up with Simpson. In late 1988, Radalj formed the sideline band The Punjabbers with Brett Ford (drums; ex-**Kryptonics**, **Lubricated Goat**), Tony Robertson (bass; ex-**Hitmen**, **New Christs**, Naked Lunch) and Tony Thewlis (guitar; ex-**Scientists**) and issued the single 'Rock'n'Roll Loveletter'/'Rock'n'Roll Loveletter' on Timberyard (December 1988). Radalj then formed the Roddy Ray'da Band with Billy Gibson (guitar; ex-**Eastern Dark**, Smelly Tongues), Chris Masuak (lead guitar; ex-**Radio Birdman**, **Hitmen**, **New Christs**, **Screaming Tribesmen**), Jim Leone (bass; from **Celibate Rifles**) and Paul Larsen (drums; from **Celibate Rifles**).

Renamed The Surfin' Caesars, the band backed Radalj on his debut solo album, the trash rock opus *Lost Lonely and Vicious* (March 1990), which was named after the 1959 American teen delinquent film of the same title. As well as producing the single 'Dynamite Party'/'Love Gun' (February), the album included a cover of The Dictators' 'Master Race Rock'. Radalj formed a new Roddy Ray'da and the Surfin' Caesars line-up with Larsen (percussion), Bob 'Dutch' Sattler (lead guitar; ex-Johnny Kannis Explosion), Richard 'Pickup' Davis (rhythm guitar; ex-Table Waiters), Phil 'Filthy' Hall (bass; ex-**Lime Spiders**) and Gye Bennetts (drums; ex-**Hitmen DTK**), and issued a second album *Orgazmatazz* (August 1991). Although hardly innovative, the album was brimming with dexterous hard rock and a healthy sense of the absurd. Tracks like 'Hammer the Motor', 'Hellcat's Howl', 'Galaxy Gals' and 'Evil Woman in a Mini Skirt' were prime examples of the Radalj trash aesthetic at work.

The Surfin' Caesars' second album, *Mouthful of Chicken*, raised more than a few eyebrows with its deliberately confrontational and explicit artwork. Once again, it was a fun and derivative album, full of schoolboy humour ('She's a Wanker', 'Gotta Hardon') and was not to be taken terribly seriously. The 18-track album combined nine new songs with the nine from the previously vinyl-only *Orgazmatazz*.

Roddy Ray'da album: *Lost Lonely and Vicious* (Regular/Festival, 1990); ***Roddy Ray'da and the***

Surfin' Caesars albums: *Orgazmatazz* (Blue Mosque/ Festival, 1991), *Mouthful of Chicken* (Shagpile/ Shock, 1993).

The Radiators

Formed: *1978*
Style: *Hard rock*
Original line-up: *Brian Nichol (lead vocals, guitar; ex-Big Swifty), Stephen 'Fess' Parker (lead guitar; ex-Big Swifty), Brendan Callinan (keyboards, vocals; ex-Big Swifty), Geoff Turner (bass, vocals; ex-Twister), Chris Tagg (drums; ex-Big Swifty)*

The emergence of Sydney band The Radiators as a force to be reckoned with on the Australian market coincided with the rise of the late 1970s new wave movement. The Radiators were initially lumped in with that scene, but in reality the band was an archetypal, hard-working pub-rock band capable of delivering tightly crafted, well-executed, hard-hitting metal-pop anthems backed by a playful sense of humour. The band toured constantly, racking up over 2500 gigs by the early 1990s.

The Radiators grew out of the ashes of Sydney hard rock band Big Swifty, which had formed in 1975 with the line-up of Brian Nichol (then on bass), Stephen Parker, Chris Tagg, Michael O'Shea (guitar) and Tony Mollo (keyboards). O'Shea left early in the piece and, when Mollo left the band in August 1978, Brendan Callinan took his place. Geoff Turner also took over from Nichol on bass. The band re-emerged as The Radiators in September. Turner's previous band, Twister, comprised Marty Barclay (guitar), Mike Davis (guitar) and Steve Rose (drums). Twister issued two singles on RCA in 1977, 'Holy Smoke'/'Midnight' (January) and the prophetically titled 'Getting Nowhere Fast'/'Saturday' (November), before splitting.

The Radiators signed to WEA and issued the single 'Comin' Home'/'Numbers' (September 1979), which reached #33 on the national chart during December. 'Fess Song'/'Gimme Head' (February 1979) and the album *Feel the Heat* (March 1979) followed, and the band supported UK visitors The Police on their Australian tour. 'Hit and Run'/'Lonely' (May) was the third single lifted from the band's debut album. *Feel the Heat* went on to sell 90 000 copies. In January 1981, The Radiators signed to 7 Records, which became Powderworks. The band's only release on 7 was the single 'Roomful of Diamonds'/'Quits' (May 1981). WEA issued its final Radiators product in June 1981, the five-track 12-inch EP *You Have the Right to Remain Silent.* The label reissued the EP in July 1982 as a mini-album.

In the meantime, Powderworks had issued the singles 'Up for Grabs'/'Brain Damage' (#37 in October) and 'Nothing's Changed'/'Automatic' (December), plus the four-track 12-inch EP *Four Grabs* (October 1981) which contained 'Up for Grabs', 'Sex', 'Roomful of Diamonds' and 'Automatic'. In 1983, The Radiators signed a new deal with EMI which resulted in the album *Scream of the Real* (#15 in May) and its singles 'No Tragedy'/'Enough's Enough' (#27 in May) and 'You'/'Driving' (July). In September, EMI (America) issued the album in the USA on the Liberty label. The Radiators kept busy during 1984 with the release of the album *Life's a Gamble*, and three singles, The Beatles' 'Revolution'/'Sitting in My Armchair' (July), 'Life's A Gamble'/'Night Slave' (October) and 'A Bit of Pain Never Hurts'/'Scream of the Real' (December). *Life's a Gamble* became the band's third platinum selling album (70 000 copies). Long-serving drummer Chris Tagg left in June 1984, to be replaced by Mick Buckley (ex-Rupert B.).

Powderworks issued a new Radiators single in June 1986, 'One Touch'/'Dangerous'. By the end of the year, The Radiators had linked up with the Mercury label (through PolyGram). The band's first album for Mercury, *Nasty Habits in Nice Children* (March 1987) produced the singles 'Bring on the Crazy'/'Three More Restless Hours' (October 1986), 'Dreaming'/'One Touch' (January 1987) and 'Love Ain't Love'/'Promise of Love' (June). That month, Brad Heaney (ex-DV8) replaced Buckley on drums. Heaney was later replaced by Mark Lucas. The March 1988 live album *Gimme . . . Live* produced the single 'Summer Holiday'/'Lonely' (April). By the early 1990s, The Radiators' brand of boogie rock had been superseded by more incendiary, alternative guitar bands. Yet, being the pub-rock warhorses that they were, The Radiators ploughed on and issued the CD EPs *Hard Core* (1991) and *Rock 'n Roll* (1993), the CD single 'Ain't that Just Like Me' (1994), plus the albums *Radiators* (October 1993) and *Stone* (September 1995).

Albums: *Feel the Heat* (WEA, 1980), *You Have the Right to Remain Silent* (mini-album, WEA, 1982), *Scream of the Real* (EMI, 1983), *Life's a Gamble* (EMI, 1984), *Nasty Habits in Nice Children* (Mercury/PolyGram, 1987), *Gimme . . . Live* (Mercury/PolyGram, 1988), *Radiators* (Mighty/MDS, 1993), *Stone* (Mighty/MDS, 1995), *In Their Element: The Best of the Radiators* (compilation, EMI, 1995).

Radio Birdman

Formed: *1974*
Style: *Rock*
Original line-up: *Rob Younger (vocals; ex-Rats),* **Deniz Tek** *(guitar, vocals; ex-TV Jones), Pip Hoyle (keyboards), Carl Rourke (bass; ex-Rats), Ron Keeley (drums; ex-Rats)*

As one of the most potent rock bands ever to emerge from Australia, Radio Birdman holds pride of place as *the* cult band of the last 25 years. The band's iconoclastic approach, uncompromising do-it-yourself ethos and outsider status in the face of overwhelming hostility remain the stuff of legend.

American-born guitarist **Deniz Tek** and fellow medical student Pip Hoyle formed Radio Birdman in Sydney during November 1974 when they joined forces with the remnants of The Rats. Carl Rourke was quickly replaced by another ex-Rats alumnus, Warwick Gilbert. From the outset, Radio Birdman played an Americanised brand of rock'n'roll that was totally honest and totally committed. The band essentially introduced Australian audiences to the music of The Stooges, MC5, New York Dolls and Blue Oyster Cult. Although generally loathed and shunned by the mainstream music industry of the day, Birdman won the *RAM (Rock Australia Magazine)*/Levi's Punk Band Thriller contest in December 1975 which cemented its cult status. By the time the band's debut EP, *Burn My Eye*, came out in October 1976, Birdman was already running its own gigs at the Oxford Tavern (later to be renamed the Oxford Funhouse) in Darlinghurst, inner-city Sydney. Alongside **The Saints'** '(I'm) Stranded' single, *Burn My Eye* kicked off the Australian new wave movement with a shower of teenage sweat and pure adrenalin.

Just after the EP came out, Hoyle left the band to be replaced by Canadian-born guitarist Chris Masuak (ex-Jackals). The new line-up completed the *Radios Appear* album which came out on the band's own Trafalgar label in June 1977. From Younger's unholy bellow at the start of the cataclysmic cover of The Stooges' 'T.V. Eye', to the closing refrains of the anthem-like 'New Race', the album remains a bona fide rock classic. In between were such archetypal Birdman cuts as 'Descent into the Maelstrom', 'Hand of Law', 'Man with Golden Helmet' and 'Love Kills'; all up, the album was testament to the band's power and conviction as an element of change.

'New Race'/'TV Eye' was issued as a single (June 1977). Inexplicably, the band came under a hail of criticism due to the supposedly 'fascist' sentiments expressed in the lyrics. This was further fuelled by the band's complex iconography (including its eagle's wings/flying saucer symbol, paramilitary appearance and 'Blitzkrieg' tours). Yet nothing could have been further from the truth. In fact Tek wrote 'New Race' as an attempt at a 'teen anthem'. Furthermore, all the various 'totems' helped create the band's mythology, as well as maintaining a sense of group solidarity.

Radio Birdman

Just as the band was starting to gain more acceptance for its brand of high-energy rock (punk had broken overseas and people began to understand what Radio Birdman was about), Pip Hoyle returned to the fold. In February 1978, the *Radios Appear (Overseas)* album came out on Trafalgar (it was issued in the US on Sire during May). Commonly referred to as *The White Album*, it combined remixed tracks from the first album, a couple of re-recorded songs and strong new material like the playfully potent single 'Aloha Steve and Danno'/'Anglo Girl Desire' (May 1978). With the album selling well in Australia, Birdman flew overseas for an extensive UK/European tour. During April 1978, the band recorded a new album at Rockfield Studios in Wales, but due to a combination of outside pressures and internal dissent, the band was on its last legs. Radio Birdman broke up following a gig at Oxford University on 10 June 1978.

Following the split, Tek, Hoyle and Keeley formed The Visitors, Masuak and Gilbert joined **The Hitmen** and Younger formed The Other Side. There was a brief Birdman reunion in August 1979 when the band (sans Rob Younger) played a one-off gig as The Comrades of War. In April 1981, Younger,

Tek and Gilbert teamed up with drummer Dennis Thompson (ex-MC5) and guitarist Ron Asheton (ex-Stooges) as **New Race** and undertook a successful tour of Australia. The blistering live album *The First and the Last* came out in September 1982. Also released in September 1982 was the Radio Birdman *Soldiers of Rock'n'Roll* audio documentary album.

Just prior to the **New Race** tour, Tek and Younger arranged for the Rockfield sessions to be issued as the *Living Eyes* album. A quarter-inch cassette safety dub was used as the source for the pressing and not the original multi-track master tapes. While the sound was not perfect, the album contained some of the most exciting and fully realised music that Birdman ever recorded, including 'Smith and Wesson Blues', 'Crying Sun', 'Hanging on' and the single 'Alone in the Endzone'/'Breaks My Heart' (March 1981).

In June 1984, Big Time Records reissued the Birdman/New Race catalogue and in December 1988 Trafalgar/WEA put out the essential *Under the Ashes* box set. *Under the Ashes* contained four albums, the live, 12-inch EP *More Fun!*, a remixed, 12-inch version of *Burn My Eye* and the single 'Aloha Steve and Danno'/'Anglo Girl Desire'. The box set reached #1 on the alternative album chart in January 1989. 'Aloha Steve and Danno' also came out separately (October 1988) and reaffirmed its status as a diamond-hard rock gem by reaching #1 on the alternative singles chart.

With the individual members of Radio Birdman still highly visible on the scene (in particular, Tek with **Deniz Tek** Group and Younger with **The New Christs**), interest in the band remained at a premium. John Foy at Red Eye Records arranged for the original, multi-track master tapes for *Living Eyes*, which had been gathering dust in the vaults at Rockfield, to be sent over to Australia. Red Eye issued a fully remastered, CD version of *Radios Appear* and a fully remixed, new version of *Living Eyes* (including previously unissued album outtakes) in October 1995. The sound on the CDs was immaculate, and *Radios Appear* and *Living Eyes* were named in the top five Best Reissue Albums in the *Rolling Stone* 1996 Readers' Poll. The remixing, in early 1995, had led to five of the members being in the studio for the first time in 17 years, which in turn was the catalyst for the Radio Birdman re-formation of January 1996. The band undertook the highly successful Radios On! national tour and also took part in the Big Day Out tour. The live, mail-order only, album *Ritualism* appeared in December 1996 on the band's own Crying Sun label, after which Birdman regrouped for another Australian tour.

Albums: *Radios Appear* (Trafalgar/WEA, 1977), *Radios Appear (Overseas)* (Trafalgar/WEA, 1978; issued in the UK and the US on Sire), *Living Eyes* (WEA, 1981), *Soldiers of Rock'n'Roll* (audio documentary, WEA, 1982), *Radios Appear* (reissue, Big Time/EMI, 1984), *Radios Appear (Overseas)/Living Eyes* (double set reissue, Big Time/EMI, 1984), *Under the Ashes* (box set, WEA/Trafalgar, 1988), *Radios Appear* (fully remastered CD version, Red Eye/Polydor, 1995), *Living Eyes* (fully remixed CD version, Red Eye/Polydor, 1995), *Ritualism* (Crying Sun/Citadel, 1996).

Further reading: *Radio Birdman* by Vivian Johnson (Sheldon Booth, 1990).

Rail

Formed: *1995*
Style: *Indie guitar pop*
Original line-up: *Dan Vertessy (vocals, guitar), Ashley Naylor (guitar, vocals; ex-Swarm), David Sayer (bass), Ian Williams (drums)*

Taking inspiration from overseas bands like Teenage Fanclub, Buffalo Tom, Dinosaur Jr and Sonic Youth, Melbourne band Rail played a melodic, languid brand of guitar pop. The band actually started life in 1993 as Sleeper, issuing the CD EP *Sleeper* (March 1994) before being forced to change its name to Fragment due to an overseas band with the same moniker. Fragment contributed 'Careering' to rooArt's *Youngblood 4* compilation (September 1994), but underwent another name change, this time to Rail. The band's contemporaries on the Melbourne inner-city scene included the likes of **Even** (Ashley Naylor's main band), **Holocene**, **Snout**, **Bodyjar**, **Hoss**, **Autohaze**, **The Earthmen**, **The Fauves** and **Dirty Three**.

Rail signed to Mushroom Records' White label, and issued its debut CD EP, 'Immune Deficiency', in August 1995. The band's debut, full-length album, *Bad Hair Life*, followed a month later. *Bad Hair Life* was a cohesive, yet modest first effort, boasting a number of cracking examples of indie guitar pop such as 'Immune Deficiency', 'Volume Creep vs Nature Boy' and 'The Coolest Thing'. The album yielded two more CD singles, 'Freebird (February 1996) and 'Never Whole' (August). In mid-1996, Rail entered the studio with world-renowned producer Don Fleming (The Posies, Dinosaur Jr, Teenage Fanclub, Sonic Youth, Gumball, the *Backbeat* soundtrack) and engineer Bil Emmons to record its second album. Naylor then left to concentrate on Even. *Goodbye Surfing Hello God!* appeared in May 1977, preceded by the CD single 'I am Awake'.

Albums: *Bad Hair Life* (White/Mushroom/Festival, 1995), *Goodbye Surfing Hello God!* (White/Mushroom/Sony, 1997).

Railroad Gin

Formed: *1968*
Style: *Soul, R&B*
1973 line-up: *Carol Lloyd (vocals), Laurie Stone (keyboards, vocals, sax, percussion), Phil Shields (lead guitar, trombone, percussion), Peter Evans (flute, sax, percussion), Dim Jansons (bass), Bob Brown (percussion), Gary Evans (drums)*

During the mid-1970s, Brisbane band Railroad Gin was the premier rock attraction on the Queensland pub/club/concert circuit. The band enjoyed #1 hit singles in its hometown, but was virtually ignored in all other states. Originally formed in the late 1960s, Railroad Gin made an impact with its sweaty, full-tilt gigs and a commercial blend of soul, brassy R&B and percussion-driven hard rock.

Laurie Stone was the driving force behind Railroad Gin, and he wrote or co-wrote most of the band's original material. Singer Carol Lloyd, however, was the band's focal point with her commanding stage presence, husky blues voice and wild mane of red hair. The band went through a number of membership changes before arriving at the recording line-up circa 1973. Early members included Geoff Fitzgibbon (vocals, flute), Frank Millward (organ, trumpet), Glen Rickwood (guitar), Danny Murphy (drums), Selwyn Wright (drums) and Trevor Fielding (drums). In 1973, Railroad Gin signed to Polydor and recorded its debut album, *A Matter of Time*. The album produced the Brisbane #1 single 'A Matter of Time'/'Don't Rile Me' (June 1974). 'A Matter of Time' featured a mixture of Shocking Blue, Jethro Tull and Steely Dan elements with its hard guitar/flute-driven sound.

The album included the band's rearrangements of The Rolling Stones' 'Ruby Tuesday' and The Beatles' 'Come Together'. Railroad Gin issued two further Brisbane #1 singles in 'Do Ya Love Me?'/'Academy Rock' (October) and 'You Told the World'/'The Driver' (March 1975). Just as Railroad Gin was enjoying its first flush of commercial success, Carol Lloyd left the band in August 1975 to pursue a solo career. She formed Tonnage, soon renamed the Carol Lloyd Band, with Peter Harvey (keyboards), Mark Moffatt (guitar, pedal steel), Gary Broadhurst (bass) and Danny Simpson (drums). The Carol Lloyd Band issued the album *Mother was Asleep at the Time* on EMI, which mixed pop, funk and country material. It produced two singles, 'Storm in My Soul'/'Blue MacKenzie' (December 1976) and 'All the Good Things'/'Don't Do Me Any Favours' (May 1977). In 1980, she issued a solo album, *Take It or Leave It* (RCA), which contained the single 'Take It or Leave It'/'Naked City' (January 1981).

In the meantime, Judee Ford (ex-Tramway) had replaced Lloyd in Railroad Gin. The band toured Sydney, Melbourne and Adelaide for the first time. The fourth Railroad Gin single, the funky 'The Keeper and the Lord'/'A Long Time Coming' (December 1975) also reached #1 in Brisbane. By that stage, Jim Dickson had replaced Jansons on bass. Railroad Gin's second album, *Journey's End* (October 1976), followed the formula set by the debut, but with a lighter, more polished Adult Oriented Rock (AOR) sound (somewhere between Chicago, Styx and Fleetwood Mac). As well as the single 'Journey's End'/'The Best I Can' (June 1976), the album again included two covers, The Doors' 'Riders on the Storm' and Steely Dan's 'Do It Again'.

At the end of 1976, Railroad Gin acquired a new rhythm section of Roger Murray (bass) and Col Wilson (drums). In early 1977, founder member Laurie Stone left, which precipitated the band's final collapse shortly after. Stone set about recording his debut album, *Life's a Carnival*, which seems never to have seen the light of day. He produced singles for Brisbane bands Moonlight, Chicks Inc and Wickety Wak before forming a partnership with Peter Moscos (ex-Sect, Burke and Wills).

Moscos and Stone issued two albums of pleasant, middle-of-the-road rock, *Moscos and Stone* (1979) and *Memorial Drive: The Story of a Kid that Survived* (1981), plus six singles: 'Captain Captain (Empty Horses)'/'Stoned on Love' (September 1978), 'Trouble in the City'/'Girls in Love' (July 1979), 'Song for You'/'Strike Up the Band' (August), 'Over and Over'/'Sharing the Days' (February 1980), 'Secrets'/'Max the Martyr' (January 1981) and 'I Wanna Sing with the Rolling Stones'/'School Days' (June). 'Captain Captain (Empty Horses)' reached #18 in Melbourne during February 1979. Stone began composing and producing music for film and television, including the drama series *The Flying Doctors*. His soundtrack work took him to Los Angeles in the early 1990s.

Railroad Gin albums: *A Matter of Time* (Polydor, 1974), *Journey's End* (Polydor, 1976); ***Carol Lloyd Band album:*** *Mother was Asleep at the Time* (EMI, 1977); ***Carol Lloyd album:*** *Take It or Leave It* (RCA,

1980); ***Moscos and Stone albums:*** *Moscos and Stone* (Image, 1979), *Memorial Drive: The Story of a Kid that Survived* (CBS, 1981).

Rainbow Theatre

Formed: *1973*
Style: *Classical rock*
Original line-up: *Keith Hoban (lead vocals, organ), Julian Browning (guitar, mellotron), Matthew Cozens (piano, organ), Steven Nash (sax, clarinet, flute), Frank Graham (trumpet, cornet, French horn), Don Santin (trombone), Ferg McKinnon (bass), Graeme Carter (drums, percussion)*

Melbourne band Rainbow Theatre was one of the pioneering independent mavericks of the mid-1970s. Led by guitarist Julian Browning (who wrote all the band's music), this classically influenced rock band recorded its debut album *The Armada* before signing a deal with the Clear Light of Jupiter label.

Often incorrectly categorised as an 'electronic' outfit, Rainbow Theatre featured the traditional rock line-up of guitar, keyboards, bass and drums augmented by a three-piece horn section and a seven-member choir. On the album, the choir comprised Sue Twigg, Helen Grad, Pauline Ashleigh, Helen Modra, Barry Skelton, Peter Cox and Evan Zachariah. As displayed on the adventurous and rare album *The Armada*, the band's music oscillated between nimble jazz rock, classical and operatic themes and several points beyond. The second side was dominated by the dramatic, 15-minute, five-suite title piece 'The Armada'. 'Petworth House'/'The Darkness Overture' was lifted as a single.

For the band's second, equally rare, album, *Fantasy of Horses*, Browning, Hoban, Graham, McKinnon and Carter were joined by new horn, woodwind and string sections. The new players were Martin West (sax, clarinet), Ian Relf (trombone), Tricia Shevenan (flute), Chris Stock (oboe), Karin McGechie (violin), Stephen Daunt (violin), Nya Murray (violin), Rowan Thomas (viola) and Sara Glenis (cello). The remarkable, 22-minute, seven-suite 'Fantasy of Horses' weaved its way through complex progressive jazz movements (akin to UK bands like King Crimson) to melancholy, minor-key classical moments. Rainbow Theatre performed the occasional concert around Melbourne, but despite the quality of music on offer, the band never attained a commercial crossover.

Albums: *The Armada* (Clear Light of Jupiter, 1975), *Fantasy of Horses* (Clear Light of Jupiter, 1976).

The Ram Jam Big Band

Formed: *1966*
Style: *Jazz, R&B, pop*
Original line-up: *Russell Smith (vocals, trumpet, trombone; ex-Bay City Set), Terry Villis (guitar, vocals; ex-Bay City Set), John Ellis (sax), Ian McPherson (organ), Joe Gorski (bass), Ray Evans (drums; ex-Bay City Set)*

Like **Cam-Pact**, The Ram Jam Big Band was a cornerstone institution and an important breeding ground for rock musicians of note on the Melbourne scene during the late 1960s/early 1970s. As Glenn A. Baker wrote, The Ram Jam Big Band started out in October 1966 as a conservative tuxedo-wearing jazz club band before emerging as one of the most respected rock groups of the late 1960s.

The band's exciting latter-day sound was influenced by US bands like Blood Sweat and Tears and Sly and the Family Stone, plus Georgie Fame/Zoot Money-styled English R&B and jazz. As well as earning a strong following around the discotheques and clubs, and making regular television appearances, The Ram Jam Big Band toured South-East Asia and the Pacific region. In early 1967, Peter Knapp replaced original bass player Joe Gorski. The move was the first of many line-up changes that plagued the band right up to its demise in late 1969. John Ellis was the next to leave when he was replaced by Mike Edwards (sax, flute; ex-**Party Machine**) in June. Soon after that, The Ram Jam Big Band signed a deal with Nat Kipner's Spin label, which resulted in the single The Temptations' 'My Girl'/'I Didn't Know' (September 1967).

For its second single 'Sunshine and I Feel Fine'/'Rainy Sunday' (December 1967), The Ram Jam Big Band comprised Smith, Villis, Knapp, Ian Clyne (organ; ex-**Loved Ones**, Black Pearls), Don Wright (sax, flute) and Stan Harris (drums). Original drummer Ray Evans went on to become one of the most respected businessmen in the Australian music industry as co-president of the Evans-Gudinski Organisation which incorporated Mushroom Records, the Premier Artists booking agency and the Frontier Touring Company. He also managed **Renée Geyer** and **Russell Morris** for many years. Following the release of *The Ram Jam Big Band* EP ('Sunshine and I Feel Fine', 'Rainy Sunday'/'My Girl', 'I Didn't Know'), the band's third single, 'I Can't Let Go of this Feeling'/'Funny How Time Slips Away', came out in March 1968. The band caused a mini-furore when Melbourne film-maker Ollie Venskevics made a film-clip to accompany the single's release. The clip used sequences of racial violence, a negro priest and a dead girl in a coffin. The clip was screened nationally on television pop show *Uptight* before concerned parents forced the Broadcasting Control Board to ban it.

In July 1968, Peter McCormack replaced Harris on drums and the band added Chris McClure on lead vocals and guitar (to allow Smith to concentrate on trumpet). By the end of 1968, Laurie Byrne (ex-Black Pearls) had replaced McCormack on drums. In early 1969, **Gary Young** (ex-Silhouettes, Rondells, Laurie Allen Revue) joined as the band's new drummer, to give a line-up of Smith, Villis, Knapp, Clyne, Wright and Young. There were a number of other horn players who passed through the band's ranks during that period: Lance Dixon (ex-**Rockwell T. James** and the Rhythm Aces, **James Taylor Move**), Liam Bradley and Bernie Payne. The new line-up issued a fourth single, a cover of Amen Corner's 'Lost and Found'/'Jamming' (May 1969), before calling it quits. The depleted line-up of Clyne, Villis, Knapp and Young, plus American singer Peter Bonner, worked for a few months as Ram Jam to tie up outstanding gig commitments. At the end of the year, Clyne, Villis, Young, Wayne Duncan (bass; ex-Rondells) and **Terry Hannagan** (lead vocals) formed a band called Turnstile which was short-lived.

In early 1970, Clyne formed the likewise short-lived Excalibur before travelling overseas. He returned in 1972 and joined **Levi Smith's Clefs**. Young and Duncan joined **Sons of the Vegetal Mother** and then **Daddy Cool**. **Hannagan** launched his solo career. In the meantime co-founder Russell Smith and latter-day sax player Lance Dixon had joined The Castaways before moving on to Luke's Walnut (the second Sydney *Hair* stage group after **Tully**). Dixon joined **Max Merritt and the Meteors** during the mid-1970s. At the end of 1972, Russell Smith and Ian Clyne reunited in Barrie McAskill's **Levi Smith's Clefs**. By December, Clyne was working with Mighty Mouse which comprised **Phil Manning** (guitar, vocals; ex-**Chain**), Mal Capewell (sax, flute; ex-Dr Kandy's Third Eye, Dada, **Company Caine**), Barry Sullivan (bass; ex-**Wild Cherries, Chain**), Barry Harvey (drums; ex-**Wild Cherries, Chain**) and Kevin Murphy (drums; ex-**Wild Cherries, Billy Thorpe** and the Aztecs, **King Harvest, Chain, Levi Smith's Clefs**). In February 1973, Mighty Mouse (sans Murphy) simply changed its name and **Chain** #15 came into being.

Since that time, Russell Smith has concentrated on session work, as well as playing with numerous groups including Powerhouse, the Vince Jones Band, **Kate Ceberano** and her Septet, The Ministry of Fun, Dianna Kiss (with **Ross Hannaford**) and Jane Clifton and the Blue Lester Trio among many others. Powerhouse played brassy soul and R&B material on the mid-1970s Melbourne pub circuit. The line-up comprised Smith, Bobby Warren (guitar, vocals), Tui Richards (guitar), David McMaster (keyboards), Miguel Carranza (trombone), Bruce Sandell (sax), Doug Williams (bass) and Doug McDonald (drums).

Lynne Randell

Style: Pop

For a brief period during the mid-1960s, Liverpool-born, Melbourne-raised singer Lynne Randell (real name Randall) (b. 1950) was the most popular female performer in the country. Randell's trendsetting clothes, 'Dollybird' looks and string of perky pop hits earned her the title of Australia's 'Miss Mod'. At the height of her popularity, she travelled to the USA and managed to make an impression on the international scene, though more by association than by hit singles.

Randell migrated to Australia with her family at age five. At 14 she was working as an apprentice hairdresser when she came to the attention of aspiring pop manager Carol West. Randell became a regular on television pop show *The Go!! Show* and began working the Melbourne discotheque and dance scene backed by the bluesy Spinning Wheels. In February 1965, she issued her debut single for EMI/HMV, a cover of Lulu's 'I'll Come Running Over'/'Hold Me'. With exposure on *Bandstand, Saturday Date* and *Sing Sing Sing,* the single took Randell into the Melbourne Top 10 a month later. Her next two singles, 'A Love Like You'/'Summertime' (May) and The Marvellettes' 'Forever'/'Be Sure' (July), made the lower reaches of the Top 40. By the end of the year, Randell had scored a 3UZ Sound Award and *The Go!! Show* award for Most Popular Female Vocalist of the Year.

In early 1966, Randell signed a new deal with CBS. 'Heart'/'That's What Love is Made of' (April) and 'Going Out of My Head'/'Take the Bitter with the Sweet' (August) returned her to the Melbourne Top 20 (#15 and #16 respectively). With *Go-Set's* inaugural Top Pop Girl Singer Award under her arm, Randell departed for the UK and the USA. In Liverpool she performed at the Cavern Club (made famous by The Beatles) and in the US she struck up a friendship with The Monkees' Davy Jones. At that time, The Monkees were just emerging as America's lastest teen idol pop sensations. Editor Gloria Stavers of the influential *16* magazine ran a photograph of Randell with her head on Jones' shoulder, which immediately labelled the singer a 'Monkee girlfriend'. Randell began recording for the US Epic label. The single 'Ciao Baby'/'Stranger in My Arms' was unsuccessful in the US, but it became her biggest, and most memorable, Australian hit when it peaked at #6 in Melbourne and #16 in Sydney during May 1967.

By that stage, Randell had opened for The Monkees on three American concerts. She went over so well, that she embarked on the quartet's first full-scale American tour as support act. Also on the bill were the likes of The 5th Dimension, Ike and Tina Turner and, for the first half-a-dozen dates, 'the wild man of rock' Jimi Hendrix. Randell's seventh single, a cover of Albert Hammond's 'That's a Hoe Down'/'I Need You Boy', made the Melbourne charts in August 1967, and the singer ended the year with her second *Go-Set* Most Popular Female Vocalist award. In February 1968, Randell settled in Los Angeles, only recording one more single (this time for Capitol), 'I Love My Dog'/'Mind Excursion' (December 1969).

Randell had already written about her adventures for *Go-Set*, and she became the paper's US correspondent during 1970 and 1971. In 1980 she returned to Australia and began performing at 1960s revival concerts (usually singing 'Ciao Baby'). In 1984, Randell commenced work as media personality Ian 'Molly' Meldrum's personal assistant, before fulfilling the same position in New York with Sire Records boss Seymour Stein. In 1986, reissue specialists Raven issued the first Lynne Randell album, *Dynamic Lynne Randell*, which combined her first seven singles (A and B sides) plus the previously unissued 'I've Got a Notion'.

Album: *Dynamic Lynne Randell* (Raven, 1986).

Ratcat

Formed: *1985*
Style: *Pop*
Original line-up: *Simon Day (guitar, vocals), Victor Levi (bass), Trevor (drums)*

As the 1980s gave way to the 1990s, Ratcat became the first band from the Sydney alternative guitar scene to reach a wider, mainstream teenypop audience. Ratcat's combination of speed-ball fuzz-pop and comic-book aesthetics was always brighter and more entertaining than its contemporaries and the results speak for themselves. Writing in *Rolling Stone*, John O'Donnell noted that in the days of precise production values, $100 000 video-clips and corporate rock strategies, Ratcat succeeded on an agenda of simple guitar-pop love songs and boyish good looks.

Ratcat

Ratcat grew out of Simon Day and Victor Levi's garage band Danger Mouse. Ratcat built-up a strong live following by playing the local haunts of the Sydney skate-punk scene alongside the likes of **Massappeal**, **The Hellmenn**, **The Hard-ons** and **Happy Hate Me Nots**. In December 1987, the Waterfront label put out the band's eponymous debut mini-LP which drew comparisons with The Buzzcocks, Jesus and Mary Chain and 1960s garage pop bands like Music Machine. *Ratcat* contained four of the band's self-penned stage favourites plus a cover of the Tommy James and the Shondells 1960s bubblegum apotheosis 'I Think We're Alone Now'.

The singles 'I Think I Love You'/'Depression' (August 1988) and 'Baby's Got a Gun'/'Purple Room' (December) followed before the band issued its debut album, *This Nightmare*, in July 1989. The album contained a treasure-trove of witty, effervescent Day-penned tracks like 'Go Go', 'True Lust', 'Baby's Got a Gun' and 'The Killing Joke', plus a cover of UK band The Darling Buds' 'If I Said'. The line-up on the album comprised Day, Andrew Polin (drums) and John McAteer (bass). 'The Killing

Joke' also appeared as a 12-inch EP (July 1989), and the band's last single for Waterfront was 'Saying Goodbye'/'Tura Satana', 'Overdrive' (March 1990). Amr Zaid replaced McAteer and the band signed a lucrative deal with the fledgling rooArt label (through PolyGram). Ratcat contributed 'You Get me By' to the label's Various Artists compilation *Youngblood II*. The *Tingles* 12-inch EP came out in November 1990, and almost immediately the frisky 'That Ain't Bad' scored mainstream radio support, which shot the EP to #1 on the Australian charts.

The 'Don't Go Now'/'The Lie' single repeated the feat in April 1991, with the result that by the time the albums *Blind Love* (July) and *Ratcat Alive* (December) came out, Ratcat was hot property indeed. Produced by Nick Mainsbridge, *Blind Love* rose effortlessly to #1 on the national chart. The band opened for Australian rock-funk veterans **INXS** on that band's massive X national tour, as well as headlining their own concerts. Ratcat's Invasion of the Dinosaur Killers tour of June 1991 saw the band supported by highly touted UK quartet Ride, plus local indie heroes **Falling Joys** and **Clouds**. The *Tingles* EP was the second biggest selling single on the Australian charts for 1991. *Blind Love* was certified gold on pre-release orders alone (35 000 copies). It was the #35 best-selling album for the year.

The next Ratcat single, 'Baby Baby' (July 1991), did not reach the national Top 40, but peaked at #15 in Sydney. In September, Ratcat headed overseas for a world tour which took in dates across the UK, Europe and the USA. The band supported the likes of Ride, Iggy Pop, Dinosaur Jr, Teenage Fanclub, Violent Femmes and The Wonder Stuff. In mid-1992, Marc Scully (ex-Love Rodeo, **Deadly Hume, Nick Barker and the Reptiles**) replaced Zaid on bass. The CD singles 'Candyman' (May 1992), 'Holiday' (October 1992) and 'The World (in a Wrapper)' (May 1993), plus the album *Insideout* (November 1992), were unable to repeat the spectacular success of their predecessors but kept Ratcat in the public eye. **Falling Joys'** Suzie Higgie sang a duet with Day on 'The World (in a Wrapper)', while The Buzzcocks' bass player, Steve Garney, made a guest appearance on 'Holiday' and the album track 'Sick of Being Down'.

In 1993, Ratcat put out two more CD EPs, 'Rain' and 'The Smiler' (which contained the radio-friendly guitar pop epic 'May You Ever'), and recorded a new album, *Easy Rider*, which finally appeared in October 1997 before slipping from view. While Ratcat's place on the Australian charts was superseded by more incendiary guitar bands like **You Am I, Spiderbait, Tumbleweed** and **Regurgitator**, there was no denying the band's pioneering efforts to elevate alternative guitar pop beyond its origins and into the mainstream charts. Simon Day was responsible for much of the band's record cover artwork (including the band's symbol) and overall image. He has had his artwork published in numerous magazines and has also held several exhibitions.

Albums: *Ratcat* (mini-LP, Waterfront, 1987), *This Nightmare* (Waterfront, 1989), *Blind Love* (rooArt/PolyGram, 1991), *Ratcat Live* (mini-album, rooArt/Warner, 1991), *Insideout* (rooArt/Warner, 1992), *Easy Rider* (rooArt/BMG, 1997).

Real Life

Formed: *1982*
Style: *Pop rock*
Original line-up: *David Sterry (vocals, guitar; ex-***Kush***), Richard Zartorski (synthesiser, sequencers, violin; ex-***Kush***), Alan Johnson (bass, bass synthesiser), Danny Simcic (drums)*

Melbourne band Real Life shot to prominence in 1983 with the airy, seductive hit single 'Send Me an Angel' which combined accessible new wave synth pop with sassy New Romantic imagery to telling effect. Real Life was one of the first Australian bands from the early 1980s that was unashamedly ambitious and international in its outlook. Everything from the band members' designer clothes (by Katie Pye) and their dyed locks to the use of high technology had been carefully arranged for maximum impact. David Sterry was one of the first musicians in Australia to use the newly designed Roland G-707 guitar synthesiser, which added to the band's overall sound. Yet, by the same token, like most other Australian rock bands, Real Life paid its dues on the pub circuit before even entering the recording studio.

Sterry and classical violinist Richard Zartorski first came into contact when they were members of the very last line-up of **Kush** at the end of 1977. By 1980, having been inspired by the then prevalent UK new wave movement, Sterry and Zartorski formed electro-pop band Wires with Alan Johnson. Initially utilising a drum machine to keep the beat, Wires added Danny Simcic in 1981 and became A Private Life. The band played the Melbourne pub circuit for a year before changing names to Real Life. At the end of 1982, Real Life signed a management and recording deal with the Wheatley organisation. Real Life issued its debut single, 'Send Me an Angel'/'Like a Gun' (through RCA), in May 1983. By June it had reached #3 in Melbourne and #6 on the national chart. Although redolent of UK bands like Ultravox, Visage, Human League and Duran Duran, it was nevertheless a confident debut. The song immediately placed Real Life at the forefront of Australian synth pop alongside the likes of **Pseudo Echo**, **Dear Enemy** and **Kids in the Kitchen**.

Englishman Steve Hillage (from hippie outfit Gong) produced Real Life's debut album, *Heartland*, which appeared in November 1983. *Heartland* reached #7 in Melbourne and #35 nationally during January 1984. It produced two further singles, 'Openhearted'/'Pick Me Up' (August 1983) and 'Catch Me I'm Falling'/'Thrill Me' (November). 'Catch Me I'm Falling' peaked at #1 in Melbourne and #13 nationally during April 1984. In late 1983, Real Life embarked on promotional tours of the UK, Europe and the USA, where the band's records had picked up considerable interest. German label Curb Records issued *Heartland* in Europe. In the USA, 'Send Me an Angel' peaked at #28 (Top 5 in Los Angeles) and 'Catch Me I'm Falling' made #40. Californian baseball team The Angels adopted 'Send Me an Angel' as its theme song. Following an American tour supporting the Eurythmics, Real Life played dates in Europe and Japan.

In all, Real Life spent two years overseas, recording a second album in Berlin in early 1985. By that stage, the critical backlash against Real Life had settled in, and the band's second album, *Flame* (November 1985), appeared to little response. The singles 'Face to Face'/'Flame' (October) and 'One Blind Love'/'Love's Not Easy' (February 1986) were not successful. In 1986, Steve Williams replaced Zartorski on keyboards. The band spent most of the late 1980s away from public view. 'Send me an Angel '89' made a showing at #26 on the US chart in June 1989. In 1990, the band signed a new deal with BMG which resulted in the singles 'God Tonight' and 'Kiss the Ground'. American audiences responded positively and 'God Tonight' became a hit in a number of territories across the USA. The Curb label also issued the album *Lifetime* in 1990.

Real Life continued its low profile well into the 1990s. Yet, ever-willing to embrace computer technology, the band set up its own World Wide Web site on the Internet which attracted the attention of Texas-based independent label Monument. Impressed with the band's resolve and perseverance, and presumably its music, Monument signed Real Life. In early 1997, plans were laid for the release of Real Life's first album in over ten years, *Happy*.

Albums: *Heartland* (Wheatley/RCA, 1983), *Master Mix* (RCA, 1984), *Flame* (RCA, 1985) *Happy* (Monument, 1997).

Johnny Rebb

Style: *Rock'n'roll*

Born John Dellbridge (in 1935), Sydney suburban butcher turned rock'n'roll singer Johnny Rebb was billed as the 'Gentleman of Rock'n'Roll'. Rebb was presented as the moral exemplar of the Australian music scene. He made all his public appearances wearing a tie and a conservative navy blue suit with a neatly folded white handkerchief in the breast pocket. Rebb also issued a string of singles, on eight different record labels. He continued working right into the 1970s.

Dellbridge started out as a country and western singer during the mid-1950s. With the advent of rock'n'roll, he adopted the American Civil War-derived stage name Johnny Rebb and formed The Rebels. The line-up comprised Sonny Neville (guitar; ex-**Alan Dale and the Houserockers**), Johnny Charters (piano; ex-**Alan Dale and the Houserockers**), Jimmy Sloggett (sax), Keith Williams (bass; ex-**Johnny O'Keefe** and the Dee Jays) and Johnny Burns (drums). In 1958, Rebb cut his debut single for EMI/Columbia, a cover of Chuck Berry's 'Johnny B. Goode'/'Rebel Rock'. From there, Rebb signed on as the first Australian artist to record for American impresario Lee Gordon's Leedon label. Johnny Rebb and the Rebels issued five singles on Leedon, 'Hey Sheriff'/'Noelene' (December 1958), 'Pathway to Paradise'/'Rock on' (June 1959), 'Bluebirds Over the Mountain'/'Say Yeah' (October), 'Highway of Love'/'It Might Have Been' (December) and 'Lonesome Road'/'We Belong Together' (April 1960); three EPs, 'Come on Let's Go' (1959), 'Highway of Love' (1960) and *Hits for Six* (1960); plus the album *Some Swing Some Sweet* (1960).

'Hey Sheriff', 'Pathway to Paradise', Bluebirds Over the Mountain' and 'Highway of Love' all made the Top 40 in Sydney. 'Pathway to Paradise' peaked at #6 and 'Highway of Love' at #8. It was during his tenure with Leedon that Rebb received his gentlemanly appellation due to his stylish attire, good manners and modesty. He became a regular on **Johnny O'Keefe's** television show *Six O'Clock Rock*. Rebb often replaced J.O.K. as compere of *Six O'Clock Rock* during the singer's periodic absences. In mid-1960, Rebb signed to the Coronet label as a solo singer. That resulted in the singles 'How will It End?'/'There You Go' (June 1960), 'Think Me a Kiss'/'L.O.V.E.V.I.L.L.E. (Sydney #10 in November) and 'Anytime You Want Me'/'She's Just Another Girl' (August 1961). Rebb then changed to the London label for 'Two Ton Tessie'/'All of Me' (December 1961) and 'Billy Blue Shoes'/'Letter a Day' (February 1962).

By 1963, Rebb was on the CBS label for the singles 'Secret'/'Done Got Over It' (June), 'Ain't I'm a Dog'/'Seeing is Believing' (November), 'Hey Now Baby'/'If You will Just Love Me' (1964), 'Girl Named Sue'/'I Just Don't Understand' (1964), 'Whirlpool'/'Then I'll Know It's Love' (1964) and 'Jessie'/'So Do I' (1964). EMI/HMV issued the Rebb singles Little Richard's 'The Girl Can't Help It'/'Pretty Thing' (May 1965), 'You Can't Judge a Book by Its Cover'/'Dreams (June) and 'Tell Me Please'/'I Just Want to Be Free' (October). By 1968, the peripatetic Rebb had signed to the Ramrod label, which issued the singles 'The Monkey Shine'/'I Need You' (February 1968), 'I Just Can't Help Believing'/'To the Patterns of the Wall' (May 1969) and 'Ding Dong'/'Summertime Blues' (1970). During the early 1970s, Rebb participated on the rock'n'roll revival circuit. He issued one final single on the Astor label, 'Playing Your Game'/'Celebrating', during 1976 before retiring from the recording business.

Albums: *Some Swing Some Sweet* (Johnny Rebb and the Rebels, Leedon/Festival, 1960), *Rock on* (compilation shared with **Barry Stanton**, Raven, 1981).

Rebecca's Empire

Formed: *1994*
Style: *Rock, pop*
Original line-up: *Rebecca Barnard (vocals, guitar; ex-Escalators,* **Stephen Cummings** *Band), Shane O'Mara (guitar; ex-***Stephen Cummings** *Band,* **Chris Wilson** *Band)*

Melbourne singer Rebecca Barnard is recognised as one of the foremost vocalists of the 1990s. As an in-demand session singer, Barnard has contributed back-up vocals to albums by the likes of **Stephen Cummings**, **Harem Scarem** and **Chris Wilson**. Since the mid-1980s, she has worked as lead vocalist with a number of Melbourne bands beginning with The Escalators.

The original line-up of The Escalators formed in 1981 with Jeff Raglus (vocals, trumpet), Steve Wilkinson (sax), Ken Leslie (guitar, vocals), Bob Reinking (bass), Billy King (drums). The Escalators' good-time hybrid of soul, reggae, pop, funk and African rhythms earned the band a strong following around the Melbourne pub circuit. The band also boasted over 30 musicians within its ranks through the years. Rebecca Barnard joined as lead vocalist in 1983. Sam Dadzi (percussion) and Michael Mildren (keyboards) also swelled the band's ranks at that time. Meanwhile, Simon Dawe had replaced Reinking, Sally Ford (ex-**Kevins**) had replaced Wilkinson and Jeff Hassle had replaced King.

It is virtually impossible to list all the line-up changes here, but other latter-day members included Clarence Bailey (drums; ex-**Dugites**), Chris Coyne (sax), Geoff Spooner (guitar), Eddie Van Roosendael (drums; ex-**Stiletto**) and Trevor Hart who replaced Raglus in 1985. The only original member to stay the distance was Ken Leslie. The Escalators issued a sole, independent single, 'Jumping in My Yard'/'The Score', in October 1986. Barnard had left by that stage, and featured vocalists were Andrea St John and Cath Wall. Leslie kept various Escalators line-ups operating until 1988.

In 1993, following stints with **Stephen Cummings'** Lovetown, Swinging Sidewalks, The Sacred Hearts of Sweet Temptation and her own Rebecca Barnard Band, Barnard and Shane O'Mara formed Rebecca's Empire as a duo. O'Mara collaborated for a number of years with **Stephen Cummings** as co-writer, producer and arranger. Like Barnard, he also worked as a session musician, playing guitar for the likes of **Andrew Pendlebury**, **Deborah Conway** and **Chris Wilson**. In 1994, Barnard contributed an excellent version of US band Pearl Jam's 'Alive' to the P.R.I.C.S. (Performers Releasing Information about Clean Syringes) album *Do It Safe*. Then, alongside **Blue Million Miles**, **Atlas Strings** and Charlotte Grace, Rebecca's Empire signed to Polydor's newly created Eternity label. Barnard and O'Mara recruited Bill McDonald (bass; ex-**Hot Half Hour**, **Deborah Conway** Band) and Peter Luscombe (drums; ex-**Stephen Cummings** Band, **Black Sorrows**) in order for the band to tour.

The CD EP *Rebecca's Empire* ('Atomic Electric') appeared at the end of 1994. In early 1995, Michael Den Elzen (ex-**Stephen Cummings** Band, Schnell Fenster) replaced McDonald (who joined **Frente!**) on bass. In June 1995, Polydor issued the 'Atomic Electric' (Fuzz Head Mix) CD EP, which included the remixed version of 'Atomic Electric', and the original version plus 'Red Dress' and 'Wasting Time' from the first EP. Over the next 18 months, Rebecca's Empire issued the CD EP *Take A Look at Happiness* (featured tracks 'Empty' and 'Alive') (September 1995), plus the CD singles 'In Deep' (May 1996) and 'So Rude' (July 1996). The band consolidated its position with the release of the excellent full-length album *Way of All Things* in August.

The album was brimming with quality songs like the ballads 'In Deep' and 'Talking Star', tough rockers like 'Way of All Things' (with its funky Lenny Kravitz-styled riff), 'So Rude' and 'Atomic Electric', plus two sterling slices of Badfinger-style guitar-pop, 'Empty' and 'Mirage'. 'So Rude' polled at #57 on the 1996 Triple J Hottest 100 list. 'Way of All Things' appeared as the band's next CD single in February 1997. As well as their own recording and touring commitments, O'Mara and Barnard found time to sing backing vocals with **Dave Graney 'n' the Coral Snakes**, while O'Mara and Luscombe toured as part of the **Paul Kelly** Band. A new Rebecca's Empire single, 'Car Radio', came out in November 1997.

Album: *Way of All Things* (Eternity/Polydor, 1996).

Helen Reddy

Style: Pop

Melbourne-born singer Helen Reddy (b. 1942) built a recording career around her interpretations of rock ballads. Reddy's biggest hit, 'I am Woman', became a feminist anthem. She has spent nearly all of her professional life in the USA, where she attained star status. After struggling for many years as an unknown, Reddy went on to score three million-selling albums, a Grammy (for 'I am Woman') and three 'Top Female Vocalist' awards from *Billboard*, *Cashbox* and *Record World* trade magazines.

Reddy is the daughter of veteran entertainers Max Reddy and Stella Lamond. In the late 1950s, she performed on television variety shows like *Swallows Juniors* and *Helen Reddy Sings*, plus in various stage productions. In 1965, Reddy took out first prize in the *Bandstand* International contest, and a year later she travelled to New York to seek fame and fortune. The promised record company auditions did not eventuate. In 1967, on the point of return, she met and married Jeff Wald from the William Morris Agency. She issued her first single on the Philips label in 1968, 'One Way Ticket'/'Go'. Reddy and Wald moved to Los Angeles. While they attempted to get her singing career underway, Reddy studied at the University of California. An appearance on the influential *Tonight Show* (with Johnny Carson) in 1970 led to a recording contract with Capitol and a hit single with 'I Don't Know How to Love Him' from Andrew Lloyd Webber and Tim Rice's *Jesus Christ Superstar*. The single (backed with 'I Believe in Music') peaked at #13 in the US in February 1971 and #2 in Australia five months later.

Capitol issued Reddy's debut album, *I Don't Know How to Love Him* (August 1971), which yielded a second, minor hit single, 'Crazy Love'/'Our House' (June). One of the album's tracks, 'I am Woman' later became her most famous recording. She had co-written the song with fellow expatriate **Ray Burton** who was working in the USA with **The Executives**. Reddy's second album, *Helen Reddy* (November), produced one single, 'No Sad Song'/'More than You Can Take', which was a minor hit. In 1972, 'I am Woman' appeared as the theme song to Jackie Cooper's feminist feature film *Stand Up and Be Counted*. Capitol issued 'I am Woman'/ 'More than You Can Take' as a single (May 1972) and it went straight to #1. American fans embraced Reddy as a passionate spokeswoman for the feminist cause. 'I am Woman' peaked at #2 in Australia during January 1973. The album of the same name reached #9 in Australia during April. The second single from the album, 'Peaceful'/'What Would They Say?' (May) was not successful nationally, but peaked at #22 in Sydney. It also reached #12 in the US.

Long Hard Climb (August 1973) produced two massive hit singles with Alex Harvey's modern country ballad 'Delta Dawn'/'If We Could Still Be Friends' (US #1, Australian #2 in July) and the sprightly 'Leave Me Alone (Ruby Red Dress)'/ 'Don't Mess with a Woman' (US #3, Australian #1 in December). *Long Hard Climb* also reached #15 in Australia and #10 in the USA. Reddy supplemented her recording career with her own television variety shows, the *Helen Reddy Show* and *Flip Wilson Presents the Helen Reddy Show*. She undertook a successful Australian tour during November. *Love Song for Jeffrey* (March 1974) produced the singles 'Keep on Singing'/'You're My Love' (Australian #25, US #15 in May) and 'You and Me Against the World'/'Love Song for Jeffrey' (US #9, June). *Free and Easy* (October) produced another US #1 hit single with the dramatic 'Angie Baby'/'I Think I'll Write a Song' (also Australian #12 and UK #5 in January 1975). The album's second single, 'Free and Easy'/'I've Been Waiting for You So Long' (January) missed the Top 40. In December 1974, Reddy obtained her US citizenship.

Reddy's seventh album, *No Way to Treat a Lady* (June 1975), and its singles, 'Bluebird'/'You Don't Need a Reason' (US #35, June), 'Ain't No Way to Treat a Lady'/'Long Time Looking' (US #8, August) and 'Somewhere in the Night'/'Ten to Eight' (November), kept her in the public eye. In fact, she attained possibly her highest profile during 1975 with a cameo role in the feature film *Airport '75* and as compere of the popular weekly television show *Midnight Special*. Her connection with the show caused the ratings to triple. She ended the year as Top Female Pop Vocalist as voted by *Billboard*, *Cashbox* and *Record World*. By mid-1976, Reddy had sold 15 million albums and ten million singles. *Billboard* and *Record World* awarded her the honour of Top Female Album Artist for 1976. Her July 1976 album *Music Music* gave rise to the singles Goffin and King's 'I Can't Hear You No More'/'Music is My Life' (US #29, July) and 'Gladiola'/'You Make It So Easy' (October). Reddy appeared with great success in cabaret at the Las Vegas MGM Grand Hotel and Lake Tahoe, and topped the bill at the London Palladium.

Reddy's ninth album for Capitol, *Ear Candy* (April 1977), featured a revival of Cilla Black's 1964 hit 'You're My World', which became her final US Top 20 (#18) entry when issued as a single backed with 'Thank You'. The album's second single, 'Long Distance Love'/'Midnight Skies' (July 1977) was not successful. Producer/svengali Kim Fowley helped Reddy with an updated sound and image on the album. Her 1978 albums were *We'll Sing in the Sunshine* (March) and *Live in London* (December), which had been culled from her Palladium shows. That year she kept busy with her first starring film role in the Walt Disney production *Pete's Dragon* alongside Mickey Rooney. Her singles during 1978 were 'Candle on the Water'/'Brazzle Dazzle Day' (February), 'We'll Sing in the Sunshine'/'I'd Rather Be Alone' (May), 'Ready or Not'/'If I Ever Had to Say Goodbye to You' (July) and 'Mama'/'West Wind Caress' (October).

Reddy (July 1979) produced the singles 'The Magic is Still There'/'Minute by Minute' (June) and 'Make Love to Me'/'Words are Not Enough' (August), while *Take What You Find* (November 1980) included the single 'Take What You Find'/'Love's Not the Question' (June). Reddy's first album for new label MCA, *Play Me Out* (produced by Joel Diamond; June 1981), gave Reddy her second UK hit (albeit a minor one) when the single 'I Can't Say Goodbye to You'/'Let's Just Stay Home Tonight' reached #43 during November. Her second MCA album, *Take It Home*, yielded the single 'Imagination'/'Don't Tell Me Tonight' (1984). In 1983, Reddy sang the theme song 'Little Boys' to the feature film *The Man Who Loved Women*.

In the mid-1980s, Reddy returned to her theatrical roots with starring roles in US productions of Cole Porter's *Anything Goes*, Irving Berlin's *Call Me Madam*, and *The Mystery of Edwin Drood*. In January 1995, she made her Broadway debut in *Blood Brothers*, Willy Russell's long-running West End musical. Later that year, Reddy took the show back to Liverpool, its city of origin. She then toured the US in another Willy Russell play, *Shirley Valentine*. Reddy continued to tour the world with her band, performing at one point on three continents in one week. During 1996, she toured in the American premiere of an Australian stage comedy, *Love, Julie*, with Millicent Martin. At the end of the year, Reddy made her debut at New York City's premier cabaret venue, Rainbow and Stars, with a four-week engagement.

Along with her world travels, Reddy issued a new album, *When I Dream*, in 1996. Active in community affairs, Reddy served for three years as Commissioner for Parks and Recreation for the State of California. Of the many honours she has received, Reddy is most proud of the tulip named for her in Holland and she grows the reddish-violet bulbs in her garden in Santa Monica, California. Despite all her other efforts over the years, 'I am Woman' continues to be Reddy's defining moment. She performed the song in 1995 on the *Late Show with David Letterman*, and again during the opening General Assembly of the Feminist Expo '96 for Woman's Empowerment held in Washington, DC.

Albums: *I Don't Know How to Love Him* (EMI/Capitol, 1971), *Helen Reddy* (EMI/Capitol, 1972), *I am Woman* (EMI/Capitol, 1972), *Long Hard Climb* (EMI/Capitol, 1973), *Love Song for Jeffrey* (EMI/Capitol, 1974), *Free and Easy* (EMI/Capitol, 1974), *No Way to Treat a Lady* (EMI/Capitol, 1975), *Greatest Hits* (EMI/Capitol, 1975), *Music Music* (EMI/Capitol, 1976), *Ear Candy* (EMI/Capitol, 1977), *We'll Sing in the Sunshine* (EMI/Capitol, 1978), *Live in London* (EMI/Capitol, 1978), *Reddy* (EMI/Capitol, 1979), *Take What You Find* (EMI/Capitol, 1980), *Play Me Out* (MCA, 1981), *Take It Home* (MCA, 1984), *Helen Reddy Greatest Hits (and More)* (EMI/Capitol, 1987), *Feel So Young* (Helen Reddy Inc, 1991), *That's All* (Helen Reddy Inc, 1991), *The Best of Helen Reddy* (EMI/Capitol, 1991), *When I Dream* (Varese Sarabande/MCA, 1996).

Jamie Redfern

Style: *Pop*

Over a three-year period during the early 1970s, child star Jamie Redfern (b. 1957) scored four Top 40 hit singles and sold more than $1.3 million worth of records. Redfern made early appearances on the television shows *Brian and the Juniors*, *Happening '70* and *Happening '71*, before establishing himself as a popular team member on the O-Ten Network's *Young Talent Time*.

Redfern possessed a booming, mature voice which belied his tender age of 14 years. *Young Talent Time* compere **Johnny Young** helped foster Redfern's burgeoning career as a solo artist. Redfern signed to Festival Records and issued his debut single, 'Little White Cloud', at the end of 1971. At the end of the year, he won the Most Outstanding Newcomer Award at the *TV Week* King of Pop ceremony. American entertainer Liberace took Redfern under his wing, which led to the youngster's first American tour in 1972. Redfern's second single, 'When You Wish Upon a Star' (from *The Wizard of Oz*), reached #31 on the national chart in February 1972. The album of the same name peaked at #12 that same month. His second album, *Sitting on Top of the World*, reached #16 in January 1973, and produced the single 'Rainbow on the River'/'We'll Meet Again' (#8 in November 1972). Redfern returned to the US to tour with Liberace for a second time in early 1973.

His hits for 1973 were a revival of Frankie Avalon's 'Venus' (#8 in June) and 'Hello Funny Face' (September). In early 1974, Redfern's third album, *Hitch a Ride on a Smile*, produced his fourth hit single, 'Hitch a Ride on a Smile' (#28 in March). Redfern took the song into the finals of the World Popular Song Festival held in Tokyo. He topped off a successful 1974 by taking out the King of Pop Award ahead of the likes of **Johnny Farnham** and **Daryl Braithwaite**. Following the release of the single 'Jenny' (October 1974) and the album *Jamie Redfern's Golden Hits* during 1975, Redfern slipped from view. By that stage his younger brother Derek had also entered the entertainment world as a member of the Young Talent Team.

Albums: *When You Wish Upon a Star* (Festival, 1971), *Sitting on Top of the World* (Festival, 1972), *Hitch a Ride on a Smile* (Festival, 1974), *Jamie Redfern's Golden Hits* (Festival, 1975).

Redgum

Formed: *1975*
Style: *Folk*
Original line-up: *John Schumann (vocals, guitar), Verity Truman (flute, sax, tin whistle, vocals), Michael Atkinson (vocals, guitar, mandolin), Chris Timms (violin)*

Aside from **Midnight Oil**, few Australian bands of the 1980s could boast such a fiercely outspoken, passionate and jingoistic outlook as that of Redgum. The band's brand of agit-folk pop earned an enormous following, but it also raised the ire of a few movers and shakers in the music industry. For example, Redgum was allegedly kicked off Willie Nelson's Australian tour for being 'too political'. Often criticised for being self-righteous, Redgum nevertheless campaigned long and hard on behalf of Vietnam War veterans, Aboriginal land rights and the unemployed. The band also attacked American ownership of Australian land, as well as railing against corrupt politicians and all manner of capitalism.

The four original members of Redgum met while studying at Adelaide's Flinders University in South Australia. The band worked on a semi-professional basis right through until 1980. Usually acoustic, though sometimes electric, Redgum used a number of musicians for its rhythm section during the late 1970s, including Dave Flett (bass; ex-**Captain Matchbox Whoopee Band**), Tom Stehlic (drums), Chris Boath (bass), Gordon McLean (drums), Geoff Gifford (drums) and Russ Coleman (drums; ex-**Tinsley Waterhouse Band**). Redgum issued its debut album, *If You Don't Fight You Lose*, on the Larrikin label in March 1978.

CBS/Epic reissued the album in September 1981 following the band's move to that label. Redgum's first album for Epic, *Virgin Ground*, produced the single 'Long Run'/'Little Hampton' (January 1981). The band's third album, *Brown Rice and Kerosene*, included the single '100 Years On'/ 'Nuclear Cop' (November). The *Redgum Songbook: Stubborn Words, Flagrant Vices* was also published in 1981. In May 1982, long-serving member Chris Timms left the band to be replaced by Hugh McDonald (violin, guitar, vocals; ex-Banshee, **Bushwackers**). The 12-inch EP *Cut to the Quick* (September 1982) contained four tracks, 'Working Girls', 'Fabulon', 'The Diamantina Drover' and 'Where Ya Gonna Run To?'.

By 1983, Redgum had reached the premier league, and was one of the biggest crowd-pulling bands on the Australian scene. The live album *Caught in the Act* (June 1983) produced the Australian classic 'I Was Only 19 (A Walk in the Light Green)'. When issued as a single in March, backed with 'Yarralumla Wine', the deeply emotional 'I Was Only 19' (about the effects of the Vietnam War) reached #1 and stayed in the Top 40 for four months. *Caught in the Act* hit #3 on the national chart, and produced two further singles, 'Long Run'/'Fabulon' (August) and 'Caught in the Act'/'Stewie', 'Lear Jets Over Kulgera' which had been included with the album as a bonus, limited edition 7-inch EP. Former folk musician **Trevor Lucas** (ex-Fairport Convention) produced *Caught in the Act*. Redgum had been performing the Lucas-penned song 'The Ballad of Ned Kelly' (under the adoptive title 'Poor Ned') for many years. The members of Redgum had always assumed the song was a traditional Australian bush ballad, until Lucas set them straight on that score.

By 1984, the Redgum line-up comprised Schumann, Truman, Atkinson, McDonald, Stephen Cooney (bass, didgeridoo, mandolin, banjo), Michael Spicer (piano) and Brian Czempinski (drums). Redgum's fifth album, *Frontline* (August 1984), produced the satirical hit single 'I've Been to Bali Too'/'Still Life' (#16 in March 1984). Two further singles were lifted from the album, 'Friday Night'/'Last Frontier' (May) and 'ASIO'/'Hira' (August). Redgum issued two singles in 1985, the topical 'Drover's Dog'/'It Doesn't Matter to Me' (#20 in May) and 'Just Another Moment on Your Own'/'Kerang' (September), plus the compilation album *Redgum's Greatest (Everything's Legal Anything Goes)* (November).

In 1985, Redgum made its first tentative foray on to the international market when CBS issued 'I Was Only 19 (A Walk in the Light Green)' in the UK. Unfortunately, the song was virtually ignored. English producer Paul Hardcastle had just reached #1 with the single 'Nineteen', which explored a similar theme, albeit in a far more brow-beating, confrontational manner. The UK press accused Redgum of ripping off the idea and the single sank without a trace.

At the end of 1985, co-founder John Schumann surprised fans by leaving the band. He signed to CBS as a solo singer, which resulted in the album *Etched in Blue* (November 1987) and its singles 'Borrowed Ground'/'Borrowed Ground' (August), 'Holy Mary'/'Coming Home' (October) and 'Safe Behind the Wire'/'He's Got the Money' (March 1988). Schumann's touring band included Mal Logan (keyboards; ex-**Healing Force**, **Renée Geyer** Band), Louis McManus (guitar, violin; ex-**Bushwackers**), David Dharamaesena (bass), Mark Peters (drums) and a trio of backing vocalists Deborah Paul, Melinda Pike and Nicky Schultz known as The Debettes. In 1989, Schumann produced a children's record, *Looby Loo*, for CBS. In September 1992 he issued the CD single 'Eyes on Fire' on Sony.

In the meantime, Truman, Atkinson, McDonald and Spicer continued on as Redgum, issuing the album *Midnight Sun* (October 1986), which yielded the single 'Running with the Hurricane'/'A Street to Die' (November). Redgum's final single was the pro-safe sex 'Roll It on Robbie'/'Empty Page', which reached #34 in May 1987. Michael Atkinson left Redgum in 1987, which precipitated the band's break-up soon after.

Albums: *If You Don't Fight You Lose* (Larrikin, 1978; reissued on CBS/Epic, 1981), *Virgin Ground* (CBS/Epic, 1980), *Brown Rice and Kerosine* (CBS/Epic, 1981), *Caught in the Act* (CBS/Epic, 1983), *Frontline* (CBS, 1984), *Redgum's Greatest (Everything's Legal Anything Goes)* (CBS/Epic, 1985), *Midnight Sun* (CBS, 1986), *Very Best of Redgum* (J&B, 1988); ***John Schumann solo albums:*** *Etched in Blue* (CBS, 1988), *Looby Loo* (CBS, 1989).

Redhouse

Formed: *1972*
Style: *Hard rock*
Original line-up: *John Ferguson (vocals), Malcolm Donnelly (guitar), Jack Green (bass), Claude Ragone (drums)*

Originally formed as Redhouse Roll Band, Geelong (Victoria) quartet Redhouse was that city's premier rock attraction during the mid-1970s. Redhouse Roll Band presented a very theatrical stage show (akin to American shock-rock pioneer Alice Cooper), which involved the band members dressing up in skeleton suits or Superman outfits.

In 1973, the band signed a deal with Atlantic which resulted in the single 'Oh! Lucky Man'/'Movin' On' (December). Taken from the British feature film of the same name, Redhouse Roll Band's version of Alan Price's 'Oh! Lucky Man' became a regional hit. Redhouse Roll Band went into hibernation in 1974, re-emerging in late 1975 as Redhouse, with a completely revamped line-up comprising Green, John Dallimore (lead guitar, vocals), Jacques De Jongh (rhythm guitar, vocals; ex-Shadowfax) and Gary Crothall (drums).

Redhouse built-up a strong following on the Melbourne pub circuit as a hard-working heavy rock group. In July 1976, De Jongh left the band to join **Hush**. Graham Matters (vocals) and Garry Quince (rhythm guitar, keyboards) took his place. Matters had already worked as an actor. He took the dual role of Wally/The Wizard in Chris Löfven's debut feature film *Oz*, which was an Australian adaptation of the *Wizard of Oz* storyline. Matters appeared on the soundtrack singing two contrasting versions of **The Missing Links'** proto-punk chestnut 'You're Driving Me Insane'. He had also played the part of Rocky in the Australian cast production of *The Rocky Horror Show*.

In September, Redhouse entered the studio with producer Gus McNeil (ex-**Nomads**) to record its debut album, *One More Squeeze*. The album failed to reflect the band's on-stage energy, presenting instead a lightweight guitar-pop sound. The album produced the singles 'I Like Dancing'/'Hot Feet' (October 1976) and 'Who's Foolin' Who?'/'I'm Just' (February 1977). 'I Like Dancing' peaked at #17 in

Melbourne during December 1976. In March 1977, Quince left to join **Finch**. Robin Riley (ex-Lois Lane) came in as his replacement.

Redhouse issued a third single, 'Thank You'/'Snap Shot' (August 1977), before Matters left to join the cast of the stage musical *A Chorus Line*. Riley left in October, and De Jongh returned briefly while **Hush** was off the road. In December, long-serving bass player Jack Green took over the band's management and Redhouse re-formed with a new line-up of Dallimore, Gary Crothall, Gary's brother Rick Crothall (bass) and Joey Amenta (lead guitar; ex-**Taste**). In March 1978, Amenta left to join the **Russell Morris** Band (before joining **Wendy and the Rocketts** and **Dear Enemy**). Redhouse continued on as a three-piece for a few months before calling it quits. In late 1978, John Dallimore and Rick Crothall formed a new band called Dallimore which comprised Robin Riley and John Lalor (drums). Dallimore was a loud, heavy rock band in the **AC/DC** and **Rose Tattoo** tradition.

Dallimore contributed two tracks, 'Heartbreaker' and 'Long Distance Frog', to the live, Various Artists album *Canned Rock* (on the Albert label) which had been recorded at Parramatta Gaol. The band issued one single on Albert, 'We Are the Kids'/'Women Together' (August 1980) and then recorded an album which never saw the light of day. The band broke up at the end of 1980. Dallimore was a talented player, and he went on to work with **Wendy and the Rocketts**, The Foster Brothers (**Jon English's** touring band during the mid-1980s), Dave Evan's Thunder Down Under, Temple of Boom, the **Brian Cadd/Max Merritt** Band and the revived **Max Merritt and the Meteors** circa 1996. Rob Riley worked with **Rose Tattoo**, **The Party Boys**, Beast, the **Jimmy Barnes** Band, The Mega Boys, Mama's Darlings, the **Angry Anderson** Band and many others.

Album: *One More Squeeze* (EMI, 1976).

The Reels

Formed: *1977*
Style: *Pop*
Original line-up: *Dave Mason (vocals), Craig Hooper (guitar, keyboards), Colin 'Polly' Newham (keyboards, sax, guitar), Paul Abrahams (bass), John Bliss (drums; ex-Thundaband)*

Originally formed in the NSW provincial city of Dubbo as Native Sons and then The Brucelanders, The Reels were one of the most original and invigorating pop bands to emerge from the Australian new wave movement of the late 1970s. Initially the band's music was almost entirely rhythm oriented, a mix of simple and contagious pop tunes (with a dark twist at times), capped off by Dave Mason's manic, clipped vocals. The band's influences ranged from English pop (XTC) and ska (Specials, Madness) to US eccentrics Devo. Gradually, the band's music took on a slower, more melancholy demeanour without losing its appeal.

The Reels moved to Sydney in late 1978. Never readily accepted by Sydney audiences more accustomed to the **Angels/Cold Chisel/Radio Birdman** style of rock, The Reels nevertheless managed to score mainstream chart success. The band's debut single for Mercury/PolyGram, 'Love will Find a Way'/'Spot the Ridge' (October 1979), peaked at #39 in January 1980. The band's Mark Opitz-produced debut album *The Reels* was full of neurotic, nervous energy and bouncy, quirky and snapping rhythms. The album's second single, 'Prefab Hearts'/'Misused Abused' (February 1980), made for a bright coupling. Karen Ansel (ex-Romantics) joined the same month on keyboards.

By that stage, the band had dispensed with all guitars in favour of a four-synthesiser (Abrahams played bass synth) and drums line-up. The Reels had also begun to replace the faster, uptempo songs with a slower, more textured sound. The new sound was first heard on the single 'After the News'/'Media Themes: Rupert Murdoch, Smokey Dawson, Ohira Tour' (July 1980) and the 12-inch EP *Five Great Gift Ideas from The Reels* (November). The EP was the band's contribution to Christmas and its most impressive cuts were covers of Jim Reeves' 1961 country song 'According to My Heart' and Freda Payne's 'Band of Gold'. During late July, 1980 the band had embarked on its ambitious The Reels by Rail tour of the eastern states.

At the end of the year, The Reels recorded their second album. Newham left the band in March 1981, the same month that the soulful single 'Shout and Deliver'/'Depression' appeared. *Quasimodo's Dream* (May 1981; #31 in June) was one of the best albums of the year, and it remains a major work in Australian pop music. Alongside previous singles cuts, 'After the News', 'According to My Heart' and 'Shout and Deliver', the album's highlight was the sparse, evocative title track. 'Quasimodo's Dream'/'Love is Here Today' also came out as a single in May. **Kate Ceberano** later included a gorgeous rendition of 'Quasimodo's Dream' on her celebrated debut solo album *Brave* (1989).

The album cut 'Kitchen Man' lent its name to The Reels' Kitchen Man tour to promote the album, which saw the stage set up like a kitchen with all the attendant trappings. The band's final release on

Mercury was the single 'No. 3'/'1, 2, 3', 'Haunted' (November 1981). In early 1982, The Reels underwent a total line-up change. Abrahams, Bliss and Ansell all left, and Mason and Hooper recruited new drummer Stefan Fidock (ex-Romantics). Abrahams and Bliss joined **The Numbers.** Ansell issued a solo single on Mushroom, 'No Commotion'/'Casa' (April 1983). She later worked in computer animation; she was one of the team of animators on the 1994 Jim Carrey feature film *The Mask*.

With significant help from the new Fairlight computer synthesiser, The Reels recorded the *Beautiful* album. Issued in October 1982 on the K-Tel label (through RCA), *Beautiful* was an entertaining diversion featuring a bevy of easy-listening, non-original love songs. It peaked at #29 on the national chart and within six months it had sold over 40 000 copies. The album produced the singles Burt Bacharach/Hal David's 'This Guy's (in Love with You)'/'Cry' (#7 in November 1982) and The 5th Dimension's 'Last Night (I Didn't Get to Sleep at All)'/'Silence is Golden' (February 1983).

In July 1983, The Reels travelled to Los Angeles and then to London. The five-track, 12-inch EP *Pitt Street Farmers* came out in September, as did the single 'Happiness'/'La Mer'. RCA issued The Reels' compilation album *Unreel* in October. The band ended 1983 with the release of the single 'Quasimodo's Dream 1983'/'Quasimodo's Dream 1980' (December). Illness forced Mason to retire from music, and to all intents and purposes that was the end of The Reels. Hooper joined **The Church** as an auxiliary member, contributing keyboards to that band's excellent 1984 mini-album *Persia*. By early 1985 he had joined Neil Finn's new band The Mullanes, but left before Finn adopted the new moniker of **Crowded House**.

By August 1985, Mason had recovered from his bout of hepatitis, and he and Hooper revived The Reels with original members John Bliss and Polly Newham. RCA ended its Reels account with a final single, 'It Must Be Love'/'My Family', in October 1985. The band's first single for new label Regular was a rearranged and radically slowed gospel rendition of Creedence Clearwater Revival's 'Bad Moon Rising'/'World's End', which reached #11 on the national chart during October 1986. Bliss left again at the end of the year and the band was down to a trio of Mason, Hooper and Newham.

Regular issued a new Reels single, a chirpy cover of Edison Lighthouse's 'Love Grows (Where My Rosemary Goes)'/'Media Themes II', in January 1987. That year The Reels instigated their Reels by Request tour with patrons calling out for the songs they wanted the band to play. In October, The Reels took the concept a little further by doing an All Australian Reels by Request tour. That concept further manifested itself with the band's first studio album in six years. *Neighbors* (November 1988) was a collection of 13 cover versions of Australian pop songs given The Reels treatment. Hence The Reels transposed **Jimmy Barnes'** macho 'Working Class Man' into a waltz with a folksy, accordion-based feel, **Dragon's** 'Are You Old Enough?' into reggae/muzak, **Cold Chisel's** 'Forever Now' into a country jaunt and **INXS**'s 'Original Sin' into a soulful ballad. The album produced the singles 'Forever Now'/'Borderless' (October 1988) and 'Are You Old Enough?'/'What's My Scene?' (February 1989). Steve Prestwich, who penned 'Forever Now', played drums on The Reels version.

At the end of 1989, Mason appeared in the Australian feature film *Ghosts . . . of the Civil Dead*. The film was set in the fictional Central Industrial Prison, and Mason played the prison queen Lilly while co-star **Nick Cave** appeared as the psychotic inmate Maynard. In September 1991, The Reels issued their first original single in five years, 'I Don't Love You Anymore', which also featured a capella and dance mixes. In November 1992, The Reels issued 'Bad Moon Rising' (Filthy Lucre Mix) as a CD single. The song had been re-mixed by the same team (Gavin Campbell and Robert Goodge) who turned **Yothu Yindi's** 'Treaty' into an epochal dance hit. The song also appeared on the 15-track 'Best of' set *Requiem* (December 1992), which coincided with the band's dissolution. Dave Mason is the son of one-time leader of the New South Wales Liberal Party John Mason.

Albums: *The Reels* (Mercury/PolyGram, 1979), *Quasimodo's Dream* (Mercury/PolyGram, 1981), *Beautiful* (K-Tel/RCA, 1982), *Pitt Street Farmers* (mini-album, RCA, 1983), *Unreel* (RCA, 1983), *Neighbors* (Regular/Festival, 1988), *Requiem* (Regular/Festival, 1992).

Regurgitator

Formed: *1993*
Style: *Rock/funk/hip-hop fusion*
Original line-up: *Quan Yeomans (guitar, bass, vocals), Benjamin Ely (bass, guitar, vocals; from Pangaea), Martin Lee (drums; ex-Brasilia)*

Alongside the likes of **You Am I, silverchair, Powderfinger** and **Spiderbait**, Brisbane outfit Regurgitator was part of a new breed of young bands that translated a fierce live reputation into respectable record sales. All five bands boasted best-selling albums and a following among local

Regurgitator

youth that would be the envy of many more established acts. Described as a cross between The Beastie Boys, Primus and any snotty punk band you care to mention, Regurgitator's appeal lay in an irreverent sense of humour and a willingness to mix and match styles (no musical genre was too sacred to plunder). And, of course, there was Quan Yeomans' penchant for donning a pink frock for live appearances.

Regurgitator formed in December 1993 when Yeomans teamed up with Benjamin Ely and Martin Lee. The band emerged out of the same scene that gave rise to **Powderfinger**, **Custard** and **Screamfeeder**. Music promoter Paul Curtis sent a Regurgitator demo tape to Warner Music, which signed the band immediately. The band's eponymous debut EP came out at the end of 1994. National youth radio network Triple J placed the track 'Like It Like That' on high rotation, resulting in a national alternative #1 hit for the band. 'Like It Like That' was four minutes of hip-hop percussion, metallic riffs, a catchy chorus and humorous lyrics.

Following a starring role on the 1995 Big Day Out tour, the band consolidated its success with the *New* CD EP (July 1995). The EP's featured track, 'Blubber Boy' mixed infectious pop with downright eccentric lyrics (a lonely Eskimo widow rubs the whale blubber likeness of her dead husband on his genitals to bring him back to life). *New* also made #1 on the alternative charts. In between touring Europe with Filter and Japan with Quicksand and another slot on the 1996 Big Day Out tour, Regurgitator found time to record its ambitious debut album, *Tu-Plang* (Thai for jukebox), in Bangkok.

The album was preceded by the bizarre 'F.S.O. (Fuck Shit Off)' single (March 1996) and another alternative #1 hit in the nifty funk/metal single 'Kong Foo Sing' (May). The release of *Tu-Plang* in May coincided with the band's support slot on US band Red Hot Chili Peppers' Australian tour. In combining fuzzed-out pop ('Rinsing', 'I Sucked a Lot of Cock to Get Where I Am') and hardcore ('F.S.O.') with hip-hop beats ('G7 Dick Electro Boogie') and surf instrumentals ('348 Hz'), Regurgitator delivered an album buzzing with creative potential. *Tu-Plang* peaked in the mainstream Top 10 during June, stayed in the Top 50 for 30 weeks and went on to achieve platinum status (70 000 copies sold). The third CD single lifted from the album, 'Miffy's Simplicity', came out in September.

Regurgitator concluded a successful 1996 by winning Best Alternative Release and Best Debut Album at the Australian Record Industry Association (ARIA) Awards, and by undertaking a second Japanese tour with local hardcore heroes Boredoms. Also, 'I Sucked a Lot of Cock to Get Where I Am' and 'Kong Foo Sing' were placed at #23 and #15 respectively on the 1996 Triple J Hottest 100 list. The band's second album, *Unit*, came out in November 1997. It made #7 on the national album listing. The CD single 'Everyday Formula' preceded the album's release a month earlier.

In between commitments to Regurgitator, Benjamin Ely has found time to work with his other band, Pangaea. Jim Sinclair (guitar), Paul Bromley (guitar) and Dave Atkins (drums) completed the line-up. Although not that dissimilar to Regurgitator in style, Pangaea traversed a more hardcore aesthetic. Pangaea's contemporaries on the Brisbane underground scene included Emporium, Elevation, Isis, Bulldozer, Shock Fungus and The Toothfaeries. Pangaea's releases have included the CD EPs *Serpent Fire* (September 1993), *Raggacore* (December 1994) and *Smile* (January 1997), the CD single 'Boys' (May) plus the full-length debut album *Freibentos* (July 1997).

Regurgitator albums: *Tu-Plang* (Warner, 1996), *Unit* (Warner, 1997); ***Pangaea album:*** *Freibentos* (Valve/East West/Warner, 1997).

Renegade Funktrain

Formed: *1994*
Style: *Hip hop, funk, rap*
Original line-up: *Rosano Martinez (rapper; ex-West Side Posse, Sound Unlimited), Tina Martinez (rapper, keyboards; ex-Sound Unlimited), Dereck Antunes (keyboards, rapper, programming, drums; ex-Slamm' Antunes), Brian 'DJ A.S.K.' Patrick (turntable scratching; ex-West Side Posse), Ramesh Sathiah (keyboards), Juan Gonzalez (guitar, rapper), Adam Dehnen (bass)*

Australia's premier groove band of the mid-1990s, Renegade Funktrain, presented a melting pot of soul, funk, hip hop, jazz and rap elements. Rosano Martinez and Brian 'DJ A.S.K.' Patrick began their association during the mid-1980s in notorious Sydney hip-hop outfit West Side Posse. Coming from multicultural backgrounds (Martinez was of Spanish descent) and influenced by American hip hop and rap, the group was one of the first in Australia to embrace overseas dance trends of the day.

Martinez's association with music went back further. He was a breakdancer with the United Break Team which supported the New York hip-hop group Rock Steady Crew on its 1984 Australian tour. In 1989, Martinez (aka 'El Assassin') formed dance/hip hop/pop outfit Sound Unlimited Posse with Vladimir 'DJ B.L.T.' Cherapanoff (ex-Digits) and rapper Alan 'Kode Blue'. CBS issued the group's debut single, 'Peace by Piece'/'Suicide', in 1990. That year, Sound Unlimited Posse supported overseas visitors Public Enemy, De La Soul and New Kids on the Block on their respective Australian tours. With the arrival of Martinez's younger sister Tina, the group adopted the shortened moniker of Sound Unlimited. Sony/Columbia then signed the band for the 12-inch EP 'Unity'/'Paradise Lost' (#36 in August 1991), the single 'Kickin' to the Undersound' (#19 in April 1992), and the album *A Postcard from the Edge of the Under-Side* (March 1993) which yielded the singles 'Saturday Night' (October 1992) and 'One More from the City' (#22 in April 1993). 'Kickin' to the Undersound' sampled **Daddy Cool's** 'Eagle Rock' and **Men at Work's** 'Downunder'.

Sound Unlimited was the proud owner of the first major release of an Australian rap album. With a dearth of appropriate local producers, Sound Unlimited had travelled to Boston to record the album with the American production team Slamm' Antunes. In early 1992, Sound Unlimited supported US visitors The Beastie Boys, Ice-T and Public Enemy on Australian tours. With the success of the group's singles, Rosano got involved in production for a number of dance acts like **Rockmelons**, the Magnificent Seven and New Zealand singer Mark Williams. Tina Martinez married the group's American producer Dereck Antunes, and by 1994 Sound Unlimited had transformed into Renegade Funktrain. In 1995, the group recorded its debut album. The CD single 'Testify' appeared, but then Renegade Funktrain had to wait nearly a year for the release of its second CD single 'Renegade Funktrain'/'I Wonder'.

The band had built 'I Wonder' around samples from the Boz Scaggs song 'Lowdown' and the American singer was reluctant to clear its use. Eventually, he relented (the group wrote him a personal letter) and 'Renegade Funktrain'/'I Wonder' reached #49 on the national chart in March 1996. The *Renegade Funktrain* album came out a month later to a positive response.

Renegade Funktrain

Sound Unlimited album: *A Postcard from the Edge of the Under-Side* (Sony/Columbia, 1993); ***Renegade Funktrain album:*** *Renegade Funktrain* (East West/Warner, 1996).

The Revelators (*see* The Black Sorrows)

Digger Revell (*see* The Denvermen)

James Reyne

Style: *Rock*

Singer/songwriter James Reyne (b. 1957) first came to public attention as frontman for popular rock band **Australian Crawl**. As the charismatic larrikin with the good looks, acerbic wit, nonchalant demeanour and idiosyncratic, clipped vocal style fronting a bunch of guitar slinging surfers, Reyne made quite an impact on the Australian music psyche. As well as his seven-year tenure with the Crawl, Reyne moonlighted with covers bands **The Party Boys** and Rocking Love Gods.

In 1983, he starred with Rebecca Gilling and Wendy Hughes in the television miniseries *Return to Eden* which was screened in September 1983. Reyne appeared in the role of playboy tennis professional Greg Marsden, and later declared he was not very good in the part, declining many acting offers since. His other acting roles to date include the part of Australian manager Roger Davies in the US telemovie *Tina* based on the life of singer Tina Turner, and in the drama series *State Coroner*. In April 1985, he issued a duet single, 'R.O.C.K.'/ 'Under My Thumb', with **Electric Pandas'** Lin Buckfield.

Three months after the break-up of **Australian Crawl** in January 1986, Reyne travelled to Los Angeles in search of an American deal. He spent the next 12 months in limbo before expatriate Australian Roger Davies (former manager of **Sherbet** and then handler for Tina Turner and **Olivia Newton-John**) put him in contact with Capitol Records and producer Davitt Sigerson (David and David). Reyne's debut solo album, *James Reyne*, boasted state-of-the-art American production values, and the cream of LA session players like Jesse Ed Davis, David Lindley and Billy Payne. Newton-John contributed backing vocals to the anti-drug song 'Hammerhead'. Reyne's core band on the album sessions comprised American Jef Scott (guitar), David Faragher (keyboards) and former Crawl drummer John Watson.

James Reyne (September 1987) reached the national Top 5 (#4) and sold over 210 000 copies (triple platinum). It yielded five singles, including three Top 10 hits, 'Fall of Rome'/'Traveller' (#3 in August 1987), 'Hammerhead'/'Coin in a Plate' (#6 in October) and 'Motor's Too Fast' (with three live cuts, 'Counting on Me', 'Mr Sandman' and 'Heaven on a Stick') (#7 in July 1988). 'Rip It Up'/'Love will Find a Way' (November 1987) also reached #21 in January 1988, while 'Heaven on a Stick'/'Submarines' (February) went Top 40. Reyne's newly formed touring band at that stage comprised Scott, Brett Kingman (guitar, ex-**Uncanny X-Men**), Simon Hussey (keyboards), Andy Cichon (bass; ex-**Rose Tattoo**) and John Watson (drums; ex-**Australian Crawl, Kevin Borich Express**). Following the national Rip It Up tour of December 1987, Reyne supported Tina Turner on her February 1988 Australian tour. Capitol issued *James Reyne* in Europe and the USA, and the singer toured those territories.

Reyne recorded his second album, *Hard Reyne*, in London with producer/mixer John Hudson. The album continued his collaboration with brother-in-law Simon Hussey, who also co-wrote a number of the songs on Reyne's debut. Hussey was known for his production work on **Daryl Braithwaite's** breakthrough debut album, *Edge*. Issued in June 1989, *Hard Reyne* was a strong, diverse rock album and repeated the success of the debut album. It reached #4, and produced the singles 'House of Cards'/ 'Walking in the Dreamtime' (#11 in June 1989), 'One More River'/'Jim Dandy' (#22 in August), 'Trouble in Paradise'/'I'm an Old Cow Hand' (October) and 'Harvest Moon'/'Five Miles Closer to the Sun' (December). Reyne embarked on a national tour (June/July 1989) with a new James Reyne Band line-up comprising Kingman, Cichon and Watson, plus Americans James Ralston (guitar, vocals; ex-Tina Turner Band) and Ollie Marland (keyboards; ex-Tina Turner Band).

Reyne was quiet for over a year before emerging in June 1991 with a new deal through Virgin and a new album, *Electric Digger Dandy*. With its colloquial pun on the Jimi Hendrix appellation 'Electric Nigger Dandy', the album was Reyne's most eclectic collection to date. It mixed the usual sophisticated guitar rock with pop, country and swamp influences (Reyne co-wrote 'Outback Woman' with American swamp king Tony Joe White). The album made its debut on the national chart at #2, and its first single, 'Slave' (co-written with Jim Vallance), peaked at #10 the same week. The next two singles, 'Any Day Above Ground' (July) and 'Some People' (September), were not successful.

One of the album's tracks, 'Company of Strangers', lent its name to a studio collaboration between Simon Hussey, Jef Scott, **Daryl Braithwaite** and James Reyne. Hussey and Scott recorded an album in December 1991 with assistance from Reyne and Braithwaite in between their own career commitments. Sony issued *Company of Strangers* in August 1992. The album contained commercial pop rock and produced the singles 'Sweet Love' (June 1992), 'Motor City (I Get Lost)' (October), 'Daddy's Gonna Make You a Star' (January 1993) and The Beatles' 'Baby You're a Rich Man' (June 1993).

In 1992, Reyne collaborated with Australian country idol James Blundell on a cover of **The Dingoes'** classic 'Way Out West'. The song appeared on Blundell's third album, *This Road*, and when issued as a single (backed with Don Walker's 'Long Yard Rider') it reached #2 on the national chart (April). To further the country connection, the James Reyne Band played the 1992 Tamworth Country Music Festival to a positive response. Reyne's backing band at that stage included guitarists Brett Goldsmith (ex-**Chantoozies**) and Paul Gildae (guitar), plus Lee Borkman (keyboards).

In 1994, Reyne signed a new deal with rooArt, and during April returned to Los Angeles to commence work on his fourth solo album, *The Whiff of Bedlam*, with high-profile producer Stuart Levine (Anita Baker, Simply Red, B.B. King). Reyne described the album as more focused and laid-back than *Electric Digger Dandy*. Indeed, the songs were based heavily around the keyboard work of former Al Jarreau sideman Neil Larsen in favour of the gritty guitar rock of Reyne's previous efforts. The album's first single, 'Red Light Avenue', reached #32 in October 1994. The next two singles, 'Day in the Sun' and 'It's Only Natural', were not successful. Reyne slipped from view again, re-emerging in May 1996 with the album *Live in Rio*.

Albums: *James Reyne* (EMI/Capitol, 1987), *Hard Reyne* (EMI/Capitol, 1989), *Electric Digger Dandy* (Virgin/EMI, 1991), *The Best* (Virgin/EMI, 1992), *The Whiff of Bedlam* (rooArt/Warner, 1994), *Live in Rio* (rooArt/Warner, 1996).

Marty Rhone

Style: *Beat pop*

In the hurly-burly world of Australian popdom circa 1966, the big names were **Billy Thorpe**, **Normie Rowe**, **Ray Brown**, **Merv Benton** and **Ronnie Burns**. One of the up and coming young hopefuls in the pop star stakes was a shy, slight guy of Dutch-Indonesian descent by the name of Marty Rhone (b. 1948). Born Carl Van Rhoon, Rhone had scored a contract with Nat Kipner's Spin label which issued his debut solo single 'Nature Boy'/'Every Minute of You' in February 1966.

The Spin roster at that time boasted **Steve & the Board**, **The Bee Gees**, **Tony Barber**, **Ronnie Burns**, **Jeff St John** and the Id and Janice Slater. For his next single, Rhone teamed up with respected beat-pop band The Soul Agents, who comprised John Green (guitar), Barry Kelly (organ), Jerry Darmick (bass) and Roger Felice-Andrews (drums). Marty Van Wynk (ex-**Throb**) later replaced Green on guitar. Marty Rhone and the Soul Agents issued two singles on Spin 'Thirteen Women'/'I Can Tell' (April 1966) and 'I Want You Back Again'/'What More Can I Do?' (June).

Rhone's fourth single, 'She is Mine'/'Village Tapestry' (September) appeared simply under his own name. None of the singles was commercially successful, although the self-penned 'Village Tapestry', in particular, is highly regarded among 1960s aficionados. The Soul Agents issued their own single, 'I Just Want to Make Love to You'/'I'm Still Mad at You' on the Downunder label around the time 'She is Mine' appeared. Rhone continued to record for Spin up to 1970 with limited success: 'No No No No'/'Tell Me Love' (July 1967), 'Green Mansions'/'Lonely Too Long' (November), 'She's Coming Home'/'Hurray Poor Working Man' (March 1968), 'Ruby with the Red Hair'/'Appeal' (July 1969) and 'So You Want to Be a Pop Singer?'/'As the Sun Goes Down' (March 1970).

At that point, Rhone was called up for national service. On his release in 1972, he enrolled in the Conservatorium of Music on a government grant for two years of study. In July 1973, he issued his first solo single in over three years, 'Goodbye in May'/'115 Sweet', on the Spiral label. In late 1974, he turned his hand to acting, taking roles in the stage play *Godspell* and the television soapies *Number 96* and *Class of '75*. In mid-1975 he revived his singing career when he signed to the M7 label. His debut single for M7, 'Denim and Lace'/'Take Me' (July), became a massive hit, peaking at #2 on the national chart on its way to becoming the second biggest selling single for the year. His next four singles, 'Star Song'/'Little Miss Demeanour' (February 1976), 'Take Away'/'Instant Coffee, Instant Tea' (July), 'Things We Did Last Night'/'Dial a Dream' (September) and 'On the Loose Again'/'You Can't Have Me' (November) were not chart hits.

The Brian Dawe/Steve Groves-penned 'On the Loose Again', however, was successful on another level. 'On the Loose Again' was the winning entry in the 1976 Australian Popular Song Festival. At the Tokyo Song Festival, the song took out the Best Song award and Rhone scored the Most Outstanding Performance prize. Rhone ended his Australian pop career with one final hit in 1977, the funky 'Mean Pair of Jeans'/'I'm Gone Again', which reached #11 during June. Rhone issued his second album, *Marty Rhone*, in July before travelling to the UK to further his singing and acting career. He landed a role in the British stage production of *The King and I* which also featured veteran actor Yul Brynner. In 1987, Rhone turned his hand to management when he became business manager for boxing champions the Waters brothers (Troy, Dean and Guy), the sons of trainer Cec Waters.

Albums: *Denim and Lace* (M7, 1975), *Marty Rhone* (M7, 1977), *Village Tapestry: The Festival File* (Festival, 1988).

Sherry Rich and the Grievous Angels (*see* Girl Monstar)

Digby 'Dig' Richards

Style: Rock'n'roll

Veteran singer Digby 'Dig' Richards (b. 1941) was the third Australian rock'n'roll artist signed to Festival by A&R man Ken Taylor (after **Johnny O'Keefe** and **Col Joye**). His combination of James Dean-type good looks, soft charm, quiet determination and spirited rock'n'roll won him many fans. He scored eight Top 40 hits in a career spanning over 20 years. He died in 1983 from cancer.

The son of a country policeman, Richards grew up in remote western New South Wales. At 17 he ventured to Sydney and found work in Waltons department store. Along with young lead guitarist Jon Hayton, Richards formed The R'Jays. Kerry Konyard (rhythm guitar), Peter Marris (sax), Roger Paulfreman (tea chest bass) and Barry Lewis (drums) completed the band's line-up. **Johnny O'Keefe**, **Col Joye** and **Alan Dale** had already established themselves as rock'n'roll stars, and Richards and the R'Jays joined other young hopefuls like **Johnny Rebb** and the Rebels, **Ray Hoff and the Off Beats**, **Barry Stanton** and the Belaires and The Stoneagers on the Sydney dance circuit.

By early 1959 The R'Jays line-up comprised Hayton, Lewis, Marris, Peter Baker (electric bass; ex-Deke Drew and the Rebel Rousers) and Jay Boogie (piano; ex-Deke Drew and the Rebel Rousers). Laurie Goodfellow soon replaced Marris on sax. Following an audition for Festival, Richards and the R'Jays issued their debut single, 'I Wanna Love You'/'Kansas City' (August 1959). It climbed into the Sydney Top 10 (#8) and catapulted Richards to stardom. 'I Wanna Love You' had been written by Richards' 15-year-old brother Doug. The band's second hit single (another Doug Richards composition), 'I'm Through'/'You are My Sunshine' (September), was a Top 40 entry.

Richards and the R'Jays became the first band ever to play live on Brian Henderson's *Bandstand*, after which they became regulars on **Johnny O'Keefe's** television show *Six O'Clock Rock* and *Teen Time*. The band supported US visitors Crash Craddock, Lloyd Price and Ricky Nelson on tour. Having established themselves, Richards and the R'Jays were lined up as support act to Lee Gordon's Fabian Big Show in October 1959 when a car accident on the Sydney Harbour Bridge put the singer in hospital. He suffered a broken hip, a broken shoulder and received 40 stitches to his face. Bowed but not beaten, Richards and the R'Jays returned with the single '(Real Gone) Annie Laurie'/'South of the Border' (January 1960) on Festival's Rex label.

By that stage, The R'Jays line-up had been revamped with Leon Isackson (ex-**Ray Hoff and the Off Beats**, Stoneagers) taking over from Lewis on drums. Other musicians came and went, including Brian Kelly (bass) and a succession of sax players: Bob Bertles, Dave Cross, Ron Patton and Brian Smith. Dig Richards and the R'Jays issued three more singles on Rex, 'Comin' Down with Love'/'Ain't She Sweet?' (#33 in June 1960), 'My Little Lover'/'Quarrels (are a Sad, Sad Thing)' (#19 in September) and 'The Gal Who Invented Kissin''/'That's How I Go for You' (March 1961), while Richards also issued two under his own name, 'You Gotta Love Me'/'My Baby's Not a Baby Anymore' (December 1960) and 'Alice (In Wonderland)'/'I'm in the Mood for Love' (#33 in June 1961).

The Rex label also issued the Richards album *Bad Boy* (with backing provided by The R'Jays and The Graduates) plus three EPs, 'Ain't She Sweet?', *Live at the Town Hall* (actually created in the studio with canned applause) and *Dig's Big Four*. Richards and the R'Jays parted ways in 1962. In 1964, The R'Jays became The Rajahs with a line-up of Hayton (guitar, vocals), Isackson (drums), Lindsay 'Nosmo' King (rhythm guitar, vocals) and Michael Lawler (bass). The Rajahs were billed as 'Australia's Beatles', and just to perpetuate the correlation the band issued the rare EP *Beatlemania* (March 1964), which contained renditions of six Beatles hits. In the meantime, The Rajahs had signed to the Leedon label and issued the singles 'Kiss Me Now'/'You'll Get Over It' (March 1964), 'Cathy's Clown'/'I Like the Look of You' (September) and 'Let Me Tell You About a Guy'/'Oh' (June 1965), plus the EP 'Kiss Me Now'. The band also backed **Johnny O'Keefe** and **Noeleen Batley** on some of their recordings. Isackson later joined **The Mighty Guys**.

Richards continued his solo career for Festival with the singles 'Dee Dee Darling'/'What'cha Gonna Do?' (September 1961), 'Dear Lady Twist'/'Do Re Mi' (February 1962), 'Raincoat in the River'/'Long Way from Home' (#19 in October), 'The Love Express'/'Whole Wild World' (April 1963) and 'Comin' Down'/'His and Hers' (December). During that time, Festival issued four more Richards EPs, 'You Gotta Love Me', *Out of the Groove*, 'Raincoat in the River' and 'The Love Express'. Richards appeared in the Christmas 1963 'surfing musical' *Once Upon a Surfie* as 'Dig the

Beatnik'. Also in the cast were Jackie Weaver as 'Gadget', **Lucky Starr**, **Bryan Davies**, Jay Justin, **Rob EG**, Jan Green and **The Delltones**. After that, Richards turned his attention to becoming an all-round entertainer. He took guitar and vocal lessons, and made his cabaret debut at Spellson's Nightclub in Sydney.

Richards issued four more singles on Festival, 'Come on and Dance with Me'/'Livin' Lovin' Wreck' (May 1964), 'Mary from the Dairy'/'No Peace of Mind' (December), 'Puff'/'Sally's Leaving in the Morning' (June 1965) and 'I was Yesterday's Hero, Today I'm a Broken Hearted Clown'/'Miss Blues' (August). He also compered his own television show, *Dig Richards' Ampol Show*, during 1965. In 1967 Richards switched to CBS for the one-off single 'Aussie Bush Hat'/'You Didn't Know Me', then headed off overseas to perform in clubs and develop his songwriting. As part of his South-East Asian tours, Richards entertained Australian troops stationed in Vietnam. Richards returned to Australia in 1971 and issued one single on EMI/Parlophone, 'Patricia Anthony'/'Man's Gotta Be Free', before signing with RCA. By that stage, Richards had moved in a country direction. As Digby Richards, he issued the acclaimed *Harlequin* album.

The album produced the singles 'A Little Piece of Peace'/'Show Me the Way' (June 1971), 'Just Loving You'/'One Voice in a Million' (September), 'People Call Me Country'/'The Dancer' (February 1972) and 'Dirty River'/'Ashton County Park' (May). 'People Call Me Country' returned Richards to the Top 40 (#27) for the first time in over nine years. 'A Little Piece of Peace' also peaked at #14 on the Sydney chart. Richards recorded his next album, *Digby Richards*, in Los Angeles. The album produced four singles, 'If I Could Write a Love Song'/'Sweetwater Valley' (December 1973), 'New York City (Send My Baby Home)'/'Dawning in the Morning' (national #31 in April 1974), 'Do the Spunky Monkey'/'Daddy was a Dance Man' (national #12 in June) and 'Be My Day'/'Be My Guitar' (September). His 1975 album *Collection* included the singles 'Mr Hard Times'/'Love Bee' (January 1975), 'Little Suzuki'/'A Girl Like You' (May) and a revival of 'Raincoat in the River'/'Having It Straight' (August).

In 1974, erstwhile R'Jays guitarist Jon Hayton re-emerged with his Farmer John persona. Farmer John's self-titled debut album on RCA (1975) featured a mix of country rock and light funk. It produced the singles 'Fat Albert'/'Rat Race' and 'Slinky'/'Jet Black'. Produced and arranged by Tweed Harris (who also contributed keyboards), the album featured musical backing from Digby Richards (vocals, guitar), **Phil Manning** (guitar), **Brian Cadd** (piano), **Mike Rudd** (mouth harp), Mike Clarke (bass) and Geoff Cox (drums). Farmer John formed a touring band which comprised Owen Booth (bass; ex-**Aesop's Fables**, Travellers), Warren Collits (guitar) and Richard Harvey (drums). Harvey later played in **Divinyls** and **The Party Boys**.

Between 1978 and 1982, Richards issued the albums *Whiskey Sundown* (December 1978), *The Thing is ...?* (January 1981) and *If You Could Read My Mind* (December 1982). His singles were 'You Can Lay Your Mind (at Rest)'/'Sweetwater Valley' (February 1976), 'Where There's Smoke'/'Falling' (1977), 'Time to Go to Bed'/'All Things Bright and Beautiful' (August 1979), 'Someone Touched Me (on the Heart Last Night)'/'In His Songs' (December 1979), 'Hong Kong Nights'/'Go for the Doctor' (July 1980), 'Beautiful to Me'/'Written in the Fire' (January 1981), 'Back to the Islands'/'Heart to Heart' (1982) and 'Stereo'/'Be My Day' (1982). Following Richards' death, Starcall issued the compilation album *Rock and Roll I Gave You All the Best Years of My Life* (September 1984) and Festival issued the Glenn A. Baker-compiled anthology *Jive After Five* (1988).

Albums: *Dig Richards and the R'Jays* (Festival, 1959), *Bad Boy* (Rex/Festival, 1960), *Harlequin* (RCA, 1971), *Digby Richards* (RCA, 1974), *Collection* (RCA, 1975), *The Best of Digby Richards* (RCA, 1977), *Whiskey Sundown* (RCA, 1978), *The Thing is . . . ?* (RCA, 1981), *If You Could Read My Mind* (EMI, 1982), *Rock and Roll I Gave You All the Best Years of My Life* (Starcall/Festival, 1984) *Jive After Five: The Festival File Volume Two* (Festival, 1988).

Ripe

Formed: *1988*
Style: *Pop*
Original line-up: *Mark Murphy (vocals, guitar), Peter Moran (guitar), Tony Cleaver (bass), Ewan McCartney (drums)*

Melbourne independent band Ripe took inspiration from UK guitar-pop bands like The Smiths, Ride, The Primitives and My Bloody Valentine in a style that mixed catchy bubblegum pop with fuzz-tone, serrated guitar melodies. Other reference points included such disparate sources as The Ramones, The Velvet Underground, The Beatles and Syd Barrett-era Pink Floyd.

In 1989, the Summershine label issued the band's limited edition debut single 'We're All Trying to Get There'/'End' (only 100 copies pressed). In 1990, Ripe signed to the Polyester label for the single 'Spacesuit 4 2'/'Little Johnny Jewel' (October) and the album *Filterfeed*. 'Little Johnny Jewel' was an unusual cover of New York band Television's debut 1975 single. Ripe also contributed a cover of **The Church's** 'Under the Milky Way' to the Various Artists album *Used and Recovered by . . .* on White/Mushroom (1990), and 'Gaze' to rooArt's *Youngblood 3* compilation (both 1991). In 1991, Jo-Anne Roberts replaced Tony Cleaver on bass. Roberts stayed with the band for a year before being replaced by Katie Dixon. Roberts later joined fellow Melbourne guitar-pop band **Holocene**. In March 1992, Ripe moved to the Shock label for the CD EP *Tough Guys Don't Dance* (title derived from the Norman Mailer novel of the same name). Shock also lifted 'The Most' from the CD EP as a 7-inch vinyl single. At the end of the year, Darren Seltmann replaced original drummer Ewan McCartney.

Ripe made its boldest statement with the full-length album *The Plastic Hassle* (August 1993), which produced a trio of excellent singles, 'Moondriven' (December 1992), 'Love Your Guts' (March 1993) and 'Something Fierce' (July). Epic album tracks like 'Centre of the Universe', 'The Plastic Hassle' and 'Daylight Wants to Kill' saw the band exploring a noisy brand of post-modernist heavy metal akin to Sonic Youth. Ripe undertook a gruelling North American tour to support the overseas release of *The Plastic Hassle*. Following the tour, Moran and Seltmann left the band. Murphy and Dixon recruited new members Mike (guitar) and Mark (drums) and recommenced playing in late 1996. Peter Moran returned to the fold in early 1997, and the band continued with new bass player Matthew Whittle (ex-**God**, Patterson's Curse).

Albums: *Filterfeed* (Polyester, 1990), *The Plastic Hassle* (Shock, 1993).

The Riptides

Formed: *1977*
Style: *Power pop*
Original line-up: *Mark 'Cal' Callaghan (vocals), Scott Matheson (rhythm guitar), Alan Reilly (lead guitar), Robert Vickers (bass), Dennis Cantwell (drums)*

Brisbane band The Riptides was one of the classic Australian new wave groups. The band's blend of diamond-hard power pop, snappy surf melodies and whomping backbeat was irresistible and eminently danceable. After becoming one of the biggest drawcards on the Australian pub circuit during the early 1980s, The Riptides called it a day in 1983. The Riptides never achieved mainstream chart success, but have proven their perennial appeal by re-forming for a number of well-received tours and albums.

The Riptides formed in 1977 as The Grudge. The band emerged from the Architecture Department of the University of Queensland. In 1978, The Grudge changed names to, firstly, The Neon Steal and then The Numbers. The Numbers were part of the burgeoning Brisbane punk/new wave scene which also gave rise to **The Leftovers**, **The Apartments**, **The Go-Betweens**, The Survivors, Razar, The Humans and The X-Men. In September 1978, The Numbers issued the rare 'Sunset Strip' EP (500 copies) on **The Go-Betweens'** Able label. The tracks 'Sunset Strip', 'Magic Castle' and 'Rules of Love' were punchy and energetic and featured a brilliant, English-flavoured 1960s-inspired pop sound.

In early 1979, Robert Vickers left The Numbers. He travelled to New York where he joined The Colors; in 1983, he joined **The Go-Betweens**. Mark Callaghan switched to bass, and The Numbers became The Riptides (in order to avoid confusion with a Sydney band also called **The Numbers**). The band remixed the 'Sunset Strip' EP and reissued it in July 1979, credited to The Riptides (in a pressing of 2000 copies). Andrew Leitch replaced Alan Reilly on guitar and keyboards and the band recorded a new single, 'Tomorrow's Tears'/'Some Other Guy'. 'Tomorrow's Tears' was a fabulous slice of 1960s-styled R&B pop, and the band issued the single on the Flat label on Valentine's Day, 14 February 1980. The band appeared on ***Countdown*** to promote the single. The Riptides made the move to Sydney during the winter of 1980 and swiftly established themselves as one of *the* best live draws in town (alongside the likes of **INXS**, **Mental as Anything**, **Sunnyboys** and **Midnight Oil**).

In March 1981, Michael Hiron (ex-**Leftovers**, **Flaming Hands**) joined on bass, which allowed Callaghan to switch to rhythm guitar. Scott Matheson had also left by that stage. The new four-piece line-up entered the studio with producer Graham 'Buzz' Bidstrup (ex-**Angels**) in mid-1981 to record the six-track mini-album *Swept Away* which appeared in November. 'Only Time' was lifted from the mini-album as a single (also November), backed by the non-album tracks 'The Riptide (Existential Stomp)' and 'Shake It'. The mini-album also included one of the band's most enduring songs, the exuberant 'Holiday Time'. With the release of *Swept Away*, Dennis Cantwell and Andrew Leitch both left the band. Callaghan and Hiron laid low for a time before re-emerging in early 1982 with a new line-up comprising Russell Parkhouse (keyboards),

Howard Shawcross (bass; ex-Last Chance Café, **Elks**) and Graeme 'Hutch' Hutchinson (drums; ex-Humans). Hiron moved to lead guitar.

Hutchinson's previous band, The Humans, had comprised Tim Collett (vocals, guitar), Paul Avenell (guitar) and Mark Purchess (bass). The Humans issued one single, 'Teen Idol'/'Gotta Run Loose' (December 1979), before Hutchinson and Purchess joined. Don Pagwell (bass) and Peter Acton (drums) were The Humans' original rhythm section. The Humans broke up in late 1981 without having made progress beyond the Brisbane live circuit. The Riptides issued a new single, 'Hearts and Flowers'/'Sandarama' (September 1982), and supported UK visitors Simple Minds on their October Australian tour. By January 1983, The Riptides had slogged around the Australian touring circuit long enough and decided to call it a day. In July, Regular issued the Callaghan-assembled anthology album *Riptides* (aka *The Last Wave*). He and Andrew Leitch had recorded a new song, 'The Wedding Song', to bring the track total up to 11.

Callaghan and Bidstrup began recording demos before being joined by Chris Bailey (bass; ex-Red Angel Panic, **Headband**, **Angels**) and Geoffrey Stapleton (guitar, keyboards; ex-**Aliens**) as **GANGgajang**. The band enjoyed several hit singles and enormous success on the live circuit. Leitch and Hiron formed Catchcry with Ross Harley (guitar, vocals), Felix Davies (bass) and Tim Seckold (drums). The band recorded two independent singles, 'Blueprint #9'/'Sometimes the Night', 'Catch 22' (1983) and 'Congratulations'/'Climatisation' (1985). By the time Catchcry recorded the mini-album *Isle of Tears* in 1988, it was essentially a studio band based around Leitch and Hiron. John Willsteed (guitar; ex-Zero), Felix Davies (bass), Geoff Stapleton (harmonica), J.J. Harris (tambourine) and Robert James (backing vocals) all contributed to *Isle of Tears*. Willsteed joined **The Go-Betweens** in 1988. Hutchinson joined Frontier Scouts with Andrew Wilson (ex-Four Gods) and Brad Allen-Waters (bass, trombone). Frontier Scouts issued the single 'When Daddy Blows His Top'/'Out of Your Shell' and the 12-inch EP *Museum Collection* on the Au-go-go label before breaking up in 1984.

In early 1987, Callaghan revived The Riptides for a reunion tour to help celebrate ten years of Brisbane pop culture. The line-up comprised Mark Callaghan, Andrew Leitch, Michael Hiron and Buzz Bidstrup. The reunion tour produced the double live album *Resurface* which came out in December 1987. The Riptides toured again in February 1988 with Callaghan, Leitch, Hiron and J.J. Harris (drums; ex-**Divinyls**).

Callaghan launched his solo career under the name of Cal with the acclaimed album *Sailors and Mermaids* (October 1988). The album produced three singles, 'Do It Rite'/'Golden Years' (September), 'I will Be with You'/'Changing Times' (March 1989) and 'Golden Years'/'Spooky' (July). Helping out on the album sessions were members of The Riptides and **GANGgajang**, plus Sean Kelly (ex-**Models**), Peter 'Maz' Maslen (drums; from **Boom Crash Opera**), Charlie McMahon (didgeridoo; from **Gondwanaland**) and English slide guitarist Chris Spedding. Callaghan toured with his solo band, which comprised Robbie James (guitar; from **GANGgajang**), The Riptides' Michael Hiron (bass) and Paul Wheeler (drums; from **Icehouse**). The singer later contributed 'Do It Rite' to the Various Artists album *Building Bridges* on CBS (1989).

In the meantime, Hiron joined inner-Sydney band The Plug Uglies. Callaghan and Hiron revived The Riptides again for successful summer tours during 1989 and 1990. In early 1991, the pair entered the studio with new guitarist Tony Adams, session drummer John James (J.J.) Hackett (ex-**Mondo Rock**) and South-African-born producer/drummer Ricky Fataar (ex-Beach Boys) to record the first full-length Riptides studio album. *Wave Rock* appeared in August 1991 and produced the singles 'Stop (Don't Start)' (May) and 'Here Comes the Sun' (August). Neil Chadwick joined as a permanent drummer and The Riptides toured once again.

Riptides albums: *Swept Away* (mini-album, Regular/Festival, 1981), *Riptides* (compilation, Regular/WEA, 1983), *Resurface* (Mercury/PolyGram, 1987), *Wave Rock* (Phonogram, 1991); ***Cal solo album:*** *Sailors and Mermaids* (Truetone/PolyGram, 1988); ***Catchcry mini-album:*** *Isle of Tears* (Red Eye, 1988).

Archie Roach

Style: *Folk, blues*

Since the release of his critically acclaimed debut album *Charcoal Lane* in 1990 Koori, singer/songwriter Archie Roach (b. 1955) has emerged as one of Australia's most gifted artists. Archie is a storyteller in the tradition of his ancestors, relaying and retelling intimate real-life stories as well as traditional 'Dreamtime' tales.

Roach's early life was difficult; forcibly removed from his family at seven, he was sent to live in a succession of white foster homes, before ending up on the streets as an alcoholic. He gave up alcohol to revive an interest in singing and songwriting. One of his early gigs was as support to **Paul Kelly**

Archie Roach

and the Messengers, and his short set made a strong impact on the audience. Under the guidance of producers Kelly and Messengers guitarist (the late) Steve Connolly, Roach constructed a debut album that was emotionally powerful in its acoustic simplicity. *Charcoal Lane* (October 1990) was a landmark release that highlighted many of the social issues that were at the forefront of Aboriginal life in Australia: alcoholism, dispossession, loss of land and culture and the continued fight for social justice. *Charcoal Lane* won Best Indigenous Album, and Roach took out Best New Talent at the 1990 Australian Record Industry Association (ARIA) Awards.

Roach also received a Human Rights and Equal Opportunity Commission award for his autobiographical debut single 'Took the Children Away' (September 1990). It was the first awarded for songwriting. This painfully honest folk song recounted the 1950s Australian government policy of 'Assimilation' in which Aboriginal children were forcibly separated from their parents and placed in white foster homes. 'Down City Streets' appeared as Roach's second single in April 1991. In 1992, Roach and his spouse **Ruby Hunter** undertook an eight-week American tour in support of *Charcoal Lane*'s release in the US (through Hightone Records). The tour included supporting Joan Armatrading for six weeks, and an opening slot for Bob Dylan for which the duo received rave reviews. *Charcoal Lane* was named in US *Rolling Stone's* Top 50 albums for 1992. Roach ended 1992 by winning the MO Award for Folk Performer of the Year.

In 1993, following a guest appearance at the Corroboree Festival at London's Southbank Centre, Roach and Hunter toured the UK for the first time. They were back for a second tour in November 1994 supporting Robyn Hitchcock and the Egyptians. Roach's second album, *Jamu Dreaming* (March 1993), continued the themes of his debut, but it was more optimistic and uplifting. Producer David Bridie (from **not drowning, waving** and **My Friend the Chocolate Cake**) imbued the record with a more varied soul, country and pop flavour that further highlighted Roach's soft, bluesy voice. Once again, songs like the title cut 'Jamu Dreaming', Hunter's 'From Paradise' and 'Walking into Doors' (both issued as CD singles) struck a strong emotional chord. The album made the national Top 40. Roach collaborated with **Shane Howard** on a cover of **Scrap Metal's** 'Nhyul Nhyul Girl', which they contributed to the Various Artists compilation *Earth Music* issued on the Mushroom label (June 1994). Publisher HarperCollins also issued a book of Roach's song lyrics, *You Have the Power.*

As a demonstration of his place in the broader Australian community, Roach was invited to appear with **Yothu Yindi** at the opening of the 1994 AFL Grand Final. He was also the only artist to have appeared at three WOMADelaide festivals to that time (1992, 1994 and 1995). In May 1995, Roach and Hunter embarked on a major international tour that took in dates across America and Europe (including an appearance at the WOMAD Festival in Spain with Van Morrison and Suzanne Vega). Roach's touring band comprised **Dave Steel** (guitar, mandolin, lap steel, vocals; ex-**Weddings, Parties, Anything**), Kerry Gilmartin (bass, vocals) and Archie Cuthbertson (drums; ex-**Hollowmen**). Roach continued to work with that line-up for the next two years.

In between his 1995 touring commitments, Roach found time to contribute the track 'Our Home, Our Land' to the ATSIC *Native Title* album, and to produce the debut release for Tasmanian Aboriginal band Rygela. Following his national tour support to international visitor Tracey Chapman in late 1996, Roach commenced work on his third solo album, *Looking for Butterboy*, with producer Malcolm Burn (Iggy Pop, Emmylou Harris, Patti Smith, Aaron Neville). Roach commenced 1997 as support to Patti

Smith's Australian tour. The first CD single from *Looking for Butterboy*, 'Hold on Tight', came out in June to coincide with a sold-out national tour. The album followed a month later to positive reviews. Roach ended the year by winning Best Indigenous Release at the 1997 ARIA Awards ceremony.

Albums: *Charcoal Lane* (Aurora/Mushroom/Festival, 1990), *Jamu Dreaming* (Aurora/Mushroom/Festival, 1993) *Looking for Butterboy* (Aurora/Mushroom/Sony, 1997).

Margret Roadknight

Style: *Folk, blues*

Acclaimed folk/blues singer Margret Roadknight began her career in 1963 around the jazz-folk clubs of Melbourne. Her soaring voice has been likened to the great blues singers of the past like Bessie Smith. Early inspiration also came from the likes of Nina Simone, Odetta and Harry Belafonte. Roadknight was a fine interpreter of songs by other artists. By the early 1970s, she had developed a wide repertoire that incorporated folk ballads, African music, blues, gospel, calypso and jazz material. She became popular at folk festivals, jazz conventions and blues concerts, as well as appearing on television shows.

The Move label issued Roadknight's debut album, the live set *People Get Ready* (recorded at Frank Traynor's Folk Club), in November 1973. It featured covers of material by the likes of Curtis Mayfield, Duke Ellington, Joni Mitchell and Malvina Reynolds. Backing musicians on the album were Martin Doley (guitars, backing vocals), Peter Doley (flute, kazoo, maracas, backing vocals), Peter Howell (bass), Bob Vinnard (piano, organ, backing vocals) and Ian Clarke (percussion). In 1974, the Jazznote label issued the split album *Australian Jazz of the 70s Vol. 5 The Blues Singers*, which Roadknight shared with **Dutch Tilders**. The Larrikin label reissued the album in 1980 under the title *Bluesmakers*.

At the end of 1974, Roadknight received a travel grant from the Australian Council of the Arts (under the auspices of Gough Whitlam's Labor government), which enabled her to study contemporary music in the USA for six months. In January 1976, Roadknight issued a cover of **Bob Hudson's** poignant 'Girls in Our Town'/'Captain Jack' as a single on the Ritz Gramophone label. It reached #21 in Melbourne during March. Her third album, *Margret Roadknight* (featuring 'Girls in Our Town'), appeared on Festival's Infinity label at the end of the year. 'Love Tastes Like Strawberries'/'I Don't Want to Play' appeared as the second single. The live track 'Margret's Blues' featured contributions from jazz players Judy Bailey (piano) and Dave Ellis (bass).

In August 1977, Roadknight embarked on a nine-month working holiday that took in appearances in the USA, Europe, the UK and the Philippines. Her fourth album, *Ice*, featured material written by Australian songwriters such as Colin Campbell ('Ice', originally recorded by folk group **Extradition** and **Tully**), **Doug Ashdown** and Jimmy Stewart ('Winter in America [Leave Love Enough Alone]') and David Bentley ('Faith Healer'), among songs by Taj Mahal, Hoyt Axton and Dory Previn. In 1978, Roadknight issued the single 'Raw Deal'/'Margret's Blues' which was the theme song to the feature film *Raw Deal*. At the end of the year, Roadknight toured the USA and also performed in China with an Australian theatrical troupe. Her 1981 album *Out of Fashion . . . Not Out of Style* yielded one single, a cover of **Spectrum**'s 'I'll Be Gone'/'Waltzing Matilda', 'Another Suitcase in Another Hall' (May).

Backing musicians on the album were Judy Bailey (keyboards), Chris Qua (bass), Willie Qua (drums), Steve Murphy (guitar) and Bob Hudson (harmonica), plus the Two Pot Screamers Jook Band (Roadknight, Hudson, Sandy Kogan: Jew's harp, washboard), and the Mount Tamborine 3-Piece Choir (Roadknight, Ellen McIllwaine, vocals, slide guitar, organ, and **Graham Lowndes**, vocals, acoustic guitar). In 1984, Festival issued the 14-track Margret Roadknight anthology album *Living in the Land of Oz*. The title track was Roadknight's version of the **Ross Wilson** song. Roadknight continued to tour, and in 1987 she worked as musical director of the Paul Robeson stage show *Deep Bells Ring*.

In January 1988, the Sandstock label issued Roadknight's first album in seven years, *Moving Target*. Once again, the album took in a remarkable breadth of styles, ranging from jazz, blues, ragtime, gospel, latin and funk to country and New Orleans R&B. Roadknight's backing band featured David Bentley (organ; ex-**Python Lee Jackson**), **Phil Manning** (guitar), Peter Walters (bass) and Robin Andrews (drums). Later in the year she represented Australia at the Houston (Texas) International Festival. In 1994, Roadknight appeared on the album *Cinderella a Cappella* alongside **Jeannie Lewis**, Moya Simpson and Blaire Greenberg.

Albums: *People Get Ready* (Move, 1973), *Australian Jazz of the 70s Vol. 5 The Blues Singers* (shared with **Dutch Tilders**, Jazznote, 1974; reissued as *Bluesmakers*, Larrikin, 1980 and again on EMI, 1981), *Margret Roadknight* (Festival/Infinity, 1976), *Ice* (Festival/Infinity, 1978), *Out of Fashion . . . Not Out of Style* (Festival/Infinity, 1981), *Living in the Land of Oz* (compilation, Festival, 1984), *Moving Target* (Sandstock, 1988), *Fringe Benefits* (Newmarket, 1993).

John Robinson (*see* Blackfeather; Duck)

Rock'n'Roll High School

Founded: *1990*

In 1990, Stephanie Bourke was teaching piano at a number of girls' schools around Melbourne when she conceived the idea for the Rock'n'Roll High School. Her students would bring sheet music of their favourite punk rock bands to learn on piano. Punk music and pianos did not necessarily mix, so Bourke procured guitars, drums and amplifiers and formed 20 of her students into four bands for a two-week crash course over the summer holidays.

The concept grew from there, to the point that by early 1993 there were over 100 students enrolled in the school with 26 bands in operation. The girls learned how to play their instruments, about writing songs and how to handle equipment. From there, the bands began to play gigs around Melbourne, and issue records. The development of the Rock'n'Roll High School corresponded with the emergence of the local 'femrock' or 'grot grrrl' movement which encompassed interstate bands like **Nitocris**, **Fur**, Mace, Gravelrash, SPDFGH, Sulk, Bittersweet, Dolljuice and others. There were some parallels to be drawn with the American 'riot grrrl' movement that encompassed Hole, Bikini Kill, Babes in Toyland, L7, etc. Irrespective of the sociological parameters at work, it gave a focus for the musicians to play the music they wanted and to address topics that affected them deeply.

Rock'n'Roll High School has given rise to bands like Midget Stooges, Bindi, Snodra, New Youth, Hecate, Gritty Kitty, Sourpuss, Leviathan, Tuff Muff, Spot the Beast, Miffy, Craw, Harey and many others. Over the years, the school has been visited by international bands likes Sonic Youth, Dinosaur Jr, Swervedriver, Rancid, Beastie Boys, The Breeders, Fugazi, Buffalo Tom, Pavement, Redd Kross, Superchunk, Ash, Rollins Band, Babes in Toyland, Bikini Kill, Sebodoh, L7 and Luscious Jackson. Sonic Youth's Thurston Moore was impressed enough to issue a Midget Stooges/Bindi split single in the USA on his own label. Bourke has issued two compilation albums featuring bands from the Rock'n'Roll High School.

Compilation albums: *Rock'n'Roll High School Volume One* (RNRHS/Shock, 1994), *Rock'n'Roll High School Volume Two* (RNRHS/Shock, 1995).

Rockmelons

Formed: *1983*
Style: *Dance pop*
Original line-up: *Ray Medhurst (keyboards), Jonathan 'Jonno' Jones (keyboards, electric dulcimer, guitar, sequencers; ex-No Heavy Lifting), Byron Jones (keyboards; ex-No Heavy Lifting)*

As Sydney's premier dance-pop band of the late 1980s/early 1990s, Rockmelons helped introduce American-influenced funk, soul and hip hop into the intensely 'rock' milieu of the Australian music scene. Utilising state-of-the-art studio technology and all manner of electronic instrumentation, the band's music combined a danceable bottom end and a seamless groove with an innate tunefulness and soulful, sunny disposition.

Formed by black music fanatic Ray Medhurst, Rockmelons started out more as a concept than a band. Having recruited the Jones brothers to put his musical ideas into practice, Medhurst was able to steer Rockmelons in the required direction. Rather than start on the pub circuit, Rockmelons mounted their own Sydney warehouse dance-parties. As well as incorporating Vinnie Dale (keyboards) into the line-up, the group hired three excellent vocalists, **Peter Blakeley**, John Kenny and Sandi Chick, to help round out the sound. In those days, the band often numbered ten or more musicians on stage, including a DJ and other guest players like Geoffrey Stapleton (keyboards, guitar; from **GANGgajang**) and Peter Kennard (guitar).

Blakeley has been acknowledged as one of the finest blue-eyed soul singers Australia has ever produced. He remained long enough to feature on the band's second single, 'Sweat It Out'/'If Tomorrow Ever Comes' (October 1986), before embarking on a solo career. Sydney independent label Phantom had issued Rockmelons' debut single 'Time Out (for Serious Fun)'/'Extremely Serious' (through Festival, February 1985), which featured Chick on lead vocals. 'Sweat It Out' was the first product of the band's new deal with the True Tone label. English producer Robin Smith (Earth Wind & Fire, 5-Star, Nolans) produced the band's third and fourth singles, a cover of Al Green's 'Rhymes'/'Hypotheque' (July 1987) and 'New Groove'/'In the Neighbourhood' (December) respectively.

'Rhymes' featured vocalist Kenny, while 'New Groove' featured **Wendy Matthews** up front; both singles reached the national Top 40. Smith completed work on Rockmelons' debut album, *Tales of the City* (May 1988), which yielded three further singles, 'What's It Gonna Be?'/'What's It Gonna Be?'

(instrumental) (February 1988), 'Thief'/'Boogie Tron' (July) and an excellent electro-funk rendition of Curtis Mayfield's 'Jump'/'Dreams in the Empty City', also sung by Matthews (October). *Tales of the City* peaked at #6 on the national chart in June. The band wrapped up the year by winning a shared (with **1927**) Australian Record Industry Association (ARIA) Award for Best Debut Album.

Rockmelons ended a lengthy period away from the scene by re-emerging in 1991 with a new vocalist **Deni Hines**. The first fruit of the new union was the hit single Bill Withers' 'Ain't No Sunshine' (November 1991), which reached #5 on the national chart during January 1992. 'That Word (L.O.V.E.)' (May 1992) followed 'Ain't No Sunshine' into the national Top 5, peaking at #4 in June. The band's self-produced second album, *Form 1 Planet* (July 1992), reached #2 on the national chart, and produced a third hit single sung by Hines, 'It's Not Over' (#15 in September). The album also featured vocal and rap contributions from Doug Williams, Eric Sebastian, Johanna Pigott (**XL-Capris**, Scribble) and Kye. **Deni Hines** embarked on a solo career. Following a fourth single lifted from the album, 'Form I Planet' (December), Rockmelons slipped from view once again.

Albums: *Tales of the City* (True Tone, 1988), *Form 1 Planet* (Mushroom/Festival, 1992).

Rocks

Formed: *1977*
Style: *Punk*
Original line-up: *Peter Davie (guitar, backing vocals), Steve Vanderschoot (bass, backing vocals), Bill Posters (drums, lead vocals)*

Alongside **X**, **The Thought Criminals**, **The Last Words**, Psycho-Surgeons, Johnny Dole and the Scabs, Filth, Blackrunner and The Hellcats, Rocks were among the leading lights of the original Sydney punk band explosion. As writer Steven Danno put it, Rocks 'churned out Ramones-inspired buzzsaw blitzkrieg'. Hardly original and as subtle as a sledgehammer, Rocks have nevertheless retained a certain cult attraction for punk aficionados.

Rocks formed in October 1977, and early gigs were at notorious inner-city punk hangouts like the Grand Hotel, the Last Resort and Blondies. In February 1978, Greg Morris (ex-Johnny Dole and the Scabs) replaced Posters on drums; Posters moved up front as lead singer. In May 1978, Rocks issued the 7-inch EP, 'You'r So Boring', on their own Point Blank label. The band managed to cram together six cuts of frantic, Ramones/Sex Pistols-derived punk mayhem on to that rare and collectable punk artefact. The Small Axe label also reissued Rocks' 'You'r So Boring' EP on 7-inch vinyl in 1996.

Rocks recorded two tracks, 'Suburban Soldiers' and 'Zero', for a proposed follow-up single, but the band broke up not long after. Davie and Morris joined The Prisoners with Bill Webb (guitar, vocals) and Ian Olive (bass). In June 1982, Rocks re-formed to record a demo entitled *The Final Assault*. The Posters/Davie/Vanderschoot/Morris line-up regrouped again in July 1984 to re-record the demo tracks. Two cuts from the latter session, 'Kamikaze Twist' and 'Migraine Headache', appeared on the Aberrant label's second Sydney punk compilation, *Not So Humdrum* (1984).

By August 1984, Rocks had settled on a new line-up of Posters (guitar, vocals), Vanderschoot (bass), Wayne Gates (vocals) and Darren Gilmore (drums). Vanderschoot, Gates and Gilmore left in 1985; Gilmore joined **Massappeal**. Peter Davie returned to Rocks to take up bass and Don McGlone took over on drums. The new three-piece line-up recorded the four-track, 12-inch EP *Final Assault* which appeared on the Waterfront label in June 1988. Steven Danno included another track from that session, 'Mental Blank', on his Various Artists album *Swingin' from the Trees* (Au-go-go, 1988).

Rocks disappeared from view again. Danno compiled 13 Rocks tracks, including four previously unissued, for inclusion on the compilation *You'r So Boring* on his Brain Salad Surgery label (1996). Danno also issued the Johnny Dole and the Scabs compilation *Scab Animal 1977* on Brain Salad Surgery. All tracks featured Scabs/Rocks drummer Greg Morris (the rest of the band comprised Johnny Dole, vocals, Peter Mullany, guitar and David Berry, bass). Three Johnny Dole and the Scabs tracks, 'Living Like an Animal', 'Psycho-Analyst' and 'Stuff Your Rules', also appeared on the third Aberrant Sydney compilation *Why March When You Can Riot?* (1985).

Album: *You'r So Boring* (compilation, Brain Salad Surgery, 1996).

The Rondells (*see* Bobby and Laurie)

Rose Tattoo

Formed: *1976*
Style: *Blues rock*
Original line-up: *Tony Lake (lead vocals),* **Peter Wells** *(slide guitar; ex-***Buffalo***), Leigh Johnston (rhythm guitar, vocals), Ian Rilen (bass, vocals; ex-***Band of Light***), Michael 'Stork' Vandersluys (drums)*

In the pantheon of Australian hard rock, Rose Tattoo stands as one of the most revered bands of all time. The Tatts played peerless, street-level heavy blues with the emphasis on slide guitar and strident lyric statements. The band's hits, like 'Bad Boy for Love' and 'We Can't Be Beaten', became anthems for disaffected suburban youth. After establishing themselves in Australia, the band members went on to earn an international reputation on the heavy metal touring circuit.

Bass player Ian Rilen is credited with the original concept for the band: blues and boogie played with passion, fire and at terminal volume, street clothes, dyed and (pre-punk) cropped hair and each member to be indelibly stamped (i.e. tattooed), all of which established a sense of group solidarity. Rilen also wrote much of the band's early material like 'Rosetta' and 'Bad Boy for Love'. The band tried out singer Tony Lake before recruiting **Gary 'Angry' Anderson** (ex-**Buster Brown**). The tiny but terrifying Angry was the perfect focal point for the band's aggressive approach. Mick Cocks also replaced original rhythm guitarist Leigh Johnston early in the piece.

Rose Tattoo made its live debut on New Year's Eve 1976. The band's early repertoire consisted of quality group originals fleshed out by suitable covers like The Rolling Stones' 'Street Fighting Man'. In mid-1977, the band entered Albert Studios with producers Vanda and Young to record its debut single. By that stage, Dallas 'Digger' Royal (ex-**Buster Brown**) had taken over the drum stool. Live favourite 'Rosetta' had been earmarked for the single A-side, but 'Bad Boy for Love'/'Snow Queen' eventually emerged in October. By that time, founder member Rilen had left the band. He went on to form infamous punk outfit **X**.

Mick Cocks switched to bass, until the band could recruit a new bass player. Ex-**Buffalo** member Chris Turner appeared as a guest guitar player until the band recruited another ex-**Buster Brown** alumnus, Geordie Leach, on bass and Cocks returned to guitar. The barnstorming 'Bad Boy for Love' peaked at #13 nationally and #10 in Sydney, and Rose Tattoo became a solid draw on the Australian pub rock circuit. By that stage, the band was competing with other Oz rock favourites like **Cold Chisel**, **The Angels**, **Dragon**, **Kevin Borich Express**, the reconstituted **Skyhooks** and **Finch** on that ever-expanding pub circuit.

Rose Tattoo completed its debut album with Vanda and Young. *Rose Tattoo* appeared in November 1978 and it remains one of *the* classic Australian rock albums. Heavy on the slide, heavy on the aggression and heavy on the atmosphere, the album was brimming with consummate street anthems like 'Bad Boy for Love', 'Rock'n'Roll Outlaw', 'Remedy', 'One of the Boys', 'Astra Wally' and the epic tale of gangland rivalries, 'The Butcher and Fast Eddy'. The album's second and third singles, 'Rock'n'Roll Outlaw'/'Remedy' (August) and 'One of the Boys'/'TV' (October), missed the national chart.

Rose Tattoo contributed two tracks, 'Bad Boy for Love' and 'Rock'n'Roll Outlaw' to the live Various Artists album *Canned Rock* recorded at Parramatta Gaol. Geordie Leach left Rose Tattoo in May 1979, to be followed by Cocks. The band went off the road, re-emerging in October with the new line-up of Anderson, Wells and Royal plus Oz rock legend **Lobby Loyde** (ex-**Purple Hearts**, **Wild Cherries**, **Billy Thorpe** and the Aztecs, **Coloured Balls**, Southern Electric) on bass guitar. The band's only record for 1980 was an independent single issued to promote the legalisation of marijuana. The Tatts' 'Realise Legalise' was combined with Colin Peterson's Bong on Aussie' (March 1980).

That year, Rose Tattoo travelled to Los Angeles and recorded an album that has never seen the light of day. By the end of the year, the band had signed international deals with Mirage in the USA, German WEA in Europe and Carrere in the UK. By September 1980, Loyde had left the band, and the line-up reverted to Anderson, Wells, Cocks, Leach and Royal. The band left for the UK in April 1981. By that stage, the 'Rock 'n' Roll Outlaw' single had already reached #5 in Germany and #2 in France; it peaked at #60 in the UK during July. Upon arrival in the UK, the press and public viewed the Tatts as a punk band, which—while not entirely accurate—did add to the band's considerable appeal and mystique. As well as two sell-out gigs at London's famous Marquee Club in late April and an appearance at the Reading Festival (alongside **Midnight Oil**, Girlschool, Gillan, Budgie, Chicken Shack, Alex Harvey and Wishbone Ash), Rose Tattoo spent most of 1981 on tour across Europe and the UK (including support slots to Ritchie Blackmore's Rainbow).

In the meantime, the band's fourth single, 'Rock'n'Roll is King'/'I Had You First' (August 1981) and second album *Assault and Battery* (September) came out in Australia. Both *Rose Tattoo* (retitled *Rock'n'Roll Outlaw* for the European market) and *Assault and Battery* reached #1 on the UK heavy metal charts. The band also garnered positive reviews in the UK rock press, with descriptions like 'Swaggering rock'n'roll desperados with hearts of gold' and 'Rose Tattoo make Motorhead look like the chorus line in a ballet' being two of the most colourful raves.

In September 1981, Robin Riley (ex-**Redhouse**,

Angry Anderson, Rose Tattoo

Dallimore) replaced Cocks (who joined **Heaven**) on guitar. The band returned to Australia in December. *Assault and Battery* (which had peaked at #28 in Australia during October) produced a second single, 'Out of this Place'/'Manzil Madness' (February 1982). The band's third album, *Scarred for Life* (November 1982), produced three singles, 'We Can't Be Beaten'/'Fightin' Sons' (#28 in December), 'Branded'/'Dead Set' (February 1983) and 'It's Gonna Work Itself Out'/'Sydney Girls' (June). The album peaked at #14 on the national chart and #4 in Melbourne. It went on to sell 70 000 copies. In the meantime, Rose Tattoo had embarked on a three-month American tour which took in support dates to Aerosmith and ZZ Top.

In early 1983, **Peter Wells**, Dallas Royal and Robin Riley all left the band. The Tatts re-emerged in June (for a tour with **Choirboys** and **The Angels**) with a new line-up: Anderson, Leach, Greg Jordan (slide guitar), John Meyer (lead guitar; ex-Fatty Lumpkin, Everest, Saracen) and Robert Bowron (drums). Scott Johnson (ex-**Jimmy and the Boys**) replaced Bowron on drums at the end of the year. In 1984, Rose Tattoo issued its fourth album, *Southern Stars* (November), which produced the singles 'I Wish'/'Wild One' (August), 'Freedom's Flame'/'Never Too Loud' (October) and 'No Secrets'/'Let Us Live' (February 1985).

Long-serving member Leach left the band in November 1984 (to join Illustrated Men), to be followed in the new year by Jordan. The new line-up of Anderson, Meyer, Johnson, plus newcomers **Tim Gaze** (slide guitar; ex-**Tamam Shud**, **Kahvas Jute**, **Ariel**, Tim Gaze Band) and Andy Cichon (bass) signed a record deal with the Mushroom label. The new line-up's first single was a cracking cover of Steppenwolf's biker anthem 'Born to Be Wild'/'Sun's Gonna Shine' (October 1985), which reached #21 on the national chart during December. That same year, Anderson moved into feature film work. His first acting role was a bit part in *Bullamakanka*. He then took the part of Ironbar Bassey in the Kennedy-Miller film *Mad Max III: Beyond Thunderdome*, alongside Mel Gibson, Tina Turner and Frank Thring.

With Rose Tattoo on hold, Meyer returned to his hometown of Perth (WA), where he rejoined his old band Saracen. The line-up featured Meyer, Jon Ryder (vocals, bass, keyboards; ex-Everest, Trilogy) and Pete Thompson (drums, vocals; ex-Trilogy). Saracen issued one accomplished hard rock album *Saracen* (1986) which sold well in Europe via a release on the French label Axe Killer. In late 1986, Saracen reverted briefly to the name of Trilogy, but Meyer left the band in the new year to join blues legends **Chain**.

The final Rose Tattoo album *Beats from a Single Drum* (November 1986) had started out as an Anderson solo album when American producer Kevin Beamish (REO Speedwagon, Starship) was brought in to oversee recording. Featuring the line-up of Anderson, Gaze, Cichon and Johnson, the album was a more polished affair than previous Tatts records. It reached #20 on the national chart in December. The album produced four singles, 'Calling'/'Win at Any Cost' (September 1986), 'Get It Right'/'Michael O'Reilly' (December), 'Falling'/'Winnie Mandela' (March 1987) and 'Suddenly'/'Falling' (August). The plaintive ballad 'Suddenly' was issued as an **Angry Anderson** solo single. It was used during the wedding of Charlene Mitchell (**Kylie Minogue**) and Scott Robinson (**Jason Donovan**) in the Ten Network's popular soapie *Neighbours*. It reached #2 on the national charts the same week that Minogue's first single 'Locomotion', sat at #1 (August 1987). The two singles swapped places a week later, with 'Suddenly' at the top and 'Locomotion' at #2. Newcomers Jake Landt (who replaced Cichon on bass) and Rick Mellick (keyboards) were used for a 1987 tour, but by the end of the year Rose Tattoo had broken up. Mushroom reissued *Beats from a Single Drum* as an Angry Anderson solo album in 1988. The legend of Rose Tattoo did not end there.

American heavy metal giants Guns N' Roses included a cover version of 'Nice Boys (Don't Play Rock'n'Roll), on their debut EP *Live Like a Suicide* (1987). The band members had always confessed their adoration for the Oz rock legends. When Guns N' Roses toured Australia in early 1993, they insisted that Rose Tattoo re-form and act as support band for their two gigs (Sydney 30 January and Melbourne 1 February). Accordingly, the line-up of Anderson, Wells, Cocks, Leach and new drummer Paul DeMarco (who replaced the late Dallas Royal) re-formed. As well as the Guns N' Roses tour, Rose Tattoo undertook a successful Australian pub tour (which saw Gunners Slash and Duff McKagan jamming with the band). In July, the Tatts played a one-off concert supporting Oz rock legends **Billy Thorpe** and the Aztecs at *Jail House Rock* held at Brisbane's infamous Boggo Road Gaol (closed down in 1992).

Aside from the compilation album *Nice Boys Don't Play Rock'n'Roll* (November 1992) and the CD EP 'Bad Boy for Love' (January 1993) issued to coincide with the re-formation tour, there was no new Rose Tattoo product forthcoming. Castle Communications announced that it was set to issue the band's legendary Reading Festival set from 1981 on CD, but nothing eventuated. Anderson returned to his television career, **Peter Wells** concentrated on his solo albums and Leach joined **The Giants**.

Albums: *Rose Tattoo* (Albert/EMI, 1978), *Assault and Battery* (Albert/EMI, 1981), *Scarred for Life* (Albert/EMI, 1982), *Southern Stars* (Albert/EMI, 1984), *Beats from a Single Drum* (Mushroom/Festival, 1986), *A Decade of Rock* (Albert/EMI, 1987), *Their Greatest Hits* (Dino, 1990), *Nice Boys Don't Play Rock'n'Roll* (Albert/Sony, 1993).

Normie Rowe

Style: Pop

During the 1960s, singer Normie Rowe (b. 1947) was Australia's original King of Pop. Between 1965 and 1967, Rowe experienced unprecedented popularity as one of the country's premier beat-pop sensations. Alongside the likes of **Ronnie Burns**, **Merv Benton**, **Bobby and Laurie**, **Billy Thorpe** and the Aztecs, **The Easybeats**, **M.P.D. Limited** and **Ray Brown and the Whispers**, Rowe created astounding scenes of mass hysteria among teenage fans that were akin to Beatlemania.

Rowe formed his first group The Valiants while still at high school. At 15 he was working as a PMG (later Telstra) trainee technician. With help from radio personality Stan Rofe and promoter Kevin McClellan, Rowe began appearing as a singer on the Melbourne dance circuit, often backed by **The Thunderbirds**, The Impostors and then The Playboys. By late 1964, he was given an ultimatum by his employers: cut his hair or resign. Naturally, he resigned to become a professional entertainer. Rowe became a regular on television shows like *The Go!! Show* and *Teen Scene*, and then signed a recording and management deal with Ivan Dayman's Sunshine organisation. Backed by The Playboys, his debut single, 'It Ain't Necessarily So'/'Gonna Leave this Town' (April 1965), was an immediate success. 'It Ain't Necessarily So' was an updated version of the song from the George Gershwin musical *Porgy and Bess*, and it came under scrutiny for its supposedly sacrilegious lyrics. Despite, or perhaps because of, an outright ban by the Catholic-owned Sydney radio station 2SM, the single shot to #1 in Melbourne and peaked at #8 in Sydney.

Rowe's second single, a cover of Ben E. King's 1963 ballad 'I (Who Have Nothing)'/'I Just Don't Understand' (June), reached #8 in Sydney and #7 in Melbourne during August. Rowe's debut album, *It Ain't Necessarily So, But It Is . . . Normie Rowe* (July), was a fine example of Aussie beat-pop. Featuring exemplary backing from The Playboys, the album boasted a cracking rendition of The Mojos' 'Everything's Alright'. Rowe's mysterious third single, 'I Confess'/'Everything's All Right' (September 1965), failed to chart. (1960s expert Dean Mittelhauser has suggested the single was never issued.) The double-sided hit 'Que Sera Sera'/'Shakin' All Over' (September) reached #1 in both Melbourne and Sydney, remaining in the Top 40 for 28 weeks and selling a (then) staggering 80 000 copies. During October, Rowe had all three hit singles in the Melbourne Top 40 at the same time. Rowe's cover of Johnny Kidd and the Pirates' 'Shakin' All Over' is considered by 1960s aficionados to be the best version cut by an Australian artist.

Rowe continued his hit run with Chuck Jackson's 'Tell Him I'm Not Home'/'Call on Me' (Melbourne #2, Sydney #5 in November), Bacharach/David's 'The Breaking Point'/'Ya Ya' (Melbourne #4, Sydney #8 in February 1966) and Marvin Gaye's 'Pride and Joy'/'The Stones that I Throw' (Melbourne #16, Sydney #11 in June). By that stage, Rowe and **The Easybeats' Stevie Wright** were the two hottest teen sensations Australia had ever seen. 'The Big Four' tour of Australia saw Normie Rowe and the Playboys, **The Easybeats**,

Normie Rowe

Bobby and Laurie and M.P.D. Limited playing to enormous crowds.

In September 1966, Rowe set his sights on the UK. On the eve of the UK trek, Rowe replaced the Playboys line-up (Graeme Trottman, drums; Phil Blackmore, organ, piano, guitar; John Cartwright, rhythm guitar; Bill Billings, lead guitar; and Neil McArthur, bass) with a new line-up containing Brian Peacock (bass; ex-Librettos) and Rod Stone (guitar; ex-Librettos). He retained the services of Trottman and Blackmore. Once in London, Rowe entered the studio with producers Trevor Kennedy and John Carter, plus a bevy of English session players like Jimmy Page, John Paul Jones, Clem Cattini and The Breakaways. The sessions produced Rowe's third Melbourne #1 hit, 'Ohh La La'/'Ain't Nobody Home' (November; also #2 in Sydney), and another Top 5 hit in Mann/Weil's 'It's Not Easy'/'Mary Mary' (Melbourne #2, Sydney #5 in December). The Playboys joined Rowe during December, and Rowe embarked on a March 1967 UK tour as support to The Troggs, Gene Pitney, Sounds Incorporated and David Garrick.

Rowe stayed in the UK for ten months, toured with Julie Driscoll, Brian Auger and the Trinity, the Spencer Davis Group and Kiki Dee, but failed to make a major breakthrough. In June 1967, he flew to North America where he supported Roy Orbison on tour in the USA, and represented Australia (alongside **The Seekers**) at Expo '67 in Montreal, Canada. He returned to Australia during July. Rowe's final UK studio sessions with Yardbirds producer/manager Giorgio Gomelsky had yielded two singles in Graham Gouldman's 'Going Home'/'I Don't Care' (Melbourne #7, Sydney #22 in April 1967) and 'But I Know'/'Sunshine Secret' (Melbourne #15, Sydney #25 in June). His first Australian single after returning, 'Turn Down Day'/'Stop to Think It Over', managed to reach the lower rungs of the Melbourne Top 40 (#38) during October.

Having lost his footing at home somewhat, Rowe suffered another blow in September when he was called up for National Service. By October 1967, The Playboys had split from the singer and evolved into **Procession**. In January 1968, Rowe was inducted into the army, where he remained until February 1970. Rowe was sent for his tour of duty in Vietnam during January 1969. At the end of 1968, Rowe had been voted Top Male Singer by *Go-Set* readers, although that acknowledgement of his popularity did not translate into record sales.

Sunshine continued to issue Rowe's singles during his army service. Of the five singles issued during 1968 and 1969, 'Penelope'/'Lucinda' (March 1968), 'Break Out'/'Born to Be by Your Side' (August), 'Walking on New Grass'/'Open Up the Skies' (October), 'Just to Satisfy You'/'Drinkin' Wine Spo-Dee-O-Dee' (March 1969) and 'You Got Style'/'Don't Say Nothin' Bad (About My Baby)' (June), only Brian Peacock's sumptuous ballad 'Penelope' made the Melbourne Top 20. Following Rowe's release from the army, the Sunshine label reissued 'Que Sera Sera'/'Let Me Tell You' (December 1970). It reached #32 in January 1971, but by that stage Rowe had left Sunshine. During his time with Sunshine, Rowe issued 13 EPs. Before signing a new deal with Festival, Rowe cut an unusual, one-off single for RCA Custom with The Jug Band. 'Rockhampton Happening'/'Rockhampton Happening' (different version) had been recorded for the Rockhampton (Queensland) Tourism Board and was accompanied by a short promotional film starring Rowe.

Rowe issued one album, *Hello* (1973), and four singles on Festival, Johnny Young's 'Hello'/'Home to Stay' (#33 in May 1970), 'Border Song'/'Come Hear My Song' (August 1971), 'Glory Road'/'Over to You Now' (April 1972) and 'Rings'/'Come Hear My Song' (August 1973), before moving to Astor. His 1975 album *That's the Way I Am* produced the singles 'Harbour for My Song'/'That's the Way I Am' (August), 'Good Morning, Good Morning'/'If You See Her' (September) and 'Elizabeth'/'A Little Ray of Sunshine' (October). At the end of the year, Rowe won the Best Song category at the Tokyo Song Festival with 'Elizabeth'.

In June 1976, Rowe issued the single 'Mother's Boy'/'Can I Get a Witness?' (written and produced by **Glenn Shorrock**) on the Rainbird label. Rowe settled on the Queensland Gold Coast where he worked in clubs, cabaret and television. In 1980, he signed a new deal with the Avenue label, which resulted in the release of five singles, 'Maybe Tomorrow'/'Help Yourself to Each Other' (January 1981), 'You've Got a Right'/'For Love' (September 1982), 'Dreaming'/'Keep It Up' (March 1983), 'Rock'n'Roll You're Beautiful'/'Does She Have a Friend?' (May) and Terry Britten's 'Don't Talk'/ 'I Need to Fall in Love Again' (May 1984), plus the album *Out of the Blue* (June 1984).

Rowe then studied acting at the Ensemble Theatre and took the role of faded pop star Vin Grey in the stage play *One Night in Julia Creek*. He also appeared in long-running television soapie *Sons and Daughters*. In 1986, reissue specialists Raven issued the comprehensive anthology album *Shakin' All Over*. A year later, Rowe took the esteemed part of Jean Valjean in the Sydney production of the stage musical *Les Miserables*. The single 'Bring Him Home'/'Do You Hear the People Sing?' (November 1987) on Festival came from the show. Due to personality clashes, however, Rowe did not accompany *Les Miserables* to Melbourne.

In 1991, Rowe was embroiled in controversy following a television appearance on *The Midday Show with Ray Martin*. Rowe got into a heated discussion with radio commentator Ron Casey over the republican issue, and the dispute erupted into an on-air punch-up between the two hotheads. Since that time, Rowe has concentrated on the 1960s revival circuit.

Albums: *It Ain't Necessarily So, But It is . . . Normie Rowe* (Sunshine, 1965), *Normie Rowe a Go Go* (Sunshine, 1965), *A Wonderful Feeling* (Sunshine, 1966), *So Much Love from Normie Rowe* (Sunshine, 1966), *Normie's Hit Happenings* (Sunshine, 1967), *Everything's Alright* (compilation of first two albums, Universal, 1968), *Normie's Top Tunes* (Summit, 1969), *Hello* (Festival, 1973), *Come Hear My Song* (Summit, 1974), *That's the Way I Am* (Astor, 1975), *Greatest Hits* (Festival, 1976), *Out of the Norm* (Astor, 1979), *Out of the Blue* (Avenue/CBS, 1984), *Piano Man* (Hammard, 1985), *Shakin' All Over* (Raven, 1986), *Count Your Blessings* (J&B, 1992).

Roxus

Formed: *1987*
Style: *Hard rock*
Original line-up: *Juno Roxas (vocals; ex-Party Pies), Dragan Stanic (guitar), Andy Shanahan (keyboards), John Nixon (bass; ex-Windsor Jamm), Darren Danielson (drums; ex-Windsor Jamm)*

Fronted by flamboyant singer Juno Roxas, Melbourne band Roxus first came to the nation's attention as support act to US glam-rockers Poison and Bon Jovi on their respective 1989 Australian tours. Roxus had been playing its blend of tuneful, Van Halenesque hard rock and Living Colour-inspired funk around the Melbourne pub circuit since 1987. The band's carefully cultivated image of black leather, ripped jeans, cowboy boots, bandannas and big hair also garnered Roxus a strong following.

Roxus caught the attention of Ian 'Molly' Meldrum, who signed the band to his Melodian label (through Mushroom). Melodian issued two Roxus singles in 1989, 'Stand Back'/'Spaghetti Wine' (July) and 'Body Heat'/'Don't Stop' (November). By 1990, the band had established itself as a popular draw on the live circuit. The live EP *That Girl* captured the sound of the band's melodic, hard rockin' gigs. In February 1991, the band entered the studio with producer Mark Opitz (**Cold Chisel, Angels, Hitmen**). In April, Roxus supported US band Warrant on an Australian tour. Roxus's debut album *Nightstreet* (September 1991) reached the national Top 10 (#7). It produced the singles 'Where are You Now?' (#11 in July) and 'Bad Boys (Need Love)' (August), both of which charted in the national Top 20.

The album mixed Warrant/Bryan Adams-like soft metal raunch ('Bad Boys', 'Rock'n'Roll Nights') with lush power ballads ('Where are You Now?', 'This Time'). 'Jimi G'/'Rock'n'Roll Nights' came out as the album's third single in October. In early 1992, Juno Roxas and Dragan Stanic travelled to Los Angeles to write new songs. They re-emerged in 1993 with a new set of players: Zack Zedras (ex-Serpentine), Craig Harnath (bass; ex-**Kids in the Kitchen, Chocolate Starfish**) and Steve Moffitt (drums). The band issued two more CD singles that year, 'Eternity' (August) and 'Almost Summer' (December). Warren Jenkins replaced Harnath on bass and Chris Doheny (guitar, vocals; ex-**Geisha**) replaced Zedras, but Roxus slipped from view.

Album: *Nightstreet* (Melodian/Mushroom/Festival, 1991).

Mike Rudd and the Heaters

Formed: *1979*
Style: *Rock*
Original line-up: *Mike Rudd (guitar, vocals; ex-Chants R&B,* **Party Machine, Spectrum, Sons of the Vegetal Mother, Ariel***), Tony Slavich (keyboards; ex-***Richard Clapton** *Band,* **Ariel, Mondo Rock***), Paul Grant (guitar; ex-Hollywood, New* **Hush***), Bill Putt (bass; ex-Lost Souls,* **Spectrum, Ariel***), Manny Paterakis (drums; ex-***Captain Matchbox Whoopee Band***, Last Chance Café)*

As leader of **Spectrum**, New Zealand-born musician Mike Rudd was one of the seminal figures behind the emergence of a mature Australian rock sound during the early 1970s. Alongside **Daddy Cool**, **Chain** and **Billy Thorpe** and the Aztecs, **Spectrum** took underground progressive rock into the mainstream charts. The band's 1971 #1 hit single, the shuffling, hypnotic 'I'll Be Gone', remains an Australian classic.

With the break-up of **Spectrum** in 1973, Rudd formed **Ariel**, which lasted until August 1977. Rudd produced Melbourne band Daniel's debut album *Last Night in the City*, which appeared on the Image label in August 1978. By that stage, Rudd had returned to the stage with his new band, Instant Replay. The line-up comprised Rudd, Bill Putt, Paul Grant, Mal Logan (keyboards; ex-**Healing Force**, **Renée Geyer** Band) and Keith Elliot (drums; ex-Ride Band). In November 1978, Tony Slavich took over from Logan on keyboards and Manny Paterakis replaced Elliot.

In July 1979, Rudd changed the band's name to Mike Rudd and the Heaters. The band played a mix of pub rock and pop (with quasi-new wave overtones) and was popular on the Melbourne scene. The band signed to Mushroom Records and issued its debut single, 'Australian Girl'/'Talking to the TV' (February 1980). In June 1980, The Heaters line-up became Rudd, Putt, Tony Fossey (keyboards) and Robert Dillon (drums; ex-Kid Gloves). The band's debut album, *The Unrealist* (January 1982), produced three singles, 'I'm an Animal'/'Head Job' (October 1981), 'Laser Love'/'Keeping Your Distance' (January 1982) and 'Love Comes and Goes'/'Models' (April 1982). The records were not successful and The Heaters broke up in June 1982.

Rudd and Putt formed electronic band W.H.Y. with John Moon (guitar; ex-**Buster Brown**, **Jim Keays** Band). Rudd switched to keyboards, and utilised the services of a drum machine dubbed Weird Harold. W.H.Y. signed to the Australian office of the German label I.C. Records (run by Klaus Schulze). Rudd took the band to Winsen, Germany to record, which resulted in the 12-inch EP 'Woman of Steel'/'Bahrain' (July 1983) and the album *Present Tense* produced by John Capek. 'Woman of Steel' presented a bright synth-pop sound but did not make the chart. *Present Tense* came out in Germany, but was never issued locally.

At the end of 1983, Rudd, Putt and Moon formed Living Legends Blues Band with Nigel Rough (drums; ex-Loose Trousers, **Jim Keays** Band) as a fun venture to play R&B material. By 1984, that band had evolved into Nuclear Dog with Rudd, Putt, Moon, Weird Harold and Tony Fossey. Next came No. 9 with Rudd, Putt, Weird Harold and David Krycer (bass, piano). In the meantime, Rudd and Putt had toured with the revived **Spectrum**. In 1988, the pair formed The Burwood Blues Band with Fossey, Gary Clarke (bass; ex-**Carson**) and a number of drummers including David Hicks and Steve Donald.

Rudd and Putt continued to play the Melbourne pub and club circuit with **Spectrum** during the early 1990s. In 1991, they were working as The Mike Rudd Quintet with Cres Crisp (keyboards), Martyn Sullivan (bass) and Manny Paterakis (drums). In 1992, Rudd and Putt began working as an acoustic duo with guest vocalist Enza Pantano. They played regularly, often utilising the services of auxiliary members like Rosie Westbrooke (bass). At the end of 1995, Mike Rudd and Bill Putt issued a new album, *Living on a Volcano*, on their own Volcano label. In late 1996, Rudd and Putt formed a fun band called The Fez with ex-**Crowded House** drummer Paul Hester. Then in August 1997, the two musicians re-formed the *Rock & Roll Scars* **Ariel** line-up (with John Lee and Harvey James) for a series of gigs.

Heaters album: *The Unrealist* (Mushroom/Festival, 1982); ***Mike Rudd and Bill Putt album:*** *Living on a Volcano* (Volcano, 1995).

Rue Morgue (*see* Vicious Circle)

The Runners

Formed: *1980*
Style: *Rock*
Original line-up: *Mark Edwards (vocals, guitar; ex-City), Trevor Reading (lead guitar; ex-City), Lester Price (keyboards), Paul McNaughton (bass; ex-City), Grant Hamston (drums)*

Popular Melbourne rock band The Runners started out as the backing outfit for 1960s pop singer

Ronnie Charles (ex-**Groop**, Atlas). Charles had been working in the UK for most of the 1970s. In 1980, he recorded a single with The Runners, 'Rock and Roll Hoodlum'/'Aim for the Stars', which came out on the Full Moon label.

In early 1981, The Runners struck out on their own, swiftly attracting a strong following on the pub circuit. Mark Greig (guitar, keyboards; ex-City, Ideals) replaced Lester Price in early 1982, and The Runners signed to Mushroom Records. The band's debut single, 'Sure Fire Thing'/'Pleasure Zone' (May), reached #16 in Melbourne. The band's second single, 'Hook Line and Sinker'/'Don't Apologise' (September), was not successful. Greig left the band at the end of 1982 to join the **Lisa Bade** Band. The Runners' debut album, *Hitting the Wall* (March 1983), produced two further singles, 'Endlessly (Hitting the Wall)'/'Logical Boy' (January) and 'Sinai'/'Midnight Flight' (May). *Hitting the Wall* reached #10 and 'Endlessly (Hitting the Wall)' #28 in hometown Melbourne during April. The album also went as high as # 39 nationally. 'Sinai' was not successful.

In July 1983, Tim Brosnan (ex-**Paul Kelly** and the Dots, **Zimmermen**) joined on rhythm guitar to allow Mark Edwards more freedom as lead singer, and John Annas (ex-**Kevin Borich Express**) replaced Hamston on drums. Mark Greig re-joined on keyboards during October. By December 1983, Michael Barclay (ex-Japanese Comix, **Little Murders**) had taken over on drums from Annas. The Runners issued one more single on Mushroom, 'Twins'/'The Penny Drops' (March 1984). The band suffered a number of line-up changes during 1984, which saw new players like Randy Bulpin (guitar; ex-**Mondo Rock**, **James Freud** and Berlin, the Darryl Cotton Band), Tony Harvey (guitar; ex-**James Freud** and the Radio Stars, Airport) and Paul Northam (guitar, bass; ex-**MEO 245**) join. The Runners struggled to survive, finally breaking up in July 1984.

Mark Edwards signed a solo deal with WEA in 1985 which resulted in a string of singles, 'Worlds Away'/'Moonbeam' (November 1985), 'Only a Love'/'So Listen' (August 1986), 'Land of the Living'/'Back in the Land of the Living' (November), 'Somebody Like You'/'One and Only' (March 1987) and 'High Times'/'Shan and Kim' (September 1987), plus one album, *Land of the Living* (November 1986). None of the records was successful and Edwards slipped from public view. In the meantime, Trevor Reading had joined the **Richard Clapton** Band, and Michael Barclay joined **Paul Kelly** and the Coloured Girls. In the late 1980s, Runners bass player Paul McNaughton also launched his solo career under the name of **Paul Norton**. His solo career got off to a flying start when his first single for Mushroom, 'Stuck on You'/'Don't Say a Word', raced up to #3 on the national chart during May 1989. Norton issued two albums on Mushroom, *Under a Southern Sky* (1990) and *Let It Fly* (1992).

Runners album: *Hitting the Wall* (Mushroom/Festival, 1983); ***Mark Edwards solo album:*** *Land of the Living* (WEA, 1986).

Ross Ryan

Style: *Folk, pop*

Best known for his soaring hit single 'I am Pegasus', American-born Ross Ryan (b. 1950) garnered considerable acclaim during the 1970s as one of Australia's foremost singer/songwriters. His local contemporaries in the troubadour field included **Glenn Cardier**, **Kevin Johnson**, **Richard Clapton** and **Mike McClellan**.

Born in Fort Leavenworth, Kansas, Ryan immigrated to Australia with his family in 1959. He grew up near Albany, Western Australia, before moving to Perth in order to further his musical career. He worked as an audio operator at the Channel Nine studios. Using the facilities available there, between July 1970 and October 1971 Ryan recorded 16 of his own songs. He had 80 copies of an album, *Homemovies*, pressed up at a cost of $500. In early 1972, Ryan issued his first single, 'Sounds of Peppermint', which came out on a split single he shared with The Statesmen's 'Keep on Truckin'. Ryan came to the attention of local entrepreneur Al Maricic, who took over his management. In September 1972, Ryan supported US visitor Roy Orbison on his Australian tour.

As a result, Ryan landed a recording deal with EMI Records via producer Peter Dawkins. EMI issued his second album, *A Poem You Can Keep* (May 1973), which produced the single 'I Don't Want to Know About It'/'Making the Same Mistakes' (July). The single took Ryan into the national Top 40 (#38) for the first time. Ryan supported UK band The Hollies (May 1973) and **Helen Reddy** (November) on their respective Australian tours. Ryan's third album, *My Name Means Horse* (#3 in April 1974), produced the singles 'I am Pegasus'/'Country Christine Waltz' (national #9, Sydney #1 in November 1973) and 'Orchestra Ladies'/'606' (March 1974). The album also contained another of Ryan's most enduring songs, 'Blood on the Microphone', which was based on his experience as support act to Shari Lewis and the puppet Lamb Chop.

At the end of 1973, he undertook a solo club

tour of the US where Capitol Records had issued *A Poem You Can Keep* and 'I Don't Want to Know About It'. Ryan appeared at the 1974 Sunbury Festival (January), and in May represented Australia at Expo '74 in Spokane, Washington (alongside **Judy Stone** and **Rolf Harris**). Back in Australia, Prime Minister Gough Whitlam presented Ryan with gold record awards for the album *My Name Means Horse* and the single 'I am Pegasus'. Ryan toured Australia with country-rock outfit Stuart and McKay, which comprised Ian Stuart (guitar, vocals), Ken McKay (guitar, vocals), John Griffin (bass) and Doug Bligh (drums). His third album, *After the Applause* (June 1975), produced the singles 'Blue Chevrolet Ballerina'/'Send Me the Pillow' (#38 in June 1975) and 'Sedel (Never Smiled at Me)'/'Love Song to You All' (August). Ryan formed a short-lived band, Cahoots, with Eric McCusker (guitar) and Sam McFerrin (bass) to promote the album.

His fourth album, *Smiling for the Camera* (April 1977), included the witty single 'Happy Birthday to Me'/'To Be Alone with You' (August 1976), plus 'Dancing'/'Anthem' (August 1977). Produced by Rick Formosa (ex-**Little River Band**) and backed by musicians like Formosa (guitar, mandolin), Tony Buchanan (sax, flute), Roger Frampton (piano), Adrian Scott (keyboards; from **Air Supply**), Les Young (bass) and Jim Duke-Yonge (drums; ex-**Pirana**), *Smiling for the Camera* was Ryan's most accomplished album to date.

It failed to chart, however, and Ryan left EMI. At the end of the year, EMI issued the Ross Ryan compilation album *Ross Ryan (1973–1976) 'I Thought This Might Happen'*. In 1977, Ryan supported US visitors Roberta Flack and Dr Hook on their respective Australian tours. In 1978, he worked on children's television show *Give 'Em Heaps* with Mike Meade. Ryan acted and sang his witty songs like 'I Love My Horse'. In 1979, he put together The Ross Ryan Brothers with Toivo Pilt (keyboards; ex-**Sebastian Hardie**), Graham Wardrop (guitar), Peter Gifford (bass; ex-Huntress) and Ace Follington (drums; ex-**Chain**, **Cleves**, Australia, **Richard Clapton** Band). James Rattray replaced Gifford in early 1980 and Ralph Cooper (ex-Windchase, **Air Supply**) replaced Follington.

In April 1980, Ryan issued a new single on PolyGram, 'Chaplin and Harlow'/'Postmark Paradise', and a final single on the 7 label (through Powderworks) in April 1981, 'Hello Stranger'/'The Ballad of the Double Bay Batman'. Ryan continued to tour, and his next band, Ross Ryan and the Redeemers, featured Toivo Pilt, Broc O'Connor (guitar), Roy Zedras (bass) and Louis Burdett (drums). In 1985, Ryan supported UK visitor Van Morrison on his Australian tour. Ryan's backing band comprised Roy Zedras, Gus McNeil (sax; ex-**Nomads**), Alex Pertout (percussion) and Marcus Holden (fiddle). Following that, Ryan settled into the folk club scene as a solo acoustic performer.

During the 1980s, Ryan issued a series of cassette albums like *The Lost Ross Ryan Album*, *The Official Ross Ryan Bootleg* and *You Can Trust Me, I'm a Musician*, which he sold at gigs. In 1990, he wrote and performed a successful revue, *Les Boys (a Masculine Sensation)*, with comedians Rod Quantock, Lynda Gibson and Geoff Brooks. EMI issued the Ross Ryan anthology, *The Greats of Ross 1973–1990*, which included old favourites and previously unissued material. Ryan experienced the most successful phase of his career during the early to mid-1970s. Nevertheless, he has continued to play and remains a gifted songwriter and performer blessed with a self-effacing sense of humour. In the mid-1990s, he set up G.I. Studios with Broc O'Connor.

Albums: *Homemovies* (private pressing, RR, 1971), *A Poem You Can Keep* (EMI, 1973), *My Name Means Horse* (EMI, 1974), *After the Applause* (EMI, 1975), *Smiling for the Camera* (EMI, 1976), *Ross Ryan (1973–1976) 'I Thought This Might Happen'* (EMI, 1977), *The Greats of Ross 1973–1990* (compilation, EMI/Axis, 1990).

S

Sacred Cowboys

Formed: *1982*
Style: *Rock*
Original line-up: *Garry Gray (vocals, ex-Reals, Negatives), Mark Ferrie (bass, guitar; ex-Myriad, Leisuremasters,* **Models***), Terry Doolan (guitar; ex-Fizzpops), Ian Forrest (keyboards; ex-True Wheels), Andrew Picouleau (bass; ex-Metronomes, Popgun Men,* **X-Ray-Z***), Janis Friedenfelds (aka Johnny Crash; ex-***Models***)*

During the early 1980s, Melbourne band Sacred Cowboys was one of the most confrontational live outfits around. In a cruel pastiche of Leatherface in the legendary horror film *The Texas Chainsaw Massacre*, lead singer Garry Gray was known for brandishing a roaring chainsaw (minus the cutting chain, of course) over the heads of audiences. Ian 'Molly' Meldrum described the Cowboys as the worst band he had encountered in five years, which instantly cemented their nefarious reputation as the local scene's *enfants terribles*. The band's music mixed post-punk moodiness and country raunch over a mutant swamp-blues backbeat.

Like their Sydney brethren **Beasts of Bourbon**, Sacred Cowboys were an inner-city supergroup of sorts. Mark Ferrie and Janis Friedenfelds had been in **Models**. Gray had fronted two early Melbourne punk combos, The Reals and The Negatives. The Reals comprised Gray, **Ian 'Ollie' Olsen** (guitar), Chris Walsh (bass) and Peter Cave (drums). With the departure of Olsen, the band recruited Michael Holmes and became The Negatives. The Negatives contributed the eerie 'Planet on the Prowl' to the Suicide Records compilation of Melbourne punk bands, *Lethal Weapons* (1978). It was one of the most interesting tracks on the album, although producer Eric Gradman added his violin without the band's knowledge. The Negatives made little headway and broke up at the end of 1978. Holmes joined Eric Gradman: Man & Machine and later **The Zimmermen**; Walsh joined The Fabulous Marquises and Champagne Edge before moving on to **The Moodists**. Ian Forrest's band True Wheels comprised Tim Brosnan (guitar), John Clifforth (guitar, vocals), Mark Pemberton (bass) and Greg Perano (drums).

Sacred Cowboys started off as a fun covers band, playing songs by their favourite artists (The Doors, Alex Chilton, The Velvet Underground, The Stranglers, Suicide, Bob Dylan). They found a ready-made audience on the Melbourne inner-city scene, and when Gray described the Cowboys as 'a show of direct hostility towards the flaccid impotence of a borrowed culture', they were on their way. In November 1982, Sacred Cowboys issued their classic debut single, 'Nothing Grows in Texas'/'Is Nothing Sacred?', on Mushroom's White subsidiary label. In July 1983, the Cowboys issued the single Alex Chilton's 'Bangkok'/'Limbo Jig' independently. A month later, the band supported Los Angeles hardcore outfit the Dead Kennedys at their Melbourne gig. The brooding 'Nothing Grows in Texas' and 'Bangkok' also appeared on the mini-album *Sacred Cowboys* (December), alongside live favourites like 'Twisted Nerve' and 'Nailed to the Cross'.

The release coincided with the arrival of new keyboard player Chris Whelan, who replaced Forrest. In 1984, Nick Rischbieth (ex-Relaxed Mechanics) replaced Picouleau on bass, while French label New Rose issued the *Sacred Cowboys* compilation album in Europe. By that stage, the band's live standing on local turf had begun to wane, and a proposed European tour was scuppered when Gray was admitted to a drug rehabilitation centre in order to kick his heroin habit. Sacred Cowboys bowed out with the album *We Love You . . . of Course We Do* which mopped up various demos and live recordings of some of the band's favourite cover songs, including 'Run Run Run' (The Velvet Underground), 'Pablo Picasso' (The Modern Lovers), 'Run Through the Jungle' (Creedence Clearwater Revival), 'Rocket USA' (Suicide), 'Highway 61' (Bob Dylan) and 'I am the Walrus' (The Beatles). Ferrie and Doolan went on to join country/gospel/roots rock outfit **The Slaughtermen**.

In late 1987, Sacred Cowboys re-formed with the line-up of Gray, Ferrie, Doolan, Rischbieth and Stefan Fidock (drums; ex-**Reels**). They signed to Sydney-based label Citadel and issued the album *Trouble from Providence* (August 1988), which was

Sacred Cowboys

one of the best independent releases of the year. The album produced the singles 'Trouble from Providence'/'Canned Goods' (July) and 'Hell Sucks'/'Trouble from Providence' (sensitive acoustic version) (December). The band toured to a positive response and German label Normal issued the album for the European market. Original member Ian Forrest rejoined in late 1990, but the band had broken up again by the end of 1991.

Gray disappeared from view while Ferrie remained active in bands like The Welcome Strangers, The Trailblazers, Long Black Limousine and country-grunge outfit Truckasaurus. The last-named comprised Ferrie, Lisa Miller (vocals; ex-Trailblazers), Ed Bates (guitar; ex-**Sports**), Nick Grant (guitar; ex-Trailblazers), Graham Lee (pedal steel; ex-**Triffids**) and Tony Thornton (drums, ex-Trailblazers). Truckasaurus issued a self-titled CD EP in October 1993. Miller went solo and issued the CD EPs 'Do that for You' (May 1995) and 'All Worked Out' (November), plus the delightful country-pop album *Quiet Girl with a Credit Card* (Shock, June 1996). Ferrie also issued a solo album, *Actual Reality*, in September 1994.

In early 1994, the Siren label issued the seven-track Sacred Cowboys compilation *Black City 1982–1993* which included the previously unissued track 'Black City'. There was still enough interest in the band for Gray, Ferrie, Doolan and Fidock to revive Sacred Cowboys with a new line-up that also included Penny Ikinger (guitar; ex-Wet Taxis, **Louis Tillett's** Aspersion Caste). In 1996, the band played a series of low-key gigs around Melbourne and issued a new album, *Things to Come*, during July. The ubiquitous Spencer P. Jones (ex-**Johnnys**, **Beasts of Bourbon**) also contributed guitar to the album. The album included covers of Bob Dylan's 'Outlaw Blues' and 'Subterranean Homesick Blues' and The Beatles' 'I am the Walrus'.

Albums: Sacred Cowboys (mini album, White/Mushroom/Festival, 1983), *We Love You . . . Of Course We Do* (Man Made, 1985), *Trouble from Providence* (Citadel, 1989), *Black City 1982–1993* (compilation, Siren, 1994), *Things to Come* (Greasy Pole/Shock, 1996).

Wendy Saddington

Style: Soul, blues

Wendy Saddington was one of Australia's premier soul/blues singers of the late 1960s/early 1970s (in the Etta James/Aretha Franklin mould). Because she was under-recorded, however, Saddington can only claim one single and one album to her credit. Saddington first came to prominence in soul/psychedelic bands like The Revolution and the **James Taylor Move**, and the original version of blues band **Chain**. In May 1969, she joined pop paper *Go-Set* as a staff writer and later joined Copperwine as co-vocalist with **Jeff St John**.

Her stay of ten months (March 1970–February 1971) motivated many changes in Copperwine's musical direction, with much of the soul-copying being replaced by a more purist blues-oriented sound. That change was heard on the album *Wendy Saddington and the Copperwine Live* which had been recorded at the Wallacia Festival during January 1971. Saddington scored her only hit single when the Warren Morgan-penned and **Billy Thorpe**/Morgan-produced 'Looking Through a Window'/'We Need a Song' reached #22 in September 1971. In 1972, Festival reissued the live album, retitled it *Looking Through a Window* and simply added the track 'Looking Through a Window'. The single was reissued in 1977 but was not successful.

In March 1973, Saddington appeared as the Nurse in the local stage production of The Who's rock opera *Tommy*. Other cast members included **Billy Thorpe**, **Daryl Braithwaite**, **Colleen Hewett**, **Broderick Smith**, **Doug Parkinson**, **Jim Keays**, **Ross Wilson** and Keith Moon. Saddington worked with a variety of bands during the mid-1970s, including Shango and Blues Assembly. She worked with the **Jeffrey Crozier** Band in New York during the late 1970s. In 1983, she formed the Wendy Saddington Band which initially comprised jazz pianist Bobby Gebert, Harvey James (guitar; ex-**Ariel**, **Sherbet**, **Swanee**), Billy Rylands (bass) and Chris Sweeney (drums). The 1987 line-up comprised Rose Bygrave (keyboards; ex-**Goanna**), Mick Liber (guitar; ex-**Python Lee Jackson**), Angelica Booth (bass) and Des McKenna (drums). Saddington spent most of her time away from the rock scene working with the Hare Krishnas. She returned to live performances in Melbourne at the start of 1996 backed by a young band called Aniseed.

Albums: *Wendy Saddington and the Copperwine Live* (Festival/Infinity, 1971), *Looking Through a Window* (reissue with the single 'Looking Through a Window' added; Festival/Infinity, 1972).

Sadistik Exekution

Formed: *1987*
Style: *Death metal*
Original line-up: *Rok (vocals), Sandy (lead guitar), Dave Slave (bass), Sloth (drums)*

The Australian death metal underground scene has given rise to a number of extreme bands like **Abramelin**, Misery, Disembowelment, Damaged, Mortality, Volatile, Manticore, Necrotomy, Blood Duster, Bestial Warlust, Destroyer 666 and, possibly the most heavily hyped of the lot, Sadistik Exekution. Even before Sadistik Exekution had played live, *Penthouse* and *Picture* magazines had run sensationalist stories on the band's evil intentions and all-corrupting, demonic influence.

The self-proclaimed 'heaviest and fastest band in the world' took its inspiration from European death metal bands like Bathory, Hellhammer, Napalm Death and Celtic Frost, and their American counterparts Morbid Angel, Death and Obituary. Sadistik Exekution issued its first record, the six-track mini-album *The Magus*, in 1991, by which time the Rev Kriss Hades had replaced Sandy on lead guitar. The 'Suspiral'/'Ipsissimus' cassette single followed in early 1992. By that stage, the band had played its first gigs to a rabid response from the converted and bemused indifference from the world at large. In August 1992, Sadistik Exekution supported US visitors Morbid Angel on that band's Australian tour. In early 1993, drummer Sloth reputedly found God, left Sadistik Exekution, renounced his nefarious past and burnt his drums. Steve the Mechanik took his place. The band contributed the track 'Ipsissimus' to Roadrunner Australia's compilation of local metal bands, *Redrum* (June 1993).

For some time, the European death metal underground had been fascinated by Sadistik Exekution, and in late 1994 French label Osmose issued the band's debut, full-length album *We are Death Fukk You*. In May 1995 the band undertook a European tour with Matt 'Skidz' Sanders from Damaged filling in on the drum stool. Very little was heard from Sadistik Exekution after that, save for the odd gig or two, until July 1997 when the band issued the album *Kaos*.

Albums: *The Magus* (mini-album, Vampire, 1991; reissued on CD in 1994), *We are Death Fukk You* (Osmose, French import only, 1994), *Kaos* (Shock, 1997).

Jeff St John

Style: *Soul, R&B*

Rock writer Glenn A. Baker made no secret of his views in his praise for Jeff St John's 'roaring, finely controlled voice'. David 'Dr Pepper' Pepperell praised St John's voice for its limitless power, its precise and meaningful phrasing and its sweetness 'like honey dripping from the hive'. Throughout the 1960s and 1970s, Jeff St John was indeed Australia's finest rock vocalist.

Born Jeffrey Leo Newton (1946), Jeff St John began his professional singing career in 1965 as a member of Sydney band The Syndicate. Peter Anson (guitar; ex-**Missing Links**), David Bentley (organ), Shane Duckham (harmonica), John Helman (bass) and Don McCormack (drums) completed the line-up. The Syndicate became The Wild Oats and then Jeff St John and the Id. Dave Montgomery replaced McCormack on drums. The band opened Sydney discotheque Rhubarbs in late 1965 and then issued its debut single, Ray Sharpe's 'Lindy Lou'/'Somebody to Love' (simply credited to The Id, February 1966), on Nat Kipner's Spin label.

By that stage, The Id comprised St John, Anson, Helman, the returned McCormack, Ian Walsh (organ), Bruce Johnson (tenor sax, flute) and King Fisher (trumpet). Bentley and Montgomery had left to form **Python Lee Jackson**. The Id issued three more singles on Spin during 1966, 'The Jerk'/'Take this Hurt Off Me' (March), Leadbelly's 'Black Girl'/'Eastern Dream' (September) and Zoot Money's 'Big Time Operator'/'Sister's Got a Boyfriend' (December), plus the 'Big Time Operator' EP (February 1967). Already established as Sydney's premier soul/R&B band, 'Big Time Operator' thrust Jeff St John and the Id into the 'Australian Top Band' bracket when the single reached #7 in Sydney and #12 in Melbourne during January 1967. By March 1967, Bob Bertles had replaced Johnson on tenor sax. A three-month residency at Sydney's Here Disco, the support slot to the Roy Orbison/Walker Brothers/Yardbirds Australian tour and an extended season at Melbourne's Thumpin' Tum had all served to cement The Id's redoubtable reputation.

The Id issued the *Big Time Operators* album (March 1967), one more single, 'You Got Me

Hummin''/'Watch Out' (April), plus the rare 'You Got Me Hummin'' EP (May). By mid-1967, however, St John had split from The Id to form Yama (a Hindi word for 'the first mortals'). The Id continued as a four-piece for a couple of months with Anson on bass and Mick Liber (ex-**Python Lee Jackson**) on guitar. The band foundered and Anson went on to **Foreday Riders** and Liber joined **Gulliver Smith** in The Noyes. Jeff St John and Yama comprised St John, Ross East (lead guitar, vocals), Virgil East (bass; ex-**Python Lee Jackson**), Wayne Myers (organ), Murray Hill (sax, flute), Keith Jenkins (trumpet) and Peter Figures (drums; ex-**Throb**). Allan English (sax) had replaced Hill and Jenkins by the time the band commenced touring. The short-lived Yama only produced one interesting single on Spin, 'Nothing Comes Easy'/'Everybody's Gone' (October 1967), before splitting.

At the end of 1967, St John entered hospital for four months of treatment on his legs (he had been afflicted with congenital spina bifida since birth). The operations were not successful and St John was confined to a wheelchair for the remainder of his career. St John returned to the live scene in February 1969 when he took his new band to Perth for a few modest bookings. Jeff St John's Copperwine comprised St John, Peter Figures, Phil Wooding (guitar; ex-**In-Sect**, quickly replaced by Ross East), Barry Kelly (piano, organ, vocals; ex-**Marty Rhone** and the Soul Agents) and Alan Ingram (bass, vocals). Copperwine swiftly developed into an uncompromising rock outfit, and once back in Sydney began to rule over the burgeoning 'head music'/concert circuit alongside the likes of **Tully** and **Tamam Shud**.

Jeff St John's Copperwine played a starring role in Australia's first rock festival, Ourimbah, Pilgrimage for Pop in January 1970. Two months later Copperwine issued the imaginative *Joint Effort* album, one of the finest Australian albums of the early 1970s. The band's influences were apparent in the covers chosen for the set: Blind Faith's 'Can't Find My Way Home', Sly and the Family Stone's 'Sing a Simple Song' and The Temptations' 'Cloud Nine'. The album was rounded out by fine band compositions like 'You Don't Have to Listen', the jazzy instrumental 'Any Orange Night' and the delicate psychedelic-infused 'Fanciful Flights (of Mind)'. The album's progressive soul single 'Cloud Nine'/'Days to Come' (February 1970) missed the charts, although the next single, a cover of Rotary Connection's surging 'Teach Me How to Fly'/'Freedom Blues' (November 1970), scored an impressive #16 placing on the national chart (#3 in Sydney and #12 in Melbourne). Spin had also issued the four-track EP, 'Sing a Simple Song' (all tracks lifted from the album), in May 1970.

By that stage, Harry Brus (ex Amazons) had replaced Ingram on bass and **Wendy Saddington** (ex-Revolution, **James Taylor Move**, **Chain**) had joined as co-lead vocalist (although she did not appear on the single). Saddington was Australia's best female blues singer of the day, and her stay of ten months (May 1970–February 1971) motivated many changes in Copperwine's musical direction. Much of the soul/jazz flavour was abandoned in favour of a more purist blues orientation on stage, as displayed on the album *Wendy Saddington and the Copperwine Live* (recorded sans St John at the Wallacia Festival in January 1971).

Jeff St John and the Copperwine were placed third behind **Fraternity** and **Sherbet** in the 1971 Hoadley's National Battle of the Sounds competition. The band issued a new single on Festival's Infinity subsidiary label, a cover of Leon Russell's 'Hummingbird'/'Keep on Growing' (August 1971), before St John fell out with the rest of the members over his songwriting role and the band's overall direction. St John left in January 1972. Copperwine recruited Glyn Mason (vocals, guitar; ex-Rebels, **Chain**) and issued one single, 'Golden Angels'/ 'What's in a Day?' (June 1972). By that stage, the line-up comprised Mason, Kelly, Figures, East and new bass player Wayne Lanham (ex-Nova Express). Copperwine folded in August 1972. Mason went on to **Home** and **Ariel**.

St John formed the Jeff St John Band and took out second place (behind **Sherbet**) at the 1972 Battle of the Sounds. St John issued his debut solo single, David Clayton Thomas's 'Yesterday's Music'/'In the Window of Your Love' (October 1972). A&M issued the single in the USA with a new B-side, 'Lady of Ginger' (April 1973). Throughout 1973, St John scored support slots to international visitors Bo Diddley, Chuck Berry and Gary Glitter. He ended the year with the Most Outstanding Vocalist of the Year award. One of the songs that St John adopted around that time was **Richard Clapton's** 'I Wanna Be a Survivor', which remained in his live set for many years.

On 27 December 1973, St John played a farewell concert at the Sydney Opera House and flew to the UK. St John's backing band for the concert comprised Ron Barry (guitar, vocals), Tony Ansell (piano), B.J. (bass) and Peter Figures (drums; ex-Copperwine). Festival/Infinity issued the concert as the *Jeff St John Live* album in May 1974. With backing provided by John A. Bird (piano; ex-**Country Radio**), Vince Melouney (guitar; ex-**Billy Thorpe** and the Aztecs, **Bee Gees**, **Fanny Adams**, **Cleves**),

Bill Twyman (bass; ex-Third Union Band, Powderhorn) and Ace Follington (drums; ex-**Chain**, Powderhorn, **Cleves**), St John played a few low-key gigs on the London pub circuit. He returned to Australia in August 1974.

In 1975, with help from producer Martin Erdman and arranger John Robinson (ex-**Blackfeather**), St John issued two singles, 'Mr Jones'/'Acapulco Lady' (May) and 'Blood Brother'/'Reach Out and Touch Me' (October). He began touring with a new backing band, Red Cloud, which comprised Russell Moran (guitar), Tony Lyon (bass) and Neil Bamford (drums). In mid-1976, St John supported Bo Diddley on his third Australian tour. In 1977, St John became the first Australian artist to sign a record deal with Warners' US Asylum label (home to The Eagles, Linda Ronstadt and Jackson Browne). This resulted in his first national chart placing since 1971 with the single 'A Fool in Love'/'Pamela's Song' (#9 in August). 'Rock'n'Roll Man'/'Dream Merchants' followed in November, but it failed to chart. Festival issued the Glenn A. Baker-compiled 'Best of' album, *Survivor 1965–1975*, at the end of the year.

The *So Far So Good* album appeared in April 1978. It was a classy album of late 1970s mainstream rock, but neither it nor its third single, 'Starbrite'/'Knock 'Em Dead Kid' (April), charted strongly. St John continued to tour and issued a couple of flop singles, Otis Redding's '(Sittin' on) the Dock of the Bay'/'High Life' (July 1979) and 'I'll Never Need Anyone More'/'Giving It All to You' (January 1983), before retiring from live performances. His 1983 touring band had comprised Nick Andrews (guitar), John Kemp (guitar), James Rattray (bass; ex-**Ross Ryan** Brothers) and Andy Buchanan (drums; ex-**Mondo Rock**).

Albums: *Big Time Operators* (Jeff St John and the Id, Spin/Festival, 1967), *Joint Effort* (Jeff St John's Copperwine, Spin/Festival, 1970), *The Best of Jeff St John* (Spin/Festival, 1972), *Jeff St John Live* (Festival/Infinity, 1972), *Survivor 1965–1975* (compilation, Festival/Infinity, 1977), *So Far So Good* (Asylum, 1978).

John St Peeters

Style: *Pop*

Italian-born John St Peeters began his professional performing career during his early teens as Johnny Lo Piccolo, playing the piano accordion on television talent quests and in clubs. In 1974, he formed John St Peeters and the Sharells with two female vocalists. The singing trio toured Australia, Canada, the USA and South-East Asia, then issued a single, 'Take Me if You Want Me'/'Romance' (October 1975), on the Astor label.

In 1976, St Peeters launched his solo career with the disco-pop single 'You Know that You're Sexy'/'School's Out at Last' (November), which made the national charts at #28. St Peeters then signed to EMI and issued the singles 'Shiny Side Up'/'Summer of Love' (June 1977), 'Fadin' Away' (October) and 'Love the Way You Move' (December). At the end of 1977, St Peeters was voted Most Popular New Talent at the *TV Week* King of Pop Awards. In 1978, St Peeters signed to RCA. His first single for RCA, the self-penned 'Deep Inside of Me'/'Every Step of the Way', became his biggest hit when it reached #10 on the national chart during September 1978. By that stage, St Peeters had established himself as Australia's version of David Essex, with his good looks and sophisticated pop releases. 'High Class Woman'/'Keep Me Up Girl' (November) peaked at #37 during December.

In 1979, St Peeters formed the John St Peeters Band in order to tour the club circuit. His debut album, *So Many Ways*, and its single, 'So Many Ways'/'Al Capone', appeared in May 1979. 'So Many Ways' was another hit, reaching #13 on the national chart. St Peeters' subsequent singles and his second album, *One Night Stand*, sold well without reaching the national Top 40. Since late 1979, his singles have included 'You Were the One'/'Such a Hold on Me' (1979), 'Wonderworld' (theme song to children's television show *Simon Townsend's Wonderworld*)/'This Time Around' (March 1980), 'Love is All You Need'/'My Favourite Smile' (July), 'Dangerous Hearts'/'Dream Breaker' (April 1981), 'Street Kids'/'Theme from *Street Kids*' (September 1983), 'I Need that Someone to Love'/'One Kiss Away' (a duet with Jane Scali, 1985) and 'Don't Make Love to Strangers'/'Power Like the Thunder' (July 1986). St Peeters also recorded an album with Jane Scali called *Lovesongs*. Since the mid-1980s, St Peeters has concentrated on club and television work.

Albums: *So Many Ways* (RCA, 1978), *One Night Stand* (RCA, 1980).

The Saints

Formed: *1974*
Style: *Rock, R&B*
Original line-up: **Chris Bailey** *(vocals)*, **Ed Kuepper** *(guitar), Ivor Hay (bass), Jeffrey Wegener (drums)*

It was Sir Bob Geldof who once said that the face of rock music in the 1970s was altered by three bands: Sex Pistols, The Ramones and The Saints.

History will record that The Saints' howling, milestone debut single '(I'm) Stranded'/'No Time' predated everything thrown up by The Damned, Sex Pistols, The Buzzcocks, The Clash and their UK punk rock contemporaries.

'(I'm) Stranded' appeared in September 1976 on the band's own Fatal Records imprint. It was all but ignored by the local industry at the time. When *Sounds* magazine in the UK declared '(I'm) Stranded' to be 'Single of this and every week', EMI (Britain) ordered EMI (Australia) to sign the band, and pronto! Fuelled by **Ed Kuepper's** relentless power chords and **Chris Bailey's** cheap'n'nasty vocal sneer, '(I'm) Stranded' was a glorious rush of kinetic energy. When Bailey snarled '*Aw-right!!*' at the end of the chorus, you knew it was a celebration: he was happy to be stranded! Writer Stuart Coupe later called '(I'm) Stranded' 'powerhouse rock'n'roll' and 'desperately exciting'. Alongside Radio Birdman's *Burn My Eye* EP, '(I'm) Stranded' kicked off the Australian late 1970s new wave movement with a shower of teenage sweat and pure adrenalin.

The Saints grew out of Brisbane garage band Kid Galahad and the Eternals which occupied Bailey, Kuepper and Ivor Hay (then on piano) between 1973 and 1974. Kenyan-born, Belfast-raised Irishman Bailey and German-born Kuepper had both emigrated to Australia with their families during the 1960s. Their vast and catholic musical tastes ran the gamut of traditional blues (Howlin' Wolf, Jimmy Reed, John Lee Hooker), 1950s rock'n'roll (Chuck Berry, Eddie Cochran), UK 1960s R&B (The Yardbirds, The Rolling Stones, The Pretty Things), US 1960s garage-punk (The Standells, The Seeds, The Count Five, ? and the Mysterians), 1960s pop (Connie Francis, Del Shannon) and proto-punk pioneers (The Velvet Underground, The Stooges, MC5, New York Dolls).

All of those early influences eventually coalesced into The Saints' own distinctive sound as defined by Kuepper's frenetic, whirlwind guitar style and Bailey's arrogant snarl. The Saints really took off at the end of 1975 when Hay replaced Jeffrey Wegener on drums and Kym Bradshaw joined on bass. Almost immediately ostracised from the Brisbane scene, The Saints found it difficult to get gigs. As a consequence, they set up their own promotions company (Eternal Promotions), their own club (the 76 Club held in their Petrie Terrace home) and record label (Fatal).

Once '(I'm) Stranded' set the roller-coaster in motion, The Saints were in big demand. They signed to EMI in November 1976, recorded their debut album, *(I'm) Stranded*, in two days flat during December, supported **AC/DC** a few weeks later and had moved to Sydney by the new year. EMI issued *(I'm) Stranded* and reissued '(I'm) Stranded'/'No Time' in February 1977. The classic *(I'm) Stranded* was full of rough, exhilarating rock'n'roll noise, and it remains one of the greatest debut albums of the era. The album mixed turbo-charged, R&B-spiced rockers like '(I'm) Stranded', 'Erotic Neurotic', a cover of **The Missing Links'** 'Wild About You' and 'Nights in Venice' with atmospheric ballads like the Stonesy 'Messin' with the Kid'. The Saints toured the east coast, and 'Erotic Neurotic'/'One Way Street' (May 1977) appeared as their second single.

Even with the band's increased profile, the local industry was still unsure of how to deal with The Saints. They made an appearance on the ABC-TV's rock show ***Countdown*** playing 'Erotic Neurotic', but were immediately banned after the outspoken Kuepper and Bailey made certain disparaging remarks in the press about the show's content. With the release of *(I'm) Stranded* in the UK on EMI/Harvest, The Saints seemed ideally placed for a prime spot amidst the burgeoning punk phenomenon. In reality, The Saints were way beyond most of the then spiky-topped UK upstarts. By the time The Saints reached London in May 1977, they were no longer hip.

The Saints supported Talking Heads and The Ramones at the London Roundhouse on their first UK gig. The band's first regional tour was successful, but after that the fashion-conscious UK audiences of the day lost interest. The Saints never considered themselves to be punks anyway, being more attuned to developing far beyond their origins in a relatively short space of time. In June, Englishman Alasdair 'Algy' Ward replaced Bradshaw (who went on to play with London punk bands The Lurkers and King). The band's fourth single, the blazing 'This Perfect Day'/'L.I.E.S.' (July) peaked at #34 on the UK mainstream charts and the band appeared on *Top of the Pops*. EMI/Harvest in the UK, also issued a 12-inch version of the single with an additional track, 'Do the Robot', added inadvertently (as the disclaimer sticker on the cover stated) 'due to an administrative error'. In October, The Saints issued the *One-Two-Three-Four* EP which matched re-recordings of two cuts from the debut album ('Demolition Girl' and 'One Way Street') with ragged but inspired covers of Ike and Tina Turner's 'River Deep Mountain High' and Connie Francis's 'Lipstick on Your Collar'.

With the next single, 'Know Your Product'/'Run

Down' (February 1978), and the second album, *Eternally Yours* (May), Kuepper began to steer the band in a new direction: Stax/Volt horn parts melded to demolition R&B riffage played through Marshall stacks. All up, there was great passion at work on the album. With the band having refined the approach of the debut album without diminishing the impact, *Eternally Yours* remains The Saints' finest hour. And, in 'Know Your Product', the band created one of the greatest R&B-fuelled rock songs of all time.

The band's third classic album, *Prehistoric Sounds*, again was a departure. The rip-snorting power rock of old had been replaced by a darker, more ponderous mood. There was a general feeling of discontent on tracks like 'Swing for the Crime, 'Church of Indifference', 'Brisbane (Security City)' and 'The Prisoner'. For the single, the band put a cover of Otis Redding's 'Security' through the meatgrinder, backed by the bluesy 'All Times Through Paradise' (November 1978). By the time the album came out in Australia during February 1979, The Saints had already called it a day. During a period of dissent throughout 1978, matters came to a head over the direction of the band. Bailey wanted to write three-chord rockers and pop songs while Kuepper was moving towards less commercial, more cerebral material. *Prehistoric Sounds* was Kuepper's attempt to move as far away from The Saints' past as possible.

With the band's break-up, **Ed Kuepper** and Ivor Hay returned to Australia. Hay immediately joined **The Hitmen** before returning to the UK in June 1979. Kuepper formed **Laughing Clowns** in April 1979. Englishman Ward joined The Damned and then heavy metal band Tank. **Chris Bailey** remained in the UK and set about assembling a new version of The Saints which initially included Hay on drums. After a spell with his own jazz-inspired combo, Wildlife Documentaries, back in Sydney, Hay rejoined Bailey in The Saints during 1985. Reissue specialists Raven issued two Saints compilations, *Scarce Saints: Hymns of Oblivion 1977–1981* (1989) and *Songs of Salvation 1976–1988* (1990). The 1995 retrospective album *The Most Primitive Band in the World (Live from the Twilight Zone Brisbane 1974)* captured The Saints in all their ragged, prototypical garage band glory.

Albums: *(I'm) Stranded* (EMI, 1977), *Eternally Yours* (EMI/Harvest, 1978), *Prehistoric Sounds* (EMI/Harvest, 1979), *Scarce Saints: Hymns of Oblivion 1977–1981* (Raven, 1989), *Songs of Salvation 1976–1988* (Raven, 1990), *The Most Primitive Band in the World (Live from the Twilight Zone Brisbane 1974)* (Hot, 1995) *Know Your Product: The Best of the Saints* (EMI, 1996).

Kim Salmon and the Surrealists

Formed: *1988*
Style: *Rock, blues, funk*
Original line-up: *Kim Salmon (guitar, vocals; ex-Cheap Nasties,* **Scientists**, **Beasts of Bourbon**, *Salamander Jim), Brian Henry Hooper (bass), Tony Pola (drums)*

Tenacious singer/guitarist Kim Salmon was one of the first musicians in Australia to embrace wholeheartedly the emergent punk phenomenon of the mid- to late 1970s. He formed Perth's first punk band, The Cheap Nasties, in August 1976. Next he formed the legendary **Scientists**, a band he fronted for eight years. During that time, **Scientists** spent three years delivering their punk/blues/noise hybrid across the UK and Europe. Salmon also found time to tour and record with the **Beasts of Bourbon.**

With **Scientists**' eventual return to Australia in March 1987, and subsequent break-up, Salmon formed his next band, The Surrealists, with the above line-up. The Surrealists' first two albums, *Hit Me with the Surreal Feel* (October 1988) and *Just Because You Can't See It ... Doesn't Mean It Isn't There* (February 1990), featured a dark, confrontational sound powered by Salmon's scratchy, neurotic guitar and snarling vocals. In March 1988, **Beasts of Bourbon** reconvened, and Salmon spent the next five years dividing his time between two bands. The Surrealists' third album, *Essence* (September 1991), produced the singles 'Lightning Scary' (originally a Salmon solo release) and 'Zero Blank'/'The Cockroach', 'Obvious is Obvious'. At once wide-ranging and sharply focused, *Essence* was the band's most fully realised album to date.

The 'Non Stop Action Groove' CD EP (November 1992) and the *Sin Factory* album (May 1993) were even better, with Salmon's steely, blues-infused guitar riffs set atop a sprightly and very funky rhythm. As displayed on tracks like 'I Fell', 'Desensitised', 'Come on Baby', 'Listen to Your Brother' and the glorious 'Rose Coloured Windscreen', Salmon had also replaced confrontation and an all-out assault with a creeping perplexity. By the time the album came out, Greg Bainbridge had replaced Tony Pola on drums. Bainbridge had previously played with a number of Melbourne bands, including Jacksworld and Ton Up Pirates. Jacksworld comprised Bainbridge, Tim Cluning (vocals, guitar), David Bilston (lead guitar) and Michael Taylor (bass). The band played a moody brand of rock that drew comparisons with the likes of Echo and the Bunnymen, The Smiths and **The Triffids.**

David Walsh replaced Taylor in mid-1985. Au-go-go Records issued the band's debut mini-album, *Lie Down on the Couch* (which included contributions from guitarist Kevin Tredrea), in early 1986. A year later, the Rampant label issued the album *Spit the Dummy*. Bainbridge and Cluning split Jacksworld to form Ton Up Pirates with Greg Rodbard-Bean (bass) and Kenny Martin (lead guitar). The band issued one 12-inch EP, 'A Dirt Road So Far', on Au-go-go in 1988.

In August 1993, The Surrealists left for a three-month tour of Europe. During November, the band played stadiums as support act to UK visitors U2 on their gigantic Zoo-TV Australian tour. In June 1994, The Surrealists supported American hardcore heroes the Rollins Band on their Australian tour. A month later, Salmon issued his acclaimed debut solo album, *Hey Believer*. The album had been recorded live with backing provided by Salmon's *other* other band, STM, which comprised Warren Ellis (violin) and Jim White (drums) from **Dirty Three** and Andrew Entsch (bass). The Surrealists re-emerged with the CD single 'What's Inside Your Box?' (February 1995) and the *Kim Salmon and the Surrealists* album (April). Both releases included a re-recording of **Scientists'** 'Frantic Romantic'. In 1996, *Sin Factory* was issued in the USA with two additional tracks, 'You'll Pay for This' and 'Something to Lean on'.

Stuart Thomas (ex-Von Trapp Family Crisis) replaced Hooper on bass and the band undertook an American tour. Hooper returned to the reconvened **Beasts of Bourbon**, although Salmon declined to rejoin. Kim Salmon and the Surrealists issued two 7-inch vinyl singles, 'Fix Me Up'/'Sugartown' and 'The World of Love'/'I Won't Tell', on their own Guilt Free label during early 1997. Salmon augmented the basic Surrealists three-piece line-up with brass players Leon De Bruin (trumpet) and Michael Redman (tenor sax). Salmon and the Surrealists then issued a new single, 'Put Your Trust in Me'/'The Crying Game' (July 1997), and album, *Ya Gotta Let Me Do My Thing* (August), on the Half a Cow label. A new CD single from the album, 'You're Such a Freak', came out in November.

Kim Salmon and the Surrealists albums: *Hit Me with the Surreal Feel* (Black Eye, 1988), *Just Because You Can't See It ... Doesn't Mean It Isn't There* (Black Eye, 1989), *Essence* (Red Eye/Polydor, 1991), *Sin Factory* (Red Eye/Polydor, 1993), *Kim Salmon and the Surrealists* (Red Eye/Polydor, 1995) *Ya Gotta let me do My Thing* (Half a Cow/MDS, 1997); ***Kim Salmon solo album:*** *Hey Believer* (Red Eye/Polydor, 1994).

Samantha Sang

Style: *Pop*

Singer Samantha Sang (b. 1951) enjoyed a successful solo career during the 1960s as Cheryl Gray. She issued six singles for EMI between 1966 and 1968: 'Real Thing'/'Move on' (December 1966), 'Brand New Woman'/'In a Woman's Eyes' (December 1966), 'You Made Me What I Am'/'You Don't Love Me Anymore' (April 1967), 'When You're Not Near'/'You're the Boy' (August 1967), 'You Were There'/'Lonely People' (1968) and 'It's Not Easy Loving You'/'I'm Gonna Try' (1968). 'You Made Me What I Am' was her biggest hit, reaching #8 in May 1967.

In 1969, Gray travelled to the UK where she issued two singles, the Barry Gibb penned 'The Love of a Woman'/'Don't Let It Happen Again' and 'Nothing in the World Like Love'/'Mia Bamba'. By the early 1970s, she had re-emerged as Samantha Sang (her real name was Cheryl Lau Sang) and signed to Polydor. She issued three singles, 'It Could Have Been', 'Raining Every Day Since Monday'/'Nothing in the World Like Love' and 'Can't You Hear the Music?'/'You've Gone Away', and an album, *Samantha Sang and Rocked the World* in 1975.

In 1977, Sang recorded the Barry and Robin Gibb song 'Emotion'/'When Love is Gone' (produced by Barry), which became an international hit (Australian #2, UK #11, US #3 in April 1978). Sang was voted Top New Female Singer at the 1978 *Cashbox-Billboard* Awards in the USA. She continued to issue singles ('You Keep Me Dancing'/'Change of Heart'; 'In the Midnight Hour'/'Now') but failed to achieve further chart success.

Albums: *Samantha Sang and Rocked the World* (Polydor, 1975), *Emotion* (Private Stock, 1978), *From Dance to Love* (UA, 1979).

S.A.S.

Formed: *1986*
Style: *Heavy metal*
Original line-up: *Rene Smit (vocals), Simon Crofts (lead guitar; ex-Dave Evans' Hot Cockerel, Fair Warning), Don Jenkins (bass, keyboards; ex-Ion Drive), Steve Mitchelmore (drums)*

The Melbourne heavy metal fraternity circa mid-to-late 1980s included S.A.S., **Bengal Tigers**, **Taramis**, Axatak, Blackjack, Ion Drive, Virgin Soldiers, Taipan, Dirty Rats, Nothing Sacred, Fair Warning and others. S.A.S. was generally considered to be the city's premier metal act, with Simon Crofts installed as the foremost guitar hero of the day.

Crofts started out in Dave Evans' Hot Cockerel. In 1984, Crofts and Hot Cockerel rhythm guitarist Nello Franceshini joined Fair Warning, which comprised Bob Topping (vocals), Craig Foster (bass) and Darell Naudi (drums). Fair Warning issued the mini-album *Love to Rock'n'Roll* in 1985. In 1986, the band sacked frontman Topping, who was replaced by Dave Franklyn. Topping joined Carmen Suite, which comprised Vic De Marco (guitar), Jim Stoitis (guitar), Paul Ioannidis (bass) and Tony De Marco (drums). Manni Fernandes also replaced Foster on bass, and Stephen Hearn replaced Crofts on lead guitar, but the new Fair Warning line-up was short-lived.

Crofts went on to form S.A.S. with Rene Smit, Don Jenkins and Steve Mitchelmore. Jenkins' previous band, Ion Drive, was one of the most underrated heavy metal bands on the Melbourne scene. S.A.S. issued one accomplished album, *Warlords*, on the Cleopatra label (August 1987). On the evidence of the album, the band's influences included overseas heavy metal acts like Judas Priest, The Scorpions and Van Halen. Bob Topping replaced Smit on lead vocals; Robyn Colbreck then replaced Topping, but S.A.S. broke up in 1989. Crofts travelled to the USA to study for a year at the Guitar Institute of Technology (GIT) after coming second in an international scholarship competition held by GIT and Fender USA. He went on to play with Melbourne tribute bands like Back in Black and Killer Queen. Jenkins joined Enseminoids, Angelica and a revived Ion Drive.

Fair Warning mini-album: *Love to Rock'n'Roll* (Cleopatra, 1985); ***S.A.S. album:*** *Warlords* (Cleopatra, 1987).

Satellite

Formed: *1993*
Style: *Hard rock*
Original line-up: *Mia Stone (vocals; ex-Pizza Sluts, Stone Circus, Dirty Strangers), Bryce Ewing (guitar), Simon Grainger (guitar), Alex Fricke (bass), Graham Scott (drums; ex-***Models***)*

Provocative singer Mia Stone was a mainstay on the Melbourne inner-city, independent scene from the mid-1980s onwards. Her bluesy, operatic-like vocals drew many comparisons with the late Janis Joplin. As Stone has commented, she would be rich if she had a dollar for every time the words 'Mia Stone' and 'Joplinesque wails' were combined in the same sentence.

Stone began her career with psychedelic noise band Pizza Sluts in 1984, worked her way through Stone Circus, Dirty Strangers, Mia Stone's Ball and Chain and then Satellite. The original Pizza Sluts line-up of Stone, Dave Jetson (guitar), Dave Dog (sax; ex-End Result), Iggy Stewart (bass) and Lindsay Brunsdon (drums; from **Ku Klux Frankenstein**) came together in July 1984. Peter Tyrrell and Dean Richter replaced Jetson on guitar in November, and Rick Fortune (a stage name for modest rock journalist and author Ian McFarlane) replaced Brunsdon on drums. Pizza Sluts played a jazzy brand of acid-grunge noise inspired by 1960s psychedelia and 1970s funk with smatterings of Hawkwind, MC5 and New York Dolls thrown into the fray. The band played the underground Melbourne circuit alongside contemporaries like **Ku Klux Frankenstein**, **Venom P. Stinger**, **Cosmic Psychos**, Bum Steers and Behind the Magnolia Curtain before breaking up in January 1986.

Stone and Tyrrell formed Stone Circus with Dave Jetson (guitar), Angela Chenoweth (bass) and Mark Costello (drums). Stone Circus took up where Pizza Sluts had left off, playing modern acid rock. Probably the only Melbourne inner-city band ever to mix the complexities of King Crimson with the visceral impact of *Ju Ju* period Siouxsie and the Banshees by way of The Soft Boys, Stone Circus built up a strong cult following. As well as contributing tracks like 'Poison Tree', 'Incest' and 'Arnold's Day' to a variety of limited edition cassette releases, Stone Circus eventually issued a single, 'Fairground'/'Chaos and Law', on the Hippy Knight label in 1990. By that stage, the line-up comprised Stone, Tyrrell, Damian Bartasek (bass) and Rick Ferrara (drums; ex-Virgins, White Elephants, Beach Nuts, Deadbeats). Jetson had left to form Melt with Penelope Black (vocals), Stuart Harrison (bass) and Peter Doumtses (drums). Melt issued one independent CD EP, *Doll Meat Fist* (1992).

In 1990, Shane Grubb (ex-Slush Puppies) replaced Bartasek on bass. Chris Widdows then replaced Grubb and Stone Circus broke up in 1991. By that stage, Mia Stone had moonlighted with DJ Stratos Pavlis's part-time outfit, Dirty Strangers. That band's 1990 single, a cover of The Rolling Stones' 'Doo Doo Doo Doo Doo (Heartbreaker)'/ 'Dirty White Boy', featured the line-up of Stone, Pavlis (guitar), Ken Martin (guitar), Adam Leaner (bass; ex-**Blue Ruin**), Paul Keane (drums; ex-Boys Keep Swinging) and John 'Hammer' Hamilton (piano). Another of Stone's side projects was cover band Mia Stone's Ball and Chain which played Janis Joplin songs. Dirty Strangers re-emerged in 1992 with Graham Scott on drums. That association eventually led to the formation of Satellite in 1993.

Satellite continued Stone's obsession with hard-edged, gothic grunge rock. She was also known to grace a stage dressed in a PVC suit, replete with fish-net stockings and platform boots. Satellite issued its debut album *Wicked Wanda* in July 1995. The album's storyline was based around Stone's aggressive, ten-armed *Wicked Wanda* character (a more subversive take on the *Tank Girl* concept), and the package came complete with a *Wicked Wanda* comic book drawn by artist Dillon Naylor (also responsible for **The Fireballs'** comic series). The music alternated between a feline-like groove and a surging, powerful, energetic roar. Satellite issued a second album, *Feed the Monster*, in November 1996.

Albums: *Wicked Wanda* (Shock, 1995), *Feed the Monster* (Shock, 1996).

Savage Garden

Formed: *1994*
Style: *Pop*
Original line-up: *Darren Hayes (vocals), Daniel Jones (guitar, keyboards)*

The pop phenomenon known as Savage Garden came together when Darren Hayes and English-born Daniel Jones formed a songwriting partnership in 1994. The two musicians met during the early 1990s on the musical netherworld of the Gold Coast (Queensland) covers band circuit. Once the pair broke away from that circuit, they recorded demos of their original songs. With absolute and single-minded faith in their songwriting and performance abilities, the pair went on to record one of the most successful Australian albums of all time.

Savage Garden enlisted the high-powered management services of John Woodruff, who had previously worked with **The Angels**, **Baby Animals** and **Diesel**. Woodruff scored the pair an Australian deal with Roadshow/Warner, and later an international deal with Columbia. Savage Garden's platinum-selling, debut CD single, 'I Want You', peaked at #4 on the national chart during September 1996. 'To the Moon and Back' followed 'I Want You' into the national Top 5 during December, attaining the top spot two weeks later. It too sold over 70 000 copies. The third CD single, 'Truly, Madly, Deeply', reached #1 in April 1997, the same week the duo's album, *Savage Garden* (produced by Charles Fisher, best known for his work with **Moving Pictures** and **1927**, and mixed by Chris Lord-Alge), made its debut at #1 on the national album listing. *Savage Garden* registered platinum status (70 000 copies) in the first week of sales alone. 'Truly, Madly, Deeply' spent eight weeks at #1 and sold over 140 000 copies.

By the end of June 1997, *Savage Garden* had been at #1 for 14 straight weeks (with sales in excess of 350 000 copies), which was the longest stay at #1 for an Australian album since **Skyhooks'** *Living in the 70's* in 1974. The commercial success of Savage Garden's album was never in doubt (it went on to sell over 700 000 copies). In combination with the duo's photogenic, youthful good looks, the album's mix of joyous pop melodies, catchy choruses and smooth beats was perfect radio fodder. The album revealed the influence of 1980s UK pop on Hayes and Jones' songwriting. Tears for Fears melodies blended seamlessly with Eurythmics-like arrangements, while Cure-styled guitar provided the icing on the cake.

Savage Garden's fourth CD single, 'Break Me, Shake Me', made its debut at #7 at the end of June 1997. At the same time, 'I Want You' sat at #15 on the USA chart and #11 in the UK. 'Truly, Madly, Deeply' went on to attain the coveted #1 spot in the USA, while the album sold over 500 000 copies. The duo won an unprecedented ten awards (including Engineer of the Year and Producer of the Year for Charles Fisher) at the 1997 Australian Record Industry Association (ARIA) presentations. Savage Garden ended the year with the release of a new CD single, 'Universe' (November).

Album: *Savage Garden* (Roadshow/Warner, 1997).

Scandal

Formed: *1976*
Style: *Pop rock*
Original line-up: *Stuart Kerrison (vocals), Chris Harriot (keyboards, vocals), Peter Watson (guitar, vocals), Michael Smith (bass, vocals), Aldo Civitico (drums)*

Adelaide band Scandal formed in February 1976, and by the end of the year had signed a deal with the Mushroom label. The band's stylish, UK-influenced rock sound drew on the likes of Supertramp, Bryan Ferry and David Bowie for inspiration. Mushroom issued Scandal's debut single, 'Best Deal in Town'/'Mountain Legend', in March 1977, followed by 'Harry'/'Read All About It' during August.

The band enjoyed its only national hit single with a cover version of Ace's smooth, soul-pop gem 'How Long?'/'My Lady's Chamber' (#23 in May 1978). Scandal's debut, self-titled album (May 1978) also produced the band's fourth single, 'She's a Lady'/'Best Deal in Town' (June). It was to be the band's final record release. Scandal broke up in December 1978, and Kerrison, Harriot and Watson formed The Extractors. By August 1979, the three musicians had revived the Scandal name for a new band with Adrian Dessent (guitar), Greg Trennery (bass) and Nat De Palma (drums; ex-20th Century, New **Hush**). De Palma's old band, 20th Century, had issued one independent single, 'Lady'/'I Wanna See the Light', on the M7 label during 1978. The new Scandal line-up was not successful. Kerrison dropped from view, while Dessent went on to work with Vixen, the **Marc Hunter** Band and **Wendy and the Rocketts**. By 1983, Watson had joined Sydney band **The Venetians**.

Album: *Scandal* (Mushroom/Festival, 1978).

Scary Mother

Formed: *1990*
Style: *Rock*
Original line-up: *Andrew Gillespie (vocals), Anthony Brown (guitar), Toby Messiter (keyboards), Dario Bortolin (bass), Tim Buchanan (drums)*

Sydney band Scary Mother played a brooding, melodic brand of rock fleshed out by sweeping, atmospheric keyboard flourishes and barely restrained passion. Frontman Andrew Gillespie's vocals were likened variously to Pearl Jam's Eddie Vedder and The Cult's Ian Astbury, which was a good indication of Scary Mother's musical gambit.

In August 1992, Scary Mother issued its debut CD EP, *Scary Mother* (through MDS), which had been recorded as a demo. Dorian West (ex-Wildland, **Boom Crash Opera**) replaced Dario Bortolin on bass and the band signed to the ATI label (through Mushroom Records). West's first band, Wildland, played a brand of synth-rock reminiscent of UK outfit Big Country. The band comprised West, Noel Zammit (vocals), Keefe West (guitar), Jeff Lenham (guitar), Toby Messiter (keyboards) and Adrian Cannon (drums). In 1989, Wildland signed to CBS, and issued the singles 'One for Unity'/'Land' (August 1989), 'Hold Me'/'Last August' (November) and 'The Sun'/'Wildland' (1990), plus the album *In this Lifetime* before calling it quits.

The new Scary Mother line-up supported US visitors Faith No More on that band's Australian tour during April/May 1993. At the same time, Scary Mother issued a new CD single, 'Lord of the Flies', which had been produced by American Matt Wallace (also Faith No More's producer). 'Who are You?' followed in July. Mushroom issued the band's third CD single, 'Looking Down', in April 1994, followed by the debut album, *Tai Laeo* (produced by Rick Will), a month later. The album's title came from a phrase that Gillespie heard during his childhood spent in Thailand. It was an expression that literally meant 'already gone'.

Album: *Tai Laeo* (ATI/Mushroom/Festival, 1994).

Scattered Aces (*see* Peter Wells)

Scattered Order

Formed: *1980*
Style: *Experimental rock*
Original line-up: *Mitch Jones (vocals, guitar, bass), Michael Tee (guitar), Patrick Gibson (guitar, synthesiser)*

In the post-punk, hurly-burly days of the early 1980s, experimentation was the norm rather than the alternative. The inner-city Sydney scene of the day was awash with experimentalists like **SPK**, **Severed Heads**, **Makers of the Dead Travel Fast**, Wet Taxis, N-Lets, The Systematics, Slugfuckers, Wild West, Seems Twice, Hiroshima Chair and possibly the most valiant of the lot, Scattered Order.

As the name implied, Scattered Order's original aim was to combine all manner of 'found sounds' and loose song structures with a perverse absurdist sense of humour (in the Snakefinger/Residents vein) and set them to a rock backing; in short, white noise with an amphetamine beat. Scattered Order started life in January 1980 as a loose conglomeration based around Mitch Jones, Michael Tee and Patrick Gibson. Scattered Order was just one of various prospects gathered under the banner of maverick independent record label and studio concern M Squared run by Jones, Tee and Gibson. Jones also worked as an in-demand live sound engineer for the likes of **The Birthday Party** and **Pel Mel**.

Early Scattered Order line-ups were never meant to be fixed, and changed from recording to recording to accommodate new members and different approaches to the studio. Scattered Order began recording, but went into semi-retirement while the trio acted as the engineering and production team for the other M Squared artists. The first Scattered Order recordings, 'Bent Up' and 'I'm Not Whole', appeared respectively on the M Squared Various Artists releases *Growing Pains* (November 1980) alongside Barons, EST, Height/Dismay, **Makers of the Dead Travel Fast**, Pleasant Pheasants and Systematics; and *A Selection* (November 1981) alongside Aural Indifference, The Limp, **Makers of the Dead Travel Fast**, Negative Reaction, **Pel Mel**, **Severed Heads**, Slugfuckers, SoliPSik, Splendid Mess, The Systematics, Tame O'Mearas and Wild West.

Scattered Order rarely performed live (nine gigs to late 1983) but did issue the four-track, 7-inch EP 'Screaming Tree' (May 1981) and the abrasive *Prat Culture* album (November 1982). Culled from both live and studio sessions, *Prat Culture* featured the line-up of Jones, Tee, Gibson and Michael Prowse (drums). Tee and Gibson left Scattered Order in late 1982. Tee, who had already been involved in The Barons and Pleasant Pheasants, formed **Ya Ya Choral**. Gibson spent some time with **Ya Ya Choral** which also included Fiona Graham (vocals) from Gibson's other band, The Systematics. That band issued the single 'Pulp Baby'/'Nuts to You', 'Product' on the Doublethink label (January 1980), plus the mini-album *Rural* (November 1980) and the EP 'My Life in the Field of Cows' (1981) on M Squared before breaking up. The Systematics' tracks 'Midnight on Balancing Day' and 'Die for My House' also appeared respectively on the compilations *Growing Pains* and *A Selection*. Gibson formed Moral Fibro.

In the meantime, the Scattered Order line-up of Jones, Prowse and Shane Fahey (synthesiser, vocals; ex-**Makers of the Dead Travel Fast**) recorded the 12-inch EP *I Feel So Relaxed with You* (October 1983). Rock writer Mark Mordue described Scattered Order on *I Feel So Relaxed with You* as 'all open guts and withered emotions' and musically akin to Public Image Ltd. The EP was all but ignored locally but sold well in Europe. Soon after, the line-up expanded with the arrival of Drusilla Johnson (soon to be Mrs Mitch Jones; synthesiser, vocals), R. Scott Holmes (vocals, guitar, synthesiser, percussion; ex-Same) and Craig Bottle (bass; ex-**Pel Mel**) who was quickly replaced by D.C. Robertson (also in **Flaming Hands** along with Michael Prowse).

Mitch Jones folded M Squared at the end of 1983 and Scattered Order signed to the Volition label. The band entered its most active phase in 1984 with east coast tours and an increase in record releases. Recorded live during January 1984, *A Dancing Foot and a Praying Knee Don't Belong on the Same Leg* featured a rhythmic brand of clattering, metallic funk. Just prior to the album's release, Fahey left Scattered Order. The band's third album, *Career of the Silly Thing* (September 1985), represented something of a breakthrough release, revealing a shift towards a more conventional and melodic yet still challenging sound. The album yielded the single 'Escape Via Cessnock'/'100 Gene Autrys' (1985). UK label Fire issued *Career of the Silly Thing* on its Ink offshoot imprint. Scattered Order toured with fellow Volition stablemates **Severed Heads** and supported US visitors The Residents on their Australian tour.

In August 1986, Geoff Holmes (guitar; ex-Wildcat Tamers) expanded the line-up to a six-piece. Ironically, his arrival heralded the departure of long-serving member Scott Holmes in early 1987. The band recorded a new 12-inch EP, *Selling the Axe to Buy the Wood*, which contained 'Loose in the House', the closest Scattered Order came to scoring a 'hit' single. Before the EP appeared in June 1987, Michael Prowse had left the band. In January 1988, Scattered Order recorded a new album, *Comfort*, which was the band's most accessible album to date. Helping out on the album sessions were guest drummers Robert Souter (from **Dynamic Hepnotics**) and Greg Fitzgerald. *Comfort* produced the single 'King of Blip'/'Comfort Five Range', 'Love is Not' (April 1988). *Comfort* was issued as a double set combined with the eight-track 'Best of' collection *1981–1987*.

The band undertook The Comfort and Joy national tour with new Volition signing **Falling Joys**. Drummer Greg Fitzgerald joined Scattered Order for the tour. Scattered Order issued its fifth album, *Professional Dead Ball* in December 1991. The band slipped from view, only to re-emerge in August 1997 with the *Chicken Hilton* album on the Rather be Vinyl label.

Albums: *Prat Culture* (M Squared, 1982), *A Dancing Foot and a Praying Knee Don't Belong on the Same Leg* (Volition, 1984), *Career of the Silly Thing* (Volition, 1985), *Comfort/1981–1987* (compilation, Volition, 1988), *Professional Dead Ball* (Volition, 1991) *Chicken Hilton* (Rather be Vinyl, 1997).

John Schumann (*see* Redgum)

Scientists

Formed: *1978*
Style: *Punk*
Original line-up: **Kim Salmon** *(guitar, vocals; ex-Cheap Nasties, Invaders)*, **Roddy Radalj** *(guitar, vocals; ex-Exterminators, Invaders), Boris Sujdovic (bass; ex-Exterminators, Invaders), James Baker (drums; ex-Geeks, Beheaded,* **Victims***)*

In August 1976, inspired by The Ramones and New York Dolls, **Kim Salmon** formed Perth's first punk band, The Cheap Nasties. Robert Porritt (vocals), Neil Fernandez (guitar), Dan Dare (bass) and Mark Betts (drums) completed the line-up. Like so many other primeval punk bands of the day, The Cheap Nasties made little headway and broke up in December 1977.

Salmon joined The Invaders, while the rest of The Cheap Nasties continued on as **Manikins**. The Invaders had started out as The Exterminators with a line-up of Mark Demetrius (vocals; replaced by Salmon), **Roddy Radalj** (guitar, vocals), Boris Sujdovic (bass) and John Dowlings (drums). The Invaders became The Scientists in May 1978 when James Baker replaced Dowlings on drums. Baker had been a member of Perth's most famous punk band, **The Victims**, alongside Dave Flick (real name Dave Faulkner). In August 1978, Sujdovic left The Scientists, and the band did not re-emerge until January 1979 with new bass player Dennis Byrne.

In April, Radalj and Byrne were replaced by Ben Juniper and Ian Sharples respectively. Radalj and Sujdovic formed The Rockets with Allan Stewart (vocals), Peter Johnson (guitar) and John Cole (drums). The Rockets issued one independent single, 'Mean Mistress'/'Little Donna' (February 1980), on the White Rider label before Radalj and Sujdovic left the band. Stewart and Johnson recruited new players and continued on until 1985.

The Scientists' debut, independent single, 'Frantic Romantic'/'Shake (Together Tonight)' (June 1979), featured the Salmon/Baker/Radalj/Byrne line-up. Along with *The Scientists* EP (February 1980), the 'Frantic Romantic' single went on to become one of the most collectable artefacts of the Australian punk rock era. The Scientists undertook two eastern states tours (December 1979 and February/March 1980). While in Melbourne, The Scientists made an appearance on the ABC-TV pop show ***Countdown***, performing The Flamin' Groovies-styled 'Last Night' (from *The Scientists* EP). In May 1980, Juniper left The Scientists and Salmon, Baker and Sharples continued on as a three-piece. By the end of the year, The Scientists had run out of steam. The band broke up after recording an album in January 1981. Baker left Perth to join Radalj and Dave Faulkner in Sydney in their new band, Le **Hoodoo Gurus**. Salmon formed Louie Louie with Kim Williams (bass) and Brett Rixon (drums; ex-Screaming Fits). By the time *The Scientists* album (commonly referred to as *The Pink Album*) came out in August 1981, Salmon had broken up Louie Louie.

In September 1981, Salmon and Sujdovic re-formed the band as Scientists and decided to move to Sydney. Rixon joined on drums and Salmon recruited Tony Thewlis (ex-**Helicopters**) on guitar. By the time Scientists arrived in Sydney, Salmon had dropped the melodic, punky power pop of old for a more malevolent, psychedelic-tinged neo-rock'n'roll. Having absorbed influences from American icons like The Cramps, The Velvet Underground, Captain Beefheart and Suicide, plus 1960s acid-punk, the band's snarling punk/blues/noise hybrid attracted a whole new audience. Scientists came to the attention of Bruce Milne, who issued the band's singles 'This is My Happy Hour'/'Swampland' (December 1982) and 'We Had Love'/'Clear Spot' (December 1983) and the consummate mini-album *Blood Red River* (September) on his Au-go-go label. *Blood Red River* was unlike any other record issued by an Australian band to that point; it remains one of the most original and influential records of the post-punk era.

Scientists were a compelling group because they manifested a sound and an attitude that captured the essence of real rock'n'roll: passionate, intense and threatening. The most publicised example of this was when the band supported Aussie pub-rock veterans **The Angels** at the Parramatta Leagues Club in Sydney's western suburbs. With their safe preconceptions having been shattered by Scientists' confrontational music, **The Angels'** audience responded to the band with a barrage of beer cans and glasses. Scientists endured the barrage for 20 minutes before leaving the stage, content in the knowledge they had ruined the entire audience's night out.

By the end of 1983, Scientists were one of the most popular independent bands on the Melbourne scene (alongside **Hunters & Collectors** and **Sacred Cowboys**). Yet, rather than consolidate their live standing on home turf, Scientists left for the UK in March 1984. Before their departure, Salmon and Sujdovic found time to tour and record with **Beasts of Bourbon**. Salmon also played with Beasts frontman **Tex Perkins** in Salamander Jim. Like **The Saints, The Birthday Party, The Go-Betweens** and **Laughing Clowns** before them (plus **The Moodists** and **The Triffids** later in the year), Scientists made an indelible impression on the UK independent scene. In October 1984, the band supported US outfit The Gun Club on that band's UK/European tour. In the meantime, Au-go-go issued the *This Heart Doesn't Run on Blood, This Heart Doesn't Run on Love* mini-album which was already a year old by the time it came out in September 1984.

Scientists' first overseas recordings appeared as the *Demolition Derby* 12-inch EP in February 1985 (only issued in Belgium, Holland and Luxembourg). The band's first overseas album, *You Get What You Deserve*, came out on the Karbon label in July 1985, followed by the single 'You Only Live Twice'/'If It's the Last Thing I Do' (September). *You Get What You Deserve* was the band's most potent statement to date, a work charged with dark emotions and dripping with primal, free-form rock'n'roll. Due to a dispute between the band and its Australian record label Au-go-go, the album also saw release locally in a different form as *Atom Bomb Baby* (July 1985). Au-go-go also issued the single 'Atom Bomb Baby'/'Backwards Man' and the compilation *Heading for a Trauma* that month.

Rixon had left the band in February 1985, and his departure marked the beginning of the implosion which continued until the band's demise in 1987. American Richard Hertz took Rixon's place, and the band supported The Sisters of Mercy and then Siouxsie and the Banshees on their respective UK tours. In December 1985, Leanne Chock replaced Hertz on drums. Scientists recorded a new album, *Weird Love*, with producer Richard Mazda (The Fall, Wall of Voodoo). *Weird Love* featured 11 re-recorded versions of some of the band's best-known songs. Sujdovic left the band after recording the album, and Salmon recruited Rob Coyne (on loan from Silver Chapter). Sujdovic returned to Australia and joined **The Dubrovniks**. *Weird Love* came out during April 1986. Coyne and Chock left in December, forcing Salmon to take over bass while Nick Combe came in on drums. The new three-piece recorded the album *Human Jukebox*, by which time Scientists had run out of steam. The band returned to Australia in April 1987 for the *Human Jukebox* tour, but broke up immediately after its completion.

As displayed on the throbbing *Human Jukebox* album, Scientists had ditched the last vestiges of melody and structure for a more experimental, minimalist sound where guitar and vocals wailed over relentless, metronomic drumming. The album appeared in October 1987, and Salmon took his new band The Surrealists (Brian Henry Hooper, bass; Tony Pola, drums) out on tour in order to promote its release. *Human Jukebox* proved to be a dry run for what Salmon achieved with the first Surrealists album *Hit Me with the Surreal Feel*. Thewlis formed **The Interstellar Villains**. In 1988, Salmon and Sujdovic joined the reconstituted **Beasts of Bourbon** for a series of notable albums and tours. The Scientists era effectively came to an end with the drug-related death of former drummer Brett Rixon in December 1993. The Salmon/Baker/Sharples/Juniper line-up re-formed for a one-off gig in Perth on 10 February 1995.

The Scientists albums: *The Scientists* (aka *The Pink Album*, EMI Custom, 1981; reissued on Easter, 1986), *The Sweetcorn Sessions* (compilation mini-album of first single and EP, Timberyard, 1988), *Pissed on Another Planet* (reissue of *The Sweetcorn Sessions*, Timberyard, 1989); ***Scientists albums:*** *Blood Red River* (mini-album, Au-go-go, 1983), *This Heart Doesn't Run on Blood, This Heart Doesn't Run on Love* (Au-go-go, 1984), *Atom Bomb Baby* (Au-go-go, 1985), *You Get What You Deserve* (UK issue of *Atom Bomb Baby*, Karbon, 1985), *Heading for a Trauma* (compilation, Au-go-go, 1985), *Weird Love* (UK import, Karbon, 1986), *The Human Jukebox* (UK import, Karbon, 1987), *Absolute* (compilation, Red Eye, 1991).

Scrap Metal

Formed: *1983*
Style: *Reggae, country*
Original line-up: *Michael Ambi (lead vocals), Stephen Pigram (vocals, guitar), Alan Pigram (guitar), Michael Teh (bass), Phillip Pigram (drums)*

Broome-based Koori band Scrap Metal played a dancey brand of rock spiced with dashes of reggae and country flavours. Formed and guided by the Pigram brothers, Stephen, Alan and Phillip, the band developed in almost complete isolation away from the Australian music industry. Situated on the remote north-western coast of Western Australia, and once the centre of a thriving pearl trade, Broome is nevertheless one of the most culturally diverse towns in Australia. The members of Scrap Metal could count Aboriginal, Filipino, Chinese, French, Irish, Indonesian, Japanese and Scottish among their immediate ancestors.

The Pigram brothers had played together since 1977, first in Crossfire and later Sunburn. Original Scrap Metal lead singer Michael Ambi drowned in 1985, and Johnny Albert joined on guitar and lead vocals. Duncan Campbell also joined on keyboards after a stint as the band's manager. Scrap Metal spent years playing to modest crowds in Broome, and occasionally making the 600-kilometre trip south to play Port Hedland and travelling over 200 kilometres to play Derby in the north. Scrap Metal recorded a self-financed cassette, *Just Looking*, which came to the attention of **Midnight Oil**. Scrap Metal suddenly found themselves supporting the Oils on their October 1987 Diesel and Dust national tour.

The members of Scrap Metal formed their own label, Jigil, and issued the debut album *Broken Down Man* in October 1988. The album produced two singles, 'Broken Down Man'/'Caught in the Wheel' (September) and 'Nimunburr (Flying Fox)'/'In the Night' (January 1989). The band also contributed 'Broken Down Man' to the Various Artists album *Burning Bridges* on CBS (1989). In 1989, Scrap Metal scored a deal with ABC Records (through PolyGram). The deal resulted in the band's second album, *Scrap Metal* (August 1990), and the singles 'Make It Work' (November) and 'Howling at the Moon' (April 1991). Scrap Metal became the first Aboriginal band to secure an international publishing deal through Warner Chappell.

In 1990, Scrap Metal participated in **Jimmy Chi's** musical play *Bran Neu Dae*. Scrap Metal performed the music alongside Chi's band Kuckles, and Stephen Pigram acted as musical director. April 1991 saw Scrap Metal featured in the ABC-TV documentary *From Broome to the Big Smoke*, which traced the band's career with live and in-the-studio footage. Scrap Metal issued a new album in May 1993, *Pub Sweat and Tears*. Since that time, very little has been heard from Scrap Metal, although the Pigram brothers recorded a new album, *Saltwater Country*, with producer **Shane Howard** in early 1997.

Albums: *Broken Down Man* (Jigil/Larrikin, 1988), *Scrap Metal* (ABC/PolyGram, 1990), *Pub Sweat and Tears* (Jigil, 1993), *Saltwater Country* (as The Pigram Brothers, Jigil, 1997).

Screamfeeder

Formed: *1991*
Style: *Indie guitar pop*
Original line-up: *Tim Stewart (guitar, vocals), Kellie Lloyd (bass, vocals), Tony Blades (drums)*

Brisbane band Screamfeeder started life as The Madmen, comprising Tim Stewart, Tony Blades, Bruce Gardner (guitar, vocals) and Jeff Johnson (bass). The Madmen formed in Townsville, Queensland during 1988, having emerged from the ashes of one of the city's only punk bands, Lethal Injection. In 1989, Cam Hurst replaced Johnson on bass and Gardner left the band. That same year, The Madmen issued a single, 'Almost Past Caring'/'That's Okay with Me' (June), on Brisbane label Bent. In 1990, The Madmen issued two more singles, 'Tower' and 'Cool Kinda Kid', plus the 12-inch EP *Thunder Egg*. With the move to Brisbane and the arrival of new bass player Kellie Lloyd during 1991, The Madmen became Screamfeeder.

Screamfeeder's formative influences included the likes of US outfits Hüsker Dü, Dinosaur Jr, Swervedriver and Redd Kross. The band played the same scene that gave rise to the likes of **Powderfinger**, **Regurgitator** and **Dreamkillers**. Sydney independent label Survival (home to **Massappeal**, **Nursery Crimes** and **Bored!**) issued the band's debut album, *Flour*, in August 1992. Screamfeeder contributed a track to rooArt's Australian grunge-pop compilation *Crack in the Sun or Fade in the Shade* (November 1992) alongside **You Am I**, **Tumbleweed**, **The Meanies**, **The Guttersnipes**, **Nursery Crimes**, **Massappeal**, Seaweed Goorillas and others.

Screamfeeder

The acclaimed *Burn Out Your Name* album and single 'Fingers and Toes' followed in August 1993. By that stage, Screamfeeder had supported overseas visitors like Rollins Band, Sonic Youth, Ride and Pavement on Australian tours. US independent label Taang! issued *Burn Out Your Name* in North America. At the end of 1993, Screamfeeder undertook a joint, six-week, 27-date European tour with **The Screaming Tribesmen** and **The Chevelles**. The band appeared on the bill of the 1994 national Big Day Out tour. A new CD EP, 'Felicitator', appeared in May 1994. At the end of the year, Screamfeeder recorded a new album with producer Wayne Connolly (**Welcome Mat**). *Fill Yourself with Music* produced the CD single 'Fill Yourself with Music' (April 1995) and the CD EP 'Who's Counting?' (September). The album confirmed the band's ability to craft guitar-heavy, but always melodic and fervent, pop rock.

Just prior to the album's release, a third promised American tour fell through, and the band severed its connection with the Taang! label. This period of frustration was further compounded by the departure of long-standing drummer Blades. Dean Shwereb came in as Blades' replacement.

Lloyd issued her debut, solo album *For Nothing and No One* at the same time as the fourth Screamfeeder album, *Kitten Licks*, appeared (August 1996). Produced by Paul McKercher (**You Am I**, **Cruel Sea**, **Tumbleweed**), *Kitten Licks* was brimming with well-crafted, off-kilter punky power pop. It contained the CD singles 'Dart' (July) and 'Static' (December), which was one of the band's best songs. Screamfeeder appeared on the bill of the Big Day Out tour (January 1997), and issued a new CD single from *Kitten Licks*, 'Gravity', during May.

Albums: *Flour* (Survival, 1992), *Burn Out Your Name* (Survival, 1993), *Fill Yourself with Music* (Hypnotized/Shock, 1995), *7 Year Glitch* (compilation of out-takes, demos and live material, Hypnotized/Shock, 1996), *Kitten Licks* (Hypnotized/Shock, 1996).

Screaming Believers

Formed: *1981*
Style: *Rock*
Original line-up: *Paul Hughes (vocals, sax; ex-Shreds), Ken Sykes (guitar, vocals; ex-Shreds), Graeme Burdett (guitar; ex-Shreds), Rees Hughes (bass; ex-Fools Apart), Craig Rodda (drums; ex-Shreds, Fools Apart)*

Despite being one of the longest-lived bands on the Adelaide independent scene of the 1980s, Screaming Believers made little impression beyond a cult following. Screaming Believers' handful of records were brimming with refined songs and highly proficient, melodic guitar thrash. That they failed to attract a wider audience is a great shame.

Screaming Believers grew out of The Shreds, which comprised Paul Hughes, Ken Sykes, Graeme Burdett, Craig Rodda and Richard Opolski (bass). Hughes had just turned 15 years of age at the time of the band's inception in early 1980. The Shreds transformed into Screaming Believers when Rees Hughes joined in mid-1981. In early 1982, Screaming Believers issued the 'Show Me Your Money' EP on the Empty Dogma label. Recorded live at the Union Hotel during September 1981, the EP featured Screaming Believers' sound in nascent form. The band honed its skills with regular gigs around Adelaide, including support slots to UK visitors like The Human League, Psychedelic Furs and John Cooper Clarke. Doug Thomas issued Screaming Believers' debut single, 'My Eyes'/'Unprofessional' on his Greasy Pop label (February 1984). Screaming Believers also shared a split single with Fools Apart, 'I Want to Have You'/'Within an Inch' (August).

Screaming Believers contributed the tracks 'I Want to Have You' and 'Unprofessional' to Greasy Pop's Various Artists cassette compilation *A Greasy Selection* (March 1985). 'My Eyes' also appeared on the Hot label's *No Worries* compilation album (1984). During the second half of 1984, Rodda moonlighted on drums with **Exploding White Mice**. He played on the band's debut, mini-album, *A Nest of Vipers*. At the end of 1984, Screaming Believers recorded their excellent debut album, *Communist Mutants from Space*, with producer/engineer Bob Allan. By the time the album appeared in June 1985, John Cavouto (ex-Innocents) had replaced Burdett on guitar. Burdett went on to join **The Garden Path** and The Psycho Daisies. Cloudi Katern (ex-Units) also replaced Rees Hughes on bass during 1985. Hughes formed The-Ists with Allan Robbins (guitar, vocals). With assistance from Rodda on drums, The-Ists recorded an album, *Rose*, which came out on Greasy Pop in 1988.

Meanwhile, Screaming Believers issued a new single, 'Sandra'/'Is Vic There?', in July 1987. Chris Lambden replaced Katern on bass, and in March 1988 the band's second album, *Refugees from the Love Generation*, appeared on Greasy Pop. Just before the album's release 16-year-old Jodie Petersen replaced Lambden. Screaming Believers recorded a new album (provisionally titled *Stories from the Other Side*) which remained unissued. They continued to tour but, having failed to snare wider acceptance, called it a day in 1991. Rodda joined **The Garden Path** but that band also split soon after.

Albums: *Communist Mutants from Space* (Greasy Pop, 1985), *Refugees from the Love Generation* (Greasy Pop, 1988).

The Screaming Jets

Formed: *1989*
Style: *Hard rock*
Original line-up: *Dave Gleeson (vocals; ex-Aspect), Grant Walmsley (guitar; ex-Aspect), Richard Lara (guitar), Paul Woseen (bass), Brad Heaney (drums; ex-DV8,* **Radiators***)*

Highly touted blue-collar hard rock band The Screaming Jets were one of the most successful outfits to emerge from Newcastle (NSW). Fronted by loud-mouthed rock'n'roll bad boy Dave Gleeson, the brash, young five-piece grew out of the ashes of high school band Aspect. Gleeson and Grant Walmsley joined forces with Richard Lara, Paul Woseen and Brad Heaney to form The Screaming Jets in January 1989.

The Jets drew capacity crowds in their hometown, and in November 1989 won the inaugural National Band Competition. By early 1990, The

Jets had relocated to Sydney where their brand of no-frills, hard blues rock attracted a good deal of industry attention. A national tour supporting **The Angels** followed, and by May 1990 The Jets had signed a deal with the rooArt label (home to **Ratcat**, **The Hummingbirds**, **Wendy Matthews**, **Absent Friends**). The band entered the studio with producer Steve James (Sex Pistols, **Mental as Anything**) in mid-1990 to record its debut album. The Screaming Jets' debut EP, *The Scorching Adventures of . . . The Screaming Jets* ('C'mon'/'Sister Tease', 'Shine on') was issued by rooArt in December 1990.

The album, *All for One* (April 1991), was a cogent and energetic release, one of the strongest debuts from an Australian hard rock band. Reference points for the album's gritty rock'n'roll included the flash of early Van Halen mixed with the traditional thunder of **AC/DC** and **The Angels**. As well as containing the three tracks from the *Scorching Adventures* EP, the album produced the singles 'Better'/'Rocket Man' (February 1991), 'Stop the World' (May) and the remixed 'Shine on' (September). 'Better' took the band into the national Top 10 (#4) for the first time. It went on to become the #20 biggest selling single in Australia during 1991.

By that stage, The Jets had earned a reputation as the local music industry's *enfants terrible*, mostly due to Gleeson's loose tongue onstage. The band was dropped from its support slot on the **Divinyls'** national tour 'officially' because of Gleeson's repeated onstage swearing, but 'unofficially' due to unsavoury comments he made of a sexual nature regarding Chrissie Amphlett. Gleeson was also known to voice his negative opinion about gays and Asians, which alienated more potential listeners. The promotional-only live *Stealth* EP contained the onstage favourite 'F.R.C.' ('Fat Rich Cunts'), which Gleeson would dedicate to the likes of Michael Gudinski or Russ Hinze on any given night.

At the end of 1991, The Jets travelled overseas for a lengthy tour of the USA and Europe. While in Los Angeles, The Jets recorded 16 demo tracks at Frank Zappa's famed Joe's Garage Studio. Gleeson also returned to Australia sporting a freshly cut mohawk hairstyle. The Jets started 1992 with the Kill Your Idols national tour. The band's third EP, 'Living in England' (June 1992), included covers of Johnny Cash's 'Folsom Prison Blues' and **AC/DC**'s 'Ain't No Fun (Waiting to Be a Millionaire)'. The EP confirmed the band's standing in hometown Newcastle when it remained at #1 on the singles chart for more than 20 weeks.

In July, the band embarked on the Living in England tour of Australia, supported by highly rated UK group The Almighty. 'Living in England' appeared on the second album, *Tear of Thought* (October 1992), which also produced the CD singles 'Think' (August), 'Shivers' (January 1993) and 'Here I Go' (July). The band's cover of The Boys Next Door's 'Shivers' peaked at #19 on the national chart. Just prior to the album's release in Australia, The Jets toured Europe and the UK with British blues-rock band Thunder (including three nights at London's legendary Hammersmith Odeon).

The Jets returned to the UK in April 1993 to support roots-rockers The Quireboys, and then to headline their own shows throughout May. UK heavy metal magazines like *Metal Hammer* and *Kerrang!* showered The Jets with rave reviews, declaring the band to be one of the best new outfits on the UK scene. 'Here I Go' featured four live cuts recorded in the UK. While on tour, Brad Heaney was dismissed from the band. British drummer Dave Holland (ex-Judas Priest) filled in on the final leg of the band's European tour supporting US brat-rockers Ugly Kid Joe. New drummer Craig Rosevear (ex-**B.B. Steal**, Angry Snuff Puppet) joined the band in July 1993, just in time for a lengthy US tour supporting Def Leppard and Ugly Kid Joe. The Jets returned to Australia in December 1993, which coincided with the release of a new

The Screaming Jets

CD single, 'Helping Hand' (from *Tear of Thought*), and the video compilation *Insanitary*.

In January 1994, Richard Lara left the band to be replaced by **Jimi 'the Human' Hocking** (ex-Spectre 7). The unexpected Top 5 success of 'Helping Hand' reactivated interest in the 18-month-old *Tear of Thought* album. During June, the album peaked at #3 on the national chart, eventually attaining platinum status (70 000 copies sold). RooArt issued a remixed version of 'Tunnel' (from *Tear of Thought* and 'Living in England') as a single during August 1994. Under the direction of producer Robbie Adams (U2), the band completed its third album, *The Screaming Jets* (September 1995). *The Screaming Jets* made its debut at #5 on the national chart, and produced the CD singles 'Friend of Mine' (October) and 'Sacrifice' (May 1996). The Jets continued to tour, recording a fourth album, *World Gone Crazy*, at the end of 1996. By the time the CD single 'Elvis (I Remember)' appeared on rooArt/BMG during June 1997, Hocking had left The Jets to return to the Melbourne pub circuit. Ismet 'Izzy' Osmanovich (ex-**Judge Mercy**) replaced Hocking. *World Gone Crazy* reached #18 on the national chart in August 1997. The album's second CD single, a cover of Barry McGuire's 'Eve of Destruction', followed in September.

Albums: *All for One* (rooArt/Phonogram, 1991), *Tear of Thought* (rooArt/Warners, 1992), *The Screaming Jets* (rooArt/Warners, 1995) *World Gone Crazy* (rooArt/BMG, 1997).

The Screaming Tribesmen

Formed: *1981*
Style: *Rock*
Original line-up: *Mick Medew (guitar, lead vocals; ex-31st), John Hartley (bass, vocals; ex-***Fun Things***), Murray Shepherd (drums, vocals; ex-***Fun Things***)*

Throughout the 1980s, The Screaming Tribesmen were one of the most revered bands on the Sydney independent scene. Led by the mercurial Mick Medew, The Tribesmen fashioned a memorable brand of 1960s-inspired pop rock that combined equal parts existential lyric angst, melodic inventiveness and strident guitar riffs. The band's handful of releases on the Citadel label are classics of their kind.

Medew had come into contact with Murray Shepherd and John Hartley when their respective bands played on the same Brisbane independent circuit during 1980. Medew's band The 31st comprised Ron Peno (vocals; ex-Hellcats), Tony Robertson (bass; ex-Credits) and Chris Walsh (drums). Brad Shepherd (lead guitar, vocals; ex-**Fun Things**) joined the band for the second half of 1980. The 31st was a straight-ahead hard rock band, and by all accounts was roundly disliked on the close-knit, post-punk, inner-city Brisbane scene. During the band's short lifespan, Peno and Medew co-wrote songs like 'Igloo' and 'A Stand Alone', which formed the foundation of The Screaming Tribesmen's early set. The 31st fell apart in early 1981. Peno and Walsh eventually ended up in **Died Pretty**; Shepherd and Robertson joined **The Hitmen** in Sydney; and Medew formed The Screaming Tribesmen.

Initially, The Tribesmen remained in Brisbane, building a grassroots following. The band issued the rare (and collectable) EP *The Screaming Tribesmen* ('I Don't Wanna Know', 'Lookin' on'/'Love Lite', 'Trans 43') on EMI Custom in early 1982. Medew made the move to Sydney in 1982 where the band cut the single 'Igloo'/'My True Love's Blood' during December with producer Chris 'Klondike' Masuak (**Radio Birdman**, **Hitmen**). John Needham issued the single on his Citadel label in October 1983, and it immediately hit #1 on the independent chart. The haunting 'Igloo' was the ultimate expression of loneliness. Rock writer J.J. Adams described 'Igloo' as 'timeless, with lyrics to equal much of Edgar Allan Poe's isolationist imagery'. Hartley and Shepherd left the band in early 1984 to return to Brisbane. Shepherd went on to join Four Horsemen with ex-members of **The Vampire Lovers**; he later played with Hydrosaurus and Harpoon.

Medew formed the short-lived Wolfgang with Janine Hall (bass; ex-Young Charlatans, **Saints**) and Michael Charles (drums; ex-Shy Impostors, **Lipstick Killers**, Angie Pepper Band). In July 1984, he recruited three ex-**Hitmen/New Christs** members, Chris Masuak (lead guitar; also ex-**Radio Birdman**), Tony Robertson (bass) and Mark Kingsmill (drums), for a new version of The Screaming Tribesmen. That line-up lasted one month until Kingsmill left to join **Hoodoo Gurus**. Robertson also left, and by November 1984 The Tribesmen had stabilised with Medew, Masuak, Michael Charles and Bob Wackley (aka Bob Hood, bass; ex-Razar, **Grooveyard**). That same month, Citadel issued The Screaming Tribesmen's second, classic single, 'A Stand Alone'/'Move a Little Closer' (recorded by the previous line-up of Medew, Hartley and Shepherd).

The new line-up issued the exceptional 'Date with a Vampyre' 12-inch EP on Citadel (September 1985) before Warwick Fraser (ex-**Feather**, Smith, Change, **Hoi Polloi**) replaced Charles on drums. UK label What Goes On issued the EP in Britain. That label had also combined the first two Citadel singles as a 12-inch EP for the European market. In September 1986, the band issued the *Top of the Town* mini-album on the Rattlesnake label. *Top of the Town* featured a more lightweight guitar-pop sound, and failed to live up to expectations. The Tribesmen returned to their hard rock roots for the consummate *Bones and Flowers* album on the Survival label (October 1987). The album included a re-recording of 'Igloo'. It also produced the singles 'I've Got a Feeling'/'Colour Me Gone' (September) and 'Casualty of Love'/'Don't Turn Away' (March 1988).

The band toured constantly across Australia, headlining its own gigs as well as supporting international visitors like The Cult, The Damned and The Flamin' Groovies. In 1988, US label Rykodisc signed the band to an American deal and issued *Bones and Flowers*. The single 'I've Got a Feeling' reached #1 on the KROQ charts in Los Angeles, and also registered #8 on Billboard's modern rock chart. The Tribesmen toured the east coast and mid-west territories of the US, including a two-week slot supporting UK reggae-pop band UB40. In April 1989, Masuak left The Tribesmen to re-form **The Hitmen**. Wackley and Fraser also departed, which left Medew to gather up the pieces. He recruited a new line-up of Glen 'Electric' Morris (lead guitar; ex-**Kings of the Sun**), 'Long' Jeff Silver (bass; ex-Volcanoes, Radio Luxembourg) and Ritchie 'the Bandit' Hine (drums; ex-Terrapins, Radio Luxembourg).

The band issued the five-track, 12-inch EP *Take Cover* (August 1989), which comprised all cover versions, including The Dictators' 'Stay with Me', **The Allusions'** 'Gypsy Woman' and Lou Reed's 'I Can't Stand It'. Morris remained with the band for nine months before returning to **Kings of the Sun**. Brian Mann (ex-**Girlies, Headstones**) took his place, and the band issued the *Blood Lust* album (March 1991) which produced the 12-inch single 'Ayla'/'Santa's Little Helper', 'A Stand Alone'. *Blood Lust* included a couple of the band's heaviest ever songs like 'High Priestess', 'Frozen Tracks', 'Something Dangerous' and 'Queen of the Night Time World'. Survival also issued The Screaming Tribesmen compilation *High Time (a Collection)* (December 1990).

German label Normal issued *Blood Lust* in Europe and the band toured there to a positive response. In late 1991, Paul Larsen (ex-**Celibate Rifles**) replaced Hine on drums. Ash Geary (ex-Lost Boys) also replaced Mann on lead guitar in 1992; Glen Morris then returned to the fold at the end of the year as replacement for Geary. The Tribesmen issued their first new album in almost three years, *Formaldehyde*, (July 1993). Tony Cardinal (drums; ex-**Candy Harlots**) replaced Larsen on drums. At the end of 1993, the band undertook a joint, six-week, 27-date European tour with **Screamfeeder** and **The Chevelles.** Medew and Cardinal re-emerged in early 1997 with a new Screaming Tribesmen line-up which included Andy Newman (bass, keyboards; ex-Trans 262, Rattlesnake Shake, Manifestations) in place of the long-standing Jeff Silver.

Albums: *Top of the Town* (mini-album, Rattlesnake, 1986), *Bones and Flowers* (Survival/CBS, 1987), *High Time (a Collection)* (Survival, 1990), *Blood Lust* (Survival, 1991), *Formaldehyde* (Survival, 1993).

Scribble (Johanna Pigott) (*see* XL-Capris)

Sea Stories

Formed: *1986*
Style: *Pop, folk*
Original line-up: *Simon Honisett (vocals, guitar), Penny Hewson (vocals, guitar), Jeremy Honisett (bass), Jonathan Williamson (drums)*

Leading lights of the late 1980s movement towards a more reflective, post-gothic folk-pop sound, alongside **The Odolites, not drowning, waving, The Hollowmen** and These Future Kings, Melbourne quartet Sea Stories created a refreshing and subtle style. Other contemporaries in the band's chosen genre included former-Perth bands like **The Triffids, Chad's Tree, The Lighthouse Keepers, The Honeys** and Rabbit's Wedding.

A year after formation, Sea Stories issued the tentative mini-album *To Light the Home Fires* (July 1987) on the Rampant label. The band contributed 'I Remember When She Had Jesus' to Rampant's Various Artists album *Running Rampant Volume 1* (1987). Robyn Clarke (ex-**Sweet Jayne**) replaced Williamson on drums and the band issued the 12-inch EP *Secret World* which appeared in early 1988. Later that year, Sea Stories recorded its debut, full-length album, but it remained on the shelf for over a year while the band sorted out a new record deal. Bypassing the Australian industry, Sea Stories signed direct to US label I.R.S. (home to bands as diverse as R.E.M. and the Lords of the New Church). *Miller's Pond* fulfilled the band's early promise with its warm, wistful and assured folk-based song arrangements. The album produced the single 'Still They Stand'/'1,000 Years' (June 1990). Sea Stories also contributed a plaintive cover of **AC/DC**'s 'You Shook Me all Night Long' to the

Various Artists tribute album *Used and Recovered by . . .* (1990).

Michael Hepworth (cello, organ) expanded the band's line-up to a five-piece. The new line-up recorded the critically acclaimed album *Wide Eyed and Dreaming*, which was further reaffirmation of the band's growth and self-confidence. It produced the single 'Gone for Sure'/'Wasted Everything', 'Here She Comes Now' (March 1991) and the four-track EP 'Wonderful Things'. The three bonus tracks included with 'Wonderful Things' were taken from a session for Triple J's *Live at the Wireless*. By the time the album appeared in April 1991, Clarke had left to be replaced temporarily by Russell Bradley (on loan from **not drowning, waving**) and Dave Shaw (ex-**Stems**), before Nick Wilson took over permanently.

Sea Stories struck a new deal with Polydor which resulted in the CD EP *Junior* and the single 'What Went Wrong?' before breaking up in late 1993. Simon Honisett and Penny Hewson re-emerged in 1994 as acoustic duo Sunglass. The duo issued the *Sunglass* album (April 1994) and the CD EP 'When Stars Collide' (June). Sunglass issued a new single, 'How Long Can You Stay Angry?' in July 1995. At the same time, Honisett and Hewson launched four-piece outfit Gigantaur to cater to their guitar pop tastes. The single 'On a Rocket'/'Trailer Trash' and CD EP *Gigantaur* (July 1995) featured bright, pacey and melodic guitar pop. Gary Aspinal (bass) and Dave Shaw (drums) augmented Honisett and Hewson on the single, after which Darren Saltman joined as permanent drummer.

Sea Stories albums: *To Light the Home Fires* (mini-album, Rampant, 1987), *Miller's Pond* (I.R.S./Liberation/Festival, 1990), *Wide Eyed and Dreaming* (I.R.S./Liberation/Festival, 1991); ***Sunglass album:*** *Sunglass* (Choc Chip, 1994).

Sebastian Hardie

Formed: *1968*
Style: *Symphonic rock*
Original line-up: **Jon English** *(vocals, rhythm guitar), Graham Ford (lead guitar), Peter Plavsic (bass), Alex Plavsic (drums)*

By and large, symphonic rock has not flourished in Australia. Sebastian Hardie was the country's first and foremost symphonic rock band. During the mid-1970s, the band enjoyed considerable success with the album *Four Moments*, but since that time has been largely forgotten on home turf. Yet in European, Japanese and American progressive rock circles, the highly revered *Four Moments* and its follow-up *Windchase* are considered to be classics of the genre.

Graham Ford formed the Sebastian Hardie Blues Band in 1967. The band played R&B and soul covers and experienced several line-up changes. The line-up included Ford, Dennis Laughlin (vocals; later in the original version of **Sherbet**), Dave Waddington (vocals), Neil Williamson (organ), John Bellamy (bass), Syd Richmond (drums) and Richard Lillico (drums). The Sebastian Hardie Blues Band became Sebastian Hardie in 1968 with the arrival of singer **Jon English** and the Plavsic brothers. All three musicians were students at Sydney's Cabramatta High School. The band went semi-professional, working the same suburban dance circuit as **The Affair**, House of Bricks, The Clik and dozens of other Sydney pop bands.

Throughout 1969, Sebastian Hardie worked as backing band for rock'n'roll legend **Johnny O'Keefe**. At the end of 1971, Sebastian Hardie broke up when English accepted the role of Judas Iscariot in the Australian stage production of the rock musical *Jesus Christ Superstar*. A year later, Ford and the Plavsics re-formed Sebastian Hardie with Steve Dunne (vocals, keyboards). At that point, the band was still playing pop covers on the dance/club circuit, with little indication of future directions. Visiting English producer Larry Page (Daniel Boone, Kincade) was impressed enough, however, to produce the band's debut single 'All Right Now'/'The Professional' (September 1973). One month after the single appeared, 19-year-old **Mario Millo** replaced Hood on lead guitar. Millo had been playing the Sydney dance circuit since 1969 with his band The Clik. The Clik comprised Millo, Brian Nicholls (organ), Vince Moult (bass) and Mark Friedland (drums). They took out first place in the 1969 2SM Pepsi Pop Poll (Battle of the Bands) held at the Sydney Stadium.

The Clik recorded two bubblegum pop singles for Festival, 'La De Da'/'Yes Sir' (November 1969) and 'Mary Mary'/'Uptight Basil' (March 1970). By 1972, The Clik comprised Millo, Garry Adams (guitar; ex-**Galadriel**), Phil Cogan (bass) and Doug Bligh (drums; ex-**Galadriel**) and had moved in a hard rock direction. Justin McCoy replaced Adams, but the band broke up when Millo joined Sebastian Hardie. McCoy later joined Sydney jazz-rock band Eight Day Clock, which issued the album *Eight Day Clock* on RCA (1975).

Millo played on Sebastian Hardie's second single, 'Day After Day'/'Mermaid on the Sand' (April 1974). By that stage, Millo had begun to write original, highly orchestrated and inventive material which helped usher in a much-needed change of direction for Sebastian Hardie. The catalyst in the band's transformation from accomplished dance-pop band to fully fledged symphonic rock band was the decision to play a 20-minute arrangement of Mike Oldfield's popular 'Tubular Bells'. Polydor Records signed the band on the strength of Millo's new material. The band supported international visitors Lou Reed and Osibisa on their respective Australian tours. At the end of 1974, classically trained musician Toivo Pilt (ex-Forever) replaced Dunne on keyboards and Millo took over lead vocals. Sebastian Hardie upstaged Dutch jazz-rock veterans Focus on their June 1975 Australian tour. With the band's increased profile, the album *Four Moments* and the single 'Rosanna'/'Openings' (edit) (both August 1975) appeared to strong critical acclaim. The album attained gold status (35 000 copies sold) after peaking at #13 on the national album chart; 'Rosanna' reached #31.

Featuring seamless, dramatic arrangements and impeccable musicianship, *Four Moments* revealed the influence of European progressive rock bands like Yes, King Crimson, Genesis and Focus. It contained just three tracks, the side-long, four suite 'Four Moments', the sensual, melancholic 'Rosanna' and the majestic 'Openings'. Millo contributed some of his most epic and graceful guitar playing to the instrumental 'Openings'. Mercury issued *Four Moments* in the USA and Japan. At the end of 1975, Sebastian Hardie undertook a very successful 63-date Australian concert tour. The band's second album, *Windchase*, appeared in February 1976 to coincide with another national tour as support to US band Santana. Like its predecessor, *Windchase* boasted superb playing and well-crafted progressive rock, but it failed to live up to expectations. It produced the single 'Life, Love and Music'/'Hello Phimistar' (February 1976).

In June 1976, the Plavsic brothers left the band amid a flurry of ill-feeling. Millo and Pilt immediately recruited a new rhythm section of New Zealander Doug Nethercote (bass; ex-Clockwork Strawberry) and Doug Bligh (drums; by then ex-Stuart & McKay), but a legal wrangle over ownership of the Sebastian Hardie name prevented the band from playing live. Peter Plavsic had registered the name Sebastian Hardie and therefore claimed legal right to its use. Millo argued because it was his music that had established the band's identity he was entitled to the name. The Plavsic brothers emerged as the successful party in the ensuing court case, and Millo was forced to rename his band Windchase. The brothers never did use the Sebastian Hardie name for their new band as intended. They recruited Graham Wardrop (guitar), John Bushell (guitar) and Rick Mellick (keyboards) in order to back rock'n'roll revival duo **The Studs**.

Windchase entered the studio during January 1977 to record a new album. Nethercote left halfway through the album session to be replaced by journeyman bass player Duncan McGuire (ex-**Doug Parkinson** In Focus, **King Harvest**, **Friends**, **Ayers Rock**). By the time the album *Symphinity* appeared in June, McGuire and Bligh had left to be replaced by the returning Nethercote and Ralph Cooper respectively. *Symphinity* saw the band moving into heavier jazz-fusion territory (akin to Al Di Meola), but it was not a chart success. It produced the singles 'Glad to Be Alive'/'No Scruples' (May 1977) and 'Flight Call'/'Horsemen to Symphinity' (October). Millo took the band on the road, but in the meantime the emergent punk and new wave movement had relegated bands like Windchase to the dinosaur scrap heap. Windchase played its last gig to 60 people in a Melbourne pub during October 1977.

Mario Millo went on to work with **Jon English** on the highly successful *Against the Wind* soundtrack, before issuing two fine, but neglected, solo albums, *Epic III* and *Human Games*. He then embarked on a successful career in television and movie soundtrack production. In 1994, the organisers of the annual US progressive rock gathering ProgFest invited Sebastian Hardie to appear on the bill. Although Millo, Pilt and the Plavsic brothers had not played together since 1976, they flew to Los Angeles in November for the festival. By all accounts, Sebastian Hardie delivered a brilliant set to which the audience responded with a standing ovation.

Sebastian Hardie albums: *Four Moments* (Polydor, 1975), *Windchase* (Polydor, 1976), *Rock Legends* (compilation, Polydor 1980), *Four Moments of the Windchase* (compilation, Polydor/Mercury, 1990); ***Windchase album:*** *Symphinity* (Festival/Infinity, 1977).

The Sect

Formed: *1966*
Style: *Pop*
Original line-up: *John Brownrigg (vocals, guitar), Carole King (vocals), Rod Harris (guitar), Stan Gospos (organ), Robin Muirhead (bass), Paul Doo (drums)*

The Sect was one of the most popular outfits on the mid-1960s Brisbane pop scene. Carole King left early in the piece to join Sydney band **The Executives**. As well as touring with the likes of **The Zoot**, **The Groop** and **The Master's Apprentices**,

The Sect backed visiting solo artists like **Johnny Farnham**, **Normie Rowe**, **Johnny Young** and Marcia Jones.

The Sect won the Queensland Battle of the Bands, and moved to Melbourne in 1969 to record for EMI/Columbia. The band issued the singles 'Lonely Road'/'I Can't Stand to Be Alone' (January 1970) and 'St John's Wood'/'Country Style' on Columbia. **Master's Apprentices** members **Jim Keays** and Doug Ford had written 'St John's Wood' for The Sect. The Masters also handled The Sect's live bookings through their own Drum agency. The Sect suffered a number of line-up changes over the years. In 1967, Neal Waddell replaced Stan Gospos; in 1968, Tom Stevens replaced Waddell; in 1968 Peter Moscos joined on second guitar; in 1971, Ron Walters replaced Moscos; in 1969, Paul Davies replaced Colin Muirhead. The band finally fell apart in 1971, but Walters, Rod Harris and Paul Doo continued on as Sect III.

Sect III issued one single, 'Everybody Sing a Song'/'In the Evening' (April 1971), on Columbia before also splitting up at the end of the year. In 1972, Brownrigg, Walters and Doo formed Star Spangled Banger. The band issued one album, *Star Spangled Banger*, and one single, 'Star Spangled Banger'/'Sailing', on the Havoc label. In keeping with the times, Star Spangled Banger went for a heavier, blues-based sound in the tradition of UK bands like Family. The album was not successful and Star Spangled Banger broke up in 1973. Brownrigg went on to produce an album for young Melbourne hard rock band Fox, *What The Hell is Going On?* (1974), to which he contributed five songs.

One-time Sect members Peter Moscos and Neal Waddell went on to form folk/soft rock band Burke and Wills with Mick Power (guitar, vocals), Warren Adams (bass, vocals) and Jamie Dunn (drums, vocals). The band was known as The Platypus for a period in late 1970 when it was resident group on Brisbane pop show *Eyeforce*. In 1972 Burke and Wills relocated to Melbourne (sans Waddell and Power) where they backed pop duo Frieze (Darryl Cotton and Beeb Birtles from **The Zoot**). Burke and Wills eventually signed to the Image label and issued two singles, 'Thank You'/'Sunshine' (April 1973) and 'Come Along with Me'/'Janine' (December). Moscos went on to work as musical director for **Ray Burgess** and Maria Mercedes before forming a duo, Moscos and Stone, in 1978 with Laurie Stone (ex-**Railroad Gin**).

Star Spangled Banger album: *Star Spangled Banger* (Havoc, 1972).

The Seekers

Formed: *1962*
Style: *Folk, pop*
Original line-up: *Ken Ray (lead vocals, guitar), Keith Potger (guitar, banjo, harmony vocals; ex-Trinamics, Escorts), Athol Guy (double bass, harmony vocals; ex-Ramblers, Escorts), Bruce Woodley (guitar, mandolin, harmony vocals; ex-Moonshine 5)*

During the mid-1960s, the phenomenally successful Seekers captivated the world with their wholesome image and bright folk-styled sound. Alongside **The Easybeats**, The Seekers were Australia's most important musical export of the decade. Judith Durham possessed a powerful, crystal clear, Joan Baez-like soprano voice and, although not the original lead singer, she became The Seekers' focal point. Before she joined The Seekers in late 1962, Durham had sung jazz, blues and gospel on the Melbourne jazz circuit. She recorded an EP, *Judy Durham with Frank Traynor's Jazz Preachers* for Melbourne label W&G. Keith Potger, Athol Guy and Bruce Woodley had played with a number of semi-professional groups before joining forces as The Seekers with Ken Ray.

From the start, The Seekers concentrated on a bright, uptempo sound, although they were too pop to be considered strictly folk and too folk to be rock. In 1963, The Seekers signed to W&G and issued the album *Introducing The Seekers*. In November, their debut single 'Waltzing Matilda'/'Just a Closer Walk with Thee' made the lower reaches of the Melbourne Top 40 chart (#37). In March 1964, The Seekers accepted an offer from the Sitmar shipping line to entertain passengers on one of its world cruises. Seven weeks later, The Seekers landed in the UK. They had intended to make their UK stay a short working vacation before rejoining the Sitmar cruise, but promoter Eddie Jarrett (from the Grade Organisation booking agency) immediately lined up gigs. He also teamed them up with songwriter/producer Tom Springfield from popular folk trio The Springfields. The Seekers made regular appearances on UK television's *The Ronnie Carroll Show*.

The Seekers' first UK single, 'Myra'/'With My Swag All on My Shoulder', appeared on the independent Oriole label. They issued two albums for the World Record Club, *The Seekers* and *Hide and Seekers*, before signing to EMI/Columbia. In November 1964, the Springfield-penned 'I'll Never Find Another You'/'Open Up Them Pearly Gates' reached #1 in Australia and the UK, and #4 in the USA. It went on to sell 1.75 million copies worldwide. Springfield's 'A World of Our Own'/ 'Sinner Man' took The Seekers to #2 in Australia, #3 in the UK and #19 in the USA during April 1965. The album *A World of Our Own* reached #5 on the UK charts during July. It was issued in Australia as *The Seekers*. The Seekers appeared on the *Ed Sullivan Show*, and then returned to Australia to tour with The Dave Clark Five.

'Morningtown Ride' reached #8 in Australia and #44 in the USA during August 1965. The Seekers re-recorded the song in 1966 for the UK market, where it reached #2 during November (backed with 'When the Stars Begin to Fall'). Another Springfield composition, 'The Carnival is Over'/'We Shall Not Be Moved', took The Seekers to #1 during November 1965 in both Australia and the UK (where it knocked The Rolling Stones' 'Get Off My Cloud' from the top spot). It became one of the group's most celebrated songs. Springfield had adapted its melody from the Russian folk song 'Stenjka Razin', and the song's elusive central characters Pierrot and Columbine have intrigued listeners for decades. **Nick Cave** later included a version of 'The Carnival is Over' on his album *Kicking Against the Pricks*.

The Seekers undertook a successful Australian tour during February 1966. A month later, the Paul Simon-penned 'Someday, Oneday' reached #4 in Australia and #11 in the UK. Woodley co-wrote another song with Simon, 'Red Rubber Ball', which The Seekers included on their second UK Top 10 album *Come the Day*. US band The Cyrkle later enjoyed a #1 American hit with the song. Springfield's 'Walk with Me' took The Seekers to #10 in the UK and #31 in Australia during October. The Tom Springfield/Jim Dale-penned 'Georgy Girl' kept The Seekers at the top when it made #1 in Australia, #3 in the UK and #1 in the USA during February 1967. It was the theme song to Silvio Narizzano's feature film *Georgy Girl* starring Lynn Redgrave and Alan Bates. 'Georgy Girl' went on to sell 3.5 million copies worldwide.

In March, The Seekers appeared before an estimated crowd of 200 000 people at the Moomba concert staged at the Myer Music Bowl. The group was onstage for only 20 minutes. The Seekers returned for a national tour in December 1967, following a successful American jaunt. They filmed two television specials during the year, *The Seekers Down Under* and *The World of The Seekers*. The Seekers were named Australians of the Year for 1967. In the meantime, 'On the Other Side' (Australian #19 in October), 'When will the Good Apples Fall?' (Australian #35, UK #11 in November) and 'Emerald City' (Australian #28, UK #50 in December) kept the group in the public eye. American producer/singer/cult figure Kim Fowley co-wrote 'Emerald City' with one 'John Martin'. Many years later, it was revealed that 'John Martin' was in fact Keith Potger.

With the release of 'Emerald City' and the *Seekers Seen in Green* album, EMI UK issued Judith Durham's second solo single, 'Again and Again'/'Memories'. Her debut single, 'The Olive Tree', had reached #33 on the UK chart during June 1967. At the start of 1968, Durham decided to leave the band. In accordance with a promise that the group members would give six months' notice, she told the others of her intention to leave. The Seekers recorded a final single, 'Days of My Life'/'Study War No More' (April 1968), with producer Mickie Most (Yardbirds, Donovan, Lulu, Herman's Hermits). Despite Most's track record on the UK charts, it was the group's least successful single in five years. The group's final album, *Live at The Talk of the Town* fared better, reaching #2 in the UK during September. Their BBC-TV special, *Farewell The Seekers*, also attracted a wide audience.

The compilation album *Best of The Seekers* reached #1 during November 1968, knocking The Beatles' *Beatles* (the 'White Album') from the top of the UK chart in the process. *Best of The Seekers* eventually stayed on the British charts for 125 weeks. With the break-up of The Seekers in July 1968, Woodley returned to Australia to concentrate on songwriting. In 1971, he recorded an album for RCA, *Just Good Friends*, and contributed four songs (alongside **Hans Poulsen** and **Billy Green**) to the soundtrack of Tim Burstall's surfing film *Getting Back to Nothing*. Guy formed a marketing and promotions company in Australia and in 1973 was elected to the NSW state Parliament as a Liberal Party candidate.

Potger stayed in the UK to form and manage The New Seekers, although he did not remain with the group for long. Potger's only hit with the group was 'What Have They Done to My Song, Ma?' (UK #44 in October 1970). With the arrival of another expatriate Australian **Peter Doyle**, The New Seekers went on to enjoy a string of worldwide hits with the likes of 'Never Ending Song of Love', 'I'd Like to Teach the World to Sing (in Perfect Harmony)' and 'You Won't Find Another Fool Like Me'.

Judith Durham launched her solo career with the album *For Christmas with Love*, followed by *A Gift of Song* and its singles 'The Light is Dark Enough' and 'Let Me Find Love', in early 1970. Durham had married musician Ron Edgeworth at the end of 1969 and he became her musical director. The album *Climb Ev'ry Mountain* and its title track single 'Climb Every Mountain' followed in 1971.

Durham began to move in a jazz/blues/ragtime direction and formed The Hottest Band in Town. Her fourth solo album, *Judith Durham and the Hottest Band in Town*, and its single, 'I Wanna Dance to Your Music', came out in 1973, followed by *Judith Durham and the Hottest Band in Town II* a year later. Durham embarked on an Australian tour with The Hottest Band in Town during January 1975. At the same time, Potger, Guy and Woodley had decided to re-form The Seekers without Durham, and recruited Dutch-born Australian Louisa Wisseling as lead singer.

The Seekers signed a new deal with the Astor label. They immediately found Australian chart success with the Woodley-penned 'Sparrow Song' (#2 in June 1975) and the album *The Seekers* (#17 in July). In September 1975, The Seekers undertook a national tour. 'Reunion'/'Break these Chains' (October), 'Where in the World?' (April 1976) and 'Giving and Taking' (June) appeared as singles. In June 1977, Woodley left the group to concentrate on songwriting and production. Former 1960s pop star **Buddy England** took his place. Athol Guy also departed in 1978, to be replaced by Peter Robinson (ex-**Strangers**). The Seekers issued a new album, *All Over the World*, in November 1978. In 1989, Woodley, Guy and Potger re-emerged as The Seekers with popular cabaret performer Julie Anthony as lead singer. The Seekers re-recorded some of their best-loved songs for the album *The Seekers Live on* later in the year. In June 1990, Anthony left to be replaced by former *Young Talent Time* team member Karen Knowles.

In the meantime, Durham had returned to live in Australia during 1977. Festival issued her new single, 'I Love You', that year. In 1978 Durham and Edgeworth travelled to New York where they appeared at the prestigious Newport Jazz Festival. The live recording of their performance formed the basis for the *Hot Jazz Duo* album (April 1981). For most of the 1980s, Durham toured internationally, but kept a low profile in Australia. In early 1990, the singer toured Australia. Then, in May 1990, Durham and Edgeworth were severely injured in a car accident just outside Melbourne. The accident put her out of action for over a year. PolyGram issued Durham's new single, 'Australia Land of Today', in January 1992. She later performed the song in front of 100 000 people at the opening of the Melbourne Cricket Ground's Great Southern Stand just before the World Cup Cricket final.

In late 1992, Durham ended years of speculation and ill-feeling by rejoining The Seekers as lead singer. The group recorded two new songs, Woodley's 'Keep a Dream in Your Pocket' and the Durham/John Young-penned 'One World Love', to coincide with the release of the 'Best of' collection *The Silver Jubilee Album*. 'Keep a Dream in Your Pocket' came out as a single in April. At the end of that month, the group embarked on the very successful Judith Durham: The Seekers Silver Jubilee Reunion tour of Australia and New Zealand. *The Silver Jubilee Album* peaked at #3 on the national chart during May 1993, eventually selling over 140 000 copies (double platinum). It was the third highest selling Australian album for 1993 behind **Jimmy Barnes'** *Heat* and **John Farnham's** *Then Again*. It also sold double platinum in New Zealand. When issued in the UK as *A Carnival of Hits*, the album peaked at #4 on the British charts.

During April 1994, Judith Durham: The Seekers performed two sell-out concerts at London's famous Royal Albert Hall. The group returned in 1995 for a full-scale UK tour. In May 1995, Durham's seventh solo album, *Let Me Find Love*, reached the Australian Top 10. In early 1997, Durham and The Seekers signed a new deal with EMI, which was the most lucrative domestic recording contract ever: each member was reportedly to receive $1 million for a two-album deal. EMI issued The Seekers' new CD single, 'Far Shore', in March 1997. EMI also put out two CD box sets, *The Seekers Complete* (five CDs of 126 Seekers songs including hits, live, rarities and previously unreleased material) and *Treasure Chest* (three CDs including the *Seekers Seen in Green* and *Live at The Talk of the Town* albums, plus the 'Far Shore' single and interviews). At the end of May 1997, Durham, **Air Supply's** Russell Hitchcock and **Yothu Yindi's** Mandawuy Yunupingu issued a collaborative CD single of the Bruce Woodley and Dobe Newton-penned 'I Am Australian'. The single peaked at #17 on the national chart during the first week of June. A month later EMI issued Durham's ninth solo album, *Always There*. Judith Durham: The Seekers' new album, *Future Road* (produced by Charles Fisher, best known for his work with **Savage Garden**), came out in October. It reached #13 on the national chart, and by the end of the year had attained platinum status (70 000 copies sold). It yielded a second CD single, 'Calling Me Home', also in October.

Seekers albums: *Introducing The Seekers* (W&G, 1963), *The Sound of the Seekers* (World Record Club/EMI, 1964), *Hide and Seekers* (World Record Club/EMI, 1964), *The Seekers Sing Their Big Hits* (W&G, 1964), *Introducing The Seekers' Big Hits* (double compilation, W&G, 1965), *The Seekers* (EMI, 1965; issued in the UK as *A World of Our Own*), *The Carnival is Over* (EMI, 1965), *Come the Day* (EMI, 1966), *Seekers Seen in Green* (EMI, 1967),

Live at The Talk of the Town (EMI, 1968), *Best of The Seekers* (EMI, 1968), *The Seekers Golden Collection* (early demos, Philips, 1969), *The Seekers* (Astor, 1975), *All Over the World* (EMI, 1978), *Australia's Own The Very Best of The Seekers* (compilation, Hammard, 1978), *The Seekers Live on* (EMI, 1989), *This is The Seekers* (compilation, EMI, 1994), *Treasure Chest* (box set, EMI, 1997), *The Seekers Complete* (box set, EMI, 1997); ***Judith Durham: The Seekers albums:*** *The Silver Jubilee Album* (EMI, 1993), *25th Anniversary Celebration Live in Concert* (EMI, 1993), *Future Road* (EMI, 1997); ***Judith Durham solo albums:*** *For Christmas with Love* (Good Year, 1968), *A Gift of Song* (EMI, 1970), *Climb Ev'ry Mountain* (Interfusion/Festival, 1971), *Judith Durham and the Hottest Band in Town* (Interfusion/Festival, 1973), *Judith Durham and the Hottest Band in Town II* (Interfusion/Festival, 1974), *Hot Jazz Duo* (Interfusion/Festival, 1981), *Let Me Find Love* (PolyGram, 1995), *Mona Lisas* (PolyGram, 1996), *Always There* (EMI, 1997).

Further reading: *Colours Of My Life: The Judith Durham Story* by Graham Simpson (Random House, 1994).

Severed Heads

Formed: *1979*
Style: *Electronic dance*
Original line-up: *Richard Fielding, Andrew Wright, Tom Ellard*

Sydney-based conceptual electronic funk outfit Severed Heads started out as an experimental project that produced radical sound collages using computers and synthesisers. With the addition of drum machine dance beats to the music, Severed Heads later became the first Australian independent band to enter the US *Billboard* Dance chart. Throughout most of its existence, Severed Heads has been primarily the work of the visionary Tom Ellard, who has also worked under the names of Mr Ellard, Coklacoma and Fusssssball. Apart from Ellard, the line-up of Severed Heads has changed a number of times. Other members have included Richard Fielding, Andrew Wright, Garry Bradbury, Paul Derring, Pete Rivett-Carnac (on loan from **Single Gun Theory**) and video-maker Steven Jones. DJ/producer (the late) Robert Rascic also worked closely with Severed Heads, being responsible for many of the group's 12-inch remixes.

Severed Heads emerged out of Fielding and Wright's experimental duo Mr and Mrs No Smoking Sign. Ellard joined Fielding and Wright at the end of 1979. They issued a number of self-financed cassettes, including *Mr and Mrs No Smoking Sign Go Cruising fer Burgers!* Having adopted the name Severed Heads, the group began issuing a series of challenging releases, either on Ellard's Terse Tapes or the Dogfood Production System imprint. Early reference points were UK outfits like Cabaret Voltaire and Throbbing Gristle. The albums *Ear Bitten/No Vowels No Bowels* (1980) and *Clean* (1981) appeared in limited edition pressings of 400 copies each. The A-side of the first album *Ear Bitten* was by Severed Heads, with the B-side by the obscure group Rhythmyx Chymx. Cassette releases on Terse around that time included *Ear Bitten* (with additional tracks), *Side 2* (recorded live), *Live 1980/81*, the mail-order only *Side 3* (featuring two Severed Heads tracks plus solo material by the three then-current members Ellard, Fielding and Bradbury), *Blubberknife* (1983) and *Since the Accident* (1983).

UK label Red Flame/Ink issued *Since the Accident* on LP for the British market, followed by *Blubberknife*. Virgin issued the *Since the Accident* album in Australia during 1984. *Since the Accident* also produced the group's first UK 12-inch EP, 'Dead Eyes Opened'/'Bullett', 'Mount' (1984). Red Flame/Ink followed that during 1985 with the four-track, 12-inch EPs 'Goodbye Tonsils', 'Stretcher' and 'Gashing the Old Mae West' plus the albums *City Slab Horror* and *Clifford Darling, Please Don't Live in the Past*. The five-track, 12-inch EP 'Dead Eyes Opened' also appeared on the Canadian label Nettwerk. In the meantime, Australian independent label Volition compiled tracks from various overseas releases for the local album *Stretcher* (November 1985). It produced Severed Heads' first 7-inch single, 'Petrol' (Short Mix)/'Petrol' (Cut Up Mix), 'Son of Petrol' (Bigot Mix). The group's next album, *The Big Bigot* (August 1986), yielded the four-track, 12-inch EP 'Propellor'.

The Canadian version of the album *Come Visit the Big Bigot* added the previously non-album track 'Twenty Deadly Diseases' (from the 'Propellor' EP), which saw release as a 12-inch EP in North America. During 1986, Ellard and Jones undertook a gruelling, 58-date European and American tour. The *Bad Mood Guy* album (October 1987) included the popular 12-inch EP 'Hot with Fleas' (September). One side of the album featured a continuous flow of Rascic's remixes. To coincide with the album's release, Volition issued the ten-track Severed Heads video collection *If I've Told You Once, I've Told You a Thousand Times*. The UK and Canadian markets each got a different video collection called *Severed Heads* which Volition issued in Australia a year later under the title *Kato Gets the Girl*. When issued in the US, 'Hot with Fleas' reached #5 on the American dance chart.

1988 saw the release of the 'Greater Reward' 12-inch EP (June) and the remix compilation *Bulkhead* (both issued in Australia on Volition and in Europe and America on Nettwerk, December). *Rotund for Success* (October 1989) included the 'All Saints' Day' 12-inch EP. The European and American markets also got the 'Big Car' 12-inch EP (from *Rotund for Success*), while the Volition album *Retread* featured various remixes of tracks like 'Big Car', 'All Saints' Day' and 'Greater Reward'. Severed Heads' November 1991 album *Cuisine* included five previously unreleased tracks taken from the scrapped *Piscatorial* project. *Cuisine* yielded the seven-track CD EP 'Twister' (September 1992). Volition also issued the second Severed Heads video collection, *I've Told You Twice and I'm Not Going to Tell You Again*, in 1992. Severed Heads headlined the techno-focused Boiler Room on the 1994 national bill of the Big Day Out tour.

Later that year, the Nippon Crown label issued the 12-track compilation *Severed Heads: Trance Techno* for the Japanese market. Local releases continued apace with the ambitious *Gigapus* album on Volition. The multimedia package *Somewhere Over the Gigapus* comprised the standard *Gigapus* CD, the video *Videpus* (a reissue of *I've Told You Twice and I'm Not Going to Tell You Again*) and the CD-ROM *Metapus*. The CD-ROM featured an interactive history of Severed Heads with excerpts from over 100 songs and 40 minutes of video. Severed Heads scored a surprise Australian hit single when Volition issued the 'Dead Eyes Opened 94' (remix) CD EP. It reached #16 on the national chart during January 1995. 'Dead Eyes Opened 94' also logged the #10 placing on Triple J's 1994 Hottest 100 list. The 'Heart of the Party' CD EP (taken from the *Gigapus* album) appeared in 1995. US label Decibel issued the *Gigapus* album for the American market during 1996. Severed Heads appeared on the Gold Coast bill of the 1997 Big Day Out (headlining the Boiler Room).

Albums: *Ear Bitten/No Vowels No Bowels* (shared LP, B-side by Rhythmyx Chymx, Terse Music/Wrong, 1980), *Clean* (Terse Tapes/Dogfood Production System, 1981), *Since the Accident* (Terse Tapes, 1983; reissued on LP Virgin, 1984), *City Slab Horror* (Ink/Red Flame, UK import, 1985), *Stretcher* (Volition/CBS, 1985), *The Big Bigot* (Volition, 1986), *Bad Mood Guy* (Volition, 1987), *Bulkhead* (remix compilation, Volition, 1988), *Rotund for Success* (Volition, 1989), *Retread* (remix compilation, Volition, 1989), *Cuisine* (Volition, 1991), *Gigapus* (Volition/Sony, 1994), *Somewhere Over the Gigapus* (multimedia package of *Gigapus* CD, *Videpus* video and *Metapus* CD-ROM) (Volition/Sony, 1994).

Mark Seymour (*see* Hunters & Collectors)

William Shakespeare

Style: Pop

In a classic case of pop reincarnation, Johnny Caves (b. 1950) became Johnny Cabe, Johnny Cabe became William Shakespeare, William Shakespeare scored two national #1 hit singles and was never heard from again. The behind-the-scenes part of the equation was the ace production/songwriting team of Vanda and Young (ex-**Easybeats**) who wrote Shakespeare's hits 'Can't Stop Myself from Loving You' and 'My Little Angel', as well as engineering his carefully contrived image.

Johnny Caves initially sang with beat band The Amazons, who recorded the single 'Ain't that Lovin' You Baby'/'You'd Better Mind' for Leedon in 1966. The rest of The Amazons included Chris Carroll (guitar), Nick Barlow (guitar), Harry Brus (bass) and Dally Carroll (drums). Caves continued singing and by the early 1970s was working the Sydney clubs as Johnny Cabe. At the beginning of 1974, he came into contact with Vanda and Young, who had just recorded the backing track for 'Can't Stop Myself from Loving You' for another singer who was unable to handle the high notes. The song seemed tailor-made for Cabe's falsetto voice, and he was signed to the Albert label.

Vanda and Young decided to create a new image for Cabe. They renamed him William Shakespeare and decked him out in glam-rock gear (à la Gary Glitter), replete with Shakespearian puffed sleeves and gaudy fake jewels. To top it all off, Shakespeare sported an immaculately coiffured, plum-coloured hairdo. 'Can't Stop Myself from Loving You'/'Goodbye Tomorrow Hello Today' came out in July 1974, and immediately hit #1 on the national chart. With the help of regular appearances on ***Countdown***, Shakespeare's second single, the Christmas-flavoured 'My Little Angel'/'Feeling Alright' (November 1974), also reached #1. Two more Vanda and Young singles followed, 'Just the Way You Are'/'On Saturday Night' (April 1975) and 'Last Night'/'Toledo Bay' (March 1976), plus the album *Can't Stop Myself from Loving You*, but none charted. While his career was in decline, Shakespeare was charged with carnal knowledge and received two years' probation.

He left Albert in 1977, and by the middle of 1979 he was back working the Sydney clubs, this time as Billy Shake. Shakespeare's career was temporarily revived in 1990 when listeners of

Melbourne radio station 3MMM voted 'My Little Angel' as the daggiest song of its generation. Around the same time, Melbourne covers band The Melody Lords were including the song in their repertoire of kitsch, 1970s glam classics. Shakespeare began headlining Dag Nights on the nostalgia circuit, and he wore his 'Top Dag' appellation like a badge of honour.

Album: *Can't Stop Myself from Loving You* (Albert, 1975).

Max Sharam

Style: *Pop*

Flamboyant singer/songwriter Max Sharam first came to the nation's attention in 1992 when she performed her song 'Coma' on television talent show *New Faces* hosted by Bert Newton. Her dramatic performance attracted the attention of a number of record companies, and she secured a deal with Warner Music Australia. Sharam cited Barbra Streisand as an influence, and her powerful, expressive vocal style, theatrical inclination and lyrical subject matter drew comparisons with the likes of Kate Bush, Nina Hagen and Tori Amos.

Sharam grew up in rural Victoria, and spent her late teen years travelling around Europe where she made a living from busking. She combined her love for theatre, art and music for the first time when she landed the lead role in an Italian rock opera *Forza Venite Gente*. The musical toured for two years, and her performance was documented in an Italian television program, *La Ragazza Con La Guitara*. Sharam then spent a year in Japan before returning to Australia. She sang with a number of small-time Sydney bands like Minx and Fleshworld, as well as performing regular solo acoustic gigs at Kinselas nightclub during 1993 (under the banner of *Max Sharam The Sounds of Sirens*). She entered *New Faces* in 1992 to make a 'statement and to break the rules' and won her heat.

Once signed to Warner, Sharam issued her debut CD EP 'Coma' in December 1994. The song's celebration of revenge and the dark side of the human spirit did not prevent it from hitting the national Top 20 (#14) during February 1995. It also logged an impressive #8 position on the 1994 Triple J Hottest 100 list. (**silverchair's** 'Tomorrow' made #5 that same year.) Sharam's compelling, full-length debut album *A Million Year Girl* (May 1995) made its debut at #10 on the national chart, and yielded two further hits in 'Be Firm' (#25 in June) and Melanie's 'Lay Down (Candles in the Rain)' (#36 in November). Produced by Daniel Denham and Nick Mainsbridge (**Ratcat**, **Tall Tales & True**, **The Sharp**), the album mixed Sharam's eclectic approach and catchy pop melodies with exotic sounds and orchestrated arrangements.

Max Sharam

Her fourth single, 'Is It OK if I Call You Mine?' (February 1996), was not successful. Sharam was nominated for an unprecedented eight Australian Record Industry Association (ARIA) Awards, although she only won Best Cover Artwork. **Tina Arena** scooped the pool that year by winning four Awards (Best Female Artist, Song of the Year, Best Pop Release and Best Album).

Album: *A Million Year Girl* (East West/Warner, 1995).

The Sharp

Formed: *1991*
Style: *Pop, rockabilly*
Original line-up: *Charlie Rooke (guitar, vocals; ex-59 Sharp), Allan Catlin (double bass, vocals), Piet Collins (drums; ex-*Hangovers*)*

Boasting double bass, stand-up drums, rockabilly-tinged guitar licks and musicians dressed in all black, Melbourne three-piece The Sharp presented a united front and an interesting twist on 1990s pop. The band cited The Kinks, The Beatles and **The Easybeats** as influences, although less overt reference points could be Dr Feelgood, The Stray Cats and the Violent Femmes. Overall, the band's aesthetic push incorporated frisky pop melodies, tight arrangements, strong harmonies and grungy guitar riffs.

The Sharp grew out of Charlie Rooke's good-time bar-band 59 Sharp. The band played 1950s rock'n'roll and rockabilly covers to a hardcore Melbourne following. With the arrival of Allan Catlin and Piet Collins, The Sharp came into being. The band issued its debut CD EP, 'Love Your Head', independently through Mushroom Distribution Services in June 1992. The Sharp then signed to Warner Music Australia's East West label for the *Spinosity* EP ('Talking Sly') (September 1992). The EP reached #28 on the national single chart during December. **Boom Crash Opera's** Peter Farnan co-produced the band's third EP, 'Train Of Thought' (May 1993), with Nick Mainsbridge (**Ratcat, Tall Tales & True**). The EP reached #32 on the national chart during July.

The exuberant 'Train of Thought' also appeared on the band's full-length, debut album *This is The Sharp* (September 1993). *This is The Sharp* made its debut at #13 on the national chart. The album produced two more minor hits, 'Scratch My Back' (#40 in October) and 'Yeah I Want You' (#44 in November). To coincide with the album's release in September, The Sharp supported US visitors The Spin Doctors on their Australian tour. The Sharp's next CD single, 'Alone Like Me', became its biggest hit, peaking at #20 on the national chart during August 1994. The single also proved to be the band's final hit. 'Alone Like Me' came from the band's second album, *Sonic Tripod* (October), which produced two more CD singles, 'Thank You Goodnight' (September) and 'Spider' (December). Adam May replaced Collins on drums in early 1995, but the band bowed out with the compilation album *Single File* (September 1995).

Albums: *This Is The Sharp* (East West/Warner, 1993), *Sonic Tripod* (East West/Warner, 1994), *Single File* (East West/Warner, 1995).

Sherbet

Formed: *1969*
Style: *Pop*
Original line-up: *Dennis Laughlin (vocals; ex-Sebastian Hardie Blues Band, Clapham Junction), Clive Shakespeare (lead guitar, vocals; ex-Downtown Roll Band), Sammy See (organ, guitar, vocals; ex-Clapham Junction), Doug Rae (bass; ex-Downtown Roll Band), Danny Taylor (drums; Downtown Roll Band)*

Alongside **Skyhooks**, Sherbet was the most successful Australian pop band of the 1970s. With a run of 20 consecutive hit singles to its credit, and 17 albums that yielded ten platinum and 40 gold disc awards, Sherbet was the first domestic act to sell a million dollars worth of records in Australia. Under the direction of astute manager Roger Davies, the band also pioneered the concept of the national rock tour by undertaking arduous, cross-country treks to play in the far-flung corners of the continent. Sherbet's carefully cultivated image tended to alienate the 'serious' music fan, although the band's ability to deliver well-crafted pop music has never been in doubt.

The original Sherbet line-up emerged from the ashes of two Sydney dance bands, Downtown Roll Band and Clapham Junction. Englishman Clive Shakespeare formed Downtown Roll Band in 1968 with Doug Rae, Danny Taylor, Pam Slater (vocals), Francis Ma (vocals) and Adrian Cuff (organ). The band played Stax/Volt soul, James Brown and Tamla Motown covers before calling it a day in March 1969. Dennis Laughlin and Sam See's previous band, Clapham Junction, ran its own discotheque called the Union Jack. There were a number of different Clapham Junction line-ups. Following Laughlin and See's departures in early 1969, the line-up of Jim Willebrandt (vocals), William Mahoney (vocals), Derek Lewis (guitar), Peter Noble (bass) and David Mills (drums) recorded a single for the Du Monde label, 'Emily on Sunday'/'Good Time Music' (November 1970).

Shakespeare formed Sherbet in April 1969. Taylor left three months later to be replaced by Alan Sandow (ex-Daisy Roots). At the end of the year, the band recorded its debut single for Festival, 'Crimson Ships'/'Everything'. By the time the single appeared in March 1970, Daryl Braithwaite (ex-Bright Lights, House of Bricks, Samael Lilith) had replaced Laughlin and Bruce Worrall (ex-Bright Lights, House of Bricks, Samael Lilith) had taken over from Rae on bass. Laughlin went on to join Toby Jugg. Well before Sherbet commenced its national touring schedule, the band had honed its performance skills with an unbelievable eight-month residency at Jonathon's discotheque in Sydney. Throughout the residency, the band played seven hours a night, four nights a week. After that, the members of Sherbet were ready to take on the world!

The next member to leave, however, was See who departed in October 1970 to join **Flying Circus**. From there he joined **Fraternity**, Greg Quill's Southern Cross, The Stockley See Mason Band, the **Jimmy Barnes** Band and the **John Farnham** Band among others. New Zealand-born Garth Porter (Hammond organ, electric piano; ex-Toby Jugg) came in as See's replacement and the band signed to Festival's new subsidiary label Infinity. 'Can You Feel It Baby?'/'The Love You Save' (#22 in August 1971) and a cover of Delaney and Bonnie's 'Free the People'/'All Our Yesterdays' (national #36, Sydney #5 in December) were the band's first national hit singles. In January 1972, Tony Mitchell (ex-Wheelbarrow, Harry Young and Sabbath) replaced Worrall on bass.

Wheelbarrow comprised Mitchell, John Ford (guitar, vocals), Charlie Wright (piano) and Jim Mitchell (drums). The band issued one single, 'Dame Zara'/'Trying So Hard' (December 1969), before Mitchell joined Harry Young and Sabbath. That band comprised Harry Young (vocals), Tony Mitchell (bass), Jim Mitchell (drums), Tony Leigh (guitar) and Tony Barton (flute, guitar). The band enjoyed minor success on the Sydney charts with three singles, 'San Bernadino'/'Sand, Sea and Sky' (December 1970), 'Wheat in the Field'/'You Can't Destroy Love' (#7, April 1971) and 'Paper Girl'/'Bus Driver's Son' (August).

1972 proved to be a watershed year in Sherbet's development. The band supported Creedence Clearwater Revival on a national tour; the singles **Ted Mulry's** 'You're All Woman'/'Back Home' (#13 in August) and 'You've Got the Gun'/'Do It' (#29 in December) were hits; the band took out first place in the Hoadley's National Battle of the Sounds final; the debut album *Time Change A Natural Progression* (December) came out; and finally Sherbet was voted Top Australian Group in the *Go-Set* Pop Poll. Sherbet issued two singles during 1973, Leiber and Stoller's 'Hound Dog'/'Can I Drive You Home?' (#21 in July) and 'Cassandra'/'Time Change' (#5 in October).

'Cassandra' came from the band's second album, *On with the Show* (#6 in November), and was the first real indication of the Porter/Shakespeare-penned pop masterpieces that were to follow. Both records made extensive use of Porter's newly acquired Mellotron, which gave Sherbet a distinctive edge and sound over other Australian pop groups of the day. The band ended the year with the Best Australian Group honour at the *TV Week* King of Pop Awards. The rocky single 'So Glad You're Mine'/'For Your Love' (March 1974) missed the national Top 40, although the next two, 'Slipstream'/'Jungle Jiver' (June) and 'Silvery Moon'/'Summer Satisfaction' (August), reached the Top 10 ('Slipstream' at #7 and 'Silvery Moon' at #9). The highly commercial *Slipstream* album reached #5 in October 1974 and went on to sell over 100 000 copies.

Braithwaite kicked off his solo career with the national #1 hit single 'You're My World'/'Princess' (October 1974). He had already taken the lead role in the local stage production of The Who's *Tommy* in March 1973, and rumours began to circular that he would leave the group. He did not leave, despite winning the *TV Week* King of Pop award for three years in a row (1975 to 1977).

Sherbet's only release on EMI, 'Summer Love'/'(You Go You're Way) I'll Go Mine', became the perfect summer hit single when it reached the national #1 spot in March 1975. 'Summer Love' was the first Sherbet single to be issued in the UK. The band's fourth album, *In Concert Live* (March), produced the single Free's 'Wishing Well'/'Freedom' (#24 in April). The band scored its first national #1 album with *Sherbet's Greatest Hits 1970–1975* (August). The band ended 1975 with the release of its most ambitious album to date, *Life ... is for Living* (#6 in November). It produced the hit singles 'Life'/'Survival' (#7 in August) and the double A-sided 'Only One You'/'Matter of Time' (#6 in November). To coincide with the album's release, the band embarked on the extensive Life national tour.

Then, in January 1976, founder member Clive Shakespeare left the band due to personal and musical differences. Initially Gunther Gorman (ex-**Home**) came in as his replacement, until Harvey James (ex-**Mississippi**, **Ariel**) took over permanently during April. Shakespeare's last recording with the band, 'Child's Play'/'Just Being You', reached #5 during February. James' first recording with the band, 'Howzat!'/'Motor of Love', became the band's biggest hit single. It reached #1 nationally in May, followed by the band's double platinum album *Howzat!* which also reached #1 (July). On the heels of the national Howzat! tour, Sherbet issued two more singles, 'Hollywood Dreaming'/'Gimme Love' (June) and 'Rock Me Gently'/'You've Got the Gun' (1976 version) (#6 in October).

In the meantime, CBS/Epic had issued *Howzat!* in the UK, Europe and South-East Asia, while MCA issued it in the USA. The 'Howzat!' single reached #4 in the UK (September) and Top 10 in South Africa, Israel, a number of European countries and various parts of South-East Asia (#2 in Thailand). Sherbet embarked on an extensive overseas tour that took in the UK, the USA and South-East Asia. The band's Australian Photoplay tour coincided with the release of the double platinum *Photoplay* album (#3 in June 1977) and its single 'Magazine Madonna'/'Still in Love with You' (#3 in June). *Photoplay* was the first release on the band's newly formed Razzle label (through Festival). The album yielded one further single, 'High Rolling'/'Mid-Summer Madness' (August). 'High Rolling' was used as the theme song to the Australian feature film of the same name.

Sherbet

The band's last single for 1977, a cover of The Beatles' 'Nowhere Man'/'Dancer' (#28 in January 1978), was lifted from the live set *Caught in the Act . . . Live* (October 1977).

In August 1977, Sherbet set off on its second overseas tour, which encompassed gigs in Thailand, the UK, Europe and the USA (supporting The Hollies). Sherbet's first single for 1978, 'Feels Like It's Slipping Away'/'Safe Water', reached #18 in March. During June 1978, the band recorded a new album with producer Jay Lewis at United Western Studios in Los Angeles. The *Sherbet* album and its single 'Another Night on the Road'/'Winnepeg Sidestep' appeared in August to coincide with the band's Another Night on the Road Australian tour. The album reached #5 in September and the single #8 in August. The album's third single, 'Beg Steal or Borrow'/'You Made a Fool' (October), failed to chart. The band's 25th single, 'Angela'/'Take My Heart' (February 1979), was taken from the soundtrack to the feature film *Snapshot* starring Sigrid Thornton.

Due to a number of delays, the *Sherbet* album did not appear in the USA until March 1979. The album came out on the RSO label (home to **The Bee Gees**) under the title of *Highway One*. The band had changed its name to Highway for the American market (at RSO's insistence) and the album's new title reflected that change. The band returned to the US for further touring but was unable to crack the American charts. The band's only Australian release under the Highway moniker was the single 'Heart Get Ready'/'Skyline' (July 1979). In 1980, the band became known as The Sherbs. The Sherbs issued three albums and nine singles. *The Skill* (October 1980) produced 'Never Surrender'/'Love You to Death' (February), 'I'm Okay'/'Into the Heat' (May), 'Juliet and Me'/'I'll Be Faster' (July) and 'I Have the Skill'/'Parallel Bars' (November). *Defying Gravity* (November 1981) produced 'Free the Sailor'/'Blood on My Hands' (October) and 'Some People'/'We Ride Tonight' (February 1982).

At the end of 1982, Tony Leigh (ex-Harry Young and Sabbath, Gillian Eastoe Band) replaced Harvey James who joined **The Party Boys**. The Sherbs' final album, *Shaping Up* (November 1982), produced the singles 'Don't Throw It All Away'/'Knowing You' (July), 'Shaping Up'/'I Don't Want to Lose You' (October) and 'The Arrow'/'Wild is the Sea' (March 1983). Despite featuring a polished, contemporary pop sound, none of The Sherbs' records made the national charts. In late 1983, the band announced its impending split. The final Sherbet single, 'Tonight will Last Forever'/'Howzat!' (February 1984), and the compilation *The Hits 1969–1984* coincided with the band's final national tour. Former members Clive Shakespeare and Harvey James made guest appearances on the tour. **Daryl Braithwaite** later embarked on a successful solo career. Sherbet was inducted into the Hall of Fame at the 1989 Australian Record Industry Association (ARIA) Awards.

Sherbet albums: *Time Change A Natural Progression* (Festival/Infinity, 1972), *On with the Show* (Festival/Infinity, 1973), *Slipstream* (Festival/Infinity, 1974), *In Concert* (Festival/Infinity, 1975), *Sherbet's Greatest Hits 1970–1975* (compilation, Festival/Infinity, 1975), *Life . . . is for Living* (Festival/Sherbet, 1975), *Howzat!* (Festival/Sherbet, 1976), *The Sherbet Collection* (compilation, Festival/Sherbet, 1976), *Photoplay* (Festival/Razzle, 1977), *Caught in the Act . . . Live* (Festival/Razzle, 1977), *Sherbet* (Festival/Razzle, 1978), *Track Record* (compilation, Festival/Razzle, 1979), *The Sherbet Phenomenon* (compilation, Hammard, 1981), *The Hits 1969–1984* (compilation, Festival/Infinity, 1984); ***Sherbs albums:*** *The Skill* (Festival/Razzle, 1980), *Defying Gravity* (Festival/Razzle, 1981), *Shaping Up* (mini-album, Festival/Razzle, 1982).

Shindiggers

Formed: *1983*
Style: *Beat pop*
Original line-up: *Bill Leggett (vocals), Pete Andrews (lead guitar; ex-***Corpse Grinders***, Twangin' Heartthrobs), Steve Agar (bass), Spud Wildman (real name Steve Andrews, drums; ex-***Dancehall Racketeers***)*

On the thriving mid-1980s Melbourne inner-city scene, Shindiggers were one of the hardest working bands around. As the city's prime beat pop merchants, the band's music was far removed from the gothic grunge or hardcore punk favoured by most Melbourne independent groups of the day. Pete Andrews' guitar riffs were twangy and upbeat instead of grungy, the rhythm section was tight and snappy instead of laborious and heavy. And in Bill Leggett the band possessed a hyperactive frontman with a neat line in James Brown dance steps. The band's Melbourne contemporaries included **Corpse Grinders**, **Olympic Sideburns**, Shower Scene from Psycho, **Huxton Creepers** and **The Slaughtermen**.

Shindiggers' influences included Carl Perkins, Screaming Lord Sutch, The Meteors, The Beatles, early Rolling Stones, The Milkshakes and Johnny Kidd and the Pirates. The band's early live set was peppered with covers like Swingin' Blue Jeans' 'Hippy Hippy Shake', Chuck Berry's 'Talking About You', Roy Head's 'Treat Her Right' and Screaming Lord Sutch's 'Til the Following Night'. Shindiggers recorded their debut, four-track EP, 'Baby Let Go' (March 1985), live, in an hour, in Graeme Thomas's lounge-room studio Bedroom Mazurka. The EP (issued on the Preston label) captured the band's raw and primitive sound in all its unembellished glory. Shindiggers issued a second EP, *Go Wild!*, and the mini-album *Beat is Back* (both on the Man Made label) during 1985. That year, Leggett and Agar also played in psychedelic outfit LSD with Jeff the Butcher (guitar) and Rodney 'Modney' McMurrich (drums; ex-**Gas Babies**).

In October 1986, Shindiggers branched out and issued the full-length album *Crash Your Party* on Sydney label Waterfront. In 1986, the band issued two gig giveaway singles, 'All I've Got to Do'/'Crash the Party', 'Xmas Massage' and 'Good Golly Miss Molly' (shared with **The Pony's** 'In the Backyard'). Shindiggers played their last gigs in February 1987. Leggett and Agar (who switched to guitar) formed neo-mod band The Joysticks with Mike Cronin (bass) and Grant Clelland (drums). The Joysticks issued one single, 'What More Can I Do?'/'Without My Say', on the Rampant label (October 1987). 'What More Can I Do?' also appeared on Rampant's Various Artists album *Running Rampant Volume 1*.

Pete Andrews played with a number of bands including Moment of Truth. In late 1996, the original Shindiggers reconvened to play gigs around Melbourne. The band also appeared under the moniker of The E-Aitches, playing gigs with other like-minded 1960s revivalists Thurston Howlers, The Exotics, **The Hekawis**, The Fudds, Driveway Service and Planet of the Apes.

Album: *Crash Your Party* (Waterfront, 1986).

Shock Poets (*see* v. Spy v. Spy)

Glenn Shorrock

Style: *Pop*

English-born singer/songwriter Glenn Shorrock (b. 1944) is one of the veterans of the Australian music industry. He got his start during the mid-1960s with **The Twilights**, before moving on to **Axiom**, **Little River Band** and a successful solo career. As a songwriter, Shorrock contributed the likes of 'Emma', 'Statue of Liberty', 'Seine City', 'Help is On Its Way', 'Cool Change', 'Shut Down, Turn Off' and 'Long Jumping Jeweller' to LRB's repertoire.

Shorrock arrived in Australia during the mid-1950s with his family as assisted-passage immigrants. The Shorrocks settled in the tough migrant suburb of Elizabeth in Adelaide, South Australia. Smitten by rock'n'roll, Shorrock formed vocal quartet The Checkmates with Mike Sykes, Paddy McCartney and Billy Volraat. In 1964, The Beatles broke in Australia and The Checkmates evolved into **The Twilights**. In terms of style and songwriting ability (if not success), **The Twilights** were the closest thing Australia had to overseas role models like The Beatles, The Rolling Stones, The Move, The Who, etc. **The Twilights** existed between 1964 and 1969, and enjoyed significant chart success with eight consecutive hit singles. With the band's break-up in early 1969, Shorrock spent three months managing Brisbane band **The Avengers**.

In May 1969, Shorrock joined highly touted 'supergroup' **Axiom**. The band ended up in the UK where the inevitable break-up came in early 1971. With assistance from manager Garry Spry (**The Groove**), Shorrock signed a UK deal with management/record/publishing company MAM, owned by Gordon Mills (manager of Tom Jones, Englebert Humperdinck and Gilbert O'Sullivan). Shorrock issued three singles on the MAM label: 'Let's Get the Band Together'/'Contemporary Caveman' (October 1971), Mann/Weil's 'Rock'n'Roll Lullaby'/'When God Plays His Guitar' (March 1972) and 'Purple Umbrella' (credited to Andre L'Escargot and His Society Syncopaters). **Twilights** producer David MacKay, then based in London, produced the sessions, with backing provided by Quartet, which comprised former Adelaide musicians Terry Britten (ex-**Twilights**), Kevin Peek, Alan Tarney and Trevor Spencer (all ex-**James Taylor Move**).

In 1972, Shorrock joined ambitious, 12-piece classical rock band Esperanto. Billed as 'the world's first international rock orchestra', Esperanto featured members from Hawaii, Belgium, Italy, England, New Zealand and Australia. The other Australian members were Brian Holloway (guitar, piano; ex-Somebody's Image) and Janice Slater (vocals). Slater had enjoyed a mildly successful solo career in Australia during the 1960s with three singles, 'Wanting You'/'Summertime' (1965) and 'I'm Gonna Live'/'He Really Cares' (1965) for Philips, plus 'Don't Let Me Be Misunderstood'/'Let the Love Come Through' (1967) for Festival/Spin. She had also been a member of Little Sammy and the In People, which had taken her to the UK in the first place.

In 1973, A&M issued Esperanto's debut album, *Esperanto Rock Orchestra*, which included a version of Shorrock's 'Statue of Liberty'. Shorrock only contributed some lyrics and backing vocals to the band's second album, *Danse Macabre* (1974). By the time the band recorded a third album, *Last Tango* (1974), Shorrock was no longer a member, but had taken over the management role. With the band's lack of success, Shorrock took his leave and began singing back-up vocals for Cliff Richard. In October 1974, Shorrock returned to Australia. In early 1975, he joined ex-**Mississippi** members Graham Goble and Beeb Birtles in their new venture **Little River Band**. LRB went on to achieve enormous international success, but Shorrock left in February 1982 to be replaced by **John Farnham**. Shorrock had already issued a Top 10 solo single, Bobby Darin's 'Dream Lover'/'Spin Me Round' (#8 in April 1979).

He recorded his debut solo album, *Villain of the Peace*, with LRB producer John Boylan in Los Angeles. The credits for the album read like a Who's Who of the American West Coast 'session mafia': Bill Payne (Little Feat), Jeff Baxter (Steely Dan, Doobie Brothers), Garth Hudson (The Band), Jimmy Fadden (Nitty Gritty Dirt Band), Timothy B. Schmit (The Eagles), Andrew Gold, David Lindley and Tom Scott. The album produced the singles 'Rock'n'Roll Soldier'/'The Duchess is Returning' (#39 in November 1982), 'Angry Words'/'Will You Stand with Me?' (December) and 'Don't Girls Get Lonely?'/'Do It Anyway' (November 1983). In late 1982, Shorrock toured Australia. He sang on **Renée Geyer's** version of the Goffin/King classic 'Going Back' which Mushroom issued as a single (backed with 'We've Got the Makings of a Fever') in February 1983. Shorrock recorded a single with **The Bushwackers**, 'We're Coming to Get You'/'We're Coming to Get You' (instrumental), which was the theme song to the feature film of the same name. It reached #6 on the national chart in October 1983. Shorrock's next recording, 'Restless', appeared on the soundtrack to the documentary film *World Safari II*.

In 1986, Shorrock issued his ninth solo single, 'American Flyer'/'The Duchess is Returning' (July) and compered the ABC-TV's rock show *Rock Arena*. He also toured with the stage show *One for the Money*. Then, in 1988, Shorrock rejoined **Little River Band** with which he remained for another three years. In 1991, Shorrock was inducted into the Australian Record Industry Association (ARIA) Hall of Fame. In 1993, he teamed up with **Brian Cadd** as The Blazing Salads and toured the club circuit. The Blazing Salads signed to EMI and issued the album *The Blazing Salads* plus the singles 'When It All Comes Down', 'De-Emphasize' and 'Little Ray of Sunshine' (all 1993). The duo's backing band included Rex Goh (guitar; ex-**Air Supply**), Kirk Lorange (guitar; ex-**Richard Clapton** Band) and Mark Kennedy (drums; ex-**Spectrum**, **Ayers Rock**, **Marcia Hines** Band).

Albums: *Villain of The Peace* (EMI/Capitol, 1982), *The First Twenty Years* (compilation with **Twilights**, **Axiom**, **Little River Band** and solo material, EMI, 1985); ***With Brian Cadd:*** *The Blazing Salads* (EMI, 1993).

Shreen (*see* Nursery Crimes)

Sick Things (*see* Fungus Brains)

Sid Rumpo

Formed: *1970*
Style: *R&B*
Original line-up: *Robert Searls (guitar, vocals), John Hood (lead guitar, vocals, harp; ex-Jelly Roll Bakers, Juke), Ken Wallace (piano), Owen Hughes (bass; ex-Jelly Roll Bakers), Noel Herridge (drums; ex-***Adderley Smith Blues Band***)*

Blues rock band Sid Rumpo formed in Perth (Western Australia) during November 1970, and made a name for itself on the eastern states festival/concert circuit with consistently powerful live performances. Original lead guitarist John Hood had been playing in blues bands since the late 1960s. Jelly Roll Bakers comprised Hood, Owen Hughes, Steve Tallis (guitar, vocals), Peter Walker (guitar) and Vic Tallis (drums). Walker joined **Bakery** in 1970. Juke comprised Hood, Steve Tallis, Vic Tallis and Steve Hogg (bass). Hogg also went on to become a member of **Bakery**. Tallis became a highly respected blues player on the Perth scene with a number of bands like Tampa Red, The Opposition and The Apache Dropouts.

In September 1972, Sid Rumpo won the West Australian Battle of the Sounds, and a month later relocated to Melbourne. The band appeared on the bill of the second annual Sunbury Festival (January 1973). The track 'Sailing' appeared on Mushroom Records triple live album set of the event, *The Great Australian Rock Festival Sunbury 1973* (April 1973). Mushroom signed Sid Rumpo, but founder member Hood departed; he later joined another Perth blues band, **The Elks**. Mick Elliott (ex-Moppa Blues, Sunshine, Tank, Sayla) came in as his replacement. The live track 'Now I'm Free' appeared on Mushroom's Various Artists album *Garrison: The Final Blow Unit 2*.

Mushroom issued the band's debut album, *First Offence* and single, 'The Riddle'/'Jump Down Step Aside', in April 1974. It was a strong album, mixing hard blues tracks like 'Spotlight' and 'Breaking My Back' with lengthy, progressive rock outings like 'Sailing' and 'Song with No Trees'. One of the unique features of the band's sound was the use of dual, harmony guitar lines which had the effect of enhancing the natural spaciousness of the music. To top it off, Searls was one of the great gravel-throated blues wailers of the day. Sid Rumpo contributed covers of Willie Dixon's 'Wang Dang Doodle' and Robert Johnson's 'Sweet Home Chicago' to the live, Various Artists album *Highlights of Sunbury '74 Part 2* issued on the Mushroom antiRipoff label. By the end of 1974, the band had called it a day.

Searls returned to Perth where he fronted The Beagle Boys and Wild Blue Yonder. Elliott joined **Jim Keays'** Southern Cross briefly before he and Herridge joined Wild Beaver Band, which comprised Snowy 'Cutmore' Townsend (vocals; ex-Moppa Blues), John Brunell (guitar), Ian Miller (guitar; ex-**Chetarca**) and Mike Crawford (bass). Although the band never issued a record under its own name, the live tracks 'What am I Doin' Here?', 'How Come All You Dudes Look Like Cowboys?' and 'Messin' Around the Town' appeared on the Various Artists album *Live at the Station* on the Lamington label (1976). Journeyman guitarist Elliott went on to work with **Bandicoot**, the Mick Elliott Band, **Western Flyer**, **Dutch Tilders'** R&B Six and The Blue Heelers. He contributed the track 'On the Cards' to the Various Artists *Australian Guitar Album* (Festival/Razzle, 1979), which also featured **Kevin Borich**, **Mario Millo**, **Ian Moss**, Chris Turner, **Lobby Loyde**, Russell Smith, Ian Miller, **Phil Manning**, Harvey James and **Rockwell T. James**.

Album: *First Offence* (Mushroom/Festival, 1974).

Sidewinder

Formed: *1990*
Style: *Indie guitar pop*
Original line-up: *Nick Craft (guitar, vocals), Pip Branson (guitar), Martin Craft (bass, vocals), Giri Fox (drums)*

Canberra band Sidewinder played an accessible brand of distortion-drenched, harmony-driven, indie guitar power pop. Various reference points abounded, including UK bands like Swervedriver, Teenage Fanclub and Stone Roses, plus local acts like **Even**, **Tumbleweed** and **Spiderbait**. With the addition of Jeremy David on viola, the inevitable comparisons with the work of John Cale in The Velvet Underground also arose.

Sidewinder formed when several members were still at high school. The band found a cult audience and issued a number of tough, yet meticulously crafted CD EPs on the Half a Cow label (alongside **Smugde**, **Godstar**, **Daisygrinders**, etc.). Half a Cow's manager Nic Dalton included an early Sidewinder track, 'Last Time', on the HAC compilation *Slice Two* (November 1992). The band kicked off with the CD EPs 'T-Star' (March 1993) and 'Yoko Icepick' (December). Sidewinder appeared on the Sydney bill of the 1994 Big Day Out tour. By that stage, David had left, and soon after Shane Melder (ex-**Hummingbirds**) replaced Giri Fox on drums. Sidewinder's third CD EP, 'The Gentle Art of Spoonbending' (March 1995) included two of the band's strongest songs in 'Up to You' and 'Day After Day'. Sidewinder also contributed the track 'Come Inside' to rooArt's *Youngblood 4* compilation (September 1994).

Sidewinder's debut, full-length album *Atlantis* (January 1996) yielded three CD singles, 'Anything You Want' (October 1995), 'Evil Eye' (January) and 'Not Coming Home' (April). *Atlantis* was brimming with unabashed, infectious rock energy and displayed a great deal of potential. To coincide with the album's release, the band scored a slot on the national bill of the 1996 Big Day Out tour. Sidewinder also undertook national tours with **Custard**, **Snout** and **The Fauves**. By that stage, Craft and Melder had also joined forces with Simon Holmes (guitar, vocals; ex-**Hummingbirds**) and Wayne Connolly (guitar, vocals; **Welcome Mat**, Knievel) as studio band Fragile.

Half a Cow issued Fragile's album *Airbrushed Perfection* (March 1996), which ran the gamut of sounds from jangly pop ('Dream Come True') to noisy Hüsker Dü-inspired rockers ('She Really Means that Much to Me', 'Resolving Conflict Situations'). Sidewinder recorded a new album, *Tangerine*, with producer Paul McKercher (**Spiderbait**, **Tumbleweed**, **You Am I**), which appeared in September 1997. The album's first CD single (issued in April), 'Titanic Days', also appeared on the soundtrack to the feature film *Blackrock*. The album's second CD single, 'Here She Comes Again', came out in August.

Albums: *Atlantis* (Half a Cow/Mercury, 1996), *Tangerine* (Mercury, 1997).

Joel Silbersher (Melonman) (*see* Hoss)

Joel Silbersher and Charlie Owen (Tendrils) (*see* Hoss)

Silver Studs

Formed: *1975*
Style: *Rock'n'roll revival*
Original line-up: *Lance Reynolds (vocals), Gino Latorre (vocals), Keith Reed (vocals)*

Lance Reynolds formed rock'n'roll revival act Silver Studs in Brisbane during 1975. The trio's act included singing, dancing and comedy. Silver Studs signed to the Philips label and issued the single 'My Teenage Dream' (February 1976). That same month, Silver Studs supported UK visitors The Hollies on their national tour. A month later, Keith Reed left to be replaced initially by Vivien Grayson and then Paul Stevens.

The trio's backing band at that stage included Mark Dozzi (guitar), Casey Steen (guitar), Chris Wilson (keyboards), Robert Glover (bass) and Phillip Smith (drums). Silver Studs scored their biggest hit single with a rendition of 'Happy Days', the theme song to popular American television comedy *Happy Days* starring Ron Howard and Henry Winkler. The single reached #4 in June 1976. 'Dance with a Dolly' was the band's second hit (#11 in September). The trio's debut album *Happy Days* (October 1976) went on to sell 50 000 copies. At the start of 1977, Stevens left to replace Frankie J. Holden in **Ol'55**. Reynolds and Latorre continued on as The Studs. The duo's backing band at that stage comprised Peter Plavsic (bass; ex-**Sebastian Hardie**), Alex Plavsic (drums; ex-**Sebastian Hardie**), Graham Wardrop (guitar), John Bushell (guitar) and Rick Mellick (keyboards).

The Studs' debut single on the Wizard label, 'Funky Feet'/'Disco Death', reached #13 on the national chart in October 1977. In the meantime, the Riva label had issued 'Funky Feet' as a single in the UK and Europe, and The Studs embarked on a promotional tour. In December, The Studs completed an album in Los Angeles. It was scheduled for release in March 1978, but did not see the light of day until November as *The New Studs Album*. Meanwhile, The Studs issued the singles 'Today I Met the Girl I'm Gonna Marry'/'I Don't Wanna Dance Matilda with You' (November 1977) and 'Dr Bop'/'Crazy Lover' (May 1978). The single lifted from *The New Studs Album*, 'One Step Too Far'/'It Don't Matter', was credited to Gino Latorre solo, as was one side of the album.

Albums: *Happy Days* (as Silver Studs, Philips, 1976), *The New Studs Album* (credited to The Studs/Gino Latorre, Wizard/Big Time, 1978).

silverchair

Formed: *1994*
Style: *Rock*
Original line-up: *Daniel Johns (guitar, vocals), Chris Joannou (bass), Ben Gilles (drums)*

As one of the most highly feted Australian rock bands of the mid-1990s, Newcastle's silverchair has enjoyed a phenomenally successful career. Led by charismatic frontman Daniel Johns, silverchair came to epitomise 1990s alternarock with a sound and style that drew as much from Led Zeppelin, Black Sabbath, Deep Purple, **AC/DC** and **Radio Birdman** as it did from Seattle grunge godheads like Nirvana, Soundgarden and Pearl Jam. The mainstream media made much of the fact that the band members were still at high school when silverchair was thrust into the limelight. Yet that hardly mattered, given the band's uncanny knack for delivering superbly crafted, dynamic, swaggering and accessible rock music. With worldwide album sales approaching six million copies, silverchair's place in Australian rock history was well assured.

Johns, Chris Joannou and Ben Gilles were all born in 1979. They formed their first band, Innocent Criminals, in 1992, along with second guitarist Tobin Finnane who left soon after due to the fact that his family was to spend a year in the UK. In early 1994, Innocent Criminals recorded demos of the songs 'Pure Massacre', 'Acid Rain', 'Cicada' and 'Tomorrow' at Terry Farrelly's Platinum Sound Studios. The band submitted 'Tomorrow' to the 'Pick Me' competition run by SBS-TV's music show *nomad* in conjunction with the ABC's national youth radio network Triple J.

Innocent Criminals emerged as the winners in April. The band re-recorded 'Tomorrow' at Triple J Studios in Sydney and the *nomad* crew filmed a low-key video which was aired on 16 June 1994.

silverchair

Triple J began to play 'Tomorrow' on a regular basis. Immediately courted by both Mushroom Records and the Murmur label (Sony's newly formed boutique, indie label headed by former music journalist John O'Donnell), the band was in big demand. Murmur eventually signed the re-named silverchair, and by October the 'Tomorrow' CD EP (issued in September) had leapt into the national Top 10. 'Tomorrow' peaked at #1 and stayed there for six weeks, selling 180 000 copies after a Top 60 stay of 28 weeks. It was the ninth biggest selling single in Australia during 1994, as well as logging the #5 spot (the highest Australian entry) on Triple J's 1994 Hottest 100 list. With 'Tomorrow' still in the Top 10, silverchair's follow-up CD EP, 'Pure Massacre', made its debut at #2 during January 1995 (kept from the top spot by Irish band The Cranberries' 'Zombie'). That same month, silverchair completed a showcase slot on the national Big Day Out tour. 'Israel's Son' reached #11 on the national chart in April.

Amidst the inevitable media jibes of 'Nirvana in pyjamas', 'silverhighchair' and 'not Soundgarden but Kindergarden', the band issued its debut, full-length album *frogstomp* (March 1995). Produced by South African Kevin 'Caveman' Shirley, *frogstomp* captured the tempo of the times with its mix of Soundgarden/Pearl Jam/Bush post-grunge noise and teenage lyrical angst. It made its debut at #1 on the national charts and went on to sell over 210 000 copies. The album's fourth single, 'Shade', reached #28 in July. Sony/Epic issued *frogstomp* in the USA, and by August it had reached the American Top 10 (on its way to selling more than two million copies). 'Tomorrow' also reached the US Top 30, and silverchair undertook two American tours (June and September, including support slots to Red Hot Chili Peppers and The Ramones). The band appeared on the bill of the MTV Music Awards at New York's Radio City Music Hall, playing 'Tomorrow' and 'Pure Massacre'.

During October 1995, silverchair took out the Australian Record Industry Association (ARIA) Awards for Best Single, Best Debut Single, Highest Selling Single ('Tomorrow'), Best Debut Album (*frogstomp*) and Best New Talent. The band also performed, in company with **You Am I's** Tim Rogers, a rendition of **Radio Birdman's** teen anthem, 'New Race', live on the television broadcast. In early 1996, silverchair appeared on the bill of the rain-sodden Homebake '96 festival (held in Byron Bay), alongside the likes of **Spiderbait**, **Tumbleweed**, **Regurgitator** and **Magic Dirt**.

silverchair returned to the USA and the UK for further bouts of touring (including an appearance on the bill of the 1996 Reading Festival). The band's next CD single, 'Freak', made its debut at #1 on the national chart in January 1997. Produced by Nick Launay (**Birthday Party**, **Models**, **Midnight Oil**), the single included a version of **Radio Birdman's** 'New Race' which featured the song's writer **Deniz Tek** on guitar and vocal 'yeah hups!'. The *Freak Show* album (produced by Launay and mixed by Andy Wallace) also made its debut at #1 (February) before slipping back down to #2 a week later. By that stage, it had already sold over 70 000 copies.

If *frogstomp* betrayed a debt to Soundgarden and Pearl Jam, then *Freak Show* and tracks like 'Freak' were firmly in Nirvana territory with a hint of Led Zeppelin's Eastern mysticism. Not a bad thing, considering the overall strengths of the album. With the platinum-selling 'Freak' still sitting at #8 after 11 weeks, the album's second single, 'Abuse Me', made its debut at #9 in April. 'Abuse Me' featured a version of **The Master's Apprentices'** R&B infused 'Undecided' (with **Deniz Tek** on guitar) as a bonus track. silverchair spent the early months of 1997 touring Australia and the USA (supported by **Automatic**).

The US tour took in an appearance on *The Late Show with David Letterman* during which the band performed 'Abuse Me'. The third CD single lifted from *Freak Show*, 'Cemetery' (June), made its debut at #5 on the Australian chart. The fourth, 'The Door', only tickled the lower reaches of the Top 40 for two weeks in November. Meanwhile, silverchair had undertaken its second UK tour. 'Pure Massacre' and 'Tomorrow' had been minor UK hits at #71 (July 1995) and #59 (September) respectively. *The Freak Box* (November 1997) comprised the four CD singles lifted from *Freak Show* (with ten non-album tracks), an interactive CD-ROM and an interview disc.

Albums: *frogstomp* (Murmur/Sony, 1995), *Freak Show* (Murmur/Sony, 1997) *The Freak Box* (CD single box set, Murmur/Sony, 1997).

Further reading: *Hi Fi Days: The Future of Australian Rock* by Craig Mathieson (Allen & Unwin, 1996).

Single Gun Theory

Formed: *1986*
Style: *Electronic dance pop*
Original line-up: *Jacqui Hunt (vocals), Kath Power (lyrics, vocal melodies, synthesiser), Peter Rivett-Carnac (guitar, synthesiser, sampling)*

Like **Severed Heads** and **Boxcar**, Sydney-based trio Single Gun Theory pioneered electronic dance music in Australia. The trio created music through technology, utilising samplers and computers as instruments. Although they rarely performed live, and were hardly prolific, the trio earned a cult following with the release of several captivating albums of dance pop.

In 1986, Single Gun Theory won a Double J (the precursor to the national Triple J network) band competition. The prize included free recording time which the band utilised to record its debut album. Before Single Gun Theory could issue the album locally, Peter Rivett-Carnac joined **Severed Heads** for their North American tour. Canadian label Nettwerk had already issued **Severed Heads'** product overseas, and the label was sufficiently impressed to release Single Gun Theory's *Exorcise this Wasteland*. The album won critical acclaim, and its limited availability in Australia as an import made the band something of a novelty. Rivett-Carnac and Jacqui Hunt put Single Gun Theory on hold while they travelled across Asia and Europe, before ending up in the UK. Kath Power studied psychiatric therapy in Sydney.

They returned to Vancouver, Canada in May 1991 to record Single Gun Theory's second album, *Like Stars in My Hands*, at Sierra Studios. Sydney-based label Volition (home to **Severed Heads**, **Scattered Order** and **Falling Joys**) issued the album locally in December. The album featured a unique blend of lush, mellow dance grooves, ethnic sampling and fragile, beguiling female vocals as epitomised by the singles 'From a Million Miles' (November 1991) and 'I am what I See' (February 1992). **Boxcar's** David Smith remixed 'I am what I See' and it became a dance floor favourite. Volition included 'I am what I See' on its dance compilation *High* (1993), and ABC-TV's *Review* program adopted the song as its theme. Single Gun Theory songs also appeared on the soundtracks for two Australian feature films, Yahoo Serious's *Reckless Kelly* and *The Heartbreak Kid*.

Single Gun Theory returned in 1994 with its third album, *Flow, River of My Soul*, which produced the infectious CD single 'Fall' (October). At the end of 1994, Single Gun Theory embarked on its first major tour in North America as support to ambient artist Sarah McLachlan. Prior to the 20-date tour, Single Gun Theory had only played a total of 11 gigs since formation. Single Gun Theory added a dancer and percussionist for its November Australian tour. Two further singles were lifted from *Flow, River of My Soul* in 1995, 'Open the Skies' (March) and 'Motherland' (August).

Albums: *Exorcise this Wasteland* (Nettwerk, Canadian import only, 1988; later issued in Australia by Volition), *Like Stars in My Hands* (Volition/Sony, 1991), *Flow, River of My Soul* (Volition/Sony, 1994).

The 69ers

Formed: *1969*
Style: *Rock'n'roll, jugband*
Original line-up: *Francis Butler (guitar, vocals, harmonica, kazoo), Brian Bethall (bass, guitar, vocals), Keith Longman (drums, vocals)*

Sydney band The 69ers played a good-time mix of vintage rock'n'roll, jugband music and country-swing that placed them somewhere between The Panama Jug Band, Bonzo Dog Doo Dah Band, Commander Cody and his Lost Planet Airmen and **Captain Matchbox Whoopee Band**. There were a number of other local bands playing a similar style at the same time, including Starving Wild Dogs, Original Battersea Heroes, Gutbucket Blues Band, Stovepipe Spasm Band and Moonshine Jug and String Band.

Yet, in retrospect, none seemed to capture the humour and downright silliness of the form in such a boisterous, zany and garrulous fashion. Billing themselves as 'The fabulous internationally famous 69ers', the band became a popular attraction on the Sydney club scene during the early 1970s. The band issued its debut single, 'On the Road Again'/'Cup of Tea Take Three', on the independent Du Monde label in late 1970. A year later, the band issued a second single, 'Morning Blues'/'Push Bike Hood' (December 1971). The single came from the band's debut album for Du Monde, *The 69ers Album*. The album included eclectic covers from the band's live set, The Kinks' 'Harry Rag', The Byrds' 'The Christian Life', Ewan MacColl's 'Dirty Old Town' and Willis and Dunn's

'Sadie Green (The Vamp of New Orleans)'. 'Harry Rag'/'Happiness is Just for Me' came out as the band's third single in August 1972.

Helping out on the album sessions were Peter Knox (vocals), Dave Ovendon (vocals), Buddy Emmons (steel guitar), Col Nolan (piano) and Keith Harris (banjo). Knox (guitar, bass, vocals) and Ovendon (drums, vocals) later joined The 69ers as full-time members. Knox had been a member of Original Battersea Heroes. Led by Terry Darmody, the Heroes had issued an album, *Little Miss Lucy and Boogie Chicken*, at the same time as *The 69ers Album* on Du Monde's sister label Violet's Holiday (although Knox did not appear on it). The 69ers' line-up of Butler, Bethall, Knox and Ovendon played a riotous set at the second annual Sunbury festival (January 1973). The 69ers' track 'Harry Rag' appeared on the triple live set *The Great Australian Rock Festival Sunbury 1973* (April 1973) issued by Mushroom. Festival also issued 'Harry Rag' as a single that month, backed with 'Blood Flash' and 'Rag Mama'. A year later, Festival/Infinity issued the band's Sunbury set as the live album *Francis Butler's 69ers Live*.

April 1973 was a busy time for the band, because that month Bethall, Knox and Ovendon sacked Butler from his own band. As Peter Knox's New Improved 69ers, Bethall, Knox and Ovendon recruited Tony Burkys (guitar; ex-Original Battersea Heroes; he did play on the *Boogie Chicken* album). The band recorded two songs for a prospective single, a cover of Shel Silverstein's 'Freakin' at the Freaker's Ball' and the self-penned 'Sailing Ship', but the single never eventuated. Butler responded by forming Francis Butler's Original 69ers which comprised Ray Ferguson (guitar, vocals, flute, kazoo; ex-Samael Lilith), Alex Smith (bass; ex-Bullet) and Peter Jarman (drums). Soon after, Terry Stacey replaced Smith on bass and John 'Ernie' McInerny (ex-**Company Caine**) replaced Jarman on drums.

In the meantime, Peter Knox's New Improved 69ers had changed names to Omnibus. A month later (November 1973), the band became known as Locoweed. Locoweed broke up in March 1974 when Knox rejoined Francis Butler's 69ers. The band issued a final single, 'Flash'/'Back Seat Drivin'', on the independent Earth label before breaking up at the end of the year. Francis Butler went on to issue an album of religious songs, *There is No Escape*, produced by Chris Neale. Musicians on the album were Grahame Wardrop (guitar), Randall Waller (guitar), Bill Grahame (bass), Phil Truscott (bass), Steve Wyatt (keyboards), Chris Neale (moog), Barry Stewart (drums) and Jim Young (drums). In 1977, Peter Knox formed Toons with Ian Willis (guitar) and Gavin Hodel (drums) before taking the stage name Izzy Foreal and forming **The Fabulous Zarsoff Bros**.

Albums: *The 69ers Album* (Du Monde/Festival, 1971), *Francis Butler's 69ers Live* (Festival/Infinity, 1974), *There is No Escape* (Francis Butler solo, Rhema, 1978).

Skunkhour

Formed: *1991*
Style: *Funk, rock*
Original line-up: *Aya Larkin (vocals), Del Larkin (rapper), Warwick Scott (guitar), Dean Sutherland (bass), Michael Sutherland (drums)*

Sydney band Skunkhour started out as an urban funk band fronted by a rapper. From there, the band incorporated all manner of styles and fusion elements into its frantic, rhythmic, groove-based attack. The Larkin brothers Del and Aya had a background in ska bands. Guitarist Warwick Scott was influenced by funk and rock. The Sutherland brothers rhythm team played rock and jazz. Common influences for all musicians were reggae, 1970s funk (James Brown, Funkadelic) and hip hop.

Originally known as Skunk, the band derived its expanded name from the poem 'The Skunkhour' by American poet Robert Lowell. Over the course of 18 months, the band became a popular live attraction on the Sydney scene. Skunkhour was amongst a clutch of new bands exploring diverse musical avenues on the traditional Australian pub-rock circuit during the early 1990s: **Juice's** hard funk, **Swoop's** soulful funk grooves, **Def FX's** techno-metal, **d.i.g.'s** acid-jazz and **Caligula's** techno-pop. In early 1993, Skunkhour supported UK acid-jazz outfit Galliano on an Australian tour, and then issued the debut, self-titled album on the Beast label. *Skunkhour* produced the CD EP 'Booty Full' (September 1993). Paul Searles (keyboards) joined the band at the end of the year. In 1994, Skunkhour signed with Id/Mercury and kept busy during the year with the release of two acclaimed CD EPs, *State* (May) and *McSkunk* (October).

The band's second album, *Feed* (April 1995), and its first for new label Sony/Epic, featured a more adventurous and varied sound than the debut. It produced two CD EPs, 'Up to Our Necks' (April) and 'Sunstone' (July). Skunkhour signed an international deal with prestigious UK label Acid Jazz, which issued the *Feed* album in Europe to a positive response. Rapper Del Larkin left in February 1996, and the band added percussionist Chris Simms for live shows. Skunkhour toured overseas during 1996, then recorded its third album, *Chin Chin*, with producer Magoo (**Regurgitator**, **Powderfinger**). The album (issued in July 1997; national #34 in August) produced the CD singles 'Breathing through my Eyes' (May), 'Weightlessness' (August) and 'Morning Rolls' (November).

Albums: *Skunkhour* (Beast, 1993; reissued by Sony/Epic in 1994), *Feed* (Sony/Epic, 1995) *Chin Chin* (Sony/Epic, 1997).

Skyhooks

Formed: *1973*
Style: *Glam pop*
Original line-up: *Steve Hill (vocals; ex-Lillee), Peter Starkie (guitar, vocals; ex-Lipp and the Double Dekker Brothers), Peter Ingliss (guitar; ex-***Captain Matchbox Whoopee Band***), Greg Macainsh (bass, vocals; ex-Reuben Tice, Frame), Freddie Strauks (drums; ex-Frame)*

The brash, rebellious and charismatic Skyhooks were a pop phenomenon in the truest sense of the label. When Skyhooks emerged from inner-city Melbourne in 1974, the Australian music industry was unprepared for the changes the band ushered in. Skyhooks irrevocably altered the guidelines by which the industry operated, in not only performance and recording standards, but also management style (under the direction of astute manager Michael Gudinski) and dealings with the press and public alike. Skyhooks validated the massive sales potential of local music by selling an unprecedented number of copies of their first two albums, *Living in the 70's* and *Ego is Not a Dirty Word.* Greg Macainsh's biting, provocative songs were the perfect expression of adolescent obsessions and frustrations. With those songs, the band made an enormous impact on Australian social life.

Skyhooks were not the first Australian band to address local themes (**Axiom**, **Fraternity** and **The Dingoes** spring to mind), but it was the way they did so that was revolutionary. In 1975 it was earth-shattering to hear a band sing about buying dope in the inner-city ('Carlton: Lygon Street Limbo'), sex in the suburbs ('Balwyn Calling'), the local gay scene ('Toorak Cowboy') and lost girlfriends in Sydney ('Somewhere in Sydney'). The seeds of creative resurgence and social and political upheaval sown during the 1960s were beginning to flower by the early 1970s. And as a power-packed, socially aware group with an uncanny knack for publicity, Skyhooks were the right band at the right time.

The origins of Skyhooks stretch back to 1971 and Eltham cult bands Reuben Tice and Frame. Inspired by the likes of **Daddy Cool**, **Company Caine**, The Rolling Stones and Gary Glitter, ex-Frame bassist Macainsh formed Skyhooks in March 1973 with the above line-up. The band came to the attention of former **Daddy Cool** frontman **Ross Wilson**, who signed Macainsh to a publishing deal with his Doo Dah Music. In August, Bob 'Bongo' Starkie (ex-Mary Jane Union) and English-born Redmond Symons (ex-Scumbag) replaced the original guitar players. (Bongo was Peter Starkie's younger brother.) The two new members had a strong theatrical flair and both added to the band's visual impact and sense of humour. At the end of the year, Skyhooks signed to Michael Gudinski's booking agency, the Australian Entertainment Exchange, which eventually led to a deal with Gudinski's Mushroom label.

In January 1974, Skyhooks appeared at the third annual Sunbury Festival. Two live tracks, 'Hey What's the Matter?' and 'Love on the Radio' appeared on the Various Artists albums *Highlights of Sunbury '74 Part 1* and *Part 2* issued on Mushroom's antiRipoff label. In March 1974, Graeme 'Shirley' Strachan (ex-Frame) replaced Steve Hill as frontman. Strachan was a natural frontman: young and gifted, loudmouthed and witty, blessed with a sweet yet powerful voice and androgynous good looks. Skyhooks played the inner-city scene alongside the likes of **Band of Light**, **The Dingoes**, **Madder Lake** and **Coloured Balls**. In June 1974, Skyhooks entered Melbourne's TCS Studios with producer **Ross Wilson** to record their debut album. By that stage, Skyhooks had built-up a huge, loyal following on the inner-city scene as well as the vast suburban dance circuit. By the time *Living in the 70's* appeared in October, there was already a groundswell of interest in this remarkable band.

Living in the 70's garnered instant critical acclaim and commercial success. Aside from the impact of the music itself and the wry social commentary of the lyrics, part of the album's success was down to the fact that the Federation of Australian Commercial Broadcasters banned from airplay six of the album's cuts. Middle-class Australia cried outrage at the use of such words as 'stoned', 'arse' and 'dope' in the songs. Macainsh's songs were the perfect reflection of the times, and the young record-buying public reacted positively. *Living in the 70's* became a national #1 hit album. It stayed on the chart for over a year, sold 226 000 copies and produced two hit singles, 'Living in the 70's'/'You're a Broken Gin Bottle, Baby' (#7 in September 1974) and 'Horror Movie'/'Carlton (Lygon Street Limbo)' (#1 in January 1975). On 19 January 1975, the ABC's new FM radio station in Sydney, Double J (precursor to the national youth radio network Triple J), commenced transmission by playing one of the banned songs, 'You Just Like Me 'Cos I'm Good in Bed'. Despite the controversy at the time, the album remains an Australian classic, and one of the most influential albums of the 1970s.

Skyhooks were also the first band to take full advantage of the television medium. With their flamboyant and colourful glam image, Skyhooks became one of the flagship acts on the ABC-TV's new pop program, ***Countdown***. Indeed, Skyhooks opened the show's first colour broadcast during January 1975 with 'Horror Movie'. That same month, Skyhooks won Single of the Year ('Horror Movie'), Record of the Year (*Living in the 70's*) and Producer of the Year (**Ross Wilson**) at the Moomba National Music Awards. With *Living in the 70's* still in the Top 10, Skyhooks hit #1 with their second album, *Ego is Not a Dirty Word* (July 1975). The album also attained triple platinum status (over 210 000 copies sold) and produced two hit singles, the incisive 'Ego is Not a Dirty Word'/'Every Chase a Steeple' (#1 in April) and the reflective 'All My Friends Are Getting Married'/'Saturday Night' (#5 in July). The album's standout cut, the bitter-sweet 'Love's Not Good Enough', was one of Macainsh's most astute observations of the human condition.

Skyhooks undertook the massive Ego national tour. By that stage, the band's concerts had become major events, attracting record crowds not seen since the days of The Beatles and **The Easybeats**. The band took 15 tonnes of equipment out on the road, including a giant mushroom which symbolically erupted at a climactic moment of the set. (It was later confiscated by 'concerned' authorities.) In October, the band's fifth single, 'Million Dollar Riff'/'Forging Ahead', reached #2 on the national chart. The band completed an enormously successful 1975 by taking out Most Popular Album Award (*Ego*), Record of the Year ('Horror Movie') and Best Songwriter Award (Greg Macainsh) at the *TV Week*/***Countdown*** King of Pop Awards. The band's manager Michael Gudinski also announced a $1.5 million American deal (for ten albums over five years) with Mercury/Phonogram. Mercury issued *Ego is Not a Dirty Word*, which featured a mix of tracks from the first two Australian albums.

In March 1976, following the band's national summer In the Heat of the Night tour the previous December, Skyhooks embarked on a 35-date American concert tour. Mercury issued a second album, *Living in the 70's* (again a mix of tracks from the first two albums), but, despite finding pockets of success in places like Boston, Massachusetts and Jacksonville, Florida, Skyhooks failed to crack the vast American market. In the days of mega-platinum arena rock à la Aerosmith, Boston and Kiss, Skyhooks' fiercely colloquial outlook and smartly arranged rock'n'roll had little relevance to contemporary American cultural values and styles.

Skyhooks

March also saw the release of the band's sixth single, Chuck Berry's 'Let It Rock'/'Saturday Night', 'Revolution' (recorded live, December 1975). It reached #13 on the national chart during April. With the US tour completed in April, Skyhooks entered the Record Plant in San Francisco with Wilson to record a new album. Back in Australia, the band embarked on the national The Brats are Back tour to coincide with the release of a new single, 'This is My City'/'Somewhere in Sydney' (#19 in August 1976). The band's American-recorded album *Straight in a Gay Gay World* displayed a more adventurous sound and style, and it reached #7 during September. 'Blue Jeans'/'Crazy Heart' peaked at #13 on the singles chart the same month. With the album selling over 100 000 copies, the band was presented with seven platinum record awards (three each for *Living in the 70's* and *Ego*, and one for *Straight*). Overall album sales had grossed an astonishing $2 million. *Living in the 70's* went on to sell 375 000 copies.

In October 1976, Shirley issued his debut solo single, a cover of Brenda Holloway's 'Every Little Bit Hurts'/'Cruisin' Out on You', which reached #3 nationally. Red Symons left the band during February 1977. Initially he issued a solo single, 'It's Only a Flipside', on the Oz label (backed with **Stiletto's** 'Nights in Parlour'). The song also appeared on the Various Artists album *Debutantes*. Symons then moved into theatre, television and radio work. He was musical director for Grahame Bond's *Boys Own McBeth* and **Jeannie Lewis's** *So U Want Blood* stage shows. In 1980, he toured as guest keyboards player for **The Sports**. He produced material for **The Globos**, Jo Kennedy, Barry Michael and the **Uncanny X-Men** (under the alias Reg 'Pinko' Sims). In 1985, he teamed up with jazz pianist Paul Grabowsky to write the soundtrack to the feature film *Wills & Burke*. He also worked with ex-Sport Martin Armiger on *The Empty Beach* film soundtrack. In 1987 he issued the single 'The Big Time' on Mushroom Records. Symons has also found notoriety as the comic hatchet man, and as part of the studio band, for popular Melbourne television variety show *Hey Hey It's Saturday*.

In the meantime, Bob Spencer (ex-**Finch**) replaced Symons on lead guitar. Spencer's arrival heralded the band's move into a straight-ahead hard rock direction. Ironically, the change in direction meant that Skyhooks lost their mass popularity, although they remained an exciting and audacious live act. Spencer's first single with the band, 'Party to End All Parties'/'Hot Rod James', peaked at #22 nationally during May 1977. The band kept busy during 1977 with three national tours, although the only other records issued during the year were Shirley's second solo single, a cover of Smokey Robinson's 'Tracks of My Tears'/'Missing You' (#18 in July), and the singles anthology *The Skyhooks Tapes*. Shirley's third and fourth singles, 'Mr Summer'/'Song for a Friend' (October 1978) and 'Nothing but the Best'/'Your Love' (March 1979) were not successful.

1978 commenced with the release of the 'Women in Uniform'/'Don't Take Your Lurex to The Laundromat', 'Do the Hook' maxi single (#8 in March). In April 1979, the UA label issued 'Women in Uniform' in the UK where it reached #73 on the charts. British heavy metal band Iron Maiden later issued a cover of 'Women in Uniform' as a single in the UK (#35 in November 1980). The song appeared on the local release of Iron Maiden's second album, *Killers*. The frantic 'Women in Uniform' was a taster for Skyhooks' classic fifth album, *Guilty Until Proven Insane*. Backed by the band's blistering hard rock firepower, the album's themes of alienation ('Hotel Hell', 'Point in the Distance') and the rigours of modern living ('Life in the Modern World', 'Twisted Innocence') packed a considerable punch. The album reached #6 nationally during April 1978, although its second single, 'Megalomania'/'BBBBBBBBBBBBoogie' (May), was the first Skyhooks single to miss the national Top 40.

In June 1978, Shirley Strachan left the band; his departure was not officially announced until January 1979. Strachan went on to enjoy a successful career in radio and television. His most prominent appearances have been in the popular children's show *Shirl's Neighbourhood* during the early 1980s and the lifestyle show *Our House* in the mid-1990s. He issued his fifth single, 'Christmas in the Neighbourhood'/'Christmas Children', in November 1979. Tony Williams (ex-Reuben Tice) replaced Strachan in early 1979. Williams was a fine singer, but Strachan proved to be a hard act to follow. In the meantime, Mushroom issued the double live album *Live! Be in It* (November 1978). Two live Skyhooks' tracks 'Somewhere in Sydney' and 'BBBBBBBBBBBBoogie' also appeared on the Various Artists in-concert album *Nightmoves II* (recorded on 25 June, just two days before Strachan's departure).

Williams' recording debut with the band was the single 'Over the Border'/'Wrong Number but the Right Girl' (April 1979). Ironically, it reached Top 10 in Queensland (the song was a dig at the policies of that state's Premier, Joh Bjelke-Petersen), but only managed #32 nationally. In November, Skyhooks played on the bill of the ambitious *Concert of the Decade* on the Sydney Opera House steps. 'Living in the 70's' appeared on the subsequent *Concert of the Decade* album (January 1980). Soon after, the *Best of Skyhooks* album made the Top 10. The band's fifth studio album, *Hot for the Orient* and its singles 'This Town is Boring'/'Is This Too Much?', (February 1980) and 'Keep the Junk in America'/'Rolls Royce' (May) all failed to live up to expectations. Skyhooks broke up after a final gig in the Western Australian mining town of Kalgoorlie on 8 June 1980.

Strauks joined **The Sports**, then **Jo Jo Zep and the Falcons** and **The Bushwackers**. Starkie became manager of The Club venue in Melbourne and played with part-time band Little Red Roosters. Macainsh went into production (**Uncanny X-Men**) and band management (Tony Catz Band, Hot Bagels). Spencer formed The Young Lions and eventually joined **The Angels** in 1986. Williams went back to being a teacher. Meanwhile, Strachan's first album, the television-promoted *Its All Rock'n'Roll to Me*, came out in December 1980.

Interest in Skyhooks did not end there. In December 1982, Mushroom issued the 'Hooked on Hooks'/'Smut' single which featured a medley of seven Skyhooks songs. It reached #21 nationally. Mushroom followed that up with *The Skyhooks Box* (the first box set for an Australian band) which contained the 'Hooked on Hooks' 12-inch single and nine albums, including two bonus LPs of rarities. On 11 April 1983, Skyhooks held a press conference to announce the re-formation of the Strachan/Symons/Starkie/Macainsh/Strauks line-up for two showcase gigs. The announcement received full press and television news coverage. Such was the demand that the band eventually did 16 shows around Australia. The first, on 23 April at the Noosa Heads Aussie Hop, attracted 21 000 fans. Supports for the show included **The Church**, **Sunnyboys**, **The Party Boys**, **Mental as Anything** and **Midnight Oil** (who said that Skyhooks were the only band they would ever support in this country).

The reunion tour produced the *Live in the 80s* album (November 1983; #18 in December). In October 1984, Skyhooks re-formed again, this time for a one-off concert at Melbourne's Olympic Park to celebrate the tenth anniversary of the release of *Living in the 70's*. The concert attracted 25 000 fans. To promote it, Mushroom issued a special commemorative edition of *Living in the 70's* which came pressed on gold vinyl and contained two bonus live tracks, 'Saturday Night' and 'Why Don't You All Get ... ?'.

After that, Macainsh toured for a year with the **John Farnham** Band, following the release of the mega-successful *Whispering Jack* album. Skyhooks re-formed for a third time during 1990 which resulted in the singles 'Jukebox in Siberia'/'Jukebox in Siberia' (karaoke version) (#1 in November 1990) and 'Tall Timber' (January 1991), plus the compilation *The Latest and Greatest*. The band undertook a national tour during December 1990. Skyhooks were inducted into the Hall of Fame at the 1991 Australian Record Industry Association (ARIA) Awards. Another Skyhooks track appeared as a single when 'Happy Hippy Hut' was combined with **Daddy Cool's** 'Ballad of Oz'. The single reached #35 nationally in August 1994. In 1996, Bongo Starkie and Freddy Strauks joined forces with **Ross Hannaford** and Wayne Duncan from **Daddy Cool**, plus Frankie J. Holden and Wilbur Wilde from **Ol'55** as Ol' Skydaddys in order to play the cabaret/club circuit.

Skyhooks albums: *Living in the 70's* (Mushroom/Festival, 1974), *Ego is Not a Dirty Word* (Mushroom/Festival, 1975), *Straight in a Gay Gay World* (Mushroom/Festival, 1976), *The Skyhooks Tapes* (Mushroom/Festival, 1977), *Guilty Until Proven Insane* (Mushroom/Festival, 1978), *Live! Be in It* (Mushroom/Festival, 1978), *Best of Skyhooks* (Mushroom/Festival, 1979), *Hot for the Orient* (Mushroom/Festival, 1980), *The Skyhooks Box* (Mushroom/Festival, 1983), *Live in the 80s* (Mushroom/Festival, 1984), *Living in the 70's (Commemorative Issue)* (Mushroom/Festival, 1984), *The Latest and Greatest* (Mushroom/Festival, 1990), *Roadcase* (box set) (Mushroom/Festival, 1994); ***Shirley Strachan solo album:*** *It's All Rock'n'Roll to Me* (Hammard, 1980).

Further reading: *Ego is Not a Dirty Word* by Jeff Jenkins (Kelly & Withers, 1994).

Skylight (*see* The Vibrants)

The Slaughtermen

Formed: *1984*
Style: *Country, gospel*
Original line-up: *'Rev' Ian Stephen (vocals, piano, organ; ex-Armchairs, Go Wild in French), Pierre Jaquinot (guitar; ex-Fabulous Nudes, Autodrifters, Leisuremasters, Go Wild in French), Rob Eastcott (piano), Peter Linden (pedal steel), Mark Ferrie (bass, vocals; ex-Myriad, Leisuremasters,* **Models**, **Sacred Cowboys***), Janis Friedenfelds (aka Johnny Crash, drums; ex-***JAB**, **Models**, **Sacred Cowboys***)*

Ian Stephen formed the original line-up of Melbourne band The Slaughtermen in order to record demos of his songs. The independent Au-go-go label issued the band's debut single, 'God's Not Dead'/'Jesus Saves White Trash' (June 1986) and then included the rollicking 'Jesus Saves White Trash' on the Various Artists album *A Slab of Vic* (1986). The band was backed by The High Spirits vocal trio of **Keith Glass**, James McDonald and Margot McDonald. By the time the single appeared, Stephen had formed a permanent line-up which comprised Mark Ferrie, **Andrew Pendlebury** (guitar, vocals; ex-Myriad, **Sports**), Terry Doolan (guitar, vocals; ex-**Sacred Cowboys**) and Des Hefner (aka Simon Monroe, drums; ex-Marching Girls, **Birthday Party**).

The members of The Slaughtermen came from diverse backgrounds. As well as having spent time with the eccentric Armchairs and the revue-styled Go Wild in French, Ian Stephen had issued an EP, *I'm Still in Two Minds About the Title*, as Ian Stephen's Schizophrenia (1979). Helping out on the recording session were Graham Barker (vocals), Randy Bulpin (guitar, from **Mondo Rock**), Robert Taylor (bass), Peter Lindley (sax) and Barry Windley (drums; ex-**Cherokees**). New Zealand-born Des Hefner had arrived in Australia as a member of punky power pop outfit The Marching Girls. The band comprised John Cooke (guitar) and Ron Perry (bass, vocals) and issued one single on the Au-go-go label, 'True Love'/'First in Line' (June 1980). Hefner had also deputised for the unavailable Mick Harvey on **The Birthday Party's** final Australian tour (1983).

Despite the implications of the band's name,

The Slaughtermen had nothing to do with psychobilly trash or heavy metal. The band's live set mixed redneck country honky tonk with southern gospel. The band belted out songs by The Kingsmen Quartet, The Lewis Family, Merle Haggard, Gram Parsons and George Jones with equal fervour. The limited edition *Live — Naturally* cassette album on Endtime failed to capture the band's true spirit. The Slaughtermen issued their debut album proper, *Still Lovin' You*, on the Cleopatra label (January 1987). Ferrie and Doolan returned to **Sacred Cowboys** when that band reconvened in late 1987. Stephen kept the band going for the album *Melbourne, Memphis and a Mansion in the Sky* (November 1988) and the 12-inch EP 'Jesus Can't Remember' (April 1989) on the Agade label.

Ferrie and Doolan returned in 1989, by which time The Slaughtermen also comprised Stephen, Martin Lubran (pedal steel, guitar; ex-**Hunters & Collectors**) and Tony Thornton (drums; ex-**Paul Kelly** and the Dots). That year, Stephen played with The Welcome Strangers which comprised Rick Dempster (guitar, dobro, harmonica), Mark Frayne (guitar), Mark Ferrie (bass) and **Gary Young** (drums). The Welcome Strangers backed country singer Rex McLean on his album *Country Paydirt*.

Stephen formed the Ian Stephen Band and issued a solo mini-album, *Working on the Nightshift*, on Agade (June 1989). He remained active on the scene with a number of bands. He issued a full-length, solo album, *King of the Cross*, in November 1994. With help from **Keith Glass** and ex-**Angels** drummer Buzz Bidstrup, Stephen crafted a good-natured slab of gospel/country and Mississippi bayou rock'n'roll. Included was a reworking of 'Jesus Saves White Trash'. Stephen re-formed The Slaughtermen in late 1994 for a series of shows. The reunion resulted in the live album *Gospel Gold* which featured one of the band's best songs, the Stephen/Pendlebury/Ferrie-penned 'Mr Wonderful'.

The Slaughtermen albums: *Still Lovin' You* (Cleopatra, 1987), *Melbourne, Memphis and a Mansion in the Sky* (Agade, 1988), *Gospel Gold* (Massive, 1995); ***Ian Stephen solo albums:*** *Working on the Nightshift* (Agade, 1989), *King of the Cross* (Massive, 1994).

Broderick Smith

Style: *Blues, country*

English-born singer/songwriter Broderick Smith (b. 1948) has been a permanent fixture on the Melbourne blues scene since the late 1960s. Blessed with a masterful blues voice, Smith has retained an interest in roots music right throughout his career. Smith immigrated to Australia with his family in 1959. He joined his first garage band at the age of 15. He then played with The Smokey Hollows, and in 1966 joined the **Adderley Smith Blues Band** which included future **Dingoes** guitarist Kerryn Tolhurst. Two years later, Smith was drafted for National Service. While stationed at Holsworthy NSW, Smith spent his spare time jamming with Sydney bands like the Peter Miller Jug Band and **The Foreday Riders**.

Upon his return to Melbourne, he sang with **Keith Glass**'s country band Sundown for a year. In June 1971, he joined boogie/blues band **Carson** with which he recorded two albums, *Blown* and *On the Air*. During early 1972, **Carson's** manager Rhett Walker decided to promote Smith as a solo artist. Smith recorded two singles for Image, 'Goin' on Down to the End of the World'/'She's Gone' (May 1972) and 'Yesterday It Rained'/'About Life' (March 1973). All four tracks had been written and produced by **Brian Cadd** (Smith did co-write 'About Life'). 'Goin' on Down to the End of the World' reached #34 on the national chart. Smith also contributed lead vocals to the **Tamam Shud** track 'First Things First' on the *Morning of the Earth* film soundtrack.

With the break-up of **Carson** in February 1973, Smith took the role of The Father in the local stage production of The Who's rock opera *Tommy*. Other cast members included **Daryl Braithwaite**, **Doug Parkinson**, **Jim Keays**, **Billy Thorpe**, **Colleen Hewett** and Keith Moon. Due to the enormity of the production, it was only ever staged twice. In April 1973, Smith formed the highly acclaimed Melbourne band **The Dingoes** with Tolhurst. Although often described as an Australian country rock band, **The Dingoes** merged R&B and country with red-hot rock'n'roll to arrive at a unique musical blend. The band's debut album *The Dingoes* remains an Australian rock classic. **The Dingoes** spent two years in the USA, and issued two further albums, *Five Times the Sun* and *Orphans of the Storm*, before breaking up.

Smith returned to Australia at the end of 1978 and formed Broderick Smith's Hired Hands. Sleepy Greg Lawrie (slide guitar; ex-**Carson**), Jose McLaughlin (keyboards; ex-**Pantha**), Ron Robertson (bass) and Adrian Payne (drums; ex-**Pantha**) completed the line-up. The band was short-lived, and by mid-1979 Smith had formed Broderick Smith's Big Combo with Robertson, Mick 'The Reverend' O'Connor (keyboards; ex-**Mark Gillespie** Band), John Ballard (guitar, sax, vocals; ex-**Phil Manning** Band) and Peter Lee (drums). In late 1979, Malcolm Eastick (guitar; ex-**Stars**) replaced Ballard, and in mid-1980, Manny Paterakis (ex-**Mike Rudd and the Heaters**, Last Chance Café) replaced Lee on drums. The band built up a strong following on the Melbourne pub scene, and signed a deal with Glenn Wheatley's Wheatley Bros label (through EMI). Big Combo recorded a single, 'Faded Roses'/'Devil Drives (Ray's Song)', but the band had broken up before the single appeared in March 1981.

Smith immediately had a new Big Combo line-up on the road in order to promote the record. 'Faded Roses' reached the Top 10 in Melbourne and peaked at #31 nationally. The new line-up of Smith, Eastick, O'Connor, Chris Wilson (piano, guitar; ex-**Buster Brown**, Ideals), Graham Thompson (bass; ex-**Stars**, **Avalanche**, **Russell Morris** Band) and John Annas (drums; ex-**Kevin Borich Express**) was a phenomenal outfit. Making full use of The Band-inspired dual keyboard approach underpinned by a tough, bluesy sound, Big Combo proffered a style unique in Australia at that time. Big Combo issued the album *Broderick Smith's Big Combo* (November 1981) and the single 'My Father's Hands'/'Mr B is Leaving Town' (October). The album peaked at #38 nationally (#12 in Melbourne), while the single reached #31 nationally and went Top 10 in Melbourne.

By that stage, Smith, Eastick and O'Connor had taken part in the *Andrew Durant Memorial Concert* which Eastick had organised in honour of former **Stars** guitarist/songwriter (the late) Andy Durant. Smith contributed heartfelt vocals to three Durant songs, 'Iceman', 'Jupiter' and 'Ocean Deep', which again boasted a soulful, Band-influenced sound. The songs appeared on the live album of the event, *The Andrew Durant Memorial Concert* (February 1981). In early 1982, O'Connor and Thompson left Big Combo. James Gillard (ex-**Western Flyer**, Tremors, **Russell Morris** and The Rubes) took over from Thompson, but O'Connor was not replaced. The band issued two more singles, 'High Rise'/'Tightrope' (February 1982) and 'Ruby in the Snow'/'I was Here' (May 1982), after which Smith broke up Big Combo.

In early 1983, Smith formed the Broderick Smith Band with Wilson, Mark Domoney (guitar), Jeremy Allsop (bass) and Robert Dillon (drums; ex-**Mike Rudd and the Heaters**). Smith issued his debut solo album, *Broderick Smith*, in June 1984. Twenty-three different musicians contributed to the recording sessions. The album produced the singles 'Vision of You'/'I'd Rather We Went Home Now' (July 1983), 'When I Swim'/'Ray of Light' (May 1984), 'Here Comes Trouble'/'I'd Rather We Went Home Now' (August) and Roy Orbison's 'Leah'/'Jungle Green' (1985). The Broderick Smith Band line-up during 1984 comprised Robert Dillon, Michael Den Elzen (guitar), Larry Groves (keyboards) and Brian Hamilton (bass, vocals; ex-**Air Supply**). Smith worked with a variety of Broderick Smith Band line-ups well into the 1990s. Some of the numerous other musicians who have passed through the band's ranks over the years are Mick O'Connor, Simon Binks (guitar; ex-**Australian Crawl**), Randy Bulpin (guitar; ex-**Mondo Rock**), Paul Gadsby (bass), Gerry Hale (mandolin, fiddle, autoharp), Mal Logan (keyboards; ex-**Healing Force**, **Renée Geyer** Band), Louis McManus (mandolin, fiddle; ex-**Bushwackers**), Sam See (guitar, keyboards; ex-**Fraternity**, **Flying Circus**, Stockley See Mason Band), Nick Smith (guitar, vocals; ex-**Kevins**), Chris Stockley (guitar; ex-**Axiom**, **Dingoes**, Stockley See Mason Band) and Paul Williams (bass; ex-**Australian Crawl**).

Broderick Smith

In 1988, Smith toured with The Noveltones, which comprised Sam See, Robert Dillon and Joe Imbrol (bass; ex-**Goanna**). In May 1991, Smith embarked on a two-month national tour with ex-**Chain** members **Matt Taylor** and **Phil Manning**, billed as Blues Power. Mick O'Connor, Peter 'Brolga' Coughlan (bass; ex-**Goanna**) and Robert Dillon completed the line-up. The band played mostly traditional blues numbers, plus a few favourites from each of the main members' past bands. At the end of the year, Smith signed a new solo deal with Mushroom which resulted in the *Suitcase* album (September 1992) and the single 'Snowblind Moon'/

'Tobacco Road' (August). Appearing on *Suitcase* were O'Connor, Dillon, Logan, Tony Naylor (guitar; ex-**Avalanche**), Randy Bulpin (guitar; ex-**Mondo Rock**), Roger McLachlan (bass; ex-**Little River Band**), Bobby Butler (piano) and David Hirschfelder (keyboards).

In 1993, Smith supported Joe Cocker on an Australian tour. In 1994, he joined the Melbourne Theatre company, undertaking four roles in the stage play *The Grapes of Wrath*. Smith furthered his acting career with parts in three television productions, *Janus*, *Blue Heelers* and *Law of the Land*. Smith's 1994 band included Gerry Hale, Michel Rose (pedal steel), Matt Walker (acoustic guitar, dobro, lap steel) and Tony Day (drums). Smith signed a new deal with Newmarket Music and issued the album *My Shiralee*. In 1995, he signed to ABC Music for two albums, *Songster* (November 1995) and *Crayon Angels* (March 1996).

Crayon Angels comprised Smith's perceptive interpretations of songs by such celebrated American songwriters as Tim Hardin ('Beautiful Dreamer'), Phil Ochs ('Jimmy Dean of Indiana'), Leonard Cohen ('The Tower of Song') and Jude Sill ('Crayon Angels'). Smith's backing band on the album, The Guild, comprised Hale, Wilson, Walker, Peter Howell (double bass), Nigel MacLean (violin), Kevin Bennett (acoustic guitar, vocals) and Laurie Ernst (drums, vocals).

Albums: *Broderick Smith's Big Combo* (Wheatley/EMI, 1981), *Broderick Smith* (Wheatley/RCA, 1984), *Suitcase* (Mushroom/Festival, 1992), *My Shiralee* (Newmarket, 1994), *Songster* (ABC, 1995), *Crayon Angels* (ABC, 1996).

Andrew 'Greedy' Smith (*see* Mental as Anything)

Gulliver Smith

Style: *Soul, R&B*

Eccentric singer/songwriter Gulliver Smith has been performing since the early 1960s. Smith drew on vintage rock'n'roll, Professor Longhair-styled New Orleans R&B, psychedelia and soul for inspiration. He was known for his outrageous stage act, which incorporated an inventive free-form approach and much evangelist-styled ad-libbing. Later on, he added a satirical Zappaesque component to his on-stage banter and lyrics with the acclaimed **Company Caine**.

Smith started out as occasional singer with **The Thunderbirds** and The Lincolns around the Melbourne dance scene. In 1965, he formed soul band Little Gulliver and the Children. The band signed to W&G's pop subsidiary label In Records and issued the singles Larry Williams' 'Short Fat Fanny'/'Oh Why' (#29 in September 1965), 'Hey Little Girl'/'Brand New Beat' (December) and Chuck Berry's 'No Money Down'/'Everything I Do is Wrong' (March 1966). W&G also issued the rare *Little Gulliver and the Children* EP in September 1966 (featuring the track 'I was Bewitched'). Smith appeared on all the television pop shows of the day like *The Go!! Show* and *Kommotion*, but the band broke up in late 1966. Smith relocated to Sydney where he became involved in the burgeoning underground psychedelic scene.

He joined psychedelic soul/R&B band Dr Kandy's Third Eye which comprised **Alison McCallum** (vocals), Dave Kain (guitar; ex-Untamed), Bob Walsh (organ), Mal Capewell (sax), Zane Hudson (sax), Kevin Patterson (trumpet), Arthur Eizenberg (bass) and Daryl McKenzie (drums). Dr Kandy's Third Eye played the Sydney discotheque circuit alongside the likes of **Jeff St John** and the Id and Nutwood Rug Band. Although the band did not release any records, Smith co-wrote a number of songs, like 'The Day Superman Got Busted', for the band which became an integral part of **Company Caine**'s repertoire.

In 1968, Smith was fired from Dr Kandy's to be replaced by Wally Mudd. The band folded soon after. Smith formed jazz-blues band The Noyes with Mick Liber (guitar; ex-**Python Lee Jackson**), John Helman (bass), Dave Ovendon (drums) and jazz pianist Bobby Gebert. Liber and Helman left to travel overseas, so Smith and Ovendon formed free-form/soul band Time and the Forest Flower with Dave Kain (guitar) and Terry Wilkins (bass). By early 1969, with Daryl McKenzie on drums and the addition of a horn section, the band had transformed into A Love Supreme. The band's radical fusion of jazz, rock and blues never really gelled. By mid-1969, Smith had returned to Melbourne. McKenzie and Wilkins left to join Red McKelvie's band Quill; McKenzie went on to Nutwood Rug Band and Wilkins joined **The Flying Circus**.

In early 1970, Smith joined forces with the remnants of **Cam-Pact** in order to form **Company Caine**. The band earned a reputation on Melbourne's burgeoning progressive rock scene as one of the most adventurous, avant-garde outfits of the day. The band issued one remarkable album, *A Product of a Broken Reality* (November 1971), before calling it a day in October 1972. After a short time spent trying to get a new band together with ex-**Daddy Cool** members **Ross Wilson** and **Ross Hannaford**, Gulliver Smith launched his solo career.

For his debut solo album, *The Band's Alright but the Singer is . . .* , Gulliver called on four ex-**Company Caine** members (Russell Smith, Jeremy Noone, Arthur Eizenberg and Ernie McInerny), Bobby Gebert plus **Lizard** members Mick Tulk (guitar) and Dave Conners (sax).

The Band's Alright but the Singer is . . . (June 1973) was basically a **Company Caine** album in everything but name. It was a very entertaining album with its uptempo mix of blues, country, psychedelia and Professor Longhair-styled New Orleans R&B elements. It produced the singles 'Such a Shame'/'Platonic Love', 'Woman Pie' (July 1973) and 'Lazy Shoe'/'Almost Freedom' (written by Greg Quill) (October 1973). In May 1973, Gulliver formed The Dead End Kids in order to promote the release of his album. The band comprised Conners, Noone, Tulk, Bruce Woodcock (piano; ex-**Sons of the Vegetal Mother**), Greg Hill (bass; ex-**Lizard**) and Greg Sheehan (drums; ex-**Blackfeather**). Later in the year, the band became known as Bad Companions.

In 1975, with help from rock writer David 'Dr Pepper' Pepperell, Gulliver Smith and Russell Smith re-formed **Company Caine**. The new line-up was superior in some respects to the original, and played the Melbourne and Sydney concert/dance circuit for a year before calling it quits again. The band recorded enough material (half studio, half live) to fill the ultra-rare *Doctor Chop* album (featuring liner notes written by Dr Pepper). In mid-1976, Smith formed Gulliver's Travels which comprised Mal Capewell (sax; ex-**Company Caine**), Gerry Joyce (guitar), John 'Groundhog Slim' Mills (keyboards; ex-**Spectrum**, **Ariel**), Wayne Duncan (bass; ex-**Daddy Cool**) and Robert Souter (drums; ex-**Lizard**). Sleepy Greg Lawrie (ex-**Carson**) replaced Joyce on guitar and Ian Mawson (keyboards; ex-**Company Caine**, **Levi Smith's Clefs**) replaced Mills in 1977. Les Stacpool (guitar; ex-**Chessmen**, **Merv Benton** and the Tamlas, **Levi Smith Clefs**, **Rockwell T. James** and the Rhythm Aces, The Browns, **Doug Parkinson** In Focus, Genesis, **Aesop's Fables**, **Country Radio**) was also a member at one stage.

During 1977, Gulliver Smith travelled to Britain where he worked for many years with the Gulliver Smith Band. In July 1980, the Gulliver Smith single 'Don't Keep Doin' It Duke'/'Dancing' appeared as part of the *Mighty Box Set* of five singles issued on Joe Camilleri's Mighty Records label. The single was withdrawn from sale a few days later at Smith's request and has never been commercially available as a separate item.

Smith returned to Australia in the late 1980s. In 1989, he formed a new version of Gulliver's Travels which comprised Andrew Reid (guitar), Steve Blau (keyboards), Allan Britton (bass; ex-**Dynamic Hepnotics**) and Robert Souter (drums; by then ex-**Dynamic Hepnotics**). In 1996, Smith issued the atmospheric album *Deux Poètes* as Gullifer Smith. The album was a collaboration between Smith and fellow writer Stephanie Hopkins. As well as seeing release in Australia, *Deux Poètes* was issued in Europe (France, Belgium, Italy, Austria, Switzerland, Germany), Canada and New Zealand. NAIRD Records in Canada also issued the track 'Could I Forget You?' as a CD single.

The album also included Smith's rendition of the song he co-penned with **Ross Wilson**, 'Touch of Paradise', which **John Farnham** included on his mega-platinum selling *Whispering Jack* album (1986). Smith's son Nick Hopkins followed in his father's footsteps when he formed raucous Sydney R&B bar-band Black Smith Hopkins in 1996. Nick Hopkins (lead vocals) numbered his influences as the blues masters like Elmore James, Lightnin' Hopkins and Howlin' Wolf, plus blues-based rock bands like The Rolling Stones, The Allman Brothers and Aerosmith. Hopkins utilised the services of such musical mainstays as **Peter Wells** (slide guitar; ex-**Buffalo**, **Rose Tattoo**), Les Stacpool (guitar), Andy Cichon (bass; ex-**Rose Tattoo**, **Judge Mercy**), Mick O'Shea (drums; ex-**Judge Mercy**) and Harold Frith (drums; ex-**Thunderbirds**), plus newcomers Chris Worrell (guitar) and Ben Chislett (guitar). Black Smith Hopkins' self-titled, debut album on the Rhythms label (1997) was one of the most exciting and dynamic blues albums ever issued in Australia.

Gulliver Smith has had a number of the songs he co-wrote with **Company Caine's** Russell Smith recorded by other Australian artists, including 'Woman with Reason' (**Steve Kilbey**), 'It's Up to You' (**Jeannie Lewis**), 'Some Other New Address' and 'With a Smile Like That (How Could We Refuse?)' (**Mighty Kong**), 'Now I'm Together' (**The Sports**) and 'Don't Hold Back that Feeling' (**The Sports**, and **Andrew Pendlebury** with **Chris Wilson**).

Albums: *The Band's Alright but the Singer is . . .* (WEA/Reprise, 1973), *Deux Poètes* (Dragon/Larrikin, 1996).

Smudge

Formed: *1991*
Style: *Indie guitar pop*
Original line-up: *Tom Morgan (guitar, vocals; ex-***Godstar***), Paul Duncan (bass), Alison Galloway (drums; ex-Jupiter,* **Godstar***)*

Three-piece Sydney brat-pop band Smudge was seen as one of the ultra-hip bands of the mid-1990s alternative scene. Aside from Smudge's snappy and accessible brand of indie guitar pop, the band came to widespread attention due to Tom Morgan's songwriting collaborations with Lemonheads' Evan Dando.

Morgan and Dando co-wrote the title track to Lemonheads' breakthrough album *It's a Shame About Ray* (1992). The Dando composition 'Alison's Starting to Happen' (purportedly concerning Alison Galloway and illicit substances) also appeared on the album. Morgan and Dando co-wrote half the songs on Lemonheads' 1993 album, *Come on Feel the Lemonheads*, including 'Divan', 'Rest Assured' and 'Down About It'. Smudge actually came about when Morgan and Galloway worked together in Nic Dalton's band **Godstar**. Dalton suggested that Morgan and Galloway should form their own band, which is exactly what they did. Later on, Dalton joined Lemonheads, and Dando also got involved in **Godstar**.

Galloway had already been a member of short-lived Sydney pop band Jupiter, which also comprised Chris Stephens (guitar) and Simon McLean (bass, vocals). Jupiter played a brand of noisy, fuzz pop that called to mind UK bands such as Ride and My Bloody Valentine. Jupiter issued the 12-inch EP *3* (1991), the single 'Leave the Ground' (1992) and the posthumous album *Arum* (1992) on the Summershine label. The album was

Smudge

a compilation of the EP and singles tracks, plus the last few tracks the band recorded. By the time the album came out, Galloway had recorded an album with **Godstar** and joined Smudge.

Dalton signed Smudge to his fledgling Half a Cow (HAC) label. The band contributed 'Tea Toast and Turmoil' to HAC's 1991 four song, 7-inch EP compilation *Slice* (alongside Jupiter's 'Meltdown', **Swirl's** 'Burning Castles' and Studley Lush and his Teenyboppers from Hell's 'Fight to Be Free'). 'Tea Toast and Turmoil' later appeared on HAC's expanded version of *Slice*, the compilation album *Slice Two* (November 1992). Smudge also contributed the track 'Leroy de Fiox' to the HAC 7-inch, giveaway compilation single alongside **Godstar** and **Swirl**.

Smudge then appeared on the bill of the inaugural Big Day Out held in Sydney during January 1992. Two months later, Smudge issued the wry, 7-inch single 'Don't Want to Be Grant McLennan'/ 'Stranglehold', 'Foccacia', followed by the CD EP/10-inch vinyl EP *Love Lust & Lemonjuice* which included 'Divan' (September 1992). Both releases set the Smudge frame of reference: rough-hewn yet sprightly power pop wrapped around witty lyrics, squalling, fuzzy guitars, urgent melodies and grungy production. Morgan described the band's sound as 'Tonka tough pop!'. A second CD EP, 'Superhero' (May 1993), appeared before the band issued its debut, full-length album *Manilow* (February 1994) and its CD single 'Impractical Joke' (November 1993). Morgan named the album *Manilow* in honour of American singer/songwriter Barry 'I Write the Songs' Manilow. Among the album's many unabashed delights was a cover of the American mid-1980s sitcom theme song 'Charles in Charge' (Smudge had previously covered 'Make All Our Dreams Come True', the theme song to *Laverne & Shirley*). Prior to recording *Manilow*, Adam Yee (ex-Headache) replaced Paul Duncan on bass.

Yee's previous band Headache comprised Jeff O'Connell (guitar, vocals) and Jaimme Rogers (drums; ex-**You Am I**). The band played a brand of grunge rock with buzzing guitars that recalled extreme US alternative outfits such as Big Black and Killdozer. Headache signed to Waterfront offshoot label Seaside and issued the single 'Stuart's Up'/'Love Without a God' at the end of 1991. Famed Seattle producer Jack Endino (Nirvana, Mudhoney) mixed the songs, and the single came in a pressing of only 500 copies. Marty O'Connell replaced Rogers in late 1991, and Headache added Nick Tkalac (guitar) at the start of 1992. The new line-up issued the CD EP 'Uma' (October 1992). In mid-1993, Gareth Lindsay replaced Yee. Headache issued 'Grate' in June 1994, by which time newer, more upbeat outfits such as **Frenzal Rhomb** had usurped the band's position in the melodic hardcore stakes.

In 1993, Morgan collaborated with Nic Dalton on irreverent studio outfit Sneeze. The duo's debut release, the double 7-inch, vinyl single set *Sneeze* (January 1994), contained 20 tunes, all under two minutes long. The music ranged from The Ramones-like thrash pop of 'Trouble in School' and 'Ripped Jeans' to The Velvet-Underground-meets-The-Shangri-Las feel of 'There He Is'. Various members of **The Hummingbirds** (Alannah Russack, Simon Holmes and Robyn St Clair), **Ratcat** (Simon Day), **Swirl** (Nicola Schultz) and Lemonheads (Evan Dando, Jesse Peretz) appeared on different tracks. *Sneeze* was later expanded to 41 songs in 47 minutes for album release (June 1996).

Meanwhile, the members of Smudge had realised one of their wildest dreams when they were introduced to Barry Manilow during the singer's Australian tour in early 1994. At the end of the year, Smudge issued its eight-track mini-album *Hot Smoke and Sassafras* (the title of which was derived from a single by 1960s Texan psychedelic band Bubble Puppy). Another CD EP, 'Big City Poontang', followed in April 1995. At the end of 1995, Smudge travelled to Chicago to record a new album and to play a handful of US shows.

In keeping with their penchant for somewhat skewed dedications, the members of Smudge re-created the cover photo of The Beach Boys' famous *Pet Sounds* album for the CD single 'Mike Love Not War' (April 1996). 'Mike Love Not War' came from Smudge's second album, *You Me Carpark . . . Now* (October 1996), which produced a second CD EP, 'Slight Return' (August). *You Me Carpark . . . Now* boasted a more confident, relaxed and varied approach to the band's trademark grungy pop.

Albums: *Manilow* (Half a Cow/Regular/Festival, 1994), *Hot Smoke and Sassafras* (Half a Cow/Mercury, 1994), *You Me Carpark . . . Now* (Half a Cow/Mercury, 1996) *Mo Poontang* (compilation, Half a Cow, 1997).

Snout

Formed: *1992*
Style: *Indie guitar pop*
Original line-up: *Ross McLennan (bass, vocals; ex-Hybrid), Rob Wolf (guitar, vocals; ex-Hybrid), Hugh Crenson (drums)*

Irreverent Melbourne band Snout played an energetic brand of guitar pop that combined 1960s US surf-pop riffs, Ramones-styled punky tempos and Small Faces/Jam-like arrangements. All up, the band's sound exuded a joyous cheekiness, yet at the heart of the matter was an acute understanding of the pop form.

Ross McLennan started out in late 1980s Melbourne band The Hybrid, which also comprised Rob Wolf, Phil Faiers (drums), Peter Caffyn (trumpet) and Drew Nelson (sax). Utilising a solid pop base, the band was able to lay catchy melodies, punky guitar riffs and blazing horn arrangements over the top, which put the listener in mind of **The Saints** circa 'Know Your Product'. The Hybrid issued the single 'The Iceman Cometh'/'Your Good Fortune' (October 1989) and the mini-album *The Getting Weird of Nigel Budweg* (1990) on the Polyester label before splitting in November 1991.

An early Snout track, 'Holiday', appeared on Sydney label Half a Cow's compilation *Slice Two* (November 1992). Meanwhile, Snout had come to the attention of Bruce Milne and Greta Moon at Melbourne's Au-go-go Records, who issued the band's debut CD EP, *Cleans and Brightens*, in July 1993. The band's contemporaries on the Melbourne scene included **The Meanies, Magic Dirt, Even, The Fauves, Hoss** and **Holocene**. McLennan also collaborated with his brother Link Meanie on the album *Muescram* (1995). Snout's debut album, *What's that Sound?* (December 1994), was brimming with offbeat songs, catchy hooks and 'biff-bang-pow!' Mod attitude. Prior to the album's release, Greg Ng (guitar) and Ewan McCartney (drums; ex-**Ripe**) replaced the original players. It proved to be a stronger line-up and McLennan's songs made the transition intact.

The first fruits of the new line-up came with the 'Night and Day' CD single (October 1995). Snout's second album, *The New Pop Dialogue* (September 1996) included live favourites like 'Matter Baby', 'Winning Smile' and 'You're the Right Kind'. It also produced the sharp, euphoric CD EP 'Cromagnon*man*' (June 1996) which was a diamond-hard pop gem in the Redd Kross vein. 'Cromagnon*man*' registered #89 on the 1996 Triple J Hottest 100 list. Snout also contributed a version of 'Karen' to the **Go-Betweens** tribute album *Right Here* on the Hippy Knight label (1996). Snout issued a second CD single from *The New Pop Dialogue* in November, 'Winning Smile', and commenced 1997 with a slot on the national bill of the Big Day Out tour. The band also contributed a cover of **Icehouse's** 'Love in Motion' to the soundtrack of David Caesar's feature film *Idiot Box* which came out in February 1997. Snout ended the year with the release of the CD single 'Hey Hey Hey'

(October), which was lifted from the band's upcoming album *Circle High and Wide* (slated for release in 1998).

Albums: *What's that Sound?* (Au-go-go, 1994), *The New Pop Dialogue* (Au-go-go, 1996).

The Someloves (*see* The Stems)

Sons of the Vegetal Mother

Formed: *1970*
Style: *Progressive rock*
Original line-up: **Ross Wilson** *(vocals, guitar; ex-***Pink Finks, Party Machine, Procession***)*, **Ross Hannaford** *(lead guitar; ex-***Pink Finks, Party Machine,** *Quinn), Mike Rudd (guitar; ex-Chants R&B,* **Party Machine, Spectrum***), Trevor Griffin (piano; ex-***Procession***), Jeremy Noone (aka Jeremy Kellock; tenor sax, piano; from* **Company Caine***), Ian Wallace (alto sax; from Lipp Arthur), Bruce Woodcock (tenor sax; from Lipp Arthur), Simon Wettenhall (trumpet; from Lipp Arthur), Wayne Duncan (bass; ex-Rondells),* **Gary Young** *(drums; ex-Silhouettes, Rondells)*

Sons of the Vegetal Mother was the brainchild of the enterprising and innovative **Ross Wilson**. The band became one of the leading lights on the burgeoning Melbourne progressive scene circa 1970. Alongside **Ross Hannaford**, Wilson had already worked in Melbourne teenage R&B outfit **The Pink Finks** and **The Party Machine**. In March 1969, Wilson received an S.O.S. call from **Procession**, then based in England. Wilson joined **Procession** in an effort to salvage the band from imminent stagnation. The scheme did not work and Wilson returned to Australia in early 1970.

In the interim, Hannaford had formed the short-lived Quinn with Mike Edwards (sax, flute; ex-**Party Machine**), Steve Edwards (bass, vocals) and Barry Windley (drums; ex-**Cherokees**). Quinn played country-influenced rock, and the band's sole single on Festival featured covers of Bob Dylan's 'Mighty Quinn' and 'I'll Be Your Baby Tonight' (January 1970). Back in Australia, Wilson formed esoteric, special occasion, progressive band Sons of the Vegetal Mother. Wilson's principal inspirations for the band were *Reuben and the Jets*-period Mothers of Invention and macrobiotic foods! Two of the band's stage favourites were 'Brown Rice is Better than White Rice' and the prototype version of 'Eagle Rock'. The Sons played at the popular 'head' venue the T.F. Much Ballroom in the inner-city Melbourne suburb of Fitzroy.

The Sons issued one of the rarest artefacts of the Australian progressive rock era, *The Garden Party* EP (November 1970), which was only ever given away at a multi-media happening/art exhibition arranged by artist Warren Knight. The lengthy, hypnotic 'Love is the Law' was based around Aleister Crowley's dictum 'to do what thou wilt shall be the whole of the law'. 'The Garden Party' was a whimsical flower pop instrumental. The primal rock rant 'Make It Begin' later appeared on Raven's essential compilation *Golden Miles: Australian Progressive Rock 1969–1974* (1994). Wilson and Hannaford abandoned The Sons' concept when they launched the popular, good-time band **Daddy Cool** during November 1970.

Sound Unlimited Posse (*see* Renegade Funktrain)

Southern Contemporary Rock Assembly (SCRA)

Formed: *1971*
Style: *Jazz rock*
Original line-up: *Micky Leyton (real name Michael Puddyfoot, vocals), Sheryl Black (vocals), Peter Martin (guitar, vocals; ex-Little Sammy and the In People), Jim Kelly (guitar; ex-***Affair, Levi Smith's Clefs***), Greg Foster (trombone, harmonica; ex-***Heart 'n' Soul***), Mike Kenny (trumpet; ex-***Levi Smith's Clefs***), Don Wright (tenor sax, flute; ex-***Ram Jam Big Band***), Dave Ellis (bass), Ian Bloxsom (percussion), Russell Dunlop (drums; ex-***Aesop's Fables, Levi Smith's Clefs***)*

Led by guitarist/arranger Peter Martin, Sydney-based band Southern Contemporary Rock Assembly (SCRA) played a blend of brassy jazz rock, R&B and soul. Obvious overseas antecedents included Blood Sweat and Tears and Chicago. A number of concurrent Australian bands like **Levi Smith's Clefs, The Ram Jam Big Band, Heart 'n' Soul, Kush** and Nova Express mined the same jazz rock/R&B vein. The band also employed dual lead singers Micky Leyton and Sheryl Black, which allowed for a wider variety of styles.

SCRA swiftly became popular on the Sydney pub/festival circuit, generally blowing up a storm with its brash, commercial sound. The band's debut album *SCRA* (December 1971), however, was a more restrained and slickly arranged work. Over half the tracks, including 'Sighin'', '(Hear the) Falling Dew' and 'Traveller', were pop ballads. Only 'Sydney Born Man', 'To Whom It May Concern', 'Roly Poly' and the traditional 'C.C. Rider' got the full rock treatment with massed horns and raunchy vocals. The album produced three singles, 'C.C. Rider'/'Traveller', 'Roly Poly'/'Sighin'' and 'Sydney

Born Man'/'(Hear the) Falling Dew', of which 'Roly Poly' became the biggest hit (Sydney #14, national #28 in April 1972). The members of SCRA also backed Digby Richards on his acclaimed country album, *Harlequin*, which came out around the same time. SCRA appeared on the bill of the inaugural Sunbury Pop Festival in January 1972. The band contributed its live version of 'Roly Poly' to the Various Artists double album *Sunbury* (EMI, 1972).

The band also featured in John Dixon's documentary film of the event, *Sunbury*. The band's steaming rendition of Willie Dixon's 'I Just Want to Make Love to You' proved that Sheryl Black was a gutsy blues singer of rare talent (despite the fact she usually only got to sing the softer songs on the band's albums). By the time 'Roly Poly' had become a hit, SCRA had relocated to the USA where its Americanised brand of 'big band' rock was well accepted. Ian Saxon (ex-Ian Saxon and the Sound) joined as third co-vocalist.

SCRA signed a deal with Atlantic Records (home to Led Zeppelin, Yes and Aretha Franklin among others). The band recorded its second album, *The Ship Album*, at The Hit Factory in New York. The band dispensed with the lighter pop moments of the debut to concentrate on a more innovative and bluesy progressive jazz-rock sound (somewhere between a heavier Blood Sweat and Tears and UK band Blodwyn Pig). The album produced the single 'Our Ship'/'Midnight' which was not successful. SCRA only issued one more single in 1972, 'It's Only a Game'/'Love is a Lonely Day', before calling it a day. Martin went on to session and production work. Leyton, Black, Ellis, Kenny, Kelly, Dunlop and Foster also did session work. Kelly also joined Mother Earth, Crossfire and the **Tommy Emmanuel** Band. Dunlop joined Mother Earth, **Johnny Rocco Band** and **Ayers Rock**.

Albums: *SCRA* (M7, 1971), *The Ship Album* (Atlantic, 1972).

Southern Cross

Formed: *1975*
Style: *Hard rock*
Original line-up: *Alan Milano (vocals; ex-***Buffalo***), John Baxter (lead guitar; ex-Head,* **Buffalo***), Michel Brouet (bass, vocals), Jeff Beacham (drums)*

Sydney-based hard rock band Southern Cross had its roots in heavy progressive rock pioneers **Buffalo**. John Baxter had been sacked from **Buffalo** at the end of 1974. Baxter's savage guitar work had virtually defined the **Buffalo** sound and approach; his departure robbed the band of its most distinctive feature and boldest asset. The band's spirit simply faded thereafter.

Initially Baxter formed Boy Racer before teaming up with original **Buffalo** singer Alan Milano in Southern Cross. Baxter wrote much of the band's early live set, although he left six months after formation. Eighteen-year-old Bruce Cumming replaced Baxter on guitar. Alongside the likes of **Finch**, **The Angels**, **Kevin Borich Express**, **Rose Tattoo** and Chariot, Southern Cross swiftly became one of the most popular hard rock bands on the Sydney scene. Southern Cross signed to the independent Living Sound/Laser label and issued its debut single, 'Stormy Lady'/'Queen of Rock'n'Roll', at the end of 1976. The funky, bluesy and heavy 'Stormy Lady' was a good indication of the band's over-the-top style. The band's self-titled debut album (1977) featured melodic, raunchy hard rock in the vein of **Billy Thorpe** and the Aztecs and UK band Bad Company. It mixed flat-out, riff-rockers ('You Need It', 'Money Maker', 'Stormy Lady') with moody rock ballads ('Jesse', 'Story Teller' and 'Games').

The album scored only minimal sales, despite its strong points. By 1978, Southern Cross had broken up and Cumming and Brouet moved on to The Press. Steve Kot (vocals) and Rick Doolan (drums) completed the line-up. The Press muscled in on the burgeoning Sydney punk rock scene, playing the inner-city circuit alongside the likes of **X**, **Rocks**, **The Thought Criminals**, Psycho-Surgeons and **XL-Capris**. Through its earlier connection to the Laser label, The Press issued its debut album, *Fodder for the Critics*, in late 1979. As an example of late 1970s heavy metal lashed with the fury of punk (predominantly in The Clash mould), the album was worth a listen. 'Alcoholic'/'Rock Capital' was issued as a single (October 1979). The Press split up soon after.

Southern Cross album: *Southern Cross* (Laser/RCA, 1977); ***The Press album:*** *Fodder for the Critics* (Laser/RCA, 1979).

Southern Electric (*see* Lobby Loyde)

Southern Sons

Formed: *1990*
Style: *Rock, pop*
Original line-up: *Jack Jones (vocals, guitar), Phil Buckle (guitar, vocals; ex-Cutters, State), Peter Bowman (guitar, vocals; ex-Cutters, State), Geoff Cain (bass; ex-State), Virgil Donati (drums; ex-***Taste***, Cutters, State)*

During the early 1990s, Melbourne band Southern Sons became one of the most popular outfits in

Australia. The band's commercial, soaring blend of Adult Oriented Rock (AOR) and pop found much favour on the concert circuit and in the charts. And in lead singer Jack Jones, the band possessed a natural, photogenic frontman.

Southern Sons grew out of the ashes of The State which had occupied Buckle, Bowman, Cain and Donati between 1987 and 1989. Prior to that, the band was known as The Cutters. Donati had also experienced pop fame with glam-rock outfit **Taste**. The State signed a deal with Glenn Wheatley's Wheatley Bros label and issued the album *Elementary* (February 1989) on BMG. The album produced three singles, 'Responsible'/'Talk Mean' (June 1988), 'Real Love'/'Not My Life' (October) and 'So Lonely Now'/'Your Eyes' (February 1989). The State supported UK visitors The Eurythmics on their 1989 Australian tour. The band's future looked promising, but there was one vital ingredient required to make the push into the big time (i.e. a good frontman and songwriter). The band found its man in New York-born, Melbourne-raised, 19-year-old guitar prodigy Jack Jones, who swiftly pushed the band in the required direction.

Southern Sons' multi-platinum, self-titled debut album (February 1991) produced three hit singles, 'Heart in Danger'/'Out of My Hands' (#5 in November 1990), 'Always and Ever'/'Stand Alone' (#16 in January 1991) and 'Hold Me in Your Arms' (#9 in May). *Southern Sons* peaked at #5 on the national chart, and became the 22nd biggest selling album in Australia during 1991. Being thrust into the premier league naturally led to increasingly prestigious gigs for Southern Sons. As well as undertaking national tours as part of Southern Sons, Jones and Buckle joined the **John Farnham** Band for his *Chain Reaction* tours of Australia and Europe. Buckle also co-wrote six of the 12 songs on *Chain Reaction*.

Following Farnham's European jaunt, Jones and Buckle returned to Southern Sons in time for the release of the *Train Tracks* EP ('Waiting for that Train'), which featured live tracks. The EP peaked at #40 during July 1991. The band's second album, *Nothing but the Truth* (November 1992), yielded three CD singles 'Lead Me to Water' (#36 in November), 'I Can't Wait Any Longer' (December) and 'You Were There' (#6 in June 1993). 'You Were There' became the #58 best selling single in Australia for 1993. The Sydney Dance Company included three Southern Sons songs in its 1993 production of *Beauty and the Beast*. The band's third album *Silent Witness* (1994) gave rise to the singles 'Sometimes' and 'Didn't Tell Me', but neither charted.

Donati found time in 1994 and 1995 to work with his jazz rock combo, On the Virg. Simon Hosford (lead guitar), Phil Turcio (keyboards) and Evripides Evripidou (bass) completed the line-up. On the Virg also toured as tribute band Theatre of Dreams, playing the music of American progressive metal band Dream Theatre. Andrew Grant (vocals) augmented the basic instrumental line-up. Southern Sons' fourth album, *Zone*, and its CD single 'Trust in Me' followed in 1996.

State album: *Elementary* (Wheatley/BMG), ***Southern Sons albums:*** *Southern Sons* (BMG/RCA, 1990), *Nothing but the Truth* (BMG/RCA, 1992), *Silent Witness* (BMG/RCA, 1994), *Zone* (BMG/RCA, 1996).

The Sparklers (*see* Sunnyboys)

Spectrum

Formed: *1969*
Style: *Progressive rock*
Original line-up: *Mike Rudd (guitar, vocals; ex-Chants R&B,* **Party Machine***), Bill Putt (bass; ex-Lost Souls), Lee Neale (organ; ex-Nineteen87), Mark Kennedy (drums)*

Alongside **Chain** and **Daddy Cool**, the valiant Spectrum was one of the first underground bands of the early 1970s to gain mainstream acceptance. Spectrum's brand of progressive rock was often built around long, complex musical passages, very much in the vein of UK bands like the post-Syd Barrett Pink Floyd, early Soft Machine and Traffic. Yet the band did embrace a commercial aesthetic at times, as its #1 hit single, the compelling 'I'll Be Gone', displayed.

New Zealand-born Mike Rudd formed Spectrum in April 1969. Rudd had come to Australia in 1966 as rhythm guitarist for Chants R&B, one of the most ferocious garage bands of the day. Chants R&B issued two astonishing singles on the Action label, 'I've Been Loving You Too Long'/'I Want Her' (March 1966) and John Mayall's 'I'm Your Witchdoctor'/'Neighbour, Neighbour' (September), but the band only survived for six months in Australia. Rudd joined **Ross Wilson**'s band **The Party Machine** on bass. **The Party Machine** found notoriety rather than success and had split up by the beginning of 1969. Bill Putt played guitar with Melbourne R&B band The Lost Souls, which won the 1966 3AK Star Seeker Contest. The band issued one single on the Sunshine label, 'This Life of Mine'/'Peace of Mind' (September 1966). In 1986, the Kavern 7 label put out *The Lost Souls* EP, which comprised four previously unissued tracks. Lee Neale's band, Nineteen87, issued one single on

EMI/Parlophone in 1968, 'Engagement Party'/'Mr John'.

The original Spectrum line-up lasted for 18 months. Just as the band was making an impression, Mark Kennedy left at the end of August 1970 to join **King Harvest** (he went on to work with **Doug Parkinson** In Focus, **Friends**, **Ayers Rock** and **Marcia Hines** among others). **Ray Arnott** (ex-Chelsea Set, The Browns, **Cam-Pact**, **Company Caine**, Genesis) took his place. Spectrum's fortunes took an upturn when the band's classic debut single 'I'll Be Gone'/'Launching Place Part II' (recorded by the Mark Kennedy line-up) came out in January 1971 on EMI's progressive subsidiary label Harvest. The shuffling, hypnotic 'I'll Be Gone' became a national #1 hit and suddenly the band was in big demand. The *Spectrum Part One* album followed in April and, although Rudd refused to allow 'I'll Be Gone' to be included on the album, it reached #10 in April 1971. Reissue specialists Raven later included the ethereal 'Superbody' on the essential compilation *Golden Miles: Australian Progressive Rock 1969–1974* (1994).

Not long after Spectrum's success, **Ross Wilson's** new band **Daddy Cool** went to #1 with 'Eagle Rock'. The two bands embarked on the joint national Aquarius tour, and Rudd noticed how **Daddy Cool** encouraged their audiences to dance around and join in the fun. In marked contrast, Rudd had presented Spectrum as a 'concert' band where the studious audience would sit and listen. Rudd decided to forego Spectrum's complex material for a much simpler, more danceable sound in order to work on the discotheque/dance circuit. In October 1971, he created a new band called The Indelible Murtceps, utilising the same musicians but with a different outlook. This allowed Spectrum to continue as a creative unit while the alter-ego Murtceps simply played for fun and profit. As Murtceps, the band enjoyed a hit single with the jaunty 'Esmeralda'/'We are Indelible' (#36 in May 1972) and issued the entertaining album *Warts Up Your Nose* (#19 in December 1972).

Meanwhile, Spectrum followed up 'I'll Be Gone' with the dramatic, though decidedly non-commercial, 'Trust Me'/'Going Home' (June 1971) and the lively 'But that's Alright'/'Play a Song that I Know' (November). Neither single charted, although 'But that's Alright' was just as catchy as 'I'll Be Gone'. The band continued to score album success when the ambitious double album *Milesago* reached #16 in January 1972. *Milesago* remains one of the landmark releases of the Australian progressive rock era. Spectrum/Indelible Murtceps appeared at the inaugural Sunbury Pop Festival over the Australia Day weekend at the end of January 1972. The Spectrum live tracks 'Some Good Advice' and 'I'll Be Gone', plus The Murtceps' 'We are Indelible', 'Be My Honey' and 'But that's Alright' appeared on the Various Artists double album *Sunbury* issued by EMI later in the year. By September, Lee Neale had left Spectrum.

Spectrum

John Mills took Neale's place, but further complications arose in March 1973 when **Ray Arnott** announced that he was leaving to join **Ross Wilson's** new band **Mighty Kong**. Rudd decided to dissolve the band, feeling that the task of re-creating the unique Spectrum/Murtceps sound and format would be too difficult. The band's final studio album, *Testimonial*, came out in July 1973 (credited to Spectrum/Indelible Murtceps; #12 in August), preceded by The Indelible Murtceps single 'The Indelible Shuffle'/'Ray's Boogie' (June). The last Spectrum/Murtceps record to see release at the time was the splendid double live set *Terminal Buzz* (December 1973), which had been recorded at the band's farewell concert on 15 April 1973.

By the time *Terminal Buzz* appeared, Rudd and Putt were already enjoying their first hit single, 'Jamaican Farewell', and album *A Strange Fantastic Dream* with their new band **Ariel**. With the break-up of **Ariel** in 1977, Rudd and Putt continued together into the 1980s with the bands Instant Replay, **Mike Rudd and the Heaters**, W.H.Y., No. 9 and The Burwood Blues Band. Spectrum next surfaced in March 1984 for a reunion tour with a new line-up of Rudd, Putt, Arnott and Tony Fossey (keyboards; ex-**Mike Rudd and the Heaters**).

EMI had issued the Spectrum compilation *Red Orange Yellow Green Blue Indigo Violet*, and it was an opportune time for Rudd to dust off the old beast. Rudd has periodically re-formed Spectrum for brief tours. The 1989 line-up comprised Rudd, Putt, Fossey, Martyn Sullivan (guitar, bass) and David Hicks (drums); the 1990 line-up saw Trevor Courtney (ex-Chants R&B, **Vibrants**, **Cam-Pact**, Skylight) replace Hicks. The 1991 line-up of Rudd, Putt, Sullivan, Courtney and Cres Crisp (keyboards) was billed as Spectrum Plays the Blues. In 1992, Raven Records compiled the first Spectrum CD collection *Ghosts: Post-Terminal Reflection*. During the early 1990s, Rudd and Putt continued to tour as an acoustic duo with various auxiliary members (including singer Enza Pantano). At the end of 1995, the duo issued a new album, *Living on a Volcano*, on their own Volcano label. In late 1996, Rudd and Putt formed a fun band called The Fez with ex-**Crowded House** drummer Paul Hester.

Albums: *Spectrum Part One* (EMI/Harvest, 1971), *Milesago* (EMI/Harvest, 1972), *Warts Up Your Nose* (as Indelible Murtceps) (EMI, 1972), *Testimonial* (as Spectrum/Indelible Murtceps) (EMI, 1973), *Terminal Buzz* (as Spectrum/Murtceps) (EMI, 1973), *Red Orange Yellow Green Blue Indigo Violet* (EMI, 1984), *Ghosts: Post-Terminal Reflection* (compilation, Raven, 1992).

Spiderbait

Formed: *1990*
Style: *Thrash pop*
Original line-up: *Damian 'Whitt' Whittey (guitar, vocals), Janet English (bass), Mark 'Kram' Maher (drums, vocals)*

In a matter of two years, Spiderbait went from cult status on an independent level to scoring Top 10 albums on the mainstream Australian charts. Alongside **You Am I**, **silverchair**, **Tumbleweed**, **Powderfinger**, **Ammonia** and **Regurgitator**, Spiderbait captured a vast new youth market that identified with the band's low-fi but uniquely hard-edged style and football obsession.

The three musicians in Spiderbait originally came from Finley (on the Victorian/NSW border), but formed the band in Melbourne during 1990. Spiderbait came to the attention of Bruce Milne and Greta Moon at Au-go-go Records, who issued the 'Circle K'/'Constipation' single (1991) and *P'tangYangKipperBangUh!!* 10-inch mini-album (January 1992). The band also contributed a live track to the 10-inch, four-track gig giveaway EP *Teeth* (December 1991), shared with Au-go-go labelmates **The Meanies**, **The Guttersnipes** and The Throw aways. Spiderbait supported US visitors Rollins Band and The Beastie Boys on their Melbourne concerts. The *ShaShaVaGlava* CD (May 1993) combined the previously vinyl only *P'TangYangKipperBangUh!!* with ten new tracks, including a funky cover of The Goodies' 'Run' which was also issued separately as a CD EP with eight bonus live tracks (March 1994). The 'Jesus'/'Home' single and a tour support to US visitors Primus followed in 1994.

Following a brilliant performance at the 1995 Big Day Out in Melbourne, Spiderbait signed a major deal with Polydor Records. *The Unfinished Spanish Galleon of Finley Lake* album (October 1995) found the band adding a jazzier touch (as on the title track) to the usually frantic, distortion-fuelled thrash-pop style. Initial copies of the album came with a bonus, five-track EP, *The Dodgy Live Disc*. National youth radio network Triple J supported the album's release with high-rotation airplay. The album reached the national Top 10 and attained gold status (35 000 copies sold). Three CD singles were culled, 'Monty' (a #44 hit in September), 'I Gotta Know' (October) and 'Sam Gribbles' (March 1996). The album's title was inspired by a failed civic beautification project in the band's hometown of Finley.

Spiderbait consolidated its success with a showcase slot on the 1996 Big Day Out tour and a second Top 10 album, *Ivy and the Big Apples* (October 1996). The album made its debut at #3 on the national album listing and, by the end of July 1997, it had spent 40 weeks on the chart and sold over 100 000 copies. The gloriously reckless CD single 'Buy Me a Pony' (September 1996) only tickled the lower reaches of the national Top 40, but was voted #1 on the 1996 Triple J Hottest 100 list (the first Australian release to attain such a position). Just as *Ivy and the Big Apples* came out, Spiderbait played shows in Canada (plus Los Angeles, New York and Seattle) in support of the album's release there.

The album's second CD single, 'Hot Water and Milk', appeared in November 1996. The third, *'Calypso' and Other Tunes For Lovers* (April 1997), became the band's biggest Australian, mainstream hit when it peaked at #13 during June. The album's fourth CD single, 'Joyce's Hut'/'Horschack Army', followed in September. The band ended the year by taking the Best Alternative Album award at the 1997 Australian Record Industry Association (ARIA) ceremony.

Albums: *P'tangYangKipperBangUh!!* (10-inch mini-LP; Au-go-go, 1992), *ShaShaVaGlava* (Au-go-go,

1993), *The Unfinished Spanish Galleon Of Finley Lake* (Polydor, 1995), *Ivy and the Big Apples* (Polydor, 1996).

Further reading: *Hi Fi Days: The Future of Australian Rock* by Craig Mathieson (Allen & Unwin, 1996).

The Spikes (*see* The Dagoes)

SPK

Formed: *1978*
Style: *Electronic, experimental*
Original line-up: *Graeme Revell (percussion, synthesiser)*

SPK has been described as one of Australia's first industrial/techno bands. Alongside the likes of **Severed Heads**, Whirlywirld, **Primitive Calculators**, →↑→ and The Slugfuckers, SPK certainly was at the forefront of the local post-punk, electronic/experimental movement of the late 1970s. Led by the indefatigable Graeme Revell, SPK has variously expanded on its acronym as SoliPsiK, Seppuku, Surgical Penis Klinik, System Planning Korporation and Sozialistisches Patienten Kollektiv. Likewise, the band's music progressed from discordant, industrial-strength metal noise to sophisticated and restrained dance-rock with strange attributes. During the 1990s, Revell moved into feature film soundtrack work.

New Zealand-born Revell formed SPK when he moved to Sydney in 1978. In 1979, SPK issued three independent 7-inch records, the *SoliPsiK* EP (April) and the singles 'Factory' (August) and 'Mekano' (November). The records featured kinetic rhythms and metallic white noise. Ugly Mirrors members David Virgin (bass) and Danny Rumour (guitar) contributed to 'Mekano'. Both went on to form Sekret Sekret, while Rumour later found commercial success with **The Cruel Sea**. SPK found little favour on the Australian scene, and Revell relocated to the UK where his music would attract a wider audience. Revell swiftly found his feet with the UK release of the album *Information Overload Unit* and the 'Slogun'/'Mekano' single (June 1980). The album's harsh, thumping sound appealed to fans of Throbbing Gristle and early Cabaret Voltaire. In Australia, the M Squared label issued the single 'See Saw'/'Chambermusik' (July 1981). The overseas albums *Leichenschrei* (1982) and *Kollective* (1983) plus the EP *Dekompositiones* (1983) kept up the metallic noise quotient, and helped pave the way for the likes of London's Test Department.

Vocalist Sinan Leong joined Revell and, by *Auto-Da-Fé* (1983), SPK had softened the approach somewhat with discernible synth melodies and dance beats coming to the fore amongst the noise. The 'Metal Dance' single (March 1984) was aptly titled. The band still managed to outrage certain factions with its anarchic Faust/Einstürzende Neubauten-influenced performance practices which incorporated swinging chains above audiences' heads, beating 10 gallon drums with lead pipes and on-stage welding. One London gig ended in a riot when officials stopped it after ten minutes for violating fire regulations.

SPK returned to Australia for a tour which attracted the curious and adventurous. While in Australia, Revell and Leong recorded a new album, *Machine Age Voodoo*, which produced the accessible single 'Junk Funk'/'High Tension' (1985). *Machine Age Voodoo* (January 1985) mixed mainstrean disco-pop and sweet vocals with electronic experimentation (sort of like Blondie meets Kraftwerk). Additional musicians on the album included Mary Bradfield-Taylor (vocals), Sam McNally (keyboards), Jeff Bartolomei (keyboards), Phil Scorgie (bass), Graham Jesse (sax) and James Kelly (guitar).

Revell and Leong returned to Australia and recruited additional vocalist Karina Hayes. SPK came even closer to mainstream acceptance with the haunting dance-pop 12-inch single 'Breathless'/'Wired for Sound' (May 1988) and the *Gold and Poison* album (June). In 1989, Revell moved into soundtrack work. He wrote the soundtrack for the stage play *Capricornia*, the television miniseries *Bangkok Hilton* (1989) and Phillip Noyce's feature film *Dead Calm* (starring Sam Neill and Nicole Kidman; 1989). Revell's work on *Dead Calm* won him an Australian Film Institute (AFI) award. Enticed by Hollywood offers, Revell and Leong relocated to Los Angeles.

Since then, Revell's film soundtrack credits have included *Til There Was You* (1990), *Deadly* (1991), *Psycho 4* (1992), Wim Wenders' *Until the End of the World* (1992), *Far Away So Close* (1993), *The Hand that Rocks the Cradle* (1994), *The Crow* (with Brandon Lee; 1994), *No Escape* (1994), Steven de Souza's *Street Fighter* (with **Kylie Minogue** and Jean-Claude Van Damme; 1995), Rachel Talalay's *Ghost in the Machine* (1994) and *Tank Girl* (with Lori Petty and Australian Naomi Watts; 1995) and *From Dusk 'til Dawn*. Much of Revell's soundtrack work has incorporated moody, well-arranged orchestral pieces, a far cry from SPK's early experimental noise excursions.

Albums: *Information Overload Unit* (Side Effects, 1980), *Leichenschrei* (Side Effects, 1982), *Kollective* (Side Effects, 1983), *Dekompositiones* (Side Effects, 1983), *Auto-Da-Fé* (Ulbricht, 1983), *Machine Age*

Voodoo (WEA, 1984), *Zamia Lehmanni* (Side Effects, 1986), *Oceania* (Side Effects, 1987), *Byzantine Flowers* (Side Effects, 1987), *Gold and Poison* (Regular/Festival, 1988), *SPK Box Set* (MDS, 1992).

Splatterheads

Formed: *1987*
Style: *Punk rock*
Original line-up: *Christo Fletcher (aka Big Guy, vocals, guitar), Sly Faulkner (aka Sly T-Bone, guitar, vocals), Adrian Carroll (guitar), Peter 'PT' Thompson (bass), Micky Scott (drums)*

Having much in common with other Sydney hardcore bands like **The Hard-Ons**, **Massappeal** and **The Hellmenn**, and their Brisbane counterparts The Insane Hombres, Splatterheads sprayed out a raucous brand of street-level punk rock'n'roll. The band formed originally in 1987 under the name of Lompoc County Splatterheads. The inspiration for the Lompoc County part of the band's name came from American cartoon series *Roger Ramjet*; Lompoc County was Ramjet's home territory.

From such cartoon beginnings, the makings of a fiery, relentless rock'n'roll beast emerged. The band's first two rough-hewn, low-fi albums, *The Filthy Mile* (January 1989) and *Ink of a Mad Man's Pen* (October 1989), presented some frantic moments, but failed to capture the band's live firepower. *Ink of a Mad Man's Pen* produced the single 'Destroyer' which, courtesy of Nick Cross's sax contribution, approximated the Stooges' free-jazz explorations on the second side of the *Funhouse* album. Other tracks like 'Self Mutilation', 'Death Ray Striplight' and 'Feel the Fear' were further indication of the band's (admittedly limited) thematic range at work, all topped off by Fletcher's tuneless vocal bark.

Guitarist Adrian Carroll had left Splatterheads by the time the band came to record *Ink of a Mad Man's Pen*. He did stay around, however, to produce and engineer the album. Splatterheads toured Melbourne a number of times (with **Bored!** and The Twenty Second Sect), and duly signed to Dave Laing's Dogmeat label which was home to **Bored!**, **Hoss**, **Powder Monkeys**, **The Sunset Strip** and The Freeloaders. Prior to that, the band issued the single The Undertones' 'Teenage Kicks'/'Seven Runes' on the Spacebeer label (March 1992). Splatterheads' third album, *Bot, the Album* (August 1993), came closer to being a truer representation of their overall sound. Marty 'Bungle' Herbert replaced original drummer Micky Scott in mid-1993, just prior to the album's release. In February 1995, Splatterheads embarked on a 40-date European tour which saw them play with US bands like NO FX, Lagwagon, Weezer and Big Chief. The tour produced a live album, *Joined at the Head*, put out by German label Subway in August 1996.

In 1990, Sly T-Bone moonlighted with his other band, Red Planet Rocketts, playing Link Wray-inspired rock'n'roll. T-Bone played drums, and George 'Mono' Boulevard (guitar, vocals; ex-Space Juniors) and Paul Kitten (bass; ex-Space Juniors) completed the line-up. Skate-punk band Space Juniors had issued the single 'Chewin''/'Chinatown' (June 1989), the mini-album *Juniorville* (1988) and the album *Zoogan* (1989) on their own Juniorville label. In 1992, Geoff Milne (ex-**Eastern Dark**, **Plunderers**) replaced T-Bone (who moved to guitar and vocals) on drums. Red Planet Rocketts issued the single 'Heaven Express' (June 1992), the mini-album *Hard Corn* (August 1992) and the CD EP *Red Planet Rocketts* (February 1994).

Albums: *The Filthy Mile* (mini-album as Lompoc County Splatterheads, Splatter Rock, 1988), *Ink of a Mad Man's Pen* (Waterfront, 1989), *Bot, the Album* (Dogmeat/Shock, 1993), *Joined at the Head* (Subway, German import, 1996).

Split Enz

Formed: *1972*
Style: *Rock, pop*
Original line-up: **Tim Finn** *(vocals, guitar, piano; ex-Stillwater), Philip Judd (guitar, vocals), Jonathan Michael Chunn (bass; ex-Stillwater), Miles Golding (violin), Mike Howard (flute)*

New Zealand band Split Enz is recognised as one of the most successful and innovative bands on the Australian music scene of the 1980s. As writer John Dix put it, Split Enz remains Kiwi Rock's most successful export. From early beginnings as an art-rock ensemble playing all-original, highly arranged material with strange and haunting embellishments, to a sleek and tasteful pop band capable of topping the charts, Split Enz had a remarkable career.

The central figure in the Split Enz saga was Brian Timothy Finn. He guided the band right up to his departure in 1984. In October 1972, Finn teamed up with the accomplished and complex Phil Judd to form Split Ends with the above line-up. Right from the outset, Finn and Judd decided to only play concert halls rather than do the usual pub grind. With financial backing from early fan (and soon to be manager) Barry Coburn, Split Ends issued its debut single, 'For You'/'Split Ends', in April 1973. By the time the single came out, Miles

Golding and Mike Howard had left. The new Split Ends line-up comprised Finn, Judd and Chunn plus newcomers Paul 'Wally' Wilkinson (lead guitar) and Geoffrey Chunn (drums; ex-Stillwater). In November 1973, EMI NZ issued the band's second single, '129'/'Sweet Talking Spoon Song'. In early 1974, Finn and Judd changed the band's name to Split Enz, and added Rob Gillies (sax) and Tony 'Eddie' Rayner (keyboards; ex-Cruise Lane, Space Waltz).

Another fan, Geoffrey Noel Crombie, began designing the band's stage costumes and stage props. That allowed Split Enz the luxury of presenting a totally theatrical show complete with a clutch of refined Finn–Judd compositions with which few other New Zealand bands of the day could hope to compete. In May 1974, Geoff Chunn and Rob Gillies left the band. Paul Emlyn Crowther (ex-Orb) joined on drums, and later in the year Noel Crombie joined the band as art director, occasional vocalist and spoon soloist! In March 1975, the band issued its third single, 'No Bother to Me', on the independent White Cloud label. A few weeks later, Split Enz left New Zealand and headed for Australia. The band swiftly found its feet, scoring support slots to local bands like **Skyhooks** and overseas visitors Roxy Music, Lou Reed, Flo and Eddie and Leo Sayer. Michael Gudinski signed the band to a management and publishing deal, plus a recording contract with his Mushroom label which resulted in the *Mental Notes* album (July 1975) and 'Maybe'/'Titus' single (September).

Mental Notes was a remarkable album, full of otherworldly, Mervyn Peake-inspired songs about death and madness ('Stranger than Fiction', 'Under the Wheel', 'Spellbound'), all offset by Judd's disturbing cover artwork. The album managed to sell 12 000 copies in Australia, reaching #19 on the album chart for one week. It also peaked at #7 in New Zealand. At the end of 1975, Wilkinson left the band and, as a result, Rob Gillies returned on sax and trumpet. In March 1976, Mushroom issued the band's second single, 'Late Last Night'/'Time for a Change'. A month later, Split Enz flew to London to record its second album with producer Phil Manzanera (from Roxy Music). Issued later in the year, *Second Thoughts* comprised four re-recorded tracks from the debut, a re-recorded 'Late Last Night', three new songs plus a re-recording of '129' as 'Matinee Idyll (129)'. 'Matinee Idyll'/'Lovey Dovey' appeared as a single (December 1976).

The band's overwhelming appearance and on-stage buffoonery merely baffled the UK press and audiences alike. Nevertheless, a cult following calling themselves Frenz of the Enz began to emerge. The band managed to score a deal with Chrysalis Records, which issued *Second Thoughts* in the UK as *Mental Notes* (September 1976). In November, Englishman Malcolm Green (ex-Love Affair, The Honeycombs, Jimmy James and the Vagabonds) replaced Crowther on drums. Split Enz returned to Australia and New Zealand in January 1977 for the Courting the Act tour, which coincided with the release of the single 'Another Great Divide'/ 'Stranger than Fiction'. Chrysalis issued *Mental Notes* (*Second Thoughts*) in the USA and Split Enz embarked on a six-week American tour. Once again, American audiences reacted with bemusement rather than acclaim. In April 1977, Tim Finn's 19-year-old younger brother Neil replaced Phil Judd on guitar and another Englishman, Nigel Griggs (ex-Octopus), replaced Michael Chunn on bass.

Split Enz began to play to growing crowds in the UK, and in June the band entered London's Air Studios to record a new album with producer Geoff Emerick. Issued in August 1977, *Dizrythmia* reached #18 for one week in Australia, while the first single, the dizzy 'My Mistake'/'Crosswords' (August), peaked at #18 during October. The second single, 'Bold as Brass'/'Sugar and Spice' (December), failed to reach the chart in Australia. Following an Australasian tour, *Dizrhythmia* reached #3 in New Zealand, and 'My Mistake' peaked at #21. Between October 1977 and February 1978 Split Enz toured throughout the UK and Europe. Phil Judd returned for a month in early 1978 (replacing Gillies), before departing for good. Split Enz spent most of 1978 without a UK record deal and without a manager. As the debts continued to mount, future prospects were grim. The band persevered, and entered Manor Studios in November to record a new album with producer Mallory Earl. That same month, Mushroom issued the whirlwind rocker 'I See Red'/'Next Exit', 'Hermit McDermot' as a single in Australia.

It eventually peaked at #15 during February 1979, by which time Split Enz had returned to live in Australia. The band's fourth album, *Frenzy*, produced the single 'Give It a Whirl'/'Frenzy' (May 1979). Although neither record charted, one song 'She Got Body She Got Soul' was later reworked for the soundtrack to the feature film *Starstruck*. The self-produced single 'Things'/'Semi Detached' (October) failed to chart. The band's fifth album, *True Colours*, was deliberately more commercial, full of contagious songs, crackerjack melodies, sweet vocals and bright instrumentation (and no strangeness!). It marked the arrival of Neil Finn as a major songwriter; his snappy, radio-friendly pop masterpiece 'I Got You' was an unqualified success.

Produced by Englishman David Tickle, *True Colours* and 'I Got You'/'Double Happy' (January 1980) simultaneously topped charts in both Australia and New Zealand during March. In Australia, the album remained at the top for ten weeks, the single for eight. 'I Got You' went on to become the highest selling single in Australia for the year. Backed by a voracious marketing campaign (different coloured jackets for each new pressing, the laser-etched edition, the video album, etc.), *True Colours* went on to sell over 250 000 copies in Australasia. A&M issued the album in the UK, Canada and the USA. 'I Got You' reached #12 on the UK charts during August and *True Colours* #42. The next single, 'I Hope I Never'/'Hypnotised', 'Carried Away' (May), made #18 on the Australian charts during June. For the first time, the band was out of debt.

Corroboree continued the winning streak. Another Australian and New Zealand #1, it produced the Neil Finn-penned singles 'One Step Ahead'/'In the Wars' (#5 in November) and 'History Never Repeats'/'Holy Smoke' (#4 in April 1981). The album's third single, 'I Don't Wanna Dance'/'Shark Attack', 'What's the Matter?' (June) failed to chart. *Corroboree* came out as *Waiata* (Maori for 'a gathering for a tribal dance') overseas. 'History Never Repeats' made #63 in the UK during May. By that stage, Noel Crombie had taken over as drummer from Mal Green, and the band took off on a world tour.

Splitz Enz

In the meantime, former Split Enz co-founder Phil Judd had launched his new band The Swingers with Bones Hillman (bass; ex-Suburban Reptiles) and Buster Stiggs (drums; ex-Suburban Reptiles). The band's debut single, 'One Good Reason' (April 1980), had reached #19 in New Zealand. The Swingers relocated to Australia and signed to Mushroom Records. Issued in January 1981, the band's next single the infectious 'Counting the Beat'/'One Good Reason', immediately leapt to #1 in both Australia and New Zealand. It was the fastest selling local single since **Daddy Cool**'s 'Eagle Rock' a decade earlier. Suddenly The Swingers were one of the top bands in the land. 'It Ain't What You Dance'/'Flak' (June 1981) went Top 5 in New Zealand, but failed to chart in Australia.

The *Practical Jokers* album and further singles 'One Track Mind'/'Distortion' (August 1981) and 'Punch and Judy'/'In the Middle of Nowhere' (April 1982) failed to live up to expectations. The Swingers appeared in Gillian Armstrong's *Starstruck* and played on the singles 'Starstruck'/'Starstruck Finale' (April 1982) and 'Starstruck Overture'/'Monkey in Me' (May) with Jo Kennedy. Judd broke up the band in May. Judd issued a solo album on Mushroom, *Private Lives*, plus two singles, 'Dreamin' Away'/'Sooner or Later' (August 1983) and 'Rendezvous'/'Private Lives' (November).

Produced by Englishman Hugh Padgham, *Time and Tide* (April 1982) became Split Enz's third successive #1 album in Australia and New Zealand. As possibly the band's finest achievement, Tim Finn's highly personalised songs dominated at the expense of Neil's more upbeat tracks. The unsettling 'Dirty Creature'/'Make Sense of It' (#6 in April), the remarkable 'Six Months in a Leaky Boat'/'Fire Drill' (#2 in June) and the reflective 'Never Ceases to Amaze Me'/'I See Red' (August) were all issued as singles. Split Enz's UK career virtually came to a standstill when radio stations refused to play 'Six Months in a Leaky Boat' due to supposed negative references to the Falklands War. The 'Best of' collection *Enz of an Era* made #8 in Australia (December) and sold 30 000 copies in New Zealand. In 1983, **Tim Finn** issued a solo album, *Escapade* (June), and won Best Songwriter at the *TV Week*/***Countdown*** Awards. Split Enz also won the Best Album (*Time and Tide*) and Most Popular Group awards.

Crombie issued a solo single, the novelty 'My Voice Keeps Changing on Me'/'Ninee Neezup' (March 1983). The Split Enz single 'Next Exit'/'Two of a Kind', 'Remember When' (March) came out as a stop-gap measure until the band could record a new album. *Conflicting Emotions* (November 1983) was a relative failure, reaching #13 on the national chart in January. Still, it was a strong album. The band's solid playing and ethereal melodies remained intact, giving the music a palpable sense of unity and purpose. Neil Finn's songs 'Straight Old Line'/'Paradise' (October), 'Message to My Girl'/'Kia Kaha Kaha' (January 1984) and 'I Wake Up Every Night'/'Conflicting Emotions' (April 1984) appeared as singles. 'Straight Old Line' peaked at #31, while the haunting 'Message to My Girl' went as high as #6 on the national chart in February.

For the Conflicting Emotions tour, Paul Hester (ex-**Deckchairs Overboard**) joined on drums, and Crombie returned to his percussion role. In June 1984, **Tim Finn** finally ended months of speculation and left the band in order to promote the release of *Escapade* in Europe. The remaining members recorded *See Ya 'Round* as a final studio album (issued November 1984). Once again, Neil's songs dominated proceedings, with 'I Walk Away'/'Overdrive' (September) and 'One Mouth is Fed'/'This is Massive' (November) appearing as singles. Having decided to end the band, Split Enz (with **Tim Finn** on board) embarked on the Enz with a Bang Australasian tour throughout October/November 1984. Split Enz played its last show on 4 December in Auckland, bringing an end to the career of New Zealand's most famous group. The live shows produced the double album *The Living Enz*, which appeared in December 1985.

By that stage, Neil Finn and Paul Hester had launched their new band, The Mullanes (soon to be **Crowded House**), and **Tim Finn** was back on the solo trail. There have been a number of Split Enz re-formations over the years, including a 1989 Australian tour, a one-off 1992 show in Sydney for the New Zealand Tourist Commission, and an Australasian tour in 1993 (which resulted in the live album *Anniversary*). Meanwhile, Eddie Rayner did session work (including tours with **Crowded House**) and then formed The Makers with Brian Baker (guitar). The Makers issued two albums on WEA, *The Makers* (1990) and *Hokey Pokey* (1993), plus six singles. Paul McCartney invited Rayner to collaborate with him on a couple of songs for his *Press to Play* album. In 1987, Phil Judd, Noel Crombie and Nigel Griggs formed Schnell Fenster with Michael Den Elzen (guitar; ex-**Broderick Smith** Band, **Tim Finn** Band). Schnell Fenster issued the albums *Sound of Trees* (1988) on EMI and *OK Alright, Ahuh* (1991) on WEA, plus five singles.

Interest in Split Enz has remained high, and in 1994 Rayner began work on the *Enzso* project which featured orchestral arrangements of 17 Split Enz songs. Rayner chose the darker, moodier numbers like 'Stranger than Fiction', 'Stuff and Nonsense' and 'I Hope I Never' at the expense of the obvious pop hits like 'I Got You'. Rayner recorded the songs with the New Zealand Symphony Orchestra in December 1995. Neil Finn sang on 'Message to My Girl', New Zealand chanteuse Annie Crummer sang 'I Hope I Never'. The *Enzso* album made its debut at #4 on the Australian chart in July 1996. It attained platinum status (70 000 copies sold) after ten weeks, remaining in the Top 40 for 15 weeks. *Enzso* re-entered the national Top 40 in February 1997 when Rayner, **Tim Finn**, Neil Finn and Noel Crombie undertook the Australian Enzso tour backed by the Adelaide Symphony Orchestra.

Albums: *Mental Notes* (Mushroom/Festival, 1975), *Second Thoughts* (Mushroom/Festival, 1976), *Dizrythmia* (Mushroom/Festival, 1977), *Frenzy* (Mushroom/Festival, 1979), *Beginning of the Enz* (compilation of early material, Mushroom/Festival, 1979), *True Colours* (Mushroom/Festival, 1980), *Corroboree* (Mushroom/Festival, 1981), *Enz of an Era* (Mushroom/Festival, 1982), *Time and Tide* (Mushroom/Festival, 1982), *Conflicting Emotions* (Mushroom/Festival, 1983), *See Ya 'Round* (Mushroom/Festival, 1984), *The Living Enz* (Mushroom/Festival, 1985), *The Best of Split Enz History Never Repeats* (Mushroom/Festival, 1989), *The Split Enz Collection 1973–1984* (compilation, Concept, 1989), *Box Set 1972–1979* (seven CDs including *Odds and Enz* rarities collection, Mushroom/Festival, 1993), *Box Set 1980–1984* (six CDs including sundries collection *Rear Enz*, Mushroom/Festival, 1993), *Anniversary* (Mushroom/ Festival, 1994), *Enzso* (Epic/Sony, 1996) *Spellbound The Very Best of Split Enz* (Mushroom/Sony, 1997).

Further reading: *Stranger than Fiction: The Life and Times of Split Enz* by Mike Chunn (GP Publications, 1992).

The Sports

Formed: *1976*
Style: *R&B, soul, rockabilly*
Original line-up: **Stephen Cummings** *(vocals, ex-***Pelaco Brothers***), Ed Bates (guitar; ex-***Pelaco Brothers***), Jim Niven (piano, ex-***Captain Matchbox Whoopee Band***), Robert Glover (bass; ex-Myriad), Paul Hitchins (drums)*

Melbourne band The Sports grew out of the ashes of cult rockabilly outfit **The Pelaco Brothers**. With the members' backgrounds in roots music so prevalent, The Sports swiftly earned a reputation as the hottest R&B/soul/rockabilly group on the Melbourne inner-city pub circuit. The band's early live set was peppered with punchy covers like 'Route 66' (Chuck Berry), 'Red Hot' (Billy Emerson), 'Chain of Fools' (Don Covay), 'Now I'm Together' (**Company Caine**) and 'White Honey' (Graham Parker), filled out by feisty Cummings–Bates originals like 'Twist Senorita', 'Cruisin' in a Citröen' and 'Put the Light On'.

In early 1977, The Sports issued the four-track *Fair Game* EP ('Right Thru Her Heart', 'Twist Senorita', 'In Trouble with the Girls' and 'Red Cadillac and a Black Moustache') on the independent Zak label. UK music paper the *New Musical Express* (NME) ran a rave review of the EP, comparing Cummings favourably with The Rolling Stones' Mick Jagger and praising Bates' Little Feat-styled slide guitar. The band contributed three **Ross Wilson**-penned tracks, 'Twist Senorita', 'Cruisin' in a Citröen' and 'In Trouble with the Girls', to the Various Artists album *Debutantes* on Wilson's Oz label (1977). **Andrew Pendlebury** (guitar; ex-Carrl Myriad Band) joined as lead guitarist in August 1977, and The Sports signed to the Mushroom label. Mushroom issued the band's modestly successful first single, 'Boys! (What Did the Detective Say?)'/'Modern Don Juan' (March 1978), which made #33 on the national chart.

The Joe Camilleri-produced debut album *Reckless* displayed plenty of charm, but failed to capture the atmosphere of the band's sweaty live shows. The album's second single, a cover of the Jackie De Shannon/The Searchers' song 'When You Walk in the Room'/'True Stories', 'Taxi Rank' (July 1978), reached #23 in July. A month later, Ed Bates had been ousted to make way for Martin Armiger (guitar, vocals; ex-**Bleeding Hearts**, High Rise Bombers). Cummings had wanted to move the band on musically, and Armiger had a more commercial outlook. In September, The Sports supported UK visitors Graham Parker and the Rumour on their Australian tour. Parker arranged for the band to tour the UK as his support in February 1979, which also led to The Sports signing a deal with the independent Stiff label (home to Elvis Costello, Wreckless Eric and Ian Dury).

Stiff issued the four-track EP 'Who Listens to the Radio?', 'Step by Step'/'So Obvious', 'Suspicious Minds'. While in the UK, The Sports recorded the four-track, 12-inch *O.K.U.K.* EP which contained a frantic reworking of **The Easybeats'** 'Wedding Ring'. Mushroom issued the EP locally in August 1979. By that stage, the band's second album, *Don't Throw Stones* (produced by Englishman Pete Solley), had come out. The album reached the national Top 10 (#9) and yielded the classic singles 'Who Listens to the Radio?'/'So Obvious' (#25 in November 1978), 'Don't Throw Stones'/'Terror Hits' (#26 in March 1979) and 'Suspicious Minds'/'Bruises' (April). Stiff issued *Don't Throw Stones* (a compilation of the first two Australian albums) in the UK during October 1979.

Arista also issued the *Don't Throw Stones* album and 'Who Listens to the Radio?' single in the USA and Japan, as did Ariola in Europe. Cummings flew to the US for a promotional tour. The band's third album, *Suddenly*, featured an even slicker, more commercial pop sound. As well as the delightful ballad 'Blue Hearts', the album included the radio-friendly singles 'Strangers on a Train'/'Can't Ever Decide' (#22 in March 1980) and 'Perhaps'/'Regular', 'Daddy's Little Thief' (April). *Suddenly* peaked at #13 in March 1980. By that stage, both Niven and Hitchins had been ousted from the band. Iain McLennan (ex-**Ariel, Mondo Rock**) took Hitchins' place, while Red Symons (ex-**Skyhooks**) filled in temporarily on keyboards for the band's national tour of March/April with Mushroom stablemates **Split Enz** (Sporting True Colours). In May 1980, McLennan came down with a recurring bout of hepatitis and was forced to leave the band. Freddy Strauks (ex-**Skyhooks**) came in as his replacement.

The band's fourth album, *Sondra* (named in honour of American actress Sondra Locke), came out in May 1981 (#20 in June). It yielded the singles 'Stop the Baby Talking'/'Big City Lights' (October 1980), 'How Come?'/'Drug Sluts' (#21 in May 1981) and 'When We Go Out Tonight'/'Some Brass Thing' (July). The album also included one of Cummings and Armiger's most affecting ballads, the sublime 'Black Stockings (for Chelsea)'. In October 1981, The Sports issued a new single, a cover of Donovan's 'Sunshine Superman'/'Cargo Cult', followed by the 10-inch mini-album *The Sports Play Dylan (and Donovan)* in November. By the end of the year, The Sports had gone their separate ways. Pendlebury joined **The Dugites, Stephen Cummings** launched a solo career, Armiger went into production and session work, Strauks joined **Jo Jo Zep and the Falcons** and Glover joined Wilbur Wilde's Big Kombi.

A year later, Mushroom issued the anthology album *All Sports*, and 'Black Stockings (for Chelsea)'/'Last House on the Left' as a farewell single. In 1988, reissue specialists Raven issued the album *Missin' Your Kissin'*. It combined live material (recorded in June 1978 at Storey Hall, Melbourne) with a selection of studio rarities including previously unissued cuts of the Cummings/Bates/Joe

Camilleri-penned 'Missin' Your Kissin'' and **Company Caine's** 'Don't Hold Back that Feeling'.

Albums: *Reckless* (Mushroom/Festival, 1978), *Don't Throw Stones* (Mushroom/Festival, 1979), *Suddenly* (Mushroom/Festival, 1980), *Sondra* (Mushroom/Festival, 1981), *All Sports* (compilation, Mushroom/Festival, 1982), *Missin' Your Kissin'* (Raven, 1988) *This is Really Something: The Complete Anthology* (Mushroom/Sony, 1997).

Rick Springfield

Style: Pop rock

Born Richard Lewis Springthorpe in Guildford, NSW (1949), singer/actor/songwriter Rick Springfield has enjoyed enormous solo success in the USA. Throughout the 1980s, Springfield issued a string of US platinum selling (one million copies) pop rock albums, as well as carving out a high profile television acting career. No doubt aided by his doe-eyed, dreamboat good looks and an ability to craft accessible, catchy power pop, Springfield remained a favourite with fans for many years.

Springfield's earliest influences included The Rolling Stones and The Beatles. He spent his formative years playing guitar in a series of local groups like Moppa Blues, Jordy Boys, Pete Watson's Rockhouse and Wickedy Wak. In late 1969, he joined **The Zoot** with which he scored a memorable hit single, a hard rock rearrangement of The Beatles' 'Eleanor Rigby'. **The Zoot** broke up in May 1971 and Springfield planned his solo career. His debut single for the Sparmac label, 'Speak to the Sky'/'I Didn't Mean to Love You', reached #5 on the national chart during November 1971. A month later, Springfield left Australia to work in the USA. In May 1972, he represented Australia at the Tokyo Song Festival with 'Speak to the Sky'. He flew to the UK with producer Robie Porter to record his debut album at London's Trident Studios. Springfield wrote all the songs on the album, as well as handling all the lead vocal, guitar, keyboard and banjo parts.

Beginnings produced two further hit singles, 'Hooky Joe'/'Why?' (#17 in July 1972) and the Beatlesque ballad 'What Would the Children Think?'/'Walking the Floor on My Hands Over You' (#40 in March 1973). In the meantime, Capitol had issued a re-make of 'Speak to the Sky' in the USA where it reached #14 during September 1972. *Beginnings* also sold a respectable 300 000 copies in the USA. Springfield based himself in Los Angeles and recorded a new album for Columbia, *Comic Book Heroes*. Columbia, was attempting to promote Springfield as a teenypop idol in the vein of David Cassidy or Donny Osmond, but *Comic Book Heroes* was an eclectic collection of mature pop songs comparable to David Bowie. The album produced two singles, the Marc Bolanesque 'I'm Your Superman'/'Mother Can You Carry Me?' (July 1973) and the hard rock 'The Liar'/'Believe in Me' (October). Springfield's producer Porter issued the album in Australia on his newly formed Wizard label.

In 1973, Springfield also scored his first US television role, albeit in cartoon form. Appearing in the Saturday morning children's cartoon show *Mission Magic!* Springfield performed a song each week which resulted in the Australian only *Mission Magic!* album. This time the album was full of infectious bubblegum pop songs, despite the presence of the cream of LA session players like Jim Keltner and Russ Kunkel on drums and Carol Kaye and Lee Sklar on bass (plus Australians **Ray Arnott**, Barry Morgan and Barry Sullivan). Springfield issued two singles in 1974, the topical 'Streaking the Australian Way'/'You'd Better Think Twice' (May) and 'Mission Magic!'/'Music to Streak By' (July). At the end of 1974, Springfield made his live, American debut at the LA Troubadour. Columbia issued a new US single, 'American Girl' and Springfield embarked on a tour supporting power pop legends The Raspberries.

Springfield's recording career, however, fell on hard times. Columbia shelved his proposed 1974 *Springfield* album, and 1976's *Wait for Night* was doomed when his new label, Chelsea, folded midway through an American concert tour. The single 'Take a Hand' did make the lower reaches of the US Top 50. Springfield utilised the services of Elton John's rhythm section, Dee Murray (bass) and Nigel Olsen (drums), for the hard rock *Wait for Night* set. The album produced three Australian singles on the Wizard label, 'Take a Hand'/'Jessica' (October 1976), 'Million Dollar Face'/'Treat Me Gently in the Morning (March 1977) and 'Archangel'/'Goldfever' (November 1979). In February 1980, Wizard issued the autobiographical 'Bruce' (about Springfield being mistaken for Bruce Springsteen) as a single (backed with 'Celebration').

Meanwhile, back in 1977, Springfield had turned to acting and enrolled in drama school under the direction of acting coaches like Vincent Chase and Malcolm McDowell. In 1978, Springfield signed a two-year contract with Universal Studios which resulted in bit parts in television adventure series like *The Six Million Dollar Man*, *Wonder Woman*, *Battlestar Gallactica* and *The Rockford Files*. In 1980, he scored a two-season stint in the popular role of Dr Noah Drake on soapie *General Hospital*.

Springfield cemented his new-found fame by signing a new recording contract with RCA. The US Top 10 album *Working Class Dog* produced the US and Australian #1 hit single 'Jessie's Girl'/'The Liar' (May 1981). 'Jessie's Girl' won Springfield a Grammy award for Best Male Rock Performance. The album's other singles were Sammy Hagar's 'I've Done Everything for You'/'Believe in Me' (US #8, Australian #31 in October) and 'Love is Alright Tonite'/'Comic Book Heroes' (US #20 in December).

Having established a formula, Springfield continued the hit run with *Success Hasn't Spoilt Me Yet* (US #2 in March 1982), which yielded the singles 'Don't Talk to Strangers'/'I'm Your Superman' (US #2, Australian #10 in May), 'What Kind of Fool'/ 'I Get Excited' (US #21 in July) and 'I Get Excited'/'Why Are You Waiting?' (US #32 in October). Springfield took the American Music Award's Favourite Male Rock Vocalist for 1982. *Living in Oz* (US #12 in May 1983) featured the singles 'Affair of the Heart'/'The Photograph' (US #9 in May), 'Me and Johnny'/'Bad Boy' (July) and 'Human Touch'/'Born Out of Time' (US #18 in August). RCA Australia also reissued 'Jessie's Girl' as a four-track, 12-inch EP (with 'Carry Me Away', 'I've Done Everything for You' and 'Everybody's Girl') (July). In 1984, Springfield took the starring role as faded pop star Jamie Roberts in Larry Peerce's feature film *Hard to Hold*.

Despite the film being lambasted by the critics, the *Hard to Hold* soundtrack album (US #16 in May) yielded three hit singles, 'Love Somebody'/'Don't You Love Your Children?' (US #5 in April), 'Don't Walk Away'/'Don't Walk Away' (US #26 in June) and 'Bop 'Til You Drop'/'Taxi Dancing' (US #20 in September). In 1984, US Mercury issued a cash-in album called *Beautiful Feelings* which featured vocal tracks Springfield had recorded in 1978 (prior to his RCA contract) with new musical backing only recently added. It reached #78 in the US. Mercury also reissued the six-year-old 'Bruce' from the album as a single which made #27 in December.

In 1985, Springfield embarked on a worldwide tour which took in sold-out concerts at London's Hammersmith Odeon and his first Australian appearances since 1971. *Tao* (US #21 in May 1985) gave rise to the singles 'Celebrate Youth'/'Stranger in the House' (US #26 in May) and a cover of **Mondo Rock's** 'State of the Heart'/'Power of Love' (US #22 in July). *Tao* sold a relatively disappointing 500 000 copies (his four previous albums had each surpassed the one million mark). After a three-year self-imposed absence, Springfield returned with the album *Rock of Life*. It was his least successful album since *Wait for Night*; *Rock of Life* only peaked at US #55 in March 1988. The album's first single, 'Rock of Life'/'Language of Love', reached #22 in the US during March, but its follow-up, 'Honeymoon in Beirut'/'Tear It All Down', was a flop. Nevertheless, his 1989 *Best Of* album returned Springfield to the US Top 10. Since that time, Springfield has issued only one album, 1993's *Rock Songs*.

Albums: *Beginnings* (Sparmac, 1972), *Comic Book Heroes* (Wizard, 1973), *Mission Magic!* (Wizard, 1974), *Wait for Night* (Wizard, 1976), *Working Class Dog* (Wizard, 1981), *Success Hasn't Spoilt Me Yet* (BMG/RCA, 1982), *Living in Oz* (BMG/RCA, 1983), *Hard to Hold* (film soundtrack, Starcall/BMG/RCA, 1984), *Beautiful Feelings* (Mercury, 1984), *Tao* (BMG/RCA, 1985), *Rock of Life* (BMG/RCA, 1988), *Best of Rick Springfield* (BMG/RCA, 1989), *Rock Songs* (BMG/RCA, 1993).

Spy v. Spy (*see* v. Spy v. Spy)

Barry Stanton

Style: *Rock'n'roll*

English-born Barry Stanton (b. 1941) was one of Australia's most overlooked rock'n'roll stars of the early 1960s. Stanton never quite achieved the success and recognition afforded the likes of **Lonnie Lee** and **Johnny Chester**, although he issued a string of competent and engaging singles. Once his career had started to fade during the mid-1960s, Stanton left the music business.

Stanton had immigrated to Sydney with his parents at age five. Like so many music fans during the mid-1950s, 15-year-old Stanton came under the spell of Elvis Presley. Stanton's first job was as an apprentice motor mechanic. He formed a number of bands, including The Boppers and The Belaires. Like **Alan Dale**, **Johnny O'Keefe** and **Col Joye** before them, Barry Stanton and the Belaires found work at the Embassy Picture Theatre (in the Sydney seaside suburb of Manly), where they would play for the kids between features. Stanton came to the attention of O'Keefe, who invited him on to his television show, *Six O'Clock Rock*. Stanton began to vie with **Lonnie Lee**, **Johnny Rebb** and **Bryan Davies** as one of the most popular young male artists of the day. He also began appearing on *Bandstand*. Soon after, Stanton split from The Belaires and teamed up with The Ark Royales. In 1960, impresario Lee Gordon signed Stanton to his Leedon label, which resulted in the EP *Barry Stanton Sings* and the single Roy Hamilton's 'Don't Let Go'/'I Got a Woman' (April 1960).

With his debut single under his belt, Stanton embarked on his first interstate tour during June 1960 with **Johnny O'Keefe**, **Lonnie Lee**, Laurel Lea, Booka Hyland and **Ray Hoff**. That was the tour that almost ended O'Keefe's life when he crashed his Belvedere returning to Sydney one early morning in late June. Stanton had already left the tour by that stage, as he was apparently too exhausted to sign on for an extra week of engagements. Stanton's second single, a cover of **Johnny O'Keefe's** 'Don't Worry About That'/'You are Gone' (September 1960), made the charts in most states and reached a peak of #37 in Sydney. Stanton's next single, Johnny 'Scat' Brown's 'Indeed I Do'/'A Teenage Idol' (1961), failed to chart. Likewise, his 'A Teenage Idol' EP was not successful.

Stanton turned to his younger brother Rod for his fourth single. Rod wrote 'Beggin' on My Knees', which when coupled with 'Solitary Confinement', gave Stanton his biggest hit. 'Beggin' on My Knees' reached the national Top 20 (#16) over the Christmas period in 1961, and is now considered by rock'n'roll aficionados to be one of the best Australian singles of the period. Rod Stanton also wrote both sides of Barry's next single, 'Back in Your Arms'/'For Now and Always' (January 1962). 'Back in Your Arms' was similar in style to 'Beggin' on My Knees', but oddly it failed to chart. An identical fate befell Stanton's next single, 'Little Miss Heartbreak'/'You'll Never Learn Will Yer?' (February 1963), and the 'Little Miss Heartbreak' EP.

Stanton maintained his regular television appearances on shows like *Sing Sing Sing* and *Bandstand*, but his recording career almost came to an end. Then in 1964, RCA's Artist and Repertoire (A&R) manager Johnny Devlin signed Stanton to a new recording contract. Stanton issued two singles on RCA, 'Tribute to the King'/'That's Right All Right' (1964) and 'Little Emmy'/'Dancing Partner' (July 1965), neither of which charted. The Johnny Devlin-penned 'Tribute to the King' consisted of 32 Elvis Presley song titles set to rocking instrumental backing provided by Devlin's backing band The Devils. Glenn A. Baker included the track on the Various Artists album *25 RCA Recycled Rock Relics* (1979).

In the meantime, with the lack of success of his RCA sides, Stanton gave up his rock'n'roll career to work as an electrician. In 1974, **Johnny O'Keefe** invited him to join his new package show called The Good Old Days of Rock'n'Roll, along with Laurel Lea, **Lonnie Lee**, Johnny Devlin, Jade Hurley and Tony Brady. It ran for four years. Stanton continued to make regular club appearances (with material predominantly culled from the Elvis Presley catalogue) and the odd television appearance into the 1980s. Stanton also issued a single on the obscure Bunyip label, 'City of Armidale'/'Big Front Door'. Reissue specialists Raven compiled most of Stanton's singles as one half of the album *Rock On!* shared with **Johnny Rebb** (1981). In 1988, the Canetoad label compiled the very first full-length album to bear Stanton's name, *A Tribute to the King*.

Albums: *Rock On!* (compilation shared with **Johnny Rebb**, Raven, 1981), *A Tribute to the King (Rare Songs 1957–1965)* (Canetoad, 1988).

Star Spangled Banger (*see* The Sect)

Lucky Starr

Style: *Rock'n'roll, country*

Born Leslie Morrison (in 1940), Lucky Starr presented an image as an 'all-Australian' teenage idol. He dressed in sharp suits and played a trademark star-shaped guitar embossed with his initials on the scratch plate beneath the strings. One of Starr's major claims to fame was that he became the first Australian performer to headline his own show in Las Vegas, with three seasons at the Flamingo Hotel. Although he was one of Australia's early rock'n'roll stalwarts, by the late 1960s Starr had moved into the country music field.

Morrison began singing in 1957 using the stage name of Les Starr. He formed The Hepparays and the band issued one of the first Australian rock'n'roll instrumental singles when 'Xmas Rock Medley'/'I Remember Xmas at Home' appeared in late 1959. After winning seven talent quests in quick succession, Les Starr became Lucky Starr. He signed to Festival and issued four singles during 1960, 'Somebody Touched Me'/'When You Come Back to Me' (January), 'The Big Hurt' (March), 'Wrong'/'Bill Bailey Won't You Please Come Home' (#40 in Sydney during May) and 'Yeah That's How (Rock'n'Roll was Born)' (#31 in September).

With two minor hit singles under his belt, Starr supported US visitors The Mouseketeers on their 1960 Australian tour. The publicity that surrounded his romance with 17-year-old Mouseketeer Cheryl Holdridge certainly helped to boost Starr's career. For a brief period in 1960, Starr compered *Six O'Clock Rock* while **Johnny O'Keefe** was in America. Starr issued his fifth single in March 1961, 'Someone Else's Roses' (Sydney #37 in May). Starr scored his first and only major hit single with the novelty tongue twister 'I've Been Everywhere', written by unsigned singer Geoff Mack. Three weeks after release, the single reached #1 in Sydney and #2 nationally (April 1962). It stayed in the charts for 15 weeks and went on to sell 45 000 copies. The B-side was Starr's own 'Cuddle Closer'. Starr issued two more singles during 1962, 'June in Junee' and 'Hot Rod', plus a couple in 1963, 'Mule Skinner Blues' and 'Come on in'.

While playing a club in Pitt Street, Sydney during early 1963, Starr met visiting jazz singer Billy Eckstine, who persuaded him to try his luck in the USA. Starr played the Nevada circuit, opening in mid-1963 at the Mapes Hotel Casino Room, Las Vegas. Although Starr signed a recording deal with local label Dot Records (one single: 'Poor Little Jimmy Brown'), the proposed American movie roles and major record deals never happened. Dot Records also issued an American version of 'I've Been Everywhere' as a single by Hank Snow. It reached #1 on the American country chart.

Starr returned to Australia in late 1963, and appeared in the Christmas 'surfing musical' *Once Upon a Surfie* with a cast that included **Dig Richards**, Jackie Weaver, **Bryan Davies**, Jay Justin, **Rob EG**, Jan Green and **The Delltones**. He issued an album in 1964, *The Silver Spade Digs Lucky*, before turning his attention to international club dates around the world including the USA, New Zealand, the Philippines, Hong Kong, Malaysia, Taiwan, Japan, Vietnam and Italy. By the late 1960s, he had moved into the country music field and took his travelling show around the Australian bush. During the late 1980s, the Lucky Starr Band included his son Craig Morrison, who went on to minor success with his own band, **De Mont**.

Album: *The Silver Spade Digs Lucky* (Festival, 1964).

Stars

Formed: *1975*
Style: *Rock, country*
Original line-up: *Mick Pealing (vocals, Flight, Nantucket, Flash), Malcolm Eastick (guitar, vocals; ex-Astra Kahn, Flash), Graham Thompson (bass), Glyn Dowding (drums; ex-Astra Kahn, Flash)*

Adelaide band Stars were originally billed as Australia's 'rock'n'roll cowboys'. Although the appellation suited the band's early image, it did become something of a millstone around their collective neck much later. Nevertheless, the band produced two fine studio albums of Southern-fried boogie and country-tinged rock'n'roll that bore a distinctly Australian flavour.

Stars formed in May 1975 out of the ashes of Flash. The band played the Adelaide pub and dance circuit before coming to the attention of **Little River Band's** Beeb Birtles. Encouraged by Birtles' interest, Stars relocated to Melbourne and scored a recording deal with Mushroom Records. Birtles produced the band's debut single, 'Quick on the Draw'/'Straight Life' (May 1976), which made the national charts (#25 in July). Guitarist/songwriter Andy Durant (ex-Astra Kahn) joined Stars in August 1976. He added a great deal to the band's strengths, becoming the major songwriter in the group. Mushroom issued a second Stars single, 'With a Winning Hand'/'Driftaway' (September), which reached #34 in October. Thompson left the band to be replaced initially by Michael Hegerty (ex-**Richard Clapton** Band) and then permanently by Roger McLachlan (ex-**Little River Band**). Thompson joined **Avalanche** and later the **Russell Morris** Band.

In mid-1977 Stars supported UK visitor Joe Cocker on his Australian tour. The tour coincided with the release of the band's third single, 'Mighty Rock'/'Jupiter Creek', which reached #22 in August. In November, Ian McDonald replaced McLachlan on bass, the same month that 'Look After Yourself'/'Red Neck Boogie' appeared. The single became Stars' biggest hit when it peaked at #21 in December. It had been lifted from the band's debut album *Paradise* (January 1978). *Paradise* sold well, reaching #11 on the national chart during February. The album produced two more singles, 'Back Again'/'Let's Get Moving' (#33 in April 1978) and 'West is the Way' (single edit)/'No Time for Crying' (June). In September, John James (J.J.) Hackett (ex-Rum Jungle, **Phil Manning** Band) replaced Glyn Dowding on drums.

The band kept up its national touring schedule (including support slots to The Beach Boys and Linda Ronstadt), then issued a new album, *Land of Fortune* (June 1979). Despite producing four singles, 'In and Out of Love'/'Song for the Road' (January), 'Land of Fortune'/'Innocent Bystanders' (May), 'Wasted Words'/'Never Coming Back' (August) and 'Last of the Riverboats'/'Gold Fever' (October), the album was not successful. By that stage, Andy Durant had been diagnosed with cancer. Coupled with the poor sales for *Land of Fortune* and the constant grind of touring, the band decided to split. Stars played their final show on 5 November 1979. The title of the band's live album, *1157* (July 1980), referred to the number of gigs Stars played in their four and a half year existence.

Andy Durant died on 6 May 1980, aged 25. Malcolm Eastick organised the *Andrew Durant Memorial Concert*, which was staged on 19 August

1980 in Melbourne. The concert featured the remaining ex-members of Stars, guest vocalists like **Broderick Smith**, **Richard Clapton**, **Jimmy Barnes** and **Renée Geyer**, plus the cream of Australian musicians like Don Walker, Kerryn Tolhurst, Rick Formosa, Glyn Mason, **Ian Moss** and Mick 'The Reverend' O'Connor. The assembled musicians played exclusively Durant's songs, with the exception of the finale, Bob Dylan's 'Knockin' on Heaven's Door'. Sales from the subsequent album release, *The Andrew Durant Memorial Concert* (#8 in March 1981), went to the Andrew Durant Cancer Research Foundation.

In the meantime, Mick Pealing had formed The Ideals. The line-up comprised Pealing, Mark Greig (guitar; ex-City), Chris Wilson (keyboards; ex-**Buster Brown**), Robbie Geappon (bass; ex-**Phil Manning** Band) and Barry Cram (drums; ex-**Avalanche**, **Russell Morris** Band, Contraband). Although Mick Pealing and the Ideals did not issue any records under their own name, The Ideals backed **Renée Geyer** on her single 'Hot Minutes'/'Tangled Up in Treachery' (July 1980). Pip Joyce (ex-Bwana) joined The Ideals in early 1981. By mid-year, the line-up comprised Pealing, Greig, Geappon, Peter Laffy (guitar; ex-**Mondo Rock**) and Alex Formosa (drums). Laffy left after three months and Derek Beattyman (ex-Mod Cons) joined, but the band broke up in late 1981. By 1983, Pealing and Mark Mannock (keyboards) had formed The Spaniards with Billy Miller (guitar, vocals; ex-**Ferrets**) and Russell Hellyer-Brown (bass).

The Spaniards utilised other players as required, including Dave Springfield (guitar; ex-**Ferrets**), Kevin Purcell (keyboards), Russell Brown (bass) and John Annas (drums; ex-**Kevin Borich Express**). The Spaniards issued three singles, 'God is a Shield'/'God is a Shield' (1984), 'Angel'/'Angel' (instrumental) (August 1985) and 'What Can I Do?'/'Memory' (1985), plus the mini-album *Locked in a Dance* (EMI, February 1986). Pealing went on to work with New Frontier, the Malcolm Eastick Band and Mick Pealing and the Method.

Malcolm Eastick carved out a career as one of the best blues guitarists in the country. With the break-up of Stars, Eastick joined **Broderick Smith's** Big Combo, appearing on the album *Broderick Smith's Big Combo* (October 1981) and four singles. From there, Eastick earned a reputation as journeyman guitarist-for-hire with the likes of **Max Merritt and the Meteors**, the **Jimmy Barnes** Band, **The Party Boys**, the Eastick–Emmanuel Band and **Matt Taylor's Chain**. In the late 1980s, Eastick formed the Mal Eastick Band which at times included vocalists Dave Tice (ex-**Buffalo**, Count Bishops, **Headhunters**) and Mick Pealing. In 1995, Eastick issued his debut album, *The Southern Line*, which included the singles 'My Life Story' (April) and 'Goin' Home Tonight' (August).

Albums: *Paradise* (Mushroom/Festival, 1978), *Land of Fortune* (Mushroom/Festival, 1979), *1157* (Mushroom/Festival, 1980), *The Andrew Durant Memorial Concert* (Various Artists, Mushroom/Festival, 1981).

The State (*see* Southern Sons)

Dave Steel

Style: *Rock, country*

Melbourne singer/songwriter Dave Steel spent his formative musical career in a number of bands playing the local pub circuit. These included Relaxed Mechanics, Moonshine, The Satellites and Fire Below. Fire Below comprised Steel, Peter Myers (guitar), Lloyd Campbell (guitar), Michael Kennedy (bass) and Nigel Harrison (drums, vocals). The band played a tough brand of pub-rock, and issued one single, 'Walk Tall'/'Bobby's Got a Gun', on its own Searchlight label in 1985. Fire Below contributed 'Johnny's Tombstone' to Au-go-go's Various Artists album *A Slab of Vic* before calling it quits in January 1986.

Steel played with **Weddings, Parties, Anything** for three years (1986–88), contributing songs like 'Big River', 'Shotgun Wedding' and 'Up for Air' to that band's oeuvre. Having relocated to Sydney in 1988, Steel launched his solo career with the single 'The Hardest Part'/'Truckin' Bosanova' (October 1988). With help from producer Graham 'Buzz' Bidstrup (ex-**Angels**), Steel recorded the acclaimed singer/songwriter album *Bitter Street* (September 1989) which yielded the single 'Hurt by You'/'In Transit' (July). Jen Anderson (**Black Sorrows**) contributed violin to the album. Steel's concise and economical arrangements, narrative style and vocal manner drew comparisons with **Paul Kelly**, albeit in a very positive light.

During 1990–91, Steel moonlighted with Sydney power pop band **The Whipper Snappers** and part-time surf band The Flaming Toxins before commencing work on his second album. Bidstrup produced Steel's second album, *Angels Never Cry* (1991), which included the singles 'Bay of Swans' and 'Angels Never Cry'. The album encompassed horn-driven boogies ('The Great Escape'), country rock ('Angels Never Cry'), epic ballads ('The Death of David Gundy'), R&B ('In My Darkest Hour') and pop rock ('Bay of Swans'). Steel also revamped 'Up for Air' for the album.

Helping out on the album sessions were Californian multi-instrumentalist Wayne Goodwin (fiddle, guitar, keyboards), Chris Bailey (bass; ex-**Angels**), James Black (keyboards; ex-**Mondo Rock**), Peter Bull (keyboards; from **Paul Kelly** and the Messengers), Michael Barclay (drums; from **Paul Kelly** and the Messengers), Charlie McMahon (didgeridoo; **Gondwanaland**), John Brewster (guitar; ex-**Angels**), Mark Denison (sax; Brasstards) and Kevin Dubber (trumpet; Brasstards). Steel's 1991 touring band comprised Goodwin, Dave Sandford (sax), Peter Howell (bass; ex-Whirling Furphies) and Graham Rankin (drums; ex-**Fish John West Reject**).

Steel's third album *The Last Radio* (August 1992) was another well-crafted set of songs, competently played by Steel (guitar, vocals), Wayne Tritton (acoustic guitar, backing vocals), Bailey (bass) and Bidstrup (keyboards, drums). It did little, however, to further Steel's status as one of the country's most promising singer/songwriters. 'Suzanne' was issued as the single in July. At the end of 1992, Steel joined The Madisons which comprised Wayne Tritton (vocals, guitar; ex-Pressmen), Clyde Bramley (bass; ex-**New Christs**, **Hoodoo Gurus**) and Brent Marks (drums; ex-Pressmen). The Madisons issued the CD EP 'Doin' Just Fine' before splitting.

In 1993, Steel formed The Roadside Prophets with Tritton, Gerry Kortesgast (bass) and Darren Gower (drums). The Roadside Prophets issued the album *Cross My Palm* (June 1993) and the CD EP 'Broken English' (March 1994). The CD EP included renditions of Marianne Faithful's gritty 'Broken English' and The Velvet Underground's 'What Goes On'. In August 1993, Steel issued a CD EP with **Pete Wells** and Bob Armstrong, 'Hard Done by You'. Steel also contributed a cover of **INXS**'s 'Don't Change' to the Various Artists compilation *Earth Music* issued on the Mushroom label (May 1994).

Without record company backing, Steel began to record a new album. The recording sessions during November 1994 and August 1995 resulted in Steel's fifth album, *Old Salt Blues* (June 1996). Former **Sports** member **Andrew Pendlebury** co-wrote two of the album's tunes with Steel, as well as contributing guitar and pedal steel. In mid-1995, Steel joined **Archie Roach** and **Ruby Hunter's** backing group, The Deadly Band, with which he toured for two years.

Albums: *Bitter Street* (WEA, 1989), *Angels Never Cry* (East West/Warner, 1991), *The Last Radio* (East West/Warner, 1992), *Cross My Palm* (with The Roadside Prophets, Ravenswood, 1993), *Old Salt Blues* (Ravenswood/Festival, 1996).

The Stems

Formed: *1984*
Style: *Power pop*
Original line-up: *Dominic Mariani (guitar, vocals; ex-Go Starts), Richard Lane (keyboards, guitar, vocals), John Shuttleworth (bass), Gary Chambers (drums)*

Maybe it had a little something to do with the (dirty) water over in the west: Perth band The Stems were one of the finest 1960s-inspired garage bands Australia ever produced. The resurgence of interest in 1960s garage-pop during the early 1980s threw up a number of paisley-clad, mop-topped, psychedelic revival bands such as **The Lime Spiders**, Wet Taxis, **Huxton Creepers** and **The Bo-Weevils**, but in retrospect none seemed to capture the flavour, the sound and the spirit of 1965 in quite the same way.

Dom Mariani's earliest influences included The Beatles, The Raspberries, Badfinger and Big Star. He formed his first band, The Go Starts, in 1981. Guido Berini (guitar, vocals), Velo Zupanovich (bass) and Ray Bacich (drums) completed the line-up. Greg Hitchcock later replaced Berini on guitar and Rob Scorer replaced Bacich on drums. The Go Starts broke up in late 1983. Zupanovich went on to The Palisades and The Someloves, Hitchcock to **The Bamboos**, The Stonefish, The Neptunes, **The Kryptonics**, **The New Christs** and **You Am I**.

Mariani formed The Stems with the above line-up. The band immediately took its cue from classic 1960s pop/R&B/garage bands like The Rolling Stones, The Kinks, The Chocolate Watch Band, The Blues Magoos, The Byrds, The Standells (of 'Dirty Water' infamy), The Count Five, The Electric Prunes and **The Easybeats**. Yet, rather than concentrate on being a 'covers band', The Stems played a solid repertoire of original material (penned by Mariani and Lane) in the 1960s vein, fleshed out with a smattering of cover songs. The Stems made their live debut in March 1984, supporting **The Saints** and **The Triffids**. In June, Shuttleworth left the band to be replaced by Julian Matthews. The Stems began promoting their own thematic gigs with titles like 'Monster Mash', 'Flowers from the Garage', 'Reverberation', 'Resurrection Rock' and 'Psychedelic Showdown'.

In May 1985, Sydney independent label Citadel (home to **Died Pretty**, **The Moffs**, **The Lime Spiders**, etc.) issued the band's debut single, 'Make You Mine'/'She's a Monster', followed by 'Tears Me in Two'/'Can't Resist' in September. Both singles were classic slices of exuberant, simplistic garage-fuzz pop that drew comparisons with everyone from The

Monkees, The Yardbirds, The Pretty Things and The Shadows of Knight to contemporary American garage bands like The Chesterfield Kings, The Fleshtones and (early) Dream Syndicate. Both singles hit the top of the independent charts (selling 5000 copies each), and The Stems toured the eastern states to a positive response. 'Make You Mine' was the second biggest selling independent single for 1985 behind **Hoodoo Gurus'** 'Like Wow-Wipeout!'

Ex-**Radio Birdman** frontman Rob Younger produced the band's four-track, 12-inch EP 'Love will Grow (Rosebuds Volume One)' which also hit #1 on the independent chart. The EP displayed the band's growing confidence with song arrangements, backed by Younger's more sophisticated production values. A month after the EP appeared in December 1985, Gary Chambers left the band to be replaced by David Huck Shaw (ex-Graverobbers). The Stems spent most of 1986 touring the country, (including major support slots to **Hoodoo Gurus** and overseas visitors The Flamin' Groovies). At the end of the year, the band signed a new deal with Mushroom's White subsidiary label. *At First Sight . . . Violets are Blue* (June 1987) produced three more independent #1 hit singles, 'At First Sight'/'Grooviest Girl in Town' (February 1987), 'For Always'/ 'Mr Misery' (May) and 'Sad Girl'/'My Beach' (September). Yahoo Serious included 'At First Sight' on the soundtrack to his feature film *Young Einstein* (1987).

Despite positive reviews and encouraging sales for the album (#10 in hometown Perth), plus a proposed European tour, The Stems called it a day in August 1987. *At First Sight . . . Violets are Blue* went on to become the third biggest selling Australian independent album for 1987 (behind **The Go-Betweens'** *Tallulah* and **Steve Kilbey**'s *Unearthed*, and ahead of **Ed Kuepper**'s *Rooms of the Magnificent*). By the time The Stems split, they had developed into one of the best live bands on the Australian scene. Citadel boss John Needham compiled the band's first two singles and EP, 'Love will Grow', for the mini-album *The Great Rosebud Hoax* (February 1988), as well as including 'Make You Mine' and 'Love will Grow' on the essential double Citadel compilation *Take Everything Leave Nothing* (March 1988).

During his time with The Stems, Mariani had moonlighted with a number of groups including The Summer Suns, The Someloves and The Stonefish. The Summer Suns comprised Mariani, Gary Chambers and Kim Williams (vocals, guitar, bass; ex-Louie Louie, Holy Rollers). The Summer Suns issued the single 'Rachel Anne'/'Honeypearl' on Williams' Easter label (October 1986). Mariani and Williams revived The Summer Suns in 1989 with Steve Kind (bass) and Martin Moon (drums; ex-Marigolds) for the single 'All Away'/'Mexican Restaurant' on Waterfront (September).

Instrumental surf outfit The Stonefish comprised Mariani, Richard Lane, Dave Shaw, Greg Hitchcock (guitar, lap steel; **Bamboos**) and Velo Zupanovich (bass). The band issued the one-off 12-inch EP *From 20,000 Fathoms* on Citadel (1987). Power pop band The Someloves comprised Mariani and Chambers, plus Sydney musicians Daryl Mather (guitar; ex-**Lime Spiders**) and Christian Houllemare (bass, vocals; from **Happy Hate Me Nots**). Citadel issued The Someloves' single 'It's My Time'/'Don't Talk About Us' (June 1986).

With the break-up of The Stems, Mariani and Mather revived The Someloves and issued a new single, 'Know You Now'/'Don't Have to Try' (September 1988). The Someloves' 1989 line-up comprised Mariani, Mather, Velo Zupanovich, Martin Moon and Tony Italiano (bass). With help from American producer Mitch Easter (Let's Active, R.E.M.) and a host of session players, Mariani and Mather completed The Someloves' debut album, *Something or Other* (May 1990). Full of shimmering power pop melodies and glittering guitar sounds, the album produced a further single, 'Melt'/'Jack Robinson' (April) and the EP 'Sunshine's Glove' (August).

Dom Mariani's Orange (Mariani, Zupanovich, Italiano and Moon) contributed the track 'Christmasonic' to the Timberyard label's Various Artists album *Rockin' Bethlehem: The Second Coming* (1990). In 1992, Mariani formed DM Three with Tony Italiano (bass) and Pascal Bartoloni (drums). Ian Campbell also played guitar as an auxiliary player. Mariani renewed his association with the Citadel label and, for a band that rarely toured, DM Three has been very prolific recording-wise. As well as two excellent pop albums, *One Times, Two Times, Three Red Light* (September 1993) and *Road to Rome* (June 1996), DM Three issued the CD singles 'Foolish' (May 1993) and 'Soultop' (May 1994) plus the CD EPs *Glovebox* (October 1994) and *Something Heavy* (September 1995).

Of the other Stems members, Dave Shaw joined surf band The Neptunes with Greg Hitchcock, James Parry (vocals), Ricky Mason (guitar, vocals) and Rob Findlay (bass, vocals). Citadel issued the band's 12-inch EP *Hydrophobia* (1988) and the album *Godfish* (1991). Shaw also joined Julian Matthews in The Shivers with Wendy Morrison (vocals) and Don Ely (guitars). Mushroom issued the band's debut single, 'Washaway'/'Dolphin Blues' (1989). Matthews and Shaw departed in 1990. With new members, Archie Larizza (bass, keyboards; ex-**Saints**) and Chris Barton (drums), The Shivers issued the album *Big Love* and the singles 'Not in Love' and 'Downtown Sister' (all 1991). The Shivers also contributed a cover of **The Angels**' 'No Secrets' to the Various Artists tribute album *Used and Recovered by . . .* (1990). Meanwhile, Shaw had joined **Sea Stories** while Matthews wrote songs. The pair reunited in 1991 to form The Catalinas with Gina Hearnden (vocals, guitar; ex-**Hollowmen**) and Phil Rowe (guitar, vocals; ex-Hooley Dooleys, Diddywah Hoodaddys).

Richard Lane formed power pop band **The Chevelles** with Duane Smith (guitar), Jeff Halley (bass; ex-**Kryptonics**) and Guy Douglas (drums). **The Chevelles** issued the EP 'The Kids Ain't Hip' (November 1990) and the single 'Be My Friend'/'She Don't Come Around' (August 1990) on Sydney independent label Zero Hour before Adrian Allen replaced Lane. The band continued on and issued the album *Gigantic* in 1993.

The final Stems single appeared in 1990 when fan George Matzkov issued three previously unissued cuts, 'Let Your Head Rest'/'Don't Let Me', 'Tears Me in Two' (demo version), on his Zero Hour label. The single came free with Matzkov's self-published book *Let Your Head Rest (The Illustrated Stems Biography)*. In 1994, Richard Lane co-compiled the Various Artists album *Bad Timing (A Perth Pop Retrospective)*, which contained rare, live and unissued tracks by Perth bands from the mid-1980s, including The Stems, **The Triffids**, **The Kryptonics**, The Graverobbers, The Neptunes, The Diddywah Hoodaddys, Chad's Tree and The Marigolds.

The Stems albums: *At First Sight . . . Violets are Blue* (White/Mushroom/Festival, 1987), *The Great Rosebud Hoax* (mini-album compilation, Citadel, 1988), *Buds* (compilation, White/Mushroom/Festival, 1993); ***Someloves album:*** *Something or Other* (White/Mushroom/Festival, 1990), ***DM Three albums:*** *One Times, Two Times, Three Red Light* (Citadel, 1993), *Road to Rome* (Citadel, 1996), *Garage Sale* (compilation of B-sides and rarities, Citadel, 1997).

Ian Stephen (*see* The Slaughtermen)

Steve & the Board

Formed: *1965*
Style: *Beat pop*
Original line-up: *Steve Kipner (vocals), Carl Keats (aka Carl Grossman, rhythm guitar), Alex Hill (lead guitar), Dennis Neville (bass), Colin Petersen (drums)*

Within the space of 18 months during the mid-1960s, Sydney beat pop/R&B band Steve & the Board produced five singles, two EPs and one highly rated album. Not a bad tally by the standards of the day, and one aided by the fact that Steve Kipner's father Nat was a record producer and the force behind the Spin label (home to **The Bee Gees**).

Steve & the Board formed in mid-1965. Drummer Colin Petersen had already been a child actor, appearing in the feature films *Smiley*, *The Scamp* and *A Cry in the Streets*. By September 1965, Steve & the Board had issued its debut single, 'Rosalyn'/'Giggle Eyed Goo' on Nat Kipner's fledgling Everybody's label. Everybody's was short-lived and a month later, Kipner had reissued the single on Spin. In 1966, the band issued three further singles on Spin, 'Margot'/'I've Just Realised' (March), 'I Call My Woman Hinges (Cause She's Something to Adore)'/'I Want' (June) and 'Now I'm Older'/'So Why Pretend?' (September), plus two EPs, *Steve & the Board* and 'I Call My Woman Hinges'. With Nat Kipner at the production helm, Steve & the Board was afforded the luxury of recording an album. *The Giggle Eyed Goo* has since assumed a reputation as one of the best, and most collectable Australian beat/R&B albums of the 1960s.

Throughout 1965 and 1966, Petersen also played drums on many of **The Bee Gees'** recordings for the Spin label. **The Bee Gees** recorded the Carl Keats (by then calling himself Carl Grossman) song 'Lonely Winter'. In turn, Steve & the Board covered Barry Gibbs' 'Little Miss Rhythm & Blues' on the album. At the end of 1966, Petersen left Steve & the Board to further his acting career in the UK. He rejoined **The Bee Gees** as their drummer when they arrived in the UK not long after. Geoff Bridgeford took Petersen's place, and Steve & the Board issued one more single, 'Sally Was a Good Old Girl'/'Good for Nothing Sue' (January 1967), before breaking up in May. Grossman later made his way to the UK, where Status Quo enjoyed a hit single with his song 'Down the Dustpipe' (UK #12 in May 1970). Bridgeford joined **The Groove**, and when he found himself out of a job when that band broke up in the UK during early 1970, he replaced Petersen in **The Bee Gees**.

Steve Kipner formed vocal harmony act the Steve and Stevie Duo with erstwhile **Kinetics** frontman Steve Groves. Steve and Stevie issued one single on Festival, 'Remains to Be Seen'/'Merry Go Round' (1968). With the arrival of another ex-**Kinetics** alumnus, John Vallins (guitar, drums, clarinet), the act became known as Rombo's World. From there, Groves and Kipner travelled to the UK and became known as Tin Tin. Adopting a very British-influenced pop sound, Tin Tin signed to Polydor. Tin Tin issued nine singles on Polydor: 'Only Ladies Play Croquet'/'He Wants to Be a Star' (1969), 'Toast and Marmalade for Tea'/'Manhattan Woman' (1970), 'Come on Over Again'/'Back to Winona' (1970), 'Is that the Way?'/ 'Swans on the Canal' (1971), 'Talking Turkey'/'The Cavalry are Coming' (1972) and 'I'm Afraid'/'Handle Me Easy' (1973), plus two albums, *Tin Tin* and *Astral Taxi*.

The Steve Groves-penned, Maurice Gibb-produced 'Toast and Marmalade for Tea' reached #10 in Australia (June 1971) and #20 in the USA. Decca issued a final Tin Tin single in 1973, 'It's a Long Way to Georgia'/'Can't Get Over You'. Vallins joined Tin Tin in May 1971, while Carl Grossman was also a latter-day member.

Steve Kipner travelled to the USA where he joined fellow Australian expatriate Darryl Cotton (ex-**Zoot**) in Friends. Friends issued a self-titled album on Warners, plus a couple of singles including 'Gonna Have a Good Time'/'Would You Laugh?' (1973). The A-side was a cover of the Vanda and Young tune which had mysteriously been credited to Vanda-Young-Cotton-Lloyd-Kipner on the record label. Kipner left Friends in 1974 and joined Skyband which recorded one unsuccessful, self-titled album for RCA in 1975. In 1979 Kipner issued a solo album, *Knock the Walls Down*, and single, 'Love is Its Own Reward', on Elektra. Both sank without a trace.

Kipner fared better when **Olivia Newton-John** turned his song 'Physical' into an international hit during 1981. In the meantime, John Vallins had formed a songwriting partnership with Nat Kipner. Johnny Mathis and Deniece Williams enjoyed a worldwide hit in March 1978 with the Kipner/Vallins composition 'Too Much Too Little Too Late'.

Album: *The Giggle Eyed Goo* (Spin/Festival, 1966; reissued on Raven in 1990 with singles tracks added).

Jon Stevens (*see* Noiseworks)

Stiletto

Formed: *1976*
Style: *Rock, pop*
Original line-up: *Jane Clifton (vocals; ex-Toads, Myriad), Janie Conway (guitar, vocals; ex-Myriad), Andrew Bell (guitar; ex-Toads), Marney Sheehan (bass; ex-Toads), Eddie Van Roosendael (drums, vocals; ex-Toads)*

Melbourne band Stiletto formed out of the ashes of pub-rock outfit Toads (which also included Martin Armiger and Eric Gradman, who went on to form **The Bleeding Hearts**). With new member Janie Conway on board, Stiletto earned a reputation as a strong feminist band. Stiletto played the inner-city pub circuit alongside the likes of the early **Sports**, **Jo Jo Zep and the Falcons**, Gulliver's Travels, **Mondo Rock**, **The Bleeding Hearts**, **Redhouse** and **Millionaires**.

By June 1977, Chris Worrall (ex-**Pelaco Brothers**, **Captain Matchbox Whoopee Band**, **Bleeding Hearts**) had replaced Conway on guitar, and Celeste Howden had replaced Marney Sheehan. Conway and Sheehan initially formed a duo, after which Conway formed Janie Conway's Scarlet. In October 1977, Stiletto provided the B-side, 'Nights in Parlour', to Red Symon's first post-**Skyhooks** single, 'It's Only a Flipside'. Stiletto also contributed three tracks 'Nights in Parlour', 'Cream' and 'The Man' to the Various Artists album *Debutantes* (1977) issued on **Ross Wilson** and Glenn Wheatley's Oz label. In early 1978, Stiletto recorded its debut album, *Licence to Rage*, with producer Peter Walker.

The album appeared in September, preceded by the singles 'Bluebirds'/'Cream' (March 1978) and 'Goodbye Johnny'/'Woman in a Man's World' (August). In late 1978, Worrall left to join **Paul Kelly** and the Dots. Chris Dyson (ex-High Rise Bombers, Cruisers) came in as his replacement, and the band supported UK visitor Elvis Costello at his Melbourne concert. By early 1979, Stiletto had split up, with the members moving on to various projects. Bell played in the backing band for the rock musical *Mickey's Moomba* at Carlton's Pram Factory, Dyson and Roosendael joined **News** briefly and then The Romantics and Clifton formed the Jane Clifton Sextet to perform predominantly Billie Holliday and Ella Fitzgerald material.

Next Clifton scored the role of Margot Gaffney in popular television drama series *Prisoner*, and in late 1982 joined the **Jo Jo Zep** big band. She sang on the tongue-in-cheek, Kid Creole and the Coconuts-styled salsa melodrama 'Taxi Mary' (which appeared as a single) and the *Cha* album. In mid-1983 she appeared in Robyn Archer's stage show *Pack of Women*. She also took roles in the feature films *The Clinic* (1983) and *A Slice of Life* (1984). In early 1984, Clifton launched her solo career with the single 'Girl on the Wall'/'Baby Wasn't It You?' (February) on the Mushroom label. She formed Jane Clifton and The Go Go Boys with five member of **The Black Sorrows**, Jeff Burstin (guitar; ex-**Jo Jo Zep and the Falcons**), Wayne Burt (guitar; ex-**Jo Jo Zep and the Falcons**), Steve Williamson (sax), Wayne Duncan (bass; ex-**Daddy Cool**) and **Gary Young** (drums, ex-**Daddy Cool**, **Jo Jo Zep and the Falcons**).

At the end of the year, she presented her solo

show, *On a Clear Day You Can See Jane Clifton*, which incorporated jazz, 1960s girl group pop, show tunes and comedy. Mushroom issued one more Clifton single, 'My Machines'/'Love's No Antidote' (July 1984), before she moved to Joe Camilleri's Spirit label for 'Turn to Dust'/'Sweet Heart' (1985). Clifton's fourth solo single, 'Might Have Been'/'Second Home' (January 1987), came out on the ABC label. Clifton continued to play Melbourne pubs and clubs in bands like The Jane Clifton Quintet, Stagefright and The Blue Lester Trio, as well as working in the theatre.

Album: *Licence to Rage* (Oz/EMI, 1978).

The Stockley See Mason Band (*see* Home)

Judy Stone

Style: *Pop, country*

During the early 1960s, singer Judy Stone became a regular on television pop show *Bandstand*, alongside the likes of **Col Joye**, **Bryan Davies**, **Lucky Starr**, **Noeleen Batley**, **Patsy Ann Noble**, The Allen Brothers, **The Delltones**, **The De Kroo Brothers**, Laurel Lea, Jimmy Hannan and Sandy Scott. Stone's duets with **Col Joye** were a popular feature of the show. She began touring with Joye and the Joyboys, and then signed a deal with Festival Records.

Stone's first two singles for Festival, 'You're Driving Me Crazy'/'It Takes a Lot To Make Me Cry' (June 1961) and 'Danger! Heartbreak Ahead'/'You're Driving Me Mad' (August), were minor hits. Her third single, 'I'll Step Down'/'Mommy and Daddy Were Twistin'' (February 1962), took her into the Sydney Top 10 for the first time when it peaked at #5 during March. Stone also issued her debut album for Festival, *I'll Step Down*, in 1962. 'Finders Keepers'/'I'm Confessing that I Love You' (June), 'I Wanna Love You'/'Where are You?' (December) and 'It Takes a Lot to Make Me Cry'/'I Cried' (July 1963) made minor impressions on the Sydney chart. It was her seventh single, however, that became Stone's most popular release of the 1960s. The heart-wrenching ballad '4,003,221 Tears from Now'/'Hello Faithless' (April 1964) peaked at #8 in Sydney and #7 in Melbourne. The 'I Cried' EP (June 1964), plus the singles 'Break My Heartache'/'Lonely People Do Foolish Things' (September), 'Hard to Say Goodnight'/'Too Much' (December) and 'In My Neighbourhood'/'This is My Prayer' (October 1965) were not so successful.

By that stage, Stone had teamed up with **Col Joye** on a number of recordings, including the EPs 'The I's Have It' and 'Clap Your Hands', and albums *Col and Judy* and *The Best of Col and Judy*, which contained cutesy material like 'Young And Healthy', 'Angry' and 'Side by Side'. In early 1965 she embarked on a two-month Japanese tour with Joye and the Joyboys. A year later, she married Leo De Kroo of **The De Kroo Brothers**. In September 1966, Stone scored her third Sydney Top 10 hit when a cover of Sandy Posey's 'Born a Woman'/'I Need You' (her first release for Joye's ATA label) peaked at #3. Stone issued five more singles on ATA, 'Don't Touch Me'/'So Softly' (February 1967), 'And the Trouble with Me is You'/'Lost Without Love' (May), 'I Might as Well Get Used to It'/'Love will Always Find a Way' (March 1968) and Janis Ian's 'Society's Child'/'I'm Not Your Woman' (March 1969), before moving to the M7 label.

Throughout the late 1960s/early 1970s, Stone consolidated on her early pop successes with regular appearances on the club and country music circuits. Her first single for M7, 'Day by Day' (from *Godspell*)/'Enough of a Woman' (November 1971) was overshadowed by **Colleen Hewett's** hit rendition, although it did peak at #6 in Sydney. Stone issued her third solo album, *Pure Stone*, in May 1972 on the Frog label. The albums *Born to Love* (1972), *The Magic of Judy Stone* (1973) and the double compilation *Judy Stone's Greatest Hits* (1974) followed. In 1974, Stone entered her most successful phase since the mid-1960s when her English-language version of 'Mare Mare Mare'/'(I Am) Only a Woman' (January 1974) and 'Would You Lay with Me in a Field of Stone?'/'Forgive Me for Saying' (June) charted in the national Top 20 (#12 and #2 respectively). With 'Would You Lay with Me in a Field of Stone?' in the Australian Top 10, Stone represented Australia at Expo '74 in Spokane, USA. Stone's first album for the M7 label was *In a Field of Stone*.

The 1975 singles 'Where are the Clowns?'/'Traveller' and 'We Two will Love'/'I Believe in Music' were not successful. Stone returned to the national chart with her version of the country standard 'Silver Wings And Golden Rings'/'We Need You' (her first release for Polydor), which reached #21 in February. 'Silver Wings and Golden Rings' had been lifted from Stone's album *A Part of Me*, which also produced the single ABBA's 'Hasta Manana'/'Runaway' (#14 in May). In 1977, Stone travelled to the UK where she had signed with recording and management company Power Exchange (which also handled Kamahl's affairs). Stone's second album for Polydor, *What are You Doing Tonight?* produced the single 'What are You Doing Tonight?'/'Don't Cry Tears for Me' (1978).

Stone issued one final single for Polydor in April 1980, 'Years'/'Magic in Your Mind'. By 1983, Stone had signed with Powderworks/RCA and issued the single 'Number One in My Heart'/'As Tears Go By' (November).

Albums: *I'll Step Down* (Festival, 1962), *Col and Judy* (with **Col Joye**, Festival, 1962), *The Best of Col and Judy* (with **Col Joye**, Festival, 1963), *Got You on My Mind* (Festival, 1964), *Pure Stone* (Frog, 1972), *Born to Love* (Summit, 1972), *The Magic of Judy Stone* (Summit, 1973), *Judy Stone's Greatest Hits* (Festival, 1974), *In a Field of Stone* (M7, 1974), *Judy Stone's Favourites* (M7, 1975), *A Part of Me* (Polydor, 1976), *What are You Doing Tonight?* (Polydor, 1978), *20 Golden Greats* (Festival, 1983), *All the Best* (Telmak, 1984).

Strange Tenants

Formed: *1981*
Style: *Ska, pop*
Original line-up: *Bruce Hearn (lead vocals, keyboards, trumpet), Ian Hearn (vocals, keyboards, guitar), John Holmes (lead guitar), Robert Calvert (sax), Paul Williamson (sax), Chris Rogers (bass), Dave Lennon (drums)*

Alongside **No Nonsense**, Strange Tenants were the instigators of the Melbourne ska movement of the early 1980s. Inspired by the original 1960s Jamaican ska pioneers like Prince Buster, The Skatalites and Desmond Dekker, plus the contemporary British 2-Tone/Bluebeat scene (Madness, Specials, Selector), Strange Tenants brought the sunny delights of ska-pop to life. Within a year of formation, Strange Tenants became one of the biggest drawcards on the Melbourne inner-city circuit.

Strange Tenants staked out inner-city hotels like the Aberdeen and the Greyhound as their home territory, spawning an entire scene and lifestyle in the process. The band's frantic dance rhythms drew a cult following of rude boys out for a good time. As the band developed, the musicians began to inject pop, jazz and soul elements plus African rhythm into the fray. Strange Tenants also infused their music with socio-political commentary as the singles 'Hard Times'/'One Thirty' (July 1983) and 'I Work at My Machine'/'The Firm' (October 1984) revealed. 'Hard Times' was one of the best independent singles of 1983.

Strange Tenants also issued two 12-inch EPs *Strange Tenants* (June 1982) and *Take One Step* (November 1983) on their own Bluebeat label before issuing the album *Movin' in* (October 1984). One-time folkie **Trevor Lucas** produced the album. As well as including 'I Work at My Machine', the album produced two more singles, 'Shoulder to Shoulder'/'Cannon Fodder' (May 1985) and 'Big Red Bus'/'Temptation' (August). The album featured new members Phil Grove who had replaced Laurence Maddick on keyboards, and Ralph Franke (ex-Invisible Mendez) who replaced Paul Williamson on sax.

The Hearn brothers also moonlighted with sideline band The Bluebeat Allstars, which produced the album *Bluebeat Party* (November 1985) on the Bluebeat label. The Bluebeat Allstars touring line-up comprised Bruce 'Boots' Hearn (vocals, trumpet, harmonica), 'Evil' Ian Hearn (vocals, guitar), Phil 'Reverend' Grove (keyboards), Robert 'Dazzler' Calvert (sax), 'Artful Dodger' Rogers (bass) and Jeff 'Bongo I Dread' Denny (drums). Strange Tenants issued the mini-album compilation *We are Stronger* (January 1986) before calling it a day. Ian Hearn revived the Strange Tenants name in 1996 for the album *Ain't that Enough?* which included a new version of one of the band's early live favourites, 'Grey Skies Over Collingwood'.

Albums: *Movin' in* (Bluebeat/EMI, 1984), *Bluebeat Party* (compilation, Bluebeat/EMI, 1993), *Ain't that Enough?* (as Ian Hearn and Strange Tenants, Bluebeat/Shock, 1996).

The Strangers

Formed: *1961*
Style: *Instrumental pop*
Original line-up: *Laurie Arthur (lead guitar; ex-***Planets**, **Chessmen***), Fred Weiland (rhythm guitar; ex-Lincolns), Peter Robinson (bass; ex-***Thunderbirds***), Graeme Thompson (drums; ex-Earls)*

Alongside **The Thunderbirds**, **The Phantoms**, The Breakaways, The Saxons, The Fabulous Blue Jays, The Marksmen and The Playboys, instrumental combo The Strangers were one of the bastions of Melbourne's early 1960s rock scene. Rather than embrace the surf craze that had enthralled Sydney counterparts like **The Atlantics**, **The Denvermen** and The Statesmen, The Strangers took their cue from British and European instrumental masters like The Shadows, The Tornados and The Spotnicks.

After forming in 1961, The Strangers worked all the major Melbourne dances. In late 1962, they signed with W&G Records, issuing their debut single, 'Cry of the Wild Geese'/'Leaving Town', in January 1963. The single reached #12 on the Melbourne chart. The Strangers issued two more singles in 1963, 'Torlido'/'Outcast' (#34 in April) and 'Undertow'/'Along the Navajo Trail' (#23 in November), followed by 'Poppa Oom Mow Mow'/'Sunday Kind of Love' in early 1964. John Farrar replaced Laurie Arthur on lead guitar, and the band began to incorporate Farrar's vocals into the sound. The Strangers' first vocal single, 'If You Gotta Make a Fool of Somebody'/'Let's Go', reached #29 in July 1964. From that point on, The Strangers became Melbourne's most popular backing group. They backed solo artists like **Merv Benton** and ex-**Thunderbirds'** sax player Colin Cook (including the single 'Heart'/'Surfin' Honeymoon' and the album *Colin Cook and the Strangers*). They also became resident group on television pop show *The Go!! Show*.

The Strangers' two 1965 singles, 'Never on a Sunday'/In My Room' and 'Put Yourself in My Place'/'Fever', did not reach the Top 40. The band made a return to the Melbourne chart with 'Western Union'/'Cool Jerk' which appeared on the Go!! label in May 1967. It peaked at #30. By that stage, Terry Walker (ex-**Glen Ingram and the Hi-Five**) had joined as lead vocalist. In 1968, Walker sang lead vocals on the **Pastoral Symphony** single 'Love Machine'/'Spread a Little Love Around' which reached #10 on the national chart during June. The Strangers signed to Philips and issued the singles 'Happy Without You'/'Take the Time' (#39 in November 1968), 'Lady Scorpio'/'California Soul' (#36 in June 1969) and 'Sweet September'/'Paper Cup' (January 1970), plus the album *The Strangers*.

With a move to Ron Tudor's Fable label, The Strangers enjoyed their biggest hit since 'Leaving Town' in 1963. 'Melanie Makes Me Smile'/'If You Think You're Groovy' reached #14 in June 1970. A month later, The Strangers broke up; Farrar travelled to the UK where he formed a partnership with Hank Marvin and Bruce Welch of The Shadows. As the vocal trio Marvin Welch and Farrar, they recorded two albums, *Marvin Welch and Farrar* (1971) and *Second Opinion* (1972). Marvin and Farrar recorded the album *Hank Marvin and John Farrar* in 1973. Then, when Marvin, Welch and bassist Brian Bennett re-formed The Shadows later in the year, Farrar joined as vocalist/rhythm guitarist. He stayed until 1975 and appeared on the albums *Rockin' with Curly Leads*, *Specs Appeal* and *Live at the Paris Olympia*.

Farrar moved to the USA and began writing, playing guitar and producing for **Olivia Newton-John** (including albums like *Olivia Newton-John*, *Have You Never Been Mellow?*, *Clearly Love*, *Don't Stop Believin'* and *Making a Good Thing Better*). As well as writing songs like 'Have You Never Been Mellow?' and 'Something Better to Do' for Newton-John, Farrar composed 'Hopelessly Devoted to You' which she sang on the *Grease* soundtrack. It became an international hit single in 1978. Farrar has also had his songs covered by Cliff Richard. In 1980, Farrar issued his debut solo album, *John Farrar*, on CBS which included the single 'Recovery'. In 1995 he produced Richard's album *Songs from Heathcliff*.

Meanwhile, back in late 1970, Strangers members Peter Robinson and Graeme Thompson recruited newcomers John Cosgrove (lead guitar; ex-Fendermen) and Bill Pyman (rhythm guitar) and continued as The New Strangers. The band issued three more singles on Fable, 'Mr President'/'Looking Through the Eyes of a Beautiful Girl' (December 1970), 'Sweet Water'/'Wishing My Life Away' (May 1971) and 'Tennessee'/'That Sunshine Feeling' (July 1972), but none was successful. Former Strangers frontman Terry Walker also issued a solo single on Fable, 'Natural Sinner'/'Sweet Inspiration' (November 1970). In March 1973, Jim Sifonious (ex-**Dove**) replaced Cosgrove on lead guitar. The New Strangers issued two more singles (on Astor), 'Hitchhike'/'Home Ain't Home Anymore' and 'Kentucky Poor Boys'/'Sweet Song of the Country', in 1975 before splitting up for good.

Albums: *Colin Cook and the Strangers* (W&G, 1966), *The Strangers* (Philips, 1969), *Best of the (Original) Strangers* (Fable, 1971), *Best of The Strangers* (Canetoad, 1997).

Dave Studdert's Mumbo Jumbo (*see* The Tactics)

Stylus

Formed: *1975*
Style: *Funk, soul*
Original line-up: *Peter Cupples (vocals, guitar, percussion, electric piano; ex-Wheatfield, Canyon, Mason's Cure), Ronnie Peers (lead guitar; ex-Mason's Cure), Sam McNally (keyboards; ex-Silver Sun, Baiyana), Ashley Henderson (bass; ex-Mason's Cure), Peter Lee (drums; ex-Mason's Cure)*

Alongside **Hot City Bump Band, Johnny Rocco Band,** Skylight and Australia, Stylus was one of the few local groups of the mid-1970s playing in a white-funk style. Unlike the limited success afforded **Hot City Bump Band**, however, Stylus scored a number of hit singles and became very popular on the Australian pub and concert circuit.

Stylus grew out of the ashes of Melbourne band Mason's Cure, formed by keyboardist Ian Mason (ex-**Kush**). Mason's Cure issued one single on Astor in early 1975, 'Let Me Love You Right'/'Back to

Reality', before Mason left the group. He joined The Bootleg Band, and went on to issue a solo single, 'Gotta Lotta Love'/'Keep It Up' (August 1978), and album, *Nobody Takes Me Seriously* (Oz/EMI, 1978). Singer Peter Cupples had been the focal point of Mason's Cure, so with Mason's departure, the band recruited Sam McNally on keyboards and became Stylus. The band toured as support to Focus, Ike and Tina Turner and **Sherbet**, scored a deal with WEA (Atlantic) and issued the single Seals and Crofts' 'Summer Breeze'/'Feelin' Blue' (July 1975). The single reached #31 in Melbourne during August. The band's second single, 'World of Make Believe'/'Just Began' (October) reached #27.

In November 1975, WEA issued the Stylus debut album *Where in the World?* (#19 in Melbourne during December). The album produced a third single, 'I'm Going Home'/'Where in the World?' (April 1976), but by that stage Stylus had left WEA. The band issued one single, 'So Much Love'/'We All Need One Another' (#30 in August 1976), on Crystal Clear, before signing a new deal with **Ross Wilson** and Glenn Wheatley's Oz label (through EMI). The album *For the Love of Music* produced the singles 'I Just Don't Wanna Fall in Love Right Now'/'Funky Fig' (October 1976) and 'Kissin'/'For the Love of Music' (June 1977). By that stage, Peter Lee had been replaced by Trevor Courtney (ex-**Vibrants**, Skylight) initially, and then by Joe Tattersalls (ex-**Ayers Rock**) by the end of the year.

Courtney played on the band's third album, *The Best Kept Secret* (April 1978), which produced the singles 'Work Out Fine'/'Natural Feeling' (March), 'Look at Me'/'You Can't Get It Out of Your Head' (July) and 'Got to Say Goodbye'/'Discover Your Life' (November). The prestigious American label Motown distributed the album in the USA (under the title *Stylus*) via the Prodigal imprint. In late 1978, Peter Roberts (ex-Ride Band) joined Stylus as co-lead vocalist. Not long after that, Mark Meyer (ex-Sailor) replaced Tattersalls on drums, and the band supported visiting American jazz guitarist George Benson on his Australian tour. The band's fourth album, *Part of It All* (August 1979), and its single, 'If You Believe in Me'/'Byron Bay' (August), were not successful and the members of Stylus parted.

Cupples went solo, forming the first version of his Peter Cupples Band in 1980 with Virgil Donati (drums; ex-**Taste**), Ross Ingliss (guitar), Robert Little (bass) and **David Hirschfelder** (keyboards). Cupples' debut album, *Fear of Thunder* (October 1981), yielded the singles 'Fear of Thunder'/'I'm into You' (September) and 'Blame It on the Weather'/'Dryin' Time' (December 1981). *Fear of Thunder* sold well in Melbourne where it peaked at #21 in March 1982. Cupples recorded a second pop album and four more singles, 'You Never Know'/'Sweet Summer Nights' (April 1982), 'All in a Day's Work'/'I Remember' (August 1982), 'Party Lights'/'In the Pits' (November 1983) and 'Love of Another World'/'On the Run' (March 1984). Cupples concentrated on becoming an all-round entertainer. He became popular on television variety shows, and on the club/cabaret circuit, but got out of the music business in the late 1980s. He returned to the studio for the 1995 album *Changes*, which included the CD singles 'Indecision' and 'The Power of Change'.

In 1980, keyboardist Sam McNally joined the **John Farnham** Band alongside **Tommy Emmanuel** (guitar; ex-Southern Star Band), Barry Sullivan (bass; ex-**Chain**) and David Jones (drums). McNally also issued a solo album, *First Chance* (February 1982, EMI), and a single, 'First Chance Romance'/'The Dance of the Funky Rabbits', 'Wonderland' (April). After that, he toured with a number of bands, including Vitabeats, the **Tommy Emmanuel** Band and the Guy Le Claire Band. McNally mostly concentrated on session work, appearing on an enormous number of albums by the likes of **Swanee**, Peter Cupples, **The Monitors**, **Tim Finn**, **Eurogliders**, **Flaming Hands**, QED, **SPK**, **Renée Geyer**, the *Street Hero* soundtrack, **Tommy Emmanuel** and **The Party Boys** among many others.

Stylus albums: *Where in the World*? (WEA, 1975), *For the Love of Music* (Oz/EMI, 1976), *The Best Kept Secret* (Oz/EMI, 1978), *Part of It All* (Oz/EMI, 1979), *Stylus Collection* (EMI, 1992); ***Peter Cupples solo albums:*** *Fear of Thunder* (Full Moon/Astor, 1981), *Half the Effort Twice the Effect* (Mercury, 1984), *Changes* (Mercury, 1995).

Suiciety

Formed: *1991*
Style: *Heavy metal*
Original line-up: *Adam Cooper (vocals), Karsten Pol (guitar), Doug Dalton (guitar), Stefan Pol (bass), Cameron McNiven (drums)*

Young Melbourne five-piece Suiciety came together under the name Ward 13 in 1990. With a name change to Suiciety in 1991, the band began attracting attention around the inner-city Melbourne scene. With influences drawn from bands as diverse as Anthrax, Nirvana, Prong, Suicidal Tendancies, Black Sabbath and Motorhead, Suiciety proffered a style of rock that mixed grunge riffs with hardcore attitude. The band was known to share gigs with heavy metal, grunge and punk groups alike.

Original guitarist Doug Dalton left early in the piece; he went on to join Sydney thrash metal band Grungeon. Ramon Varela took his place. Suiciety's first recording, 'Saddam Hussein', appeared on the Various Artists album *From Brunswick to Babylon*, a compilation of Melbourne acts put out by the independent Nomad label in 1991. The band's 1992 demos, *Suiciety* and *That's My Excuse*, led to a deal with Shock Records' hard music label Shagpile.

Shagpile issued Suiciety's debut album *Deeper Vision* in July 1993, and over the next year the band scored tour supports to overseas visitors Kreator, Fear Factory, Bolt Thrower, Sepultura and Body Count. German label Forge issued *Deeper Vision* in Europe to a positive response. The CD EP 'Shades of Grey' appeared in June 1994, followed by the band's second album, *Primrose Path* (November). *Primrose Path* displayed a greater variety in the music and stronger songs all up. It produced the CD single 'T.C.P.' (November). In 1995, Suiciety signed a major deal with BMG Records which finally resulted in the five-track CD EP *Cell* ('Once Again') in February 1996. The band also contributed a sturdy, thrash-styled rendition of 'Night Prowler' to the **AC/DC** tribute album *Fuse Box: The Alternative Tribute* (on BMG, May 1995). Suiciety set about writing and recording a new album, but nothing eventuated and the band slipped from view.

Albums: *Deeper Vision* (Shagpile/Shock, 1993), *Primrose Path* (Shagpile/Shock, 1994).

Sunday Painters

Formed: *1979*
Style: *Avant pop*
Original line-up: *Peter Raengel (vocals, guitar, bass, keyboards; ex-Winged Death, Art Throbs), Bruce Ellis (synthesisers; ex-Art Throbs), Peter MacKinnon (guitar), Katherine Lorenc (vocals, flute, keyboards)*

Hailing from the steel town of Wollongong, on the New South Wales coast 100 kilometres south of Sydney, Sunday Painters operated on the very periphery of the Australian independent scene. Sunday Painters seldom toured, but did issue a steady stream of records on their own Terminal label (with its motto of 'obscurum per obscurius').

The band's startling music drew inspiration from late 1970s UK punk (Wire, Buzzcocks), American pioneers such as The Velvet Underground and several points beyond. Rock writer Clinton Walker described the band's approach as 'musical schizophrenia — part-pop/rock garage band, part-classical experimentalists, and sometimes somewhere in between'. Underpinning it all was a political manifesto that explored themes of oppression, alienation, pain and the search for identity. Peter Raengel and Bruce Ellis had played in a number of high school/garage bands before formulating plans for Sunday Painters. Sunday Painters issued two strangely appealing EPs during 1980, 'Like a Reptile'/'Venus (Bathed in Misogyny)', 'Heart of a Siren' (aka *Alternatives To Perfection*; April) and 'In My Dreams'/'Rebel Rebel', 'Part Two' (aka *Painting by Numbers*; October) which displayed their garage band/primitive, neo-Velvet Underground roots. As described by the band, the EPs were an 'attempt to provide both radical entertainment and alternative politics'.

A third EP, *Three Kinds of Escapism* (1981), the album *Something to Do* (1982) and the live cassette release *On the Beach* (1983) furthered the band's cause on an independent level. *Something to Do* displayed an extraordinary breadth of stylistic reference, from the frantic Wire-like 'Emotion Sickness' to the sprawling epic 'ECT', which would not have sounded out of place on a Faust or Neu! record circa 1973. Both tracks appeared on *Beyond the Southern Cross* (1984), a compilation of Australian bands (including **The Triffids**, **Tactics**, **Severed Heads**, Whirlywirld and Mad Room) put out by UK-based label Red Flame on its subsidiary Ink imprint. By that stage, the band had suffered a number of line-up changes: Bruce Ellis and Katherine Lorenc had left, and Dennis Kennedy had joined on bass. The line-up of Raengel, MacKinnon and Kennedy recorded the album *Fourth Annual Report* in May 1983. At the end of 1983, Allan Coop replaced Dennis Kennedy on bass and Ed Zeidan joined on alto sax.

Fourth Annual Report appeared in 1984, by which time co-founder MacKinnon had also departed. The album was divided into the *Surface Paradise* side and *Music for Riot Control* side, and once again the music ranged from the abrasive ('God is My Biro', 'Concertina') and the eerie ('Surface Paradise') to soundscapes of the epic kind ('Through a Shattered Lens'). *Fourth Annual Report* brought Sunday Painters' first 'Five Year Plan' to a close, and, although various other musicians joined (Kerrie Erwin, bass; Tony Tziolas, bass; and Chris

Flannagan, drums), the band did not issue any more records before splitting in 1986.

Albums: *Something to Do* (Terminal, 1982), *Fourth Annual Report* (Terminal, 1984).

Sunglass (*see* Sea Stories)

Sunnyboys

Formed: *1980*
Style: *Power pop*
Original line-up: *Jeremy Oxley (guitar, vocals), Richard Burgman (lead guitar; ex-Shy Impostors), Peter Oxley (bass; ex-Shy Impostors), Bil Bilson (drums; ex-Playboy Lords)*

Sydney quartet Sunnyboys remains one of the most highly regarded and best-loved bands of the Australian post-punk era. Fronted by the enigmatic, expressive 18-year-old singer/songwriter/guitarist Jeremy Oxley, Sunnyboys breathed some freshness and vitality into the divergent Sydney scene.

Essentially Sunnyboys were a post-punk guitar band with influences rooted in 1960s pop (The Kinks, The Beatles, The Remains, The Flamin' Groovies) with a dash of Detroit muscle added. Sunnyboys were young and energetic and their brand of finely crafted, melodic power pop packed a hell of a dance beat. As a consequence, the band was rewarded with an immediate positive response. Things happened very quickly for Sunnyboys, from playing inner-city Sydney venues supporting the likes of **The Lipstick Killers** and Trans Love Energies to being snapped up by, and scoring hit singles for, the prestigious Mushroom label all within a year of formation. What set the band apart in many ways were Oxley's intrinsic songwriting abilities and the internal chemistry between the four players.

The Oxley brothers and Bil Bilson hailed from the northern New South Wales town of Kingscliff where they had formed garage band Wooden Horse. Richard Burgman came from Wagga Wagga. Peter Oxley, Bilson and Burgman met in Sydney during 1979. Bilson joined The Playboy Lords with Darcy Condon (vocals), Paul Thirkell (guitar) and Stephen Mather (bass). Oxley and Burgman joined Shy Impostors with Penny Ward (vocals) and Michael Charles (drums). Shy Impostors recorded one excellent single, 'At the Barrier'/'Seein' Double' (issued posthumously on the Phantom label), before breaking up in early 1980. 'Seein' Double' and the previously unissued 'When the Night Comes in' later turned up on Phantom's Various Artists album *Paths of Pain to Jewels of Glory* (alongside Sunnyboys' 'Love to Rule; 1984).

Jeremy Oxley joined brother Peter, Burgman and Bilson in their new band Sunnyboys in July 1980. In October, Sunnyboys recorded four songs with redoubtable producer **Lobby Loyde**, 'Love to Rule', 'Alone with You', 'What You Need' and 'The Seeker'. The songs appeared on the band's independent, four-track debut EP *Sunnyboys*, issued by Phantom in December. The EP was an immediate success, selling out its pressing of 1000 copies in two weeks. Phantom later reissued the EP as a 'Special Limited Edition Remixed' 12-inch record. Sunnyboys signed to Mushroom Records in early 1981, and by July had cracked the mainstream charts with the high-spirited single 'Happy Man'/'Tomorrow will Be Fine' (national #26, Sydney #18). Mushroom also issued 'Happy Man' as Australia's first cassette single which contained two bonus live tracks, 'Thrill' and 'Why Do I Cry?'. That same month, Sunnyboys issued their own independent, gig giveaway EP *Happy Birthday* ('What You Need', 'Why Do I Cry?/'I Want to Be Alone', 'Let You Go') pressed on red vinyl, which was handed out to patrons attending their first anniversary concert.

Lobby Loyde also produced the band's debut album, *Sunnyboys* (September 1981). *Sunnyboys* reached #13 on the national album chart in October, eventually selling over 50 000 copies. It remains an Australian rock classic, an album brimming with infectious, danceable R&B-spiced rock'n'roll, impassioned, dynamic songs, a marvellously light-hearted disposition and lashings of youthful exuberance. The album produced a second hit single, 'Alone with You'/'Stop & Think', 'To the Bone' (national #26, Sydney #15 in November). The album came in two versions. The standard issue featured 'Happy Man', while a 'Limited Edition' release (2000 copies pressed on sunshine yellow vinyl) replaced that song with the otherwise unavailable track 'Tell Me What You Say'. The limited edition album was aimed at fans who already had the 'Happy Man' single.

The album established Sunnyboys as a bona fide headlining attraction, and they spent the next year touring constantly. In between the heavy touring schedule, they found time to record a second album *Individuals* (issued May 1982) with **Lobby Loyde**. The album peaked at #19 on the national chart during July, but of its two singles, 'You Need a Friend'/'No Love Around' (April) and 'This is Real'/'Pain' (August), only 'You Need a Friend' charted briefly (#38 in June). After further live work, Sunnyboys issued their fifth single, 'Show Me Some Discipline'/'Guts of Iron' (June 1983), which charted in Sydney (#30). Meanwhile, Sunnyboys travelled to the UK to re-evaluate their future and to record a new album. The band played two sold-out shows at London's famous Marquee Club before entering Ridgefarm Studios, Surrey and Townhouse Studios, London with English producer Nick Garvey (ex-Motors).

The recording sessions involved more planning in the pre-production stage, and the resultant album, *Get Some Fun* (April 1984), displayed a greater diversity in the songs and more confident musicianship. To coincide with the album's release, Sunnyboys embarked on their first national tour since May 1983. Unfortunately, neither the album, nor its singles 'Love in a Box'/'Physical Jerk' (March 1984) and 'Comes as No Surprise'/'Bottom of My Heart' (May) charted strongly enough. Internal dissent also began to plague the band, and Sunnyboys announced their break-up in June 1984. The band's farewell tour produced the album *Real Live* (November 1984), which had been recorded over two nights in Sydney, 29 and 30 June. In 1985, French label Closer combined Sunnyboys' first two albums as the double set *Days are Gone* for the European market. The band's singles had become sought-after items within European collectors circles.

With Sunnyboys' break-up, Jeremy Oxley immediately launched his new band Chinless Elite which comprised Marcus Phelan (guitar; ex-Numbers, **v. Spy v. Spy**, **Hoi Polloi**), Jon Schofield (bass; ex-**Grooveyard**), Mark Fuccilli (sax), Sean McEleogue (trumpet) and Andrew Robertson (drums). Chinless Elite signed to the Big Time label and issued the single 'I Got to Get to California'/'I Heard It Through the Grapevine' (November 1985) and the mini-album *Chinless Elite* before splitting up at the end of the year. Oxley formed three-piece outfit The Fishermen with Andrew Denison (bass, backing vocals) and Ian Potterton (drums). The Fishermen earned a lively following around Sydney and managed to issue one single, 'Can't You Stop?'/'City Opera' (January 1987), on the Waterfront label before going their separate ways.

In the meantime, Richard Burgman had joined **Chris Bailey's Saints** before moving on to **Weddings, Parties, Anything** in 1988. He later emigrated to Canada. Peter Oxley and Bil Bilson formed soul-pop band The Sparklers with another Oxley sibling, Melanie (vocals; ex-Sweet Nothings), **Chris Abrahams** (piano; ex-Benders), Gerard Corben (guitar; ex-**Lime Spiders**) and Ernie Finch (guitar). There were a number of line-up changes over the years: in late 1986, Colin Bloxsom (guitar; ex-Pop Rivets, **John Kennedy's Love Gone Wrong**) replaced Corben (who rejoined **Lime Spiders**); Phil Grove (keyboards; ex-**Strange Tenants**) replaced **Chris Abrahams** in 1987; and Dave Harden replaced Bilson in 1989.

The Sparklers issued one single on the Phantom label, 'Overworking'/'Baby Baby' (October 1986), before signing to the Mighty Boy label. The band went on to issue four more singles, 'So Often Dreaming'/'Can't Take Anymore' (January 1987), 'Heart and Soul'/'The Middle of Time' (September 1988), 'Merry Go Round'/'When You're Alone' (December) and 'Don't Go Changing'/'Overworking' (February 1989), plus the Les Karski-produced album *Persuasion* (October 1988) on the Mighty Boy label before breaking up in June 1989. Oxley and Abrahams formed a partnership which resulted in the 12-inch EP 'Resisting Calm' for jazz label Spiral Scratch. Since then, the duo has issued two moody, emotive soul/pop albums, *Welcome to Violet* (Remote/MDS, 1992) and *Coal* (Remote/MDS, 1994).

In late 1987, Jeremy Oxley attempted to relive past glories by reviving the Sunnyboys name with a new line-up. The new line-up comprised Oxley (vocals, guitar), Nick Freedman (guitar), Phil Smith (bass) and Peter Hinchenbergs (drums). Sunnyboys signed a new deal with RCA and issued the Garth Porter-produced album *Wildcat* in August 1989. It yielded the singles 'Too Young to Despair'/'I'm Changing' (December 1988), 'Sinful Me'/'Baby Did Leave' (June 1989) and 'Sad Girl'/'Sorrow is Mine' (October). Despite a couple of strong moments, the album failed to convince old Sunnyboys fans that the band had well and truly risen from the dead. That version of Sunnyboys broke up in 1990.

In July 1991, Mushroom issued the compilation album *Play the Best*, and the original line-up of Jeremy and Peter Oxley, Richard Burgman and Bil Bilson reunited for a national tour. The reunion tour, produced the 'official bootleg' live album *Shakin'*: Live August 1991 issued by Phantom in December 1992. Following the reunion tour, Oxley the younger launched a brief solo career as Jeremy 'Ponytail' Oxley which resulted in the CD EP *A Little Bit of Me in You* on the Yellow label through Shock (October 1992).

Sunnyboys albums: *Sunnyboys* (Mushroom/Festival, 1981), *Individuals* (Mushroom/Festival, 1982), *Get Some Fun* (Mushroom/Festival, 1984), *Real Live* (Mushroom/Festival, 1984), *Wildcat* (RCA, 1989), *Play the Best* (Mushroom/Festival, 1991), *Shakin': Live August 1991* (Phantom, 1992); ***Sparklers album:*** *Persuasion* (Mighty Boy, 1988).

The Sunset Strip

Formed: *1985*
Style: *Rock*
Original line-up: *Warwick Brown (lead guitar, vocals, ex-Behind the Magnolia Curtain), Wayne Arnold (bass, vocals; ex-Behind the Magnolia Curtain), Les Butrims (drums; ex-Behind the Magnolia Curtain)*

The Sunset Strip was one of the great 'underground' underground bands of the late 1980s/early 1990s. Originally from the harbourside city of Geelong (70 kilometres south west of Melbourne), The Sunset Strip was essentially a loud, psychedelic guitar band steeped in electric, fuzz-blues. Hampered by frequent line-up changes and long periods of inactivity (which affected record sales), the band nevertheless was a popular live attraction on the inner-city circuit.

The Sunset Strip grew out of the ashes of seminal Geelong outfit Behind the Magnolia Curtain, a wild Cramps/Stooges/MC5/Panther Burns/13th Floor Elevators covers band that existed for two years (early 1984 to early 1986). The original line-up comprised Dean F. Bateup (vocals), Warwick Brown (guitar), John Nolan (guitar), Jeff Schipple (bass) and Andy Turner (drums; ex-Psych-Out). Bateup, Schipple and Turner all left at the end of 1984. With a new line-up of Brown, Nolan, Simon Kerger (vocals), Wayne Arnold (bass) and Les Butrims (drums), the band developed a penchant for extended psychedelic guitar jams in the Quicksilver Messenger Service/Television mould. Behind the Magnolia Curtain fell apart in February 1986, having only issued the 'Movin' On'/'You're Gonna Miss Me' flexi disc (given away with Issue #4 of *The Livin' End* fanzine) and contributing '1,000 Miles' to Au-go-go Records' Various Artists compilation *A Slab of Vic* (October 1986).

John Nolan joined **Bored!** and later on **Powder Monkeys**. Brown, Arnold and Butrims formed The Sunset Strip. Matt Cadusch joined on guitar in May 1986 and the band recorded the single 'Going Home'/'Yesterday's Gone'. By the time the single appeared in February 1987, the line-up was Brown, Butrims, Andy Turner (guitar), Paul Ryan (bass; ex-Endangered Species) and Ian Hill (Hammond organ; ex-**Crackajacks**, **Olympic Sideburns**, **Bo-Weevils**). Two weeks after formation (October 1986), that line-up supported American visitors the Dream Syndicate in Melbourne. 'Going Home' reached #2 on the national alternative chart. Described as sounding like a garage band version of Buffalo Springfield, the single displayed Brown's whining, off-key vocals and sweetly ragged, Neil Young-inspired guitar work and the band's steady loping beat.

In September 1987, Kerrie Hickin (ex-**Ku Klux Frankenstein**, Fire) replaced Ryan on bass. The band's debut album, *Sunset Strip*, finally appeared in April 1988. Recorded by previous line-ups between March and December 1986, it was a flawed, erratic offering with a hotch-potch of styles and only a handful of standouts (the lengthy 'Run On', a poppy re-recording of 'Going Home' and the bluesy 'Morning Comes'). **Chris Wilson** contributed sax and harmonica to the 12-minute epic 'The Rising Wind' and 'Shotgun Blues'. An off-shoot band known as Magnolia Strip comprising Brown (guitar), Turner (drums) and Hickin (bass) plus Dean F. Bateup (vocals) and Dave Thomas (guitar; from **Bored!**) contributed a blistering rendition of 'Dirt' to Au-go-go Records' double Stooges tribute album *Hard to Beat* (1988). The Sunset Strip also contributed a cover of The Standells' 'Riot on Sunset Strip' to Au-go-go's Various Artists giveaway single *Going to Au-go-go* (December 1987).

Hill left The Sunset Strip in early 1988 (although he still recorded with the band) and the four-piece line-up remained stable until February 1989. The 10-inch EP 'Holocaust' (recorded July 1988, issued August 1989) featured covers of The Rolling Stones' 'Child of the Moon', Alice Cooper's 'Caught in a Dream' and Alex Chilton's 'Holocaust' (with **The Zimmermen**'s John Dowler on lead vocals), plus one tasty original, 'I'd Die Instead'. Brown and Turner reactivated The Sunset Strip in November 1989 with a new rhythm section of Paul Ryan (bass) and Rod McMurrich (drums; ex-End Result, **Gas Babies**, LSD, Funhouse). The new line-up proved to be the most powerful aggregation to date. The band completed work on its second album, *Move Right In*, which came out in early 1991.

Once again recorded in several sessions spread over 18 months (late 1988 to mid-1990), the album was nevertheless a minor masterpiece of multi-layered guitar riffing and dark, acid-blues/avant sludge rock. It remains one of the most underrated independent albums ever issued in Australia. Paula Henderson contributed sax to '20th Century Girl' and **Chris Wilson** played harp on 'Crawl Around'.

The Sunset Strip went into another period of inactivity, Brown and Turner only re-emerging in 1992 with Tim Hemensley (from **Powder Monkeys**) and Michael Glenn (from **Hoss**) helping out on bass and drums respectively. The Dog Meat label issued the CD EP 'Scrap It Out' (April 1993), which saw a refinement of The Sunset Strip's adventurous approach. Joel Silbersher (from **Hoss**) contributed lead vocals to the title track and Robert Jackson sax to the title track and the jazzy 'The Grass is Not Always Greener on the Other Side'. A previously unissued version of 'The Rising Wind' (dating from March 1986) appeared as a bonus track.

The CD EP 'Nothing Lost, Nothing Gained' (November 1993) was even better, boasting several of the band's finest-ever songs, the brooding, psychedelic-infused 'While My Light Still Burns', the frenzied 'Mercy Killing' and the astonishingly acerbic riff-rocker 'Monday Morning'. Helping out again were Silbersher, Hemensley, Glenn, Jackson and Jim Thompson (drums on one track). The previously unissued 'Here She Comes' (recorded in 1988) appeared as a bonus track. Brown and Turner took so long to complete work on the third Sunset Strip album *Stone Lazy* that the Dog Meat label had folded (early 1997) before it could be issued.

Albums: *Sunset Strip* (Au-go-go, 1988), *Move Right In* (Au-go-go, 1991; reissued on CD combined with the 'Holocaust' EP, 1994).

The Superjesus

Formed: *1994*
Style: *Indie guitar rock*
Original line-up: *Sarah McLeod (vocals, guitar), Chris Tennent (guitar), Stuart Rudd (bass), Paul Berryman (drums)*

For young Adelaide band The Superjesus, the trip to the upper echelons of the Australian alternative scene was a swift and convincing one. Formed in late 1994, initially under the name of Hell's Kitchen, the band's sound was based around the juxtaposition of Sarah McLeod's captivating voice and melodic rhythm guitar, and Chris Tennent's vicious, radically down-tuned guitar riffs. The mix of alternative crunch and commercial hooks drew inspiration from bands as diverse as The Beatles, Cheap Trick and Smashing Pumpkins.

Virtually from the outset, The Superjesus became a popular live attraction, although the band took a full year to perfect its repertoire and stage craft. The band appeared on the Adelaide bill of the 1996 Big Day Out, and began to tour the eastern states (including the Heavy Weight Kings of Rock tour during August with **Front End Loader** and New Zealand's Shihad). The additional exposure (plus the demo *The Superjesus*) led to a distribution deal with Warner Music Australia which issued the CD EP *Eight Step Rail* (on the Aloha imprint; August 1996). The CD EP reached #2 on the national alternative chart and sold a respectable 4000 copies. The featured track 'Shut My Eyes' logged #81 on the 1996 Triple J Hottest 100 list.

The Superjesus

The Superjesus consolidated its live standing with national tour supports to **Clouds**, **Hoodoo Gurus** and UK visitors Bush, plus a slot on the 1997 national Big Day Out jaunt. In April 1997, The Superjesus travelled to the USA in order to record its debut album, *Sumo* (slated for release in early 1998), with producer Matt Serletic (Collective Soul) and engineer Jeff Tomei (Smashing Pumpkins, Hole). At the 1997 Australian Record Industry Association (ARIA) awards ceremony, The Superjesus took out Best New Band and Best Debut Single ('Shut My Eyes'). Two CD singles preceded the release of *Sumo*, 'Down Again' (national #30 in October) and 'Saturation' (November).

Supernaut

Formed: *1974*
Style: *Glam pop*
Original line-up: *Gary Twinn (vocals; ex-Sidewinder, Moby Dick), Chris Burnham (guitar; ex-Moby Dick), Randall Murphy (bass), Joey Burnham (drums; ex-Moby Dick)*

For a brief period during 1976, Supernaut rivalled the likes of **Hush**, **Sherbet** and **Skyhooks** as the most popular Australian band of the day. Supernaut scored four hit singles and a best-selling debut album that sold over 50 000 copies. Gary Twinn and the Burnham brothers, Chris and Joey, were all born in England and had migrated to Perth, Western

Australia with their families. The Burnhams formed pub band Moby Dick. Twinn joined Moby Dick in late 1974 and the band soon evolved into Supernaut (named after the song 'Supernaut' by British heavy metal outfit Black Sabbath).

Despite the heavyweight name, the band Supernaut developed a commercially minded glam rock style that relied as much on visual impact as the sound of the music. In February 1976, Supernaut relocated to Melbourne and Ian 'Molly' Meldrum produced the band's debut single, 'I Like It Both Ways'/'Lightning' (May 1976). With the aid of regular appearances on the ABC-TV rock show ***Countdown*** (Meldrum was the show's talent co-ordinator), the risqué, Australian glam apotheosis 'I Like It Both Ways' reached #14 on the national chart in June (#3 in Melbourne). 'Too Hot to Touch'/'Lick My Lolly' (September) repeated that national chart feat in October (also #12 in Melbourne) and Supernaut was hot property.

Murphy left the band in late June, and session bass player Little Russ Silver (real name Argentino Russo) joined for two months to help keep the band on the road. Phil Foxman joined at the end of August, and Supernaut entered Armstrongs Studios with producer Tony Cohen to complete its debut album *Supernaut.* Upon release in December 1976, *Supernaut* shot into the Top 20 (peaking at #13 nationally and #11 in Melbourne). Supernaut took out the *TV Week* King of Pop award for Most Popular New Talent. Three further singles appeared in 1977, 'Young and Innocent'/'Goodbye' (April), 'The Kids are Out Tonight'/'Why?' (July) and The Rolling Stones' 'Let's Spend the Night Together'/ 'Space Angel' (November). 'Young and Innocent' reached #27 and 'The Kids are Out Tonight' reached #22 on the national chart.

By the end of 1977, Supernaut's popularity had subsided. Work on the band's second album (originally to be titled *Exile*, then *Test Pressing*) dragged out for over a year. Eventually the band scrapped the album as too dated. By early 1978, Supernaut had adopted a quasi-punk/new wave direction. The first example of the band's newly established sound and style was the 'Unemployed'/'Exile' (April 1978) single. The band relocated to Sydney and began to play the inner-city new wave circuit. In mid-1978, Supernaut signed a new deal with the Wizard label which resulted in the single 'Spies'/'Misfits' (December). By that stage, the band had added Noel Kennedy on keyboards and the live repertoire included cover versions of material by David Bowie, The Stranglers, XTC and The Doors. In April 1979, Supernaut became The Nauts.

The band completed work on its long-overdue second album, which appeared in December as *The Nauts*, along with the single 'Black Market World'/ 'I Don't Want to Be Like You' (September). The Nauts travelled to the UK but had broken up by March 1980. Twinn remained in the UK where he joined rock revivalists Twenty Flight Rockers which featured ex-members of The Damned. Foxman later joined UK-based outfit Illustrated Man with Roger Mason (ex-**James Freud's** Berlin) and Rob Dean (ex-Japan). Joey Burnham appeared as session drummer on Illustrated Man's 1984 self-titled mini-album for EMI. Chris Burnham returned to Australia and joined **Chris Bailey's Saints** with whom he stayed until late 1984 (appearing on the album *A Little Madness to Be Free* and the single 'Ghost Ship'). Following that, he and Joey formed This is This with Stephen Mather (bass; ex-**Lipstick Killers**) and then joined R&B band Stupidity.

Supernaut albums: *Supernaut* (Polydor, 1976), *I Like It Both Ways* (compilation, Shock, 1995); ***Nauts album:*** *The Nauts* (Wizard, 1979).

Swanee

Style: *Rock*

Journeyman singer/drummer John 'Swanee' Swan (b. 1952) was famous for his raucous rock voice and his dogged determination to succeed in the face of overwhelming odds. Swanee eventually became a popular live performer, scoring a number of mainstream hit singles. Swanee was born in Glasgow, Scotland. His family emigrated to Australia when he was eight years old. The family (including younger brother James, aka **Jimmy Barnes**) settled in the tough migrant working-class suburb of Elizabeth in Adelaide, South Australia. Swanee joined the army in 1969, but was discharged two years later. He joined his first band, Adelaide blues outfit Hard Time Killing Floor, as drummer in 1971.

He got his first break when he joined the legendary **Fraternity** as replacement singer for the departing Bon Scott. Swanee switched to drums when his younger brother Jimmy joined as lead singer briefly in mid-1975. By that stage, **Fraternity** was on its last legs and Swanee left to join **Jim Keays'** Southern Cross as drummer. The line-up comprised Keays (ex-**Master's Apprentices**), Swanee, Mick Elliot (guitar; ex-**Sid Rumpo**) and Ron Robinson (bass). In November 1976, Swanee joined Sydney hard rock band **Feather** as singer with whom he remained for 18 months.

In November 1978, John Swan launched his own band under the name of Swanee. The original line-up comprised Swanee, Kelly Haese (lead guitar; ex-Karl Taylor's Huntress), Gary Norbis (piano, sax), Bill McMahon (bass) and Peter McFarlane (drums; ex-**Finch**). Swanee built-up a strong following around Sydney with a mix of Led Zeppelin and Bad Company covers, plus a clutch of confident, melodic hard rock songs like 'The Road Keeps Moving Sideways', 'Matthew' and 'Crazy Dreams'. Swanee signed to WEA and issued its debut single, 'Crazy Dreams'/'Johnny the Rocker', in August 1979. By early 1980, the line-up comprised Swan, Kelly, McFarlane, Bronte Wade (lead guitar; ex-Cunning Stunts), David Spell (piano; ex-Squeeze, **Ray Arnott's** Rude Dudes) and Peter Webb (bass; ex-Cunning Stunts). Kelly then left to join **Heaven**.

The new line-up of Swan, Wade, Webb, Jon Cooke (lead guitar; ex-Cunning Stunts, Gillian Eastoe and King Dog), Peter Kekel (keyboards; ex-Gillian Eastoe and King Dog), Greg Plimmer (drums; ex-Gillian Eastoe and King Dog) and Taya Verkuil (backing vocals) completed Swanee's debut album *Into the Night* (October 1980). Produced by Mark Moffatt, Mark Opitz and John Swan, the album yielded the singles 'Ol' Rosie'/'Late News' (September), 'Linda'/'Beware' (November) and 'Matthew'/'Crazy Dreams' (January 1981). Guest players on the album included **Tommy Emmanuel** (acoustic guitar), Tony Buchanan (sax), Buzz Bidstrup (backing vocals) and **Jimmy Barnes** (backing vocals). None of the records charted in the national Top 40, although Swanee continued to draw capacity crowds around the pub circuit.

1981 saw the commercial breakthrough for which Swanee had worked so hard the previous two and a half years. His cover of Tim Hardin's 'If I Were a Carpenter'/'Play' (July 1981) peaked at #5 on the national singles chart. 'Samantha'/'Ginny' (November 1981) was not successful, but 'Temporary Heartache'/'I'll Come Home' (April 1982) reached #18. 'Temporary Heartache' came from Swanee's second album, *This Time It's Different* (May 1982). The album peaked at #20 on the national chart, while its second single, 'Lady What's Your Name?'/'I was Lonely' (July) reached #13. Swanee, Kekel, Plimmer and Verkuil had recorded the album with assistance from a string of top session players like Emmanuel (acoustic guitar), Kirk Lorange (guitar; ex-**Richard Clapton** Band), **Renée Geyer** (backing vocals), Clive Harrison (bass), Steve Hopes (drums), Mark Kennedy (drums; ex-Spectrum, **Ayers Rock**, **Marcia Hines** Band) and Englishman David Skinner (keyboards), who also produced the album.

The Swanee line-up at the time of the album's release comprised Swanee, Kekel, Plimmer and Verkuil, plus newcomers Mark Evans (bass; ex-**AC/DC**, **Finch**) and Dennis Wilson (lead guitar; ex-**Kahvas Jute**, **Chariot**, Dennis Wilson Band). Peter Northcote (sax), Mick Thornton (trombone) and Wayne Emery (sax) were added for live shows. By the end of 1982, the Swanee line-up consisted of Swanee, Verkuil, Evans, Harvey James (lead guitar; ex-**Mississippi**, **Ariel**, **Sherbet**), Stuart Fraser (guitar; ex-**Feather**) and John Lalor (drums; ex-Dallimore). That line-up recorded the single 'Sail Away'/ 'Change Your Mind' (July 1983). The next line-up of Swanee, Verkuil, Dennis Wilson, Mark Tinson (guitar; ex-**Rabbit**, Heroes), Coz Russo (keyboards; ex-**Richard Clapton** Band), John Strangio (bass; ex-**Dingoes**, **Chariot**, **Rockwell T. James** and the Rhythm Aces) and Phil Screen (drums; ex-**Rabbit**, Heroes), recorded the album *Ready for Action! Live in the Snow* which came out in October 1983. The album yielded the single 'Motor Down'/'Tin Soldier' (December 1983). Swanee's first single for 1984, 'I'm Ready'/'Carrie Ann', came out in March. He wrapped up his deal with WEA by issuing the compilation album *Days Gone By* (October 1984).

In 1985 he signed a new deal with RCA which resulted in the *Bushido* album (April) and its singles 'You Oughta Know by Now'/'Country Boys' (March) and 'Turn Away'/'Gone for Me' (May). *Bushido* was essentially a John Swan solo album. Musical backing on the album was provided by session players: guitarists Mark Tinson, Dennis Wilson, Ken Francis and **Tommy Emmanuel**; bass players Andy Sidari, Gus Fenwick and Clive Harrison; drummers Buzz Bidstrup, Mark Kennedy, Mark Meyers, John Swan himself and Joe Tattersall; keyboard players Rick Mellick, Ashley Irwin and Jamie McKinley; backing vocalists Linda Barnes, Shauna Jensen, Bernie Lynch, **Renée Geyer**, Jon Stevens, Venetta Fields, Shirley Williams, Maggie McKinney and Mark Williams.

In 1985, John Swan also issued his first single under that name, 'It Could Have Been You'/ 'Theme from an Indecent Obsession' (July). He signed to Mushroom and issued two more John Swan singles 'Say You'll Do Something'/'Letter to Home' (October 1985) and 'Angel'/Back Home' (July 1986). His touring band comprised Bruno Renzella (guitar; ex-**Heaven**), John MacKay (keyboards), Gus Fenwick (bass; ex-**Healing Force**, **Band of Talabene**) and Peter Heckenberg (drums; ex-Boss). In early 1987, Swan joined popular covers band **The Party Boys**. His arrival ushered in the band's most successful phase which included a #1 hit single with a cover of John Kongas' 'He's Gonna Step On You Again' (June 1987).

Just as the band's success was peaking, Swan left to work on a feature film called *Chase the Moon* (which did not eventuate). He returned for **The Party Boys'** support to **AC/DC**'s February 1988 Australian tour. He left again to revive his solo career which resulted in the single 'Lucille' for Mushroom during 1989. The John Swan Band at that stage comprised John Jurkovic (guitar), Ben Little (guitar), Mark Evans (bass; by then ex-**Heaven**) and Mick O'Shea (drums). Swanee issued a new single, 'Blood is Thicker than Water', in June 1990.

Albums: *Into the Night* (WEA, 1980), *This Time It's Different* (WEA, 1982), *Ready for Action! Live in the Snow* (WEA, 1983), *Days Gone By: The Best of Swanee* (WEA, 1984), *Bushido* (RCA, 1985).

Sweet Jayne

Formed: *1977*
Style: *Heavy rock*
Original line-up: *Chris Scheri (vocals, flute), Cris Bonacci (lead guitar; ex-Vixen), Sally Zylstra (bass), Robyn Clarke (drums)*

Melbourne band Sweet Jayne was the very first all-girl heavy metal outfit to gain widespread attention in Australia. Sweet Jayne was known for its note-perfect covers of material by Thin Lizzy, Heart, Led Zeppelin, Joe Walsh and Black Sabbath, as well as an extensive repertoire of fine, original songs in the same vein.

Teenage guitar prodigy Cris Bonacci formed Sweet Jayne in early 1977. Bonacci had played with Vixen, which comprised Robyn Youlten (vocals, lead guitar) Glenda Hunt (bass) and Wendy Hemmings (drums). Youlten had pioneered the concept of all-girl rock bands in Australia when she formed Screeming Heep in 1973 with Hemmings, Angie Adams (guitar, vocals) and Frances Mills (bass). Youlten sang with the nascent Sweet Jayne but left before the band played any gigs. Chris Scheri became Sweet Jayne's lead singer and flute player, and the band made an impression around Melbourne by taking out first place in the 1978 Yamaha/3XY Battle of the Bands competition.

Sweet Jayne issued the five-track, 7-inch *Sweet Jayne* EP which appeared in January 1980. The tracks were 'Ambiguous Girl', 'Omniscience'/'Some People', 'State of Mind' and 'Crushed and Crazy'. The band described its sound as 'sweet and heavy rock' and the EP certainly highlighted Bonacci's crunching guitar riffs offset by Scheri's melodic vocals and lilting flute lines. The band also sold the 14-track cassette *Sweet Jayne (The T.C.S. Tapes)* (1978) and the nine-track cassette *The Belgrave Tapes* (1980) at gigs. Not long after the EP appeared, Sweet Jayne became Scheri, Bonacci, Brendan O'Shea (bass) and John Zaffarese (drums). The new line-up recorded the single 'Icarus'/'State of Mind', which appeared on the Cleopatra label in October 1981. Fab Versace then replaced Zaffarese on drums, and Billy George in turn replaced Versace in 1982.

Always a popular live attraction on the Australian pub circuit, Sweet Jayne nevertheless broke up in January 1983. Scheri and Bonacci had received an invitation from acclaimed British musician Mike Oldfield to work with him in the UK. They travelled to the UK but worked with Oldfield only briefly. Scheri and Bonacci recorded a single 'Pictures on the Wall'/'Heartbeat', which appeared as a Chris Scheri solo release on the Possum label in 1986. By that stage, Scheri had returned to Melbourne and she set up Studio Seven. She then issued the cassingle 'Guardian Angel'/'Eloquent Eyes' in 1987. Bonacci joined all-girl outfit She before scoring a gig in late 1984 with Britain's most famous all-girl heavy metal band, Girlschool.

Bonacci remained with Girlschool until 1989, appearing on the albums *Running Wild* (1985), *Nightmare at Maple Cross* (1986) and *Take a Bite* (1988), plus singles like the band's cover of Gary Glitter's 'I'm the Leader of the Gang (I am)' (May 1986). Since leaving Girlschool, Bonacci has become a high-profile guitarist for the likes of Bryan Ferry, **Jason Donovan**, Robert Plant and Samantha Fox.

In the meantime, Bonacci's partner in Vixen, Robyn Youlten, had assembled Butterfly which comprised Josie Jason (guitar, vocals), Ackie Helmer (bass), and Michelle Brown (drums). Jackie Morrison replaced Brown on drums at the end of 1979. The band played original material in the vein of Led Zeppelin and Jimi Hendrix. The band issued an independent single, 'Strange Kind of Loving'/'Ulterior Motives' (November 1980), on its own Butterfly label. Towards the end of the band's life, Youlten switched to bass, and ex-Sweet Jayne member Robyn Clarke took over on drums to be followed by Colin Trott.

In 1983, Youlten and Jason formed Final Outcome with Peter Paolini (bass) and another ex-Sweet Jayne alumnus, John Zaffarese (drums). Final Outcome issued the cassette album *Live at the Jam Tin* in 1985. Tim Campbell took over from Paolini on bass and Greg Aldridge replaced Zaffarese on drums, after which Final Outcome went their separate ways. Josie Jason went on to play with

Dirty Rats and **Jimi 'The Human'** and Spectre 7 before forming her own group, popular Melbourne hard rock band Josie Jason and the Argonauts. Youlten later teamed up with erstwhile Sweet Jayne singer Chris Scheri in the Wild Orchids, playing rock, folk and blues; the duo issued the *Past All the Edges* album on the Dreamful Ease label in 1996.

Wild Orchids album: *Past All the Edges* (Dreamful Ease, 1996).

Swirl

Formed: *1991*
Style: *Indie guitar pop*
Original line-up: *Ben Aylward (guitar, vocals), Nicola Schultz (bass, vocals), David Lord (drums)*

Sydney band Swirl was one of the leading lights, along with contemporaries **Sidewinder**, **Smudge**, **Godstar**, **The Daisygrinders**, Fragile and SPDFGH, on Nic Dalton's Half a Cow label. A very prolific outfit, Swirl's brand of UK-inspired, noisy guitar pop stamped the band as a popular drawcard on the alternative scene.

Swirl's first appearance on record was the track 'Burning Castles' on Half a Cow's 1991 four-track, 7-inch vinyl EP compilation *Slice* (alongside **Smudge**, Jupiter and Studley Lush and his Teeny-boppers from Hell). 'Burning Castles' later appeared on HAC's expanded version of *Slice*, the compilation album *Slice Two* (November 1992). Swirl also contributed a cover of Klaatu's 'Calling Occupants' to the HAC 7-inch, giveaway compilation single alongside **Godstar** and **Smudge**. In quick succession, Swirl issued the 12-inch vinyl EP 'People I Know' (December 1991), the album *Aurora* (May 1992), the CD single 'Tears' (October) and the CD EP 'Touch' (May 1993). The band supported UK visitors My Bloody Valentine and Ride on their respective Australian tours.

Swirl's second album, *The Last Unicorn* (April 1995), produced the CD EP *The Last Unicorn* ('Night of the Unicorn') (July). The songs on *The Last Unicorn* album ranged from soft, jangly moments ('Strangelands') to bursts of sonic guitar squalls ('Dark Star', 'Last of the Unicorns'). The US-based Dirt label issued the CD EP 'Fade Away' and the compilation *Touch* for the American market. Swirl issued a new CD EP, 'On My Own', in November 1996 and commenced work on a third album.

Albums: *Aurora* (Half a Cow, 1992), *The Last Unicorn* (Half a Cow/Mercury, 1995).

Swoop

Formed: *1991*
Style: *Funk, rap, soul*
Original line-up: *Roland P. Kapferer (vocals), Joshua Beagley (guitar, keyboards)*

Sydney-based band Swoop was one of a number of young outfits that emerged during the early 1990s exploring diverse musical avenues on the traditional Australian pub-rock scene: **d.i.g.**'s acid jazz, **Juice**'s hard funk, **Def FX**'s techno-metal, **Skunkhour**'s funk'n'rap and **Caligula**'s techno-pop. Swoop started out as a funk and rap duo based around Adelaide musicians Roland P. Kapferer and Joshua Beagley.

With the recruitment of a full band, Swoop's sound began to take on a soulful, funky groove with a rock backing. Swoop issued two independent records in 1992 on the Freakzone label, the 12-inch EP *Positivity's Groove* (May) and the single 'Jelly Funk' (August). By that stage, Fiona Ta'akimoeaka had joined as lead vocalist. Her crystal-clear, tuneful vocals lifted the band's appeal considerably. Swoop's second single, 'Everybody Loves The Sunshine' (December), featured relaxed and catchy melodies.

Swoop's debut, full-length album *Thriller* (October 1993) produced the CD single 'Do It' (August) and the CD EP *Raw Funk Power* ('Everything I Do from Now on is Going to Be Funky') (November). 'Do It' became a surprise hit in Japan when it topped the disco charts. Swoop undertook a tour of Japan in early 1995. The band appeared on the compilation *Undertones Vol. 1* (1993), a collection of Australian soul, funk and jazz tracks from U.T.E., Banana, Wicked Beats, Step It Up, Fonké Knomaads, Urban Poets and the Carl Orr Band.

At the end of 1994, Swoop signed to Mushroom Records. The deal resulted in the album *The Woxo Principle*, which came out in November 1995. The album gave rise to the CD EPs 'Neighbourhood Freak' (November 1994), 'Rock Dog' (July 1995) and the super cool'n'funky 'Apple Eyes' (November). In January 1996, 'Apple Eyes' reached the national mainstream Top 10 (peaking at #9). The song also logged #32 on the 1995 Triple J Hottest 100 list. The Swoop line-up on *The Woxo Principle* was Kapferer, Beagley, Ta'akimoeaka, Breadman St Ledger III (keyboards), Alex 'Gob' Hewettson (bass), Chris O'Brien (drums) and Armando Gomez (percussion). Swoop issued a new CD single in September 1996, a cover of the Captain and Tennille's 1970s hit 'Do that to Me (One More Time)'.

Albums: *Thriller* (Freakzone, 1993), *The Woxo Principle* (Mushroom/Festival, 1995).

Swordfish

Formed: *1990*
Style: *Rock, funk*
Original line-up: *James Dixon (vocals, guitar, keyboards), Peter Hickson (guitar, keyboards), Peter Marley (bass, vocals), Rob Hodgson (drums)*

Sydney-based quartet Swordfish drew inspiration from such disparate sources as Jimi Hendrix, Neil Young, The Beatles, 1960s psychedelia and 1970s funk to arrive at a suitably eccentric, yet energetic, accessible and groove-based rock hybrid. The band issued its debut single, 'Wrap'/'Let It Be Me', on the independent Fishface label not long after formation.

In 1991, Swordfish signed to the Volition label (home to the likes of **Falling Joys, Severed Heads** and **Scattered Order**) for the mini-album *Paralytic.* **Ian 'Ollie' Olsen** (Third Eye, **Max Q**) and Tony Cohen produced the band's debut album, *Strange Tractor* (November 1992), which yielded two CD singles, the funky pop 'Lucy' (September) and the conga-driven jungle stomp 'Missing Factor' (December), plus the CD EP 'Hey Chicken' (July). Swordfish issued one more CD EP, 'Genii' (March 1994), before a car accident in June, while the band was on tour, claimed the life of drummer Rob Hodgson.

James Dixon re-emerged in early 1996 with his low-key, limited edition solo album *Pure Dope.* The album was given away at Dixon's solo gigs and sold on mail order. With his new, eclectic backing outfit, Supagroup, Dixon signed to Mushroom's development label Infectious. Infectious issued Supagroup's CD EP/10-inch vinyl EP 'Creamy Cruiser' (July 1996). A new CD EP, 'Warm is in', came out in March 1997. As well as Dixon, Supagroup comprised another ex-Swordfish alumnus, Peter Marley (bass), with guests like Greg Wales (**Verys**), Tom Jackman (Ricaine), Chris Cobb (**Drop City**), Dave Ashton (Trout Fishing in Quebec) and Ian Williams (**Rail**) helping out on drums. Dixon co-produced **Drop City's** *This Heavenly Machine* in collaboration with Greg Wales.

Albums: *Paralytic* (mini-album, Volition, 1991), *Strange Tractor* (Volition, 1992).

T

Tactics

Formed: *1977*
Style: *Post-punk pop*
Original line-up: *David Studdert (lead vocals, rhythm guitar), Angus Douglas (lead guitar), Geoff Marsh (bass, vocals), Robert Whittle (drums)*

The small new wave scene centred around Canberra during the late 1970s gave rise to a number of bands like Young Docteurs, The Naturals, No Concept, Quintrex Bop, The Word and the most unconventional and adventurous of the lot, Tactics. Although not punk in the traditional sense, Tactics' music was closer in spirit to the art-punk of the likes of New York band Talking Heads, and UK outfits like Wire and Gang Of Four.

The band's hyperkinetic sound was unlike anything heard in Australia at the time. Writer Clinton Walker described it as 'psychedelic/reggae influenced post-punk pop', which was as close as anyone got to an accurate description. Singer David Studdert's spiky 'strangled cat' vocal style was definitely unusual. He had formed the band in 1977, and its quirky, embryonic sound met with virtual indifference in Canberra. Tactics moved to Sydney in September 1978 (at the invitation of **The Thought Criminals**) and built an inner-city cult following. Ingrid Spielman joined on piano.

The band's early records, the 'Long Weekend' EP (on the band's own Folding Chair label, June 1979) and the single 'Hole in My Life'/'Outdoors' (on Doublethink, July 1980), suffered from poor sound quality and really only hinted at the band's potential. A much punchier, re-recorded version of 'Buried Country' (from 'Long Weekend') was included on the band's acclaimed debut album, *My Houdini*, on the GREEN label (issued February 1981). The album was full of frantic energy, scratchy guitars, uneasy melodies, challenging songs and astute lyrical observations. It produced the single 'Second Language'/'Long Story' (March 1981).

The band's second album, *Glebe* and its single 'Standing by the Window'/'Gold Watch' (November 1981) were departures from the earlier sound, featuring a stronger reggae/dub influence. The 1982 Tactics line-up comprised Studdert, Douglas, Marsh, Duncan McKenzie (keyboards) and Michael Farmer (drums). *The Bones of Barry Harrison* album (August 1982) comprised live cuts from 1979 to 1982, but the overall effect was lessened due to the low-fi sound on offer. Studdert broke the band up in 1983, but re-emerged a year later with a new line-up comprising Angus Douglas, Nicky Baruch (vocals, percussion, flute), Snajik (bass) and Tony Donohue (drums; ex-Same). That line-up issued the single 'Fat Man'/'Shark Bed Rally' (July 1985) on the Waterfront label.

The November 1986 album *Blue and White Future Whale* produced the single 'Coat Tails'/'Committee of Love'. By the time Tactics entered the studio in 1989 to record their fifth album, the line-up comprised Studdert, Snajik, Gary Manley (guitar, piano) and Malcolm MacCallum (drums, keyboards), with **Go-Between** Amanda Brown and Robert (surname not known) guesting on violin and backing vocals, and trumpet respectively. *The Great Gusto* (November 1989) was another ambitious release, but it sank without a trace. It produced the singles 'Coalface'/'Birthday Girl', 'Know it All' (October) and 'Turn' (March 1990).

Studdert laid Tactics to rest in 1990 and flew to the UK at the invitation of now-defunct English independent label Red Flame (which had issued albums by **The Moodists** and **Laughing Clowns**). The Red Flame deal fell through, and Studdert played with a number of bands on the London scene. He eventually formed Dave Studdert's Mumbo Jumbo with Adam Blake (guitars), Louis Vause (piano, organ; ex-**Dave Graney** with the Coral Snakes), Louise Elliot (sax, flute; ex-**Laughing Clowns**), Paul Jayashina (trumpet), Chris Lee (trumpet), Paul Pember (bass) and Chris Wyles (drums). Mumbo Jumbo issued its debut CD EP, *The Dead Man's Hat*, in late 1994. Studdert followed that up with the *Post Hypnotic Suggestion* album and the 'Addicted Police Dog' CD EP in October 1996. Both releases featured a blend of jazz, reggae, rock and psychedelia which was ironic and driven, yet funky, accessible, intelligent and entertaining. The band undertook a brief tour of Australia in November, which also coincided with the release of the Tactics anthology *The History of the Sky*.

Tactics albums: *My Houdini* (GREEN, 1981), *Glebe* (GREEN, 1982), *The Bones Of Barry Harrison* (GREEN, 1982), *Blue and White Future Whale* (Folding Chair, 1986), *The Great Gusto* (Regular/Festival, 1990), *The History of the Sky* (compilation, Folding Chair/PolyGram, 1996); ***Dave Studdert's Mumbo Jumbo album:*** *Post Hypnotic Suggestion* (Folding Chair/PolyGram, 1996).

Tall Tales & True

Formed: *1983*
Style: *Rock, folk*
Original line-up: *Matthew de la Hunty (vocals, guitar), Paul Miskin (bass), Dave Rashleigh (drums)*

Highly touted three-piece Tall Tales & True grew out of Perth-born musician Matthew de la Hunty's desire to tackle a broad spectrum of musical styles and arrangements. His earliest influences ranged from Bob Dylan, The Beatles and The Rolling Stones, right through to late-1970s punk/new wave bands like Sex Pistols, Siouxsie and the Banshees and The Cure. Also, experiencing Perth bands like **The Triffids**, **Scientists** and **The Victims** first hand provided the inspiration for de la Hunty to form his own band.

He travelled to Sydney and formed Tall Tales & True in 1983. The band became a regular attraction on the inner-city circuit, but did not enter the studio until late 1985. Engineer/producer Nick Mainsbridge worked with the band on its debut, mini-album *Tall Tales & True* (on the Survival label), which produced the single 'Wasted Life'/'Good Heart Gone Bad' (August 1986). Tall Tales & True issued two four-track 12-inch EPs on Survival, 'Up Our Street' (1987) and 'You've Got Your Troubles' (1988), before coming to the attention of fledgling independent label rooArt.

Tall Tales & True contributed a remixed version of 'You've Got Your Troubles' to rooArt's inaugural *Youngblood* compilation (September 1988), alongside material from **The Trilobites**, **Martha's Vineyard**, **Crash Politics**, **Hipslingers**, **The Hummingbirds**, Violet Town and others. That led to a full recording contract which resulted in the *Shiver* album (May 1989). Again produced by Nick Mainsbridge, the album highlighted the dramatic sweep of de la Hunty's songwriting and his earnest vocal delivery. *Shiver* produced the singles 'Trust'/'Heaven Knows' (April 1989) and 'Hold on'/'Lullaby Number 1' (June). The 12-inch version of 'Trust' added a third track, 'Loser's Game', while likewise the 'Hold On' 12-inch added 'Love is Gone'. Tall Tales & True's debut rooArt release, however, was the 1988 promotional split single 'You've Got Your Troubles', which the band shared with **The Trilobites'** 'All Hail the New Right'.

Two years later, following extensive touring locally and overseas, Tall Tales & True returned with the powerful EP 'Superstition Highway' (April 1991). **Triffids** member David McComb contributed to the blustering title track. The band also added Vanessa Lucas on violin around that time. The band embarked on the Trilogy tour with rooArt labelmates **The Hummingbirds** and Canadian band The Pursuit of Happiness. Tall Tales & True issued two new singles in the second-half of 1991, 'Lifeboat' and 'Summer of Love', the second of which reached #51 on the national chart. Both tracks were lifted from the band's second album, *Revenge* (May 1992). *Revenge* featured tracks recorded with long-time producer Mainsbridge in Sydney and London. Former **Triffids** violin player Rob McComb contributed to the London sessions, as well as touring with the band. The album gave rise to two more singles, 'Watching the Wind Blow' (May) and 'Looking for a Place' (October), after which the band slipped from view for another two years.

Recorded in a Sydney warehouse in mid-1994 with Mainsbridge, the album *Tilt* featured the band revisiting its garage-band roots with a noisy, ragged edge to proceedings. *Tilt* produced two CD EPs, 'You Sleep I'll Drive' (October 1994) and 'Moonshine' (January 1995).

Albums: *Tall Tales & True* (mini-album, Survival, 1986), *Shiver* (rooArt/PolyGram, 1989), *Revenge* (rooArt/Warner, 1992), *Tilt* (rooArt/Warner, 1995).

Tamam Shud

Formed: *1968*
Style: *Progressive rock*
Original line-up: *Lindsay Bjerre (vocals, guitar; ex-Strangers, Sunsets), Alex 'Zac' Zytnik (lead guitar; ex-Four Strangers, Strangers, Sunsets), Peter Barron (bass), Dannie Davidson (drums; ex-Four Strangers, Strangers, Sunsets)*

Sydney band Tamam Shud was one of the first local bands to embrace the late 1960s psychedelic sounds of Cream, The Jimi Hendrix Experience, Pink Floyd, Eric Burdon and The (New) Animals, plus the San Francisco stylings of The Grateful Dead and their ilk. As an outgrowth of the acid-rock movement, Tamam Shud was able to translate the music into a uniquely Australian context. Tamam Shud became inextricably linked with the surfing fraternity, with audiences seemingly transfixed by the band's enveloping acid-surf progressive rock.

In the Persian language, the term 'tamam shud' simply means 'the very end'. Lindsay Bjerre took the name from eleventh century Persian poet Omar Khayyám's book *The Rubáiyát.* As Glenn A. Baker has suggested, it would not be an exaggeration to describe Tamam Shud as the **Midnight Oil** of its day. Bjerre formed the Shud around an aura of social and musical credibility, the band quickly commanding a loyal following on the concert circuit.

The roots of Tamam Shud go back to Newcastle (NSW) instrumental combo The Four Strangers which comprised teenagers Alex 'Zac' Zytnik (lead guitar), Gary Johns (rhythm guitar), Eric Connell (bass) and Dannie Davidson (drums). The band cut one highly regarded surf instrumental single for Astor, 'The Rip'/'Pearl Diver', in 1964 before Lindsay Bjerre replaced Johns at the end of the year. With a name change to The Strangers, Bjerre steered the band in a more strident Stones/R&B direction. The Strangers issued the gritty R&B single 'Sad and Lonely'/'You'll Be Mine' on Festival in 1965. Reissue specialists Raven later included 'Sad and Lonely' on the seminal collection of Australian 1960s garage-punk artefacts *Ugly Things* (1980). At the end of 1965, The Strangers became The Sunsets. With regular trips to Sydney to play Surf City, the Star Club and the Sunset discotheque (alongside the likes of **Billy Thorpe** and the Aztecs, **Ray Brown and the Whispers** and **Max Merritt and the Meteors**), The Sunsets drew a strong following.

The Sunsets issued two singles on Lee Gordon's Leedon label, 'Bye Bye Goodbye'/'It's the End' (October 1965) and 'When I Found You'/ 'Don't Get Around Anymore' (March 1966), three singles on Festival, 'A Life in the Sun Theme'/ 'Windansea' (Sydney #18 in January 1967), 'Love's Face'/'I Want Love' (June) and 'The Hot Generation'/'That is What It is All About' (August), plus an EP on Festival, 'A Life in the Sun'. 'A Life in the Sun' and the thumping, R&B-fuelled rocker 'The Hot Generation' appeared on the soundtracks to the surfing films of the same names. Raven also included 'I Want Love' on *Ugly Things.* Peter Barron replaced Eric Connell in late 1967. With the advent of acid-rock, The Sunsets' music changed almost overnight with the band moving in a heavier direction. Tamam Shud emerged from the ashes of The Sunsets in early 1968. The band's debut show as Tamam Shud was at the Intermedia Circus in Sydney.

At the end of the year, Tamam Shud recorded its debut album, *Evolution.* Recorded in two and a half hours on primitive equipment, it was nevertheless one of the first wholly original rock albums produced in Australia. Film-maker Paul Witzig financed the album session in return for being able to use four tracks on the soundtrack to his surfing film of the same name. The album was leased to CBS, and its popularity resulted in the band signing to Warner Brothers in 1970. *Evolution* produced the single 'Lady Sunshine'/'Evolution' (also issued on CBS). Raven included 'Lady Sunshine' on the excellent *Golden Miles Australian Progressive Rock 1969–1974* compilation (1994).

With the album out, Tamam Shud spearheaded Australia's burgeoning progressive rock movement, alongside the likes of **Tully**, **Levi Smith's Clefs**, **Jeff St John's** Copperwine, **Chain** and **Spectrum**. Zytnik left the band at the end of 1969 to be replaced by 16-year-old guitar prodigy **Tim Gaze** (ex-Stonehenge). Zytnik went on to work with **Graham Lowndes'** band Bootleg and **Blackfeather**. With Gaze on board, Tamam Shud recorded its second album, *Goolutionites and the Real People.* Issued in October 1970, *Goolutionites* is the band's masterpiece, an ambitious concept suite, a carefully crafted song cycle of cosmic enlightenment and cascading acid-rock. The Goolutionites were the polluters of the world, and the album's precursory environmental message remains pertinent in the 1990s. The album yielded the single 'Stand in the Sunlight'/'I Love You All' (November 1970). Before the album's release, both Davidson and Gaze left Tamam Shud to join new band **Kahvas Jute**. Gaze only stayed long enough to appear on **Kahvas Jute**'s album *Wide Open*, before returning to the Shud fold in October.

While Gaze was absent, Bjerre and Barron recruited jazz players Kevin Stephenson (sax, flute, clarinet) and Kevin Sinnott (drums). They left when Gaze returned, and the new Shud line-up was completed by 18-year-old Nigel Macara (drums; ex-Stonehenge, Bootleg). At the end of the year, conga player Larry Duryea (aka Larry Taylor; ex-**Heart 'n' Soul**) joined, and jazz pianist Bobby Gebert appeared as an auxiliary player. Tamam Shud toured regularly throughout 1971, and added Richard Lockwood (sax, flute, clarinet; ex-**Tully**) towards the end of the year. The band issued a new single, 'Got a Feeling'/'My Father Told Me' (January 1972), on Warner, and then contributed three tracks to the Various Artists *Morning of the Earth* soundtrack.

Produced by **G. Wayne Thomas**, the tracks were 'First Things First', 'Bali Waters' and the propulsive 'Sea the Swells' (one of the best songs the Shud ever recorded). **Carson** singer **Broderick Smith** contributed lead vocals to the delicate, pastoral 'First Things First'. *Morning of the Earth* was best known for Thomas's hit single 'Open Up Your Heart'. 'Bali Waters' was also combined with the single cuts 'Got a Feeling' and 'My Father Told Me' for the rare 'Bali Waters' EP. The Shud continued to tour with the likes of **MacKenzie Theory**, **Spectrum**, **Carson**, **Chain**, **Friends** and **Lizard**, but Bjerre broke up the band in August 1972. He wanted to explore a softer country-rock mode, and duly formed Albatross with Barron. Lindsay Bjerre re-emerged in the late 1970s with the romantic **Bjerre** persona and the hit single 'She Taught Me How to Love Again'.

Gaze and Macara formed Miss Universe with New Zealand musicians Phillip Pritchard (guitar; ex-Highway) and George Limbidis (bass; ex-Highway). In early 1973, Gaze and Macara briefly linked up with **Ross Wilson** (ex-**Daddy Cool**) in a new band which never got off the ground (it eventually became **Mighty Kong**). Gaze and Macara then formed a short-lived, three-piece power trio with Steve Hogg (bass; ex-**Bakery**) before abandoning that in April to join Mike Rudd's post-**Spectrum** outfit **Ariel**. Gaze left **Ariel** in April 1974; he went on to work with **Stevie Wright** and the All Stars, Dayride, Tim Gaze Rock Ensemble, Tim Gaze Band, **Rose Tattoo**, **Gyan**, The Sultans, the **Peter Wells** Band and **The Bushwackers**. Barron played with The Bilgola Bop Band for most of the 1970s. Macara toured with **Ariel** and **Air Supply** before opening a record store.

In March 1993, Tamam Shud re-formed with Bjerre, Gaze, Barron and Macara. The band signed to Polydor and issued the CD single 'Stay'/'Election Day', 'The Fire' (June 1994). The funky 'Stay' caught the attention of the programmers at ABC national youth radio network Triple J and it became something of a radio hit. The *Permanent Culture* album followed in August, with a second CD single 'Shaking Out the Stones'/'What's Your Problem?' arriving in October. *Permanent Culture* was the sound of a revitalised Shud making its way in the 1990s. Excellent songs like 'Stay', 'Shaking Out the Stones', 'It's My Time' and 'Ain't No City' featured tough, simple, direct and energetic rock arrangements and playing. Polydor duly dropped Tamam Shud when the album failed to chart significantly. With touring commitments ceasing in April 1995, Tamam Shud broke up for a second time.

Albums: *Evolution* (CBS, 1969), *Goolutionites and the Real People* (Warner 1970), *Permanent Culture* (Polydor, 1994).

Taramis

Formed: *1985*
Style: *Heavy metal*
Original line-up: *Shane 'Joel' Southby (vocals), Craig Robertson (guitar), Danny Komorr (bass), Dave Browne (drums)*

Melbourne band Taramis was one of the first local groups to play a brand of 'progressive' heavy metal in the style of overseas acts like Iron Maiden, Rush, Queensryche, Manowar, Mercyful Fate and Fate's Warning. Another influence, though less apparent, was Yes. Taramis infused its esoteric music with an epic, mystical feel. Man-mountain frontman Joel Southby also possessed a booming rock voice which added an edge to the band's billowing, blustering song arrangements.

Taramis began life in 1983 as an Iron Maiden/Manowar covers band called Prowler (a name derived from the opening track on the debut Iron Maiden album). The line-up comprised Southby, Craig Robertson, Danny Komorr, Mick Lights (guitar) and Joe Cordina (drums). Andrew Rigo replaced Lights on guitar; Rigo's stay was brief. In 1985, Dave Browne replaced Cordina on drums. As the band began to add original material, the name change to Taramis (derived from the film *Conan the Destroyer*) came about. The band's contemporaries on the Melbourne heavy metal scene included the likes of **S.A.S.**, Fair Warning, New Religion, Blackjack, Ion Drive, Virgin Soldiers, Taipan, Nothing Sacred and Tyrus. Taramis recorded its debut album, *Queen of Thieves*, in late 1986. By the time the album appeared in August 1987, Evan Harris had replaced Komorr on bass. The band toured interstate and built-up a strong following. The band scored a licensing deal with US label Metal Blade for the release of *Queen of Thieves* in North America. The album came out there in mid-1988 with new cover artwork.

In early 1990, George Larin replaced Robertson on guitar. Larin's experience extended to stints with Melbourne bands New Religion and Nothing Sacred, as well as bands in the UK and Germany (one of which, Backwater, was an early contemporary of Kreator and Destruction). Larin immediately lent his more inventive and forceful playing style to the band's sound. The second Taramis album, *Stretch of the Imagination* finally appeared in April 1992. The album was licensed to the Rising Sun label for distribution in Europe and the USA. Taramis supported Brazilian thrash/hardcore band Sepultura at its Melbourne concert in July 1992. With overseas interest still bubbling underneath,

Taramis set its sights on Europe but eventually slipped from view.

Albums: *Queen of Thieves* (Metal for Melbourne, 1987), *Stretch of the Imagination* (Rising Sun, import only, 1992).

Taste

Formed: *1975*
Style: *Glam rock*
Original line-up: *Ken Murdoch (vocals, guitar, keyboards), Joey Amenta (lead guitar, vocals), Michael Gemini (bass), Virgil Donati (drums)*

Melbourne band Taste was an archetypal glam-rock outfit that hedged its bets by catering to pop fans and hard rock fans alike. On the one hand, Taste scored hit singles with commercial glam-pop singles, appeared on ***Countdown*** and played suburban dances to crowds of adoring teenage fans. On the other hand, the band filled out its albums with screaming hard rock songs (in the vein of Queen and the heavier side of The Sweet), and enjoyed a strong following on the pub-rock circuit. Musical stagnation eventually caused the band's break-up in late 1977.

Taste began life as Cloud Nine, which Ken Murdoch and Michael Gemini formed in 1970 while still at high school. Cloud Nine issued its debut single on Warner Brothers, 'Say Goodbye'/'Rock'n'Roll Highway', in 1973. Virgil Donati and Tony Faramond (vocals) joined in 1974 and the band signed to RCA. Cloud Nine issued the album *We're Good Friends, So Rock On* and the singles 'Take My Hand'/'Hi There' and Eddie Cochran's 'Summertime Blues'/'Little Darlin' on RCA. In 1975, Joey Amenta replaced Faramond and the band became known as Taste. At the end of the year, Taste signed to the Bootleg label. Taste's debut album, *Tickle Your Fancy* (July 1976), produced the singles 'Tickle Your Fancy'/'Rock And Roll Superstar' (February) and 'Degenerate Fool'/'Lone Ranger' (July). 'Tickle Your Fancy' reached #22 in Melbourne during June. 'Boys will Be Boys'/'Love Ya Babe' (November 1976) became the band's biggest chart hit when it peaked at #14 in Melbourne during January 1977.

The band's final single for Bootleg, 'A Little Romance'/'Same Old Story' (February 1977), reached #24 in April. At that stage, Taste signed a new deal with the Philips label which reissued 'A Little Romance' and then put out the *Knights of Love* album (August). The album also included 'Boys will Be Boys' and a third single, 'Rebecca'/'Teenage Anthem' (July). Taste played its last gigs during October 1977 as a three-piece (Amenta, Gemini, Donati). Ken Murdoch had left to join Melbourne boogie band Texas. Joey Amenta went on to **Redhouse**, the **Russell Morris** Band, the Darryl Cotton Band, **Wendy and the Rocketts**, **Dear Enemy** and **Uncanny X-Men** among others. Donati joined the Peter Cupples Band, Cosy Connection, The Cutters, Loose Change, The State and **Southern Sons**.

Texas evolved out of Fat Daddy which comprised Tony Catz (lead guitar, vocals), Max Vella (vocals, rhythm guitar, harmonica), Mick Stilo (bass, vocals) and Carl Stanley (drums). The members of Fat Daddy used the gimmick of stage costumes and troll masks until they had established their self-styled 'fat funky rock'n'roll' on the Melbourne pub circuit. Fat Daddy issued one single 'Roll Daddy Roll'/'Help Me' on the Bootleg label in July 1976. By the end of the year, Fat Daddy had evolved into Texas.

With the arrival of Murdoch, Texas was able to broaden its scope. Texas issued the singles 'Good Morning'/'Ain't No Place Like Home' (1978), 'I Wanna Dance with You'/'Life Ain't Meant to Be Easy' (June 1979) and 'I Won't Say No'/'Infatuation' (November), plus the live album *Real to Reel* (1979) on Festival's Infinity label. By 1980, Texas had evolved into The Torpedoes with a line-up of Murdoch, Vella and Stilo, plus newcomers Mark Smith (guitar) and Vic Lamnek (drums). Ian Langford replaced Lamnek in 1981, after which The Torpedoes broke up. Murdoch, Stilo and Smith formed Primal Tears with Gary McFarlane (keyboards; ex-**La Femme**) and Craig Waugh (drums). Murdoch went on to work the Melbourne club and pub circuit with numerous bands. Craig Waugh went on to **Uncanny X-Men** and **Horsehead**.

In the meantime, Tony Catz had formed pub outfit the Tony Catz Band which comprised Phil George (guitar, vocals), Tony Allan (bass, vocals) and Vince Leighton (drums). By 1986, the band was known as Wildcatz. In 1984, Max Vella formed his own band, Relax with Max, which became a popular attraction on the Melbourne pub rock circuit. The band had up to 40 members pass through its ranks by the early 1990s.

Cloud Nine album: *We're Good Friends, So Rock On* (RCA, 1974); ***Taste albums:*** *Tickle Your Fancy* (Bootleg, 1976), *Knights Of Love* (Philips/Phonogram, 1977); ***Texas album:*** *Real to Reel* (Festival/Infinity, 1979).

Matt Taylor

Style: *Blues*

Indefatigable Australian blues master Matt Taylor (b. 1948) has been spreading the blues gospel since the mid-1960s. Inspired by the original blues masters like John Lee Hooker, Robert Johnson, Elmore James, B.B. King, Howlin' Wolf, Muddy Waters and Willie Dixon, Taylor has been able to translate the traditional blues idiom into a uniquely Australian context. Born in Brisbane, Queensland, Taylor's first band, **Bay City Union**, is generally acknowledged, alongside Melbourne's **Adderley Smith Blues Band** and Sydneysiders **The Foreday Riders**, as one of the earliest traditional Chicago blues bands formed in Australia. Formed in March 1966, **Bay City Union** issued one single, 'Mo'reen'/'Mary Mary' (April 1968), on Festival before folding in July 1968 due to a lack of interest in blues bands at that time.

Taylor sang with **The Wild Cherries** for two weeks before forming The Horse with Stewie Stewart (guitar), Ian Robinson (drums; ex-Running Jumping Standing Still) and an unknown bass player. Tinsley Waterhouse also played drums in The Horse at one stage. Taylor also filled in as lead singer with **Cam-Pact** for a two-week tour of Sydney during early 1970, before joining Genesis in February. Genesis comprised Taylor, Les Stacpool (guitar; ex-**Chessmen**, **Merv Benton** and the Tamlas, **Levi Smith's Clefs**, **Rockwell T. James** and the Rhythm Aces, Browns, **Doug Parkinson** In Focus), Reno Tehei (guitar; ex-Compulsion, Luke's Walnut), John 'Yuk' Harrison (bass; ex-**Levi Smith's Clefs**, **Max Merritt and the Meteors**) and Laurie Pryor (drums; ex-**Twilights**, Luke's Walnut).

Billed as a 'New Blues Super Group', Genesis found success on the Melbourne discotheque/pub circuit. By the end of April 1970, both Tehei and Stacpool had left the band, to join **La De Das** and **Aesop's Fables** respectively. Tim Piper (ex-Chants R&B, Electric Heap, **Wild Cherries**, Savage Rose Blues Band, **Chain**) came in as the band's new guitarist. A month later, the Genesis line-up of Taylor, Piper and Harrison joined forces with **Carson** County Band members Sleepy Greg Lawrie (slide guitar) and John Capek (piano), plus Trevor Courtney (drums; ex-Chants R&B, **Cam-Pact**), to record a one-off single as The Meating. Issued on the Rebel label during August, the resultant single 'Bad Luck Feeling'/'Back Home' was a fine example of Australian hard blues.

In the meantime, **Ray Arnott** (ex-Chelsea Set, Browns, **Cam-Pact**, **Company Caine**) had replaced Pryor on drums during July 1970. Pryor went on to join **Healing Force**. Genesis toured until the end of August when Taylor received an invitation to join **Chain** in Brisbane. **Chain** enjoyed considerable success with the hit single 'Black and Blue'/'Lightning Ground' (March 1971) and the ground-breaking album *Toward the Blues* (September). Taylor has worked with **Chain** on and off since that time.

Taylor left **Chain** in October 1971 and retired from the music industry to live on a farm in Beechworth, Victoria for a year. In January 1973, Taylor made an appearance at the 1973 Sunbury festival backed by members of Mighty Mouse (**Phil Manning**, Barry Sullivan, Barry Harvey and Kevin Murphy). The nine-minute 'From Brisbane to Beechworth' appeared on Mushroom's triple live album set of the event *The Great Australian Rock Festival Sunbury 1973* (April 1973). Another live Taylor track, 'Roberta' (recorded June 1973), appeared on the Various Artists album *Garrison the Final Blow Unit 2*. He also appeared on **Chain's** 'Grab a Snatch and Hold It' from the same album.

Taylor recorded his debut solo album with help from Manning, Sullivan and Harvey, plus **Carson's** Sleepy Greg Lawrie. The sessions resulted in the album *Straight as a Die* and the single 'I Remember When I was Young'/'Krishna Loves You, Too' (September 1973) on the Mushroom label. The autobiographical 'I Remember When I was Young' became Mushroom's first Top 10 hit single in Melbourne. It had been recorded in an open paddock at Kingston Park Farm, just outside of Frankston, Victoria. To help promote the album (which reached #15 nationally), Taylor embarked on a tour with Mushroom labelmates **The Dingoes** and **Madder Lake**. Taylor performed at Sunbury 1974, and the live track 'We'll Never Do the Same Again' appeared on the Various Artists album *Highlights of Sunbury '74 Part 2* (May 1974).

Taylor's second album, *Music* (August 1974), produced the single 'Fair Dinkum Aussie Blues'/'Alone' (May). In August 1975, Taylor supported UK visitors Jethro Tull on that band's Australian tour, as well as supporting Willie Dixon throughout Australia and New Zealand. Taylor issued his third solo album, *Old, New, Intuitive*, and third single, 'Somebody Stole My Hair'/'Hound Dog Dust Bug', in September 1975, before retiring once again to a commune at Balingup, Western Australia. In 1977 Taylor formed **Western Flyer** with Brian Peacock (bass, vocals; ex-Librettos, Playboys, **Procession**, **Gerry and the Joy Band**). Taylor stayed with **Western Flyer** until August 1979. In Perth, he formed the Matt Taylor Band with ace slide guitarist **Dave Hole**, Paul Poole (bass; ex-Manteca) and Ric Whittle (drums; ex-Fatty Lumpkin, Manteca). For the next year, The Matt Taylor Band featuring Dave Hole toured the country to packed venues. At the height of new wave (when everything pre-1976 was considered passé), Taylor and Hole were playing some of the most electrifying blues music ever heard in Australia. The band had the potential to be as popular as **Chain**, but broke up before committing anything to vinyl.

In December 1980, Taylor and **Phil Manning** formed the Matt Taylor Phil Manning Band with Whittle and Roy Daniel (bass). The band issued the rare and excellent *Oz Blues* album (June 1981) and one single, 'Spring Hill'/'The Line'. Taylor and Manning supported US guitarist Roy Buchanan on his Australian tour, before breaking up in December 1981. In January 1982, the 'Black and Blue' version of **Chain** re-formed for the Mushroom Evolution Concert to celebrate the tenth anniversary of Mushroom Records. Taylor formed a new version of the Matt Taylor Band with Roy Daniel, **Chris Finnen** (lead guitar) and Paul Keane (drums). That line-up issued the album *Always Land on Your Feet* in February 1983. The Matt Taylor Band broke up in December 1983, which provided an opportune time for **Chain** to re-form with Taylor, **Phil Manning**, Barry Sullivan and Barry Harvey. Taylor kept various line-ups of **Chain** on the road until 1995.

In April 1991, Taylor and Manning joined forces with **Broderick Smith** (vocals, harmonica; ex-**Carson**, **Dingoes**, Big Combo), Mick 'The Reverend' O'Connor (organ; ex-Big Combo), Peter 'Brolga' Coughlan (bass; ex-**Goanna**) and Robert Dillion (drums; ex-**Mike Rudd and the Heaters**, **Broderick Smith** Band) as Blues Power for a national tour. The band played a mix of blues classics, plus material from each of the principal members' pasts. At the end of 1993, Taylor flew to Germany to tour with a band called The Booze Brothers. From there he played in the UK, then played a couple of shows in the USA supporting the John Heussenstenn Band and Walter Trout Band.

Taylor issued his fourth solo album, *Pyramids and Spirals*, in March 1995. Backing Taylor was a studio band comprising Wayne Burt (guitar; ex-**Jo Jo Zep and the Falcons**, **Giants**), Wayne Duncan (bass; ex-**Daddy Cool**), Mick O'Connor (organ), Gerry Hale (mandolin, fiddle) and Alex Burns (bottleneck guitar; ex-Orphans). Taylor has continued to work with various line-ups of **Chain**, as well as touring as a solo artist. He recorded his fifth solo album, *The Awakening*, in early 1997 for release later in the year.

Albums: *Straight as a Die* (Mushroom/Festival, 1973), *Music* (Mushroom/Festival, 1974), *Old, New, Intuitive* (Mushroom/Festival, 1975), *Pyramids and Spirals* (Newmarket, 1995), *The Awakening* (Forever, 1997); ***Matt Taylor Band album:*** *Always Land on Your Feet* (Forever/Monash, 1983); ***Matt Taylor Phil Manning Band album:*** *Oz Blues* (Full Moon/Astor, 1981).

Matt Taylor Phil Manning Band (*see* Matt Taylor; Phil Manning)

→↑→ (Tch Tch Tch) (*see* Philip Brophy)

Teen Queens

Formed: *1992*
Style: *Pop*
Original line-up: *Kelly Hoggart (vocals), Liza Watt (vocals), Roxanne Clarke (vocals)*

Kelly Hoggart, Liza Watt and Roxanne Clarke were three models/actresses/singers who appeared in the short-lived 1992 television series *Teen Queens*. The show (produced by the same company which developed popular soapie *E Street*) was set in the early 1960s. The girls win a talent competition in the country and move to the city in an attempt to make it as the new Supremes. To help promote the show, the girls issued a couple of CD singles on the *E Street*-affiliated Westside Records which sold very well. The trio's cover of The Ronettes' 'Be My Baby' reached #6 on the national chart during May 1992. The Four Tops' 'I Can't Help Myself' made #12 in August, followed by 'Love How You Love Me' at #16 during November. Teen Queens emerged at the same time as other dance pop acts like **Girlfriend**, **Dannii Minogue**, **Melissa**, **Peter Andre** and **Euphoria** were making an impact on the Australian charts. Teen Queens issued two full-length albums before slipping from view.

Albums: *Get Happy* (Westside/Phonogram, 1992), *Get Happy II* (Westside/Phonogram, 1993).

Teenage Radio Stars

Formed: *1977*
Style: *Glam punk*
Original line-up: **James Freud** *(lead vocals, guitar), Sean Kelly (guitar, vocals), Graeme Schiavello (bass), Peter Kidd (drums)*

School friends **James Freud** and Sean Kelly formed Melbourne punk band Teenage Radio Stars at the end of 1977. Originally known as Spred, the band made its live debut on New Year's Eve as part of the *Punk Gunk* festival (alongside The Boys Next Door, Babeez and →↑→) which was played out on a Carlton footpath. Spred became Teenage Radio

Stars in January 1978 and signed to the Suicide label (a Mushroom subsidiary through RCA).

With a new rhythm section of Pierre Voltaire (bass) and Dave Osbourne (drums), Teenage Radio Stars contributed two tracks to Suicide's punk compilation *Lethal Weapons* (alongside The Boys Next Door, Negatives, **JAB**, **X-Ray-Z**, etc.). The band also issued the single 'Wanna Be Ya Baby'/'Sweet Boredom' on Suicide (April 1978) and appeared on the ABC-TV pop show ***Countdown*** to promote its release. 'Wanna Be Ya Baby' was a straight rewrite of UK band The Vibrators' 'Baby Baby'. Along with The Boys Next Door, Teenage Radio Stars was one of the first punk/new wave bands to appear on ***Countdown***. The rhythm section changed again in May with Mick Prague (bass) and Mark Graeme (drums) taking over from Voltaire and Osbourne. Voltaire joined **JAB** and Osbourne joined pub-rock band Fastbuck. Outspoken vocalist Richard Grist, Wayne Sullivan (bass) and Vic Crump (guitar) completed the Fastbuck line-up. The band issued the rough-hewn mini-album *Drinking with the Boys* (Funny Melon, 1980), which boasted a blend of pub-rock and R&B. Latter-day Fastbuck members included Howard Croft (keyboards), Steve Donald (drums) and Dave Rowe (bass).

In the meantime, Freud began to steer Teenage Radio Stars in a glam punk direction (as much influenced by Marc Bolan and David Bowie as Sex Pistols and Iggy Pop). In August 1978, Tony Harvey replaced Kelly, who left to form **Models** with three ex-members of **JAB** (including Voltaire). Teenage Radio Stars became The Radio Stars, then James Freud's Ego, but by the end of 1978 Freud had decided to break-up the band. Freud formed a new band called **James Freud** and the Radio Stars which had a hit with 'Modern Girl' in June 1980. By the beginning of 1982, Freud had rejoined Sean Kelly in his band **Models**. Harvey played with Keith Lamb's band Airport in 1979.

Deniz Tek

Style: Rock

Ann Arbor (Michigan, USA) native Deniz Tek came to prominence in Australia as lead guitarist/visionary with Sydney cult legends **Radio Birdman**. Tek has not been resident in Australia for many years (he runs a medical practice in Billings, Montana), but through his tireless efforts over the years, he made a significant contribution to Australian rock'n'roll. Tek arrived in Australia during February 1972 to study medicine at Sydney University. In 1973 he formed TV Jones with Chris Jones (guitar), Giles Van der Werf (bass) and Gerry Jones (drums). Tek had experienced the Detroit rock scene (MC5, The Stooges, SRC, Alice Cooper, Rationals, etc., as well as Motown) first hand, and he brought those influences with him.

Deniz Tek

TV Jones was one of the first local bands to cover material by such rarefied US icons as The Stooges and Alice Cooper. One of the only other bands around at the time aware of that musical genre were The Rats, which comprised Rob Younger (vocals), Warwick Gilbert (guitar), Mick Lyne (guitar), Carl Rourke (bass) and Ron Keeley (drums). When TV Jones and The Rats both broke up in late 1974, it was an opportune time for various ex-members to join forces. Accordingly, **Radio Birdman** rose from the ashes in November 1974 with a line-up of Tek, Younger, Gilbert, Rourke, Keeley, plus Tek's fellow medical student Pip Hoyle (klavier). Birdman broke up in June 1978 following its ill-fated European tour.

In December 1978, Tek formed The Visitors with old Birdman cohorts Pip Hoyle, Ron Keeley and the band's Minister of Defence Mark Sisto (vocals). Steve Harris (bass; on loan from **The**

Passengers) completed the line-up. Because Tek had to return to the US in August 1979 to commence his internship at a Detroit hospital, The Visitors were designed as an 'event' with in-built obsolescence. Over a period of nine months, The Visitors played exactly 12 gigs around Sydney (with the likes of **The Lipstick Killers**, **The Hitmen**, **The Passengers**, **The Thought Criminals** and Rob Younger's new band The Other Side) and recorded an album's worth of material.

In September 1980, Sydney independent label Phantom issued the excellent four-track EP *The Visitors* which contained a couple of the band's classic stage numbers in the hard-driving 'Brother John' and the chilling 'Journey by Sledge'. Much later, John Needham (the subject of 'Brother John') at Citadel issued the album *The Visitors* (August 1985), which contained 11 tracks (including 'Journey by Sledge' and 'Brother John') the band had recorded at Palm Studios in July 1979. 'Euro Girls' appeared on Citadel's essential double compilation album *Take Everything Leave Nothing* (March 1988). Red Eye reissued the album on CD as *Visitation '79* (September 1994) with the previously unissued cut 'Skimp the Pimp' added.

In the meantime, Tek had returned to Australia to partake in the **New Race** national tour of April 1981. Once that tour was over, Tek joined the Angie Pepper Band, fronted by Tek's wife-to-be Angie Pepper (ex-**Passengers**). The Angie Pepper Band comprised Pepper, Tek, Steve Harris (keyboards), Clyde Bramley (bass; ex-**Hitmen**, Other Side, **New Christs**) and Ivor Hay (drums; ex-**Saints**), who was later replaced by Michael Charles (ex-Shy Impostors, **Lipstick Killers**). In early 1982, the band commenced work on an album but the sessions were never completed. Only two songs from the sessions ever saw the light of day when Citadel issued the evocative 'Frozen World'/'Why Tell Me?' as an Angie Pepper solo single (February 1984). Citadel also issued the Deniz Tek solo single '100 Fools'/'Alien Skies' (a previously unissued **Radio Birdman** track) (May 1984). 'Frozen World' and '100 Fools' appeared on *Take Everything Leave Nothing*.

Tek retired from rock music in 1982 to commence a ten-year career as a jet fighter pilot and squadron doctor with the US Navy. In 1989, French label Revenge Records issued a Deniz Tek album called *Orphan Tracks* and a single 'Destination Void'/'Steel Bridge' which came from demo sessions Tek had recorded circa 1980/1981. In early 1991, Tek contributed guitar to **Hitmen** DTK's album *Moronic Inferno*, and toured Australia as the band's guest guitarist at the end of the year. By that stage Tek had set up his medical practice in Montana. He also began working with a part-time band called Zero Hour.

Next he assembled a studio band, dubbed The World Shakers, to record his official debut album. The band comprised Chris 'Klondike' Masuak (guitar, keyboards; ex-**Radio Birdman**, **Hitmen**, **New Christs**, **Screaming Tribesmen**), Phil 'Dust' Petersen (bass), Scott 'Rock Action' Asheton (drums; ex-Stooges, Sonic's Rendezvous Band) and Angie Pepper (backing vocals). The album, *Take It to the Vertical*, came out on the Red Eye label in September 1992. The album reflected Tek's current listening tastes for R&B, as well as the country leanings of Masuak and Asheton. It afforded the CD EP *Good 'Nuff* (October 1992).

To coincide with the album's release, Tek toured Australia (with The World Shakers supplemented by Pip Hoyle) for the first time in over ten years. A year later, Tek returned to Australia to record a new album. Backed by Kent Steedman (guitar; from **Celibate Rifles**) and the crack rhythm section of Jim Dickson (bass; ex-**Railroad Gin**, Survivors, **Passengers**, Barracudas, **New Christs**) and Nik Rieth (drums; from **Celibate Rifles**), Tek could not put a foot wrong. Chris Masuak (guitar), Pip Hoyle (keyboards) and Angie Pepper (vocals) also contributed to Tek's second album.

With surging tracks like 'Blood from a Stone', 'Condition Black' and 'Searching', *Outside* (March 1994) was one of the best Australian albums of the year. Early copies of the album included a four-track Limited Edition CD EP, *Insideout*, which contained unissued cuts. To coincide with the album's release, Tek toured Australia (backed by Steedman, Dickson and Rieth) to a positive response. Tek returned to Australia in January 1995 to supervise (with Rob Younger) the remastering of the **Radio Birdman** back catalogue. The Deniz Tek Group appeared on the Sydney bill of the 1995 Big Day Out, and commenced recording a new album for Red Eye. Only the CD EP *4-4 The Number of the Beat* came out of those sessions. During June, The Deniz Tek Group embarked on a European tour.

In January 1996, Tek took part in the **Radio Birdman** Radios On! reunion tour of Australia. During July, The Deniz Tek Group toured Europe for a second time. Tek's fourth album, *Le Bonne Route*, appeared on the Citadel label in November 1996. Once again backed by Dickson, Steedman and Rieth, the album maintained the quality of *Outside* balanced out by some of Tek's most unusual, adventurous songs like 'Lunatics at the Edge of the World, 'Salted Leeches' and 'Rabbit's Foot'. The limited edition CD EP *The Italian Tour EP '96* (which included 'Tubular Dreams' and 'Lunatics at the Edge of the World' from *Le Bonne Route*) was available briefly in Australia at the same time. The Deniz Tek Group toured Australia for the fourth time (November), then during January 1997 Tek was back on the road with **Radio Birdman**. Citadel also issued the six-track Deniz Tek Group CD EP 'Bad Road' (May 1997), which included previously unissued tracks and live cuts.

In early 1997, US label Alive Records issued the album *Dodge Main*. Recorded in Hollywood during 1996 by an all-star cast of musicians, including Deniz Tek, Wayne Kramer (guitar; ex-MC5) and Scott Morgan (vocals; ex-Rationals), plus Paul Ill (bass) and Brock Avery (drums) from Kramer's band, the album was a fiery romp through covers of material made famous by various Detroit groups. Songs included 'Future/Now' and 'Over and Over' by MC5, 'I Got a Right' by Iggy and the Stooges and 'City Slang' by Sonic's Rendezvous Band, plus a gritty update on Tek's '100 Fools'. The album was dedicated to late Detroit musicians Rob Tyner, Fred 'Sonic' Smith and Dave Alexander.

Deniz Tek albums: *Take It to the Vertical* (Red Eye/Polydor, 1992), *Outside* (Red Eye/Polydor, 1994), *Le Bonne Route* (Citadel, 1996); ***Visitors albums:*** *The Visitors* (Citadel, 1985), *Visitation '79* (Red Eye/Polydor, 1994).

Tex Don and Charlie (*see* Catfish/Don Walker; Tex Perkins)

Texas (*see* Taste)

These Immortal Souls (*see* Crime and The City Solution)

Things of Stone and Wood

Formed: *1989*
Style: *Folk, rock*
Original line-up: *Greg Arnold (lead vocals, acoustic guitar; ex-Thirteen at Midnight), Justin Brady (violin, mandolin, harmonica; ex-Crown of Thorns), Michael Allen (bass, vocals; ex-Thirteen at Midnight), Tony Floyd (drums, percussion; ex-Vince Jones Band)*

Melbourne band Things of Stone and Wood (ToSaW) comprised four young troubadours who shared a love for rootsy Celtic folk and acoustic song arrangements. As a rock band with a folk mood and a left-wing sensibility, both musically and politically, ToSaW built-up a large following on the Australian scene. The band's simple, well-crafted and uplifting songs garnered critical praise, radio airplay and strong sales alike.

ToSaW grew out of the ashes of Melbourne independent band Thirteen at Midnight. That band comprised Greg Arnold, Michael Allen (who had replaced original bass player Russell Hall), Byron Smith (lead guitar) and Peter Pilley (drums). Smith was a rock journalist with *Juke* magazine. The band issued the album *Warring Tribes* (February 1988) and one single, a cover of The Cult's 'She Sells Sanctuary'/'Shine' (June), on the Cleopatra label before disintegrating.

Arnold's formative influences included Bob Dylan, Billy Bragg, The Beatles, Elvis Costello, Sex Pistols and **Paul Kelly**. He formed ToSaW in 1989 with the intention of performing one song at his girlfriend Helen's 21st birthday party. From there the band's rise to national prominence came about through long residencies and tireless interstate touring on the Australian pub/concert circuit. ToSaW issued its debut EP, 'The Hopeful'/'Sweet Conversation', 'My Vision', in September 1991 which gave an indication of the band's early promise and Arnold's confident songwriting at work. In 1992, the band recorded its debut album. Produced by manager James Black (ex-**Russell Morris** Band, **Mondo Rock**, Revelators, **Mark Gillespie** Band), the album was the culmination of three years' hard work. Once the album was completed, the band signed a record deal with Sony Music who issued the single 'Share this Wine'/'In Our Home' (October) and the CD EP 'Happy Birthday Helen' (December). 'Share this Wine' peaked at #46 on the national chart in October.

Then, backed by mass radio support, the ebullient 'Happy Birthday Helen' leapt into the national Top 10 at #8 in February 1993. With a raised profile, ToSaW scored tour support slots to **Midnight Oil**, **Paul Kelly** and UK visitor Luka Bloom. ToSaW's debut album, *The Yearning*, came out in March 1993 and it reached the national Top 10 (#8) in April. The album's next two singles, 'Rock this Boat' (March) and 'Single Perfect Raindrop' (July), were minor hits at #51 and #50 respectively. 'Happy Birthday Helen' logged a #91 placing on the 1993 Triple J Hottest 100 list. In late 1993, Sony Music issued *The Yearning* in the UK and Europe, and ToSaW embarked on their first overseas tour. One of the band's gigs in the UK was supporting **Midnight Oil** at the Forum. While the band was overseas, Greg Arnold was named Songwriter of the Year by the Australian Performing Right Association (APRA).

ToSaW's next CD single, 'Wildflowers', came out in September 1994. Sony Music initially baulked at issuing 'Wildflowers' as the first single from the band's all-important second album due to the word 'Nazis' in the song's cheery chorus hook. Arnold insisted on the release of 'Wildflowers' and, although it did not chart higher than #41, it became the most played Australian single on radio during October. It also was placed at #93 on the 1994 Triple J Hottest 100 list. The band's second album, *Junk Theatre* (March 1995), produced another, minor hit single, 'Churchill's Black Dog' (#34 in March). The album highlighted the band's eternal capacity for adventurous folk-pop arrangements, mellifluous melodies and Arnold's astute and sometimes acrid lyrical observations. The album's third single, 'Crazy Shadow' (April), was not a chart success.

By the end of 1995, ToSaW had parted ways with Sony Music. Free of corporate restraints, the band issued the independent, mail-order only album *The Man with the Perfect Hair* (November). Aimed at the dedicated ToSaW fan, the album comprised a pleasantly relaxed, single-take, 'unplugged' session that featured new songs, reworked B-sides and a dodgy Beatles cover, 'I've Just Seen a Face'. The band ended 1996 with the release of its fourth album, *Whirligig* (October), which included another batch of joyful folk-pop such as the Beatlesque 'Blink'. *Whirligig* produced the CD singles 'Blink' (July) and 'Half Way Round the World' (March 1997). By that stage, Justin Brady had left the band and ToSaW toured with fill-in players Mel Pinkerton (guitar, cello; from The Anyones) and Cameron McKenzie (guitar; from Horsehead).

Albums: *The Yearning* (Sony, 1993), *Junk Theatre* (Sony, 1995), *The Man with the Perfect Hair* (Things, 1995), *Whirligig* (Things/Shock, 1996), *Live at The Espy* (Things, 1996).

Third Eye (*see* Ian 'Ollie' Olsen)

This Is Serious Mum (TISM)

Formed: *1983*
Style: *Electro-funk*
Original line-up: *Ron Hitler-Barassi (vocals), Leak Van Vlalen (guitar), Eugene De La Hotcroix Bun (keyboards), Jock Cheese (bass), Humphrey B. Flaubert (drum machine programming), Les Miserables (performance artist), John St Peenis (performance artist)*

More a concept than a band, the provocative This Is Serious Mum (TISM) remain something of an enigma. Despite a series of popular releases since 1986, and an entertaining 'Theatre of the Absurd' stage show, the group members remain anonymous. Rumour has it that they actually serve in various public offices (e.g. lawyers) and are pillars of the community. Yet, as all cultural terrorists know, to make an impact one must have the courage of one's convictions. So, on stage and record, the world of TISM exploded with a shower of nagging sarcasm, grotesque parody, gratuitous obscenity and relentless electro-funk noise. Writing in *Rolling Stone*, Howard Stringer stated that TISM 'appointed themselves stormtroopers against establishment garishness, slapping the wrists of cultural icons'. TISM steadfastly refused to be interviewed in the conventional manner, and thought nothing of haranguing the press with a barrage of scathing and obnoxious media releases and stunts that ruffled more than a few feathers.

Musically, TISM was reminiscent of US eccentrics like Devo and The Residents, and UK group Pop Will Eat Itself. Like The Residents, TISM dressed in a variety of disguises ranging from black balaclava and urban guerilla stage gear, to more elaborate Ku Klux Klan-inspired outfits and facemasks or white smocks with billowing headpieces filled with balloons. TISM made its live debut in August 1985, and within a year was drawing capacity audiences on the Melbourne inner-city pub circuit. In July 1986, TISM issued the single 'Defecate on My Face'/'Death Death Death', 'Art Income Dialectic' on the Elvis label. Lyrically, 'Defecate on My Face' explored the sexual interplay between Adolf Hitler and Eva Braun in Nazi Germany, and it became a dance club favourite. TISM followed that up with the mini-album *Form and Meaning* (December 1986) and the 12-inch single '40 Years — Then Death'/'The Back Upon Which Jezza Jumped' (October 1987).

TISM's independent #1 double album *Great Truckin' Songs of the Renaissance* (October 1988) produced the singles 'Ballad of John Bonham's Coke Roadie'/'(I Think I've Got) Mick Jagger Worked Out' (May 1988), 'I'm Interested in Apathy'/'Gas! Gas! An Ecstasy of Fumbling' (October), 'Saturday Night Palsy'/'Pus' (March 1989) and 'Martin Scorcese is Really Quite a Jovial Fellow'/'Babies Bite Back' (July). The album also included a dance mix of 'Defecate on My Face' and a re-recorded version of '40 Years — Then Death'. 'I'm Interested in Apathy' won Best Independent Release at the 1988 Australian Record Industry Association (ARIA) Awards. TISM issued one single during 1989 'I Don't Want TISM, I Want a Girlfriend'/'I'll 'ave Ya' (December). In late 1990, Phonogram issued TISM's second album, *Hot Dogma*, which produced the singles 'The History of Western Civilisation' (October) and 'Let's Form a Company'.

TISM moved to the Shock label for a trio of

CD EPs, *Gentlemen, Start Your Egos* (December 1991), *Beasts of Suburban* (August 1992) and *Australia, The Lucky Cunt* ('Lose Your Delusion I') (August 1993). Just as the last-named hit the stores, the Ken Done Group took legal action against the band for its bastardisation of a Done image on the cover. Shock was forced to recall all stock, reprint the cover and reissue it as *Censored Due to Legal Advice*. Toward the end of the year, TISM entered the studio with producer Paul McKercher to record its first full-length album in three years.

TISM appeared on the bill of the 1995 Big Day Out tour. *Machiavelli and the Four Seasons* (May 1995) gave rise to the CD singles 'Jung Talent Time' (February), '(He'll Never Be an) Ol' Man River' (June), 'Greg! The Stop Sign!!' (August) and 'Garbage' (January 1996). '(He'll Never Be an) Ol' Man River' took TISM into the national mainstream chart for the first time when it reached #23. TISM also scored well on the 1995 Triple J Hottest 100 list when '(He'll Never Be an) Ol' Man River' and 'Greg! The Stop Sign!!' logged the #9 and #10 placings respectively. Since its initial release, *Machiavelli and the Four Seasons* has been repackaged on two different occasions. The first reissue featured a limited edition bonus disc *Gold! Gold! Gold! for Australia* which comprised 15 tracks of remixed and previously unissued material which had been recorded as part of the sessions that produced *Machiavelli*. Then *Machiavelli* came with a bonus live disc called *Machines Against the Rage*. TISM issued two CD singles in 1997, 'Shut Up, the Footy's on the Radio' (May) and 'Yob' (November).

Albums: *Form and Meaning* (mini-album, Elvis, 1986), *Great Truckin' Songs of the Renaissance* (Elvis, 1988), *Hot Dogma* (Phonogram, 1990), *Machiavelli and the Four Seasons* (Genre B. Goode/Shock, 1995), *Complete Recordings 1986–1993* (four-CD box set, Genre B. Goode/Shock, 1995), *Machiavelli and the Four Seasons/Gold! Gold! Gold! For Australia* (reissue, Genre B. Goode/Shock, 1996), *Machiavelli and the Four Seasons/Machines Against the Rage* (reissue, Genre B. Goode/Shock, 1996).

G. Wayne Thomas

Style: *Pop, rock*

New Zealand-born singer/songwriter/producer G. Wayne Thomas made a name for himself during the early 1970s with a series of finely crafted, soaring pop ballads like 'Open Up Your Heart' and 'Everything in You'. Thomas arrived in Australia during 1968, and began his musical career writing commercials for Eveready, Pepsi and Rheem. He issued his debut solo single on Warner Brothers, 'Take It Easy'/'You're Not Alone', in November 1971. It reached #33 in Sydney. W.E.A. also signed Thomas on as a producer, and one of his earliest pop productions was the **Autumn** album *Comes Autumn* (1971).

At the end of 1971, Thomas produced the soundtrack to Albert Falzon's surfing film *Morning of the Earth*. The project had initially started out as a full album by Sydney band **Tamam Shud**, but Thomas brought in other singer/songwriters such as **Brian Cadd**, **Terry Hannagan** and **John J. Francis** to contribute, thus cutting the Shud's song tally back to three. Thomas also included three of his own songs, 'Morning of the Earth', 'Open Up Your Heart' and 'Day Comes'. The *Morning of the Earth* soundtrack album (May 1972) produced Thomas's second single, the memorable 'Open Up Your Heart'/'Morning of the Earth' (March), which reached #22 nationally and #14 in Sydney during June. *Morning of the Earth* went on to achieve gold record status. Next Thomas produced the album *Laid* by studio outfit **Duck** which comprised John Robinson (ex-**Blackfeather**), **Jon English** and **Bobbi Marchini** among others. At the start of 1973, Thomas formed his own record label, Warm & Genuine. As well as being executive producer for **Jon English's** debut album *Wine Dark Sea* on Warm & Genuine, Thomas issued his own album in 1973.

The delicate, romantic *G. Wayne Thomas* album included the singer's previous singles 'Take It Easy' and 'Open Up Your Heart', as well as producing his third single, 'Everything in You'/'Call My Name' (February 1973). In 1973, Thomas produced and sang on the *Crystal Voyager* motion picture soundtrack album. Thomas formed a studio band for the album session which comprised Bobby Gebert (piano), Mick Liber (guitar; ex-**Python Lee Jackson**), Rod Coe (bass) and John Proud (drums) with assistance from Michael Carlos (keyboards; ex-**Tully**). Thomas sang and played rhythm guitar. Dubbed the Crystal Voyager Band, Thomas took the band on the road for live appearances. The *Crystal Voyager* soundtrack album produced the singles 'Hollywood'/'Morning Light' and 'Changes'/'Into the Blue'. Thomas issued a final single on Warm & Genuine, 'Mercy for the Innocent'/'Junkyard' (1975), before moving to Polydor for 'Just to Love You'/'How Can I Tell You?' (March 1976).

Thomas returned to writing commercials, before teaming up with Peter Bailey. The duo signed to Polydor and issued four singles, 'The Last Laugh'/'It's Alright' (1979), 'Missing Persons'/'Loving You' (1979), 'I Don't Want to Spoil Your Party'/'Half Way Home' (March 1980) and 'Tobacco

Road'/'They Loved Their Lives Away' (September 1980), plus the album *Missing Persons* (1979). Thomas then slipped from view.

Albums: *Morning of the Earth* (soundtrack shared with other artists, Warner, 1972), *G. Wayne Thomas* (Warm & Genuine, 1973), *Crystal Voyager* (soundtrack, Warm & Genuine, 1974), *Open Up Your Heart* (reissue of *G. Wayne Thomas*, Warm & Genuine, 1974), *Missing Persons* (with Peter Bailey, Polydor, 1979).

Billy Thorpe

Style: Rock

The indefatigable Billy Thorpe (b. 1946) is one of the true legends of Australian rock'n'roll. Ever the journeyman rock'n'roll chameleon, Thorpie evolved from child star, beat pop sensation and cuddly pop crooner to finally emerge as the country's wildest and heaviest blues rocker. By the early 1970s, fronting the umpteenth version of his ever-changing Aztecs, Thorpie was the unassailable monarch of Australian rock music.

Growing tired of the faded denims and the 'suck more piss' Aussie pub rock ethos, Thorpie left Australia in 1976 to try his luck in Los Angeles. He produced a series of inventive, futuristic concept albums which sold remarkably well in the USA, but were overlooked locally. He returned to Australia in 1994 as a conquering hero, issued the three-CD box set *Lock Up Your Mothers*, was interviewed on *60 Minutes* and relaunched himself on the Australian pub and concert circuit. There have been few more remarkable careers in Australian rock'n'roll.

Thorpie was born in Manchester, England. He immigrated to Australia with his family when he was nine, and settled in Brisbane, Queensland. By the time he was ten years old, Thorpie was performing on Brisbane television (billed as Little Rock Allen). He toured country areas with singer Reg Lindsay. By the time he was 15, Thorpie had worked in stage shows, variety television, clubs and even vaudeville at Brisbane's Theatre Royal with George Wallace. He also toured with the likes of **Johnny O'Keefe** and **Col Joye**. In late 1963, as a seasoned 17-year-old, Thorpie moved to Sydney and joined his first band The Aztecs. The original Aztecs line-up comprised Vince Maloney (lead guitar; ex-Vibratones), Val Jones (rhythm guitar), John 'Bluey' Watson (bass; ex-Vibratones) and Col Baigent (drums). Just prior to Thorpie's arrival, The Aztecs had issued a surf instrumental single, 'Smoke and Stack'/'Board Boogie', on the Linda Lee label (January 1964). Billy Thorpe and the Aztecs became a major attraction at promoter John Harrigan's Surf City discotheque.

Englishman **Tony Barber** (guitar, vocals) replaced Jones, and the band issued its next single, 'Blue Day'/'You Don't Love Me', on Linda Lee (April 1964). Written by Barber, the single scraped into the lower reaches of the Sydney Top 40. Two days before The Aztecs were to record two more of his songs for the next single, Barber received The Rolling Stones' first British EP, *Rolling Stones*, sent over by his brother from England. The Aztecs heard The Stones' version of Leiber and Stoller's 'Poison Ivy' and decided to record it themselves. Backed by Barber's 'Broken Things', 'Poison Ivy' became The Aztecs' first #1 hit single in June 1964. The single heralded the arrival of beat music in Australia, and Thorpie and the Aztecs became the country's biggest pop sensations. In Melbourne, where The Beatles had played to 52 000 screaming kids, Thorpie and The Aztecs drew 63 000 at the Myer Music Bowl.

In July, the band signed to the Albert Organisation (home to **The Easybeats**). The Aztecs' first single for EMI/Parlophone, 'Mashed Potato'/'Don'cha Know' (August), reached the Top 10 in most states. 'Sick and Tired'/'About Love' (October) followed 'Mashed Potato' into the Top 10 (#2 in Sydney, #7 in Melbourne and #3 in Adelaide). The band recorded its debut album *Billy Thorpe and the Aztecs*, and ended a successful 1964 with the release of the schmaltzy ballad 'Over the Rainbow' taken from the film *The Wizard of Oz*. 'Over the Rainbow'/'That I Love' reached #1 in Sydney during December, which precipitated Tony Barber's departure. By the beginning of 1965, Maloney, Watson and Baigent had all left The Aztecs, leaving Thorpie to assemble a new line-up. **Tony Barber** initially joined forces with Maloney in Vince and Tony's Two (with John Shields on bass and Jimmy Thompson on drums), before striking out as a solo artist. Maloney formed The Vince Maloney Sect, before travelling to the UK where he joined **The Bee Gees** as lead guitarist. He returned to Australia with **Fanny Adams** in late 1970.

Meanwhile, Thorpie had his new Aztecs on the road: Col Risby (lead guitar; ex-**Ray Hoff and the Off Beats**), Mike Downes (rhythm guitar; ex-**Ray Hoff and the Off Beats**), Jimmy Taylor (piano; ex-**Ray Hoff and the Off Beats**), Teddy Toi (bass; ex-**Max Merritt and the Meteors**) and Johnny Dick (drums; ex-**Max Merritt and the Meteors**). Tony Buchanan (sax) also joined in 1966. Following the success of 'Over the Rainbow', Thorpie's next run of singles were all ballads. Marty Robbins' 'I Told the Brook'/'Funny Face' (June 1965) was #1 in

Sydney and #4 in Melbourne. The Platters' 'Twilight Time'/'My Girl Josephine' (July) was #3 in both Sydney and Melbourne. 'Baby Hold Me Close'/'Hallelujah I Love Her So' (September) went Top 5 (#4) in Sydney, but only managed #24 in Melbourne. Ketty Lester's 'Love Letters'/'Dancing in the Street' (December) reached #2 in Sydney.

In March 1966, Thorpie was given his own television show, *It's All Happening*, on the Seven Network in Sydney. With The Aztecs installed as house band and Rory Thomas as musical director, *It's All Happening* is still considered to be one of the best pop shows of the 1960s. Thorpie's tenth single, 'The Word for Today'/'The New Breed', reached #14 in Sydney during July. Despite his high profile during 1966, however, the next single, 'I've Been Wrong Before'/'Wee Bit More of Your Lovin'' (October), failed to chart. At the end of 1966, the Seven Network took *It's All Happening* off the air, and by early 1967 The Aztecs had broken up. Thorpie kept busy during 1967, but only issued one (flop) single on Festival, a cover of Roy Orbison's 'Dream Baby'/'You Don't Live Twice' (Sydney #36 in October). By 1968 he had ditched the middle-of-the-road crooner bit, and adopted a 'General Custer' look replete with moustache and fringed jacket. In January, he formed a new backing band with Johnny Dick, Mick Liber (guitar; ex-**Python Lee Jackson**) and Dave McTaggert (bass) who was soon replaced by Paul 'Sheepdog' Wheeler (ex-**Affair**).

In August 1968, Thorpie accepted a few lowly gigs in Melbourne, and ended up staying for eight years. On the eve of the Melbourne trip, Liber and Dick quit. Thorpie recruited Jimmy Thompson (ex-Vince Maloney Sect, **Tony Worsley and the Fabulous Blue Jays**) on drums. Reverting to the Billy Thorpe and the Aztecs name, the band played as a trio for four months with Thorpie handling all guitar and vocals for the first time. Australian guitar legend **Lobby Loyde**, freshly departed from **The Wild Cherries**, joined The Aztecs as lead guitarist in December 1968. Under Loyde's direction, The Aztecs spearheaded the burgeoning Melbourne underground blues and heavy rock movement. Alongside the likes of **Chain**, **Spectrum**, **Company Caine**, **Carson** and a host of other new bands, The Aztecs began to rule over the southern club and pub circuit.

With Thorpie's spirits revitalised and his music changed forever, The Aztecs became the loudest and heaviest blues band of the day *and* the biggest drawcard in the land. Thorpie's voice became a guttural, ferocious roar. Few groups of the day could hope to match The Aztecs for sheer volume, visceral impact and raw energy. 'Aztecs Energy' it was dubbed at the time, and Thorpie and the Aztecs became festival mainstays. The band appeared at Australia's first rock festival, Pilgrimage for Pop, held at a farm near Ourimbah, NSW over the Australia Day weekend in January 1970. That was followed by an appearance at 'The Odyssey' Festival, Wallacia (NSW) in January 1971 and, most famous of all, the Sunbury Pop Festival in January 1972.

The first recorded example of Thorpie and the Aztecs' raucous, blues-rock sound was the single Willie Dixon's 'Good Mornin' Little School Girl'/'Rock Me Baby' on Festival (March 1970). B.B. King's 'Rock Me Baby' became an Aztecs live staple, as did the likes of Ma Rainey's 'C.C. Rider' and the 18-minute showstopper 'Ooh Poo Pa Doo'. By the time the single appeared, Kevin Murphy (ex-**Wild Cherries**, Rush) had replaced Thompson on drums. Warren 'Pig' Morgan (piano, vocals; ex-**Chain**) joined The Aztecs in July 1970, and in September the band cut the live-in-the-studio album, *The Hoax is Over*, for Festival's new progressive label Infinity. Issued in January 1971, the album contained just two long, bluesy jams (including Johnny 'Guitar' Watson's 'Gangster of Love') and two short, rocky tracks. Only Loyde's fiery guitar work saved the album from being monotonous and tedious. Nevertheless, it reached the national Top 10 (#7) and achieved gold status.

By the time of its release, **Lobby Loyde** had left to record his solo album *Plays with George Guitar* and to form a new version of **The Wild Cherries** with Toi and Dick. He formed **Coloured Balls** in March 1972. Murphy had likewise moved on to join **King Harvest**. Thorpie took over all guitar duties, and Gil 'Rats' Matthews replaced Murphy on drums in May (preceded by a two-month period with fill-in drummer Steve Innis). As a child drumming prodigy, Matthews had toured the USA with The Mouseketeers. He started in rock music with John Konrad's Kaydets in 1960, moving on to The Silhouettes and The Scorpions before joining Max Hamilton and The Impacts as lead guitarist in 1965.

That popular Melbourne R&B band also comprised Max Hamilton (vocals), Ron Sheedy (guitar), Ron Cork (bass) and Daryl Feddon (drums). The band issued three singles on EMI/HMV, Little Richard's 'Jenny Jenny'/'Shake with Me' (September 1965), 'I'm Blue'/'Bull Moose' (April 1966) and 'Foolish Little Boy'/'Now Hear This' (June 1966) before breaking up in 1967. Matthews spent time with a number of bands like **Levi Smith's Clefs** and The John Rupert Group before joining The Aztecs. Matthews also issued a solo single in 1971, 'Little Dove'/'Gil's Thing' (December).

In June 1971, The Aztecs headlined a concert at Melbourne Town Hall, which resulted in the *Aztecs — Live* album (December 1971). The album came out on the band's new label, Havoc, and reached the national Top 10 (#8). The lush 'Dawn Song'/'Time to Live' (October) also returned Thorpie to the Top 40 singles chart (#29) for the first time in five years. Morgan left The Aztecs in August to form the duo Pilgrimage with **Phil Manning** (guitar; ex-**Chain**). Bruce Howard (ex-**La De Das, Levi Smith's Clefs**) took Morgan's place on keyboards.

Thorpie and the Aztecs' legendary performance at the inaugural Sunbury Pop Festival in January 1972 spawned the Top 5 hit album *Aztecs Live! At Sunbury*. The album peaked at #3 on the national chart during September, sold over 80 000 copies and remains a milestone in the annals of Australian heavy rock. The crunching 'Mamma' also appeared on the Various Artists live album *Sunbury*, issued by EMI. Just after Sunbury, alongside **La De Das** and **Friends**, The Aztecs were responsible for drawing one of the largest crowds ever assembled in Australia at Melbourne's Myer Music Bowl (estimated at over 200 000 people).

Billy Thorpe

The perennial and autobiographical 'Most People I Know (Think that I'm Crazy)'/'Regulation 3 Puff' (March 1972) reached #3 on the national chart (#1 in Sydney). The follow-up, 'Believe It Just Like Me'/'Get to Hell Out of Here' (October) peaked at #21. Meanwhile, the RAK label issued 'Most People I Know (Think that I'm Crazy)'/'Regulation 3 Puff' in the UK during June, and the band duly left for an English tour in November. By all accounts, the English punters found it difficult to contend with The Aztecs' massive sound, and the band made little headway. Thorpie was back in Australia in time to headline at Sunbury 1973. The live track, 'Going Back Home', appeared on Mushroom's triple album set *The Great Australian Rock Festival Sunbury 1973* (April 1973).

Warren Morgan rejoined The Aztecs, and he and Thorpe issued the album *Thump'n Pig & Puff'n Billy* which yielded one of the best singles of 1973, the pounding rocker 'Captain Straightman'/'Bow My Head' (#26 in April). Although only credited to the infamous duo, the album featured Gil Matthews, in addition to **Chain's Phil Manning** (guitar) and Barry Sullivan (bass). 'Captain Straightman' later won Thorpie an award at the 1975 American Music Festival.

Paul Wheeler was sacked from The Aztecs in April 1973. Teddy Toi (by then ex-**Wild Cherries, Duck**) took his place on bass. The band also signed a new deal with WEA (Atlantic) and issued the singles 'Movie Queen'/'Mame' (June 1973) and 'Don't You Know?'/'Yes I'm Tired' (August). 'Don't You Know?' was the first single lifted from the band's next studio album, *More Arse than Class* (May 1974). With raunchy blues/boogie tracks like 'Boogie Woogie' and 'Back on the Road Again', *More Arse than Class* was the most successful studio album the band issued. It peaked at #12 on the national chart during July.

In November 1973, The Aztecs became the first rock band to perform at the prestigious Sydney Opera House. The concert spawned the band's third live set, *Steaming at the Opera House*, and the single 'Cigarettes and Whiskey'/'Back Home in Australia' (August 1974). At Sunbury 1974 Thorpie revived 'Over the Rainbow', and when issued as a single, backed with the rip-roarin' 'Let's Have a Party' (April), it provided him with another Top 30 hit (#27). The hard-driving rendition of Eddie Hodges' 'New Orleans' appeared on the Various Artists live album *Highlights of Sunbury '74 Part 1*.

In March 1974, Johnny Dick rejoined The Aztecs, giving a dual drum line-up. There was a short-lived three-piece line-up of Thorpie, Toi and Matthews in early 1975, but soon after the singer disbanded The Aztecs to lay plans for his move to the USA. By that stage, Thorpie no longer saw himself as the manic blues rocker. He had cut his hair and dispensed with the faded denims for more stylish attire, and was not content to sit on his laurels. His next two albums, *Million Dollar Bill* and *Pick Me Up and Play Me Loud*, featured a sophisticated mix of funk, Adult Oriented Rock (AOR), country and blues with a definite American slant. *Million Dollar Bill* produced the delightfully breezy single 'It's Almost Summer'/'Drive My Car' (November 1975) which was a minor hit in Melbourne and Sydney (#39). 'Do the Best You Can'/'Mama Told Her' (March 1976) was the second single. The basic line-up on the album was Thorpe, Matthews and New Zealander Billy Kristian (bass; ex-**Max Merritt and the Meteors**), aided by the likes of Warren Morgan (keyboards, by then a member of **John Paul Young** and the All Stars).

Thorpie and Matthews formed a touring band, dubbed Million Dollar Bill, with Kristian, Derek Griffiths (lead guitar) and John Le Vine (keyboards). That line-up reverted to the Billy Thorpe and the Aztecs name when Morgan returned to the fold in April 1976. The new line-up recorded *Pick Me Up and Play Me Loud*, which produced the single 'Blue Mary'/'Good Night Out' (August 1976). Between July and November 1976, Thorpie worked live with the revived Aztecs line-up of Morgan, Toi and Matthews before splitting the band and moving to Los Angeles in December. Back in Australia during December 1977, Thorpie and the Morgan/Toi/Matthews Aztecs embarked on a four-week national tour. Following that, Matthews went on to work with **Mondo Rock, Cybotron** and Southern Electric among others, and as an in-demand engineer/producer.

In 1979, Thorpie signed a deal with American producer Spencer Proffer's Pasha Music Organisation, and recorded the science fiction/rock opera concept album *Children of the Sun*. One side featured AM radio-styled pop rock, with the second side being taken up with the spacey, side-long 'Children of the Sun' suite. Backing musicians on the album were American session legends Leland Sklar (bass), Alvin Taylor (drums), Larry Brown (synthesiser) and Mike Boddicker (synthesiser), with an appearance by Australian expatriate Steve Kipner on backing vocals. It produced the singles 'Wrapped in the Chains of Your Love'/'Goddess of the Night' (July, 1979) and 'Children of the Sun'/'Simple Life' (September). *Children of the Sun* reached #1 in Dallas, Memphis and New Orleans, before climbing into the American Top 20. Thorpie toured arenas across the American mid-west, and the album sold 500 000 copies before the distribution label Capricorn Records (home to The Allman Brothers) went bankrupt. For his second American-recorded album, *21st Century Man*, Thorpie called on Gil Matthews to play drums. It also attained US gold status (500 000 copies) and gave rise to the single 'In My Room'/'She's Alive' (February 1981) which went Top 10 in Canada.

Stimulation and the single 'Just the Way I Like It'/'Rock Until You Drop' (October 1981) featured the basic line-up of Thorpie (guitar, vocals, synthesisers) and Matthews (drums) plus American session players. Thorpie returned to Australia in October for a tour, which took in an appearance at the Tanelorn Rock Festival. Thorpie's fourth American album, *East of Eden's Gate* (1982), was not issued in Australia. Thorpie undertook one more Australian tour (January 1983) with Matthews and Americans Bruce Turgon (bass) and Jeff Northrup (guitar) before retiring from the music business in 1984. He concentrated on a new business developing electronics for companies such as Disney, Mattel and Universal. His work took him to Hong Kong, Taiwan and Japan, and he spent six months living in Beijing, China.

By 1986 he had set up a production and recording facility in Los Angeles and began writing and scoring music for many Disney, Paramount, Universal and Lorimar TV shows such as *War of the Worlds*, *Star Trek*, *Colombo*, *Eight is Enough* and *Hard Times on Planet Earth*. In 1987 he formed a partnership with **Tony Barber** in the Sunshine Friends soft toy company, and together they issued a series of children's books, cassettes and videos. That year he also recorded three new songs which were combined with the 'Children of the Sun' suite and 'East of Eden's Gate' as the album *Children of the Sun . . . Revisited*. In 1990, he joined Fleetwood Mac drummer Mick Fleetwood in his band The Zoo, which also featured singer Bekka Bramlett. The band issued the *Shakin' the Cage* album and single (March 1991), and toured Australia. That year Thorpie was inducted into the Australian Record Industry Association (ARIA) Hall of Fame.

On 31 July 1993, Thorpie re-formed The Aztecs line-up of Warren Morgan, Paul Wheeler and Gil Matthews for a one-off showcase gig at the Jail House Rock concert held at Brisbane's infamous Boggo Road Gaol (closed down in 1992). The Aztecs were back for an Australian tour in October. Thorpie assembled the box set *Lock Up Your Mothers*, which contained 38 prime Aztecs tracks (some previously unissued) spanning the 1969–73 period. The Aztecs toured again and the box set reached the Melbourne Top 10 in August 1994, launching a

Thorpie revival to rival the peak of his popularity during the 1970s. His return resulted in front-page news articles and extensive television coverage, culminating in appearances on top-rating television shows such as *Hey Hey It's Saturday*, *Denton* and *60 Minutes*. ('Was it really all sex and drugs and rock'n'roll, Billy?' cooed reporter Tracey Curro.) Riding on a wave of nostalgia, Thorpie took The Aztecs on the road for a successful national tour over the 1994/95 summer.

The Aztecs also recorded three new songs, 'Rock'n'Roll City', 'Southern Comfort' and 'Let Love Show the Way', which were included on the 15-track compilation *The Best of and the Rest of Lock Up Your Mothers* (December 1994). In 1996, Thorpie assembled the Billy Thorpe Band with Randall Waller (guitar, vocals, keyboards; ex-**Avion**), Steve Edmonds (guitar, vocals; ex-**Head Hunters**), Andy Cichon (bass, guitar, keyboards, vocals; ex-**Rose Tattoo**, **James Reyne** Band, **Peter Wells** Band, **Judge Mercy**) and Paul DeMarco (drums; ex-Scattered Aces, **Rose Tattoo**, **Head Hunters**, **Peter Wells** Band). Thorpie returned to Australia in July 1996 for a national tour with his new band. In November, Pan Macmillan Australia published Thorpie's first book, *Sex and Thugs and Rock'n'Roll: A Year in Kings Cross 1963–1964*. Its release also coincided with a profile of Thorpie's life and career on television show *This is Your Life*. Thorpie was back in Australia during 1997 for a tour, and to write his second book, *Most People I Know (Think that I'm Crazy)*.

Billy Thorpe and the Aztecs albums: *Poison Ivy and Introducing ... Johnny Noble* (split album shared with Johnny Noble, Linda Lee/Festival, 1964), *Billy Thorpe and the Aztecs* (EMI/Parlophone, 1965), *The Best of Billy Thorpe* (EMI/Parlophone, 1965), *Don't You Dig this Kind of Beat?* (EMI/Parlophone, 1965), *Great Hits* (compilation, Calendar/Festival, 1971), *Gold* (compilation, Atlantic, 1975), *It's All Happening* (compilation, Albert/EMI, 1981), *Live at Sunbury* (reissue of *Aztecs Live! At Sunbury*, Ultimate, 1989), *20 Greatest Hits* (CD reissue of *It's All Happening*, Sony, 1994), *Lock Up Your Mothers* (box set, Mushroom/Festival, 1994), *The Best of and the Rest of Lock Up Your Mothers* (compilation, Mushroom/Festival, 1994); ***Aztecs albums:*** *The Hoax is Over* (Festival/Infinity, 1971), *Aztecs — Live* (Havoc, 1971), *Aztecs Live! At Sunbury* (Havoc, 1972), *More Arse than Class* (Atlantic, 1974), *Steaming at the Opera House* (Atlantic, 1974); ***Thump'n Pig and Puff'n Billy album:*** *Thump'n Pig and Puff'n Billy* (Atlantic, 1973); ***Billy Thorpe albums:*** *The Billy Thorpe Rock Classics* (compilation, M7, 1974), *Million Dollar Bill* (Festival/Infinity, 1975), *Pick Me Up and Play Me Loud* (Festival/Infinity, 1976), *Children of the Sun* (Festival/Interfusion/Capricorn, 1979), *21st Century Man* (Mushroom/Festival, 1980), *Time Traveller* (compilation, Blue Goose, 1980), *Stimulation* (Mushroom/Festival, 1981), *East of Eden's Gate* (US only, CBS, 1982). *Children of the Sun . . . Revisited* (US only, CBS, 1987).

Further reading: *Sex and Thugs and Rock'n'Roll: A Year in Kings Cross 1963–1964* by Billy Thorpe (Pan Macmillan, 1996).

The Thought Criminals

Formed: *1977*
Style: *Punk*
Original line-up: *Bruce Warner (vocals), Stephen Philip (guitar), Roger Grierson (bass), Derik Wappilspoon (drums)*

Sydney band The Thought Criminals were one of the most enterprising outfits on the late 1970s independent scene. As one of the first punk bands to exist in Sydney outside the **Radio Birdman** coterie, The Thought Criminals were able to set up their own alternative record label and booking agency, Doublethink. Under the Doublethink banner, The Thought Criminals helped foster the talents of younger, less established bands such as **Tactics**, Popular Mechanics, Sekret Sekret, Seems Twice, Suicide Squad, Rejex and many others.

The Thought Criminals came together in late 1977. The band's name (like the term Doublethink, and the name of the band's producer Winston Smith) was derived from George Orwell's novel *1984*. The band issued its debut 7-inch EP 'Hilton Bomber' in June 1978 as the inaugural Doublethink release. The EP was a good example of the band's jagged, frantic sound. A year after formation, Ken Doyle replaced Derik Wappilspoon on drums and John Hoey (ex-X-Men) joined on keyboards. Doyle and Hoey later played on **The New Christs'** debut single 'Face a New God'/'Waiting World' (August 1981). The *Food for Thoughtcrimes* EP (July 1979) contained probably The Thought Criminals' best known song, the hyper-kinetic 'More Suicides Please'. The band's debut album, *Speed. Madness.. Flying Saucers...* (February 1980), comprised tracks recorded in three separate sessions spread over a year and a half. The album's crude production values tended to focus on Philip's wiry guitar sound, although songs like 'Lonely One', 'Termination' and 'Oceania Oceania' were delivered with fiery passion.

Following the release of the single 'Edge of Time'/'Equidistance' (August 1980), The Thought Criminals retired from live performances. Their final gig on 29 August provided the band's rarest release, the one-sided, live single 'Land of the Living Room', 'Oceania Oceania' (300 copies), which was given away to punters on the night. The second album, *You Only Think Twice* (October 1981) revealed the band expanding its scope with a more considered and diverse approach (sounding somewhere between UK bands like Wire and The Fall, and US eccentrics The Residents). By the end of 1981, The Thought Criminals had parted ways. Stephen Philip joined **Do Ré Mi** and later Lupi. John Hoey joined **Died Pretty** in 1988, while the band's resident business expert, Roger Grierson, helped set up the GREEN label with rock journalist Stuart Coupe. Grierson also worked in band and tour management, before taking on the prestigious job of Managing Director with PolyGram Music Publishing.

Albums: *Speed. Madness.. Flying Saucers...* (Doublethink, 1980), *You Only Think Twice* (GREEN/ Larrikin, 1981).

The Throb

Formed: *1965*
Style: *R&B*
Original line-up: *John Bell (vocals, rhythm guitar), Marty Van Wynk (lead guitar; ex-Geoff Doyle and the Resonettes, No Names), Denny Burgess (bass, vocals; ex-Mystery Men), Peter Figures (drums; ex-Geoff Doyle and the Resonettes, No Names)*

Sydney R&B band The Throb's main claim to fame is the cover of an obscure Rolling Stones track, 'The Fortune Teller' that outstripped The Stones' own version in more ways than one. First, The Throb's gritty rendition knocked The Stones' tentative one for six. Second, The Throb's version outsold The Stones' when it was also issued as a single in Australia.

The Throb evolved out of surf instrumental band Geoff Doyle and the Resonettes. In 1964, The Resonettes became The No Names with the line-up of Geoff Doyle (vocals), Marty Van Wynk (guitar), Paul Reay (guitar), Geoff MacWalters (bass) and Peter Figures (drums). The No Names signed to Polydor and issued two beat singles in 1964, 'She is Mine'/'All Because of You' and 'Charlie Brown'. The No Names also backed singer Janice Slater on her two singles for Philips, 'Wanting You'/'Summertime' and 'I'm Gonna Live'/'He Really Cares'. In May 1965, John Bell and Denny Burgess replaced Doyle, Reay and MacWalters in The No Names. Englishman Bell had known Harry Vanda and George Young at the Villawood Migrant Hostel and occasionally sang with the nascent **Easybeats** before the arrival of **Stevie Wright**. Burgess brought a stronger R&B influence (à la The Rolling Stones and The Animals) into the band. By December, The No Names had signed to Albert Productions and had renamed themselves The Throb.

As Glenn A. Baker wrote, Albert saw The Throb as a 'poor man's Easybeats', with their Dutch and English members and tough image. Ted Albert and The Easybeats' manager Mike Vaughan suggested The Throb record a Rolling Stones album track, 'The Fortune Teller' (written by Allen Toussaint as Naomi Neville), as its debut single. 'The Fortune Teller'/'Believe in Me' came out on EMI/Parlophone in February 1966 and immediately went to #4 in Sydney and #2 in Melbourne. The Throb became a hot live draw on the discotheque circuit. The band's contemporaries included **The Allusions, The Missing Links, Marty Rhone** and the Soul Agents, **Steve & the Board** and **Jeff St John** and the Id. As a follow-up to 'The Fortune Teller', The Throb adapted an old folk song, 'Black is the Colour of My True Love's Hair'. The band's mournful, demonic reworking of 'Black' (backed with 'Turn My Head', August 1966) proved too much for the band's fans. It stalled in the lower reaches of the Sydney Top 40 (#38), but remains a remarkable achievement nonetheless.

By that stage, Van Wynk had left to join The Soul Agents. The Throb continued on as a three-piece for a short time, until Burgess left in October. He formed psychedelic band Honeybunch with his brother Colin Burgess (drums; ex-Untamed), Joe Travers (guitar; ex-Untamed) and Bill Verbaan (bass; ex-Morloch). Bell and Figures recruited two new players for The Throb, Paul 'Dog' Wylde (organ, piano) and Bob Daisley (bass; ex-Dennis Williams and the Delawares, Gino Affair). That line-up broke up in January 1967. Figures replaced Daryl McKenzie in The Square Circle, which also comprised Dave Kain (guitar; ex-Untamed), Laurie Crooks (vocals), Paul Sine (keyboards) and Arthur Eizenberg (bass). The Square Circle became resident group at Sydney 'mod discotheque' Suzie Wong's (where The Throb had also played), and Denny Burgess joined for a couple of months. He returned to Honeybunch, which became known as The Haze at the end of 1967.

Colin Burgess joined **The Master's Apprentices** in January 1968, which brought The Haze to an end. Denny Burgess spent several months with Brisbane blues band Thursday's Children during mid-1968. He turned up in the 1970 line-up of **Ray Brown**'s old band The Whispers before travelling to the UK. There he joined the final, three-piece line-up of **The Master's Apprentices** with Doug Ford (guitar, vocals) and Colin Burgess (drums) circa 1972. That line-up recorded the track 'Freedom Seekers', which remained unissued until reissue specialists Raven included it on the **Master's Apprentices** rarities album *Jam It Up!* (1987). Raven also included the Throb tracks 'The Fortune Teller' and 'Black', plus The No Names' 'She is Mine' on an EP shared with **The Wild Cherries** (in the *Australian Rock Archives* series, 1979).

In the meantime, Figures had joined **Jeff St John** and Yama (and later Copperwine). Van Wynk joined **The Cherokees**, who were just entering their most popular phase with hits like 'Oh Monah' and 'Minnie the Moocher'. He remained with **The Cherokees** for a year, during which time he co-wrote 'Hide and Seek' with Doug Trevor. The song became a hit for Somebody's Image. Van Wynk next joined Bobby Bright's new band Penny Arcade in 1968, and by the end of 1968 he was playing in the Elliot Gordon Union. In 1983, Denny and Colin Burgess formed hard rock band His Majesty with Japanese singer Yukiko Davis and Spike Williams (guitar). His Majesty launched itself in a blaze of publicity, but neither the singles 'Glory Boys'/'Champagne Cocaine' (November 1983) and 'C Me Comin''/'Randy' (February 1985, on the Regal label) nor its live shows attracted sufficient interest from the public. His Majesty broke up in 1987.

Album: *The Raven EP LP Vol. 1* (compilation shared with **The Purple Hearts**, **The Wild Cherries** and **The Missing Links**; Raven, 1982).

Thug (*see* Tex Perkins)

Thumpin' Pig and Puffin' Billy (*see* Billy Thorpe)

The Thunderbirds

Formed: *1957*
Style: *Rock'n'roll*
Original line-up: *Laurie Bell (lead guitar, vocals), Mickey Borg (guitar, vocals), Don Henderson (rhythm guitar), Marion Grossman (piano, vocals), Frank Tenni (sax), Harold Frith (drums)*

Alongside **The Phantoms**, **The Strangers**, **The Chessmen**, The Breakaways, The Saxons, The Fabulous Blue Jays, The Marksmen and The Playboys, The Thunderbirds were one of the bastions of Melbourne's early 1960s rock scene. The Thunderbirds backed many solo singers on the Melbourne dance circuit, and virtually became resident band for Ron Tudor's W&G label during the early 1960s. The Thunderbirds were not the first Melbourne rock'n'roll group to record (Henri Bource All Stars hold that distinction), but they achieved an enormous level of popularity.

Drummer Harold Frith formed the first line-up of The Thunderbirds in September 1957. That line-up was short-lived. In early 1958, Frith and Bell re-formed The Thunderbirds with Murray Robertson (piano) and Peter Robinson (bass). **Colin Cook** (ex-Sapphires) then joined on sax. Graham Lyall (sax, flute; ex-Sapphires) joined towards the end of 1958. By that stage, The Thunderbirds had also incorporated three featured vocalists into the line-up, Billy Owens, Billy O'Rourke and **Judy Cannon**. The Thunderbirds became resident group at Earl's Court in St Kilda. In late 1959, The Thunderbirds signed to Festival's Rex label which resulted in the release of two EPs and two singles. Owens, O'Rourke and Cannon sang a song each on the band's debut EP, *Rex 4 Star* (completed by one instrumental track, Duane Eddy's 'Peter Gunn'). Owens and O'Rourke sang two songs each on the second EP, *The Thunderbirds*, and the debut single 'Running Bear'/'Blue Woman' (1959). **Judy Cannon** took vocal honours on the second single, 'Ma, He's Making Eyes at Me'/'Laughing on the Outside' (April 1960).

By the end of 1960, The Thunderbirds' line-up comprised Frith and Robertson, plus newcomers Henri Bource (sax, flute; ex-Henri Bource All Stars), Gordon Onley (bass; ex-Malcolm Arthur and the Knights) and 17-year-old Charles Gauld (guitar). The Henri Bource All Stars are credited with having issued the very first Australian rock'n'roll album, *Rock'n'Roll Party*, on the Planet label in 1958. Peter Robinson joined **The Strangers** in 1961, remaining with them for over ten years. **Colin Cook** went on to enjoy a very successful solo career. The Thunderbirds left Rex and, with help from top Melbourne DJ Stan Rofe, signed a new deal with the W&G label. The Thunderbirds recorded for W&G as an instrumental outfit. The band's run of singles comprised a cover of The Rockin' Rebels' 'Wild Weekend'/'Theme from the Rat Race' (February 1961), 'New Orleans Beat'/'Delilah' (April 1961), The Riptides' 'Machine Gun'/'Teen Scene' (June 1961), The Royaltones' 'Royal Whirl'/'Yippee Hoedown' (December 1961), 'Dardanella'/'What Me Worry?' (1962), 'Wild Weekend'/'Yippee Hoedown' (reissued 1962), The Markeys' 'One Degree North'/'Amarillo Stomp' (1962) and 'Pink Dominoes'/'Walk on the Wild Side' (1962).

'Wild Weekend', 'New Orleans Beat' and 'Machine Gun' were all hits in Melbourne, reaching

#13, #10 and #16 respectively. All six sides of those three singles appeared as the EP *The Thunderbirds' Big 6* in late 1961. English label Oriole issued the 'Wild Weekend' and 'New Orleans Beat' singles in the UK. The Melbourne label also issued 'Wild Weekend' in the USA. 'Wild Weekend' must rank alongside **The Atlantics** 1963 hit 'Bombora' as one of the most successful Australian instrumental singles of all-time. At the end of 1961, The Thunderbirds supported Roy Orbison, Ray Peterson and Dion on their package tour of Australia. That was followed with a support slot to Cliff Richard and the Shadows, alongside The Allen Brothers, Andy Ellis and **Judy Stone**. In 1962 The Thunderbirds appeared on the live album *Quite a Party* issued on W&G's budget Gem label. The band featured on three instrumental tracks, as well as providing backing for **Johnny Chester**, Noel Watson and Jillian Buckley.

By that stage, The Thunderbirds had backed a number of solo artists both on record and on tour. They included **Johnny Chester**, Colin Buckley, **Betty McQuade** ('Midnight Bus'), **Bobby Cookson** and the Thin Men. Tony Buchanan (ex-Premiers, **Planets**) played sax on the Thin Men's single 'Here She Comes'/'Sorry (I Ran All the Way Home)' having replaced Henri Bource, who joined **The Planets**. **Normie Rowe** and Marcia Jones also began their singing careers fronting The Thunderbirds at the Preston Town Hall dances. The Thunderbirds were augmented by a brass section of Ken Jones (baritone sax), Norman Robertson (tenor sax) and Ivan Cocking (trombone) for their appearances at Preston Town Hall. The Thunderbirds went on to appear with Helen Shapiro, Fabian, **Lonnie Lee**, **Johnny O'Keefe**, **Lucky Starr** and **The Bee Gees** at various concerts.

In 1964, Terry Clark replaced Murray Robertson on piano. A year later, Clark and Gordon Onley left The Thunderbirds and by the end of 1965, the band had called it a day. Gauld and Frith formed The Charlie Gauld Trio with Frank McMahon (bass; ex-**Chessmen**). Noel Tresider (ex-Premiers) later joined on keyboards. Gauld went on to be resident guitar player for W&G Records, and lead guitarist and musical arranger for the Brian May ABC Show Band. Frith played with Nite Train, Doctor Feelgood, The Promised Land and 1970s country-rock band Saltbush. Bource performed with **The Planets** and The Johnny Donohue Quartet before retiring following a near-fatal shark attack in November 1964. Murray Robertson became musical director for **Merv Benton**, and in 1983 he and Bource formed The Allstars. Billed as 'Australia's most authentic 1950s group', The Allstars included former members of **The Planets**, **The Blue Echoes**, **The Chessmen**, **Jigsaw** and The Thunderbirds.

In 1983, The Thunderbirds re-formed briefly for a 1960s revival concert. The line-up comprised Charles Gauld, Henri Bource, Murray Robertson, Gordon Onley and Harold Frith. The night also included performances by **Judy Cannon, Betty McQuade**, Malcolm Arthur and Billy Owens. In 1990, the Canetoad label included 17 Thunderbirds' tracks on the collection *The W&G Instrumental Story*. Other bands featured were **The Strangers**, **The Cherokees**, **The Phantoms**, The Breakaways, The Marksmen and The Saxons. Canetoad also compiled most of The Thunderbirds' best-known tracks for the collection *The W&G Instrumental Story Volume Two*. In the mid-1990s, Frith, Peter Robinson, Danny Robinson (vocals; ex-**Wild Cherries**) and another Melbourne mainstay, Les Stacpool (ex-**Chessmen**, **Merv Benton** and the Tamlas, **Levi Smith's Clefs**, **Rockwell T. James** and the Rhythm Aces), formed Alright on the Night. In 1997, Frith and Robinson re-formed The Thunderbirds to record new material.

Albums: *Quite a Party* (Gem/W&G, 1962), *The W&G Instrumental Story* (compilation shared with other bands, Canetoad, 1990), *The W&G Instrumental Story Volume Two* (Canetoad, 1990).

Tiddas

Formed: *1991*
Style: *Folk pop*
Original line-up: *Lou Bennett (vocals, acoustic guitar), Sally Dastey (vocals, acoustic guitar), Amy Saunders (vocals, percussion)*

Lou Bennett, Sally Dastey and Amy Saunders came together in 1990 as backing singers for Saunders' brother Richard Franklin's band Djaambi. In 1991, the trio struck out on their own to unexpected and wide-ranging success. Koori singer **Ruby Hunter** suggested the trio call themselves Tiddas from an Aboriginal word meaning 'sisters'. The Tiddas stock in trade was heartfelt, honest and remarkably powerful songs and exquisite three-part vocal harmonies.

By combining traditional Aboriginal instrumentation, spirituality and folk songs with Western acoustic guitar and rock influences, Tiddas created a unique yet accessible musical legacy. Shorthand reference points include the likes of The Indigo Girls and The Roches. The trio's music has warmed international audiences and allowed them to cross racial and social barriers. Tiddas stand proud alongside **Archie Roach**, **Ruby Hunter**, **Kev Carmody**,

Warumpi Band and **Yothu Yindi** in the growing body of contemporary Aboriginal music.

The trio's debut release, the modest CD EP *Inside My Kitchen* (on Id/Mercury, October 1992), brought instant acclaim and two nominations for Best New Talent and Best Indigenous Record at the 1992 Australian Record Industry Association (ARIA) Awards. Tiddas supported groups as disparate as US harmony singers Sweet Honey in the Rock and **Midnight Oil**. The trio added didgeridoo player Tim 'Froggie' Holtze, and recorded their debut, full-length album *Sing About Life*. Issued in late 1993, *Sing About Life* was a simple, unadorned acoustic folk album. It went on to achieve gold status (35 000 copies sold), and won Best Indigenous Record at the 1993 ARIA Awards.

Tiddas toured nationally (including the Big Day Out tour) and then headed overseas for extensive tours across Europe and North America. They supported UK singer Billy Bragg, and performed at two WOMAD concerts in Britain (Reading, Bath) and a third in Granada, Spain where they shared the stage with the likes of Suzanne Vega and Van Morrison. Back in Australia, Tiddas performed at the 1995 WOMADelaide Festival alongside the likes of Sierra Maestra, Papa Wemba, Nusrat Fateh Ali Khan and Australia's **Cruel Sea**. *Sing About Life* came out in the USA in September 1995, and Tiddas embarked on a second (five month) tour of North America (supporting Billy Bragg, Arlo Guthrie and Robyn Hitchcock) and Europe.

In early 1996, Tiddas recorded their second album with producer Joe Camilleri (from **Black Sorrows**) and engineer Laurence Maddick. Backing musicians on the album sessions included **The Black Sorrows'** Jen Anderson (violin), Peter Luscombe (drums) and Steven Hadley (bass), **Weddings, Parties, Anything's** Mark 'Squeezebox Wally' Wallace (piano accordion) and Kavisha Mazzella. Camilleri also contributed sax to the track 'Waving Goodbye'. Issued in August 1996, *Tiddas* was a mature, polished and dynamic album. It reached the National Top 40, and spawned the single 'Ignorance is Bliss' (June). That song had been inspired by a 'heated' discussion with Sir Bob Geldof while on tour in 1993. Other standouts on the album included 'Anthem', written by Dan Warner from Melbourne band Overnight Jones, the traditional Torres Strait Island folk song 'No Goon No Pah' and the delicate 'Burdens to Bear'. Tiddas commenced 1997 with an appearance on the national bill of the Big Day Out tour, and a new CD single, 'Walk Alone' (April).

Albums: *Sing About Life* (Id/Mercury, 1993), *Tiddas* (Id/Mercury, 1996).

Dutch Tilders

Style: *Blues, folk*

Dutch-descended singer/guitarist/songwriter Mathew 'Dutch' Tilders (b. 1939) has been a stalwart fixture on the local blues scene since the 1960s. Tilders has rarely courted mainstream success, despite his reputation as one of the country's foremost blues exponents.

Tilders migrated to Australia from the Netherlands in 1955. According to Noel McGrath, Tilders made his first record in 1961, a 10-inch album which he had recorded at a friend's home studio. In 1962, Tilders teamed up with Shane Duckham, and the duo became popular on the Sydney folk–blues circuit. Tilders spent much of the 1960s away from the music business. In September 1970, he appeared on Melbourne television talent show *New Faces*. One of the judges on the night, Fable label manager Ron Tudor, was impressed enough to sign Tilders to the Bootleg label in 1972. Tilders' debut solo album *Dutch Tilders* proved the man's mastery of the blues form. One side featured Tilders playing down-home Mississippi delta acoustic blues, the flip Chicago electric blues with backing provided by members of **Chain**. Tilders played all the rock clubs and pubs of the day, as well as appearing at Sunburys 1973 and 1974. The live track 'Sweet Marie' appeared on the Various Artists album *Garrison The Final Blow Unit 2* on Mushroom (1973).

In 1974, Tilders toured with UK bluesman John Mayall, and issued a split album with folk-blues singer **Margret Roadknight**, *Australian Jazz of the 70s Vol. 5 The Blues Singers*, on the Jazznote label. The Larrikin label reissued the album in 1980 under the title *Bluesmakers*. Tilders recorded his debut album for the Eureka label, *Break*, live to two-track. His backing band comprised Phil Colson (guitar; **Foreday Riders**), Don Reid (sax), Keith Dubber (trumpet, flugel horn), John Power (bass; **Company Caine**) and Rick Lock (drums; **Foreday Riders**). As well as four Tilders originals, the album included blues covers like Lightnin' Hopkins' 'Lonesome Dog Blues', Leadbelly's 'Good Morning Blues' and Blind Blake's 'Diddie Wa Diddie'. 'I'm a Mean Mistreater'/'21st Birthday Rag' appeared as a single. In 1976, Tilders supported visiting blues masters Sonny Terry and Brownie McGhee, and B.B. King, on their respective Australian tours. Tilders' fourth album, *Working Man*, featured contributions from backing musicians Jim Conway (harp; **Captain Matchbox Whoopee Band**), Kerryn Tolhurst (mandolin, dobro; **Dingoes**), John Dubois (bass; **Dingoes**), **Ray Arnott** (drums; **Dingoes**) and Jeff

King (dobro; **Foreday Riders**). *Working Man* gave rise to one single, a cover of Leadbelly's 'Goodnight Irene'/'Working Man' (February 1977).

In January 1979, Tilders recorded his next album using the direct-to-disc process, which involved recording live in the studio and cutting the music direct to a master disc. *Direct* came out on Eureka in May. Tilders' backing musicians were Jim Conway (mouth harp), Bob Bertles (alto, soprano saxes) and Peter Howell (bass). In August 1980, Tilders entered the studio with the **Kevin Borich Express** to record the album *The Blues Had a Baby* using the direct-to-disc process. The Express comprised Kevin Borich (lead guitar, vocals), Michael Deep (bass) and John Watson (drums), with Bob Bertles contributing sax. The album produced the single 'Bad Books'/'The Blues Had a Baby' (April 1981).

Tilders remained active on the scene for the remainder of the 1980s, but did not issue any albums during that period. In 1989, he formed The Blues Club with **Geoff Achison** (lead guitar), Martin Corcoran (baritone sax), Terry Noone (tenor sax), Barry Hills (bass) and Winston Galea (drums). Dutch Tilders and the Blues Club issued two albums, *The Blues is My Life* (April 1990) and *Live* (1993). The band also contributed a track to the compilation album *Real Australian Blues* (Blues Club, 1992). In 1994, Tilders was working with The Holey Soles: Anthony Harkin (harmonica), Barry Hills (bass) and Ian Clarke (drums). The second Holey Soles line-up comprised Clarke, Luke Keoh (harmonica) and Peter Howell (bass). The Dutch Tilders Band circa early 1996 consisted of Greg Dodd (guitar), Barry Hills (bass) and Winston Galea (drums).

Dutch Tilders albums: *Dutch Tilders* (Bootleg, 1973), *Australian Jazz of the 70s Vol. 5 The Blues Singers* (shared with **Margret Roadknight**, Jazznote, 1974; reissued as *Bluesmakers*, Larrikin, 1980 and again on EMI, 1981), *Break* (Eureka, 1975), *Working Man* (Eureka, 1977), *Direct* (Eureka, 1979), *Eureka Files 1975–1980* (Blues Club, 1992); ***Borich'n'Tilders album:*** *The Blues Had a Baby* (with **Kevin Borich Express**, Eureka, 1980); ***Dutch Tilders and the Blues Club albums:*** *The Blues is My Life* (Blues Club, 1990), *Live* (Blues Club, 1993).

Louis Tillett

Style: *Rock*

Sydney-based singer/songwriter/pianist Louis Tillett (b. 1959) has earned a reputation as a solo artist of considerable imagination, authority and confidence, and as a sideman of redoubtable stature. Tillett has lent his resonant vocals, distinctive piano technique and powerful songwriting skills to groups like Wet Taxis, No Dance, Paris Green and The Aspersion Caste, to say nothing of his work as a backing musician with **Catfish** (Don Walker), **Ed Kuepper**, **The New Christs** and **Tex Perkins**.

Tillett's first band, Wet Taxis, started out as an experimental outfit in the manner of fellow Sydneysiders **Severed Heads**, **Scattered Order** and Negative Reaction. Wet Taxis issued one cassette, *Taxidermy* (1980), on **Severed Heads'** Terse Tapes label, and contributed tracks to the *Terse Sampler* EP (December 1980). By 1981, Tillett was steering Wet Taxis in a tougher 1960s-influenced direction. The line-up comprised Tillett (vocals, piano), Simon Knuckey (guitar), Tim Knuckey (bass) and Gary Bradbury (drum machine). Nick Fisher replaced Bradbury on drums in 1982. Peter Watt also joined on rhythm guitar, to be replaced by Penny Ikinger a year later. The band's repertoire by that stage comprised predominantly covers of material by American 1960s garage-punk bands such as We the People, The Moving Sidewalks, The Lemon Fog and The Chocolate Watch Band. The band's debut single on the Hot label, 'C'Mon'/'Clock On the Wall' (May 1984), featured such an authentic 1960s garage/R&B sound that few people realised 'C'Mon' had originally been issued by **The Atlantics** in 1967 (as 'Come on'). Wet Taxis also issued the appropriately named *From the Archives* album at the end of 1984.

One of Tillett's first sideline ventures was studio band No Dance with **Died Pretty**'s Brett Myers and **The Celibate Rifles'** Damian Lovelock. No Dance eschewed the electric rock framework of the musicians' respective bands for a more acoustic and melodic approach. The trio recorded the EP *Carnival of Souls*, which came out on Hot in March 1984. Tillett contributed 'Swimming in the Mirror', Myers 'Just Skin' and Lovelock 'You Say'. Towards the end of 1984, Tillett also began to play with a loose aggregation of musicians under the name of Paris Green (he eventually put Wet Taxis on hold in February 1985). Based around Tillett, Raoul Hawkins (bass) and Jeffrey Wegener (drums; ex-**Laughing Clowns**), Paris Green was designed as a jamming outfit where other musicians would get up for a blow. Driven by an enormous energy and desire to create according to their own rules, the musicians accepted no boundaries. The band covered material ranging from Mose Allison to John Coltrane, Ray Charles to Nina Simone, and on any given night there was as many as nine or ten musicians on stage.

Inevitably Paris Green operated on an irregular

Louis Tillett

basis, and Tillett resurrected Wet Taxis in January 1986 with the line-up of Fisher, Ikinger, Jason Kain (lead guitar; ex-Relatives), Rod Howard (bass) and Dr Bronstantine Karlarka (keyboards). Dianne Spence (sax), Kathy Wemyss (trumpet) and Glad Reed (trombone) later augmented the band on stage and record. Spence and Reed had been members of the final **Laughing Clowns** line-up at the end of 1984. Spence had started out in 1982 with Great White Noise. Michael Tinney (guitar), Lenny Bastiaans (bass, vocals) and Tony Buck (drums) completed the line-up. Great White Noise was an important part of the Sydney-based, post-punk jazz improvisation movement of the early 1980s, which also included Kill The King and Upside Down House. Great White Noise issued a self-titled cassette, and a couple of tracks from it appeared on the Various Artists compilation album *March of the Five Limbs*. The track 'Parent Apparent' appeared on the UK compilation of Australian bands *Beneath the Southern Cross* on the Red Flame subsidiary label Ink (1984). The band broke up in 1984. After working with **Laughing Clowns**, and before joining Wet Taxis, Spence played with a band called Carnival of Souls.

Wet Taxis undertook several Australian tours (including supporting former Velvet Underground chanteuse Nico), and issued a new single, 'Sailor's Dream'/'Ambulance Ride', on the Citadel label (May 1987). Produced by Rob Younger, 'Sailor's Dream' was an amazing slice of horn-driven R&B. The band broke up mid-year, and Tillett lost no time in recording his debut solo album, *Ego Tripping at the Gates of Hell*, for Citadel (issued in November). Tillett utilised the services of a stellar array of backing musicians for the album, including Charlie Owen (lead guitar; ex-Tango Bravo, Paris Green, **New Christs**), Lenny Bastiaans (bass), Dianne Spence (sax) and Louis Burdett (drums; ex-Benders, Paris Green, **New Christs**). The album traversed jazz, blues, R&B, pop and rock, making for fascinating and engrossing listening. Tillett toured with a 12-piece backing band, The Ego Trippers from Hell, in support of the album's release.

In 1989, Tillett formed The Aspersion Caste, with Owen, Bastiaans, Ikinger (by then ex-Kings of the World), Burdett, James Greening (trombone), Miroslav Bukovsky (trumpet) and Jason Morphett (sax). The band's debut single for the Blue Mosque label (through Festival), 'Condemned to Live'/'Midnight Witch' (January 1990), was an astonishing gut-bucket blues that packed a considerable punch. The single was a taster from the album *A Cast of Aspersions* (April 1990), another eclectic set of material driven by Tillett's booming baritone voice and smouldering organ, Owen's jagged guitar lines and the swinging brass arrangements. Mary-Ellen Stringer (ex-Kings of the World) contributed backing vocals. 'Carousel'/'Persephone's Dance' was lifted as the album's second single (August 1990). Tillett took The Aspersion Caste out on the road in Australia, before undertaking a tour of Europe, where the album had garnered considerable praise and respectable sales.

The 1991 Aspersion Caste line-up consisted of Colin Watson (guitar), **Jackie Orszaczky** (bass; ex-Syrius), Dianne Spence (sax) and Nick Fisher (drums). Damian Kennedy then replaced Orszaczky on bass. In 1992, Tillett dispensed with The Aspersion Caste for his second solo album, *Letters to a Dream* (October). The album was structured as a series of replies to dreams. Many of the songs were built around just Tillett's voice and piano, with minimal embellishment from Mary-Ellen Stringer and Peter Boyd (sax). In 1995, Tillett collaborated with old cohort Charlie Owen on the album *Midnight Rain*, which came out in October. Tillett and Owen toured in support of the album's release. In August 1996, Tillett and Owen joined Ken Gormly (bass) and Jim Elliot (drums) as backing musicians for **Tex Perkins** on tour to promote his solo album *Far Be It from Me*.

Wet Taxis album: *From the Archives* (Hot, 1984); ***Louis Tillett solo albums:*** *Ego Tripping at the Gates of Hell* (Citadel, 1987), *Letters to a Dream* (Blue Mosque/Festival, 1992); ***Louis Tillett and the Aspersion Caste album:*** *A Cast of Aspersions* (Blue Mosque/Festival, 1990); ***Louis Tillett and Charlie Owen album:*** *Midnight Rain* (Red Eye/Polydor, 1995).

TISM (*see* This Is Serious Mum)

TMG (*see* Ted Mulry Gang)

Toys Went Beserk (*see* Box of Fish)

The Town Criers

Formed: *1967*
Style: *Pop*
Original line-up: *Andy Agtoft (lead vocals), Sam Dunnin (lead guitar; ex-Gemini 5), George Kurtiss (keyboards), Mark Demajo (bass; ex-Gemini 5), Chris Easterby (drums)*

Melbourne band The Town Criers made a name for themselves with a melodious, commercial pop sound and squeaky-clean teen idol image. The group formed in July 1967 and in February 1968 issued its debut single on the Astor label. The band's version of Love Affair's 'Everlasting Love'/ 'I Can't Help Myself' reached #17 in Melbourne and #16 in Sydney during March.

George Kurtiss left in May 1968 to be replaced by John Taylor (ex-Strings Unlimited). The band's second single, 'Unexpectedly'/'It's Hurting Badly' (September 1968), failed to reach the Top 40. In November, The Town Criers embarked on a tour of South-East Asia to entertain American troops stationed in Vietnam. The band also travelled to the US and made an appearance on the *Bob Hope Christmas Special.* In early 1969, Andy Agtoft and John Taylor left the band. Taylor joined Sydney soul/pop band Daisy Clover which comprised Greg Hunt (vocals), Nick Kvenos (guitar, vocals) and Jimmy Maxwell (drums). Daisy Clover issued two singles on Festival, 'Tell Me'/'Butterflies' (July 1969) and 'Penny Brown Girl'/'Barbara' (November 1969). Bernadette O'Neill (ex-Browns) joined at the start of 1970, but a few months later Daisy Clover parted ways. Hunt and Maxwell re-formed Daisy Clover in 1971 with a new line-up.

The remaining three members of The Town Criers took on new frontman Barry Smith to replace Agtoft. The Town Criers signed a new deal with Festival records for the singles 'Any Old Time'/'Rene' (March 1969), 'Love Me Again'/'Hey Girl' (October) and 'Living in a World of Love'/'Roundabout' (May 1970). 'Love Me Again' managed to reach #35 in Melbourne, but the other singles were not successful. In October 1970, The Town Criers moved over to EMI's His Master's Voice (HMV) label for the singles 'Laughing Man'/'Living in a Dream World' (May 1971) and 'Love Love Love'/'Chorus Girl' (November). By the end of 1971, The Town Criers' sound had become outmoded, and the members went their separate ways.

As well as the singles listed, The Town Criers issued two EPs, 'Everlasting Love' (1968) and 'Love Me Again' (1969). Reissue specialists Raven included the chirpy 'Everlasting Love' on the compilation *Kicks (The Great Lost Australian 60s Pop Album)* (1984) alongside tracks by **Procession, Pastoral Symphony, The Iguana, Ronnie Charles**, The Virgil Brothers, Somebody's Image, Nineteen87 and The Playboys.

The Triffids

Formed: *1978*
Style: *Pop, folk, country*
Original line-up: *David McComb (vocals, bass, guitar, keyboards), Phillip Kakulas (guitar, vocals), Alsy MacDonald (drums, vocals, piano)*

Perth, Western Australia band The Triffids remain one of Australia's best-loved, post-punk groups. Frontman David McComb was an authoritative singer and accomplished songwriter and, while his influences were mostly American, he infused his melancholy songs with stark yet beautiful and uniquely Australian imagery. Few songwriters managed to capture the feeling of isolation and fatalistic sense of despair of the Australian countryside as did McComb with songs like 'Hell of a Summer', 'Raining Pleasure' and the evocative 'Wide Open Road'. Like **The Saints, The Birthday Party, The Go-Betweens, Laughing Clowns, The Moodists** and **Scientists** before them, The Triffids left Australia in 1984 to reside in the UK where they garnered considerable acclaim.

David McComb and Alsy MacDonald formed Dalsy in 1976 while still at high school. The Triffids emerged from Blok Musik in May 1978. McComb had started out on bass so, when Byron Sinclair took over bass during September, he moved to rhythm guitar. Within two years of formation, and armed with over 100 McComb originals, The Triffids had issued six independent cassette albums and become Perth's most popular non-covers band. Fired by such disparate sources as Bob Dylan, Talking Heads,

Television, folk, country and blues, McComb was even then a prolific songwriter. Phillip Kakulas and Sinclair left in 1979 to be replaced by Robert McComb (violin, guitar) and Will Akers (bass). Margaret Gillard also joined on keyboards in 1980. Kakulas later went to join **Martha's Vineyard** and **The Blackeyed Susans**.

At the end of 1980, The Triffids won first prize in a song competition held by Perth radio station 6NR. The prize resulted in the recording of the band's debut single, 'Stand Up'/'Farmers Never Visit Nightclubs', which came out on the Shake Some Action label in July 1981. Mark Peters played drums on the single as MacDonald left for two months in early 1981. In August 1981, the band recorded the delightful four-track EP 'Reverie', 'Place in the Sun'/'Joan of Arc', 'This Boy' which appeared on the Resonant label in April 1982. By that stage, The Triffids were resident in Sydney. Gillard and Akers left in February 1982 to be replaced by Jill Yates (keyboards; ex-Teeny Weenies) and the returning Sinclair. By mid-year, Martyn Casey had replaced Sinclair on bass.

The four-piece line-up of David and Robert McComb, MacDonald and Casey moved to Melbourne where they signed to Mushroom's White label. The Triffids issued their second single, 'Spanish Blue'/'Twisted Brain', initially on the No label (through EMI Custom), before White reissued it in October 1982. The acclaimed '*Bad Timing' and Other Stories* EP ('Bad Timing', 'Left to Rot'/'Being Driven', 'Snake Pit') came out on White in April 1983, by which time The Triffids were back in Sydney. Jill Burt had also joined on organ and vocals. With the EP out, The Triffids began to build up a large and enthusiastic following on the inner-city circuit.

The self-produced album *Treeless Plain* appeared on the Hot label in November 1983. Although the brilliant and justly acclaimed album yielded no singles, it contained a number of live favourites like 'Red Pony', 'My Baby Thinks She's a Train' and 'Hell of a Summer'. Hot issued the single 'Beautiful Waste'/'Property is Condemned' (February 1984), after which the band entered the studio with producer Nick Mainsbridge (who had engineered *Treeless Plain*) to record the mini-album *Raining Pleasure*. Issued in July 1984, it was another superb release highlighted by the shimmering title track 'Raining Pleasure' (sung by Burt), the atmospheric country-blues of 'Jesus Calling' and a mournful rendering of the traditional blues tune 'St James Infirmary'. The last two may have been the inspiration behind the sideline project Lawson Square Infirmary, a one-off aggregation comprising David, Robert, MacDonald, Rob Snarski (bass), James Peterson (piano) and Graham Lee (dobro, pedal steel). The group came together through a mutual love of country music. Hot issued the *Lawson Square Infirmary* mini-album in October 1984.

By that stage, The Triffids had returned to Perth from where they flew to London. The Triffids had already built up a cult following in the UK via a distribution deal with the Rough Trade label. *Treeless Plain* and *Raining Pleasure* garnered positive reviews from the usually fickle British rock press. The band's first UK recording session in November 1984 resulted in the three-track, 12-inch EP 'Field of Glass' (February 1985). 'Bright Lights Big City' and 'Monkey on My Back' furthered McComb's more reflective songwriting processes, while the epic 'Field of Glass' was nine minutes of rumbling rhythms, eerie organ flows, crashing guitars and sheer lyrical invective.

When The Triffids returned to Australia in early 1985, 'Evil' Graham Lee (ex-Lawson Square Infirmary, **John Kennedy's Love Gone Wrong**) joined on acoustic guitar and pedal steel. Hot issued a new Triffids single, William Bell's 'You Don't Miss Your Water (Till Your Well Runs Dry)'/'Convent Walls', in August 1985. That same month, The Triffids entered the studios in London with producer Gil Norton and engineer Nick Mainsbridge to record their third album. *Born Sandy Devotional* (March 1986) appeared to almost universal praise, and produced the classic single 'Wide Open Road'/'Time of Weakness' (February). *Born Sandy Devotional* was full of some of the most lonely, spacious songs ever written, and it remains one of the best Australian albums of the 1980s. It peaked at #26 on the UK mainstream charts.

With the local release of the album, The Triffids returned to Australia in order to tour. During April, the band set up an eight-track recording desk in an isolated shearing shed 600 kilometres south east of Perth on the edge of the Nullarbor Plain. The recording sessions resulted in the album *In the Pines* (January 1987) which evoked the spirit of The Band, Gram Parsons and the softer side of The Velvet Underground with a wonderfully relaxed, offbeat and uncontrived set of songs. The Triffids undertook a British tour in late 1986, after which they returned to Australia for the ambitious Australian Made tour (January 1987) alongside **Mental as Anything, The Saints, I'm Talking, Models, Jimmy Barnes** and **INXS**. Having signed to the prestigious Island label (home to the likes of Free, Fairport Convention, Nick Drake, Bob Marley and U2), The Triffids returned to the UK to record a new album with Craig Leon. The sessions were abandoned, and Gil Norton took over from Leon to complete the album.

Calenture (February 1988) was the band's most ambitious and expensive project to date. It produced two lush singles, 'Bury me Deep in Love'/'Baby can I Walk You Home' (December 1987) and 'A Trick of the Light'/'Love the Fever (March 1988). 'A Trick of the Light' became The Triffids' only single to chart in the British mainstream listings when it peaked at #73 for one week. The 12-inch version of 'Bury me Deep in Love' added the non-album track 'Region Unknown', while the 12-inch of 'A Trick of the Light' likewise added the non-album tracks 'Bad News Always Reminds Me of You' and 'Everything You Touch Turns to Time'. Island also issued the UK-only, 12-inch EP 'Holy Water', 'Raining Pleasure'/'Good Morning, Good Morning', 'Red Pony'.

The album's release locally coincided with the band's fourth annual Australian tour. The second Island album, *The Black Swan* (June 1989), yielded the wistful pop single 'Goodbye Little Boy'/'Go Home Eddie' (June) sung by Burt (the 12-inch added 'Shell of the Man') and the rap-influenced single 'Falling Over You'/'Can't Help Falling in Love' (September). In June, The Triffids were back in Australia for a tour, after which David McComb and MacDonald moonlighted with one-time Triffids member Phil Kakulas (bass; ex-**Martha's Vineyard**), plus Rob Snarski (guitar, vocals; ex-**Chad's Tree**) and Ross Bolleter (keyboards) as **The Blackeyed Susans.**

The Triffids returned to the UK once again, but by the end of 1989 had parted ways. The band's final album, *Stockholm Live* (February 1990), had been recorded for Swedish National Radio and concentrated on early material such as 'Property is Condemned', 'Hell of a Summer' and 'Wide Open Road'. McComb recorded the single 'I Don't Need You' with latter-day Triffids arranger Adam Peters, plus the solo single 'The Message' before returning to Australia in 1991. He and Graham Lee joined **The Blackeyed Susans** on a permanent basis. McComb appeared on the albums *Welcome Stranger* (1992) and *All Souls Alive* (1993), after which he recorded his debut solo album *Love of Will.*

McComb's studio band The Red Ponies comprised one-time Triffids alumni Lee, Martyn Casey (by that stage a member of **Nick Cave's** band The Bad Seeds) and Will Akers, plus Bruce Haymes (keyboards; ex-**Stephen Cummings** Band, **Bachelors from Prague**), Peter Luscombe (drums; from **Black Sorrows**) and **The Blackeyed Susans'** Phil Kakulas and Rob Snarski on backing vocals. Warren Ellis from **The Blackeyed Susans** and **Dirty Three** joined on violin when the band toured. *Love of Will* (December 1993) produced the CD singles 'Setting You Free' (November) and 'Clear Out My Mind' (January 1994). McComb set out on tour with the Red Ponies in order to promote the album (including a trip to the UK). The compilation *Australian Melodrama* (November 1994) drew together 19 classic Triffids songs covering the period 1983 to 1989.

Triffids albums: *Treeless Plain* (Hot, 1983), *Raining Pleasure* (mini-album, Hot, 1984), *Born Sandy Devotional* (White Hot/Mushroom/Festival, 1986), *In the Pines* (White Hot/Mushroom/Festival, 1987), *Love in Bright Landscapes* (compilation, White Hot/Mushroom/Festival, 1987), *Calenture* (White Hot/Mushroom/Festival, 1988), *The Black Swan* (White Hot/Mushroom/Festival, 1989), *Stockholm Live* (White/Mushroom/Festival, 1990), *Australian Melodrama* (compilation, White Hot/Mushroom/Festival, 1994); ***David McComb solo album:*** *Love of Will* (Mushroom/Festival, 1994); ***Lawson Square Infirmary mini-album:*** *Lawson Square Infirmary* (Hot, 1984).

The Trilobites

Formed: *1984*
Style: *Rock*
Original line-up: *Mike Dalton (vocals), Paul Skates (guitar), Martin Martini (guitar), Scott Leighton (bass), Paul Styman (drums)*

Sydney five-piece The Trilobites grew out of that city's push towards the kind of guitar-driven raunch'n'roll which was directly descended from Detroit bands like MC5 and The Stooges. Yet The Trilobites always infused their aggressive, garage rock sound with a punchy, 1960s-influenced power pop sensibility that highlighted the tuneful harmonies and strong melodies on offer.

The Citadel label issued the band's first two, classic singles, 'Venus in Leather'/'Amphetamine Dream' (October 1985) and 'American TV'/'Legacy of Morons' (August 1986). Both singles reached #1 on the alternative charts, and the band toured to a strong response. 'Venus in Leather' and 'Legacy of Morons' appeared on Citadel's essential compilation *Take Everything Leave Nothing* (March 1988). In the meantime, The Trilobites had signed a new deal with the Big Time label which resulted in the single 'Night of The Many Deaths'/'Living by a Different Yardstick' (May 1987).

At the end of the year, the band issued its debut album, the live set *Turn It Around*, on the Waterfront label (December). Waterfront also put out the band's fourth single, 'Jenny's Wake'/'I Can See' (June 1988). At that stage, The Trilobites came to

The Trilobites

the attention of the fledgling rooArt label. The band contributed 'All Hail the New Right' to rooArt's inaugural *Youngblood* compilation (September 1988), alongside material from **Tall Tales & True**, **Martha's Vineyard**, **Crash Politics**, **Hipslingers**, **The Hummingbirds**, Violet Town and others.

That led to a full recording contract which resulted in the 12-inch EP/CD EP 'I Can't Wait for Summer to End' (March 1989). The Trilobites also appeared on a split, promotional single which combined 'All Hail the New Right' with **Tall Tales & True's** 'You've Got Your Troubles' (December 1988). Englishman Steve James produced The Trilobites' debut studio album, *Savage Mood Swing* (March 1990), which yielded the controversial 12-inch single 'Fuck=Love'/'Little Death', 'Legacy of Morons ('89 mix) (September 1989) and the single 'New Head'/'Minibar of Oblivion' (February 1990). Between recording the album (March 1989) and its release, The Trilobites also undertook a successful European tour (late 1989).

In 1991, frontman Mike Dalton left the band to concentrate on his career as a television producer. One of his Executive Producer roles was with the Australian edition of the American-devised *MTV* (Music Television). Gary Slater (ex-Voodoo Lust) took his place. Glen Abbott also replaced Styman on drums, and The Trilobites returned to the Citadel label for the single 'Tear You Apart'/'Don't Hide' (October 1991) and the mini-album *Lost Generation* (February 1992). Citadel also combined the single and mini-album for the eight-track CD *Lost Generation*. The band continued to tour locally, but made little further impact.

Albums: *Turn It Around* (Waterfront, 1987), *Savage Mood Swing* (rooArt/PolyGram, 1990), *Lost Generation* (Citadel, 1992).

Trilogy (*see* Black Alice)

Tully

Formed: *1968*
Style: *Progressive rock, folk*
Original line-up: *Terry Wilson (vocals, flute), Michael Carlos (organ, piano; ex-Little Sammy and the In People,* **Levi Smith's Clefs***), Richard Lockwood (sax, flute, clarinet, piano; ex-***Levi Smith's Clefs***), John Blake (bass;* **Levi Smith's Clefs***), Robert Taylor (drums; ex-***Levi Smith's Clefs***)*

If the late 1960s was a time of radical social and musical change, when rock musicians went in search of cosmic enlightenment by mingling Eastern philosophies with Western ideals, then Sydney band Tully was the first local manifestation of that search for Nirvana. Alongside the likes of **Tamam Shud** and **Spectrum**, Tully helped usher in a bold new era of Australian rock music.

To put it all in a historical context, when Tully formed, the local scene was still dominated by teen idol pop stars and all the attendant fan hysteria. Tully's members were serious musicians, willing to experiment and explore sound through intellectual stimulus and emotional feedback. Improvisation and the mood of the moment were the keys to expanded consciousness. To facilitate their search for spiritual awareness, the members of Tully combined rock, jazz, psychedelia and the European symphonic tradition with a large dash of Eastern mysticism that placed the idea of love and self-knowledge at the core of existence. If such a metaphysical aesthetic now seems intolerably pompous and a flight of pure hippie fancy, then remember that Tully was a product of its time, a time when people believed they could change the world. And, for a while, Tully's innovative and creative musical expression really did make a difference.

Tully emerged at the end of 1968 from the ranks of R&B band **Levi Smith's Clefs**. Having recruited singer Terry Wilson, Tully took a residency at Sydney's Caesar's Palace discotheque. The band had to leave a month later because the patrons could not dance to the music. Tully staged a series of concerts at Paddington Town Hall where a hip new generation of self-styled flower children were willing to embrace the band's more avant-garde sound and approach. The lifting refrains of Tully, by all accounts, were best appreciated sitting cross-legged (and somewhat stoned) on the floor. In July 1969, Tully became resident backing band for director Jim Sharman's Australian production of the American 'tribal love-rock musical' *Hair*. Tully appeared on the Original Cast soundtrack album of *Hair* which came out at the end of 1969 on the Spin label. Tully stayed with the stage show for six months, during which time the band also appeared at a series of successful concerts at Sydney Town Hall and the Mandala Theatre.

In late 1969, Tully starred in its own television series, *Fusions*, a program of six half-hour shows produced by the ABC that highlighted the band's live prowess and musical adventurousness. As one of Australia's foremost concert attractions, Tully naturally played a leading role in Australia's first rock festival, Pilgrimage for Pop, Ourimbah, held over the Australia Day weekend, January 1970. By that stage, John Blake had left the band. Graham Conlan (ex-White Wine) and Murray Wilkins (ex-**Chain**) each filled in on a temporary basis until Ken Firth took over permanently.

In February 1970, Tully achieved a new measure of acclaim by being invited to play with the Sydney Symphony Orchestra under the conductorship of John Hopkins. The occasion was the Sydney Prom concerts and the work was composer Peter Sculthorpe's *Love 200*. The band's highly acclaimed debut album *Tully* came out in July 1970. The album's spacious, reverential and lyrical sense of arrangement owed very little to the burgeoning boogie, blues and hard rock movement. It sold surprisingly well, spending ten weeks on the Australian chart after reaching a peak placing of #8.

Tully's concerts at the time were billed as 'Tully and the Moog', with the band becoming the first local group to use the new musical instrument the Moog synthesiser. In December 1970, Terry Wilson and Robert Taylor left the band. The departures were alleged to have been due to the fact that they were the only members not involved in the religious sect Meher Baba. Prior to the departures, Richard Lockwood and Ken Firth worked with Tully's sister band **Extradition** on its debut album. **Extradition's** ultra-rare folk album *Hush* came out in June 1971. By that time, Colin Campbell (acoustic guitar) and Shayna Stewart (nee Shayna Karlin, vocals), both from **Extradition**, had been performing with Tully for six months. The new, drummerless Tully line-up issued the delicate single 'Krishna Came'/'Lord Baba' (May 1971), which reflected the band's religious leanings. Tully's second album, *Sea of Joy* (June 1971), was the soundtrack to Paul Witzig's surfing film of the same name. As such, *Sea of Joy* featured a collection of finely crafted musical themes rather than self-contained songs, although the esoteric, folksy mood of the music suited the film's themes of peace, beauty, simplicity and freedom.

Just before the album appeared, Michael Carlos left Tully to re-join **Levi Smith's Clefs**. Several months later, Tully broke up, and Lockwood joined **Tamam Shud**. Tully's final album, *Loving is Hard* (recorded with Carlos), finally appeared in May 1972. In October 1971, former members Terry Wilson and Robert Taylor launched a new band, Space. Dave Kain (guitar; ex-Dr Kandy's Third Eye), Bobby Gebert (piano), Adrian Falk (cello) and Ian Rilen (bass) completed the line-up. At first the band was wrongly billed as Tully in Space. The band's sound combined the electrified cello with electric blues rock, a unique combination. Space, however, proved to be short-lived. By early 1972, Kain had joined **Company Caine**.

Canadian-born Carlos went on to carve out a respectable career as an in-demand session player and musical arranger for the likes of **Jeannie Lewis**, **Jon English**, **Ross Ryan** and Judy Henderson. Carlos was musical director with the backing band utilised for the 1972 local production of Andrew Lloyd Webber and Tim Rice's rock musical *Jesus Christ Superstar*. The *Superstar* band also included Mike Wade (guitar; ex-Climax), Jamie McKinley (piano), Bruce Worrall (bass; ex-**Sherbet**) and Greg Henson (drums; ex-**Levi Smith's Clefs**). That line-up appeared on the *Jesus Christ Superstar* Original Cast album issued on MCA. Carlos later composed soundtracks for feature films like *Sunday Too Far Away* (1975), *Storm Boy* (1977), *Listen to the Lion* (1977), *Blue Fin* (1978), *The Long Weekend* (1978), *Dawn!* (1979), *The Odd Angry Shot* (1979) and *The Dark Room* (1982). Firth later joined pop band **The Ferrets**.

Albums: *Hair* (Original Cast recording, Spin/Festival, 1969), *Tully* (EMI/Columbia, 1970), *Sea Of Joy* (soundtrack, EMI/Harvest, 1971), *Loving is Hard* (EMI/Harvest, 1972).

Tumbleweed

Formed: *1990*
Style: *Rock*
Original line-up: *Richie Lewis (vocals; ex-Proton Energy Pills), Lenny Curley (guitar; ex-Proton Energy Pills), Paul Hausmeister (guitar; ex-Unheard), Jay Curley (bass; ex-Proton Energy Pills), Steve O'Brien (drums; ex-Unheard)*

With a look and sound that mixed the Fabulous Furry Freak Brothers with The Grateful Dead and Black Sabbath, Tarrawanna (near Wollongong, NSW) five-piece Tumbleweed was the ultimate stoner's band for the 1990s. From within a post-psychedelic underground haze that evoked the spirit of 1969, Tumbleweed came on with lashings of fuzz-drenched wah wah guitar riffs, hard-driving beats, languid vocal melodies and more hair than any band had a right to possess! To further the quasi-psychedelic connection, the band lifted its artwork almost intact from that of famed San Francisco poster artist Rick Griffin. As the saying goes, imitation is the sincerest form of flattery.

Tumbleweed grew out of the ashes of Proton Energy Pills which comprised Davey Curley (vocals), Lenny Curley (guitar), Jay Curley (bass), Stewy Cunningham (guitar) and Richie Lewis (drums). Proton Energy Pills derived their name from American cartoon series *Roger Ramjet* (the proton energy pills gave Ramjet his extraordinary strength). The band played a form of heavy retro-grunge that drew on US bands like Blue Oyster Cult, MC5 and Mudhoney for inspiration. Local bands that the Pills aspired to included **Radio Birdman, The Celibate Rifles** and **The New Christs**. Sydney independent label Waterfront issued two Proton Energy Pills singles, 'Survival'/'Symmetry' (September 1989) and '(Less than I) Spend'/'Strawberry Patch' (March 1990), and the mini-album *Proton Energy Pills*. By the time the mini-album appeared in October 1990, Proton Energy Pills had evolved into Tumbleweed with the line-up listed above. Tumbleweed entered the studio in December 1990 with American producer 'Freewheelin'' Mark Arm (from Seattle band Mudhoney) to record its debut single.

Waterfront issued 'Captain's Log'/'Space Friends' (August 1991), which was a distorted slice of voodoo acid-rock. Tumbleweed followed that swiftly with the single 'Stoned'/'Holy Moses' (January 1992) and the 12-inch EP *Tumbleweed* ('Carousel', 'Millenium', 'Shakedown') (April). *Tumbleweed* was also combined with both sides of the 'Stoned' single to make up the five-track CD EP *Theatre of Gnomes* (also April). The five-track *Weedseed* double 7-inch single/CD EP (with booklet) followed in August. *Weedseed* contained the tracks 'Fish Out of Water', 'The Sky is High', 'Fritz, 'Come and Get It' and 'Rainbow Waterwillow'.

By that stage, Tumbleweed had signed an American deal with Atlantic's new subsidiary Seed label. Waterfront continued to issue Tumbleweed's records locally, and 1992 ended with the release of the 'Acid Rain' CD single (November) and the *Tumbleweed* full-length album produced by American Doug Colson (December). Tumbleweed also contributed the track 'Lullaby' to rooArt's Australian heavy grunge-pop compilation *Crack in the Sun or Fade in the Shade* (November 1992), alongside the likes of **You Am I, Guttersnipes, Screamfeeder, Nursery Crimes, Massappeal, The Meanies** and Seaweed Goorillas.

The Seed label combined all the tracks from *Theatre of Gnomes*, *Weedseed* and 'Acid Rain' for release as Tumbleweed's international debut album. In October 1992, Tumbleweed embarked on a five-week world tour which took in dates across the USA and Europe. Tumbleweed appeared on the Sydney bill of the 1993 Big Day Out, then spent a good

Tumbleweed

deal of the year touring locally and overseas (four shows a week for nine months). The band undertook the joint Tune In Turn On Sell Out Australian tour with **You Am I** (May to June). Tumbleweed's releases for 1993 were the CD EP 'Sundial (Mary Jane)' (March) which was lifted from *Tumbleweed*, and the CD single 'Daddy Longlegs' (December). 'Sundial' reached #35 on the national mainstream chart, while 'Daddy Longlegs' managed #53 (and #35 in Sydney). 'Daddy Longlegs' also registered #50 on the 1993 Triple J Hottest 100 list.

Tumbleweed was added to the national bill of the 1994 Big Day Out tour. Then, after spending most of 1994 in limbo, the band entered Sydney's Electric Avenue Studios during September with producer Paul McKercher to record a new album. Tumbleweed signed a new deal with Polydor who issued 'Gyroscope' (December 1994) as the first CD EP from the album *Galactaphonic*. 'Gyroscope' reached #50 on the mainstream chart. Tumbleweed again appeared on the national bill of the January 1995 Big Day Out tour. *Galactophonic* came out in May, and it spawned two CD singles, 'Hang Around' (#48 in April) and 'Armchair Ride' (August). *Galactaphonic* was Tumbleweed's epic masterwork, a strident album full of fierce, booming metal-boogie and catchy, hard-edged rock'n'roll. As well as the band's formative influences, *Galactophonic* also revealed a debt to the likes of Monster Magnet, The Stooges, Sonic Youth and even The Beatles. Tumbleweed included a rendition of Pink Floyd's 'Interstellar Overdrive' (recorded during a spontaneous jam session) as a hidden, bonus track on the album.

At the end of 1995, Paul Hausmeister and Steve O'Brien left the band to be replaced by David Achille (ex-Full Tab) and Nick Rieth (on loan from **Celibate Rifles** and the **Deniz Tek** Group) respectively. Tumbleweed made its fourth appearance on the (1996) Big Day Out tour. Having already supported overseas visitors like Nirvana (January 1992) and the Rollins Band (June 1994), Tumbleweed supported US retro-metal kings Monster Magnet on that band's February/March 1996 Australian tour.

Tumbleweed's third album *Return to Earth* came out in September 1996. It reached #11 on the national mainstream chart, but slipped out of the Top 40 two weeks later. The limited edition (2500 copies) CD single 'Lavabread' and CD EP 'I Remember' preceded the album's release in July and August respectively. Initial copies of *Return to Earth* contained a limited edition, bonus ten-track disc, *Ready by Wednesday*. The band embarked on the Return to Earth national tour (October/November 1996) with support band **Magic Dirt**. The album's next CD single, 'Silver Lizard' (October), logged a #59 placing on the 1996 Triple J Hottest 100 list. Tumbleweed commenced 1997 with its fifth appearance on the Big Day Out.

In the meantime, Proton Energy Pills' frontman Dave Curley had formed Zambian Goat Herders in 1992. Greg (guitar), Brent (guitar), Matt (bass) and Dillon (drums) completed the line-up. The Zambian Goat Herders issued the album *Endorphin* on the Redback label (through MDS, July 1993), followed by *Awake* (August 1994).

Tumbleweed albums: *Tumbleweed* (Waterfront/Festival, 1992), *Galactaphonic* (Polydor, 1995), *Return to Earth* (Polydor, 1996); ***Zambian Goat Herders albums:*** *Endorphin* (Redback/MDS, 1993), *Awake* (Redback/MDS, 1994).

The Twilights

Formed: *1964*
Style: *Beat pop*
Original line-up: **Glenn Shorrock** *(lead vocals; ex-Checkmates), Clem 'Paddy' McCartney (lead vocals; ex-Checkmates), Kevin Peek (lead guitar; ex-Hurricanes), Peter Brideoake (rhythm guitar; ex-Hurricanes), John Bywaters (bass; ex-Hurricanes) and Frank Barnard (drums; ex-Hurricanes)*

In terms of style, musicianship and songwriting ability (if not success), Adelaide's favourite sons The Twilights were the closest thing Australia had to overseas role models like The Beatles, The Move, The Who, etc. As Glenn A. Baker wrote, when *every* young Australian rock band in 1965 struggled to sound like The Beatles, The Twilights hardly had to try. They were able to copy their Liverpool idols with faultless, note-for-note accuracy. Before the inevitable split came in 1969, The Twilights enjoyed significant chart success with eight consecutive hit singles.

The Twilights grew out of Adelaide vocal quartet The Checkmates, which comprised English-born **Glenn Shorrock**, Irish-born Paddy McCartney, Mike Sykes and Billy Volraat. In 1964, The Beatles broke in Australia and The Checkmates (sans Volraat) merged with crack instrumental outfit The Hurricanes to became The Twilights. Kevin Peek left early in the piece to be replaced by 19-year-old English-born Terry Britten. Peek went on to join Adelaide's top R&B outfit Johnny Broome and the Handels, followed by **James Taylor Move**, Quartet and John Williams' classical rock group Sky.

By the end of 1965, The Twilights had become Adelaide's most popular band. The singles 'I'll Be Where You Are'/'I Don't Know Where the Wind

The Twilights

Will Blow Me' (June 1965) and The Hollies' 'Come On Home'/'Wanted to Sell' (October) charted in their hometown. At the end of the year, manager Gary Spry took The Twilights to Melbourne where they swiftly became the 'in' band to see at discotheques like Pinnochio's and Opus. The Twilights also managed to draw enormous crowds on the suburban dance circuit. The band's third single, 'If She Finds Out'/'John Hardy' (February 1966), reached #13 on the Melbourne chart. By that stage, Laurie Pryor (ex-Johnny Broome and the Handels) had replaced original drummer Frank Barnard. The band scored its first major hits with 'Baby, Let Me Take You Home'/'You've Really Got a Hold on Me' (#23 in May) and Larry Williams' 'Bad Boy'/'It's Dark' (Top 10 in Adelaide, Melbourne, Perth and Brisbane during July).

That same month, The Twilights took out first place in the 1966 Hoadley's National Battle of the Sounds final. Their prize was a trip to the UK, and on 26 September The Twilights left Australia on the cruise ship *Castel-Felice*. In the meantime, the band scored a smash hit with The Velvelettes' 'Needle in a Haystack'/'I Won't be the Same Without Her' which reached #1 in Melbourne and #6 in Sydney during September. The Twilights' debut album, *The Twilights*, appeared in December 1966. It was a strong collection of mod-rock covers (The Who's 'La La La Lies', The Rolling Stones' 'Satisfaction'), R&B tunes (Mose Allison's 'I'm Not Talking', Willie Dixon's 'Diddy Wa Diddy') and a handful of appealing originals. 'You've Got Soul'/'Yes I Will' was lifted as the album's second single (after 'Needle in a Haystack') and it reached the National Top 30 in January 1967.

While in the UK, The Twilights recorded three tracks at EMI's Abbey Road Studios with producer Norman 'Hurricane' Smith: The Hollies' 'What's Wrong with the Way I Live?', Britten's '9.50' and Pryor's 'Young Girl'. With the release of 'What's Wrong with the Way I Live?'/'9.50' in February 1967, The Twilights returned to Australia. The single took the band back into the Top 5 in most states (#2 in Adelaide) during March. The Twilights saw out 1967 as the country's most popular band, with two more hit singles, 'Young Girl'/'Time and Motion Study Man' (#11 in Melboure, #26 in Sydney during May) and 'The Way They Play'/'Cathy Come Home' (Top 5 in Melbourne, Adelaide and Brisbane and #18 in Sydney during November). Near-perfect psychedelic pop gems like '9.50', 'Time and Motion Study Man', 'The Way They Play' and 'Cathy Come Home' remain some of the finest moments in Australia's 1960s musical legacy.

No doubt due to their UK sojourn, The Twilights' repertoire and stage show during 1967 had taken on a new dimension. The band played the entire Beatles' *Sergeant Pepper's Lonely Hearts Club Band* and The Small Faces' *Ogden's Nut Gone Flake* albums on stage with exacting perfection, as well as complex pieces by Cream, The Move, Traffic and Vanilla Fudge. In early 1968, The Twilights commenced work on a proposed television series featuring the band in musical and comedy situations, not unlike *The Monkees* show. The band completed a pilot episode of *Once Upon a Twilight . . .*, but with no sponsors willing to invest money in the venture, it was shelved. While manager Gary Spry was attempting to get the series up and running the band scored another hit, but this time under a cloak of anonymity. As faceless studio backing musicians, The Twilights appeared on **Pastoral Symphony's** single 'Love Machine' which reached #10 in June 1968.

The Twilights' own singles at that time fared poorly, as did their second album, *Once Upon a Twilight . . .* (June 1968). Of the three singles issued during 1968, 'Always'/'What a Silly Thing to Do' (May), 'Comin' on Down'/'Tell Me Goodbye' (August) and 'Sand in the Sandwiches'/'Lotus' (December), only 'Always' managed to crack the

Top 40 (and then only at #40 for two weeks). In January 1969, Pryor refused to undertake another UK trip, and the band parted company.

Glenn Shorrock worked with the AMBO agency and managed the (Brisbane) **Avengers** for three months before joining much vaunted 'supergroup' **Axiom** in May. He eventually went on to work with Esperanto in the UK and **Little River Band** before pursuing a successful solo career. Pryor went on to work with the likes of Luke's Walnut (the second Sydney *Hair* house band after **Tully**), Genesis, **Healing Force**, **Chain** and **Ray Brown's** One Ton Gypsy.

Britten issued a solo single on EMI, '2,000 Weeks'/'Bargain Day' (March 1969), which was the (unused) theme song to the Australian feature film *2,000 Weeks*. He returned to the UK where Cliff Richard had covered a couple of his songs ('Mr Nice', 'Take Action'). In the UK, he joined forces with fellow Aussie expatriates Kevin Peek, Trevor Spencer and Allan Tarney (all ex-**James Taylor Move**) as Quartet. Quartet recorded two singles for Decca, 'Now'/'Will My Lady Come?' (December 1969) and 'Joseph'/'Mama Where Did You Fall?' (May 1970). The band also recorded an album which never saw the light of day. With the break-up of Quartet, Britten became an in-demand session player for the likes of Cliff Richard (for whom he co-wrote 'Devil Woman'), Tina Turner and Mike Hugg. In 1977, Britten returned to Australia to write and produce songs for **Christie Allen**. He later co-wrote two of Tina Turner's biggest hits, 'What's Love Got to Do with It?' and 'We Don't Need Another Hero'.

Albums: *The Twilights* (EMI/Columbia, 1966; reissued on Music For Pleasure, 1968), *Once Upon a Twilight . . .* (EMI/Columbia, 1968), *Best of the Twilights* (EMI/HMV, 1969), *The Way They Played* (compilation, EMI, 1978; reissued on Raven, 1989), *Twilight Time* (previously unissued live tracks, Raven, 1983).

Tymepiece (*see* The Black Diamonds)

Tyrnaround

Formed: *1984*
Style: *Psychedelic pop*
Original line-up: *Michael Phillips (lead vocals), Peter Fidler (guitar, vocals), Ken Gardner (keyboards), Leigh Underhill (bass, vocals), Gavin Gray (drums, vocals).*

The Melbourne inner-city scene circa the mid-1980s gave rise to a number of 1960s-influenced bands including Tyrnaround, **The Gas Babies**, **The Bo-Weevils**, **Shindiggers**, **The Arctic Circles**, The Wet Ones and Too Much Hair for the BBC. Tyrnaround's stock in trade was a diamond-hard blend of beat pop and psychedelia that was redolent of UK 1960s bands like (Syd Barrett-era) Pink Floyd, Tomorrow, Creation, The Accent, The Timebox, The Smoke, The Syndicats and dozens of other obscure outfits gathered together on compilations like *Chocolate Soup for Diabetics*, *The Perfumed Garden*, *The British Psychedelic Trip* and *Rubble*.

Tyrnaround issued its debut 12-inch EP *Colour Your Mind* in late 1985, to be followed by the single 'Want of a Rhyme'/'Hello or Goodbye' (January 1988). Tyrnaround made its strongest statement with the album *Succeeds when Daylight Fails* (1989), which featured a series of well-crafted psychedelic pop gems like 'As I Walk with You', 'This Time', 'Vox 1 (What I Need)' and the single 'Uncle Sydney'/'Uncle Jack'. Leigh Underhill and Gavin Gray also played in The Playground with Carol Taweel (vocals, keyboards) and Colin Badger (guitar, vocals). The Playground issued the flexi-disc 'Tell You What I Want'/'Do or Die' (1988), the vinyl single 'Pandemonium'/'I am the Walrus' (1991) and the album *Surreal* (1992).

Albums: *Succeeds when Daylight Fails* (Polyester, 1989), *Go Back* (Polyester, 1992).

U

Ultrasound (*see* Deborah Conway)

Uncanny X-Men

Formed: *1981*
Style: *Pop*
Original line-up: *Brian Mannix (vocals), Chuck Hargreaves (guitar), Ron Thiessen (guitar), Steve Harrison (bass), Nick Manthandos (drums)*

Melbourne five-piece Uncanny X-Men started out as a hard-edge guitar pop band that built-up a strong following on the pub circuit. Fronted by the hyperactive, mischievous Brian Mannix, the band became known for its comic send-ups of other well-known artists. As more commercial concerns beckoned, the band began to temper its sound and approach, which resulted in a series of catchy hit singles.

Mushroom Records signed Uncanny X-Men towards the end of 1982. The band recorded a live-in-the-studio mini-album, *'Salive One!* which appeared in November. As the record sat at #15 on the Melbourne chart, Uncanny X-Men supported US visitors Joan Jett and the Blackhearts on tour. In early 1983, John Kirk replaced original bass player Steve Harrison. **Skyhooks'** Greg Macainsh wrote and co-produced (with David Briggs, ex-**Little River Band**) Uncanny X-Men's debut single 'How Do You Get Your Kicks?'/'Superhero' (March 1983). 'How Do You Get Your Kicks?' reached the Melbourne Top 20 (#17) in April. A couple of months later, Craig Waugh (ex-Primal Tears) replaced Nick Manthandos on drums. The band's second single, 'Time Goes So Fast'/'Up to You' (September), peaked at #31 in Melbourne during November. The band spent most of 1984 on tour, only releasing one record, the 12-inch EP *Beach Party* (July) which contained 'Everybody Wants to Work'.

1985 proved to be Uncanny X-Men's biggest year with the national success of their debut album *'Cos Life Hurts* (#2 in June) and three hit singles, 'The Party'/'The Slug' (#17 in March), '50 Years'/'Best Looking Gut' (#6 in June) and 'Still Waiting'/'Time Goes So Fast' (live) (August). Ron Thiessen left the band in early 1986 to join **Kings of the Sun.** Joey Amenta (guitar; ex-**Taste**, **Redhouse**, **Russell Morris Band**, **Wendy and the Rocketts**) helped out temporarily until Brett Kingman (ex-Adventure) took over full-time. Uncanny X-Men signed a new deal with CBS which resulted in the album *What You Give is What You Get!* (#11, November 1986) and the singles 'I Am'/'Treat Me Nice', 'Children' (#10 in May), 'Don't Wake Me'/'Truckin' on into Alice' (September), 'Nothing Touches My World'/'Playing the *Titanic*' (January 1987) and 'Start Believing'/'Sullivans' (June). Kingman and Amenta shared guitar duties, and session players on the album included Andy Thompson (sax) and Michael Caruna (keyboards). By the end of 1987, Uncanny X-Men had run out of steam and the band parted ways.

Mannix, Kingman and Waugh recruited new bass player Derek O'Leary and formed the short-lived Dead Legends. In 1990, Mannix performed in the stage play *Bad Boy Johnny and the Prophets of Doom*, along with Daniel Abineri, Nadine Garner and Wendy Stapleton, and appeared on the soundtrack album. At the end of the year, he issued a self-titled solo album which produced the single 'Beautiful People'. He also kept busy singing in a number of Melbourne pub bands like The Bang Gang and The Atomic Dining Club. Of the other Uncanny X-Men members, Chuck Hargreaves joined **Daryl Braithwaite** Band, Kingman joined **James Reyne** Band, **Daryl Braithwaite** Band, Gas and Bigger than Jesus and Waugh joined **Horsehead.**

Uncanny X-Men albums: *'Salive One!* (mini-album, Mushroom/Festival, 1982), *'Cos Life Hurts* (Mushroom/Festival, 1985), *What You Give is What You Get!* (Mushroom/Festival, 1986); ***Brian Mannix solo album:*** *Brian Mannix* (Musicland, 1990).

Underground Lovers

Formed: *1990*
Style: *Pop*
Original line-up: *Phillipa Nihill (vocals, keyboards, guitar; ex-McGuffins), Vince Giarrusso (vocals, guitar), Glen Bennie (vocals, guitar), Maurice Argiro (bass; ex-***No Nonsense***), Richard Andrew (drums)*

Highly touted Melbourne quintet Underground Lovers played its first gig in May 1990. Two gigs

Underground Lovers

later the band recorded its debut album, the starkly beautiful *Underground Lovers* (aka *Get To Notice*), which appeared in March 1991 on the Shock label. It featured melancholy guitar pop ('Girl Afraid', 'Wasted'), rhythmic dance pop ('Yes I Do', 'Round and Round') and reflective, acoustic folk ('My American Accent').

As well as yielding the singles 'Round and Round' (February 1991) and 'Looking for Rain' (April), the album revealed a debt to the band's formative influences. They included UK groups Echo and the Bunnymen, Joy Division, New Order and The Cure, plus hometown luminaries like **Equal Local** and Essendon Airport. 'Lick the Boot' appeared as a limited edition single in August 1991. 'Lick the Boot' also became the band's first release in the UK. Underground Lovers contributed the track 'Ripe' to rooArt's *Youngblood 3* compilation. The band's final release for 1991 was the four-track EP *Nice* which came out in October.

Underground Lovers won the 1991 Australian Record Industry Association (ARIA) award for Best New Artist. Having established their redoubtable promise, Underground Lovers signed a major deal with Polydor Records. The band entered Melbourne's Paradise Studio in January 1992 with producer Wayne Connolly (from **The Welcome Mat**) to record its second album. *Leaves Me Blind* emanated a haunting, brooding intensity, with the songs creating a range of moods from serene to sinister. 'Ladies Choice' (August) and 'I was Right' (November) were lifted as singles. During 1992, the band supported UK visitors My Bloody Valentine and The Cure on their respective Australian tours.

While *Leaves Me Blind* came out locally in December 1992, British label 4AD (home to **The Birthday Party, Dead Can Dance**) had already issued the album on its Guernica offshoot during August. The album garnered critical acclaim in the UK press, and also sold well in the USA as an import release. Following the release of the CD EP 'Promenade' (March 1993), Underground Lovers embarked on an overseas tour which took in shows across the UK and North America. In August 1993, Underground Lovers issued the single 'Your Eyes' (from *Leaves Me Blind*), which had been remixed by Robert Goodge (ex-Essendon Airport, **I'm Talking**) and **David Chesworth** (also ex-Essendon Airport). Goodge and Chesworth also produced the band's lush and atmospheric third album, *Dream It Down*, and its singles, 'Las Vegas' (May 1994) and 'Losin' It' (August). By that stage, Derek Yuen had replaced original drummer Richard Andrew (who went on to join Sydney band **Crow**).

Underground Lovers left Polydor in 1995 and set up their own independent label Mainstream. They recorded their fourth album at the end of 1995 with producer Wayne Connolly. Phillipa Nihill left during the recording sessions (she appeared on two tracks) to pursue a solo career. Underground Lovers continued on as a four-piece, embarking on a second American tour in early 1996. With the release of *Rushall Station* in April 1996, the band undertook an Australian tour. *Rushall Station* yielded the CD single 'Takes You Back' (July). Nihill's debut CD EP on Mainstream, *Dead Sad* (November 1996), highlighted her beautiful voice and gentle songs. Underground Lovers issued their fifth album, *Ways T' Burn*, in July 1997, preceded by the CD single 'Starsigns' in June. The second CD single, 'Common Box', followed in November.

Albums: *Underground Lovers* (Shock, 1991), *Leaves Me Blind* (Polydor, 1992), *Dream It Down* (Polydor, 1994), *Rushall Station* (Mainstream/Shock, 1996), *Ways T' Burn* (Mainstream/Rubber, 1997).

Ups and Downs

Formed: *1983*
Style: *Pop*
Original line-up: *Greg Atkinson (bass, vocals; ex-42nd Street), John Flade (guitar), Darren Atkinson (drums, vocals; ex-42nd Street)*

Brisbane band Ups and Downs played a brand of ethereal, well-crafted, jangly guitar pop that called to mind Australian post-punk icons **The Church**. The band's influences also extended to overseas groups like Cocteau Twins, R.E.M., Siouxsie and the Banshees and The Flamin' Groovies. Indeed, the name Ups and Downs was derived from a track on that band's 1978 album *Now*.

Brothers Greg and Darren Atkinson got their start in late 1970s power pop band 42nd Street. Ken Allen (guitar) and Neil Coombe (guitar) completed the line-up. 42nd Street issued one single, 'Work It Out'/'Afraid of the Dark', on the Virgo Seven label (1979) and also contributed a track, 'Mistaken Identity', to radio station 4IP's Various Artists compilation album *That's Queensland*. 42nd Street made little impact beyond the Brisbane scene. In 1983, the Atkinson brothers formed Ups and Downs as a three-piece, with Peter Hamilton-Shaw (guitar; ex-Furious Turtles) joining soon after to round out the sound.

The band issued its debut single, 'Living Inside My Head'/'Out of the Darkness' (December 1984), on the Basketcase label. Ups and Downs issued a second single, 'Perfect Crime'/'Never Ending', on Basketcase before venturing down to Sydney. The Waterfront label reissued the 'Perfect Crime' single in September 1985, by which time Ups and Downs had built-up a strong cult following on the Sydney inner-city scene. The band's second single on Waterfront, 'In the Shadows'/'Wonder', 'Treah' (April 1986), was a gorgeous slice of harmony-drenched guitar pop and one of the best independent singles for the year. Ups and Downs signed a new deal with the True Tone label (through PolyGram) which resulted in the release of the mini-album *Sleepless* (August 1986) and the single 'The Living Kind'/'Painted Sad' (July). To coincide with the single's release, Ups and Downs supported US visitors The Flamin' Groovies on their Australian tour.

In 1987, Trevor O'Neil (ex-21 Faces) joined Ups and Downs on keyboards, which gave the band an even more spacious sound. O'Neil's previous band, 21 Faces, had issued one single on the Pagan label in November 1985, 'Red Hearts'/'Michelle's in Love'. By the end of 1987, Ups and Downs had signed with the Mushroom label. The band entered Sydney's Paradise Studios in March 1988 to record its debut album, *Underneath the Watchful Eye*. Mushroom issued the singles 'Lit by the Fuse'/'Househunting' (June 1988) and 'Moments Away'/'Pleasant' (October) before the album appeared in November. *Underneath the Watchful Eye* was a strong showcase for the band's songwriting skills and musical adventurousness. Founder member John Flade left the band in June 1989. Ups and Downs ended its Mushroom association later in the year, and moved to the Volition label for the 12-inch EP *Rash* (1990). By the end of the year, the Atkinsons had split Ups and Downs to form the decidedly noisier outfit **Big Heavy Stuff**.

Albums: *Sleepless* (mini-album, True Tone/PolyGram, 1986), *Underneath the Watchful Eye* (Mushroom/Festival, 1988).

V

V Capri

Formed: *1984*
Style: *Pop, rock*
Original line-up: *Tod Johnson (vocals; ex-Manic D), Damian Ward (guitar; ex-Flavours, Perfect Strangers), Lance Karapetcoff (keyboards; ex-Harlequin Tears), Michael O'Brien (bass; ex-Harlequin Tears), Alan Simpson (drums; ex-Harlequin Tears)*

Stylish pop rock band V Capri was a popular attraction in its hometown of Perth, Western Australia but, despite a big push from the Mushroom label and several national tours, the band failed to make an impact on the eastern states. V Capri came together with the above line-up in 1984. Having established a strong position in Perth, the band issued its debut single, the one-sided 'Only a Movie' (May 1985) on the independent Theatre label. It reached the Perth Top 10.

Mushroom signed V Capri on the strength of its hometown following. The band's debut single for Mushroom was also a one-sided release, 'Haunting Me' (August 1985). The record featured a limited edition photo of the band on the flipside. 'Haunting Me' went all the way to #1 in Perth. V Capri issued three singles during 1986, 'That's the Way'/'In My World' (January; another Perth #1), 'Nights and Days'/'Smiling Words' (July) and 'Love is Such a Lonely Song'/'Memories' (October) plus its debut album *In My World* (October). The singles all made the Top 10 in Perth.

By the time the album appeared, Clint Arnold (ex-Frames) had replaced original guitarist Damian Ward (who returned to Perfect Strangers). Arnold's previous band, The Frames comprised Dean Denton (vocals), Tim Count (keyboards), Mark Donohoe (bass) and John Crothers (drums). That ambitious band was one of the most popular outfits on the Perth scene during the early 1980s. The Frames won the Masters of Music band competition run by Perth radio station 6IX. Early members included Boyd Wilson (guitar), Ray Vine (sax) and Max Kittler (drums). The independent single 'Please Listen to Me'/'Never Coming Home' charted in Perth, after which The Frames focused their attention on touring the Eastern States.

In 1984, CBS issued the single 'Funny Situation' and the band relocated to Sydney. The Frames issued one more single, 'Shadows'/'Night by Night', before calling it a day in 1985. With Arnold on board, V Capri issued one more single for Mushroom, 'Time is Always Changing'/'Book of Life' (June 1987). Despite regular touring, V Capri found it difficult to crack the national charts and eventually called it a day at the end of the year. V Capri briefly made a comeback in 1988 for gigs as a four-piece around Johnson, Karapetcoff, O'Brien and Simpson. Arnold returned to the re-formed The Frames briefly during 1988 for a tour with a line-up of Denton, Donohoe, Tim Count (keyboards) and Mark Kittler (drums). Arnold then formed Clutch Cargo with Mark Kittler, Dave Cook (guitar), John Webster (keyboards) and Tom Jennis (bass). Clutch Cargo won the 1989 Yamaha/Juke Battle of the Unsigned Bands contest.

Album: *In My World* (Mushroom/Festival, 1986).

v. Spy v. Spy

Formed: *1980*
Style: *Rock, ska*
Original line-up: *Mike Weiley (guitar, vocals), Craig Bloxom (bass, vocals), Cliff Grigg (drums)*

Formed in 1981 amidst the squats and slums of inner-city Sydney (Glebe), tenacious three-piece v. Spy v. Spy forged an identity as one of Australia's most outspoken bands. The issues of racism and the plight of the homeless were recurrent themes in the band's strongly politicised lyrics. With fire in their bellies, anger in their hearts and a commitment to change in their heads, the members of v. Spy v. Spy made a considerable impact on the Australian scene.

Englishman Mike Weiley, American Craig Bloxom and Australian Cliff Grigg formed the band originally under the name Spy v. Spy. The band was later forced to modify its name to v. Spy v. Spy in order to avoid legal action from the publishers of

v. Spy v. Spy

Mad magazine which featured the comic strip *Spy vs Spy*. The band's earliest records, the single 'Do What You Say'/'Table Tea and Mix' (April 1982) and the EP *Four Fresh Lemons* (August) on the GREEN label bore the Spy v. Spy moniker. Those early records displayed a strong ska inflection which found the band instant favour amongst the rude boys who packed into Sydney pubs like the Sussex Hotel. The band gradually replaced its ska leanings with a more effective, primal, no-nonsense pub rock sound.

Having made a minor impact throughout 1982, the members of v. Spy v. Spy went their separate ways in early 1983. Bloxom joined **The Numbers** in March, remaining with that band until July. At that point, v. Spy v. Spy reconvened with second guitar player Marcus Phelan (also ex-**Numbers**). 1983 was not a good year for the band. First Weiley took ill and was confined to a hospital bed for an extended period. Second, the band's gear was stolen and finally Phelan left. Undaunted, v. Spy v. Spy acquired a manager in the shape of Gary Morris (**Midnight Oil**) and entered 1984 with renewed vigour. Nevertheless, the mini-album *Meet Us Inside* (October 1984) and its single, 'One of a Kind'/'Where are We Going?' (November), were tentative and somewhat stilted.

The band's debut, full-length album, *Harry's Reasons* (March 1986), was much stronger with a clear socio-political focus. The title track was inspired by a friend's misuse of heroin ('Harry' being a euphemism for the drug); 'Give Us Something' was directed at the media; and 'Injustice' was dedicated to the Aboriginal Arts Council. Those three songs appeared as the singles 'Injustice'/'The Wait' (August 1985), 'Give Us Something'/'Dangerman' (February 1986) and 'Harry's Reasons'/'All Over the World' (May). The band later contributed 'Injustice' to the Various Artists album *Burning Bridges* on CBS (1989).

The band signed a new deal with WEA and followed up *Harry's Reasons* with the album *A.O. Mod. T.V. Ver.* in November 1986. Once again, the album produced three singles, 'Don't Tear It Down'/'Go to Work' (November), 'Sallie-Anne'/'Use Your Head' (March) and 'Credit Cards'/'The Wait' (July). The strident 'Don't Tear It Down' was written in protest at the demolition of Sydney's historic buildings. It became the band's biggest, and most memorable, hit when it peaked at #11 on the national chart. *A.O. Mod T.V. Ver.* also reached #11 in February 1987 and went on to attain platinum status (70 000 copies sold).

Issued during Australia's Bicentennial Year of 1988, *Xenophobia (Why?)* (March) was a timely release, a reminder to all that change was needed before celebration. The album included three singles, 'Forget About the Working Week'/'Flares' (December 1987), 'Clarity of Mind'/'Mingle'n'Mix' (May 1988) and 'Waiting'/'Back on the Track' (August). *Xenophobia (Why?)* peaked at #14 in Australia, and was strong enough for WEA to issue it in 14 countries. In early 1989, v. Spy v. Spy travelled to the UK in order to record its fifth album at The Manor Studio with Craig Leon (The Ramones, Blondie, The Bangles). *Trash the Planet* (November 1989) was the band's most refined and cohesive release. The singles 'Hardtimes'/'A New Start' (November), 'Clear Skies'/'Asleep at the Wheel' (February 1990), 'Our House'/'Hooligans' (May) and 'Oceania' (August 1990) still displayed the inspirational power that the band continued to muster on stage.

Cliff Grigg left the band at the end of 1991 to be replaced by Mark Cuffe (ex-Ludwigs). Grigg joined Mixed Relations as guest percussionist. Following a year's absence from the live scene, v. Spy v. Spy set out on tour in support of the June 1992 'Best of' collection, *The Spy File*. The band signed a new deal with Sony for the album *Fossil* (May

1993), which produced the CD singles 'Comes a Time' (March) and 'One Way Street' (June).

With the break-up of v. Spy v. Spy in 1994, Bloxom and Cuffe began experimenting with new approaches. Cuffe stepped out from behind his drums to take up guitar and vocals. The pair recruited Paul Wheeler (drums; ex-**Icehouse**) to form Shock Poets. The band travelled to the USA to play gigs in New York, which resulted in a meeting with producer Jim Nickel. Nickel subsequently produced the band's debut album, *Bait*, in his Pachyderm Studios in Minneapolis (where Soul Asylum recorded its debut record). *Bait* and its CD single 'Never Should Have Bothered You' appeared in November 1995, and the band returned to Australia to tour.

v. Spy v. Spy albums: *Meet Us Inside* (mini-album, Powderworks, 1984), *Harry's Reasons* (Powderworks, 1986), *A.O. Mod. T.V. Ver.* (WEA, 1986), *Xenophobia (Why?)* (WEA, 1988), *Trash the Planet* (WEA, 1989), *The Best of v. Spy v. Spy: The Spy File* (East West/ Warner, 1992), *Fossil* (Sony, 1993); ***Shock Poets album:*** *Bait* (Roadshow/Warner, 1995).

The Valentines

Formed: *1966*
Style: *Pop*
Original line-up: *Bon Scott (lead vocals; ex-Spektors), Vince Lovegrove (lead vocals; ex-Winztons), Wyn Milson (lead guitar; ex-Spektors), Ted Ward (aka Ted Junko, rhythm guitar; ex-Winztons), John Cooksey (bass; ex-Winztons), Warwick Findlay (drums; ex-***Ray Hoff and the Off Beats***)*

When Bon Scott made an impact on the international hard rock market as frontman for the awesome **AC/DC**, he was already a bona fide Oz Rock veteran. During the 1960s, he had commanded the attention of hordes of hysterical fans as a fluffy, cuddly scream-dream pop idol with The Valentines. With the dawning of the 1970s, the adaptable Scott eschewed the bubblegum pop format in favour of the solid thumping rock and metaphysical progressive stylings of **Fraternity**. From there, it was just a short leap into the no bullshit power rock world of **AC/DC**.

Scott's first band was Perth (Western Australia) beat group The Spektors, which he formed in 1965 with friends John Collins (vocals, drums), Wyn Milson (guitar) and Brian Gannon (bass). Scott was co-drummer and co-lead singer; he and Collins would play half a set each in their respective roles. Although The Spektors did not release any records, three tracks recorded in October 1965 for Perth television show *Club 17* appeared on a CD EP *Bon Scott and the Spektors*, issued in 1992 by UK label See for Miles. The tracks were covers of Them's 'Gloria', Chuck Berry's 'On My Mind' and The Beatles' 'Yesterday'.

In mid-1966, Scott and Milson joined forces with members of rival band The Winztons to form The Valentines. Like Adelaide's **Twilights**, The Valentines were fronted by two lead singers, Scott and Vince Lovegrove. The Valentines wore matching suits, and their early repertoire comprised soul covers by Sam and Dave and Wilson Pickett, plus mod staples by the likes of The Who, the Spencer Davis Group and The Small Faces. By 1967, The Valentines were Perth's top pop band. The Clarion label issued the band's debut single, Arthur Alexander's 'Every Day I Have to Cry'/'I Can't Dance Without You' (May 1967), followed by Vanda and Young's 'She Said'/'To Know You is to Love You' (August).

The singles charted locally and The Valentines won the WA state final of the Hoadley's National Battle of the Sounds. The band flew to Melbourne to compete in the national finals, only to be beaten by **The Groop**. The Valentines had made enough of an impression to move to Melbourne permanently in October 1967. Clarion continued to issue The Valentines' singles into 1968: 'I Can Hear the Raindrops'/'Why Me?' (February) and Vanda and Young's 'Peculiar Hole in the Sky'/'Love Makes Sweet Music' (July). 'Peculiar Hole in the Sky', with its psychedelic overtones, was the band's most adventurous single to date. ('Love Makes Sweet Music' on the flip was originally by UK psychedelic band Soft Machine.) Nevertheless, the single failed to chart. Doug Lavery (ex-Andy James Asylum, Running Jumping Standing Still, **Doug Parkinson** In Focus) replaced original drummer Warwick Findlay as the single appeared. At the end of 1968, The Valentines signed a deal with Ron Tudor's June Productions, which then leased the band's next three singles to Philips.

Vanda and Young's 'My Old Man's a Groovy Old Man'/'Ebeneezer' (issued on Valentine's Day, 14 February 1969) took the band into the Top 40 for the first time when it peaked at #12 in Sydney and #23 in Melbourne. 'My Old Man's a Groovy Old Man' was pure bubblegum pop, sugary and vacuous but fun all the same. The Valentines donned matching frilly orange shirts, flares and beads, worked out a choreographed stage act and began to rival **The Zoot** (with their 'Think Pink' campaign) and **New Dream** as the most popular bubblegum act of the day.

In May 1969, Doug Lavery left The Valentines

to join **Axiom**. New Zealander Paddy Beach (ex-Compulsion) took his place on drums. In July, The Valentines lost out to **Doug Parkinson** In Focus in their second Battle of the Sounds appearance. The band's next single, 'Nick Nack Paddy Wack'/'Getting Better', came out in September. That same month, the band embarked on the ambitious Operation Starlift national tour with the cream of Australian pop of the day: **Russell Morris, Johnny Farnham, Ronnie Burns, Johnny Young, Doug Parkinson** In Focus, **The Zoot** and **The Master's Apprentices**. John Cooksey then left the band, and Ted Ward took over on bass.

At the end of September, The Valentines became the first Australian band to be arrested for the possession of marijuana. The band members each received a fine of $150 and a good behaviour bond. Although The Valentines had started to make an impact on the discotheque circuit, and were in the process of toughening up their sound and image (swapping the orange suits for jeans and T-shirts), the band was on the verge of breaking up. The band's seventh single, 'Juliette'/'Hoochie Coochie Billy' (March 1970), managed to reach #28 in Melbourne during April. The Valentines struggled on until August 1970, with Bon Scott immediately joining **Fraternity** in Sydney.

Of the other Valentines, Wyn Milson became a live sound engineer and helped pioneer the use of huge P.A. systems on stage in Australia. Lovegrove worked as a writer for *Go-Set* magazine and compered a television show in Adelaide called *Move*. He also issued a solo single on the independent Pepper label in 1971, 'Livestock'/'Rented Room Blues', and one on Raven, 'Get Myself Out of This Place'/'That's Alright Mama' (1972). 'Livestock' had been written by **Fraternity's** Mick Jurd and John Bissett. Lovegrove also worked as an Adelaide booking agent, in which capacity he was instrumental in Bon Scott joining **AC/DC** during 1974. In the late 1970s, he worked as youth affairs reporter on the Nine Network's *A Current Affair* program and produced *The Don Lane Show*. He managed **Divinyls** for many years. In the late 1980s, he produced a documentary, *Susie's Story*, which chronicled the AIDS-related death of his second wife. He also produced *A Kid Called Troy* (about his son) along similar lines. The documentaries served to heighten community awareness of the disease and the problems faced by AIDS sufferers.

Albums: *Bon Scott: Seasons of Change 1968–72* (compilation shared with **Fraternity**, Raven, 1988), *Bon Scott: The Early Years 1967–72* (UK-only compilation shared with **Fraternity**, See for Miles, 1992).

The Vampire Lovers

Formed: *1982*
Style: *Garage punk*
Original line-up: *Axel 'Axe Babe' Conrad (vocals), Matt Nasty (real name Matt Le Noury, guitar), Shane Cooke (bass), Dave Chamberlain (drums)*

Notorious Brisbane punk band The Vampire Lovers gained some measure of international attention when Jello Biafra, lead singer with Californian hardcore band the Dead Kennedys, pushed their 'Buzzsaw Popstar' single on the US college radio circuit. The Vampire Lovers were never really in a position to capitalise on the exposure. Despite their intermittent break-ups and infrequent gigs, The Vampire Lovers have enjoyed a cult status all the same.

The Vampire Lovers formed in 1982 as a third-generation garage-punk outfit. Brisbane had already produced the likes of **The Saints, The Leftovers**, The Numbers, Razar, **Young Identities** and **The Fun Things**. The Vampire Lovers' contemporaries on the early 1980s Brisbane punk scene included **The Screaming Tribesmen**, Mystery of Sixes, Public Execution and Pictish Blood. The Vampire Lovers issued their debut EP, 'Buzzsaw Popstar', 'Gothic School of Twilight Punk'/'Rubber Sex (This Way) Rubber Sex (That Way)', 'Freaks', on the Sundown label in 1983. The single featured a glam/punk edge (it was dedicated to T-Rex and Generation X). The band's second single, 'Sweetheart's Blown Mindless'/'Long Awaited Justice' (July 1984), on the Rubber label boasted a heavier Iggy and the Stooges (circa *Raw Power*) style. By early 1985, The Vampire Lovers had broken up, and Matt Le Noury and Shane Cooke formed Four Horsemen with Nick Lee (vocals) and Murray Shepherd (drums, vocals; ex-**Fun Things, Screaming Tribesmen**).

Although short-lived, Four Horsemen did manage to issue one single, 'World to End All Wars'/'Perfect Sound', on Sundown during 1986. In keeping with the members' previous directions, the Chris Masuak-produced single featured tough, guitar rock'n'roll. With the break-up of the band later in the year, Le Noury joined Flying Tigers, and Shepherd played in Hydrosuarus and (briefly) **Died Pretty** in 1992. Cooke joined **The Girlies** and **Hitmen DTK**. Lee formed The Adorable Ones with Peter DeHesse (guitar, vocals), Lex Weddell (bass) and Don Dawson (drums). The Adorable Ones issued one single, 'Rita'/'Rising Sun', in February 1988. Lee then joined Big Lummox.

In the meantime, Sundown had reissued

'Buzzsaw Popstar'/'Sweetheart's Blown Mindless', 'Long Awaited Justice' as a 12-inch single (December 1987). 'Buzzsaw Popstar' also appeared on the Rubber Records Various Artists compilation *At the Solicitor's Request* (alongside tracks by **The Leftovers**, **Young Identities**, **The End**, Kicks, Section Urbane, Razar, Mystery of Sixes and Public Execution). The releases were incentive enough for Conrad, Cooke (concurrently in **The Girlies**) and Le Noury to reform The Vampire Lovers with newcomers Jason Shepherd (guitar; younger brother of Brad and Murray Shepherd) and Ziggy Staten (drums).

The new line-up recorded the single 'Heavy Planet Fuzz'/'2nd Generation Psychopath', which came out on the Bent label in November 1988. By that stage, The Vampire Lovers had moved to Sydney where their brand of tough rock'n'roll found some favour on the inner-city circuit. Le Noury went off to join **Hitmen DTK**, while the Conrad/Cooke/Shepherd/Staten line-up completed an album, *Acid Commandos from Planet Fuzz*, which came out on the Shock Valve label in 1991.

Album: *Acid Commandos from Planet Fuzz* (Shock Valve, 1991).

Peggy Van Zalm (*see* Martha's Vineyard)

Vanda and Young (*see* The Easybeats; Flash and the Pan)

Vanilla Chainsaws

Formed: *1986*
Style: *Rock*
Original line-up: *Simon Drew (vocals, guitar; ex-An Aged Photograph), Mark Alexander (guitar; ex-An Aged Photograph), Cameron Lee (bass), Peter Kelly (drums; ex-***Flies***)*

Like a number of other independent Australian bands from the 1980s, Sydney quartet Vanilla Chainsaws enjoyed more success in European territories such as Germany and France than on home soil. The band's powerful guitar rock nevertheless found some favour on the local inner-city circuit.

A year after formation, Vanilla Chainsaws issued their debut single 'T.S. (Was It Really Me?)'/'Everything' (August 1987) on the Phantom label. The band followed that up with 'Like You'/'Onslaught' (March 1988). By that stage, Duilio Hernandez (ex-**No Man's Land**) had replaced Peter Kelly on drums. Kelly took Hernandez's place in **No Man's Land**. The new Vanilla Chainsaws line-up recorded the mini-album *Wine Dark Sea* which produced the single 'Wine Dark Sea'/'The Journey' (August 1988). In October 1988, Vanilla Chainsaws appeared on a rare gig giveaway album *Assorted Desecrations and Magnificent Mutations*, as part of Phantom's tenth anniversary celebrations. The Chainsaws covered songs by former Phantom bands **The Dagoes** ('Ten Years on') and **Machinations** ('Average Inadequacy'). There was enough interest in Vanilla Chainsaws at that time for the band to undertake an overseas tour in 1989. German label Glitterhouse issued the album *Vanilla Chainsaws*, which was a compilation of the *Wine Dark Sea* mini-album and the band's first two singles.

By that stage, only Drew and Alexander remained, so with Drew on bass and new drummer Andrew Marks on board, the band toured the US East Coast and the UK. Marks then left the band, so Drew and Alexander employed the services of German musicians Henning Woarner (bass) and Chekov Helmke (drums) in order to complete the European leg of the tour. **Cosmic Psychos'** drummer Bill Walsh appeared on the band's German-recorded mini-album *Thousand*, which Glitterhouse issued throughout Europe. Drew and Alexander returned to Australia in late 1990.

With the original Vanilla Chainsaws rhythm section of Cameron Lee and Peter Kelly back on board, the band undertook an Australian tour in April 1991. Peter 'D.J.' Kelly (not the same person as Peter Kelly the drummer) also joined on bass, allowing Lee to move to third guitar. Phantom issued the album *Red Lights* (December) and in early 1992 drummer Peter Kelly left to join The Snow Leopards and then **The New Christs**. Gerard Presland (ex-**Hitmen DTK**, Bloodshot) joined on drums and Vanilla Chainsaws issued a new CD EP, 'Watching Me', in December 1992.

Albums: *Wine Dark Sea* (mini-album, Phantom, 1988), *Vanilla Chainsaws* (Glitterhouse, German import only, 1989), *Thousand* (mini-album, Glitterhouse, Geman import only, 1990), *Red Lights* (Phantom, 1991).

The Venetians

Formed: *1983*
Style: *Rock*
Original line-up: *Rik Swinn (vocals), Peter Watson (guitar, bass, synthesiser, vocals; ex-***Scandal***, Extractors), Dave Skeet (guitar, bass, synthesiser, vocals), Matthew Hughes (keyboards; ex-Gotham City), Tim Powles (drums; ex-***Ward 13***)*

The Venetians began as a studio concept rather than a touring band. English immigrant Rik Swinn arrived in Australia in 1982 with the mastertapes for a batch of songs he had recorded in the UK with producer Vic Coppersmith-Heaven. Under the name The Venetians, Swinn signed to Festival's Parole label which saw the release of the singles 'Sound on Sound'/'Son Sur Son' (May 1983) and 'Chinese I's'/'Fundamental Principles' (November).

The singles featured an accessible synth-pop sound akin to contemporary UK bands like Ultravox, Orchestral Manoeuvres in the Dark (OMD), Heaven 17 and The Fixx. By July 1983, Swinn had formed a touring line-up of The Venetians with the above musicians. The band set about establishing an identity on the pub circuit, and issued a third single 'Ooh La La'/'Things' (November 1984). With the release of the album *Step Off the Edge* in May 1985, The Venetians began to transcend their cult following. *Step Off the Edge* produced the single 'Shine the Light'/'If London Were Venice' (February).

If *Step Off the Edge* had been somewhat tentative, the band's second album, *Calling in the Lions*, was a marked improvement. It was full of dense, swirling pop like the singles 'So Much for Love'/'10' (December 1985), 'Inspiration'/'Here Comes the Rain' (March 1986), 'If Somebody Loves You'/'Voices' (June) and 'Let It All Go'/'Ooh La La' (October). 'So Much for Love' took the band into the national Top 10 for the first time when it peaked at #3 during March. The Venetians set off on tour with **The Church** to a positive response. Chrysalis Records issued *Calling in the Lions* and 'So Much for Love' in the USA. The band continued to tour, but Matthew Hughes left in 1987. The Venetians came off the road for a year to write and record their third album, *Amazing World*, as a quartet (Swinn, Watson, Skeet, Powles). With the album's release in July 1988, Swinn added Lee Borkman (keyboards; ex-Pink Slips, Scribble) and Steve Ball (bass) for live work.

Amazing World produced three singles, 'Amazing World' (November 1987), 'Bitter Tears'/'Heartbeat' (May 1988) and 'Must Believe'/'Looks Like Love' (September). By then, The Venetians had developed into a seasoned, mature and accomplished rock band. Nevertheless, they were unable to sustain a hold on the charts, and Swinn dissolved the group in 1989. Swinn appeared with The Grubbs, a one-off concert band assembled to help launch the *Burning Bridges* album. The band comprised other local luminaries like Mark Callaghan (**Riptides**, **GANGgajang**), Geoffrey Stapleton (**GANGgajang**), Robbie James (**GANGgajang**), Rob Hirst (**Midnight Oil**), Craig Hooper (**Reels**), James Valentine (**Models**), Rick Grossman (**Hoodoo Gurus**) and Michael Hiron (**Riptides**). New Zealand-born Tim Powles went on to work with **Divinyls**, Johnny Batchelor, **Angry Anderson**, **Ana Christensen** and **Steve Kilbey**.

Albums: *Step Off the Edge* (Parole/Festival, 1985), *Calling in the Lions* (Parole/Festival, 1986), *Amazing World* (Parole/Festival, 1988).

Venom P. Stinger

Formed: *1985*
Style: *Avant-rock*
Original line-up: *Dugald MacKenzie (vocals; ex-Sick Things, Brainshack), Mick Turner (guitar; ex-Sick Things,* **Fungus Brains**, **Moodists***), Alan Secher-Jensen (bass; ex-Brainshack, Beachnuts), Jim White (drums; ex-People with Chairs Up Their Noses,* **Feral Dinosaurs***)*

The members of Melbourne band Venom P. Stinger all had considerable experience on the inner-city scene under their collective belts when they joined forces in 1985. Sick Things were one of Melbourne's pioneering hardcore bands of the early 1980s. **Fungus Brains** played a mix of proto-grunge and jazzy avant no-wave noise. Venom P. Stinger took the experimental avant-garde route to its logical conclusion with an unnerving sound that thrived on raw energy, a complex rhythmic base and unconventional song structures.

Venom P. Stinger earned a strong following on the Melbourne inner-city circuit, and issued its debut album, *Meet My Friend Venom*, in January 1987. Album tracks like 'P.C.P. Crazy' and 'Venom P. Stinger' were clattering slices of avant-rock with absolutely no concession to commercial gains. The band's next record, the single 'Walking About'/'26 Milligrams' appeared on the Aberrant label in July 1988. In 1989 Turner reactivated **Fungus Brains** for the album *I'm So Glad*. Turner, Secher-Jensen and White re-formed Venom P. Stinger with new singer Nick Palmer in 1991.

Aberrant issued the band's second album, *What's Yours is Mine* (October 1990), and the Au-go-go label issued the band's four-track CD EP *Waiting Room* in November 1991. The band toured the USA and issued the album *Live (in Davis)* in 1992. At the end of the year Turner and White put Venom P. Stinger on hold when they formed **Dirty Three** with Warren Ellis (violin). While the three musicians were getting that band off the ground, White and Ellis also toured and recorded with **The Blackeyed Susans**. Secher-Jensen formed Come the Rubber Pig, and later became involved with running the independent Vulgar Tongue label.

Venom P. Stinger regrouped at the end of 1993

to record the sludge-rock single 'Thick-skin'/'Tearbucketer' for the Death Valley label (issued in August 1994). Venom P. Stinger recorded one more album, *Tear Bucket*, which was only issued in Australia as a US import release. As **Dirty Three's** star continued to rise, Turner and White finally laid Venom P. Stinger to rest.

Albums: *Meet My Friend Venom* (No Master's Voice, 1986), *What's Yours is Mine* (Aberrant, 1990), *Live (in Davis)* (Anopheles, 1992), *Tear Bucket* (US import, 1996).

Vertical Hold

Formed: *1980*
Style: *Pop*
Original line-up: *Mick Michalopoulos (guitar, vocals), Jim Mountzouris (bass, vocals), Hillary Frost (cello, keyboards), Noel Forth (drums)*

Adelaide band Vertical Hold played a bouncy brand of pop which earned the group a strong following on home territory. Despite intermittent bouts of interstate touring, Vertical Hold remained virtually unknown throughout the rest of Australia. Classically trained Hillary Frost added a touch of musical class to the band's bright, accessible sound.

Vertical Hold's debut single, 'My Imagination'/'You Send Me', on RCA (October 1981) reached #1 in Adelaide, which helped consolidate the band's live popularity. WEA signed the band to a new deal in 1982 which resulted in the band's second #1 hit in Adelaide, 'Tears of Emotion'/'In Your Life' (October 1982). Vertical Hold's debut, self-titled album (May 1984) produced three singles, 'Shot Down (in Love)'/'Night Bite' (October 1983), 'This Must Be Love'/'She Comes to Me' (February 1984) and 'United States of America (USA)'/'Teacher Teach Me' (July). Once again the records sold well in South Australia, but continued indifference from audiences further afield led to Vertical Hold's break-up in 1985.

Album: *Vertical Hold* (WEA, 1984).

The Verys

Formed: *1992*
Style: *Indie guitar pop*
Original line-up: *Tim Oxley (vocals, guitar; ex-Humdingers), Anthony 'Bazz' Barrett (guitar, vocals), Matt Day (bass), Greg Wales (drums)*

Sydney band The Verys played a punchy brand of guitar pop that placed them in the same bracket as contemporaries like **Clouds**, **Pollyanna** and **Drop City**. Drummer Greg Wales has also worked as a producer and engineer for **feedtime**, **Smudge**, **Crow**, **Even**, **Pollyanna** and **Drop City**. The Verys had difficulty with bass players: Matt Day, Adrian Workman and Lino Romeo all served time with the band before veteran Greg Hitchcock (ex-**Bamboos**, **Kryptonics**, Neptunes, **New Christs**) joined in 1995.

Tim Oxley's previous band, The Humdingers, played a hard-edged brand of rock. The original line-up also comprised John Mitting (guitar, vocals), Karl Bergensen (bass) and Stuart Eadie (drums). Jeff Ryan replaced Bergensen in 1987. The band issued the single 'A Little Love on the Side'/'We Have Got It All' (October 1987), the mini-album *Sign in the City* (1988) and the 12-inch EP *Big Brutha* (1988) on the Waterfront label. Eadie went on to join **Clouds**.

The Verys issued one CD EP, 'That's a Moray' (May 1993), before signing to Sydney independent label Red Eye. The band's debut album *Twentieth Century Fix* (April 1994) produced the CD singles 'Colour Blue' (April) and 'Pushes' (November). The CD EP *Free Wheelin' Surgical Monster* (June 1995) featured the lead cut 'You Can'. The Verys recorded one more CD EP, 'No Landing Gear' (October), with producer Paul McKercher (**Tumbleweed**) before calling it a day at the end of 1995. Hitchcock joined **You Am I** as auxiliary guitar and keyboards player.

Album: *Twentieth Century Fix* (Red Eye/Polydor, 1994).

The Vibrants

Formed: *1962*
Style: *Soul, R&B*
Original line-up: *Bobby James (vocals), Geoff Skewes (organ), Terry Osmond (guitar), Terry Radford (guitar), Brenton Hay (sax), Jeff Gurr (bass), Rick Kent (drums)*

Adelaide band The Vibrants started out as backing group for singer Bobby James. Bobby James and the Vibrants cut one single for EMI/Columbia, 'Jezabel'/'Tossin' and Turnin'', in 1965 before James went off to form the Bobby James Syndicate. That band issued the excellent 'Hey Hey Hey'/'Short Sam' single on the Go!! label (May 1967). James and the Vibrants had also cut 'I've Learned', which was an R&B rave-up in the vein of **The Missing Links**. The Vibrants backed other, visiting solo performers like **Bev Harrell** and **Johnny O'Keefe** at suburban dances. The Vibrants also issued a single on the W&G label, 'Furry Legs'/'Maybe Tomorrow' (May 1965).

In April 1966, Geoff Skewes formed a new line-up of The Vibrants that comprised Rick Kent, plus newcomers John Rupert Perry (vocals), Mike Wade (guitar), Bill Pfeifer (bass) and John Hossin (sax). The Vibrants moved to Melbourne in July 1966, where Mick Hamilton (ex-Moods) replaced Wade on guitar. The new line-up issued its debut single, 'I've Got to Go'/'Somebody Help Me' (September 1966), on EMI/Columbia. Like **The Groove** and fellow Adelaide band The Clefs, The Vibrants were highly proficient exponents of white soul/R&B, which earned them respect on the dance and discotheque circuit.

The band made its biggest impact with the dynamic, soul-stirring cover of the Four Tops' 'Something About You Baby'/'Danger Zone' (January 1967), which reached #17 on the Melbourne chart in April. The band's second single 'The Letter Song'/'How Sweet It Is' (June), kept up the standard of 'Something About You Baby', but it failed to reach the Top 40. A somewhat vacuous cover of the chestnut 'My Prayer'/'Don't Let Your Left Hand Know' (September) took the band back into the charts when it peaked at #5 in November. Perry left in February 1968 to form his own band, The John Rupert Group. That band issued one single, 'Put a Bar in My Car'/'Tightrope' (August 1968).

Deep-voiced Marc Leon (ex-Impulse) took Rupert's place and, not long after, Barry Rogers took over on bass from Bill Pfeifer. The band issued a new single, **The Bee Gees'** 'Terrible Way to Treat You Baby'/'I Don't Need Nobody' (March 1968). In October, Leon, Hossin and Rogers split from The Vibrants to form Graduate. Skewes, Hamilton and Kent formed a 'new' Vibrants that included Penny Parsons (vocals) and Bob Flynn (bass). The Vibrants worked the club and cabaret circuit, and issued two singles on the Air label, 'I Can't Let Go of Your Love'/'Looking for Someone' (1970) and 'Give Me Just a Little More'/'I'm Gonna Be a Man Someday' (1971). By that stage, Ken Leroy (ex-John Rupert Group) had taken over from Flynn on bass and Trevor Courtney (ex-Chants **R&B**, **Cam-Pact**) had replaced long-serving drummer Rick Kent. The Vibrants broke up at the end of 1971, but a new band rose out of its ashes.

Skylight featured Geoff Skewes, Trevor Courtney, Bonnie Lever (vocals), Greg Cook (guitar, organ; ex-**Cam-Pact, Mixtures**), Mike Clarke (bass, guitar) and Sunil De Silva (percussion). Skylight continued to play soul with a stronger 1970s rock inflection. The band signed to EMI Records in 1973, which resulted in the album *Skyhigh*, plus the singles 'Get It Happening'/'Skyhigh' (June 1974) and 'Too Many People'/'Give Me Your Love' (September). Skylight broke up in 1975 and Skewes went on to manage **Stars**. Of the other Vibrants members, Mick Hamilton concentrated on session and club work until he joined rockabilly band **The Mighty Guys** in 1980. Courtney worked with **Stylus**.

Vibrants album: *Five by 4 Volume 2* (compilation shared with **Ronnie Burns**, **The Groove**, **The Cherokees**, Raven, 1982); ***Skylight album:*** *Skyhigh* (EMI, 1974).

Vicious Circle

Formed: *1983*
Style: *Hardcore punk*
Original line-up: *Paul Lindsay (vocals), Les Rumincik (lead guitar; ex-Politburo), Alby Brovedani (bass, guitar; ex-Politburo), Michael (drums)*

Alongside **Depression**, Melbourne band Vicious Circle was that city's most influential hardcore punk band of the 1980s. Vicious Circle also proved to be a very prolific recording outfit, and while the band's records sold to a dedicated few in Australia, they sold in reasonable quantities in places like the US west coast.

Perth-born drummer Russell Hopkinson replaced original drummer Michael in 1984. The earliest Vicious Circle recordings ('Blood Race', 'Police Brutality') appeared on the Various Artists punk compilation *Eat Your Head* (No Master's Voice, 1984). The compilation also included tracks by Civil Dissident, Murder Murder Suicide, End Result, Royal Flush, **I Spit on Your Gravy**, Bodies, Permanent Damage and Madflowers. Vicious Circle issued its debut EP, *Search for the Solution*, on Phil McDougall's Reactor label. *Search for the Solution* sold 1000 copies, incentive enough for the band to record its debut album *The Price of Progress* (September 1985). The album was a ground-breaking release in the annals of the local hardcore scene. US label Children of the Revolution licensed the album for the American market (November).

The US connection led to Vicious Circle issuing a split album with American band Youth Brigade (April 1986). That same month, Reactor issued the band's first single, 'A Nightmare So Quick'/'Viewing Time'. By that stage, David Ross had replaced Hopkinson on drums and Keith Chatham (ex-Death Sentence) had come in on bass to allow Alby Brovedani to concentrate on rhythm guitar. By the time the band came to record its second album *Reflections*, Chatham had left and Brovedani was back on bass. *Reflections* (October 1986) charted the band's progress, with elements of melody seeping into the band's all-out thrash approach. Californian label Boner issued the album on the American market. Vicious Circle undertook a three-month US tour which took in support gigs to west coast hardcore bands like GBH, Agnostic Front, MDC and Attitude Adjustment.

At the end of 1986, James Lynch (ex-Children of Sorrow) replaced Ross on drums. Vicious Circle issued one more record on Reactor, the 12-inch EP *Hope and Wait* (September 1987), before linking up with Sydney-based label Waterfront for the album *Into the Void* (August 1988). Vicious Circle continued to play the Melbourne inner-city scene, but broke up in 1990. Lindsay and Rumincik formed a new band, Rue Morgue, during 1991. Rue Morgue also comprised Peter (guitar), Gary (bass) and Danny (drums; ex-**Depression**). The band's sound incorporated an eclectic mix of hardcore punk, death metal and skate-core elements.

Rue Morgue contributed the track 'Romance of Death' to Roadrunner Australia's compilation of local metal bands *Redrum* (June 1993). The band's debut album, *Soul Museum*, followed at the end of 1993. Rue Morgue issued a second album, *Freak Nation* (January 1995), but by the middle of the year Lindsay and Rumincik had revived Vicious Circle. The reunion resulted in the retrospective compilation *Reactivate* on the Def label (July 1995). In March 1996, Vicious Circle issued a new CD EP, *Fixated*. By early 1997, the Vicious Circle line-up had stabilised with Lindsay and Rumincik joined by Gary (guitar), Chris (bass; ex-Buttjuice) and Stu (drums; ex-Extreme Forces). That line-up issued a new album in May 1997, *Internal Headstrength*.

Vicious Circle albums: *Price of Progress* (Reactor, 1985), *Vicious Circle/Youth Brigade* (split album, Reactor, 1986), *Reflections* (Reactor, 1986), *Into the Void* (Waterfront, 1988), *Reactivate* (compilation, Def, 1995), *Internal Headstrength* (Spent, 1997); ***Rue Morgue albums:*** *Soul Museum* (Def, 1993), *Freak Nation* (Def, 1995).

The Victims

Formed: *1977*
Style: *Punk*
Original line-up: *Dave Flick (real name Dave Faulkner, guitar, vocals; ex-Beagle Boys), Rudolph V (bass), James Baker (drums; ex-Beheaded/The Geeks)*

The late 1970s punk rock explosion spread its tentacles far and wide across Australia. Perth (Western Australia) was the centre of a small but vibrant punk scene. The Victims were Perth's third punk band following on from The Cheap Nasties (with **Kim Salmon**) and Beheaded/The Geeks. By all accounts, James Baker was a New York Dolls/Stooges/MC5 devotee, whose powerful, furious drumming was legendary around Perth.

When his band The Geeks broke up in May 1977, Baker teamed up with Dave Flick and Rudolph V to form one of the legendary Australian punk outfits, The Victims. The Victims' acknowledged mentors included US pioneers like New York Dolls, The Stooges, The Heartbreakers and The Flamin' Groovies. With their frantic, explosive sound backed by a solid melodic bent, The Victims became the premier punk band on the Perth scene. The Victims staked out such punk haunts as the Governor Broome Hotel and Hernando's Hideaway as their own. They consolidated their fierce live reputation with the release of one of the first Australian punk singles, 'Television Addict'/'(I'm) Flipped Out Over You' (April 1978).

'Television Addict' ranks with the first records by the likes of **The Saints**, **Radio Birdman**, **The Leftovers**, **Scientists**, **News** and **The Fun Things** as one of *the* great singles of the Aussie punk rock era. 'Television Addict' later appeared on the Missing Link label's Various Artists album *Inner Sanctum* (1979). Just as 'Television Addict' hit the record shops, The Victims decided to break-up. The band's final recordings appeared as the five-track EP *The Victims* ('I Understand', 'Open Your Eyes', 'High School Girls'/'T.V. Freak', 'Disco Junkies') in August 1978. Some copies of the EP came in hand-drawn and painted sleeves; these are ultra-rare and highly prized collector's items. All the tracks from the single and the EP (plus the previously unissued 'Perth is a Culture Shock') were later compiled on the album *All Loud on the Western Front* (December 1989).

With the break-up of The Victims, Baker joined **Kim Salmon's** band **Scientists**, where he remained until January 1981. Faulkner joined fellow Perth band Midget and The Farrellys, before travelling to the USA for an extended holiday. On the eve of his departure for the USA in early 1979, Faulkner re-formed The Victims in order to play a farewell gig for their fans. Following his return to Australia in late 1979, Faulkner joined another Perth band, **Manikins**. At the end of 1980, he travelled to Sydney where he formed Le **Hoodoo Gurus** with Baker and **Roddy Radalj** (ex-**Scientists**, Rockets). Baker has since played with **Beasts of Bourbon**, **The Dubrovniks** and Satellite 5. Rudolph V went on to join the Stooges-influenced Love Assassins with John Rowlings (vocals), Mark Hutchinson (guitar) and Marc Siddall (drums).

Album: *All Loud on the Western Front* (compilation, Timberyard, 1989).

The Visitors (*see* Deniz Tek)

Steve Maxwell Von Braund (*see* Cybotron)

W

Wa Wa Nee

Formed: *1985*
Style: *Funk, pop*
Original line-up: *Paul Gray (vocals, keyboards), Steve Williams (guitar, vocals)*

Before **Savage Garden** there was Wa Wa Nee. Fronted by the songwriting duo of Paul Gray and Steve Williams, Sydney band Wa Wa Nee found instant favour on the mainstream charts with a string of bubblegum white funk singles that were at turns sophisticated, commercial, calculated and ephemeral in the best pop tradition. Inevitably eyed with suspicion by pub-rock veterans and the alternative cognoscenti alike, the members of Wa Wa Nee were nevertheless genuine scream-dream pop idols who were more than capable of holding their own in the live arena. If there was an element of shameless narcissism and gaucherie in the Wa Wa Nee approach, then it was offset by a firm grasp of the dynamics of dance music, and a natural talent for song arrangement and melodic construction. Like Prince, Wa Wa Nee was able to overlay a good funk groove with heavy metalesque lead guitar work, and make it work with seamless ease.

As a duo, Wa Wa Nee signed a deal with CBS Records in late 1985. In January 1986, Gray and Williams formed a full touring line-up which comprised Geoff Lundren (bass), Elizabeth Lord (keyboards, backing vocals) and American Chris Sweeney (drums). Soon after, Gray's younger brother, Mark, replaced Lundren on bass, and Phil Witchett joined as additional keyboard player. The band's self-titled debut album yielded the singles 'Stimulation'/'Headlines' (April 1986), 'I Could Make You Love Me'/'Meelapolar May' (August), 'Sugar Free'/'Wild Days and Windy Nights' (November) and 'One and One (Ain't I Good Enough?)'/'Rubber Cookie' (May 1987). 'One and One (Ain't I Good Enough?)' also appeared as a limited edition double single pack with 'Mind Over Matter'/'Playtime'. The album's four singles all made the national Top 20, with 'Stimulation' peaking at #2, 'I Could Make You Love Me' at #5, 'Sugar Free' at #10 and 'One and One' at #19. *Wa Wa Nee* went on to attain platinum status (over 70 000 copies sold) and the band undertook its own headlining national tours. In October 1987, Wa Wa Nee undertook a promotional tour of the USA where 'Sugar Free' had reached the Top 30.

By the time Wa Wa Nee issued a new single in November 1988, 'Can't Control Myself'/'Happy Part 1', interest in the band had subsided somewhat. 'Can't Control Myself' reached #17 on the national chart, and was a taster for the band's second album, *Blush* (April 1989). Although *Blush* reached #20 on the national chart in June, and produced two more singles, 'So Good'/'The Other Side' (#28 in April 1989) and 'I Want You' (July), Wa Wa Nee's chart run was over. After the band came to a natural end in 1989, Steve Williams joined the **James Freud** Band. He went on to work with Mama's Darlings and Skunk. Paul Gray appeared as a session player on Maybe Dolls' 1992 album *Propaganda* and produced a series of singles for **Danni'elle Gaha**. Bass player Mark Gray worked with the Tania Bowra Band, the **James Reyne** Band and **Indecent Obsession**.

Albums: *Wa Wa Nee* (CBS, 1986), *Wa Wa Nee Ultra Mixes* (CBS, 1987), *Blush* (CBS, 1989).

Ward 13

Formed: *1978*
Style: *Rock*
Original line-up: *John Arthurs (lead vocals), Ron Roberts (lead guitar, keyboards), Leigh Hamilton Johnston (rhythm guitar, vocals; ex-***Rose Tattoo***), Peter Mullens (bass), Stephen Walls (drums)*

Sydney band Ward 13 started out as a brash, 1960s influenced, hard rock'n'roll band. Later on, the band eschewed the raunchy rock stylings of its onstage sound for a more textured, varied approach on record. Of the original Ward 13 line-up, only Leigh Johnston had any amount of experience, having been a member of the nascent **Rose Tattoo**.

Ward 13 worked the Sydney pub circuit for 18 months before issuing the five-track, 12-inch EP *Robot Wizards* in mid-1980. Issued on the Survival label (through EMI), the EP consolidated the band's live following. With tracks like 'Star System 5' on the EP, Ward 13 was unjustly accused of emulating **Mi-Sex**, who had just hit with the album *Space Race*. Undaunted, Ward 13 returned with the album *Flash as a Rat* (April 1981) and its two punchy singles 'See Venice and Die'/'Cold Hearted Lover' (March) and 'News for You'/'Idle Chatter' (July). Ward 13 ended the year with a third single, 'Slow Dancer'/'Time We Live' (November).

In early 1982, Ward 13 signed a new deal with Mercury/PolyGram which resulted in the single 'Midnight Caravan'/'Private Eye' (June). By the time the band came to record the mini-album *Too Much Talk*, only Arthurs, Roberts and Mullens remained from the original line-up. Newcomers Steve Lunn (guitar, sax; ex-Tigers, Think), Andrew Ross (keyboards, sax; ex-Kid Royal, **Marcia Hines** Band) and Tim Powles (drums; ex-Flight X7) completed the new line-up. *Too Much Talk* (December 1982) produced the single 'Drift Away'/'Can't Say No' (also October). Ward 13 broke up in 1983. Tim Powles joined **The Venetians**.

Albums: *Flash as a Rat* (Survival/EMI, 1981), *Too Much Talk* (mini-album, Mercury/PolyGram, 1982).

Dave Warner's From the Suburbs

Formed: *1977*
Style: *Rock*
Original line-up: *Dave Warner (vocals), John Dennison (keyboards, vocals), John Ryan (aka Johnny Leopard, lead guitar), Hayden Pickersgill (bass), Stuart Davies-Slate (drums)*

The garrulous Dave Warner was Australia's first and foremost exponent of 'Suburban Rock'. Fuelled by his pronounced strine accent and an acerbic wit, Warner's biting lyrics celebrated as well as satirised Australian suburban culture (e.g. 'Convict Streak', 'Suburban Boy', 'Mug's Game', 'Half Time at the Football'). His backing band, From the Suburbs, delivered a competently executed brand of pub rock that was the perfect launching pad for Warner's attack on the morals and mores of Australian society. Writing in *Rolling Stone*, Mark Demetrius suggested that Warner's great skill was to hone in on 'popular delusions or pretensions and demoralise them in one telling phrase'.

Dave Warner's From the Suburbs commenced playing live in January 1977. The band's debut single 'Australian Heat'/'Summer '78' appeared on their own Bicton label in early 1978. The single sold well in Warner's hometown of Perth, Western Australia, where From the Suburbs had become a major pub attraction. 'Summer '78' later appeared on Missing Link's Various Artists album *Inner Sanctum* (1979). In 1978, with the addition of Tony Durant (guitar, pedal steel, vocals) and the replacement of Pickersgill by Paul Noonan and Davies-Slate by Howie 'Ali' Johnstone, From the Suburbs toured the eastern states and signed with the Mushroom label. *Mug's Game* (November 1978) comprised half live and half studio material. The 13-minute 'Mug's Game' was Warner's epic tale of sexual frustration. The album was preceded by the single 'Suburban Boy'/'Clarke's Bolero', which reached #24 on the national chart.

Dave Warner's From the Suburbs' first single for 1979 was the good-time rocker '(We Got) Nothing to Lose'/'African Summer' (February). The band's second album, *Free Kicks* (April 1979), was another live set. The A-side of the next single, 'Free Kicks'/'Kangaroo Hop' (October), was a studio recording which had not appeared on the album of the same name. 'Kangaroo Hop' nevertheless had already been heard on the album. By that stage, Warner had parted ways with From the Suburbs and was utilising the services of fellow Perth band **The Dugites** as his backing band. Warner's next band, The Racquet, comprised two **Dugites**, Peter Crosbie (keyboards) and Gunther Berghoffer (guitar), plus ex-From the Suburbs members Paul Noonan and Ali Johnstone. Noonan went on to join **The Dugites** in 1980.

In the meantime, Warner issued the first album under his own name, *Correct Weight*, in November 1979. 'Wimbledon'/'On the Weekend' was lifted as the single; neither it nor the album lived up to expectations. Warner left Australia in early 1980 and travelled overseas for a year. Following his return in 1981, Warner issued the single 'Half Time at the Football'/'Lonely Bar Room Crawler' on the Bicton label before signing a new deal with Mercury/PolyGram. The new deal resulted in the album *This is My Planet* (October 1981) and its singles 'Kookaburra Girl'/'Little Miss Dynamite' (August) and 'Bicton vs Brooklyn'/'Carpark' (November). The Dave Warner Band at that stage comprised Ali Johnstone, Robert Searls (guitar; ex-**Sid Rumpo**), Phillip Bailey (bass; ex-**Dugites**) and Neville Dowling (keyboards). By 1983, Warner's backing band included three ex-members of From the Suburbs, Johnstone, Johnny Leopard and Tony Durant, plus newcomer Michael Parks (bass; ex-**Jimmy and the Boys**).

Warner was quiet on the recording front for most of the 1980s. He concentrated on writing comedy stage revues (including *Flappers*, *Broadway, Babylon and Bust* and *60s and All that Pop*), film scripts and the musical *Planet Pres* (which made its debut in October 1986). In the late 1980s, Warner issued the album *The Dark Side of the Scrum* under the name of Dave Warner and the Happy Hookers. Howard Shawcross (bass), Andrew Bell (guitar) and Bill Deane (drums) comprised The Happy Hookers. In late 1987, Warner revived the From the Suburbs moniker for a national tour. The line-up included Johnny Leopard and Greg Macainsh (bass; ex-**Skyhooks**, **John Farnham** Band).

Warner issued the five-track, 12-inch EP *Meanwhile in the Suburbs* (on Musicland) in March 1989. Produced by Macainsh, the EP was a strong return to form. As displayed on the title track, 'Meanwhile in the Suburbs', the erudite poem 'Australia Two' and the epic 'Half Time at the Football' (reworked to satirise the contemporary trend for high flying millionaires), Warner had lost none of his sharp wit. Mushroom issued the 18-track Dave Warner's From the Suburbs compilation album *Suburban Sprawl* in 1990. Warner issued a new album, *Surplus and Dearth*, in 1995.

After that he turned his hand to writing crime novels. His first, *City of Light* (Fremantle Arts Press, 1996), won the Western Australian Premier's Award for Fiction. He followed that in 1997 with *Big Bad Blood* (Vintage Press). Warner also wrote *Footy's Hall of Shame* (1996), 'the only book in Australian Rules Football literature that celebrated the Dull, the Dud and the Dead'.

Dave Warner's From the Suburbs albums: *Mug's Game* (Mushroom/Festival, 1978), *Free Kicks* (Mushroom/Festival, 1979), *Suburban Sprawl* (compilation, Mushroom/Festival, 1990); ***Dave Warner albums:*** *Correct Weight* (Mushroom/Festival, 1979), *This is My Planet* (Mercury/PolyGram, 1981), *Surplus and Dearth* (Anthem, 1995); ***Dave Warner and the Happy Hookers album:*** *The Dark Side of the Scrum* (J&B, 1988).

Warumpi Band

Formed: *1982*
Style: *Roots rock*
Original line-up: *George Rurrambu (born Kumanjayi Rurrambu II Burrarrawanga, vocals, didgeridoo),* **Neil Murray** *(rhythm guitar, backing vocals), Sammy Jabanangka Butcher (guitar, bass), Gordon Jabanangka Butcher (drums)*

Formed in Papunya, a remote Aboriginal community 150 miles west of Alice Springs, the Warumpi Band was one of Australia's pioneering Aboriginal rock groups. George Rurrambu was a Gumatj clan member from Galiwinku on Elcho Island (Northern Territory). Sammy and Gordon Butcher were both Luritja clansmen from Papunya. Another Butcher brother, Brian, also played bass with the Warumpis in 1983. White Australian singer/songwriter/guitarist **Neil Murray** was raised on a farm at Lake Bolac, near Ararat in western Victoria. In 1980, he travelled to the Northern Territory, and worked as a teacher, supply truck driver and outstation worker at Papunya and Kintore.

Murray was instrumental in getting the Warumpi Band off the ground. The band members started out playing covers of vintage rock'n'roll songs before writing original material that reflected their own experiences and celebrated Aboriginal cultural values. The Warumpis were voted best band at the Aboriginal Country Music Festival in 1983, and later in the year issued their debut single, 'Jailanguru Pakarnu (Out from Jail)'/'Kintorelaktu', on Sydney independent label Hot (October). It was the first rock song ever sung in an Aboriginal dialect (Luritja). The Warumpis came to the attention of **Midnight Oil**, which led to the critically acclaimed album *Big Name, No Blankets* appearing on the Oils' Powderworks label (April 1985).

Big Name, No Blankets featured the single 'Blackfella Whitefella'/'Fitzroy Crossing', which came out during October. Grounded in early American R&B and boogie as it was, the album was nevertheless an honest, enduring and bare-boned slice of indigenous country music. **Midnight Oil** then invited the Warumpis to join the historical Blackfella/Whitefella tour playing to remote Aboriginal communities in the Northern Territory. While the two bands were on the tour (July 1986), the Warumpi Band's 'Blackfella/Whitefella' appeared on the flipside of **Midnight Oil**'s 12-inch single 'Dead Heart' (alongside **Coloured Stone**'s 'This Land').

The Warumpis issued one more single on Powderworks, 'Sit Down Money'/'Warm Fire' (October 1986), before signing to Festival Record's Parole label. The Butcher brothers left the band, and the line-up of Rurrambu, Murray, Kenny Smith (bass, backing vocals) and American Allen Murphy (drums) recorded the album *Go Bush!* in October/November 1986. By the time the album appeared in April 1987, Murray Cook had joined on keyboards. As well as including a re-recorded version of 'Jailanguru Pakarnu (Out from Jail)', the album produced two singles, 'My Island Home'/'Didjeridoo Blue' (February 1987) and 'No Fear'/'Tjiluru Tjiluru' (May).

At the end of 1988, **Neil Murray** left the band to pursue a solo career which effectively meant the end of the Warumpi Band. Murray reunited with Rurrambu and Sammy Butcher in 1995, and the reconstituted Warumpi Band embarked on a

European tour. The album *Too Much Humbug* followed in April 1996. It boasted slicker production values than either of its predecessors. Standout tracks included the sparse 'Djulpan', the hard-rocking 'Stompin' Ground', the delicate 'Hold Me in Your Arms' (sweetened by the voices of Amy Saunders and Sally Dastey from **Tiddas**) and a re-recording of 'Blackfella/'Whitefella'.

Albums: Big Name, No Blankets (Powderworks/RCA, 1985), *Go Bush!* (Festival/ Parole, 1987), *Too Much Humbug* (CAAMA/Shock, 1996).

The Tinsley Waterhouse Band

Formed: *1980*
Style: *R&B*
Original line-up: *Tinsley Waterhouse (vocals), Gerry Joyce (guitar; ex-Gulliver's Travels), John Ballard (tenor sax, guitar; ex-***Phil Manning** *Band,* **Broderick Smith's** *Big Combo), Steve Ewart (trombone), Sean O'Sullivan (trumpet), Neil Hodgson (bass; ex-Fox), Noel Herridge (drums; ex-***Sid Rumpo**, *Wild Beaver Band, One Armed Bandit)*

Throughout the 1980s and into the 1990s, gravel-voiced R&B veteran Tinsley Waterhouse led ever-changing line-ups of his Tinsley Waterhouse Band. The band boasted over 50 musicians through its ranks over the years. Among all the changes in personnel, Waterhouse managed to issue three albums of tough, roadhouse R&B material.

Waterhouse played drums in late 1960s blues bands The Gravy Train and The Horse, plus a brief stint in the final version of New Zealand band Chants R&B circa mid-1967. In 1979, he formed Tinsley Waterhouse's Old Tracks which had evolved into The Tinsley–Townsend Band (with Snowy 'Cutmore' Townsend, ex-Wild Beaver Band) by April 1980, and The Tinsley Waterhouse Band by July. The line-up listed above recorded the 7-inch EP *Full of Ink an' Talkin' Shorthand* ('I've Been Dreamin', 'Ain't Got You'/'If You Love Me Like You Say', 'Hard to Handle'), which came out on Project 9 Records in February 1981. The Tinsley Waterhouse Band worked the Melbourne pub circuit, and issued its debut album, *After the Mudd You've Got ... The Tinsley Waterhouse Band*, in October 1982.

By that stage, the line-up comprised Waterhouse and Ballard, plus Mick 'The Reverend' O'Connor (Hammond organ), Ron Robertson (bass) and Peter Lee (drums), all of whom had previously played with **Broderick Smith's** Big Combo. By March 1983, the line-up comprised Waterhouse, Robertson, Gerry Joyce, Chris Stockley (guitar; ex-**Cam-Pact**, **Axiom**, **Dingoes**, Stockley See Mason Band, Rock Doctors), Neil Wyatt (sax; ex-**Dutch Tilders**, Keith Lamb's Airport) and Paul Hitchins (drums; ex-**Sports**, Nighthawks). The August 1983 line-up featured Waterhouse, Stockley, Robertson, Leigh Horton (sax; ex-Saxons, Pete Watson's Rockhouse) and Barry Cram (drums; ex-Michael Turner In Session, **Avalanche**, **Russell Morris** Band, Contraband, Ideals).

In early 1984, Michael Bright replaced Chris Stockley on guitar. By November, Ray Davies had taken Bright's place, and Horton had also left to be replaced by Dean Hilson (sax) and Dave Wright (trombone). The Tinsley Waterhouse Band's second album, *Hangin' Around* (1985), had been recorded in three sessions (March 1983, June 1984 and November 1984). As well as covers of a number of R&B staples like Robert Johnson's 'Sweet Home Chicago' and Jimmy Witherspoon's 'What Becomes of the Broken Hearted?', the album included the single 'Don't Get Mad'/'Holy Cow'. The Tinsley Waterhouse Band's third album, *I've Been Dreaming*, featured the line-up of Waterhouse, Cram, Ron 'Groper' Trinder (guitar), Paul Gatcham (sax), Ron Anderson (sax) and Tim Ayres (bass; ex-**Kevin Borich Express**).

Albums: After the Mudd You've Got . . . The Tinsley Waterhouse Band (EMI Custom, 1982), *Hangin' Round* (EMI Custom, 1985), *I've Been Dreaming* (Cleopatra, 1988).

Weddings, Parties, Anything

Formed: *1984*
Style: *Rock, folk, country*
Original line-up: *Michael Thomas (vocals, guitar, bass; ex-Never Never Band), Paul Clarke (guitar), Wendy Joseph (piano accordion, violin, vocals), David Adams (drums)*

As writer Clinton Walker put it, Weddings, Parties, Anything united two great Australian music traditions: post-punk pub rock and folk/bush balladry. The band's affection for traditional Australian songs and the Celtic roots behind those tunes, combined with a left-wing political stance, engendered the music with a uniquely Australian flavour and identity.

Weddings, Parties, Anything (WPA) founder Michael Thomas started out with Geelong group the Never Never Band in 1978. Joe Nadoh (guitar), Wendy Harrison (bass) and Archie Cuthbertson (drums) completed the line-up. The Never Never Band issued one independent single, 'It Doesn't Mean Anything'/'On the Beach' (February 1981), before breaking up. Thomas developed an interest in folk music, and began to lace his songs with colloquialism and local references to time and place. Using that as a basis, Thomas formed WPA in late 1984, based around the idea of combining traditional folk narrative structures and the melodic sound of the piano accordion with a rock-solid guitar backing. He derived the band's name from a throwaway lyric line at the end of The Clash's 'Revolution Rock'. Thomas also decided to sing in his natural Australian accent. WPA slogged around the Melbourne pub circuit and slowly began to build a cult following. Irish band The Pogues and English guitarist Richard Thompson were often mentioned in any attempt to categorise the WPA approach, and if not entirely accurate, then the form and intent was cognate.

Mark 'Squeezebox Wally' Wallace became an important addition to the band when he replaced Wendy Joseph on piano accordion, keyboards and vocals in early 1985. In December 1985, WPA issued its independent, four-track debut EP, *Weddings, Parties, Anything*, on the Suffering Tram label. The EP contained a number of the band's early live classics like 'Summons in the Morning' and 'Roaring Days'. WPA also issued a cover of Tex Morton's 'Sergeant Small'/'Go, Move, Shift' as a single on Suffering Tram in late 1986. By that stage, the WPA line-up comprised Thomas, Wallace, **Dave Steel** (guitar, vocals; ex-Relaxed Mechanics, Fire Below), Janine Hall (bass, vocals; ex-Young Charlatans, **Saints**, Wolfgang) and Marcus Schintler (drums). WPA began recording its debut album with producer/engineer Alan Thorne with the intention of issuing it independently.

WEA stepped in with a recording deal, and WPA's debut album, *Scorn of the Women* (April 1987), came out to critical acclaim. That refreshing and distinctive debut produced three excellent singles, 'Away Away'/'Bourgeois Blues' (March), 'Shotgun Wedding'/'Bells of Rhymney', 'Australia Goodnight' (June) and 'Hungry Years'/'The Swan's Return' (September). The album contained eight Thomas originals, three from Steel ('Lost Boys', 'Up for Air', 'Shotgun Wedding') and an adaptation of the Bertolt Brecht poem 'The Infanticide of Marie Farrar'. The band later contributed 'Hungry Years' to the Various Artists album *Building Bridges* on CBS (1989). WPA toured extensively in support of *Scorn of the Women*, eventually taking out the 1987 Australian Record Industry Association (ARIA) award for Best New Talent. Janine Hall left the band in August 1987, just as WPA was in the process of recording a new album. Peter Lawler (bass, mandolin, harp) took Hall's place and completed the album. Hall joined Kings of the World. In January 1988, WPA supported The Pogues on that band's Australian tour.

The 14-track album *Roaring Days* (April 1988) included the singles 'Say the Word'/'Bright Lights Tonight' (March) and 'Tilting at Windmills'/'Misfits' (July). **Dave Steel** left the band in mid-1988 to be replaced by Richard Burgman (ex-Shy Impostors, **Sunnyboys**, **Saints**). WPA left Australia at that point for its first American tour. The band had been invited to Houston, Texas to participate in an International Music Festival, which they followed up with dates across the USA and Canada. While WPA was overseas, the five-track, 12-inch EP *Goat Dancing on the Tables* came out (November). The EP contained **Paul Kelly's** 'Laughing Boy', 'Tough Time in the Old Town Tonight', 'Goat Dance (at Falaffel Beach)' and 'Sergeant Small' (live).

WPA's third album, *The Big Don't Argue* (recorded with veteran American producer Jim Dickinson), featured some of Thomas's most heart-wrenching and passionate songwriting. Issued in October 1989, WEA promoted the album using the catchphrase '11 songs about love, loneliness and cannibalism'. 'Streets of Forbes'/'Missing in Action' (September 1989), 'The Wind and the Rain'/'Marie Provost' (November) and 'Darling Please'/'Ticket in Tatts' (March 1990) were issued as singles. WPA supported international visitors U2 and The Men They Couldn't Hang on their respective October 1989 Australian tours. *The Big Don't Argue* won WPA Best Indigenous Record at the 1989 ARIA Awards.

In early 1990, WPA parted ways with its record company WEA. Burgman also left the band to be replaced by Paul Thomas (ex-**Huxton Creepers**). WPA recorded its next record independently, although it came out on the Virgin label. The mini-

Weddings, Parties, Anything

album *The Weddings Play Sports (and Falcons)* (October 1990) featured five covers of songs by Melbourne pub rock stalwarts **The Sports** and one by **Jo Jo Zep and the Falcons** ('So Young'). It was a parody of the 10-inch mini-album *The Sports Play Dylan (and Donovan)*. **The Sports'** guitarist **Andrew Pendelbury** contributed the lead guitar solo to WPA's version of 'Reckless'. Virgin issued 'Reckless'/'The Great North West' as a single. Although issued as a stop-gap measure, the mini-album made for enjoyable listening and was generally well received. WPA contributed a version of **The Triffids'** 'Wide Open Road' to the Various Artists album *Used and Recovered by* issued on Mushroom's White label (1990).

With WPA's fortunes at something of a low ebb, Thomas took the band off the road to write new material for the next album. In late 1991, WPA entered Platinum Studios in Melbourne with producer Alan Thorne to record *Difficult Loves* (the title derived from a short story by American novelist Gabriel García Márquez). Only with the completion of the album did WPA sign a new deal, with the rooArt label. *Difficult Loves* came out in July 1992, preceded by the CD single 'Father's Day' (May), which took WPA into the national Top 40 (#29) for the first time. *Difficult Loves* also hit the national Top 30 when it peaked at #23 in August. The August follow-up CD single, 'Step In, Step Out' (featuring a duet with **Clouds'** Trish Young), maintained the momentum. The Top 40 success of 'Father's Day' pushed the album close to gold record status (over 30 000 copies sold), and earned the band the 1992 ARIA Award for Best Single along the way.

In early 1993, WPA undertook its second North American tour, and then entered **Tim Finn's** Periscope Studios in Melbourne to record its fifth album, *King Tide*, with producer Paul Kosky. Hugh Jones mixed the finished tapes in London. *King Tide* (October 1993) produced the CD singles 'Monday's Experts' (August), 'The Rain in My Heart' (December) and 'Island of Humour' (August 1994). 'Island of Humour' featured UK singer/songwriter Billy Bragg. With its full allotment of beautifully crafted songs, the album revealed a shift in sound to a more reflective, radio-friendly approach without sacrificing either Thomas's astute and compassionate lyrical observations or the deftness of the musicianship in the process. *King Tide* took the band into the national album Top 20 for the first time.

WPA contributed a cover of **Hell to Pay's** 'Saints and Kings' to the Various Artists compilation *Earth Music* issued on the Mushroom label (June 1994). By that stage, Jen Anderson (ex-Kings of the World, **Black Sorrows**) had joined on violin. At the end of 1994, Stephen 'Irish' O'Prey (ex-**Badloves**) replaced Lawler on bass. In 1995, Thomas and WPA found themselves without a record deal once more. Demand for the band's music was still at a premium among fans. To rectify the situation, WPA issued its sixth album, *Donkey Serenade*, as a mail-order only release. Among well-chosen covers like **The Triffids'** 'Wide Open Road' and **Strange Tenants'** 'Grey Skies Over Collingwood', the album boasted such memorable Thomas originals as 'Where the Highway Meets the Cane' and 'In Your Memory'. Michael Barclay (ex-**Little Murders**, **Zimmermen**, **Paul Kelly** and the Messengers) then replaced long-serving drummer Schintler.

With the release of the album *River'esque* on Mushroom (September 1996), WPA recommenced touring. The album was another top-notch release, mixing storming rockers with pristine ballads. Anderson's gypsy violin also served to flesh out the band's honest and direct songs. *River'esque* produced the CD singles 'Luckiest Man' (August 1996) and 'Don't Need Much' (March 1997). Mushroom reissued the *River'esque* album in November 1997, replete with a bonus disc of new material called *Garage Sale*.

Albums: *Scorn of the Women* (WEA, 1987), *Roaring Days* (WEA, 1988), *The Big Don't Argue* (WEA, 1989), *The Weddings Play Sports (and Falcons)* (mini-album, Virgin, 1990), *Difficult Loves* (rooArt/Warner, 1992), *King Tide* (rooArt/Sony, 1993), *Donkey Serenade* (mail-order only, WPA, 1995), *River'esque* (Mushroom/Festival, 1996), *Life's Great Adventure* (compilation, rooArt/Shock, 1996) *River'esque* (reissue with bonus disc *Garage Sale*, Mushroom/Sony, 1997).

The Welcome Mat

Formed: *1990*
Style: *Indie guitar pop*
Original line-up: *Wayne Connolly (guitar, vocals; ex-***John Kennedy's Love Gone Wrong***), Cory Messenger (guitar, vocals; ex-***John Kennedy's Love Gone Wrong***), Dave Moss (bass), Pete Bennett (drums; ex-Fiction Romance)*

Sydney band The Welcome Mat started out as a chirpy, jangly guitar pop outfit before heading in a tougher, though still melodic and harmony-laced, power pop direction. Wayne Connolly, Cory Messenger and Pete Bennett all had extensive experience under their collective belts when they formed the band in late 1990. Leo Mullins (ex-Benedicts) replaced original bass player Dave Moss in May 1991, and thus the classic Welcome Mat line-up came into being.

The Welcome Mat issued its modest, independent debut single 'Last of the Great Letdowns' in late 1990, followed by the six-track CD EP *Fairydust* in November 1991. The EP displayed the band's more characteristic power pop, hook-heavy sound. The band signed a deal with Regular Records, issuing the well-received EP *Spare* (July 1992) which topped the independent charts. The EP revealed Mullins' literary interests; the two songs he wrote on *Spare* had been inspired by Norman Mailer's *The Executioner's Song* ('Somewherelse') and Kurt Vonnegut's *Breakfast of Champions* ('The Big Show is Inside My Head').

The band supported local acts like **Hoodoo Gurus** and **Died Pretty**, as well as American visitors Buffalo Tom on tour. At the end of 1992, The Welcome Mat entered the studio with American producers Paul Kolderie and Sean Slade (best known for their work with Boston bands like Lemonheads, Buffalo Tom and Dinosaur Jr) to record its debut album. *Gram* (April 1993) and its CD singles 'Hell Hoping' (March) and 'Play Me' (July) highlighted the band's ready grasp of traditional song structures and the elements of melody backed by bursts of acerbic guitar. By that stage, Connolly had proven himself as a noted producer in his own right. His production credits have included the likes of Billy Baxter, The Benedicts, **Custard**, **Underground Lovers**, **You Am I** and **The Fauves**.

Despite the strengths and diversity displayed on *Gram*, the album was not a big seller and failed to propel The Welcome Mat into the premier league. The band disappeared from view, and Connolly formed Knievel with Tracy Ellis (bass) and Nick Kennedy (drums; ex-Templebears). Knievel signed to Sony's Murmur label (home to **silverchair** and **Ammonia**) for the album *We Fear Change* (July 1995), which was crammed full of simple, exuberant, well-crafted guitar pop. The album produced the singles 'Might as Well Be Gone' (May) and 'Let It Go' (September).

Connolly also joined forces with Simon Holmes (guitar, vocals, ex-**Hummingbirds**), Shane Melder (then in **Sidewinder**) and Martin Craft (bass; also from **Sidewinder**) in Holmes' new band, Fragile. The Half a Cow label issued Fragile's album *Airbrushed Perfection* (March 1996), which ran the gamut of sounds from jangly pop ('Dream Come True') to noisy Hüsker Dü-inspired rockers ('She Really Means that Much to Me', 'Resolving Conflict Situations'). Connolly, Messenger, Mullins and Bennett re-formed The Welcome Mat, and re-emerged with the album *Lap of Honour* (July 1996) and its CD single, 'Hey! Illusion'. Paul McKercher (best known for his work with **Tumbleweed**) produced the album, and **Hoodoo Gurus'** Brad Shepherd added extra guitar grunt where necessary. Knievel reappeared with the CD EP, 'Something Good Must Come' (October 1997), and album, *Steep Hill Climb* (November).

Welcome Mat albums: *Gram* (Regular/Festival, 1993), *Lap of Honour* (Id/Mercury, 1996); ***Knievel albums:*** *We Fear Change* (Murmur/Sony, 1995), *Steep Hill Climb* (MDS, 1997).

Peter Wells

Style: R&B, country

Legendary slide guitar expert Peter Wells (b. 1946) has earned a place in the hearts of a diverse range of music fanatics. His work with such rough'n' tumble, ornery outfits as **Buffalo**, **Rose Tattoo** and Romeo Dog has engendered him to dedicated fans seeking brain damage by way of slashing guitar riffs and pounding rhythms. On the contrary, his solo albums indicated a preference for worldly bar-room blues and rueful country ballads (which suited Wells' drawling, whisky-laced vocals). Either way, Wells remains master of his own destiny and a pivotal figure in the history of the Australian pub-rock tradition.

Wells got his start as bass player with Brisbane blues band Head, before moving on to Sydney's lumbering, heavy progressive monster **Buffalo**. After playing bass on four **Buffalo** albums (*Dead Forever ...* , *Volcanic Rock*, *Only Want You for Your Body*, *Mother's Choice*), Wells left the band in 1976. He converted to slide guitar and helped form seminal hard blues outfit **Rose Tattoo**. The Tatts went on to build an international reputation as one of the greatest street-level, outlaw Australian bands of all time. Wells left the Tatts in 1983 after three classic albums, *Rose Tattoo*, *Assault and Battery* and *Scarred for Life*, and several international tours. In August, Wells formed Scattered Aces with Ronnie Peel (bass, vocals; ex-**Missing Links**, **Pleazers**, **Rockwell T. James** and the Rhythm Aces, **La De Das**, **John Paul Young** and the All Stars, **Cheetah**), Chris Turner (guitar, vocals; ex-Drain, **Buffalo**) and Fred Zeppelin (real name Paul DeMarco, drums; ex-Chris Turner Band). The band toured into 1984 and issued the mini-album *Six Pack* (April 1984) and the single Eddie Cochran's 'C'mon Everybody'/'Waltzing Matilda' on the Big Rock label.

In November 1984, Wells formed Illustrated Men with other ex-**Rose Tattoo** alumni Ian Rilen (vocals; **X**), Mick Cocks (guitar; also ex-**Heaven** by that stage), Geordie Leach (bass) and Dallas 'Digger' Royal (drums). Illustrated Men played loud, barnstorming rock'n'roll in the **Rose Tattoo** tradition. Most of the songs in the band's repertoire had been written by Rilen, including such early **Rose Tattoo** classics as 'Bad Boy for Love'. Illustrated Men was designed to be a short-term touring venture, so by 1985 Wells had joined blues outfit the Lucy De Soto Band with Lucy De Soto (lead vocals, piano, Hammond organ), Fast Eddie (real name Geordie Leach, bass) and Ross Mercer (drums).

Tony Zuell replaced Mercer on drums for the album *Three Girls and a Sailor* on the Chase label. For the album *Help Me Rhonda, My Boyfriend's Back* (August 1986), the Lucy De Soto Band line-up comprised De Soto, Wells, Leach and Charlie Watts (no relation) on drums. Wells and De Soto went into semi-retirement living in the foothills behind the Gold Coast, only appearing for the occasional gig with old sparring partners like Chris Turner. In January 1990, Wells and De Soto formed Heart Attack with Mick Cocks (guitar), Mick Strutt (bass) and Paul DeMarco (drums). Heart Attack attracted a strong live following, but the band did not record in the studio. By mid-1990, Wells had entered the studio with producer Kevin Shirley to record his debut solo album *Everything You Like Tries to Kill You*.

Issued in late 1990, the album gave full vent to Wells' wry, sardonic world-view. It produced the singles 'Between the Saddle and the Ground'/'Pirate Song' and 'Darling Please Don't Fight with Me'/'Something for the Rabbit'. The album also included a terrific reworking of the old **Rose Tattoo** chestnut 'Rock'n'Roll Outlaw'. Helping out in the studio were De Soto, Mark Meyer (drums; ex-**Richard Clapton** Band, **Moving Pictures**, **Mark Gillespie** Band), **Noiseworks'** Stuart Fraser (guitar) and Ted Pepper (sax) plus **Noiseworks'** Jon Stevens and **The Angels'** Jim Hilbun on backing vocals. In early 1991, Wells hit the road in support of the album's release with the Peter Wells Band. The line-up comprised Wells, De Soto, **Tim Gaze** (guitar; ex-**Tamam Shud**, **Kahvas Jute**, **Ariel**, **J.P.Y.** and the All Stars, the **Tim Gaze** Band, **Rose Tattoo**), Michael Vidale (bass; ex-**Jimmy and the Boys**) and Warwick Fraser (drums; ex-**Feather**, **Screaming Tribesmen**). While the album had mixed country, bluesy boogies and laid-back rock'n'roll, the Peter Wells Band in the live situation played raunchy, traditional Aussie pub rock. Over the next year and a half, Wells scored tour supports to international visitors Marianne Faithfull, Jeff Healey, The Stray Cats and Bob Dylan.

Wells' July 1992 album *The Meaning of Life* was more straight-up rock'n'blues, and featured the line-up of De Soto, **Tim Gaze**, Mick Strutt (bass), Bernie Bremond (sax; ex-**Johnny Diesel** and the Injectors) and Scott Johnson (drums; ex-**Jimmy and the Boys**, **Rose Tattoo**). The album produced the CD single 'The Meaning of Life'/'Baby's Burning Bright' (June). In early 1993, Wells put his solo career on hold while **Rose Tattoo** re-formed in order to support American heavyweights Guns N' Roses on their two Australian concerts (Sydney, 30 January and Melbourne, 1 February). As well as the Guns N' Roses tour, **Rose Tattoo** undertook a successful Australian pub tour (which saw Gunners Slash and Duff McKagan jamming with the band).

For his third solo album, *No Hard Feelings* (June 1993), Wells gathered together De Soto, Geordie Leach, Bernie Bremond and Paul DeMarco. He also recorded a CD EP, 'Hard Done by You', with **Dave Steel** and Bob Armstrong which came out in August 1993. In early 1994, Wells revived the Heart Attack name to play the Melbourne pub circuit. As well as Wells and De Soto, the line-up comprised Leach and Steve Donald (drums; ex-Fastbuck, **Wendy and the Rocketts**). Once again, Heart Attack did not record and Wells and De Soto formed a new version of the Peter Wells Band with Chris Turner, Mark Evans (bass; ex-**AC/DC**, **Finch**, **Heaven**) and Mick O'Shea (drums; ex-**Swanee**, **Judge Mercy**). By 1995, the Peter Wells Band featured De Soto, DeMarco, Cocks and Andy Cichon (bass; ex-**Rose Tattoo**, **James Reyne** Band, **Judge Mercy**). Wells issued a new album, *Orphans* (June 1995), which included the CD single 'Crisis Point Casino' (April).

Around that time, Wells travelled to Germany where he recorded the album *Romeo Dog* with studio band Romeo Dog which featured American singer Andy Anderson. Cichon and O'Shea completed the line-up. *Romeo Dog* mixed raucous bar-room blues with hard rock grunt, and was the most powerful recording Wells had been involved in since the days of **Rose Tattoo**. The album was only ever available as an import from German label Down South. Wells and De Soto also comprised one-third of part-time, Melbourne R&B 'supergroup' Blues Hangover, which featured Dave Hogan (vocals, harp), Nigel Rough (guitar) and Ken Farmer (drums; all from **The Paramount Trio**) plus John Stax (original bass player with 1960s UK R&B kings The Pretty Things). The band's passionate, gritty brand of R&B was heard to good effect on two albums issued on the Dog Meat label, *Blues Hangover* (1995) and *Roadrunner* (1996).

In 1996, Wells and De Soto worked with **Powder Monkeys'** rhythm section Tim Hemensley (bass) and Timmy Jack Ray (drums). That line-up of the Peter Wells Band recorded the album *Go Ahead, Call the Cops*, which came out on the Dog Meat label in October 1996. Wells revisited his past again with covers of the Tatts' 'One of the Boys' and 'Nice Boys (Don't Play Rock'n'Roll)'. The album also included a languid cover of Bob Dylan's 'From a Buick 6' and a song called 'Romeo Dog', no doubt in homage to Wells' involvement with studio band Romeo Dog. Wells also found time to play slide guitar with promising Sydney R&B bar-band Black Smith Hopkins, fronted by Nick Hopkins.

Peter Wells solo albums: *Everything You Like Tries to Kill You* (Big Stars!/Mushroom/Festival, 1990), *The Meaning of Life* (Big Stars!/Mushroom/Festival, 1992), *No Hard Feelings* (Big Stars!/MDS, 1993), *Orphans* (Big Stars!/MDS,1995); ***Peter Wells Band album:*** *Go Ahead, Call the Cops* (Dog Meat/Shock, 1996); ***Lucy De Soto Band albums:*** *Three Girls and a Sailor* (Chase, 1985), *Help Me Rhonda, My Boyfriend's Back* (Chase, 1986); ***Scattered Aces mini-album:*** *Six Pack* (Big Rock, 1984); ***Romeo Dog album:*** *Romeo Dog* (Down South, import only, 1994).

Wendy and the Rocketts

Formed: *1980*
Style: *Rock*
Original line-up: *Wendy Stapleton (lead vocals), Mark Chew (guitar, keyboards; ex-Southern Transit), Victor Crump (guitar; ex-Fastbuck), Wayne Sullivan (bass; ex-Fastbuck), Steve Donald (drums; ex-Fastbuck)*

Singer Wendy Stapleton fronted a number of bands during the late 1970s (including Souled Out, Incession, Southern Transit and the Bill Livingstone Trio) before moving into session work. She signed a solo deal with Festival Records for the release of her debut single, a cover of The Rolling Stones' 'Heart of Stone'/'I Need You' (September 1979). In August 1980, Stapleton formed Wendy and the Rocketts and hit the Melbourne pub rock trail.

Wendy and the Rocketts signed to the Mushroom label, and the original line-up listed above recorded the singles 'Reputation'/'Let the Boy Go' (June 1981) and 'Tonite'/'The Brighton Creeper' (September). 'Reputation' peaked at #40 for one week during August. In March 1982, Stapleton launched a new Wendy and the Rocketts line-up with Steve Donald, plus newcomers Joey Amenta (lead guitar, vocals; ex-**Taste**, **Redhouse**, **Russell Morris** Band, Darryl Cotton Band), Adrian Dessent (rhythm guitar, vocals; ex-**Scandal**, Vixen, **Marc Hunter** Band) and Noel Beare (bass; ex-Misfits, Routinos). Dessent's previous band, Vixen, comprised Jann Baxter (vocals), Jude Owen (bass), Michael Elkington-Allen (keyboards) and Nick Thurm (drums). The band issued two independent singles, 'Cover Up Job'/'Machine' (1980) and 'I'm in Love Again'/'Do It Again' (1981), on the Alternative label (through Festival) before calling it quits.

Wendy and the Rocketts' third single, 'Your Place or Mine?'/'In Your Eyes' (March 1982), reached #35 in Melbourne for one week during May. By that stage, however, the band had built-up a strong live following. The mini-album *Live* (September 1982) managed to capture some of the band's onstage excitement. In early 1983, Wendy and the Rocketts travelled to the UK to record their debut album *Dazed for Days*. The album appeared in July 1983. It gave rise to the singles 'Play the Game'/'I Can't Tell You (May), 'Have You Been Telling Me Lies?'/'How Come You're Still Hanging Around?' (August) and 'Security'/'Nightflyer' (November). 'Play the Game' was a minor national hit (#28 in June) and the album went as high as #26.

The A&M label issued *Dazed for Days* in the UK and Europe, and in September 1983 Wendy and the Rocketts undertook a tour of those territories (which took in supports to Bryan Adams and ZZ Top). In November 1984, John Dallimore (ex-**Redhouse**, Dallimore, **Jon English** and the Foster Brothers) replaced Amenta (who joined **Moving Pictures**) and Brian Hamilton replaced Beare on bass. Wendy and the Rocketts toured into 1985, but no further recordings were forthcoming. With the break-up of the band in March 1985, Stapleton returned to session work.

In 1989, she appeared in the stage play *Bad Boy Johnny and the Prophets of Doom* (alongside Daniel Abineri, Brian Mannix and Nadine Garner), which yielded the soundtrack of the same name. In 1990, Stapleton joined her spouse **Paul Norton's** (real name Paul McNaughton) backing band in support of his solo album *Under a Southern Sky*. Mark Greig (guitar; ex-**Runners**), Tim Millikan (bass; ex-**Chantoozies**) and Derek Pellici (drums; ex-**Little River Band**) completed the Paul Norton Band line-up. In 1995, Stapleton turned her talents again to musical theatre. She took the part of Dusty Springfield in the long-running Australian production of *I Only Want to Be with You (The Dusty Springfield Story)*, which opened during May. Stapleton was a natural for the part, and she revived her role when the musical returned for a new season in July 1997.

Albums: *Live* (mini-album, Mushroom/Festival, 1982), *Dazed for Days* (Mushroom/Festival, 1983).

Western Flyer

Formed: *1977*
Style: *Country rock, blues*
Original line-up: Matt Taylor *(vocals, harmonica; ex-* Bay City Union, *Genesis,* Chain*), Brian Peacock (guitar, vocals; ex-Librettos,* Normie Rowe *and the Playboys,* Procession, Gerry and the Joy Band*), Vance Burrows (lead guitar; ex-Piers Partridge Band), James Gillard (bass; ex-Piers Partridge Band), Bruce Devenish (drums; ex-*Phil Manning *Band)*

Journeyman singer/songwriter **Matt Taylor** has been spreading the blues gospel throughout Australia since the 1960s. He enjoyed considerable acclaim and success with legendary blues band **Chain**, as well as pursuing a rewarding solo career. In 1975, he retired from the music business to live on a commune in Balingup, Western Australia. A year later, he moved to the Nannup Plains near Perth where he struck up a friendship with another veteran singer/songwriter, Brian Peacock.

New Zealander Peacock had arrived in Australia during the 1960s as a member of The Librettos, before travelling to the UK as one of **Normie Rowe's** Playboys. Peacock helped form pioneering psychedelic pop band **Procession**. That band broke up at the end of 1969, and by late 1971 Peacock had joined **Gerry and the Joy Band**. Like Taylor, Peacock retired from the music business for a time, but by 1976 was ready to return to the fray. In 1977, Taylor and Peacock gathered together American Vance Burrows, 19-year-old James Gillard and Bruce Devenish to record a one-off single. The session proved so enjoyable that the duo decided to form a band and record an album, hence the birth of Western Flyer. With the combination of Taylor's blues influences, Peacock's pop leanings and the rock and country flavours from the other members, Western Flyer emerged as one of the finest country-rock bands in Australia since **The Dingoes**.

Western Flyer recorded its debut album *First Flight* at Will Upson Studios in Fremantle during October 1977. The debut single 'Western Towns'/'Fish Jumps' came out in November, and the band made its first appearance that same month as support to US visitor Michael Nesmith in Perth. Nesmith was so impressed that he wanted to issue the band's album on his Pacific Arts Corp label in the USA, but nothing eventuated. Festival/Infinity issued *First Flight* in Australia during June 1978, and the band embarked on a national tour throughout July and August. The album produced the singles 'Providence'/'Pieces' (June) and 'Doublegee Queen'/'Ocean Dancer' (November). The album was tuneful and genial, although Peacock's closer adherence to a pensive, West Coast American country rock sound tended to smooth out Taylor's trademark bluesy rawness. Vance Burrows contributed excellent electric and acoustic guitar work throughout. Session player Alan Eammons assisted with plaintive pedal steel on the two Taylor-penned ballads 'Make Up' and 'Pieces'.

In late 1978, Western Flyer hit the eastern states again for an extensive tour (October through December). At the beginning of 1979, Mick Elliot (ex-**Sid Rumpo**, Wild Beaver Band, **Jim Keays'** Southern Cross, **Bandicoot**) replaced Burrows on guitar. Keyboardist John Poole-Johnson also served to fill out the sound when he joined at the same time. The non-album single 'Last of the Lovers'/'Blue Rinse Tour' came out in May, and that same month Western Flyer recorded its second album in front of a studio audience. *Live to Survive* (August 1979) and its accompanying single 'Throw Me a Line'/'Sunburst' succeeded in capturing the live essence of the band, but the records received less attention than the debut album. That hardly mattered, because Taylor left straight after the album's release in order to relaunch his solo career. He wanted to return to his traditional blues roots and duly formed the **Matt Taylor** Band with slide guitar master **Dave Hole**.

In the meantime, foundering under the familiar pressures of restrictive economics and a lack of direction, Western Flyer quietly broke up at the end of the year. Gillard went on to work with The Tremors, **Russell Morris** and the Rubes and **Mondo Rock**. Both Western Flyer albums were later coupled together on the one cassette release (on Taylor's Forever label) replete with the bonus, non-album track 'Blue Rinse Tour'. Peacock applied his extensive knowledge and experience gained in the music industry to the field of band management. Between 1980 and 1987, he looked after the affairs of **The Dugites**, **Eurogliders**, **Redgum**, **Deckchairs Overboard** and **Wa Wa Nee**. In the early 1990s, Peacock became managing director of Export Music Australia (EMA), which launched the Wizards of Oz showcase in 1993.

Albums: *First Flight* (Festival/Infinity, 1978), *Live to Survive* (Festival/Infinity, 1979).

The Wet Ones (*see* Girl Monstar)

Wet Taxis (*see* Louis Tillett)

The Whipper Snappers

Formed: *1986*
Style: *Pop*
Original line-up: *Annette Crowe (bass, vocals), Joy Howard (rhythm guitar, vocals), Tim Eaton (lead guitar), Frank Zaknich (drums)*

Sydney band The Whipper Snappers were practitioners of a delightful brand of chiming pop fleshed out by strong melodies, sweet, mellifluous harmonies and diamond-hard guitars. The band did not attain widespread recognition, but always lived up to audience expectations with its crystalline delivery.

The Whipper Snappers issued their debut single 'You Never Look'/'Love Elixir' (June 1988) on the Green Fez label. The band played the Sydney pub circuit on a regular basis, but no further singles were forthcoming at that stage. In 1989, The Whipper Snappers appeared on the ABC-TV show *The Money or the Gun* playing their harmony-drenched power pop version of Led Zeppelin's 'Stairway to Heaven'. Each week, presenter Andrew Denton introduced an artist doing a version of 'Stairway to Heaven' in their own style. Thus **Rolf Harris** played it with a throwaway semi-reggae lilt (complete with wobbleboard!), the Australian Doors Show as a brooding, druggie epic and **Robyne Dunn** as a dramatic torch song. In 1990, The Whipper Snappers contributed a refreshing cover of 'Sure Know Something' to the Waterfront label's Kiss tribute album *Hard to Believe*. By that stage, Tim Eaton had left the band, and 'Rock Hard' (otherwise known as Brad Shepherd from **Hoodoo Gurus**) contributed lead guitar to the song.

Singer/songwriter **Dave Steel** then augmented the basic Whipper Snappers line-up as lead guitarist in the live situation. Annette Crowe and Joy Howard worked as session singers on albums by the likes of **Dave Steel**, **Porcelain Bus**, **G.W. McLennan** and **Paul Kelly**. At the end of 1990, with assistance from Steel, Peter Bull (from Kelly's Messengers) on keyboards and percussionist Darren Gower, The Whipper Snappers contributed a cover of **Russell Morris**'s, 'Sweet Sweet Love' to the Various Artists album *Used and Recovered by* on Mushroom's White label. 'Sweet Sweet Love' also appeared as a single, backed with **The Hollowmen's** rendition of **God**'s 'My Pal' (February 1991).

Later in the year, Joy Howard left the band, and Annette Crowe assembled a new Whipper Snappers line-up which comprised Steve Waters (keyboards), Christian Powers (guitar), Lara Goodridge (backing vocals, violin) and Tim Seckold (drums; ex-**Crystal Set**). The new line-up recorded the CD EP *See My Finger, See My Thumb*, which came out in August 1992. The Aberrant label also issued The Whipper Snappers' version of 'Stairway to Heaven' as a CD single in November. The Whipper Snappers issued one more CD EP, *Dragster* (December 1993), before disappearing from view.

Whirlywirld (*see* Ian 'Ollie' Olsen)

White Cross

Formed: *1985*
Style: *Rock, folk*
Original line-up: *Tanya Davies (vocals; ex-Soft Ones), Peter Mather (12-string acoustic guitar, vocals; ex-Soft Ones), Nigel Harford (bass, vocals; ex-Stray Tapes, German Humour), Ashley Davies (drums; ex-Soft Ones)*

Although formed in Melbourne (Victoria), White Cross had its roots in a number of Perth (Western Australia) bands: Soft Ones, Stray Tapes and German Humour. The Stray Tapes line-up of Nigel Harford (vocals, guitar), Peter Bates (guitar, vocals), Andrew Chambers (keyboards), Mark O'Loughlin (bass) and Ross Philpott (drums) recorded the single 'Flashcube'/'Lights On', 'One of the Crowd' for the Resonant label. Neither Soft Ones nor German Humour issued any recordings.

Tanya Davies left White Cross early in the piece, and the band began playing the Melbourne inner-city pub circuit as a trio. White Cross mixed acoustic folk and country elements with a rock-solid backing. The band's simple, emotive songs and passionate delivery struck a responsive chord on a Melbourne scene then besotted with heavy grunge and awash with angst-ridden goth rock bands. White Cross found much favour with support slots to the likes of **X** and **Hunters & Collectors**. Artists as disparate as John Martyn, Van Morrison, Tim Buckley and New Zealand bands on the Flying Nun label (The Chills, The Bats) were mentioned as reference points for the band's music.

Paula Henderson (sax; ex-Ghostriders) joined in January 1986 to add instrumental colour and flesh out the sound. White Cross issued its debut mini-album *When the Fabric's Torn* in June 1986 on the Crash label (through Monash distribution). Among five brash and beguiling originals, White Cross threw in a somewhat misguided cover of the traditional folk song 'Michael Row the Boat Ashore'. White Cross also backed **X** frontman Steve Lucas on his debut solo album *Double Cross* and single 'City Song'/'Mr Anfenger's Fish' (October 1987). In 1987, White Cross also issued its critically acclaimed, full-length debut album *The Bride*. The album displayed the band's growth, and was a smoother, more fully realised work than the debut. The band then moved to the Mighty Boy label for the single 'Don't Break Their Hearts'/'Lonely Man' (August 1988). Later in the year, Harford and Henderson left White Cross, and Mather and Davies kept the band going with new players. These included Tony Hicks (sax), Pasquale Monea (bass) and Kerri Simpson (vocals, piano accordion).

White Cross issued one more single, 'How Deep is the Ocean?' and the CD EP 'White Boy' (both on the Higher Love label) in 1991 before calling it a day. Kerri Simpson was a well-established jazz/soul singer in her own right. She fronted a number of her own bands, like The Kerri Simpson Quintet, The Golden Gods of Rhythm, Kerri Simpson Band and Vévé. Kerri Simpson and Vévé issued the CD EP *Vévé* and the albums *The Arousing* (June 1995) and *Speak* (September 1996). Of the other White Cross members, Harford played with Ton Up Pirates and **Maurice Frawley's** Big City Burnout. Ashley Davies went on to work with a number of Melbourne groups including Barbara Waters and the Rough Diamonds, **Wild Pumpkins at Midnight** and the Lisa Miller Band. Henderson joined **Fungus Brains** and contributed sax to **Sunset Strip's** glorious *Move Right In* album.

Albums: *When the Fabric's Torn* (Crash, 1986), *The Bride* (Crash, 1987).

The Whitlams

Formed: *1993*
Style: *Pop*
Original line-up: *Tim Freedman (keyboards, vocals; ex-Olive Branch), Stevie Plunder (guitar; ex-***Gadflys, Plunderers, New Christs***), Andy Lewis (double bass; ex-***Gadflys, Plunderers**, *Olive Branch).*

Popular Sydney band The Whitlams emerged in 1993 playing a vigorous and diverse blend of indie guitar pop, jazz and bluegrass. Stevie Plunder (real name Anthony Hayes) had spent eight years with trash pop outfit **The Plunderers**, and a year with **The New Christs**, before joining forces with singer/songwriter Tim Freedman. Freedman and Andy Lewis had previously worked together in The Olive Branch with ex-**Clouds** drummer Stuart Eadie. The Whitlams issued the albums *Introducing . . . The Whitlams* (October 1993) and *Undeniably The Whitlams* (February 1995), plus the CD EPs 'Met My Match' (October 1994) and 'I Make Hamburgers' (October 1995). Stevie Plunder died on 24 January 1996 at the age of 32. Freedman kept The Whitlams going with additional members, and recorded a new album, *Eternal Nightcap*, which produced the CD singles 'You Sound Like Louis Burdett' (May 1997) and 'No Aphrodisiac' (August). The haunting, dramatic 'No Aphrodisiac' was voted #1 on the 1997 Triple J Hottest 100 list. *Eternal Nightcap* also took the band into the national Top 20 for the first time, when it peaked at #16.

Albums: *Introducing . . . The Whitlams* (Black Yak/Phantom, 1993), *Undeniably The Whitlams* (Black Yak/Phantom, 1995), *Stupor Ego (Live)* (Black Yak/Phantom, 1996, *Eternal Nightcap* (Phantom/MDS, 1997).

The Widdershins (*see* The Lighthouse Keepers)

The Wiggles (*see* The Cockroaches)

The Wild Cherries

Formed: *1964*
Style: *R&B, psychedelia*
Original line-up: *John Bastow (vocals), Malcolm McGee (lead guitar, vocals), Rob Lovett (guitar, vocals), Les Gilbert (bass), Kevin Murphy (drums)*

The original version of The Wild Cherries was a jazz/R&B band that came together in Melbourne during 1964. The band broke up in 1965 without having recorded anything for posterity. Rob Lovett joined **The Loved Ones**; Malcolm McGee joined **Python Lee Jackson**, with both later reuniting in The Virgil Brothers. Kevin Murphy went on to work with numerous bands, including **Billy Thorpe** and the Aztecs, **Chain, King Harvest** and **Levi Smith's Clefs**.

In January 1967, Les Gilbert switched to organ and revived The Wild Cherries with a new, more notorious line-up comprising guitar wizard **Lobby Loyde** (born Barry Lyde, ex-**Purple Hearts**), Danny Robinson (vocals), Peter Eddy (bass; ex-Weird Mob) and Keith Barber (drums). As Glenn A. Baker has noted, The Wild Cherries swiftly earned a reputation as the most relentlessly experimental psychedelic band on the Melbourne discotheque/dance scene. The band's four singles for the Festival label, 'Krome Plated Yabby'/'Everything I Do is Wrong' (June 1967), 'That's Life'/'Try Me' (November 1967), 'Gotta Stop Lying'/'Time Killer' (April 1968) and 'I Don't Care'/'Theme for a Merry Go Round' (September 1968) were exciting, revolutionary excursions into a musical void with no concessions to commercial demands. Only 'That's

Life' made the charts (#38 in Melbourne), but all remain classic examples of hard guitar psychedelia.

In early 1968, John Phillips (ex-Running Jumping Standing Still) replaced Peter Eddy. In October, Barber, Robinson and Phillips all left, to be replaced by **Matt Taylor** (fresh from the break-up of **Bay City Union**) and three ex-members of Brisbane blues band Thursday's Children: Barry Sullivan (rhythm guitar), Steve Pristash (bass) and Barry Harvey (drums). Robinson replaced McGee in The Virgil Brothers, and later sang with studio group **Duck**. One month later, Gilbert, Loyde and Taylor all moved on. Loyde joined **Billy Thorpe** and the Aztecs. Brian Wilson joined as frontman, and Sullivan played lead guitar for four weeks until Tim Piper (ex-Chants R&B, Electric Heap) joined in December. Pristash left and Sullivan switched to bass but that line-up split in April 1969. Piper went on to join all manner of bands, including Savage Rose Blues Band, **Chain**, Genesis, **Ray Brown's** One Ton Gypsy, **Blackfeather**, Alta Mira and the **Ray Burton** Band. Sullivan and Harvey joined **Chain** in October 1969.

Brian Wilson went on to front heavy blues band Sunshine which comprised Ralph Boyd (guitar), Ian Holding (bass) and Wally Edwards (drums). Sunshine issued one single, 'Luke McCoy'/'Sweet Little Mama' (1971), on RCA. Loyde spent two years with **Billy Thorpe** and the Aztecs, after which he revived The Wild Cherries' name at the beginning of 1971 for a three-piece hard rock outfit featuring Teddy Toi (bass; ex-**Max Merritt and the Meteors**, **Billy Thorpe** and the Aztecs, **Fanny Adams**) and Johnny Dick (drums; ex-**Max Merritt and the Meteors**, **Billy Thorpe** and the Aztecs, **Fanny Adams**). The new line-up came about when Loyde recorded his classic solo album *Plays with George Guitar* utilising the services of the ex-Aztecs/**Fanny Adams** rhythm section.

The Wild Cherries issued one single on the Havoc label, 'I am the Sea (Stop Killing Me)'/'Daily Planet' (November 1971), which was atypical of the overall repertoire, being a rousing acoustic tune with a precursory environmental message. Reissue specialists Raven included 'I am the Sea (Stop Killing Me)' on the essential compilation *Golden Miles: Australian Progressive Rock 1969–1974* (1994). The band appeared at the inaugural Sunbury Pop Festival (January 1972), but broke up a month later. Loyde formed **Coloured Balls** in March 1972, while Dick and Toi later re-joined **Billy Thorpe** and the Aztecs.

Album: *The Raven EP LP Vol. 1* (compilation shared with **The Purple Hearts**, **The Throb** and **The Missing Links**; Raven, 1982).

Wild Orchids (*see* Sweet Jayne)

Wild Pumpkins at Midnight

Formed: *1984*
Style: *Roots rock*
Original line-up: *Debra Manskey (vocals, guitar), Michael Turner (guitar, vocals), Dan Tuffy (bass, vocals)*

Tasmanian band Wild Pumpkins at Midnight played a politically motivated brand of semi-acoustic roots rock (blues, folk and rockabilly). After relocating to Melbourne in 1987, the band members made the bold move of basing themselves in Europe where their music was readily accepted by a cult following. Wild Pumpkins at Midnight had much in common with like-minded bands such as **Weddings, Parties, Anything** and fellow Tasmanian expatriates **The Fish John West Reject**.

In 1988, Wild Pumpkins at Midnight issued their self-titled mini-album and single, 'Birth of a Nation', on Melbourne label Major. At the end of the year, the band signed with Sydney-based Mighty Boy Records for the albums *Living* (April 1989), *This Machine is Made of People* (August) and *Little Victories* (1990), plus the single 'Watermelon Patch'/'Sheba' (March 1989). *This Machine is Made of People* won the 1989 Australian Record Industry Association (ARIA) award for Best Independent Release. The band contributed 'Birth of a Nation' to the Various Artists album *Burning Bridges* on CBS (1989).

Original lead singer Debra Manskey left in early 1990, and the band expanded its base with the addition of drummer Ashley Davies (ex-**White Cross**). With live sound engineer Melanie Fazackerley in tow, Wild Pumpkins at Midnight left Australia in June 1990 headed for London. From there, the band relocated to Amsterdam, capital city of the Netherlands, before finally settling in the small town of Wangeningen, one-and-a-half hours south east of the capital. Using that as a base, the band toured extensively throughout Europe, and issued the CD EP *Sending a Vampire* (October 1992) plus the albums *Strangeways* (May 1993), and *Going Sick* (1994) along the way. In late 1993 Davies returned to Australia to be replaced by Greg Hyne. The band also added another Tasmanian expatriate, Nick Larkins, on guitar.

Wild Pumpkins at Midnight returned to Australia in 1995 and issued the album *Low-Fi Lucy's Mobile Temple* (November 1995). They toured Australia (including a slot on the 1996 Big Day Out bill) and issued a new album in July 1996, *Sad Trees*.

The album comprised six studio tracks (produced by Tony Cohen) and nine live cuts (recorded at Melbourne's Continental Cafe). In February 1997, Hot Records combined selected tracks from both *Low-Fi Lucy's Mobile Temple* and *Sad Trees* for the CD release *The Secret of the Sad Tree*. It had been specifically compiled for the European and North American markets, although Hot also issued it in Australia. In June 1997, Wild Pumpkins at Midnight embarked on a European tour which saw the band reacquainting old fans with some delightful yet boisterous sounds.

Albums: *Wild Pumpkins at Midnight* (mini-album, Major, 1988), *Living* (Mighty Boy, 1989), *This Machine is Made of People* (Mighty Boy, 1989), *Little Victories* (Mighty Boy, 1990), *Strangeways* (Current/MDS, 1993), *Going Sick* (MDS, 1994), *Low-Fi Lucy's Mobile Temple* (Way Over There, 1995), *Sad Trees* (Way Over There, 1996), *The Secret of the Sad Tree* (Hot, 1997).

Warren Williams

Style: *Rock'n'roll*

Inspired by Bill Haley and His Comets' 'Rock Around the Clock' (from the groundbreaking juvenile delinquent film *Blackboard Jungle*), Gene Vincent and the Blue Caps, Little Richard and Jerry Lee Lewis, singer Warren Williams (b. 1940) formed one of Sydney's first rock'n'roll bands The Squares. Warren Williams and the Squares played their first dance in January 1958 at the Malabar Community Hall. By April, they were attracting 600 kids to Friday night dances at the Mascot Masonic Hall.

The first line-up of The Squares comprised Williams (vocals, guitar), Ronnie Patton (tenor sax, flute), Jimmy Taylor (piano) and Bert Goebe (drums). Billy Hucker then replaced Taylor, who had left to join **Dig Richard**'s R'Jays. By the end of 1959, the line-up had altered to contain Williams, Patton and Goebe plus newcomers Des Ebejer (guitar), Peter Butler (sax) and Al Schwer (bass). Williams made his television debut in July 1959 on *Six O'Clock Rock* after meeting compere **Johnny O'Keefe**. He went on to become a regular on *Six O'Clock Rock*, *Bandstand* and *Teen Time*. Williams was chosen by music impresario Lee Gordon as one of the Australian supports, alongside **Col Joye** and the Joy Boys, Johnny Devlin and the Devils, **Lonnie Lee**, **Dig Richards**, **Johnny Rebb** and the Rebels, **The Delltones**, **The Crescents** and The Graduates, at Fabian's Big Show in October 1959.

By that stage, Williams had signed to Festival Records and recorded his debut single, 'My Teenage Love'/'Where My Baby Goes (She Goes with Me)', which came out in December 1959. The single made the Top 10 (#7) in Sydney. He followed that with 'Kath-a-Leen'/'What's a Happenin' Baby?' (April 1960). As well as playing at Sydney's top dance spot, the famous Trocadero, Williams and the Squares appeared on a second Lee Gordon Big Show, this time with Americans Crash Craddock, Duane Eddy, The Diamonds, Johnny Restivo and Santo and Johnny, plus local hero **Johnny O'Keefe** (January 1960). At the end of 1960, Williams left Festival and also parted ways with The Squares. He issued a one-off single on EMI, 'My Little Girl'/'Lovely Lovely Habit' (October), which failed to chart. He ended the year by being voted the sixth most popular artist on *Six O'Clock Rock* behind **Lonnie Lee**, **Johnny O'Keefe**, **Dig Richards**, **Barry Stanton** and **The Crescents**.

In 1961, with encouragement from O'Keefe, Williams signed to Lee Gordon's Leedon, label. Williams' first single on Leedon, the ballad 'A Star Fell from Heaven'/'Why Do They Doubt Our Love?' (September), took him into both the Sydney and Melbourne Top 30 charts. Williams issued eight more singles on Leedon, Gene Pitney's 'Beautiful as You'/'Look Out It's Me' (December 1961), 'The First and Last Time'/'Absence Makes the Heart Grow Fonder' (March 1962), 'Girls Were Made to Love and Kiss'/'Too Proud to Cry' (June), 'Stand There and Cry'/'Absence Makes the Heart Grow Fonder' (October), 'Speak to Me of Love'/'Heartache Queen' (March 1963), 'Just Like a Child'/'Where My Baby Goes' (November), 'It's Party Time'/'Great Balls of Fire' (March 1964) and 'Come to Me'/'She's a Pretty One' (February 1965). Of those, 'Girls Were Made to Love and Kiss' reached #15 in Sydney and #25 in Melbourne, 'Just Like a Child' #32 in Sydney and 'It's Party Time' #35 in Melbourne.

Williams was a prolific songwriter. He recorded many of his own compositions during his heyday, including 'My Teenage Love (co-written with Des Ebejer), 'Too Proud to Cry', 'Absence Makes the Heart Grow Fonder', 'Look Out It's Me', 'Stand There and Cry', 'Heartache Queen', 'It's Party Time' and others. Local singers like **Betty McQuade** ('My Boy'), **Digger Revell** ('Just Call on Me') and **Judy Cannon** also recorded Williams' songs. British singer Petula Clarke later recorded a French language version of 'It's Party Time'. In 1962, Williams formed a music publishing company, Williams-Conde Music Pty Ltd, with Franz Conde.

Throughout his pop career, Williams retained a love for other musical pursuits, and one of his most popular EP releases was *Warren Williams Sings*

Famous Tenor Solos ('A Star Fell from Heaven', 'Girls Were Made to Love and Kiss', 'Vienna, City of My Dreams' and 'Pedro The Fisherman'). In fact, Williams' earliest singing experience was as a member of the local church choir. At the age of five, the young soprano took out a City of Sydney Eisteddfod prize, and later made an appearance as a choir boy in the feature film *Wherever She Goes* on the life of pianist Eileen Joyce.

In March 1964, Williams began to work with The Courtmen, who comprised Ronnie Wilton (guitar), Peter Rowan (sax), Con Serrafis (bass) and Joe Skurnik (drums). The Courtmen backed Williams on 'It's Party Time'. By that stage, Beatlemania had broken out in Australia. With the likes of **Billy Thorpe** and the Aztecs, **The Easybeats**, **M.P.D. Limited**, **Normie Rowe** and **Ray Brown** and the Whispers riding a wave of beat-pop hysteria, Williams' popularity began to decline sharply (as indeed did that of other early rock'n'roll singers like **Col Joye**, **Johnny Chester** and **Johnny O'Keefe**). In 1966, Williams signed with CBS for whom he issued the singles 'You're Breaking My Heart'/'Only a Rose' (1966) and 'Goodbye'/'Wimoweh' (1967).

After that, Williams concentrated on club and cabaret work. In the 1970s and 1980s, Williams resurfaced as one of the most popular performers on the nostalgia circuit. He appeared on shows like **Lonnie Lee's** Rock'n'Remember Show, the Rockerina Show and the J.O'K Memorial Show. He also issued two independent singles, the country-tinged 'Jimmy Brown the News Boy'/'The Long Black Veil' (on the Troubadour label, 1978) and 'I was There'/'Just Call on Me' (on Pomegranate, 1982). In 1984, Williams formed a family troupe called The Williams Family Show which featured his sons Warren Jr, Darren and Andy.

Warren Williams' brother Dennis Williams also led his own band, The Delawares. The original Delawares line-up comprised Michael Morris (rhythm guitar, vocals), Bruce Davis (lead guitar, vocals), Terry Smith (bass) and Laurie Wardsman (drums). Dennis Williams and the Delawares became popular at Sydney discotheques such as Surf City, and issued two singles in 1965 on EMI/HMV, 'Bad Girl'/'They Say' and 'Walk'/'Don't Try and Change My Ways'. By the time the band recorded the singles, Leith Ryan had replaced Morris on rhythm guitar and Bill Swindles had replaced Smith on bass. The Delawares also provided instrumental backing for some of the earliest **Bee Gees** recordings. Bob Daisley (bass; ex-Roundabouts) joined in February 1966, replacing Swindles. Tony Bowman also replaced Ryan on rhythm guitar. The Delawares broke up in August 1966, with Davis moving on to **The Allusions.** Daisley and Bowman worked briefly with Gino Cunnico in The Gino Affair, before Daisley went on to work with **The Throb,** Barrington Davis and the Powerpact, Mecca and **Kahvas Jute**.

Album: *Teenage Love: The Festival File Volume Four* (Festival, 1988).

Marty Willson-Piper (*see* The Church)

Chris Wilson

Style: *Blues, country, folk*

Acclaimed singer/songwriter/multi-instrumentalist Chris Wilson (b. 1956) is the owner of an enormous, booming voice. His pitch, range and raw vocal power remain virtually unmatched in Australia. And when Wilson blows into a harmonica or a saxophone, the music around him takes on a guttural authority and unearthly dimension. Wilson has mostly worked in the blues idiom, albeit with a folksy country slant, and has earned a reputation as a passionate performer and gifted songwriter. Wilson has played a pivotal role in the development of the Melbourne music scene since the mid-1980s. He started out in R&B-revue band The Sole Twisters in 1984, before joining neo-blues rockers **Harem Scarem** and appearing on the excellent *Pilgrim's Progress* album. Wilson then gained notoriety by guesting with **Paul Kelly** and the Coloured Girls (with whom he toured the USA in 1987), **X** (with which he played for a year), **Hunters & Collectors** and **Blue Ruin**.

In 1987 Wilson formed his own band, Crown of Thorns. The band's sparsely recorded debut mini-album, *Gnawing on the Bones of Elvis* (April 1988) mixed one side of electric blues including Willie Dixon's 'Bring It on Home', and one side of acoustic folk tunes not unlike Tim Buckley. Engineer Graeme Thomas recorded the album in his lounge-room studio. Joining Wilson on the record were Barry Palmer (guitar; from **Harem Scarem**), Chris Rodgers (double bass) and Ken Farmer (washboard). Wilson formed a permanent Crown of Thorns line-up with Palmer, Rodgers, Barbara Waters (guitar, vocals, mandolin; ex-**Hollowmen**), Justin Brady (violin) and Peter Jones (drums; also concurrently in **Harem Scarem**). That line-up recorded the first full-length Crown of Thorns album, *Carnival*, which was a more fully realised work than the debut. *Carnival* (February 1989) mixed blues, country and folk with a great deal of verve and authority.

Among the album's highlights was Wilson's

Chris Wilson

spectacular blues/gospel ballad 'The Ballad of Slim Boy Fat'. Crown of Thorns recorded one more album, *Babylon* (1990), with a line-up of Wilson, Rogers, Waters and Ashley Davies (drums; ex-**White Cross**) before Wilson abandoned the group concept for a solo career. Barb Waters formed The Rough Diamonds and issued the album *Not Until the Next Time Anyway* (April 1992) and single 'The Great Divide' (October). Under his own name, Wilson issued the CD EPs 'The Big One' (May 1992) and 'Alimony Blues' (October 1992), plus the critically acclaimed albums *Landlocked* (June 1992) and *Live at The Continental* (October 1994). Wilson's interpretation of Booker T. Jones' 'Born Under a Bad Sign' (from 'Alimony Blues'), backed by Shane O'Mara's blistering guitar work, was one of the finest renditions ever committed to record.

Backing Wilson on *Landlocked* were long-standing sidemen Chris Rodgers and Shane O'Mara (ex-**Stephen Cummings** Band), plus Peter Luscombe (drums; **Black Sorrows**), Graham Lee (pedal steel; ex-**Triffids**), Jen Anderson (violin; **Black Sorrows**) and Rebecca Barnard (backing vocals; ex-**Stephen Cummings** Band). *Live at The Continental* also featured O'Mara plus Jex Saarelaht (keyboards). Wilson collaborated with guitarist **Diesel** on *Short Cool Ones* (April 1996), an album of 15 soul and R&B standards (including four Willie Dixon songs) and a sole original, 'Other Man'. The CD EP 'I Can't Stand the Rain' was issued at the same time. 'Strangelove' appeared as a CD single in June.

As well as pursuing his own career, Wilson has played on dozens of album sessions, including **Paul Kelly** and the Coloured Girls' *Gossip*, **Hunters & Collectors'** *What's a Few Men?*, **Sacred Cowboys'** *Trouble from Providence*, **Boom Crash Opera's** *These Here are Crazy Times*, **Sunset Strip's** *Move Right in*, Richard Pleasance's *Galleon* and **Crowded House's** *Woodface*. In 1990, Wilson was part of the ad-hoc **Chris Bailey** Combo featuring **Saints** mainman Bailey (guitar, vocals), Dror Erez (piano), Paul Hester (drums; from **Crowded House**), Nick Seymour (bass; from **Crowded House**) and Tony Norris (trumpet).

Crown of Thorns albums: *Gnawing on the Bones of Elvis* (mini-album; Crawdaddy, 1988), *Carnival* (Crawdaddy, 1989), *Babylon* (Crawdaddy, 1990); ***Chris Wilson solo albums:*** *Landlocked* (Aurora/Mushroom/Festival, 1992); *Live at The Continental* (Aurora/Mushroom/Festival, 1994); ***Wilson/Diesel album:*** *Short Cool Ones* (Aurora/Mushroom/Festival, 1996).

Dennis D. Wilson (*see* Chariot, Kahvas Jute)

Ross Wilson

Style: *R&B, rock*

The tenacious Ross 'The Boss' Wilson (b. 1947) has given more to the institution of Australian rock and pop than can ever possibly be repaid. Through his valiant efforts over the course of 35 years, Wilson has participated in the transformation of a fledgling industry into an enormously successful and well-respected force on the international stage. Wilson has achieved recognition across four decades, with perhaps only the likes of **John Farnham, Jimmy Barnes, Col Joye, Billy Thorpe**, the late **Johnny O'Keefe** and **Paul Kelly** outstripping him in terms of overall sales and popularity.

For most of his career, Wilson has led rock bands, although he has periodically taken to the stage as a solo artist. By the time he was 16 years old, Wilson was already an R&B devotee. He got his start in Melbourne teenage R&B band **The Pink Finks** during 1965. From there, he fronted **The Party Machine** which lasted until 1969 when Wilson received an SOS call from the members of

Procession then resident in the UK. Wilson flew to London in an effort to revive **Procession's** flagging spirits but to no avail. When he arrived back in Australia during early 1970, Wilson teamed up again with his **Pink Finks/Party Machine** cohort **Ross Hannaford** in esoteric, special occasion progressive band **Sons of the Vegetal Mother**.

That band spawned the wondrous **Daddy Cool**, one of the most fondly remembered Australian bands of the early 1970s. **Daddy Cool** helped usher in an exciting new phase in the development of Australian rock music. By applying a commercial outlook to the prevailing underground trends of the day, **Daddy Cool** made a major impact on the local charts. Interestingly, Wilson had launched **Daddy Cool** as a bit of a joke. **Daddy Cool** was basically a rock'n'roll revival outfit, a humorous and entertaining diversion from the serious business of advancing the horizons of rock music. Wilson took the band's name from The Rays' 1957 hit, and it was a chance for him to indulge his passion for vintage Los Angeles rock'n'roll. The public caught on quickly and **Daddy Cool** soon became Australia's top group.

The band's bold, exuberant debut album, *Daddy Who? Daddy Cool!*, and single, the Australian dance classic 'Eagle Rock', both attained national #1 chart positions. The album set a new yardstick by which Australian rock success could be measured by selling an unprecedented 60 000 copies. As well as containing covers of Slay and Crewe's 'Daddy Cool' and Chuck Berry's 'School Days', plus more obscure R&B songs like 'Guided Missiles', 'Good Rockin' Daddy' and 'Cherry Pie', the album contained clever, appealing Wilson-penned originals like 'Eagle Rock', 'Come Back Again', 'Blind Date' and 'Bom Bom'. The album retains a freshness and charm to this day.

Wilson broke up the original **Daddy Cool** in August 1972. He then formed **Mighty Kong** which lasted until December 1973. As he was getting **Mighty Kong** off the ground, Wilson took the part of Cousin Kevin in the local stage production of The Who's rock opera *Tommy*. Other cast members included **Billy Thorpe, Daryl Braithwaite, Colleen Hewett, Broderick Smith, Doug Parkinson, Linda George** and Keith Moon. In January 1974, Wilson revived **Daddy Cool**, but the band ground to a halt in September 1975. By that stage, younger and more boisterous bands like **Skyhooks** and **AC/DC** had stolen **Daddy Cool's** thunder. Wilson took an instant shine to **Skyhooks**, and signed the band's songwriter, Greg Macainsh, to a publishing deal with his Doo Dah Music.

Wilson produced **Skyhooks'** two groundbreaking albums, *Living in the 70's* and *Ego is Not a Dirty Word*. Both albums went on to break **Daddy Cool's** local sales record in an equally bold fashion. He also produced the *Straight in a Gay Gay World* album (1976), which was not so successful. Having established his production credentials, Wilson went on to produce **Company Caine** (*Doctor Chop*), **Ray Burgess** (*Not So Pretty*), **Jo Jo Zep and the Falcons** (*Don't Waste It, Whip It Out*), **Gary Young** and the Rocking Emus (*Gary Young and the Rocking Emus*), **The Dynamic Hepnotics** (*Strange Land*), **The Johnnys** (*Highlights of a Dangerous Life, Grown Up Wrong*) and the *Street Hero* film soundtrack.

With the final break-up of **Daddy Cool** in September 1975, Wilson took time off to sort out legal wranglings with his former record company, Wizard. He then set up his own label Oz Records (through EMI) with **Little River Band** manager Glenn Wheatley. Oz issued some of the earliest material recorded by the likes of **Mondo Rock, The Sports, Jo Jo Zep and the Falcons, Stiletto** and **Mark Gillespie**. Wilson launched his solo career with the release of the single 'Living in the Land of Oz'/'Who's Gonna Love You Tonight?' (August 1976) on Oz. The single was one of the first ever to deal with the issue of Aboriginal land rights. It charted at #30 in Melbourne during October. Folk/blues singer **Margret Roadknight** later recorded a version of the song.

'Living in the Land of Oz' was used as the theme song to Chris Löfven's feature film *Oz*, which was an antipodean adaptation of the *Wizard of Oz* story-line. Wilson produced and arranged the soundtrack album which included other Wilson-penned tracks like 'The Mood', 'Greaseball' and 'Who's Gonna Love You Tonight?'. **Jo Jo Zep and the Falcons** contributed two songs, and the soundtrack also included a reworking of **The Missing Links'** garage-punk chestnut 'You're Drivin' Me Insane'. 'Living in the Land of Oz' and 'Greaseball' also appeared on the Oz sampler album *Living in the Land of Oz*. Wilson later contributed 'Living In The Land Of Oz' to the Various Artists album *Building Bridges* on CBS (1989).

Just as the 'Living in the Land of Oz' single appeared, Wilson launched his new band, **Mondo Rock**. By way of ceaseless touring and the release of a series of sophisticated pop rock albums, Wilson was able to establish **Mondo Rock** as one of the most popular acts in Australia during the early 1980s. One of Wilson's sideline ventures during his tenure with **Mondo Rock** was Ross Wilson's Rockhouse. Rockhouse comprised Wilson's old **Daddy Cool** partner **Ross Hannaford** (lead guitar), Bruce Allen (sax; ex-**Ol'55, Dynamic Hepnotics**), Craig Watson (sax), Dave Wray (sax), Mike Gubb (keyboards; ex-**Dynamic Hepnotics**), Graham Gibb (bass) and Martin McHighland (drums). Rockhouse played the Melbourne pub circuit during late 1985, with a repertoire that comprised exclusively post-war R&B material. **Mondo Rock** took a break in 1988. That same year, Wilson was inducted into the Hall of Fame at the Australian Record Industry Association (ARIA) Awards ceremony.

At that point, Wilson took the opportunity to record his autobiographical debut solo album, *Dark Side of the Man*. Production credits for the album were shared among Mark Moffatt, Ricky Fataar and jazz pianist/arranger Paul Grabowsky. The album appeared in July 1989 and mixed country rock with jazz-blues material. It bore little resemblance to his work with **Mondo Rock**, yielding the singles 'Bed of Nails'/'Visit To America' (#20 in August 1989) and 'Dark Side of the Man' (September). *Dark Side of the Man* was moderately successful (#24 in August), and Wilson revived **Mondo Rock** for the 1990 album *Why Fight It?*

That album failed to live up to past glories, and Wilson was unable to re-establish his band at the forefront of Australian music. He dissolved **Mondo Rock** in late 1991 in order to work the local pub circuit with his new venture, RAW. The line-up comprised Michael Sheridan (guitar; ex-No), Barry Deenik (bass) and Craig Waugh (drums; ex-**Uncanny X-Men**). RAW played an aggressive blend of rock and funk but, aside from building up a strong cult following on the Australian pub circuit, the band did not issue any recordings before breaking up in 1993. Wilson contributed a cover of Spencer P. Jones' 'The World's Got Everything in It' to the Various Artists compilation *Earth Music* issued on the Mushroom label (June 1994). Wilson continued to work in production, and then in July 1997 appeared as guest singer on **The Angels**' Lounge Lizards acoustic tour.

A number of other artists have recorded Ross Wilson's songs. The highest profile example is **John Farnham's** version of 'Touch of Paradise', which Wilson co-wrote with **Gulliver Smith**. Also, **Def** FX covered **Daddy Cool's** 'Make Your Stash' on the CD EP *Water* (June 1991), while **You Am I** included 'All I Wanna Do is Rock' (**Mighty Kong**) on the single 'Berlin Chair' (February 1994).

Another of Wilson's extracurricular activities was overseeing the career of his spouse Pat Wilson. During the mid-1970s, Pat had fronted Melbourne R&B band Rock Granite and the Profiles, which comprised Wayne Burt (guitar, vocals), Jeff Burstin (guitar; ex-Gutbucket), Chris Stafford (bass), who was later replaced by Wayne Duncan (ex-**Daddy Cool**), and Bob Bickerton (drums). The Profiles did not issue any records, but the various members went on to achieve a great deal of success with a number of different bands. Burt went on to **Daddy Cool**, **Jo Jo Zep and the Falcons** and **The Giants** among others. Burstin was a long-time musical accomplice to Joe Camilleri in **Jo Jo Zep and the Falcons** and **The Black Sorrows**. Pat also fronted The Marvels in 1980 with Ed Bates (guitar; ex-**Sports**), Neil McPherson (keyboards; ex-**Billy T**), Neil Hodgson (bass; ex-Fox) and Paul Hitchins (drums; ex-**Sports**).

In August 1983, Pat Wilson issued the Ross Wilson-penned and produced 'Bop Girl'/'Tacky' single on WEA. The single became a great success, reaching #2 nationally and #3 in Melbourne. It stayed in the Melbourne Top 10 for ten weeks. Pat followed that up with another Ross Wilson-penned single, 'Strong Love'/'Tacky Two' (April 1984), and the mini-album *Strong Love*. 'Strong Love' was not so successful, only reaching #25 in Melbourne and #19 in Sydney during May.

Albums: *Retrospective* (EMI, 1988), *Dark Side of the Man* (WEA, 1989).

Windchase (*see* Sebastian Hardie)

Tony Worsley and the Fabulous Blue Jays

Formed: *1964*
Style: *Beat pop*
Original line-up: *Tony Worsley (vocals), Mal Clarke (rhythm guitar; ex-Mustangs), Ray Eames (lead guitar), Paul Shannon (sax), Royce Nicholls (bass), Bob Johnson (drums)*

English-born singer Tony Worsley migrated to Australia with his parents at the age of 13. He started his singing career on the Brisbane dance circuit during 1963 when he was 18. A year later (around May 1964), he teamed up with popular Melbourne rock'n'roll band The Blue Jays who had been together since 1959.

The original Blue Jays line-up comprised Frankie Brent (vocals, rhythm guitar), Chris Lawson (lead guitar), Doug Stirling (piano) and Bob Johnson (drums). The band's first single, 'Maori's Farewell'/'Everybody Loves Saturday Night', came out on the Crest label in October 1961. The Blue Jays issued the album *Arthur Murray's Twist Party* on Crest in 1962. By that stage, the line-up comprised Brent, Johnson, Laurie Allen (vocals, guitar, piano; ex-Malcolm Arthur and the Knights), Johnny Cosgrove (vocals, lead guitar), Alan Easterbrook (vocals, sax) and Ray Houston (bass). Laurie Allen and the

Blue Jays issued the single 'Wolfman'/'Kept a Broken Heart in Broken Hill' in January 1962. In 1963, the line-up became Allen, Johnson, Easterbrook, Mal Clarke (rhythm guitar), Dennis Tucker (bass) and Doug Flower (lead guitar). Allen left in 1963 and eventually joined up with Bobby Bright as **Bobby and Laurie**. By early 1964, the line-up was Johnson, Clarke, Ray Eames (lead guitar), Paul Shannon (sax) and Royce Nicholls (bass).

After promoter Ivan Dayman matched Worsley with the already established Blue Jays, the union proceeded to score a series of hit singles. The band's first release on Dayman's Sunshine label, however, was the instrumental 'Jaywalker'/'Pathfinder' (sans Worsley and credited to The Fabulous Blue Jays, October 1964). A month later, Tony Worsley and the Fabulous Blue Jays issued the single 'I Sure Know a Lot About Love'/'Me You Gotta Teach' on Sunshine. The single peaked at #25 in Brisbane, which provided the band with a stepping stone on to the local scene. The Fabulous Blue Jays issued their second single without Worsley, 'Motivate'/'We're Friends', in January 1965. That same month, Worsley and the Fabulous Blue Jays supported UK visitors The Kinks, Manfred Mann, The Honeycombs and Tony Sheveton on The Big Show package tour. Worsley and the Fabulous Blue Jays' second single, 'Just a Little Bit'/'If I', reached #23 in Sydney during March. The Fabulous Blue Jays' third single, 'Zoom Gonk'/'Hey! Jack', also came out in March.

Sunshine issued the band's self-titled debut album, with one side dedicated to Worsley's songs and the flip to The Fabulous Blue Jays (sans Worsley). Of the album's 16 tracks, ten had already been issued as A and B-sides of singles. Eames left the band around that time to be replaced by Jimmy Cerezo (ex-**Pleazers**). The Fabulous Blue Jays backed Worsley on his third single, Chuck Berry's 'Talkin' About You'/'I Dream of You' (June 1965), although their name was dropped from the label credit. The Fabulous Blue Jays issued their final single, 'Beat Out Dat Rhythm'/'I'll Make You Cry', at the same time. Dayman began pushing Worsley as a solo artist, so his next three singles on Sunshine appeared credited to Tony Worsley.

They were 'Velvet Waters'/'Rock-a-Billy' (September 1965), 'Missing You'/'Lonely City' (January 1966) and 'Something's Got a Hold on Me'/'Something' (March). Although the bulk of Worsley's material was rocky and uptempo, the ballad 'Velvet Waters' provided him with the biggest hit of his career. It reached #5 in Sydney and #14 in Melbourne during October. A second ballad, 'Missing You', failed to replicate that success (#28 in Sydney). Sunshine issued Worsley's second album, *Velvet Waters and Other Great Songs*, in late 1965. 'Something's Got a Hold on Me' returned Worsley to more upbeat material, but it too failed to chart. Not long after the single's release, Worsley and the Fabulous Blue Jays parted company. The last Worsley record to feature The Fabulous Blue Jays on a couple of tracks was the album *My Time of Day* (November 1966).

Worsley formed a new, short-lived version of The Fabulous Blue Jays with **Phil Manning** (lead guitar), Brian Patterson (rhythm guitar), Brian Saunders (bass) and Jimmy Thompson (drums). By 1967, Manning had joined The Laurie Allen Revue, before going on to work with celebrated blues band **Chain**. Worsley's last three singles for Sunshine, 'Raining in My Heart'/'Knocking on Wood' (May 1966), 'No Worries'/'Humpty Dumpty' (January 1967) and 'Reaching Out'/'Do You Mind?' (October 1967), sank without a trace, and Worsley disappeared from view. He joined a Brisbane band, Hands Down, in 1969, but virtually retired from the music industry soon after. In the early 1990s, Worsley issued three singles on the local Enrec label, 'Heartache for You', 'High on Love' and 'Hey Hey Little Girl'.

During their time with Sunshine, Worsley and the Blue Jays issued eight EPs: 'Pathfinder' and 'Jaywalk' (The Fabulous Blue Jays), 'I Sure Know a Lot About Love' (Tony Worsley and the Fabulous Blue Jays), 'Motivate' (The Fabulous Blue Jays), 'If I' (Tony Worsley and the Fabulous Blue Jays), 'Velvet Waters' (Tony Worsley), 'Missing You' (Tony Worsley), 'Something's Got a Hold on Me' (Tony Worsley) and 'Raining in My Heart' (Tony Worsley). Of The Fabulous Blue Jays members, Bob Johnson and Paul Shannon formed Grandma's Tonic with erstwhile Blue Jays member Ray Houston (bass) plus Dennis Whitehead (guitar). Grandma's Tonic backed solo singer **Peter Doyle** for a time, and also issued two singles on the Astor label, The Troggs' 'Hi Hi Hazel'/'Johnny the Hammer' (October 1966) and the punkish 'Lost Girl'/'I Know' (April 1967).

Royce Nicholls formed a folk-blues duo with English-born, Brisbane-bred singer Toni McCann. The Fabulous Blue Jays had already backed the teenage McCann on her astonishing debut single for Sunshine 'No'/'My Baby' (July 1965). McCann issued a second single, 'Saturday Date'/'If You Don't Come Back', which came out on the Everybody's label in December 1965. Both singles are among the wildest garage/R&B releases of the era (indeed, in the words of the late Dean Mittelhauser, 'Australia had never heard a girl singer quite like

Toni McCann before!'). There is some conjecture as to whether it was The Fabulous Blue Jays, or **Steve & the Board** that backed McCann on 'Saturday Date'. Either way, it was McCann's riotous vocal delivery (in that boisterous Wanda Jackson vein), and the rough-hewn sound quality on offer, that precluded any notion of chart success for the singles.

McCann recorded a third solo single, 'Buy Some Love'/'Look on', which was due out on CBS in December 1966, but never seems to have appeared. Toni and Royce issued two singles on CBS, 'On The Road'/'Happiness is Just a State of Mind' (May 1967) and 'The Streets are Not Deserted Now' /'Even I Can Hear the Grass Grow' (February 1968), before disappearing from view. Mal Clarke went on to work with **Ray Brown** and Moonstone, the **Ray Burton** Band, **Chariot** and Bullamakanka.

Albums: *Tony Worsley and the Fabulous Blue Jays* (Sunshine, 1965), *Velvet Waters and Other Great Songs* (Sunshine, 1965), *My Time of Day* (Sunshine, 1966).

The Wreckery

Formed: *1985*
Style: *Rock, blues*
Original line-up: *Hugo Race (vocals, guitar; ex-Plays with Marionettes,* **Nick Cave and the Bad Seeds***), Edward Clayton-Jones (guitar, organ, vocals; ex-Fabulous Marquises, Plays with Marionettes, Horla,* **Nick Cave and the Bad Seeds***), Charles Todd (sax, organ; ex-Wild Dog Rodeo,* **Cattletruck***), Tadeusz O'Biegly (bass), Robin Casinader (drums, piano, Hammond organ, guitar, violin; ex-Plays with Marionettes, Horla)*

Melbourne inner-city angst kings The Wreckery proffered a lurching brand of gutbucket St Kilda blues by way of the Mississippi delta. It was a fiery sound totally unique in Australia at the time, although **The Birthday Party** was an obvious antecedent. Led by the enigmatic, petulant Hugo Race, whose bleak visions stabbed at the heart of the human condition, The Wreckery defied conventional approaches to plough a deep furrow of dark romantic melodrama.

The Wreckery had its roots in Melbourne band Plays with Marionettes. Formed in 1980 and also led by Race, Plays with Marionettes played an aggravating style of jazzy no-wave noise. The band was popular on the inner-city/Crystal Ballroom circuit already mapped out by the likes of **The Birthday Party**. Plays with Marionettes shared one side of a 7-inch single ('Witchen Kopf') with fellow Melbourne band People with Chairs Up Their Noses on the Au-go-go label (1982). Another track, 'Hellbelly', surfaced on the Various Artists compilation *This is Hot* on the Sydney-based Hot label in 1984. The band's bass player Nick Seymour went on to play with **Crowded House** and **deadstar**.

Edward Clayton-Jones' first band, The Fabulous Marquises, virtually had 'inner-city supergroup' status from the outset. As well as Clayton-Jones, the band comprised Mr Pierre (real name Peter Sutcliffe; vocals, guitar; ex-**Teenage Radio Stars**, **JAB**, **Models**), Chris Walsh (bass; ex-Negatives) and Katherine Denney (piano, organ). The band formed after Mr Pierre had been ousted from the nascent **Models** in late 1978. The Marquises' sound was sparse and electronic. The band's solitary single, 'Honeymoon'/'1,2,3, Factory' (September 1980), was initially included as part of the Unforgettable Music Box Set of three singles, alongside Ron Rude's Piano Piano and Microfilm. Ron Rude (head of the Unforgettable Music label) produced the Marquises' single. Rude also included the Marquises' track 'From My Heart to My Hands' on the Various Artists album *From Belgrave with Love* (1981). Walsh was later in **The Moodists**.

Plays with Marionettes broke up in February 1984 when Race joined former **Birthday Party** frontman Nick Cave's new band Nick Cave: Man or Myth? for an Australian tour. Redubbed **Nick Cave and the Bad Seeds**, the band flew to London to complete work on Cave's debut album, *From Her to Eternity*. The band then embarked on an extensive tour of the UK, Europe and the USA, winding up in Los Angeles in July 1984. Clayton-Jones joined The Bad Seeds on the European leg of the tour, deputising for the unavailable Blixa Bargeld. It was during this time that Race and Clayton-Jones laid plans for their new venture The Wreckery.

When Race had joined The Bad Seeds, Clayton-Jones and multi-instrumentalist Robin Casinader formed The Horla with Brian McMahon (keyboards) and Nick Seymour (bass; ex-Plays with Marionettes, Bang). With Race's return to Melbourne in late 1984, he began to assemble The Wreckery. The line-up listed above stabilised in January 1985, and three months later The Wreckery entered the studio to record its debut mini-album. The Hot label issued the rough-hewn *I Think this Town is Nervous* in December 1985, by which time Nick Barker (ex-Curse, Reptile Smile) had replaced original bass player Tadeusz O'Biegly.

By 1986, The Wreckery had earned considerable infamy on the Melbourne scene as a cathartic live experience. The band also attracted television exposure when the ABC-TV's rock show *Edge of the Wedge* and SBS's *The Noise* both screened Wreckery concerts. The Rampant label reissued *I Think this*

Town is Nervous in 1986, and the band returned to the studio in April to record a second mini-album, *Yeh My People*. The mini-album and its single, 'No Shoes for this Road'/'You is My Smoke', appeared in January 1987 to a positive response. Race wrote the bulk of the band's material, although one of the standout tracks on *Yeh My People* was Clayton-Jones' tremulous 'Overload'.

In early 1987, Race helped co-write the screenplay for director John Hillcoat and producer Evan English's feature film *Ghosts ... of the Civil Dead*. Set in the fictional Central Industrial Prison, the film starred **Nick Cave** and **The Reels'** Dave Mason. It had its premiere in early 1989. By that stage Race had also played the role of sociopath Mack in the film *Mack the Knife*, which never seems to have been officially released. In August 1987, The Wreckery issued its debut, full-length album, *Here at Pain's Insistence*, which was a consolidation of the band's thematic approach. It yielded the beguiling single, 'Everlasting Sleep'/'Damned is Hard' (November). The 12-inch EP 'Ruling Energy' (February 1988) was four more slices of moody, rough-shod R&B. Rampant assembled the ten-track Wreckery compilation album *The Collection*, which came out in October.

By that stage, The Wreckery had signed a new deal with Citadel (only the second Melbourne band to join that Sydney-based label) for the album *Laying Down Law* (October 1988) and its single 'Good to Be Gone'/'Laying Down Law' (August). *Laying Down Law* displayed a refinement of the traditional Wreckery approach without sacrificing one ounce of power and passion in the process. There were moments of great beauty to be found amongst the album's chilling atmospherics, making it the band's most accessible album to date. To allow Casinader freer rein to concentrate on piano and organ in the studio, session drummer Peter Jones (ex-**Harem Scarem**) played on five of the album's ten tracks.

Laying Down Law proved to be the band's final album, because soon after recording it in early 1988, Barker, Clayton-Jones and Todd had all left. Casinader moved to guitar and keyboards, and Race recruited new bass player Brian Colechin (ex-Marching Girls) and veteran drummer John Murphy (ex-**News**, Whirlywirld, Associates, Slub). That line-up toured in support of the album's release, but Race had split the band by mid-1989. By that stage, Nick Barker had relaunched himself as frontman with the commercially minded **Nick Barker and the Reptiles**. Casinader issued a solo album, *All This will Be Yours* (August 1991), and went on to play keyboards in **Dave Graney 'n' the Coral Snakes**.

During a lull in The Wreckery's schedule circa 1987, Race, Casinader and Barker (with guests **Chris Wilson**, harmonica, Brian Colechin, bass and John Murphy, percussion) had recorded under the name of The True Spirit. The True Spirit track 'Certified Fool' appeared on Rampant's 1987 compilation of local bands, *Melbourne Stuff* (which also included The Wreckery cut 'Seven Day Spell'). The sessions also produced Race's debut solo album, *Rue Morgue Blues* (June 1988).

At the end of 1989, Race relocated to Berlin, Germany, where he revived The True Spirit name. He issued two True Spirit albums, *Earl's World* (1990) and *Second Revelator* (January 1992), on German label Normal. Appearing on *Second Revelator* was long-time friend Mick Harvey from **Nick Cave and the Bad Seeds**, plus members of German bands Einsturzende Neubauten and Die Haut. Race returned to Australia in December 1991 to promote *Second Revelator*. For the tour, The True Spirit comprised ex-Wreckery alumni Robin Casinader, Edward Clayton-Jones, Brian Colechin and new drummer Chris Hughes (ex-Once Upon a Time). With the re-release of *Second Revelator* in February 1993, Hugo Race The True Spirit undertook another Australian tour. *Stations of the Cross* followed in 1994. Race re-emerged in February 1996 with his first release on an Australian label (Roadshow) for almost seven years, *Valley of Light*. Race paid homage to one of his formative influences, Captain Beefheart, by covering 'Clear Spot' on *Valley of Light*. Hugo Race The True Spirit followed that up with the album *Wet Dream* (June 1997), which was described as 'industrial trance blues'.

Wreckery albums: *I Think this Town is Nervous* (mini-album, Hot, 1985; reissued on Rampant, 1986), *Yeh My People* (mini-album, Rampant, 1986), *Here at Pain's Insistence* (Rampant, 1987), *The Collection* (compilation, Rampant, 1988), *Laying Down Law* (Citadel, 1988); ***Hugo Race The True Spirit albums:*** *Rue Morgue Blues* (Rampant 1988), *Earl's World* (Normal/Shock, 1990), *Second Revelator* (Normal/ Survival, 1992; reissued 1993), *Stations of the Cross* (Normal, 1994), *Valley of Light* (Roadshow/Warner, 1996), *Wet Dream* (Glitterhouse, German import, 1997).

Stevie Wright

Style: *Rock, pop*

At one point during the 1960s, 'Little' Stevie Wright (b. 1948) was the hottest teen sensation in the country. As frontman for the chart-busting **Easybeats**, Wright helped ignite scenes of fan hysteria the likes of which Australia had never witnessed before. He got a second bite of the apple in 1974 when the dramatic, 11-minute Vanda and Young-penned epic 'Evie Parts I, II and III' took him to the top of the charts. Yet Wright always seemed to be his own worst enemy, and when his much-publicised drug addiction got the better of him, he disappeared from view.

Wright was born on 20 December 1948 in Leeds, England. He migrated to Australia with his family at the age of nine. The Wright family settled in Melbourne before moving to Sydney in 1960. Before joining **The Easybeats** in 1964, Wright sang with local combos The Outlaws and Chris Langdon and the Langdells. **The Easybeats** went on to become one of Australia's most celebrated 1960s rock bands, enjoying international success with the working-class anthem 'Friday on My Mind'. While Harry Vanda and George Young came to prominence as **The Easybeats'** hit-making, songwriting team, it was the Wright/Young combination which fashioned the band's earliest hits. They included 'For My Woman', 'She's So Fine', 'Women (Make You Feel Alright)', 'Come and See Her' and 'Sorry'. **The Easybeats** broke up in late 1969 following an Australian tour.

When Vanda and Young returned to the UK to further their production and songwriting work, Wright remained in Australia. He formed backing band Rachette, helped set up Sydney label Musical Expression and produced local band Bootleg's debut single for that label, 'Whole World Should Slow Down'. Stevie Wright and Rachette made an appearance at the Odyssey Music Festival (Wallacia, NSW) in January 1971. In late 1971, Wright travelled to Perth, Western Australia where he joined an ambitious rock'n'roll revue band called Likefun. The line-up included Wright, **Ray Hoff** (vocals; ex-Off Beats), Shirley Reid (vocals), Morri Pierson (vocals), John Tucak (bass) and Alan Wilkes (organ). Wright worked with Likefun only briefly, before returning to Sydney where he took the part of Simon Zealotes in the Australian production of the Andrew Lloyd-Webber/Tim Rice rock musical *Jesus Christ Superstar* (directed by Jim Sharman). Wright stayed with the production for two years and he appeared on the Original Australian Cast album which came out on MCA Records in 1973. During 1972, Wright also sang with a band called Black Tank with Rory O'Donoghue (guitar; ex-Pogs), Ken Firth (bass; ex-**Tully**) and Greg Henson (drums; ex-**Levi Smith Clefs**).

At the end of 1973, Wright signed to the Albert label and commenced work on his debut solo album, *Hard Road*, with producers Vanda and Young. *Hard Road* (April 1974) proved to be an excellent rock album with Wright in fine form. The Vanda and Young-penned tracks 'Hard Road', 'Didn't I Take You Higher?' and 'Evie' saw Wright in full-blooded rock mode, while his own compositions like 'Movin' On Up', 'Commando Line', 'Life Gets Better' and 'Dancing in the Limelight' were cut from a slightly less frantic blues mould. The single 'Evie' (May 1974) peaked at #2 on the national chart during July. It did even better in Melbourne, where it remained at #1 for seven weeks. *Hard Road* also peaked at #5 nationally and #1 in Melbourne. Suzi Quatro later covered 'Evie', while Rod Stewart included his version of 'Hard Road' on the *Smiler* album. *Hard Road* also came out on Atlantic in the USA and Polydor in the UK.

Wright hit the road with The All Stars, which contained such well-known local rock luminaries as Warren Morgan (piano; ex-**Chain**, **Billy Thorpe** and the Aztecs), **Tim Gaze** (lead guitar; ex-**Tamam Shud**, **Kahvas Jute**, **Ariel**) and Johnny Dick (drums; ex-**Billy Thorpe** and the Aztecs). Wright headed back into the studio with Vanda and Young for his second solo album, *Black Eyed Bruiser*, which produced the singles 'Guitar Band'/'Hard Road' (November 1974), 'You'/'My Kind of Music' (March 1975) and 'Black Eyed Bruiser'/'Help Help' (May). 'Guitar Band' reached #8 in Melbourne, and #8 nationally during December 1974. Wright ended the year by performing three concerts at the Sydney Opera House with backing produced by Vanda, Young and **AC/DC**'s Malcolm Young. *Black Eyed Bruiser* was a punchy album of blues-rock, soul and country-tinged material, but it failed to chart. While Wright had dominated the charts in 1974, he disappeared from view in 1975.

By May 1975, The All Stars had departed to back **John Paul Young** and Wright formed the Stevie Wright Band with Russell Johnson (guitar; ex-**Mississippi, Country Radio**), Peter White (keyboards), Billy Rylands (bass; ex-**Lotus**, Wolfe), Larry Duryea (percussion; ex-**Heart 'n' Soul, Tamam Shud**) and Tony Bolton (drums; ex-**Aesop's Fables**, Luke's Walnut, Traine, **Freshwater, Country Radio**). Wright played a few gigs around Sydney during mid-1976 with a band called Sacha, but over the ensuing years he sought treatment for his drug addiction.

On 4 November 1979, Wright performed 'Evie' at the Concert of the Decade in front of 100 000 people on the steps of the Sydney Opera House. Other acts who appeared that day included **Cheetah, Russell Morris, Jim Keays, Doug Parkinson, Hush, Stars, Marcia Hines, Max Merritt, Jo Jo Zep and the Falcons, Norman Gunston, Split Enz, Richard Clapton, Skyhooks, Jon English** and **Sherbet**. Mushroom issued the double live album of the event, *Concert of the Decade*, in 1980.

In 1982, Wright joined Vanda and Young's studio

band **Flash and the Pan** for the album *Headlines* and its singles 'Where were You?'/'Hey Jimmy' (July 1982) and 'Waiting for a Train'/'Don't Vote' (December 1982). When issued overseas during April 1983, 'Waiting for a Train'/"A" became a smash hit, reaching #7 in the UK. *Headlines* was **Flash and The Pan's** third #1 album in Scandinavia. In 1983, Wright worked with backing band The Street Beat Band, but nothing came out of the project. In January 1984, Wright appeared in Penrith Court charged with attempted housebreaking. He had signed himself out of Westmount drug rehabilitation centre only days before he attempted to break into the house. Wright was also arrested for heroin use that same month, after being found unconscious in a hotel toilet. He had been using heroin since 1973.

In October 1986, **The Easybeats** re-formed for a six-week national tour. That same month, Albert reissued the 'You' single with a new B-side, '20 Dollar Bill'. In 1988, Wright formed Hard Rain which comprised Peter Northcote (sax), Bruno Renzella (guitar), Vic Young (bass) and Paul DeMarco (drums; ex-Scattered Aces). Hard Rain became the Stevie Wright Band, and Glenn Goldsmith replaced Renzella on guitar. To celebrate 25 years in music, Wright issued a new album, *Striking It Rich*, on the Laser label in 1991. It featured seven new songs, a new version of 'Evie' and six re-workings of old **Easybeats** material. In April 1992, Wright performed a concert at Selina's in Sydney. By that stage, Wright's health had deteriorated to such a degree that he disappeared from view again.

Albums: *Hard Road* (Albert/EMI, 1974), *Black-eyed Bruiser* (Albert/EMI, 1975), *Facing the Music (Greatest Hits)* (compilation, Albert/EMI, 1986), *Striking It Rich* (Laser, 1991).

Ross D. Wyllie

Style: Pop

Brisbane-born entertainer Ross D. Wyllie (b. 1948) joined his first band, The Kodiaks, in 1964 at the age of 16. In 1967, Wyllie signed to Ivan Dayman's Sunshine label and recorded the single 'Short Skirts'/'Paper Bunnies' backed by The Escorts (who had their own singles on Sunshine, 'The House on Soul Hill'/'The Sound of Your Voice' and 'On a Day Like Today'/'Sitting by a Tree').

Entrepreneur David Joseph offered Wyllie the opportunity to compere a new Melbourne television pop show, *Uptight*. Wyllie accepted and moved to Melbourne for the pilot episode, which screened on 28 October 1967. Wyllie signed a new deal with Festival Records, although his debut single 'Smile'/'Faces' (April 1968) was not successful. 1969 proved to be Wyllie's most successful year when the singles Ray Stevens' 'Funny Man'/'Last Day in Town' (June) and **Johnny Young's** 'The Star'/'Do the Uptight' (September) took the singer into the Top 20 for the first time. 'Funny Man' peaked at #17 during May, and 'The Star' did even better by going all the way to #1 in October. In March 1970 *Uptight* was replaced by *Happening '70* which Wyllie also compered. One month later, Wyllie issued his fifth single, 'Free Born Man'/'My Little Girl', which was only a moderate hit. Wyllie left *Happening '70* and Melbourne in late 1970 to return to Brisbane.

In the new year he signed to Ron Tudor's Fable label, which resulted in the singles 'He Gives Us All His Love'/'Life' (April 1971), 'It Takes Time'/'Child's Dream' (August) and 'Sweet White Dove'/'Going Home' (May 1972). By that stage, Wyllie was concentrating on projecting a more mature image, and he began working on the club circuit. He also went into business by setting up the production and public relations companies Paladin Productions (with **Ronnie Burns** and Jeff Joseph) and Paladin Public Relations (with Tony Healy). During the late 1970s, Wyllie returned to Melbourne television as presenter of the late-night movies for the 0-10 Network.

Album: *Smile: The Festival Files Volume Ten* (Festival, 1988).

X

X

Formed: *1977*
Style: *Punk rock*
Original line-up: *Steve Lucas (vocals), Ian Krahe (guitar), Ian Rilen (bass; ex-Space,* **Band of Light, Rose Tattoo***), Steve Cafiero (drums)*

The legendary X was one of the most notorious bands ever to emerge from the Sydney inner-city scene. Following on from the pioneering wake of **Radio Birdman**, and alongside the likes of **The Thought Criminals**, **The Last Words**, **Rocks**, Psycho-Surgeons, Johnny Dole and the Scabs, Filth and The Hellcats, X was among the leading lights of the original Sydney punk band explosion.

Driven by the ferocious bass lines of the venerable Ian Rilen, the raucous bawling of lead singer Steve Lucas and a melange of screaming guitars, X was long revered as *the* punk band to experience live. X-music was rock'n'roll stripped down to the bare essentials of noise, raw power and pure energy; in short, the band's music was tough, simplistic and incredibly loud. Writing in *Rolling Stone*, Clinton Walker once described X as 'the eternal outsiders'. X also had one of the most turbulent histories imaginable. Original guitarist Ian Krahe died in his sleep in May 1978; the band was constantly banned from city venues, subjected to regular harassment from the local constabulary, and suffered several line-up changes, but X was persistent enough to eventually release a number of records.

Ian Rilen had been instrumental in getting the original **Rose Tattoo** off the ground. He left the Tatts in mid-1977 just as they were establishing a formidable reputation as an influential, street-wise hard rock band. Rilen had in mind an even more elemental and cathartic sound for his new band, initially dubbed Evil Rumours. That band comprised Rilen, Lucas, Krahe, Geoff Holmes (guitar) and Eddie Fisher (drums). Evil Rumours never got out of the rehearsal studio and, in September 1977, Rilen unveiled X with Lucas, Krahe and Steve Cafiero. During a period of uncertainty over Cafiero's position in the band, Eddie Fisher and Nino (ex-Filth) both filled in on drums. X staked out such infamous Sydney punk hangouts as the Grand Hotel, the Paris Theatre and the Stagedoor Tavern as their own territory, laying down a sound that was short, sharp and brutally honest. As well as a smattering of cover songs like Del Shannon's 'Runaway', **The Easybeats'** 'She's So Fine' and The Rolling Stones' 'Paint It Black', the band's early repertoire consisted of original material of the calibre of 'Degenerate Boy', 'Slash Your Wrists, 'You Don't Like Me', 'One Last Chance', 'Home is Where the Floor Is' and 'Hate City' (originally written for **Rose Tattoo**).

With Krahe's death, X recruited Evil Rumours guitarist Geoff Holmes as his replacement. Although the original X line-up with Krahe did not issue any records, the band recorded three demo tracks, 'Home is Where the Floor Is', 'Hate City' and 'TV Cabaret Roll', which later appeared on the third Aberrant compilation of Sydney punk bands *Why March When You Can Riot?* (1985). Peter Coutanche (ex-Kamikaze Kidz) replaced Holmes in early 1979. Although the band continued to attract a fanatical following, as Steve Lucas put it, 'something in the core of X's being was lacking'. In mid-1979, Lucas took up guitar (to replace Coutanche) and the band continued as a three-piece.

That line-up entered Trafalgar Studios in late 1979 with redoubtable producer **Lobby Loyde** to record an album. The classic single 'I Don't Wanna Go Out'/'Waiting' (December 1979) preceded the album *X-Aspirations* which appeared in early 1980. Recorded in just five hours, *X-Aspirations* remains raw and unnerving. There was no light and shade across the record, just stark black and white. The energy levels teetered constantly on the edge, so the overall effect was akin to a sledgehammer applied methodically to the guts. Despite the rough-hewn quality, tracks like 'Suck Suck', 'Delinquent Cars', 'I Don't Wanna Go Out' and 'Dipstick' are among the band's best. At the start of 1980, X brought Coutanche back into the fold, and the band held down a residency at the Heritage Hotel for a couple of months. By mid-1980, X had called it a day. Lucas, Coutanche (who switched to bass) and Cafiero played one gig as The Stand before Lucas formed Harold Holt and the Sharks with Michael Orland (bass) and Ken Wylie (drums). In mid-1982, Lucas formed The Feel with Peter Copeland (bass) and Chris Gormly (drums; ex-Local Product). Lucas and Cafiero, plus guest player Stuart Dunlop on bass, played one gig as X in October 1982.

In the meantime, Rilen had switched to guitar and formed Sardine v with his spouse Stephanie Rilen (vocals, keyboards), Phil Hall (bass) and Greg Skehill (drums). That line-up lasted from December 1980 to December 1981. For Sardine v, Rilen adopted a more stylish persona, replete with an impeccably tailored powder-blue suit and slicked-back hair. Likewise, the band's music eschewed the aggressive assault of X for a more refined and melodic yet brooding approach that recalled UK bands like The Cure, Public Image Ltd and Gang of Four. In late 1981, Sardine v issued the single 'Sabotage'/'Sudan' on the EMI Custom label. Mushroom's White label reissued the single in March 1982, by which time Johanna Pigott (ex-**XL-Capris**) had replaced Hall on bass and New Zealander Barton Price (ex-Crocodiles) had taken over from Skehill on drums. Price left in April to join **Models**, and John Lloyd (ex-**Paul Kelly** and The Dots, Flowers, **Icehouse**) took his place. Pigott left in June to be replaced by Craig Rossi (on loan from **Box of Fish**). In November, Lloyd left, so Rossi switched to drums and Stuart Dunlop came in on bass.

The new line-up recorded the excellent five-track, 12-inch EP 'I Hate You'. Tracks like 'I Hate You', 'Pictures' and 'Minutes' displayed a remarkable flair, and were equal to anything produced by The Cure to that point. Not long after the EP appeared on the Phantom label in June 1983, Rilen broke up Sardine v to revive X. The X line-up of Rilen, Lucas and Cafiero lasted until November 1984. That month, X issued its second independent single, a cover of John Lennon's 'Mother'/'Half Way 'Round the World'. X relocated to Melbourne where Cathy Green (ex-Cough Cough, Horla) replaced Cafiero.

In early 1985, X recorded its second album, *At Home with You.* Once again produced by **Lobby Loyde**, the album (issued during October) displayed a breadth and sense of dynamics only previously hinted at in the band's music. A lot had to do with the freshness and vitality, to say nothing of the rhythmic swing, that Green contributed to the band. The album included reworkings of 'Half Way 'Round The World' and 'Degenerate Boy'. For the next five years, X built-up a reputation as one of Melbourne's finest bands. Every X gig was an event, with packed houses being the order of the day. Renowned Melbourne bluesman **Chris Wilson** became a regular guest on sax and harmonica for the band's live shows.

In 1987, X signed to the White label, which issued the single Roy Orbison's 'Dream Baby'/'I Don't Wanna Go Out' (July 1987). The single also appeared in 12-inch format with an additional track, 'Without You', added. Fans had to wait another two years before X issued its third Loyde-produced album, *And More* (July 1989), and fourth single, 'And More'/'Getting Wet' (June). Unfortunately, the album failed to live up to the band's illustrious past, and was a disappointing release. The album was dedicated to the memory of the late Steve Cafiero, who had died in December 1988.

Rilen broke up X for a second time, and he and Green formed **Hell to Pay** with Spencer P. Jones (guitar, vocals; ex-Cuban Heels, **Johnnys**, **Beasts of Bourbon**) and Tony Biggs (drums; ex-Black Assassins). **Hell to Pay** remained together until 1993 and issued the single 'Saints and Kings'/'Would You Believe It?', 'Starting All Over' (May 1991), the album *Steal It* (August 1992) and the CD EP 'Two Days Off (Five Days On)' (November 1992) on the Red Eye label. In the meantime, Lucas had formed a part-time outfit called The Groody Frenzy with Herbie Mayhem (keyboards), Anthony Ragg (bass; ex-**Kings of the Sun**) and Doug Falconer (drums; on loan from **Hunters & Collectors**). Lucas also issued his third solo album, *All Too Human* (Novem-

X

ber 1990), and its single, 'Count Yourself Lucky', on the Mighty Boy label. During his time with X, Lucas had issued the single 'City Song'/'Mr Anfenger's Fish' (October 1987), plus the albums *Double Cross* (backed by Melbourne band **White Cross**; April 1987) and *Bought and Sold* (January 1989). The albums displayed a gentler side to Lucas's talents as a songwriter. Lucas went on to issue another solo album, *Bread and Water* (1995).

In 1992, Lucas joined another high-powered Melbourne band, Bigger than Jesus, which comprised Hank Oudendyk (guitar; ex-Law), Brett Kingman (guitar; ex-Adventure, **Uncanny X-Men**, the **James Reyne** Band, Gas), Kevin McMahon (bass) and Craig Whitelock (drums). Bigger than Jesus was not afraid to court controversy via its bold use of religious iconography. Hence the name (derived from John Lennon's aside about The Beatles being 'bigger than Jesus') and a penchant for burning six-foot crosses onstage. Lucas was also known to appear on stage wrapped entirely in bandages from head to foot. Oudendyk's previous band, The Law, issued two independent singles, 'Some Girl'/'White Man's Law' (December 1985) and 'Hang the Jury'/'Shadow' (September 1987). Bigger than Jesus' debut album, *Killervision* (April 1993), mixed thrash metal riffs and break-neck tempos with a solid production sound. The 1995 CD EP 'Soul Feast' and October 1996 CD single 'PC'/'In God We Trust' furthered the cause (although Tony Kopa, ex-Truth, had replaced Lucas as lead singer by that stage).

Such was X's legendary status that US label Amphetamine Reptile re-issued *X-Aspirations* on CD for the North American market. In June 1993, Rilen and Lucas revived X once more with new drummer Stefan Berg. The band held down a three-month residency at St Kilda's Prince of Wales Hotel, which attracted hordes of dedicated fans. X continued to play on an irregular basis with Cathy Green back in the drum seat. X supported UK outfit The Damned on that band's Australian tour of April 1997. Green then joined a new band, Universe, which comprised former **Noiseworks** member and **Electric Hippy** Steve Balbi (guitar, vocals), Big Bird (real name Matt McCormack, guitar; ex-Starworld), Jim Denley (flute) and Cath Synnerdahl (drums; ex-Mother Hubbard). As with **Hell to Pay**, Green played bass in Universe. The band issued its debut CD EP, *Above Water*, on the Phantom label during September 1997.

X albums: *X-Aspirations* (X-Records, 1980), *At Home with You* (Major, 1985), *And More* (White/Mushroom/Festival, 1989) *X Live 8 July 1978* (Spiral Scratch, 1997); ***Steve Lucas solo albums:*** *Double Cross* (Rampant, 1987), *Bought and Sold* (Rampant, 1989), *All Too Human* (Mighty Boy, 1990), *Bread and Water* (Mighty Boy, 1995); ***Bigger than Jesus album:*** *Killervision* (Frank/Shock, 1993).

XL-Capris

Formed: *1978*
Style: *Rock*
Original line-up: *Errol Cruz (real name Tim Gooding, guitar, vocals), Däg Rattler (real name Kimble Rendall, guitar, vocals), Alligator Bagg (real name Johanna Pigott, bass, vocals), Nancy Serapax (real name Julie Anderson, drums)*

For a time, XL-Capris was slated as the chicest, most consistently artistic and loony band in Sydney. What the members initially lacked in musical competence, they made up for in energy and bizarre lyric fun. XL-Capris made their live debut on 1 January 1979, and exactly one year later issued their debut single, 'My City of Sydney'/'Dead Budgies', on the Axle label.

'My City of Sydney' was a noisy, perverse stamping all over the old Tommy Leonetti standard (which was the closing theme for the Seven Network in Sydney for many years). The single received strong local airplay, and even some attention overseas when influential London DJ John Peel was reported to have quipped 'If that's what Australia's like, I don't want to go there'. Another track recorded in late 1979, 'Skylab (Son of Telstar)', later appeared on the Aberrant label's third Sydney punk compilation *Why March When You Can Riot?* (1985).

Julie Anderson left the band in April 1980 to be replaced by Michael Farmer. The band's second single, 'World War 3'/'Dusty' (October 1980), was not quite so raucous as 'My City of Sydney'. The band had developed a more tempered, diverse sound as displayed on the album *Where is Hank?* (March 1981) and its single, 'Red Bikini Runaway'/'K-Tel City' (April). By the time the album appeared, Rendall had left the band to join Dave Faulkner, James Baker and **Roddy Radalj** in the original line-up of Le **Hoodoo Gurus**. Todd Hunter (ex-**Dragon**) had replaced Rendall on guitar in November 1980. Michael Churnside also joined on bass to allow Johanna Pigott to concentrate on vocals, keyboards and guitar. The new line-up recorded the album *Weeds* and fourth single 'Igloos'/'Elevator' in June 1981. Barry Blackler then joined the band as second drummer in time for the release of 'Igloos' (September) and *Weeds* (October). XL-Capris played their last gig on 1 January 1982, three years to the day from their debut appearance.

In March 1982, Pigott replaced Phil Hall in Ian Rilen's band Sardine v. Pigott toured with Sardine v until June, when she and Tim Gooding turned their talents to television. They devised and wrote the ABC-TV series *Sweet and Sour*, which starred David Reyne (ex-**Australian Crawl**) and Tracy Mann. *Sweet and Sour* followed the trials and tribulations of fictional Sydney band The Takeaways as they went about the task of breaking into the Australian music industry. In late 1982, Todd Hunter joined the re-formed **Dragon**, and Pigott went on to co-write, with Todd and Marc Hunter, five tracks on the band's comeback album, *Body and the Beat*, including the #2 hit 'Rain' (August 1983). One of the tracks, 'Wilderworld', also appeared on the *Street Hero* soundtrack. Pigott also launched her solo career under the name of Scribble, playing winsome, witty pop.

The mini-album *Scribble* and its single, 'Silly Girl'/'Mr Calico' (November 1983), featured Pigott singing and playing guitar, piano and synthesiser, with Todd Hunter on bass and synthesiser. Guest players were Jeff Oakes (sax), Keith Stirling (trumpet) and Michel Rose (pedal steel). 'Adaptability'/'B4' came out in November 1984, and Pigott's label Regular issued the compilation album *So Far* in December 1985. By that stage, Pigott had formed a touring line-up of Scribble which comprised Hunter, Mike Caen (guitar, backing vocals; ex-Pink Slips), Lee Borkman (keyboards; ex-Pink Slips) and Tim Powles (drums; ex-**Ward 13**, on loan from **Venetians**).

That line-up recorded the album *Pop Art* and its three singles, 'Sunday School'/'Lowdown' (April 1986), 'Don't Give Your Heart Away'/'Blues Again' (July) and 'Alligator'/'Laws of Motion' (November). Iva Davies from **Icehouse** and **The Reels'** Dave Mason contributed to a number of tracks; Davies also mixed five tracks. By the end of 1986, Scribble comprised Mark Bell (guitar), Nicolette Boaz (keyboards), Jeff Zundren (bass) and Bill Heckenberg (drums). Pigott folded Scribble in 1987, after which she concentrated on her songwriting partnership with Todd Hunter. Their best-known song 'Age of Reason' became a #1 hit single for **John Farnham** (July 1988).

XL-Capris albums: *Where is Hank?* (Axle, 1981), *Weeds* (Axle, 1981); ***Scribble albums:*** *Scribble* (mini-album, Regular/WEA, 1983), *So Far 1983–1985* (Regular/Festival, 1985), *Pop Art* (Regular/Festival, 1986).

X-Ray-Z

Formed: *1977*
Style: *New wave*
Original line-up: *Peter Rich (real name Peter Dooley, vocals, sax; ex-Rufus Red), Mike D'Art (real name Martin Dooley, guitar, keyboards; ex-Rufus Red), James Wave (real name James Lloyd, bass; ex-Rufus Red), Jon Ray (real name Jon Wilkinson, drums; ex-Spare Change, Rufus Red)*

X-Ray-Z is recognised as one of Australia's pioneering new wave outfits. The band had its roots in Adelaide pub band Rufus Red, which moved to Melbourne in early 1977. Sensing a change in the musical climate, the band members adopted a 'poor image', renamed themselves X-Ray-Z and set about establishing an identity on the Melbourne inner-city pub circuit.

X-Ray-Z supported US visitor Lou Reed on his October 1977 Australian tour, and then signed to Mushroom Records for a one-off single, 'Poor Image'/'Sledgehammer Hit', 'Citizen John' (November). 'Poor Image' was a chunky rocker with a kinetic guitar riff, and the storming 'Sledgehammer Hit' boasted a punkish snarl. The band members made up a few picture sleeves for the single (probably less than 100), which they distributed to shops themselves. In early 1978, X-Ray-Z signed to Suicide Records and contributed 'Three Glorious Years' and 'Valium' to the Melbourne punk compilation *Lethal Weapons* (alongside The Boys Next Door, **Teenage Radio Stars**, The Negatives, **JAB**, The Survivors and Wasted Daze). X-Ray-Z played around Melbourne with The Boys Next Door, **Teenage Radio Stars**, The Negatives and **JAB** as part of Suicide's package tours. By the end of 1978, X-Ray-Z had mutated into Popgun Men.

Popgun Men comprised Peter Rich, Mauri Bund (aka Martin Dooley, guitar, vocals, synth), Dis Naylor (guitar), Andrew Picoleau (bass, vocals) and Errol Senol (real name Errol Selimi, drums). Popgun Men played in a hard-edged electro-pop vein and issued one independent single, 'Behind Dark Glasses'/'Modern Man' (February 1980). Rich and Bund also contributed sax and synth respectively to The Metronomes' single 'Saturday Night'/'Sunday Morning' (May 1980), the connection being Picoleau who was also a member of that band. By mid-1980, Popgun Men had transformed back into X-Ray-Z with a line-up of Rich, Bund,

Picoleau and Selimi. X-Ray-Z played the Melbourne scene until early 1982, after which Picoleau joined **Sacred Cowboys**. Before splitting, X-Ray-Z recorded studio demos and live material which the Polyester label combined with the three tracks from the 'Poor Image' single and 'Three Glorious Years' for the compilation *X-Ray-Z*.

Album: *X-Ray-Z* (Polyester, 1988).

Y

Ya Ya Choral

Formed: *1982*
Style: *Electronic to hard rock*
Original line-up: *Fiona Graham (keyboards, vocals; ex-Systematics), Patrick Gibson (keyboards, rhythm box, vocals; ex-***Scattered Order***, Systematics), Michael Tee (keyboards, guitar, vocals; ex-***Scattered Order***)*

Ya Ya Choral grew out of the early 1980s Sydney experimental/electronic movement which spawned **Scattered Order, SPK, Severed Heads, Makers of the Dead Travel Fast**, Wet Taxis, The Systematics, The N-Lets, Slugfuckers, Wild West, Seems Twice and Hiroshima Chair. By the end of the decade, the band had transformed into a solid hard rock outfit which owed an allegiance to the likes of **AC/DC**, Led Zeppelin, Aerosmith and Metallica.

As well as their involvement with studio band/production team **Scattered Order**, Michael Tee and Patrick Gibson also ran the M Squared label with the third **Scattered Order** member, Mitch Jones. Gibson and Fiona Graham first worked together as The Systematics, which included Michael Filewood on guitar. The Systematics, played mutant electro-pop and issued the single 'Pulp Baby'/'Nuts to You' on the Doublethink label (January 1980) and the mini-album *Rural* (November 1980) on M Squared. Ya Ya Choral issued the three-track EP *Such a Dutchman* ('Waiting Time'/'Gods Buzzsaw', 'Nonsense') on M Squared in 1982, followed by the mini-album *What's a Quaver?* in July 1983. Former Systematic Filewood (lead guitar) replaced Gibson and Ya Ya Choral issued the single 'Two Lines'/'White City' on the Red Eye label (August 1985). In 1986, the band was chosen for the inaugural Band of the Week series by Double J/ABC-TV's *Beatbox*. The band recorded 'Who's the King?' and 'Lonesome No More' with an accompanying video screened nationally on *Beatbox*.

Ya Ya Choral broke up for a time, but Graham, Tee and Filewood revived the band in 1987 with a new line-up of Joanna Urbanik (bass) and Dave Kelly (drums). Having finetuned its blend of hard rock and pop, Ya Ya Choral proceeded to attract a new audience by way of support gigs with the likes of **The Lime Spiders, The Radiators, Sunnyboys, The New Christs, The Hard-Ons, The Screaming Tribesmen, Candy Harlots** and Fester Fanatics. Ya Ya Choral issued the five-track 12-inch EP *Grunts* on its own Màèlströmm label (July 1988). The EP included a tensile cover of **AC/DC**'s 'Touch Too Much', and was later expanded with bonus live tracks for the cassette release *Extra Grunt*. The band entered IQ Sound in October 1988 to record its live-in-the-studio debut album, *One Small Step for Mankind*, which came out in March 1989. The album garnered positive reviews in the UK heavy metal press (*Kerrang!, Metal Hammer*) and the band set its sights overseas.

Ya Ya Choral left Australia in late 1989 bound for the UK. The band played small shows around England, built-up a cult following, but generally found the going tough. In early 1990, Ya Ya Choral took on the new name Fear of Angels, but the band was unable to scale the upper reaches of the UK hard rock scene. Despite a lack of widespread success, Ya Ya Choral/Fear of Angels should be remembered for its doggered determination in a field where few bands dared venture.

Albums: What's a Quaver? (mini-album, M-Squared, 1983), *One Small Step for Mankind* (Survival, 1989).

Yothu Yindi

Formed: *1986*
Style: *Rock, dance*
Original line-up: *Mandawuy Yunupingu (born Bakamana Yunupingu, vocals, guitar), Gurrumul 'The Guru' Yunupingu (keyboards, guitar, percussion), Witiyana Marika (manikay or traditional vocals, bilma or ironwood clapsticks, dance), Milkayngu Mununggurr (yidaki or didgeridoo), Cal Williams (guitar; ex-Swamp Jockeys), Stuart Kellaway (bass; ex-Swamp Jockeys), Andrew Belletty (drums; ex-Swamp Jockeys)*

Yothu Yindi hailed from the north eastern Arnhem Land community of Yirrkala in northern Australia. The band consisted of both Yolngu (as the people of Arnhem Land refer to themselves) and Balanda (non-Aboriginal) musicians and embodied a sharing of cultures. Other Aboriginal bands like **Coloured Stone**, the **Warumpi Band** and **No Fixed Address** had already utilised the sounds and instrumentation of Western rock'n'roll, but Yothu Yindi was the first to combine that with ancient song cycles and traditional dance performances.

By working those indigenous songs and dances into the context of a contemporary performance, Yothu Yindi created a unique example of world music. The name Yothu Yindi ('yo-thoo-yin-dee') translates from Yolngu 'matha' (Aboriginal language) to English as 'child and mother' or 'children of the earth' and is essentially a kinship term referring to the connection that the Yolngu clans of north east Arnhem Land have between themselves. In his role as principal of the Yirrkala Community School, lead singer Mandawuy Yunupingu implemented a radical two-way curriculum which combined Western and Aboriginal educational processes designed to present students with the best aspects of both cultures. Yunupingu was named 1992 Australian of the Year in recognition of his commitment to forging greater understanding between Aboriginal and non-Aboriginal Australians.

Yunupingu came from the Gumatj tribe and he formed Yothu Yindi in 1986. Yunupingu and Witiyana Marika also toured with Cal Williams and Stuart Kellaway's band The Swamp Jockeys. Even before Yothu Yindi had signed a recording contract, the band had gained valuable exposure around the world. In August 1988, the band was invited to perform at the South Pacific Festival of Arts in Townsville, Queensland. In September, the band represented Australia at the Cultural Olympics in Seoul, South Korea. In early 1989, Yothu Yindi performed at the inaugural Aboriginal Rock Music Festival in Darwin, which was recorded and filmed by a joint ABC/Central Australian Aboriginal Media Association (CAAMA) venture for the documentary *Sing Loud Play Strong.*

Yothu Yindi

In late 1988, Yothu Yindi supported **Midnight Oil** on the 36-date Diesel and Dust to Big Mountain tour of the USA and Canada. Upon returning to Australia, Yothu Yindi signed a deal with Mushroom Records which resulted in the release of the groundbreaking debut album *Homeland Movement* (May 1989) and its single 'Mainstream'/'Gudurrka (Brolga)' (March). Produced by Leszek Karski and recorded in one day, the album featured one side of politicised rock and one side of traditional songs. 'Djapana (Sunset Dreaming)'/'Gunumarra' was lifted as a second single in August. Yothu Yindi also contributed 'Gudurrka (Brolga)' to the Various Artists album *Burning Bridges* on CBS. By that stage, Yothu Yindi had added Bart Willoughby (ex-**No Fixed Address, Coloured Stone**) on drums.

Between 1989 and 1991, Yothu Yindi toured extensively throughout Australia (including a tour support to Neil Young), as well as performing in Papua New Guinea, Hong Kong, New Zealand (with Tracey Chapman) and the UK (at the Edinburgh Fringe Festival and the European Focus Festival in Glasgow). By 1991, the line-up comprised Mandawuy Yunupingu, Gurrumul Yunupingu, Marika, Mununggurr, Williams and Kellaway, plus Hughie Benjamin (drums; ex-Lifesavers, **Big Storm, Steve Hoy** Band), Makuna Yunupingu (yidaki, vocals, bilma), Mangatjay Yunupingu (dance), Sophie Garrkali (dance) and Julie Gungunbuy (dance). In August 1991, the band was invited to play three showcase gigs at the New Music Seminar in New York, securing a six-album American deal with Hollywood Records (a division of the Disney organisation) in the process.

Yothu Yindi gained national recognition when it became the first Aboriginal band to achieve a Top 40 hit in Australia with the epochal 'Treaty'/'Yolngu Boy' single. Featuring a dance re-mix by the Filthy Lucre production team (which included Robert Goodge, ex-Essendon Airport, **I'm Talking**), 'Treaty' (Filthy Lucre mix) peaked at #11 nationally in September 1991. Mandawuy Yunupingu collaborated with **Paul Kelly** and **Midnight Oil's** Peter Garrett in writing 'Treaty'. The 'Treaty' video won the Australian Video Award at the International MTV Awards held in Los Angeles. 'Treaty' was lifted from the band's second album, *Tribal Voice* (October 1991), which sold 20 000 copies within three weeks and initially made the national Top 20.

It went on to peak at #3 in June 1992 and, after a Top 40 stay of 41 weeks, it had sold over 140 000 copies (double platinum). Produced by Mark Moffatt, *Tribal Voice* yielded two further singles, a re-recorded version of 'Djapana (Sunset Dreaming)' (#13 in May 1992) and 'Tribal Voice' (#51 in October). As well as Benjamin, veteran South African producer Ricky Fataar (ex-Beach Boys, Rutles) and American Allen Murphy contributed drums to the album sessions.

Tribal Voice won the band Best Indigenous Record at the 1991 Australian Record Industry Association (ARIA) Awards. The group also took out ARIAs for Best Record Cover, Song of the Year and Best Single ('Treaty'). After receiving a $30 000 grant from Australian Prime Minister Paul Keating in early 1992, the band performed at the United Nations in New York to help launch the International Year for the World's Indigenous People. To top off a successful 1992, Keating's federal Labor government named Mandawuy Yunupingu as Australian of the Year on Australia Day, 26 January 1993.

With the release of the band's third critically acclaimed album, *Freedom* (November 1993), Yothu Yindi won three major MO Awards: Australian Performers of the Year, Australian Showbusiness Ambassadors of the Year and Rock Performers of the Year. *Freedom* produced the CD singles 'World Turning' (October 1993), which reached #56 in November, 'Timeless Land' (December) and 'Dots on the Shells' (March 1994). On the album, Mandawuy collaborated with **Crowded House's** Neil Finn ('Dots on the Shells'), **not drowning, waving's** David Bridie ('Timeless Land') and **INXS**'s Andrew Farriss ('Our Generation'). The Yothu Yindi line-up on *Freedom* comprised Mandawuy, Gurrumul, Makuna and Mangatjay Yunupingu, Marika, Williams, Kellaway, Benjamin and Mununggurr plus newcomers Banula Marika (vocals, dance), Bunimburr Marika (yidaki), Natalie Gillespie (vocals) and Jodie Cockatoo (vocals). Gumatj clan leader and Chairman of the Northern Lands Council Galarrwuy Yunupingu also contributed bilma and vocals. Session players included Americans Bernie Worrall (Hammond organ) and Allen Murphy, plus Andrew Belletty, who had been the band's original drummer.

On a historical note, Galarrwuy Yunupingu had actually issued a single, 'Gurindji Blues', on RCA in July 1971. It was released to raise money for the Gurindji tribe in their fight for land rights. Galarrwuy pleaded his case on 'Gurindji Blues' over didgeridoo and bilma backing.

During November 1993, Yothu Yindi joined **Rick Price** and New Zealand singer Margaret Urlich as part of Export Music Australia's (EMA) Wizards of Oz showcase concert tour of Japan. Following a hectic touring schedule for the first six months of 1994, which took in dates across Australia, the USA, Canada and Europe, long-time guitarist Cal Williams left the band. Colin Simpson took his place. Yothu Yindu also added two Papua New Guinean musicians, Ben Hakalitz (drums; ex-Sanguma Band, **not drowning, waving**) and Baruka Tau-Matagu (keyboards; ex-Sanguma Band).

Apart from a gritty reworking of 'Jailbreak' contributed to the **AC/DC** tribute album *Fuse Box: The Alternative Tribute* (on BMG, May 1995), Yothu Yindi was quiet on the scene for the next two years. The absence was broken in August 1996 with the release of the band's fourth album, *Wild Honey (Birrkuta)*, and its single, 'Super Highway'. *Wild Honey* continued *Freedom's* move towards a broader musical horizon while retaining a strong commercial appeal. Yothu Yindi contributed 'Gapu' (from *Freedom*) to the *Mantra Mix* compilation, Australia's first Tibet benefit album. The compilation album saw release during the Australian visit of His Holiness the Dalai Lama when he conferred the historic Kalachakra Initiation in Sydney.

Albums: *Homeland Movement* (Mushroom/Festival, 1989), *Tribal Voice* (Mushroom/Festival, 1991), *Freedom* (Mushroom/Festival, 1993), *Wild Honey (Birrkuta)* (Mushroom/Festival, 1996).

You Am I

Formed: *1989*
Style: *Rock*
Original line-up: *Tim Rogers (vocals, guitar, mellotron, Hammond organ), Nick Tischler (bass), Jaimme Rogers (drums)*

Alongside the likes of **Regurgitator**, **silverchair**, **Spiderbait**, **Powderfinger** and **Tumbleweed**, Sydney band You Am I holds pride of place as one of the best, and most successful, Australian guitar bands of the 1990s. And in the tenacious Tim Rogers the band possessed a gifted songwriter whose spirited and insightful songs were at the heart of You Am I's success. To top it off, Rogers was able to combine the guitar swagger of Keith Richards with the power chord, windmilling arm action appropriated from the young Pete Townshend to telling effect.

Rogers formed his first band, The Pleasureheads, while studying arts/law at the Australian National University in Canberra. Rogers returned to Sydney, where he joined Glazed Expression before forming the first version of You Am I in December 1989 with school friend Nick Tischler and older brother Jaimme Rogers. From early on, You Am I mixed the gritty raunch of early 1970s The Who, The Rolling Stones and The Faces with the frenzied kick of The Clash, The Jam and The Replacements. The band gained valuable experience playing supports to Sydney contemporaries like **Box the Jesuit**, **Massappeal**, **Falling Joys** and **The Hard-Ons**. Jaimme Rogers left at the end of 1990 to be replaced by Mark Tunaley.

In May 1991, You Am I issued its rough-hewn debut, 12-inch EP, 'Snake Tide', on the Timberyard label. Through manager Kate Stewart's work connections with promoter Ken West, the band appeared at the first, Sydney-only, Big Day Out held at the Sydney Showground (Hordern Pavilion) on 25 January 1992. A second EP on Timberyard, *Goddamn*, followed in May 1992. One month before the EP came out, the band's live sound engineer, New Zealand-born Andy Kent (ex-Pupils of Love), replaced Tischler on bass. By that stage, Rogers had established his credentials as a fine songwriter and the band a reputation as an exciting, dynamic live act.

You Am I signed a new deal with rooArt Records' subsidiary label Ra, which resulted in the CD EP *Can't Get Started* (November 1992). With the CD EP's release, You Am I set off on a national tour supporting **Hoodoo Gurus**. The band ended a successful 1992 by contributing the track 'Alembic' to rooArt's Australian grunge-pop compilation *Crack in the Sun or Fade in the Shade* (November 1992) alongside the likes of **Nursery Crimes**, **Guttersnipes**, **Screamfeeder**, **Massappeal**, **The Meanies**, **Tumbleweed** and Headache. You Am I appeared on the bill of the inaugural national Big Day Out tour in January 1993. Lee Renaldo from US band Sonic Youth (also on the BDO bill) was impressed enough to produce You Am I's next release (with engineering assistance from **The Welcome Mat's** Wayne Connolly). The CD EP *Coprolalia* (April) was bursting with kinetic energy and first-rate songs like 'Cool Hand Luke' and 'Last Thing You Can Depend On'. You Am I then embarked on the joint Tune In Turn On Sell Out Australian tour with **Tumbleweed** (May to June).

The members of You Am I spent eight days recording their debut album, *Sound as Ever*, at Pachyderm Studios in Cannon Falls, Minnesota with Renaldo and Connolly, after which they played a handful of American showcase gigs. One month before the release of *Sound as Ever* (November 1993), Tunaley was ousted from the band. At that point, Rogers considered folding the band, but instead asked journeyman drummer Russell 'Rusty' Hopkinson (ex-**Vicious Circle**, **Bamboos**, Cremator, **Kryptonics**, Killing Time, **Nursery Crimes**) to join. Hopkinson supplied the boost of confidence required for You Am I to make the leap into the premier league of Australian rock. *Sound as Ever* gave rise to three CD singles, 'Adam's Ribs' (October 1993), 'Berlin Chair' (February 1994) and 'Jaimme's Got a Gal' (May). 'Adam's Ribs' logged the #50 spot on the 1993 Triple J Hottest 100 list. 'Berlin Chair' was one of the most popular singles of 1994 and it logged the #23 placing on the 1994 Triple J Hottest 100 list, while 'Jaimme's Got a Gal' appeared at #77. *Sound as Ever* also won You Am I the 1993 Australian Record Industry Association (ARIA) award for Best Alternative Release.

One of Hopkinson's first major engagements with You Am I was the second Big Day Out national tour in January 1994. The band came into contact with BDO headliners Soundgarden, who invited You Am I to fill the opening slot on their next American tour. Following an Australian tour supporting **Hoodoo Gurus** and US visitors Redd Kross during April, You Am I spent six weeks supporting Soundgarden across North America (July–August). You Am I linked up with Lee Renaldo again during September to record a new album at Green Street Studios, New York. *Hi Fi Way* (February 1995) remains one of the finest Australian albums of the 1990s. Full of audacious, incisive and tuneful rock'n'roll it made its debut at #1 on the mainstream national chart and went on to sell over 35 000 copies. One track, 'Gray', was a tribute to Rogers' friend, the late Stephen 'Goose' Gray from **Box the Jesuit**. The first pressing of *Hi Fi Way* featured a limited edition, seven-track bonus live CD EP, *Someone Else's Crowd*. *Hi Fi Way* won You Am I its second ARIA award for Best Alternative Album.

Hi Fi Way produced the limited edition, double vinyl single *How Much is Enough When You Got Dry?* (November 1994), plus the CD singles 'Cathy's Clown' (January 1995), 'Jewels and Bullets' (April) and 'Purple Sneakers' (June). The double single featured the tracks 'When You Got Dry'/'Ken (The Mother Nature's Son)' and 'How Much is Enough?'/ 'Bitter Young Man of the Fanzine Press'. 'When You Got Dry' and 'Bitter Young Man of the Fanzine Press' were both non-album cuts. The double single is one of You Am I's rarest releases. Due to a pressing fault, only 449 copies were ever produced out of what was to be a run of 1000.

'Cathy's Clown' took You Am I into the national Top 40 singles chart for the first time when it reached #36 in February 1995. 'Cathy's Clown' logged #84 on the 1995 Triple J Hottest 100 list. 'Jewels and Bullets' came in at #93, while 'Purple

You Am I

Sneakers' performed even better by appearing at #24. Such was You Am I's live popularity by 1995 that the band was able to headline four sold-out shows at Sydney's Metro Theatre in April. By that stage, You Am I had added Greg Hitchcock (ex-**Bamboos**, Neptunes, **Kryptonics**, **New Christs**, **Verys**) as auxiliary guitar and keyboards player. The band also completed its fourth Big Day Out tenure as part of the January 1995 national bill.

You Am I entered Sydney's Q Sound Studios in December 1995 to record a new album with engineers Wayne Connolly and Paul McKercher (best known for his work with **Tumbleweed**). *Hourly, Daily* (July 1996) was another album of urgent, adventurous, unabashed pure pop. Like *Hi Fi Way*, it made its debut at #1 on the national album chart. It remained in the Top 40 for 18 weeks and went on to sell over 35 000 copies. It re-entered the Top 40 during December, where it remained in the lower reaches for another seven weeks. The first pressing of *Hourly, Daily* came packaged with another limited edition, bonus seven-track live CD EP, *Beat Party*, which included covers of **The Easybeats'** 'She's So Fine', Creation's 'Makin' Time' and Iggy and The Stooges' 'Search and Destroy'. *Hourly, Daily* produced the punchy CD singles 'Mr Milk' (November 1995) and 'Good Mornin'' (September 1996) plus the CD EP/7-inch vinyl EP 'Soldiers' ('Soldiers', 'Boulder Fair'/'Six', 'Count to Four') (July 1996). 'Mr Milk' reached #50 on the national singles chart during December, while 'Soldiers' went as high as #33 in August 1996. 'Good Mornin'' included a cover of **The Easybeats'** 'I'll Make You Happy'. 'Soldiers' and 'Good Mornin'' logged the #80 and #84 positions respectively on the 1996 Triple J Hottest 100 list.

You Am I scooped the pool at the 1996 ARIA Awards by walking away with six awards, including Best Album (*Hourly, Daily*), Best Independent Release (*Hourly, Daily*), Best Group, Producer of the Year (the band itself) and Engineer of the Year (Paul McKercher and Wayne Connolly for *Hourly, Daily*). The band continued to tour locally and overseas for most of 1996. If appearing on the bill of the American 'alternarock' festival Lollapalooza and touring throughout the UK and Europe with Lemonheads was not enough for Tim Rogers, he also found time early in the year to co-produce (with Englishman Nick Launay) the soundtrack to David Caesar's feature film *Idiot Box*.

You Am I contributed the tracks 'Idiot Box I', 'Cats and Dogs', 'Idiot Box II', 'Gasoline for Two', 'Idiot Box III' and a cover of **The Victims'** 'Television Addict' to the soundtrack album (February 1997). You Am I's cover of **Beasts of Bourbon's** 'Drop Out' also appeared on the first single, **The Mark of Cain's** cover of **X**'s 'Degenerate Boy'. The other bands on the soundtrack were **Hoss**, **Snout**, **Magic Dirt** and **Crow**. At the end of 1996, You Am I recorded in Los Angeles with American producer George Drakoulias (Black Crowes). In March 1997, Ra/BMG issued the international version of *Hourly, Daily* which featured two of the freshly recorded tracks 'Trike' and 'Opportunities', in place of 'Someone Else's Home' and 'Moon Shines on Trubble'. The album came out locally in July. A third track recorded with Drakoulias, 'Who Turned Out the Lights?' was earmarked for an American soundtrack album.

You Am I commenced 1997 with its fifth appearance on the Big Day Out bill. The four-track 'Tuesday' CD single came out in February. It also included the previously released 'When You Got Dry' plus a cover of Peter Townshend's 'Circles'. With the single and the *Idiot Box* soundtrack in the shops, You Am I headed overseas again for an American tour with Lemonheads. The three American recorded tracks were coupled with covers of The Move's 'I Can Hear the Grass Grow' and the Gamble/Huff song '(There's Gonna be a) Showdown' for the local release of the 'Trike' CD EP (June 1997). You Am I recorded a new album with Drakoulias for release in 1998.

Albums: *Sound as Ever* (Ra/rooArt/WEA, 1993), *Hi Fi Way* (Ra/rooArt/WEA, 1995), *Hourly, Daily* (Ra/rooArt/Shock, 1996), *Idiot Box* (original soundtrack album shared with other artists, rooArt/BMG, 1997).

Further reading: *Hi Fi Days: The Future of Australian Rock* by Craig Mathieson (Allen & Unwin, 1996).

Gary Young

Style: *Country, rockabilly*

Veteran drummer Gary Young was born in New York, USA (in 1947), and grew up in Melbourne, Victoria. Young's first band was high school outfit The Fenders, followed by the delightful Shadows-inspired Silhouettes. The Silhouettes comprised Young, Roger Treble (lead guitar), Gil Matthews (guitar), Ed Nantes (guitar) and Ian Allen (bass). By 1963, The Silhouettes had transformed into The Lincolns with Young, Treble, Nantes and Wayne Duncan (bass; ex-Ramrods).

With the arrival of beat music in Australia during 1964, The Lincolns took on lead singer Bob Johnson. The Lincolns became popular on the Melbourne dance circuit, but Young left in early 1965 to form vocal duo Double Trouble with New Zealander Issy Di. That soon fell apart, and Young and his old friends Treble and Duncan joined The Rondells, then backing outfit for beat hit-makers **Bobby and Laurie**. Just prior to Young's arrival, The Rondells enjoyed their own, minor hit single on the Go!! label when their cover of Chuck Berry's 'Talkin' 'Bout You'/'Baby Don't Hide' reached #31 in Melbourne during June 1965.

The Rondells line-up of John Sullivan (rhythm guitar), Treble, Duncan and Young toured with **Bobby and Laurie** until the duo broke up in early 1967. Young, Treble and Duncan joined pop outfit The Changing Times, which featured Alex Opitz (vocals) and Jenny Johnson (organ). Opitz and Johnson went off to form The Dream (later known as **New Dream**) in October 1967. Young and Duncan joined erstwhile **Bobby and Laurie** singer Laurie Allen in his ambitious Laurie Allen Revue.

The Laurie Allen Revue issued three singles for Festival: 'Beautiful Brown Eyes'/'Saved' (recorded before Young's arrival and issued August 1967), 'Any Little Bit'/'Cool Jerk' (April 1968) and 'As Long as I Got You'/'Born to Follow' (June 1968). In early 1969, **Bobby and Laurie** reunited, so Young moved on to popular Melbourne R&B/jazz institution **The Ram Jam Big Band**. Young played on the final **Ram Jam Big Band** single, a cover of Amen Corner's 'Lost and Found'/'Jamming' (May 1969), before the band fell apart. The depleted line-up of Ian Clyne, Terry Villis, Peter Knapp and Young, plus American singer Peter Bonner, worked for a few months as Ram Jam to tie up outstanding gig commitments. At the end of 1969, Clyne, Villis, Young, Wayne Duncan (bass; ex-Rondells) and **Terry Hannagan** (lead vocals) formed a band called Turnstile which was short-lived.

By early 1970, Young and Duncan had become members of **Ross Wilson** and **Ross Hannaford's** esoteric, special occasion band **Sons of the Vegetal Mother**. The Sons became one of the leading lights on Melbourne's burgeoning, underground progressive rock scene. In November 1970, Wilson unveiled the rollicking **Daddy Cool**, which featured Hannaford, Duncan and Young. **Daddy Cool** helped usher in an exciting new era of Australian rock when the band's exuberant debut album, *Daddy Who? Daddy Cool!*, and single, the dance classic 'Eagle Rock', both soared effortlessly to #1 on the charts. Initially **Daddy Cool** played a good-time combination of vintage rock'n'roll, doo wop and R&B. Up to that point, Young's influences had specifically been British invasion bands of the 1960s (Beatles, Kinks, Rolling Stones, Who) and English jazz/R&B outfits like Georgie Fame and the Blue Flames and Zoot Money's Big Roll Band. Wilson introduced Young to the delights of roots rock (country, blues and rockabilly).

Young began writing songs in that vein, and **Daddy Cool** issued two of his earliest compositions as the single 'Rock'n'Roll Lady'/'Cadillacin"(October 1972). Young also sang lead vocals on those two cuts, and the single was credited to Gary Young with Daddy Cool. The band recorded another Young composition, 'Rock-a-Billy Beatin' Boogie Band', which remained unissued until it was included on the rarities collection *The Missing Masters* (1980). **Daddy Cool** broke up in August 1972. Young formed Hot Dog with Wayne Duncan (who had switched to lap steel guitar), Dannie Bourne (piano), Paul Pyle (bass; ex-**Johnny O'Keefe** Band) and Peter Reed (drums; ex-**New Dream**, **Johnny O'Keefe** Band). Young also switched to lead vocals and rhythm guitar, and he used Hot Dog specifically as an outlet for his rockabilly/country influenced songwriting. Gary Young's Hot Dog issued two singles, 'Rock-a-Billy Beatin' Boogie Band'/'You Can't Shake the Boogie in Worn Down Rockin' Shoes' (April 1973) and 'The Saga of the Three Pigs'/'With You Tonight' (October).

By that stage, Young's label Wizard had issued the **Daddy Cool** live album *The Last Drive-in Movie Show*, which had been taped at the band's farewell performance the previous August. Young sang lead vocals on four cuts, 'Cadillacin'', Jambalaya', 'One Night' and 'Rock-a-Billy Beatin' Boogie Band'. Wizard also issued the single 'One Night'/ 'Cadillacin'' (July 1973) as Gary Young with Daddy Cool. 'Jambalaya' (credited to Daddy Cool featuring Gary Young) appeared as the B-side to the single 'Duke of Earl' (credited to Daddy Cool featuring Ross Wilson; September 1973).

Young broke up Hot Dog, and in January 1974 joined the re-formed **Daddy Cool**. The band lasted until September 1975. Young became a founder member of popular Melbourne R&B outfit **Jo Jo Zep and The Falcons**. In 1976, Young collaborated with **Ross Wilson** and Wayne Burt on assembling the soundtrack album for Chris Löfven's feature film *Oz*. Young also played sessions, which took in appearances on **Mándu's** *To the Shores of His Heaven* album and **Bandicoot's** 1976 album *Bandicoot*. Melbourne roots rockers **The Pelaco Brothers** also recorded one of Young's songs, 'Rockabilly Heaven', which Missing Links later included on the Various Artists album *The Autodrifters and The Relaxed Mechanics Meet The Fabulous Nudes and The Pelaco Bros* (June 1978).

Young remained with **Jo Jo Zep and the Falcons** until 1981, appearing on such classic records as the *So Young* mini-album and the band's most successful album, *Screaming Targets*. During his time with The Falcons, Young issued two solo singles, Charles Underwood's 'Ubangi Stomp'/'Mystery' (July 1980) on the Mighty Boy label and 'Running Late for Wandong'/'Rockabilly Heaven' (February 1981) on Mushroom. When Young left the Falcons in June 1981, he formed The Rocking Emus with Jeff Burstin (guitar; **Jo Jo Zep and The Falcons**), **Ross Hannaford** (guitar; ex-**Daddy Cool**, **Billy T**, Lucky Dog), Wayne Duncan (bass) and Peter Reed (drums). The Rocking Emus was essentially a studio band and only played a couple of gigs. Gary Young and the Rocking Emus recorded one single, 'Keep Your Hands Off My Baby'/'Rollin' Home' (February 1982), and the album *Gary Young and the Rocking Emus* (May 1982) for Mushroom. Mushroom also reissued 'Running Late for Wandong'/'Rockabilly Heaven' as a double A-sided single (June 1982) credited to Gary Young and the Rocking Emus.

By that stage, Young was touring with Chris Stockley (guitar, vocals; ex-**Cam-Pact**, **Axiom**, **Dingoes**, Stockley See Mason Band) and John Power (bass, vocals; ex-**Company Caine**, **Jo Jo Zep and the Falcons**) in Rock Doctors, which also comprised Wayne Burt (guitar, vocals; ex-**Jo Jo Zep and the Falcons**, Living Legends, **Fabulaires**) and Steve Williams (sax, vocals; ex-Full Boar). Rock Doctors issued one mini-album, *Now Hear This!* (August 1982), which had been recorded live. By early 1983, Young was a member of The **Phil Manning** Rock'n'Roll Trio with Wayne Duncan. It was the first time Young and Duncan had played in a strict Chicago blues/Muddy Waters-influenced band. Young deputised for the unavailable Steve Prestwich in **Cold Chisel** for a six-week tour in early 1983. The **Phil Manning** Rock'n'Roll Trio broke up at the end of the year after touring constantly but getting nowhere. They had also spent time backing soul/jazz/blues singer **Renée Geyer**.

In 1984, Young joined Joe Camilleri's new zydeco-influenced outfit **The Black Sorrows**. Young played on the albums *Sonola* and *Rockin' Zydeco*, after which Peter Luscombe took his place. In 1986, Young joined Melbourne cajun/country swing band **Dancehall Racketeers**, with whom he remained for a year. Young played on the album *Dancehall Racketeers* which came out on RCA in late 1986. **Dancehall Racketeers** was the last band Young played in as a mainstream career. He moved into radio broadcasting (co-presenting the *Chicken Mary* show on community radio station 3RRR), but still played gigs on a freelance basis with all sorts of roots music/rockabilly bands. They included Bongo Starkie's Little Red Roosters (1986), Melbourne pub band Relax with Max (1986) and The Prestones (1987), which was a spin-off from **Dancehall Racketeers** featuring Graham Thomas (bass). Thomas was running the Preston label, and The Prestones were virtually the resident studio band for Preston. As a result, Young played on dozens of sessions for the label.

After that, Young played with pub rockers The Beat Boys for 12 months (1988). The Beat Boys comprised Steve Williams (sax), Jimmy Fewings (bass; ex-Relax with Max), who was replaced by Paul Gadsby (ex-**Paul Kelly** and the Dots, **Broderick Smith** Band) and Chris Wilson (keyboards; ex-**Buster Brown**, **Broderick Smith** Band). Young joined The Midnight Trio in 1989. That band had been formed to play R&B at Madigan's Club and also contained James Black (keyboards, guitar, vocals; ex-**Mondo Rock**) and at various times either Graham Thomas or Paul Pyle on double bass. The Welcome Strangers comprised Young, Ian Stephen (vocals, piano, ex-**Slaughtermen**), Rick Dempster (guitar, dobro, harmonica; ex-Autodrifters, **Dancehall Racketeers**), Mark Frayne (guitar) and Mark Ferrie (bass; ex-**Models**, **Sacred Cowboys**, **Slaughtermen**).

The Welcome Strangers backed country singer Rex McLean on his album *Country Paydirt.*

Next Young played with The Cool Healers backing country singer Leslie Avril. Young played with blues boogie band Southern Lightning for ten months throughout 1991. Andy Baylor's Cajun Combo circa 1992 to 1993 featured Young, Duncan, Andy Baylor (guitar, fiddle; ex-**Dancehall Racketeers**), Peter Linden (pedal steel), Jimi Baeck (sax), Brendan Sheaston (guitar), Sam Lemann (guitar), George Butrimlis (piano accordion; ex-**Black Sorrows**) and Lisa Miller (vocals). That line-up recorded the *Andy Baylor's Cajun Combo* album (1992). The Mick Hamilton Trio (1992–97) comprised Young, Mick Hamilton (guitar, vocals; ex-**Vibrants**, **Mighty Guys**) and Peter Robinson (bass; ex-**Strangers**). Young sat in with ex-Swinging Sidewalks' bass player Steve Purcell's band The R&B Double Agents, before rejoining Southern Lightning in 1997. The line-up was Dave Hogan (vocals, harmonica; also in **Paramount Trio**), Manny Seddon (guitar), Geordie Leach (bass; ex-**Buster Brown**, **Rose Tattoo**, **Giants**) and Gary Young. Young has also recorded albums with the Glass Hamilton Young Band (alongside **Keith Glass** and Mick Hamilton).

Gary Young and the Rocking Emus album: *Gary Young and the Rocking Emus* (Mushroom/Festival, 1982).

John Paul Young

Style: Pop

Singer John Paul Young (b. 1950) was one of the most popular stars of the 1970s. Affectionately known by his fans as 'Squeak', Young came to the attention of an enormous audience via his regular appearances on the ABC-TV's pop show ***Countdown***. Under the guidance of the venerable songwriting/ production team of Vanda and Young, who fashioned for him a string of sprightly, reckless and downright catchy pop hits like 'Yesterday's Hero', 'I Hate the Music', 'Standing in the Rain' and 'Love is in the Air', Young was never far from the charts. He also toured with his crack backing band The All Stars, with whom he gained valuable exposure on the concert and pub circuit.

John Young was born in Glasgow, Scotland and he migrated to Australia with his parents in 1966. After completing school, Young took an apprenticeship as a sheetmetal worker. By night and on the weekends, he sang in Sydney band Elm Tree, which comprised Andy Imlah (co-lead vocals), Oli Chojnacki (guitar), Ron Mazurkiewicz (keyboards), Roger 'Slim' Barnett (bass) and Geoff Watts (drums). Elm Tree cut one single for producer Martin Erdman's Du Monde label, a cover of Marmalade's 'Rainbow'/'Lonely Nights' (November 1970), but never broke out of the suburban dance circuit. The band broke up at the end of 1971, and Young took the role of Annas in the Australian stage production of Andrew Lloyd-Webber and Tim Rice's rock musical *Jesus Christ Superstar*. At the same time, visiting English producer Simon Napier-Bell (Yardbirds, Move, T-Rex) took Young into the studio to record the Vanda and Young composition 'Pasadena' (with lyrics written by English actor David Hemmings). When issued as a single on the Albert label in March 1972, 'Pasadena'/'Better Go Back to Bed' took Young into the Sydney Top 10 (#10).

Young stayed with *Jesus Christ Superstar* until February 1974, during which time he issued a second single on Albert, 'You Drive Me Crazy'/'For My Love' (February 1973). 'It's Only Love'/'Bad Trip' followed in March 1974. In the meantime, Vanda and Young had returned from the UK and, fully ensconced in Albert's Sydney recording complex, took charge of Young's career. They came up with the rambunctious 'Yesterday's Hero' as Young's next single. Issued in March 1975 (with 'The Next Time' as the flip), the single leapt to the national #1 spot and John Young became a scream-dream pop sensation. 'Yesterday's Hero' stayed at #1 on the Melbourne chart for six weeks before being knocked off the top spot by **Hush's** 'Boney Maroney'.

'Yesterday's Hero' also charted at a respectable #42 on the US *Cashbox* charts. Young's next single, the rollicking 'The Love Game'/'St Louis' (August 1975) appeared under his new John Paul Young appellation. It became Young's second national Top 5 hit (#5 in September), as well as peaking at #9 in Melbourne during October. By mid-year, Young had linked up with The All Stars (who had been working with **Stevie Wright**), which included veteran musicians Warren Morgan (piano, vocals; ex-**Chain**, **Billy Thorpe** and the Aztecs), **Kevin Borich** (lead guitar; ex-**La De Das**), Ian 'Willie' Winter (guitar; ex-**Carson**, **Daddy Cool**), Ronnie Peel (bass; ex-**Pleazers**, **Missing Links**, **Rockwell T. James** and the Rhythm Aces, One Ton Gypsy, **La De Das**) and Johnny Dick (drums; ex-**Max Merritt and the Meteors**, **Billy Thorpe** and the Aztecs, **Fanny Adams**, **Wild Cherries**). Young completed work on his Vanda and Young produced and written debut album *Hero*, which reached #20 in November 1975. Ray Goodwin (guitar; ex-**Dragon**) then replaced Borich in

The All Stars. Goodwin also left in the new year to join Punkz (who became **Cheek**).

Young's second album, *J.P.Y.*, produced the singles 'I Hate the Music'/'My Name is Jack' (March 1976) and 'Keep on Smilin''/'If I Could Live My Life Again' (October 1976). 'I Hate the Music' reached #3 nationally in April and 'Keep on Smilin'' peaked at #14. *J.P.Y.* reached #10 on the album chart and went on to achieve platinum status (70 000). The album featured the first of many John Paul Young/Warren Morgan compositions ('Won't Let this Feeling Go By', 'Give It Time' and 'The Painting') that would balance out all the Vanda and Young tunes on subsequent albums. During 1976, various members of The All Stars issued solo records. Warren Morgan teamed up with drummer Gil Matthews (from **Billy Thorpe** and the Aztecs) for the single 'Endless Winter Nights'/'Raw Love' (November). Johnny Dick issued the single 'The Warrior'/'She was My Baby' (January). Ronnie Peel (under his **Rockwell T. James** persona) issued the singles 'Come on Home (A Song for Anna)'/'Belinda' (May) and 'Roxanne'/'Hey Mama' (October).

In January 1977, Winter left The All Stars to join **Ross Wilson's Mondo Rock**. Peel switched to rhythm guitar, Dallas McDermott joined on bass and legendary blues guitarist **Phil Manning** (ex-**Chain**) took over on lead guitar. The new line-up recorded the album *Green*, which came out in May. The album featured five J.P. Young/Morgan compositions, four by Vanda/Young and one by Warren Morgan. *Green* produced the singles 'I Wanna Do It with You'/'The Painting' (February 1977) and 'Here We Go'/'Shake that Thing' (April). 'I Wanna Do It With You' reached #8 nationally and #11 in Melbourne, but 'Here We Go' was not successful. Following a national tour, Manning left The All Stars in June. Producer Ian Miller (ex-**Chetarca**, Wild Beaver Band) took over as lead guitarist.

In the meantime, Young's singles had begun to chart overseas. The discofied 'Standing in the Rain' (from the *J.P.Y.* album) reached #6 in Germany, and Young left for a European promotional tour. It was in South Africa, however, that Young experienced his greatest success. Four singles, 'Yesterday's Hero', 'Keep on Smilin'', 'I Hate the Music' and 'I Wanna Do It with You', all made the Top 10. In September, Young and the All Stars embarked on a South African tour that produced wild scenes of fan hysteria the likes of which had not been seen before in that country. The band played 32 concerts to a total audience of 70 000 people. When Young left the country, 'The Painting' was sitting at #1 on the South African charts.

Young's next Australian single, 'Where the Action Is'/'Down on My Knees' (September 1977), failed to chart nationally, peaking at #23 in Sydney. 'Where the Action Is' appeared on the compilation album *All the Best* (December 1977). Young's eleventh Australian single, 'Standing in the Rain'/'Same Old Thing' (January 1978), reached #13 nationally during March and #4 in Melbourne during May. By that stage, Jacques De Jongh (bass; ex-**Redhouse**, **Hush**) had replaced McDermott. The new line-up recorded the album *Love is in the Air*, which produced the hit singles 'Love is in the Air'/'Won't Let this Feeling Go By' (#3 in June 1978), 'The Day that My Heart Caught Fire'/'Lazy Days' (#18 in September) and 'Fool in Love'/'It's All Over' (December).

'Standing in the Rain' made #1 in South Africa, the Top 10 in Germany and Holland, Top 40 in France and the lower reaches of the US Top 100. The breezy, seductive 'Love is in the Air' did even better by reaching #1 in South Africa and Bangkok, #2 in Norway, Sweden and Holland, #3 in Germany, #5 in the UK and Top 40 in the USA, as well as selling well in France, Switzerland and Italy. Young undertook extensive promotional tours of Europe, the UK (where he appeared on the television pop show *Top of the Pops*) and the USA.

Following a successful Australian tour, Young completed a monumental 1978 by winning the *TV Week* King of Pop award. 1979, however, proved to be a quiet year for Young. His two albums, *John Paul Young 1974–1979* (on the budget Hammard label) and *Heaven Sent* (November), plus the single 'Heaven Sent'/'Don't You Walk that Way' (August 1979) were not successful. The All Stars line-up on *Heaven Sent* comprised Morgan, Miller, Tony Buchanan (sax; ex-**Thunderbirds**, Cool Bananas, **Johnny Rocco Band**) and **Ray Arnott** (drums; ex-**Company Caine**, **Spectrum**, **Mighty Kong**, **Dingoes**), plus Harry Vanda and George Young. Multi-instrumentalist Billy Rogers (ex-**Dragon**) and John Young (bass; ex-**Ayers Rock**) joined in January 1980.

Young's sixteenth single, 'Hot for You Baby'/'I Don't Want to Lose You' (January 1980), was his last for the Albert label. In 1981, Young recorded an album of 1960s rock and pop favourites, *The Singer*, for Hammard. Jagger/Richards' 'Out of Time'/'Hold Me' came out as a single (September 1981). Session musicians on the album were Jim Doyle (ex-**Ayers Rock**) and Stuart Fraser (ex-**Feather**) on guitars, Rex Bullen (keyboards; ex-**Bakery**), Ralph White (trumpet; ex-Fugitives), Les Young (bass; ex-**Chessmen**) and Russell Dunlop (drums, percussion, synthesiser; ex-**Levi Smith's Clefs**, **SCRA**, **Johnny Rocco Band**, **Ayers Rock**).

In 1981, Young assembled a new All Stars with

Vince Melouney (guitar; ex-**Billy Thorpe** and the Aztecs, **Bee Gees**, **Fanny Adams**), Peter Northcote (sax, keyboards) and **Ray Arnott** (drums). He issued the single 'Oh No No'/'You Can Do Anything' (July 1982) on the Southern Cross label. In 1983, Young signed to the Australian branch of German label I.C. Records. He flew to Germany with producer/keyboards player John Capek (ex-**Carson**) to record a new album in Horus Sound Studios, Hannover and Union Studios, Munich. They completed the album with sessions in Los Angeles, AAV Studios Melbourne and Albert Studio 2 Sydney. The resultant album *One Foot in Front* (March 1984; renamed *Soldier of Fortune* for the European market) produced four singles, 'Soldier of Fortune'/'Sirens' (September 1983), 'War Games'/'Come on Down' (January 1984), 'L.A. Sunset'/'Cryin' Eyes' (1984) and 'Call the Night'/'L.A. Sunset' (1984).

The album displayed a contemporary electro-pop sound. Most of the material had been written by John Capek and Canadian Marc Jordan, with one Young/Morgan composition 'Cryin' Eyes'. 'Soldier of Fortune' returned Young to the Australian Top 20 for the first time in five years when it reached #15 in December. 'Soldier of Fortune' was picked as the theme song for the 1984 Disabled Olympics held in New York, and it also went on to be a hit in Germany. The album put Young back in the spotlight for a while, but apart from two more singles, 'Spain'/'Money to Burn' (on EMI, October 1986) and 'Don't Sing that Song'/'Here We Go' (for CBS, June 1989), he essentially retired from the music business. One Vanda and Young song, the whimsical acoustic tune 'Lazy Days' (from the *Love is in the Air* album) summed up Young's philosophy best: amongst the hurly-burly of pop stardom, Young would rather be sitting on his sail boat with fishing line in hand and sipping wine.

In 1992, Young came to the attention of a new generation when 'Love is in the Air' was used as the theme song to director Baz Luhrmann's internationally acclaimed feature film *Strictly Ballroom*. 'Love is in the Air (The Ballroom Mix)' came out as a CD single on Albert/Sony (August 1992) and peaked at #4 in October. Young came out of retirement to record a new album, *Now*, which consisted of a re-recorded version of 'Love is in the Air', plus old chestnuts like The Young Rascals' 'Groovin', 'Fats Domino's 'Ain't that a Shame' and **The Easybeats'** 'St Louis'. It also yielded a new single, 'Happy the Man' in August 1996.

Albums: *Hero* (Albert/EMI, 1975), *J.P.Y.* (Albert/EMI, 1976), *Green* (Albert/EMI, 1977), *All the Best of John Paul Young* (Albert/EMI, 1977), *Love is in the Air* (Albert/EMI, 1978), *John Paul Young 1974–1979* (Hammard, 1979), *Heaven Sent* (Albert/EMI, 1979), *The Singer* (Hammard, 1981), *One Foot in Front* (I.C./EMI, 1984), *Classic Hits* (Albert/EMI, 1986), *The War Years* (CD reissue of *One Foot in Front*, Boulevarde, 1992), *Now* (Albert/EMI, 1996).

Johnny Young

Style: Pop

During the 1970s and 1980s, Johnny Young (b. 1945) was best known as the grinning compere of television variety show *Young Talent Time*. The show groomed the likes of **Debra Byrne**, Rod Kirkham, **Jamie Redfern**, Jane Scali, Phillip Gould, Karen Knowles, **Tina Arena**, Joey Perone and **Dannii Minogue** for their contribution to the Australian entertainment world. During the 1960s, however, Young was a bona fide pop star himself, dishing out a string of frantic beat hits like 'Step Back' and 'Cara-lyn'. He also became a well-respected songwriter, penning hits for **Russell Morris**, **Ross D. Wyllie**, **Ronnie Burns**, Lionel Rose and even UK popsters Herman's Hermits.

Young was born John De Jong in Indonesia. He grew up in Kalamunda, Western Australia. When he left school, Young began work as a trainee disc jockey on Perth radio, and began singing around the local dances with The Nomads. In 1965, he became host of local television pop show *Club 17*. He also issued two singles, 'Club 17'/'Hi Ho' (January) and 'Go Johnny Go' (March) on the 7 Teen label. In 1966, Young signed to Martin Clarke's local Clarion label, and formed backing band Kompany which comprised John Eddy (guitar), Tony Sommers (guitar), Jim Griffiths (bass) and Warwick Findlay (drums; ex-**Ray Hoff and the Off Beats**).

Visiting Sydney band **The Easybeats** presented Young with a song to record, 'Step Back'. When issued as a single (backed by a stomping cover of The Strangeloves' 'Cara-lyn', May 1966), it became a smash #1 hit in Perth, Sydney and Melbourne. The 'Let It Be Me' EP soared to #1 in Sydney and #4 in Melbourne during October, and suddenly Johnny Young and Kompany were the hottest band in the land. With a move to Melbourne, Young's fortunes continued to rise. Mike Wade (guitar, organ; ex-**Vibrants**) joined Kompany at the end of 1966. The next single, a cover of the Everly Brothers' 'When will I Be Loved?'/'Kiss Me Now' (January 1967), gave Young and Kompany another double-sided hit when it reached #3 in Melbourne and #10 in Sydney. Soon after, Young dispensed with the services of his sterling Kompany cohorts to go solo. Sommers joined **The Master's Apprentices**.

Young compered the short-lived television pop show *Too Much* before taking over the reins from the departing Ian 'Turps' Turpie as compere of the popular *Go!! Show*. The EP 'All My Lovin'' reached the Top 10 in Sydney during April, and 'Lady'/'Good Evening Girl' peaked at #34 three months later. Soon after, Young set off for the UK. Young's farewell concert at Sydney's Trocadero discotheque featured the cream of local bands in support: Gus and **the Nomads**, Julian Jones, **Jeff St John** and the Id, **Sebastian Hardie** Blues Band, **Phil Jones and the Unknown Blues** and **The Master's Apprentices**. In London, Young recorded several Barry Gibb songs, 'Craise Finton Kirk', 'I am the World' and 'Every Christian Lionhearted Man will Show You'. Young's next single, 'Craise Finton Kirk'/'I am the World' (August 1967), took him back into the national Top 30 (#14 in Melbourne and #29 in Sydney) during September, but the next single, 'Every Christian Lionhearted Man will Show You'/'Wonderful World', failed to chart.

Young returned to Australia briefly during September, and returned to the UK with ex-**M.P.D. Limited** drummer Danny Findley in tow. In the UK, Young and Findley assembled a new band, Danny's Word, with English musicians Rob Alexander (guitar), Mick (surname not known, organ) and Pete Piper (bass). Young failed to make a major impression on the UK scene, and he returned to Australia in January 1968. That same month, Young issued a new single, 'Unconscientious Objector'/'Epitaph to Mr Simon, Sir'. Young's third album, *Surprises . . .* , was culled from sessions he had recorded in the UK during late 1967.

In April 1968, Young joined Melbourne radio station 3XY as the weekday drive-time DJ. He also issued his last hit single, 'It's a Sunny Day'/'My World', which reached #31 in Sydney during August. Young recorded two more singles for Clarion, 'Mrs Willoughby'/'123' and 'Love Song'/'The Trip', in 1969, but his pop star days were over. Instead Young concentrated on songwriting and, over the next few years, he wrote hit singles for **Russell Morris** ('The Real Thing'), **Ronnie Burns** ('Smiley'), **Ross D. Wyllie** ('The Star'), Lionel Rose ('I Thank You') and Herman's Hermits ('Here Comes the Star'). With the aid of producer Ian 'Molly' Meldrum's audacious studio embellishments and driving backing from **The Groop**, Morris transformed the modest 'The Real Thing' into a reverberating psychedelic epic. It soared to #1 on the charts in May 1969 and remains an Australian classic.

In 1970, Young teamed up with Kevin Lewis from Festival Records to form Lewis–Young Productions. Their first outings were the television pop shows *Happening '70* and *Happening '71*, followed by *Young Talent Time* in early 1971. As well as appearing on a series of *Young Talent Time* albums, Young recorded the album *A Young Man And His Music* and single 'Just Another Rock and Roller'/'Another One of These Songs' (April 1973) for the Festival label. He went on to record several albums of contemporary and easy listening pop favourites. *Young Talent Time* remained on the air until 1986, and for most of the 1970s and 1980s Young also operated a successful school of music.

Albums: *Young Johnny* (as Johnny Young and Kompany, Clarion/Festival, 1966), *It's a Wonderful World* (Clarion/Festival, 1967), *Surprises . . .* (Clarion/Festival, 1968), *A Young Man and His Music* (Festival, 1972), *A Musical Portrait* (L&Y, 1974), *The Best of Johnny Young* (Calendar/Festival, 1974), *Mother's Favourites* (Harlequin/Festival, 1976), *All My Loving* (Pisces, 1978), *Step Back with Johnny Young and Kompany: The Festival Files Volume Eight* (Festival, 1988).

Young Homebuyers (*see* The Fabulaires)

Young Identities

Formed: *1978*
Style: *Punk*
Original line-up: *Clayton McLeod (vocals), Rod McLeod (guitar), Gavin McLeod (bass), Paul Murray (drums)*

Following in the pioneering wake of the likes of **The Saints** and **The Leftovers**, Brisbane band Young Identities was among the second generation of punk outfits formed in that city. The band's contemporaries included The Numbers (soon to be renamed **The Riptides**), The Aliens (later on **The Fun Things**), Razar, The X-Men and The Survivors. That Australia's most conservative city should give rise to such a seditious sub-cultural coterie is a sociological phenomenon yet to be fully explored.

Suffice it to say that when the McLeod siblings formed Young Identities, they were still too young to play the pub circuit (such as it was in Brisbane at that time). With an average age of around 16 years, Young Identities displayed plenty of youthful energy, belligerent spirit and all-important punk attitude. Young Identities issued two rare EPs of ultra-primitive, snot-nosed punk: *Young Identities* ('Positive Thinking Negative Reaction'/'Convulsions [Let's All Have]', 'Mass Appeal') which came out in November 1979, followed by *New Trends* ('New Trends'/'Instant Feelings', 'Threats') in April

1980. Both appeared on the independent Shake Music imprint.

Rod and Gavin McLeod also collaborated with John Hunter (vocals) on The Bodysnatchers' single, 'Frantic'/'Mystery (Solve It)', on Shake (April 1980). Rod McLeod was part of studio band Just Urbain circa 1979–1980. Peter Miller (vocals), Robert Lewis (bass) and Dave Holiday (drums) completed the line-up. Just Urbain issued two rare punk EPs on Shake: 'Burning' ('Burning', 'Part Two'/'Guns and Guitars') (November 1979) and *Everybody Loves Just Urbain* ('Hospital Bed'/'End', 'Everybody Loves') (April 1980). By 1980, Young Identities had evolved into Kicks with Clayton, Rod and Gavin McLeod, plus Mark Young (drums). Kicks had toned down the frenzied punk attack somewhat for a more varied post-punk sound as displayed on the single 'The Secret'/'Return of the Action Men' in late 1980.

In 1983, Rod McLeod, Miller, Lewis and Holiday revived Just Urbain under the name of Section Urbane with Wolfgang Kuepper added on synthesiser. Section Urbane issued the EP *Final Program* ('I'd Rather Stay at Home and Watch TV', 'Obsession'/'Goddess', 'In that Case') on Shake in 1984. 'I'd Rather Stay at Home and Watch TV' and 'Obsession' had been recorded by Just Urbain in 1980. In 1985, the Rubber label issued the Brisbane punk compilation *At the Solicitor's Request*, which included Young Identities' 'Threats', the previously unissued Kicks song 'In Fear of God' and Just Urbain's 'I'd Rather Stay at Home and Watch TV'.

In 1986, Rod McLeod joined The Pineapples from the Dawn of Time, which comprised Marco Halstead (guitar, vocals; ex-Disposable Fits, Tex Deadly and the Dum Dums, Kingswoods), Clem Lukey (drums, ex-Tex Deadly and the Dum Dums), Michael Hiron (guitar; ex-**Leftovers**, **Riptides**), Peter Krool (bass, ex-Kingswoods), John Downie (drums, ex-Kingswoods), Michael Gilmore and Kim Watling. The band issued one single, 'Too Much Acid'/'Saha' (1986), and an album, *Shocker*, (on the Pineapple label, 1987) before breaking up.

Young Modern

Formed: *1977*
Style: *Power pop*
Original line-up: *John Dowler (vocals; ex-Spare Change), Vic Yates (guitar), Michael Jones (guitar), Andrew Richards (bass), Mark Kohler (drums)*

Led by the stylish John Dowler, Adelaide band Young Modern was one of Australia's pioneering power pop/new wave bands of the late 1970s. Dowler derived the band's name from *Young Modern* magazine (published by Rupert Murdoch between 1962 and 1965). Naturally, the band's music was an entertaining amalgam of 1965 Beatles, Rolling Stones, Kinks, Byrds and Who, with lashings of The Flamin' Groovies and Alex Chilton's Big Star thrown in for good measure.

Dowler formed Young Modern in late 1977 after his previous band, the would-be Roxy Music-styled Spare Change, imploded in Melbourne. Spare Change had recorded an album which remained unissued for three years. Dowler's first mission was to imbue Young Modern's music with a sprightly, tuneful and accessible pop sheen, in contrast to the harder-edged kick of the emergent punk movement. The band members decked themselves out in sharp suits, white shirts and black ties. Dowler was also the first singer in Australia to adopt the Brian Jones/Keith Relf haircut as a way of life!

Young Modern played its first show on 26 November 1977, supporting Sydney legends **Radio Birdman** at Adelaide's Unley Town Hall. The band gradually became an Adelaide institution, with regular appearances at inner-city venues like The Tivoli. In May 1978, Young Modern recorded an album's worth of demos. In August, the members of Young Modern ventured to Melbourne where they put down a single at Richmond Recorders under the direction of producer **Stephen Cummings** (from **The Sports**). 'She's Got the Money'/'Automatic' came out on the Top Gear label in October 1978. The single sounded lightweight, lacking the punch of the band's live shows, but it nevertheless remains a cult classic of the late 1970s Australian power pop movement alongside The Numbers'/**Riptides**' 'Sunset Strip', **The Go-Betweens**' 'Lee Remick' and **Little Murders**' 'Things will Be Different'. Mark Carroll replaced original guitar player Michael Jones around that time.

By the time the single appeared, Young Modern had relocated to Sydney to join the Dirty Pool Agency (which also booked **Cold Chisel** and **The Angels**). Young Modern failed to make an impact on a Sydney scene still besotted by the spectre of **Radio Birdman**, and in which **Cold Chisel, The Angels** and **The Radiators** currently held court. The band broke up following a gig during July 1979. Dowler moved to Melbourne, where he eventually formed **The Zimmermen** in 1983.

Vic Yates and Mark Kohler attempted to keep the Young Modern flame alight with new players Peter Laverick (vocals), Peter Hilton (guitar) and Mike Donovan (bass), but that line-up was short-lived. Andrew Richard joined Sydney band The

Singles, which issued two singles 'Stay'/'Sad Clown', 'Love of Loves' (on Doublethink, July 1980) and 'That's Just Someone that I Knew'/'If You'll Only' (on Basilisk, February 1981). Yates, Kohler and Donovan returned to Adelaide, where they formed Acrylic Chewies with original Young Modern guitarist Michael Jones and Kerry Short (guitar, vocals). In 1982, Peter Spooner replaced Donovan on bass, and David Long joined on keyboards in place of the departing Jones. Acrylic Chewies lasted until 1983, and folded without making significant headway.

In the meantime, the enterprising Local label had assembled Young Modern's May 1978 demos and both sides of the 'She's Got the Money' single for release as the album *Play Faster* (December 1979). The quality of the demos was rough, but they captured some of the band's spirit. The album contained a handful of the band's best tunes (although live favourites like 'New Wave' and 'Do You Care?' went unrecorded). The album's title was derived from the taunts to which the band was subjected when playing Sydney venues: 'Play faster, ya wimps, play faster!'

Album: *Play Faster* (Local, 1979).

Z

Zambian Goat Herders (*see* Tumbleweed)

The Zimmermen

Formed: *1983*
Style: *Rock, country*
Original line-up: *John Dowler (vocals; ex-Spare Change,* **Young Modern**, *Glory Boys, Talk Show), Mick Holmes (guitar, vocals; ex-Negatives, Eric Gradman: Man & Machine, Romantics,* **Paul Kelly** *and the Dots, Fatal Attraction), Tim Brosnan (guitar; ex-***Millionaires**, *True Wheels, Romantics,* **Paul Kelly** *and the Dots), Peter 'Pedro' Steele (bass; ex-Fatal Attraction), Trevor Upton (drums; ex-Lipservice, Fatal Attraction)*

Singer/songwriter John Dowler fronted one of the great power pop bands of the late 1970s, **Young Modern**. Despite boundless promise and a swag of snappy, finely crafted pop songs on which to call, **Young Modern** never quite made the leap into the big time. Dowler went on to form The Zimmermen, another group of undoubted charm and appeal that earned a strong cult following. Although his efforts have rarely translated into major record sales, Dowler is recognised as one of Australia's most underrated songwriters. Dowler's formative influences, Big Star's Alex Chilton and Lou Reed, have always informed his work without him sounding slavish in the process.

With the break-up of **Young Modern** in Sydney during mid-1979, Dowler ended up in Melbourne. In early 1980, he joined The Glory Boys with Chris Langman (guitar, vocals; ex-Spare Change, **Parachute**, High Rise Bombers, **Paul Kelly** and the Dots), Robert Kretschmer (guitar; ex-Spare Change, **Parachute**, Eric Gradman: Man & Machine), Nick Seymour (bass; ex-Romantics) and Jon Wilkinson (drums; ex-Spare Change, **X-Ray-Z**). The Glory Boys played a handful of gigs before changing names to Talk Show. After that, Dave Cahill replaced Seymour on bass and Graeme Perry (ex-Spare Change, **Parachute**, Eric Gradman: Man & Machine) replaced Wilkinson on drums. Seymour went on to play with Scratch Record Scratch, Bang, Plays with Marionettes and **Crowded House**. Kretchmer went on to become an integral member of **Icehouse**.

By mid-1980, Talk Show had split, and Dowler commenced recording an abortive solo album with producer Martin Armiger (from **The Sports**). Dowler and Armiger completed 11 tracks, but the album remained unissued. By mid-1981, Dowler was working with Everybody's So Glad with Bill Darling (guitar, vocals), Steve Pike (guitar), Bob Delfonia (bass) and Steve Shears (drums). Dowler left Everybody's So Glad in December 1981, after which the band became known as Chamber Rhymes. By June 1983, Dowler had managed to formulate a permanent line-up for his new band. Dubbed The Zimmermen as a pun based on Bob Dylan's real name (Robert Zimmerman), the band began to rehearse. Even before they had played a gig, The Zimmermen suffered their first line-up change when Tim Brosnan left to join **The Runners** in July 1983.

Dowler recruited Steve Connolly (guitar, vocals; ex-Cuban Heels, Rare Things) and the band began to play gigs. The Zimmermen's brand of melodic, country-influenced rock was at odds with prevailing trends on the Melbourne scene (shockabilly, goth-rock, hard funk), but the band picked up a following on the inner-city pub circuit by playing supports with the likes of **Hoodoo Gurus** and **Sunnyboys**. In late 1983, Michael Barclay (ex-Japanese Comix, **Little Murders, Runners**) replaced Upton on drums. By that stage, Dowler had written a batch of first-rate pop songs, and he began making plans for The Zimmermen's debut album.

Towards the end of 1984, Connolly and Barclay both left to join the **Paul Kelly** Band, which had evolved into The Coloured Girls by 1985. Peter Tulloch (guitar, vocals; ex-Wrecked Jets) came in as Connolly's replacement, although it took some time for Dowler to find a suitable drummer. Graeme Perry helped out on drums when The Zimmermen entered the studio in January 1985 to record their debut single, 'Don't Go To Sydney'. By mid-1985, Neil Osborn (ex-Wrecked Jets) had joined as permanent drummer. Tulloch and Osborn's previous band, Wrecked Jets, also comprised Mick McGinley (guitar, vocals) and Keith Nunn (bass). Wrecked Jets played the Carlton/inner-city circuit between 1979 and 1981, and issued one single, 'Can I Go Home?'/'The Howling Life', on the Au-go-go label in 1980.

The Zimmermen's debut single, 'Don't Go To Sydney'/'A Spy in the House of Love' came out on Au-go-go in December 1985. 'Don't Go to Sydney' was an instant classic, an exceptional slice of harmony-drenched guitar pop. It became one of the most successful independent singles for 1986. Steve Connolly contributed guitar to the song, with Barclay on backing vocals and Peter 'Pedro' Bull (from Coloured Girls) on organ. 'A Spy in the House of Love' also appeared on Au-go-go's Various Artists Melbourne compilation *A Slab of Vic* (August 1986). The band's critically acclaimed debut album, *Rivers of Corn*, and its second single, 'Ordinary Man'/'Are You Still Alone?' (February 1987), followed. As well as newer material, the album included two earlier tracks recorded by the Dowler/Holmes/Bull/Connolly/Barclay line-up, 'Shake Down' and 'I Shall Return'.

Having established a strong identity on the Australian independent scene, The Zimmermen began to record a second album in early 1987. By mid-1987, Alan Brooker (bass; ex-Clean Cut, **Paul Kelly** and the Dots, **Little Murders**) had replaced Bull on bass, and Graeme Perry had replaced Osborn on drums. Dissatisfied with the album recorded by the previous line-up, Dowler took the band back into the studio with producer **Lobby Loyde** during November 1988 to re-record the entire set. Having signed a new deal with Mushroom Records, The Zimmermen issued a new single, 'What Really Hurts'/'Waltz' (February 1989), followed by the wryly titled album *Way Too Casual* in April. The album was a more balanced effort than the debut, displaying a depth, freshness and sense of humour that made for excellent listening. The album contained several of Dowler's most fully realised compositions, such as 'What Really Hurts', 'Ties that Bind' and 'Corsican Dreams'. Guitarist Peter Tulloch also weighed in with a couple of delightful love songs in 'All the Boys Need Love' and 'Waiting'. Bruce Haymes (from **Bachelors from Prague**) contributed piano and organ to the album.

The Zimmermen embarked on a national tour in support of the album's release; however, by early 1990 the band had run its course. Dowler retired from live performances; he issued a solo album in late 1993. *Low Society* included new versions of 'Ordinary Man' and 'Don't Go to Sydney', plus an ambitious cover of Alex Chilton's 'Holocaust'.

Zimmermen albums: *Rivers of Corn* (Au-go-go, 1986), *Way Too Casual* (Mushroom/Festival, 1989); ***John Dowler solo album:*** *Low Society* (In Law/Siren, 1993).

The Zoot

Formed: *1967*
Style: *Pop*
Original line-up: *Darryl Cotton (lead vocals), John D'Arcy (guitar, vocals), Beeb Birtles (born Gerard Birtlekamp, bass, vocals), Teddy Higgins (drums)*

The original Zoot line-up came together in Adelaide during 1966 under the name of Down the Line. School friends Darryl Cotton and Dutch-descended Gerard Birtlekamp joined forces with a recent arrival from Manchester, England, guitarist John D'Arcy. Adelaide had already produced the likes of **The Twilights** and **The Master's Apprentices**, and the young band no doubt had designs on following in the footsteps of such distinguished company.

With a name change to The Zoot in 1967, the band became the premier 'mod' group on the Adelaide dance scene, playing note-for-note renditions of new material by British bands such as The Move, The Small Faces and The Hollies. In early 1968, D'Arcy left to be replaced by Steve Stone. In mid-1968, The Zoot relocated to Melbourne where EMI/Columbia sent the band into the studio to record its debut single, 'You Better Get Going Now'/'Three Jolly Little Dwarfs' (August). The Zoot launched the single at Berties discotheque, with owner Tony Knight and the band's new manager Wayne de Gruchy decking out the venue, and the band, in total pink. It was the start of The Zoot's 'Think Pink—Think Zoot' promotional campaign, a ploy which was to haunt them in later years.

The Zoot's second single, written and produced by **The Twilights'** Terry Britten, 'One Times, Two Times, Three Times, Four'/'Sailing' (January 1969) became a moderate hit in Melbourne when it peaked at #32. Soon after, Higgins and Stone left the band to be replaced by Rick Brewer (drums; ex-Third Party) and Roger Hicks (guitar) respectively. The band became regulars on Melbourne pop show *Uptight*. Single number three, **Hans Poulsen** and **Seekers'** Bruce Woodley's 'Monty and Me'/'Little Roland Lost' (produced by Ian 'Molly' Meldrum) only managed #33 in Melbourne during June, but soared to #1 in Brisbane. By that stage, The Zoot was spearheading Australia's emergent bubblegum pop movement, vying with the likes of **The Valentines**, **The Flying Circus** and **New Dream** for a place on the charts and in the hearts of hysterical teenage girls.

Guitarist **Rick Springfield** (ex-Wickedy Wak) replaced Roger Hicks, who joined Brisbane band **The Avengers**. Springfield was a talented musician and songwriter, and with him on board the band gradually began to move in a more musically substantial direction. In September 1969, The Zoot joined the cream of Australian popdom (**Russell Morris**, **Johnny Farnham**, **Johnny Young**, **Ronnie Burns**, **The Valentines**, **The Master's Apprentices** and **Doug Parkinson** In Focus) on the ambitious Operation Starlift tour of capital cities. EMI issued The Zoot's fourth single, 'It's About Time'/'Sha La La' (October 1969), without the band's consent. It was not successful. The Zoot ended the year by being voted Top Australian Group in the *Go-Set* Pop Poll.

In early 1970, The Zoot ceremoniously burned all the pink gear before the cameras of *Happening '70*. The band's next single, 'Hey Pinky'/'Strange Things' (April), was an unsubtle dig at the just-discarded pop image. The single was promoted in the pages of *Go-Set* by a beefcake shot of the members of The Zoot displaying their bared bums for all to see. While the photo may have fluttered the hearts and stirred the loins of a few of the band's young female fans, the single failed to chart. Under Springfield's direction, the band recorded its debut album, *Just Zoot* (August 1970), which emerged as a creditable effort. One month before its release, The Zoot took out second spot to **The Flying Circus** in Hoadley's National Battle of the Sounds final.

In December 1970, The Zoot issued a thunderous re-working of The Beatles' 'Eleanor Rigby'/'Turn Your Head' as a single. It became the band's biggest hit when it reached #4 on the national chart (March 1971). 'Eleanor Rigby' was just one of a number of contemporary songs that the band re-arranged in a suitably heavy fashion for live appearances. They included The Beatles' 'Hello Goodbye', Joni Mitchell's 'Woodstock' and Donovan's 'Hurdy Gurdy Man'. The single stayed on the charts for 21 weeks, but ironically sales fell just short of attaining gold status. That occurred when EMI finally re-issued 'Eleanor Rigby' in 1979.

In the meantime, The Zoot followed that up with another hard rock single, 'The Freak'/'Evil Child' (April 1971), which only managed to reach #27 in Melbourne. By that stage, frustrations had come to a head when The Zoot was unable to throw off the shackles of its teenypop past. The Zoot parted ways in May 1971. **Rick Springfield** signed to Robie Porter's Sparmac label and launched his solo career with the single 'Speak to the Sky'/'I Didn't Mean to Love You' (October 1971). Springfield went on to attain superstar status in the USA as a highly visible solo performer and television actor.

Darryl Cotton and Beeb Birtles formed the duo Darryl and Beeb, playing harmony-laden soft rock. The Frieze clothing company offered the duo a sponsorship on the condition, as Noel McGrath wrote, that they wear the company's clothing and perform under the name Frieze. Frieze issued a cover of Mann–Weil's 'Feelings'/'Young Man's Lament' (September 1971) as a single on the Sparmac label. Utilising Burke and Wills as its backing band, Frieze recorded the album *1972 BC* for Warner Brothers. Cotton's debut solo single, 'Why Do Little Children Have to Die?'/'Jimmie and Jessie', was lifted from the *1972 BC* album. Cotton and Birtles dissolved the partnership in May 1972. Birtles joined **Mississippi** and later enjoyed considerable acclaim in Australia and the USA with **Little River Band**.

Cotton left Australia in July 1972, and travelled to the UK where he worked with Mick Flynn, (ex-**Mixtures**). In early 1973 he received an offer to join a band in the US called Friends with American Michael Lloyd and fellow Aussie expatriate Steve Kipner (ex-**Steve & the Board**). Friends signed to Warners and issued one self-titled album, plus a couple of singles including 'Gonna Have a Good Time'/'Would You Laugh?' (1973). The A-side was a cover of the Vanda and Young tune 'Good Times', which had mysteriously been credited to Vanda-Young-Cotton-Lloyd-Kipner on the record label. Cotton and Lloyd continued as Cotton Lloyd and Christian with new member Chris Christian. The vocal trio recorded a self-titled album for 20th Century which was also used as the soundtrack to the 1976 US teen film *The Pom Pom Girls* directed by Joseph Ruben. Cotton Lloyd and Christian issued the single 'Crying in the Rain' in April 1977. Cotton toured as guitar player and backing vocalist for **Olivia Newton-John** before returning to Australia in early 1978.

On returning to Australia, Cotton signed to **Ross Wilson** and Glenn Wheatley's Oz label (through EMI) and issued the single 'Don't Let It Get to You'/'Can't Face the Music' (August 1978). The single peaked at #22 in Melbourne during October. In January 1979, Cotton was in Adelaide hosting the television pop show *Summer Rock* for the Nine Network. He issued two more singles on Oz, a cover of Hall and Oates' 'I Don't Want to Lose You'/'Let the Music Take You Away' (February 1979) and

'Glamour Girl'/'Childish Games and Foolish Pride' (July) before turning to acting. Cotton appeared in the Nine Network's soapie *Young Doctors* for a season, before hosting another series of *Summer Rock*. In 1980, he signed to EMI and enjoyed his biggest solo hit when 'Same Old Girl'/'What'cha Gonna Do?' (February 1980) reached #6 on the national chart in April. The single came from his debut solo album *Best Seat in the House*, which had been produced by his old partner from the US, Chris Christian.

Cotton formed a backing band, dubbed The Charts, which comprised Joey Amenta (lead guitar; ex-**Taste**, **Redhouse**, **Russell Morris** Band), Randy Bulpin (guitar; ex-**Mondo Rock**), Terry Davidson (keyboards), Simon Gyllies (bass; ex-**Mondo Rock**) and Andy Buchanan (drums). The band toured the Australian pub circuit to some success. Cotton issued three more singles on EMI, 'Here Comes Another Heartache'/'Dance' (June 1980), Burt Bacharach and Hal David's 'Little Red Book'/'Rollin' Over' (May 1981) and 'Nice Girls'/'All Nite', 'Break Out Tonight' (November). Cotton's 1981 touring band, The Divers, comprised Amenta, Davidson, Spiro Philipas (bass) and Robert Ross (drums).

In July 1983, Cotton issued a duet single with Heather Favell on CBS, 'Baby You're Changing'/'No One Wants to Dance'. In 1984, he recorded an album of rock'n'roll and pop chestnuts for the Hammard label called *Rockin' Good Fun*. Cotton retired from live performances and returned to television to host the Ten Network's Saturday morning children's show *The Early Bird Show* (sharing the limelight with Marty the Monster). During 1996, Cotton joined up with fellow 1960s veterans **Russell Morris** and **Ronnie Burns** to play the revival circuit. The three singers issued a self-titled album during the year which comprised nine original solo recordings, plus three new recordings by the trio.

Zoot albums: *Just Zoot* (EMI/Columbia, 1970), *Zoot Out* (compilation, EMI/Columbia, 1971), *Zoot Locker* (compilation, EMI, 1980); ***Frieze album:*** *1972 BC* (Warner, 1972); ***Darryl Cotton solo albums:*** *Best Seat in the House* (EMI, 1980), *Rockin' Good Fun* (Hammard, 1984), *Let the Children Sing* (DC, 1994).

Stop Press!

Since I finished writing this book in late November 1997, the Australian music industry has rolled ever onwards. A lot has happened in 1998. The year's biggest success story belongs to former *Neighbours* star Natalie Imbruglia, whose #1 album, *Left of the Middle*, spawned three Australian hit singles: 'Torn' (#3, March 1998), 'Big Mistake' (#7, June) and 'Wishing I Was There' (#24, July). All three also hit big in the UK, and *Left of the Middle* went on to sell close to five million copies worldwide. Imbruglia walked away with six Australian Record Industry Association (ARIA) awards for Best Single ('Torn'), Best Female Artist, Best New Talent, Best Debut Album (*Left of the Middle*), Best Debut Single ('Torn') and Best Pop Release (*Left of the Middle*).

Savage Garden not only continued to dominate the local charts, but also toured overseas to wide acclaim. The Brisbane duo's enormously successful #1 debut album, *Savage Garden*, left the Australian Top 40 chart in May, after a stay of 60 weeks and sales of over 700 000 copies. It re-entered the Top 40 in September, peaking at #28. Darren Hayes and Daniel Jones also scored well at the ARIAs with awards for Highest-selling Album and Outstanding Achievement.

The success rate for local acts continued apace, with albums by **You Am I** (*You Am I's #4 Record*), Neil Finn (*Try Whistling This*), **Powderfinger** (*Internationalist*), the re-formed **Cold Chisel** (*The Last Wave of Summer*) and Melbourne-based rockabilly punks The Living End (*The Living End*) all making their debut at #1 on the Australian album chart. The Living End burst onto the national scene with the #3 hit 'Second Solution'/'Prisoner of Society', which took the Highest-selling Single award at the ARIA ceremony. The follow-up single, 'Save the Day', peaked at #24 in October. **Cold Chisel**'s first single in three years, 'The Things I Love in You', went as high as #11 in September. The first single lifted from **Powderfinger**'s *Internationalist*, 'The Day You Come', made #24 in August. Neil Finn repeated his local success with the release of *Try Whistling This* in the UK.

Kylie Minogue's platinum-selling *Impossible Princess* album also attained the #1 spot in the wake of her successful Australian tour. The album's second single, 'Did it Again', had already reached #21 in December 1997, and went as high as #16 in February. The next two singles, 'Breathe' and 'Cowboy Style', were minor hits at #23 (April) and #32 (October) respectively. **Nick Cave and the Bad Seeds** had their best showing on the national chart when *The Best of Nick Cave & the Bad Seeds* entered at #2 in June.

Regurgitator's platinum-selling *Unit* album reached #3, and yielded three more singles: 'Black Bugs' (#43, March), 'Polyester Girl' (#14, July) and '! The Song Formerly Known As' (#46, October). *Unit* also took out the ARIA awards for Best Album, Best Cover Artwork, Best Alternative Release and Producer of the Year (Magoo and Regurgitator). When re-issued as *Unit Re-booted* in October, the album made its debut at #13. **Kate Ceberano**'s jubilant single, 'Pash', hit #11 in March; the album of the same name reached #23 in May. **Grinspoon**'s *Guide to Better Living* had initially made #12 on the national chart in October 1997; it was still selling strong enough to peak at #16 in April 1998. The album's fourth single, 'Just Ace', reached #21 in February. The band's latest release, the 'Pushing Buttons' EP, hit #10 in October.

Young Perth band Jebediah issued its debut album, *Slightly Odway*, in late 1997 (national #16 in September). It swiftly fell out of the chart, but with singles like 'Military Strongman', 'Leaving Home' and 'Teflon (Slippin' Along)' (#41 in April 1998) on board, the album re-entered the Top 40 in March 1998. It eventually peaked at #14 in May. Another successful alternative band, Cordrazine, made its debut on the national mainstream Top 40 at #9 (May) with the album *From Here to Wherever*. **The Superjesus** consolidated on initial interest with the national Top 10 placement (#6 in March) of the debut album *Sumo*. The album's third single 'Now and Then' managed #40 in April. The band re-issued the album in October as *Sumo II* with a bonus disc of live material added. **The Whitlams**' popular (and platinum-selling) *Eternal Nightcap* album peaked at #12 in February. The band ended a successful year with the ARIA awards for Best Group, Best Independent Release (*Eternal Nightcap*) and Song of the Year ('No Aphrodisiac'). At the awards ceremony, former Prime Minister Gough

Whitlam announced the band's award for Song of the Year with the off-the-cuff quip 'It's my family!'. The band responded appropriately with a down-on-the-knees 'we're not worthy!' routine.

Melbourne's latest grunge-pop heroes **The Mavis's** scored well on the national charts with their second album, *Pink Pills* (#12 in April), and its infectious 'Cry' single (#13 in May). Veterans **The Cruel Sea** returned to the national charts when their first album in three years, *Over Easy*, hit #10 in August. Likewise, seasoned Aussie pub rockers **The Angels** came back with the high-tensile *Skin and Bone* album (#27, March), and found themselves inducted into the ARIA Hall of Fame (alongside **The Master's Apprentices**). **Paul Kelly** followed up the success of his triple platinum-selling anthology, *Songs From the South: Paul Kelly's Greatest Hits*, with the release of his seventh solo album, *Words and Music* (#17, May).

Big-voiced newcomer Marie Wilson scored her first hits with the anthemic single 'Next Time' (#21, May) and debut album *Real Life* (#7, October). Former ARIA recipient **Tina Arena** followed up her triple platinum-selling *In Deep* album with two more hit singles, 'Now I Can Dance' (#13, May) and 'I Want to Know What Love Is' (#41, September). Harmony quartet **Human Nature** scored with the singles 'People Get Ready' (#35, December 1997) and 'Cruel' (#13, September 1998). The duo Bachelor Girl was another surprise success with two radio-friendly hit singles, 'Buses and Trains' (#3, September) and 'Treat Me Good' (#40, November). Dance-pop sensation **Peter Andre** managed one hit in 1998, 'All Night All Right' (#30, April). Satirist Pauline Pantsdown overcame the threat of legal action from politician Pauline Hanson to score big with the playful 'I Don't Like It' single (#4, October).

A couple of big name acts struggled for attention throughout 1998. **Hunters & Collectors**' final studio album, *Juggernaut*, suffered a brief two-week stay in the Top 40 after making its debut at #38 (February). The perennial **Midnight Oil** was unable to capitalise on the success of its double platinum-selling *20,000 Watt R.S.L.—The Midnight Oil Collection*, when *Redneck Wonderland* failed to chart convincingly. Likewise, **Mental as Anything** watched their first album in three years, *Garage*, disappear without trace; **TISM** did the same with *www.tism.wanker.com*. After a promising beginning, Leonardo's Bride has yet to follow-up the success of its evocative hit single 'Even When I'm Sleeping' (#4, July 1997; and winner of the Australian Performing Right Association Song of the Year award) and album *Angel Blood* (#25, August 1997).

Other album releases up to November 1998 have included: **Dirty Three** (*Ocean Songs*), **Bodyjar** (*No Touch Red*), **Died Pretty** (*Using My Gills as a Roadmap*), **Colin Hay** (*Transcendental Highway*), **Chain** (*The First 30 Years*), **The Killjoys** (*Sun Bright Deep*), Ricaine (*The Clarity of Distance*), **Magic Dirt** (*Young and Full of the Devil*), **Chris Wilson** (*The Long Weekend*), **Ammonia** (*Eleventh Avenue*), Richard Davies (*Telegraph*), The Onyas (*Six*), Snout (*Circle High and Wide*), **Ed Kuepper** and His Oxley Creek Playboys (*Cloudland* and *Live!*), **The Paradise Motel** (*Flight Paths*), Peter Koppes (*Love Era/Irony*), The Necks (*Piano Bass Drums*), Sandpit (*On Second Thought*), Something for Kate (*Elsewhere for 8 Minutes*), **Autohaze** (*Counter Clockwise*), Boo Boo and Mace (*Sublimely Pointless*), **Cactus Child** (*Earthgirl*), **Renée Geyer** (*The Best of 1973–1998*), **The Fauves** (*Lazy Highway*), Suzie Higgie and Conway Savage (*Soon Will be Tomorrow*), Christopher Marshall (*Strange Waters, Small Mercies*), Hot Rollers (*Hot Rollers*), **Effigy** (*Century Collapsing*), Gondwana (*Xenophon*), **Olivia Newton-John** (*Back With a Heart*), Melanie Oxley and **Chris Abrahams** (*Jerusalem Bay*), **Deniz Tek** (*Equinox*), **Weddings, Parties, Anything** (*The Best of Weddings, Parties, Anything: Trophy Night*), Happyland (*Welcome To . . .*), **The Church** (*Hologram of Baal*), **Fini Scad** (*Wider Screen*), **Coloured Stone** (*The Best of Coloured Stone*), **Deni Hines** (*Remix Your Imagination*), Not From There (*Sand on Seven*), Violetine (*Small Speaker Joyland*), **Merrill Bainbridge** (*Between the Days*), **Even** (*Come Again*), **Dave Graney** (*The Dave Graney Show*), **d.i.g.** (*Curvystrasse*), Astrid Munday (*Astrid Munday*), The Simpletons (*Popcore*), Tendrils (*Soaking Red*), **Hunters & Collectors** (*Under One Roof Live*), **Hoodoo Gurus** (*Bite the Bullet Live*), **Gaslight Radio** (*Hitch on the Leaves*), **The Jackson Code** (*The Second Greatest Story Ever Told*), **Painters and Dockers** (*Advance Australia Where?*) and Pollen (*The Glorious Couch Life*).

Mushroom Records celebrated 25 years of Australian music with the release of *The Mushroom Story* series of CD compilations, the book *25 Years of Mushroom Records* written by **Dave Warner** and the gigantic *Mushroom 25* concert at the Melbourne Cricket Ground on 14 November. Mushroom boss Michael Gudinski may have sold his rights in the company he set up in 1973 to the majority shareholder, Rupert Murdoch, but it did not stop him from celebrating the label's achievements. On a sadder note, Australian music bade farewell to **Marc Hunter**, who lost his battle with throat cancer, The Freeloaders' Guy Lucas and to one of the country's pioneering rock'n'rollers Henri Bource (The Henri Bource All Stars, **The Thunderbirds**, **The Planets**), who died from leukemia in September.

Ian McFarlane
20 November 1998

References

Books

Baker, Glenn A. *Australian Made: Gonna Have a Good Time Tonight.* Fontana/Collins, 1987.

——*External Combustion.* Horwitz Grahame, 1990.

Baker, Glenn A., and Coupe, Stuart. *The New Music.* Bay Books, 1980.

——*The New Rock'n'Roll: The A–Z of Rock in the '80s.* Omnibus Press, 1983.

Barnes, Jim and Scanes, Stephen. *The Book (Top 40 Research 1956–1994)*, 3rd edn. Barscan Music Research, 1995.

Breen, Marcus (ed.). *Missing in Action: Australian Popular Music in Perspective.* Verbal Graphics, 1987.

Brokenmouth, Robert. *Nick Cave: The Birthday Party and Other Epic Adventures.* Omnibus Press, 1996.

Brown, Jenny. *Skyhooks: Million Dollar Riff.* Dingo Press, 1975.

Bryden-Brown, John. *JO'K: The Official Johnny O'Keefe Story.* Doubleday, 1982.

Creswell, Toby. *Jimmy Barnes: Too Much Ain't Enough.* Random House, 1993.

Dewey, Karen. *Angry: Scarred for Life.* Ironbark/Pan Macmillan, 1994.

Dix, John. *Stranded in Paradise: New Zealand Rock'n'Roll 1955–1988.* Paradise Publications, 1988.

Forbes, Clark. *Whispering Jack: The John Farnham Story.* Hutchison Australia, 1989.

Hayton, Jon, and Isackson, Leon. *Behind the Rock.* Select Books, 1990.

Hayward, Philip (ed.). *From Pop to Punk to Postmodernism.* Allen & Unwin, 1992.

Hutchinson, Tracee. *Your Name's on the Door: 10 Years of Australian Music.* ABC Publishing, 1992.

Hutton, Doug and Sawford, Gavin. *Out of the Unknown.* Time Out Publications, 1989.

Jenkins, Jeff. *Ego is Not a Dirty Word: The Skyhooks Story.* Kelly and Withers, 1994.

Johnson, Vivien. *Radio Birdman.* Sheldon Booth, 1990.

Kelton, Tim. *Underground in the City of Churches.* The Printing House, 1986.

Larkin, Colin (gen. ed.). *The Guinness Who's Who of Blues*, 2nd edn. Guinness Publishing, 1995.

——*The Guinness Who's Who of Indie and New Wave Music.* Guinness Publishing, 1992.

Latta, David. *Australian Country Music.* Random House Australia, 1991.

McLean, David (comp.). *Canetoad Records Presents Collected Stories on Australian Rock'n'Roll.* A Canetoad Publication, 1991.

McGrath, Noel. *Noel McGrath's Australian Encyclopedia of Rock.* Outback Press, 1978.

——*Noel McGrath's Australian Encyclopedia of Rock 1978–79 Yearbook.* Outback Press, 1979.

——*Noel McGrath's Australian Encyclopedia of Rock & Pop.* Rigby, 1984.

——*Noel McGrath's Book of Australian Rock.* Lothian Publishing, 1988.

McMillan, Andrew. *Strict Rules.* Hodder and Stoughton, 1988.

Mathieson, Craig. *Hi Fi Days: The Future of Australian Rock.* Allen & Unwin, 1996.

Murray, Scott (ed.). *Australian Film 1978–1994.* Oxford University Press, 1995.

Nichols, David. *The Go-Betweens.* Allen & Unwin, 1997.

Rawlins, Adrian. *Festivals in Australia: An Intimate History.* DTE Publishing, 1983.

Rice, Tim, Gambaccini, Paul, and Rice, Jonathan (comp.). *British Hit Singles*, 10th edn. Guinness Publishing, 1995.

Robbins, Ira (ed.). *The New Music Record and Tape Guide.* Omnibus Press, 1987.

——*The Trouser Press Guide to '90s Rock.* Fireside, 1997.

Rogers, Bob and O'Brien, Denis. *Rock 'n Roll Australia: The Australian Pop Scene 1954–1964.* Cassell Australia, 1975.

Scatena, Dino. *Kylie.* Penguin Books, 1997.

Simpson, Graham. *Colours of My Life: The Judith Durham Story.* Random House, 1994.

Smith, David and Peters, Neal. *Peter Allen: 'Between the Moon and New York City'.* Delilah Communications, 1983.

Spencer, Chris (comp.). *An Australian Rock Discography.* Moonlight Publications, 1990.

——*The Various Artist in Australia: A Rock Discography*. Moonlight Publications, 1990.
Spencer, Chris, Nowara, Zbig and McHenry, Paul (comp.). *Who's Who of Australian Rock*, 4th edn. The Five Mile Press, 1996.
St John, Ed (ed.). *The Big Australian Rock Book*. Megabooks, 1985.
Strong, M.C. *The Great Rock Discography*, 3rd edn. Canongate Books, 1996.
Sturma, Michael. *Australian Rock'n'Roll: The First Wave*. Kangaroo Press, 1991.
Thorpe, Billy. *Sex and Thugs and Rock'n'Roll: A Year in Kings Cross 1963–1964*. Pan Macmillan, 1996.
Virgin Publishing, *Peter Andre: The Unofficial Book*, 1997.
Walker, Clinton (ed.). *Inner City Sound*. Wild & Woolley, 1982.
——*The Next Thing: Contemporary Australian Rock*. Kangaroo Press, 1984.
Walker, Clinton. *Highway to Hell: The Life & Times of AC/DC Legend Bon Scott*. Sun/Pan Macmillan, 1994.
——*Stranded: The Secret History of Australian Independent Music 1977–1991*. Pan Macmillan, 1996.
Wilmoth, Peter. *Glad All Over: The Countdown Years 1974–1987*. McPhee Gribble, 1993.

Magazines

The Age EG (Entertainment Guide). Syme Media.
Ausmusic News. Ausmusic.
Big Backyard News, 1992–95.
Countdown. Countdown Publications.
The Edge. Century Magazines, 1989–90.
Fast Forward (cassette magazine). 1980–1982.
From the Vault. Ed: Glenn Terry, From the Vault Publications, 1986–90.
Go-Set. Go-Set Publications, 1966–74.
Hot Metal/HM Magazine. Pacific Publications, 1989–97.
International Record Buyers Guide. Wide World Publications, 1980–81.
It: The Australian Record Collectors Magazine, Ed: David Gibson, 1994–97.
Jmag. Gore & Osment Publications.
Juice. Terraplane Press, 1993–97.
Juke. Syme Media Pty Ltd, 1975–93.
Loudmouth. Blunt Publications, 1997.
RAM (Rock Australian Magazine). Soundtracks Publishing, 1975-1989.
Rhythms. Rhythms Publications, 1990–97.
Roadrunner. Roadrunner Publications, 1978–81.
Rolling Stone (Australian edition). Next Publishing, 1975–97.
Sound Blast, David Frith Publications, 1972.
The Trip. Triple R Broadcasters Ltd.
Virgin Press. Virgin Press Publishing, 1980–1981.
Vox Muzpaper. Vox Publications, 1981.

Street Press

Beat Magazine
Drum Media
In-Press
On the Street

Fanzines

Australian Music Museum. Ed: Chris Spencer, Moonlight Publishing, 1993–97.
The Australian New Music Record Guide 1976–80. Ed/writer: Ian McFarlane, Pristine Productions, 1992.
The Australian Progressive, Hard Rock and Blues Record Guide, 1969–77. Ed/writer: Ian McFarlane, Third Stone Press, 1996.
Australian Punk Rock 1976–1983, Henry Weld, 1994.
B-Side. Ed: Simon Lonergan, 1983–87.
Caddie (Brian Cadd). Paul McHenry, Moonlight Publishing, 1996.
DNA. Ed: Harry Butler, 1979–97.
Form Guide. Ed: Richard, The Punters Club, 1993–97.
Freedom Train: Australian Progressive Rock 1970–76. Ed/writer: Ian McFarlane, Third Stone Press, 1993–96.
Lemon. Ed: Louise Dickinson, 1990–94.
The Livin' End. Ed: Dean Mittelhauser, 1983–89.
Russell Morris. Paul McHenry, Moonlight Publishing, 1995.
Party Fears. Ed: David Gerard, 1986–92.
Hans Poulsen: Troubadour. Paul McHenry, Moonlight Publishing, 1996.
Prehistoric Sounds: Australian Independent Music 1976–90. Ed/writer: Ian McFarlane, Dark City Press, 1993–96.
Pulp. Eds: Bruce Milne and Clinton Walker, 1977.
Resistant Harmony. Ed: Scotti, 1987–95.
Ross Ryan (Thought this Might Happen). Paul McHenry, Moonlight Publishing, 1996.
Shakin' Street. Ed: Jim Wylie, 1986.
Spleen. Ed: Damien Power, 1993–96.
Thorpie!. Paul McHenry, Moonlight Publishing, 1994.
Underworld. Eds: Martin Newman, David Higgins, 1996.
Vicious Kitten. Ed: Denis Gray, Kristabell Productions, 1995–97.

Credits

Photos by Tony Mott: Peter Garrett (frontispiece); Doc Neeson (The Angels); Christine Anu; Tina Arena; Baby Animals; Chris Bailey; Nick Barker; Jimmy Barnes; Beasts of Bourbon; Joe Camilleri (The Black Sorrows); Box the Jesuit; Don Walker (Catfish); Nick Cave; Kate Ceberano; Celibate Rifles; Steve Kilbey (The Church); Clouds; The Cruel Sea; Def FX; Died Pretty; Dirty Three; Christina Amphlett (Divinyls); Electric Hippies; Even; The Fauves; Neil and Tim Finn; Robert Forster; Frente!; Dave Graney; The Hard-ons; Holocene; Dave Faulkner, Hoodoo Gurus; The Hummingbirds; Iva Davies, Icehouse; Michael Hutchence (INXS); Paul Kelly; The Killjoys; Ed Kuepper; Magic Dirt; Nina Grant (Mantissa); The Mark of Cain; Wendy Matthews; The Meanies; Peter Garrett (Midnight Oil); Dannii Minogue; Moler; Ian Moss; Jon Stevens (Noiseworks); The Paradise Motel; Tex Don and Charlie; The Plunderers; Pollyanna; Powder Monkeys; Powderfinder; Ratcat; Regurgitator; Archie Roach; Angry Anderson (Rose Tattoo); Screamfeeder; The Screaming Jets; silverchair; Louis Tillett; Tumbleweed; Underground Lovers; v. Spy v. Spy; Weddings, Parties, Anything; Chris Wilson; X; Yothu Yindi; You Am I.

Other credits: Ayers Rock: David Parker; CDB: Isamu Sawa; Daddy Cool: Glenn A. Baker Archives; The Easybeats: Glenn A. Baker Archives; John Farnham: *TV Week*; Godstar: Robyn Murphy; Grinspoon: Sophie Howarth; Shane Howard: Simon O'Dwyer; Johnny O'Keefe: Glenn A. Baker Archives; Ol'55: *TV Week*; Sacred Cowboys: Peter Milne; Smudge: Robin Murphy; Spectrum: Glenn A. Baker Archives; Deniz Tek: Peter Wise; Billy Thorpe: *TV Week*; The Twilights: Glenn A. Baker Archives. All other photographs are publicity shots, courtesy of the relevant artists' record companies.